Massachusetts Criminal Law Sourcebook & Citator

2017 EDITION

Hon. R. Marc Kantrowitz

Timothy E. Maguire

Helle Sachse

MCLE
NEW ENGLAND
Keep raising the bar.®

2170144B27

Printed in the United States of America

This publication should be cited: Hon. R. Marc Kantrowitz, Timothy E. Maguire, Esq., and Helle Sachse, Esq., *Massachusetts Criminal Law Sourcebook & Citator 2017* (MCLE, Inc. 2016).

ISBN: 1-57589-984-1
ISSN: 2154-591X

Massachusetts Continuing Legal Education, Inc.
Ten Winter Place, Boston, MA 02108-4751
800-966-6253 I Fax 617-482-9498 I www.mcle.org

Foreword

The 2017 Edition of the *Massachusetts Criminal Law Sourcebook & Citator* was written to assist attorneys handling criminal matters in the Massachusetts trial courts. Hopefully, this book will provide answers to questions that commonly arise during the process of handling a criminal matter—from arraignment (or even before) through trial and beyond. While this work cannot replace the necessity of thorough preparation at every step of the process, it will serve as a quick reference in responding to the various questions that inevitably arise.

As the *Sourcebook & Citator* is updated annually, we encourage you to contact us, via MCLE, with your comments on how to improve it.

> Hon. R. Marc Kantrowitz
> Timothy E. Maguire, Esq.
> Helle Sachse, Esq.
> September 2016

About the Authors

R. MARC KANTROWITZ retired from the Massachusetts Appeals Court bench in August 2015. From there he returned to his alma mater, Ohio University, as a visiting professor during the 2015 fall semester. Previously, he served as an associate justice of the Massachusetts Juvenile Court, in private practice in Boston, and an assistant district attorney with the Suffolk County District Attorney's Office. He is the most heavily published author of state law in the Commonwealth, having written books on criminal law, evidence, mental health law, juvenile law, and civil litigation, as well as legal chapters and articles. He served, from its inception until 2013, as editor-in-chief of the *Massachusetts Guide to Evidence*. He also writes a monthly column, "Law 'n History," which is published by *Lawyers Weekly*. Currently he is an adjunct professor in Northeastern University's School of Law. He also continues to write and lectures on his latest book, *Old Whiskey and Young Women: American True Crime Tales of Murder, Sex and Scandal*, which was released in the United States and Europe in October 2015.

TIMOTHY E. MAGUIRE is a staff attorney at the Massachusetts Appeals Court. Previously, he was in private practice for over fifteen years, working out of the Boston offices of national law firms Greenberg Traurig LLP, Seyfarth Shaw LLP, and Schnader Harrison Segal & Lewis LLP, and concentrating on complex business, securities and financial litigation, fraud prevention, and white-collar and other criminal defense. Prior to that, he was an attorney with the Massachusetts Department of Correction for two years. He has extensive litigation, trial, and appellate experience. Mr. Maguire is a graduate of Suffolk University Law School and the University of Massachusetts at Amherst.

HELLE SACHSE is an assistant district attorney in the appeals unit at the Suffolk County District Attorney's Office. After graduating from Boston College Law School she served as law clerk to the Honorable Paul A. Suttell, Chief Justice of the Rhode Island Supreme Court, and the Honorable R. Marc Kantrowitz of the Massachusetts Appeals Court. Before embarking on her legal career, she received a Ph.D. in art history from the University of Witten/Herdecke in Germany.

Acknowledgments

I am deeply indebted to MCLE's executive director, and my good friend, Jack Reilly. I also wish to thank MCLE's Board of Trustees for their continuing support. Appreciation also goes to Alexis J. LeBlanc for her editorial assistance and to the staff of MCLE's Production Department for bringing this book to print.

Special thanks to my wonderful coauthors: Tim Maguire, a scholar with whom it continues to be a pleasure to work, and Helle Sachse, who continues to provide superb work and serves as the backbone of this book. As I am now in the next phase of my career—writing, teaching, and lecturing—I realize that it is time to leave some former projects, sadly including the *Sourcebook*. While I will no longer be involved in its annual updates, I am confident that Helle and Tim will continue its fine tradition. When I first published the book in 1985, then called the *Compendium of Massachusetts Criminal Law*, I had no idea that for over thirty years it would remain a mainstay in our courts. I am heartened by its success.

For the final time, I wish to thank all those who made the practice of law challenging and enjoyable—John Galvin, Steve Connolly, Kevin Driscoll, Joe Burke, Peter Klein, Bob Schilling, Chuck McGowan, Dave Downes, Jay Carney, Kevin Manganaro, Amal Bala, Roger Witkin, the late John Ruby, Tom Connors, Rosemary Minehan, Gina DeMetrio, and my former colleagues on the Appeals and Juvenile Court, as well as those with whom I worked on the *Massachusetts Guide to*

Evidence. Undoubtedly I have forgotten to include some who should be listed here. To those whom I have unintentionally neglected, I apologize. Last and best of all, I wish to thank my family, most notably my wife, Marianne, to whom this book is dedicated.

R. Marc Kantrowitz
September 2016

I want to again thank Judge Kantrowitz for offering me the opportunity to work on the *Massachusetts Criminal Law Sourcebook & Citator*. I also want to thank Attorney Helle Sachse for all of her work on this latest edition. Indeed, this edition, like other recent ones, is almost exclusively the product of her time and effort.

My sincerest thanks also go out to the following: all of the attorneys, staff, and judges at the Appeals Court; my former colleagues Peter Alley, Mark Berthiaume, Peter Brooks, Rob Carpenter, Brian Cheever, Jessica Cook, John Galvin, Sue Gelwick, Dan Less, and Mary Murray; and former University of Massachusetts at Amherst Professor Dean Alfange. I also want to thank my wife, Christine.

Tim Maguire
September 2016

I would like to thank Judge Kantrowitz for giving me the unique opportunity to work on the *Massachusetts Criminal Law Sourcebook & Citator*, and for being such a wonderful mentor, teacher, and friend. His input and advice for the *Sourcebook* will be deeply missed in the future. My thanks also go to Tim Maguire, with whom it has been a great pleasure to work on this edition of the *Sourcebook*, and to Alexis J. LeBlanc at MCLE for all her work on this latest edition.

I am very grateful to District Attorney Daniel F. Conley, and to all of my colleagues in the appeals unit at the Suffolk County District Attorney's Office, particularly my fabulous boss, Jack Zanini, all of whom teach me so much and make it a pleasure to come to work every day. Most of all, I would like to thank my family, especially my husband Wolfram.

Helle Sachse
September 2016

A Note on Usage

This book was prepared for press in August 2016. Case law and statutory amendments are current through August 31, 2016.

Many section headings reflect the common usage the authors noted in ongoing criminal practice and, therefore, depart from headings found in the official statutory compilation.

Criminal practitioners should note the controlling law at the time the crime was committed in order to consult the appropriate edition of the *Criminal Law Sourcebook & Citator* (or its predecessor, the *Compendium of Massachusetts Criminal Law*).

While every effort was made to provide the most current information available, practitioners are reminded to update their reference use of this book with attention to legislative and case law developments.

If a statute has been amended, added, or repealed by the Massachusetts legislature since 2011, a reference to the relevant chapter and section of the Massachusetts Acts and Resolves will be noted right after the title to the statute. In order to keep the *Sourcebook* manageable, however, there is generally no indication as to how specifically a statute has been amended. Counsel will have to conduct further research to ascertain exactly what effect the legislative act had on the statute.

The case law contained in the notes following the statutes and rules, as well as that reflected in the evidence section (Part 11), is not necessarily fully comprehensive of the topic covered, but rather, represents an accumulation of the relevant case law that has come out since the first edition of this book was published.

Contents

Part 1   Selected Statutes 1

                Constitution of Massachusetts 1

Chapter 6   Officers of the Commonwealth; Criminal Offender Record
                Information System Sex Offender Registration Act 1

Chapter 12   Department of the Attorney General and the District Attorneys 16

Chapter 18   Department of Transitional Assistance 17

Chapter 22C   Department of State Police 19

Chapter 22E   State DNA Database 20

Chapter 23K   The Massachusetts Gaming Commission 22

Chapter 89   Law of the Road 24

Chapter 90   Motor Vehicles and Aircraft 28

Chapter 90B   Motorboats and Other Vessels 83

Chapter 90C   Procedure for Motor Vehicle Offenses 92

Chapter 90D   Motor Vehicle Certificates of Title 98

Chapter 94C   Controlled Substances Act 99

Chapter 111   Public Health 122

Chapter 111B   Alcoholism 122

Chapter 111E   Drug Rehabilitation 123

Chapter 112   Registration of Certain Professions and Occupations 127

Chapter 113A   Uniform Anatomical Gift Act 129

Chapter 119   Protection and Care of Children, and Proceedings Against Them 129

Chapter 123   Mental Health 153

Chapter 123A   Care, Treatment and Rehabilitation of Sexually Dangerous Persons 162

Chapter 131   Inland Fisheries and Game and Other Natural Resources 171

Chapter 138   Alcoholic Liquors 172

Chapter 140   Licenses 174

Chapter 159A½ Transportation Network Companies 207

Chapter 208   Divorce 207

Chapter 209   Husband and Wife 209

Chapter 209A   Abuse Prevention 210

Chapter 212   The Superior Court 220

Chapter 218   District Courts 220

Chapter 221   Clerks, Attorneys and Other Officers of Judicial Courts 224

Chapter 233   Witnesses and Evidence 224

Chapter 234   Juries 238

Chapter 234A   Office of Jury Commissioner 238

Chapter 258B   Rights of Victims and Witnesses of Crime 243

Chapter 258C   Compensation of Victims of Violent Crimes 247

Chapter 258E   Harassment Prevention Orders 251

Chapter 261   Costs in Civil Actions 255

Part 2   Crimes, Punishments, and Proceedings in Criminal Cases 259

Chapter 263   Rights of Persons Accused of Crime 259

Chapter 263A   Witness Protection in Criminal Matters 262

Chapter 264   Crimes Against Governments 264
Chapter 265   Crimes Against the Person 267
Chapter 266   Crimes Against Property 312
Chapter 267   Forgery and Crimes Against the Currency 360
Chapter 267A   Money Laundering 366
Chapter 268   Crimes Against Public Justice 367
Chapter 268A   Conduct of Public Officials and Employees 377
Chapter 268B   Financial Disclosure by Certain Public Officials and Employees 391
Chapter 269   Crimes Against Public Peace 396
Chapter 270   Crimes Against Public Health 411
Chapter 271   Crimes Against Public Policy 421
Chapter 271A   Enterprise Crime 434
Chapter 272   Crimes Against Chastity, Morality, Decency and Good Order 435
Chapter 273   Desertion, Non-Support and Illegitimacy 472
Chapter 274   Felonies, Accessories and Attempts to Commit Crimes 476
Chapter 275   Proceedings to Prevent Crimes 479
                   Commentary on Chapter 276 Search and Seizure 481
Chapter 276   Search Warrants, Rewards, Fugitives from Justice, Arrest, Examination,
                   Commitment and Bail, Probation Officers and Board of Probation 505
Chapter 276A   District Court Pretrial Diversion of Selected Offenders 553
Chapter 277   Indictments and Proceedings Before Trial 556
Chapter 278   Trials and Proceedings Before Judgment 571
Chapter 278A   Post Conviction Access to Forensic and Scientific Analysis 580
Chapter 279   Judgment and Execution 584
Chapter 280   Fines and Forfeitures 596

Part 3 Massachusetts Rules of Criminal Procedure 599

Rule 1   Title; Scope 599
Rule 2   Purpose; Construction; Definition of Terms 599
Rule 3   Complaint and Indictment: Waiver of Indictment; Probable Cause Hearing 600
Rule 3.1   Determination of Probable Cause for Detention 601
Rule 4   Form and Contents of Complaint or Indictment; Amendment 601
Rule 5   The Grand Jury 601
Rule 6   Summons to Appear; Arrest Warrant 602
Rule 7   Initial Appearance and Arraignment 603
Rule 8   Assignment of Counsel 605
Rule 9   Joinder of Offenses or Defendants 605
Rule 10   Continuances 606
Rule 11   Pretrial Conference and Pretrial Hearing 606
Rule 12   Pleas and Plea Agreements 608
Rule 13   Pretrial Motions 615
Rule 14   Pretrial Discovery 619
Rule 15   Interlocutory Appeal 626
Rule 16   Dismissal by the Prosecution 628
Rule 17   Summonses for Witnesses 628
Rule 18   Presence of Defendant 630
Rule 19   Trial by Jury or by the Court 630

Rule 20   Trial Jurors 630

Rule 21   Sequestration of Witnesses.. 632

Rule 22   Objections... 633

Rule 23   Stipulations... 633

Rule 24   Opening Statements; Arguments; Instructions to Jury. 634

Rule 25   Motion for Required Finding of Not Guilty 635

Rule 26   Requests for Rulings.. 636

Rule 27   Verdict.. 636

Rule 28   Judgment 637

Rule 29   Revision or Revocation of Sentence.. 637

Rule 30   Post Conviction Relief.. 640

Rule 31   Stay of Execution; Relief Pending Review 641

Rule 32   Filing and Service of Papers.. 642

Rule 33   Counsel for Defendants Indigent and Indigent but Able to Contribute 642

Rule 34   Report 642

Rule 35   Depositions to Perpetuate Testimony 642

Rule 36   Case Management 643

Rule 37   Transfer of Cases... 645

Rule 38   Disability of Judge... 646

Rule 39   Records of Foreign Proceedings and Notice of Foreign Law 646

Rule 40   Proof of Official Records 646

Rule 41   Interpreters and Experts... 647

Rule 42   Clerical Mistakes... 647

Rule 43   Summary Contempt.. 647

Rule 44   Contempt 649

Rule 45   Removal of the Disruptive Defendant 649

Rule 46   Time 649

Rule 47   Special Magistrates.. 649

Rule 48   Sanctions 650

Part 4   Rules of the Superior Court 651

Rule 1   Effect of These Rules 651

Rule 2   Appearances 651

Rule 3   Authority to Appear.. 651

Rule 4   Postponement 651

Rule 5   Jurors 652

Rule 6   Peremptory Challenges of Jurors 652

Rule 7   Openings; Use of Pleadings... 652

Rule 8   Objections to Evidence... 652

Rule 8A   Notes by Jurors 652

Rule 9   Motions and Interlocutory Matters 652

Rules 9A–E   Omitted... 652

Rule 10   Extra Charges by Officers 652

Rule 11   Attorney Not to Become Bail or Surety 652

Rule 12   Attorneys as Witnesses... 653

Rule 13   Hospital Records 653

Rule 14   Exhibits Other than Hospital Records...653
Rule 15   Eliminating Requirement for Verification by Affidavit......................653
Rule 16   Writ of Protection 653
Rule 17   Recording Devices 653
Rules 18–52   Omitted 653
Rule 53   Assignment of Counsel 653
Rule 54   Experts in Criminal Cases 653
Rule 55   Experts in Criminal and Delinquent Children Cases.......................653
Rule 56   Conditions of Probation 654
Rule 57   Term of Probation 654
Rule 58   Term of Orders for Payment 654
Rule 59   Waiver of Indictment 654
Rule 60   Plea of Not Guilty 654
Rule 61   Motions for Return of Property and to Suppress Evidence 654
Rule 61A   Motions for Post-Conviction Relief 654
Rule 62   Withdrawal of Appearance 655
Rule 63   Court Reporter in Grand Jury Proceedings 655
Rule 64   Appellate Division Procedure and Forms 655
Rule 65   Claim of Appeal..655
Rules 66–67   Repealed..655
Rule 68   Arguments...656
Rule 69   Examination of Witnesses...656
Rule 70   Requests for Instructions or Rulings 656
Rule 71   Depositions—Commissions...656
Rule 72   Depositions—Manner of Taking..656
Rules 73–77   Omitted 656
Standing Order 1-15 Participation in Juror Voir Dire by Attorneys and Self-Represented Parties 656
Standing Order 2-15 Exceptions to Notice Requirement of Trial Court Rule VIII, Uniform Rules
                   on Impoundment Procedure (URIP)..658
Standing Order 2-86 (Amended) Criminal Case Management..658
Standing Order 2-86 Criminal Case Management 661

Part 5   **District/Municipal Court Rules of Criminal Procedure 665**

Rule 1   Applicability 665
Rule 2   Issuance of Complaint; Police Statement..665
Rule 3   Arraignment 665
Rule 4   Pretrial Hearing..666
Rule 5   Hearing Date for Discovery Compliance and Jury Waiver Election...................667
Rule 6   Pretrial Motions 667
Rule 7   Trials 667
Rule 8   [Reserved] 667
Rule 9   Sanctions..667
Rule 10   Title..668
Standing Order 1-09 (Amended) For the Sealing of Three or More Dismissals
                   and Non-Conviction Criminal Records..668

Part 6   **Massachusetts Rules of Appellate Procedure** **669**

Rule 1	Scope of Rules: Definitions	669
Rule 2	Suspension of Rules	669
Rule 3	Appeal—How Taken	669
Rule 4	Appeal—When Taken	670
Rule 5	Report of a Case for Determination	671
Rule 6	Stay or Injunction Pending Appeal	671
Rule 7	Disability of a Member of the Lower Court	672
Rule 8	The Record on Appeal	672
Rule 9	Assembly and Transmission of the Record: Exhibits	675
Rule 10	Docketing the Appeal	676
Rule 11	Direct Appellate Review	676
Rule 11.1	Transfer from Supreme Judicial Court	677
Rule 12	Proceedings in Forma Pauperis	677
Rule 13	Filing and Service	677
Rule 14	Computations and Extensions of Time	677
Rule 15	Motions	678
Rule 16	Briefs	678
Rule 17	Briefs of an Amicus Curiae	679
Rule 18	Appendix to the Briefs	679
Rule 19	Filing and Service of Briefs and Motions	681
Rule 20	Form of Briefs, Appendices, and Other Papers	681
Rule 21	Prehearing Conference	682
Rule 22	Oral Argument	682
Rule 23	Issuance of Rescript: Stay of Rescript	683
Rule 24	Justices' Participation	683
Rule 24.1	Divided Vote on Further Appellate Review	683
Rule 25	Damages for Delay	683
Rule 26	Costs	683
Rule 27	Petition for Rehearing	683
Rule 27.1	Further Appellate Review	684
Rule 28	Entry of Judgment Following Rescript	684
Rule 29	Voluntary Dismissal	684
Rule 30	Substitution of Parties	685
Rule 31	Duties of Clerks	685
Rule 32	Title	685

Part 7   **District/Municipal Courts Rules for Probation Violation Proceedings** **687**

Rule 1	Scope and Purpose	687
Rule 2	Definition of Terms	688
Rule 3	Commencement of Violation Proceedings: Charged Criminal Conduct	689
Rule 4	Commencement of Violation Proceedings: Violations Other than a New Criminal Complaint	693
Rule 5	Probation Detention Hearings	694
Rule 6	Conduct of Violation Hearings	697

Rule 7   Hearsay Evidence..701
Rule 8   Finding and Disposition 703
Rule 9   Violation of Conditions of a "Continuance Without a Finding"...................706

Part 8   Issues in Probation and Probation Revocation Hearings 709

I.   Preamble: Guidelines for Probation Violation Proceedings in
            the Superior Court..710
II.   Probation in Massachusetts 713
III.   Probation Conditions...720
IV.   Probation Revocations 731
V.   Conclusion 750

Part 9   Elements and Penalties of Selected Crimes 753

Part 10   Schedule of Assessments for Civil Motor Vehicle Infractions............773

Table of Citable Motor Vehicle Offenses...773
Alphabetical Index of Citable Motor Vehicle Offenses.........................798

Part 11   Alphabetical References to Evidence 803

Part 12   Reference Tables 859

Table of Cases...859
Index 871

ELECTRONIC MATERIALS DOWNLOAD

All of the content of this book is available for download as a PDF file from the MCLE website. **You must be signed into the account used to purchase this book to access the downloadable ebook.**

To download the ebook, go to

www.mcle.org/forms

and enter Forms Download Code (case sensitive):

BdtSnWLG

This code applies only to the 2017 Edition of the *Massachusetts Criminal Law Sourcebook & Citator.* You may download the ebook in PDF format, and may return to the download page anytime while this edition remains in print.

Use Note:
The ebook is an electronic version of the content as it appears in the book—there is no interactive software that deletes information or fills in blank lines in the forms included in the book. For court forms and other standardized forms, be sure to check with the original source to obtain the most recent version and any special instructions.

If you have any questions or problems accessing your ebook download, please contact MCLE's Customer Service at **customerservice@mcle.org** or by phone at 1-800-966-6253.

PART 1

Selected Statutes

Constitution of Massachusetts

Part 1
Art. 12 Regulation of prosecutions; right of trial by jury in criminal cases
Art. 14 Freedom from unreasonable searches and seizures; warrants

PART 1, ARTICLE 12
Regulation of prosecutions; right of trial by jury in criminal cases

No subject shall be held to answer for any crimes or offence, until the same is fully and plainly, substantially and formally, described to him; or be compelled to accuse, or furnish evidence against himself. And every subject shall have a right to produce all proofs, that may be favorable to him; to meet the witnesses against him face to face, and to be fully heard in his defence by himself, or his counsel, at his election. And no subject shall be arrested, imprisoned, despoiled, or deprived of his property, immunities, or privileges, put out of the protection of the law, exiled, or deprived of his life, liberty, or estate, but by the judgment of his peers, or the law of the land. And the legislature shall not make any law that shall subject any person to a capital or infamous punishment, excepting for the government of the army and navy, without trial by jury.

NOTE 1   See Note following G.L. c. 263, § 5.

NOTE 2   See Note 2 following G.L. c. 278, § 16D.

NOTE 3   **Self-incrimination.** "Today we hold that a custodian of corporate records may invoke his art. 12 right against self-incrimination in response to a subpoena for those corporate records when the act of production itself would be self-incriminating." *Commonwealth v. Doe*, 405 Mass. 676, 678 (1989). The SJC also noted that "Article 12 applies only to evidence of a testimonial or communicative nature." *Commonwealth v. Doe*, 405 Mass. at 679. Accordingly, "[n]ontestimonial evidence can be demanded." *Commonwealth v. Doe*, 405 Mass. at 681.

NOTE 4   **Defendant's Failure to Testify.** "The law in this Commonwealth has long been that art. 12 prohibits any comment by the judge which can be fairly understood as permitting the jury

to draw an inference adverse to the defendant from the fact of his failure to testify." *Commonwealth v. Pope*, 406 Mass. 581, 589 (1990) (citations and quotation marks omitted).

NOTE 5   "We therefore conclude that a trial judge has no discretion to permit a witness to appear before a jury for the sole purpose of properly invoking his or her privilege against self-incrimination. Article 12 requires nothing to the contrary. We further conclude that the defendant was not entitled to enter in evidence his subpoena of Marotta, or to ask the jury to consider why Marotta did not testify. Each of these alternatives is merely an indirect attempt to put before the jury information—namely, the fact that Marotta had invoked his Fifth Amendment privilege not to testify—that we have determined may not be put before them directly. The judge committed no error when she ruled against the defendant on each of these three requests." *Commonwealth v. Gagnon*, 408 Mass. 185, 198 (1990) (footnotes and citations omitted).

PART 1, ARTICLE 14
Freedom from unreasonable searches and seizures; warrants

Every subject has a right to be secure from all unreasonable searches, and seizures, of his person, his houses, his papers, and all his possessions. All warrants, therefore, are contrary to this right, if the cause or foundation of them be not previously supported by oath or affirmation; and if the order in the warrant to a civil officer, to make search in suspected places, or to arrest one or more suspected persons, or to seize their property, be not accompanied with a special designation of the persons or objects of search, arrest, or seizure: and no warrant ought to be issued but in cases, and with the formalities prescribed by the laws.

NOTE 1   "From time to time, we have noted that art. 14 might provide greater protection against search and seizure than the Fourth Amendment does." *Commonwealth v. Madera*, 402 Mass. 156, 160 (1988).

NOTE 2   See "Chapter 276. Search and Seizure Special Commentary" & G.L. c. 276, §§ 1–3A.

Chapter 6. Officers of the Commonwealth; Criminal Offender Record Information System Sex Offender Registration Act

Section
178C   Definitions
178D   Sex offender registry
178E   Transmission of registration data to Criminal History Systems Board, police departments, and FBI
178F   Annual verification of registration data; homeless sex offenders; juveniles; disclosure of information
178F½   Registration by personal appearance; level 2 or level 3 sex offenders
178F¾   Global positioning system device to be worn by homeless sex offender
178G   Termination of obligation to register

178H   Failure to register, verify registration information or provide change of address notice; providing false information; penalties
178I   Report identifying sex offender; request for information; confidentiality
178J   Request for sex offender information; notice of penalty for misuse; data required to receive report
178K   Sex offender registry board; member qualifications; guidelines to assess risk of re-offense; notification
178L   Classification of sex offenders by board; hearings; right to counsel
178M   Judicial review of board's final classification and registration requirements; confidential proceedings and records
178N   Misuse of information; penalties

178O   Liability of police officials and public employees for sex
        offender registry information
178P   Failure to comply with registration requirements; right to arrest
178Q   Sex offender registry fee

SECTION 178C
Definitions
(Amended by 2011 Mass. Acts c. 178, §§ 1–3, effective Nov. 21, 2011.)

As used in sections 178C to 178P, inclusive, the following words shall have the following meanings:

"Agency", an agency, department, board, commission or entity within the executive or judicial branch, excluding the committee for public counsel services, which has custody of, supervision of or responsibility for a sex offender as defined in accordance with this chapter, including an individual participating in a program of any such agency, whether such program is conducted under a contract with a private entity or otherwise. Each agency shall be responsible for the identification of such individuals within its custody, supervision or responsibility. Notwithstanding any general or special law to the contrary, each such agency shall be certified to receive criminal offender record information maintained by the department for the purpose of identifying such individuals.

"Employment", includes employment that is full-time or part-time for a period of time exceeding fourteen days or for an aggregate period of time exceeding thirty days during any calendar year, whether compensated or uncompensated.

"Institution of higher learning", a post secondary institution.

"Mental abnormality", a congenital or acquired condition of a person that affects the emotional or volitional capacity of such person in a manner that predisposes that person to the commission of criminal sexual acts to a degree that makes such person a menace to the health and safety of other persons.

"Predatory", an act directed at a stranger or person with whom a relationship has been established, promoted or utilized for the primary purpose of victimization.

"Secondary addresses," the addresses of all places where a sex offender lives, abides, lodges, or resides for a period of 14 or more days in the aggregate during any calendar year and which is not a sex offender's primary address; or a place where a sex offender routinely lives, abides, lodges, or resides for a period of 4 or more consecutive or nonconsecutive days in any month and which is not a sex offender's permanent address, including any out-of-state address.

"Sentencing court", the court that sentenced a sex offender for the most recent sexually violent offense or sex offense or the superior court if such sentencing occurred in another jurisdiction or the sex offender registry board to the extent permitted by federal law and established by the board's regulations.

"Sex offender", a person who resides, has secondary addresses, works, or attends an institution of higher learning in the commonwealth and who has been convicted of a sex offense or who has been adjudicated as a youthful offender or as a delinquent juvenile by reason of a sex offense or a person released from incarceration or parole or probation supervision or custody with the department of youth services for such a conviction or adjudication or a person who has been adjudicated a sexually dangerous person under section 14 of chapter 123A, as in force at the time of adjudication, or a person released from civil commitment pursuant to section 9 of said chapter 123A, whichever last occurs, on or after August 1, 1981.

"Sex offender registry", the collected information and data that is received by the department pursuant to sections 178C to 178P, inclusive, as such information and data is modified or amended by the sex offender registry board or a court of competent jurisdiction pursuant to said sections 178C to 178P, inclusive.

"Sex offense", an indecent assault and battery on a child under 14 under section 13B of chapter 265; aggravated indecent assault and battery on a child under the age of 14 under section 13B½ of said chapter 265; a repeat offense under section 13B¾ of said chapter 265; indecent assault and battery on a mentally retarded person under section 13F of said chapter 265; indecent assault and battery on a person age 14 or over under section 13H of said chapter 265; rape under section 22 of said chapter 265; rape of a child under 16 with force under section 22A of said chapter 265; aggravated rape of a child under 16 with force under section 22B of said chapter 265; a repeat offense under section 22C of said chapter 265; rape and abuse of a child under section 23 of said chapter 265; aggravated rape and abuse of a child under section 23A of said chapter 265; a repeat offense under section 23B of said chapter 265; assault with intent to commit rape under section 24 of said chapter 265; assault of a child with intent to commit rape under section 24B of said chapter 265; kidnapping of a child under section 26 of said chapter 265; enticing a child under the age of 16 for the purposes of committing a crime under section 26C of said chapter 265; enticing a child under 18 via electronic communication to engage in prostitution, human trafficking or commercial sexual activity under section 26D of said chapter 265; trafficking of persons for sexual servitude under section 50 of said chapter 265; a second or subsequent violation of human trafficking for sexual servitude under section 52 of chapter 265; enticing a child under the age of 16 for the purposes of committing a crime under section 26C of said chapter 265; enticing away a person for prostitution or sexual intercourse under section 2 of chapter 272; drugging persons for sexual intercourse under section 3 of said chapter 272; inducing a minor into prostitution under section 4A of said chapter 272; living off or sharing earnings of a minor prostitute under section 4B of said chapter 272; second and subsequent adjudication or conviction for open and gross lewdness and lascivious behavior under section 16 of said chapter 272, but excluding a first or single adjudication as a delinquent juvenile before August 1, 1992; incestuous marriage or intercourse under section 17 of said chapter 272; disseminating to a minor matter harmful to a minor under section 28 of said chapter 272; posing or exhibiting a child in a state of nudity under section 29A of said chapter 272; dissemination of visual material of a child in a state of nudity or sexual conduct under section 29B of said chapter 272; possession of child pornography under section 29C of said chapter 272; unnatural and lascivious acts with a child under 16 under section 35A of said chapter 272; aggravated rape under section 39 of chapter 277; and any attempt to commit a violation of any of the aforementioned sections pursuant to section 6 of chapter 274 or a like violation of the laws of another state, the United States or a military, territorial or Indian tribal authority.

"Sex offense involving a child", an indecent assault and battery on a child under 14 under section 13B of chapter 265; aggravated indecent assault and battery on a child under the age of 14 under section 13B½ of said chapter 265; a repeat offense under section 13B¾ of said chapter 265; rape of a child under 16 with force under section 22A of said chapter 265; aggravated rape of a child under 16 with force under section 22B of said chapter 265; a repeat offense under section 22C of said chapter 265; rape and abuse of a child under section 23 of said chapter 265; aggravated rape and abuse of a child under section 23A of said chapter 265; a repeat offense under section 23B of said chapter 265; assault of a child with intent to commit rape under section 24B of said chapter 265; kidnapping of a child under the age of 16 under section 26 of said chapter 265; enticing a child under 18 via electronic communication to engage in prostitution, human trafficking or commercial sexual activity under section 26D of said chapter 265; trafficking of persons for sexual servitude upon a person under 18 years of age under subsection (b) of section 50 of said chapter 265; enticing a child under the age of 16 for the purposes of committing a crime under section 26C of said chapter 265; inducing a minor into prostitution under section 4A of chapter 272; living off or sharing earnings of a minor prostitute under section 4B of said chapter 272; disseminating to a minor matter harmful to a minor under section 28 of said chapter 272; posing or exhibiting a child in a state of nudity under section 29A of said chapter 272; dissemination of visual material of a child in a state of nudity or sexual conduct under section 29B of said chapter 272; unnatural and lascivious acts with a child under 16 under section 35A of said chapter 272; aggravated rape under section 39 of chapter 277; and any attempt to commit a violation of any of the aforementioned sections pursuant to section 6 of chapter 274 or a like violation of the laws of another state, the United States or a military, territorial or Indian tribal authority.

"Sexually violent offense", indecent assault and battery on a child under 14 under section 13B of chapter 265; aggravated indecent assault and battery on a child under the age of 14 under section 13B½ of said chapter 265; a repeat offense under section 13B¾ of said chapter 265; indecent assault and battery on a mentally retarded person under section 13F of said chapter 265; rape under section 22 of said chapter 265; rape of a child under 16 with force under section 22A of said chapter 265; aggravated rape of a child under 16 with force under section 22B of said chapter 265; a repeat offense under section 22C of said chapter 265; assault with intent to commit rape under section 24 of said chapter 265; assault of a child with intent to commit rape under section 24B of said chapter 265; enticing a child under 18 via electronic communication to engage in prostitution, human trafficking or commercial sex activity under section 26D of said chapter 265; trafficking of persons for sexual servitude under section 50 of chapter 265; a second or subsequent violation of human trafficking for sexual servitude under section 52 of chapter 265; drugging persons for sexual intercourse under section 3 of chapter 272; unnatural and lascivious acts with a child under 16 under section 35A of said chapter 272; aggravated rape under section 39 of chapter 277; and any attempt to commit a violation of any of the aforementioned sections pursuant to section 6 of chapter 274 or a like violation of the law of another state, the United States or a military, territorial or Indian tribal authority, or any other offense that the sex offender registry board determines to be a sexually violent offense pursuant to the Jacob Wetterling Crimes Against Children and Sexually Violent Offender Registration Act, 42 U.S.C. section 14071.

"Sexually violent predator", a person who has been convicted of a sexually violent offense or who has been adjudicated as a youthful offender or as a delinquent juvenile by reason of a sexually violent offense, or a person released from incarceration, parole, probation supervision or commitment under chapter 123A or custody with the department of youth services for such a conviction or adjudication, whichever last occurs, on or after August 1, 1981, and who suffers from a mental abnormality or personality disorder that makes such person likely to engage in predatory sexually violent offenses.

NOTE 1   Facial Constitutionality. When asked by the Legislature to conduct a facial review of the then proposed Sex Offender Registry bill, the Supreme Judicial Court, answering four (4) specific questions, held as follows:

(1) The community notification provisions of the bill did not "violate the prohibitions against ex post facto laws under Clause 1 of Section 10 of Article I of the United States Constitution and Article XXIV of the Massachusetts Constitution as applied to a person adjudicated or convicted of a sex offense committed prior to the effective date of th[e] proposed act";

(2) The community notification provisions of the bill did not "violate the due process rights guaranteed by the Fifth and Fourteenth Amendments of the United States Constitution and Article 1 of the Massachusetts Constitution of a person who was convicted or adjudicated of committing a sex offense either before or after the effective date of [the bill] or violate the terms of a plea agreement of a person sentenced for a sex offense after the enactment of the [the bill]";

(3) The provisions of the bill did not "unconstitutionally violate the Fourteenth Amendment of the United States Constitution or Article I of the Massachusetts Constitution which guarantee equal protection under the law or violate the protections granted by the Fourteenth Amendment of the United States Constitution against invasion of privacy"; and

(4) The provisions of the bill did not "violate the Eighth Amendment of the United States Constitution prohibiting cruel and unusual punishment or violate double jeopardy principles protected under the Fifth Amendment of the United States Constitution."
Opinion of the Justices, 423 Mass. 1201, 1224–42 (1996).

NOTE 2   Homeless Sex Offenders. "The statute does not define the term 'home address.' . . . We conclude that the term 'home address' in the statute refers to an offender's primary place of residence. . . . [Nonetheless,] a violation of the statutory obligation to register can also arise from a defendant's failure to report any secondary addresses, or changes thereto." *Commonwealth v. Bolling*, 72 Mass. App. Ct. 618, 623–25 (2008).

SECTION 178D
Sex offender registry
(Amended by 2013 Mass. Acts c. 38, § 7, effective July 1, 2013.)

The sex offender registry board, known as the board, in cooperation with the department, shall establish and maintain a central computerized registry of all sex offenders required to register pursuant to sections 178C to 178P, inclusive, known as the sex offender registry. The sex offender registry shall be updated based on information made available to the board, including information acquired pursuant to the registration provisions of said sections 178C to 178P, inclusive. The file on each sex offender required to register pursuant to said sections 178C to 178P, inclusive, shall include the following information, hereinafter referred to as registration data:

(a) the sex offender's name, aliases used, date and place of birth, sex, race, height, weight, eye and hair color, social security number, home address, any secondary address and work address and, if the sex offender works at or attends an institution of higher learning, the name and address of the institution;

1

(b) a photograph and set of fingerprints;

(c) a description of the offense for which the sex offender was convicted or adjudicated, the city or town where the offense occurred, the date of conviction or adjudication and the sentence imposed;

(d) any other information which may be useful in assessing the risk of the sex offender to reoffend; and

(e) any other information which may be useful in identifying the sex offender.

Notwithstanding sections 178C to 178P, inclusive, or any other general or special law to the contrary and in addition to any responsibility otherwise imposed upon the board, the board shall make the sex offender information contained in the sex offender registry, delineated below in subsections (i) to (viii), inclusive, available for inspection by the general public in the form of a comprehensive database published on the internet, known as the "sex offender internet database"; provided, however, that no registration data relating to a sex offender given a level 1 designation by the board under section 178K shall be published in the sex offender internet database but may be disseminated by the board as otherwise permitted by said sections 178C to 178P, inclusive; and provided further, that the board shall keep confidential and shall not publish in the sex offender internet database any information relating to requests for registration data under sections 178I and 178J:

(i) the name of the sex offender;

(ii) the offender's home address and any secondary addresses;

(iii) the offender's work address;

(iv) the offense for which the offender was convicted or adjudicated and the date of the conviction or adjudication;

(v) the sex offender's age, sex, race, height, weight, eye and hair color;

(vi) a photograph of the sex offender, if available;

(vii) whether the sex offender has been designated a sexually violent predator; and

(viii) whether the offender is in compliance with the registration obligations of sections 178C to 178P, inclusive.

All information provided to the general public through the sex offender internet database shall include a warning regarding the criminal penalties for use of sex offender registry information to commit a crime or to engage in illegal discrimination or harassment of an offender and the punishment for threatening to commit a crime under section 4 of chapter 275. The sex offender internet database shall be updated regularly, based on information available to the board and shall be open to searches by the public at any time without charge or subscription. The board shall promulgate rules and regulations to implement, update and maintain such a sex offender internet database, to ensure the accuracy, integrity and security of information contained therein, to ensure the prompt and complete removal of registration data for persons whose duty to register has terminated or expired under section 178G, 178L or 178M or any other law and to protect against the inaccurate, improper or inadvertent publication of registration data on the internet.

The board shall develop standardized registration and verification forms, which shall include registration data as required pursuant to sections 178C to 178P. The board shall make blank copies of such forms available to all agencies having custody of sex offenders and all city and town police departments; provided, however, that the board shall determine the format for the collection and dissemination of registration data, which may include the electronic transmission of data. Records maintained in the sex offender registry shall be open to any law enforcement agency in the commonwealth, the United States or any other state. The board shall promulgate rules and regulations to implement the provisions of sections 178C to 178P, inclusive. Such rules and regulations shall include provisions which may permit police departments located in a city or town that is divided into more than one zip code to disseminate information pursuant to the provisions of section 178J categorized by zip code and to disseminate such information limited to one or more zip codes if the request for such dissemination is so qualified; provided, however, that for the city of Boston dissemination of information may be limited to one or more police districts.

The board may promulgate regulations further defining in a manner consistent with maintaining or establishing eligibility for federal funding pursuant to the Jacob Wetterling Crimes Against Children and Sexually Violent Offender Registration Act, 42 U.S.C. § 14071, the eligibility of sex offenders to be relieved of the obligation to register, including but not limited to, regulations limiting motions under subsection (e) of section 178E, section 178G and relief from registration pursuant to paragraph (d) of subsection (2) of section 178K.

NOTE 1   Sex Offender Registry Board (SORB) Documents—Not Testimonial. "The Supreme Judicial Court has recently stated that a copy of a 'notice of the defendant's license revocation . . . created and kept in the ordinary course' of the registry of motor vehicles' affairs is not testimonial. *[Commonwealth v.] Parenteau*, 460 Mass. 1, 10 (2011). . . . The same is true of the SORB documents at issue here. The documents were not created for the 'purpose of establishing an essential fact at trial.' *See Parenteau*, [460 Mass. at 10.] These records are maintained for administrative purposes, such as keeping an updated registry of biographical data regarding sex offenders, including their names, photographs, fingerprints, and addresses, so that the public may obtain information about dangerous sex offenders who live or work in each community, and so that law enforcement can access and distribute information about sex offenders to prevent further victimization. *See* G.L. c. 6, § 178D. Nor is 'the regularly conducted business activity' of SORB for which these documents were created 'the production of evidence for use at trial.' *Melendez-Diaz [v. Massachusetts*, 129 S. Ct. 2527,] 2538 (2009). . . . The introduction of the SORB records at issue here in the absence of a SORB witness did not violate the Sixth Amendment." *Commonwealth v. Fox*, 81 Mass. App. Ct. 244, 245–46, *rev. denied*, 462 Mass. 1106 (2012).

NOTE 2   Retroactivity. "We declare unconstitutional the retroactive application of the amendments to G.L. c. 6, §§ 178D and 178K, that became effective on July 12, 2013, to the extent they would require the Internet publication of the registry information of individuals who were finally classified as level two sex offenders on or before July 12, 2013." *Moe v. Sex Offender Registry Bd.*, 467 Mass. 598, 616 (2014).

SECTION 178E

Transmission of registration data to Criminal History Systems Board, police departments, and FBI

(a) Within 5 days of receiving upon sentence any sex offender required to register under sections 178C to 178Q, inclusive, the agency which has custody of the sex offender, including the department of correction, the department of youth services and each of the houses of correction, shall transmit to the board said sex offender's registration data, which shall include identifying factors, anticipated future residence, any anticipated secondary addresses, offense history, documentation of any treatment received for a mental abnormality, the official version of any sex offenses, the mittimus, any prior incarceration history, and the projected maximum release date and the earliest possible release date for the sex offender. All custodial agencies shall inform the board immediately of any transfers of sex offenders so that there may be contact with the offender throughout the classification process. The bureau shall classify such a sex offender at least 10 days before the offender's earliest possible release date. The board shall promptly transmit the registration data to the police departments in the municipalities where the sex offender intends to live, maintain any secondary address and work and where the offense was committed and to the Federal Bureau of Investigation. The sex offender shall be informed by, and shall acknowledge in writing to, the agency which has custody of the sex offender of the duty to register in the commonwealth and in any state where he resides, is employed, carries on a vocation or is a student, to verify registration information, to give notice of change of address or intended change of address within the commonwealth or in another state and the penalties for failure to do so and for giving false registration information, and of his right to submit to the board, according to section 178L, documentary evidence relative to his risk of reoffense, the degree of dangerousness posed to the public and of his duty to register under this section. If such sex offender is a juvenile at the time of such notification, notification shall also be mailed to such sex offender's legal guardian or agency having custody of the juvenile in the absence of a legal guardian and his most recent attorney of record. The agency shall transmit such acknowledgment to the board within ten days of receipt of such acknowledgment. Not later than two days before his release from custody, a sex offender shall register by mailing to the board on a form approved by the board and signed under the pains and penalties of perjury, the sex offender's name, date of birth, home address or intended home address, any secondary addresses or intended secondary addresses, work address or intended work address and, if the sex offender is or intends to become a part-time or full-time employee of an institution of higher learning, the name and address of the institution, and, if the sex offender is or intends to become a part-time or full-time student of an institution of higher learning, the name and address of the institution. No sex offender shall be released from custody unless such registration has been filled out, signed, and mailed to the board.

(b) An agency that has supervision of a sex offender required to register pursuant to sections 178C to 178P, inclusive, on probation or parole shall, within five days of assuming supervision of such sex offender, transmit to the board such sex offender's registration data which, for purposes of this paragraph, shall include identifying factors, residential address or anticipated future residence, secondary addresses or anticipated secondary addresses, work address, offense history, documentation of any sex offender treatment, and documentation of any treatment received for a mental abnormality. The agency shall also report any changes of address of any sex offender required to register pursuant to said sections 178E to 178P, inclusive, within its jurisdiction to the board. The board shall promptly transmit the registration data to the police departments in the municipalities where such sex offender intends to live and work and where the offense was

committed and to the Federal Bureau of Investigation. The sex offender shall be informed by, and shall acknowledge in writing to, the agency which has custody of the sex offender of the duty to register in the commonwealth and in any state where he resides, has any secondary addresses, is employed, carries on a vocation, or is a student, to verify registration information and to give notice of change of address, or any secondary addresses or intended change of address within the commonwealth or in another state and the penalties for failure to do so and for giving false registration information, and of his right to submit to the board, according to section 178L, documentary evidence relative to his risk of reoffense, the degree of dangerousness posed to the public and his duty to register under this section. If such sex offender is a juvenile at the time of such notification, notification shall also be mailed to such sex offender's legal guardian or agency having custody of the juvenile in the absence of a legal guardian, and his most recent attorney of record. A sex offender shall, within two days of receiving such notice, register by mailing to the board on a form approved by the board and signed under the pains and penalties of perjury, the sex offender's name, date of birth, home address or intended home address, any secondary addresses or intended secondary addresses, work address or intended work address and, if the sex offender is or intends to become a part-time or full-time employee of an institution of higher learning, the name and address of the institution, and, if the sex offender is or intends to become a part-time or full-time student of an institution of higher learning, the name and address of the institution.

(c) Any court which enters a conviction for a sex offense or adjudication as a youthful offender or as a delinquent juvenile by reason of a sex offense, but does not impose a sentence of confinement of 90 days or more to be served immediately shall inform the sex offender and require the sex offender to acknowledge, in writing, his duty to register in the commonwealth and in any state where he resides, is employed, carries on a vocation, or is a student, to verify registration information and to give notice of change of address or intended change of address within the commonwealth or in another state and the penalties for failure to do so and for giving false registration information, and of his right to submit to the board, according to section 178L, documentary evidence relative to his risk of reoffense, the degree of dangerousness posed to the public and of his duty to register under this section. If such sex offender is a juvenile at the time of such adjudication, the legal guardian or agency having custody of the juvenile and his most recent attorney of record shall also be required to acknowledge, in writing, such information. The court shall cause such sex offender's registration data which, for purposes of this paragraph, shall include identifying factors, anticipated future residence, any anticipated secondary addresses, offense history and documentation of any treatment received for a mental abnormality to be transmitted to the board within five days of sentencing. The board shall promptly transmit the registration data to the police departments in the municipalities where such sex offender intends to live and work and where the offense was committed and to the Federal Bureau of Investigation. A sex offender shall, within two days of receiving such notice or of release from confinement, whichever is later, register by mailing to the board on a form approved by the board and signed under the pains and penalties of perjury, the sex offender's name,

1

date of birth, home address or intended home address, any secondary addresses or intended secondary addresses, work address or intended work address and, if the sex offender is or intends to become a part-time or full-time employee of an institution of higher learning, the name and address of the institution, and, if the sex offender is or intends to become a part-time or full-time student of an institution of higher learning, the name and address of the institution.

(d) Any court which accepts a plea for a sex offense shall inform the sex offender prior to acceptance and require the sex offender to acknowledge, in writing, that such plea may result in such sex offender being subject to the provisions of sections 178C to 178P, inclusive. Failure to so inform the sex offender shall not be grounds to vacate or invalidate the plea.

(e) Upon written motion of the commonwealth, a court which enters a conviction or adjudication of delinquent or as a youthful offender may, at the time of sentencing, having determined that the circumstances of the offense in conjunction with the offender's criminal history does not indicate a risk of reoffense or a danger to the public, find that a sex offender shall not be required to register under sections 178C to 178P, inclusive. Such motion by the commonwealth shall state the reasons for such motion with specificity. The court may not make such a finding if the sex offender has been determined to be a sexually violent predator; has been convicted of two or more sex offenses defined as sex offenses pursuant to the Jacob Wetterling Crimes Against Children and Sexually Violent Offender Registration Act, 42 U.S.C. section 14071, committed on different occasions; has been convicted of a sex offense involving a child or a sexually violent offense; or if the sex offender is otherwise subject to minimum or lifetime registration requirements as determined by the board pursuant to section 178D.

(f) In the case of a sex offender who has been convicted of a sex offense or adjudicated as a youthful offender or as a delinquent juvenile by reason of a sex offense, on or after December 12, 1999, and who has not been sentenced to immediate confinement, the court shall, within 14 days of sentencing, determine whether the circumstances of the offense in conjunction with the offender's criminal history indicate that the sex offender does not pose a risk of reoffense or a danger to the public. If the court so determines, the court shall relieve such sex offender of the obligation to register under sections 178C to 178P, inclusive. The court may not make such a determination or finding if the sex offender has been determined to be a sexually violent predator; has been convicted of two or more sex offenses defined as sex offenses pursuant to the Jacob Wetterling Crimes Against Children and Sexually Violent Offender Registration Act, 42 U.S.C. section 14071, committed on different occasions; has been convicted of a sex offense involving a child or a sexually violent offense; or if the sex offender is otherwise subject to minimum or lifetime registration requirements as determined by the board pursuant to section 178D.

(g) A sex offender who moves into the commonwealth from another jurisdiction shall, within two days of moving into the commonwealth, register by mailing to the board on a form approved by the board and signed under the pains and penalties of perjury, the sex offender's name, date of birth, home address or intended home address, any secondary addresses or intended secondary addresses, work address or intended work address and, if the sex offender is or intends to

become a part-time or full-time employee of an institution of higher learning, the name and address of the institution, and, if the sex offender is or intends to become a part-time or full-time student of an institution of higher learning, the name and address of the institution. The board shall transmit the registration data to the police department in the municipality where such sex offender intends to live and work and, if the sex offender intends to work at or become a student at an institution of higher learning, to the police departments in the municipalities where the sex offender will work or attend such institution and shall transmit the same to the Federal Bureau of Investigation.

(h) A sex offender required to register pursuant to sections 178C to 178P, inclusive, who intends to move to a different city or town within the commonwealth shall, not later than ten days prior to establishing such new residence, register by mailing to the board on a form approved by the board and signed under the pains and penalties of perjury, the sex offender's name, date of birth, home address or intended home address, any secondary addresses or intended secondary addresses, work address or intended work address and, if the sex offender is or intends to become a part-time or full-time employee of an institution of higher learning, the name and address of the institution, and, if the sex offender is or intends to become a part-time or full-time student of an institution of higher learning, the name and address of the institution. The board shall transmit notice of such change of address to all the police departments in the municipalities where the offense was committed, where the sex offender last registered and where the sex offender intends to live or attend an institution of higher learning and shall transmit the same to the Federal Bureau of Investigation. A sex offender required to register pursuant to said sections 178C to 178P, inclusive, who intends to change his address within a city or town shall notify the board in writing not later than ten days prior to establishing such new residence. The board shall transmit notice of the change of address to the police departments within such city or town, in the municipality where the offense was committed and to the Federal Bureau of Investigation.

(i) A sex offender required to register pursuant to sections 178C to 178P, inclusive, who intends to move out of the commonwealth shall notify the board not later than ten days before leaving the commonwealth. The board shall transmit notice of the change of address to the police departments in the municipalities where such sex offender last registered, where the offense was committed and to the Federal Bureau of Investigation. The board shall notify such sex offender of the duty to register in the new jurisdiction and shall forward a copy of his registration data to the appropriate law enforcement agency in such new jurisdiction.

(j) A sex offender required to register pursuant to sections 178C to 178P, inclusive, who intends to change his work address shall notify the board in writing not later than ten days prior to establishing the new work address. The board shall transmit notice of the change of address and, if the sex offender is or intends to become employed part-time or full-time at an institution of higher learning, the name and address of the institution to the police department in the municipalities where such sex offender previously worked, where such sex offender intends to work, where such sex offender resides or intends to reside, and where the offense was committed. The board shall transmit notice of the change of address to the Federal Bureau of Investigation.

(k) The registrar of motor vehicles shall inform a person applying for or renewing a license to operate a motor vehicle that he has a duty to register with the board if such person is a sex offender, pursuant to regulations established by the board.

(l) Except as hereinbefore provided, a sex offender residing or working in the commonwealth or working at or attending an institution of higher learning in the commonwealth shall, within ten days of the effective date of this section, register by mailing to the board on a form approved by the board and signed under the pains and penalties of perjury, the sex offender's name, date of birth, home address or intended home address, any secondary addresses or intended secondary addresses, work address or intended work address and, if the sex offender is or intends to become a part-time or full-time employee of an institution of higher learning, the name and address of the institution, and, if the sex offender is or intends to become a part-time or full-time student of an institution of higher learning, the name and address of the institution. The board shall promptly transmit the registration data to the police departments where the sex offender intends to live and work, where the offense was committed and, if the sex offender intends to work at or become a student at an institution of higher learning, to the police departments in the municipalities where the sex offender will work or attend such institution and to the Federal Bureau of Investigation. The board shall send written notification of the requirements of sections 178C to 178P, inclusive, to the last known address of all sex offenders residing in the commonwealth who, prior to the effective date of this section, have been released from all custody and supervision. If any such sex offender is a juvenile at the time of such notification, notification shall also be mailed to such sex offender's legal guardian or the agency having custody of the juvenile in the absence of a legal guardian and his most recent attorney of record.

(m) Upon registering, verifying registration information, or giving notice of change of address or intended change of address under this section, a sex offender shall provide independent written verification of the address at which he is registered or, if changing address, will be registered.

(n) Registration data received by the board and disseminated to law enforcement pursuant to this section shall not be disseminated to the public except in accordance with sections 178D, 178I, 178J, and 178K.

(o) A sex offender who plans to work at or attend an institution of higher learning part-time or full-time in the commonwealth shall, within 10 days prior to commencing employment or enrollment in classes at an institution of higher learning, register by mailing to the board on a form approved by the board and signed under the pains and penalties of perjury, the sex offender's name, date of birth, home address or intended home address, any secondary addresses or intended secondary addresses, work address or intended work address, and the name and address of the institution of higher learning. The board shall transmit notice of such change of address to all police departments in the municipalities where the sex offender plans to work or attend an institution of higher learning and shall transmit the same to the Federal Bureau of Investigation.

(p) A sex offender required to register pursuant to section 178C to 178P, inclusive, who intends to transfer from the institution of higher learning he is attending or stop attending shall notify the board in writing not later than 10 days before leaving the present institution of higher learning and shall provide the board with the name and address of the new institution of higher learning, if applicable. The board shall transmit notice of any such change of address to all police departments in the municipalities where the sex offender previously attended an institution of higher learning and, if applicable, to the police department in the municipality where the sex offender plans to attend an institution of higher learning. The board shall transmit notice of any change of address for the institution of higher learning to the Federal Bureau of Investigation.

(q) Any nonresident person enrolled on a full-time or part-time basis, in any public or private education institution in the commonwealth, including any secondary school, trade or professional institution, shall register with the board if such person is required to register as a sex offender in the state in which he resides. Such student shall, within 10 days of attending such institution, register by mailing to the board on a form approved by the board and signed under the pains and penalties of perjury, the student's name, date of birth, home address, any secondary addresses, and the name and address of the educational institution he is attending.

NOTE 1   No State Due Process Violation in Requirement that Sex Offender Provide Information to SORB Prior to Individualized Hearing and SORB's Transmission of that Data to Law Enforcement Authorities. "We conclude that persons convicted of a sex offense may be required to provide the sex offender registry board (board) with their names and addresses prior to conducting individualized hearings, and that the board may transmit registration data to law enforcement authorities, as these two initial steps of the 1999 statute do not offend the due process requirements of art. 12 of the Massachusetts Declaration of Rights." *Roe v. Attorney General*, 434 Mass. 418, 419–20 (2001).

NOTE 2   Burden of Proof. "[T]he language of G.L. 6, § 178E(f), suggests that the burden of proof should rest on the sex offender: '[T]he court shall . . . determine whether the circumstances of the offense in conjunction with the offender's criminal history indicate that the sex offender does not pose a risk.'" *Commonwealth v. Ronald R.*, 450 Mass. 262, 269 (2007).

NOTE 3   Notice of Registration Requirement at Time of Plea Not Required. The defendants both pled delinquent to, among other charges, indecent assault and battery on a child under 14, G.L. c. 265, § 13B. While the defendants were on probation, the Legislature passed the Sex Offender Registry Act, which required them to register. The defendants sought to withdraw their pleas as constitutionally defective. The court ruled against the defendants, holding that a plea is not defective even if a defendant is not told of its contingent or collateral consequences. *Commonwealth v. Albert A.*, 49 Mass. App. Ct. 269 (2000).

NOTE 4   Registration Requirement Upon Revocation of Probation. "The defendant is a sex offender who, after pleading guilty to one indictment charging possession of child pornography, was placed on probation by a judge in the Superior Court and relieved of his obligation to register as a sex offender with the Sex Offender Registry Board (SORB), pursuant to G.L. c. 6, § 178E(f). The question in this case is whether a second judge, after finding the defendant in violation of his probation, may on that basis and consistent with the Sex Offender Registry Act, G.L. c. 6, §§ 178C–178Q (act), order him to register with SORB. We hold that she may not." *Commonwealth v. Ventura*, 465 Mass. 202, 202–03 (2013).

1

SECTION 178F
Annual verification of registration data; homeless sex offenders; juveniles; disclosure of information

Except as provided in section 178F½ for a sex offender finally classified by the board as a level 2 or a level 3 sex offender, a sex offender required to register pursuant to sections 178C to 178P, inclusive, shall annually verify that the registration data on file with the board remains true and accurate by mailing to the board on a form approved by the board and signed under the pains and penalties of perjury, the sex offender's name, date of birth, home address or intended home address, any secondary addresses or intended secondary addresses, work address or intended work address and, if the sex offender is or intends to become a part-time or full-time employee of an institution of higher learning, the name and address of said institution and, if the sex offender is a part-time or full-time student at an institution of higher learning or intends to become a part-time or full-time student of an institution of higher learning, the name and address of said institution of higher learning. A homeless sex offender shall verify registration data every 30 days with the board by mailing to the board on a form approved by the board and signed under the pains and penalties of perjury the sex offender's name, date of birth, home address, any secondary addresses, and work address. A homeless shelter receiving state funding shall cooperate in providing information in the possession of or known to such shelter, when a request for information is made to such shelter by the board; provided, however, that such request for information shall be limited to that which is necessary to verify an offender's registration data or a sex offender's whereabouts. A shelter that violates the provisions of this paragraph shall be punished by a fine of $100 a day for each day that such shelter continues to violate the provisions of this paragraph. In addition, in each subsequent year during the month of birth of any sex offender required to register, the board shall mail a nonforwardable verification form to the last reported address of such sex offender. If such sex offender is a juvenile at the time of such notification, notification shall also be mailed to such sex offender's legal guardian or the agency having custody of the juvenile in the absence of a legal guardian and his most recent attorney of record. Such sex offender shall, within five days of receipt, sign the verification form under the penalties of perjury and mail it back to the board. The board shall periodically, and at least annually, send written notice to a city or town police department regarding any sex offender required to register whose last known address was in such city or town or who gave notice of his intent to move to or is otherwise believed to live or work or attend an institution of higher learning in such city or town, but who has failed to register or verify registration information as required.

The board shall examine through electronic transfer of information the tax returns, wage reports, child support enforcement records, papers, or other documents on file with the commissioner of revenue or any other entity within the executive branch when there is reason to believe a sex offender required to register has not so registered in accordance with this chapter or where the address of such sex offender cannot be verified through other means; provided, however, that nothing herein shall be construed to authorize the disclosure, directly or indirectly, of any information other than the address of such sex offender.

See Note 4 following Section 178E, above.

SECTION 178F½
Registration by personal appearance; level 2 or level 3 sex offender
(Amended by 2013 Mass. Acts c. 63, effective Aug. 7, 2013.)

An incarcerated sex offender finally classified by the board as a level 2 or level 3 sex offender who is required to register under sections 178C to 178P, inclusive, shall appear in person within 2 days of release from the custody of an agency, including the department of correction, the department of youth services or any of the houses of correction, at the local police department in the city or town in which the sex offender lives, or if the sex offender does not reside in the commonwealth, in the city or town in the commonwealth in which the sex offender has a secondary address, works or attends an institution of higher learning, to register; but no such obligation to register in person shall arise where the pertinent address is the same as that provided to the board by the offender before his release under subsection (a) of section 178E. The sex offender shall be informed by, and shall acknowledge in writing to, the agency that has custody of the sex offender of the duty to comply with this section. A sex offender who is finally classified by the board as a level 2 or level 3 offender and who is required to register under said sections 178C to 178P, inclusive, shall appear in person annually at the local police department in the city or town in which the sex offender lives or, if the sex offender does not reside in the commonwealth, in the city or town in the commonwealth in which the sex offender has a secondary address, works or attends an institution of higher learning, to verify that the registration data on file remains true and accurate. At such time, the sex offender's photograph and fingerprints shall be updated. Such sex offender who has been determined to be a sexually violent predator under paragraph (c) of subsection (2) of section 178K shall also appear in person at such police department every 45 days to verify, under the pains and penalties of perjury, that the registration data on file remains true and accurate. A homeless sex offender shall appear in person at such police department every 30 days to verify, under the pains and penalties of perjury, that the registration data on file remains true and accurate. A homeless shelter receiving state funding shall cooperate in providing information in the possession of or known to such shelter, when a request for information is made to such shelter by the board or such local police department; provided, however, that such request for information shall be limited to that which is necessary to verify an offender's registration data or a sex offender's whereabouts. A shelter that violates the provisions of this paragraph shall be punished by a fine of $100 a day for each day that such shelter continues to violate the provisions of this paragraph. In addition, in each subsequent year during the month of birth of any sex offender required to register, the board shall mail a nonforwardable verification form to the last reported address of such sex offender. If such sex offender is a juvenile at the time of such notification, notification shall also be mailed to such sex offender's legal guardian or the agency having custody of the juvenile in the absence of a legal guardian and his most recent attorney of record. Such sex offender shall, within five days of receipt, sign the verification form under the penalties of perjury and register in person at the police department in the municipality in which such sex offender lives, or if such sex offender does not reside in the commonwealth, in the city or town in which such sex offender has a secondary address, works, or attends an institution of higher learning. The board shall periodically, and at least annually, send written notice to a city or town police department regarding any sex offender required to register whose last known address was in such city or town or who gave notice of his intent to move to or is otherwise believed to live or work in such city or town, but who has failed to register or verify registration information as required. A sex offender finally classified as a level 2 or level 3 offender shall also comply with the provisions of paragraphs (g) to (j), inclusive, of section 178E, but the offender shall give the required notice in person at the police department in the city or town where such sex offender resides, or if such sex offender does not reside in the commonwealth, in the city or town in which such sex offender has a secondary address, works or attends an institution of higher learning.

The board shall examine through electronic transfer of information the tax returns, wage reports, child support enforcement records, papers, or other documents on file with the commissioner of revenue or any other entity within the executive branch when there is reason to believe a sex offender required to register has not so registered in accordance with this chapter or where the address of such sex offender cannot be verified through other means; provided, however, that nothing herein shall be construed to authorize the disclosure, directly or indirectly, of any information other than the address of such sex offender, except as otherwise provided by sections 178C to 178P, inclusive.

SECTION 178F¾
Global positioning system device to be worn by homeless sex offender

A homeless sex offender shall wear a global positioning system device, or any comparable device, administered by the commissioner of probation.

SECTION 178G
Termination of obligation to register

The duty of a sex offender required to register pursuant to this chapter and to comply with the requirements hereof shall, unless sooner terminated by the board under section 178L, end 20 years after such sex offender has been convicted or adjudicated or has been released from all custody or supervision, whichever last occurs, unless such sex offender was convicted of two or more sex offenses defined as sex offenses pursuant to the Jacob Wetterling Crimes Against Children and Sexually Violent Offender Registration Act, 42 U.S.C. § 14071, committed on different occasions, has been convicted of a sexually violent offense; has been determined by the sentencing court to be a sexually violent predator, or if such sex offender is otherwise subject to lifetime registration requirements as determined by the board pursuant to section 178D, in which cases the duty to register shall never be terminated. A person required to register with the sex offender registry board may make an application to said board to terminate the obligation upon proof, by clear and convincing evidence, that the person has not committed a sex offense within ten years following conviction, adjudication or release from all custody or supervision, whichever is later, and is not likely to pose a danger to the safety of others. For so long as

such sex offender is under a duty to register in the commonwealth or in any other state where the offender resides or would be under such a duty if residing in the commonwealth, such sex offender shall not be entitled to relief under the provisions of section 100A or 100B of chapter 276.

SECTION 178H
Failure to register, verify registration information or provide change of address notice; providing false information; penalties

(a) A sex offender required to register pursuant to this chapter who knowingly: (i) fails to register; (ii) fails to verify registration information; (iii) fails to provide notice of a change of address; or (iv) who knowingly provides false information shall be punished in accordance with this section.

(1) A first conviction under this subsection shall be punished by imprisonment for not less than six months and not more than two and one-half years in a house of correction nor more than five years in a state prison or by a fine of not more than $1,000 or by both such fine and imprisonment.

A person convicted under this paragraph, who has been adjudicated or convicted of any of the offenses set forth in sections 13B, 13B½, 13B¾, 13F, 22A, 22B, 22C, 23, 23A, 23B, 24B, and 26 of chapter 265 or for conspiracy to commit any of these offenses, or as an accessory thereto, or a like violation of the laws of another state, the United States or a military, territorial or Indian tribal authority shall, in addition to the term of imprisonment authorized by this section, be punished by a term of community parole supervision for life, to be served under the jurisdiction of the parole board, as set forth in section 133D of said chapter 127. The sentence of community parole supervision for life shall commence immediately upon the expiration of the term of imprisonment imposed upon such person by the court or upon such person's release from probation or parole supervision or upon the expiration of a continuance without a finding or upon discharge from commitment to the treatment center pursuant to section 9 of chapter 123A, whichever first occurs.

(2) A second and subsequent conviction under this subsection shall be punished by imprisonment in the state prison for not less than five years.

Any person convicted under this paragraph who is a level 2 or level 3 offender shall, in addition to the term of imprisonment authorized by this paragraph, be punished by a term of community parole supervision for life, to be served under the jurisdiction of the parole board, as set forth in said section 133D of said chapter 127. The sentence of community parole supervision for life shall commence immediately upon the expiration of the term of imprisonment imposed upon such person by the court or upon such person's release from probation or parole supervision or upon the expiration of a continuance without a finding or upon discharge from commitment to the treatment center pursuant to section 9 of chapter 123A, whichever first occurs.

(3) Any person convicted under this subsection who is a level 2 or level 3 sex offender shall, in addition to the term of imprisonment authorized by this subsection, be subject to community parole supervision for life, to be served under the jurisdiction of the parole board, as set forth in section 133D of chapter 127. The sentence of community parole supervision for life shall commence immediately upon the expiration of the term of imprisonment imposed upon such person by the

court or upon such person's release from any post-release supervision or upon the expiration of a continuance without a finding or upon discharge from commitment to the treatment center under section 9 of chapter 123A, whichever first occurs.

(b) Violations of this section may be prosecuted and punished in any county where the offender knowingly (i) fails to register; (ii) fails to verify registration information; (iii) fails to provide notice of a change of address; or (iv) knowingly provides false information.

NOTE 1   Registration Requirement. "[T]he judge who accepted the plea reported . . . two questions of law concerning the regulation: '1. If an individual is classified as a level 2 or 3 sex offender pursuant to [G.L. c. 6, §§ 178C–178P], and incarcerated in the Commonwealth of Massachusetts, must that individual report in person with the police department in the city or town where he plans to reside within two days of release from incarceration? '2. Does failure to comply with 803 [Code Mass. Regs. §] 1.04(7)(b) as promulgated by the Sex Offender Registry Board, pursuant to G.L. c. 6, § 178D, constitute a violation of G.L. c. 6, § 178[H]?' . . .

"The regulation at issue imposes an additional registration obligation but provides no information or security that the statute, standing alone, does not provide. Because it does not implement the statutory registration requirements but rather adds to them, and because the board is not vested with any authority to create new registration requirements, 803 Code Mass. Regs. § 1.04(7)(b) is outside the board's authority and is invalid. . . .

"[W]e answer the first reported question, 'No,' and order that the defendant's sentence and conviction be vacated. Because we conclude that the regulation is invalid, we answer the second question, 'No,' as well." *Commonwealth v. Maker*, 459 Mass. 46, 47, 49, 51–52 (2011).

NOTE 2   CPSL Is Unconstitutional. "The issue presented on appeal is whether community parole supervision for life (CPSL) violates our separation of powers doctrine, articulated in art. 30 of the Massachusetts Declaration of Rights, by improperly delegating to the parole board, an entity of the executive branch, the exercise of the judicial power to impose sentences. We conclude that CPSL grants to the parole board a quintessential judicial power, the power to determine whether a defendant should be sentenced to additional terms of imprisonment, and therefore violates art. 30." *Commonwealth v. Cole*, 468 Mass. 294, 295 (2014).

NOTE 3   CPSL Sentences Must Be Vacated. "Therefore, we strike [G.L. c. 127,] § 133D in its entirety and order that CPSL sentences, whether imposed pursuant to G.L. c. 6, § 178H(a), or G.L. c. 265, § 45, be vacated." *Commonwealth v. Cole*, 468 Mass. 294, 308–09 (2014).

SECTION 178I
Report identifying sex offender; request for information; confidentiality

Any person who is 18 years of age or older and who states that he is requesting sex offender registry information for his own protection or for the protection of a child under the age of 18 or another person for whom the requesting person has responsibility, care, or custody shall receive at no cost from the board a report to the extent available pursuant to sections 178C to 178P, inclusive, which indicates whether an individual identified by name, date of birth, or sufficient personal identifying characteristics is a sex offender with an obligation to register pursuant to this chapter, the offenses for which he was convicted or adjudicated and the dates of such convictions or adjudications. Any records of inquiry shall be kept confidential, except that the records may be disseminated to assist or defend in a criminal prosecution.

Information about an offender shall be made available pursuant to this section only if the offender is a sex offender who has been finally classified by the board as a level 2 or level 3 sex offender.

All reports to persons making inquiries shall include a warning regarding the criminal penalties for use of sex offender registry information to commit a crime or to engage in illegal discrimination or harassment of an offender and the punishment for threatening to commit a crime under section 4 of chapter 275.

The board shall not release information identifying the victim by name, address, or relation to the offender.

NOTE   Judge may order preliminary injunction to enjoin the Commonwealth from enforcing 178I as it pertains to the defendant who was convicted of two relatively minor sex offenses (open and gross lewdness) as "[t]he potential harm to the plaintiff in his employment or in his community, or both, from the use of such information for other than personal protection is substantial." *Doe v. Attorney General (No. 2)*, 425 Mass. 217, 221 n.7, 222 (1997).

SECTION 178J
Request for sex offender information; notice of penalty for misuse; data required to receive report

(a) A person who requests sex offender registry information shall:

(1) be 18 years of age or older;

(2) appear in person at a city or town police station and present proper identification;

(3) require sex offender registry information for his own protection or for the protection of a child under the age of 18 or another person for whom such inquirer has responsibility, care or custody, and so state; and

(4) complete and sign a record of inquiry, designed by the board, which shall include the following information: the name and address of the person making the inquiry, the person or geographic area or street which is the subject of the inquiry, the reason for the inquiry, and the date and time of the inquiry.

Such records of inquiries shall include a warning regarding the criminal penalties for use of sex offender registry information to commit a crime or to engage in illegal discrimination or harassment of an offender and the punishment for threatening to commit a crime under the provisions of section 4 of chapter 275. Such records of inquiries shall state, before the signature of the inquirer, as follows: "I understand that the sex offender registry information disclosed to me is intended for my own protection or for the protection of a child under the age of 18 or another person for whom I have responsibility, care, or custody." Such records of inquiries shall be kept confidential, except that such records may be disseminated to assist in a criminal prosecution.

(b) The person making the inquiry may either:

(1) identify a specific individual by name or provide personal identifying information sufficient to allow the police to identify the subject of the inquiry; or

(2) inquire whether any sex offenders live, work, or attend an institution of higher learning within the same city or town at a specific address including, but not limited to, a residential address, a business address, school, after-school program, child care center, playground, recreational area, or other identified address and inquire in another city or town whether any sex offenders live, work, or attend an institution of higher learning within that city or town, upon a reasonable

showing that the sex offender registry information is requested for his own protection or for the protection of a child under the age of 18 or another person for whom the inquirer has responsibility, care, or custody; or

(3) inquire whether any sex offenders live, work, or attend an institution of higher learning on a specific street within the city or town in which such inquiry is made.

(c) If the search of the sex offender registry results in the identification of a sex offender required to register pursuant to this chapter who has been finally classified by the board as a level 2 or level 3 offender under section 178K, the police shall disseminate to the person making the inquiry:

(1) the name of the sex offender;

(2) the home address and any secondary address if located in the areas described in clause (2) or (3) of subsection (b);

(3) the work address if located in the areas described in said clause (2) or (3) of said subsection (b);

(4) the offense for which he was convicted or adjudicated and the dates of such conviction or adjudication;

(5) the sex offender's age, sex, race, height, weight, eye and hair color; and

(6) a photograph of the sex offender, if available;

(7) the name and address of the institution of higher learning where the sex offender works or is enrolled as a student, if located in the areas described in clause (2) or (3) of subsection (b).

The police shall not release information identifying the victim by name, address, or the victim's relation to the offender.

SECTION 178K
Sex offender registry board; member qualifications; guidelines to assess risk of reoffense; notification
(Amended by 2013 Mass. Acts c. 38, §§ 9, 10, effective July 1, 2013.)

(1) There shall be, in the executive office of public safety and security, a sex offender registry board which shall consist of seven members who shall be appointed by the governor for terms of six years, with the exception of the chairman, and who shall devote their full time during business hours to their official duties. The board shall include one person with experience and knowledge in the field of criminal justice who shall act as chairman; at least two licensed psychologists or psychiatrists with special expertise in the assessment and evaluation of sex offenders and who have knowledge of the forensic mental health system; at least one licensed psychologist or psychiatrist with special expertise in the assessment and evaluation of sex offenders, including juvenile sex offenders and who has knowledge of the forensic mental health system; at least two persons who have at least five years of training and experience in probation, parole or corrections; and at least one person who has expertise or experience with victims of sexual abuse. Members shall be compensated at a reasonable rate subject to approval of the secretary of administration and finance.

The chairman shall be appointed by and serve at the pleasure of the governor and shall be the executive and administrative head of the sex offender registry board, shall have the authority and responsibility for directing assignments of members of said board and shall be the appointing and removing authority for members of said board's staff. In the case of the absence or disability of the chairman, the governor may designate one of the members to act as chairman during such absence or disability. The chairman shall, subject

to appropriation, establish such staff positions and employ such administrative, research, technical, legal, clerical, and other personnel and consultants as may be necessary to perform the duties of said board. Such staff positions shall not be subject to section 9A of chapter 30 or chapter 31.

The governor shall fill any vacancy for the unexpired term. As long as there are four sitting members, a vacancy shall not impair the right of the remaining members to exercise the powers of the board.

The sex offender registry board shall promulgate guidelines for determining the level of risk of reoffense and the degree of dangerousness posed to the public or for relief from the obligation to register and shall provide for three levels of notification depending on such risk of reoffense and the degree of dangerousness posed to the public; apply the guidelines to assess the risk level of particular offenders; develop guidelines for use by city and town police departments in disseminating sex offender registry information; devise a plan, in cooperation with state and local law enforcement authorities and other appropriate agencies, to locate and verify the current addresses of sex offenders including, subject to appropriation, entering into contracts or interagency agreements for such purposes; and conduct hearings as provided in section 178L. The attorney general and the chief counsel of the committee for public counsel services, or their designees, shall assist in the development of such guidelines. Factors relevant to the risk of reoffense shall include, but not be limited to, the following:

(a) criminal history factors indicative of a high risk of reoffense and degree of dangerousness posed to the public, including:

(i) whether the sex offender has a mental abnormality;

(ii) whether the sex offender's conduct is characterized by repetitive and compulsive behavior;

(iii) whether the sex offender was an adult who committed a sex offense on a child;

(iv) the age of the sex offender at the time of the commission of the first sex offense;

(v) whether the sex offender has been adjudicated to be a sexually dangerous person pursuant to section 14 of chapter 123A or is a person released from civil commitment pursuant to section 9 of said chapter 123A; and

(vi) whether the sex offender served the maximum term of incarceration;

(b) other criminal history factors to be considered in determining risk and degree of dangerousness, including:

(i) the relationship between the sex offender and the victim;

(ii) whether the offense involved the use of a weapon, violence, or infliction of bodily injury;

(iii) the number, date and nature of prior offenses;

(c) conditions of release that minimize risk of reoffense and degree of dangerousness posed to the public, including whether the sex offender is under probation or parole supervision, whether such sex offender is receiving counseling, therapy or treatment and whether such sex offender is residing in a home situation that provides guidance and supervision, including sex offender-specific treatment in a community-based residential program;

(d) physical conditions that minimize risk of reoffense including, but not limited to, debilitating illness;

(e) whether the sex offender was a juvenile when he committed the offense, his response to treatment and subsequent criminal history;

(f) whether psychological or psychiatric profiles indicate a risk of recidivism;

(g) the sex offender's history of alcohol or substance abuse;

(h) the sex offender's participation in sex offender treatment and counseling while incarcerated or while on probation or parole and his response to such treatment or counseling;

(i) recent behavior, including behavior while incarcerated or while supervised on probation or parole;

(j) recent threats against persons or expressions of intent to commit additional offenses;

(k) review of any victim impact statement; and

(l) review of any materials submitted by the sex offender, his attorney or others on behalf of such offender.

(2) The guidelines shall provide for three levels of notification depending on the degree of risk of reoffense and the degree of dangerousness posed to the public by the sex offender or for relief from the obligation to register:

(a) Where the board determines that the risk of reoffense is low and the degree of dangerousness posed to the public is not such that a public safety interest is served by public availability, it shall give a level 1 designation to the sex offender. In such case, the board shall transmit the registration data and designation to the police departments in the municipalities where such sex offender lives and works and attends an institution of higher learning or, if in custody, intends to live and work and attend an institution of higher learning upon release and where the offense was committed and to the Federal Bureau of Investigation. The police shall not disseminate information to the general public identifying the sex offender where the board has classified the individual as a level 1 sex offender. The police and the board may, however, release such information identifying such sex offender to the department of correction, any county correctional facility, the department of youth services, the department of children and families, the parole board, the department of probation and the department of mental health, all city and town police departments and the Federal Bureau of Investigation.

(b) Where the board determines that the risk of reoffense is moderate and the degree of dangerousness posed to the public is such that a public safety interest is served by public availability of registration information, it shall give a level 2 designation to the sex offender. In such case, the board shall transmit the registration data and designation to the police departments in the municipalities where the sex offender lives and works and attends an institution of higher learning or, if in custody, intends to live and work and attend an institution of higher learning upon release and where the offense was committed and to the Federal Bureau of Investigation. The public shall have access to the information regarding a level 2 offender in accordance with the provisions of sections 178D, 178I and 178J. The sex offender shall be required to register and to verify registration information pursuant to section 178F½.

(c) Where the board determines that the risk of reoffense is high and the degree of dangerousness posed to the public is such that a substantial public safety interest is served by active dissemination, it shall give a level 3 designation to the sex offender. In such case, the board shall transmit the registration data and designation to the police departments in the municipalities where the sex offender lives and works and attends an institution of higher learning or, if in custody, intends to live and work and attend an institution of higher learning upon release and where the offense was committed and to the Federal Bureau of Investigation. A level 3 community notification plan shall require the police department to notify organizations in the community which are likely to encounter such sex offender and individual members of the public who are likely to encounter such sex offender. The sex offender shall be required to register and to verify registration information pursuant to section 178F½. Neighboring police districts shall share sex offender registration information of level 3 offenders and may inform the residents of their municipality of a sex offender they are likely to encounter who resides in an adjacent city or town. The police or the board shall actively disseminate in such time and manner as such police department or board deems reasonably necessary the following information:

(i) the name of the sex offender;

(ii) the offender's home address;

(iii) the offender's work address;

(iv) the offense for which the offender was convicted or adjudicated and the date of the conviction or adjudication;

(v) the sex offender's age, sex, race, height, weight, eye and hair color; and

(vi) a photograph of the sex offender, if available; provided, that such active dissemination may include publication of such information on the internet by the police department at such time and in such manner as the police or the board deem reasonably necessary; and provided further that the police or the board shall not release information identifying the victim by name, address, or relation to the sex offender. All notices to the community shall include a warning regarding the criminal penalties for use of sex offender registry information to commit a crime or to engage in illegal discrimination or harassment of an offender and the punishment for threatening to commit a crime under section 4 of chapter 275; and

(vii) the name and address of the institution of higher learning that the sex offender is attending.

The public shall have access to the information regarding a level 3 offender in accordance with sections 178D, 178I, and 178J.

If the board, in finally giving an offender a level 3 classification, also concludes that such sex offender should be designated a sexually violent predator, the board shall transmit a report to the sentencing court explaining the board's reasons for so recommending, including specific identification of the sexually violent offense committed by such sex offender and the mental abnormality from which he suffers. The report shall not be subject to judicial review under section 178M. Upon receipt from the board of a report recommending that a sex offender be designated a sexually violent predator, the sentencing court, after giving such sex offender an opportunity to be heard and informing the sex offender of his right to have counsel appointed, if he is deemed to be indigent in accordance with section 2 of chapter 211D, shall determine, by a preponderance of the evidence, whether such sex offender is a sexually violent predator. An attorney employed or retained by the board may make an appearance, subject to section 3 of chapter 12, to defend the board's recommendation. The board shall be notified of the determination. A determination that a sex offender should not be designated a sexually violent predator shall not invalidate such sex offender's classification. Where the sentencing court determines that such sex offender is a sexually violent predator, dissemination of the sexually violent predator's registration data shall be in accordance with a level 3 community notification plan; provided, however, that such dissemination shall include such sex offender's designation as a sexually violent predator.

(d) The board may, upon making specific written findings that the circumstances of the offense in conjunction with the offender's criminal history do not indicate a risk of reoffense or a danger to the public and the reasons therefor, relieve such sex offender of any further obligation to register, shall remove such sex offender's registration information from the registry and shall so notify the police departments where said sex offender lives and works or if in custody intends to live and work upon release, and where the offense was committed and the Federal Bureau of Investigation. In making such determination the board shall consider factors, including but not limited to, the presence or absence of any physical harm caused by the offense and whether the offense involved consensual conduct between adults. The burden of proof shall be on the offender to prove he comes within the provisions of this subsection. The provisions of this subsection shall not apply if a sex offender has been determined to be a sexually violent predator; if a sex offender has been convicted of two or more sex offenses defined as sex offenses pursuant to the Jacob Wetterling Crimes Against Children and Sexually Violent Offender Registration Act, 42 U.S.C. § 14071, committed on different occasions; or has been convicted of a sexually violent offense. The provisions of this subsection shall also not apply if a sex offender has been convicted of a sex offense involving a child or a sexually violent offense, and such offender has not already registered pursuant to this chapter for at least ten years, or if the sex offender is otherwise subject to lifetime or minimum registration requirements as determined by the board pursuant to section 178D.

(e) No sex offender classified as a level 3 offender shall knowingly and willingly establish living conditions within, move to, or transfer to any convalescent or nursing home, infirmary maintained in a town, rest home, charitable home for the aged or intermediate care facility for the mentally retarded which meets the requirements of the department of public health under section 71 of chapter 111. Any sex offender who violates this paragraph shall, for a first conviction, be punished by imprisonment for not more than 30 days in a jail or house of correction; for a second conviction, be punished by imprisonment for not more than 2½ years in a jail or house of correction nor more than 5 years in a state prison or by a fine of not more than $1,000, or by both such fine and imprisonment; and for a third and subsequent conviction, be punished by imprisonment in a state prison for not less than 5 years; provided, however, that the sentence imposed for such third or subsequent conviction shall not be reduced to less than 5 years, nor suspended, nor shall any person sentenced herein be eligible for probation, parole, work release or furlough, or receive any deduction from his sentence for good conduct until he shall have served 5 years. Prosecutions commenced hereunder shall neither be continued without a finding nor placed on file.

(3) The sex offender registry board shall make a determination regarding the level of risk of reoffense and the de-gree of dangerousness posed to the public of each sex offender listed in said sex offender registry and shall give immediate priority to those offenders who have been convicted of a sex offense involving a child or convicted or adjudicated as a delinquent juvenile or as a youthful offender by reason of a sexually violent offense or of a sex offense of indecent assault and battery upon a mentally retarded person pursuant to section 13F of chapter 265, and who have not been sentenced to incarceration for at least 90 days, followed, in order of priority, by those sex offenders who (1) have been released from incarceration within the past 12 months, (2) are currently on parole or probation supervision, and (3) are scheduled to be released from incarceration within six months. All agencies shall cooperate in providing files to the sex offender registry board and any information the sex offender registry board deems useful in providing notice under sections 178C to 178P, inclusive, and in assessing the risk of reoffense and the degree of dangerousness posed to the public by the sex offender. All agencies from which registration data, including data within the control of providers under contract to such agencies, is requested by the sex offender registry board shall make such data available to said board immediately upon request. Failure to comply in good faith with such a request within 30 days shall be punishable by a fine of not more than $1,000 per day.

(4) The sex offender registry board, in cooperation with the executive office of public safety and security, and with the consultation of the offices of the district attorneys, the department of probation, the department of children and families and the Massachusetts Chiefs of Police Association Incorporated, shall establish and maintain a system of procedures for the ongoing sharing of information that may be relevant to the board's determination or reevaluation of a sex offender's level designation among the board, the offices of the district attorneys and any department, agency or office of the commonwealth that reports, investigates or otherwise has access to potentially relevant information, including, but not limited to, the department of youth services, the department of children and families, the department of mental health, the department of developmental services, the department of correction, the department of probation, the department of early education and care, the department of public health and the office of the child advocate.

The board shall promulgate any rules or regulations necessary to establish, update and maintain this system including, but not limited to, the frequency of updates, measures to ensure the comprehensiveness, clarity and effectiveness of information, and metrics to determine what information may be relevant. When sharing information through this system, all members shall have discretion to delay sharing information where it is reasonably believed that disclosure would compromise or impede an investigation or prosecution or would cause harm to a victim.

(5) The sex offender registry board shall have access to any information that is determined to be relevant to the board's determination or reevaluation of a sex offender's level designation, as defined in subsection (4), through the system of procedures established in said subsection (4).

NOTE 1a   Classification Hearing, Burden of Proof, Findings of Fact, Appeal. In *Doe v. Sex Offender Registry Board*, 428 Mass. 90 (1998), the Supreme Judicial Court held that an offender is entitled to an evidentiary hearing before the Sex Offender Registry

Board, to be held pursuant to the State Administrative Procedure Act (G.L. c. 30A), at which the board shall have the burden of proving, by a preponderance of the evidence, the offender's risk classification. The board is further required to "make particularized, specific, and detailed findings, guided by the factors set forth in [Section] 178K, to demonstrate that close attention has been given to the evidence as to each offender and that the classification for each is appropriate." *Doe v. Sex Offender Registry Bd.*, 428 Mass. at 102. The offender is then entitled to appeal the board's decision to the Superior Court pursuant to the provisions of Section 178M. *Doe v. Sex Offender Registry Bd.*, 428 Mass. at 91.

NOTE 1b   "We now conclude that sex offenders are entitled to the effective assistance of counsel at classification hearings and that the civil formulation of the *Saferian* standard governs claims of ineffectiveness." *Poe v. Sex Offender Registry Bd.*, 456 Mass. 801, 811 (2010).

NOTE 2   Evidence. "While the board, under its regulations, is not bound by the rules of evidence observed by courts but may receive and consider evidence of a kind 'on which reasonable people are accustomed to rely in the conduct of serious affairs,' 803 Code Mass. Regs. § 119(1), a non-eyewitness police report, standing alone, cannot constitute substantial evidence within the meaning of G.L. c. 30A. However, particular narratives related therein may be admissible in board hearings depending on the general plausibility and consistency of the victim's or witness's story, the circumstances under which it is related, the degree of detail, the motives of the narrator, the presence or absence of corroboration and the like. The victim's story, contained in the police reports, was plausible, consistent and highly detailed. It was corroborated by the petitioner's testimony wherein he admitted that he had taken the victim to a house in the neighborhood and engaged in sexual intercourse with the victim." *Doe v. Sex Offender Registry Bd.*, 70 Mass. App. Ct. 309, 312–13 (2007) (citations omitted).

NOTE 3a   Due Process. In *Doe v. Sex Offender Registry Board*, 447 Mass. 750, 759–62 (2006), the Supreme Judicial Court concluded that G.L. c. 6, § 178K(2)(d) and 803 C.M.R. § 1.37A do not, on their face, violate substantive or procedural due process protections.

NOTE 3b   Due Process Violated. "We conclude that [G.L. c. 6, § 178K(2)(e)] infringes on the plaintiff's protected liberty and property interests and violates his right to due process; because the statute fails to provide for an individualized determination that the public safety benefits of requiring him to leave the rest home outweigh the risks to the plaintiff of such a removal, the statute is unconstitutional as applied to the plaintiff." *Doe v. Police Comm'r of Boston*, 460 Mass. 342, 342–43 (2011).

NOTE 4   Procedure for Determining Classification Level. In *Doe v. Sex Offender Registry Board*, 447 Mass. 768, 774–77 (2006), the Supreme Judicial Court concluded that G.L. c. 6, § 178K and 803 C.M.R. §§ 1.38–1.40 do not vest untrammeled discretion in the Sex Offender Registry Board over the classification level so as to render the procedure arbitrary and contrary to law.

NOTE 5   CWOF. "While a hearing examiner may not consider a CWOF a 'prior offense' in relation to the classification factor that looks at the dates, number, and nature of prior offenses, he is permitted to take into account the misconduct underlying the CWOF on the issue whether the sex offender's conduct was repetitive and compulsive." *Doe v. Sex Offender Registry Bd.*, 452 Mass. 764, 777 (2008) (footnote omitted).

NOTE 6   Retroactivity. "We declare unconstitutional the retroactive application of the amendments to G.L. c. 6, §§ 178D and 178K, that became effective on July 12, 2013, to the extent they would require the Internet publication of the registry information of individuals who were finally classified as level two sex offenders on or before July 12, 2013." *Moe v. Sex Offender Registry Bd.*, 467 Mass. 598, 616 (2014).

NOTE 7   Composition of Board. "The plaintiff['s] . . . primary claims arise from the fact that, at all times relevant to his case, the composition of the seven-member board failed to include . . . two licensed psychologists or psychiatrists who have special expertise in the assessment and evaluation of sex offenders and knowledge of the forensic mental health system. According to the plaintiff, the deficiency in the qualifications of its membership deprived the board of subject matter jurisdiction. . . . The board did not lack subject matter jurisdiction at any time relevant to this case. General Laws c. 6, § 178K(1), specifically states that '[a]s long as there are four sitting members, a vacancy shall not impair the right of the remaining members to exercise the powers of the board.' Significantly, that statute does not limit the types of board members that must comprise the 'four sitting members.' The board, therefore, is authorized to carry out its legislatively mandated duties, regardless of whether it is fully constituted with two licensed psychologists or psychiatrists." *Doe v. Sex Offender Registry Bd.*, 452 Mass. 784, 785–86, 790–91 (2008).

SECTION 178L
Classification of sex offenders by board; hearings; right to counsel
(Amended by 2013 Mass. Acts c. 38, § 11, effective July 1, 2013.)

(1) Upon review of any information useful in assessing the risk of reoffense and the degree of dangerousness posed to the public by the sex offender, including materials described in the board guidelines and any materials submitted by the sex offender, the board shall prepare a recommended classification of each offender. Such recommendation may be made by board staff members upon written approval by one board member; provided, however, that if the sex offender was a juvenile at the time of the offense, written approval must be given by a board member who is a licensed psychologist or psychiatrist with special expertise in the assessment and evaluation of juvenile sex offenders.

(a) Not less than 60 days prior to the release or parole of a sex offender from custody or incarceration, the board shall notify the sex offender of his right to submit to the board documentary evidence relative to his risk of reoffense and the degree of dangerousness posed to the public and his duty to register according to the provisions of section 178E. If the sex offender is a juvenile at the time of such notification, notification shall also be mailed to the sex offender's legal guardian or agency having custody of the juvenile in the absence of a legal guardian and his most recent attorney of record. Such sex offender may submit such evidence to the board within 30 days of receiving such notice from the board. Upon a reasonable showing, the board may extend the time in which such sex offender may submit such documentary evidence. Upon reviewing such evidence, the board shall promptly notify the sex offender of the board's recommended sex offender classification, his duty to register, if any, his right to petition the board to request an evidentiary hearing to challenge such classification and duty, his right to retain counsel to represent him at such hearing and his right to have counsel appointed for him if he is found to be indigent as determined by the board using the standards under chapter 211D; provided, however, that such indigent offender may also apply for and the board may grant payment of fees for an expert witness in any case where the board in its classification proceeding intends to rely on the testimony or report of an expert witness prepared specifically for the purposes of the classification proceeding. Such sex offender shall petition the board for such hearing within 20 days of receiving such notice. The board shall conduct such hearing in a reasonable time according to the provisions of subsection (2). The failure timely to petition the board for such hearing shall result in a waiver of such right and the registration requirements, if any, and the board's recommended classification shall become final.

(b) The district attorney for the county where such sex offender was prosecuted may, within ten days of a conviction or adjudication of a sexually violent offense, file a motion with the board to make an expedited recommended classification upon a showing that such sex offender poses a grave risk of imminent reoffense. If the petition is granted, the board shall make such recommendation within ten days of the expiration of the time to submit documentary evidence. If the petition is not granted, the board shall make such recommended classification as otherwise provided in this section.

(c) In the case of any sex offender not in custody, upon receiving registration data from the agency, the police department at which the sex offender registered, the sentencing court or by any other means, the board shall promptly notify the sex offender of his right to submit to the board documentary evidence relative to his risk of reoffense and the degree of dangerousness posed to the public and his duty to register, if any, according to section 178E. If such sex offender is a juvenile at the time of such notification, notification shall also be mailed to such sex offender's legal guardian or agency having custody of the juvenile in the absence of a legal guardian and his most recent attorney of record. Such sex offender may submit such evidence to the board within 30 days of receiving such notice from the board. Upon a reasonable showing, the board may extend the time in which a sex offender may submit such documentary evidence. Upon reviewing such evidence, the board shall promptly notify such sex offender of the board's recommended sex offender classification, his duty to register, if any, and his right to petition the board to request an evidentiary hearing to challenge such classification and duty, his right to retain counsel to represent him at such hearing and his right to have counsel appointed for him if he is found to be indigent as determined by the board using the standards under chapter 211D; provided, however, that such indigent offender may also apply for and the board may grant payment of fees for an expert witness in any case where the board in its classification proceeding intends to rely on the testimony or report of an expert witness prepared specifically for the purposes of the classification proceeding. Such sex offender shall petition the board for such hearing within 20 days of receiving such notice. The board shall conduct such hearing in a reasonable time according to the provisions of subsection (2). The failure timely to petition the board for such hearing shall result in a waiver of such right and the registration requirements, if any, and the board's recommended classification shall become final.

(2) If an offender requests a hearing in accordance with subsection (1), the chair may appoint a member, a panel of three board members or a hearing officer to conduct the hearing, according to the standard rules of adjudicatory procedure or other rules which the board may promulgate, and to determine by a preponderance of evidence such sex offender's duty to register and final classification. The board shall inform offenders requesting a hearing under the provisions of subsection (1) of their right to have counsel appointed if a sex offender is deemed to be indigent as determined by the board using the standards under chapter 211D. If the sex offender does not so request a hearing, the recommended classification and determination of duty to register shall become the board's

final classification and determination and shall not be subject to judicial review. All offenders who are juveniles at the time of notification shall be represented by counsel at the hearing.

(3) The board may, on its own initiative or upon written request by a police department or district attorney, seek to reclassify any registered and finally classified sex offender in the event that new information, which is relevant to a determination of a risk of reoffense or degree of dangerousness, is received. The board shall promulgate regulations defining such new information and establishing the procedures relative to a reclassification hearing held for this purpose; provided that (i) the hearing is conducted according to the standard rules of adjudicatory procedure or other rules which the board may promulgate, (ii) the hearing is conducted in a reasonable time, and (iii) the sex offender is provided prompt notice of the hearing, which includes: the new information that led the board to seek reclassification of the offender, the offender's right to challenge the reclassification, the offender's right to submit to the board documentary evidence relative to his risk of reoffense and the degree of dangerousness posed to the public, the offender's right to retain counsel for the hearing, and the offender's right to have counsel appointed if the offender is indigent, as determined by the board using the standards in chapter 211D. An indigent offender may also apply for and the board may grant payment of fees for an expert witness in any case in which the board intends to rely on the testimony or report of an expert witness prepared specifically for the purposes of the reclassification proceeding. The failure of the offender to attend the hearing may result in a waiver of the offender's rights and the board's recommended reclassification becoming final.

All offenders who are juveniles at the time of notification shall be represented by counsel at the hearing and notification shall also be mailed to the sex offender's legal guardian or agency having custody of the juvenile in the absence of a legal guardian and the offender's most recent attorney of record.

NOTE 1   **Expert Testimony.** In *Doe v. Sex Offender Registry Board*, 447 Mass. 779, 784–86 (2006), the Supreme Judicial Court concluded that, under G.L. c. 6, § 178L, the Sex Offender Registry Board's use of expert testimony to support its position before the hearing examiner is discretionary, not mandatory. See Note 1 following G.L. c. 6, § 178K.

NOTE 2   **Motion for Funds.** "We conclude that § 178L (1) gives the board discretion to grant a motion for funds filed by an indigent sex offender . . . even though the board itself does not intend to rely on the testimony or report of an expert witness." *Doe v. Sex Offender Registry Bd.*, 452 Mass. 764, 765 (2008).

Compare: "In connection with his appeal from the board's classification decision to the Superior Court, Doe filed and then renewed a motion pursuant to G.L. c. 261, § 27B, for $3,000 in funds to retain an expert witness. The judge denied the motion, reasoning that any funds sought under § 27B must relate to a pending trial or appeal, and that the funds Doe sought related to the underlying administrative proceeding before the board . . . . The judge's ruling was correct. Doe's civil action in the Superior Court was in substance an appeal, under G.L. c. 6, § 178M, and c. 30A, § 14, from the board's adjudicatory decision." *Doe v. Sex Offender Registry Bd.*, 452 Mass. at 778–79 (footnote omitted).

NOTE 3   **Hearing.** "The Legislature acted carefully to protect a sex offender's due process rights, and declared that a sex offender waives the right to a classification hearing only where the offender does not ask the board to be put to its burden to justify the classification. See G.L. c. 6, § 178L (1). We conclude, therefore, that the board's regulation [803 Code Mass. Regs. § 1.13(2)

[(2002)] exceeds the scope of its legislative mandate by declaring that a sex offender who has asked that the board be put to its burden and whose attorney is present and prepared to challenge the recommended classification waives the right to a classification hearing by failing to appear without good cause." *Doe v. Sex Offender Registry Bd.*, 460 Mass. 336, 341 (2011).

SECTION 178M
Judicial review of final classification
(Amended by 2013 Mass. Acts c. 38, § 12, effective July 1, 2013.)

An offender may seek judicial review, in accordance with section 14 of chapter 30A, of the board's final classification, reclassification and registration requirements. The court shall, if requested, appoint counsel to represent the sex offender in the proceedings if such sex offender is deemed indigent in accordance with section 2 of chapter 211D. An attorney employed or retained by the board may make an appearance, subject to section 3 of chapter 12, to defend the board's decision. The court shall reach its final decision within 60 days of such sex offender's petition for review. The court shall keep proceedings conducted pursuant to this paragraph and records from such proceedings confidential and such proceedings and records shall be impounded, but the filing of an action under this section shall not stay the effect of the board's final classification.

NOTE   See Note 1 following G.L. c. 6, § 178K.

SECTION 178N
Misuse of information; penalties

Information contained in the sex offender registry shall not be used to commit a crime against a sex offender or to engage in illegal discrimination or harassment of an offender. Any person who uses information disclosed pursuant to the provisions of sections 178C to 178P, inclusive, for such purpose shall be punished by not more than two and one-half years in a house of correction or by a fine of not more than $1,000 or by both such fine and imprisonment.

SECTION 178O
Liability of police officials and public employees for sex offender registry information

Police officials and other public employees acting in good faith shall not be liable in a civil or criminal proceeding for any dissemination of sex offender registry information or for any publication on the internet under section 178D or other act or omission pursuant to the provisions of sections 178C to 178P, inclusive.

SECTION 178P
Failure to comply with registration requirements; right to arrest
(Amended by 2013 Mass. Acts c. 63, effective Aug. 7, 2013.)

Whenever a police officer has probable cause to believe that a sex offender has failed to comply with the registration requirements of sections 178C to 178P, inclusive, such officer shall have the right to arrest such sex offender without a warrant and to keep such sex offender in custody.

Whenever a police officer, district attorney or agent, employee or representative of the executive office of health and human services has information indicating that a sex offender is at risk to reoffend, the police department, district attorney or, to the extent permitted by federal law, the executive office of health and human services agent, employee or representative shall forward that information to the board; but a police department or district attorney shall not forward information to the board that the police department or district attorney believes will compromise an ongoing investigation. The board, after consulting the executive office of health and human services, shall adopt regulations to provide specific guidance concerning the type and location of information that might indicate that a sex offender is at risk to reoffend and the circumstances that require disclosure.

SECTION 178Q
Sex offender registry fee

The sex offender registry board shall assess upon every sex offender a sex offender registration fee of $75, hereinafter referred to as a sex offender registry fee. Said offender shall pay said sex offender registry fee upon his initial registration as a sex offender and annually thereafter on the anniversary of said registration; provided, however, that no such fee shall be assessed or collected until the offender has either (1) waived his right to petition for an evidentiary hearing to challenge his duty to register as a sex offender as set forth in section 178L or (2) has completely exhausted the legal remedies made available to him to so challenge said duty to register pursuant to sections 178L and 178M and has not prevailed in his attempt to eliminate said duty. A sex offender's duty to pay the fee established by this section shall only terminate upon the termination of said offender's duty to register as a sex offender as set forth in section 178G.

The sex offender registry board may waive payment of said sex offender registry fee if it determines that such payment would constitute an undue hardship on said person or his family due to limited income, employment status, or any other relevant factor. Any such waiver so granted shall be in effect only during the period of time that said person is determined to be unable to pay the sex offender registry fee. The sex offender registry board shall establish procedures relative to the collection and waiver of such fee by regulation. Said sex offender registry fee shall be collected and retained by the sex offender registry board. The sex offender registry board shall account for all such fees received and report said fees annually to the secretary of administration and finance and the house and senate committees on ways and means.

Chapter 12. Department of the Attorney General and the District Attorneys

---

SECTION 11H
Violations of constitutional rights; civil actions by attorney general; venue
(Amended by 2014 Mass. Acts c. 197, § 1, effective July 30, 2014.)

Whenever any person or persons, whether or not acting under color of law, interfere by threats, intimidation or coercion, or attempt to interfere by threats, intimidation or coercion, with the exercise or enjoyment by any other person or persons of rights secured by the constitution or laws of the United States, or of rights secured by the constitution or laws of the commonwealth, the attorney general may bring a civil action for injunctive or other appropriate equitable relief in order to protect the peaceable exercise or enjoyment of the right or rights secured. Said civil action shall be brought in the name of the commonwealth and shall be instituted either in the superior court for the county in which the conduct complained of occurred or in the superior court for the county in which the person whose conduct complained of resides or has his principal place of business.

If the attorney general prevails in an action under this section, the attorney general shall be entitled to: (i) an award of compensatory damages for any aggrieved person or entity; and (ii) litigation costs and reasonable attorneys' fees in an amount to be determined by the court. In a matter involving the interference or attempted interference with any right protected by the constitution of the United States or of the commonwealth, the court may also award civil penalties against each defendant in an amount not exceeding $5,000 for each violation.

NOTE 1   Massachusetts Civil Rights Act. "On appeal, Guilfoyle contends that (1) G.L. c. 12, §§ 11H & 11J, are inapplicable to minors, (2) the sanction imposed was unreasonable in scope and duration, (3) the judge erroneously denied Guilfoyle's motion for a trial by jury, and (4) the judge erroneously used the 'preponderance of the evidence' standard of proof when the proper standard was 'beyond a reasonable doubt.' We affirm the judgment." *Commonwealth v. Guilfoyle*, 402 Mass. 130, 133 (1988).

NOTE 2 "[A] curse does not violate any civil rights *unless* it rises to the level of a threat or an attempt to intimidate." *Tatro v. Kervin*, 41 F.3d 9, 19 (1st Cir. 1994).

Chapter 18. Department of Transitional Assistance

Section
5B   False representations or failure to disclose facts; penalty
5E   Return of unlawful payments
5F   Father's leaving family to obtain assistance; penalty
5J   Preventing electronic benefit transfer transactions for certain purchases made using direct cash assistance funds; penalty
5K   Obtaining or receiving Department of Transitional Assistance property through embezzlement, theft or fraud; penalty
5L   Food stamp benefits trafficking; penalty
5M   Organizational food stamp benefits trafficking; penalty
5N   Fraud hotline; display

SECTION 5B

False representations or failure to disclose facts; penalty

Any person or institution which knowingly makes a false representation or, contrary to a legal duty to do so, knowingly fails to disclose any material fact affecting eligibility or level of benefits to the department of public welfare or its agents, for the purpose of causing any person, including the person making such representations, to be supported in whole or in part by the commonwealth, or for the purpose of procuring a payment under any assistance program administered by the department, shall be punished by a fine of not less than two hundred nor more than five hundred dollars or by imprisonment for not more than one year.

Nothing in this section shall be construed as preventing the institution of criminal proceedings for the violation of any other law of the commonwealth.

NOTE   Venue. "[F]or the crime of public assistance fraud, G.L. c. 18, § 5B, '[t]he venue question . . . is one of common law.'" *Commonwealth v. Wright*, 88 Mass. App. Ct. 82, 87 (2015) (citation omitted).

SECTION 5E

Return of unlawful payments

Any recipient or vendor who receives payment under any assistance program administered by the department, to which he is not entitled, shall return such payment to the commonwealth by paying the same to the state treasurer as soon as demand is made upon him.

SECTION 5F

Father's leaving family to obtain assistance; penalty

A father who leaves his family for the purpose of qualifying them for assistance under any of the programs administered by the department shall be punished by a fine of not less than two hundred dollars nor more than five hundred dollars or by imprisonment for not more than three months.

SECTION 5J

Preventing electronic benefit transfer transactions for certain purchases made using direct cash assistance funds; penalty

(Amended by 2011 Mass. Acts c. 84, effective July 28, 2011; stricken & replaced by 2012 Mass. Acts c. 161, § 2, effective July 27, 2012.)

(a) The department shall maintain policies and practices as necessary to prevent cash assistance provided under this chapter from being used in any electronic benefit transfer transaction at: liquor stores; casinos, gambling casinos or gaming establishments licensed pursuant to chapter 23K; retail establishments which provide adult-oriented entertainment in which performers disrobe or perform in an unclothed state for entertainment, as 564 defined in Section 408(a) of the Social Security Act, as amended; adult bookstores or adult paraphernalia stores, as defined in section 9A of chapter 40A; firearms dealers licensed under section 122 of chapter 140 and ammunitions dealers licensed pursuant to section 122B of chapter 40; tattoo parlors; manicure shops or aesthetic shops registered pursuant to chapter 112; rent-to-own stores; jewelry stores; or on cruise ships. Such establishments shall not accept electronic benefits transfer cards. A store owner who knowingly allows a prohibited electronic benefit transfer transaction in violation of this section or subsection (b) of section 5I shall be punished by a fine of not more than $500 for a first offense, by a fine of not less than $500 nor more than $2,500 for a second offense and by a fine of not less than $2,500 for a third or subsequent offense.

(b) A store owner who knowingly violates this section and who also possesses a license to sell alcoholic beverages under section 12 of chapter 138 shall be referred to the appropriate licensing authority for possible disciplinary action pursuant to section 64 of said chapter 138.

(c) A store owner who knowingly violates this section and who also possesses a license to sell lottery tickets under sections 26 and 27 of chapter 10 shall be referred to the director of the state lottery for possible disciplinary action.

SECTION 5K
Obtaining or receiving Department of Transitional Assistance property through embezzlement, theft or fraud; penalty
(Amended by 2011 Mass. Acts c. 84, effective July 28, 2011.)

Notwithstanding any general or special law to the contrary, whoever embezzles, steals or obtains by fraud any funds, assets or property provided by the department of transitional assistance and whoever receives, conceals or retains such funds, assets or property for his own interest knowing such funds, assets or property have been embezzled, stolen or obtained by fraud shall, if such funds, assets or property are of a value of $100 or more, be punished by a fine of not more than $25,000 or by imprisonment in a jail or house of correction for not more than 2½ years, or imprisonment in the state prison for not more than 5 years, or both such fine and imprisonment, or if such funds, assets or property are of a value of less than $100, by a fine of not more than $1,000 or by imprisonment in a jail or house of correction for not more than 1 year, or both such fine and imprisonment.

SECTION 5L
Food stamp benefits trafficking; penalty
(Added by 2012 Mass. Acts c. 161, § 3, effective July 27, 2012.)

(a) As used this section and section 5M, "food stamp benefits" shall mean benefits issued pursuant to the federal Food and Nutrition Act of 2008, 7 U.S.C. §§ 2011 to 2029, inclusive, as amended, including such benefits contained on an electronic benefit transfer card.

(b) An individual commits the offense of food stamp benefits trafficking if the individual knowingly: (1) presents for payment or redemption or transfers food stamp benefits in any form, including transfers to another, who does not, or does not intend to, use the food stamp benefits for the benefit of the household for whom the benefits were intended, as defined in the regulations of the department; or (2) possesses, buys, sells, uses, alters, accepts or transfers food stamp benefits in any manner not authorized by the Food and Nutrition Act of 2008, 7 U.S.C. § 2011, as amended.

(c) An individual who traffics food stamp benefits, as described in subsection (b), shall: (1) if the food stamp benefits are of a value of less than $250 or if the item used, transferred, acquired, altered or possessed has a value of less than $250, be punished by imprisonment in a jail or house of correction for not more than 1 year or by a fine of not more than $1,000, or both such fine and imprisonment; or (2) if the food stamp benefits are of a value of $250 or more or the item used, transferred, acquired, altered or possessed has a value of $250 or more, be punished by imprisonment in a jail or house of correction for not more than 2 years or by imprisonment in a state prison for not more than 5 years or by a fine of not more than $5,000, or both fine and imprisonment.

(d) If a person is alleged to have committed the offense of trafficking in food stamp benefits 2 or more times within a 6-month period, those offenses may be aggregated and charged in a single count and the offenses so aggregated and charged shall constitute a single offense; provided, however, that, if the aggregate value of the food stamp benefits alleged to be trafficked is $250 or more, the person shall be subject to the penalties prescribed in clause (2) of subsection (c).

(e) Crimes under this section may be prosecuted and punished in any county where a defendant used, transferred, acquired or possessed food stamp benefits or in the county in which the state agency responsible for administering food stamp benefits is headquartered.

SECTION 5M
Organizational food stamp benefits trafficking; penalty
(Added by 2012 Mass. Acts c. 161, § 3, effective July 27, 2012.)

(a) As used in this section, "organization" shall mean a corporation for profit or not-for-profit, partnership, limited partnership, joint venture, unincorporated association, estate, trust or other commercial or legal entity; provided, however, that "organization" shall not include an entity organized as or by a governmental agency for the execution of a governmental program.

(b) An organization commits the offense of organizational food stamp benefits trafficking if the organization knowingly; (i) uses, sells, transfers, acquires, alters or possesses food stamp benefits or electronic benefit transfer cards in any manner not authorized by the Food and Nutrition Act of 2008, 7 U.S.C. § 2011, as amended, or the regulations of the department; or (2) presents for payment or redemption food stamp benefits that have been received, transferred, altered or used in violation of this section shall guilty of organizational food stamp benefits trafficking.

(c) If an organization is alleged to have committed the offense of organizational food stamp benefits trafficking 2 or more times within a 6-month period, any of those offenses may be aggregated and charged in a single count and the offenses so aggregated and charged shall constitute a single offense.

(d) An organization that commits food stamp benefits trafficking as described in subsection (c) shall: (1) if it is the organization's first offense under this section, be punished by a fine of not less than $5,000; (2) if it is the organization's second offense under this section, be punished by a fine of not less than $10,000; or (3) if it is the organization's third or subsequent offense under this section, be punished by a fine of not less than $50,000.

(e) A retail or wholesale organization owner who is convicted of organizational food stamp benefits trafficking and who also possesses a license to sell alcoholic beverages under section 12 of chapter 138 shall be referred to the appropriate licensing authority for possible disciplinary action pursuant to section 64 of said chapter 138.

(f) A retail or wholesale organization owner who is convicted of organizational food stamp benefits trafficking and who also possesses a license to sell lottery tickets under sections 26 and 27 of chapter 10 shall be referred to the director of the state lottery for possible disciplinary action.

(g) Crimes under this section may be prosecuted and punished in any county where defendant used, transferred, acquired or possessed food stamp benefits, or the county in which the state agency responsible for administering food stamp benefits is headquartered.

SECTION 5N
Fraud hotline; sign display
(Added by 2012 Mass. Acts c. 161, § 3, effective July 27, 2012.)

The department shall develop and make available on its website for download a sign specifying the department's fraud hotline. Business associations may also maintain a downloadable form of the sign on the business associations' websites. Such sign shall be posted in a conspicuous area in any business accepting electronic benefits transfer cards as a form of payment. Any business accepting electronic benefit transfer cards as a form of payment shall maintain a list of categories of prohibited products under section 5I at each cash register.

Chapter 22C. Department of State Police

Section
39   Chemist's analysis of drugs; certificate of results; prima facie evidence
39A   Analysis of samples of alcoholic beverages
39B   Procedural rules and policies for testing and analysis of drug samples
41   Chemist's analysis for presence of sperm cells; certificate of results; prima facie evidence
42   Motor vehicle ownership records; certified copies; prima facie evidence

SECTION 39

Chemist's analysis of drugs; certificate of results; prima facie evidence
(Amended by 2012 Mass. Acts c. 139, § 56, effective July 1, 2012.)

(a) The department shall, free of charge, or the University of Massachusetts Medical School shall, under section 36B of chapter 75, make a chemical analysis of any narcotic drug, any synthetic substitute for the same, any preparation containing the same, or any salt or compound thereof, and of any poison, drug, medicine or chemical submitted to it by police authorities, as the department shall approve for this purpose; provided, however, that neither the department nor the medical school shall conduct such analysis unless it is satisfied that the analysis submitted to it is to be used in connection with the enforcement of law.

(b) A certificate by a chemist or analyst or other designated employee of the department or of the University of Massachusetts medical school of the result of the chemist's or analyst's or other designated employee's analysis, signed and sworn to by that chemist or analyst or other designated employee, shall be prima facie evidence of the composition, quality and, when appropriate, net weight of the substance or any mixture containing the substance.

(c) A signed certificate of drug analysis furnished by an analyst, assistant analyst or other designated employee of the Drug Enforcement Administration of the United States Department of Justice which conforms with the requirements of this section shall be prima facie evidence of the composition, quality and, when appropriate, net weight of the substance or any mixture containing the substance.

SECTION 39A

Analysis of samples of alcoholic beverages
(Added by 2012 Mass. Acts c. 139, § 56, effective July 1, 2012.)

The department shall analyze, in accordance with sections 36 to 39, inclusive, of chapter 138, all samples of alcoholic beverages, as defined in section 1 of said chapter 138, submitted to it for that purpose by police authorities as provided in said section 36 if satisfied that the analysis is to be used in enforcing the laws.

SECTION 39B

Procedural rules and policies for testing and analysis of drugs
(Added by 2012 Mass. Acts c. 139, § 56, effective July 1, 2012.)

The director of the crime laboratory within the department shall establish procedural rules and policies governing the department's testing and analysis of drug samples and shall establish a quality assurance program for the department, which shall include proficiency standards for its laboratories and analysts responsible for performing drug testing and analysis. The procedural rules and quality assurance program shall be compatible with the laboratory's accreditation procedural rules and shall establish compatible laboratory techniques, laboratory equipment, supplies, computer software and acceptance criteria for laboratory accreditation.

SECTION 41

Chemist's analysis for presence of sperm cells; certificate of results; prima facie evidence

A certificate by a chemist of the department of the result of analysis made by him for the presence of a sperm cell or cells or seminal fluid on or in any material or substance furnished him by a police officer of any department, signed and sworn to by such chemist, shall be prima facie evidence of the presence of a sperm cell or cells or seminal fluid on or in such material or substance.

NOTE   "Although the statutory language used [in G.L. c. 22C, § 41] refers to the admissibility of the certificate as prima facie evidence of the presence of a sperm cell or cells or seminal fluid, the statute was obviously intended to provide for the admissibility of the results of the police chemist's examination by means of a certificate for the presence, as well as the absence, of sperm or seminal fluid." *Commonwealth v. Juzba*, 46 Mass. App. Ct. 319, 322 (1999).

SECTION 42

Motor vehicle ownership records; certified copies; prima facie evidence

In proceedings under sections twenty-seven A, twenty-eight, twenty-nine, one hundred and eleven A and one hundred and thirty-nine of chapter two hundred and sixty-six, certified copies of any motor vehicle or trailer ownership records, including computer records, in the possession of the registrar of motor vehicles, attested by the registrar or his designee or, if the motor vehicle or trailer is registered or titled in another state, such records similarly certified by the keeper of records of the appropriate motor vehicle department, shall be admissible as proof of ownership of a motor vehicle or trailer and shall be prima facie evidence that the use of the motor vehicle or trailer was unauthorized. If the defendant rebuts such evidence, the commonwealth may be granted a reasonable continuance to enable the owner of the vehicle to be brought into court to testify.

Chapter 22E. State DNA Database

Section
1   Definitions
2   State DNA database; director
3   Submission of DNA sample
4   Collection of DNA samples; civil liability; costs
5   Collection materials
6   Filing and storage of DNA records
7   Laboratories and facilities
8   Rules for testing and analysis; quality assurance program; independent forensic laboratories
9   Confidentiality of records
10   Furnishing of records by director
11   Refusal to provide DNA sample; penalty
12   Unauthorized disclosure of records; penalty
13   Obtaining records without proper authority; penalty
14   Tampering with DNA sample or DNA record; penalty
15   Expungement of record

SECTION 1

Definitions

As used in this chapter, the following words shall have the following meanings, unless the context clearly requires otherwise:—

"CODIS" or "combined DNA index system", the Federal Bureau of Investigation's national DNA identification index system which facilitates the storage and exchange of DNA records submitted by state and local criminal justice and law enforcement agencies.

"Colonel", the colonel of state police.

"DNA", deoxyribonucleic acid.

"DNA analysis", DNA typing tests that generate numerical identification information and are obtained from a DNA sample.

"DNA record", DNA information that is derived from a DNA sample and DNA analysis and is stored in the state DNA database or in CODIS, including all records pertaining to DNA analysis.

"DNA sample", biological evidence of any nature that is utilized to conduct DNA analysis.

"Department", the department of state police.

"Director", the director of the crime laboratory within the department of state police.

"FBI", the Federal Bureau of Investigation within the United States department of justice.

"State DNA database", the DNA identification records system maintained and administered by the director.

SECTION 2

State DNA database; director

There is hereby established within the department of state police a state DNA database under the direction of the director. The director shall be a person knowledgeable in the field of forensic sciences and shall be paid an annual salary which shall be set by the colonel in consultation with the secretary of public safety and the secretary for administration and finance. Such salary shall be competitive with comparable or similar positions in other jurisdictions. The director shall have responsibility for DNA analysis and the management and administration of the state DNA database.

SECTION 3

Submission of DNA sample

(Amended by 2012 Mass. Acts c. 192, § 1, effective Aug. 2, 2012.)

Any person who is convicted of an offense that is punishable by imprisonment in the state prison and any person adjudicated a youthful offender by reason of an offense that would be punishable by imprisonment in the state prison if committed by an adult shall submit a DNA sample to the department within one year of such conviction or adjudication or, if incarcerated, before release from custody, whichever occurs first. The trial court and probation department shall work in conjunction with the director to establish and implement a system for the electronic notification to the department whenever a person is convicted of an offense that requires the submission of a DNA sample under this section. The sample shall be collected by a person authorized under section 4, in accordance with regulations or procedures established by the director. The results of such sample shall become part of the state DNA database. The submission of such DNA sample shall not be stayed pending a sentence appeal, motion for new trial, appeal to an appellate court or other post conviction motion or petition.

NOTE   **Constitutionality.** DNA law, G.L. c. 22E, requiring convict to provide DNA sample for State DNA database, constitutional. *Landry v. Attorney General*, 429 Mass. 336 (1999); *see also Murphy v. Dep't of Corr.*, 429 Mass. 736 (1999).

SECTION 4

Collection of DNA samples; civil liability; costs

(Amended by 2012 Mass. Acts c. 192, §§ 2–4, effective Aug. 2, 2012.)

(a) The director may establish regulations or procedures for the collection of DNA samples, including standards for training and licensing personnel who may collect such samples. A physician, registered professional nurse, licensed practical nurse, phlebotomist, health care worker with phlebotomist training or a person approved and trained by the director shall collect DNA samples pursuant to section 3. No person authorized under this section to collect DNA samples, including buccal swabs and blood samples, shall be subject to civil liability for the act of withdrawing blood, or any other act directly related to the taking of a DNA sample; provided, however, that they shall employ recognized medical procedures and comply with all regulations or procedures promulgated by the director for the collection of DNA samples. Duly authorized law enforcement and correction personnel may employ reasonable force to assist in collecting DNA samples in cases where an individual refuses to submit to such collection as required under this chapter; provided, further, that such law enforcement and correction personnel shall not be subject to criminal prosecution or civil liability for the use of such reasonable force.

(b) The cost of preparing, collecting and processing a DNA sample shall be assessed against the person required to submit a DNA sample, unless such person is indigent as defined in section 27A of chapter 261. The cost of preparing, collecting and processing a DNA sample shall be determined by the secretary for administration and finance in consultation with the director and shall be paid to the department and retained by it to offset costs associated with creating, maintaining and administering the state DNA database.

SECTION 5
Collection materials

The department shall provide all blood sample vials, collection tubes, mailing tubes, other DNA sample collection materials, labels and instructions for the collection of DNA samples pursuant to this chapter.

SECTION 6
Filing and storage of DNA records

All DNA samples collected pursuant to sections 3 and 4 shall be forwarded to the director for the purpose of DNA analysis. The director shall provide for the receipt and analysis of DNA samples and for the filing and storage of DNA records derived from such DNA analysis in the state DNA database. The director shall promulgate regulations governing the collection, submission, receipt, identification, storage and disposal of DNA samples.

SECTION 7
Laboratories and facilities

The department is hereby authorized to establish such laboratories and facilities within the commonwealth as may be necessary to conduct forensic and DNA analysis. Notwithstanding the provisions of any general or special law to the contrary, the department is hereby authorized to enter into such contracts, agreements or partnerships with governmental or nongovernmental entities, including educational, scientific, medical, or not for profit entities, as the director may deem necessary to meet the purposes of this chapter.

SECTION 8
Rules governing testing and analysis; quality assurance program; independent forensic laboratories

The director shall establish procedural rules governing the testing and analysis of DNA samples and a quality assurance program, which shall include proficiency standards for laboratories and analysts responsible for performing DNA testing and analysis. Such procedural rules and quality assurance program shall be compatible with the procedural rules and quality assurance program utilized by the FBI and shall establish compatible laboratory techniques, laboratory equipment, supplies, computer software and acceptance criteria for DNA records in CODIS. The director may employ independent forensic laboratories to perform the DNA analysis required under section 3; provided, however, that such laboratories shall comply with the regulations established pursuant to this section and the procedural rules and quantity assurance program established pursuant to this section. With respect to any independent forensic laboratory that performs or seeks to perfume the DNA analysis required under section 3, the director may audit such laboratory for compliance with such regulations or procedures as may be adopted under this chapter and may revoke such laboratory's right to create and exchange DNA records on the ground that such laboratory has failed to comply with any regulations, procedures, rules or quality assurance programs established pursuant to this section.

SECTION 9
Confidentiality of records

All DNA records collected pursuant to this chapter shall be confidential and shall not be disclosed to any person or agency unless such disclosure shall be authorized by this chapter. DNA records shall not be stored in a criminal offender record information system operated by the department of criminal justice information services pursuant to sections 167 to 178, inclusive, of chapter 6.

SECTION 10
Furnishing of records by director

(a) The director shall furnish records in his possession, including DNA records and analysis, to police departments in cities and towns, to the department, to the department of correction, to a sheriff's department, to the parole board or to prosecuting officers within the commonwealth upon request in writing or electronically.

(b) The director shall make DNA records available upon written or electronic request to: (1) local, state and federal criminal justice and law enforcement and prosecuting agencies, including forensic laboratories serving such agencies, for identification purposes in order to further official criminal investigations or prosecutions; provided, however, that any DNA sample obtained directly from a person not otherwise required to provide a DNA sample under this chapter and delivered to the director for comparison with DNA records in the state DNA database shall have been obtained pursuant to a warrant; (2) the FBI for storage and maintenance in CODIS; and (3) any person who has been identified and charged with a criminal offense as a result of a search of DNA records stored in the state DNA database; provided, however, that such access shall be limited to DNA information pertaining to such individual.

(c) The director shall make DNA records upon written or electronic request to meet such purposes or comply with such statutory obligations as may be required under federal law as a condition to obtaining federal grants or funding.

(d) The director may, in his discretion, make DNA records available to authorized persons or organizations, upon written or electronic request, for the limited purpose of (1) advancing DNA analysis methods and supporting statistical interpretation of DNA analysis, including development of population databases; provided, however, that personal identifying information shall be removed from DNA records disclosed for such purposes; (2) assisting in the identification of human remains from mass disasters; (3) assisting the identification and recovery of missing persons; and (4) advancing other humanitarian purposes.

SECTION 11
Refusal to provide DNA sample; penalty
(Amended by 2012 Mass. Acts c. 192, § 5, effective July 1, 2013, see 2012 Mass. Acts c. 192, § 50.)

Any person required to provide a DNA sample pursuant to this chapter and who, after receiving written notice, fails to provide such DNA sample within 1 year of conviction, adjudication or release from custody, as required by section 3, whichever occurs first, shall be subject to punishment by a fine of not more than $1,000 or imprisonment in a jail or house of correction for not more than six months or both.

SECTION 12
Unauthorized disclosure of records; penalty

Any person who, by virtue of employment or official position, has possession of, or access to, a DNA sample or record or portion thereof contained in the state DNA database and who purposely discloses such record or portion thereof in any manner to any person or agency not authorized to receive such record or portion thereof shall be subject to punishment by a fine of not more than $1,000 or imprisonment in a jail or house of correction for not more than six months or both.

SECTION 13
Obtaining records without proper authority; penalty

Any person who, without proper authorization, willfully obtains a DNA record or a portion thereof contained in the state DNA database shall be subject to punishment by a fine of not more than $1,000 or imprisonment in a jail or house of correction for not more than six months or both.

SECTION 14
Tampering with DNA sample or records; penalty

Any person who tampers with or attempts to tamper with a DNA sample or DNA record with the intent to interfere with DNA analysis shall be subject to punishment by a fine of not more than $5,000 or imprisonment in the state prison for not more than five years or in a jail or house of correction for not more than two and a half years or both such fine and imprisonment.

SECTION 15
Expungement of record

Any person whose DNA record has been included in the state DNA database may apply to the superior court to have such record expunged on the grounds that the conviction or judicial determination that resulted in the inclusion of the person's DNA record in the state DNA database has been reversed and the case dismissed; provided, however, that one year shall have elapsed from the date the judgment reversing or dismissing the conviction became final or such person shall have obtained, in writing, authorization from the district attorney that no further prosecution is contemplated under the original offense for which such person was convicted or for which the original judicial determination was entered.

Chapter 23K. The Massachusetts Gaming Commission

Section
2   Definitions [excerpt]
37   Unlawful conduct or operation of game or gaming device
38   Resisting, preventing, impeding, etc., performance of duties of agent or employee of the bureau, commission or division; penalty
39   Cheating and swindling; penalty
40   Possession of cheating and swindling device or game; penalty
41   Manufacture, distribution, sale or service of gaming device for purpose of defrauding, cheating or stealing; penalty
42   Seizure and forfeiture of device, game or gaming device possessed, used, manufactured, etc. in violation of chapter
43   Playing, placing of wagers or collecting winnings from game in a gaming establishment by or on behalf of person under 21 years of age; penalty

SECTION 2
Definitions [excerpt]
(Added by 2011 Mass. Acts c. 194, § 16, effective Nov. 22, 2011.)

"Gambling", the playing of a game by a patron of a gaming establishment.

"Game", a banking or percentage game played with cards, dice, tiles, dominoes or an electronic, electrical or mechanical device or machine played for money, property, checks, credit or any other representative of value which has been approved by the commission.

"Gaming", dealing, operating, carrying on, conducting, maintaining or exposing any game for pay.

"Gaming device" or "gaming equipment", an electronic, electrical or mechanical contrivance or machine used in connection with gaming or a game.

SECTION 37
Unlawful conduct or operation of game or gaming device
(Added by 2011 Mass. Acts c. 194, § 16, effective Nov. 22, 2011.)

(a) Whoever conducts or operates, or permits to be conducted or operated, any game or gaming device in violation of this chapter or the regulations adopted under this chapter shall be punished by imprisonment in the state prison for not more than 5 years or imprisonment in the house of correction for not more than 2½ years, or by a fine not to exceed $25,000, or both, and in the case of a person other than a natural person, by a fine not to exceed $100,000.

(b) Whoever employs, or continues to employ, an individual in a position, the duties of which require a license or registration under this chapter, who is not so licensed or registered, shall be punished by imprisonment in the house of correction for not more than 6 months or by a fine not to exceed $10,000, or both, and in the case of a person other than a natural person, by a fine not to exceed $100,000.

(c) Whoever works or is employed in a position, the duties of which require licensing or registration under this chapter, without the required license or registration, shall be punished by imprisonment in the house of correction for not more than 6 months or a fine not to exceed $10,000, or both.

(d) A gaming licensee who, without the permission of the commission: (i) places a game or gaming device into play or displays a game or gaming device in a gaming establishment; or (ii) receives, directly or indirectly, any compensation or reward or any percentage or share of the revenue for keeping, running or carrying on a game, or owning the real property upon, or the location within which any game occurs, shall be punished by imprisonment in the house of correction for not more than 2½ years or by a fine not to exceed $25,000, or both, and in the case of a person other than a natural person, by a fine not to exceed $100,000.

(e) Whoever conducts or operates any game or gaming device after the person's gaming license has expired and prior to the actual renewal of the gaming license shall be punished by imprisonment in the house of correction for not more than 1½ years or a fine not to exceed $25,000, or both, and in the case of a person other than a natural person, by a fine not to exceed $100,000.

(f) A gaming licensee who knowingly fails to exclude from the licensee's gaming establishment any person placed by the commission on the list of excluded persons shall be punished by a fine not to exceed $5,000 or by imprisonment in the house of correction for not more than 1 year, or both, and in the case of a person other than a natural person, by a fine not to exceed $100,000.

(g) Whoever willfully: (i) fails to report, pay or truthfully account for and pay over a license fee or tax imposed by this chapter or by the regulations adopted under this chapter; or (ii) evades or defeats, or attempts to evade or defeat, a license fee or tax or payment of a license fee or tax shall be punished by imprisonment in the state prison for not more than 5 years or in the house of correction for not more than 2½ years or a fine not to exceed $100,000, or both, and in the case of a person other than a natural person, by a fine not to exceed $5,000,000.

SECTION 38
Resisting, preventing, impeding, etc., performance of duties of agent or employee of the bureau, commission or division; penalty
(Added by 2011 Mass. Acts c. 194, § 16, effective Nov. 22, 2011.)

Whoever willfully resists, prevents, impedes, interferes with or makes any false, fictitious or fraudulent statement or representation to the bureau, commission or division or to agents or employees of the bureau, commission or division in the lawful performance of the agent's or employee's duties under this chapter shall be punished by imprisonment in the state prison for not more than 5 years or in the house of correction for not more than 2½ years or by a fine not to exceed $25,000, or both.

SECTION 39
Cheating and swindling; penalty
(Added by 2011 Mass. Acts c. 194, § 16, effective Nov. 22, 2011.)

(a) Whoever, during a game in a gaming establishment, knowingly and by any trick or sleight of hand performance or by a fraud or fraudulent scheme, cards, dice or other gaming device, for himself, for another or for a representative of either: (i) wins, or attempts to win, money or property; or (ii) reduces, or attempts to reduce, a losing wager in a gaming establishment shall be guilty of cheating and swindling.

(b) Whoever knowingly uses a cheating and swindling device or game in a gaming establishment shall be guilty of cheating and swindling.

(c) Whoever commits the offense of cheating and swindling shall be punished as follows:

(i) if the value of the money, property or wager cheated and swindled is $75,000 or more, by imprisonment in the state prison for not more than 10 years or in the house of correction for not more than 2½ years or by a fine not to exceed $1,000,000, or both, and in the case of a person other than a natural person, by a fine not to exceed $10,000,000;

(ii) if the value of the money, property or wager cheated and swindled is $10,000 or more but less than $75,000, by imprisonment in the state prison for not more than 5 years or in the house of correction for not more than 2½ years or by a fine not to exceed $500,000, or both, and in the case of a person other than a natural person, by a fine not to exceed $5,000,000;

(iii) if the value of the money, property or wager cheated and swindled is $1,000 or more but less than $10,000, by imprisonment in the state prison for not more than 3 years or in the house of correction for not more than 2½ years or by a fine not to exceed $100,000, or both, and in the case of a person other than a natural person, by a fine not to exceed $1,000,000;

(iv) if nothing of value was obtained in violation of this subsection or if the value of the money, property or wager cheated and swindled is less than $1,000, by imprisonment in the house of correction for not more than 2½ years or by a fine not to exceed $10,000, or both, and in the case of a person other than a natural person, by a fine not to exceed $100,000.

(d) Each episode or transaction of swindling and cheating may be the subject of a separate prosecution and conviction. In the discretion of the commonwealth, multiple episodes or transactions of swindling and cheating committed as part of a single scheme or course of conduct may be treated as a single offense and the amounts involved in acts of swindling and cheating committed according to a scheme or course of conduct, whether by the same person or several persons, may be aggregated in determining the value of money, property or wager involved in the offense.

(e) A gaming licensee, or an employee of a gaming licensee, who, in a gaming establishment, knowingly: (i) conducts or operates any game using a cheating and swindling device or game; (ii) displays for play a cheating and swindling game; or (iii) permits to be conducted, operated or displayed, any cheating and swindling device or game shall be punished by imprisonment in the state prison for not more than 5 years or imprisonment in the house of correction for not more than 2½ years, or by a fine not to exceed $25,000, or both, and in the case of a person other than a natural person, by a fine not to exceed $100,000.

SECTION 40
Possession of cheating and swindling device or game; penalty
(Added by 2011 Mass. Acts c. 194, § 16, effective Nov. 22, 2011.)

(a) Whoever possesses a cheating and swindling device or game, with the intent to defraud, cheat or steal, shall be punished by imprisonment in the house of correction for not more than 2½ years or by a fine not to exceed $10,000, or both, and in the case of a person other than a natural person, by a fine not to exceed $100,000.

(b) Possession of a cheating and swindling device or game within a gaming establishment shall constitute prima facie evidence of an intent to defraud, cheat or steal, except possession by a gaming licensee or an employee of a gaming licensee, acting lawfully in furtherance of such person's employment within the gaming establishment, and shall be punished by imprisonment in the house of correction for not more than 2½ years or a fine not to exceed $10,000, or both.

SECTION 41
Manufacture, distribution, sale or service of gaming device for purpose of defrauding, cheating or stealing; penalty
(Added by 2011 Mass. Acts c. 194, § 16, effective Nov. 22, 2011.)

Whoever manufactures, distributes, sells or services a gaming device, in violation of this chapter or regulations adopted under this chapter and for the purpose of defrauding, cheating or stealing from a person playing, operating or conducting a game in a gaming establishment, shall be punished by imprisonment in the state prison for not more than 5 years or imprisonment in the house of correction for not more than 2½ years or by a fine not to exceed $25,000, or both, and in the case of a person other than a natural person, by a fine not to exceed $150,000.

SECTION 42
Seizure and forfeiture of device, game or gaming device possessed, used, manufactured, etc. in violation of chapter
(Added by 2011 Mass. Acts c. 194, § 16, effective Nov. 22, 2011.)

Any device, game or gaming device possessed, used, manufactured, distributed, sold or serviced in violation of this chapter shall be subject to seizure and forfeiture by the division or bureau. Forfeiture proceedings shall be conducted as provided in subsections (b) to (j), inclusive, of section 47 of chapter 94C. For purposes of subsection (d) of said section 47 of said chapter 94C, the commission shall be considered a police department and shall be entitled to a police department's distribution of forfeiture proceedings.

SECTION 43
Playing, placing of wagers or collecting winnings from game in a gaming establishment by or on behalf of person under 21 years of age; penalty
(Added by 2011 Mass. Acts c. 194, § 16, effective Nov. 22, 2011.)

(a) Whoever, being under 21 years old, plays, places wagers at or collects winnings from, whether personally or through an agent, a game in a gaming establishment shall be punished by a fine not to exceed $1,000.

(b) Whoever, being a gaming licensee or an employee of a gaming licensee, who knowingly allows a person under the age of 21 to play, place wagers at, or collect winnings from a game in a gaming establishment, whether personally or through an agent, shall be punished, for a first offense, by imprisonment in the house of correction for not more than 1 year or a fine not to exceed $10,000, or both, and in the case of a person other than a natural person, by a fine not to exceed $500,000 and, for a second or subsequent offense, by imprisonment in the house of correction for not more than 2 years or a fine not to exceed $50,000, or both, and in the case of a person other than a natural person, by a fine not to exceed $1,000,000.

(c) Whoever knowingly plays, places wagers at or collects winnings from a game in a gaming establishment for or on behalf of a person under 21 years of age shall be punished by imprisonment in a house of correction for not more than 6 months or by a fine of not more than $1,000 or both.

Chapter 89. Law of the Road

Section
1	Meeting vehicles
2	Passing vehicle traveling in same direction
3	Sleigh or sled; bells
4	Keeping to right while view obstructed
4A	Driving vehicles in a single lane; motorcycles, riding and passing
4B	Driving in lane nearest right side of way
4C	Heavy trucks; driving in right-hand lane on multi-lane highways
5	Penalties; exceptions
6	Applicability of rules of road to street railway cars
6A	Stopping of street railway cars for passage of fire apparatus
7	Right of way of fire engines, patrol vehicles and ambulances; obstruction; penalties
7A	Restrictions on use of ways upon approach of emergency vehicles
7B	Operation of emergency vehicles
7C	Lane change upon approach of stationary emergency response vehicle; highway maintenance vehicle or recovery vehicle; penalty
8	Right of way at intersecting ways; turning on red signals
9	Designation of highways as through ways; traffic control signs and devices
10	Violation of one-way traffic; civil liability
11	Marked crosswalks; yielding right of way to pedestrians; penalty

SECTION 1
Meeting vehicles

When persons traveling with vehicles meet on a way, each shall seasonably drive his vehicle to the right of the middle of the traveled part of such way, so that the vehicles may pass without interference, except that the department of highways may modify such restriction by pavement markings on state highways, on ways leading thereto and on all main highways between cities and towns. The department may by permit, revocable upon notice, authorized cities and towns to modify such restriction by pavement markings. All markings shall be in accordance with accepted standards of engineering practice, as provided in section two of chapter eighty-five.

The provisions of this section shall not be construed as prohibiting a vehicle from crossing a solid center pavement marking line or lines in making a left turn into or from a private way.

SECTION 2
Passing vehicle traveling in same direction

Except as herein otherwise provided, the driver of a vehicle passing another vehicle traveling in the same direction shall drive a safe distance to the left of such other vehicle and shall not return to the right until safely clear of the overtaken vehicle; and, if the way is of sufficient width for the two vehicles to pass, the driver of the leading one shall not unnecessarily obstruct the other. If it is not possible to overtake a bicycle or other vehicle at a safe distance in the same lane, the overtaking vehicle shall use all or part of an adjacent lane if it is safe to do so or wait for a safe opportunity to overtake. Except when overtaking and passing on the right is permitted, the driver of an overtaken vehicle shall give way to the right in favor of the overtaking vehicle on visible signal and shall not increase the speed of his vehicle until completely passed by the overtaking vehicle.

The driver of a vehicle may, if the roadway is free from obstruction and of sufficient width for two or more lines of moving vehicles, overtake and pass upon the right of another vehicle when the vehicle overtaken is (a) making or about to make a left turn, (b) upon a one way street, or (c) upon any roadway on which traffic is restricted to one direction of movement.

SECTION 3
Sleigh or sled; bells

No person shall travel on a way with a sleigh or sled drawn by a horse, unless there are at least three bells attached to some part of the harness.

SECTION 4
Keeping to right while view obstructed

Whenever on any way, public or private, there is not an unobstructed view of the road for at least four hundred feet, the driver of every vehicle shall keep his vehicle on the right of the middle of the traveled part of the way, whenever it is safe and practicable so to do, except that the department of highways may alter this provision by the use of restrictive pavement markings in areas of limited sight distance, at intersections and at obstructions in the highway, on state highways, on ways leading thereto and on all main highways between cities and towns; and may by permit, revocable upon notice, authorize cities and towns to alter said provision by the use of such restrictive pavement markings; provided, that such markings shall be in accordance with accepted standards of engineering practice; but, notwithstanding the foregoing provisions, every driver of a slow moving vehicle, while ascending a grade shall reasonably keep said vehicle in the extreme right-hand lane until the top of such grade has been reached.

SECTION 4A
Driving vehicles in a single lane; motorcycles, riding and passing

When any way has been divided into lanes, the driver of a vehicle shall so drive that the vehicle shall be entirely within a single lane, and he shall not move from the lane in which he is driving until he has first ascertained if such movement can be made with safety. The operators of motorcycles shall not ride abreast of more than one other motorcycle, shall ride single file when passing, and shall not pass any other motor vehicle within the same lane, except another motorcycle.

SECTION 4B
Driving in lane nearest right side of way

Upon all ways the driver of a vehicle shall drive in the lane nearest the right side of the way when such lane is available for travel, except when overtaking another vehicle or when preparing for a left turn. When the right lane has been constructed or designated for purposes other than ordinary travel, a driver shall drive his vehicle in the lane adjacent to the right lane except when overtaking another vehicle or when preparing for a left or right turn; provided, however, that a driver may drive his vehicle in such right lane if signs have been erected by the department of highways permitting the use of such lane.

SECTION 4C
Heavy trucks; driving in right-hand lane on multi-lane highways

On any highway with more than one passing lane in the same direction, heavy commercial vehicles, except buses, shall be restricted in ordinary operation to the right-hand travel lane, and in overtaking and passing shall be restricted to the next adjacent passing or travel lane, and shall not use any other lanes except in an emergency. For the purpose of this section, heavy commercial vehicles shall be defined as those in excess of two and one half tons used for transportation of goods, wares, and merchandise.

SECTION 5
Penalties; exceptions

Whoever violates any of the provisions of sections one to four C, inclusive, except as otherwise provided herein, shall, upon complaint made within three months after the commission of the offense, forfeit not more than one hundred dollars and whoever drives in the right lane which has been constructed or designated for purposes other than ordinary travel as set forth in section four B shall, upon complaint made within three months after the commission of the offense, forfeit not more than one hundred dollars.

Notwithstanding any provisions of the law to the contrary, the provisions of sections one to four C, inclusive, shall not apply to a person acting in conformity with the direction of a police officer or to a driver of a vehicle actually engaged in authorized work upon a highway under construction, repair or during maintenance operations when the nature of the work necessitates a departure from normal operational practices or to any operator of a motor vehicle when construction or repair is being performed which prohibits passage in the ordinary travel lane or lanes on a highway.

SECTION 6
Applicability of rules of road to street railway cars

In construing rules, by-laws and regulations concerning the use and operation of vehicles on ways, street railway cars or other cars moving upon rails shall not be considered to be vehicles within the provisions of the five preceding sections, unless it is expressly so provided.

SECTION 6A
Stopping of street railway cars for passage of fire apparatus

Every motorman of a car upon a street railway shall, upon the approach of any fire apparatus going to a fire or responding to an alarm, immediately stop said car and keep the same at a standstill until such apparatus has passed. Violation of any provision of this section shall be punished by a fine of not more than twenty-five dollars.

SECTION 7
Right of way of fire engines, patrol vehicles and ambulances; obstruction; penalties

The members and apparatus of a fire department while going to a fire or responding to an alarm, police patrol vehicles and ambulances, and ambulances on a call for the purpose of hospitalizing a sick or injured person shall have the right of way through any street, way, lane or alley. Whoever wilfully obstructs or retards the passage of any of the foregoing in the exercise of such right shall be punished by a fine of fifty dollars or by imprisonment for not more than three months for the first offense and by a fine of not more than five hundred dollars or by imprisonment for up to one year for a second and subsequent offenses; provided, however, that for a third or subsequent offense the court or the registry of motor vehicles, in addition to any such fine or imprisonment, may suspend the license of the person so convicted and may order mandatory classroom retraining in motor vehicle and traffic laws.

SECTION 7A
Restrictions on use of ways upon approach of emergency vehicles

Upon the approach of any fire apparatus, police vehicle, ambulance or disaster vehicle which is going to a fire or responding to call, alarm or emergency situation, every person driving a vehicle on a way shall immediately drive said vehicle as far as possible toward the right-hand curb or side of said way and shall keep the same at a standstill until such fire apparatus, police vehicle, ambulance or disaster vehicle has passed. No person shall drive a vehicle over a hose of a fire department without the consent of a member of such department. No person shall drive a vehicle within three hundred feet of any fire apparatus going to a fire or responding to an alarm, nor drive said vehicle, or park or leave the same unattended, within eight hundred feet of a fire or within the fire lanes established by the fire department, or upon or beside any traveled way, whether public or private, leading to the scene of a fire, in such a manner as to obstruct the approach to the fire of any fire apparatus or any ambulance, safety or police vehicle, or of any vehicle bearing an official fire or police department designation. Authorized police or fire department personnel may tow a vehicle found to be in violation of the provisions of this section or which is illegally parked or standing in a fire lane as established by the fire department, whether or not a fire is in progress, and such personnel shall not be subject to the provisions of section one hundred and twenty D of chapter two hundred and sixty-six. No person shall operate a motor vehicle behind any such fire apparatus, ambulance, safety or police vehicle, or any vehicle bearing an official fire or police department designation which is operating with emergency systems on, for a distance of three hundred feet. Violation of any provision of this section shall be punished by a fine of not more than one hundred dollars.

SECTION 7B
Operation of emergency vehicles

The driver of a vehicle of fire, police or recognized protective department and the driver of an ambulance shall be subject to the provisions of any statute, rule, regulation, ordinance or by-law relating to the operation or parking or vehicles, except that a driver of fire apparatus while going to a fire or responding to an alarm, or the driver of a vehicle of a police or recognized protective department or the driver of an ambulance, in an emergency and while in performance of a public duty or while transporting a sick or injured person to a hospital or other destination where professional medical services are available, may drive such vehicle at a speed in excess of the applicable speed limit if he exercises caution and due regard under the circumstances for the safety of persons and property, and may drive such vehicle through an intersection of ways contrary to any traffic signs or signals regulating traffic at such intersection if he first brings such vehicle to a full stop and then proceeds with caution and due regard for the safety of persons and property, unless otherwise directed by a police officer regulating traffic at such intersection. The driver of any such approaching emergency vehicle shall comply with the provisions of section fourteen of chapter ninety when approaching a school bus which has stopped to allow passengers to alight or board from the same, and whose red lamps are flashing.

SECTION 7C
Lane change upon approach of stationary emergency response vehicle, highway maintenance vehicle or recovery vehicle; penalty

(a) As used in this section the following words shall, unless the context clearly requires otherwise, have the following meanings:

"Emergency response vehicle", a fire apparatus, police vehicle, ambulance, or disaster vehicle.

"Highway maintenance vehicle", a vehicle used for the maintenance of highways and roadways: (1) that is owned or operated by the executive office of transportation and public works, a county, a municipality or any political subdivision thereof; or (2) that is owned or operated by a person under contract with the executive office of transportation and public works, a county, a municipality or any political subdivision thereof.

"Operator", any person who operates a motor vehicle as defined in section 1 of chapter 90.

"Person", a natural person, corporation, association, partnership or other legal entity.

"Recovery vehicle", a vehicle that is specifically designed to assist a disabled vehicle or to tow a disabled vehicle.

(b) Upon approaching a stationary emergency vehicle, highway maintenance vehicle or recovery vehicle with flashing lights an operator shall:

(1) proceed with due caution, reduce the speed of the vehicle to that of a reasonable and safe speed for road conditions, and, if practicable and on a highway having at least 4 lanes with not less than 2 lanes proceeding in the same direction as the operator's vehicle, yield the right-of-way by making a lane change into a lane not adjacent to that of the emergency response vehicle, highway maintenance vehicle or recovery vehicle; or

(2) if changing lanes is impracticable, proceed with due caution and reduce the speed of the vehicle to that of a reasonable and safe speed for road conditions.

(c) Violation of this section shall be punished by a fine of not more than $100.

SECTION 8
Right of way at intersecting ways; turning on red signals

When two vehicles approach or enter an intersection of any ways, as defined in section one of chapter ninety, at approximately the same instant, the operator of the vehicle on the left shall yield to the right-of-way to the vehicle on the right. Any operator intending to turn left, in an intersection, across the path or lane of vehicles approaching from the opposite direction shall, before turning, yield the right-of-way until such time as the left turn can be made with reasonable safety. Any operator of a vehicle entering a rotary intersection shall yield the right-of-way to any vehicle already in the intersection. The foregoing provisions of this section shall not apply when an operator is otherwise directed by a police officer, or by a traffic regulating sign, device or signal lawfully erected and maintained in accordance with the provisions of section two of chapter eighty-five and, where so required with the written approval of the department of highways and while such approval is in effect.

At any intersection on ways, as defined in section one of chapter ninety, in which vehicular traffic is facing a steady red indication in a traffic control signal, the driver of a vehicle which is stopped as close as practicable at the entrance to the crosswalk or the near side of the intersections or, if none, then at the entrance to the intersection in obedience to such red or stop signal, may make either (1) a right turn or (2) if on a one-way street may make a left turn to another one-way street, but shall yield the right-of-way to pedestrians and other traffic proceeding as directed by the signal at said intersection, except that a city or town, subject to section two of chapter eighty-five, by rules, orders, ordinances, or by-laws, or the department of highways on state highways or on ways at their intersections with a state highway, may prohibit any such turns against a red or stop signal at any such intersection, and such prohibition shall be effective when a sign is erected at such intersection giving notice thereof. Any person who violates the provisions of this paragraph shall be punished by a fine of not less than thirty-five dollars.

SECTION 9

Designation of highways as through ways; traffic control signs and devices

The department of highways may designate any state highway or part thereof as a through way and may designate intersections or other roadway junctions with state highways at which vehicular traffic on one or more roadways should stop or yield and stop before entering the intersection or junction, and the department may, after notice, revoke any such designation. The department of highways on any state highway or part thereof so designated as a through way, or on any way where the department has designated such way as intersecting or joining with a state highway, shall erect and maintain stop signs, yield signs and other traffic control devices.

The local authorities of a city or town authorized to enact ordinances or bylaws, or make rules, orders or regulations under the provisions of section twenty-two of chapter forty may in accordance with the provisions of section two of chapter eighty-five of the General Laws, including department approval when required, designate any way or part thereof under the control of such city or town as a through way and may designate intersections or other roadway junctions at which vehicular traffic on one or more roadways shall stop or yield and stop before entering the intersection or junction, and may, after notice and like department approval, when required, revoke any such designation. Such local authorities of a city or town having control of any way or part thereof so designated as a through way shall erect and maintain stop signs, yield signs and other traffic control devices at such designated intersections or junctions.

Except when directed to proceed by a police officer, every driver of a vehicle approaching a stop sign or a flashing red signal indication shall stop at a clearly marked stop line, but if none, before entering the crosswalk on the near side of the intersection, or, if none, then at the point nearest the intersecting roadway where the driver has a view of approaching traffic on the intersecting roadway before entering it. After having stopped, the driver shall yield the right of way to any vehicle in the intersection or approaching on another roadway so closely as to constitute an immediate hazard during the time when such driver is moving across or within the intersection or junction of roadways.

The driver of a vehicle approaching a yield sign shall in obedience to such sign slow down to a speed reasonable for the existing conditions and, if required for safety to stop, shall stop at a clearly marked stop line, but if none, before entering the crosswalk on the near side of the intersection, or, if none, then at the point nearest the intersecting roadway where the driver has a view of approaching traffic on the intersecting roadway before entering it. After slowing or stopping, the driver shall yield the right of way to any vehicle in the intersection or approaching on another roadway so closely as to constitute an immediate hazard during the time such driver is moving across or within the intersection or junction of roadways; provided, however, that if such a driver is involved in a collision with a vehicle in the intersection or junction of roadways, after driving past yield sign without stopping, such collision shall be deemed prima facie evidence of his failure to yield the right of way.

The driver of a motor vehicle shall not cross or enter an intersection, which it is unable to proceed through, without stopping and thereby blocking vehicles from traveling in a free direction. A green light is no defense to be blocking the intersection. The driver must wait another cycle of the signal light, if necessary.

For the purposes of this section the word, "vehicle", shall include a trackless trolley.

Any person violating the provisions of this section shall be punished by a fine not to exceed $150 for each offense.

SECTION 10

Violation of one-way traffic; civil liability

The violation by the operator or driver of a motor or other vehicle of any rule, regulation, ordinance or by-law limiting traffic on any specified way to traffic moving in one direction shall not, in respect to any civil liability, render such operator or driver, or such vehicle or any occupant thereof, a trespasser upon said way.

SECTION 11

Marked crosswalks; yielding right of way to pedestrians; penalty

When traffic control signals are not in place or not in operation the driver of a vehicle shall yield the right of way, slowing down or stopping if need be so to yield, to a pedestrian crossing the roadway within a crosswalk marked in accordance with standards established by the department of highways if the pedestrian is on that half of the traveled part of the way on which the vehicle is traveling or if the pedestrian approaches from the opposite half of the traveled part of the way to within 10 feet of that half of the traveled part of the way on which said vehicle is traveling.

No driver of a vehicle shall pass any other vehicle which has stopped at a marked crosswalk to permit a pedestrian to cross, nor shall any such operator enter a marked crosswalk while a pedestrian is crossing or until there is a sufficient space beyond the crosswalk to accommodate the vehicle he is operating, notwithstanding that a traffic control signal may indicate that vehicles may proceed.

Whoever violates any provision of this section shall be punished by a fine of not more than $200.

Whenever a pedestrian is injured by a motor vehicle in a marked crosswalk, the department of state police or the municipal police department with jurisdiction of the street, in consultation with department of state police if deemed appropriate, shall conduct an investigation into the cause of the injury and any violation of this section or other law or ordinance and shall issue the appropriate civil or criminal citation or file an application for the appropriate criminal complaint, if any. This section shall not limit the ability of a district attorney or the attorney general to seek an indictment in connection with the operation of a motor vehicle which causes injury or death and which violates this section.

Chapter 90. Motor Vehicles and Aircraft

Section

1	Definitions
1B	Motorized bicycles; operation regulations
6	Display of number plates; temporary number plates
7	Brakes, braking systems, mufflers, horns, lights, audible warning systems and other equipment; compliance with safety standards; stickers and emblems
7AA	Child passenger restraints; fine; violation as evidence in civil action
9	Operation of unregistered or improperly equipped motor vehicles, tractors, trailers, etc.
10	Operation of motor vehicle without license; members of armed forces; nonresidents; suspension or revocation of license
11	Carrying certificate of registration and license; presentation after accident upon request
12	Employing or allowing unlicensed operator to operate motor vehicle; permitting person with suspended or revoked license to operate motor vehicle; permitting person with ignition interlock device license restriction to operate motor vehicle without device; penalties
12A	Use of mobile telephone, hands-free mobile telephone or other mobile electronic device by operator of vehicle or vessel used in public transportation prohibited; penalties; affirmative defenses
13	Safety precautions for proper operation and parking of vehicles and buses
13A	Seat belt use required; exemptions; penalty
13B	Composing, sending or reading of electronic messages while operating a motor vehicle prohibited; penalties
14	Precautions for safety of other travelers
14A	Protection of blind pedestrians crossing or attempting to cross ways
14B	Uniform stopping and turning signals on ways
16	Offensive or illegal operation of motor vehicles
17	Speed limits
17B	Drag racing; penalties
20	Penalties and punishments
20A	Parking regulations; violations; notice to appear; failure to appear; adjudication by mail
20A½	Cities of Boston and Cambridge; parking violations; tags; appearance; failure to appear; adjudication by mail
20C	Nature of proceedings under Secs. 20A and 20A½; fines
20D	Tampering or destruction of parking tags; penalty
21	Arrest without warrant
22	Suspension or revocation of certificate of registration or license; notice
22½	Suspension of right to operate based upon violation of Sec. 32E of chapter 94C
22B	Abandonment of motor vehicles; penalties; non-criminal proceedings
22D	Suspension of license for automobile law violation; reinstatement
22E	Abandoned vehicles; removal of parts; penalty
22F	Habitual traffic offender; revocation of license; reinstatement
22G	Littering; suspension of license
22H	Safe transportation of animals
22I	Suspension of license upon report of health care provider or law enforcement officer of operator's cognitive or functional impairment or incapability to operate motor vehicle safely; contents of report; immunity from liability; review by registrar; confidentiality of report
23	Operation of motor vehicle after suspension or revocation of license; concealment of identity of motor vehicle
24	Driving while under influence of intoxicating liquor, etc.; second and subsequent offenses; punishment; treatment programs; reckless and unauthorized driving; failure to stop after collision
24½	Ignition interlock device license restriction; revocation of license for failure to install or maintain device; revocation of license for attempt to operate motor vehicle with elevated blood alcohol level
24A	Use of motor vehicles in commission of felony, larceny or other crimes
24B	Stealing, forging or other falsification of a learner's permit, operator's license, certificate of registration or inspection sticker; use or possession; penalties; suspension and reinstatement of license or right to operate motor vehicle
24D	Probation of persons convicted of driving under the influence; driver alcohol education program; alcohol treatment and rehabilitation programs; fees; indigents; gifts and grants; report
24E	Dismissal of charges upon compliance with terms of probation; records; report
24F	Civil liability to owner for unauthorized use of motor vehicle
24G	Homicide by motor vehicle; punishment
24H	Removal of abandoned or stolen vehicles from public places; towing vehicles; machines that crush, mutilate or destroy vehicles; salvage or junk yard owners or agents
24I	Possession of alcoholic beverages in motor vehicles
24J	Inquiry of defendant convicted of driving under influence of intoxicating liquors as to establishment serving alcohol
24K	Chemical breath analysis; validity; testing procedures; report forms
24L	Serious bodily injury by motor vehicle while under influence of intoxicating substance; penalties
24M	Training for law enforcement personnel regarding alcohol-related offenses; alcohol sensitive selective traffic enforcement program
24N	Suspension of operator's license upon issuance of complaint; hearing
24O	Statement to defendant regarding further violations
24P	Minors; further violations; education and treatment programs
25	Refusal to submit to police officer
26	Accident reports; supplemental report; penalty for violation
26A	Licenses and learner's permit; reporting changes of name and address
34J	Operating motor vehicle without liability policy, bond or security deposit

SECTION 1
Definitions

(Amended by 2014 Mass. Acts c. 62, § 20, effective July 2, 2014; 2016 Mass. Acts c. 133, §§ 50–52, effective July 1, 2016.)

The following words used in this chapter shall have the following meanings, unless a different meaning is clearly apparent from the language or context, or unless such construction is inconsistent with the manifest intention of the legislature:

"Alternative fuel", an energy source used to power a vehicle that does not meet the definition of fuel in section 1 of chapter 64A and is not diesel motor fuel.

"Alternative fuel vehicle," a vehicle powered by alternative fuel with the following attributes:

(a) the capability of operating only on alternative fuel;

(b) its original use was commenced with the taxpayer;

(c) acquired by the taxpayer for use or lease, but not for resale;

(d) is designed to use and uses alternative fuel for a significant portion of the total fuel used for propulsion energy for the vehicle; and

(e) when operating on petroleum fuel, the vehicle model's miles per gallon rating from the United States Environmental Protection Agency exceeds the agency's corporate average fuel economy requirement for the class of vehicles, whether cars or light trucks, in which the vehicle model is classified. The model specification shall include characteristics that affect fuel economy and for which the United States Environmental Protection Agency issues distinct miles per gallon ratings, such as transmission type and engine size.

"Ambulance", a motor vehicle equipped and used exclusively for the transportation of sick, injured or wounded persons, or a motor vehicle operated by a society incorporated under the laws of the commonwealth for the prevention of cruelty to animals, or for the care and protection of harmless or suffering animals, and used exclusively for the transportation of stray and neglected, sick, injured or wounded animals.

"Application", an application by mail or otherwise to the registrar or any agent designated by him for the purpose, upon a blank provided by the registrar, and with which is deposited the fee provided in section thirty-three.

"Articulated bus", a bus consisting of two units, connected in such a way as to permit the safe and convenient passage of passengers while allowing the bus to bend and have some vertical movement at the pivot point, with the design capability of being locked at the pivot point.

"Auto home", any motor vehicle originally designed or permanently altered and equipped for human habitation which is not used to transport property other than that property used for human habitation or camping purposes. A motor vehicle designed primarily to transport property which has been temporarily altered or equipped for human habitation shall not be deemed to be an auto home.

"Automobile", any motor vehicle except a motor cycle.

"Automobile transporter", any vehicle combination, including a stinger-steered automobile transporter and a low-boy automobile transporter, designed and used specifically for the transport of assembled, capable of being driven, highway vehicles. The highway vehicles being transported may be carried on the power unit on an over-cab rack and behind the cab and on the semi-trailer or low-boy.

"Boat transporter", any vehicle combination including a stinger-steered boat transporter and a low-boy boat transporter, designed and used specifically for the transport of assembled boats and boat hulls. The boats may be partially disassembled to facilitate transportation. Boats may be carried on the tractor so long as the length and width restrictions of the vehicle and load are not exceeded.

"B-train assembly", a rigid frame extension attached to the rear frame of a first semi-trailer which allows for a fifth wheel connection point for a second semi-trailer in a tractor semi-trailer-semi-trailer unit.

"B-train assembly unit", a motor vehicle composed of a tractor, semitrailer and semi-trailer with the semi-trailers connected by a B-train assembly.

"Bus or motor bus", any motor vehicle operated upon a public way in any city or town for the carriage of passengers for hire in such a manner as to afford a means of transportation similar to that afforded by a railway company by indiscriminately receiving and discharging passengers along the route on which the vehicle is operated or may be running, or for transporting passengers for hire as a business between fixed and regular termini, or transporting passengers for hire under a charter license, special service or school service permit issued by the department.

"Dealer", any person who is engaged principally and substantially in the business of buying, selling or exchanging motor vehicles or trailers or motor vehicle bodies who maintains a facility dedicated to carrying out said business and, except for a person who exchanges such vehicles on a wholesale basis, is open to the public.

"Department", the division of highways.

"Electronic message", a piece of digital communication that is designed or intended to be transmitted between a mobile electronic device and any other electronic device; provided, however, that electronic message shall include, but not be limited to, electronic mail, electronic message, a text mes-

sage, an instant message, a command or request to access an internet site, or any message that includes a keystroke entry sent between mobile devices.

"Licensed private driver school", a person, partnership or corporation licensed by the registrar to give instruction for hire in the operation of motor vehicles.

"Farmer", a person substantially engaged in the occupation of farming which shall include, but not be limited to, farming in all its branches, the cultivation and tillage of the soil, dairying, the production, cultivation, growing and harvesting of any agricultural, aquacultural, floricultural or horticultural commodities, the growing and harvesting of forest products upon forest land, the raising of livestock including horses, the keeping of horses as a commercial enterprise, the keeping and raising of poultry, swine, cattle and other domesticated animals used for food purposes, bees, fur-bearing animals, and any forestry or lumbering operations, performed by a farmer engaged in agriculture or farming as herein defined, or on a farm as an incident to or in conjunction with such farming operations including, but not limited to, preparations for market, delivery to storage or to market or to carriers for transportation to market.

"Farming", the tillage or use of the soil to raise food for man or beast, the raising of tobacco, or the propagation and growing of trees, shrubs, vines and plants for transplanting and sale.

"Fullmount", a smaller vehicle mounted completely on the frame of either the first or last vehicle in a saddlemount combination.

"Garage", any place where five or more motor vehicles are stored or housed at any one time for pay, except only such places in which motor vehicles are kept by the owners thereof without payment for storage.

"Gross vehicle weight rating", the gross vehicle weight rating established by a manufacturer when applied to a motor vehicle, trailer, semi-trailer or semi-trailer unit, including the gross combination weight rating, if any, when applied to a semi-trailer unit or to a tractor-trailer combination.

"Hands-free mobile telephone", a hand-held mobile telephone that has an internal feature or function, or that is equipped with a hands-free accessory, whether or not permanently part of such hand-held mobile telephone, by which a user engages in a call without the use of either hand, whether or not the use of either hand is necessary to activate, deactivate or initiate a telephone call.

"Heavy duty platform trailer", a trailer other than a semi-trailer, especially constructed for transporting machinery, contractors' equipment, or other heavy or clumsy units. The top surface of the deck or platform of such a vehicle shall not be more than thirty-six inches above the surface on which the wheels of the vehicle rest.

"House trailer", a vehicle having no motive power of its own, originally designed or permanently altered and equipped for human habitation which is not used to transport property other than property used for human habitation or camping purposes. A trailer designed primarily to transport property which has been temporarily altered or equipped for human habitation shall not be deemed to be a house trailer.

"Hybrid vehicle", a vehicle (a) which draws propulsion energy from onboard sources of stored energy which are both: (1) an internal combustion or heat engine using combustible fuel; and (2) a rechargeable energy storage system;

or (b) which, in the case of a passenger vehicle, medium duty passenger vehicle or light truck: (1) for model year 2002 and later model year vehicles, has received a certificate of conformity under the Clean Air Act and meets or exceeds the equivalent qualifying California low emission vehicle standard adopted under section 243(e)(2) of said Clean Air Act for that make and model year; (2) for model year 2004 and later model vehicles, has received a certificate that the vehicle meets or exceeds the Tier II Bin 5 emission level established in regulations prescribed by the Administrator of the United States Environmental Protection Agency under section 202(i) of said Clean Air Act for that make and model year vehicle; and (3) achieves an increase of 25 per cent fuel efficiency as compared to the average vehicle of its class as defined by the United States Environmental Protection Agency.

"Incompetent person", a person lacking legal qualification, ability or fitness to operate motor vehicles or to hold a certificate of motor vehicle registration.

"Intersecting way", any way which joins another at an angle, whether or not it crosses the other.

"Killed in action", a casualty classification determined by the United States Department of Defense when a member of the armed forces of the United States has been killed while performing military operations while serving the United States in a conflict recognized by the United States Department of Defense.

"Lawful presence", persons who have: (i) lawful status in the United States; or (ii) documentation of lawful presence in the United States satisfactory to the registrar, in consultation with the United States Department of Homeland Security.

"Lawful status", the same meaning as defined in 6 C.F.R. 37.3.

"Like offense", as used in sections twenty-four and twenty-four D, shall mean any violation of subparagraph (1) of paragraph (a) of subsection (1) of section twenty-four, or any violation of paragraph (1) of subsection (a) of section eight of chapter ninety B or any violation of the comparable laws of any other jurisdiction.

"Like violation", as used in sections twenty-four and twenty-four D, shall mean any violation of subparagraph (1) of paragraph (a) of subsection (1) of section twenty-four, or any violation of paragraph (1) of subsection (a) of section eight of chapter ninety B or any violation of the comparable laws of any other jurisdiction.

"Low-boy automobile transporter", a semi-trailer unit in which the trailer is designed and used specifically for the transport of assembled, capable of being driven, highway vehicles. The top surface of the deck platform of such semi-trailer shall not be more than thirty-six inches above the surface on which the wheels of the vehicle rest.

"Low-boy boat transporter", a semi-trailer unit in which the trailer is designed and used specifically for the transport of assembled boats and hulls. The top surface of the deck platform of such semi-trailer shall not be more than thirty-six inches above the surface on which the wheels of the vehicle rest.

"Low-speed motor vehicle" or "low-speed vehicle", a motor vehicle as defined in 49 C.F.R. § 571.3 as a vehicle that is 4-wheeled, whose speed attainable in 1 mile is more than 20 miles per hour and not more than 25 miles per hour on a paved level surface and whose gross vehicle weight rating is less than 3,000 pounds. All low-speed motor vehicles shall comply with the standards established in 49 C.F.R.

§ 571.500, as amended, and pursuant thereto, shall be equipped with headlamps, front and rear turn signal lamps, tail lamps, stop lamps, an exterior mirror mounted on the driver's side of the vehicle and either an exterior mirror mounted on the passenger's side of the vehicle or an interior mirror, a parking brake, a windshield that conforms to the federal standards on glazing materials, a vehicle identification number that conforms to the requirements of 49 C.F.R. pt 565 for such numbers, a Type 1 or Type 2 seat belt assembly conforming to 49 C.F.R. § 571.209, installed at each designated seating position and reflex reflectors; provided, that 1 reflector is red on each side as far to the rear as practicable and 1 reflector is red on the rear. A low speed motor vehicle that meets the requirements of 49 C.F.R. § 571.500, as amended, and is equipped as herein provided, may be registered in the commonwealth, subject to inspection and insurance requirements.

"Manufacturer", any person who is engaged principally and substantially in the business of manufacturing motor vehicles, trailers, motor vehicle bodies or complete mechanical units for excavating or carrying materials and does not incidentally sell used motor vehicles.

"Massachusetts identification card", an identification card that is not issued in compliance with the standards established by the United States Department of Homeland Security in 6 C.F.R. 37

"Massachusetts license", a license to operate motor vehicles that is not issued in compliance with the standards established by the United States Department of Homeland Security in 6 C.F.R. 37.

"Mobile construction crane", any motor vehicle having a construction type crane, including such a motor vehicle which exceeds the dimensional or weight limits imposed by sections nineteen and nineteen A of this chapter or by sections thirty or thirty A of chapter eighty-five.

"Mobile electronic device", any hand-held or other portable electronic equipment capable of providing data communication between 2 or more persons, including, without limitation, a mobile telephone, a text messaging device, a paging device, a personal digital assistant, a laptop computer, electronic equipment that is capable of playing a video game or digital video disk, equipment on which digital photographs are taken or transmitted or any combination thereof, or equipment that is capable of visually receiving a television broadcast; provided, however, that mobile electronic device shall not include any audio equipment or any equipment installed, or affixed, either temporarily or permanently, in a motor vehicle for the purpose of providing navigation or emergency assistance to the operator of such motor vehicle or video entertainment to the passengers in the rear seats of such motor vehicle.

"Mobile telephone", a handheld or portable cellular, analog, wireless, satellite or digital telephone, including a telephone with 2-way radio functionality, capable of sending or receiving telephone communications and with which a user initiates, terminates or engages in a call using at least 1 hand. For the purposes of this chapter, "mobile telephone" shall not include amateur radios operated by those licensed by the Federal Communications Commission to operate such radios, or citizen band radios.

"Motorcycle", any motor vehicle having a seat or saddle for the use of the rider and designed to travel on not more than three wheels in contact with the ground, including any bicycle with a motor or driving wheel attached, except a tractor or a motor vehicle designed for the carrying of golf clubs and not more than four persons, an industrial three-wheel truck, a motor vehicle on which the operator and passenger ride within an enclosed cab, or a motorized bicycle.

"Motorcycle split service brake system", a motorcycle brake system consisting of two or more subsystems actuated by a single control designed so that a leakage-type failure of a pressure component in a single subsystem, except structural failure of a housing that is common to all subsystems, shall not impair the operation of the other subsystems.

"Motorized bicycle", a pedal bicycle which has a helper motor, or a non-pedal bicycle which has a motor, with a cylinder capacity not exceeding fifty cubic centimeters, an automatic transmission, and which is capable of a maximum speed of no more than thirty miles per hour.

"Motorized scooter", any 2 wheeled tandem or 3 wheeled device, that has handlebars, designed to be stood or sat upon by the operator, powered by an electric or gas powered motor that is capable of propelling the device with or without human propulsion. The definition of "motorized scooter" shall not include a motorcycle or motorized bicycle or a 3 wheeled motorized wheelchair.

"Motor vehicles", all vehicles constructed and designed for propulsion by power other than muscular power including such vehicles when pulled or towed by another motor vehicle, except railroad and railway cars, vehicles operated by the system known as trolley motor or trackless trolley under chapter one hundred and sixty-three or section ten of chapter five hundred and forty-four of the acts of nineteen hundred and forty-seven, vehicles running only upon rails or tracks, vehicles used for other purposes than the transportation of property and incapable of being driven at a speed exceeding twelve miles per hour and which are used exclusively for the building, repair and maintenance of highways or designed especially for use elsewhere than on the travelled part of ways, wheelchairs owned and operated by invalids and vehicles which are operated or guided by a person on foot; provided, however, that the exception for trackless trolleys provided herein shall not apply to sections seventeen, twenty-one, twenty-four, twenty-four I, twenty-five and twenty-six. The definition of "Motor vehicles" shall not include motorized bicycles. In doubtful cases, the registrar may determine whether or not any particular vehicle is a motor vehicle as herein defined. If he determines that it should be so classified, he may require that it be registered under this chapter, but such determination shall not be admissible as evidence in any action at law arising out of the use or operation of such vehicle previous to such determination.

"Non-resident", any person whose legal residence is not within the commonwealth.

"Number plate", the sign or marker furnished by the registrar on which is displayed the register number or mark of a motor vehicle assigned to such motor vehicle by the registrar.

"Operator", any person who operates a motor vehicle or trackless trolley.

"Owner", a person, other than a lien holder, having title to a vehicle. The term includes a person entitled to the use and possession of a vehicle subject to a security interest in another person, but excludes a lessee under a lease not intended as security and a bailee of any description; but, the term shall include the commonwealth and its political subdivisions for the purpose of registering a vehicle that is on loan from the United States or from a motor vehicle manufacturer or distributor.

"Owner-contractor", any person who is not a manufacturer, dealer or repairman who owns a fleet of ten or more vehicles, trailers, special mobile equipment, mobile construction cranes or combination thereof, which is used or leased exclusively by him in his principal business and who maintains an establishment with facilities for the repair, alteration or equipment of such vehicles or trailers.

"Persons", wherever used in connection with the registration of a motor vehicle, all persons who own or control such vehicles as owners, or for the purpose of sale, or for renting, as agents, salesmen or otherwise.

"Police officer" or "officer", any constable or other officer authorized to make arrest or serve process, provided he is in uniform or displays his badge of office.

"REAL ID Act", the REAL ID Act of 2005, 49 U.S.C. 30301.

"REAL ID-compliant identification card", a license or identification card issued in compliance with the standards established by the United States Department of Homeland Security at 6 C.F.R. 37.

"REAL ID-compliant license", a license to operate motor vehicles issued in compliance with the standards established by the United States Department of Homeland Security at 6 C.F.R. 37.

"Register number", the letter or letters, mark or marks, arabic numeral or numerals, or combinations thereof assigned by the registrar to a motor vehicle or trailer.

"Registrar", the registrar of motor vehicles.

"Repairman", any person who is principally and substantially engaged in the business of repairing, altering, reconditioning, equipping or towing motor vehicles or trailers for the public and who maintains an established place of business, as defined in this section.

"Retread or recap", any tire, designed for use on motor vehicles or trailers, which has had its original tread removed and replaced with new tread rubber.

"Other than first Quality", any tire which has been sold or designated by the manufacturer thereof as not meeting its standard quality or appearance specifications for such brand of tire. Nothing herein shall be deemed to authorize the offering or sale of tires which do not meet any minimum safety standards established by or under the laws of the commonwealth or of the United States which may be applicable to such tires.

"Right to operate", the privilege of operating motor vehicles on the ways of the commonwealth conferred by a license issued under section eight, a learner's permit issued under section eight B, or by reciprocity to nonresidents under sections three and ten, including the right of residents of the commonwealth who are at least sixteen years of age to apply for such license or learner's permit.

"Routes of reasonable access", routes of access, as designated by the department as provided in section nineteen G, between the National Network, as defined in section nineteen F, and such terminals, facilities for food, fuel, repair and rest as are located more than one road-mile in distance from the National Network.

"Saddlemount combination", a combination of vehicles in which a truck tractor tows one or more trucks or truck tractors,

1

each connected by a saddle to the frame or fifth wheel of the vehicle in front of it. The saddle is a mechanism which connects the front axle of the towed vehicle to the frame or fifth wheel of the vehicle in front and functions like a fifth wheel kingpin connection. When two vehicles are towed in this manner the combination is called a double saddlemount combination and when three vehicles are so towed the combination is called a triple saddlemount combination. Such combinations may include one fullmount.

"School bus", any motor vehicle used for the transportation of school pupils and school personnel to and from school or for the transportation of children enrolled in a camp or recreational program, while so used, but not including any such motor vehicle used for not more than five days in case of emergency or a motor vehicle while also used for the common carriage of the public under a certificate and permit issued under sections seven and eight of chapter one hundred and fifty-nine A, or a motor vehicle having permanent seating accommodations for and carrying not more than eight persons in addition to the operator, or a motor vehicle used to transport vocational students participating in a work project to and from a work site and having permanent seating accommodations for not more than fourteen persons in addition to the operator.

"School pupil", any person enrolled in any school, kindergarten through grade twelve, or enrolled in any program for child care services, or in any program for children with special needs as defined in section one of chapter seventy-one B, or in any organized day or summer camp program or any activity supported by said schools.

"Semi-trailer", a trailer so designed and used in combination with a tractor that some part of the weight of such trailer and that of its load rests upon and is carried by, the tractor.

"Semi-trailer unit", a motor unit composed of a tractor and a semi-trailer.

"Stinger-steered automobile transporter", an automobile transporter configured as a semi-trailer combination wherein the fifth wheel is located on a drop frame located behind and below the rear-most axle of the power unit.

"Stinger-steered boat transporter", a boat transporter configured as a semi-trailer combination wherein the fifth wheel is located on a drop frame located behind and below the rear-most axle of the power unit.

"Student", every person enrolled full time in a school, college or university, but not including any fully registered medical practitioner or any person enrolled in a school, college or university for the purpose of pursuing advanced or postgraduate studies or on the job training under any fellowship program, grant or other program which provides such person with any salary or compensation beyond the actual tuition costs of such schooling. In doubtful cases, the registrar may determine whether or not this definition applies.

"Tandem unit", a motor vehicle composed of a tractor, semi-trailer and trailer.

"Terminal", any location where: freight either originates, terminates, or is handled in the transportation process; or commercial motor carriers maintain operating facilities.

"Truck-trailer boat transporter", a boat transporter combination consisting of a truck towing a trailer using typically a ball and socket connection and where the trailer axle is located substantially at the trailer center of gravity, rather than at the rear of the trailer, but so as to maintain a downward force on the trailer tongue.

"Thickly settled or business district", the territory contiguous to any way which is built up with structures devoted to business, or the territory contiguous to any way where the dwelling houses are situated at such distances as will average less than two hundred feet between them for a distance of a quarter of a mile or over.

"Trackless trolley", an electrically operated, rubber wheeled vehicle receiving power from a fixed overhead electrical source by way of a trolley mechanism.

"Tractor", a motor vehicle with or without a carrying capacity of its own but which is primarily designed and used for drawing another vehicle or for industrial or agricultural purposes.

"Trailer", any vehicle or object on wheels and having no motive power of its own, but which is drawn by, or used in combination with, a motor vehicle. It shall not include a pole dolly or pole dickey, so called, nor a pair of wheels commonly used as an implement for other purposes than transportation, nor a portable, collapsible or separate two wheel tow dolly limited only to the purpose of transporting or towing a registered vehicle, nor farm machinery or implements when used in connection with the operation of a farm or estate, nor any vehicle when towed behind a farm tractor and used in connection with the operation of a farm or estate.

"Antique motor car", any motor vehicle over twenty-five years old which is maintained solely for use in exhibitions, club activities, parades and other functions of public interest and which is not used primarily for the transportation of passengers or goods over any way, provided that the application for registration thereof is accompanied by an affidavit upon a form provided by the registrar which shall include a statement of the age and intended use of such motor vehicle.

"Transporter", any person principally and substantially engaged in the business of transporting or delivering motor vehicles under their own power not owned by him and who possesses a valid license for said business issued by the department of telecommunications and energy, or any person or agent thereof, licensed to engage in the business of financing the purchase of or insuring motor vehicles who is required to take into possession such motor vehicles by foreclosure or subrogation of title.

"Way", any public highway, private way laid out under authority of statute, way dedicated to public use, or way under the control of park commissioners or body having like powers.

"Certificate of inspection", a serially numbered, adhesive sticker, device, or symbol, as may be prescribed by the registrar, indicating a motor vehicle has met the inspection requirements established by the registrar for issuance of a certificate. The registrar may prescribe the use of one or more categories of certificate of inspection.

"Certificate of rejection", a serially numbered, adhesive sticker, device or symbol, as may be prescribed by the registrar indicating a motor vehicle has failed to meet the inspection requirements as established by the registrar.

"Certificate of waiver", a serially numbered device or symbol, as may be prescribed by the registrar, indicating that the requirement of passing the inspection has been waived for a vehicle pursuant to the provisions of this chapter.

"Certified inspector", an individual certified by the commissioner as properly trained to perform an emissions inspection as delineated by the manufacturer of the emissions analyzer.

"Child Passenger restraint", a specifically designed seating system which meets the United States Department of Transportation Federal Motor Vehicle Safety Standards, as established in 49 C.F.R. 571.213, which is either permanently affixed to a motor vehicle or is affixed to such vehicle by a safety belt or a universal attachment system.

"Commissioner", commissioner of the department of environmental protection.

"Fleet inspection station", a proprietorship, partnership or corporation which owns or maintains a fleet of at least twenty-five motor vehicles and maintains a garage for the repair and maintenance of those vehicles and is licensed by the registrar to perform the inspections on said motor vehicles.

"Inspection station", a proprietorship, partnership, or corporation licensed by the registrar to perform inspections on motor vehicles.

"Licensee", a fleet inspection station or inspection station.

"Referee station", a location designated by the registrar to verify the accuracy of inspections performed by licensed inspection stations and to grant certificates of waiver.

"Special mobile equipment", a motor vehicle which is principally designed to conduct excavations or lift building materials at a public or private construction site and is operated on a way for the sole purpose of transportation to or from said construction site and has a gross vehicle weight of at least twelve thousand pounds. This definition shall not include a motor vehicle which is designed to carry passengers, or any load, on a way.

"Established place of business", a permanently enclosed premises owned or leased exclusively by a repairman which is open to the general public. Unless said business is limited solely to the towing of motor vehicles or trailers for the public, said repairman shall possess the necessary tools and facilities reasonably necessary to conduct a repair business. If more than one business is located within the same building or structure and the other businesses are not owned or controlled by the same principals, the repair business shall maintain a separate and exclusive entrance.

NOTE   1986 Mass. Acts c. 35, § 10 provides:

> Upon the effective date of this act, all automobile law violations, as defined in section one, for which the assessment, heretofore considered a penalty or fine, does not exceed one hundred dollars for the first offense and does not provide for a penalty of imprisonment, excepting operation of a motor vehicle in violation of the first paragraph of section ten of chapter ninety, or violation of section twenty-five of chapter ninety, shall be deemed civil motor vehicle infractions and not criminal offenses, and all statutes, ordinances, bylaws or regulations heretofore providing for such automobile law violations shall be so interpreted. Appearances and proceedings pursuant to this subsection shall not be deemed criminal, and payments, heretofore considered penalties or fines, made, whether after hearing or otherwise, shall be deemed civil assessments and not criminal penalties or fines. The violator shall not be required to report to a probation officer and no record of the case shall be entered in any probation records except as prescribed by the commissioner of probation.

SECTION 1B
Motorized bicycles; operation regulations

A motorized bicycle shall not be operated upon any way, as defined in section one within the commonwealth by any person under sixteen years of age, nor at a speed in excess of twenty-five miles per hour. A motorized bicycle shall not be operated on any way by any person not possessing a valid driver's license or learner's permit. Every person operating a motorized bicycle upon a way shall have the right to use all public ways in the commonwealth except limited access or express state highways where signs specifically prohibiting bicycles have been posted, and shall be subject to the traffic laws and regulations of the commonwealth and the regulations contained in this section, except that: (1) the motorized bicycle operator may keep to the right when passing a motor vehicle which is moving in the travel lane of the way, and (2) the motorized bicycle operator shall signal by either hand his intention to stop or turn. Motorized bicycles may be operated on bicycle lanes adjacent to the various ways, but shall be excluded from offstreet recreational bicycle paths.

Every person operating a motorized bicycle or riding as a passenger on a motorized bicycle shall wear protective headgear conforming with such minimum standards of construction and performance as the registrar may prescribe, and no person operating a motorized bicycle shall permit any other person to ride a passenger on such a motorized bicycle unless such passenger is wearing such protective headgear.

A person convicted of a violation of this section shall be punished by a fine of not more than twenty-five dollars for the first offense, not less than twenty-five nor more than fifty dollars for a second offense, and not less than fifty nor more than one hundred dollars for subsequent offenses committed.

SECTION 6
Display of number plates; temporary number plates

Every motor vehicle or trailer registered under this chapter when operated in or on any way in this commonwealth shall have its register number displayed conspicuously thereon by the number plates furnished by the registrar in accordance with section two or five or by temporary number plates authorized by the register as hereinafter provided, one number plate to be attached at the front and one at the rear of said motor vehicle, and one number plate to be attached at the rear of said trailer, but if the registrar issues but one number plate it shall be attached to the rear of the vehicle so that it shall always be plainly visible. The said number plates shall be kept clean with numbers legible and shall not be obscured in any manner by the installation of any device obscuring said numbers, and during the period when the vehicle or trailer is required to display lights the rear register number shall be illuminated so as to be plainly visible at a distance of sixty feet. No number plates other than such as are procured from the registrar or such as may be authorized by him for temporary use, except as provided in section three, shall be displayed on any motor vehicle or trailer so operated; provided, that a motor vehicle or trailer which by reason of its interstate operation is registered in this commonwealth and elsewhere may display the register number plates of this and any other state or country in which it is registered, if, while being operated on the ways of this commonwealth, the number plates furnished by the registrar, or temporary number plates authorized by him as hereinafter provided, are displayed as required hereby. If any number plate supplied by the registrar is lost or mutilated or if the register number thereon becomes illegible, the owner or person in control of the vehicle for which said number plate was furnished shall make application for a new number plate, and thereupon the registrar shall issue to such applicant a permit allowing him to place a temporary number plate bearing his register number on said vehicle until a number plate of the regular design is made and delivered to said applicant; provided, that all such temporary number plates and the register numbers thereon shall conform to the regular number plates and be displayed as nearly as may be as herein provided for said regular number plates. Any motor vehicle or trailer may, if duly registered, be operated, pushed, drawn or towed or remain upon any way between the hours of twelve o'clock noon on the date on which its registration expires and twelve o'clock noon on the following day, if the following day is the first day of the new registration period, and if such vehicle or trailer displays its register number for either registration period as otherwise required by this section.

SECTION 7
Brakes, braking systems, mufflers, horns, lights, audible warning systems and other equipment; compliance with safety standards; stickers and emblems

Every motor vehicle operated in or upon any way shall be provided with brakes adequate to control the movement of such vehicle and conforming to rules and regulations made by the registrar, and such brakes shall at all times be maintained in good working order. Every automobile shall be provided with at least two braking systems, one of which shall be the service brake system, and the other shall be the parking brake system, each with a separate means of application, each operating directly or indirectly on at least two wheels and each of which shall suffice alone to stop said automobile within a proper distance as defined in said rules and regulations; provided, that if such systems are connected, combined or have any part in common, such systems shall be so constructed that a breaking of any one element thereof will not leave the automobile without brakes acting directly or indirectly on at least two wheels; and provided, further, that a tractor having a draw-bar pull rating of ten horse power or less and capable of a maximum speed of not more than eighteen miles an hour and designed specially for use elsewhere than on the traveled part of ways may be operated thereon if equipped with a single braking system which shall suffice to stop such tractor within a proper distance as aforesaid. Every automobile equipped with an hydraulic braking system whether or not assisted by other means, which provides braking action on four or more wheels, shall be equipped with a service brake system so arranged as to provide separate systems for at least two wheels and so designed and constructed that rupture or leakage-type failure of any single pressure component of the service brake system, except structural failures of the brake master cylinder body, effectiveness indicator body, or other housing common to the divided system, will not result in complete loss of function of the vehicle brakes when force on the brake pedal is continued. "Pressure component" means any internal component of the brake master cylinder or master control unit, wheel brake cylinder, brake line, brake hose, or equivalent, except vacuum assist components. Except in the case of a school bus or fire apparatus, every motor vehicle and every tractor which is designed and used for drawing another vehicle, having an unladen weight of more than ten thousand pounds, shall be equipped with full air brakes or hydraulic brakes with vacuum power assist or air power assist. All braking systems shall be constructed and designed so as to permit modulated control of brake application and release by the operator from the normal operating position. Every trailer or semi-trailer having an unladen weight of more than ten thousand pounds shall be equipped with air or electric brakes. One braking system shall be so constructed that it can be set to hold the automobile stationary. Each motorcycle shall have either a split service brake system or two independently actuated service brake systems. Any motorcycle which has a number or registration plate issued under the provisions of section 6A of said chapter 90 or which was not manufactured with either a split service brake system or two independently actuated service brake systems, shall be required to have one brake system adequate to stop said motorcycle within a proper distance, as defined in rules and regulations made by the registrar. Every automobile used on a way by a person in giving driving instruction for compensation shall be equipped with dual brake controls whereby he may apply the brake while the pupil is driving. Every motor vehicle so operated shall be provided with a muffler or other suitable device to prevent unnecessary noise and with a suitable bell, horn or other means of signalling, with suitable lamps, and with a lock, key or other device to prevent such vehicle from being set in motion by unauthorized persons, or otherwise contrary to the will of the owner or person in charge thereof. Every automobile operated during the period from one half an hour after sunset to one half an hour before sunrise, and during any other period when visibility is reduced by atmospheric conditions so as to render dangerous further operation without lights being displayed, shall display at least two lighted white headlamps with at least one mounted at each side of the front of the vehicle or if parked within the limits of a way at least one white or amber light on the side of the automobile nearer the center of the way, and every motorcycle so operated at least one white headlamp and every such motorcycle with a sidecar attached, in addition, one such light on the front of the sidecar, and every motor truck, trailer and commercial motor vehicle used solely as such, having a carrying capacity of three tons or over, in addition, an amber light attached to the extreme left of the front of such vehicle, so attached and adjusted as to indicate the extreme left lateral extension of the vehicle or load, which shall in all cases aforesaid be visible not less than two hundred feet in the direction toward which the vehicle is proceeding or facing; provided, that an automobile need display no light when parked within the limits of a way in a space in which unlighted parking is permitted by the rules or regulations of the board or officer having control of such way. Every motor vehicle and trailer so operated shall be equipped with two rear lights mounted one at each side of the rear of the vehicle so as to show two red lights from behind and a white light so arranged as to illuminate and not obscure the rear number plate and shall be equipped with two stop lights mounted and displayed in a like manner of a type complying with minimum standards for construction and performance as the registrar may prescribe; provided, however, that a two-wheeled motorcycle, an antique motor car and a farm tractor need be equipped with only one such rear red light and one suitable stop light in addition to the number plate illuminator; and provided, further, that a trailer having a gross weight of three thousand pounds or less which does not obscure the required lights of the towing vehicle need be equipped with only one such rear red light and one white light so arranged as to illuminate and not obscure the rear number plate. No motor vehicle so operated shall mount or display a flashing, rotating or oscillating light in any direction except pursuant to section 7E of this chapter; provided, however, that this shall not apply to the use of rear directional signals nor to the proper use of vehicle hazard warning signals as provided for by this section. In no event, however, shall the registrar prohibit any commercial auto parts dealer, motor vehicle repair shop or station from selling, offering for sale or installing quartz-halogen headlamps which receive a certificate of approval from the American Association of Motor Vehicles Administrators or which meet the standards of the Canadian Standard Association (CSA) nor shall any provision of this section prohibit any person from using, purchasing or installing a quartz-halogen headlamp as herein described. Every motor vehicle or trailer so operated which carries a load or object extending four feet or more beyond the cab or body of such vehicle shall display at the extreme rear end of such load or object a red light plainly visible from a distance of at least five hundred feet to the sides and rear, and shall display in place thereof a red flag or cloth not less than twelve inches square during the period when motor vehicles are not required to display lights. Every commercial motor vehicle or trailer weighing, with its load, more than twelve thousand pounds, shall, in addition to such rear light, be equipped with a red reflector of a type complying with such minimum standards for construction and performance as the registrar may prescribe, so placed at the rear of such vehicle as to reflect rays of light thrown upon such reflector from behind. No headlamp or rear lamp shall be used on any motor vehicle so operated unless such headlamp or rear lamp is of a type complying with such minimum standards for construction and performance as the registrar may prescribe. Every motor vehicle shall be equipped with at least one mirror so placed and adjusted as to afford the operator a clear, reflected view of the highway to the rear and left side of the vehicle. Every motor vehicle or trailer, excepting passenger motor vehicles, operated in or upon any way shall be equipped with suitable guards which will effectively reduce the spray or splash to the rear of mud, water or slush caused by the rear wheels thereof. Every passenger motor vehicle which is equipped with tires which extend beyond the fenders or body of such vehicle and which is operated in or upon any way shall be equipped with flaps or suitable guards to reduce such spray or splash to the rear and sides. Every motor vehicle registered in the commonwealth which is privately owned and operated and designed for the carriage of passengers and which is used primarily for pleasure or for pleasure and business, including every such vehicle furnished for hire by a rental car agency but excluding every such vehicle used for public or commercial purposes, shall be equipped with two seat safety belts for the use of occupants of the front seats. No safety belt installed in a motor vehicle in accordance with the provisions of this section or in accordance with the provisions of federal law or the rules or regulations issued by the United States Department of Transportation, shall be removed from said motor vehicle except for the purpose of repairs. Every motor vehicle registered in the commonwealth shall be equipped with a device to permit the

front and rear directional signals to flash simultaneously, said device to be operated only when the vehicle is disabled or stopped in the event of emergency on or at the side of any way. Every person operating a motorcycle or riding as a passenger on a motorcycle or in a sidecar attached to a motorcycle shall wear protective head gear conforming with such minimum standards of construction and performance as the registrar may prescribe, and no person operating a motorcycle shall permit any other person to ride as a passenger on such motorcycle or in a sidecar attached to such motorcycle unless such passenger is wearing such protective head gear, except that no protective head gear shall be required if the motorcyclist is participating in a properly permitted public parade and is 18 years of age or older. If a motorcycle is not equipped with a windshield or screen, the operator of such motorcycle shall wear eye glasses, goggles or a protective face shield when operating such vehicle. Every motor vehicle truck with dump bodies shall be equipped with an adequate audible warning system to alert the operator when the dump body is in an upright and elevated position. No person operating a motorcycle shall permit any person to ride as a passenger, unless such motorcycle is designed to carry more than one person; and no person operating a motorcycle shall permit a passenger to ride in front of said operator.

Every commercial motor vehicle, or trailer weighing, with its load, more than twelve thousand pounds, and used to deliver gasoline or other flammable material, shall be equipped with an audible warning system when the vehicle's transmission is in reverse. For the purpose of this paragraph, the term commercial motor vehicle or trailer shall mean a bulk tank carrier delivering gasoline or other flammable material.

Every trailer, except a semi-trailer, shall, in addition to a regular hitch, be fastened by safety chains to prevent it from breaking away from the towing vehicle. Such chains shall comply with such minimum standards for construction and performance as the registrar may prescribe.

Notwithstanding the preceding provisions of this section, any commercial motor vehicle, semi-trailer or trailer, used in interstate commerce, which shall conform as to its equipment with the regulations established from time to time by the bureau of motor carrier safety of the United States department of transportation, shall be deemed to conform to the requirements of this section.

No person shall sell, offer for sale or install on, or in, any motor vehicle or trailer, any component, device or substance, other than quartz-halogen lights, which does not comply with the federal motor vehicle safety standard, if any, established for such component, device or substance. Nothing in this act shall prevent the registrar from prescribing minimum standards for any component, device, or substance for which no federal motor vehicle safety standard is or has been established and no persons shall sell, offer for sale or install on, or in, any motor vehicle or trailer, any such component, device or substance which does not comply with the said standards so prescribed.

Any tractor or other self propelled vehicle used exclusively for agricultural or farming purposes, excepting automobiles and trucks, the use of which is declared by the owner or person in control thereof to be restricted to the period from a half hour before sunrise to a half hour after sunset, and which is operated in or upon any way during said period shall be equipped with one stop light or a flashing red light to the rear and with brakes as manufactured, including a stationary brake with ratchet and pawl. Upon declaration by the owner or person in control of such vehicle that the use of such vehicle is to be so restricted, the person making the periodic inspection of motor vehicles and trailers, as provided under section seven A, may, notwithstanding the failure of such restricted tractor or other vehicle to have the necessary lights and other equipment required by the first paragraph of this section, issue a windshield sticker, so called, if the stop light or such flashing light and brakes are in good order. Any windshield sticker so issued shall state thereon that such vehicle is to be used upon the ways of the commonwealth only during the period from a half hour before sunrise to half hour after sunset.

The registrar shall adopt standards and specifications for size, design, mounting, creation and use of a distinctive slow moving vehicle emblem. Every horse-drawn vehicle and every other vehicle designed to operate at twenty-five miles an hour or less, every implement of husbandry, every farm tractor, each piece of special mobile equipment and other machinery, including all road construction and maintenance machinery and every low-speed motor vehicle, traveling on a public way during day or night shall display on the rear of the vehicle such emblem. The use of such emblem shall be in addition to any lighting devices, flags or other equipment required by law. Use of such emblem as a clearance marker or on wide machinery or on stationary objects on the highways is prohibited.

NOTE   "Operating with defective equipment under G.L. c. 90, § 7, is not among the motor vehicle offenses for which G.L. c. 90, § 21, allows arrest without warrant." *Commonwealth v. Zorrilla*, 38 Mass. App. Ct. 77, 79 n.3 (1995).

SECTION 7AA
Child passenger restraints; fine; violation as evidence in civil action

A passenger in a motor vehicle on any way who is under the age of 8 shall be fastened and secured by a child passenger restraint, unless such passenger measures more than 57 inches in height. The child passenger restraint shall be properly fastened and secured according to the manufacturer's instructions.

Unless required to be properly fastened and secured by a child passenger restraint under the preceding paragraph, a passenger in a motor vehicle on any way that is under the age of 13 shall wear a safety belt which is properly adjusted and fastened according to the manufacturer's instructions.

The provisions of this section shall not apply to any such child who is: (1) riding as a passenger in a motor vehicle in which all seating positions equipped with safety belts or child passenger restraints are occupied by other passengers who are using said restraints; (2) riding as a passenger in a motor vehicle used to transport passengers for hire; (3) riding as a passenger in a motor vehicle not equipped with safety belts; (4) physically unable to use safety belts or child passenger restraints. Any operator of a motor vehicle who violates the provisions of this section shall be subject to a fine of not more than twenty-five dollars; provided, however, that such fine may be waived if the court is satisfied that the defendant has purchased a child passenger restraint as defined in section one.

A violation of this section shall not be used as evidence of contributory negligence in any civil action.

A person who receives a citation for a violation of any of the provisions of this section may contest such citation pursuant to section three of chapter ninety C. A violation of this section shall not be deemed to be a conviction of a moving violation of the motor vehicle laws for the purpose of determining surcharges on motor vehicle premiums pursuant to section one hundred and thirteen B of chapter one hundred and seventy-five.

SECTION 9
Operation of unregistered or improperly equipped motor vehicles, tractors, trailers, etc.

No person shall operate, push, draw or tow any motor vehicle or trailer, and the owner or custodian of such a vehicle shall not permit the same to be operated, pushed, drawn or towed upon or to remain upon any way except as authorized by section three, unless such vehicle is registered in accordance with this chapter and carries its register number displayed as provided in section six, and, in the case of a motor vehicle, is equipped as provided in section seven. A motor vehicle which is being towed or drawn by a motor vehicle designed to draw or tow such vehicles need not be so registered if (a) the towing vehicle is properly registered and displays a valid repair plate issued pursuant to section five, (b) said towing vehicle maintains insurance which also provides coverage for the motor vehicle being towed, and (c) said towing vehicle has been issued a certificate by the department of public utilities pursuant to paragraph (b) of section three of chapter one hundred and fifty-nine B. A tractor, trailer or truck may be operated without such registration upon any way for a distance not exceeding one-half mile, if said tractor, trailer or truck is used exclusively for agricultural purposes, or between one-half mile and ten miles if said tractor, trailer or truck is used exclusively for agricultural purposes and the owner thereof maintains in full force a policy of liability insurance which conforms to the provisions of section one hundred and thirteen A of chapter one hundred and seventy-five or for a distance not exceeding three hundred yards, if such tractor, trailer or truck is used for industrial purposes other than agricultural purposes, for the purpose of going from property owned or occupied by the owner of such tractor, trailer or truck to other property so owned or occupied. A new automobile being delivered to a dealer by means of a tractor and trailer may be unloaded on a public way and driven by the person so delivering or his agents or servants without such registration to a dealer's premises over a public way for a distance not exceeding three hundred feet provided that the person so delivering, with respect to such new automobile, shall have filed with the registrar a motor vehicle liability policy or bond in compliance with the provisions of this chapter. A motor vehicle designed for the carrying of golf clubs and not more than four persons may be operated without such registration upon any way if such motor vehicle is being used solely for the purpose of going from one part of the property of a golf course, provided that the owner of such motor vehicle shall have filed with the registrar a public liability policy or bond providing for the payment of damages to any person to the amount provided by section thirty-four A due to injuries sustained as a result of the operation of such vehicle. A motor vehicle owned by a cemetery may be operated without such registration upon any way if such motor vehicle is being used solely for the purpose of going from one part of the property of a cemetery to another part of the property of said cemetery, provided that such vehicle shall not travel more than one mile on any public way and the owner of such motor vehicle shall have filed with the registrar a public liability policy or bond providing for the payment of damages to any person to the amount provided by section thirty-four A due to injuries sustained as a result of the operation of such vehicle. An earth-moving vehicle used exclusively for the building, repair and maintenance of highways which exceed the dimensions or weight limits imposed by section nineteen and the weight limits imposed by section thirty of chapter eighty-five may be operated without such registration for a distance not exceeding three hundred yards on any way adjacent to any highway or toll road being constructed, relocated or improved under contract with the commonwealth or any agency or political subdivision thereof or by a public instrumentality, provided that a permit authorizing the operation of such a vehicle in excess of the stated weight or dimension limits has been issued by the commissioner of public works or the board or officer having charge of such way, and provided that such earth-moving vehicle shall be operated under such permit only when directed by an officer authorized to direct traffic at the location where such earth-moving vehicle is being operated. The operation of such an earth-moving vehicle shall conform to any terms or conditions set forth in such permit, and any person to whom any such permit is issued shall provide indemnity for his operation by means of a motor vehicle liability policy or bond conforming to the requirements of this chapter and shall furnish a certificate conforming to the requirements of section thirty-four A with each such application for a permit. Violation of this section shall not be deemed to render the motor vehicle or trailer a nuisance or any person a trespasser upon a way and shall not constitute a defense to, or prevent a recovery in, an action of tort for injuries suffered by a person, or for the death of a person, or for damage to property, unless such violation by the person injured or killed or sustaining the damage was in fact a proximate cause of such injury, death or damage, but violation of this section shall be deemed evidence of negligence on the part of the violator. A motor vehicle or trailer shall be deemed to be registered in accordance with this chapter notwithstanding any mistake in so much of the description thereof contained in the application for registration or in the certificate required to be filed under section thirty-four B as relates to the type of such vehicle or trailer or to the identifying number or numbers required by the registrar or any mistake in the statement of residence of the applicant contained in said application or certificate. A person convicted of a violation of this section shall be punished by a fine of not more than one hundred dollars for the first offense and not more than one thousand dollars for any subsequent offense.

SECTION 10
Operation of motor vehicle without license; members of armed forces; nonresidents; suspension or revocation of license

No person under sixteen years of age shall operate a motor vehicle upon any way. No other person shall so operate unless licensed by the registrar unless he possesses a receipt issued under section eight for persons licensed in another state or country or unless he possesses a valid learner's permit issued under section eight B, except as is otherwise herein provided or unless he is the spouse of a member of the armed forces of the United States who is accompanying such member on military or naval assignment to this commonwealth and who has a valid operator's license issued by another state, or unless he is on active duty in the armed forces of the United States and has in his possession a license to operate motor vehicles issued by the state where he is domiciled, or unless he is a member of the armed forces of the United States returning from active duty outside the United States, and has in his possession a license to operate motor vehicles issued by said armed forces in a foreign country, but in such case for a period of not more than forty-five days after his return. The motor vehicle of a nonresident may be operated on the ways of the commonwealth in accordance with section three by its owner or by any nonresident operator without a license from the registrar if the nonresident operator is duly licensed under the laws of the state or country where such vehicle is registered and has such license on his person or in the vehicle in some easily accessible place. Subject to the provisions of section three, a nonresident who holds a license under the laws of the state or country in which he resides may operate any motor vehicle of a type which he is licensed to operate under said license, duly registered in this commonwealth or in any state or country; provided, that he has the license on his person or in the vehicle in some easily accessible place, and that, as finally determined by the registrar, his state or country grants substantially similar privileges to residents of this commonwealth and prescribes and enforces standards of fitness for operations of motor vehicles substantially as high as those prescribed and enforced by this commonwealth.

Notwithstanding the foregoing provisions, no person shall operate on the ways of the commonwealth any motor vehicle, whether registered in this commonwealth or elsewhere, if the registrar shall have suspended or revoked any license to operate motor vehicles issued to him under this chapter, or shall have suspended his right to operate such vehicles, and such license or right has not been restored or a new license to operate motor vehicles has not been issued to him. Operation of a motor vehicle in violation of this paragraph shall be subject to the same penalties as provided in section twenty-three for operation after suspension or revocation and before restoration or issuance of a new license or the restoration of the right to operate.

NOTE   See Note following G.L. c. 90, § 1.

SECTION 11
Carrying certificate of registration and license; presentation after accident upon request

Every person operating a motor vehicle shall have the certificate of registration for the vehicle and for the trailer, if any, and his license to operate, upon his person or in the vehicle, in some easily accessible place, except that the certificates of registration of dealers, manufacturers, repairmen, owner-repairmen, farmers or dealers in both boats and boat trailers need not so be carried; provided, however, that the certificate of registration of a person who is operating a motor vehicle in accordance with the provisions of the last sentence of the fifth paragraph of section two need not so be carried; and, provided further, that in the case of a rental vehicle, a photostat copy of the certificate of registration, accompanied by the rental agreement, shall be sufficient to comply with the provisions of this section. If for any reason the registrar or his agents are unable to issue promptly to an applicant the certificate of registration or the license applied for, they may issue a receipt for the fee paid, and said receipt shall be carried in lieu of the certificate or license as the case may be, and for a period of sixty days from the date of its issue said receipt shall have the same force and effect given to the certificate or license by this chapter. If, in compliance with a written demand of the registrar or any of his authorized agents, a certificate of registration or license to operate is returned for inspection or for any other purpose, except for suspension or revocation, such written demand shall be carried in lieu of the certificate or license, as the case may be, and for the period of sixty days from its date said demand shall have the same force and effect given to the certificate or license by this chapter. Any operator who knowingly collides with or causes injury to any person or damage to any property shall, upon the request of the person injured or the person owning or in charge of the property damaged, plainly exhibit to such person his license and, if required under the provisions of this chapter to carry the certificate of registration for the vehicle upon his person or in the vehicle, such certificate.

SECTION 12
Employing unlicensed motor vehicle operator; permitting person with suspended or revoked license to operate motor vehicle; permitting person with ignition interlock device license restriction to operate motor vehicle without device; penalties
(Amended by 2012 Mass. Acts c. 139, § 93, effective July 1, 2012.)

(a) Whoever knowingly employs for hire as a motor vehicle operator any person not licensed in accordance with this chapter shall be punished for a first offense by a fine of not more than $1,000 and, for a second or subsequent violation, by a fine of not less than $1,000 nor more than $1,500 or imprisonment in the house of correction for not more than 1 year, or both such fine and imprisonment.

(b) Whoever, being the owner or person in control of a motor vehicle, knowingly permits such motor vehicle to be operated by a person who is unlicensed or whose license has been suspended or revoked shall be punished for a first offense of a fine of not more than $1,000 or imprisonment in a house of correction for not more than 1 year or, for a second or subsequent offense by a fine of not less than $1,000 nor more than $1,500 or imprisonment in a house of correction for not more than 2½ years, or both such fine and imprisonment.

(c) Whoever knowingly permits a motor vehicle owned by him or under his control, which is not equipped with a functioning ignition interlock device, to be operated by a person who has an ignition interlock restricted license shall be punished by 1 year in the house of correction and a fine of not more than $500 for a first offense or, for a second or subsequent offense by a fine of not more than $1,000 or imprisonment in a house of correction for not more than 2½ years, or both. For the purposes of this section the term "certified ignition interlock device" shall mean an alcohol breath screening device that prevents a vehicle from starting if it detects a blood alcohol concentration over a preset limit of .02 or 20 mg of alcohol per 100 ml of blood.

(d) The registrar may suspend for not more than 1 year the motor vehicle registration of a vehicle used in the commission of a violation of this section or the license or right to operate of the person who commits a violation of this section, or both.

SECTION 12A
Use of mobile telephone, hands-free mobile telephone or other mobile electronic device by operator of vehicle or vessel used in public transportation prohibited; penalties; affirmative defenses

(a) No operator of a vehicle or vessel used in public transportation, including a train, passenger bus, school bus or other vehicle used to transport pupils, passenger ferry boat, water shuttle or other equipment used in public transportation owned by, or operated under the authority of the Massachusetts Bay Transportation Authority, the Woods Hole, Martha's Vineyard and Nantucket Steamship Authority, Massachusetts Port Authority, or the Massachusetts Department of Transportation, shall use a mobile telephone, hands-free mobile telephone or other mobile electronic device while operating such vehicle or vessel; provided, however that this section shall not apply to the operator of a vehicle or vessel used in public transportation using a mobile telephone, hands-free mobile telephone or mobile electronic device in the performance of the operator's official duties; provided, however, that in order for the use of any such device to be made "in the performance of the operator's official duties," such use must have been made in conformance with applicable written guidelines issued by a public entity listed in this paragraph relative to circumstances when operators are permitted to use said devices in the performance of their official duties or pursuant to directives from federal authorities having regulatory jurisdiction over such public entity's operations.

Whoever violates this section shall be punished by a fine of $500. A violation of this section shall not be a moving violation for purposes of the safe driver insurance plan under section 113B of chapter 175.

(b) It shall be an affirmative defense for an operator under this section to produce evidence that the use of a mobile telephone that is the basis of the alleged violation was in the case of an emergency. For the purpose of this paragraph, an emergency shall mean that the operator needed to communicate with another to report any of the following: (1) that the vehicle or vessel was disabled; (2) that medical attention or assistance was required on the vehicle or vessel; (3) that police intervention, fire department or other emergency services was necessary for the personal safety of a passenger or to otherwise ensure the safety of the passengers; or (4) that a disabled vehicle or an accident was present on a roadway.

SECTION 13
Safety precautions for proper operation and parking of vehicles and buses

No person, when operating a motor vehicle, shall permit to be on or in the vehicle or on or about his person anything which may interfere with or impede the proper operation of the vehicle or any equipment by which the vehicle is operated or controlled, except that a person may operate a motor vehicle while using a federally licensed 2-way radio or mobile telephone, except as provided in sections 8M, 12A and 13B, as long as 1 hand remains on the steering wheel at all times. No person having control or charge of a motor vehicle, except a person having control or charge of a police, fire or other emergency vehicle in the course of responding to an emergency or a person having control or charge of a motor vehicle while engaged in the delivery or acceptance of goods, wares or merchandise for which the vehicle's engine power is necessary for the loading or unloading of such goods, wares or merchandise, shall allow such vehicle to stand in any way and remain unattended without stopping the engine of said vehicle, effectively setting the brakes thereof or making it fast, and locking and removing the key from the locking device and from the vehicle. Whenever a bus having a seating capacity of more than seven passengers, a truck weighing, unloaded, more than four thousand pounds, or a tractor, trailer, semi-trailer or combination thereof, shall be parked on a way, on a grade sufficient to cause such vehicle to move of its own momentum, and is left unattended by the operator, one pair of adequate wheel safety chock blocks shall be securely placed against the rear wheels of such vehicle so as to prevent movement thereof. The provisions of the preceding sentence shall not apply to a vehicle equipped with positive spring-loaded air parking brakes. No person shall drive any motor vehicle equipped with any television viewer, screen or other means of visually receiving a television broadcast which is located in the motor vehicle at any point forward of the back of the driver's seat, or which is visible to the driver while operating such motor vehicle. Whoever operates a motorcycle on the ways of the commonwealth shall ride only upon the permanent and regular seat attached thereto, and he shall not carry any other person, nor allow any other person to ride, on such motorcycle unless it is designed to carry more than one person, in which case a passenger may ride upon the permanent and regular seat if such seat is designed for two persons, or upon another seat which is intended for a passenger and is firmly attached to the motorcycle to the rear of the operator if proper foot rests are provided for the passenger's use, or upon a seat which is intended for a passenger and is firmly attached to the motorcycle in a side car. No person shall operate a motor vehicle, commonly known as a pick-up truck, nor shall the owner permit it to be operated, for a distance more than five-miles, in excess of five-miles per hour, with persons under twelve years of age in the body of such truck, unless such truck is part of an official parade, or has affixed to it a legal "Owner Repair" or "Farm" license plate or a pick-up truck engaged in farming activities. No person, except firefighters or garbage collectors, or operators of fire trucks or garbage trucks, or employees of public utility companies, acting pursuant to and during the course of their duties, or such other persons exempted by regulation from the application of this section or by limited application by special permit granted by the selectmen in a town or of the city council in a city, shall hang onto the outside of, or the rear-end of any vehicle, and no person on a pedacycle, motorcycle, roller skates, sled, or any similar device, shall hold fast or attach the device to any moving vehicle, and no operator of a motor vehicle shall knowingly permit any person to hang onto or ride on the outside or rear-end of the vehicle or streetcar, or allow any person on a pedacycle, motorcycle, roller skates, sled, or any similar device, to hold fast or attach the device to the motor vehicle operated on any highway. No person or persons, except firefighters acting pursuant to their official duties, shall occupy a trailer or semi-trailer while such trailer or semi-trailer is being towed, pushed or drawn or is otherwise in motion upon any way. No person shall operate a motor vehicle while wearing headphones, unless said headphones are used for communication in connection with controlling the course or movement of said vehicle.

SECTION 13A
Seatbelt use required; exemptions; penalty

No person shall operate a private passenger motor vehicle or ride in a private passenger motor vehicle, a vanpool vehicle or truck under eighteen thousand pounds on any way unless such person is wearing a safety belt which is properly adjusted and fastened; provided, however, that this provision shall not apply to:

(a) any child less than twelve years of age who is subject to the provisions of section seven AA;

(b) any person riding in a motor vehicle manufactured before July first, nineteen hundred and sixty-six;

(c) any person who is physically unable to use safety belts; provided, however, that such condition is duly certified by a physician who shall state the nature of the handicap, as well as the reasons such restraint is inappropriate; provided, further, that no such physician shall be subject to liability in any civil action for the issuance or for the failure to issue such certificate;

(d) any rural carrier of the United States Postal Service operating a motor vehicle while in the performance of his duties; provided, however, that such rural mail carrier shall be subject to department regulations regarding the use of safety belts or occupant crash protection devices;

(e) anyone involved in the operation of taxis, liveries, tractors, trucks with gross weight of eighteen thousand pounds or over, buses, and passengers of authorized emergency vehicles.

(f) the side facing seat on which the factory did not install a seat belt in any car owned for the purpose of antique collection.

Any person who operates a motor vehicle without a safety belt, and any person sixteen years of age or over who rides as a passenger in a motor vehicle without wearing a safety belt in violation of this section, shall be subject to a fine of twenty-five dollars. Any operator of a motor vehicle shall be subject to an additional fine of twenty-five dollars for each person under the age of sixteen and no younger than twelve who is a passenger in said motor vehicle and not wearing a safety belt. The provisions of this section shall be enforced by law enforcement agencies only when an operator of a motor vehicle has been stopped for a violation of the motor vehicle laws or some other offense.

Any person who receives a citation for violating this section may contest such citation pursuant to section three of chapter ninety C. A violation of this section shall not be considered as a conviction of a moving violation of the motor vehicle laws for the purpose of determining surcharges on motor vehicle premiums pursuant to section one hundred and thirteen B of chapter one hundred and seventy-five.

SECTION 13B
Composing, sending or reading of electronic messages while operating a motor vehicle prohibited; penalties

(a) No operator of a motor vehicle shall use a mobile telephone, or any handheld device capable of accessing the internet, to manually compose, send or read an electronic message while operating a motor vehicle. For the purposes of this section, an operator shall not be considered to be operating a motor vehicle if the vehicle is stationary and not located in a part of the public way intended for travel.

(b) A violation of this section shall be punishable by a fine of $100 for a first offense, by a fine of $250 for a second offense and by a fine of $500 for a third or subsequent offense.

(c) A penalty under this section shall not be a surchargeable offense under section 113B of chapter 175.

SECTION 14
Precautions for safety of other travelers

Every person operating a motor vehicle shall bring the vehicle and the motor propelling it immediately to a stop when approaching a cow, horse or other draft animal being led, ridden or driven, if such animal appears to be frightened and if the person in charge thereof shall signal so to do; and, if traveling in the opposite direction to that in which such animal is proceeding, said vehicle shall remain stationary so long as may be reasonable to allow such animal to pass; or, if traveling in the same direction, the person operating shall use reasonable caution in thereafter passing such animal. In approaching or passing a person on a bicycle the operator of a motor vehicle shall slow down and pass at a safe distance and at a reasonable and proper speed. In approaching or passing a car of a street railway which has been stopped to allow passengers to alight from or board the same, the person operating a motor vehicle shall not drive such vehicle within eight feet of the running board or lowest step of the car then in use by passengers for the purpose of alighting or boarding, except by the express direction of a traffic officer or except at points where passengers are protected by safety zones. When approaching a vehicle which displays a sign bearing the words "SCHOOL BUS" and which is equipped with front and rear alternating flashing red signal lamps which are flashing, as provided in section seven B, and which has been stopped to allow pupils to alight from or board the same, a person operating a motor vehicle or trackless trolley shall, except when approaching from the opposite direction on a divided highway, bring his vehicle or trackless trolley to a full stop before reaching said school bus and shall not thereafter proceed until the warning signals are deactivated, unless directed to the contrary by a police officer duly authorized to control the movement of traffic. Any person who violates the preceding sentence shall be punished by a fine of not less than $250; and for a second offense by a fine of not less than $500 nor more than $1,000; and for a third or subsequent offense by a fine of not less than $1,000 nor more than $2,000. A second conviction or third or subsequent conviction as set forth in the preceding sentence shall be reported forthwith by the court or magistrate to the registrar who shall revoke immediately the license or right to operate of the person so convicted and no appeal, motion for a new trial or exceptions, shall operate to stay the revocation of the license or right to operate; provided, however, that no license or right to operate shall be issued by the registrar to any person convicted of a second such offense until 6 months after the date of revocation following said conviction or to any person convicted of a third or subsequent such offense until 1 year after the date of revocation following said conviction; and provided, further, that if the prosecution against such person has terminated in his favor the registrar shall forthwith reinstate his license or right to operate. No person shall operate a motor vehicle within a distance of 100 feet behind a school bus. Every school bus shall have the words "keep back 100 feet" prominently displayed on the back of the bus, in type large and dark enough so that the words are legible at a distance of 100 feet. Upon approaching a pedestrian who is upon the traveled part of any way and not upon a sidewalk, every person operating a motor vehicle shall slow down. The person operating a motor vehicle on any way or a curve or a corner in said way where his view is obstructed shall slow down and keep to the right and upon approaching any junction of said way with an intersecting way shall, before entering the same, slow down and keep to the right of the center line. When turning to the right, an operator shall do so in the lane of traffic nearest to the right-hand side of the roadway and as close as practicable to the right-hand curb or edge of roadway. No person operating a vehicle that overtakes and passes a bicyclist proceeding in the same direction shall make a right turn at an intersection or driveway unless the turn can be made at a safe distance from the bicyclist at a speed that is reasonable and proper. When approaching for a left turn on a two-way street, an operator shall do so in the lane of traffic to the right of and nearest to the center line of the roadway and the left turn shall be made by passing to the right of the center line of the entering way where it enters the intersection from his left. When turning to the left within an intersection or into an alley, private road or driveway an operator shall yield the right of way to any vehicle approaching from the opposite direction, including a bicycle on the right of the other approaching vehicles, which is within the intersection or so close thereto as to constitute an immediate hazard. It shall not be a defense for a motorist causing an accident with a bicycle that the bicycle was to the right of vehicular traffic. When approaching for a left turn on a one-way street, an operator shall do so in the lane of traffic nearest to the left-hand side of the roadway and as close as practicable to the left-hand curb or edge of roadway. No person shall open a door on a motor vehicle unless it is reasonably safe to do so without interfering with the movement of other traffic, including bicyclists and pedestrians. Whoever violates the preceding sentence shall be punished by a fine of not more than $100.

The department, on ways within their control and at the intersection of state highways, and other ways, the metropolitan district commission, on ways within their control and at the intersection of metropolitan district commission roadways, except state highways, and other ways, the traffic and parking commission of the city of Boston, the traffic commission or traffic director of any city or town having such a commission or director with authority to promulgate traffic rules, the city council of any other city, and the board of selectmen of any other town may provide for the placing of traffic control devices in accordance with department standards to indicate the course to be traveled by vehicles turning at such intersections. Such course may be other than as is prescribed by the requirements for lane usage set forth in this section.

Such regulations and devices shall be, so far as applicable, subject to the provisions of section two of chapter eighty-five.

SECTION 14A
Protection of blind pedestrians crossing or attempting to cross ways

Whenever a totally or partially blind pedestrian, guided by a guide dog or carrying in a raised or extended position a cane or walking stick which is white in color or white tipped with red, crosses or attempts to cross a way, the driver of every vehicle approaching the place where such pedestrian is crossing or attempting to cross shall bring his vehicle to a full stop, and before proceeding shall take such precautions as may be necessary to avoid injuring such pedestrian. A person who owns an animal shall restrain and control such animal on a leash when in proximity to a guide dog that is on a public or private way. Nothing contained in this section shall be construed to deprive any totally or partially blind person, not carrying such a cane or walking stick or not being guided by a dog, of the rights and privileges conferred by law upon pedestrians crossing ways, nor shall the failure of such blind person to carry a cane or walking stick or to be guided by a guide dog while on the ways of this commonwealth be held to constitute or be evidence of contributory negligence. Whoever violates any provision of this section shall be punished by a fine of not more than one hundred nor more than five hundred dollars.

SECTION 14B
Uniform stopping and turning signals on ways

Every person operating a motor vehicle, before stopping said vehicle or making any turning movement which would affect the operation of any other vehicle, shall give a plainly visible signal by activating the brake lights or directional lights or signal as provided on said vehicle; and in the event electrical or mechanical signals are not operating or not provided on the vehicle, a plainly visible signal by means of the hand and arm shall be made. Hand and arm signals shall be made as follows:—

1. An intention to turn to the left shall be indicated by hand and arm extended horizontally.

2. An intention to turn to the right shall be indicated by hand and arm extended upward.

3. An intention to stop or decrease speed shall be indicated by hand and arm extended downward.

Whoever violates any provision of this section shall be punished by a fine of not less than twenty-five dollars for each offense.

SECTION 16
Offensive or illegal operation of motor vehicles

No person shall operate a motor vehicle, nor shall any owner of such vehicle permit it to be operated, in or over any way, public or private, whether laid out under authority of law or otherwise, which motor vehicles are prohibited from using, provided notice of such prohibition is conspicuously posted at the entrance to such way. No person shall operate a motor vehicle, nor shall any owner of such vehicle permit it to be operated upon any way, except fire department and fire patrol apparatus, unless such motor vehicle is equipped with a muffler to prevent excessive or unnecessary noise, which muffler is in good working order and in constant operation, and complies with such minimum standards for construction and performance as the registrar may prescribe. No person shall use a muffler cut-out or by-pass. No person shall operate a motor vehicle on any way which motor vehicle is equipped (1) with a muffler from which the baffle plates, screens or other original internal parts have been removed and not replaced; or (2) with an exhaust system which has been modified in a manner which will amplify or increase the noise emitted by the exhaust. No person operating a motor vehicle shall sound a bell, horn or other device, nor in any manner

operate such motor vehicle so as to make a harsh, objectionable or unreasonable noise, nor permit to escape from such vehicle smoke or pollutants in such amounts or at such levels as may violate motor vehicle air pollution control regulations adopted under the provisions of chapter one hundred and eleven. No siren shall be mounted upon any motor vehicle except fire apparatus, ambulances, vehicles used in official line of duty by any member of the police or fire fighting forces of the commonwealth or any agency or political subdivision thereof, and vehicles owned by call fire fighters or by persons with police powers and operated in official line of duty, unless authorized by the registrar. No person shall use on or in connection with any motor vehicle a spot light, so called, the rays from which shine more than two feet above the road at a distance of thirty feet from the vehicle, except that such a spot light may be used for the purpose of reading signs, and as an auxiliary light in cases of necessity when the other lights required by law fail to operate.

No person, except a duly authorized person driving an emergency fire vehicle, shall operate a motor vehicle equipped with metal studded tires upon a public way between May the first and November the first; provided, however, the registrar may authorize the use of such tires before November the first, if weather conditions require the use thereof. Whoever violates the provisions of this paragraph shall be punished by a fine of not more than fifty dollars.

SECTION 17
Speed limits

No person operating a motor vehicle on any way shall run it at a rate of speed greater than is reasonable and proper, having regard to traffic and the use of the way and the safety of the public. Unless a way is otherwise posted in accordance with the provisions of section eighteen, it shall be prima facie evidence of a rate of speed greater than is reasonable and proper as aforesaid (1) if a motor vehicle is operated on a divided highway outside a thickly settled or business district at a rate of speed exceeding fifty miles per hour for a distance of a quarter of a mile, or (2) on any other way outside a thickly settled or business district at a rate of speed exceeding forty miles per hour for a distance of a quarter of a mile, or (3) inside a thickly settled or business district at a rate of speed exceeding thirty miles per hour for a distance of one-eighth of a mile, or (4) within a school zone which may be established by a city or town as provided in section two of chapter eighty-five at a rate of speed exceeding twenty miles per hour. Operation of a motor vehicle at a speed in excess of fifteen miles per hour within one-tenth of a mile of a vehicle used in hawking or peddling merchandise and which displays flashing amber lights shall likewise be prima facie evidence of a rate of speed greater than is reasonable and proper. If a speed limit has been duly established upon any way, in accordance with the provisions of said section, operation of a motor vehicle at a rate of speed in excess of such limit shall be prima facie evidence that such speed is greater than is reasonable and proper; but, notwithstanding such establishment of a speed limit, every person operating a motor vehicle shall decrease the speed of the same when a special hazard exists with respect to pedestrians or other traffic, or by reason of weather or highway conditions. Any person in violation of this section, while operating a motor vehicle through the parameters of a marked construction zone or construction area, at a speed which exceeds the posted limit, or at a speed that is greater than is reasonable and proper, shall be subject to a fine of 2 times the amount currently in effect for the violation issued. Except on a limited access highway, no person shall operate a school bus at a rate of speed exceeding forty miles per hour, while actually engaged in carrying school children.

NOTE 1a   Radar. The radar speedmeter is an accurate and reliable means of measuring velocity and results therefrom are admissible if some foundation to the accuracy of the particular radar instrument is laid. *Commonwealth v. Whynaught*, 377 Mass. 14, 14–19 (1979).

NOTE 1b Where the issue of the accuracy of the radar instrument is raised by the defendant, the trial judge has discretion to determine when a sufficient showing has been made. The judge should "closely examine the nature of all testing procedures and . . . will be guided in [his or her] admission decisions by the quality of the tests performed, rather than by their quantity. At the same time, we expect that the testing requirements judges impose will not be so onerous as to make use of radar devices a practical impossibility." *Commonwealth v. Whynaught*, 377 Mass. at 19 (citation and footnote omitted).

NOTE 2 A 13-year-old boy testified (1) he saw a car travel 60 feet before coming to a stop; and (2) "that he had ridden in an automobile with his father and had made observations of speed." As such, "[i]t could not have been ruled as a matter of law that this witness had no opportunity whatever to form a judgment of speed." *Logan v. Goward*, 313 Mass. 48, 51 (1943).

NOTE 3 "One mode of proving that a traveller was driving at an unusual, improper and unsafe rate of speed is by witnesses who saw him at or near the time and place in question. . . . But to limit such testimony to witnesses who were looking at the driver at the very moment and spot of the accident would render it practically unavailable." *Smith v. Neibauer Bus Co.*, 328 Mass. 624, 627 (1952) (quoting *Stone v. Hubbardston*, 100 Mass. 49, 55–56 (1868)).

SECTION 17B
Drag racing; penalties

No person shall operate a motor vehicle, nor shall any owner of such vehicle permit it to be operated, in a manner where the owner or operator accelerates at a high rate of speed in competition with another operator, whether or not there is an agreement to race, causing increased noise from skidding tires and amplified noise from racing engines. Whoever violates this section shall be punished by imprisonment in the house of correction for not more than 2½ years or by a fine of not more than $1,000. The registrar shall suspend such violator's license for a period of not less than 30 days for a first offense and for not less than 180 days for any subsequent violation.

Notwithstanding the penalties provided in the first paragraph, a holder of a junior operator's license or learner's permit who commits a violation of this section shall be punished by a fine of not less than $250 for a first offense and the registrar shall suspend the junior operator's license or learner's permit for 1 year. A subsequent violation shall be punished by a fine of not less than $500 and the registrar shall suspend the junior operator's license or learner's permit for 3 years. A holder of a junior operator's license or learner's permit who commits a violation under this section shall also be required to complete the state courts against road rage program sponsored by the trial court and the department of state police.

The registrar shall impose a $500 reinstatement fee upon a junior operator who seeks to have his license or learner's permit reinstated following suspension for a first offense under this section and a $1,000 reinstatement fee shall be imposed upon a junior operator who seeks to have his license or learner's permit reinstated following suspension for a subsequent violation under this section. A junior operator whose license is suspended under this section shall not be eligible for license reinstatement until he also completes a program selected by the registrar that encourages attitudinal changes in young drivers who have committed a violation of the motor vehicle laws and until he successfully completes a driving test as required by the registrar. A junior operator whose learner's permit is suspended under this section shall be required to complete a program selected by the registrar that encourages attitudinal changes in young drivers who have committed a violation of the motor vehicle laws and shall be required to reapply for his learner's permit before he may be issued a license to operate a motor vehicle pursuant to section 8.

SECTION 20
Penalties and punishments
(Amended by 2012 Mass. Acts c. 139, § 95, effective July 1, 2012, § 96, effective July 1, 2013.)

A person convicted of a violation of any provision of this chapter the punishment for which is not otherwise provided, or of a violation of any rule or regulation of the registrar made under authority of section thirty-one, shall be punished by a fine of not more than thirty-five dollars for the first offense, not less than thirty-five nor more than seventy-five dollars for a second offense, and not less than seventy-five nor more than one hundred and fifty dollars for subsequent offenses committed during any twelve-month period; provided, however, that any person convicted of operating a motor vehicle without having been issued a license by the registrar shall be punished by a fine of not more than $500 for a first offense, by a fine of not less than $500 nor more than $1,000, for a second offense and by a fine of not less than $1,000 nor more than $2,000, for any subsequent offense.; provided, however, that any person convicted of operating or permitting the operation of a school bus carrying passengers in excess of the number authorized under section seven B shall be punished by a fine of not more than one hundred dollars or by imprisonment for not more than thirty days, or both, and that any person convicted of violating any of the provisions of section sixteen shall be punished by a fine of not less than twenty nor more than one hundred dollars, and that any person convicted of operating a motor vehicle, trailer, semitrailer, semitrailer unit or tandem unit in violation of section nineteen shall be punished by a fine of not more than one hundred dollars and that any person convicted of knowingly operating a motor vehicle, trailer, semitrailer, semitrailer unit or tandem unit or any owner or bailee convicted of requiring or permitting the operation thereof in violation of section nineteen A or of the terms of any permit issued under sections thirty and thirty A of chapter eighty-five shall be punished by a fine of forty dollars for each one thousand pounds of weight or fraction thereof by which the gross weight of such motor vehicle, trailer, semitrailer, semitrailer unit or tandem unit as operated exceeds either that permitted by said section nineteen A or by permit issued for such motor vehicle, trailer, semitrailer, semitrailer unit or tandem unit under sections thirty and thirty A of chapter eighty-five, whichever is greater; provided, further, that if the total of such excess weight is greater than ten thousand pounds, the fine shall be eighty dollars for each one thousand pounds or fraction thereof over said ten thousand pounds; and, provided further, that in a case of so-called irreducible loads, if the owner or bailee of the motor vehicle, trailer, semitrailer, semitrailer unit or tandem unit, or his agent, servant or employee did not have reasonable means or opportunity to ascertain the weight of the load prior to applying for the permit, then the fine shall be ten dollars for each one thousand pounds of weight by which the gross weight of such motor vehicle, trailer, semitrailer, semitrailer unit or tandem unit as operated exceeds either that permitted by said section nineteen A or section thirty A of the gross weight specified in such permit but in no event more than five hundred dollars.

Any person convicted of a violation of the provisions of section seventeen, or of a violation of a special regulation lawfully made under the authority of section eighteen shall be punished by a fine of not less than fifty dollars. Where said conviction is for operating a vehicle at a rate of speed exceeding ten miles per hour over the speed limit for the way upon which the person was operating, an additional fine of ten dollars for each mile per hour in excess of the ten miles per hour shall be assessed.

Any person convicted of a violation of the provisions of section seventeen while operating any motor vehicle, trailer, semitrailer, semitrailer unit or tandem unit under a permit issued under sections thirty and thirty A of chapter eighty-five and while the weight of such motor vehicle, trailer, semitrailer, semitrailer unit or tandem unit exceeds the limits provided in section nineteen A, exclusive of the additional limits provided in such permit, shall be punished by a fine of not more than one hundred dollars for the first offense, not less than one hundred dollars nor more than one hundred and fifty dollars for a second offense committed in any twelve-month period, and not less than one hundred and fifty nor more than three hundred dollars for subsequent offenses committed in any twelve-month period, and complaints of such violations, notwithstanding the subsequent provisions of this section shall not be placed on file by the court.

There shall be a surcharge of $50. on a fine assessed against a person convicted or found responsible of a violation of section 17 or a violation of a special regulation lawfully made under the authority of section 18. The first $37.50 of each surcharge shall be transferred by the registrar of motor vehicles to the state treasurer for deposit into the Head Injury Treatment Services Trust Fund. The remaining amount shall be transferred by the registrar to the state treasurer for deposit in the General Fund.

Upon a third or subsequent conviction in the same twelve month period of a violation of section 16 or section 17 or of a regulation made under section 18 said violation having occurred in the same year, the registrar shall forthwith revoke the license of the person convicted, and no new license shall be issued to such person for at least thirty days after the date of such revocation, nor thereafter except in the discretion of the registrar; provided, however, that a holder of a learner's permit who is convicted of a violation under section 17 or section 17A, or under a special regulation under section 18, shall, in addition to any other penalty, fine, suspension, revocation or requirement that may be imposed for such violation, have his learner's permit suspended for 90 days for a first offense and for 1 year for a subsequent offense and the person

shall be required to reapply for his learner's permit before he may be issued a license to operate a motor vehicle pursuant to section 8; and provided further that a holder of a junior operator's license who is convicted of a violation under section 17 or section 17A, or under a special regulation under section 18 shall, in addition to any other penalty, fine, suspension, revocation or requirement that may be imposed for such violation, have such license suspended for 90 days for a first offense and 1 year for a subsequent offense and the junior operator shall also be required to complete the state courts against road rage program sponsored by the trial court and the department of the state police. The registrar shall impose a $500 reinstatement fee upon a junior operator who seeks to have his license reinstated following a suspension under this paragraph. A junior operator whose license is suspended pursuant to this paragraph shall not be eligible for license reinstatement until he also completes a program selected by the registrar that encourages attitudinal changes in young drivers who have committed a violation of the motor vehicle laws and until he successfully completes a driving test as required by the registrar. In addition to any reinstatement fee, there shall be a surcharge of $50, assessed against a person who seeks to have his license reinstated following a revocation or suspension under this paragraph. The first $25 of each surcharge shall be transferred by the registrar of motor vehicles to the state treasurer for deposit into the Spinal Cord Injury Trust Fund. The remaining amount shall be transferred by the registrar to the state treasurer for deposit in the General Fund.

Any person who operates and any person who owns or permits to be operated a motor vehicle or trailer that fails to meet the safety standards established by the registrar pursuant to section 7A shall be punished by a fine of $25. Any person who owns and fails to have inspected a motor vehicle owned by him, as required pursuant to section 7A or 7V of this chapter or sections 142J and 142M of chapter 111 or any person who operates or permits a motor vehicle owned by him to be operated without a certificate of inspection or a certificate of rejection displayed in accordance with the provisions of said section 7A or 7V or said sections 142J or 142M and the rules and regulations promulgated thereunder shall be punished by a fine of $50. Any motor vehicle which is required to be inspected pursuant to the provisions of said section 7A and said section 142J or 142M and fails to meet the requirements of such inspection and has not been issued a certificate of waiver under the provisions of clause (b) of the first paragraph of said section 7V or said section 142M shall be subject to suspension or revocation of the certificate of registration as may be prescribed by the registrar under section 22.

SECTION 20A
Parking regulations; violations; notice to appear; failure to appear; adjudication by mail
(Amended by 2010 Mass. Acts c. 454, § 44, effective Jan. 14, 2011.)

In any city or town accepting the provisions of this section, each city manager in a city having a Plan D or E form of charter or the mayor with the approval of the city council or board of aldermen in any other city or the town council or board of selectmen of a town shall designate or appoint a parking clerk, who may also perform other municipal functions except police functions. The parking clerk shall be directly responsible to said city manager, mayor, town council or board of selectmen and shall supervise and coordinate the processing of parking notices in such city or town. The parking clerk shall have the authority, subject to the approval of the city manager or mayor in a city or town manager or board of selectmen in a town, to hire or designate such personnel and organize such divisions as he may deem necessary or contract, by competitive bidding, for such services subject to appropriation to carry out the provisions of this section.

It shall be the duty of any police officer, except in cities and towns subject to the provisions of section twenty A½, who takes cognizance of a violation of any provision of any rule, regulation, order, ordinance or by-law regulating the parking of motor vehicles established by any city or town, forthwith to give to the offender a notice to appear before the parking clerk of the city or town wherein the violation occurred at any time during regular office hours, not later than twenty-one days after the time of said violation.

Said notice must be made in triplicate and one copy shall be affixed securely to the motor vehicle and shall contain, but shall not be limited to, the following information: the make, color, registration number and state of issuance of said registration number of the vehicle involved, the date, time and place of the violation, the specific violation charged and, if a meter violation, the number of said meter, the name and badge number of the officer and his division, a schedule of established fines, instructions for the return of the notice and a notice which reads as follows: This notice may be returned by mail, personally or by an authorized person. A hearing may be obtained upon the written request of the registered owner. Failure to obey this notice within twenty-one days after the date of violation may result in the non-renewal of the license to drive and the certificate of registration of the registered owner.

Whenever it is not possible to deliver a copy of said notice to the offender at the time and place of the violation by affixing it to the motor vehicle, said copy shall be sent by the officer, or by his commanding officer or any person authorized by said commanding officer, in the case of a violation involving a motor vehicle registered under the laws of this commonwealth, within five days of the offense, and in the case of any motor vehicle registered under the laws of another state or country, within ten days thereof, exclusive, in either case, of Sundays and holidays, to the address of the registrant of the motor vehicle registered under the laws of this commonwealth, in the records of the registry of motor vehicles, or, in the case of a motor vehicle registered under the laws of another state or country, in the records of the official in such state or country having charge of the registration of such motor vehicle. Such notice mailed by the officer, his commanding officer, or the person so authorized, to the last address of such registrant as appearing as aforesaid, shall be deemed as sufficient notice, and a certificate of the officer or person so mailing such notice that it has been mailed in accordance with this section shall be deemed prima facie evidence thereof and shall be admissible in any judicial or administrative proceeding as to the facts contained therein. At or before the completion of each tour of duty the officer shall give to his commanding officer those copies of each notice of such a violation taken cognizance of during such tour which have not already been delivered or mailed by him as aforesaid. Said commanding officer shall retain and safely preserve one of such copies and shall, at a time not later than the end of the second business day of the city or town after said delivery or mailing, deliver another of such copies to the parking clerk before whom the offender has been notified to appear. The parking clerk shall maintain a docket of all such notices to appear.

Any person notified to appear before the parking clerk, as provided herein, may appear before such parking clerk or his designee and confess the offense charged, either personally or through an agent duly authorized in writing or by mailing to such parking clerk the notice and the fine provided herein, such payment to be made only by postal note, money order or check made out to the parking clerk. If it is the first violation subject to this section committed by such person in a particular city or town in the calendar year, the parking clerk shall dismiss the charge without the payment of any fine; if it is the second, third or fourth violation so committed in such city or town in the calendar year, payment to the parking clerk of a fine of five dollars for each such violation shall operate as a final disposition of the case; and if it is the fifth or subsequent violation so committed in such city or town in the calendar year, payment to the parking clerk of a fine of ten dollars for each such violation shall operate as a final disposition of the case; provided, however, that the provisions of this sentence shall not apply to any violation subject to this section committed in any city or town wherein the city council or board of aldermen, town council, board of selectmen, or traffic commission or traffic director having authority to promulgate traffic rules shall have established by municipal rule, regulation, ordinance or by-law a schedule of fines for such violations. The schedule of fines shall be uniform for the same offense committed in the same zone or district, if any, and shall not exceed $25 if paid within 21 days, $35 if paid thereafter but before the parking clerk reports to the registrar as provided below, and $50 if paid thereafter; provided, however, that the fine for the violation of parking a motor vehicle within a posted bus stop shall be $100. Notice affixed to a motor vehicle as provided in this section shall be deemed a sufficient notice, and a certificate of the officer affixing such notice that it has been affixed thereto, in accordance with this section, shall be deemed prima facie evidence thereof and shall be admissible in any judicial or administrative proceeding as to the facts contained therein. Whenever it becomes necessary to ascertain whether a person owning two or more motor vehicles is chargeable as such owner with a first, second, third, fourth, fifth or subsequent violation hereunder, such question shall, in the case of vehicles singly registered, be determined separately with respect to the particular vehicle involved in such violation and, in the case of vehicles subject to section five, with respect to the particular number plate or plates used on the vehicle involved in such violation at the time thereof.

Should any person notified to appear hereunder fail to appear and, if a fine is provided hereunder, to pay the same, or having appeared desire not to avail himself of the benefits of the procedure established by this section, the parking clerk shall forthwith schedule the matter before a person hereafter referred to as a hearing officer, said hearing officer to be the parking clerk of the city or town wherein the violation occurred or such other person or persons as the parking clerk may designate. Written notice of the date, time and place of said hearing shall be sent by first-class mail to the registered owner. Said hearing shall be informal, the rules of evidence shall not apply and the decision of the hearing officer shall be final subject to judicial review as provided by section fourteen of chapter thirty A.

If any person fails to appear in accordance with said notice, the parking clerk shall notify the registrar of motor vehicles who shall place the matter on record and, upon receipt of two or more such notices, shall not renew the license to operate a motor vehicle of the registered owner of the vehicle or the registration of said vehicle until after notice from the parking clerk that all such matters have been disposed of in accordance with law. Upon such notification to the registrar, an additional twenty dollar charge, payable to the registrar of motor vehicles, shall be assessed against the registered owner of said vehicle. It shall be the duty of the parking clerk to notify the registrar forthwith that such case has been disposed of in accordance with law, provided however, that a certified receipt of full and final payment from the parking clerk of the city or town in which the violation occurred shall also serve as legal notice to the registrar that said violation has been so disposed of. The notice to appear provided herein shall be printed in such form as the registrar of motor vehicles may approve. The parking clerk shall distribute such notices to the commanding officer of the police department of the city or town upon request, and shall take a receipt therefor. The registrar shall approve such other forms as he deems appropriate to implement this section, and said forms shall be printed and used by the cities and towns.

If any person shall have failed to appear in accordance with five or more said notices, notwithstanding any notification to the registrar, the parking clerk may notify the chief of police or director of traffic or parking of said city or town that the vehicle involved in said multiple violations shall be removed and stored, or otherwise immobilized by a mechanical device, at the expense of the registered owner of said vehicle until such time as the matter has been disposed of in accordance with law.

As used in this section, the words "motor vehicle" shall, so far as apt, include trailer, semi-trailer and semi-trailer unit.

The provisions of this section shall apply to violations of rules and regulations relative to the use of parking areas subject to the control of the county commissioners adjacent to or abutting county buildings, and county commissioners are hereby authorized to make said rules and regulations.

Any person notified to appear before the parking clerk, as provided herein, without waiving his right to a hearing before the parking clerk or hearing officer as provided by this section, and also without waiving judicial review as provided by section fourteen of chapter thirty A, may challenge the validity of the parking violation notice and receive a review and disposition of the violation from the parking clerk or a hearing officer by mail. The alleged parking violator may, upon receipt of the notice to appear, send a signed statement explaining his objections to the violation notice as well as signed statements from witnesses, police officers, government officials and any other relevant parties. Photographs, diagrams, maps and other documents may also be sent with the statements. Any such statements or materials sent to the parking clerk for review shall have attached the persons' name and address as well as the ticket number and the date of the violation. The parking clerk or hearing officer shall, within twenty-one days of receipt of said material, review the material and dismiss or uphold the violation and notify, by mail, the alleged violator of the disposition of the hearing. If the outcome of the hearing is against the alleged violator, the parking clerk or hearing officer shall explain the reasons for the outcome on the notice. Such review and disposition handled by mail shall be informal, the rules of evidence shall not apply, and the decision of the parking clerk shall be final subject to any hearing provisions provided by this section or to judicial review as provided by section fourteen of chapter thirty A. Each parking violation issued shall carry a statement explaining the procedure to adjudicate the violation by mail.

SECTION 20A½
Cities of Boston and Cambridge; parking violations; tags; appearance; failure to appear; adjudication by mail
(Amended by 2010 Mass. Acts c. 454, § 45, effective Jan. 14, 2011.)

In the cities of Boston and Cambridge and in any city or town which accepts the provisions of this section, each manager in a city having a Plan D or E form of charter or the mayor, with the approval of the city council or board of aldermen in any other city, or the town council or board of selectmen of a town shall designate or appoint a parking clerk. The parking clerk shall report to the council or aldermen of a city, the council or board of selectmen of a town and shall supervise and coordinate the processing of parking notices in such city or town. The parking clerk shall have the authority, after such authorization by the mayor and city council in a city or town council or selectmen in a town, to hire and designate such personnel as may be necessary or contract by competitive bid for such services, subject to appropriation, to implement the provisions of this section; provided, however, that such positions shall be filled in the city of Boston and Cambridge by granting preference to persons who had been employees of said cities in the fire, police or traffic crossing guard service, and all such positions in said city of Boston and Cambridge shall be subject to chapter thirty-one, and in no case in the city of Boston and Cambridge shall the amount expended for administration of this section exceed eleven per cent of the total amount of the annual receipts collected by the parking clerk.

It shall be the duty of every police officer who takes cognizance of a violation of any provision of any rule, regulation, order, ordinance or by-law regulating the parking of motor vehicles established for their respective city or town, forthwith to give the offender a notice, which shall be in tag form as provided in this section, to appear before the parking clerk of the city or town wherein the violation occurred at any time during regular office hours, not later than twenty-one days after the date of such violation. All tags shall be prepared in triplicate and shall be prenumbered.

Said tag shall be affixed securely to the motor vehicle and shall contain, but shall not be limited to, the following information: the make, color and registration number of the vehicle involved and the state of issuance of said registration number, the date, time and place of the violation, the specific violation charged and, if a meter violation, the number of said meter, the name and badge number of the officer and his division, a schedule of established fines, instructions for the return of the tag and a notice which reads: This notice may be returned by mail, personally or by an authorized person. A hearing may be obtained upon the written request of the registered owner. Failure to obey this notice within twenty-one days after the date of violation may result in the non-renewal of the license to drive and the registration of the registered owner.

At or before the completion of each tour of duty, the officer shall give to his commanding officer those copies of each notice of such violation taken cognizance of during such tour. Said commanding officer shall retain and safely preserve one of such copies and shall at a time no later than the beginning of the next business day of the city or town after receipt of such notice deliver another of such copies to the parking clerk before whom the offender has been notified to appear. The parking clerk shall maintain a docket of all such notices to appear.

Any person notified to appear before the parking clerk, as provided herein, may appear before such parking clerk, or his designee, and confess the offense charged, either personally or through an agent duly authorized in writing or by mailing to such parking clerk the notice accompanied by the fine provided therein, such payment to be made only by postal note, money order or check made out to the parking clerk. Payment of the fine established shall operate as a final disposition of the case. Notice affixed to a motor vehicle as provided in this section, shall be deemed a sufficient notice, and a certificate of the officer affixing such notice that it has been affixed thereto, in accordance with this section, shall be deemed prima facie evidence thereof and shall be admissible in any judicial or administrative proceeding as to the facts contained therein.

The traffic and parking commission of the city of Boston, the traffic commission or traffic director of any other city or town having such a commission or director with authority to promulgate traffic rules, the city council of any other city, and the board of selectmen of any other town, shall, from time to time, establish by rule or regulation a schedule of fines for violations subject to this section committed within such city or town; provided, however, that all such fines shall be uniform for the same offense committed in the same zone or district, if any; and provided, further, that the fine for the violation of the parking of motor vehicles within ten feet of a fire hydrant shall not be more than one hundred dollars, and provided, further, that the fine for the violation of parking a motor vehicle within a posted bus stop shall be $100; and provided further, that any fine established under the provisions of this section for all other parking violations shall not exceed $50, if paid within 21 days, nor shall it exceed $55, if paid thereafter, but before the parking clerk reports to the registrar, as provided below and shall not exceed $75 if paid thereafter.

Should any person notified to appear hereunder fail to appear and, if a fine is provided hereunder, to pay the same, or having appeared desire not to avail himself of the benefits of the procedure established by this section, the parking clerk shall forthwith schedule the matter before a person hereafter referred to as a hearing officer, said hearing officer to be the parking clerk of the city or town wherein the violation occurred or such other person or persons as the parking clerk may designate. Written notice of the date, time and place of said hearing shall be sent by first-class mail to the registered owner. Said hearing shall be informal, the rules of evidence shall not apply and the decision of the hearing officer shall be final subject to judicial review as provided by section fourteen of chapter thirty A.

If any person fails to appear in accordance with said notice, the parking clerk shall notify the registrar of motor vehicles who shall place the matter on record and, upon receipt of two or more such notices, shall not renew the license to operate a motor vehicle of the registered owner of the vehicle or the registration of said vehicle until after notice from the parking clerk that all such matters have been disposed of in accordance with law. Upon such notification to the registrar, an additional twenty dollar charge, payable to the registrar of motor vehicles, shall be assessed against the registered owner of said vehicle. It shall be the duty of the parking clerk to notify the registrar forthwith that such case has been so disposed of in accordance with law, provided however, that a certified receipt of full and final payment from the parking clerk of the city or town in which the violation occurred shall also serve as legal notice to the registrar that said violation has been disposed of. The notice to appear provided herein shall be printed in such form as the registrar of motor vehicles may approve. The parking clerk shall distribute such notices to the commanding officer of the police department of the city or town upon request, and shall take a receipt therefor. The registrar shall approve such other forms as he deems appropriate to implement this section, and said forms shall be printed and used by the cities and towns.

If any person shall have failed to appear in accordance with five or more said notices, notwithstanding any notification to the registrar, the parking clerk may notify the chief of police or director of traffic and parking of said city or town that the vehicle involved in said multiple violations shall be removed and stored, or otherwise immobilized by a mechanical device, at the expense of the registered owner of said vehicle until such time as the matter has been disposed of in accordance with law.

As used in this section, the words "motor vehicle" shall, so far as apt, include trailer, semi-trailer and semi-trailer unit.

The provisions of this section shall apply to violations of rules and regulations relative to the use of parking areas subject to the control of the county commissioners adjacent to or abutting county buildings, and county commissioners are hereby authorized to make such rules and regulations. Said provisions shall also apply to violations of rules and regulations relative to the parking of motor vehicles established by any commission or body empowered to make such rules and regulations.

Any person notified to appear before the parking clerk, as provided herein, without waiving his right to a hearing before the parking clerk or hearing officer as provided by this section, and also without waiving judicial review as provided by section fourteen of chapter thirty A, may challenge the validity of the parking violation notice and receive a review and disposition of the violation from the parking clerk or a hearing officer by mail. The alleged parking violator may, upon receipt of the notice to appear, send a signed statement explaining his objections to the violation notice as well as signed statements from witnesses, police officers, government officials and any other relevant parties. Photographs, diagrams, maps and other documents may also be sent with the statements. Any such statements or materials sent to the parking clerk for review shall have attached the persons' name and address as well as the ticket number and the date of the violation. The parking clerk or hearing officer shall, within twenty-one days of receipt of said material, review the material and dismiss or uphold the violation and notify, by mail, the alleged violator of the disposition of the hearing. If the outcome of the hearing is against the alleged violator, the parking clerk or hearing officer shall explain the reasons for the outcome on the notice. Such review and disposition handled by mail shall be informal, the rules of evidence shall not apply, and the decision of the parking clerk shall be final subject to any hearing provisions provided by this section or to judicial review as provided by section fourteen of chapter thirty A. Each parking violation issued shall carry a statement explaining the procedure to adjudicate the violation by mail.

SECTION 20C
Nature of proceedings under Secs. 20A and 20A½; fines

Proceedings under sections twenty A or twenty A½ of this chapter shall not be deemed criminal. Whenever there are outstanding against the registered owner of a motor vehicle more than five unpaid parking violations issued by a city or town, said owner or city or town may apply to the clerk of the division of the district or municipal court having jurisdiction to have the matter of these alleged violations treated criminally, and the district or municipal court shall take jurisdiction of the matter. The matter shall thereafter be deemed criminal and the procedures established for criminal cases be followed, provided, however, that the provisions of the second and third paragraphs of section thirty-five A of chapter two hundred and eighteen shall not apply to such cases. Any such fine imposed by the court shall not exceed double the maximum fine provided for in any city or town. Said fine imposed by the court shall be paid back to the said cities or towns where the violation occurred.

SECTION 20D
Tampering or destruction of parking tags; penalty

Whoever unlawfully tampers with or removes from a motor vehicle, or unlawfully changes, mutilates or destroys any notice affixed to such motor vehicle in accordance with section twenty A or twenty A½ shall be punished by a fine of not more than fifty dollars, or by imprisonment in jail for not more than one month, or by both such fine and imprisonment.

SECTION 21
Arrest without warrant

Any officer authorized to make arrests may arrest without a warrant and keep in custody for not more than twenty-four hours, unless a Saturday, Sunday or a legal holiday intervenes, any person who, while operating a motor vehicle on any way, as defined in section one, violates the provisions of the first paragraph of section ten of chapter ninety. Any arrest made pursuant to this paragraph shall be deemed an arrest for the criminal offense or offenses involved and not for any civil motor vehicle infraction arising out of the same incident.

Any officer authorized to make arrests, provided such officer is in uniform or conspicuously displaying his badge of office, may arrest without a warrant and keep in custody for not more than twenty-four hours, unless Saturday, Sunday or legal holiday intervenes, any person, regardless of whether or not such person has in his possession a license to operate motor vehicles issued by the registrar, if such person upon any way or in any place to which the public has the right of access, or upon any way or in any place to which members of the public have access as invitees, operates a motor vehicle after his license or right to operate motor vehicles in this state has been suspended or revoked by the registrar, or whoever upon any way or in any place to which the public has the right of access, or upon any way or in any place to which members of the public have access as invitees, or who the

officer has probable cause to believe has operated or is operating a motor vehicle while under the influence of intoxicating liquor, marihuana or narcotic drugs, or depressant or stimulant substances, all as defined in section one of chapter ninety-four C, or under the influence of the vapors of glue, carbon tetrachloride, acetone, ethylene, dichloride, toluene, chloroform, xylene or any combination thereof, or whoever uses a motor vehicle without authority knowing that such use is unauthorized, or any person who, while operating or in charge of a motor vehicle, violates the provisions of section twenty-five of chapter ninety, or whoever operates a motor vehicle upon any way or in any place to which members of the public have a right of access as invitees or licensees and without stopping and making known his name, residence and the register number of his motor vehicle goes away after knowingly colliding with or otherwise causing injury to any person, or whoever operates a motor vehicle recklessly or negligently so that the lives or safety of the public might be endangered in violation of paragraph (a) of subdivision (2) of section 24 and by such operation causes another person seriously bodily injury as defined in section 24L, or whoever commits motor vehicle homicide in violation of subsection (a) or (b) of section 24G.

Any person who is arrested pursuant to this section shall, at or before the expiration of the time period prescribed, be brought before the appropriate district court and proceeded against according to the law in criminal or juvenile cases, as the case may be, provided, however, that any violation otherwise cognizable as a civil infraction shall retain its character as, and be treated as, a civil infraction notwithstanding that the violator is arrested pursuant to this section for a criminal offense in conjunction with said civil infraction.

An investigator or examiner appointed under section twenty-nine may arrest without a warrant, keep in custody for a like period, bring before a magistrate and proceed against in like manner, any person operating a motor vehicle while under the influence of intoxicating liquor or marihuana, narcotic drugs, depressants or stimulant substances, all as defined in section one of chapter ninety-four C, irrespective of his possession of a license to operate motor vehicles issued by the registrar.

NOTE 1   Deputy sheriffs "cannot arrest without a warrant, even for those violations specifically enumerated in s. 21, if there is no concomitant breach of the peace." *Commonwealth v. Baez,* 42 Mass. App. Ct. 565, 569 (1997).

NOTE 2   See Note 15 following G.L. c. 90, § 24.

SECTION 22
Suspension or revocation of certificate of registration or license; notice
(Amended by 2016 Mass. Acts c. 64, § 1, effective Mar. 30, 2016.)

(a) The registrar may suspend or revoke without a hearing any certificate of registration or any license issued under this chapter whenever the holder thereof has committed a violation of the motor vehicle laws of a nature which would give the registrar reason to believe that continuing operation by such holder is and will be so seriously improper as to constitute an immediate threat to the public safety. Upon such suspension or revocation, the registrar shall forthwith send written notice thereof to the licensee or registrant, as the case may be. Such notice shall specify the time and place of the violation. The registrar may order the license of such operator or the registration certificate and number plates to be delivered to him; and neither the certificate of registration nor the license shall be reissued unless, upon examination or investigation, or after a hearing, the registrar determines that the operator shall again be permitted to operate. Said operator shall be entitled to a hearing within thirty days of the suspension or revocation, and the registrar shall so advise him in his notice of suspension or revocation. The registrar, under the same conditions and for the same cause, may also suspend the right of any person to operate motor vehicles in the commonwealth under section ten until he shall have received a license from the registrar or until his right to operate has been restored by the registrar.

(b) The registrar may, after due hearing, suspend or revoke any certificate of registration or any license issued under this chapter, when he has reason to believe the holder thereof is an incompetent person to operate motor vehicles, or is operating a motor vehicle improperly. The registrar may also, after due hearing, suspend or revoke any certificate of registration issued under this chapter, when a certificate of title issued by him under chapter ninety D has been suspended or revoked. At least fourteen days prior to any such suspension or revocation, the registrar shall notify the operator in writing of his intention to suspend or revoke his license as of a specified date. Said notice shall specify the reasons for the intended suspension or revocation and shall inform the operator of his right to request in writing a hearing within fourteen days after the date of such notice on the question of whether there is just cause for such suspension or revocation. If he so requests, the registrar shall grant him a hearing, shall notify him of the date of such hearing and he shall not suspend or revoke the license or registration prior to the completion of the hearing. If, after such hearing, the registrar determines that there is just cause for suspension or revocation, he may suspend or revoke the license but, except as provided by law, or except when he finds that the operator is physically or mentally incapable of operating a motor vehicle, no suspension under this subsection shall be for a period in excess of thirty days. Failure on the part of the operator to request a hearing as aforesaid shall constitute a waiver of his right to a hearing and the registrar may thereafter suspend or revoke the license or certificate on the date originally specified.

(c) If the registrar receives official notice, in any form which the registrar deems appropriate, including electronic transmissions, that a resident of the commonwealth or any person licensed to operate a motor vehicle under the provisions of this chapter has been convicted in another state, county, or jurisdiction of a motor vehicle violation, the registrar shall give the same effect to said conviction for the purposes of suspension, revocation, limitation or reinstatement of the right to operate a motor vehicle, as if said violation had occurred in the commonwealth.

As used in this section "motor vehicle violation" shall mean a violation of law, regulation, by-law, or ordinance, except a violation related to parking, the nature of which would have been reported to the registrar pursuant to chapters eighty-nine, ninety, ninety C, or one hundred and seventy-five, if said violation had occurred in the commonwealth.

If the registrar receives official notice, in any form which the registrar deems appropriate, including electronic transmissions, that a resident of the commonwealth, or any person licensed to operate a motor vehicle under the provisions of

chapter ninety, or any applicant therefor has had a license or right to operate suspended or revoked in another state, county, or jurisdiction, the registrar shall not issue a license to said person, and if a license has already been issued the registrar shall immediately revoke said license, without a prior hearing. However, if said license or right to operate is subsequently reinstated by such other state, county, or jurisdiction the person may apply to the registrar for reinstatement of said license in the commonwealth.

(d) Notice to any person whose license or registration certificate or right to operate is suspended or revoked under this section or notice to any person of intention to revoke or suspend his license or registration certificate under this section shall be in writing, shall be mailed by the registrar or any person authorized by him to the last address as appearing on the registrar's records or to his last and usual place of abode and a certificate of the registrar that such notice has been mailed in accordance with this section shall be deemed prima facie evidence and shall be admissible in any court of the commonwealth as to the facts contained therein.

If during the period of any such suspension or revocation and prior to its termination by the registrar a new or duplicate learner's permit, license or certificate of registration, or any renewal thereof, is issued, such learner's permit, license or certificate of registration shall be void and of no effect.

(e) The registrar may, suspend the license or right to operate and the certificate of registrations of any person for up to six months, whenever the registrar, after a hearing, has reason to believe that said person has violated the provisions of section thirty-four B of chapter one hundred and thirty-eight.

Upon a conviction of said section thirty-four B, the court shall notify the registrar, who shall immediately revoke the license, right to operate or registration for one year.

[Section (f) repealed effective Mar. 30, 2016.]

(g) Upon receipt of notice, as specified by the registrar, from the department of revenue that a final determination of child support delinquency to suspend or prohibit issuance or renewal of a license has been issued against a resident of the commonwealth or an individual licensed to operate a motor vehicle under this chapter, after a hearing or an opportunity therefor pursuant to section 16 of chapter 119A, the registrar, without opportunity for further hearing, shall suspend or prohibit issuance or renewal of such license, learner's permit, right to operate a motor vehicle or certificate of motor vehicle registration held by such individual and forward any notice required by paragraph (d) to such individual. Notwithstanding any other provisions of this chapter, the opportunity for a hearing provided by the department of revenue pursuant to section 16 of chapter 119A shall constitute the exclusive administrative remedy to contest the existence of a child support arrearage which is the basis for action by the department of revenue to effect the suspension, nonissuance or nonrenewal of a license, learner's permit, right to operate a motor vehicle or certificate of motor vehicle registration. The registrar shall reinstate, issue or renew such license, learner's permit or right to operate a motor vehicle or allow the registration of a motor vehicle if the department of revenue provides to the registrar a notice, as specified by the registrar, stating that the resident or other individual is in compliance with a subpoena, warrant, summons or judgment or order for child support, including any agreement with or regulation issued by the department of revenue governing payment of arrears or upon order by the reviewing court, if the individual is otherwise entitled thereto. Notices between the department of revenue and the registrar under this subsection may be made in any form, including electronic transmission. Upon exhaustion of administrative remedies provided in section 16 of chapter 119A, an individual aggrieved by a final determination of the department of revenue, as adopted or acted upon by the registrar, may seek judicial review of the final determination issued by the department of revenue in the court where the child support order was issued, which has jurisdiction to register the order, or which issued the subpoena, warrant or summons, within 45 days of the date of the registrar's notice to such individual that his license, learner's permit, right to operate a motor vehicle or certificate of motor vehicle registration is subject to suspension, nonissuance or nonrenewal; provided, however, that a request for judicial review shall be by action against the department of revenue and not the registrar and shall be accompanied by a copy of the department of revenue's final determination. Such review shall constitute the exclusive remedy for individuals aggrieved by a final determination as adopted or acted upon by the registrar under section 16 of chapter 119A; provided, however, that such review shall not limit an individual's appellate remedies. The provisions of section 28 shall not apply.

(h) The registrar shall not issue, renew or reinstate a license to operate of any person against whom a default or arrest warrant issued by any court in the commonwealth is outstanding. Evidence of the outstanding warrant appearing in the warrant management system, established by section twenty-three A of chapter two hundred and seventy-six, shall be sufficient grounds for such action by the registrar.

(i) The registrar shall suspend the license to operate motor vehicles of a person against whom an arrest or default warrant issued by any court in the commonwealth is outstanding. Evidence of the outstanding warrant appearing in the warrant management system shall be sufficient grounds for such action by the registrar. The person shall receive notice that his license shall be suspended in 90 days due to an outstanding warrant unless such person furnishes proof to the registrar that such warrant has been recalled or does not exist. A person whose license has been suspended due to an outstanding warrant may petition for reinstatement of such license at any time if he can furnish sufficient proof as determined by the registrar that such warrant has been recalled. The registrar shall promulgate regulations to implement this section, which shall include the opportunity for a hearing to challenge the existence of the outstanding warrant. If a hearing is requested, the law enforcement agency responsible for the warrant shall be notified of the time, place, date of hearing and the subject of the warrant. An affidavit from the law enforcement agency responsible for the warrant or from the colonel of the state police may be introduced as prima facie evidence of the existence of a warrant without the need for members of that law enforcement agency to attend any hearings held under this section.

(j) Upon receipt of notice, as specified by the registrar, from the sex offender registry board, that a sex offender has failed to comply with the registration requirements of sections 178C to 178P, inclusive, of chapter 6, the registrar shall suspend or prohibit issuance or renewal of a license, learner's permit, right to operate a motor vehicle or certificate of motor vehicle registration held by such sex offender. The sex offender shall receive notice that the registrar shall suspend or prohibit renewal of such a license, learner's permit, right to operate a motor vehicle or certificate of motor vehicle registration in 90 days due to his failure to comply with the registration requirements of said sections 178C to 178P, inclusive, of said chapter 6, unless the sex offender furnishes proof to the registrar that he has complied with his sex offender registration requirements. A sex offender whose license, learner's permit, right to operate a motor vehicle or certificate of motor vehicle registration has been suspended due to his failure to comply with the registration requirements of said sections 178C to 178P, inclusive of said chapter 6 may petition for reinstatement of his license, learner's permit, right to operate a motor vehicle or certificate of motor vehicle registration at any time if he produces sufficient proof, as determined by the registrar, that he is in compliance with his sex offender registration requirements. The registrar shall promulgate regulations to implement this subsection, which shall include the opportunity for a hearing to challenge the lack of sex offender registration compliance. If a hearing is requested, the sex offender registry board shall be notified of the time, place, date of hearing and the identity of the sex offender. An affidavit from the sex offender registry board may be introduced as prima facie evidence of the lack of sex offender registration compliance and members or employees of the sex offender registry board need not attend any hearings held under this subsection.

The registrar shall reinstate, issue or renew such license, learner's permit or right to operate a motor vehicle or the registration of a motor vehicle if the sex offender registry board provides to the registrar a notice, as specified by the registrar, stating that the sex offender is in compliance with the registration requirements of said sections 178C to 178P, inclusive, of said chapter 6 and such sex offender shall be assessed a $100 sex offender registry reinstatement fee which shall be transmitted by the registrar to the treasurer for deposit into the general fund. Notices between the sex offender registry board and the registrar under this subsection may be made in any form, including electronic transmission.

NOTE 1   Notice   Mailed—Testimonial. "[W]e consider whether a District Court judge erred by admitting in evidence, pursuant to G.L. c. 90, § 22 (d) a certificate from the registry of motor vehicles (registry) attesting to the fact that a notice of license suspension or revocation was mailed to the defendant. . . . We conclude that the registry certificate, like a certificate of drug analysis, is testimonial in nature. It is a solemn declaration made by the registrar for the purpose of establishing the fact that a notice of license revocation was mailed to the defendant on May 2, 2007, and, by inference, was received by him. The registry certificate was dated July 24, 2009, nearly two months after the criminal complaint for operating a motor vehicle after license revocation had issued against the defendant. As such, it plainly was made for use at the defendant's trial as prima facie evidence that he was notified of his license revocation, an essential element of the charged crime that the Commonwealth was required to prove. The certificate did not simply attest to the existence and authenticity of records kept by the registry but made a factual representation based on those records that a particular action had been performed—notice had been mailed on a specified date. . . . [T]he actual notice of the defendant's license revocation . . . constitutes a business record of the registry, created and kept in the ordinary course of its affairs. However, there is no evidence of the existence of a contemporaneous business record showing that the notice was mailed on that date. If such a record had been created at the time the notice was mailed and preserved by the registry as

1

part of the administration of its regular business affairs, then it would have been admissible at trial." *Commonwealth v. Parenteau,* 460 Mass. 1, 2, 9–10 (2011) (footnotes and citations omitted).

SECTION 22½
Suspension of right to operate based upon violation of Sec. 32E of chapter 94C
(Added by 2016 Mass. Acts c. 64, § 2, effective Mar. 30, 2016.)

The registrar shall suspend, without a hearing, the license or right to operate of a person who is convicted of a violation of subsection (b), (c) or (c½) of section 32E of chapter 94C or adjudged a delinquent child by reason of having violated said subsection (b), (c) or (c½) of said section 32E of said chapter 94C; provided, however, that the period of such suspension shall not exceed 5 years from the date of conviction; and provided further, that the person may, after the completion of any time served, apply for and shall be granted a hearing before the registrar to request the issuance of a new license for employment or educational purposes or for any other hardship purpose for the balance of the license suspension. The registrar may issue such license under such terms or conditions as the registrar may prescribe. If the registrar denies the applicant's request for a hardship license, the registrar shall issue written findings supporting the denial.

SECTION 22B
Abandonment of motor vehicles; penalties; non-criminal proceedings

(a) Whoever abandons a motor vehicle registered or unregistered, upon any public or private way or upon any property other than his own without the permission of the owner or lessee of said property shall be fined two hundred and fifty dollars for the first such abandonment and five hundred dollars for each such abandonment thereafter. A conviction of a violation of this section shall be reported forthwith by the court to the registrar, who may revoke, for a period not exceeding three months, the license of the person so convicted, and if the motor vehicle is registered in his name or was last registered in his name he shall be prohibited from registering another motor vehicle for one year, and no appeal, motion for new trial or exceptions shall operate to stay the revocation of the license or the prohibition of registration.

This subsection shall not apply in a city or town which accepts the provisions of subsection (b) to (k), inclusive.

Subsection (b) to (k), inclusive, shall apply in any city or town which accepts the provisions of said subsections in accordance with the provisions of section four of chapter four.

(b) Notwithstanding the provisions of subsection (a), or any other general or special law to the contrary, proceedings under the provisions of subsections (b) to (k), inclusive, shall be deemed non-criminal.

As used in subsections (b) to (k), inclusive, the word "owner" shall mean the person or entity registered as the owner of a motor vehicle in the records of the registry of motor vehicles or the person or entity who last had custody or possession of a motor vehicle, legally or otherwise, including, without limitation, operators and owners of automobile graveyards or junkyards as defined in section one of chapter one hundred and forty B; provided, however, that the owner of a motor vehicle which has been stolen from said owner and subsequently abandoned shall not be subject to the penalties provided for in this section.

(c) There shall be in any city or town which accepts the provisions of subsections (b) to (k), inclusive, a parking clerk designated or appointed in the same manner as provided in section twenty A. Said parking clerk, in addition to other duties provided by law, shall supervise and coordinate the processing of abandoned motor vehicles.

Said parking clerk shall have the authority to hire personnel, or may contract by competitive bid for services necessary to implement the provisions of this section.

(d) A person who abandons a motor vehicle, registered or unregistered, upon any public or private way, or upon the property of another, without the permission of the owner or lessee of said property, shall pay a civil penalty of two hundred and fifty dollars for the first such abandonment and five hundred dollars for each such abandonment thereafter and, in addition thereto shall be liable for costs incurred by a city or town in removing or disposing of such motor vehicle, including, but not limited to, towing, storage, processing and disposal charges.

(e) A police officer, or a person assigned responsibility for abandoned motor vehicles by the parking clerk, who determines that a motor vehicle has been abandoned shall attach a tag to said vehicle containing, but not limited to, the following information: the current date, the location of said vehicle, its make, color, registration number, if any, and its vehicle identification number; a telephone number or address at which the owner may obtain information regarding the status of the motor vehicle; the hearing procedure regarding abandoned motor vehicles, as provided herein; and, a statement that after a specified period of time, the vehicle may be towed and disposed of.

(f) After said tag has been affixed to such vehicle, if the owner's identity is ascertained and the motor vehicle is still deemed to be abandoned pursuant to section twenty-two C, the parking clerk or his designee shall send a written notice in a form approved by the registrar of motor vehicles by first class mail to the owner's last known address as contained in records of said registrar of motor vehicles. Such notice shall be deemed sufficient, whether or not actually received by the addressee, if mailed to the address furnished by said registrar. Such notice shall contain, but not be limited to, the following information regarding the abandoned vehicle: the current date, the location of said vehicle, make, color, registration number, if any, and its vehicle identification number; the amount of the fine and costs assessed for the offense and the scheduled date, time and place of the hearing before a hearing officer. Notwithstanding the hearing scheduled by the parking clerk, the owner shall be granted a hearing prior to the scheduled hearing date by appearing at the office of the parking clerk during its regular business hours and requesting an immediate hearing regarding the apparently abandoned motor vehicle. Notwithstanding the hearing scheduled by the parking clerk, the owner may elect to have the matter adjudicated in accordance with the provisions of subsection (h).

(g) All such hearings shall be held before a person hereinafter referred to as a hearing officer who shall be the parking clerk or a designee of said parking clerk. Such hearings shall be informal, the rules of evidence shall not apply and decisions of the hearing officer shall be subject to judicial review as provided by section fourteen of chapter thirty A. No appeal or exception shall operate to stay the imposition of the fine and costs, the revocation or nonrenewal of the license or the prohibition of registration as provided for herein.

(h) A person so notified to appear before the hearing officer may appear and contest or confess the alleged violation, either personally or through an agent duly authorized in writing or in the alternative, may confess the alleged violation by mailing to the parking clerk the notice accompanied by the fine and any costs assessed; provided, however, that such payment shall be made only by postal note, money order or registered check made payable to the city or town in which the violation occurred.

(i) If the owner fails to appear at a hearing, or fails to pay the fine and costs, the parking clerk shall, in the case of a person, notify the registrar of motor vehicles who shall place the matter on record and not renew the license of such person to operate a motor vehicle, and in the case of an entity, notify the appropriate person to revoke or not renew the owner's license or permit to operate a business pertaining to the towing, storing, servicing or dismantling of motor vehicles including, without limitation, automobile graveyards and junkyards. If the abandoned motor vehicle is registered in such owner's name or was last registered in his name, the registrar shall prohibit the registration and renewal of registration of any such motor vehicle under such owner's name. Such notice shall be in a form approved by the registrar of motor vehicles. Upon notification to the registrar of the owner's name, an additional ten dollar charge shall be assessed against such owner of the abandoned vehicle. Said ten dollar charge shall be collected by the city or town and notification of such collection shall be made to the registrar of motor vehicles each month. On or before September first of each year, the registrar shall certify the total number of ten dollar charges to be assessed against the city or town. This number shall equal the total number of notifications of actual collections by said city or town. The registrar shall transmit such certified assessments to the treasurer of the commonwealth who shall include such assessments in the warrants prepared in accordance with section twenty of chapter fifty-nine. All such actions taken by the registrar shall remain in effect until said registrar receives notice from the parking clerk that the matter has been disposed of in accordance with the law.

(j) Notwithstanding any other general or special law, ordinance or regulation to the contrary, if an owner has abandoned a motor vehicle on three occasions and has incurred a fine therefor, each subsequent abandonment, in addition to the fines and costs assessed herein, shall result, in the case of a person, in the revocation for one year of the owner's license to operate a motor vehicle, and in the case of an entity, in the revocation for one year of the owner's license or permit to operate a business pertaining to the towing, storing, servicing or dismantling of motor vehicles including, without limitation, automobile graveyards and junkyards. Such one year time period shall commence on the date on which the parking clerk's records indicate that a hearing was held and a fourth or subsequent abandonment was found or that a fine was received in the mail confessing a fourth or subsequent abandonment.

(k) Notwithstanding any other provisions of this section, whenever the clerk or a person designated or appointed by said clerk, shall deem that an abandoned motor vehicle is worth less than the cost of its removal, transportation and three days storage and expenses incidental to its disposal, said clerk or designee shall direct a carrier to take possession of

such motor vehicle and dispose of it as refuse. A record of such disposal shall be made and kept in the office of said clerk for a period of two years. Neither said clerk, carrier nor the city or town shall be liable for such disposal. The owner of such vehicle shall be notified as hereinbefore provided and shall pay to said carrier all charges for removal, transportation, storage and disposal of such vehicle within fourteen days after the mailing of said notice or shall be subject to the fine herein provided as well as nonrenewal of such owner's license to operate and registration of a motor vehicle.

SECTION 22D
Suspension of license for automobile law violation; reinstatement

Notwithstanding the provisions of section twenty-two, if the registrar has suspended or revoked any license issued under this chapter solely or in part because of an automobile law violation, as defined in section one of chapter ninety C, he shall forthwith reinstate such license if the holder thereof is later found not guilty of such automobile law violation by a court of competent jurisdiction, and the registrar shall not suspend or revoke any license issued under this chapter solely or in part because of an automobile law violation, as so defined, of which the holder of such license has been found not guilty by a court of competent jurisdiction.

SECTION 22E
Abandoned vehicles; penalty for removal of parts

Whoever takes any part or accessory from an abandoned motor vehicle standing upon a public or private way or standing upon any property without the permission of the owner or lessee thereof shall be punished by a fine of not less than fifty nor more than three hundred dollars.

SECTION 22F
Habitual traffic offender; revocation of license; reinstatement

A person shall be deemed an habitual traffic offender when records maintained by the registrar show that such person has accumulated the following convictions within a five-year period; provided, however, that when a person who has no prior record of an automobile law violation, as defined in section one of chapter ninety C, is convicted of more than one of the violations referred to in this section, if such offenses all occurred within a six-hour period, such convictions shall for the purposes of this section be treated as a single conviction:—(1) three or more convictions, singularly or in combination, of operating a motor vehicle while under the influence of intoxicating liquor or narcotic drugs in violation of paragraph (a) of subdivision (1) of section twenty-four; operating a motor vehicle recklessly or negligently so that the lives and safety of the public might be endangered; making a false statement in an application for a learner's permit or motor vehicle operator's license or in an application for registration of a motor vehicle; going away without making known his name, residence and the registration number of his vehicle after knowingly colliding with or otherwise causing injury to any person, other vehicle or property, all in violation of paragraph (a) of subdivision (2) of section twenty-four; operating a motor vehicle after suspension or revocation of the person's motor vehicle operator's license or his right to operate motor vehicles in violation of section twenty-three; operating a motor vehicle without a license in violation of section ten; or the commission of any felony in the commission of which a motor vehicle is used; or twelve or more convictions of offenses which are required by any provision of law to be reported to the registrar and for which the registrar is authorized or required to suspend or revoke the person's license or right to operate motor vehicles for a period of thirty days or more, including convictions of the offenses listed above.

When the records of the registrar on any person contain reports of such convictions as will constitute such person an habitual traffic offender, the registrar shall hold a hearing within six months from such third conviction, and shall give notice to such person that such hearing will be held to show cause why such person should not be designated as an habitual traffic offender. Such notice shall be sent not less than twenty-one days prior to the date for such hearing, shall contain a list of the person's convictions, and shall otherwise be in such form as the registrar shall prescribe. If the person named in such notice is a nonresident, such notice shall be sent to his last known address of which the registrar has a record; or, if none, to the motor vehicle department of any state in which such person resides or which has issued a motor vehicle operator's license or permit to such person. If such person denies he was convicted of any offense necessary for a determination that he is an habitual offender, and if the registrar cannot, on the evidence available to him, make such determination, the registrar may refer the decision of such issue to the court in which such conviction was made. The said court shall forthwith conduct a hearing to determine such issue and send a certified copy of its final order determining such issue to the registrar.

If the registrar finds that such person is not the same person named in the records of conviction, or that he is otherwise not an habitual offender under this section, no action shall be taken; but if the registrar finds that such person is the same person named in the record of conviction and that such person is an habitual offender, the registrar shall immediately revoke such person's license or right to operate. The registrar, after having revoked the license or right to operate of any person under this section, shall not issue a new license or reinstate the right to operate to such person for a period of four years from the date of revocation, nor until such person has satisfactorily completed a driver improvement course approved by the registrar and has passed such examination as to his competence to operate motor vehicles as the registrar may require; provided, however, that such person may, after the expiration of one year, apply for and shall be granted a hearing before the registrar for the purpose of requesting the issuance of a new license on a limited basis on the sole grounds of hardship, and the registrar may, in his discretion, issue such a license under such terms and conditions as he deems appropriate and necessary. An appeal to the superior court may be had, in accordance with the provisions of chapter thirty A, from any order of the registrar of motor vehicles made under the provisions of this section.

SECTION 22G
Littering; suspension of license

The registrar may, after due hearing, suspend for a period not exceeding seven days the license or permit to operate motor vehicles or the right of a person to operate motor vehicles in the commonwealth of any person who litters, or who knowingly permits, as the operator, occupants of his vehicle to litter, public or private property through the disposal of trash or garbage from said motor vehicle.

SECTION 22H
Transport of animals

No person shall transport an animal in the back of a motor vehicle in a space intended for a load on the vehicle on a public way unless such space is enclosed or has side and tail racks to a height of at least 46 inches extending vertically from the floor, the animal is cross tethered to the vehicle, the animal is protected by a secured container or cage or the animal is otherwise protected in a manner which will prevent the animal from being thrown or from falling or jumping from the vehicle. Whoever violates the provisions of this section shall be punished by a fine of not less than $50.

SECTION 22I
Suspension of license upon report of health care provider or law enforcement officer of operator's cognitive or functional impairment or incapability to operate motor vehicle safely; contents of report; immunity from liability; review by registrar; confidentiality of report

(a) For the purposes of this section, "health care provider" shall mean a registered nurse, licensed practical nurse, physician, physician assistant, psychologist, occupational therapist, physical therapist, optometrist, ophthalmologist, osteopath or podiatrist who is a licensed health care provider under chapter 112.

(b) If a health care provider acting in his professional capacity or law enforcement officer has reasonable cause to believe that an operator is not physically or medically capable of safely operating a motor vehicle or has a cognitive or functional impairment that will affect that person's ability to safely operate a motor vehicle, the health care provider or officer may make a report to the registrar, requesting medical evaluation of the operator's ability to safely operate a motor vehicle; provided, however, that such report shall not be made solely on the basis of age. The report shall state the health care provider's or officer's good faith belief that the operator cannot safely operate a motor vehicle and shall disclose the medical information underlying his good faith belief in his report to the registrar. The good faith belief shall be based upon personal observation, physical evidence, or, in the case of a law enforcement officer, an investigation which shall be described in the report. A report regarding an operator's ability to safely operate a motor vehicle shall not be based solely on the diagnosis of a medical condition or cognitive or functional impairment, but shall be based on observations or evidence of the actual affect of that condition or impairment on the operator's ability to safely operate a motor vehicle.

A health care provider or law enforcement officer who reports, in good faith, pursuant to this section shall be immune from civil liability that might otherwise result from making the report. A health care provider or law enforcement officer who does not report shall be immune from civil liability that might otherwise result from not making the report.

(c) Not later than 30 days after receipt of the report, the registrar shall conduct a review to determine the operator's capacity for continued licensure to operate a motor vehicle. The commissioner of public health shall, in consultation with the registrar and with medical experts on cognitive or functional impairments, and with the medical advisory board established in section 8C, promulgate regulations designating the cognitive or functional impairments that are likely to affect a person's ability to safely operate a motor vehicle. The registrar shall consider information contained in a report under subsection (b) in determining whether to issue or suspend a license to operate a motor vehicle.

(d) A report to the registry pursuant to this section shall be confidential and shall be used by the registrar only to determine a person's qualifications to operate a motor vehicle. All reports made and all medical records reviewed and maintained by the registry under this section shall be confidential, or upon written request of the respondent to examine any medical records or reports made about the respondent under this section.

A report made under this section shall not be a public record as defined in section 7 of chapter 4.

The registrar shall include the information about the procedures authorized in this section on the electronic website of the registrar.

SECTION 23
Operation of motor vehicle after suspension or revocation of license; concealment of identity of motor vehicle

Any person convicted of operating a motor vehicle after his license to operate has been suspended or revoked, or after notice of the suspension or revocation of his right to operate a motor vehicle without a license has been issued by the registrar and received by such person or by his agent or employer, and prior to the restoration of such license or right to operate or to the issuance to him of a new license to operate, and any person convicted of operating or causing or permitting any other person to operate a motor vehicle after the certificate of registration for such vehicle has been suspended or revoked and prior to the restoration of such registration or to the issuance of a new certificate of registration for such vehicle, or whoever exhibits to an officer authorized to make arrests, when requested by said officer to show his license, a license issued to another person with intent to conceal his identity, shall, except as provided by section twenty eight of chapter two hundred and sixty-six, be punished for a first offense by a fine of not less than five hundred nor more than one thousand dollars or by imprisonment for not more than ten days, or both, and for any subsequent offense by imprisonment for not less than sixty days nor more than one year, and any person who attaches or permits to be attached to a motor vehicle or trailer a number plate assigned to another motor vehicle or trailer, or who obscures or permits to be obscured the figures on any number plate attached to any motor vehicle or trailer, or who fails to display on a motor vehicle or trailer the number plate and the register number duly issued therefor, with intent to conceal the identity of such motor vehicle or trailer, shall be punished by a fine of not more than one hundred dollars or by imprisonment for not more than ten days, or both. Any person convicted of operating a motor vehicle after his license to operate has been revoked by reason of his having been found to be an habitual traffic offender, as provided in section twenty-two or after notice of such revocation of his right to operate a motor vehicle without a license has been issued by the registrar and received by such person or by his agent or employer, and prior to the restoration of such license or right to operate or the issuance to him of a new license to operate shall be punished by a fine of not less than five hun-

dred nor more than five thousand dollars or by imprisonment for not more than two years, or both.

Notwithstanding the preceding paragraph or any other general or special law to the contrary, whoever has not been previously found responsible for or convicted of, or against whom a finding of delinquency or a finding of sufficient facts to support a conviction has not been rendered on, a complaint charging a violation of operating a motor vehicle after his license to operate has been suspended or revoked, or after notice of the suspension or revocation of his right to operate a motor vehicle without a license has been issued by the registrar and received by such person or by his agent or employer, and prior to the restoration of such license or right to operate or to the issuance to him of a new license to operate shall be punished by a fine of not more than $500. This paragraph shall not apply to any person who is charged with operating a motor vehicle after his license to operate has been suspended or revoked pursuant to a violation of paragraph (a) of subdivision (1) of section 24, or section 24D, 24E, 24G, 24L or 24N of this chapter, subsection (a) of section 8 or section 8A or 8B of chapter 90B, section 8, 9 or 11 of chapter 90F or after notice of such suspension or revocation of his right to operate a motor vehicle without a license has been issued and received by such person or by his agent or employer, and prior to the restoration of such license or right to operate or the issuance to him of a new license or right to operate because of any such violation.

Any person convicted of operating a motor vehicle after his license to operate has been suspended or revoked pursuant to a violation of paragraph (a) of subdivision (1) of section twenty-four, or pursuant to sections twenty-four D, twenty-four E, twenty-four G, twenty-four L, or twenty-four N of this chapter, or pursuant to subsection (a) of section eight, or pursuant to a violation of section eight A or section eight B of chapter ninety B, or pursuant to a violation of section eight, nine, or eleven of chapter ninety F, or after notice of such suspension or revocation of his right to operate a motor vehicle without a license has been issued and received by such person or by his agent or employer, and prior to the restoration of such license or right to operate or the issuance to him of a new license to operate shall be punished by a fine of not less than one thousand nor more than ten thousand dollars and by imprisonment in a house of correction for not less than sixty days and not more than two and one-half years; provided, however, that the sentence of imprisonment imposed upon such person shall not be reduced to less than sixty days, nor suspended, nor shall any such person be eligible for probation, parole, or furlough or receive any deduction from his sentence for good conduct until he shall have served sixty days of such sentence; provided, further, that the commissioner of correction may, on the recommendation of the warden, superintendent, or other person in charge of a correctional institution, or the administrator of a county correctional institution, grant to an offender committed under this paragraph a temporary release in the custody of an officer of such institution for the following purposes only: to attend the funeral of a relative; to visit a critically ill relative; to obtain emergency medical or psychiatric services unavailable at said institution; or to engage in employment pursuant to a work release program. The provisions of section eighty-seven of chapter two hundred and seventy-six shall not apply to a person charged with a violation of this paragraph. Prosecution commenced under this paragraph shall not be placed on file or continued without a finding.

Whoever operates a motor vehicle in violation of paragraph (a) of subdivision (1) of section 24, sections 24G or 24L, subsection (a) of section 8 of chapter 90B, sections 8A or 8B of chapter 90B or section 13½ of chapter 265, while his license or right to operate has been suspended or revoked, or after notice of such suspension or revocation of his right to operate a motor vehicle has been issued and received by such person or by his agent or employer, and prior to the restoration of such license or right to operate or the issuance to him of a new license or right to operate, pursuant to paragraph (a) of subdivision (1) of section 24, sections 24G or 24L, subsection (a) of section 8 of chapter 90B, sections 8A or 8B of chapter 90B or section 13½ of chapter 265 shall be punished by a fine of not less than $2,500 nor more than $10,000 and by imprisonment in a house of correction for a mandatory period of not less than 1 year and not more than 2½ years, with said sentence to be served consecutively to and not concurrent with any other sentence or penalty. Such sentence shall not be suspended, nor shall any such person be eligible for probation, parole, or furlough or receive any deduction from his sentence for good conduct until he shall have served said 1 year of such sentence; provided, however, that the commissioner of correction may, on the recommendation of the warden, superintendent or other person in charge of a correctional institution, or of the administrator of a county correctional institution, grant to an offender committed under this paragraph a temporary release in the custody of an officer of such institution only to obtain emergency medical or psychiatric services unavailable at said institution or to engage in employment pursuant to a work release program. Section 87 of chapter 276 shall not apply to any person charged with a violation of this paragraph. Prosecutions commenced under this paragraph shall not be placed on file or continued without a finding.

A certificate of the registrar or his authorized agent that a license or right to operate motor vehicles or a certificate of registration of a motor vehicle has not been restored or that the registrar has not issued a new license so to operate to the defendant or a new certificate of registration for a motor vehicle the registration whereof has been revoked, shall be admissible as evidence in any court of the commonwealth to prove the facts certified to therein, in any prosecution hereunder wherein such facts are material. A certificate of a clerk of court that a person's license or right to operate a motor vehicle was suspended for a specified period shall be admissible as prima facie evidence in any court of the commonwealth to prove the facts certified to therein in any prosecution commenced under this section.

Upon a conviction of operating after suspension or revocation of license or right to operate under the first paragraph, the registrar shall extend said suspension or revocation for an additional sixty days. Upon a conviction of operating after suspension or revocation of license or right to operate under the second paragraph, the registrar shall extend said suspension or revocation for an additional year.

If a person operating a motor vehicle after suspension or revocation of a license to operate or the right to operate a motor vehicle under the first or second paragraphs of this section, is found by the registrar to have operated a vehicle registered to another in violation of said suspension or revocation, the registrar shall, after hearing, revoke the certificate of registration of said motor vehicle for up to thirty days. Pursuant to said hearing, the certificate of registration and the number plates shall be immediately surrendered to the registrar.

NOTE 1   "We conclude that there is no statutory authority to arrest an individual for operating a motor vehicle with a revoked registration." *Commonwealth v. Ubilez*, 88 Mass. App. Ct. 814, 815 (2016).

NOTE 2   The Commonwealth must offer, among other elements in an operating after suspension or revocation case, proof of receipt of either the notice of suspension or the intention to suspend. *Commonwealth v. Crosscup*, 369 Mass. 228, 231 (1975).

NOTE 3   The Commonwealth may rely on the "rule" that the proper mailing of a letter is prima facie evidence of its receipt by the addressee. The defendant, on the other hand, may introduce relevant evidence tending to show nonreceipt. *Commonwealth v. Crosscup*, 369 Mass. at 240–41. *See also Commonwealth v. Koney*, 421 Mass. 295, 303–04 (1995).

NOTE 4   "At issue is whether the complaint is defective and must be dismissed for failure to allege that he operated the motor vehicle *on a public way*. We hold that the statute does not require that the violation occur on a public way." *Commonwealth v. Murphy*, 409 Mass. 665 (1991).

NOTE 5   "Although that crime requires proof that the defendant was operating a motor vehicle while under the influence of alcohol 'after his license to operate ha[d] been suspended or revoked for a prior similar crime,' G.L. c. 90, § 23, as appearing in St. 1954, c. 74, the 'reason for the suspension or revocation of the license—operating a motor vehicle while under the influence of alcohol—is an element of the crime with which the defendant was charged,' *ibid.*, and is not a sentencing enhancement. Also, the fact that the Legislature has provided for a separate and distinct sentence for conviction of this crime demonstrates that, like the school zone statute, § 23 creates a freestanding crime and is not a sentencing enhancement provision. Thus, bifurcation is not compelled." *Commonwealth v. Beaulieu*, 79 Mass. App. Ct. 100, 102 (2011).

NOTE 6   **Actual Knowledge.** Of course, proof of a defendant's actual knowledge of the revocation of his or her license is sufficient. *See Commonwealth v. Deramo*, 436 Mass. 40, 51–52 (2002), wherein the court held that "the defendant's statement to the officer, claiming that he was going to see his attorney to get a 'Cinderella license,' constituted an admission that he knew that his license had been revoked. . . . Where, as here, the defendant's actual knowledge of license revocation has been proved by his own admission, there is no further requirement that the Commonwealth prove precisely how that actual knowledge was acquired."

NOTE 7   **Copy of Original Attestation.** "Merely making a copy of the original attestation along with a copy of the underlying record does not serve the purpose of the attestation requirement, as the copied attestation no longer signifies that the official in question is vouching for the authenticity of the copy that has just been made. . . .

"The requirement that the responsible official be the one to attest to the authenticity of a copy is not some minor technicality." *Commonwealth v. Deramo*, 436 Mass. 40, 48 (2002) (further noting that "[w]here, as here, the parties and the judge have themselves compared an authenticated record with a copy, the copy may be admitted to the extent that it is identical to the authenticated document").

NOTE 8   **Registry Records.** "From other entries in the properly authenticated set of registry records it was clear that the defendant's license had been revoked for operating a motor vehicle while under the influence of alcohol. . . . These entries established that the defendant's license had been revoked for operating while under the influence of alcohol, without resort to the information contained in the notice of that revocation." *Commonwealth v. Deramo*, 436 Mass. 40, 50 (2002).

NOTE 9   New License. "[T]he defendant argued, and the trial judge agreed, that he could not be indicted for a violation of § 23 because the registry had issued him a new license. We concur. Although 'new license' is not defined in § 23, the type of license he was granted—a hardship license—is described in G.L. c. 90, § 24(1)(c)(3), as 'a new license' subject to certain restrictions." *Commonwealth v. Murphy*, 68 Mass. App. Ct. 152, 153 (2007) (footnote omitted).

SECTION 24
Driving while under influence of intoxicating liquor, etc.; second and subsequent offenses; punishments; treatment programs; reckless and unauthorized driving; failure to stop after collision

(Amended by 2012 Mass. Acts c. 139, §§ 97–100, effective July 1, 2012, effective date of 2012 Mass. Acts c. 139, § 97, extended to July 1, 2013 by 2012 Mass. Acts c. 239, § 49; by 2013 Mass. Acts c. 38, § 80, effective Mar. 1, 2014.)

(1)(a)(1) Whoever, upon any way or in any place to which the public has a right of access, or upon any way or in any place to which members of the public have access as invitees or licensees, operates a motor vehicle with a percentage, by weight, of alcohol in their blood of eight one-hundredths or greater, or while under the influence of intoxicating liquor, or of marijuana, narcotic drugs, depressants or stimulant substances, all as defined in section one of chapter ninety-four C, or the vapors of glue shall be punished by a fine of not less than five hundred nor more than five thousand dollars or by imprisonment for not more than two and one-half years, or both such fine and imprisonment.

There shall be an assessment of $250 against a person who is convicted of, is placed on probation for, or is granted a continuance without a finding for or otherwise pleads guilty to or admits to a finding of sufficient facts of operating a motor vehicle while under the influence of intoxicating liquor, marijuana, narcotic drugs, depressants or stimulant substances under this section; provided, however, that but $187.50 of the amount collected under this assessment shall be deposited monthly by the court with the state treasurer for who shall deposit it into the Head Injury Treatment Services Trust Fund, and the remaining amount of the assessment shall be credited to the General Fund. The assessment shall not be subject to reduction or waiver by the court for any reason.

There shall be an assessment of $50 against a person who is convicted, placed on probation or granted a continuance without a finding or who otherwise pleads guilty to or admits to a finding of sufficient facts for operating a motor vehicle while under the influence of intoxicating liquor or under the influence of marihuana, narcotic drugs, depressants or stimulant substances, all as defined by section 1 of chapter 94C, pursuant to this section or section 24D or 24E or subsection (a) or (b) of section 24G or section 24L. The assessment shall not be subject to waiver by the court for any reason. If a person against whom a fine is assessed is sentenced to a correctional facility and the assessment has not been paid, the court shall note the assessment on the mittimus. The monies collected pursuant to the fees established by this paragraph shall be transmitted monthly by the courts to the state treasurer who shall then deposit, invest and transfer the monies, from time to time, into the Victims of Drunk Driving Trust Fund established in section 66 of chapter 10. The monies shall then be administered, pursuant to said section 66 of said chapter 10, by the victim and witness assistance board for the purposes set forth in said section 66. Fees paid by an individual into the Victims of Drunk Driving Trust Fund pursuant to this section shall be in addition to, and not in lieu of, any other fee imposed by the court pursuant to this chapter or any other chapter. The administrative office of the trial court shall file a report detailing the amount of funds imposed and collected pursuant to this section to the house and senate committees on ways and means and to the victim and witness assistance board not later than August 15 of each calendar year.

If the defendant has been previously convicted or assigned to an alcohol or controlled substance education, treatment, or rehabilitation program by a court of the commonwealth or any other jurisdiction because of a like violation preceding the date of the commission of the offense for which he has been convicted, the defendant shall be punished by a fine of not less than six hundred nor more than ten thousand dollars and by imprisonment for not less than sixty days nor more than two and one-half years; provided, however, that the sentence imposed upon such person shall not be reduced to less than thirty days, nor suspended, nor shall any such person be eligible for probation, parole, or furlough or receive any deduction from his sentence for good conduct until such person has served thirty days of such sentence; provided, further, that the commissioner of correction may, on the recommendation of the warden, superintendent, or other person in charge of a correctional institution, or the administrator of a county correctional institution, grant to an offender committed under this subdivision a temporary release in the custody of an officer of such institution for the following purposes only: to attend the funeral of a relative; to visit a critically ill relative; to obtain emergency medical or psychiatric services unavailable at said institution; to engage in employment pursuant to a work release program; or for the purposes of an aftercare program designed to support the recovery of an offender who has completed an alcohol or controlled substance education, treatment or rehabilitation program operated by the department of correction; and provided, further, that the defendant may serve all or part of such thirty day sentence to the extent such resources are available in a correctional facility specifically designated by the department of correction for the incarceration and rehabilitation of drinking drivers.

If the defendant has been previously convicted or assigned to an alcohol or controlled substance education, treatment, or rehabilitation program by a court of the commonwealth, or any other jurisdiction because of a like offense two times preceding the date of the commission of the offense for which he has been convicted, the defendant shall be punished by a fine of not less than one thousand nor more than fifteen thousand dollars and by imprisonment for not less than one hundred and eighty days nor more than two and one-half years or by a fine of not less than one thousand nor more than fifteen thousand dollars and by imprisonment in the state prison for not less than two and one-half years nor more than five years; provided, however, that the sentence imposed upon such person shall not be reduced to less than one hundred and fifty days, nor suspended, nor shall any such person be eligible for probation, parole, or furlough or receive any deduction from his sentence for good conduct until he shall have served one hundred and fifty days of such sentence; provided, further, that the commissioner of correction may, on the recommendation of the warden, superintendent, or other person in charge of a correctional institution, or the administrator of a county correctional institution, grant to an offender committed under this subdivision a temporary release in the custody of an officer of such institution for the following purposes only: to attend the funeral of a relative, to visit a critically ill relative; to obtain emergency medical or psychiatric services unavailable at said institution; to engage in employment pursuant to a work release program; or for the purposes of an aftercare program designed to support the recovery of an offender who has completed an alcohol or controlled substance education, treatment or rehabilitation program operated by the department of correction; and provided, further, that the defendant may serve all or part of such one hundred and fifty days sentence to the extent such resources are available in a correctional facility specifically designated by the department of correction for the incarceration and rehabilitation of drinking drivers.

If the defendant has been previously convicted or assigned to an alcohol or controlled substance education, treatment, or rehabilitation program by a court of the commonwealth or any other jurisdiction because of a like offense three times preceding the date of the commission of the offense for which he has been convicted the defendant shall be punished by a fine of not less than one thousand five hundred nor more than twenty-five thousand dollars and by imprisonment for not less than two years nor more than two and one-half years, or by a fine of not less than one thousand five hundred nor more than twenty-five thousand dollars and by imprisonment in the state prison for not less than two and one-half years nor more than five years; provided, however, that the sentence imposed upon such person shall not be reduced to less than twelve months, nor suspended, nor shall any such person be eligible for probation, parole, or furlough or receive any deduction from his sentence for good conduct until such person has served twelve months of such sentence; provided, further, that the commissioner of correction may, on the recommendation of the warden, superintendent, or other person in charge of a correctional institution, or the administrator of a county correctional institution, grant to an offender committed under this subdivision a temporary release in the custody of an officer of such institution for the following purposes only: to attend the funeral of a relative; to visit a critically ill relative; to obtain emergency medical or psychiatric services unavailable at said institution; to engage in employment pursuant to a work release program; or for the purposes of an aftercare program designed to support the recovery of an offender who has completed an alcohol or controlled substance education, treatment or rehabilitation program operated by the department of correction; and provided, further, that the defendant may serve all or part of such twelve months sentence to the extent that resources are available in a correctional facility specifically designated by the department of correction for the incarceration and rehabilitation of drinking drivers.

If the defendant has been previously convicted or assigned to an alcohol or controlled substance education, treatment or rehabilitation program by a court of the commonwealth or any other jurisdiction because of a like offense four or more times preceding the date of the commission of the offense for which he has been convicted, the defendant shall be punished by a fine of not less than two thousand nor more than fifty thousand dollars and by imprisonment for not less than two and one-half years or by a fine of not less than two thousand nor more than fifty thousand dollars and by impris-

onment in the state prison for not less than two and one-half years nor more than five years; provided, however, that the sentence imposed upon such person shall not be reduced to less than twenty-four months, nor suspended, nor shall any such person be eligible for probation, parole, or furlough or receive any deduction from his sentence for good conduct until he shall have served twenty-four months of such sentence; provided, further, that the commissioner of correction may, on the recommendation of the warden, superintendent, or other person in charge of a correctional institution, or the administrator of a county correctional institution, grant to an offender committed under this subdivision a temporary release in the custody of an officer of such institution for the following purposes only: to attend the funeral of a relative; to visit a critically ill relative; to obtain emergency medical or psychiatric services unavailable at said institution; to engage in employment pursuant to a work release program; or for the purposes of an aftercare program designed to support the recovery of an offender who has completed an alcohol or controlled substance education, treatment or rehabilitation program operated by the department of correction; and provided, further, that the defendant may serve all or part of such twenty-four months sentence to the extent that resources are available in a correctional facility specifically designated by the department of correction for the incarceration and rehabilitation of drinking drivers.

A prosecution commenced under the provisions of this subparagraph shall not be placed on file or continued without a finding except for dispositions under section twenty-four D. No trial shall be commenced on a complaint alleging a violation of this subparagraph, nor shall any plea be accepted on such complaint, nor shall the prosecution on such complaint be transferred to another division of the district court or to a jury-of-six session, until the court receives a report from the commissioner of probation pertaining to the defendant's record, if any, of prior convictions of such violations or of assignment to an alcohol or controlled substance education, treatment, or rehabilitation program because of a like offense; provided, however, that the provisions of this paragraph shall not justify the postponement of any such trial or of the acceptance of any such plea for more than five working days after the date of the defendant's arraignment. The commissioner of probation shall give priority to requests for such records.

At any time before the commencement of a trial or acceptance of a plea on a complaint alleging a violation of this subparagraph, the prosecutor may apply for the issuance of a new complaint pursuant to section thirty-five A of chapter two hundred and eighteen alleging a violation of this subparagraph and one or more prior like violations. If such application is made, upon motion of the prosecutor, the court shall stay further proceedings on the original complaint pending the determination of the application for the new complaint. If a new complaint is issued, the court shall dismiss the original complaint and order that further proceedings on the new complaint be postponed until the defendant has had sufficient time to prepare a defense.

If a defendant waives right to a jury trial pursuant to section twenty-six A of chapter two hundred and eighteen on a complaint under this subdivision he shall be deemed to have waived his right to a jury trial on all elements of said complaint.

(2) Except as provided in subparagraph (4) the provisions of section eighty-seven of chapter two hundred and seventy-six shall not apply to any person charged with a violation of subparagraph (1) and if said person has been convicted of or assigned to an alcohol or controlled substance education, treatment or rehabilitation program because of a like offense by a court of the commonwealth or any other jurisdiction preceding the commission of the offense with which he is charged.

(3) Notwithstanding the provisions of section six A of chapter two hundred and seventy-nine, the court may order that a defendant convicted of a violation of subparagraph (1) be imprisoned only on designated weekends, evenings or holidays; provided, however, that the provisions of this subparagraph shall apply only to a defendant who has not been convicted previously of such violation or assigned to an alcohol or controlled substance education, treatment or rehabilitation program preceding the date of the commission of the offense for which he has been convicted.(4) Notwithstanding the provisions of subparagraphs (1) and (2), a judge, before imposing a sentence on a defendant who pleads guilty to or is found guilty of a violation of subparagraph (1) and who has not been convicted or assigned to an alcohol or controlled substance education, treatment or rehabilitation program by a court of the commonwealth or any other jurisdiction because of a like offense two or more times of the date of the commission of the offense for which he has been convicted, shall receive a report from the probation department of a copy of the defendant's driving record, the criminal record of the defendant, if any, and such information as may be available as to the defendant's use of alcohol and may, upon a written finding that appropriate and adequate treatment is available to the defendant and the defendant would benefit from such treatment and that the safety of the public would not be endangered, with the defendant's consent place a defendant on probation for two years; provided, however, that a condition for such probation shall be that the defendant be confined for no less than fourteen days in a residential alcohol treatment program and to participate in an out patient counseling program designed for such offenders as provided or sanctioned by the division of alcoholism, pursuant to regulations to be promulgated by said division in consultation with the department of correction and with the approval of the secretary of health and human services or at any other facility so sanctioned or regulated as may be established by the commonwealth or any political subdivision thereof for the purpose of alcohol or drug treatment or rehabilitation, and comply with all conditions of said residential alcohol treatment program. Such condition of probation shall specify a date before which such residential alcohol treatment program shall be attended and completed.

Failure of the defendant to comply with said conditions and any other terms of probation as imposed under this section shall be reported forthwith to the court and proceedings under the provisions of section three of chapter two hundred and seventy-nine shall be commenced. In such proceedings, such defendant shall be taken before the court and if the court finds that he has failed to attend or complete the residential alcohol treatment program before the date specified in the conditions of probation, the court shall forthwith specify a second date before which such defendant shall attend or complete such program, and unless such defendant shows ex-traordinary and compelling reasons for such failure, shall forthwith sentence him to imprisonment for not less than two days; provided, however, that such sentence shall not be reduced to less than two days, nor suspended, nor shall such person be eligible for furlough or receive any reduction from his sentence for good conduct until such person has served two days of such sentence; and provided, further, that the commissioner of correction may, on the recommendation of the warden, superintendent, or other person in charge of a correctional institution, or of the administrator of a county correctional institution, grant to an offender committed under this subdivision a temporary release in the custody of an officer of such institution for the following purposes only: to attend the funeral of a relative; to visit a critically ill relative; to obtain emergency medical or psychiatric services unavailable at said institution; or to engage in employment pursuant to a work release program. If such defendant fails to attend or complete the residential alcohol treatment program before the second date specified by the court, further proceedings pursuant to said section three of said chapter two hundred and seventy-nine shall be commenced, and the court shall forthwith sentence the defendant to imprisonment for not less than thirty days as provided in subparagraph (1) for such a defendant.

The defendant shall pay for the cost of the services provided by the residential alcohol treatment program; provided, however, that no person shall be excluded from said programs for inability to pay; and provided, further, that such person files with the court, an affidavit of indigency or inability to pay and that investigation by the probation officer confirms such indigency or establishes that payment of such fee would cause a grave and serious hardship to such individual or to the family of such individual, and that the court enters a written finding thereof. In lieu of waiver of the entire amount of said fee, the court may direct such individual to make partial or installment payments of the cost of said program.

(b) A conviction of a violation of subparagraph (1) of paragraph (a) shall revoke the license or right to operate of the person so convicted unless such person has not been convicted of or assigned to an alcohol or controlled substance education, treatment or rehabilitation program because of a like offense by a court of the commonwealth or any other jurisdiction preceding the date of the commission of the offense for which he has been convicted, and said person qualifies for disposition under section twenty-four D and has consented to probation as provided for in said section twenty-four D; provided, however, that no appeal, motion for new trial or exceptions shall operate to stay the revocation of the license or the right to operate. Such revoked license shall immediately be surrendered to the prosecuting officer who shall forward the same to the registrar. The court shall report immediately any revocation, under this section, of a license or right to operate to the registrar and to the police department of the municipality in which the defendant is domiciled. Notwithstanding the provisions of section twenty-two, the revocation, reinstatement or issuance of a license or right to operate by reason of a violation of paragraph (a) shall be controlled by the provisions of this section and sections twenty-four D and twenty-four E.

(c) (1) Where the license or right to operate has been revoked under section twenty-four D or twenty-four E, or revoked under paragraph (b) and such person has not been convicted of a like offense or has not been assigned to an alcohol or controlled substance education, treatment or rehabilitation program because of a like offense by a court of the commonwealth or any other jurisdiction preceding the date of the commission of the offense for which he has been convicted, the registrar shall not restore the license or reinstate the right to operate to such person unless the prosecution of such person has been terminated in favor of the defendant, until one year after the date of conviction; provided, however, that such person may, after the expiration of three months from the date of conviction, apply for and shall be granted a hearing before the registrar for the purpose of requesting the issuance of a new license for employment or educational purposes, which license shall be effective for not more than an identical twelve hour period every day on the grounds of hardship and a showing by the person that the causes of the present and past violations have been dealt with or brought under control, and the registrar may, in his discretion, issue such license under such terms and conditions as he deems appropriate and necessary; and provided, further, that such person may, after the expiration of six months from the date of conviction, apply for and shall be granted a hearing before the registrar for the purpose of requesting the issuance of a new license on a limited basis on the grounds of hardship and a showing by the person that the causes of the present and past violations have been dealt with or brought under control and the registrar may, in his discretion, issue such a license under such terms and conditions as he deems appropriate and necessary.

(2) Where the license or the right to operate of a person has been revoked under paragraph (b) and such person has been previously convicted of or assigned to an alcohol or controlled substance education, treatment or rehabilitation program by a court of the commonwealth or any other jurisdiction because of a like violation preceding the date of the commission of the offense for which such person has been convicted, the registrar shall not restore the license or reinstate the right to operate of such person unless the prosecution of such person has been terminated in favor of the defendant, until two years after the date of the conviction; provided, however, that such person may, after the expiration of 1 year from the date of conviction, apply for and shall be granted a hearing before the registrar for the purpose of requesting the issuance of a new license for employment or education purposes, which license shall be effective for not more than an identical twelve hour period every day on the grounds of hardship and a showing by the person that the causes of the present and past violations have been dealt with or brought under control and that such person shall have successfully completed the residential treatment program in subparagraph (4) of paragraph (a) of subdivision (1), or such treatment program mandated by section twenty-four D, and the registrar may, in his discretion, issue such license under such terms and conditions as he deems appropriate and necessary; and provided, further, that such person may, after the expiration of 18 months from the date of conviction, apply for and shall be granted a hearing before the registrar for the purpose of requesting the issuance of a new license on a limited basis on the grounds of hardship and a showing by the person that the causes of the present and past violations have been dealt with or brought under control and the registrar may, in his discretion, issue such a license under such terms and conditions as he deems appropriate and necessary. A mandatory restriction on a hardship license granted by the registrar under this sub-

paragraph shall be that such person have an ignition interlock device installed on each vehicle owned, each vehicle leased and each vehicle operated by the licensee for the duration of the hardship license.

(3) Where the license or right to operate of any person has been revoked under paragraph (b) and such person has been previously convicted or assigned to an alcohol or controlled substance education, treatment or rehabilitation program because of a like offense by a court of the commonwealth or any other jurisdiction two times preceding the date of the commission of the crime for which he has been convicted or where the license or right to operate has been revoked pursuant to section twenty-three due to a violation of said section due to a prior revocation under paragraph (b) or under section twenty-four D or twenty-four E, the registrar shall not restore the license or reinstate the right to operate to such person, unless the prosecution of such person has terminated in favor of the defendant, until eight years after the date of conviction; provided however, that such person may, after the expiration of two years from the date of the conviction, apply for and shall be granted a hearing before the registrar for the purpose of requesting the issuance of a new license for employment or education purposes, which license shall be effective for not more than an identical twelve hour period every day, on the grounds of hardship and a showing by the person that the causes of the present and past violations have been dealt with or brought under control and the registrar may, in his discretion, issue such license under such terms and conditions as he deems appropriate and necessary; and provided, further, that such person may, after the expiration of four years from the date of conviction, apply for and shall be granted a hearing before the registrar for the purpose of requesting the issuance of a new license on a limited basis on the grounds of hardship and a showing by the person that the causes of the present and past violations have been dealt with or brought under control and the registrar may, in his discretion, issue such a license under such terms and conditions as he deems appropriate and necessary. A mandatory restriction on a hardship license granted by the registrar under this subparagraph shall be that such person have an ignition interlock device installed on each vehicle owned, each vehicle leased and each vehicle operated by the licensee for the duration of the hardship license.

(3½) Where the license or the right to operate of a person has been revoked under paragraph (b) and such person has been previously convicted of or assigned to an alcohol or controlled substance education, treatment or rehabilitation program by a court of the commonwealth or any other jurisdiction because of a like violation three times preceding the date of the commission of the offense for which such person has been convicted, the registrar shall not restore the license or reinstate the right to operate of such person unless the prosecution of such person has been terminated in favor of the defendant, until ten years after the date of the conviction; provided, however, that such person may, after the expiration of five years from the date of the conviction, apply for and shall be granted a hearing before the registrar for the purpose of requesting the issuance of a new license for employment or education purposes which license shall be effective for an identical twelve hour period every day on the grounds of hardship and a showing by the person that the causes of the present and past violations have been dealt with or brought under control and the registrar may, in his discretion, issue such license under such terms and conditions as he deems appropriate and necessary; and provided, further, that such person may, after the expiration of eight years from the date of conviction, apply for and shall be granted a hearing before the registrar for the purpose of requesting the issuance of a new license on a limited basis on the grounds of hardship and a showing by the person that the causes of the present and past violations have been dealt with or brought under control and the registrar may, in his discretion, issue such a license under the terms and conditions as he deems appropriate and necessary. A mandatory restriction on a hardship license granted by the registrar under this subparagraph shall be that such person have an ignition interlock device installed on each vehicle owned, each vehicle leased and each vehicle operated by the licensee for the duration of the hardship license.

(3¾) Where the license or the right to operate of a person has been revoked under paragraph (b) and such person has been previously convicted of or assigned to an alcohol or controlled substance education, treatment or rehabilitation program by a court of the commonwealth or any other jurisdiction because of a like violation four or more times preceding the date of the commission of the offense for which such person has been convicted, such person's license or right to operate a motor vehicle shall be revoked for the life of such person, and such person shall not be granted a hearing before the registrar for the purpose of requesting the issuance of a new license on a limited basis on the grounds of hardship; provided, however, that such license shall be restored or such right to operate shall be reinstated if the prosecution of such person has been terminated in favor of such person. An aggrieved party may appeal, in accordance with the provisions of chapter thirty A, from any order of the registrar of motor vehicles under the provisions of this section.

(4) In any prosecution commenced pursuant to this section, introduction into evidence of a prior conviction or a prior finding of sufficient facts by either certified attested copies of original court papers, or certified attested copies of the defendant's biographical and informational data from records of the department of probation, any jail or house of corrections, the department of correction, or the registry, shall be prima facie evidence that the defendant before the court had been convicted previously or assigned to an alcohol or controlled substance education, treatment, or rehabilitation program by a court of the commonwealth or any other jurisdiction. Such documentation shall be self-authenticating and admissible, after the commonwealth has established the defendant's guilt on the primary offense, as evidence in any court of the commonwealth to prove the defendant's commission of any prior convictions described therein. The commonwealth shall not be required to introduce any additional corrob[or]ating evidence, nor live witness testimony to establish the validity of such prior convictions.

(d) For the purposes of subdivision (1) of this section, a person shall be deemed to have been convicted if he pleaded guilty or admits to a finding of sufficient facts or was found or adjudged guilty by a court of competent jurisdiction, whether or not he was placed on probation without sentence or under a suspended sentence or the case was placed on file, and a license may be revoked under paragraph (b) hereof notwithstanding the pendency of a prosecution upon appeal or otherwise after such a conviction. Where there has been more than one conviction in the same prosecution, the date of the first conviction shall be deemed to be the date of conviction under paragraph (c) hereof.

(e) In any prosecution for a violation of paragraph (a), evidence of the percentage, by weight, of alcohol in the defendant's blood at the time of the alleged offense, as shown by chemical test or analysis of his blood or as indicated by a chemical test or analysis of his breath, shall be admissible and deemed relevant to the determination of the question of whether such defendant was at such time under the influence of intoxicating liquor; provided, however, that if such test or analysis was made by or at the direction of a police officer, it was made with the consent of the defendant, the results thereof were made available to him upon his request and the defendant was afforded a reasonable opportunity, at his request and at his expense, to have another such test or analysis made by a person or physician selected by him; and provided, further, that blood shall not be withdrawn from any party for the purpose of such test or analysis except by a physician, registered nurse or certified medical technician. Evidence that the defendant failed or refused to consent to such test or analysis shall not be admissible against him in a civil or criminal proceeding, but shall be admissible in any action by the registrar under paragraph (f) or in any proceedings provided for in section twenty-four N. If such evidence is that such percentage was five one-hundredths or less, there shall be a permissible inference that such defendant was not under the influence of intoxicating liquor, and he shall be released from custody forthwith, but the officer who placed him under arrest shall not be liable for false arrest if such police officer had reasonable grounds to believe that the person arrested had been operating a motor vehicle upon any such way or place while under the influence of intoxicating liquor; provided, however, that in an instance where a defendant is under the age of twenty-one and such evidence is that the percentage, by weight, of alcohol in the defendant's blood is two one-hundredths or greater, the officer who placed him under arrest shall, in accordance with subparagraph (2) of paragraph (f), suspend such defendant's license or permit and take all other actions directed therein, if such evidence is that such percentage was more than five one-hundredths but less than eight one-hundredths there shall be no permissible inference. A certificate, signed and sworn to, by a chemist of the department of the state police or by a chemist of a laboratory certified by the department of public health, which contains the results of an analysis made by such chemist of the percentage of alcohol in such blood shall be prima facie evidence of the percentage of alcohol in such blood.

(f) (1) Whoever operates a motor vehicle upon any way or in any place to which the public has right to access, or upon any way or in any place to which the public has access as invitees or licensees, shall be deemed to have consented to submit to a chemical test or analysis of his breath or blood in the event that he is arrested for operating a motor vehicle while under the influence of intoxicating liquor; provided, however, that no such person shall be deemed to have consented to a blood test unless such person has been brought for treatment to a medical facility licensed under the provisions of section 51 of chapter 111; and provided, further, that no person who is afflicted with hemophilia, diabetes or any other condition requiring the use of anticoagulants shall be deemed to have consented to a withdrawal of blood. Such test shall be administered at the direction of a police officer, as defined in section 1 of chapter 90C, having reasonable grounds to believe that the person arrested has been operating a motor vehicle upon such way or place while under the influence of intoxicating liquor. If the person arrested refuses to submit to such test or analysis, after having been informed that his license or permit to operate motor vehicles or right to operate motor vehicles in the commonwealth shall be suspended for a period of at least 180 days and up to a lifetime loss, for such refusal, no such test or analysis shall be made and he shall have his license or right to operate suspended in accordance with this paragraph for a period of 180 days; provided, however, that any person who is under the age of 21 years or who has been previously convicted of a violation under this section, subsection (a) of section 24G, operating a motor vehicle with a percentage by weight of blood alcohol of eight one-hundredths or greater, or while under the influence of intoxicating liquor in violation of subsection (b) of said section 24G, section 24L or subsection (a) of section 8 of chapter 90B, section 8A or 8B of said chapter 90B, or section 13½ of chapter 265 or a like violation by a court of any other jurisdiction or assigned to an alcohol or controlled substance education, treatment or rehabilitation program by a court of the commonwealth or any other jurisdiction for a like offense shall have his license or right to operate suspended forthwith for a period of 3 years for such refusal; provided, further, that any person previously convicted of, or assigned to a program for, 2 such violations shall have the person's license or right to operate suspended forthwith for a period of 5 years for such refusal; and provided, further, that a person previously convicted of, or assigned to a program for, 3 or more such violations shall have the person's license or right to operate suspended forthwith for life based upon such refusal. If a person refuses to submit to any such test or analysis after having been convicted of a violation of section 24L, the re[g]istrar shall suspend his license or right to operate for 10 years. If a person refuses to submit to any such test or analysis after having been convicted of a violation of subsection (a) of section 24G, operating a motor vehicle with a percentage by weight of blood alcohol of eight one-hundredths or greater, or while under the influence of intoxicating liquor in violation of subsection (b) of said section 24G, or section 13½ of chapter 265, the registrar shall revoke his license or right to operate for life. If a person refuses to take a test under this paragraph, the police officer shall:

(i) immediately, on behalf of the registrar, take custody of such person's license or right to operate issued by the commonwealth;

(ii) provide to each person who refuses such test, on behalf of the registrar, a written notification of suspension in a format approved by the registrar; and

(iii) impound the vehicle being driven by the operator and arrange for the vehicle to be impounded for a period of 12 hours after the operator's refusal, with the costs for the towing, storage and maintenance of the vehicle to be borne by the operator.

The police officer before whom such refusal was made shall, within 24 hours, prepare a report of such refusal. Each report shall be made in a format approved by the registrar and shall be made under the penalties of perjury by the police officer before whom such refusal was made. Each report shall set forth the grounds for the officer's belief that the person

arrested had been operating a motor vehicle on a way or place while under the influence of intoxicating liquor, and shall state that such person had refused to submit to a chemical test or analysis when requested by the officer to do so, such refusal having been witnessed by another person other than the defendant. Each report shall identify the police officer who requested the chemical test or analysis and the other person witnessing the refusal. Each report shall be sent forthwith to the registrar along with a copy of the notice of intent to suspend in a form, including electronic or otherwise, that the registrar deems appropriate. A license or right to operate which has been confiscated pursuant to this subparagraph shall be forwarded to the registrar forthwith. The report shall constitute prima facie evidence of the facts set forth therein at any administrative hearing regarding the suspension specified in this section.

The suspension of a license or right to operate shall become effective immediately upon receipt of the notification of suspension from the police officer. A suspension for a refusal of either a chemical test or analysis of breath or blood shall run consecutively and not concurrently, both as to any additional suspension periods arising from the same incident, and as to each other.

No license or right to operate shall be restored under any circumstances and no restricted or hardship permits shall be issued during the suspension period imposed by this paragraph; provided, however, that the defendant may immediately, upon the entry of a not guilty finding or dismissal of all charges under this section, section 24G, section 24L, or section 13½ of chapter 265, and in the absence of any other alcohol related charges pending against said defendant, apply for and be immediately granted a hearing before the court which took final action on the charges for the purpose of requesting the restoration of said license. At said hearing, there shall be a rebuttable presumption that said license be restored, unless the commonwealth shall establish, by a fair preponderance of the evidence, that restoration of said license would likely endanger the public safety. In all such instances, the court shall issue written findings of fact with its decision.

(2) If a person's blood alcohol percentage is not less than eight one-hundredths or the person is under twenty-one years of age and his blood alcohol percentage is not less than two one-hundredths, such police officer shall do the following:

(i) immediately and on behalf of the registrar take custody of such person's drivers license or permit issued by the commonwealth;

(ii) provide to each person who refuses the test, on behalf of the registrar, a written notification of suspension, in a format approved by the registrar; and

(iii) immediately report action taken under this paragraph to the registrar. Each report shall be made in a format approved by the registrar and shall be made under the penalties of perjury by the police officer. Each report shall set forth the grounds for the officer's belief that the person arrested has been operating a motor vehicle on any way or place while under the influence of intoxicating liquor and that the person's blood alcohol percentage was not less than .08 or that the person was under 21 years of age at the time of the arrest and whose blood alcohol percentage was not less than .02. The report shall indicate that the person was administered a test or analysis, that the operator administering the test or analysis was trained and certified in the administration of the test or analysis, that the test was performed in accordance with the regulations and standards promulgated by the secretary of public safety, that the equipment used for the test was regularly serviced and maintained and that the person administering the test had every reason to believe the equipment was functioning properly at the time the test was administered. Each report shall be sent forthwith to the registrar along with a copy of the notice of intent to suspend, in a form, including electronic or otherwise, that the registrar deems appropriate. A license or right to operate confiscated under this clause shall be forwarded to the registrar forthwith.

The license suspension shall become effective immediately upon receipt by the offender of the notice of intent to suspend from a police officer. The license to operate a motor vehicle shall remain suspended until the disposition of the offense for which the person is being prosecuted, but in no event shall such suspension pursuant to this subparagraph exceed 30 days.

In any instance where a defendant is under the age of twenty-one years and such evidence is that the percentage, by weight, of alcohol in the defendant's blood is two one-hundredths or greater and upon the failure of any police officer pursuant to this subparagraph, to suspend or take custody of the driver's license or permit issued by the commonwealth, and, in the absence of a complaint alleging a violation of paragraph (a) of subdivision (1) or a violation of section twenty-four G or twenty-four L, the registrar shall administratively suspend the defendant's license or right to operate a motor vehicle upon receipt of a report from the police officer who administered such chemical test or analysis of the defendant's blood pursuant to subparagraph (1). Each such report shall be made on a form approved by the registrar and shall be sworn to under the penalties of perjury by such police officer. Each such report shall set forth the grounds for the officer's belief that the person arrested had been operating a motor vehicle on a way or place while under the influence of intoxicating liquor and that such person was under twenty-one years of age at the time of the arrest and whose blood alcohol percentage was two one-hundredths or greater. Such report shall also state that the person was administered such a test or analysis, that the operator administering the test or analysis was trained and certified in the administration of such test, that the test was performed in accordance with the regulations and standards promulgated by the secretary of public safety, that the equipment used for such test was regularly serviced and maintained, and that the person administering the test had every reason to believe that the equipment was functioning properly at the time the test was administered. Each such report shall be endorsed by the police chief as defined in section one of chapter ninety C, or by the person authorized by him, and shall be sent to the registrar along with the confiscated license or permit not later than ten days from the date that such chemical test or analysis of the defendant's blood was administered. The license to operate a motor vehicle shall thereupon be suspended in accordance with section twenty-four P.

(g) Any person whose license, permit or right to operate has been suspended under subparagraph (1) of paragraph (f) shall, within fifteen days of suspension, be entitled to a hearing before the registrar which shall be limited to the following issues: (i) did the police officer have reasonable grounds to believe that such person had been operating a motor vehicle while under the influence of intoxicating liquor upon any way or in any place to which members of the public have a right of access or upon any way to which members of the public have a right of access as invitees or licensees, (ii) was such person placed under arrest, and (iii) did such person refuse to submit to such test or analysis. If, after such hearing, the registrar finds on any one of the said issues in the negative, the registrar shall forthwith reinstate such license, permit or right to operate. The registrar shall create and preserve a record at said hearing for judicial review. Within thirty days of the issuance of the final determination by the registrar following a hearing under this paragraph, a person aggrieved by the determination shall have the right to file a petition in the district court for the judicial district in which the offense occurred for judicial review. The filing of a petition for judicial review shall not stay the revocation or suspension. The filing of a petition for judicial review shall be had as soon as possible following the submission of said request, but not later than thirty days following the submission thereof. Review by the court shall be on the record established at the hearing before the registrar. If the court finds that the department exceeded its constitutional or statutory authority, made an erroneous interpretation of the law, acted in an arbitrary and capricious manner, or made a determination which is unsupported by the evidence in the record, the court may reverse the registrar's determination.

Any person whose license or right to operate has been suspended pursuant to subparagraph (2) of paragraph (f) on the basis of chemical analysis of his breath may within ten days of such suspension request a hearing and upon such request shall be entitled to a hearing before the court in which the underlying charges are pending or if the individual is under the age of twenty-one and there are no pending charges, in the district court having jurisdiction where the arrest occurred, which hearing shall be limited to the following issue; whether a blood test administered pursuant to paragraph (e) within a reasonable period of time after such chemical analysis of his breath, shows that the percentage, by weight, of alcohol in such person's blood was less than eight one-hundredths or, relative to such person under the age of twenty-one was less than two one-hundredths. If the court finds that such a blood test shows that such percentage was less than eight one-hundredths or, relative to such person under the age of twenty-one, that such percentage was less than two one-hundredths, the court shall restore such person's license, permit or right to operate and shall direct the prosecuting officer to forthwith notify the department of criminal justice information services and the registrar of such restoration.

(h) Any person convicted of a violation of subparagraph (1) of paragraph (a) that involves operating a motor vehicle while under the influence of marihuana, narcotic drugs, depressants or stimulant substances, all as defined in section one of chapter ninety-four C, or the vapors of glue, may, as part of the disposition in the case, be ordered to participate in a driver education program or a drug treatment or drug rehabilitation program, or any combination of said programs. The court shall set such financial and other terms for the participation of the defendant as it deems appropriate.

(2)(a) Whoever upon any way or in any place to which the public has a right of access, or any place to which members of the public have access as invitees or licensees, operates a motor vehicle recklessly, or operates such a vehicle negligently so that the lives or safety of the public might be endangered, or upon a bet or wager or in a race, or whoever operates a motor vehicle for the purpose of making a record and thereby violates any provision of section seventeen or any regulation under section eighteen, or whoever without stopping and making known his name, residence and the register number of his motor vehicle goes away after knowingly colliding with or otherwise causing injury to any other vehicle or property, or whoever loans or knowingly permits his license or learner's permit to operate motor vehicles to be used by any person, or whoever makes false statements in an application for such a license or learner's permit, or whoever knowingly makes any false statement in an application for registration of a motor vehicle or whoever while operating a motor vehicle in violation of section 8M, 12A or 13B, such violation proved beyond a reasonable doubt, is the proximate cause of injury to any other person, vehicle or property by operating said motor vehicle negligently so that the lives or safety of the public might be endangered, shall be punished by a fine of not less than twenty dollars nor more than two hundred dollars or by imprisonment for not less than two weeks nor more than two years, or both; and whoever uses a motor vehicle without authority knowing that such use is unauthorized shall, for the first offense be punished by a fine of not less than fifty dollars nor more than five hundred dollars or by imprisonment for not less than thirty days nor more than two years, or both, and for a second offense by imprisonment in the state prison for not more than five years or in a house of correction for not less than thirty days nor more than two and one half years, or by a fine of not more than one thousand dollars, or by both such fine and imprisonment; and whoever is found guilty of a third or subsequent offense of such use without authority committed within five years of the earliest of his two most recent prior offenses shall be punished by a fine of not less than two hundred dollars nor more than one thousand dollars or by imprisonment for not less than six months nor more than two and one half years in a house of correction or for not less than two and one half years nor more than five years in the state prison or by both fine and imprisonment. A summons may be issued instead of a warrant for arrest upon a complaint for a violation of any provision of this paragraph if in the judgment of the court or justice receiving the complaint there is reason to believe that the defendant will appear upon a summons.

There shall be an assessment of $250 against a person who, by a court of the commonwealth, is convicted of, is placed on probation for or is granted a continuance without a finding for or otherwise pleads guilty to or admits to a finding of sufficient facts of operating a motor vehicle negligently so that the lives or safety of the public might be endangered under this section, but $250 of the $250 collected under this assessment shall be deposited monthly by the court with the state treasurer, who shall deposit it in the Head Injury Treatment Services Trust Fund, and the remaining amount of the assessment shall be credited to the General Fund. The assessment shall not be subject to reduction or waiver by the court for any reason.

(a½)(1) Whoever operates a motor vehicle upon any way or in any place to which the public has right of access, or upon any way or in any place to which members of the public shall have access as invitees or licensees, and without stopping and making known his name, residence and the registra-

tion number of his motor vehicle, goes away after knowingly colliding with or otherwise causing injury to any person not resulting in the death of any person, shall be punished by imprisonment for not less than six months nor more than two years and by a fine of not less than five hundred dollars nor more than one thousand dollars.

(2) Whoever operates a motor vehicle upon any way or in any place to which the public has a right of access or upon any way or in any place to which members of the public shall have access as invitees or licensees and without stopping and making known his name, residence and the registration number of his motor vehicle, goes away to avoid prosecution or evade apprehension after knowingly colliding with or otherwise causing injury to any person shall, if the injuries result in the death of a person, be punished by imprisonment in the state prison for not less than two and one-half years nor more than ten years and by a fine of not less than one thousand dollars nor more than five thousand dollars or by imprisonment in a jail or house of correction for not less than one year nor more than two and one-half years and by a fine of not less than one thousand dollars nor more than five thousand dollars. The sentence imposed upon such person shall not be reduced to less than one year, nor suspended, nor shall any person convicted under this paragraph be eligible for probation, parole, or furlough or receive any deduction from his sentence until such person has served at least one year of such sentence; provided, however, that the commissioner of correction may on the recommendation of the warden, superintendent or other person in charge of a correctional institution, or the administrator of a county correctional institution, grant to an offender committed under this paragraph, a temporary release in the custody of an officer of such institution for the following purposes only: to attend the funeral of a relative; to visit a critically ill relative; to obtain emergency medical or psychiatric services unavailable at said institution or to engage in employment pursuant to a work release program.

(3) Prosecutions commenced under subparagraph (1) or (2) shall not be continued without a finding nor placed on file.

(b) A conviction of a violation of paragraph (a) or paragraph (a½) of subdivision (2) of this section shall be reported forthwith by the court or magistrate to the registrar, who may in any event, and shall unless the court or magistrate recommends otherwise, revoke immediately the license or right to operate of the person so convicted, and no appeal, motion for new trial or exceptions shall operate to stay the revocation of the license or right to operate. If it appears by the records of the registrar that the person so convicted is the owner of a motor vehicle or has exclusive control of any motor vehicle as a manufacturer or dealer or otherwise, the registrar may revoke the certificate of registration of any or all motor vehicles so owned or exclusively controlled.

(c) The registrar, after having revoked the license or right to operate of any person under paragraph (b), in his discretion may issue a new license or reinstate the right to operate to him, if the prosecution has terminated in favor of the defendant. In addition, the registrar may, after an investigation or upon hearing, issue a new license or reinstate the right to operate to a person convicted in any court for a violation of any provision of paragraph (a) or (a½) of subdivision (2); provided, however, that no new license or right to operate shall be issued by the registrar to: (i) any person convicted of a violation of subparagraph (1) of paragraph (a½) until one year after the date of revocation following his conviction if for a first offense, or until two years after the date of revocation following any subsequent conviction; (ii) any person convicted of a violation of subparagraph (2) of paragraph (a½) until three years after the date of revocation following his conviction if for a first offense or until ten years after the date of revocation following any subsequent conviction; (iii) any person convicted, under paragraph (a) of using a motor vehicle knowing that such use is unauthorized, until one year after the date of revocation following his conviction if for a first offense or until three years after the date of revocation following any subsequent conviction; and (iv) any person convicted of any other provision of paragraph (a) until sixty days after the date of his original conviction if for a first offense or one year after the date of revocation following any subsequent conviction within a period of three years. Notwithstanding the forgoing, a person holding a junior operator's license who is convicted of operating a motor vehicle recklessly or negligently under paragraph (a) shall not be eligible for license reinstatement until 180 days after the date of his original conviction for a first offense or 1 year after the date of revocation following a subsequent conviction within a period of 3 years. The registrar, after investigation, may at any time rescind the revocation of a license or right to operate revoked because of a conviction of operating a motor vehicle upon any way or in any place to which the public has a right of access or any place to which members of the public have access as invitees or licensees negligently so that the lives or safety of the public might be endangered. The provisions of this paragraph shall apply in the same manner to juveniles adjudicated under the provisions of section fifty-eight B of chapter one hundred and nineteen.

(3) The prosecution of any person for the violation of any provision of this section, if a subsequent offence, shall not, unless the interests of justice require such disposition, be placed on file or otherwise disposed of except by trial, judgment and sentence according to the regular course of criminal proceedings; and such a prosecution shall be otherwise disposed of only on motion in writing stating specifically the reasons therefor and verified by affidavits if facts are relied upon. If the court or magistrate certifies in writing that he is satisfied that the reasons relied upon are sufficient and that the interests of justice require the allowance of the motion, the motion shall be allowed and the certificate shall be filed in the case. A copy of the motion and certificate shall be sent by the court or magistrate forthwith to the registrar.

(4) In any prosecution commenced pursuant to this section, introduction into evidence of a prior conviction or prior finding of sufficient facts by either original court papers or certified attested copy of original court papers, accompanied by a certified attested copy of the biographical and informational data from official probation office records, shall be prima facie evidence that a defendant has been convicted previously or assigned to an alcohol or controlled substance education, treatment, or rehabilitation program because of a like offense by a court of the commonwealth one or more times preceding the date of commission of the offense for which said defendant is being prosecuted.

NOTE 1a   **Way.** See definition in Section 1 of this chapter.

NOTE 1b   **Proof of Existence of a Public Way.**

(1) G.L. c. 233 § 79F. "A certificate by the secretary of the public works commission in the case of a state highway, or the secretary of the metropolitan district commission in the case of a highway under the control of said commission, or by a city or town clerk in the case of a city or town way, that a particular way is a public way as a matter of record shall be admissible as prima facie evidence that such a way is a public way."

(2) Public way may be shown by evidence such as lights, curbs, crossroads, houses, traffic, hydrants, railroad tracks, concrete paving, and connecting roads. *Commonwealth v. Mara*, 257 Mass. 198 (1926).

(3) Stipulation between the parties on this point is a common practice.

(4) "Although the judge found that the owners of the property took no affirmative steps to exclude the public from their lots, and that there were no barriers preventing access to the property, he also found that the public use of the property 'was without the permission of the owners'; that the property had been posted with 'No Trespassing' signs (which were vandalized over the years); and that the owners had notified the local police, who said that they would patrol the area.

"In light of these findings, it is more reasonable to conclude for the purposes of this criminal case that members of the public had access to the property only as trespassers, who enter land 'without a privilege to do so, created by the possessor's consent or otherwise.' Restatement (Second) of Torts § 329 (1965)." *Commonwealth v. Callahan*, 405 Mass. 200, 204 (1989) (citations omitted).

(5) "It is the status of the way, not the status of the driver, which the statute defines. Moreover, it is the objective appearance of the way that is determinative of its status, rather than the subjective intent of the property owner. It is sufficient if the physical circumstances of the way are such that members of the public may reasonably conclude that it is open for travel to invitees or licensees." *Commonwealth v. Smithson*, 41 Mass. App. Ct. 545, 549–50 (1996) (quoting *Commonwealth v. Hart*, 26 Mass. App. Ct. 235, 237–38 (1988)). "We conclude that the physical circumstances surrounding the gravel haul road running through Brewster Sand & Gravel on [Memorial day] . . . were not sufficient to create a reasonable expectation among members of the public that, on that particular day, they were welcome to drive through the main gate of the facility, and continue along the gravel haul road some 650 feet, past the office and utility buildings and into the sand pit area." *Commonwealth v. Smithson*, 41 Mass. App. Ct. at 551–52.

NOTE 1c   "[T]hough members of the general public are invited to become licensees of the campground, they are not allowed into the campground unless or until they have acquired such a license. Even more than the fact of that limitation, the gate makes its reality abundantly clear to any putative visitor. . . . In the present case, registered campers and their guests have access to the ways within the campground, but members of the public who have not acquired that status do not. . . . By plainly restricting access of the general public to the campground, the owner has made it clear to all visitors that it is a private facility, accessible only to a limited class of persons, and not the general public." *Commonwealth v. Stoddard*, 74 Mass. App. Ct. 179, 183 (2009).

NOTE 2a   **Operation.** "To operate a motor vehicle upon a way in violation of the statute, it is not necessary that the engine should be running. The engine of a motor vehicle may cease to run while it is going down a hill, but the vehicle may remain within the control of the driver and he may operate it, under these conditions." *Commonwealth v. Clarke*, 254 Mass. 566, 568 (1926).

NOTE 2b   The shifting of gears which causes the car to move is operation notwithstanding the fact that the car engine is *not* on. *Commonwealth v. Clarke*, 254 Mass. 566, 568 (1926).

NOTE 2b(1)   "It has long been recognized that 'a vehicle may be operated when standing still.' *Commonwealth v. Clarke*, 254 Mass. 566, 568 (1926)." *Commonwealth v. Sudderth*, 37 Mass. App. Ct. 317, 320 (1994) (driver asleep behind the wheel of a legally parked car, with the engine running).

NOTE 2b(2)   "A person operates a motor vehicle . . . when, in the vehicle, he intentionally does any act or makes use of any mechanical or electrical agency which alone or in sequence will set in motion the motive power of that vehicle." *Commonwealth v. Uski*, 263 Mass. 22, 24 (1928).

NOTE 2b(3) "Under the *Uski* definition, turning the key in the ignition to the 'on' setting could be found to be part of a sequence that would set the vehicle's engine in motion and that would, thus, constitute operation." *Commonwealth v. McGillivary*, 78 Mass. App. Ct. 644, 646 (2011).

NOTE 2c   Operation may be proven by circumstantial evidence. In *Wood*, immediately after a collision, the defendant was found, alone, slumped over the driver's seat. The car was neither moving nor was its engine running. Conviction affirmed. *Commonwealth v. Wood*, 261 Mass. 458 (1927).

NOTE 2d   "The only evidence on the contested issue of operation in this case was the defendant's admissions to Keenan and Higgins that he was driving. These statements were made while the defendant was highly intoxicated. . . .

"In *Commonwealth v. Forde*, 392 Mass. 453, 457 (1984), we stated, as to an extrajudicial confession, that we would adopt the majority rule of this nation that an uncorroborated confession is 'insufficient to prove guilt' . . .

"The only contested issue of fact was whether he had operated the vehicle. Apart from his statements, there was no such evidence. The Commonwealth claims that his demand that his wife 'give . . . back' the keys, together with the wife's cigarettes being found on the floor of the passenger side of the front compartment, suffice to corroborate the defendant's statements. We are unpersuaded. . . .

"Returning to *Forde*, we noted that the corroborative evidence we would require is 'some evidence, besides the confession, that the criminal act was committed by someone, that is, that the crime was real and not imaginary.' *Id.* at 458. There was no such evidence in this case. Thus, it was error to deny the defendant's motions for a required finding of not guilty."

Commonwealth v. Leonard, 401 Mass. 470, 472–73 (1988). *Cf. Commonwealth v. O'Connor*, 420 Mass. 630, 632 (1995) ("The officer confirmed the defendant's version of the accident with other witnesses. The finder of fact could infer operation from the facts and circumstances surrounding the accident and from the defendant's cooperation with the field sobriety tests."). *See also Commonwealth v. Adams*, 421 Mass. 289, 291 (1995) and *Commonwealth v. Manning*, 41 Mass. App. Ct. 18 (1996).

NOTE 2e   See also *State v. Pritchett*, 53 Del. 583, 598–99 (Del. Super. Ct. 1961), which was favorably quoted in *Hilton*, 398 Mass. at 67–68 as follows:

"[OUI cases] are not to be tried with an ostrich like attitude - one's head in the sand. Defendant's car didn't reach the position where it was found by some magical process; no figure from outer space dropped it from the sky to Memorial Drive at its intersection with Bizarre Avenue, where it was found by the State Trooper; it had to have been 'operated' by someone to get to the place where the Trooper found it, with defendant in it. The evidence clearly indicated it was practically, if not wholly, impossible to conceive that any person, other than the defendant, could have gotten into the driver's seat, manipulated the gears and driven it to the spot where it was found, with the defendant sitting as he was in relation to the driver's seat and with his feet situated as they were."

NOTE 3a   **Operating Under the Influence—Section 24(1)(a).** The Commonwealth need not prove that the defendant actually drove in an unsafe or erratic manner, but it must prove a diminished capacity to operate safely. *Commonwealth v. Connolly*, 394 Mass. 169, 173 (1985).

NOTE 3a(1) Factors. "That a defendant was belligerent, unsteady on his feet and smelled of alcohol are factors that may support an inference of diminished capacity to operate due to intoxication. The opinion testimony of police who observed the defendant may also be taken into account. Evidence of use of obscenities is probative on the issue of whether the defendant was intoxicated." *Commonwealth v. Sudderth*, 37 Mass. App. Ct. 317, 321 (1994).

NOTE 3b   Lay Opinion. "[A] lay witness in a case charging operation of a motor vehicle while under the influence of alcohol may offer his opinion regarding a defendant's level of sobriety or intoxication but may not opine whether a defendant operated a motor vehicle while under the influence of alcohol or whether the defendant's consumption of alcohol diminished his ability to operate a motor vehicle safely." *Commonwealth v. Canty*, 466 Mass. 535, 544 (2013).

NOTE 3c   Any liquor, including 3.2 beer, is intoxicating if it in fact is capable of subjecting a person to its alcoholic influence. *Commonwealth v. Bridges*, 285 Mass. 572 (1934).

NOTE 3d   Additional Substances. The Defendant Was Arrested for OUI. His breathalyzer was a .07. A postarrest search revealed five yellow pills which contained PCP.

"A defendant may be found guilty of driving while under the influence of intoxicating liquor if the defendant's ability to operate a vehicle safely is diminished, and alcohol is one contributing cause of the diminished ability . . . It is not necessary that alcohol be the sole or exclusive cause. It is enough if the defendant's capacity to operate a motor vehicle is diminished because of alcohol, even though other, concurrent causes contribute to that diminished capacity. Case law in other jurisdictions supports this conclusion."

In similar circumstances the court suggested the proper jury instruction:

"You are instructed that, if the defendant's ability to operate safely was diminished by alcohol, the defendant has violated the statute even though some other cause, also operating on the defendant while he or she was driving, tended to magnify the effect of the liquor or concurred in causing the defendant's diminished capacity to operate safely. It is no defense, under the statute, to show the existence of such concurring cause, so long as the influence of the liquor remained as one of the causes of the defendant's diminished capacity. See 3 Erwin, Defense of Drunk Driving Cases § 40.05 (3d ed. 1985)." *Commonwealth v. Stathopoulos*, 401 Mass. 453, 456–57 (1988) (citation and footnote omitted).

NOTE 3e   Admission. "Although there was no direct evidence that the defendant had more than two drinks of intoxicating liquor, there was an opportunity for him to have had more, and there was evidence of his admission that he had had 'one too many.' That in substance was an admission that he was operating while under the influence of intoxicating liquor, and that is a crime." *Hallett v. Rimer*, 329 Mass. 61, 62–63 (1952).

NOTE 3f   Marijuana. "Here, the officer smelled the odor of burnt marijuana and recovered two small bags of it from Tayetto, who explained that the smell was the result of others using marijuana at a party. While the officer was not required to credit this explanation, the Commonwealth elicited no testimony that Tayetto showed any signs of impairment during their encounter. The officer did not testify that Tayetto's eyes were red or glassy, that her speech or movements were unusual, or that her responses to questioning were inappropriate or uncooperative. He did not perform any tests to assess her physical and mental acuity. Indeed, he instructed her to move her vehicle herself to allow traffic to pass. In short, there was no indication that her 'judgment, alertness, and ability to respond promptly and effectively to unexpected emergencies [were] diminished' by the consumption of marijuana. *Commonwealth v. Connolly*, [394 Mass. 169, 172–73 (1985)]." *Commonwealth v. Daniel*, 464 Mass. 746, 756–57 (2013) (footnote omitted).

NOTE 4   Purpose of Statute. The Supreme Judicial Court rejected the defendant's argument that "public policy considerations dictate that an intoxicated motorist not be punished for choosing to stop his automobile and sleep, rather than attempting to proceed. . . .

"This same argument was answered well by the Supreme Court of North Dakota. '[The defendant] argues that to sustain convictions of [operating] a vehicle while intoxicated in cases where the defendant has voluntarily stopped his vehicle off the road after realizing his inability to drive safely is to discourage such behavior in the future. He argues that convictions under these circumstances will encourage drivers aware of their impaired driving capability to continue driving rather than risk conviction . . . should they pull off the highway to await other transportation.

"'While we believe such behavior should be encouraged, the real purpose of the statute is to deter individuals who have been drinking intoxicating liquor from getting into their vehicles, except as passengers. . . . One who has been drinking intoxicating liquor should not be encouraged to test his driving ability on the highway, even for a short distance, where his life and the lives of others hang in the balance'. *State v. Ghylin*, 250 N.W.2d 252, 255 (N.D. 1977)." *Commonwealth v. Otmishi*, 398 Mass. 69, 70, 71–72 (1986).

NOTE 5a   **Breathalyzer—Section 24(1)(e) & (f).** "G.L. c. 90, § 24(1)(e) and (f), requires a defendant's actual consent to breath and blood testing as a condition of admissibility of the results in evidence. The consent required is not the 'knowing, voluntary and intelligent' consent required for waiver of constitutional rights, but the consent of customary usage indicated by criteria such as verbal agreement to undergo, lack of objection to, or cooperation in the performance of, the blood testing. . . . The statute requires a suspect's consent, and whether the defendant consented . . . is a question of fact." *Commonwealth v. Carson*, 72 Mass. App. Ct. 368, 370–71 (2008) (citations and footnote omitted).

NOTE 5b   (1) Admission of evidence of defendant's refusal to take the breathalyzer is prejudicial error in clear contravention of G.L. c. 90, § 24(1)(e). *Commonwealth v. Scott*, 359 Mass. 407 (1971).

"Would the provisions of Senate No. 717 which permits a defendant's failure or refusal to submit to a chemical test or analysis of his breath to be admissible as evidence in a criminal proceeding violate the self-incrimination clause of Article XII of Part the First of the Constitution of the Commonwealth in that the defendant is therefore compelled to furnish evidence against himself?" The Supreme Judicial Court answered "yes." *Opinion of the Justices*, 412 Mass. 1201 (1992).

(1)(a) Failed efforts to take breath test are admissible. "[T]he defendant did not refuse to take the breathalyzer test; had he done so, evidence of that refusal would have been inadmissible against him. Instead, he signed a form indicating that he *consented* to take the test. What followed—a series of physical actions—was properly the subject of the observing police officer's testimony. . . . Accordingly we conclude that the evidence was properly admitted." *Commonwealth v. Curley*, 78 Mass. App. Ct. 163, 168 (2010) (footnotes omitted).

(2) Having a sufficient basis for finding that the Commonwealth's witness, a police sergeant, who had administered the breathalyzer to the defendant, was qualified to testify as an expert (he had taken a 40-hour course of instruction on the operation of the breathalyzer machine and had used the machine 100 times), shortcomings with respect to that witness' knowledge and skill in administering the test did *not* put his testimony out of the case, although it might have affected its weight. *Commonwealth v. Shea*, 356 Mass. 358, 361 (1969).

(3) "[G.L. c.] 90, § 24(1)(e), does no more than regulate the admissibility and effect of chemical tests of blood alcohol content. If the police administer a blood alcohol content test, the section imposes certain requirements which must be met if the test is to be admissible on the issue whether the defendant was intoxicated. It does not establish a right to a police administered test." *Commonwealth v. Alano*, 388 Mass. 871, 875 (1983).

(4) "The sole issue in this appeal of the Commonwealth from the allowance of a motion to dismiss is whether, under the United States Constitution or the Massachusetts Constitution, an arrested person has a due process right to counsel prior to deciding whether to take a breathalyzer test. Admittedly, there is no statutory right. We hold that there is no such constitutional right." *Commonwealth v. Brazelton*, 404 Mass. 783 (1989).

(5) Breathalyzer. "[Defendant] claims that the judge erred by failing to find explicitly that the Commonwealth had sustained its burden of showing that the breath test procedure used in this case was scientifically reliable. The defendant also charges that the admission of the single breath test result, without the benefit of a

second breath test or a simulator test, violated his State and Federal due process rights to challenge the accuracy of evidence against him. We conclude that the judge made a preliminary finding of fact that the breath test evidence was sufficiently reliable to be admitted in evidence, and that the admission of the single breath test result did not deprive the defendant of any of his due process rights." *Commonwealth v. Durning*, 406 Mass. 485, 489–90 (1990).

"The statute and the regulations read together require that there be a periodic testing program as well as an annual certification, and that the annual certification is valid only insofar as it comports with the requirements of the periodic program. We conclude, therefore, that prior to the admission of a breathalyzer result, the Commonwealth must prove the existence of and compliance with, the requirements of a periodic testing program." *Commonwealth v. Barbeau*, 411 Mass. 782, 786 (1992). *See also Morris v. Commonwealth*, 412 Mass. 861 (1992) (promulgated standards written as a result of *Barbeau* sufficient).

(6) An article appearing in the *Massachusetts Law Review* asserts that one's blood alcohol concentration may increase after an arrest so that one, who at the time of arrest was not legally intoxicated, may become so during the period of delay between the arrest and the test. E.F. Fitzgerald & D.N. Hume, "The Single Chemical Test for Intoxication: A Challenge to Admissibility," 66 *Mass. L. Rev.* 23 (1981).

Retrograde Extrapolation. "Our conclusion that breathalyzer test results are admissible in OUI prosecutions, without the necessity of retrograde extrapolation, is limited to cases where the tests have been conducted within a reasonable time of the operation of a motor vehicle. . . . We conclude that the passage of up to three hours between testing and operation is a reasonable time for this purpose. The facts and circumstances in particular cases may establish that a lesser or greater time period ought to be applied. Such determinations fall within the sound discretion of the trial judge.

"Finally, if the *per se* and impaired ability theories of criminal liability are charged in the alternative (as they were here) and so tried, we see no prejudice in the admission of breathalyzer test results without expert testimony establishing the significance of the test level to the degree of intoxication or impairment of the defendant. . . . If, however, the Commonwealth were to proceed only on a theory of impaired operation and offered a breathalyzer test result of .08 or greater, without evidence of its relationship to intoxication or impairment and without the statutorily permissible inference of intoxication eliminated by the 2003 amendments, the jury would be left to guess at its meaning. . . . While it is difficult to envision a situation in which the Commonwealth would proceed in this fashion, if it chooses to do so, it must present expert testimony establishing a relationship between the test results and intoxication as a foundational requirement of the admissibility of such results." *Commonwealth v. Colturi*, 448 Mass. 809, 816–18 (2007).

(7) G.L. c. 24(1)(e) jury instruction improper. The jury instruction concerning why a breathalyzer was not taken mandated in G.L. c. 24(1)(e) "unconstitutionally compels an accused to furnish evidence against himself or herself." *Commonwealth v. Zevitas*, 418 Mass. 677 (1994).

(8) Acceptable Instruction Regarding Lack of Evidence of Breathalyzer. In *Commonwealth v. Downs*, 53 Mass. App. Ct. 195 (2001), *review denied*, 435 Mass. 1108 (2002), the Appeals Court upheld the giving of the following instruction by the trial court judge: "You are not to mention or consider in any way whatsoever, either for or against either side, that there is no evidence of a breathalyzer. Do not consider that in any way. Do not mention it. And put it completely out of your mind." *Commonwealth v. Downs*, 53 Mass. App. Ct. at 198. The Appeals Court reasoned as follows:

> We cannot close our eyes to the fact that there is widespread public information and common knowledge about breathalyzer testing. . . . It was, therefore, not incorrect for the trial judge to conclude that he should give some instruction to the jury about the absence of evidence of breathalyzer test results.

... Unlike the impermissible instruction mandate by § 24(1)(e), the limiting instruction delivered in the instant case made no mention either of a defendant's legal right to refuse to take the breathalyzer or the possible reasons for any refusal. It is this difference which leads us to conclude that the instruction did not violate the defendant's art. 12 rights.

Commonwealth v. Downs, 53 Mass. App. Ct. at 199–200.

NOTE 5c   Breathalyzer Test—No Right to Counsel. "We now revisit our holding in [*Commonwealth v. Brazelton*, 404 Mass. 783 (1989)] to determine whether the creation of a 'per se' violation theory under G.L. c. 90, § 24, transforms the decision whether to submit to a breathalyzer test into a critical stage in the criminal justice process. We conclude that, despite the creation of a 'per se' violation theory, there is no constitutional right to counsel under the Sixth Amendment or art. 12 when deciding whether to submit to a breathalyzer test." *Commonwealth v. Neary-French*, 475 Mass. 167, 170 (2016).

NOTE 5d   Observation of Defendant Taking Breathalyzer Test. "We believe that the regulation does not preclude observation of an arrestee by the breathalyzer operator outside the breathalyzer room." *Commonwealth v. Pierre*, 72 Mass. App. Ct. 230, 232 (2008).

NOTE 5e   Breathtest as Search Incident to Arrest. "Because breath tests are significantly less intrusive than blood tests and in most cases amply serve law enforcement interests, we conclude that a breath test, but not a blood test, may be administered as a search incident to a lawful arrest for drunk driving. As in all cases involving reasonable searches incident to arrest, a warrant is not needed in this situation." *Birchfield v. North Dakota*, 136 S. Ct. 2160, 2185 (2016).

NOTE 5f   Blood Test. Medical. "[N]either G.L. c. 90, § 24(1)(e), nor art. 12 renders inadmissible evidence of the defendant's refusal to consent to a blood test requested by medical professionals for medical purposes, even where the defendant is in custody and police may have an interest in the results of the tests." *Commonwealth v. Arruda*, 73 Mass. App. Ct. 901, 904 (2008).

NOTE 5g   Lower Breathalyzer Reading. "[A] District Court judge concluded that, in accordance with statutory and regulatory requirements, the Commonwealth in its prosecution of the OUI offense could only introduce evidence of the lower of the two breath sample results (or, stated another way, only the lower blood alcohol level result and not, as the Commonwealth wanted, both blood alcohol level results) . . . We agree with the District Court judge." *Commonwealth v. Steele*, 455 Mass. 209, 210 (2009) (footnotes omitted).

NOTE 6a   Proof of Substance. Codeine. "We agree with the Appeals Court that the trial judge could have taken judicial notice that codeine is a derivative of opium." *Commonwealth v. Green*, 408 Mass. 48, 50 (1990) (footnote omitted).

NOTE 6b   Heroin. Absent evidence that heroin is a narcotic drug, or judicial notice of that fact, essential element not proven. *Commonwealth v. Finegan*, 45 Mass. App. Ct. 921 (1998).

NOTE 6c   Prescription Drugs. Where the defendant had reason to know of a prescription drug's possible effects on driving ability, criminal liability can be imposed if intoxication is demonstrated beyond a reasonable doubt. *Commonwealth v. Reynolds*, 67 Mass. App. Ct. 215, 222 (2006).

NOTE 6d   Amphetamines. "There was no foundation to support the theory that the amphetamine use was the cause of the accident. To be properly admitted, the evidence of amphetamines in the defendant's system in this case required, at a minimum, (1) reliable evidence as to the amount or concentration of the drug in the defendant's system; and (2) expert testimony indicating that the concentration of the drug in the defendant's system would impair her ability to operate a motor vehicle." *Commonwealth v. Shellenberger*, 64 Mass. App. Ct. 70, 76 (2005).

NOTE 6e   Failure of Proof (drugs). "The evidence was ample that the defendant was operating a motor vehicle on a public way while under the influence of the CNS depressants Klonopin and amitriptyline. Likewise, the evidence was sufficient to establish that the defendant's capacity to operate her vehicle was impaired by these substances. Given the statutory requirements, however, it was simply not enough to establish that the defendant was operating her vehicle under the influence of a depressant substance without also establishing that the substance in question is a drug that 'contains any quantity of a substance which the United States Attorney General has by regulation designated as having a potential for abuse because of its depressant . . . effect on the central nervous system or its hallucinogenic effect.' G.L. c. 94C, § 1. . . . [N]othing in the evidence established directly, or by inference, that Klonopin or amitriptyline are such substances." *Commonwealth v. Ferola*, 72 Mass. App. Ct. 170, 173 (2008) (citation omitted).

NOTE 7   Effect of Medication. "[W]e hold that it was error to preclude the defendant from introducing evidence that he did not know of the possible effects of the medication on his driving ability, that he did not receive warnings as to its use, and that he had no reason to anticipate the effects which the drug induced.[15] His failure to receive warnings from his physician and pharmacist, if there is evidence of such failure, is relevant both to the charge of driving under the influence of drugs (G.L. c. 90, sec. 24(1)(a)) and to the charge of negligence (G.L. c. 90, sec. 24(2)(a))." *Commonwealth v. Wallace*, 14 Mass. App. Ct. 358, 365 & n.15 (1982).

> [15] "We do not imply that a jury could not in some instances find that a defendant had information sufficient to place on him a duty of inquiring of his doctor as to the possible effects of a prescription drug. In such circumstances, a conviction under Section 24(1)(a) would be proper if it is found that the defendant was negligent in not asking, and hence not knowing, of such possible effects on his driving."

NOTE 8a   Field Sobriety Tests (FST). Refusal to take field sobriety tests should not be admitted into evidence "since its use violate[s] the defendant's privilege against self-incrimination secured by art. 12." *Commonwealth v. McGrail*, 419 Mass. 774, 780 (1995).

NOTE 8b   Admissibility of FST. Traditional field sobriety tests—heel-to-toe, one-legged standing and alphabet recitation—admissible into evidence. *Vanhouton v. Commonwealth*, 424 Mass. 327 (1997), *aff'd in part, rev'd in part*, 522 U.S. 834 (1997).

NOTE 8c   Horizontal Gaze Nystagmus Test—Inadmissible Absent Expert Testimony. *Commonwealth v. Sands*, 424 Mass. 184 (1997).

NOTE 8d   No right to refuse to take field sobriety tests. After declaring that the police need not advise an OUI suspect that he or she has the right to refuse to take field sobriety tests, the Supreme Judicial Court clarified that an individual who is lawfully arrested or detained does not have a right to refuse to take such tests in the first place. *Commonwealth v. Blais*, 428 Mass. 294 (1998). The unresolved issue is what, if anything, can be done to compel compliance if a person so refuses. The Supreme Judicial Court noted that "because a person is under an obligation to perform the tests . . . does not necessarily imply that he may be forced to comply. Whether and what steps may be taken to compel compliance will depend on the circumstances." *Commonwealth v. Blais*, 428 Mass. at 301. Compliance cannot be compelled at gunpoint or by use or threats of force. *Commonwealth v. Blais*, 428 Mass. at 301 n.6. The court did indicate that the Legislature could, as they have in the case of a refusal to take a breathalyzer, pass a law suspending an individual's license for refusing to take field sobriety tests. *Commonwealth v. Blais*, 428 Mass. 294 (1998) (referring to G.L. c. 90, § 24(1)(f)).

NOTE 8e   Reasonable Suspicion Standard. "[I]t is appropriate for an officer with reasonable suspicion [not probable cause] that a person is operating a vehicle while under the influence of drugs or alcohol to take the brief, scarcely burdensome steps involved in administering these tests in order to assure himself that he is not turning loose a drunk driver on the traveling public." *Commonwealth v. Blais*, 428 Mass. 294, 298 (1998) (citations omitted).

NOTE 8f   Lack of FST. "The judge properly instructed the jury that the police were not obligated to conduct field sobriety tests at the time they arrested the defendant, but that the jury could consider the absence of such tests in deciding whether the defendant was under the influence of intoxicating liquor." *Commonwealth v. Ames*, 410 Mass. 603, 609 (1991).

NOTE 9a   Miranda. "Without being advised of his rights under *Miranda v. Arizona*, 384 U.S. 436, he was taken to a Booking Center where, as was the routine practice, he was told that his actions and voice would be videotaped. He then answered seven questions regarding his name, address, height, weight, eye color, date of birth, and current age, stumbling over two responses. He was also asked, and was unable to give, the date of his sixth birthday. In addition, he made several incriminating statements while he performed physical sobriety tests and when he was asked to submit to a breathalyzer test" (syllabus). Held:

1) "Muniz's answers to direct questions are not rendered inadmissible by *Miranda* merely because the slurred nature of his speech was incriminating" (syllabus).

2) "However, Muniz's response to the sixth birthday question was incriminating not just because of his delivery, but also because the *content* of his answer supported an inference that his mental state was confused. His response was testimonial because he was required to communicate an express or implied assertion of fact or belief, and, thus, was confronted with the 'trilemma' of truth, falsity, or silence, the historical abuse against which the privilege against self-incrimination was aimed" (syllabus).

3) "Muniz's incriminating utterances during the sobriety and breathalyzer tests were not prompted by an interrogation within the meaning of *Miranda* and should not have been suppressed. The officer's dialogue with Muniz concerning the physical sobriety tests consisted primarily of carefully scripted instructions as to how the tests were to be performed that were not likely to be perceived as calling for any verbal response. Therefore, they were not 'words or actions' constituting custodial interrogation, and Muniz's incriminating utterances were 'voluntary'" (syllabus).

4) "Muniz's answers to these first seven questions are nonetheless admissible because the questions fall within a 'routine booking question' exception which exempts from *Miranda*'s coverage questions to secure the 'biographical data necessary to complete booking or pretrial services.'"

The Court did not decide whether counting (or not) itself in performing field sobriety tests was testimonial within the meaning of the privilege against self-incrimination. *Pennsylvania v. Muniz*, 496 U.S. 582, 600, 604 n.17 (1990).

"[W]here an arrestee's employment status may prove incriminatory, the police must give Miranda warnings before asking questions about employment." *Commonwealth v. Woods*, 419 Mass. 366, 372 (1995) (footnote omitted).

NOTE 9b   FST/Miranda. Miranda warnings are not required prior to conducting field sobriety tests. *Commonwealth v. Cameron*, 44 Mass. App. Ct. 912, 914 (1998). Furthermore, "[t]he fact that the defendant was not free to leave (at least until the performance of field sobriety tests) did not render the interrogation custodial." *Commonwealth v. Cameron*, 44 Mass. App. Ct. at 915 (quoting *Commonwealth v. Ayre*, 31 Mass. App. Ct. 17, 20 (1991)).

NOTE 9c   Alcohol/Miranda. "The question about whether the defendant had been drinking constituted general on-the-scene questioning and did not require the officer to administer Miranda warnings." *Commonwealth v. Sauer*, 50 Mass. App. Ct. 299, 301 (2000) (citations, quotation marks, and punctuation omitted).

NOTE 9d   Drugs/Miranda. "The subsequent question as to whether the defendant had taken any of the percocets is, we think, the narcotics equivalent of asking someone stopped in similar circumstances whether he has been drinking [and, as such, Miranda is not required]." *Commonwealth v. Sauer*, 50 Mass. App. Ct. 299, 302 (2000).

NOTE 10   Videotape of Booking. The defendant unsuccessfully argued that a videotape of the booking procedure was erroneously admitted into evidence in violation of his Fourth, Fifth, and Sixth Amendment rights and *Miranda*.

The Supreme Judicial Court ruled "that videotapes are 'on balance a reliable evidentiary resource'. Consequently, videotapes should be admissible as evidence if they are relevant, they provide a fair representation of that which they purport to depict, and they are not otherwise barred by an exclusionary rule." *Commonwealth v. Mahoney*, 400 Mass. 524, 527 (1987) (citations omitted).

NOTE 11   Prior Determination of Guilt. "We conclude that as used in the statute, 'convicted' references only dispositions of criminal charges that include a determination of guilt. . . .

"[T]he Legislature did not intend an admission to sufficient facts to be treated as a conviction pursuant to G.L. c. 90, § 24(1)(f)(1). Accordingly, the registrar was not authorized pursuant to that statute to suspend the plaintiff's driver's license for more than 180 days on account of his refusal to take a breathalyzer test, because the plaintiff had not previously been convicted of a violation of G.L. c. 90, § 24." *Souza v. Registrar of Motor Vehicles*, 462 Mass. 227, 228, 235 (2012).

NOTE 12a   Driving to Endanger—Section 24(2)(a). All surrounding circumstances are important to consider, i.e., speed, opportunity to see oncoming traffic, distance, opportunity to avoid a collision, distance vehicles moved as a result of a collision, vehicles weight, and the conduct of the driver. *Commonwealth v. Gurney*, 261 Mass. 309 (1927). Other factors include the condition of the car as well as the road, the presence of other cars and people, the strength and vision of the defendant, and so on. *Commonwealth v. Vartanian*, 251 Mass. 355, 358 (1925).

**NOTE 12b   "[I]t is not the duration of negligent operation or the proximity of the public, but the operation of the vehicle itself that is the crime." *Commonwealth v. Ferreira*, 70 Mass. App. Ct. 32, 35 (2007) (citation and quotation marks omitted).

**NOTE 12c   "It is [the] act which is penalized. The intent with which the act is done is an immaterial factor." *Commonwealth v. Pentz*, 247 Mass. 500, 509 (1924).

**NOTE 12d   A person may be found guilty of reckless driving although no one was upon the street. *Commonwealth v. Horsfall*, 213 Mass. 232, 235 (1913).

**NOTE 12e   Juvenile defendant may be bound over for trial as an adult for operating to endanger as the charge is an offense involving the infliction or threat of serious bodily harm within the meaning of G.L. c. 119, § 61. "The crucial fact is that the crime involves a threat of serious bodily harm, not that the person charged intended such a threat." *Commonwealth v. A Juvenile*, 383 Mass. 877, 878 (1981), *aff'g* 10 Mass. App. Ct. 385 (1980).

**NOTE 12f   Evidence that the defendant was travelling in the wrong direction in a traffic rotary and speeding sufficient to warrant a conviction for operating to endanger. *Commonwealth v. Charland*, 338 Mass. 742 (1959).

**NOTE 12g   "The defendant also urges that his two convictions of operating so as to endanger are duplicative. . . . As it is the conduct of operating a vehicle in a negligent manner so as to endanger the public that is proscribed, not the act of harming another, the defendant can be convicted only once of operating so as to endanger although more than one person was killed. Therefore, we conclude it was error and gives rise to a substantial risk of a miscarriage of justice to convict the defendant twice of this offense, rather than once, and to sentence him to concurrent terms of probation." *Commonwealth v. Constantino*, 443 Mass. 521, 526–27 (2005).

NOTE 13a   Use Without Authority—Section 24(2)(a). Elements are (1) use (2) of a motor vehicle (3) on a public way (4) without authority (5) knowing that such use is unauthorized. *Commonwealth v. Giannino*, 371 Mass. 700, 702 (1977).

(1) Use. A passenger may be found guilty of "using" a motor vehicle under this statute. "One uses a machine if he rides in it, although he rides as a passive invited guest. It is not necessary

that there be active control or operation on his part." *Commonwealth v. Coleman*, 252 Mass. 241, 243 (1925).

(2) Motor vehicle—defined in G.L. c. 90, § 1.

(3) Public way—see annotation 1 above.

(4) Without authority. Authority may come from the owner or by one lawfully in control of the vehicle. *Commonwealth v. Coleman*, 252 Mass. 241, 243 (1925).

(5) Knowing that such use is unauthorized.

(a) "[K]nowledge of the wrongful character of the act is an essential element of the offense." *Commonwealth v. Giannino*, 371 Mass. at 704.

(b) "The testimony of the owner that he had not authorized [either the driver or the passenger] to use the motor vehicle is not enough, without more, to convict the defendant passenger of knowledge that its use was unauthorized." *Commonwealth v. Boone*, 356 Mass. 85, 87 (1969).

(c) Mere presence of the defendant in a stolen car is insufficient to support an inference of knowledge on his part that the use of the vehicle was unauthorized. *Commonwealth v. Boone*, 356 Mass. 85, 87 (1969).

(d) Presence supplemented by other incriminating evidence will serve to tip the scales in favor of sufficiency. *Commonwealth v. Johnson*, 6 Mass. App. Ct. 956 (1978).

NOTE 13b "[T]he 'public way' language found in the first portion of the section, which ends in a semicolon, does not modify the crime of use without authority found in the next, independent clause of the section. . . . We conclude that public way is not an element of the crime of use of a motor vehicle without authority." *Commonwealth v. Morris M.*, 70 Mass. App. Ct. 688, 695–96 (2007).

NOTE 13c Failure to issue a citation to one charged with use without authority is *not* a defense as provided in G.L. c. 90C, § 2. Chapter 90C, § 2 is inapplicable to one so charged. *Commonwealth v. Giannino*, 371 Mass. at 702.

NOTE 13d Use without authority is a lesser included offense of larceny of a motor vehicle, G.L. c. 266, § 28. *Costarelli v. Commonwealth*, 374 Mass. 677 (1978).

NOTE 13e Use without authority is not a lesser included offense of receiving a stolen motor vehicle, G.L. c. 266, § 28. *Commonwealth v. Lewis*, 41 Mass. App. Ct. 910–11 (1996).

NOTE 14a **Leaving the Scene—Section 24(2)(a).** The obvious purpose of the statute is to enable those in any way injured by the operation of an automobile upon a public way to obtain forthwith accurate information as to the person in charge of the automobile. Active and positive duties are imposed upon the operator of the vehicle. *Commonwealth v. Horsfall*, 213 Mass. 232, 236 (1913).

NOTE 14b This statute relates to the driver of the car only and not to the owner, who is not the operator. *Nager v. Reid*, 240 Mass. 211, 214 (1921).

NOTE 14c **Leaving the Scene—Section 24(2)(a½).** "[T]he proper 'unit of prosecution' under the statute is the act of leaving the scene of the accident, not the number of victims . . . .

"The object of G.L. c. 90, § 24(2)(a½)(2), is the failure of an involved driver to stop at the scene of an accident resulting in injury or death. Although this accident caused two deaths, there was but one accident scene and one failure to stop. Accordingly, we conclude that convicting the defendant of two violations, rather than one, and sentencing him to consecutive terms in a house of correction was error and gives rise to a substantial risk of a miscarriage of justice." *Commonwealth v. Constantino*, 443 Mass. 521, 524, 526 (2005).

NOTE 14d **Lesser Included.** Leaving the scene of an accident after causing injury, G.L. c. 90, § 24(2)(a½)(1), is a lesser included offense of leaving the scene of an accident after causing death, G.L. c. 90, § 24(2)(a½)(2). *Commonwealth v. Muir*, 84 Mass. App. Ct. 635, 638 (2013).

NOTE 14e **"Knowingly Collide".** "Here, the uncontested facts are that the defendant knew he had a collision. The judge, as the trier of fact, determined the Commonwealth did not prove beyond

a reasonable doubt that the defendant knew he had collided with a person. Therefore, the defendant did not knowingly collide with a person or otherwise injure a person, resulting in death, within the meaning of G.L. c. 90, § 24(2)(a½)(2). . . . Based on the plain language of the statute, we conclude that leaving the scene of an accident causing injury to a person, resulting in that person's death, requires the Commonwealth to prove that the defendant knew he collided with a person 'or otherwise' caused injury to a person." *Commonwealth v. Daley*, 463 Mass. 620, 626 (2012).

NOTE 15a **Roadblocks.** "Whether, as a precondition to the admission of evidence obtained as a result of a sobriety checkpoint or roadblock operated by law enforcement personnel, the Commonwealth is required to prove that there was no less intrusive alternative to the checkpoint or roadblock which would have been effective to accomplish the legitimate public safety goals of the Commonwealth." The Supreme Judicial Court answered in the negative. *Commonwealth v. Shields*, 402 Mass. 162, 163 (1988). *See also Commonwealth v. Lovelace*, 402 Mass. 1002 (1988) (rescript).

NOTE 15b "The roadblock was conducted pursuant to State police General Order TRF-15. . . . We conclude that TRF-15 falls within constitutional parameters, because its guidelines permit a vehicle to be diverted to secondary screening only when the officer has a reasonable suspicion, based on articulable facts, that the driver has committed an OUI violation or another violation of law. . . . [A]s a result of the orders and instructions in the operations plan that governed this sobriety checkpoint and supplemented the guidance provided by TRF-15, the discretion provided to the initial screening officers in greeting motorists was appropriately limited to pass constitutional muster." *Commonwealth v. Murphy*, 454 Mass. 318, 319–20 (2009); *see also Commonwealth v. Swartz*, 454 Mass. 330 (2009).

NOTE 15c The judge ruled that, in extending the roadblock [fifteen minutes] beyond 2 a.m., the state police deviated from "the specific plan which was in operation for this roadblock." The Supreme Judicial Court affirmed the judge's suppression order. *Commonwealth v. Anderson*, 406 Mass. 343, 344 (1989).

The Supreme Judicial Court in *Anderson* reviewed the various roadblock cases.

"Since *Trumble*, the constitutionality of such roadblocks under the Fourth and Fourteenth Amendments and under the adequate and independent State constitutional ground of arts. 12 and 14 has been measured by the officers' compliance with these guidelines. See *Commonwealth v. Shields, supra* at 164–165 ("where the Commonwealth shows a roadblock employed to enforce c. 90, §24, was operated in accordance with the established guidelines, the accompanying seizures, although not conducted on the basis of individualized suspicion, are reasonable under the Fourth Amendment and art. 14"); *Commonwealth v. Amaral, supra* at 100 ("roadblocks stand or fall based on some set of neutral criteria governing the officers in the field," quoting *State v. Jones*, 483 So. 2d 433, 438 [Fla. 1986], in which that court required a written set of uniform guidelines be followed to render a roadblock stop constitutional). . . .

"Adherence to a neutrally devised, preplanned blueprint in order to eliminate arbitrariness and discretion has been this court's principal prerequisite for abandoning the requirement of individualized suspicion in roadblock stops. *Commonwealth v. Shields, supra* at 165. In *Commonwealth v. Amaral, supra* at 100, we noted with approval the position of other courts that control over the discretion of officers in the field is the key constitutional requirement. *People v. Bartley*, 109 Ill. 2d 273, 289 (1985), *cert. denied sub nom. Bartley v. Illinois*, 475 U.S. 1068 (1986). In *Commonwealth v. Trumble, supra* at 90, it was stressed that the officers at the scene were instructed that no deviation from the procedures set forth in the guidelines would be permitted. In *Commonwealth v. McGeoghegan, supra* at 143, we stated that, in a constitutionally reasonable roadblock, 'assurance must be given that the procedure is being conducted pursuant to a plan devised by law enforcement supervisory personnel.' To allow the Commonwealth to do anything short of complying in full with its own guidelines would inject an element of discretion into the roadblock procedures and thus undercut the very foundation upon which the roadblock seizure is constitutionally justified.

"This court has also specifically pointed to the importance of the requirement that the 'roadblock be planned in advance by supervisory personnel [and such] plans must include "date, location, *time, duration, and set patterns of cars to be stopped*"' *Commonwealth v. Trumble, supra* at 89. As we have noted, the department's own procedure requires that the plans be in writing and disseminated prior to implementation. See section 5 of the procedure. We conclude, therefore, that the Commonwealth must adhere to the requirements of its own guidelines for establishing the duration of a roadblock in order that the possibility of arbitrariness and discretion of officers in the field be eliminated." [Emphasis added.]

The cases alluded to above include *Commonwealth v. Shields*, 402 Mass. 162 (1988); *Commonwealth v. Amaral*, 398 Mass. 98 (1986); *Commonwealth v. Trumble*, 396 Mass. 81 (1985); *Commonwealth v. McGeoghegan*, 389 Mass. 137 (1983).

NOTE 16a Fresh and Continued Pursuit Outside Jurisdiction. A trial judge dismissed an OUI complaint on the grounds that (1) the arresting police officer was outside of his jurisdiction and not in "fresh and continued pursuit" of the defendant at the time of making the arrest, G.L. c. 41, § 98A; and (2) a private citizen has no authority to arrest for traffic violations or OUI. The SJC affirmed the dismissal. *Commonwealth v. Grise*, 398 Mass. 247, 248 (1986).

For a different result, *see Commonwealth v. Morrissey*, 422 Mass. 1, 3–4 (1996) ("We concluded in *Grise* that the arrest was unlawful because it occurred outside the arresting officer's jurisdiction, and that the evidence which would not have been obtained but for the arrest should be suppressed. Here, [the arresting officer] stopped the defendant at the request of a police officer whose jurisdiction included the place where the stop occurred.") and *Commonwealth v. Callahan*, 428 Mass. 335, 338 (1998) ("[The SJC stated in *Grise, supra* at 252–253, that 'police departments, where practical, may take the precaution of having their officers sworn in as special officers on the police forces of neighboring cities and towns in order to validate extra-territorial arrests.' Pepperell [permissibly] took that precaution when it appointed Officer Turgeon as a special police officer [pursuant to G.L. c. 41, § 99], granting him the authority to make arrests in Pepperell."); *see also Commonwealth v. Claiborne*, 423 Mass. 275, 280 (1996). ("When a police officer makes a warrantless arrest outside of his jurisdiction, and not in 'fresh and continued pursuit' of the suspect within the meaning of the G.L. c. 41, s. 98A, then he acts as a private citizen, and the arrest will be held valid only if a private citizen would be justified in a making the arrest under the same circumstances. . . . [T]o make a citizen's arrest, [police] officers need[ ] only probable cause to believe that a felony has been committed and that the person arrested ha[s] committed it." (citation and quotation marks omitted)).

NOTE 16a(1) Other "fresh and continued pursuit" cases include: *Commonwealth v. LeBlanc*, 407 Mass. 70, 71 (1990); *Commonwealth v. O'Hara*, 30 Mass. App. Ct. 608 (1991); *Commonwealth v. Zirpolo*, 37 Mass. App. Ct. 307 (1994).

NOTE 16b Deputy Sheriffs May Arrest. The authority of a deputy sheriff "to stop the defendant's vehicle and to arrest him for operating a motor vehicle while under the influence of intoxicating liquor" "is recognized by statute [G.L. c. 90, § 21; G.L. c. 37, § 13; and G.L. c. 268, § 24]." *Commonwealth v. Howe*, 405 Mass. 332, 333–34 (1989) (footnote omitted).

NOTE 16c Extraterritorial Stop/Arrest. Police officer observed defendant speeding and pass a red light in the town of Natick. He followed the defendant's car and stopped him in the town of Framingham. Ultimately, the defendant was arrested for OUI.

Held, both the extraterritorial stop and arrest were without lawful authority. Concerning the legality of the arrest the court stated: "The officer must have some reason to believe that the suspect has committed an arrestable offense before he can pursue and arrest an individual pursuant to § 98A."

Concerning the legality of the stop: "A police officer's authority is limited to the territorial jurisdiction of his appointment, barring a statutory exception. [See, e.g., § 95 (1988 ed.) (extraterritorial authority to convey weapons); G.L. c. 41, § 98A (extraterritorial fresh pursuit for arrestable offenses)]." There was no statutory exception here. *Commonwealth v. LeBlanc*, 407 Mass. 70, 73–74 (1990).

NOTE 16d "It appears to us that the legislature was fully aware that it was conferring a relatively broad scope of jurisdiction on the police officers when it provided that MWRA [Massachusetts Water Resources Authority] ownership, management or control of property within a town or city can confer jurisdiction to the MDC police within the entire city or town in which the property lies. . . . Because the MWRA owns and operates underground waterpipes in Woburn, Woburn is a city under the statute in which MDC police officers have jurisdiction." *Commonwealth v. Maher*, 408 Mass. 34, 37, 38 (1990).

NOTE 16e "Because Boston and Somerville are both listed in G.L. c. 92, § 33, they are within the metropolitan parks district. And because MDC police officers have authority 'within the metropolitan parks district' under G.L. c. 92, § 61, Officer Scalese was acting within his territorial jurisdiction when he stopped the defendant in Somerville and Boston and when he arrested the defendant in Boston." *Commonwealth v. Whelan*, 408 Mass. 29, 33 (1990).

NOTE 16f Out of State Special Police Officer. "[A] Hollis, New Hampshire police officer stopped the defendant in Pepperell, after pursuing him across the New Hampshire border. The officer had been appointed a special police officer in Pepperell pursuant to G.L. c. 41, § 99."

Held, stop valid as "G.L. c. 41, § 99, is broad, and provides that special police officers 'shall have the authority of constables and police officers within the limits of such city or town, except as to the service of civil process.'" *Commonwealth v. Callahan*, 428 Mass. 335, 336–37 (1998). *Cf. Commonwealth v. Mullen*, 40 Mass. App. Ct. 404 (1996), where the Appeals Court held that a campus police officer, who was specially sworn in as a special State police officer, was found to lack proper authority to stop a motor vehicle for a civil infraction. The case is inapposite. The authorizing statute at issue there did not confer 'all the powers of a State police officer' on the campus security officer. *Id.* at 407." *Callahan*, 428 Mass. at 337.

NOTE 17a Subsequent Offenses. Second Offense. "A 'complaint [of OUI] should set forth any former conviction that may be relied on to justify greater punishment on conviction . . . [but] [a] prior offense is not part of the crime charged; it relates only to punishment . . . A defendant, if convicted of a charge, will be entitled to a separate trial on the issue whether he had been convicted of a prior, like offense. G.L. c. 278, § 11A.' (Citations omitted.) *Commonwealth v. Murphy*, 389 Mass. 316, 320–321 (1983)." *Daley v. Board of Appeal on Motor Vehicle Liab. Policies & Bonds*, 406 Mass. 857, 860 (1990).

NOTE 17b Third Offense. "[T]hird offense OUI conviction is invalid because the judge failed to conduct a jury waiver colloquy or procure a written waiver from the defendant. A defendant's right to a trial by jury is ensured by the Sixth and Fourteenth Amendments to the United States Constitution. A defendant may waive this right, but a conviction based on such waiver cannot stand if the waiver is not voluntarily and intelligently made. *Ciummei v. Commonwealth*, 378 Mass. 504, 507–509 (1979).

"[W]hile a defendant may waive a jury trial on the subsequent offense portion of a trial, the procedural safeguards mandated under *Ciummei* are required in the second portion of the bifurcated proceedings." *Commonwealth v. Dussault*, 71 Mass. App. Ct. 542, 548 (2008).

NOTE 17c Identity of Name for Subsequent Offense. "It was incumbent on the Commonwealth to prove, as part of its case on the subsequent offense charge, that the defendant, Roger A. Koney, who was in the courtroom, was the same Roger A. Koney named in the three prior convictions. *See Commonwealth v. Ierardi*, 17 Mass. App. Ct. 297, 302–03 (1983). . . . Mere identity of name is not sufficient to indicate an identity of person." *Commonwealth v. Koney*, 421 Mass. 295, 301–02 (1995).

"Read into § 24(4) is the additional requirement that the documentation reflecting a conviction be linked to the defendant before such documentation can be prima facie evidence of a conviction. While 'identity of name' alone is insufficient, when the conviction records 'include more identifying information than merely the offender's name, . . . this requirement will be met.' The conviction records here satisfied the Commonwealth's burden. The records matched the defendant's full name, including his middle initial, and the judge also took into account the fact that the defendant's last name was an unusual one. The court records provided additional biographical information that correlated with the defendant's identity, including date of birth and town of residence. The addresses on both convictions also were associated with the defendant: the address for one conviction correlated with the address listed on the defendant's probation records, and the address listed for the other conviction matched the address of the registered third-party owner of the vehicle the defendant was driving. Accordingly, the judge properly concluded that the Commonwealth satisfied its burden of proof." *Commonwealth v. Dussault*, 71 Mass. App. Ct. 542, 546–47 (2008) (citations omitted).

NOTE 17d   Documentary Evidence. Documentary evidence may "be sufficient to sustain a finding of a prior conviction when it demonstrates, through corroborating identifying information such as date of birth, address, social security number, or distinguishing physical characteristics, that the defendant is the same person as that named in the prior conviction." *Commonwealth v. Maloney*, 447 Mass. 577, 579, 592 (2006).

NOTE 17e   Melanie's Law. "Melanie's Law has authorized a variety of types of evidence that will constitute prima facie evidence. It permits the Commonwealth to use prior convictions alone or various criminal justice records to prove the prior offenses. The statement that no live witness testimony is required codifies prior law, and is thus not superfluous." *Commonwealth v. Bowden*, 447 Mass. 593, 601 (2006).

NOTE 17f The application of Melanie's Law (2005 Mass. Acts c. 122, § 6A, amending G.L. c. 90, § 24) to cases now pending does not violate the ex post facto, due process, or confrontation clauses of the federal or state Constitutions. *Commonwealth v. Maloney*, 447 Mass. 577, 579, 592 (2006).

NOTE 18   Lost/Ill Motorists. Police stopped to assist a motorist thought to be ill. Held, OUI conviction upheld. *Commonwealth v. Leonard*, 422 Mass. 504 (1996). Police stopped to assist lost motorist. Held, OUI conviction reversed. *Commonwealth v. Canavan*, 40 Mass. App. Ct. 642 (1996).

NOTE 19   Admissibility of hospital records. Admissibility of hospital records showing defendant's blood alcohol content as determined by a test performed as a routine medical practice in the course of treatment is *not* barred by confidentiality and privacy rights of the defendant. Judge has discretion to admit/not admit. *Commonwealth v. Dube*, 413 Mass. 570 (1992).

NOTE 20   Copy of Original Attestation of Court Papers. "The requirement that the responsible official be the one to attest to the authenticity of a copy is not some minor technicality." *Commonwealth v. Deramo*, 436 Mass. 40, 48 (2002) (further noting that "[w]here, as here, the parties and the judge have themselves compared an authenticated record with a copy, the copy may be admitted to the extent that it is identical to the authenticated document").

NOTE 21   Chain of Custody. "The defendant's objection that the Commonwealth did not adequately show the custody of the two vials [of blood] goes to the weight of the evidence of test results, not to their admissibility." *Commonwealth v. Howe*, 405 Mass. 332, 335 (1989).

NOTE 22   Closing Argument. "The defendant objected to the prosecutor's closing argument to the jury that the existence of a blood alcohol content of 0.18% was 'completely inconsistent' with

the defendant's testimony that he had only three twelve-ounce cups of 'lite' beer at the race track."

Held, "[a]lthough there was no expert testimony concerning the effect on blood alcohol content of the consumption of three twelve-ounce beers in the circumstances of this case, the prosecutor's argument was proper. The inference that, because of the results of his blood alcohol tests, the defendant had more than three twelve-ounce cups of beer was one that the prosecutor was warranted in asking the jury to draw."

Commonwealth v. Howe, 405 Mass. 332, 335–36 (1989) (footnote omitted).

NOTE 23   Stay of License Revocation Pending Appeal. "[A] judge in his discretion may stay a license revocation pending appeal." *Commonwealth v. Yameen*, 401 Mass. 331, 334–35 (1987) (citation omitted).

NOTE 24   Restitution. "The Commonwealth does not take issue with the order of restitution which, in its view, was supported by the record. *See Commonwealth v. McIntyre*, 436 Mass. 829, 831–836 (2002) (discussing proper scope of restitution imposed as condition of probation); *Commonwealth v. Casanova*, 65 Mass. App. Ct. 750, 754–755 n.7 (2006) (stating that lost tuition 'would appear to fall within the ambit of available restitution on proper proof of causal connection'). The single justice concluded that the 'order of restitution was properly calibrated to the losses incurred by [the victim],' as required by *Commonwealth v. Rotonda*, 434 Mass. 211, 221 (2001)." *Commonwealth v. McCulloch*, 450 Mass. 483, 485 n.3 (2008).

SECTION 24½

Ignition interlock device license restriction; revocation of license for failure to install or maintain device; revocation of license for attempt to operate motor vehicle with elevated blood alcohol level

No person whose license has been suspended in the commonwealth or any other jurisdiction by reason of: an assignment to an alcohol or controlled substance education, treatment or rehabilitation program; or a conviction for violating paragraph (a) of subdivision (1) of section 24, subsection (a) of section 24G, operating a motor vehicle with a percentage by weight of blood alcohol of eight one-hundredths or greater, or while under the influence of intoxicating liquor in violation of subsection (b) of said section 24G, section 24L, section 13½ of chapter 265, subsection (a) of section 8 of chapter 90B, section 8A or 8B of chapter 90B or, in the case of another jurisdiction, for any like offense, shall be issued a new license or right to operate or have his license or right to operate restored if he has previously been so assigned or convicted, unless a certified ignition interlock device has been installed on each vehicle owned, each vehicle leased and each vehicle operated by that person as a precondition to the issuance of a new license or right to operate or the restoration of such person's license or right to operate. A certified ignition interlock device shall be installed on all vehicles owned, leased and operated by the licensee for a period of 2 years and person restricted by a certified ignition interlock device shall have such device inspected, maintained and monitored in accordance with such regulations as the registrar shall promulgate. The registrar may, after hearing, revoke for an extended period or for life, the license of whoever removes such device or fails to have it inspected, maintained or monitored on at least 2 occasions during the period of the restricted license or right to operate if the licensee has operated or attempted to operate a vehicle with a blood alcohol level that caused the certified ignition interlock device to prohibit a vehicle from starting on at least 2 occasions or that recorded a blood alcohol level in excess of .02 on at least 2 occasions. A person aggrieved by a decision of the registrar pursuant to this section may file an appeal in the superior court of the trial court department. If the court determines that the registrar abused his discretion, the court may vacate the suspension or revocation of a license or right to operate or reduce the period of suspension or revocation as ordered by the registrar.

SECTION 24A
Use of motor vehicles in commission of felony, larceny or other crimes

If a motor vehicle is used in connection with the commission of a felony, of any larceny, or of any offence punishable under any provision of sections twenty-two, one hundred and thirteen to one hundred and seventeen, inclusive, and one hundred and twenty of chapter two hundred and sixty-six, or section thirteen of chapter two hundred and sixty-nine, of which a person is convicted, the material facts relative to such use, including the registration number of the vehicle, so far as disclosed in the proceedings, shall be reported forthwith to the registrar by the clerk of the court in which the conviction occurs.

SECTION 24B
Stealing, forging or other falsification of learner's permit, operator's license, disability placard, certificate of registration or inspection sticker; use or possession; penalties; suspension and reinstatement of license or right to operate motor vehicle
(Amended by 2012 Mass. Acts c. 139, § 101, effective July 1, 2012.)

Whoever falsely makes, steals, alters, forges or counterfeits or procures or assists another to falsely make, steal, alter, forge or counterfeit a learner's permit, a license to operate motor vehicles, an identification card issued under section eight E, a special parking identification disability placard, a certificate of registration of a motor vehicle or trailer, or an inspection sticker, or whoever forges or without authority uses the signature, facsimile of the signature, or validating signature stamp of the registrar or deputy registrar upon a genuine, stolen or falsely made, altered, forged or counterfeited learner's permit, license to operate motor vehicles, certificate of registration of a motor vehicle or trailer or inspection sticker, or whoever has in his possession, or utters, publishes as true or in any way makes use of a falsely made, stolen, altered, forged or counterfeited learner's permit, license to operate motor vehicles, an identification card issued under section eight E, a special parking identification disability placard, certificate of registration of a motor vehicle or trailer or inspection sticker, and whoever has in his possession, or utters, publishes as true, or in any way makes use of a falsely made, stolen, altered, forged or counterfeited signature, facsimile of the signature or validating signature stamp of the registrar or deputy registrar, shall be punished by a fine of not more than five hundred dollars or by imprisonment in the state prison for not more than five years or in jail or house of correction for not more than two years.

Whoever falsely makes, steals, forges or counterfeits a learner's permit, a license to operate motor vehicles or an identification card issued under section 8E with the intent to distribute such learner's permit, license to operate motor vehicles or identification card shall be punished as follows: (i) for acts involving any combination of 5 or fewer learner's permits, licenses to operate or identification cards, by a fine of not more than $500 or by imprisonment in the house of correction for not more than 1 year, or both such fine and imprisonment; (ii) for acts involving 6 to 10 such documents, by a fine of not more than $1,000 or by imprisonment in the state prison for not more than 5 years or in the house of correction for not more than 2 1/2 years, or both such fine and imprisonment; (iii) for acts involving more than 10 such documents, by a fine of not more than $10,000 or by imprisonment in the state prison for not more than 10 years, or both such fine and imprisonment.

Whoever falsely impersonates the person named in an application for a license or learner's permit to operate motor vehicles, or procures or assists another to falsely impersonate the person named in such an application whether of himself or of another, or uses a name other than his own to falsely obtain such a license or whoever has in his possession, or utters, publishes as true, or in any way makes use of a license or learner's permit to operate motor vehicles that was obtained in such a manner shall be punished by a fine of not more than five hundred dollars or by imprisonment in the state prison for not more than five years or in a jail or house of correction for not more than two years.

A conviction of a violation of this section shall be reported forthwith by the court or magistrate to the registrar who shall suspend immediately the license or right to operate of the person so convicted, and no appeal, motion for new trial or exceptions shall operate to stay the suspension of the license or right to operate. The registrar after having suspended the license or right to operate in accordance with this paragraph shall not terminate such suspension nor reinstate the right to operate to such person until one year after the date of suspension following said conviction; provided, however, that if the prosecution against such person has terminated in his favor, the registrar shall forthwith reinstate his license or right to operate.

SECTION 24D
Probation of persons convicted of driving under the influence; driver alcohol education program; alcohol treatment and rehabilitation programs; fees; indigents; gifts and grants; report

Any person convicted of or charged with operating a motor vehicle with a percentage, by weight, of alcohol in their blood of eight one-hundredths or greater, or while under the influence of intoxicating liquor, controlled substance or the vapors of glue, may if such person consents, be placed on probation for not more than two years and shall, as a condition of probation, be assigned to a driver alcohol education program as provided herein and, if deemed necessary by the court, to an alcohol or controlled substance abuse treatment or rehabilitation program or to both, and such person's license or right to operate shall be suspended for a period of no less than forty-five nor more than ninety days; provided, however, that if such person was under the age of twenty-one when the offense was committed, the person's license or right to operate shall be suspended for two hundred and ten days, and such person shall be assigned to a program specifically designed by the department of public health for the education and treatment of drivers who operates[1] a motor vehicle after or while consuming alcohol, controlled substances or the vapors of glue, except for a person aged 17 to 21, inclusive, whose blood alcohol percentage, by weight, was not less than .20, in which case such person shall be assigned to a driver alcohol treatment and rehabilitation program known as the "14-day second offender in-home program". Such order of probation shall be in addition to any penalties imposed as provided in subparagraph (1) of paragraph (a) of subdivision (1) of section twenty-four and shall be in addition to any requirements imposed as a condition for any suspension of sentence. Said person shall cooperate in an investigation conducted by the probation staff of the court for supervision of cases of operating under the influence and operating with a blood alcohol percentage of eight one-hundredths or greater, or in such manner as the commissioner of probation shall determine. A defendant not otherwise prohibited by this section, upon conviction after a trial on the merits, shall be presumed to be an appropriate candidate for the above mentioned programs; provided, however, that a judge who deems that the defendant is not a suitable candidate for said programs shall make such findings in writing.

[¹ G.L. c. 111B, § 1 et seq.]

This section shall apply to any person who has never been convicted of operating a motor vehicle while under the influence of intoxicating liquor or assigned to an alcohol or controlled substance education, treatment or rehabilitation program because of a like offense by a court of the commonwealth or any other jurisdiction. This section shall also apply to any person convicted of or charged with operating a motor vehicle while under the influence of intoxicating liquor who has been convicted of such offense or assigned to an alcohol or controlled substance education, treatment or rehabilitation program because of a single like offense by a court of the commonwealth or any other jurisdiction 10 years or more before the date of the commission of the offense for which he is to be sentenced, once in his lifetime. If, after receiving a sentence for a second disposition pursuant to this paragraph, a person is convicted of an additional operating under the influence of intoxicating liquor all prior convictions or assignments to an alcohol or controlled substances program by a court of the commonwealth or any other jurisdiction shall be counted for purposes of sentencing under subdivision (1) of section 24.

This section shall not apply to any person who caused serious personal injury to or the death of another person during the events that gave rise to the complaint or indictment for operating under the influence of alcohol.

Upon each disposition under this section, the defendant will surrender any Massachusetts drivers license or permit in his possession to the probation department of that court. The probation department will dispose of the license, and the court shall report the disposition in the case in a manner as determined by the registrar. Notwithstanding the provisions of subparagraph (1) of paragraph (c) of subdivision (2) of section 24, subparagraph (1) of paragraph (f) of subdivision (1) of section 24, and section 24P, a defendant may immediately upon entering a program pursuant to this section apply to the registrar for consideration of a limited license for hardship purposes. The registrar, at his discretion, may issue such license under such terms and conditions as he may prescribe. Any such license shall be valid for an identical 12 hour period, 7 days a week. This provision shall also apply to any other suspensions due to the same incident that may be in effect pursuant to said subparagraph (1) of paragraph (c) of subdivision (2) of section 24, said subparagraph (1) of paragraph (f) of subdivision (1) of said section 24 and section 24P of this chapter. Nothing in this section shall be construed to authorize hardship eligibility if the person is suspended or revoked, or to be suspended or revoked, under any other statute not referenced in this section, or due to any other incident. Failure of the operator to complete his obligations to the program, or remain in compliance with court probation, shall be cause for immediate revocation of the hardship license. In these and all cases where a hardship license is sought by an operator, the probation office for the court where the offender is on probation will, upon request, furnish the registry with documentation verifying the person's status with probation.

Driver alcohol education programs utilized under the provisions of this section shall be established and administered by the department of public health in consultation with the registrar and the secretary of public safety. The department of public health may adopt rules and regulations to carry out its powers and duties to establish and administer driver alcohol education programs in the commonwealth. Any person who is qualified for a disposition under this section, and who at the time of disposition is legally domiciled out-of-state, or is a full-time student residing out-of-state, may at the discretion of the court, be assigned to an out-of-state driver alcohol education program. The out-of-state program must be licensed by the appropriate state authority in the jurisdiction where the person is legally domiciled or is a full-time student. If the out-of-state driver alcohol education program contains fewer treatment service hours than is required by the department of public health, additional service treatment hours must be obtained to achieve equivalence with the driver alcohol education program requirement of the commonwealth.

Alcohol or controlled substance abuse treatment, rehabilitation program or alcohol or controlled substance abuse treatment and rehabilitation programs utilized under the provisions of this section shall include any public or private outpatient clinic, hospital, employer or union-sponsored program, self-help group, or any other organization, facility, service or program which the department of public health has accepted as appropriate for the purposes of this section. The department of public health shall prepare and publish annually a list of all such accepted alcohol treatment, rehabilitation programs and alcohol treatment and rehabilitation programs in the commonwealth, shall make this list available upon request to members of the public, and shall from time to time furnish each court in the commonwealth, the registrar, and the secretary of public safety with a current copy of such list. The list shall also include the single state authority contacts for other states that operate driver alcohol education programs.

Each person placed in a program of driver alcohol or controlled substance abuse education and, if deemed necessary by the court, a program of alcohol or controlled substance abuse treatment, rehabilitation, or alcohol or controlled substance abuse treatment and rehabilitation pursuant to this section shall pay directly to such program a fee in an amount to be determined by the department of public health. The department of public health shall establish and may from time to time revise a schedule of uniform fees to be charged by such programs which shall not exceed the actual cost per client of running said programs after notice and a public hearing, provided that until such time as the department of public health establishes a schedule of such fees pursuant to this section the fee for such programs shall be two hundred dollars. The department of public health shall promulgate regulations relative to the methodology of setting such fees. No person may be excluded from said program for inability to pay the stated fee, provided that such person files an affidavit of indigency or inability to pay with the court within ten days of the date of disposition, that investigation by the probation officer confirms such indigency or establishes that the payment of such fee would cause a grave and serious hardship to such individual or to the family of such individual, and that the court enters a written finding thereof. In lieu of waiver of the entire amount of said fee, the court may direct such individual to make partial or installment payments of such fee when appropriate. Subject to appropriation, the department of public health shall reimburse each program for the costs of services provided to persons for whom payment of a fee has been waived on the grounds of indigency.

The state treasurer may accept for the commonwealth for the purpose of driver alcohol or controlled substance abuse education, treatment, or rehabilitation any gift or bequest of money or property and any grant, loan, service, payment of property from a governmental authority. Any such money received shall be deposited in the state treasury for expenditure by the department of public health subject to appropriation for the support of said driver alcohol or controlled substance abuse treatment or rehabilitation programs in accordance with the conditions of the gift, grant, or loan. Any federal legislation generating funds for driver alcohol or controlled substance abuse education or treatment or rehabilitation shall be used by the department of public health to the extent possible to support the purposes of this section.

An additional fee of two hundred and fifty dollars shall be paid to the chief probation officer of each court by each person placed in a program of driver alcohol or controlled substance abuse education pursuant to this section and all such fees shall be deposited with the state treasurer, subject to appropriation, for the support of programs operated by the secretary of public safety, the alcohol beverage control commission, and the department of public health for the investigation, enforcement, treatment and rehabilitation of those persons convicted of or charged with driving under the influence of intoxicating liquor or drugs.

No such fee shall be collected from any person who, after the filing of an affidavit of indigency or inability to pay with the court within ten days of disposition and investigation by the probation officer confirming such indigency or establishing that the payment of such fee would cause a grave and serious hardship to such individual or to the family thereof, is determined by the court to be indigent, provided that the court enters a written finding thereof. In lieu of waiver of the entire amount of said fee, the court may direct such individual to make partial or installment payments of such fee when appropriate. Failure to pay the fees required under this section shall, unless excused, constitute sufficient basis for a finding by the court at a hearing held pursuant to section twenty-four E that the person has failed to satisfactorily comply with the program.

The commissioner of probation shall report in writing at least once annually to the department of public health on the total number of persons who have received disposition hereunder and on the number of such persons who have been determined by the court to require alcohol or controlled substance abuse treatment or rehabilitation, or both. Said commissioner and the chief justices of the district courts and the Boston municipal court shall make further written report at least once annually to said department of public health on the resources available for alcohol or controlled substance abuse treatment or rehabilitation, or alcohol or controlled substance abuse treatment and rehabilitation, of alcohol-impaired or controlled substance abuse-impaired drivers, which report shall evaluate the existing resources and shall make recommendation as to additional necessary resources. Said department of public health shall take such reports into consideration in the development, implementation, and review of the state's alcoholism or controlled substance abuse plan and in the preparation of the division's annual budget in a manner consistent with the Alcoholism Treatment and Rehabilitation Law.[1]

[[1] G.L. c. 111B, § 1 et seq.]

When imposing a sentence pursuant to subparagraph (1) of paragraph (a) of section twenty-four or this section, the court may consider requiring the defendant, as a condition of probation, to serve a minimum of thirty hours in public service or in a community work project.

NOTE 1   "[T]he judge, pursuant to G.L. c. 90, § 24N, suspended the defendant's operator's license for ninety days or until earlier disposition of his case." The defendant was convicted and "in connection with sentence, [the judge] suspended the defendant's license for the minimum period of forty-five days (the maximum being ninety days), . . . The defendant asked the judge to exercise discretion and 'relate back' the forty-five days to the earlier ninety-day suspension, thus reducing the current suspension to zero, but the judge held that he had no such discretion under § 24D. . . . We agree with the judge." *Commonwealth v. Callen*, 26 Mass. App. Ct. 920, 921 (1988) (rescript).

NOTE 2   Loss of License for Second Offender Who Qualifies for 24D Disposition. "Absent language resolving the ambiguity between § 24 and § 24D, second offenders who qualify for a disposition under § 24D should be treated no differently from first offenders. Limiting their loss of license to a maximum of ninety days comports with the plain wording of § 24D, as amended, as well as that section's historical purpose of providing an incentive to persons who 'have a potential for rehabilitation' to opt for probation and alcohol treatment. At the same time, our holding leaves intact the dispositional provisions of § 24 for first and second offenders to whom a § 24D disposition would not apply." *Commonwealth v. Cahill*, 442 Mass. 127, 134, (2004) (applying forty-five to ninety day suspension under 24D instead of two year suspension under 24(1)(b) and (1)(c)(2)) (citation omitted).

SECTION 24E
Dismissal of charges upon compliance with terms of probation; records; reports

The provisions of and this section shall apply to any person convicted of or charged with operating a motor vehicle while with a percentage, by weight, of alcohol in their blood of eight one-hundredths or greater or under the influence of intoxicating liquor provided said person is qualified for a disposition under section twenty-four D. The provisions of this section shall not apply where notice from the registrar of intention to suspend or revoke a person's license or right to operate is pending prior to the date of complaint on the offense before the court.

In order to qualify for a disposition under this section such person shall, in the judgment of the court, have cooperated fully with the investigation as described in section twenty-four D and shall be and have been in full compliance with such order as the court may have made for a one year term of probation as provided therein, including participation in such driver alcohol education programs, alcohol treatment or alcohol treatment and rehabilitation programs as the court may have ordered.

Nothing in this section shall be construed to prevent the exercise by a court of its authority under law to make any other disposition of a case of operating under the influence of intoxicating liquor.

Where a person has been charged with operating a motor vehicle under the influence of intoxicating liquor, and where the case has been continued without a finding and such person has been placed on probation with his consent and where such person is qualified for disposition under this section, a hearing shall be held by the court at any time after sixty days but not later than ninety days from the date where the case has been continued without a finding to review such person's compliance with the program ordered as a condition of probation and to determine whether dismissal of the charge is warranted.

At said hearing the probation officer shall submit to the courts a written report which shall include but shall not be limited to a written statement by the supervisor of any program of alcohol education and of any program of alcohol treatment and of any program of alcohol treatment, rehabilitation, or alcohol treatment and rehabilitation to which the court has assigned such person. Such statement shall consider such person's participation and attendance in each such court ordered program. The registrar shall submit a written report to the judge at said hearing regarding any entries made on said person's driving record in the period following placement in the program. If the court finds sufficient basis to conclude that said person has not satisfactorily completed or is not satisfactorily complying with such program, the court may notify the registrar and the registrar shall revoke the person's license or right to operate forthwith. If the judge finds that the person is satisfactorily complying with the conditions of probation, the judge may enter a dismissal of the charges and issue appropriate orders relative to said person's participation in a program or relative to a later hearing, subject to the duration of the term of probation. The court shall cause to be entered and to be maintained upon the probation record of said person notice of a dismissal of charges under this section. The probation officer supervision a person pursuant to the provisions of this section shall make a written report to the court if at any time such person has failed to satisfactorily comply with a court ordered program or if such person's operation of a motor vehicle constitutes a threat to the public safety. Upon receipt of such report the court shall forthwith hold a hearing on the matter. If at such hearing the court determines that said person has failed to satisfactorily comply with such program or that the said operation of a motor vehicle constitutes such a threat, the court may notify the registrar and the registrar shall with further hearing revoke said person's license or right to operate. Such revocation shall be for the remainder of the period from the date of conviction provided in subparagraph (1) of paragraph (c) of subdivision (1) of section twenty-four. Said person shall thereafter be subject to the same conditions for issuance of a new license or right to operate as any person applying for a new license or right to operate following revocation as provided in subparagraph (1) of paragraph (c) of said subdivision (1).

Where an order of probation has been revoked by the court, the court shall forthwith so notify the registrar in writing and the registrar shall forthwith revoke said person's operator's license or right to operate which was restored under this section and without further hearing.

SECTION 24F
Civil liability to owner for unauthorized use of motor vehicle

Persons convicted of using a motor vehicle without authority under the provisions of paragraph (a) of subdivision (2) of section twenty-four shall be liable in a civil action to the owner of such vehicle, if it is recovered, for all towing and storage charges necessitated and all property damage caused to said vehicle by such use without authority.

SECTION 24G
Homicide by motor vehicle; punishment

(a) Whoever, upon any way or in any place to which the public has a right of access, or upon any way or in any place to which members of the public have access as invitees or licensees, operates a motor vehicle with a percentage, by weight, of alcohol in their blood of eight one-hundredths or greater or, while under the influence of intoxicating liquor, or of marihuana, narcotic drugs, depressants, or stimulant substances, all as defined in section one of chapter ninety-four C, or the vapors of glue, and so operates a motor vehicle recklessly or negligently so that the lives or safety of the public might be endangered, and by any such operation so described causes the death of another person, shall be guilty of homicide by a motor vehicle while under the influences of an intoxicating substance, and shall be punished by imprisonment in the state prison for not less than two and one-half years or more than fifteen years and a fine of not more than five thousand dollars, or by imprisonment in a jail or house of correction for not less than one year nor more than two and one-half years and a fine of not more than five thousand dollars. The sentence imposed upon such person shall not be reduced to less than one year, nor suspended, nor shall any person convicted under this subsection be eligible for probation, parole, or furlough or receive any deduction from his sentence until such person has served at least one year of such sentence; provided, however, that the commissioner of correction may, on the recommendation of the warden, superintendent, or other person in charge of a correctional institution, or the administrator of a county correctional institution, grant to an offender committed under this subsection a temporary release in the custody of an officer of such institution for the following purposes only: to attend the funeral of a relative; to visit a critically ill relative; to obtain emergency medical or psychiatric services unavailable at said institution; or to engage in employment pursuant to the work release program. Prosecutions commenced under this section shall neither be continued without a finding nor placed on file.

The provisions of section eighty-seven of chapter two hundred and seventy-six, shall not apply to any person charged with a violation of this subsection.

(b) Whoever, upon any way or in any place to which the public has a right of access or upon any way or in any place to which members of the public have access as invitees or licensees, operates a motor vehicle with a percentage, by weight, of alcohol in their blood of eight one-hundredths or greater or, while under the influence of intoxicating liquor, or of marihuana, narcotic drugs, depressants or stimulant substances, all as defined in section one of chapter ninety-four C, or the vapors of glue, or whoever operates a motor vehicle recklessly or negligently so that the lives or safety of the public might be endangered and by any such operation causes the death of another person, shall be guilty of homicide by a motor vehicle and shall be punished by imprisonment in a jail or house of correction for not less than thirty days nor more than two and one-half years, or by a fine of not less than three hundred nor more than three thousand dollars, or both.

(c) The registrar shall revoke the license or right to operate of a person convicted of a violation of subsection (a) or (b) for a period of fifteen years after the date of conviction for a first offense. The registrar shall revoke the license or right to operate of a person convicted for a subsequent violation of this section for the life of such person. No appeal, motion for a new trial or exceptions shall operate to stay the revocation of the license or of the right to operate; provided, however, such license shall be restored or such right to operate shall be reinstated if the prosecution of such person ultimately terminates in favor of the defendant.

NOTE 1   Model Jury Instructions on Homicide. The Supreme Judicial Court has adopted revised Model Jury Instructions on Homicide (approved Mar. 21, 2013). The instructions are available at http://www.mass.gov/courts/docs/sjc/docs/model-jury-instructions-homicide.pdf and in *Massachusetts Superior Court Criminal Model Jury Instructions* (MCLE, Inc. 2nd ed. 2013).

NOTE 2a   Accident. "The elements necessary to find criminal culpability for vehicular homicide . . . are: '(1) operation of a motor vehicle, (2) upon a public way, (3) recklessly or negligently so as to endanger human life or safety, (4) thereby causing the death of a person.' *Commonwealth v. Angelo Todesca Corp.*, 446 Mass. 128, 137 (2006). There is no requirement in the trial of a motor vehicle homicide indictment that the Commonwealth prove that the defendant intentionally caused the deaths of the victims. Because the defendant's intent is not an essential element of the crime of motor vehicle homicide, the defense of accident is not available. *See Commonwealth v. Figueroa*, 56 Mass. App. Ct. 641, 648 (2002) (accident is only exculpatory if the crime requires proof that the consequences were intended)." *Commonwealth v. Doyle*, 73 Mass. App. Ct. 304, 309 (2008).

NOTE 2b   "'The mere happening of an accident between a motor vehicle and a pedestrian, where the circumstances immediately preceding it are left to conjecture, is not sufficient to prove negligence on the part of the operator of the vehicle.' *Callahan v. Lach*, 338 Mass. 233, 235 (1958)." *Aucella v. Commonwealth*, 406 Mass. 415, 418 (1990).

NOTE 3a   "Although we decline to hold that vehicular homicide is a lesser-included crime of manslaughter, we nonetheless conclude that in the present situation, which in fact did involve operation of a motor vehicle on a public way, the two offenses are sufficiently closely related so as to preclude punishment on both." *Commonwealth v. Jones*, 382 Mass. 387, 394 (1981).

**NOTE 3b   **Defendant found guilty of vehicular homicide, driving under the influence, and driving to endanger. "As we read the *Jones* case . . . we are of the opinion that the reasoning of the decision requires the dismissal of both the lesser included charges [operating under the influence and driving to endanger] where there has been a conviction under § 24G arising from a single accident and where [the defendant] had been found guilty of each of the statutory included offenses." *Commonwealth v. Atencio*, 12 Mass. App. Ct. 747, 753 (1981).

**NOTE 4   **Vehicular homicide stands as a middle ground between driving to endanger and manslaughter. *Commonwealth v. Jones*, 382 Mass. 387, 389 (1981).

NOTE 5   Lesser included offense. "As all of the elements of felony motor vehicle homicide are included within the elements of OUI manslaughter [G.L. c. 265, § 13½], it is a lesser included offense." *Commonwealth v. Guaman*, 90 Mass. App. Ct. 36, 47 (2016).

**NOTE 6   **"A finding of ordinary negligence suffices to establish a violation of sec. 24G. . . . [T]he proper standard of causation for this offense is the standard of proximate cause enunciated in the law of torts." *Commonwealth v. Berggren*, 398 Mass. 338, 340, 342 (1986).

**NOTE 7   **"[The defendant] filed a motion to dismiss, alleging that the mandatory sentencing provisions of sec. 24G(a) violate Federal and State provisions against cruel and unusual punishment, violate his rights to due process, and offend the doctrine of separation of powers under art. 30 of the Massachusetts Declaration of Rights." The Supreme Judicial Court disagreed. *Commonwealth v. Therriault*, 401 Mass. 237 (1987).

NOTE 8   Search and Seizure. "[T]here can be no reasonable expectation of privacy in the equipment and safety features of an involved vehicle in the rightful possession of the police. We conclude that the defendant did not have an objectively reasonable expectation of privacy in the brakes of his truck after the truck was involved in the fatal accident and was removed from the highway by the police. We therefore conclude also that Sergeant Streeter's examination and testing of the brakes, even though conducted after the defendant's request that his vehicle be returned to him, was not a search within the meaning of the Fourth Amendment." *Commonwealth v. Mamacos*, 409 Mass. 635, 640 (1991).

NOTE 9   Registry Revocation/Under Age 21 or 18. General Laws c. 90, § 24P should be referred to for license suspensions for defendants under the ages of 21 and 18 who either (1) fail or refuse to take a breathalyzer or blood test or (2) are convicted under this section (G.L. c. 90, § 24G).

NOTE 10   CWOF inapplicable. A continuance without a finding is not a sentencing option for one charged under this section, whether dealing with subsection (a) (felony) or subsection (b) (misdemeanor). *Commonwealth v. Millican*, 449 Mass. 298 (2007).

SECTION 24H
Removal of abandoned or stolen vehicles from public places; towing vehicles; machines that crush, mutilate or destroy vehicles; salvage or junk yard owners or agents

No person shall remove an abandoned or stolen motor vehicle on a public way or in any place to which the public has right of access without the express consent of the owner of such vehicle or without the written permission of the police department. The owner or operator of a motor vehicle that is designed to carry or tow another vehicle shall be licensed for that specific purpose or as a towing service.

The owner of any machine that is designed to crush, mutilate or destroy a motor vehicle, whether the machine be mobile or affixed permanently, shall have that machine listed with the registry of motor vehicles.

If the owner or agent of a salvage or junk yard transports crushed or mutilated vehicles without the commonwealth for purposes of resale, the operator of the transporting vehicle shall carry a list of the vehicles being transported, and a copy of such list shall be forwarded to said registrar.

Any person convicted of violation of any provision of this section shall forfeit any license issued which is related to such violation and shall be punished by a fine of not less than one thousand dollars or by imprisonment for not less than two years, or both.

SECTION 24I
Possession of alcoholic beverages in motor vehicles

(a) As used in this section, the following words shall have the following meanings:

"Open container," a bottle, can or other receptacle used to contain a liquid that has been opened or has a broken seal or the contents of which have been partially removed or consumed; provided, however, that a bottle resealed pursuant to section 12 of chapter 138 shall not be considered an open container; provided further, that a resealed bottle shall not be transported in the passenger area.

"Passenger area," the area designed to seat the driver and passengers while the motor vehicle is in operation and any area that is readily accessible to the driver or a passenger while in a seated position including, but not limited to, the glove compartment; provided, however, that the passenger area shall not include a motor vehicle's trunk or a locked glove compartment or, if a motor vehicle is not equipped with a trunk, the area behind the last upright seat or an area not normally occupied by the driver or passenger.

(b) Whoever, upon any way or in any place to which the public has a right of access, or upon any way or in any place to which members of the public have access as invitees or licensees, possesses an open container of alcoholic beverage in the passenger area of any motor vehicle shall be punished by a fine of not less than $100 nor more than $500.

(c) This section shall not apply to (1) the passengers of a motor vehicle designed, maintained and used for the transportation of persons for compensation, or (2) the living quarters of a house coach or house trailer.

(d) Notwithstanding this section, the driver of any motor vehicle, including but not limited to a house coach or house trailer, shall not possess an open container of alcoholic beverage.

NOTE   **Registry Revocation/Under Age 21 or 18.** General Laws c. 90, § 24P should be referred to for license suspensions for defendants under the ages of 21 and 18 who are convicted under this section (G.L. c. 90, § 24I).

SECTION 24J
Inquiry of defendant convicted of driving under influence of intoxicating liquors as to establishment serving alcohol

In every case of a conviction of or a plea of guilty to a violation of subdivision (1) of section twenty-four involving operating a motor vehicle with a percentage, by weight, of alcohol in their blood of eight one-hundredths or greater or, under the influence of intoxicating liquor, or a disposition under section twenty-four D, the court shall inquire of the defendant, before sentencing, regarding whether he was served alcohol prior to his violation of said section at an establishment licensed to serve alcohol on the premises and the name and location of said establishment.

Any information so acquired by the court shall be transmitted by the clerk's office to the alcohol beverage control commission, the office of the attorney general, the office of the district attorney for the district in which the establishment is located, and such establishment.

SECTION 24K
Chemical breath analysis; validity; testing procedures; report forms

Chemical analysis of the breath of a person charged with a violation of this chapter shall not be considered valid under the provisions of this chapter, unless such analysis has been performed by a certified operator, using infrared breath-testing devices according to methods approved by the secretary of public safety. The secretary of public safety shall promulgate rules and regulations regarding satisfactory methods, techniques and criteria for the conduct of such tests, and shall establish a statewide training and certification program for all operators of such devices and a periodic certification program for such breath testing devices; provided, however, that the secretary may terminate or revoke such certification at his discretion.

Said regulations shall include, but shall not be limited to the following: (a) that the chemical analysis of the breath of a person charged be performed by a certified operator using a certified infrared breath-testing device in the following sequence: (1) one adequate breath sample analysis; (2) one calibration standard analysis; (3) a second adequate breath sample analysis; (b) that no person shall perform such a test unless certified by the secretary of public safety; (c) that no breath-testing device mouthpiece or tube shall be cleaned with any substance containing alcohol.

The secretary of public safety shall prescribe a uniform form for reports of such chemical analysis to be used by law enforcement officers and others acting in accordance with the provisions of this chapter. Such forms shall be sequentially numbered. Each chief of police or other officer or official having charge or control of a law enforcement agency shall be responsible for the furnishing and proper disposition of such uniform forms. Each party so responsible shall prepare or cause to be prepared such records and reports relating to such uniform forms and their disposition in such manner and at such times as the secretary of public safety shall prescribe.

NOTE   "The regulations promulgated pursuant to G.L. c. 90, § 24K, establish an office of alcohol testing (OAT) within the State police crime laboratory. 501 Code Mass. Regs. § 2.10. The OAT is charged with maintaining a list of approved breathalyzer machines, subject to several enumerated criteria. 501 Code Mass. Regs. § 2.38. In order to effectuate the requirement that all breathalyzer tests are conducted on certified devices, the regulations provide that OAT must annually certify that any breathalyzer machine in use is compliant with certain regulatory criteria. 501 Code Mass. Regs. §§ 2.39 and 2.40. . . .

"[W]e conclude that the OAT certification records are nontestimonial, and their admission without the live testimony of the technician who prepared them did not violate the confrontation clause of the Sixth Amendment." *Commonwealth v. Zeininger*, 459 Mass. 775, 779, 788–89 (2011) (footnotes omitted).

SECTION 24L
Serious bodily injury by motor vehicle while under influence of intoxicating substance; penalties

(1) Whoever, upon any way or in any place to which the public has a right of access, or upon any way or in any place to which members of the public have access as invitees or licensees, operates a motor vehicle with a percentage, by weight, of alcohol in their blood of eight one-hundredths or greater or, while under the influence of intoxicating liquor, or marihuana, narcotic drugs, depressants, or stimulant substances, all as defined in section one of chapter ninety-four C, or the vapors of glue, and so operates a motor vehicle recklessly or negligently so that the lives or safety of the public might be endangered, and by any such operation so described causes serious bodily injury, shall be punished by imprisonment in the state prison for not less than two and one-half years nor more than ten years and by a fine of not more than five thousand dollars, or by imprisonment in a jail or house or correction for not less than six months nor more than two and one-half years and by a fine of not more than five thousand dollars.

The sentence imposed upon such person shall not be reduced to less than six months, nor suspended, nor shall any person convicted under this subsection be eligible for probation, parole, or furlough or receive any deduction from his sentence until such person has served at least six months of such sentence; provided, however, that the commissioner of correction may, on the recommendation of the warden, superintendent, or other person in charge of a correctional institution, or of the administrator of a county correctional institution, grant to an offender committed under this subsection a temporary release in the custody of an officer of such institution for the following purposes only: to attend the funeral of a relative; to visit a critically ill relative; to obtain emergency medical or psychiatric services unavailable at said institution; or to engage in employment pursuant to a work release program. Prosecutions commenced under this subdivision shall neither be continued without a finding nor placed on file.

The provisions of section eighty-seven of chapter two hundred and seventy-six shall not apply to any person charged with a violation of this subdivision.

(2) Whoever, upon any way or in any place to which the public has a right of access or upon any way or in any place to which members of the public have access as invitees or licensees, operates a motor vehicle with a percentage, by weight, of alcohol in their blood of eight one-hundredths or greater or, while under the influence of intoxicating liquor, or of marihuana, narcotic drugs, depressants or stimulant substances, all as defined in section one of chapter ninety-four C, or vapors of glue, and by any such operation causes serious bodily injury, shall be punished by imprisonment in a jail or house of correction for not more than two and one-half years, or by a fine of not less than three thousand dollars, or both.

(3) For the purposes of this section "serious bodily injury" shall mean bodily injury which creates a substantial risk of death or which involves either total disability or the loss or substantial impairment of some bodily function for a substantial period of time.

(4) The registrar shall revoke the license or right to operate of a person convicted of a violation of subdivision (1) or (2) for a period of two years after the date of conviction. No appeal, motion for a new trial or exception shall operate to stay the revocation of the license or the right to operate; provided, however, such license shall be restored or such right to operate shall be reinstated if the prosecution of such person ultimately terminates in favor of the defendant.

NOTE   **Registry Revocation/Under Age 21 or 18.** General Laws c. 90, § 24P should be referred to for license suspensions for defendants under the ages of 21 and 18 who either (1) fail or refuse to take a breathalyzer or blood test or (2) are convicted under this section.

SECTION 24M
Training for law enforcement personnel regarding alcohol related offenses; alcohol sensitive selective traffic enforcement program
(Amended by 2011 Mass. Acts c. 93, § 16, effective July 1, 2012.)

The officials and agencies designated in this section are hereby directed to perform the duties specified in this section and any other action within their authority in order to ensure effective enforcement of sections twenty-four to twenty-four O, inclusive.

(1) The municipal police training committee established in section one hundred and sixteen of chapter six shall provide training, including but not limited to alcohol education and education concerning the aforesaid sections, to all law enforcement personnel throughout the commonwealth.

(2) The chief justice of the trial court department shall provide training, including but not limited to alcohol education and education concerning the aforesaid sections, to all appropriate court personnel throughout the commonwealth, including, but not limited to, judges, district attorneys and probation officers.

(3) The courts of the commonwealth shall give priority to the speedy and effective disposition of all matters arising under the aforesaid sections.

(4) The executive office of public safety shall establish and implement an alcohol sensitive selective traffic enforcement program.

SECTION 24N
Suspension of operator's license upon issuance of complaint; hearing
Upon the issuance of a complaint alleging a violation of paragraph (a) of subdivision (1) of section 24 or a violation of section 24G or 24L of this chapter, or a violation of paragraph (1) of subsection (a) of section eight, or a violation of section 8A or section 8B of chapter 90B, the judge, in addition to any other terms of bail or recognizance, shall, upon the failure of any police officer to suspend or take custody of the drivers license or permit issued by the commonwealth of any such defendant under paragraph (f) of subdivision (1) of section 24, immediately suspend the defendant's license or right to operate a motor vehicle or vessel in the following instances: (i) if the prosecutor makes a prima facie showing at the arraignment that said defendant was operating a motor vehicle while the percentage, by weight, of alcohol in his blood was eight one-hundredths or more, or, relative to any defendant under the age of 21, while the percentage by weight, of alcohol in his blood was two one-hundredths or more, as shown by chemical test or analysis of his blood or breath, and presents written certification of oral testimony from the person administering to the defendant such chemical test or analysis of his blood or breath that the defendant was administered such a test or analysis, that the operator administering the test or analysis of his blood or breath was trained and certified in the administration of such tests, that the test was performed in accordance with regulations and standards promulgated by the secretary of public safety, that the equipment used for such test was regularly serviced and maintained, and that the person administering the test had every reason to believe the equipment was functioning properly at the time the test was administered. Such certification shall be prima facie evidence of the facts so certified. Upon such a showing and presentation, the judge shall take immediate physical possession of such defendant's license or permit issued by the commonwealth to operate a motor vehicle, and shall direct the prosecuting officer to forthwith notify the department of criminal justice information services and the registrar of such suspension by the most expeditious means available. The defendant's license or permit to operate a motor vehicle shall remain suspended until the disposition of the offense for which said defendant is being prosecuted, but in no event shall such suspension pursuant to this section exceed 30 days; or (ii) if the

prosecutor makes a prima facie showing at arraignment that said defendant was arrested on the charge of driving a motor vehicle on any such way or place while under the influence of intoxicating liquor, and said defendant refused to submit to a chemical test or analysis of his breath or blood. Upon such a showing and presentation, the judge shall take immediate physical possession of such defendant's license or permit issued by the commonwealth to operate a motor vehicle, and shall direct the prosecuting officer to forthwith notify the department of criminal justice information services and the registrar of such suspension by the most expeditious means available. The defendant's license or permit to operate a motor vehicle shall remain suspended for a period of 180 days; provided, however, that any person who is under the age of 21 or who has been previously convicted of a violation under section 24 or a like violation by a court of any other jurisdiction shall have his license or right to operate suspended forthwith for a period of 1 year for such refusal; provided, further, that any person previously convicted 2 or more times of a violation under section 24 of a like violation by a court of any other jurisdiction shall have his license or right to operate suspended forthwith for a period of 18 months for such refusal. No license shall be restored under any circumstances and no restricted or hardship permits shall be issued during the suspension period imposed by this paragraph; provided, however, that the defendant may immediately, upon entry of a not guilty finding or dismissal of all charges under section 24, sections 24G and 24L, and in the absence of any other alcohol related charges pending against said defendant, apply for and be granted a hearing forthwith before the court which shall have entered said finding for the purpose of requesting the restoration of said license. At said hearing, there shall be a rebuttable presumption that said license be restored, unless the commonwealth shall establish, by a fair preponderance of the evidence that restoration of said license would likely endanger the public safety. In all such instances, the court shall issue written findings of fact with its decision.

Any person whose license or right to operate has been suspended pursuant to this section on the basis of chemical analysis of his breath may within ten days of such suspension request a hearing and upon such request shall be entitled to a hearing before the court in which the underlying charge is pending, which hearing shall be limited to the following issue: whether a blood test administered pursuant to paragraph (e) of subdivision (1) of section 24, within a reasonable period of time after such chemical analysis of his breath, shows that the percentage, by weight, of alcohol in such person's blood was less than eight one-hundredths, or, relative to such person under the age of 21 was less than two one-hundredths. If the court finds that such a blood test shows that such percentage was less than eight one-hundredths, or, relative to such person under the age of 21, that such percentage was less than two one-hundredths, the court shall restore such person's license or right to operate and shall direct the prosecuting officer to forthwith notify the department of criminal justice information services and the registrar of such restoration.

Any person whose right to operate has been suspended pursuant to this section on the basis of the failure of such person to submit to a chemical test or analysis of his breath or blood may within ten days of his suspension request a hearing and upon such request shall be entitled to a hearing before the court in which the underlying charges are pending, which

hearing shall be limited to the following issues: (1) did the police officer have reasonable grounds to believe that such person had been operating a motor vehicle while under the influence of intoxicating liquor upon any way or in any place to which members of the public have a right of access or upon any way to which members of the public have a right of access as invitees or licensees, (2) was such person placed under arrest, and (3) did such person refuse to submit to such test or analysis. If, after such hearing, the court finds on any one of the said issues in the negative, the court shall restore such person's license or right to operate and shall direct the prosecuting officer to forthwith notify the criminal history systems board and the registrar of such restoration.

NOTE   OUI. This section is constitutional. The questions reported to the Supreme Judicial Court in one case included:

"'1. Whether the provisions of Massachusetts General Laws, Chapter 90, Section 24N provide the Defendant with adequate procedural due process protection?

'2. Whether the provisions of Massachusetts General Laws, Chapter 90, Section 24N deny the defendant substantive due process right to the presumption of innocence?

'3. Whether the provisions of Massachusetts General Laws, Chapter 90, Section 24N in practice deny the defendant his substantive due process right to a trial by jury because of undue pressure imposed upon the defendant to dispose of his case without a trial for the sole purpose of regaining his driving privileges?

'4. Whether the defendant, if found guilty, is entitled to credit for the period of suspension pursuant to Chapter 90, Section 24N imposed on the defendant?

'5. Whether the defendant is entitled to a dismissal of his case where the police failed to inform the defendant that his license would be suspended for up to ninety (90) days if he submitted to a breathalizer exam and received a reading of .10 or above?

'6. Whether, in the context of question 5, in lieu of dismissal, the defendant is entitled to have the results of the breathalizer excluded from evidence?'

We answer question one 'yes,' and all the rest 'no.'"

Commonwealth v. Crowell, 403 Mass. 381, 382 n.2 (1988).

SECTION 24O
Statement to defendant regarding further violations

Upon conviction of any violation of the provisions of this chapter, the defendant shall be provided by the probation office in the court in which said conviction was entered a statement in writing prepared by the secretary of public safety of the statutory provisions that apply to any further violation of this chapter.

NOTE 1   Lack of written notice not a defense to enhanced penalties under G.L. c. 90, § 23. *Commonwealth v. Dowler*, 414 Mass. 212 (1993).

NOTE 2   Registry/Revocation of License. The defendant, a second offender, pleaded guilty to so much of the complaint as alleged a first offender and was given the G.L. c. 90, § 24O disposition, including a ninety-day license suspension.

"When the ninety-day suspension expired, the plaintiff sought to retrieve his license from the registrar of motor vehicles. The registrar refused, relying on G.L. c. 90, § 24 (1988 ed.), which provides for a two-year license revocation for those who have been convicted twice of O.U.I. within a six-year period. The plaintiff appealed to the defendant Board of Appeal on Motor Vehicle Liability Policies and Bonds (board), and a hearing was held. The board affirmed the registrar's decision."

The Supreme Judicial Court affirmed, stating that 24O was inapplicable "because the plaintiff had been convicted of a 'like offense' within six years.

"Instead, c. 90, § 24 (1)(c)(2) applies [instructing the Registrar to suspend the defendant's license for two years.]" *Daley v. Bd. of*

Appeal on Motor Vehicle Liab. Policies & Bonds, 406 Mass. 857, 858–59 (1990).

SECTION 24P
Minors; license suspension; education and treatment programs

(a) Upon evidence that a person under the age of 21, after having been arrested for or charged with a violation under section 24, 24G or 24L, had a blood alcohol percentage of two one-hundredths or greater or upon evidence that such person refused to submit to a chemical test or analysis of his breath or blood under section 24, notwithstanding the finding upon any such charge, such person shall have his license or permit to operate a motor vehicle suspended by the registrar for a period of 180 days; provided, however, that any such person who is less than 18 years of age at the time of such violation shall have his license suspended by the registrar for one year. Such suspension by the registrar shall be imposed in addition to any penalty, license suspension or revocation imposed upon such person by the court as required by said section 24, 24G or 24L.

If a person has not been previously arrested for or charged with a violation under said section 24, 24G or 24L, such person shall, if he consents, be assigned to a program specifically designed by the department of public health for the treatment of underage drinking drivers; provided, however, that such assignment shall not be precluded by a finding or disposition upon a charge against such person under said section 24, 24G or 24L. Upon entry into such program, as authorized by this section or as otherwise required under any disposition pursuant to section 24D, the suspension of a license or permit to operate as required by this section shall be waived by the registrar for a person under 21 years of age but over 18 years of age; provided, however, that such suspension shall be for a period of 180 days for such person who was under the age of 18 at the time of such violation. Upon the failure of a person under the age of 21 to successfully complete such program, the registrar shall forthwith suspend such license or permit to operate for 180 days; provided, however, that upon such failure to successfully complete such program by a person who was under the age of 18 at the time of such violation, the registrar shall forthwith suspend the license or permit to operate for one year.

(b) The license or permit to operate of a person convicted of any violation under section 24, 24G, 24I or 24L who was under the age of 18 at the time of such violation and whose license or permit to operate was not suspended under subsection (a) for such violation shall have such license or permit suspended for a period of 180 days for a first offense and for a period of one year for a second or subsequent offense.

SECTION 24Q
Alcohol or drug assessment as condition for certain sentences imposed under chapter

A mandatory condition of any sentence imposed for: (1) a conviction or an assignment to an alcohol or controlled substance education, treatment or rehabilitation program if evidence in the prosecution of a violation of this chapter or chapter 90B was that a person's blood alcohol percentage, by weight, was not less .20 or (2) an assignment to an alcohol or controlled substance education, treatment or rehabilitation program or a conviction for violating paragraph (a) of subdivision (1) of section 24, subsection (a) of section 24G, operating a motor vehicle with a percentage by weight of blood alcohol of eight one-hundredths or greater, or while under the influence of intoxicating liquor in violation of subsection (b) of said section 24G, section 24L, subsection (a) of section 8 of chapter 90B, section 8A or 8B of chapter 90B, or section 13½ of chapter 265 or, in the case of any other jurisdiction, for any like offense, if the person being sentenced has previously been so assigned or convicted of a like offense, shall be that such person complete an alcohol or drug assessment conducted by the department of public health or other court-approved program. The assessment shall include, but not be limited to, an assessment of the level of the offender's addiction to alcohol or drugs, and the department's recommended course of treatment. Such assessment and recommended course of treatment shall be reported to the offender's probation or parole officer. No person shall be excluded from an assessment for inability to pay if the offender files an affidavit of indigency or inability to pay with the court and an investigation by the probation or parole officer confirms such indigency or establishes that such payment would cause a grave and serious hardship to the offender or his family, and the court enters written findings relative thereto. The commissioner of public health may make such rules and regulations as are necessary or proper to carry out this section.

SECTION 24R
Revocation for life of license or right to operate

(a) Notwithstanding section 24 or section 24D, the registrar shall revoke for life the license or right to operate of a person assigned to an alcohol or controlled substance education, treatment, or rehabilitation program or convicted of a violation of subsection (a) of section 24G, operating a motor vehicle with a percentage by weight of blood alcohol of eight one-hundredths or greater, or while under the influence of intoxicating liquor in violation of subsection (b) of said section 24G, section 24L, section 8A or 8B of chapter 90B, or section 13½ of chapter 265 who has previously been convicted of a violation of subdivision (a) of section 24 or a like violation in another jurisdiction.

(b) Notwithstanding section 24, the registrar shall revoke for life the license or right to operate of any person convicted of a violation of subdivision (a) of section 24G who has previously been assigned to an alcohol or controlled substance education, treatment, or rehabilitation program by a court of the commonwealth, or convicted of violation of paragraph (a) of subdivision (1) of section 24, subsection (a) of section 24G, operating a motor vehicle with a percentage by weight of blood alcohol of eight one-hundredths or greater, or while under the influence of intoxicating liquor in violation of subsection (b) of said section 24G, section 24L, subsection (a) of section 8 of chapter 90B, or section 8A or 8B of chapter 90B, section 13½ of chapter 265 or a like violation in another jurisdiction.

SECTION 24S
Operation of motor vehicle on public way in violation of ignition interlock device license restriction; penalties

(a) Whoever, upon any way or place to which the public has a right of access, or upon any way or place to which members of the public have access as invitees or licensees, operates a motor vehicle that is not equipped with a certified functioning ignition interlock device while his license or right to operate has been restricted to operating only motor vehicles equipped with such device shall be punished by fine of not less than $1,000 nor more than $15,000 and by imprisonment for not less than 180 days nor more than 2½ years or by a fine of not less than $1,000 nor more than $15,000 and by imprisonment in the state prison for not less than 2½ years nor more than 5 years. The sentence imposed upon such person shall not be reduced to less than 150 days, nor suspended, nor shall any such person be eligible for probation, parole or furlough or receive any deduction from his sentence for good conduct until he shall have served 150 days of such sentence. The commissioner of correction may, on the recommendation of the warden, superintendent, or other person in charge of a correctional institution, or the administrator of a county correctional institution, grant to an offender committed under this subsection a temporary release in the custody of an officer of such institution for the following purposes only: to attend the funeral of a relative; to visit a critically ill relative; to obtain emergency medical or psychiatric services unavailable at that institution; to engage in employment pursuant to a work release program; or for the purposes of an aftercare program designed to support the recovery of an offender who has completed an alcohol or controlled substance education, treatment or rehabilitation program operated by the department of correction. The defendant may serve all or part of such 150-day sentence, to the extent such resources are available, in a correctional facility specifically designated by the department of correction for the incarceration and rehabilitation of drinking drivers.

(b) For the purposes of this section the term "certified ignition interlock device" shall mean an alcohol breath screening device that prevents a vehicle from starting if it detects a blood alcohol concentration over a preset limit of .02 or 20 mg of alcohol per 100 ml of blood.

SECTION 24T
Tampering with ignition interlock device; penalties

(a) Whoever interferes with or tampers with a certified ignition interlock device, with the intent to disable such device, shall be punished by imprisonment in the house of correction for not less than 6 months nor more than 2½ years or by imprisonment in the state prison for not less than 3 years nor more than 5 years.

(b) For the purposes of this section the term "certified ignition interlock device" shall mean an alcohol breath screening device that prevents a vehicle from starting if it detects a blood alcohol concentration over a preset limit of .02 or 20 mg of alcohol per 100 ml of blood.

SECTION 24U
Starting motor vehicle equipped with ignition interlock device for another person under a restricted license

(a)(1) Whoever knowingly breathes into a certified ignition interlock device as defined in section 24T or starts a motor vehicle equipped with such a device for the purpose of providing an operable motor vehicle to a person whose license or right to operate a vehicle is restricted to the operation of vehicles equipped with a certified ignition interlock device shall be punished by a fine not less than $1,000 nor more than $5,000 or imprisonment in a house of correction for not less than 6 months nor more than 2½ years in the house of correction and, for a second or subsequent conviction, by imprisonment in a state prison for not less than 3 nor more than 5 years.

(2) A certified copy of an acknowledgement of the existence and terms of certified ignition interlock device restriction, executed by a person alleged to have violated this section shall be admissible as evidence to prove the existence of such knowledge by the person who executed the document.

[There is no subsection (b).]

SECTION 24V
Child endangerment while operating a motor vehicle or vessel under the influence; penalties; suspension of license

(a) Whoever violates paragraph (a) of subdivision (1) of section 24, subsection (a) of section 24G, operating a motor vehicle with a percentage by weight of blood alcohol of eight one-hundredths or greater, or while under the influence of intoxicating liquor in violation of subsection (b) of said section 24G, section 24L, subsection (a) of section 8 of chapter 90B, or section 8A or 8B of chapter 90B, or section 13½ of chapter 265 with a child 14 years of age or younger in the motor vehicle or vessel shall also be guilty of child endangerment while operating a motor vehicle or vessel under the influence and shall be punished by an enhanced penalty of a fine of not less than $1,000 nor more than $5,000 and by imprisonment in the house of correction for not less than 90 days nor more than 2½ years. If a defendant has previously violated this subsection or a like offense in another jurisdiction preceding the date of the commission of the offense for which he has been convicted, he shall be punished by a fine of not less than $5,000 nor more than $10,000 and by imprisonment in the house of correction for not less than 6 months nor more than 2½ years or by imprisonment in state prison for not less than 3 years but not more than 5 years. The sentence of imprisonment imposed upon such person shall not be reduced to less than 6 months, nor suspended, nor shall any such person be eligible for probation, parole, or furlough or receive any deduction from his sentence for good conduct until he shall have served at least 6 months of such sentence but the commissioner of correction may, on the recommendation of the warden, superintendent or other person in charge of a correctional institution, or of the administrator of a county correctional institution, grant to an offender committed under this subsection a temporary release in the custody of an officer of such institution for the following purposes only: to attend the funeral of a relative; to visit a critically ill relative; to obtain emergency medical or psychiatric services unavailable at the institution; or to engage in employment pursuant to a work release program. A sentence imposed under this subsection shall be served consecutively to and not concurrently with the predicate violation of said paragraph (a) of subdivision (1) of section 24, subsection (a) of section 24G, subsection (b) of section 24G, section 24L, subsection (a) of section 8 of chapter 90B, or section 8A or 8B of chapter 90B, section 13½ of chapter 265. Section 87 of chapter 276 and sections 1 to 9, inclusive, of chapter 276A shall not apply to a person charged with a violation of this subsection. Prosecutions commenced under this subsection shall not be placed on file or continued without a finding.

(b) The registrar shall suspend the license or right to operate of person who violates this section for a period of 1 year for a first offense, and for a period of 3 years for a second or subsequent violation.

SECTION 24W
Forfeiture of motor vehicle owned by certain drunk driving offenders; procedure; Operating Under the Influence Deterrent Trust Fund

(a) A motor vehicle or vessel owned by a person who has been assigned to an alcohol or controlled substance education, treatment or rehabilitation program or who was convicted of a violation of paragraph (a) of subdivision (1) of section 24, subsection (a) of section 24G, operating a motor vehicle with a percentage by weight of blood alcohol of eight one-hundredths or greater, or while under the influence of intoxicating liquor in violation of subsection (b) of said section 24G, section 24L, subsection (a) of section 8 of chapter 90B, section 8A or 8B of chapter 90B, or section 13½ of chapter 265 or, in the case of another jurisdiction, for any like offense, if owned by such operator, may be forfeited to the commonwealth if such person has been so assigned or so convicted previously at least 3 times.

(b) A district attorney or the attorney general may petition the superior or district court in the name of the commonwealth in the nature of a proceeding in rem to order forfeiture of such motor vehicle or vessel. The petition shall be filed in the court having jurisdiction over the criminal proceeding brought under this section. The proceeding shall be deemed a civil suit in equity. In all such actions where the motor vehicle or vessel is jointly owned before the date of the second or subsequent operating under the influence offense committed by the defendant by either a parent, spouse, child, grandparent, brother, sister, or parent of the spouse living in the defendant's household, the commonwealth shall have the burden of proving to the court the existence of probable cause to institute the action, and the claimant shall have the burden of proving to the court's satisfaction that the property is not forfeitable because the claimant is dependent on the motor vehicle or vessel for his livelihood or the maintenance of his family. The court shall order the commonwealth to give notice by certified or registered mail to the owners of the motor vehicle or vessel and to such other persons or entities who appear to have an interest therein, and the court shall promptly, but not less than 2 weeks after notice, hold a hearing on the petition. Upon the motion of an owner of the motor vehicle or vessel, the court may continue the hearing on the petition pending the outcome of a criminal trial related to a charge of operating under the influence in violation of this chapter or chapter 90B. During the pendency of the proceedings, the court may issue at the request of the commonwealth ex parte any preliminary order or process as is necessary to seize or secure the property for which forfeiture is sought and to provide for its custody. Process for seizure of the property shall issue only upon a showing of probable cause, and the application therefore and the issuance, execution and return thereof shall be subject to chapter 276, as applicable.

(c) At a hearing under this section, the court shall hear evidence and make findings of fact and conclusions of law, and shall thereon issue a final order from which the parties shall have such right of appeal as from a decree in equity. No forfeiture under this section shall extinguish a perfected security interest held by a creditor in the property at the time of the filing of the forfeiture action. In all actions where a final order results in forfeiture, the final order shall provide for disposition of the property by the commonwealth or any sub-division thereof in any manner not prohibited by law, including official use by an authorized law enforcement or other agency, or at sale at public auction or by competitive bidding, with such sale being conducted by the office of the district attorney or the attorney general that obtained the final order of forfeiture.

(d) The final order of the court shall provide that the proceeds of any such sale shall be used to pay the reasonable expenses of the forfeiture proceedings, seizure, storage, maintenance of custody, advertising and notice, and the balance of any such sale shall be distributed equally among the prosecuting district attorney or attorney general, the city, town or state police department involved in the forfeiture and the Victims of Drunk Driving Trust Fund established in section 66 of chapter 10. If more than 1 department was substantially involved in the seizure, the court having jurisdiction over the forfeiture proceeding shall distribute the portion for law enforcement equitably among the departments.

(e) There shall be established within the office of the state treasurer a separate Operating Under the Influence Deterrent Trust Fund for each district attorney and for the attorney general. All monies and proceeds received by a prosecuting district attorney or attorney general pursuant to this section shall be deposited in the fund and shall be expended without further appropriation to defray the costs of investigations, to provide additional technical equipment or expertise, to provide matching funds to obtain federal grants, or for such other law enforcement purposes as the district attorney or attorney general deems appropriate. Any program seeking to be an eligible recipient of the funds shall file an annual audit report with the local district attorney and attorney general. Such report shall include, but not be limited to, a listing of the assets, liabilities, itemized expenditures and board of directors of the program. Within 90 days of the close of the fiscal year, each district attorney and the attorney general shall file an annual report with the house and senate committees on ways and means on the use of the monies in the trust fund for the purposes of deterring operating under the influence programs.

(f) All moneys and proceeds received by a police department shall be deposited into the fund and shall be expended without further appropriation to defray the costs of investigations, to provide additional technical equipment or expertise, to provide matching funds to obtain federal grants, or to accomplish such other law enforcement purposes as the chief of police of such city or town, or the colonel of state police deem appropriate, but such funds shall not be considered a source of revenue to meet the operating needs of such department.

SECTION 24X
Cancellation of registration for motor vehicles owned by certain drunk driving offenders

The registration of a motor vehicle owned by a person who is assigned to an alcohol or controlled substance education, treatment or rehabilitation program or who is convicted of a violation of paragraph (a) of subdivision (1) of section 24, subsection (a) of section 24G, operating a motor vehicle with a percentage by weight of blood alcohol of eight one-hundredths or greater, or while under the influence of intoxicating liquor in violation of subsection (b) of section 24G, section 24L, subsection (a) of section 8 of chapter 90B, section 13½ of chapter 265, or section 8A or 8B of chapter 90B, or, in the case of another jurisdiction, for any like offense, may be cancelled and the registration plates for such vehicle seized for the period of the suspension or revocation of the license or right to operate due to such assignment or conviction, if the person has been so assigned or so convicted previously at least 2 times. No new registration shall be issued to such person during the period of the suspension or revocation of the license or right to operate.

SECTION 25
Refusal to submit to police officer

Any person who, while operating or in charge of a motor vehicle, shall refuse, when requested by a police officer, to give his name and address or the name and address of the owner of such motor vehicle, or who shall give false name or address, or who shall refuse or neglect to stop when signalled to stop by any police officer who is in uniform or who displays his badge conspicuously on the outside of his outer coat or garment, or who refuses, on demand of such officer, to produce his license to operate such vehicle or his certificate of registration, or to permit such officer to take the license or certificate in hand for the purpose of examination, or who refuses, on demand of such officer, to sign his name in the presence of such officer, and any person who on the demand of an officer of the police or other officer mentioned in section twenty-nine or authorized by the registrar, without a reasonable excuse fails to deliver his license to operate motor vehicles or the certificate of registration of any motor vehicle operated or owned by him or the number plates furnished by the registrar for said motor vehicle, or who refuses or neglects to produce his license when requested by a court or trial justice, shall be punished by a fine of one hundred dollars.

NOTE 1   See Note following G.L. c. 90, § 1.

NOTE 2   Although the detective was in plain clothes and not displaying his badge on the outside of his coat or garment, "[b]y activating his 'strobe lights' and displaying his badge, the defendant was effectively notified that he was being told to stop by a police officer." *Commonwealth v. Gray*, 423 Mass. 293, 295 (1996).

NOTE 3   "While a literal reading would require that, in order to establish a violation of the statute, the Commonwealth must prove that the officer in question was either in uniform or displayed his badge on his coat or garment, *see Commonwealth v. Materia*, 350 Mass. 785 (1966), '[w]e will not adopt a literal construction of a statute if the consequences of such construction are absurd or unreasonable.' *Commonwealth v. Gray*, 423 Mass. 293, 296 . . . . One purpose of the statute 'is to ensure that the motorist is informed that the person demanding that he stop has the authority to make such a demand.' . . . Through the officer's activation of the siren, blue lights, and strobe lights, along with repeated attempts to pull alongside the car and at least one request to pull over, 'the defendant was effectively notified that he was being told to stop by a police officer.' *Id.* at 295." *Commonwealth v. Ross*, 73 Mass. App. Ct. 181, 183–84 (2008) (some citations omitted).

SECTION 26
Accident reports; supplemental report; penalty for violation

Every person operating a motor vehicle which is involved in an accident in which any person is killed or injured or in which there is damage in excess of one thousand dollars to any one vehicle or other property shall, within five days after such accident, report in writing to the registrar on a form approved by him and send a copy thereof to the police department having jurisdiction on the way where such accident occurred; provided, however, that such police department

shall accept a report filed by an owner or operator whose vehicle has been damaged in an accident in which another person has unlawfully left the scene of such accident. Such report shall not be required during the period of incapacity of any person who is physically incapable of making a report. If the operator is not the owner of the vehicle and is physically incapable of making such written report, the owner shall within five days after the accident make such report based on such knowledge as he may have and such information as he can obtain regarding the accident.

The registrar may require any such operator or owner to file a supplementary written report whenever in the opinion of the registrar the original report is insufficient.

The registrar may revoke or suspend the license of any person violating any provision of this section.

NOTE   "[W]hile a c. 90, § 26, accident report is in most cases nonincriminating and primarily aimed at noncriminal, regulatory governmental objectives, where the authorities seeking to compel the defendant to submit a report were the very authorities who had already instituted a criminal prosecution against him [for vehicular homicide and for failure to yield to a pedestrian within a crosswalk], the defendant was clearly faced with a real and substantial danger that the evidence supplied would incriminate him. Under the circumstances, *any* information provided by the defendant on the report would tend to incriminate him; the threat of incrimination was not merely a remote possibility or unlikely contingency, but an actual and present danger, against which the defendant was constitutionally protected." *Commonwealth v. Sasu*, 404 Mass. 596, 601 (1989) (citation and quotation marks omitted).

SECTION 26A
Licenses and learner's permits; reporting changes of name and address

(a) A person in whose name a motor vehicle or trailer has been registered under the provisions of this chapter and a person to whom a learner's permit or a license to operate motor vehicles has been granted by the registrar shall report a change of name, residential address or mailing address in writing to said registrar within 30 days after the date on which any such change was made. Said registrar may revoke or suspend the license or certificate of registration or learner's permit of a person violating the provisions of this subsection.

(b) Said registrar may use reasonable sources of information regarding addresses including, but not limited to, municipal excise records, insurance company records and United Stated Post Office change of address records to update address information contained in registry records and such updated records shall constitute the official records of said registrar for purpose of giving any notice as provided in this chapter or for any other purpose. If the registrar obtains information from the department of revenue, he shall have access only to individuals' names and addresses.

(c) Said registrar shall not be required to mail a notice pursuant to this chapter to more than one address; provided, however, that such address was obtained pursuant to subsection (a) or (b).

SECTION 34J
Operating motor vehicle without liability policy, bond or security deposit

Whoever operates or permits to be operated or permits to remain on a public or private way a motor vehicle which is subject to the provisions of section one A during such time as the motor vehicle liability policy or bond or deposit required by the provisions of this chapter has not been provided and maintained in accordance therewith shall be punished by a fine of not less than five hundred nor more than five thousand dollars or by imprisonment for not more than one year in a house of correction, or both such fine and imprisonment; provided, however, that any municipality that enforces the provisions of this section shall retain such fine. This section shall not apply to a person who operates a motor vehicle leased under any system referred to in section thirty-two C without knowledge that the lessor thereof has not complied with the provisions of section thirty-two E relative to providing indemnity, protection or security for property damage.

In proceedings under this section, written certification by the registrar of motor vehicles that the registry of motor vehicles has no record of a motor vehicle liability policy or bond or deposit in effect at the time of the alleged offense as required by the provisions of this chapter for the motor vehicle alleged to have been operated in violation of this section, shall be admissible as evidence in any court of the commonwealth and shall raise a rebuttable presumption that no such motor vehicle liability policy or bond or deposit was in effect for said vehicle at the time of the alleged offense. Such presumption may be rebutted and overcome by evidence that a motor vehicle liability policy or bond or deposit was in effect for such vehicle at the time of the alleged offense.

Any person who is convicted of, or who enters a plea of guilty to a violation of this section shall be liable to the plan organized pursuant to section one hundred and thirteen H of chapter one hundred and seventy-five in the amount of the greater of five hundred dollars or one year's premium for compulsory motor vehicle insurance for the highest rated territory and class or risk in effect at the time of the commission of the offense. Said liability shall be in addition to all other liabilities imposed on the person so convicted or so

pleading whether civil or criminal. The said plan shall apply any sums collected hereunder, to defray its costs of collection and to defray in whole or in part its expenses for preventing fraud and arson. Furthermore, any person who is convicted of, or enters a plea of guilty to a violation of this section shall have his or her license or right to operate a motor vehicle suspended for sixty days by the registrar of motor vehicles upon the registrar's receipt of notification from the clerk of any court which enters any conviction hereunder or which accepts such plea of guilty. The clerk of any court which enters any conviction hereunder or which accepts such plea shall promptly notify the registrar of motor vehicles and the Commonwealth Auto Reinsurers pursuant to section one hundred and thirteen of chapter one hundred and seventy-five or any successor thereto of such entry of acceptance of such plea. For any second or subsequent said conviction or plea of guilty within a six year period the offender's license or right to operate a motor vehicle shall be suspended for one year by the registrar upon the registrar's receipt of such notification by the clerk of any such court.

Notwithstanding any general or special law to the contrary, whoever violates this section and has not been previously determined responsible for or convicted therefore, or against whom a finding of delinquency or a finding of sufficient facts to support a conviction has not been previously rendered, on a complaint charging a violation of this section shall be punished by fine of not more than $500.

NOTE "[T]he Commonwealth must prove as an element of the crime charged that the motor vehicle was in fact uninsured." The rationale of the court was that "insurance is an element of the crime charged, not a mere license or authority. Therefore, the issue of insurance cannot be viewed as an affirmative defense and, of course, it cannot be removed from jury consideration." *Commonwealth v. Munoz*, 384 Mass. 503, 507 (1981).

Chapter 90B. Motorboats and Other Vessels

Section
1   Definitions
4A   Altering, forging or counterfeiting certificates of number; penalty
4B   Removal, defacing, etc. of identification number of motorboat, motor or engine; penalties
8   Operation of a vessel under influence of intoxicating liquor or narcotics, etc.; breath or blood testing; water skiing; professional exhibitions
8A   Operation of a vessel while under the influence of controlled substances causing serious bodily injury; penalties; parole, probation or furlough; license revocation
8B   Operation of a vessel under the influence of a controlled substance causing death; penalties; probation, parole or furlough; license revocation
9A   Jet ski, surf jet or wetbike operation
13   Arrest without warrant; entry upon private lands
14   Penalties; proceedings

SECTION 1
Definitions
(Amended by 2012 Mass. Acts c. 153, § 1, effective Oct. 16, 2012.)

In this chapter, unless the context otherwise requires, the following words shall have the following meanings:

"Amphibious landing vehicle", a motor vehicle that can travel on land and water.

"Boating accident", an occurrence in which a waterborne vessel subject to this chapter is involved, whether or not there

has been any actual collision, and which results in damages by or such vessel or its equipment, or by or to an object or person being towed, pushed or propelled by such vessel, or in which there in an injury to any person, loss of life, or disappearance of any person under circumstances which indicate the possibility of death or injury or disappearance of a vessel other than by theft.

"Certificate of Number", a document issued by the director, upon application therefor, stating the name and address of the owner of, and the number awarded to a vessel subject to this chapter, except such vessels, other than livery boats, owned by a manufacturer of or dealer in boats.

"Commissioner", the commissioner of the department of fisheries, wildlife and environmental law enforcement.

"Department", the department of fisheries, wildlife and environmental law enforcement of the executive office of environmental affairs.

"Director", the director of the division of law enforcement of the department of fisheries, wildlife and environmental law enforcement.

"Division", the division of law enforcement of the department of fisheries, wildlife and environmental law enforcement.

"Horsepower", the aggregate rated horsepower of all propellant machinery at maximum operating revolutions per minute.

"Identification number", the number awarded to a vessel subject to this chapter and upon approval of an application for a certificate of number.

"Jet skis", a ski propelled by machinery and designed to travel over water.

"Length", the extreme deck fore-and-aft measurement of a vessel.

"Like offense", as used in subsection (a) of section eight, shall mean any violation of paragraph (1) of subsection (a) of section eight, or any violation of subparagraph (1) of paragraph (a) of subsection (1) of section twenty-four of chapter ninety.

"Liver boat", a boat hired or available for hire from a person who offers boats for hire as a regular business.

"Machinery", all inboard and outboard engines and all other types of motors or mechanical devices capable of propelling vessels.

"Motorboat", any vessel propelled by machinery whether or not such machinery is the principal source of propulsion, but not a vessel which has a valid marine document issued by the Bureau of Customs of the United States government or any federal agency successor thereto.

"Operate", navigate or otherwise use a motorboat or vessel.

"Operator", a person who operates or who has a charge of the navigation or use of a motorboat or vessel.

"Owner", the person who claims lawful possession of a vessel by virtue of legal title or equitable interest therein which entitles him to possession.

"Person", a natural person, corporation, association, partnership or other legal entity or other legal agency or political subdivision.

"Personal floatation devices", TYPE I, a coast guard approved device designed to turn an unconscious person in the water from a face downward position to a vertical or slightly backward position, and to have more than twenty pounds of buoyancy. Acceptable for all size boats. TYPE II, a coast guard approved device designed to turn an unconscious person in the water from a face downward position to vertical or slightly backward position and have at least fifteen and five-tenths pounds of buoyancy. Acceptable for all size boats. TYPE III, a coast guard approved device designed to keep a conscious person in a vertical or slightly backward position and to have at least fifteen and five-tenths pounds of buoyancy. While having the same buoyancy as TYPE II, the TYPE III has a lesser turning ability to allow for a comfortable design for water activities such as water skiing. Acceptable for all size boats. TYPE IV, a coast guard approved devise designed to be thrown to a person in the water and not worn. It is designed to have at least sixteen and five-tenths pounds of buoyancy. Acceptable for all boats as a throwable device only.

"Registrar", the registry of motor vehicles.

"Secretary", the Secretary of the Department of the United States government in which the coast guard is operating.

"Ship's lifeboats", boats carried aboard a vessel and used solely for lifesaving purposes, but not including dinghies, tenders, speedboats or other types of craft carried about a vessel and used for other than lifesaving purposes.

"Surf jet", a surfboard propelled by machinery and designed to travel over water.

"Underway", not an anchor, made fast to the shore or aground.

"Vessel", watercraft of every description, except a seaplane on the water or capable of being used as a means of transportation on water.

"Waters of the commonwealth", all coastal and inland waters as defined in section one of chapter one hundred and thirty-one except ponds less than ten acres in area and owned by one person, and is not open to the public.

"Wet bike", a vessel designed to travel over water, supported by skis propelled by machinery.

SECTION 4A
Altering, forging or counterfeiting certificates of number; penalty

Whoever falsely makes, alters, forges, or counterfeits, or procures or assists another to falsely make, alter, forge or counterfeit, a certificate of number of a motorboat, facsimile of the signature, or validating signature stamp of the director of the division of law enforcement upon a genuine or falsely made, altered, forged or counterfeited certificate of number of a motorboat, and whoever has in his possession or utters, publishes as true, or in any way makes use of a falsely made, altered, forged or counterfeited signature, facsimile of the signature or validation signature stamp of the director of the division of law enforcement, shall be punished by a fine of not more than one hundred dollars.

SECTION 4B
Removal, defacing, etc. of identification number of motorboat, motor or engine; penalties

Whoever removes, defaces, alters, changes, destroys, obliterates or mutilates, or causes to be removed or destroyed or in any way defaced, altered, changed, obliterated or mutilated, the identifying number or numbers of the manufacturer of a motorboat or the identification number of the manufacturer of a motor or engine designed for use in a boat with intent thereby to conceal the identity of such motorboat, motor or engine shall be punished by a fine of not more than five hundred dollars or by imprisonment for not more than one year, or both; and possession of any motorboat or any such motor or engine or of any part thereof, the identifying number or numbers of which have been so removed, defaced, altered, changed, destroyed, obliterated or mutilated shall be prima facie evidence of a violation of the foregoing provision. Whoever sells or otherwise disposes of or attempts to sell or otherwise dispose of such motorboat, motor or engine, knowing or having reason to believe that the identifying number or numbers of said motorboat, motor or engine have been so removed, defaced, altered, changed, destroyed, obliterated or mutilated, shall be punished by the same fine or imprisonment, or both.

SECTION 8
Operation of a vessel under influence of intoxicating liquor or narcotics, etc.; breath or blood testing; water skiing; professional exhibitions

(a)(1) No person shall operate any vessel on the waters of the commonwealth with a percentage, by weight, of alcohol in their blood of eight one-hundredths or greater, or while such person is under the influence of intoxicating liquor or marijuana, narcotic drugs, depressant or stimulant substances, as defined in chapter ninety-four C, or the vapors of glue.

(A) If a person arrested for operating a vessel while under the influence of intoxicating liquor refuses to submit to such test or analysis, after having been informed that his license, permit or right to operate motor vehicles shall be suspended and any certificate or numbers may be revoked for a period of one hundred and twenty days for such refusal, no such test or analysis shall be made, but the officer before whom such refusal was made shall immediately prepare a written report of such refusal. Each report shall be made on a form approved by the registrar, and shall be sworn to under the penalties of perjury by the officer before whom such refusal was made. Each such report shall set forth the grounds for the officer's belief that the person arrested had been operating a vessel while under the influence of intoxicating liquor, and shall state that such person had refused to submit to such chemical test or analysis when requested by such officer to do so[,] such refusal having been witnessed by another person other than the defendant. Each such report shall identify which police officer requested said chemical test or analysis, and the other person witnessing said refusal. Each such report shall be sent forthwith to the registrar and to the director along with a copy of the notice of intent to suspend in any form, including electronic or otherwise, that the registrar deems appropriate. Upon receipt of such report, the registrar shall suspend any license or permit to operate motor vehicles issued to such person under chapter ninety or the right of such person to operate motor vehicles in the commonwealth under section ten for a period of one hundred and twenty days, and the director may revoke any and all certificates of number of any vessel such person [sic] and may refuse to issue any certificate of number to such vessels for a period of one hundred and twenty days. Said report shall constitute prima facie evidence of the facts set forth therein at any administrative hearing regarding any suspension specified in this section.

If the defendant has been previously convicted or assigned to an alcohol education or rehabilitation program by a court of the commonwealth because of a like offense within six years preceding the date of the commission of the offense for which he has been convicted, the defendant shall be punished by a fine of not less than three hundred nor more than one thousand dollars and by imprisonment for not less than fourteen days nor more than two and one-half years, provided that the sentence imposed upon such person shall not be reduced to less than fourteen days, nor suspended, nor shall any such person be eligible for probation, parole, or furlough or receive any deduction from his sentence for good conduct until he shall have served fourteen days of such sentence; provided, however, that the commissioner of correction may, on the recommendation of the warden, superintendent, or other person in charge of a correctional institution, or the administrator of a county correctional institution, grant to an offender committed under this paragraph a temporary release in the custody of an officer of such institution for the following purposes only: to attend the funeral of a relative; to visit a critically ill relative, to obtain emergency medical or psychiatric services unavailable at said institution, or to engage in employment pursuant to a work release program.

If the defendant has been previously convicted or assigned to an alcohol education or rehabilitation program by a court of the commonwealth because of a like offense two times within six years preceding the date of the commission of the offense for which he has been convicted, the defendant shall be punished by a fine of not less than five hundred nor more than one thousand dollars and by imprisonment for not less than six months nor more than two and one-half years, provided that the sentence imposed upon such person shall not be reduced to less than six months, nor suspended, nor shall any person be eligible for probation, parole, or furlough or receive any deduction from his sentence for good conduct until he shall have served six months of such sentence; provided, however, that the commissioner of correction may, on the recommendation of the warden, superintendent, or other person in charge of a correctional institution, or the administrator of a county correctional institution, grant to an offender committed under this paragraph a temporary release in the custody of an officer of such institution for the following purposes only: to attend the funeral of a relative; to visit a critically ill relative; to obtain emergency medical or psychiatric services unavailable at said institution; or to engage in employment pursuant to a work release program; provided, further, that the defendant shall serve such six month sentence in a correctional facility specifically designated by the department of correction for the incarceration and rehabilitation of those who operate while under the influence of intoxicating liquor.

If the defendant has been previously convicted or assigned to an alcohol education or rehabilitation program by a court of the commonwealth because of a like offense three times within ten years preceding the date of the commission of the offense for which he has been convicted, the defendant shall be punished by a fine of not less than five hundred nor more than one thousand dollars and by imprisonment in the state prison for not less than two and one-half years nor more than ten years or by such fine and imprisonment in a jail or house of correction for not less than one year nor more than two and one-half years; provided, however, that the sentence imposed upon such person shall not be reduced to less than one year nor suspended, nor shall any person be eligible for probation, parole, or furlough or receive any deduction from his sentence for good conduct until he shall have served one year of such sentence; provided, further, that the commissioner of correction may, on the recommendation of the warden, superintendent, or other person in charge of a correctional institution, or of the administrator of a county correctional institution, grant to an offender committed under this paragraph a temporary release in the custody of an officer of such institution for the following purposes only: to attend the funeral of a relative; to visit a critically ill relative; to obtain emergency medical or psychiatric services unavailable at said institution; or to engage in employment pursuant to a work release program.

If the defendant has been previously convicted or assigned to an alcohol education or rehabilitation program by a court of the commonwealth because of a like offense four or more times within ten years preceding the date of the commission of the offense for which he has been convicted, the defendant shall be punished by a fine of not less than one thousand nor more than one thousand five hundred dollars and by imprisonment in the state prison for not less than two and one-half years nor more than ten years, or by such fine and imprisonment in a jail or house of correction for not less than two years nor more than two and one-half years; provided, however, that the sentence imposed upon such person shall not be reduced to less than two years nor suspended, nor shall any such person be eligible for probation, parole, or furlough or receive any deduction from his sentence for good conduct until he shall have served two years of such sentence; provided, further, that the commissioner of correction may, on the recommendation of the warden, superintendent, or other person in charge of a correctional institution, or of the administrator of a county correctional institution, grant to an offender committed under this paragraph a temporary release in the custody of an officer of such institution for the following purposes only: to attend the funeral of a relative; to visit a critically ill relative; to obtain emergency medical or psychiatric services unavailable at said institution; or to engage in employment pursuant to a work release program.

(B) A prosecution commenced under the provisions of this paragraph shall not be placed on file or continued without a finding. No trial shall be commenced on a complaint alleging a violation of this paragraph, nor shall any plea be accepted on such a complaint, nor shall the prosecution on such a complaint be transferred to another division of the district court or to a jury-of-six session, until the court receives a report from the commissioner of probation pertaining to the defendant's record, if any, of prior convictions of like offenses or of assignment to an alcohol education or rehabilitation program because of a like offense; provided, however, that the provisions of this paragraph shall not justify the postponement of any such trial or of the acceptance of any such plea for more than five working days after the date of the defendant's arraignment. The commissioner of probation shall give priority to requests for such records.

(C) At any time before the commencement of a trial or acceptance of a plea on a complaint alleging a violation of this paragraph, the prosecutor may apply for the issuance of a new complaint pursuant to section thirty-five A of chapter two hundred and eighteen alleging a violation of this paragraph and one or more prior like offenses. If such application is made upon motion of the prosecutor, the court shall stay further proceedings on the original complaint pending the determination of the application for the new complaint. If a new complaint is issued, the court shall dismiss the original complaint and order that further proceedings on the new complaint be postponed until the defendant has had sufficient time to prepare a defense.

(D) If a defendant waives right to a jury trial pursuant to section twenty-six A of chapter two hundred and eighteen on a complaint under this paragraph he shall be deemed to have waived right to a jury trial on all elements of said complaint subject to the right to appeal pursuant to section twenty-seven A of said chapter two hundred and eighteen.

(E) Except as provided herein the provisions of section eighty-seven of chapter two hundred and seventy-six shall not apply to any person charged with a violation of this paragraph if said person has been convicted of or assigned to an alcohol education or rehabilitation program because of a like offense by a court of the commonwealth within a period of six years immediately preceding the commission of the offense with which he is charged.

(F) Notwithstanding the provisions of section six A of chapter two hundred and seventy-nine, the court may order that a defendant convicted of a violation of this subparagraph be actually imprisoned only on designated weekends, eve-

nings or holidays; provided, however, that the provisions of this paragraph shall apply only to a defendant who has not been convicted previously of a like offense or assigned to an alcohol education or rehabilitation program within six years preceding the date of the commission of the offense for which he has been convicted.

(2)(a) In any prosecution for a violation of paragraph (1), evidence of the percentage, by weight, of alcohol in the defendant's blood at the time of the alleged offense, as shown by chemical test or analysis of his blood or as indicated by chemical test or analysis of his breath, shall be admissible, and such failure or refusal shall be admissible in any action by the registrar under this section or in any proceedings provided for in section twenty-four N of chapter ninety, and deemed relevant to the determination of the question of whether the defendant was at such time under the influence of intoxicating liquor; provided, however, that if such test or analysis was made by or at the direction of a law enforcement officer, it was made with the consent of the defendant, the results thereof were made available to the defendant upon his request and the defendant was afforded a reasonable opportunity, at his request and at his expense, to have another such test or analysis made by a person or physician selected by him; and provided, further, that blood shall not be withdrawn from any person for the purpose of such test or analysis except by a physician, registered or certified medical technician; and, provided further, that a chemical test or analysis of the defendant's breath shall be by means of equipment which has been calibrated within thirty days of its use.

Evidence that the defendant failed or refused to consent to such test or analysis shall not be admissible against him in a civil or criminal process but any failure of the law enforcement officer to attempt to administer or have administered such test or analysis, shall be so admissible, and such failure or refusal shall be admissible in any action by the registrar under this section or in any proceedings provided for in section twenty-four N of chapter ninety. If such evidence is that such percentage was five one-hundredths or less, there shall be a presumption that such defendant was not under the influence of intoxicating liquor, and he shall be released from custody forthwith, but the officer who placed him under arrest shall not be liable for false arrest, if such law enforcement officer had reasonable grounds to believe that the person arrested had been operating a vessel while under the influence of intoxicating liquor; if such evidence is that such percentage was more than five one-hundredths but less than eight one-hundredths, there shall be no presumption; A certificate, signed and sworn to, by a chemist of the department of state police or by a chemist of a laboratory certified by the department of public health, or a reading from a device certified by said department as providing accurate readings of the percentage of alcohol in blood, and signed and sworn to by the law enforcement officer who administered such test which contains the results of an analysis of the percentage of alcohol in such blood shall be prima facie evidence of the percentage of alcohol in such blood.

Whoever operates a vessel on the waters of the commonwealth shall be deemed to have consented to submit to a chemical test or analysis of his breath or blood in the event that he is arrested for operating while under the influence of intoxicating liquor; provided, however, that no person shall be deemed to have consented to a blood test unless such person has been brought for treatment to a medical facility licensed under the provisions of section fifty-one of chapter one hundred and eleven; and provided, further, that no person who is afflicted with hemophilia, diabetes or any other condition requiring the use of anticoagulants shall be deemed to have consented to a withdrawal of blood. Such test shall be administered at the direction of a law enforcement officer, having reasonable grounds to believe that the person arrested has been operating a vessel under the influence of intoxicating liquor.

(A) If a person arrested for operating a vessel while under the influence of intoxicating liquor refuses to submit to such test or analysis, after having been informed that his license, permit or right to operate motor vehicles shall be suspended and any certificate or [sic] numbers may be revoked for a period of one hundred and twenty days for such refusal, no such test or analysis shall be made, but the officer before whom such refusal was made shall immediately prepare a written report of such refusal. Each such report shall be made on a form approved by the registrar, and shall be sworn to under the penalties of perjury by the officer before whom such refusal was made. Each such report shall set forth the grounds for the officer's belief that the person arrested had been operating a vessel while under the influence of intoxicating liquor, and shall state that such person had refused to submit to such chemical test or analysis when requested by such officer to do so such refusal having been witnessed by another person other than the defendant. Each such report shall identify which police officer requested said chemical test or analysis, and the other person witnessing said refusal. Each such report shall be sent forthwith to the registrar or to the director along with a copy of the notice of intent to suspend in any form, including electronic or otherwise, that the registrar deems appropriate. Upon receipt of such report, the registrar shall suspend any license or permit to operate motor vehicles issued to such person under chapter ninety or the right of such person to operate motor vehicles in the commonwealth under section ten for a period of one hundred and twenty days, and the director may revoke any and all certificates of number of any vessel such person [sic] and may refuse to issue any certificate of number to such vessels for a period of one hundred and twenty days. Said report shall constitute prima facie evidence of the facts set forth therein at any administrative hearing regarding any suspension specified in this section.

(B) Any person whose license, permit or right to operate motor vehicles has been suspended or whose certificate of number has been revoked under this paragraph shall be entitled to a hearing before the registrar which shall be limited to the following issues: (i) did the officer have reasonable grounds to believe that such person had been operating a vessel while under the influence of intoxicating liquor on the waters of the commonwealth, (ii) was such person placed under arrest and (iii) did such person refuse to submit to such test or analysis. If, after such hearing, the registrar finds on any one of the said issues in the negative, the registrar shall reinstate such license, permit or right to operate motor vehicles of such person and shall notify the registrar of such reinstatement. Upon receipt of such notification, the director shall reinstate such certificate of number to the vessel of such person.

Notwithstanding any of the foregoing, any person whose certificate of number has been revoked under this paragraph may at any time apply for and shall, within fifteen days, be granted a hearing before the director for the purpose of requesting the issuance of a certificate of number on the grounds of hardship and the director may, in his discretion, issue such certificate of number under such terms and conditions as he deems appropriate and necessary.

If a person fails to pay a civil administrative penalty assessed pursuant to this section within ninety days of the time it becomes final, such person shall be liable to the commonwealth for up to three times the amount of such penalty, together with the costs, plus interest from the time the civil administrative penalty became final, including all costs and attorney's fees incurred directly in the collection thereof. The rate of interest shall be the rate set forth in section six C of chapter two hundred and thirty-one. The director shall refuse to issue an original certificate of number or to renew the certificate of number for any boat owned by a person who fails to pay such civil administrative penalty and any related penalties or costs, until such payment is made in full.

(3)(A) Notwithstanding any of the foregoing, any person convicted of or charged with a violation of paragraph (1) and who has not been previously convicted or assigned to an alcohol education or rehabilitation program because of a like offense, may, if he consents, be placed on probation for not more than two years and shall, as a condition of probation, be ordered to complete a boating safety education course, if he has not previously completed one and received a certificate of same and, if deemed necessary by the court, to complete an alcohol education or rehabilitation program provided or sanctioned by the division of alcoholism, and comply with all conditions of said alcohol education or rehabilitation program. Such conditions of probation shall specify a date before which such boating safety education course and alcohol education or rehabilitation program must be attended and completed. Such order of probation shall be in addition to any penalties imposed as provided in paragraph (1) of this subsection.

Notwithstanding any of the above provisions, a judge, before imposing sentence on a defendant who pleads guilty to or is found guilty of a violation of paragraph (1) and who has not been convicted or assigned to an alcohol education or rehabilitation program by a court of the commonwealth because of a like offense two or more times within ten years of the date of the commission of the offense for which he has been convicted shall receive a report from the probation staff of the court which shall include, but not be limited to, a copy of the defendant's operating record, the criminal record of the defendant, if any, and such information as may be available as to the defendant's use of alcohol and may, upon a written finding that appropriate and adequate treatment is available to the defendant and that the defendant would benefit from such treatment and that the safety of the public would not be endangered, with the defendant's consent, place a defendant on probation for two years, provided that a condition of such probation shall be that the defendant be confined for no less than fourteen days in a residential alcohol treatment program, as provided by or sanctioned by the division of alcoholism, pursuant to regulations to be promulgated by said division in consultation with the department of correction and with the approval of the secretary of health and human services or at any other facility so sanctioned or regulated as may be established by the commonwealth or any political subdivision thereof for the purpose of alcohol or drug treatment or rehabilitation, and comply with all conditions of said residential alcohol treatment program. Such condition of probation shall specify a date before which such residential alcohol treatment program shall be attended and completed.

Failure of the defendant to comply with said conditions and any other terms of probation as imposed under this section shall be reported forthwith to the court and proceedings under the provisions of section three of chapter two hundred and seventy-nine shall be commenced. In such proceedings, such defendant shall be taken before the court and if the court finds that he has failed to attend or complete the residential alcohol treatment program before the date specified in the conditions of probation, the court shall forthwith specify a second date before which such defendant shall attend or complete such program and, unless such defendant shows extraordinary and compelling reasons for such failure, shall forthwith specify a second date before which such defendant shall attend or complete such program and, unless such defendant shows extraordinary and compelling reasons for such failure, shall forthwith sentence him to imprisonment for not less than two days; provided, however, that such sentence shall not be reduced to less than two days, nor suspended, nor shall such person be eligible for furlough or receive any deduction from his sentence for good conduct until he shall have served two days of such sentence; and provided, further, that the commissioner of correction may, on the recommendation of the warden, superintendent, or other person in charge of a correctional institution, or of the administrator of a county correctional institution, grant to an offender committed under this paragraph a temporary release in the custody of an officer of such institution for the following purposes only: to attend the funeral of a relative; to visit a critically ill relative; to obtain emergency medical or psychiatric services unavailable at said institution; or to engage in employment pursuant to a work release program. If such defendant fails to attend or complete the residential alcohol education or rehabilitation program before the second date specified by the court, further proceedings pursuant to said section three of said chapter two hundred and seventy-nine shall be commenced, and the court shall forthwith sentence the defendant to imprisonment for not less than fourteen days; provided, however, that such sentence shall not be reduced to less than fourteen days, nor suspended, nor shall such person be eligible for furlough or receive any deduction from his sentence for good conduct until he shall have served fourteen days of such sentence; and provided further that the commissioner of correction may, on the recommendation of the warden, superintendent, or other person in charge of a correctional institution, or of the administrator of a county correctional institution, grant to an offender committed under this paragraph a temporary release in the custody of an officer of such institution for the following purposes only: to attend the funeral of a relative; to visit a critically ill relative; to obtain emergency medical or psychiatric services unavailable at said institution; or to engage in employment pursuant to a work release program.

(B) The defendant shall pay for the cost of the services provided by the boating safety education course, the alcohol education or rehabilitation program, and the residential alcohol treatment program; however, no person shall be excluded from said programs for inability to pay, provided that such person files an affidavit of indigency or inability to pay with the court, that investigation by the probation officer confirms

such indigency or establishes that the payment of such fee would cause a grave and serious hardship to such individual or to the family of such individual, and that the court enters a written finding thereof. In lieu of waiver of the entire amount of said fee, the court may direct such individual to make partial or installment payments of the cost of said program.

(4)(a) A conviction of a violation of paragraph (1) shall revoke the license or right to operate motor vehicles and may, in the discretion of the director, revoke the certificate of number of the person so convicted, and no appeal, motion for new trial or exceptions shall operate to stay the revocation of the license, right to operate, or certificate of number. Such revoked license and certificate of number shall immediately be surrendered to the prosecuting officer who shall forward the license to the director and the certificate of number to the director. The court shall report immediately any revocation, under this paragraph, of a license or right to operate to the registrar and to the police department of the municipality in which the defendant is domiciled and any revocation, under this paragraph, of a certificate of number to the director.

(b) Where the license, right to operate, or certificate of number has been revoked under this paragraph, and such person has not been convicted of a like offense by a court of the commonwealth within a period of ten years preceding the date of the commission of the offense for which he has been convicted, the registrar shall not restore the license or reinstate the right to operate to such person and the director may refuse to issue a certificate of number to the vessel of such person unless the prosecution of such person has terminated in favor of the defendant, until one year after the date of conviction; provided, however, that if such person has been placed under probation as provided by paragraph (3) of this subsection and has successfully completed all terms of such probation, the registrar shall not restore the license or reinstate the right to operate to such person and the director may refuse to issue a certificate of number to the vessel of such person until forty-five days after the date of conviction.

Where the license, right to operate or certificate of number of a person has been revoked under this paragraph, and such person has been previously convicted of or assigned to an alcohol education or rehabilitation program by a court of the commonwealth because of a like offense within a period of ten years preceding the date of the commission of the offense for which such person has been convicted, the registrar shall not restore the license or reinstate the right to operate and the director may refuse to issue a certificate of number to the vessel of such person unless the prosecution of such person has terminated in favor of the defendant, until two years after the date of the conviction; provided, however, that such person may, after the expiration of one year from the date of conviction, apply for and shall be granted a hearing before the registrar for the purpose of requesting the issuance of a new license on a limited basis on the grounds of hardship and a showing by the person that the causes of the present and past like offenses have been dealt with or brought under control and the registrar may, in his discretion, issue such a license under such terms and conditions as he deems appropriate and necessary.

Where the license, right to operate or certificate of number of a person has been revoked under this paragraph, and such person has been previously convicted or assigned to an alcohol education or rehabilitation program because of a like offense by a court of the commonwealth two times within a period of ten years preceding the date of commission of the offense for which he has been convicted or where the license or right to operate has been revoked pursuant to section twenty-three of chapter ninety due to a violation of said section due to a prior revocation for a like offense, the registrar shall not restore the license or reinstate the right to operate and the director may refuse to issue a certificate of number to the vessel of such person, unless the prosecution of such person has terminated in favor of the defendant, until five years after the date of conviction; provided, however, that such person may, after the expiration of two years from the date of conviction, apply for and shall be granted a hearing before the registrar for the purpose of requesting the issuance of a new license on a limited basis on the grounds of hardship and a showing by the person that the causes of the present and past violations have been dealt with or brought under control and the registrar may, in his discretion, issue such a license under such terms and conditions as he deems appropriate and necessary.

Where the license, right to operate, or certificate of number of a person has been revoked under this paragraph and such person has been previously convicted or assigned to an alcohol education or rehabilitation program by a court of the commonwealth because of a like offense three times within a period of ten years preceding the date of the commission of the offense for which such person has been convicted, the registrar shall not restore the license or reinstate the right to operate and the director may refuse to issue a certificate of number to the vessel of such person unless the prosecution of such person has terminated in favor of the defendant, until ten years after the date of the conviction; provided, however, that such person may, after the expiration of five years from the date of conviction, apply for and shall be granted a hearing before the registrar for the purpose of requesting the issuance of a new license on a limited basis on the grounds of hardship and a showing by the person that the causes of the present and past violations have been dealt with or brought under control and the registrar may, in his discretion, issue such a license under such terms and conditions as he deems appropriate and necessary.

Where the license, right to operate, or certificate of number of a person has been revoked under this paragraph and such person has been previously convicted or assigned to an alcohol education or rehabilitation program by a court of the commonwealth because of a like offense four or more times within a period of ten years preceding the date of the commission of the offense for which such person has been convicted, the registrar shall not restore the license or reinstate the right to operate and the director may refuse to issue a certificate of number to the vessel of such person unless the prosecution of such person has terminated in favor of the defendant, until fifteen years after the date of the conviction; provided, however, that such person may, after the expiration of seven years from the date of conviction, apply for and shall be granted a hearing before the registrar for the purpose of requesting the issuance of a new license on a limited basis on the grounds of hardship and a showing by the person that the causes of the present and past violations have been dealt with or brought under control and the registrar may, in his discretion, issue such a license under such terms and conditions as he deems appropriate and necessary.

Notwithstanding the foregoing, no new license shall be issued or right to operate be reinstated by the registrar to any person convicted of a violation of paragraph (1) until ten years after the date of conviction in case the registrar determines upon investigation and after hearing that the action of the person so convicted in committing such offense caused an accident resulting in the death of another, nor at any time after a subsequent conviction of such an offense, whenever committed, in case the registrar determines in the manner aforesaid that the action of such person, in committing the offense of which he was so subsequently convicted, caused an accident resulting in the death of another.

Notwithstanding any of the foregoing, any person whose certificates of number has been revoked under this paragraph may at any time apply for and shall within fifteen days be granted a hearing for the purpose of requesting the issuance of certificates of number on the grounds of hardship and the director may, in his discretion, issue such certificates of number under such terms and conditions as he deems appropriate and necessary.

For the purposes of this subsection, a person shall be deemed to have been convicted if he pleaded guilty or nolo contendere or was found or adjudged guilty by a court of competent jurisdiction, whether or not he was placed on probation without sentence or under a suspended sentence or the case was placed on file, and a license may be revoked under this subsection notwithstanding the pendency of a prosecution upon appeal or otherwise after such a conviction. Where there has been more than one conviction in the same prosecution, the date of the first conviction shall be deemed to be the date of conviction under this paragraph.

There shall be an assessment of $250 against a person who is convicted of, placed on probation for, or otherwise pleads guilty to or admits to a finding of sufficient facts of operating a vessel while under the influence of intoxicating liquor or marijuana, narcotic drugs, depressant or stimulant substances or the vapors of glue; provided, however, that $150 of the $250 collected under this assessment shall be deposited by the court with the state treasurer into the Head Injury Treatment Services Trust Fund, established by section 59 of chapter 10, and the remaining amount of the assessment shall be credited to the General Fund. The assessment shall not be subject to reduction or waiver by the court for any reason.

(b) No person shall use any water skis, surfboard or similar device on the waters of the commonwealth negligently so as to endanger the lives or safety of the public, or use any water skis, surfboard or similar device thereon in the nighttime.

(c) No person shall operate any motorboat on the waters of the commonwealth towing a person or persons on water skis, a surfboard or other similar device, unless there is in such motorboat a person who has attained age twelve in addition to the operator in a position to observe the person or persons being towed, and unless such motorboat is equipped with a ladder, steps or similar means by which any person being towed can be taken from the water.

(d) So much of the provisions of subsection (b) as prohibit the use of water skis, surfboards or similar devices in the nighttime, and the provisions of subsections (c) and (d), shall not apply to a performer engaged in a professional exhibition which has previously been approved by the director.

(e)(1) Whoever upon any waters of the commonwealth, operates a vessel recklessly, or operates a vessel negligently so that the lives or safety of the public might be endangered, or upon a bet or wager or in a race, or whoever operates a vessel for the purpose of making a record and thereby violates any speed regulation, or whoever without stopping and making known his name, residence and the identification number of his vessel goes away after knowingly colliding with or otherwise causing injury to any other vessel or property, or whoever knowingly makes any false statement in an application for a certificate of number of a vessel shall be punished by a fine of not less than fifty dollars nor more than five hundred dollars or by imprisonment for not less than thirty days nor more than two years, or both.

Whoever uses a vessel without authority knowing that such use is unauthorized shall, for the first offense be punished by a fine or not less than fifty dollars nor more than five hundred dollars or by imprisonment for not less than thirty days nor more than two years, or both, and for a second offense by imprisonment in the state prison for not more than five years or in a house of correction for not less than thirty days nor more than two and one-half years, or by a fine of not more than one thousand dollars, or by both such fine and imprisonment; and whoever is found guilty of a third or subsequent offense of such use without authority committed within five years of the earliest of his two most recent prior offenses shall be punished by a fine or not less than two hundred dollars nor more than one thousand dollars or by imprisonment for not less than six months nor more than two and one-half years in a house of correction or for not less than two and one-half years nor more than five years in the state prison or by both fine and imprisonment.

Whoever upon any waters of the commonwealth operates a vessel and, without stopping and making known his name, residence and the identification number of his vessel, goes away after knowingly colliding with or otherwise causing injury to any person shall be punished by imprisonment for not less than two months nor more than two years.

A summons may be issued instead of a warrant for arrest upon a complaint for a violation of any provision of this paragraph if in the judgment of the court or justice receiving the complaint there is reason to believe that the defendant will appear upon a summons.

(2) A conviction of a violation of this subsection shall be reported forthwith by the court or magistrate to the registrar, who may in any event, and shall unless the court or magistrate recommends otherwise, revoke immediately the license or right to operate and to the director, who may immediately revoke the certificates of number of the person so convicted, and no appeal, motion for a new trial or exceptions shall operate to stay the revocation of such license, right to operate or certificates of number. If it appears by the records of the director that the person so convicted is the owner of a vessel or has exclusive control of any vessel as a manufacturer or dealer or otherwise, the director may revoke the certificates of number of any or all vessels so owned or exclusively controlled.

(3) The registrar, after having revoked the license or right to operate of any person under this subsection, in his discretion, may issue a new license or reinstate the right to operate and the director may issue a new certificate of number, if the prosecution of such person in the superior court has terminated in favor of the defendant or after an investigation or upon hearing, the registrar may issue a new license or reinstate the right to operate and the director may issue a new

certificate of number to a person convicted in any court of the violation of any provision of this subsection; provided, that no license shall be issued by the registrar to any person convicted of going away without stopping and making known his name, residence and the certificate of number of his vessel after having, while operating such vessel upon any such waters, knowingly collided with or otherwise caused injury to any person, or to any person adjudged a delinquent child by reason thereof under the provisions of section fifty-eight B of chapter one hundred and nineteen, until one year after the date of revocation following his original conviction or adjudication if for a first offense or until three years after the date of revocation following any subsequent conviction or adjudication, or to any person convicted of using a vessel knowing that such use is unauthorized, until one year after the date of revocation following his original conviction or adjudication if for a first offense or until three years after the date of revocation following any subsequent conviction or adjudication, or to any person convicted of violating any other provision of this subsection until sixty days after the date of revocation following his original conviction if for a first offense, or one year after the date of revocation following any subsequent conviction within a period of three years. But the registrar, after investigation, may at any time rescind the revocation of a license or right to operate revoked because of a conviction of operating a vessel upon any such waters negligently so that the lives or safety of the public might be endangered and the director, after investigation, may at any time rescind the revocation of a certificate of number revoked because of a conviction of operating a vessel upon any such waters negligently so that the lives or safety of the public might be endangered.

Notwithstanding any of the foregoing, any person whose certificate of number has been revoked under this subsection may at any time and shall within fifteen days be granted a hearing for the purpose of requesting the issuance of a certificate of number on the grounds of hardship and the director may, in his discretion, issue such certificate of number under such terms and conditions as he deems appropriate and necessary.

(4) The prosecution of any person for the violation of any provision of this subsection, if a subsequent offense, shall not, unless the interests of justice require such disposition, be placed on file or otherwise disposed of except by trial, judgment and sentence according to the regular course of criminal proceedings; and such a prosecution shall be otherwise disposed of only on motion in writing stating specifically the reasons therefor and verified by affidavits if facts are relied upon. If the court or magistrate certifies in writing that it is satisfied that the reasons relied upon are sufficient and that the interests of justice require the allowance of the motion, the motion shall be allowed and the certificate shall be filed in the case. A copy of the motion and certificate shall be sent by the court or magistrate forthwith to the director.

(f) In any prosecution commenced pursuant to this section, introduction into evidence of a prior conviction or prior finding of sufficient facts by either original court papers or certified attested copy of original court papers, accompanied by a certified attested copy of the biographical and informational data from official probation office records, shall be prima facie evidence that a defendant has been convicted previously or assigned to an alcohol education or rehabilitation program because of a like offense by a court of the commonwealth one or more times within a period of six years preceding the date of commission of the offense for which said defendant is being prosecuted.

SECTION 8A
Operation of a vessel while under the influence of controlled substances causing serious bodily injury; penalties; parole, probation or furlough; license revocation

(1) Whoever operates a vessel on the waters of the commonwealth with a percentage, by weight, of alcohol in their blood of eight one-hundredths or greater, or while under the influence of intoxicating liquor, or marihuana, narcotic drugs, depressants, or stimulant substances, all as defined in chapter ninety-four C, or the vapors of glue, and so operates said vessel recklessly or negligently so that the lives or safety of the public might be endangered, and by any such operation so described causes serious bodily injury, shall be punished by imprisonment in the state prison for not less than two and one-half years nor more than ten years and by a fine of not more than five thousand dollars, or by imprisonment in a jail or house or correction for not less than six months nor more than two and one-half years and by a fine of not more than five thousand dollars.

The sentence imposed upon such person shall not be reduced to less than six months, nor suspended, nor shall any person convicted under this paragraph be eligible for probation, parole, or furlough or receive any deduction from his sentence until such person has served at least six months of such sentence; provided, however, that the commissioner of correction may, on the recommendation of the warden, superintendent, or other person in charge of a correctional institution, grant to an offender committed under this paragraph a temporary release in the custody of an officer of such institution for the following purposes only: to attend the funeral of a relative; to visit a critically ill relative; to obtain emergency medical or psychiatric services unavailable at said institution; or to engage in employment pursuant to a work release program. Prosecutions commenced under this paragraph shall neither be continued without a finding nor placed on file.

The provisions of section eighty-seven of chapter two hundred and seventy-six shall not apply to any person charged with a violation of this section.

(2) Whoever operates a vessel on the waters of the commonwealth while under the influence of intoxicating liquor, or of marihuana, narcotic drugs, depressants, or stimulant substances, all as defined in chapter ninety-four C, or vapors of glue, and by any such operation causes serious bodily injury, shall be punished by imprisonment in a jail or house of correction for not less than thirty days nor more than two and one-half years, or by a fine or not less than three thousand dollars, or both.

(3) For the purposes of this section "serious bodily injury" shall mean bodily injury which creates a substantial risk of death or which involves either total disability or the loss or substantial impairment of some bodily function for a substantial period of time.

(4) The registrar shall revoke the license or right to operate and the director shall revoke the certificate of number of a person convicted of a violation of this section for a period of two years after the date of conviction. No appeal, motion for new trial or exception shall operate to stay the revocation of said license, right to operate or certificate of number provid-

ed, however, that such license, right to operate and certificate of number shall be restored if the prosecution of such person ultimately terminates in favor of the defendant.

Notwithstanding the foregoing, any person whose certificate of number has been revoked under this section may at any time apply for and shall within fifteen days be granted a hearing for the purpose of requesting the issuance of a certificate of number on the grounds of hardship and the director may, in his discretion, issue such certificate of number under such terms and conditions as he deems appropriate and necessary.

SECTION 8B
Operation of a vessel under the influence of a controlled substance causing death; penalties; probation, parole or furlough; license revocation

Whoever operates a vessel on the waters of the commonwealth with a percentage, by weight, of alcohol in their blood of eight one-hundredths or greater, or while under the influence of intoxicating liquor, or of marihuana, narcotic drugs, depressants, or stimulant substances, all as defined in chapter ninety-four C, or the vapors of glue, and so operates said vessel recklessly or negligently so that the lives or safety of the public might be endangered, and by any such operation so described causes the death of another person, shall be guilty of homicide by a vessel while under the influence of an intoxicating substance, and shall be punished by imprisonment in the state prison for not less than two and one-half years nor more than fifteen years and a fine of not more than five thousand dollars, or by imprisonment in a jail or house of correction for not less than one year nor more than two and one-half years and a fine of not more than five thousand dollars. The sentence imposed upon such person shall not be reduced to less than one year, nor suspended, nor shall any person convicted under this paragraph be eligible for probation, parole, or furlough or receive any deduction from his sentence until such person has served at least one year of such sentence; provided, however, that the commissioner of correction may, on the recommendation of the warden, superintendent, or other person in charge of a correctional institution, or the administrator of a county correctional institution, grant to an offender committed under this paragraph a temporary release in the custody of an officer of such institution for the following purposes only: to attend the funeral of a relative; to visit a critically ill relative; to obtain emergency medical or psychiatric services unavailable at said institution; or to engage in employment pursuant to a work release program. Prosecutions commenced under this section shall neither be continued without a finding nor placed on file.

The provisions of section eighty-seven of chapter two hundred and seventy-six, shall not apply to any person charged with a violation of this section.

(2) Whoever operates a vessel on the waters of the commonwealth with a percentage, by weight, of alcohol in their blood of eight one-hundredths or greater, or while under the influence of intoxicating liquor, or of marihuana, narcotic drugs, depressants or stimulant substances, all as defined in chapter ninety-four C, or the vapors of glue, or whoever operates a vessel recklessly or negligently so that the lives or safety of the public might be endangered and by any such operation causes the death of another person, shall be guilty of homicide by a vessel and shall be punished by imprisonment in a jail or house of correction for not less than thirty days nor

more than two and one-half years, or by a fine of not less than three hundred nor more than three thousand dollars, or both.

(3) The registrar shall revoke the license or right to operate and the director shall revoke the certificate of number of a person convicted of a violation of this section for a period of ten years after the date of conviction for a first offense. The registrar shall revoke the license or the right to operate and the director shall revoke the certificate of a person convicted for a subsequent violation of this section for the life of such person. No appeal, motion for a new trial or exception shall operate to stay the revocation of the license, right to operate, or certificate provided, however, such license, right to operate and certificate of number shall be restored if the prosecution of such person ultimately terminates in favor of the defendant.

Notwithstanding the foregoing, any person whose certificate of number has been revoked under this section may at any time apply for and shall within fifteen days be granted a hearing for the purpose of requesting the issuance of a certificate of number on the grounds of hardship and the director may, in his discretion, issue such certificate of number under such terms and conditions as he deems appropriate and necessary.

SECTION 9A
Jet ski, surf jet or wetbike operation

No person shall operate a jet ski, surf jet or wetbike (a) on waters of the commonwealth unless the person is sixteen years of age or older, (b) within one hundred and fifty feet of a swimmer, shore or moored vessel, except at headway speed, (c) on waters of the commonwealth of less than seventy-five acres, (d) without wearing an approved personal flotation device or (e), between sunset and sunrise. For the purposes of this section, the term, "headway speed," shall mean the slowest speed at which a personal watercraft, jet ski, surf jet or wetbike can be operated and maintain steerage way.

SECTION 13
Arrest without warrant; entry upon private lands

Any officer empowered to enforce this chapter may arrest without a warrant any person who the officer has probable cause to believe has violated or is violating any provision of this chapter or any rule or regulation made under authority hereof. All officers empowered to enforce this chapter may in the performance of their duties enter upon and pass through or over private lands and property whether or not covered by water.

SECTION 14
Penalties; proceedings

(a) Whoever violates any provision of section two, three, four, six or nine A or of any rule or regulation pertaining thereto shall be punished by a fine of not more than fifty dollars, except as hereinafter provided. Any person against whom a complaint has been issued for a violation of section two or of any rule or regulation pertaining thereto may, if it is the first offense committed by such person in violation of the provisions of this chapter or of any rule or regulation made under authority hereof, appear in person or through an attorney or agent duly authorized in writing, before the clerk of the court having jurisdiction of the offense, and confess the offense charged. In the alternative, any person against whom a compliant has been issued for violation of section five, five A, six or nine A may waive a trial and plead guilty by mailing to the clerk of the court having jurisdiction of the offense, payment in the amount of ten dollars for each offense, by postal note, money order, or certified check made payable to said clerk. Payment by such a person to such clerk of a fine of ten dollars and costs shall operate as a final disposition of the case. Proceedings so disposed of by such clerk of court as provided herein shall be required to report to any probation officer and no record of the case shall be entered in the probation records. Such clerk shall, within three days of such payment, forward to the director a certified copy of such proceedings. For the purpose of counting violations such disposition shall operate as if a finding of guilty had been made in court.

(b) Whoever as a scuba diver, so-called or boat operator violates any provision of section five, five A, seven, subsection (b) of section nine, twelve A or thirteen A or of any rule or regulation pertaining thereto shall be punished by a fine of not less than ten nor more than fifty dollars.

(c) Whoever violates any provision of subsections (b), (c), or (d) of section eight or any rules or regulations pertaining to section eight shall be punished by a fine of not more than five hundred dollars or by imprisonment for not more than six months, or both.

Chapter 90C. Procedure for Motor Vehicle Offenses

Section

1	Definitions
2	Citations and citation books
2A	Citation issuing authority of campus police; record keeping and data collection requirements
3	Issuance of citations; hearing; appeal; summons or warrant; complaint; trial; license or permit suspension
4	Criminal complaint; arrest without warrant; effect of conviction; access to records of offenders
5	Citation not deemed writ
6	Printing and distribution of citation books; audit sheets
7	Reciprocal and mutual agreements with other states
7A	Electronic communication between courts and registry
8	Construction of chapter
9	Disposal of citation, copy or record of issuance
10	Penalty for falsification or disposal of citation, copy or record of issuance
11	Severability

SECTION 1
Definitions

In this chapter, unless the context otherwise requires, the following words shall have the following meanings:

"Appellate division", in the case of the district and Boston municipal court departments, the appellate divisions of such departments established by section one hundred and eight of chapter two hundred and thirty-one; in the case of the juvenile court department, those justices appointed by the chief justice to sit in one or more districts in panels of three justices in order to fulfill within such department the functions assigned by this chapter to the appellate division.

"Audit sheet", a list of consecutive numbers assigned to the citations in a particular citation book or books, in such form as the registrar shall determine.

"Automobile law violation", any violation of any statute, ordinance, by-law or regulation relating to the operation or control of motor vehicles other than a violation (1) of any rule, regulation, order, ordinance or by-law regulating the parking of motor vehicles established by any city or town or by any commission or body empowered by law to make such rules and regulations therein, or (2) of any provision of chapter one hundred and fifty-nine B. A recreation vehicle and a snow vehicle, both as defined in section 20 of chapter 90B, a motorized bicycle and motorized scooter, both as defined in section 1 of chapter 90, shall be considered a motor vehicle for the purposes of this chapter. A motor boat, as defined in section one of chapter ninety B, shall not be considered a motor vehicle for purposes of this chapter.

"Citation", a notice upon which a police officer shall record an occurrence involving all automobile law violations by the person cited. Each citation shall be numbered consecutively and shall be in such form and such parts as determined jointly by the administrative justice of the district court department and the registrar.

"Citation book", not less than twenty citations, stapled or bound together in book form. Each such book shall be consecutively numbered.

"Civil Motor Vehicle Infraction", an automobile law violation for which the maximum penalty does not provide for imprisonment, excepting: (a) operation of a motor vehicle in violation of the first paragraph of section 10 of chapter 90; (b) a violation of sections 23, 25, or 34J of chapter 90; and (c) any automobile law violation committed by a juvenile who does not hold a valid operator's license.

"Criminal", shall include a delinquency matter under chapter one hundred and nineteen.

"District court", a division of the district court department or a session thereof for holding court or a division of the Boston municipal court department or a session thereof for holding court. It shall also include the divisions of the juvenile court department with respect to automobile law violations that are treated as a delinquency matter in such department and with respect to civil motor vehicle infractions that are recorded in conjunction with and that arise from the same occurrence as automobile law violations that are treated as a delinquency matter in such department.

"Division", a division of the district court department or juvenile court department or a division of the Boston municipal court department.

"Magistrate" the clerk-magistrate of a district court, or an assistant clerk who has been designated as a magistrate pursuant to section sixty-two B or chapter two hundred and twenty-one. With the approval of the administrative justice of the department, in a particular division the term "magistrate" may include a justice.

"Police chief", the chief or the head of the organized police department of a city or town, the commissioner of public safety, the colonel of state police, the state superintendent of buildings, the chairman of the Massachusetts Department of Transportation, or the director of environmental law enforcement within the executive office of energy and environmental affairs, a person appointed by the trustees of the University of Massachusetts as chief of the police officers appointed under section 32A of chapter 75, a person appointed by the trustees at each of the commonwealth's state universities and community colleges as chief of the police officers appointed under section

22 of chapter 15A, persons designated by the commissioner of mental health at each institution of the department of mental health, or by the commissioner of developmental services at each institution of the department of developmental services as the chief of the special police officers appointed under section 59 of chapter 22C, or the chief of the Massachusetts Bay Transportation Authority police department.

"Police Officer," any officer, other than an investigator or examiner of the transportation division of the department of telecommunications and energy, authorized to make arrests or serve criminal process, any person appointed by the registrar under section 29 of chapter 90, any person appointed by the trustees of the University of Massachusetts under section 32A of chapter 75, any person appointed by the trustees at each of the commonwealth's state universities and community colleges under section 22 of chapter 15A, and any person appointed by the colonel of state police under section 59 of chapter 22C.

"Registrar", the registrar of motor vehicles.

"Scheduled assessment", the amount of the civil assessment for a particular civil motor vehicle infraction, as established jointly by the chief justice of the district court department and the registrar. A scheduled assessment shall not exceed the maximum assessment or fine established by law for each such violation. A schedule of such assessments shall be visibly posted in each office of the registry of motor vehicles and in the clerk-magistrate's office of each district court.

"Violator", a person, corporation, society, association or partnership accused of an automobile law violation.

SECTION 2
Citations and citation books

Each police chief shall issue citation books to each permanent full-time police officer of his department whose duties may or will include traffic duty or traffic law enforcement, or directing or controlling traffic, and to such other officers as he at his discretion may determine. Each police chief shall obtain a receipt on a form approved by the registrar from such officer to whom a citation book has been issued. Each police chief shall also maintain citation books at police headquarters for the recording of automobile law violations by police officers to whom citation books have not been issued.

Each police chief appointed by the trustees of the commonwealth's state universities and community colleges under section 22 of chapter 15A shall certify to the registrar, on or before January first of each year, that:

(a) the police officers appointed by the trustees at the state university or community college have been issued a current first aid/CPR certificate;

(b)(i)(A) 51 per cent of such police officers have completed either the basic full-time recruit academy operated or certified by the municipal police training committee or the campus police academy operated by the Massachusetts state police, or

(B) 51 per cent of the police officers have completed a basic reserve/intermittent police officer training course approved by the municipal police training committee and have had at least 5 years experience issuing citations pursuant to this chapter; and

(ii) the remaining 49 per cent of police officers have completed a minimum of a basic reserve/intermittent police officer training course approved by the municipal police training committee;

(c) such officers have completed annual in-service training of no less than 40 hours;

(d) such officers meet the same firearms qualification standards as set from time to time by the municipal police training committee if such officers have been authorized by the board of trustees of the state university or community college to carry firearms;

(e) the state university or community college police department submits uniform crime reports to the FBI;

(f) a memorandum of understanding has been entered into with the police chief of the municipality wherein the state university or community college is located outlining the policies and procedures for utilizing the municipality's booking and lock-up facilities, fingerprinting, and breathalyzer equipment if the state university or community college police department does not provide booking and lock-up facilities, fingerprinting, or breathalyzer equipment; and

(g) the state university or community college police department has policies and procedures in place for use of force, pursuit, arrest, search and seizure, racial profiling, and motor-vehicle law enforcement.

Notwithstanding the previous paragraph, nothing in this section shall limit the authority granted to the police chiefs and police officers at the state universities and community colleges under said section 22 of said chapter 15A or section 18 of chapter 73.

Notwithstanding the provisions of any general or special law, other than a provision of this chapter, to the contrary, any police officer assigned to traffic enforcement duty shall, whether or not the offense occurs within his presence, record the occurrence of automobile law violations upon a citation, filling out the citation and each copy thereof as soon as possible and as completely as possible and indicating thereon for each such violation whether the citation shall constitute a written warning and, if not, whether the violation is a criminal offense for which an application for a complaint as provided by subsection B of section three shall be made, whether the violation is a civil motor-vehicle infraction which may be disposed of in accordance with subsection (A) of said section three, or whether the violator has been arrested in accordance with section twenty-one of chapter ninety. Said police officer shall inform the violator of the violation and shall give a copy of the citation to the violator. Such citation shall be signed by said police officer and by the violator, and whenever a citation is given to the violator in person that fact shall be so certified by the police officer. The violator shall be requested to sign the citation in order to acknowledge that is [it] has been received. If a written warning is indicated, no further action need be taken by the violator. No other form of notice, except as provided in this section, need be given to the violator.

A failure to give a copy of the citation to the violator at the time and place of the violation shall constitute a defense in any court proceeding for such violation, except where the violator could not have been stopped or where additional time was reasonably necessary to determine the nature of the violation or the identity of the violator, or where the court finds that a circumstance, not inconsistent with the purpose of this section to create a uniform, simplified and non-criminal method for disposing of automobile law violations, justifies the failure. In such case the violation shall be recorded upon a

citation as soon as possible after such violation and the citation shall be delivered to the violator or mailed to him at his residential or mail address or to the address appearing on his license or registration as appearing in registry of motor vehicles records. The provisions of the first sentence of this paragraph shall not apply to any complaint or indictment charging a violation of section twenty-four, twenty-four G or twenty-four L of chapter ninety, providing such complaint or indictment relates to a violation of automobile law which resulted in one or more deaths.

At or before the completion of his tour of duty, a police officer to whom a citation book has been issued and who has recorded the occurrence of an automobile law violation upon a citation shall deliver to his police chief or to the person duly authorized by said chief all remaining copies of such citation, duly signed, except the police officer's copy which shall be retained by him. If the police officer has directed that a written warning be issued, the part of the citation designated as the registry of motor vehicles record shall be forwarded forthwith by the police chief or person authorized by him to the registrar and shall be kept by the registrar in his main office.

If the police officer has not directed that a written warning be issued and has not arrested the violator, the police chief or a person duly authorized by him shall retain the police department copy of each citation, and not later than the end of the sixth business day after the date of the violation:

(a) in the case of citations alleging only one or more civil motor vehicle infractions, shall cause all remaining copies of such citations to be mailed or delivered to the registrar; or

(b) in the case of citations alleging one or more criminal automobile law violations, shall cause all remaining copies of such citations to be delivered to the clerk-magistrate of the district court for the judicial district where the violation occurred. Failure to comply with the provisions of this paragraph shall not constitute a defense to any complaint or indictment charging a violation of section twenty-four, twenty-four G, or twenty-four L of chapter ninety if such violation resulted in one or more deaths. Each clerk-magistrate shall maintain a record in the form prescribed by the chief justice of the district court department of such citations and shall notify the registrar of the disposition of such citations in accordance with the provisions of section twenty-seven of said chapter ninety. If a citation is spoiled, mutilated, or voided, it shall be endorsed with a full explanation thereof by the police officer voiding such citation, and shall be returned to the registrar forthwith and shall be duly accounted for upon the audit sheet for the citation book from which said citation was removed.

NOTE 1a If no citation is given to the defendant at the time and place of an accident, "the burden [is] on the Commonwealth to establish that one of the exceptions in § 2 justified the prosecution of the defendant." *Commonwealth v. Mullins*, 367 Mass. 733, 734–35 (1975).

NOTE 1b Motor vehicle citation written 15 days after the offense took place valid due to the wilful evasion by the defendant. *Commonwealth v. McCarthy*, 11 Mass. App. Ct. 655 (1981).

NOTE 1c Crisis and confusion at the scene and the necessity to collect additional information needed to determine the nature of the violation justified the four and one-half hour delay between the accident and the giving of a citation. *Commonwealth v. Pappas*, 384 Mass. 428 (1981).

NOTE 1d The off duty police officer was not in uniform and did not have his citation book with him when he stopped the defendant for motor vehicle violations. The officer returned home, filled out the required citation and delivered it to the defendant's home the following day. Conviction upheld. *Commonwealth v. Pizzano*, 357 Mass. 636, 638–39 (1970).

NOTE 2   "An arrest, accompanied by the arrested person's awareness that he is being charged with a motor vehicle violation," negates the necessity of the issuance and "delivery of a citation at the time and place of the offense." *Commonwealth v. Gorman*, 356 Mass. 355, 358 (1969).

NOTE 3   "The Commonwealth is not required, as part of its case, to prove the procedural fact that the defendant has received the citation as required by the statute." *Commonwealth v. Freeman*, 354 Mass. 685, 687 (1968).

NOTE 4   See Note following G.L. c. 90, § 1.

SECTION 2A
Citation issuing authority of campus police; record keeping and data collection requirements

The authority for police officers appointed by the trustees of the Commonwealth's state universities and community colleges under section 22 of chapter 15A to issue citations under this chapter shall be limited to the issuance of citations for violations occurring on the property of state universities and community colleges. Separate record keeping and data collection, including, but not limited to, racial or gender profiling data collection and analysis required under chapter 228 of the acts of 2000, shall be performed by such campus police departments, separate from those conducted by any municipal police department or said state police.

SECTION 3
Issuance of citations; hearing; appeal; summons or warrant; complaint; trial; license or permit suspension
(Amended by 2011 Mass. Acts c. 93, § 17, effective July 1, 2012.)

(A)(1) If a police officer observes or has brought to the officer's attention the occurrence of a civil motor vehicle infraction, the officer may issue a written warning or may cite the violator for a civil motor vehicle infraction in accordance with this subsection. If the officer issues a citation solely for one or more civil motor vehicle infractions without any associated criminal violations, the officer shall indicate on the citation the scheduled assessment for each civil motor vehicle infraction alleged.

(2) The citation shall notify the violator that within twenty days of the date of the citation the violator must, for each civil motor vehicle infraction alleged, either pay the scheduled assessment or contest responsibility for the infraction by requesting a noncriminal hearing before a magistrate of the district court.

(3) The violator shall pay the assessment indicated by the officer for each such infraction within twenty days of the date of the citation: (a) by mailing the total amount of the indicated assessment, along with the citation appropriately marked, to the registrar at the address indicated on the citation, or (b) by delivering, personally or through an agent duly authorized in writing, the total amount of the indicated assessment, along with the citation appropriately marked, to any office of the registrar during normal business hours. Payment may be made in such forms, including payment by credit card or other recognized form of electronic payment, as the registrar shall determine.

Payment of the indicated assessment shall operate as a final disposition of the matter. The violator shall not be required to report to any probation officer, and no record of the matter shall be entered in any criminal or probation records of any court. The payment of the indicated assessment shall not be admissible as an admission of guilt, responsibility or negligence in any criminal or civil proceeding, except that such payment shall be an admission of responsibility and shall operate as a conviction for purposes of any action by the registrar pursuant to chapter ninety and for purposes of the safe driver insurance plan established by section one hundred and thirteen B of chapter one hundred and seventy-five.

(4) A violator may contest responsibility for the infraction by making a signed request for a noncriminal hearing on the back of the citation, and mailing such citation to the registrar at the address indicated on the citation within twenty days of the date of the citation. If a violator requests a noncriminal hearing, he shall pay a fee of $25 to the court prior to the commencement of the hearing before the clerk magistrate; provided, however, that the registrar may retain from the court filing fees an amount not greater than $200,000 for fiscal year 2011 for information technology associated with the implementation of this section; and provided, further that the registrar may retain an amount not greater than $100,000 annually for personnel costs associated with the processing of those filing fees.

A violator who does not, within twenty days of the date of the citation, request a noncriminal hearing shall not thereafter be given such a hearing, unless the registrar shall determine that the failure to make such a hearing, unless the registrar shall determine that the failure to make such a request timely was for good cause that was not within the control of the violator. The registrar's determination of such issue shall be final.

The registrar shall notify the clerk-magistrate of the district court for the judicial district in which the infraction occurred of such request for a noncriminal hearing, in such manner as the chief justice of the district court department and the registrar shall jointly determine. Unless a hearing date and time has already been assigned pursuant to procedures jointly established by the chief justice of the district court department and the registrar, the clerk-magistrate shall notify the police agency concerned and the violator of the date and time of the hearing before a magistrate of the court.

If the hearing is conducted by a magistrate other than a justice, either the violator or the police agency concerned may appeal the decision of the magistrate to a justice, who shall hear the case de novo. Any violator so appealing the decision of a magistrate shall be responsible for paying a fee of $50 prior to the scheduling of the appeal hearing before a justice. There shall be no right of jury trial for civil motor vehicle infractions.

In any such hearing before a magistrate or justice, the citation shall be admissible and shall be prima facie evidence of the facts stated therein. Compulsory process for witnesses may be had by either party in the same manner as in criminal cases. On a showing of need in advance of such hearing, the magistrate or justice may direct that the violator be permitted to inspect specific written documents or materials in the possession of the police officer or agency concerned that are essential to the violator's defense.

At the conclusion of the hearing, the magistrate or justice shall announce a finding of responsible or not responsible. The magistrate or justice shall enter a finding of responsible if it was shown by a preponderance of the credible evidence that the violator committed the infraction alleged; otherwise the magistrate or justice shall enter a finding of not responsible. No other disposition shall be permitted, and such matters shall not be continued without a finding, dismissed, or filed.

If the violator is found responsible after a noncriminal hearing, the magistrate or justice shall require the violator to pay to the registrar an assessment which shall not exceed the scheduled assessment for that infraction. Such assessment shall be in accordance with any guidelines promulgated by the chief justice of that department of the trial court, which shall be binding on magistrates and justices, to the end that such assessments are made as uniformly as possible, and which may include provisions requiring a prescribed or a minimum assessment for specified civil motor vehicle infractions.

The violator shall pay to the registrar the assessment imposed by the magistrate or justice within twenty days of the date the violator is personally notified or is mailed notice of the decision of the magistrate or justice, unless for good cause the magistrate or justice allows the violator a longer time to pay the imposed assessment.

The violator's obligation to pay such imposed assessment shall automatically be stayed during the pendency of any timely appeal to the appellate division or any subsequent appeal to an appellate court. The violator shall be required to pay such imposed assessment to the registrar within twenty days of the date the appellate division or the appellate court renders a decision that is adverse to the violator and that has not been further appealed.

(5) Questions of law arising in the disposition of a civil motor vehicle infraction in a noncriminal hearing before a justice may be appealed to the appellate division. Such appeals shall be governed by a simplified method of appeal established by rules promulgated by the chief justice of the district court department, subject to the approval of the supreme judicial court. Claims of appeal shall be accompanied by an entry fee in an amount established by the chief justice of the trial court. Proceedings under this chapter shall not be reviewable by a civil action in the nature of certiorari.

(6)(a) If a violator:

(i) fails either to pay the full amount of the scheduled assessment to the registrar or to request a noncriminal hearing within twenty days of the date of the citation plus such grace period as the registrar shall allow, or

(ii) fails to appear for a noncriminal hearing before a magistrate or a justice at the time required after having been given notice of such hearing either personally or by first class mail directed to such violator's mail address as reported to the registrar and after notice of such failure has been given to the registrar by the clerk-magistrate, the registrar shall notify such violator by first class mail directed to such violator's mail address that unless and until the violator pays to the registrar the full amount of the scheduled or imposed assessments for such civil motor vehicle infractions, plus any late fees or other administrative fees provided for by law or regulation:

(i) in the case of an operator violation, such violator's operators license, learners permit or right to operate will be suspended by operation of law and without further notice or hearing at the expiration of thirty days from the date of the mailing of such notice, and any license to operate a motor vehicle issued to such violator by the registrar will not be renewed upon or after the expiration date of such license; or

(ii) in the case of an owner violation, any registration of a motor vehicle issued to such violator will be suspended by operation of law and without further notice or hearing at the expiration of thirty days from the date of the mailing of such notice, and any registration of a motor vehicle issued to such violator by the registrar will not be renewed upon or after the expiration date of such registration.

Unless such notice is sooner canceled by the registrar, in the case of an operator violation, such violator's operators license, learners permit or right to operate, or in the case of an owner violation any registration of a motor vehicle issued to such violator by the registrar, shall be deemed suspended by operation of law on the date indicated on the notice mailed by the registrar, and shall remain suspended until reinstated by the registrar upon payment of the scheduled or imposed assessments for such civil motor vehicle infractions, plus any late fees or other administrative fees which he registrar is required or authorized by law or regulation to impose, unless such fees are waived in whole or in part by the registrar.

(b) If a violator attempts to pay a scheduled assessment with a check, credit card, debit card, or any other payment method that is returned unpaid or rejected, or fails to pay the full amount of an assessment imposed by a magistrate or justice pursuant to this section within the time allowed plus such grace period as the registrar shall allow, the registrar shall revoke any operator's license, learner's permit, certificate of registration or title, number plate, sticker, decal or other item issued by the registrar and held by the violator and order the return thereof forthwith.

(c) Payment of a scheduled assessment or an assessment imposed by a magistrate or justice pursuant to this section, plus any late fees or other administrative fees provided for by law or regulation, shall operate as a final disposition of the matter. The violator shall not be required to report to any probation officer, and no record of the matter shall be entered in any criminal or probation records of any court.

(B)(1) If a police officer observes or has brought to the officer's attention the occurrence of an automobile law violation that constitutes a criminal offense, the police officer: (a) may direct that a written warning be issued; (b) may arrest the violator without a warrant in accordance with the provisions and limitations of section twenty-one of chapter ninety for such offenses as are specified in that section; or (c) may determine that an application for criminal complaint shall be filed.

(2) If the police officer determines that an application for criminal complaint shall be filed, the officer shall so indicate on the citation. The citation shall notify the violator that a violator accused of a misdemeanor, with no accompanying felony, will be granted a hearing before such complaint issues, as provided in section thirty-five A of chapter two hundred and eighteen, if the violator so requests in writing within four days of the violation to the clerk-magistrate of the district court for the judicial district where the offense occurred. Such notification on the citation shall satisfy the notice requirements of section thirty-five A or chapter two hundred and eighteen.

The citation shall serve as the application for criminal complaint, supplemented if necessary with such additional information as shall be required by the administrative justice of the district court department. If a criminal complaint is issued, the procedure established for criminal cases shall then be followed. Each police chief may, from time to time, designate one person to sign all such complaints.

(3) If a violator in the case of a citation which alleges one or more criminal automobile law violations:

(a) fails without good cause to appear in court as required after having been summonsed or after having been given notice to appear either personally or by first class mail directed to such person's mail address as reported to the registrar, or such person's last known address as furnished by such person to the citing officer or to the court; or

(b) fails to pay within the time allowed the full amount of a fine, penalty, assessment, or other lawful amount required by a justice pursuant to law; or

(c) attempts to pay such fine, penalty, assessment, or other lawful amount with a check that is returned, unpaid, the clerk-magistrate shall notify the registrar. Such notice to the registrar may be given more than once in the same case if necessary.

Upon receipt of such notice, the registrar shall revoke any operators license, learners permit, certificate of registration or title, number plate, sticker, decal or other item issued by the registrar and held by the violator and order the return thereof forthwith. Such violator may not apply for or receive any operators license, learners permit, certificate of registration or title, number plate, sticker, decal or other item issued by the registrar unless and until the violator presents the registrar with a certificate of the clerk-magistrate of the court that the matter has been fully disposed of in accordance with the law or, in the case of a matter still pending before the court, that the violator is attending to the matter to the satisfaction of the court. The court shall not unreasonably withhold such certificate. The registrar may cancel such revocation, and so notify the court, if satisfied that it resulted through error of the registrar or the court.

Nothing herein shall limit the availability to the court of other enforcement mechanisms in addition to notice to the registrar, including the issuance of additional written notices, summonses or warrants, including warrants of distress as provided for in section forty-two of chapter two hundred and seventy-nine, or proceedings for civil or criminal contempt. Civil contempt actions shall be prosecuted by the district attorney or police prosecutor and heard by a justice pursuant to rules of court. Any summons or warrant issued pursuant to this subsection may be served by any officer authorized to service criminal process.

(C) If a violator is cited for a civil motor vehicle infraction in conjunction with and arising from the same occurrence as an automobile law violation that constitutes a criminal offense, both shall be recorded on the same citation whenever feasible and all parts of the citation shall be deposited with the clerk-magistrate as provided in section two.

The civil motor vehicle infraction shall retain its character as such and shall be decided and disposed of under the same general procedures and with the same provisions as to disposition and assessments as provided in subsection (A), with the following exceptions:

(1) The violator may not dispose of the civil motor vehicle infraction by paying the scheduled assessment to the registrar until there has been an adjudication of the associated automobile law violation.

(2) The violator may request a noncriminal hearing on such civil motor vehicle infraction by making a written request therefor at any time prior to the commencement of trial on the associated criminal automobile law violation. Such noncriminal hearing shall be conducted by a justice, and either may be conducted simultaneously with the criminal trial, or may be severed from the trial of the associated criminal automobile law violation if justice so requires. If the violator exercises the right to trial by jury in the first instance with respect to the associated criminal automobile law violation, the noncriminal hearing shall be conducted by the justice presiding over such trial.

(3) If the violator has been found guilty of, and is simultaneously being sentenced on, the criminal automobile law violation, the justice may order filed without imposition of an assessment any associated civil motor vehicle infraction as to which the violator admits responsibility or has been found responsible. In all other cases, if the violator admits responsibility of has been found responsible for the civil motor vehicle infraction, the justice shall require the violator to pay a civil assessment in accordance with subsection (A). Such civil assessment shall be paid directly to the registrar, or shall be paid to the clerk-magistrate and then paid over to the registrar, as the registrar and the chief justice of the district court shall jointly determine.

If the violator in such a case defaults solely on the portion of such citation that constitutes one or more civil motor vehicle infractions, such default shall be dealt with as indicated in subsection (A). If the violator in such a case defaults on the portion of such citation that constitutes one or more criminal automobile law violations, such default shall be dealt with as indicated in subsection (B).

NOTE 1   See Note following G.L. c. 90, § 1.

NOTE 2   "We agree with the town and the Commonwealth that [former] G.L. c. 90C, § 3(A), fifth par., does not constitute a statutory mandate that the police officer who issued the citation attend and present evidence at the clerk magistrate's hearing under sanction of having the charge against the defendant dismissed." *Town of Reading v. Murray*, 405 Mass. 415, 417 (1989).

SECTION 4
Criminal complaint; arrest without warrant; effect of conviction; access to records of offenders

Nothing in this chapter shall prevent a person other than a police officer from applying for a criminal complaint for an offense that constitutes a criminal automobile law violation under subsection (B) of section three of this chapter, and such person need not show that the violator has been issued a citation in connection with such violation.

Nothing in this chapter shall be construed to prevent a police officer from arresting any person without a warrant pursuant to the provisions of section twenty-one of chapter ninety for such criminal offenses and in such circumstances as are specified in said section. If any such arrest is made, it shall be noted on the citation and all copies of the citation except the police officer's copy and the police department copy shall be forwarded to the clerk-magistrate of the appropriate district court and one copy of same shall serve as the application for complaint. The police chief may from time to time designate one person to sign all such complaints. If such arrest is made in good faith, the arresting officer shall not be liable in civil proceedings arising from such arrest.

Any provisions of this chapter to the contrary notwithstanding, any payment of a penalty, fine or assessment made pursuant to the provisions of this chapter, including the payment of an assessment for a civil motor vehicle infraction, shall operate as a conviction for purposes of registry of motor vehicles action pursuant to chapter ninety and for purposes of the safe driver insurance plan established pursuant to section one hundred and thirteen B of chapter one hundred and seventy-five.

Nothing in this chapter shall be construed to prevent access by probation officers to driving records of offenders maintained by the registrar or by the motor vehicle insurance merit rating board.

NOTE   See Note following G.L. c. 90, § 1.

SECTION 5
Citation not deemed writ

A citation issued pursuant to this chapter shall not be deemed a writ as comprehended under the provisions of Article V of Chapter VI of Part the Second of the Constitution of Massachusetts.

SECTION 6
Printing and distribution of citation books; audit sheets

The registrar shall print citation books and distribute the same to each police chief, and shall obtain receipts therefor. Each police chief shall accept and be responsible for all citation books issued to that department. The registrar shall also furnish two copies of an audit sheet for each citation book, with the same number as the citation book.

When a citation has been completed the police chief or an officer of a rank not less than sergeant, or in the case of the state police of a rank not less than corporal and who is in charge of a state police barracks, shall record the issuance and disposition of said citation upon the audit sheet in such manner as the registrar shall prescribe, including but not limited to the name of the police officer who utilized the citation, and whether any citation was spoiled, mutilated or otherwise voided by an agent of the police department or organization. When all citations in a citation book are issued or used, the police chief shall sign and return one copy of the completed audit sheet to the registrar, keeping the other copy for the files of that department. The registrar shall determine the form and content, and the method of transmitting, such audit sheets. The registrar may at any time demand and inspect any citation, citation book or audit sheet used by any police department or police chief.

SECTION 7
Reciprocal and mutual agreements with other states

The registrar is hereby authorized to enter into reciprocal and mutual agreements with other states with regard to the interstate enforcement of motor vehicle violations and all other matters relating to motorists and motor vehicles, upon approval by the secretary of public safety.

NOTE   See Note following G.L. c. 90, § 1.

SECTION 7A
Electronic communication between courts and registry

The chief justice of the district court department and the registrar may jointly determine that any communication between the courts and the registry required to implement chapter ninety or this chapter may be accomplished solely by electronic means. The registrar may determine that any other communication by or to the registry required to implement chapter ninety or this chapter may be accomplished solely by electronic means.

SECTION 8
Construction of chapter

Nothing in this chapter shall be construed to supercede the powers and duties of the registrar as provided in chapter ninety.

SECTION 9
Disposal of citation, copy or record of issuance

It shall be unlawful and official misconduct to dispose of a citation or copies thereof, or of the record of the issuance of same in a manner other than as required by the provisions of this chapter.

SECTION 10
Penalty for falsification or disposal of citation, copy or record of issuance

Whoever knowingly falsifies a citation or copies thereof or a record of the issuance of same, or disposes of such citation, copy, or record, in a manner other than as required by the provisions of this chapter, or attempts so to falsify or dispose, or attempts to incite or procure another so to falsify or dispose shall be punished by a fine of not more than five hundred dollars or by imprisonment for a term not to exceed one year, or both such fine and imprisonment.

SECTION 11
Severability

If any of the provisions of this chapter, or the application of such provision to any persons or circumstances, shall be held invalid, the remainder thereof, or the application of such provision to persons or circumstances other than those wherein it is held invalid, shall not be affected thereby.

Chapter 90D. Motor Vehicle Certificates of Title

SECTION 32
Punishment

(a) Whoever falsely makes, alters, forges, or counterfeits a certificate of title or salvage title; or alters or forges an assignment of a certificate of title or salvage title, or supporting documents, or an assignment or release of a security interest on a certificate of title or a form the registrar prescribes; or has possession of or uses a certificate of title or salvage title, knowing it to have been altered, forged, or counterfeited; or uses a false or fictitious name or address, or makes a material false statement or fails to disclose a security interest, or conceals any other material fact, in an application for a certificate of title or salvage title; or supporting documents, shall be punished by a fine of not more than one thousand dollars or by imprisonment in the state prison for not more than five years, or in a jail or house of correction for not more than two years, or both.

(b) Whoever permits another not entitled thereto, to use or have possession of a certificate of title or salvage title or fails to mail or deliver a certificate of title, salvage title or application therefor to the registrar within ten days after the time required by this chapter, or whoever fails to deliver to the transferee or the registrar a certificate of title or salvage title within ten days after the time required by this chapter, or violates any other provision of the chapter, except as provided for in paragraph (a), shall be punished by a fine of not less than five hundred dollars nor more than one thousand dollars or by imprisonment in a jail or house of correction for not more than six months, or both.

(c) Notwithstanding subsections (a) and (b), a lienholder who is found to be in violation of section 24 in accordance with the procedures set forth in section 24A shall be punished by a fine of not less than $500 for a first offense. For each successive violation, the fine shall not be less than $1,000 nor more than $2,000; but, if the lienholder has been cited and punished by the registrar for noncompliance 5 or more times in the preceding 12 month period, the penalty shall not be less than $5,000 for each subsequent offense.

Chapter 94C. Controlled Substances Act

Section
1   Definitions
27   Sale of hypodermic syringes or hypodermic needles
27A   Collection and disposal of spent non-commercially generated hypodermic needles and lancets
31   Classes of controlled substances; establishment of criminal penalties for violations of this chapter
32   Class A controlled substances; unlawful manufacture, distribution, dispensing or possession with intent to manufacture, etc.; eligibility for parole
32A   Class B controlled substances; unlawful manufacture, distribution, dispensing or possession with intent to manufacture, etc.; eligibility for parole
32B   Class C controlled substances; unlawful manufacture, distribution, dispensing or possession with intent to manufacture, etc.; eligibility for parole
32C   Class D controlled substances; unlawful manufacture, distribution, dispensing, cultivation or possession with intent to manufacture, etc.
32D   Class E controlled substances; unlawful manufacture, distribution, dispensing or possession with intent to manufacture, etc.
32E   Trafficking in marihuana, cocaine, heroin, morphine, opium, etc., eligibility for parole
32F   Unlawful manufacture, distribution, dispensing or possession with intent to manufacture, etc. of controlled substances in classes A to C to minors
32G   Counterfeit substances; unlawful creation, distribution, dispensing or possession with intent to distribute or dispense
32H   Prosecutions not to be continued or placed on file; suspension or reduction of sentence; eligibility for parole, etc.
32I   Drug paraphernalia; sale, possession or manufacture with intent to sell; penalty; sale of tobacco rolling papers
32J   Controlled substances violations in, on, or near school property; eligibility for parole
32K   Inducing or abetting minor to distribute or sell controlled substances
32L   Possession of one ounce or less of marihuana; civil penalty and forfeiture; other sanctions or disqualifications prohibited
32M   Possession of one ounce or less of marihuana; drug awareness program
32N   Possession of one ounce or less of marihuana; enforcement consistent with non-criminal disposition provisions of Sec. 21D of Chapter 40; duty of police department; notice; failure to file certificate of completion of drug awareness program
33   Unlawful use of registration numbers in manufacture or distribution, or fraudulently obtaining possession of controlled substances; criminal penalties
34   Unlawful possession of particular controlled substances, including heroin and marihuana
34A   Immunity from prosecution under Secs. 34 or 35 for persons seeking medical assistance for self or other experiencing drug-related overdose
35   Unlawful presence at a place where heroin is kept or being in company of person in possession thereof
36   Protective custody of children found present where controlled substances are unlawfully kept or possessed
37   Theft of controlled substances from persons authorized to dispense or possess
38   Violation of Secs. 24(a), 25, 26 or 27
40   Conspiracy
41   Arrest without warrant
44   Violations of Sec. 34; acquittal, dismissal or indictment nol prossed; sealing of records
45   Photographing and fingerprinting of person charged with felony
47   Forfeiture of property
47A   Seized controlled substances and narcotic drugs; custodian; mailing for chemical analysis; destruction or disposal upon completion of trial

NOTE   General Laws c. 90, § 22 provides that persons convicted of a drug offense under Chapter 94C can lose their licenses for up to five years. Counsel is wise to check with the Registry of Motor Vehicles to ascertain the length of time a client's license may be revoked upon conviction of a specific statute found in Chapter 94C.

SECTION 1
Definitions
(Amended by 2014 Mass. Acts c. 165, § 130, effective July 15, 2014; 2015 Mass. Acts c. 46, § 80, effective July 17, 2015; 2016 Mass. Acts c. 52, § 19, effective Mar. 14, 2016.)

As used in this chapter, the following words shall, unless the context clearly requires otherwise, have the following meanings:

"Administer", the direct application of a controlled substance whether by injection, inhalation, ingestion, or any other means to the body of a patient or research subject by—

(a) a practitioner, or

(b) a nurse at the direction of a practitioner in the course of his professional practice, or

(c) an ultimate user or research subject at the direction of a practitioner in the course of his professional practice.

"Agent", an authorized person who acts on behalf of or at the direction of a manufacturer, distributor, or dispenser; except that such term does not include a common or contract carrier, public warehouseman, or employee of the carrier or warehouseman, when acting in the usual and lawful course of the carrier's or warehouseman's business.

"Bureau", the Bureau of Narcotics and Dangerous Drugs, United States Department of Justice, or its successor agency.

"Class", the lists of controlled substances for the purpose of determining the severity of criminal offenses under this chapter.

"Commissioner", the commissioner of public health.

"Controlled substance", a drug, substance, controlled substance analogue or immediate precursor in any schedule or class referred to in this chapter.

"Controlled substance analogue", (i) a drug or substance with a chemical structure substantially similar to the chemical structure of a controlled substance in Class A, B, C, D or E, listed in section 31 and which has a stimulant, depressant or hallucinogenic effect on the central nervous system that is substantially similar to or greater than the stimulant, depressant or hallucinogenic effect on the central nervous system of a controlled substance in Class A, B, C, D or E, listed in said section 31; or (ii) a drug or substance with a chemical structure substantially similar to the chemical structure of a controlled substance in Class A, B, C, D or E, listed in said section 31 and with respect to a particular person, which such person represents or intends to have a stimulant, depressant or hallucinogenic effect on the central nervous system that is substantially similar to or greater than the stimulant, depressant or hallucinogenic effect on the central nervous system of a controlled substance in Class A, B, C, D or E, listed in said section 31; provided, however, that "controlled substance analogue" shall not include: (1) a controlled substance; (2) any substance for which there is an approved new drug application; (3) with respect to a particular person, any substance for which there is an exception in effect for investigational use for that person, under section 8, to the extent conduct with respect to the substance is pursuant to such exemption; or (4) any substance not intended for human consumption before such an exemption takes effect with respect to that substance; provided, however, that for the purposes of this chapter, a "controlled substance analogue" shall be treated as the Class A, B, C, D or E substance of which it is a controlled substance analogue.

"Counterfeit substance", a substance which is represented to be a particular controlled drug or substance, but which is in fact not that drug or substance.

"Deliver", to transfer, whether by actual or constructive transfer, a controlled substance from one person to another, whether or not there is an agency relationship.

"Department", the department of public health.

"Depressant or stimulant substance",

(a) a drug which contains any quantity of barbituric acid or any of the salts of barbituric acid; or any derivative of barbituric acid which the United States Secretary of Health, Education, and Welfare has by regulation designated as habit forming; or

(b) a drug which contains any quantity of amphetamine or any of its optical isomers; any salt of amphetamine or any salt of an optical isomer of amphetamine; or any substance which the United States Attorney General has by regulation designated as habit forming because of its stimulant effect on the central nervous system; or

(c) lysergic acid diethylamide; or

(d) any drug except marihuana which contains any quantity of a substance which the United States Attorney General has by regulation designated as having a potential for abuse because of its depressant or stimulant effect on the central nervous system or its hallucinogenic effect.

"Dispense", to deliver a controlled substance to an ultimate user or research subject or to the agent of an ultimate user or research subject by a practitioner or pursuant to the order of a practitioner, including the prescribing and administering of a controlled substance and the packaging, labeling, or compounding necessary for such delivery.

"Distribute", to deliver other than by administering or dispensing a controlled substance.

"Drug",

(a) substances recognized as drugs in the official United States Pharmacopoeia, official Homeopathic Pharmacopoeia of the United States, or official National Formulary, or any supplement to any of them;

(b) substances intended for use in the diagnosis, cure, mitigation, treatment, or prevention of disease in man or animals;

(c) substances, other than food, intended to affect the structure, or any function of the body of man and animals; or

(d) substances intended for use as a component of any article specified in clauses (a), (b) or (c), exclusive of devices or their components, parts or accessories.

"Drug paraphernalia", all equipment, products, devices and materials of any kind which are primarily intended or designed for use in planting, propagating, cultivating, growing, harvesting, manufacturing, compounding, converting, producing, processing, preparing, testing, analyzing, packaging, repackaging, storing, containing, concealing, ingesting, inhaling or otherwise introducing into the human body a controlled substance in violation of this chapter. It includes, but is not limited to:

(1) kits used, primarily intended for use or designed for use in planting, propagating, cultivating, growing or harvesting of any species of plant which is a controlled substance or from which a controlled substance can be derived;

(2) kits used, primarily intended for use or designed for use in manufacturing, compounding, converting, producing, processing or preparing controlled substances;

(3) isomerization devices used, primarily intended for use or designed for use in increasing the potency of any species of plant which is a controlled substance;

(4) testing equipment used, primarily intended for use or designed for use in identifying or in analyzing the strength, effectiveness or purity of controlled substances;

(5) scales and balances used, primarily intended for use or designed for use in weighing or measuring controlled substances;

(6) diluents and adulterants, such as quinine hydrochloride, mannitol, mannite, dextrose and lactose, used, primarily intended for use or designed for use in cutting controlled substances;

(7) separation gins and sifters used, primarily intended for use or designed for use in removing twigs and seeds from or in otherwise cleaning or refining marihuana;

(8) blenders, bowls, containers, spoons and mixing devices used, primarily intended for use or designed for use in compounding controlled substances;

(9) capsules, balloons, envelopes and other containers used, primarily intended for use or designed for use in packaging small quantities of controlled substances;

(10) containers and other objects used, primarily intended for use or designed for use in storing or concealing controlled substances;

(11) deleted [effective July 13, 2006];

(12) objects used, primarily intended for use or designed for use in ingesting, inhaling, or otherwise introducing marihuana, cocaine, hashish or hashish oil into the human body, such as:

(a) metal, wooden, acrylic, glass, stone, plastic or ceramic pipes, which pipes may or may not have screens, permanent screens, hashish heads or punctured metal bowls;

(b) water pipes;

(c) carburetion tubes and devices;

(d) smoking and carburetion masks;

(e) roach clips; meaning objects used to hold burning material, such as a marihuana cigarette that has become too small or too short to be held in the hand;

(f) miniature cocaine spoons and cocaine vials;

(g) chamber pipes;

(h) carburetor pipes;

(i) electric pipes;

(j) air-driven pipes;

(k) chillums;

(l) bongs;

(m) ice pipes or chillers;

(n) wired cigarette papers;

(o) cocaine freebase kits.

In determining whether an object is drug paraphernalia, a court or other authority should consider, in addition to all other logically relevant factors, the following:

(a) the proximity of the object, in time and space, to a direct violation of this chapter;

(b) the proximity of the object to controlled substances;

(c) the existence of any residue of controlled substances on the object;

(d) instructions, oral or written, provided with the object concerning its use;

(e) descriptive materials accompanying the object which explain or depict its use;

(f) national and local advertising concerning its use;

(g) the manner in which the object is displayed for sale;

(h) whether the owner, or anyone in control of the object, is a supplier of like or related items to the community, such as a licensed distributor or dealer of tobacco products;

(i) direct or circumstantial evidence of the ratio of sales of the object to the total sales of the business enterprise;

(j) the existence and scope of legitimate uses for the object in the community;

(k) expert testimony concerning its use.

For purposes of this definition, the phrase "primarily intended for use" shall mean the likely use which may be ascribed to an item by a reasonable person. For purposes of this definition, the phrase "designed for use" shall mean the use a reasonable person would ascribe to an item based on the design and features of said item.

"Extended-release long-acting opioid in a non-abuse deterrent form", a drug that is: (i) subject to the United States Food and Drug Administration's extended release and long-acting opioid analgesics risk evaluation and mitigation strategy; (ii) an opioid approved for medical use that does not meet the requirements for listing as a drug with abuse deterrent properties pursuant to section 13 of chapter 17; and (iii) identified by the drug formulary commission pursuant to said section 13 of said chapter 17 as posing a heightened level of public health risk.

"Immediate precursor", a substance which the commissioner has found to be and by rule designates as being a principal compound commonly used or produced primarily for use, and which is an immediate chemical intermediary used or likely to be used in the manufacture of a controlled substance, the control of which is necessary to prevent, curtail, or limit manufacture.

"Isomer", the optical isomer, except that wherever appropriate it shall mean the optical, position or geometric isomer.

"Manufacture", the production, preparation, propagation, compounding, conversion or processing of a controlled substance, either directly or indirectly by extraction from substances of natural origin, or independently by means of chemical synthesis, including any packaging or repackaging of the substance or labeling or relabeling of its container except that this term does not include the preparation or compounding of a controlled substance by an individual for his own use or the preparation, compounding, packaging, or labeling of a controlled substance:

(a) by a practitioner as an incident to his administering a controlled substance in the course of his professional practice, or

(b) by a practitioner, or by his authorized agent under his supervision, for the purpose of, or as an incident to, research, teaching or chemical analysis and not for sale, or

(c) by a pharmacist in the course of his professional practice.

"Marihuana", all parts of the plant Cannabis sativa L., whether growing or not; the seeds thereof; and resin extracted from any part of the plant; and every compound, manufacture, salt, derivative, mixture, or preparation of the plant, its seeds or resin. It does not include the mature stalks of the plant, fiber produced from the stalks, oil, or cake made from the seeds of the plant, any other compound, manufacture salt derivative, mixture, or preparation of the mature stalks, except the resin extracted therefrom, fiber, oil, or cake or the sterilized seed of the plant which is incapable of germination.

"Narcotic drug", any of the following, whether produced directly or indirectly by extraction from substances of vegetable origin, or independently by means of chemical synthesis, or by a combination of extraction and chemical synthesis:

(a) Opium and opiate, and any salt, compound, derivative, or preparation of opium or opiate;

(b) Any salt, compound, isomer, derivative, or preparation thereof which is chemically equivalent or identical with any of the substances referred to in clause (a), but not including the isoquinoline alkaloids of opium;

(c) Opium poppy and poppy straw;

(d) Coca leaves and any salt, compound, derivative, or preparation of coca leaves, and any salt, compound, isomer, derivative, or preparation thereof which is chemically equivalent or identical with any of these substances, but not including decocainized coca leaves or extractions of coca leaves which do not contain cocaine or ecgonine.

"Nuclear pharmacy", a facility under the direction or supervision of a registered pharmacist which is authorized by the board of registration in pharmacy to dispense radiopharmaceutical drugs.

"Nurse", a nurse registered or licensed pursuant to the provisions of section seventy-four or seventy-four A of chapter one hundred and twelve, a graduate nurse as specified in section eighty-one of said chapter one hundred and twelve or a student nurse enrolled in a school approved by the board of registration in nursing.

"Nurse anesthetist", a nurse with advanced training authorized by the board of registration in nursing as a nurse anesthetist in an advanced practice nursing role as provided in section 80B of chapter 112.

"Nurse practitioner", a nurse with advanced training who is authorized to practice by the board of registration in nursing as a nurse practitioner, as provided for in section eighty B of chapter one hundred and twelve.

"Opiate", any substance having an addiction-forming or addiction-sustaining liability similar to morphine or being capable of conversion into a drug having addiction-forming or addiction-sustaining liability. It does not include, unless specifically designated as controlled under section two, the dextrorotatory isomer of 3-methoxy-n-methyl-morphinan and its salts, dextromethorphan. It does include its racemic and levorotatory forms.

"Opium poppy", the plant of the species Papaver somniferum L., except its seeds.

"Oral prescription", an oral order for medication which is dispensed to or for an ultimate user, but not including an order for medication which is dispensed for immediate administration to the ultimate user by a practitioner, registered nurse, or practical nurse.

"Outsourcing facility," an entity at 1 geographic location or address that: (i) is engaged in the compounding of sterile drug preparations; (ii) has registered with the federal Food and Drug Administration as an outsourcing facility pursuant to 21 U.S.C. section 353b; and (iii) has registered with the board of registration in pharmacy pursuant to section 36E of chapter 112.

"Person", individual, corporation, government, or governmental subdivision or agency, business trust, estate, trust, partnership or association, or any other legal entity.

"Pharmacist", any pharmacist registered in the commonwealth to dispense controlled substances, and including any other person authorized to dispense controlled substances under the supervision of a pharmacist registered in the commonwealth.

"Pharmacy", a facility under the direction or supervision of a registered pharmacist which is authorized to dispense controlled substances, including but not limited to "retail drug business" as defined below.

"Physician assistant", a person who is a graduate of an approved program for the training of physician assistants who is supervised by a registered physician in accordance with sections nine C to nine H, inclusive, of chapter one hundred and twelve.

"Poppy straw", all parts, except the seeds of the opium poppy, after mowing.

"Practitioner",

(a) A physician, dentist, veterinarian, podiatrist, scientific investigator, or other person registered to distribute, dispense, conduct research with respect to, or use in teaching or chemical analysis, a controlled substance in the course of professional practice or research in the commonwealth;

(b) A pharmacy, hospital, or other institution registered to distribute, dispense, conduct research with respect to or to administer a controlled substance in the course of professional practice or research in the commonwealth.

(c) An optometrist authorized by sections 66 and 66B of chapter 112 and registered pursuant to paragraph (h) of section 7 to utilize and prescribe therapeutic pharmaceutical agents in the course of professional practice in the commonwealth.

"Prescription drug", any and all drugs upon which the manufacturer or distributor has, in compliance with federal law and regulations, placed the following: "Caution, Federal law prohibits dispensing without prescription."

"Production", includes the manufacture, planting, cultivation, growing, or harvesting of a controlled substance.

"Radiopharmaceutical drug", any drug which is radioactive as defined in the Federal Food, Drug and Cosmetic Act.

"Registrant", a person who is registered pursuant to any provision of this chapter.

"Registration", unless the context specifically indicates otherwise, such registration as is required and permitted only pursuant to the provisions of this chapter.

"Registration number", such registration number or numbers, either federal or state, that are required with respect to practitioners by appropriate administrative agencies.

"Retail drug business", a store for the transaction of "drug business" as defined in section thirty-seven of chapter one hundred and twelve.

"Schedule", the list of controlled substances established by the commissioner pursuant to the provisions of section two for purposes of administration and regulation.

"State", when applied to a part of the United States other than Massachusetts includes any state, district, commonwealth, territory, insular possession thereof, and any area subject to the legal authority of the United States of America.

"Tetrahydrocannabinol", tetrahydrocannabinol or preparations containing tetrahydrocannabinol excluding marihuana except when it has been established that the concentration of delta-9 tetrahydrocannabinol in said marihuana exceeds two and one-half percent.

"Ultimate user", a person who lawfully possesses a controlled substance for his own use or for the use of a member of his household or for the use of a patient in a facility licensed by the department or for administering to an animal owned by him or by a member of his household.

"Written prescription", a lawful order from a practitioner for a drug or device for a specific patient that is communicated directly to a pharmacist in a licensed pharmacy; provided, however, that "written prescription" shall not include an order for medication which is dispensed for immediate administration to the ultimate user by a practitioner, registered nurse or licensed practical nurse.

SECTION 27
Sale of hypodermic syringes or hypodermic needles

Hypodermic syringes or hypodermic needles for the administration of controlled substances by injection may be sold in the commonwealth, but only to persons who have attained the age of 18 years and only by a pharmacist or wholesale druggist licensed under the provisions of chapter 112, a manufacturer of or dealer in surgical supplies, or a manufacturer of or dealer in embalming supplies. When selling hypodermic syringes or hypodermic needles without a prescription, a pharmacist or wholesale druggist must require proof of identification that validates the individual's age.

SECTION 27A
Collection and disposal of spent noncommercially generated hypodermic needles and lancets

(a) Notwithstanding any general or special law to the contrary, the department of environmental protection and the department of public health, in conjunction with other relevant state and local agencies and government departments, shall design, establish and implement or cause to be implemented a program for the collection and disposal of spent non-commercially generated, hypodermic needles and lancets. The program shall be designed to protect the public health and the environment by providing for the safe, secure, and accessible collection and disposal of hypodermic needles and lancets. The departments may collaborate with private companies as well as not-for-profit agencies when designing, establishing and implementing this program.

(b)(1) Sharps disposal programs may include, but are not limited to the following:

(i) a program for safe, secure home sharp disposal;

(ii) the establishing sharps collection centers in medical facilities and pharmacies;

(iii) establishing sharps collection centers in municipal facilities, including, but not limited to, fire stations, police stations, and public health offices; provided that sharps collection centers may be located at senior centers only for the purpose of disposing of medically necessary hypodermic needles; and

(iv) medical waste mail-back programs approved by the United States Postal Service.

(2) Medical facilities, pharmacies, and participating municipal facilities may work with the department of public health and the department of environmental protection to determine the proper program for sharps disposal implementation within each community.

(c) For the purposes of this section, a "sharps collection center" shall be an identified site within a community which:

(1) uses only collection containers that meet the requirements of the federal Occupational Safety and Health Administration and the federal Department of Transportation and is marked with the international biohazard symbol;

(2) provides secure, accessible collection containers on site;

(3) accepts sharps from sharps users that are in leak-proof, rigid, puncture-resistant and shatterproof containers;

(4) provides appropriate transfer containers for sharps users who fail to bring their sharps in suitable containers for placement in the collection container;

(5) has a written agreement with a medical waste transporter providing for regularly scheduled waste pickups;

(6) stores, handles, transports and treats the collected waste in accordance with department of public health regulations.

(d) The program shall be designed to protect the public health and the environment by providing for the safe, secure and accessible collection and disposal of hypodermic needles and lancets. The department of public health, in consultation with the department of environmental protection, shall adopt regulations to ensure the safe, secure, and accessible collection and disposal of hypodermic needles and lancets, and shall provide recommendations for legislative action to the joint committee on public health, the senate and house committees on ways and means, and the clerks of the senate and house of representatives. Included in the recommendations for legislative action shall be recommended punishments and fines for the inappropriate, unsafe or unlawful disposal of the hypodermic needles and lancets.

SECTION 31
Classes of controlled substances; establishment of criminal penalties for violations of this chapter
(Amended by 2012 Mass. Acts c. 244, § 9, effective Jan. 1, 2013; 2014 Mass. Acts c. 165, § 133, effective July 15, 2014; 2016 Mass. Acts c. 52, § 30, effective Mar. 14, 2016.)

For the purposes of establishing criminal penalties for violation of a provision of this chapter, there are established the following five classes of controlled substances:

CLASS A
(a) Unless specifically excepted or unless listed in another schedule, any of the following opiates, including their isomers, esters, ethers, salts, and salts of isomers, esters and ethers, whenever the existence of such isomers, esters, ethers and salts is possible within the specific chemical designation:

(1) Acetylmethadol
(2) Allylprodine
(3) Alphacetylmethadol
(4) Alphameprodine
(5) Alphamethadol
(6) Benzethidine
(7) Betacetylmethadol
(8) Betameprodine
(9) Betamethadol
(10) Betaprodine
(11) Clonitazene
(12) Dextromoramide
(13) Dextrorphan
(14) Diampromide
(15) Diethylthiambutene
(16) Dimenoxadol
(17) Dimepheptanol
(18) Dimethylthiambutene
(19) Dioxaphetylbutyrate
(20) Dipipanone
(21) Ethylmethylthiambutene
(22) Etonitazene
(23) Etoxeridine
(24) Furethidine
(25) Hydroxypethidine
(26) Ketobemidone
(27) Levomoramide
(28) Levophenacylmorphan
(29) Morpheridine
(30) Noracymethadol
(31) Norlevorphanol
(32) Normethadone
(33) Norpipanone
(34) Phenadoxone
(35) Phenampromide
(36) Phenomorphan
(37) Phenoperidine
(38) Piritramide
(39) Proheptazine
(40) Properidine
(41) Racemoramide
(42) Trimeperidine

(b) Unless specifically excepted or unless listed in another schedule, any of the following opium derivatives, their salts, isomers, and salts of isomers whenever the existence of such salts, isomers, and salts of isomers is possible within the specific chemical designation:

(1) Acetorphine
(2) Acetyldihydrocodeine
(3) Benzylmorphine
(4) Codeine methylbromide
(5) Codeine-N-Oxide
(6) Cyprenorphine
(7) Desomorphine
(8) Dihydromorphine
(9) Etorphine
(10) Heroin
(11) Hydromorphinol
(12) Methyldesorphine
(13) Methylhydromorphine
(14) Morphine methylbromide
(15) Morphine methylsulfonate
(16) Morphine-N-Oxide
(17) Myrophine
(18) Nicocodeine
(19) Nicomorphine
(20) Normorphine
(21) Pholcodine
(22) Thebacon

(c) Unless specifically excepted or unless listed in another schedule, any material, compound, mixture or preparation that contains any quantity of the following substances including its salts, isomers and salts of isomers whenever the existence of such salts, isomers and salts of isomers is possible within the specific chemical designations:

(1) Flunitrazepam
(2) Gamma Hydroxy Butyric Acid
(3) Ketamine.

CLASS B

(a) Unless specifically excepted or unless listed in another schedule, any of the following substances whether produced directly or indirectly by extraction from substances of vegetable origin, or independently by means of chemical synthesis, or by a combination of extraction and chemical synthesis:

(1) Opium and opiate, and any salt, compound, derivative, or preparation of opium or opiate

(2) Any salt, compound, derivative, or preparation thereof which is chemically equivalent or identical with any of the substances referred to in paragraph (1) except that these substances shall not include the isequinoline alkaloids of opium

(3) Opium poppy and poppy straw

(4) Coca leaves and any salt, compound, derivative, or preparation of coca leaves, and any salt, compound, derivative, or preparation thereof which is chemically equivalent or identical with any of these substances, except that the substances shall not include decocainized coca leaves or extraction of coca leaves, which extractions do not contain cocaine or ecgonine.

(5) Phenyl-2-propanone (P2P)
(6) Phenylcyclohexylamine (PCH)
(7) Piperidinocyclohexanecarbonitrile (PCC)
(8) 3, 4-methylenedioxy methamphetamine (MDMA)

(b) Unless specifically excepted or unless listed in another schedule, any of the following opiates, including isomers, esters, ethers, salts, and salts of isomers, esters, and ethers, whenever the existence of such isomers, esters, ethers and salts is possible within the specific chemical designation:

(1) Acetyl fentanyl
(1½) Alphaprodine

(2) Anileridine
(3) Bezitramide
(4) Dihydrocodeine
(5) Diphenoxylate
(6) Fentanyl
(7) Isomethadone
(8) Levomethorphan
(9) Levorphanol
(10) Metazocine
(11) Methadone
(12) Methadone-Intermediate, 4-cyano-2-dimethylamino-4, 4-diphenyl butane
(13) Moramide-Intermediate, 2-methyl-3 morpholine-1, 1-diphenylpropane carboxylic acid
(14) Pethidine
(15) Pethidine-Intermediate-A, 4-cyano-1-methyl-4-phenylpiperidine
(16) Pethidine-Intermediate-B, ethyl-4-phenyl-piperidine-4-carboxyl ate
(17) Pethidine-Intermediate-C, 1-methyl-4-phenyl-piperidine-4-carboxylic acid
(18) Phenazocine
(19) Piminodine
(20) Racemethorphan
(21) Racemorphan

(c) Unless specifically excepted or unless listed in another schedule, any material, compound, mixture, or preparation which contains any quantity of the following substances having a stimulant effect on the central nervous system:

(1) Amphetamine, its salts, optical isomers, and salts of its optical isomers.

(2) Any substance which contains any quantity of methamphetamine, including its salts, isomers and salts of isomers.

(3) Phenmetrazine and its salts.

(4) Methylphenidate.

(d) Unless specifically excepted or unless listed in another schedule, any material, compound, mixture or preparation which contains any quantity of the following substances having a depressant effect on the central nervous system:

(1) Any substance which contains any quantity of a derivative of barbituric acid, or any salt of a derivative of barbituric acid.

(2) Any substance which contains any quantity of methaqualone, or any salt or derivative of methaqualone.

(e) Unless specifically excepted or listed in another schedule, any material, compound, mixture, or preparation, which contains any quantity of the following hallucinogenic substances or which contains any of their salts, isomers, and salts of isomers whenever the existence of such salts, isomers, and salts of isomers is possible within the specific chemical designation:

(1) Lysergic acid
(2) Lysergic acid amide
(3) Lysergic acid diethylamide
(4) Phencyclidine.

CLASS C

(a) Unless specifically excepted or unless listed in another schedule, any material, compound, mixture, or preparation which contains any quantity of the following substances having a depressant effect on the central nervous system:

(1) Chlordiazepoxide
(2) Chlorhexadol

(3) Clonazepam

(4) Clorazepate

(5) Diazepam

(6) Flurazepam

(7) Glutethimide

(8) Lorazepam

(9) Methyprylon

(10) Oxazepam

(11) Prazepam

(12) Sulfondiethylmethane

(13) Sulfonethylmethane

(14) Sulfonmethane

(15) Temazepam.

(b) Nalorphine

(c) Unless specifically excepted or unless listed in another schedule, any material, compound, mixture, or preparation containing limited quantities of any of the following narcotic drugs, or any salts thereof:

(1) Not more than 1.8 grams of codeine per 100 milliliters or not more than 90 milligrams per dosage unit with an equal or greater quantity of an isoquinoline alkaloid of opium.

(2) Not more than 1.8 grams of codeine per 100 milliliters or not more than 90 milligrams per dosage unit, with one or more active, nonnarcotic ingredients in recognized therapeutic amounts.

(3) Not more than 300 milligrams of dihydrocodeinone per 100 milliliters or not more than 15 milligrams per dosage unit, with a fourfold or greater quantity of an isoquinoline alkaloid of opium.

(4) Not more than 300 milligrams of dihydrocodeinone per 100 milliliters or not more than 15 milligrams per dosage unit, with one or more active nonnarcotic ingredients in recognized therapeutic amounts.

(5) Not more than 1.8 grams of dihydrocodeine per 100 milliliters or not more than 90 milligrams per dosage unit, with one or more active nonnarcotic ingredients in recognized therapeutic amounts.

(6) Not more than 300 milligrams of ethylmorphine per 100 milliliters or not more than 15 milligrams per dosage unit with one or more active, nonnarcotic ingredients in recognized therapeutic amounts.

(7) Not more than 500 milligrams of opium per 100 milliliters or per 100 grams, or not more than 25 milligrams per dosage unit, with one or more active, nonnarcotic ingredients in recognized therapeutic amounts.

(8) Not more than 50 milligrams of morphine per 100 milliliters or per 100 grams with one or more active nonnarcotic ingredients in recognized therapeutic amounts.

(e) Unless specifically excepted or listed in another schedule, any material, compound, mixture, or preparation, which contains any quantity of the following hallucinogenic substances, or which contains any of their salts, isomers, and salts of isomers whenever the existence of such salts, isomers, and salts of isomers is possible within the specific chemical designation:

(1) 3, 4-methylenedioxy amphetamine

(2) 5-methoxy-3, 4-methylenedioxy amphetamine

(3) 3, 4, 5-trimethoxy amphetamine

(4) Bufotenine

(5) Diethyltryptamine

(6) Dimethyltryptamine

(7) 4-methyl-2, 5-dimethoxyamphetamine

(8) Ibogaine

(9) Mescaline

(10) Peyote

(11) N-ethyl-3-piperidyl benzilate

(12) N-methyl-3-piperidyl benzilate

(13) Psilocybin

(14) Psilocyn

(15) Tetrahydrocannabinols

(16) 4-Bromo-2, 5-Dimethoxy-amphetamine

(17) 3, 4-methylenedioxymethcathinone, MDMC

(18) 3, 4-methylenedioxypyrovalerone, MDPV

(19) 4-methylmethcathinone, 4-MMC

(20) 4-methoxymethcathinone, bk-PMMA, PMMC

(21) 3, 4-fluoromethcathinone, FMC

(22) Napthylpyrovalerone, NRG-1

(23) Beta-keto-N-methylbenzodioxolylpropylamine

(24) 2-(methylamino)-propiophenone OR alpha-(methyl-amino)-propiophenone

(25) 3-methoxymethcathinone

(26) 4-methyl-alpha-pyrrolidinobutyrophenone

(27) 2-(methylamino)-1-phenylpropan-1-one

(28) 4-ethylmethcathinone

(29) 3,4-Dimethylmethcathinone

(30) alpha-Pyrrolidinopentiophenone

(31) beta-Keto-Ethylbenzodioxolylbutanamine

(32) 3,4-methylenedioxy-N-ethylcathinone.

(f) Unless specifically excepted or listed in another schedule, any material, compound, mixture or preparation, which contains any quantity of the following hallucinogenic substances or cannabimimetic agents within the structural classes identified below:

(1) 2-(3-hydroxycyclohexyl) phenol with substitution at the 5-position of the phenolic ring by alkyl or alkenyl, whether or not substituted on the cyclohexyl ring to any extent;

(2) 3-(1-naphthoyl) indole or 3-(1-naphthyl) indole by substitution at the nitrogen atom of the indole ring, whether or not further substituted on the indole ring to any extent, whether or not substituted on the naphthoyl or naphthyl ring to any extent;

(3) 3-(1-naphthoyl) pyrrole by substitution at the nitrogen atom of the pyrrole ring, whether or not further substituted in the indole ring to any extent, whether or not substituted on the naphthoyl ring to any extent;

(4) 1-(1-naphthylmethyl) indene by substitution of the 3-position of the indene ring, whether or not further substituted in the indene ring to any extent, whether or not substituted on the naphthyl ring to any extent;

(5) 3-phenylacetylindole or 3-benzoylindole by substitution at the nitrogen atom of the indole ring, whether or not further substituted in the indole ring to any extent, whether or not substituted on the phenyl ring to any extent;

(6) 5-(1,1-dimethylheptyl)-2-[(1R,3S)-3-hydroxycyclohexyl]-phenol (CP-47,497);

(7) 5-(1,1-dimethyloctyl)-2-[(1R,3S)-3-hydroxycyclohexyl]-phenol (cannabicyclohexanol or CP-47,497 C8-homolog);

(8) 1-pentyl-3-(1-naphthoyl) indole (JWH-018 and AM678);

(9) 1-butyl-3-(1-naphthoyl) indole (JWH-073);

(10) 1-hexyl-3-(1-naphthoyl) indole (JWH-019);

(11) 1-[2-(4-morpholinyl)ethyl]-3-(1-naphthoyl) indole (JWH-200);

(12) 1-pentyl-3-(2-methoxyphenylacetyl) indole (JWH-250);

(13) 1-pentyl-3-[1-(4-methoxynaphthoyl)] indole (JWH-081);

(14) 1-pentyl-3-(4-methyl-1-naphthoyl) indole (JWH-122);

(15) 1-pentyl-3-(4-chloro-1-naphthoyl) indole (JWH-398);

(16) 1-(5-fluoropentyl)-3-(1-naphthoyl) indole (AM2201);

(17) 1-(5-fluoropentyl)-3-(2-iodobenzoyl) indole (AM694);

(18) 1-pentyl-3-[(4-methoxy)-benzoyl] indole (SR-19 and RCS-4);

(19) 1-cyclohexylethyl-3-(2-methoxyphenylacetyl) indole (SR-18 and RCS-8); and

(20) 1-pentyl-3-(2-chlorophenylacetyl) indole (JWH-203).

CLASS D

(a)

(1) Barbital

(2) Chloral betaine

(3) Chloral hydrate

(4) Ethchlorvynol

(5) Ethinamate

(6) Methohexital

(7) Meprobamate

(8) Methylphenorbarbital

(9) Paraldehyde

(10) Petrichloral

(11) Phenobarbital

(b) Unless specifically excepted or unless listed in another schedule, any material, compound, mixture, or preparation, which contains any quantity of the following substances, or which contains any of their salts, isomers, and salts of isomers whenever the existence of such salts, isomers, and salts of isomers is possible within the specific chemical designation:

(1) Marihuana

(2) Butyl Nitrite

(3) Isobutyl Nitrite

(4) 1-Nitrosoxy-Methyl-Propane.

CLASS E

(a) Any compound, mixture, or preparation containing any of the following limited quantities of narcotic drugs, which shall include one or more nonnarcotic active medicinal ingredients in sufficient proportion to confer upon the compound, mixture, or preparation valuable medicinal qualities other than those possessed by the narcotic drug alone:

(1) Not more than 200 milligrams of codeine per 100 milliliters or per 100 grams

(2) Not more than 100 milligrams of dihydrocodeine per 100 milliliters or per 100 grams

(3) Not more than 100 milligrams of ethylmorphine per 100 milliliters or per 100 grams

(4) Not more than 2.5 milligrams of diphenoxylate and not less than 25 micrograms of atropine sulfate per dosage unit

(5) Not more than 100 milligrams of opium per 100 milliliters or per 100 grams

(b) Prescription drugs other than those included in Classes A, B, C, D, and subsection (a) of this Class.

SECTION 32

Class a controlled substances; unlawful manufacture, distribution, dispensing or possession with intent to manufacture, etc., eligibility for parole

(Amended by 2010 Mass. Acts c. 256, § 67, effective May 4, 2012; 2012 Mass. Acts c. 192, § 12, effective Aug. 2, 2012.)

(a) Any person who knowingly or intentionally manufactures, distributes, dispenses, or possesses with intent to manufacture, distribute or dispense a controlled substance in Class A of section thirty-one shall be punished by imprisonment in the state prison for not more than ten years or in a jail or house of correction for not more than two and one-half years or by a fine of not less than one thousand nor more than ten thousand dollars, or both such fine and imprisonment.

(b) Any person convicted of violating this section after one or more prior convictions of manufacturing, distributing, dispensing or possessing with the intent to manufacture, distribute, or dispense a controlled substance as defined by section thirty-one of this chapter under this or any prior law of this jurisdiction or of any offense of any other jurisdiction, federal, state, or territorial, which is the same as or necessarily includes the elements of said offense shall be punished by a term of imprisonment in the state prison for not less than 3½ nor more than fifteen years. No sentence imposed under the provisions of this section shall be for less than a mandatory minimum term of imprisonment of 3½ years and a fine of not less than two thousand and five hundred nor more than twenty-five thousand dollars may be imposed but not in lieu of the mandatory minimum 3½ year term of imprisonment, as established herein.

(c) Any person serving a mandatory minimum sentence for violating any provision of this section shall be eligible for parole after serving one-half of the maximum term of the sentence if the sentence is to the house of correction, except that such person shall not be eligible for parole upon a finding of any 1 of the following aggravating circumstances:

(i) the defendant used violence or threats of violence or possessed a firearm, rifle, shotgun, machine gun or a weapon described in paragraph (b) of section 10 of chapter 269, or induced another participant to do so, during the commission of the offense;

(ii) the defendant engaged in a course of conduct whereby he directed the activities of another who committed any felony in violation of chapter 94C; or

(iii) the offense was committed during the commission or attempted commission of a violation of section 32F or section 32K of chapter 94C.

A condition of such parole may be enhanced supervision; provided, however, that such enhanced supervision may, at the discretion of the parole board, include, but shall not be limited to, the wearing of a global positioning satellite tracking device or any comparable device, which shall be administered by the board at all times for the length of the parole.

NOTE 1a "When knowledge is an essential element of an offense, it can be proved by circumstantial evidence." *Commonwealth v. Nichols*, 4 Mass. App. Ct. 606, 613 (1976). In *Nichols* there was evidence of heroin in various generally inaccessible locations in the defendant's apartment, i.e., behind a linen closet shelf and under the kitchen sink. As such "the jury could have inferred that the defendant had placed it there or had at least known of its existence." *Commonwealth v. Nichols*, 4 Mass. App. Ct. at 613.

NOTE 1b "The Commonwealth may prove that the defendant had knowledge of the contraband by circumstantial evidence, if the evidence warrants a reasonable inference to that effect. Discovery of contraband in the same automobile with the defendant, without more, is not sufficient evidence to warrant a finding of possession. Presence in the same vehicle supplemented by other incriminating evidence, however, may suffice to show knowledge or intent to control." *Commonwealth v. Garcia*, 409 Mass. 675, 686–87 (1991) (citations omitted). *See also Alicea v. Commonwealth*, 410 Mass. 384, 388 (1991) ("The fact that the defendant was operating a vehicle with a 'popped' ignition and containing heroin worth thousands of dollars tends to show his knowledge of the presence of the drugs.").

NOTE 2   See annotations dealing with knowledge following G.L. c. 269, § 10.

NOTE 3   The District Court also has jurisdiction of an offense commenced under paragraph (a) of this section. *See* G.L. c. 218, § 26.

NOTE 4   "To warrant a finding of constructive possession it must be shown that the defendant could exercise dominion or control over the heroin." *Commonwealth v. Lee*, 2 Mass. App. Ct. 700, 704 (1974).

NOTE 5a   **With Intent to Distribute.** "The quantity of heroin [100 some-odd bags] whether taken in conjunction with or considered apart from the cutting paraphernalia, was sufficient to warrant a finding of possession with intent to distribute." *Commonwealth v. Gill*, 2 Mass. App. Ct. 653, 657 (1974).

NOTE 5b   Police found 56 glassine bags of heroin worth about $560, several empty sheets of glassine bags, a bag of heroin, and equipment for processing heroin. They arrested two men coming from the defendant's house and recovered "a bundle" of heroin. Conviction for possession of Cl. A with intent affirmed. *Commonwealth v. Ellis*, 356 Mass. 574 (1970).

NOTE 5c   "In order to convict a defendant of possession with intent to 'distribute' the Commonwealth must prove that the defendant delivered or intended to deliver the substance 'other than by administering or dispensing a controlled substance.' G.L. c. 94C, § 1 (1990 ed.). The term '[d]eliver' is defined as 'to transfer, whether by actual or constructive transfer, a controlled substance from one person to another, whether or not there is an agency relationship.' *Commonwealth v. Ellis*, 356 Mass. 574 (1970). Thus, to purchase the substance, even with friends' money, intending to transfer it to them, constitutes distribution within the meaning of the trafficking statute. *See Commonwealth v. Poole*, 29 Mass. App. Ct. 1003, 1004 (1990) (defendant's storing marijuana with intention 'to transfer' it back to owner constituted distribution)." *Commonwealth v. Johnson*, 413 Mass. 598, 604–05 (1992).

NOTE 5d   **Intent to Distribute 2 Grams.** "While 2.04 grams is a small amount, the defendant's intent to distribute could be inferred not from the amount but from the manner of the packing and the general circumstances, including the fact that the defendant was spotted at a location high in drug activity, and the vigor of his attempt to avoid apprehension—an attempt that could reasonably be thought excessive for a mere user." *Commonwealth v. Martin*, 48 Mass. App. Ct. 391, 392–93 (1999).

NOTE 5e   "Where the evidence is sufficient to support a guilty verdict as to the indictment alleging distribution of heroin, that same evidence is sufficient to support a conviction on the indictment alleging possession of heroin with intent to distribute. It is reasonable to infer that, where the defendant had just sold one packet of heroin from the bundle of similar packets he possessed, he intended to sell more heroin from the same bundle." *Commonwealth v. Clark*, 446 Mass. 620, 624 (2006).

NOTE 6   **Expert Testimony.** It need not be shown that the evidence the expert will offer is essential to the jury; it is enough that the evidence will aid the jury in their deliberations. In *Nichols* it was permissible to admit "the opinion testimony of an experienced narcotics officer to the effect that the size of the tinfoil containing traces of heroin which had been found in the defendant's apartment was an indication that the foil had once contained a large quantity of heroin." *Commonwealth v. Nichols*, 4 Mass. App. Ct. 606, 609 (1976).

NOTE 7   A substance may be identified as a controlled drug, as defined in G.L. c. 94C, § 31, through the testimony of experienced police officers or the users of the drug rather than through laboratory analysis or testimony by a qualified chemist, but "[w]e suspect it would be a rare case in which a witness's statement that a particular substance looked like a controlled substance would alone be sufficient to support a conviction." *Commonwealth v. Dawson*, 399 Mass. 465, 467 (1987).

"Proof that a substance is a particular drug need not be made by chemical analysis and may be made by circumstantial evidence." *Commonwealth v. Alisha A.*, 56 Mass. App. Ct. 311, 313 (2002) (quoting *Dawson*, 399 Mass. at 467).

NOTE 8   **Chain of Custody.** "If there were weaknesses in the chain, that would go to the weight of the evidence rather than to its admissibility." *Commonwealth v. White*, 353 Mass. 409, 419–20 (1967), *cert. denied*, 391 U.S. 968 (1968).

NOTE 9a   **Duplicative Convictions.** Defendant convicted of distributing one bag of heroin and of possessing seven other bags of heroin with intent to distribute them. Conviction affirmed as "the defendant had completed one heroin sale, and was holding a separate cache of the drug for future distributions." *Commonwealth v. Diaz*, 383 Mass. 73, 84 (1981); *see also Commonwealth v. Richardson*, 37 Mass. App. Ct. 482, 489 (1994) ("In this case, the charges were based on distinct quantities of cocaine, the trafficking indictment being based on the eighty packets thrown out the rear window and the distribution charge arising from the bag sold to Detective Grice [ten minutes before].").

NOTE 9b   Conviction for possession and possession with intent to distribute the same drug will not lie. *Kuklis v. Commonwealth*, 361 Mass. 302, 307–08 (1972).

NOTE 10a   **Complaint/Indictments.** It is no defense that the word "knowingly" is omitted from the indictment. *Commonwealth v. Sepulveda*, 6 Mass. App. Ct. 868, 869 (1978).

NOTE 10b   It is no defense that the word "unlawful" is omitted from the complaint. *Commonwealth v. Munoz*, 11 Mass. App. Ct. 30, 31 (1980) (a second charge dealing with a motor vehicle violation which was affirmed at this level was reversed by the Supreme Judicial Court at 384 Mass. 503 (1981)).

NOTE 11   **Location of Contraband.** "'When contraband is found in a dwelling shared by a defendant and one or more other persons, a finder of fact may properly infer that the defendant is in possession of the contraband . . . from evidence that the contraband was found in proximity to personal effects of the defendant in areas of the dwelling, such as a bedroom or closet, to which other evidence indicates the defendant has a particular relationship.' *Commonwealth v. Rarick*, 23 Mass. App. Ct. 912, 912 (1986), and cases cited." *Commonwealth v. Pratt*, 407 Mass. 647, 652 (1990).

NOTE 12   **Beepers.** A message beeper is an item associated with the sale of drugs. While there are legitimate uses of beepers, an item not primarily designed for drug use may take on characteristics of drug paraphernalia by virtue of particular circumstances. *Commonwealth v. Sanchez*, 40 Mass. App. Ct. 411, 417 (1996) (quotation marks and citations omitted).

NOTE 13   **Related Statutes.**

G.L. c. 277, § 38—Allegations, bill of particulars, presumption and proof in prosecutions under Chapter 94C.

G.L. c. 111, § 13—Drug reports and analysis (contained elsewhere in this chapter).

G.L. c. 277, § 79—Form of indictment.

SECTION 32A

Class b controlled substances; unlawful manufacture, distribution, dispensing or possession with intent to manufacture, etc.; eligibility for parole

(Amended by 2012 Mass. Acts c. 192, §§ 13–14, effective Aug. 2, 2012.)

(a) Any person who knowingly or intentionally manufactures, distributes, dispenses, or possesses with intent to manufacture, distribute or dispense a controlled substance in Class B of section thirty-one shall be punished by imprisonment in the state prison for not more than ten years, or in a jail or house of correction for not more than two and one-half years, or by a fine of not less than one thousand nor more than ten thousand dollars, or both such fine and imprisonment.

(b) Any person convicted of violating this section after one or more prior convictions of manufacturing, distributing, dispensing, or possessing with the intent to manufacture, distribute or dispense a controlled substance as defined by section thirty-one of this chapter under this or any other prior law of this jurisdiction or of any offense of any other jurisdiction, federal, state, or territorial, which is the same as or necessarily includes the elements of said offense shall be punished by a term of imprisonment in the state prison for not less than 2 nor more than ten years. No sentence imposed under the provisions of this section shall be for less than a mandatory minimum term of imprisonment of 2 years and a fine of not less than two thousand and five hundred nor more than twenty-five thousand dollars may be imposed but not in lieu of the mandatory minimum term of imprisonment, as established herein.

(c) Any person who knowingly or intentionally manufactures, distributes, dispenses or possesses with intent to manufacture, distribute or dispense phencyclidine or a controlled substance defined in clause (4) of paragraph (a) or in clause (2) of paragraph (c) of class B of section thirty-one shall be punished by a term of imprisonment in the state prison for not less than two and one-half nor more than ten years or by imprisonment in a jail or house of correction for not less than one nor more than two and one-half years. No sentence imposed under the provisions of this section shall be for less than a mandatory minimum term of imprisonment of one year and a fine of not less than one thousand nor more than ten thousand dollars may be imposed but not in lieu of the mandatory minimum one year term of imprisonment, as established herein.

(d) Any person convicted of violating the provisions of subsection (c) after one or more prior convictions of manufacturing, distributing, dispensing or possessing with the intent to manufacture, distribute, or dispense a controlled substance, as defined in section thirty-one or of any offense of any other jurisdiction, either federal, state or territorial, which is the same as or necessarily includes, the elements of said offense, shall be punished by a term of imprisonment in the state prison for not less than 3 1/2 nor more than fifteen years and a fine of not less than two thousand five hundred nor more than twenty-five thousand dollars may be imposed but not in lieu of the mandatory minimum term of imprisonment, as established herein.

(e) Any person serving a mandatory minimum sentence for violating this section shall be eligible for parole after serving one-half of the maximum term of the sentence if the sentence is to the house of correction, provided that said person shall not be eligible for parole upon a finding of any one of the following aggravating circumstances:

(i) the defendant used violence or threats of violence or possessed a firearm, rifle, shotgun, machine gun or a weapon described in paragraph (b) of section 10 of chapter 269, or induced another participant to do so, during the commission of the offense;

(ii) the defendant engaged in a course of conduct whereby he directed the activities of another who committed any felony in violation of chapter 94C; or

(iii) the offense was committed during the commission or attempted commission of a violation of section 32F or section 32K of chapter 94C.

A condition of such parole may be enhanced supervision; provided, however, that such enhanced supervision may, at the discretion of the parole board, include, but shall not be limited to, the wearing of a global positioning satellite tracking device or any comparable device, which shall be administered by the board at all times for the length of the parole.

NOTE 1   See Notes following G.L. c. 94C, § 32.

NOTE 2   "The legislature has enacted two statutory provisions making the possession of cocaine with the intent to distribute it unlawful. The two provisions [G.L. c. 94C, §§ 32A(a) and (c)] set forth somewhat inconsistent potential penalties for conviction of that crime. . . . Although these are considerable similarities in the sentencing options available to a judge under the two statutes, § 32A(c) requires the imposition on conviction of 'a mandatory minimum term of imprisonment of one year,' whereas § 32A(a) contains no mandatory minimum prison term. . . .

"The only question . . . is whether there is any constitutional weakness because the prosecutor can elect whether to proceed against a defendant under § 32A (a) in the District Court or under § 32A (c) in the Superior Court (perhaps after a probable cause hearing in the District Court).5 [Footnote 5 reads: 'The District Court has original jurisdiction over a complaint charging a violation of § 32A (a) but does not have original jurisdiction over a charge of violating § 32A (c). See G.L. c. 218, § 26 (1986 ed.).]' . . .

"In the absence of any showing that individual prosecutors have acted arbitrarily or unfairly in exercising their discretion, we see no violation of State due process principles resulting from the coexistence of § 32A (a) and § 32A (c).

Cedeno v. Commonwealth, 404 Mass. 190, 190–91, 194 (1989) (citation omitted).

NOTE 3a   **Mandatory Sentence: 3 or 5 Years?** "The district attorney argued that the cocaine distribution conviction was under § 32A(c), with the consequence that the defendant faced a mandatory minimum term of five years for the repeat offender conviction under § 32A(d). Defense counsel argued that the cocaine distribution conviction was under § 32A(a), and thus that the repeat offender conviction was under § 32A(b), with a minimum mandatory term of only three years." The trial judge agreed with the District Attorney and the Appeals Court affirmed, finding that the indictment tracked the language of 32A(c), rather than 32A(a). Also, as "this indictment charged the defendant with possession with intent to distribute, not just a Class B controlled substance, but rather cocaine specifically, it put the defendant on notice that he was exposed to the more stringent penalties of subsection (c)." *Commonwealth v. Ortiz*, 39 Mass. App. Ct. 70, 73 (1995) (quoting *Commonwealth v. Zwickert*, 37 Mass. App. Ct. 364, 365–66 (1994)).

NOTE 3b   **Sentencing.** "In this case, we consider whether the mandatory minimum sentence required under G.L. c. 94C, § 32A(d) (§ 32A[d]), which was reduced effective August 2, 2012, by St. 2012, c. 192, §§ 14 and 48 (Crime Bill), applies to a defendant who committed an offense prior to the effective date of the reduction, but whose conviction and sentencing did not occur until after that effective date. We conclude that to interpret the statute amending the mandatory minimum sentence in § 32A(d) not to apply to the defendant would be inconsistent with the manifest intent of the Legislature that the benefits of the sentence reductions in the Crime Bill broadly apply to all those serving or subject to serving such sentences." *Commonwealth v. Galvin*, 466 Mass. 286, 286–87 (2013).

NOTE 4   **Duplicative Convictions.** "The defendant was convicted both of possession of cocaine with intent to distribute, G.L. c. 94C § 32A, and possession of cocaine, G.L. c. 94C § 34, for which he apparently received separate concurrent sentences. Insofar as the latter is a lesser included offense of the former, the two convictions cannot stand." *Commonwealth v. Clermy*, 37 Mass. App. Ct. 774, 778 (1995).

NOTE 5   Subsection (d). Section 32A(d) is not an independent crime. Rather, it "provides for an enhanced sentence for a person convicted of violating G.L. c. 94C, § 32A(c), after one or more convictions of certain drug-related crimes. . . . The provisions of G.L. c. 278, § 11A, indicate that the Legislature did not intend the belated imposition of an enhanced sentence in the circumstances of this case. The Legislature has prescribed a procedure that does not permit the imposition of a sentence for the underlying offense, and then, years later in a separate proceeding, the imposition of a harsher sentence because the offense was a repeat offense." *Bynum v. Commonwealth*, 429 Mass. 705, 708–10 (1999).

SECTION 32B
Class C controlled substances; unlawful manufacture, distribution, dispensing or possession with intent to manufacture, etc.; eligibility for parole
(Amended by 2012 Mass. Acts c. 192, §§ 15–16, effective Aug. 2, 2012.)

(a) Any person who knowingly or intentionally manufactures, distributes, dispenses, or possesses with intent to manufacture, distribute, or dispense a controlled substance in Class C of section thirty-one, shall be imprisoned in state prison for not more than five years or in a jail or house of correction for not more than two and one-half years, or by a fine of not less than five hundred nor more than five thousand dollars, or both such fine and imprisonment.

(b) Any person convicted of violating this section after one or more prior convictions of manufacturing, distributing, dispensing or possessing with the intent to manufacture, distribute or dispense a controlled substance as defined by section thirty-one under this or any prior law of this jurisdiction or of any offense of any other jurisdiction, federal, state, or territorial, which is the same as or necessarily includes the elements of said offense shall be punished by a term of imprisonment in the state prison for not less than two and one-half nor more than ten years, or by imprisonment in a jail or house of correction for not less than 18 months nor more than two and one-half years. No sentence imposed under the provisions of this section shall be for less than a mandatory minimum term of imprisonment of 18 months and a fine of not less than one thousand nor more than ten thousand dollars may be imposed, but not in lieu of the mandatory minimum term of imprisonment, as established herein.

(c) Any person serving a mandatory minimum sentence for violating this section shall be eligible for parole after serving one-half of the maximum term of the sentence if the sentence is to the house of correction, except that such person shall not be eligible for parole upon a finding of any 1 of the following aggravating circumstances:

(i) the defendant used violence or threats of violence or possessed a firearm, rifle, shotgun, machine gun or a weapon described in paragraph (b) of section 10 of chapter 269, or induced another participant to do so, during the commission of the offense;

(ii) the defendant engaged in a course of conduct whereby he directed the activities of another who committed any felony in violation of chapter 94C; or

(iii) the offense was committed during the commission or attempted commission of a violation of section 32F or section 32K of chapter 94C.

A condition of such parole may be enhanced supervision; provided, however, that such enhanced supervision may, at the discretion of the parole board, include, but shall not be limited to, the wearing of a global positioning satellite tracking device or any comparable device, which shall be administered by the board at all times for the length of the parole.

NOTE   See Notes following G.L. c. 94C, § 32.

SECTION 32C
Class D controlled substances; unlawful manufacture, distribution, dispensing, cultivation or possession with intent to manufacture, etc.

(a) Any person who knowingly or intentionally manufactures, distributes, dispenses or cultivates, or possesses with intent to manufacture, distribute, dispense or cultivate a controlled substance in Class D of section thirty-one shall be imprisoned in a jail or house of correction for not more than two years or by a fine of not less than five hundred nor more than five thousand dollars, or both such fine and imprisonment.

(b) Any person convicted of violating this section after one or more prior convictions of manufacturing, distributing, dispensing, cultivating or possessing with intent to manufacture, distribute, dispense or cultivate a controlled substance as defined by section thirty-one under this or any prior law of this jurisdiction or of any offense of any other jurisdiction, federal, state, or territorial, which is the same as or necessarily includes the elements of said offense shall be punished by a term of imprisonment in a jail or house of correction for not less than one nor more than two and one-half years, or by a fine of not less than one thousand nor more than ten thousand dollars, or both such fine and imprisonment.

NOTE 1   See Notes following G.L. c. 94C, § 32.

NOTE 2a   Smell of Burnt Marijuana. "Given our conclusion that G.L. c. 94C, §§ 32L–32N, has changed the status of possessing one ounce or less of marijuana from a crime to a civil violation, without at least some other additional fact to bolster a reasonable suspicion of actual criminal activity, the odor of burnt marijuana alone cannot reasonably provide suspicion of criminal activity to justify an exit order." *Commonwealth v. Cruz*, 459 Mass. 459, 472 (2011).

NOTE 2b   Smell of Unburnt Marijuana. "[W]e hold that [the] odor [of unburnt marijuana], standing alone, does not provide probable cause to search an automobile.

"In sum, we are not confident, at least on this record, that a human nose can discern reliably the presence of a criminal amount of marijuana, as distinct from an amount subject only to a civil fine." *Commonwealth v. Overmyer*, 469 Mass. 16, 17, 23 (2014).

NOTE 3   "We conclude that the passage of G.L. c. 94C, § 32L, did not repeal the offense of possession of marijuana with intent to distribute, G.L. c. 94C, § 32C(a), where the amount of marijuana possessed is one ounce or less. We also determine that, while the sale of any amount of marijuana remains a criminal offense under G.L. c. 94C, § 32L, third par., a prosecution under G.L. c. 94C, § 32C(a), is not limited solely to situations where the 'distribut[ion]' involves a sale." *Commonwealth v. Keefner*, 461 Mass. 507, 508 (2012).

NOTE 4   Social Sharing of Marijuana. "We now decide that the social sharing of marijuana is akin to simple possession, and does not constitute the facilitation of a drug transfer from seller to buyer that remains the hallmark of drug distribution. Cf. *Garcia-Echaverria v. United States*, 376 F.3d 507, 514 n.5 (6th Cir. 2004) ('casual sharing of marijuana' in social setting 'is akin to mere possession rather than distribution'). We therefore conclude that the social sharing of marijuana does not violate the distribution statute." *Commonwealth v. Jackson*, 464 Mass. 758, 764–65 (2013) (footnote omitted).

NOTE 5   Cultivation of Marijuana. "[W]e hold that the cultivation of one ounce or less of marijuana, regardless of its intended use, is a criminal offense under § 32C(a)." *Commonwealth v. Palmer*, 464 Mass. 773, 779 (2013).

NOTE 6   Federal Prohibition. "Where the 2008 initiative decriminalized possession of one ounce or less of marijuana under State law, and accordingly removed police authority to arrest individuals for civil violations, *see* G.L. c. 94C, § 32N, it also must be read as curtailing police authority to enforce the Federal prohibition of possession of small amounts of marijuana." *Commonwealth v. Craan*, 469 Mass. 24, 33 (2014).

SECTION 32D
Class E controlled substances; unlawful manufacture, distribution, dispensing or possession with intent to manufacture, etc.

(a) Any person who knowingly or intentionally manufactures, distributes, dispenses, or possesses with intent to manufacture, distribute, or dispense a controlled substance in Class E of section thirty-one shall be imprisoned in a jail or house of correction for not more than nine months, or by a fine of not less than two hundred and fifty nor more than two thousand and five hundred dollars, or both such fine and imprisonment.

(b) Any person convicted of violating this section after one or more prior convictions of manufacturing, distributing, dispensing or possessing with the intent to manufacture, distribute or dispense a controlled substance as defined by section thirty-one under this or any prior law of this jurisdiction or of any offense of any other jurisdiction, federal, state, or territorial which is the same as or necessarily includes the elements of said offense shall be punished by a term of imprisonment in a jail or house of correction for not more than one and one-half years, or by a fine of not less than five hundred nor more than five thousand dollars, or both such fine and imprisonment.

NOTE   See Notes following G.L. c. 94C, § 32.

SECTION 32E
Trafficking in marihuana, cocaine, heroin, morphine, opium, etc.; eligibility for parole
(Amended by 2012 Mass. Acts c. 139, § 102, effective July 1, 2012; 2012 Mass. Acts c. 192, §§ 17–27, effective Aug. 2, 2012; 2014 Mass. Acts c. 165, §§ 134–135, effective July 15, 2014; 2015 Mass. Acts c. 136, effective Feb. 22, 2016.)

(a) Any person who traffics in marihuana by knowingly or intentionally manufacturing, distributing, dispensing, or cultivating or possessing with intent to manufacture, distribute, dispense, or cultivate, or by bringing into the commonwealth a net weight of fifty pounds or more of marihuana or a net weight of fifty pounds or more of any mixture containing marihuana shall, if the net weight of marihuana or any mixture thereof is:—

(1) Fifty pounds or more, but less than one hundred pounds, be punished by a term of imprisonment in the state prison for not less than two and one-half nor more than fifteen years or by imprisonment in a jail or house of correction for not less than one nor more than two and one-half years. No sentence imposed under the provisions of this section shall be for less than a mandatory minimum term of imprisonment of one year and a fine of not less than five hundred nor more than ten thousand dollars may be imposed but not in lieu of the mandatory minimum one year term of imprisonment, as established herein.

(2) One hundred pounds or more, but less than two thousand pounds, be punished by a term of imprisonment in the state prison for not less than 2 nor more than fifteen years. No sentence imposed under the provisions of this section shall be for less than a mandatory minimum term of imprisonment of 2 years and a fine of not less than two thousand and five hundred nor more than twenty-five thousand dollars may be imposed but not in lieu of the mandatory minimum term of imprisonment, as established herein.

(3) Two thousand pounds or more, but less than ten thousand pounds, be punished by a term of imprisonment in the state prison for not less than 3½ nor more than fifteen years. No sentence imposed under the provisions of this section shall be for less than a mandatory minimum term of imprisonment of 3½ years and a fine of not less than five thousand nor more than fifty thousand dollars may be imposed but not in lieu of the mandatory minimum term of imprisonment, as established herein.

(4) Ten thousand pounds or more, be punished by a term of imprisonment in the state prison for not less than 8 nor more than fifteen years. No sentence imposed under the provisions of this section shall be for less than a mandatory minimum term of imprisonment of 8 years and a fine of not less than twenty thousand nor more than two hundred thousand dollars may be imposed but not in lieu of the mandatory minimum term of imprisonment, as established herein.

(b) Any person who traffics in a controlled substance defined in clause (4) of paragraph (a), clause (2) of paragraph (c) or in clause (3) of paragraph (c) of Class B of section thirty-one by knowingly or intentionally manufacturing, distributing or dispensing or possessing with intent to manufacture, distribute or dispense or by bringing into the commonwealth a net weight of 18 grams or more of a controlled substance as so defined, or a net weight of 18 grams or more of any mixture containing a controlled substance as so defined shall, if the net weight of a controlled substance as so defined, or any mixture thereof is:—

(1) Eighteen grams or more but less than 36 grams, be punished by a term of imprisonment in the state prison for not less than 2 nor more than 15 years. No sentence imposed under this clause shall be for less than a minimum term of imprisonment of 2 years, and a fine of not less $2,500 nor more than $25,000 may be imposed but not in lieu of the mandatory minimum term of imprisonment, as established herein.

(2) Thirty-six grams or more, but less than 100 grams, be punished by a term of imprisonment in the state prison for not less than 3½ nor more than 20 years. No sentence imposed under this clause shall be for less than a mandatory minimum term of imprisonment of 3½ years, and a fine of not less than $5,000 nor more than $50,000 may be imposed but not in lieu of the mandatory minimum term of imprisonment, as established herein.

(3) One hundred grams or more, but less than two hundred grams, be punished by a term of imprisonment in the state prison for not less than 8 nor more than twenty years. No sentence imposed under the provisions of this clause shall be for less than a mandatory minimum term of imprisonment of 8 years and a fine of not less than ten thousand nor more than one hundred thousand dollars may be imposed but not in lieu of the mandatory minimum term of imprisonment, as established herein.

(4) Two hundred grams or more, be punished by a term of imprisonment in the state prison for not less than 12 nor more than twenty years. No sentence imposed under the provisions of this clause shall be for less than a mandatory min-

imum term of imprisonment of 12 years and a fine of not less than fifty thousand nor more than five hundred thousand dollars may be imposed but not in lieu of the mandatory minimum term of imprisonment, as established herein.

(c) Any person who traffics in heroin or any salt thereof, morphine or any salt thereof, opium or any derivative thereof by knowingly or intentionally manufacturing, distributing or dispensing or possessing with intent to manufacture, distribute, or dispense or by bringing into the commonwealth a net weight of 18 grams or more of heroin or any salt thereof, morphine or any salt thereof, opium or any derivative thereof or a net weight of 18 grams or more of any mixture containing heroin or any salt thereof, morphine or any salt thereof, opium or any derivative thereof shall, if the net weight of heroin or any salt thereof, morphine or any salt thereof, opium or any derivative thereof or any mixture thereof is:—

(1) Eighteen grams or more but less than 36 grams, be punished by a term of imprisonment in the state prison for not less than 3½ nor more than 30 years. No sentence imposed under this clause shall be for less than a mandatory minimum term of imprisonment of 3½ years, and a fine of not less than $5,000 nor more than $50,000 may be imposed but not in lieu of the mandatory minimum term of imprisonment, as established herein.

(2) Thirty-six grams or more but less than 100 grams, be punished by a term of imprisonment in the state prison for not less than 5 nor more than 30 years. No sentence imposed under this clause shall be for less than a mandatory minimum term of imprisonment of 5 years, and a fine of not less than $5,000 nor more than $50,000 may be imposed, but not in lieu of the mandatory minimum term of imprisonment, as established herein.

(3) One hundred grams or more but less than two hundred grams, be punished by a term of imprisonment in the state prison for not less than 8 nor more than 30 years. No sentence imposed under the provisions of this clause shall be for less than the mandatory minimum term of imprisonment of 8 years, and a fine of not less than ten thousand nor more than one hundred thousand dollars may be imposed but not in lieu of the mandatory minimum term of imprisonment, as established therein.

(4) Two hundred grams or more, be punished by a term of imprisonment in the state prison for not less than 12 nor more than 30 years. No sentence imposed under the provisions of this clause shall be for less than a mandatory minimum term of imprisonment of 12 years and a fine of not less than fifty thousand nor more than five hundred thousand dollars may be imposed but not in lieu of the mandatory minimum term of imprisonment, as established therein.

(c½) Any person who traffics in fentanyl, by knowingly or intentionally manufacturing, distributing, dispensing or possessing with intent to manufacture, distribute or dispense or by bringing into the commonwealth a net weight of more than 10 grams of fentanyl shall be punished by a term of imprisonment in state prison for not more than 20 years.

For purposes of this subsection, "fentanyl" shall include any derivative of fentanyl and any mixture containing more than 10 grams of fentanyl or a derivative of fentanyl.

(d) Any person serving a mandatory minimum sentence for violating this section shall be eligible for parole after serving one-half of the maximum term of the sentence if the sentence is to the house of correction, except that such person shall not be eligible for parole upon a finding of any 1 of the following aggravating circumstances:

(i) the defendant used violence or threats of violence or possessed a firearm, rifle, shotgun, machine gun or a weapon described in paragraph (b) of section 10 of chapter 269, or induced another participant to do so, during the commission of the offense;

(ii) the defendant engaged in a course of conduct whereby he directed the activities of another others [sic] who committed any felony in violation of chapter 94C; or

(iii) the offense was committed during the commission or attempted commission of a violation of section 32F or section 32K of chapter 94C.

A condition of such parole may be enhanced supervision; provided, however, that such enhanced supervision may, at the discretion of the parole board, include, but shall not be limited to, the wearing of a global positioning satellite tracking device or any comparable device, which shall be administered by the board at all times for the length of the parole.

NOTE 1   See Notes following G.L. c. 94C, § 32.

NOTE 2   "In our view, a reasonable juror could have understood the jury instructions to mean either that the burden was on the defendant to prove that the bags did not contain 88.02 grams of heroin or that the certificates conclusively established that the bags did contain that amount. The instructions, therefore, were not correct." *Commonwealth v. Claudio*, 405 Mass. 481, 484 (1989). *But cf. Commonwealth v. Johnson*, 405 Mass. 488, 490 (1989) ("The only live dispute between the parties was whether the defendant had possessed the substance in question at all. Thus, there is little risk that a properly instructed jury would have chosen to disbelieve the evidence contained in the certificate of analysis.").

NOTE 3   **Registry of Motor Vehicles License Suspension.** Upon conviction of a violation or an adjudication of delinquency under subsections (b), (c), or (c½) of this section, the Registry of Motor Vehicles is statutorily required to suspend the defendant's license or right to operate for a period not to exceed five years from the date of conviction. G.L. c. 90, § 22½. The defendant may apply for a hardship license after completing any time served. G.L. c. 90, § 22½.

SECTION 32F
Unlawful manufacture, distribution, dispensing or possession with intent to manufacture, etc. of controlled substances in classes A to C to minors

(a) Any person who knowingly or intentionally manufactures, distributes, dispenses, or possesses with intent to manufacture, distribute, or dispense a controlled substance in Class A of section thirty-one to a person under the age of eighteen years shall be punished by a term of imprisonment in the state prison for not less than five nor more than fifteen years. No sentence imposed under the provisions of this section shall be for less than a mandatory term of imprisonment of five years and a fine of not less than one thousand nor more than twenty-five thousand dollars may be imposed but not in lieu of the mandatory minimum term of imprisonment, as established herein.

(b) Any person who knowingly or intentionally manufactures, distributes, dispenses, or possesses with intent to manufacture, distribute, or dispense a controlled substance in Class B of section thirty-one to a person under the age of eighteen years shall be punished by a term of imprisonment in the state prison for not less than three nor more than fifteen years. No sentence imposed under the provisions of this section shall be for less than a mandatory term of imprisonment of three years and a fine of not less than one thousand nor more than twenty-five thousand dollars may be imposed but not in lieu of the mandatory minimum term of imprisonment, as established herein.

(c) Any person who knowingly or intentionally manufactures, distributes, dispenses, or possesses with intent to manufacture, distribute, or dispense a controlled substance in Class C of section thirty-one to a person under the age of eighteen years shall be punished by a term of imprisonment in the state prison for not less than two and one-half nor more than fifteen years or in a jail or house of correction for not less than two nor more than two and one-half years. No sentence imposed under the provisions of this section shall be for less than a mandatory minimum term of imprisonment of two years and a fine of not less than one thousand nor more than twenty-five thousand dollars may be imposed but not in lieu of the mandatory minimum two year term of imprisonment, as established herein.

(d) Any person who knowingly or intentionally manufactures, distributes, dispenses, or possesses with intent to manufacture, distribute or dispense a controlled substance as defined in clause (4) of paragraph (a) of class B of section thirty-one, to a person under the age of eighteen years shall be punished by a term of imprisonment in the state prison for not less than five nor more than fifteen years. No sentence imposed under the provisions of this section shall be for less than a minimum term of imprisonment of five years, and a fine of not less than one thousand nor more than twenty-five thousand dollars may be imposed but not in lieu of the mandatory minimum term of imprisonment, as established herein.

NOTE 1   See Notes following G.L. c. 94C, § 32.

NOTE 2   **Related Statute.** Inducing delinquency of a child—G.L. c. 119, § 63.

SECTION 32G
Counterfeit substances; unlawful creation, distribution, dispensing or possession with intent to distribute or dispense

Any person who knowingly or intentionally creates, distributes, dispenses or possesses with intent to distribute or dispense a counterfeit substance shall be punished by imprisonment in a jail or house of correction for not more than one year or by fine of not less than two hundred and fifty nor more than two thousand and five hundred dollars, or both such fine and imprisonment.

NOTE   See Notes following G.L. c. 94C, § 32.

SECTION 32H
Prosecutions not to be continued or placed on file; suspension or reduction of sentence; eligibility for parole, etc.

(Amended by 2012 Mass. Acts c. 192, §§ 28–29, effective Aug. 2, 2012; 2013 Mass. Acts c. 84, § 4, effective Sept. 18, 2013.)

A prosecution commenced under paragraph (b) of section thirty-two, paragraphs (b), (c) and (d) of section thirty-two A, paragraph (b) of section thirty-two B, sections thirty-two E thirty-two F and thirty-two J shall not be placed on file or continued without a finding, and the sentence imposed upon a person convicted of violating any provision of said sections shall not be reduced to less than the mandatory minimum term of imprisonment as established in said section, nor shall any sentence of imprisonment imposed upon any person

be suspended or reduced until such person shall have served said mandatory minimum term of imprisonment.

A person convicted of violating said sections shall not, until he shall have served the mandatory minimum term of imprisonment established in said sections, be eligible for probation, furlough, work release or receive any deduction from his sentence for good conduct under sections 129C and 129D of chapter 127, nor shall he be eligible for parole except as authorized pursuant to subsection (c) of Section 32, subsection (e) of section 32A, subsection (c) of section 32B, subsection (d) of section 32E, or section 32J; provided, however, that the commissioner of correction, on the recommendation of the warden, superintendent or other person in charge of the correctional institution, or a sheriff, on the recommendation of the administrator of a county correctional institution, may grant to said offender a temporary release, subject to the rules and regulations of the institution and under the direction, control and supervision of the officers thereof for the following purposes: (1) to attend the funeral of a relative, to visit a critically ill relative, to obtain emergency medical or psychiatric services unavailable at said institution; (2) to participate in education, training, or employment programs established under section 48 of chapter 127; (3) to participate in a program to provide services under section 49B or 49C of chapter 127; or (4) to engage in employment under a work release program under sections 49, 49A, 86F or 86G of chapter 127. Section 87 of chapter 276 shall not apply to any person, 17 years of age or older, charged with a violation of said sections, or to any child between age 14 and 18, so charged by indictment under section 54 of chapter 119.

SECTION 32I
Drug paraphernalia; sale, possession or manufacture with intent to sell; penalty; sale of tobacco rolling papers

(a) No person shall sell, possess, or purchase with intent to sell, or manufacture with intent to sell drug paraphernalia, knowing, or under circumstances where one reasonably should know, that it will be used to plant, propagate, cultivate, grow, harvest, manufacture, compound, convert, produce, process, prepare, test, analyze, pack, repack, store, contain, conceal, ingest, inhale, or otherwise introduce into the human body a controlled substance in violation of this chapter. Whoever violates any provision of this paragraph shall be punished by imprisonment in jail or house of correction for not less than one nor more than two years, or by a fine of not less than five hundred nor more than five thousand dollars, or both.

(b) Any person who violates the foregoing provision by selling drug paraphernalia to a person under eighteen years of age shall be imprisoned in the state prison for not less than three nor more than five years, or by a fine of not less than one thousand nor more than five thousand dollars, or both.

(c) On any premises where tobacco rolling papers are sold, the person in control of such premises shall cause to be displayed in a prominent place therein a printed warning that such papers shall not be used in conjunction with the possession of a controlled substance, the possession of which is punishable by a fine or imprisonment. Whoever violates the provisions of this subsection shall be punished by fine of not less than fifty nor more than two hundred dollars.

(d) This section shall not apply to the sale of hypodermic syringes or hypodermic needles to persons over the age of eighteen pursuant to section 27.

NOTE 1   Neither Section 32I(a) nor the definition of drug paraphernalia in G.L. c. 94C, § 1 are constitutionally vague. *Commonwealth v. Jasmin*, 396 Mass. 653 (1986).

NOTE 2   "The Commonwealth need not introduce evidence bearing individually on each factor listed for consideration in the definition of drug paraphernalia." *Commonwealth v. Jasmin*, 396 Mass. at 658.

NOTE 3   "Although the indictment referred only to possession of scales, pipes and rolling papers, evidence of the defendant's possession of other objects was properly admitted. One dispositive reason is that the presence of other objects found in the shop was relevant to whether the items referred to in the indictment were drug paraphernalia and whether the defendant possessed intending to sell them." *Commonwealth v. Jasmin*, 396 Mass. at 659.

SECTION 32J
Controlled substances violations in, on, or near school property; penalties
(Amended by 2012 Mass. Acts c. 192, §§ 30–31, effective Aug. 2, 2012.)

Any person who violates the provisions of section thirty-two, thirty-two A, thirty-two B, thirty-two C, thirty-two D, thirty-two E, thirty-two F or thirty-two I while in or on, or within 300 feet of the real property comprising a public or private accredited preschool, accredited headstart facility, elementary, vocational, or secondary school if the violation occurs between 5:00 a.m. and midnight, whether or not in session, or within one hundred feet of a public park or playground shall be punished by a term of imprisonment in the state prison for not less than two and one-half nor more than fifteen years or by imprisonment in a jail or house of correction for not less than two nor more than two and one-half years. No sentence imposed under the provisions of this section shall be for less than a mandatory minimum term of imprisonment of two years. A fine of not less than one thousand nor more than ten thousand dollars may be imposed but not in lieu of the mandatory minimum two year term of imprisonment as established herein. In accordance with the provisions of section eight A of chapter two hundred and seventy-nine such sentence shall begin from and after the expiration of the sentence for violation of section thirty-two, thirty-two A, thirty-two B, thirty-two C, thirty-two D, thirty-two E, thirty-two F or thirty-two I.

Lack of knowledge of school boundaries shall not be a defense to any person who violates the provisions of this section.

Any person serving a mandatory minimum sentence for violating this section shall be eligible for parole after serving one-half of the maximum term of the sentence if the sentence is to a house of correction, except that such person shall not be eligible for parole upon a finding of any 1 of the following aggravating circumstances:

(i) the defendant used violence or threats of violence or possessed a firearm, rifle, shotgun, machine gun or a weapon described in paragraph (b) of section 10 of chapter 269, or induced another participant to do so, during the commission of the offense;

(ii) the defendant engaged in a course of conduct whereby he directed the activities of another who committed any felony in violation of chapter 94C.

(iii) the offense was committed during the commission or attempted commission of the a violation of section 32F or section 32K of chapter 94C.

A condition of such parole may be enhanced supervision; provided, however, that such enhanced supervision may, at the discretion of the parole board, include, but shall not be limited to, the wearing of a global positioning satellite tracking device or any comparable device, which shall be administered by the board at all times for the length of the parole.

NOTE 1   **Statute Is Constitutional.** *Commonwealth v. Alvarez*, 413 Mass. 224 (1992). *See also Commonwealth v. Taylor*, 413 Mass. 243 (1992).

NOTE 2   **Retroactivity.** "We ... hold that St. 2012, c. 192, § 30, applies to all cases alleging a school zone violation for which a guilty plea had not been accepted or conviction entered as of August 2, 2012, regardless of whether the alleged violation was committed before August 2, 2012." *Commonwealth v. Bradley*, 466 Mass. 551, 552 (2013).

NOTE 3   "Although some schools are not clearly recognizable as such from all points within the 1000 foot radius, the dealers bear the burden of ascertaining where schools are located and removing their operations from those areas or face enhanced penalties. . . .

"Section 32J does not require that the real property comprising a school be owned by the school." *Commonwealth v. Klusman*, 46 Mass. App. Ct. 919, 920 (1999).

NOTE 4   Issue: "[W]hether G.L. c. 94C, § 32J, applies if, within a school zone, a defendant is shown to have possessed cocaine with the intent to distribute it somewhere, whether within or outside the zone."

The Supreme Judicial Court answered "yes."
Commonwealth v. Roucoulet, 413 Mass. 647, 650 (1992).

NOTE 5   **Measurement.** Determined by "a straight line from the school's boundary line to the site of the illegal drug activity." *Commonwealth v. Spano*, 414 Mass. 178, 181 (1993).

NOTE 6   "Here, the evidence . . . as to the nature of the school was provided by several witnesses who were familiar with the city, the neighborhood, and the school itself. Indeed, the evidence came from those who had been inside the school, driven by it on a daily basis and had grandchildren who attended it for several years. *See Commonwealth v. Gonzales*, 33 Mass. App. Ct. 728, 730 n.1 (1992) (officers may use their personal knowledge to categorize the school). Children were seen carrying books, arriving on school buses, or being conveyed to and from the school by parents, and assisted by crossing guards." *Commonwealth v. Laro*, 68 Mass. App. Ct. 556, 559 (2007).

NOTE 7   **Place of Offense Dictates, Not of Arrest.** "The defendant contends that the judge erred in denying his motion for required finding of not guilty because the Commonwealth failed to provide sufficient evidence to prove beyond a reasonable doubt that he committed a drug offense within 1,000 feet of a school. The defendant argues that all that the Commonwealth established in this regard was a distance of 680 feet between the school and the place of his *arrest*. Because the arrest did not occur at the same location as the drug transaction eighteen days before, the defendant argues that the Commonwealth failed to establish that the *drug transaction* had occurred within 1,000 feet of a school. We agree." *Commonwealth v. Williams*, 54 Mass. App. Ct. 236, 244–45 (2002).

NOTE 8   "The statute requires only that the land in question be real property 'comprising' a school. It says nothing about ownership or claim of right. It is unnecessary to resolve questions about title, leases, licenses, easements and the like. . . . The Commonwealth need not establish that the point in question was on land owned by the school or any particular entity. Nor need the point be at or in a school building or structure. It is sufficient to show that the point was on land used for school purposes. Stated differently, the Commonwealth need not show the exact point at which the school's 'boundary' is located, so long as it may reasonably be inferred that the point at which the measurement is taken would fall within that boundary, i.e., that the point is located on property used for school purposes." *Commonwealth v. Johnson*, 53 Mass. App. Ct. 732, 734–35 (2002) (citations omitted).

NOTE 9a   Secondary School Defined. "Dictionary definitions of the term 'secondary school' are not vague and include 'a school more advanced in grade than an elementary school and offering general, technical, vocational, or college-preparatory courses,' Webster's Third New Int'l Dictionary 2051 (1993); 'a school intermediate between elementary school and college and usu[ally] offering general, technical, vocational, or college-preparatory courses,' Webster's Ninth New Collegiate Dictionary 1060 (1989); '[a] school that is intermediate in level between elementary school and college and that usually offers general, technical, vocational, or college-preparatory curricula,' The American Heritage Dictionary 1630 (3d ed.1996)." *Commonwealth v. Bell*, 442 Mass. 118, 124, 126, (2004) (directing the trial court to use one or more of these dictionary definitions in the jury charge).

NOTE 9b   Alternative Education Program is Secondary School. "[A]n alternative education program located in Boston, ABCD University High School, can be a 'secondary school' within the meaning of G.L. c. 94C, § 32J." *Commonwealth v. Bell*, 442 Mass. 118, 118–19 (2004).

NOTE 9c   "[A]ccreditation of a public preschool is not a requirement, and consequently the judge correctly omitted it as an element that the Commonwealth had to prove. The defendant points out correctly that the judge misspoke in referring to the Keith School as an elementary school when the evidence showed that it was a preschool. Acknowledging that the term 'elementary school' may not encompass a 'preschool,' the judge's slip could not have created a substantial risk of a miscarriage of justice. The statute applies equally to public preschools and public elementary schools; the evidence warranted a finding that the Keith School is a public preschool; and the jury got the point." *Commonwealth v. Thomas*, 71 Mass. App. Ct. 323, 326 (2008).

NOTE 9d   Child Care Center. "[T]he primary issue is whether a child care facility that enrolls younger than school aged children can qualify as a 'preschool' within the meaning of the school zone statute." The court concluded that it can. *Commonwealth v. Cruz*, 90 Mass. App. Ct. 60, 60–61 (2016).

NOTE 10   Public Playground. "[W]e interpret the word 'public' to modify both 'park' and 'playground,' such that the statute applies only to public playgrounds. . . . [As such,] privately owned playgrounds fall outside the scope of § 32J." *Commonwealth v. Gopaul*, 86 Mass. App. Ct. 685, 689, 690 (2014).

SECTION 32K
Inducing or abetting minor to distribute or sell controlled substances

Any person who knowingly causes, induces or abets a person under the age of eighteen to distribute, dispense or possess with the intent to distribute or dispense any controlled substance as defined herein, or to accept, deliver or possess money used or intended for use in the procurement, manufacture, compounding, processing, delivery, distribution or sale of any such controlled substance shall be punished by imprisonment in the state prison for not less than five years nor more than fifteen years. No sentence imposed under the provisions of this section shall be for less than a mandatory minimum term of imprisonment of five years and a fine of not less than one thousand nor more than one hundred thousand dollars may be imposed but not in lieu of the mandatory minimum five year term of imprisonment established herein.

NOTE   ". . . [Section] 32K does not require the prosecution to prove that the defendant knew the age of the youth employed in drug dealing; it is sufficient to prove the age of that youth." *Commonwealth v. Montalvo*, 50 Mass. App. Ct. 85, 89 (2000).

SECTION 32L
Possession of one ounce or less of marihuana; civil penalty and forfeiture; other sanctions or disqualifications prohibited

Notwithstanding any general or special law to the contrary, possession of one ounce or less of marihuana shall only be a civil offense, subjecting an offender who is eighteen years of age or older to a civil penalty of one hundred dollars and forfeiture of the marihuana, but not to any other form of criminal or civil punishment or disqualification. An offender under the age of eighteen shall be subject to the same forfeiture and civil penalty provisions, provided he or she completes a drug awareness program which meets the criteria set forth in Section 32M of this Chapter. The parents or legal guardian of any offender under the age of eighteen shall be notified in accordance with Section 32N of this Chapter of the offense and the availability of a drug awareness program and community service option. If an offender under the age of eighteen fails within one year of the offense to complete both a drug awareness program and the required community service, the civil penalty may be increased pursuant to Section 32N of this Chapter to one thousand dollars and the offender and his or her parents shall be jointly and severally liable to pay that amount.

Except as specifically provided in "An Act Establishing A Sensible State Marihuana Policy," neither the Commonwealth nor any of its political subdivisions or their respective agencies, authorities or instrumentalities may impose any form of penalty, sanction or disqualification on an offender for possessing an ounce or less of marihuana. By way of illustration rather than limitation, possession of one ounce or less of marihuana shall not provide a basis to deny an offender student financial aid, public housing or any form of public financial assistance including unemployment benefits, to deny the right to operate a motor vehicle or to disqualify an offender from serving as a foster parent or adoptive parent. Information concerning the offense of possession of one ounce or less of marihuana shall not be deemed "criminal offender record information," "evaluative information," or "intelligence information" as those terms are defined in Section 167 of Chapter 6 of the General Laws and shall not be recorded in the Criminal Offender Record Information system.

As used herein, "possession of one ounce or less of marihuana" includes possession of one ounce or less of marihuana or tetrahydrocannabinol and having cannabinoids or cannibinoid metabolites in the urine, blood, saliva, sweat, hair, fingernails, toe nails or other tissue or fluid of the human body. Nothing contained herein shall be construed to repeal or modify existing laws, ordinances or bylaws, regulations, personnel practices or policies concerning the operation of motor vehicles or other actions taken while under the influence of marihuana or tetrahydrocannabinol, laws concerning the unlawful possession of prescription forms of marihuana or tetrahydrocannabinol such as Marinol, possession of more than one ounce of marihuana or tetrahydrocannabinol, or selling, manufacturing or trafficking in marihuana or tetrahydrocannabinol. Nothing contained herein shall prohibit a political subdivision of the Commonwealth from enacting ordinances or bylaws regulating or prohibiting the consumption of marihuana or tetrahydrocannabinol in public places and providing for additional penalties for the public use of marihuana or tetrahydrocannabinol.

NOTE 1a   Smell of Burnt Marijuana. "Given our conclusion that G.L. c. 94C, §§ 32L–32N, has changed the status of possessing one ounce or less of marijuana from a crime to a civil violation, without at least some other additional fact to bolster a reasonable suspicion of actual criminal activity, the odor of burnt marijuana alone cannot reasonably provide suspicion of criminal activity to justify an exit order." *Commonwealth v. Cruz*, 459 Mass. 459, 472 (2011).

NOTE 1b   Smell of Unburnt Marijuana. "[W]e hold that [the] odor [of unburnt marijuana], standing alone, does not provide probable cause to search an automobile.

"In sum, we are not confident, at least on this record, that a human nose can discern reliably the presence of a criminal amount of marijuana, as distinct from an amount subject only to a civil fine." *Commonwealth v. Overmyer*, 469 Mass. 16, 17, 23 (2014).

NOTE 1c   Reasonable Suspicion Not Enough for Motor Vehicle Stop. "[W]e conclude that in a case such as the present one, where the only factor leading an officer to conclude that an individual possesses marijuana is the smell of burnt marijuana, this factor supports a reasonable suspicion that that individual is committing the civil offense of possession of a small quantity of marijuana, but not probable cause to believe that he or she is committing the offense. Therefore, the question in this case is whether the Fourth Amendment and art. 14 permit police to stop a vehicle where they have reasonable suspicion, but not probable cause, to believe that a civil, infractionary offense of marijuana possession is occurring or has occurred." The court answered in the negative. *Commonwealth v. Rodriguez*, 472 Mass. 767, 775 (2015).

NOTE 2   Possession with Intent to Distribute. "We conclude that the passage of G.L. c. 94C, § 32L, did not repeal the offense of possession of marijuana with intent to distribute, G.L. c. 94C, § 32C(a), where the amount of marijuana possessed is one ounce or less. We also determine that, while the sale of any amount of marijuana remains a criminal offense under G.L. c. 94C, § 32L, third par., a prosecution under G.L. c. 94C, § 32C(a), is not limited solely to situations where the 'distribut[ion]' involves a sale." *Commonwealth v. Keefner*, 461 Mass. 507, 508 (2012).

NOTE 3   Social Sharing of Marijuana. "We now decide that the social sharing of marijuana is akin to simple possession, and does not constitute the facilitation of a drug transfer from seller to buyer that remains the hallmark of drug distribution. *Cf. Garcia-Echaverria v. United States*, 376 F.3d 507, 514 n.5 (6th Cir. 2004) ('casual sharing of marijuana' in social setting 'is akin to mere possession rather than distribution'). We therefore conclude that the social sharing of marijuana does not violate the distribution statute." *Commonwealth v. Jackson*, 464 Mass. 758, 764–65 (2013) (footnote omitted).

NOTE 4   Cultivation of Marijuana. "[W]e hold that the cultivation of one ounce or less of marijuana, regardless of its intended use, is a criminal offense under § 32C(a)." *Commonwealth v. Palmer*, 464 Mass. 773, 779 (2013).

NOTE 5   Federal Prohibition. "Where the 2008 initiative decriminalized possession of one ounce or less of marijuana under State law, and accordingly removed police authority to arrest individuals for civil violations, *see* G.L. c. 94C, § 32N, it also must be read as curtailing police authority to enforce the Federal prohibition of possession of small amounts of marijuana." *Commonwealth v. Craan*, 469 Mass. 24, 33 (2014).

SECTION 32M
Possession of one ounce or less of marihuana; drug awareness program
(Added by 2013 Mass. Acts c. 84, § 5, effective Sept. 18, 2013.)

An offender under the age of eighteen is required to complete a drug awareness program within one year of the offense for possession of one ounce or less of marihuana. In addition to the civil penalties authorized by Section 32L and 32N of this Chapter, the failure of such an offender to com-

plete such a program may be a basis for delinquency proceedings for persons under the age of 18 at the time of their offense. The drug awareness program must provide at least four hours of classroom instruction or group discussion and ten hours of community service. In addition to the programs and curricula it must establish and maintain pursuant to Section 7 of Chapter 18A of the General Laws, the bureau of educational services within the department of youth services or any successor to said bureau shall develop the drug awareness programs. The subject matter of such drug awareness programs shall be specific to the use and abuse of marihuana and other controlled substances with particular emphasis on early detection and prevention of abuse of substances.

SECTION 32N
Possession of one ounce or less of marihuana; enforcement consistent with non-criminal disposition provisions of Sec. 21D of chapter 40; duty of police department; notice; failure to file certificate of completion of drug awareness program

The police department serving each political subdivision of the Commonwealth shall enforce Section 32L in a manner consistent with the non-criminal disposition provisions of Section 21D of Chapter 40 of the General Laws, as modified in this Section.

The person in charge of each such department shall direct the department's public safety officer or another appropriate member of the department to function as a liaison between the department and persons providing drug awareness programs pursuant to Section 32M of this Chapter and the Clerk-Magistrate's office of the District Court serving the political subdivision. The person in charge shall also issue books of non-criminal citation forms to the department's officers which conform with the provisions of this Section and Section 21D of Chapter 40 of the General Laws.

In addition to the notice requirements set forth in Section 21D of Chapter 40 of the General Laws, a second copy of the notice delivered to an offender under the age of eighteen shall be mailed or delivered to at least one of that offender's parents having custody of the offender, or, where there is no such person, to that offender's legal guardian at said parent or legal guardian's last known address. If an offender under the age of eighteen, a parent or legal guardian fails to file with the Clerk of the appropriate Court a certificate that the offender has completed a drug awareness program in accordance with Section 32M within one year of the relevant offense, the Clerk shall notify the offender, parent or guardian and the enforcing person who issued the original notice to the offender of a hearing to show cause why the civil penalty should not be increased to one thousand dollars. Factors to be considered in weighing cause shall be limited to financial capacity to pay any increase, the offender's ability to participate in a compliant drug awareness program and the availability of a suitable drug awareness program. Any civil penalties imposed under the provisions of "An Act Establishing A Sensible State Marihuana Policy" shall inure to the city or town where the offense occurred.

1

SECTION 33
Unlawful use of registration numbers in manufacture or distribution, or fraudulently obtaining possession of controlled substances; criminal penalties

(a) No person shall knowingly or intentionally use in the course of the manufacture or distribution of a controlled substance a registration number which is fictitious, revoked, suspended, or issued to another person.

(b) No person shall utter a false prescription for a controlled substance, nor knowingly or intentionally acquire or obtain possession of a controlled substance by means of forgery, fraud, deception or subterfuge, including but not limited to the forgery or falsification of a prescription or the nondisclosure of a material fact in order to obtain a controlled substance from a practitioner.

(c) Whoever violates any provision of this section shall be punished by imprisonment in the state prison for not more than four years or in a house of correction for not more than two and one half years or by a fine of not more than twenty thousand dollars, or by both such fine and imprisonment. Whoever violates any provision of this section after one or more prior convictions of a violation of this section, or of a felony under any other provision of this chapter, or under a provision of prior law relative to the sale or manufacture of a narcotic drug or a harmful drug as defined in said earlier law shall be punished by imprisonment in the state prison for not more than eight years or in a jail or house of correction for not more than two and one-half years, or by a fine of not more than thirty thousand dollars or by both such fine and imprisonment.

SECTION 34
Unlawful possession of particular controlled substances, including heroin and marihuana
(Amended by 2015 Mass. Acts c. 46, § 90, effective July 17, 2015.)

No person knowingly or intentionally shall possess a controlled substance unless such substance was obtained directly, or pursuant to a valid prescription or order, from a practitioner while acting in the course of his professional practice, or except as otherwise authorized by the provisions of this chapter. Except as provided in Section 32L of this Chapter or as hereinafter provided, any person who violates this section shall be punished by imprisonment for not more than one year or by a fine of not more than one thousand dollars, or by both such fine and imprisonment. Any person who violates this section by possessing heroin shall for the first offense be punished by imprisonment in a house of correction for not more than two years or by a fine of not more than two thousand dollars, or both, and for a second or subsequent offense shall be punished by imprisonment in the state prison for not less than two and one-half years nor more than five years or by a fine of not more than five thousand dollars and imprisonment in a jail or house of correction for not more than two and one-half years. Any person who violates this section by possession of more than one ounce of marihuana or a controlled substance in Class E of section thirty-one shall be punished by imprisonment in a house of correction for not more than six months or a fine of five hundred dollars, or both. Except for an offense involving a controlled substance in Class E of section thirty-one, whoever violates the provisions of this section after one or more convictions of a violation of this section or of a felony under any other provisions

of this chapter, or of a corresponding provision of earlier law relating to the sale or manufacture of a narcotic drug as defined in said earlier law, shall be punished by imprisonment in a house of correction for not more than two years or by a fine of not more than two thousand dollars, or both.

If any person who is charged with a violation of this section has not previously been convicted of a violation of any provision of this chapter or other provision of prior law relative to narcotic drugs or harmful drugs as defined in said prior law, or of a felony under the laws of any state or of the United States relating to such drugs, has had his case continued without a finding to a certain date, or has been convicted and placed on probation, and if, during the period of said continuance or of said probation, such person does not violate any of the conditions of said continuance or said probation, then upon the expiration of such period the court may dismiss the proceedings against him, and may order sealed all official records relating to his arrest, indictment, conviction, probation, continuance or discharge pursuant to this section; provided, however, that departmental records which are not public records, maintained by police and other law enforcement agencies, shall not be sealed; and provided further, that such a record shall be maintained in a separate file by the department of probation solely for the purpose of use by the courts in determining whether or not in subsequent proceedings such person qualifies under this section. The record maintained by the department of probation shall contain only identifying information concerning the person and a statement that he has had his record sealed pursuant to the provisions of this section. Any conviction, the record of which has been sealed under this section, shall not be deemed a conviction for purposes of any disqualification or for any other purpose. No person as to whom such sealing has been ordered shall be held thereafter under any provision of any law to be guilty of perjury or otherwise giving a false statement by reason of his failure to recite or acknowledge such arrest, indictment, conviction, dismissal, continuance, sealing, or any other related court proceeding, in response to any inquiry made of him for any purpose.

Notwithstanding any other penalty provision of this section, any person who is convicted for the first time under this section for the possession of marihuana or a controlled substance in Class E and who has not previously been convicted of any offense pursuant to the provisions of this chapter, or any provision of prior law relating to narcotic drugs or harmful drugs as defined in said prior law shall be placed on probation unless such person does not consent thereto, or unless the court files a written memorandum stating the reasons for not so doing. Upon successful completion of said probation, the case shall be dismissed and records shall be sealed.

It shall be a prima facie defense to a charge of possession of marihuana under this section that the defendant is a patient certified to participate in a therapeutic research program described in chapter ninety-four D, and possessed the marihuana for personal use pursuant to such program.

Notwithstanding any general or special law to the contrary, a laboratory may possess, store, analyze, process and test medical marijuana and medical marijuana-infused products; provided, however, that such laboratory shall do so in accordance with the department's regulations and written guidelines governing procedures for quality control and testing of products for potential contaminants.

NOTE 1   See Notes following G.L. c. 94C, § 32.

NOTE 2   **Criminal Responsibility.** "[W]e reject both drug addiction and the normal consequences of the consumption of drugs as a basis for a claim of lack of criminal responsibility." *Commonwealth v. Sheehan*, 376 Mass. 765, 772 (1978).

NOTE 3   Being present where heroin is found (Section 35) is *not* a lesser included offense of possession of heroin (this section). *Commonwealth v. Rodriguez*, 11 Mass. App. Ct. 379 (1981).

NOTE 4   "If any ambiguity exists in § 34, it is the use of the term 'notwithstanding' at the beginning of paragraph three. . . . Paragraph three begins with the language, '[N]otwithstanding any other penalty provision of this section . . . .' We interpret this as precluding imposition of any penalty otherwise authorized by paragraph one of § 34. Mandatory probation is the exclusive punishment that may be imposed on a consenting first offender convicted of possession of marihuana or a controlled substance in Class E, unless the judge files a written memorandum explaining his reasons for doing otherwise." *Commonwealth v. Lupo*, 394 Mass. 644, 649–50 (1985).

NOTE 5   **Marihuana.** "The Nissenbaums follow the church's teachings, including its laws concerning dress and diet. Coptics regard marihuana (ganja) as the body and blood of Christ and use it as a sacrament. . . .

"[T]he courts have uniformly determined that the First Amendment does not protect the possession of controlled substances from the reach of criminal statutes." *Commonwealth v. Nissenbaum*, 404 Mass. 575, 576, 579 (1989).

NOTE 6   If one is acquitted, or if the case is dismissed or nol prossed, the record should be sealed. *See* G.L. c. 94C, § 44.

NOTE 7   "Notwithstanding the provisions of any general or special law to the contrary, the department of environmental protection and the office of the attorney general shall work in cooperation with the office of seized property management within the division of capital planning and operations, created pursuant to paragraph (2) of subsection (f) of section forty-seven of chapter ninety-four C of the General Laws, to identify and obtain a vessel forfeited pursuant to the provisions of said section forty-seven, suitable to meet the needs of the department in enforcing the provisions of chapter ninety-one of the General Laws and regulations promulgated thereunder." 1996 Mass. Acts c. 15, § 49.

SECTION 34A

Immunity from prosecution under Secs. 34 or 35 for persons seeking medical assistance for self or other experiencing drug-related overdose
(Added by 2012 Mass. Acts c. 192, § 32, effective Aug. 2, 2012.)

(a) A person who, in good faith, seeks medical assistance for someone experiencing a drug related overdose shall not be charged or prosecuted for possession of a controlled substance under sections 34 or 35 if the evidence for the charge of possession of a controlled substance was gained as a result of the seeking of medical assistance.

(b) A person who experiences a drug-related overdose and is in need of medical assistance and, in good faith, seeks such medical assistance, or is the subject of such a good faith request for medical assistance, shall not be charged or prosecuted for possession of a controlled substance under said sections 34 or 35 if the evidence for the charge of possession of a controlled substance was gained as a result of the overdose and the need for medical assistance.

(c) The act of seeking medical assistance for someone who is experiencing a drug-related overdose may be used as a mitigating factor in a criminal prosecution under the Controlled Substance Act, 1970 P.L. 91-513, 21 U.S.C. section 801, et seq.

(d) Nothing contained in this section shall prevent anyone from being charged with trafficking, distribution or possession of a controlled substance with intent to distribute.

(e) A person acting in good faith may receive a naloxone prescription, possess naloxone and administer naloxone to an individual appearing to experience an opiate-related overdose.

SECTION 35

Unlawful presence at a place where heroin is kept or being in company of person in possession thereof

Any person who is knowingly present at a place where heroin is kept or deposited in violation of the provisions of this chapter, or any person who is in the company of a person, knowing that said person is in possession of heroin in violation of the provisions of this chapter, shall be punished by imprisonment for not more than one year or by a fine of not more than one thousand dollars, or both; provided, however, that the provisions of the third paragraph of section thirty-four relative to probation sealing of the records and repeated violations shall apply to him.

NOTE   See Note 3 following G.L. c. 94C, § 34.

SECTION 36

Protective custody of children found present where controlled substances are unlawfully kept or possessed
(Amended by 2013 Mass. Acts c. 84, § 6, effective Sept. 18, 2013.)

Notwithstanding the provisions of section thirty-five, if a police officer finds a child present where said officer finds a substance which he reasonably believes to be a controlled substance listed in Class A, B, or C of section thirty-one kept or possessed in violation of any provision of this chapter, and if the police officer reasonably believes that the child has not reached his eighteenth birthday and that the child knew of the presence of such controlled substance, the police officer may lawfully take such child into protective custody for a period not to exceed four hours. Persons having custody of a child under this section shall make reasonable efforts to notify the child's parent or guardian or other person having lawful custody. Such persons shall be considered to be acting in the conduct of their official duties and shall not be held criminally or civilly liable for such acts. A child detained pursuant to the provisions of this section shall not be considered to have been arrested or to have a criminal record for any purpose; however, only a departmental record of custody shall be made by the officer indicating the circumstances of custody. The procedures and processes provided by this section for the care, protection, and custody of children are not exclusive but are in addition to all others provided by law.

SECTION 37

Theft of controlled substances from persons authorized to dispense or possess

Whoever steals a controlled substance from a registered manufacturer, wholesale druggist, pharmacy or other person authorized to dispense or possess any controlled substance shall be punished by imprisonment in the state prison for not more than ten years or in a jail or house of correction for not more than two and one-half years or by a fine of not more than five hundred dollars.

SECTION 38
Violation of Secs. 24(a), 25, 26 or 27

Any person who knowingly violates any provision of subsection (a) of section twenty-four, or of section twenty-five, twenty-six or twenty-seven shall be punished by imprisonment for not more than one year or by a fine of not more than one thousand dollars, or both. Whoever violates any of the provisions of any of said sections after one or more prior convictions of a violation of any provision of this chapter or of a provision of prior law relating to the sale or manufacture of narcotic drugs or harmful drugs as defined in said prior law shall be punished by imprisonment for not more than two years or by a fine of not more than two thousand dollars, or both.

SECTION 40
Conspiracy

Whoever conspires with another person to violate any provision of this chapter shall be punished by imprisonment or fine, or both, which punishment shall not exceed the maximum punishment described for the offense, the commission of which was the object of the conspiracy.

NOTE 1   "The heart of a conspiracy is the formulation of the unlawful agreement or combination. *Attorney Gen. v. Tufts*, 239 Mass. 458, 493–494 (1921). The law of the Commonwealth does not require an overt act to complete a conspiracy. The Commonwealth must prove, however, that the defendants combined with the intention to [commit the object crime], and the evidence and inferences permitted to be drawn therefrom must be of sufficient force to bring minds of ordinary intelligence and sagacity to the persuasion of [guilt] beyond a reasonable doubt.

"A conspiracy may be proved by circumstantial evidence, and this is the usual mode of proving it, since it is not often that direct evidence can be had. The acts of different persons who are shown to have known each other, or to have been in communication with each other, directed towards the accomplishment of the same object, especially if by the same means or in the same manner, may be satisfactory proof of a conspiracy."
Commonwealth v. Cantres, 405 Mass. 238, 244 (1989) (quotation marks and citations omitted).

NOTE 2   District Court lacks jurisdiction on conspiracy to distribute heroin (a 10 year felony) complaint. G.L. c. 218, § 26 confers jurisdiction upon the district court over all felonies punishable in the state prison for not more than 5 years. Also, the "maximum penalty is dispositive in determining whether district court has jurisdiction over those felonies not specifically made part of its jurisdiction." *Commonwealth v. Grace*, 425 Mass. 1108 (1997) (citation omitted).

SECTION 41
Arrest without warrant

A police officer shall have the authority to arrest without a warrant:

(a) any person committing in his presence any offense set forth in this chapter;

(b) any person who he has probable cause to believe has committed or is committing a felony set forth under the provisions of this chapter; or

(c) any person who he has probable cause to believe has committed or is committing a violation of the provisions of sections twenty-seven, thirty-two, thirty-two A, thirty-two B, thirty-two C, thirty-two D, thirty-two E, thirty-two F, thirty-three, thirty-four, thirty-five, thirty-seven and forty.

NOTE 1   Police officer searching third floor of factory for intruders; looked through window of third floor apartment across the street; saw defendant and two men packing green herb from large bag into smaller bags. Officers went to apartment building; downstairs door open; hallway door unlocked; defendant's apartment door partially open; music blaring and odor of marijuana from apartment. Police entry, seizure of marijuana and arrest. Held, search and seizure *invalid* as there were no exigent circumstances justifying the warrantless search. Exigent circumstances requires evidence of the defendant being armed, possibly fleeing or being aware of the police presence; the threats of removing or destroying evidence or of the time to secure a warrant thwarting the arrest are other considerations. *Commonwealth v. Huffman*, 385 Mass. 122 (1982).

NOTE 2   **Related Statutes.**
Search warrants—*See* G.L. c. 276, § 1 et seq.
Arrest without warrant—(for theft, etc.)—G.L. c. 276, § 28.

SECTION 44
Violations of Sec. 34; acquittal, dismissal or indictment nol prossed; sealing of records

If any person is found not guilty of the violation of any provision of section thirty-four or if a complaint against him is dismissed or an indictment nol prossed for a violation of said section, the court shall order all official records relating to his arrest, indictment, conviction, continuance or discharge to be sealed; provided, however, that departmental records maintained by police and other law enforcement agencies which are not public records shall not be sealed.

No person as to whom such sealing has been ordered shall be held thereafter under any provision of any law to be guilty of perjury or otherwise making a false statement by reason of his failure to recite or acknowledge such arrest, indictment, disposition, sealing or any other related court proceeding, in response to any inquiry made of him for any purpose.

SECTION 45
Photographing and fingerprinting of person charged with felony

Any person arrested for or charged with the criminal violation of any provision of this chapter which constitutes a felony may at the time of arrest or as soon thereafter as is practicable be photographed and fingerprinted according to the system of the state bureau of identification, and upon conviction any such fingerprints and photographs shall be made a part of permanent records of the police department of the municipality where the arrest took place, and without delay two copies of the fingerprints and photographs shall be forwarded, with such other description as may be required and a written history of the offense, to the state bureau of identification.

SECTION 47
Forfeiture of property

(a) The following property shall be subject to forfeiture to the commonwealth and all property rights therein shall be in the commonwealth:

(1) All controlled substances which have been manufactured, delivered, distributed, dispensed or acquired in violation of this chapter.

(2) All materials, products, and equipment of any kind which are used, or intended for use, in manufacturing, compounding, processing, delivering, dispensing, distributing, importing, or exporting any controlled substance in violation of this chapter.

(3) All conveyances, including aircraft, vehicles or vessels used, or intended for use, to transport, conceal, or otherwise

facilitate the manufacture, dispensing, distribution of or possession with intent to manufacture, dispense or distribute, a controlled substance in violation of any provision of section thirty-two, thirty-two A, thirty-two B, thirty-two C, thirty-two D, thirty-two E, thirty-two F, thirty-two G, thirty-two I, thirty-two J, or forty.

(4) All books, records, and research, including formulas, microfilm, tapes and data which are used, or intended for use, in violation of this chapter.

(5) All moneys, negotiable instruments, securities or other things of value furnished or intended to be furnished by any person in exchange for a controlled substance in violation of this chapter, all proceeds traceable to such an exchange, including real estate and any other thing of value, and all moneys, negotiable instruments, and securities used or intended to be used to facilitate any violation of any provision of section thirty-two, thirty-two A, thirty-two B, thirty-two C, thirty-two D, thirty-two E, thirty-two F, thirty-two G, thirty-two I, thirty-two J, or forty.

(6) All drug paraphernalia.

(7) All real property, including any right, title, and interest in the whole of any lot or tract of land and any appurtenances or improvements thereto, which is used in any manner or part, to commit or to facilitate the commission of a violation of any provision of section thirty-two, thirty-two A, thirty-two B, thirty-two C, thirty-two D, thirty-two E, thirty-two F, thirty-two G, thirty-two I, thirty-two J or forty.

(8) All property which is used, or intended for use, as a container for property described in subparagraph (1) or (2).

(9) No forfeiture under this section shall extinguish a perfected security interest held by a creditor in a conveyance or in any real property at the time of the filing of the forfeiture action.

(b) Property subject to forfeiture under subparagraphs (1), (2), (4), (5), (6), (7) and (8) of subsection (a) shall, upon motion of the attorney general or district attorney, be declared forfeit by any court having jurisdiction over said property or having final jurisdiction over any related criminal proceeding brought under any provision of this chapter. Property subject to forfeiture under subparagraph (1) of subsection (a) shall be destroyed, regardless of the final disposition of such related criminal proceeding, if any, unless the court for good cause shown orders otherwise.

(c) The court shall order forfeiture of all conveyances subject to the provisions of subparagraph (3) and of all real property subject to the provisions of subparagraph (7) of subsection (a) of this section, except as follows:

(1) No conveyance used by any person as a common carrier in the transaction of business as a common carrier shall be forfeited unless it shall appear that the owner or other person in charge of such conveyance was a consenting party or privy to a violation of this chapter.

(2) No conveyance shall be forfeited by reason of any act or omission established by the owner thereof to have been committed or omitted by any person other than such owner while such conveyance was unlawfully in the possession of a person other than the owner in violation of the criminal laws of the United States, or of the commonwealth, or of any state.

(3) No conveyance or real property shall be subject to forfeiture unless the owner thereof knew or should have known that such conveyance or real property was used in and for the business of unlawfully manufacturing, dispensing, or distributing controlled substances. Proof that the conveyance or real property was used to facilitate the unlawful dispensing, manufacturing, or distribution of, or possession with intent unlawfully to manufacture, dispense or distribute, controlled substances on three or more different dates shall be prima facie evidence that the conveyance or real property, was used in and for the business of unlawfully manufacturing, dispensing, or distributing controlled substances.

(4) No conveyance or real property used to facilitate the unlawful manufacturing, dispensing, or distribution of, or the possession with intent unlawfully to manufacture, dispense, or distribute marihuana or a substance, not itself a controlled substance, containing any marihuana shall be forfeited if the net weight of the substance so manufactured, dispensed, or distributed or possessed with intent to manufacture, dispense, or distribute, is less than ten pounds in the aggregate.

(d) A district attorney or the attorney general may petition the superior court in the name of the commonwealth in the nature of a proceeding in rem to order forfeiture of a conveyance, real property, moneys or other things of value subject to forfeiture under the provisions of subparagraphs (3), (5), and (7) of subsection (a). Such petition shall be filed in the court having jurisdiction over said conveyance, real property, monies or other things of value or having final jurisdiction over any related criminal proceeding brought under any provision of this chapter. In all such suits where the property is claimed by any person, other than the commonwealth, the commonwealth shall have the burden of proving to the court the existence of probable cause to institute the action, and any such claimant shall then have the burden of proving that the property is not forfeitable pursuant to subparagraph (3), (5), or (7) of said subsection (a). The owner of said conveyance or real property, or other person claiming thereunder shall have the burden of proof as to all exceptions set forth in subsections (c) and (i). The court shall order the commonwealth to give notice by certified or registered mail to the owner of said conveyance, real property, moneys or other things of value and to such other persons as appear to have an interest therein, and the court shall promptly, but not less than two weeks after notice, hold a hearing on the petition. Upon the motion of the owner of said conveyance, real property, moneys or other things of value, the court may continue the hearing on the petition pending the outcome of any criminal trial related to the violation of this chapter. At such hearing the court shall hear evidence and make conclusions of law, and shall thereupon issue a final order, from which the parties shall have a right of appeal. In all such suits where a final order results in a forfeiture, said final order shall provide for disposition of said conveyance, real property, moneys or any other thing of value by the commonwealth or any subdivision thereof in any manner not prohibited by law, including official use by an authorized law enforcement or other public agency, or sale at public auction or by competitive bidding. The proceeds of any such sale shall be used to pay the reasonable expenses of the forfeiture proceedings, seizure, storage, maintenance of custody, advertising, and notice, and the balance thereof shall be distributed as further provided in this section.

The final order of the court shall provide that said moneys and the proceeds of any such sale shall be distributed equally between the prosecuting district attorney or attorney general and the city, town or state district police department involved in the seizure. If more than one department was substantially involved in the seizure, the court having jurisdiction over the forfeiture proceeding shall distribute the fifty percent equitably among these departments.

There shall be established within the office of the state treasurer separate special law enforcement trust funds for each district attorney and for the attorney general. All such monies and proceeds received by any prosecuting district attorney or attorney general shall be deposited in such a trust fund and shall then be expended without further appropriation to defray the costs of protracted investigations, to provide additional technical equipment or expertise, to provide matching funds to obtain federal grants, or such other law enforcement purposes as the district attorney or attorney general deems appropriate. The district attorney or attorney general may expend up to ten percent of the monies and proceeds for drug rehabilitation, drug education and other anti-drug or neighborhood crime watch programs which further law enforcement purposes. Any program seeking to be an eligible recipient of said funds shall file an annual audit report with the local district attorney and attorney general. Such report shall include, but not be limited to, a listing of the assets, liabilities, itemized expenditures, and board of directors of such program. Within ninety days of the close of the fiscal year, each district attorney and the attorney general shall file an annual report with the house and senate committees on ways and means on the use of the monies in the trust fund for the purposes of drug rehabilitation, drug education, and other anti-drug or neighborhood crime watch programs.

All such moneys and proceeds received by any police department shall be deposited in a special law enforcement trust fund and shall be expended without further appropriation to defray the costs of protracted investigations, to provide additional technical equipment or expertise, to provide matching funds to obtain federal grants, or to accomplish such other law enforcement purposes as the chief of police of such city or town, or the colonel of state police deems appropriate, but such funds shall not be considered a source of revenue to meet the operating needs of such department.

(e) Any officer, department, or agency having custody of any property subject to forfeiture under this chapter or having disposed of said property shall keep and maintain full and complete records showing from whom it received said property, under what authority it held or received or disposed of said property, to whom it delivered said property, the date and manner of destruction or disposition of said property, and the exact kinds, quantities and forms of said property. Said records shall be open to inspection by all federal and state officers charged with enforcement of federal and state drug control laws. Persons making final disposition or destruction of said property under court order shall report, under oath, to the court the exact circumstances of said disposition or destruction.

(f)(1) During the pendency of the proceedings the court may issue at the request of the commonwealth ex parte any preliminary order or process as is necessary to seize or secure the property for which forfeiture is sought and to provide for its custody, including but not limited to an order that the commonwealth remove the property if possible, and safeguard it in a secure location in a reasonable fashion; that monies be deposited in an interest-bearing escrow account; and, that a substitute custodian be appointed to manage such property or a business enterprise. Property taken or detained under this section shall not be repleviable, but once seized shall be deemed to be lawfully in the custody of the commonwealth pending forfeiture, subject only to the orders and decrees of the court having jurisdiction thereof. Process for seizure of said property shall issue only upon a showing of probable cause, and the application therefor and the issuance, execution, and return thereof shall be subject to the provisions of chapter two hundred and seventy-six, so far as applicable.

(2) There shall be created within the division of capital asset management and maintenance an office of seized property management to which a district attorney or the attorney general may refer any real property, and any furnishings, equipment and related personal property located therein, for which seizure is sought. The office of seized property management shall be authorized to preserve and manage such property in a reasonable fashion and to dispose of such property upon a judgment ordering forfeiture issued pursuant to the provisions of said section (d), and to enter into contracts to preserve, manage and dispose of such property. The office of seized property management may receive initial funding from the special law enforcement trust funds of the attorney general and each district attorney established pursuant to subsection (d) and shall subsequently be funded by a portion of the proceeds of each sale of such managed property to the extent provided as payment of reasonable expenses in subsection (d).

(g) Species of plants from which controlled substances in Schedules I and II may be derived which have been planted or cultivated in violation of this chapter, or of which the owners or cultivators are unknown, or which are wild growths may be seized by any police officer and summarily forfeited to the commonwealth.

(h) The failure, upon demand by a police officer of the person in occupancy or in control of land or premises upon which the species of plants are growing to produce an appropriate registration, or proof that he is a holder thereof, constitutes authority for the seizure and forfeiture of the plants.

(i) The owner of any real property which is the principal domicile of the immediate family of the owner and which is subject to forfeiture under this section may file a petition for homestead exemption with the court having jurisdiction over such forfeiture. The court may, in its discretion, allow the petition exempting from forfeiture an amount allowed under section one of chapter one hundred and eighty-eight. The value of the balance of said principal domicile, if any, shall be forfeited as provided in this section. Such homestead exemption may be acquired on only one principal domicile for the benefit of the immediate family of the owner.

(j) A forfeiture proceeding affecting the title to real property or the use and occupation thereof or the buildings thereon shall not have any effect except against the parties thereto and persons having actual notice thereof, until a memorandum containing the names of the parties to such proceeding, the name of the town where the affected real property lies, and a description of such real property sufficiently accurate for identification is recorded in the registry of deeds for the county or district where the real property lies. At any time after a judgment on the merits, or after the discontinuance, dismissal or other final disposition is recorded by the court having jurisdiction over such matter, the clerk of such court shall issue a certificate of the fact of such judgment, discontinuance, dismissal or other final disposition, and such certificate shall be recorded in the registry in which the original memorandum recorded pursuant to this section was filed.

NOTE 1   Lawfulness of Judgment. The defendant challenged the lawfulness of a forfeiture judgment as it was entered in the criminal proceedings themselves and not in connection with an independent petition brought by the Commonwealth under G.L. c. 94C, § 47 (d).

The Supreme Judicial Court disagreed with the defendant, ruling that "the provision in § 47 (b) for the forfeiture of property on order of a judge has independent significance and permits a judge to enter a judgment of forfeiture without the Commonwealth first filing a petition under § 47 (d)." *Commonwealth v. Goldman,* 398 Mass. 201, 202 (1986).

"Fundamental due process considerations entitle the defendant to a hearing on the question of the connection, if any, between his illegal drug operations and the funds seized." *Commonwealth v. Goldman,* 398 Mass. at 204.

NOTE 2   Initiation of Proceedings. "The statute contemplates two methods by which forfeiture proceedings may be initiated by the Commonwealth: either by petition in the nature of a proceeding in rem filed in the Superior Court, G.L. c. 94C, § 47(d), or . . . by motion filed in a related criminal proceeding, G.L. c. 94C, § 47(b)." *Commonwealth v. Brown,* 426 Mass. 475, 480 (1998). In the latter situation, seven days' notice is required.

"The Commonwealth's burden under the forfeiture statute is to prove probable cause to proceed, in the form of sound reason to believe that the money-drug nexus exists. . . . The Commonwealth must show only that the money was probably derived from illegal drug activity." *Commonwealth v. Brown,* 426 Mass. at 478–79 (citations, quotation marks, and footnote omitted).

NOTE 3   Nature of Proceeding. A civil action brought under G.L. c. 94C, § 47(d) seeking forfeiture of proceeds from unlawful drug sales was not punitive in nature, but rather was remedial or preventive, where it was shown to be intended to recover illegally obtained funds or to prevent purchases of illicit drugs. *Commonwealth v. Fourteen Thousand Two Hundred Dollars,* 421 Mass. 1 (1995).

NOTE 4   Burden. "[W]e hold that the Commonwealth need not demonstrate in its forfeiture complaint the existence of probable cause, but rather, the showing of probable cause is its burden at the trial on the complaint." *Commonwealth v. One 2004 Audi Sedan Auto.,* 73 Mass. App. Ct. 311, 318 (2008).

At the pleading stage "[t]he question of a pleading's sufficiency pursuant to the Massachusetts Rules of Civil Procedure turns on whether the complaint provides enough information to give the defendant notice of what the dispute is about and asserts a right to recovery cognizable on some acceptable legal theory. A complaint is sufficient unless it appears beyond doubt that the plaintiff can prove no set of facts in support of his claim which would entitle him to relief. Therefore, we examine the sufficiency of the [Commonwealth's] claims in light of the principles that the allegations of the complaint, as well as such inferences as may be drawn therefrom in the [Commonwealth's] favor, are to be taken as true." *Commonwealth v. One 2004 Audi Sedan Auto.,* 73 Mass. App. Ct. at 320 (citations, footnotes, and quotation marks omitted).

NOTE 5   Evidence insufficient to support inference that monies seized were drug proceeds. "[T]he Commonwealth presented no evidence that the Nissenbaums had been involved in selling marihuana or were conducting an ongoing drug business. No ledger books, packaging materials, or safety deposit box keys were found in the thorough search of the Nissenbaum residence. No sales of marihuana had been observed by the investigating officers and no controlled purchases had been arranged so that there would be identifiable funds among the monies seized." *Commonwealth v. Seven Thousand Two Hundred Forty-Six Dollars,* 404 Mass. 763, 766 (1989).

NOTE 6   "Ownership" "[A] person with a financial stake in an automobile does not possess a sufficient ownership interest to contest its forfeiture unless the person also exercises dominion and control over the vehicle." *Commonwealth v. One 1986 Volkswagen GTI Automobile,* 417 Mass. 369, 375–76 (1994).

NOTE 7   Destination of Funds. "[M]oney ordered forfeited under G.L. c. 94C, § 47, is properly directed to the prosecuting district attorney or Attorney General and the investigating police department, as specified in § 47 (d), even when the forfeiture is sought and obtained in the District Court by means of a motion brought pursuant to § 47 (b)." *District Attorney for the Northwestern Dist. v. Eastern Hampshire Div. of the Dist. Court Dep't,* 452 Mass. 199, 200 (2008).

SECTION 47A
Seized controlled substances and narcotic drugs; custodian; mailing for chemical analysis; destruction or disposal upon completion of trial
(Amended by 2012 Mass. Acts c. 139, §§ 103–06, effective July 1, 2012.)

The police commissioner, chief superintendent or other officer or board at the head of each police department in the commonwealth shall appoint a police officer to act as custodian of all controlled substances and narcotic drugs seized in the course of any arrest or investigation. Such custodian shall be designated as the "evidence officer."

Notwithstanding the provisions of any general or special law or rule or regulation to the contrary, controlled substances or narcotic drugs seized in cases under the provisions of this chapter where the violation is a misdemeanor and requiring chemical analyses which are to be performed at a laboratory operated by the department of state police or the University of Massachusetts medical center may be mailed to or from the place of such analyses by using the registered mail service of the United States Postal Service, and testimony from a law enforcement officer that he mailed or received such substances or narcotic drugs by registered mail together with the return receipts accompanying such mailing shall be prima facie evidence that said substances or drugs are the substances or drugs so seized.

At any time after the seizure of a controlled substance or narcotic drug, a district attorney or the attorney general may petition the superior court in the name of the commonwealth to order the destruction of said controlled substance or narcotic drug seized in the course of any arrest or investigation. The court shall order the commonwealth to give notice by certified or registered mail to the known defendant and his attorney and shall promptly, but not less than two weeks after notice, hold a hearing on the petition. At such hearing, the court shall hear evidence from the parties on the issue of destruction, the extent of the proposed destruction, the preservation of samples, the inspection, examination and testing of the controlled substance or narcotic drugs. The court, after such hearing, shall have the power to order the forfeiture and destruction of such controlled substance or narcotic drug as it so determines, under procedures and to the extent as so determined by the court, with the remainder to be kept under the provisions of this section and shall thereupon issue a final order in writing.

Such final order shall provide for the analysis of representative and fair samples of such forfeited controlled substances or narcotic drugs by a chemist of the department of state police or by a chemist at the University of Massachusetts medical school who shall issue a signed certificate, on oath, of the results of such analysis. Such certificate shall be sworn to before a justice of the peace or a notary public and shall be prima facie evidence of the composition and quality of such controlled substances or narcotic drugs when introduced as evidence before a grand jury or any court proceeding in the commonwealth. Upon completion of such analysis, such order shall direct the evidence officer to deliver such controlled substances or narcotic drugs ordered destroyed to the department of state police for such destruction or disposition in any way not prohibited by law; provided, however, that the evidence officer shall make proper provisions for maintaining and securing such samples as may be directed by the court.

The court having jurisdiction shall, upon completion of a trial or other disposition by the trial court and after the expiration of the period for an appeal from that trial or disposition, in writing, order such forfeited controlled substances or narcotic drugs not destroyed prior thereto to be caused to be delivered forthwith by the evidence officer to the department of state police for destruction or disposition in any way not prohibited by law. In the event of an appeal as prescribed by law, the evidence officer shall retain possession of such controlled substances or narcotic drugs until final disposition of the case, at which time, the district attorney or attorney general may petition the superior court for summary destruction of such controlled substances or narcotic drugs.

The department of state police shall keep a record of the place where such controlled substances or narcotic drugs were seized, of the kinds and quantities of drugs received, by whose order the controlled substance or narcotic drugs were received, by whom the controlled substance or narcotic drugs were delivered and received, the date and manner of destruction or disposition of such controlled substances or narcotic drugs, and a report under oath of such destruction or disposition shall be made to the court, which record shall be open to inspection by attorneys of record in the case and by all federal and state officers charged with enforcement of federal and state narcotic laws.

The department of state police shall keep a complete record of all drugs received and of all drugs disposed of, showing the exact kinds, quantities and forms of such drugs; the persons from whom received and the dates of receipt, disposal or destruction, which record shall be open to inspection by all federal and state officers charged with enforcement of federal and state narcotic laws.

Chapter 111. Public Health

Section
9   Inspectors, analysts and chemists; appointment; removal; power and authority; interference with
10   Repealed
11-13   Repealed

DUTIES OF THE DEPARTMENT OF PUBLIC HEALTH

SECTION 9
Inspectors, analysts and chemists; appointment; removal; power and authority; interference with

In the performance of the duties relative to the sale of drugs and food the commissioner may appoint and remove inspectors, analysts and chemists. Such inspectors shall, in addition to the powers given by sections one hundred and twenty-one to one hundred and twenty-three, inclusive, of chapter ninety-four, have the same power and authority relative to drugs, fish, food and milk as is given inspectors of milk by sections thirty-five and sixty of said chapter. Such inspectors shall, in the enforcement of laws relative to controlled substances as defined in section one of chapter ninety-four C, have all the powers and authority of police officers and constables except the power to serve civil process. Inspectors assigned to investigate violations of laws relative to controlled substances as defined in section one of chapter ninety-four C may at the request of the commissioner carry revolvers, billies, clubs, handcuffs and any other paraphernalia necessary for their protection and the enforcement of such laws. Whoever hinders, obstructs or in any way interferes with any such inspector, analyst or chemist in the performance of his official duty shall for the first offence be punished by a fine of not more than fifty dollars, and for a subsequent offence by a fine of not more than one hundred dollars.

SECTION 10
Repealed

SECTIONS 11–13
Repealed
(2012 Mass. Acts c. 139, § 107, effective July 1, 2012.)

Chapter 111B. Alcoholism

SECTION 8
Incapacitated persons; assistance to facility or protective custody

Any person who is incapacitated may be assisted by a police officer with or without his consent to his residence, to a facility or to a police station. To determine for purposes of this chapter only, whether or not such person is intoxicated, the police officer may request the person to submit to reasonable tests of coordination, coherency of speech, and breath.

Any person assisted by a police officer to a police station shall have the right, and be informed in writing of said right, to request and be administered a breathalyzer test. Any person who is administered a breathalyzer test shall be presumed intoxicated if evidence from said test indicates that the percentage of alcohol in his blood is ten one hundredths or more and shall be placed in protective custody at a police station or transferred to a facility. Any person who is administered a breathalyzer test, under this section, shall be presumed not to be intoxicated if evidence from said test indicates that the percentage of alcohol in his blood is five one hundredths or less and shall be released from custody forthwith. If any person who is administered a breathalyzer test, under this section, and evidence from said test indicates that the percentage of alcohol in his blood is more than five one hundredths and is less than ten one hundredths there shall be no presumption made based solely on the breathalyzer test. In such instance a reasonable test of coordination or speech coherency must be administered to determine if said person is intoxicated. Only when such test of coordination or speech coherency indicates said person is intoxicated shall he be placed in protective custody at a police station or transferred to a facility.

Any person presumed intoxicated and to be held in protective custody at a police station shall, immediately after such presumption, have the right to be informed of said right to make one phone call at his own expense and on his own behalf. Any person assisted by a police officer to a facility under this section shall have the right to make one phone call at his own expense or his own behalf and shall be informed forthwith upon arriving at the facility of said right. The parent or guardian of any person, under the age of eighteen, to be held in protective custody at a police station shall be notified forthwith upon his arrival at said station or as soon as possible thereafter.

If any incapacitated person is assisted to a police station, the officer in charge or his designee shall notify forthwith the nearest facility that the person is being held in protective custody. If suitable treatment services are available at a facility, the department shall thereupon arrange for the transportation of the person to the facility in accordance with the provisions of section seven.

No person assisted to a police station pursuant to this section shall be held in protective custody against his will; provided, however, that if suitable treatment at facility is not available, an incapacitated person may be held in protective custody at a police station until he is no longer incapacitated or for a period of not longer than twelve hours, whichever is shorter.

A police officer acting in accordance with the provisions of this section may use such force as is reasonably necessary to carry out his authorized responsibilities. If the police officer reasonably believes that his safety or the safety of other persons present so requires, he may search such person and his immediate surroundings, but only to the extent necessary to discover and seize any dangerous weapons which may on that occasion be used against that officer or other person present; provided, however, that if such person is held in protective custody at a police station all valuables and all articles which may pose a danger to such person or to others may be taken from him for safekeeping and if so taken shall be inventoried.

A person assisted to a facility or held in protective custody by the police pursuant to the provisions of this section, shall not be considered to have been arrested or to have been charged with any crime. An entry of custody shall be made indicating the date, time, place of custody, the name of the assisting officer, the name of the officer in charge, whether the person held in custody exercised his right to make a phone call, whether the person held in custody exercised his right to take a breathalyzer test, and the results of the breathalyzer test if taken, which entry shall not be treated for any purpose, as an arrest or criminal record.

NOTE 1   Reasonable Suspicion Standard. "The reasonable suspicion standard is . . . appropriate to G.L. c. 111B, § 8, the protective custody statute. Pursuant to that law, the police may take an individual into protective custody if they determine that the person is 'incapacitated'" *Commonwealth v. McCaffery*, 49 Mass. App. Ct. 713, 716 (2000).

NOTE 2   Incapacitated. "[D]efined as the condition of an intoxicated person who, by reason of the consumption of intoxicating liquor is (1) unconscious, (2) in need of medical attention, (3) likely to suffer or cause physical harm or damage property, or (4) disorderly." *Commonwealth v. McCaffery*, 49 Mass. App. Ct. 713, 716 (2000) (citation and quotation marks omitted).

NOTE 3   Field Sobriety Tests. "Section 8 . . . states that, in order to determine whether or not [a] person is intoxicated, the police officer may request the person to submit to reasonable tests of coordination, coherency of speech, and breath." *Commonwealth v. McCaffery*, 49 Mass. App. Ct. 713, 716 (2000) (citation and quotation marks omitted).

Chapter 111E. Drug Rehabilitation

Section

9A   Incapacitated person; protective custody
10   Defendant charged with drug offense; request for examination; stay of proceedings; report of findings; assignment; hearing; discharge or transfer; quarterly reports; juveniles; review
11   Defendant charged with other than drug offense; request for examination; evidence; report; treatment; consent; hearing; order
12   Probation of drug dependent persons; treatment; urinalysis program; reports
13   Juveniles and youthful offenders; examination; admission; inpatient or outpatient treatment; report; department of youth services; jurisdiction
13A   Children referred by department of children and families or juvenile court; examination; report; treatment; jurisdiction

SECTION 9A

Incapacitated person; protective custody

(Added by 2016 Mass. Acts c. 161, § 1, effective July 1, 2016.)

For purposes of this section, "incapacitated" shall mean the condition of a person who, by reason of the consumption of a controlled substance or toxic vapor or other substance other than alcohol is: (i) unconscious; (ii) in need of medical attention; (iii) likely to suffer or cause physical harm or damage property; or (iv) disorderly.

Any person who is incapacitated may be placed into protective custody by a police officer without the person's consent for the purpose of immediately transporting the person to an acute care hospital or satellite emergency facility as defined in section 51½ of chapter 111 or otherwise immediately obtaining appropriate emergency medical treatment. For the purposes of this section, to determine whether or not a person is incapacitated, a police officer may request the person to submit to reasonable tests of coordination, coherency of speech and breath. A police officer may place the person into protective custody when such tests or other information or observations indicate that the person is incapacitated. Whenever a police officer places into protective custody a person under the age of 18 in accordance with this section, the police officer shall notify the parent or guardian of that person forthwith.

A person may not be held in protective custody against the person's will beyond the time required to complete the person's immediate transport to an acute care hospital or satellite emergency facility as defined in section 51½ of chapter 111, or to otherwise immediately obtain appropriate emergency medical treatment.

A police officer acting in accordance with this section may use such force as is reasonably necessary to carry out the officer's authorized responsibilities. If the police officer reasonably believes that there may be a risk to the safety of the incapacitated person, the safety of the officer or the safety of other persons present, the police officer may search the person and the immediate surroundings of the person placed into protective custody but only to the extent necessary to discover and seize any items or weapons which may pose a danger. Any item taken shall be inventoried and, unless the item is contraband or otherwise unlawfully possessed, shall be returned to the person when the person is no longer incapacitated.

A person placed under protective custody in accordance with this section shall not be considered to have been arrested or to have been charged with any crime. An entry of custody shall be made indicating the date, time, place of custody, the name of the assisting officer and the name of the officer in charge. No such entry shall be treated as an arrest or criminal record for any purpose.

SECTION 10
Defendant charged with drug offense; request for examination; stay of proceedings; report of findings; assignment; hearing; discharge or transfer; quarterly reports; juveniles; review

Any defendant who is charged with a drug offense shall, upon being brought before the court on such charge, be informed that he is entitled to request an examination to determine whether or not he is a drug dependent person who would benefit by treatment, and that if he chooses to exercise such right he must do so in writing within five days of being in so informed.

If the defendant requests such an examination, the court may in its discretion determine that the defendant is a drug dependent person, who would benefit by treatment, without ordering the examination. In such event, the court shall inform the defendant that he may request assignment to a drug treatment facility, and advise him of the consequences of assignment and that if he is so assigned the court proceedings shall be stayed for the term of such assignment.

The court proceedings shall be stayed for the period during which a request made under this section is under consideration by the court. If the defendant requests an examination, the court shall, unless the court has already determined that the defendant is a drug dependent person, appoint a psychiatrist, or if it is, in the discretion of the court, impracticable to do so, a physician, to conduct the examination at an appropriate location designated by it. In no event shall the request for such an examination or any statement made by the defendant during the course of the examination, or any finding of the psychiatrist or physician be admissible against the defendant in any court proceedings.

The psychiatrist or physician shall report his findings in writing to the court within five days after the completion of the examination, stating the facts upon which the findings are based and the reasons therefor.

If the defendant is also charged with a violation of any law other than a drug offense, the stay of the court proceedings may be vacated by the court upon the report of the psychiatrist or physician, whereupon the report shall be considered upon disposition of the charges in accordance with sections eleven and twelve, and the remaining provisions of this chapter shall not apply. If the defendant is charged with a drug offense only and if the psychiatrist or physician reports that the defendant is a drug dependent person who would

benefit by treatment, the court shall inform the defendant that he may request assignment to a drug treatment facility, and advise him of the consequences of the assignment and that if he is so assigned the court proceedings shall be stayed for the term of such assignment.

If the defendant requests assignment and if the court determines that he is a drug dependent person who would benefit from treatment the court may stay the court proceedings and assign him to a drug treatment facility.

An order assigning a person under this section shall specify the period of assignment, which shall not exceed eighteen months or the period of time equal to the maximum sentence he could have received had he been found guilty of every count alleged in the complaint or indictment, whichever is shorter.

In determining whether or not to grant a request for assignment under this section, the court shall consider the report, the past criminal record of the defendant, the availability of adequate and appropriate treatment at a facility, the nature of the offense with which the defendant is charged including, but not limited to, whether the offense charged is that of a sale or sale to a minor, and any other relevant evidence.

In the event that the defendant requests assignment and if the court determines that the defendant is a drug dependent person who would benefit by treatment, and the defendant is charged for the first time with a drug offense not involving the sale or manufacture of dependency related drugs, and there are no continuances outstanding with respect to the defendant pursuant to this section, the court shall order that the defendant be assigned to a drug treatment facility without consideration of any other factors.

Before such assignment, the court shall consult with the facility or the division, to determine that adequate and appropriate treatment is available.

If the defendant requests assignment, and if the court determines that the defendant is a drug dependent person who would benefit by treatment, and the defendant is charged for the first time with a drug offense not involving the sale or manufacture of dependency related drugs, and there are no continuances outstanding with respect to the defendant pursuant to this section, and adequate and appropriate treatment at a facility is not available, the stay of court proceedings shall remain in effect until such time as adequate and appropriate treatment at a facility is available.

In all other cases, an assignment order shall not be made unless, after consultation with the facility or the division, the court determines that adequate and appropriate treatment is available, provided, however, that the court may in its discretion order that the stay of court proceedings remain outstanding until such time as adequate and appropriate treatment is available.

In the event that the stay of the court proceedings remains in effect for the reason that adequate and appropriate treatment at a facility is not available, the issue of the availability of adequate and appropriate treatment at a facility may be reopened at any time by the court on its own motion, or on motion by the prosecutor, or the defendant.

In no event shall any defendant be assigned pursuant to this section unless the defendant consents in writing to the terms of the assignment order.

If the psychiatrist or physician reports that the person is not a drug dependent person who would benefit by treatment, the defendant shall be entitled to request a hearing to determine whether or not he is a drug dependent person who would benefit by treatment. The court may on its own motion, or shall, upon request of the defendant or his counsel, appoint an independent psychiatrist, or if it is impracticable to do so, an independent physician to examine the defendant and testify at the hearing. If the court determines that the defendant is a drug dependent person who would benefit by treatment, the procedures and standards applicable to a defendant who is determined by the court, following the report of the first examining psychiatrist or physician to be a drug dependent person who would benefit by treatment, shall apply to the defendant.

If the court does not assign the defendant to a facility, the stay of the court proceedings shall be vacated.

At any time during the term of assignment, the administrator may transfer any inpatient, to an outpatient program if he finds that the patient is a proper subject for an outpatient program; provided, however, that the administrator may retransfer the patient to an inpatient program if he finds that the person is not suitable for outpatient treatment, and provided further that immediately upon such transfer the administrator shall notify in writing the assigning court and the director of such transfer.

Any patient assigned under this section may apply in writing to the assigning court for discharge or transfer either from inpatient or outpatient treatment or from one facility to another; provided, however, that not more than one such application may be made in any three month period. Upon receipt of an application for discharge or transfer, the court shall give written notice to the patient of his right to a hearing and to be represented by counsel at the hearing.

Within ten days of the receipt by the court of an application for discharge, the administrator and an independent psychiatrist, or, if none is available, an independent physician, designated by the court to make an examination of the patient shall report to the court as to whether or not the patient would benefit from further treatment at a facility. If the court determines that the patient would no longer so benefit, the patient's application for discharge shall be granted. If the court does not so determine, said application shall be denied.

Within ten days of the receipt by the court of an application for transfer, the administrator shall report to the court as to whether the patient is a proper subject for the transfer for which he has made application. If the court determines that the patient is a proper subject for the transfer, the patient's application for transfer shall be granted and the assigning court shall be so notified. If the court does not so determine, said application shall be denied.

Throughout the period of assignment at a facility pursuant to this section, the administrator of said facility shall provide quarterly written reports on the progress being made in treatment by the defendant to the assigning court. Failure to comply may be grounds for suspension of the facility's license. At the end of the assignment period, or when the patient is discharged by the administrator, or when the patient prematurely terminates treatment at a facility, whichever occurs first, the administrator shall notify in writing the assigning court and the director of such termination, and further shall state the reasons for such termination, including whether the defendant successfully completed the treatment program.

In reaching its determination of whether or not the defendant successfully completed the treatment program, the court shall consider, but shall not be limited to, whether the defendant cooperated with the administrator and complied with the terms and conditions imposed on him during this assignment. If the report states that the defendant successfully completed the treatment program, or if the defendant completes the term of treatment ordered by the court, the court shall dismiss the charges pending against the defendant. If the report does not so state, or if the defendant does not complete the term of treatment ordered by the court, then, based on the report and any other relevant evidence, the court may take such action as it deems appropriate, including the dismissal of the charges or the revocation of the stay of the court proceedings.

As to any defendant determined by the court pursuant to this section to be a drug dependent person who would benefit by treatment, concerning whom the court does not order assignment in lieu of prosecution, the court may in the event that such person is convicted of the criminal charges, order that he be afforded treatment pursuant to either section eleven or twelve. The provisions of this chapter shall apply to juveniles in the same manner and under the same terms and conditions as adults; provided that no juvenile shall be committed to a facility without the consent of his parents or guardian.

The provisions of this section shall apply to proceedings in the superior court provided, however, that no defendant who has been examined for his drug dependency pursuant to this section in a district court shall have the right to a new examination if his case is bound over or appealed to the superior court; provided, however, that a superior court judge may, in his discretion, grant a second such drug examination.

During any stays authorized by this section, the court may in its discretion place the defendant in the care of a probation officer until he is accepted at a facility. For the purposes of this section, the term "facility" shall include federal facilities. The provisions of this section shall not apply to a person charged with violating sections thirty-two to thirty-two G, inclusive, of chapter ninety-four C of the General Laws.

SECTION 11
Defendant charged with other than drug offense; request for examination; evidence; report; treatment; consent; hearing; order

Any person found guilty of a violation of any law other than a drug offense, who prior to disposition of the charge, states that he is a drug dependent person, and requests an examination shall be examined by a psychiatrist or, if, in the discretion of the court, it is impracticable to do so, by a physician, to determine whether or not he is a drug dependent person who is a drug addict who would benefit by treatment or a drug dependent person who is not a drug addict but who would benefit by treatment.

If the defendant has previously been examined, pursuant to a request for an examination made in accordance with section ten, the report of the physician or psychiatrist who conducted the examination shall serve at the examination provided for under this section.

The examination shall be conducted at any appropriate location upon appropriate order of the court. In no event shall the request for such examination or any statement made by the defendant during the course of the examination or any finding of the psychiatrist or physician be admissible against the defendant in any criminal proceeding. The psychiatrist or physician shall report in writing to the court within five days after the completion of the examination, stating the facts upon which the report is based and the reasons therefor.

If the report states that the defendant is a drug dependent person who would benefit by treatment and if the court orders that the defendant be confined to a jail, house of correction, prison, or other correctional institution, the court may further order that the defendant be afforded treatment at a penal facility for the whole or any part of the term of imprisonment; provided, however, that the court shall determine the term of treatment to be afforded with the advice of the administrator of the penal facility; and provided, further, that the court shall not order that the defendant be afforded treatment at a penal facility unless the defendant consents to the order in writing. The administrator may terminate treatment of the defendant at such time as he determines the defendant will no longer benefit by treatment.

If the report states that the defendant is not a drug dependent person who would benefit by treatment, the defendant shall be entitled to request a hearing on whether or not he is a drug dependent person who would benefit by treatment. If the court determines that he is a drug dependent person who would benefit by treatment, and if the court orders that the defendant be confined to a jail, house of correction, prison, or other correctional institution, the court may order that the defendant be afforded treatment at a penal facility in accordance with the standards and procedures set forth in this section.

If the court does not order that the defendant be confined to a jail, house of correction, prison, or other correctional institution, the court may order that the defendant be afforded treatment pursuant to section twelve.

SECTION 12
Probation of drug dependent persons; treatment; urinalysis program; reports
(Bracketed text added by 2014 Mass. Acts c. 165, § 147, effective June 1, 2015.)

Any court may, in placing on probation a defendant who is a drug dependent person who would benefit by treatment, impose as a condition of probation that the defendant receive treatment in a facility as an inpatient or outpatient; provided, however, that the court shall not impose such a condition of probation unless, after consulting with the facility, it determines that adequate and appropriate treatment is available. The defendant shall receive treatment at the facility for so long as the administrator of the facility deems that the defendant will benefit by treatment, but in no event shall he receive treatment at the facility for a period longer than the period of probation ordered by the court. A periodic program of urinalysis may be employed as a condition of probation to determine the drug free status of the probationer. The cost of the administration of such program shall be borne by the commonwealth. [If the court requires as a condition of probation that the defendant shall reside in alcohol and drug free housing, the judge issuing the order shall require the probation officer to refer the defendant only to alcohol and drug free housing certified pursuant to section 18A of chapter 17 and the probation officer shall require the defendant to reside in housing so certified in order to satisfy such condition if such certified housing is available.] If at any time during the period of treatment the defendant does not cooperate with the administrator or the probation officer, or does not conduct

himself in accordance with the order or conditions of his probation, the administrator or the probation officer may make a report thereon to the court which placed him on probation, which may consider such conduct as a breach of probation.

Throughout the period of probation at a facility pursuant to this section, the administrator of said facility shall provide quarterly written reports on the progress being made in treatment by the defendant to the defendant's probation officer.

SECTION 13
Juveniles and youthful offenders; examination; admission; inpatient or outpatient treatment; report; department of youth services; jurisdiction

The division shall accept for referral juveniles and youthful offenders referred to the division by the department of youth services. Application by the department of youth services for such referral shall be made to the director.

Upon receipt by the director of a request for referral from the youth service board, he shall, unless the person has been examined pursuant to section ten, designate a psychiatrist or, if in the discretion of the director it is impracticable to do so, a physician, to make an examination of the person to be referred to determine whether or not he is a drug dependent person who would benefit by treatment. The psychiatrist or physician shall report his findings in writing to the director after the completion of the examination, stating the facts upon which the findings are based and the reasons therefor.

If the director finds that the person is a drug dependent person who would benefit by treatment and that adequate treatment is available at an appropriate facility, he may recommend to the department of youth services that the person be admitted to the facility as an inpatient or an outpatient.

In determining whether to admit to a facility a person who is reported to be a drug dependent person who would benefit by treatment, the director shall consider the past record of treatment, if any, afforded the person at a facility, and whether or not the person complied with the terms of any prior admission.

If the director decides to admit to a facility a juvenile or youthful offender pursuant to this section, he shall recommend to the department of youth services the period deemed necessary to accomplish adequate and appropriate treatment but in no case shall the period exceed one year. The director shall also notify the department of youth services of the nature of the treatment to be afforded and the facility to which the person will be admitted. If the department of youth services consents in writing to admission to the facility, to the nature of the treatment to be afforded, and to the period deemed necessary to accomplish treatment, the person shall be admitted to the facility.

If the director decides that the referral to the division is to be refused because the juvenile or youthful offender is not a drug dependent person who would benefit by treatment or because adequate treatment is not available at an appropriate facility, he shall make known in writing to the department of youth services the basis for this decision.

The referral to the division shall terminate at the conclusion of the period of treatment to which the department of youth services consents, or upon a determination by the director that the juvenile or youthful offender will no longer benefit by treatment, whichever first occurs. If the director determines before the conclusion of the period of treatment to which the department of youth services consents that the juvenile or youthful offender will no longer benefit by treatment, he shall make known in writing to the department of youth services the basis for his decision.

Juveniles and youthful offenders referred to the division pursuant to this section shall remain subject to the jurisdiction and control of the department of youth services for all purposes, including, but not limited to, discharge and release; provided, however, that the treatment to be afforded the juvenile and youthful offenders referred to the division shall be within the jurisdiction and control of the division. In no event, however, shall a juvenile or youthful offender be referred for a period longer than the period during which he is subject to the jurisdiction and control of the department of youth services.

SECTION 13A
Children referred by department of children and families or juvenile court; examination; report; treatment; jurisdiction

The division shall, in accordance with the provisions of this section, accept for referral children determined to be in need of services under section 39G of chapter 119 and referred to the division by the department of children and families, hereinafter referred to as the department, or the juvenile court. Such referral shall be made to the director of the division.

Upon receipt by the director of a request for referral he may, unless the child has been examined pursuant to section ten, designate a qualified physician to make an examination of the child to determine whether or not he is a drug dependent child who would benefit from treatment.

The physician designated shall report his findings in writing to the director stating the facts upon which the findings are based and the reasons therefore, and said report shall be kept confidential by the division and shall not be disclosed to any person, other than the department or the court, without the written approval of the child or his parent or legal guardian.

If the director finds that the child is a drug dependent person who would benefit from treatment and that adequate treatment is available at an appropriate drug treatment facility, he may recommend to the department or the court that the child be admitted to the facility on an inpatient or an outpatient basis.

The director may also recommend to the department or the juvenile court the period of time necessary to accomplish adequate and appropriate treatment, not to exceed one year; the nature of the treatment to be afforded and the facility to which the child could be admitted. If the department or court determines that admission to the facility, the nature of the treatment to be afforded and the period deemed necessary to accomplish treatment are appropriate and the child and his parent or legal guardian agree to the treatment, the child may, subject to the availability of funds appropriated for that purpose, be admitted to the facility for such treatment. Said determination shall be provided in writing.

If the director decides that referral to the division is inappropriate because the child is not a drug dependent person who would benefit by treatment or because adequate treatment is not available at an appropriate facility, he shall make known in writing to said department or said court the basis for this decision.

The referral to the division shall terminate at the conclusion of the period of treatment to which the department or the court consents, or upon a determination by the director that the child will no longer benefit by treatment, whichever first occurs. If the director determines before the conclusion of such period of treatment that the child will no longer benefit by treatment, he shall make known in writing to the department or the court the basis for his decision.

Children in need of services referred to the division pursuant to this section shall remain subject to the jurisdiction and control of the department or the court for all purposes, including, but not limited to, discharge and release; provided, however, that the treatment to be afforded the child in need of services referred to the division shall be within the jurisdiction and control of the division. In no event, however, shall a child in need of services be referred for a period longer than the period during which he is subject to the jurisdiction and control of the department or the court.

Chapter 112. Registration of Certain Professions and Occupations

Section
135   Definitions
135A Confidential communications; exceptions
135B Confidential communications; testimonial privilege

SECTION 135
Definitions

As used in this section and sections one hundred and thirty-five A and one hundred and thirty-five B the following words shall have the following meanings, unless the context clearly indicates otherwise:—

"Client", a person with whom a social worker has established a social worker-client relationship.

"Communications", includes conversations, correspondence, actions and occurrences regardless of the client's awareness of such conversations, correspondence, actions and occurrences and any records, memoranda or notes of the foregoing.

"Reasonable precautions", reasonable efforts to take one or more of the following actions as would be taken by a reasonably prudent social worker under the same or similar circumstances:

(a) communicates a threat of death or serious bodily injury to any reasonably identified victim or victims;

(b) notifies an appropriate law enforcement agency in the vicinity where the client or any potential victim resides;

(c) arranges for the client to be hospitalized voluntarily; or

(d) takes appropriate steps, within the legal scope of social work practice, to initiate proceedings for involuntary hospitalization.

SECTION 135A
Confidential communications; exceptions

All communications between a social worker licensed pursuant to the provisions of section one hundred and thirty-two or a social worker employed in a state, county or municipal governmental agency, and a client are confidential. During the initial phase of the professional relationship, such social worker shall inform the client of such confidential communications and the limitations thereto as set forth in this section and section one hundred and thirty-five B, in accordance with sound professional practice.

No such social worker, colleague, agent or employee of any social worker, whether professional, clerical, academic or therapeutic, shall disclose any information acquired or revealed in the course of or in connection with the performance of the social worker's professional services, including the fact, circumstances, findings or records of such services, except under the following circumstances:

(a) pursuant to the provisions of this section and section one hundred and thirty-five B or any other law;

(b) upon express, written consent of such client or, in the event of a client incompetent to consent, of a guardian appointed to act in the client's behalf;

(c) upon the need to disclose that information which is necessary to protect the safety of the client or others if

(1) the client presents a clear and present danger to himself and refuses explicitly to voluntarily accept further appropriate treatment. In such circumstances, where the social worker has a reasonable basis to believe that a client can be committed to a hospital pursuant to section twelve of chapter one hundred and twenty-three, the social worker shall take appropriate steps within the legal scope of social work practice, to initiate proceedings for involuntary hospitalization. The social worker may also contact members of the client's family or other individuals if in the social worker's opinion, it would assist in protecting the safety of the client;

(2) the client has communicated to the social worker an explicit threat to kill or inflict serious bodily injury upon a reasonably identified victim or victims and the client has the apparent intent and ability to carry out the threat or has a history of physical violence which is known to the social worker and the social worker has a reasonable basis to believe that there is a clear and present danger that the client will attempt to kill or inflict serious bodily injury against a reasonably identified victim or victims. In either of such circumstances, any duty owed by a social worker to warn or in any other way protect a potential victim or victims shall be discharged if the social worker takes reasonable precautions. No cause of action shall lie against, nor shall legal liability be imposed against, a social worker for failure to warn or in any other way protect a potential victim or victims, unless the social worker fails to take such reasonable precautions. Nothing in this paragraph shall require a social worker to take any actions which, in the exercise of reasonable professional judgment, would endanger such social worker or increase the danger to a potential victim or victims;

(d) in order to collect amounts owed by the client for professional services rendered by the social worker or his employees; provided, however, that the social worker may disclose only the nature of services provided, the dates of services, the amount due for services and other relevant financial information; and, provided, further, that if the client raises as a defense to said action substantive assertions concerning the competence of the social worker or the quality of the services provided, the social worker may disclose whatever information is necessary to rebut such assertions;

(e) to initiate a proceeding under paragraph C of section twenty-three or section twenty-four of chapter one hundred

and nineteen, or section three of chapter two hundred and ten or to give testimony in connection therewith;

(f) [stricken]

(g) where the social worker has acquired the information while acting as an elder protective services worker for a designated protective services agency as defined in section fourteen of chapter nineteen A and has acquired the information while conducting an assessment in accordance with section eighteen of said chapter nineteen A;

(h) where the social worker has acquired the information while conducting an investigation pursuant to subsections (b) and (c) of section four or section five of chapter nineteen C;

(i) in the case of marital therapy, family therapy or consultation in contemplation of such therapy, with the written consent of each adult patient participant.

The provision of information acquired by a social worker from a client to any insurance company, nonprofit hospital service corporation, medical service corporation or health maintenance organization or to a board established pursuant to section twelve of chapter one hundred and twenty-six B, pertaining to the administration or provision of benefits, including utilization review or peer review, provided for expenses arising from the out-patient diagnosis or treatment or both, of mental or nervous conditions, shall not constitute a waiver or breach of any right to which said client is otherwise entitled under this section.

No provision of this section shall be construed to prevent a nonprofit hospital service or medical service corporation from inspecting and copying, in the ordinary course of determining eligibility for or entitlement to benefits, any and all records relating to diagnosis, treatment or other services provided to any person, including a minor or incompetent, for which coverage, benefit or reimbursement is claimed, so long as the policy or certificate under which the claim is made provides that such access to such records is permitted. No provision of this section shall be construed to prevent access to any such records in connection with any coordination of benefits, subrogation, workers' compensation, peer review, utilization review or benefit management procedures applied and implemented in good faith.

NOTE 1   Unlicensed Social Workers. "Since the Legislature has authorized the practice of social work by unlicensed governmental agents (G.L. c. 112, § 134), there would be no reason not to apply the provision of secs. 135A and 135B to such individuals . . ." *Bernard v. Commonwealth*, 424 Mass. 32, 35 (1996).

NOTE 2   "The social worker-client privilege is qualified rather than absolute. When the issue of privilege is raised, it falls to the judge to determine the nature and extent of the privilege. Notwithstanding the fact that the referral to the social worker was apparently made by a physician, the judge could have found that the statements in question were made not for the purpose of diagnosis and treatment but were part of the continuing scheme of insurance fraud." *Commonwealth v. Wojcik*, 43 Mass. App. Ct. 595, 608 (1997) (citations, quotation marks, and punctuation omitted).

NOTE 3   See Psychiatric, Psychological, Privileged Records in Alphabetical References to Evidence section of this volume.

SECTION 135B
Confidential communications; testimonial privilege

Except as hereinafter provided, in any court proceeding and in any proceeding preliminary thereto and in legislative and administrative proceedings, a client shall have the privilege of refusing to disclose and of preventing a witness from disclosing, any communication, wherever made, between said client and a social worker licensed pursuant to the provisions of section one hundred and thirty-two of chapter one hundred and twelve, or a social worker employed in a state, county or municipal governmental agency, relative to the diagnosis or treatment of the client's mental or emotional condition.

If a client is incompetent to exercise or waive such privilege, a guardian shall be appointed to act in the client's behalf under this section. A previously appointed guardian shall be authorized to so act.

Upon the exercise of the privilege granted by this section, the judge or presiding officer shall instruct the jury that no adverse inference may be drawn therefrom.

The privilege granted hereunder shall not apply to any of the following communications:

(a) If a social worker, in the course of making a diagnosis or treating the client, determines that the client is in need of treatment in a hospital for mental or emotional illness or that there is a threat of imminently dangerous activity by the client against himself or another person, and on the basis of such determination discloses such communication either for the purpose of placing or retaining the client in such hospital; provided, however, that the provisions of this section shall continue in effect after the client is in said hospital, or placing the client under arrest or under the supervision of law enforcement authorities;

(b) If a judge finds that the client, after having been informed that the communications would not be privileged, has made communications to a social worker in the course of a psychiatric examination ordered by the court; provided, however, that such communications shall be admissible only on issues involving the client's mental or emotional condition but not as a confession or admission of guilt;

(c) In any proceeding, except one involving child custody, adoption or adoption consent, in which the client introduces his mental or emotional condition as an element of his claim or defense, and the judge or presiding officer finds that it is more important to the interests of justice that the communication be disclosed than that the relationship between the client and the social worker be protected;

(d) In any proceeding after the death of a client in which his mental or emotional condition is introduced by any party claiming or defending through or as a beneficiary of the client as an element of the claim or defense, and the judge or presiding officer finds that it is more important to the interests of justice that the communication be disclosed than that the relationship between client and social worker be protected;

(e) In the initiation of proceedings under paragraph C of section twenty-three or under section twenty-four of chapter one hundred and nineteen, or section three of chapter two hundred and ten or to give testimony in connection therewith;

(f) In any proceeding whereby the social worker has acquired the information while conducting an investigation pursuant to section fifty-one B of chapter one hundred and nineteen.

(g) In any other case involving child custody, adoption or the dispensing with the need for consent to adoption in which, upon a hearing in chambers, the judge, in the exercise of his discretion, determines that the social worker has evidence bearing significantly on the client's ability to provide suitable care or custody, and that it is more important to the welfare of the child that the communication be disclosed than that the relationship between client and social worker be protected; provided, however, that in such case of adoption or the dispensing with the need for consent to adoption, a judge shall determine that the client has been informed that such communication would not be privileged; or

(h) In any proceeding brought by the client against the social worker and in any malpractice, criminal or license revocation proceeding in which disclosure is necessary or relevant to the claim or defense of the social worker.

NOTE 1   Records Unprivileged Absent Affirmative Assertion by Patient. "Absent an affirmative assertion [by the patient] of the privileges established by G.L. c. 233, § 20B, and G.L. c. 112, § 135B, the [trial] court must treat such records as if they [are] unprivileged." *Commonwealth v. Oliviera*, 438 Mass. 325, 337 (2002).

NOTE 2   No In Camera Review Absent Assertion of Privilege. "There is no reason to conduct an in camera *Bishop* review for 'relevance' in the absence of any asserted privilege." *Commonwealth v. Oliviera*, 438 Mass. 325, 340 (2002).

Chapter 113A. Uniform Anatomical Gift Act

SECTION 17
Other prohibited acts
(Added by 2012 Mass. Acts c. 39, § 3, effective Feb. 22, 2012.)

A person who, in order to obtain a financial gain, intentionally falsifies, forges, conceals, defaces or obliterates a document of gift, an amendment or revocation of a document of gift or a refusal to make a gift shall be punished by imprisonment in the state prison for not more than 5 years or in a house of correction for not more than 2½ years or by a fine of not more than $50,000 or by both such fine and imprisonment.

Chapter 119. Protection and Care of Children, and Proceedings Against Them

Section
21   Definitions applicable to Secs. 22–51H
39   Abandonment of infant under age of ten
39½   Placement of newborn into foster care
39E   Petitions seeking determination that child is in need of services; jurisdiction; standing
39F   Right to counsel; determination of indigency; assessment of costs
39G   Hearing; determination of child requiring assistance
39H   Custodial protection of child; notification and placement; bail; detention; right of appeal
39I   Appeal; rights and procedures

39J   Repealed
39K   Child welfare service needs of sexually exploited children
39L   Children in violation of prohibition against common night walking or common streetwalking; petition for care and protection; appointment of guardian ad litem; stay of juvenile delinquency or criminal proceedings; failure of child to comply with requirements
51A   Reporting of suspected abuse or neglect; mandated reporters; collection of physical evidence; penalties; content of reports; liability; privileged communication

51B	Investigation of report of abuse filed under Sec. 51A; removal of child; transmissions and filing of written reports; notice to district attorney; disclosure of information by mandated reporter
51C	Custody of injured child pending transfer to department or pending hearing
51D	Powers and duties of area directors; multi-disciplinary service teams
51E	Reports of injured children; files; confidentiality; penalties
51F	Central registry of information; confidentiality; penalties
51G	Severability of Secs. 51A–51F
52	Definitions
53	Liberal construction; nature of proceedings
54	Complaint; indictment; examination of complainant; summons; warrant
55	Summoning of parent or guardian
55A	Jury trials; discovery orders; jury-waived trials; appointment of stenographer
55B	Plea; disposition request; pretrial motions
56	Adjournments; jury sessions; appointment of stenographer
57	Investigation by probation officer; record of performance; reports
58	Adjudication as delinquent child or youthful offender
58A	Repealed
58B	Motor vehicle violations; disposition; admissibility of adjudication and disposition as evidence in other proceedings
59	Violation of terms of probation
60	Admissibility of adjudication in subsequent proceeding; disqualification for public service
60A	Inspection of records in youthful offender and delinquency cases
61	Repealed
62	Restitution or reparation by child to injured person
63	Inducing or abetting delinquency of child
64	Powers of commissioner of probation; annual report
65	Juvenile sessions; presence of minors; exclusion of public
66	Detention of child in police station; commitment to jail, house of correction or state farm
67	Notice of arrest of child to probation officer and parent or guardian; detention
68	Commitment of children held for examination or trial
68A	Diagnostic study by department of youth services; report and recommendations
68B	Special foster homes; detention homes; transfer of child
68C	Diagnostic services by department of youth services
69	Information and reports of superintendents of schools and teachers
69A	Information of probation officers, police and school authorities
70	Summoning of parent or guardian during case
71	Failure to appear on summons; capias
72	Continuance of jurisdiction of courts in juvenile sessions
72A	Proceedings upon apprehension after nineteenth birthday
72B	Persons between the ages of fourteen and eighteen convicted of murder; penalties
73	Repealed
74	Limitation on criminal proceedings against children
75–83	Repealed
84	Warrant of commitment to department of youth services
85	Department employees reporting animal cruelty, abuse or neglect; immunity from liability

PROTECTION OF CHILDREN

SECTION 21

Definitions applicable to Secs. 22–51H
(Amended by 2011 Mass. Acts c. 178, §§ 6–8, effective Nov. 21, 2011; 2012 Mass. Acts c. 240, effective Nov. 5, 2012; 2013 Mass. Acts c. 3, § 5B, effective Feb. 15, 2013.)

As used in sections 21 to 51H, inclusive, the following words shall have the following meanings, unless the context clearly otherwise requires:

"51A report", a report filed with the department under section 51A that details suspected child abuse or neglect.

"Advocate", an employee of a governmental or nongovernmental organization or entity providing appropriate services, or a similar employee of the department of children and families who has been trained to work and advocate for the needs of sexually exploited children.

"Appropriate services", the assessment, planning and care provided by a state agency or nongovernmental organization or entity, through congregate care facilities, whether publicly or privately funded, emergency residential assessment services, family-based foster care or the community, including food, clothing, medical care, counseling and appropriate crisis intervention services, provided: (i) that such agency, organization or entity has expertise in providing services to sexually exploited children or children who are otherwise human trafficking victims; and (ii) that such services are provided in accordance with such regulations that the department of children and families may adopt or the policies of such department.

"Child", a person under the age of 18.

"Child advocate", the child advocate appointed under chapter 18C.

"Child requiring assistance", a child between the ages of 6 and 18 who: (i) repeatedly runs away from the home of the child's parent, legal guardian or custodian; (ii) repeatedly fails to obey the lawful and reasonable commands of the child's parent, legal guardian or custodian, thereby interfering with their ability to adequately care for and protect the child; (iii) repeatedly fails to obey the lawful and reasonable regulations of the child's school; (iv) is habitually truant; or (v) is a sexually exploited child.

"Commissioner", the commissioner of children and families.

"Custody", the power to: (1) determine a child's place of abode, medical care and education; (2) control visits to a child; and (3) consent to enlistments, marriages and other contracts otherwise requiring parental consent. If a parent or guardian objects to the carrying out of any power conferred by this paragraph, that parent or guardian may take application to the committing court and the court shall review and make an order on the matter.

"Department", the department of children and families.

"Family requiring assistance", a parent, guardian, custodian, sibling and any relative or caretaker responsible for a child requiring assistance.

"Habitually truant", a school-aged child, not excused from attendance under the lawful and reasonable regulations of such child's school, who willfully fails to attend school for more than 8 school days in a quarter.

"Mandated reporter", a person who is: (i) a physician, medical intern, hospital personnel engaged in the examination, care or treatment of persons, medical examiner, psychologist, emergency medical technician, dentist, nurse, chiropractor, podiatrist, optometrist, osteopath, allied mental health and human services professional licensed under section 165 of chapter 112, drug and alcoholism counselor, psychiatrist or clinical social worker; (ii) a public or private school teacher, educational administrator, guidance or family counselor, child care worker, person paid to care for or work with a child in any public or private facility, or home or program funded by the commonwealth or licensed under chapter 15D that provides child care or residential services to children or that provides the services of child care resource and referral agencies, voucher management agencies or family child care systems or child care food programs, licensor of the department of early education and care or school attendance officer; (iii) a probation officer, clerk-magistrate of a district court, parole officer, social worker, foster parent, firefighter, police officer; (iv) a priest, rabbi, clergy member, ordained or licensed minister, leader of any church or religious body, accredited Christian Science practitioner, person performing official duties on behalf of a church or religious body that are recognized as the duties of a priest, rabbi, clergy, ordained or licensed minister, leader of any church or religious body, accredited Christian Science practitioner, or person employed by a church or religious body to supervise, educate, coach, train or counsel a child on a regular basis; (v) in charge of a medical or other public or private institution, school or facility or that person's designated agent; or (vi) the child advocate.

"Parent", a mother or father, unless another relative has been designated as a parent as defined in section 1 of chapter 118 for the purposes of receiving benefits from the department of transitional assistance.

"Relative", the father or mother of a child; a stepfather, stepmother, stepbrother, stepsister, or any blood relative of a child, including those of the half blood, except cousins who are more distantly related than first cousins; any adoptive relative of equal propinquity to the foregoing; or a spouse of any such persons.

"Serious bodily injury", bodily injury which involves a substantial risk of death, extreme physical pain, protracted and obvious disfigurement or protracted loss or impairment of the function of a bodily member, organ or mental faculty.

"Sexually exploited child", any person under the age of 18 who has been subjected to sexual exploitation because such person: (1) is the victim of the crime of sexual servitude pursuant to section 50 of chapter 265 or is the victim of the crime of sex trafficking as defined in 22 United States Code 7105; (2) engages, agrees to engage or offers to engage in sexual conduct with another person in return for a fee, in violation of subsection (a) of section 53A of chapter 272, or in exchange for food, shelter, clothing, education or care; (3) is a victim of the crime, whether or not prosecuted, of inducing a minor into prostitution under by section 4A of chapter 272; or (4) engages in common night walking or common street-walking under section 53 of chapter 272.

"Young adult", a person between the ages of 18 and 22.

SECTION 39
Abandonment of infant under age of ten

Whoever abandons an infant under the age of ten within or without any building, or, being its parent, or being under a legal duty to care for it, and having made a contract for its board or maintenance, absconds or fails to perform such contract, and for four weeks after such absconding or breach of his contract, if of sufficient physical and mental ability, neglects to visit or remove such infant or notify the department of his inability to support such infant, shall be punished by imprisonment in a jail or house of correction for not more than two years; or, if the infant dies by reason of such abandonment, by imprisonment in a jail or house of correction for not more than two and one half years of in the state prison for not more than five years.

SECTION 39½
Placement of newborn into foster care

Subject to appropriation, the department of children and families shall accept for placement into foster care any newborn infant 7 days of age or less that is voluntarily placed with a hospital, police department or manned fire station, hereinafter "designated facility" by a parent of said newborn infant. Such a voluntary placement under this section shall not constitute, in an of itself, an automatic termination of parental rights or an abrogation of the parental rights or responsibilities but shall, for purposes of authorizing the department to initiate a petition to terminate parental rights under chapter 210, be presumed to be an abandonment of the newborn infant that has been so placed.

Voluntary abandonment of a newborn infant 7 days of age or younger to an appropriate person at a hospital, police department or manned fire station shall not by itself constitute either a finding of abuse or neglect or a violation of any criminal statu[t]e for child abuse or neglect or for abandonment. If child abuse or neglect, that is not based solely on the newborn infant having been left in the hospital, police department or manned fire station is suspected, hospital, police or fire department personnel who are mandated reporters under section 51A shall report the abuse or neglect.

The designated facility receiving a newborn infant shall immediately notify the department of the placement of the newborn infant at the facility. Upon receipt of such notice, the department shall take immediate custody of the newborn infant and shall initiate all actions authorized by law to achieve the safety and permanent placement of the newborn infant in a manner that is consistent with the best interests of the child.

The person accepting a newborn infant at a designated facility shall make every effort to solicit the following information from the parent placing the newborn infant: (1) the name of the newborn infant; (2) the name and address of the parent placing the newborn infant; (3) the location of the newborn infant's birthplace; (4) information relative to the newborn infant's medical history and his or her biological family's medical history, if available; and (5) and any other information that might reasonably assist the department or the court in current or future determinations of the best interests of the child, including whether the parent or guardian plans on returning to seek future custody of the child. The person receiving the newborn infant shall encourage the parent to provide the information but the parent shall not be required to provide such information.

The department shall develop and implement a public information program to inform the general public of the provisions of this section, teen pregnancy prevention programs and adoption information. The department shall also work in conjunction with other departments and agencies of the commonwealth and the Massachusetts Hospital Association relative to development of the program. The program may include, but not be limited to, educational and informational materials in print, audio video, electronic and other media, public service announcements and advertisements and the establishment of a toll-free hotline.

For purposes of this section only, the following term shall be defined in the following manner unless the context shall clearly indicate a different meaning or intent:– "hospital", a hospital that is licensed under section 51 of chapter 111, or operated by the teaching hospital of the University of Massachusetts Medical School.

The department shall explore the possibility of expending funds received from the United States Department of Health and Human Services pursuant to the Promoting Safe and Stable Families Program, as most recently amended by the Promoting Safe and Stable Families of 2001, in order to implement the public information program required by this section and to alleviate the burden said information program may have on the department's appropriation from the commonwealth. When implementing its public information program, the department shall prioritize those areas of the commonwealth that have been identified by the department of public health as having the highest teen pregnancy rates.

The department of children and families, in conjunction with a designee of the juvenile court, the probate and family court, the center for adoption research at the University of Massachusetts, Massachusetts Families for Kids, Massachusetts Children's Trust Fund, Massachusetts Society for the Prevention of Cruelty to Children, Alliance on Teen Pregnancy and the department of early care and education, shall report every 2 years on the overall effectiveness of the program of voluntary placement of newborn infants established pursuant to this section. The report shall include, but not be limited to, the following: (1) an analysis of this section's effectiveness in decreasing the number of newborns that are abandoned in an unsafe manner in the commonwealth; (2) the department's success or failure in permanently placing in the adoption process any newborn placed with a designated facility pursuant to this section; (3) the average length of time that newborns remain in foster care after being so placed; (4) any issues arising from the termination of parental rights following the placement of a newborn pursuant to this section; (5) the success or failure of any public information campaign implemented by the department pursuant to this section; (6) any increased administrative burdens that may be placed upon any department or agency of the commonwealth as a result of this section; (7) issues with regard to the eligibility of any newborn infant placed pursuant to this section for federal entitlements such as foster care or adoption subsidies under Title IV-E of the United State Social Security Act or any other applicable federal law; and (8) the frequency or infrequency with which a parent placing a newborn at a designated facility supplies the facility with the information sought by the facility pursuant to the fourth paragraph of this section and any negative effects the lack of medical or background information on the child or parents may have had on facilitating the temporary or permanent placement of the child through the foster care or adoption process. The report, including any legislative recommendations, shall be submitted to the joint committee on children, families and persons with disabilities and the house and senate committees on ways and means on or before December 1, 2008 and not later than December 1 of each even numbered year thereafter.

SECTION 39E
Petitions seeking determination that child is in need of services; jurisdiction; standing
(Amended by 2012 Mass. Acts c. 240, §§ 5–12, effective Nov. 5, 2012.)

The divisions of the juvenile court department may receive and hear requests for assistance stating there is a child requiring assistance or a family requiring assistance as defined in section twenty-one, in accordance with the provisions of this section and of sections thirty-nine F to thirty-nine I, inclusive. Proceedings pursuant to sections thirty-nine E to thirty-nine I, inclusive, shall not be deemed criminal proceedings and any record of these proceedings, including the filing of an application for assistance and creation of a docket, shall

not be entered in the criminal offender record information system. Notwithstanding any general or special law to the contrary, no record pertaining to the child involved in the proceedings shall be maintained or remain active after the application for assistance is dismissed. The identity and record of any child for which an application for assistance is filed shall not be submitted to the department of criminal justice information services, criminal offender record information system, court activity record index or any other criminal record information system. Proceedings under sections 39E to 39I, inclusive, shall be confidential and not open to the public. The jurisdiction of the Boston juvenile court for the subject matter of this section shall extend to the territorial limits of Suffolk county.

A parent, legal guardian, or custodian of a child having custody of such child, may initiate an application for assistance in one of said courts stating that said child repeatedly runs away from the home of said parent or guardian or repeatedly runs away from the home of said parent or guardian or persistently refuses to obey the lawful and reasonable commands of said parent or guardian resulting in said parent's or guardian's inability to adequately care for and protect said child.

A school district may initiate an application for assistance in said court stating that said child is not excused from attendance in accordance with the lawful and reasonable regulations of such child's school, has willfully failed to attend school for more than 8 school days in a quarter or repeatedly fails to obey the lawful and reasonable regulations of the child's school. The application for assistance shall also state whether or not the child and the child's family have participated in the truancy prevention program, if one is available, and a statement of the specific steps taken under the truancy prevention program to prevent the child's truancy; and if the application for assistance states that a child has repeatedly failed to obey the lawful and reasonable regulations of the school, a statement of the specific steps taken by the school to improve the child's conduct.

When an application for assistance is presented to the clerk for filing, the clerk shall inform the petitioner that the petitioner may delay filing the request and choose to have the child and the child's family referred to a family resource center, community-based services program or other entity designated by the secretary of health and human services to provide community-based services in the juvenile court district where the child resides and return to court at a later time to file an application for assistance, if needed. The clerk shall prepare, publish and disseminate to each petitioner educational material relative to available family resource centers, community-based services programs and other entities designated by the secretary of health and human services. If the petitioner is a parent, legal guardian or custodian the clerk shall provide to the petitioner informational materials, prepared by the court that explain the court process and shall include the types of orders that the court may issue and the possibility of changes in the custody of the child and may include an explanation of the services available through the court process, including language translation services and the manner in which those services are delivered.

Whenever an application for assistance is initiated, the clerk shall set a date for a hearing as soon as possible, but not later than 15 days after the request is presented to the clerk for filing, to determine whether assistance is needed, shall notify the child of such hearing and shall request the chief probation officer or a designee to conduct an immediate inquiry to determine whether in the officer's opinion the best interest of the child require that assistance be given. The court shall hold a hearing in which it shall receive the recommendation of the probation officer and shall either (i) decline to accept the application for assistance because there is no probable cause to believe that the child and family are in need of assistance; (ii) decline to accept the application for assistance because it finds that the interests of the child would best be served by informal assistance, in which case the court shall, with the consent of the child and the child's parents or guardian, refer the child to a probation officer for assistance; or (iii) accept the application for assistance and schedule a fact-finding hearing. If the child is brought in on custodial protection, the court shall accept an application for assistance unless one has already been filed, and the court shall immediately request the probation officer promptly to make like inquiry and thereafter report to the court the probation officer's recommendation as to whether the interests of the child can best be served by informal assistance without a fact-finding hearing. Upon receiving such recommendation, the court may hold a hearing and shall decide whether to proceed with a fact-finding hearing or to refer the child to the care of a probation officer for assistance.

When an application for assistance is dismissed under this section, the court shall enter an order directing expungement of any records of the request and related proceedings maintained by the clerk, the court, the department of criminal justice information services, the court activity record index and the probation department that directly pertain to the application for assistance.

Whenever a child is referred to a probation officer for assistance, such officer may: refer the child to an appropriate public or private organization or person for psychiatric, psychological, educational, occupational, medical, dental or social services; and may conduct conferences with the child and the child's family to effect adjustments or agreements which are calculated to resolve the situation which formed the basis of the application for assistance and which will eliminate the need for a fact finding hearing. During the pendency of such referrals or conferences, neither the child nor the child's parents may be compelled to appear at any conferences, produce any papers or visit any place. However, if the child or the child's parents fail to participate in good faith in the referrals or conferences arranged by the probation officer, the probation officer shall so certify in writing, and the clerk shall accept the application for assistance if one has not already been accepted and shall set a date for a fact finding hearing. The judge who conducted the hearing on the acceptance of the application for assistance shall not preside at any subsequent hearing. Conferences and referrals arranged under this section may extend for a period not to exceed 90 days from the date that the application for assistance was initially filed, unless the parent and child voluntarily agree in writing to a continuation of such conferences or referrals for an additional period not to exceed 90 days from the expiration of the original period. Upon the expiration of the initial 90 day period, or of such additional 90 day period, the application for assistance, if any, shall be dismissed and the child and his parents discharged from any further obligation to participate in such conferences

and referrals, or an application for assistance shall, if not already accepted, be accepted and a date set for a fact-finding hearing. No statements made by a child or by any other person during the period of inquiries, conferences or referrals may be used against the child at any subsequent hearing to determine that the child requires assistance, but such statements may be received by the court after the fact finding hearing for the purpose of disposition.

The commissioner of probation shall establish a system to collect data on all requests for assistance made and how they are resolved under sections 39E to 39I, inclusive. Said system shall maintain the privacy of clients served, assist the court in addressing the needs of the population to be served and collect information related to: the racial and ethnic identity of the child; the insurance status and coverage of clients served; the length of time a child is receiving assistance from a probation officer, including the time prior to and subsequent to the filing of an application for assistance; the identity of any public or private organization to whom a probation officer has referred a child or family for services; and any other information that may assist the commissioner and the court in evaluating the availability and effectiveness of services for children who are the subjects of requests for assistance under this section. The probation officer shall gather information concerning each child and family referred to the officer including, but not limited to, insurance status and coverage and other information that may assist the commissioner of probation and the court in evaluating the availability and effectiveness of services for children who are the subjects of requests for assistance under this section.

Upon the filing of an application for assistance under this section, the court may issue a summons, to which a copy of the application for assistance shall be attached, requiring the child named in such application to appear before said court at the time set forth in the summons. If such child fails to obey the summons, said court may issue a warrant reciting the substance of the petition and requiring the officer to whom it is directed forthwith to take and bring such child before said court. Notice of the hearing shall be given to the department of children and families and the department of youth services.

Where the court summons such child, the court shall in addition issue a summons to both parents of the child, if both parents are known to reside in the commonwealth, or to one parent if only one is known to reside within the commonwealth, or, if there is no parent residing in the commonwealth, then to the parent having custody or to the lawful guardian of such child. Said summons shall require the person served to appear at a time and place stated therein at a hearing to determine whether or not such child is in need of assistance.

Unless service of the summons required by this section is waived in writing, such summons shall be served by the constable or police officer, either by delivering it personally to the person to whom addressed, or by leaving it with a person of proper age to receive the same, at the place of residence or business of such person, and said constable or police officer shall immediately make return to the court of the time and manner of service.

SECTION 39F
Right to counsel; determination of indigency; assessment of costs
(Amended by 2012 Mass. Acts c. 240, §§ 13–15, effective Nov. 5, 2012.)

When an application for assistance stating the a [sic] child and family are in need of assistance is initiated the child shall be informed that he has a right to counsel at all hearings, and if said child is not able to retain counsel, the court shall appoint counsel for said child. The clerk shall cause a copy of the application for assistance and notice of the time and place of the any scheduled hearing or proceeding to be delivered to counsel at the time of appointment. When the application for assistance is filed, each parent, legal guardian or custodian of the child shall be informed of the right to be heard in any proceeding under sections 39E to 39I, inclusive, involving the child and that a parent or legal guardian has the right to counsel at any hearing or proceeding regarding custody of such child. If said parent or legal guardian is indigent, the court shall appoint counsel for said parent or legal guardian. The court shall determine whether the parent or guardian of a child stated to require assistance is indigent. If the court determines that the parent or guardian is not indigent, the court shall assess a $300 fee against the parent or guardian to pay for the cost of appointed counsel. If the parent is determined to be indigent but is still able to contribute toward the payment of some of said costs, the court shall order the parent to pay a reasonable amount toward the cost of appointed counsel.

SECTION 39G
Hearing; determination of child requiring assistance
(Amended by 2012 Mass. Acts c. 240, §§ 16–23, effective Nov. 5, 2012.)

At any hearing to determine whether a child and family require assistance, said child and the child's attorney shall be present and the parent, legal guardian or custodian shall be given an opportunity to be heard. The petitioner and any party may file a motion to dismiss the request for assistance at any time prior to a hearing to determine the disposition of a request for assistance. The judge, upon a filing of a motion to dismiss, may order that the request for assistance be dismissed upon a showing that the dismissal is in the best interests of the child or if all parties agree to the dismissal. A probation officer may at any time recommend to the court that the request for assistance be dismissed upon a showing that dismissal is in the best interests of the child.

Upon making a finding that a child requires assistance after a fact finding hearing, the court shall convene and may participate in a conference of the probation officer who conducted the preliminary inquiry, a representative from a family resource center or other community-based services program, if involved with the family, the petitioner, a representative from the child's school, the child's parent, legal guardian or custodian, the child and the child's attorney, a representative of the department of children and families, if involved with the family, and any other person who may be helpful in determining the most effective assistance available to be offered to the child and family. The probation officer shall present written recommendations and other persons at the conference may present written recommendations to the court to advise the court on appropriate treatment and services for the child and family, appropriate placement for the child, and appropriate conditions and limitations of such placement.

At the conference and subsequent hearing on disposition, the child and the child's attorney shall be present and the parents, legal guardian or custodian, and the child and petitioner shall be given an opportunity to be heard. The court may receive evidence as to the best disposition from all persons who participate in the conference and any other person who may be helpful in determining an appropriate disposition.

If the court finds the statements in the application for assistance have been proved at the hearing beyond a reasonable doubt, it may determine the child to be in need of assistance. Upon making such determination, the court, taking into consideration the physical and emotional welfare of the child, may make any of the following orders of disposition:

(a) subject to any conditions and limitations the court may prescribe, including provision for medical, psychological, psychiatric, educational, occupational and social services, and for supervision by a court clinic or by any public or private organization providing counseling or guidance services, permit the child to remain with his parents, legal guardian or custodian;

(b) subject to such conditions and limitations as the court may prescribe, including, but no limited to provisions for those services described in clause (a), place the child in the care of any of the following:

(1) a relative, probation officer, or other adult individual who, after inquiry by the probation officer or other person or agency designated by the court, is found to be qualified to receive and care for the child; (2) a private charitable or childcare agency or other private organization, licensed or otherwise authorized by law to receive and provide care for such children; or (3) a private organization which, after inquiry by the probation officer or other person or agency designated by the court, is found to be qualified to receive and care for the child; or

(c) subject to the provisions of sections 32 and 33 and with such conditions and limitations as the court may recommend, place the child in the custody of the department of children and families. At the same time, the court shall consider the provisions of section 29C and shall make the written certification and determinations required by said section 29C. The department shall give due consideration to the recommendations of the court. The department may not refuse out-of-home placement of a child if the placement is recommended by the court provided that the court has made the written certification and determinations required by said section 29C. The department shall direct the type and length of such out-of-home placement. The department shall give due consideration to the requests of the child that the child be placed outside the home of a parent or guardian where there is a history of abuse and neglect in the home by the parent or guardian.

If the family or child are directed by the court to participate in treatment or services which are eligible for coverage by an insurance plan or other third-party payer, payment for such services shall not be denied if the treatment or services otherwise meet the criteria for coverage.

A child who is the subject of an application for assistance may not be confined in shackles or similar restraints or in a court lockup facility in connection with any proceedings under sections 39E to 39I, inclusive. A child who is the subject of an application for assistance shall not be placed in a locked facility or any facility designated or operated for juveniles who are alleged to be delinquent or who have been adjudicated delinquent. Such child may, however, be placed in a facility which operates as a group home to provide therapeutic care for juveniles, regardless of whether juveniles adjudicated delinquent are also provided care in such facility.

Any order of disposition pursuant to this section shall continue in force for not more than 120 days; provided, however, that the court which entered the order may, after a hearing, extend its duration for up to 3 additional periods, each such period not to exceed 90 days if the court finds that the purposes of the order have not been accomplished and that such extension would be reasonable likely to further those purposes.

No order shall continue in effect after the eighteenth birthday of a child named in an application for assistance authorized to be filed by a parent, a legal guardian or custodian or a police officer or after the sixteenth birthday of a child named in a petition authorized to be filed by a school district.

SECTION 39H

Custodial protection of child; notification and placement; bail; detention; right of appeal

(Amended by 2012 Mass. Acts c. 240, §§ 24–30, effective Nov. 5, 2012.)

A child may be taken into custodial protection for engaging in the behavior described in the definition of "Child requiring assistance" in section 21, only if such child has failed to obey a summons issued pursuant to section thirty-nine E, or if the law enforcement officer initiating such custodial protection has probable cause to believe that such child has run away from the home of his parents or guardian and will not respond to a summons.

After a law enforcement officer has taken a child into custodial protection, the officer shall immediately notify the parent, other person legally responsible for the child's care or the person with whom the child is domiciled, that such child is under the custodial protection of the officer and a representative of the department of children and families, if the law enforcement officer has reason to believe that the child is or has been in the care or custody of such department, and shall inquire into the case.

The law enforcement officer, in consultation with the probation officer, shall then immediately make all reasonable diversion efforts so that such child is delivered to the following types of placements, and in the following order of preference:

(i) to one of the child's parents, or to the child's guardian or other responsible person known to the child, or to the child's legal custodian including the department of children and families or the child's foster home upon the written promise, without surety, of the person to whose custody the child is released that such parent, guardian, person or custodian will bring the child to the court on the next court date;

(ii) forthwith and with all reasonable speed take the child directly and without first being taken to the police station house, to a temporary shelter facility licensed or approved by the department of early education and care, a shelter home approved by a temporary shelter facility licensed or approved by said department of early education and care or a family foster care home approved by a placement agency licensed or approved by said department of early education and care; or

(iii) take the child directly to the juvenile court in which the act providing the reason to take the child into custodial protection occurred if the officer affirms on the record that the officer attempted to exercise the options identified in clauses (i) and (ii), was unable to exercise these options and the reasons for such inability.

A child in custodial protection may not be confined in shackles or similar restraints or in a court lockup facility in connection with any proceedings under sections 39E to 39I, inclusive. A child who is the subject of an application for assistance shall not be placed in a locked facility or a facility designated or operated for juveniles who are alleged to be delinquent or who have been adjudicated delinquent. Such child may, however, be placed in a facility which operates as a group home to provide therapeutic care for juveniles, regardless of whether juveniles adjudicated delinquent are also provided care in such facility.

Notwithstanding the foregoing requirements for placement, any such child who is taken into custodial protection shall, if necessary, to be taken to a medical facility for treatment or observation.

If the court finds that a child stated to require assistance by reason of repeatedly refusing to obey the lawful and reasonable commands of such child's parents, legal guardian or custodian or is likely not to appear at the fact finding or disposition hearing, the court may order the child to be released upon such terms and conditions as it determines to be reasonable or, if the standards below are met, may place the child in the temporary custody of the department of children and families. The court shall not order the child to be placed in the custody of the department of youth services. Prior to the court granting temporary custody to the department of children and families, the court shall make a written certification and determination that it is contrary to the best interests of the child for the child to be in the child's home or current placement and that the department of children and families has made reasonable efforts to prevent removal of the child from the child's home or the existing circumstances indicate that there is an immediate risk of harm or neglect which precludes the provision of preventative services as an alternative to removal. An order placing a child with the department under this section shall be valid for not more than 15 days upon which the child and the child's parents, legal guardians or custodians, represented by counsel, shall be brought again before the court for a hearing on whether such order should be continued for another 15 day period based on the preponderance of the evidence. If the court decides to continue said order, it shall note in writing the detailed reasons for its decision; provided, however that no child shall be placed with the department under this section for more than 45 days.

SECTION 39I

Appeal; rights and procedures

(Amended by 2012 Mass. Acts c. 240, § 31, effective Nov. 5, 2012; 2013 Mass. Acts c. 118, § 10, effective Oct. 29, 2013.)

A child, parent, legal guardian or custodian may appeal from any order or determination, whether final or not final, made under sections 39E to 39H, inclusive. Pending the appeal, the juvenile court shall retain jurisdiction and may enter any order under this chapter to meet the needs of the child. Notwithstanding any general or special law to the contrary, the appeal shall be to a single justice of the appeals court under section 118 of chapter 231 and shall proceed in accordance with the procedures governing petitions to a single justice.

SECTION 39J

Repealed

(Repealed by 2012 Mass. Acts c. 240, § 32, effective Nov. 5, 2012.)

1

SECTION 39K
Child welfare service needs of sexually exploited children
(Added by 2011 Mass. Acts c. 178, § 9, effective Nov. 21, 2011.)

(a) Notwithstanding any general or special law to the contrary, the department of children and families, in collaboration with the department of mental health and other appropriate state agencies, shall: (i) provide for the child welfare services needs of sexually exploited children including, but not limited to, services for sexually-exploited children residing in the commonwealth at the time they are taken into custody by law enforcement or are identified by the department as sexually-exploited children, for the duration of any legal or administrative proceeding in which they are either the complaining witness, defendant or the subject child; and (ii) provide appropriate services to a child reasonably believed to be a sexually exploited child in order to safeguard the child's welfare. If a child reasonably believed to be a sexually exploited child declines services or is unable or unwilling to participate in the services offered, the department or any person may file a care and protection petition under section 24. Sexually exploited children shall have access to an advocate. The advocate or a member of the multidisciplinary service team established under section 51D shall accompany the child to all court appearances and may serve as a liaison between the service providers and the court.

(b) The services that shall be provided under this section shall be available to all sexually exploited children, whether they are accessed voluntarily, through a court proceeding under this section or through a referral, which may be made by any person.

(c) In determining the need for and capacity of the services that may be provided under this section, the department of children and families shall recognize that sexually exploited youth have separate and distinct service needs according to gender and appropriate services shall be made available while ensuring that an appropriate continuum of services exists.

(d) The commissioner of the department may, subject to appropriation, contract with nongovernmental organizations or entities with experience working with sexually exploited children to train law enforcement officials likely to encounter sexually exploited children in the course of their law enforcement duties. The training shall include, but not be limited to, awareness and compliance with the provisions of this section, identification of, access to, and the provision of services for sexually-exploited children and any other services the department deems necessary.

(e) The department may apply to the victim and witness assistance board for grants from the Victims of Human Trafficking Trust Fund, established in section 66A of chapter 10, grants from the United States Department of Justice's Office of Juvenile Justice and Delinquency Prevention or any other federal agency, or grants from any other private source to fund the law enforcement training and services for sexually-exploited children.

(f) The department shall adopt regulations to carry out this section.

SECTION 39L
Children in violation of prohibition against common night walking or common streetwalking; petition for care and protection; appointment of guardian ad litem; stay of juvenile delinquency or criminal proceedings; failure of child to comply with requirements
(Added by 2011 Mass. Acts c. 178, § 9, effective Nov. 21, 2011.)

(a) Before or after arraignment in any juvenile delinquency or criminal proceeding against a sexually exploited child alleging that such juvenile or such defendant violated the prohibition against common night walking or common streetwalking under section 53 of chapter 272 or the provisions of subsection (a) of section 53A of said chapter 272, there shall be a presumption that a care and protection petition on behalf of such child, or a child in need of services petition under section 39E, shall be filed. Any person, including the juvenile, may file a care and protection petition on behalf of such child, including a petition for emergency commitment under section 24, or a parent or a police officer may file a child in need of services petition under section 39E.

(b) The court may appoint a guardian ad litem and shall hold a hearing on such petition. The court may allow a reasonable delay in the proceedings, including any arraignment, to consider the petition. The necessary findings of fact to support the court's decision shall be reduced to writing and made part of the court record.

(c) Upon a motion by a party to the juvenile delinquency or criminal proceeding or by a guardian ad litem, unless the district attorney or the attorney general objects, and upon a finding that a child alleged to be a juvenile delinquent by reason of violating section 53 of chapter 272 or subsection (a) of section 53A of said chapter 272 is a child in need of care and protection or a child in need of services, the court shall, if arraignment has not yet occurred, indefinitely stay arraignment and place the proceeding on file. If the court finds that the child has failed to substantially comply with the requirements of services or that the child's welfare or safety so requires, the court may remove the proceeding from file, arraign the child and restore the delinquency or criminal complaint to the docket for trial or further proceedings in accordance with the regular course of such proceedings. If arraignment has already occurred, unless the district attorney or the attorney general objects, the court shall place the child on pretrial probation under section 87 of chapter 276. If appropriate, the conditions of such probation shall include, but not be limited to, requiring the child to substantially comply with all lawful orders of the court, including orders relating to any care and protection or child in need of services proceeding, and the child shall also comply with the guidance and services of the department or any designated non-governmental service provider. If the child fails to substantially comply with the conditions of probation or if the child's welfare or safety so requires, the court may in its discretion restore the delinquency or criminal complaint to the docket for trial or further proceedings in accordance with the regular course of such proceedings.

SECTION 51A
Reporting of suspected abuse or neglect; mandated reporters; collection of physical evidence; penalties; content of reports; liability; privileged communication
(Amended by 2011 Mass. Acts c. 178, § 10, effective Nov. 21, 2011.)

(a) A mandated reporter who, in his professional capacity, has reasonable cause to believe that a child is suffering physical or emotional injury resulting from: (i) abuse inflicted upon him which causes harm or substantial risk of harm to the child's health or welfare, including sexual abuse; (ii) neglect, including malnutrition; (iii) physical dependence upon an addictive drug at birth, shall immediately communicate with the department orally and, within 48 hours, shall file a written report with the department detailing the suspected abuse or neglect; or (iv) being a sexually exploited child; or (v) being a human trafficking victim as defined by section 20M of chapter 233.

If a mandated reporter is a member of the staff of a medical or other public or private institution, school or facility, the mandated reporter may instead notify the person or designated agent in charge of such institution, school or facility who shall become responsible for notifying the department in the manner required by this section.

A mandated reporter may, in addition to filing a report under this section, contact local law enforcement authorities or the child advocate about the suspected abuse or neglect.(b) For the purpose of reporting under this section, hospital personnel may have photographs taken of the areas of trauma visible on the child without the consent of the child's parents or guardians. These photographs or copies thereof shall be sent to the department with the report.

If hospital personnel collect physical evidence of abuse or neglect of the child, the local district attorney, local law enforcement authorities, and the department shall be immediately notified. The physical evidence shall be processed immediately so that the department may make an informed determination within the time limits in section 51B. If there is a delay in processing, the department shall seek a waiver under subsection (d) of section 51B.

(c) Notwithstanding subsection (g), whoever violates this section shall be punished by a fine of not more than $1,000. Whoever knowingly and willfully files a frivolous report of child abuse or neglect under this section shall be punished by: (i) a fine of not more than $2,000 for the first offense; (ii) imprisonment in a house of correction for not more than 6 months and a fine of not more than $2,000 for the second offense; and (iii) imprisonment in a house of correction for not more than 2½ years and a fine of not more than $2,000 for the third and subsequent offenses.

Any mandated reporter who has knowledge of child abuse or neglect that resulted in serious bodily injury to or death of a child and willfully fails to report such abuse or neglect shall be punished by a fine of up to $5,000 or imprisonment in the house of correction for not more than 2½ years or by both such fine and imprisonment; and, upon a guilty finding or a continuance without a finding, the court shall notify any appropriate professional licensing authority of the mandated reporter's violation of this paragraph.

(d) A report filed under this section shall contain: (i) the names and addresses of the child and the child's parents or other person responsible for the child's care, if known; (ii) the child's age; (iii) the child's sex; (iv) the nature and extent of the child's injuries, abuse, maltreatment or neglect, including any evidence of prior injuries, abuse, maltreatment or neglect; (v) the circumstances under which the person required to report first became aware of the child's injuries, abuse, maltreatment or neglect; (vi) whatever action, if any, was taken to treat, shelter or otherwise assist the child; (vii) the name of the person or persons making the report; (viii) any other information that the person reporting believes might be helpful in establishing the cause of the injuries; (ix) the identity of the person or persons responsible for the neglect or injuries; and (x) other information required by the department.

(e) A mandated reporter who has reasonable cause to believe that a child has died as a result of any of the conditions listed in subsection (a) shall report the death to the district attorney for the county in which the death occurred and the office of the chief medical examiner as required by clause (16) of section 3 of chapter 38. Any person who fails to file a report under this subsection shall be punished by a fine of not more than $1,000.

(f) Any person may file a report under this section if that person has reasonable cause to believe that a child is suffering from or has died as a result of abuse or neglect.

(g) No mandated reporter shall be liable in any civil or criminal action for filing a report under this section or for contacting local law enforcement authorities or the child advocate, if the report or contact was made in good faith, was not frivolous, and the reporter did not cause the abuse or neglect. No other person filing a report under this section shall be liable in any civil or criminal action by reason of the report if it was made in good faith and if that person did not perpetrate or inflict the reported abuse or cause the reported neglect. Any person filing a report under this section may be liable in a civil or criminal action if the department or a district attorney determines that the person filing the report may have perpetrated or inflicted the abuse or caused the neglect.

(h) No employer shall discharge, discriminate or retaliate against a mandated reporter who, in good faith, files a report under this section, testifies or is about to testify in any proceeding involving child abuse or neglect. Any employer who discharges, discriminates or retaliates against that mandated reporter shall be liable to the mandated reporter for treble damages, costs and attorney's fees.

(i) Within 30 days of receiving a report from a mandated reporter, the department shall notify the mandated reporter, in writing, of its determination of the nature, extent and cause or causes of the injuries to the child and the services that the department intends to provide to the child or the child's family.

(j) Any privilege relating to confidential communications, established by sections 135 to 135B, inclusive, of chapter 112 or by sections 20A and 20B of chapter 233, shall not prohibit the filing of a report under this section or a care and protection petition under section 24, except that a priest, rabbi, clergy member, ordained or licensed minister, leader of a church or religious body or accredited Christian Science practitioner need not report information solely gained in a confession or similarly confidential communication in other religious faiths. Nothing in the general laws shall modify or limit the duty of a priest, rabbi, clergy member, ordained or licensed minister, leader of a church or religious body or accredited Christian Science practitioner to report suspected child abuse or neglect under this section when the priest, rabbi, clergy member, ordained or licensed minister, leader of a church or religious body or accredited Christian Science practitioner is acting in some other capacity that would otherwise make him a mandated reporter.

(k) A mandated reporter who is professionally licensed by the commonwealth shall complete training to recognize and report suspected child abuse or neglect.

SECTION 51B
Investigation of report of abuse filed under Sec. 51A; removal of child; transmission and filing of written reports; notice to district attorney; disclosure of information by mandated reporter
(Amended by 2011 Mass. Acts c. 178, §§ 11–12, effective Nov. 21, 2011; 2012 Mass. Acts c. 459, §§ 8–8A, effective Apr. 10, 2013.)

(a) Upon receipt of a report filed under section 51A, the department shall investigate the suspected child abuse or neglect, provide a written evaluation of the household of the child, including the parents and home environment and make a written determination relative to the safety of and risk posed to the child and whether the suspected child abuse or neglect is substantiated. The department shall immediately report to the district attorney and local law enforcement authorities, a sexually exploited child or a child who is otherwise a human trafficking victim, regardless of whether the child is living with a parent, guardian or other caretaker.

(b) The investigation shall include: (i) a home visit at which the child is viewed, if appropriate; (ii) a determination of the nature, extent and cause or causes of the injuries; (iii) the identity of the person or persons responsible therefore; (iv) the name, age and condition of other children in the same household; (v) an evaluation of the parents and the home environment; and (vi) all other pertinent facts or matters. The department shall coordinate with other agencies to make all reasonable efforts to minimize the number of interviews of any potential victim of child abuse or neglect. Upon completion of the investigation and evaluation, the department shall make a written determination relative to: (i) the safety of the child and risk of physical or emotional injury to that child and the safety of and risk thereto of any other children in the household; and (ii) whether the suspected child abuse or neglect is substantiated.

(c) If the department has reasonable cause to believe a child's health or safety is in immediate danger from abuse or neglect, the department shall take a child into immediate temporary custody if it has reasonable cause to believe that the removal is necessary to protect the child from abuse or neglect. The investigation and evaluation shall commence within 2 hours of initial contact and an interim report with an initial determination regarding the child's safety and custody shall be completed as soon as possible but not more than 24 hours after initial contact. The final report required under this section shall be complete within 5 business days of initial contact. If a child is taken into immediate temporary custody, the department shall make a written report stating the reasons for such removal and shall file a care and protection petition under section 24 on the next court day.

(d) If the department does not have reasonable cause to believe that a child's health or safety is in immediate danger from abuse or neglect, the investigation and evaluation shall commence within 2 business days of initial contact and a determination shall be made within 15 business days, unless a waiver has been approved by the area director or requested by law enforcement.

(e) Notwithstanding subsection (c), whenever the department has reasonable cause to believe that removal is necessary to protect a child from abuse or neglect, it shall take the child into immediate temporary custody. If a child is taken into immediate temporary custody, the department shall make a written report stating the reasons for such removal and shall file a care and protection petition under section 24 on the next court day.

(f) If a child named in a report filed under section 51A is in an out-of-home placement and the suspected child abuse or neglect is substantiated, the department shall notify his parents that such report was filed and has been substantiated by the department. If the child died or suffered serious bodily injury, the department shall notify the parents, including the biological parents, if the department determines that such notification is in the best interest of the child or of another child in the same placement. The department shall consult with these parents in decisions about removal or further placement. These notifications and consultations shall not be required if the commissioner determines that such notifications or consultations are not appropriate or in the best interests of a child.

(g) The department shall offer appropriate services to the family of any child which it has reasonable cause to believe is suffering from any of the conditions described in the report to prevent further injury to the child, to safeguard his welfare, and to preserve and stabilize family life whenever possible. If the family declines or is unable to accept or to participate in the offered services, the department or any person may file a care and protection petition under section 24.

(h) The department shall file in the central registry, established under section 51F, a written report containing information sufficient to identify each child whose name is reported under this section or section 51A. A notation shall be sent to the central registry whenever further reports on each such child are filed with the department. If the department determines during the initial screening period of an investigation that a report filed under section 51A is frivolous, or other absolute determination that abuse or neglect has not taken place, such report shall be declared as "allegation invalid". If a report is declared "allegation invalid", the name of the child, or identifying characteristics relating to the child, or the names of his parents or guardian or any other person relevant to the report, shall not be placed in the central registry or in any other computerized program utilized in the department.

(i) The department may purchase and utilize such protective services of private and voluntary agencies as it determines necessary.

(j) The department shall adopt regulations to implement the sections 51A to 51F, inclusive.

(k) The department shall notify and shall transmit copies of substantiated 51A reports and its written evaluations and written determinations under subsection (a) or (b) to the district attorney for the county in which the child resides and for the county in which the suspected abuse or neglect occurred, and to the local law enforcement authorities in the city or town in which the child resides and in the city or town in which the suspected abuse or neglect occurred when the department has reasonable cause to believe that 1 of the conditions listed below resulted from abuse or neglect.

The department shall immediately report to the district attorney and local law enforcement authorities listed above when early evidence indicates there is reasonable cause to believe that 1 of the conditions listed below resulted from abuse or neglect:

(1) a child has died or has suffered brain damage, loss or substantial impairment of a bodily function or organ, substantial disfigurement, or serious physical injury including, but not limited to, a fracture of any bone, a severe burn, an impairment of any organ or an injury requiring the child to be placed on life-support systems;

(2) a child has been sexually assaulted, which shall include a violation of section 13B, 13B½, 13B¾, 13H, 22, 22A, 22B, 22C, 23, 23A, 23B, 24 or 24B of chapter 265 or section 35A of chapter 272;

(3) a child has been sexually exploited, which shall include a violation of section 4A, 4B or 29A of said chapter 272 or is a sexually exploited child or a child who is otherwise a human trafficking victim; or

(4) any other disclosure of physical abuse involving physical evidence which may be destroyed, any current disclosure by a child of sexual assault, or the presence of physical evidence of sexual assault.

Within 45 days of the notification under the first paragraph, the department shall further notify the district attorney of a service plan, if any, developed for such child and his family.

No provision of chapter 66A, sections 135 to 135B, inclusive, of chapter 112, or sections 51E and 51F of this chapter relating to confidential data or confidential communications shall prohibit the department from making such notifications or from providing to the district attorney or local law enforcement authorities any information obtained under this section. No person providing notification or information to a district attorney or local law enforcement authorities under this section shall be liable in any civil or criminal action by reason of such action. Nothing herein shall be construed to prevent the department from notifying a district attorney relative to any incident reported to the department under section 51A or to limit the prosecutorial power of a district attorney.

(l) If the department substantiates a report alleging that abuse or neglect occurred at a facility approved, owned, operated or funded, in whole or in part, or was committed by an individual the department has reason to believe was licensed by the department of elementary and secondary education, the department of early education and care, the department of mental health, the department of developmental services, the department of public health or the department of youth services, the department shall notify the office of the child advocate and the affected department, in writing, by transmitting a copy of the report filed under section 51A and the department's written evaluation and written determination.

If the department substantiates a report alleging that abuse or neglect was committed by an individual who was employed at a facility approved or licensed by the department of early education and care, then the department shall notify the office of the child advocate and the department of early education and care, in writing, by transmitting a copy of the report filed under section 51A and the department's written evaluation and written determination.

If the department is aware of a licensing violation in any such facility, the department shall immediately notify the affected department.

No provision of chapter 66A, sections 135 to 135B, inclusive, of chapter 112, or sections 51E and 51F, or any other provision of law shall prohibit: (i) the department from transmitting copies of reports filed under section 51A or its written evaluations and written determinations to the office of the child advocate or the affected departments; (ii) the department, the office of the child advocate and the affected departments from coordinating activities and sharing information for the purposes of this section or for investigating a licensing violation; or (iii) the department's employees from testifying at administrative hearings held by the affected department in connection with a licensing violation.

(m) Notwithstanding any privilege created by statute or common law relating to confidential communications or any statute prohibiting the disclosure of information but subject to subsection (j) of section 51A, a mandated reporter shall answer questions and provide information posed by the department relating to an investigation conducted under this section, whether or not that person filed the 51A report being investigated. A statutory or common law privilege shall not preclude the admission of any such information in any civil proceeding concerning abuse or neglect of a child, placement or custody of a child.

(n) No person required to provide such information under this section or permitted to disclose information under section 5A of chapter 119A shall be liable in any civil or criminal action for providing such information.

(o) No employer shall discharge, discriminate or retaliate against a mandated reporter who, in good faith, provides such information, testifies or is about to testify in any proceeding involving child abuse or neglect unless such person perpetrated or inflicted such abuse or neglect. Any employer who discharges, discriminates or retaliates against such a person shall be liable to such person for treble damages, costs and attorney's fees.

(p) If the department determines that a 51A report is not substantiated, the department shall notify in writing any and all sources or recipients of information in connection with the investigation that the report of abuse or neglect has not been substantiated, unless the target of the investigation requests that such notification not occur.

(q) The department and the private agencies under contract with it, shall conduct periodic and regular training and education to caseworkers, screeners of 51A reports, and administrators of the department and the agencies regarding their duties and obligations under section 51A and 51B.

(r) There shall be a review by a regional clinical review team when 3 or more 51A reports involving separate incidents have been filed on any child in a family within 3 months and a review by an area clinical review team when 3 or more 51A reports involving separate incidents have been filed on any child in a family within 1 year.

SECTION 51C
Custody of injured child pending transfer to department or pending hearing

If a parent or other person requests the release from a hospital of a child reported pursuant to section fifty-one A, the presiding judge of the juvenile court of the judicial district in which such hospital is located may, if he believes such release would be detrimental to the child's health or safety, authorize the hospital and the attending physician, by any means of communication, to keep such a child in the hospital until custody is transferred to the department or until a hearing may be held relative to the care and custody of such child.

Any other physician treating a child reported pursuant to section fifty-one A may be so authorized by the court to keep such child in his custody until such time as the custody of the child has been transferred to the department or until a hearing may be held relative to the care and custody of such child.

SECTION 51D
Powers and duties of area directors; multi-disciplinary service teams
(Amended by 2011 Mass. Acts c. 178, §§ 13–14, effective Nov. 21, 2011.)

Each area director of the department shall be responsible for implementing subsection (k) of section 51B. Each area director shall, in cooperation with the appropriate district attorney, establish 1 or more multi-disciplinary service teams to review the provision of services to the children and families who are the subject of 51A reports that meet the conditions of subsection (k).

Each team shall consist of the department's caseworker for the particular case, 1 representative of the appropriate district attorney, and at least 1 other member appointed by the area director who is not an employee of either office. The additional member shall have training and experience in the fields of child welfare or criminal justice and, as far as practicable, be involved with the provision of services to these families. No members of a team shall receive any compensation, or in the case of a state employee, any additional compensation, for service on the team.

The team shall review and monitor the service plan developed by the department under subsection (g) of section 51B. The team shall evaluate the effectiveness of the service plan in protecting the child from further abuse or neglect. The team shall make recommendations regarding amendments to the service plan, the advisability of prosecuting members of the family, and the possibility of utilizing diversionary alternatives. If the team finds that services required under such plan are not provided to the family, the case shall be referred to the commissioner.

For 51A reports specifically involving a sexually exploited child or a child who is otherwise a human trafficking victim, the multi-disciplinary service team may consist of a team of professionals trained or otherwise experienced and qualified to assess the needs of sexually exploited children or children who are otherwise human trafficking victims including, but not limited to, a police officer, as defined by section 1 of chapter 90C, or other person designated by a police chief, as defined in said section 1 of said chapter 90C, an employee of the department of children and families, a representative of the appropriate district attorney, a social service provider, a medical professional or a mental health professional.

The team shall have full access to the service plan and any personal data known to the department which is directly related to the implementation of the plan, notwithstanding sections 51E and 51F, chapter 66A, and section 135 of chapter 112. The members of the team shall be considered to be employees of the department for purposes of protecting the confidentiality of the data and the data shall be utilized solely to carry out the provisions of this section; provided, however, that the team may report to the district attorney if the family has failed to participate in the plan.

Each area director shall file a monthly report with the commissioner regarding the activities in the area which have occurred in the previous month pursuant to this section. The report shall be written on a form prescribed by the commissioner and shall include, but not be limited to, the number of cases reported under said subsection (k) of said section 51B, the activities of the teams, the availability of services described in the service plans, and the number of family members that are subject of the reports that have been prosecuted. The commissioner, after deleting all personal identifying information, shall combine these area reports into a monthly report that shall be filed with the secretary of health and human services, each district attorney, the joint committee on children, families and persons with disabilities, and the house and senate committees on ways and means.

For 51B reports specifically involving a sexually exploited child, the purpose of the multi-disciplinary service team shall be to determine whether the child has been sexually exploited or is otherwise a human trafficking victim and to recommend a plan for services to the department that may include, but shall not be limited to, shelter or placement, mental health and medical care needs and other social services.

SECTION 51E
Reports of injured children; files; confidentiality; penalties

The department shall maintain a file of the written reports prepared under this section and sections 51A to 51D, inclusive. These written reports shall be confidential. Upon request and with the approval of the commissioner, copies of written reports of initial investigations may be provided to: (i) the child's parent, guardian, or counsel, (ii) the reporting person or agency, (iii) the appropriate review board, (iv) a child welfare agency of another state for the purpose of assisting that agency in determining whether to approve a prospective foster or adoptive parent, or (v) a social worker assigned to the case. No such report shall be made available to any persons other than those specified in this section without the written and informed consent of the child's parent or guardian, the written approval of the commissioner, or an order of a court of competent jurisdiction. Pursuant to chapter 18C, the child advocate shall have access to these reports.

A child welfare agency of another state may, upon request, and upon the approval of the commissioner, receive a copy of the written report of the initial investigation if the agency has a need for such information in order to carry out its responsibilities under law to protect children from abuse and neglect.

The name and all other identifying information relating to any child, or to his parents or guardian, shall be removed from said reports 1 year after the department determines that the allegation of serious physical or emotional injury resulting from abuse or neglect cannot be substantiated, or, if said allegations are substantiated, when the child reaches the age of 18, or 1 year after the date of termination of services to the child or his family, whichever date occurs last; provided, however, that the department may retain information on unsubstantiated reports to assist in future risk and safety assessments of children and families and may release said information to the child welfare agencies of other states upon request of said child welfare agency for the purpose of assisting said child welfare agency in determining whether to approve a prospective foster or adoptive parent.

Any person who permits any information in the files to be released to persons other than those specified in this section shall be punished by a fine of not more than $1,000 or by imprisonment for not more than 2½ years, or both.

SECTION 51F
Central registry of information; confidentiality; penalties

The department shall maintain a central registry of information sufficient to identify children whose names are reported pursuant to section fifty-one A or fifty-one B. Data and information relating to individual cases in the central registry shall be confidential and shall be made available only with the approval of the commissioner or upon court order; provided, however, that the department may release this data and information to a child welfare agency of another state for the purpose of assisting that agency in determining whether to approve a prospective foster or adoptive parent. The commissioner shall establish rules and regulations governing the availability of such data and information. Pursuant to chapter 18C, the child advocate shall have access to the information in the registry.

A child welfare agency of another state may, upon request, and upon the approval of the commissioner, receive information from the central registry if the agency has a need for such information in order to carry out its responsibilities under law to protect children from abuse and neglect.

The name and all other identifying characteristics relating to any child which is contained in the central registry, or to his parents or guardian, shall be removed 1 year after the department determines, after investigation, that the allegation of serious physical or emotional injury resulting from abuse or neglect cannot be substantiated or, if said allegations are substantiated, when the child reaches the age of 18, or 1 year after the date of termination of services to the child or his family, whichever date occurs last. If the department determines during the initial screening period of an investigation that said report under section 51A is frivolous, or other absolute determination that abuse or neglect has not taken place, then said report shall be declared as "allegation invalid". If such reports are declared "allegation invalid", the name of the child, or identifying characteristics relating to the child, or the names of his parents or guardian or any other person relevant to the report, shall not be placed in the central registry, nor under any other computerized program utilized in the department. Nothing in this section shall prevent the department from keeping information on unsubstantiated reports to assist in future risk and safety assessments of children and families.

Any person employed in the central registry who permits the data and information stored in the registry to be released without authorization to persons other than those specified in the rules and regulations shall be punished by a fine of not more than $1,000 or by imprisonment for not more than 2½ years, or both.

SECTION 51G
Severability of Secs. 51A–51F

Sections fifty-one A to fifty-one F, inclusive, are severable and the invalidity of any of said sections shall not affect the continuing validity of any other of said sections.

SECTION 51H
Protective alerts; transport of child to another state or country

Notwithstanding any general or special law to the contrary, the department may send to, or receive from, any other state or country a protective alert containing any information about a child related to a substantiated report of child abuse or neglect if the department reasonably believes that the child has been or will be transported to another state or country.

DELINQUENT CHILDREN

SECTION 52
Definitions
(Amended by 2013 Mass. Acts c. 84, § 7, effective Sept. 18, 2013.)

The following words are used in the following sections shall, except as otherwise specifically provided, have the following meanings:

"Court", a division of the juvenile court department.

"Delinquent child", a child between seven and 18 who violates any city ordinance or town bylaw or who commits any offense against a law of the commonwealth.

"Probation officer", a probation officer or assistant probation officer of the court having jurisdiction of the pending case.

"Punishment as is provided by law", any sentences which may be imposed upon an adult by a justice of the district court or superior court.

"Youthful offender", a person who is subject to an adult or juvenile sentence for having committed, while between the ages of fourteen and 18, an offense against law of the commonwealth which, if he were an adult, would be punishable by imprisonment in the state prison, and (a) has previously been committed to the department of youth services, or (b) has committed an offense which involves the infliction or threat of serious bodily harm in violation of law, or (c) has committed a violation of paragraph (a), (c) or (d) of section ten or section ten E of chapter two hundred and sixty-nine; provided that, nothing in this clause shall allow for less than the imposition of the mandatory commitment periods provided in section fifty-eight of chapter one hundred and nineteen.

SECTION 53
Liberal construction; nature of proceedings

Sections fifty-two to sixty-three, inclusive, shall be liberally construed so that the care, custody and discipline of the children brought before the court shall approximate as nearly as possible that which they should receive from their parents, and that, as far as practicable, they shall be treated, not as criminals, but as children in need of aid, encouragement and guidance. Proceedings against children under said sections shall not be deemed criminal proceedings.

SECTION 54
Complaint; indictment; examination of complainant; summons; warrant
(Amended by 2013 Mass. Acts c. 84, § 8, effective Sept. 18, 2013.)

If complaint is made to any court that a child between seven and 18 years of age is a delinquent child, said court shall examine, on oath, the complainant and the witnesses, if any, produced by him, and shall reduce the complaint to writing, and cause it to be subscribed by the complainant.

If said child is under twelve years of age, said court shall first issue a summons requiring him to appear before it at the time and place named therein, and such summons shall be issued in all other cases, instead of a warrant, unless the court has reason to believe that he will not appear upon summons, in which case, or if such a child has been summoned and did not appear, said court may issue a warrant reciting the substance of the complaint, and requiring the officer to whom it is directed forthwith to take such child and bring him before said court, to be dealt with according to law, and to summon the witnesses named therein to appear and give evidence at the examination.

The commonwealth may proceed by complaint in juvenile court or in a juvenile session of a district court, as the case may be, or by indictment as provided by chapter two hundred and seventy-seven, if a person is alleged to have committed an offense against a law of the commonwealth while between the ages of fourteen and 18 which, if he were an adult, would be punishable by imprisonment in the state prison, and the person has previously been committed to the department of youth services, or the offense involves the infliction or threat of serious bodily harm in violation of law or the person has committed a violation of paragraph (a), (c), or (d) of section ten or section ten E of chapter two hundred and sixty-nine. The court shall proceed on the complaint or the indictment, as the case may be, in accordance with sections fifty-five to seventy-two, inclusive. Complaints and indictments brought against persons for such offenses, and for other criminal offenses properly joined under Massachusetts Rules of Criminal Procedure 9(a)(1), shall be brought in accordance with the usual course and manner of criminal proceedings.

NOTE 1   "The juvenile's position of authority [uncle; babysitter], age difference between the juvenile [15] and the victim [6], and the vulnerability of the victim are sufficient to support a youthful offender indictment [under G.L. c. 265, § 23 (statutory rape)]." *Commonwealth v. Clint C.*, 430 Mass. 219, 226 (1999) (The SJC also indicated, at 224, that "absent an error of law, a judge may not dismiss an indictment brought under G.L. c. 119, § 54.").

NOTE 2   The Commonwealth may proceed by complaint against a juvenile even if the grand jury has returned a no bill. *Commonwealth v. Dale D.*, 431 Mass. 757, 761 (2000).

NOTE 3   "The issue thus is whether, when the Commonwealth indicts a juvenile as a youthful offender and improperly joins a companion indictment on a misdemeanor charge against the same juvenile, and, after trial, the juvenile is adjudicated a youthful offender on the misdemeanor charge, the proper remedy is to vacate the misdemeanor adjudication and dismiss the indictment (as the Appeals Court ordered in this case) or to order the entry of a delinquency finding on that misdemeanor offense. We conclude that the entry of an adjudication of delinquency should be ordered in such circumstances." *Commonwealth v. Lamont L.*, 438 Mass. 842, 843 (2003).

NOTE 4   **Threat.** "[W]e hold that the definition of 'threat' in the juvenile offender statute requires a communication or declaration, explicit or implicit, of an actual threat of physical injury by the juvenile. . . [P]ossession of heroin with the intent to distribute . . . is not what the Legislature intended when setting forth the 'threat' requirement for a youthful offender indictment." *Felix F., a juvenile v. Commonwealth*, 471 Mass. 513, 516 (2015).

NOTE 5   **Dismissal Before Arraignment.** "[A] Juvenile Court judge, in his or her discretion, may allow a motion to dismiss before the arraignment of a juvenile where the judge concludes that prearraignment dismissal is in both the best interests of the child and the interests of justice." *Commonwealth v. Humberto H.*, 466 Mass. 562, 563 (2013).

NOTE 6   **Transfer Hearing.** "We . . . determine whether a transfer hearing pursuant to G.L. c. 119, § 72A (§ 72A), must be held before the Commonwealth may seek an indictment pursuant to G.L. c. 119, § 54 (§ 54), against a defendant who is alleged to have committed offenses when he was between fourteen and seventeen years of age, but was not apprehended until after his eighteenth birthday. [W]e conclude that the clear language of § 72A requires that a hearing be held prior to the Commonwealth's proceeding on an indictment pursuant to § 54." *Commonwealth v. Nanny*, 462 Mass. 798, 798–99 (2012).

NOTE 7a   **Retroactivity.** "This case requires us to decide whether St. 2013, c. 84 (act), which extended the Juvenile Court's jurisdiction to persons who are seventeen years of age at the time of committing an offense, applies retroactively to persons who were seventeen years of age when they committed an offense and against whom criminal proceedings had begun and were pending on September 18, 2013, the effective date of the act. We conclude that the act is not retroactive to criminal cases begun and pending before September 18, 2013, against persons who were seventeen years of age at the time of the alleged offense." *Watts v. Commonwealth*, 468 Mass. 49, 49–50 (2014).

NOTE 7b   The act [2013 Mass. Acts c. 84] does not apply retroactively to a defendant who commits an offense prior to his or her eighteenth birthday for which a criminal proceeding commenced prior to the effective date of the act [September 18, 2013]. *Commonwealth v. Freeman*, 472 Mass. 503, 509 (2015).

SECTION 55
Summoning of parent or guardian

If a child has been summoned to appear or is brought before such court upon a warrant, as provided in section fifty-four, a summons shall be issued to at least one of its parents, if either of them is known to reside within the commonwealth, and, if there is no such parent, then to its lawful guardian, if there is one known to be so resident, and if not, then to the person with whom such child resides, if known. Said summons shall require the person served to appear at a time and place stated therein, and show cause why such child should not be adjudged a delinquent child and why it is not in such child's best interest that he be removed from his home and whether reasonable efforts were made to prevent or eliminate the need for removal from his home. If there is no such parent, guardian or person who can be summoned as aforesaid, the court may appoint a suitable person to act for such child. A parent, guardian or person with whom such child resides who is summoned to appear before the court to show cause why such child shall not be adjudged a delinquent child by reason of having committed the offense of wilful or malicious destruction or wanton destruction of property, in violation of the provisions of section one hundred and twenty-seven or one hundred and twenty-seven A of chapter two hundred and sixty-six, and who wilfully fails to so appear shall be punished by a fine of not less than two hundred nor more than three hundred dollars.

If such child is summoned, the time for appearance fixed in the summons to a parent, guardian or other person, as herein provided, shall, when practicable, be that fixed for the appearance of said child.

A summons required by this and said section fifty-four, unless service thereof is waived in writing, shall be served by a constable or police officer, by delivering it personally to the person to whom addressed, or by leaving it with a person of proper age to receive the same, at the place of residence or business of such person; and said constable or officer shall immediately make return to the court of the time and manner of the service.

If the court shall be of the opinion that the interests of the child require the attendance at any proceedings of an agent of the department of youth services and shall request such attendance by reasonable notice to the commissioner of youth services, such agent shall attend to protect the interests of said child.

SECTION 55A
Jury trials; discovery orders; jury-waived trials; appointment of stenographer

Trial of a child complained of as a delinquent child or indicted as a youthful offender in a division of the juvenile court department shall be by a jury, unless the child files a written waiver and consent to be tried by the court without a jury. Such waiver shall not be received unless the child is represented by counsel or has filed, through his parent or guardian, a written waiver of counsel. No decision on such waiver shall be received until after the completion of a pretrial conference and a hearing on the results of such conference and until after the disposition of any pretrial discovery motions and compliance with any order of the court pursuant to said motions. Such waiver shall be filed in accordance with the provisions of section six of chapter two hundred and sixty-three; provided, however, that defense counsel shall execute a certificate signed by said counsel indicating that he has made all the necessary explanations and determinations regarding such waiver. The form of such certificates shall be prescribed by the chief justice for the juvenile court department.

In the juvenile court department upon the motion of a child consistent with criminal procedure, or upon the court's own motion, the judge shall issue an order of discovery requiring the prosecutor to provide in writing any information to which the child is entitled and also requiring that the child be permitted to discover, inspect, and copy any material and relevant evidence, documents, statements of persons, or reports of physical or mental examinations of any person or of scientific tests or experiments, within the possession, custody, or control of the prosecutor or persons under his direction or control. Upon motion of the child the judge shall order the production by the commonwealth of the names and addresses of the prospective witnesses and the production by the commonwealth of the names and addresses of the prospective witnesses and the production by the probation department of the record of prior convictions of any such witnesses. The commonwealth shall be entitled to reciprocal discovery as set forth in Rule 14(a)(1)(3) of the Massachusetts Rules of Criminal Procedure.

Trial by jury in the juvenile court department shall be in those jury sessions designated in accordance with section fifty-six. Where the child has properly filed a waiver and consented to be tried without a jury, as hereinbefore provided, trial shall proceed in accordance with the provisions of law applicable to jury-waived trials in the superior court; provided, however, that at the option of the child, the trial may be before a judge who has not rejected an agreed upon recommendation or disposition request made by the child pursuant to the provisions of section fifty-five B. Review in such cases may be had directly by the appeals court, by appeal, report or otherwise in the same manner provided for trials of criminal cases in the superior court.

The justice presiding over such jury-waived trial in the juvenile court department shall have and exercise all the powers which a justice sitting in the superior court department has and may exercise in the trial and disposition of criminal cases including the power to report questions of law to the appeals court.

The justice presiding at such jury-waived session in the juvenile court department shall, upon the request of the child, appoint a stenographer; provided, however, that where the child claims indigence, such appointment is determined to be reasonably necessary in accordance with the provisions of sections twenty-seven A to twenty-seven G, inclusive, of chapter two hundred and sixty-one. Such stenographer shall be sworn, and shall take stenographic notes of all the testimony given at the trial, and shall provide the parties thereto with a transcript of his notes or any part thereof taken at the trial or hearing for which he shall be paid by the party requesting it at the rate fixed by the chief justice of the juvenile court department; provided, however, that such rate shall not exceed the rate provided pursuant to section eighty-eight of chapter two hundred and twenty-one. Said chief justice may make regulations not inconsistent with law relative to the assignments, duties and services of stenographers appointed for sessions in his department and any other matter relative to stenographers. The compensation and expenses of a stenographer shall be paid by the commonwealth.

The request for the appointment of a stenographer to preserve the testimony at a trial in the juvenile court department shall be given to the clerk of the court by the child in writing no later than forty-eight hours prior to the proceeding for which the stenographer has been requested. The child shall file with such request an affidavit of indigence and request for payment by the commonwealth of the cost of the transcript and the court shall hold a hearing on such request prior to appointing a stenographer, in those cases where the child alleges that he will be unable to pay said cost. Said hearing shall be governed by the provisions of sections twenty-seven A to twenty-seven G, inclusive, of chapter two hundred and sixty-one, and the cost of such transcript shall be considered an extra cost as provided therein. If the court is unable, for any reason, to provide a stenographer, the proceedings may be recorded by electronic means. The original recording of proceedings in the juvenile court department made with a recording device under the exclusive control of the court shall be the official record of such proceedings. Said record or a copy of all or a part thereof, certified by the presiding justice or his designee, to be an accurate electronic reproduction of said record or part thereof, or a typewritten transcript of all or part of said record or copy thereof, certified to be accurate by the court or by the preparer of said transcript, or stipulated to by the parties, shall be admissible in any court as evidence of testimony given wherever proof of such testimony is otherwise competent. The child may request payment by the commonwealth of the cost of said transcript subject to the same provisions regarding a transcript of a stenographer as provided hereinbefore.

SECTION 55B
Plea; disposition request; pretrial motions
(Amended by 2011 Mass. Acts c. 178, § 15, effective Nov. 21, 2011.)

A child who is before the juvenile court on a delinquency complaint or an indictment within the court's jurisdiction shall plead not delinquent, or that he should not be adjudged as a youthful offender, as the case may be. Such plea shall be submitted by the child and acted upon by the court; provided, however that a child with whom the commonwealth cannot reach agreement for a recommended disposition shall be allowed to tender a plea together with a request for a specific disposition. Such request may include any disposition or dispositional terms within the court's jurisdiction, including, unless otherwise prohibited by law, a disposition request that a finding not be entered, but rather the case be continued without a finding to a specific date thereupon to be dismissed, such continuance conditioned upon compliance with specific terms and conditions or that the child be placed on probation pursuant to the provisions of section 57; provided, however, that a complaint alleging a child to be a delinquent child by reason of having violated the provisions of section 13B, 13B½, 13B¾, section 22A, 22B, 22C or section 23, 23A, 23B or section 50 of chapter 265 shall not be placed on file or continued without a finding. If a plea, with an agreed upon recommendation or with a disposition request by the child, is tendered, the court shall inform the child that it will not impose a disposition that exceeds the terms of the agreed upon recommendation or the disposition request by the child, whichever is applicable, without giving the child the right to withdraw the plea.

Notwithstanding the foregoing requirements, if a child attempts to enter a plea or statement consisting of an admission of facts sufficient for a finding of delinquency or adjudication as a youthful offender, or some similar statement, such admission shall be deemed a tender of plea for purposes of the procedures set forth in this section.

Any pretrial motion filed in a delinquency case or case in which the commonwealth has proceeded by indictment pending in the juvenile court and decided before entry of the child's decision on waiver of the right to jury trial shall not be refiled or reheard thereafter, except in the discretion of the court as substantial justice requires. Any such pre-trial motion not filed or filed but not decided prior to entry of the child's decision on waiver of the right to jury trial may be filed thereafter but not later than twenty-one days after entry of said decision on waiver of the right to jury trial, except for good cause shown.

SECTION 56
Adjournments; jury sessions; appointment of stenographer

Hearings upon cases arising under sections fifty-two to eighty-four, inclusive, may be adjourned from time to time; provided however, that no adjournment shall exceed fifteen days at any one time against the objection of the child. Section thirty-five of chapter two hundred and seventy-six relative to recognizance in cases continued shall apply to cases arising under sections fifty-two to eighty-four, inclusive.

(a) Every division of the juvenile court department shall be authorized to hold jury sessions for the purpose of conducting jury trials of cases commenced in the several courts of offenses over which the juvenile courts have original jurisdiction.

(b) The chief justice of the juvenile court department shall designate at least one division in each county or an adjourning county for the purpose of conducting jury trials.

The chief justice of the juvenile court department may also designate one or more divisions in each county for the purpose of conducting jury-waived trials of cases commenced

in any court of said county consistent with the requirements of the proper administration of justice.

(c) A child in any division of the juvenile court who waives his right to jury trial as provided in section fifty-five A shall be provided a jury-waived trial in the same division.

A child in any division of the juvenile court who does not waive his right to jury trial as provided in section fifty-five A shall be provided a jury trial in a jury session in the same division if such session has been established in said division. If such session has not been so established, the child shall be provided a jury trial in a jury session in an adjoining county as designated by the clerk in the division where the case is pending. In cases where the child declines to waive the right to jury trial, the clerk shall forthwith transfer the case for trial in the appropriate jury session. Such transfer shall be governed by procedures to be established by the chief justice for the juvenile court department.

(d) The justice presiding over a jury session shall have and exercise all the powers and duties which a justice sitting in the superior court department has and may exercise in the trial and disposition of criminal cases including the power to report questions of law to the appeals court. No justice so sitting shall act in a case in which he has sat or held an inquest or otherwise taken part in any proceeding therein.

(e) Trials by juries shall proceed in accordance with the provisions of law applicable to trials by jury in the superior court. The commonwealth shall be entitled to as many challenges as equal the whole number to which all the children in the case are entitled. Trial by jury shall be by juries of six persons, except that in cases where the commonwealth has proceeded by indictment, said child shall be entitled to a jury of twelve.

(f) For the jury sessions, jurors shall be provided by the office of the jury commissioner in accordance with the provisions of chapter two hundred and thirty-four A.

(g) The district attorney for the district in which the alleged offense or offenses occurred shall appear for the commonwealth in the trial of all cases in which the right to jury trial has not been waived and may appear in any other case. The chief justice for the juvenile court department shall arrange for the sittings of the jury sessions of the juvenile court department and shall assign justices thereto, to the end that speedy trials may be provided. Review may be had directly by the appeals court, by appeal, report or otherwise in the same manner provided for trials of criminal cases in the superior court. A claim of trial by jury under this section may be withdrawn before trial, in which event trial and disposition of the case shall be by a justice in a jury session sitting without a jury.

(h) The justice presiding at such session in the juvenile court department shall, upon request of the child, appoint a stenographer in accordance with section fifty-five A herein.

The request for the appointment of a stenographer to preserve the testimony at a trial in the juvenile court department shall be given to the clerk of the court by the child in writing no later than forty-eight hours prior to the proceeding for which the stenographer has been requested. The child shall file with such request an affidavit of indigence and request for payment by the commonwealth of the cost of the transcript and the court shall hold a hearing on such request prior to appointing a stenographer, in those cases where the child alleges that he will be unable to pay said cost. Said hearing shall be governed by the provisions of sections twenty-seven

A to twenty-seven G, inclusive, of chapter two hundred and sixty-one, and the cost of such transcript shall be considered an extra cost as provided therein. If the court is unable, for any reason, to provide a stenographer, the proceedings may be recorded by electronic means. The original recording of proceedings in the juvenile court department made with a recording device under the exclusive control of the court shall be the official record of such proceedings. Said record or a copy of all or a part thereof, certified by the presiding justice or his designee, to be an accurate electronic reproduction of said record or part thereof, or a typewritten transcript of all or part of said record or copy thereof, certified to be accurate by the court or by the preparer of said transcript, or stipulated to by the parties, shall be admissible in any court as evidence of testimony given wherever proof of such testimony is otherwise competent. The child may request payment by the commonwealth of the cost of said transcript subject to the same provisions regarding a transcript of a stenographer as provided hereinbefore.

SECTION 57
Investigation by probation officer; record of performance; reports

Every case of a delinquent child shall be investigated by the probation officer, who shall make a report regarding the character of such child, his school record, home surroundings and the previous complaints against him, if any. In every case involving a child attending a special class authorized by law, he shall secure from the bureau of special education a record of performance of said child. He shall be present in court at the trial of the case, and furnish the court with such information and assistance as shall be required. At the end of the probation period of a child who has been placed on probation, the officer in whose care he has been shall make a report as to his conduct during such period.

SECTION 58
Adjudication as delinquent child or youthful offender
(Amended by 2011 Mass. Acts c. 178, § 16, effective Nov. 21, 2011; 2013 Mass. Acts c. 84, §§ 9–11, effective Sept. 18, 2013.)

At the hearing of a complaint against a child the court shall hear the testimony of any witnesses who appear and take such evidence relative to the case as shall be produced. If the allegations against a child are proved beyond a reasonable doubt, he may be adjudged a delinquent child, or in lieu thereof, the court may continue the case without a finding and, with the consent of the child and at least one of the child's parents or guardians, place said child on probation; provided, however, that any such probation may be imposed until such child reaches age eighteen or age nineteen in the case of a child whose case is disposed of after he has attained his eighteenth birthday or age 20 in the case of a child whose case is disposed of after he has attained his nineteenth birthday; provided further, that a complaint alleging a child to be a delinquent child by reason of having violated the provisions of section 13B, 13B½, 13B¾, section 22A, 22B, 22C, 23, 23A, section 23B or section 50 of chapter 265 shall not be placed on file or continued without a finding. Said probation may include a requirement, subject to agreement by the child and at least one of the child's parents or guardians, that the child do work or participate in activities of a type and for a period of time deemed appropriate by the court.

If a child is adjudicated a delinquent child on a complaint, the court may place the case on file or may place the child in the care of a probation officer for such time and on such conditions as it deems appropriate or may commit him to the custody of the department of youth services, but the probationary or commitment period shall not be for a period longer than until such child attains the age of eighteen, or nineteen in the case of a child whose case is disposed of after he has attained his eighteenth birthday or age 20 in the case of a child whose case is disposed of after he has attained his nineteenth birthday.

If a child is adjudicated a youthful offender on an indictment, the court may sentence him to such punishment as is provided by law for the offense. The court shall make a written finding, stating its reasons therefor, that the present and long-term public safety would be best protected by:

(a) a sentence provided by law; or

(b) a combination sentence which shall be a commitment to the department of youth services until he reaches the age of twenty-one, and an adult sentence to a house of correction or to the state prison as is provided by law for the offense. The adult sentence shall be suspended pending successful completion of a term of probation, which shall include, but not be limited to, the successful completion of the aforementioned commitment to the department of youth services. Any juvenile receiving a combination sentence shall be under the sole custody and control of the department of youth services unless or until discharged by the department or until the age of twenty-one, whichever occurs first, and thereafter under the supervision of the juvenile court probation department until the age of twenty-one and thereafter by the adult probation department; provided, however, that in no event shall the aggregate sentence imposed on the combination sentence exceed the maximum adult sentence provided by law; or

(c) a commitment to the department of youth services until he reaches the age of twenty-one.

In making such determination the court shall conduct a sentencing recommendation hearing to determine the sentence by which the present and long-term public safety would be best protected. At such hearing, the court shall consider, but not be limited to, the following factors: the nature, circumstances and seriousness of the offense; victim impact statement; a report by a probation officer concerning the history of the youthful offender; the youthful offender's court and delinquency records; the success or lack of success of any past treatment or delinquency dispositions regarding the youthful offender; the nature of services available through the juvenile justice system; the youthful offender's age and maturity; and the likelihood of avoiding future criminal conduct. In addition, the court may consider any other factors it deems relevant to disposition. No such sentence shall be imposed until a pre-sentence investigation report has been filed by the probation department and made available to the parties no less than seven days prior to sentencing.

A youthful offender who is sentenced as is provided by law either to a state prison or to a house of correction but who has not yet reached his eighteenth birthday shall be held in a youthful offender unit separate from the general population of adult prisoners; provided, however, that such youthful offender shall be classified at a facility other than the reception and diagnostic center at the Massachusetts Correctional Institution, Concord, and shall not be held at the Massachusetts

Correctional Institution, Cedar Junction, prior to his eighteenth birthday.

If it is alleged in the complaint upon which the child is so adjudged that a penal law of the commonwealth, a city ordinance or a town by-law has been violated, the court may commit such child to the custody of the commissioner of youth services and authorize him to place such child in the charge of any person, and, if at any time thereafter the child proves unmanageable, to transfer such child to that facility or training school which in the opinion of said commissioner, after study, will best serve the needs of the child. The department of youth services shall provide for the maintenance, in whole or in part, of any child so placed in the charge of any person.

Notwithstanding any other provisions of this chapter, a person adjudicated a delinquent child by reason of a violation of paragraphs (a), (c) or (d) of section ten or ten E of chapter two hundred and sixty-nine, shall be committed to the custody of the commissioner of youth services who shall place such child in the custody of a facility supported by the commonwealth for the care, custody and training of such delinquent children for a period of at least one hundred and eighty days or until such child attains his eighteenth birthday or his nineteenth birthday in the case of a child whose case is disposed of after he has attained his eighteenth birthday, whichever first occurs, provided, however, that said period of time shall not be reduced or suspended.

Upon the second or subsequent violation of said paragraphs (a), (c) or (d) of said section ten or ten E of said chapter two hundred and sixty-nine, the commissioner of youth services shall place such child in the custody of a facility supported by the commonwealth for the care, custody and training of such delinquent child for not less than one year; provided, however that said period of time shall not be reduced or suspended.

The court may make an order for payment by the child's parents or guardian from the child's property, or by any other person responsible for the care and support of said child, to the institution, department, division, organization or person furnishing care and support at times to be stated in an order by the court of sums not exceeding the cost of said support after ability to pay has been determined by the court; provided, however, that no order for the payment of money shall be entered until the person by whom payments are to be made shall have been summoned before the court and given an opportunity to be heard. The court may from time to time, upon petition by, or notice to the person ordered to pay such sums of money, revise or alter such order or make a new order, as the circumstances may require.

The court may commit such delinquent child to the department of youth services, but it shall not commit such child to any institution supported by the commonwealth for the custody, care and training of delinquent children or juvenile offenders.

Except in cases in which the child has attained the age of the majority, whenever a court of competent jurisdiction adjudicates a child as delinquent and commits the child to the department of youth services, the court, in order to comply with the requirements contained in the federal Adoption Assistance and Child Welfare Act of 1980 and any amendments thereto, shall receive evidence in order to determine whether continuation of the child in his home is contrary to his best interest, and whether reasonable efforts were made prior to the commitment of the child to the department, to prevent or eliminate the need for removal from his home; or whether an emergency situation existed making such efforts impossible. No such determination shall be made unless the parent or guardian of the delinquent shall have been summoned before the court and, if present, given an opportunity to be heard. The court, in its discretion, may make its determinations concerning said best interest and reasonable efforts in written form, but in the absence of a written determination to the contrary, it shall be presumed that the court did find that continuation of the child in his home was contrary to his best interest and that reasonable efforts to prevent or eliminate the need for removal of the child from his home did occur. Nothing in this section shall diminish the department's responsibility to prevent delinquent acts and to protect the public safety.

NOTE   "This case . . . requires us to decide whether G.L. c. 119, § 58, empowers a Juvenile Court judge to continue a delinquency case without a finding and place the juvenile under the supervision of the probation department, notwithstanding a jury's prior verdict of delinquency. Based on the text of the statute, its placement within the broader statutory scheme, and the underlying philosophy of our juvenile justice system, we conclude that it does." *Commonwealth v. Magnus M.*, 461 Mass. 459, 459 (2012).

SECTION 58A
Repealed

SECTION 58B
Motor vehicle violations; disposition; admissibility of adjudication and disposition as evidence in other proceedings

If, under the provisions of section fifty-eight, a child is adjudged a delinquent child by reason of having violated any statute, by-law, ordinance or regulation relating to the operation of motor vehicles, the court may place the case on file, or may place the child in the care of a probation officer, or may commit him to the custody of the department of youth services, as provided in section fifty-eight, and may require restitution as provided in section sixty-two; and in addition to or in lieu of such disposition, the court may impose upon such child a fine not exceeding the amount of the fine authorized for the violation of such statute, by-law, ordinance or regulation. Any fine imposed under the authority of this section shall be collected, recovered and paid over in the manner provided by chapters two hundred and seventy-nine and two hundred and eighty; provided, however, that if any child shall neglect, fail or refuse to pay a fine imposed under this section, he may be arrested upon order of the court and brought before the court, which may thereupon place him in the care of a probation officer or commit him to the custody of the department of youth services; but no such child shall be committed to any jail, house of correction, or correctional institution of the commonwealth. The provisions of section sixty and sixty A shall apply to any case disposed of under this section; provided, however, that the court shall provide the registrar of motor vehicles with an abstract of every such adjudication and disposition in the manner provided by section twenty-seven of chapter ninety; and provided, further, that such adjudication and disposition shall be admissible as evidence in any proceeding for the revocation or restoration of the child's license or right to operate a motor vehicle and for the cancellation of a motor vehicle insurance policy covering the vehicle operated by such child, and in any action of tort arising out of the negligent operation of a motor vehicle by said child, to the same extent that such evidence would be admissible if said child were an adult.

SECTION 59
Violation of terms of probation

If a child has been placed in care of a probation officer, said officer, at any time before the final disposition of the case, may arrest such child without a warrant and take him before the court, or the court may issue a warrant for his arrest. When such child is before the court, it may make any disposition of the case which it might have made before said child was placed on probation, or may continue or extend the period of probation.

SECTION 60
Admissibility of adjudication in subsequent proceeding; disqualification for public service

An adjudication of any child as a delinquent child under sections fifty-two to fifty-nine, inclusive, or any disposition thereunder of any child so adjudicated, or any evidence given in any case arising against any child under said sections fifty-two to fifty-nine, or any records in cases arising against any child under said sections fifty-two to fifty-nine shall not be received in evidence or used against such child for any purpose in any proceedings in any court except in subsequent delinquency or criminal proceedings against the same person; nor shall such adjudication or disposition or evidence operate to disqualify a child in any future examination, appointment, or application for public service under the government either of the commonwealth or of any political subdivision thereof; provided, however, that adjudication of delinquency by reason of the child having committed an offense against the commonwealth may be used for impeachment purposes in subsequent delinquency or criminal proceedings in the same manner and to the same extent as prior criminal convictions.

NOTE 1a   "[W]e conclude that the State's desire that Green [the juvenile] fulfill his public duty to testify free from embarrassment and with his reputation unblemished must fall before the right of petitioner to seek out the truth in the process of defending himself. The State's policy interest in protecting the confidentiality of a juvenile offender's record cannot require yielding of so vital a constitutional right as the effective cross-examination for bias of an adverse witness." *Commonwealth v. Ferrara*, 368 Mass. 182, 190 (1975) (quoting *Davis v. Alaska*, 415 U.S. 308, 320 (1974)).

NOTE 1b   *Compare Commonwealth v. A Juvenile (No. 2)*, 384 Mass. 390, 395 (1981): "In this case, the defendant asserts that because the case against him rested on the credibility of the juvenile victim's testimony, the defendant should have been allowed to attack that credibility through use of the victim's juvenile record. We have already rejected such a general contention. *Commonwealth v. Santos*, [376 Mass. 920,] 923–924 (1978)."

NOTE 1c   "[T]he provisions of § 60 must yield to countervailing constitutional considerations, such as where the records would be relevant to the issue of bias resulting from the witness's susceptibility to government pressure." *Commonwealth v. A Juvenile (No. 2)*, 384 Mass. at 394.

NOTE 2   It would be reversible error for the prosecutor to question the defendant and his mother on their prior testimony in Juvenile Court. *Commonwealth v. Franklin*, 366 Mass. 284, 291 (1974).

NOTE 3   "The *Davis [v. Alaska*, 415 U.S. 308 (1974),] decision held that, if information contained in a juvenile record indicated that the witness's testimony may be the product of official pressure or inducement, a claim that the record was confidential can-

not prevail over the defendant's right to use the record to impeach the witness for bias. *See Commonwealth v. Ferrara*, 368 Mass. 182, 189–190 (1975). . . .

"The *Davis* and *Ferrara* decisions fashioned a general rule on the use of a juvenile record to show bias, but they did not provide a defendant an absolute right to impeach a witness by proof of past delinquencies. See *Davis v. Alaska, supra* at 321 (Stewart, J., concurring); *Commonwealth v. Ferrara, supra* at 186–187; *Commonwealth v. Santos*, 376 Mass. 920, 924 (1978). When the issue arises, the principal inquiry is whether the witness's juvenile record has a rational tendency to show bias on his or her part. *Commonwealth v. Ferrara, supra* at 187. If the record has no such tendency, it is not error to exclude it.

"In deciding the issue several considerations may apply. First, does the record disclose the commission of 'relatively serious delinquencies?' *Commonwealth v. Ferrara, supra* at 189. Second, are those delinquencies recent enough to support an inference of bias? *Commonwealth v. DiRoma*, 5 Mass. App. Ct. 853, 853–854 (1977). Third, what do the facts show with respect to the probationary status of the witness, whether some suspicion focused on the witness, and the witness's motives to please the prosecution? *Commonwealth v. Santos*, 376 Mass. 920, 924 (1978). Fourth, did the witness prior to the delinquency furnish a pretrial statement or testimony consistent in material respects with his or her testimony at trial? *Commonwealth v. Haywood*, 377 Mass. 755, 761–763 (1979). These considerations do not constitute an exhaustive list because, in the given case, other factors may also be relevant, such as the extent it was brought out to the jury that the witness may have had a dislike for the defendant and a motive to testify against him."

Commonwealth v. Bembury, 406 Mass. 552, 557–59 (1990).

SECTION 60A
Inspection of records in youthful offender and delinquency cases
(Amended by 2013 Mass. Acts c. 84, §§ 12–13, effective Sept. 18, 2013.)

The records of a youthful offender proceeding conducted pursuant to an indictment shall be open to public inspection in the same manner and to the same extent as adult criminal court records. All other records of the court in cases of delinquency arising under sections fifty-two to fifty-nine, inclusive, shall be withheld from public inspection except with the consent of a justice from such court; provided, however, that such records shall be open, at all reasonable times, to inspection by the child proceeded against, his parents, guardian or attorney; provided further, that nothing herein shall be construed to provide access to privileged or confidential communications and information; and provided further, that said protections shall be construed to include information and communications entered at the indictment.

Notwithstanding the provisions of this section, the name of a child shall be made available to the public officer without such consent if the child is: alleged to have committed an offense while between his fourteenth and eighteenth birthdays; and has previously been adjudicated delinquent on at least two occasions for acts which would have been punishable by imprisonment in the state prison if such child had been age 18 or older; and is charged with delinquency by reason of an act which would be punishable by imprisonment in the state prison if such child were age 18 or older.

NOTE   Notwithstanding this section, a juvenile, who is found delinquent of a sexual offense, as per the Sexual Offender Act, G.L. c. 6, § 178C–O, must register as a sexual offender. *Doe v. Attorney General (No. 1)*, 425 Mass. 210 (1997). (Note: All youthful offender records are, under 60A, open to the public. Any juvenile adjudicated a youthful offender for having committed a sex offense also must register.)

SECTION 61
Repealed

SECTION 62
Restitution or reparation by child to injured person

If, in adjudging a person a delinquent child, the court finds, as an element of such delinquency, that he has committed an act involving liability in a civil action, and such delinquent child is placed on probation, the court may require, as a condition thereof, that he shall make restitution or reparation to the injured person to such an extent and in such sum as the court determines. If the payment is not made at once, it shall be made to the probation officer, who shall give a receipt therefor, keep a record of the payment, pay the money to said injured person, and keep on file his receipt therefor.

SECTION 63
Inducing or abetting delinquency of child

Any person who shall be found to have caused, induced, abetted, or encouraged or contributed toward the waywardness or delinquency of a child, or to have acted in any way tending to cause or induce such waywardness or delinquency, may be punished by a fine of not more than five hundred dollars or by imprisonment of not more than one year, or both. The court may release on probation under section eighty-seven of chapter two hundred and seventy-six, subject to such orders as it may make as to future conduct tending to cause, induce or contribute to such delinquency, or it may suspend sentence under section one of chapter two hundred and seventy-nine, or before trial, with the defendant's consent, it may allow the defendant to enter into a recognizance, in such penal sum as the court may fix, conditioned to comply with such terms as the court may order for the promotion of the future welfare of the child, and the said case may then be placed on file. The provisions for recognizance in section fifty-six shall be applicable to cases arising hereunder. The divisions of the juvenile court department shall, within their respective territorial limits, have exclusive jurisdiction over complaints alleging violations of this section.

NOTE 1   This charge may be heard in the Juvenile Court or, if indicted, in the Superior Court. *Commonwealth v. Lender*, 47 Mass. App. Ct. 164, 165–66 (1999).

NOTE 2   "[T]ruancy is not comprehended within the phrase 'delinquency of a child,' as used in § 63 . . ." Conviction reversed. *Commonwealth v. Santos*, 47 Mass. App. Ct. 639, 643 (1999).

SECTION 63A
Aiding or abetting violation of juvenile court order; concealing or harboring child; penalties; defenses
(Amended by 2013 Mass. Acts c. 84, § 14, effective Sept. 18, 2013.)

Whoever is 19 years of age or older and: (i) knowingly and willfully aids or abets a child under the age of 18, to violate an order of a juvenile court; or (ii) knowingly and willfully conceals or harbors a child who has taken flight from the custody of the court, a parent, a legal guardian, the department of children and families or the department of youth services shall be punished by a fine of not more than $500 or by imprisonment in the house of correction for not more than 1 year, or by both such fine and imprisonment.

It shall be a defense to a violation of clause (ii) if the defendant concealed or harbored a child in the reasonable good faith belief that the child would be at risk of physical or sexual abuse if the child returned to his custodial residence, unless the defendant concealed or harbored such child with intent to abuse the child or if the defendant committed abuse on that child.

The court may release on probation under section 87 of chapter 276, subject to such orders as it may make as to future conduct tending to cause, induce or contribute to a person's status as a child in need of services or delinquency, or it may suspend sentence under section 1 of chapter 279, or before trial, with the defendant's consent, it may allow the defendant to enter into a recognizance, in such penal sum as the court may fix, conditioned to comply with such terms as the court may order for the promotion of the future welfare of the child, and the case may then be placed on file. The provisions for recognizance in section 56 of chapter 276 shall be applicable to cases arising hereunder.

The divisions of the juvenile court department shall, within their respective territorial limits, have exclusive jurisdiction over complaints alleging a violation of this section.

SECTION 64
Powers of commissioner of probation; annual report

The commissioner of probation may supervise the probation work for wayward and delinquent children, and make necessary inquiries in regard to the same, and in his annual report may make such recommendations as he considers advisable for the improvement of methods of dealing with such children.

PROVISIONS COMMON TO ALL PROCEEDINGS AGAINST CHILDREN

SECTION 65
Juvenile sessions; presence of minors; exclusion of public
(Amended by 2013 Mass. Acts c. 84, § 15, effective Sept. 18, 2013.)

Courts shall designate suitable times for the hearing of cases of children under 18 years of age, which shall be called the juvenile session, for which a separate docket and record shall be kept. Said session shall be separate from that for the trial of criminal cases, shall not, except as otherwise expressly provided, be held in conjunction with other business of the court, and shall be held in rooms not used for criminal trials; and in places where no separate juvenile courtroom is provided, hearings, so far as possible, shall be held in chambers. The court shall exclude the general public from the juvenile sessions admitting only such persons as may have a direct interest in the case, except in cases where the commonwealth has proceeded by indictment. A complaint under section sixty-three may be heard in such juvenile session.

SECTION 66
Detention of child in police station; commitment to jail, house of correction or state farm
(Amended by 2013 Mass. Acts c. 84, § 16, effective Sept. 18, 2013.)

Except as otherwise provided in section sixty-seven and in section twelve of chapter one hundred and twenty, no child under 18 years of age shall be detained by the police in a lockup, police station or house of detention pending arraignment, examination or trial by the court. No child under 18 years of age shall be committed by the court to a jail or house of correction or to the state farm, pending further examination or trial by the court or pending any continuance of his case or, except as otherwise provided in sections fifty-two through eighty-four upon adjudication as a youthful offender.

SECTION 67
Notice of arrest of child to probation officer and parent or guardian; detention
(Amended by 2013 Mass. Acts c. 84, § 17, effective Sept. 18, 2013.)

Except for children in need of service arrested pursuant to section thirty-nine H, whenever a child between seven and 18 years of age is arrested with or without a warrant, as provided by law, the officer in charge of the police station or town lockup to which the child has been taken shall immediately notify the probation officer of the district court or of the juvenile court, if there is one, within whose judicial district such child was arrested and at least one of the child's parents, or, if there is no parent, the guardian or person with whom it is stated that such child resides, and shall inquire into the case. Pending such notice and inquiry, such child shall be detained. Upon the acceptance by the officer in charge of said police station or town lockup of the written promise of said parent, guardian or any other reputable person to be responsible for the presence of such child in court at the time and place when such child is to appear or upon the receipt of such officer in charge from said probation officer of a request for the release of such child to him, such child shall be released to said person giving such promise or to said probation officer making such request; provided, that, if the arresting officer requests in writing that a child between fourteen and 18 years of age be detained, and if the court issuing a warrant for the arrest of a child between fourteen and 18 years of age directs in the warrant that such child shall be held in safekeeping pending his appearance in court, or, if the probation officer shall so direct, such child shall be detained in a police station or town lockup, or place of temporary custody commonly referred to as a detention home of the department of youth services, or any other home approved by the department of youth services pending his appearance in court. In the event any such child is so detained the officer in charge at the police station or town lockup shall notify the probation officer and parent or parents, guardian, or person with whom it stated that such child resides of the detention of such child. Nothing contained in this section shall prevent the admitting of such child to bail in accordance with law. Said probation officer or officer in charge at the police station or town lockup shall notify such child and his parent or parents or guardian or person with whom it is stated that such child resides of the time and place of the hearing of his case. No child between fourteen and 18 years of age shall be detained in a police station or town lockup unless the detention facilities for children at such police station or town lockup have received the approval in writing of the commissioner of youth services. The department of youth services shall make inspection at least annually of police stations or town lockups wherein children are detained. If no such approved detention facilities exist in any city or town, such city or town may contract with an adjacent city or town for the use of approved detention facilities in order to prevent children who are detained from coming in contact with adult prisoners. Nothing in this section shall permit a child between fourteen and 18 years of age being detained in a jail or house of correction. A separate and distinct place shall be provided in police stations, town lockups or places of detention for such children.

SECTION 68
Commitment of children held for examination or trial
(Amended by 2013 Mass. Acts c. 84, § 18, effective Sept. 18, 2013.)

A child who has attained the age of seven but not yet attained the age of 18 held by the court for further examination, trial or continuance, or for indictment and trial, if unable to furnish bail, shall be committed by the court to the care of the department of youth services or to a probation officer, a parent, guardian, or other responsible person who shall provide for his safekeeping; provided, however, that the appearance at such examination or trial, shall be the responsibility of the court for which he is being held in safekeeping.

The court may recommend that a child who has attained the age of fourteen and who is committed to the care of the department shall be held in a secure detention facility if the court further determines that the child (a) is a fugitive from another jurisdiction on a delinquency petition; or (b) is charged with an offense for which the commonwealth may proceed by indictment in accordance with the provisions of section fifty-four; provided, however, that such child is already detained or on conditional release in conjunction with another delinquency proceeding, or has demonstrated a recent record of willful failure to appear at juvenile court proceedings, or has demonstrated a recent record of violent conduct resulting in physical injury to others.

The court shall forward such recommendation and the reasons therefor, in writing, to the department. Such recommendation shall not be binding upon the department, but if the department chooses not to comply with such recommendation, the department shall inform the court within two business days.

The department may provide special foster homes, and places of temporary custody commonly referred to as detention homes of the department of youth services for the care, maintenance and safekeeping of such children who may be committed by the court to said department under this section; provided, however, that no more than five such children shall be detained in any such special foster home at any one time.

A child between seven and 18 years of age so committed by the court to the department to await further examination or trial by the court shall be returned thereto within fifteen days after the date of the order of such commitment, and final disposition of the case shall thereupon be made by adjudication or otherwise, unless, in the opinion of the court, the interest of the child and the public otherwise require.

The provisions of section twenty-four of chapter two hundred and twelve, relative to the precedence of cases of persons actually confined in prison and awaiting trial, shall apply to children held in detention facilities of the department of youth services under this section.

Said probation officer shall have the same authority, rights and powers in relation to a child committed to his care under this section, and in relation to a child released to him as provided in section sixty-seven, as he would have if he were surety on the recognizance of such child.

A person who at the time of the offense had attained the age of fourteen but had not attained the age of 18, and who is charged with murder in the first or second degree and is held by the superior court for trial or continuance, or for indictment and trial, if unable to furnish bail, shall be committed by the court to the custody of the sheriff of the county in which the court is situated; provided, however, that the appearance of the person at such examination or trial shall be the responsibility of the court for which he is being held in safekeeping.

SECTION 68A
Diagnostic study by department of youth services; report and recommendations
(Amended by 2013 Mass. Acts c. 84, § 19, effective Sept. 18, 2013.)

A child between seven and 18 years of age, held by the court for further examination, trial or continuance, or for indictment and trial, may at the discretion of the court be referred to the department of youth services, any court clinic, or the department of mental health, with its consent, and with the consent of the parents or guardian, for diagnostic study on an inpatient or outpatient basis; and, upon completion of such study, the department of youth services, court clinic or department of mental health, as the case may be, shall forward a report and recommendations to the court. In default of bail, any such child may be committed by the court to the department of youth services for a period not to exceed thirty days while undergoing diagnostic study. At the expiration of such period, such child shall be returned to the court, together with the report and recommendations to the department of youth services.

SECTION 68B
Special foster homes; detention homes; transfer of child

The department of youth services may use or provide special foster homes and places of temporary custody commonly referred to as detention homes, at various places in the commonwealth which shall be completely separate from any police station, town lockup or jail, and which shall be used solely for the temporary care, custody and study of children committed to the care of the department of youth services. Nothing in this section shall prevent the department from using or providing alternative placements and employing alternative measures which, in its discretion, will reasonably assure the appearance of the children before the court.

SECTION 68C
Diagnostic services by department of youth services

The department of youth services shall maintain and provide diagnostic services for the purpose of providing the diagnostic studies and making the reports and recommendations provided for under section sixty-eight A, and the department may provide offices and facilities for such diagnostic services, at such places in the commonwealth as will best serve the needs of the several courts.

SECTION 69
Information and reports of superintendents of schools and teachers

The superintendent of the public schools in any town, any teacher therein, and any person in charge of a private school, or any teacher therein, shall furnish to any court from time to time any information and reports requested by any justice thereof relating to the attendance, conduct and standing of any pupil enrolled in such school, if said pupil is at the time awaiting examination or trial by the court or is under the supervision of the court.

SECTION 69A
Information of probation officers, police and school authorities

When a person has been committed to the department of youth services, the court, the probation officers, and other public and police authorities, the school authorities, and other public officials shall make available to said department all pertinent information in their possession in respect to the case.

SECTION 70
Summoning of parent or guardian during case
(Amended by 2013 Mass. Acts c. 84, § 20, effective Sept. 18, 2013.)

At any time during the pendency of any case before a court or trial justice against a child under 18 years of age, whether pending adjudication or during continuances or probation or after the case has been taken from the files, the court or trial justice may summon any parent or guardian of said child, or any person with whom the child resides, in the manner provided in section fifty-five.

SECTION 71
Failure to appear on summons; capias

If any person to whom a summons is issued under the preceding section or section forty-two or fifty-five fails to appear in response to such summons, the court issuing the summons may issue a capias to compel the attendance of such person, and such capias shall be issued and served in the same manner as a capias to compel the attendance of witnesses who have failed to appear on a subpoena issued in behalf of the commonwealth in a criminal case.

SECTION 72
Continuance of jurisdiction of courts in juvenile sessions
(Amended by 2013 Mass. Acts c. 84, §§ 21–22A, effective Sept. 18, 2013; 2014 Mass. Acts c. 165, § 153, effective July 15, 2014.)

(a) The divisions of the juvenile court department shall continue to have jurisdiction over children who attain their eighteenth birthday pending final adjudication of their cases, including all remands and retrials following appeals from their cases, or during continuances or probation, or after their cases have been placed on file, or for any other proceeding arising out of their cases. Except as provided in subsection (b), nothing herein shall authorize the commitment of a person to the department of youth services after he has attained his twentieth birthday.

If a child commits an offense prior to his eighteenth birthday, and is not apprehended until between such child's eighteenth and nineteenth birthday, the court shall deal with such child in the same manner as if he has not attained his eighteenth birthday, and all provisions and rights applicable to a child under 18 shall apply to such child.

(b) If the commonwealth has proceeded by indictment, the divisions of the juvenile court department shall continue to have jurisdiction over such persons who attain their eighteenth birthday pending the final adjudication of their cases, including all remands and retrials following appeals from their cases, or pending the determination allowed under section 58, or during continuances or probation, or after their cases have been placed on file, or for any other proceeding arising out of their cases. Nothing herein shall authorize the commitment of a youthful offender to the department of youth services after he has attained his twenty-first birthday.

NOTE "We conclude that, where a person commits a criminal offense before the age of fourteen years and is apprehended after the person has reached the age of eighteen years, the Superior Court has jurisdiction to try the person for that offense under G.L. c. 119, § 72A, after indictment, provided that a judge in the Juvenile Court has determined that there is probable cause to believe that the person committed the offense charged and that the interests of the public require that the person be tried for the offense instead of being discharged." *Commonwealth v. Porges*, 460 Mass. 525, 526 (2011).

SECTION 72A
Proceedings upon apprehension after nineteenth birthday
(Amended by 2013 Mass. Acts c. 84, § 23, effective Sept. 18, 2013.)

If a person commits an offense or violation prior to his eighteenth birthday, and is not apprehended until after his nineteenth birthday, the court, after a hearing, shall determine whether there is probable cause to believe that said person committed the offense charged, and shall, in its discretion, either order that the person be discharged, if satisfied that such discharge is consistent with the protection of the public; or, if the court is of the opinion that the interests of the public require that such person be tried for such offense or violation instead of being discharged, the court shall dismiss the delinquency complaint and cause a criminal complaint to be issued. The case shall thereafter proceed according to the usual course of criminal proceedings and in accordance with the provisions of section thirty of chapter two hundred and eighteen and section eighteen of chapter two hundred and seventy-eight. Said hearing shall be held prior to, and separate from, any trial on the merits of the charges alleged.

NOTE 1 "We . . . determine whether a transfer hearing pursuant to G.L. c. 119, § 72A (§ 72A), must be held before the Commonwealth may seek an indictment pursuant to G.L. c. 119, § 54 (§ 54), against a defendant who is alleged to have committed offenses when he was between fourteen and seventeen years of age, but was not apprehended until after his eighteenth birthday. [W]e conclude that the clear language of § 72A requires that a hearing be held prior to the Commonwealth's proceeding on an indictment pursuant to § 54." *Commonwealth v. Nanny*, 462 Mass. 798, 798–99 (2012).

NOTE 2 "We conclude that the commencement of process marks the point of apprehension, provided the individual is available to the court at that time. We answer the [question whether an individual may be indicted as a youthful offender after he has turned 18, for offenses he allegedly committed between the ages of 14 and 17] in the negative and, . . . we conclude that a youthful offender indictment may not issue against an individual after his or her eighteenth birthday, regardless of whether a delinquency complaint on the same facts has been filed before the individual's eighteenth birthday." *Commonwealth v. Mogelinski*, 466 Mass. 627, 629 (2013).

NOTE 3 "In *Mogelinski I*, we held for purposes of G.L. c. 119, §§ 72 and 72A, that apprehension occurs upon commencement of process, provided that the defendant is available to the court. Commencement of process is in this context ordinarily achieved by the issuance of a summons, which serves as a notification of the pending charges. Insofar as G.L. c. 119, § 72A, required that the defendant not be 'apprehended until after his eighteenth birthday,' and the defendant here was summonsed on the 2014 complaint when he was twenty years old, the second statutory predicate would appear to be satisfied. The defendant, however, maintains that his apprehension in 2011 on identical complaints where nolle prosequi have been entered precludes the apprehension contemplated by G.L. c. 119, § 72A, either because that section contemplated that the first apprehension on the charged offenses occur only after the defendant has turned eighteen, or because the 2014 complaint is in reality a continuation of the 2011 complaints

on which apprehension occurred before his eighteenth birthday. For the reasons that follow, neither contention is correct, and we conclude that the Juvenile Court has jurisdiction over the 2014 complaint.

"We are confirmed in our view that, given its raison d'être, G.L. c. 119, § 72A, confers jurisdiction in circumstances where, as here, a defendant otherwise would face no possibility of prosecution for the offenses in question." *Commonwealth v. Mogelinski*, 473 Mass. 164, 168–69, 171 (2015).

SECTION 72B
Persons between the ages of fourteen and eighteen convicted of murder; penalties
(Amended by 2013 Mass. Acts c. 84, §§ 24–24A, effective Sept. 18, 2013; 2014 Mass. Acts c. 189, § 2, effective July 25, 2014.)

If a person is found guilty of murder in the first degree committed on or after his fourteenth birthday and before his eighteenth birthday under the provisions of section one of chapter two hundred and sixty-five, the superior court shall commit the person to such punishment as is provided by law for the offense.

If a person is found guilty of murder in the second degree committed on or after his fourteenth birthday and before his eighteenth birthday under the provisions of section one of chapter two hundred and sixty-five, the superior court shall commit the person to such punishment as is provided by law. Said person shall be eligible for parole under section one hundred and thirty-three A of chapter one hundred and twenty-seven when such person has served fifteen years of said confinement. Thereafter said person shall be subject to the provisions of law governing the granting of parole permits by the parole board.

The superior court shall not suspend the commitment of a person found guilty of murder in the first or second degree, nor shall the provisions of section one hundred and twenty-nine C or one hundred and twenty-nine D of chapter one hundred and twenty-seven apply to such commitment. In all cases where a person is alleged to have violated section one of chapter two hundred and sixty-five, the person shall have the right to an indictment proceeding under section four of chapter two hundred and sixty-three.

A person who is found guilty of murder and is sentenced to a state prison but who has not yet reached his eighteenth birthday shall be held in a youthful offender unit separate from the general population of adult prisoners; provided, however, that such person shall be classified at a facility other than the reception and diagnostic center at the Massachusetts Correctional Institution, Concord, and shall not be held at the Massachusetts Correctional Institution, Cedar Junction, prior to his eighteenth birthday.

The department of correction shall not limit access to programming and treatment including, but not limited to, education, substance abuse, anger management and vocational training for youthful offenders, as defined in section 52, solely because of their crimes or the duration of their incarcerations. If the youthful offender qualifies for placement in a minimum security correctional facility based on objective measures determined by the department, the placement shall not be categorically barred based on a life sentence.

If the defendant is not found guilty of murder in the first or second degree, but is found guilty of a lesser included offense or a criminal offense properly joined under Massachusetts Rules of Criminal Procedure 9(a)(1), then the superior court shall make its disposition in accordance with section fifty-eight.

NOTE   "We . . . hold that mandatory life without parole for those under the age of 18 at the time of their crimes violates the Eighth Amendment's prohibition on 'cruel and unusual punishments.'" *Miller v. Alabama*, 132 S. Ct. 2455, 2460 (2012).

CRIMINAL PROCEEDINGS

SECTION 73
Repealed

SECTION 74
Limitations on criminal proceedings against children
(Amended by 2013 Mass. Acts c. 84, §§ 25–26, effective Sept. 18, 2013.)

Except as hereinafter provided and as provided in sections fifty-two to eighty-four, inclusive, no criminal proceeding shall be begun against any person who prior to his eighteenth birthday commits an offense against the laws of the commonwealth or who violates any city ordinance or town by-law, provided, however, that a criminal complaint alleging violation of any city ordinance or town by-law regulating the operation of motor vehicles, which is not capable of being judicially heard and determined as a civil motor vehicle infraction pursuant to the provisions of chapter ninety C may issue against a child between sixteen and 18 years of age without first proceeding against him as a delinquent child.

The juvenile court shall not have jurisdiction over a person who had at the time of the offense attained the age of fourteen but not yet attained the age of 18 who is charged with committing murder in the first or second degree. Complaints and indictments brought against persons for such offenses, and for other criminal offenses properly joined under Massachusetts Rules of Criminal Procedure 9(a)(1), shall be brought in accordance with the usual course and manner of criminal proceedings.

SECTIONS 75–83
Repealed

SECTION 84
Warrant of commitment to department of youth services
(Amended by 2013 Mass. Acts c. 84, § 27, effective Sept. 18, 2013.)

Whenever a person is committed to the department of youth services by a court under section fifty-six, fifty-eight or eighty-three, a warrant of commitment shall be issued in substance as follows:

THE COMMONWEALTH OF MASSACHUSETTS
(COUNTY) ss.

To the Sheriff of the County of _____ or his Deputy, or any Constable or Police Officer in said County, and to the Department of Youth Services at

GREETING:

Whereas, (name of person committed) of _____ in the county of _____, a boy (or girl) between seven and eighteen (or nineteen) years of age, has this day been brought before the _____ court of _____ by virtue of a summons (or warrant) issued to (against) him (or her) on the complaint of _____ of _____ in the county of _____ who therein, upon oath, says that said defendant, at _____ in the county of _____ on the _____ day of _____ in the year one thousand nine hundred and _____ was guilty of _____ as is more fully alleged in said complaint.

And after hearing all matters and things concerning the same, and all persons entitled thereto having been summoned and notified of the pendency of said complaint, as required by law, it is adjudged by said court that said defendant is delinquent and that he (or she) is of the age of _____ years and _____ months, and is a suitable subject for commitment to the custody of the department of youth services, and that his (or her) moral welfare and best interest and the good of society require that he (or she) should be sent thereto for diagnosis, treatment and training; and said court shall also find that reasonable efforts were made to prevent or eliminate the need for the defendant's removal from his home or that an emergency situation made such efforts impossible and it is thereupon ordered by said court that said defendant stand committed to the custody of the department of youth services during his (or her) minority, or until he (or she) be discharged according to law.

You are therefore hereby required, in the name of the Commonwealth of Massachusetts, to take said defendant and him (or her) carry to the department of youth services and him (or her) deliver to the (designated officer) thereof, together with an attested copy thereof, and thereafterward forthwith to return this warrant with your doings thereon into said court.

And you, the department of youth services, are alike required to receive said defendant into your custody, and him (or her) safely keep for diagnosis, treatment, instruction and training until the expiration of said term of his (or her) minority, or he (or she) be discharged according to law.

Witness, _____ at said _____ this _____ day of _____ in the year one thousand nine hundred and _____.

Clerk
A true copy.   (Constable of _____)
Attest: (Sheriff of _____)

No variance from said form shall be considered material if it sufficiently appears upon the face thereof that the person is committed by the court in the exercise of the powers conferred by this chapter. The warrant may be executed by any officer qualified to serve civil or criminal process in the county where the case is heard. Accompanying the warrant, the court or magistrate shall transmit to the designated officer of the department of youth services, by the officer serving it, a statement of the substance of the complaint and testimony given in the case, and such other particulars relative to the person committed as can be ascertained.

SECTION 85
Department employees reporting animal cruelty, abuse or neglect; immunity from liability

(a) During any investigation or evaluation reported under section 51A, any employee of the department or person employed pursuant to a contract with the department, when acting in his professional capacity or within the scope of his or her employment, who has knowledge of or observes an animal whom he knows or reasonably suspects has been the victim of animal cruelty, abuse or neglect, may report the known or suspected animal cruelty, abuse or neglect to the entities that investigate reports of animal cruelty, abuse or neglect, as described in section 57 of chapter 22C, or any local animal control authority.

(b) The report may be made within two working days of receiving the information concerning the animal, by facsimile transmission or a written report or by telephone. In cases where an immediate response may be necessary in order to protect the health and safety of the animal, the report should be made by telephone as soon as possible.

(c) When two or more employees of the department are present and jointly have knowledge of known or reasonably suspected animal cruelty, abuse or neglect, and where there is agreement among them, a report may be made by 1 person by mutual agreement. Any reporter who has knowledge that the person designated to report has failed to do so may thereafter make the report.

(d) No person making such report shall be liable in any civil or criminal action by reason of such report if it was made in good faith. Any privilege established by sections 135A and 135B of chapter 112 or by section 20B of chapter 233, relating to confidential communications, shall not prohibit the filing of a report pursuant to this section.

(e) Nothing in this section shall impose a duty on the department to investigate known or reasonably suspected animal cruelty, abuse or neglect.

(f) Nothing in this section shall prevent the department, area office or subdivision from entering into an agreement, contract or memorandum of understanding with the entities that investigate reports of animal cruelty, abuse or neglect as described in section 57 of chapter 22C, to require such reports or to engage in training in identification and reporting of animal abuse, cruelty and neglect.

Chapter 123. Mental Health

Section
1   Definitions
5   Commitment or retention hearings; right to counsel; medical examination; notice
6   Retention of persons; validity of orders; hearing
7   Commitment and retention of dangerous persons; petition; notice; hearing
8   Proceedings to commit dangerous persons; notice; hearing; orders; jurisdiction
8A   Repealed
8B   Treatment of committed persons with antipsychotic medication; petition; notice; hearing; guardian
9   Review of matters of law; application for discharge; notice; hearing
15   Competence to stand trial or criminal responsibility; examination; period of observation; reports; hearing; commitment; delinquents
16   Hospitalization of persons incompetent to stand trial or not guilty by reason of mental illness; examination period; commitment; hearing; restrictions; dismissal of criminal charges
17   Periodic review of incompetence to stand trial; petition; hearing; continued treatment; defense to charges; release
18   Hospitalization of mentally ill prisoners; examination; reports; hearings; commitment; voluntary admission; reduction of sentence; discharge
19   Parties or witnesses; determination of mental condition
33   Expenses of apprehension, examination, hearing, commitment or delivery; certification; audit; payment; fees
34   Commitment or transfer to Veterans Administration or other federal agency
35   Commitment of alcoholics or substance abusers
36A   Court records of examination or commitment; privacy
36B   Duty of licensed mental health professional to warn patient's potential victims; cause of action
36C   Report of commitment order to department of criminal justice information services

SECTION 1
Definitions

The following words as used in this section and sections two to thirty-seven, inclusive, shall, unless the context otherwise requires, have the following meanings:

"Commissioner", the commissioner of mental health.

"Department", the department of mental health.

"Dependent funds", those funds which a resident is unable to manage or spend himself as determined by the periodic review.

"District court", the district court within the jurisdiction of which a facility is located.

"Facility", a public or private facility for the care and treatment of mentally ill persons, except for the Bridgewater State Hospital.

"Fiduciary", any guardian, conservator, trustee, representative payee as appointed by a federal agency, or other person who receives or maintains funds on behalf of another.

"Funds", all cash, checks, negotiable instruments or other income or liquid personal property, and governmental and private pensions and payments, including payments pursuant to a Social Security Administration program.

"Independent Funds", those funds which a resident is able to manage or spend himself as determined by the periodic review.

"Licensed mental health professional", any person who holds himself out to the general public as one providing mental health services and who is required pursuant to such practice to obtain a license from the commonwealth.

"Likelihood of serious harm", (1) a substantial risk of physical harm to the person himself as manifested by evidence of, threats of, or attempts at, suicide or serious bodily harm; (2) a substantial risk of physical harm to other persons as manifested by evidence of homicidal or other violent behavior or evidence that others are placed in reasonable fear of violent behavior and serious physical harm to them; or (3) a very substantial risk of physical impairment or injury to the person himself as manifested by evidence that such person's judgment is so affected that he is unable to protect himself in the community and that reasonable provision for his protection is not available in the community.

"Patient", any person with whom a licensed mental health professional has established a mental health professional-patient relationship.

"Psychiatric nurse", a nurse licensed pursuant to section seventy-four of chapter one hundred and twelve who specializes in mental health or psychiatric nursing.

"Psychiatrist", a physician licensed pursuant to section two of chapter one hundred and twelve who specializes in the practice of psychiatry.

"Psychologist", an individual licensed pursuant to section one hundred and eighteen to one hundred and twenty-nine, inclusive, of chapter one hundred and twelve.

"Qualified physician", a physician who is licensed pursuant to section two of chapter one hundred and twelve who is designated by and who meets the qualifications required by the regulations of the department; provided that different qualifications may be established for different purposes of this chapter. A qualified physician need not be an employee of the department or of any facility of the department.

"Qualified psychiatric nurse mental health clinical specialist", a psychiatric nurse mental health clinical specialist authorized to practice as such under regulations promulgated pursuant to the provisions of section eighty B of chapter one hundred and twelve who is designated by and meets qualifications required by the regulations of the department, provided that different qualifications may be established for different purposes of this chapter. A qualified psychiatric nurse mental health clinical specialist need not be an employee of the department or of any facility of the department.

"Qualified psychologist", a psychologist who is licensed pursuant to sections one hundred and eighteen to one hundred and twenty-nine, inclusive, of chapter one hundred and twelve who is designated by and who meets qualifications required by the regulations of the department, provided that different qualifications may be established for different purposes of this chapter. A qualified psychologist need not be an employee of the department or of any facility of the department.

"Reasonable precautions", any licensed mental health professional shall be deemed to have taken reasonable precautions, as that term is used in section thirty-six B, if such professional makes reasonable efforts to take one or more of the following actions as would be taken by a reasonably prudent member of his profession under the same or similar circumstances:—

(a) communicates a threat of death or serious bodily injury to the reasonably identified victim or victims;

(b) notifies an appropriate law enforcement agency in the vicinity where the patient or any potential victim resides;

(c) arranges for the patient to be hospitalized voluntarily;

(d) takes appropriate steps, within the legal scope of practice of his profession, to initiate proceedings for involuntary hospitalization.

"Restraint", bodily physical force, mechanical devices, chemicals, confinement in place of seclusion other than the placement of an inpatient or resident in his room for the night, or any other means which unreasonably limit freedom of movement.

"Social worker", an individual licensed pursuant to sections one hundred and thirty to one hundred and thirty-two, inclusive, of chapter one hundred and twelve.

"Superintendent", the superintendent or other head of public or private facility.

SECTION 5
Commitment or retention hearings; right to counsel; medical examination; notice

Whenever the provisions of this chapter require that a hearing be conducted in any court for the commitment or further retention of a person to a facility or to the Bridgewater state hospital or for medical treatment including treatment with antipsychotic medication, it shall be held as hereinafter provided. Such person shall have the right to be represented by counsel and shall have the right to present independent testimony. The court shall appoint counsel for such person whom it finds to be indigent and who is not represented by counsel, unless such person refuses the appointment of counsel. The court may provide an independent medical examination for such indigent person upon request of his counsel or upon

his request if he is not represented by counsel. The person shall be allowed not less than two days after the appearance of his counsel in which to prepare his case and a hearing shall be conducted forthwith after such period unless counsel requests a delay. Notice of the time and place of hearing shall be furnished by the court to the department, the person, his counsel, and his nearest relative or guardian. The court may hold the hearing at the facility or said hospital.

SECTION 6
Retention of persons; validity of orders; hearing

(a) No person shall be retained at a facility or at the Bridgewater state hospital except under the provisions of paragraph (a) of section ten, the provisions of paragraphs (a), (b) and (c) of section twelve, section thirteen, paragraph (e) of section sixteen and section thirty-five or except under a court order or except during the pendency of a petition for commitment or to the pendency of a request under section fourteen. A court order of commitment to a facility or to the Bridgewater state hospital shall be valid for the period stipulated in this chapter or, if no such period is so stipulated, for one year. A petition for the commitment of a person may not be issued except as authorized under the provisions of this chapter.

(b) Following the filing of a petition for a commitment to a facility or to the Bridgewater state hospital, a hearing shall be held unless waived in writing by the person after consultation with his counsel. In the event the hearing is waived, the person may request a hearing for good cause shown at any time during the period of commitment.

SECTION 7
Commitment and retention of dangerous persons; petition; notice; hearing

(a) The superintendent of a facility may petition the district court or the division of the juvenile court department in whose jurisdiction the facility is located for the commitment to said facility and retention of any patient at said facility whom said superintendent determines that the failure to hospitalize would create a likelihood of serious harm by reason of mental illness.

(b) The medical director of the Bridgewater state hospital, the commissioner of mental health, or with the approval of the commissioner of mental health, the superintendent of a facility, may petition the district court or the division of the juvenile court department in whose jurisdiction the facility or hospital is located for the commitment to the Bridgewater state hospital of any male patient at said facility or hospital when it is determined that the failure to hospitalize in strict security would create a likelihood of serious harm by reason of mental illness.

(c) Whenever a court receives a petition filed under any provisions of this chapter for an order of commitment of a person to a facility or to the Bridgewater state hospital, such court shall notify the person, and his nearest relative or guardian, of the receipt of such petition and of the date a hearing on such petition is to be held. The hearing on a petition brought for commitment pursuant to paragraph (e) of section 15, and sections 16 and 18, or for a subsequent commitment pursuant to paragraph (d) of section 8 shall be commenced within 14 days of the filing of the petition, unless a delay is requested by the person or his counsel. For all other persons, the hearing shall be commenced within 5 days of the filing of the petition, unless a delay is requested by the person or his counsel. The period of time prescribed or allowed under the provisions of this section shall be computed pursuant to Rule 6 of the Massachusetts Rules of Civil Procedure.

SECTION 8
Proceedings to commit dangerous persons; notice; hearing; orders; jurisdiction

(a) After a hearing, unless such hearing is waived in writing, the district court or the division of the juvenile court department shall not order the commitment of a person at a facility or shall not renew such order unless it finds after a hearing that (1) such person is mentally ill, and (2) the discharge of such person from a facility would create a likelihood of serious harm.

(b) After a hearing, unless such hearing is waived in writing, the district court or the division of the juvenile court department shall not order the commitment of a person at the Bridgewater state hospital or shall not renew such order unless it finds that (1) such person is mentally ill; (2) such person is not a proper subject for commitment to any facility of the department; and (3) the failure to retain such person in strict custody would create a likelihood of serious harm. If the court is unable to make the findings required by this paragraph, but makes the findings required by paragraph (a), the court shall order the commitment of the person to a facility designated by the department.

(c) The court shall render its decision on the petition within ten days of the completion of the hearing, provided, that for reasons stated in writing by the court, the administrative justice for the district court department may extend said ten day period.

(d) The first order of commitment of a person under this section shall be valid for a period of six months and all subsequent commitments shall be valid for a period of one year; provided that if such commitments occur at the expiration of a commitment under any other section of this chapter, other than a commitment for observation, the first order of commitment shall be valid for a period of one year; and provided further, that the first order of commitment to the Bridgewater state hospital of a person under commitment to a facility shall be valid for a period of six months. If no hearing is held before the expiration of the six months commitment, the court may not recommit the person without a hearing.

(e) In the event that the hearing is waived and on the basis of a petition filed under the authority of this chapter showing that a person is mentally ill and that the discharge of the person from a facility would create a likelihood of serious harm, the district court or the division of the juvenile court department which has jurisdiction over the commitment of the person may order the commitment of the person to such facility.

(f) In the event that the hearing is waived and on the basis of a petition filed under the authority of this chapter showing that a person is mentally ill, that the person is not a proper subject for commitment to any facility of the department and that the failure to retain said person in strict security would create a likelihood of serious harm, the district court or the division of the juvenile court department which has jurisdiction over a facility, if a person is retained in a facility, or the Brockton district court if a person is retained in the Bridge-water state hospital, may order the commitment of the person to said hospital.

SECTION 8A
Repealed

SECTION 8B
Treatment of committed persons with antipsychotic medication; petition; notice; hearing; guardian

(a) With respect to any patient who is the subject of a petition for a commitment or an order of a commitment for care and treatment under the provisions of sections seven, eight, fifteen, sixteen or eighteen, the superintendent of a facility or medical director of the Bridgewater state hospital may further petition the district court or the division of the juvenile court department in whose jurisdiction the facility is located (i) to adjudicate the patient incapable of making informed decisions about proposed medical treatment, (ii) to authorize, by an adjudication of substituted judgment, treatment with antipsychotic medications, and (iii) to authorize according to the applicable legal standards such other medical treatment as may be necessary for the treatment of mental illness.

(b) A petition filed under this section shall be separate from any pending petition for commitment and shall not be heard or otherwise considered by the court unless the court has first issued an order of commitment on the pending petition for commitment.

(c) Whenever a court receives a petition filed under the provisions of this section, such court shall notify the person, and his nearest relative or guardian of the receipt of such petition and of the date a hearing on such petition is to be held. The hearing shall be commenced within fourteen days of the filing of the petition unless a delay is requested by the person of his counsel, provided that the commencement of such hearing shall not be delayed beyond the date of the hearing on the commitment petition if the petition was filed concurrently with a petition for commitment.

(d) After a hearing on the petition regarding antipsychotic medication treatment the court shall not authorize medical treatment unless it (i) specifically finds that the person is incapable of making informed decisions concerning the proposed medical treatment, (ii) upon application of the legal substituted judgment standard, specifically finds that the patient would accept such treatment if competent, and (iii) specifically approves and authorized a written substituted judgment treatment plan. The court may base its findings exclusively upon affidavits and other documentary evidence if it (i) determines, after careful inquiry and upon representations of counsel, that there are not contested issues of fact and (ii) includes in its findings the reasons that oral testimony was not required.

(e) The court may delegate to a guardian who has been duly appointed by a court of competent jurisdiction the authority to monitor the antipsychotic medication treatment process to ensure that an antipsychotic medication treatment plan is followed, provided such a guardian is readily available for such purpose. Approval of a treatment plan shall not be withheld, however, because such a guardian is not available to perform such monitoring. In such circumstances, the court shall monitor the treatment process to ensure that the treatment plan is followed.

(f) Any authorization for treatment that is ordered pursuant to the provisions of this section shall expire at the same time as the expiration of the order of commitment that was in effect when the authorization for treatment was ordered; provided that subsequent authorizations may be ordered and any party may at any time petition the court for modification of a medical treatment authorization that has been ordered pursuant to the standards and procedures established in this section.

(g) An adjudication of competency or incompetency with respect to treatment for mental illness by a court pursuant to this section shall be binding upon the juvenile court department in any subsequent guardianship proceedings only with respect to matters which were the subject of the district court or juvenile court department adjudication.

(h) Any privilege established by section one hundred and thirty-five of chapter one hundred and twelve or by section twenty B of chapter two hundred and thirty-three, relating to confidential communications, shall not prohibit the filing of reports or affidavits, or the giving of testimony, pursuant to this section, for the purpose of obtaining treatment of a patient, provided that such patient has been informed prior to making such communications that they may be used for such purpose and has waived the privilege.

SECTION 9
Review of matters of law; application for discharge; notice; hearing

(a) Matters of law arising in commitment hearings, antipsychotic medication hearings or incompetency for trial proceedings in a district court may be reviewed by the appellate division of the district courts in the same manner as the civil cases generally.

(b) Any person may make a written application to a justice of superior court at any time and in any county, stating that he believes or has reason to believe that a person named in such application is retained in a facility or the Bridgewater state hospital, who should no longer be so retained, or that a person named in such application is the subject of a medical treatment order issued by a district court or a division of the juvenile court department and should not be so treated, giving the names of all persons interested in his confinement or medical treatment and requesting his discharge or other relief. The justice within seven days thereof shall order notice of the time and place for hearing to be given to the superintendent or medical director and to such other persons as he considers proper; and such hearing shall be given promptly before a justice of the superior court in any county. The justice shall appoint an attorney to represent any applicant whom he finds to be indigent. The alleged mentally ill person may be brought before the justice at the hearing upon a writ of habeas corpus, upon a request approved by the justice. Pending the decision of the court such person may be retained in the custody of the superintendent or medical director. If the justice decides that the person is not mentally ill or that failure to retain the person in a facility or the Bridgewater state hospital would not create a likelihood of serious harm; has not engaged in repeated and recent incidents of serious self-destructive behavior or assaultive behavior as an inpatient at a facility or an inmate of a place of detention; can be properly treated in any other facility licensed, operated or regulated by the department, said person shall be discharged. If the justice decides that a patient at the Bridgewater state hospital does not require strict security, he shall be transferred to a facility. If the justice decides that a person who is the subject of a medical treatment order issued by a district court or a division of the juvenile court department pursuant to section eight B should not be treated, the justice shall issue an appropriate order modifying or vacating such order and, where such previous order is modified, the court shall monitor said modified order by means of a guardian or otherwise as provided in paragraph (e) of section eight B.

SECTION 15
Competence to stand trial or criminal responsibility; examination; period of observation; reports; hearing; commitment; delinquents

(a) Whenever a court of competent jurisdiction doubts whether a defendant in a criminal case is competent to stand trial or is criminally responsible by reason of mental illness or mental defect, it may at any stage of the proceedings after the return of an indictment or the issuance of a criminal complaint against the defendant, order an examination of such defendant to be conducted by one or more qualified physicians or one or more qualified psychologists. Whenever practicable, examinations shall be conducted at the court house or place of detention where the person is being held. When an examination is ordered, the court shall instruct the examining physician or psychologist in the law for determining mental competence to stand trial and criminal responsibility.

(b) After the examination described in paragraph (a), the court may order that the person be hospitalized at a facility or, if such person is a male and appears to require strict security, at the Bridgewater state hospital, for a period not to exceed twenty days for observation and further examination, if the court has reason to believe that such observation and further examination are necessary in order to determine whether mental illness or mental defect have so affected a person that he is not competent to stand trial or not criminally responsible for the crime or crimes with which he has been charged. Copies of the complaints or indictments and the physician's or psychologist's report under paragraph (a) shall be delivered to the facility or said hospital with the person. If, before the expiration of such twenty day period, an examining qualified psychologist believes that observation for more than twenty days is necessary, he shall so notify the court and shall request in writing an extension of the twenty day period, specifying the reason or reasons for which such further observation is necessary. Upon the receipt of such request, the court may extend said observation period, but in no event shall the period exceed forty days from the date of the initial court order of hospitalization; provided, however, if the person requests continued care and treatment during the pendency of the criminal proceedings against him and the superintendent or medical director agrees to provide such care and treatment, the court may order the further hospitalization of such person at the facility or the Bridgewater state hospital.

(c) At the conclusion of the examination or the observation period, the examining physician or psychologist shall forthwith give to the court written signed reports of their findings, including the clinical findings bearing on the issue of competence to stand trial or criminal responsibility. Such reports shall also contain an opinion, supported by clinical findings, as to whether the defendant is in need of treatment and care offered by the department.

(d) If on the basis of such reports the court is satisfied that the defendant is competent to stand trial, the case shall continue according to the usual course of criminal proceedings; otherwise the court shall hold a hearing on whether the defendant is competent to stand trial; provided that at any time before trial any party to the case may request a hearing on whether the defendant is competent to stand trial. A finding of incompetency shall require a preponderance of the evidence. If the defendant is found incompetent to stand trial, trial of the case shall be stayed until such time as the defendant becomes competent to stand trial, unless the case is dismissed.

(e) After a finding of guilty on a criminal charge, and prior to sentencing, the court may order a psychiatric or other clinical examination and, after such examination, it may also order a period of observation in a facility, or at the Bridgewater state hospital if the court determines that strict security is required and if such person is male. The purpose of such observation or examination shall be to aid the court in sentencing. Such period of observation or examination shall not exceed forty days. During such period of observation, the superintendent or medical director may petition the court for commitment of such person. The court, after imposing sentence on said person, may hear the petition as provided in section eighteen, and if the court makes the necessary findings as set forth in section eight, it may in its discretion commit the person to a facility or the Bridgewater state hospital. Such order of commitment shall be valid for a period of six months. All subsequent proceedings for commitment shall take place under the provisions of said section eighteen in the district court which has jurisdiction of the facility or hospital. A person committed to a facility or Bridgewater state hospital pursuant to this section shall have said time credited against the sentence imposed as provided in paragraph (c) of said section eighteen.

(f) In like manner to the proceedings under paragraphs (a), (b), (c), and (e) of this section, a court may order a psychiatric or psychological examination or a period of observation for an alleged delinquent in a facility to aid the court in its disposition. Such period shall not exceed forty days.

NOTE 1   Issue: "Whether a defendant, who has been charged with a crime(s), and has been found incompetent by a Superior Court Justice by reason of mental retardation (and not mental illness), and for whom the medical evidence indicates that there is no expectation that he will ever become competent to stand trial, and who has a Guardian appointed pursuant to M.G.L. c. 201, § 6A, can offer to enter a plea of guilty through his Guardian on an agreed upon plea bargaining and recommendation of sentence, and have it accepted by the Superior Court pursuant to the doctrine of substituted judgment."

The Supreme Judicial Court answered "No."

Commonwealth v. DelVerde, 398 Mass. 288, 291 (1986).

NOTE 2   At arraignment, the judge ordered a competency hearing. None was ever done. Fifteen months later the defendant went to trial and was found guilty.

Conviction affirmed especially since trial counsel never raised the issue nor was there anything in the trial record indicating a lack of competency.

The key question is whether the defendant is competent to stand trial at the actual time of trial. It was also noted that, once the question is raised, the burden is upon the Commonwealth to establish competency.

Commonwealth v. Dias, 402 Mass. 645 (1988).

NOTE 3   **Judge's Determination.** "We give substantial deference to a trial judge's determination of a defendant's compe-

tence to stand trial, see *Commonwealth v. Lyons*, 426 Mass. 466, 469 (1998), recognizing that the judge has had the 'opportunity to observe the defendant's demeanor during the trial,' *Commonwealth v. Russin*, 420 Mass. 309, 317 (1995)." *Commonwealth v. McMahon*, 443 Mass. 409, 423 (2005).

SECTION 16

Hospitalization of persons incompetent to stand trial or not guilty by reason of mental illness; examination period; commitment; hearing; restrictions; dismissal of criminal charges

(Amended by 2015 Mass. Acts c. 46, § 108, effective July 17, 2015; 2015 Mass. Acts c. 112, effective Oct. 30, 2015.)

(a) The court having jurisdiction over the criminal proceedings may order that a person who has been found incompetent to stand trial or not guilty by reason of mental illness or mental defect in such proceedings be hospitalized at a facility for a period of forty days for observation and examination; provided that, if the defendant is a male and if the court determines that the failure to retain him in strict security would create a likelihood of serious harm by reason of mental illness, or other mental defect, it may order such hospitalization at the Bridgewater state hospital; and provided, further, that the combined periods of hospitalization under the provisions of this section and paragraph (b) of section fifteen shall not exceed fifty days.

(b) During the period of observation of a person believed to be incompetent to stand trial or within sixty days after a person is found to be incompetent to stand trial or not guilty of any crime by reason of mental illness or other mental defect, the district attorney, the superintendent of a facility or the medical director of the Bridgewater state hospital may petition the court having jurisdiction of the criminal case for the commitment of the person to a facility or to the Bridgewater state hospital. However, the petition for the commitment of an untried defendant shall be heard only if the defendant is found incompetent to stand trial or if the criminal charges are dismissed after commitment. If the court makes the findings required by paragraph (a) of section eight, it shall order the person committed to a facility; if the court makes the findings required by paragraph (b) of section eight, it shall order the commitment of the person to the Bridgewater state hospital; otherwise the petition shall be dismissed and the person discharged. An order of commitment under the provisions of this paragraph shall be valid for six months. In the event a period of hospitalization under the provisions of paragraph (a) has expired, or in the event no such period of examination has been ordered, the court may order the temporary detention of such person in a jail, house of correction, facility or the Bridgewater state hospital until such time as the findings required by this paragraph are made or a determination is made that such finding cannot be made.

(c) After the expiration of a commitment under paragraph (b) of this section, a person may be committed for additional one-year periods under the provisions of sections seven and eight of this chapter, but no untried defendant shall be so committed unless in addition to the findings required by sections seven and eight the court also finds said defendant is incompetent to stand trial. If the person is not found incompetent, the court shall notify the court with jurisdiction of the criminal charges, which court shall thereupon order the defendant returned to its custody for the resumption of criminal proceedings. All subsequent proceedings for the further commitment of a person committed under this section shall be in the court which has jurisdiction of the facility or hospital.

(d) The district attorney for the district within which the alleged crime or crimes occurred shall be notified of any hearing conducted for a person under the provisions of this section or any subsequent hearing for such person conducted under the provisions of this chapter relative to the commitment of the mentally ill and shall have a right to be heard at such hearings.

(e) Any person committed to a facility under the provisions of this section may be restricted in his movements to the buildings and grounds of the facility at which he is committed by the court which ordered the commitment. If such restrictions are ordered, they shall not be removed except with the approval of the court. If the superintendent seeks removal or modification of such restriction, the superintendent shall notify the district attorney who has or had jurisdiction of the relevant criminal case. If, after the superintendent communicates the superintendent's intention to remove or modify such restriction in writing to the court and the district attorney who has or had jurisdiction of the relevant criminal case, neither the court nor the district attorney makes written objection to such removal or modification within 14 days of receipt of the notice, such restrictions shall be removed by the superintendent. If the superintendent or medical director of the Bridgewater state hospital intends to discharge a person committed under this section or at the end of a period of commitment intends not to petition for his further commitment, he shall notify the court and district attorney which have or had jurisdiction of the criminal case. Within thirty days of the receipt of such notice, the district attorney may petition for commitment under the provisions of paragraph (c). During such thirty day period, the person shall be held at the facility or hospital. This paragraph shall not apply to persons originally committed after a finding of incompetence to stand trial whose criminal charges have been dismissed.

(f) If a person is found incompetent to stand trial, the court shall send notice to the department of correction which shall compute the date of the expiration of the period of time equal to the time of imprisonment which the person would have had to serve prior to becoming eligible for parole if he had been convicted of the most serious crime with which he was charged in court and sentenced to the maximum sentence he could have received, if so convicted. For purposes of the computation of parole eligibility, the minimum sentence shall be regarded as one half of the maximum potential sentence. Where applicable, the provisions of sections one hundred and twenty-nine, one hundred and twenty-nine A, one hundred and twenty-nine B and one hundred and twenty-nine C of chapter one hundred and twenty-seven shall be applied to reduce such period of time. On the final date of such period, the court shall dismiss the criminal charges against such person, or the court in the interest of justice may dismiss the criminal charges against such person prior to the expiration of such period.

NOTE 1   Mental Illness. "'For purposes of involuntary commitment . . . "mental illness" shall mean a substantial disorder of thought, mood, perception, orientation, or memory which grossly impairs judgment, behavior, capacity to recognize reality or ability to meet the ordinary demands of life. . . .' 104 Code Mass. Regs. § 3.01(1)(a) (1986). *Commonwealth v. Nassar*, [380 Mass. 908 (1980)] at 913 n.6. In addition, c. 123, § 1 (1986 ed.), provides that a mentally retarded person may not be adjudged mentally ill 'solely

by virtue of his mental retardation.'" *Commonwealth v. DelVerde*, 401 Mass. 447, 449–50 (1988) (footnote omitted).

NOTE 2   Calculating Period of Pendency of Criminal Charges. "This case raises a question of statutory interpretation: Whether G.L. c. 123, § 16(f), mandates the dismissal of charges pending against an incompetent criminal defendant on the final date of the period prescribed under the statute and computed on the basis of the maximum sentence for the single most serious crime charged or on the basis of the maximum consecutive sentences of all of the crimes charged of equal seriousness. . . .

"We conclude that the plain meaning of G.L. c. 123, § 16(f), requires the Department of Correction to calculate the period of the pendency of criminal charges against an incompetent defendant on the basis of the single most serious crime charged and on the single maximum sentence allowable." *Foss v. Commonwealth*, 437 Mass. 584, 584–85 (2002).

SECTION 17
Periodic review of incompetence to stand trial; petition; hearing; continued treatment; defense to charges; release

(a) The periodic review of a person found incompetent to stand trial shall include a clinical opinion with regard to the person's competence to stand trial, which opinion shall be noted in writing on the patient's record. If any person found incompetent to stand trial is determined by the superintendent of the facility or the medical director of the Bridgewater state hospital to be no longer incompetent, the superintendent or medical director shall notify the court, which shall without delay hold a hearing on the person's competency to stand trial. Any person found incompetent to stand trial may at any time petition the court for a hearing on his competency. Whenever a hearing is held and the court finds that the person is competent to stand trial, his commitment, if any, to a facility or to the Bridgewater state hospital shall be terminated and he shall be returned to the custody of the court for trial. However, if the person requests continued care and treatment during the pendency of the criminal proceedings against him and the superintendent or medical director agrees to provide such care and treatment, the court may order the further hospitalization of such person at the facility or the Bridgewater state hospital.

(b) If either a person or counsel of a person who has been found to be incompetent to stand trial believes that he can establish a defense of not guilty to the charges pending against the person other than the defense of not guilty by reason of mental illness or mental defect, he may request an opportunity to offer a defense thereto on the merits before the court which has criminal jurisdiction. The court may require counsel for the defendant to support the request by affidavit or other evidence. If the court in its discretion grants such a request, the evidence of the defendant and of the commonwealth shall be heard by the court sitting without a jury. If after hearing such petition the court finds a lack of substantial evidence to support a conviction it shall dismiss the indictment or other charges or find them defective or insufficient and order the release of the defendant from criminal custody.

(c) Notwithstanding any finding of incompetence to stand trial under the provisions of this chapter, the court having jurisdiction may, at any appropriate stage of the criminal proceedings, allow a defendant to be released with or without bail.

SECTION 18
Hospitalization of mentally ill prisoners; examination; reports; hearings; commitment; voluntary admission; reduction of sentence; discharge

(a) If the person in charge of any place of detention within the commonwealth has reason to believe that a person confined therein is in need of hospitalization by reason of mental illness at a facility of the department or at the Bridgewater state hospital, he shall cause such prisoner to be examined at such place of detention by a physician or psychologist, designated by the department as qualified to perform such examination. Said physician or psychologist shall report the results of the examination to the district court which has jurisdiction over the place of detention or, if the prisoner is awaiting trial, to the court which has jurisdiction of the criminal case. Such report shall include an opinion, with reasons therefore, as to whether such hospitalization is actually required. The court which receives such report may order the prisoner to be taken to a facility or, if a male, to the Bridgewater state hospital to be received for examination and observation for a period not to exceed thirty days. After completion of such examination and observation, a written report shall be sent to such court and to the person in charge of the place of detention. Such report shall be signed by the physician or psychologist conducting such examination, and shall contain an evaluation, supported by clinical findings, of whether the prisoner is in need of further treatment and care at a facility or, if a male, the Bridgewater state hospital by reason of mental illness. The person in charge of the place of detention shall have the same right as a superintendent of a facility and the medical director of the Bridgewater state hospital to file a petition with the court which received the results of the examination for the commitment of the person to a facility or to the Bridgewater state hospital; provided, however, that, notwithstanding the court's failure, after an initial hearing or after any subsequent hearing, to make a finding required for commitment to the Bridgewater state hospital, the prisoner shall be confined at said hospital if the findings required for commitment to a facility are made and if the commissioner of correction certifies to the court that confinement of the prisoner at said hospital is necessary to insure his continued retention in custody. An initial court order of commitment issued subject to the provisions of this section shall be valid for a six-month period, and all subsequent commitments during the term of the sentence shall take place under the provisions of sections seven and eight and shall be valid for one year.

(b) Notwithstanding any contrary provision of general or special law, a prisoner who is retained in any place of detention within the commonwealth and who is in need of care and treatment in a facility may, with the approval of the person in charge of such place of detention apply for voluntary admission under the provisions of paragraph (a) of section ten.

(c) At the commencement of hospitalization under the provisions of paragraph (a) or paragraph (b) the department of correction shall enter in the patient record of such prisoner the date of the expiration of the sentence of the prisoner. Where applicable, the provisions of sections one hundred and twenty-nine, one hundred and twenty-nine A, one hundred and twenty-nine B and one hundred and twenty-nine C of chapter one hundred and twenty-seven may be applied to reduce such sentence, and on such date the prisoner shall be discharged; provided, however, that if the superintendent or other head of a facility or the medical director of the Bridgewater state hospital determines that the discharge of the prisoner committed subject to the provisions of paragraph (a) would create a likelihood of serious harm by reason of mental illness, he shall petition the district court having jurisdiction over the facility prior to the date of expiration to order the commitment of such person to a facility or to the Bridgewater state hospital under the provisions of this chapter other than paragraph (a); and provided, further, that any prisoner resident in a facility subject to the provisions of paragraph (b) shall be free to leave such facility subject to the provisions of section eleven.

(d) In the event the provisions of this chapter require the release of a prisoner from a facility or from the Bridgewater state hospital prior to the date of expiration of his sentence calculated under the provisions of paragraph (c), such prisoner shall be forthwith returned to the place of detention from which he was transferred to such facility or to said hospital.

SECTION 19
Parties or witnesses; determination of mental condition

In order to determine the mental condition of any party or witness before any court of the commonwealth, the presiding judge may, in his discretion, request the department to assign a qualified physician or psychologist, who, if assigned shall make such examinations as the judge may deem necessary.

SECTION 33
Expenses of apprehension, examination, hearing, commitment or delivery; certification; audit; payment; fees
(Amended by 2012 Mass. Acts c. 224, § 137, effective Nov. 4, 2012.)

All necessary expenses attending the apprehension, examination, hearing, commitment or delivery of a mentally ill person, or an alleged alcoholic shall be allowed and certified by the judge if said person is committed pursuant to this chapter, and presented as often as once a year to the comptroller, who shall examine and audit the same. Necessary expenses attending the apprehension, examination or hearing of any person sought to be committed pursuant to this chapter but not so committed shall be so presented, examined and audited if they have been allowed in the discretion of the judge and certified by him. All expenses certified, examined and audited as provided in this section shall be paid by the commonwealth. If application is made for the commitment of a person whose expenses and support are not to be paid by the commonwealth, said expenses shall be paid by the applicant or by a person in his behalf. The compensation of the physicians and officers taking part in the commitment or admission of persons to facilities in accordance with this chapter shall be as follows: The fee for each physician making an authorized mental examination and for making a written report thereon to the court, or for making a medical certificate, shall be twenty-five dollars, and twenty cents for each mile traveled one way or such other rate as may be set by the executive office of health and human services or governmental unit designated by the executive office. Any physician required to appear before a judge or justice in any commitment proceedings in which such physician has made an examination, shall receive a fee of twenty-five dollars, and twenty cents for each mile traveled one way for such appearance before the court, or such other rate as may be set by the executive office of health and human services or governmental unit designated by the executive office. The fees for officers servicing process shall be the same as are allowed by law in like cases.

SECTION 34
Commitment or transfer to Veterans Administration or other federal agency

(a) The judgment or order of commitment by a court of competent jurisdiction of another state or of the District of Columbia, committing a person to the Veterans Administration or other agency of the United States government for care or treatment shall have the same force and effect as to the committed person while in this commonwealth as in the jurisdiction in which is situated the court entering the judgment or making the order; and the courts of the committing state, or of the District of Columbia, shall be deemed to have retained jurisdiction of the person so committed for the purpose of inquiring into the mental condition of such person, and of determining the necessity for continuance of his restraint. The law of the committing state or district shall govern with respect to the authority of the chief officer of any facility of said Veterans Administration or of any institution operated in this commonwealth by any other agency of the United States to retain custody of, or transfer, trial visit, or discharge, the committed person.

(b) Whenever, in any proceeding under the laws of this commonwealth for the commitment of a person alleged to be of unsound mind or otherwise in need of care and treatment in a facility or other institution for his proper care, it is determined after such adjudication of the status of such person as may be required by law that commitment to a facility for the mentally ill or other institution is necessary for care and treatment and it appears that such person is eligible for care or treatment by said Veterans Administration or other agency of the United States government, the court, upon receipt of certificate from said Veterans Administration or such other agency showing that facilities are available and that such person is eligible for care or treatment therein, may commit such person to said Veterans Administration or other agency. The person whose commitment is sought shall be personally served with such notice of the pending commitment proceedings as is required, and in such manner as is provided, by the laws of the commonwealth; and nothing in this section shall affect his right to appear and be heard in the proceedings. Upon commitment, such person, when admitted to any facility operated by any such agency within or without this commonwealth shall be subject to the rules and regulations of said Veterans Administration or other agency. The chief officer of any facility of said Veterans Administration or institution operated by any other agency of the United States to which the person is so committed shall with respect to such person be vested with the same powers as the department with respect to retention of custody, transfer, parole or discharge. Jurisdiction is retained in the committing or other appropriate court of the commonwealth at any time to inquire into the mental condition of the person so committed, and to determine the necessity for continuance of his restraint, and all commitments pursuant to this section are so conditioned.

(c) Upon receipt of a certificate of said Veterans Administration or such other agency of the United States that facilities are available for the care or treatment of any person committed to any facility for the mentally ill or other institu-

tion for the care or treatment of persons similarly afflicted and that such person is eligible for care or treatment, the department or the committing court may cause the transfer of such person to said Veterans Administration or other agency of the United States for care or treatment. Upon effecting any such transfer, the committing court or proper officer thereof shall be notified thereof by the transferring agency. No person shall be transferred to said Veterans Administration or other agency of the United States if he is confined pursuant to conviction of any felony or misdemeanor or if he has been acquitted of the charge solely on the grounds of insanity, unless prior to transfer the court or other authority originally committing such person shall enter an order for such transfer after appropriate motion and hearing. Any person transferred as provided in this subsection shall be deemed to be committed to said Veterans Administration or other agency of the United States pursuant to the original commitment.

SECTION 35
Commitment of alcoholics or substance abusers
(Amended by 2011 Mass. Acts c. 142, § 18, effective July 1, 2012; 2014 Mass. Acts c. 284, § 15, effective Jan. 1, 2015; 2016 Mass. Acts c. 8, §§ 1–4, effective Apr. 24, 2016; 2016 Mass. Acts c. 52, § 40, effective July 1, 2016 per § 71.)

For the purposes of this section the following terms shall, unless the context clearly requires otherwise, have the following meanings:

"Alcohol use disorder", the chronic or habitual consumption of alcoholic beverages by a person to the extent that (1) such use substantially injures the person's health or substantially interferes with the person's social or economic functioning, or (2) the person has lost the power of self-control over the use of such beverages.

"Facility", a public or private facility that provides care and treatment for a person with an alcohol or substance use disorder.

"Substance use disorder", the chronic or habitual consumption or ingestion of controlled substances or intentional inhalation of toxic vapors by a person to the extent that: (i) such use substantially injures the person's health or substantially interferes with the person's social or economic functioning; or (ii) the person has lost the power of self-control over the use of such controlled substances or toxic vapors.

Any police officer, physician, spouse, blood relative, guardian or court official may petition in writing any district court or any division of the juvenile court department for an order of commitment of a person whom he has reason to believe has an alcohol or substance use disorder. Upon receipt of a petition for an order of commitment of a person and any sworn statements the court may request from the petitioner, the court shall immediately schedule a hearing on the petition and shall cause a summons and a copy of the application to be served upon the person in the manner provided by section twenty-five of chapter two hundred and seventy-six. In the event of the person's failure to appear at the time summoned, the court may issue a warrant for the person's arrest. Upon presentation of such a petition, if there are reasonable grounds to believe that such person will not appear and that any further delay in the proceedings would present an immediate danger to the physical well-being of the respondent, said court may issue a warrant for the apprehension and appearance of such person before it. If such person is not immediately presented before a judge of the district court, the warrant shall continue day after day for up to 5 consecutive days, excluding Saturdays, Sundays and legal holidays, or until such time as the person is presented to the court, whichever is sooner; provided, however that an arrest on such warrant shall not be made unless the person may be presented immediately before a judge of the district court. The person shall have the right to be represented by legal counsel and may present independent expert or other testimony. If the court finds the person indigent, it shall immediately appoint counsel. The court shall order examination by a qualified physician, a qualified psychologist or a qualified social worker.

If, after a hearing which shall include expert testimony and may include other evidence, the court finds that such person is an individual with an alcohol or substance use disorder and there is a likelihood of serious harm as a result of the person's alcohol or substance use disorder, the court may order such person to be committed for a period not to exceed 90 days to a facility designated by the department of public health, followed by the availability of case management services provided by the department of public health for up to 1 year; provided, that a review of the necessity of the commitment shall take place by the superintendent on days 30, 45, 60 and 75 as long as the commitment continues. A person so committed may be released prior to the expiration of the period of commitment upon written determination by the superintendent of the facility that release of that person will not result in a likelihood of serious harm. Such commitment shall be for the purpose of inpatient care for the treatment of an alcohol or substance use disorder in a facility licensed or approved by the department of public health or the department of mental health. Subsequent to the issuance of a commitment order, the superintendent of a facility may authorize the transfer of a patient to a different facility for continuing treatment; provided, that the superintendent shall provide notification of the transfer to the committing court.

If the department of public health informs the court that there are no suitable facilities available for treatment licensed or approved by the department of public health or the department of mental health, or if the court makes a specific finding that the only appropriate setting for treatment for the person is a secure facility, then the person may be committed to: (i) a secure facility for women approved by the department of public health or the department of mental health, if a female; or (ii) the Massachusetts correctional institution at Bridgewater, if a male; provided, however, that any person so committed shall be housed and treated separately from persons currently serving a criminal sentence. The person shall, upon release, be encouraged to consent to further treatment and shall be allowed voluntarily to remain in the facility for such purpose. The department of public health shall maintain a roster of public and private facilities available, together with the number of beds currently available and the level of security at each facility, for the care and treatment of alcohol use disorder and substance use disorder and shall make the roster available to the trial court.

Nothing in this section shall preclude a facility, including the Massachusetts correctional institution at Bridgewater, from treating persons on a voluntary basis.

The court, in its order, shall specify whether such commitment is based upon a finding that the person is a person with an alcohol use disorder, substance use disorder, or both. The court, upon ordering the commitment of a person found to be a person with an alcohol use disorder or substance use disorder pursuant to this section, shall transmit the person's name and nonclinical identifying information, including the person's social security number and date of birth, to the department of criminal justice information services. The court shall notify the person that such person is prohibited from being issued a firearm identification card pursuant to section 129B of chapter 140 or a license to carry pursuant to sections 131 and 131F of said chapter 140 unless a petition for relief pursuant to this section is subsequently granted.

After 5 years from the date of commitment, a person found to be a person with an alcohol use disorder or substance use disorder and committed pursuant to this section may file a petition for relief with the court that ordered the commitment requesting that the court restore the person's ability to possess a firearm, rifle or shotgun. The court may grant the relief sought in accordance with the principles of due process if the circumstances regarding the person's disqualifying condition and the person's record and reputation are determined to be such that: (i) the person is not likely to act in a manner that is dangerous to public safety; and (ii) the granting of relief would not be contrary to the public interest. In making the determination, the court may consider evidence from a licensed physician or clinical psychologist that the person is no longer suffering from the disease or condition that caused the disability or that the disease or condition has been successfully treated for a period of 3 consecutive years.

If the court grants a petition for relief pursuant to this section, the clerk shall provide notice immediately by forwarding a certified copy of the order for relief to the department of criminal justice information services, who shall transmit the order, pursuant to paragraph (h) of section 167A of chapter 6, to the attorney general of the United States to be included in the National Instant Criminal Background Check System.

A person whose petition for relief is denied may appeal to the appellate division of the district court for a de novo review of the denial.

SECTION 36A
Court records of examination or commitment; privacy
(Second paragraph added by 2014 Mass. Acts c. 284, § 16, effective Jan. 1, 2015.)

All reports of examinations made to a court pursuant to sections one to eighteen, inclusive, section forty-seven and forty-eight shall be private except in the discretion of the court. All petitions for commitment, notices, orders of commitment and other commitment papers used in proceedings under sections one to eighteen and section thirty-five shall be private except in the discretion of the court. Each court shall keep a private docket of the cases of persons coming before it believed to be mentally ill, including proceedings under section thirty-five; provided that nothing in this section shall prevent public inspection of any complaints or indictments in a criminal case, or prevent any notation in the ordinary docket of criminal cases concerning commitment proceedings under sections one to eighteen against a defendant in a criminal case. Notwithstanding the provisions of this paragraph, any person who is the subject of an examination or a commitment proceeding, or his counsel, may inspect all reports and papers filed with the court in a pending proceeding, and the prosecutor in a criminal case may inspect all reports and papers concerning commitment proceedings that are filed with the court in a pending case.

Notwithstanding this section, a court may, pursuant to section 35 and section 36C, transmit information contained in court records to the department of criminal justice information services to provide: (i) licensing authorities as defined under section 121 of chapter 140 with information required or permitted to be considered under state or federal law to conduct background checks for firearm sales or licensing; and (ii) the attorney general of the United States with information required or permitted under federal law to be included in the National Instant Criminal Background Check System maintained to conduct background checks for firearms sales or licensing; provided, however, that the court shall not transmit information solely because a person seeks voluntary treatment or is involuntarily hospitalized for assessment or evaluation. Information transmitted to the department of criminal justice information services pursuant to this section and sections 35 and 36C shall not be considered public records pursuant to section 10 of chapter 66 and clause Twenty-sixth of section 7 of chapter 4.

SECTION 36B
Duty of licensed mental health professional to warn patient's potential victims; cause of action

(1) There shall be no duty owed by a licensed mental health professional to take reasonable precautions to warn or in any other way protect a potential victim or victims of said professional's patient, and no cause of action imposed against a licensed mental health professional for failure to warn or in any other way protect a potential victim or victims of such professional's patient unless: (a) the patient has communicated to the licensed mental health professional an explicit threat to kill or inflict serious bodily injury upon a reasonably identified victim or victims and the patient has the apparent intent and ability to carry out the threat, and the licensed mental health professional fails to take reasonable precautions as that term is defined in section one; or (b) the patient has a history of physical violence which is known to the licensed mental health professional and the licensed mental health professional has a reasonable basis to believe that there is a clear and present danger that the patient will attempt to kill or inflict serious bodily injury against a reasonably identified victim or victims and the licensed mental health professional fails to take reasonable precautions as that term is defined by said section one. Nothing in this paragraph shall be construed to require a mental health professional to take any action which, in the exercise of reasonable professional judgment, would endanger such mental health professional or increase the danger to potential victim or victims.

(2) Whenever a licensed mental health professional takes reasonable precautions, as that term is defined in section one of chapter one hundred and twenty-three, no cause of action by the patient shall lie against the licensed mental health professional for disclosure of otherwise confidential communications.

SECTION 36C
Report of commitment order to department of criminal justice information services
(Added by 2014 Mass. Acts c. 284, § 17, effective Jan. 1, 2015.)

(a) A court that orders the commitment of a person pursuant to sections 7, 8 or 18 or subsection (e) of section 12 or subsection (b) of section 15 or subsection (b) or (c) of section 16, shall transmit the person's name and nonclinical, identifying information, including the person's social security number and date of birth to the department of criminal justice information services. The court shall notify the person that such person is prohibited from being issued a firearm identification card pursuant to section 129B of chapter 140 or a license to carry pursuant to sections 131 and 131F of said chapter 140 unless a petition for relief is subsequently granted pursuant to subsection (b).

(b) After 5 years from the date of commitment, a person committed pursuant to sections 7, 8 or 18 or subsection (e) of section 12 or subsection (b) of section 15 or subsection (b) or (c) of section 16 may file a petition for relief with the court that ordered the commitment requesting the court to restore the person's ability to possess a firearm. The court may grant the relief sought in accordance with the principles of due process if the circumstances regarding the person's disqualifying condition and the person's record and reputation are determined to be such that: (i) the person is not likely to act in a manner that is dangerous to public safety; and (ii) the granting of relief would not be contrary to the public interest. In making the determination, the court may consider evidence from a licensed physician or clinical psychologist that the person is no longer suffering from the disease or condition that caused the disability or that the disease or condition has been successfully treated for a period of 3 consecutive years.

(c) When the court grants a petition for relief pursuant to subsection (b), the clerk shall immediately forward a copy of the order for relief to the department of criminal justice information services.

(d) A person whose petition for relief is denied pursuant to subsection (b) may appeal to the appellate division of the district court for a de novo review of the denial.

Chapter 123A. Care, Treatment and Rehabilitation of Sexually Dangerous Persons

Section	
1	Definitions
2	Nemansket Correctional Center; treatment and rehabilitation personnel
2A	Transfer to a correctional institution; provision of voluntary treatment services
3–6	Repealed
6A	Most appropriate level of security; participation in community access program; notice required
7–8	Repealed
9	Petitions for examination and discharge
9A–B	Repealed
10–11	Repealed
12	Notification of persons adjudicated delinquent juvenile or youthful offender by reason of a sexual offense; petitions for classification as sexually dangerous person; hearings
13	Temporary commitment of prisoner or youth to treatment center; right to counsel; psychological examination
14	Trial by jury; right to counsel; admissibility of evidence; commitment to treatment; temporary commitments pending disposition of petitions
15	Competence to stand trial; hearing
16	Annual reports describing treatments offered

SECTION 1
Definitions

As used in this chapter the following words shall, except as otherwise provided, have the following meanings:

"Agency with jurisdiction", the agency with the authority to direct the release of a person presently incarcerated, confined or committed to the department of youth services, regardless of the reason for such incarceration, confinement or commitment, including, but not limited to a sheriff, keeper, master or superintendent of a jail, house of correction or prison, the director of a custodial facility in the department of youth services, the parole board and, where a person has been found incompetent to stand trial, a district attorney.

"Community access board", a board consisting of five members appointed by the commissioner of correction, whose function shall be to consider a person's placement within a community access program and conduct an annual review of a person's sexual dangerousness.

"Community Access Program", a program established pursuant to section six A that provides for a person's reintegration into the community.

"Conviction", a conviction of or adjudication as a delinquent juvenile or a youthful offender by reason of sexual offense, regardless of the date of offense or date of conviction or adjudication.

"Mental abnormality", a congenital or acquired condition of a person that affects the emotional or volitional capacity of the person in a manner that predisposes that person to the commission of criminal sexual acts to a degree that makes the person a menace to the health and safety of other persons.

"Personality disorder", a congenital or acquired physical or mental condition that results in a general lack of power to control sexual impulses.

"Qualified examiner" a physician who is licensed pursuant to section two of chapter one hundred and twelve who is either certified in psychiatry by the American Board of Psychiatry and Neurology or eligible to be so certified, or a psychologist who is licensed pursuant to sections one hundred and eighteen to one hundred and twenty-nine, inclusive, of chapter one hundred and twelve; provided, however, that the examiner has had two years of experience with diagnosis or treatment of sexually aggressive offenders and is designated by the commissioner of correction. A "qualified examiner" need not be an employee of the department of correction or of any facility or institution of the department.

"Sexual offense", includes any of the following crimes: indecent assault and battery on a child under fourteen under the provisions of section thirteen B of chapter two hundred and sixty-five; aggravated indecent assault and battery on a child under the age of 14 under section 13B½ of chapter 265; a repeat offense under section 13B¾ of chapter 265; indecent assault and battery on a mentally retarded person under the provisions of section thirteen F of chapter two hundred and sixty-five; indecent assault and battery on a person who has obtained the age of fourteen under the provisions of section thirteen H of chapter two hundred and sixty-five; rape under the provisions of section twenty-two of chapter two hundred and sixty-five; rape of a child under sixteen with force under the provisions of section twenty-two A of chapter two hundred and sixty-five; aggravated rape of a child under 16 with force under section 22B of chapter 265; a repeat offense under section 22C of chapter 265; rape and abuse of a child under sixteen under the provisions of section twenty-three of chapter two hundred and sixty-five; aggravated rape and abuse of a child under section 23A of chapter 265; a repeat offense under section 23B of chapter 265; assault with intent to commit rape under the provisions of section twenty-four of chapter two hundred and sixty-five; assault on a child with intent to commit rape under section 24B of chapter 265; kidnapping under section 26 of said chapter 265 with intent to commit a violation of section 13B, 13B½, 13B¾, 13F, 13H, 22, 22A, 22B, 22C, 23, 23A, 23B, 24 or 24B of said chapter 265; enticing away a person for prostitution or sexual intercourse under section 2 of chapter 272; drugging persons for sexual intercourse under section 3 of chapter 272; inducing a person under 18 into prostitution under section 4A of said chapter 272; living off or sharing earnings of a minor prostitute under section 4B of said chapter 272; open and gross lewdness and lascivious behavior under section 16 of said chapter 272; incestuous intercourse under section 17 of said chapter 272 involving a person under the age of 21; dissemination or possession with the intent to disseminate to a minor matter harmful to a minor under section 28 of said chapter 272; posing or exhibiting a child in a state of nudity under section 29A of said chapter 272; dissemination of visual material of a child in a state of nudity or sexual conduct under section 29B of said chapter 272; purchase or possession of visual material of a child depicted in sexual conduct under section 29C of said chapter 272; dissemination of visual material of a child in the state of nudity or in sexual conduct under section 30D of chapter 272; unnatural and lascivious acts with a child under the age of sixteen under the provisions of section thirty-five A of chapter two hundred and seventy-two; accosting or annoying persons of the opposite sex and lewd, wanton and lascivious speech or behavior under section 53 of said chapter 272; and any attempt to commit any of the above listed crimes under the provisions of section six of chapter two hundred and seventy-four or a like violation of the laws of another state, the United States or a military, territorial or Indian tribal authority; and any other offense, the facts of which, under the totality of the circumstances, manifest a sexual motivation or pattern of conduct or series of acts of sexually-motivated offenses.

"Sexually dangerous person", any person who (i) has been convicted of or adjudicated as a delinquent juvenile or youthful offender by reason of a sexual offense and who suffers from a mental abnormality or personality disorder which makes the person likely to engage in sexual offenses if not confined to a secure facility; (ii) has been charged with a sexual offense and was determined to be incompetent to stand trial and who suffers from a mental abnormality or personality disorder which makes such person likely to engage in sexual offenses if not confined to a secure facility; or (iii) a person previously adjudicated as such by a court of the commonwealth and whose misconduct in sexual matters indicates a general lack of power to control his sexual impulses, as evidenced by repetitive or compulsive sexual misconduct by either violence against any victim, or aggression against any victim under the age of 16 years, and who, as a result, is likely to attack or otherwise inflict injury on such victims because of his uncontrolled or uncontrollable desires.

NOTE 1   **Review of 1999 Amendments to Chapter 123A.** In *Commonwealth v. Bruno*, 432 Mass. 489 (2000), the Supreme

1

Judicial Court reviewed many aspects of the 1999 amendments to Chapter 123A.

NOTE 2   Retroactivity of 1999 Amendments. "The defendants maintain that the application of the amended c. 123A to them is unconstitutional because it was triggered by an event, namely, a conviction of a sexual offense, that occurred before [the amendment's] effective date. They assert that the statute may only be applied to persons (unlike themselves) whose convictions of sexual offenses occur on or after the effective date of the 1999 amendments. We disagree because we conclude that the statute operates prospectively. . . ."

"[T]he conduct triggering the statute's application is not the prior conviction of a sexual offense, but the current mental condition of a defendant. The focus of the definition of 'sexually dangerous person' and the statute's various sections relating to the procedures governing commitment is a defendant's current mental condition."

"That a person, in addition to possessing the requisite current mental condition, must have been convicted of a sexual offense, only identifies and limits the class of persons subject to potential commitment under c. 123A. The Legislature may, of course, choose to classify or reclassify a thing, and provided the new definition is applied only to determine status for the purpose of matters arising in the future, the prohibition on retroactive laws is not violated. A law is not made retroactive because it alters the existing classification of a thing. Nor is a law retroactive if it draws upon antecedent facts for its operation. Because the requisite sexual offense convictions determine only the persons eligible for potential civil commitment, and is not the basis for commitment, the statute is not retroactive in application." *Commonwealth v. Bruno*, 432 Mass. 489, 497–98 (2000) (citations and quotation marks omitted).

NOTE 3   Ex Post Facto—1999 Amendments. "The defendants argue that various features of c. 123A render the statute punitive in both intent and effect, and thus, an unconstitutional ex post facto law under art. 24 of the Massachusetts Declaration of Rights. They point to the following features of the statute as punitive: (1) the commitment and treatment occurs after a sexually dangerous person has served his sentence; (2) the statute does not permit less restrictive alternatives to commitment; and (3) the treatment center is operated by the department [of correction], instead of the Department of Mental Health, as previously had been the case. We reject these contentions. The statute is neither punitive in intent or effect, nor does it constitute an ex post facto law." *Commonwealth v. Bruno*, 432 Mass. 489, 499 (2000) (citations and footnote omitted).

NOTE 4   Due Process—1999 Amendments. "While commitment proceedings under c. 123A are civil proceedings, the potential deprivation of liberty to those persons subjected to these proceedings mandates that due process protections apply. The defendants argue that temporary commitment of an indeterminate duration pending a probable cause hearing, pursuant to G.L. c. 123A, § 12(e), violates their substantive due process rights because the temporary restraint does not occur in narrowly circumscribed situations. They maintain that the temporary restraint is not imposed in narrowly circumscribed situations because the 'district attorneys' discretion to initiate proceedings is not informed by meaningful guidelines; a district attorney can file a petition for commitment of any person who has been convicted of a single sex offense.' The defendants also claim that this lack of guidelines violates their procedural due process rights. We reject these contentions." *Commonwealth v. Bruno*, 432 Mass. 489, 502–03 (2000) (citations omitted).

NOTE 5   Probation—From and After Probation Does Not Commence Until After Release from Treatment Center. In *Commonwealth v. Sheridan*, 51 Mass. App. Ct. 74 (2001), the defendant had been convicted and sentenced in 1976 to twelve to twenty years on two counts of rape. Two years later, the defendant, while incarcerated, was convicted on two charges of assault and battery and given a suspended sentence and three years probation to be served "from and after" the sentences he was then

serving on the rape convictions. In 1984, while still serving the criminal sentence, the defendant was found to be a sexually dangerous person and civilly committed to the Treatment Center for one day to life under the provisions of Chapter 123A. In 1994, the defendant completed serving the criminal sentence, but remained civilly committed as a sexually dangerous person. Five years later, in 1999, the defendant was released from his civil commitment. At that time, the Commonwealth contended that the defendant still had to serve his three year probationary period. The defendant countered that his probation had started to run in 1994 when he completed his criminal sentence and had expired three years later in 1997. The Appeals Court rejected "the defendant's argument that his probationary sentence ran concurrently with his commitment at the treatment center. While committed to the treatment center, the defendant was separated from society and in an institutionalized setting that eliminated any need for the supervision of a probation officer. . . . The two goals of probation—rehabilitation under the supervision of a probation officer and the protection of society—are only brought into play when the offender is released into the community." *Commonwealth v. Sheridan*, 51 Mass. App. Ct. at 77 (citation omitted).

NOTE 6   Incompetent Defendant. "The defendant argues that trial of a petition to commit an incompetent person under § 14 would violate principles of due process. We disagree. 'Minimum due process varies with context.' *Commonwealth v. Torres*, 441 Mass. 499, 502 (2004), quoting from *Spence v. Gormley*, 387 Mass. 258, 274 (1982)." *Commonwealth v. Nieves*, 446 Mass. 583, 590 (2006).

"Due process is not offended by subjecting [an incompetent] defendant, with the assistance of counsel, to trial of the Commonwealth's [G.L. c. 123A] petition as provided in § 14.

"The defendant incorrectly presumes that the severity of his limitations, and the judge's recognition that his limitations may have 'had some effect' on the outcome of the case, precludes a conclusion, beyond a reasonable doubt, that the defendant committed the charged offenses. This is not accurate. To the contrary, the language of § 15 expresses an intent, on the part of the Legislature, that G.L. c. 123A commitment proceedings go forward against an incompetent person, even one who may have limited comprehension of the proceedings.

"We now turn to the constitutional question presented—whether an individual, who has been charged with a sexual offense but, due to incompetency, has not been tried and convicted of that charge, may nevertheless, consistent with principles of due process and equal protection, be subject to G.L. c. 123A commitment proceedings as a sexually dangerous person based on a judge's determination, after a hearing pursuant to § 15, that he committed the sexual offense, or offenses, charged.

"The defendant's interest is weighty. If committed, his loss of liberty would be total. G.L. c. 123A, § 6A. Commitment is for an indeterminate period, § 14, and he has a strong interest in avoiding such commitment. However, the defendant's interest must, with appropriate safeguards, yield to the Commonwealth's paramount interest in protecting its citizens. We see no reason why the public interest in committing sexually dangerous persons to the care of the treatment center must be thwarted by the fact that one who is sexually dangerous also happens to be incompetent." *Commonwealth v. Burgess*, 450 Mass. 366, 367, 370–73 (2008).

NOTE 7   "Likely" Defined. "The judge dismissed the petition . . . because he concluded that the Commonwealth had failed to prove beyond a reasonable doubt that Boucher was 'likely' to commit new sexual offenses unless confined to a secure facility. He based this conclusion on his interpretation of the term 'likely' in the statute to mean 'more likely than not,' or, stated otherwise, that the Commonwealth had the burden of proving that the risk of Boucher committing an additional sexual offense was 'at least fifty percent'. . . .

". . . [W]e conclude that these terms have different meanings . . . .

"'Likely' is not defined in G.L. c. 123A, nor is it understood to be a term of art requiring a specific and limited interpretation. . . .

We conclude that something is 'likely' if it is reasonably to be expected in the context of the particular facts and circumstances at hand.

"In assessing the risk of reoffending, it is for the fact finder to determine what is 'likely.' Such a determination must be made on a case-by-case basis, by analyzing a number of factors, including the seriousness of the threatened harm, the relative certainty of the anticipated harm, and the possibility of successful intervention to prevent that harm. . . . The degree of likelihood necessary to support commitment may depend on many factors'). While 'likely' indicates more than a mere propensity or possibility, it is not bound to the statistical probability inherent in a definition such as 'more likely than not,' and the terms are not interchangeable. To conclude that 'likely' amounts to a quantifiable probability, absent a more specific statutory expression of such a quantity, is to require mathematical precision from a term that, by its plain meaning, demands contextual, not statistical, analysis.

"'More likely than not' is most familiar as a standard of proof equivalent to fifty per cent plus one. As used in the statute, however, the term 'likely' is not intended as a standard or burden of proof. Rather, it is descriptive of one characteristic ('likely to engage in sexual offenses') of a sexually dangerous person. While the Commonwealth is required to prove beyond a reasonable doubt that a person is sexually dangerous, that is, has all the characteristics of such a person as defined in G.L. c. 123A, § 1, it is not required to prove to any particular mathematical quantum the likelihood of his committing another sexual offense.

". . . There is little question that, in the circumstances of our statute, proof that a person is likely to commit another sexual offense need not be established to a mathematical certainty above fifty per cent in order to distinguish the dangerous sexual offender from 'the dangerous but typical recidivist convicted in an ordinary criminal case.'

". . . [T]here is nothing in the statute or its history to suggest that the Legislature intended that 'likely' be interpreted to mean 'more likely than not.' As a matter of legislative intent, such an interpretation would be incongruous given the unmitigated use of the word 'likely' in the statute. If the Legislature had intended to restrict 'likely' to a usage less broad than its commonly understood meaning, the Legislature would have done so." *Commonwealth v. Boucher*, 438 Mass. 274, 275–78 (2002).

NOTE 8a   **Non-contact Offenses.** "The first question we must address is whether G.L. c. 123A, properly construed, permits a finding that this defendant is sexually dangerous, where the judge found that because of his exhibitionism he is likely to commit only a 'hands-off, noncontact sex[ual] offense[ ] involving exposing himself and masturbating in front of unsuspecting strangers.'" . . . Where the judge found no evidence that the defendant had ever stalked, lured, approached, confined, or touched a victim, that there was no reason to believe he would target children, and that there was no reason to believe the defendant's future sexual offenses would escalate into contact offenses, the judge should have concluded that, as a matter of law, the manner in which the defendant would likely commit a future 'sexual offense,' i.e., open and gross lewdness and lascivious behavior, would not render him a 'menace to the health and safety of other persons.' G.L. c. 123A, § 1 (definition of '[m]ental abnormality')." *Commonwealth v. Suave*, 460 Mass. 582, 586, 588 (2011).

NOTE 8b   "We now hold that a defendant may be determined to be a 'menace' where he is likely to commit only noncontact sexual offenses." *Commonwealth v. Fay*, 467 Mass. 574 (2014).

SECTION 2
Nemansket correctional center; treatment and rehabilitation personnel

The commissioner of correction shall maintain subject to the jurisdiction of the department of correction a treatment program or branch thereof at a correctional institution for the care, custody, treatment and rehabilitation of persons adjudicated as being sexually dangerous. Said facility shall be known as the "Nemansket Correctional Center". The commissioner of correction shall appoint a chief administrative officer who shall have responsibility for providing personnel with respect to the treatment and rehabilitation of the sexually dangerous persons, consistent with public safety. The commissioner of correction shall have the authority to promulgate regulations consistent with the provisions of this chapter.

SECTION 2A
Transfer to a correctional institution; provision of voluntary treatment services

An individual committed as sexually dangerous and who has also been sentenced for a criminal offense and said sentence has not expired may be transferred from the treatment center to another correctional institution designated by the commissioner of correction. In determining whether a transfer to a correctional institution is appropriate the commissioner of correction may consider the following factors:

(1) the person's unamenability to treatment:

(2) the person's unwillingness or failure to follow treatment recommendations;

(3) the person's lack of progress in treatment at the center or branch thereof;

(4) the danger posed by the person to other residents or staff at the Treatment Center or branch thereof;

(5) the degree of security necessary to protect the public.

The department of correction shall promulgate regulations establishing a transfer board and procedures governing transfer, including notification of hearing, opportunity to be heard, written decision notification of decision, opportunity for appeal, and periodic review of placement.

The commissioner of correction shall make available to the remanded individuals a program of voluntary treatment services. An annual review shall be conducted of the current sexual dangerousness of each transferred individual and a report prepared which shall be admissible in a hearing under section nine of this chapter. Upon completion of said person's criminal sentence, he shall be returned to the treatment center and considered for participation in the community access program. Existing civil commitments to the treatment center shall not be vacated by the transfer to a correctional institution.

SECTIONS 3–6
Repealed

SECTION 6A
Most appropriate level of security; participation in community access program; notice required

Any person committed as a sexually dangerous person to the treatment center or a branch thereof under the provisions of this chapter shall be held in the most appropriate level of security required to ensure protection of the public, correctional staff, himself and others. Any juvenile who is committed as a sexually dangerous person to the treatment center or a branch thereof under the provisions of this chapter shall be segregated from any adults held at such facility.

Only a person whose criminal sentence has expired or upon whom a criminal sentence was never imposed shall be entitled to apply for participation in a community access program once in every twelve months. Said program shall be administered pursuant to the rules and regulations promulgated by the department of correction. As part of its program of community access the department of correction shall establish a board known as the community access board which board shall consist of five members appointed by the commissioner of correction, consistent with the rules and regulations of the department. Membership shall include three department of correction employees and two persons who are not department of correction employees, but who may be independent contractors or consultants. The non-employee members shall consist of psychiatrists or psychologists licensed by the commonwealth. The board shall evaluate residents for participation in the community access program and establish conditions to ensure the safety of the general community. The board shall have access to all records of the person being evaluated and shall give a report of its findings including dissenting views, to the chief administrative officer of the center. Such report shall be admissible in any hearing under section nine of this chapter. The board shall also conduct annual reviews of and prepare reports on the current sexual dangerousness of all persons at the treatment center, including those whose criminal sentences have not expired. The reports shall be admissible in a hearing under section nine of this chapter.

Any person participating in a community access program under this section shall continue to reside within the secure confines of MCI-Bridgewater and be under daily evaluation by treatment center personnel to determine if he presents a danger to the community. Upon approval of a person for participation in a community access program, notice shall be given to the colonel of state police, to the attorney general, to the district attorney in the district from which the person's criminal commitment originated, to the police department of the city or town from which the commitment originated, the police department of the town of Bridgewater, the police department where such person's participation in the community access program will occur the employer of persons participating in the access program, and any victim of the sexual offense from which the commitment originated. If such victim is deceased at the time of such program participation, notice of the person's participation in a community access program shall be given to the parent, spouse or other member of the immediate family of such deceased victim.

SECTIONS 7–8
Repealed

SECTION 9
Petitions for examination and discharge

Any person committed to the treatment center shall be entitled to file a petition for examination and discharge once in every twelve months. Such petition may be filed by either the committed person, his parents, spouse, issue, next of kin or any friend. The department of correction may file a petition at any time if it believes a person is no longer a sexually dangerous person. A copy of any petition filed under this subsection shall be sent within fourteen days after the filing thereof to the department of the attorney general and to the district attorney for the district where the original proceedings were commenced. Said petition shall be filed in the district of the superior court department in which said person was committed. The petitioner shall have a right to a speedy hearing on a date set by the administrative justice of the superior court department. Upon the motion of the person or upon its own motion, the court shall appoint counsel for the person.

The hearing may be held in any court or any place designated for such purpose by the administrative justice of the superior court department. In any hearing held pursuant to the provisions of this section, either the petitioner or the commonwealth may demand that the issue be tried by a jury. If a jury is demanded, the matter shall proceed according to the practice of trial in civil cases in the superior court.

The court shall issue whatever process is necessary to assure the presence in court of the committed person. The court shall order the petitioner to be examined by two qualified examiners, who shall conduct examinations, including personal interviews, of the person on whose behalf such petition is filed and file with the court written reports of their examinations and diagnoses, and their recommendations for the disposition of such person. Said reports shall be admissible in a hearing pursuant to this section. If such person refuses, without good cause, to be personally interviewed by a qualified examiner appointed pursuant to this section, such person shall be deemed to have waived his right to a hearing on the petition and the petition shall be dismissed upon motion filed by the commonwealth. The qualified examiners shall have access to all records of the person being examined. Evidence of the person's juvenile and adult court and probation records, psychiatric and psychological records, the department of correction's updated annual progress report of the petition, including all relevant materials prepared in connection with the section six A process, and any other evidence that tends to indicate that he is a sexually dangerous person shall be admissible in a hearing under this section. The chief administrative officer of the treatment center or his designee may testify at the hearing regarding the annual report and his recommendations for the disposition of the petition. Unless the trier of fact finds that such person remains a sexually dangerous person, it shall order such person to be discharged from the treatment center. Upon such discharge, notice shall be given to the chief administrative officer, to the commissioner of correction and the colonel of state police, to the attorney general, to the district attorney in the district from which the commitment originated, to the police department of the city or town from which the commitment originated, the police department of the town of Bridgewater, the police department where such person is anticipated to take up residency, any employer of the resident, the department of criminal justice information services, and any victim of the sexual offense from which the commitment originated; provided, however, that said victim has requested notification pursuant to section three of chapter two hundred and fifty-eight B. If such victim is deceased at the time of such discharge, notice of such discharge shall be given to the parent, spouse or other member of the immediate family of such deceased victim.

NOTE 1   "Section 9 provides that at any hearing on such a petition, the written reports prepared by the designated qualified examiners of their examinations of the petitioner are admissible in evidence, as are written annual reviews of the petitioner prepared by the community access board (CAB) under G.L. c. 123A, § 6A, as well as the petitioner's 'psychiatric and psychological records.' The question presented is whether § 9 also renders admissible the written reports of expert witnesses retained by a § 9 petitioner for purposes of the § 9 proceeding." The Supreme Judicial Court responded in the affirmative. *Santos, petitioner*, 461 Mass. 565, 565–66 (2012) (footnotes omitted).

NOTE 2   "While the petitioner claims that he made significant progress in treatment, this contention misrepresents the witnesses' ultimate conclusions, which were that the petitioner had not sufficiently completed sex offender treatment. Specifically, there was testimony that '[t]he treatment team in his treatment is recommending that he continue to engage in behavioral treatment which would be focused on deviant sexual arousal'; '[h]e has been engaged in sex offender treatment for many years, but no one has reported, at least at the treatment center or his treatment team, that he has completed his treatment or [is] close to completing his treatment; [and,] [n]ow, notwithstanding [the petitioner's prior treatment] achievements, as I evaluated [the petitioner] and as I looked at all of his behavior, I found myself seeing him as a man who had difficulty translating the abstract concepts of things that he had learned in the treatment programs into real-life, day-to-day, concrete, observable, sustained changes in his behavior. . . . I decided, in my opinion, he had not yet fully completed the sex offender treatment available to him.' The witnesses also opined that further avenues of necessary treatment include seeking additional treatment for anger management and deviant sexual arousal and for developing a realistic release plan. Also noted was the absence of treatment on the petitioner's association of physical violence and women. Lastly, while the jury heard evidence that the petitioner passed twenty-nine classes, they also heard that he did not pass twenty-six.

"Here, the evidence demonstrated that the petitioner had previously been convicted of enumerated sex offenses, that he had personality disorders, and that he was likely to reoffend if not confined to a secure facility. See G.L. c. 123A, § 1. The evidence was overwhelming that the petitioner remained sexually dangerous. In light of all these factors, we conclude that even if the instruction were deemed error, there was no reversible error.

"In sum, we conclude that in pretrial and final instructions in § 9 discharge proceedings, the better practice is that judges should not charge the jury that every twelve months the petitioner has a statutory right to file a petition for examination and discharge (nor should the Commonwealth or petitioner allude to that statutory right in their presentation of the evidence). Rather, the jurors should be instructed that their responsibility is solely to determine whether the Commonwealth has met its burden of establishing that, as of the time of the hearing, the petitioner remains sexually dangerous." *Miller, petitioner*, 71 Mass. App. Ct. 625, 634–35 (2008) (citation omitted).

SECTION 9A–B
Repealed

SECTION 10–11
Repealed

SECTION 12
Notification of persons adjudicated as delinquent juveniles or youthful offender by reason of a sexual offense; petitions for classification as sexually dangerous person; hearings

(a) Any agency with jurisdiction of a person who has ever been convicted of or adjudicated as a delinquent juvenile or a youthful offender by reason of a sexual offense as defined in section 1, regardless of the reason for the current incarceration, confinement or commitment, or who has been charged with such offense but has been found incompetent to stand trial, or who has been charged with any offense, is currently incompetent to stand trial and has previously been convicted of or adjudicated as a delinquent juvenile or a youthful offender by reason of a sexual offense, shall notify in writing the district attorney of the county where the offense occurred and the attorney general six months prior to the release of such person, except that in the case of a person who is returned to prison for no more than six months as a result of a revocation of parole or who is committed for no more than

six months, such notice shall be given as soon as practicable following such person's admission to prison. In such notice, the agency with jurisdiction shall also identify those prisoners or youths who have a particularly high likelihood of meeting the criteria for a sexually dangerous person.

(b) When the district attorney or the attorney general determines that the prisoner or youth in the custody of the department of youth services is likely to be a sexually dangerous person as defined in section 1, the district attorney or the attorney general at the request of the district attorney may file a petition alleging that the prisoner or youth is a sexually dangerous person and stating sufficient facts to support such allegation in the superior court where the prisoner or youth is committed or in the superior court of the county where the sexual offense occurred.

(c) Upon the filing of a petition under this section, the court in which the petition was filed shall determine whether probable cause exists to believe that the person named in the petition is a sexually dangerous person. Such person shall be provided with notice of, and an opportunity to appear in person at, a hearing to contest probable cause.

(d) At the probable cause hearing, the person named in the petition shall have the following rights:

(1) to be represented by counsel;

(2) to present evidence on such person's behalf;

(3) to cross-examine witnesses who testify against such person; and

(4) to view and copy all petitions and reports in the court file.

(e) If the person named in the petition is scheduled to be released from jail, house of correction, prison or a facility of the department of youth services at any time prior to the court's probable cause determination, the court, upon a sufficient showing based on the evidence before the court at that time, may temporarily commit such person to the treatment center pending disposition of the petition. The person named in the petition may move the court for relief from such temporary commitment at any time prior to the probable cause determination.

NOTE 1   See Notes 1–4 following G.L. c. 123A, § 1.

NOTE 2a   **Standard of Proof for Temporary Commitment Under § 12(c).** "[T]he Commonwealth's burden of proof at the probable cause hearing under § 12(c) is the same as that required for a probable cause, or bind-over, hearing held pursuant to G.L. c. 276, § 38. It is referred to as the 'directed verdict' standard." *Commonwealth v. Bruno*, 432 Mass. 489, 509 (2000) (citation omitted).

NOTE 2b   **The *Bruno* Directed Verdict Standard.** "Taking into account the preliminary nature of the § 12(c) probable cause hearing, the screening function that the hearing performs, the substantial public safety and liberty interests that are at stake, and the need to consider not only the Commonwealth's evidence but also the cross-examination of witnesses by the defendant and any evidence he may introduce, we are of the opinion that implementation of the 'directed verdict' decision-making process requires a two-part inquiry, one part of which is quantitative and the other qualitative. The judge must be satisfied, first, that the Commonwealth's admissible evidence, if believed, satisfied all of the elements of proof necessary to prove the Commonwealth's case. Second, she must be satisfied that the evidence on each of the elements is not so incredible, insubstantial or otherwise of such a quality that no reasonable person could rely on it to conclude that the Commonwealth had met its burden of proof. The second part of the inquiry, of necessity, involves, inter alia, an assessment of credibility. In conducting this credibility assessment, the judge is not to look to whether she is herself persuaded by the evidence. Instead, the judge is to determine whether the evidence before her is of suitable quality to allow the action to proceed further along a course that was legislatively designed ultimately to place the matter before a trier of fact." *Commonwealth v. Blanchette*, 54 Mass. App. Ct. 165, 174–75 (2002).

NOTE 2c   Consideration of Credibility at Probable Cause Hearing. "The centrality of the screening function . . . can only be effectuated by an adversary hearing where the defendant is given a meaningful opportunity to challenge the credibility of the prosecution's witnesses and to raise any affirmative defenses he may have. [*Myers v. Commonwealth*, 363 Mass. 843, 852 (1973)]. What this unavoidably entails for the hearing judge is that she make some assessment of the credibility of the evidence that is presented when making the determination as to whether sufficient evidence has been presented to warrant further proceedings. This is an exercise requiring a very deft touch and considerable restraint on the part of the judge. The proceeding is a preliminary one, and the evidence, of necessity, is often quite hastily cobbled together; to expect a trial-quality presentation would be unrealistic and contrary to the role which the hearing plays in the overall scheme. The preliminary nature of the hearing—to be followed in many instances . . . by a sixty-day commitment for evaluation and then possible trial . . . —dictates that ultimate credibility determinations are ordinarily to be reserved for a subsequent trier of fact.

"[T]he judicial role in pretrial screening involves weighing and judgment rather than a wooden comparison of the testimony with the elements of the crime. Although credibility ordinarily is a matter for the jury, and it is not expected that judges will normally resolve testimonial conflicts at the preliminary hearing, cases do occasionally arise in which a witness's testimony is so weak or contradicted by sufficiently clear facts that the judge should have the power to dismiss the case. "*Myers v. Commonwealth*, 363 Mass. at 853 n.12, quoting from A Model Code of Pre-Arraignment Procedure (T.D. No. 5) at 91 (Model Code). At the same time, the judge's role remains considerably greater at such a hearing than that of the proverbial potted plant: to make the requisite determination, the judge must be permitted to consider 'the credibility of the witnesses and the quality of the evidence introduced. *Myers*, supra at 853, quoting Model Code, § 330.5(3)." *Commonwealth v. Blanchette*, 54 Mass. App. Ct. 165, 173–74 (2002) (footnotes and internal quotation marks omitted).

NOTE 3   Standard of Proof for Temporary Commitment Under § 12(e). The Commonwealth's burden at the temporary commitment hearing under § 12(e) is the probable cause to arrest standard articulated in *Jenkins v. Chief Justice of the District Court Department*, 416 Mass. 221 (1993). *Commonwealth v. Bruno*, 432 Mass. 489, 507–10 (2000).

NOTE 4   Expert Evidence at Temporary Commitment Hearing Under § 12(e). "[P]robable cause to commit a person temporarily under G.L. c. 123A, § 12(e), exists when the evidence presented, assuming it is true, is sufficient to warrant a judge in believing that the person is a sexually dangerous person. The evidence must meet this standard as to each element of proof, which includes proof that the person currently 'suffers from a mental abnormality or personality disorder which makes such person likely to engage in sexual offenses.' G.L. c. 123A, § 1. Whether a person suffers from a mental abnormality or personality defect, as well as the predictive behavioral question of the likelihood that a person suffering from such a condition will commit a sexual offense, are matters beyond the range of ordinary experience and require expert testimony."

"Because the hearing is ex parte, the expert evidence required for a temporary commitment need not be in the form of live testimony, and need not be extensive, but it must establish probable cause as to those elements of proof." *Commonwealth v. Bruno*, 432 Mass. 489, 510–11 (2000) (citations omitted).

NOTE 5   Expert Evidence at Probable Cause Hearing. Expert evidence is required at a probable cause hearing for the

same reasons it is required at a temporary commitment hearing under § 12(e). *Commonwealth v. Bruno*, 432 Mass. 489, 513 (2000).

NOTE 6   Duration of Temporary Commitment Under § 12(e) Absent Expert Evidence. "In his third reported question the judge asks how long a temporary commitment may be ordered if the Commonwealth fails to adduce expert evidence. He ruled that such a commitment may only last twenty-four hours. Wilson argues that he was correct. We agree, but caution that even a twenty-four hour commitment can be justified only on a showing that is the equivalent of probable cause to arrest. If a petition for commitment under § 12(e) is made without expert evidence meeting the requirements [set forth earlier in this opinion], it must be represented to the judge that such evidence exists, is not immediately available for presentation, but will be forthcoming." *Commonwealth v. Bruno*, 432 Mass. 489, 511 (2000) (citations omitted).

NOTE 7   Duration of Temporary Commitment Pending Hearing Under § 12(c) and (d). "The fourth reported question asks how long a person may be temporarily committed under § 12(e) pending commencement of the probable cause hearing under § 12(c) and (d). The statute does not address the matter. . . . We conclude that absent unusual circumstances, a probable cause hearing should commence no later than ten business days after a temporary commitment order is made under § 12(e)." *Commonwealth v. Bruno*, 432 Mass. 489, 511–12 (2000).

NOTE 8a   Not Applicable to Persons Serving Sentences for Crimes Not Statutorily Enumerated. In *Commonwealth v. McLeod*, 437 Mass. 286 (2002), the Supreme Judicial Court considered "whether the provisions of G.L. c. 123A, § 12, apply to persons convicted of sexual offenses who have completed and been released from those sentences but who are later serving sentences for crimes that are not statutorily enumerated 'sexual offenses.'" The court held that Section 12 does not apply in such cases.

NOTE 8b   Not Applicable to Committed Persons Not Serving Sentence and Having No Charges Pending. "Individuals who are not serving any criminal sentence and have no charges pending against them, but who have been civilly committed to Bridgewater State Hospital under G.L. c. 123, §§ 7 and 8, following a period of incarceration, are [not] subject to SDP commitment." *Commonwealth v. Gillis*, 448 Mass. 354, 355 (2007).

NOTE 8c   Custody. "We conclude that the Commonwealth may file an SDP petition under § 12 against a person who has been convicted of a sexual offense only where the person is in custody because of a criminal conviction, an adjudication as a delinquent juvenile or youthful offender, or a judicial finding that the person is incompetent to stand trial. The Commonwealth may not file such a petition where, as here, the defendant is in custody only because he is awaiting trial, unless a judge has found the defendant incompetent to stand trial." *Commonwealth v. Libby*, 472 Mass. 93, 94 (2015).

NOTE 9a   Commonwealth's Right of Appeal of Finding of No Probable Cause. "Blanchette maintains that the Commonwealth may not appeal from the judge's determination that no probable cause exists to believe he is a sexually dangerous person, basing this contention on the absence of any statutory provision expressly conferring such a right of appeal. Because we think that *Wyatt, petitioner*, 428 Mass. 347, 351 (1998), and *Hill, petitioner*, 422 Mass. 147, 151, 155, cert. denied, 519 U.S. 867 (1996), foreclose any serious contention that the Commonwealth cannot appeal, we do not further address the point other than to observe that the current incarnation of G.L. c. 123A was enacted after *Wyatt* and *Hill* and did not revoke or limit *Wyatt's* broad holding that '[t]he Commonwealth may appeal any ruling or judgment adverse to it in a c. 123A proceeding.' See *Wyatt*, supra at 351." *Commonwealth v. Blanchette*, 54 Mass. App. Ct. 165, 167 n.3 (2002).

NOTE 9b   Appeal Must Be Expeditious. "While the Commonwealth has the right to appeal from adverse rulings in c. 123A proceedings . . . , in instances involving detention beyond the discharge date, we think that, in view of [*Commonwealth v. Kennedy*,

435 Mass. 527 (2002)], it must henceforth obtain necessary transcripts and in all other respects prosecute the appeal in an expeditious fashion or risk dismissal of the appeal." *Commonwealth v. Blanchette*, 54 Mass. App. Ct. 165, 167 n.4 (2002).

NOTE 9c   Consideration of Supervised Probation During Pendency of Appeal. "[P]ending such appeals (and, in this case, during the pendency of the proceedings on remand), consideration should be given by the trial court judge in appropriate cases to devising and imposing conditions of supervised probation in lieu of detention in the Treatment Center." *Commonwealth v. Blanchette*, 54 Mass. App. Ct. 165, 167 n.4 (2002).

SECTION 13
Temporary commitment of prisoner or youth to treatment center; right to counsel; psychological examination

(a) If the court is satisfied that probable cause exists to believe that the person named in the petition is a sexually dangerous person, the prisoner or youth shall be committed to the treatment center for a period not exceeding 60 days for the purpose of examination and diagnosis under the supervision of two qualified examiners who shall, no later than 15 days prior to the expiration of said period, file with the court a written report of the examination and diagnosis and their recommendation of the disposition of the person named in the petition.

(b) The court shall supply to the qualified examiners copies of any juvenile and adult court records which shall contain, if available, a history of previous juvenile and adult offenses, previous psychiatric and psychological examinations and such other information as may be pertinent or helpful to the examiners in making the diagnosis and recommendation. The district attorney or the attorney general shall provide a narrative or police reports for each sexual offense conviction or adjudication as well as any psychiatric, psychological, medical or social worker records of the person named in the petition in the district attorney's or the attorney general's possession. The agency with jurisdiction over the person named in the petition shall provide such examiners with copies of any incident reports arising out of the person's incarceration or custody.

(c) The person named in the petition shall be entitled to counsel and, if indigent, the court shall appoint an attorney. All written documentation submitted to the two qualified examiners shall also be provided to counsel for the person named in the petition and to the district attorney and attorney general.

(d) Any person subject to an examination pursuant to the provisions of this section may retain a psychologist or psychiatrist who meets the requirements of a qualified examiner, as defined in section 1, to perform an examination on his behalf. If the person named in the petition is indigent, the court shall provide for such qualified examiner.

NOTE 1a   Strict Adherence to Time Limits Post Discharge from Criminal Sentence. "Where . . . the G.L. c. 123A proceedings are still ongoing and the defendant is detained beyond his discharge date, the liberty interests at stake compel strict adherence to the time frames set forth in the statute." *Commonwealth v. Kennedy*, 435 Mass. 527, 531 (2002) (dismissing petition for civil commitment where no qualified examiner's report was on file within the time required).

NOTE 1b   "The case before us presents a different question, namely, whether any violation of § 13(a) that results in a confinement exceeding sixty days requires dismissal of the Commonwealth's belated petition for trial. We now hold that it does, unless there are extraordinary circumstances justifying an extremely brief delay." *Commonwealth v. Parra*, 445 Mass. 262, 265 (2005).

NOTE 1c   "The sixty-day deadline in § 13(a) is mandatory to protect a defendant's liberty interest, and any delay by the Commonwealth that results in a confinement exceeding sixty days is a violation of the statute." *Commonwealth v. Alvarado*, 452 Mass. 194, 196 (2008) (citations and quotation marks omitted).

NOTE 2   Privileged Documents. "G.L. c. 123A, § 13(b), contains no authority for a judge to order the production of *privileged* documents for use by the qualified examiners." *Commonwealth v. Callahan*, 440 Mass. 436, 439 (2003). The particular privileges that were applicable in *Callahan* were the patient-psychotherapist (G.L. c. 233, § 20B) and client-social worker (G.L. c. 112, § 135B).

NOTE 3   Testimony by Examiners. "[T]o permit the defendant to offer his own expert testimony, based on personal interviews, while refusing to submit to interviews with court-appointed experts, would offend basic notions of fairness in such proceedings." *Commonwealth v. Connors*, 447 Mass. 313, 317 (2006).

NOTE 4   Counsel. "[T]here is no right to counsel at an interview with a qualified examiner under G.L. c. 123A." The court did note, however, that "[a] judge may, in his or her discretion, permit counsel to be present during a psychiatric examination." *Commonwealth v. Sargent*, 449 Mass. 576, 577, 579 n.5 (2007).

SECTION 14
Trial by jury; right to counsel; admissibility of evidence; commitment to treatment; temporary commitments pending disposition of petitions

(a) The district attorney, or the attorney general at the request of the district attorney, may petition the court for a trial. In any trial held pursuant to this section, either the person named in the petition or the petitioning party may demand, in writing, that the case be tried to a jury and, upon such demand, the case shall be tried to a jury. Such petition shall be made within 14 days of the filing of the report of the two qualified examiners. If such petition is timely filed within the allowed time, the court shall notify the person named in the petition and his attorney, the district attorney and the attorney general that a trial by jury will be held within 60 days to determine whether such person is a sexually dangerous person. The trial may be continued upon motion of either party for good cause shown or by the court on its own motion if the interests of justice so require, unless the person named in the petition will be substantially prejudiced thereby. The person named in the petition shall be confined to a secure facility for the duration of the trial.

(b) The person named in the petition shall be entitled to the assistance of counsel and shall be entitled to have counsel appointed if he is indigent in accordance with section 2 of chapter 211D. In addition, the person named in the petition may retain experts or professional persons to perform an examination on his behalf. Such experts or professional persons shall be permitted to have reasonable access to such person for the purpose of the examination as well as to all relevant medical and psychological records and reports of the person named in the petition. If the person named in the petition is indigent under said section 2 of said chapter 211D, the court shall, upon such person's request, determine whether the expert or professional services are necessary and shall determine reasonable compensation for such services. If the court so determines, the court shall assist the person named in the petition in obtaining an expert or professional person to perform an examination and participate in the trial on such person's behalf. The court shall approve payment for such services upon the filing of a certified claim for compensation supported by a written statement specifying the time expended, services rendered, expenses incurred and compensation received in the same case or for the same services from any other source. The court shall inform the person named in the petition of his rights under this section before the trial commences. The person named in the petition shall be entitled to have process issued from the court to compel the attendance of witnesses on his behalf. If such person intends to rely upon the testimony or report of his qualified examiner, the report must be filed with the court and a copy must be provided to the district attorney and attorney general no later than ten days prior to the scheduled trial.

(c) Juvenile and adult court probation records, psychiatric and psychological records and reports of the person named in the petition, including the report of any qualified examiner, as defined in section 1, and filed under this chapter, police reports relating to such person's prior sexual offenses, incident reports arising out of such person's incarceration or custody, oral or written statements prepared for and to be offered at the trial by the victims of the person who is the subject of the petition and any other evidence tending to show that such person is or is not a sexually dangerous person shall be admissible at the trial if such written information has been provided to opposing counsel reasonably in advance of trial.

(d) If after the trial, the jury finds unanimously and beyond a reasonable doubt that the person named in the petition is a sexually dangerous person, such person shall be committed to the treatment center or, if such person is a youth who has been adjudicated as a delinquent, to the department of youth services until he reaches his twenty-first birthday, and then to the treatment center for an indeterminate period of a minimum of one day and a maximum of such person's natural life until discharged pursuant to the provisions of section 9. The order of commitment, which shall be forwarded to the treatment center and to the appropriate agency with jurisdiction, shall become effective on the date of such person's parole or in all other cases, including persons sentenced to community parole supervision for life pursuant to section 133C of chapter 127, on the date of discharge from jail, the house of correction, prison or facility of the department of youth services.

(e) If the person named in the petition is scheduled to be released from jail, house of correction, prison or a facility of the department of youth services at any time prior to the final judgment, the court may temporarily commit such person to the treatment center pending disposition of the petition.

NOTE 1   Petition for Trial. Under G.L. c. 123A, § 14(a), if a petition for trial is not filed with the court within 14 days of the filing of the qualified examiner's report, the case does not proceed to trial. *Commonwealth v. Gross*, 447 Mass. 691, 694 (2006). In addition, § 14(a) requires "the filing of a distinct petition for trial after the qualified examiner's reports have been filed. A request for trial in the original § 12(b) petition, or a trial petition filed prior to the filing of the qualified examiner's reports, is not effective, as it would fail to serve all of the purposes that are to be served by the petition for trial. If the Commonwealth does not file a timely petition for trial, the case is to be dismissed." *Commonwealth v. Gross*, 447 Mass. at 700.

NOTE 2   Time limits. Under G.L. c. 123A, § 14(a), "ordinary violations of the fourteen-day deadline, like violations of the forty-five day deadline, do not result in prejudice to the defendant's liberty interest, and do not require dismissal." *Commonwealth v. Alvarado*, 452 Mass. 194, 196–97 (2008).

NOTE 3   Police Report for Offense Not Prosecuted. "In *Commonwealth v. Markvart*, [437 Mass. 331 (2002)], the Supreme Judicial Court held that a police report relating to a sexual assault by the defendant that resulted in an indictment that was later nol prossed did not constitute a police report 'relating to such person's prior sexual offenses' and, thus, was not admissible at trial under the statute. The court also stated that such a report was not admissible as 'any other evidence' tending to show that the defendant is or is not sexually dangerous as that phrase is used in G.L. c. 123A, § 14(c). *Markvart*, [437 Mass.] at 335 n.3. The portion of the police report to which objection was made here does not, as it did not in *Markvart*, 'relate to' a 'prior sexual offense' of the defendant because he had not been charged, much less convicted, of any offense involving the alleged assault on the unidentified six year old boy." *Commonwealth v. Given*, 59 Mass. App. Ct. 390, 394 (2003) (certain quotation marks omitted).

"The entire police report could be used by the experts in formulating their opinions, because the information in the report was otherwise admissible." *Commonwealth v. Given*, 59 Mass. App. Ct. at 394 n.6 (citing *Commonwealth v. Markvart*, 437 Mass. at 337).

NOTE 4   Jury waiver. "If a defendant wishes to waive his right to a jury trial and proceed jury-waived, the better practice, as for criminal cases, is for the judge to engage in a colloquy with the defendant and for the defendant to execute a written jury waiver." *Commonwealth v. Dresser*, 71 Mass. App. Ct. 454 (2008).

SECTION 15
Competence to stand trial; hearing

If a person who has been charged with a sexual offense has been found incompetent to stand trial and his commitment is sought and probable cause has been determined to exist pursuant to section 12, the court, without a jury, shall hear evidence and determine whether the person did commit the act or acts charged. The hearing on the issue of whether the person did commit the act or acts charged shall comply with all procedures specified in section 14, except with respect to trial by jury. The rules of evidence applicable in criminal cases shall apply and all rights available to criminal defendants at criminal trials, other than the right not to be tried while incompetent, shall apply. After hearing evidence the court shall make specific findings relative to whether the person did commit the act or acts charged; the extent to which the cause of the person's incompetence to stand trial affected the outcome of the hearing, including its effect on the person's ability to consult with and assist counsel and to testify on his own behalf; the extent to which the evidence could be reconstructed without the assistance of the person; and the strength of the prosecution's case. If the court finds, beyond a reasonable doubt, that the person did commit the act or acts charged, the court shall enter a final order, subject to appeal by the person named in the petition and the court may proceed to consider whether the person is a sexually dangerous person according to the procedures set forth in sections 13 and 14. Any determination made under this section shall not be admissible in any subsequent criminal proceeding.

SECTION 16
Annual reports describing treatments offered

The department of correction and the department of youth services shall annually prepare reports describing the treatment offered to each person who has been committed to the treatment center or the department of youth services as a sexually dangerous person and, without disclosing the identity of such persons, describe the treatment provided. The annual reports shall be submitted, on or before January 1, 2000 and every November 1 thereafter, to the clerk of the house of representatives and the clerk of the senate, who shall forward the same to the house and senate committees on ways and means and to the joint committee on criminal justice. The treatment center shall submit on or before December 12, 1999 its plan for the administration and management of the treatment center to the clerk of the house of representatives and the clerk of the senate, who shall forward the same to the house and senate committees on ways and means and to the joint committee on criminal justice. The treatment center shall promptly notify said committees of any modifications to said plan.

Chapter 131. Inland Fisheries and Game and Other Natural Resources

SECTION 80A
Leghold traps and certain other devices restricted; punishment

Notwithstanding any other provision of this chapter, a person shall not use, set, place, maintain, manufacture or possess any trap for the purpose of capturing furbearing mammals, except for common type mouse and rat traps, nets, and box or cage type traps, as otherwise permitted by law. A box or cage type trap is one that confines the whole animal without grasping any part of the animal, including Hancock or Bailey's type live trap for beavers. Other than nets and common type mouse or rat traps, traps designed to capture and hold a furbearing mammal by gripping the mammal's body, or body part are prohibited, including steel jaw leghold traps, padded leghold traps, and snares.

The above provision shall not apply to the use of prohibited devices by federal and state departments of health or municipal boards of health for the purpose of protection from threats to human health and safety. A threat to human health and safety may include, but shall not be limited to:

(a) beaver or muskrat occupancy of a public water supply;

(b) beaver or muskrat-caused flooding of drinking water wells, well fields or water pumping stations;

(c) beaver or muskrat-caused flooding of sewage beds, septic systems or sewage pumping stations;

(d) beaver or muskrat-caused flooding of a public or private way, driveway, railway or airport runway or taxi-way;

(e) beaver or muskrat-caused flooding of electrical or gas generation plants or transmission or distribution structures or facilities, telephone or other communications facilities or other public utilities;

(f) beaver or muskrat-caused flooding affecting the public use of hospitals, emergency clinics, nursing homes, homes for the elderly or fire stations;

(g) beaver or muskrat-caused flooding affecting hazardous waste sites or facilities, incineration or resource recovery plants or other structures or facilities whereby flooding may result in the release or escape of hazardous or noxious materials or substances;

(h) the gnawing, chewing, entering, or damage to electrical or gas generation, transmission or distribution equipment, cables, alarm systems or facilities by any beaver or muskrat;

(i) beaver or muskrat-caused flooding or structural instability on property owned by the applicant if such animal problem poses an imminent threat of substantial property damage or income loss, which shall be limited to: (1) flooding of residential, commercial, industrial or commercial buildings or facilities; (2) flooding of or access to commercial agricultural lands which prevents normal agricultural practices from being conducted on such lands; (3) reduction in the production of an agricultural crop caused by flooding or compromised structural stability of commercial agricultural lands; (4) flooding of residential lands in which the municipal board of health, its chair or agent or the state or federal department of health has determined a threat to human health and safety exists. The department of environmental protection shall make any determination of a threat to a public water supply.

An applicant or his duly authorized agent may apply to the municipal board of health for an emergency permit to immediately alleviate a threat to human health and safety, as defined in the previous paragraph. If the municipal board of health determines that such a threat exists, it shall immediately issue said emergency permit to alleviate the existing threat to human health and safety, for a period not exceeding ten days. If denied, the applicant or his duly authorized agent may appeal said emergency permit application to the state department of public health or director. If the state department of public health or director determines that such a threat exists, it shall immediately issue said emergency permit to alleviate the existing threat to human health and safety, for a period not exceeding ten days.

The aforementioned emergency permit authorizes the applicant or his duly authorized agent to immediately remedy the threat to human health and safety by one or more of the following options: (a) the use of conibear or box or cage-type traps, subject to the regulations promulgated by the division; (b) the breaching of dams, dikes, bogs or berms, so-called, subject to determinations and conditions of municipal conservation commissions under section 40; and (c) employing any nonlethal management or water-flow devices, subject to determinations and conditions of municipal conservation commissions under section 40.

If said threat to human health and safety has not been alleviated within said ten days, the applicant or his duly authorized agent in conjunction with the municipal board of health, shall apply to the director for an extension permit to continue the use of alleviation techniques, specified in this section, for a period not exceeding 30 days. If the director determines that such a threat to human health or safety exists, as defined in this section, the director shall immediately issue an extension permit.

If the director determines that said extension permit should be continued for 30 days, the director shall within 30 days of such decision develop, with the assistance of the applicant or his duly authorized agent, municipal board of health and municipal conservation commission, a plan to abate the beaver or muskrat problem using alternative, nonlethal management techniques in combination with water-flow devices, where possible, subject to the determinations and conditions of municipal conservation commissions under section 40, and if necessary, box and cage type-traps in order to provide a long-term solution. The director shall take reasonable steps to implement the plan within this 30-day period.

Compliance with the provisions of any or all of the previous four paragraphs shall not preclude the applicant or his duly authorized agent from applying to the municipal board of health for an additional emergency permit, provided the applicant (a) states in writing that there exists on the property an animal problem which poses a threat to human health and safety, as defined in this section, which cannot reasonably be abated by the use of alternative, nonlethal management techniques or box or cage traps, and that the applicant has attempted to abate the animal problem using alternative, nonlethal management techniques or box or cage traps, or (b) is awaiting the director's approval for an extension permit.

An applicant or his duly authorized agent under clause (b) shall be eligible for only two additional emergency permits, the first of which shall entitle the applicant or his duly authorized agent the use of all or any of the alleviation techniques previously allowed under the initial emergency permit. Said first additional emergency permit shall expire in ten days. If the director still has not acted within this ten day period, the applicant or his duly authorized agent shall be eligible for a second additional emergency permit. Said second additional emergency permit shall entitle the applicant or his duly authorized agent the use of all alleviation techniques previously allowed in this section, except for the use of conibear traps. The second additional emergency permit shall expire on the rendering of a decision by the director regarding the extension permit.

The division shall provide a report annually to the joint committee on natural resources and agriculture on the creation, implementation and efficiency of such animal problem plans.

A person or his duly authorized agent may apply to the director for a special permit to use otherwise prohibited traps on property owned by such person. Issuance of such special permits shall be governed by rules and regulations adopted by the director pursuant to chapter 30A. Such rules and regulations shall include, but not be limited to, provisions relative to the following:

The applicant shall apply to the director in writing and shall state that there exists on the property an animal problem which cannot be reasonably abated by the use of traps other than those prohibited by this section, and that the applicant has attempted to abate the problem using traps permitted under this section. If the director determines that the applicant has complied with sections 37 and 80, if required to do so, and any other laws regarding trapping, and that such an animal problem exists which cannot reasonably be abated by the use of alternative, nonlethal management techniques or traps other than those prohibited by this section, the director may authorize the use, setting, placing or maintenance of such traps, not including leghold traps, for a period not exceeding 30 days during which time the applicant shall remain in compliance with the procedures for obtaining a special permit as set forth in regulations adopted pursuant to this section.

Whoever violates any provisions of this section, or any rule or regulation made under the authority thereof, shall be punished by a fine of not less than $300 nor more than $1,000, or by imprisonment for not more than six months, or by both such fine and imprisonment for each trap possessed, used, set, placed, maintained, or manufactured. Each day of violation shall constitute a separate offense. A person found guilty of, or convicted of, or assessed in any manner after a plea of nolo contendere, or penalized for, a second violation of this section shall surrender to an officer authorized to enforce this chapter any trapping license and problem animal control permit issued to such person and shall be barred forever from obtaining a trapping license and a problem animal control permit.

NOTE   "The defendant was charged . . . with using a 'steel jaw leghold trap' in violation of G.L. c. 131, § 80A (1986 ed.). Pursuant to Mass.R.Crim.P. 13, 379 Mass. 871 (1978), the defendant moved to dismiss the complaint arguing that his trap, a Woodstream Soft Catch Trapping System, is not a 'steel jaw leghold trap' prohibited by § 80A. After hearing argument on the motion, examining the trap in question, and reviewing the affidavits and memoranda of law submitted by the parties, the District Court judge found that the 'soft catch trapping system' is not a 'steel jaw leghold trap' and it is not designed to cause injury or suffering to the trapped animal, and therefore granted the defendant's motion to dismiss. The Commonwealth appealed the dismissal pursuant to Mass.R.Crim.P. 15 (a), 378 Mass. 882 (1979). We transferred the case here on our own motion. We affirm." *Commonwealth v. Black*, 403 Mass. 675, 676–77 (1989) (footnotes omitted).

Chapter 138. Alcoholic Liquors

Section

34	Sale, delivery or furnishing alcoholic beverages to persons under twenty-one years of age; employment of persons under eighteen years of age
34A	Persons under twenty-one years; purchase or attempt to purchase alcoholic beverages
34B	Liquor purchase identification cards
34C	Minors; operation of motor vehicle containing alcoholic beverage; suspension of driver's license
34D	Posting notices of penalties for driving while under influence and driving while drinking from open container of alcohol
35	Omitted
36	Analysis of alcoholic beverages by department of public health
37	Certificate accompanying sample of beverages to be analyzed; contents

SECTION 34
Sale, delivery or furnishing alcoholic beverages to persons under twenty-one years of age; employment of persons under eighteen years of age

No person shall receive a license or permit under this chapter who is under 21 years of age. Whoever makes a sale or delivery of any alcoholic beverage or alcohol to any person under 21 years of age, either for his own use or for the use of his parent or any other person, or whoever, being a patron of an establishment licensed under section 12 or 15, delivers or procures to be delivered in any public room or area of such establishment if licensed under section 12, 15, 19B, 19C or 19D or in any area of such establishment if licensed under said section 15, 19B, 19C or 19D any such beverages or alcohol to or for use by a person who he knows or has reason to believe is under 21 years of age or whoever procures any such beverage or alcohol for a person under 21 years of age in any establishment licensed under section 12 or procures any such beverage or alcohol for a person under 21 years of age who is not his child, ward or spouse in any establishment licensed under said section 15, 19B, 19C or 19D or whoever furnishes any such beverage or alcohol for a person under 21 years of age shall be punished by a fine of not more than $2,000 or by imprisonment for not more than one year or both. For the purpose of this section the word "furnish" shall mean to knowingly or intentionally supply, give, or provide to or allow a person under 21 years of age except for the children and grandchildren of the person being charged to possess alcoholic beverages on premises or property owned or controlled by the person charged. Nothing in this section shall be construed to prohibit any person licensed under this chapter from employing any person 18 years of age or older for the direct handling or selling of alcoholic beverages or alcohol.

Notwithstanding the provisions of clause (14) of section 62 of chapter 149, a licensee under this chapter may employ a person under the age of 18 who does not directly handle, sell, mix or serve alcohol or alcoholic beverages.

NOTE   **Age of Defendant.** Age is not a limiting factor under § 34; a defendant may be charged with furnishing alcohol to a person under twenty-one even if the defendant himself is under the age of twenty-one. *Commonwealth v. Kneram*, 63 Mass. App. Ct. 371 (2005).

SECTION 34A
Persons under twenty-one years; purchase or attempt to purchase alcoholic beverages

Any person under twenty-one years of age who purchases or attempts to purchase alcoholic beverages or alcohol, or makes arrangements with any person to purchase or in any way procure such beverages, or who willfully misrepresents his age, or in any way alters, defaces or otherwise falsifies his identification offered as proof of age, with the intent of purchasing alcoholic beverages, either for his own use or for the use of any other person shall be punished by a fine of three hundred dollars and whoever knowingly makes a false statement as to the age of a person who is under twenty-one years of age in order to procure a sale or delivery of such beverages or alcohol to such person under twenty-one years of age, either for the use of the person under twenty-one years of age or for the use of some other person, and whoever induces a person under twenty-one years of age to make a false statement as to his age in order to procure a sale or delivery of such beverages or alcohol to such person under twenty-one years of age, shall be punished by a fine of three hundred dollars. A conviction of a violation of this section shall be reported forthwith to the registrar of motor vehicles by the court. Upon receipt of such notice the registrar shall thereupon suspend for 180 days the defendant's license or right to operate a motor vehicle.

The commission shall prepare and distribute to business establishments which sell, serve or otherwise dispense alcohol or alcoholic beverages to the general public, posters to be displayed therein in a conspicuous place. Said posters shall contain a summary and explanation of this section.

SECTION 34B
Liquor purchase identification cards
(Amended by 2012 Mass. Acts c. 170, §§ 2–3, effective Oct. 28, 2012.)

Any person who shall have attained age twenty-one and does not hold a valid operator's license issued by the registry of motor vehicles, pursuant to section eight of chapter ninety, may apply for a liquor purchase identification card. Such cards shall be valid for five years and shall be issued by the registry of motor vehicles pursuant to regulations prescribed by the registrar with the advice of the commission and shall bear the name, signature, date of birth, address and photograph of such person. The registry of motor vehicles shall require payment of a twenty-five dollar fee for any card issued pursuant to this section.

Any licensee, or agent or employee thereof, under this chapter who reasonably relies on such a liquor purchase identification card or motor vehicle license issued pursuant to section eight of chapter ninety or on an identification card issued under section 8E of chapter 90, or on a valid passport issued by the United States government, or by the government, recognized by the United States government, of a foreign country, or a valid United States issued military identification card, for proof of a person's identity and age shall not suffer any modification, suspension, revocation or cancellation or such license, nor shall he suffer any criminal liability, for delivering or selling alcohol of alcoholic beverages to a person under twenty-one years of age. Any licensee, or agent or employee thereof, under this chapter, who reasonably relies on such a liquor purchase identification card, or an identification card issued under section 8E of chapter 90, or motor vehicle license issued pursuant to said section eight, for proof of a person's identity and age shall be presumed to have exercised due care in making such delivery or sale of alcohol or alcoholic beverages to a person under twenty-one years of age. Such presumption shall be rebuttable; provided, however, that nothing contained herein shall affect the applicability of section sixty-nine.

Any person in a licensed premises shall, upon request of an agent of the commission or the local licensing authorities, state his name, age, and address. Whoever, upon such request, refuses to state his name, age or address, or states a false name, age, or address, including a name or address which is not his name or address in ordinary use, shall be guilty of a misdemeanor and shall be punished by a fine of not more than five hundred dollars.

Any person who transfers, alters or defaces any such card or license, or who makes, uses, carries, sells or distributes a false identification card or license, or uses the identification card or motor vehicle license of another, or furnishes false information in obtaining such card or license, shall be guilty of a misdemeanor and shall be punished by a fine of not more than two hundred dollars or by imprisonment for not more than three months.

Any person who is discovered by a police officer or special police officer in the act of violating the provisions of this section may be arrested without a warrant by such police officer or special police officer and held in custody, in jail or otherwise, until a complaint is made against him for such offense, which complaint shall be made as soon as practicable and in any case within twenty-four hours, Sundays and legal holidays excepted.

NOTE   **Registry of Motor Vehicles License Suspension.** Upon belief, after a hearing, that an individual has committed a violation under this section, the Registry of Motor Vehicles may suspend the defendant's license or right to operate. G.L. c. 90,

§ 22(e). Upon notice of a conviction of a violation under this section, the Registry of Motor Vehicles is required to immediately suspend the defendant's license or right to operate. G.L. c. 90, § 22(e).

SECTION 34C
Minors; operation of motor vehicle containing alcoholic beverage; suspension of driver's license

Whoever, being under twenty-one years of age and not accompanied by a parent or legal guardian, knowingly possesses, transports or carries on his person, any alcohol or alcoholic beverages, shall be punished by a fine of not more than fifty dollars for the first offense and not more than one hundred and fifty dollars for a second or subsequent offense; provided, however, that this section shall not apply to a person between the age of eighteen and twenty-one who knowingly possesses, transports or carries on his person, alcohol or alcoholic beverages in the course of his employment. A police officer may arrest without a warrant any person who violates this section. A conviction of a violation of this section shall be reported forthwith to the registrar of motor vehicles by the court, and said registrar shall thereupon suspend for a period of ninety days the license of such person to operate a motor vehicle.

SECTION 34D
Posting notices of penalties for driving while under influence and driving while drinking from open container of alcohol

Any establishment which sells alcoholic beverages to be drunk on the premises, shall post a copy of the penalties set forth in subdivision (1) of section twenty-four of chapter ninety for driving under the influence. Any establishment which sells alcoholic beverages not to be drunk on the premises shall post a copy of the penalties set forth in section twenty-four I of said chapter ninety for operating a motor vehicle while drinking from an open container of alcohol. Said copies shall be posted conspicuously by the owner or person in charge of the respective establishment, and whoever violates this provision shall be punished by a fine of not more than fifty dollars. Any person unlawfully removing a copy so posted shall be punished by a fine of fifty dollars. Said copies, printed in letters not less in size than eighteen point capitals, boldface, shall be prepared by the commission and distributed to business establishments which sell, serve or otherwise dispense alcohol or alcoholic beverages to the general public.

SECTION 35
Omitted

SECTION 36
Analysis of alcoholic beverages by department of public health
(Amended by 2012 Mass. Acts c. 139, § 123, effective July 1, 2012.)

The analyst or assistant analyst of the department of state police shall upon request make, free of charge, an analysis of all alcoholic beverages sent to it by the licensing authorities or by police officers or other officers authorized by law to make seizures of alcoholic beverages, if the department is satisfied that the analysis requested is to be used in connection with the enforcement of the laws of the commonwealth. The said department shall return to such police or other officers, as soon as may be, a certificate, signed by the analyst or assistant analyst making such analysis, of the percentage of alcohol which such samples of beverages contain, and, if the commission so requests, of the composition and quality of such beverages as shown by the samples submitted. Such certificate shall be prima facie evidence of the composition and quality of the alcoholic beverages to which it relates, and the court may take judicial notice of the signature of the analyst or the assistant analyst, and of the fact that he is such.

SECTION 37
Certificate accompanying sample of beverages to be analyzed; contents
(Amended by 2012 Mass. Acts c. 139, § 124, effective July 1, 2012.)

A certificate shall accompany each sample of beverages sent for analysis by an officer to the department of state police stating from whom the beverages were seized, the date of the seizure and the name and residence of the officer who seized said beverages. Said department shall note upon said certificate the date of the receipt and the analysis of said alcoholic beverages and the percentage of the alcohol or the composition and quality of said beverages, as the case may be, as required by section thirty-six on a form prescribed by said department of state police.

Chapter 140. Licenses

Section

121	Firearms sales; definitions; antique firearms; application of law; exceptions
121A	Identification of firearms; certificate by ballistics expert as prima facie evidence
122	Licenses; contents; fingerprints of applicants; procedure on refusal of license; fees; punishment for improper issuance
122A	Record of licenses; notice to department of criminal justice information services; sales record books
122B	Sale of ammunition; license; fees; rules and regulations; refusal, suspension or revocation of license; judicial review; penalties
122C	Self-defense spray; licensing; possession; fine
122D	Purchase and possession of self-defense spray; persons prohibited
123	Conditions of licenses
124	Term of licenses
125	Forfeiture or suspension of licenses; notice
126	Placards, signs or advertisements; prima facie evidence
127	Transfer of licenses
128	Penalty for violation of statute on selling, renting or leasing weapons; evidence on sale of machine gun
128A	Application of Sec. 128
128B	Unauthorized purchase of firearms; report to commissioner; penalties
129	Fictitious name or address and other false information; penalties
129A	Repealed
129B	Firearm identification cards; conditions and restrictions
129C	Application of Sec. 129B; ownership or possession of firearms or ammunition; transfers; report to commissioner; exemptions; exhibiting license to carry, etc. on demand
129D	Surrender of firearms and ammunition to licensing authority upon denial of application for, or revocation of, identification card or license; right to transfer; sale by colonel of state police; rules and regulations
130	Sale or furnishing weapons or ammunition to aliens or minors; penalty; exceptions
130½	Furnishing weapons to minors for hunting, recreation

130A   Repealed
130B   Firearm licensing review board; members; license applicants; hearings
131   License to carry firearms; Class A and B; conditions and restrictions
131½   Gun control advisory board
131¾   Roster of large capacity rifles, shotguns, firearms, and feeding devices
131A   Permits to purchase, rent or lease firearms, or to purchase ammunition; fee; penalties
131B   Penalty for loan of money secured by weapons
131C   Carrying of firearms in a vehicle
131D   Repealed
131E   Purchase by residents; licenses; firearm identification cards; purchase for use of another; penalties; revocation of licenses or cards; reissuance
131F   Nonresidents or aliens; temporary license to carry firearms or ammunition
131F½   Theatrical productions; carrying firearms and blank ammunition
131G   Carrying of firearms by nonresidents; conditions
131H   Ownership or possession of firearms by aliens; penalties; seizure and disposition
131I   Falsifying firearm license or identification card; penalty
131J   Sale or possession of electrical weapons; penalties
131K   Firearms or large capacity weapons without safety devices; liability
131L   Weapons stored or kept by owner; inoperable by any person other than owner or lawfully authorized user; punishment
131M   Assault weapon or large capacity feeding device not lawfully possessed on September 13, 1994; sale, transfer or possession; punishment
131N   Covert weapons; sale, transfer or possession; punishment
131O   Colonel of state police; statewide firearms surrender program
131P   Basic firearms safety certificate; instructors
131Q   Firearm used to carry out criminal act, tracing to licensing authority, reporting of statistical data
185A   Resale of tickets; necessity, term and transfer of license; information in application; definition of resale; restrictions

SALE OF FIREARMS

SECTION 121
Firearms sales; definitions; antique firearms; application of law; exceptions
(Amended by 2014 Mass. Acts c. 284, §§ 20–21, effective Aug. 11, 2014; 2014 Mass. Acts c. 284, § 19, effective Jan. 1, 2015.)

As used in sections 122 to 131Q, inclusive, the following words shall, unless the context clearly requires otherwise, have the following meanings:—

"Ammunition", cartridges or cartridge cases, primers (igniter), bullets or propellant powder designed for use in any firearm, rifle or shotgun. The term "ammunition" shall also mean tear gas cartridges.

"Assault weapon", shall have the same meaning as a semiautomatic assault weapon as defined in the federal Public Safety and Recreational Firearms Use Protection Act, 18 U.S.C. section 921(a)(30), as appearing in such section on September 13, 1994 and shall include, but not be limited to, any of the weapons, or copies or duplicates of the weapons, of any caliber, known as: (i) Avtomat Kalishnikov (AK) (all models); (ii) Action Arms Israeli Military Industries UZI and Galil; (iii) Beretta Ar70 (SC-70); (iv) Colt AR-15; (v) Fabrique National FN/FAL, FN/LAR and FNC; (vi) SWD M-10, M-11, M-11/9 and M-12; (vi) Steyr AUG; (vii) INTRATEC TEC-9, TEC-DC9 and TEC-22; and (viii) revolving cylinder shotguns, such as, or similar to, the Street Sweeper and Striker 12; provided, however, that the term assault weapon shall not include: (i) any of the weapons, or replicas or duplicates of such weapons, specified in appendix A to 18 U.S.C. section 922, as appearing in such appendix on September 13, 1994 as such weapons were manufactured on October 1, 1993; (ii) any weapon that is operated by manual bolt, pump, lever of slide action; (iii) any weapon that has been rendered permanently inoperable or otherwise rendered permanently unable to be designated a semiautomatic assault weapon; (iv) any weapon that was manufactured prior to the year 1899; (v) any weapon that is an antique or relic, theatrical prop or other weapon that is not capable of firing a projectile and which is not intended for use as a functional weapon and cannot be readily modified through a combination of available parts into an operable assault weapon; (vi) any semiautomatic rifle that cannot accept a detachable magazine that holds more than five rounds of ammunition; or (vii) any semiautomatic shotgun that cannot hold more than five rounds of ammunition in a fixed or detachable magazine.

"Conviction", a finding or verdict of guilt or a plea of guilty, whether or not final sentence is imposed.

"Deceptive weapon device", any device that is intended to convey the presence of a rifle, shotgun or firearm that is used in the commission of a violent crime, as defined in this section, and which presents an objective threat of immediate death or serious bodily harm to a person of reasonable and average sensibility.

"Firearm", a pistol, revolver or other weapon of any description, loaded or unloaded, from which a shot or bullet can be discharged and of which the length of the barrel or barrels is less than 16 inches or 18 inches in the case of a shotgun as originally manufactured; provided, however, that the term firearm shall not include any weapon that is: (i) constructed in a shape that does not resemble a handgun, short-barreled rifle or short-barreled shotgun including, but not limited to, covert weapons that resemble key-chains, pens, cigarette-lighters or cigarette-packages; or (ii) not detectable as a weapon or potential weapon by x-ray machines commonly used at airports or walk-through metal detectors.

"Gunsmith", any person who engages in the business of repairing, altering, cleaning, polishing, engraving, blueing or performing any mechanical operation on any firearm, rifle, shotgun or machine gun.

"Imitation firearm", any weapon which is designed, manufactured or altered in such a way as to render it incapable of discharging a shot or bullet.

"Large capacity feeding device", (i) a fixed or detachable magazine, box, drum, feed strip or similar device capable of accepting, or that can be readily converted to accept, more than ten rounds of ammunition or more than five shotgun shells; or (ii) a large capacity ammunition feeding device as defined in the federal Public Safety and Recreational Firearms Use Protections Act, 18 U.S.C. section 921(a)(31) as appearing in such section on September 13, 1994. The term "large capacity feeding device" shall not include an attached tubular device designed to accept, and capable of operating only with, .22 caliber ammunition.

"Large capacity weapon", any firearm, rifle or shotgun: (i) that is semiautomatic with a fixed large capacity feeding device; (ii) that is semiautomatic and capable of accepting, or readily modifiable to accept, any detachable large capacity feeding device; (iii) that employs a rotating cylinder capable of accepting more than ten rounds of ammunition in a rifle or firearm and more than five shotgun shells in the case of a shotgun or firearm; or (iv) that is an assault weapon. The term "large capacity weapon" shall be a secondary designation and shall apply to a weapon in addition to its primary designation as a firearm, rifle or shotgun and shall not include: (i) any weapon that was manufactured in or prior to the year 1899; (ii) any weapon that operates by manual bolt, pump, lever or slide action; (iii) any weapon that is a single-shot weapon; (iv) any weapon that has been modified so as to render it permanently inoperable or otherwise rendered permanently unable to be designated a large capacity weapon; or (v) any weapon that is an antique or relic, theatrical prop or other weapon that is not capable of firing a projectile and which is not intended for use as a functional weapon and cannot be readily modified through a combination of available parts into an operable large capacity weapon.

"Length of barrel" or "barrel length", that portion of a firearm, rifle, shotgun or machine gun through which a shot or bullet is drive, guided or stabilized and shall include the chamber.

"Licensing authority", the chief of police or the board or officer having control of the police in a city or town, or persons authorized by them.

"Machine gun", a weapon of any description, by whatever name known, loaded or unloaded, from which a number of shots or bullets may be rapidly or automatically discharged by one continuous activation of the trigger, including a sub-machine gun.

"Purchase" and "sale" shall include exchange; the word "purchaser" shall include exchanger; and the verbs "sell" and "purchase", in their different forms and tenses, shall include the verb exchange in its appropriate form and tense.

"Rifle", a weapon having a rifled bore with a barrel length equal to or greater than 16 inches and capable of discharging a shot or bullet for each pull of the trigger.

"Sawed-off shotgun", any weapon made from a shotgun, whether by alteration, modification or otherwise, if such weapon as modified has one or more barrels less than 18 inches in length or as modified has an overall length of less than 26 inches.

"Semiautomatic", capable of utilizing a portion of the energy of a firing cartridge to extract the fired cartridge case and chamber the next round, and requiring a separate pull of the trigger to fire each cartridge.

"Shotgun", a weapon having a smooth bore with a barrel length equal to or greater than 18 inches with an overall length equal to or greater than 26 inches, and capable of discharging a shot or bullet for each pull of the trigger.

"Violent crime", shall mean any crime punishable by imprisonment for a term exceeding one year, or any act of juvenile delinquency involving the use or possession of a deadly weapon that would be punishable by imprisonment for such term if committed by an adult, that: (i) has as an element the use, attempted use or threatened use of physical force or a deadly weapon against the person of another; (ii) is burglary, extortion, arson or kidnapping; (iii) involves the use of explosives; or (iv) otherwise involves conduct that presents a serious risk of physical injury to another.

"Weapon", any rifle, shotgun or firearm.

Where the local licensing authority has the power to issue licenses of cards under this chapter, but no such licensing authority exists, any resident or applicant may apply for such license or firearm identification card directly to the colonel of state police and said colonel shall for this purpose be the licensing authority.

The provisions of sections 122 to 129D, inclusive, and sections 131, 131A, 131B and 131E shall not apply to:

(A) any firearm, rifle or shotgun manufactured in or prior to the year 1899;

(B) any replica of any firearm, rifle or shotgun described in clause (A) if such replica: (i) is not designed or redesigned for using rimfire or conventional centerfire fixed ammunition; or (ii) uses rimfire or conventional centerfire fixed ammunition which is no longer manufactured in the United States and which is not readily available in the ordinary channels of commercial trade; and

(C) manufacturers or wholesalers of firearms, rifles, shotguns or machine guns.

NOTE   **Related statutes.** G.L. c. 269, § 10 (see Notes there) and G.L. c. 269, §§ 12–12E.

SECTION 121A
Identification of firearms; certificate by ballistics expert as prima facie evidence

A certificate by a ballistics expert of the department of the state police or of the city of Boston of the result of an examination made by him of an item furnished him by any police officer, signed and sworn to by such expert, shall be prima facie evidence of his findings as to whether or not the item furnished is a firearm, rifle, shotgun, machine gun, sawed off shotgun or ammunition, as defined by section one hundred and twenty-one, provided that in order to qualify as an expert under this section he shall have previously qualified as an expert in a court proceeding.

SECTION 122
Licenses; contents; fingerprints of applicants; procedure on refusal of licenses; fees; punishment for improper issuance

The chief of police or the board or officer having control of the police in a city or town, or persons authorized by them, may, after an investigation into the criminal history of the applicant to determine eligibility for a license under this section, grant a license to any person except an alien, a minor, a person who has been adjudicated a youthful offender, as defined in section fifty-two of chapter one hundred and nineteen, including those who have not received an adult sentence, or a person who has been convicted of a felony or of the unlawful use, possession or sale of narcotic or harmful drugs, to sell, rent or lease firearms, rifles, shotguns or machine guns, or to be in business as a gunsmith. Every license shall specify the street and number of the building where the business is to be carried on, and the license shall not protect a licensee who carries on his business in any other place. The licensing authority to whom such application is made shall cause one copy of said applicant's fingerprints to be forwarded to the department of the state police, who shall within a reasonable time thereafter advise such authority in writing of any criminal record of the applicant. The taking of fingerprints shall not be required in issuing a renewal of a license, if the fingerprints of said applicant are on file with the department of the state police. The licensing authority to whom such application is made shall cause one copy of such application to be forwarded to the commissioner of the department of criminal justice information services. Any person refused a license under this section may within ten days thereafter apply to the colonel of state police for such license, who may direct that said licensing authorities grant said license, if, after a hearing, he is satisfied there were no reasonable grounds for the refusal to grant such license and that the applicant was not barred by the provisions of law from holding such a license. The fee for an application for a license issued under this section shall be $100, which shall be payable to the licensing authority and shall not be prorated or refunded in case of revocation or denial. The licensing authority shall retain $25 of the fee; $50 of the fee shall be deposited into the general fund of the commonwealth; and $25 of the fee shall be deposited in the Firearms Fingerprint Identity Verification Trust Fund. A person licensed to sell, rent or lease firearms, rifles, shotguns or machine guns shall not be assessed any additional fee for a gunsmith's license. Whoever knowingly issues a license in violation of this section shall be punished by imprisonment for not less than six months nor more than two years in a jail or house of correction.

NOTE   See Note 2 following G.L. c. 276, § 100A.

SECTION 122A
Record of licenses; notice to department of criminal justice information services; sales record books

The licensing authority, under section one hundred and twenty-two, shall record all issued licenses in books, forms or electronic files kept for that purpose, and upon the granting of any such license or renewal thereof or renewal of an expired license shall send notice thereof to the department of criminal justice information services in a manner prescribed by the commissioner of the department of criminal justice information services; provided, however, that said executive director shall promulgate rules and regulations to ensure the prompt collection, exchange, dissemination, and distribution of such license information. The commissioner of the department of criminal justice information services, upon the application of the licensee, at a price not in excess of the cost thereof, shall furnish said licensee with the necessary sales record books to be kept by him as provided in section one hundred and twenty-three.

SECTION 122B
Sale of ammunition; license; fees; rules and regulations; refusal, suspension or revocation of license; judicial review; penalties

No person shall sell ammunition in the commonwealth unless duly licensed. The chief of police or the board or officer having control of the police in a city or town, or persons authorized by them, may, after an investigation into the criminal history of the applicant to determine eligibility to be licensed under this section, grant a license to any person, except an alien, a minor, a person who has been adjudicated a youthful offender, as defined in section fifty-two of chapter one hundred and nineteen, including those who have not received an adult sentence, or a person who has been convicted of a felony in any state or federal jurisdiction, or of the unlawful use, possession or sale of narcotic or harmful drugs, to sell ammunition. Every license shall specify the street and number, if any, of the building where the business is to be carried on. The licensing authority to whom such application is made shall cause one copy of the application to be forwarded to the commissioner of the department of criminal justice information services, who shall within a reasonable time thereafter advise such authority in writing of any crimi-

nal record disqualifying the applicant. The fee for an application for a license to sell ammunition shall be $100, which shall be payable to the licensing authority and shall not be prorated or refunded in case of revocation or denial. The licensing authority shall retain $25 of the fee; $50 of the fee shall be deposited into the general fund of the commonwealth; and $25 of the fee shall be deposited in the Firearms Fingerprint Identity Verification Trust Fund. The licensing authority to whom such application is made shall cause one copy of any approved application to be forwarded to the commissioner of the department of criminal justice information services.

Any lawfully incorporated sporting or shooting club shall, upon application, be licensed to sell or supply ammunition for regulated shooting on their premises, as for skeet, target or trap shooting; provided, however, that such club license shall, in behalf of said club, be issued to and exercised by an officer or duly authorized member of the club who himself possesses a firearm identification card or a license to carry a firearm and who would not be disqualified to receive a license to sell ammunition in his own right. The licensing authority may revoke or suspend a license to sell ammunition for violation of any provision of this chapter.

The secretary of the executive office of public safety may establish such rules and regulations as he may deem necessary to carry out the provisions of this section.

Any person refused a license under this section or once issued a license under this section has had said license suspended or revoked may obtain a judicial review of such refusal, suspension or revocation by filing within thirty days of such refusal, suspension or revocation a petition for review thereof in the district court having jurisdiction in the city or town in which the applicant filed for such license, and a justice of said court, after a hearing, may direct that a license be issued the applicant if satisfied there was no reasonable ground for refusing such license and that the applicant was not prohibited by law from holding the same.

Whoever not being licensed, as hereinbefore provided, sells ammunition within the commonwealth shall be punished by a fine of not less than five hundred nor more than one thousand dollars or by imprisonment for not less than six months nor more than two years.

NOTE   See Note 2 following G.L. c. 276, § 100A.

SECTION 122C
Self-defense spray; licensing; possession; fine
(Added by 2014 Mass. Acts c. 284, § 22, effective Aug. 11, 2014.)

(a) As used in this section and section 122D, "self-defense spray" shall mean chemical mace, pepper spray or any device or instrument which contains, propels or emits a liquid, gas, powder or other substance designed to incapacitate.

(b) Whoever, not being licensed as provided in section 122B, sells self-defense spray shall be punished by a fine of not more than $1,000 or by imprisonment in a house of correction for not more than 2 years.

(c) Whoever sells self-defense spray to a person younger than 18 years of age, if the person younger than 18 years of age does not have a firearms identification card, shall be punished by a fine of not more than $300.

(d) A person under 18 years of age who possesses self-defense spray and who does not have a firearms identification card shall be punished by a fine of not more than $300.

1

SECTION 122D
Purchase and possession of self-defense spray; persons prohibited
(Added by 2014 Mass. Acts c. 284, § 22, effective Aug. 11, 2014.)

No person shall purchase or possess self-defense spray who:

(i) in a court of the commonwealth, has been convicted or adjudicated a youthful offender or delinquent child as defined in section 52 of chapter 119 for the commission of: (A) a felony; (B) a misdemeanor punishable by imprisonment for more than 2 years; (C) a violent crime as defined in section 121; (D) a violation of a law regulating the use, possession, ownership, transfer, purchase, sale, lease, rental, receipt or transportation of weapons or ammunition for which a term of imprisonment may be imposed; or (E) a violation of a law regulating the use, possession or sale of a controlled substance as defined in section 1 of chapter 94C including, but not limited to, a violation under said chapter 94C; provided, however, that except for the commission of a violent crime or a crime involving the trafficking of controlled substances, if the person has been so convicted or adjudicated or released from confinement, probation or parole supervision for such conviction or adjudication, whichever occurs last, for 5 or more years immediately preceding the purchase or possession, that person may purchase or possess self-defense spray;

(ii) in another state or federal jurisdiction, has been convicted or adjudicated a youthful offender or delinquent child for the commission of: (A) a felony; (B) a misdemeanor punishable by imprisonment for more than 2 years; (C) a violent crime as defined in section 121; (D) a violation of a law regulating the use, possession, ownership, transfer, purchase, sale, lease, rental, receipt or transportation of weapons or ammunition for which a term of imprisonment may be imposed; or (E) a violation of a law regulating the use, possession or sale of a controlled substance as defined in section 1 of chapter 94C; provided, however, that, except for the commission of a violent crime or a crime involving the trafficking of weapons or controlled substances, if the person has been so convicted or adjudicated or released from confinement, probation or parole supervision for such conviction or adjudication, whichever occurs last, for 5 or more years immediately preceding the purchase or possession and that applicant's right or ability to possess a rifle or shotgun has been fully restored in the jurisdiction wherein the subject conviction or adjudication was entered, then that person may purchase or possess self-defense spray;

(iii) has been committed to any hospital or institution for mental illness unless the person obtains, prior to purchase or possession, an affidavit of a licensed physician or clinical psychologist attesting that such physician or psychologist is familiar with the applicant's mental illness and that in the physician's or psychologist's opinion the applicant is not disabled by such an illness in a manner that shall prevent the applicant from possessing self-defense spray;

(iv) is or has been in recovery from or committed based upon a finding that the person is a person with an alcohol use disorder or a substance use disorder or both unless a licensed physician or clinical psychologist deems such person to be in recovery from such condition, in which case, such person may purchase or possess self-defense spray after 5 years from the date of such confinement or recovery; provided, however, that prior to such purchase or possession of self-defense spray, the applicant shall submit an affidavit issued by a li-censed physician or clinical psychologist attesting that such physician or psychologist knows the person's history of treatment and that in that physician's or psychologist's opinion the applicant is in recovery;

(v) at the time of the application, is younger than 15 years of age;

(vi) at the time of the application, is at least 15 years of age but less than 18 years of age unless the applicant submits with the application a certificate from the applicant's parent or guardian granting the applicant permission to apply for a card;

(vii) is an alien who does not maintain lawful permanent residency or is an alien not residing under a visa pursuant to 8 U.S.C. § 1101(a)(15)(U), or is an alien not residing under a visa pursuant to 8 U.S.C. § 1154(a)(1)(B)(ii)(I) or is an alien not residing under a visa pursuant to 8 U.S.C. § 1101(a)(15)(T)(i)(I)–(IV);

(viii) is currently subject to: (1) an order for suspension or surrender issued pursuant to section 3B or 3C of chapter 209A or section 7 of chapter 258E; or (2) a permanent or temporary protection order issued pursuant to chapter 209A or section 7 of chapter 258E; or

(ix) is currently the subject of an outstanding arrest warrant in any state or federal jurisdiction.

Whoever purchases or possesses self-defense spray in violation of this section shall be punished by a fine of not more than $1,000 or by imprisonment in a house of correction for not more than 2 years or both such fine and imprisonment.

SECTION 123
Conditions of licenses
(Amended by 2014 Mass. Acts c. 284, § 26, effective Aug. 11, 2014; 2014 Mass. Acts c. 284, § 25, effective Jan. 1, 2015. Bracketed text stricken by 2014 Mass. Acts c. 284, §§ 23, 24, effective Jan. 1, 2021.)

A license granted under section one hundred and twenty-two shall be expressed to be and shall be subject to the following conditions:—First, That the provisions in regard to the nature of the license and the building in which the business may be carried on under it shall be strictly adhered to. Second, That every licensee shall, before delivery of a firearm, rifle or shotgun, make or cause to be made a true, legible entry in a sales record book to be furnished by the commissioner of the department of criminal justice information services and to be kept for that purpose, specifying the complete description of the firearm, rifle or shotgun, including the make, serial number, if any, type of firearm, rifle or shotgun, and designation as a large capacity weapon, if applicable, whether sold, rented or leased, the date of each sale, rental or lease, the license to carry firearms number or permit to purchase number and the identification card number in the case of a firearm or the identification card number or the license to carry firearms number in the case of a rifle or shotgun, the sex, residence and occupation of the purchaser, renter or lessee, and shall before delivery, as aforesaid, require the purchaser, renter or lessee personally to write in said sales record book his full name. Said book shall be open at all times to the inspection of the police. Third, That the license or a copy thereof, certified by the official issuing the same, shall be displayed on the premises in a position where it can easily be read. Fourth, That no firearm, rifle or shotgun, or machine gun shall be displayed in any outer window of said premises or in any other place where it can readily be seen from the outside. Fifth, That the licensee shall submit a record of all sales, rentals and leases forthwith at the time of such sale, rental or lease via electronic communication link to the commissioner of the department of criminal justice information services. Sixth, That every firearm, rifle or shotgun shall be unloaded when delivered. Seventh, That no delivery of a firearm shall be made to any person not having a license to carry firearms issued under the provisions of section one hundred and thirty-one nor shall any delivery of a rifle or shotgun or ammunition be made to any minor nor to any person not having a license to carry firearms issued under the provisions of section one hundred and thirty-one or a firearm identification card issued under the provisions of section one hundred and twenty-nine B nor shall any large capacity firearm or large capacity feeding device therefor be delivered to any person not having a [Class A] license to carry firearms issued under section 131 nor shall any large capacity rifle or shotgun or large capacity feeding device therefor be delivered to any person not having a [Class A or Class B] license to carry firearms issued under section 131; provided, however, that delivery of a firearm by a licensee to a person possessing a valid permit to purchase said firearm issued under the provisions of section one hundred and thirty-one A and a valid firearm identification card issued under section one hundred and twenty-nine B may be made by the licensee to the purchaser's residence or place of business, subject to the restrictions imposed upon such permits as provided under section 131A. Eighth, That no firearm shall be sold, rented or leased to a minor or a person who has not a permit then in force to purchase, rent or lease the same issued under section one hundred and thirty-one A, and a firearm identification card issued under the provisions of section one hundred and twenty-nine B, or unless such person has a license to carry firearms issued under the provisions of section one hundred and thirty-one; nor shall any rifle or shotgun be sold, rented or leased to a person who has not a valid firearm identification card as provided for in section one hundred and twenty-nine B, or has a license to carry firearms as provided in section one hundred and thirty-one; that no large capacity firearm nor large capacity feeding device therefor shall be sold, rented, leased or transferred to any person not having (i) a [Class A] license to carry firearm issued under section 131 or (ii) a proper permit issued under section 131A and a firearm identification card issued under section 129B; that no large capacity rifle or shotgun nor large capacity feeding device therefor shall be sold to any person not having a [Class A or Class B] license to carry firearms issued under said section 131; and that no machine gun shall be sold, rented or leased to any person who has not a license to possess the same issued under section one hundred and thirty-one. Ninth, That upon the sale, rental or lease of a firearm, subject to a permit to purchase issued under the provisions of section one hundred and thirty-one A, the licensee under section one hundred and twenty-two shall take up such permit to purchase and shall endorse upon it the date and place of said sale, rental or lease, and shall transmit the same to the commissioner of the department of criminal justice information services; and that upon the sale, rental or lease of a machine gun shall endorse upon the license to possess the same the date and place of said sale, rental or lease, and shall within seven days transmit notice thereof to said executive director. In case of a sale under the provisions of section one hundred and thirty-one E the licensee under section one hundred and twenty-two shall write in the sales rec-

ord book the number of the license to carry firearms issued the purchaser under the provisions of section one hundred and thirty-one, or the number of the firearm identification card issued the purchaser under the provisions of section one hundred and twenty-nine B, whichever is applicable under the provisions of condition Eighth of this section. Tenth, That this license shall be subject to forfeiture as provided in section one hundred and twenty-five for breach of any of its conditions, and that, if the licensee hereunder is convicted of a violation of any such conditions, this license shall thereupon become void. Eleventh, That the second, fifth, eighth and ninth conditions shall not apply to a gunsmith with regard to repair or remodeling or servicing of firearms, rifles or shotguns unless said gunsmith has manufactured a firearm, rifle or shotgun for the purchaser, but said gunsmith shall keep records of the work done by him together with the names and addresses of his customers. Such records shall be kept open for inspection by the police at all times. Twelfth, That any licensee shall keep records of each sale, rental or lease of a rifle or shotgun, specifying the description of said rifle or shotgun, together with the name and address of the purchaser, renter or lessee, and the date of such transaction. Thirteenth, That the current validity of any firearm identification card, license to carry firearms or permit to purchase, rent or lease firearms presented, and that the person presenting said card, license or permit is the lawful holder thereof, shall be verified by the licensee prior to any sale, rental or lease of a rifle, shotgun, firearm or large capacity feeding device; and, upon being presented with such card or license that is expired, suspended or revoked, the licensee shall notify the licensing authority of the presentment of such expired, suspended or revoked card, license or permit; and further, the licensee may take possession of such card or license provided that, in such case, such licensee shall: (i) issue a receipt, in a form provided by the executive director of the criminal history systems board, to the holder thereof which shall state that the holder's card or license is expired, suspended or revoked, was taken by such licensee and forwarded to the licensing authority by whom it was issued and such receipt shall be valid for the date of issuance for the purpose of providing immunity from prosecution under section 10 of chapter 269 for unlawfully possessing a firearm, rifle or shotgun or large capacity weapon; (ii) notify the cardholder or licensee of his requirement to renew said card or license; and (iii) forward such expired card or license to the licensing authority forthwith; provided, however, that such licensee shall be immune from civil and criminal liability for good faith compliance with the provisions herein. Fourteenth, That the licensee shall conspicuously post at each purchase counter the following warning in bold type not less than one inch in height: "IT IS UNLAWFUL TO STORE OR KEEP A FIREARM, RIFLE, SHOTGUN OR MACHINE GUN IN ANY PLACE UNLESS THAT WEAPON IS EQUIPPED WITH A TAMPER-RESISTANT SAFETY DEVICE OR IS STORED OR KEPT IN A SECURELY LOCKED CONTAINER.", and that such licensee shall provide said warning, in writing, to the purchaser or transferee of any firearm, rifle, shotgun or machine gun in bold type not less than one-quarter inch in height, and further that the licensee shall conspicuously post and distribute at each purchase counter a notice providing information on suicide prevention developed and provided by the division on violence and injury prevention within the department of public health. The department of public health shall develop and make available on its website for download a sign providing the information on suicide prevention. Fifteenth, That all licensees shall maintain a permanent place of business that is not a residence or dwelling wherein all transactions described in this section shall be conducted and wherein all records required to be kept under this section shall be so kept. Sixteenth, That no licensee shall sell, lease, rent, transfer or deliver or offer for sale, lease, rent, transfer or delivery to any person any assault weapon or large capacity feeding device that was not otherwise lawfully possessed on September 13, 1994. Seventeenth, That any licensee from whom a rifle, shotgun, firearm or machine gun is lost or stolen shall report such loss or theft to the licensing authority and the executive director of the criminal history systems board forthwith. Such report shall include a complete description of the weapon, including the make, model, serial number and caliber and whether such weapon is a large capacity weapon. Eighteenth, That no licensee shall sell, rent, lease, transfer or deliver or offer for sale, lease, transfer or delivery any firearm, to any purchaser in the commonwealth unless such sale is to a business entity that is primarily a firearm wholesaler and the sale, by its terms, prohibits the purchaser from reselling such firearm to a firearm retailer or consumer in the commonwealth if such firearm has a frame, barrel, cylinder, slide or breechblock that is composed of: (i) any metal having a melting point of less than 900 degrees Fahrenheit; (ii) any metal having an ultimate tensile strength of less than 55,000 pounds per square inch; or (iii) any powdered metal having a density of less than 7.5 grams per cubic centimeter. This clause shall not apply to any make and model of firearm for which a sample of three firearms in new condition all pass the following test: Each of the three samples shall fire 600 rounds, stopping every 100 rounds to tighten any loose screws and to clean the gun if required by the cleaning schedule in the user manual, and as needed to refill the empty magazine or cylinder to capacity before continuing. For any firearm that is loaded in a manner other than via a detachable magazine, the tester shall also pause every 50 rounds for ten minutes. The ammunition used shall be the type recommended by the firearm manufacturer in its user manual or, if none recommended, any standard ammunition of the correct caliber in new condition. A firearm shall pass this test if it fires the first 20 rounds without a malfunction, fires the full 600 rounds with not more than six malfunctions and completes the test without any crack or breakage of an operating part of the firearm. The term "crack" or "breakage" shall not include a crack or breakage that does not increase the danger of injury to the user. For purposes of evaluating the results of this test, malfunction shall mean any failure to feed, chamber, fire, extract or eject a round or any failure to accept or eject a magazine or any other failure which prevents the firearm, without manual intervention beyond that needed for routine firing and periodic reloading, from firing the chambered round or moving a new round into position so that the firearm is capable of firing the new round properly. "Malfunction" shall not include a misfire caused by a faulty cartridge the primer of which fails to detonate when properly struck by the firearm's firing mechanism. Nineteenth, That no licensee shall sell, rent, lease, transfer or deliver or offer for sale, lease, transfer or delivery any firearm to any purchaser in the commonwealth unless such sale is to a business entity that is primarily a firearms wholesaler, and the

sale, by its terms, prohibits such purchaser from reselling such firearm to a firearm retailer or consumer in the commonwealth if such firearm is prone to accidental discharge which, for purposes of this clause, shall mean any make and model of firearm for which a sample of five firearms in new condition all undergo, and none discharge during, the following test: Each of the five sample firearms shall be: (a) test loaded; (b) set so that the firearm is in a condition such that pulling the trigger and taking any action that must simultaneously accompany the pulling of the trigger as part of the firing procedure would fire the handgun; and (c) dropped onto a solid slab of concrete from a height of one meter from each of the following positions: (i) normal firing position; (ii) upside down; (iii) on grip; (iv) on the muzzle; (v) on either side; and (vi) on the exposed hammer or striker or, if there is no exposed hammer or striker, the rearmost part of the firearm. If the firearms is designed so that its hammer or striker may be set in other positions, each sample firearm shall be tested as above with the hammer or striker in each such position but otherwise in such condition that pulling the trigger, and taking any action that must simultaneously accompany the pulling of the trigger as part of the firing procedure, would fire the firearm. Alternatively, the tester may use additional sample firearms of the same make and model, in a similar condition, for the test of each of three hammer striker settings. Twentieth, That no licensee shall sell, rent, lease, transfer or deliver or offer for sale, lease, transfer or delivery, any firearm to any purchaser in the commonwealth unless such sale is to a business entity that is primarily a firearm wholesaler, and the sale, by its terms, prohibits the purchaser from reselling such firearm to a firearm retailer or consumer in the commonwealth if such firearm is prone to: (i) firing more than once per pull of the trigger; or (ii) explosion during firing. Twenty-first, That no licensee shall sell, rent, lease, transfer or deliver or offer for sale, lease, transfer or delivery any firearm to any purchaser in the commonwealth unless such sale is to a business entity that is primarily a firearm wholesaler and the sale, by its terms, prohibits the purchaser from reselling such firearm to a firearm retailer or consumer in the commonwealth if such firearm has a barrel less than three inches in length, unless the license discloses in writing, prior to the transaction, to the prospective buyer, lessee, deliveree or transferee the limitations of the accuracy of the particular make and model of the subject firearm, by disclosing the make and model's average group diameter test result at seven yards, average group diameter test result at 14 years and average group diameter test result at 21 yards. For purposes of this clause, "average group diameter test result" shall mean the arithmetic mean of three separate trials, each performed as follows on a different sample firearm in new condition of the make and model at issue. Each firearm shall fire five rounds at a target from a set distance and the largest spread in inches between the centers of any of the holds made in a test target shall be measured and recorded. This procedure shall be repeated two more times on the firearm. The arithmetic mean of each of the three recorded results shall be deemed the result of the trial for that particular sample firearm. The ammunition used shall be the type recommended by the firearm manufacturer in its user manual or, if none is recommended, any standard ammunition of the correct caliber in new condition. No licensee shall sell any rifle or shotgun, contrary to the provisions of section one hundred and thirty or section 131E.

Clauses Eighteenth to Twenty-first, inclusive, of the first paragraph shall not apply to: (i) a firearm lawfully owned or possessed under a license issued under this chapter on or before October 21, 1998; (ii) a firearm designated by the secretary of public safety, with the advice of the gun control advisory board, established pursuant to section 131½ of chapter 140, as a firearm solely designed and sold for formal target shooting competition; or (iii) a firearm designated by the secretary of public safety, with the advice of the gun control advisory board, established pursuant to section 131½ of chapter 140, as a firearm or pistol solely designed and sold for Olympic shooting competition. The secretary of public safety shall compile lists, on a bi-annual basis, of firearms designated as "formal target shooting firearms" and "Olympic competition firearms" in accordance with this paragraph. Such lists shall be made available for distribution by the executive office of public safety and security.

No person licensed under the provisions of section 122 or section 122B shall sell, rent, lease, transfer or deliver any rifle, shotgun or firearm or ammunition or ammunition feeding device contrary to the provisions of section 130 or section 131E; and no such licensee shall sell, rent, lease, transfer or deliver any rifle, shotgun or firearm or ammunition or ammunition feeding device to any person who does not have in his possession the required firearm identification card or proof of exemption therefrom, license to carry firearms or permit to purchase, rent or lease firearms and who does not present such card, proof, license or permit to the licensee in person at the time of purchase, rental or lease. No person licensed under the provisions of section 122 or section 122B shall fill an order for such weapon, ammunition or ammunition feeding device that was received by mail, facsimile, telephone or other telecommunication unless such transaction or transfer includes the in-person presentation of the required card, proof, license or permit as required herein prior to any sale, delivery or any form of transfer of possession of the subject weapon, ammunition or ammunition feeding device. Transactions between persons licensed under section 122 or between federally licensed dealers shall be exempt from the provisions of this paragraph.

The licensing authority shall enter, one time per calendar year, during regular business hours, the commercial premises owned or leased by any licensee, wherein such records required to be maintained under this section are stored or maintained, and inspect, in a reasonable manner, such records and inventory for the purpose of enforcing provisions of this section. If such records and inventory contain evidence of violations of this section, the inspecting officer shall produce and take possession of copies of such records and, in the event that the licensee subject to inspection does not possess copying equipment, the inspecting officer shall arrange to have copied, in a reasonable time and manner, such records that contain evidence of such violations and the costs for such copying shall be assessed against the owner of such records. Licensees found to be in violation of this section shall be subject to the suspension or permanent revocation of such license issued under section 122 and to the provisions of section 128. Nothing herein shall prohibit the licensing authority or the department of state police from conducting such inspections pursuant to a valid search warrant issued by a court of competent jurisdiction.

Notwithstanding the provisions of this section, a person licensed under the provisions of section one hundred and twenty-two, or section one hundred and twenty-two B, may sell or transfer firearms, rifles, shotguns, machine guns or ammunition at any regular meeting of an incorporated collectors club or at a gun show open to the general public; provided, however, that all other provisions of this section are complied with and that such sale or transfer is in conformity with federal law or regulations applicable to the transfer or sale of firearms, rifles, shotguns, machine guns or ammunition, including the restrictions imposed upon firearm identification cards issued under section 129B, licenses to carry firearms issued under section 131 and permits to purchase, lease or rent firearms issued under section 131A.

NOTE 1   **Clause Fifth.** Not applicable to any person licensed under G.L. c. 140, § 122 until September 1, 1999. 1998 Mass. Acts c. 180, § 77.

NOTE 2   **Clause Fifteenth.** Not applicable to any licensee holding a valid license issued pursuant to G.L. c. 140, § 122 until September 1, 1999. 1998 Mass. Acts c. 180, § 78.

NOTE 3   **Clauses Eighteenth to Twenty-First.** Not applicable to any firearm lawfully owned or possessed under a license issued under G.L. c. 140 on the effective date of this act. 1998 Mass. Acts c. 180, § 79 [July 23, 1998].

SECTION 124
Term of licenses

Licenses issued under sections one hundred and twenty-two and one hundred and twenty-two B shall expire three years from the date of issuance.

SECTION 125
Forfeiture or suspension of licenses; notice

The officials authorized to issue a license under section one hundred and twenty-two, after due notice to the licensee and reasonable opportunity for him to be heard, may declare his license forfeited, or may suspend his license for such period of time as they may deem proper, upon satisfactory proof that he has violated or permitted a violation of any condition thereof or has violated any provision of this chapter, or has been convicted of a felony. The pendency of proceedings before a court shall not suspend or interfere with the power to declare a forfeiture. If the license is declared forfeited, the licensee shall be disqualified to receive a license for one year after the expiration of the term of the license so forfeited. The commissioner of the department of criminal justice information services shall be notified in writing of any forfeiture under this section.

SECTION 126
Placards, signs or advertisements; prima facie evidence

If there is exposed from, maintained in or permitted to remain on any vehicle or premises any placard, sign or advertisement purporting or designed to announce that firearms, rifles, shotguns or machine guns are kept in or upon such vehicle or premises or that an occupant of any vehicle or premises is a gunsmith, it shall be prima facie evidence that firearms, rifles, shotguns or machine guns are kept in or upon such vehicle or premises for sale or that the occupant is engaged in business as a gunsmith.

SECTION 127
Transfer of licenses

The officials authorized to issue a license under section one hundred and twenty-two may transfer licenses from one location to another within the city or town in which the licenses are in force, but such transfer shall be granted only to the original licensee and upon the same terms and conditions upon which the license was originally granted. The commissioner of the department of criminal justice information services shall be notified in writing of any transfers made under this section.

SECTION 128
Penalty for violation of statute on selling, renting or leasing weapons; evidence on sale of machine gun
(Amended by 2014 Mass. Acts c. 284, § 27, effective Jan. 1, 2015.)

Any licensee under a license described in section one hundred and twenty-three, and any employee or agent of such a licensee, who violates any provision of said section required to be expressed in the second, fourth, sixth, seventh, eighth, ninth, sixteenth, seventeenth, eighteenth, nineteenth, twentieth or twenty-first condition of said license, and except as provided in section one hundred and twenty-eight A, any person who, without being licensed as hereinbefore provided, sells, rents or leases a firearm, rifle, shotgun or machine gun, or is engaged in business as a gunsmith, shall be punished by a fine of not less than $1,000 nor more than $10,000, or by imprisonment for not less than one year nor more than ten years, or by both such fine and imprisonment.

Evidence that a person sold or attempted to sell a machine gun without being licensed under section one hundred and twenty-three shall, in a prosecution under this section, constitute prima facie evidence that such person is engaged in the business of selling machine guns.

SECTION 128A
Application of Sec. 128
(Amended by 2014 Mass. Acts c. 284, §§ 28–29, effective Mar. 1, 2015.)

The provisions of section one hundred and twenty-eight shall not apply to any person who, without being licensed as provided in section one hundred and twenty-two, sells or transfers a firearm, rifle or shotgun to a person licensed under said section one hundred and twenty-two, or to a federally licensed firearms dealer, or to a federal, state or local historical society, museum or institutional collection open to the public. The provisions of section one hundred and twenty-eight shall not apply to any resident of the commonwealth who, without being licensed as provided in section one hundred and twenty-two, sells or transfers to other than a federally licensed firearms dealer or organization named above not more than four firearms, including rifles and shotguns in any one calendar year; provided, however, that the seller has a firearm identification card or a license to carry firearms, is an exempt person under the conditions of clauses (n), (o), (r) and (s) of the fourth paragraph of section one hundred and twenty-nine C, or is permitted to transfer ownership under the conditions of section one hundred and twenty-nine D and the purchaser has, in the case of sale or transfer of a firearm, a permit to purchase issued under the provisions of section one hundred and thirty-one A and a firearm identification card issued under section one hundred and twenty-nine B, or has such permit to purchase and is an exempt person under the provisions of section one hundred and twenty-nine C, or has

been issued a license to carry firearms under the provisions of section one hundred and thirty, or in the case of sale or transfer of a rifle or shotgun, the purchaser has a firearm identification card or a license to carry firearms or is an exempt person as hereinbefore stated. Any sale or transfer conducted pursuant to this section shall comply with section 131E and shall, prior to or at the point of sale, be conducted over a real time web portal developed by the department of criminal justice information services. The department of criminal justice information services shall require each person selling or transferring a firearm, shotgun or rifle pursuant to this section to electronically provide, though the portal, such information as is determined to be necessary to verify the identification of the seller and purchaser and ensure that the sale or transfer complies with this section. Upon submission of the required information, the portal shall automatically review such information and display a message indicating whether the seller may proceed with the sale or transfer and shall provide any further instructions for the seller as determined to be necessary by the department of criminal justice information services. The department of criminal justice information services shall keep a record of any sale or transfer conducted pursuant to this section and shall provide the seller and purchaser with verification of such sale or transfer.

SECTION 128B
Unauthorized purchase of firearms; report to commissioner; penalties

Any resident of the commonwealth who purchases or obtains a firearm, rifle or shotgun or machine gun from any source within or without the commonwealth, other than from a licensee under section one hundred and twenty-two or a person authorized to sell firearms under section one hundred and twenty-eight A, and any nonresident of the commonwealth who purchases or obtains a firearm, rifle, shotgun or machine gun from any source within or without the commonwealth, other than such a licensee or person, and receives such firearm, rifle, shotgun or machine gun, within the commonwealth shall within seven days after receiving such firearm, rifle, shotgun or machine gun, report, in writing, to the commissioner of the department of criminal justice information services the name and address of the seller or donor and the buyer or donee, together with a complete description of the firearm, rifle, shotgun or machine gun, including the caliber, make and serial number. Whoever violates any provision of this section shall for the first offense be punished by a fine of not less than $500 nor more than $1,000 and for any subsequent offense by imprisonment in the state prison for not more than ten years.

SECTION 129
Fictitious name or address and other false information; penalties

Whoever in purchasing, renting or hiring a firearm, rifle, shotgun or machine gun, or in making application for any form of license or permit issued in connection therewith, or in requesting that work be done by a gunsmith, gives a false or fictitious name or address or knowingly offers or gives false information concerning the date or place of birth, his citizenship status, occupation, or criminal record, shall for the first offense be punished by a fine of not less than five hundred nor more than one thousand dollars, or by imprisonment for not more than one year, or both; and for a second or subsequent offense, shall be punished by imprisonment for not less than two and one half years nor more than five years in the state prison.

SECTION 129A
Repealed

SECTION 129B
Firearm identification cards; conditions and restrictions
(Amended by 2010 Mass. Acts c. 466, § 1, effective Apr. 14, 2011; 2011 Mass. Acts c. 9, §§ 14–15, effective Apr. 11, 2011; 2011 Mass. Acts c. 68, § 93, effective July 11, 2011; 2014 Mass. Acts c. 284, §§ 32, 35, 37, effective Aug. 11, 2014; 2014 Mass. Acts c. 284, §§ 30, 31, 34, 36, 38, 39, effective Jan. 1, 2015; 2014 Mass. Acts c. 284, § 33, effective Jan. 1, 2021. Bracketed text in paragraphs (7) and (9B) added by 2014 Mass. Acts c. 284, § 35, effective Aug. 11, 2014 and stricken effective Jan. 1, 2021 by 2014 Mass. Acts c. 284, §§ 35A, 35B.)

A firearm identification card shall be issued and possessed subject to the following conditions and restrictions:

(1) Any person residing or having a place of business within the jurisdiction of the licensing authority or any person residing in an area of exclusive federal jurisdiction located within a city or town may submit to the licensing authority an application for a firearm identification card, or renewal of the same, which the licensing authority shall issue if it appears that the applicant is not a prohibited person. A prohibited person shall be a person who:

(i) has ever, in a court of the commonwealth, been convicted or adjudicated a youthful offender or delinquent child, or both as defined in section 52 of chapter 119, for the commission of: (A) a felony; (B) a misdemeanor punishable by imprisonment for more than 2 years ; (C) a violent crime as defined in section 121; (D) a violation of any law regulating the use, possession, ownership, transfer, purchase, sale, lease, rental, receipt or transportation of weapons or ammunition for which a term of imprisonment may be imposed; (E) a violation of any law regulating the use, possession or sale of controlled substances, as defined in section 1 of chapter 94C, including, but not limited to, a violation under said chapter 94C; or (F) a misdemeanor crime of domestic violence as defined in 18 U.S.C. 921(a)(33); provided, however, that, except for the commission of a felony, a misdemeanor crime of domestic violence, a violent crime or a crime involving the trafficking of controlled substances, if the applicant has been so convicted or adjudicated or released from confinement, probation or parole supervision for such conviction or adjudication, whichever occurs last, for 5 or more years immediately preceding such application, then the applicant's right or ability to possess a non-large capacity rifle or shotgun shall be deemed restored in the commonwealth with respect to such conviction or adjudication and that conviction or adjudication shall not disqualify the applicant for a firearm identification card;

(ii) has, in any other state or federal jurisdiction, been convicted or adjudicated a youthful offender or delinquent child for the commission of: (A) a felony; (B) a misdemeanor punishable by imprisonment for more than 2 years; (C) a violent crime as defined in section 121; (D) a violation of any law regulating the use, possession, ownership, transfer, purchase, sale, lease, rental, receipt or transportation of weapons or ammunition for which a term of imprisonment may be imposed; (E) a violation of any law regulating the use, possession or sale of controlled substances, as defined in section 1 of chapter 94C, including, but not limited to, a violation under said chapter 94C; or (F) a misdemeanor crime of domestic violence as defined in 18 U.S.C. 921(a)(33); provided, however, that, except for the commission of felony, a misdemeanor crime of domestic violence, a violent crime or a crime involving the trafficking of weapons or controlled substances, if the applicant has been so convicted or adjudicated or released from confinement, probation or parole supervision for such conviction or adjudication, whichever occurs last, for 5 or more years immediately preceding such application and the applicant's right or ability to possess a rifle or shotgun has been fully restored in the jurisdiction wherein the conviction or adjudication was entered, then the conviction or adjudication shall not disqualify such applicant for a firearm identification card;

(iii) is or has been: (A) except in the case of a commitment pursuant to sections 35 or 36C of chapter 123, committed to any hospital or institution for mental illness, alcohol or substance abuse, unless after 5 years from the date of the confinement, the applicant submits with the application an affidavit of a licensed physician or clinical psychologist attesting that such physician or psychologist is familiar with the applicant's mental illness, alcohol or substance abuse and that in the physician's or psychologist's opinion the applicant is not disabled by a mental illness, alcohol or substance abuse in a manner that should prevent the applicant from possessing a firearm, rifle or shotgun; (B) committed by an order of a court to any hospital or institution for mental illness, unless the applicant was granted a petition for relief of the court's order pursuant to said section 36C of said chapter 123 and submits a copy of the order for relief with the application; (C) subject to an order of the probate court appointing a guardian or conservator for a incapacitated person on the grounds that that applicant lacks the mental capacity to contract or manage affairs, unless the applicant was granted a petition for relief pursuant to section 56C of chapter 215 and submits a copy of the order for relief with the application; or (D) found to be a person with an alcohol use disorder or substance use disorder or both and committed pursuant to said section 35 of said chapter 123, unless the applicant was granted a petition for relief of the court's order pursuant to said section 35 of said chapter 123 and submits a copy of the order for relief with the application;

(iv) is at the time of the application younger than 14 years of age; provided however that the applicant shall not be issued the card until the applicant reaches the age of 15.

(v) is at the time of the application more than 14 but less than 18 years of age, unless the applicant submits with the application a certificate of a parent or guardian granting the applicant permission to apply for a card;

(vi) is an alien who does not maintain lawful permanent residency;

(vii) is currently subject to: (A) an order for suspension or surrender issued pursuant to section 3B or 3C of chapter 209A or a similar order issued by another jurisdiction; or (B) a permanent or temporary protection order issued pursuant to chapter 209A, a similar order issued by another jurisdiction, including an order described in 18 U.S.C. 922(g)(8);

(viii) is currently the subject of an outstanding arrest warrant in any state or federal jurisdiction;

(ix) has been discharged from the armed forces of the United States under dishonorable conditions;

(x) is a fugitive from justice; or

(xi) having been a citizen of the United States, has re-nounced that citizenship.

(1½) (a) Notwithstanding paragraph (1) to the contrary, the licensing authority may file a petition to request that an applicant be denied the issuance or renewal of a firearm identi-fication card, or to suspend or revoke such a card in the district court of jurisdiction. If the licensing authority files any such petition it shall be accompanied by written notice to the ap-plicant describing the specific evidence in the petition. Such petition shall be founded upon a written statement of the rea-sons for supporting a finding of unsuitability pursuant to sub-section (d).

(b) Upon the filing of a petition to deny the issuance or renewal of a firearm identification card, the court shall within 90 days hold a hearing to determine if the applicant is unsuit-able under subsection (d) of this paragraph. Such a petition shall serve to stay the issuance or renewal of the firearm identi-fication card pending a judicial determination on such petition.

(c) Upon the filing of a petition to suspend or revoke a firearm identification card, the court shall within 15 days determine whether there is sufficient evidence to support a finding that the applicant is unsuitable. Such petition shall serve to effect the suspension or revocation pending a judicial determination on the sufficiency of evidence. If a court de-termines that insufficient evidence exists to support a finding of unsuitability, the licensing authority shall not file a petition under this subsection for the same applicant within 75 days of the licensing authority's previous petition for that applicant. If a court determines that sufficient evidence exists to support a finding of unsuitability, the court shall within 75 days hold a hearing to determine if the applicant is unsuitable under subsection (d); provided, however, that such initial suspen-sion or revocation shall remain in effect pending a judicial determination thereon.

(d) A determination of unsuitability shall be based on a preponderance of evidence that there exists: (i) reliable, artic-ulable, and credible information that the applicant has exhib-ited or engaged in behavior to suggest the applicant could potentially create a risk to public safety; or (ii) existing fac-tors that suggest that the applicant could potentially create a risk to public safety. If a court enters a judgment that an ap-plicant is unsuitable the court shall notify the applicant in a writing setting forth the specific reasons for such determina-tion. If a court has not entered a judgment that an applicant is unsuitable under this clause within 90 days for petitions under clause (ii) or within 75 days under clause (iii), the court shall enter a judgment that the applicant is suitable for the purposes of this paragraph.

(2) Within seven days of the receipt of a completed ap-plication for a card, the licensing authority shall forward one copy of the application and one copy of the applicant's fin-gerprints to the colonel of state police, who shall, within 30 days, advise the licensing authority, in writing, of any dis-qualifying criminal record of the applicant arising from with-in or without the commonwealth and whether there is reason to believe that the applicant is disqualified for any of the foregoing reasons from possessing a card; provided, however, that the taking of fingerprints shall not be required in issuing the renewal of a card if the renewal applicant's fingerprints are on file with the department of state police. In searching for any disqualifying history of the applicant, the colonel shall utilize, or cause to be utilized, files maintained by the

department of mental health, department of probation and statewide and nationwide criminal justice, warrant and pro-tection order information systems and files including, but not limited to, the National Instant Criminal Background Check System. If the information available to the colonel does not indicate that the possession of a non-large capacity rifle or shotgun by the applicant would be in violation of state or federal law, he shall certify such fact, in writing, to the licens-ing authority within such 30 day period. The licensing author-ity shall provide to the applicant a receipt indicating that it received the applicant's application. The receipt shall be pro-vided to the applicant within 7 days by mail if the application was received by mail or immediately if the application was made in person; provided, however, that the receipt shall in-clude the applicants' name, address, current firearm identifi-cation card number, if any, the current card's expiration date, if any, the date when the application was received by the li-censing authority, the name of the licensing authority and its agent that received the application, the licensing authority's address and telephone number, the type of application and whether it is an application for a new card or for renewal of an existing card; and provided further, that a copy of the re-ceipt shall be kept by the licensing authority for not less than 1 year and a copy shall be furnished to the applicant if re-quested by the applicant.

(3) The licensing authority may not prescribe any other condition for the issuance of a firearm identification card issued pursuant to subclause (vi) of clause (1) of section 122D and shall, within 40 days from the date of application, either approve the application and issue the license or deny the application and notify the applicant of the reason for such denial in writing; provided, however, that no such card shall be issued unless the colonel has certified, in writing, that the information available to him does not indicate that the pos-session of a rifle or shotgun by the applicant would be in vio-lation of state or federal law.

(4) A firearm identification card shall be revoked or sus-pended by the licensing authority or his designee upon the occurrence of any event that would have disqualified the holder from being issued such card or from having such card renewed or for a violation of a restriction provided under this section. Any revocation or suspension of a card shall be in writing and shall state the reasons therefor. Upon revocation or suspension, the licensing authority shall take possession of such card and receipt for fee paid for such card, and the per-son whose card is so revoked or suspended shall take all ac-tion required under the provisions of section 129D. No appeal or postjudgment motion shall operate to stay such revocation or suspension. Notices of revocation and suspension shall be forwarded to the commissioner of the department of criminal justice information services and the commissioner of proba-tion and shall be included in the criminal justice information system. A revoked or suspended card may be reinstated only upon the termination of all disqualifying conditions.

(5) Any applicant or holder aggrieved by a denial, revo-cation or suspension of a firearm identification card, unless a hearing has previously been held pursuant to chapter 209A, may, within either 90 days after receipt of notice of such de-nial, revocation or suspension or within 90 days after the ex-piration of the time limit in which the licensing authority is required to respond to the applicant, file a petition to obtain judicial review in the district court having jurisdiction in the

city or town wherein the applicant filed or was issued such card. A justice of such court, after a hearing, may direct that a card be issued or reinstated to the petitioner if the justice finds that such petitioner is not prohibited by law from possessing such card.

[Paragraph (6) as effective through Dec. 31, 2020:]

(6) A firearm identification card shall not entitle a holder thereof to possess: (i) a large capacity firearm or large capacity feeding device therefor, except under a Class A license to a shooting club as provided under section 131 or under the direct supervision of a holder of a Class A license issued to an individual under section 131 at an incorporated shooting club or licensed shooting range; or (ii) a non-large capacity firearm or large capacity rifle or shotgun or large capacity feeding device therefor, except under a Class A license issued to a shooting club as provided under section 131 or under the direct supervision of a holder of a Class A or Class B license issued to an individual under section 131 at an incorporated shooting club or licensed shooting range. A firearm identification card shall not entitle a holder thereof to possess any rifle or shotgun that is, or in such manner that is, otherwise prohibited by law. A firearm identification card shall be valid for the purpose of purchasing and possessing chemical mace, pepper spray or other similarly propelled liquid, gas or powder designed to temporarily incapacitate. Except as otherwise provided herein, a firearm identification card shall not be valid for the use, possession, ownership, transfer, sale, lease, rental or transportation of a rifle or shotgun if such rifle or shotgun is a large capacity weapon as defined in section 121.

[Paragraph (6) as amended effective Jan. 1, 2021:]

A firearm identification card shall not entitle a holder thereof to possess: (i) a large capacity firearm or large capacity feeding device therefor, except under a license issued to a shooting club as provided under section 131 or under the direct supervision of a holder of a license issued to an individual under said section 131 at an incorporated shooting club or licensed shooting range; or (ii) a non-large capacity firearm or large capacity rifle or shotgun or large capacity feeding device therefor, except under a license issued to a shooting club as provided under said section 131 or under the direct supervision of a holder of a license issued to an individual under said section 131 at an incorporated shooting club or licensed shooting range. A firearm identification card shall not entitle a holder thereof to possess any rifle or shotgun that is, or in such manner that is, otherwise prohibited by law. A firearm identification card issued pursuant to subclause (vi) of clause (1) of section 122D, shall be valid to purchase and possess chemical mace, pepper spray or other similarly propelled liquid, gas or powder designed to temporarily incapacitate. Except as otherwise provided herein, a firearm identification card shall not be valid for the use, possession, ownership, transfer, purchase, sale, lease, rental or transportation of a rifle or shotgun if such rifle or shotgun is a large capacity weapon as defined in section 121.

(7) A firearm identification card shall be in a standard form provided by the commissioner of the department of criminal justice information services in a size and shape equivalent to that of a license to operate motor vehicles issued by the registry of motor vehicles pursuant to section 8 of chapter 90 and shall contain an identification number, name, address, photograph, fingerprint, place and date of birth, height, weight, hair color, eye color and signature of the cardholder and shall be marked "Firearm Identification Card" and shall provide in a legible font size and style the phone numbers for the National Suicide Prevention Lifeline and the Samaritans Statewide Helpline. If a firearm identification card is issued [pursuant to clause (vi) of section 122D] for the sole purpose of purchasing or possessing chemical mace, pepper spray or other similarly propelled liquid, gas or powder designed to temporarily incapacitate, such card shall clearly state that such card is valid for such limited purpose only. The application for such card shall be made in a standard form provided by the commissioner of the department of criminal justice information services which shall require the applicant to affirmatively state, under the pains and penalties of perjury, that he is not disqualified on any of the grounds enumerated in clauses (i) to (ix), inclusive, from being issued such card.

(8) Any person who knowingly files an application containing false information shall be punished by a fine of not less than $500 nor more than $1,000 or by imprisonment for not less than six months nor more than two years in a house of correction, or by both such fine and imprisonment.

(9) A firearm identification card shall be valid, unless revoked or suspended, for a period of not more than 6 years from the date of issuance, except that if the cardholder applied for renewal before the card expired, the card shall remain valid after the expiration date on the card for all lawful purposes, until the application for renewal is approved or denied; provided, however, if the cardholder is on active duty with the armed forces of the United States on the expiration date of the card, the card shall remain valid until the cardholder is released from active duty and for a period of not less than 180 days following such release, except that if the cardholder applied for renewal prior to the end of such period, the card shall remain valid after the expiration date on the card for all lawful purposes, until the application for renewal is approved or denied. A card issued on February 29 shall expire on March 1. The commissioner of criminal justice information services shall send electronically or by first class mail to the holder of a firearm identification card, a notice of the expiration of the card not less than 90 days before its expiration and shall enclose with the notice a form for the renewal of the card. The form for renewal shall include an affidavit whereby the applicant shall verify that the applicant has not lost a firearm or had a firearm stolen from the applicant's possession since the date of the applicant's last renewal or issuance. The commissioner of criminal justice information services shall include in the notice all pertinent information about the penalties that may be imposed if the firearm identification card is not renewed. The commissioner of criminal justice information services shall provide electronic notice of expiration only upon the request of a cardholder. A request for electronic notice of expiration shall be forwarded to the department on a form furnished by the commissioner. Any electronic address maintained by the department to provide electronic notice of expiration shall be considered a firearms record and shall not be disclosed except as provided in section 10 of chapter 66.

(9A) Except as provided in paragraph (9B), the fee for an application for a firearm identification card shall be $100, which shall be payable to the licensing authority and shall not be prorated or refunded in the case of revocation or denial. The licensing authority shall retain $25 of the fee; $50 of the fee shall be deposited in the General Fund; and $25 of the fee shall be deposited in the Firearms Fingerprint Identity Verification Trust Fund. Notwithstanding any general or special law to the contrary, licensing authorities shall deposit quarterly that portion of the firearm identification card application fee which is to be deposited into the General Fund, not later than January 1, April 1, July 1 and October 1 of each year.

(9B) The application fee for a firearm identification card issued [pursuant to clause (vi) of section 122D] for the sole purpose of purchasing or possessing chemical mace, pepper spray or other similarly propelled liquid, gas or powder designed to temporarily incapacitate shall be $25, which shall be payable to the licensing authority and shall not be prorated or refunded in the case of revocation or denial. The licensing authority shall retain 50 per cent of the fee and the remaining portion shall be deposited in the General Fund. Notwithstanding any general or special law to the contrary, licensing authorities shall deposit quarterly that portion of the firearm identification card application fee which is to be deposited into the General Fund, not later than January 1, April 1, July 1 and October 1 of each year. There shall be no application fee for the renewal of a firearm identification card issued under this paragraph.

A firearm identification card issued under this paragraph shall display, in clear and conspicuous language, that the card shall be valid only for the purpose of purchasing or possessing chemical mace, pepper spray or other similarly propelled liquid, gas or powder designed to temporarily incapacitate.

(9C) Except as provided in paragraph (9B), the fee for an application for a firearm identification card for any person under the age of 18 shall be $25, which shall be payable to the licensing authority and shall not be prorated or refunded in the case of revocation or denial. The licensing authority shall retain 50 percent of the fee and the remaining portion shall be deposited into the General Fund. Notwithstanding any general or special law to the contrary, licensing authorities shall deposit quarterly that portion of the firearm identification card application fee which is to be deposited into the General Fund, not later than January 1, April 1, July 1, and August 1 of each year.

(10) Any person over the age of 70 shall be exempt from the requirement of paying a renewal fee for a firearm identification card.

(11) A cardholder shall notify, in writing, the licensing authority that issued such card, the chief of police into whose jurisdiction such cardholder moves and the executive director of the criminal history systems board of any change of address. Such notification shall be made by certified mail within 30 days of its occurrence. Failure to so notify shall be cause for revocation or suspension of such card.

(12) Notwithstanding the provisions of section 10 of chapter 269, any person in possession of a non-large capacity rifle or shotgun whose firearm identification card issued under this section is invalid for the sole reason that it has expired, not including licenses that remain valid under paragraph (9) because the licensee applied for renewal before the license expired, but who shall not be disqualified from renewal upon application therefor under this section, shall be subject to a civil fine of not less than $100 nor more than $5,000 and the provisions of said section 10 of said chapter 269 shall not apply; provided, however, that the exemption from the provisions of said section 10 of said chapter 269

provided herein shall not apply if: (i) such firearm identification card has been revoked or suspended, unless such revocation or suspension was caused by failure to give notice of a change of address as required under this section; (ii) revocation or suspension of such firearm identification card is pending, unless such revocation or suspension was caused by failure to give notice of a charge of address as required under this section; or (iii) an application for renewal of such firearm identification card has been denied. Any law enforcement officer who discovers a person to be in possession of a rifle or shotgun after such person's firearm identification card has expired, meaning after 90 days beyond the stated expiration date on the card, or has been revoked or suspended solely for failure to give notice of a change of address shall confiscate any rifle or shotgun and such expired or suspended card then in possession, and such officer shall forward such card to the licensing authority by whom it was issued as soon as practicable. Any confiscated weapon shall be returned to the owner upon the renewal or reinstatement of such expired or suspended card within one year of such confiscation or such weapon may otherwise be disposed of in accordance with the provisions of section 129D. Pending the issuance of a renewed firearm identification card, a receipt for the fee paid, after five days following issuance, shall serve as a valid substitute and any rifle or shotgun so confiscated shall be returned, unless the applicant is disqualified. The provisions of this paragraph shall not apply if such person has a valid license to carry firearms issued under section 131 or 131F.

(13) Upon issuance of a firearm identification card under this section, the licensing authority shall forward a copy of such approved application and card to the executive director of the criminal history systems board, who shall inform the licensing authority forthwith of the existence of any disqualifying condition discovered or occurring subsequent to the issuance of a firearm identification card under this section.

(14) Nothing in this section shall authorize the purchase, possession or transfer of any weapon, ammunition or feeding device that is, or in such manner that is, prohibited by state or federal law.

(15) The secretary of the executive officer of public safety, or his designee, may promulgate regulations to carry out the purposes of this section.

NOTE   "Notwithstanding the provisions of any general or special law or rule or regulation to the contrary, all firearm identification cards issued under section 129B of chapter 140 of the General Laws prior to the effective date of this act shall expire on the following schedule: if a person's anniversary of birth is between July 1 and December 31, inclusive, such card shall expire on the cardholder's anniversary of birth in 1999; if a person's anniversary of birth is between January 1 and June 30, inclusive, such card shall expire on the holder's anniversary of birth in 2000. Any such card issued to an applicant born on February 29, for the purposes described herein, shall expire on March 1. A firearm identification card lawfully possessed on the effective date of this act shall be valid, unless revoked or suspended, until it expires under this section for the purpose of possessing large capacity rifles or shotguns or large capacity feeding devices therefor or possessing any firearm or feeding device lawfully owned on the effective date of this act that was purchased with a permit issued under section 131A of said chapter 140; provided, however, that such card shall not be valid for the purpose of purchasing, leasing or otherwise receiving through transfer large capacity rifles or shotguns or large capacity feeding devices. Nothing herein shall prohibit such person from possessing, purchasing, leasing or otherwise receiving through transfer nonlarge capacity rifles, shotguns or ammunition feeding devices therefor or from applying for a license to carry firearms pursuant to the provisions of said section 131 of said chapter 140.

"Any person who lawfully owns a large capacity or nonlarge capacity firearm or feeding device therefor, on the effective date of this act that was purchased with a permit issued under said section 131A of said chapter 140 shall, unless such firearm and feeding device are transferred in accordance with the provisions of said chapter 140, apply for a firearm identification card under the provisions of section 129B of said chapter 140. Unless such applicant is disqualified under the provisions of said section 129B, such card shall be issued; provided, however, that if such card may not be issued, all firearms, ammunition and ammunition feeding devices therefor shall be surrendered in accordance with the provisions of section 129D of said chapter 140; provided further, that the requirements for obtaining a card under said section 129B shall not apply to such person that possesses valid proof of exemption under the provisions of section 129C of said chapter 140. Nothing herein shall permit such person to possess or carry any firearm outside his residence or business unless such person obtains a Class A or Class B license to carry firearms pursuant to the provisions of said section 131 of said chapter 140.

"Any license to carry firearms lawfully possessed on the effective date of this act shall be valid, unless revoked or suspended, until the stated expiration date of such license for all lawful purposes for which it was issued and such license shall be deemed a Class A license.

"The secretary of the executive office of public safety or his designee shall promulgate regulations necessary to implement the provisions of this act, and shall ensure that notice be provided through the most effective means possible to each such cardholder and licensee of the upcoming expiration dates of such cards and licenses, and instructing such holders with regard to renewal procedures, entitlements and restrictions provided under this act including, but not limited to, entitlements and restrictions relative to large capacity weapons and ammunition feeding devices."

1998 Mass. Acts c. 358, § 11.

SECTION 129C
Application of Sec. 129B; ownership or possession of firearms or ammunition; transfers; report to commissioner; exemptions; exhibiting license to carry, etc. on demand
(Amended by 2010 Mass. Acts c. 466, § 2, effective Apr. 14, 2011; 2014 Mass. Acts c. 284, § 40, effective Jan. 1, 2015, 2014 Mass. Acts c. 284, § 41, effective Jan. 1, 2021.)

No person, other than a licensed dealer or one who has been issued a license to carry a pistol or revolver or an exempt person as hereinafter described, shall own or possess any firearm, rifle, shotgun or ammunition unless he has been issued a firearm identification card by the licensing authority pursuant to the provisions of section one hundred and twenty-nine B.

No person shall sell, give away, loan or otherwise transfer a rifle or shotgun or ammunition other than (a) by operation of law, or (b) to an exempt person as hereinafter described, or (c) to a licensed dealer, or (d) to a person who displays his firearm identification card, or license to carry a pistol or revolver.

A seller shall, within seven days, report all such transfers to the commissioner of the department of criminal justice information services according to the provisions set forth in section one hundred and twenty-eight A, and in the case of loss, theft or recovery of any firearm, rifle, shotgun or machine gun, a similar report shall be made forthwith to both the commissioner of the department of criminal justice information services and the licensing authority in the city or town where the owner resides. Whoever fails to report the loss or theft of a firearm, rifle, shotgun or machine gun or the recov-

ery of a firearm, rifle, shotgun or machine gun previously reported lost or stolen to the commissioner of the department of criminal justice information services and the licensing authority in the city or town where the owner resides shall be punished by a fine of not less than $500 nor more than $1,000 for a first offense, by a fine of not less than $2,500 nor more than $7,500 for a second offense and by a fine of not less than $7,500 nor more than $10,000 or imprisonment for not less than 1 year nor more than 5 years, or by both such fine and imprisonment, for a third or subsequent offense. Failure to so report shall be a cause for suspension or permanent revocation of a person's firearm identification card or license to carry firearms, or both. Notwithstanding this paragraph or any general or special law to the contrary, no person, who in good faith, reports a loss or theft under this paragraph for the first time shall be subject to suspension, revocation or be considered unsuitable under section 131 for the renewal of a lawfully held firearm identification card or license to carry firearms; provided, however, that persons reporting loss or theft under this paragraph or under section 129B on a second or subsequent occasion may be subject to suspension, revocation or be considered unsuitable under said section 131 for the renewal of a lawfully held firearm identification card or license to carry firearms.

The provisions of this section shall not apply to the following exempted persons and uses:

(a) Any device used exclusively for signalling or distress use and required or recommended by the United States Coast Guard or the Interstate Commerce Commission, or for the firing of stud cartridges, explosive rivets or similar industrial ammunition;

(b) Federally licensed firearms manufacturers or wholesale dealers, or persons employed by them or by licensed dealers, or on their behalf, when possession of firearms, rifles or shotguns is necessary for manufacture, display, storage, transport, installation, inspection or testing;

(c) To a person voluntarily surrendering a firearm, rifle or shotgun and ammunition therefor to a licensing authority, the colonel of the state police or his designee if prior written notice has been given by said person to the licensing authority or the colonel of the state police, stating the place and approximate time of said surrender;

(d) The regular and ordinary transport of firearms, rifles or shotguns as merchandise by any common carrier;

(e) Possession by retail customers for the purpose of firing at duly licensed target concessions at amusement parks, fairs and similar locations, provided that the firearms, rifles or shotguns to be so used are firmly chained or affixed to the counter and that the proprietor is in possession of a firearm identification card or license to carry firearms;

(f) Possession of rifles and shotguns and ammunition therefor by nonresident hunters with valid nonresident hunting licenses during hunting season;

(g) Possession of rifles and shotguns and ammunition therefor by nonresidents while on a firing or shooting range;

(h) Possession of rifles and shotguns and ammunition therefor by nonresidents traveling in or through the commonwealth, providing that any rifles or shotguns are unloaded and enclosed in a case;

(i) Possession of rifles and shotguns and ammunition therefor by nonresidents while at a firearm showing or display organized by a regularly existing gun collectors' club or association;

(j) Any resident of the commonwealth returning after having been absent from the commonwealth for not less than 180 consecutive days or any new resident moving into the commonwealth, with respect to any firearm, rifle or shotgun and any ammunition therefor then in his possession, for 60 days after such return or entry into the commonwealth.

(k) Any person under the age of fifteen with respect to the use of a rifle or shotgun by such person in hunting or target shooting, provided that such use is otherwise permitted by law and is under the immediate supervision of a person holding a firearm identification card or license to carry firearms, or a duly commissioned officer, noncommissioned officer or enlisted member of the United States Army, Navy, Marine Corps, Air Force or Coast Guard, or the National Guard or military service of the commonwealth or reserve components thereof, while in the performance of his duty;

(l) The possession or utilization of any rifle or shotgun during the course of any television, movie, stage or other similar theatrical production, or by a professional photographer or writer for examination purposes in the pursuit of his profession, providing such possession or utilization is under the immediate supervision of a holder of a firearm identification card or a license to carry firearms;

(m) The temporary holding, handling or firing of a firearm for examination, trial or instruction in the presence of a holder of a license to carry firearms, or the temporary holding, handling or firing of a rifle or shotgun for examination, trial or instruction in the presence of a holder of a firearm identification card, or where such holding, handling or firing is for a lawful purpose;

(n) The transfer of a firearm, rifle or shotgun upon the death of an owner to his heir or legatee shall be subject to the provisions of this section, provided that said heir or legatee shall within one hundred and eighty days of such transfer, obtain a firearm identification card or a license to carry firearms if not otherwise an exempt person who is qualified to receive such or apply to the licensing authority for such further limited period as may be necessary for the disposition of such firearm, rifle or shotgun;

(o) Persons in the military or other service of any state or of the United States, and police officers and other peace officers of any jurisdiction, in the performance of their official duty or when duly authorized to possess them;

(p) Carrying or possession by nonresidents of so-called black powder rifles, shotguns, and ammunition therefor as described in such paragraphs (A) and (B) of the third paragraph of section 121, and the carrying or possession of conventional rifles, shotguns, and ammunition therefor by nonresidents who meet the requirements for such carrying or possession in the state in which they reside;

[(q) DELETED]

(r) Possession by a veteran's organization chartered by the Congress of the United States, chartered by the commonwealth or recognized as a nonprofit tax-exempt organization by the Internal Revenue Service and possession by the members of any such organization when on official parade duty or ceremonial occasions.

(s) Possession by federal, state and local historical societies, museums, and institutional collections open to the public, provided such firearms, rifles or shotguns are unloaded, properly housed and secured from unauthorized handling;

(t) the possession of firearms, rifles, shotguns, machine guns and ammunition, by banks or institutional lenders, or their agents, servants or employees, when the same are possessed as collateral for a secured commercial transaction or as a result of a default under a secured commercial transaction.

(u) Any nonresident who is eighteen years of age or older at the time of acquiring a rifle or shotgun from a licensed firearms dealer; provided, however, that such nonresident must hold a valid firearms license from his state of residence; provided, further, that the licensing requirements of such nonresident's state of residence are as stringent as the requirements of the commonwealth for a firearm identification card, as determined by the colonel of the state police who shall, annually, publish a list of those states whose requirements comply with the provisions of this clause.

Any person, exempted by clauses (o), (p) and (q), purchasing a rifle or shotgun or ammunition therefor shall submit to the seller such full and clear proof of identification, including shield number, serial number, military or governmental order or authorization, military or other official identification, other state firearms license, or proof of nonresidence, as may be applicable.

Nothing in this section shall permit the sale of rifles or shotguns or ammunition therefor to a minor under the age of eighteen in violation of section one hundred and thirty nor may any firearm be sold to a person under the age of 21 nor to any person who is not licensed to carry firearms under section one hundred and thirty-one unless he presents a valid firearm identification card and a permit to purchase issued under section one hundred and thirty-one A, or presents such permit to purchase and is a properly documented exempt person as hereinbefore described.

[Seventh paragraph effective through Dec. 31, 2020:]

Nothing in this section shall permit the sale or transfer of any large capacity rifle or shotgun or large capacity feeding device therefor to any person not in possession of a Class A or Class B license to carry firearms issued under section 131, or of any large capacity firearm or large capacity feeding device therefor to any person not in possession of a Class A license to carry firearms issued under section 131.

[Seventh paragraph effective Jan. 1, 2021:]

Nothing in this section shall permit the sale or transfer of a large capacity rifle, shotgun or firearm or large capacity feeding device therefor to a person not in possession of a license to carry firearms issued pursuant to section 131.

The possession of a firearm identification card issued under section one hundred and twenty-nine B shall not entitle any person to carry a firearm in violation of section ten of chapter two hundred and sixty-nine and, the possession of a firearm identification card issued under section 129B shall not entitle any person to possess any large capacity rifle or shotgun or large capacity feeding device therefor in violation of subsection (m) of said section 10 of said chapter 269.

Any person who, while not being within the limits of his own property or residence, or such person whose property or residence is under lawful search, and who is not exempt under this section, shall on demand of a police officer or other law enforcement officer, exhibit his license to carry firearms, or his firearm identification card or receipt for fee paid for such card, or, after January first, nineteen hundred and seventy, exhibit a valid hunting license issued to him which shall bear the number officially inscribed of such license to carry or card if any. Upon failure to do so such person may be required to surrender to such officer said firearm, rifle or shotgun which shall be taken into custody as under the provisions of section one hundred and twenty-nine D, except that such firearm, rifle or shotgun shall be returned forthwith upon presentation within thirty days of said license to carry firearms, firearm identification card or receipt for fee paid for such card or hunting license as hereinbefore described. Any person subject to the conditions of this paragraph may, even though no firearm, rifle or shotgun was surrendered, be required to produce within thirty days said license to carry firearms, firearm identification card or receipt for fee paid for such card, or said hunting license, failing which the conditions of section one hundred and twenty-nine D will apply. Nothing in this section shall prevent any person from being prosecuted for any violation of this chapter.

NOTE 1   "We hold that as a matter of law § 129C, par. 4(h), does not require that a rifle be enclosed in a case that is specifically manufactured as a gun case to the exclusion of all other intended uses for such a container. . . ." *Commonwealth v. Lee*, 10 Mass. App. Ct. 518, 522 (1980).

NOTE 2   Ammunition. "The possession of ammunition is an indictable offense if the person in possession does not have either a firearm identification card or a license to carry firearms. G.L. c. 140, § 129C, G.L. c. 269 § 10(h)." *Commonwealth v. Corridori*, 11 Mass. App. Ct. 469, 478–79 (1981).

NOTE 3a   Miranda. "The Miranda warnings are designed to protect the integrity of a suspect's privilege against self-incrimination. Although this privilege protects a suspect's testimonial communications, it does not permit a suspect to refuse to produce real or physical evidence (such as a license) when lawfully ordered to do so. It would serve no purpose to advise a suspect that he has a right to remain silent when the police are only demanding the production of physical evidence that the suspect may not withhold. The police, therefore, need not administer Miranda warnings before demanding that a suspect in custody produce one of the documents listed in § 129C." *Commonwealth v. Haskell*, 438 Mass. 790, 796 (2003) (citations omitted).

NOTE 3b   "The problem in this case, however, is one of form. Lieutenant Reilly did not order the defendant to produce or exhibit a license to possess the revolver found in his car; he asked the defendant whether he had such a license. As subtle as this distinction may seem, Lieutenant Reilly's question was an invitation to relate a factual assertion or disclose information, specifically, an admission that the defendant was in violation of G.L. c. 140, § 129C. It was therefore a request for a testimonial communication that entitled the defendant to the Fifth Amendment's protections, including the right to refuse to answer. Given our assumption that the defendant was in custody for Miranda purposes when Lieutenant Reilly questioned him, and the fact that the defendant was not given the required warnings, the defendant's answer must therefore be suppressed." *Commonwealth v. Haskell*, 438 Mass. 790, 796 (2003) (citations omitted).

NOTE 4   See Notes following G.L. c. 269, § 10.

SECTION 129D
Surrender of firearms and ammunition to licensing authority upon denial of application for, or revocation of, identification card or license; right to transfer; sale by colonel of state police; rules and regulations
(Amended by 2014 Mass. Acts c. 284, §§ 42–44, effective Jan. 1, 2015.)

Upon revocation, suspension or denial of an application for a firearm identification card pursuant to section 129B or for any firearms license if the firearm identification card is not then in force or for any machine gun license, the person whose application was so revoked, suspended or denied shall without delay deliver or surrender to the licensing authority where the person resides all firearms, rifles, shotguns and machine guns and ammunition which the person then possesses unless an appeal of the revocation or suspension is pending. The person or the person's legal representative shall have the right, at any time up to 1 year after the delivery or surrender, to transfer the firearms, rifles, shotguns and machine guns and ammunition to any licensed dealer or any other person legally permitted to purchase or take possession of the firearms, rifles, shotguns and machine guns and ammunition and, upon notification in writing by the purchaser or transferee and the former owner, the licensing authority shall within 10 days deliver the firearms, rifles, shotguns and machine guns and ammunition to the transferee or purchaser and the licensing authority shall observe due care in the receipt and holding of any such firearm, rifle, shotgun or machine gun and ammunition; provided, however, that the purchaser or transferee shall affirm in writing that the purchaser or transferee shall not in violation of section 129C transfer the firearms, rifles, shotguns or machine guns or ammunition to the former owner. The licensing authority shall at the time of delivery or surrender inform the person in writing of the authority's ability, within 1 year after delivery or surrender, to transfer the firearms, rifles, shotguns and machine guns and ammunition to any licensed dealer or other person legally permitted to purchase or take possession.

The licensing authority, after taking possession of any firearm, rifle, shotgun, machine gun or ammunition by any means, may transfer possession of such weapon for storage purposes to a federally and state licensed dealer of such weapons and ammunition who operates a bonded warehouse on the licensed premises that is equipped with a safe for the secure storage of firearms and a weapon box or similar container for the secure storage of other weapons and ammunition; provided, however, that the licensing authority shall not transfer to such dealer possession of any weapon that is or may be evidence in any current or pending criminal case concerning a violation of any general or special law, rule or regulation governing the use, possession or ownership of such weapon. Any such dealer that takes possession of a weapon under the provision of this section shall: (i) inspect such weapon; (ii) issue to the owner a receipt indicating the make, model, caliber, serial number and condition of each weapon so received; and (iii) store and maintain all weapons so received in accordance with such regulations, rules or guidelines as the secretary of the executive office of public safety may establish under this section. The owner shall be liable to such dealer for reasonable storage charges and may dispose of any such weapon as provided under this section by transfer to a person lawfully permitted to purchase or take possession of such weapon.

Firearms, rifles, shotguns or machine guns and ammunition not disposed of after delivery or surrender according to the provisions of this section shall be sold at public auction by the colonel of the state police to the highest bidding person legally permitted to purchase and possess said firearms, rifles, shotguns or machine guns and ammunition and the proceeds shall be remitted to the state treasurer. Any such weapon that is stored and maintained by a licensed dealer as provided under this section may be so auctioned at the direction of: (i) the licensing authority at the expiration of one year following initial surrender or delivery to such licensing authority; or (ii) the dealer then in possession, if the storage charges for such weapon have been in arrears for 90 days; provided, however, that in either case, title shall pass to the licensed dealer for the purpose of transferring ownership to the auctioneer; and provided, further, that in either case, after deduction and payment for storage charges and all necessary costs associated with such surrender and transfer, all surplus proceeds, if any, shall be immediately returned to the owner of such weapon; provided, however, that no firearm, rifle, shotgun or machine gun or ammunition classified as having been used to carry out a criminal act pursuant to section 131Q shall be sold at public auction pursuant to this section.

If the licensing authority cannot reasonably ascertain a lawful owner within 180 days of acquisition by the authority, the authority may, in its discretion, trade or dispose of surplus, donated, abandoned or junk firearms, rifles, shotguns or machine guns or ammunition to properly licensed distributors or firearms dealers. The proceeds of the sale or transfer shall be remitted or credited to the municipality in which the authority presides to purchase weapons, equipment or supplies or for violence reduction or suicide prevention; provided, however, that no firearm, rifle, shotgun or machine gun or ammunition classified as having been used to carry out a criminal act pursuant to section 131Q shall be considered surplus, donated, abandoned or junk for the purposes of this section.

The secretary of the executive office of public safety may make and promulgate such rules and regulations as are necessary to carry out the provisions of this section.

SECTION 130
Sale or furnishing weapons or ammunition to aliens or minors; penalty; exceptions
(Stricken & replaced by 2014 Mass. Acts c. 284, § 45, effective Jan. 1, 2015.)

Whoever sells or furnishes a rifle, shotgun or ammunition to any alien 18 years of age or older who does not hold a permit card issued to that alien pursuant to section 131H or, except as provided in this section or section 131E, whoever sells or furnishes any alien or any person under 18 years of age a rifle, shotgun, machine gun or ammunition, or whoever sells or furnishes to any person under 21 years of age a firearm or large capacity rifle or shotgun or ammunition therefor shall have the license to sell firearms, rifles, shotguns, machine guns or ammunition revoked and shall not be entitled to apply for such license for 10 years from the date of such revocation and shall be punished by a fine of not less than $1,000 nor more than $10,000, or by imprisonment in a state prison for not more than 10 years or by imprisonment in a house of correction for not more than 2½ years or by both such fine and imprisonment.

SECTION 130½
Furnishing weapons to minors for hunting, recreation
(Added by 2014 Mass. Acts c. 284, § 45, effective Jan. 1, 2015.)

Notwithstanding section 130 or any general or special law to the contrary, it shall be lawful to furnish a weapon to a minor for hunting, recreation, instruction and participation in shooting sports while under the supervision of a holder of a valid firearm identification card or license to carry appropriate for the weapon in use; provided, however, that the parent or guardian of the minor granted consent for such activities.

SECTION 130A
Repealed

SECTION 130B
Firearm licensing review board; members; license applicants; hearings

(a) There shall be a firearm licensing review board, established within the department of criminal justice information services, in this section called the board, comprised of seven members, one of whom shall be a member of the department of criminal justice information services appointed by the commissioner and who shall be the chair, one of whom shall be the secretary of public safety or his designee, one of whom shall be the colonel of state police or his designee, one of whom shall be appointed by the Massachusetts Chiefs of Police Association, one of whom shall be the attorney general or his designee, one whom shall be an attorney with litigation experience in firearm licensing cases and appointed by the governor from a list of qualified persons submitted to the governor by the Massachusetts Bar Association, and one of whom shall be a retired member of the judiciary and appointed by the governor.

(b) An applicant for a firearm identification card or license to carry who has been convicted of or adjudicated a delinquent child or youthful offender by reason of an offense or offenses punishable by two and a half years imprisonment or less when committed under the laws of the commonwealth which was not an assault or battery on a family member or household member, as defined by section 1 of chapter 209A, except that the determination to be made under clause (e) of said section 1 of said chapter 209A shall be made by the review board, may, after the passage of five years from conviction, adjudication as a youthful offender or a delinquent child or release from confinement, commitment, probation or parole supervision for such conviction or adjudication, whichever is last occurring, file a petition for review of eligibility with the firearm licensing review board.

(c) The petitioner shall provide to the board a copy of a completed firearm identification card or license to carry application, which application shall have previously been submitted to the licensing authority or be submitted to the licensing authority contemporaneously with the petition filed with the board. The petitioner shall have the burden to prove his suitability to receive a firearm identification card or a license to carry by clear and convincing evidence. The board shall set a reasonable filing fee to file the petition.

(d) If the board determines, by two-thirds vote, that: (i) the sole disqualifier for the petitioner is any conviction or adjudication as a youthful offender or a delinquent child for an offense or offenses punishable by two and a half years imprisonment or less when committed under the laws of the commonwealth, arising out of a single incident and which does not otherwise disqualify the petitioner under subclauses (a), (d) or (e) of clause (i) or clauses (ii) to (ix), inclusive, of paragraph (1) of section 129B or subclauses (a), (d) or (e) of clause (i) or clauses (ii) to (vii), inclusive, of paragraph (d) of section 131, and which was not an assault or battery on a family member or household members, as defined by section 1 of chapter 209A, except that the determination to be made under clause (e) of said section 1 of said chapter 209A shall be made by the board; (ii) five years has passed since such conviction or adjudication or release from confinement, commitment, probation or parole supervision for such conviction or adjudication, whichever is last occurring; and (iii) by clear and convincing evidence, that the petitioner is a suitable person to be a firearm identification card or license to carry holder, the board shall determine that the petitioner's right or ability to possess a firearm is fully restored in the commonwealth with respect to such conviction or adjudication and that such conviction or adjudication shall not prohibit such petitioner from applying to a licensing authority for a firearm identification card or license to carry. The board shall make a determination on a petition within 60 days after receipt of the petition.

(e) The board shall hold hearings at such times and places as in its discretion it reasonably determines to be required, but not less than once every 90ninety days, and shall give reasonable notice of the time and place of the hearing to the petitioner. The board shall have the power to compel attendance of witnesses at hearings.

(f) All hearings shall be conducted in an informal manner, but otherwise according to the rules of evidence, and all witnesses shall be sworn by the chair. If requested by the petitioner and payment for stenographic services, as determined by the board, accompanies such request, the board shall cause a verbatim transcript of the hearing to be made. The board's decisions and findings of facts therefore shall be communicated in writing to the petitioner and to the licensing authority to whom the petitioner has applied or intends to apply within twenty days of rendering a decision.

(g) Members of the board shall serve without compensation, but shall be entitled to reasonable subsistence and travel allowances in the performance of their duties.

SECTION 131
License to carry or possess firearms; Class A and B; conditions and restrictions
(Amended by 2010 Mass. Acts c. 466, § 3, effective Apr. 14, 2011; 2011 Mass. Acts c. 9, §§ 16–17, effective Apr. 11, 2011; 2014 Mass. Acts c. 284, § 55, effective Aug. 11, 2014; 2014 Mass. Acts c. 284, §§ 48, 50, 51, 53, 56, 57, effective Jan. 1, 2015.)

(For text of Section 131 as amended by 2014 Mass. Acts c. 284, §§ 46, 47, 49, 52, 54, effective Jan. 1, 2021, see below.)

All licenses to carry firearms shall be designated Class A or Class B, and the issuance and possession of any such license shall be subject to the following conditions and restrictions:

(a) A Class A license shall entitle a holder thereof to purchase, rent, lease, borrow, possess and carry: (i) firearms, including large capacity firearms, and feeding devices and ammunition therefor, for all lawful purposes, subject to such restrictions relative to the possession, use or carrying of firearms as the licensing authority deems proper; and (ii) rifles and shotguns, including large capacity weapons, and feeding devices and ammunition therefor, for all lawful purposes; provided, however, that the licensing authority may impose such restrictions relative to the possession, use or carrying of large capacity rifles and shotguns as it deems proper. A violation of a restriction imposed by the licensing authority under the provisions of this paragraph shall be cause for suspension or revocation and shall, unless otherwise provided, be punished by a fine of not less than $1,000 nor more than $10,000; provided, however, that the provisions of section 10 of chapter 269 shall not apply to such violation.

The colonel of state police may, after an investigation, grant a Class A license to a club or facility with an on-site shooting range or gallery, which club is incorporated under the laws of the commonwealth for the possession, storage and use of large capacity weapons, ammunition therefor and large capacity feeding devices for use with such weapons on the premises of such club; provided, however, that not less than one shareholder of such club shall be qualified and suitable to be issued such license; and provided further, that such large capacity weapons and ammunition feeding devices may be used under such Class A club license only by such members that possess a valid firearm identification card issued under section 129B or a valid Class A or Class B license to carry firearms, or by such other persons that the club permits while under the direct supervision of a certified firearms safety instructor or club member who, in the case of a large capacity firearm, possesses a valid Class A license to carry firearms or, in the case of a large capacity rifle or shotgun, possesses a valid Class A or Class B license to carry firearms. Such club shall not permit shooting at targets that depict human figures, human effigies, human silhouettes or any human images thereof, except by public safety personnel performing in line with their official duties.

No large capacity weapon or large capacity feeding device shall be removed from the premises except for the purposes of: (i) transferring such firearm or feeding device to a licensed dealer; (ii) transporting such firearm or feeding device to a licensed gunsmith for repair; (iii) target, trap or skeet shooting on the premises of another club incorporated under the laws of the commonwealth and for transporting thereto; (iv) attending an exhibition or educational project or event that is sponsored by, conducted under the supervision of or approved by a public law enforcement agency or a nationally or state recognized entity that promotes proficiency in or education about semiautomatic weapons and for transporting thereto and therefrom; (v) hunting in accordance with the provisions of chapter 131; or (vi) surrendering such firearm or feeding device under the provisions of section 129D. Any large capacity weapon or large capacity feeding device kept on the premises of a lawfully incorporated shooting club shall, when not in use, be secured in a locked container, and shall be unloaded during any lawful transport. The clerk or other corporate officer of such club shall annually file a report with the colonel of state police and the commissioner of the department of criminal justice information services listing all large capacity weapons and large capacity feeding devices owned or possessed under such license. The colonel of state police or his designee, shall have the right to inspect all firearms owned or possessed by such club upon request during regular business hours and said colonel may revoke or suspend a club license for a violation of any provision of this chapter or chapter 269 relative to the ownership, use or possession of large capacity weapons or large capacity feeding devices.

(b) A Class B license shall entitle a holder thereof to purchase, rent, lease, borrow, possess and carry: (i) non-large capacity firearms and feeding devices and ammunition therefor, for all lawful purposes, subject to such restrictions relative to the possession, use or carrying of such firearm as the licensing authority or any law enforcement officer employed by the licensing authority deems proper; provided, however, that a Class B license shall not entitle the holder thereof to carry or possess a loaded firearm in a concealed manner in any public way or place; and provided further, that a Class B license shall not entitle the holder thereof to possess a large capacity firearm, except under a Class A club license issued under this section or under the direct supervision of a holder of a valid Class A license at an incorporated shooting club or licensed shooting range; and (ii) rifles and shotguns, including large capacity rifles and shotguns, and feeding devices and ammunition therefor, for all lawful purposes; provided, however, that the licensing authority may impose such restrictions relative to the possession, use or carrying of large capacity rifles and shotguns as he deems proper. A violation of a restriction provided under this paragraph, or a restriction imposed by the licensing authority under the provisions of this paragraph, shall be cause for suspension or revocation and shall, unless otherwise provided, be punished by a fine of not less than $1,000 nor more than $10,000; provided, however, that the provisions of section 10 of chapter 269 shall not apply to such violation.

A Class B license shall not be a valid license for the purpose of complying with any provision under this chapter governing the purchase, sale, lease, rental or transfer of any weapon or ammunition feeding device if such weapon is a large capacity firearm or if such ammunition feeding device is a large capacity feeding device for use with a large capacity firearm, both as defined in section 121.

(c) Either a Class A or Class B license shall be valid for the purpose of owning, possessing, purchasing and transferring nonlarge capacity rifles and shotguns, and for purchasing and possessing chemical mace, pepper spray or other similarly propelled liquid, gas or powder designed to temporarily incapacitate, consistent with the entitlements conferred by a firearm identification card issued under section 129B.

(d) Any person residing or having a place of business within the jurisdiction of the licensing authority or any law enforcement officer employed by the licensing authority or any person residing in an area of exclusive federal jurisdiction located within a city or town may submit to the licensing authority or the colonel of state police, an application for a Class A license to carry firearms, or renewal of the same, which the licensing authority or the colonel may issue if it appears that the applicant is not a prohibited person, as set forth in this section, to be issued a license and has good reason to fear injury to the applicant or the applicant's property or for any other reason, including the carrying of firearms for use in sport or target practice only, subject to the restrictions expressed or authorized under this section.

A prohibited person shall be a person who:

(i) has, in a court of the commonwealth, been convicted or adjudicated a youthful offender or delinquent child, both as defined in section 52 of chapter 119, for the commission of (A) a felony; (B) a misdemeanor punishable by imprisonment for more than 2 years; (C) a violent crime as defined in section 121; (D) a violation of any law regulating the use, possession, ownership, transfer, purchase, sale, lease, rental, receipt or transportation of weapons or ammunition for which a term of imprisonment may be imposed; (E) a violation of any law regulating the use, possession or sale of a controlled substance as defined in section 1 of chapter 94C including, but not limited to, a violation of said chapter 94C; or (F) a misdemeanor crime of domestic violence as defined in 18 U.S.C. 921(a)(33);

(ii) has, in any other state or federal jurisdiction, been convicted or adjudicated a youthful offender or delinquent child for the commission of (A) a felony; (B) a misdemeanor punishable by imprisonment for more than 2 years; (C) a violent crime as defined in section 121; (D) a violation of any law regulating the use, possession, ownership, transfer, purchase, sale, lease, rental, receipt or transportation of weapons or ammunition for which a term of imprisonment may be imposed; (E) a violation of any law regulating the use, possession or sale of a controlled substance as defined in said section 1 of said chapter 94C including, but not limited to, a violation of said chapter 94C; or (F) a misdemeanor crime of domestic violence as defined in 18 U.S.C. 921(a)(33);

(iii) is or has been (A) committed to a hospital or institution for mental illness, alcohol or substance abuse, except a commitment pursuant to sections 35 or 36C of chapter 123, unless after 5 years from the date of the confinement, the applicant submits with the application an affidavit of a licensed physician or clinical psychologist attesting that such physician or psychologist is familiar with the applicant's mental illness, alcohol or substance abuse and that in the physician's or psychologist's opinion, the applicant is not disabled by a mental illness, alcohol or substance abuse in a manner that shall prevent the applicant from possessing a firearm, rifle or shotgun; (B) committed by a court order to a hospital or institution for mental illness, unless the applicant was granted a petition for relief of the court order pursuant to said section 36C of said chapter 123 and submits a copy of the court order with the application; (C) subject to an order of the probate court appointing a guardian or conservator for a incapacitated person on the grounds that the applicant lacks the mental capacity to contract or manage the applicant's affairs, unless the applicant was granted a petition for relief of the order of the probate court pursuant to section 56C of chapter 215 and submits a copy of the order of the probate court with the application; or (D) found to be a person with an alcohol use disorder or substance use disorder or both and committed pursuant to said section 35 of said chapter 123, unless the applicant was granted a petition for relief of the court order pursuant to said section 35 and submits a copy of the court order with the application;

(iv) is younger than 21 years of age at the time of the application;

(v) is an alien who does not maintain lawful permanent residency;

(vi) is currently subject to: (A) an order for suspension or surrender issued pursuant to sections 3B or 3C of chapter 209A or a similar order issued by another jurisdiction; or (B) a permanent or temporary protection order issued pursuant to said chapter 209A or a similar order issued by another jurisdiction, including any order described in 18 U.S.C. 922(g)(8);

(vii) is currently the subject of an outstanding arrest warrant in any state or federal jurisdiction;

(viii) has been discharged from the armed forces of the United States under dishonorable conditions;

(ix) is a fugitive from justice; or

(x) having been a citizen of the United States, has renounced that citizenship.

The licensing authority may deny the application or renewal of a license to carry, or suspend or revoke a license issued under this section if, in a reasonable exercise of discretion, the licensing authority determines that the applicant or licensee is unsuitable to be issued or to continue to hold a license to carry. A determination of unsuitability shall be based on: (i) reliable and credible information that the applicant or licensee has exhibited or engaged in behavior that suggests that, if issued a license, the applicant or licensee may create a risk to public safety; or (ii) existing factors that suggest that, if issued a license, the applicant or licensee may create a risk to public safety. Upon denial of an application or renewal of a license based on a determination of unsuitability, the licensing authority shall notify the applicant in writing setting forth the specific reasons for the determination in accordance with paragraph (e). Upon revoking or suspending a license based on a determination of unsuitability, the licensing authority shall notify the holder of a license in writing setting forth the specific reasons for the determination in accordance with paragraph (f). The determination of unsuitability shall be subject to judicial review under said paragraph (f).

(e) Within seven days of the receipt of a completed application for a license to carry or possess firearms, or renewal of same, the licensing authority shall forward one copy of the application and one copy of the applicant's fingerprints to the colonel of state police, who shall within thirty days advise the licensing authority, in writing, of any disqualifying criminal record of the applicant arising from within or without the commonwealth and whether there is reason to believe that the applicant is disqualified for any of the foregoing reasons from possessing a license to carry or possess firearms. In searching for any disqualifying history of the applicant, the colonel shall utilize, or cause to be utilized, files maintained by the department of probation and statewide and nationwide criminal justice, warrant and protection order information systems and files including, but not limited to, the National Instant Criminal Background Check System. The colonel shall inquire of the commissioner of the department of mental health relative to whether the applicant is disqualified from being so licensed. If the information available to the colonel does not indicate that the possession of a firearm or large capacity firearm by the applicant would be in violation of state or federal law, he shall certify such fact, in writing, to the licensing authority within said thirty day period.

The licensing authority may also make inquiries concerning the applicant to: (i) the commissioner of the department of criminal justice information services relative to any disqualifying condition and records of purchases, sales, rentals, leases and transfers of weapons or ammunition concerning the applicant; (ii) the commissioner of probation relative to any record contained within the department of probation or the statewide domestic violence record keeping system concerning the applicant; and (iii) the commissioner of the department of mental health relative to whether the applicant is a suitable person to possess firearms or is not a suitable person to possess firearms. The director or commissioner to whom the licensing authority makes such inquiry shall provide prompt and full cooperation for that purpose in any investigation of the applicant.

The licensing authority shall, within forty days from the date of application, either approve the application and issue the license or deny the application and notify the applicant of the reason for such denial in writing; provided, however, that no such license shall be issued unless the colonel has certified, in writing, that the information available to him does not indicate that the possession of a firearm or large capacity

firearm by the applicant would be in violation of state or federal law.

The licensing authority shall provide to the applicant a receipt indicating that it received the application. The receipt shall be provided to the applicant within 7 days by mail if the application was received by mail or immediately if the application was made in person; provided, however, that the receipt shall include the applicant's name and address; current license number and license expiration date, if any; the date the licensing authority received the application; the name, address and telephone number of the licensing authority; the agent of the licensing authority that received the application; the type of application; and whether the application is for a new license or a renewal of an existing license. The licensing authority shall keep a copy of the receipt for not less than 1 year and shall furnish a copy to the applicant if requested by the applicant.

(f) A license issued under this section shall be revoked or suspended by the licensing authority, or his designee, upon the occurrence of any event that would have disqualified the holder from being issued such license or from having such license renewed. A license may be revoked or suspended by the licensing authority if it appears that the holder is no longer a suitable person to possess such license. Any revocation or suspension of a license shall be in writing and shall state the reasons therefor. Upon revocation or suspension, the licensing authority shall take possession of such license and the person whose license is so revoked or suspended shall take all actions required under the provisions of section 129D. No appeal or post-judgment motion shall operate to stay such revocation or suspension. Notices of revocation and suspension shall be forwarded to the executive director of the criminal history systems board and the commissioner of probation and shall be included in the criminal justice information system. A revoked or suspended license may be reinstated only upon the termination of all disqualifying conditions, if any.

Any applicant or holder aggrieved by a denial, revocation, suspension or restriction placed on a license, unless a hearing has previously been held pursuant to chapter 209A, may, within either 90 days after receiving notice of the denial, revocation or suspension or within 90 days after the expiration of the time limit during which the licensing authority shall respond to the applicant or, in the case of a restriction, any time after a restriction is placed on the license pursuant to this section, file a petition to obtain judicial review in the district court having jurisdiction in the city or town in which the applicant filed the application or in which the license was issued. If after a hearing a justice of the court finds that there was no reasonable ground for denying, suspending, revoking or restricting the license and that the petitioner is not prohibited by law from possessing a license, the justice may order a license to be issued or reinstated to the petitioner or may order the licensing authority to remove certain restrictions placed on the license.

(g) A license shall be in a standard form provided by the commissioner of the department of criminal justice information services in a size and shape equivalent to that of a license to operate motor vehicles issued by the registry of motor vehicles pursuant to section 8 of chapter 90 and shall contain a license number which shall clearly indicate whether such number identifies a Class A or Class B license, the name, address, photograph, fingerprint, place and date of birth, height, weight, hair color, eye color and signature of the licensee. Such license shall be marked "License to Carry Firearms" and shall clearly indicate whether the license is Class A or Class B. The application for such license shall be made in a standard form provided by the executive director of the criminal history systems board, which form shall require the applicant to affirmatively state under the pains and penalties of perjury that such applicant is not disqualified on any of the grounds enumerated above from being issued such license.

(h) Any person who knowingly files an application containing false information shall be punished by a fine of not less than $500 nor more than $1,000 or by imprisonment for not less than six months nor more than two years in a house of correction, or by both such fine and imprisonment.

(i) A license to carry or possess firearms shall be valid, unless revoked or suspended, for a period of not more than 6 years from the date of issue and shall expire on the anniversary of the licensee's date of birth occurring not less than 5 years nor more than 6 years from the date of issue; provided, however, that, if the licensee applied for renewal before the license expired, the license shall remain valid after its expiration date for all lawful purposes until the application for renewal is approved or denied. If a licensee is on active duty with the armed forces of the United States on the expiration date of the license, the license shall remain valid until the licensee is released from active duty and for a period not less than 180 days following the release; provided, however, that, if the licensee applied for renewal prior to the end of that period, the license shall remain valid after its expiration date for all lawful purposes until the application for renewal is approved or denied. An application for renewal of a Class B license filed before the license has expired shall not extend the license beyond the stated expiration date; provided, that the Class B license shall expire on the anniversary of the licensee's date of birth occurring not less than 5 years nor more than 6 years from the date of issue. Any renewal thereof shall expire on the anniversary of the licensee's date of birth occurring not less than five years but not more than six years from the effective date of such license. Any license issued to an applicant born on February 29 shall expire on March 1. The fee for the application shall be $100, which shall be payable to the licensing authority and shall not be prorated or refunded in case of revocation or denial. The licensing authority shall retain $25 of the fee; $50 of the fee shall be deposited into the general fund of the commonwealth and not less than $50,000 of the funds deposited into the General Fund shall be allocated to the Firearm Licensing Review Board, established in section 130B, for its operations and that any funds not expended by said board for its operations shall revert back to the General Fund; and $25 of the fee shall be deposited in the Firearms Fingerprint Identity Verification Trust Fund. For active and retired law enforcement officials, or local, state, or federal government entities acting on their behalf, the fee for the application shall be set at $25, which shall be payable to the licensing authority and shall not be prorated or refunded in case of revocation or denial. The licensing authority shall retain $12.50 of the fee, and $12.50 of the fee shall be deposited into the general fund of the commonwealth. Notwithstanding any general or special law to the contrary, licensing authorities shall deposit such portion of the license application fee into the Firearms Record Keeping Fund quarterly, not later than January 1, April 1, July 1 and October 1 of each

year. Notwithstanding any general or special law to the contrary, licensing authorities shall deposit quarterly such portion of the license application fee as is to be deposited into the General Fund, not later than January 1, April 1, July 1 and October 1 of each year. For the purposes of section 10 of chapter 269, an expired license to carry firearms shall be deemed to be valid for a period not to exceed 90 days beyond the stated date of expiration, unless such license to carry firearms has been revoked.

Any person over the age of 70 and any law enforcement officer applying for a license to carry firearms through his employing agency shall be exempt from the requirement of paying a renewal fee for a Class A or Class B license to carry.

(j)(1) No license shall be required for the carrying or possession of a firearm known as a detonator and commonly used on vehicles as a signaling and marking device, when carried or possessed for such signaling or marking purposes.

(2) No license to carry shall be required for the possession of an unloaded large capacity rifle or shotgun or an unloaded feeding device therefor by a veteran's organization chartered by the Congress of the United States, chartered by the commonwealth or recognized as a nonprofit tax-exempt organization by the Internal Revenue Service, or by the members of any such organization when on official parade duty or during ceremonial occasions. For purposes of this subparagraph, an "unloaded large capacity rifle or shotgun" and an "unloaded feeding device therefor" shall include any large capacity rifle, shotgun or feeding device therefor loaded with a blank cartridge or blank cartridges, so-called, which contain no projectile within such blank or blanks or within the bore or chamber of such large capacity rifle or shotgun.

(k) Whoever knowingly issues a license in violation of this section shall be punished by a fine of not less than $500 nor more than $1,000 or by imprisonment for not less than six months nor more than two years in a jail or house of correction, or by both such fine and imprisonment.

(l) The executive director of the criminal history systems board shall send electronically or by first class mail to the holder of each such license to carry firearms, a notice of the expiration of such license not less than 90 days prior to such expiration and shall enclose therein a form for the renewal of such license. The form for renewal shall include an affidavit in which the applicant shall verify that the applicant has not lost any firearms or had any firearms stolen from the applicant since the date of the applicant's last renewal or issuance. The taking of fingerprints shall not be required in issuing the renewal of a license if the renewal applicant's fingerprints are on file with the department of the state police. Any licensee shall notify, in writing, the licensing authority who issued said license, the chief of police into whose jurisdiction the licensee moves and the executive director of the criminal history systems board of any change of address. Such notification shall be made by certified mail within 30 days of its occurrence. Failure to so notify shall be cause for revocation or suspension of said license. The commissioner of criminal justice information services shall provide electronic notice of expiration only upon the request of a cardholder. A request for electronic notice of expiration shall be forwarded to the department on a form furnished by the commissioner. Any electronic address maintained by the department for the purpose of providing electronic notice of expiration shall be considered a firearms record and shall not be disclosed except as provided in section 10 of chapter 66.

(m) Notwithstanding the provisions of section 10 of chapter 269, any person in possession of a firearm, rifle or shotgun whose license issued under this section is invalid for the sole reason that it has expired, not including licenses that remain valid under paragraph (i) because the licensee applied for renewal before the license expired, but who shall not be disqualified from renewal upon application therefor pursuant to this section, shall be subject to a civil fine of not less than $100 nor more than $5,000 and the provisions of section 10 of chapter 269 shall not apply; provided, however, that the exemption from the provisions of said section 10 of said chapter 269 provided herein shall not apply if: (i) such license has been revoked or suspended, unless such revocation or suspension was caused by failure to give notice of a change of address as required under this section; (ii) revocation or suspension of such license is pending, unless such revocation or suspension was caused by failure to give notice of a change of address as required under this section; or (iii) an application for renewal of such license has been denied. Any law enforcement officer who discovers a person to be in possession of a firearm, rifle or shotgun after such person's license has expired, meaning after 90 days beyond the stated expiration date on the license, has been revoked or suspended, solely for failure to give notice of a change of address, shall confiscate such firearm, rifle or shotgun and the expired or suspended license then in possession and such officer, shall forward such license to the licensing authority by whom it was issued as soon as practicable. The officer shall, at the time of confiscation, provide to the person whose firearm, rifle or shotgun has been confiscated, a written inventory and receipt for all firearms, rifles or shotguns confiscated and the officer and his employer shall exercise due care in the handling, holding and storage of these items. Any confiscated weapon shall be returned to the owner upon the renewal or reinstatement of such expired or suspended license within one year of such confiscation or may be otherwise disposed of in accordance with the provisions of section 129D. The provisions of this paragraph shall not apply if such person has a valid license to carry firearms issued under section 131F.

(n) Upon issuance of a license to carry or possess firearms under this section, the licensing authority shall forward a copy of such approved application and license to the executive director of the criminal history systems board, who shall inform the licensing authority forthwith of the existence of any disqualifying condition discovered or occurring subsequent to the issuance of a license under this section.

(o) No person shall be issued a license to carry or possess a machine gun in the commonwealth, except that a licensing authority or the colonel of state police may issue a machine gun license to:

(i) a firearm instructor certified by the municipal police training committee for the sole purpose of firearm instruction to police personnel;

(ii) a bona fide collector of firearms upon application or upon application for renewal of such license.

(p) The executive director of the criminal history systems board shall promulgate regulations in accordance with chapter 30A to establish criteria for persons who shall be classified as bona fide collectors of firearms.

(q) Nothing in this section shall authorize the purchase, possession or transfer of any weapon, ammunition or feeding device that is, or in such manner that is, prohibited by state or federal law.

(r) The secretary of the executive office of public safety or his designee may promulgate regulations to carry out the purposes of this section.

[*Text of Section 131 as effective Jan. 1, 2021:*]

The issuance and possession of a license to carry firearms shall be subject to the following conditions and restrictions:

(a) A license shall entitle a holder thereof of a license to purchase, rent, lease, borrow, possess and carry: (i) firearms, including large capacity firearms, and feeding devices and ammunition therefor, for all lawful purposes, subject to such restrictions relative to the possession, use or carrying of firearms as the licensing authority considers proper; and (ii) rifles and shotguns, including large capacity weapons, and feeding devices and ammunition therefor, for all lawful purposes; provided, however, that the licensing authority may impose such restrictions relative to the possession, use or carrying of large capacity rifles and shotguns as it considers proper. A violation of a restriction imposed by the licensing authority under this paragraph shall be cause for suspension or revocation and shall, unless otherwise provided, be punished by a fine of not less than $1,000 nor more than $10,000; provided, however, that section 10 of chapter 269 shall not apply to a violation of this paragraph.

(b) The colonel of state police may, after an investigation, grant a license to a club or facility with an on-site shooting range or gallery, which club is incorporated under the laws of the commonwealth for the possession, storage and use of large capacity weapons, ammunition therefor and large capacity feeding devices for use with such weapons on the premises of the club; provided, however, that not less than 1 shareholder of the club shall be qualified and suitable to be issued a license; and provided further, that such large capacity weapons and ammunition feeding devices may be used under the club license only by a member that possesses a valid firearm identification card issued pursuant to section 129B or a valid license to carry firearms, or by such other person that the club permits while under the direct supervision of a certified firearms safety instructor or club member who, in the case of a large capacity firearm, possesses a valid license to carry firearms or, in the case of a large capacity rifle or shotgun, possesses a valid license to carry firearms. The club shall not permit shooting at targets that depict human figures, human effigies, human silhouettes or any human images thereof, except by public safety personnel performing in line with their official duties.

No large capacity weapon or large capacity feeding device shall be removed from the premises except to: (i) transfer the firearm or feeding device to a licensed dealer; (ii) transport the firearm or feeding device to a licensed gunsmith for repair; (iii) target, trap or skeet shoot on the premises of another club incorporated under the laws of the commonwealth and to transport thereto; (iv) attend an exhibition or educational project or event that is sponsored by, conducted under the supervision of or approved by a public law enforcement agency or a nationally or state recognized entity that promotes proficiency in or education about semiautomatic weapons and to transport thereto and therefrom; (v) hunt pursuant to chapter 131; or (vi) surrender the firearm or feeding device pursuant to section 129D. Any large capacity weapon or large capacity feeding device kept on the premises of a lawfully incorporated shooting club shall, when not in use, be secured in a locked container and shall be unloaded during any lawful transport. The clerk or other corporate officer of the club shall annually file a report with the colonel of state police and the commissioner of criminal justice information services listing all large capacity weapons and large capacity feeding devices owned or possessed under the license. The colonel or a designee may inspect all firearms owned or possessed by the club upon request during regular business hours and the colonel may revoke or suspend a club license for a violation of this chapter or chapter 269 relative to the ownership, use or possession of large capacity weapons or large capacity feeding devices.

(c) A license to carry firearms shall be valid to own, possess, purchase and transfer non-large capacity rifles and shotguns, consistent with the entitlements conferred by a firearm identification card issued under section 129B.

(d) A person residing or having a place of business within the jurisdiction of the licensing authority or any law enforcement officer employed by the licensing authority or any person residing in an area of exclusive federal jurisdiction located within a city or town may submit to the licensing authority or the colonel of state police an application for a license to carry firearms, or renewal of the same, which the licensing authority or the colonel may issue if it appears that the applicant is not a prohibited person as set forth in this section to be issued a license and that the applicant has good reason to fear injury to the applicant or the applicant's property or for any other reason, including the carrying of firearms for use in sport or target practice only, subject to the restrictions expressed or authorized under this section.

A prohibited person shall be a person who:

(i) has, in a court of the commonwealth, been convicted or adjudicated a youthful offender or delinquent child, both as defined in section 52 of chapter 119, for the commission of (A) a felony; (B) a misdemeanor punishable by imprisonment for more than 2 years; (C) a violent crime as defined in section 121; (D) a violation of any law regulating the use, possession, ownership, transfer, purchase, sale, lease, rental, receipt or transportation of weapons or ammunition for which a term of imprisonment may be imposed; (E) a violation of any law regulating the use, possession or sale of a controlled substance as defined in section 1 of chapter 94C including, but not limited to, a violation of said chapter 94C; or (F) a misdemeanor crime of domestic violence as defined in 18 U.S.C. 921(a)(33);

(ii) has, in any other state or federal jurisdiction, been convicted or adjudicated a youthful offender or delinquent child for the commission of (A) a felony; (B) a misdemeanor punishable by imprisonment for more than 2 years; (C) a violent crime as defined in section 121; (D) a violation of any law regulating the use, possession, ownership, transfer, purchase, sale, lease, rental, receipt or transportation of weapons or ammunition for which a term of imprisonment may be imposed; (E) a violation of any law regulating the use, possession or sale of a controlled substance as defined in said section 1 of said chapter 94C including, but not limited to, a violation of said chapter 94C; or (F) a misdemeanor crime of domestic violence as defined in 18 U.S.C. 921(a)(33);

(iii) is or has been (A) committed to a hospital or institution for mental illness, alcohol or substance abuse, except a commitment pursuant to sections 35 or 36C of chapter 123, unless after 5 years from the date of the confinement, the applicant submits with the application an affidavit of a licensed physician or clinical psychologist attesting that such physician or psychologist is familiar with the applicant's mental illness, alcohol or substance abuse and that in the physician's or psychologist's opinion, the applicant is not disabled by a mental illness, alcohol or substance abuse in a manner that shall prevent the applicant from possessing a firearm, rifle or shotgun; (B) committed by a court order to a hospital or institution for mental illness, unless the applicant was granted a petition for relief of the court order pursuant to said section 36C of said chapter 123 and submits a copy of the court order with the application; (C) subject to an order of the probate court appointing a guardian or conservator for a incapacitated person on the grounds that the applicant lacks the mental capacity to contract or manage the applicant's affairs, unless the applicant was granted a petition for relief of the order of the probate court pursuant to section 56C of chapter 215 and submits a copy of the order of the probate court with the application; or (D) found to be a person with an alcohol use disorder or substance use disorder or both and committed pursuant to said section 35 of said chapter 123, unless the applicant was granted a petition for relief of the court order pursuant to said section 35 and submits a copy of the court order with the application;

(iv) is younger than 21 years of age at the time of the application;

(v) is an alien who does not maintain lawful permanent residency;

(vi) is currently subject to: (A) an order for suspension or surrender issued pursuant to sections 3B or 3C of chapter 209A or a similar order issued by another jurisdiction; or (B) a permanent or temporary protection order issued pursuant to said chapter 209A or a similar order issued by another jurisdiction, including any order described in 18 U.S.C. 922(g)(8);

(vii) is currently the subject of an outstanding arrest warrant in any state or federal jurisdiction;

(viii) has been discharged from the armed forces of the United States under dishonorable conditions;

(ix) is a fugitive from justice; or

(x) having been a citizen of the United States, has renounced that citizenship.

The licensing authority may deny the application or renewal of a license to carry, or suspend or revoke a license issued under this section if, in a reasonable exercise of discretion, the licensing authority determines that the applicant or licensee is unsuitable to be issued or to continue to hold a license to carry. A determination of unsuitability shall be based on: (i) reliable and credible information that the applicant or licensee has exhibited or engaged in behavior that suggests that, if issued a license, the applicant or licensee may create a risk to public safety; or (ii) existing factors that suggest that, if issued a license, the applicant or licensee may create a risk to public safety. Upon denial of an application or renewal of a license based on a determination of unsuitability, the licensing authority shall notify the applicant in writing setting forth the specific reasons for the determination in accordance with paragraph (e). Upon revoking or suspending a license based on a determination of unsuitability, the licensing authority shall notify the holder of a license in writing setting forth the specific reasons for the determination in accordance with paragraph (f). The determination of unsuitability shall be subject to judicial review under said paragraph (f).

(e) Within seven days of the receipt of a completed application for a license to carry or possess firearms, or renewal of same, the licensing authority shall forward one copy of the application and one copy of the applicant's fingerprints to the colonel of state police, who shall within thirty days advise the licensing authority, in writing, of any disqualifying criminal record of the applicant arising from within or without the commonwealth and whether there is reason to believe that the applicant is disqualified for any of the foregoing reasons from possessing a license to carry or possess firearms. In searching for any disqualifying history of the applicant, the colonel shall utilize, or cause to be utilized, files maintained by the department of probation and statewide and nationwide criminal justice, warrant and protection order information systems and files including, but not limited to, the National Instant Criminal Background Check System. The colonel shall inquire of the commissioner of the department of mental health relative to whether the applicant is disqualified from being so licensed. If the information available to the colonel does not indicate that the possession of a firearm or large capacity firearm by the applicant would be in violation of state or federal law, he shall certify such fact, in writing, to the licensing authority within said thirty day period.

The licensing authority may also make inquiries concerning the applicant to: (i) the commissioner of the department of criminal justice information services relative to any disqualifying condition and records of purchases, sales, rentals, leases and transfers of weapons or ammunition concerning the applicant; (ii) the commissioner of probation relative to any record contained within the department of probation or the statewide domestic violence record keeping system concerning the applicant; and (iii) the commissioner of the department of mental health relative to whether the applicant is a suitable person to possess firearms or is not a suitable person to possess firearms. The director or commissioner to whom the licensing authority makes such inquiry shall provide prompt and full cooperation for that purpose in any investigation of the applicant.

The licensing authority shall, within forty days from the date of application, either approve the application and issue the license or deny the application and notify the applicant of the reason for such denial in writing; provided, however, that no such license shall be issued unless the colonel has certified, in writing, that the information available to him does not indicate that the possession of a firearm or large capacity firearm by the applicant would be in violation of state or federal law.

The licensing authority shall provide to the applicant a receipt indicating that it received the application. The receipt shall be provided to the applicant within 7 days by mail if the application was received by mail or immediately if the application was made in person; provided, however, that the receipt shall include the applicant's name and address; current license number and license expiration date, if any; the date the licensing authority received the application; the name, address and telephone number of the licensing authority; the agent of the licensing authority that received the application; the type of application; and whether the application is for a new license or a renewal of an existing license. The licensing authority shall keep a copy of the receipt for not less than 1 year and shall furnish a copy to the applicant if requested by the applicant.

(f) A license issued under this section shall be revoked or suspended by the licensing authority, or his designee, upon the occurrence of any event that would have disqualified the holder from being issued such license or from having such license renewed. A license may be revoked or suspended by the licensing authority if it appears that the holder is no longer a suitable person to possess such license. Any revocation or suspension of a license shall be in writing and shall state the reasons therefor. Upon revocation or suspension, the licensing authority shall take possession of such license and the person whose license is so revoked or suspended shall take all actions required under the provisions of section 129D. No appeal or post-judgment motion shall operate to stay such revocation or suspension. Notices of revocation and suspension shall be forwarded to the executive director of the criminal history systems board and the commissioner of probation and shall be included in the criminal justice information system. A revoked or suspended license may be reinstated only upon the termination of all disqualifying conditions, if any.

Any applicant or holder aggrieved by a denial, revocation, suspension or restriction placed on a license, unless a hearing has previously been held pursuant to chapter 209A, may, within either 90 days after receiving notice of the denial, revocation or suspension or within 90 days after the expiration of the time limit during which the licensing authority shall respond to the applicant or, in the case of a restriction, any time after a restriction is placed on the license pursuant to this section, file a petition to obtain judicial review in the district court having jurisdiction in the city or town in which the applicant filed the application or in which the license was issued. If after a hearing a justice of the court finds that there was no reasonable ground for denying, suspending, revoking or restricting the license and that the petitioner is not prohibited by law from possessing a license, the justice may order a license to be issued or reinstated to the petitioner or may order the licensing authority to remove certain restrictions placed on the license.

(g) A license shall be in a standard form provided by the commissioner of criminal justice information services in a size and shape equivalent to that of a license to operate motor vehicles issued by the registry of motor vehicles pursuant to section 8 of chapter 90 and shall contain a license number which shall clearly indicate the name, address, photograph, fingerprint, place and date of birth, height, weight, hair color, eye color and signature of the licensee. The license shall be clearly marked "License to Carry Firearms". The license shall provide in a legible font size and style the phone numbers for the National Suicide Prevention Lifeline and the Samaritans Statewide Helpline. The application for such license shall be made in a standard form provided by the executive director of the criminal history systems board, which form shall require the applicant to affirmatively state under the pains and penalties of perjury that such applicant is not disqualified on any of the grounds enumerated above from being issued such license.

(h) Any person who knowingly files an application containing false information shall be punished by a fine of not less than $500 nor more than $1,000 or by imprisonment for not less than six months nor more than two years in a house of correction, or by both such fine and imprisonment.

(i) A license to carry or possess firearms shall be valid, unless revoked or suspended, for a period of not more than 6 years from the date of issue and shall expire on the anniversary of the licensee's date of birth occurring not less than 5 years nor more than 6 years from the date of issue; provided, however, that, if the licensee applied for renewal before the license expired, the license shall remain valid after its expiration date for all lawful purposes until the application for renewal is approved or denied. If a licensee is on active duty with the armed forces of the United States on the expiration date of the license, the license shall remain valid until the licensee is released from active duty and for a period not less than 180 days following the release; provided, however, that, if the licensee applied for renewal prior to the end of that period, the license shall remain valid after its expiration date for all lawful purposes until the application for renewal is approved or denied. Any renewal thereof shall expire on the anniversary of the licensee's date of birth occurring not less than five years but not more than six years from the effective date of such license. Any license issued to an applicant born on February 29 shall expire on March 1. The fee for the application shall be $100, which shall be payable to the licensing authority and shall not be prorated or refunded in case of revocation or denial. The licensing authority shall retain $25 of the fee; $50 of the fee shall be deposited into the general fund of the commonwealth and not less than $50,000 of the funds deposited into the General Fund shall be allocated to the Firearm Licensing Review Board, established in section 130B, for its operations and that any funds not expended by said board for its operations shall revert back to the General Fund; and $25 of the fee shall be deposited in the Firearms Fingerprint Identity Verification Trust Fund. For active and retired law enforcement officials, or local, state, or federal government entities acting on their behalf, the fee for the application shall be set at $25, which shall be payable to the licensing authority and shall not be prorated or refunded in case of revocation or denial. The licensing authority shall retain $12.50 of the fee, and $12.50 of the fee shall be deposited into the general fund of the commonwealth. Notwithstanding any general or special law to the contrary, licensing authorities shall deposit such portion of the license application fee into the Firearms Record Keeping Fund quarterly, not later than January 1, April 1, July 1 and October 1 of each year. Notwithstanding any general or special law to the contrary, licensing authorities shall deposit quarterly such portion of the license application fee as is to be deposited into the General Fund, not later than January 1, April 1, July 1 and October 1 of each year. For the purposes of section 10 of chapter 269, an expired license to carry firearms shall be deemed to be valid for a period not to exceed 90 days beyond the stated date of expiration, unless such license to carry firearms has been revoked.

Any person over the age of 70 and any law enforcement officer applying for a license to carry firearms through his employing agency shall be exempt from the requirement of paying a renewal fee for a Class A or Class B license to carry.

(j)(1) No license shall be required for the carrying or possession of a firearm known as a detonator and commonly used on vehicles as a signaling and marking device, when carried or possessed for such signaling or marking purposes.

(2) No license to carry shall be required for the possession of an unloaded large capacity rifle or shotgun or an unloaded feeding device therefor by a veteran's organization chartered by the Congress of the United States, chartered by the commonwealth or recognized as a nonprofit tax-exempt organization by the Internal Revenue Service, or by the members of any such organization when on official parade duty or during ceremonial occasions. For purposes of this subparagraph, an "unloaded large capacity rifle or shotgun" and an "unloaded feeding device therefor" shall include any large capacity rifle, shotgun or feeding device therefor loaded with a blank cartridge or blank cartridges, so-called, which contain no projectile within such blank or blanks or within the bore or chamber of such large capacity rifle or shotgun.

(k) Whoever knowingly issues a license in violation of this section shall be punished by a fine of not less than $500 nor more than $1,000 or by imprisonment for not less than six months nor more than two years in a jail or house of correction, or by both such fine and imprisonment.

(l) The executive director of the criminal history systems board shall send electronically or by first class mail to the holder of each such license to carry firearms, a notice of the expiration of such license not less than 90 days prior to such expiration and shall enclose therein a form for the renewal of such license. The form for renewal shall include an affidavit in which the applicant shall verify that the applicant has not lost any firearms or had any firearms stolen from the applicant since the date of the applicant's last renewal or issuance. The taking of fingerprints shall not be required in issuing the renewal of a license if the renewal applicant's fingerprints are on file with the department of the state police. Any licensee shall notify, in writing, the licensing authority who issued said license, the chief of police into whose jurisdiction the licensee moves and the executive director of the criminal history systems board of any change of address. Such notification shall be made by certified mail within 30 days of its occurrence. Failure to so notify shall be cause for revocation or suspension of said license. The commissioner of criminal justice information services shall provide electronic notice of expiration only upon the request of a cardholder. A request for electronic notice of expiration shall be forwarded to the department on a form furnished by the commissioner. Any electronic address maintained by the department for the purpose of providing electronic notice of expiration shall be considered a firearms record and shall not be disclosed except as provided in section 10 of chapter 66.

(m) Notwithstanding the provisions of section 10 of chapter 269, any person in possession of a firearm, rifle or shotgun whose license issued under this section is invalid for the sole reason that it has expired, not including licenses that remain valid under paragraph (i) because the licensee applied for renewal before the license expired, but who shall not be disqualified from renewal upon application therefor pursuant to this section, shall be subject to a civil fine of not less than $100 nor more than $5,000 and the provisions of section 10 of chapter 269 shall not apply; provided, however, that the exemption from the provisions of said section 10 of said chapter 269 provided herein shall not apply if: (i) such license has been revoked or suspended, unless such revocation or suspension was caused by failure to give notice of a change of address as required under this section; (ii) revocation or suspension of such license is pending, unless such revocation or suspension was caused by failure to give notice of a change of address as required under this section; or (iii) an application for renewal of such license has been denied. Any law enforcement officer who discovers a person to be in possession of a firearm, rifle or shotgun after such person's license has expired, meaning after 90 days beyond the stated expiration date on the license, has been revoked or suspended, solely for failure to give notice of a change of address, shall confiscate such firearm, rifle or shotgun and the expired or suspended license then in possession and such officer, shall forward such license to the licensing authority by whom it was issued as soon as practicable. The officer shall, at the time of confiscation, provide to the person whose firearm, rifle or shotgun has been confiscated, a written inventory and receipt for all firearms, rifles or shotguns confiscated and the officer and his employer shall exercise due care in the handling, holding and storage of these items. Any confiscated weapon shall be returned to the owner upon the renewal or reinstatement of such expired or suspended license within one year of such confiscation or may be otherwise disposed of in accordance with the provisions of section 129D. The provisions of this paragraph shall not apply if such person has a valid license to carry firearms issued under section 131F.

(n) Upon issuance of a license to carry or possess firearms under this section, the licensing authority shall forward a copy of such approved application and license to the executive director of the criminal history systems board, who shall inform the licensing authority forthwith of the existence of any disqualifying condition discovered or occurring subsequent to the issuance of a license under this section.

(o) No person shall be issued a license to carry or possess a machine gun in the commonwealth, except that a licensing authority or the colonel of state police may issue a machine gun license to:

(i) a firearm instructor certified by the municipal police training committee for the sole purpose of firearm instruction to police personnel;

(ii) a bona fide collector of firearms upon application or upon application for renewal of such license.

(p) The executive director of the criminal history systems board shall promulgate regulations in accordance with chapter 30A to establish criteria for persons who shall be classified as bona fide collectors of firearms.

(q) Nothing in this section shall authorize the purchase, possession or transfer of any weapon, ammunition or feeding device that is, or in such manner that is, prohibited by state or federal law.

(r) The secretary of the executive office of public safety or his designee may promulgate regulations to carry out the purposes of this section.

NOTE 1   See Note 2 following G.L. c. 276, § 100A.
NOTE 2   See Notes following G.L. c. 269, § 10.
NOTE 3   See Note following G.L. c. 140, § 129B.

SECTION 131½
Gun control advisory board

The governor shall appoint a gun control advisory board, hereinafter referred to as the board. The board shall consist of seven individuals, one of whom shall be a member of the gun owners action league, one of whom shall be a police chief selected from a list of four selected by the police chiefs association and one of whom shall be the director of the firearms record bureau within the department of criminal justice information services. It shall be the responsibility of the board to advise the executive office of public safety on matters relating to the implementation of sections 121 and 131P, inclusive, and section 2SS of chapter 29. The board shall serve without compensation and shall adopt operating rules and procedures for its organization and activities.

SECTION 131¾
Roster of large capacity rifles, shotguns, firearms and feeding devices

The secretary of public safety shall, with the advice of the gun control advisory board established pursuant to the provisions of section 131½, compile and publish a roster of large capacity rifles, shotguns, firearms, and feeding devices, all as defined in section 121, and such weapons referred to in clauses Eighteenth to Twenty-first, inclusive of section 123.

The secretary shall, not less than three times annually, publish the roster in newspapers of general circulation throughout the commonwealth, and shall send a copy thereof to all dealers licensed in the commonwealth under the provisions of said section 122 of said chapter 140; and further, the licensing authority shall furnish said roster to all cardholders and licensees upon initial issuance and upon every renewal of the same.

The secretary may amend the roster upon his own initiative or with the advice of said board. A person may petition the secretary to place a weapon on, or remove a weapon from, the roster, subject to the provisions of this section. A person who so petitions shall give the reasons why the roster should be so amended.

A petition to amend the roster shall be submitted in writing to the secretary and shall be in the form and manner prescribed by the secretary. Upon receipt of the petition to place a weapon on the roster, the secretary shall, within 45 days of receipt of the petition, either notify the petitioner by certified mail that the petition is denied, or it shall modify the roster. An addition to the roster shall be effective on the date it is included in the next publication in newspapers of general circulation as provided under this section.

The secretary may promulgate rules and regulations relative to the appeal of a decision on a petition to modify the roster and any other regulations consistent with the provisions of this section and sections 2SS of chapter 29, sections 11 and 14 of chapter 131, sections 121, 122, 122B, 123, 128, 128A, 129B, 129B, 129C, 129D, 130, 131, 131A, 131E, 131F and 131K of chapter 140 to effectuate the purposes of each said section.

SECTION 131A
Permits to purchase, rent or lease firearms, or to purchase ammunition; fee; penalties

A licensing authority under section one hundred and thirty-one, upon the application of a person qualified to be granted a license thereunder by such authority, may grant to such a person, other than a minor, a permit to purchase, rent or lease a firearm if it appears that such purchase, rental or lease is for a proper purpose, and may revoke such permit at will. The colonel of the state police or a person authorized by him, upon the application of a person licensed under section one hundred and thirty-one F, may grant to such licensee, other than a minor, a permit to purchase, rent or lease a firearm, rifle or shotgun, or to purchase ammunition therefor, if it appears that such purchase, rental or lease is for a proper purpose, and may revoke such permit at will. Such permits shall be issued on forms furnished by the commissioner of the department of criminal justice information services, shall be valid for not more than ten days after issue, and a copy of every such permit so issued shall within one week thereafter be sent to the said executive director. The licensing authority may impose such restrictions relative to caliber and capacity of the firearm to be purchased, rented or leased as he deems proper. Whoever knowingly issues a permit in violation of this section shall be punished by a fine of not less than five hundred nor more than one thousand dollars and by imprisonment for not less than six months nor more than two years in a jail or house of correction.

The fee for the permits shall be $100, which shall be payable to the licensing authority and shall not be prorated or refunded in case of revocation or denial. The licensing authority shall retain $25 of the fee; $50 of the fee shall be deposited into the general fund of the commonwealth; and $25 of the fee shall be deposited in the Firearms Fingerprint Identity Verification Trust Fund.

NOTE   See Note following G.L. c. 140, § 129B.

SECTION 131B
Penalty for loan of money secured by weapons

Whoever loans money secured by mortgage, deposit or pledge of a firearm, rifle, shotgun or machine gun shall be punished by a fine of not more than five hundred dollars or by imprisonment for not more than one year, or by both; provided, however that nothing herein shall prohibit a bank or other institutional lender from loaning money secured by a mortgage, deposit, or pledge of a firearm, rifle, shotgun or machine gun to a manufacturer, wholesaler, or dealer of firearms, rifles, or shotguns. The provisions of section one hundred and twenty-three shall not be applicable to any such mortgage, deposit or pledge unless or until the lender takes possession of the collateral upon default or the collateral is removed from the premises of the debtor.

SECTION 131C
Carrying of firearms in a vehicle
(Amended by 2014 Mass. Acts c. 284, § 58, effective Jan. 1, 2021.)
  [Text of section as effective through Dec. 31, 2020:]

(a) No person carrying a loaded firearm under a Class A license issued under section 131 or 131F shall carry the same in a vehicle unless such firearm while carried therein is under the direct control of such person. Whoever violates the provisions of this subsection shall be punished by a fine of $500.

(b) No person carrying a firearm under a Class B license issued under section 131 or 131F shall possess the same in a vehicle unless such weapon is unloaded and contained within the locked trunk of such vehicle or in a locked case or other secure container. Whoever violates the provisions of this subsection shall be punished by a fine of $500.

(c) No person possessing a large capacity rifle or shotgun under a Class A or Class B license issued under section 131 or 131F shall possess the same in a vehicle unless such weapon is unloaded and contained within the locked trunk of such vehicle or in a locked case or other secure container. Whoever violates the provisions of this subsection shall be punished by a fine of not less than $500 nor more than $5,000.

(d) The provisions of this section shall not apply to (i) any officer, agent or employee of the commonwealth or any state or the United States; (ii) any member of the military or other service of any state or of the United States; (iii) any duly authorized law enforcement officer, agent or employee of any municipality of the commonwealth; provided, however, that any such person described in clauses (i) to (iii), inclusive, is authorized by a competent authority to carry or possess the weapon so carried or possessed and is acting within the scope of his duties.

(e) A conviction of a violation of this section shall be reported forthwith by the court or magistrate to the licensing authority who shall immediately revoke the card or license of the person so convicted. No new such card or license may be issued to any person until one year after the date of revocation.

  [Text of section as effective on Jan. 1, 2021:]

(a) No person carrying a loaded firearm under a license issued pursuant to section 131 or 131F shall carry the loaded firearm in a vehicle unless the loaded firearm while carried in the vehicle is under the direct control of the person. Whoever violates this subsection shall be punished by a fine of $500.

(b) No person possessing a large capacity rifle or shotgun under a license issued pursuant to section 131 or 131F shall possess the large capacity rifle or shotgun in a vehicle unless the large capacity rifle or shotgun is unloaded and contained within the locked trunk of the vehicle or in a locked case or other secure container. Whoever violates this subsection shall be punished by a fine of not less than $500 nor more than $5,000.

(c) This section shall not apply to: (i) an officer, agent or employee of the commonwealth, any state or the United States; (ii) a member of the military or other service of any state or of the United States; (iii) a duly authorized law enforcement officer, agent or employee of a municipality of the commonwealth; provided, however, that a person described in clauses (i) to (iii), inclusive, is authorized by a competent authority to carry or possess the weapon so carried or possessed and is acting within the scope of the person's official duties.

(d) A conviction of a violation of this section shall be reported immediately by the court or magistrate to the licensing authority. The licensing authority shall immediately revoke the firearm identification card or license of the person convicted of a violation of this section. No new firearm identification card or license may be issued to a person convicted of a violation of this section until 1 year after the date of revocation of the firearm identification card or license.

NOTE   See Notes following G.L. c. 269, § 10.

SECTION 131D
Repealed

SECTION 131E
Purchase by residents; licenses; firearm identification cards; purchase for use of another; penalties; revocation of licenses or cards; reissuance
(Amended by 2014 Mass. Acts c. 284, § 59, effective Jan. 1, 2021.)
[Text of section as effective through Dec. 31, 2020:]

Any resident of the commonwealth may purchase firearms, rifles, shotguns and ammunition feeding devices from any dealer licensed under section 122, or from such person as shall be qualified under section 128A, or ammunition from a licensee under section 122B, subject to the following conditions and restrictions:

(a) rifles, shotguns and feeding devices therefor may be so purchased only upon presentment of: (i) a valid firearm identification card issued under section 129B; or (ii) a valid Class A or Class B license to carry firearms issued under section 131; or (iii) valid proof of exempt status under section 129C; provided, however, that large capacity rifles and shotguns and large capacity feeding devices therefor may be so purchased only upon presentment of a Class A or Class B license to carry firearms issued under said section 131; and provided, further, that no rifle or shotgun or ammunition or ammunition feeding device therefor shall be sold to any person less than 18 years of age; and provided further, that no large capacity rifle or shotgun or large capacity feeding device therefor shall be sold to any person less than 21 years of age;

(b) firearms and feedings devices therefor may be so purchased only upon presentment of: (i) a valid Class A or Class B license to carry firearms issued under section 131; or (ii) a valid firearm identification card issued under section 129B together with a valid permit to purchase a firearm issued under section 131A; or (iii) a valid permit to purchase a firearm issued under section 131A together with a valid proof of exempt status under section 129C; provided, however, that large capacity firearms and large capacity feeding devices therefor may be so purchased only upon presentment of: (i) a valid Class A license to carry firearms issued under section 131; or (ii) a valid firearm identification card issued under section 129B together with a valid and proper permit to purchase a firearm issued under section 131A; or (iii) a valid and proper permit to purchase a firearm issued under section 131A together with valid proof of exempt status under section 129C; and provided further, that neither a firearm identification card issued under section 129B, nor proof of exempt status under section 129C, shall be valid for the purpose of purchasing any firearm or ammunition feeding device therefor without being presented together with a valid and proper permit to purchase issued under section 131A; and provided further, that an alien permit to possess a rifle or shotgun shall not be valid for the purpose of purchasing firearms or ammunition or ammunition feeding devices therefor; and provided further, that no firearm or ammunition or ammunition feeding device therefor shall be sold to any person less than 21 years of age. Any person who uses said license to carry firearms or firearm identification card for the purpose of purchasing a firearm, rifle or shotgun for the unlawful use of another, or for resale to or giving to an unlicensed person, shall be punished by a fine of not less than one thousand nor more than fifty thousand dollars, or by imprisonment for not less than two and one-half years nor more than ten years in a state prison, or by both such fine and imprisonment. A conviction of a violation of this section shall be reported forthwith by the court to the licensing authority which issued the license or firearm identification card, which shall immediately revoke the license or firearm identification card of such person. No new license or firearm identification card under section one hundred and twenty-nine B or section one hundred and thirty-one shall be issued to any such person within two years after the date of said revocation.

[Text of section as effective on Jan. 1, 2021:]

A resident of the commonwealth may purchase firearms, rifles, shotguns and ammunition feeding devices from a dealer licensed pursuant to section 122 or from a person qualified pursuant to section 128A or may purchase ammunition from a licensee under section 122B subject to the following conditions and restrictions:

(a) rifles, shotguns and feeding devices therefor may be so purchased only upon presentment of: (i) a valid firearm identification card issued pursuant to section 129B; (ii) a valid license to carry firearms issued pursuant to section 131; or (iii) valid proof of exempt status under section 129C; provided, however, that large capacity rifles and shotguns and large capacity feeding devices therefor may be so purchased only upon presentment of a license to carry firearms issued pursuant to said section 131; and provided further, that no rifle, shotgun, ammunition or ammunition feeding device therefor shall be sold to a person younger than 18 years of age; and provided further, that no large capacity rifle, shotgun or large capacity feeding device therefor shall be sold to a person younger than 21 years of age; and

(b) firearms and feeding devices therefor, including large capacity firearms and large capacity feeding devices therefor, may be so purchased only upon presentment of: (i) a valid license to carry firearms issued pursuant to section 131; (ii) a valid firearm identification card issued pursuant to section 129B; or (iii) valid proof of exempt status under section 129C; provided, however, that neither a firearm identification card issued pursuant to said section 129B nor proof of exempt status under said section 129C shall be valid to purchase a firearm or ammunition feeding device therefor, including large capacity firearms and large capacity feeding devices therefor, without being presented together with a valid and proper permit to purchase issued under section 131A; and provided further, that an alien permit to possess a rifle or shotgun shall not be valid to purchase firearms, ammunition or ammunition feeding devices therefor; and provided further, that no firearm, ammunition or ammunition feeding device therefor shall be sold to a person younger than 21 years of age.

A firearms collector, licensed pursuant to 18 U.S.C. 923(b), may purchase a rifle, shotgun or firearm that was not previously owned or registered in the commonwealth from a dealer licensed under section 122 if that rifle, shotgun or firearm is a curio or relic as defined in 27 CFR 478.11.

A person who uses a license to carry firearms or a firearm identification card to purchase a firearm, rifle or shotgun for the unlawful use of another or for resale to or giving to an unlicensed person shall be punished by a fine of not less than $1,000 nor more than $50,000 or by imprisonment for not less than 2½ years nor more than 10 years in a state prison or by both such fine and imprisonment. A conviction of a violation of this section shall be reported immediately by the court to the licensing authority that issued the license or firearm identification card. The licensing authority shall immediately revoke the license or firearm identification card pursuant to said section 129B or said section 131 and no license shall be issued to a person convicted of a violation of this section within 2 years after the date of the revocation of the license or firearm identification card.

SECTION 131F

Nonresidents or aliens; temporary license to carry firearms or ammunition

(Amended by 2014 Mass. Acts c. 284, §§ 61–62, effective Jan. 1, 2015; bracketed text is stricken effective Jan. 1, 2021 by 2014 Mass. Acts

c. 284, § 60; fourth paragraph amended by 2014 Mass. Acts c. 284, § 63, effective Jan. 1, 2021.)

A [Class A or Class B] temporary license to carry firearms or feeding devices or ammunition therefor, within the commonwealth, may be issued by the colonel of state police, or persons authorized by him, to a nonresident or any person not falling within the jurisdiction of a local licensing authority or to an alien that resides outside the commonwealth for purposes of firearms competition and subject to such terms and conditions as said colonel may deem proper; provided, however, that no license shall be issued to a person who:

(i) has, in any state or federal jurisdiction, been convicted or adjudicated a youthful offender or delinquent child for the commission of (A) a felony; (B) a misdemeanor punishable by imprisonment for more than 2 years; (C) a violent crime as defined in section 121; (D) a violation of any law regulating the use, possession, ownership, transfer, purchase, sale, lease, rental, receipt or transportation of weapons or ammunition for which a term of imprisonment may be imposed; (E) a violation of any law regulating the use, possession or sale of a controlled substance as defined in section 1 of chapter 94C; or (F) a misdemeanor crime of domestic violence as defined in 18 U.S.C. 921(a)(33);

(ii) has been confined to any hospital or institution for mental illness, unless the applicant submits with his application an affidavit of a registered physician attesting that such physician is familiar with the applicant's mental illness and that in such physician's opinion the applicant is not disabled by such an illness in a manner that should prevent such applicant from possessing a firearm;

(iii) is or has been under treatment for or confinement for drug addiction or habitual drunkenness, unless such complaint is deemed to be cured of such condition by a licensed physician, and such applicant may make application for said license after the expiration of five years from the date of such confinement or treatment and upon presentment of an affidavit issued by such physician stating that such physician knows the applicant's history of treatment and that in such physician's opinion the applicant is deemed cured;

(iv) is currently subject to: (A) an order for suspension or surrender issued pursuant to section 3B or 3C of chapter 209A or a similar order issued by another jurisdiction; or (B) a permanent or temporary protection order issued pursuant to chapter 209A or a similar order issued by another jurisdiction;

(v) is currently the subject of an outstanding arrest warrant in any state or federal jurisdiction;

(vi) has been discharged from the armed forces of the United States under dishonorable conditions;

(vii) is a fugitive from justice;

(viii) having been a citizen of the United States, has renounced that citizenship;

(ix) not being a citizen or national of the United States, is illegally or unlawfully in the United States; or

(x) not being a citizen or national of the United States, has been admitted to the United States under a nonimmigrant visa as defined in 8 U.S.C. 1101(a)(26), unless the person has been admitted to the United States for lawful hunting or sporting purposes or is in possession of a hunting license or permit lawfully issued in the United States or another exception set forth in 18 U.S.C. 922(y)(2) applies.

Such license shall be valid for a period of one year but the colonel may renew such license, if in his discretion, such renewal is necessary.

The colonel may also issue such license, subject to such terms and conditions as he deems proper, to any resident of the commonwealth for the purposes of sports competition.

[Fourth paragraph as effective through Dec. 31, 2020:]

A temporary license issued under this section shall be marked "Temporary License to Carry Firearms", shall clearly indicate whether it is Class A or Class B and shall not be used to purchase firearms in the commonwealth as provided under section 131E. Neither a large capacity firearm nor large capacity feeding device therefor may be carried unless such person has been issued a Class A license; provided, however, that the colonel may permit a Class A or Class B licensee to possess large capacity rifles or shotguns or both, and such entitlement shall be clearly indicated on such license. The fee for an application for the license shall be $100, which shall be payable to the licensing authority and shall not be prorated or refunded in case of revocation or denial. The licensing authority shall retain $25 of the fee; $50 of the fee shall be deposited into the general fund of the commonwealth; and $25 of the fee shall be deposited in the Firearms Fingerprint Identity Verification Trust Fund. A license issued under the provisions of this section to a non-resident who is in the employ of a bank, public utility corporation, or a firm engaged in the business of transferring monies, or business of similar nature, or a firm licensed as a private detective under the provisions of chapter 147, and whose application is endorsed by his employer, or who is a member of the armed services and is stationed within the territorial boundaries of the commonwealth and has the written consent of his commanding officer, may be issued for any term not to exceed two years, and said licenses shall expire in accordance with the provisions of section one hundred and thirty-one.

[Fourth paragraph as effective on Jan. 1, 2021:]

A temporary license issued pursuant to this section shall be clearly marked "Temporary License to Carry Firearms" and shall not be used to purchase firearms in the commonwealth as provided in section 131E. A large capacity firearm and a large capacity feeding device therefor may be carried if the person has been issued a license. The colonel may permit a licensee to possess a large capacity rifle or shotgun or both; provided, however, that this entitlement shall be clearly indicated on the license. The fee for an application for the license shall be $100, which shall be payable to the licensing authority and shall not be prorated or refunded in case of revocation or denial. The licensing authority shall retain $25 of the fee; $50 of the fee shall be deposited into the general fund of the commonwealth; and $25 of the fee shall be deposited in the Firearms Fingerprint Identity Verification Trust Fund. A license issued under the provisions of this section to a non-resident who is in the employ of a bank, public utility corporation, or a firm engaged in the business of transferring monies, or business of similar nature, or a firm licensed as a private detective under the provisions of chapter 147, and whose application is endorsed by his employer, or who is a member of the armed services and is stationed within the territorial boundaries of the commonwealth and has the written consent of his commanding officer, may be issued for any term not to exceed two years, and said licenses shall expire in accordance with the provisions of section one hundred and thirty-one.

A license, otherwise in accordance with provisions of this section, may be issued to a nonresident employee, whose application is endorsed by his employer, of a federally licensed Massachusetts manufacturer of machine guns to possess within the commonwealth a machine gun for the purpose of transporting or testing relative to the manufacture of machine guns, and the license shall be marked "temporary license to possess a machine gun" and may be issued for any term not to exceed two years and shall expire in accordance with the provisions of section one hundred and thirty-one.

NOTE   See Notes following G.L. c. 269, § 10.

SECTION 131F½
Theatrical productions; carrying firearms and blank ammunition

Notwithstanding the provisions of subsection (a) of section ten of chapter two hundred and sixty-nine of the General Laws or any other law to the contrary, the carrying or possession of a firearm and blank ammunition therefor, during the course of any television, movie, stage or other similar theatrical production, by a person within such production, shall be authorized; provided, however, that such carrying or possession of such firearm shall be under the immediate supervision of a person licensed to carry firearms.

SECTION 131G
Carrying of firearms by nonresidents; conditions

Any person who is not a resident of the commonwealth may carry a pistol or revolver in or through the commonwealth for the purpose of taking part in a pistol or revolver competition or attending any meeting or exhibition of any organized group of firearm collectors or for the purpose of hunting; provided, that such person is a resident of the United States and has a permit or license to carry firearms issued under the laws of any state, district or territory thereof which has licensing requirements which prohibit the issuance of permits or licenses to persons who have been convicted of a felony or who have been convicted of the unlawful use, possession or sale of narcotic or harmful drugs; provided, further, that in the case of a person traveling in or through the commonwealth for the purpose of hunting, he has on his person a hunting or sporting license issued by the commonwealth or by the state of his destination. Police officers and other peace officers of any state, territory or jurisdiction within the United States duly authorized to possess firearms by the laws thereof shall, for the purposes of this section, be deemed to have a permit or license to carry firearms as described in this section.

NOTE   See Notes following G.L. c. 269, § 10.

SECTION 131H
Ownership or possession of firearms by aliens; penalties; seizure and disposition

No alien shall own or have in his possession or under his control a firearm, except as provided in section one hundred and thirty-one F or a rifle or shotgun except as provided in this section or section one hundred and thirty-one F. The colonel of the state police may, after an investigation, issue a permit to an alien to own or have in his possession or under his control a rifle or shotgun; subject to such terms and conditions as said colonel may deem proper. The fee for the permit shall be $100, which shall be payable to the licensing authority and shall not be prorated or refunded in case of revocation

or denial. The licensing authority shall retain $25 of the fee; $50 of the fee shall be deposited into the general fund of the commonwealth; and $25 of the fee shall be deposited in the Firearms Fingerprint Identity Verification Trust Fund. Upon issuing such permit said colonel shall so notify, in writing, the chief of police or the board or officer having control of the police in the city or town in which such alien resides. Each such permit card shall expire at twelve midnight on December thirty-first next succeeding the effective date of said permit, and shall be revocable for cause by said colonel. In case of revocation, the fee for such permit shall not be prorated or refunded. Whenever any such permit is revoked, said colonel shall give notification as hereinbefore provided. The permit issued to an alien under this section shall be subject to sections one hundred and twenty-nine B and one hundred and twenty-nine C except as otherwise provided by this section.

Violation of any provision of this section shall be punished by a fine of not less than five hundred nor more than one thousand dollars, and by imprisonment for not more than six months in a jail or house of correction. If, in any prosecution for violation of this section, the defendant alleges that he has been naturalized, or alleges that he is a citizen of the United States, the burden of proving the same shall be upon him. Any firearm, rifle or shotgun owned by an alien or in his possession or under his control in violation of this section shall be forfeited to the commonwealth. Any such firearm, rifle or shotgun may be the subject of a search warrant as provided in chapter two hundred and seventy-six.

The director of law enforcement of the department of fisheries, wildlife and environmental law enforcement, deputy directors of enforcement, chiefs of enforcement, deputy chiefs of enforcement, environmental police officers and deputy environmental police officers, wardens as defined in section one of chapter one hundred and thirty-one and members of the state police in areas over which they have jurisdiction, and all officers qualified to serve criminal process shall arrest, without a warrant, any person found with a firearm, rifle or shotgun in his possession if they have reason to believe that he is an alien and if he does not have in his possession a valid permit as provided in this section.

SECTION 131I
Falsifying firearm license or identification card; penalty

Whoever falsely makes, alters, forges or counterfeits or procures or assists another to falsely make, alter, forge or counterfeit a license to carry a firearm or a firearm identification card, or whoever forges, or without authority uses the signature, facsimile of the signature, or validating signature stamp of the licensing authority or its designee, or whoever possesses, utters, publishes as true or in any way makes use of a falsely made, altered, forged or counterfeited license to carry a firearm or a firearm identification card, shall be punished by imprisonment in a state prison for not more than five years or in a jail or house of correction for not more than two years, or by a fine of not less than five hundred dollars, or both such fine and imprisonment.

SECTION 131J
Sale or possession of electrical weapons; penalties

No person shall possess a portable device or weapon from which an electrical current, impulse, wave or beam may be directed, which current, impulse, wave or beam is designed to incapacitate temporarily, injure or kill, except: (1) a federal, state or municipal law enforcement officer, or member of a special reaction team in a state prison or designated special operations or tactical team in a county correctional facility, acting in the discharge of his official duties who has completed a training course approved by the secretary of public safety in the use of such a devise or weapon designed to incapacitate temporarily; or (2) a supplier of such devices or weapons designed to incapacitate temporarily, if possession of the device or weapon is necessary to the supply or sale of the device or weapon within the scope of such sale or supply enterprise. No person shall sell or offer for sale such device or weapon, except to federal, state or municipal law enforcement agencies. A device or weapon sold under this section shall include a mechanism for tracking the number of times the device or weapon has been fired. The secretary of public safety shall adopt regulations governing who may sell or offer to sell such devices or weapons in the commonwealth and governing law enforcement training on the appropriate use of portable electrical weapons.

Whoever violates this section shall be punished by a fine of not less than $500 nor more than $1,000 or by imprisonment in the house of correction for not less than six months nor more than two and a half years, or by both such fine and imprisonment. A law enforcement officer may arrest without a warrant any person whom he has probable cause to believe has violated this section.

SECTION 131K
Firearms or large capacity weapons without safety devices; liability

Any firearm or large capacity weapon, both as defined in section 121, sold within the commonwealth without a safety device designed to prevent the discharge of such weapon by unauthorized users and approved by the colonel of state police including, but not limited to, mechanical locks or devices designed to recognize and authorize, or otherwise allow the firearm to be discharged only by its owner or authorized user, by solenoid use-limitation devices, key activated or combination trigger or handle locks, radio frequency tags, automated fingerprint identification systems or voice recognition, provided, that such device is commercially available, shall not be defective and the sale of such a weapon shall constitute a breach of warranty under section 2-314 of chapter 106 and an unfair or deceptive trade act or practice under section 2 of chapter 93A. Any entity responsible for the manufacture, importation or sale as inventory item or consumer good, both as defined in section 9-102 of chapter 106, of such a weapon that does not include or incorporate such a device shall be individually and jointly liable to any person who sustains person injury or property damage resulting from the failure to include or incorporate such a device. If death results from such personal injury, such entities shall be liable in an amount including, but not limited to, that provided under chapter 229. Contributory or comparative negligence shall not be valid defenses to an action brought under this section in conjunction with section 2 of chapter 93A or section 2-314 of chapter 106 or both; provided, however, that nothing herein shall prohibit such liable parties from maintaining an action for indemnification or contribution against each other or against the lawful owner or other authorized user of said weapon.

Any disclaimer, limit or waiver of the liability provided under this section shall be void.

No entity responsible for the manufacture, importation or sale of such a weapon shall be liable to any person for injuries caused by the discharge of such weapon that does not include or incorporate a safety device as required under this section if such injuries were: (i) self-inflicted, either intentionally or unintentionally, unless such injuries were self-inflicted by a person less than 18 years of age; (ii) inflicted by the lawful owner or other authorized user of said weapon; (iii) inflicted by any person in the lawful exercise of self-defense; or (iv) inflicted upon a co-conspirator in the commission of a crime.

This section shall not apply to any weapon distributed to an officer of any law enforcement agency or any member of the armed forces of the United States or the organized militia of the commonwealth; provided, however, that such person is authorized to acquire, possess or carry such a weapon for the lawful performance of his official duties; and provided, further, that any such weapon so distributed is distributed solely for use in connection with such duties. This section shall not apply to any firearm manufactured in or prior to the year 1899, or to any replica of such a firearm if such replica is not designed or redesigned for using rimfire or conventional centerfire fixed ammunition.

SECTION 131L
Weapons stored or kept by owner; inoperable by any person other than owner or lawfully authorized user; punishment
(Amended by 2014 Mass. Acts c. 284, § 64, effective Jan. 1, 2015.)

(a) It shall be unlawful to store or keep any firearm, rifle or shotgun including, but not limited to, large capacity weapons, or machine gun in any place unless such weapon is secured in a locked container or equipped with a tamper-resistant mechanical lock or other safety device, properly engaged so as to render such weapon inoperable by any person other than the owner or other lawfully authorized user. For purposes of this section, such weapon shall not be deemed stored or kept if carried by or under the control of the owner or other lawfully authorized user.

(b) A violation of this section shall be punished, in the case of a firearm, rifle or shotgun that is not a large capacity weapon, by a fine of not less than $1000 nor more than $7,500 or by imprisonment for not more than 1½ years or by both such fine and imprisonment and, in the case of a large capacity weapon or machine gun, by a fine of not less than $2,000 nor more than $15,000 or by imprisonment for not less than 1½ years nor more than 12 years or by both such fine and imprisonment.

(c) A violation of this section shall be punished, in the case of a rifle or shotgun that is not a large capacity weapon and the weapon was stored or kept in a place where a person younger than 18 years of age who does not possess a valid firearm identification card issued under section 129B may have access without committing an unforeseeable trespass, by a fine of not less than $2,500 nor more than $15,000 or by imprisonment for not less than 1½ years nor more than 12 years or by both such fine and imprisonment.

(d) A violation of this section shall be punished, in the case of a rifle or shotgun that is a large capacity weapon, firearm or machine gun that was stored or kept in a place where a person younger than 18 years of age may have access without committing an unforeseeable trespass, by a fine of not less than $10,000 nor more than $20,000 or by imprisonment for not less than 4 years nor more than 15 years or by both such fine and imprisonment.

(e) A violation of the provisions of this section shall be evidence of wanton or reckless conduct in any criminal or civil proceeding if a person under the age of 18 who was not a trespasser or was a foreseeable trespasser acquired access to a weapon, unless such person possessed a valid firearm identification card issued under section 129B and was permitted by law to possess such weapon, and such access results in the person injury to or the death of any person.

(f) This section shall not apply to the storage or keeping of any firearm, rifle or shotgun with matchlock, flintlock, percussion cap or similar type of ignition system manufactured in or prior to the year 1899, or to any replica of any such firearm, rifle or shotgun if such replica is not designed or redesigned for using rimfire or conventional centerfire fixed ammunition.

NOTE 1   "[N]either the statute nor our case law requires a gun owner who keeps a firearm 'secured in a locked container' to also store that container in a secure *location*." *Commonwealth v. Lojko*, 77 Mass. App. Ct. 82, 85 (2010).

NOTE 2   "We hold that, because § 131L(a) is consistent with the right to bear arms in self-defense in one's home and is designed to prevent those who are not licensed to possess or carry firearms from gaining access to firearms, it falls outside the scope of the Second Amendment. As a result, it is subject only to rational basis analysis, which it easily survives. Therefore, we conclude that § 131L(a) is constitutional under the Supreme Court's holdings and analysis in *Heller* and *McDonald*, and that Massachusetts may enforce § 131L(a) to protect the health, safety, and welfare of its citizens." *Commonwealth v. McGowan*, 464 Mass. 232, 244 (2013).

SECTION 131M
Assault weapon or large capacity feeding device not lawfully possessed on September 13, 1994; sale, transfer or possession; punishment
(Amended by 2014 Mass. Acts c. 284, § 65, effective Aug. 11, 2014.)

No person shall sell, offer for sale, transfer or possess an assault weapon or a large capacity feeding device that was not otherwise lawfully possessed on September 13, 1994. Whoever not being licensed under the provisions of section 122 violates the provisions of this section shall be punished, for a first offense, by a fine of not less than $1,000 nor more than $10,000 or by imprisonment for not less than one year nor more than ten years, or by both such fine and imprisonment, and for a second offense, by a fine of not less than $5,000 nor more than $15,000 or by imprisonment for not less than five years nor more than 15 years, or by both such fine and imprisonment.

The provisions of this section shall not apply to: (i) the possession by a law enforcement officer; or (ii) the possession by an individual who is retired from service with a law enforcement agency and is not otherwise prohibited from receiving such a weapon or feeding device from such agency upon retirement.

SECTION 131N
Covert weapons; sale, transfer or possession; punishment

No person shall sell, offer for sale, transfer or possess any weapon, capable of discharging a bullet or shot, that is: (i) constructed in a shape that does not resemble a handgun, short-barreled rifle or short-barreled shotgun including, but not limited to, covert weapons that resemble key-chains, pens, cigarette-lighters or cigarette-packages; or (ii) not detectable as a weapon or potential weapon by x-ray machines commonly used at airports or walk-through metal detectors. Whoever violates the provisions of this section shall be punished, for a first offense, by a fine of not less than $1,000 nor more than $10,000 or by imprisonment for not less than one year nor more than ten years, or by both such fine and imprisonment, and for a second offense, by a fine of not less than $5,000 nor more than $15,000 or by imprisonment of not less than five years nor more than 15 years, or by both such fine and imprisonment.

SECTION 131O
Colonel of state police; statewide firearms surrender program

Notwithstanding any general or special law, rule or regulation to the contrary, the colonel of state police, in conjunction with the secretary of the executive office of public safety, shall promulgate rules and regulations implementing a statewide firearms surrender program. In conjunction with this program only, any citizen of the commonwealth who complies with the policies set forth by the colonel shall not be asked for identification and shall be immune from prosecution for possession of such firearm; provided, however, that nothing herein shall prohibit the prosecution of any person for the unlawful possession of a firearm who is not in compliance with the conditions and procedures established by the colonel; and provided further, that nothing herein shall prohibit the prosecution of any person for any other offense committed within the commonwealth.

Any firearm surrendered in accordance with the provisions of this program that is reported stolen shall be returned to its lawful owner; provided, however, that any firearm suspected to be evidence in a crime shall remain in the custody and control of the department of state police in the same manner as any other such firearm lawfully seized by the department of state police. The department of state police may test-fire and preserve any and all firearms voluntarily surrendered. All weapons that have been voluntarily surrendered that are not suspected to be evidence of criminal activity and have not been reported stolen shall be disposed of in accordance with procedures established by the colonel.

SECTION 131P
Basic firearm safety certificate; instructors
(Amended by 2014 Mass. Acts c. 284, §§ 66–67, effective Aug. 11, 2014; 2014 Mass. Acts c. 284, § 69, effective Jan. 1, 2015; bracketed text stricken by 2014 Mass. Acts c. 284, § 68, effective Jan. 1, 2021.)

(a) Any person making application for the issuance of a firearms identification card under section 129B, a [Class A or Class B] license to carry firearms under section 131 or 131F, or a permit to purchase under section 131A, who was not licensed under the provisions of this chapter on June 1, 1998, shall, in addition to the requirements set forth in said sections 129B, 131, 131A or 131F submit to the licensing authority a basic firearms safety certificate; provided, however, that a certificate issued by the division of fisheries and wildlife pursuant to the provisions of section 14 of chapter 131, evidencing satisfactory completion of a hunting safety course, shall serve as a valid substitute for a basic firearms safety certificate required under this section. Persons lawfully possessing a firearm identification card or license to carry firearms on June 1, 1998 shall be exempt from the provisions of this section upon expiration of such card or license and when applying for licensure as required under this chapter. No application for the issuance of a firearm identification card or license to carry shall be accepted or processed by the licensing authority without such certificate attached thereto; provided, however, that the provisions of this section shall not apply to (i) any officer, agent or employee of the commonwealth or any state of the United States; (ii) any member of the military or other service of any state or of the United States; (iii) any duly authorized law enforcement officer, agent or employee of any municipality of the commonwealth; provided, however, that any such person described in clauses (i) to (iii), inclusive, is authorized by a competent authority to carry or possess the weapon so carried or possessed and is acting within the scope of his duties.

A current member of the United States military or the Massachusetts National Guard who has not been prohibited under said section 129B from owning a firearm and has received adequate training while serving in the military shall be exempt from being required to submit a basic firearms safety certificate to the licensing authority upon submitting a copy of the member's most current military identification form.

(b) The colonel of state police shall promulgate rules and regulations governing the issuance and form of basic firearms safety certificates required by this section. Said colonel shall certify certain persons as firearms safety instructors and shall certify safety course curriculum. Such certification shall be for a period of ten years, unless sooner revoked by reason of unsuitability, in the discretion of said colonel. The department of state police may impose a fee of $50 for initial issuance of such certification to offset the cost of certifying instructors. The fee for certification renewal shall be $10. Firearms safety instructors shall be any person certified by a nationally recognized organization that fosters safety in firearms, or any other person in the discretion of said colonel, to be competent to give instruction in a basic firearms safety course. Applicants for certification as instructors under the provisions of this section shall not be exempt from the requirement of this chapter or any other law or regulation of the commonwealth or the United States. Upon application to the colonel of state police, said colonel may, in his discretion, certify as a firearms safety instructor any person who operates a firearms safety course or program which provides in its curriculum: (a) the safe use, handling and storage of firearms; (b) methods of securing and childproofing firearms; (c) the applicable laws relating to the possession, transportation and storage of firearms; and (d) knowledge of operation, potential dangers and basic competency in the ownership and usage of firearms.

(c) Any firearms safety instructor certified under the provisions of this section may, in his discretion, issue a basic firearms safety certificate to any person who successfully completes the requirements of a basic firearms safety course approved by the colonel. No firearms safety instructor shall issue or cause to be issued any basic firearms safety certificate to any person who fails to meet minimum requirements of the prescribed course of study including, but not limited to, demonstrated competency in the use of firearms. Instructors certified under the provisions of this section shall forward to the department of state police the names of those persons who have received basic firearms safety certificates. Local licens-

ing authorities, as defined in section 121, shall, upon receipt of an application for a firearm identification card of a [Class A or Class B] license to carry firearms, make inquiry to the department of state police to confirm the issuance to the applicant of a basic firearms safety certificate.

(d) Any person applying for licensure under the provisions of this chapter who knowingly files or submits a basic firearms safety certificate to a licensing authority which contains false information shall be punished by a fine of not less than $1,000 nor more than $5,000 or by imprisonment for not more than two years in a house of correction, or by both such fine and imprisonment.

(e) Any firearms safety instructor who knowingly issued a basic firearms safety certificate to a person who has not successfully completed a firearms safety course approved by the colonel shall be punished by a fine of not less than $5,000 nor more than $10,000 or by imprisonment for not more than two years in a house of correction, or by both such fine and imprisonment.

(f) The colonel of state police shall produce and distribute public service announcements to encourage and educate the general public about: (i) safe storage and transportation of weapons pursuant to sections 131C and 131L; and (ii) importance of firearms safety education and training, including information on places and classes that a person may attend to obtain firearms safety education and training.

SECTION 131Q
Firearm used to carry out criminal act, tracing to licensing authority, reporting of statistical data
(Added by 2014 Mass. Acts c. 284, § 70, effective Jan. 1, 2015.)

A firearm, rifle or shotgun, large capacity weapon, machine gun or assault weapon used to carry out a criminal act shall be traced by the licensing authority for the city or town in which the crime took place. The licensing authority shall report statistical data, when the data is readily available as determined by the chief of police, including, but not limited to: (i) the make, model, serial number and caliber of the weapon used; (ii) the type of crime committed; (iii) whether an arrest or conviction was made; (iv) whether fingerprint evidence was found on the firearm; (v) whether ballistic evidence was retrieved from the crime scene; (vi) whether the criminal use of the firearm was related to known gang activity; (vii) whether the weapon was obtained illegally; (viii) whether the weapon was lost or stolen; and (ix) whether the person using the weapon was otherwise a prohibited person.

The data shall be reported to the commonwealth fusion center or the criminal firearms and trafficking unit within the division of investigation and intelligence in the department of state police established pursuant to section 6 of chapter 22C. The colonel of state police shall produce an annual report by December 31 of each year regarding crimes committed in the commonwealth using firearms, rifles or shotguns, large capacity weapons, machine guns or assault weapons, including all of the categories of data contained in this section, and shall submit a copy of the report to the joint committee on public safety and homeland security, the clerks of the house of representatives and the senate and, upon request, to criminology, public policy and public health researchers and other law enforcement agencies.

SECTION 185A
Resale of tickets; necessity, term and transfer of license; information in application; definition of resale; restrictions

No person shall engage in the business of reselling any ticket or tickets of admission or other evidence of right of entry to any theatrical exhibition, public show or public amusement or exhibition required to be licensed under sections 181 and 182 of this chapter or under chapter 128A, whether such business is conducted on or off the premises on which such ticket or other evidence is to be used, without being licensed therefor by the commissioner of public safety, in this and the six following sections called the commissioner. A license shall be granted only upon a written application setting forth such information as the commissioner may require. Each license issued under this section shall be in force until the first day of January next after its date, unless sooner revoked. No such license may be transferred or assigned except upon written permission of the commissioner. The sale of a ticket or pass, entitling the holder thereof to admission to any such theatrical exhibition, public show or public amusement or exhibition upon payment either of nothing or a sum less than that demanded of the public generally, shall be deemed to be a resale thereof within the meaning of this section.

No person shall engage in or have any interest, as a stockholder or otherwise, in any such business in the conduct of which is or are resold any ticket or tickets of admission or other evidence or evidences of right of entry to any theatrical exhibition, public show or public amusement or exhibition of which said person is the owner or in which he has any interest, as a stockholder or otherwise.

Chapter 159A½. Transportation Network Companies

SECTION 7
Title
(Added by 2016 Mass.)

(a) A driver providing transportation network services who is not in compliance with subsection (b) of section 2 or sections 4 or 5 shall be deemed to have committed a civil motor vehicle infraction, as defined in section 1 of chapter 90C. State or local law enforcement officials may issue a citation for any such violation in the manner provided for in said chapter 90C. If the driver is cited under this subsection, every transportation network company that allows the driver to provide transportation network services shall be subject to a fine of $500.

(b) A driver providing transportation network services who knowingly or willfully allows another individual to use that driver's certificate or identity to provide transportation network services or a driver who is using a transportation network driver certificate belonging to another individual or is misrepresenting a driver's identity to riders or potential riders by means of a digital network shall be punished by a fine of not more than $500 for a first offense, by a fine of not more than $750 for a second offense and by a fine of not more than $1,000 or by imprisonment in the house of correction for not more than 6 months for a third or subsequent offense.

(c) A driver who violates section 3 or any other person who, by soliciting, accepting, arranging or providing transportation network services in any other manner, including through street hails, cruising or street solicitations, shall be deemed to have committed a civil motor vehicle infraction, as defined in section 1 of chapter 90C. State or local law enforcement officials may issue a citation for any such violation in the manner provided for in said chapter 90C to the transportation network driver and may assess a fine of $500.

(d) A driver who fails to produce proof of a transportation network driver certificate and a background check clearance certificate upon request by law enforcement shall be punished by a fine of not more than $100 for a first offense, by a fine of not more than $500 for a second offense and not more than $1,000 for a third or subsequent offense.

Chapter 208. Divorce

Section
18   Pendency of action for divorce; protection of personal liberty of spouse; restraint orders authorized
34B   Order to vacate marital home
34C   Orders to vacate marital home and orders of restraint; notice to law enforcement agencies; procedures; violations
34D   Request for restraining order or order to vacate marital home; information provided to petitioner upon filing; domestic violence record search; outstanding warrants
40   Cohabitation after divorce
41   Personation
42   Procurement of unlawful divorce
43   Advertisement to procure divorce
44   Certificate of divorce; unlawful issuance
45   Criminal offenses; notice to district attorney

LIBELS FOR DIVORCE

SECTION 18
Pendency of action for divorce; protection of personal liberty of spouse; restraint orders authorized

The probate court in which the action for divorce is pending may, upon petition of the wife, prohibit the husband, or upon petition of the husband, prohibit the wife from imposing any restraint upon her or his personal liberty during the pendency of the action for divorce. Upon the petition of the husband or wife or the guardian of either, the court may make such further order as it deems necessary to protect either party or their children, to preserve the peace or to carry out the purposes of this section relative to restraint on personal liberty.

GENERAL PROVISIONS

SECTION 34B
Order to vacate marital home

Any court having jurisdiction of actions for divorce, or for nullity of marriage or of separate support or maintenance, may, upon commencement of such action and during the pendency thereof, order the husband or wife to vacate forthwith the marital home for a period of time not exceeding ninety days, and upon further motion for such additional certain period of time, as the court deems necessary or appropriate if the court finds, after a hearing, that the health, safety or welfare of the moving party or any minor children residing with the parties would be endangered or substantially impaired by a failure to enter such an order. The opposing party shall be given at least three days' notice of such hearing and may appear and be heard either in person or by his attorney. If the moving party demonstrates a substantial likelihood of immediate danger to his or her health, safety or welfare or to that of such minor children from the opposing party, the court may enter a temporary order without notice, and shall immediately thereafter notify said opposing party and give him or her an opportunity to be heard as soon as possible but not later than five days after such order is entered on the question of continuing such temporary order. The court may issue an order to vacate although the opposing party does not reside in the marital home at the time of its issuance, or if the moving party has left such home and has not returned there because of fear for his or her safety or for that of any minor children.

SECTION 34C
Orders to vacate marital home and orders of restraint; notice to law enforcement agencies; procedures; violations

Whenever a division of the probate and family court department issues an order to vacate under the provisions of section thirty-four B, or an order prohibiting a person from imposing any restraint on the personal liberty of another person under section eighteen or under the provisions of section thirty-two of chapter two hundred and nine or section three, four or five of chapter two hundred and nine A or section fifteen or twenty of chapter two hundred and nine C or an order for custody pursuant to any above abuse prevention action, the register shall transmit two certified copies of each order forthwith to the appropriate law enforcement agency which shall serve one copy of each such order upon the defendant. Unless otherwise ordered by the court, service shall be by delivering a copy in hand to the defendant. Law enforcement officers shall use every reasonable means to enforce such order. Law enforcement agencies shall establish procedures adequate to insure that an officer at the scene of an alleged violation of such order may be informed of the existence and terms of such order.

The court shall notify the appropriate law enforcement agency in writing whenever any such order is vacated by the court and shall direct the agency to destroy all records of such vacated order and such agency shall comply with such directive.

Any violation of such order shall be punishable by a fine of not more than five thousand dollars or by imprisonment for not more than two and one-half years in the house of correction, or both such fine and imprisonment. Each such order

issued shall contain the following statement: VIOLATION OF THIS ORDER IS A CRIMINAL OFFENSE.

Any such violation may be enforced in the superior or district or Boston municipal court departments. Criminal remedies provided herein are not exclusive and do not preclude any other available civil or criminal remedies. The superior, probate and family, district and Boston municipal court departments may each enforce by civil contempt procedure a violation of its own court order.

SECTION 34D
Request for restraining order or order to vacate marital home; information provided to petitioner upon filing; domestic violence record search; outstanding warrants

Upon the filing of a request for a restraining order pursuant to section eighteen or for an order for a spouse to vacate the marital home pursuant to section thirty-four B, a petitioner shall be informed that the proceedings hereunder are civil in nature and that violations of orders issued hereunder are criminal in nature. Further, a petitioner shall be given information prepared by the appropriate district attorney's office that other criminal proceedings may be available and such petitioner shall be instructed by such district attorney's office relative to the procedures required to initiate such criminal proceedings including, but not limited to, the filing of a complaint for a violation of section forty-three of chapter two hundred and sixty-five. Whenever possible, a petitioner shall be provided with such information in the petitioner's native language.

When considering a request for a restraining order pursuant to section eighteen or for an order for a spouse to vacate the marital home pursuant to section thirty-four B, a judge shall cause a search to be made of the records contained within the statewide domestic violence record keeping system maintained by the office of the commissioner of probation and shall review the resulting data to determine whether the named defendant has a civil or criminal record involving domestic or other violence. Upon receipt of information that an outstanding warrant exists against the named defendant, a judge shall order that the appropriate law enforcement officials be notified and shall order that any information regarding the defendant's most recent whereabouts shall be forwarded to such officials. In all instances where an outstanding warrant exists, a judge shall make finding, based upon all of the circumstances, as to whether an imminent threat of bodily injury exists to the petitioner. In all instances where such an imminent threat of bodily injury is found to exist, the judge shall notify the appropriate law enforcement officials of such finding and such officials shall take all necessary actions to execute any such outstanding warrant as soon as is practicable.

CRIMINAL PROVISIONS

SECTION 40
Cohabitation after divorce

Persons divorced from each other cohabiting as husband and wife or living together in the same house shall be held to be guilty of adultery.

SECTION 41
Personation

Whoever falsely personates another or wilfully and fraudulently procures a person so to do, or fraudulently procures false testimony to be given, or makes a false or fraudulent return of service of process in an action for divorce or in any proceeding connected therewith, shall be punished by a fine of not more than one thousand dollars or by imprisonment for not more than two years.

SECTION 42
Procurement of unlawful divorce

Whoever knowingly procures or obtains or assists another to procure or obtain any false, counterfeit or fraudulent divorce or judgment of divorce, or any divorce or judgment of divorce from a court of another state for or in favor of a person who at the time of making application therefor was a resident of this commonwealth, such court not having jurisdiction to grant such judgment, shall be punished by a fine of not more than two hundred dollars or by imprisonment for not more than six months.

SECTION 43
Advertisement to procure divorce

Whoever writes, prints or publishes, or solicits another to write, print or publish, any notice, circular or advertisement soliciting employment in the business of procuring divorces or offering inducements for the purpose of procuring such employment shall be punished by a fine of not more than two hundred dollars or by imprisonment for not more than six months.

SECTION 44
Certificate of divorce; unlawful issuance

Whoever, except in compliance with an order of a court of competent jurisdiction, gives, signs or issues any writing purporting to grant a divorce to persons who are husband and wife according to the laws of the commonwealth, or purporting to be a certificate that a divorce has been granted to such persons, shall be punished by a fine of not more than one thousand dollars, or by imprisonment for not more than three years, or both.

SECTION 45
Criminal offenses; notice to district attorney

If a divorce is granted for a cause constituting a crime, committed within the commonwealth and within the time provided by law for making complaints and finding indictments therefor, the court granting the divorce may, in its discretion, cause notice of such facts to be given by the clerk of the court or register of probate to the district attorney for the district where such crime was committed, with a list of the witnesses proving such crime and any other information which it considers proper and thereupon the district attorney may cause complaint therefor to be made before a magistrate having jurisdiction thereof, or may present the evidence thereof to the grand jury.

Chapter 209. Husband and Wife

SECTION 32
Order prohibiting restraint of personal liberty of spouse; support, custody and maintenance orders; information provided to complainant; domestic violence record search; investigations; factors determining support amount

If a spouse fails, without justifiable cause, to provide suitable support of the other spouse, or deserts the other spouse, or if a married person has justifiable cause for living apart from his spouse, whether or not the married person is actually living apart, the probate court may, upon the complaint of the married person, or if he is incompetent due to mental illness or mental retardation upon the complaint of the guardian or next friend, prohibit the spouse from imposing any restraint upon the personal liberty of the married person during such time as the court by its order may direct or until further order of the court thereon. Upon the complaint of any such party or guardian of a minor child made in accordance with the Massachusetts Rules of Civil Procedure the court may make further orders relative to the support of the married person and the care, custody and maintenance of minor children, may determine with which of the parents the children or any of them shall remain and may, from time to time, upon similar complaint revise and alter such judgment or make a new order or judgment as the circumstances of the parents or the benefit of the children may require.

Upon the filing of a complaint pursuant to this section to prohibit a spouse from imposing any restraint upon the complainant's personal liberty, a complainant shall be informed that proceedings hereunder are civil in nature and that violations of orders issued hereunder are criminal in nature. Further, a complainant shall be given information prepared by the appropriate district attorney's office that other criminal proceedings may be available and shall be instructed by such district attorney's office relative to the procedures required to initiate criminal proceedings including, but not limited to, the filing of a complaint for a violation of section forty-three of chapter two hundred and sixty-five. Whenever possible, a complainant shall be provided with such information in the complainant's native language.

When considering a complaint to prohibit a spouse from imposing any restraint upon the complainant's personal liberty under this section, a judge shall cause a search to be made of the records contained within the statewide domestic violence record keeping system maintained by the office of the commissioner of probation and shall review the resulting data to determine whether the named defendant has a civil or criminal record involving domestic or other violence. Upon receipt of information that an outstanding warrant exists against the named defendant, a judge shall order that the appropriate law enforcement officials be notified and shall order that any information regarding the defendant's most recent whereabouts shall be forwarded to such officials. In all instances where an outstanding warrant exists, a judge shall make a finding, based upon all of the circumstances, as to whether an imminent threat of bodily injury exists to the petitioner. In all instances where such an imminent threat of bodily injury is found to exist, the judge shall notify the appropriate law enforcement officials of such finding and such officials shall take all necessary actions to execute any such outstanding warrant as soon as is practicable.

Upon request by the court, the state police, local police or probation officers shall make an investigation in relation to any proceedings and report to the court. Every such report shall be in writing and shall become part of the record of such proceedings.

In determining the amount of a support order, if any, to be made, the court shall consider, but is not limited to, the following factors, to the extent pertinent and raised by the parties: (a) the net income, assets, earning ability, and other obligations of the obligor; (b) the number and ages of the persons to be supported; (c) the expenses incurred by the obligor and the persons to be supported for the necessities of life, and the usual standard of living of the persons to be supported; (d) the assets and net earnings, including a deduction for the provision for childcare, of the persons to be supported; (e) the marriage or remarriage of any person being supported; (f) the responsibilities of the obligor for the maintenance or support of any other children of the obligor, even if a court order for such maintenance or support does not exist, or for any preexisting order for the maintenance or support of any other children from a previous marriage, or for any preexisting order for the maintenance or support of any other children born out of wedlock and that said obligor is fulfilling such responsibility; and (g) the capacity of any person being supported or having custody of supported children, except persons under eighteen years of age, to work or to make reasonable efforts to obtain employment, including the extent of employ-

ment opportunities in fields in which such person is suited for employment, the necessity for and availability to said person of job training programs, and the extent to which said person is needed during business hours by members of the family and the availability to said person of child care services and the extent to which such person needs to attend school to obtain skills necessary for employment. When the court makes an order for maintenance or support on behalf of a spouse or child, said court shall determine whether the obligor under such order has health insurance or other health coverage available to him through an employer or organization or has health insurance or other health coverage available to him at reasonable cost that may be extended to cover the spouse or child for whom support is ordered. When said court has determined that the obligor has such insurance or coverage available to him, said court shall include in the support order a requirement that the obligor exercise the option of additional coverage in favor of the spouse and child or obtain coverage for the spouse and child.

No order shall leave an obligor with less money than is required to provide him minimum subsistence, including food, shelter, utilities, clothing and the reasonable expenses necessary to travel to or obtain employment.

Chapter 209A. Abuse Prevention

Section

1   Definitions
2   Venue
3   Remedies; period of relief
3A   Nature of proceedings and availability of other criminal proceedings; information required to be given to complainant upon filing
3B   Order for suspension and surrender of firearms license or firearms identification card; surrender of firearms; petition for review; hearing
3C   Continuation or modification of order for suspension or surrender
3D   Suspension or surrender issued pursuant to sections 3B or 3C; reporting to department of criminal justice information services
4   Temporary orders; notice; hearing
5   Granting of relief when court closed; certification
5A   Protection order issued by another jurisdiction; enforcement; filing; presumption of validity
6   Powers of police
7   Abuse prevention orders; domestic violence record search; service of order; enforcement; violations
8   Confidentiality of records
9   Form of complaint; promulgation
10   Assessments against persons referred to certified batterers' treatment program as condition of probation
11   Possession, care and control of domesticated animal owned by persons involved in certain protective orders; notice to law enforcement upon finding of imminent threat to household member or animal

SECTION 1
Definitions

As used in this chapter the following words shall have the following meanings:

"Abuse", the occurrence of one or more of the following acts between family or household members:

(a) attempting to cause or causing physical harm;

(b) placing another in fear of imminent serious physical harm;

(c) causing another to engage involuntarily in sexual relations by force, threat or duress.

"Court", the superior, probate and family, district or Boston municipal court departments of the trial court, except when the petitioner is in a dating relationship when "Court" shall mean district, probate, or Boston municipal courts.

"Family or household members", persons who:

(a) are or were married to one another;

(b) are or were residing together in the same household;

(c) are or were related by blood or marriage;

(d) having a child in common regardless of whether they have ever married or lived together; or

(e) are or have been in a substantive dating or engagement relationship, which shall be adjudged by district, probate or Boston municipal courts consideration of the following factors:

(1) the length of time of the relationship; (2) the type of relationship; (3) the frequency of interaction between the parties; and (4) if the relationship has been terminated by either person, the length of time elapsed since the termination of the relationship.

"Law officer", any officer authorized to serve criminal process.

"Protection order issued by another jurisdiction", any injunction or other order issued by a court of another state, territory or possession of the United States, the Commonwealth of Puerto Rico, or the District of Columbia, or tribal court that is issued for the purpose of preventing violent or threatening acts or harassment against, or contact or communication with or physical proximity to another person, including temporary and final orders issued by civil and criminal courts filed by or on behalf of a person seeking protection.

"Vacate order", court order to leave and remain away from a premises and surrendering forthwith any keys to said premises to the plaintiff. The defendant shall not damage any of the plaintiff's belongings or those of any other occupant and shall not shut off or cause to be shut off any utilities or mail delivery to the plaintiff. In the case where the premises designated in the vacate order is a residence, so long as the plaintiff is living at said residence, the defendant shall not interfere in any way with the plaintiff's right to possess such residence, except by order or judgment of a court of competent jurisdiction pursuant to appropriate civil eviction proceedings, a petition to partition real estate, or a proceeding to divide marital property. A vacate order may include in its scope a household, a multiple family dwelling and the plaintiff's workplace. When issuing an order to vacate the plaintiff's workplace, the presiding justice must consider whether the plaintiff and defendant work in the same location or for the same employer.

NOTE 1   For a case discussing the definition of "abuse," see *Commonwealth v. Jacobsen*, 419 Mass. 269 (1995).

NOTE 2   **Substantive Dating Relationship.** "Chapter 209A must be interpreted to protect all who are in a substantive dating relationship from abuse, regardless of whether the relationship was developed or conducted by the use of technology." *E.C.O. v. Compton*, 464 Mass. 558, 565 (2013).

SECTION 2
Venue

Proceedings under this chapter shall be filed, heard and determined in the superior court department or the Boston municipal court department or respective divisions of the probate and family or district court departments having venue over the plaintiff's residence. If the plaintiff has left a residence or household to avoid abuse, such plaintiff shall have the option of commencing an action in the court having venue over such prior residence or household, or in the court having venue over the present residence or household.

NOTE   Chapter 209A is constitutional. *Frizado v. Frizado*, 420 Mass. 592 (1995).

SECTION 3
Remedies; period of relief
(Amended by 2014 Mass. Acts c. 260, §§ 12–13, effective Aug. 8, 2014.)

A person suffering from abuse from an adult or minor family or household member may file a complaint in the court requesting protection from such abuse, including, but not limited to, the following orders:

(a) ordering the defendant to refrain from abusing the plaintiff, whether the defendant is an adult or minor;

(b) ordering the defendant to refrain from contacting the plaintiff, unless authorized by the court, whether the defendant is an adult or minor;

(c) ordering the defendant to vacate forthwith and remain away from the household, multiple family dwelling, and workplace. Notwithstanding the provisions of section thirty-four B of chapter two hundred and eight, an order to vacate shall be for a fixed period of time, not to exceed one year, at the expiration of which time the court may extend any such order upon motion of the plaintiff, with notice to the defendant, for such additional times as it deems necessary to protect the plaintiff from abuse;

(d) awarding the plaintiff temporary custody of a minor child; provided, however, that in any case brought in the probate and family court a finding by such court by a preponderance of the evidence that a pattern or serious incident of

abuse, as defined in section 31A of chapter 208, toward a parent or child has occurred shall create a rebuttable presumption that it is not in the best interests of the child to be placed in sole custody, shared legal custody or shared physical custody with the abusive parent. Such presumption may be rebutted by a preponderance of the evidence that such custody award is in the best interests of the child. For the purposes of this section, an "abusive parent" shall mean a parent who has committed a pattern of abuse or a serious incident of abuse;

For the purposes of this section, the issuance of an order or orders under chapter 209A shall not in and of itself constitute a pattern of serious incident of abuse; nor shall an order or orders entered ex parte under said chapter 209A be admissible to show whether a pattern or serious incident of abuse has in fact occurred; provided, however, that an order or orders entered ex parte under said chapter 209A may be admissible for other purposes as the court may determine, other than showing whether a pattern or serious incident of abuse has in fact occurred; provided further, that the underlying facts upon which an order or orders under said chapter 209A was based may also form the basis for a finding by the probate and family court that a pattern or serious incident of abuse has occurred.

If the court finds that a pattern or serious incident of abuse has occurred and issues a temporary or permanent custody order, the court shall within 90 days enter written findings of fact as to the effects of the abuse on the child, which findings demonstrate that such order is in the furtherance of the child's best interests and provides for the safety and well-being of the child.

If ordering visitation to the abusive parent, the court shall provide for the safety and well-being of the child and the safety of the abused parent. The court may consider:

(a) ordering an exchange of the child to occur in a protected setting or in the presence of an appropriate third party;

(b) ordering visitation supervised by an appropriate third party, visitation center or agency;

(c) ordering the abusive parent to attend and complete, to the satisfaction of the court, a certified batterer's treatment program as a condition of visitation.

(d) ordering the abusive parent to abstain from possession or consumption of alcohol or controlled substances during the visitation and for 24 hours preceding visitation;

(e) ordering the abusive parent to pay the costs of supervised visitation;

(f) prohibiting overnight visitation;

(g) requiring a bond from the abusive parent for the return and safety of the child;

(h) ordering an investigation or appointment of a guardian ad litem or attorney for the child; and

(i) imposing any other condition that is deemed necessary to provide for the safety and well-being of the child and the safety of the abused parent.

Nothing in this section shall be construed to affect the right of the parties to a hearing under the rules of domestic relations procedure or to affect the discretion of the probate and family court in the conduct of such hearing.

(e) ordering the defendant to pay temporary support for the plaintiff or any child in the plaintiff's custody or both, when the defendant has a legal obligation to support such person. In determining the amount to be paid, the court shall apply the standards established in the child support guidelines.

Each judgment or order of support which is issued, reviewed or modified pursuant to this chapter shall conform to and shall be enforced in accordance with the provisions of section 12 of chapter 119A;

(f) ordering the defendant to pay to the person abused monetary compensation for the losses suffered as a direct result of the abuse. Compensatory losses shall include, but not be limited to, loss of earnings or support, costs for restoring utilities, out-of-pocket losses for injuries sustained, replacement costs for locks or personal property removed or destroyed, medical and moving expenses and reasonable attorney's fees;

(g) ordering information in the case record to be impounded in accordance with court rule;

(h) ordering the defendant to refrain from abusing or contacting the plaintiff's child, or child in plaintiff's care or custody, unless authorized by the court;

(i) the judge may recommend to the defendant that the defendant attend a batterer's intervention program that is certified by the department of health.

No filing fee shall be charged for the filing of the complaint. Neither the plaintiff nor the plaintiff's attorney shall be charged for certified copies of any orders entered by the court, or any copies of the file reasonably required for future court action or as a result of the loss or destruction of plaintiff's copies.

Any relief granted by the court shall be for a fixed period of time not to exceed one year. Every order shall on its face state the time and date the order is to expire and shall include the date and time that the matter will again be heard. If the plaintiff appears at the court at the date and time the order is to expire, the court shall determine whether or not to extend the order for any additional time reasonably necessary to protect the plaintiff or to enter a permanent order. When the expiration date stated on the order is on a weekend day or holiday, or a date when the court is closed to business, the order shall not expire until the next date that the court is open to business. The plaintiff may appear on such next court business day at the time designated by the order to request that the order be extended. The court may also extend the order upon motion of the plaintiff, for such additional time as it deems necessary to protect from abuse the plaintiff or any child in the plaintiff's care or custody. The fact that abuse has not occurred during the pendency of an order shall not, in itself, constitute sufficient ground for denying or failing to extend the order, of allowing an order to expire or be vacated, or for refusing to issue a new order.

The court may modify its order at any subsequent time upon motion by either party. When the plaintiff's address is in accessible to the defendant as provided in section 8 of this chapter and the defendant has filed a motion to modify the court's order, the court shall be responsible for notifying the plaintiff. In no event shall the court disclose any such inaccessible address.

No order under this chapter shall in any manner affect title to any real property.

No court shall compel parties to mediate any aspect of their case. Although the court may refer the case to the family service office of the probation department or victim/witness advocates for information gathering purposes, the court shall not compel the parties to meet together in such information gathering sessions.

A court shall not deny any complaint filed under this chapter solely because it was not filed within a particular time period after the last alleged incident of abuse.

A court may issue a mutual restraining order or mutual no-contact order pursuant to any abuse prevention action only if the court has made specific written findings of fact. The court shall then provide a detailed order, sufficiently specific to apprise any law officer as to which party has violated the order, if the parties are in or appear to be in violation of the order.

Any action commenced under the provisions of this chapter shall not preclude any other civil or criminal remedies. A party filing a complaint under this chapter shall be required to disclose any prior or pending actions involving the parties for divorce, annulment, paternity, custody or support, guardianship, separate support or legal separation, or abuse prevention.

If there is a prior or pending custody support order from the probate or family court department of the trial court, an order issued in the superior, district or Boston municipal court departments of the trial court pursuant to this chapter may include any relief available pursuant to this chapter including orders for custody or support; provided, however, that upon issuing an order for custody or support, the superior, district or Boston municipal court shall provide a copy of the order to the probate and family court department of the trial court that issued the prior or pending custody or support order immediately; provided further, that such order for custody or support shall be for a fixed period of time, not to exceed 30 days; and provided further, that such order may be superseded by a subsequent custody or support order issued by the probate and family court department, which shall retain final jurisdiction over any custody or support order. This section shall not be interpreted to mean that superior, district or Boston municipal court judges are prohibited or discouraged from ordering all other necessary relief or issuing the custody and support provisions of orders pursuant to this chapter for the full duration permitted under subsection (c).

If the parties to a proceeding under this chapter are parties in a subsequent proceeding in the probate and family court department for divorce, annulment, paternity, custody or support, guardianship or separate support, any custody or support order or judgment issued in the subsequent proceeding shall supersede any prior custody or support order under this chapter.

NOTE 1   Abuse Prevention Order; Evidence Required. "We conclude that when, at a contested hearing, a plaintiff fails to prove that 'abuse' has occurred, a judge may not continue an ex parte order that directs the defendant to vacate and remain away from the household because of subjective concerns that violence may occur if both remain in the same household." *Corrado v. Hedrick*, 65 Mass. App. Ct. 477, 477 (2006).

NOTE 2a   Extension of an Order; Standard. "'The inquiry at an extension hearing is whether the plaintiff has shown by a preponderance of the evidence that an extension of the order is necessary to protect her from the likelihood of 'abuse' as defined in G.L. c. 209A, § 1' . . .

"In determining whether abuse, as defined in G.L. c. 209A, § 1(b) exists, a judge must ascertain whether the applicant's fear of imminent serious physical harm is objectively reasonable. 'In evaluating whether a plaintiff has met her burden, a judge must consider the totality of the circumstances of the parties' relationship . . . . The judge is to consider the basis for the initial order in evaluating the risk of future abuse should the existing order expire. This does not mean that the restrained party may challenge the evidence underlying the initial order.'" *Vittone v. Clairmont*, 64 Mass. App. Ct. 479, 485–86 (2005) (citations to *Iamele v. Asselin*, 444 Mass. 734 (2005) omitted).

NOTE 2b   The standard for extension of a protective order under G.L. c. 209A is the same as the standard for initially obtaining a 209A order. "The language 'reasonably necessary to protect the plaintiff' is not intended to alter the criteria for issuing a protective order. That phrase simply modifies 'additional time,' the words immediately preceding it." *Iamele v. Asselin*, 444 Mass. 734, 737 (2005).

NOTE 3   **Request to Vacate Order Retroactively; Standard.** "Where, as here, a party seeks through asserted 'new evidence' to vacate retroactively an abuse prevention order, we think that principles analogous to those applicable to Mass. R. Dom. P. 60(b)(2) . . . and to the identical Mass. R. Civ. P. 60(b)(2), 365 Mass. 828 (1974), provide a useful guide to judges deciding whether to grant the relief sought . . . .

"Applying the foregoing concepts, we think that a motion that seeks to vacate retroactively an order issued under c. 209A 'on the ground of newly discovered evidence cannot properly be granted unless it is found that the evidence relied on was not available to the party seeking [relief] for introduction at the original trial by the exercise of reasonable diligence, and that such evidence is material not only in the sense that it is relevant and admissible but also in the sense that it is important evidence of such a nature' that it likely would have affected the result had it been available at the time. *DeLuca v. Boston. Elev. Ry.*, 312 Mass. 495, 497 (1942)." *Mitchell v. Mitchell*, 62 Mass. App. Ct. 769, 775 (2005).

NOTE 4   **Request for Relief from Prospective Application of Order.** "[T]he standard for determining whether prospective relief from a c. 209A order is warranted must be a flexible one. The level of impact on the underlying risk from harm that a c. 209A order seeks to protect against will vary from case to case . . . A request to modify a provision of the order that bears only tangentially on the safety of the protected party (e.g., certain for visitation or support) will fall at one end of the continuum, whereas a defendant's request to terminate an abuse prevention order in its entirety will fall at the other end. The greater the likelihood that the safety of the protected party may be put at risk by a modification, the more substantial the showing the party seeking relief must make.

"In deciding whether to grant or deny a party's request for relief, the basis on which the order was initially issued is not subject to review or attack. Rather, the court must consider the nature of the relief sought keeping in mind the primary purpose of a 209A order: to protect a party from harm or the fear of imminent serious harm.

"The husband's claims amounted to a collateral attack on an abuse prevention order that, at least for the one-year period of its duration, was final. Such an abuse prevention order, entered after a hearing that satisfies due process requirements . . . should be set aside only in the most extraordinary circumstances and where it has been clearly and convincingly established that the order is no longer needed to protect the victim from harm or the reasonable fear of serious harm. Furthermore, if the judge determines that it is appropriate to allow a motion to vacate or terminate a c. 209A order, the decision should be supported by findings of fact." *Mitchell v. Mitchell*, 62 Mass. App. Ct. 769, 780–81 (2005).

NOTE 5   **Timeliness.** "Notwithstanding that Capuano faced a potentially difficult choice between testifying in the c. 209A case or asserting his privilege against self-incrimination, Singh was nevertheless entitled to a prompt evidentiary hearing on her claim under c. 209A." *Singh v. Capuano*, 468 Mass. 328, 332–33 (2014).

SECTION 3A
Nature of proceedings and availability of other criminal proceedings; information required to be given to complainant upon filing

Upon the filing of a complaint under this chapter, a complainant shall be informed that the proceedings hereunder are civil in nature and that violations of orders issued hereunder

are criminal in nature. Further, a complainant shall be given information prepared by the appropriate district attorney's office that other criminal proceedings may be available and such complainant shall be instructed by such district attorney's office relative to the procedures required to initiate criminal proceedings including, but not limited to, a complaint for a violation of section forty-three of chapter two hundred and sixty-five. Whenever possible, a complainant shall be provided with such information in the complainant's native language.

NOTE   "The guarantee of Art. 12 that 'no subject shall be . . . deprived of his property . . . but by the judgment of his peers,' is not violated when, without a jury trial, a court enters an order under G.L. c. 209A, provided that in its implementation, the order does not confiscate property as punishment for the commission of a crime." *Frizado v. Frizado*, 420 Mass. 592, 594 (1995).

SECTION 3B
Order for suspension and surrender of firearms license; surrender of firearms; petition for review; hearing

Upon issuance of a temporary or emergency order under section four or five of this chapter, the court shall, if the plaintiff demonstrates a substantial likelihood of immediate danger of abuse, order the immediate suspension and surrender of any license to carry firearms and or firearms identification card which the defendant may hold and order the defendant to surrender all firearms, rifles, shotguns, machine guns and ammunition which he then controls, owns, or possesses in accordance with the provisions of this chapter and any license to carry firearms or firearms identification cards which the defendant may hold shall be surrendered to the appropriate law enforcement officials in accordance with the provisions of this chapter and, said law enforcement official may store, transfer or otherwise dispose of any such weapon in accordance with the provisions of section 129D of chapter 140; provided however, that nothing herein shall authorize the transfer of any weapons surrendered by the defendant to anyone other than a licensed dealer. Notice of such suspension and ordered surrender shall be appended to the copy of abuse prevention order served on the defendant pursuant to section seven. Law enforcement officials, upon the service of said orders, shall immediately take possession of all firearms, rifles, shotguns, machine guns, ammunition, any license to carry firearms and any firearms identification cards in the control, ownership, or possession of said defendant. Any violation of such orders shall be punishable by a fine of not more than five thousand dollars, or by imprisonment for not more than two and one-half years in a house of correction, or by both such fine and imprisonment.

Any defendant aggrieved by an order of surrender or suspension as described in the first sentence of this section may petition the court which issued such suspension or surrender order for a review of such action and such petition shall be heard no later than ten court business days after the receipt of the notice of the petition by the court. If said license to carry firearms or firearms identification card has been suspended upon the issuance of an order issued pursuant to section four or five, said petition may be heard contemporaneously with the hearing specified in the second sentence of the second paragraph of section four. Upon the filing of an affidavit by the defendant that a firearm, rifle, shotgun, machine gun or ammunition is required in the performance of the defendant's employment, and upon a request for an expedited hearing, the court shall order said hearing within two business days of receipt of such affidavit and request but only on the issue of surrender and suspension pursuant to this section.

SECTION 3C
Continuation or modification of order for suspension or surrender
(Bracketed text deleted by 2014 Mass. Acts c. 284, § 71, effective Jan. 1, 2021.)

Upon the continuation or modification of an order issued pursuant to section 4 or upon petition for review as described in section 3B, the court shall also order or continue to order the immediate suspension and surrender of a defendant's license to carry firearms[, including a Class A or Class B license,] and firearms identification card and the surrender of all firearms, rifles, shotguns, machine guns or ammunition which such defendant then controls, owns or possesses if the court makes a determination that the return of such license to carry firearms, including a Class A or Class B license, and firearms identification card or firearms, rifles, shotguns, machine guns or ammunition presents a likelihood of abuse to the plaintiff. A suspension and surrender order issued pursuant to this section shall continue so long as the restraining order to which it relates is in effect; and, any law enforcement official to whom such weapon is surrendered may store, transfer or otherwise dispose of any such weapon in accordance with the provisions of section 129D of chapter 140; provided, however, that nothing herein shall authorize the transfer of any weapons surrendered by the defendant to anyone other than a licensed dealer. Any violation of such order shall be punishable by a fine of not more than $5,000 or by imprisonment for not more than two and one-half years in a house of correction or by both such fine and imprisonment.

NOTE **Jurisdiction over Out-of-State Defendant.** "[T]hat portion of the order that requires the defendant to surrender his firearms imposes an affirmative duty. Such an obligation may only be imposed by a court with personal jurisdiction over the defendant, and accordingly, that portion of the order is invalid." *Caplan v. Donovan*, 450 Mass. 463, 472 (2008).

SECTION 3D
Suspension or surrender issued pursuant to sections 3B or 3C; reporting to department of criminal justice information services
(Added by 2014 Mass. Acts c. 284, § 72, effective Jan. 1, 2015.)

Upon an order for suspension or surrender issued pursuant to sections 3B or 3C, the court shall transmit a report containing the defendant's name and identifying information and a statement describing the defendant's alleged conduct and relationship to the plaintiff to the department of criminal justice information services. Upon the expiration, cancellation or revocation of the order, the court shall transmit a report containing the defendant's name and identifying information, a statement describing the defendant's alleged conduct and relationship to the plaintiff and an explanation that the order is no longer current or valid to the department of criminal justice information services who shall transmit the report, pursuant to paragraph (h) of section 167A of chapter 6, to the attorney general of the United States to be included in the National Instant Criminal Background Check System.

SECTION 4
Temporary orders; notice; hearing
Upon the filing of a complaint under this chapter, the court may enter such temporary orders as it deems necessary to protect a plaintiff from abuse, including relief as provided in section three. Such relief shall not be contingent upon the filing of a complaint for divorce, separate support, or paternity action.

If the plaintiff demonstrates a substantial likelihood of immediate danger of abuse, the court may enter such temporary relief orders without notice as it deems necessary to protect the plaintiff from abuse and shall immediately thereafter notify the defendant that the temporary orders have issued. The court shall give the defendant an opportunity to be heard on the question of continuing the temporary order and of granting other relief as requested by the plaintiff no later than ten court business days after such orders are entered.

Notice shall be made by the appropriate law enforcement agency as provided in section seven.

If the defendant does not appear at such subsequent hearing, the temporary orders shall continue in effect without further order of the court.

NOTE For a case discussing sufficiency of evidence at the trial of a complaint for violation of a protective order issued pursuant to G.L. c. 209A, see *Commonwealth v. Robicheau*, 421 Mass. 176 (1995).

SECTION 5
Granting of relief when court closed; certification
(Amended by 2011 Mass. Acts c. 93, § 40, effective July 1, 2012.)

When the court is closed for business or the plaintiff is unable to appear in court because of severe hardship due to the plaintiff's physical condition, any justice of the superior, probate and family, district or Boston municipal court departments may grant relief to the plaintiff as provided under section four if the plaintiff demonstrates a substantial likelihood of immediate danger of abuse. In the discretion of the justice, such relief may be granted and communicated by telephone to an officer or employee of an appropriate law enforcement agency, who shall record such order on a form of order promulgated for such use by the chief justice of the trial court and shall deliver a copy of such order on the next court day to the clerk-magistrate of the court having venue and jurisdiction over the matter. If relief has been granted without the filing of a complaint pursuant to this section of this chapter, then the plaintiff shall appear in court on the next available business day to file said complaint. If the plaintiff in such a case is unable to appear in court without severe hardship due to the plaintiff's physical condition, then a representative may appear in court on the plaintiff's behalf and file the requisite complaint with an affidavit setting forth the circumstances preventing the plaintiff from appearing personally. Notice to the plaintiff and defendant and an opportunity for the defendant to be heard shall be given as provided in said section four.

Any order issued under this section and any documentation in support thereof shall be certified on the next court day by the clerk-magistrate or register of the court issuing such order to the court having venue and jurisdiction over the matter. Such certification to the court shall have the effect of commencing proceedings under this chapter and invoking the other provisions of this chapter but shall not be deemed necessary for an emergency order issued under this section to take effect.

SECTION 5A
Protection order issued by another jurisdiction; enforcement; filing; presumption of validity

Any protection order issued by another jurisdiction, as defined in section one, shall be given full faith and credit throughout the commonwealth and enforced as if it were issued in the commonwealth for as long as the order is in effect in the issuing jurisdiction.

A person entitled to protection under a protection order issued by another jurisdiction may file such order in the superior court department or the Boston municipal court department or any division of the probate and family or district court departments by filing with the court a certified copy of such order which shall be entered into the statewide domestic violence record keeping system established pursuant to the provisions of section seven of chapter one hundred and eighty-eight of the acts of nineteen hundred and ninety-two and maintained by the office of the commissioner of probation. Such person shall swear under oath in an affidavit, to the best of such person's knowledge, that such order is presently in effect as written. Upon request by a law enforcement agency, the register or clerk of such court shall provide a certified copy of the protection order issued by the other jurisdiction.

A law enforcement officer may presume the validity of, and enforce in accordance with section six, a copy of a protection order issued by another jurisdiction which has been provided to the law enforcement officer by any source; provided, however, that the officer is also provided with a statement by the person protected by the order that such order remains in effect. Law enforcement officers may rely on such statement by the person protected by such order.

SECTION 6
Powers of police

Whenever any law officer has reason to believe that a family or household member has been abused or is in danger of being abused, such officer shall use all reasonable means to prevent further abuse. The officer shall take, but not be limited to the following action:

(1) remain on the scene of where said abuse occurred or was in danger of occurring as long as the officer has reason to believe that at least one of the parties involved would be in immediate physical danger without the presence of a law officer. This shall include, but not be limited to remaining in the dwelling for a reasonable period of time;

(2) assist the abused person in obtaining medical treatment necessitated by an assault, which may include driving the victim to the emergency room of the nearest hospital, or arranging for appropriate transportation to a health care facility, notwithstanding any law to the contrary;

(3) assist the abused person in locating and getting to a safe place; including but not limited to a designated meeting place for a shelter or a family member's or friend's residence. The officer shall consider the victim's preference in this regard and what is reasonable under all the circumstances;

(4) give such person immediate and adequate notice of his or her rights. Such notice shall consist of handing said person a copy of the statement which follows below and reading the same to said person. Where said person's native language is not English, the statement shall be then provided in said person's native language whenever possible.

"You have the right to appear at Superior, Probate and Family, District or Boston Municipal Court, if you reside within the appropriate jurisdiction, and file a complaint requesting any of the following applicable orders: (a) an order restraining your attacker from abusing you; (b) an order directing your attacker to leave your household, building or workplace; (c) an order awarding you custody of a minor child; (d) an order directing your attacker to pay support for you or any minor child in your custody, if the attacker has a legal obligation of support; and (e) an order directing your attacker to pay you for losses suffered as a result of abuse, including medical and moving expenses, loss of earnings or support, costs for restoring utilities and replacing locks, reasonable attorney's fees and other out-of-pocket losses for injuries and property damage sustained.

For an emergency on weekends, holidays, or weeknights the police will refer you to a justice of the superior, probate and family, district, or Boston municipal court departments.

You have the right to go to the appropriate district court or the Boston municipal court and seek a criminal complaint for threats, assault and battery, assault with a deadly weapon, assault with intent to kill or other related offenses.

If you are in need of medical treatment, you have the right to request that an officer present drive you to the nearest hospital or otherwise assist you in obtaining medical treatment.

If you believe that police protection is needed for your physical safety, you have the right to request that the officer present remain at the scene until you and your children can leave or until your safety is otherwise ensured. You may also request that the officer assist you in locating and taking you to a safe place, including but not limited to a designated meeting place for a shelter or a family member's or a friend's residence, or a similar place of safety.

You may request a copy of the police incident report at no cost from the police department."

The officer shall leave a copy of the foregoing statement with such person before leaving the scene or premises.

(5) assist such person by activating the emergency judicial system when the court is closed for business;

(6) inform the victim that the abuser will be eligible for bail and may be promptly released; and

(7) arrest any person a law officer witnesses or has probable cause to believe has violated a temporary or permanent vacate, restraining, or no-contact order or judgment issued pursuant to section eighteen, thirty-four B or thirty-four C of chapter two hundred and eight, section thirty-two of chapter two hundred and nine, section three, three B, three C, four or five of this chapter, or sections fifteen or twenty of chapter two hundred and nine C or similar protection order issued by another jurisdiction. When there are no vacate, restraining, or no-contact orders or judgments in effect, arrest shall be the preferred response whenever an officer witnesses or has probable cause to believe that a person:

(a) has committed a felony;

(b) has committed a misdemeanor involving abuse as defined in section one of this chapter;

(c) has committed an assault and battery in violation of section thirteen A of chapter two hundred and sixty-five.

The safety of the victim and any involved children shall be paramount in any decision to arrest. Any officer arresting both parties must submit a detailed, written report in addition to an incident report, setting forth the grounds for dual arrest.

No law officer investigating an incident of domestic violence shall threaten, suggest, or otherwise indicate the arrest of all parties for the purpose of discouraging requests for law enforcement intervention by any party.

No law officer shall be held liable in any civil action regarding personal injury or injury to property brought by any party to a domestic violence incident for an arrest based on probable cause when such officer acted reasonably and in good faith and in compliance with this chapter and the statewide policy as established by the secretary of public safety.

Whenever any law officer investigates an incident of domestic violence, the officer shall immediately file a written incident report in accordance with the standards of the officer's law enforcement agency and, wherever possible, in the form of the National Incident-Based Reporting System, as defined by the Federal Bureau of Investigation. The latter information may be submitted voluntarily by the local police on a monthly basis to the crime reporting unit of the department of criminal justice information services.

The victim shall be provided a copy of the full incident report at no cost upon request to the appropriate law enforcement department.

When a judge or other person authorized to take bail bails any person arrested under the provisions of this chapter, he shall make reasonable efforts to inform the victim of such release prior to or at the time of said release.

When any person charged with or arrested for a crime involving abuse under this chapter is released from custody, the court of the emergency response judge shall issue, upon the request of the victim, a written no-contact order prohibiting the person charged or arrested from having any contact with the victim and shall use all reasonable means to notify the victim immediately of release from custody. The victim shall be given at no cost a certified copy of the no-contact order.

NOTE   "On this record alone, we cannot say that the defendant's actions constitute 'abuse' as defined in § 1 of G.L. c. 209A. As such, we conclude that G.L. c. 209A may not presently be relied on to justify the warrantless arrest of the defendant. We point out, however, that a warrantless arrest for 'abuse' properly may be made under G.L. c. 209A § 6(7), if a police officer has reason to believe that a defendant's conduct with respect to a person protected under G.L. c. 209A, placed the person in fear of imminent serious physical harm." *Commonwealth v. Jacobsen*, 419 Mass. 269, 274 (1995).

SECTION 7
Abuse prevention orders; domestic violence record search; service of order; enforcement; violations
(Amended by 2014 Mass. Acts c. 260, §§ 14–15, effective Aug. 8, 2014.)

When considering a complaint filed under this chapter, a judge shall cause a search to be made of the records contained within the statewide domestic violence record keeping system maintained by the office of the commissioner of probation and shall review the resulting data to determine whether the named defendant has a civil or criminal record involving domestic or other violence. Upon receipt of information that an outstanding warrant exists against the named defendant, a judge shall order that the appropriate law enforcement officials be notified and shall order that any information regarding the defendant's most recent whereabouts shall be forwarded to such officials. In all instances where an outstanding warrant exists, a judge shall make a finding, based upon all of the circumstances, as to whether an imminent threat of bodily

injury exists to the petitioner. In all instances where such an imminent threat of bodily injury is found to exist, the judge shall notify the appropriate law enforcement officials of such finding and such officials shall take all necessary actions to execute any such outstanding warrant as soon as is practicable.

Whenever the court orders under sections eighteen, thirty-four B, and thirty-four C of chapter two hundred and eight, section thirty-two of chapter two hundred and nine, sections three, four and five of this chapter, or sections fifteen and twenty of chapter two hundred and nine C, the defendant to vacate, refrain from abusing the plaintiff or to have no contact with the plaintiff or the plaintiff's minor child, the register or clerk-magistrate shall transmit two certified copies of each such order and one copy of the complaint and summons forthwith to the appropriate law enforcement agency which, unless otherwise ordered by the court, shall serve one copy of each order upon the defendant, together with a copy of the complaint, order and summons and notice of any suspension or surrender ordered pursuant to section three B of this chapter. Law enforcement agencies shall establish adequate procedures to ensure that, when effecting service upon a defendant pursuant to this paragraph, a law enforcement officer shall, to the extent practicable: (i) fully inform the defendant of the contents of the order and the available penalties for any violation of an order or terms thereof and (ii) provide the defendant with informational resources, including, but not limited to, a list of certified batterer intervention programs, substance abuse counseling, alcohol abuse counseling and financial counseling programs located within or near the court's jurisdiction. The law enforcement agency shall promptly make its return of service to the court.

Law enforcement officers shall use every reasonable means to enforce such abuse prevention orders. Law enforcement agencies shall establish procedures adequate to insure that an officer on the scene of an alleged violation of such order may be informed of the existence and terms of such order. The court shall notify the appropriate law enforcement agency in writing whenever any such order is vacated and shall direct the agency to destroy all record of such vacated order and such agency shall comply with that directive.

Each abuse prevention order issued shall contain the following statement: VIOLATION OF THIS ORDER IS A CRIMINAL OFFENSE.

Any violation of such order or a protection order issued by another jurisdiction shall be punishable by a fine of not more than five thousand dollars, or by imprisonment for not more than two and one-half years in a house of correction, or by both such fine and imprisonment. In addition to, but not in lieu of, the forgoing penalties and any other sentence, fee, or assessment, including the victim witness assessment in section 8 of chapter 258B, the court shall order persons convicted of a crime under this statute to pay a fine of $25 that shall be transmitted to the treasurer for deposit into the General Fund. For any violation of such order, or as a condition of a continuance without a finding, the court shall order the defendant to complete a certified batterer's intervention program unless, upon good cause shown, the court issues specific written findings describing the reasons that batterer's intervention should not be ordered or unless the batterer's intervention program determines that the defendant is not suitable for intervention. The court shall not order substance abuse or anger management treatment or any other form of treatment as a substitute for certified batterer's intervention. If a defendant ordered to undergo treatment has received a suspended sentence, the original sentence shall be reimposed if the defendant fails to participate in said program as required by the terms of his probation. If the court determines that the violation was in retaliation for the defendant being reported by the plaintiff to the department of revenue for failure to pay child support payments or for the establishment of paternity, the defendant shall be punished by a fine of not less than one thousand dollars and not more than ten thousand dollars and by imprisonment for not less than sixty days; provided, however, that the sentence shall not be suspended, nor shall any such person be eligible for probation, parole, or furlough or receive any deduction from his sentence for good conduct until he shall have served sixty days of such sentence.

When a defendant has been ordered to participate in a treatment program pursuant to this section, the defendant shall be required to regularly attend a certified or provisionally certified batterer's treatment program. To the extent permitted by professional requirements of confidentiality, said program shall communicate with local battered women's programs for the purpose of protecting the victim's safety. Additionally, it shall specify the defendant's attendance requirements and keep the probation department informed of whether the defendant is in compliance.

In addition to, but not in lieu of, such orders for treatment, if the defendant has a substance abuse problem, the court may order appropriate treatment for such problem. All ordered treatment shall last until the end of the probationary period or until the treatment program decides to discharge the defendant, whichever comes first. When the defendant is not in compliance with the terms of probation, the court shall hold a revocation of probation hearing. To the extent possible, the defendant shall be responsible for paying all costs for court ordered treatment.

Where a defendant has been found in violation of an abuse prevention order under this chapter or a protection order issued by another jurisdiction, the court may, in addition to the penalties provided for in this section after conviction, as an alternative to incarceration and, as a condition of probation, prohibit contact with the victim through the establishment of court defined geographic exclusion zones including, but not limited to, the areas in and around the complainant's residence, place of employment, and the complainant's child's school, and order that the defendant to wear a global positioning satellite tracking device designed to transmit and record the defendant's location data. If the defendant enters a court defined exclusion zone, the defendant's location data shall be immediately transmitted to the complainant, and to the police, through an appropriate means including, but not limited to, the telephone, an electronic beeper or a paging device. The global positioning satellite device and its tracking shall be administered by the department of probation. If a court finds that the defendant has entered a geographic exclusion zone, it shall revoke his probation and the defendant shall be fined, imprisoned or both as provided in this section. Based on the defendant's ability to pay, the court may also order him to pay the monthly costs or portion thereof for monitoring through the global positioning satellite tracking system.

In each instance where there is a violation of an abuse prevention order or a protection order issued by another jurisdiction, the court may order the defendant to pay the plaintiff for all damages including, but not limited to, cost for shelter or emergency housing, loss of earnings or support, out-of-pocket losses for injuries sustained or property damaged, medical expenses, moving expenses, cost for obtaining an unlisted telephone number, and reasonable attorney's fees.

Any such violation may be enforced in the superior, the district or Boston municipal court departments. Criminal remedies provided herein are not exclusive and do not preclude any other available civil or criminal remedies. The superior, probate and family, district and Boston municipal court departments may each enforce by civil contempt procedure a violation of its own court order.

The provisions of section eight of chapter one hundred and thirty-six shall not apply to any order, complaint or summons issued pursuant to this section.

NOTE 1   Elements of Violation. "[A] defendant may be convicted under G.L. c. 209A, § 7, if it is shown that (1) a c. 209A order had been entered and was in effect when the alleged violation occurred; (2) the defendant knew about the order; and (3) he violated it by abusing the alleged victim." *Commonwealth v. Collier*, 427 Mass. 385, 388 (1998) (citing *Commonwealth v. Delaney*, 425 Mass. 587, 595 (1997)).

NOTE 2a   Violation of No Contact by Telephone Order. "[W]e hold that violation of an order not to contact by telephone is established by proof of unexcused conversation with a protected party over the telephone and without proof that the protected party was placed in fear." *Commonwealth v. Mendonca*, 50 Mass. App. Ct. 684, 688 (2001).

NOTE 2b   Incidental Contact. "A no-contact order like this one would not be violated when a father has to speak on the telephone with a protected woman, in order to speak with his children, and he does so briefly, and in a direct and non-abusive way. Such contact would be a lawful incident of the order because there may be no other way for the father to exercise his right to reach his children. This brief and inevitable contact, however, cannot be used as an occasion to harass, threaten, or intimidate the protected party. That form of conduct crosses the line between lawful incidental conversation, permitted by the order, and a substantive violation of its terms." *Commonwealth v. Silva*, 431 Mass. 194, 198 (2000).

NOTE 3   Intent. "[A] violation of G.L. c. 209A, prosecuted under § 7, does not require proof that the defendant actually intended to abuse the victim." *Commonwealth v. Collier*, 427 Mass. 385, 388 (1998) (citing *Commonwealth v. Delaney*, 425 Mass. 587 (1997)). *See also Commonwealth v. Silva*, 431 Mass. 194, 200 (2000).

NOTE 4a   Accidental, Mistaken, Unknowing Contact. "The[ ] cases suggest, as does common sense, that a defendant cannot be convicted of violating a 'no contact' order issued under c. 209A where the contact occurs in circumstances where the defendant did not know, and could not reasonably have been expected to know, that the protected person would be present. We view this proposition as nothing more than an application of the principle enunciated by the Supreme Judicial Court in *Commonwealth v. Silva*, [431 Mass. 194 (2000)]. It is consistent with the traditional view that, in the absence of specific language to the contrary, the Legislature does not intend to make accidents and mistakes crimes." *Commonwealth v. Raymond*, 54 Mass. App. Ct. 488, 493 (2002).

NOTE 4b "In cases of nonnegligent, inadvertent contact, failure to end the encounter as soon as reasonably possible is a substantive element of the offense. Massachusetts cases instruct that '[h]appening on a protected person whom one did not, and could not reasonably, know to be present *is not a violation*, but the party subject to the order must end the encounter by leaving' (emphasis supplied)." *Commonwealth v. Stoltz*, 73 Mass. App. Ct. 642, 645–46 (2009) (quoting *Commonwealth v. Kendrick*, 446 Mass. 72, 76 (2006)).

NOTE 5   Acts Committed by Third Party. "[I]n those comparatively rare situations where a third party is involved in the act that results in the violation, to obtain a conviction under G.L. c. 209A, § 7, the Commonwealth is required to prove beyond a reasonable doubt an intentional act by the defendant which led to the violation of the c. 209A order. We reaffirm the principle . . . that . . . the Commonwealth is not required to show that the defendant intended to violate the order." *Commonwealth v. Collier*, 427 Mass. 385, 388 (1998) (citing *Commonwealth v. Delaney*, 425 Mass. 587 (1997)).

NOTE 6a   Service. "When the appropriate law enforcement agency has made a conscientious and reasonable effort to serve the statutorily specified documents on the defendant, but has nevertheless failed, the agency should promptly notify the court so that a judge, if satisfied after a hearing that an appropriate effort has been made, may order that service be made by some other identified means reasonably calculated to reach the defendant. Where such substituted service appears unlikely to notify the defendant, the judge may excuse service." *Zullo v. Goguen*, 423 Mass. 679, 681 (1996).

NOTE 6b   Proof of Service. "[P]roof of service is not required in a prosecution under G.L. c. 209A, § 7. . . . What is necessary in such a prosecution is that the Commonwealth prove that a valid order was in effect, and that the defendant had fair notice of what the order prohibited." *Edge v. Commonwealth*, 451 Mass. 74, 77–78 (2008).

NOTE 6c   Actual Knowledge. "Even if we assume a failure of service, the evidence was sufficient to show the defendant had actual knowledge of the order's terms. Shirley testified she told the defendant 'a few times' that he was not supposed to call, and he responded that he 'didn't believe' in restraining orders and said 'to hell with them.' Her daughter essentially corroborated this testimony." *Commonwealth v. Mendonca*, 50 Mass. App. Ct. 684, 688 (2001) (citation omitted).

NOTE 6d   Admissibility of Improperly Served Order in Prosecution. "[T]he improper service does not render the order inadmissible in a prosecution for an alleged criminal violation of the order . . . . It is settled that failure of service is not fatal to a conviction, although it may be relevant to whether the defendant had the requisite knowledge. *Commonwealth v. Delaney*, 425 Mass. 587, 593 (1997)." *Commonwealth v. Griffen*, 444 Mass. 1004, 1005 (2005).

NOTE 7   Service of Affidavit Not Required. Plaintiff "argues that the affidavit in support of the issuance of the complaint should have been but was not served on him with the G.L. c. 209A order. There is no statutory or constitutional requirement that a G.L. c. 209A complainant's affidavit be served with the order." *Flynn v. Warner*, 421 Mass. 1002, 1002 (1995).

NOTE 8   Confrontation Clause. "A District Court judge . . . reported the following question: 'Can the commonwealth prove that the defendant was served a G.L. c. 209A [order] by the return of service filed by an out of state law enforcement officer without direct testimonial evidence that the defendant was in fact the person served?' The report subsumes two distinct questions: first, does the completed return of service form fall within an exception to the hearsay rule and, second, if so, is it testimonial for purposes of the confrontation clause of the Sixth Amendment to the United States Constitution. We answer the reported question, 'Yes,' and hold that a c. 209A completed return of service is admissible under the public records exception to the hearsay rule and that it is nontestimonial for purposes of the confrontation clause." *Commonwealth v. Shangkuan*, 78 Mass. App. Ct. 827, 827–28 (2011).

NOTE 9   Stay Away Order vs. No-Contact Order. "[T]he two terms are not interchangeable, but a 'no contact' order includes a 'stay away' order, Pursuant to a 'stay away' order, the defendant may not come within a specified distance of the protected party, usually stated in the order, but written or oral contact between the parties is not prohibited. By contrast, a 'no contact' order mandates that the defendant not communicate by any means with the protected party, in addition to remaining physically separated. Thus, a 'no contact' order is broader than a 'stay away' order. . . . Violations of a no contact order (including stay away provisions) may be prosecuted under § 7 because the Legislature has so provided." *Commonwealth v. Finase*, 435 Mass. 310, 314–15 (2001) (citations omitted).

NOTE 10   Only Enumerated Criminal Violations of G.L. c. 209A Covered by Section 7. "We continue to read § 7 as limiting to the enumerated offenses those actions that will constitute a criminal violation of G.L. c. 209A." *Commonwealth v. Finase*, 435 Mass. 310, 315 (2001) (citation omitted).

"It does not appear that *all* violations of any c. 209A order are criminalized. Section 3 authorizes the court to issue numerous other types of orders, such as ordering the defendant to pay temporary support for the plaintiff and ordering the defendant to pay the person abused monetary compensation for the losses suffered as a direct result of such abuse. The terms of § 7 do not encompass these latter types of orders." *Commonwealth v. Finase*, 435 Mass. 310, 314 n.2 (2001).

NOTE 11   No Lesser Included Offense. "[W]e conclude that a violation of an abuse prevention order that contains a mandate to refrain from abuse is not a lesser included offense of assault and battery on a person protected by an abuse prevention order." *Commonwealth v. Torres*, 468 Mass. 286, 287 (2014).

NOTE 12   Duration. "[N]either a defendant's visitation rights nor the pendency of criminal proceedings is an appropriate consideration in establishing the duration of a G.L. c. 209A order. The exclusive focus must be on the applicant's need for protection." *Singh v. Capuano*, 468 Mass. 328, 334 (2014).

NOTE 13   Promptness. "It is essential, among other things, that hearings be held promptly. Neither the pendency of criminal proceedings against the defendant nor a judicial preference that the matter be decided in another forum is an appropriate consideration in deciding whether to continue a hearing. Decisions to grant, deny, extend, modify, or vacate orders must be based on the evidence, after hearings, and only upon proper considerations, and orders that are granted must be of sufficient duration to protect the plaintiff, for whose benefit they are issued." *Singh v. Capuano*, 468 Mass. 328, 334–35 (2014).

NOTE 14   Expungement. "We therefore conclude that a judge has the inherent authority to expunge a record of a 209A order from the Statewide domestic violence registry system in the rare and limited circumstance that the judge has found through clear and convincing evidence that the order was obtained through fraud on the court." *Comm'r of Prob. v. Adams*, 65 Mass. App. Ct. 725, 737 (2006).

NOTE 15a   Out-of-State Defendant. "We consider in this case whether a Massachusetts court has jurisdiction to issue an abuse prevention order under G.L. c. 209A in favor of a plaintiff who alleges that she has fled to this State to escape the abuse of her domestic partner who remains in their home in Florida. We conclude that a court may issue such an order of prevention and protection even without personal jurisdiction over the defendant, but may not impose affirmative obligations on the defendant if there is no personal jurisdiction." *Caplan v. Donovan*, 450 Mass. 463, 463–64 (2008).

"The defendant does not argue that he was denied reasonable notice or an opportunity to be heard, nor could he, because he was personally served in Florida with a notice of the order and a hearing was held (in Massachusetts) at which his attorney appeared. The order's prohibition against the defendant's abusing, contacting, or approaching the plaintiff or their child contains no affirmative obligation, and therefore it does not require personal jurisdiction. The defendant does not contest the District Court's jurisdiction to grant custody of the child to the plaintiff, but even if he did, jurisdiction can be found in G.L. c. 209B, § 2(a)(3), which allows the exercise of jurisdiction for purposes of determining emergency custody of a child present in the Commonwealth. *See Lamarche v. Lussier*, 65 Mass. App. Ct. 887, 894 n.13 (2006), citing *Umina v. Malbica*, 27 Mass. App. Ct. 351, 359 (1989)." *Caplan v. Donovan*, 450 Mass. at 472.

NOTE 15b   **Out-of-State Order.** "We conclude that, where an out-of-State abuse protection order is allegedly violated in Massachusetts and prosecuted under c. 209A, the violation is governed by Massachusetts law and the jury should be instructed in accordance with Massachusetts law." *Commonwealth v. Shea*, 467 Mass. 788, 792 (2014).

NOTE 16   **Jurisdiction.** *See* G.L. c. 277, § 62A.

SECTION 8
Confidentiality of records

The records of cases arising out of an action brought under the provisions of this chapter where the plaintiff or defendant is a minor shall be withheld from public inspection except by order of the court; provided, that such records shall be open, at all reasonable times, to the inspection of the minor, said minor's parent, guardian, attorney, and to the plaintiff and the plaintiff's attorney, or any of them.

The plaintiff's residential address, residential telephone number and workplace name, address and telephone number, contained within the court records of cases arising out of an action brought by a plaintiff under the provisions of this chapter, shall be confidential and withheld from public inspection, except by order of the court, except that the plaintiff's residential address and workplace address shall appear on the court order and accessible to the defendant and the defendant's attorney unless the plaintiff specifically requests that this information be withheld from the order. All confidential portions of the records shall be accessible at all reasonable times to the plaintiff and plaintiff's attorney, to others specifically authorized by the plaintiff to obtain such information, and to prosecutors, victim-witness advocates as defined in section 1 of chapter 258B, domestic violence victim's counselors as defined in section 20K of chapter 233, sexual assault counselors as defined in section 20J of chapter 233, and law enforcement officers, if such access is necessary in the performance of their duties. The provisions of this paragraph shall apply to any protection order issued by another jurisdiction, as defined in section 1, that is filed with a court of the commonwealth pursuant to section 5A. Such confidential portions of the court records shall not be deemed to public records under the provisions of clause twenty-sixth of section 7 of chapter 4.

SECTION 9
Form of complaint; promulgation

The administrative justices of the superior court, probate and family court, district court, and the Boston municipal court departments shall jointly promulgate a form of complaint for use under this chapter which shall be in such form and language to permit a plaintiff to prepare and file such complaint pro se.

SECTION 10
Assessments against persons referred to certified batterers' treatment program as condition of probation

The court shall impose an assessment of three hundred and fifty dollars against any person who has been referred to a certified batterers' treatment program as a condition of probation. Said assessment shall be in addition to the cost of the treatment program. In the discretion of the court, said assessment may be reduced or waived when the court finds that the person is indigent or that payment of the assessment would cause the person, or the dependents of such person, severe financial hardship. Assessments made pursuant to this section shall be in addition to any other fines, assessments, or restitution imposed in any disposition. All funds collected by the court pursuant to this section shall be transmitted monthly to the state treasurer, who shall deposit said funds in the General Fund.

SECTION 11
Possession, care and control of domesticated animal owned by persons involved in certain protective orders; notice to law enforcement upon finding of imminent threat to household member or animal
(Added by 2012 Mass. Acts c. 193, § 50, effective Oct. 31, 2012.)

(a) Whenever the court issues a temporary or permanent vacate, stay away, restraining or no contact order or a judgment under section 18, 34B or 34C of chapter 208, or under section 32 of chapter 209, or under section 3, 4 or 5 of this chapter, or under section 15 or 20 of chapter 209C, or under section 3 to 7, inclusive, of chapter 258E or a temporary restraining order or preliminary or permanent injunction relative to a domestic relations, child custody, domestic abuse or abuse prevention proceeding, the court may order the possession, care and control of any domesticated animal owned, possessed, leased, kept or held by either party or a minor child residing in the household to the plaintiff or petitioner. The court may order the defendant to refrain from abusing, threatening, taking, interfering with, transferring, encumbering, concealing, harming or otherwise disposing of such animal.

(b) A party to any proceeding listed in subsection (a) may petition the court for an order authorized by said subsection (a).

(c) Whenever the court issues a warrant for a violation of a temporary or permanent vacate, stay away, restraining or no contact order or a judgment issued under section 18, 34B or 34C of chapter 208, or under section 32 of chapter 209, or under section 3, 4 or 5 of this chapter, or under section 15 or 20 of chapter 209C, or section 3 to 7, inclusive, of chapter 258E or otherwise becomes aware that an outstanding warrant for such a violation has been issued against a person before the court, the judge may make a finding, based upon the totality of the circumstances, as to whether there exists an imminent threat of bodily injury to any party to such judgment or the petitioner of any such protective order, a member of the petitioner's family or household or to a domesticated animal belonging to the petitioner or to a member of the petitioner's family or household. If the court makes a finding that such an imminent threat of bodily injury to a person or domesticated animal exists, the court shall notify the appropriate law enforcement officials of such finding and the law enforcement officials shall take all necessary actions to execute any such outstanding warrant as soon as is practicable.

Chapter 212. The Superior Court

SECTION 6
Criminal Jurisdiction

The court shall have original jurisdiction of all crimes. Crimes committed in that part of Scituate described in chapter three hundred and ninety-four of the acts of nineteen hundred and twelve shall be within the territorial jurisdiction of the court both in Norfolk county and in Plymouth county, and arrests and service of process in such cases may be made by an officer qualified to serve criminal process in Cohasset. Crimes committed in any part of Cambridge, Watertown or Newton lying in the Charles river basin shall be within the territorial jurisdiction of the court both in Middlesex county and in Suffolk county.

Chapter 218. District Courts

Section

26	General provisions
26A	Trial by jury; discovery; jury-waived trial; record of proceedings; probation
27	Imposition of penalties
27A	Jury sessions
28	Recognizances to keep peace
29	Repealed
30	Binding over to superior court
31	Repealed
32	Complaints and warrants
33	Warrants and process; power of clerks to issue
34	Arrest without warrant; endorsement of complaint by arresting officer
35	Complaints, warrants and process; power to issue; disqualification to hear case; destruction of applications for complaints
35A	Process; issuance on complaints for misdemeanors; consideration of criminal records and domestic violence records; right to hearing
36	Justice of peace; taking bail
37	Process for witnesses and defendants in criminal and juvenile cases; direction and service

CRIMINAL JURISDICTION

SECTION 26
General provisions
(Amended by 2014 Mass. Acts c. 260, § 19, effective Aug. 8, 2014.)

The district courts and the divisions of the Boston municipal court department shall have original jurisdiction, concurrent with the superior court, of the following offenses, complaint of which shall be brought in the court of the district court department, or in the Boston municipal court department, as the case may be, within which judicial district the offense was allegedly committed or is otherwise made punishable: all violations of by-laws, orders, ordinances, rules and regulations, made by cities, towns and public officers, all misdemeanors, except libels, all felonies punishable by imprisonment in the state prison for not more than five-years, the crimes listed in paragraph (1) of subsection (a) of section eight of chapter ninety B, subparagraph (1) of paragraph (a) of subdivision (1) of section twenty-four, paragraph (a) of section twenty-four G and paragraph (1) of section twenty-four L of chapter ninety, paragraph (a) of section thirty-two and paragraph (a) of section thirty-two A of chapter ninety-four C and section thirty-two J of chapter ninety-four C, section 38B of chapter 127, section one hundred and thirty-one E of chapter one hundred and forty, sections thirteen K, 15A, 15D, 21A and 26 of chapter two hundred and sixty-five and sections sixteen, seventeen, eighteen, nineteen, twenty-eight, thirty, forty-nine and one hundred and twenty-seven of chapter two hundred and sixty-six, and sections one, fifteen and fifteen A of chapter two hundred and seventy-three, and the crimes of malicious destruction of personal property under section one hundred and twenty-seven of chapter two hundred and sixty-six, indecent assault and battery on a child under fourteen years of age, intimidation of a witness or juror under section thirteen B of chapter two hundred and sixty-eight, escape or attempt to escape from any penal institution, forgery of a promissory note, or of an order for money or other property, and of uttering as true such a forged note or order, knowing the same to be forged. They shall have jurisdiction of proceedings referred to them under the provisions of section four A of chapter two hundred and eleven.

NOTE   Despite the District Court judge reducing rape and assault and battery by means of a dangerous weapon to assault and battery and convicting the defendants, this did *not* ban the subsequent convictions of the defendants in Superior Court on the original counts as the District Court lacked the jurisdiction to try the defendants on the original charges. *Commonwealth v. Nazarro*, 7 Mass. App. Ct. 859 (1979).

SECTION 26A
Trial by jury; discovery; jury-waived trial; record of proceedings; probation

Trial of criminal offenses in the Boston municipal court department and in the district court department shall be by a jury of six persons, unless the defendant files a written waiver and consent to be tried by the court without a jury. Such waiver shall not be received unless the defendant is represented by counsel or has filed a written waiver of counsel. No decision on such waiver shall be received until after the completion of a pretrial conference and a hearing on the results of such conference and until after the disposition of any pretrial discovery motions and compliance with any order of the court pursuant to said motions. Such waiver shall be filed in accordance with the provisions of section six of chapter two hundred and sixty-three; provided, however, that defense counsel shall execute a certificate signed by said counsel indicating that he has made all the necessary explanations and determinations regarding such waiver. The form of such certificate shall be prescribed by the chief justice for the district court department.

In the Boston municipal court department and the district court department upon the motion of a defendant consistent with criminal procedure, or upon the court's own motion, the judge shall issue an order of discovery requiring any information to which the defendant is entitled and also requiring that the defendant be permitted to discover, inspect, and copy any material and relevant evidence, documents, statements of persons, or reports of physical or mental examinations of any person or of scientific tests or experiments, within the possession, custody, or control of the prosecutor or persons under his direction and control. Upon motion of the defendant the judge shall order the production by the commonwealth of the names and addresses of the prospective witnesses and the production by the probation department of the record of prior convictions of any such witness.

Trial by jury in the Boston municipal court department and the district court department shall be in those jury sessions designated in accordance with section twenty-seven A. Where the defendant has properly filed a waiver and consented to be tried without a jury, as hereinbefore provided, trial shall proceed in accordance with provisions of law applicable to jury-waived trials in the superior court; provided, however, that at the option of the defendant, the trial may be before a judge who has not rejected an agreed recommendation or dispositional request made by the defendant pursuant to the provisions of section eighteen of chapter two hundred and seventy-eight. Review in such cases may be had directly by the appeals court, by appeal, report or otherwise in the same manner provided for trials of criminal cases in the superior court.

The justice presiding over such jury-waived trial in the Boston municipal court department or the district court department shall have and exercise all of the powers and duties which a justice sitting in the superior court department has and may exercise in the trial and disposition of criminal cases including the power to report questions of law to the appeals court, but in no case may he impose a sentence to the state prison.

The justice presiding at such jury-waived session in the Boston municipal court department or the district court department shall, upon the request of the defendant, appoint a stenographer; provided, however, that where the defendant claims indigency, such appointment is determined to be reasonably necessary in accordance with the provisions of sections twenty-seven A to twenty-seven G, inclusive, of chapter two hundred and sixty-one. Such stenographer shall be sworn, and shall take stenographic notes of all the testimony given at the trial, and shall provide the parties thereto with a transcript of his notes or any part thereof taken at the trial or hearing for which he shall be paid by the party requesting it at the rate fixed by the chief justice of the Boston municipal court department or for the district court department as the case may be; and provided, further, that such rate shall not exceed the rate provided by section eighty-eight of chapter two hundred and twenty-one. Said chief justice may make regulations not inconsistent with law relative to the assignments, duties and services of stenographers appointed for sessions in his department and any other matter relative to stenographers. The compensation and expenses of a stenographer shall be paid by the commonwealth.

The request for the appointment of a stenographer to preserve the testimony at a trial in the Boston municipal court department or district court department shall be given to the clerk of the court by the defendant in writing no later than forty-eight hours prior to the proceeding for which the stenographer has been requested. The defendant shall file with such request an affidavit of indigency and request for payment by the commonwealth of the cost of the transcript and the court shall hold a hearing on such request prior to appointing a stenographer, in those cases where the defendant alleges that he will be unable to pay said cost. Said hearing shall be governed by the provisions of sections twenty-seven A to twenty-seven G, inclusive, of chapter two hundred and sixty-one, and the cost of such transcript shall be considered an extra cost as provided therein. If the court is unable, for any reason, to provide a stenographer, the proceedings may be recorded by electronic means. The original recording of proceedings in the Boston municipal court department or of a division of the district court department made with a recording device under the exclusive control of the court shall be the official record of such proceedings. Said record or a copy of all of a part thereof, certified by the chief justice for the Boston municipal court department or a district court department, or his designee, to be an accurate electronic reproduction of said record or part thereof, or a typewritten transcript of all or a part of said record or copy thereof, certified to be accurate by the court or by the preparer of said transcript, or stipulated to by the parties, shall be admissible in any court as evidence of testimony given whenever proof of such testimony is otherwise competent. The defendant may request payment by the commonwealth of the cost of said transcript subject to the same provisions regarding a transcript of a stenographer as provided hereinbefore.

In any case heard in a jury waived session in the Boston municipal court department or a district court department where a defendant is placed on probation or placed under probation supervision, he shall thereafter be supervised by the probation officer of the court in which the case originated, unless the trial justice shall order otherwise and unless the regulations of the commissioner of probation provide otherwise.

NOTE 1   "Based on our interpretation of the language of the relevant statutes and the Legislature's intent in prioritizing the policy interests promoted by the sealing statute, the mandatory discovery provisions of G.L. c. 218, § 26A, and Mass. R. Crim. P. 14(a)(1)(D) do not apply to a criminal record sealed under G.L. c. 276, § 100A." *Wing v. Commissioner of Probation*, 473 Mass. 368, 378 (2015).

NOTE 2   **Related statute.** Pleas and pretrial motions in the district court. G.L. c. 278, § 18.

SECTION 27
Imposition of penalties

The district court may impose the same penalties as the superior court for all crimes of which they have jurisdiction, except that they may not impose a sentence to the state prison; provided, however, that the divisions of the juvenile court department shall have the authority to hear cases and impose penalties in accordance with the provisions of sections fifty-two through eighty-four of chapter one hundred and nineteen, and section one through nineteen of chapter one hundred and twenty.

SECTION 27A
Jury sessions

(a) Every division of the district court department is authorized to hold jury sessions for the purpose of conducting jury trials of cases commenced in the several courts of criminal offenses over which the district courts have original jurisdiction under the provisions of section twenty-six. The Boston municipal court department shall also be authorized for the purpose of conducting jury trials in cases commenced in said department and for the purpose of conducting jury trials of cases commenced in the divisions of the district court department in Suffolk county.

(b) The chief justice for the district court department shall designate at least one division in each county or an adjoining county for the purpose of conducting jury trials; provided, however, that jury trials in cases commenced in the courts within Suffolk county shall be held in the Boston municipal court department or district courts in Suffolk county or with the approval of the chief justice, may be held in such divisions of the district court department the judicial districts of which adjoin Suffolk county as are designated by said chief justice; and jury trials in cases commenced in the divisions for Dukes county and Nantucket county may be held in Barnstable county or Bristol county; and provided further that, with the approval of the chief justice for the superior court department, facilities of said superior court may be designated by the chief justice for administration and management of the trial court for jury trials in cases commenced in the district court department or in the Boston municipal court department. Jurors shall be drawn from the county in which trial is held.

The chief justice of the district court department may also designate one or more divisions in each county for the purpose of conducting jury-waived trials of cases commenced in any court of said county consistent with the requirements of the proper administration of justice.

(c) A defendant in any division of the district court who waives his right to jury trial as provided in section twenty-six A shall be provided a jury-waived trial in the same division.

A defendant in any division of the district court who does not waive his right to jury trial as provided in section twenty-six A shall be provided a jury trial in a jury session in the same division if such has been established in said division. If such session has not been so established, the defendant shall be provided a jury trial in a jury session as hereinbefore designated. In cases where the defendant declines to waive the right to jury trial, the clerk shall forthwith transfer the case for trial in the appropriate jury session. Such transfer shall be governed by procedures to be established by the chief justice for the district court department.

(d) The justice presiding over a jury session shall have and exercise all the powers and duties which a justice sitting in the superior court department has and may exercise in the trial and disposition of criminal cases including the power to report questions of law to the appeals court, but in no case may he impose a sentence to the state prison. No justice so sitting shall act in a case in which he has sat or held an inquest or otherwise taken part in any proceeding therein.

(e) Trials by juries of six persons shall proceed in accordance with the provisions of law applicable to trials by jury in the superior court except that the number of peremptory challenges shall be limited to two to each defendant. The commonwealth shall be entitled to as many challenges as equal the whole number to which all the defendants in the case are entitled.

(f) For the jury sessions, jurors shall be provided by the office of the jury commissioner in accordance with the provisions of chapter two hundred and thirty-four A.

(g) The district attorney for the district in which the alleged offense or offenses occurred shall appear for the commonwealth in the trial of all cases in which the right to jury trial has not been waived and may appear in any other case. The chief justice for the district court department and the Boston municipal court department shall arrange for the sittings of the jury sessions of their respective departments and shall assign justices thereto, to the end that speedy trials may be provided. Review may be had directly by the appeals court, by appeals, report or otherwise in the same manner provided for trials of criminal cases in the superior court.

(h) The justice presiding at such jury session in the Boston municipal court department or district court department shall, upon the request of the defendant, appoint a stenographer; provided, however, that where the defendant claims indigency, such appointment is determined to be reasonably necessary in accordance with the provisions of chapter two hundred and sixty-one. Such stenographer shall be sworn, and shall take stenographic notes of all the testimony given at the trial, and shall provide the parties thereto with a transcript of his notes or any part thereof taken at the trial or hearing for which he shall be paid by the party requesting it at the rate fixed by the chief justice for the department where the case is tried; and provided, further, that such rate shall not exceed the rate provided by section eighty-eight of chapter two hundred and twenty-one. Said chief justice may make regulations not inconsistent with law relative to the assignments, duties and services of stenographers appointed for sessions in his department and any other matter relative to stenographers. The compensation and expenses of a stenographer shall be paid by the commonwealth.

The request for the appointment of a stenographer to preserve the testimony at a trial shall be given to the clerk of the court by the defendant in writing no later than forty-eight hours prior to the proceeding for which the stenographer has been requested. In the Boston municipal court department, the defendant shall file with such request an affidavit of indigency and request for payment by the commonwealth of the cost of the transcript and the court shall hold a hearing on such request prior to appointing a stenographer, in those cases where the defendant alleges that he will be unable to pay said cost. Said hearing shall be governed by the provisions of sections twenty-seven A to twenty-seven G, inclusive, of chapter two hundred and sixty-one, and the cost of such transcript shall be considered an extra cost as provided therein. If the court is unable, for any reason, to provide a stenographer, the proceedings may be recorded by electronic means. The original recording of proceedings in the Boston municipal court department or the district court department made with a recording device under the exclusive control of the court shall be the official record of such proceedings. Said record or a copy of all or a part thereof, certified by the chief justice for the Boston municipal court department or the district court department, or his designee, to be an accurate electronic reproduction of said record or part thereof, or a typewritten transcript of all or a part of said record or copy thereof, certified to be accurate by the court or by the preparer of said transcript, or stipulated to by the parties, shall be admissible in any court as evidence of testimony given whenever proof of such testimony is otherwise competent. The defendant may request payment by the commonwealth of the cost of said transcript subject to the same provisions regarding a transcript of a stenographer as provided hereinbefore.

(i) In any case heard in a jury session where a defendant is found guilty and placed on probation, he shall thereafter be supervised by the probation officer of the court in which the case originated, unless the trial justice shall order otherwise and unless the regulations of the commissioner of probation provide otherwise.

NOTE   **Related statute.** Pleas and Pretrial Motions in the District Court. G.L. c. 278, § 18.

SECTION 28
Recognizances to keep peace

District courts may require persons found guilty of any crime within their final jurisdiction, except a violation of by-laws, orders, ordinances, rules and regulations, made by cities, towns and public officers, or of the laws and regulations relative to the public health or relative to defective highways, in addition to the punishment prescribed by law, to recognize with sureties, in a reasonable sum, to keep the peace or be of good behavior, or both, for not more than one year, and to stand committed until they so recognize. Sections thirteen, sixteen and seventeen of chapter two hundred and seventy-five shall apply to recognizances so taken.

SECTION 29
Repealed

SECTION 30
Binding over to superior court

They shall commit or bind over for trial in the superior court persons brought before them who appear to be guilty of crimes not within their final jurisdiction, and may so commit or bind over persons brought before them who appear to be guilty of crimes within their final jurisdiction. If such a person is committed for failure to recognize as ordered, the superior court shall thereupon have jurisdiction of the case against such person for the purpose of revising the amount of bail theretofore fixed.

SECTION 31
Repealed

SECTION 32
Complaints and warrants

District courts may receive complaints and issue warrants and other processes for the apprehension of persons charged with crime and found within their county, or who after committing crime therein escape therefrom, returnable before a court of the county having jurisdiction of the trial or examination of the person charged with the crime.

SECTION 33
Warrants and process; power of clerks to issue

A clerk, assistant clerk, temporary clerk or temporary assistant clerk, may receive complaints, administer to complainants the oath required thereto, and issue warrants, search warrants and summonses, returnable as required when such process are issued by said courts. No other person, except a judge, shall be authorized to issue warrants, search warrants or summonses.

SECTION 34
Arrest without warrant; endorsement of complaint by arresting officer

Said courts may dispense with the issuing of a warrant if the person charged with a crime has been arrested without a warrant and brought before the court or admitted to bail; but in such case the officer making the arrest shall endorse upon the complaint a statement of his doings.

SECTION 35
Complaints, warrants and process; power to issue; disqualification to hear case; destruction of applications for complaints

A justice or special justice of a district court, or a justice of the peace who is also a clerk or assistant clerk of such a court, may at any time receive complaints and issue warrants and summonses, under his own hand and seal, and such justice or special justice may likewise issue search warrants, returnable before a court or trial justice having jurisdiction of the trial or examination of the person charged with the crime. If, after a hearing on the issuance of a complaint or a request for a search warrant, by a justice or special justice of a district court he issues such complaint or warrant, he shall be disqualified from presiding over a trial on the merits of any matter brought to trial because of such complaint or warrant if the defendant objects to his sitting before any evidence is taken.

If such an application for the issuance of a complaint is denied, the clerk of the district court wherein such application was made shall destroy such application one year after the date such application was filed, unless a justice of such court or the chief justice of the district courts shall for good cause order that such application be retained on file for a further period of time. The clerk shall enter on the face of any application so denied a conspicuous notation to that effect, and such applications shall be maintained separately from other records of such court. The provisions of this paragraph relating to the destruction of such applications shall not apply to applications filed pursuant to section twenty C of chapter ninety.

NOTE   **Role of the Prosecutor.** "A district attorney has wide discretion in determining whether to prosecute an individual, just as he has wide discretion in determining whether to discontinue a prosecution once commenced." *Manning v. Mun. Court of the Roxbury Dist.*, 372 Mass. 315, 318 (1977).

SECTION 35A
Process; issuance on complaints for misdemeanors; consideration of criminal records and domestic violence records; right to hearing

If a complaint is received by a district court, or by a justice, associate justice or special justice thereof, or by a clerk, assistant clerk, temporary clerk or temporary assistant clerk thereof under section 32, 33 or 35, as the case may be, the person against whom such complaint is made, if not under arrest for the offense for which the complaint is made, shall, in the case of a complaint for a misdemeanor or a complaint for a felony received from a law enforcement officer who so requests, and may, in the discretion of any said officers in the case of a complaint for a felony which is not received from a law enforcement officer, be given an opportunity to be heard personally or by counsel in opposition to the issuance of any process based on such complaint unless there is an imminent threat of bodily injury, of the commission of a crime, or of flight from the commonwealth by the person against whom such complaint is made. The court or said officers referred to above shall consider the named defendant's criminal record and the records contained within the statewide domestic violence record keeping system maintained by the office of the commissioner of probation in determining whether an imminent threat of bodily injury exists. Unless a citation as defined in section 1 of chapter 90C has been issued, notice shall also be given of the manner in which he may be heard in opposition as provided herein.

The court, or said officer thereof, may upon consideration of the evidence, obtained by hearing or otherwise, cause process to be issued unless there is no probable cause to believe that the person who is the object of the complaint has committed the offense charged.

The term district court as used in this section shall include the Boston municipal court department and the juvenile court department.

NOTE 1 If a person is charged with a misdemeanor, barring exigent circumstances, he or she is entitled to notice and an opportunity to be heard in opposition to the issuance of a criminal complaint, the denial of which calls for a dismissal without prejudice. *Commonwealth v. Tripolone*, 44 Mass. App. Ct. 23, 27–28 (1997).

NOTE 2 "'[A] previous adjudication of delinquency' for a violation of G.L. c. 269, § 10(a), (c), or (d), as that term is used in G.L. c. 119, §§ 52–63, is a 'conviction' as that term is used in G.L. c. 269, § 10(d). We emphasize that our holding is a narrow one, limited to those specific statutory provisions." *Commonwealth v. Connor C.*, 432 Mass. 635, 646 (2000).

NOTE 3 **No De Novo Review of Clerk-Magistrate's Finding of Probable Cause.** "[A] District Court or a BMC judge may not conduct a de novo evidentiary hearing to review a clerk-magistrate's finding of probable cause to issue process on an application for a criminal complaint." *Commonwealth v. DiBennadetto*, 436 Mass. 310, 310 (2002).

NOTE 4 There is no First Amendment right to public access to "show cause" hearings, held pursuant to G.L. c. 218, § 35A. *Eagle-Tribune Publ'g Co. v. Clerk-Magistrate of the Lawrence Div. of the Dist. Court Dep't*, 448 Mass. 647, 647–48 (2007).

SECTION 36
Justice of peace; taking bail

The governor, with the advice and consent of the council, may from time to time, upon the petition of the aldermen or the selectmen of any town within the judicial district of a district court, except a town in which the clerk of such court resides, designate and commission a justice of the peace residing in such town to take bail in criminal cases arising within said judicial district.

SECTION 37
Process for witnesses and defendants in criminal and juvenile cases; direction and service

District courts, justices, special justices, clerks, assistant clerks, temporary clerks and temporary assistant clerks thereof may issue summonses and other processes for witnesses in criminal cases, and at all hearings upon applications for complaints wherein a person may be charged with the commission of a crime, and such processes and likewise warrants and other processes in such cases, issued by said courts or persons, may be directed to a court officer or probation officer of the court issuing the process, or either specifically or in general terms to any person in the commonwealth qualified to serve criminal process, and any such process may be served and executed in any part of the commonwealth by the person to whom it is delivered for that purpose. This section shall apply to summonses, warrants and other processes for parties and witnesses in cases of wayward, delinquent or neglected children.

Chapter 221. Clerks, Attorneys and Other Officers of Judicial Courts

STENOGRAPHERS

SECTION 91B
Employment of stenographer by defendant; admissibility of transcripts of notes; application of section

At any hearing or proceeding in connection with a criminal case, including a hearing on the issuance of a complaint, at which a court appointed stenographer is not present, the defendant or the person against whom such complaint is filed may have the proceedings taken by a stenographer provided at his own expense. The judge or other officer presiding at such hearing or proceeding shall provide a suitable place in which such stenographer may hear and take notes of all testimony, arguments and rulings. The transcripts of notes taken by stenographers provided under authority of this section shall be admissible in accordance with the provisions of section eighty of chapter two hundred and thirty-three, except that the provisions of this section shall not be applicable to grand jury proceedings.

NOTE **Related Statute.** Transcripts from stenographic notes. G.L. c. 233, § 80.

Chapter 233. Witnesses and Evidence

Section	
20	Competency of witnesses; husband and wife; criminal defendant; parent and child
20A	Privileged communications; communications with clergymen
20B	Privileged communications; patients and psychotherapists; exceptions
20C	Immunity from prosecution; privilege against self-incrimination
20D	Crimes subject to immunity
20E	Application for witness immunity by attorney general or district attorney; hearing; representation of witness; notice or waiver; transcript
20F	Repealed
20G	Scope of immunity; copies of transcript of testimony compelled and documents furnished; availability to witness
20H	Contempt of court; punishment; appeal
20I	Necessity of corroborating testimony of, or evidence produced by, person granted immunity
20J	Sexual assault; confidential communications with sexual assault counsellor; disclosure; discovery
20K	Domestic violence victims' counselors; confidential communications
20L	Confidentiality of domestic violence victims' program and rape crisis center locations
20M	Disclosure of confidential communication regarding human trafficking victim by caseworker
20N	Disclosure of social worker home address and service of process procedures
21	Proof of conviction of crime to affect credibility
21A	Evidence of reputation
21B	Evidence of sex crime victim's sexual conduct; admission hearing; findings

23   Impeachment of party's own witness

23B   Accused; statements made while undergoing psychiatric examination; admissibility

23E   Alternative procedure for determining competency of witnesses with intellectual disability

23F   Admissibility of past physical, sexual or psychological abuse of defendant

69   Records of courts of other states or United States

70   Judicial notice of foreign law

75   Admissibility of printed copies of acts of legislative and administrative bodies

76   Admissibility of authenticated records of governmental departments

77   Authenticated copies of records of banks and trust companies

77A   Bank account statement together with legible copy of check; prima facie proof of payment

78   Entry, writing or record made in regular course of business; impeachment

79   Records and copies of records of hospitals and certain institutions; admissibility in evidence

79A   Certified copies of public and private records

79B–C Omitted

79D   Photographic copies of newspaper in library; prints from photographic films

79E   Reproductions of public or business records

79F   Proof of public way

79G   Medical and hospital records; evidence

79H–I   Omitted

79J   Business records required to be produced in court; certification, admissibility and inspection; copies

79K   Duplicate of computer data file or program file; admissibility

80   Transcripts from stenographic notes

81   Criminal proceedings; out-of-court statements describing sexual contact; admissibility

NOTE   See also Alphabetical References to Evidence section of this volume.

WITNESSES

SECTION 20

Competency of witnesses; husband and wife; criminal defendant; parent and child

Any person of sufficient understanding, although a party, may testify in any proceeding, civil or criminal, in court or before a person who has authority to receive evidence, except as follows:

First, Except in a proceeding arising out of or involving a contract made by a married woman with her husband, a proceeding under chapter two hundred and nine D and in a prosecution begun under sections one to ten, inclusive, of chapter two hundred and seventy-three, any criminal proceeding in which one spouse is a defendant alleged to have committed a crime against the other spouse or to have violated a temporary or permanent vacate, restraining, or no-contact order or judgment issued pursuant to section eighteen, thirty-four B or thirty-four C of chapter two hundred and eight, section thirty-two of chapter two hundred and nine, section three, three B, three C, four, or five of chapter two hundred and nine A, or sections fifteen or twenty of chapter two hundred and nine C, or a similar protection order issued by another jurisdiction, obtained by the other spouse, and except in a proceeding involving abuse of a person under the age of eighteen, including incest, neither husband nor wife shall testify as to private conversations with the other.

Second, Except as otherwise provided in section seven of chapter two hundred and seventy-three and except in any proceeding relating to child abuse, including incest, neither husband nor wife shall be compelled to testify in the trial of an indictment, complaint or other criminal proceeding against the other.

Third, the defendant in the trial of an indictment, complaint or other criminal proceeding shall, at his own request, but not otherwise, be allowed to testify; but his neglect or refusal to testify shall not create any presumption against him.

Fourth, An unemancipated, minor child, living with a parent, shall not testify before a grand jury, trial of an indictment, complaint or other criminal proceeding, against said parent, where the victim in such proceeding is not a member of said parent's family and who does not reside in the said parent's household. For the purposes of this clause the term "parent" shall mean the natural or adoptive mother or father of said child.

NOTE 1   One must "voluntarily and intelligently waive . . . his rights under G.L. c. 233, § 20, with respect to any statements made by him to the [experts]." *Commonwealth v. DelVerde*, 401 Mass. 447, 449 (1988) (citing *Commonwealth v. Lamb*, 365 Mass. 265, 270 (1974)).

NOTE 2   **Husband/Wife.** "To determine whether the [marital] disqualification should yield to the invoked constitutional rights we look to whether the evidence at issue if admitted might have a significant impact on the result of the trial. Stated otherwise, we look to whether the excluded evidence was sufficiently relevant, material, and not cumulative." *Commonwealth v. Perl*, 50 Mass. App. Ct. 445, 453 (2000) (quotation marks and citations omitted).

NOTE 3   **Test for Competency.** "In this Commonwealth, courts apply a two-prong test to determine competency: (1) whether the witness has the general ability or capacity to observe, remember, and give expression to that which she has seen, heard, or experienced; and (2) whether she has understanding sufficient to comprehend the difference between truth and falsehood, the wickedness of the latter and the obligation and duty to tell the truth, and, in a general way, belief that failure to perform the obligation will result in punishment." *Commonwealth v. Monzon*, 51 Mass. App. Ct. 245, 248 (2001) (citations and quotation marks omitted); *see also Commonwealth v. Thibeault*, 77 Mass. App. Ct. 419, 423–24 (2010) (quoting *Monzon*).

NOTE 4   **Judicial Discretion/Clearly Erroneous.** "Whether a witness is competent is first determined by the judge. . . . [I]t is seldom that the discretion of the trial judge can be revised; its exercise must have been clearly erroneous to justify action." *Commonwealth v. Monzon*, 51 Mass. App. Ct. 245, 248–49 (2001) (citations and quotation marks omitted).

SECTION 20A

Privileged communications; communications with clergymen

A priest, rabbi or ordained or licensed minister of any church or an accredited Christian Science practitioner shall not, without the consent of the person making the confession, be allowed to disclose a confession made to him in his professional character, in the course of discipline enjoined by the rules or practice of the religious body to which he belongs; nor shall a priest, rabbi or ordained or licensed minister of any church or an accredited Christian Science practitioner testify as to any communication made to him by any person in seeking religious or spiritual advice or comfort, or as to his advice given thereon in the course of his professional duties or in his professional character, without the consent of such person.

NOTE   Documents submitted to the Catholic Church in connection with an annulment may well have "literally involved 'seeking religious or spiritual advice or comfort' but, in any event, the process appears to fall within the scope of what the legislature was seeking to protect by § 20A." *Ryan v. Ryan*, 419 Mass. 86, 95 (1994).

SECTION 20B
Privileged communications; patients
and psychotherapists; exceptions

The following words as used in this section shall have the following meanings:—

"Patient", a person who, during the course of diagnosis or treatment, communicates with a psychotherapist;

"Psychotherapist", a person licensed to practice medicine, who devotes a substantial portion of his time to the practice of psychiatry. "Psychotherapist" shall also include a person who is licensed as a psychologist by the board of registration of psychologists; a graduate of, or student enrolled in, a doctoral degree program in psychology at a recognized educational institution as that term is defined in section 118, who is working under the supervision of a licensed psychologist; or a person who is a registered nurse licensed by the board of registration in nursing whose certificate of registration has been endorsed authorizing the practice of professional nursing in an expanded role as a psychiatric nurse mental health clinical specialist, pursuant to the provisions of section eighty B of chapter one hundred and twelve.

"Communications" includes conversations, correspondence, actions and occurrences relating to diagnosis or treatment before, during or after institutionalization, regardless of the patient's awareness of such conversations, correspondence, actions and occurrences, and any records, memoranda or notes of the foregoing.

Except as hereinafter provided, in any court proceeding and in any proceeding preliminary thereto and in legislative and administrative proceedings, a patient shall have the privilege of refusing to disclose, and of preventing a witness from disclosing, any communication, wherever made, between said patient and a psychotherapist relative to the diagnosis or treatment of the patient's mental or emotional condition. This privilege shall apply to patients engaged with a psychotherapist in marital therapy, family therapy, or consultation in contemplation of such therapy.

If a patient is incompetent to exercise or waive such privilege, a guardian shall be appointed to act in his behalf under this section. A previously appointed guardian shall be authorized to so act.

Upon the exercise of the privilege granted by this section, the judge or presiding officer shall instruct the jury that no adverse inference may be drawn therefrom.

The privilege granted hereunder shall not apply to any of the following communications:—

(a) If a psychotherapist, in the course of his diagnosis or treatment of the patient, determines that the patient is in need of treatment in a hospital for mental or emotional illness or that there is a threat of imminently dangerous activity by the patient against himself or another person, and on the basis of such determination discloses such communication either for the purpose of placing or retaining the patient in such hospital, provided however that the provisions of this section shall continue in effect after the patient is in said hospital, or placing the patient under arrest or under the supervision of law enforcement authorities.

(b) If a judge finds that the patient, after having been informed that the communications would not be privileged, has made communications to a psychotherapist in the course of a psychiatric examination ordered by the court, provided that such communications shall be admissible only on issues involving the patient's mental or emotional condition but not as a confession or admission of guilt.

(c) In any proceeding, except one involving child custody, adoption or adoption consent, in which the patient introduces his mental or emotional condition as an element of his claim or defense, and the judge or presiding officer finds that it is more important to the interests of justice that the communication be disclosed than that the relationship between patient psychotherapist be protected.

(d) In any proceeding after the death of a patient in which his mental or emotional condition is introduced by any party claiming or defending through or as a beneficiary of the patient as an element of the claim or defense, and the judge or presiding officer finds that it is more important to the interests of justice that the communication be disclosed than that the relationship between patient and psychotherapist be protected.

(e) In any case involving child custody, adoption or the dispensing with the need for consent to adoption in which, upon a hearing in chambers, the judge, in the exercise of his discretion, determines that the psychotherapist has evidence bearing significantly on the patient's ability to provide suitable care or custody, and that it is more important to the welfare of the child that the communication be disclosed than that the relationship between patient and psychotherapist be protected; provided, however, that in such cases of adoption or the dispensing with the need for consent to adoption, a judge shall determine that the patient has been informed that such communication would not be privileged.

(f) In any proceeding brought by the patient against the psychotherapist, and in any malpractice, criminal or license revocation proceeding, in which disclosure is necessary or relevant to the claim or defense of the psychotherapist.

The provision of information acquired by a psychotherapist relative to the diagnosis or treatment of a patient's emotional condition, to any insurance company, nonprofit hospital service corporation, medical service corporation, or health maintenance organization, or to a board established pursuant to section twelve of chapter one hundred and seventy-six B, pertaining to the administration or provision of benefits, including utilization review or peer review, for expenses arising from the out-patient diagnosis or treatment, or both, of mental or nervous conditions, shall not constitute a waiver or breach of any right to which said patient is otherwise entitled under this section and section thirty-six B of chapter one hundred and twenty-three.

NOTE 1   See Psychiatric, Psychological, Privileged Records in Alphabetical References to Evidence section of this volume.

NOTE 2   "The judge stated: 'I'm not going to let this record go to the jury, since it contains communications which are protected by the privilege, the statutory privilege. I would only override the privilege, in the interests of justice, if it's helpful to the jury. At this point, I see no basis for my concluding that it would be helpful to the jury'. . . .

"We conclude that the defendant suffered prejudice as a result of the judge's exclusion of the evidence. The Commonwealth's case depended almost entirely on the testimony of the complainant. Exclusion of the statement left the jury completely ignorant of the fact that six weeks prior to the incident the complainant had claimed to hear the voice of the defendant telling her to do things. [T]he proffered evidence, if believed, might have had a significant impact on the outcome of the trial."

Commonwealth v. Fayerweather, 406 Mass. 78, 82–84 (1989) (quotation marks, punctuation, and citations omitted).

NOTE 3 "General Laws c. 233, § 20B (1990 ed.), confers on a patient 'the privilege of refusing to disclose, and of preventing a witness from disclosing, any communication, wherever made, between said patient and a psychotherapist relative to the diagnosis or treatment of the patient's mental or emotional condition.' The privilege does not apply to communications made pursuant to a court-ordered examination where the patient has been warned in advance that his communications would not be privileged. G.L. c. 233, § 20B (1990 ed.)." *Commonwealth v. Benoit*, 410 Mass. 506, 518 (1991).

NOTE 4 "The findings that (1) the defendant was referred not to Dr. Purcell but to a physician at the Center for Mental Health in Waltham because of his suicidal thoughts; (2) the defendant cooperated with Dr. Purcell in order to minimize the legal impact of the charges and the impact of the charges on his family and job; and (3) Dr. Purcell told the defendant that he was not promising confidentiality, strongly suggest, although we do not decide the question, that the defendant did not consult Dr. Purcell for treatment or diagnosis incidental to treatment, and that therefore the relationship was not that of patient and psychotherapist and G.L. c. 233, § 20B, did not apply.

"If the statute were to apply, and we were to consider whether the defendant waived the privilege, we are at least doubtful as to whether we would agree with the judge that the defendant waived the privilege. It must be remembered that the statutory privilege is to prevent the psychotherapist from testifying in a Court proceeding. It is surely arguable that the defendant's acquiescence in Dr. Purcell's asserted reservation of the right to report his communication to the department and the district attorney in no way amounted to an irrevocable relinquishment of the privilege to prevent Dr. Purcell's testimony at trial."

Commonwealth v. Berrio, 407 Mass. 37, 42–43 (1990).

NOTE 5 "The judge ruled that the defendant's conversations with Dr. Scott did not fall within the statutory bounds of the psychotherapist-patient privilege, G.L. c. 233, § 20B (1988 ed.), because Dr. Scott has a doctoral degree in education, not a doctoral degree in the field of psychology. The patient-psychotherapist privilege has never been recognized at common law. We are thus not inclined here to extend the patient-psychotherapist privilege beyond the bounds established by the Legislature. There was no error." *Commonwealth v. Rosenberg*, 410 Mass. 347, 353 (1991) (citations omitted).

NOTE 6 "The exercise of the privilege established by G.L. c. 233, § 20B, does not preclude admission of such parts of a psychiatric record as are conclusions based on objective indicia rather than on communications from the mother. The extent to which the psychiatrist based her testimony on objective facts or data as distinguished from communications by the mother to a treating psychotherapist is not clear. To the extent that the psychiatrist's opinions may have been grounded on such a mixed foundation, the recommended approach would be for the mother's counsel to request a voir dire to determine the basis of the expert opinion." *Adoption of Seth*, 29 Mass. App. Ct. 343, 353 (1990) (citations and quotation marks omitted).

NOTE 8 **Standard.** "[T]he heightened *Fuller* standard of relevance applies when a defendant seeks information protected by G.L. c. 233, § 20B." *Commonwealth v. Oliveira*, 431 Mass. 609, 616 (2000).

NOTE 9 **Records Unprivileged Absent Affirmative Assertion by Patient.** "Absent an affirmative assertion [by the patient] of the privileges established by G.L. c. 233, § 20B, and G.L. c. 112, § 135B, the [trial] court must treat such records as if they [are] unprivileged." *Commonwealth v. Oliviera*, 438 Mass. 325, 337 (2002).

NOTE 10 **No In Camera Review Absent Assertion of Privilege.** "There is no reason to conduct an in camera *Bishop* review for 'relevance' in the absence of any asserted privilege." *Commonwealth v. Oliviera*, 438 Mass. 325, 340 (2002).

NOTE 11 **Dwyer.** "[W]e replaced the Bishop-Fuller protocol with a protocol set forth in *Commonwealth v. Dwyer*, 448 Mass. 122 (2006) (Dwyer). The Dwyer protocol is applicable to all criminal cases tried after issuance of the rescript in that case, *id.* at 124, and therefore applies to this case. We vacate the Superior Court judge's order. Records privileged pursuant to G.L. c. 112, § 135B, G.L. c. 233, § 20B, or any other statute, were subject to the Bishop-Fuller protocol, and are subject to the Dwyer protocol, regardless of their subject matter." *Martin v. Commonwealth*, 451 Mass. 113, 114 (2008).

SECTION 20C
Immunity from prosecution; privilege against self-incrimination

In any investigation or proceeding before a grand jury, or in a criminal proceeding in the supreme judicial court, appeals court or superior court involving any offense listed in section 20D, a witness shall not be excused from testifying or from producing books, papers or other evidence on the ground that the testimony or evidence required of him may tend to incriminate him or subject him to a penalty or forfeiture, if he has been granted immunity with respect to the transactions, matters or things concerning which he is compelled, after having claimed his privilege against self-incrimination, to testify or produce evidence by a justice of the supreme judicial court, appeals court or superior court, as provided in section 20E.

NOTE See Self-Incrimination in Alphabetical References to Evidence section of this volume.

SECTION 20D
Crimes subject to immunity

A witness who is called or who may be called to testify before a grand jury or in a criminal proceeding in the supreme judicial court, appeals court or superior court may, in the manner provided in section twenty E, be granted immunity in any proceeding or investigation involving the following crimes: abortion, arson, assault and battery to collect a loan, assault and battery by means of a dangerous weapon, assault to murder, breaking and entering a dwelling house or a building, bribery, burning of a building or dwelling house or other property, burglary, counterfeiting, deceptive advertising, electronic eavesdropping, embezzlement, extortion, firearm violations, forgery, fraudulent personal injury and property damage claims, violation of the gaming laws, gun registration violations, intimidation of a witness or of a juror, insurance law violations, kidnapping, larceny, lending of money or thing of value in violation of the general laws, liquor law violations, mayhem, murder, violation of the narcotic or harmful drug laws, perjury, prostitution, violations of environmental control laws (pollution), violations of conflicts of interest laws, consumer protection laws, pure food and drug law violations, receiving stolen property, robbery, subornation of perjury, uttering, or any felony, being an accessory to any of the foregoing offenses and conspiracy or attempt or solicitation to commit any of the foregoing offenses.

SECTION 20E
Application for witness immunity by attorney general or district attorney; hearing; representation of witness; notice or waiver; transcript

(a) A justice of the supreme judicial court, appeals court or superior court shall, at the request of the attorney general or a district attorney, and after a hearing, issue an order granting immunity to a witness, provided that such justice finds that the investigation or proceeding before the grand jury or the criminal proceeding in the supreme judicial court, appeals court or superior court involves an offense listed in section 20D and that the witness did validly refuse, or is likely to refuse, to answer questions or produce evidence on the grounds that such testimony or such evidence might tend to incriminate him. If such justice so finds, such justice shall order the witness to answer the questions or produce the evidence requested and, if he so orders, such order and the order granting immunity shall be in writing and shall become effective upon the refusal of the witness to answer any question or produce any evidence requested on the bases of his privilege against self-incrimination.

(b) The witness shall be entitled to representation by an attorney at the hearing, which shall not be open to the public. The court may appoint counsel for the witness.

(c) An application filed pursuant to this section shall, at the request of the attorney general or a district attorney, act to stay any criminal proceedings in the supreme judicial court, appeals court or superior court, but not grand jury proceedings, until such time as a justice acts upon such application; provided, however, that a justice shall conduct an expedited hearing when such application is brought after the impanelment of a jury in the superior court.

(d) When the attorney general or a district attorney brings such application, he shall, at least three days before the date fixed for hearing on his application, send by certified mail or deliver a copy of such application to the attorney general and to each other district attorney in the commonwealth. The attorney general and any of the district attorneys may waive, either orally or in writing, his right to be served with such application. The attorney general and any such district attorney may file an appearance and have the right to be heard at the hearing as herein provided.

(e) An affidavit of proof of service or, in the alternative, waiver of such service, upon each district attorney and the attorney general shall be filed with the court.

(f) A transcript shall be made of the proceedings at the hearing and a certified copy of said transcript shall be transmitted to the grand jury or the court, whichever is appropriate.

NOTE   "We determine that a proper grant of immunity protects a witness from prosecution on the basis of the immunized testimony in any court in the Commonwealth, and must be recognized in the Juvenile Court." *Commonwealth v. Austin A.*, 450 Mass. 665, 666 (2008).

SECTION 20F
Repealed

SECTION 20G
Scope of immunity; copies of transcript of testimony compelled and documents furnished; availability to witness

A witness who has been granted immunity as provided in section twenty E shall not be prosecuted or subjected to any penalty or forfeiture for or on account of any transaction matter, or thing concerning which he is so compelled, after having claimed his privilege against self-incrimination, to testify or produce evidence, nor shall testimony so compelled be used as evidence in any criminal or civil proceeding against him in any court of the commonwealth, except in a prosecution for perjury or contempt committed while giving testimo-

ny or producing evidence under compulsion, pursuant to sections twenty C or twenty F.

A witness who has been granted immunity shall be given a certified copy of the transcript, if he so requests, of any testimony that he furnished in compliance with an order of the court to testify, and shall be given a copy of all documents he has furnished in compliance with such order.

A transcript of said testimony and copies of said documents shall be maintained by the supreme court, appeals court or superior court, and shall be available at the request of such witness in any subsequent proceeding involving the witness.

SECTION 20H
Contempt of court; punishment; appeal

If a witness has been granted immunity pursuant to the provisions of section twenty E by a justice of the supreme judicial court, appeals court or superior court and thereafter refuses to testify or produce evidence after being so ordered by such justice, the attorney general or district attorney shall institute contempt proceedings against such witness in the court where the alleged contempt occurred, and, after hearing or trial, if such witness is adjudged in contempt of court, he shall be punished by imprisonment in the house of correction for a term not to exceed one year or until he complies with the order of the court, whichever occurs first. The rules of practice and procedure relative to criminal appeals as provided by the Massachusetts Rules of Criminal Procedure and the Massachusetts Rules of Appellate Procedure shall apply to appeals under this section.

NOTE   An immunized witness refused to testify before the grand jury. A Superior Court judge held the witness in contempt under both G.L. c. 233, § 20H and Mass.R.Crim.P. 43.

The Supreme Judicial Court affirmed, noting, however, that the Section 20H route is the proper one, not Rule 43. *Commonwealth v. Steinberg*, 404 Mass. 602 (1989).

SECTION 20I
Necessity of corroborating testimony of, or evidence produced by, person granted immunity

No defendant in any criminal proceeding shall be convicted solely on the testimony of, or the evidence produced by, a person granted immunity under the provisions of section twenty E.

NOTE   "The purpose of the statute is to require support for the credibility of the immunized witness. That support may come as much in the form of corroboration of evidence of the commission of the crime as it does from proof that the defendant was a participant." *Commonwealth v. Fernandes*, 425 Mass. 357, 359 (1997) (quoting *Commonwealth v. DeBrosky*, 363 Mass. 718, 730 (1973), citing J. Wigmore, *Evidence* § 2059, at 327 (3d ed. 1940)).

SECTION 20J
Sexual assault; confidential communications with sexual assault counsellor; disclosure; discovery

As used in this section the following words, unless the context clearly requires otherwise, shall have the following meaning:—

"Rape crisis center", any office, institution or center offering assistance to victims of sexual assault and the families of such victims through crisis intervention, medical and legal counseling.

"Sexual assault counsellor", a person who is employed by or is a volunteer in a rape crisis center, has undergone thirty-five hours of training, who reports to and is under the direct control and supervision of a licensed social worker, nurse, psychiatrist, psychologist or psychotherapist and whose primary purpose is the rendering of advice, counseling or assistance to victims of sexual assault.

"Victim", a person who has suffered a sexual assault and who consults a sexual assault counsellor for the purpose of securing advice, counseling or assistance concerning a mental, physical or emotional condition caused by such sexual assault.

"Confidential communication", information transmitted in confidence by and between a victim of sexual assault and a sexual assault counsellor by a means which does not disclose the information to a person other than a person present for the benefit of the victim, or to those to whom disclosure of such information is reasonably necessary to the counseling and assisting of such victim. The term includes all information received by the sexual assault counsellor which arises out of and in the course of such counseling and assisting, including, but not limited to reports, records, working papers or memoranda.

A sexual assault counsellor shall not disclose such confidential communication, without the prior written consent of the victim; provided, however, that nothing in this chapter shall be construed to limit the defendant's right of cross-examination of such counsellor in a civil or criminal proceeding if such counsellor testifies with such written consent.

Such confidential communications shall not be subject to discovery and shall be inadmissible in any criminal or civil proceeding without the prior written consent of the victim to whom the report, record, working papers or memorandum relates.

NOTE 1   See Psychiatric, Psychological, Privileged Records in Alphabetical References to Evidence section of this volume.

NOTE 2   "The judge concluded correctly that the portion of the records that sets forth the time, date, and fact of a communication between the complainant and the rape counselor on the 'hotline' is not protected by the sexual assault counselor privilege." *Commonwealth v. Neumyer*, 432 Mass. 23, 29 (2000).

SECTION 20K
Domestic violence victims' counselors; confidential communications

As used in this section the following words shall unless the context clearly requires otherwise have the following meanings:—

"Abuse", causing or attempting to cause physical harm; placing another in fear of imminent physical harm; causing another to engage in sexual relations against his will by force, threat of force, or coercion.

"Confidential communication", information transmitted in confidence by and between a victim and a domestic violence victims' counselor by a means which does not disclose the information to a person other than a person present for the benefit of the victim, or to those to whom disclosure of such information is reasonably necessary to the counseling and assisting of such victim. The term includes all information received by the domestic violence victims' counselor which arises out of and in the course of such counseling and assisting, including, but not limited to reports, records, working papers, or memoranda.

"Domestic violence victims' counselor", a person who is employed or volunteers in a domestic violence victims' program, who has undergone a minimum of twenty-five hours of training and who reports to and in under the direct control and supervision of a direct service supervisor of a domestic violence victims' program, and whose primary purpose is the rendering of advice, counseling or assistance to victims of abuse.

"Domestic violence victims' program", any refuge, shelter, office, safe home, institution or center established for the purpose of offering assistance to victims of abuse through crisis intervention, medical, legal or support counseling.

"Victim", a person who has suffered abuse and who consults a domestic violence victims' counselor for the purpose of securing advice, counseling or assistance concerning a mental, physical or emotional condition caused by such abuse.

A domestic violence victims' counselor shall not disclose such confidential communication without the prior written consent of the victim, except as hereinafter provided. Such confidential communication shall not be subject to discovery in any civil, legislative or administrative proceeding without the prior written consent of the victim to whom such confidential communication relates. In criminal actions such confidential communication shall be subject to discovery and shall be admissible as evidence but only to the extent of information contained therein which is exculpatory in relation to the defendant; provided, however, that the court shall first examine such confidential communication and shall determine whether or not such exculpatory information is therein contained before allowing such discovery or the introduction of such evidence.

NOTE 1   "The heightened *Fuller* standard of relevance applies when a defendant seeks information protected by G.L. c. 233, § 20K." *Commonwealth v. Oliveira*, 431 Mass. 609, 617 (2000). "Before a judge should undertake an in camera review of privileged records, the defendant must demonstrate a good faith, specific, and reasonable basis for believing that the records will contain exculpatory evidence that is relevant and material to the defendant's guilt." *Commonwealth v. Tripolone*, 425 Mass. 487, 489 (1997).

NOTE 2   **Dwyer.** "[W]e replaced the Bishop-Fuller protocol with a protocol set forth in *Commonwealth v. Dwyer*, 448 Mass. 122 (2006) (Dwyer). The Dwyer protocol is applicable to all criminal cases tried after issuance of the rescript in that case, *id.* at 124, and therefore applies to this case. We vacate the Superior Court judge's order. Records privileged pursuant to G.L. c. 112, § 135B, G.L. c. 233, § 20B, or any other statute, were subject to the Bishop-Fuller protocol, and are subject to the Dwyer protocol, regardless of their subject matter." *Martin v. Commonwealth*, 451 Mass. 113, 114 (2008).

SECTION 20L
Confidentiality of domestic violence victims' program and rape crisis center locations

The location and street address of all domestic violence victims' programs, as defined in section twenty K and rape crisis centers, as defined in section twenty J, shall be absolutely confidential and shall not be required to be revealed in any criminal or civil proceeding.

SECTION 20M
Disclosure of confidential communication regarding human trafficking victim by caseworker
(Added by 2011 Mass. Acts c. 178, § 17, effective Nov. 21, 2011.)

(a) As used in this section, the following words shall, unless the context clearly requires otherwise, have the following meanings:—

"Confidential communication", information transmitted in confidence by and between a victim and a victim's caseworker by a means which does not disclose the information to a person other than a person present for the benefit of the victim, or to those to whom disclosure of such information is reasonably necessary to the counseling and assisting of such victim. The term confidential communication shall include all information received by a victim's caseworker which arises out of and in the course of such counseling and assisting including, but not limited to, reports, records, working papers or memoranda.

"Human trafficking victim" or "victim", a person who is subjected to the conduct prohibited under sections 50 or 51 of chapter 265.

"Human trafficking victims' caseworker," a person who is employed by or volunteers with a program serving human trafficking victims, who has undergone a minimum of 25 hours of training and who reports to and is under the direct control and supervision of a direct service supervisor of a human trafficking victim program, and whose primary purpose is the rendering of advice, counseling or assistance to human trafficking victims.

"Human trafficking victims' program", any refuge, shelter, office, safe house, institution or center established for the purpose of offering assistance to human trafficking victims through crisis intervention, medical, legal or support counseling.

(b) A human trafficking victims' caseworker shall not disclose any confidential communication without the prior written consent of the victim, or the victim's guardian in the case of a child, except as hereinafter provided. Such confidential communication shall not be subject to discovery in any civil, legislative or administrative proceeding without the prior written consent of the victim, or victim's guardian in the case of a child, to whom such confidential communication relates. In criminal actions such confidential communication shall be subject to discovery and shall be admissible as evidence but only to the extent of information contained therein which is exculpatory in relation to the defendant; provided, however, that the court shall first examine such confidential communication and shall determine whether or not such exculpatory information is contained in the communication before allowing such discovery or the introduction of such evidence.

(c) During the initial meeting between a caseworker and victim, the caseworker shall inform the human trafficking victim and any guardian thereof of the confidentiality of communications between a caseworker and victim and the limitations thereto.

SECTION 20N
Disclosure of social worker home address and service of process procedures
(Added by 2015 Mass. Acts c. 46, § 126, effective July 17, 2015.)

(a) No court shall permit or require the disclosure of the home address or personal telephone number of a social worker employed by the department of children and families; and no witness shall be required to disclose such social worker's home address or personal telephone number in any court proceeding or in any proceeding preliminary thereto or in any documents filed with the court, except as otherwise ordered by the court, for good cause shown; provided, however, that an order of the court shall include, if possible, conditions to limit the disclosure of any such address or phone number so as to protect the privacy and safety of the social worker.

(b) Service of process, summons or subpoena upon a department of children and families social worker in any court proceeding and in any proceeding preliminary thereto shall be made upon the agency employing the social worker and in accordance with the Massachusetts Rules of Civil Procedure or the Massachusetts Rules of Criminal Procedure governing any such service of process, summons or subpoena. For the purpose of making such service, the employing agency, upon request, shall certify to the summoning party the name and work address of any such social worker as disclosed by its records, and a summoning party may serve the social worker at the work address so certified.

SECTION 21
Proof of conviction of crime to affect credibility
(Amended by 2010 Mass. Acts c. 256, § 105, effective May 4, 2012.)

The conviction of a witness of a crime may be shown to affect his credibility, except as follows:

First, The record of his conviction of a misdemeanor shall not be shown for such purpose after five years from the date on which sentence on said conviction was imposed, unless he has subsequently been convicted of a crime within five years of the time of his testifying.

Second, The record of his conviction of a felony upon which no sentence was imposed or a sentence was imposed and the execution thereof suspended, or upon which a fine only was imposed, or a sentence to a reformatory prison, jail, or house of correction, shall not be shown for such purpose after ten years from the date of conviction, if no sentence was imposed, or from the date on which sentence on said conviction was imposed, whether the execution thereof was suspended or not, unless he has subsequently been convicted of a crime within ten years of the time of his testifying. For the purpose of this paragraph, a plea of guilty or a finding or verdict of guilty shall constitute a conviction within the meaning of this section.

Third, The record of his conviction of a felony upon which a state prison sentence was imposed shall not be shown for such purpose after ten years from the date of expiration of the minimum term of imprisonment imposed by the court, unless he has subsequently been convicted of a crime within ten years of the time of his testifying.

Fourth, The record of his conviction for a traffic violation upon which a fine only was imposed shall not be shown for such purpose unless he has been convicted of another crime or crimes within five years of the time of his testifying.

For the purpose of this section, any period during which the defendant was a fugitive from justice shall be excluded in determining time limitations under the provisions of this section.

Upon order of the court, a party may obtain a witness's criminal offender record information from the department of criminal justice information services.

NOTE 1   "Prior convictions may be introduced in the discretion of the judge, who weighs the danger of unfair prejudice that might result from the admission of such evidence against its probative value for impeachment purposes. The admission of a large number of convictions does not by itself create a risk of prejudice sufficient to warrant reversal." *Commonwealth v. Brown*, 451 Mass. 200, 202–03 (2008) (citation omitted).

NOTE 2   "The certified records of the defendant's prior convictions included docket entries which showed defaults, warrants issued, arrests on warrant, and violations of probation. The admission of unexpurgated records was error. We agree with the Appeals Court that where certified records of prior conviction are used to impeach, G.L. c. 233, sec. 21 (1984 ed.), 'they should hew to the convictions, and extraneous entries should not pass to the jury as part of the exhibits.' If, as the judge believed, masking the extraneous material risked inducing the jury to speculate about the missing portions of the records, to the defendant's prejudice, he should have denied the Commonwealth request to mark the records as exhibits." *Commonwealth v. Ford*, 397 Mass. 298, 300 (1986) (citations omitted).

NOTE 3   "In *Commonwealth v. Walker*, 401 Mass. 338, 345–46 (1987), we said that the trial judge did not abuse his discretion in allowing impeachment of the defendant with a prior unarmed robbery conviction when he was on trial for armed robbery as well as for other crimes. In that case, a prior larceny conviction was also available for use, and was in fact used, for impeachment purposes. We conclude that the judge in the present case acted within his discretion in denying the defendant's motion in limine [to preclude impeachment by prior convictions of offenses . . . similar to the crimes for which he was being tried]." *Commonwealth v. Smith*, 403 Mass. 489, 498, 497 (1988).

NOTE 4   "While a conviction for assault by means of a dangerous weapon does not involve conduct directly demonstrating dishonesty or untruthfulness, we have recognized that 'a defendant's earlier disregard for the law may suggest to the fact finder similar disregard for the courtroom oath.' *Commonwealth v. Fano*, [400 Mass. 296, 302–03 (1987)] (quoting *Commonwealth v. Roucoulet*, 22 Mass. App. Ct. 603, 608 (1986)). We have indicated that substantial similarity of the crimes is an important factor in determining whether the danger of unfair prejudice exists. The prior conviction for assault by means of a dangerous weapon and the crime of aggravated rape for which the defendant was being tried bear no such substantial similarity. The fact that the dangerous weapon involved in the prior conviction was a knife and that there was evidence here that one of the assailants held a knife does not establish such substantial similarity. Therefore, admission of evidence of a prior conviction for assault by means of a dangerous weapon did not create the danger that the defendant would be convicted by 'proof of his . . . propensity to commit similar crimes.' *Commonwealth v. Fano, supra*, quoting *Commonwealth v. DiMarzo*, 364 Mass. 669, 681 (1974) (Hennessey, J., concurring)." *Commonwealth v. Cordeiro*, 401 Mass. 843, 854–55 (1988) (citations omitted).

NOTE 5   "[A] defendant need not testify to preserve for review a claim that a motion to exclude impeachment evidence of a prior conviction was improperly denied. . . .

"Armed robbery is not an offense substantially similar to offenses charged. When presented with the identical issue in the appeal of a codefendant at the first trial, this court stated that '[t]here is a substantial difference between armed robbery and murder, even if that murder is committed in the course of armed robbery.' *Commonwealth v. Andrews*, 403 Mass. 441 (1988). There was no abuse of discretion."

Commonwealth v. Feroli, 407 Mass. 405, 407–08 (1990).

NOTE 6a   "The general rule is that, when a record of a witness's conviction of a crime has been introduced to impeach him, the conviction must be left unexplained. The guilt or innocence of the witness cannot be revisited and the jury should not be distracted by the collateral matter of the witness's prior crimes. The proponent of the witness, then, generally is not entitled to present on redirect examination the circumstances of prior convictions by which its witness is impeached. When, however, as in this case, cross-examination goes beyond simply establishing that the witness is the person named in the record of conviction, the proponent of the witness may, in the judge's discretion, properly inquire on redirect examination about those collateral matters raised during the cross-examination." *Commonwealth v. McGeoghean*, 412 Mass. 839, 843 (1992) (citations and quotation marks omitted).

NOTE 6b   "Here, the length and consecutive nature of Bonilla's sentences were relevant to explain why, after giving four statements to police in which he essentially denied killing Simmons, he would come forward and seemingly without explanation confess to the killing. The fact that he expected to spend the rest of his life in prison was evidence of a motive to lie for his friend, the defendant, and a willingness to shoulder the entire responsibility for the killing. The prosecutor's questions were not designed solely for impeachment under G.L. c. 233, § 21, but for another, permissible reason." *Commonwealth v. Bly*, 444 Mass. 640, 652 (2005).

NOTE 7   Presumption of Representation. "[W]e see no reason to continue the requirement that the Commonwealth, as a condition of seeking, under G.L. c. 233, § 21, Second, to introduce a felony conviction to impeach a defendant (or to revive an otherwise time-barred conviction), affirmatively show that the defendant had or waived counsel. The rule henceforth will presume that the counsel requirement was fulfilled, and the Commonwealth will not have to come forward with proof on the point unless the defendant first makes a showing that the conviction in issue was obtained without representation by, or waiver of, counsel." *Commonwealth v. Saunders*, 435 Mass. 691, 695–96 (2002).

NOTE 8   Where "probation officer was allowed to testify, over objection, that she was supervising the defendant for a 'felony' conviction[,] . . . [t]he better course would have been to allow the probation officer to testify that she was supervising the defendant 'for a crime.'" *Commonwealth v. Crouse*, 447 Mass. 558, 566 (2006) (footnote omitted).

NOTE 9   Misdemeanor/Probation. "Probation on a conviction of a misdemeanor is not a sentence for the purposes of G.L. c. 233, § 21." *Commonwealth v. Stewart*, 422 Mass. 385, 387 (1996) (citation omitted).

NOTE 10   Witness. "The duty of the judge to exercise discretion regarding impeachment by prior convictions applies equally to the testimony of parties and of other witnesses. It is the duty of the judge to exercise discretion, and it is error as a matter of law to refuse to exercise it." *Commonwealth v. Manning*, 47 Mass. App. Ct. 923 (1999) (citations, quotation marks, and punctuation omitted).

NOTE 11   The judge excluded evidence of a prior conviction for carrying a firearm. The defendant basically testified, at his murder trial, that he had never carried a firearm before. "[W]hen the defendant answered untruthfully that he had never carried a gun, he opened the door to admission of the evidence of his prior conviction for gun possession." Evidence may be admitted "to rebut specific portions of the defendant's testimony." *Commonwealth v. Roderick*, 429 Mass. 271, 274–75 (1999).

NOTE 12   Use of Other Person's Prior Convictions. "We do not discount the possibility that a case might arise in which a judge, within discretion, could permit the use of someone else's conviction in cross-examination to test the accuracy of a witness's perception. This is not such a case since the witness in question, Hession, had long concluded her testimony before the defense tried to bring in Clifford's plea and conviction. The judge acted within his discretion in excluding the Clifford conviction at a time when the witness to be impeached by it was no longer on the stand." *Commonwealth v. Supplee*, 45 Mass. App. Ct. 265, 268 (1998).

NOTE 13   Records Need Not be Admitted. "The defendant argues that the judge erred by refusing to admit certified copies of three convictions used to impeach . . . . There was no error. 'The impeachment was complete on reading the records and establishing that the witness was the subject of them . . . The judge was not obliged to admit the records as exhibits, though he could have chosen to do so.'" *Commonwealth v. Thomas*, 439 Mass. 362, 364 (2003) (quoting *Commonwealth v. St. Pierre*, 377 Mass. 650, 664 (1979)).

NOTE 14   "The defendant has a right to testify. He does not have a right to testify free of the effects of impeachment by prior conviction." *Commonwealth v. Deberry*, 57 Mass. App. Ct. 93, 99 (2003).

NOTE 15   Rape-Shield Statute. *See* G.L. c. 233, § 21, note 3.

SECTION 21A
Evidence of reputation

Evidence of the reputation of a person in a group with the members of which he has habitually associated in his work or business shall be admissible to the same extent and subject to the same limitations as is evidence of such reputation in a community in which he has resided.

SECTION 21B
Evidence of sex crime victim's sexual conduct; admission hearing; findings
(Amended by 2011 Mass. Acts c. 178, § 18, effective Nov. 21, 2011.)

Evidence of the reputation of a victim's sexual conduct shall not be admissible in an investigation or proceeding before a grand jury or a court of the commonwealth for a violation of sections 13B, 13B½, 13B¾, 13F, 13H, 22, 22A, 22B, 22C, 23, 23A, 23B, 24, 24B, 50 or 51 of chapter 265 . Evidence of specific instances of a victim's sexual conduct in such an investigation or proceeding shall not be admissible except evidence of the victim's sexual conduct with the defendant or evidence of recent conduct of the victim alleged to be the cause of any physical feature, characteristic, or condition of the victim; provided, however, that such evidence shall be admissible only after an in camera hearing on a written motion for admission of same and an offer of proof. If, after said hearing, the court finds that the weight and relevancy of said evidence is sufficient to outweigh its prejudicial effect to the victim, the evidence shall be admitted; otherwise not. If the proceeding is a trial with jury, said hearing shall be held in the absence of the jury. The finding of the court shall be in writing and filed but shall not be made available to the jury.

NOTE 1   "Pursuant to G.L. c. 233, § 21B (the rape-shield statute), the defendant filed a pretrial motion in limine requesting a ruling on the admissibility of testimony relating to sexual activity of the complainant. The sexual activity that the defendant referred to was intercourse with the defendant in the weeks following April 19, 1988 and intercourse with her boyfriend before and after April 19. The defendant argued in the motion that this testimony was admissible on the issues of consent, bias and motive to falsify.

"The defendant argues that the judge erred in precluding cross-examination designed to uncover evidence that the complainant was biased and motivated to lie because she did not want her parents to learn that she was sexually active. We agree with the defendant that the judge's restriction on cross-examination was reversible error.

"Because bias is intimately related to credibility, a defendant has the right to cross-examine a prosecution witness in order to reveal bias. A judge may not restrict cross-examination of a material witness by foreclosing inquiry into a subject that could show bias or prejudice [or motive to lie] on the part of the witness. If a defendant believes that the judge improperly restrained his cross-examination of a witness, the defendant must demonstrate that the judge abused his discretion and that he was prejudiced by such restraint.

"The principles protecting a defendant's right to cross-examination are particularly important when the charge is rape, because the right to cross-examine a complainant in a rape case to show a false accusation may be the last refuge of an innocent defendant."

Commonwealth v. Stockhammer, 409 Mass. 867, 873–74, 875 (1991) (citations and quotation marks omitted).

NOTE 2   "[T]he judge erred in invoking the rape-shield statute to forbid defense counsel from asking the complainant whether she had sexual relations with someone else on the night of the incident. Rape-shield statutes are aimed at eliminating a common defense strategy of trying the complaining witness rather than the defendant. The result of this strategy was harassment and further humiliation of the victim as well as discouraging victims of rape from reporting the crimes to law enforcement authorities. The rape-shield statute is principally designed to prevent defense counsel from eliciting evidence of the victim's promiscuity as part of a general credibility attack.

"Contrary to the Commonwealth's assertions, the defendant was not seeking to use the evidence for any of the purposes that the rape-shield statute forbids. It was expected that the question would have produced a negative answer. The intended examination would not have suggested that the complainant was promiscuous and did not amount to a general attack on her credibility. Rather, the evidence tended to support the defendant's theory of the case: that someone else had attacked the complainant and she had wrongly accused the defendant. The inquiry was relevant and outside of the prohibition of the rape-shield statute."

Commonwealth v. Fitzgerald, 412 Mass. 516, 523–24 (1992) (footnote and citation omitted).

NOTE 3   Convictions for Sex-Related Offenses. "[I]f the convictions are for sex-related offenses . . . [w]e conclude that it is within the judge's discretion to admit evidence of such convictions pursuant to G.L. c. 233, § 21, but that the exercise of that discretion must take into consideration the objectives of the rape-shield statute . . . .

"The judge should thus consider the potential that the jury may misuse the conviction of a sexual offense as indicative of the complaining witness's consent, and the risk that the complaining witness may be subjected to needless humiliation."

In a footnote, the court also noted, "The judge should also consider whether the defendant has available other impeachment evidence, in particular, whether there are other convictions of non sexual offenses that may be used to impeach the complainant . . . . And, as is customary, if the prior conviction is admitted in evidence under § 21, an appropriate limiting instruction should be given." *Commonwealth v. Harris*, 443 Mass. 714, 715, 727–28 (2005).

NOTE 4   Courtroom Closure. "While we agree with the motion judge that the statute provides for mandatory closure of the rape shield hearing, we conclude that the mandatory closure rule is impermissible. In reaching that conclusion, we emphasize at the outset that we do not question the compelling interest underlying the rape shield statute. That statute, like similar statutes in other States, was enacted in response to the pervasive practice of attacking a victim's testimony that she did not consent to sex with evidence of the victim's 'lack of chastity.' *Commonwealth v. Joyce*, 382 Mass. 222, 227–28 (1981) ('The major innovative thrust of the rape-shield statute is found in the first sentence, which reverses the common law rule under which evidence of the complainant's general reputation for unchastity was admissible'). And although '[t]he primary purpose of the statute is to prevent a general credibility attack of a victim with evidence of his or her promiscuity,' *Commonwealth v. Mountry*, 463 Mass. [80, 86 (2012)], the statute's requirement for an 'in camera hearing' on the admissibility of evidence of sexual conduct reflects a legitimate interest in guarding against the public 'revelation of facts that can only smear' a rape victim, and in 'protecting complainants and encouraging victim cooperation in bringing suspected assailants to trial.'

"We also stress the narrowness of our holding: we do not determine that this particular rape shield hearing should have been open to the public, much less that all rape shield hearings must be open to the public. Instead, we merely conclude that, before a judge may order the court room closed for a rape shield hearing, the judge must make a case-by-case determination in accordance with the four-prong framework articulated by the United States Supreme Court in *Waller* [*v. Georgia*, 467 U.S. 39, 48 (1984)], decided after the enactment of the rape shield law at issue here." *Commonwealth v. Jones*, 472 Mass. 707, 722 (2015) (citation omitted).

SECTION 23
Impeachment of party's own witness

The party who produces a witness shall not impeach his credit by evidence of bad character, but may contradict him by other evidence, and may also prove that he has made at other times statements inconsistent with his present testimony; but before proof of such inconsistent statements is given, the circumstances thereof sufficient to designate the particular occasion shall be mentioned to the witness, and he shall be asked if he has made such statements, and, if so, shall be allowed to explain them.

NOTE 1   "In *Commonwealth v. Cadwell*, 374 Mass. 308 (1978), we held that it was permissible for the prosecution to elicit its own witness's prior criminal record on direct examination. 'The essential import of *Cadwell* is that the jury are entitled to information regarding the witness's prior conviction as that information bears on his credibility, but that neither party has an unalterable prerogative to bring out these facts at a particular time and "in a perhaps more dramatic way.'" *Commonwealth v. Coviello*, 378 Mass. 530, 533 (1979) (quoting *Commonwealth v. Cadwell, supra* at 312). Similarly, evidence of an agreement for leniency between the witness and the prosecution may be introduced by either party at the discretion of the trial judge." *Commonwealth v. Griffith*, 404 Mass. 256, 265–66 (1989).

NOTE 2   "There is nothing improper in interviewing a witness before trial, or, subject to the judge's discretion, in cross-examining a witness concerning discrepancies between his in-court and out-of-court statements. Indeed, where the witness is one's own, such questions may be a prerequisite to the admission of prior inconsistent statements for the purpose of impeaching that witness. . . . [I]f no third person is present during a conversation between the witness and the prosecutor, the prosecutor has no basis for introducing the witness's prior inconsistent statement unless he obtains leave to withdraw from the case in order to do so.'" *Commonwealth v. White*, 367 Mass. 280, 284 (1975); *see also Commonwealth v. Johnson*, 412 Mass. 318, 326 (1992).

NOTE 3   "Although G.L. c. 233, § 23, permits a party to impeach its own witness with prior inconsistent statements, 'a party cannot rely on this statutory right to call a witness whom he knows beforehand will offer no testimony relevant to an issue at trial solely for the purpose of impeaching that witness.'" *Commonwealth v. Maldonado*, 466 Mass. 742, 758 (2014) (quoting *Commonwealth v. McAfee*, 430 Mass. 483, 489–90 (1999)).

SECTION 23B
Accused; statements made while undergoing psychiatric examination; admissibility

In the trial of an indictment or complaint for any crime, no statement made by a defendant therein subjected to psychiatric examination pursuant to sections fifteen or sixteen of chapter one hundred and twenty-three for the purposes of such examination or treatment shall be admissible in evidence against him on any issue other than that of his mental condition, nor shall it be admissible in evidence against him on that issue if such statement constitutes a confession of guilt of the crime charged.

SECTION 23E
Alternative procedure for determining competency of witnesses with an intellectual disability

(a) For the purposes of this section, the following words shall have the following meanings, unless the context clearly requires otherwise:—

"Witnesses with an intellectual disability", a witness in a proceeding whom the presiding justice has found after hearing, as provided in paragraph (1) of subsection (b), to have an intellectual disability.

"Intellectual disability", substantial limitations in present functioning manifesting before age eighteen and characterized by significantly subaverage intellectual functioning, existing concurrently with related limitations in two or more of the following applicable skill areas: communication, self-care, home living, social skills, community use, self-direction, health and safety, functional academics, leisure and work.

(b)(1) In any judicial proceeding in which a witness with an intellectual disability will testify, the court, on its own motion or on motion of the proponent of the witness with an intellectual disability and after hearing on the witness's competency to testify, may order the use of alternative procedures for taking testimony of the witness with an intellectual disability; provided, however, that the court finds at the time of the order, by clear and convincing evidence in the case of a criminal proceeding, and by a preponderance of the evidence in the case of a noncriminal proceeding, that the witness with an intellectual disability is likely, as a result of submitting to usual procedures for determining competency or as a result of testifying in open court, as the case may be, (i) to suffer severe psychological or emotional trauma; or (ii) to suffer a temporary loss of or regression in cognitive or behavioral functioning or communicative abilities, such that his ability to testify will be significantly impaired. If the court so finds, the court may order the use of alternative procedures for determining competency to testify or for taking testimony of the witness with an intellectual disability including, but not limited to, the following:

(i) permitting a person familiar to the witness, such as a family member, clinician, counselor, social worker or friend, to sit near or next to such witness;

(ii) permitting the witness with mental retardation to testify in court but off the witness stand; provided, however, that if the proceeding is a bench proceeding, testimony may be taken at another location within the courthouse but outside the courtroom; and, provided further, that if the proceeding is a jury trial, testimony may be taken on videotape out of the presence of the jury or in a location chosen by the court or by agreement of the parties; or

(iii) combining alternative procedures provided in clauses (i) and (ii).

(c) When the proceedings are not criminal or juvenile delinquency related, testimony taken by videotape pursuant to an order under paragraph (1) of subsection (b) shall be taken in the presence of the judge, counsel for all parties and such other persons as the court may allow. Counsel shall be given the opportunity to examine or cross-examine the witness with mental retardation to the same extent as he would be permitted if ordinary procedures had been followed.

(d) When the proceedings are criminal or juvenile delinquency related, the defendant shall have the right to be present during the taking of the testimony, to have an unobstructed view of the witness with an intellectual disability, and to have the witness's view of the defendant be unobstructed.

(e) If the court orders that the testimony of the witness with an intellectual disability be videotaped out of the presence of the jury, the videotape shall be shown in court to the jury in the presence of the judge, the parties and the parties' counsel. The videotape shall be marked as an exhibit and retained by the court as part of the record of the case.

(f) Testimony taken by alternative procedures authorized by this section shall be admissible as substantive evidence to the same extent as and in lieu of live testimony by the witness in any proceeding in which such testimony is taken.

(g) The witness requesting that testimony be taken by videotape shall bear the responsibility of producing an acceptable videotape of the testimony. The commonwealth shall reimburse such witness for reasonable costs of producing such videotape. Each party shall be afforded an opportunity to view the recording before it is shown in the courtroom.

(h) The fact that the witness with an intellectual disability has been found in a court proceeding to be incompetent to make informed decisions of a personal, medical or financial nature or that he is under a guardianship or conservatorship shall not preclude such witness from testifying if he is found to be competent to testify and shall not preclude a determination of competency to testify.

(i) A witness shall not be denied the benefit of appropriate alternative procedures provided by this section and the court shall allow such additional time or continuances to permit application of such procedures.

(j) A person with expertise in persons with an intellectual disability may be called by the proponent of the witness to testify in all relevant matters, including the competency determination of such witness.

(k) Nothing in this section shall be construed to prohibit a court from using other appropriate means consistent with this section and any other general or special law and with the defendant's rights to accomplish the purposes of this section.

SECTION 23F
Admissibility of past physical, sexual or psychological abuse of defendant

In the trial of criminal cases charging the use of force against another where the issue of defense of self or another, defense of duress or coercion, or accidental harm is asserted, a defendant shall be permitted to introduce either or both of the following in establishing the reasonableness of the defendant's apprehension that death or serious bodily injury was imminent, the reasonableness of the defendant's belief that he had availed him of all available means to avoid physical combat or the reasonableness of a defendant's perception of the amount of force necessary to deal with the perceived threat:

(a) evidence that the defendant is or has been the victim of acts of physical, sexual or psychological harm or abuse;

(b) evidence by expert testimony regarding the common pattern in abusive relationships; the nature and effects of physical, sexual or psychological abuse and typical responses thereto, including how those effects relate to the perception of the imminent nature of the threat of death or serious bodily harm; the relevant facts and circumstances which form the basis for such opinion; and evidence whether the defendant displayed characteristics common to victims of abuse.

Nothing in this section shall be interpreted to preclude the introduction of evidence or expert testimony as described in clause (a) or (b) in any civil or criminal action where such evidence or expert testimony is otherwise now admissible.

PROOF OF STATUTES, LAWS, ETC.

SECTION 69
Records of courts of other states or United States

The records and judicial proceedings of a court of another state or of the United States shall be admissible in evidence in this commonwealth, if authenticated by the attestation of the clerk or other officer who has charge of the records of such court under its seal.

SECTION 70
Judicial notice of foreign law

The courts shall take judicial notice of the law of the United States or of any state, territory or dependency thereof or of a foreign country whenever the same shall be material.

SECTION 75
Admissibility of printed copies of acts of legislative and administrative bodies

The printed copies of all statutes, acts and resolves of the commonwealth, public or private, which are published under its authority, and copies of the ordinances of a city, the by-laws of a town or of the rules and regulations of a board of aldermen, if attested by the clerk of such city or town, shall be admitted as sufficient evidence thereof in all courts of law and on all occasions. Printed copies of rules and regulations purporting to be issued by authority of any department, commission, board or officer of the commonwealth or of any city or town having authority to adopt them, or printed copies of any city ordinances or town by-laws or printed copies of the United States Code Annotated or the United States Code Service and all federal regulations, and the titles, chapters, subchapters, parts and sections thereof, shall be admitted without certification or attestation, but, if their genuineness is questioned, the court shall require such certification or attestation thereof as it deems necessary.

SECTION 76
Admissibility of authenticated records of governmental departments

Copies of books, papers, documents and records in any department of the commonwealth or of any city or town, authenticated by the attestation of the officer who has charge of the same, shall be competent evidence in all cases equally with the originals thereof; provided, that, except in the case of books, papers, documents and records of the department of public utilities or the department of telecommunications and cable in matters relating to common carriers, and of the registry of motor vehicles, the genuineness of the signature of such officer shall be attested by the secretary of the commonwealth under its seal or by the clerk of such city or town, as the case may be.

NOTE   Copy of Original Attestation. "Merely making a copy of the original attestation along with a copy of the underlying record does not serve the purpose of the attestation requirement, as the copied attestation no longer signifies that the official in question is vouching for the authenticity of the copy that has just been made. . . .

"The requirement that the responsible official be the one to attest to the authenticity of a copy is not some minor technicality." *Commonwealth v. Deramo*, 436 Mass. 40, 48 (2002) (further noting that "[w]here, as here, the parties and the judge have themselves compared an authenticated record with a copy, the copy may be admitted to the extent that it is identical to the authenticated document").

SECTION 77
Authenticated copies of records of banks and trust companies

Copies from the records, books and accounts of a trust company, cooperative bank, national bank or savings bank, doing business in the commonwealth, shall be competent evidence in all cases, equally with the originals thereof, if there is annexed to such copies an affidavit, taken before a clerk of a court of record or notary public, under the seal of such court or notary, stating that the affiant is the officer having charge of the original records, books and accounts, and that the copy is correct and is full so far as it relates to the subject matter therein mentioned.

SECTION 77A
Bank account statement together with legible copy of check; prima facie proof of payment

A statement of account of a bank showing payment of a check or other item, together with a legible copy of the check or other item, shall be competent evidence in all cases to constitute prima facie proof of the payment in the amount of the check or other item. For the purposes of this section, the terms "bank," "check" and "item" shall have the meanings set forth in Article 4 of chapter 106.

SECTION 78
Entry, writing or record made in regular course of business; impeachment

An entry in an account kept in a book or by a card system or by any other system of keeping accounts, or a writing or record, whether in the form of an entry in a book or otherwise, made as a memorandum or record of any act, transaction, occurrence or event, shall not be inadmissible in any civil or criminal proceeding as evidence of the facts therein stated because it is transcribed or because it is hearsay or self-serving, if the court finds that the entry, writing or record was made in good faith in the regular course of business and before the beginning of the civil or criminal proceeding aforesaid and that it was the regular course of such business to make such memorandum or record at the time of such act, transaction, occurrence or event or within a reasonable time thereafter. For the purposes hereof, the word "business", in addition to its ordinary meaning, shall include profession, occupation and calling of every kind. The court, in its discretion, before admitting such entry, writing or record in evidence, may, to such extent as it deems practicable or desirable, but to no greater extent than the law required before April eleventh, nineteen hundred and thirteen, require the party offering the same to produce and offer in evidence the original entry, writing, document or account or any other form which the entry, writing or record offered or the facts therein stated were transcribed or taken, and to call as his witness any person who made the entry, writing or record offered or the original or any other entry, writing, document or account from which the entry, writing or record offered or the facts therein stated were transcribed or taken, or who has personal knowledge of the facts stated in the entry, writing or record offered. When any such entry, writing or record is admitted, all other circumstances of the making thereof, including lack of personal knowledge by the entrant or maker, may be

shown to affect its weight and when such entry, writing or record is admitted in a criminal proceeding all questions of fact which must be determined by the court as the basis for the admissibility of the evidence involved shall be submitted to the jury, if a jury trial is had for its final determination.

NOTE   "The judge did not err in admitting the laboratory report that showed that Johnson's urine tested positive for cocaine. The chain of custody, although less than perfectly shown, was sufficiently established to justify admission of the evidence. The results of the laboratory test were properly admitted as a business record." *Johnson v. MBTA*, 418 Mass. 783, 786 (1994).

SECTION 79
Records and copies of records of hospitals and certain institutions; admissibility in evidence

Records kept by hospitals, dispensaries or clinics, and sanatoria under section seventy of chapter one hundred and eleven shall be admissible, and records which the court finds are required to be kept by the laws of any other state or territory, or the District of Columbia, or by the laws and regulations of the United States of America pertaining to the department of national defense and the veterans administration, by hospitals, dispensaries or clinics, and sanatoria similarly conducted or operated or which, being incorporated, offer treatment free of charge, may be admitted by the court, in its discretion, as evidence in the courts of the commonwealth so far as such records relate to the treatment and medical history of such cases and the court may, in its discretion, admit copies of such records, if certified by the persons in custody thereof to be true and complete; but nothing therein contained shall be admissible as evidence which has reference to the question of liability. Copies of photographic or microphotographic records so kept by hospitals, dispensaries or clinics, or sanatoria, when duly certified by the person in charge of the hospital, dispensary or clinic, or sanitorium, shall be admitted in evidence equally with the original photographs or microphotographs.

A record kept by any hospital, dispensary or clinic, or sanatorium under section seventy of chapter one hundred and eleven which is required to be produced in court by any party shall be certified by the affidavit of the person in custody thereof to be a true and complete record, and shall be delivered by such hospital, dispensary or clinic, or sanitorium to the clerk of such court, who shall keep the same in his custody until its production is called for at the trial or hearing by the party requiring the said record. Such record, so certified and delivered shall be deemed to be sufficiently identified to be admissible in evidence if admissible in all other respects. The party requiring the production of said record and, in the discretion of the court, any other party may examine said record in the custody of the clerk at any time before it is produced in court. The clerk upon completion of such trial or hearing shall notify such hospital that said record is no longer required and will be returned to the hospital by certified mail unless an authorized representative of the hospital calls for the same at the office of said clerk within seven days of said notice.

NOTE 1   Redaction/Sanitization of Medical Records. "The defendant also alleges that it was error for the Malden Hospital emergency room records to be 'sanitized' to remove the defendant's self-diagnosis. . . .

"The redaction appears to have been carried out in accordance with G.L. c. 233, § 79. The statute operates as an exception to the hearsay rule, permitting 'admission of the substantive content of hospital records because of the presumption of reliability which attaches to statements relating to treatment and medical history in these records.' *Bouchie v. Murray*, 376 Mass. 524, 527–28 (1978). 'Hence entries made in the regular course of the institution's operation from the personal knowledge of the recorder or from a compilation of the personal knowledge of those who have an obligation in the course of their employment to transmit that medical information to the recorder are admissible under the exception. Any other statements in the record which relate to treatment and medical history and which are offered for the truth of the matter contained therein must fall within some other exception to the hearsay rule in order to be admissible.' *Bouchie v. Murray*, 376 Mass. at 528–29. The excised statements thus are not admissible under G.L. c. 233, § 79, nor has the defendant referred us to any other exception to the hearsay rule that covers them. There was no error either on the part of the trial judge in excluding the hearsay portions of the records, or on the part of counsel in failing to take other steps to save the evidence."

Commonwealth v. Hartman, 404 Mass. 306, 316–17 (1989).

NOTE 2   Presumption of Reliability Defeated. "We conclude that the presumption of reliability that attaches to the content of hospital records is defeated where the record explicitly indicates that the results of a toxicology screen are 'presumptive based only on screening methods and have not been confirmed by a second independent chemical method.'" *Commonwealth v. Wall*, 469 Mass. 652, 668 (2014).

SECTION 79A
Certified copies of public and private records

Copies of public records, of records described in sections five, seven and sixteen, respectively, of chapter sixty-six, and of records of banks, trust companies, insurance companies and hospitals, whether or not such records or copies are made by the photographic or microphotographic process, shall, when duly certified by the person in charge thereof, be admitted in evidence equally with the originals.

SECTIONS 79B–C
Omitted

SECTION 79D
Photographic copies of newspaper in library; prints from photographic films

Copies of any newspaper, or part thereof made by the photographic or microphotographic process deposited in any public library or a library of any college or university located in the commonwealth, shall, when duly certified by the person in charge thereof, be admitted in evidence equally with the originals.

A print, whether enlarged or not, from any photographic film, including any photographic plate, microphotographic film, photostatic negative or reproduction of any original record, document, instrument, plan, book or paper destroyed, lost or for any reason unavailable after such film was taken, shall be admissible in evidence in all instances that the original record, document, instrument, plan, book or paper might have been admitted in evidence, and shall have the full force and effect of said original if it is proved that (a) such reproduction was made in the regular course of any business and that it was the regular course of any such business to make such reproductions; (b) said photographic film, microphotographic, photostatic or similar reproduction was taken in order to keep a permanent record of the original; and (c) the said original was subsequently destroyed, lost or is unavailable.

SECTION 79E
Reproductions of public or business records

If any business, institution, member of a profession or calling, or any department or agency of government, in the regular course of business or activity, has kept or recorded any memorandum, writing entry, print, representation or combination thereof of any act, transaction, occurrence or event, and in the regular course of business has caused any or all of the same to be recorded, copied or reproduced by any photographic, photostatic, microfilm, microcard, miniature photographic or other process which accurately reproduces or forms a durable medium for so reproducing the original, the original may be destroyed in the regular course of business unless its preservation is required by law. Such reproduction, when satisfactorily identified, shall be as admissible in evidence as the original itself in any judicial or administrative proceeding whether the original is in existence or not and an enlargement or facsimile of such reproduction shall be likewise admissible in evidence if the original reproduction is in existence and available for inspection under direction of the court. The introduction of a reproduced record, enlargement or facsimile, shall not preclude admission of the original.

SECTION 79F
Proof of public way

A certificate by the secretary of the public works commission in the case of a state highway, or the secretary of the metropolitan district commission in the case of a highway under the control of said commission, or by a city or town clerk in the case of a city or town way, that a particular way is a public way as a matter of record shall be admissible as prima facie evidence that such a way is a public way.

SECTION 79G
Medical and hospital records; evidence

In any proceeding commenced in any court, commission or agency, an itemized bill and reports, including hospital medical records, relating to medical, dental, hospital services, prescriptions, or orthopedic appliances rendered to or prescribed for a person injured, or any report of any examination of said injured person, including, but not limited to hospital medical records subscribed and sworn to under the penalties of perjury by the physician, dentist, authorized agent of a hospital or health maintenance organization rendering such services or by the pharmacist or retailer of orthopedic appliances, shall be admissible as evidence of the fair and reasonable charge for such services or the necessity of such services or treatments, the diagnosis of said physician or dentist, the prognosis of such physician or dentist, the opinion of such physician or dentist as to proximate cause of the condition so diagnosed, the opinion of such physician or dentist as to disability or incapacity, if any, proximately resulting from the condition so diagnosed; provided, however, that written notice of the intention to offer such bill or report as such evidence, together with a copy thereof, has been given to the opposing party or parties, or to his or their attorneys, by mailing the same by certified mail, return receipt requested, not less than ten days before the introduction of same into evidence, and that an affidavit of such notice and the return receipt is filed with the clerk of the court, agency or commission forthwith after said receipt has been returned. Nothing contained in this section shall be construed to limit the right of any party to the action to summon, at his own expense, such physician, dentist, pharmacist, retailer of orthopedic appliances or agent of such hospital or health maintenance organization or the records of such hospital or health maintenance organization for the purpose of cross examination with respect to such bill, record and report or to rebut the contents thereof, or for any other purpose, nor limit the right of any party to the action or proceeding to summon any other person to testify in respect to such bill, record or report or for any other purpose.

The words "physician" and "dentist" shall not include any person who is not licensed to practice as such under the laws of the jurisdiction within which such services were rendered, but shall include chiropodists, chiropractors, optometrist, osteopaths, physical therapists, podiatrists, psychologists and other medical personnel licensed to practice under the laws of the jurisdiction within which such services were rendered.

The word "hospital" shall mean any hospital required to keep records under section seventy of chapter one hundred and eleven, or which is in any way licensed or regulated by the laws of any other state, or by the laws and regulations of the United States of America, including hospitals of the Veterans Administration or similar type institutions, whether incorporated or not.

The words "health maintenance organization" shall have the same meaning as defined in section one of chapter one hundred and seventy-six G.

SECTIONS 79H–I
Omitted

SECTIONS 79J
Business records required to be produced in court; certification, admissibility and inspection; copies

A record kept by any business which is required to be produced in court by any party shall be certified by the affidavit of the person in custody thereof to be a true and complete record and shall be delivered by such business to the clerk of such court who shall keep the same in his custody until its production is called for at the trial or hearing by the party requiring the said record. Such record, so certified and delivered shall be deemed to be sufficiently identified to be admissible in evidence if admissible in all other respects. The party requiring the production of said record and, in the discretion of the court, any other party may examine said record in the custody of the clerk at any time before it is produced in court. The clerk upon completion of such trial or hearing shall notify such business that said record is no longer required and will be returned by mail unless an authorized representative of the business calls for the same at the office of said clerk within seven days of said notice.

A copy of such record made by the photographic process may be delivered to the clerk of such court in place of the original and, if certified as hereinbefore provided, shall be admitted in evidence equally with the original.

SECTION 79K
Duplicate of computer data file or program file; admissibility

A duplicate of a computer data file or program file shall be admissible in evidence as the original itself unless (1) a genuine question is raised as to the authenticity of the original or (2) in the circumstances it would be unfair to admit the duplicate in lieu of the original.

For the purposes of this section, if data is stored in a computer or similar device, any printout or other output readable by sight, shown to reflect the data accurately, shall be an original.

A "duplicate of a computer data file or program file" shall mean a file produced by the same impression as the original, or from the same matrix, or by mechanical or electronic recording, in the normal way such a duplicate is produced on a computer, or by other equivalent techniques that accurately reproduce the original.

STENOGRAPHIC TRANSCRIPTS

SECTION 80
Transcripts from stenographic notes

Transcripts from stenographic notes duly taken under authority of law in any court proceeding by a stenographer duly appointed for the purpose and sworn, when verified by the certificate of such stenographer, shall be admissible as evidence of testimony given whenever proof of such testimony is otherwise competent.

NOTE **Related Statute.** Stenographer employed by defendant; admissibility of transcript. G.L. c. 221, § 91B.

SECTION 81
Criminal proceedings; out-of-court statements describing sexual contact; admissibility

(a) An out-of-court statement of a child under the age of ten describing an act of sexual contact performed on or with the child, the circumstances under which it occurred, or which identifies the perpetrator shall be admissible as substantive evidence in any criminal proceeding; provided, however, that the statement is offered as evidence of a material fact and is more probative on the point for which it is offered than any other evidence which the proponent can procure through reasonable efforts; the person to whom the statement was made or who heard the child make the statement testifies; the judge finds pursuant to subsection (b) that the child is unavailable as a witness: and the judge finds pursuant to subsection (c) that the statement is reliable.

(b) The proponent of such statement shall demonstrate a diligent and good faith effort to produce the child and shall bear the burden of showing unavailability. A finding of unavailability shall be supported by specific findings on the record, describing facts with particularity, demonstrating that:

(1) the child is unable to be present or to testify because of death or physical or mental illness or infirmity; or

(2) by a ruling of the court, the child is exempt on the ground of privilege from testifying concerning the subject matter of such statement; or

(3) the child testifies to a lack of memory of the subject matter of such statement; or

(4) the child is absent from the hearing and the proponent of such statement has been unable to procure the attendance of the child by process or by other reasonable means; or

(5) the court finds, based upon expert testimony from a treating psychiatrist, psychologist, or clinician, that testifying would be likely to cause severe psychological or emotional trauma to the child; or

(6) the child is not competent to testify.

(c) If a finding of unavailability is made, the out-of-court statement shall be admitted if the judge further finds: (1) after holding a separate hearing, that such statement was made under oath, that it was accurately recorded and preserved, and there was sufficient opportunity to cross-examine; or (2) after holding a separate hearing and, where practicable and where not inconsistent with the best interests of the child, meeting with the child, that such statement was made under circumstances inherently demonstrating a special guarantee or reliability.

For the purposes of finding circumstances demonstrating reliability pursuant to clause (2) of subsection (c), a judge may consider whether the relator documented the child witness's statement, and shall consider the following factors:

(i) the clarity of the statement, meaning, the child's capacity to observe, remember, and give expression to that which such child has seen, heard, or experienced; provided, however, that a finding under this clause shall be supported by expert testimony from a treating psychiatrist, psychologist, or clinician;

(ii) the time, content and circumstances or the statement;

(iii) the child's sincerity and ability to appreciate the consequences of such statement.

(d) An out-of-court statement which is admissible by common law or by statute shall remain admissible notwithstanding the provisions of this section.

NOTE 1   Generally. "We believe that, if a child witness's out-of-court statements are to be admitted substantively, there must be other evidence, independently admitted, that corroborates those hearsay statements." *Commonwealth v. Colin C., a juvenile,* 419 Mass. 54, 62 (1994).

NOTE 2   Procedure. In addition to the statutory procedures, to which a judge "must strictly adhere", (1) "the Commonwealth must give prior notice to the criminal defendant that it will seek to use such hearsay statements"; (2) "the Commonwealth must show, by more than a mere preponderance of evidence, a compelling need for use of such a procedure"; (3) "any separate hearing regarding the reliability of a child witness's out-of-court statement be on the record, and that the judge's determination that the child's statement is reliable be supported by specific findings on the record. Where possible without causing severe emotional trauma to the child witness, the defendant, and defense counsel should be given the opportunity to be present at the hearing. Expert testimony may aid the trial judge in determining whether the defendant's and defense counsel's presence at the hearing would severely traumatize the child witness."; and (4) "there must be other independently admitted evidence that corroborates those out-of-court statements." *Commonwealth v. Colin C., a juvenile,* 419 Mass. at 64–66.

NOTE 3   Related Statutes. G.L. c. 233, §§ 82 and 83. Section 81 deals with criminal proceedings; section 82 with civil proceedings; section 83 with care and protection proceedings. *See Care and Prot. of Rebecca,* 419 Mass. 67 (1994).

Chapter 234. Juries

(Repealed by 2016 Mass. Acts c. 36, effective May 10, 2016.)

Chapter 234A. Office of Jury Commissioner

Section

3	Juror service
4	Disqualification from juror service
22	Confidential juror questionnaire included with summons
23	Use of juror questionnaire during voir dire
27A	Questioning of summoned juror
30A	Talesmen
32	Wilful misrepresentations in juror questionnaire
39	Deferment or advancement of, or excuse from, juror service; term limitations; dismissal or discharge of juror
42	Enforcement of chapter
43	Delinquency notice
44	Criminal complaint for delinquent juror
60	Employer liability for failure to pay juror-employee
61	Violation of Sec. 60; harassment, etc. of employee
67A	Examination of jurors
67B	Peremptory challenges
67C	Certain interests not to disqualify
67D	Voir dire procedures
68	Additional jurors impanelled; alternate jurors
68A	Foreperson
68B	Number of jurors required to render verdict; instructions on sufficient numbers
68C	Failure of jury to agree
69A	View by jury
71	Fraud in processing or selection of jurors or prospective jurors
73	Challenge of array
74	Irregularities or defects causing mistrial or verdict to be set aside
74A	Gratuities

SECTION 3
Juror service

Juror service in the participating counties shall be a duty which every person who qualifies under this chapter shall perform when selected. All persons selected for juror service on grand and trial juries shall be selected at random from the population of the judicial district in which they reside. All persons shall have equal opportunity to be considered for juror service. All persons shall serve as jurors when selected and summoned for that purpose except as hereinafter provided. No person shall be exempted or excluded from serving as a grand or trial juror because of race, color, religion, sex, national origin, economic status, or occupation. Physically handicapped persons shall serve except where the court finds such service is not feasible. The court shall strictly enforce the provisions of this section.

SECTION 4
Disqualification from juror service

Any citizen of the United States who is a resident of the judicial district or who lives within the judicial district more than fifty per cent of the time, whether or not he is registered to vote in any state or federal election, shall be qualified to serve as a grand or trial juror in such judicial district unless one of the following grounds for disqualification applies:

1. Such person is under the age of eighteen years.

2. Such person is seventy years of age or older and indicates on the juror confirmation form an election not to perform juror service.

3. Such person is not able to speak and understand the English language.

4. Such person is incapable, by reason of a physical or mental disability, of rendering satisfactory juror service. Any

person claiming this disqualification must submit a letter from a registered physician stating the nature of the disability and the physician's opinion that such disability prevents the person from rendering satisfactory juror service. In reaching such opinion, the physician shall apply the following guideline: a person shall be capable of rendering satisfactory juror service if such person is able to perform a sedentary job requiring close attention for six hours per day, with short work breaks in the morning and afternoon sessions, for three consecutive business days. If, according to the aforementioned guideline, a person shall be permanently incapable of rendering satisfactory jury service during the person's lifetime, the person claiming such permanent disqualification shall submit a letter from a registered physician stating the nature of the disability and the physician's opinion that such disability will permanently prevent the person from rendering satisfactory jury service. If the jury commissioner determines that the person is permanently disabled, then the person shall be considered permanently ineligible for jury service, and the person's name and physician's letter shall be placed on record with the office of jury commissioner. The jury commissioner shall make a decision on such matter promptly upon receipt of the aforementioned letter. For the purposes of this section, "physician" shall include any accredited Christian Science practitioner.

5. Such person is solely responsible for the daily care of a permanently disabled person living in the same household and the performance of juror service would cause a substantial risk of injury to the health of the disabled person. Any person claiming this disqualification must submit a letter from a registered physician stating the name, address, and age of the disabled person, the nature of the daily care provided by the prospective juror, and the physician's opinion that the performance of juror service would cause a substantial risk of injury to the health of the disabled person. Any person who is regularly employed at a location other than that of his household shall not be entitled to this disqualification.

6. Such person is outside the judicial district and does not intend to return to the judicial district at any time during the following year.

7. Such person has been convicted of a felony within the past seven years or is a defendant in pending felony case or is in the custody of a correctional institution.

8. Such person has served as a grand or trial juror in any state or federal court within the previous three years or the person is currently scheduled to perform such service. Any person claiming this disqualification must submit a letter or certificate from the appropriate clerk of court or jury commissioner verifying such prior or pending juror service unless such service was performed or is pending in a court of the commonwealth.

SECTION 22
Confidential juror questionnaire included with summons

Enclosed with the juror summons shall be a confidential juror questionnaire. The information elicited by the questionnaire shall be such information as is ordinarily raised in *voir dire* examinations of jurors, including the juror's name, sex, age, residence, marital status, number and ages of children, education level, occupation, employment address, spouse's occupation, spouse's employment address, previous service as a juror, present or past involvement as a party to civil or criminal litigation, relationship to a police or law enforcement officer, and such other information as the jury commissioner deems appropriate. The questionnaire shall contain the prospective juror's declaration that the information supplied in the completed questionnaire is true to the best of his knowledge and that he understands that a wilful misrepresentation of a material fact therein is a crime, which, upon conviction, may be punished by a fine of not more than two thousand dollars. Immediately below such declaration, the questionnaire shall contain a place for the signature of the juror. A notice of the confidentiality of the completed questionnaire shall appear prominently on the face of the questionnaire.

SECTION 23
Use of juror questionnaire during voir dire

Unless the court orders otherwise, the clerk of court or an assistant clerk shall provide copies of the appropriate completed questionnaires to the trial judge and counsel for use during *voir dire*. Except for disclosures made during *voir dire* or unless the court orders otherwise, the information inserted by jurors in the questionnaires shall be held in confidence by the court, the clerk or assistant clerk, the parties, trial counsel, and their authorized agents. Upon completion of *voir dire*, the parties and their counsel shall return all copies of the completed questionnaire to the clerk or the assistant clerk. The clerk of court shall retain in a secure place all original completed questionnaires for each impanelled jury and alternate jurors until final disposition of the case. These completed questionnaires shall not constitute a public record. All copies of juror questionnaire, other than the copy retained by the trial judge and the original retained by the clerk, shall be destroyed as soon as practicable after the completion of *voir dire*.

SECTION 27A
Questioning of summoned juror
(Added by 2016 Mass. Acts c. 36, § 2, effective May 10, 2016.)

After a summons has been received by a juror, no person shall, except as otherwise provided by law, question any juror so summoned for the purpose of obtaining information as to the juror's background in connection with the juror's jury duty.

SECTION 30A
Talesmen
(Added by 2016 Mass. Acts c. 36, § 3, effective May 10, 2016.)

If, by challenge or otherwise, a sufficient number of jurors duly drawn and summoned cannot be obtained for the trial of a case, the court shall cause jurors to be returned from the bystanders or from the county at large, to complete the panel, if there are on the jury not fewer than 7 of the jurors who were originally drawn and summoned.

Before causing additional jurors to be returned for service the jury pool officer shall file an affidavit with the court stating that more than the usual number of jurors are required on the case and that the jury pool has been exhausted. The judge sitting on the case shall make a finding as to the accuracy of said affidavit prior to the return of additional jurors.

The jurors from the bystanders shall be returned by the sheriff or the sheriff's deputy or by a disinterested person appointed by the court, and shall be qualified and liable to be drawn as jurors.

SECTION 32
Wilful misrepresentations in juror questionnaire

Any juror or other person who wilfully misrepresents a material fact in the confidential questionnaire for the purpose of either avoiding or securing service as a grand or trial juror shall be guilty of a crime, and, upon conviction, may be punished by a fine of not more than two thousand dollars.

SECTION 39
Deferment or advancement of, or excuse from, juror service; term limitations; dismissal or discharge of juror

The court or the office of jury commissioner shall have authority to defer or advance any term of grand or trial juror service upon a finding of hardship, inconvenience, or public necessity provided the juror recognizes his firm obligation to perform juror service on the new date. The court shall have authority to excuse a grand juror from juror service, in part or in full, upon a finding of hardship, inconvenience, or public necessity, taking into consideration the length of grand juror service. The court shall have authority to excuse a trial juror from juror service, in part or in full, upon a finding of extreme hardship; the court shall exercise this authority strictly. Notwithstanding the fact that a juror has been summoned as a grand or trial juror, with or without right of postponement of service, the court shall have the discretionary authority to require the juror to serve either as a grand or trial juror, immediately or at a future date, at the original court location or at a different court location. The court may impose reasonable conditions and limitations, including appropriate time limitations, upon a term of juror service. It shall be the policy of this chapter that every trial juror shall be prepared to serve three trial days; the court shall not grant term limitations of less than three trial days except upon a finding that extreme hardship would be imposed upon the juror in the absence of such limitation. The court shall have the discretionary authority to dismiss a juror at any time in the best interests of justice. The court shall have authority to excuse and discharge an impanelled juror prior to jury deliberations after a hearing upon a finding of extreme hardship. The court shall have authority to excuse and discharge a juror participating in jury deliberations after a hearing only upon a finding of an emergency or other compelling reason. The court shall have authority to discharge an impanelled juror who has not appeared for juror service upon a finding that there is a strong likelihood that an unreasonable delay in the trial would occur if the court were to await the appearance of the juror. At any time during the trial, the court shall discharge any juror whose term limitation has expired upon the demand of the juror except where the court finds unusual circumstances; such discharge shall not be a ground for mistrial or objection by any party. The court may exercise any authority granted in this section at any time before or during a juror's term of service.

NOTE   Compelling Reason for Excusing. Supreme Judicial Court found "compelling reason" for excusing juror where "juror's son was housed at the same institution as the defendant and . . . 'pressure' could be brought against the juror through her son [and also due to fact] that a palpable conflict existed in that the juror's son was arrested, held in jail, and awaiting prosecution by the same district attorney's office prosecuting the defendant." *Commonwealth v. Garrey*, 436 Mass. 422, 431 n.5 (2002).

SECTION 42
Enforcement of chapter

The court shall take whatever actions are appropriate to enforce the provisions of this chapter. Upon a finding by the court that a juror will not appear to perform or complete juror service or in response to the court's order, the court may issue a warrant for the arrest of the juror or may take such other appropriate actions as are likely to compel the juror to appear before the court. Any grand or trial juror who fails to appear for juror service or who fails to perform any condition of his juror service shall be guilty of a crime, and upon conviction thereof, may be punished by a fine of not more than two thousand dollars.

SECTION 43
Delinquency notice

The office of jury commissioner may send a delinquency notice by certified or first-class mail or by delivery by a sheriff or constable to any grand or trial juror who has failed to appear for juror service based upon the records in the office of jury commissioner; provided, however, that the purpose of the delinquency notice shall be only to notify the juror of his delinquency status and to rectify the problem by appropriate means. The office of jury commissioner shall have discretionary authority to resolve problems with delinquent jurors or with jurors appearing to be delinquent in accordance with guidelines approved by the committee.

SECTION 44
Criminal complaint for delinquent juror

The office of jury commissioner may prepare an application for the issuance of a criminal complaint against any grand or trial juror who has not been removed from delinquency status by the office of jury commissioner within thirty days after the date of a delinquency notice sent to such juror. The application shall aver that the named person was duly selected and summoned to perform trial or grand juror service at a specified location on a specified date and that such person has failed to appear for jury service without justifiable excuse in violation of section forty-two. The information provided in the application shall be based upon the records of the office of jury commissioner. The application shall contain the name, address, and identification number of the juror and a summary of all official transactions between the juror and the office of jury commissioner that have occurred as of the date of the application. At the bottom of the application, there shall be a certificate signed by the legal counsel for the office of jury commissioner declaring that the information provided in the application is true and complete to the best of his knowledge and belief. The application shall contain such further information as deemed appropriate by the jury commissioner with the approval of the jury management advisory committee. The application may be submitted by mail or personal delivery to any superior or district court having criminal jurisdiction over such juror. The office of jury commissioner shall send a copy of this application to the juror by first-class or certified mail. The legal counsel or his delegate shall be authorized to represent the jury commissioner and the office of jury commissioner in all judicial proceedings arising out of any application for the issuance of a criminal complaint under this section or otherwise.

SECTION 60
Employer liability for failure to pay juror-employee

Any employer who fails to compensate a juror-employee under the applicable provisions of this chapter and who has not been excused from such duty or compensation shall be liable to the juror-employee in tort. Upon the expiration of thirty days after the tender of the juror service certificate to the employer, the juror may commence a civil action in any superior or district court having jurisdiction over the parties. Extreme financial hardship on the employer shall not be a defense to this action. The court may award treble damages and reasonable attorney fees to the juror upon a finding of wilful conduct by the employer.

SECTION 61
Violation of Sec. 60; harassment, etc. of employee

Any willful violation of section sixty of this chapter by an employer shall also constitute a violation of this section. A juror seeking a civil remedy against an employer shall have an election to proceed either under section sixty or under this section. An employer shall not deprive a juror-employee of his employment or any incidents or benefits thereof, nor shall an employer harass, threaten, or coerce an employee because the employee has received a juror summons, responds thereto, performs any obligation or election of juror service as a grand or trial juror, or exercises any right under any section of this chapter. An employer shall not impose compulsory work assignments upon any juror-employee nor shall the employer do any other intentional act which will substantially interfere with the availability, effectiveness, attentiveness, or peace of mind of the employee during the performance of his juror service. Any employer who violates this section shall be guilty of a crime and, upon conviction, may be punished by a fine of not more than five thousand dollars. Any employer who violates this section also shall be liable in tort to the juror-employee. The juror-employee may commence a civil action in the superior court for such damages and injunctive relief as may be appropriate. The court may award treble damages and reasonable attorney's fees to the juror upon a finding of willful conduct by the employer. The legal counsel for the office of jury commissioner may submit an application for the issuance of a criminal complaint in any court of competent jurisdiction against an employer who has violated this section or section sixty.

SECTION 67A
Examination of jurors
(Added by 2016 Mass. Acts c. 36, § 4, effective May 10, 2016.)

Upon motion of either party, the court shall, or the parties or their attorneys may under the direction of the court, examine on oath a person who is called as a juror, to learn whether the juror related to either party or has any interest in the case, or has expressed or formed an opinion, or is sensible of any bias or prejudice. The objecting party may introduce other competent evidence in support of the objection. If the court finds that the juror does not stand indifferent in the case, another juror shall be called in. In a criminal case such examination shall include questions designed to learn whether such juror understands that a defendant is presumed innocent until proven guilty, that the commonwealth has the burden of proving guilt beyond a reasonable doubt, and that the defendant need not present evidence on the defendant's behalf. If the court finds that such juror does not so understand, another juror shall be called in.

To determine whether a juror stands indifferent in the case, if it appears that, as a result of the impact of considerations which may cause a decision to be made in whole or in part upon issues extraneous to the case, including, but not limited to, community attitudes, possible exposure to potentially prejudicial material or possible preconceived opinions toward the credibility of certain classes of persons, the juror may not stand indifferent, the court shall, or the parties or their attorneys may, with the permission and under the direction of the court, examine the juror specifically with respect to such considerations, attitudes, exposure, opinions or any other matters which may cause a decision to be made in whole or in part upon issues extraneous to the issues in the case. Such examination may include a brief statement of the facts of the case, to the extent the facts are appropriate and relevant to the issue of such examination and shall be conducted individually and outside the presence of other persons about to be called as jurors or already called.

SECTION 67B
Peremptory challenges
(Added by 2016 Mass. Acts c. 36, § 4, effective May 10, 2016.)

In a civil case each party shall be entitled to 4 peremptory challenges. Such challenges shall be made before the commencement of the trial and may be made after it has been determined that a person called to serve as a juror stands indifferent in the case.

SECTION 67C
Certain interests not to disqualify
(Added by 2016 Mass. Acts c. 36, § 4, effective May 10, 2016.)

In indictments and penal actions for the recovery of a forfeiture, it shall not be a challenge for cause to a juror that the juror is liable to pay taxes in a county, city or town which may be benefited by such recovery.

SECTION 67D
Voir dire procedures
(Added by 2016 Mass. Acts c. 36, § 4, effective May 10, 2016.)

Notwithstanding section 67A, the following procedures shall govern in all criminal and civil superior court jury trials:

(1) In addition to whatever jury voir dire of the jury venire is conducted by the court, the court shall permit, upon the request of any party's attorney or a self-represented party, the party's attorney or self-represented party to conduct an oral examination of the prospective jurors at the discretion of the court.

(2) The court may impose reasonable limitations upon the questions and the time allowed during such examination, including, but not limited to, requiring pre-approval of the questions.

(3) In criminal cases involving multiple defendants, the commonwealth shall be entitled to the same amount of time as that to which all defendants together are entitled.

(4) The court may promulgate rules to implement this section, including, but not limited to, providing consistent policies, practices and procedures relating to the process of jury voir dire.

SECTION 68
Additional jurors impanelled; alternate jurors

In every twelve-person jury case, the court shall impanel at least two additional jurors. In every six-person jury case, the court shall impanel at least one additional juror. Alternate jurors shall not be identified until immediately prior to jury deliberations in accordance with the following. If, at the time of the submission of the case by the court to the jury for its deliberations upon a verdict, more than the number of jurors required for deliberation are available, the court shall direct the clerk to place the names of all of the available jurors except the foreperson into a box or drum and to select at random the names of the appropriate number of jurors necessary to reduce the jury to the proper number of members required for deliberation in the particular case. The jurors so selected shall not be discharged, but shall be known as alternate jurors. The alternate jurors shall be kept separate from the jury in some convenient location, subject to the same rules and procedures as govern the jury during its deliberations, until the jury has agreed upon a verdict or has been otherwise discharged. If at any time after the submission of the case by the court to the jury for its deliberation upon a verdict, a juror is discharged by the court for any reason, the court shall direct the clerk to place all of the names of the alternate jurors in a box or drum and to select at random the name of an alternate juror. The alternate juror so selected shall take the place of the discharged juror on the jury. The jury, so constituted, shall begin its deliberations anew with full authority to render a verdict in the case. The court shall have jurisdiction to receive the verdict of the jury, as constituted under the provisions of this section, and shall have jurisdiction and full authority to render judgment in the case. Whenever it is appropriate for the court to direct a verdict, the court may do so without first reducing the number of jurors to the proper number required for deliberation in the case. Upon a finding of cause, the trial judge may impanel a lesser number of jurors than specified under this section. Nothing in this section shall prevent the court from rendering a valid judgment based upon a verdict rendered by fewer jurors than required under this section where all parties have by stipulation agreed to this procedure. Nothing in this section shall prevent the court from entering a valid judgment based upon a verdict rendered by fewer or more jurors than required under this section or based upon procedures other than that specified in this section where all parties have by stipulation agreed to such a number of jurors or to such procedures.

SECTION 68A
Foreperson
(Added by 2016 Mass. Acts c. 36, § 5, effective May 10, 2016.)

After a jury has been impanelled and sworn, the court shall appoint a foreperson.

SECTION 68B
Number of jurors required to render verdict; instructions on sufficient numbers
(Added by 2016 Mass. Acts c. 36, § 5, effective May 10, 2016.)

In any civil action the jury shall be instructed that the agreement of 5/6 of its members shall be sufficient to render any special or general verdict.

SECTION 68C
Failure of jury to agree
(Added by 2016 Mass. Acts c. 36, § 5, effective May 10, 2016.)

If a jury, after due and thorough deliberation, returns to court without having agreed on a verdict, the court may state anew the evidence or any part of the evidence, explain to them anew the law applicable to the case and send them out for further deliberation; but if they return a second time without having agreed on a verdict, they shall not be sent out again without their own consent, unless they ask from the court some further explanation of the law.

SECTION 69A
View by jury
(Added by 2016 Mass. Acts c. 36, § 6, effective May 10, 2016.)

The court may, upon motion, allow the jury in a civil case to view the premises or place in question or any property, matter or thing relative to the case if the party making the motion advances an amount sufficient to defray the expenses of the jury and the officers who attend them in taking the view, which shall be taxed as costs, if the party who advanced them prevails. The court may order a view by a jury impanelled to try a criminal case.

SECTION 71
Fraud in processing or selection of jurors or prospective jurors

Whoever is guilty of fraud in the processing or selection of jurors or prospective jurors either by causing any name to be inserted into any list wrongfully, or by causing any name to be deleted from any list wrongfully, including wrongful data entry or the altering of any data processing machine or any set of instructions or programs which control data processing equipment for such wrongful purpose, shall have committed the crime of jury tampering, and, upon conviction thereof, may be punished by a fine of not more than ten thousand dollars, or imprisonment for not more than two years, or both. This section shall not limit any other provisions of law concerning the crime of jury tampering.

SECTION 73
Challenge of array

A party may challenge the composition of the juror pool by a motion for appropriate relief. This challenge shall be made and decided before any individual juror is examined, unless the court orders otherwise. The challenge shall be in writing, supported by affidavit, and shall specify the facts and demographic data constituting the ground of the challenge. The challenge shall be tried by the court and may, within the discretion of the court, be decided on the basis of the affidavits filed with the challenge. Upon the trial of such a challenge, witnesses may be examined on oath by the court and may be so examined by either party. If the challenge is sustained, the court shall discharge the entire juror pool.

SECTION 74
Irregularities or defects causing mistrial or verdict to be set aside

Any irregularity in compiling any list of jurors or prospective jurors; or any irregularity in qualifying, selecting, summoning, confirming, postponing, excusing, cancelling, instructing, impanelling, challenging, discharging, or managing jurors; or any irregularity in limiting any term of juror service, in length or other incident of the term; or the fact that a juror shall be found to be not qualified under section four of this chapter; or any defect in any procedure performed under this chapter shall not be sufficient to cause a mistrial or to set aside a verdict unless objection to such irregularity or defect has been made as soon as possible after its discovery or after it should have been discovered and unless the objecting party has been specially injured or prejudiced thereby.

SECTION 74A
Gratuities
(Added by 2016 Mass. Acts c. 36, § 7, effective May 10, 2016.)

If either party to a case at the sitting at which a verdict is returned, either before or after the trial, gives to any of the jurors who try the case anything by way of treat or gratuity, the court may, upon motion of the adverse party, set aside the verdict and award a new trial.

Chapter 258B. Rights of Victims and Witnesses of Crime

Section
1   Definitions
2   Eligibility of victim for services
3   Rights afforded victims, witnesses or family members
4   Victim and witness assistance board
5   Programs created and maintained by district attorney; services
6   Program plan
7   Interagency cooperation
8   Assessments imposed by court
9   Deposit of assessments
10   Construction
11   Duration of rights and duties
12   Assurance of rights; assistance by criminal justice agencies
13   Failure to provide rights, privileges, or notice to victim; no grounds for appeal of or objection to conviction

SECTION 1
Definitions

The following words as used in this chapter shall have the following meanings, unless the context otherwise requires:—

"Board", the victim and witness assistance board as established in section four;

"Court", a forum established under the General Laws for the adjudication of criminal and delinquency complaints, indictments and civil motor vehicle infractions.

"Crime", an act committed in the commonwealth which would constitute a crime if committed by a competent adult including any act which may result in an adjudication of delinquency;

"Disposition", the sentencing or determination of penalty or punishment to be imposed upon a person convicted of a crime or found delinquent or against whom a finding of sufficient facts for conviction or finding of delinquency is made;

"Family member", a spouse, child, stepchild, sibling, parent, stepparent, dependent, as defined in section one of chapter two hundred and fifty-eight C, or legal guardian of a victim, unless such family member has been charged in relation to the crime against the victim;

"Prosecutor", the attorney general, assistant attorneys general, district attorney, assistant district attorneys, police prosecutors, other attorneys specially appointed to aid in the prosecution of a case, law students approved for practice pursuant to and acting as authorized by the rules of the supreme judicial court, or any other person acting on behalf of the commonwealth, including victim-witness advocates;

"Restitution", money or services which a court orders a defendant to pay or render to a victim as part of the disposition;

"Victim", any natural person who suffers direct or threatened physical, emotional or financial harm as the result of the commission or attempted commission of a crime or delinquency offense, as demonstrated by the issuance of a complaint or indictment, the family members of such person if the person is a minor, incompetent or deceased, and, for relevant provisions of this chapter, a person who is the subject of a case reported to a prosecutor pursuant to section eighteen of chapter nineteen A, sections five and nine of chapter nineteen C, and section fifty-one B of chapter one hundred and nineteen, and the family members of such person if the person is a minor, incompetent or deceased;

"Victim-witness advocate", an individual employed by a prosecutor, the board, or other criminal justice agency to provide necessary and essential services in carrying out policies and procedures under this chapter;

"Witness", any person who has been or is expected to be summoned to testify for the prosecution whether or not any action or proceeding has yet been commenced.

SECTION 2
Eligibility of victim for services

Prosecutors shall not be precluded from providing, subject to appropriation, services under this chapter to any natural person or family member of such natural person who suffers direct or threatened physical, emotional or financial harm as the result of the commission or attempted commission of a crime or delinquency offense in which complaints or indictments have not been issued.

SECTION 3
Rights afforded victims, witnesses or family members
(Amended by 2012 Mass. Acts c. 139, § 138, effective July 1, 2012.)

To provide victims a meaningful role in the criminal justice system, victims and witnesses of crime, or in the event the victim is deceased, the family members of the victim, shall be afforded the following basic and fundamental rights, to the greatest extent possible and subject to appropriation and to available resources, with priority for services to be provided to victims of crimes against the person and crimes where physical injury to a person results:

(a) for victims, to be informed by the prosecutor about the victim's rights in the criminal process, including but not limited to the rights provided under this chapter. At the beginning of the criminal justice process, the prosecutor shall provide an explanation to the victim of how a case progresses through the criminal justice system, what the victim's role is in the process, what the system may expect from the victim, why the system requires this, and, if the victim requests, the prosecutor shall periodically apprise the victim of significant developments in the case;

(b) for victims and family members, to be present at all court proceedings related to the offense committed against the victim, unless the victim or family member is to testify and the court determines that the person's testimony would be materially affected by hearing other testimony at trial and orders the person to be excluded from the courtroom during certain other testimony;

(c) for victims and witnesses, to be notified by the prosecutor, in a timely manner, when a court proceeding to which they have been summoned will not go on as scheduled, provided that such changes are known in advance. In order to notify victims and witnesses, a form shall be provided to them by the prosecutor for the purpose of maintaining a current telephone number and address. The victim or witness shall thereafter maintain with the prosecutor a current telephone number and address;

(d) for victims and witnesses, to be provided with information by the prosecutor as to the level of protection available and to receive protection from the local law enforcement agencies from harm and threats of harm arising out of their cooperation with law enforcement and prosecution efforts;

(e) for victims, to be informed by the prosecutor of financial assistance and other social services available to victims, including information relative to applying for such assistance or services;

(f) for victims and witnesses, to a prompt disposition of the case in which they are involved as a victim or a witness;

(g) for victims, to confer with the prosecutor before the commencement of the trial, before any hearing on motions by the defense to obtain psychiatric or other confidential records, and before the filing of a nolle prosequi or other act by the commonwealth terminating the prosecution or before the submission of the commonwealth's proposed sentence recommendation to the court. The prosecutor shall inform the court of the victim's position, if known, regarding the prosecutor's sentence recommendation. The right of the victim to confer with the prosecutor does not include the authority to direct the prosecution of the case;

(h) for victims and witnesses, to be informed of the right to request confidentiality in the criminal justice system. Upon the court's approval of such request, no law enforcement agency, prosecutor, defense counsel, or parole, probation or corrections official may disclose or state in open court, except among themselves, the residential address, telephone number, or place of employment or school of the victim, a victim's family member, or a witness, except as otherwise ordered by the court. The court may enter such other orders or conditions to maintain limited disclosure of the information as it deems appropriate to protect the privacy and safety of victims, victims' family members and witnesses;

(i) for victims, family members and witnesses, to be provided, by the court as provided in section 17 of chapter 211B, with a secure waiting area or room which is separate from the waiting area of the defendant or the defendant's family, friends, attorneys or witnesses and separate from the district attorney's office; provided, however, that the court shall designate a waiting area at each courthouse; and provided further, that designation of those areas shall be made in accordance with the implementation plan developed by the task force;

(j) for victims and witnesses, to be informed by the court and the prosecutor of procedures to be followed in order to apply for and receive any witness fee to which they are entitled;

(k) for victims and witnesses, to be provided, where appropriate, with employer and creditor intercession services by the prosecutor to seek employer cooperation in minimizing employees' loss of pay and other benefits resulting from their participation in the criminal justice process, and to seek consideration from creditors if the victim is unable, temporarily, to continue payments;

(l) for victims or witnesses who have received a subpoena to testify, to be free from discharge or penalty or threat of discharge or penalty by his employer by reason of his attendance as a witness at a criminal proceeding. A victim or witness who notifies his employer of his subpoena to appear as a witness prior to his attendance, shall not on account of his absence from employment by reason of such witness service be subject to discharge or penalty by his employer. Any employer or agent of said employer who discharges or disciplines or continues to threaten to discharge or discipline a victim or witness because that victim or witness is subpoenaed to attend court for the purpose of giving testimony may be subject to the sanctions stated in section fourteen A of chapter two hundred and sixty-eight;

(m) for victims and witnesses, to be informed of the right to submit to or decline an interview by defense counsel or anyone acting on the defendant's behalf, except when responding to lawful process, and, if the victim or witness decides to submit to an interview, the right to impose reasonable conditions on the conduct of the interview;

(n) for victims, to confer with the probation officer prior to the filing of the full presentence report. If the victim is not available or declines to confer, the probation officer shall record that information in the report. If the probation officer is not able to confer with the victim or the victim declines to confer, the probation officer shall note in the full presentence report the reason why the probation officer did not make contact with the victim;

(o) for victims, to request that restitution be an element of the final disposition of a case and to obtain assistance from the prosecutor in the documentation of the victim's losses. If restitution is ordered as part of a case disposition, the victim has the right to receive from the probation department a copy of the schedule of restitution payments and the name and telephone number of the probation officer or other official who is responsible for supervising the defendant's payments. If the offender seeks to modify the restitution order, the offender's supervising probation officer shall provide notice to the victim and the victim shall have the right to be heard at any hearing relative to the proposed modification.

(p) for victims, to be heard through an oral and written victim impact statement at sentencing or the disposition of the case against the defendant about the effects of the crime on the victim and as to a recommended sentence, pursuant to section four B of chapter two hundred and seventy-nine, and to be heard at any other time deemed appropriate by the court. The victim also has a right to submit the victim impact statement to the parole board for inclusion in its records regarding the perpetrator of the crime;

(q) for victims, to be informed by the prosecutor of the final disposition of the case, including, where applicable, an explanation of the type of sentence imposed by the court and a copy of the court order setting forth the conditions of probation or other supervised or unsupervised release within thirty days of establishing the conditions, with the name and telephone number of the probation officer, if any, assigned to the defendant;

(r) for victims, to have any personal property that was stolen or taken for evidentiary purposes, except contraband, property subject to evidentiary analysis, and property the ownership of which is disputed, returned by the court, the prosecutor or law enforcement agencies within ten days of its taking or recovery if it is not needed for law enforcement or prosecution purposes or as expeditiously as possible when said property is no longer needed for law enforcement or prosecution purposes;

(s) for victims, to be informed by the parole board of information regarding the defendant's parole eligibility and status in the criminal justice system;

(t) for victims, to be informed in advance by the appropriate custodial authority whenever the defendant receives a temporary, provisional or final release from custody, whenever a defendant is moved from a secure facility to a less-secure facility, and whenever the defendant escapes from custody. The victim shall be informed by the prosecutor about notification rights and the certification process required to access the criminal offender record information files. Persons requesting such notice must provide the appropriate authority with current information as to their address and telephone number;

(u) for victims, to be informed that the victim may have a right to pursue a civil action for damages relating to the crime, regardless of whether the court has ordered the defendant to make restitution to the victim.

(v) for one family member of a victim of a homicide, which the matter before the court is related, to possess in the courtroom a photograph, that is not of itself of an inflammatory nature, of the deceased victim that is not larger than eight by ten inches; provided, however, that at no time may the photograph be exposed or in anyway displayed in the presence of any member of the jury, or the jury pool from which a jury is to be selected in a particular matter; provided, further, that nothing in this section shall preclude the admission into evidence of a photograph that the court deems relevant and material.

(w) Where the victim or witness is an employee of the department of youth services, no law enforcement agency, prosecutor, defense counsel or parole, probation or corrections official shall disclose or state the residential address, telephone number or place of employment or school of the victim, a victim's family member or a witness, except as otherwise ordered by the court. The court may enter such other orders or conditions to maintain limited disclosure of the information as it deems appropriate to protect the privacy and safety of victims, victims' family members and witnesses.

There shall be conspicuously posted in all courthouses and police stations a summary of the rights afforded under this section. The victim and witness assistance board, pursuant to section 4, shall devise and provide posters to satisfy this requirement to court officials and police station personnel, and, upon request and at the discretion of the office and board, to any other institution or organization to post and maintain in space accessible to the general public. The board shall develop such posters in a variety of languages as determined by the Massachusetts office for victim assistance. Upon request, the board will respond, to the extent possible, to any requests for additional language translations of such posters.

NOTE 1   "[A] defendant's right to cross-examine a witness about his current address and place of employment may be restricted when the judge determines that a threat to the witness' safety from disclosure of this information outweighs the defendant's need for it." *Commonwealth v. Francis*, 432 Mass. 353, 357–58 (2000).

NOTE 2   Restitution/No Need for Insurance Claim. "The statute does not provide that in order to obtain restitution, the victim is first required to submit a claim under an insurance policy that might cover the loss. Moreover, such a requirement would run counter to the purpose of restitution, which is not only to compensate the victim for his or her economic loss tied to the defendant's conduct, but also to make the defendant pay for the damage he or she caused as a punitive and rehabilitative sanction." *Commonwealth v. Williams*, 57 Mass. App. Ct. 917, 918 (2003) (rescript).

SECTION 4
Victim and witness assistance board

There is hereby established a victim and witness assistance board, to consist of five members who shall serve without compensation. Notwithstanding any provision of section six of chapter two hundred and sixty-eight A to the contrary, the board shall consist of the attorney general or his designee who shall be chairman, two district attorneys who shall be appointed by the governor, and two members of the public who shall be appointed by the governor, of whom one shall be a victim. The members of the board first appointed shall serve as follows: of the district attorneys appointed by the governor, one shall serve for three years, and one shall serve for one year, of the members of the public appointed by the governor, one shall serve for three years and one shall serve for two years. The successor of each such member shall serve for a term of three years and until his successor is duly appointed and qualified, except that any person appointed to fill a vacancy shall serve only for the unexpired term. Any member of the board shall be eligible for reappointment.

The board shall by majority vote of its members, appoint an executive director who shall serve, subject to appropriation, at such rate of compensation as the board directs for a term of three years unless removed for cause by a vote of four members of the board. The executive director, subject to appropriation, shall have the power to hire such staff, subject to the approval of the board, as is needed to fulfill the powers and duties of the board. The executive director shall have such other powers and duties as the board may delegate to him.

The provisions of chapter thirty-one shall not apply to the executive director or any employee of the board.

The board shall review program plans, annual reports, and the implementation and operation of programs as described in this chapter. The board shall promulgate rules for the preparation and review of such program plans and annual reports.

In addition to the foregoing, the board shall:

(a) have printed and shall make available to social service agencies, medical facilities, and law enforcement agencies, cards, posters, brochures or other materials explaining the victim and witness rights and services established under this chapter;

(b) assist hospitals, clinics and other medical facilities, whether public or private, in disseminating information giving notice of the rights established under this chapter. This assistance may include providing informational materials including posters suitable to be displayed in emergency and waiting rooms;

(c) assist law enforcement agencies in familiarizing all of their officers and employees with the crime victims' rights as provided under this chapter. This assistance may include supplying informational literature on this subject to be utilized as part of the training curriculum for all trainee officers; and

(d) assist all local law enforcement agencies in establishing procedures whereby expedient notification is given to victims and witnesses, as defined under this chapter, of the rights provided under this chapter. In municipalities which do not have a local law enforcement agency, the board shall establish procedures whereby it, in cooperation with the state police, shall give notice to victims of crimes as provided in this section.

SECTION 5
Programs created and maintained by district attorney; services

Each district attorney shall create and maintain, to the extent reasonably possible and subject to the available resources, a program to afford victims and witnesses of crimes the rights and services described in this chapter. Those services shall include but not be limited to the following:

(a) court appearance notification services, including cancellations of appearances;

(b) informational services relative to the availability and collection of witness fees, victim compensation and restitution;

(c) escort and other transportation services related to the investigation or prosecution of the case, if necessary;

(d) case process notification services;

(e) employer intercession services;

(f) expedited return of property services;

(g) protection services;

(h) family support services including child and other dependent care services;

(i) waiting facilities; and

(j) social service referrals.

SECTION 6
Program plan

Each district attorney shall submit annually on January fifteenth to the board, the secretary of administration and finance and the house and senate committees on ways and means, a program plan to be implemented within the district attorney's jurisdiction. The program plan shall include, but not be limited to: a description of the services to be provided to victims and witnesses in each judicial district within the district attorney's jurisdiction; the personnel or agencies responsible for providing individual services and related administrative programs; proposed staffing for the program; proposed education, training and experience requirements for program staff and, where appropriate, the staff of agencies providing individual services and related administrative services; and a proposed budget for implementing the program. The district attorney shall include in the annual program plan a detailed report on the operation of the program, as well as a detailed report of deposits and expenditures of all funds made available to said district attorney for the preceding fiscal year and the current fiscal year, and proposed for the upcoming fiscal year, pursuant to section nine.

SECTION 7
Interagency cooperation

The district attorney, local law enforcement agencies, local social service agencies, and court shall cooperate to afford victims and witnesses of crimes, the rights and services described in this chapter.

SECTION 8
Assessments imposed by court
(Amended by 2014 Mass. Acts c. 260, §§ 20–21, effective Aug. 8, 2014.)

The court shall impose an assessment of no less than $90 against any person who has attained the age of seventeen years and who is convicted of a felony or against whom a finding of sufficient facts for a conviction is made on a complaint charging a felony. The court shall impose an assessment of $50 against any person who has attained the age of seventeen and who is convicted of a misdemeanor or against whom a finding of sufficient facts for a conviction is made on a complaint charging a misdemeanor. The court shall impose an assessment of $45 against any person who has attained the age of fourteen years and who is adjudicated a delinquent child or against whom a finding of sufficient facts for a finding of delinquency is made. The court shall impose an additional domestic violence prevention and victim assistance assessment of $50 for: (i) any violation of an order issued pursuant to sections 18 or 34B of chapter 208, section 32 of chapter 209, sections 3, 4 or 5 of chapter 209A or section 15 or 20 of chapter 209C; (ii) a conviction or adjudication for an act which would constitute abuse, as defined in section 1 of chapter 209A; or (iii) a violation of section 13M or 15D of chapter 265, which shall be deposited in the Domestic and Sexual Violence Prevention and Victim Assistance Fund, established in section 20 of chapter 17. The court, including the clerk-magistrate, or the registrar of motor vehicles shall impose an assessment of $45 against any violator who fails to pay the scheduled civil assessment for a civil motor vehicle infraction or to request a noncriminal hearing within the twenty day period provided for in subsection (A) of section three of chapter ninety C, except where the person is required by law to exercise the right to pay before a justice. When multiple civil motor vehicle infractions arising from a single incident are charged, the total assessment shall not exceed $75; provided, however, that the total assessment against a person who has not attained seventeen years shall not exceed thirty dollars. In the discretion of the court or the clerk magistrate in the case of a civil motor vehicle infraction that has not been heard by or brought before a justice, a civil motor vehicle assessment imposed pursuant to this section which would cause the person against whom the assessment is imposed severe financial hardship, may be reduced or waived. If it is determined by a written finding of fact that an assessment, other than for a civil motor vehicle infraction imposed by this section would impose a severe financial hardship upon the person against whom the assessment is imposed, the court may waive the fee or structure a payment plan in order to ensure compliance with payment; provided, however, that the court may order a person required to pay a domestic violence prevention and victim assistance assessment to complete at least 8 hours of community service in order to satisfy such assessment, if a structured payment would continue to impose a severe financial hardship. Such a finding shall be made independently of a finding of indigency for purposes of appointing counsel. If the person is sentenced to a correctional facility in the commonwealth and the assessment has not been paid, the court shall note the assessment on the mittimus.

All such assessments made shall be collected by the court or by the registrar, as the case may be, and shall be transmitted monthly to the state treasurer. If the person convicted is sentenced to a correctional facility in the commonwealth, the superintendent or sheriff of the facility shall deduct any part or all of the monies earned or received by any inmate and held by the correctional facility, to satisfy the victim and witness assessment, and shall transmit such monies to the court monthly. The assessment from any conviction or adjudication of delinquency which is subsequently overturned on appeal shall be refunded by the court to the person whose conviction or adjudication of delinquency is overturned. Said court shall deduct such funds from the assessments transmitted to the state treasurer. Assessments pursuant to this section shall be in addition to any other fines or restitution imposed in any disposition.

When a determination of the order of priority for payments required of a defendant must be made by the court or other criminal justice system personnel required to assess and collect such fines, assessments or other payments, the victim and witness assessment and the domestic violence prevention and victim assistance assessment mandated by this section shall be the defendant's first obligation.

SECTION 9
Deposit of assessments

Any assessment imposed pursuant to section eight shall be deposited in the Victim and Witness Assistance Fund, established by section forty-nine of chapter ten. In addition, the board may also apply for and accept on behalf of the commonwealth any private grants, bequests, gifts or contributions to further aid in financing programs or policies of the division. Such funds shall be received by the state treasurer on behalf of the commonwealth and deposited into said fund; provided, that said board shall submit to the house and senate committees on ways and means, as necessary, a report detailing all such amounts as deposited into said fund. All monies deposited into said fund that are unexpended at the end of the year shall not revert to the General Fund. The proceeds of the fund shall be made available, subject to appropriation, to the district attorney victim and witness programs, to the attorney general and the parole board for programs serving crime victims and witnesses.

SECTION 10
Construction

Nothing in this chapter shall be construed as creating an entitlement or a cause of action on behalf of any person against any public employee, public agency, the commonwealth or any agency responsible for the enforcement of rights and provision of services set forth in this chapter.

SECTION 11
Duration of rights and duties

The rights and duties established under this chapter shall continue to be enforceable until the final disposition of the

charges, including acquittal or dismissal of charges, all post-conviction release proceedings, post-conviction relief proceedings, all appellate proceedings, and the discharge of all criminal proceedings relating to restitution. If a defendant's conviction or adjudication of delinquency is reversed and the case is returned to the trial court for further proceedings, the victim shall have the same rights that applied to the criminal or delinquency proceedings that led to the appeal or other post-conviction relief proceeding.

SECTION 12
Assurance of rights; assistance by criminal justice agencies

Law enforcement agencies, prosecutors, judges, probation officers, clerks and corrections officials shall assure that victims of crime are afforded the rights established in this chapter.

Unless specifically stated otherwise, the requirements to provide information to the victim may be satisfied by either written or oral communication with the victim. The person responsible for providing such information shall do so in a timely manner and shall advise the victim of any significant changes in such information.

The board shall assist the prosecutors in providing the rights set forth in this chapter by preparing for distribution to victims written materials explaining the rights and services to which they are entitled.

A victim or family member may request assistance from the board in obtaining the rights provided under this chapter by the court or by any criminal justice agency responsible for implementing such rights. In order to address the victim's concerns, the board may seek assistance from the district attorney governing the jurisdiction in which the crime against the victim is alleged to have been committed or from the attorney general.

A victim or family member may request assistance from the district attorney or the attorney general in obtaining the rights provided under this chapter by the court or by any criminal justice agency responsible for implementing such rights.

SECTION 13
Failure to provide rights, privileges, or notice to victim; no grounds for appeal of or objection to conviction

A defendant or person convicted of a criminal or delinquency offense against the victim shall have no standing to object to any failure to comply with this chapter, and the failure to provide a right, privilege or notice to a victim under this chapter shall not be grounds for the defendant or person convicted of a criminal or delinquency offense to seek to have the conviction or sentence set aside.

Chapter 258C. Compensation of Victims of Violent Crimes

Section
1   Definitions
2   Eligibility for compensation
3   Maximum award; compensable expenses
4   Division of victim compensation and assistance; program director; powers and duties
5   Filing and proof of claims; civil investigative demands
6   Notification by claimant of change in address
7   Notice to claimant; payment of compensation
8   Request for reconsideration of award or denial
9   Judicial review
10   Amounts received by claimant from other sources; offset
11   Subrogation
12   Misrepresentations or concealment; fines and damages
13   "Good Samaritans"; liability

SECTION 1
Definitions

As used in this chapter, the following words shall, unless the context clearly requires otherwise, have the following meanings:—

"Claim", an application for compensation under this chapter.

"Claimant", a person who files a claim for compensation under this chapter.

"Crime", an act committed by a person which, if committed by a mentally competent, criminally responsible adult who has no legal exemption or defense, would constitute a crime. Crime shall apply to an act occurring within the commonwealth, and to an act of terrorism, as defined in 18 USC section 2331, occurring outside the United States or territories against a resident of the commonwealth.

"Crime scene cleanup", the removal of, or the attempted removal of, blood or other stains that are the direct result of the commission of a crime or other dirt or debris caused by the processing of the crime scene; provided, however, that crime scene cleanup shall not include the replacement or repair of property damaged during the commission of the crime in accordance with section 4.

"Department", the department of the attorney general.

"Dependent", mother, father, spouse, spouse's mother, spouse's father, child, grandchild, adopted child, child born out of wedlock, brother, sister, niece or nephew, or other person who is wholly or partially dependent for support upon the victim at the time of his injury or death due to a crime alleged in a claim made pursuant to this chapter.

"Division," the division of victim compensation and assistance within the department of the attorney general, established in section 11K of chapter 12.

"Family", the spouse, parent, grandparent, stepmother, stepfather, child, grandchild, brother, sister, half brother, half sister, adopted child of parents, or spouse's parents of the victim.

"Medical care", the medical, psychological, surgical, dental, optometric, chiropractic, podiatric and hospital care provided to a victim including, but not limited to, medicines, medical, dental and surgical supplies, crutches, artificial members and appliances and training in the use of artificial members and appliances.

"Offender", an adult or juvenile person who commits a crime as defined in this section for which a claimant seeks compensation.

"Out-of-pocket loss", unreimbursed or unreimbursable expenses for services eligible for compensation pursuant to this chapter.

"Security measures", the replacement, repair or installation of locks, windows or other security devices deemed to be reasonably necessary for the promotion of the victim's safety by the program director after taking into consideration the nature of the crime in accordance with section 4.

"State", a state of the United States, the district of Columbia, the commonwealth of Puerto Rico or any other possession or territory of the United States.

"Victim", a person who suffers personal physical or psychological injury or death:

(a) as a direct result of a crime as defined in this section;

(b) as a result of attempting to assist a person against whom a crime was attempted or committed; or

(c) as a result of efforts to prevent a crime or an attempted crime from occurring in his presence or to apprehend a person who had committed a crime in his presence.

SECTION 2
Eligibility for compensation

(a) No compensation shall be paid under this chapter unless the division finds that a crime was committed and that such crime directly resulted in personal physical or psychological injury to, or death of, the victim.

(b) No compensation shall be paid under this chapter unless the claimant demonstrates that the crime was reported to the police or other law enforcement authorities or to an agency or entity obligated by law to report complaints of criminal misconduct to law enforcement authorities. Except in the case where the division finds such report to have been delayed for good cause, such report shall have been made within five days after the occurrence of such crime.

(c) A claimant shall be eligible for compensation only if such claimant cooperates with law enforcement authorities in the investigation and prosecution of the crime in which the victim was injured or killed unless the claimant demonstrates that he possesses or possessed a reasonable excuse for failing to cooperate.

(d) A claimant shall not be eligible for compensation if such compensation would unjustly benefit the offender; provided, however, that a claimant shall not, except pursuant to regulations enacted in accordance with section four to prevent unjust enrichment, be denied compensation because of such claimant's or victim's familial relationship with the offender or because of the sharing of a residence by the victim or claimant and the offender.

(e) An offender or an accomplice of an offender shall not be eligible to receive compensation with respect to a crime committed by an offender. To the extent that the victim's acts or conduct provoked or contributed to the injuries, the division shall reduce or deny an award to the claimant or claimants in accordance with regulations enacted pursuant to section four.

[Subsection (f) repealed.]

(g) The claimant may retain counsel under this chapter. Attorneys fees shall be deducted from, and not in addition to, the total award for compensation. No attorneys fees shall be paid unless the attorney submits an affidavit which sets forth the hours worked and the services rendered for representing the claimant in the claim for compensation. The division may include as part of its award, reasonable attorneys fees to be determined by the division in an amount not to exceed fifteen percent of the total award for compensation.

SECTION 3
Maximum award; compensable expenses
(Amended by 2012 Mass. Acts c. 224, § 224, effective Nov. 4, 2012.)

(a) The maximum award for compensation to a claimant under this chapter shall be twenty-five thousand dollars. If there are two or more claimants eligible for compensation arising out of a crime committed against one individual for the same crime, each claimant shall be entitled to receive compensation to the extent of out-of-pocket loss, in proportion to the out-of-pocket losses of every other claimant. The cumulative total of all awards based on such crime shall not exceed twenty-five thousand dollars.

(b) Except as otherwise provided in this chapter, the following expenses are compensable in accordance with this section:

(1)(A) The maximum award or compensation for funeral and burial expenses shall be $6,500. A legal guardian, dependent or other family member of the victim or a person who actually incurs funeral and burial expenses directly related to the death of a victim shall be eligible for compensation for such funeral and burial expenses.

(B) The maximum award or compensation for expenses other than funeral and burial expenses associated with the interment of a victim whose death is the direct result of a crime shall be $800. For purposes of this subsection compensable expenses shall include, but not be limited to, transportation of the victim to the location of interment, travel of a legal guardian or family member to accompany the victim to the location of interment, memorial markers at the location of interment or other associated expenses as determined by the program director in accordance with section 4.

(2)(A) Expenses incurred for hospital services as the direct result of injury to the victim shall be compensable in accordance with this chapter; provided, however, that when claiming compensation for hospital expenses, the claimant must demonstrate an out-of-pocket loss or a legal liability for payment of said expenses. No hospital expenses shall be paid if the expense is reimbursable by Medicaid or if the services are covered by chapter 118E. Every claim for compensation for hospital services shall include a certification by the hospital that the services are not reimbursable by Medicaid and that the services are not covered by chapter 118E. In no event shall the amounts awarded for hospital services exceed the rates for services established by the executive office of health and human services or a governmental unit designated by the executive office if rates have been established for such services.

(B) Expenses incurred for physician, dental, ambulance, or other medically necessary services or prosthetic devices as the direct result of injury to the victim shall be compensable in accordance with this chapter; provided however, that when claiming compensation for such expenses, the claimant must demonstrate an out-of-pocket loss or legal liability for payment of such expenses. No physician, dental, ambulance or other necessary services or prosthetic device shall be paid where the services were reimbursable by medicaid. Every claim for compensation for physician, dental, ambulance or other medically necessary services or for prosthetic devices shall include a certification by the health care provider that the expense was not reimbursable by medicaid.

(C) A victim, parent or legal guardian of a victim who is a minor in accordance with section 4 or, where death results from the crime, the dependents and family members of the victim, shall be eligible for compensation for reasonable mental health counseling obtained as a result of the crime.

(D) If the victim was employed or had received a bona fide employment offer at the time of the crime, he shall be eligible for compensation for loss of actual earnings due to disability from work as the result of injuries caused by the crime. In order to be eligible for lost earnings, the victim must demonstrate medical disability and causal relationship to the crime. The amount of compensation shall be based on the victim's net earnings or expected net earnings as a result of an employment offer at the time of the crime. If the victim is a minor at the time of the crime, he shall be eligible for future lost earnings due to disability from future employment as a result of injuries caused by the crime.

(E) If the sole occupation of the victim at the time of the crime and for the preceding one year was limited to performing the duties and responsibilities of a homemaker, the victim or his dependents shall be eligible for reimbursement for the reasonable costs of maintaining such services. In order to be eligible for compensation for homemaker services in non-homicide cases, the victim must demonstrate a medical disability which is causally related to the crime.

(F) In the case of the death of the victim as a direct result of the crime, a dependent of a victim shall be eligible for compensation for loss of the victim's support. No compensation for loss of support shall be paid unless the claimant demonstrates either that the dependent was living with the victim at the time of the crime or, in the case of minor children of a deceased victim who were not residing in the victim's household at the time of the crime, that the minor children received financial support directly from the victim prior to the crime or were legally entitled to receive such support, such entitlement having been established by a court order or a judicially enforceable agreement. An award for loss of support shall be based upon the victim's actual earnings and the life expectancy of the victim.

(G) Expenses incurred for professional crime scene cleanup services necessary as the direct result of the commission of a crime at a private residence or in a motor vehicle that is owned or leased by a victim, family member or other dependent shall be compensable in accordance with this chapter; provided, however, that the maximum amount of compensation shall not exceed $1,500.

(H) A victim shall be eligible for compensation for the reasonable replacement costs of clothing and bedding seized as evidence or rendered unusable as the result of a criminal investigation that is the direct result of a crime; provided, however, that the maximum compensable amount shall not exceed $250.

(I) A victim or a family member residing with the victim at the time a crime is committed, shall be eligible for compensation for the costs associated with the implementation of security measures; provided, however, that the maximum compensable amount shall not exceed $500.

SECTION 4
Division of victim compensation and assistance; program director; powers and duties

(a) The division of victim compensation and assistance shall administer the provisions of this chapter. Subject to appropriation, the attorney general shall designate a program director of said division. Said program director may appoint and remove, subject to the approval of the attorney general, such investigative, legal and clerical or other staff as the work of the division requires.

(b) The program director shall have the authority to promulgate rules and regulations pursuant to chapter thirty A as may be necessary to carry out the provisions of this chapter.

(c) The program director shall be authorized to apply for and receive sums which may be transmitted to the victim compensation fund maintained by the treasurer and for any other such funds as may become available to administer the requirements of this chapter.

SECTION 5
Filing and proof of claims; civil investigative demands

(a)(1) A claim for compensation under this chapter shall be filed within three years of the date of the crime.

(2) The claimant has the burden of proving by a preponderance of the evidence that he is eligible to receive compensation.

(3) A claim under this chapter shall be made on a claim form prescribed by the division. The claim shall be accompanied by copies of bills and other documentation supporting the claim, and shall be signed under the pains and penalties of perjury. Any claim for loss of support or other expenses incurred as the result of the death of a victim must be accompanied by proof of dependency of the claimant upon the victim. All claims must contain a release of information necessary to investigate the claim.

Law enforcement agencies, district attorneys, the department of children and families and the department of transitional assistance, hospitals, physicians and other service providers shall cooperate with the department in the investigation of claims filed under this chapter.

(b) Upon receipt of a claim hereunder, the division shall acknowledge receipt of same, in writing, to the claimant or counsel of record. The division shall, thereafter, conduct an investigation of the claim to verify the information contained on the application.

The division shall be authorized to issue a written civil investigative demand, issue interrogatories, under oath, and requests for production of documents, and take oral testimony, under oath, in order to obtain information necessary to verify a claim. All information collected by the division shall be kept in accordance with the provisions of chapters four, sixty-six and sixty-six A.

A civil investigative demand may be served by certified mail, return receipt requested, and first class mail shall be returned within twenty days from the date of service. Failure to comply with this provision may result in dismissal of the claim for compensation.

Whenever a person fails to comply with a civil investigative demand served upon him pursuant to this section, the attorney general may petition the district court of any county in which such person resides, is found, or transacts business, to enter such orders as may be necessary to carry into effect the provisions of this section. A failure to comply with an order entered under this section shall be punished as a contempt of court.

SECTION 6
Notification by claimant of change in address

The claimant shall have a continuing obligation to notify the division of a change in address. Failure to comply with this requirement may result in the dismissal of the claim for compensation or the termination of a proceeding set forth in this chapter.

SECTION 7
Notice to claimant; payment of compensation

(a) Within fifteen days of completion of the investigation, the program director shall mail notice to the claimant or the attorney of record stating the amount of compensation to be paid or denied, and the reasons therefor, and the payees, if any. The program director may direct that warrant for pay-

ment by the department of the attorney general be made jointly to the claimant and to a provider. The notice shall contain information regarding the right of the claimant to petition for judicial review of the decision of the program director.

(b) Upon receipt of the notice of assent by a claimant, the division shall present the notice to the department of the attorney general for payment. Subject to the availability of funds appropriated for this purpose, said department of the attorney general shall cause payment to be made in accordance with the division's award without further authorization.

SECTION 8
Request for reconsideration of award or denial

(a) Within 20 days of the date of mailing of the notice of award or denial, a claimant aggrieved by the program director's decision may request, in writing, a reconsideration of such decision. Said program director shall reconsider any order for which a request for reconsideration is received. Said program director may in his discretion reconsider a decision granting or denying an award or the amount of an award where there has been no request for reconsideration. After reconsideration of the award, said program director shall affirm the decision or issue an amended notice of award or denial.

(b) The program director shall notify the claimant by certified mail, return receipt required, and first class mail of the decision upon reconsideration within 30 days of the claimant's request for reconsideration. Such notice shall include information regarding the claimant's right to a petition for judicial review of the decision of the program director.

SECTION 9
Judicial review
(Amended by 2011 Mass. Acts c. 93, § 111, effective July 1, 2012.)

(a) Within thirty days of the date of mailing of the notice of award or denial by the program director, the claimant may petition for judicial review in the district court within the judicial district in which the claimant resides or, in the case of a nonresident claimant, in the Boston municipal court. Where the claimant requests reconsideration of the decision of the program director, the petition for judicial review shall be filed within 30 days from the date of mailing of the decision of reconsideration. If no petition is filed within the time specified, the decision of the program director shall be final.

(b) The program director shall, in response to the aforesaid, within thirty days, file in such court a copy of his official decision.

(c) The district court shall schedule the matter for hearing and shall notify the parties of the date and time thereof.

(d) The review shall be conducted by the district court without a jury.

(e) For the purpose of determining the amount of compensation payable pursuant to this chapter, the chief justice of the trial court shall formulate standards for the uniform application of this chapter. The court shall take into consideration the provisions of this chapter, the rates and amounts of compensation payable for injuries and death under other laws of the commonwealth and of the United States, excluding pain and suffering. All decisions of the court on claims heard under this chapter shall be in writing, setting forth the name of the claimant, the amount of compensation and the reasons for the decision. The clerk of the court shall immediately notify the claimant in writing of the decision and shall forward to the department of the attorney general a certified copy of the decision. The department of the attorney general without further authorization shall, subject to appropriation, pay the claimant the amount determined by the court.

In determining the amount of compensation payable, the court shall determine whether because of his conduct the victim contributed to the infliction of his injury; and the court shall reduce the amount of the compensation or deny the claim altogether, in accordance with such determination; provided, however, that the court may disregard the responsibility of the victim for his own injury where such responsibility was attributable to efforts by the victim to aid a victim, or to prevent a crime or an attempted crime from occurring in his presence or to apprehend a person who had committed a crime in his presence or had in fact committed a felony.

(f) Judicial review of the finding and decisions of the program director shall be a de novo hearing of the claim.

SECTION 10
Amounts received by claimant from other sources; offset

No compensation shall be awarded or paid unless the out-of-pocket expenses or legal liability of the claimant for services rendered as the result of the crime exceeds any and all of the amounts received, applied for, or to be applied for as the result of the crime from any of the following or any combination of the following:

(a) insurance, including, but not limited to, homeowner's insurance, renter's insurance, automobile insurance, disability;

(b) workers' compensation, unemployment compensation, social security benefits, veteran's benefits, retirement benefits;

(c) medicaid, medicare, free care, any other forms of public assistance including aid to families with dependent children and assistance to the aged and disabled or any successor thereto;

(d) restitution in the criminal action;

(e) proceeds from a civil suit; or

(f) institutional gifts.

SECTION 11
Subrogation

Acceptance of any compensation under this chapter shall subrogate the commonwealth, to the extent of such compensation paid, to any right or right of action accruing to the claimant or to the victim to recover payments on account of losses resulting from the crime with respect to which the compensation has been paid, and the claimant has a continuing obligation to so notify the attorney general of such recovery. The attorney general may enforce the subrogation, and he shall bring suit to recover from any person to whom compensation is paid, to the extent of compensation actually paid under this chapter, any amount received by the claimant from any source exceeding the actual loss to the victim.

SECTION 12
Misrepresentation or concealment; fines and damages

Any person who: (a) submits a false or fraudulent application or claim for an award; (b) intentionally makes or causes to be made any false statement or representation of a material fact in relation to any claim pending before the division; or (c) intentionally conceals or fails to disclose information affecting the amount of or the initial or continued right to any such award shall be punished by a fine of not more than one thousand dollars or by imprisonment in a house of correction for not more than six months, or both.

The commonwealth shall, in addition, have a civil cause of action for relief against any person who violates the provisions of this chapter for the amount of damages which the commonwealth sustains by reason of such violation which shall include costs of the action and attorneys fees and, in addition, for punitive damages of not more than triple the amount of damages which the commonwealth sustains, and interest. The attorney general may bring any such action necessary to enforce this section.

Any amount reimbursed or any fine or damages paid pursuant to this section shall be paid to the victim compensation fund maintained by the treasurer.

SECTION 13
"Good Samaritans"; liability

No person who, in good faith, provides or obtains, or attempts to provide or obtain, assistance for a victim of a crime as defined in section one, shall be liable in a civil suit for damages as a result of any acts or omissions in providing or obtaining, or attempting to provide or obtain, such assistance unless such acts or omissions constitute willful, wanton or reckless conduct.

Chapter 258E. Harassment Prevention Orders

Section

1	Definitions
2	Jurisdiction
3	Filing of complaint; impounding of case record information; filing fee; expiration of order; modification of order; time for filing; nonexclusivity of remedy
4	Notice of nature of proceedings and availability of other criminal proceedings
5	Temporary orders
6	Granting of relief without the filing of a complaint
7	Enforcement of protection order issued by another jurisdiction
8	Law officer emergency response to prevent further abuse or harassment
9	Review and filing of records within court activity record information system and statewide domestic violence recordkeeping system; execution of outstanding warrants; service upon defendant; order for payment of damages
10	Confidentiality of records
11	Adoption of suitable form of complaint
12	Assessment against persons referred to a treatment program as condition of probation

SECTION 1
Definitions

As used in this chapter the following words shall, unless the context clearly requires otherwise, have the following meanings:—

"Abuse", attempting to cause or causing physical harm to another or placing another in fear of imminent serious physical harm.

"Harassment", (i) 3 or more acts of willful and malicious conduct aimed at a specific person committed with the intent to cause fear, intimidation, abuse or damage to property and that does in fact cause fear, intimidation, abuse or damage to property; or (ii) an act that: (A) by force, threat or duress causes another to involuntarily engage in sexual relations; or (B) constitutes a violation of section 13B, 13F, 13H, 22, 22A, 23, 24, 24B, 26C, 43 or 43A of chapter 265 or section 3 of chapter 272.

"Court", the district or Boston municipal court, the superior court or the juvenile court departments of the trial court.

"Law officer", any officer authorized to serve criminal process.

"Malicious", characterized by cruelty, hostility or revenge.

"Protection order issued by another jurisdiction", an injunction or other order issued by a court of another state, territory or possession of the United States, the Commonwealth of Puerto Rico, or the District of Columbia, or a tribal court that is issued for the purpose of preventing violent or threatening acts, abuse or harassment against, or contact or communication with or physical proximity to another person, including temporary and final orders issued by civil and criminal courts filed by or on behalf of a person seeking protection.

SECTION 2
Jurisdiction
(Amended by 2014 Mass. Acts c. 284, § 74, effective Aug. 11, 2014.)

Proceedings under this chapter shall be filed, heard and determined in the superior court department or the respective divisions of the district court department or the Boston municipal court department having venue over the plaintiff's residence. The juvenile court department shall have exclusive jurisdiction of proceedings under this chapter in which the defendant is under the age of 18. Such proceedings shall be filed, heard and determined in the division of the juvenile court department having venue over the plaintiff's residence.

SECTION 3
Filing of complaint; impounding of case record information; filing fee; expiration of order; modification of order; time for filing; nonexclusivity of remedy

(a) A person suffering from harassment may file a complaint in the appropriate court requesting protection from such harassment. A person may petition the court under this chapter for an order that the defendant:

(i) refrain from abusing or harassing the plaintiff, whether the defendant is an adult or minor;

(ii) refrain from contacting the plaintiff, unless authorized by the court, whether the defendant is an adult or minor;

(iii) remain away from the plaintiff's household or workplace, whether the defendant is an adult or minor; and

(iv) pay the plaintiff monetary compensation for the losses suffered as a direct result of the harassment; provided, however, that compensatory damages shall include, but shall not be limited to, loss of earnings, out-of-pocket losses for injuries sustained or property damaged, cost of replacement of locks, medical expenses, cost for obtaining an unlisted phone number and reasonable attorney's fees.

(b) The court may order that information in the case record be impounded in accordance with court rule.

(c) No filing fee shall be charged for the filing of the complaint. The plaintiff shall not be charged for certified copies of any orders entered by the court, or any copies of the file reasonably required for future court action or as a result of the loss or destruction of plaintiff's copies.

(d) Any relief granted by the court shall not extend for a period exceeding 1 year. Every order shall, on its face, state the time and date the order is to expire and shall include the date and time that the matter will again be heard. If the plaintiff appears at the court at the date and time the order is to expire, the court shall determine whether or not to extend the order for any additional time reasonably necessary to protect the plaintiff or to enter a permanent order. When the expiration date stated on the order is on a date when the court is closed to business, the order shall not expire until the next date that the court is open to business. The plaintiff may appear on such next court business day at the time designated by the order to request that the order be extended. The court may also extend the order upon motion of the plaintiff, for such additional time as it deems necessary to protect the plaintiff from harassment. The fact that harassment has not occurred during the pendency of an order shall not, in itself, constitute sufficient ground for denying or failing to extend the order, or allowing an order to expire or be vacated or for refusing to issue a new order.

(e) The court may modify its order at any subsequent time upon motion by either party; provided, however, that the non-moving party shall receive sufficient notice and opportunity to be heard on said modification. When the plaintiff's address is inaccessible to the defendant as provided in section 10 and the defendant has filed a motion to modify the court's order, the court shall be responsible for notifying the plaintiff. In no event shall the court disclose any such inaccessible address.

(f) The court shall not deny any complaint filed under this chapter solely because it was not filed within a particular time period after the last alleged incident of harassment.

(g) An action commenced under this chapter shall not preclude any other civil or criminal remedies. A party filing a complaint under this chapter shall be required to disclose any prior or pending actions involving the parties; including, but not limited to, court actions, administrative proceedings and disciplinary hearings.

SECTION 4
Notice of nature of proceedings and availability of other criminal proceedings

Upon the filing of a complaint under this chapter, a complainant shall be informed that the proceedings hereunder are civil in nature and that violations of orders issued hereunder are criminal in nature. Further, a complainant shall be given information prepared by the appropriate district attorney's office that other criminal proceedings may be available and such complainant shall be instructed by such district attorney's office relative to the procedures required to initiate criminal proceedings including, but not limited to, a complaint for a violation of section 13B, 13F, 13H, 22, 22A, 23, 24, 24B, 26C, 43 and 43A of chapter 265 or section 3 of chapter 272. Whenever possible, a complainant shall be provided with such information in the complainant's native language.

SECTION 5
Temporary orders

Upon the filing of a complaint under this chapter, the court may enter such temporary orders as it deems necessary to protect a plaintiff from harassment, including relief as provided in section 3.

If the plaintiff demonstrates a substantial likelihood of immediate danger of harassment, the court may enter such temporary relief orders without notice as it deems necessary to protect the plaintiff from harassment and shall immediately thereafter notify the defendant that the temporary orders have been issued. The court shall give the defendant an opportunity to be heard on the question of continuing the temporary order and of granting other relief as requested by the plaintiff not later than 10 court business days after such orders are entered.

Notice shall be made by the appropriate law enforcement agency as provided in section 9.

If the defendant does not appear at such subsequent hearing, the temporary orders shall continue in effect without further order of the court.

SECTION 6
Granting of relief without the filing of a complaint
(Amended by 2011 Mass. Acts c. 93, § 113, effective July 1, 2012.)

When the court is closed for business or the plaintiff is unable to appear in court because of severe hardship due to the plaintiff's physical condition, the court may grant relief to the plaintiff as provided under section 5 if the plaintiff demonstrates a substantial likelihood of immediate danger of harassment. In the discretion of the justice, such relief may be granted and communicated by telephone to an officer or employee of an appropriate law enforcement agency, who shall record such order on a form of order promulgated for such use by the chief justice of the trial court and shall deliver a copy of such order on the next court day to the clerk or clerk-magistrate of the court having venue and jurisdiction over the matter. If relief has been granted without the filing of a complaint pursuant to this section, the plaintiff shall appear in court on the next available business day to file a complaint. If the plaintiff in such a case is unable to appear in court without severe hardship due to the plaintiff's physical condition, a representative may appear in court, on the plaintiff's behalf and file the requisite complaint with an affidavit setting forth the circumstances preventing the plaintiff from appearing personally. Notice to the plaintiff and defendant and an opportunity for the defendant to be heard shall be given as provided in said section 5.

Any order issued under this section and any documentation in support thereof shall be certified on the next court day by the clerk or clerk-magistrate of the court issuing such order to the court having venue and jurisdiction over the matter. Such certification to the court shall have the effect of commencing proceedings under this chapter and invoking the other provisions of this chapter but shall not be deemed necessary for an emergency order issued under this section to take effect.

NOTE   "We . . . determine whether appeals of expired harassment protection orders issued pursuant to G.L. c. 258E should be dismissed as moot. [W]e conclude that appeals of such orders should be reviewed on their merits even if the orders have expired during the pendency of the appeal." *Seney v. Morhy*, 467 Mass. 58 (2014).

SECTION 7
Enforcement of protection order issued by another jurisdiction

Any protection order issued by another jurisdiction shall be given full faith and credit throughout the commonwealth and enforced as if it were issued in the commonwealth for as long as the order is in effect in the issuing jurisdiction.

A person entitled to protection under a protection order issued by another jurisdiction may file such order with the appropriate court by filing with the court a certified copy of such order. Such person shall swear under oath in an affidavit, to the best of such person's knowledge, that such order is presently in effect as written. Upon request by a law enforcement agency, the clerk or clerk-magistrate of such court shall provide a certified copy of the protection order issued by the other jurisdiction.

A law officer may presume the validity of, and enforce in accordance with section 8, a copy of a protection order issued by another jurisdiction which has been provided to the law officer by any source; provided, however, that the officer is also provided with a statement by the person protected by the order that such order remains in effect. Law officers may rely on such statement by the person protected by such order.

SECTION 8
Law officer emergency response to prevent further abuse or harassment

Whenever a law officer has reason to believe that a person has been abused or harassed or is in danger of being abused or harassed, such officer shall use all reasonable means to prevent further abuse or harassment. Law officers shall make every reasonable effort to do the following as part of the emergency response:

(1) assess the immediate physical danger to the victim and provide assistance reasonably intended to mitigate the safety risk;

(2) if there is observable injury to the victim or if the victim is complaining of injury, encourage the victim to seek medical attention and arrange for medical assistance or request an ambulance for transport to a hospital;

(3) if a sexual assault has occurred, notify the victim that there are time-sensitive medical or forensic options that may be available, encourage the victim to seek medical attention and arrange for medical assistance or request an ambulance for transport to a hospital;

(4) provide the victim with referrals to local resources that may assist the victim in locating and getting to a safe place;

(5) provide adequate notice to the victim of the victim's rights including, but not limited to, obtaining a harassment prevention order; provided, however, that the notice shall consist of providing the victim with a copy of the following statement before the officer leaves the scene or premises and after reading the statement to the victim; provided further, that if the victim's native language is not English, the statement shall be then provided in the victim's native language whenever possible:

"You have the right to appear at the Superior, Juvenile (only if the attacker is under 17), District or Boston Municipal Court, if you reside within the appropriate jurisdiction, and file a complaint requesting any of the following applicable orders: (i) an order restraining your attacker from harassing or abusing you; (ii) an order directing your attacker to refrain from contacting you; (iii) an order directing your attacker to stay away from your home and your workplace; (iv) an order directing your attacker to pay you for losses suffered as a result of the harassment or abuse, including loss of earnings, out-of-pocket losses for injuries sustained or property damaged, costs of replacement of locks, medical expenses, cost for obtaining an unlisted phone number, and reasonable attorneys' fees. For an emergency on weekends, holidays or weeknights, the police will assist you in activating the emergency response system so that you may file a complaint and request a harassment prevention order.

You have the right to go to the appropriate court and apply for a criminal complaint for sexual assault, threats, criminal stalking, criminal harassment, assault and battery, assault with a deadly weapon, assault with intent to kill or other related offenses.

If you are in need of medical treatment, you have the right to request that an officer present drive you to the nearest hospital or otherwise assist you in obtaining medical treatment.

If you believe that police protection is needed for your physical safety, you have the right to request that the officer present remain at the scene until you can leave or until your safety is otherwise ensured. You may also request that the officer assist you in locating and taking you to a safe place including, but not limited to, a designated meeting place for a shelter or a family member's or a friend's residence or a similar place of safety.

You may request and obtain a copy of the police incident report at no cost from the police department.";

(6) assist the victim by activating the emergency judicial system when the court is closed for business;

(7) inform the victim that the abuser will be eligible for bail and may be promptly released; and

(8) arrest any person that a law officer witnessed or has probable cause to believe violated a temporary or permanent vacate, restraining, stay-away or no-contact order or judgment issued under this chapter or similar protection order issued by another jurisdiction; provided, however, that if there are no vacate, restraining, stay-away or no-contact orders or judgments in effect, arresting the person shall be the preferred response if the law officer witnessed or has probable cause to believe that a person: (i) has committed a felony; (ii) has committed a misdemeanor involving harassment or abuse as defined in section 1; or (iii) has committed an assault and battery in violation of section 13A of chapter 265; provided further, that the safety of the victim shall be paramount in any decision to arrest; and provided further, that if a law officer arrests both parties, the law officer shall submit a detailed, written report in addition to an incident report, setting forth the grounds for arresting both parties.

No law officer shall be held liable in a civil action for personal injury or property damage brought by a party to an incident of abuse or for an arrest based on probable cause when such officer acted reasonably and in good faith and in compliance with this chapter.

Whenever a law officer investigates an incident of harassment, the officer shall immediately file a written incident report in accordance with the standards of the law officer's law enforcement agency and, wherever possible, in the form of the National Incident-Based Reporting System, as defined by the Federal Bureau of Investigation. The latter information may be submitted voluntarily by the local police on a monthly basis to the crime reporting unit of the state police crime reporting unit established in section 32 of chapter 22C.

The victim shall be provided with a copy of the full incident report at no cost upon request to the appropriate law enforcement department.

When a judge or other person authorized to take bail bails any person arrested under this chapter, reasonable efforts shall be made to inform the victim of such release prior to or at the time of the release. When any person charged with or arrested for a crime involving harassment under this chapter is released from custody, the court or the emergency response judge shall issue, upon the request of the victim, a written no-contact order or stay-away order prohibiting the person charged or arrested from having any contact with the victim and shall use all reasonable means to notify the victim immediately of release from custody. The victim shall be provided, at no cost, with a certified copy of the no-contact or stay-away order.

SECTION 9
Review and filing of records within court activity record information system and statewide domestic violence recordkeeping system; execution of outstanding warrants; service upon defendant; order for payment of damages

When considering a complaint filed under this chapter, the court shall order a review of the records contained within the court activity record information system and the statewide domestic violence recordkeeping system, as provided in chapter 188 of the acts of 1992 and maintained by the commissioner of probation, and shall review the resulting data to determine whether the named defendant has a civil or criminal record involving violent crimes or abuse. Upon receipt of information that an outstanding warrant exists against the named defendant, a judge shall order that the appropriate law enforcement officials be notified and shall order that any information regarding the defendant's most recent whereabouts shall be forwarded to such officials. In all instances in which an outstanding warrant exists, the court shall make a finding, based upon all of the circumstances, as to whether an imminent threat of bodily injury exists to the petitioner. In all instances in which such an imminent threat of bodily injury is found to exist, the judge shall notify the appropriate law enforcement officials of such finding and such officials shall take all necessary actions to execute any such outstanding warrant as soon as is practicable.

Whenever the court orders that the defendant refrain from harassing the plaintiff or have no contact with the plaintiff under section 3, 5 or 6, the clerk or clerk-magistrate shall transmit: (i) to the office of the commissioner of probation information for filing in the court activity record information system or the statewide domestic violence recordkeeping system as provided in said chapter 188 of the acts of 1992 or in a recordkeeping system created by the commissioner of probation to record the issuance of, or violation of, prevention orders issued pursuant to this chapter; and (ii) 2 certified copies of each such order and 1 copy of the complaint and summons forthwith to the appropriate law enforcement agency which, unless otherwise ordered by the court, shall serve 1 copy of each order upon the defendant, together with a copy of the complaint and order and summons. The law enforcement agency shall promptly make its return of service to the court. The commissioner of probation may develop and implement a statewide harassment prevention order recordkeeping system.

Law officers shall use every reasonable means to enforce such harassment prevention orders. Law enforcement agencies shall establish procedures adequate to ensure that an officer on the scene of an alleged violation of such order may be informed of the existence and terms of such order. The court shall notify the appropriate law enforcement agency in writing whenever any such order is vacated and shall direct the agency to destroy all record of such vacated order and such agency shall comply with that directive.

Each harassment prevention order issued shall contain the following statement: VIOLATION OF THIS ORDER IS A CRIMINAL OFFENSE.

Any violation of such order or a protection order issued by another jurisdiction shall be punishable by a fine of not more than $5,000, or by imprisonment for not more than 2½ years in a house of correction, or both. In addition to, but not in lieu of, the foregoing penalties and any other sentence, fee or assessment, including the victim witness assessment in section 8 of chapter 258B, the court shall order persons convicted of a violation of such an order to pay a fine of $25 that shall be transmitted to the treasurer for deposit into the General Fund. For any violation of such order, the court may order the defendant to complete an appropriate treatment program based on the offense.

In each instance in which there is a violation of a harassment prevention order or a protection order issued by another jurisdiction, the court may order the defendant to pay the plaintiff for all damages including, but not limited to, loss of earnings, out-of-pocket losses for injuries sustained or property damaged, cost of replacement locks, medical expenses, cost for obtaining an unlisted telephone number and reasonable attorney's fees.

Any such violation may be enforced by the court. Criminal remedies provided herein are not exclusive and do not preclude any other available civil or criminal remedies. The court may enforce by civil contempt procedure a violation of its own court order.

Section 8 of chapter 136 shall not apply to any order, complaint or summons issued pursuant to this section.

SECTION 10
Confidentiality of records

The records of cases arising out of an action brought under this chapter in which the plaintiff or defendant is a minor shall be withheld from public inspection except by order of the court; provided, however, that such records shall be open, at all reasonable times, to the inspection of the minor, such minor's parent, guardian and attorney and to the plaintiff and the plaintiff's attorney.

The plaintiff's residential address, residential telephone number and workplace name, address and telephone number, contained within the court records of cases arising out of an action brought by a plaintiff under this chapter, shall be confidential and withheld from public inspection, except by order of the court; provided, however, that the plaintiff's residential address and workplace address shall appear on the court order and be accessible to the defendant and the defendant's attorney unless the plaintiff specifically requests that this information be withheld from the order. All confidential portions of the records shall be accessible at all reasonable times to the plaintiff and plaintiff's attorney, to others specifically authorized by the plaintiff to obtain such information and to prosecutors, victim-witness advocates as defined in section 1 of chapter 258B, sexual assault counselors as defined in section 20J of chapter 233 and law officers, if such access is necessary in the performance of their duties. This paragraph shall apply to any protection order issued by another jurisdiction filed with a court of the commonwealth pursuant to section 7. Such confidential portions of the court records shall not be deemed to be public records under clause Twenty-sixth of section 7 of chapter 4.

SECTION 11
Adoption of suitable form of complaint
(Amended by 2011 Mass. Acts c. 93, § 114, effective July 1, 2012.)

The chief justice of the trial court shall adopt a form of complaint for use under this chapter which shall be in such form and language to permit a plaintiff to prepare and file such complaint pro se.

SECTION 12
Assessment against persons referred to a treatment program as condition of probation

The court shall impose an assessment of $350 against any person who has been referred to a treatment program as a condition of probation. Such assessment shall be in addition to the cost of the treatment program. In the discretion of the court, such assessment may be reduced or waived if the court finds that such person is indigent or that payment of the assessment would cause the person, or the dependents of such person, severe financial hardship. Assessments made pursuant to this section shall be in addition to any other fines, assessments or restitution imposed in any disposition. All funds collected by the court pursuant to this section shall be transmitted monthly to the state treasurer, who shall deposit such funds into the General Fund.

Chapter 261. Costs in Civil Actions

Section
27A　Definitions applicable to Secs. 27A to 27G
27B　Affidavit of indigency; waiver; substitution or state payment of fees or costs; supplementary affidavits
27C　Granting requests for waiver, substitution or state payment
27D　Appeal; notice; record; speedy hearing; stay of proceedings; decision final
27E　Repayment; deductions from judgment or settlement; notice; procedure
27F　Substitute documents, services or objects at less cost; court order
27G　Payment procedure; public record; report of expenditures

COURT COSTS OF INDIGENT PERSONS

SECTION 27A
Definitions applicable to Secs. 27A to 27G

As used in sections twenty-seven A to twenty-seven G, inclusive, the following words shall have the following meanings:

"Indigent", (a) a person who receives public assistance under aid to families with dependent children, program of emergency aid for elderly and disabled residents or veterans' benefits programs or who receives assistance under Title XVI of the Social Security Act or the medicaid program, 42 U.S.C.A. 1396, et seq.; (b) a person whose income, after taxes, is 125 per cent or less of the current poverty threshold established annually by the Community Services Administration pursuant to section 625 of the Economic Opportunity Act, as amended; or (c) a person who is unable to pay the fees and costs of the proceeding in which he is involved or is unable to do so without depriving himself or his dependents of the necessities of life, including food, shelter and clothing, but an inmate shall not be adjudged indigent pursuant to section 27C unless the inmate has complied with the procedures set forth in section 29 and the court finds that the inmate is incapable of making payments under the plans set forth in said section 29.

"Fees and costs", fees and costs shall not include attorneys' fees.

"Normal fees and costs", the fees and costs a party normally is required to pay in order to prosecute or defend the particular type of proceeding in which he is involved shall include, but not be limited to, the following: in all civil cases, filing or entry fees, including the surcharges required by section four C of chapter two hundred and sixty-two; fees and related costs for service of process, including publications of a citation when publication is ordered; fees and costs for the issuance or service of a subpoena and witness fees for trial or deposition; jury trial fees; removal fees; costs assessed in a bill of costs; in equity, fees for the issuance of an injunction, restraining order, writ or other process; in the probate and family court department, fees for an amendment of record.

"Extra fees and costs", the fees and costs, in addition to those a party is normally required to pay in order to prosecute or defend his case, which result when a party employs or responds to a procedure not necessarily required in the particular type of proceeding in which he is involved. They shall include, but not necessarily be limited to, the cost of transcribing a deposition, expert assistance and appeal bonds and appeal bond premiums.

"Clerk", the clerk or an assistant clerk or the register or an assistant register.

"Inmate", a person committed to, held by or in the custody of the department of correction or a state, county or federal correctional facility or the treatment center under chapter 123A.

SECTION 27B
Affidavit of indigency; waiver; substitution or state payment of fees or costs; supplementary affidavits

Upon or after commencing or answering to any civil, criminal or juvenile proceeding or appeal in any court, including but not limited to civil actions, proceedings for divorce or separate support, summary and supplementary processes, and proceedings upon petitions to vacate, for review or, upon appeal in a criminal case, any party may file with the clerk an affidavit of indigency and request for waiver, substitution or payment by the commonwealth of fees and costs upon a form prescribed by the chief justice of the supreme judicial court and in accordance with the standards set forth in sections twenty-seven C to twenty-seven F, inclusive, and sworn to under oath by the affiant.

An indigent party may subsequently file one or more supplementary affidavits requesting the waiver, substitution or payment by the commonwealth of fees and costs not previ-

ously granted at any time while the case is still pending in the original court or elsewhere.

SECTION 27C
Granting requests for waiver, substitution or state payment
(Amended by 2011 Mass. Acts c. 68, § 120, effective July 11, 2011.)

(1) If the affidavit is filed with the complaint or other paper initiating the proceeding, the clerk shall receive the complaint or other paper for filing and proceed as if all regular filing fees had been paid. Such filing shall be conditional until either (a) the affidavit is granted or (b) if the affidavit is denied, the payment of necessary and regular filing fees is made within five days of the denial of the affidavit, or such further time as the court may allow, or within five days of the denial of any appeal relating to the affidavit, whichever is later.

(2) If the affidavit appears regular and complete on its face and indicates that the affiant is indigent, as defined in section twenty-seven A, and requests a waiver, substitution or payment by the commonwealth, of normal fees and costs, the clerk shall grant such request forthwith without hearing and without the necessity of appearance of any party or counsel.

(3) If the affidavit does not appear to satisfy the condition of paragraph (2), the clerk or register shall forthwith bring the affidavit to the attention of the justice or judge, as the case may be. The justice or judge may grant such request forthwith or may have the clerk or register notify the affiant that a hearing will be held on the affidavit within five days. If it appears at the hearing that there is a serious question as to the affiant's indigency, as defined in section twenty-seven A, then before making a finding of indigency, the court shall consider the following facts with respect to the applicant as of the time of hearing, in the immediate past and with respect to the immediate future; his age, education, training, physical and mental ability and number of dependents; gross and net income; regular and extraordinary expense, if any; assets and liabilities; whether or not he is a recipient of public assistance and for what purposes; and any other facts which are relevant to the applicant's ability to pay court costs.

(4) If the court makes a finding of indigency, it shall not deny any request with respect to normal fees and costs, and it shall not deny any request with respect to extra fees and costs if it finds the document, service or object is reasonably necessary to assure the applicant as effective a prosecution, defense or appeal as he would have if he were financially able to pay. The court shall not deny any request without first holding a hearing thereon; and if there is an appeal pursuant to section twenty-seven D following a denial, the court shall, within three days, set forth its written findings and reasons justifying such denial, which document shall be part of the record on appeal.

(5) The clerk of each court shall conspicuously post in the part of his office open to the public a notice informing the public in plain language of the availability of waiver, substitution or payment by the commonwealth of fees and costs for indigent persons.

(6) If the court makes a finding that the applicant could reasonably pay part of the normal fees and costs or extra fees and costs, the court may assess a reasonable partial payment towards said fees or costs and a date by which same is to be paid by the applicant. The court shall not order partial payment without first holding a hearing thereon, and if there is an

appeal pursuant to section 27D following such an order, the court shall, within 3 days, set forth its written findings and reasons justifying the order of partial payment, which document shall be part of the record on appeal.

NOTE 1   "Prosecutors serve neither the judicial process nor the interests of justice by impeding the indigent defendant's efforts to obtain funds pursuant to G.L. c. 261, § 27C. We take this opportunity to state that the prosecution has no proper role to play in a defendant's motion for defense funds unless the judge requests the prosecution's participation." *Commonwealth v. Dotson*, 402 Mass. 185, 187 (1988).

NOTE 2   "[G.L. c.] 261, § 27C(4) assures an indigent defendant of those costs 'reasonably necessary to assure [him] as effective a prosecution, defense or appeal as he would have if he were financially able to pay.' The defendant's motion for costs, however, is not aimed at a 'prosecution, defense or appeal;' it contemplates a possible motion for a new trial after the defendant's initial, unsuccessful defense and appeal. Thus, the defendant's motion for the costs of PCR testing is not cognizable under G.L. c. 261, § 27C(4), because the funds sought are not related to a pending trial or appeal." *Commonwealth v. Davis*, 410 Mass. 680, 684 (1991) (footnote omitted).

NOTE 3   "The standard is essentially one of reasonableness; whether the item is reasonably necessary to prevent the party from being subjected to a disadvantage in preparing or presenting his case adequately. The test is not whether an item might conceivably contribute some assistance to the defense, nor whether such an item would be acquired by a defendant who had unlimited resources. In assessing a request for funds, a judge should look to whether a defendant who was able to pay and was paying the expenses himself, would consider the service sufficiently important that he would choose to obtain it in preparation for trial." *Commonwealth v. Clarke*, 418 Mass. 207, 213 (1994) (citations and punctuation omitted).

NOTE 4   "General Laws c. 261, § 27C, does not cover the costs associated with a motion for a new trial. Under rule 30(c)(5) a judge has 'discretion to allow the defendant costs associated with the preparation and presentation of a motion' for a new trial." *Commonwealth v. Dubois*, 451 Mass. 20, 33 (2008) (citations omitted).

SECTION 27D
Appeal; notice; record; speedy hearing; stay of proceedings; decision final

In any case where the court denies a request for waiver, substitution or payment by the commonwealth of fees and costs, pursuant to section twenty-seven C or any other provision of law, the applicant may take an appeal as hereinafter provided. If the matter arises in the superior, the land, the probate or the housing court departments, the appeal shall be to a single justice of the appeals court at the next sitting thereof. If the matter arises in the juvenile court department, the appeal shall be to the superior court sitting in the nearest county or in Suffolk county. If the matter arises in the district court or Boston municipal court departments, the appeal shall be to the appellate division. Upon being notified of the denial the applicant shall also be advised of his right of appeal, and he shall have seven days thereafter to file a notice of appeal with the clerk or register. Upon receipt of notice of appeal timely filed the clerk or register shall forthwith notify the judge or justice, who shall within three days set forth his written findings and reasons as provided in paragraph (4) of section twenty-seven C. The court denying the request may, with or without motion, stay proceedings pending appeal or issue any other order or process to preserve the rights of the parties pending the appeal. The clerk or register shall then forward the affidavit and request, the court's findings and reasons for denial and any other documents on file relevant to the appeal, to the clerk of the court deciding the appeal, who, upon receipt thereof, shall refer the matter to the court for speedy decision and shall promptly notify the applicant of such decision. The court deciding the appeal may enter a stay or revoke an existing stay or other order, and its decision shall be final with respect to such request.

NOTE   "[T]he decision of the single justice of the Appeals Court is, in accordance with G.L. c. 261, § 27D, 'final.' Moreover, we have repeatedly declined to review a decision of a single justice of the Appeals Court affirming a trial judge's denial of a motion for funds or for a waiver of fees." *Sinath IM v. Commonwealth*, 432 Mass. 1018, 1019 (2000) (citation and quotation marks omitted).

SECTION 27E
Repayment; deductions from judgment or settlement; notice; procedure

Any party on whose behalf any fees or costs have been waived or paid by the commonwealth pursuant to sections twenty-seven C or twenty-seven F, or both, shall repay the total amount thereof to the clerk or register of the court if said party shall have recovered, as a result of the proceeding in which said fees or costs were waived or paid, an amount in excess of three times the total amount of said fees and costs. In any case in which any fees or costs have been so waived or paid, the court, upon the waiver or payment of any such fees or costs shall notify all parties of the total amount of said fees and costs to date and that any money judgment or settlement in favor of the party for whom said fees or costs were waived or paid which exceeds three times the total amount thereof shall be deposited with the clerk or register of the court in the following manner. Any party obligated to pay any judgment or settlement exceeding three times the total amount of said fees and costs, or any portion of such a judgment or settlement, shall pay to the clerk or register the total amount of said fees or costs, or if more than one party is so obligated, his proportional share thereof, and deduct the same from such judgment or settlement. The clerk or register shall notify all parties when the total amount of fees and costs has been so reimbursed. When said notification is received by the party obligated to pay such judgment or settlement or portion thereof, or if no such notification is received after the expiration of thirty days after the payment by said party of such fees or costs or his share thereof, said party shall promptly forward the remainder of the judgment or settlement to the party entitled to it. This procedure shall not be construed to excuse any person on whose behalf any fees or costs have been waived or paid from the obligation to repay the same as provided in this section.

SECTION 27F
Substitute documents, services or objects at less cost; court order

The court may, upon its own motion or that of any party, order that the document, service or object for which a normal or extra fee or cost would be charged shall be provided by an alternative means at lower or no cost, if the substitute thereby provided is substantially equivalent and the provision thereof does not materially impair the rights of any party. In any such order the court may direct payment by the commonwealth of the cost of any substitute to the same extent that the court would but for this section have ordered payment by the commonwealth for the document, service or object in question.

SECTION 27G
Payment procedure; public record; report of expenditures
(Amended by 2011 Mass. Acts c. 93, § 115, effective July 1, 2012.)

The clerk shall receive from any indigent party or his attorney all bills and vouchers for any document, service or object rendered to said party for which an order for payment by the commonwealth has been issued, and shall transmit said bills and vouchers and an attested copy of said order to the office of the court administrator who shall make prompt payment thereon.

The office of the court administrator shall keep a record of all payments or waivers made pursuant to this section and of all repayments made pursuant to section twenty-seven E, including therein the name of the party, his attorney if any, the names and addresses of the person or persons to whom payment is made, the dates each was rendered to the party and the charge for each, and the dates payment was made by the office of the court administrator. This record shall be a public record.

The office of the court administrator shall on or before December first of each year make a written report to the general court indicating the amounts and purposes of all expenditures under sections twenty-seven A to twenty-seven G, inclusive, and making such recommendations for change in the law as he deems necessary.

PART 2

Crimes, Punishments, and Proceedings in Criminal Cases

2

Chapter 263. Rights of Persons Accused of Crime

Section
1   Nature of crime; right to be informed; penalty
1A   Fingerprinting and photographing
2   Arrest on false pretense; penalty
3   False imprisonment; actions against officers
4   Prosecution of crimes; manner
4A   Waiver of indictment; procedure
5   Counsel; right of accused
5A   Driving while intoxicated; right to medical examination; notice
6   Conviction; manner; waiver of jury trial
7   Acquittal; effect on subsequent charges
8   Acquittal on defective pleadings; subsequent indictment
8A   Acquittal on merits in district court or housing courts of city of Boston and counties of Hampden and Worcester; effect
9   Punishment; conditions precedent

SECTION 1
Nature of crime; right to be informed; penalty

Whoever is arrested by virtue of process, or whoever is taken into custody by an officer, has a right to know from the officer who arrests or claims to detain him the true ground on which the arrest is made; and an officer who refuses to answer a question relative to the reason for such arrest, or answers such question untruly, or assigns to the person arrested an untrue reason for the arrest, or neglects upon request to exhibit to the person arrested, or to any other person acting in his behalf, the precept by virtue of which such arrest has been made, shall be punished by a fine of not more than one thousand dollars or by imprisonment for not more than one year.

SECTION 1A
Fingerprinting and photographing

Whoever is arrested by virtue of process, or is taken into custody by an officer, and charged with the commission of a felony shall be fingerprinted, according to the system of the bureau of investigation and intelligence in the department of state police, and may be photographed. Two copies of such fingerprints and photographs shall be forwarded within a reasonable time to the colonel of state police by the person in charge of the police department taking such fingerprints and photographs.

NOTE   "[W]e construe G.L. c. 263, § 1A, to include an individual who is arrested for an offense classified as a felony but who is later charged with delinquency because of age." *Commonwealth v. Shipps*, 399 Mass. 820, 832–33 (1987) (footnote and citation omitted).

SECTION 2
Arrest on false pretense; penalty

An officer who arrests or takes into or detains in custody a person, pretending to have a process if he has none, or pretending to have a different process from that which he has,

shall be punished by a fine of not more than one thousand dollars or by imprisonment for not more than one year.

SECTION 3
False imprisonment; actions against officers

No action, except for use of excessive force, shall lie against any officer other than the arresting officer, by reason of the fact that, in good faith and in the performance of his duties, he participates in the arrest or imprisonment of any person believed to be guilty of a crime unless it can be shown that such other officer in the performance of his duties took an active part in the arrest or imprisonment as aforesaid, either by ordering or directing that said arrest or imprisonment take place or be made, or by actually initiating the making and carrying out of said arrest and imprisonment. No action, except for use of excessive force, shall lie against any bystander assisting an officer in making an arrest, at the request of the officer.

SECTION 4
Prosecution of crimes; manner

No person shall be held to answer in any court for an alleged crime, except upon an indictment by a grand jury or upon a complaint before a district court, the housing court of the city of Boston, the western division of the housing court department, the northeastern division of the housing court department, the southeastern division of the housing court department; the housing court of the county of Worcester or in proceedings before a court-martial.

A defendant charged with an offense punishable by imprisonment in state prison shall have the right to be proceeded against by indictment except when the offense charged is within the concurrent jurisdiction of the district and superior courts and the district court retains jurisdiction.

No juvenile shall be sentenced to any punishment as is provided by law for the offense by a juvenile court or a juvenile session of a district court, as the case may be, unless he has been proceeded against by indictment or has waved indictment pursuant to section four A of chapter two hundred and sixty-three, except as otherwise provided in section seventy-two A of chapter one hundred and nineteen. The clerk of the superior court in which an indictment of such juvenile is returned shall promptly remit the indictment to the clerk of the juvenile court or the juvenile session of the district court, as the case may be, in which such indictment is to be tried.

2

SECTION 4A
Waiver of indictment; procedure

A defendant charged in the district court with an offense as to which he has the right to be proceeded against by indictment shall have the right, except when the offense charged is a capital crime, to waive that right, whereupon the court shall have as full jurisdiction of the complaint as if an indictment had been found. If a defendant is so charged and requests a probable cause hearing in district court, that request shall constitute a waiver of the right to be proceeded against by indictment and the prosecution may proceed upon the complaint. If a defendant waives the right to be proceeded against by indictment, a probable cause hearing shall be held in the district court unless the defendant waives the probable cause hearing or unless the prosecutor elects to proceed by indictment pursuant to the Massachusetts Rules of Criminal Procedure.

If the district attorney desires to charge a defendant who waives indictment hereunder with an additional non-capital crime which is not charged in the complaint upon which the prosecution is proceeding and as to which there is the right to be proceeded against by indictment, the district attorney may prepare an additional complaint charging such additional crime and serve that complaint upon the defendant so as to give the defendant an opportunity to waive indictment upon such additional charge.

NOTE   No Written Waiver Required. "While we have held that a defendant's waiver of his right to indictment must be explicit, *Commonwealth v. Perry*, 418 Mass. 808, 812–813 (1994), and voluntarily and intelligently made, *De Golyer v. Commonwealth*, [314 Mass. 626 (1943)], we have not held that the execution of a written waiver is constitutionally required for it to be effective . . . .

"General Laws c. 263, § 4A, however, does not require that the waiver of indictment be in writing. Contrast G.L. c. 263, § 6 (written waiver required to waive jury trial)." *Commonwealth v. Peterson*, 445 Mass. 782, 785–86 (2006).

SECTION 5
Counsel; right of accused

A person accused of crime shall at his trial be allowed to be heard by counsel, to defend himself, to produce witnesses and proofs in his favor and to meet the witnesses produced against him face to face.

**NOTE   **Does "the language of art. 12 and G.L. c. 263, § 5 (1986 ed.), provide[ ] the defendant with more protection against the introduction of a witness's previously recorded testimony than does the Sixth Amendment? We conclude that in these circumstances the specific language of art. 12 and G.L. c. 263, § 5, does not impose a stricter standard than that of the Sixth Amendment." *Commonwealth v. Siegfriedt*, 402 Mass. 424, 430 (1988).

SECTION 5A
Driving while intoxicated; right to medical examination; notice

A person held in custody at a police station or other place of detention, charged with operating a motor vehicle while under the influence of intoxicating liquor, shall have the right, at his request and at his expense, to be examined immediately by a physician selected by him. The police official in charge of such station or place of detention, or his designee, shall inform him of such right immediately upon being booked, and shall afford him a reasonable opportunity to exercise it. Such person shall, immediately upon being booked, be given a copy of this section unless such a copy is

posted in the police station or other place of detention in a conspicuous place to which such person has access.

**NOTE 1   **"[U]nder G.L. c. 263, § 5A, the police must not prevent or hinder an individual's timely, reasonable attempts to obtain an independent examination, but they need not assist him. They need only inform him of his rights and allow him access to a telephone." *Commonwealth v. Alano*, 388 Mass. 871, 879 (1983).

NOTE 2a   Remedy. "Where a defendant's right under § 5A has been violated, the violation itself is prima facie evidence that the defendant has been prejudiced in that his opportunity to obtain and present potentially exculpatory evidence has been restricted or destroyed. This presumption of prejudice, however, may be overcome by overwhelming evidence of intoxication . . . or by other evidence indicating that the omission was not prejudicial in the circumstances." *Commonwealth v. King*, 429 Mass. 169, 180–81 (1999).

**NOTE 2b   **"Thus, G.L. c. 263, § 5A, creates a right to obtain evidence that is available for only a short period of time, and also seeks to protect this right by requiring that the defendant be informed of its existence. In contrast, G.L. c. 276, § 33A is not primarily concerned with ensuring access to evidence which has a short period of availability. Consequently, while suppression of unfavorable evidence is an appropriate remedy for violations of a defendant's rights under § 33A, suppression of evidence will not always be an effective remedy for a violation of a defendant's rights under G.L. c. 263, § 5A, since a violation of § 5A may actually prevent exculpatory evidence from being revealed. For example, in this case, the police officers did not conduct a breathalyzer examination. Therefore, there is no unfavorable evidence to suppress. Nevertheless, the defendant might still be unfairly prejudiced by the police officers' violation of his § 5A rights because, had an independent examination been conducted, evidence which exculpated him may have emerged." *Commonwealth v. Andrade*, 389 Mass. 874, 881–82 (1983).

NOTE 3   Bail. "[W]hen the bail commissioner is notified that an individual has been arrested and wishes to exercise his right to an independent medical examination under § 5A, the bail commissioner must respond as promptly as he is able . . . . In cases where the defendant has not asserted his § 5A right, the general rule of promptness, loosely delimited by the six-hour guideline, still holds. . . . [I]t is crucial that [the bail commissioner] be aware when a defendant has asserted the § 5A right." *Commonwealth v. King*, 429 Mass. 169, 176 (1999).

NOTE 4   Lost Blood Sample. After the defendant was informed of his rights, a police officer drove him, at his request, to a nearby hospital to have a blood sample drawn. Said sample was subsequently inexplicably lost by the hospital. Under these facts, there was no violation of this statute. *Commonwealth v. Lindner*, 395 Mass. 144 (1985).

**NOTE 5   **"We again hold that police have no obligation under G.L. c. 263, § 5A, to transport a defendant to a doctor, hospital or clinic to obtain an independent examination. . . . [The defendant] requested an opportunity to make a telephone call in order to exercise that right and telephoned a hospital to arrange for the test. The hospital told him that they would administer the test if he went to the hospital, but that they would not be able to perform it at the barracks. The police refused to transport him to the hospital. . . . If the judge dismissed the complaint because of the conceded refusal of the police to transport the defendant to the hospital, he was in error. Our cases clearly demonstrate that 'under G.L. c. 263, § 5A, the police must not prevent or hinder an individual's timely, reasonable attempts to obtain an independent examination, but they need not assist him.' *Commonwealth v. Alano*, 388 Mass. 871, 879 (1983). . . . If the police did in fact obstruct the defendant's attempts to get released on bail, his G.L. c. 263, § 5A, rights were violated." *Commonwealth v. Rosewarne*, 410 Mass. 53, 54–55 (1991); see also *Commonwealth v. McIntyre*, 36 Mass. App. Ct. 193, 202–04 (1994) ("The fact that the hospital was nearby or that the police were available to transport the defendant to the hospital, or to go to the hospital at his request, is not relevant. It is clear that the police are not under any duty to assist a defendant in obtaining a physical examination or a blood alcohol content test." *Id.* at 204).

NOTE 6　　Drugs—No Right to be Advised of Option to Arrange for Independent Medical Examination. Article 12 of the Massachusetts Declaration of Rights and the 6th and 14th Amendment to the United States Constitution do not require that an individual arrested for operating under the influence of drugs be advised by the police that he or she can arrange for an independent medical examination. *Commonwealth v. Mandell*, 61 Mass. App. Ct. 526 (2004).

SECTION 6
Conviction; manner; waiver of jury trial

A person indicted for a crime shall not be convicted thereof except by confessing his guilt in open court, by admitting the truth of the charge against him by his plea or demurrer or by the verdict of a jury accepted and recorded by the court or, in any criminal case other than a capital case, by the judgment of the court. Any defendant in a criminal case other than a capital case, whether begun by indictment or upon complaint, may, if he shall so elect, when called upon to plead, or later and before a jury has been impanelled to try him upon such indictment or complaint, waive his right to trial by jury by signing a written waiver thereof and filing the same with the clerk of the court. If the court consents to the waiver, he shall be tried by the court instead of by a jury, but not, however, unless all the defendants, if there are two or more charged with related offenses, whether prosecuted under the same or different indictments or complaints shall have exercised such election before a jury has been impanelled to try any of the defendants; and in every such case the court shall have jurisdiction to hear and try such cause and render judgment and sentence thereon. Except where there is more than one defendant involved as aforesaid, consent to said waiver shall not be denied in the district court or the Boston municipal court if the waiver is filed before the case is transferred for jury trial to the appropriate jury session, as provided in section twenty-seven A of chapter two hundred and eighteen.

NOTE 1　　Related Statute. G.L. c. 278, § 2—Trial of issues of fact.

NOTE 2　　Waiver Requirements. "The rule we laid down in *Ciummei v. Commonwealth*, [378 Mass. 504 (1979)], requiring an oral colloquy in addition to a written waiver, has been termed a 'bright line rule.' . . . A waiver obtained without observing both requirements is ineffective." *Commonwealth v. Osborne*, 445 Mass. 776, 781 (2006).

NOTE 3　　Written jury trial waiver. "There is no requirement that, when accepting a defendant's tender of a guilty plea, a defendant's waiver of the right to a trial with or without a jury be in writing. . . . The absence of a written jury trial waiver does not violate G.L. c. 263, § 6, or rule 19 (a), and does not provide a basis to invalidate the defendant's pleas. . . . The rule, by its express terms, applies only in circumstances where a defendant chooses to be tried by a judge instead of a jury." *Commonwealth v. Hubbard*, 457 Mass. 24, 26, 28 (2010).

SECTION 7
Acquittal; effect on subsequent charges

A person shall not be held to answer on a second indictment or complaint for a crime of which he has been acquitted upon the facts and merits; but he may plead such acquittal in bar of any subsequent prosecution for the same crime, not-

withstanding any defect in the form or substance of the indictment or complaint on which he was acquitted.

NOTE 1　　Double Jeopardy; Insufficient Evidence. The defendant moved to dismiss on double jeopardy grounds arguing that there was insufficient evidence at the first trial to warrant a guilty verdict. The judge declined to do so, and the Supreme Judicial Court affirmed, ruling that "this evidence [from the first trial], if offered at a retrial of the indictment, will be sufficient to take the case to a jury even without defendant's confession. *Cf. Commonwealth v. Campbell*, 378 Mass. 680, 688–690 (1979).

"Furthermore, dismissal is not now warranted. It would be premature to assume that the prosecution, on retrial will not rely on evidence that has developed since the trial, or evidence that it elected not to pursue at the defendant's first trial." *Commonwealth v. Sperrazza*, 404 Mass. 19, 21 (1989) (citations omitted).

"When a defendant's trial ends in a mistrial because the jury are unable to reach a verdict, double jeopardy principles do not bar retrial as long as the Commonwealth presented evidence at trial legally sufficient to warrant a conviction. In making a determination whether the Commonwealth presented sufficient evidence to support a finding of guilt, we apply the standard articulated in *Commonwealth v. Latimore*, 378 Mass. 671, 677–78 (1979), and used in reviewing the denial of a motion for a required finding of not guilty." *Cramer v. Commonwealth*, 419 Mass. 106, 109 (1994) (citations omitted).

Cf. Aucella v. Commonwealth, 406 Mass. 415, 416 (1990). After a hung jury and mistrial, the defendant "moved to dismiss the indictments on the ground that the prosecutor's evidence at trial was legally insufficient, and that retrial was therefore barred by double jeopardy principles as articulated in *Berry v. Commonwealth*, 393 Mass. 793 (1985)." The Supreme Judicial Court agreed.

**NOTE 2　　** See also Note 1 following Mass.R.Crim.P. 24.

**NOTE 3　　** "The defendant then moved for a mistrial which the judge allowed. The defendant argues that double jeopardy bars retrial after a mistrial has been declared. Under both Federal and Massachusetts law, the protection against double jeopardy bars a retrial after a mistrial is declared on a defendant's motion if 'the prosecutor intended to provoke a mistrial or otherwise engaged in 'overreaching' or 'harassment.' *Commonwealth v. Smith*, 404 Mass. 1, 4 (1989)." *Mercedes v. Commonwealth*, 405 Mass. 693, 696 (1989).

**NOTE 4　　** "Today we decide whether the double jeopardy clause of the Fifth Amendment to the United States Constitution and the corresponding protections against double jeopardy provided by State law bar retrial after conviction on one indictment is reversed, where the wording of the indictment is identical to the wording of another indictment on which the defendant was acquitted, and the defendant has shown that it cannot be determined on which alleged offense the jury acquitted him and on which they convicted him. Because we determine that, in these circumstances, the Commonwealth should bear the risk that identically-worded indictments will later cause the defendant to be subjected to a retrial on an acquitted charge, we hold that the judge erred in failing to dismiss the two indictments charging the defendant, Peter Hrycenko, with aggravated rape and reverse his convictions on these indictments. We reach this conclusion even though the uncertainty regarding a retrial may have been avoided if the defendant had exercised his right to request a bill of particulars prior to the first trial." *Commonwealth v. Hrycenko*, 417 Mass. 309, 310 (1994).

**NOTE 5　　** See Note 15 Duplicative Convictions following G.L. c. 265, § 22.

SECTION 8
Acquittal on defective pleadings; subsequent indictments

If a person has been acquitted by reason of a variance between the indictment or complaint and the proof, or by reason of a defect of form or substance in the indictment or complaint, he may be again arraigned, tried and convicted for the same

2

crime on a new indictment or complaint, notwithstanding such former acquittal.

SECTION 8A
Acquittal on merits in district court or housing courts of city of Boston and counties of Hampden and Worcester; effect

A person shall not be held to answer in a district court or the housing court of the city of Boston, the western division of the housing court department, the northeastern division of the housing court department, the southeastern division of the housing court department, or the housing court of the county of Worcester to a second complaint for an offense for which he has already been tried upon the merits in a district court or in the housing court of the city of Boston, the housing court of the county of Hampden, the northeastern division of the housing court department, the southeastern division of the housing court department, or the housing court of the county of Worcester.

SECTION 9
Punishment; conditions precedent

A person shall not be punished for a crime unless he has been legally convicted thereof by a court having competent jurisdiction of the cause and of the person.

Chapter 263A. Witness Protection in Criminal Matters

Section
1   Definitions
2   Witness protection board; composition; powers and duties
3   Petition requesting witness protection services
4   Temporary action based on exigent circumstances without prior approval by board
5   Protective services provided to critical witnesses; notice to defense counsel
6   Written memorandum of understanding; persons required to sign; contents
7   Refusal of protective services; revocation of services upon violation of memorandum of understanding
8   Relocation of critical witness within public housing system
9   Relocation of critical witness to another public school
10   Entitlement or private right of action not available; governmental immunity
11   Liaison with United States Marshal's office; pursuit of federal resources and funding
12   Confidentiality of records
13   Disclosure of identity or location of witness or other sensitive information; penalties

SECTION 1
Definitions

For the purposes of this chapter, the following words shall have the following meanings:—

"Board", the witness protection board established in section 2.

"Prosecuting officer", the attorney general or a district attorney from each county.

"Critical witness", any person who is participating in a criminal investigation, or has received a subpoena or who is reasonably expected to give testimony that is, in the judgment of the prosecuting officer, essential to a criminal investigation or proceeding or such person's relatives, guardians, friends or associates who are reasonably endangered by such person's participation in the criminal investigation or proceeding.

SECTION 2
Witness protection board; composition; powers and duties

There is hereby established a witness protection board within the executive office of public safety consisting of the secretary of public safety, the attorney general, the auditor, a chief of police appointed by the Massachusetts Chiefs of Police Association, and a district attorney appointed by the Massachusetts District Attorney's Association, or any member's respective designees. The board shall oversee the commonwealth's witness protection program and coordinate the efforts of state, county and law enforcement agencies to protect the health, safety and welfare of witnesses including, but not limited to, the administration and approval of funding for witness protection services. The board shall promulgate rules and regulations for the administration of the commonwealth's witness protection program and establish procedures to maximize federal funds for witness protection services.

SECTION 3
Petition requesting witness protection services

In any criminal investigation or proceeding, the prosecuting officer with jurisdiction over the investigation or proceeding may file a petition with the board requesting witness protection services for a critical witness if the prosecuting officer certifies that such witness's participation in the investigation or proceeding places the witness at risk of harm including, but not limited to, intimidation or retaliatory violence. The petition shall include a proposed plan for protective services which shall include, but not be limited to, projected costs, method of protection and likely duration of services. The board shall review the petition as soon as possible and if, by a vote of 3 or more board members, finds that the petition and plan comply with the rules and regulations established by the board, the board shall assist the prosecuting officer to coordinate the efforts of state, county and local agencies to secure witness protection services. The board shall, subject to appropriation, reimburse the prosecuting officer for any witness protection related costs that comply with the regulations and guidelines established by the board.

SECTION 4
Temporary action based on exigent circumstances without prior approval by board

If a prosecuting officer determines that exigent circumstances exist regarding an imminent threat to the safety of a critical witness, he may take any appropriate temporary action he determines is necessary to protect the safety of the witness without prior approval of the board. The prosecuting officer shall inform the board of the action taken and the related costs within 48 hours. Any such costs, which would otherwise be in compliance with the rules and regulations established by the board pursuant to section 2, may be reimbursed to the prosecuting officer.

SECTION 5
Protective services provided to critical witnesses; notice to defense counsel

Protective services provided to a critical witness may include, but not be limited to:—

(a) any necessary armed protection or escort, marked or unmarked surveillance or periodic visits or contact by law enforcement officials prior, during or subsequent to a criminal proceeding;

(b) physical relocation to an alternate shelter, housing or residence;

(c) reasonable housing expenses;

(d) transportation or storage of personal possessions;

(e) basic living expenses; and

(f) petition for a protective order on any individual identified as a threat to a critical witness.

Any protective services provided to a critical witness shall be made known to defense counsel pursuant to Rule 14 of the Massachusetts Rules of Criminal Procedure.

SECTION 6
Written memorandum of understanding; persons required to sign; contents

Before providing witness protection services to any critical witness under this chapter, except where it is determined that temporary protective services are necessary pursuant to section 4, the prosecuting officer shall enter into a written memorandum of understanding with such witness. If temporary protective services have been provided pursuant to section 4, a written memorandum of understanding shall be entered into as soon as practicable. The written memorandum of understanding shall be signed by: the prosecuting officer or his designee; the witness to be afforded protective services; the witness' guardian if the witness is a minor; and the witness' attorney if the witness is represented by counsel. Such written memorandum of understanding shall not be considered a grant of immunity. The written memorandum of understanding shall include:—

(a) The responsibilities agreed to by the witness while receiving protective services, shall include, but not limited to, an agreement to:—

(i) provide complete and truthful information to all relevant law enforcement officials related to all relevant investigations, and to testify completely and truthfully in all appropriate proceedings;

(ii) not commit any crime;

(iii) take all necessary precautions to avoid making known to others his participation in the witness protection program or the provision of protective services under such program;

(iv) comply with any legal obligations or civil judgments against the witness;

(v) cooperate with all reasonable requests of officers and employees of the commonwealth who are providing protective services under this chapter;

(vi) designate another person to act as an agent for the service of process. Under no circumstances shall the person so designated be an employee of the prosecuting officer or other law enforcement agency, or be a member of or perform duties on behalf of the witness protection board;

(vii) make a sworn statement of all outstanding legal obligations, including obligations concerning child custody and visitation, and child support;

(viii) disclose any probation or parole conditions, obligations, or responsibilities; and

(ix) regularly inform the prosecuting officer of the activities and current address of the witness.

(b) The responsibilities agreed to by the commonwealth while providing protective services shall include, but not be limited to:

(i) The names and telephone numbers of representatives of the prosecuting officer or law enforcement personnel to contact if the witness has questions or concerns related to the protective services or the witness' safety;

(ii) The protective services that the prosecuting officer has determined will be requested, and, if authorized, to be provided to the witness under this chapter; and

(iii) The procedures to be followed, if there is a determination by the prosecuting officer that there has occurred a material breach of the memorandum of understanding, as established by the prosecuting officer.

SECTION 7
Refusal of protective services; revocation of services upon violation of memorandum of understanding

If a witness, after being offered protective services under this chapter, at any time declines to receive such services, the prosecuting officer shall request that the witness make such refusal in writing, or, if the witness refuses to document such refusal of services in writing, the prosecuting officer shall document the refusal and inform the witness protection board forthwith that the witness has declined protective services. If a witness violates the terms of the memorandum of understanding set forth in section 6 or any other condition of receiving witness protection services under this chapter, the prosecuting officer may revoke and terminate all protective services, and shall so advise the witness in writing. The prosecuting officer shall notify the board forthwith of such revocation and grounds therefore.

SECTION 8
Relocation of critical witness within public housing system

Notwithstanding any general or special law to the contrary, or any regulation, rule or ordinance, if a petition and plan for witness protection, approved by the board, requires relocation of a critical witness within the public housing system, such relocation shall be effectuated without regard to any impediment including, but not limited to, any existing waiting list.

SECTION 9
Relocation of critical witness to another public school

Notwithstanding any general or special law to the contrary, or any regulation, rule or ordinance, if a petition and plan for witness protection, approved by the witness protection board, requires relocation of a critical witness to another public school within or without of the witness's current school system, such relocation shall be effectuated without regard to any impediment including, but not limited to, class capacity limits and jurisdictional boundaries of any given school district.

2

SECTION 10
Entitlement or private right of action not available; governmental immunity

Nothing in this section shall be construed as creating a right, entitlement or cause of action on behalf of any person against any public employee, public agency, the commonwealth, or any agency responsible for the provision of services set forth in this chapter. The commonwealth, its officers and employees, and law enforcement personnel shall have immunity from suit based on any decision, act or omission related to this chapter.

SECTION 11
Liaison with United States Marshal's office; pursuit of federal resources and funding

The board shall establish a liaison with the United States Marshal's office in order to facilitate the legal processes over which the federal government has sole authority. The liaison shall coordinate all requests for federal assistance relating to witness protection.

The board shall pursue all federal sources that may be available for implementing this chapter. For that purpose, the board shall establish a liaison with the United States Department of Justice.

The board shall, in conjunction with the executive office of administration and finance and the senate and house ways and means committees, establish procedures to maximize federal funding for witness protection services.

SECTION 12
Confidentiality of records

Records of the board and all records relating to petitions and filed with the board shall be confidential and shall not be public records. Section 11A and section 11A½ of chapter 30A shall not apply to meetings, discussions or deliberations of the board.

SECTION 13
Disclosure of identity or location of witness or other sensitive information; penalties

(a) A prosecuting officer may disclose or refuse to disclose the identity or location of a protected witness, or any other matter concerning a protected witness or the program, after balancing the danger such disclosure may pose to the protected witness, the detriment it may cause to the general effectiveness of the program, and the benefit it may afford to the public or the person seeking discovery, except that a prosecuting officer shall, upon the request of a federal, state or local law enforcement official, or pursuant to a court order, disclose to such official the identity, location and criminal records relating to the protected witness when the prosecuting officer knows, or the request from such official indicates, that the protected witness is under criminal investigation for, or has been arrested for, or charged with, a felony.

(b) Whoever, without the express written authorization of the prosecuting officer, knowingly discloses any information received from the prosecuting officer or generated in connection with witness protection services and which poses a risk of harm: to a program participant; of disclosure of any person's participation in such program; or of jeopardizing the objectives of the program shall be punished by imprisonment in the house of correction for not more than 2½ years or by a fine of not more than $5,000, or by both such fine and imprisonment. This section shall not apply to: any members of the board; members of the attorney general's office; members of the district attorneys' offices; law enforcement; or agents thereof, acting in the lawful discharge of their duties.

Chapter 264. Crimes Against Governments

Section

1	Treason defined
2	Penalty for treason
3	Misprision of treason; penalty
4	Treason; manner of conviction
5	Flag; penalty for misuse
6	Flag; use in print in certain cases
7	Foreign flags; misuse; penalty
8	Foreign flag; display; penalty; exception
9	National anthem; manner of playing
10	Repealed
10A	Uniforms; penalty for unlawful use
11	Promotion of anarchy; prohibition
12–14	Repealed
14A	Educational activities; participation; exchange teachers; necessity of oath
15	Repealed
16	Subversive organization defined
16A	Communist Party
17	Subversive organizations; prohibition
18	Subversive organizations; actions to enjoin; duty of attorney general
19	Subversive organization; knowingly becoming or remaining member; penalty
20	Public office; ineligibility of certain persons; removal of disability
21	Subversive organizations; destruction or concealment of books; penalty
22	Subversive organizations; knowingly permitting to use building; penalty
23	Subversive organizations; contribution; penalty

SECTION 1
Treason defined

Treason against the commonwealth shall consist only in levying war against it, or in adhering to the enemies thereof, giving them aid and comfort; it shall not be bailable.

SECTION 2
Penalty for treason

Whoever commits treason against the commonwealth shall be punished by imprisonment in the state prison for life.

SECTION 3
Misprision of treason; penalty

Whoever, having knowledge of the commission of treason, conceals the same and does not as soon as may be disclose and make known such treason to the governor, or to a justice of the supreme judicial or superior court, shall be guilty of misprision of treason, and shall be punished by a fine of not more than one thousand dollars or by imprisonment in the state prison for not more than five years, or in jail for not more than two years.

SECTION 4
Treason; manner of conviction

No person shall be convicted of treason except by the testimony of two witnesses to the same overt act of treason whereof he stands indicted, unless he confesses the same in open court.

SECTION 5
Flag; penalty for misuse

Whoever publicly burns or otherwise mutilates, tramples upon, defaces or treats contemptuously the flag of the United States or of Massachusetts, whether such flag is public or private property, or whoever displays such flag or any representation thereof upon which are words, figures, advertisements or designs, or whoever causes or permits such flag to be used in a parade as a receptacle for depositing or collecting money or any other article or thing, or whoever exposes to public view, manufactures, sells, exposes for sale, gives away or has in his possession for sale or to give away or for use for any purpose, any article or substance, being an article of merchandise or a receptacle of merchandise or articles upon which is attached, through a wrapping or otherwise, engraved or printed in any manner, a representation of the United States flag, or whoever uses any representation of the arms or the great seal of the commonwealth for any advertising or commercial purpose, shall be punished by a fine of not less than one hundred dollars or by imprisonment for not more than one year, or both. Words, figures, advertisements or designs attached to, or directly or indirectly connected with, such flag or any representation thereof in such manner that such flag or its representation is used to attract attention to or advertise such words, figures, advertisements or designs, shall for the purposes of this section be deemed to be upon such flag. Notwithstanding the foregoing, there may be attached to the staff bearing a flag of the United States or of Massachusetts belonging to an organization of veterans of the Civil War, to a camp of the United Spanish War Veterans, to a post or department of the American Legion, or to a post or department of the Veterans of Foreign Wars of the United States, or to a post or department of the Jewish War Veterans of the United States, or to a camp or department of the Sons of Union Veterans of the Civil War, or to a barracks or department of the Veterans of World War I of the U.S.A., or belonging to or used in the service of the United States or the commonwealth, a streamer having inscribed thereon the names of battles and the name and number of the organization to which such flag belongs. For the purposes of this section, a flag shall be deemed to continue to belong to any organization of veterans hereinbefore specified, although such organization has ceased to exist, during such time as it remains in the lawful ownership or custody of any other of the aforesaid organizations or of the commonwealth or of any political subdivision thereof, or of any patriotic or historical society incorporated under the laws of the commonwealth or determined by the adjutant general to be a proper custodian thereof. For the purposes of this section the term "flag of the United States" shall mean any flag which has been designated by Act or Resolution of the Congress of the United States as the national emblem, whether or not such designation is currently in force.

SECTION 6
Flag; use in print in certain cases

The preceding section shall not apply to publications issued solely for the purpose of giving information in relation to the flag, or of promoting patriotism or of encouraging the study of American history, or to any newspaper, periodical, book, pamphlet, certificate, diploma, warrant, or commission of appointment to office, ornamental picture, article of jewelry, or stationery for use in correspondence, on which is printed, painted, or placed the flag of the United States not connected with any advertisement and not used for advertising purposes, or to any article of jewelry upon which is placed a representation of the arms or flag of the commonwealth not connected with any advertisement and not used for advertising purposes; but no words, figures, designs or other marks of any kind shall be placed upon the flag of the United States or of the commonwealth or representation thereof, or upon any representation of the arms of the commonwealth.

SECTION 7
Foreign flags; misuse; penalty

Whoever publicly mutilates, tramples upon, defaces or treats contemptuously the flag or emblem of a foreign country at peace with the United States, whether such flag or emblem is public or private property, or whoever displays such flag or emblem or any representation thereof upon which are words, figures, advertisements or designs, shall be punished by a fine of not less than five nor more than fifty dollars.

SECTION 8
Foreign flag; display; penalty; exception

Whoever displays the flag or emblem of a foreign country upon the outside of a state, county, city or town building or public schoolhouse shall be punished by a fine of not more than twenty dollars; but, except as to public schoolhouses, this section shall not apply when a citizen of such foreign country becomes the guest of the United States or of the commonwealth, or when a diplomatic representative of a foreign country is a guest at said public building and, if the governor by proclamation authorizes the flag of the country of which such guest is a citizen to be displayed upon public buildings.

SECTION 9
National anthem; manner of playing

Whoever plays, sings or renders the "Star Spangled Banner" in any public place, theater, motion picture hall, restaurant or cafe, or at any public entertainment, other than as a whole and separate composition or number, without embellishment or addition in the way of national or other melodies, or whoever plays, sings or renders the "Star Spangled Banner", or any part thereof, as dance music, as an exit march or as a part of a medley of any kind, shall be punished by a fine of not more than one hundred dollars.

SECTION 10
Repealed

SECTION 10A
Uniforms; penalty for unlawful use

Whoever wears the uniform, or any distinctive part thereof, of the United States army, navy, marine corps, revenue cutter service, or coast guard, or of the national guard, or of any organization enumerated in section seventy of chapter two hundred and sixty-six, or wears a hat, cap or other apparel similar to or resembling the hat, cap or other distinctive part of any such uniform, while engaged, for personal profit, in soliciting alms, in selling merchandise or taking orders for the same, in seeking or receiving contributions in support of any cause, enterprise or undertaking or in soliciting or receiving subscriptions to any book, paper or magazine, shall be punished by a fine of not more than one hundred dollars, or by imprisonment for not more than three months; provided, that this section shall not apply to the sale of property or any other act or transaction conducted under authority of the government of the United States, and provided further, that no person shall be subject to prosecution hereunder for wearing the uniform, or any distinctive part thereof, while engaged as aforesaid, of any organization enumerated in said section seventy if he so acted under authority of such organization or any post, camp or other unit thereof.

SECTION 11
Promotion of anarchy; prohibition

Whoever by speech or by exhibition, distribution or promulgation of any written or printed document, paper or pictorial representation advocates, advises, counsels or incites assault upon any public official, or the killing of any person, or the unlawful destruction of real or personal property, or the overthrow by force or violence or other unlawful means of the government of the commonwealth or of the United States, shall be punished by imprisonment in the state prison for not more than three years, or in jail for not more than two and one half years, or by a fine of not more than one thousand dollars; provided, that this section shall not be construed as reducing the penalty now imposed for the violation of any law. It shall be unlawful for any person who shall have been convicted of a violation of this section, whether or not any sentence shall have been imposed, to perform the duties of a teacher or of an officer of administration in any public or private educational institution, and the superior court, in a suit by the commonwealth, shall have jurisdiction in equity to restrain and enjoin any such person from performing such duties thereafter; provided, that any such restraining order or injunction shall be forthwith vacated if such conviction shall be set aside.

SECTIONS 12–14
Repealed

SECTION 14A
Educational activities; participation; exchange teachers; necessity of oath

Any city or town of the commonwealth may, through its school committee, participate in the educational activities under the United States Educational Program conducted by the department of state pursuant to Public Law 584, 79th Congress, and Public Law 402, 80th Congress, whereby there is an interchange of teaching positions between a teacher of such city or town and a teacher from abroad under an arrangement or agreement which provides that each teacher shall continue to receive his salary from his own school. The salary may be paid by such city or town notwithstanding that the teacher to whom it is paid is not actually rendering service within the schools thereof. The exchange teacher from abroad shall not be required to take or subscribe to any oaths or pledge of allegiance which is inconsistent with his citizenship in a foreign country.

SECTION 15
Repealed

SECTION 16
Subversive organization defined

The term "subversive organization" as used in sections seventeen, eighteen, nineteen, twenty-one, twenty-two and twenty-three of this chapter shall mean any form of association of three or more persons, however named or characterized, and by whatever legal or nonlegal entity or non-entity it be established, and whether incorporated or otherwise for the common purpose of advocating, advising, counseling or inciting the overthrow by force or violence, or by other unlawful means, of the government of the commonwealth or of the United States.

SECTION 16A
Communist Party

The Communist Party is hereby declared to be a subversive organization.

SECTION 17
Subversive organizations; prohibition

A subversive organization is hereby declared to be unlawful.

SECTION 18
Subversive organizations; actions to enjoin; procedure; duty of attorney general

The attorney general shall bring an action in the superior court by an information or petition in equity against any organization which he has reasonable cause to believe is a subversive organization. The fact that such information or petition has been or is to be filed shall not be made public until an order of notice, hereinafter referred to, is issued.

A justice of the superior court shall, upon a summary examination of the information or petition and such supporting depositions, other testimony or evidence as he may require, if he is of the opinion that there is reasonable cause to believe that such organization is subversive, issue an order of notice against such organization to show cause why there should not be an adjudication to that effect. Notice of such order of notice shall be sent by registered mail to such officers of such organization as are known to the court, and to any other persons, including members, as the court may order, at least fourteen days before the return day of said order of notice. Notice of such order shall also be given by publication once a week for two successive weeks in a daily newspaper published in the city of Boston. Any officer or member of any such organization or its attorney may appear and answer on its behalf on or before the return day or such later time as the court may allow. The respondent shall have the right to claim a trial by jury within the time allowed for filing its answer or within such further time as the court may allow within its discretion. If no person appears and answers the court may on its own motion or upon motion of the petitioner default the organization. If an appearance is entered and answer filed the case shall be set down for a speedy hearing.

Such hearing shall be conducted in accordance with the usual course of proceedings in equity, including all rights of exception and appeal. Upon such hearing or upon default the court may make an adjudication that the organization is a subversive organization and may enjoin such organization from acting further as such, may order the dissolution of the organization and shall cause the secretary of state to be notified of the finding of the court; provided, however, that the effectiveness of any such adjudication, injunction and order shall be stayed pending determination by the supreme judicial court of any exceptions or appeals; or the court may find that the organization is not a subversive organization. Upon any final determination that the organization is subversive notice thereof shall be published by the secretary of state once each week for two successive weeks in a daily newspaper published in the city of Boston and the court shall order any funds or property of such organization turned over to the treasurer of the commonwealth which shall then be considered escheated. The fact that proceedings have begun or findings or decision made under this section shall not be admissible in evidence in any action brought under the provisions of sections eleven, nineteen, twenty-one or twenty-three.

SECTION 19
Subversive organization; knowingly becoming or remaining member; penalty

Any person who becomes or remains a member of any organization knowing it to be a subversive organization shall be punished by imprisonment in the state prison for not more than three years or in jail for not more than two and one half years or by a fine of not more than one thousand dollars, provided that this section shall not be construed as reducing the penalty now imposed for the violation of any law.

SECTION 20
Public office; ineligibility of certain persons; removal of disability

No person who has been convicted of a violation of the provisions of section eleven, nineteen or twenty-three shall be eligible to election or appointment to any public office, or employment, nor as a teacher in any public or private educational institution, nor shall any person continue to hold any such office after final conviction. The superior court on petition of the attorney general shall have jurisdiction in equity to restrain and enjoin any such person from performing such

duties thereafter and to prevent any such person's name being placed on any ballot for election to any office. The court may upon petition in its discretion after a lapse of five years from the date of final conviction under sections eleven, nineteen or twenty-three remove the disability if in its opinion such person can then be adjudged to be loyal to the government of the commonwealth and the United States.

SECTION 21
Subversive organizations; destruction or concealment of books; penalty

Whoever destroys or conceals books, records, files, membership lists or funds belonging to an organization which he knows to be a subversive organization shall be punished by imprisonment in the state prison for not more than three years or in jail for not more than two and one half years or by a fine of not more than one thousand dollars; provided, that this section shall not be construed as reducing the penalty now imposed for the violation of any law.

SECTION 22
Subversive organizations; knowingly permitting to use building; penalty

Whoever being in charge of an auditorium, hall or other building shall knowingly permit it to be used by the Communist Party or by an organization which has been adjudicated a subversive organization under the provisions of section eighteen shall be punished by a fine of not more than one thousand dollars or by imprisonment for not more than one year, or both.

SECTION 23
Subversive organizations; contribution; penalty

Whoever contributes money or any other property having a value in money to an organization which he knows to be a subversive organization shall be punished by imprisonment in the state prison for not more than three years or in jail for not more than two and one half years or by a fine of not more than one thousand dollars.

Chapter 265. Crimes Against the Person

Section
1   Murder
2   Punishment for murder
3   Duel; wound without and death within state; venue
4   Accessory in duel
5   Duel; conviction or acquittal in foreign state; effect
6–8   Repealed
9   Prize fighting; engaging
10   Prize fight; aiding or promoting
11   Prize fight; appointment within and fight without state
12   Boxing; kickboxing; mixed martial arts or other unarmed combative sporting matches or sparring exhibitions; penalty
13   Manslaughter
13½   Manslaughter while operating a motor vehicle
13A   Assault or assault and battery
13B   Indecent assault and battery on child under 14
13B½   Aggravated indecent assault and battery on child under 14
13B¾   Indecent assault and battery on child under 14, subsequent offense
13C   Assault and battery to collect loan
13D   Assault and battery upon public employees
13D½   Injury to firefighter resulting from willful burning of property or reckless burning of woods

13E   Repealed
13F   Indecent assault and battery on person with an intellectual disability; assault and battery
13G   Commission of a felony for hire; additional punishment
13H   Indecent assault and battery on person 14 or older; penalties
13I   Assault or assault and battery on emergency medical technician, ambulance operator , ambulance attendant or health care provider
13J   Assault and battery upon a child; liability of person having custody; penalties
13K   Assault and battery on elderly or disabled person
13L   Reckless endangerment to children
13M   Assault and battery on a family or household member; second or subsequent offense: penalty
13N   Misdemeanor offense including use or attempted use of physical force or threatened use of deadly weapon against family or household member; reporting to department of criminal justice information services
14   Mayhem
15   Assault with intent to murder or maim
15A   Assault and battery by means of a dangerous weapon
15B   Assault with dangerous weapon
15C   Assault by means of hypodermic syringe or needle; assault and battery by means of hypodermic syringe or needle

2

15D   Strangling or suffocating another person
15E   Assault and battery by discharging firearm
15F   Attempted assault and battery by discharging firearm
16   Attempt to murder
17   Armed robbery
18   Armed assault with intent to rob or murder
18A   Armed assault in dwelling house
18B   Use of firearms while committing a felony
18C   Home invasion; persons present within; weapons
19   Unarmed robbery
20   Assault with intent to rob or steal
21   Stealing by confining or putting in fear
21A   Carjacking
22   Rape, generally; penalties; eligibility for furlough, education, training or employment programs
22A   Rape of a child under 16
22B   Aggravated rape of a child under 16
22C   Rape of a child under 16, subsequent offense
23   Statutory rape
23A   Aggravated statutory rape
23B   Statutory rape, subsequent offense
24   Assault with intent to commit rape
24A   Venue
24B   Assault of child with intent to commit rape
24C   Victim's name; confidentiality
25   Attempted extortion
26   Kidnapping
26A   Kidnapping of minor or incompetent by relative
26B   Drugging persons for kidnapping
26C   Enticing children
26D   Enticement of child under age 18 to engage in prostitution, human trafficking or commercial sexual activity
27   Kidnapping; venue
27A   Kidnapping of minor by relative venue
28   Poison
29   Assault with intent to commit felony
30   Gross negligence by common carrier
31   Repealed
32   Glass; throwing in public streets and beaches
33   Repealed
34   Tattooing body of person by other than qualified physician
35   Throwing or dropping objects onto public way
36   Throwing or dropping objects at sporting events
37   Violations of constitutional rights
38   Repealed
39   Assault or battery for purpose of intimidation due to race, etc.
40   Willful or reckless cause of serious bodily injury to participants in physical exercise training programs
41   Sentences for violation of this chapter; inclusion in record of reasons for non-imposition of sentence of imprisonment
42   Use of radio or boom box without using earphones on public conveyance; sale of evidence at public auction
43   Stalking
43A   Criminal harassment
44   Coercion of child under 18 into criminal conspiracy
45   Lifetime parole; probation or treatment center sentence
46   Taking from deceased victim's estate prohibited
47   Global positioning system device to be worn by certain sex offender probationers
48   Sex offenders prohibited from ice cream truck vending
49   Definitions applicable to Secs. 50 to 51
50   Trafficking of persons for sexual servitude; persons under 18; trafficking by business entities; penalties; tort actions by victims
51   Trafficking of persons to forced servitude; victims under 18; trafficking by business entities; penalties; tort actions by victims
52   Subsequent violations of Sec. 50 or 51; penalties; evidence of prior adjudication or conviction
53   Organ trafficking, victims under 18, penalties
54   Transmittal of fines to state treasurer
55   Forfeiture of funds use to facilitate violation of Sec. 50 or 51; victim restitution
56   Property subject to forfeiture resulting from violations of Secs. 50 or 51; procedure; exceptions; records; preliminary orders for seizure; referral to office of seized property management; homestead exemptions; recording of certificate of fact of final judgment
57   Victim of human trafficking as affirmative defense to charges of common night walking or common streetwalking
58   Possession of a deceptive weapon device during commission of violent crime

SECTION 1
Murder

Murder committed with deliberately premeditated malice aforethought, or with extreme atrocity or cruelty, or in the commission or attempted commission of a crime punishable with death or imprisonment for life, is murder in the first degree. Murder which does not appear to be in the first degree is murder in the second degree. Petit treason shall be prosecuted and punished as murder. The degree of murder shall be found by the jury.

NOTE 1   Model Jury Instructions on Homicide. The Supreme Judicial Court has adopted revised Model Jury Instructions on Homicide as of March 21, 2013. They are available at http://www.mass.gov/courts/sjc/model-jury-instructions-homicide.html or in *Massachusetts Superior Court Criminal Practice Jury Instructions* (MCLE, Inc. 2d ed. 2013).

NOTE 2a   "Murder is the unlawful killing of a human being with malice aforethought and if a killing is caused by the intentional use of a deadly weapon malice may be inferred unless by the circumstances it is disproved. The burden of proof is on the Commonwealth to prove every element of the offense charged." *Commonwealth v. McCauley*, 355 Mass. 554, 559 (1969) (citations and quotations omitted). *See also* G.L. c. 277, § 39 (definition of murder).

NOTE 2b   Three Prongs of Malice. "Malice as an element of murder may be proved by evidence establishing any one of three facts beyond a reasonable doubt: if, without justification or excuse, (1) the defendant intended to kill the victim (the so-called first prong of malice), or (2) the defendant intended to do the victim grievous bodily harm (the second prong), or (3) in the circumstances known to the defendant, a reasonably prudent person would have known that, according to common experience, there was a plain and strong likelihood that death would follow the contemplated act (the third prong)." *Commonwealth v. Sneed*, 413 Mass. 387, 388 n.1 (1992) (citing *Commonwealth v. Grey*, 399 Mass. 469, 470 n.1 (1987)).

NOTE 2b(1)   The Second Prong. "'[W]here deaths were caused by gunshot or by some other dangerous instrument and there was no appellate issue concerning the severity of any intended bodily harm, the court has used a summary definition of the second prong of malice that does not refer to the grievousness of the intended bodily injury.' *Commonwealth v. Sneed*, [413 Mass. 387, 392 (1992)]." *Commonwealth v. Pierce*, 419 Mass. 28, 36 n.9 (1994).

NOTE 2b(2)   The Third Prong. "The third prong of malice has both a subjective and objective component. 'When deliberating as to whether the Commonwealth has proved the knowledge aspect of malice aforethought under the third prong, a jury should consider: (1) the nature and extent of the defendant's knowledge of the circumstances at the time he acted; (2) whether, in the circumstances known by the defendant, a reasonably prudent person would have recognized that the defendant's conduct would create a plain and strong likelihood of death or injury.'" *Commonwealth v. Pierce*, 419 Mass. 28, 36–37 (1994) (quoting *Commonwealth v. Sama*, 411 Mass. 293, 298 (1991)).

NOTE 2b(2)(a)   "We have recently reiterated that the third prong of the malice definition can only be satisfied by proof that there was a plain and strong likelihood of death." *Commonwealth v. Fuller*, 421 Mass. 400, 412 (1995) (quotation marks and citations omitted).

NOTE 2b(2)(b)   The third prong of malice is not applicable to deliberate premeditation or felony murder. *Commonwealth v. Shanahan*, 422 Mass. 631, 633 (1996); *Commonwealth v. Morgan*, 422 Mass. 373 (1996).

NOTE 2b(2)(c) "The difference between the elements of the third prong of malice and wanton and reckless conduct amounting to involuntary manslaughter lies in the degree of risk of physical harm that a reasonable person would recognize was created by particular conduct, based on what the defendant knew. The risk for purposes of the third prong of malice is that there was a plain and strong likelihood of death. The risk that will satisfy the standard for willful and wanton conduct amounting to involuntary manslaughter involves a high degree of likelihood that substantial harm will result to another." *Commonwealth v. Robinson*, 48 Mass. App. Ct. 329, 339 (1999) (citations, quotation marks, and punctuation omitted).

NOTE 2b(2)(d) "[I]t is not required that the defendant subjectively know that his actions would create a substantial risk of death. It is enough that based on what the defendant knew, a reasonable person would objectively realize the risk of death." *Commonwealth v. Lyons*, 444 Mass. 289, 299 (2005).

NOTE 2c   Inference of Malice from Intentional Use of Dangerous Weapon. "The defendant contends that the judge improperly instructed that the jury are 'permitted to infer that a person who intentionally uses a dangerous weapon on another person is acting with malice.' He claims that this created a mandatory presumption of malice from the use of a dangerous weapon. The jury were told that they were 'permitted to infer,' not that they must infer. This instruction (now contained in the Model Jury Instructions on Homicide 61 [1999]) was proper." *Commonwealth v. Obershaw*, 435 Mass. 794, 808–09 (2002).

NOTE 3 "Murder in the second degree is an unlawful killing with malice aforethought; malice includes any intent to inflict injury on another without legal excuse or palliation." *Commonwealth v. Casale*, 381 Mass. 167, 171–72 (1980).

NOTE 4   Malice/"Frame of Mind." "In recent cases, this court has consistently discouraged use of the frame of mind definition, which describes malice as a 'frame of mind which includes not only anger, hatred and revenge, but also any other unlawful and unjustifiable motive.' . . . Malice should be defined by reference to the three prongs described in *Commonwealth v. Grey*[, 399 Mass. 469 (1987)]." *Commonwealth v. Williams*, 428 Mass. 383, 389 (1998) (citations and quotation marks omitted).

NOTE 5a   Deliberate Premeditation. "[W]hile it must be shown that a plan to murder was formed after the matter had been made a subject of deliberation and reflection . . . the law cannot set any limit to the time. . . . It is not so much a matter of time as of logical sequence. First the deliberation and premeditation, the resolution to kill, and lastly the killing in pursuance of the resolution; and all this may occur in a few seconds." *Commonwealth v. Tucker*, 189 Mass. 457, 494–95 (1905) (quote from syllabus).

NOTE 5b "[D]eliberate premeditation requires either a specific intent to kill that equates with express malice . . . or . . . an intent to kill, combined with planning how to effectuate that desire and an evaluation of the pros and cons of proceeding." *Commonwealth v. Jiles*, 428 Mass. 66, 72 (1998) (citation and quotation marks omitted).

NOTE 5c "Deliberately" does not mean slowly. Instead it has reference to the purposeful character of the premeditated malice rather than to the time spent in premeditation. *Commonwealth v. Brooks*, 308 Mass. 367, 369 (1941).

NOTE 5d   Inference of Premeditation from Gun. "We have stated that, where a defendant brings a gun to the scene of the crime, there is sufficient evidence to support an inference of premeditation." *Commonwealth v. Ruci*, 409 Mass. 94, 96–97 (1991) (citations omitted).

NOTE 5e   Consciousness of Guilt and Premeditation. "Evidence of consciousness of guilt is rarely relevant to the issue of premeditation. . . . [W]here a judge gives correct instructions on consciousness of guilt and correct instructions on deliberate premeditation, there is no need to further instruct the jury as to limitations on the use of consciousness of guilt with respect to the issue of premeditation." *Commonwealth v. Dagenais,* 437 Mass. 832, 843 (2002) (citations and quotation marks omitted).

NOTE 6a   Extreme Atrocity or Cruelty—Factors that Can Be Considered. "We have delineated a number of factors which a jury can consider in deciding whether a murder was committed with extreme atrocity or cruelty. These include indifference to or taking pleasure in the victim's suffering, consciousness and degree of suffering of the victim, extent of physical injuries, number of blows, manner and force with which delivered, instrument employed, and disproportion between the means needed to cause death and those employed." *Commonwealth v. Cunneen*, 389 Mass. 216, 227 (1983).

NOTE 6b   Extreme Atrocity or Cruelty—Unanimity Not Required as to Underlying Factors. "[T]he factors underlying the theory of extreme atrocity or cruelty, *see Commonwealth v. Cunneen*, [389 Mass. 216, 227 (1983)], are neither elements of the crime nor separate theories of culpability, but 'evidentiary considerations' that guide a jury in determining whether a murder was committed with extreme atrocity or cruelty. Because they are not elements of the offense, unanimity is not required. *See Commonwealth v. Obershaw*, 435 Mass. 794, 809 (2002).

". . . Here, the jury determined that the defendant murdered Jenkins with extreme atrocity or cruelty, and they were instructed that extreme atrocity or cruelty had to be proved beyond a reasonable doubt. The requirement that the jury base their determination on one or more of the *Cunneen* factors does not transform those factors into elements of the offense." *Commonwealth v. Moses*, 436 Mass. 598, 606 (2002) (rejecting arguments that (1) "extreme atrocity or cruelty, as an element of murder in the first degree, is unconstitutionally vague" and (2) "the absence of a requirement that the jury be unanimous as to the applicable *Cunneen* factors violates principles of due process").

NOTE 6c   Atrocity/Cruelty. Knowledge of Weapon. "'When the theory of first degree murder is murder by extreme atrocity or cruelty, knowledge of a joint venturer's possession of a weapon is not necessary.' *Commonwealth v. Colon-Cruz*, 408 Mass. 533, 546, 555 (1990) (not necessary that jury be instructed regarding defendant's knowledge that codefendants were armed because such knowledge not essential to proof of murder by deliberate premeditation or extreme atrocity or cruelty)." *Commonwealth v. Semedo*, 422 Mass. 716, 723 (1996). Compare with felony-murder cases in which typically "the possession of a weapon [is] an element of the underlying felony." *Commonwealth v. Semedo*, 422 Mass. at 723.

NOTE 6d   Atrocity/Cruelty. Photographs. "The photographs of the victim, showing all seventy-nine stab wounds and the gunshot to the head, supported the Commonwealth's theory of murder in the first degree based on extreme atrocity and cruelty." *Commonwealth v. Allison*, 434 Mass. 670, 684 (2001) (citations omitted).

NOTE 7a   Felony Murder. "Although the law provides that a homicide committed in the commission of a felony is murder at common law, it is only by reason of G.L. c. 265, § 1, that murder perpetrated in the commission or attempted commission of a crime punishable by death or imprisonment for life becomes murder in the first degree. Murder perpetrated during the commission or attempt of some other felony is murder in the second degree." *Commonwealth v. Ambers*, 370 Mass. 835, 839–40 (1976) (citations omitted).

NOTE 7b   Predicate Offenses. "Whether a crime qualifies as a predicate offense for purposes of first degree felony-murder depends on whether the offense is punishable by death or life imprisonment." *Commonwealth v. Jackson*, 432 Mass. 82, 89 (2000) (citing *Commonwealth v. Fluker*, 377 Mass. 123, 128 (1979)).

NOTE 7b(1)   Two Categories of Predicate Offenses. "Predicate offenses then fall into two categories; those that are inherently dangerous to human life, and those that are not." *Commonwealth v. Jackson*, 432 Mass. 82, 89 (2000).

NOTE 7b(2)   Dismissal of Predicate Felony. "[T]rial judges have the authority, at the time of sentencing, to order a predicate felony dismissed, subject, of course, to affirmance of a defendant's felony-murder conviction. A predicate felony should be dismissed

2

where there were no other theories of murder in the first degree for which he was convicted, and there was only one predicate felony." *Commonwealth v. Vives*, 447 Mass. 537, 544 (2006) (citations omitted).

NOTE 7b(3) No dismissal needed. "By contrast, where, as here, a defendant is convicted of murder in the first degree on a theory of felony-murder, and also is convicted of murder in the first degree on another theory, and where we affirm the convictions on both theories, the conviction of the predicate felony is not duplicative, and the felony conviction stands." *Commonwealth v. Foster*, 471 Mass. 236, 244 (2015).

NOTE 7c   Inherently Dangerous to Human Life. "If an offense is inherently dangerous to human life, commission of the crime that causes death constitutes first degree felony-murder." *Commonwealth v. Jackson*, 432 Mass. 82, 89 (2000).

NOTE 7c(1) Use of Dangerous Weapon. "An inherently dangerous crime does not necessarily require the use of a dangerous weapon." *Commonwealth v. Jackson*, 432 Mass. 82, 89 (2000).

NOTE 7c(2) Case-by-Case Basis. "The determination whether a particular felony is inherently dangerous to human life, for purpose of felony-murder, is made on a case-by-case basis." *Commonwealth v. Jackson*, 432 Mass. 82, 89 (2000) (citation omitted).

NOTE 7c(3) Aggravated Rape. "For example, aggravated rape is an inherently dangerous felony for purposes of first degree felony-murder, and it need not be committed with a weapon." *Commonwealth v. Jackson*, 432 Mass. 82, 89 (2000) (citing *Commonwealth v. Troy*, 405 Mass. 253, 263 (1989)).

NOTE 7c(4) Rape. "For the purposes of the felony-murder doctrine, the common-law felony of rape [like arson] is inherently dangerous." *Commonwealth v. Baez*, 427 Mass. 630, 634 (1998) (citations omitted).

NOTE 7c(5) Armed Robbery. "We have delineated several felonies, including armed robbery, as 'inherently dangerous.'" *Commonwealth v. Scott*, 428 Mass. 362, 364 (1998) (citations omitted)

NOTE 7c(6) Armed Assaultive Burglary. "[A]n assaultive burglary under G.L. c. 266, § 14, while armed, [is] an inherently dangerous offense." *Commonwealth v. Jackson*, 432 Mass. 82, 89 (2000) (citing *Commonwealth v. Claudio*, 418 Mass. 103, 105–09 (1994)).

NOTE 7c(7) Unarmed Assaultive Burglary. "We conclude that unarmed assaultive burglary is a felony inherently dangerous to human life for purposes of first degree felony-murder." *Commonwealth v. Jackson*, 432 Mass. 82, 90 (2000).

NOTE 7c(8) Inherently dangerous "felonies, as a matter of law, may support a conviction of felony murder. There is no need to show a 'conscious disregard for human life' because the risk is implicit in the intent required for the felony." *Commonwealth v. Scott*, 428 Mass. 362, 364 (1998) (citations omitted).

NOTE 7c(9) Substitute for Malice Aforethought. "Once such a felony [one inherently dangerous to human life] and a homicide in the course of the commission of that felony are proven, the intent to commit the underlying felony is, in effect, substituted for the malice aforethought otherwise necessary to support a verdict of guilty of murder in the first degree." *Commonwealth v. Bourgeois*, 404 Mass. 61, 64 (1989) (citations omitted).

NOTE 7d   Conscious Disregard for Human Life. "If an offense is not inherently dangerous, then the Commonwealth must prove that the circumstances under which it was committed show that the defendant 'consciously disregarded risk to human life.'" *Commonwealth v. Jackson*, 432 Mass. 82, 89 (2000) (citing *Commonwealth v. Moran*, 387 Mass. 644, 651 (1982)).

NOTE 7d(1) Unarmed Robbery. "The judge did err in telling the jury that the crime of unarmed robbery was inherently dangerous to human life. *Commonwealth v. Moran*, 387 Mass. 644, 651 (1982) ('Unarmed robbery is not inherently dangerous to human life')." *Commonwealth v. Bourgeois*, 404 Mass. 61, 64 (1989).

NOTE 7e   Joint Enterprise. "Under the felony-murder rule, 'a homicide committed during the commission or attempted commission of a felony is murder.' *Commonwealth v. Silva*, 388 Mass. 495, 503 (1983). 'Once it is determined that a defendant is a joint venturer in a felony and that a homicide occurred in the commission or attempted commission of that felony, complicity in the underlying felony is sufficient to establish guilt of murder in the first or second degree (see G.L. c. 265, § 1) if the homicide followed naturally and probably from the carrying out of the joint enterprise.' *Commonwealth v. Ambers*, 370 Mass. 835, 839 (1976). There must be evidence that the defendant intentionally assisted Hamilton in the commission or attempted commission of the crime of armed robbery, sharing with Hamilton the mental state required for that crime. *Commonwealth v. Watson*, 388 Mass. 536, 544–545 n.7 (1983), S.C., 393 Mass. 297 (1984). '[O]ne who aids, commands, counsels, or encourages commission of a crime while sharing with the principal the mental state required for the crime is guilty as a principal. . . . The jury may infer the requisite mental state from the defendant's knowledge of the circumstances and subsequent participation in the offense.' *Commonwealth v. Williams*, 399 Mass. 60, 69–70 (1987), quoting *Commonwealth v. Soares*, 377 Mass. 461, 470, cert. denied, 444 U.S. 881 (1979)." *Commonwealth v. Pope*, 406 Mass. 581, 584–85 (1990).

NOTE 7e(1) "Even if a killing were not intended, a participant in an underlying felony which poses an inherent risk to human life is responsible for a killing which is a natural and probable consequence of the felony. . . . As a joint venturer, the defendant was responsible for the natural and foreseeable consequences of the robbery, regardless of whether his attempt to throw a punch and his use of the couch cushion were the proximate causes of the victim's death." *Commonwealth v. Nichypor*, 419 Mass. 209, 215 (1994).

NOTE 7f "It is not necessary for the Commonwealth to show that the homicide occurred while the armed robbery was still in progress, as long as the homicide was connected with and incident to the armed robbery and as long as the armed robbery and the homicide took place at substantially the same time and place. *Commonwealth v. Ortiz*, [408 Mass. 463, 466 (1990)]." *Commonwealth v. Gordon*, 422 Mass. 816, 850 (1996) (parenthesis omitted).

NOTE 7g "Where the felony-murder rule applies, generally the defendant is not entitled to an instruction on manslaughter." *Commonwealth v. Selby*, 426 Mass. 168, 172 (1997) (citation and quotation marks omitted).

NOTE 7h "For a felony murder conviction there must be a felony independent of the homicide. Therefore, the conduct which constitutes the felony must be separate from the acts of personal violence which constitute a necessary part of the homicide itself." *Commonwealth v. Robinson*, 48 Mass. App. Ct. 329, 333 (1999) (citations and quotation marks omitted).

NOTE 7i "The primary issue in this appeal is whether a defendant who joins with others to commit an armed robbery may be found guilty of murder on the theory of felony-murder for the killing of his accomplice by someone resisting the armed robbery. We conclude that he may not." *Commonwealth v. Tejeda*, 473 Mass. 269, 270 (2015).

NOTE 8a   Intoxication. Defendant's intoxication at time of killing did not relieve his actions of their malicious quality in law. *Commonwealth v. McGuirk*, 376 Mass. 338, 346 (1978), cert. denied, 439 U.S. 1120 (1979).

NOTE 8b Voluntary intoxication is not an excuse, justification or extenuation of crime. *Commonwealth v. Hawkins*, 3 Gray 463, 466, 69 Mass. 463, 466 (1855).

NOTE 8c "The voluntary consumption of alcohol bears on the defendant's capacity to have a specific intent to do something. . . . The Commonwealth, however, did not have to prove that the defendant was not intoxicated. Voluntary intoxication is merely 'an evidentiary factor which the jury can consider' on questions of premeditation and malice." *Commonwealth v. Kelcourse*, 404 Mass. 466, 469 (1989) (citations omitted).

NOTE 8d   Intoxication/Jury Instruction Not Required Absent "Debilitating Intoxication." "An instruction on voluntary intoxication is not required absent evidence of 'debilitating intoxication.'" *Commonwealth v. Moses*, 436 Mass. 598, 603 (2002) (quoting *Commonwealth v. Chaleumphong*, 434 Mass. 70, 78 (2001) and *Commonwealth v. Erdely*, 430 Mass. 149, 152 (1999)).

In *Moses*, the Supreme Judicial Court upheld the trial court's decision not to instruct the jury on voluntary intoxication, since "[n]o evidence was introduced to demonstrate how much or how long the defendant had been drinking on the night in question, or what effect it had on him. Although the defendant testified that he was 'drinking and smoking weed,' a fact corroborated by other witnesses, there was nothing to support the inference that, at the time of the killing, intoxication impaired the defendant's ability to form any requisite criminal intent. The defendant had no difficulty accounting for his actions and emotions on the night in question. His clear recollection of events at trial belies his claim on appeal that he was debilitated at the time. The judge correctly refused to instruct on voluntary intoxication." *Commonwealth v. Moses*, 436 Mass. 598, 603 (2002) (citation omitted).

NOTE 8e   Intoxication/Jury Instruction. "While the judge did not state explicitly that voluntary intoxication could be the basis of reducing the degree of murder, he correctly instructed the jurors that they could consider voluntary intoxication on premeditation and extreme atrocity or cruelty theories of murder in the first degree. We have never required more than a simple instruction that the jury may consider voluntary intoxication when considering state of mind." *Commonwealth v. Raymond*, 424 Mass. 382, 387 (1997).

NOTE 8f   Expert Testimony. "[T]he trial judge erred in excluding expert testimony, offered in the form of an opinion, that the defendant's blood alcohol level impaired his mental capacity. That evidence was relevant to the jury's consideration of the defendant's culpability for first-degree murder." *Commonwealth v. Cruz*, 413 Mass. 686, 686 (1992).

"The judge should deny a request to instruct the jury that an individual with a blood alcohol level exceeding .10 percent can be found to be intoxicated. We do not think the percentage of blood alcohol level that applies to motor vehicle cases should become the basis of an instruction in a first-degree murder case on the effects of intoxication." *Commonwealth v. Cruz*, 413 Mass. at 691–92.

NOTE 8g See Notes for Intoxication following G.L. c. 265, § 13 (manslaughter).

NOTE 9   Mental illness and drugs or alcohol. "[W]e set forth an appropriate instruction that may be used in this case and in future homicide cases as warranted where there is evidence that a defendant had a mental disease or defect and consumed drugs or alcohol:

'A defendant's lack of criminal responsibility cannot be solely the product of intoxication caused by her voluntary consumption of alcohol or another drug. *Commonwealth v. Sheehan*, 376 Mass. 765, 770 (1978). However, a defendant is not criminally responsible if you have a reasonable doubt as to whether, when the crime was committed, the defendant had a latent mental disease or defect that became activated by the voluntary consumption of drugs or alcohol, or an active mental disease or defect that became intensified by the voluntary consumption of drugs or alcohol, which activated or intensified mental disease or defect then caused her to lose the substantial capacity to appreciate the wrongfulness of her conduct or the substantial capacity to conform her conduct to the requirements of the law. If you have a reasonable doubt as to whether the defendant was criminally responsible, you shall find the defendant not guilty by reason of lack of criminal responsibility.' *Commonwealth v. Herd*, 413 Mass. 834, 841 (1992). *Commonwealth v. McGrath*, 358 Mass. 314 (1970).

Where a defendant has an active mental disease or defect that caused her to lose the substantial capacity to appreciate the wrongfulness of her conduct or the substantial capacity to conform her conduct to the requirements of the law, the defendant's consumption of alcohol or another drug cannot preclude the defense

of lack of criminal responsibility.'" *Commonwealth v. Berry*, 457 Mass. 602, 617–18 (2010) (footnote and quotation marks omitted).

The court further stated: "Where the Commonwealth offers evidence that the defendant knew or had reason to know of the effects of drugs or alcohol on her latent mental disease or defect, or on the intensification of her active mental disease or defect, the following instruction must be added: 'However, if the Commonwealth has proved beyond a reasonable doubt that the defendant consumed drugs or alcohol knowing or having reason to know that the drugs or alcohol would activate a latent mental disease or intensify an active mental disease, causing her to lose the substantial capacity to appreciate the wrongfulness of her conduct or the substantial capacity to conform her conduct to the requirements of the law, then you would be warranted in finding the defendant criminally responsible for a crime in which you find she knowingly participated. In deciding what the defendant had reason to know about the consequences of her consumption of drugs or alcohol, you should consider the question solely from the defendant's point of view, including her mental capacity and her past experience with drugs or alcohol.'" *Commonwealth v. Berry*, 457 Mass. at 617 n.9.

NOTE 10a   Provocation. "The judge's first error was that he failed to tell the jury that, if the Commonwealth had not proved the absence of provocation beyond a reasonable doubt, there could be no finding of malice and hence no conviction of murder. Malice and adequate provocation are mutually exclusive. . . .

"In the view of a lay person, one who acts on reasonable provocation could still deliberately premeditate his intention to kill or do grievous bodily harm. The law says, however, that the crime is voluntary manslaughter, not murder, if malice is negated by reasonable provocation or sudden combat (or at least by a reasonable doubt whether those conditions were absent)."

Commonwealth v. Boucher, 403 Mass. 659, 661–63 (1989).

NOTE 10b "The correct rule is that, where the evidence raises the possibility that the defendant may have acted on reasonable provocation, the Commonwealth must prove, and the jury must find, beyond a reasonable doubt, that the defendant did not act on reasonable provocation." *Commonwealth v. Acevedo*, 427 Mass. 714, 716 (1998) (citation omitted).

NOTE 10c "The general rule is that words alone are insufficient provocation to reduce murder to manslaughter. We have recognized an exception to this general rule, however, where the words convey inflammatory information to the defendant. A sudden oral revelation of infidelity may be sufficient provocation to reduce murder to manslaughter. But the revelation which is said to have precipitated the homicide must constitute a 'sudden discovery' in order to reduce the degree of culpability." *Commonwealth v. LeClair*, 429 Mass. 313, 316–17 (1999) (citations omitted).

NOTE 11a   Self-Defense. "The right reasonably to use a nondeadly force, such as one's fists, in self-defense, arises at a somewhat lower level of danger (a reasonable concern for personal safety) than the right to use a dangerous weapon (deadly force may be used only where the person has 'a reasonable apprehension of great bodily harm and a reasonable belief that no other means would suffice to prevent such harm')." *Commonwealth v. Bastarache*, 382 Mass. 86, 105 (1980) (citation and footnote omitted).

NOTE 11b Once the defendant introduces evidence that he acted in self-defense, the Commonwealth has the burden of proof beyond a reasonable doubt that the defendant did not act in self-defense. *Commonwealth v. Rodriguez*, 370 Mass. 684, 687–88 (1976).

NOTE 11c "In passing upon the reasonableness of the force used by the defendant, again on the hypothesis that he was acting in self-defence, the jury should consider evidence of the relative physical capabilities of the combatants, the characteristics of the weapons used, and the availability of maneuver room in, or means of escape from, the area. The right of self-defence does not accrue to a person until he has availed all proper means to avoid physical combat. The right of self-defence arises from necessity, and ends when the necessity ends." *Commonwealth v. Kendrick*, 351 Mass. 203, 212 (1966) (citations omitted).

NOTE 11d The question of how far one may go in self-defense is a question for the jury. *Kendrick*, 351 Mass. at 211.

NOTE 11e "In explaining self-defense the judge first correctly told the jury that, '[i]f the government proves beyond a reasonable doubt that there was no necessity to avoid grievous, serious bodily harm, there's no more consideration of self-defense.' *See Commonwealth v.* Stokes, 374 Mass. 583, 591 (1978) (burden of proof); *Commonwealth v. Houston*, 332 Mass. 687, 690 (1955); *Commonwealth v. Woodward*, 102 Mass. 155, 161 (1869). He then added, also correctly, that one 'may use only that amount of force that's reasonably necessary to avoid the grievous bodily harm.' *Commonwealth v. Kendrick*, 351 Mass. 203, 211 (1966). Nowhere, however, did the judge tell the jury that, if the defendant was privileged to use force to defend himself but the Commonwealth proved beyond a reasonable doubt that the defendant used excessive force, the defendant would be guilty only of manslaughter, not murder. See *Commonwealth v. Burbank*, 388 Mass. 789, 795 (1983); *Commonwealth v. Stokes, supra* at 593–594."

This required that the defendant's conviction for first degree murder be reversed.

Commonwealth v. Boucher, 403 Mass. 659, 663 (1989).

NOTE 11f "A defendant is not entitled to a jury instruction on self-defense unless the evidence warrants at least a reasonable doubt that he had 'reasonable ground to believe, and actually did believe that he was in imminent danger of death or serious bodily harm.' *Commonwealth v. Harrington*, 379 Mass. 446, 450 (1980). In general, self-defense is unavailable to the person who initiates the fray." *Commonwealth v. Carrion*, 407 Mass. 263, 268 (1990) (citation omitted).

The court also noted that "[i]nsults or quarrelling alone cannot provide a reasonable provocation." *Commonwealth v. Carrion*, 407 Mass. at 267 (citations and quotation marks omitted).

NOTE 11g "In such situations, where the level of force used cannot be determined as a matter of law, instructions on both deadly force and nondeadly force may be appropriate." *Commonwealth v. Tirado*, 65 Mass. App. Ct. 571, 575 (2006).

NOTE 12 **First Aggressor.** "[W]here the identity of the first aggressor is in dispute and the victim has a history of violence, we hold that the trial judge has the discretion to admit evidence of specific acts of prior violent conduct that the victim is reasonably alleged to have initiated, to support the defendant's claim of self-defense." *Commonwealth v. Adjutant*, 443 Mass. 649, 664 (2005).

NOTE 13 Defense for killing or injuring a person unlawfully in a dwelling. *See* G.L. c. 278, § 8A.

NOTE 14 **Duress.** "In [*Commonwealth v. Vasquez*, 462 Mass. 827, 835 (2012)], we concluded that duress was not an available defense to intentional murder. Nonetheless, the defendant claims that it was error to foreclose the defense to a juvenile offender because of the fundamental differences between adults and juveniles. . . . We take this opportunity to clarify that our holding does foreclose such a defense for both classes of offender." *Commonwealth v. Jackson*, 471 Mass. 262, 266 (2015).

NOTE 15 **Juvenile Defendants and Mitigating Circumstances.** "In future cases, where the Commonwealth seeks to indict a juvenile for murder and where there is substantial evidence of mitigating circumstances or defenses (other than lack of criminal responsibility) presented to the grand jury, the prosecutor shall instruct the grand jury on the elements of murder and on the significance of the mitigating circumstances and defenses. The instructions are to be transcribed as part of the transcription of the grand jury proceedings." *Commonwealth v. Walczak*, 463 Mass. 808, 810 (2012).

NOTE 16 Given the advances of medical science, the "year and a day" rule is anachronistic, no longer supportable in reason, and its abolition could be accomplished by judicial decision. *Commonwealth v. Lewis*, 381 Mass. 411, 418 (1980). *See also Commonwealth v. Casanova*, 429 Mass. 293, 299 (1999) ("We decline

to adopt a rule providing a specific interval between injury and death after which the injuring party cannot be held legally responsible for the death . . .").

NOTE 17 **Homicide of a Viable Fetus.** "In *Commonwealth v. Cass*, 392 Mass. 799, 807 (1984), we held that the 'infliction of prenatal injuries resulting in the death of a viable fetus, before or after it is born, is homicide.'" *Commonwealth v. Lawrence*, 404 Mass. 378, 383–84 (1989).

NOTE 18a **Motive.** "Evidence of a hostile relationship between a defendant and his spouse may be admitted as relevant to the defendant's motive to kill the victim's spouse. The evidence was admissible for this purpose even if it tended to show prior bad acts on the part of the Defendant . . . .

"Moreover, the question of remoteness was a matter within the discretion of the trial judge."

Commonwealth v. Nardone, 406 Mass. 123, 128 (1989) (citations omitted).

NOTE 18b **Motive/Abuse Prevention Order.** "Evidence that a victim has obtained an abuse prevention order against the defendant is admissible to demonstrate the existence of a hostile relationship, as the relationship may be relevant to the defendant's motive to kill." *Commonwealth v. Eugene*, 438 Mass. 343, 348 (2003) (citing *Commonwealth v. Sarourt Nom*, 426 Mass. 152, 160 (1997)).

NOTE 19 **Joint Venture. Knowledge of Weapon.** "'The Commonwealth is not required to prove that a defendant who was not armed with a dangerous weapon, for example, a knife, knew that a codefendant was armed with a knife. However, the Commonwealth is required to prove beyond a reasonable doubt that a defendant who was not armed with a [dangerous weapon] acted with malice, and that he himself intended to inflict grievous bodily harm on [the victim], or he intended to kill [the victim], or he intended to commit an act which would create a strong likelihood that death would follow the contemplated act.'" *Commonwealth v. Barros*, 425 Mass. 572, 586 (1997) (quoting *Commonwealth v. Semedo*, 422 Mass. 716, 722–23 n.4 (1996)).

NOTE 20 **Intervening Act.** "[W]e have never ruled out the argument that reckless medical care can be an intervening cause of death. The general rule is that the intervening conduct of a third party will relieve a defendant of culpability only if such an intervening response was not reasonably foreseeable." *Commonwealth v. Niemic*, 427 Mass. 718, 727 (1998) (citations and quotation marks omitted).

NOTE 21 Solicitation to Commit Murder. "Conviction of the common-law crime of solicitation to commit murder requires proof that the defendant solicited, counseled, advised, or otherwise enticed another to commit murder and that the defendant intended that the person in fact commit the murder." *Commonwealth v. Lenahan*, 50 Mass. App. Ct. 180, 186 (2000).

NOTE 22 **Mode of Commission.** "[W]hen a single crime can be committed in various ways, jurors need not agree upon the mode of commission. . . . When a woman's charred body has been found in a burned house, and there is ample evidence that the defendant set out to kill her, it would be absurd to set him free because six jurors believe he strangled her to death . . . while six others believe he left her unconscious and set the fire to kill her." *Commonwealth v. Cyr*, 433 Mass. 617, 623 (2001) (citations omitted).

NOTE 23 **Venue.** G.L. c. 277, §§ 60–62.

NOTE 24 **Related Statutes.**

G.L. c. 272, § 22—Concealment by parent of death of child born out of wedlock.

G.L. c. 272, § 23—Joinder of charges of murder and offence under Section 22.

SECTION 2
Punishment for murder
(Amended by 2014 Mass. Acts c. 189, § 5, effective July 25, 2014.)

(a) Except as provided in subsection (b), any person who is found guilty of murder in the first degree shall be punished by imprisonment in the state prison for life and shall not be eligible for parole pursuant to section 133A of chapter 127.

(b) Any person who is found guilty of murder in the first degree who committed the offense on or after the person's fourteenth birthday and before the person's eighteenth birthday shall be punished by imprisonment in the state prison for life and shall be eligible for parole after the term of years fixed by the court pursuant to section 24 of chapter 279.

(c) Any person who is found guilty of murder in the second degree shall be punished by imprisonment in the state prison for life and shall be eligible for parole after the term of years fixed by the court pursuant to section 24 of chapter 279.

(d) Any person whose sentence for murder is commuted by the governor and council pursuant to section 152 of chapter 127 shall thereafter be subject to the laws governing parole.

NOTE 1   The death penalty, as most recently amended in 1982, is unconstitutional. *Commonwealth v. Colon-Cruz*, 393 Mass. 150 (1984). *See also District Attorney for the Suffolk Dist. v. Watson*, 381 Mass. 648 (1980).

NOTE 2   **DNA Database.** A conviction of an offense under this section or of an attempt or conspiracy to commit such an offense results in the defendant being required to submit a DNA sample to the state's DNA database. *See* G.L. c. 22E, § 3.

NOTE 3a   **Punishment—Juvenile Defendants.** "We . . . hold that mandatory life without parole for those under the age of 18 at the time of their crimes violates the Eighth Amendment's prohibition on 'cruel and unusual punishments.'" *Miller v. Alabama*, 132 S. Ct. 2455, 2460 (2012).

NOTE 3b   **Retroactivity.** "The Court now holds that *Miller* announced a substantive rule of constitutional law. The conclusion that *Miller* states a substantive rule comports with the principles that informed *Teague*. *Teague* sought to balance the important goals of finality and comity with the liberty interests of those imprisoned pursuant to rules later deemed unconstitutional. *Miller's* conclusion that the sentence of life without parole is disproportionate for the vast majority of juvenile offenders raises a grave risk that many are being held in violation of the Constitution.

"Giving *Miller* retroactive effect, moreover, does not require States to relitigate sentences, let alone convictions, in every case where a juvenile offender received mandatory life without parole. A State may remedy a *Miller* violation by permitting juvenile homicide offenders to be considered for parole, rather than by resentencing them." *Montgomery v. Louisiana*, 136 S. Ct. 718, 736 (2016).

NOTE 3c   "[W]e conclude that the Supreme Court's decision in *Miller* has retroactive application to cases on collateral review. We further conclude that the mandatory imposition of a sentence of life in prison without the possibility of parole on individuals who were under the age of eighteen when they committed the crime of murder in the first degree violates the prohibition on 'cruel or unusual punishments' in art. 26 of the Massachusetts Declaration of Rights, and that the discretionary imposition of such a sentence on juvenile homicide offenders also violates art. 26 because it is an unconstitutionally disproportionate punishment when viewed in the context of the unique characteristics of juvenile offenders." *Diatchenko v. Dist. Attorney for the Suffolk Dist.*, 466 Mass. 655, 658–59 (2013).

NOTE 3d   "We now hold that [the defendant] is entitled to the benefit of *Miller* and *Diatchenko* and that he may not be sentenced to life without parole. He may only be sentenced to the lesser punishment under G.L. c. 265, § 2, of mandatory life in prison with the possibility of parole set pursuant to the parole eligibility statute in effect at the time of [his] crime, G.L. c. 127, § 133A, as amended through St. 2000, c. 159, § 230, providing for parole eligibility in fifteen years." *Commonwealth v. Brown*, 466 Mass. 676, 678 (2013).

NOTE 4   See G.L. c. 279, § 24.

SECTION 3
Duel; wound without and death within state; venue

An inhabitant or resident of this commonwealth who, by previous appointment or engagement made within the same, fights a duel outside its jurisdiction, and in so doing inflicts a mortal wound upon a person whereof he dies within the commonwealth shall be guilty of murder within this commonwealth, and may be indicted, tried and convicted in the county where the death occurs.

SECTION 4
Accessory in duel

An inhabitant or resident of this commonwealth who, by previous appointment or engagement made within the same, becomes the second of either party in such duel and is present as a second when a mortal wound is inflicted upon a person whereof he dies within this commonwealth shall be an accessory before the fact to murder in this commonwealth, and may be indicted, tried and convicted in the county where the death occurs.

SECTION 5
Duel; conviction or acquittal in foreign state; effect

A person indicted under either of the two preceding sections may plead a former conviction or acquittal of the same crime in any other state or country; and if his plea is admitted or established, it shall be a bar to all further proceedings against him for the same crime within this commonwealth.

SECTIONS 6–8
Repealed

SECTION 9
Prize fighting; engaging

Whoever, except as provided in sections thirty-two to fifty, inclusive, of chapter one hundred and forty-seven, by previous appointment or arrangement, engages in a fight with another person shall be punished by imprisonment in the state prison for not more than ten years or by a fine of not more than five thousand dollars.

SECTION 10
Prize fight; aiding or promoting

Whoever, except as provided in sections thirty-two to fifty, inclusive, of chapter one hundred and forty-seven, is present at such fight as an aid, second or surgeon, or advises, encourages or promotes such fight, shall be punished by imprisonment in the state prison for not more than five years or by a fine of not more than one thousand dollars and by imprisonment in jail for not more than two and one half years.

SECTION 11
Prize fight; appointment within and fight without state

An inhabitant or resident of this commonwealth who, by previous appointment or engagement made in the same, leaves the same and engages in a fight with another person outside the limits thereof shall be punished by imprisonment in the state prison for not more than five years or by a fine of not more than five thousand dollars.

SECTION 12
Boxing; kickboxing; mixed martial arts or other unarmed combative sporting matches or sparring exhibitions; penalty

Whoever directly or indirectly, except as provided in sections 32 to 50A, inclusive, of chapter 147, gives, promotes or engages in a public boxing, kickboxing, mixed martial arts or other unarmed combative sporting match or sparring exhibition, or engages in a private boxing, kickboxing, mixed martial arts or other unarmed combative sporting event match or sparring exhibition, for which the contestants have received or have been promised any pecuniary reward, remuneration or consideration whatsoever shall be punished by imprisonment in the house of corrections for not more than 3 months or by a fine of not more than $5,000, or both such fine and imprisonment.

SECTION 13
Manslaughter

Whoever commits manslaughter shall, except as hereinafter provided, be punished by imprisonment in the state prison for not more than twenty years or by a fine of not more than one thousand dollars and imprisonment in jail or a house of correction for not more than two and one half years. Whoever commits manslaughter while violating the provisions of sections 102 to 102C, inclusive, of chapter 266 shall be imprisoned in the state prison for life or for any term of years.

NOTE 1   Model Jury Instructions on Homicide. The Supreme Judicial Court has adopted revised Model Jury Instructions on Homicide as of March 21, 2013. They are available at http://www.mass.gov/courts/sjc/model-jury-instructions-homicide.html or in *Massachusetts Superior Court Criminal Practice Jury Instructions* (MCLE, Inc. 2d ed. 2013).

NOTE 2a "Manslaughter is the unlawful killing of another without malice." *Commonwealth v. Beaulieu*, 333 Mass. 640, 643 (1956).

NOTE 2b Manslaughter may be found if act causing death was intentionally done, even if death was accidental. *Commonwealth v. Campbell*, 352 Mass. 387, 397 (1967).

NOTE 2c Manslaughter is a battery which causes death. *Commonwealth v. Sostilio*, 325 Mass. 143, 145 (1949).

NOTE 3a   Involuntary Manslaughter. "There are two aspects of involuntary manslaughter. One aspect involves wanton and reckless conduct causing death. The other concerns an unintentional killing resulting from a battery not amounting to a felony which the defendant knew or should have known endangered human life . . . An instruction on involuntary manslaughter is required where any view of the evidence will permit a finding of manslaughter and not murder . . . When it is obvious, however, that the risk of physical harm to the victim created a plain and strong likelihood that death will follow, an instruction on involuntary manslaughter is not required." *Commonwealth v. Fryar*, 425 Mass. 237, 248–49 (1997) (quotation marks and citation omitted).

NOTE 3b A person who handles a dangerous weapon in such a manner as to make the killing or physical injury of another a natural and probable result of such conduct can be found guilty of involuntary manslaughter, although he or she did not contemplate such a result. *Commonwealth v. Bouvier*, 316 Mass. 489, 494 (1944).

NOTE 3c   Omission/Failure to Act. "Wanton or reckless conduct usually consists of an affirmative act like driving an automobile or discharging a firearm. An omission, however, may form the basis of a manslaughter conviction where the defendant has a duty to act. . . .

". . . [A] duty to prevent harm to others arises when one creates a dangerous situation, whether that situation was created intentionally or negligently. . . .

"Our law, both civil and criminal, imposes on people a duty to act reasonably. . . . The civil law creates a specific duty that we may apply to the situation in this case. . . . If the actor does an act, and subsequently realizes or should realize that it has created an unreasonable risk of causing physical harm to another, he is under a duty to exercise reasonable care to prevent the risk from taking effect. . . . When a person places another in a position of danger, and then fails to safeguard or rescue that person, and the person subsequently dies as a result of this omission, such an omission may be sufficient to support criminal liability.

". . . It is consistent with society's general understanding that certain acts need to be accompanied by some kind of warning by the actor. . . . [W]here one's actions create a life-threatening risk to another, there is a duty to take reasonable steps to alleviate the risk. The reckless failure to fulfil this duty can result in a charge of manslaughter.

"Where a defendant's failure to exercise reasonable care to prevent the risk he created is reckless and results in death, the defendant can be convicted of involuntary manslaughter. Public policy requires that one who creates, by his own conduct . . . a grave risk of death or injury to others has a duty and obligation to alleviate the danger. We are not faced with the situation of a mere passerby who observes a fire and fails to alert authorities; the defendants started the fire and then increased the risk of harm from that fire by allowing it to burn without taking adequate steps either to control it or to report it to the proper authorities.

"Whether a defendant has satisfied this duty will depend on the circumstances of the particular case and the steps that the defendant can reasonably be expected to take to minimize the risk. Although, in this case, the defendants apparently could not have successfully put out the fire, they could have given reasonable notice of the danger they created. It was for the grand jury (and later, the petit jury) to decide whether the defendants' failure to take additional steps was reasonable, and if not, whether the defendants' omission constituted wanton or reckless conduct." *Commonwealth v. Levesque*, 436 Mass. 443, 448–51 (2002) (citations and quotation and punctuation marks omitted).

NOTE 3d   Verbal Conduct. "In sum, we conclude that there was probable cause to show that the coercive quality of the defendant's verbal conduct overwhelmed whatever willpower the eighteen year old victim had to cope with his depression, and that but for the defendant's admonishments, pressure, and instructions, the victim would not have gotten back into the truck and poisoned himself to death. Consequently, the evidence before the grand jury was sufficient for a finding of probable cause that the defendant, by wanton or reckless conduct, caused the victim's death." *Commonwealth v. Carter*, 474 Mass. 624, 635–36 (2016).

NOTE 4a Voluntary manslaughter is a slaying without malice in the heat of passion or anger. Involuntary manslaughter is a slaying through wanton or reckless conduct. *Commonwealth v. Lewinski*, 367 Mass. 889, 896–97 (1975).

NOTE 4b "Provocation is not an element of voluntary manslaughter, but is rather a defense to murder. More specifically, provocation is one of the mitigating circumstances that negate malice, an element of murder. Malice and adequate provocation or mitigation are mutually exclusive. . . . It would, therefore, have been error in a case where only manslaughter was charged to add a third element to the crime, namely, that the Commonwealth must prove that the defendant killed the victim in the heat of passion." *Commonwealth v. Baker*, 67 Mass. App. Ct. 760, 770–71 (2006) (quotations and citations omitted).

NOTE 4c "Words, alone, cannot provide a reasonable provocation" and basis for reducing murder to manslaughter. *Commonwealth v. Leate*, 352 Mass. 452, 458 (1967).

NOTE 4d "[A] manslaughter instruction based on reasonable provocation was warranted, even where no physical contact by the victim preceded the defendant's attack. . . . [W]e hold that the judge's instruction to the jury that physical contact was required for heat of passion upon reasonable provocation was error." *Commonwealth v. Morales*, 70 Mass. App. Ct. 526, 532–33 (2007).

2

NOTE 5   "Murder may be committed without any actual intent, either to kill or to do grievous bodily harm." *Commonwealth v. Parsons*, 195 Mass. 560, 570 (1907).

NOTE 6a   Intoxication. (See also Notes following Murder, G.L. c. 265, § 1).

"The fact that the defendant was drunk at the time of the shooting might have rendered him incapable of conceiving a deliberately premeditated intention to kill necessary to be present in an indictment for murder in the first degree. But it would not transfer into manslaughter an act, which, if committed while the defendant was sober, would have been murder." *Commonwealth v. Soaris*, 275 Mass. 291, 299–300 (1931) (citation omitted).

NOTE 6b   Judge permitted to reduce jury's verdict of second degree murder to manslaughter as there was evidence that the killing was in the heat of uncontrolled anger and that the defendant's conduct was influenced by her alcoholic consumption. *Commonwealth v. Gaulden*, 383 Mass. 543, 557–58 (1981).

NOTE 7a   Wanton or Reckless Conduct. "A defendant's omission when there is a duty to act can constitute manslaughter if the omission is wanton or reckless. . . . The words 'wanton' and 'reckless' constitute conduct that is 'different in kind' than negligence or gross negligence. It has been defined as 'intentional conduct . . . involv[ing] a high degree of likelihood that substantial harm will result to another.' To constitute wanton or reckless conduct, the risk of death or grave bodily injury must be known or reasonably apparent, and the harm must be a probable consequence of the defendant's election to run that risk or of his failure reasonably to recognize it. Under Massachusetts law, recklessness has an objective component as well as a subjective component. A defendant can be convicted of manslaughter even if he was so stupid or so heedless that in fact he did not realize the grave danger if an ordinary normal man under the same circumstances would have realized the gravity of the danger." *Commonwealth v. Levesque*, 436 Mass. 443, 451–52 (2002) (citations and certain quotation and punctuation marks omitted).

NOTE 7b   "The defendant argues that he cannot be convicted of involuntary manslaughter unless the Commonwealth proves 'wanton or reckless' conduct on his part. Conversely, the Commonwealth relies on our long-standing rule that an assault and battery causing a death is sufficient to support a conviction for involuntary manslaughter."

Held, conviction affirmed. *Commonwealth v. Sheppard*, 404 Mass. 774, 775 (1989).

NOTE 8a   Battery/Manslaughter. "For a battery resulting in death to be battery manslaughter, there must have been a battery not amounting to a felony, when the defendant knew or should have known that the battery he was committing endangered human life. This court has also described battery manslaughter as requiring a showing that the defendant knew, or should have known, that his conduct created a high degree of likelihood that substantial harm would result to another." *Commonwealth v. Williams*, 428 Mass. 383, 390 (1998) (citations and quotation marks omitted).

NOTE 8b   "An instruction on battery manslaughter is required where there is evidence that the victim died as a result of a battery not amounting to a felony." *Commonwealth v. Reed*, 427 Mass. 100, 104 (1998) (citations and quotation marks omitted).

NOTE 9   Statutory offense of vehicular homicide, G.L. c. 90, § 24G, did not implicitly repeal the common law crime of involuntary manslaughter resulting from the wanton or reckless operation of a motor vehicle. *Commonwealth v. Jones*, 382 Mass. 387, 391–92 (1981).

NOTE 10   There is no crime of attempted manslaughter. *Commonwealth v. Hebert*, 373 Mass. 535, 537 (1977).

NOTE 11   Self-Defense. See Notes following Murder, G.L. c. 265, § 1, and Assault and Battery, G.L. c. 265, § 13A.

NOTE 12   Accident. "On the facts of this case, telling the jury that the Commonwealth had to prove beyond a reasonable doubt that the death was not an accident adequately presented the jury with the question whether the Commonwealth had proved beyond a reasonable doubt that the intervention by Sales was a reasonably foreseeable response to the situation that the defendant had recklessly created. The charge would have benefited from an additional statement that the Commonwealth had to prove that the defendant's conduct was the efficient cause that necessarily set in motion the factors that caused the victim's death (*see Commonwealth v. Rhoades*, 379 Mass. 810, 825 [1980]), and that, if Sales's response was not shown to be a reasonably foreseeable one, the defendant's conduct was not the legal or proximate cause of the victim's death." *Commonwealth v. Askew*, 404 Mass. 532, 535 (1989).

NOTE 13   "It is well established that a manslaughter charge should be given if, on any view of the evidence, a finding of manslaughter would be warranted. *See, e.g., Commonwealth v. Garabedian*, 399 Mass. 304, 313 (1987)." *Commonwealth v. Parker*, 402 Mass. 333, 343–44 (1988).

NOTE 14   "On his manslaughter contention the defendant directs attention to the decisions which require a judge to instruct a jury on a lesser offense if any view of the evidence in the case, without regard to its ultimate credibility, provides a rational basis for acquitting a defendant of the crime charged and convicting him of the lesser offense." *Commonwealth v. Freeman*, 407 Mass. 279, 285 (1990).

NOTE 15   Corporation. "May a corporation be found guilty of involuntary manslaughter under General Laws chapter 265 section 13 based upon a theory of collective knowledge and conduct of multiple of its employees, in the absence of one specific employee who is criminally liable for the commission of that crime?" The court answered "No." *Commonwealth v. Life Care Ctrs. of Am., Inc.*, 456 Mass. 826, 827–28 (2010).

NOTE 16   Verdict. "[I]n a case where the evidence would warrant a guilty verdict of manslaughter or some other crime on more than one theory, a guilty verdict should state the theory on which guilt was found." *Commonwealth v. Accetta*, 422 Mass. 642, 646–47 (1996).

NOTE 17   DNA Database. A conviction of an offense under this section or of an attempt or conspiracy to commit such an offense results in the defendant being required to submit a DNA sample to the state's DNA database. *See* G.L. c. 22E, § 3.

NOTE 18   Venue. G.L. c. 277, §§ 60–62.

SECTION 13½

Manslaughter while operating a motor vehicle

Whoever commits manslaughter while operating a motor vehicle in violation of paragraph (a) of subdivision (1) of section 24 of chapter 90 or section 8A of chapter 90B, shall be punished by imprisonment in the state prison for not less than 5 years and not more than 20 years, and by a fine of not more than $25,000. The sentence of imprisonment imposed upon such person shall not be reduced to less than 5 years, nor suspended, nor shall any such person be eligible for probation, parole or furlough or receive a deduction from his sentence for good conduct until he shall have served 5 years of such sentence. The commissioner of correction may, on the recommendation of the warden, superintendent or other person in charge of a correctional institution, or of the administrator of a county correctional institution, grant to an offender committed under this section a temporary release in the custody of an officer of such institution for the following purposes only: to attend the funeral of a relative; to visit a critically ill relative; to obtain emergency medical or psychiatric services unavailable at said institution; or to engage in employment pursuant to a work release program. Upon receipt of notice of a conviction under this section, the registrar may

2

suspend the license or right to operate of such person for any extended period up to life, provided that such suspension be at least a 15 year period. A person aggrieved by a decision of the registrar pursuant to this section may file an appeal in the superior court of the trial court department. If the court determines that the registrar abused his discretion, the court may vacate the suspension or revocation of a license or right to operate and reduce the period of suspension or revocation as ordered by the registrar, but in no event may the reduced period of suspension be for less than 15 years.

SECTION 13A
Assault or assault and battery

(a) Whoever commits an assault or an assault and battery upon another shall be punished by imprisonment for not more than 2½ years in a house of correction or by a fine of not more than $1,000.

A summons may be issued instead of a warrant for the arrest of any person upon a complaint for a violation of any provision of this subsection if in the judgment of the court or justice receiving the complaint there is reason to believe that he will appear upon a summons.

(b) Whoever commits an assault or an assault and battery:

(i) upon another and by such assault and battery causes serious bodily injury;

(ii) upon another who is pregnant at the time of such assault and battery, knowing or having reason to know that the person is pregnant; or

(iii) upon another who he knows has an outstanding temporary or permanent vacate, restraining or no contact order or judgment issued pursuant to section 18, section 34B or 34C of chapter 208, section 32 of chapter 209, section 3, 4 or 5 of chapter 209A, or section 15 or 20 of chapter 209C, in effect against him at the time of such assault or assault and battery; shall be punished by imprisonment in the state prison for not more than 5 years or in the house of correction for not more than 2½ years, or by a fine of not more than $5,000, or by both such fine and imprisonment.

(c) For the purposes of this section, "serious bodily injury" shall mean bodily injury that results in a permanent disfigurement, loss or impairment of a bodily function, limb or organ, or a substantial risk of death.

NOTE 1   Assault and Battery—Two Alternative Theories. "The crime of assault and battery is defined as the intentional and unjustified use of force upon the person of another, however slight, or the intentional doing of a wanton or grossly negligent act causing personal injury to another." *Commonwealth v. Moore*, 36 Mass. App. Ct. 455, 459 (1994); *Commonwealth v. Ford*, 424 Mass. 709 (1997).

NOTE 2a   Battery. A battery is an intentional, unpermitted contact with another person. *Matter of Spring*, 8 Mass. App. Ct. 831, 836 n.5 (1979), *findings revised* 380 Mass. 629 (1980).

NOTE 2b "In *Commonwealth v. Ford*, 424 Mass. [709,] 711 [(1997),] the court explained that 'it is incorrect to instruct the jury that the defendant may be convicted on a finding that the defendant intentionally did the act which resulted in the touching.' The correct formulation of intent requires a finding that the defendant intended to touch the victim." *Commonwealth v. Mitchell*, 67 Mass. App. Ct. 556, 564–65 (2006).

NOTE 3a   Assault. An assault is "an attempt or offer to do bodily harm to another by force and violence; or simply, an attempt to commit battery." *Commonwealth v. Slaney*, 345 Mass. 135, 138 (1962).

NOTE 3b   Two Subcategories. "The crime of assault breaks down into two subcategories: an attempted battery (e.g., intentionally swinging at a person with a bat and missing) or a threatened battery (e.g., waving a baseball bat toward a person in an overt and objectively menacing way)." *Commonwealth v. Chambers*, 57 Mass. App. Ct. 47, 48 (2003) (citations omitted).

NOTE 3c An attempted battery, like any crime of attempt, requires proof both of a specific intent and an overt act; mere preparation is not enough. *People v. Miller*, 42 P.2d 308, 309 (Cal. 1935).

NOTE 3d "In the case of an attempted battery type of assault, although the Commonwealth must prove that the defendant attempted to do bodily harm, there is no requirement that the victim be aware of the attempt or be put in fear by it." *Commonwealth v. Gorassi*, 432 Mass. 244, 248 (2000). *See also Commonwealth v. Chambers*, 57 Mass. App. Ct. 47, 48 (2003).

NOTE 3e   Threatened Battery—Elements. "In the case of a threatened battery type of assault, the Commonwealth must prove that the defendant engaged in 'objectively menacing' conduct with the intent to put the victim in fear of immediate bodily harm." *Commonwealth v. Gorassi*, 432 Mass. 244, 248 (2000). *See also Commonwealth v. Chambers*, 57 Mass. App. Ct. 47, 49 (2003).

NOTE 3f   Words. As a general rule words are not sufficient to constitute an assault, simple or aggravated; what is needed is an act placing another in reasonable apprehension that force may be used. *Commonwealth v. Delgado*, 367 Mass. 432, 436 (1975).

NOTE 3g   Victim Asleep. One may be found guilty of assault even if his victim is asleep. *Commonwealth v. Richards*, 363 Mass. 299, 303 (1973).

NOTE 4a   The Second Prong—Wanton/Reckless Conduct. If by wanton or reckless conduct bodily injury is caused to another, the person guilty of such conduct is guilty of assault and battery.

"'Wanton or reckless conduct' is intentional conduct, by way either of commission or of omission where there is a duty to act, which conduct involves a high degree of likelihood that substantial harm will result to another." *Commonwealth v. Sostillo*, 325 Mass. 143, 145 (1949) (citations omitted).

NOTE 4b   Actual Physical Injury Required. "We have never defined what degree of physical injury must be shown to prove a charge of assault and battery based on the reckless conduct theory. All our reported cases concerning reckless conduct have involved serious injuries to the victims, but the stated rule has not required proof of more than personal or bodily injury. . . .

"We accept the requirement that the Commonwealth must prove an injury that interfered with the health or comfort of the victim. It need not have been permanent, but it must have been more than transient and trifling. For example, if an alleged victim were shaken up but by his own admission not injured, or if an alleged victim were to have a sore wrist for only a few minutes, the 'injury' in each instance would be transient and trifling at most."

Commonwealth v. Burno, 396 Mass. 622, 626–27 (1986) (citations omitted); *see also Commonwealth v. Moore*, 36 Mass. App. Ct. 455, 459 (1994).

NOTE 5   Harm. The trial judge erroneously instructed the jury "that the Commonwealth had to prove, among other elements, that the defendant intended to physically harm the victim. The Commonwealth bear no such burden in a case of assault and battery; it need only prove that the touching, however slight, was intentional and not accidental." *Commonwealth v. Pease*, 49 Mass. App. Ct. 539, 543 (2000) (footnote omitted).

NOTE 6   Psychological Harm. "Under the threatened battery prong of assault, we have not recognized an attempt to inflict psychological harm as an assault and, in fact, the victim's apprehension of, or fear created by, the attempt is immaterial to whether an assault has occurred." *Commonwealth v. Gorassi*, 432 Mass. 244, 248 (2000).

NOTE 7a   Lesser Included Offenses. Assault is a lesser included offense of both assault and battery, and assault with a dangerous weapon, G.L. c. 265, § 15B. *Commonwealth v. Eaton*, 2 Mass. App. Ct. 113, 118–19 (1974).

NOTE 7b   If a defendant is accused of unarmed robbery by assaulting and placing the victim in fear, i.e., constructive force, then the elements of assault would make up some of the elements of unarmed robbery, and assault would remain a lesser included offense. But where the defendant is accused of unarmed robbery by use of actual, as opposed to constructive, force, then Massachusetts law provides that apprehension is not a necessary element of the crime and the defendant may be convicted of unarmed robbery even though the victim had no fear of being harmed. In this circumstance, unarmed robbery by use of actual force, assault is *not* a lesser included offense. *Brown v. Genakos*, 405 F.Supp. 381, 384 (D. Mass. 1975).

NOTE 7c   "[W]e conclude that a violation of an abuse prevention order that contains a mandate to refrain from abuse is not a lesser included offense of assault and battery on a person protected by an abuse prevention order." *Commonwealth v. Torres*, 468 Mass. 286, 287 (2014).

NOTE 8a   **Defenses.** "An actor is justified in using force against another to protect a third person (a) when a reasonable person in the actor's position would believe his intervention to be necessary for the protection of the third person and (b) in the circumstances as that reasonable person would believe them to be, the third person would be justified in using such force to protect himself. The reasonableness of such belief may depend in part on the relationships among the persons involved. . . . The actor's justification is lost if he uses excessive force, e.g., aggressive or deadly force unwarranted for the protective purpose." *Commonwealth v. Martin*, 369 Mass. 640, 649 (1976).

NOTE 8b   **Self-Defense.** "'The right of self-defense ordinarily *cannot be claimed by a person who provokes or initiates an assault unless* that person withdraws in good faith from the conflict and announces *his intention to retire*.' Annot., Withdrawal, After Provocation of Conflict, as Reviving Right of Self-Defense, 55 A.L.R.3d 1000, 1003 (1974)." *Commonwealth v. Naylor*, 407 Mass. 333, 335 (1990) (citations omitted and emphasis added).

See self-defense annotations following Murder, G.L. c. 265, § 1.

NOTE 8c   **Consent Not a Defense.** "[T]o commit a battery upon a person with such violence that bodily harm is likely to result is unlawful, and consent thereto is immaterial . . . [B]odily harm has its ordinary meaning and includes any hurt or injury calculated to interfere with the health or comfort of the [victim]. Such hurt or injury need not be permanent but must be more than merely transient or trifling." *Commonwealth v. Farrell*, 322 Mass. 606, 620–21 (1948) (citations omitted).

NOTE 8d   **Parental Privilege.** "[W]e hold that a parent or guardian may not be subjected to criminal liability for the use of force against a minor child under the care and supervision of the parent or guardian, provided that (1) the force used against the minor child is reasonable; (2) the force is reasonably related to the purpose of safeguarding or promoting the welfare of the minor, including the prevention or punishment of the minor's misconduct; and (3) the force used neither causes, nor creates a substantial risk of causing, physical harm (beyond fleeting pain or minor, transient marks), gross degradation, or severe mental distress." *Commonwealth v. Dorvil*, 472 Mass. 1, 12 (2015).

NOTE 8e   **In loco parentis.** The court "consider[ed] whether *Dorvil* left open the possibility that one acting in loco parentis may raise a parental discipline defense." It answered in the affirmative. *Commonwealth v. Packer*, 88 Mass. App. Ct. 585, 590 (2015).

NOTE 9   **Accord and Satisfaction.** *See* G.L. c. 276, § 55.

NOTE 10   **Related Statute.** G.L. c. 275, § 2—threats.

NOTE 11   **Spitting.** "On appeal, the defendant contends that spitting on another, intentionally and without consent, does not amount to a prohibited touching under the statute. To the contrary, we conclude that such conduct does constitute an assault and battery." *Commonwealth v. Cohen*, 55 Mass. App. Ct. 358, 358 (2002).

NOTE 12a   **Serious Bodily Injury.** The modifier "permanent" in the definition of "serious bodily injury" under G.L. c. 265, § 13A(c), applies only to "disfigurement," "loss or impairment of a bodily function, limb, or organ" need not be permanent to be a serious bodily injury. *Commonwealth v. Jean-Pierre*, 65 Mass. App. Ct. 162, 162–63 (2005).

NOTE 12b   Serious Bodily Injury—Medical Testimony Required. "While medical testimony may not be required in every instance to establish that a victim has suffered serious injury resulting in impairment to an organ, the Commonwealth bears the burden of establishing the severity of an injury through its impact on the structure of the victim's organ and its consequent effect on the ability of the organ to perform its usual function. Medical records containing technical terminology that require jurors to speculate on the meaning of key terms will be insufficient, without more, to meet this burden." *Commonwealth v. Scott*, 464 Mass. 355, 364 (2013).

SECTION 13B
Indecent assault and battery on child under 14

Whoever commits an indecent assault and battery on a child under the age of 14 shall be punished by imprisonment in the state prison for not more than 10 years, or by imprisonment in the house of correction for not more than 2½ years. A prosecution commenced under this section shall neither be continued without a finding nor placed on file.

In a prosecution under this section, a child under the age of 14 years shall be deemed incapable of consenting to any conduct of the defendant for which such defendant is being prosecuted.

NOTE 1a   "The test for indecent assault and battery . . . is an objective one that is bounded by contemporary moral values . . . The measure of indecency is common understanding and practices. A touching is indecent when, judged by the normative standard of societal mores, it is violative of social and behavioral expectations . . . in a manner which [is] fundamentally offensive to contemporary moral values . . . [and] which the common sense of society would regard as immodest, immoral and improper." Examples include touching one's private areas, e.g., breasts, abdomen, buttocks, inner thighs, genitals and pubic area. *Commonwealth v. Lavigne*, 42 Mass. App. Ct. 313, 314–15 (1997) (citations omitted).

NOTE 1b   "[A]n unwanted kiss on the mouth may constitute indecent conduct, where it involves forced insertion of the tongue. While a brief kiss not involving the insertion of the tongue is not generally criminally indecent, we do not require that there always be tongue involvement for an act that might be characterized as a kiss to be found indecent, as the attendant circumstances may allow the trier of fact rationally to determine that the kiss was an indecent act." *Commonwealth v. Miozza*, 67 Mass. App. Ct. 567, 572 (2006) (quotations and citations omitted).

NOTE 2   This section did not create the crime of indecent assault. An indecent assault is punishable as simple assault under G.L. c. 265, § 13A. *Commonwealth v. Eaton*, 2 Mass. App. Ct. 113, 116 (1974).

NOTE 3a   The victim's consent is of no consequence. *Commonwealth v. Hannaford*, 10 Mass. App. Ct. 903, 904 (1980).

NOTE 3b   **Lack of Consent.** "Although manifest objection by the victim would have made this a simpler case, we do not require an explicit verbal or physical rebuff to prove lack of consent. Instead, we analyze lack of consent based on the totality of the circumstances. Here, the jury had sufficient evidence to conclude that the fifteen-year-old victim did not consent to her forty-seven-year-old employer's sudden grabbing of her breast in the back of the pharmacy where he employed her." *Commonwealth v. Shore*, 65 Mass. App. Ct. 430, 433 (2006).

NOTE 4a   Indecent assault and battery is a lesser included offense of forcible rape. *Commonwealth v. Sanchez*, 405 Mass.

2

369, 381 (1989) (citing *Commonwealth v. Egerton*, 396 Mass. 499, 503 n.3 (1986)).

NOTE 4b   "The conviction of indecent assault and battery on a child under fourteen years (G.L. c. 265, § 13B) may not stand for resentencing as a conviction of indecent assault and battery on a person fourteen years or over (G.L. c. 265, § 13H), or, indeed, of simple assault and battery (G.L. c. 265, § 13A), because those offenses (§§ 13A and 13H), both having as an element lack of consent by the victim, are not lesser included within the § 13B offenses, to which consent or lack thereof was made immaterial by St. 1986, c. 187." *Commonwealth v. Traynor*, 40 Mass. App. Ct. 527, 529 (1996).

NOTE 5   **Touching.** A defendant who induces a child under the age of fourteen to touch the defendant in an indecent manner may be convicted of indecent assault and battery on a child under the age of fourteen. *Commonwealth v. Davidson*, 68 Mass. App. Ct. 72, 72–73 (2007).

NOTE 6   **Statute Constitutional.** G.L. c. 265, § 13B is not unconstitutionally vague. *Commonwealth v. Miozza*, 67 Mass. App. Ct. 567, 570 (2006).

NOTE 7   **Juvenile Disposition.** As is the case with an adult/criminal prosecution commenced under this section, a complaint alleging a child to be a delinquent child by reason of having violated the provisions of this section shall not be placed on file or continued without a finding. G.L. c. 119, §§ 55B, 58.

NOTE 8   **Sex Offender Registry.** A conviction or adjudication of delinquency of an offense under this section or of an attempt to commit such an offense (*see* G.L. c. 274, § 6) renders the defendant subject to the requirements of the sex offender registry law. *See* G.L. c. 6, §§ 178C–178Q.

NOTE 9   **DNA Database.** A conviction of an offense under this section or of an attempt or conspiracy to commit such an offense results in the defendant being required to submit a DNA sample to the state's DNA database. *See* G.L. c. 22E, § 3.

NOTE 10   **Sexually Dangerous Person Commitment.** A conviction or adjudication of delinquency of an offense under this section or of an attempt to commit such an offense (*see* G.L. c. 274, § 6) can serve as a predicate "sexual offense" for civil commitment as a "sexually dangerous person." *See* G.L. c. 123A, §§ 1–15.

NOTE 11   District and superior courts have concurrent jurisdiction. G.L. c. 218, § 26.

NOTE 12   **Related statutes.** G.L. c. 265, § 13F—Indecent assault and battery on a mentally retarded person; G.L. c. 265, § 13H—Indecent assault and battery of a child fourteen or over; G.L. c. 265, § 22A—Rape of a child under sixteen; G.L. c. 265, § 23—Statutory rape; G.L. c. 272, § 35A—Unnatural acts, etc., with child under sixteen.

SECTION 13B½
Aggravated indecent assault and battery on child under 14

Whoever commits an indecent assault and battery on a child under the age of 14 and:

(a) the indecent assault and battery was committed during the commission or attempted commission of the following offenses:—(1) armed burglary as set forth in section 14 of chapter 266; (2) unarmed burglary as set forth in section 15 of said chapter 266; (3) breaking and entering as set forth in section 16 of said chapter 266; (4) entering without breaking as set forth in section 17 of said chapter 266; (5) breaking and entering into a dwelling house as set forth in section 18 of said chapter 266; (6) kidnapping as set forth in section 26 of chapter 265; (7) armed robbery as set forth in section 17 of said chapter 265; (8) unarmed robbery as set forth in section 19 of said chapter 265; (9) assault and battery with a dangerous weapon or assault with a dangerous weapon, as set forth in

sections 15A and 15B of said chapter 265; (10) home invasion as set forth in section 18C of said chapter 265; or (11) posing or exhibiting child in state of nudity or sexual conduct as set forth in section 29A of chapter 272; or

(b) at the time of commission of said indecent assault and battery, the defendant was a mandated reporter as is defined in section 21 of chapter 119, shall be punished by imprisonment in the state prison for life or for any term of years, but not less than 10 years. The sentence imposed on such person shall not be reduced to less than 10 years, or suspended, nor shall any person convicted under this section be eligible for probation, parole, work release, or furlough or receive any deduction from his sentence for good conduct until he shall have served 10 years of such sentence. Prosecutions commenced under this section shall neither be continued without a finding nor placed on file.

In a prosecution under this section, a child under the age of 14 years shall be deemed incapable of consenting to any conduct of the defendant for which such defendant is being prosecuted.

SECTION 13B¾
Indecent assault and battery on child under 14, subsequent offense

Whoever commits an indecent assault and battery on a child under the age of 14 and has been previously convicted of or adjudicated delinquent or as a youthful offender for: indecent assault and battery on a child under 14 as set forth in section 13B; aggravated indecent assault and battery on a child under 14 as set forth in section 13B½; indecent assault and battery on a person 14 or older as set forth in section 13H; assault of a child with intent to commit rape as set forth in section 24B; rape of a child with force as set forth in section 22A; aggravated rape of a child with force as set forth in section 22B; rape and abuse of a child as set forth in section 23; aggravated rape and abuse of a child as set forth in section 23A; rape as set forth in section 22 or; a like violation of the laws of another state, the United States or a military, territorial or Indian tribal authority, shall be punished by imprisonment in the state prison for life or for any term of years, but not less than 15 years. The sentence imposed on such person shall not be reduced to less than 15 years, or suspended, nor shall any person convicted under this section be eligible for probation, parole, work release or furlough or receive any deduction from his sentence for good conduct until he shall have served 15 years of such sentence. Prosecutions commenced under this section shall neither be continued without a finding nor placed on file.

In any prosecution commenced pursuant to this section, introduction into evidence of a prior adjudication or conviction or a prior finding of sufficient facts by either certified attested copies of original court papers, or certified attested copies of the defendant's biographical and informational data from records of the department of probation, any jail or house of correction or the department of correction shall be prima facie evidence that the defendant before the court had been convicted previously by a court of the commonwealth or any other jurisdiction. Such documentation shall be self-authenticating and admissible, after the commonwealth has established the defendant's guilt on the primary offense, as evidence in any court of the commonwealth to prove the defendant's commission of any prior conviction described therein. The commonwealth shall not be required to introduce any additional corroborating evidence or live witness testimony to establish the validity of such prior conviction.

SECTION 13C
Assault and battery to collect loan

Whoever commits an assault and battery upon another for the purpose of collecting a loan shall for the first offense be punished by imprisonment in the state prison for not less than three nor more than five years or by imprisonment for not more than two and one half years in a jail or house of correction; and for a second or subsequent offense, by imprisonment in the state prison for not less than five nor more than ten years. Except in the case of a conviction for the first offense for violation of this section, the imposition or execution of the sentence shall not be suspended and no probation or parole shall be granted until the minimum imprisonment herein provided for the offense shall have been served.

NOTE   **Loan for Drugs.** "Webster's . . . defines loan as including 'something lent for the borrower's temporary use on condition that it or its equivalent be returned. . . . Black's . . . defines 'loan' to include 'the creation of debt by a credit to an account with the lender upon which the debtor is entitled to draw immediately.' . . . Burton's Legal Thesaurus cites 'extension of credit as a synonym for 'loan.' . . . Providing another with drugs on the condition that payment for those drugs be made at a later date surely fits within these definitions." *Commonwealth v. Thompson*, 56 Mass. App. Ct. 710, 712 (2002).

SECTION 13D
Assault and battery upon public employees; penalties
(Amended by 2014 Mass. Acts c. 165, § 177, effective July 15, 2014; bracketed text added by 2014 Mass. Acts c. 284, § 75, effective Jan. 1, 2015.)

Whoever commits an assault and battery upon any public employee when such person is engaged in the performance of his duties at the time of such assault and battery, shall be punished by imprisonment for not less than ninety days nor more than two and one-half years in a house of correction or by a fine of not less than five hundred nor more than five thousand dollars. [Whoever commits an offense under this section and which includes an attempt to disarm a police officer in the performance of the officer's duties shall be punished by imprisonment in the state prison for not more than 10 years or by a fine of not more than $1,000 and imprisonment in a jail or house of correction for not more than 2½ years.]

An officer authorized to make arrests may arrest any person upon probable cause and without a warrant if the person has committed an offense under this section upon a public employee when the public employee was operating a public transit vehicle and the officer may keep the person in custody during which period the officer shall seek the issuance of a complaint and request a bail determination with all reasonable promptness.

NOTE 1   Defendant must know alleged victim is an officer "engaged in the performance of his duty." That knowledge may be inferred from all of the relevant facts, including evidence that the officer and defendant were known to each other prior to the incident. *Commonwealth v. Sawyer*, 142 Mass. 530, 532–33 (1886).

NOTE 2   An officer has the right to use force which is reasonably necessary to overcome resistance by the person sought to be arrested. If the circumstances merit it, deadly force may be used. *Commonwealth v. Young*, 326 Mass. 597, 601–02 (1950).

NOTE 3   Police officer stopped an erratically driven car; heard a woman scream from within the car as he stood by the driver's side door. The defendant (the driver) swung the door on the driver's side open, knocking the officer down, and sped off. Held: The factfinder may infer that the defendant intentionally struck the officer with the door.

Further, the officer chased the car for three or four miles, shooting its tires, thereby forcing it to stop. As the officer attempted to remove the defendant from the car, the defendant kicked and punched him repeatedly. Held: A second assault occurred. Accordingly, guilty finding for assault and battery with a deadly weapon and assault and battery upon a police officer were upheld, as were sentences on both incidents.

Commonwealth v. LeBlanc, 3 Mass. App. Ct. 780 (1975).

NOTE 4   Evidence: Police filed charges against the defendant after the defendant had applied for civil complaints against the officer. Held: Officers may be cross-examined on this point in order to show bias of the officers against the defendant. *Commonwealth v. Ahearn*, 370 Mass. 283, 286 (1976).

NOTE 5a   **Defense.** The failure to charge the defendant for the offense for which he was originally arrested is *no* defense to a resultant assault and battery upon a police officer. *Commonwealth v. Tobin*, 108 Mass. 426, 429, 11 AR 375, 378 (1871).

NOTE 5b   "[I]n the absence of excessive or unnecessary force by an arresting officer, a person may not use force to resist an arrest by one who he knows or has good reason to believe is an authorized police officer, engaged in the performance of his duties, regardless of whether the arrest was unlawful in the circumstances. . . . [W]here the officer uses excessive or unnecessary force to subdue the arrestee, regardless of whether the arrest is lawful or unlawful, the arrestee may defend himself by employing such force as reasonably appears to be necessary. . . . Moreover, once the arrestee knows or reasonably should know that if he desists from using force in self-defense, the officer will cease using force, the arrestee must desist. Otherwise, he will forfeit his defense." *Commonwealth v. Moreira*, 388 Mass. 596, 601–02 (1983) (citations omitted). *See also Commonwealth v. Montes*, 49 Mass. App. Ct. 789, 792–93 (2000).

SECTION 13D½
Injury to firefighter resulting from willful burning of property or reckless burning of woods

Whoever commits an offense set forth in section one, two, five or seven of chapter two hundred and sixty-six where said offense results in injury to a firefighter in the performance of his duty, shall be punished by imprisonment in the state prison for not more than ten years, or by a fine of not more than one thousand dollars and imprisonment in a jail or house of correction for not more than two and one-half years.

SECTION 13E
Repealed

SECTION 13F
Indecent assault and battery on person with an intellectual disability; assault and battery

Whoever commits an indecent assault and battery on a person with an intellectual disability knowing such person to have an intellectual disability shall for the first offense be punished by imprisonment in the state prison for not less than five years or not more than ten years; and for a second or subsequent offense, by imprisonment in the state prison for not less than ten years. Except in the case of a conviction for the first offense for violation of this section, the imposition or execution of the sentence shall not be suspended, and no probation or parole shall be granted until the minimum imprisonment herein provided for the offense shall have been served. This section shall not apply to the commission of an indecent assault and battery by a person with an intellectual disability upon another person with an intellectual disability.

2

Whoever commits an assault and battery on a person with an intellectual disability knowing such person to have an intellectual disability shall for the first offense be punished by imprisonment in a house of correction for not more than two and one-half years or by imprisonment in the state prison for not more than five years; and, for a second or subsequent offense, by imprisonment in the state prison for not more than ten years. This section shall not apply to the commission of an assault and battery by a mentally retarded person upon another mentally retarded person.

NOTE 1   "[W]e conclude that the term 'intellectual disability' is sufficiently clear and definite and is therefore not unconstitutionally vague. The legislative history of § 13F, makes it clear that the Legislature's intent was merely to change the nomenclature and not the substance of the statute." *Commonwealth v. St. Louis*, 473 Mass. 350, 356 (2015).

NOTE 2   No abuse of discretion in admitting the testimony of examining pediatrician, who had extensive experience in cases of child abuse, as to the function of "reality testing" and its relationship to retarded children or in admitting his opinion relating to the imagination of children. However the expert may not testify that "it was my impression that she was telling the truth." *Commonwealth v. Carter*, 9 Mass. App. Ct. 680, 681–82 (1980).

NOTE 3   **Sex Offender Registry.** A conviction or adjudication of delinquency of an offense under this section or of an attempt to commit such an offense (*see* G.L. c. 274, § 6) renders the defendant subject to the requirements of the sex offender registry law. *See* G.L. c. 6, §§ 178C–178Q.

NOTE 4   **DNA Database.** A conviction of an offense under this section or of an attempt or conspiracy to commit such an offense results in the defendant being required to submit a DNA sample to the state's DNA database. *See* G.L. c. 22E, §§ 1–15.

NOTE 5   **Sexually Dangerous Person Commitment.** A conviction or adjudication of delinquency of an offense under this section or of an attempt to commit such an offense (*see* G.L. c. 274, § 6) can serve as a predicate "sexual offense" for civil commitment as a "sexually dangerous person". *See* G.L. c. 123A, §§ 1–15.

SECTION 13G
Commission of a felony for hire; additional punishment

Whoever, for the payment of consideration or for the promise of the payment of such consideration, commits a felony, shall be punished by imprisonment in the state prison for not more than five years. The punishment imposed by this section shall be in addition to the punishment provided by law for the commission of a felony so committed.

SECTION 13H
Indecent assault and battery on person 14 or older; penalties

Whoever commits an indecent assault and battery on a person who has attained age fourteen shall be punished by imprisonment in the state prison for not more than five years, or by imprisonment for not more than two and one-half years in a jail or house of correction.

Whoever commits an indecent assault and battery on an elder or person with a disability, as defined in section 13K, shall be punished by imprisonment in the state prison for not more than 10 years, or by imprisonment in the house of correction for not more than 2½ years, and whoever commits a second or subsequent such offense shall be punished by imprisonment in the state prison for not more than 20 years. A prosecution commenced under this paragraph shall not be placed on file nor continued without a finding.

NOTE 1   See Notes accompanying G.L. c. 265, §§ 13B and 22.

NOTE 2   **Sex Offender Registry.** A conviction or adjudication of delinquency of an offense under this section or of an attempt to commit such an offense (*see* G.L. c. 274, § 6) renders the defendant subject to the requirements of the sex offender registry law. *See* G.L. c. 6, §§ 178C–178Q.

NOTE 3   **DNA Database.** A conviction of an offense under this section or of an attempt or conspiracy to commit such an offense results in the defendant being required to submit a DNA sample to the state's DNA database. *See* G.L. c. 22E, § 3.

NOTE 4   **Sexually Dangerous Person Commitment.** A conviction or adjudication of delinquency of an offense under this section or of an attempt to commit such an offense (*see* G.L. c. 274, § 6) can serve as a predicate "sexual offense" for civil commitment as a "sexually dangerous person". *See* G.L. c. 123A, §§ 1–15.

SECTION 13I
Assault or assault and battery on emergency medical technician, ambulance operator, ambulance attendant or health care provider

Whoever commits an assault or assault and battery on an emergency medical technician, an ambulance operator, an ambulance attendant, or a health care provider as defined in section 1 of chapter 111, while the technician, operator, attendant or provider is treating or transporting a person in the line of duty shall be punished by imprisonment in the house of correction for not less than 90 days nor more than 2 and one-half years or by a fine of not less than $500 nor more than $5,000, or both.

SECTION 13J
Assault and battery upon a child; liability of person having custody; penalties

(a) For the purposes of this section, the following words shall, unless the context indicates otherwise, have the following meanings:

"Bodily injury", substantial impairment of the physical condition including any burn, fracture of any bone, subdural hematoma, injury to any internal organ, any injury which occurs as the result of repeated harm to any bodily function or organ including human skin or any physical condition which substantially imperils a child's health or welfare.

"Child", any person under fourteen years of age.

"Person having care and custody", a parent, guardian, employee of a home or institution or any other person with equivalent supervision or care of a child, whether the supervision is temporary or permanent.

"Substantial bodily injury", bodily injury which creates a permanent disfigurement, protracted loss or impairment of a function of a body member, limb or organ, or substantial risk of death.

(b) Whoever commits an assault and battery upon a child and by such assault and battery causes bodily injury shall be punished by imprisonment in the state prison for not more than five years or imprisonment in the house of correction for not more than two and one-half years.

Whoever commits an assault and battery upon a child and by such assault and battery causes substantial bodily injury shall be punished by imprisonment in the state prison for not more than fifteen years or imprisonment in the house of correction for not more than two and one-half years.

Whoever, having care and custody of a child, wantonly or recklessly permits bodily injury to such child or wantonly or recklessly permits another to commit an assault and battery upon such child, which assault and battery causes bodily injury, shall be punished by imprisonment for not more than two and one-half years in the house of correction.

Whoever, having care and custody of a child, wantonly or recklessly permits substantial bodily injury to such child or wantonly or recklessly permits another to commit an assault and battery upon such child, which assault and battery causes substantial bodily injury, shall be punished by imprisonment in the state prison for not more than five years, or by imprisonment in a jail or house of correction for not more than two and one-half years.

NOTE   "The evidence was such that it was not clear who had committed the batteries upon the infant. It could have been either parent, the babysitter, or the cousin who lived with them. For this reason, the judge properly entered required findings of not guilty [on the A&B, c. 265, § 13A, charges].

"[However, u]nder c. 265, § 13J, it does not matter who committed the batteries, and each person having the care and custody of the child may be found guilty of permitting anyone to commit an assault and battery." *Commonwealth v. Garcia*, 47 Mass. App. Ct. 419, 423–24 (1999).

SECTION 13K
Assault and battery on elderly or disabled person

(a) For the purpose of this section the following words shall, unless the context requires otherwise, have the following meanings:—

"Abuse", physical contact which either harms or creates a substantial likelihood of harm.

"Bodily injury", substantial impairment of the physical condition, including, but not limited to, any burn, fracture of any bone, subdural hematoma, injury to any internal organ, or any injury which occurs as the result of repeated harm to any bodily function or organ, including human skin.

"Caretaker", a person with responsibility for the care of an elder or person with a disability, which responsibility may arise as the result of a family relationship, or by a fiduciary duty imposed by law, or by a voluntary or contractual duty undertaken on behalf of such elder or person with a disability. A person may be found to be a caretaker under this section only if a reasonably person would believe that such person's failure to fulfill such responsibility would adversely affect the physical health of such elder or person with a disability. Minor children and adults adjudicated incompetent by a court of law may not be deemed to be caretakers under this section.

(i) "Responsibility arising from a family relationship", it may be inferred that a husband, wife, son, daughter, brother, sister, or other relative of an elder or person with a disability is a caretaker if the person has provided primary and substantial assistance for the care of the elder or person with a disability as would lead a reasonable person to believe that failure to provide such care would adversely affect the physical health of the elder or person with a disability.

(ii) "Responsibility arising from a fiduciary duty imposed by law", it may be inferred that the following persons are caretakers of an elder or person with a disability to the extent that they are legally required to apply the assets of the estate of the elder or person with a disability to provide the necessities essential for the physical health of the elder or person with a disability: (i) a guardian of the person or assets of an elder or person with a disability; (ii) the conservator of an elder or person with a disability, appointed by the probate court pursuant to chapter two hundred and one; and (iii) an attorney-in-fact holding a power of attorney or durable power of attorney pursuant to chapter two hundred and one B.

(iii) "Responsibility arising from a contractual duty", it may be inferred that a person who receives monetary or personal benefit or gain as a result of a bargained-for agreement to be responsible for providing primary and substantial assistance for the care of an elder or person with a disability is a caretaker.

(iv) "Responsibility arising out of the voluntary assumption of the duties of caretaker", it may be inferred that a person who has voluntarily assumed responsibility for providing primary and substantial assistance for the physical care of an elder or person with a disability is a caretaker if the person's conduct would lead a reasonable person to believe that failure to provide such care would adversely affect the physical health of the elder or person with a disability, and at least one of the following criteria is met: (i) the person is living in the household of the elder or person with a disability, or present in the household on a regular basis; or (ii) the person would have reason to believe, as a result of the actions, statements or behavior of the elder or person with a disability, that he is being relied upon for providing primary and substantial assistance for care.

"Elder", a person sixty years of age or older.

"Mistreatment", the use of medications or treatments, isolation, or physical or chemical restraints which harms or creates a substantial likelihood of harm.

"Neglect", the failure to provide treatment or services necessary to maintain health and safety and which either harms or creates a substantial likelihood of harm.

"Person with disability", a person with a permanent or long-term physical or mental impairment that prevents or restricts the individual's ability to provide for his or her own care or protection.

"Serious bodily injury", bodily injury which results in a permanent disfigurement, protracted loss or impairment of a bodily function, limb or organ, or substantial risk of death.

(a½) Whoever commits an assault and battery upon an elder or person with a disability shall be punished by imprisonment in the state prison for not more than 3 years or by imprisonment in a house of correction for not more than 2½ years, or by a fine of not more than $1,000, or both such fine and imprisonment.

(b) Whoever commits an assault and battery upon an elder or person with a disability and by such assault and battery causes bodily injury shall be punished by imprisonment in the state prison for not more than five years or in the house of correction for not more than two and one-half years or by a fine of not more than one thousand dollars or by both such fine and imprisonment.

(c) Whoever commits an assault and battery upon an elder or person with a disability and by such assault and battery causes serious bodily injury shall be punished by imprisonment in the state prison for not more than ten years or in the house of correction for not more than two and one-half years or by a fine of not more than five thousand dollars or by both such fine and imprisonment.

(d) Whoever, being a caretaker of an elder or person with a disability, wantonly or recklessly permits bodily injury to such elder or person with a disability, or wantonly or recklessly permits another to commit an assault and battery upon

2

such elder or person with a disability which assault and battery causes bodily injury, shall be punished by imprisonment in the state prison for not more than five years or in the house of correction for not more than two and one-half years or by a fine of not more than five thousand dollars or by both such fine and imprisonment.

(d½) Whoever, being a caretaker of an elder or person with a disability, wantonly or recklessly commits or permits another to commit abuse, neglect or mistreatment upon such elder or person with a disability, shall be punished by imprisonment in the state prison for not more than 3 years, or imprisonment in the house of correction for not more than 2½ years, or by a fine of not more than $5,000, or by both such fine and imprisonment.

(e) Whoever, being a caretaker of an elder or person with a disability, wantonly or recklessly permits serious bodily injury to such elder or person with a disability, or wantonly or recklessly permits another to commit and assault and battery upon such elder or person with a disability which assault and battery causes serious bodily injury, shall be punished by imprisonment in the state prison for not more than ten years or by imprisonment in the house of correction for not more than two and one-half years or by a fine of not more than ten thousand dollars or by both such fine and imprisonment.

(f) Conduct shall not be construed to be wanton or reckless conduct under this section if directed by a competent elder or person with a disability, or for the sole reason that, in lieu of medical treatment, an elder or person with a disability is being furnished or relies upon treatment by spiritual means through prayer if such treatment is in accordance with the tenets and practices of the established religious tradition of such elder or person with a disability, and is provided at the direction of such elder or person with a disability, who shall be competent, or pursuant to the direction of a person who is properly designated a health care proxy under chapter two hundred and one D.

NOTE "Contrary to the defendant's claim, the difference between § 13K(d½) and § 13K(e) is not a matter of degree. While § 13K(d½) encompasses conduct that constitutes 'abuse, neglect or mistreatment,' § 13K(e) applies more broadly to any conduct that results in serious bodily injury. As such, each offense 'requires proof of an additional fact that the other does not.' *Edge v. Commonwealth*, 451 Mass. 74, 75 (2008). Put another way, a violation of § 13K(e) does not necessarily constitute a violation of § 13K(d½). Certainly, engaging in conduct that constitutes abuse, neglect, or mistreatment is not the only way by which a caretaker can permit serious bodily injury to an elder. Accordingly, § 13K(d½) is not a lesser included offense of § 13K(e), and the defendant's convictions are not duplicative." *Commonwealth v. Cruz*, 88 Mass. App. Ct. 206, 211–12 (2015) (citations omitted).

SECTION 13L
Reckless endangerment to children

For the purposes of this section, the following words shall have the following meanings:—

"Child", any person under 18 years of age.

"Serious bodily injury", bodily injury which results in a permanent disfigurement, protracted loss or impairment of a bodily function, limb or organ, or substantial risk of death.

"Sexual abuse", an indecent assault and battery on a child under 14 under section 13B of chapter 265; aggravated indecent assault and battery on a child under 14 under section 13B½ of said chapter 265; a repeat offense under section 13B¾ of said chapter 265; indecent assault and battery on a

person age 14 or over under section 13H of said chapter 265; rape under section 22 of said chapter 265; rape of a child under 16 with force under section 22A of said chapter 265; aggravated rape of a child under 16 with force under section 22B of said chapter 265; a repeat offense under section 22C of said chapter 265; rape and abuse of a child under section 23 of said chapter 265; aggravated rape and abuse of a child under section 23A of said chapter 265; a repeat offense under section 23B of said chapter 265; assault with intent to commit rape under section 24 of said chapter 265; and assault of a child with intent to commit rape under section 24B of said chapter 265.

Whoever wantonly or recklessly engages in conduct that creates a substantial risk of serious bodily injury or sexual abuse to a child or wantonly or recklessly fails to take reasonable steps to alleviate such risk where there is a duty to act shall be punished by imprisonment in the house of correction for not more than 2½ years.

For the purposes of this section, such wanton or reckless behavior occurs when a person is aware of and consciously disregards a substantial and unjustifiable risk that his acts, or omissions where there is a duty to act, would result in serious bodily injury or sexual abuse to a child. The risk must be of such nature and degree that disregard of the risk constitutes a gross deviation from the standard of conduct that a reasonable person would observe in the situation.

NOTE 1 **Preamble.** The Legislature, in enacting Section 13L as 2002 Mass. Acts c. 322, included the following preamble:

The general court finds that the majority of state criminal codes and the model penal code include reckless endangerment offenses. These crimes punish reckless conduct that creates a risk of, but do not necessarily result in, serious physical injury. These crimes do not punish a particular injury or outcome, but seek to prevent and penalize the risk that is created. While examples of offenses from states that have adopted reckless endangerment statutes often involve physical acts, such offenses include conduct that does not involve the performance of a physical act. Several states limit the statutes' application to creating a risk of serious physical injury to children.

The general court further finds that there are growing numbers of complaints concerning the sexual abuse of minors by non-custodial adults who have been recklessly placed or retained in positions of trust and authority. The general court recognizes that reckless behavior may serve as the basis for criminal liability for certain crimes committed in the commonwealth. The general court hereby finds that there is a significant public interest and urgent necessity to protect children from physical and sexual abuse by penalizing reckless behavior that creates a risk of serious physical injury or sexual abuse to a child. It is the intention of the general court to penalize reckless behavior, including the failure to act where civil or criminal law has imposed a duty on persons to act in a certain manner, which results in a risk of serious physical injury or sexual abuse to a child.

NOTE 2 The statute is constitutional. *Commonwealth v. Hendricks*, 452 Mass. 97, 104 (2008).

NOTE 3 "[B]ecause each element of § 13J(b), fourth par. [wantonly and recklessly permitting an assault and battery on a child that causes the child substantial bodily injury], encompasses a corresponding element of § 13L, and because there are no additional elements in § 13L that are not in § 13J(b), fourth par., § 13L is a lesser included offense of § 13J(b), fourth par." *Commonwealth v. Roderiques*, 462 Mass. 415, 424 (2012).

SECTION 13M
Assault and battery on a family or household member; second or subsequent offense; penalty
(Amended by 2014 Mass. Acts c. 260, § 23, effective Aug. 8, 2014.)

(a) Whoever commits an assault or assault and battery on a family or household member shall be punished by imprisonment in the house of correction for not more than 2½ years or by a fine of not more than $5,000, or both such fine and imprisonment.

(b) Whoever is convicted of a second or subsequent offense of assault or assault and battery on a family or household member shall be punished by imprisonment in the house of correction for not more than 2½ years or by imprisonment in the state prison for not more than 5 years.

(c) For the purposes of this section, "family or household member" shall mean persons who (i) are or were married to one another, (ii) have a child in common regardless of whether they have ever married or lived together or (iii) are or have been in a substantive dating or engagement relationship; provided, that the trier of fact shall determine whether a relationship is substantive by considering the following factors: the length of time of the relationship; the type of relationship; the frequency of interaction between the parties; whether the relationship was terminated by either person; and the length of time elapsed since the termination of the relationship.

(d) For any violation of this section, or as a condition of a continuance without a finding, the court shall order the defendant to complete a certified batterer's intervention program unless, upon good cause shown, the court issues specific written findings describing the reasons that batterer's intervention should not be ordered or unless the batterer's intervention program determines that the defendant is not suitable for intervention.

SECTION 13N
Misdemeanor offense including use or attempted use of physical force or threatened use of deadly weapon against family or household member; reporting to department of criminal justice information services
(Added by 2014 Mass. Acts c. 284, § 76, effective Jan. 1, 2015.)

Upon entry of a conviction for any misdemeanor offense that has as an element the use or attempted use of physical force or the threatened use of a deadly weapon the court shall determine whether the victim or intended victim was a family or household member, as defined in section 1 of chapter 209A, of the defendant. If the victim or intended victim was a family or household member of the defendant, the court shall enter the offense, the chapter, section and subsection, if any, of the offense and the relationship of the defendant to the victim or intended victim upon the records and this entry shall be forwarded to the department of criminal justice information services for inclusion in the criminal justice information system and to provide the attorney general of the United States with information required or permitted under federal law to be included in the National Instant Criminal Background Check System or any successor system maintained to conduct background checks for firearm sales or licensing.

SECTION 14
Mayhem

Whoever, with malicious intent to maim or disfigure, cuts out or maims the tongue, puts out or destroys an eye, cuts or tears off an ear, cuts, slits or mutilates the nose or lip, or cuts off or disables a limb or member, of another person, and whoever is privy to such intent, or is present and aids in the commission of such crime, or whoever, with intent to maim or disfigure, assaults another person with a dangerous weapon, substance or chemical, and by such assault disfigures, cripples or inflicts serious or permanent physical injury upon such person, and whoever is privy to such intent, or is present and aids in the commission of such crime, shall be punished by imprisonment in the state prison for not more than twenty years or by a fine of not more than one thousand dollars and imprisonment in jail for not more than two and one half years.

NOTE 1a   "Maim" means to disfigure, cripple or to inflict serious or permanent injury; "to disable, wound, cause bodily hurt or disfigurement to the body." "Cripple" is "to deprive of the use of a limb, particularly of a leg or foot, to lame, to deprive of strength, activity, or capability for service." *Commonwealth v. Farrell*, 322 Mass. 606, 618–19 (1948).

NOTE 1b   Burns caused by a lighted cigarette may constitute maiming. *Farrell*, 322 Mass. at 618–19.

NOTE 2a   **Dangerous Weapon.** Mayhem includes an assault with a dangerous weapon which results in disfiguring, crippling, or infliction of serious or permanent injury. *Farrell*, 322 Mass. at 618.

NOTE 2b   A lighted cigarette may be a dangerous weapon. This is a question of fact to be decided by the factfinder. *Farrell*, 322 Mass. at 614–15.

NOTE 2c   For further material on dangerous weapons see the notes following G.L. c. 265, § 15A.

NOTE 3   In reading the mayhem statute, it is readily apparent that the crime may be prosecuted under one of two theories. Under the first theory ("Whoever . . . cuts out or maims the tongue), ABDW is not a lesser included offense. Under the second theory ("Whoever . . . assaults another person with a dangerous weapon), ABDW is a lesser included offense. *Commonwealth v. Martin*, 425 Mass. 718, 721–23 (1997).

NOTE 4   **Consent.** "To commit a battery upon a person with such violence that bodily harm is likely to result is unlawful, and consent thereto is immaterial." *Farrell*, 322 Mass. at 620.

NOTE 5a   **Intent.** To be found guilty of mayhem, specific intent to maim or disfigure must be shown. Such intent may be established by showing intent to inflict serious bodily injury. *Commonwealth v. Hogan*, 7 Mass. App. Ct. 236, 244 (1979), *aff'd*, 379 Mass. 190, 192–93 (1979).

NOTE 5b   Defendant stayed in car while two codefendants entered an apartment with clubs and beat the victim. Held: evidence did not warrant conviction for mayhem for defendant as he did not share or know of codefendants intent to maim or disfigure the victim. Defendant, however, still may be found guilty of assault and battery by means of a dangerous weapon. *Commonwealth v. Hogan*, 379 Mass. 190, 193 (1979), *aff'g*, 7 Mass. App. Ct. 236 (1979).

NOTE 5c   "The evidence warranted a finding that the victim suffered 'serious or permanent physical injury' (under G.L. c. 265, § 14) to her right eye as a result of the defendant's repeatedly rubbing handfuls of dirt into her eyes and striking the right side of her face in the area of the eye with his fist. The specific intent to maim or disfigure was inferable from the sustained nature of the assault in the eyes. As applied to so delicate an organ such as the eye, dirt can be found to be a dangerous substance within the meaning of this statute." *Commonwealth v. Tucceri*, 9 Mass. App. Ct. 844, 845 (1980) (citations omitted). *See also Commonwealth v. Cleary*, 41 Mass. App. Ct. 214 (1996) (single blow of ax handle to eye, causing permanent loss of sight, insufficient as no direct or inferential evidence of specific intent to maim or disfigure) and *Commonwealth v. Sparks*, 42 Mass. App. Ct. 915 (1997) (inference of intent to maim from prolonged attack, five minutes, and the nature of the victim's eye injuries).

2

NOTE 6   DNA Database. A conviction of an offense under this section or of an attempt or conspiracy to commit such an offense results in the defendant being required to submit a DNA sample to the state's DNA database. *See* G.L. c. 22E, § 3.

SECTION 15

Assault with intent to murder or maim

Whoever assaults another with intent to commit murder, or to maim or disfigure his person in any way described in the preceding section, shall be punished by imprisonment in the state prison for not more than ten years or by a fine of not more than one thousand dollars and imprisonment in jail for not more than two and one half years.

NOTE 1   Assault with intent to murder is a crime requiring specific intent, while assault and battery by means of a dangerous weapon requires general intent. *Commonwealth v. Jones*, 6 Mass. App. Ct. 750, 757 (1978).

NOTE 2   "There was evidence to show that the defendant was five miles off shore with no boats in sight when he threw the women overboard. The water was fifty-two degrees, and the waves were one to two feet high. Because the defendant had jumped into the water to hold one of the women under, he knew it was cold and choppy. For all he knew, they could not swim. This evidence of the defendant's conduct was sufficient to warrant the reasonable inference that he intended that the victims drown." *Commonwealth v. Shea*, 38 Mass. App. Ct. 7, 14 (1995).

NOTE 3a   Malice Definition Different Than for Murder. "[I]n the context of assault with intent to murder, malice has a different definition: the absence of justification, excuse, or mitigation. That definition should be included in the jury instruction on assault with intent to murder. *Commonwealth v. Boateng*, 438 Mass. 498, 517 (2003) (citations and quotation marks omitted).

NOTE 3b   "We clarify that mental impairment is not a factor that mitigates an otherwise proved offense, and hold that, where no evidence of justification, excuse, or traditionally recognized mitigation, is introduced at a trial of a charge of assault with intent to murder, a judge need not instruct on malice." *Commonwealth v. Johnston*, 446 Mass. 555, 555–56 (2006).

NOTE 4   See Notes following G.L. c. 265, § 13A (assault; assault and battery).

NOTE 5   DNA Database. A conviction of an offense under this section or of an attempt or conspiracy to commit such an offense results in the defendant being required to submit a DNA sample to the state's DNA database. *See* G.L. c. 22E, § 3.

SECTION 15A

Assault and battery by means of a dangerous weapon

(Amended by 2014 Mass. Acts c. 284, §§ 77–78, effective Aug. 11, 2014.)

(a) Whoever commits assault and battery upon a person sixty years or older by means of a dangerous weapon shall be punished by imprisonment in the state prison for not more than ten years or by a fine of not more than one thousand dollars or imprisonment in jail for not more than two and one-half years.

Whoever, after having been convicted of the crime of assault and battery upon a person sixty years or older, by means of a dangerous weapon, commits a second or subsequent such crime, shall be punished by imprisonment for not less than two years. Said sentence shall not be reduced until two years of said sentence have been served nor shall the person convicted be eligible for probation, parole, furlough, work release or receive any deduction from his sentence for good conduct until he shall have served two years of such sentence; provided, however, that the commissioner of correction may, on the recommendation of the warden, superintendent, or other person in charge of a correctional institution, or the

administrator of a county correctional institution, grant to said offender a temporary release in the custody of an officer of such institution for the following purposes only: to attend the funeral of next of kin or spouse; to visit a critically ill close relative or spouse; or to obtain emergency medical services unavailable at said institution. The provisions of section eighty-seven of chapter two hundred and seventy-six relating to the power of the court to place certain offenders on probation shall not apply to any person 18 years of age or over charged with a violation of this subsection.

(b) Whoever commits an assault and battery upon another by means of a dangerous weapon shall be punished by imprisonment in the state prison for not more than 10 years or in the house of correction for not more than 2½ years, or by a fine of not more than $5,000, or by both such fine and imprisonment.

(c) Whoever:

(i) by means of a dangerous weapon, commits an assault and battery upon another and by such assault and battery causes serious bodily injury;

(ii) by means of a dangerous weapon, commits an assault and battery upon another who is pregnant at the time of such assault and battery, knowing or having reason to know that the person is pregnant;

(iii) by means of a dangerous weapon, commits an assault and battery upon another who he knows has an outstanding temporary or permanent vacate, restraining or no contact order or judgment issued pursuant to section 18, section 34B or section 34C of chapter 208, section 32 of chapter 209, section 3, 4 or 5 of chapter 209A, or section 15 or 20 of chapter 209C, in effect against him at the time of such assault and battery; or

(iv) is 18 years of age or older and, by means of a dangerous weapon, commits an assault and battery upon a child under the age of 14;

shall be punished by imprisonment in the state prison for not more than 15 years or in the house of correction for not more than 2½ years, or by a fine of not more than $10,000, or by both such fine and imprisonment.

(d) For the purposes of this section, "serious bodily injury" shall mean bodily injury which results in a permanent disfigurement, loss or impairment of a bodily function, limb or organ, or a substantial risk of death.

NOTE 1   See Notes following G.L. c. 265, § 13A (assault; assault and battery) and G.L. c. 265, § 15 (assault with intent to murder/maim).

NOTE 2   "[T]he offense of assault and battery by means of a dangerous weapon . . . requires that the elements of assault be present, that there be a touching, however slight, that touching be by means of a weapon, and that the battery be accompanied by use of an inherently dangerous weapon, or by use of some other object in a dangerous or potentially dangerous fashion." *Commonwealth v. Appleby*, 380 Mass. 296, 308 (1980) (citations omitted).

NOTE 3a   Dangerous Weapons. There are two categories of dangerous weapons:

(a) Dangerous weapons per se—an instrumentality designed and constructed to produce death or great bodily harm. Examples include firearms, daggers, stilettos, and brass knuckles. Excluded are pocket-knives, razors, hammers, wrenches, and cutting tools. *Commonwealth v. Appleby*, 380 Mass. at 303.

(b) Weapons which may be used in a dangerous fashion. Examples include a lighted cigarette, door of car, kitchen-type knife, German shepherd dog, walking stick, chair, microphone cord, jackknife, broomstick, flashlight, lighter fluid, straight razor, and riding crop. Generally it is a question for the factfinder to determine whether the instrument was so used in a particular case. *Commonwealth v. Appleby*, 380 Mass. at 304.

NOTE 3b "The essential question, when an object which is not dangerous per se [such as sneakers] is alleged to be a dangerous weapon . . . is whether the object, as used by the defendant, is capable of producing serious bodily harm. Resolution of these questions is invariably for the fact finder . . . and involves not only consideration of any evidence as to the nature and specific features of the object but also attention to the circumstances surrounding the assault and the use of the object, and the manner in which it was handled or controlled." *Commonwealth v. Tevlin*, 433 Mass. 305, 310 (2001) (citations and quotation and punctuation marks omitted).

NOTE 3c **Standard.** "The dangerousness of an object which is not inherently dangerous turns on the manner in which it is used (objective test), not the intention of the actor when using it (subjective test). . . . The relevant contrast is to the criminal intent, or scienter, required for conviction of this crime. The jury must find an *intentional* touching without consent, excuse, or justification." *Commonwealth v. Connolly*, 49 Mass. App. Ct. 424, 425 (2000).

NOTE 3d Human teeth and other parts of the body are *not* dangerous weapons. *Commonwealth v. Davis*, 10 Mass. App. Ct. 190 (1980). Where the defendant threw two women overboard five miles offshore, the ocean, which "in its natural state cannot be possessed or controlled," could not be a dangerous weapon within the meaning of the statute. *Commonwealth v. Shea*, 38 Mass. App. Ct. 7, 16 (1995).

NOTE 3e **Shod Foot.** Defendant stomped on the female victim's hands and fingers with his shoe-covered foot and additionally beat her with a rubber hose for 30 minutes in order to coerce the victim into working as a prostitute for him. Held: Defendant may be found guilty of assault and battery by means of a dangerous weapon (shod foot). *Commonwealth v. Durham*, 358 Mass. 808, 809 (1970).

NOTE 3f **Mace.** "The particular device used here, a canister that sprays mace, is dangerous per se because it was designed for the sole purpose of bodily assault or defense and was constructed to inflict serious bodily harm through incapacitation, and because, in these circumstances, the defendant used it in a manner consistent with its design." *Commonwealth v. Lord*, 55 Mass. App. Ct. 265, 269–70 (2002).

NOTE 3g *Commonwealth v. Sexton*, 425 Mass. 146 (1997) (concrete paving may be a dangerous weapon).

NOTE 3h **Natural Gas.** "Today we hold that natural gas, as used here, is a dangerous weapon. . . . Here, the defendant uncapped the gas line and turned it on, releasing gas into the house, where he knew several people were sleeping. The gas line, and hence the gas itself, was entirely under the defendant's control while he used it in a manner foreign to its intended use." *Commonwealth v. Lednum*, 75 Mass. App. Ct. 722, 722, 724 (2009).

NOTE 4 **Intent.** Section 15A requires only general intent to do the act causing injury, not specific intent to injure. *Commonwealth v. Appleby*, 380 Mass. 296, 307 (1980).

NOTE 5 **Consent.** Defendant and victim involved in a homosexual, sadomasochistic relationship. Defendant beat the victim with a riding crop. Held, as one cannot consent to become a victim of an assault and battery by means of a dangerous weapon, the private, consensual relationship between the parties was *not* a defense to the charge. *Commonwealth v. Appleby*, 380 Mass. at 312.

NOTE 6 **Self-Defense.** "In order to raise the issue of self-defense, '[t]here must be evidence warranting at least a reasonable doubt that the defendant: (1) had reasonable ground to believe and actually did believe that he was in imminent danger of death or serious bodily harm, from which he could save himself only by using deadly force, (2) had availed himself of all proper means to avoid physical combat before resorting to the use of deadly force, and (3) used no more force than was reasonably necessary in all

circumstances of the case.' *Commonwealth v. Harrington, supra*, at 450, [379 Mass. 446 (1980)]. *Commonwealth v. Burbank*, 388 Mass. 789, 794 (1983)." *Commonwealth v. Barber*, 394 Mass. 1013 (1985).

NOTE 7 **Lesser Included.** "Assault and battery by means of a dangerous weapon fails the test to be a lesser included offense of murder. A conviction of murder does not require proof of all of the elements of assault and battery by means of a dangerous weapon, which has as an element that an actual battery be accomplished by means of a dangerous weapon. . . . [This is u]nlike assault and battery—which *is* a lesser included offense of murder." *Commonwealth v. Pimental*, 454 Mass. 475, 482 & n.5 (2009).

SECTION 15B
Assault with dangerous weapon
(Amended by 2014 Mass. Acts c. 284, § 79, effective Aug. 11, 2014.)

(a) Whoever, by means of a dangerous weapon, commits an assault upon a person sixty years or older, shall be punished by imprisonment in the state prison for not more than five years or by a fine of not more than one thousand dollars or imprisonment in jail for not more than two and one-half years.

Whoever, after having been convicted of the crime of assault upon a person sixty years or older, by means of a dangerous weapon, commits a second or subsequent such crime, shall be punished by imprisonment for not less than two years. Said sentence shall not be reduced until one year of said sentence has been served nor shall the person convicted be eligible for probation, parole, furlough, work release or receive any deduction from his sentence for good conduct until he shall have served one year of such sentence; provided, however, that the commissioner of correction may, on the recommendation of the warden, superintendent, or other person in charge of a correctional institution, or the administrator of a county correctional institution, grant to said offender a temporary release in the custody of an officer of such institution for the following purposes only: to attend the funeral of next of kin or spouse; to visit a critically ill close relative or spouse; or to obtain emergency medical services unavailable at said institution. The provisions of section eighty-seven of chapter two hundred and seventy-six relative to the power of the court to place certain offenders on probation shall not apply to any person 18 years of age or over charged with a violation of this subsection.

For the purposes of prosecution, a conviction obtained under subsection (a) of section fifteen A or paragraph (a) of section 18 shall count as a prior criminal conviction for the purpose of prosecution and sentencing as a second or subsequent conviction.

(b) Whoever, by means of a dangerous weapon, commits an assault upon another shall be punished by imprisonment in the state prison for not more than five years or by a fine of not more than one thousand dollars or imprisonment in jail for not more than two and one-half years.

NOTE 1 See Notes following G.L. c. 265, § 13A (assault; assault and battery) and G.L. c. 265, § 15A (assault and battery by means of a dangerous weapon).

NOTE 2a The thrust of the offense is the outward demonstration of force with an apparent ability to injure. *Commonwealth v. Appleby*, 380 Mass. 296, 305 (1980).

NOTE 2b "The essence of the assault is the outward menacing gesture. It is not necessary to demonstrate that the victim was in fear or apprehensive of harm as a result of the use of the dangerous weapon. The criminal law punishes the overt act without regard to the victim's state of mind." 32 J.R. Nolan and Bruce R.

Henry, Massachusetts Practice, *Criminal Law*, § 323 at 241–42 (1988, 1996).

NOTE 2c   "The crime of assault by means of a dangerous weapon requires proof of an overt act undertaken with the intention of putting another person in fear of bodily harm and reasonably calculated to do so, whether or not the defendant actually intended to harm the victim." *Commonwealth v. Melton*, 50 Mass. App. Ct. 637, 640 (2001), *aff'd*, 436 Mass. 291 (2002) (citation omitted).

NOTE 3   Although firearm was loaded with blanks, the victim did not know this and as such a conviction for assault by means of a dangerous weapon was proper. *Commonwealth v. Henson*, 357 Mass. 686, 693–94 (1970).

NOTE 4   "It is beyond dispute that a charge of assault and battery is not a lesser included offense within a charge of assault by means of a dangerous weapon. However, the offense of assault is a lesser included offense within such a charge. . . ." *A Juvenile v. Commonwealth*, 404 Mass. 1001 (1984) (rescript) (citations and footnote omitted).

NOTE 5   One Shot, Four Counts. "The defendant argues that he cannot be found guilty of four counts of assault by means of a dangerous weapon because there was not sufficient evidence of any intent to batter all four alleged victims. Because it would have been physically impossible to hit all four victims with a single shot, he contends that the perpetrator could not have had the intent to batter four people. The defendant's argument misapprehends our jurisprudence on the element of intent.

". . .

"Under the attempted battery theory, the Commonwealth must prove that the defendant intended to commit a battery, took some overt step toward accomplishing that intended battery, and came reasonably close to doing so. *See Commonwealth v. Musgrave*, [38 Mass. App. Ct. 519, 520 n.2 (1995)], quoting Model Jury Instructions for Criminal Offenses Tried in the District Court Department § 5.402 (1988). The defendant concedes, as he must, that a single act can result in multiple convictions if there are multiple victims. '[T]he appropriate 'unit of prosecution' for such crimes [of violence] is the person assaulted or killed, not the underlying criminal act.' *Commonwealth v. Crawford*, 430 Mass. 683, 686–687 (2000), quoting *Commonwealth v. Donovan*, 395 Mass. 20, 31 (1985). *See Commonwealth v. Gordon*, 41 Mass. App. Ct. 459, 465 (1996); *Commonwealth v. Dello Iacono*, 20 Mass. App. Ct. 83, 89–90 (1985)." *Commonwealth v. Melton*, 436 Mass. 291, 294–95 (2002).

SECTION 15C
Assault by means of hypodermic syringe or needle; assault and battery by means of hypodermic syringe or needle

(a) Whoever commits an assault upon another, by means of a hypodermic syringe, hypodermic needle, or any instrument adapted for the administration of controlled or other substances by injection, shall be punished by imprisonment in the state prison for not more than 10 years or in the house of correction for not more than 2½ years, or by a fine of not more than $1,000, or by both such fine and imprisonment.

(b) Whoever commits an assault and battery upon another, by means of a hypodermic syringe, hypodermic needle, or any instrument adapted for the administration of controlled or other substances by injection, shall be punished by imprisonment in the state prison for not more than 15 years or in the house of correction for not more than 2½ years, or by a fine of not more than $5,000, or by both such fine and imprisonment.

SECTION 15D
Strangling or suffocating another person
(Added by 2014 Mass. Acts c. 260, § 24, effective Aug. 8, 2014.)

(a) For the purposes of this section the following words shall have the following meanings, unless the context clearly indicates otherwise:

"Serious bodily injury", bodily injury that results in a permanent disfigurement, loss or impairment of a bodily function, limb or organ or creates a substantial risk of death.

"Strangulation", the intentional interference of the normal breathing or circulation of blood by applying substantial pressure on the throat or neck of another.

"Suffocation", the intentional interference of the normal breathing or circulation of blood by blocking the nose or mouth of another.

(b) Whoever strangles or suffocates another person shall be punished by imprisonment in state prison for not more than 5 years or in the house of correction for not more than 2½ years, or by a fine of not more than $5,000, or by both such fine and imprisonment.

(c) Whoever: (i) strangles or suffocates another person and by such strangulation or suffocation causes serious bodily injury; (ii) strangles or suffocates another person, who is pregnant at the time of such strangulation or suffocation, knowing or having reason to know that the person is pregnant; (iii) is convicted of strangling or suffocating another person after having been previously convicted of the crime of strangling or suffocating another person under this section, or of a like offense in another state or the United States or a military, territorial or Indian tribal authority; or (iv) strangles or suffocates another person, with knowledge that the individual has an outstanding temporary or permanent vacate, restraining or no contact order or judgment issued under sections 18 or 34B of chapter 208, section 32 of chapter 209, sections 3, 4 or 5 of chapter 209A or sections 15 or 20 of chapter 209C, in effect against such person at the time the offense is committed, shall be punished by imprisonment in state prison for not more than 10 years, or in the house of correction for not more than 2½ years, and by a fine of not more than $10,000.

(d) For any violation of this section, or as a condition of a continuance without a finding, the court shall order the defendant to complete a certified batterer's intervention program unless, upon good cause shown, the court issues specific written findings describing the reasons that batterer's intervention should not be ordered or unless the batterer's intervention program determines that the defendant is not suitable for intervention.

SECTION 15E
Assault and battery by discharging firearm
(Added by 2014 Mass. Acts c. 284, § 80, effective Jan. 1, 2015.)

(a) Whoever commits an assault and battery upon another by discharging a firearm, large capacity weapon, rifle, shotgun, sawed-off shotgun or machine gun, as defined in section 121 of chapter 140, shall be punished by imprisonment in the state prison for not more than 20 years or by imprisonment in the house of correction for not more than 2½ years or by a fine of not more than $10,000, or by both such fine and imprisonment.

SECTION 15F
Attempted assault and battery by discharging firearm
(Added by 2014 Mass. Acts c. 284, § 80, effective Jan. 1, 2015.)

(a) Whoever attempts to commit an assault and battery upon another by means of discharging a firearm, large capacity weapon, rifle, shotgun, sawed-off shotgun or machine gun, as defined in section 121 of chapter 140, shall be punished by imprisonment in the state prison for not more than 15 years or by imprisonment in the house of correction for not more than 2½ years or by a fine of not more than $10,000, or by both such fine and imprisonment.

SECTION 16
Attempt to murder

Whoever attempts to commit murder by poisoning, drowning or strangling another person, or by any means not constituting an assault with intent to commit murder, shall be punished by imprisonment in the state prison for not more than twenty years or by a fine of not more than one thousand dollars and imprisonment in jail for not more than two and one half years.

NOTE 1 "The elements of attempt, whether general attempt or attempted murder, are (1) the specific intent to commit the substantive crime at issue, and (2) an overt act toward completion of the substantive crime . . . [but] nonachievement of murder is not an element of attempted murder." *Commonwealth v. LaBrie*, 473 Mass. 754, 764–65 (2016).

NOTE 2 **DNA Database.** A conviction of an offense under this section or of an attempt or conspiracy to commit such an offense results in the defendant being required to submit a DNA sample to the state's DNA database. *See* G.L. c. 22E, § 3.

SECTION 17
Armed robbery

Whoever, being armed with a dangerous weapon, assaults another and robs, steals or takes from his person money or other property which may be the subject of larceny shall be punished by imprisonment in the state prison for life or for any term of years; provided, however, that any person who commits any offence described herein while masked or disguised or while having his features artificially distorted shall, for the first offence be sentenced to imprisonment for not less than five years and for any subsequent offence for not less than ten years. Whoever commits any offense described herein while armed with a firearm, shotgun, rifle, machine gun or assault weapon shall be punished by imprisonment in the state prison for not less than five years. Any person who commits a subsequent offense while armed with a firearm, shotgun, rifle, machine gun or assault weapon shall be punished by imprisonment in the state prison for not less than 15 years.

NOTE 1 "Larceny is the unlawful taking and carrying away of personal property of another with specific intent to deprive the person of the property permanently. Robbery includes all of the elements of larceny and in addition requires that force and violence be used against the victim or that the victim be put in fear." *Commonwealth v. Johnson*, 379 Mass. 177, 181 (1979) (citations omitted). *See also* G.L. c. 277, § 39 (definition of robbery).

NOTE 1a "A larceny may be converted into a robbery if, as here, an assault is committed on a person who, having some protective concern for the goods taken interferes with the completion of the theft." *Commonwealth v. Rajotte*, 23 Mass. App. Ct. 93, 94 (1986).

NOTE 1b See Notes following G.L. c. 265, § 13A (assault and assault and battery); G.L. c. 265, § 15A, (assault and battery by means of a dangerous weapon); and G.L. c. 265, § 15B (assault by means of a dangerous weapon).

NOTE 2 "Deliberate premeditation is not an element of robbery . . . all that must be shown to prove specific intent is an inference, based on defendant's conduct, that he intended to steal the property wrongfully taken." *Commonwealth v. Sheehan*, 5 Mass.

App. Ct. 754, 759 n.6 (1977), *aff'd*, 376 Mass. 765, 776 (1978) (citations omitted).

NOTE 3 "It is not necessary to show the use of a dangerous weapon in proving the offense of robbery while armed. The gist of the offense is being armed, not the use of the weapon." *Commonwealth v. Goldman*, 5 Mass. App. Ct. 635, 637 (1977) (citations omitted).

NOTE 4 A dangerous weapon for purposes of armed robbery is determined by the factfinder, who will decide "[w]hether the instrumentality under the control of the perpetrator has the apparent ability to inflict harm, whether the victim reasonably so perceived it, and whether the perpetrator by use of the instrumentality intended to elicit fear in order to further the robbery." *Commonwealth v. Tarrant*, 367 Mass. 411, 417 (1975).

NOTE 5a The only evidence of any gun was the words of the defendant, "Hold him or I'm going to shoot him." Conviction of armed robbery upheld. *Commonwealth v. Delgado*, 367 Mass. 432, 436–37 (1975).

NOTE 5b Cf. *Commonwealth v. Howard*, 386 Mass. 607, 610 (1982). "[T]he defendant's statement alone, implying that he had a gun, where no gun was seen or found and *he had no opportunity or reason to dispose of it*, cannot be sufficient to warrant a conviction of robbery while 'armed with a dangerous weapon.'" (Emphasis added.)

NOTE 5c "[A] woman, later identified as the defendant, entered the Store 24 . . . . [T]he sole clerk on duty, stood opposite her at a counter and asked how he could help her. She replied that she needed one hundred fifty dollars. Unflinchingly, he told her that he could not give her any money. With more insistence, she repeated her demand. 'I want one hundred fifty dollars, now.' [The clerk] told her that the money was not his to give. Then the defendant replied, 'I have a gun.' From behind the counter, [the clerk] was not in a position to see her left hand. So with much trepidation, he allowed her—presumably with her right hand—to reach into the cash drawer of the register and remove all of the bills. . . .

" . . .

"Here, what the defendant said, by itself, may not be sufficient for a petit jury to draw an inference that she, in fact, possessed a weapon. This aspect troubled the motion judge who concluded, on the basis of *Commonwealth v. Howard*, 386 Mass. 607, 608–609 (1982), that the 'armed' aspect of the robbery could not be inferred. The assessment made in the *Howard* case came after a full trial. In this case, we conclude that it was premature for the motion judge to reach this conclusion.

"A motion to dismiss an indictment based on evidentiary irregularities before a grand jury does not permit a court [to] review the competency or sufficiency of the evidence. Evidence before a grand jury will be considered to be legally sufficient if it meets the less strict probable cause to arrest standard. Perhaps more to the point, here the defendant claimed to be armed and held one hand out of [the clerk's] line of sight. It was reasonable for [the clerk] to assume from the circumstances that she could well have a weapon. In the final analysis, it remains for a petit jury, properly instructed, to determine whether the Commonwealth can satisfy the *Commonwealth v. Latimore*, 378 Mass. 671, 678–679 (1979), standard with respect to the 'armed' element of the charged offense. *See Commonwealth v. Delgado*, 367 Mass. 432, 435–437 (1975); *Commonwealth v. Drew*, 4 Mass. App. Ct. 30, 32 (1976)." *Commonwealth v. Simpson*, 54 Mass. App. Ct. 477, 477–80 (2002) (certain citations and punctuation marks omitted).

NOTE 6 Variance between indictment charging that the defendant committed armed robbery with a knife and evidence showing that the armed robbery was committed with a gun was *not* material; the particular type of weapon with which the crime was committed not being on essential element of the crime. *Commonwealth v. Harris*, 9 Mass. App. Ct. 708, 710–12 (1980). *See also* G.L. c. 277, § 21.

NOTE 7 **BB Gun.** "[W]e conclude that a BB gun does not satisfy the statutory requirement of a 'firearm' within the meaning

2

of G.L. c. 265, § 17." *Commonwealth v. Garrett*, 473 Mass. 257, 258 (2015).

NOTE 8   Masks. The mask need not totally cover or conceal facial features that the wearer cannot be identified or recognized. It is sufficient if the true character of the face is screened or concealed to such an extent that recognition is materially or substantially obstructed. *Commonwealth v. Flynn*, 362 Mass. 455, 477–78 (1972).

NOTE 9   Fear. "Although [the victim] maintained that he was not afraid, the jury could have rejected this portion of his testimony as 'false bravado,'" in light of the defendant's "objectively menacing conduct," where he demanded all money while brandishing a gun, to which the victim "responded by immediately handing over the cash drawer." *Commonwealth v. Joyner*, 467 Mass. 176, 188 (2014).

NOTE 10   Examples of *asportation* include:

(a) Victim handing over sack containing drugs and an envelope containing money. *Commonwealth v. Talbot*, 5 Mass. App. Ct. 857, 858 (1977) (rescript).

(b) Transfer of money or goods from victim's control to robber's, even if done by the victim at the robber's direction. *Commonwealth v. Flowers*, 1 Mass. App. Ct. 415, 418–19 (1973).

(c) Victim thrown to floor, punched, pockets searched; defendant arrested; victim arose from the floor and saw his wallet on the floor. The Court found a momentary transfer of control over the victim's wallet from the victim to the defendant. *Commonwealth v. Bradley*, 2 Mass. App. Ct. 804, 805 (1974) (rescript).

NOTE 11   Honest But Mistaken Belief. "[T]he specific intent to steal is negated by a finding that a defendant held an honest, albeit mistaken, belief that he was entitled to the property he took. . . . [A]n honest belief need not be objectively reasonable to negate the specific intent required for larceny. . . . Evidence of reasonableness may, however, be considered by the jury to assist in their determination whether to credit a defendant's honest belief. Neither juries nor judges are required to divorce themselves of common sense, but rather should apply to facts which they find proven such reasonable inferences as are justified in the light of their experience as to the natural inclinations of human beings." *Commonwealth v. Liebenow*, 470 Mass. 151, 157, 160, 161 (2014).

NOTE 12   Self-Defense. "The right to claim self-defense is forfeited by one who commits armed robbery." *Commonwealth v. Vives*, 447 Mass. 537, 544 (2006).

NOTE 13a   Joint Enterprise. *Knowledge of nonprincipal.* "Where a defendant is charged as an aider and abettor of an aggravated robbery, requiring proof of use of a dangerous weapon, 'the Government must show that the accomplice knew a dangerous weapon would be used or at least he was on notice of the likelihood of its use.'" *Commonwealth v. Watson*, 388 Mass. 536, 544 n.6 (1983) (citing numerous cases).

NOTE 13b   Joint Enterprise—Felony Murder. "The primary issue in this appeal is whether a defendant who joins with others to commit an armed robbery may be found guilty of murder on the theory of felony-murder for the killing of his accomplice by someone resisting the armed robbery. We conclude that he may not." *Commonwealth v. Tejeda*, 473 Mass. 269, 270 (2015).

NOTE 14   Related Statute. G.L. c. 266, § 21—Refusal to deliver stolen property.

NOTE 15   DNA Database. A conviction of an offense under this section or of an attempt or conspiracy to commit such an offense results in the defendant being required to submit a DNA sample to the state's DNA database. *See* G.L. c. 22E, § 3.

SECTION 18

Armed assault with intent to rob or murder

(Amended by 2014 Mass. Acts c. 284, § 81, effective Aug. 11, 2014.)

(a) Whoever, being armed with a dangerous weapon, assaults a person sixty or older with intent to rob or murder shall be punished by imprisonment in the state prison for not more than twenty years. Whoever commits any offense described herein while armed with a firearm, shotgun, rifle, machine gun or assault weapon shall be punished by imprisonment in the state prison for not less than ten years.

Whoever, after having been convicted of the crime of assault upon a person sixty years or older with intent to rob or murder while being armed with a dangerous weapon, commits a second or subsequent such crime, shall be punished by imprisonment for not less than two years. Said sentence shall not be reduced until two years of said sentence have been served nor shall the person convicted be eligible for probation, parole, furlough, work release or receive any deduction from his sentence for good conduct until he shall have served two years of such sentence; provided, however, that the commissioner of correction may, on the recommendation of the warden, superintendent, or other person in charge of a correctional institution, or the administrator of a county correctional institution, grant to said offender a temporary release in the custody of an officer of such institution for the following purposes only: to attend the funeral of next of kin or spouse; to visit a critically ill close relative or spouse; or to obtain emergency medical services unavailable at said institution. The provisions of section eighty-seven of chapter two hundred and seventy-six relating to the power of the court to place certain offenders on probation shall not apply to any person 18 years of age or over charged with a violation of this subsection. Whoever, after having been convicted of the crime of assault upon a person 60 years or older with intent to rob or murder while armed with a firearm, shotgun, rifle, machine gun or assault weapon commits a second or subsequent such crime shall be punished by imprisonment in the state prison for not less than 20 years.

(b) Whoever, being armed with a dangerous weapon, assaults another with intent to rob or murder shall be punished by imprisonment in the state prison for not more than twenty years. Whoever, being armed with a firearm, shotgun, rifle, machine gun or assault weapon assaults another with intent to rob or murder shall be punished by imprisonment in the state prison for not less than five years and not more than 20 years.

NOTE 1   See Notes following G.L. c. 265, § 13A (assault; assault and battery); G.L. c. 265, § 15A (assault and battery by means of a dangerous weapon); and G.L. c. 265, § 15B (assault by means of a dangerous weapon).

NOTE 2   The offense of assault with intent to murder while armed with a dangerous weapon does *not* require proof that the assault was committed by use of the weapon but does require proof of an intent to murder. *Commonwealth v. Burkett*, 5 Mass. App. Ct. 901, 903 (1977) (rescript).

NOTE 3   Assault by means of a dangerous weapon is *not* a lesser included offense of armed assault with intent to murder; assault by means of a dangerous weapon requires proof that the assault was committed by the use of a weapon. "Use" need not be shown in assault with intent to murder. *Burkett*, 5 Mass. App. Ct at 901, 903.

NOTE 4   Related Statute. G.L. c. 266, § 21—Refusal to deliver stolen property.

NOTE 5   "[I]n addition to malice the crime of assault with intent to murder requires proof of a specific intent to kill." *Commonwealth v. Henson*, 394 Mass. 584, 590 (1985).

NOTE 6   "The question before us is whether the trial judge impermissibly relieved the Commonwealth of its burden of proof by allowing the jury to presume this intent to murder from the fact that the defendant had fired his gun. *See Commonwealth v. Zezima*,

387 Mass. 748, 754–55 (1982) (*Sandstrom [v. Montana*, 442 U.S. 510 (1979)], error where judge allowed a jury to presume that defendant intended the natural consequences of his use of a deadly weapon); *DeJoinville v. Commonwealth*, 381 Mass. 246, 252–54 (1980) (Sandstrom error where judge instructed jury that defendant is presumed to have intended natural consequences of voluntary act). . . .

"We agree that the trial judge's instructions in this case created an unconstitutional presumption of intent."

Commonwealth v. Burkett, 396 Mass. 509, 513 (1986) (footnote omitted).

NOTE 7　　Intoxication. "It is time to announce that where proof of a crime requires proof of a specific criminal intent and there is evidence tending to show that the defendant was under the influence of alcohol or some other drug at the time of the crime, the judge should instruct the jury, if requested, that they may consider evidence of the defendant's intoxication at the time of the crime in deciding whether the Commonwealth has proved that specific intent beyond a reasonable doubt. If the judge gives such an instruction, he should further instruct the jury that, if they find beyond a reasonable doubt that the defendant had the required specific intent, the defendant's intoxication, if any, is not an excuse or justification for his actions." *Commonwealth v. Henson*, 394 Mass. 584, 593–94 (1985).

NOTE 8　　"It would have been better if the judge had stated explicitly that proof of both an intent to kill and of malice (i.e., in this context, the absence of justification, excuse, and mitigation) is required in order to prove the crime of assault with intent to murder." *Commonwealth v. Bourgeois*, 404 Mass. 61, 65 (1989) (citations omitted).

NOTE 9　　DNA Database. A conviction of an offense under this section or of an attempt or conspiracy to commit such an offense results in the defendant being required to submit a DNA sample to the state's DNA database. *See* G.L. c. 22E, § 3.

SECTION 18A
Armed assault in dwelling house

Whoever, being armed with a dangerous weapon, enters a dwelling house and while therein assaults another with intent to commit a felony shall be punished by imprisonment in the state prison for life, or for a term of not less than ten years. No person imprisoned under this paragraph shall be eligible for parole in less than five years.

Whoever, being armed with a dangerous weapon defined as a firearm, shotgun, rifle or assault weapon, enters a dwelling house and while therein assaults another with intent to commit a felony shall be punished by imprisonment in the state prison for a term of not less than ten years. Such person shall not be eligible for parole prior to the expiration of ten years.

NOTE 1　　"Making a case under G.L. c. 265, § 18A, requires that the government prove (1) entry of a dwelling while armed; (2) an assault on someone in the dwelling; and (3) a purpose accompanying the assault to commit a felony." *Commonwealth v. Fleming*, 46 Mass. App. Ct. 394, 395–96 (1999) (citations and footnote omitted).

NOTE 2　　Entry. "An entry, i.e., going in, by an armed person into a dwelling [a place of habitation] in response to an invitation from a person living there rather obviously is not a violation of the statute. . . . Inherent in the idea of criminal trespass is an unwarranted intrusion, one that the actor was not privileged or licensed to make." *Commonwealth v. Fleming*, 46 Mass. App. Ct. at 396 (citations and footnote omitted).

NOTE 3　　Weapon. "[The statute requires] that the perpetrator be armed with a dangerous weapon but not that it be *used*." *Commonwealth v. Hawkins*, 21 Mass. App. Ct. 766, 768 & n.4 (1986) (emphasis in original). *See also Commonwealth v. Werner*, 73 Mass. App. Ct. 97, 102 (2008).

NOTE 4　　Dwelling House. *See* G.L. c. 266, § 1.

NOTE 5　　See Notes following G.L. c. 265, § 13A (assault; assault and battery); G.L. c. 265, § 15A (assault and battery by means of a dangerous weapon); G.L. c. 265, § 15B (assault by means of a dangerous weapon); G.L. c. 265, § 18 (armed assault with intent to rob or murder).

NOTE 6　　Not Lesser Included Offense. "Armed assault in a dwelling [G.L. c. 265, § 18A] is not a lesser included offense of aggravated burglary [G.L. c. 266, § 14] because armed assault in a dwelling requires an element not required in either armed burglary or burglary with assault—the intent to commit a felony at the time of the assault. Neither armed burglary nor burglary with assault is a lesser included offense of armed assault in a dwelling, because both armed burglary and burglary with assault require two elements not required in armed assault in a dwelling—the intent to commit a felony at the time of entry into the dwelling, and breaking and entering in the nighttime. Because each offense has an element not shared by the other, neither is a lesser included offense of the other, and the two convictions are not duplicative." *Commonwealth v. Negron*, 462 Mass. 102, 110–11 (2012).

NOTE 7　　DNA Database. A conviction of an offense under this section or of an attempt or conspiracy to commit such an offense results in the defendant being required to submit a DNA sample to the state's DNA database. *See* G.L. c. 22E, § 3.

SECTION 18B
Use of firearms while committing a felony
(Amended by 2014 Mass. Acts c. 284, § 82, effective Aug. 11, 2014.)

Whoever, while in the commission of or the attempted commission of an offense which may be punished by imprisonment in the state prison, has in his possession or under his control a firearm, rifle or shotgun shall, in addition to the penalty for such offense, be punished by imprisonment in the state prison for not less than five years; provided, however, that if such firearm, rifle or shotgun is a large capacity weapon, as defined in section 121 of chapter 140, or if such person, while in the commission or attempted commission of such offense, has in his possession or under his control a machine gun, as defined in said section 121, such person shall by punished by imprisonment in the state prison for not less than ten years. Whoever has committed an offense which may be punished by imprisonment in the state prison and had in his possession or under his control a firearm, rifle or shotgun including, but not limited to, a large capacity weapon or machine gun and who thereafter, while in the commission or the attempted commission of a second or subsequent offense which may be punished by imprisonment in the state prison, has in his possession or under his control a firearm, rifle or shotgun shall, in addition to the penalty for such offense, be punished by imprisonment in the state prison for not less than 20 years; provided, however, that if such firearm, rifle or shotgun is a large capacity semiautomatic weapon or if such person, while in the commission or attempted commission of such offense, has in his possession or under his control a machine gun, such person shall be punished by imprisonment in the state prison for not less than 25 years.

A sentence imposed under this section for a second or subsequent offense shall not be reduced nor suspended, nor shall any person convicted under this section be eligible for probation, parole, furlough or work release or receive any deduction from his sentence for good conduct until he shall have served the minimum term of such additional sentence; provided, however, that the commissioner of correction may, on the recommendation of the warden, superintendent or other person in charge of a correctional institution or the administrator of a

2

county correctional institution, grant to such offender a temporary release in the custody of an officer of such institution for the following purposes only: (i) to attend the funeral of a spouse or next of kin; (ii) to visit a critically ill close relative or spouse; or (iii) to obtain emergency medical services unavailable at such institution. Prosecutions commenced under this section shall neither be continued without a finding nor placed on file. The provisions of section 87 of chapter 276 relative to the power of the court to place certain offenders on probation shall not apply to any person 18 years of age or over charged with a violation of this section.

NOTE 1   Commission of a Felony. "[The defendant] contends that his possession of a loaded .40 caliber Smith and Wesson handgun in a locked safe in the bedroom of his apartment, where a quantity of unlawful drugs and the key to the safe were found, does not, as matter of law, constitute the unlawful possession of a firearm 'in the commission of a felony' (the felony being the unlawful possession of cocaine with intent to distribute) within the meaning of G.L. c. 265, § 18B."

The Supreme Judicial Court disagreed, holding that "[t]he 'commission' element consists of the unlawful possession of the defendant's large cache of forty-nine individually wrapped pieces of crack cocaine with, as the jury could find, based on the packaging and quantity of the crack cocaine, the intent to distribute them.

"The statute, admittedly, sweeps in a broad range, speaking generally of any felony combined with the possession of, or control over, a firearm. Some nexus between the felony and the firearm in terms of proximity, and logical relation to the nature of the felony itself, must ordinarily exist before conviction can result. The existence of the requisite nexus necessarily will be determined on a case-by-case basis." *Commonwealth v. Hines*, 449 Mass. 183, 184, 188, 190 (2007).

NOTE 2   Sentencing. "We agree with the Commonwealth that the statute prohibits the disposition of probation . . . . [We] reject the Commonwealth's contention that the statute requires a mandatory minimum State prison sentence of five years . . . . When resentencing the defendant, the judge should 'fix a maximum and a minimum term' in accordance with G.L. c. 279, § 24." *Commonwealth v. Hines*, 449 Mass. 183, 190, 191–192 (2007).

NOTE 3   DNA Database. A conviction of an offense under this section or of an attempt or conspiracy to commit such an offense results in the defendant being required to submit a DNA sample to the state's DNA database. *See* G.L. c. 22E, § 3.

NOTE 4   Related Statutes.
G.L. c. 140, § 121—Firearms sales.
G.L. c. 269, § 10—Carrying dangerous weapons.

SECTION 18C

Home invasion; persons present within; weapons

Whoever knowingly enters the dwelling place of another knowing or having reason to know that one or more persons are present within or knowingly enters the dwelling place of another and remains in such dwelling place knowing or having reason to know that one or more persons are present within while armed with a dangerous weapon, uses force or threatens the imminent use of force upon any person within such dwelling place shall be punished by imprisonment in the state prison for life or for any term of not less than twenty years.

NOTE 1   Elements. "The crime of armed house invasion has four elements. To obtain a conviction of the crime, the Commonwealth must show that the defendant (1) knowingly entered the dwelling place of another; (2) knowing or having reason to know that one or more persons are present within (or entered without such knowledge but then remained in the dwelling place after acquiring or having reason to acquire such knowledge); (3) while armed with a dangerous weapon; (4) used such force or threatened the imminent use of force upon any person within such

dwelling place whether or not injury occurred, or intentionally caused any injury to any person within such dwelling place." *Commonwealth v. Doucette*, 430 Mass. 461, 465–66 (1999) (citations, quotations, and punctuation marks omitted).

NOTE 2   Self-Defense. This defense is not available to a charge framed under G.L. c. 265, § 18C. *Commonwealth v. Doucette*, 430 Mass. 461, 471 (1999).

NOTE 3   This statute only applies where a defendant is armed at the time of entry, not where a defendant arms himself after entering a home. *Commonwealth v. Ruiz*, 426 Mass. 391 (1998).

NOTE 4   DNA Database. A conviction of an offense under this section or of an attempt or conspiracy to commit such an offense results in the defendant being required to submit a DNA sample to the state's DNA database. *See* G.L. c. 22E, § 3.

NOTE 5   Unit of Prosecution. "Claiming that the home invasion statute is an 'anomaly,' and that its plain meaning, and the interpretation of 'closely related statutes,' indicate that its 'purpose is to deter home invasions,' the defendant asks that we interpret it, as the armed burglary statute, G.L. c. 266, § 14, has been, to permit only one conviction for entry in a dwelling, no matter how many assaults follow. *Compare Commonwealth v. Gordon*, 42 Mass. App. Ct. 601, 604–05 (1997). No Massachusetts appellate decision has analyzed whether multiple convictions may be sustained under the home invasion statute, G.L. c. 265, § 18C.

"In addressing the issue, we are mindful of the proscription of the double jeopardy clause of the Fifth Amendment to the United States Constitution, but 'few, if any, limitations are imposed by that clause on the legislative power to define offenses.' *Commonwealth v. Levia*, 385 Mass. 345, 347 (1982). . . .

"The defendant acknowledges that the 'teaching of our cases is that, where the intent of the Legislature in the enactment of a criminal statute is primarily to protect the safety of individuals, as opposed to one's possessory interest in property, the number of victims determines the number of units of legitimate prosecution.' *Commonwealth v. Melton*, 50 Mass. App. Ct. 637, 643 (2001), S.C., 436 Mass. 291, 295 (2002).

"'The appropriate inquiry in a case like this . . . asks what "unit of prosecution" was intended by the Legislature as the punishable act. . . . The inquiry requires us look to the language and purpose of the statutes, to see whether they speak directly to the issue of the appropriate unit of prosecution . . . keeping in mind that any ambiguity that arises in the process must be resolved, under the rule of lenity, in the defendant's favor.' *Commonwealth v. Rabb*, 431 Mass. 123, 128 (2000).

"In *Commonwealth v. Dunn*, 43 Mass. App. Ct. 58 (1997), the court determined that G.L. c. 265, § 18C, is not constitutionally vague and does not impose cruel and unusual punishment, taking into consideration the 'nature of the offense of home invasion and the degree of harm to society that the statute seeks to prevent.' *Id.* at 63. The court stated that while the crime of home invasion is 'akin to that of armed burglary, G.L. c. 266, § 14, and armed assault within a dwelling, G.L. c. 265, § 18A[,] . . . [w]hat sets home invasion apart from the other two crimes—and we think legitimately triggers a longer minimum sentence—is the additional element that the armed intruder knows, or should know, that an occupant is present before he enters the dwelling.' *Id.* at 63–64. 'The home invasion statute punishes more severely the armed intruder who invades another's dwelling while knowing that one or more individuals are present and then proceeds to assault those individuals.' *Id.* at 64.

"'These scienter requirements distinguish § 18C from § 18A.' *Commonwealth v. Ruiz*, 426 Mass. 391, 393 (1998). Sections 18A and 18C 'are functionally much closer than sections 18C and G.L. c. 266, § 14.' *Id.* at 394 n.4.

"Placement in the General Laws is a legitimate indication of the Legislature's intent. *Commonwealth v. Levia*, 385 Mass. at 347, considered whether the Legislature intended that the taking of money from two individuals in a single episode would constitute one or two robberies under G.L. c. 265, § 17. The court noted that the armed robbery statute appears in the 'chapter of the General

Laws entitled "Crimes against the Person," rather than under the chapter (c. 266) entitled "Crimes against Property."' *Id.* at 348. The court also noted it had 'previously stressed the assault aspect of the crime' in *Commonwealth v. Weiner*, 255 Mass. 506 (1926). *Ibid*. The *Levia* court concluded, '[i]n light of the emphasis that the [Legislature] and this court have placed on the assault element of the crime of robbery, we conclude that the "offense" is against the person assaulted, and not against the entity that owns or possesses the property taken.' *Id.* at 350–351.

"Here, the Legislature placed G.L. c. 265, § 18C, in c. 265, Crimes Against the Person. 'Influential [in *Levia*] was the text of the defining statute which spoke of the "person" as the object of protection; so also the fact that armed robbery falls under the statutory heading "Crimes Against the Person."' *Commonwealth v. Dello Iacono*, 20 Mass. App. Ct. 83, 89–90 (1985). So, too, we conclude in this case that the home invasion statute clearly and unambiguously is concerned with the assault of persons in the invaded dwelling. Moreover, the language of § 18C sets it apart from G.L. c. 266, § 14, and, when viewed in the light of *Levia*, we conclude that the unit of prosecution is the person assaulted." *Commonwealth v. Antonmarchi*, 70 Mass. App. Ct. 463, 466–68 (2007) (footnotes omitted).

NOTE 6   **Person entering after defendant.** "At issue on appeal is whether G.L. c. 265, § 18C, applies to an assault of an individual who entered a dwelling after the defendant and codefendant had entered the dwelling and already had assaulted the persons who were present. This individual was not a legal occupant or legal resident of the apartment. We hold it does, so we affirm." *Commonwealth v. Martinez*, 85 Mass. App. Ct. 288 (2014).

NOTE 7   **Probationary sentence.** "In light of the successive changes the Legislature has made to § 18C since 1998, we find the statute ambiguous with respect to whether it currently permits a sentence of probation. The rule of lenity, *see Commonwealth v. Crosscup*, 369 Mass. 228, 234 (1975), therefore comes into play, and we are constrained to conclude that § 18C in its present form does allow a judge to impose a probationary sentence." *Commonwealth v. Zapata*, 455 Mass. 530, 531 (2009).

SECTION 19
Unarmed robbery
(Amended by 2014 Mass. Acts c. 284, § 83, effective Aug. 11, 2014.)

(a) Whoever, not being armed with a dangerous weapon, by force and violence, or by assault and putting in fear, robs, steals or takes from the person of a person sixty years or older, or from his immediate control, money or other property which may be the subject of larceny, shall be punished by imprisonment in the state prison for life or for any term of years.

Whoever, after having been convicted of said crime, commits a second or subsequent such crime, shall be punished by imprisonment for not less than two years. Said sentence shall not be reduced until two years of said sentence have been served nor shall the person convicted be eligible for probation, parole, furlough, work release or receive any deduction from his sentence for good conduct until he shall have served two years of such sentence; provided, however, that the commissioner of correction may, on the recommendation of the warden, superintendent, or other person in charge of a correctional institution, or administrator of a county correctional institution, grant to said offender a temporary release in the custody of an officer of such institution for the following purposes only: to attend the funeral of next of kin or spouse; to visit a critically ill close relative or spouse; or to obtain emergency medical services unavailable at said institution. The provisions of section eighty-seven of chapter two hundred and seventy-six relative to the power of the court to place certain offenders on probation shall not apply to any person 18 years of age or over charged with a violation of this subsection.

(b) Whoever, not being armed with a dangerous weapon, by force and violence, or by assault and putting in fear, robs, steals or takes from the person of another, or from his immediate control, money or other property which may be the subject of larceny, shall be punished by imprisonment in the state prison for life or for any term of years.

NOTE 1   See Notes following G.L. c. 265, § 13A (assault; assault and battery); G.L. c. 265, § 15A (assault and battery by means of a dangerous weapon); G.L. c. 265, § 15B (assault by means of a dangerous weapon); G.L. c. 265, § 17 (armed robbery).

NOTE 2   General Laws c. 265, § 19(b), "permits a conviction for unarmed robbery in either of two ways: by force applied to the person, with intent to steal, or by an assault putting the person in fear, with the same intent. There is no requirement that the fear be for MaCakathi himself. The jury could find: (1) objectively menacing conduct by the defendant, undertaken with the intent to put MaCakathi in fear for the purpose of stealing the bank's money; and (2) this conduct resulted in reasonable fear or apprehension on MaCakathi's part and thereby facilitated the theft. They were also warranted in concluding that MaCakathi turned over the money because he feared that if he did not comply with the defendant's request, a customer standing near the defendant might get hurt. Even if the threatening gestures against MaCakathi did not cause him to fear for himself, they induced him to hand over the money because they reasonably caused him to fear for the customer's safety. We see no reason to limit the rationale . . . to the situation where acts of violence are committed on third persons. MaCakathi's reasonable fear for the customer was sufficient to satisfy the statute." *Commonwealth v. Davis*, 70 Mass. App. Ct. 314, 317 (2007) (citations and footnote omitted).

NOTE 3   Purse snatching, without more, could constitute robbery if the actual force involved in the taking was sufficient to produce awareness, although the action may be so swift as to leave the victim momentarily in a dazed condition. *Brown v. Genakos*, 405 F. Supp. 381, 384 (D. Mass. 1975) (examining *Commonwealth v. Jones*, 362 Mass. 83, 87 (1972)); *Commonwealth v. Zangari*, 42 Mass. App. Ct. 931, 932 (1997).

NOTE 4   "The ordinary pickpocket is guilty of larceny from the person, rather than robbery, because there is neither violence nor intimidation involved in the perpetration of the theft. The force used to bring about the theft is only that amount of force needed to lift and remove the property and is not of the class of violence essential to robbery. Pickpocketing characteristically involves stealth and a lack of awareness of the taking by the victim." Awareness of a theft does *not* constitute the essential difference between larceny and robbery. Rather, it is the exertion of force, actual or constructive, that remains the principal distinguishing characteristic of the offense of robbery. *Commonwealth v. Davis*, 7 Mass. App. Ct. 9, 11 (1979) (citations omitted).

NOTE 5   "A larceny may be converted to a robbery where the assault is committed on a victim who has a protective concern for the goods and where the victim interferes with the completion of the theft. See Commonwealth v. Mavredakis, 430 Mass. 848, 854–855 (2000). Here, a rational jury could have found that the Honda was taken from Adams's person as the robbery was not complete when the defendant was still fleeing the scene while being pursued by Adams. The defendant accelerated the car and pushed at Adams's hands to attempt to remove the car from Adams's grasp and to complete the theft." *Commonwealth v. Cruzado*, 73 Mass. App. Ct. 803, 805 (2009).

NOTE 6   "Of course, '[t]he exertion of force, actual or constructive, remains the principal distinguishing characteristic' between a robbery and the underlying larceny. *Commonwealth v. Jones*, 362 Mass. 83, 86 (1972). Also, where force is used, 'the degree of force is immaterial so long as it is sufficient to obtain the victim's property "against his will."' *Id.* at 87. Hamilton testified that the defendant 'took [the T-shirts] from my left arm and he pushed me back forward a little bit.' Hamilton also testified that the defendant's push 'made me move off balance' and 'I fell back a little bit. . . .' Hamilton's testimony warranted the finding that the taking was 'against his will' and that the defendant used at least some force to facilitate the larceny.

"The defendant argues that, because the alleged pushing must have followed the taking, there is no causal connection between the defendant's use of violence and his acquisition of Hamilton's property. Even if the jury believed that the defendant pushed Hamilton immediately after the defendant actually took the shirts, the jury were free to draw the reasonable inference that the defendant used the force to facilitate the larceny."

Commonwealth v. Sheppard, 404 Mass. 774, 778 (1989).

NOTE 7   **Related Statute.** G.L. c. 266, § 21—Refusal to deliver stolen property.

SECTION 20
Assault with intent to rob or steal

Whoever, not being armed with a dangerous weapon, assaults another with force and violence and with intent to rob or steal shall be punished by imprisonment in the state prison for not more than ten years.

NOTE 1   See Notes following G.L. c. 265, § 13A (assault; Assault and battery); G.L. c. 265, § 17 (armed robbery); G.L. c. 265, § 18 (armed assault with intent to rob or murder); and G.L. c. 265, § 19 (unarmed robbery).

NOTE 2   The words "with force and violence" in this section mean actual violence, as distinguished from merely constructive force and arms. *Commonwealth v. Crowley*, 167 Mass. 434 (1897).

NOTE 3   The defendant's actions in grabbing at the money while the victim resisted by tugging back constituted an assault with sufficient force and violence under this Section. *Commonwealth v. Ramos*, 6 Mass. App. Ct. 955 (1978) (rescript).

SECTION 21
Stealing by confining or putting in fear

Whoever, with intent to commit larceny or any felony, confines, maims, injures or wounds, or attempts or threatens to kill, confine, maim, injure or wound, or puts any person in fear, for the purpose of stealing from a building, bank, safe, vault or other depository of money, bonds or other valuables, or by intimidation, force or threats compels or attempts to compel any person to disclose or surrender the means of opening any building, bank, safe, vault or other depository of money, bonds, or other valuables, shall whether he succeeds or fails in the perpetration of such larceny or felony, be punished by imprisonment in the state prison for life or for any term of years.

NOTE 1   **Confinement.** The bank manager, by threats and force, was removed at gunpoint from a burglar alarm in her own office and restricted, until the police arrived, to a fixed area in the lobby. This constitutes confinement under this section. *Commonwealth v. Balakin*, 356 Mass. 547, 553 (1969).

NOTE 2   "Evidence was presented at trial that the defendant and another man intimidated victims into withdrawing funds from an automated teller machine (ATM) and handing those funds over to the defendant and the unidentified coventurer. The defendant argues that these facts do not support a finding that he had the purpose required by G.L. c. 265, § 21. We reject this argument.

"We share the view, articulated by the United States Court of Appeals for the Seventh Circuit, that '[i]f the depositor is robbed of the money he has just withdrawn after he leaves the bank, that is not a [robbery from the bank]. But if . . . the robber forces the bank's customer to withdraw the money, the customer becomes the unwilling agent of the robber . . . .'" *Commonwealth v. McGhee*, 470 Mass. 638, 639, 642 (2015) (citations omitted).

SECTION 21A
Carjacking
(Amended by 2014 Mass. Acts c. 284, § 84, effective Jan. 1, 2015.)

Whoever, with intent to steal a motor vehicle, assaults, confines, maims or puts any person in fear for the purpose of stealing a motor vehicle shall, whether he succeeds or fails in the perpetration of stealing the motor vehicle be punished by imprisonment in the state prison for not more than fifteen years or in a jail or house of correction for not more than two and one-half years and a fine of not less than one thousand nor more than fifteen thousand dollars; provided, however, that any person who commits any offense described herein while being armed with a dangerous weapon shall be punished by imprisonment in the state prison for not more than twenty years or in a jail or house of correction for not less than one year nor more than two and one-half years and a fine of not less than five nor more than fifteen thousand dollars. Whoever commits any offense described in this section while armed with a firearm, rifle, shotgun, machine gun or assault weapon, shall be punished by imprisonment in the state prison for not less than 7 years.

NOTE   Carjacking and kidnapping are not duplicative offenses; so too with unarmed robbery and carjacking ("carjacking requires proof that an automobile was the object of the defendant's desire, while unarmed robbery . . . requires proof of asportation." However, "where the indictment specifies that a car was the object of the unarmed robbery, carjacking might, in fact, be a lesser included offense of unarmed robbery"). *Commonwealth v. Smith*, 44 Mass. App. Ct. 394, 395, 396, 397 n.2 (1998).

SECTION 22
Rape, generally; penalties; eligibility for furlough, education, training or employment programs

(a) Whoever has sexual intercourse or unnatural sexual intercourse with a person, and compels such person to submit by force and against his will, or compels such person to submit by threat of bodily injury and if either such sexual intercourse or unnatural sexual intercourse results in or is committed with acts resulting in serious bodily injury, or is committed by a joint enterprise, or is committed during the commission or attempted commission of an offense defined in section fifteen A, fifteen B, seventeen, nineteen or twenty-six of this chapter, section fourteen, fifteen, sixteen, seventeen or eighteen of chapter two hundred and sixty-six or section ten of chapter two hundred and sixty-nine shall be punished by imprisonment for life or for any term of years.

No person serving a sentence for a second or subsequent such offense shall be eligible for furlough, temporary release, or education, training or employment programs established outside a correctional facility until such person shall have served two-thirds of such minimum sentence or if such person has two or more sentences to be served otherwise than concurrently, two thirds of the aggregate of the minimum terms of such several sentences.

For the purposes of prosecution, the offense described in subsection (b) shall be a lesser included offense to that described in subsection (a).

(b) Whoever has sexual intercourse or unnatural sexual intercourse with a person and compels such person to submit by force and against his will, or compels such person to submit by threat of bodily injury, shall be punished by imprisonment in the state prison for not more than twenty years; and whoever commits a second or subsequent such offense shall be punished by imprisonment in the state prison for life or for any term or years.

Whoever commits any offense described in this section while armed with a firearm, shotgun, rifle, machine gun or assault weapon, shall be punished by imprisonment in the state prison for not less than ten years. Whoever commits a second or subsequent such offense shall be punished by imprisonment in the state prison for life or for any term of years, but not less than 15 years.

No person serving a sentence for a second or subsequent such offense shall be eligible for furlough, temporary release, or education, training or employment programs established outside a correctional facility until such person shall have served two-thirds of such minimum sentence or if such person has two or more sentences to be served otherwise than concurrently, two-thirds of the aggregate of the minimum terms of such several sentences.

For the purposes of prosecution, the offense described in subsection (b) shall be a lesser included offense to that described in subsection (a).

NOTE 1 See Notes accompanying G.L. c. 265, §§ 13B, 22A and 24.

NOTE 2 Sexual intercourse connotes the traditional common law notion of rape, the penetration of the female sex organ by the male sex organ, with or without emission. *Commonwealth v. Gallant*, 373 Mass. 577, 584 (1977).

NOTE 3 Unnatural sexual intercourse refers to oral and anal intercourse, including fellatio, cunnilingus, and other intrusions of a part of a person's body or other object into the genital or anal opening of another person's body. *Commonwealth v. Gallant*, 373 Mass. 577, 584 (1977).

NOTE 4 **Penetration.** "Although the victim had testified simply that the defendant had touched her vagina with his penis in an attempt to insert it in her, intrusion into the vagina is not required to prove penetration; just a touching of the vulva or labia is sufficient." *Commonwealth v. Gichel*, 48 Mass. App. Ct. 206, 213 (1999). Other examples of penetration include semen, a piece of twine, and dirt found in the victim's vagina and "six year old's testimony that her 'privacy' was made to feel bad, by evidence of defendant's lubricating victim's 'private parts' and doctor's testimony about injury to the victim's hymen." *Commonwealth v. Fowler*, 431 Mass. 30, 33 (2000).

NOTE 5 A female can be convicted under this statute by either proving male-to-female rape through a joint venture with the male actors, or female-to-female rape, or both. *Commonwealth v. Whitehead*, 379 Mass. 640, 646–50 (1980).

NOTE 6 Evidence of the reputation of or of specific instances of a victim's past sexual conduct generally not admissible. *Rape shield provision.* G.L. c. 233, § 21B. *But see Commonwealth v. Harris*, 443 Mass. 714 (2005).

NOTE 7a **First Complaint/Fresh Complaint.** The fresh complaint doctrine was supplanted by the first complaint doctrine, as announced by the Supreme Judicial Court in *Commonwealth v. King*, 445 Mass. 217 (2005). The first complaint doctrine provides as follows:

- the recipient of a complainant's first complaint of an alleged sexual assault may testify about the fact of the first complaint and the circumstances surrounding the making of that first complaint;
- the witness may also testify about the details of the complaint;
- the complainant may likewise testify to the details of the first complaint (i.e., what he or she told the first complaint witness);
- the complainant may also testify as to why the complaint was made at that particular time;

- testimony from additional complaint witnesses is not admissible;
- the limited purpose for which first complaint testimony may be admitted is to assist the jury in determining whether to credit the complainant's testimony about the alleged sexual assault;
- the first complaint testimony may not be admitted in order to prove the truth of the complainant's allegations, and the jury must be so instructed when the "first complaint" witness testifies and again when the court gives its final instructions;
- first complaint evidence will not be disqualified by the complainant's timing in making a complaint; however, timing may be taken into consideration by the jury when deciding whether the first complaint testimony supports the complainant's credibility or reliability; and
- first complaint evidence will be considered presumptively relevant to a complainant's credibility in most sexual assault cases where the fact of the assaout or the issue of consent is contested. However, first complaint testimony is not relevant and therefore not admissible, where, for example, the sole issue is the identity of the perpetrator.

NOTE 7b **Modification of Scope of Review; No Longer Evidentiary Rule.** "Six years after the adoption of the first complaint doctrine . . . [w]e now conclude that the doctrine should be retained, but that the scope of appellate review of decisions on the admissibility of first complaint evidence should be modified.

"We remain concerned with the fact that sexual assault victims, particularly children, often do not promptly report or disclose such crimes for a variety of reasons, including fear, shame, psychological trauma, or concern that they will not be believed. *See* [*Commonwealth v.*] *King*, 445 Mass. 217, 237–238, 240 [(2005), cert. denied, 546 U.S. 1216 (2006)]. *See also Commonwealth v. Licata*, 412 Mass. 654, 657 (1992) ('It is not difficult to understand a rape victim's reluctance to discuss with others, particularly strangers, the uncomfortably specific details of a sexual attack'). The primary goals of the first complaint doctrine were, and still are, to 'refute any false inference that silence is evidence of a lack of credibility on the part of [sexual assault] complainants,' *King*, [445 Mass.] at 243, and 'to give the jury as complete a picture as possible of how the accusation of sexual assault first arose.' *Id.* at 247. We continue to believe that by allowing in evidence all the details of the first complaint, the doctrine gives the fact finder 'the maximum amount of information with which to assess the credibility of the . . . complaint evidence as well as the over-all credibility of the victim.' *Commonwealth v. Licata*, [412 Mass.] at 659, quoting Graham, *The Cry of Rape: The Prompt Complaint Doctrine and the Federal Rules of Evidence*, 19 Willamette L. Rev. 489, 511 (1983). The fact finder should not be left to speculate on the evidence or to draw erroneous inferences due to incomplete information. *See King*, [445 Mass.] at 244–245.

"Until now, we have considered the first complaint doctrine to be an 'evidentiary *rule*' that is designed 'to give support to a complainant's testimony of a sexual assault in cases where the credibility of the accusation is a contested issue at trial' (emphasis added). [*Commonwealth v.*] *Arana*, 453 Mass. [214, 228 (2009)]. The admission of evidence in violation of such evidentiary rule, that is, in violation of the established parameters of the first complaint doctrine, will always be deemed error. *See, e.g., id.* at 222–223; *Commonwealth v. Lyons*, 71 Mass. App. Ct. 671, 673–74 (2008). Where a defendant has objected to the admission of the evidence, an appellate court then will determine whether the error was prejudicial, *see Arana*, [453 Mass.] at 228, and where a defendant has not raised an objection, an appellate court will determine whether the error created a substantial risk of a miscarriage of justice. *See Commonwealth v. McCoy*, 456 Mass. 838, 850–852 (2010).

"As our post-*King* jurisprudence has developed, it has become apparent that trial judges need greater flexibility to deal with the myriad factual scenarios that arise in the context of purported first complaint evidence. Rules, because of their inherent inflexibility, tend to break down when it becomes necessary to address factual circumstances not yet contemplated by the established rubric. Rather than considering the first complaint doctrine as an evidentiary 'rule,' it makes greater sense to view the doctrine as a body of governing principles to guide a trial judge on the admissibility of first complaint evidence. . . . The judge who is evaluating the facts of a particular case is in the best position to determine the scope of admissible evidence, keeping in mind the underlying goals of the first complaint doctrine, our established first complaint jurisprudence, and our guidelines for admitting or excluding relevant evidence. *See* Mass. G. Evid. §§ 401–403 (2011). *See also Commonwealth v. Kebreau*, 454 Mass. 287, 296 (2009) ('Any determination concerning first complaint testimony is fact-specific and requires, in the first analysis, a careful evaluation of the circumstances by the trial judge'); *Commonwealth v. Murungu*, 450 Mass. 441, 445–47 (2008) (judge warranted in determining whether witness other than very first person to whom victim spoke about sexual assault should be permitted to testify as substituted first complaint witness). Once a judge has carefully and thoroughly analyzed these considerations, and has decided that proposed first complaint evidence is admissible, an appellate court shall review that determination under an abuse of discretion standard.

"The modification we announce today in no way should be construed as a relaxation or erosion of our first complaint jurisprudence. Our observation in *King*, [445 Mass.] at 243, that '[t]he testimony of multiple complaint witnesses likely serves no additional corroborative purpose, and may unfairly enhance a complainant's credibility as well as prejudice the defendant by repeating for the jury the often horrific details of an alleged crime,' remains relevant and significant. The importance of maintaining a balance between the interests of a complainant (who still may be a child) 'in having her credibility fairly judged on the specific facts of the case' and the interests of a defendant 'in receiving a trial free from irrelevant and potentially prejudicial testimony' cannot be overstated.[10] *Arana*, [453 Mass. at 228].

"FN10 While the first complaint doctrine prohibits the 'piling on' of multiple complaint witnesses, *Commonwealth v. Murungu*, 450 Mass. 441, 442-43 (2008), it does not exclude testimony that is 'otherwise independently admissible' and serves a purpose 'other than to repeat the fact of a complaint and thereby corroborate the complainant's accusations.' *Commonwealth v. Arana*, 453 Mass. 214, 220–21, 229 (2009). The modification that we announce today does not impact the admissibility of such evidence because it is outside the scope of the first complaint doctrine. *See id.* at 220. *See also Commonwealth v. Dargon*, 457 Mass. 387, 399 (2010) (certain evidence may be admissible 'under an evidentiary rubric other than first complaint')."
Commonwealth v. Aviles, 461 Mass. 60, 71–73 (2011).

**NOTE 7c	Exceptions to First Complaint.** "We stated in the King case that in certain circumstances a judge, in his discretion, could permit someone other than and 'in lieu of, the very "first" complaint witness' to testify, *Commonwealth v. King*, 445 Mass. 217, 243 (2005), and we provided some specific examples of when such substitutions could occur. For example, 'where the first person told of the alleged assault is unavailable, incompetent, or too young to testify meaningfully, the judge may exercise discretion in allowing one other complaint witness to testify.' *Id.* at 243–244. Thus, we left open the possibility that, on unusual occasions, the first person the victim informs of the incident may not be required to be the first complaint witness. We did not attempt to set forth an exhaustive list of appropriate substitutions. Other exceptions are permissible based on the purpose and limitations of the first complaint doctrine.

"The present case provides us an opportunity to detail two such additional exceptions. The first is when the encounter that the victim has with the first person does not constitute a complaint, when, for example, the victim expresses to that person unhappiness, upset or other such feelings, but does not actually state that she has been sexually assaulted. The second is when there is such a complaint, but the listener has an obvious bias or motive to minimize or distort the victim's remarks.

"We endorse these exceptions because they are consistent with the purposes of the first complaint doctrine as enunciated in the *King* case. The exceptions permit the Commonwealth to rebut any suggestion that the victim's silence was indicative of fabrication, while still avoiding the 'piling on' of complaint witnesses. *Id.* at 243–245. On the other hand, always requiring the Commonwealth to proceed with the first complaint witness regardless of the content of the conversation or the motivation of the witness may undermine the purpose for which the hearsay is permitted. Testimony of a vague conversation that does not 'complain' that a sexual assault occurred or testimony by a hostile first complaint witness may communicate to the jury that the victim in fact did not complain at all and that, if she had indeed been assaulted, she would have complained with more force and in greater detail.

"By permitting these exceptions to the first complaint doctrine, we do not suggest a relaxation of that doctrine so that the Commonwealth may pick and choose among various complaint witnesses to locate the one with the most complete memory, the one to whom the complainant related the most details, or the one who is likely to be the most effective witness. We conclude only that a judge, in situations such as we have described, may substitute a later complaint witness as the first complaint witness. The substituted witness should in most cases be the next complaint witness, absent compelling circumstances justifying further substitution." *Commonwealth v. Murungu*, 450 Mass. 441, 445–46 (2008).

"[W]here there was both ongoing abuse over a period of many years and escalating abuse during that period, with disclosures at two widely separated intervals, the judge's decision to allow two first complaint witnesses was appropriate." *Commonwealth v. Kebreau*, 454 Mass. 287, 296 (2009).

**NOTE 7d	Scope.** "The scope of the first complaint doctrine is not without limits. It does not, of course, prohibit the admissibility of evidence that, while barred by that doctrine, is otherwise independently admissible. *See Commonwealth v. Montanez*, [439 Mass. 441, 456 (2003)] (Sosman, J., concurring) ('Obsession with the strictures imposed on [first] complaint testimony should not blind us to the fact that [first] complaint is not the only basis for admitting such evidence'). *See also Commonwealth v. Lyons*, 71 Mass. App. Ct. 671, 674 n.4 (2008)." *Commonwealth v. Arana*, 453 Mass. 214, 220–21 (2009).

**NOTE 7e	Jury Instructions.** "A proper instruction to the jury will now read:
'In sexual assault cases we allow testimony by one person the complainant told of the alleged assault. We call this 'first complaint' evidence. The complainant may have reported the alleged sexual assault to more than one person. However, our rules normally permit testimony only as to the complainant's first report. The next witness will testify about the complainant's 'first complaint.' You may consider this evidence only for specific limited purposes: to establish the circumstances in which the complainant first reported the alleged offense, and then to determine whether that first complaint either supports or fails to support the complainant's own testimony about the crime. You may not consider this testimony as evidence that the assault in fact occurred. The purpose of this 'first complaint' evidence is to assist you in your assessment of the credibility and reliability of the complainant's testimony here in court. In assessing whether this 'first complaint' evidence supports or detracts from the complainant's credibility or reliability, you may consider all the circumstances in which the first complaint was made. The length of time between the alleged crime and the report of the complainant to this witness is one factor you may consider in evaluating the complainant's testimony, but you may also consider that sexual assault complainants may delay reporting the crime for a variety of reasons.'

"As is the current practice, these instruction should be given to the jury contemporaneously with the first complaint testimony, and again during the final instructions." *Commonwealth v. King*, 445 Mass. 217, 247–48 (2005).

**NOTE 7f	Investigative process.** The first complaint doctrine does not permit "description of the investigative process. . . . The fact that the Commonwealth brought its resources to bear on this incident creates the imprimatur of official belief in the complainant. It is unnecessary and irrelevant to the issue of the defendant's guilt, and is extremely prejudicial." *Commonwealth v. Stuckich*, 450 Mass. 449, 457 (2008).

NOTE 8a   Intoxication. "Diminished capacity resulting from the voluntary use of intoxicating liquor is not a defense to rape." *Commonwealth v. Rahilly*, 10 Mass. App. Ct. 911, 913 (1980) (citations omitted).

NOTE 8b   A man who has "carnal intercourse with a woman, without her consent, and while she was as he knew [insensible and] incapable of consenting," is guilty of rape. *Commonwealth v. Burke*, 105 Mass. 376, 380–81 (1870).

NOTE 8c   "[W]here there is no element of specific intent, a defendant is not entitled to an instruction on the effect intoxication may have had on the defendant's ability to form intent.

"The crime of rape is a general intent crime and therefore voluntary intoxicating has no mitigating effect." *Commonwealth v. Troy*, 405 Mass. 253, 260 (1989) (citations omitted).

NOTE 8d   "The Commonwealth may satisfy the required element of lack of consent by proof that the complainant was incapable of consenting, but as we hold today in *Commonwealth v. Blache*, to do so the Commonwealth must establish beyond a reasonable doubt that "because of the consumption of drugs or alcohol or for some other reason (for example, sleep, unconsciousness, mental retardation, or helplessness), the complainant was so impaired as to be incapable of consenting to intercourse." *Commonwealth v. Urban*, 450 Mass. 608, 613 (2008) (quoting *Commonwealth v. Blache*, 450 Mass. 583 (2008)) (citation omitted).

NOTE 9a   Lesser Included Offense. Assault and battery is a lesser included offense of rape. *Commonwealth v. McCan*, 277 Mass. 199, 202–03 (1931).

NOTE 9b   Indecent assault and battery is a lesser included offense of rape. *Commonwealth v. Thomas*, 400 Mass. 676, 681 (1987).

NOTE 10   See Notes following G.L. c. 265, § 22A (rape of a child under sixteen).

NOTE 11   *See* G.L. c. 277, § 39 (definition of rape).

NOTE 12   Related Statutes.
G.L. c. 272, § 3—Drugging person for sexual intercourse.
G.L. c. 272, § 35—Unnatural and lascivious acts.

NOTE 13a   Consent. In *Commonwealth v. Goldenberg*, 338 Mass. 377 (1959), "[t]he court reasoned that the 'essence of the crime is not the fact of intercourse but the injury and outrage to the feelings of the [victim] by the forceful penetration of her person. . . . Fraud cannot be allowed to supply the place of the force which the statute makes mandatory.' *Id.* at 384. In *Goldenberg*, the court specifically stated: 'This is not a case where a woman is incapable of consent by reason of stupefaction, unconsciousness or helplessness, and the amount of force required to commit the crime may be only that sufficient to effect the intercourse. *Commonwealth v. Burke*, 105 Mass. 376.' *Id.* at 383." *Commonwealth v. Helfant*, 398 Mass. 214, 221 (1986). The court in footnote 5 stated "[I]t may be questioned whether that reasoning is consistent with *Burke* and whether the injury and outrage to the personal integrity of the victim is any less when consent is fraudulently obtained. However, we need not decide whether *Goldenberg* is still good law, because it is inapposite to the facts of the case." *See also Suliveres v. Commonwealth*, 449 Mass. 112, 118 (2007) ("Fraudulently obtaining consent to sexual intercourse does not constitute rape as defined in our statute.") (footnote omitted); *Commonwealth v. Keevan*, 400 Mass. 557, 563 (1987).

NOTE 13b   "The law does not require that the complainant have been rendered 'unconscious or nearly so' before she may be deemed past the point of consent. We conclude that an instruction concerning capacity to consent should be given in any case where the evidence would support a finding that because of the consumption of drugs or alcohol or for some other reason (for example, sleep, unconsciousness, mental retardation, or helplessness),

the complainant was so impaired as to be incapable of consenting to intercourse. If the jury find the Commonwealth has proved beyond a reasonable doubt the complainant's incapacity according to this standard, that finding satisfies the element of lack of consent, and as a corollary, the Commonwealth need only prove the amount of force necessary to accomplish intercourse." "As *Burke* and its progeny reflect, a case in which the jury find that the complainant lacked the capacity to consent obviously represents one instance where the Commonwealth has no obligation to prove the use of force by the defendant beyond what is required for the act of penetration. *See Commonwealth v. Lopez*, 433 Mass. at 728–729. It thus makes sense to reemphasize the second principle suggested by [*Commonwealth v. Burke*, 105 Mass. 376 (1870)], and affirm that in such a case, the Commonwealth must prove that the defendant knew or reasonably should have known that the complainant's condition rendered her incapable of consenting to the sexual act. A proposed instruction that covers incapacity to consent, its effect on the elements of force and lack of consent, and the defendant's knowledge is set forth in the margin" (footnotes omitted).

The court in footnote 19 provided the following instruction: "In this case, there has been evidence that the complainant [had consumed alcohol; had consumed drugs; was unconscious; etc.]. If, because of the consumption of drugs or alcohol or for some other reason (for example, sleep, unconsciousness, mental retardation, or helplessness), a person is so impaired as to be incapable of consenting to sexual intercourse, then intercourse occurring during such incapacity is without that person's consent. If you find that the Commonwealth has proved beyond a reasonable doubt that the complainant was so impaired as to be incapable of consenting as I have just described, and if you further find that the Commonwealth has proved beyond a reasonable doubt that the defendant knew, or reasonably should have known, that the complainant's condition rendered her [or him] incapable of consenting, then the Commonwealth has proved the element of lack of consent, and, on the element of force, the Commonwealth need only prove that the defendant used the degree of force necessary to accomplish the sexual intercourse—that is, to effect penetration. However, if the Commonwealth has not proved that the complainant lacked the capacity to consent, or if the Commonwealth has not proved that the defendant knew or reasonably should have known of such incapacity, then in order to find the defendant guilty of rape, you must find that the Commonwealth has proved the elements of lack of consent and force as I have defined these elements for you earlier. This instruction would, in cases where it is relevant, supplement the basic instruction on the elements of force and lack of consent." *Commonwealth v. Blache*, 450 Mass. 583, 591–92, 593–95 & n.19 (2008).

NOTE 13c   "In *Commonwealth v. Blache*, 450 Mass. 583, 589 (2008), we held that where the Commonwealth relies on evidence that a rape victim was incapable of consent to establish the element of lack of consent and thereby reduce the degree of required force to that which is needed to effect penetration, 'the Commonwealth should also prove the defendant's knowledge of the complainant's incapacitated state.' Today we hold that a defendant in such a case is entitled to have the jury instructed that they may consider credible evidence of his mental incapacity, by intoxication or otherwise, when deciding whether the Commonwealth has met its burden of proof as to his knowledge of the victim's incapacity to consent." *Commonwealth v. Mountry*, 463 Mass. 80, 81 (2012).

NOTE 14   "One theory of the defense in this case was that the complainant, in her intoxicated state, misidentified the defendant as the man who raped her. It was fundamental to this defense that the defendant have the opportunity to rebut the Commonwealth's chemical evidence by offering evidence tending to show that he was not the source of the seminal fluid found in or near the victim. We have held that, '[w]hen evidence concerning a critical issue is excluded and when that evidence might have had a significant impact on the result of the trial, the right to present a full defense has been denied.' *Commonwealth v. Bohannon*, 376 Mass. 90, 94 (1978), s.c., 385 Mass. 733 (1982). *See Commonwealth v. Jewett*,

2

392 Mass. 558, 562 (1984) (right to present witnesses to establish a defense is fundamental element of due process)." *Commonwealth v. Fitzgerald*, 402 Mass. 517, 521 (1988).

NOTE 15a   Prior Complaint of Rape. "In *Bohannon*, [376 Mass. 90 (1978)] we recognized an exception to the general rule that prior bad acts may not be used to impeach a witness's credibility and held that, in the circumstances of that case, the denial of the defendants' request to cross-examine the victim on the central issue of consent, by asking about prior false allegations of rape and thereby testing her credibility on this issue, deprived the defendants of a full and fair opportunity to present their defense to the jury. In the instant case, the defendants argue that, where, under cross-examination, the victim denied the 1981 incident or any recollection of it, the reasoning of *Bohannon* requires admission of the document itself.

"We would agree, but for the critical fact that, as was found by the judge, the hospital record itself provides no evidence that the allegation of rape was indeed false."
Commonwealth v. Vieira, 401 Mass. 828, 839 (1988).

NOTE 15b   "[T]he exception in *Bohannon* is a narrow one. A necessary circumstance for this exception is that there is a basis in independent third-party records for concluding that the prior accusations of the same type of crime had been made and were false. Evidence that the victim failed to pursue a claim is not evidence that the claim was falsely made." *Commonwealth v. Hrycenko*, 417 Mass. 309, 319 (1994) (citations and quotation marks omitted).

NOTE 15c   "The defendant is entitled to cross-examine an alleged victim about a pattern of false accusations or 'crying wolf'. . . . [T]he allegation of sexual misconduct against a single individual (the stepgrandfather) fell short of suggesting the pattern of similar accusations in *Bohannon*. . . . [E]vidence of a false allegation of rape is relevant only on the issue of a witness's ability, readiness, or proclivity to lie and fabricate." *Commonwealth v. Haynes*, 45 Mass. App. Ct. 192, 199–200 (1998) (citations, quotation marks, and punctuation omitted).

NOTE 16   Duplicative Convictions. "[T]here is a distinction between cases where the indecent assault and battery and the rape are "'so closely related in fact as to constitute in substance but a single crime,' [and situations where] the indecent assault and battery constituted a separate and incidental act." Victim C testified that the defendant "tore" down her pants and put his penis into her rectum. When Victim C cried out in pain, the defendant took his penis out of her rectum and put it into her vagina. Victim C also testified that the defendant inserted his tongue into her mouth. There is evidence of two distinct acts of rape and one act of indecent assault and battery in this scenario. Thus, the indecent assault and battery could have been held to constitute a wholly separate act and not a lesser included offense. In *Commonwealth v. Sanchez*, 405 Mass. 369, 381–82 (1989), a case analogous to the instant case, we held that the indecent assault and battery conviction had to be reversed. In *Sanchez*, however, '[t]he Commonwealth [did] not argue . . . that it was a wholly separate act.' *Id.* at 381. Here, the prosecutor consistently highlighted the different actions of the defendant. If the defendant had requested an instruction that each conviction must be based on separate acts, or had objected to the lack of such an instruction, we might reverse the conviction of the lesser included offense."
Commonwealth v. Mamay, 407 Mass. 412, 418–19 (1990) (citations omitted).

NOTE 17   Expert Testimony. "The defendant argues that it was improper to admit the testimony of Ann W. Burgess, who was qualified as an expert in the field of rape and sexual assault syndrome. A trial judge has broad discretion with respect to the admissibility of expert testimony. . . . Expert testimony is admissible if, in the judge's discretion, the subject is not within the common knowledge or common experience of the jury.

"Burgess testified that not all victims of rape and sexual assault will report the event immediately. Often the first person they will tell is someone close to them. Burgess also said that, in the

context of a trust relationship, such as a doctor-patient relationship, some victims may return to the trusted relationship for further contact with the perpetrator of the assault Burgess's testimony did not relate to the victims in this case. It was simply testimony relating to rape and sexual assault syndrome generally. . . . It was within the judge's discretion properly to conclude that it was beyond the jury's common knowledge to know why a victim would return to a situation in which she had been sexually assaulted or raped.

"The defendant contends that there is a lack of scientific evidence (1) that rape trauma syndrome, so called, occurs in cases of mere indecent assault and battery, or (2) that the syndrome occurs in trust relationships. Burgess testified, based on her extensive studies in the area of rape trauma syndrome, that medical science recognizes the syndrome; and that it extends to victims of 'nonconsensual sexual assault.' A number of other Courts and commentators, . . . have recognized the scientific basis of rape trauma syndrome. . . .

". . . Thus, there was a clear basis from which the judge could conclude that the medical community has generally recognized the existence of rape trauma syndrome."
Commonwealth v. Mamay, 407 Mass. 412, 421–22 (1990) (quotation marks and citations omitted). *See also Commonwealth v. Hudson*, 417 Mass. 536 (1994).

NOTE 18   Evidence—Weapons. "The defendant argues that it was reversible error for the judge to admit in evidence seven small pocket knives seized from the defendant's house. There was evidence that all of the knives were found near the sofa bed where the alleged crimes were committed. Nevertheless, the defendant argues that at least six of the knives had no relevance to the case.

"'The fact that, at or about the time of a crime, a defendant had a weapon that could have been used in committing the crime is admissible in the judge's discretion.' *Commonwealth v. Toro*, 395 Mass. 354, 356 (1985). '[I]t is commonly competent to show the possession by a defendant of an instrument capable of being used in the commission of the crime, without direct proof that particular instrument was in fact the one used.'"
Commonwealth v. Ascolillo, 405 Mass. 456, 461 (1989).

NOTE 19   Evidence of Force. "[W]e conclude there was evidence of force and constraint of the victim's will. The evidence indicates that the defendant wore a gun; that he ordered the victim into his car; that he named a number of police officers; that he gave her a false name; and that he told her he was a police officer and would imprison her if she did not obey him. The defendant made the complainant beg him not to 'lock her up.' The facts indicate that the woman was 'petrified' by the defendant's threats that he would 'lock her up.' The issue whether, in light of the circumstances, the victim's obedience or submission to the defendant's threats was by force and against her will is for the petit jury."
Commonwealth v. Caracciola, 409 Mass. 648, 654 (1991).

NOTE 20a   "Committed With." "While the language 'committed with,' of course, implies some logical nexus between time and place, the words do not specifically require that the physical force precede the rape or that the injuries be inflicted to overcome a victim's will to resist. If this were true, a person who savagely beat his victim following a sexual attack, as here, would be punished less severely than one who inflicted the beating before penetration, even though both rape victims sustained identical injuries." *Commonwealth v. McCourt*, 438 Mass. 486, 493 (2003).

NOTE 20b   "The Legislature's choice of the flexible terms 'committed with' and 'committed during,' rather than terms indicating a restrictive causal relationship, such as 'accomplished by' or 'facilitated by,' demonstrates its intent to avoid a limiting temporal distinction." *Commonwealth v. McCourt*, 438 Mass. 486, 493 (2003).

NOTE 20c   "The critical point is not whether the aggravating acts served to compel a victim's submission, but whether the rape victim sustained serious bodily injuries, or was subjected to other felonious conduct, during the same criminal episode. The Legislature, by enacting G.L. c. 265, § 22(a), intended that rapists who inflict serious bodily injury or commit other crimes against their victims, will be dealt with severely. It is neither appropriate nor consistent with the Legislature's purpose to draw an artificial bright line between the ending of the sexual offense and aggravating conduct that occurs immediately thereafter. We conclude that the language of G.L. c. 265, § 22(a), is sufficiently broad to encompass a rape that precedes a brutal beating that inflicts serious bodily injury on the victim, so long as the rape and the beating constituted one continuous episode and course of conduct." *Commonwealth v. McCourt*, 438 Mass. 486, 495–96 (2003) (citation and quotation omitted).

NOTE 21   Records. "In addition to rejecting the assumptions that support the federal standard, we note that section 20B of G.L. c. 233 and section 135 of G.L. c. 112, are not statements of absolute privilege, unlike certain other statutory testimonial privileges such as G.L. c. 233, § 20A (priest/penitent) and G.L. c. 233, § 20J (sexual assault counselor/victim). . . .

"Accordingly, we conclude that, under Article 12 of the Massachusetts Declaration of Rights, counsel for the defendant is entitled to review the records of the complainant's treatment at the New York Hospital and with the Greenwich, Connecticut, social worker to search for evidence of bias, prejudice or motive to lie. The judge then shall conduct an in-camera hearing concerning the admissibility of any information in the records that counsel may wish to use at trial. In his discretion. the judge also shall enter any orders that are deemed appropriate to ensure that the information contained in the records will not be disclosed beyond the defendant's need to prepare and present his defense." *Commonwealth v. Stockhammer*, 409 Mass. 867, 883–84 (1991).

See also Psychiatric, Psychological, Privileged Records in Alphabetical References to Evidence section of this volume.

NOTE 22   Prior Bad Acts. "[W]hen a defendant is charged with any form of illicit sexual intercourse, evidence of the commission of similar crimes by the same parties though committed in another place, if not too remote in time, is competent to prove an inclination to commit the acts charged in the indictment and is relevant to show the probable existence of the same passion or emotion at the time in issue. Evidence of similar misconduct may also be used to show the relationship between the defendant and the victim." *Commonwealth v. Barrett*, 418 Mass. 788, 794 (1994) (citations and punctuation omitted).

NOTE 23   Common Law Presumption That Child Under 14 Is Incapable of Rape Not Applicable in Massachusetts. The Supreme Judicial Court declined to adopt in Massachusetts the common law presumption that a child under the age of fourteen is conclusively presumed incapable of committing rape, noting that it saw "no sound legal or medical basis for [such] a presumption." *Commonwealth v. Walter R.*, 414 Mass. 714, 715–18 (1993).

NOTE 24   Sex Offender Registry. A conviction or adjudication of delinquency of an offense under this section or of an attempt to commit such an offense (*see* G.L. c. 274, § 6) renders the defendant subject to the requirements of the sex offender registry law. *See* G.L. c. 6, §§ 178C–178Q.

NOTE 25   DNA Database. A conviction of an offense under this section or of an attempt or conspiracy to commit such an offense results in the defendant being required to submit a DNA sample to the state's DNA database. *See* G.L. c. 22E, § 3.

NOTE 26   Sexually Dangerous Person Commitment. A conviction or adjudication of delinquency of an offense under this section or of an attempt to commit such an offense (*see* G.L. c. 274, § 6) can serve as a predicate "sexual offense" for civil commitment as a "sexually dangerous person". *See* G.L. c. 123A, §§ 1–15.

SECTION 22A
Rape of a child under 16

Whoever has sexual intercourse or unnatural sexual intercourse with a child under 16, and compels such child to submit by force and against his will or compels such child to submit by threat of bodily injury, shall be punished by im-

prisonment in the state prison for life or for any term of years. A prosecution commenced under this section shall neither be continued without a finding nor placed on file.

NOTE 1a   A finger is comprehended within the meaning of the words "a part of a person's body" as used in the construction of the words "unnatural sexual intercourse" and thus allegation that defendant had forcefully and unlawfully penetrated sexual organs of victim, a female child, by means of his hand and/or fingers stated a crime under this statute. *Commonwealth v. Mamay*, 5 Mass. App. Ct. 708, 710 (1977).

NOTE 1b   A 12-year-old was charged with rape based upon the digital penetration of a five-year-old victim. The defendant unsuccessfully argued that a child under 14 was, at common law, conclusively presumed incapable of committing rape.

Held, "The defendant here is not charged with rape as defined at common law, but rather with conduct that falls within the proscriptive phrase 'unnatural sexual intercourse.' . . . Since the act upon which the rape charge is based did not constitute rape at common law the presumption can have no application here." *Commonwealth v. A Juvenile*, 399 Mass. 451, 453 (1987).

NOTE 1c   Oral Penetration. "As a matter of law, evidence that a male forced a female to perform fellatio on him and made her 'lick' his penis, is sufficient to support a jury's finding of penetration and thus a conviction of forcible rape of a child.

"While some degree of penetration is required to sustain a conviction under the statute, a jury may infer penetration on the basis of licking a penis." *Commonwealth v. King*, 445 Mass. 217, 222–23 (2005).

NOTE 2   The crime of statutory rape, punishable under G.L. c. 265, § 23, is also a crime included within the crime of forcible rape, punishable under G.L. c. 265, § 22A. *Commonwealth v. Franks*, 365 Mass. 74, 78–79, *appeal after remand*, 369 Mass. 608 (1976), *appeal after remand*, 372 Mass. 866 (1977) (appeals after remand dealt with sentencing); *see also Commonwealth v. Thayer*, 418 Mass. 130, 132 (1994).

NOTE 3   Medical records generally admissible into evidence on question of treatment and diagnosis. G.L. c. 233, § 79; Proposed Mass.R.Evid. (rejected) 803 (4); *Commonwealth v. Franks*, 359 Mass. 577, 580 (1971).

NOTE 4   Expert Testimony. "*Expert testimony on the general characteristics of sexually abused children.* The defendant challenges the admission in evidence of Dr. Brant's expert testimony on the general behavioral characteristics of sexually abused children. He argues that such testimony should have been in response to a hypothetical question related to the facts of the case, whether assumed or in evidence. We disagree."

Evidence child "lies a lot." "The defendant argues that, although a five year old boy cannot have a general reputation in a community, the statement that the boy 'lies a lot' was admissible because it suggests a poor reputation for truth and veracity within his foster family. We disagree."

Commonwealth v. Dockham, 405 Mass. 618, 627–28, 630 (1989).

NOTE 5   "We conclude that the admission in evidence of a 'child battering profile' is reversible error due to its irrelevance and its inherent prejudicial impact on the defendant." *Commonwealth v. Day*, 409 Mass. 719, 724 (1991).

NOTE 6   Specificity of Date of Offense. See Note 3 following G.L. c. 277, § 20.

NOTE 7   Individual Juror Voir Dire. "[I]n cases . . . involving sexual offenses against minors, on request, the judge must interrogate individually each prospective juror as to whether the juror has been a victim of a childhood sexual offense." *Commonwealth v. Flebotte*, 417 Mass. 348, 353 (1994).

NOTE 8   Related statutes.

G.L. c. 272, § 4—Inducing person under eighteen to have sexual intercourse.

G.L. c. 272, § 35A—Unnatural and lascivious acts with a child under sixteen.

NOTE 9   Sex Offender Registry. A conviction or adjudication of delinquency of an offense under this section or of an attempt to commit such an offense (*see* G.L. c. 274, § 6) renders the defendant subject to the requirements of the sex offender registry law. *See* G.L. c. 6, §§ 178C–178Q.

NOTE 10   DNA Database. A conviction of an offense under this section or of an attempt or conspiracy to commit such an offense results in the defendant being required to submit a DNA sample to the state's DNA database. *See* G.L. c. 22E, § 3.

NOTE 11   Juvenile Disposition. As is the case with an adult/criminal prosecution commenced under this section, a complaint alleging a child to be a delinquent child by reason of having violated the provisions of this section shall not be placed on file or continued without a finding. G.L. c. 119, §§ 55B, 58.

NOTE 12   Sexually Dangerous Person Commitment. A conviction or adjudication of delinquency of an offense under this section or of an attempt to commit such an offense (*see* G.L. c. 274, § 6) can serve as a predicate "sexual offense" for civil commitment as a "sexually dangerous person". *See* G.L. c. 123A, §§ 1–15.

SECTION 22B
Aggravated rape of a child under 16

Whoever has sexual intercourse or unnatural sexual intercourse with a child under 16, and compels such child to submit by force and against his will or compels such child to submit by threat of bodily injury and:

(a) the sexual intercourse or unnatural sexual intercourse is committed during the commission or attempted commission of any of the following offenses: (1) armed burglary as set forth in section 14 of chapter 266; (2) unarmed burglary as set forth in section 15 of said chapter 266; (3) breaking and entering as set forth in section 16 of said chapter 266; (4) entering without breaking as set forth in section 17 of said chapter 266; (5) breaking and entering into a dwelling house as set forth in section 18 of said chapter 266; (6) kidnapping as set forth in section 26 of chapter 265; (7) armed robbery as set forth in section 17 of said chapter 265; (8) unarmed robbery as set forth in section 19 of said chapter 265; (9) assault and battery with a dangerous weapon or assault with a dangerous weapon as set forth in sections 15A and 15B of said chapter 265; (10) home invasion as set forth in section 18C of said chapter 265; or (11) posing or exhibiting child in state of nudity or sexual conduct as set forth in section 29A of chapter 272;

(b) the sexual intercourse or unnatural sexual intercourse results in, or is committed by means of an act or acts resulting in, substantial bodily injury as defined in section 13J;

(c) the sexual intercourse or unnatural sexual intercourse is committed while the victim is tied, bound or gagged;

(d) the sexual intercourse or unnatural sexual intercourse is committed after the defendant administered, or caused to be administered, alcohol or a controlled substance by injection, inhalation, ingestion, or any other means to the victim without the victim's consent;

(e) the sexual intercourse or unnatural sexual intercourse is committed by a joint enterprise; or

(f) the sexual intercourse or unnatural sexual intercourse was committed in a manner in which the victim could contract a sexually transmitted disease or infection of which the defendant knew or should have known he was a carrier, shall be punished by imprisonment in the state prison for life or for any term of years, but not less than 15 years. The sentence imposed on such person shall not be reduced to less than 15 years, or suspended, nor shall any person convicted under this section be eligible for probation, parole, work release or furlough or receive any deduction from his sentence for good conduct until he shall have served 15 years of such sentence. Prosecutions commenced under this section shall neither be continued without a finding nor placed on file. Whoever has sexual intercourse or unnatural sexual intercourse with a child under 16, and compels such child to submit by force and against his will or compels such child to submit by threat of bodily injury, shall be punished by imprisonment in the state prison for life or for any term of years. A prosecution commenced under this section shall neither be continued without a finding nor placed on file.

SECTION 22C
Aggravated rape of a child under 16; subsequent offenses

Whoever has sexual intercourse or unnatural sexual intercourse with a child under 16, and compels such child to submit by force and against his will or compels such child to submit by threat of bodily injury, and has been previously convicted of or adjudicated delinquent or as a youthful offender for: indecent assault and battery on a child under 14 as set forth in section 13B; aggravated indecent assault and battery on a child under 14 as set forth in section 13B½; indecent assault and battery on a person 14 or older as set forth in section 13H; assault of a child with intent to commit rape as set forth in section 24B; rape of a child with force as set forth in section 22A; aggravated rape of a child with force as set forth in section 22B; rape and abuse of a child as set forth in section 23; aggravated rape and abuse of a child as set forth in section 23A; rape as set forth in section 22; or a like violation of the laws of another state, the United States or a military, territorial or Indian tribal authority, shall be punished by imprisonment in the state prison for life or for any term of years, but not less than 20 years. The sentence imposed on such person shall not be reduced to less than 20 years, or suspended, nor shall any person convicted under this section be eligible for probation, parole, work release or furlough or receive any deduction from his sentence for good conduct until he shall have served 20 years of such sentence. Prosecutions commenced under this section shall neither be continued without a finding nor placed on file.

In any prosecution commenced pursuant to this section, introduction into evidence of a prior adjudication or conviction or a prior finding of sufficient facts by either certified attested copies of original court papers, or certified attested copies of the defendant's biographical and informational data from records of the department of probation, any jail or house of correction or the department of correction, shall be prima facie evidence that the defendant before the court has been convicted previously by a court of the commonwealth or any other jurisdiction. Such documentation shall be self-authenticating and admissible, after the commonwealth has established the defendant's guilt on the primary offense, as evidence in any court of the commonwealth to prove the defendant's commission of any prior conviction described therein. The commonwealth shall not be required to introduce any additional corroborating evidence or live witness testimony to establish the validity of such prior conviction.

SECTION 23
Statutory rape

Whoever unlawfully has sexual intercourse or unnatural sexual intercourse, and abuses a child under 16 years of age, shall be punished by imprisonment in the state prison for life or for any term of years or, except as otherwise provided, for any term in a jail or house of correction. A prosecution commenced under this section shall neither be continued without a finding nor placed on file.

NOTE 1   "Statutory rape is a strict liability crime. The only element the Commonwealth must prove are (1) sexual intercourse or unnatural sexual intercourse with (2) a child under 16 years of age."
"A reasonable mistake as to the age [or identity] of the victim is not a defense."
Commonwealth v. Knap, 412 Mass. 712, 714 (1992).

NOTE 2   Consent. The consent of a child is immaterial in a trial under this section. *Commonwealth v. Ellis*, 321 Mass. 669 (1947). She is incapable, as a matter of law, of giving any effective consent. *Glover v. Callahan*, 299 Mass. 55, 58–59 (1937).

NOTE 3   Statute of Limitations. See Notes following G.L. c. 277, § 63.

NOTE 4   See Notes following G.L. c. 265, § 22 (rape) and G.L. c. 265, § 22A (rape of child under 16).

NOTE 5   Related Statutes.
G.L. c. 272, § 4—Inducing person under eighteen to have sexual intercourse.
G.L. c. 272, § 35A—Unnatural and lascivious acts with child under sixteen.

NOTE 6   Sex Offender Registry. A conviction or adjudication of delinquency of an offense under this section or of an attempt to commit such an offense (*see* G.L. c. 274, § 6) renders the defendant subject to the requirements of the sex offender registry law. *See* G.L. c. 6, §§ 178C–178Q.

NOTE 7   DNA Database. A conviction of an offense under this section or of an attempt or conspiracy to commit such an offense results in the defendant being required to submit a DNA sample to the state's DNA database. *See* G.L. c. 22E, § 3.

NOTE 8   Juvenile Disposition. As is the case with an adult/criminal prosecution commenced under this section, a complaint alleging a child to be a delinquent child by reason of having violated the provisions of this section shall not be placed on file or continued without a finding. G.L. c. 119, §§ 55B, 58.

NOTE 9   Sexually Dangerous Person Commitment. A conviction or adjudication of delinquency of an offense under this section or of an attempt to commit such an offense (*see* G.L. c. 274, § 6) can serve as a predicate "sexual offense" for civil commitment as a "sexually dangerous person". *See* G.L. c. 123A, §§ 1–15.

SECTION 23A
Aggravated statutory rape

Whoever unlawfully has sexual intercourse or unnatural sexual intercourse, and abuses a child under 16 years of age and:

(a) there exists more than a 5 year age difference between the defendant and the victim and the victim is under 12 years of age;

(b) there exists more than a 10 year age difference between the defendant and the victim where the victim is between the age of 12 and 16 years of age; or

(c) at the time of such intercourse, was a mandated reporter as defined in section 21 of chapter 119, shall be punished by imprisonment in the state prison for life or for any term of years, but not less than 10 years. The sentence imposed on such person shall not be reduced to less than 10 years, or suspended, nor shall any person convicted under this section be eligible for probation, parole, work release, or furlough or receive any deduction from his sentence for good conduct until he shall have served 10 years of such sentence. Prosecutions commenced under this section shall neither be continued without a finding nor placed on file.

SECTION 23B
Statutory rape, subsequent offense

Whoever unlawfully has sexual intercourse or unnatural sexual intercourse, and abuses a child under 16 years of age and has been previously convicted of or adjudicated delinquent or as a youthful offender for: indecent assault and battery on a child under 14 under section 13B; aggravated indecent assault and battery on a child under 14 under section 13B½; indecent assault and battery on a person 14 or older under section 13H; assault of a child with intent to commit rape under section 24B; rape of a child with force under section 22A; aggravated rape of a child with force under section 22B; rape and abuse of a child under section 23; aggravated rape and abuse of a child under section 23A; rape under section 22; or a like violation of the laws of another state, the United States or a military, territorial or Indian tribal authority, shall be punished by imprisonment in the state prison for life or for any term of years, but not less than 15 years. The sentence imposed on such person shall not be reduced to less than 15 years, or suspended, nor shall any person convicted under this section be eligible for probation, parole, work release, or furlough or receive any deduction from his sentence for good conduct until he shall have served 15 years of such sentence. Prosecutions commenced under this section shall neither be continued without a finding nor placed on file.

In any prosecution commenced pursuant to this section, introduction into evidence of a prior adjudication or conviction or a prior finding of sufficient facts by either certified attested copies of original court papers, or certified attested copies of the defendant's biographical and informational data from records of the department of probation, any jail or house of correction or the department of correction, shall be prima facie evidence that the defendant before the court has been convicted previously by a court of the commonwealth or any other jurisdiction. Such documentation shall be self-authenticating and admissible, after the commonwealth has established the defendant's guilt on the primary offense, as evidence in any court of the commonwealth to prove the defendant's commission of any prior conviction described therein. The commonwealth shall not be required to introduce any additional corroborating evidence or live witness testimony to establish the validity of such prior conviction.

SECTION 24
Assault with intent to commit rape

Whoever assaults a person with intent to commit a rape shall be punished by imprisonment in the state prison for not more than twenty years or by imprisonment in a jail or house of correction for not more than two and one-half years; and whoever commits a second or subsequent such offense shall be punished by imprisonment in the state prison for life or for any term of years. Whoever commits any offense described in this section while armed with a firearm, shotgun, rifle, machine gun or assault weapon, shall be punished by imprisonment in

2

the state prison for not less than five years. Whoever commits a second or subsequent such offense shall be punished by imprisonment in the state prison for life or for any term of years, but not less than 20 years.

No person serving a sentence for a second or subsequent such offense shall be eligible for furlough, temporary release, or education, training or employment programs established outside a correctional facility until such person shall have served two-thirds of such minimum sentence or if such person has two or more sentences to be served otherwise than concurrently, two-thirds of the aggregate of the minimum terms of such several sentences.

NOTE 1   Whether there was an intent to commit rape is a question for the factfinder. Some factors which might help make that determination include evidence of (a) an assault and battery, (b) an attempt to restrain the complainant; (c) a struggle; (d) sexual advances to the victim against her will. *Commonwealth v. Brattman*, 10 Mass. App. Ct. 579, 582 (1980).

NOTE 2   First complaint evidence applicable here. See Note 6 following G.L. c. 265, § 22.

NOTE 3   **Prior Bad Acts.** "There must be a uniqueness of technique, a distinctiveness, or a particularly distinguishing pattern of conduct common to the current and former incidents to warrant the admission of evidence of prior bad acts as tending to prove that the defendant was the person who committed the crime charged."

Footnote 7 indicated, among other things, that "a defendant may show that someone else had recently committed such a crime in the same distinct manner."

Commonwealth v. Brusgulis, 406 Mass. 501, 506 (1990); *see also Commonwealth v. Jackson*, 417 Mass. 830, 835–42 (1994).

NOTE 4   **Statute of Limitations.** See Note 2 following G.L. c. 277, § 63.

NOTE 5   See Notes on assault following G.L. c. 265, § 13A (assault; assault and battery); G.L. c. 265, § 15A (assault and battery by means of a dangerous weapon); G.L. c. 265, § 15B (assault by means of a dangerous weapon); G.L. c. 265, § 17 (armed robbery); and Rape, G.L. c. 265, §§ 22, 22A and 23 (rape).

NOTE 6   **Related Statute.** G.L. c. 272, § 35—Unnatural and lascivious acts.

NOTE 7   **Sex Offender Registry.** A conviction or adjudication of delinquency of an offense under this section or of an attempt to commit such an offense (*see* G.L. c. 274, § 6) renders the defendant subject to the requirements of the sex offender registry law. *See* G.L. c. 6, §§ 178C–178Q.

NOTE 8   **DNA Database.** A conviction of an offense under this section or of an attempt or conspiracy to commit such an offense results in the defendant being required to submit a DNA sample to the state's DNA database. *See* G.L. c. 22E, § 3.

NOTE 9   **Sexually Dangerous Person Commitment.** A conviction or adjudication of delinquency of an offense under this section or of an attempt to commit such an offense (*see* G.L. c. 274, § 6) can serve as a predicate "sexual offense" for civil commitment as a "sexually dangerous person." *See* G.L. c. 123A, §§ 1–15.

SECTION 24A
Venue

If, in connection with the alleged commission of a crime described in section thirteen B, 13B½, 13B¾, thirteen F, thirteen H, twenty-two, twenty-two A, twenty-three, twenty-four or twenty-four B of this chapter or in section five of chapter two hundred and seventy-two, the person against whom said crime is alleged to have been committed has been conveyed from one county or judicial district into another, said crime

may be alleged to have been committed, and may be prosecuted and punished, in the county or judicial district where committed or from which such person was so conveyed.

NOTE   "With respect to the offenses of kidnapping and rape, there is a wide latitude in trying a defendant in either the county from which or the county to which the victim was taken." *Commonwealth v. Libby*, 358 Mass. 617, 620 n.2 (1971).

SECTION 24B
Assault of child with intent to commit rape

Whoever assaults a child under sixteen with intent to commit a rape, as defined in section thirty-nine of chapter two hundred and seventy-seven, shall be punished by imprisonment in the state prison for life or for any term of years; and whoever over the age of eighteen commits a subsequent such offense shall be punished by imprisonment in the state prison for life or for any term of years but not less than five years.

Whoever commits any offense described in this section while armed with a firearm, shotgun, rifle, machine gun or assault weapon shall be sentenced to state prison for life or for any term of years, but not less than ten years. Whoever over the age of 18 commits a second or subsequent such offense shall be punished by imprisonment in the state prison for life or for any term of years, but not less than 15 years.

NOTE 1   See Notes following G.L. c. 265, § 22 (rape); G.L. c. 265, § 22A (rape of a child); G.L. c. 265, § 23 (statutory rape); and G.L. c. 265, § 24 (assault to rape).

NOTE 2   **Related Statute.** G.L. c. 272, § 35A—Unnatural and lascivious acts with a child under sixteen.

NOTE 3   **Sex Offender Registry.** A conviction or adjudication of delinquency of an offense under this section or of an attempt to commit such an offense (*see* G.L. c. 274, § 6) renders the defendant subject to the requirements of the sex offender registry law. *See* G.L. c. 6, §§ 178C–178Q.

NOTE 4   **DNA Database.** A conviction of an offense under this section or of an attempt or conspiracy to commit such an offense results in the defendant being required to submit a DNA sample to the state's DNA database. *See* G.L. c. 22E, § 3.

NOTE 5   **Sexually Dangerous Person Commitment.** A conviction or adjudication of delinquency of an offense under this section or of an attempt to commit such an offense (*see* G.L. c. 274, § 6) can serve as a predicate "sexual offense" for civil commitment as a "sexually dangerous person". *See* G.L. c. 123A, §§ 1–15.

SECTION 24C
Victim's name; confidentiality
(Amended by 2011 Mass. Acts c. 178, § 21, effective Nov. 21, 2011.)

That portion of the records of a court or any police department of the commonwealth or any of its political subdivisions, which contains the name of the victim in an arrest, investigation or complaint for rape or assault with intent to rape under section thirteen B, 13B½, 13B¾, twenty-two, twenty-two A, 22B, 22C, twenty-three, 23A, 23B, twenty-four or twenty-four B, inclusive, of chapter two hundred and sixty-five, or an arrest, investigation or complaint for trafficking of persons under section 50 of chapter 265 shall be withheld from public inspection, except with the consent of a justice of such court where the complaint or indictment is or would be prosecuted.

Said portion of such court record or police record shall not be deemed to be a public record under the provisions of section seven of chapter four.

Except as otherwise provided in this section, it shall be unlawful to publish, disseminate or otherwise disclose the name of any individual identified as an alleged victim of any of the offenses described in the first paragraph. A violation of this section shall be punishable by a fine of not less than two thousand five hundred dollars nor more than ten thousand dollars.

SECTION 25
Attempted extortion

Whoever, verbally or by a written or printed communication, maliciously threatens to accuse another of a crime or offence, or by a verbal or written or printed communication maliciously threatens an injury to the person or property of another, or any police officer or person having the powers of a police officer, or any officer, or employee of any licensing authority who verbally or by a written or printed communication maliciously and unlawfully uses or threatens to use against another the power or authority vested in him, with intent thereby to extort money or any pecuniary advantage, or with intent to compel any person to do any act against his will, shall be punished by imprisonment in the state prison for not more than fifteen years, or in the house of correction for not more than two and one half years, or by a fine of not more than five thousand dollars, or both.

NOTE 1   "The elements of the crime are (1) a malicious threat (2) made to a named person (3) to accuse someone of a crime or to injure someone's person or property (4) with intent to extort money." *Commonwealth v. Miller*, 385 Mass. 521, 526 (1982) (citations omitted).

Note that the threat may be made to anyone.

NOTE 2   "If the threat was wilfully made, with the intent to extort money, it was a malicious act, and the fact that the charge was true would be immaterial." *Commonwealth v. Buckley*, 148 Mass. 27, 28 (1888).

NOTE 3   "The victim's fear confirms the capacity of the threats to create apprehension and is thus probative of defendant's intent to intimidate." *Commonwealth v. Winter*, 9 Mass. App. Ct. 512, 528 (1980).

NOTE 4   The same individual threatening the same victim on two separate occasions over a sum of money owed may be charged twice. *Commonwealth v. DeVincent*, 358 Mass. 592, 594–95 (1971).

NOTE 5   Defendant threatened, unless he was paid money, to tell victim's parents of their sexual relationship and to circulate in victim's neighborhood naked pictures of her. Held, conviction affirmed as the victim would have suffered a blow to her reputation of such magnitude as to cause her severe mental anguish which would constitute injury to the person. "Simply stated, an injury to a person's reputation is an injury to the person." *Commonwealth v. Miller*, 385 Mass. at 526–28.

NOTE 6   "The statute is clear that for a violation, an officer must threaten a person with a power or authority *vested* in the officer. The statute is penal and therefore must be construed narrowly. No arrest power was vested in Kerr at the time of the threat. Accordingly, he should have been found not guilty.

"The legislature may want to consider amending G.L. c. 265, § 25 to make it punishable for a police officer with *apparent authority*, as here, to commit these reprehensible acts." *Commonwealth v. Kerr*, 409 Mass. 284, 287–88 (1991).

SECTION 26
Kidnapping

Whoever, without lawful authority, forcibly or secretly confines or imprisons another person within this common-

wealth against his will, or forcibly carries or sends such person out of this commonwealth, or forcibly seizes and confines or inveigles or kidnaps another person, with intent either to cause him to be secretly confined or imprisoned in this commonwealth against his will, or to cause him to be sent out of this commonwealth against his will or in any way held to service against his will, shall be punished by imprisonment in the state prison for not more than ten years or by a fine of not more than one thousand dollars and imprisonment in jail for not more than two years. Whoever commits any offence described in this section with the intent to extort money or other valuable thing thereby shall be punished by imprisonment in the state prison for life or for any term of years.

Whoever commits any offense described in this section while armed with a firearm, rifle, shotgun, machine gun or assault weapon shall be punished by imprisonment in the state prison for not less than ten years or in the house of correction for not more than two and one-half years. The provisions of the preceding sentence shall not apply to the parent of a child under 18 years of age who takes custody of such child. Whoever commits such offense described in this section while being armed with a firearm, rifle, shotgun, machine gun or assault weapon with the intent to extort money or other valuable thing thereby shall be punished by imprisonment in the state prison for life or for any term of years but not less than 20 years.

Whoever commits any offense described in this section while armed with a dangerous weapon and inflicts serious bodily injury thereby upon another person or who sexually assaults such person shall be punished by imprisonment in the state prison for not less than 25 years. For purposes of this paragraph the term "serious bodily injury" shall mean bodily injury which results in a permanent disfigurement, protracted loss or impairment of a bodily function, limb or organ or substantial risk of death. For purposes of this paragraph, the term "sexual assault" shall mean the commission of any act set forth in sections 13B, 13B½, 13B¾, 13F, 13H, 22, 22A, 22B, 23, 23A, 23B, 24, or 24B.

Whoever, without lawful authority, forcibly or secretly confines or imprisons a child under the age of 16 within the commonwealth against his will or forcibly carries or sends such person out of the commonwealth or forcibly seizes and confines or inveigles or kidnaps a child under the age of 16 with the intent either to cause him to be secretly confined or imprisoned in the commonwealth against his will or to cause him to be sent out of the commonwealth against his will or in any way held to service against his will, shall be punished by imprisonment in the state prison for not more than 15 years. The provisions of the preceding sentence shall not apply to the parent of a child under 16 years of age who takes custody of such child.

NOTE 1   "The act of holding the victim hostage for a period of time after the arrival of the police had interrupted the robbery was beyond those acts which were merely incidental to the commission of the robbery and warranted a guilty verdict on the kidnapping charge." *Commonwealth v. Talbot*, 5 Mass. App. Ct. 857 (1977).

NOTE 2   Victim taken from a bus stop to a room in abandoned dwelling and raped. Court found that there was sufficient evidence concerning the defendant's confinement of the victim at the bus station and while on the way to the abandoned house some distance away to warrant the jury finding that a kidnapping had occurred, separate and apart from the commission of the rape. *Commonwealth v. Vasquez*, 11 Mass. App. Ct. 261, 268 (1981).

2

NOTE 3   "Within the context of the crime of kidnapping, the concept of 'confinement' has been broadly interpreted to mean any restraint of a person's movement." *Commonwealth v. Lent*, 46 Mass. App. Ct. 705, 710 (1999).

NOTE 4a   Minor Victim. "Even though an essential element of the crime is that the taking must be against the victim's will, if a kidnapping victim is of such age as to be incapable of having a recognizable will, the confinement must then be against the will of the parents or legal guardian of the victim." *Commonwealth v. Moyles*, 45 Mass. App. Ct. 350, 354 (1998) (citations, quotation marks and punctuation omitted).

NOTE 4b   Tender Years Doctrine. A 12-year-old child falls within the "tender years doctrine" and cannot consent, as a matter of law, to leaving the custody of his or her parent or legal guardian. The doctrine holds that "a child of tender years is incapable of assenting to forcible removal from the legal custody of his or her parents." *Commonwealth v. Colon*, 431 Mass. 188, 191 (2000) (citation and quotation marks omitted).

NOTE 5   "[T]he first clause of § 26 'states a crime which may be proved by objective facts concerning the use of force and confinement and does not require proving a specific criminal intent.' *Commonwealth v. Saylor*, 27 Mass. App. Ct. 117, 121–122 (1989), citing both *Commonwealth v. Ware*, 375 Mass. at 120, and *Commonwealth v. Dean*, 21 Mass. App. Ct. at 181–182. *See also Commonwealth v. Lent*, 46 Mass. App. Ct. 705, 709 (1999). These authorities unequivocally hold that the Commonwealth need not prove that a defendant had a specific intent to violate the first clause of G.L. c. 265, § 26." *Commonwealth v. Bibby*, 54 Mass. App. Ct. 158, 161 (2002).

NOTE 6   Sex Offender Registry. A conviction or adjudication of delinquency of an offense under this section or of an attempt to commit such an offense (*see* G.L. c. 274, § 6) renders the defendant subject to the requirements of the sex offender registry law. *See* G.L. c. 6, §§ 178C–178Q.

NOTE 7   DNA Database. A conviction of an offense under this section or of an attempt or conspiracy to commit such an offense results in the defendant being required to submit a DNA sample to the state's DNA database. *See* G.L. c. 22E, § 3.

SECTION 26A
Kidnapping of minor by relative

Whoever, being a relative of a child less than eighteen years old, without lawful authority, holds or intends to hold such a child permanently or for a protracted period, or takes or entices such a child from his lawful custodian, or takes or entices from lawful custody any incompetent person or other person entrusted by authority of law to the custody of another person or institution shall be punished by imprisonment in the house of correction for not more than one year or by a fine of up to one thousand dollars, or both. Whoever commits any offence described in this section by taking or holding said child outside the commonwealth or under circumstances which expose the person taken or enticed from lawful custody to a risk which endangers his safety shall be punished by a fine of not more than five thousand dollars, or by imprisonment in the state prison for not more than five years, or by both such fine and imprisonment.

NOTE   "The question before us is whether the phrase 'without lawful authority,' within the meaning of G.L. c. 265, § 26A, includes the action of a parent who takes his or her children from the other parent prior to a court proceeding. The Commonwealth argues that the phrase 'without lawful authority' necessarily includes within its definition the act of a parent who takes his or her children away from the other parent by leaving with the children even if the parent does not act in violation of an existing custody order. The defendant argues that the phrase 'without lawful authority' fails to provide 'fair warning' that the action of a parent in

these circumstances constitutes a crime. We agree with the defendant's argument." *Commonwealth v. Beals*, 405 Mass. 550, 552 (1989).

SECTION 26B
Drugging persons for kidnapping

Whoever applies, administers to or causes to be taken by a person any drug, matter or thing with the intent to stupefy or overpower such person so as to, without lawful authority, forcibly or secretly confine or imprison another person within the commonwealth against his will or to forcibly carry or send such person out of the commonwealth, or to forcibly seize and confine or inveigle or kidnap such person with intent to cause him to be secretly confined or imprisoned in the commonwealth against his will, or to cause him to be sent out of the commonwealth against his will or in any way held to service against his will, shall be punished by imprisonment in the state prison for life or for any term of years not less than ten years. Whoever violates the provisions of this section with the intent to extort money or other valuable thing thereby shall be punished by imprisonment in the state prison for life or for any term of years not less than 15 years.

SECTION 26C
Enticing children

(a) As used in this section, the term "entice" shall mean to lure, induce, persuade, tempt, incite, solicit, coax or invite.

(b) Any one who entices a child under the age of 16, or someone he believes to be a child under the age of 16, to enter, exit or remain within any vehicle, dwelling, building, or other outdoor space with the intent that he or another person will violate section 13B, 13B½, 13B¾, 13F, 13H, 22, 22A, 22B, 23, 23A, 23B, 24 or 24B of chapter 265, section 4A, 16, 28, 29, 29A, 29B, 29C 35A, 53 or 53A of chapter 272, or any offense that has as an element the use or attempted use of force, shall be punished by imprisonment in the state prison for not more than 5 years, or in the house of correction for not more than 2½ years, or by both imprisonment and a fine of not more than $5,000.

NOTE 1   The statute is constitutional. *Commonwealth v. Disler*, 451 Mass. 216 (2008).

NOTE 2   "[W]here a defendant is charged with child enticement, the Commonwealth must prove not only that the defendant enticed a person under the age of sixteen, or someone he believed to be under the age of sixteen, but also that the defendant so acted with the intent to violate one or more of the enumerated criminal statutes. When the statute the defendant is alleged to have intended to violate is a strict liability statute, . . . the Commonwealth is required to prove beyond a reasonable doubt, as an element of the crime of child enticement, that the defendant intended that his advances be directed to an underage person. . . . A defendant may introduce his own evidence [or] rely on evidence presented by the Commonwealth in its case-in-chief . . . that tends to negate proof of the requisite criminal intent, that is, evidence tending to show that he did not intend that the object of his advances be underage. The burden, of course, always remains with the Commonwealth to prove the requisite intent. In this case, . . . there was evidence that, if believed, could have negated the Commonwealth's evidence of the requisite criminal intent." *Commonwealth v. Filopoulos*, 451 Mass. 234, 238–39 (2008) (citations omitted).

NOTE 3   Kidnapping. "The kidnapping statute, G.L. c. 265, § 26 . . . is an offense that has an element which requires the use of force. *Commonwealth v. LaPlante*, 73 Mass. App. Ct. 199, 202–03 (2008).

2

SECTION 26D
Enticement of child under age 18 to engage in prostitution, human trafficking or commercial sexual activity
(Added by 2011 Mass. Acts c. 178, § 22, effective Nov. 21, 2011.)

(a) As used in this section, the term "entice" shall mean to lure, induce, persuade, tempt, incite, solicit, coax or invite.

(b) As used in this section, the term "electronic communication" shall include, but not be limited to, any transfer of signs, signals, writing, images, sounds, data or intelligence of any nature transmitted in whole or in part by a wire, radio, electromagnetic, photo-electronic or photo-optical system.

(c) Whoever, by electronic communication, knowingly entices a child under the age of 18 years, to engage in prostitution in violation of section 50 or section 53A of chapter 272, human trafficking in violation of section 50, 51, 52 or 53 or commercial sexual activity as defined in section 49, or attempts to do so, shall be punished by imprisonment in a house of correction for not more than 2½ years or in the state prison for not more than 5 years or by a fine of not less than $2,500, or by both such fine and imprisonment.

(d) Whoever, after having been convicted of, or adjudicated delinquent by reason of a violation of this section, commits a second or subsequent such violation, shall be punished by imprisonment in the state prison for not less than 5 years and by a fine of not less than $10,000. Such sentence shall not be reduced to less than 5 years, or suspended, nor shall any person convicted under this subsection be eligible for probation, parole, work release or furlough or receive any deduction from the sentence for good conduct until that person has served 5 years of such sentence.

SECTION 27
Kidnapping; venue

A crime described in section twenty-six may be tried in the county where committed or in any county in or to which the person so seized, inveigled, or kidnapped is confined, held, carried or brought; and upon the trial of any such crime, the consent thereto of the person so seized, inveigled, kidnapped or confined shall not be a defence unless the jury finds that such consent was not obtained by fraud or extorted by duress or threats.

NOTE   See Note following G.L. c. 265, § 24A (venue).

SECTION 27A
Kidnapping of minor by relative; venue

A crime described in section twenty-six A may be tried in the county where committed or in a county in or to which the person so taken or enticed is held, carried to, or brought.

NOTE   See Note following G.L. c. 265, § 24A (venue).

SECTION 28
Poison

Whoever mingles poison with food, drink or medicine with intent to kill or injure another person, or wilfully poisons any spring, well or reservoir of water with such intent, shall be punished by imprisonment in the state prison for life or for any term of years.

NOTE 1a   Substances That Have Beneficial Uses. "[I]n addition to 'per se' poisons, there are substances that have beneficial uses, but when used improperly, may have the capacity to act as a poison." *Commonwealth v. Walker*, 442 Mass. 185, 195 (2004) (citations omitted).

SECTION 29
Assault with intent to commit felony

Whoever assaults another with intent to commit a felony shall, if the punishment of such assault is not hereinbefore provided, be punished by imprisonment in the state prison for not more than ten years or by a fine of not more than one thousand dollars and imprisonment in jail for not more than two and one half years.

NOTE   See Notes following G.L. c. 265, § 13A (assault; assault and battery).

SECTION 30
Gross negligence by common carrier

Whoever, having the management or control of or over a steamboat or other public conveyance used for the common carriage of persons, is guilty of gross negligence in or relative to the management or control of such steamboat or other public conveyance, while being so used for the common carriage of persons, shall be punished by a fine of not more than five thousand dollars or by imprisonment in jail for not more than two and one half years.

SECTION 31
Repealed

SECTION 32
Glass; throwing in public streets and beaches

Whoever throws or drops glass on a public way, or on or near a bathing beach, or on a public way, sidewalk or reservation in the immediate neighborhood of a bathing beach, shall be punished by a fine of not more than one hundred dollars or by imprisonment for not more than one month.

SECTION 33
Repealed

SECTION 34
Tattooing body of person by other than qualified physician

Whoever, not being registered as a qualified physician under section two of chapter one hundred and twelve, or corresponding provisions of earlier laws, marks the body of any person by means of tattooing, shall be punished by a fine or not more than three hundred dollars or by imprisonment for not more than one year, or both.

SECTION 35
Throwing or dropping objects onto public way

Whoever willfully or negligently drops, throws or otherwise releases any object, missile or other article onto any way as defined in section one of chapter ninety, the turnpike as defined in clause (b) of section four of chapter three hundred and fifty-four of the acts of nineteen hundred and fifty-two or the tunnels as defined in clause (d) of section one of chapter five hundred and ninety-eight of the acts of nineteen hundred and fifty-eight so that the lives or safety of the public might be endangered shall be punished by a fine of not more than one hundred dollars, or by imprisonment for not more than one year, or both.

SECTION 36
Throwing or dropping objects at sporting events

Any person who willfully drops, throws or otherwise releases any object, missile or other article at any sporting event with the intent to injure any person at such event shall be

2

punished by a fine of not more than five hundred dollars or by imprisonment in the house of correction for not more than one year, or both.

SECTION 37
Violations of constitutional rights

No person, whether or not acting under color of law, shall by force or threat of force, willfully injure, intimidate or interfere with, or attempt to injure, intimidate or interfere with, or oppress or threaten any other person in the free exercise or enjoyment of any right or privilege secured to him by the constitution or laws of the commonwealth or by the constitution or laws of the United States. Any person convicted of violating this provision shall be fined not more than one thousand dollars or imprisoned not more than one year or both; and if bodily injury results, shall be punished by a fine of not more than ten thousand dollars or by imprisonment for not more than ten years, or both.

NOTE   Jurisdiction. "The language [in the second and last sentence of the statute] preceding the semicolon describes a misdemeanor, i.e., an offense comfortably within the jurisdiction of the District Court. . . . The portion of s. 37 after the semicolon . . . provides for more severe punishment—imprisonment up to ten years—should bodily injury result. . . ." The District Court does not have jurisdiction over this. *Commonwealth v. Zawatsky*, 41 Mass. App. Ct. 392, 395–97 (1996).

SECTION 38
Repealed

SECTION 39
Assault or battery for purpose of intimidation due to race, etc.
(Amended by 2011 Mass. Acts c. 93, § 117, effective July 1, 2012; 2011 Mass. Acts c. 199, § 8, effective July 1, 2012.)

(a) Whoever commits an assault or a battery upon a person or damages the real or personal property of a person with the intent to intimidate such person because of such person's race, color, religion, national origin, sexual orientation, gender identity, or disability shall be punished by a fine of not more than five thousand dollars or by imprisonment in a house of correction for not more than two and one-half years, or by both such fine and imprisonment. The court may also order restitution to the victim in any amount up to three times the value of property damage sustained by the owners of such property. For the purposes of this section, the term "disability" shall have the same meaning as "handicap" as defined in subsection 17 of section one of chapter one hundred and fifty-one B; provided, however, that for purposes of this section, the term "disability" shall not include any condition primarily resulting from the use of alcohol or a controlled substance as defined in section one of chapter ninety-four C.

(b) Whoever commits a battery in violation of this section and which results in bodily injury shall be punished by a fine of not more than ten thousand dollars or by imprisonment in the state prison for not more than five years, or by both such fine and imprisonment. Whoever commits any offense described in this section while armed with a firearm, shotgun, rifle, machine gun or assault weapon shall be punished by imprisonment in the state prison for not more than ten years or in the house of correction for not more than two and one-half years. For purposes of this section, "bodily injury" shall mean substantial impairment of the physical condition, including, but not limited to, any burn, fracture of any bone,

subdural hematoma, injury to any internal organ, or any injury which occurs as the result of repeated harm to any bodily function or organ, including human skin.

There shall be a surcharge of one hundred dollars on a fine assessed against a defendant convicted of a violation of this section; provided, however, that moneys from such surcharge shall be delivered forthwith to the treasurer of the commonwealth and deposited in the Diversity Awareness Education Trust Fund established under the provisions of section thirty-nine Q of chapter ten. In the case of convictions for multiple offenses, said surcharge shall be assessed for each such conviction.

A person convicted under the provisions of this section shall complete a diversity awareness program designed by the secretary of the executive office of public safety in consultation with the Massachusetts commission against discrimination and approved by the chief justice of the trial court. A person so convicted shall complete such program prior to release from incarceration or prior to completion of the terms of probation, whichever is applicable.

NOTE 1   "[W]e analyze G.L. c. 265, § 39, to determine whether the racial animus necessary for conviction under the statute must be quantified. . . . By requiring proof that a defendant's actions were specifically motivated by racial animus, the Legislature has ensured that the 'hate crime' classification is not applied to individuals whose actions do not fall within the purview of G.L. c. 265, § 39—that is to say, individuals who committed an assault or a battery in circumstances where the race of the victim did not play a role in the perpetration of the crime." *Commonwealth v. Kelly*, 470 Mass. 682, 688, 689–90 (2015) (citations omitted).

NOTE 2   Civil Remedy. *See* G.L. c. 266, § 127B.

SECTION 40
Willful or reckless cause of serious bodily injury to participants in physical exercise training programs

Whoever, having the direct management or direct control over the conduct of physical exercise as part of a course of study or training program at any public or private institution, agency or entity, willfully, wantonly and recklessly causes serious bodily injury to a person participating in a course of study or training program involving physical exercise, shall be punished by a fine of not more than five thousand dollars or by imprisonment in a jail or house of correction for not more than two and one-half years or both.

For the purposes of this section "serious bodily injury" shall mean bodily injury which creates a substantial risk of death or which involves either total disability or the loss or substantial impairment of some bodily function for a substantial period of time.

SECTION 41
Sentences for violation of this chapter; inclusion in record of reasons for non-imposition of sentence of imprisonment

In sentencing a person for a violation of any provision of this chapter, the penalty for which includes imprisonment, a judge sitting in superior court or in a jury of six session who does not impose such sentence of imprisonment shall include in the record of the case specific reasons for not imposing a sentence of imprisonment. Notwithstanding any general or special law to the contrary, the record of such reasons shall be a public record.

SECTION 42
Use of radio or boom box without using earphones on public conveyance; sale of evidence at public auction

Whoever uses a radio or boom box, so-called, or similar broadcasting equipment without the use of earphones or other apparatus on a public conveyance used for the common carriage of persons, shall be punished by a fine of not less than one hundred dollars nor more than five hundred dollars or by imprisonment for not more than one month. Evidence seized pursuant to this section shall be sold at public auction and the proceeds therefrom may be applied against outstanding fines and court costs.

SECTION 43
Stalking
(Amended by 2014 Mass. Acts c. 284, § 85, effective Aug. 11, 2014.)

(a) Whoever (1) willfully and maliciously engages in a knowing pattern of conduct or series of acts over a period of time directed at a specific person which seriously alarms or annoys that person and would cause a reasonable person to suffer substantial emotional distress, and (2) makes a threat with the intent to place the person in imminent fear of death or bodily injury, shall be guilty of the crime of stalking and shall be punished by imprisonment in the state prison for not more than 5 years or by a fine of not more than $1,000, or imprisonment in the house of correction for not more than 2½ years or by both such fine and imprisonment. The conduct, acts or threats described in this subsection shall include, but not be limited to, conduct, acts or threats conducted by mail or by use of a telephonic or telecommunication device or electronic communication device including, but not limited to, any device that transfers signs, signals, writing, images, sounds, data, or intelligence of any nature transmitted in whole or in part by a wire, radio, electromagnetic, photo-electronic or photo-optical system, including, but not limited to, electronic mail, internet communications, instant messages or facsimile communications.

(b) Whoever commits the crime of stalking in violation of a temporary or permanent vacate, restraining, or no-contact order or judgment issued pursuant to sections eighteen, thirty-four B, or thirty-four C of chapter two hundred and eight; or section thirty-two of chapter two hundred and nine; or sections three, four, or five of chapter two hundred and nine A; or sections fifteen or twenty of chapter two hundred and nine C or a protection order issued by another jurisdiction; or a temporary restraining order or preliminary or permanent injunction issued by the superior court, shall be punished by imprisonment in a jail or the state prison for not less than one year and not more than five years. No sentence imposed under the provisions of this subsection shall be less than a mandatory minimum term of imprisonment of one year.

A prosecution commenced hereunder shall not be placed on file or continued without a finding, and the sentence imposed upon a person convicted of violating any provision of this subsection shall not be reduced to less than the mandatory minimum term of imprisonment as established herein, nor shall said sentence of imprisonment imposed upon any person be suspended or reduced until such person shall have served said mandatory term of imprisonment.

A person convicted of violating any provision of this subsection shall not, until he shall have served the mandatory minimum term of imprisonment established herein, be eligible for probation, parole, furlough, work release or receive any deduction from his sentence for good conduct under sections one hundred and twenty-nine, one hundred and twenty-nine C and one hundred and twenty-nine D of chapter one hundred and twenty-seven; provided, however, that the commissioner of correction may, on the recommendation of the warden, superintendent, or other person in charge of a correctional institution, grant to said offender a temporary release in the custody of an officer of such institution for the following purposes only: to attend the funeral of next of kin or spouse; to visit a critically ill close relative or spouse; or to obtain emergency medical services unavailable at said institution. The provisions of section eighty-seven of chapter two hundred and seventy-six relating to the power of the court to place certain offenders on probation shall not apply to any person 18 years of age or over charged with a violation of this subsection. The provisions of section thirty-one of chapter two hundred and seventy-nine shall not apply to any person convicted of violating any provision of this subsection.

(c) Whoever, after having been convicted of the crime of stalking, commits a second or subsequent such crime shall be punished by imprisonment in a jail or the state prison for not less than two years and not more than ten years. No sentence imposed under the provisions of this subsection shall be less than a mandatory minimum term of imprisonment of two years.

A prosecution commenced hereunder shall not be placed on file or continued without a finding, and the sentence imposed upon a person convicted of violating any provision of this subsection shall not be reduced to less than the mandatory minimum term of imprisonment as established herein, nor shall said sentence of imprisonment imposed upon any person be suspended or reduced until such person shall have served said mandatory term of imprisonment.

A person convicted of violating any provision of this subsection shall not, until he shall have served the mandatory minimum term of imprisonment established herein, be eligible for probation, parole, furlough, work release or receive any deduction from his sentence for good conduct under sections one hundred and twenty-nine, one hundred and twenty-nine C and one hundred and twenty-nine D of chapter one hundred and twenty-seven; provided, however, that the commissioner of correction may, on the recommendation of the warden, superintendent, or other person in charge of a correctional institution, grant to said offender a temporary release in the custody of an officer of such institution for the following purposes only: to attend the funeral of next of kin or spouse; to visit a critically ill close relative or spouse; or to obtain emergency medical services unavailable at said institution. The provisions of section eighty-seven of chapter two hundred and seventy-six relating to the power of the court to place certain offenders on probation shall not apply to any person 18 years of age or over charged with a violation of this subsection. The provisions of section thirty-one of chapter two hundred and seventy-nine shall not apply to any person convicted of violating any provision of this section.

NOTE 1a   "In a case brought under G.L. c. 265, § 43 (1994 ed.), the Commonwealth is entitled to present to a jury admissible evidence of the totality of the defendant's conduct toward the victim. That the content of the letters or other communications may offend the sensibilities of the jury does not render the communications unduly prejudicial in view of the statutory definition of harassment, which requires the Commonwealth to prove the victim's alarm or annoyance, and the likelihood that a reasonable person

2

in the victim's position would suffer substantial emotional distress. *See* G.L. c. 265, § 43(d)." *Commonwealth v. Matsos*, 421 Mass. 391, 393 n.3 (1995).

NOTE 1b   Intent to Commit Stalking. "The defendant asserts that the Commonwealth failed to prove that he intended to commit the felony of stalking on the night he broke into and entered the victim's home. Essentially, he argues that it is legally impossible to commit a stalking during the course of a single event because that crime requires a pattern of conduct or series of acts involving more than two incidents of harassment or following . . . .

"... The trial judge properly and thoroughly instructed the jury on this point, stating twice that 'what the Commonwealth has to prove is that the defendant specifically intended to commit an act *which in the circumstances, when considered in conjunction with other actions of the defendant,* would constitute an act of stalking.'" *Commonwealth v. Bibbo*, 50 Mass. App. Ct. 648, 652–54 (2001) (emphasis in original).

NOTE 2   Facebook Posting. "This case raises the question whether a posting to the Web site Facebook may constitute a threat within the meaning of the stalking statute, G.L. c. 265, § 43(a). We conclude that . . . content posted to Facebook may qualify as a threat as defined in the statute." *Commonwealth v. Walters*, 472 Mass. 680, 681 (2015).

NOTE 3   Subsection d of Section 43 was deleted by 1997 Mass. Acts c. 238, § 2.

NOTE 4   Jurisdiction. *See* G.L. c. 277, § 62B.

NOTE 5   Lesser included offense. "[Section] 43(a) is a lesser included offense of § 43(b)." *Edge v. Commonwealth*, 451 Mass. 74, 76 (2008).

NOTE 6   Double Jeopardy. "[A] prosecution under § 43(b) implicates double jeopardy concerns if the Commonwealth relies on conduct previously the subject of [a defendant's] convictions of violating [a] 209A order." *Edge v. Commonwealth*, 451 Mass. 74, 78 (2008).

SECTION 43A
Criminal harassment

(a) Whoever willfully and maliciously engages in a knowing pattern of conduct or series of acts over a period of time directed at a specific person, which seriously alarms that person and would cause a reasonable person to suffer substantial emotional distress, shall be guilty of the crime of criminal harassment and shall be punished by imprisonment in a house of correction for not more than 2½ years or by a fine of not more than $1,000, or by both such fine and imprisonment. The conduct or acts described in this paragraph shall include, but not be limited to, conduct or acts conducted by mail or by use of a telephonic or telecommunication device or electronic communication device including, but not limited to, any device that transfers signs, signals, writing, images, sounds, data or intelligence of any nature transmitted in whole or in part by a wire, radio, electromagnetic, photo-electronic or photo-optical system, including, but not limited to, electronic mail, internet communications, instant messages or facsimile communications.

(b) Whoever, after having been convicted of the crime of criminal harassment, commits a second or subsequent such crime, or whoever commits the crime of criminal harassment having previously been convicted of a violation of section 43, shall be punished by imprisonment in a house of correction for not more than two and one-half years or by imprisonment in the state prison for not more than ten years.

NOTE 1a   Constitutionality. "[W]e believe the Legislature, in carefully crafting the statute, intended the statute to be applied solely to constitutionally unprotected speech. Any attempt to pun-

ish an individual for speech not encompassed within the 'fighting words' doctrine (or within any other constitutionally unprotected category of speech) would of course offend our Federal and State Constitutions." *Commonwealth v. Welch*, 444 Mass. 80, 99 (2005).

NOTE 1b   Speech as Conduct. "[T]he criminal harassment statute was intended to proscribe harassing conduct encompassing 'speech' or 'statements' . . ." *Commonwealth v. Welch*, 444 Mass. 80, 87 (2005).

NOTE 1c   Cyberharassment. "[A] pattern of harassing conduct that includes both communications made directly to the targets of the harassment and false communications made to third parties through Internet postings solely for the purpose of encouraging those parties also to engage in harassing conduct toward the targets [is] constitutionally proscribed by the statute." *Commonwealth v. Johnson*, 470 Mass. 300, 301 (2014).

NOTE 2a   "[P]attern of conduct or series of acts." "We determine today that the phrase 'pattern of conduct or series of acts' requires the Commonwealth to prove three or more incidents of harassment . . ." *Commonwealth v. Welch*, 444 Mass. 80, 99 (2005). *See also Commonwealth v. Robinson*, 444 Mass. 102 (2005) (more than three incidences of "glaring" and threatening words sufficient to show harassment); *Commonwealth v. Paton*, 63 Mass. App. Ct. 215 (2005) (visiting victim's place of employment and asking for her more than twenty times sufficient to show harassment).

NOTE 2b   Subjective and Objective Components. "There are also both subjective and objective components to the harm to be proved: the acts must 'seriously alarm' the person to whom they are directed. G.L. c. 265, § 43A(a). If the acts would not 'cause a reasonable person to suffer substantial emotional distress,' the subjective reaction is insufficient." *Commonwealth v. Braica*, 68 Mass. App. Ct. 244, 246 (2007) (citations omitted).

NOTE 3   Malice. "The defendant made no explicit threats and, after that first evening in the bar, never even spoke to the victim, so there is no verbal basis from which to assess his conduct. However, the defendant' behavior alone was sufficient in this case for a rational trier of fact to conclude that the defendant had acted maliciously. The defendant's staring at the victim in the bar without speaking and then unexpectedly appearing in proximity to her in other places had an ominous, menacing, even sinister quality that caused the victim anxiety and apprehension. Conduct 'directed at a specific person, which seriously alarms that person,' is proscribed by the criminal harassment statute. See G.L. c. 265, § 43A(a). The defendant's acts were injurious without justification and demonstrated cruel, hostile, and retaliatory or revengeful purposes. Evaluated under the foregoing principles, they constitute legally malicious conduct. The defendant's persistence in initiating such encounters even after he was advised that the victim found them alarming further illustrates that his purpose was not benign." *Commonwealth v. Paton*, 63 Mass. App. Ct. 215, 219–20 (2005). *Contra Commonwealth v. Clemens*, 61 Mass. App. Ct. 915 (2004) (although defendant visited victim's places of employment five times, the statute was violated only by the fifth visit, where an intimation of anger demonstrated malice).

NOTE 4   Substantial Emotional Distress. "The judge's instruction could have been interpreted by the jury as meaning either that anything even slightly 'more than trifling or passing emotional distress' would qualify as 'substantial,' or it could have been understood as a mere comparison between the two types of emotional distress from which they would understand that mere 'trifling or passing emotional distress' would not suffice. To that extent the instruction was ambiguous and, if the first interpretation were adopted, erroneous. To describe 'substantial emotional distress' as anything at all above 'trifling or passing' gives the word 'substantial' less than its traditional meaning, i.e., 'considerable in amount, value, or worth,' Webster's Third New Int'l Dictionary . . . 2280 [(1993)], or 'of real worth and importance; of considerable value . . . . Synonymous with material.' Black's Law Dictionary 1428 (6th ed. 1990).

"While the judge's formulation of this portion of the instruction was error, it did not create a substantial risk of a miscarriage of justice because it did not affect the defense that the defendant chose to pursue . . . .

"In the future, judges should define 'substantial emotional distress' more specifically, in line with the dictionary definition, detailed supra, emphasizing that emotional distress that is merely trifling or passing is not enough to satisfy this element, but must be markedly greater than that commonly experienced as part of ordinary living." *Commonwealth v. Robinson*, 444 Mass. 102, 106, 108 (2005).

SECTION 44
Assault and battery on child to join gang

Whoever commits an assault and battery on a child under the age of eighteen for the purpose of causing or coercing such child to join or participate in a criminal conspiracy in violation of section seven of chapter two hundred and seventy-four, including but not limited to a criminal street gang or other organization of three or more persons which has a common name, identifying sign or symbol and whose members individually or collectively engage in criminal activity, shall, for the first offense, be punished by imprisonment in the state prison for not less than three nor more than five years or by imprisonment in the house of correction for not more than two and one-half years; and for a second or subsequent offense by imprisonment in the state prison for not less than five nor more than ten years.

SECTION 45
Lifetime parole

Any person who commits indecent assault and battery on a child under 14 under section 13B, indecent assault and battery on a mentally retarded person under the first paragraph of section 13F or indecent assault and battery on a person who has attained the age of 14 under section 13H may, in addition to the term of imprisonment authorized by such section, be punished by a term of community parole supervision for life to be served under the jurisdiction of the parole board, as set forth in section 133C of chapter 127. Any person who commits rape under section 22; rape of a child under 16 with force under section 22A; rape and abuse of a child under section 23; assault with intent to commit rape under section 24; assault of a child under 16 with intent to commit rape under section 24B; kidnapping a child under the age of 16 under section 26; drugging persons for sexual intercourse under section 3 of chapter 272; unnatural and lascivious acts with a child under 16 under section 35A of said chapter 272; or commits an attempt to violate any such section pursuant to section 6 of chapter 274, shall, except as provided for in section 18 of chapter 275, and in addition to the term of imprisonment authorized by such section, receive a sentence of community parole supervision for life to be served under the jurisdiction of the parole board, as set forth in section 133D of chapter 127. Any person convicted of violating section 13B, 13B½, 13B¾, 13F, 13H, 22, 22A, 22B, 22C, 23, 23A, 24, 24B or 26 of this chapter or of an attempt to violate any of such sections pursuant to section 6 of chapter 274, after one or more prior convictions of indecent assault and battery, rape, assault with intent to commit rape, unnatural and lascivious acts, drugging for sex, kidnap or of any offense which is the same as or necessarily includes the same elements of said offense shall, in addition to the term of imprisonment authorized by such section, be punished by a term of community parole supervision for life, to be served under the jurisdiction of the parole board, as set forth in said section 133D of said chapter 127. The sentence of community parole supervision for life shall commence immediately upon the expiration of the term of imprisonment imposed upon such person by the court or upon such person's release from probation supervision or upon discharge from commitment to the treatment center pursuant to section 9 of chapter 123A, whichever first occurs.

NOTE 1   CPSL Is Unconstitutional. "The issue presented on appeal is whether community parole supervision for life (CPSL) violates our separation of powers doctrine, articulated in art. 30 of the Massachusetts Declaration of Rights, by improperly delegating to the parole board, an entity of the executive branch, the exercise of the judicial power to impose sentences. We conclude that CPSL grants to the parole board a quintessential judicial power, the power to determine whether a defendant should be sentenced to additional terms of imprisonment, and therefore violates art. 30. *Commonwealth v. Cole*, 468 Mass. 294, 295 (2014).

NOTE 2   CPSL Sentences Must Be Vacated. "Therefore, we strike [G.L. c. 127,] § 133D in its entirety and order that CPSL sentences, whether imposed pursuant to G.L. c. 6, § 178H(a), or G.L. c. 265, § 45, be vacated." *Commonwealth v. Cole*, 468 Mass. 294, 295, 308–09 (2014).

SECTION 46
Taking from deceased victim's estate prohibited

The court shall prohibit any person charged with the unlawful killing of the decedent from taking from the decedent's estate through its distribution and disposition, including property held between the person charged and the decedent in joint tenancy or by tenancy in the entirety. The court shall consider any person convicted of the unlawful killing of the decedent as predeceasing the decedent for the purpose of distribution and disposition of the decedent's estate including property held between the person charged and the decedent in joint tenancy or by tenancy in the entirety. The bar to succession shall apply only to murder in the first degree, murder in the second degree, or manslaughter; it shall not include vehicular homicide or negligent manslaughter in the death of the decedent. No court shall distribute the accused's share of the decedent's assets until a verdict or finding on the charge has been rendered in open court. If the court determines the accused not guilty of the unlawful killing of the decedent, the accused may take by decent or distribution from the decedent's estate under law. The provisions of this section and any order of a court entered pursuant thereto, shall not have any effect on title to real property, except against the person charged with an offense to which this section applies, or that person's heirs and devisees, until a memorandum that recites the name of that person is recorded in the manner provided in section 15 of chapter 184, and no order so entered shall divest any person who has given fair consideration for any interest in such property before such recording.

SECTION 47
Global positioning system device to be worn by certain sex offender probationers

Any person who is placed on probation for any offense listed within the definition of "sex offense," a "sex offense involving a child," or a "sexually violent offense," as defined in section 178C of chapter 6, shall, as a requirement of any term of probation, wear a global positioning system device, or any comparable device, administered by the commissioner of probation, at all times for the length of his probation for any such offense. The commissioner of probation, in addition to any other conditions, shall establish defined geographic exclusion zones including, but not limited to, the areas in and around the victim's residence, place of employment and school and other areas defined to minimize the probationer's contact with children, if applicable. If the probationer enters an excluded zone, as defined by the terms of his probation, the probationer's location data shall be immediately transmitted to the police department in the municipality wherein the violation occurred and the commissioner of probation, by telephone, electronic beeper, paging device or other appropriate means. If the commissioner or the probationer's probation officer has probable cause to believe that the probationer has violated this term of his probation, the commissioner or the probationer's probation officer shall arrest the probationer pursuant to section 3 of chapter 279. Otherwise, the commissioner shall cause a notice of surrender to be issued to such probationer.

The fees incurred by installing, maintaining and operating the global positioning system device, or comparable device, shall be paid by the probationer. If an offender establishes his inability to pay such fees, the court may waive them.

NOTE 1   Not Applicable to Pretrial Probation. "We conclude that G.L. c. 265, § 47, does not apply to persons placed on probation prior to trial and prior to conviction or entry of a plea of guilty or admission to facts sufficient for a finding of guilt (admission to sufficient facts). Because the defendant, with his consent, has been placed on pretrial probation under G.L. c. 276, § 87, without a guilty plea or admission to sufficient facts, it follows that G.L. c. 265, § 47, has no application to him." *Commonwealth v. Raposo*, 453 Mass. 739, 740 (2009).

NOTE 2   Not Applicable to CWOF. "We conclude that § 47 does not apply to cases that are continued without a finding, and that a judge is not required in such cases to order that a defendant wear a global positioning system device that will monitor his or her whereabouts (GPS monitoring) as a condition of probation." *Commonwealth v. Doe*, 473 Mass. 76, 77 (2015).

NOTE 3   Applicable to Postconviction Probation. "We conclude that G.L. c. 265, § 47, by its terms applies to the defendant, because he was 'placed on' postconviction probation following the statute's effective date of December 20, 2006. We further conclude, however, that G.L. c. 265, § 47, is punitive in effect, and under the ex post facto provisions of the United States and Massachusetts Constitutions, may not be applied to persons who are placed on probation for qualifying sex offenses committed before the statute's effective date." *Commonwealth v. Cory*, 454 Mass. 559, 560 (2009).

NOTE 4   GPS Monitoring Not Discretionary. "[W]e conclude that G.L. c. 265, § 47, affords judges no discretion to decide whether GPS monitoring should apply in any particular set of circumstances; where a defendant is convicted of a qualifying offense and is sentenced to a term of probation, the sentencing judge must impose GPS monitoring as a condition of that probation." *Commonwealth v. Guzman*, 469 Mass. 492, 496 (2014).

NOTE 5   GPS Monitoring Not Mandatory for Juveniles. "The issue presented in this case is whether a Juvenile Court judge is required under G.L. c. 265, § 47, to order a juvenile to wear a global positioning system device that will monitor his whereabouts (GPS monitoring) as a condition of probation where a juvenile is adjudicated delinquent and placed on probation for committing a 'sex offense,' a 'sex offense involving a child,' or a 'sexually violent offense,' as defined in G.L. c. 6, § 178C. We conclude that, when § 47 is read in its entirety, it is not apparent that the Legislature intended to apply mandatory GPS monitoring to juveniles placed on probation as a result of having been adjudicated delinquent and thereby eliminate the discretion granted to Ju-

venile Court judges to render individualized dispositions consistent with the best interests of the child. We also conclude that, where the Legislature has established the statutory principle that, 'as far as practicable, [juveniles] shall be treated, not as criminals, but as children in need of aid, encouragement and guidance,' G.L. c. 119, § 53, we will not interpret a statute affecting the delinquency adjudications of juveniles to conflict with this principle in the absence of clear legislative intent. Here, where such clear legislative intent is absent, we conclude that a Juvenile Court judge retains the discretion, based on the totality of the circumstances, to determine whether GPS monitoring should be imposed as a condition of probation for a juvenile who is adjudicated delinquent after committing a sex offense." *Commonwealth v. Hanson H.*, 464 Mass. 807, 807–08 (2013).

SECTION 48

Sex offenders prohibited from ice cream truck vending
(Added by 2010 Mass. Acts c. 256, § 119, effective May 4, 2012.)

A sex offender, as defined by section 178C of chapter 6, who engages in ice cream truck vending, as defined in section 25 of chapter 270, shall be punished by imprisonment in the house of correction for not more than 2½ years or by a fine of $1,000, or by both such fine and imprisonment. A police officer or officer authorized to serve criminal process may arrest, without a warrant, any person whom he has probable cause to believe has violated this section.

SECTION 49

Definitions applicable to Secs. 50 to 51
(Added by 2011 Mass. Acts c. 178, § 23, effective Nov. 21, 2011.)

As used in sections 50 to 51, inclusive, the following words shall, unless the context clearly requires otherwise, have the following meanings:

"Commercial sexual activity", any sexual act on account of which anything of value is given, promised to or received by any person.

"Financial harm", a detrimental position in relation to wealth, property or other monetary benefits that occurs as a result of another person's illegal act including, but not limited to, extortion under by section 25, a violation of section 49 of chapter 271 or illegal employment contracts.

"Forced services", services performed or provided by a person that are obtained or maintained by another person who: (i) causes or threatens to cause serious harm to any person; (ii) physically restrains or threatens to physically restrain another person; (iii) abuses or threatens to abuse the law or legal process; (iv) knowingly destroys, conceals, removes, confiscates or possesses any actual or purported passport or other immigration document, or any other actual or purported government identification document, of another person; (v) engages in extortion under section 25; or (vi) causes or threatens to cause financial harm to any person.

"Services", acts performed by a person under the supervision of or for the benefit of another including, but not limited to, commercial sexual activity and sexually-explicit performances.

"Sexually-explicit performance", an unlawful live or public act or show intended to arouse or satisfy the sexual desires or appeal to the prurient interests of patrons.

SECTION 50

Trafficking of persons for sexual servitude; persons under 18; trafficking by business entities; penalties; tort actions by victims
(Added by 2011 Mass. Acts c. 178, § 23, effective Nov. 21, 2011.)

(a) Whoever knowingly: (i) subjects, or attempts to subject, or recruits, entices, harbors, transports, provides or obtains by any means, or attempts to recruit, entice, harbor, transport, provide or obtain by any means, another person to engage in commercial sexual activity, a sexually-explicit performance or the production of unlawful pornography in violation of chapter 272, or causes a person to engage in commercial sexual activity, a sexually-explicit performance or the production of unlawful pornography in violation of said chapter 272; or (ii) benefits, financially or by receiving anything of value, as a result of a violation of clause (i), shall be guilty of the crime of trafficking of persons for sexual servitude and shall be punished by imprisonment in the state prison for not less than 5 years but not more than 20 years and by a fine of not more than $25,000. Such sentence shall not be reduced to less than 5 years, or suspended, nor shall any person convicted under this section be eligible for probation, parole, work release or furlough or receive any deduction from his sentence for good conduct until he shall have served 5 years of such sentence. No prosecution commenced under this section shall be continued without a finding or placed on file.

(b) Whoever commits the crime of trafficking of persons for sexual servitude upon a person under 18 years of age shall be punished by imprisonment in the state prison for life or for any term of years, but not less than 5 years. No person convicted under this subsection shall be eligible for probation, parole, work release or furlough or receive any deduction from his sentence for good conduct until he shall have served 5 years of such sentence.

(c) A business entity that commits trafficking of persons for sexual servitude shall be punished by a fine of not more than $1,000,000.

(d) A victim of subsection (a) may bring an action in tort in the superior court in any county wherein a violation of subsection (a) occurred, where the plaintiff resides or where the defendant resides or has a place of business. Any business entity that knowingly aids or is a joint venturer in trafficking of persons for sexual servitude shall be civilly liable for an offense under this section.

NOTE   **Statute Constitutional.** "[W]e conclude that G.L. c. 265, § 50, is constitutional.

"[W]e conclude that because G.L. c. 265, § 50(a), is sufficiently clear and definite, it did not violate the defendants' rights to due process under the Fifth and Fourteenth Amendments and art. 12. The words of the statute have commonly accepted and readily understood meanings in the English language, and the phrase 'commercial sexual activity' is amply defined in G.L. c. 265, § 49." *Commonwealth v. McGhee*, 472 Mass. 405, 408, 415 (2015).

SECTION 51
Trafficking of persons to forced servitude; victims under 18; trafficking by business entities; penalties; tort actions by victims
(Added by 2011 Mass. Acts c. 178, § 23, effective Nov. 21, 2011.)

(a) Whoever knowingly: (i) subjects, or attempts to subject, another person to forced services, or recruits, entices, harbors, transports, provides or obtains by any means, or attempts to recruit, entice, harbor, transport, provide or obtain by any means, another person, intending or knowing that such person will be subjected to forced services; or (ii) benefits, financially or by receiving anything of value, as a result of a violation of clause (i), shall be guilty of trafficking of persons for forced services and shall be punished by imprisonment in the state prison for not less than 5 years but not more than 20 years and by a fine of not more than $25,000. Such sentence shall not be reduced to less than 5 years, or suspended, nor shall any person convicted under this section be eligible for probation, parole, work release or furlough or receive any deduction from his sentence for good conduct until he shall have served 5 years of such sentence. No prosecution commenced under this section shall be continued without a finding or placed on file.

(b) Whoever commits the crime of trafficking of persons for forced services upon a person under 18 years of age shall be punished by imprisonment in the state prison for life or for any term of years, but not less than 5 years. No person convicted under this subsection shall be eligible for probation, parole, work release or furlough or receive any deduction from his sentence for good conduct until he shall have served 5 years of such sentence.

(c) A business entity that commits trafficking of persons for forced labor services shall be punished by a fine of not more than $1,000,000.

(d) A victim of subsection (a) may bring an action in tort in the superior court in any county wherein a violation of subsection (a) occurred, where the plaintiff resides or where the defendant resides or has a place of business. Any business entity that knowingly aids or is a joint venturer in trafficking of person for forced labor or services shall be civilly liable for an offense under this section.

SECTION 52
Subsequent violations of Sec. 50 or 51; penalties; evidence of prior adjudication or conviction
(Added by 2011 Mass. Acts c. 178, § 23, effective Nov. 21, 2011.)

(a) Whoever, after having been convicted of or adjudicated delinquent by reason of a violation of section 50 or 51, commits a second or subsequent violation of either section 50 or 51, shall be punished by imprisonment in the state prison for life or for any term of years, but not less than 10 years. Such sentence shall not be reduced to less than 10 years, or suspended, nor shall any person convicted under this section be eligible for probation, parole, work release or furlough or receive any deduction from his sentence for good conduct until he shall have served 10 years of such sentence. No prosecutions commenced under this section shall be continued without a finding or placed on file.

(b) In any prosecution commenced pursuant to this section, introduction into evidence of a prior adjudication or conviction or a prior finding of sufficient facts by either certified attested copies of original court papers, or certified attested copies of the defendant's biographical and informational data from records of the department of probation, any jail or house of correction or the department of correction, shall be prima facie evidence that the defendant before the court has been convicted previously by a court of the commonwealth or any other jurisdiction. Such documentation shall be self-authenticating and admissible, after the commonwealth has established the defendant's guilt on the primary offense, as evidence in any court of the commonwealth to prove the defendant's prior conviction described therein. The commonwealth shall not be required to introduce any additional corroborating evidence or live witness testimony to establish the validity of such prior conviction.

2

SECTION 53
Organ trafficking, victims under 18, penalties
(Added by 2011 Mass. Acts c. 178, § 23, effective Nov. 21, 2011.)

(a) Whoever: (i) recruits, entices, harbors, transports, delivers or obtains by any means, another person, intending or knowing that an organ, tissue or other body part of such person will be removed for sale, against such person's will; or (ii) knowingly receives anything of value, directly or indirectly as a result of a violation of clause (i) shall be guilty of organ trafficking and punished by imprisonment in the state prison for not more than 15 years or by a fine of not more than $50,000, or both.

(b) Whoever commits the crime of organ trafficking upon a person under 18 years of age shall be punished by imprisonment in the state prison for 5 years. Such sentence shall not be reduced to less than 5 years, or suspended, nor shall any person convicted under this subsection be eligible for probation, parole, work release, or furlough or receive any deduction from such sentence for good conduct until having served 5 years of such sentence.

SECTION 54
Transmittal of fines to state treasurer
(Added by 2011 Mass. Acts c. 178, § 23, effective Nov. 21, 2011.)

The court shall transmit fines collected pursuant to sections 50 and 51 to the state treasurer. The treasurer shall deposit such fines into the Victims of Human Trafficking Trust Fund established in section 66A of chapter 10.

SECTION 55
Forfeiture of funds use to facilitate violation of Sec. 50 or 51; victim restitution
(Added by 2011 Mass. Acts c. 178, § 23, effective Nov. 21, 2011.)

All monies furnished or intended to be furnished by any person in exchange for forced labor or services or sexual servitude, and all monies used or intended to be used to facilitate any violation of section 50 or 51 shall be subject to forfeiture to the commonwealth and shall be made available by the court to any victim ordered restitution by the court pursuant to section 3 of chapter 258B.

SECTION 56
Property subject to forfeiture resulting from violations of Secs. 50 or 51; procedure; exceptions; records; preliminary orders for seizure; referral to office of seized property management; homestead exemptions; recording of certificate of fact of final judgment
(Added by 2011 Mass. Acts c. 178, § 23, effective Nov. 21, 2011.)

(a) The following property shall be subject to forfeiture to the commonwealth and all property rights therein shall be in the commonwealth:

(i) all conveyances, including aircraft, vehicles or vessels used, or intended for use, to transport, conceal or otherwise facilitate a violation of section 50 or 51;

(ii) all books, records and research, including microfilm, tapes and data which are used, or intended for use, in violation of section 50 or 51;

(iii) all negotiable instruments, securities or other things of value furnished or intended to be furnished by any person in exchange for forced labor or services or sexual servitude, all proceeds traceable to such an exchange, including real estate and any other thing of value, and all negotiable instruments and securities used or intended to be used to facilitate any violation of section 50 or 51; and

(iv) all real property, including any right, title and interest in the whole of any lot or tract of land and any appurtenances or improvements thereto, which is used in any manner or part to commit or to facilitate any violation of section 50 or 51.

No forfeiture under this section shall extinguish a perfected security interest held by a creditor in a conveyance or in any real property at the time of the filing of the forfeiture action.

(b) Property subject to forfeiture pursuant to clauses (i) to (iv), inclusive, of subsection (a) shall, upon motion of the attorney general or district attorney, be declared forfeit by any court having jurisdiction over said property or having final jurisdiction over any related criminal proceeding brought under this section.

(c) The court shall order forfeiture of all conveyances and real property subject to forfeiture under this section, except as follows:

(i) no conveyance used by any person as a common carrier in the transaction of business as a common carrier shall be forfeited unless it shall appear that the owner or other person in charge of such conveyance was a consenting party or privy to a violation of section 50 or 51;

(ii) no conveyance shall be forfeited by reason of any act or omission established by the owner thereof to have been committed or omitted by any person other than such owner while such conveyance was unlawfully in the possession of a person other than the owner in violation of the criminal laws of the United States, of the commonwealth or of any state; and

(iii) no conveyance or real property shall be subject to forfeiture unless the owner thereof knew or should have known that such conveyance or real property was used in violation of section 50 or 51.

(d) A district attorney or the attorney general may petition the superior court in the name of the commonwealth in the nature of a proceeding in rem to order forfeiture of a conveyance, real property or other things of value subject to forfeiture under subsection (a). Such petition shall be filed in the court having jurisdiction over the conveyance, real property or other things of value or having final jurisdiction over any related criminal proceeding brought under section 50 or 51. In all such suits in which the property is claimed by any person, other than the commonwealth, the commonwealth shall have the burden of proving to the court the existence of probable cause to institute the action, and any such claimant shall then have the burden of proving that the property is not forfeitable pursuant to subsection (c). The owner of the conveyance or real property, or other person claiming thereunder, shall have the burden of proof as to all exceptions set forth in subsections (c) and (j). The court shall order the commonwealth to give notice by certified or registered mail to the owner of the conveyance, real property or other things of value and to such other persons as appear to have an interest therein, and the court shall promptly, but not less than 2 weeks after notice, hold a hearing on the petition. Upon the motion of the owner of the conveyance, real property or other things of value, the court may continue the hearing on the petition pending the outcome of any criminal trial related to the violation of sections 50 or 51. At such hearing, the court shall hear evidence and make conclusions of law, and shall thereupon issue a final order from which the parties shall have a right of appeal.

In all such suits in which a final order results in a forfeiture, the final order shall provide for disposition of the conveyance, real property or any other thing of value by the commonwealth or any subdivision thereof in any manner not prohibited by law, including official use by an authorized law enforcement or other public agency, or sale at public auction or by competitive bidding. The proceeds of any such sale shall be used to pay the reasonable expenses of the forfeiture proceedings, seizure, storage, maintenance of custody, advertising and notice and the balance thereof shall be distributed as further provided in this section.

(e) The final order of the court shall be deposited into the Victims of Human Trafficking Trust Fund established in section 66A of chapter 10.

(f) Any officer, department, or agency having custody of any property subject to forfeiture under this section or having disposed of the property shall keep and maintain full and complete records showing from whom it received the property, under what authority it held or received or disposed of said property, to whom it delivered the property, the date and manner of disposition of the property, and the exact kinds, quantities and forms of the property. The records shall be open to inspection by all federal and state officers charged with enforcement of federal and state human trafficking laws. Persons making final disposition of the property under court order shall report, under oath, to the court the exact circumstances of such disposition.

(g) During the pendency of the proceedings, the court may issue at the request of the commonwealth ex parte any preliminary order or process as is necessary to seize or secure the property for which forfeiture is sought and to provide for its custody including, but not limited to: an order that the commonwealth remove the property if possible and safeguard it in a secure location in a reasonable fashion; that monies be deposited in an interest-bearing escrow account; and that a substitute custodian be appointed to manage such property. Property taken or detained under this section shall not be repleviable, but once seized shall be deemed to be lawfully in the custody of the commonwealth pending forfeiture, subject only to the orders and decrees of the court having jurisdiction thereof. Process for seizure of the property shall issue only upon a showing of probable cause, and the application therefore and the issuance, execution and return thereof shall be subject to chapter 276, so far as applicable.

(h) A district attorney or the attorney general may refer any real property, and any furnishings, equipment and related personal property located therein, for which seizure is sought, to the division of capital asset management and maintenance office of seized property management, established under section 47 of chapter 94C. The office of seized property management shall preserve and manage the property in a reasonable fashion and dispose of the property upon a judgment ordering forfeiture, and to enter into contracts to preserve, manage and dispose of the property. The office of seized property management may receive initial funding from the special law enforcement trust funds of the attorney general and each district attorney under paragraph (f) and shall subsequently be funded by a portion of the proceeds of each sale of such managed property to the extent provided as payment of reasonable expenses in paragraph (d).

(i) The owner of any real property which is the principal domicile of the immediate family of the owner and which is subject to forfeiture under this section may file a petition for homestead exemption with the court having jurisdiction over such forfeiture. The court may, in its discretion, allow the petition exempting from forfeiture an amount allowed under section 1 of chapter 188. The value of the balance of the principal domicile, if any, shall be forfeited as provided in this section. Such homestead exemption may be acquired on only 1 principal domicile for the benefit of the immediate family of the owner.

(j) A forfeiture proceeding affecting the title to real property or the use and occupation thereof or the buildings thereon shall not have any effect except against the parties thereto and persons having actual notice thereof, until a memorandum containing the names of the parties to such proceeding, the name of the town wherein the affected real property lies, and a description of the real property sufficiently accurate for identification is recorded in the registry of deeds for the county or district wherein the real property lies. At any time after a judgment on the merits, or after the discontinuance, dismissal or other final disposition is recorded by the court having jurisdiction over such matter, the clerk of such court shall issue a certificate of the fact of such judgment, discontinuance, dismissal or other final disposition, and such certificate shall be recorded in the registry in which the original memorandum recorded pursuant to this section was filed.

SECTION 57
Victim of human trafficking as affirmative defense to charges of common night walking or common streetwalking
(Added by 2011 Mass. Acts c. 178, § 23, effective Nov. 21, 2011.)

In any prosecution or juvenile delinquency proceeding of a person who is a human trafficking victim, as defined by section 20M of chapter 233, it shall be an affirmative defense to charges of engaging in common night walking or common streetwalking in violation of section 53 of chapter 272 and to a violation of section 53A of said chapter 272 that, while a human trafficking victim, such person was under duress or coerced into committing the offenses for which such person is being prosecuted or against whom juvenile delinquency proceedings have commenced.

SECTION 58
Possession of a deceptive weapon device during commission of violent crime
(Added by 2014 Mass. Acts c. 284, § 86, effective Aug. 11, 2014.)

Any person who is in possession of a deceptive weapon device as defined in section 121 of chapter 140 during the commission of a violent crime as defined in said section 121 of said chapter 140 shall be deemed to be armed and shall be punishable by penalties set forth in this chapter.

Chapter 266. Crimes Against Property

Section

1 Arson (dwelling)
2 Arson (building)
3–4 Repealed
5 Arson (wood and other property)
5A Attempted arson
6 Repealed
7 Woods; wanton or reckless injury or destruction by fire
8 Injury by fire; negligent use
9 Injury by fire; negligent use in town
10 Insured property; burning with intent to defraud
11 Fire alarm, engine or apparatus; injury before fire
12 Fire alarm, engine or apparatus; injury during fire to prevent alarm or extinction of fire
13 Fire engines; wanton or malicious injury
13A Duty of hotel manager, etc., to notify fire department and sound alarm; penalty
14 Burglary; armed assault on occupants
15 Burglary; unarmed
16 Breaking and entering at night
16A Building, vessel or vehicle; breaking and entering with intent to commit a misdemeanor
17 Entering without breaking at night; breaking and entering in day time
18 Dwelling house; entry at night; breaking and entering in day time
18A Entering dwelling house by false pretenses; intent to commit felony; larceny; punishment
19 Railroad car; breaking and entering
20 Stealing in building, ship or railroad car
20A Breaking and entering of trucks, tractors, trailers or freight containers
20B Stealing in trucks, tractors, trailers or freight containers
21 Stolen property; refusal to surrender
22 Poultry thieves; detention by owner
23 Embezzlement of property at fire
24 Stealing at a fire
25 Larceny from the person
26 Repealed
27 Theft of tools of contractors, builders or mechanics; stealing
27A Motor vehicle fraud
28 Motor vehicle theft
29 Statement concerning theft: recovery of vehicles; restitution
29A Repealed
29B Burning motor vehicle; owner's statement to fire department
30 Larceny
30A Shoplifting
30B Distribution or possession of theft detection shielding device
30C Counterfeiting of retail sales or return receipt or price ticket
30D Organized retail crime
31 Signature; obtaining under false pretenses
32 Fraudulent conversion of property by captain of vessel
33 Larceny; false pretenses relating to contracts, banking transactions or credit
33A Intent to defraud commercial computer service; penalties
34 Larceny; inducement to part with property
35 Nonapplicability of sections 30, 31 and 34
36 Repealed
37 Fraudulent checks, etc.; drawing or uttering
37A Misuse of credit cards; definitions
37B Misuse of credit cards; penalties; multiple possession; presumption; arrest
37C Fraudulent use of credit cards to obtain money, goods or services; false embossment of credit cards, multiple possession, presumption; arrest
37D Publishing credit card numbering or coding systems
37E Identity fraud
38 Larceny; wrongful detention of money by carriers
38A Construction loan; misapplication
39 Wills; destruction or concealment
40 Common and notorious thief
41 Larceny of bicycles; second conviction
42 Larceny of paper designated for bank bills

43 Paper designated for bank bills; retention by printer with intent to pass
44–46 Repealed
47 Dogs; wrongful removal of collar; poisoning; penalty
48 Stolen goods; duty of arresting officers to secure
49 Possession of burglarious tools
50 State treasury; fraud or embezzlement by employee
51 City, town or county officers; fraud or embezzlement
52 Bank officers or employees; fraud or embezzlement
53 Bank officers or employees; prosecution for fraud or embezzlement; evidence
53A Bank officers and employees; misconduct; penalty
54 Receipt of deposits by insolvent banks; penalty
55 Liquidating agent or receiver; embezzlement
56 Brokers or agents; embezzlement
57 Fiduciaries; embezzlement
58 Larceny; embezzlement from voluntary association
59 Simple larceny; embezzlement from voluntary association
60 Stolen goods; buying or receiving
60A Stolen trade secrets; buying or selling
60B Jurisdiction
61 Stolen property; restitution; effect
62 Stolen goods; common receiver
63 Unlawful taking or use of transportation media
64 Fraudulent hiring of transportation media
65 Stock; unauthorized issue
66 Stock; fraudulent issue or transfer
67 Corporate books; false entries with intent to defraud
67A Departments, agencies and public instrumentalities; fraud in procurement of supplies; penalty
67B Presentation of false claims
67C Capital facility construction projects, etc.; false entries in records; penalties
68 Corporate books as evidence
69 Insignia of societies; unlawful use
69A Fraudulent use of labor union seal, trademark or insignia
70 Insignia of veteran organizations; unlawful use
71 Signature, money or membership; obtaining under false pretenses
71A Individuals and corporations; false use of names of benevolent organizations
72 Fraternal names; use in publication
73 Obtaining goods under false pretenses
74 Corporate credit; fraudulent use
75 Obtaining property by trick
75A Gambling devices and vending machines; fraudulent use
75B Slugs; manufacture and sale
75C Gift certificates; expiration dates; failure to redeem
75D Imposition of certain fees reducing total value amount of gift certificate; penalty
75E Printed notice required for certain fees associated with gift certificates; penalty for violation
75F Deduction of gratuity from gift certificate without consent; penalty
76 Gross fraud or cheat at common law; punishment
77 Sterling and coin silver; contents; sale; penalty
78 Articles made of gold; false marking; prohibition
79 Imitation furs; false representation; prohibition
80 Encumbered land; conveyance without notice
81 Attached land; conveyance without notice
82 Concealment of mortgaged personalty; use of rented personalty as container for illegal sale of liquor
83 Personalty; sale by mortgagor without consent
84 Personalty; sale by hirer without consent
85 Collateral security; sale before debt due
86 Hired property; buying or receiving with intent to defraud
87 Larceny of leased or rented property
87A Stolen leased or rented motor vehicles; report dissemination of information by police
88 Consignee or factor; fraudulent deposit or pledge of property
89 Degrees; pretending to hold or conferring without authority; use of designation "university" or "college"

2

90 Endorsement or approval; penalty for false claim
91 Untrue and misleading advertisements; prohibitions
91A Merchandise, commodities and service; advertisement regulated; penalty
91B Deceptive advertising of merchandise for sale; injunction
92 False or exaggerated statements; making or publishing; prohibition
92A Motor vehicles; sale in certain condition; written disclosure on bill of sale; penalty
93 Animals; obtaining or giving false pedigree
94 Boundary monuments and miscellaneous markers; malicious destruction
95 Historical monuments; malicious destruction or injury
96 State building; defacement or injury
97 County buildings; defacement
98 Schoolhouse or church; defacement or injury
98A Public park or playground equipment; destruction, defacement or injury
99 Libraries; definitions
99A Libraries; theft of materials or property; destruction of records
100 Libraries; mutilation or destruction of materials or property
101 Definitions related to sections 101–102D
102 Possession or control of incendiary device or material; possession of hoax device or material; penalty
102A Throwing, secreting, launching or placing of incendiary device; intent, punishment
102A½ Repealed
102B Malicious explosion
102C Biological, chemical or nuclear weapon or delivery system; possession; punishment
102D Notice of seizure of explosive or incendiary device resulting from a violation of sections 102–102C; restitution
103 Oil of vitriol or other substances; throwing into house, building, or vessel
104 Buildings; destruction or injury
104A Goal posts; penalty for destruction
104B Research animals; unauthorized removal
105 Stone walls or fences; unauthorized removal
106 Ice ponds; injury
107 Bridge or canal; injury
108 Vessel; destruction to injure or defraud owner or insurer; punishment; restitution
109 Vessel; fitting out with intent to destroy
110 False invoice of cargo; intent to defraud insurer
111 False affidavit or protest; penalty for making
111A Insurance policies; penalties for fraudulent claims
111B Motor vehicle insurance policies; penalty for fraudulent claims
111C Fraudulent Motor Vehicle Insurance Claims—Runners
112 Domestic animals; malicious killing or injury
113 Timber, wood and shrubs; wilful cutting and destruction on land of another
114 Trees and fences; malicious injury
115 Trespass in orchards and gardens
116 Repealed
116A Protection of certain flowers
117 Orchards and gardens; entry with intent to injure or destroy
118 Domestic animals; trespass on land
119 Pests; bringing into state; penalty; exception
120 Trespass
120A Motor vehicle; parking on private way; prosecution; evidence
120B Entry on land by abutting property owners not constituting trespass law
120C Entry upon adjoining lands by surveyors not constituting trespass
120D Removal of motor vehicles from private ways or property; procedure; penalties; liability for removal and storage charges; release of vehicle
120E Obstruction of entry to or departure from medical facility; injunctive relief; damages
120E½ Reproductive health care facility; buffer zone; penalties
120F Unauthorized access to computer system; penalties
121 Entry on land with firearms
121A Trespasses involving motor vehicles and other powered devices
122 Notice against trespassers; penalty for defacement
123 Land of state and county institutions; institutions of higher education; trespass

123A Willful trespass upon public source of water, water supply facility or land
124 Legal notice; penalty for malicious injury
125 Show bill or advertisement; penalty for malicious injury
126 Natural scenery; penalty for defacement
126A Walls, signs, gravestones, etc.; penalty for defacement
126B Walls, signs, gravestones, etc.; penalty for "tagging"
127 Personalty; malicious or wanton injuries
127A Destruction of place of worship, etc.; punishment
127B Action for civil rights violations; liability
128 Milk cans; defacement
129 Correctional institutions; injury to property
130 Penal institutions; injury to property
131 Sunday trespassers; arrest and detention without warrant
132 Pigeons; killing or frightening
133 Humane society; injury to property
134 Repealed
135 Vessels; mooring the buoy; beacon or floating guide; penalty
136 Repealed
137 Injury to mill by raising water
138 Dams or reservoirs; malicious injury
138A Irrigation equipment; malicious injury
139 Motor vehicles or trailers; defacement, etc., of identifying numbers; penalties; arrests
139A Machines, or electrical or mechanical devices; alteration or obliteration of identifying numbers; possession as prima facie evidence; sale or attempt; punishment
140 Sale or offer for sale of master keys; penalty
141 Tampering with odometer of motor vehicle prohibited acts; intent to defraud; civil remedy; treble damages; costs and fees; violation as unfair competition; definitions; repair or replacement excepted
141A Misrepresentation of mileage of motor vehicle by turning back or readjusting speedometer or odometer; criminal penalty
142 Records of purchases by dealers in scrap copper wire; inspection; penalty
142A Gold, silver and platinum dealers; records; penalty
143 Definitions applicable to sections 143A–143E
143A Unauthorized reproduction and transfer of sound recordings
143B Unauthorized reproduction and sale of live performances
143C Manufacture, rental, or sale of recorded devices in packaging not bearing reproducer's name and address
143D Violations of sections 143–143C; punishment
143E Penalties
143F Unauthorized Recording of Motion Picture in Theater
143G Detaining of Suspected Violators of Section 143F Permitted
143H Destruction of Recordings and Recording Devices
144 Carrying away or conversion of certain milk containers without permission of owners
145 Theft of public records
146 Disposal of unlawful solid waste
147 Items or services bearing or identified by counterfeit mark; sales; penalties

SECTION 1

Arson (dwelling)

Whoever wilfully and maliciously sets fire to, burns, or causes to be burned, or whoever aids, counsels or procures the burning of, a dwelling house, or a building adjoining or adjacent to a dwelling house, or a building by the burning whereof a dwelling house is burned, whether such dwelling house or other building is the property of himself or another and whether the same is occupied or unoccupied, shall be punished by imprisonment in the state prison for not more than twenty years, or by imprisonment in a jail or house of correction for not more than two and one half years, or by a fine of not more than ten thousand dollars, or by both such fine and imprisonment. The words "dwelling house", as used in this section, shall mean and include all buildings used as dwellings such as apartment houses, tenement houses, hotels, boarding houses, dormitories, hospitals, institutions, sanatoria, or other buildings where persons are domiciled.

2

NOTE 1   **Malice.** "The malice which is a necessary element in the crime of arson need not be express, but may be implied; it need not take the form of malevolence or ill will, but it is sufficient if one deliberately and without justification or excuse sets out to burn the dwelling house of another." *Commonwealth v. Lamothe*, 343 Mass. 417, 419 (1961) (quoting *State v. Pisano*, 141 A. 660, 661 (Conn. 1928)).

NOTE 2   "Wilfully and maliciously" are essential words forming the substance of the crime without which no crime is set forth. *Commonwealth v. Cooper*, 264 Mass. 378, 380 (1928).

NOTE 3   A necessary element for proof of arson that the structure be burned in some way was met when the Commonwealth established a charring of the kitchen floor. *Commonwealth v. McIntosh*, 10 Mass. App. Ct. 924, 925 (1980).

NOTE 4   **Sections 1 and 10—Not Duplicative.** Arson of a dwelling under G.L. c. 266, § 1 and arson with intent to defraud an insurer under G.L. c. 266, § 10 are not duplicative offenses. The offenses have mutually exclusive elements—§ 1 requires proof that a dwelling was burned, while § 10 requires proof of intent to defraud an insurer. *Commonwealth v. Anolik*, 27 Mass. App. Ct. 701, 712 (1989).

NOTE 5   **Related Statutes.** G.L. c. 277, § 25—Description of ownership.

SECTION 2
Arson (building)

Whoever wilfully and maliciously sets fire to, burns, or causes to be burned, or whoever aids, counsels or procures the burning of, a meeting house, church, court house, town house, college, academy, jail or other building which has been erected for public use, or a banking house, warehouse, store, manufactory, mill, barn, stable, shop, outhouse or other building, or an office building, lumber yard, ship, vessel, street car or railway car, or a bridge, lock, dam, flume, tank, or any building or structure or contents thereof, not included or described in the preceding section, whether the same is the property of himself or of another and whether occupied, unoccupied or vacant, shall be punished by imprisonment in the state prison for not more than ten years, or by imprisonment in a jail or house of correction for not more than two and one half years.

NOTE 1   See Notes following G.L. c. 266, § 1 (arson).

NOTE 2a   **Variances.** *See* G.L. c. 277, § 35.

NOTE 2b   Where it was alleged that a building and its contents belonged to one person but proven that while the building did belong to that person the contents did not, there was *not* a fatal variance between the allegations and proof. *Commonwealth v. Brailey*, 134 Mass. 527 (1883).

NOTE 3   This section is a lesser included offense of G.L. c. 266, § 10. *Commonwealth v. Ploude*, 44 Mass. App. Ct. 137, 142 (1998).

SECTIONS 3–4
Repealed

SECTION 5
Arson (wood and other property)

Whoever wilfully and maliciously sets fire to, or burns or otherwise destroys or injures by burning, or causes to be burned or otherwise so destroyed or injured, or whoever aids, counsels or procures the burning of, a pile or parcel of wood, boards, timber or other lumber, or any fence, bars or gate, or a stack of grain, hay or other vegetable product, or any vegetable product severed from the soil and not stacked, or any standing tree, grain, grass or other standing product of the

soil, or the soil itself, or any personal property of whatsoever class or character exceeding a value of twenty-five dollars, of another, or any boat, motor vehicle as defined in section one of chapter ninety, or other conveyance, whether of himself or another, shall be punished by imprisonment in the state prison for not more than three years, or by a fine of not more than five hundred dollars and imprisonment in a jail or house of correction for not more than one year.

NOTE 1   "To obtain convictions under G.L. c. 266, § 5, the Commonwealth was required to prove that the defendant had procured the burning of his automobile. *See* G.L. c. 266, § 5. By procuring another to commit a felony, the defendant became an accessory before the fact." *Commonwealth v. Jones*, 59 Mass. App. Ct. 157, 160 (2003) (citation omitted).

NOTE 2   **Sections 5 and 10—Not Duplicative.** Arson of motor vehicle under G.L. c. 266, § 5 and arson with intent to defraud an insurer under G.L. c. 266, § 10 are not duplicative offenses. The offenses "have mutually exclusive elements—§ 5 requires proof that an automobile was burned, while § 10 requires proof of intent to defraud an insurer . . . ." *Commonwealth v. Jones*, 59 Mass. App. Ct. 157, 161–63 (2003) ("Section 10 is aimed at protecting personal property, and embodies a public safety component as well; § 10, by contrast, punishes what is at bottom an economic crime, which has widespread impact among members of the insurer's risk pool.").

NOTE 3   See Notes following G.L. c. 266, § 1 (arson).

SECTION 5A
Attempted arson

Whoever wilfully and maliciously attempts to set fire to, or attempts to burn, or aids, counsels or assists in such an attempt to set fire to or burn, any of the buildings, structures or property mentioned in the foregoing sections, or whoever commits any act preliminary thereto or in furtherance thereof, shall be punished by imprisonment in the state prison for not more than ten years, or by imprisonment in a jail or house of correction for not more than two and one half years or by a fine of not more than one thousand dollars.

The placing or distributing of any flammable, explosive or combustible material or substance or any device in or against any building, structure or property mentioned in the foregoing sections in an arrangement or preparation with intent eventually to wilfully and maliciously set fire to or burn such building, structure or property, or to procure the setting fire to or burning of the same shall, for the purposes of this section, constitute an attempt to burn such building, structure or property.

NOTE 1   See Notes following G.L. c. 266, § 1 (arson).

NOTE 2   The defendant "placed turpentine in a building preparatory to the execution of his intention to burn that building in two to three weeks. It cannot be held as a matter of law that an intention to burn a building three weeks hence is too remote under the statute." *Commonwealth v. Ali*, 7 Mass. App. Ct. 120, 123 (1979).

NOTE 3   The malice now essential under G.L. c. 266, § 5A (attempted arson), comparable, if not identical, to the malice of this section, "is not necessarily against the owner of the building, but that malice which 'characterizes all acts done with an evil disposition, a wrong and unlawful motive or purpose; the wilful doing of an injurious act without lawful excuse.'" *Commonwealth v. Lamothe*, 343 Mass. 417, 420 (1961) (quoting *Commonwealth v. Mehales*, 284 Mass. 412, 415 (1933)).

SECTION 6
Repealed

SECTION 7
Woods; wanton or reckless injury or destruction by fire

Whoever by wantonly or recklessly setting fire to any material, or by increasing a fire already set, causes injury to, or the destruction of, any growing or standing wood of another shall be punished by a fine of not more than one thousand dollars or by imprisonment for not more than two years.

SECTION 8
Injury by fire; negligent use

Whoever, not being a tenant thereof, sets or increases a fire upon land of another whereby the property of another is injured, or whoever negligently or wilfully suffers any fire upon his own land to extend beyond the limits thereof whereby the woods or property of another are injured, shall be punished by a fine of not more than one thousand dollars or by imprisonment for not more than two years, and the town where such fire occurred may recover in an action of tort, brought within two years after the cause of action accrues, against any such person the expense of extinguishing such fire.

SECTION 9
Injury by fire; negligent use in town

Whoever, in a town which accepts this section or has accepted corresponding provisions of earlier laws, sets a fire on land which is not owned or controlled by him and before leaving the same neglects to entirely extinguish such fire, or whoever wilfully or negligently sets a fire on land which is not owned or controlled by him whereby property is endangered or injured, or whoever wilfully or negligently suffers a fire upon his own land to escape beyond the limits thereof to the injury of another, shall be punished by a fine of not more than one hundred dollars or imprisonment in jail for not more than one month, or both, and shall also be liable for all damages caused thereby. Such fine shall be equally divided between the complainant and the town. This section shall not apply to cities.

SECTION 10
Insured property; burning with intent to defraud

Whoever, wilfully and with intent to defraud or injure the insurer, sets fire to, or attempts to set fire to, or whoever causes to be burned, or whoever aids, counsels or procures the burning of, a building, or any goods, wares, merchandise or other chattels, belonging to himself or another, and which are at the time insured against loss or damage by fire, shall be punished by imprisonment in the state prison for not more than five years or in a jail or house of correction for not more than two and one half years.

NOTE 1 "In order to establish its charge the Commonwealth must prove (1) that the defendant made the attempt to burn the property described; (2) that the property was insured; and (3) that the defendant had an intent to injure the insurer." *Commonwealth v. Cooper*, 264 Mass. 368, 371–72 (1928).

NOTE 2 Although the property may be insured by more than one insurer, only one charge may be brought against the defendant who burns the property with an intent to injure the insurers. *Commonwealth v. Goldstein*, 114 Mass. 272, 277–78 (1873).

NOTE 3 "A direct benefit to the defendant is *not* a necessary element of the crime." *Commonwealth v. Kaplan*, 238 Mass. 250, 254 (1921).

NOTE 4 **Variance.** Property alleged to belong to the defendant. In fact it belonged to a partnership, of which the defendant was a member. Held, no variance. *Commonwealth v. Goldstein*, 114 Mass. at 277.

NOTE 5 **Sections 1 and 10—Not Duplicative.** Arson of a dwelling under G.L. c. 266, § 1 and arson with intent to defraud an insurer under G.L. c. 266, § 10 are not duplicative offenses. The offenses have mutually exclusive elements—§ 1 requires proof that a dwelling was burned, while § 10 requires proof of intent to defraud an insurer. *Commonwealth v. Anolik*, 27 Mass. App. Ct. 701, 712 (1989).

NOTE 6 **Sections 5 and 10—Not Duplicative.** Arson of motor vehicle under G.L. c. 266, § 5 and arson with intent to defraud an insurer under G.L. c. 266, § 10 are not duplicative offenses. The offenses "have mutually exclusive elements—§ 5 requires proof that an automobile was burned, while § 10 requires proof of intent to defraud an insurer . . . ." *Commonwealth v. Jones*, 59 Mass. App. Ct. 157, 161–63 (2003) ("Section 10 is aimed at protecting personal property, and embodies a public safety component as well; § 10, by contrast, punishes what is at bottom an economic crime, which has widespread impact among members of the insurer's risk pool.").

SECTION 11
Fire alarm, engine or apparatus; injury before fire

Whoever, within twenty-four hours prior to the burning of a building or other property, wilfully, intentionally and without right cuts or removes a bell rope or a wire or conduit connected with a fire alarm signal system or injures or disables any fire alarm signal box or any part of such system in the vicinity of such building or property, or cuts, injures or destroys an engine, hose or other fire apparatus in said vicinity shall be punished by a fine of not more than five hundred dollars or by imprisonment for not more than two years.

NOTE **Related Statutes.**
G.L. c. 268, § 32—Tampering with police or fire signal systems.
G.L. c. 268, § 32A—Interference with fire fighting operations.
G.L. c. 269, § 13—False alarm of fires.

SECTION 12
Fire alarm, engine or apparatus; injury during fire to prevent alarm or extinction of fire

Whoever, during the burning of a building or other property, wilfully and maliciously cuts or removes a bell rope or a wire or conduit connected with a fire alarm signal system or injures or disables any fire alarm signal box or any part of such system in the vicinity of such building or property, or otherwise prevents an alarm being given, or whoever cuts, injures or destroys an engine, hose or other fire apparatus, in said vicinity, or otherwise wilfully and maliciously prevents or obstructs the extinction of a fire shall be punished by imprisonment in the state prison for not more than seven years or in jail for not more than two and one half years or by a fine of not more than one thousand dollars.

NOTE See Note following G.L. c. 266, § 11.

SECTION 13
Fire engines; wanton or malicious injury

Whoever wantonly or maliciously injures a fire engine or other fire apparatus shall be punished by a fine of not more than five hundred dollars or by imprisonment for not more than two years, and shall be further ordered to recognize with sufficient surety or sureties for his good behavior during such term as the court shall order.

2

SECTION 13A
Duty of hotel manager, etc., to notify fire department and sound alarm; penalty

The manager of a hotel or family hotel or such other person as may be in charge of the premises in the absence of the manager, shall, as soon as he becomes aware that there is a fire therein, notify the fire department and, if such fire, or heat, smoke or gas therefrom, threatens to spread to rooms occupied by guests, sound the alarm system required by the state building code.

Whoever violates any provision of this section shall be punished by imprisonment in a jail or house of correction for not more than two and a half years or by a fine of not more than one thousand dollars.

SECTION 14
Burglary; armed assault on occupants

Whoever breaks and enters a dwelling house in the night time, with intent to commit a felony, or whoever, after having entered with such intent, breaks such dwelling house in the night time, any person being then lawfully therein, and the offender being armed with a dangerous weapon at the time of such breaking or entry, or so arming himself in such house, or making an actual assault on a person lawfully therein, shall be punished by imprisonment in the state prison for life or for any term of not less than ten years.

Whoever commits any offense described in this section while armed with a firearm, shotgun, rifle, machine gun or assault weapon, shall be punished by imprisonment in the state prison for life or for any term of years, but not less than 15 years. Whoever commits a subsequent such offense shall be punished by imprisonment in the state prison for life or for any term of years, but not less than 20 years.The sentence imposed upon a person who, after being convicted of any offense mentioned in this section, commits the like offense, or any other of the offenses therein mentioned, shall not be suspended, nor shall he be placed on probation.

NOTE 1a   **Break.** "[T]he opening of a closed but unlocked door or window is a breaking. . . . But passing through an unobstructed entrance is not." *Commonwealth v. Tilley*, 355 Mass. 507, 508 (1969) (quoting *Commonwealth v. Lewis*, 346 Mass. 373, 377 (1963)).

NOTE 1b   "[E]ntry through an open window not apparently intended, or useable in due course, as a means of entry is within the intent of the statute." *Commonwealth v. Tilley*, 355 Mass. at 509. *See also Commonwealth v. Hall*, 48 Mass. App. Ct. 727 (2000).

NOTE 1c   "The reasonable inference was that for the intruders to enter in the course of their joint enterprise one or both had moved to a material degree something that barred the way. This, we rule, was a breaking." *Commonwealth v. Tilley*, 355 Mass. at 508.

NOTE 1d   The Commonwealth need *not* prove that all windows were closed or locked. *Commonwealth v. Tilley*, 355 Mass. at 508–09.

NOTE 1e   The opening of an interior door constitutes a break. *Commonwealth v. Lewis*, 346 Mass. at 377.

NOTE 1f   The word "breaks" as it appears in this Section (G.L. c. 266, § 14) as well as other statutory forms of that word includes the doctrine of constructive breaking. Thus there was a break when the defendant gained entrance to the victim's apartment by pretending to be her brother. *Commonwealth v. Labare*, 11 Mass. App. Ct. 370, 377 (1981).

NOTE 1g   **Sunroof.** "Scrambling onto the top of a car and slipping through an open sunroof is as surreptitiously intrusive a violation of the security of one of the several physical spaces intended to be protected by G.L. c. 266, § 18, as is crawling down a chimney or scaling a wall to clamber through a window high above the ground." *Commonwealth v. Cextary (No. 1)*, 68 Mass. App.Ct. 752, 757 (2007) (footnotes omitted).

NOTE 1h   **One Break/Several Victims.** "In *Commonwealth v. Gordon*, 42 Mass. App. Ct. 601, 602 & n.1 (1997), the Commonwealth indicted the defendant on multiple counts of burglary under G.L. c. 266, § 14, each naming a different victim, despite the fact that the counts arose out of a single breaking and entering . . . [T]he single act of breaking and entering could support only one conviction. . . ." *Commonwealth v. Cruz*, 430 Mass. 182, 196 (1999).

NOTE 2a   **Enter.** It is sufficient entry when any part of the defendant's body is within any part of the dwelling. *Commonwealth v. Lewis*, 346 Mass. at 377 (citing *Commonwealth v. Glover*, 111 Mass. 395, 402 (1873)).

NOTE 2b   "[T]he locked storm door is a part of the 'protected enclosure,' and the defendant's presence between the previously locked door and the front door, with his hands on the front door handle, is enough to constitute an entry." *Commonwealth v. Porter*, 70 Mass. App. Ct. 901, 901 (2007) (citations omitted).

NOTE 2c   **Victim's Presence After Entry.** "We conclude that the phrase 'any person being then lawfully therein' does not preclude a defendant from being convicted under G.L. c. 266, § 14, merely because the victim came home after the defendant broke and entered her home. Although the victim was not present in the dwelling at the time of the defendant's breaking and entry, she was lawfully present during the course of the burglary. The victim of an assault is 'present' at the time of the assault, and it is the time of the assault that is relevant, not the time of the entry." *Commonwealth v. Mitchell*, 67 Mass. App. Ct. 556, 563 (2006) (footnote omitted).

NOTE 3a   **Dwelling House.** See G.L. c. 266, § 1 (arson) for general guidance.

NOTE 3b   "G.L. c. 266, § 14 permits only one burglary conviction per dwelling." *Commonwealth v. Bolden*, 470 Mass. 274, 275 (2014).

NOTE 3c   The defendant argued that the apartment in question was *not* a dwelling house at the time of the break-in because it had no furniture or other personal property in it and no one was actually living in it. The court rejected this as the new tenants had taken possession of the apartment with an intention to live there. They had a right of access and a right to move in at the time of the break-in. One tenant who testified stated he considered the apartment as his place of residence. Lastly, it was the tenants who confronted the defendant in the apartment. The absence of any personal property from the apartment is *not* dispositive. *Commonwealth v. Kingsbury*, 378 Mass. 751, 757 (1979).

NOTE 3d   Issue: Whether the locked common hallway was a part of the victim's 'dwelling house'? The Appeals Court answered in the affirmative. "We conclude that, for purposes of G.L. c. 266, § 14, an apartment dweller's 'dwelling house' does include secured common hallways. However, as the physical features of a multi-family residential structure will vary from case to case, so too will the determination whether the common areas of that structure, even if locked, constitute the tenant's 'dwelling house.'" *Commonwealth v. Goldoff*, 24 Mass. App. Ct. 458, 463 (1987). *See also Commonwealth v. Doucette*, 430 Mass. 461, 467 (1999).

NOTE 4a   **Nighttime.** The time between one hour after sunset on one day and one hour before sunrise on the next day. G.L. c. 278, § 10.

NOTE 4b   While there was evidence that a break-in occurred between 6 p.m. and 7 p.m. on October 31, there was no evidence as to the precise time of sunset on that day. Held, this is a question for the jury, who are entitled to rely on their general knowledge of matters commonly known within the community. *Commonwealth v. Kingsbury*, 378 Mass. at 753–54.

NOTE 5a　Intent to Commit a Felony. Felony—A crime punishable by death or imprisonment in the state prison. G.L. c. 274, § 1.

NOTE 5b "When a person, by the use of force, enters a dwelling house or building in the middle of the night it may ordinarily be presumed, in the absence of evidence to the contrary, that his intent is to steal." *Commonwealth v. Ronchetti*, 333 Mass. 78, 81 (1955); *Commonwealth v. Eppich*, 342 Mass. 487, 493 (1961).

NOTE 5c As the defendant was charged with burglary, the amount of property stolen or its value is immaterial. *Commonwealth v. Grace*, 265 Mass. 119 (1928).

NOTE 5d The Commonwealth must prove the specific intent with which the break was committed. *Commonwealth v. Wygrzywalski*, 362 Mass. 790, 791 (1973); *Commonwealth v. Perron*, 11 Mass. App. Ct. 915 (1981).

NOTE 5e "[P]roof of the actual commission of larceny is decisive proof of the intent with which the entry was made. The overt act leaves no room for doubt as to the felonious purpose with which the previous criminal act was perpetrated." *Commonwealth v. Carter*, 306 Mass. 141, 149 (1940).

NOTE 5f "We are aware of no case that, in circumstances such as these, requires a trial judge to define the elements of the intended felony. Indeed, as we have already noted, a burglary indictment need not even specify the intended felony by name, as the identity of the felony is not an element of the crime and the jury can find an intent to commit an unspecified felony. Thus, although here the trial judge did not define the elements of larceny in a building, she was not required to do so. All that was required was that she instruct the jury that they must find, beyond a reasonable doubt, that the defendant had the intent to commit some felony." *Commonwealth v. Willard*, 53 Mass. App. Ct. 650, 656–57 (2002) (citation omitted).

NOTE 6　Dangerous Weapon. *See* G.L. c. 265, § 15A (assault and battery by means of a dangerous weapon); G.L. c. 265, § 15B (assault by mean of a dangerous weapon); G.L. c. 265, § 17 (armed robbery); and G.L. c. 265, § 18 (armed assault with intent to rob or murder).

NOTE 7　Assault. *See* G.L. c. 265, § 13A (assault; assault and battery); G.L. c. 265, § 15A (assault and battery by means of a dangerous weapon); and G.L. c. 265, § 15B (assault by means of a dangerous weapon).

NOTE 8a　Lesser Included Offenses. Burglary (G.L. c. 266, § 15) is a lesser included offense of this section. *Commonwealth v. Powell*, 10 Mass. App. Ct. 57, 58–59 (1980).

NOTE 8b General Laws c. 266, §§ 17 and 18 define lesser included offenses where there is no evidence of any form of breaking, actual or constructive. *Commonwealth v. Labare*, 11 Mass. App. Ct. at 377.

NOTE 8c "Armed assault in a dwelling [G.L. c. 265, § 18A] is not a lesser included offense of aggravated burglary [G.L. c. 266, § 14] because armed assault in a dwelling requires an element not required in either armed burglary or burglary with assault—the intent to commit a felony at the time of the assault. Neither armed burglary nor burglary with assault is a lesser included offense of armed assault in a dwelling, because both armed burglary and burglary with assault require two elements not required in armed assault in a dwelling—the intent to commit a felony at the time of entry into the dwelling, and breaking and entering in the nighttime. Because each offense has an element not shared by the other, neither is a lesser included offense of the other, and the two convictions are not duplicative." *Commonwealth v. Negron*, 462 Mass. 102, 110–11 (2012).

NOTE 9 If an indictment for a crime involving the commission or attempted commission of an injury to property describes the property with sufficient certainty in other respects to identify the act, it need not allege the name of the owner. G.L. c. 277, § 25. *See also* G.L. c. 278, § 9 (proof of ownership of property).

NOTE 10a A defendant may be found to have committed a break even if, in the course of a joint venture, his partner was the one who did the actual break. *Commonwealth v. Tilley*, 355 Mass. at 508. *See also Commonwealth v. Lowrey*, 158 Mass. 18, 19–20 (1893).

NOTE 10b If the defendant by prearrangement was stationed in a position where he might render his comrades who did the actual breaking and entering aid and encouragement, as a lookout to give warning, or as a decoy to beguile the police and others from possible suspicions, or as an ally in making an escape, then he was equally guilty with the perpetrators of the crimes. *Commonwealth v. Conroy*, 333 Mass. 751, 754–55 (1956).

NOTE 11　Self Defense. "Self-defense is not an available defense to a charge of armed assault in a dwelling house with intent to rob." *Commonwealth v. Doucette*, 430 Mass. 461, 470 (1999) (citation and quotation marks omitted).

NOTE 12　Recently Stolen Property. "[T]he defendant's mere possession of recently stolen property may be relied upon by the jury as evidence that he had stolen it." *Commonwealth v. Latney*, 44 Mass. App. Ct. 423, 425 (1998) (B&E conviction affirmed for defendant, in possession of property stolen from a burglarized house, which was 200 yards away).

NOTE 13 See Notes following G.L. c. 266, § 16.

NOTE 14　Related Statute. G.L. c. 265, § 18A—Armed assault in a dwelling house.

NOTE 15　DNA Database. A conviction of an offense under this section or of an attempt or conspiracy to commit such an offense results in the defendant being required to submit a DNA sample to the state's DNA database. *See* G.L. c. 22E, § 3.

SECTION 15
Burglary; unarmed

Whoever breaks and enters a dwelling house in the night time, with the intent mentioned in the preceding section, or, having entered with such intent, breaks such dwelling house in the night time, the offender not being armed, nor arming himself in such house, with a dangerous weapon, nor making an assault upon a person lawfully therein, shall be punished by imprisonment in the state prison for not more than twenty years and, if he shall have been previously convicted of any crime named in this or the preceding section, for not less than five years.

NOTE 1　Jurisdiction. The District Court cannot find one guilty of a crime over which it lacks jurisdiction, e.g., unarmed burglary (G.L. c. 266, § 15). If it mistakenly does, double jeopardy principles do not apply, and the Superior Court may try the defendant for the same offense. *Commonwealth v. Lovett*, 374 Mass. 394, 397 (1978).

NOTE 2 See Notes following G.L. c. 266, § 14.

NOTE 3　DNA Database. A conviction of an offense under this section or of an attempt or conspiracy to commit such an offense results in the defendant being required to submit a DNA sample to the state's DNA database. *See* G.L. c. 22E, § 3.

SECTION 16
Breaking and entering at night

Whoever, in the night time, breaks and enters a building, ship, vessel or vehicle, with intent to commit a felony, or who attempts to or does break, burn, blow up or otherwise injures or destroys a safe, vault or other depository of money, bonds or other valuables in any building, vehicle or place, with intent to commit a larceny or felony, whether he succeeds or fails in the perpetration of such larceny or felony, shall be punished by imprisonment in the state prison for not more than twenty years or in a jail or house of correction for not more than two and one-half years.

NOTE 1   See Notes following G.L. c. 266, § 14.

NOTE 2a   **Ownership.** G.L. c. 278, § 9 (Proof of ownership of property).

NOTE 2b   Although the complaint stated that "Ward" owned the building, there was no evidence presented on the point. Conviction upheld. "The gravamen of the crime alleged against the defendant is not that the building allegedly broken and entered belonged to Ward, but rather that the defendant broke and entered a building not his own. . . . [A]ll the Commonwealth was required to prove as to ownership was that the building was owned by someone other than the defendant." The Commonwealth need not bring in title or registry records, but may rely upon the circumstances of the case, i.e., statements and actions by the defendant. *Commonwealth v. Kalinowski*, 360 Mass. 682, 684–85 (1971).

NOTE 2c   *Cf. Commonwealth v. DeRome*, 6 Mass. App. Ct. 900, 901 (1978). Indictment alleged that "Turin" owned the victimized building. Proof showed that (1) the building was in fact owned by Plotkin; and (2) the only break which occurred was in the second floor which was leased to the defendant's brother. The variance was fatal and the conviction(s) for breaking and entering (and arson) was set aside.

NOTE 3   **Nature of Building.** "[T]he locked, fenced-in delivery hall is part of the Home Depot building and under the protection of G.L. c. 266, § 16. . . . The fact that the delivery hall lacks a roof is not determinative, where its other physical characteristics, including its contiguity to the roofed portion, shared wall, restricted access, and use for storage of valuable merchandise sold there, indicate that it is an integral part of the building proper." *Commonwealth v. Rudenko*, 74 Mass. App. Ct. 396, 400 (2009) (citation omitted).

NOTE 4   **Intent.** "Although the value of any item actually taken may be relevant on intent, especially if the item actually taken was visible at the time of the breaking and entering, it was not necessary for the Commonwealth to present evidence of the value of the property actually stolen, or, in fact, that any property was actually stolen. A defendant's intent to commit a felonious larceny may be proved in a number of ways." *Commonwealth v. Hill*, 57 Mass. App. Ct. 240, 247 (2003).

NOTE 5   "The judge in his jury instructions considered any larceny to constitute the felony element of G.L. c. 266, § 16. This was error. Under G.L. c. 266, § 30, a larceny is not a felony unless the value of the property stolen exceeds $250." *Commonwealth v. Hill*, 57 Mass. App. Ct. 240, 249 (2003).

NOTE 6a   **Lesser Included Offense.** Breaking and entering in the daytime (G.L. c. 266, § 18) is a lesser included offense of breaking and entering in the nighttime (G.L. c. 266, § 16). *Commonwealth v. Sitko*, 372 Mass. 305, 307 (1977).

NOTE 6b   "The fact that the indictment failed to state the time of day the offense was committed is immaterial, except that the accused could only be punished for the lesser offense." *Carr v. Lanagan*, 50 F.Supp. 41, 43 (D.Mass. 1943); *see also Commonwealth v. Reynolds*, 122 Mass. 454, 457 (1877).

NOTE 7   "The 'intent to commit a felony' is a specific element within G.L. c. 266, § 16. The Commonwealth must prove the specific intent with which the defendant committed the breaking and entering. That intent must exist at the time of the breaking and entering." *Commonwealth v. Hill*, 57 Mass. App. Ct. 240, 248–49 (2003) (citations omitted).

SECTION 16A
Building, vessel or vehicle; breaking and entering with intent to commit a misdemeanor

Whoever in the nighttime or daytime breaks and enters a building, ship, vessel or vehicle with intent to commit a misdemeanor shall be punished by a fine of not more than two

hundred dollars or by imprisonment for not more than six months, or both.

NOTE 1   See Notes following G.L. c. 266, §§ 14 and 16.

NOTE 2   **Misdemeanor.** A crime punishable by death or imprisonment in the state prison is a felony. All other crimes are misdemeanors. G.L. c. 274, § 1.

NOTE 3   **Underlying offense.** "To the extent that the defendant argues that intent to commit a trespass cannot be the underlying intended misdemeanor for a breaking and entering conviction, the Supreme Judicial Court has ruled otherwise in *Rogan v. Commonwealth*, 415 Mass. 376, 379 (1993). The defendant argues that the judge, in permitting the case to proceed at the close of the Commonwealth's evidence, erred because 'it is inherent that a trespass appears to be subsumed into a [b]reaking and [e]ntering and therefore[] cannot be the sole independent intended misdemeanor necessary to support the charge.' To be sure, 'there is no such crime as "breaking and entering" unaccompanied by intent to commit a felony or a misdemeanor. See G.L. c. 266, §§ 14, 15, 16, 17, 18, 19, & 20A. There is such a thing as criminal trespass. It consists of entry of, or remaining in, a dwelling house (among other places) without right after having been forbidden so to do. G.L. c. 266, § 120.' *Commonwealth v. Vinnicombe*, 28 Mass. App. Ct. 934, 935 (1990). '[C]riminal trespass . . . contains elements which need not be found for breaking and entry with intent to commit a [misdemeanor], notably entering or remaining after having been forbidden so to do.' Ibid. Here, the evidence presented by the Commonwealth—that after breaking and entering into a building, the defendant was seen walking down the stairs of a hallway—was sufficient for the jury to determine that he had broken and entered the building with the intent to commit a trespass therein." *Commonwealth v. Scott*, 71 Mass. App. Ct. 596, 604 (2008).

SECTION 17
Entering without breaking at night; breaking and entering in day time
(Amended by 2014 Mass. Acts c. 284, § 87, effective Jan. 1, 2015.)

Whoever, in the night time, enters without breaking, or breaks and enters in the day time, a building, ship, vessel or vehicle, with intent to commit a felony, the owner or any other person lawfully therein being put in fear, shall be punished by imprisonment in the state prison for not more than ten years. Whoever commits any offense described in this section while armed with a firearm, rifle, shotgun, machine gun or assault weapon shall be punished by imprisonment in the state prison for not less than 7 years or in the house of correction for not less than 2 years nor more than 2½ years.

NOTE 1   See Notes following G.L. c. 266, §§ 14 and 16.

NOTE 2   A dwelling home is a "building" within the meaning of this section. *Commonwealth v. Swahn*, 5 Mass. App. Ct. 642, 645–48 (1977).

SECTION 18
Dwelling house; entry at night; breaking and entering in day time
(Amended by 2014 Mass. Acts c. 284, § 88, effective Jan. 1, 2015.)

Whoever, in the night time, enters a dwelling house without breaking, or breaks and enters in the day time a building, ship or motor vehicle or vessel, with intent to commit a felony, no person lawfully therein being put in fear, shall be punished by imprisonment in the state prison for not more than ten years or by a fine of not more than five hundred dollars and imprisonment in jail for not more than two years. Whoever commits any offense described in this section while armed with a firearm, rifle, shotgun, machine gun or assault weapon shall be punished by imprisonment in the state prison for not less than 7 years or by imprisonment in the house of correction for not less than 2 years nor more than 2½ years.

NOTE 1   See Notes following G.L. c. 266, §§ 14 and 16.

NOTE 2   **Double Jeopardy.** See Note 1 following G.L. c. 263, § 7.

NOTE 3   **Restitution.** "[A] defendant may be ordered to pay restitution, even where he was acquitted of larceny, so long as the restitution is significantly causally related to the crime of conviction." *Commonwealth v. Palmer P.*, 61 Mass. App. Ct. 230, 232 (2004) (citing *Commonwealth v. McIntyre*, 436 Mass. 829, 835–36 (2002)). In *Palmer P.*, the defendant was convicted under G.L. c. 266, § 18.

SECTION 18A
Entering dwelling house by false pretenses; intent to commit felony; larceny; punishment

Whoever enters a dwelling house by false pretenses, without breaking and with the intent to commit a felony, no person lawfully therein being put in fear, or whoever enters a dwelling house by false pretenses, without breaking and, after having entered, commits a larceny, as defined in section 30, no person lawfully therein being put in fear, shall be punished by imprisonment in the state prison for not more than ten years or by a fine of not more than $5,000 and imprisonment in a house of correction for not more than two years, or by both such fine and imprisonment.

SECTION 19
Railroad car; breaking and entering

Whoever breaks and enters, or enters in the night time without breaking, a railroad car, with intent to commit a felony, shall be punished by imprisonment in the state prison for not more than ten years or by a fine of not more than five hundred dollars and imprisonment in the house of correction for not more than two years.

SECTION 20
Stealing in building, ship or railroad car

Whoever steals in a building, ship, vessel or railroad car shall be punished by imprisonment in the state prison for not more than five years or by a fine of not more than five hundred dollars or by imprisonment in jail for not more than two years.

NOTE 1   "For over 100 years, it has been held that in order to obtain a conviction for the crime of larceny in a building, it is not enough for the Commonwealth to prove that the property was in a building at the time of the theft, and that the defendant was the thief. It is necessary to show also that the property was under the protection of the building, placed there for safe keeping, and not under the eye or personal care of some one in the building." *Commonwealth v. Cruz*, 430 Mass. 182, 190 (1999) (citations and quotation marks omitted).

NOTE 2   Charge of shoplifting improper under this section as the property is under the protection of the storeowner's servants rather than that of the building. *McDermott v. W.T. Grant Co.*, 313 Mass. 736, 737 (1943).

NOTE 3   Value of property stolen is immaterial. *Commonwealth v. Williams*, 56 Mass. (2 Cush.) 582, 588 (1849).

SECTION 20A
Breaking and entering of trucks, tractors, trailers or freight containers

Whoever breaks and enters, or enters without breaking, a truck, tractor/trailer unit, trailer, semi-trailer or freight container with intent to commit a felony, shall be punished by imprisonment in the state prison for not more than ten years

or by a fine of not more than five hundred dollars and imprisonment in the house of correction for not more than two years.

NOTE   See Notes following G.L. c. 266, §§ 14 and 16.

SECTION 20B
Stealing in trucks, tractors, trailers or freight containers

Whoever steals in a truck, tractor/trailer unit, trailer, semi-trailer or freight container shall be punished by imprisonment in the state prison for not more than five years or by a fine of not more than five hundred dollars or by imprisonment in jail for not more than two years.

NOTE   See Notes following G.L. c. 266, § 20.

SECTION 21
Stolen property; refusal to surrender

Whoever, having been convicted, either as principal or accessory, of burglary or robbery, or of any of the crimes described in sections seventeen to twenty, inclusive, of chapter two hundred and sixty-five, or of breaking and entering or of entering a building with intent to commit robbery or larceny, has in his possession or control money, goods, bonds or bank notes, or any paper of value, or any property of another, which was obtained or taken by means of such crime, and, upon being requested by the lawful owner thereof to deliver the same to him, refuses or fails so to do while having power to deliver the same, shall be punished by imprisonment in the state prison for not more than five years or in jail or house of correction for not more than two years.

SECTION 22
Poultry thieves; detention by owner

Whoever, with intent to commit larceny, breaks or enters or enters in the night without breaking any building or enclosure wherein is kept or confined any kind of live poultry, may be detained or kept in custody in a convenient place by the owner of the poultry, or by his agent or employee, for not more than twenty-four hours, Sunday excepted, until a complaint can be made against him for the offense and he be taken upon a warrant issued upon such complaint, and, upon conviction of such trespassing or breaking or entering shall be punished by imprisonment in the state prison for not more than three years, or by a fine of not more than five hundred dollars and imprisonment in the house of correction for not more than two years.

SECTION 23
Embezzlement of property at fire

Whoever steals, conveys away or conceals any furniture, goods, chattels, merchandise or effects of persons whose houses or buildings are on fire or are endangered thereby, and does not, within two days thereafter, restore the same or give notice of his possession thereof to the owner, if known, or, if unknown, to the mayor or one of the aldermen, selectmen or firewards of the place, shall be guilty of larceny.

SECTION 24
Stealing at a fire

Whoever steals in a building which is on fire, or steals property which has been removed in consequence of an alarm caused by fire, shall be punished by imprisonment in the state prison for not more than five years or by a fine of not more than five hundred dollars and imprisonment in jail for not more than two years.

2

SECTION 25
Larceny from the person

(a) Whoever commits larceny by stealing from the person of a person sixty-five years or older shall be punished by imprisonment in the state prison for not more than five years or in jail for not more than two and one-half years.

Whoever, after having been convicted of said crime commits a second or subsequent such crime, shall be punished by imprisonment for not less than two years. Said sentence shall not be reduced until one year of said sentence has been served nor shall the person convicted be eligible for probation, parole, furlough, work release or receive any deduction from his sentence for good conduct until he shall have served one year of such sentence; provided, however, that the commissioner of correction may, on the recommendation of the warden, superintendent, or other person in charge of a correctional institution, or the administrator of a county correctional institution, grant to said offender a temporary release in the custody of an officer of such institution for the following purposes only: to attend the funeral of next of kin or spouse; to visit a critically ill close relative or spouse; or to obtain emergency medical services unavailable at said institution. The provisions of section eighty-seven of chapter two hundred and seventy-six relating to the power of the court to place certain offenders on probation shall not apply to any person seventeen years of age or over charged with a violation of this subsection.

(b) Whoever commits larceny by stealing from the person of another shall be punished by imprisonment in the state prison for not more than five years or in jail for not more than two and one-half years.

NOTE 1   Larceny from the person is the theft, without the element of force or fear, of property under the protection of the victim. Property is under a person's protection if it is attached to him or his clothing or under his immediate guard. Perkins, *Criminal Law*, 235 (1957).

NOTE 2   To be found guilty under this section, it is *not* necessary that the taking be either openly or violently, or privily or fraudulently; but if it is with the knowledge, though without dissent or resistance, of the owner, the offense is committed, provided the taking is with an intention, on the part of the defendant, to deprive the owner of his property. *Commonwealth v. Dimond*, 57 Mass. (3 Cush.) 235, 238 (1849).

NOTE 3   Value of stolen property immaterial and need not be proved or found by the factfinder. *Commonwealth v. Burke*, 94 Mass. 182, 183 (1866).

NOTE 4a   **Attempted Larceny from the Person.** *See* G.L. c. 274, § 6 (attempt to commit crime).

NOTE 4b   One may be found guilty of this offense despite the fact that his victim had no property on his person capable of being stolen. *Commonwealth v. Sherman*, 105 Mass. 169, 170–71 (1870).

NOTE 4c   One may be found guilty of this offense despite the fact that the victim/owner is unknown. The offense is made out upon proof of a general intent to commit a crime, and the doing of overt acts toward its accomplishment. *Commonwealth v. Cline*, 213 Mass. 225 (1913).

NOTE 5   **Pickpocketing.** See Note 4 following G.L. c. 265, § 19 (unarmed robbery).

NOTE 6   **Joint Enterprise.** Although only one defendant may handle the property all those who associated themselves together in the crime may be found guilty of this crime. *Commonwealth v. Fortune*, 105 Mass. 592, 593 (1870).

NOTE 7   See Notes following G.L. c. 266, § 30 (larceny).

SECTION 26
Repealed

SECTION 27
Theft of tools of contractors, builders or mechanics; stealing

Whoever steals any tool belonging to any contractor, builder or mechanic from any building during the course of its construction, completion, alteration or repair, shall, for a first offense be punished by a fine of not more than one hundred dollars or by imprisonment for not more than six months, or both, and for a subsequent offense by a fine of one hundred dollars or by imprisonment for six months, or both.

NOTE   Restitution. *See* G.L. c. 276, § 92a.

SECTION 27A
Motor vehicle fraud

Whoever, with intent to defraud the insurer, removes or conceals a motor vehicle or trailer belonging to himself or another which is at the time insured against theft, or whoever, with intent as aforesaid, aids or abets in such removal or concealment, shall be punished by imprisonment in the state prison for not more than five years or by imprisonment in jail or house of correction for not less than one year nor more than two and one-half years, and a fine of not less than five hundred or more than five thousand dollars.

The court shall, after conviction, conduct an evidentiary hearing to ascertain the extent of the damages or financial loss suffered as a result of the defendant's crime. A person found guilty of violating this section shall, in all cases, upon conviction, in addition to any other punishment, be ordered to make restitution to the insurer for any financial loss sustained as a result of the commission of the crime; provided, however, that restitution shall not be ordered to a party whom the court determines to be aggrieved without that party's consent. Restitution shall be imposed in addition to incarceration or fine, and not in lieu thereof; provided, however, the court shall consider the defendant's present and future ability to pay in its determinations regarding a find; provided, further, that, whenever possible subject to the constraints of this paragraph and the preceding paragraph, the amount of a fine imposed for a violation of this section shall equal twice the amount of damages or financial loss suffered as a result of the defendant's crime.

In determining the amount, time and method of payment of restitution, the court shall consider the financial resources of the defendant and the burden restitution will impose on the defendant. Upon a real or impending change in financial circumstances, a defendant ordered to pay restitution may petition the court for a modification of the amount, time or method of payment of restitution. If the court finds that because of any such change the payment of restitution will impose an undue financial hardship on the defendant or his family, the court may modify the amount, time or method of payment, buy may not grant complete remission from payment of restitution.

If a defendant who is required to make restitution defaults in any payment of restitution or installment thereof, the court shall hold him in contempt unless said defendant has made a good faith effort to pay such restitution. If said defendant has made a good faith effort to pay such restitution, the court may modify the amount, time or method of payment, but may not grant complete remission from payment of restitution.

A prosecution commenced under this section shall not be placed on file, or continued without a finding and the sentence imposed upon a person convicted of violating this section for a second or subsequent offense shall not be reduced to less than one year nor shall any sentence of imprisonment imposed upon any person be suspended or reduced until such person shall have served one year of such sentence if convicted of a second or subsequent offense.

A person convicted of a second or subsequent offense of violating the provisions of this section shall not be eligible for probation, parole, furlough or work release; provided, however that the commissioner of correction may, on the recommendation of the warden, superintendent, or other person in charge of a correctional institution, grant to said offender a temporary release in the custody of an officer of such institution for the following purposes: to attend the funeral of next of kin or spouse; to visit a critically ill close relative or spouse; or to obtain emergency medical services unavailable at said institutions.

NOTE 1   See Note 3 following G.L. c. 266, § 28.

NOTE 2   Testimony of owner and witnesses in stolen motor vehicle cases. G.L. c. 278, § 6A.

SECTION 28
Motor vehicle theft

(a) Whoever steals a motor vehicle or trailer, whoever maliciously damages a motor vehicle or trailer, whoever buys, receives, possesses, conceals, or obtains control of a motor vehicle or trailer, knowing or having reason to know the same to have been stolen, or whoever takes a motor vehicle without the authority of the owner and steals from it any of its parts or accessories, shall be punished by imprisonment in the state prison for not more than fifteen years or by imprisonment in a jail or house of correction for not more than two and one-half years or by a fine of not more than fifteen thousand dollars, or by both such fine and imprisonment.

Evidence that an identifying number or numbers of a motor vehicle or trailer or part thereof has been intentionally and maliciously removed, defaced, altered, changed, destroyed, obliterated, or mutilated, shall be prima facie evidence that the defendant knew or had reason to know that the motor vehicle, or trailer or part thereof had been stolen.

A prosecution commenced under this subdivision shall not be placed on file or continued without a finding and the sentence imposed upon a person convicted of violating this subdivision for a second or subsequent offense shall not be reduced to less than one year imprisonment, nor shall any sentence imposed upon any person be suspended, or reduced, until such person shall have served one year of such sentence if convicted of a second or subsequent such offense.

A person convicted of a second or subsequent offense of violating the provisions of this subdivision shall not be eligible for probation, parole, furlough or work release; provided, however that the commissioner of correction may, on the recommendation of warden, superintendent, or other person in charge of a correctional institution, or the administrator of a county correctional institution, grant to said offender a temporary release in the custody of an officer of such institution for the following purposes: to attend the funeral of next of kin or spouse; to visit a critically ill close relative or spouse; or to obtain emergency medical services unavailable at said institution.

(b) Whoever conceals any motor vehicle or trailer thief knowing him to be such, shall be punished by imprisonment for not more than ten years or by imprisonment in jail or house of correction for not more than two and one-half years or by a fine of not more than five thousand dollars, or both.

(c) A conviction of a violation of this section or any adjudication that a person is a delinquent child by reason thereof shall be reported forthwith by the court or magistrate to the registrar of motor vehicles who shall revoke immediately the license to operate motor vehicles or the right to operate motor vehicles of the person so convicted or adjudged, and no appeal, motion for new trial or exceptions shall operate to stay the revocation of such license or right to operate. The registrar of motor vehicles after having revoked the license or right to operate of any such person so convicted or adjudged shall issue a new license or reinstate such right to operate, if the prosecution of such person is finally terminated in his favor; otherwise, no new license shall be issued nor shall such right to operate be reinstated until one year after the date of revocation following his original conviction or adjudication if for a first offense, or until five years after the date of revocation following any subsequent conviction or adjudication.

NOTE 1   **Related Statute.** G.L. c. 90, § 24(2)(a)—Use without authority.

NOTE 2   Failure to issue a citation does not provide a defense to a defendant charged with larceny of a motor vehicle under this section. *Commonwealth v. Boos*, 357 Mass. 68, 71 (1970).

NOTE 3   "In proceedings under sections twenty-seven A, twenty-eight, twenty-nine, one hundred and eleven A and one hundred and thirty-nine of chapter two hundred and sixty-six, certified copies of any motor vehicle or trailer ownership records, including computer records, in the possession of the registrar of motor vehicles, attested by the registrar or his designee or, if the motor vehicle or trailer is registered or titled in another state, such records similarly certified by the keeper of records of the appropriate motor vehicle department, shall be admissible as proof of ownership of a motor vehicle or trailer and shall be prima facie evidence that the use of the motor vehicle or trailer was unauthorized. If the defendant rebuts such evidence, the commonwealth may be granted a reasonable continuance to enable the owner of the vehicle to be brought into court to testify." G.L. c. 22C, § 42.

NOTE 4   **Jurisdiction.** G.L. c. 277, § 58A.

NOTE 5   **Restitution.** G.L. c. 276, § 92A.

NOTE 6   **Description of Ownership.** G.L. c. 277, § 25.

NOTE 7   **Proof of Ownership of Property.** G.L. c. 278, § 9.

NOTE 8   Testimony of owner and witnesses in stolen motor vehicle cases. G.L. c. 278, § 6A.

NOTE 9   "Because 'reason to know' as used in G.L. c. 266, sec. 28(a), can be read as referring exclusively to subjective knowledge or belief that a vehicle is stolen, the statute is constitutional." *Commonwealth v. Dellamano*, 393 Mass. 132, 140 (1984). *See also Commonwealth v. Boris*, 317 Mass. 309, 313 (1944).

NOTE 10   Use without authority, G.L. c. 90, § 24, is not a lesser included offense of receiving a stolen motor vehicle. *Commonwealth v. Lewis*, 41 Mass. App. Ct. at 910–11 (1996).

NOTE 11   **ATV is Motor Vehicle.** An ATV "may be deemed a motor vehicle for the purposes of G.L. c. 266, § 28." *Commonwealth v. Gonsalves*, 56 Mass. App. Ct. 506, 508 (2002).

NOTE 12   **Possession.** "A person's presence in a vehicle as a passenger, without more, is insufficient to prove that he possessed the vehicle. See *Commonwealth v. Campbell*, 60 Mass. App. Ct. 215, 217 (2003), citing *Commonwealth v. Johnson*, 7 Mass. App. Ct. 191, 193 (1979). To establish possession, the prosecution must show that the defendant exercised 'dominion and control'

2

over the automobile. *Commonwealth v. McArthur*, [55 Mass. App. Ct. 596, 598 (2002)]. See *Commonwealth v. Gonsalves*, 56 Mass. App. Ct. 506, 511 (2002) ('requisite control')." *Commonwealth v. Darnell D.*, 445 Mass. 670, 673 (2005).

SECTION 29
Statement concerning theft: recovery of vehicles; restitution

Whenever a motor vehicle is stolen or misappropriated, the owner of record shall sign and submit to the appropriate police authority a statement under the penalties of perjury on a form containing such information relating to the theft or misappropriation of the vehicle as is prescribed by the registrar of motor vehicles.

Whenever a stolen or misappropriated motor vehicle is recovered by a police officer or other law enforcement officer, the police department shall notify the registry of motor vehicles, the owner of record and the storage facility if any, as soon as possible after the identity of the owner is determined. Such notification may be made by letter, telephone call or personal visit to the owner and shall include information as to the location of the recovered vehicle. In the event the vehicle is placed in a garage or other storage facility, the owner of said facility shall lose his lien for the reasonable charges for storage and towing unless he notifies the owner of record of the vehicle by certified mail and return receipt requested within five days of the date of said recovery or his actual knowledge of the identity of the owner of record. Said notice shall contain the information on the location of the vehicle and the amount of charge due on said vehicle.

The court shall, after a defendant is convicted of a violation of subsection (a) of section twenty-eight, conduct an evidentiary hearing to ascertain the extent of the damages or financial loss suffered as a result of the defendant's crime. A person found guilty of violating subsection (a) of section twenty-eight shall in all cases, upon conviction, in addition to any other punishment, be ordered to make restitution to the insurer for any financial loss sustained as a result of the commission of the crime; provided, however, that restitution shall not be ordered to a party whom the court determines to be aggrieved without that party's consent. Restitution shall be imposed in addition to incarceration or fine, and not in lieu thereof; provided, however, the court shall consider the defendant's present and future ability to pay in its determinations regarding a fine; provided, further, that, whenever possible subject to the constraints of this paragraph and the first paragraph of said subsection (a) of section twenty-eight, the amount of a fine imposed for a violation of said subsection (a) of section twenty-eight shall equal twice the amount of damages or financial loss suffered as a result of the defendant's crime.

In determining the amount, time and method of payment of restitution, the court shall consider the financial resources of the defendant and the burden restitution will impose on the defendant. Upon a real or impending change in financial circumstances, a defendant ordered to pay restitution may petition the court for a modification of the amount, time or method of payment of restitution. If the court finds that because of any such change the payment of restitution will impose an undue financial hardship on the defendant or his family, the court may modify the amount, time or method of payment, but may not grant complete remission from payment of restitution.

If a defendant who is required to make restitution defaults in any payment of restitution or installment thereof, the court shall hold him in contempt unless said defendant has made a good faith effort to pay such restitution. If said defendant has made a good faith effort to pay such restitution, the court may modify the amount, time or method of payment, but may not grant complete remission from payment of restitution.

NOTE   See Notes following G.L. c. 266, § 28.

SECTION 29A
Repealed

SECTION 29B
Burning motor vehicle; owner's statement to fire department

Whenever a motor vehicle is burned, the owner of record of such vehicle shall submit to the appropriate fire department a statement signed under the penalties of perjury containing such information concerning the burning of such vehicle as the state fire marshall shall require.

SECTION 30
Larceny

(1) Whoever steals, or with intent to defraud obtains by false pretense, or whoever unlawfully, and with intent to steal or embezzle, converts, or secretes with intent to convert, the property of another as defined in this section, whether such property is or is not in his possession at the time of such conversion or secreting, shall be guilty of larceny, and shall, if the property stolen is a firearm, as defined in section one hundred and twenty-one of chapter one hundred and forty, or if the value of the property exceeds two hundred and fifty dollars, be punished by imprisonment in the state prison for not more than five years, or by a fine of not more than twenty-five thousand dollars and imprisonment in jail for not more than two years; or, if the value of the property stolen other than a firearm as so defined, does not exceed two hundred and fifty dollars, shall be punished by imprisonment in jail for not more than one year or by a fine of not more than three hundred dollars; or, if the property was stolen from the conveyance of a common carrier or of a person carrying on an express business, shall be punished for the first offence by imprisonment for not less than six months nor more than two and one-half years, or by a fine of not less than fifty nor more than six hundred dollars, or both, and for a subsequent offense, by imprisonment for not less than eighteen months nor more than two and one-half years, or by a fine of not less than one hundred and fifty nor more than six hundred dollars, or both.

(2) The term "property", as used in the section, shall include money, personal chattels, a bank note, bond, promissory note, bill of exchange or other bill, order or certificate, a book of accounts for or concerning money or goods due or to become due or to be delivered, a deed or writing containing a conveyance of land, any valuable contract in force, a receipt, release or defeasance, a writ, process, certificate of title or duplicate certificate issued under chapter one hundred and eighty-five, a public record, anything which is of the realty or is annexed thereto, a security deposit received pursuant to section fifteen B of chapter one hundred and eighty-six, electronically processed or stored data, either tangible or intangible, data while in transit, telecommunications services, and any domesticated animal, including dogs, or a beast or bird which is ordinarily kept in confinement.

2

(3) The stealing of real property may be a larceny from one or more tenants, sole, joint, or in common, in fee, for life or years, at will or sufferance, mortgagors or mortgagees, in possession of the same, or who may have an action of tort against the offender for trespass upon the property, but not from one having only the use or custody thereof. The larceny may be from a wife in possession, if she is authorized by law to hold such property as if sole, otherwise her occupation may be the possession of the husband. If such property which was of a person deceased is stolen, it may be a larceny from any one or more heirs, devisees, reversioners, remaindermen or others, who have a right upon such deceased to take possession, but not having entered, as it would be after entry. The larceny may be from a person whose name is unknown, if it would be such if the property stolen were personal, and may be committed by those who have only the use or custody of the property, but not by a person against whom no action of tort could be maintained for acts like those constituting the larceny.

(4) Whoever steals, or with intent to defraud obtains by a false pretense, or whoever unlawfully, and with intent to steal or embezzle, converts, secretes, unlawfully takes, carries away, conceals or copies with intent to convert any trade secrets of another, regardless of value, whether such trade secret is or is not in his possession at the time of such conversion or secreting, shall be guilty of larceny, and shall be punished by imprisonment in the state prison for not more than five years, or by a fine of not more than twenty-five thousand dollars and imprisonment in jail for not more than two years. The term "trade secret" as used in the paragraph means and includes anything tangible or intangible or electronically kept or stored, which constitutes, represents, evidences or records a secret scientific, technical, merchandising, production or management information, design, process, procedure, formula, invention or improvement.

(5) Whoever steals or with intent to defraud obtains by a false pretense, or whoever unlawfully, and with intent to steal or embezzle, converts, or secretes with intent to convert, the property of another, sixty years of age or older, or of a person with a disability as defined in section thirteen K of chapter two hundred and sixty-five, whether such property is or is not in his possession at the time of such conversion or secreting, shall be guilty of larceny, and shall, if the value of the property exceeds two hundred and fifty dollars, be punished by imprisonment in the state prison for not more than ten years or in the house of correction for not more than two and one-half years, or by a fine of not more than fifty thousand dollars or by both such fine and imprisonment; or if the value of the property does not exceed two hundred and fifty dollars, shall be punished by imprisonment in the house of correction for not more than two and one-half years or by a fine of not more than one thousand dollars or by both such fine and imprisonment. The court may order, regardless of the value of the property, restitution to be paid to the victim commensurate with the value of the property.

NOTE 1   Theft offenses, e.g., larceny, embezzlement, larceny by false pretenses, have been merged into this section. G.L. c. 277, §§ 39, 41.

NOTE 2   Definition. Stealing, Larceny—The criminal taking, obtaining or converting of personal property, with intent to defraud or deprive the owner permanently of the use of it; including all forms of larceny, criminal embezzlement and obtaining by criminal false pretenses. G.L. c. 277, § 39.

NOTE 3a   Larceny. The taking and carrying away of the personal property of another with the intent unlawfully to deprive that other permanently of the use of it. *Commonwealth v. Johnson*, 379 Mass. 177, 181 (1979); *Rich v. United Material Fire Ins. Co.*, 328 Mass. 133, 134 (1951).

NOTE 3b   Taking.
(1) The trespassory taking is against possession, not necessarily title; thus one may steal from a thief, or steal contraband. R. Stearns, *The Massachusetts Criminal Law: A District Court Prosecutor's Guide*, at 114, Criminal Justice Training Council (1979); *Commonwealth v. Rourke*, 64 Mass. (10 Cush.) 397, 399 (1852); *Commonwealth v. Coffee*, 75 Mass. (9 Gray) 139 (1857).

(2) One with title to property may steal it from one in lawful possession, e.g., repairman with a mechanic's lien. R. Stearns, *The Massachusetts Criminal Law: A District Court Prosecutor's Guide*, Criminal Justice Training Council (1979) (citing Perkins, *Criminal Law*, 196 (1957)).

(3) Possession by the owner may be constructive; thus the complaint may allege theft from the owner or the bailee. *Id.*; *Commonwealth v. Sullivan*, 104 Mass. 552, 553–54 (1870).

(4) See Note 3e (7) below.

NOTE 3c   Carrying Away (Asportation). A momentary transfer from the victim to the defendant of control over the victim's property satisfies this requirement. *Commonwealth v. Bradley*, 2 Mass. App. Ct. 804 (1974). *See also Commonwealth v. Davis*, 41 Mass. App. Ct. 901 (1996) ("[T]aking goods beyond a store's premises is not a necessary precondition to a conviction for larceny. . . . Asportation requires] that the defendant remove the stolen goods from the store's control to his own.").

NOTE 3d   Personal Property.
(1) *See* G.L. c. 266, §§ 30(2), 30(4).

(2) Proof at trial of object stolen must correspond with description of object in the complaint. *Commonwealth v. Baker*, 368 Mass. 58, 67 (1975). *Compare* G.L. c. 277, § 37 (variances).

(a) It is well settled that the insufficiency of the description of certain articles has no other effect than to strike them out of the indictment and the verdict is to be applied to the remaining property which is properly and sufficiently charged to have been stolen. *Commonwealth v. Williams*, 56 Mass. (2 Cush.) 582, 588 (1849).

(3) Value.

(a) While a thing stolen must be of some value, it need not be an article having any special, appreciable, or market value. *Commonwealth v. Cabot*, 241 Mass. 131, 140 (1922).

(b) The precise value of the property need not be proven; value is a question of fact for the jury. *Riggs*, 80 Mass. (14 Gray) 376, 378 (1860); *Commonwealth v. Cabot*, 241 Mass. at 141.

(d) **The $250 Threshold.**
(1) A complaint need not be any more specific than "over $250" if a felony is charged or "under $250" for a misdemeanor. G.L. c. 277, § 24.

(2) In a continuous larcenous scheme carried out over a period of time involving, in the aggregate, property worth more than $250, larceny over (a felony) may be charged in a single complaint. That the value of the property involved in any single taking may have been more or less than $250 is immaterial. *Commonwealth v. England*, 350 Mass. 83 (1966); *Commonwealth v. Pina*, 1 Mass. App. Ct. 411 (1973). *See also* G.L. c. 277, § 31 (alternative allegations).

(a) *Cf. Commonwealth v. Donovan*, 395 Mass. 20, 27–31 (1985). Two defendants placed a false night deposit bank box on the wall of a bank building. Seven individuals, on the same evening, placed their deposits into the bank box. Defendants each charged, convicted and sentenced consecutively for seven counts of larceny. Held, a single crime, not seven distinct crimes, occurred.

NOTE 3e   Of Another.
(1) The larceny may be from an unknown person. G.L. c. 266, § 30 (3).

(2) See Note 3a above.

(3) Proof of ownership of property. G.L. c. 278, § 9.

(4) Description of ownership. G.L. c. 277, § 25.

(5) Variance. G.L. c. 277, § 35.

(6) By way of analogy, see ownership notes following G.L. c. 266, § 16.

(7) The complaint need not allege the true owner of the property, merely a person or entity with a property right superior to that of the thief. R. Stearns, *The Massachusetts Criminal Law: A District Court Prosecutor's Guide*, Criminal Justice Training Council (1988) (citing *Commonwealth v. Abbott Eng'g, Inc.*, 351 Mass. 568, 571 (1967)).

(8) "It is an essential element of the crime charged that the property stolen must be 'the property of another'. It is sufficient if the evidence and the permissible inferences from that evidence 'are sufficient to bring minds of ordinary intelligence and sagacity to the persuasion' that the Commonwealth has established beyond a reasonable doubt that the property belonged to someone other than the defendant." *Commonwealth v. Casale*, 381 Mass. 167, 168 (1980). *Commonwealth v. Latimore*, 378 Mass. 671, 676–77 (1979).

"Direct proof of ownership, though preferable, is not essential, since the statute only requires a showing that the defendant was not the owner." *Commonwealth v. Souza*, 397 Mass. 236, 238 (1986).

NOTE 3f(1)   With Intent to Deprive Permanently.

(a) Intent is to be ascertained by the factfinder by an analysis of all the evidence and circumstances disclosed at the trial. *Commonwealth v. Schraffa*, 2 Mass. App. Ct. 808, 809 (1974). In *Schraffa* the jury could have found that the defendant intended to steal whatever the truck contained although its contents may have been unknown to him when the truck was taken.

(b) **Lost or Mislaid Property.** "The finder of lost goods may lawfully take them into his possession, and if he does so without any felonious intent at that time, a subsequent conversion of them to his own use, by whatever intent that conversion is accompanied, will not constitute larceny. But if, at the time of first taking them into his possession, he has a felonious intent to appropriate them to his own use and to deprive the owner of them, and then knows or has the reasonable means of knowing or ascertaining, by marks on the goods or otherwise, who the owner is, he may be found guilty of larceny." *Commonwealth v. Titus*, 116 Mass. 42, 44–45 (1874).

(c) **Intent to Steal.** Intent to steal may be inferred "from his having torn off the magnetic sticker, hidden it behind other merchandise, and carried goods for which he had no means of paying past the cash registers and the alarm stanchions into the unsecured hallway area giving unimpeded access to the garage and the outdoors." *Commonwealth v. Davis*, 41 Mass. App. Ct. 901 (1996).

NOTE 3f(2)   "The intent to deprive the owner permanently *may* be found where the defendant uses or disposes of the vehicle so 'as to show indifference' whether the owner recovers possession of it." *Commonwealth v. Souza*, 428 Mass. 478, 491 (1998) (quoting *Commonwealth v. Salerno*, 356 Mass. 642, 648 (1970)).

NOTE 3g   Compare the Model Penal Code § 233.5 (1962). ("[A] person who is aware that property is lost, mislaid, or mistakenly delivered is guilty of larceny unless he takes reasonable steps to restore it to its owner.") R. Stearns, *The Massachusetts Criminal Law: A District Court Prosecutor's Guide* (1988) at 237.

NOTE 4   Larceny from person v. larceny from building.
"Larceny from a person and larceny in a building are distinguished from each other in large part based upon the circumstances in which the stolen property was safeguarded prior to its theft. We have recently noted the distinction between the two forms of larceny:

'On many occasions, the property in question will have been placed in the control, or under the supervision, of one or more individuals. It will, at least for a certain period of time, be in the possession of those persons. At other times, personal property will not be left in the control of individuals, but rather will be placed within a secured structure with the expectation on the part of the owner that the structure itself will provide the desired protection against theft.'

Commonwealth v. Barklow, 52 Mass. App. Ct. 765, 767 (2001). Moreover, the structure need not be vacant for property to be 'under the protection of the building.' Ibid. All that is required is that

the property be under the protection of the building 'rather than under the protection of the person or persons who are present.' Ibid." *Commonwealth v. Willard*, 53 Mass. App. Ct. 650, 654–55 (2002).

NOTE 5a   Larceny by False Pretenses.   G.L. c. 266, § 30 provides that "[w]hoever steals, or with intent to defraud obtains by a false pretense . . . the property of another," shall be guilty of larceny. This requires proof that (1) a false statement of fact has been made; (2) known or believed by the defendant to be false; (3) made with the intent that the person to whom it was made should rely upon its truth; and (4) that such person did rely upon it as true and parted with property as a result of such reliance. *Commonwealth v. Leonard*, 352 Mass. 636, 644–45 (1967). *See also Commonwealth v. Lewis*, 48 Mass. App. Ct. 343, 350 (1999).

"To establish larceny by embezzlement, the prosecution must prove beyond a reasonable doubt (a) that the defendant fraudulently converted to [her] personal use, (b) property under her control by virtue of a position of trust or confidence, (c) with the intent to deprive the owner of the property permanently. The distinctive gist of embezzlement is the betrayal of the trust placed in the embezzler by the victim." *Commonwealth v. Caparella*, 70 Mass. App. Ct. 506, 510 (2007) (citations and quotation marks omitted).

NOTE 5b   Under the common law a distinction was drawn between larceny by trick (a felony wherein deceit was used to gain possession, but not title to property) and obtaining property by false pretenses (a misdemeanor in which both possession and title to property were gained). Today both are treated as false pretenses without regard to the niceties of possession and/or title. R. Stearns, *The Massachusetts Criminal Law: A District Court Prosecutor's Guide* (1988) at 238.

NOTE 5c   False Statement of Fact.

(1) It is for the jury to say whether a representation made is intended as an expression of an opinion (not punishable) or as a statement of fact. *Commonwealth v. Quinn*, 222 Mass. 504, 513–14 (1916).

(2) A false statement need not be made directly by the defendant to the victim; rather it may be made through a third party. *Commonwealth v. Leonard*, 352 Mass. 636, 644–46 (1967); *Commonwealth v. Camelio*, 1 Mass. App. Ct. 296, 299–300 (1973) (joint enterprise).

(3) Defendant's knowledge that a statement was false may be inferred from all of the evidence. *Commonwealth v. Leonard*, 352 Mass. at 646.

NOTE 5d   Intent. The intent of the accused to cheat, injure or defraud a particular person is not a requisite of larceny by false pretenses. Under such circumstances all that is necessary to establish the crime is proof that a false statement was made with the intention to commit a fraud, and money or property was thereby obtained. *Commonwealth v. Camelio*, 1 Mass. App. Ct. 296, 299–300 (1973).

NOTE 5e   Defenses.

(1) "[I]t was no defense to show that (the defendant) might have obtained other moneys from other persons by similar pretenses, and omitted to do so; or that in cases where she had obtained other moneys, either by false pretenses or otherwise, she had repaid the same." *Commonwealth v. Howe*, 132 Mass. 250, 260 (1882).

(2) It is *no* defense that the victimized party also made false representations as to his goods, which he exchanged with the defendants. *Commonwealth v. Morrill*, 62 Mass. (8 Cush.) 571, 573–74 (1851).

(3) **Variance.** It is *no* defense that the value of the goods are worth less than alleged in the complaint. *Commonwealth v. Morrill*, 62 Mass. at 574.

NOTE 6a   Embezzlement. Embezzlement is the fraudulent conversion of property of another in the defendant's possession in violation of a trust. *Commonwealth v. Hays*, 80 Mass. (14 Gray) 62, 64 (1859).

2

NOTE 6b The essence of embezzlement is the breach of trust or violation of a confidence intentionally reposed by one party and voluntarily assumed by the other. *Commonwealth v. Hays*, 80 Mass. (14 Gray) 62, 65 (1859).

(1) Accordingly, the following examples, while resembling embezzlement, do *not* constitute it:

(a) Property received by mistake. *Commonwealth v. Hays*, 80 Mass. at 65.

(b) Debtor-creditor relationship. *Commonwealth v. Snow*, 284 Mass. 426, 430–32 (1933).

NOTE 6c "[T]he existence of a confidential or fiduciary relationship between the embezzler and the victim has always been at the heart of th[e] crime [of embezzlement]." *Commonwealth v. Mills*, 436 Mass. 387, 394 (2002).

NOTE 6d **Elements.** "Pursuant to Instruction 5.415 of the Model Jury Instructions for Use in the District Court (1997), in order to establish embezzlement, the Commonwealth must prove: (1) 'That the defendant, while in a position of trust or confidence, was entrusted with possession of personal property belonging to another person'; (2) 'That the defendant took that property, or hid it, or converted it to his (her) own use, without the consent of the owner'; and (3) 'That the defendant did so with the intent to deprive the owner of the property permanently' (emphasis added)." *Commonwealth v. Mills*, 436 Mass. 387, 394 n.4 (2002).

NOTE 6e Fraudulent intent is an essential element of the crime. Without it, while misconduct may exist, there is no criminality. This question, along with that of conversion, is one for the jury. "Fraudulently" well defines the character of the conversion or taking to be proved, that is, there must be some deceit, concealment or breach of trust. *Commonwealth v. O'Brien*, 305 Mass. 393, 397 (1940).

NOTE 6f "[F]raud may be defined to be any artifice whereby he who practices it gains, or attempts to gain, some undue advantage to himself, or to work some wrong or do some injury to another, by means of a representation which he knows to be false, of an act which he knows to be against right or in violation of some positive duty." *Commonwealth v. O'Brien*, 305 Mass. at 397–98 (quoting *Commonwealth v. Tuckerman*, 76 Mass. (10 Gray) 173, 203 (1857)).

NOTE 6g **Defenses.**

(1) It is *no* defense that the property (money) entrusted to the defendant was for an illegal purpose. *Commonwealth v. Cooper*, 130 Mass. 285, 288 (1881).

(2) Intending to return the stolen property or the value thereof is not a defense. R. Stearns, *The Massachusetts Criminal Law: A District Court Prosecutor's Guide*, (1988) at 240; *Commonwealth v. Stovall*, 22 Mass. App. Ct. 737, 642 (1986).

NOTE 7a **Honest But Mistaken Belief.** "[T]he specific intent to steal is negated by a finding that a defendant held an honest, albeit mistaken, belief that he was entitled to the property he took. . . . [A]n honest belief need not be objectively reasonable to negate the specific intent required for larceny. . . . Evidence of reasonableness may, however, be considered by the jury to assist in their determination whether to credit a defendant's honest belief. Neither juries nor judges are required to divorce themselves of common sense, but rather should apply to facts which they find proven such reasonable inferences as are justified in the light of their experience as to the natural inclinations of human beings." *Commonwealth v. Liebenow*, 470 Mass. 151, 157, 160, 161 (2014).

NOTE 7b "Where, as here, a defendant asserts a claim of right defense that allows for an honest, but mistaken, belief in the defendant's legal right to take property, we hold that it is not enough that the Commonwealth prove that the defendant should have known of the victim's incapacity. Instead, if the defendant meets his or her burden of production, the Commonwealth must prove beyond a reasonable doubt that the defendant knew that the victim lacked the mental capacity to consent to the transaction." *Commonwealth v. St. Hilaire*, 470 Mass. 338, 348 (2015).

NOTE 8 **Larceny Versus Receiving Stolen Goods.** While a defendant may be charged with both larceny and receiving stolen goods, he may only be convicted of one. *Commonwealth v. Pettingel*, 10 Mass. App. Ct. 916 (1980).

NOTE 9 **Possession of Recently Stolen Goods.** See Notes 3a et seq. following G.L. c. 266, § 60.

NOTE 10 **Date.** If the precise date of the offense is not known, "on or about" a certain date will suffice. *Commonwealth v. Corcoran*, 348 Mass. 437, 442 (1965); *see also* G.L. c. 277, §§ 20, 34 and 35.

NOTE 11 **Joint Enterprise.** "It is very obvious that several persons may associate themselves together in an attempt to steal from one's person. In such cases, they are all principals, and may be jointly indicted. Though but one of them thrusts his hand into the pocket, all may be equally guilty; and though the indictment alleges that they all did so, yet proof that one did so is sufficient." *Commonwealth v. Fortune*, 105 Mass. 592, 593 (1870) (citations omitted).

NOTE 12 **Venue.** G.L. c. 277, §§ 58 and 59.

NOTE 13 **Related Statutes.** There are numerous statutes contained within this Chapter which relate to larceny. See the table of contents of this Chapter.

The more commonly utilized statutes include:

(1) G.L. c. 266, § 20—Stealing in building, ship or railroad car.

G.L. c. 266, § 20B—Stealing in truck, tractors, etc.

G.L. c. 266, § 21—Refusal to surrender stolen property.

G.L. c. 266, §§ 23 and 24—Theft at fires.

G.L. c. 266, § 25—Larceny from the person.

G.L. c. 266, § 28—Motor vehicle theft.

G.L. c. 266, § 37—Drawing or uttering fraudulent checks, drafts, etc.

G.L. c. 266, §§ 37A, 37B, 37C and 37D—Misuse of credit cards.

G.L. c. 266, § 40—Common and notorious thief.

G.L. c. 266, § 41—Larceny of a bicycle (second offense).

G.L. c. 266, § 47—Theft or abuse of dogs.

G.L. c. 266, § 49—Possession of burglarious implements.

G.L. c. 266, § 60—Receiving stolen goods.

G.L. c. 266, § 62—Common receiver of stolen or embezzled goods.

G.L. c. 266, § 63—Unlawful use of boat, vehicle, or animal.

G.L. c. 266, § 75—Obtaining property by trick.

G.L. c. 266, § 87—Larceny, etc. of certain leased or rented property.

(2) G.L. c. 265, § 19—Unarmed robbery.

G.L. c. 265, § 20—Assault with intent to rob.

(3) G.L. c. 277, § 30—Intent to injure or defraud.

G.L. c. 277, § 41—Indictment for criminal dealing with personal property.

G.L. c. 277, § 79—Form of pleading.

NOTE 14a **Restitution.** "There is no question that restitution is an appropriate consideration in a criminal sentencing. The procedure used to determine the amount of restitution or reparation must be reasonable and fair. . . . If the record reveals an arbitrary method of determining the amount of restitution, the order cannot stand. . . . The hearing need not be elaborate; a forum for both sides to air their views and cross-examine is sufficient." *Commonwealth v. Nawn*, 394 Mass. 1, 6–7 (1985).

NOTE 14b "Where items are stolen from a retail store, the actual loss to the victim is the replacement value of the items, that is, their wholesale price, unless the Commonwealth proves by a preponderance of the evidence that the items would have been sold were they not stolen, in which event the actual loss would be the retail price of the items." *Commonwealth v. Henry*, 475 Mass. 117, 129 (2016).

NOTE 15 **Continuing Larcenous Scheme.** "In two indictments containing a total of 180 counts, the defendant was charged with larceny from his corporate employer, and in two other indictments containing 128 counts, he was charged with making false entries in his corporate employer's books with intent to defraud.

2

Each count alleges a separate incident of larceny or false entry. . . .

"The defendant moved for a dismissal of the indictments on the ground that the offenses charged by the larceny indictments constituted only one crime of continuing larceny, and the offenses charged in the other indictments constituted only one continuing crime of false entry."

The Supreme Judicial Court agreed with the Commonwealth.

"Thus, if the defendant obtained his employer's money by the use of a forged check with larcenous intent 180 times, he committed 180 crimes of larceny. The same is true with respect to the alleged making of 128 false entries with intent to defraud."

Commonwealth v. Murray, 401 Mass. 771, 771–72 (1988).

SECTION 30A
Shoplifting

Any person who intentionally takes possession of, carries away, transfers or causes to be carried away or transferred, any merchandise displayed, held, stored or offered for sale by any store or other retail mercantile establishment with the intention of depriving the merchant of the possession, use of benefit of such merchandise or converting the same to the use of such person without paying to the merchant the value thereof; or

any person who intentionally conceals upon his person or otherwise any merchandise offered for sale by any store or other retail mercantile establishment with the intention of depriving the merchant of proceeds, use or benefit of such merchandise or converting the same to the use of such person without paying to the merchant the value thereof; or

any person who intentionally alters, transfers or removes any label, price tag or marking indicia of value or any other markings which aid in determining value affixed to any merchandise displayed, held, stored or offered for sale by any store or other retail mercantile establishment and to attempt to purchase such merchandise personally or in consort with another at less than the full retail value with the intention of depriving the merchant of all or some part of the retail value thereof; or

any person who intentionally transfers any merchandise displayed, held, stored or offered for sale by any store or other retail mercantile establishment from the container in or on which the same shall be displayed to any other container with intent to deprive the merchant of all or some part of the retail value thereof; or

any person who intentionally records a value for the merchandise which is less than the actual retail value with the intention of depriving the merchant of the full retail value thereof; or

any person who intentionally removes a shopping cart from the premises of a store or other retail mercantile establishment without the consent of the merchant given at the time of such removal with the intention of permanently depriving the merchant of the possession, use or benefit of such cart, and

where the retail value of the goods obtained is less than one hundred dollars, shall be punished for a first offense by a fine not to exceed two hundred and fifty dollars, for a second offense by a fine of not less than one hundred nor more than five hundred dollars and for a third or subsequent offense by a fine of not more than five hundred dollars or imprisonment in a jail for not more than two years, or by both such fine and imprisonment. Where the retail value of the goods obtained equals or exceeds one hundred dollars, any violation of this

section shall be punished by a fine of not more than one thousand dollars or by imprisonment in the house of correction for not more than two and one-half years, or by both such fine and imprisonment.

If the retail value of the goods obtained is less than one hundred dollars, this section shall apply to the exclusion of section thirty.

Law enforcement officers may arrest without warrant any person he has probable cause for believing has committed the offense of shoplifting as defined in this section. The statement of a merchant or his employee or agent that a person has violated a provision of this section shall constitute probable cause for arrest by any law enforcement officer authorized to make an arrest in such jurisdiction.

NOTE **Implied Repeal.** "The Commonwealth argues that the judge erred in dismissing the complaint charging the defendant with larceny, G.L. c. 266, § 30(1), because the shoplifting statute, G.L. c. 266, § 30A, did not repeal the larceny statute as it relates to the theft of merchandise offered for sale. We agree, and therefore vacate the order of dismissal.

"The defendant's argument, apparently adopted by the judge, is that, because both the larceny and shoplifting statutes prohibit the same conduct in some instances, the subsequent shoplifting statute impliedly repealed the application of the general larceny statute to conduct punishable under the shoplifting statute, G.L. c. 266, § 30A.

"Where two statutes deal with the same subject they should be interpreted harmoniously to effectuate a consistent body of law. We note, moreover, the well-settled principle that there is a very strong presumption against implied repeal."

Commonwealth v. Hudson, 404 Mass. 282, 285–86 (1989) (footnote, citations and quotation marks omitted). (It should be noted that under the 1996 amendment shoplifted merchandise worth less than $100 should be prosecuted under G.L. c. 266, § 30A, not the larceny statute, G.L. c. 266, § 30.)

SECTION 30B
Unlawful distribution, possession, or deactivation of theft detection shielding device
(Added by 2014 Mass. Acts c. 451, § 2, effective Apr. 6, 2015.)

(a) A person shall be guilty of unlawful distribution of a theft detection shielding device if the person knowingly manufactures, sells, offers for sale or distributes a laminated or coated bag or other device intended to shield merchandise from detection by an electronic or magnetic theft detector.

(b) A person shall be guilty of unlawful possession of a theft detection shielding device if the person, with the intent to commit, aid or abet a theft, knowingly possesses a laminated or coated bag or device intended to shield merchandise from detection by an electronic or magnetic theft detector.

(c) A person shall be guilty of unlawful possession of a theft detection device deactivator or remover if the person knowingly possesses any tool or device designed or adapted to either: (i) allow the deactivation of a theft detection device, with the intent to use such tool or device to deactivate a theft detection device on merchandise without the permission of the merchant or person owning or lawfully holding said merchandise; or (ii) allow the removal of a theft detection device from merchandise, with the intent to use such tool or device to remove a theft detection device from merchandise without the permission of the merchant or person owning or lawfully holding said merchandise.

(d) A person shall be guilty of unlawful distribution of a theft detection device deactivator or remover if the person knowingly manufactures, sells, offers for sale or distributes a tool or device designed or adapted to allow the deactivation of a theft detection device or to allow the removal of a theft detection device from merchandise, without the permission of the merchant or person owning or lawfully holding said merchandise.

(e) A person shall be guilty of unlawful deactivation or removal of a theft detection device if the person intentionally deactivates or removes a theft detection device from merchandise prior to purchase, in a retail establishment, with the intent to steal said merchandise.

(f) A violation of this section shall be punished by imprisonment in a house of correction for not more than 2½ years or by imprisonment in the state prison for not more than 5 years or by a fine of not more than $25,000, or by both such fine and imprisonment.

SECTION 30C
Counterfeiting of retail sales or return receipt or price ticket
(Added by 2014 Mass. Acts c. 451, § 2, effective Apr. 6, 2015.)

A person who, with intent to cheat or defraud a retailer, possesses, uses, utters, transfers, makes, alters, counterfeits or reproduces a retail sales or return receipt, price ticket or universal product code label shall be punished by imprisonment in a house of correction for not more than 2½ years or by imprisonment in the state prison for not more than 5 years or by a fine of not more than $10,000, or by both such fine and imprisonment.

SECTION 30D
Organized retail crime
(Added by 2014 Mass. Acts c. 451, § 2, effective Apr. 6, 2015.)

(a) For purposes of this section, "retail merchandise" shall mean 1 or more items of tangible personal property displayed, held, stored or offered for sale in a retail establishment.

(b) A person commits an organized retail crime if the person, acting in concert with 2 or more persons and within a 180 day period steals, embezzles or obtains by fraud, false pretense or other illegal means retail merchandise valued at more than $2,500 to resell or otherwise reenter such retail merchandise into commerce; provided, that a series of thefts from 1 or more mercantile establishments may be aggregated; provided further, that said person may be prosecuted in any county where a theft from a mercantile establishment occurred.

A violation of this subsection shall be punished by imprisonment in a state prison for not more than 10 years.

(c) A person commits an aggravated organized retail crime if the person, acting in concert with 2 or more persons and within a 180 day period, steals, embezzles or obtains by fraud, false pretense or other illegal means retail merchandise valued at more than $10,000 to resell or otherwise reenter such retail merchandise into commerce; provided, that a series of thefts from 1 or more mercantile establishments may be aggregated; provided further, that said person may be prosecuted in any county where a theft from a mercantile establishment occurred.

A violation of this subsection shall be punished by imprisonment in a state prison for not more than 15 years.

(d) A person shall be a leader of an organized retail theft enterprise if the person conspires with others as an organizer, supervisor, financier or manager, to commit an organized retail crime or an aggravated organized retail crime. A leader of organized retail crime may be punished by a fine of not

more than $250,000 or 5 times the retail value of the merchandise seized at the time of the arrest, whichever is greater, or imprisonment in state prison for not more than 20 years, or both such fine and imprisonment.

SECTION 31
Signature; obtaining under false pretenses
Whoever by a false pretence, with intent to defraud, obtains the signature of a person to a written instrument, the false making whereof would be a forgery, shall be punished by imprisonment in the state prison for not more than ten years, or by a fine of not more than five hundred dollars and imprisonment in the jail for not more than two years.

NOTE   Venue. *See* G.L. c. 277, § 59.

SECTION 32
Fraudulent conversion of property by captain of vessel
Whoever, being a captain of a vessel, embezzles or fraudulently converts or appropriates money, goods or property, held or possessed by or delivered to him, which belong wholly or in part to the crew of such vessel, the owners of the vessel, or to those who have furnished supplies to the vessel, although he is a joint charterer or co-partner with the members of the crew or with the owners of the vessel, or with the person who furnished the supplies, shall be guilty of larceny.

SECTION 33
Larceny; false pretenses relating to contracts, banking transactions or credit
(1) Whoever, with intent to defraud, obtains by a false pretence the making, acceptance or endorsement of a bill of exchange or promissory note, the release or substitution of collateral or other security, an extension of time for the payment of an obligation, or the release or alteration of the obligation of a written contract, or (2) whoever, with intent to defraud, by a false statement in writing respecting the financial condition, or means or ability to pay, of himself or of any other person, obtains for himself or for any other person credit from any bank or trust company or any banking institution or any mortgage lender, as defined in section 1 of chapter 255E, or any retail seller of goods or services accustomed to give credit in any form whatsoever shall be guilty of larceny.

NOTE 1   General Laws c. 266, § 30 and this section declare distinct offenses although both are classified as larcenies. In Section 30 it is the theft of property as defined in the statute which is penalized; here it is the fraudulent obtaining of credit. As such the defendant could *not*, as a matter of right, demand that the Commonwealth elect on which of the two counts go to the jury. It is a matter within the discretion of the judge. *Commonwealth v. Greenberg*, 339 Mass. 557, 572–73 (1959).

NOTE 2   "[W]e conclude that the instructions fairly distinguished between obtaining credit by false written statements (§ 33[2]) and inducing the bank to part with money by false pretenses (§ 34) and that therefore the convictions were not duplicative based on the law of the case as established by the judge's instructions." *Commonwealth v. Duddie Ford, Inc.*, 409 Mass. 387, 397 (1991).

SECTION 33A
Intent to defraud commercial computer service; penalties
Whoever, with intent to defraud, obtains, or attempts to obtain, or aids or abets another in obtaining, any commercial computer service by false representation, false statement, unauthorized charging to the account of another, by installing

2

or tampering with any facilities or equipment or by any other means, shall be punished by imprisonment in the house of correction for not more than two and one-half years or by a fine of not more than three thousand dollars, or both. As used in this section, the words "commercial computer service" shall mean the use of computers, computer systems, computer programs or computer networks, or the access to or copying of the data, where such use, access or copying is offered by the proprietor or operator of the computer, system, program, network or data to others on a subscription or other basis for monetary consideration.

SECTION 34
Larceny; inducement to part with property
Whoever, with intent to defraud and by a false pretence, induces another to part with property of any kind or with any of the benefits described in sections 33 and 33A shall be guilty of larceny.

SECTION 35
Nonapplicability of Secs. 30, 31 and 34
Sections thirty, thirty-one and thirty-four shall not apply to a purchase of property by means of a false pretence relative to the purchaser's means or ability to pay, if, by the terms of the purchase, payment therefor is not to be made upon or before the delivery of the property purchased, unless such pretence is made in writing and is signed by the person to be charged.

SECTION 35A
False material statements or omissions during or in connection with mortgage lending process; penalties; mitigating factors with respect to sentencing
(a) As used in this section, the following words shall have the following meanings, unless the context clearly otherwise requires:—

"Funds", shall include, but not be limited to, a commission, fee, yield spread premium or compensation in any form.

"Material omission", the omission or concealment of a material fact necessary to prevent a statement from being misleading, in the light of the circumstances under which the statement is made.

"Mortgage lending process", the process through which a person seeks or obtains a residential mortgage loan including, but not limited to, solicitation, application, origination, negotiation of terms, third-party provider services, underwriting, signing and closing, and funding of the loan; provided, however, that documents involved in the mortgage lending process shall include, but not be limited to, uniform residential loan applications or other loan applications, appraisal reports, HUD-1 settlement statements, supporting personal documentation for loan applications such as W-2 forms, verification of income and employment, bank statements, tax returns and payroll stubs and any required disclosures.

"Pattern of residential mortgage fraud", violation of subsection (b) in connection with 3 or more residential properties.

"Person", a natural person, corporation, company, limited liability company, partnership, real estate trust, association or any other entity.

"Residential mortgage loan", a loan or agreement to extend credit made to a person, which loan is secured by a mortgage, security interest, deed to secure debt, deed of trust, or other document representing a security interest or lien upon any interest in a 1 to 4 family residential property located in the commonwealth, including the renewal or refinancing of any such loan.

(b) Whoever intentionally: (1) makes or causes to be made any material statement that is false or any statement that contains a material omission, knowing the same to be false or to contain a material omission, during or in connection with the mortgage lending process, with the intent that such statement be relied upon by a mortgage lender, borrower or any other party to the mortgage lending process; (2) uses, or facilitates the use of, any material statement that is false or any statement that contains a material omission, knowing the same to be false or to contain a material omission, during or in connection with the mortgage lending process, with the intent that such statement be relied upon by a mortgage lender, borrower or any other party to the mortgage lending process; (3) receives any proceeds or any other funds in connection with a residential mortgage closing, knowing such proceeds or funds were obtained in violation of clause (1) or (2); or (4) files or causes to be filed with a registrar of deeds any document that contains a material statement that is false or a material omission, knowing such document to contain a material statement that is false or a material omission, shall be punished by imprisonment in the state prison for not more than 5 years or by imprisonment in the house of correction for not more than 2 and one-half years or by a fine of not more than $10,000 in the case of a natural person or not more than $100,000 in the case of any other person, or by both such fine and imprisonment.

Any person who engages in a pattern of residential mortgage fraud shall be punished by imprisonment in the state prison for not more than 15 years or by a fine of not more than $50,000, in the case of a natural person, or not more than $500,000 in the case of any other person, or by both such fine and imprisonment.

(c) If a defendant is convicted of a violation of this section as a result of conduct or an omission by an employee or agent of the defendant the court may consider the following mitigating factors with respect to sentencing:

(1) that the defendant had instituted and maintained at the time of the violation, and continues to have, a written policy including:

(i) a prohibition against conduct that violates this section by employees and agents of the defendant;

(ii) penalties or discipline for violation of the policy;

(iii) a process for educating employees and agents concerning the policy and consequences of a violation thereof; and

(iv) with respect to a defendant authorized to conduct criminal history checks for the employee's or agent's position, a requirement for a criminal history check before employing an employee or engaging an agent and a requirement that the defendant will not employ or engage an individual who has been convicted of a crime involving fraud;

(2) a demonstration that the defendant enforces the policy described in clause (1); and

(3) prior to the violation of this section the defendant provided a copy of the policy described in clause (1), including a description of the consequences for violating the policy, to the employee or agent who committed the violation.

SECTION 36
Repealed

SECTION 37
Fraudulent checks, etc.; drawing or uttering

Whoever, with intent to defraud, makes, draws, utters or delivers any check, draft or order for the payment of money upon any bank or other depositary, with knowledge that the maker or drawer has not sufficient funds or credit at such bank or other depositary for the payment of such instrument, although no express representation is made in reference thereto, shall be guilty of attempted larceny, and if money or property or services are obtained thereby shall be guilty of larceny. As against the maker or drawer thereof, the making, drawing, uttering or delivery of such a check, draft or order, payment of which is refused by the drawee, shall be prima facie evidence of intent to defraud and of knowledge of insufficient funds in, or credit with, such bank or other depositary, unless the maker or drawer shall have paid the holder thereof the amount due thereon, together with all costs and protest fees, within two days after receiving notice that such check, draft or order has not been paid by the drawee. The word "credit", as used herein, shall be construed to mean an arrangement or understanding with the bank or depositary for the payment of such check, draft or order.

NOTE   "Most States' statutes require (like Massachusetts) that property or something of value be obtained in exchange for a fraudulent check, and cases decided under substantially all such statutes have concluded that the statute does not apply to a check tendered in payment of an antecedent debt." *Commonwealth v. Goren*, 72 Mass. App. Ct. 678, 682 (2008).

SECTION 37A
Misuse of credit cards; definitions

As used in sections thirty-seven A to thirty-seven C, inclusive, the following words shall have the following meanings, unless the context otherwise requires:

"Cardholder", the person named on the face of a credit card to whom or for whose benefit the credit card is issued by an issuer.

"Credit card", any instrument or device, whether known as a credit card, credit plate, or by any other name, issued with or without fee by an issuer for the use of the cardholder in obtaining money, goods, services or anything else of value on credit.

"Expired credit card", a credit card which is no longer valid because the term shown on its face has elapsed.

"Falsely embosses", completion of a credit card, without the authorization of the named issuer, by adding any of the matter, other than the signature of the cardholder, which an issuer requires to appear on the credit card before it can be used by a cardholder.

"Falsely makes", making or drawing, in whole or in part, a device or instrument which purports to be the credit card of a named issuer but which is not such a credit card because the issuer did not authorize the making or drawing, or altering a credit card which was validly issued.

"Incomplete credit card", a credit card that does not contain all of the matter that must be stamped, embossed, imprinted or written on said card other than the signature, as required by the issuer before it can be used by a cardholder.

"Issuer", the business organization or financial institution which issues a credit card or his duly authorized agent.

"Receives" or "receiving", acquiring possession or control or accepting as security for a loan.

"Revoked credit card", a credit card which is no longer valid because permission to use it has been suspended or terminated by the issuer.

SECTION 37B
Misuse of credit cards; penalties; multiple possession; presumption; arrest

Whoever, with intent to defraud, (a) makes or causes to be made, either directly or indirectly, any false statement as to a material fact in writing, knowing it to be false and with intent that it be relied on, respecting his identity or that of any other person, or his financial condition or that of any other person, for the purpose of procuring the issuance of a credit card, or (b) takes a credit card from the person, possession, custody or control of another without the cardholder's consent by any conduct which would constitute larceny, or who, with knowledge that it has been so taken, receives the credit card with intent to use it or to sell it, or to transfer it to a person other than the issuer or cardholder, or (c) receives a credit card that he knows to have been lost, mislaid, or delivered under a mistake as to the identity or address of the cardholder, and who retains possession with intent to use it or to sell it or to transfer it to a person other than the issuer or the cardholder, or (d) being a person other than the issuer or his authorized agent, sells a credit card, or buys a credit card from a person other than the issuer or his authorized agent, or (e) being a person other than the cardholder or a person authorized by him, signs a credit card, or (f) uses, for the purpose of obtaining money, goods, services or anything else of value, a credit card obtained or retained in violation of clauses (b) to (e), inclusive, or a credit card which he knows is forged, expired or revoked, where the value of money, goods or services obtained in violation of this section is not in excess of two hundred and fifty dollars, or (g) obtains money, goods, services or anything else of value by representing without the consent of the cardholder that he is said cardholder or by representing that he is the holder of a card and such card has not in fact been issued, where the value of money, goods or services obtained is not in excess of two hundred and fifty dollars, (h) being a person authorized by an issuer to furnish money, goods, services or anything else of value upon presentation of a credit card by the cardholder, or any agent or employees of such person, furnishes money, goods, services or anything else of value upon presentation of a credit card which he obtained or retained in violation of clauses (b) to (e), inclusive, or credit card which he knows is forged, expired or revoked where the value of the goods or services obtained is not in excess of two hundred and fifty dollars, or (i) being a person who is authorized by an issuer to furnish money, goods, or services or anything else of value upon presentation of a credit card by the cardholder, or any agent or employee of such person, fails to furnish money, goods, services or anything else of value which he represents in writing to the issuer that he has furnished, and the difference between the value of all money, goods, services and anything else of value actually furnished and the value represented to the issuer to have been furnished does not exceed two hundred and fifty dollars, or (j) receives money, goods, services or anything else of value obtained in violation of clauses (f) to (i), inclusive or (k) makes a false statement in reporting a credit card to be lost or stolen, shall be punished by a fine of

2

not more than five hundred dollars or by imprisonment in a jail or house of correction for not more than one year or both.

Whoever has in his possession or under his control stolen credit cards issued in the names of four or more other persons shall be presumed to have violated clause (b).

Whoever is discovered by a police officer in the act of violating this section, while such officer is lawfully at or within the place where such violation occurs, may be arrested without warrant by such police officer.

SECTION 37C
Fraudulent use of credit cards to obtain money, goods or services; false embossment of credit cards, multiple possession, presumption; arrest

Whoever, with intent to defraud, (a) obtains control over a credit card as security for debt, or (b) receives a credit card which he knows was taken or retained under circumstances which constitute credit card theft or a violation of clauses (a) or (d) of section thirty-seven B or clause (a) of this section, or (c) falsely makes or falsely embosses a purported credit card or utters such a credit card, or (d) obtains money, goods, services or anything else of value by use of a credit card obtained or retained in violation of clauses (b) to (e), inclusive, of section thirty-seven B, or by use of a credit card which he knows is forged, expired or revoked, where the value of the money, goods or services obtained in violation of this section is in excess of two hundred and fifty dollars, or (e) obtains money, goods or services or anything else of value by representing without the consent of the cardholder that he is said cardholder or by representing that he is the holder of a card and such card has not in fact been issued, where the value of money, goods or services obtained in violation of this section is in excess of two hundred and fifty dollars, or (f) being a person authorized by an issuer to furnish money, goods, services or anything else of value upon presentation of a credit card which he knows was obtained in violation of subsections (b) to (e), inclusive, of section thirty-seven B, or a credit card which he knows is forged, expired or revoked, when the value of the money, goods or services obtained is in excess of two hundred and fifty dollars, or (g) being a person authorized by an issuer to furnish money, goods, services or anything else of value upon presentation of a credit card by the cardholder or any agent or employee of such person, fails to furnish money, goods or services or anything else of value which he represents in writing to the issuer that he has furnished, and the difference between the value of all money, goods, services and anything else of value actually furnished and the value represented to the issuer to have been furnished exceeds two hundred and fifty dollars, or (h) receives money, goods, services or anything else of value obtained in violation of subsections (f) or (g) of section thirty-seven B, or (i) possesses one or more incomplete credit cards, intending to complete them without the consent of the issuer, or (j) possesses, with knowledge of its character, machinery, plates or any other contrivance designed to reproduce instruments purporting to be the credit cards of an issuer who has not consented to the preparation of such credit cards, shall be punished by a fine of not more than two thousand dollars, or by imprisonment in jail or house of correction for not more than two and one half years or in the state prison for not more than five years, or by both such fine and imprisonment.

Whoever has in his possession or under his control four or more credit cards which are falsely embossed shall be presumed to have violated clause (c).

Whoever is discovered by a police officer in the act of violating this section, while such officer is lawfully at or within the place where such violation occurs, may be arrested without warrant by such police officer.

NOTE   "A cardholder may consent to another person using his or her credit card. See G.L. c. 266, § 37C(e)." *Commonwealth v. Liotti*, 49 Mass. App. Ct. 641, 642 (2000).

SECTION 37D
Publishing credit card numbering or coding systems

Whoever publishes or causes to be published the number or code of an existing, canceled, revoked, expired, or nonexistent credit card issued by a public utility company or the numbering or coding system which is employed in the issuance of such credit cards, or any method, scheme, instruction or information on how to fraudulently avoid payment for telecommunication services, with the intent that such number or coding system or information be used or with knowledge that such system or information are to be used to fraudulently avoid the payment of any lawful charges imposed by a public utility company shall be punished by a fine not exceeding two thousand dollars or by imprisonment for not more than twelve months, or both.

As used in this section, "publishes" means the communication of information to any one or more persons, either orally, in person, or by telephone, radio, or television, or in a writing of any kind, including a letter or memorandum, circular, poster, or handbill, newspaper or magazine article or book with the intent that such information be used or employed in violation of this section.

SECTION 37E
Identity fraud

(a) For purposes of this section, the following words shall have the following meanings:-

"Harass", willfully and maliciously engage in an act directed at a specific person or persons, which act seriously alarms or annoys such person or persons and would cause a reasonable person to suffer substantial emotional distress.

"Personal identifying information", any name or number that may be used, alone or in conjunction with any other information, to assume to identity of an individual, including any name, address, telephone number, driver's license number, social security number, place of employment, employee identification number, mother's maiden name, demand deposit account number, savings account number, credit card number or computer password identification.

"Pose", to falsely represent oneself, directly or indirectly, as another person or persons.

"Victim", any person who has suffered financial loss or any entity that provided money, credit, goods, services or anything of value and has suffered financial loss as a direct result of the commission or attempted commission of a violation of this section.

(b) Whoever, with intent to defraud, poses as another person without the express authorization of that person and uses such person's personal identifying information to obtain or to attempt to obtain money, credit, goods, services, anything of value, any identification card or other evidence of such person's identity, or to harass another shall be guilty of identity fraud and shall be punished by a fine of not more than $5,000 or imprisonment in a house of correction for not more than two and one-half years, or by both such fine and imprisonment.

(c) Whoever, with intent to defraud, obtains personal identifying information about another person without the express authorization of such person, with the intent to pose as such person or who obtains personal identifying information about a person without the express authorization of such person in order to assist another to pose as such person in order to obtain money, credit, goods, services, anything of value, any identification card or other evidence of such person's identity, or to harass another shall be guilty of the crime of identity fraud and shall be punished by a fine of not more than $5,000 or imprisonment in a house of correction for not more than two and one-half years, or by both such fine and imprisonment.

(d) A person found guilty of violating any provisions of this section shall, in addition to any other punishment, be ordered to make restitution for financial loss sustained by a victim as a result of such violation. Financial loss may include any costs incurred by such victim in correcting the credit history of such victim or any costs incurred in connection with any civil or administrative proceeding to satisfy any debt or other obligation of such victim, including lost wages and attorney's fees.

(e) A law enforcement officer may arrest without warrant any person he has probable cause to believe has committed the offense of identity fraud as defined in this section.

(f) A law enforcement officer shall accept a police incident report from a victim and shall provide a copy to such victim, if requested, within 24 hours. Such police incident reports may be filed in any county where a victim resides, or in any county where the owner or license holder of personal information stores or maintains said personal information, the owner's or license holder's principal place of business or any county in which the breach of security occurred, in whole or in part.

NOTE   "In . . . the variation of identity fraud at issue here, a conviction under G.L. c. 266, § 37E(b), 'requires that the Commonwealth prove beyond a reasonable doubt four elements, specifically, that a defendant (1) posed as another person; (2) did so without that person's express authorization; (3) used the other person's identifying information to obtain, or attempt to obtain, something of value; and (4) did so with the intent to defraud.' *Commonwealth v. Giavazzi*, 60 Mass. App. Ct. 374, 376 (2004).

"[This] variation of identity fraud under G.L. c. 266, § 37E(b) . . . 'is necessarily accomplished on commission of the greater crime[s]' of the variations of credit card fraud under G.L. c. 266, §§ 37C(e) and 37B(g), of which the defendant was convicted, and so it is a lesser included offense." *Commonwealth v. Thompson*, 89 Mass. App. Ct. 456, 462–63 (2016).

SECTION 38
Larceny; wrongful detention of money by carriers

Whoever, being engaged in the business of transporting merchandise, parcels or other property for hire, accepts from a consignor or his agent or from a connecting carrier any merchandise, parcel or other property for delivery to a consignee upon payment by the consignee of an amount of money for said merchandise, parcel or other property, and embezzles or fraudulently converts to his own use, or with intent to use or embezzle, takes, secretes or otherwise disposes of, or fraudulently withholds, appropriates, lends, invests or other-

wise uses or applies such money in whole or in part or any substitute therefor received by him from such consignee, contrary to the instructions or without the consent of the consignor, shall be deemed guilty of larceny. A member or employee of a co-partnership, or any officer or employee of a corporation, engaged in said business of transporting merchandise, parcels or other property for hire who so disposes of such money in whole or in part or any substitute therefor for his own use or for the use of said co-partnership or corporation, contrary to the instructions or without the consent of the consignor, shall be guilty of larceny.

SECTION 38A
Construction loan; misapplication

Whoever obtains a building or construction loan, secured by a mortgage of real estate, for the payment for labor furnished or to be furnished and/or materials used and/or employed or to be used and/or employed in the construction, repair, removal or alteration of a building or other structure which is attached or is to be attached to such real estate, and, before payment in full for all labor furnished or to be furnished and/or materials used or to be used and/or employed or to be employed as aforesaid, applies the proceeds of such loan, or any part thereof, to any use other than payment for labor and/or materials as aforesaid, shall be punished by a fine of not more than five hundred dollars or by imprisonment in jail for not more than one year, or both.

SECTION 39
Wills; destruction or concealment

Whoever steals or for any fraudulent purpose destroys, mutilates or conceals a will, codicil or other testamentary instrument shall be punished by imprisonment in the state prison for not more than five years or in the house of correction for not more than two years. An indictment for a violation of this section need not contain any allegation of value or ownership; and in the trial of such an indictment, no disclosure made by any person under section fourteen of chapter one hundred and ninety-one shall be used in evidence against him.

SECTION 40
Common and notorious thief

Whoever, having been convicted, upon indictment, of larceny or of being accessory to larceny before the fact, afterward commits a larceny or is accessory thereto before the fact, and is convicted thereof upon indictment, and whoever is convicted at the same sitting of the court, as principal or accessory before the fact, of three distinct larcenies, shall be adjudged a common and notorious thief, and shall be punished by imprisonment in the state prison for not more than twenty years or in jail for not more than two and one half years.

NOTE   See Note 1 following G.L. c. 278, § 11A.

SECTION 41
Larceny of bicycles; second conviction

Whoever is convicted of a second offense of the larceny of a bicycle shall, if the value of the bicycle stolen exceeds ten dollars, be punished by imprisonment in the state prison for not more than five years or by a fine of not more than two hundred dollars or by imprisonment in jail for not more than two years.

2

SECTION 42
Larceny of paper designated for bank bills

Whoever commits larceny of a printed piece of paper or blank designed for issue by any incorporated bank or banking company in the United States as a bank bill, certificate or promissory note, or printed by means of an engraved plate designed for printing such pieces of paper or blanks, with intent to injure or defraud either by uttering or passing the same, or causing or allowing the same to be uttered or passed as true, either with or without alteration or addition, shall be punished by imprisonment in the state prison for life or for any term of years.

SECTION 43
Paper designated for bank bills; retention by printer with intent to pass

Whoever, having been employed to print or having assisted in printing a printed piece of paper or blank described in the preceding section, or having been intrusted with the care or custody thereof, retains it in his possession without the knowledge and consent of the corporation for which it was printed, with intent to injure or defraud either by uttering or passing it or causing or allowing it to be uttered or passed as true, either with or without alteration or addition, shall be punished by imprisonment in the state prison for life or for any term of years.

SECTIONS 44–46
Repealed

SECTION 47
Dogs; wrongful removal of collar; poisoning; penalty

Whoever wrongfully removes the collar from a dog which is licensed and collared as provided in chapter one hundred and forty shall be punished by a fine of not more than one hundred dollars, or by six months' imprisonment, or both.

NOTE   **Related Statute.** G.L. c. 272, § 85A—Removal of dog license tag.

SECTION 48
Stolen goods; duty of arresting officers to secure

An officer who arrests a person charged as a principal or accessory in a robbery or larceny shall secure the property which is alleged to have been stolen, annex a schedule thereof to his return and be answerable for the same; and, upon conviction of the offender, it shall be restored to the owner.

SECTION 49
Possession of burglarious tools

Whoever makes or mends, or begins to make or mend, or knowingly has in his possession, an engine, machine, tool or implement adapted and designed for cutting through, forcing or breaking open a building, room, vault, safe or other depository, in order to steal therefrom money or other property, or to commit any other crime, knowing the same to be adapted and designed for the purpose aforesaid, with intent to use or employ or allow the same to be used or employed for such purpose, or whoever knowingly has in his possession a master key designed to fit more than one motor vehicle, with intent to use or employ the same to steal a motor vehicle or other property therefrom, shall be punished by imprisonment in the state prison for not more than ten years or by a fine of not more than one thousand dollars and imprisonment in jail for not more than two and one half years.

NOTE 1a   Possession may be either actual or constructive. *Commonwealth v. Tivnon*, 74 Mass. (8 Gray) 375, 381 (1857).

NOTE 1b   In a joint enterprise, a lookout, who never entered the building nor actually used the tools, can nonetheless be found guilty of not only the breaking and entering, but the possession of burglarious tools as well. *Commonwealth v. Conroy*, 333 Mass. 751, 754–55 (1956).

NOTE 2a   A burglarious intention can doubtless be inferred from the mere possession of tools uniquely or very highly adapted to burglarious purposes, i.e., pry bars, sledge hammers, skeleton keys, explosives, and possibly dent pullers; but an intention to use ordinary tools, i.e., screwdrivers and wirecutters, must appear clearly from the circumstances in which they are found. *Commonwealth v. Dellinger*, 10 Mass. App. Ct. 549, 561 (1980), *reversed on other grounds on appeal after remand*, 383 Mass. 780, 781 (1981).

NOTE 2b   A battering ram, used to gain entrance for the purposes of a criminal trespass (a sit-in) to the discomfort or exclusion of the usual occupant, is a burglarious tool. *Commonwealth v. Krasner*, 358 Mass. 727, 730, aff'd, 360 Mass. 848, 849 (1971).

NOTE 2c   "[T]he words 'tool' and 'implement' refer to man-made, rather than naturally occurring, items. . . . [T]he indictment failed to identify an implement 'adapted and designed' for breaking into a building, G.L. c. 266, § 49, because a rock is not a tool or implement within the meaning of § 49." *Commonwealth v. Dykens*, 473 Mass. 635, 647–48 (2016).

NOTE 3a   This statute does *not* require the depository to be located in a building or that it be annexed to real estate. A car trunk, thus, is a depository and within the provision of this section. *Commonwealth v. Tilley*, 306 Mass. at 415–16.

NOTE 3b   "Building, room, . . ." does not only refer to places where goods susceptible of theft may be found or deposited, but also to places (buildings and rooms) which humans ordinarily occupy. *Commonwealth v. Krasner*, 358 Mass. at 730.

NOTE 3c   **Bike Locks.** "[A] bike lock attached to a parking meter is not a depository within the meaning of G.L. c. 266, s. 49." *Commonwealth v. Hogan*, 41 Mass. App. Ct. 73, 75 (1996).

NOTE 4a   If an indictment fails to charge the defendant with possession of such tools or implements for the purpose of committing any other crime the Commonwealth is confined in its proof to the language in the complaint. *Commonwealth v. Armenia*, 4 Mass. App. Ct. 33, 38 (1976). In *Armenia* these crucial words were deleted. As such the defendant's conviction for possession of a screwdriver and hammer, used to punch out a car's ignition switch, was reversed as sufficient evidence was lacking to infer an intent to steal *from* the automobile. *Commonwealth v. Armenia*, 4 Mass. App. Ct. at 38–39.

NOTE 5a   The offense is complete when the tools are procured with a design to use them for a burglarious purpose. A general intent is sufficient. *Commonwealth v. Tivnon*, 74 Mass. (8 Gray) 375, 381 (1857).

NOTE 5b   Defendants caught with a screwdriver, kitchen knife, and gloves emerging from a dwelling. A pane of glass above the door lock was found broken. There were no jimmy marks or fingerprints. Held, the intent to use the tools to break and enter is reasonably inferable. That there was *no* evidence that the tools were in fact so used does *not* bar the inference. (note: the gloves, although *not* burglarious instruments, were useful to avoid leaving finger marks). *Commonwealth v. Jones*, 355 Mass. 170, 177 (1969).

NOTE 5c   Out-of-state car seen, with engine running, by fur store. Car driven around and stopped almost in front of fur store. Codefendant seen bent down in front of store window, looking under papers which were placed over whatever was in the window. Defendant also seen looking into the window and conversing with the codefendant. When questioned, defendant said he was

2

waiting for his girlfriend who worked nearby. Police found tools and marked map in rear seat of car and arrested the defendants for possession of burglarious tools. Further evidence at trial that defendant had been in the store as a possible customer and had been in its basement, using the restroom. Held, conviction for possession of burglarious tools affirmed as the inference was strong that the intent was to use the tools to enter the fur store to steal furs. *Cortellesso v. Commonwealth*, 354 Mass. 514, 515–16 (1968).

NOTE 6a   Opinion Evidence. Police officer allowed to testify that chisel and bags of cartridges are ordinarily used by burglars and found upon or with them. *Commonwealth v. Johnson*, 199 Mass. 55, 62 (1908).

NOTE 6b   Police officer testified that a door had been "jimmied," there were "scuff marks" on the floor showing that the "safe had been dragged . . . across the floor. There were also scuff marks on the window . . . and . . . there was a safe laying . . . [on the] roof to the garage. Obviously . . . [the safe] had been pushed over and landed on the roof." Lastly he testified that tools found in the defendant's car were a "pretty complete set of safe cracker's tools." Held, evidence admissible. *Commonwealth v. Garreffi*, 355 Mass. 428, 432 (1969).

NOTE 6c   Police expert on explosives (12 years dealing with explosives and 38 years as a chemist) permitted to testify as an expert on the adaptability of the tools and implements in question (dynamite, nitroglycerine, wire, fuses, detonators, gloves, punches, drills, chisels, a bitstock, hammer, pocket knife, padlock, keys, two thumb screws and pistol cartridges) for cutting through and breaking open buildings and other depositories. *Commonwealth v. Anderson*, 245 Mass. 177, 185 (1923).

NOTE 7   See Note 4 accompanying G.L. c. 263, § 7.

SECTION 50
State treasury; fraud or embezzlement by employee

A person employed in the treasury of the commonwealth who commits a fraud or embezzlement therein shall be punished by a fine of not more than two thousand dollars or by imprisonment in the state prison for life or for any term of years.

SECTION 51
City, town or county officers; fraud or embezzlement

A county, city or town officer who embezzles or fraudulently converts, or who fraudulently takes or secretes with intent so to do, effects or property which belong to or are in possession of said county, city or town, shall be punished by imprisonment in the state prison for not more than ten years or by a fine of not more than one thousand dollars and imprisonment in jail for not more than two years.

SECTION 52
Bank officers or employees; fraud or embezzlement

An officer, director, trustee, agent or employee of a bank, as defined in section one of chapter one hundred and sixty-seven, who fraudulently converts, or fraudulently takes and secretes with intent so to do, any bullion, money, note, bill or other security for money which belongs to and is in possession of such bank, or which belongs to any person and is deposited therein, shall, whether intrusted with the custody thereof or not, be guilty of larceny from said bank. Any such officer, director, trustee, agent or employee so guilty of larceny and any person who knowingly aids, counsels or procures such larceny to be committed shall be punished by imprisonment in the state prison for not more than fifteen years, or by a fine of not more than two thousand dollars and imprisonment in jail for not more than two and one half years.

SECTION 53
Bank officers or employees; prosecution for fraud or embezzlement; evidence

In prosecutions for such crimes, the fraudulent taking or receiving by any person of bullion, money, notes, bills or other security for money which belongs to such bank, by reason of an unlawful confederacy or agreement between him and an officer of said bank or any person in the employment thereof, with intent to defraud the same, shall be deemed to be a fraudulent taking by such officer or person in the employment of the bank to his own use, within the meaning of the preceding section; and it shall not be necessary, upon the trial, to identify the particular bullion, money, note, bill or security for money which is so taken or received. Upon the trial of the crime of embezzling, fraudulently converting or fraudulently converting or fraudulently taking and secreting, with intent so to embezzle or convert, the bullion, money, notes, bank notes, checks, drafts, bills of exchange, obligations or other securities for money of any person, bank, corporation, partnership, county, city or town by a cashier or other officer, clerk, agent or servant of such person, bank, corporation, partnership, county, city or town, evidence may be given of any such embezzlement, fraudulent conversion or taking with such intent committed within six months after the time stated in the indictment.

SECTION 53A
Bank officers and employees; misconduct; penalty

An officer, director, trustee, agent or employee of a bank, as defined in section one of chapter one hundred and sixty-seven, who wilfully misapplies otherwise than as described in section fifty-two or fifty-three, any of the moneys, funds, credits or other property of such bank; or who, without authority from the directors or trustees of such bank, executes or issues a certificate of deposit, order or bill of exchange, or makes an acceptance, purporting to be executed, issued or made by such bank; or who, without such authority, assigns any note, bond, draft, bill of exchange, mortgage, judgment, decree or other property of such bank; or who loans the funds or credit of such bank to any individual, corporation, joint stock company, trust, association or partnership when the assets of such borrower are known by such officer, director, trustee, agent or employee to be less than all the liabilities of such borrower other than debts subordinated to such loan, unless such loan is adequately secured or is necessary for the protection of existing loans; or who knowingly receives or accepts for such bank any fictitious, valueless, inadequate or irresponsible obligation directly or as security or endorsement unless the consideration or security is otherwise sufficient, or unless it shall be necessary to prevent loss upon a debt previously contracted in good faith; or who certifies any check drawn upon such bank unless the drawer then has on deposit with the bank and entered to his credit on its books not less than the amount of money specified in the check; or who resorts to any fictitious or colorable loan, transfer or device to avoid any provision of law relating to such bank; or who knowingly makes or causes to be made any false entry in any book, report or statement of such bank; and any person who knowingly aids or abets any violation of this section shall be punished by a fine of not more than ten thousand dollars or by imprisonment in the state prison for not more than ten years, or in a jail or house of correction for not more than two and one half years, or by both such fine and imprisonment.

2

SECTION 54
Receipt of deposits by insolvent banks; penalty

Any officer or employee of a bank, as defined in section one of chapter one hundred and sixty-seven, who receives or permits the receipt of any deposit knowing that such bank is insolvent, shall be punished by imprisonment for not more than two and one half years or by a fine of not more than five thousand dollars, or both.

SECTION 55
Liquidating agent or receiver; embezzlement

An agent appointed by the commissioner of banks for the purpose of liquidating the affairs of a bank, as defined in section one of chapter one hundred and sixty-seven, or a person employed by said commissioner under section twenty-six of said chapter, or a receiver or other officer appointed by a court of record, who embezzles or fraudulently converts, or fraudulently takes and secretes with intent so to do, or wilfully misapplies, moneys, funds, credits or other property in his possession by virtue of his appointment or employment, shall be guilty of larceny and shall be punished by imprisonment in the state prison for not more than ten years, or by a fine of not more than one thousand dollars and imprisonment in a jail or house of correction for not more than two years.

SECTION 56
Brokers or agents; embezzlement

A broker, or officer, manager or agent of a corporation doing the business of brokers, who, having been intrusted, solely or jointly, with money, stock or security for the payment of money, with any direction in writing to invest, dispose of, apply, pay or deliver such money, stock or security, or any part thereof, or the proceeds or any part of the proceeds thereof, in any manner, for any purpose or to any person mentioned or specified in such direction in violation of good faith and contrary to the terms of such direction, embezzles or fraudulently converts such money, stock or security, or any part thereof, or the proceeds or any part of the proceeds thereof, shall be punished by imprisonment in the state prison for not more than five years or in jail for not more than two and one half years or by a fine of not more than five hundred dollars.

SECTION 57
Fiduciaries; embezzlement

A trustee under an express trust created by a deed, will or other instrument in writing, or a guardian, conservator, executor or administrator, or any person upon or to whom such a trust has devolved or come, who embezzles or fraudulently converts or appropriates money, goods or property held or possessed by him for the use or benefit, either wholly or partially, of some other person or for a public or charitable purpose, to or for his own use or benefit or to or for the use or benefit of any person other than such person as aforesaid, or for any purpose other than such public or charitable purpose as aforesaid, or who otherwise fraudulently disposes of or destroys such property, shall be punished by imprisonment in the state prison for not more than ten years or by a fine of not more than two thousand dollars and imprisonment in jail for not more than two years.

NOTE   Venue. G.L. c. 277, § 58B.

SECTION 58
Larceny; embezzlement from voluntary association

Whoever, being an officer, agent, clerk or servant of a voluntary association or society, embezzles or fraudulently converts, or fraudulently takes or secretes with intent so to do, effects or property which belong to such association or society, or which have come to his possession or are under his care by virtue of his office or employment, shall be guilty of larceny.

SECTION 59
Simple larceny; embezzlement from voluntary association

Whoever embezzles or fraudulently converts, or secretes with intent to embezzle or fraudulently convert, money, goods or property or any part thereof which has been delivered to him, which may be the subject of larceny and which belong to any organization of the volunteer militia, post of the Grand Army of the Republic, or other voluntary association, shall be guilty of simple larceny, although he is a member of such organization or voluntary association and, as such, entitled to an interest in the property thereof. In a prosecution under this section, it shall be sufficient to describe such organization or association by the name by which it is generally known and as a voluntary association.

SECTION 60
Stolen goods; buying or receiving
(Stricken & replaced by 2014 Mass. Acts c. 451, § 3, effective Apr. 6, 2015.)

Whoever buys, receives or aids in the concealment of stolen or embezzled property, knowing it to have been stolen or embezzled, or whoever with intent to defraud buys, receives or aids in the concealment of property, knowing it to have been obtained from a person by false pretense of carrying on a business in the ordinary course of trade or whoever obtains or exerts control over property in the custody of any law enforcement agency, or any individual acting on behalf of a law enforcement agency, which is explicitly represented to such person by any law enforcement officer or any individual acting on behalf of a law enforcement agency as being stolen and who intends to deprive its rightful owner permanently of the use and enjoyment of said property shall be punished as follows: if the value of such property does not exceed $250, for a first offense by imprisonment in the house of correction for not more than 2½ years or by a fine of not more than $1,000; if the value of such property does not exceed $250, for a second or subsequent offense by imprisonment in the house of correction for not more than 2½ years or by imprisonment in the state prison for not more than 5 years or by a fine of not more than $5,000 or by both such fine and imprisonment; or if the value of such property exceeds $250 by imprisonment in the house of correction for not more than 2½ years or by imprisonment in the state prison for not more than 5 years or by a fine of not more than $5,000 or by both such fine and imprisonment.

It shall not be a defense that the property was obtained by means other than through the commission of a theft offense if the property was explicitly represented to the accused as having been obtained through the commission of a theft offense.

NOTE 1a   **The Elements.** The name of the original thief need not be alleged nor proved; the defendant need not have received the goods from the thief. All that is necessary is that the defendant knowingly received stolen goods. *Commonwealth v. Grossman*, 261 Mass. 68, 70–71 (1927). *See also* G.L. c. 277, § 42.

NOTE 1b   The complaint may use the words "buy, receive, or aid" and the Commonwealth need *not* elect, despite a bill of particulars, among the three. *Commonwealth v. Colella*, 2 Mass. App. Ct. 706, 708 (1974).

NOTE 1c   Possession may be constructive. *Commonwealth v. Kuperstein*, 207 Mass. 25, 27 (1910).

NOTE 1d   In order to constitute the crime of aiding in the concealment of stolen goods, it is not necessary that there be actual hiding, but only such conduct as might render their discovery difficult. *Commonwealth v. Kuperstein*, 207 Mass. at 27.

NOTE 2a   **Stolen Property.** The Commonwealth must prove the goods were actually stolen. *Commonwealth v. Budreau*, 372 Mass. 641, 643 (1977). In *Budreau*, the defendant was charged with receiving two speakers and an eight track unit. The items bore no serial numbers nor distinguishing marks or features and were not in any cartons or boxes when they were seized by the police. Conviction reversed. *Commonwealth v. Budreau*, 372 Mass. at 643–44.

NOTE 2b   Compare *Commonwealth v. Rossi*, 15 Mass. App. Ct. 950, 952 (1983). "The jury could infer that the meat had been stolen from a Food Mart, Inc., store from the following evidence: (a) at one point Tillman saw the taller man in his store with packaged meats in a shopping basket; (b) Tillman lost sight of this man for about five minutes; (c) this man got into the defendant's car, and the defendant drove off without turning on his headlights; (d) a bag of meat and seafood was thrown from the defendant's car as he drove to a poorly lighted section of the church parking lot with Officer Shumway in pursuit; (e) unbagged packages of meat were in the back of the car; (f) no saleslips or receipts were found with those items or in the retrieved bag; and (g) Tillman identified the meat which is the subject of the compliant as having come from a Food Mart, Inc., store. *See Commonwealth v. Peopcik*, 251 Mass. 369, 371 (1925); *Commonwealth v. Ryan*, 11 Mass. App. Ct. 906 (1981)."

NOTE 3a   **Knowledge (That the Goods Were Stolen).** Inference involving recently stolen goods. Knowledge on the part of the defendant that the goods which he possessed were stolen is an essential element of the crime, which must be proved by the Commonwealth. A person's knowledge, however, like his intent, is a matter of fact, which may not be [capable] of proof by direct evidence. In that event resort must be had, and frequently is had, to proof by inference from all the facts and circumstances developed at the trial. [The factfinder] may infer that the defendant had knowledge, if the Commonwealth has proved beyond a reasonable doubt that the defendant possessed recently stolen goods and if the facts and circumstances in this case warrant an inference that the defendant knew that the goods were stolen. [The factfinder] should consider all the facts and circumstances surrounding the defendant's possession of stolen goods in drawing the inference and in deciding whether the Commonwealth has proved beyond a reasonable doubt that the defendant knew the goods he possessed were stolen. [The factfinder] may, but [is] not required, to draw the inference of knowledge." *Commonwealth v. Burns*, 388 Mass. 178, 183–84 n.11 (1983) (quotation marks and citation omitted).

NOTE 3b   **Recency.** There is no uniform period of time on the expiration of which stolen property ceases to be stolen. That decision must be made on the basis of the facts and circumstances of each case and it is a question of fact for the factfinder, except in those cases where the theft was so recent or so remote as to permit the judge to rule on the question as a matter of law. *Commonwealth v. Sandler*, 368 Mass. 729, 744 (1975).

NOTE 3c   Fifty-four days between the robbery and the date of the defendant's proved possession is *not* too long, as a matter of law, to permit the jury to draw an inference of guilty knowledge, especially if "much more" evidence exists other than the mere possession of stolen money. *Commonwealth v. Kelley*, 333 Mass. 191, 194 (1955).

NOTE 3d   One may be found guilty of receiving stolen goods even if knowledge of the property being stolen comes *after* the goods come into the possession of the defendant so long as the defendant undertook to deprive the owner of his rightful use of it. *Commonwealth v. Kronick*, 196 Mass. 286, 288 (1907).

NOTE 3e   "[The defendant] suspected from the start that the gun was stolen. This may be the equivalent of belief that theft had occurred, which, though short of knowledge, is enough for § 60." *Comm'r of Pub. Safety v. Treadway*, 368 Mass. 155, 160 (1975). It should be noted here that belief turned into knowledge when the defendant, a state trooper, learned of the break-in and theft of the gun, which he had earlier recovered and kept. *Comm'r of Pub. Safety v. Treadway*, 368 Mass. at 160.

NOTE 3f   **No Ownership Identity Required.** "The defendant seeks to add another . . . element[ ], contending that, in order to prove that the property is stolen and the defendant's possession thereof unlawful, the Commonwealth perforce must prove some particular and identifiable ownership interest associated with the property, either by the owner identifying the property or by particular identifying markings on the property itself. In support of this proposition, the defendant compiles cases in which evidence was adduced linking the allegedly stolen goods to an owner, and argues that these cases demonstrate ownership linkage as an element. While the cases reflect evidence adduced concerning owners reporting loss of, and identification of, discrete items of stolen goods, none of the cited cases stands for the proposition that ownership by a particular identified person is an element of proof for the crime of receiving stolen property. The defendant does not point to, and research has not disclosed, any case holding as a matter of law that a conviction for receiving stolen property requires the Commonwealth to prove that the received property belongs to an identified owner or has unique ownership identifying markings. We also note that ownership is not an element of proof in the Model Penal Code definition of the crime of receiving stolen property. *See* Model Penal Code and Commentaries § 223.6 (1980)." *Commonwealth v. Cromwell*, 53 Mass. App. Ct. 662, 664–66 (2002).

NOTE 4a   **Value.** While a thing stolen must be of some value to be the subject of an indictment for larceny or receiving stolen goods, it need not be an article having any special, appreciable or market value. *Commonwealth v. Cabot*, 241 Mass. 131, 140 (1922).

NOTE 4b   G.L. c. 277, § 24. Description of value or price.

NOTE 5   It is no defense that the defendants thought that their conduct was justifiable. *Commonwealth v. Cabot*, 241 Mass. at 143–44.

NOTE 6a   **Larceny v. Receiving Stolen Goods.** While a defendant may be charged with both crimes, he may be convicted only of one. *Commonwealth v. Pettingel*, 10 Mass. App. Ct. 916 (1980). Note, however, that a conviction for breaking and entering in the nighttime is not duplicative of a conviction for receiving stolen property because although these crimes may arise out of the same course of conduct, they contain no elements in common. *Commonwealth v. Cabrera*, 449 Mass. 825 (2007).

NOTE 6b   One may be found guilty of receiving stolen goods, even if the evidence equally supported a finding that he was the thief. *Commonwealth v. Obshatkin*, 2 Mass. App. Ct. 1, 4 (1974). *See also Commonwealth v. Corcoran*, 69 Mass. App. Ct. 123, 127 (2007) ("[W]here evidence would support a conviction of larceny, it does not prevent an alternative conviction of receipt of stolen goods arising from the same events if the evidence supports that conviction as well.[5]" Footnote 5 reads: ". . . the obverse would be equally true, so long as there is but one conviction.").

NOTE 7   **Statute of Limitations.** Dismissal of receiving stolen goods complaint, by reason of statute of limitations, was improper, even though the property had been stolen more than six years before, where an act in concealment of stolen property could have occurred within six years of date of indictment. *Commonwealth v. Ciesla*, 380 Mass. 346, 349 (1980).

NOTE 8a   Jurisdiction. One may be convicted of receiving stolen goods in Massachusetts despite the fact that the goods were stolen in another state. *Commonwealth v. White*, 123 Mass. 430, 433 (1877).

NOTE 8b   Receiving stolen goods indictment may be prosecuted in the same jurisdiction in which the larceny or embezzlement of any property involved in the crime may be prosecuted. G.L. c. 277, § 58A.

NOTE 9   Related Statutes.

G.L. c. 266, § 37B—Misuse of (receiving stolen) credit cards.

G.L. c. 266, § 62—Common receiver of stolen goods.

G.L. c. 277, § 25—Description of ownership.

G.L. c. 277, § 31—Alternative allegations.

G.L. c. 278, § 9—Proof of ownership of property.

SECTION 60A
Stolen trade secrets; buying or selling

Whoever buys, receives, conceals, stores, barters, sells or disposes of any trade secret, or pledges or accepts as security for a loan any trade secret, regardless of value, knowing the same to have been stolen, unlawfully converted, or taken, shall be punished by imprisonment for not more than five years or by a fine of not more than five hundred dollars and imprisonment in jail for not more than two years. The term "trade secret" as used in this section shall have the same meaning as is set forth in section thirty.

SECTION 60B
Jurisdiction
(Added by 2014 Mass. Acts c. 451, § 4, effective Apr. 6, 2015.)

Crimes committed in different counties or the territorial jurisdiction of different courts in violation of this chapter, if the crimes may be joined for trial under the Massachusetts Rules of Criminal Procedure but for venue and jurisdiction, may be charged and prosecuted in any court having jurisdiction of at least 1 of the crimes.

SECTION 61
Stolen property; restitution; effect

If, upon a first conviction under the preceding section, it is shown that the act of stealing the property was a simple larceny, and if the person convicted makes restitution to the person injured to the full value of the property stolen and not restored, he shall not be imprisoned in the state prison.

NOTE   Burden of proof is upon the defendant as "[t]his is not an instance where previous conviction is an essential part of the offence charged and must accordingly be laid in the indictment and proved as charged." *Harding v. Commonwealth*, 283 Mass. 369, 371 (1933).

SECTION 62
Stolen goods; common receiver

Whoever is convicted of buying, receiving or aiding in the concealment of stolen or embezzled property, knowing it to have been stolen or embezzled, having been before convicted of the like offence, and whoever is convicted at the same sitting of the court of three or more distinct acts of buying, receiving or aiding in the concealment of money, goods or property stolen or embezzled as aforesaid, shall be adjudged a common receiver of stolen or embezzled goods and shall be punished by imprisonment in the state prison for not more than ten years.

SECTION 63
Unlawful taking or use of transportation media

Whoever wilfully, mischievously and without right takes or uses a boat or vehicle, other than a motor vehicle, or takes, drives, rides or uses any draught animal which is the property of another, without the consent of the owner or other person who has the legal custody, care or control thereof, shall be punished by a fine of not more than three hundred dollars or by imprisonment for not more than six months; but this section shall not apply to the property of another taken with intent to steal it, or under a claim of right, or with the presumed consent of the owner or other person who has the legal control, care or custody thereof.

SECTION 64
Fraudulent hiring of transportation media

Whoever hires a horse, carriage or other vehicle, and, with intent to cheat or defraud the owner thereof, makes to him or to his agent at the time of such hiring a false statement of the distance which he proposes to travel with such horse, carriage or other vehicle, or whoever, with such intent, makes to the owner or his agent, after the use of a horse, carriage or other vehicle, a false statement of the distance which he has actually traveled with such horse, carriage or other vehicle, and whoever, with such intent, refuses to pay for the use of a horse, carriage or other vehicle the lawful fare established therefor by any town, shall be punished by a fine of not more than twenty dollars or by imprisonment for not more than two months, or both.

SECTION 65
Stock; unauthorized issue

An officer, agent, clerk or servant of a corporation, or any other person, who issues or signs with intent to issue a certificate of stock in a corporation, or who issues, signs or endorses with intent to issue, a bond, note, bill or other obligation or security in the name of such corporation, beyond the amount authorized by law or limited by the legal votes of such corporation or its proper officers, or negotiates, transfers of disposes of such certificate with intent to defraud, shall be punished by imprisonment in the state prison for not more than ten years or in the house of correction for not more than one year.

SECTION 66
Stock; fraudulent issue or transfer

An officer, agent, clerk or servant of a corporation, or any other person, who fraudulently issues or transfers a certificate of the stock of a corporation to a person who is not entitled thereto, or who fraudulently signs such certificate, in blank or otherwise, with intent that it shall be so issued or transferred by himself or any other person, shall be punished by imprisonment in the state prison for not more than ten years or in the house of correction for not more than one year.

NOTE   This section prohibits the manual making out and handling over of the physical thing known as a certificate of stock and is not aimed at directors voting to instruct the proper officers to issue stock to promoters who, by receiving the same in return for property sold by them to the corporation at a secret profit, violate their fiduciary obligations to the corporation. *Commonwealth v. Dyer*, 243 Mass. 472, 496–97 (1922).

SECTION 67
Corporate books; false entries with intent to defraud

An officer of a corporation or an agent, clerk or servant of a person, firm or corporation who makes a false entry or omits to make a true entry in any book of such person, firm or corporation, with intent to defraud, and any person whose duty it is to make a record or entry of the transfer of stock, or of the issuing or cancelling of certificates thereof, or of the amount of stock issued by a corporation, in any book thereof, who, with intent to defraud, omits to make a true record or entry thereof, shall be punished by imprisonment in the state prison for not more than ten years or in the house of correction for not more than one year.

NOTE   "In a prosecution under § 67, the Commonwealth must prove that the defendant made, with intent to defraud, a false entry in the books of a 'corporation.' The statute does not define the term 'corporation.' Massport is a 'body politic and corporate.' *See* St. 1956, c. 465, § 2 (establishing 'a body politic and corporate to be known as the Massachusetts Port Authority'). We conclude that the term 'corporation' in § 67 encompasses the entity Massport." *Commonwealth v. Biagiotti*, 451 Mass. 599, 601 (2008).

SECTION 67A
Departments, agencies and public instrumentalities; fraud in procurement of supplies; penalty

Whoever, in any matter, relative to procurement of supplies, services or construction, as defined in section one of chapter twelve A, within the jurisdiction of any department, agency or public instrumentality of the commonwealth, or of any political subdivision thereof, intentionally:

(1) makes a material statement that is false;

(2) omits or conceals a material fact in a written statement;

(3) submits or invites reliance on a material writing or recording that is false, forged, altered, or otherwise lacking in authenticity;

(4) submits or invites reliance on a sample, specimen, map, photograph, boundary-mark, or other object that is misleading in a material respect; or

(5) uses any trick, scheme, or device that is misleading in a material respect;

shall be punished by a fine of not more than ten thousand dollars or by imprisonment in the state prison for not more than five years, or in the house of correction for not more than two and one-half years, or both.

SECTION 67B
Presentation of false claims

Whoever makes or presents to any employee, department, agency or public instrumentality of the commonwealth, or of any political subdivision thereof, any claim upon or against any department, agency, or public instrumentality of the commonwealth, or any political subdivision thereof, knowing such claim to be false, fictitious, or fraudulent, shall be punished by a fine of not more than ten thousand dollars or by imprisonment in the state prison for not more than five years, or in the house of correction for not more than two and one-half years, or both.

SECTION 67C
Capital facility construction projects, etc.; false entries in records; penalties

Any person who knowingly and wilfully, directly or indirectly makes, or knowingly and wilfully causes to be made, a false entry or omission of a true entry in any books, record or account subject to the provisions of section thirty-nine R of chapter thirty shall be punished by a fine of not more than five thousand dollars, or by imprisonment in the state prison for not more than five years, or in the house of correction for not more than two years, or both.

SECTION 68
Corporate books as evidence

Upon the trial of a person for a crime under the three preceding sections, the books of any person, firm or corporation to which he had access or the right of access shall be admissible in evidence.

SECTION 69
Insignia of societies; unlawful use

Whoever, not being a member of a society, association or labor union, for the purpose of representing that he is a member thereof, wilfully wears or uses the insignia, ribbon, badge, rosette, button or emblem thereof, if it has been registered in the office of the state secretary, shall be punished by a fine of not more than twenty dollars or by imprisonment for not more than one month, or both.

SECTION 69A
Fraudulent use of labor union seal, trademark or insignia

Whoever knowingly and fraudulently displays or otherwise uses, in any manner whatsoever, the seal, trademark or insignia of any labor organization as defined by subsection (5) of section two of chapter one hundred and fifty A shall be punished by a fine of not more than one thousand dollars.

SECTION 70
Insignia of veteran organizations; unlawful use

Whoever, not being a member and without authority of the Military Order of the Loyal Legion of the United States, the Grand Army of the Republic, the Sons of Union Veterans of the Civil War, the Woman's Relief Corps, the American Gold Star Mothers, Inc., the Union Veterans' Union, the Union Veteran Legion, the Military and Naval Order of the Spanish-American War, the United Spanish War Veterans, the American Officers of the Great War, the Veterans of Foreign Wars of the United States, the Military Order of Foreign Wars of the United States, the Disabled American Veterans of the World War, the Yankee Division Veterans' Association, The American Legion, the Army and Navy Union, U.S.A., the American Veterans of World War II, AMVETS, the American Veterans' Committee, Inc., the Franco-American War Veterans, Inc., the Military Order of the Purple Heart, the Seabee Veterans of America, Inc.—Department of Massachusetts, the Italian American War Veterans of the United Sates, Incorporated, the PT Veterans Association, Inc., the Fleet Reserve Association, United States Navy, the American Portuguese War Veterans Association, Polish-American Veterans of Massachusetts, Inc., and its affiliated posts, the Navy Club of the United States of America, or the Marine Corps League or the Veterans of World War I of the U.S.A., wilfully wears or uses the insignia, distinctive ribbons or membership rosette or button thereof for the purpose of representing that he is a member thereof or displays on his property or permits to be displayed thereon any such insignia, distinctive ribbon, membership rosette or button, or any sign or statement for the purpose of falsely representing that such property

2

is occupied by or is the quarters of any such veterans' organization, shall be punished by a fine of not more than twenty dollars or by imprisonment for not more than one month, or both.

SECTION 71
Signature, money or membership; obtaining under false pretenses

Whoever wilfully, by color or aid of any false token or writing, or other false pretense or false statement, verbal or written, or without authority of the grand or supreme governing lodge, council, union or other governing body hereinafter mentioned, obtains the signature of any person to any written application, or obtains any money or property for any alleged or pretended degree, or for any alleged or pretended membership in any fraternity, association, society, order, organization or union having a grand or supreme governing lodge, council, union or other governing body in the commonwealth, or in any subordinate lodge or body thereof, shall be punished by imprisonment for not more than one year or by a fine of not more than five hundred dollars, or both.

SECTION 71A
Individuals and corporations; false use of names of benevolent organizations

No person, society, association or corporation shall knowingly assume, adopt or use the name of a benevolent, humane, fraternal, charitable or labor organization, whether incorporated or unincorporated, or a name so nearly resembling the name of such incorporated or unincorporated organization as to be a colorable imitation thereof or calculated to deceive persons not members with respect to such organizations. Whoever violates this section shall be punished by a fine of not more than two hundred dollars or by imprisonment for not more than one year or by both such fine and imprisonment. The superior court shall have jurisdiction in equity to enjoin any violation of this section.

SECTION 72
Fraternal names; use in publication

Whoever, in a newspaper or other publication, or in any written or printed letter, notice, matter or device, without authority of the grand or supreme governing lodge, council, union or other governing body, fraudulently uses or aids in any way in the use of the name, title or common designation of any fraternity, association, society, order, organization or union which has such a governing body, having priority in such use in the commonwealth, or by any name, title or designation so nearly resembling the same as to be calculated or likely to deceive; and whoever, without such authority, fraudulently publishes, sells, circulates or distributes any written or printed letter, notice, matter or device, in any way soliciting members of such fraternity, association, society, order, organization or union, for any alleged or pretended fraternity, association, society, order, organization or union, using any such name, title, designation, or near resemblance thereto; and whoever therein or thereby in any way, without such authority, fraudulently offers to sell, confer, communicate or give information where, of whom or by what means any degree or work, in whole or in part, of such fraternity, association, society, order, organization or union, or of any alleged or pretended fraternity, association, society, order, organization or union using any such name, title or designation or near re-

semblance thereto, can or may be obtained, conferred or communicated, shall be punished by imprisonment for not more than one year or by a fine of not more than five hundred dollars, or both.

SECTION 73
Obtaining goods under false pretenses

Whoever, with intent to defraud, by a false pretense of carrying on business and dealing in the ordinary course of trade, obtains from any person goods or chattels shall be punished by imprisonment in the state prison for not more than five years or by a fine of not more than five hundred dollars and imprisonment in jail for not more than two years.

SECTION 74
Corporate credit; fraudulent use

An officer, agent, clerk or servant of a corporation organized or doing business in the commonwealth, who wilfully uses the name of such corporation, or his own name as such officer, agent, clerk or servant, to obtain money upon the credit of such corporation for his own use or benefit, without authority from such corporation, or who fraudulently lends, invests or appropriates the money or disposes of the property of such corporation, or fraudulently converts it, shall be punished by imprisonment in the state prison for not more than ten years.

NOTE   This section is intended to prohibit breaches of trust by which faithless corporate officers or agents appropriate the corporation's property to their own use, and is not confined in its scope to a prohibition of the crime of embezzlement. *Commonwealth v. Dow*, 217 Mass. 473, 476–77 (1914).

SECTION 75
Obtaining property by trick

Whoever, by a game, device, sleight of hand, pretended fortune telling or by any trick or other means by the use of cards or other implements or instruments, fraudulently obtains from another person property of any description shall be punished as in the case of larceny of property of like value.

SECTION 75A
Gambling devices and vending machines; fraudulent use

Whoever operates or causes to be operated, or attempts to operate or to cause to be operated, any automatic vending machine, slot machine, turnstile, coin-box telephone or other receptacle designed to receive lawful coin of the United States or tokens provided by the person entitled to the coin-contents or token-contents of such receptacle in connection with the sale, use or enjoyment of property, transportation or other service, by means of a slug or any false, counterfeited, mutilated or sweated coin or token or by any means, method, trick or device whatsoever not lawfully authorized by the owner, lessee or licensee of such machine, turnstile, coin-box telephone or receptacle; or whoever takes, obtains or receives from or in connection with any automatic vending machine, slot machine, turnstile, coin-box telephone or other receptacle designed to receive lawful coin of the United States or tokens provided by the person entitled to the coin-contents or token-contents of such receptacle in connection with the sale, use of or enjoyment of property or service, any goods, wares, merchandise, transportation, gas, electric current, article of value, or the use or enjoyment of any transportation or any telephone or telegraph facilities or service, or of any musical instrument, phonograph or other property, without depositing in and surrendering to such machine, turnstile, coin-box telephone or other receptacle lawful coin or a token or tokens to the amount or value required therefor by the owner, lessee or licensee of such machine, turnstile, coin-box telephone or receptacle, shall be punished by a fine of not more than one hundred dollars or by imprisonment in the house of correction for not more than thirty days, or both. The word "person" as used in this section shall include any municipal corporation or political subdivision of the commonwealth.

SECTION 75B
Slugs; manufacture and sale

Whoever manufactures for sale, advertises for sale, sells, offers for sale, or gives away any slug, device or substance whatsoever, designed or calculated to be placed or deposited in any automatic vending machine, slot machine, turnstile, coin-box telephone or other such receptacle, depository or contrivance, designed to receive lawful coin of the United States or tokens provided by the person entitled to the coin-contents or token-contents of such receptacle, depository or contrivance in connection with the sale, use or enjoyment of property or service, with intent that such slug, device or substance shall be used to cheat or defraud the person entitled to the contents of any such machine, turnstile, coin-box telephone or other such receptacle, depository or contrivance, shall be punished by a fine of not more than five hundred dollars, or by imprisonment in the house of correction for not more than one year, or both. The word "person" as used in this section shall include any municipal corporation or political subdivision of the commonwealth.

SECTION 75C
Gift certificates; expiration dates; failure to redeem

Whoever sells or offers to sell a gift certificate as defined in section 1 of chapter 255D, which imposes a time limit of less than 7 years within which such certificate may be redeemed, shall be punished by a fine of not more than $300. This section shall not apply when the purchaser of the gift certificate is not obligated to pay for it until the time of use. Whoever, after having sold a gift certificate refuses to redeem the certificate before it has reached the expiration date, shall be punished by a fine of not more than $300.

SECTION 75D
Imposition of certain fees reducing total value amount of gift certificate; penalty

Whoever sells or offers to sell a gift certificate, as defined in section 1 of chapter 255D, which imposes dormancy fees, latency fees, administrative fees, periodic fees, service fees or other fees that have the effect of reducing the total value amount for which the holder may redeem such gift certificate, shall be punished by a fine of not more than $300 per violation.

SECTION 75E
Printed notice required for certain fees associated with gift certificates; penalty for violation

Whoever sells or offers to sell a gift certificate, as defined in section 1 of chapter 255D, which imposes any fees or charges including, but not limited to, purchase fees, activation fees, renewal fees or cancellation fees, shall provide to consumers notice of any such fees, in writing, on the gift certifi-

cate, on the packaging of the gift certificate, or on both. Failure to print such notice shall be punished by a fine of not more than $300 per violation.

SECTION 75F
Deduction of gratuity from gift certificate without consent; penalty

Whoever redeems a gift certificate, as defined in section 1 of chapter 255D and deducts a gratuity therefrom without the consent of the holder of the gift certificate, shall be punished by a fine of not more than $300 per violation.

SECTION 76
Gross fraud or cheat at common law; punishment

Whoever is convicted of any gross fraud or cheat at common law shall be punished by imprisonment in the state prison for not more than ten years or in jail for not more than two years or by a fine of not more than four hundred dollars.

SECTION 77
Sterling and coin silver; contents; sale; penalty

Whoever makes or sells, or offers to sell or dispose of, or has in his possession with intent so to do, any article of merchandise marked, stamped or branded with the words "sterling", "sterling silver", "coin" or "coin silver", or encased or enclosed in any box, package, cover or wrapper or other thing in or by which the said article is packed, enclosed or otherwise prepared for sale or disposition, having thereon any engraving or printed label, stamp, imprint, mark or trade mark, indicating or denoting by such marking, stamping, branding, engraving or printing, that such article is silver, sterling silver, solid silver, coin or coin silver, shall, unless nine hundred and twenty-five one thousandths of the component parts of the metal of which the said article so marked, stamped or branded with the words "sterling" or "sterling silver" is manufactured are pure silver, or unless nine hundred one-thousandths of the component parts of the metal of which the article so marked, stamped or branded with the words "coin" or "coin silver" is manufactured, are pure silver, be punished by a fine of not more than one hundred dollars.

SECTION 78
Articles made of gold; false marking; prohibition

Whoever makes or sells, or offers for sale or disposes of, or has in his possession with intent so to do, any article constructed in whole or in part of gold or alloy of gold, or of any metal resembling gold, having marked thereon or upon any tag or label attached thereto, or upon any package, cover or wrapper in which such article is enclosed or wrapped, any word or mark indicating or designed or intended to indicate that the gold or alloy of god in said article, or in the plating, surface or any other part of said article is of a greater degree or carat of fineness by more than one carat than the actual quality or fineness of such gold or alloy of gold, or any so-called gold filled, rolled gold plated or electro gold plated article having marked thereon, or upon any tag or label attached thereto, or upon any package, cover or wrapper in which such article is enclosed or wrapped, any word or mark indicating or designed or intended to indicate that the gold or alloy of gold upon such article is of a greater percentage of weight of the article by more than one per cent than the actual percentage of gold or alloy of gold, shall be punished by a fine of not more than five hundred dollars. The word or mark

2

upon the article or upon the tag or label attached thereto, or upon the package, cover or wrapper in which such article is enclosed, shall be held to apply to the whole article, all the gold, alloys, solder and base metals being assayed as one piece, unless the word or mark plainly indicates that it applies to the plating, surface or other particular part of such article.

SECTION 79
Imitation furs; false representation; prohibition

Whoever, himself, or by his agent or servant, or as the agent or servant of another person, sells or exchanges, or has in his custody or possession with intent so to do, or exposes for sale or exchange, any manufactured imitations of furs or furbearing animals, representing the same to be the genuine fur of certain animals, shall be punished by a fine of not less than two hundred nor more than five hundred dollars.

SECTION 80
Encumbered land; conveyance without notice

Whoever conveys land, knowing that an encumbrance exists thereon, without informing the grantee, before the consideration is paid, of the existence and nature of such encumbrance, so far as he has knowledge thereof, shall be punished by imprisonment for not more than one year or by a fine of not more than one thousand dollars.

SECTION 81
Attached land; conveyance without notice

Whoever, knowing that his land is attached on mesne process, sells and conveys it without giving notice of the attachment to the grantee, and with intent to defraud, shall be punished by imprisonment in the state prison for not more than three years or in jail for not more than one year.

SECTION 82
Concealment of mortgaged personalty; use of rented personalty as container for illegal sale of liquor

Whoever, with a fraudulent intent to place personal property which is subject to a mortgage beyond the control of the mortgagee, removes or conceals or aids or abets in removing or concealing the same, and a mortgagor of such property who assents to such removal or concealment, or whoever shall use rented, leased or mortgaged personal property as a container or implement of sale of intoxicating liquor contrary to law, shall be punished by a fine of not more than one thousand dollars or by imprisonment for not more than one year.

SECTION 83
Personalty; sale by mortgagor without consent

A mortgagor of personal property who sells or conveys the same or any part thereof without the written consent of the mortgagee, and without informing the vendee or grantee that the same is mortgaged, shall be punished by a fine of not more than one hundred dollars or by imprisonment for not more than one year.

SECTION 84
Personalty; sale by hirer without consent

A hirer or lessee of personal property who sells or conveys the same or any part thereof without the written consent of the owner or lessor, and without informing the vendee or grantee that it is so hired or leased, shall be punished by a fine of not more than one hundred dollars or by imprisonment for not more than one year.

SECTION 85
Collateral security; sale before debt due

Whoever, holding collateral security deposited with him for the payment of a debt which may be due to him, sells, pledges, lends or in any way disposes of the same before such debt becomes due and payable, without the authority of the depositor thereof, shall be punished by a fine of not more than five hundred dollars or by imprisonment in jail for not more than two years.

SECTION 86
Hired property; buying or receiving with intent to defraud

Whoever, with intent to defraud, buys, receives or aids in concealing personal property, knowing it to be hired or leased or held as collateral security, shall be punished by a fine of not more than one hundred dollars or by imprisonment for not more than one year.

SECTION 87
Larceny of leased or rented property

Any person leasing or renting personal property who, with the intent to place such property beyond the control of the owner, conceals or aids or abets the concealment of such property or any part thereof, or fails or refuses to return such property to the owner within ten days after expiration of the lease or rental agreement, or sells, conveys or pledges such property or any part thereof without the written consent of the owner, shall be guilty of larceny of leased or rented personal property.

Any person convicted of larceny of leased or rented personal property shall be punished by a fine of not more than one thousand dollars or imprisonment of not more than one year, or both. A person found guilty of violating this section shall, in all cases upon conviction in addition to any other punishment, be ordered to make restitution to the owner for any financial loss.

It shall be prima facie evidence of intent to place such property beyond the control of the owner when a person in obtaining such property presents identification or information which is materially false, fictitious, misleading or not current with respect to such person's name, address, place of employment or any other material matter or fails to return such property to the owner or his representative within ten days after proper notice to return such property. For purposes of this section proper notice shall be actual notice or a written demand sent by certified or registered mail to such person at the address given at the time of making the lease or rental agreement.

It shall be a defense to prosecution for conversion of leased or rented property that the defendant was unaware the property belonged to another or that he had a right to acquire or dispose of the property as he did.

SECTION 87A
Stolen leased or rented motor vehicles; report; dissemination of information by police

The owner or lessee of a leased or rented motor vehicle which has been stolen or placed beyond his control shall report the loss of the same to the police department of the city or town wherein said vehicle was leased or rented or stolen.

Notwithstanding any provision of law to the contrary, a police department receiving a report of said stolen vehicle shall list the same as stolen and shall, by the use of radio, teletype, computer or other communication, disseminate the information concerning said stolen vehicle using the same standards as applicable to other stolen motor vehicles.

SECTION 88
Consignee or factor; fraudulent deposit or pledge of property

A consignee or factor who, in violation of good faith and with intent to defraud the owners thereof, deposits or pledges, as security for money borrowed by him, a negotiable instrument received by him, merchandise consigned or intrusted to him, or a bill of lading, certificate or order for the delivery of merchandise; or who, in like violation and with like intent, disposes of or applies such property or evidence of property to his own use; or who, in like violation and with like intent, disposes of or applies to his own use money which has been raised or a negotiable instrument which has been acquired by the sale or other disposition of such property or evidence of property, shall be punished by a fine of not more than five thousand dollars and imprisonment for not more than five years.

SECTION 89
Degrees; pretending to hold or conferring without authority; use of designation "university" or "college"

Whoever, in a book, pamphlet, circular, advertisement or advertising sign, or by a pretended written certificate or diploma, or otherwise in writing, knowingly and falsely pretends to have been an officer or teacher, or to be a graduate or to hold any degree, of a college or other educational institution of this commonwealth or elsewhere, which is authorized to confer degrees, or of a public school of this commonwealth, and whoever, without having lawful authority to confer degrees, offers or confers degrees as a school, college or as a private individual, alone or associated with others, shall be punished by a fine of not more than one thousand dollars or by imprisonment for not more than one year, or both. Any individual, school, association, corporation or institution of learning, not having lawful authority to confer degrees, using the designation of "university" or "college" shall be punished by a fine on one thousand dollars; but this shall not apply to any educational institution whose name on July ninth, nineteen hundred and nineteen, included the word "university" or "college".

SECTION 90
Endorsement or approval; penalty for false claim

Whoever, in a book, pamphlet, circular, advertisement or advertising sign, or otherwise in writing, makes any false and fraudulent statement or assertion of endorsement, authority, approval or sanction of an incorporated college, university or professional school in this commonwealth or elsewhere, or of officers or instructors thereof, as a commendation or advertisement of a person or of his services, or of goods, wares, commodities, processes or treatment, shall be punished by a fine of not more than one thousand dollars or by imprisonment for not more than one year, or both.

SECTION 91
Untrue and misleading advertisements; prohibitions

Any person who, with intent to sell or in any way dispose of merchandise, securities, service, or anything offered by such person, directly or indirectly, to the public for sale or distribution, or who, with intent to increase the consumption of or demand for such merchandise, securities, service or other thing, or to induce the public in any manner to enter into any obligation relating thereto, or to acquire title thereto, or an interest therein, makes, publishes, disseminates, circulates or places before the public, or causes, directly or indirectly, to be made, published, disseminated, circulated or placed before the public within the commonwealth, in a newspaper or other publication, or in the form of a book, notice, handbill, poster, bill, circular, pamphlet or letter, or in any other way, an advertisement of any sort regarding merchandise, securities, service or anything so offered to the public, which advertisement contains any assertion, representation or statement of fact which is untrue, deceptive or misleading, and which such person knew, or might on reasonable investigation have ascertained to be untrue, deceptive or misleading, shall be punished by a fine of not less than one thousand nor more than two thousand dollars; provided, that this section shall not apply to any owner, publisher, printer, agent or employee of a newspaper or other publication, periodical or circular, or to any agent of the advertiser who in good faith and without knowledge of the falsity or deceptive character thereof publishes, causes to be published, or participates in the publication of such advertisement.

Whoever violates the provisions of this section may be enjoined therefrom by a petition in equity brought by the attorney general or any aggrieved party.

SECTION 91A
Merchandise, commodities and service; advertisement regulated; penalty

Any person who offers for sale merchandise, commodities or service by making, publishing, disseminating, circulating or placing before the public within the commonwealth, in a newspaper or other publication, or in the form of a book, notice, handbill, poster, bill, circular, pamphlet or letter, or in any other way, an advertisement describing the said merchandise, commodities or service, as part of a plan or scheme with the intent not to sell said merchandise, commodities or service so advertised at the price stated therein, or with intent not to sell said merchandise, commodities or service so advertised, shall be punished by a fine of not less than five hundred nor more than one thousand dollars or by imprisonment for not more than one year.

SECTION 91B
Deceptive advertising of merchandise for sale; injunction

Any person offering for sale merchandise, commodities or service by making, publishing, disseminating, circulating or placing before the public within the commonwealth in any manner an advertisement of merchandise, commodities, or service, with the intent, design or purpose not to sell the merchandise, commodities, or service so advertised at the price stated therein or otherwise communicated, or with the intent not to sell the merchandise, commodities, or service so advertised may be enjoined from such advertising by a bill in equity in the superior court brought by the attorney general or any aggrieved party; provided, however, that the provisions of this section shall not apply to any medium for the printing, publishing, or disseminating of advertising, or any owner, agent or employee thereof, nor to any advertising agency or owner, agent, or employee thereof, nor to any radio or television station, or owner, agent, or employee thereof for printing, publishing, or disseminating or causing to be printed, published, or disseminated such advertisement in good faith and without knowledge of the deceptive character thereof.

SECTION 92
False or exaggerated statements; making or publishing; prohibition

Whoever wilfully and with intent to defraud makes or publishes, or causes or permits to be made or published in any way whatever, any book, prospectus, notice, report, statement, exhibit, advertisement or other publication of or concerning the affairs, financial condition, property or assets of any corporation, joint stock association, partnership or individual, which said book, prospectus, notice, report, statement, exhibit, advertisement or other publication contains any statement which is false or wilfully exaggerated and which shall have a tendency to give a less or greater apparent value to the shares, bonds, property or assets of such corporation, joint stock association, partnership or individual, or any part of said shares, bonds, property or assets, than said shares, bonds, property or assets or any part thereof shall really and in fact possess, shall be punished by a fine of not more than five thousand dollars or by imprisonment for not more than ten years, or both.

SECTION 92A
Motor vehicles; sale in certain condition; written disclosure on bill of sale; penalty

Whoever sells a motor vehicle knowing that its engine or electrical parts have been submerged in water, or knowing that it has been used as a police car, a taxicab, a rental vehicle by a motor vehicle rental agency, or a leased vehicle which has been leased to any corporation, individual or entity, other than a motor vehicle rental company, without indicating such fact in writing on the bill of sale, and whoever, other than the commonwealth or any political subdivision thereof, sells any such police car to an ultimate user for other than police purposes without first having obliterated all evidence of distinctive police insignias or markings thereon, and painting the exterior of every marked state police vehicle thereof one solid color, shall be punished by a fine of not less than ten nor more than five hundred dollars.

SECTION 93
Animals; obtaining or giving false pedigree

Whoever, by a false pretense, obtains from any club, association, society or company for improving the breed of cattle, horses, sheep, swine or other domestic animals, the registration, or a certificate thereof, of any animal in the herd register, or any other register of such club, association, society or company, or a transfer of such registration, or a certificate thereof, of any animal in the herd register, or any other register of such club, association, society or company, or a transfer of such registration, or whoever knowingly makes, exhibits or gives a false pedigree in writing of any animal, shall be punished by imprisonment for not more than two years or by a fine of not more than five hundred dollars, or both.

SECTION 94
Boundary monuments and miscellaneous markers; malicious destruction

Whoever wilfully, intentionally and without right breaks down, injures, removes or destroys a monument erected for the purpose of designating the boundaries of a town or of a tract or lot of land, or a tree which has been marked for that purpose, or so breaks down, injures, removes or destroys a milestone, mileboard or guideboard erected upon a public way or railroad, or wilfully, intentionally and without right defaces or alters the inscription on any such stone or board, or wilfully, intentionally and without right mars or defaces a building or signboard, or extinguishes a light or breaks, destroys or removes a lamp, lamp post, railing or post erected on a bridge, sidewalk, public way, court or passage, or wilfully, intentionally and without right defaces or otherwise injures, removes, interferes with or destroys any traffic regulating sign, light, signal, marking or device lawfully erected or placed under public authority on any public way, shall be punished by imprisonment for not more than six months or by a fine of not more than two hundred dollars. Any person convicted under the provisions of this section shall, in addition to any imprisonment or fine, make restitution.

SECTION 95
Historical monuments; malicious destruction or injury

Whoever wilfully or maliciously removes, displaces, destroys, defaces, mars or injures any monument, tablet or other device erected to mark an historic place or to commemorate an historic event shall be punished by a fine of not more than one thousand dollars or by imprisonment for not more than two years. Any person convicted under the provisions of this section shall, in addition to any fine assessed, reimburse the commonwealth for the total amount of damage incurred.

SECTION 96
State building; defacement or injury

Whoever wilfully, intentionally and without right defaces, mars or injures the walls, wainscoting or any other part of any building belonging to the commonwealth, or the appurtenances thereof, by cutting, writing or otherwise, shall be punished by a fine of not less than one hundred nor more than one thousand dollars or by imprisonment for not more than two years. Any person convicted under the provisions of this section shall, in addition to any fine assessed, reimburse the commonwealth for the total amount of damages incurred.

SECTION 97
County buildings; defacement

Whoever wilfully mars of injures the walls, wainscoting or any other part of a court house, jail or house of correction, or of any other building or room used for county business, or the appurtenances thereof, by cutting, writing or otherwise, shall be punished by imprisonment for not more than two years or by a fine of not less than one hundred nor more than one thousand dollars. Any person convicted under the provisions of this section shall, in addition to any fine assessed, reimburse the county for the total amount of damage incurred.

SECTION 98
Schoolhouse or church; defacement or injury

Whoever wilfully, intentionally and without right, or wantonly and without cause, destroys, defaces, mars or injures a schoolhouse, church or other building erected or used for purposes of education or religious instruction, or for the general diffusion of knowledge, or an outbuilding, fence, well or appurtenance of such schoolhouse, church or other building, or furniture, apparatus or other property belonging thereto or connected therewith, shall be punished by a fine of not more than one thousand dollars, or by imprisonment for not more than two years, or both.

SECTION 98A
Public park or playground equipment; destruction, defacement or injury

Whoever wilfully, intentionally and without right, or wantonly and without cause destroys, defaces, mars or injures any playground apparatus or equipment located in a public park or playground shall be punished by a fine of not more than one thousand dollars.

SECTION 99
Libraries; definitions

As used in sections ninety-nine A and one hundred, the following words shall have the following meanings:—

"Library materials and property", any book, plate, picture, portrait, photograph, broadside, engraving, painting, drawing, map, specimen, print, lithograph, chart, musical score, catalog card, catalog record, statue, coin, medal, computer software, film, periodical, newspaper, magazine, pamphlet, document, manuscript, letter, archival material, public record, microform, sound recording, audio-visual material in any format, magnetic or other tape, tape recorder, film projector or other machinery or equipment, electronic data-processing record, artifact or other documentary written or printed material regardless of the physical form or characteristics which is a constituent element of a library's collection or any part thereof, belonging to, on loan to or otherwise in the custody of any library. Library materials and property shall also include the walls, wainscotting or any part of the library, or any other building or room used for library business or the appurtenances thereof, including furnishings.

"Library premises", the interior of the building, structure or other enclosure in which a library is located, bookmobiles and kiosks, the exterior appurtenances to such building, structure or enclosure is located.

SECTION 99A
Libraries; theft of materials or property; destruction of records

Whoever wilfully conceals on his person or among his belongings any library materials or property and removes said library materials or property, if the value of the property stolen exceeds two hundred and fifty dollars, shall be punished by imprisonment in the state prison for not more than five years, or by a fine of not less than one thousand nor more than twenty-five thousand dollars, or both; or, if the value of the property stolen does not exceed two hundred and fifty dollars, shall be punished by imprisonment in jail for not more than one year or by a fine of not less than one hundred nor more than one thousand dollars, or both, and ordered to pay the replacement value of such library materials or property, including all reasonable processing costs, as determined by the governing board of said library.

Any person who has properly charged out any library materials or property, and who, upon neglect to return the same within the time required and specified in the by-laws, rules or regulations of the library owning the property, after receiving notice from the librarian or other proper custodian of the property that the same is overdue, shall willfully fail to return the same within thirty days from the date of such notice shall pay a fine of not less than one hundred nor more than five hundred dollars and shall pay the replacement value of such library materials or property, including all reasonable processing costs, as determined by said governing board. Each piece of library property shall be considered a separate offense.

The giving of a false identification or fictitious name, address or place of employment with the intent to deceive, or borrowing or attempting to borrow any library material or property by: the use of a library card issued to another without the other's consent; the use of a library card knowing that it is revoked, canceled or expired; or, the use of a library card knowing that it is falsely made, counterfeit or materially altered shall be punished by a fine of not less than one hundred dollars nor more than one thousand dollars.

The willful alteration or destruction of library ownership records, electronic or catalog records retained apart from or applied directly to the library materials or property shall be punished by imprisonment in the state prison for not more than five years or by a fine of not less than one thousand nor more than twenty-five thousand dollars, or both, and shall pay the replacement value of such library materials or property, including all reasonable processing costs, as determined by the governing board having jurisdiction.

SECTION 100
Libraries; mutilation or destruction of materials or property

Whoever willfully, maliciously or wantonly writes upon, injures, defaces, tears, cuts, mutilates or destroys any library material or property, shall make restitution in full replacement value of the library materials or property, and, in addition, shall be punished by imprisonment in a house of correction for not more than two years or by a fine of not less than one hundred nor more than one thousand dollars, or both.

A law enforcement officer may arrest without warrant any person he has probable cause to believe has violated the provisions of section ninety-nine A and this section. The statement of an employee or agent of the library, eighteen years of age or older, that a person has violated the provisions of said section ninety-nine A and this section shall constitute probable cause for arrest by a law enforcement officer authorized to make an arrest in such jurisdiction. The activation of an electronic anti-theft device shall constitute probable cause for believing that a person has violated the provisions of this section.

A library shall prepare posters to be displayed therein in a conspicuous place. Said posters shall contain a summary and explanation of said section ninety-nine A and this section.

SECTION 101
Definitions related to Secs. 101–102D

For the purposes of sections 101 to 102D, inclusive, the following terms shall have the following meanings, unless otherwise clearly required:—

"Ammunition", cartridges or cartridge cases, primers (igniter), bullets or propellant powder designed for use in any weapon utilizing a propellant including, but not limited to,

2

ammunition produced by or for the military for national defense and security.

"Biological weapon", any microorganism, virus, infectious substance or biological product that may be engineered as a result of biotechnology, or any naturally occurring or bioengineered component of any such microorganism, virus, infectious substance or biological product, except if intended for a purpose not prohibited under this chapter or chapter 265, specifically prepared in a manner to cause death, disease or other biological malfunction in a human, animal, plant or another living organism, deterioration of food, water, equipment supplies or material of any kind, or deleterious alteration of the environment.

"Black powder", a compound or mixture of sulfur, charcoal and an alkali nitrate including, but not limited to, potassium or sodium nitrate.

"Chemical weapon", (i) a toxic chemical or substance, including the precursors to any toxic chemical or substance; and (ii) ammunition or a device designed to cause death or bodily harm by means of the release of a toxic chemical or substance.

"Delivery system", any equipment designed or adapted for use in connection with the deployment of chemical, biological or nuclear weapons.

"Denial of access", contamination to an area, including any structures thereon, which poses a health risk to humans, animals or plants and which precludes the safe use of such area until the contaminant becomes inactive, decays or is removed.

"Destructive or incendiary device or substance", an explosive, article or device designed or adapted to cause physical harm to persons or property by means of fire, explosion, deflagration or detonation and consisting of substance capable of being ignited, whether or not contrived to ignite or explode automatically.

"Element", a substance that is made entirely from 1 type of atom.

"Explosive", any element, compound or mixture that is manufactured, designed or used to produce an explosion and that contains an oxidizer, fuel or other ingredient, in such proportion, quantity or packing that an ignition by fire, friction, concussion, percussion or detonation of the element or of any part of the compound or mixture may cause such a sudden generation of highly heated gases that the resultant gaseous pressures, release of heat or fragmentation is capable of producing destructive effects on contiguous objects or of destroying life or causing bodily harm including, but not limited to, all material which is classified as division 1.1, 1.2, 1.3, 1.4, 1.5 or 1.6 explosives by the United States Department of Transportation or listed pursuant to 18 U.S.C. 841(d) and 27 C.F.R. 555.23. Explosive shall not include a pyrotechnic, small arms ammunition, small arms ammunition primers, smokeless powder weighing less than 50 pounds and black powder weighing less than 5 pounds, unless possessed or used for an illegal purpose.

"Hoax explosive", "hoax destructive or incendiary device or substance" or "hoax chemical, biological or nuclear weapon", any device, article or substance that would cause a person to reasonably believe that such device, article or substance is: (i) an explosive; (ii) a destructive or incendiary device or substance; or (iii) a chemical, biological or nuclear weapon, harmful radioactive substance or poison capable of causing bodily injury which is actually an inoperable facsimile.

"Nuclear weapon", a device designed for the purpose of causing bodily injury, death or denial of access through the release of radiation or radiological material either by propagation of nuclear fission or by means of any other energy source.

"Oxidizer", a substance that yields oxygen readily to stimulate the combustion of organic matter or other fuel.

"Pyrotechnic", any commercially manufactured combustible or explosive composition or manufactured article designed and prepared for the purpose of producing an audible effect or a visible display and regulated by chapter 148 including, but not limited to: (i) fireworks, firecrackers; (ii) flares, fuses and torpedoes, so-called, and similar signaling devices.

"Small arms ammunition", any shotgun, rifle, pistol, or revolver cartridge, and cartridges for propellant-actuated power devices and industrial guns.

"Smokeless powder", a rapid-burning solid material containing nitrocellulose used as a propellant.

SECTION 102
Possession or control of incendiary device or material; possession of hoax device or material; penalty

(a) Whoever, without lawful authority, has in his possession or under his control:

(i) any substance, material, article, explosive or ingredient which, alone or in combination, could be used to make a destructive or incendiary device or substance and who intends to make a destructive or incendiary device or substance; or

(ii) any substance, material, article, explosive or ingredient which, alone or in combination, could be used to make a chemical, biological or nuclear weapon and who intends to make a chemical, biological or nuclear weapon, shall be punished by imprisonment in the house of correction for not more than 2 and one-half years or in state prison for not less than 5 years nor more than 10 years or by a fine of not more than $25,000, or by both such fine and imprisonment. It shall not be a defense to a violation of this subsection that the defendant did not possess or have under his control every substance, material, article, explosive or ingredient, or combination thereof, required to make a complete and functional destructive or incendiary device or substance or chemical, biological or nuclear weapon.

(b) Whoever, without lawful authority, has in his possession or uses or places, or causes another to knowingly or unknowingly possess, use or place, any hoax explosive, hoax destructive or incendiary device or substance or any hoax chemical, biological or nuclear weapon, with the intent that such hoax explosive, device or substance or weapon be used to cause anxiety, unrest, fear or personal discomfort to any person or group of persons, shall be punished by imprisonment in the house of correction for not more than 2 and one-half years or by imprisonment in the state prison for not more than 5 years or by a fine of not more than $10,000, or by both such fine and imprisonment.

(c) Whoever, without lawful authority, has in his possession or under his control any explosive or any destructive or incendiary device or substance shall be punished by imprisonment for not more than 2 and one-half years in the house of correction or for not less than 10 years nor more than 20 years in the state prison or by a fine of not more than $25,000, or by both such fine and imprisonment.

2

SECTION 102A
Throwing, secreting, launching or placing of incendiary device; intent; punishment

Whoever, without lawful authority, secretes, throws, launches or otherwise places an explosive or a destructive or incendiary device or substance with the intent: (i) to cause fear, panic or apprehension in any person; or (ii) to ignite, explode or discharge such explosive or such destructive or incendiary device or substance; or (iii) to release or discharge any chemical, biological or nuclear weapon, shall be punished by imprisonment for not more than 2 and one-half years in the house of correction or for not less than 10 years nor more than 25 years in the state prison or by a fine of not more than $25,000, or by both such fine and imprisonment.

SECTION 102A½
Repealed

SECTION 102B
Malicious explosion

Whoever, without lawful authority, willfully discharges, ignites or explodes any destructive or incendiary device or substance shall be punished by imprisonment in the state prison by not less than 15 years nor more than 25 years or by a fine of $50,000 or by both such fine and imprisonment.

SECTION 102C
Biological, chemical or nuclear weapon or delivery system; possession; punishment

Whoever, without lawful authority, knowingly develops, produces, stockpiles, acquires, transports, possesses, controls, places, secretes or any biological, chemical or nuclear weapon or delivery system, with the intent to cause death, bodily injury or property damage, shall be punished by imprisonment in the house of correction for not more than 2 and one-half years or by imprisonment in the state prison for not more than 25 years or by a fine of not more than $50,000, or by both such fine and imprisonment.

SECTION 102D
Notice of seizure of explosive or incendiary device resulting from a violation of Secs. 102–102C; restitution

(a) Notice of the seizure of an explosive, destructive or incendiary device or substance, any weapon or the component parts thereof, in violation of any provision of section 102 to 102C, inclusive, shall be sent forthwith to the state fire marshal by the officer who made such seizure. The marshal may, in his sole discretion, render safe or direct any other official to assist him in rendering safe any item so seized, if such item cannot be safely kept pending trial. Upon final conviction of such person, such explosive, device, substance or weapon, or component parts thereof, shall be adjudged forfeited to the commonwealth and be disposed of by the marshal or his authorized representative.

(b) Upon conviction for a violation of sections 102 to 102C, inclusive, the court shall conduct a hearing to ascertain the extent of costs incurred, damages and financial loss suffered by local, county or state public safety agencies and the amount of property damage caused as a result of the violation of this section, if any. A person found guilty of violating sections 102 to 102C, inclusive, shall, in all cases, in addition to any other punishment, be ordered to make restitution to the local, county or state government for any costs incurred, damages and financial loss sustained as a result of the commission of such offense. Restitution shall be imposed in addition to incarceration or fine; provided, however, that the court shall consider the defendant's present and future ability to pay in its determinations regarding a fine. In determining the amount, time and method of payment of restitution, the court shall consider the financial resources of the defendant and the burden restitution will impose on the defendant.

SECTION 103
Oil of vitriol or other substances; throwing into house, building, or vessel

Whoever wilfully, intentionally and without right throws into, against or upon a dwelling house, office, shop or other building, or vessel, or puts or places therein or thereon oil of vitriol, coal tar or other noxious or filthy substance, with intent unlawfully to injure, deface or defile such dwelling house, office, shop, building or vessel, or any property therein, shall be punished by imprisonment in the state prison for not more than five years or in jail for not more than two and one half years or by a fine of not more than three hundred dollars.

SECTION 104
Buildings; destruction or injury

Whoever wilfully, intentionally and without right destroys, injures, defaces or mars a dwelling house or other building, whether upon the inside or outside, shall be punished by imprisonment for not more than two months or by a fine of not more than fifty dollars.

SECTION 104A
Goal posts; penalty for destruction

Whoever wilfully and without right destroys, injures or removes a goal post on a football field shall be punished by a fine of not less than fifty nor more than two hundred dollars.

SECTION 104B
Research animals; unauthorized removal

Whoever enters any premises in which animals are being housed or used in research by a research institution and, without authority, injures, damages, commits any trespass upon, removes or carries away any data, equipment, facility or property or injures, damages, removes, carries away, interferes with or releases any animal shall, if such injury, damage, trespass, removal, carrying away, interference or release is malicious and wilful, be punished by imprisonment in the state prison for not more than ten years or by a fine of not more than twenty-five thousand dollars and imprisonment in a jail or house of correction for not more than two and one-half years; or is such injury, damage, trespass, removal, carrying away, interference or release is wilful but not malicious, be punished by imprisonment in the state prison for not more than five years or a fine of not more than ten thousand dollars and imprisonment in jail or house of correction for not more than two and one-half years.

SECTION 105
Stone walls or fences; unauthorized removal

Whoever wilfully and without right pulls down or removes any portion of a stone wall or fence which is erected or maintained for the purpose of enclosing land shall be punished by a fine of not more than ten dollars. Natural resource officers and deputy natural resource officers of the office of the secretary of the executive office of environmental affairs, may arrest without a warrant any person found violating this section.

SECTION 106
Ice ponds; injury

Whoever wilfully, intentionally and without right or license, cuts, injures, mars or otherwise damages or destroys ice upon waters from which ice is or may be taken as an article of merchandise, whereby the taking thereof is hindered or the value thereof diminished for that purpose, shall be punished by a fine of not more than one hundred dollars.

SECTION 107
Bridge or canal; injury

Whoever wilfully, intentionally and without right breaks down, injures, removes or destroys a public bridge, or a lock, culvert or embankment of a canal, or wilfully, intentionally and without right makes an aperture or breach in such embankment with intent to destroy or injure the same, shall be punished by imprisonment in the state prison for not more than five years or by a fine of not more than five hundred dollars and imprisonment in jail for not more than two years.

SECTION 108
Vessel; destruction to injure or defraud owner or insurer; punishment; restitution

Whoever casts away, burns, sinks or otherwise destroys a ship or vessel, with intent to injure or defraud an owner thereof, or of any property laden on board the same, or an insurer of such ship, vessel or property, or of any part thereof, shall be punished by imprisonment in the state prison for not more than ten years or imprisonment in a jail for not more than two and one-half years.

A person found guilty of violating this section shall, in addition to any other punishment, be ordered to make restitution to the insurer or owner for any financial loss sustained as a result of the commission of the crime except as hereinafter provided. Restitution shall be imposed in addition to incarceration or fine. In the case of an indigent defendant, the court may determine that the interests of the victim and of justice would not be served by ordering such restitution. In such case, the court shall make specific written findings of the evidence presented which militated against the imposition of restitution.

The courts shall, after conviction, conduct an evidentiary hearing to ascertain the extent of the damages or financial loss suffered as a result of the defendant's crime and may then determine the amount and method of restitution. In so determining, the court shall consider the financial resources of the defendant and the burden restitution will impose on the defendant. The defendant's present and future ability to make such restitution shall be considered.

A defendant ordered to make restitution may petition the court for remission from any payment of restitution or from any unpaid portion thereof. If the court finds that the payment of restitution due will impose an undue financial hardship on the defendant or his family, the court may grant remission from any payment of restitution or modify the time and method of payment.

If a defendant who is required to make restitution defaults in any payment of restitution or installment thereof, the court may hold him in contempt unless said defendant has made a good faith effort to make restitution. If the defendant

has made such good faith effort, the court may, upon motion of the defendant, modify the order requiring restitution by:

(a) providing for additional time to make any payment in restitution;

(b) reducing the amount of any payment in restitution or installment thereof;

(c) granting a remission from any payment of restitution or part thereof.

Restitution shall not be authorized to a party whom the court determines to be aggrieved, without such party's consent.

SECTION 109
Vessel; fitting out with intent to destroy

Whoever lades, equips or fits out, or assists in lading, equipping or fitting out, a ship or vessel, with intent that it shall be wilfully cast away, burnt, sunk or otherwise destroyed, and with intent to injure or defraud an owner or insurer of such ship or vessel, or of any property laden on board the same, shall be punished by imprisonment in the state prison for not more than twenty years or by a fine of not more than five thousand dollars and imprisonment in jail for not more than two and one half years.

SECTION 110
False invoice of cargo; intent to defraud insurer

An owner of a ship or vessel, or of property laden or pretended to be laden on board the same, or any other person concerned in the lading or fitting out of a ship or vessel, who makes out or exhibits, or causes to be made out or exhibited, a false or fraudulent invoice, bill of lading, bill or parcels or other false estimates of any goods or property laden or pretended to be laden on board such ship or vessel, with intent to injure or defraud an insurer of such ship, vessel or property or of any part thereof, shall be punished by imprisonment in the state prison for not more than ten years or by a fine of not more than five thousand dollars and imprisonment in jail for not more than two years.

SECTION 111
False affidavit or protest; penalty for making

A master, officer or mariner of a ship or vessel who makes or causes to be made or swears to a false affidavit or protest, or an owner of or other person concerned in such ship or vessel, or the owner of or the person concerned in the goods or property laden on board the same, who procures such false affidavit or protest to be made, or exhibits the same, with intent to injure, deceive or defraud an insurer of such ship or vessel, or of any goods or property laden on board the same, shall be punished by imprisonment in the state prison for not more than ten years or by a fine of not more than five thousand dollars and imprisonment in jail for not more that two years.

SECTION 111A
Insurance policies; penalties for fraudulent claims

Whoever, in connection with or in support of any claim under any policy of insurance issued by any company, as defined in section one of chapter one hundred and seventy-five, and with intent to injure, defraud or deceive such company, presents to it, or aids or abets in or procures the presentation to it of, any notice, statement, proof of loss, bill of lading, bill of parcels, invoice, schedule, account or other written document, whether or not the same is under oath or is required or authorized by law or by the terms of such policy, knowing that such notice, statement, proof of loss, bill of lading, bill of parcels, invoice, schedule, account or other written document contains any false or fraudulent statement of representation of any fact or thing material to such claim, or whoever with intent as aforesaid makes, prepares or subscribes, or aids or abets in or procures the making, preparation or subscription of, any such notice, statement, proof of loss, bill of lading, bill of parcels, invoice, schedule, account or other written document intended to be presented to any such company in connection with or in support of any claim under any such policy issued by it knowing that such notice, statement, proof of loss, bill of lading, bill of parcels, invoice, schedule, account or other written document contains any false or fraudulent statement or representation as aforesaid, shall, except as provided in section one hundred and ten or one hundred and eleven, be punished by imprisonment in the state prison for not more than five years or by imprisonment in jail for not less than six months nor more than two and one half years or by a fine of not less than $500 nor more than $10,000, or by both such fine and imprisonment in jail.

NOTE　　See Notes following G.L. c. 266, § 28.

SECTION 111B
Motor vehicle insurance policies; penalty for fraudulent claims

Whoever, in connection with or in support of any application for or claim under any motor vehicle, theft or comprehensive insurance policy issued by an insurer, and with intent to injure, defraud or deceive such insurer knowingly presents to it, or aids or abets in or procures the presentation to it of, any notice, statement, or proof of loss, whether or not the same is under oath or is required or authorized by law or the terms of such policy, knowing such notice, statement or proof of loss contains any false or fraudulent statement or representation of any fact or thing material to such application or claim, shall be punished by imprisonment in the state prison for not more than 5 years or by imprisonment in the house of correction for not less than 6 months nor more than 2½ years or by a fine of not less than $1,000 nor more than $10,000, or by both such fine and imprisonment.

A person licensed as a motor vehicle damage appraiser pursuant to section eight G of chapter twenty-six or registered as a motor vehicle repair shop pursuant to chapter one hundred A who violates this section, by fraudulently inflating an appraisal of damage to a motor vehicle or the charges for repairing a damaged motor vehicle or otherwise, shall be punished by the additional penalty of revocation of such license or registration for a period not to exceed two years.

The court shall, after conviction, conduct an evidentiary hearing to ascertain the extent of damages or financial loss suffered as a result of the defendant's crime. A person found guilty of violating this section shall, in all cases, upon conviction, in addition to any other punishment, be ordered to make restitution to the insurer for any financial loss sustained as a result of the commission of the crime; provided, however, that restitution shall not be ordered to a party whom the court determines to be aggrieved without that party's consent. Restitution shall be imposed in addition to incarceration or fine, and not in lieu thereof; provided, however, the court shall consider the defendant's present and future ability to pay in its determinations regarding a fine; provided, further, that,

whenever possible subject to the constraints of this paragraph and the first paragraph of this section, the amount of a fine imposed for a violation of this section shall equal twice the amount of damages or financial loss suffered as a result of the defendant's crime.

In determining the amount, time and method of payment of restitution, the court shall consider the financial resources of the defendant and the burden restitution will impose on the defendant. Upon a real or impending change in financial circumstances, a defendant ordered to pay restitution may petition the court for a modification of the amount, time or method of payment of restitution. If the court finds that because of any such change the payment of restitution will impose an undue financial hardship on the defendant or his family, the court may modify the amount, time or method of payment, but may not grant complete remission from payment of restitution.

If a defendant who is required to make restitution defaults in any payment of restitution or installment thereof, the court shall hold him in contempt unless said defendant has made a good faith effort to pay such restitution. If said defendant has made a good faith effort to pay such restitution, the court may modify the amount, time or method of payment, but may not grant complete remission from payment of restitution.

NOTE 1　　**Restitution.** *See* G.L. c. 276, § 92A.

NOTE 2　　See Notes following G.L. c. 266, § 28.

SECTION 111C
Fraudulent motor vehicle insurance claims—runners

(a) As used in this section, the following words shall have the following meanings:—

"Provider", an attorney, a health care professional licensed pursuant to chapter 112, an owner or operator of a health care practice or facility, any person who creates the impression that he or his practice or facility can provide legal or health care services, or any person employed or acting on behalf of any of the aforementioned persons.

"Public media", telephone directories, professional directories, newspapers and other periodicals, radio and television, billboards and mailed or electronically transmitted written communications that do not involve in-person contact with a specific prospective client, patient or customer.

"Runner", a person who, for a pecuniary benefit, procures or attempts to procure a client, patient or customer at the direction of, request of, or in cooperation with a provider whose purpose is to seek to fraudulently obtain benefits under a contract of insurance or fraudulently assert a claim against an insured or an insurance carrier for providing services to the client, patient or customer. "Runner" shall not include a person who procures or attempts to procure clients, patients or customers for a provider through public media or a person who refers clients, patients or customers to a provider as otherwise authorized by law.

(b) Whoever knowingly acts as a runner or uses, solicits, directs, hires or employs another to act as a runner for the purpose of defrauding an insured or an insurance carrier shall be punished by imprisonment in the state prison for not more than 5 years, by imprisonment in a jail or house of correction for not less than 6 months nor more than 2½ years or by a fine of not less than $1,000 nor more than $4,000.

2

SECTION 112
Domestic animals; malicious killing or injury
(Amended by 2014 Mass. Acts c. 293, § 2, effective Nov. 18, 2014.)

Whoever wilfully and maliciously kills, maims or disfigures any horse, cattle or other animal of another person, or wilfully and maliciously administers or exposes poison with intent that it shall be taken or swallowed by any such animal, shall be punished by imprisonment in the state prison for not more than 7 years in state prison or imprisonment in the house of correction for not more than 2½ years or by a fine of not more than $5,000 or by both fine and imprisonment; provided, however, that a second or subsequent offense shall be punished by imprisonment in the state prison for not more than 10 years or by a fine of not more than $10,000 or by both such fine and imprisonment.

SECTION 113
Timber, wood and shrubs; wilful cutting and destruction on land of another

Whoever wilfully cuts down or destroys timber or wood standing or growing on the land of another, or carries away any kind of timber or wood cut down or lying on such land, or digs up or carries away stone, ore, gravel, clay, sand, turf or mould from such land, or roots, nuts, berries, grapes or fruit of any kind or any plant there being, or cuts down or carries away sedge, grass, hay or any kind of corn, standing, growing or being on such land, or cuts or takes therefrom any ferns, flowers or shrubs, or carries away from a wharf or landing place any goods in which he has no interest or property, without the license of the owner thereof, shall be punished by imprisonment for not more than six months or by a fine of not more than five hundred dollars; and if the offense is committed on Sunday, or in disguise, or secretly in the night time, the imprisonment shall not be for less than five days nor the fine less than five dollars.

SECTION 114
Trees and fences; malicious injury

Whoever wilfully and maliciously or wantonly breaks glass in a building which is not his own, or whoever wilfully and maliciously breaks down, injures, mars or defaces a fence belonging to or enclosing land which is not his own, or wilfully and maliciously throws down or opens a gate, bars or fence, and leaves the same down or open, or maliciously and injuriously severs from the freehold of another any produce thereof or anything attached thereto, shall be punished by imprisonment for not more than six months or by a fine of not more than five hundred dollars.

SECTION 115
Trespass in orchards and gardens

Whoever wilfully and maliciously enters an orchard, nursery, garden or cranberry meadow, and takes away, mutilates or destroys a tree, shrub or vine, or steals, takes and carries away any fruit or flower, without the consent of the owner thereof, shall be punished by a fine of not more than five hundred dollars or by imprisonment for not more than six months.

SECTION 116
Repealed

SECTION 116A
Protection of certain flowers

No person shall pull up or dig up the plant of a wild azalea, wild orchid or cardinal flower (lobelia cardinalis), or any part thereof, or injure any such plant or any part thereof except in so far as is reasonably necessary in procuring the flower therefrom, within the limits of any state highway or any other public way or place, or upon the land of another person without written authority from him, and no person shall buy or sell, or offer or expose for sale, any such flower, or the whole or any part of the plant thereof, knowing, or having reasonable cause to believe, that in procuring such flower or plant the foregoing provisions have been violated. Violation of any provision of this section shall be punished by a fine of not more than five dollars.

SECTION 117
Orchards and gardens; entry with intent to injure or destroy

Whoever wilfully, intentionally and without right enters upon the orchard, garden or other improved land of another, with intent to cut, take, carry away, destroy or injure the trees, grain, grass, hay, fruit or vegetables there growing or being, shall be punished by imprisonment for not more than six months or by a fine of not more than five hundred dollars; and if the offence is committed on Sunday, or in disguise, or secretly in the night time, the imprisonment shall not be for less than five days nor the fine less than five dollars.

SECTION 118
Domestic animals; trespass on land

Whoever, having the charge or custody of sheep, goats, cattle, horses, swine or fowl, wilfully suffers or permits them to enter or remain on or pass over any orchard, garden, mowing land or other improved or enclosed land of another, after being forbidden so to do in writing or by notice posted thereon by the owner or occupant, shall be punished by a fine of not more than ten dollars.

SECTION 119
Pests; bringing into state; penalty; exception

Whoever knowingly brings into the commonwealth, or transports from one town to another therein, any pest referred to in section eleven or twenty-five of chapter one hundred and thirty-two, or the eggs, nests, larvae or pupae thereof, except when engaged in research work for the commonwealth or for the United States department of agriculture, and for the purpose of suppressing such pests, or whoever knowingly evades the requirements of a quarantine regulation duly established under any provision of said chapter one hundred and thirty-two, shall be punished by fine of not more than two hundred dollars, or imprisonment for not more than two months, or both.

SECTION 120
Trespass

Whoever, without right enters or remains in or upon the dwelling house, buildings, boats or improved or enclosed land, wharf, or pier of another, or enters or remains in a school bus, as defined in section 1 of chapter 90 after having been forbidden so to do by the person who has lawful control of said premises, whether directly or by notice posted thereon, or in violation of a court order pursuant to section thirty-four

B of chapter two hundred and eight or section three or four of chapter two hundred and nine A, shall be punished by a fine of not more than one hundred dollars or by imprisonment for not more than thirty days or both such fine and imprisonment. Proof that a court has given notice of such a court order to the alleged offender shall be prima facie evidence that the notice requirement of this section has been met. A person who is found committing such trespass may be arrested by a sheriff, deputy sheriff, constable or police officer and kept in custody in a convenient place, not more than twenty-four hours, Sunday excepted, until a complaint can be made against him for the offense, and he be taken upon a warrant issued upon such complaint.

This section shall not apply to tenants or occupants of residential premises who, having rightfully entered said premises at the commencement of the tenancy or occupancy, remain therein after such tenancy or occupancy has been or is alleged to have been terminated. The owner or landlord of said premises may recover possession thereof only through appropriate civil proceedings.

NOTE 1   "[A] trespasser is a person who enters or remains upon land in the possession of another without a privilege to do so created by the possessor's consent or otherwise.' *Restatement (Second) of Torts* § 329 (1965). He is in brief someone who lacks any right at all to be on another's property." *Monterosso v. Gaudette*, 8 Mass. App. Ct. 93, 99–100 (1979).

NOTE 2   Although there was no posted notice and no evidence that the defendant had been orally forbidden entrance, the conviction was affirmed because entry to the premises (a stadium) was forbidden as the property was secured with fences or walls and locked gates or doors. *Commonwealth v. A Juvenile (No. 1)*, 6 Mass. App. Ct. 106, 108 (1978).

NOTE 3   One may be found guilty of trespass even though the defendant was given lawful access to another part of the building. *Commonwealth v. Krasner*, 360 Mass. 848, 849 (1971).

NOTE 4   This section covers public, as well as private, property. *Commonwealth v. Egleson*, 355 Mass. 259, 262 (1969).

NOTE 5   **Boston Housing Authority.** "We address here the question whether *Commonwealth* v. *Richardson*, 313 Mass. 632 (1943), which involved a private landlord, applies equally to the Boston Housing Authority (BHA). Concluding that it does, we reverse the defendant's conviction of criminal trespass, G.L. c. 266, § 120. . . . [T]he BHA public housing lease throughout acknowledges that residents are entitled to have guests in their apartments. . . . As a result, a conviction for trespass cannot stand against a defendant who is found to be passing through the halls of BHA property in order to reach a tenant's apartment at the tenant's invitation. The guest must be passing through, not lingering or loitering. Here, the trial judge found that the defendant was present at the invitation of McCall, and there was no evidence that the defendant had lingered or loitered in the hall." *Commonwealth v. Nelson*, 74 Mass. App. Ct. 629, 630, 633 (2009).

NOTE 6   "It is not necessary that the person entering should actually see the notices posted, if they were reasonably distinct and were posted in reasonably suited places, so that by the exercise of due care they would be seen by persons who come upon the land." *Fitzgerald v. Lewis*, 164 Mass. 495, 501 (1895).

NOTE 7   **Related Statute.** G.L. c. 277, § 25—Description of ownership.

SECTION 120A
Motor vehicle; parking on private way; prosecution; evidence

In any prosecution for committing the crime of trespass by parking a motor vehicle upon a private way or upon im-

proved or enclosed land, proof that the defendant named in the complaint was at the time of such parking the registered owner of such vehicle shall be prima facie evidence that the defendant was the person who parked such vehicle upon such way or land at such time.

SECTION 120B
Entry on land by abutting property owners not constituting trespass

Whoever, being the owner of land abutting that of another, the building or buildings on which are so close to the land of such other person as to require an entry on said abutting land for the purpose of maintaining or repairing said building or buildings in order to prevent waste, shall not be deemed guilty of trespass or liable civilly for damages, provided that such entry is made expeditiously and in the exercise of due care and that no damage is caused by such entry to the land or buildings of said abutting owner. Before such entry said owner shall notify the chief or other officer in charge of the police department of the city or town in which the land is located that he has requested permission to enter on adjoining land from the owner or occupants thereof for the purpose of maintaining or repairing a building or buildings and that such permission has been refused, and that he intends to enter under the provisions of this section. Before entering on said land, said owner shall post bond with the chief of police in the amount of one thousand dollars to protect the adjoining land owner from damage caused by said entry. No person so entering on land of another shall store material or tools thereon for more than eight hours in any one day nor shall he continue to enter thereon for more than thirty days in the aggregate in any calendar year. After said entry, said owner shall in all respects restore said adjoining land to the condition in which it was prior to said entry.

SECTION 120C
Entry upon adjoining lands by surveyors not constituting trespass

Whenever a land surveyor registered under chapter one hundred and twelve deems it reasonably necessary to enter upon adjoining lands to make surveys of any description included under "Practice of land surveying", as defined in section eighty-one D of said chapter one hundred and twelve, for any private person excluding any public authority, public utility or railroad, the land surveyor or his authorized agents or employees may, after reasonable notice, enter upon lands, waters and premises, not including buildings, in the commonwealth, within a reasonable distance from the property line of the land being surveyed, and such entry shall not be deemed a trespass. Nothing in this act shall relieve a land surveyor of liability for damage caused by entry to adjoining property by himself or his agents or employees.

SECTION 120D
Removal of motor vehicles from private ways or property; procedure; penalties; liability for removal and storage charges; release of vehicle

No person shall remove a motor vehicle which is parked or standing on a private way or upon improved or enclosed property unless the operator of such vehicle has been forbidden so to park or stand, either directly or by posted notice, by the person who has lawful control of such way or property.

2

No vehicle shall be removed from such way or property without the consent of the owner of such vehicle unless the person who has lawful control of such way or property shall have notified the chief of police or his designee in a city or town, or, in the city of Boston the police commissioner, or a person from time to time designated by said police commissioner, that such vehicle is to be removed. Such notification shall be made before any such vehicle shall be removed, and shall be in writing unless otherwise specified by such chief of police or police commissioner and shall include the address from which the vehicle is to be removed, the address to which the vehicle is to be removed, the registration number of the vehicle, the name of the person in lawful control of the way or property from which such vehicle is being removed, and the name of the person or company or other business entity removing the vehicle. Vehicles so removed shall be stored in a convenient location. Neither the city or town, nor its chief of police or police commissioner or his designee, shall be liable for any damages incurred during the removal or storage of any such vehicle removed under this section. Any person who, without notifying the chief of police or his designee, or the police commissioner or his designee, or without obtaining the consent of the owner, removes a vehicle from a private way or from improved or enclosed property as aforesaid, shall, in addition to any other penalty of law, be punished by a fine of not more than one hundred dollars. The employer of such person if any, shall also be punished by a fine of not more than one hundred dollars.

Any person who purports to authorize the removal of a vehicle from a way or property as aforesaid without having fully complied with the provision of this section shall be punished by a fine of not more than one hundred dollars.

In addition to any other penalty provided by law, the registered owner of a vehicle illegally parked or standing on a private way or upon improved or enclosed property shall be liable for charges for the removal and storage of such vehicle; provided, however, that the liability so imposed shall not exceed the following, and provided, further, that the vehicle has been removed after compliance with the provisions of this section:

(1) the maximum amount for towing or transportation of motor vehicles established by the department of public utilities for motor vehicles towed away when such towing is ordered by the police or other public authority under the provisions of section six B of chapter one hundred and fifty-nine B; and

(2) the maximum charge for storage of noncommercial passenger motor vehicles with a maximum capacity of nine persons, shall be not more than the maximum storage charge allowed under the provisions of said section six B of said chapter one hundred and fifty-nine B.

A person lawfully holding a vehicle removed under the provisions of this section may hold such vehicle until the registered owner pays the removal and storage charges.

Any person who is called to remove by towing a vehicle illegally parked or standing on a private way or upon improved or enclosed property may, at his discretion, if the owner appears to remove said vehicle before the towing is completed, charge said owner one half of the fee usually charged for such towing.

Any person who removes a vehicle illegally parked or standing on a private way or upon improved or enclosed property, or holds such a vehicle after its removal, and who has not complied in full with the provisions of this section, shall release such vehicle to its owner without assessing any charges for its removal or storage.

SECTION 120E
Obstruction of entry to or departure from medical facility; injunctive relief; damages

As used in this section, the following words shall have the following meanings:—

"Medical facility", any medical office, medical clinic, medical laboratory, or hospital.

"Notice", (i) receipt of or awareness of the contents of a court order prohibiting blocking of a medical facility; (ii) oral request by an authorized representative of a medical facility, or law enforcement official to refrain from obstructing access to a medical facility; or (iii) written posted notice outside the entrance to a medical facility to refrain from obstructing access to a medical facility.

Whoever knowingly obstructs entry to or departure from any medical facility or who enters or remains in any medical facility so as to impede the provision of medical services, after notice to refrain from such obstruction or interference, shall be punished for the first offense by a fine of not more than one thousand dollars or not more than six months in jail or a house of correction or both, and for each subsequent violation of this section by a fine of not less than five hundred dollars and not more than five thousand dollars or not more than two and one-half years in jail or a house of correction or both. These penalties shall be in addition to any penalties imposed for violation of a court order.

A person who knowingly obstructs entry to or departure from such medical facility or who enters or remains in such facility so as to impede the provision of medical services after notice to refrain from such obstruction or interference, may be arrested by a sheriff, deputy sheriff, constable, or police officer.

Any medical facility whose rights to provide services under the provisions of this section have been violated or which has reason to believe that any person or entity is about to engage in conduct proscribed herein may commence a civil action for injunctive and other equitable relief, including the award of compensatory and exemplary damages. Said civil action shall be instituted either in superior court for the county in which the conduct complained of occurred, or in the superior court for the county in which any person or entity complained of resides or has a principal place of business. An aggrieved facility which prevails in an action authorized by this paragraph, in addition to other damages, shall be entitled to an award of the costs of the litigation and reasonable attorney's fees in an amount to be fixed by the court.

Nothing herein shall be construed to interfere with any rights provided by chapter one hundred and fifty A or by the federal Labor-Management Act of 1947 or other rights to engage in peaceful picketing which does not obstruct entry or departure.

SECTION 120E½
Reproductive health care facility; buffer zone; penalties
(Amended by 2014 Mass. Acts c. 197, § 2, effective July 30, 2014.)

(a) As used in this section, the following words shall have the following meanings unless the context clearly requires otherwise:

"Driveway", an entry from a public street to a public or private parking area used by a reproductive health care facility.

"Entrance", a door to a reproductive health care facility that directly abuts the public sidewalk; provided, however, that if the door does not directly abut the public sidewalk, the "entrance" shall be the point at which the public sidewalk intersects with a pathway leading to the door.

"Impede", to obstruct, block, detain or render passage impossible, unsafe or unreasonably difficult.

"Law enforcement official", a duly authorized member of a law enforcement agency, including a member of a municipal, metropolitan or state police department, sheriffs or deputy sheriffs.

"Reproductive health care facility", a place, other than within or upon the grounds of a hospital, where abortions are offered or performed including, but not limited to, the building, grounds and driveway of the facility and a parking lot in which the facility has an ownership or leasehold interest.

(b) A law enforcement official may order the immediate withdrawal of 1 or more individuals who have on that day substantially impeded access to or departure from an entrance or driveway to a reproductive health care facility. A withdrawal order issued pursuant to this section shall be in writing and shall include the following statements: (i) the individual or individuals have substantially impeded access to or departure from the reproductive health care facility; (ii) the individual or individuals so ordered shall, under the penalty of arrest and prosecution, immediately withdraw and cease to stand or be located within at least 25 feet of an entrance or driveway to the reproductive health care facility; and (iii) the order shall remain in place for 8 hours or until the close of business of the reproductive health facility, whichever is earlier. This subsection shall apply during the business hours of a reproductive health care facility. This subsection shall also apply only if the 25-foot boundary is clearly marked and subsections (a) through (c), inclusive, of this section are posted outside of the reproductive health care facility.

(c) A person who fails to comply with a withdrawal order pursuant to subsection (b) shall be punished, for the first offense, by a fine of not more than $500 or not more than 3 months in a jail or house of correction or by both such fine and imprisonment and, for each subsequent offense, by a fine of not less than $500 nor more than $5,000 or not more than 2½ years in a jail or house of correction or by both such fine and imprisonment.

(d) A person who, by force, physical act or threat of force, intentionally injures or intimidates or attempts to injure or intimidate a person who attempts to access or depart from a reproductive health care facility shall be punished, for the first offense, by a fine of not more than $2,000 or not more than 1 year in a jail or house of correction or by both such fine and imprisonment and, for each subsequent offense, by a fine of not less than $10,000 nor more than $50,000 or not more than 2½ years in a jail or house of correction or not more than 5 years in a state prison or by both such fine and imprisonment. For the purpose of this subsection, "intimidate" shall mean to place a person in reasonable apprehension of bodily harm to that person or another.

(e) A person who impedes a person's access to or departure from a reproductive health care facility with the intent to interfere with that person's ability to provide, support the provision of or obtain services at the reproductive health care facility shall be punished, for the first offense, by a fine of not more than $1,000 or not more than 6 months in a jail or house of correction or by both such fine and imprisonment and, for each subsequent offense, by a fine of not less than $5,000 nor more than $25,000 or not more than 2½ years in a jail or house of correction or not more than 5 years in the state prison or by both such fine and imprisonment.

(f) A person who knowingly impedes or attempts to impede a person or a vehicle attempting to access or depart from a reproductive health care facility shall be punished, for the first offense, by a fine of not more than $500 or not more than 3 months in a jail or house of correction or by both such fine and imprisonment and, for each subsequent offense, by a fine of not less than $1,000 nor more than $5,000 or not more than 2½ years in a jail or house of correction or by both such fine and imprisonment.

(g) A person who recklessly interferes with the operation of a vehicle that attempts to enter, exit or park at a reproductive health care facility shall be punished, for the first offense, by a fine of not more than $500 or not more than 3 months in a jail or house of correction or by both such fine and imprisonment and, for each subsequent offense, by a fine of not less than $1,000 nor more than $5,000 or not more than 2½ years in a jail or house of correction or by both such fine and imprisonment.

(h) A person who fails to comply with a withdrawal order pursuant to said subsection (b) or who is found in violation of subsection (c), (d), (e), (f) or (g) may be arrested without a warrant by a law enforcement official.

(i) If a person or entity fails to comply with a withdrawal order pursuant to subsection (b) or who is found in violation of subsection (c), (d), (e), (f) or (g), an aggrieved person or entity or the attorney general or both may commence a civil action. The civil action shall be commenced either in the superior court for the county in which the conduct complained of occurred or in the superior court for the county in which the person or entity complained of resides or has a principal place of business.

(j) In an action pursuant to subsection (i), a court may award as remedies: (1) temporary, preliminary and permanent injunctive relief; (2) compensatory and punitive damages; and (3) costs, attorneys' fees and expert witness fees. In an action brought by the attorney general pursuant to subsection (i), the court may also award civil penalties against each defendant in an amount not exceeding: (A) $5,000 for a nonviolent violation and $7,500 for other first violations; and (B) $7,500 for a subsequent nonviolent violation and $12,500 for any other subsequent violation.

(k) A violation of an injunction entered by a court in an action brought pursuant to subsection (i) shall be a criminal offense under section 11J of chapter 12.

SECTION 120F
Unauthorized access to computer system; penalties

Whoever, without authorization, knowingly accesses a computer system by any means, or after gaining access to a computer system by any means knows that such access is not authorized and fails to terminate such access, shall be punished by imprisonment in the house of correction for not more than thirty days or by a fine of not more than one thousand dollars, or both.

The requirement of a password or other authentication to gain access shall constitute notice that access is limited to authorized users.

SECTION 121
Entry on land with firearms

Whoever, without right, enters upon the land of another with firearms, with intent to fire or discharge them thereon, and, having been requested by the owner or occupant of such land or by his agent to leave such land, remains thereon, shall be punished by a fine of not more than two hundred dollars or by imprisonment for not more than two months, or both.

SECTION 121A
Trespasses involving motor vehicles and other powered devices

Whoever, without right, enters upon the private land of another, whether or not such land be posted against trespass, and in so entering makes use of or has in his immediate possession or control any vehicle, machine, or device which includes an internal combustion engine or other source of mechanical power, shall be punished by a fine of not more than two hundred and fifty dollars.

The provisions of this section shall not apply to such an entry at the junction of a public way with a paved private roadway, unless said private roadway is distinguished from the public way by a sign, gatepost, or the display of a street number or the name of the occupant of the premises, or by the improvement of adjacent land, the type of construction of the roadway, or other distinguishing feature, or unless such entry has been forbidden by the person having lawful control of said private roadway.

Nothing herein shall in any way restrict the operation of power boats on waterways not otherwise restricted.

SECTION 122
Notice against trespassers; penalty for defacement

Whoever wilfully tears down, removes or defaces any notice posted on land, or other property described in section one hundred and twenty, by the owner, lessee or custodian thereof, warning persons not to trespass thereon, shall be punished by a fine of not more than twenty-five dollars.

SECTION 123
Land of state and county institutions; institutions of higher education; trespass

Whoever willfully trespasses upon land or premises belonging to the commonwealth, or to any authority established by the general court for purposes incidental to higher education, appurtenant to a public institution of higher education, any correctional institution of the commonwealth, Tewksbury hospital, Soldiers' Home in Massachusetts, Soldiers' Home in Holyoke, any public institution for the care of mentally ill and developmentally disabled persons, any Massachusetts training school or state charitable institution, or upon land or premises belonging to any county and appurtenant to a jail, house of correction or courthouse, or whoever, after notice from an officer of any of said institutions to leave said land, remains thereon, shall be punished by a fine of not more than fifty dollars or by imprisonment for not more than three months.

SECTION 123A
Willful trespass upon public source of water, water supply facility or land
(Added by 2012 Mass. Acts c. 446, § 4, effective Apr. 9, 2013.)

(a) Whoever willfully trespasses upon any public source of water or public water supply facilities or land after having been forbidden to do so by a person who has lawful control of the water, facilities or land, or an agent of such a person, whether directly or by notice posted on such water supply facility or land, shall be punished by a fine of not less than $250 nor more than $1,000.

(b) Whoever commits any offense described in subsection (a) with the intent to corrupt, pollute or defile such public source of water shall be punished by a fine of not less than $1,000 nor more than $5,000 or by imprisonment in the house of correction for not more than 2 years or in state prison for not more than 5 years or by both such fine and imprisonment. Whoever is convicted of a second or subsequent violation of this subsection shall be punished by a fine of not less than $1,000 nor more than $10,000 or by imprisonment in state prison for not less than 5 years nor more than 10 years or by both such fine and imprisonment.

(c) In addition to the punishments outlined in subsections (a) and (b), restitution in the amount of costs associated with water quality analysis and any subsequent investigation to determine water safety and security of the facilities or land may be ordered by a court after a hearing relative to such restitution.

(d) A law enforcement officer may arrest, without a warrant, any person that the officer has probable cause to believe has violated this section.

SECTION 124
Legal notice; penalty for malicious injury

Whoever wilfully and maliciously, or wantonly and without cause, tears down, removes or defaces a warrant for a town meeting, list of jurors or other notice or paper which has been posted in compliance with law shall, except as otherwise provided, be punished by a fine of not more than ten dollars.

SECTION 125
Show bill or advertisement; penalty for malicious injury

Whoever wilfully and maliciously removes, destroys or mutilates a show bill, placard, program or other advertisement posted upon a wall, fence, billboard or structure not lawfully under his control, of an exhibition, show or amusement licensed under section one hundred and eighty-one of chapter one hundred and forty, before such exhibition, show or amusement has taken place, shall be punished by a fine of not more than ten dollars.

SECTION 126
Natural scenery; penalty for defacement

Whoever paints, or puts upon, or in any manner affixes to, any fence, structure, pole, rock or other object which is public property or the property of another, whether within or without the limits of the highway, any words, device, trade mark, advertisement or notice which is not required by law to be posted thereon, without first obtaining the written consent of the municipal or public officer in charge thereof or the owner or tenant of such property, shall, upon complaint of such municipal or public officer, or of such owner or tenant, be punished by a fine of not less than ten nor more than one hundred dollars, and in addition shall forfeit to the use of the public or private owner of such property or the tenant thereof the cost of removing or obliterating such defacement to be recovered in an action of tort. Any word, device, trade mark, advertisement or notice which has been painted, put up or affixed within the limits of a highway in violation of this section shall be considered a public nuisance, and may be forthwith removed or obliterated and abated by any person.

SECTION 126A
Walls, signs, gravestones, etc.; penalty for defacement

Whoever intentionally, willfully and maliciously or wantonly, paints, marks, scratches, etches or otherwise marks, injures, mars, defaces or destroys the real or personal property of another including but not limited to a wall, fence, building, sign, rock, monument, gravestone or tablet, shall be punished by imprisonment in a state prison for a term of not more than three years or by imprisonment in a house of correction for not more than two years or by a fine of not more than fifteen hundred dollars or not more than three times the value of the property so marked, injured, marred, defaced or destroyed, whichever is greater, or both imprisonment and fine, and shall also be required to pay for the removal or obliteration of such painting, marking, scratching or etching, or to remove or obliterate such painting, marking, scratching or etching; provided, however, that when a fine is levied pursuant to the value of the property marked, injured, marred, defaced or destroyed or when the cost of removal or obliteration is assessed, the court shall, after conviction, conduct an evidentiary hearing to ascertain the value of the property so marked, injured, marred, defaced or destroyed or to ascertain the cost of the removal or obliteration; and provided, however, that if the property marked, injured, marred, defaced or destroyed is a war or veterans' memorial, monument or gravestone, the fine under this section shall be doubled and the person convicted shall be ordered to perform not less than 500 hours of court-approved community service. A police officer may arrest any person for commission of the offenses prohibited by this section without a warrant if said police officer has probable cause to believe that said person has committed the offenses prohibited by this section.

Upon conviction for said offense the individual's driver's license shall be suspended for one year. If the individual convicted of defacing or vandalizing the real or personal property of another is under the age of sixteen then one year shall be added to the minimum age eligibility for driving.

SECTION 126B
Walls, signs, gravestones, etc.; penalty for "tagging"

Whoever sprays or applies paint or places a sticker upon a building, wall, fence, sign, tablet, gravestone, monument or other object or thing on a public way or adjoined to it, or in public view, or on private property, such person known or commonly known as "taggers" and such conduct or activity known or commonly known as "tagging", or other words or phrases associated to such persons, conduct or activity, and either as an individual or in a group, joins together with said group, with the intent to deface, mar, damage, mark or destroy such property, shall be punished by imprisonment in a house of correction for not more than two years or by a fine of not less than fifteen hundred dollars or not more than three times the value of such damage to the property so defaced,

marked, marred, damaged or destroyed, whichever is greater, or both fine and imprisonment and shall also be required to pay for the removal or obliteration of such "tagging" or to obliterate such "tagging"; provided, however, that when a fine is levied pursuant to the value of the property marred, defaced, marked, damaged or destroyed or where the cost of removal or obliteration is assessed the court shall, after conviction, conduct an evidentiary hearing to ascertain the value of the property so defaced, marked, marred, damaged or destroyed or to ascertain the cost of the removal or obliteration. A police officer may arrest any person for commission of the offenses prohibited by this section without a warrant if said police officer has probable cause to believe that said person has committed the offenses prohibited by this section.

Upon conviction for said offense the individual's drivers license shall be suspended for one year. If the individual convicted of defacing or vandalizing the real or personal property of another is under the age of sixteen then one year shall be added to the minimum age eligibility for driving.

SECTION 127
Personalty; malicious or wanton injuries

Whoever destroys or injures the personal property, dwelling house or building of another in any manner or by any means not particularly described or mentioned in this chapter shall, if such destruction or injury is wilful and malicious, be punished by imprisonment in the state prison for not more than ten years or by a fine of three thousand dollars or three times the value of the property so destroyed or injured, whichever is greater and imprisonment in jail for not more than two and one-half years; or if such destruction or injury is wanton, shall be punished by a fine of fifteen hundred dollars or three times the value of the property so destroyed or injured, whichever is greater, or by imprisonment for not more than two and one-half years; if the value of the property so destroyed or injured is not alleged to exceed two hundred and fifty dollars, the punishment shall be by a fine of three times the value of the damage or injury to such property or by imprisonment for not more than two and one-half months; provided, however, that where a fine is levied pursuant to the value of the property destroyed or injured, the court shall, after conviction, conduct an evidentiary hearing to ascertain the value of the property so destroyed or injured. The words "personal property", as used in this section, shall also include electronically processed or stored data, either tangible or intangible, and data while in transit.

NOTE 1a   Wilful and Malicious. Wilful "means intentional and by design in contrast to that which is thoughtless or accidental. Malic[ious], on the other hand, refers to a state of mind of cruelty, hostility or revenge." Both are necessary elements. J. Nolan, Criminal Law, § 427 at 259, 325–30, Massachusetts Practice Series (1976).

"The word 'wilful' means intentional and by design in contrast to that which is thoughtless or accidental. Malice, on the other hand, refers to a state of mind of cruelty, hostility or revenge." *Commonwealth v. Morris M.*, 70 Mass. App. Ct. 688, 691 (2007).

NOTE 1b   "To establish the defendant's guilt on the wilful and malicious destruction charge, the Commonwealth had to prove that the defendant, in addition to participation in the venture, had or shared the requisite mental state for that crime. Wilful and malicious destruction of property (G.L. c. 266, § 127) is a specific intent to crime. Wilfulness requires a showing that the defendant intended both the conduct and its harmful consequences, *Commonwealth v. Schuchardt*, 408 Mass. 347, 352 (1990); wilful conduct is 'intentional and by design in contrast to that which is thoughtless or accidental.' *Commonwealth v. Peruzzi*, 15 Mass. App. Ct. 437, 443 (1983) quoting J.R. Nolan, Criminal Law § 427, at 259 (1976). Malice requires a showing that the defendant's conduct was 'motivated by 'cruelty, hostility or revenge.' *Commonwealth v. Schuchardt*, 408 Mass. 347, 352 (1990), quoting *Commonwealth v. Peruzzi*, 15 Mass. App. Ct. 437, 443 (1983)." *Commonwealth v. Armand*, 411 Mass. 167, 170 (1991).

NOTE 2a   Wanton. "The words 'wanton' and 'reckless' are practically synonymous terms although the word 'wanton' may contain a suggestion of arrogance or insolence or heartlessness which is lacking in the word 'reckless.' But intentional conduct to which either word applies is followed by the same legal consequences as though both words applied." *Commonwealth v. Welansky*, 316 Mass. 383, 398 (1944).

NOTE 2b   Wanton or reckless conduct may consist either of an affirmative act or an intentional failure to take proper care in disregard of the probable harmful consequences. *Commonwealth v. Welansky*, 316 Mass. at 397.

NOTE 2c   Wanton conduct is more serious than negligence or gross negligence. *Commonwealth v. Welansky*, 316 Mass. at 399–400.

NOTE 2d   Not a Lesser Included Offense. "The short answer to the question whether wantonly destroying or injuring property is a lesser included offense of wilfully and maliciously doing so is that, in order to convict a defendant of wilful and malicious conduct, there need not be a finding, as is required for wantonness, that the likely effect of the defendant's conduct was substantial harm. Since wanton criminality requires proof of elements not required for proof of wilful and malicious destruction or injury, the former crime is not included in the latter. We conclude that the defendants were not charged with wanton destruction of, or injury to, property and that therefore as to those convictions, the judgments must be reversed and the verdicts set aside." *Commonwealth v. Schuchardt*, 408 Mass. 347, 352 (1990).

NOTE 3a   Value. Although there was no evidence at trial as to the value of the property (cars), "[a]s a matter of common experience a jury could find that each of the cars was worth more than $15" thus necessitating a more serious penalty under the statute as it appeared, prior to amendment, in 1926. *Commonwealth v. Hosman*, 257 Mass. 379, 386 (1926).

NOTE 3b   Value Is Element of Felony. "Under G.L. c. 266, § 127, the value of the property destroyed is the factor that distinguishes a felony conviction . . . from a misdemeanor. . . . In view of the significantly increased sentencing range triggered by a finding that the value of the destroyed property exceeds $250, we conclude that the value of the property must be treated as an element of the felony of malicious destruction of property . . . and that a value in excess of $250 must be found by a jury beyond a reasonable doubt." *Commonwealth v. Beale*, 434 Mass. 1024, 1025 (2001) (citation omitted) (rescript).

NOTE 3c   Total Valuation Method. "In adopting a 'total valuation' methodology at trial, it appears that both parties relied on *Commonwealth v. Pyburn*, 26 Mass. App. Ct. 967 (1988). In *Pyburn*, the court held that the felony threshold under G.L. c. 266, § 127, was not properly calculated based upon repair bills for fixing a truck. '[I]t is the value of the 'property so destroyed or injured' that must be found to exceed [two hundred fifty dollars], not the amount of damage to the property that must exceed [that amount].' *Id.* at 969 (emphasis in original). The *Pyburn* court noted, however, that, apart from the repair bills, had the jury been so instructed, the evidence would have warranted a finding that the truck's value was more than the statutory threshold. Thus, *Pyburn* may be read—as both the Commonwealth and the defendant did at trial—to endorse valuation of the truck as a whole, in lieu of valuation limited to the specific parts of the truck that the maliciously destructive acts affected. This reading of total valuation finds further support in *Commonwealth v. Walters*, 12 Mass. App. Ct. 389, 392 (1981) (although only vehicle windshield was struck with a club as object of the malicious destruction, 'the jury could

have inferred that the truck was worth [the then statutory threshold of] more than one hundred dollars'). *See* Nolan, Criminal Law § 427 (2001). *But see Commonwealth v. Cimino*, 34 Mass. App. Ct. 925, 927–28 (1993) (where injury to property limited to automobile windows shot out by BB gun, felony sentences vacated and vehicle value as a whole not considered)." *Commonwealth v. Lauzier*, 53 Mass. App. Ct. 626, 632 n.8 (2002).

NOTE 3d   "Where only a portion of property has been damaged, it is possible to consider three definitions for the 'value of the property': the fair market value of the whole property (here the house) (as the Commonwealth urges); the fair market value of so much of the property as is destroyed or injured (here the wall) (as the defendant urges); or the pecuniary loss (here measured by the reasonable cost of repair) (as most other States do). We conclude, consistent with our duty to construe ambiguous terms in light of the Legislature's probable intent, that where damage is caused to a portion of the property as a whole and may be replaced or repaired, the value of the property is to be measured by the pecuniary loss, in this case the reasonable cost of repair necessitated by the malicious conduct." *Commonwealth v. Deberry*, 441 Mass. 211, 212–13 (2004).

NOTE 4   The complaint need not specify the means or mode of injury, nor charge more specifically the guilty knowledge of the defendant. *Commonwealth v. Falvey*, 108 Mass. 304, 307 (1871).

NOTE 5   The charge, of poisoning 14 hens, was brought under this statute. Although the crime is more particularly described or mentioned in another section of the same chapter (wilful and malicious destruction of horses, cattle or other beasts by . . . poisoning) a conviction may nonetheless lie. *Commonwealth v. Falvey*, 108 Mass. at 307.

NOTE 6   Related Statutes.

There are nearly 40 different sections within this chapter dealing with the destruction of another's property. Please refer to the table of contents. Also see:

G.L. c. 272, §§ 73–75—Injury to cemetery property.

G.L. c. 277, § 25—Description of ownership.

G.L. c. 159, § 103—Common carriers, injury to signals, tracks, cars, etc.

Whoever unlawfully and intentionally injures, molests or destroys any signal of a railroad corporation or railway company, or any line, wire, post or other structure or mechanism used in connection with such signal, or prevents or in any way interferes with the proper working of such signal, or whoever unlawfully and intentionally injures, molests, meddles or tampers with or destroys a track, car, motor bus or trackless trolley vehicle or any part, appliance or appurtenance thereof, of a railroad corporation or railway company, or the mechanism or apparatus used in the operation of any such car, or motor bus or trackless trolley vehicle, or whoever without right operates any such car, motor bus or trackless trolley vehicle or any mechanism or appliance thereof, shall be punished by a fine of not more than five hundred dollars or by imprisonment for not more than two years, or both.

G.L. c. 159, § 104—Throwing missiles, etc.

Whoever wilfully throws or shoots a missile at a locomotive engine, or railroad or railway car or train, or at a motor bus or trackless trolley vehicle, or at a school bus, or at a person on such engine, car, train, motor bus or trackless trolley vehicle, or school bus, or in any way assaults or interferes with a conductor, engineer, brakeman, motorman or operator while in the performance of his duty on or near such engine, car, train, motor bus or trackless trolley vehicle, or school bus, shall be punished by a fine of not more than five hundred dollars or by imprisonment for not more than one year, or both. A person so offending may be arrested without a warrant by an officer authorized to serve criminal process, or by any railroad, railway or railway express police officer, and kept in custody in jail or other convenient place not more than twenty-four hours, Sundays and legal holidays excepted, at or before the expiration of which time he shall be taken before a proper court or magistrate and proceeded against according to law. If such person commits such offense in the presence of such officer and refuses to state his name and address at the request of such officer, he may be arrested by him without a warrant.

NOTE 7   The district court has jurisdiction over both wanton destruction and wilful and malicious destruction of property. G.L. c. 218, § 26 (contained in this book).

NOTE 8   Venue. See G.L. c. 277, § 58A½.

SECTION 127A
Destruction of place of worship, etc.; punishment

Whoever willfully, intentionally and without right, or wantonly and without cause, destroys, defaces, mars, or injures a church, synagogue or other building, structure or place used for the purpose of burial or memorializing the dead, or a school, educational facility or community center or the grounds adjacent to and owned or leased by any of the foregoing or any personal property contained in any of the foregoing shall be punished by a fine of not more than two thousand dollars or not more than three times the value of the property so destroyed, defaced, marred or injured, whichever is greater, or by imprisonment in a house of correction for not more than two and one-half years or both; provided, however, that if the damage to or loss of such property exceeds five thousand dollars, such person shall be punished by a fine of not more than three times the value of the property so destroyed, defaced, marred or injured or by imprisonment in a state prison for not more than five years, or both.

Whoever threatens to burn, deface, mar, injure, or in any way destroy a church, synagogue or other building, structure, or place of worship, shall be punished by a fine of not more than one thousand five hundred dollars, or by imprisonment in a jail or house of correction for not more than one year, or both.

SECTION 127B
Action for civil rights violations; liability

Any person incurring injury to his person or damage or loss to his property as a result of conduct in violation of section one hundred and twenty-seven A or of section thirty-nine of chapter two hundred and sixty-five shall have a civil action to secure injunctive relief, special and general damages, reasonable attorney fees and costs against the person whose conduct has violated said section one hundred and twenty-seven A of this chapter or of section thirty-nine of chapter two hundred and sixty-five. In any such action the burden of proof shall be the same as in other civil actions for similar relief.

Notwithstanding any other provisions of law to the contrary, the parent or legal guardian of an unemancipated minor child shall be liable for any judgment rendered against such minor under the provisions of this section.

SECTION 128
Milk cans; defacement

Whoever, without the consent of the owner thereof, knowingly and wilfully effaces, alters or covers over, or procures to be effaced, altered or covered over, the name, initial or device of any dealer in milk, marked or stamped upon a milk can, or whoever, with intent to defraud and without such consent, detains or uses in his business any such can having the name, initial or device of any dealer in milk so marked or stamped thereon, shall be punished by a fine of not more than ten dollars.

SECTION 129
Correctional institutions; injury to property

An inmate of a correctional institution of the commonwealth who wilfully and maliciously destroys or injures the property of the commonwealth at such correctional institution, or the property of any person who furnishes materials for the employment of the prisoners, may be sentenced to the state prison for not more than three years.

SECTION 130
Penal institutions; injury to property

Whoever, being a prisoner at a jail or house of correction, wilfully and maliciously injures or destroys any public property or any materials furnished for the employment of prisoners in such jail or house of correction may be punished by imprisonment for not less than six months nor more than two and one half years.

SECTION 131
Sunday trespassers; arrest and detention without warrant

Whoever is discovered in the act of wilfully injuring a fruit or forest tree or of committing any kind of malicious mischief on Sunday may be arrested without a warrant by a sheriff, deputy sheriff, constable, police officer or other person, and detained in jail or otherwise until a complaint can be made against him for the offence, and he be taken upon a warrant issued upon such complaint; but such detention without warrant shall not continue beyond the following day.

SECTION 132
Pigeons; killing or frightening

Whoever wilfully kills pigeons upon, or frightens them from, beds which have been made for the purpose of taking them in nets, by any method, within one hundred rods of the same, except on land lawfully occupied by himself, shall be punished by imprisonment for not more than one month or by a fine of not more than twenty dollars, and shall also be liable for the actual damages to the owner or occupant of such beds.

NOTE   Related Statute. G.L. c. 272, § 87—Bird shooting.

SECTION 133
Humane society; injury to property

Whoever unlawfully enters a house, boat house or hut which is the property of the Humane Society of the Commonwealth of Massachusetts and wilfully injures, removes or carries away any property belonging to said society, or wilfully injures or unlawfully uses or commits any trespass upon the property of said society which is intended or kept for the purpose of saving or preserving human life, or commits any trespass upon such house, hut or boat house, shall be punished by a fine of not more than two hundred dollars or by imprisonment for not more than six months; but the penalties of this section shall not apply to persons for whose use said boats, houses and other property are intended and kept. Pilots, sheriffs and their deputies, and constables shall make complaint against all persons guilty of a violation of this section. One half of any fine paid hereunder shall be paid to the person who gives information upon which a conviction is obtained.

SECTION 134
Repealed

2

SECTION 135
Vessels; mooring the buoy; beacon or floating guide; penalty

Whoever moors or in any manner makes fast a vessel, scow, boat or raft to a buoy, beacon or floating guide placed by the government of the United States in the navigable waters of the commonwealth shall be punished by a fine of not more than fifty dollars; and whoever wilfully destroys, injures or removes any such beacon or guide shall be punished by a fine of not more than one hundred dollars or by imprisonment for not more than three months. One third of all fines which accrue under this section shall be paid to the complainant and two-thirds to the commonwealth.

SECTION 136
Repealed

SECTION 137
Injury to mill by raising water

Whoever, by erecting or maintaining a dam, either within or without the commonwealth, knowingly causes the water of a river or stream so to be raised as to flow upon or injure a mill lawfully existing in the commonwealth and belonging to a citizen thereof, without right as against the owner of such mill, shall be punished by a fine of not more than one thousand dollars or by imprisonment for not more than six months; but this section shall not apply to cases in which the courts of the commonwealth have jurisdiction to abate a dam so raised or maintained.

SECTION 138
Dams or reservoirs; malicious injury

Whoever wilfully, intentionally and without right breaks down, injures, removes or destroys a dam, reservoir, canal or trench, or a gate, flume, flashboards or other appurtenances thereof, or a wheel, or mill gear, or machinery of a water mill or steam mill, or wilfully or wantonly, without color of right, draws off the water contained in a mill pond, reservoir, canal or trench, or obstructs such water from flowing out of the same, shall be punished by imprisonment in the state prison for not more than five years or by a fine of not more than five hundred dollars and imprisonment in jail for not more than two years.

SECTION 138A
Irrigation equipment; malicious injury

Whoever wilfully, intentionally and without right damages or renders unusable machinery or equipment used in the transmission of water for agricultural purposes shall be punished by imprisonment in state prison for not more than five years or by a fine of not more than five hundred dollars and imprisonment in jail for not more than two years.

SECTION 139
Motor vehicles or trailers; defacement, etc., of identifying numbers; penalties; arrests

(a) Whoever intentionally and maliciously removes, defaces, alters, changes, destroys, obliterates or mutilates or causes to be removed or destroyed or in any way defaced, altered, changed, obliterated or mutilated, the identifying number or numbers of a motor vehicle or trailer shall be punished by a fine of not more than one thousand dollars or by imprisonment in the state prison for not more than three years, or both. The possession of any motor vehicle or trailer by a person who knows, should know, or has reason to know that the identifying number or numbers of such vehicle has been removed, defaced, altered, changed, destroyed, obliterated or mutilated shall be a prima facie evidence of a violation of this paragraph.

(b) Whoever sells, transfers, distributes, dispenses or otherwise disposes of or attempts to sell, transfer, distribute, dispense or otherwise dispose of any motor vehicle or trailer or motor vehicle part knowing or having reason to believe that the identifying number or numbers to said motor vehicle, trailer, or vehicle part have been so removed, defaced, altered, changed, destroyed, obliterated, or mutilated, unless authorized by law to do so, shall be punished by a fine of not more than one thousand dollars or by imprisonment in the state prison for not more than three years, or both.

(c) Whoever buys, receives, possesses, or obtains control of a motor vehicle, trailer, or motor vehicle part knowing or having reason to believe that an identifying number to said vehicle, trailer, or vehicle part has been removed, obliterated, tampered with, or altered, unless authorized by law to do so, shall be punished by a fine of not more than five hundred dollars or by imprisonment in a house of correction for not more than two years, or both.

The phrase "identifying number or numbers", as used in this section, shall mean the manufacturer's number or numbers identifying the motor vehicle, trailer or motor vehicle part as required to be contained in an application for registration by section two of chapter ninety, including the identifying number or numbers as restored or substituted under authority of section thirty-two A of said chapter ninety or similar law of another state.

An officer authorized to make arrests may arrest without warrant any person who he has probable cause to believe has committed or is committing a violation of the provisions of this section.

A conviction of a violation of this section or any adjudication that a person is a delinquent child by reason thereof shall be reported forthwith by the court or magistrate to the registrar of motor vehicles who shall revoke immediately the license to operate motor vehicles or the right to operate motor vehicles of the person so convicted or adjudged, and no appeal, motion for a new trial or exceptions shall operate to stay the revocation of such license or right to operate. The registrar of motor vehicles after having revoked the license or right to operate of any such person so convicted or adjudged shall issue a new license or reinstate such right to operate; if the prosecution of such person is finally terminated in his favor; otherwise, no new license shall be issued nor shall such right to operate be reinstated until sixty days after the date of revocation following his original conviction or adjudication if for a first offense, or until one year after the date of revocation following any subsequent conviction or adjudication.

Whoever takes and carries away the registration plate that is attached to the vehicle of another or is assigned by the registry of motor vehicles to another shall be punished by a fine of not less than $500 nor more than $1,000 or imprisonment in the house of correction for not more than 2½ years, or both.

NOTE 1   See Note 3 following G.L. c. 266, § 28.

NOTE 2   **Restitution.** *See* G.L. c. 276, § 92A.

NOTE 3   Testimony of owner and witnesses in motor vehicle cases. G.L. c. 278, § 6A.

SECTION 139A
Machines, or electrical or mechanical devices; alteration or obliteration of identifying numbers; possession as prima facie evidence; sale or attempt; punishment

Whoever removes, defaces, alters, changes, destroys, obliterates or mutilates or causes to be removed or destroyed or in any way defaced, altered, changed, obliterated or mutilated, the identifying number or numbers of any machine or any electrical or mechanical device, with intent thereby to conceal its identity, to defraud the manufacturer, seller, or purchaser, to hinder competition in the areas of sales and servicing, or to prevent the detection of a crime shall be punished by a fine of not more than five hundred dollars or by imprisonment in a jail or house of correction for not more than one year or by both such fine and imprisonment. Possession of any machine or electrical or mechanical device the identifying number or numbers of which have been so removed, defaced, altered, changed, destroyed, obliterated or mutilated shall be prima facie evidence of a violation of the foregoing provision.

Whoever sells or otherwise disposes of or attempts to sell or otherwise dispose of a machine or an electrical or a mechanical device, knowing or having reason to believe that the identifying number or numbers of the same have been so removed, defaced, altered, changed, destroyed, obliterated or mutilated, shall be punished by a fine of not more than five hundred dollars or by imprisonment for not more than one year in a jail or house of correction or by both such fine and imprisonment.

SECTION 140
Sale or offer for sale of master keys; penalty

Whoever sells or offers to sell or solicits offers to purchase a master key designed to fit more than one motor vehicle knowing, or having reasonable cause to believe, that said key will be used for an illegal purpose shall be punished by a fine of not more than five hundred dollars or by imprisonment for not more than one year, or both.

SECTION 141
Tampering with odometer of motor vehicle prohibited acts; intent to defraud; civil remedy; treble damages; costs and fees; violation as unfair competition; definitions; repair or replacement excepted

Whoever advertises for sale, sells, uses, installs or has installed any device which causes an odometer to register any mileage other than the true mileage driven, or whoever resets, or alters the odometer of any motor vehicle with the intent to change the number of miles indicated thereon, or whoever, with the intent to defraud, operates a motor vehicle on any street or highway knowing that the odometer of such vehicle is disconnected to nonfunctional, shall be liable in a civil action of tort or contract in an amount equal to the sum of three times the amount of actual damages sustained or one thousand five hundred dollars, whichever is the greater, plus the costs of the action together with reasonable attorney fees as determined by the court.

A violation of the provisions of this section shall constitute an unfair method of competition under chapter ninety-three A.

For the purposes of this section, the true mileage driven shall be that mileage traveled by the motor vehicle as registered by the odometer within the manufacturer's designed tolerance.

The term "odometer", as used in this section and in section one hundred and forty-one A, shall mean an instrument for measuring and recording the actual distance a motor vehicle travels while in operation; but shall not include any auxiliary odometer designed to be reset by the operator of the motor vehicle for the purpose of recording mileage on trips.

Nothing in this section and section one hundred and forty-one A shall prevent the service, repair or replacement of an odometer, provided the mileage indicated thereon remains the same as before the service, repair or replacement. Where the odometer is incapable of registering the same mileage as before such service, repair or replacement, the odometer shall be adjusted to read zero and a notice in writing shall be attached to the left door frame of the vehicle by the owner or his agent specifying the mileage prior to repair or replacement of the odometer and the date on which it was repaired or replaced.

NOTE   General Laws c. 266, § 141 roughly parallels Section 409(a) of the Motor Vehicle Information and Cost Savings Act, 15 U.S.C. § 1989(a), in that civil liability attaches to what the used car trade calls an "odometer spinback." The principle difference between the two is that in G.L. c. 266, § 141 intent to defraud need not be proved except when driving a car "knowing that the odometer of . . . [the] vehicle is disconnected [or] nonfunctional." Liability under the federal statute comes only upon a showing of intent to defraud. *Commonwealth v. Colonial Motor Sales, Inc.*, 11 Mass. App. Ct. 800, 802–03 (1981).

SECTION 141A
Misrepresentation of mileage of motor vehicle by turning back or readjusting speedometer or odometer; criminal penalty

Whoever, with the intent to misrepresent to a prospective or eventual purchaser the number of miles traveled by a motor vehicle, turns back or readjusts the speedometer or odometer thereof shall be punished by a fine of not less than five hundred nor more than one thousand dollars, or by imprisonment in a jail or house of correction for not less than thirty days nor more than two years, or both. In a prosecution under this section, evidence that a dealer, as defined in section one of chapter ninety, or a person required to be licensed under the provisions of section fifty-nine of chapter one hundred and forty, by himself or by another turned back or readjusted the speedometer or odometer shall constitute prima facie evidence of such intent to misrepresent.

SECTION 142
Records of purchases by dealers in scrap copper wire; inspection; penalty

Whoever is in the business of purchasing copper line wire or scrap copper wire shall enter in a book kept for that purpose a description of the same, the quantity purchased, the purchase price and a name and address of the seller. Said book shall at all times be open to the inspection of the chief of police of a city or town or any other officer having similar duties or any officer authorized by either of them, or a state police officer. Whoever violates any provision of this section shall be punished by a fine of not more than fifty dollars.

2

SECTION 142A
Gold, silver and platinum dealers; records; penalty

Whoever is in the business of purchasing gold, silver or platinum shall enter in a book kept for that purpose a description of the item, quantity purchased, the purchase price and the name and address of the seller; provided that the purchase price of such item is at least fifty dollars. Any person who sells gold, silver or platinum shall be required to show to the buyer prior to said sale identification which includes a photograph of said seller. Said book shall at all times be open to the inspection of the chief of police of a city or town or of any other officer having similar duties or any officer authorized by either of them, or a state police officer. Whoever violates any provision of this section shall be punished by a fine of not more than one thousand dollars or imprisonment of not more than one year, or both such fine and imprisonment.

SECTION 143
Definitions applicable to Secs. 143A–143H

As used in sections 143A to 143H, inclusive, the following words shall have the following meanings:—

"Article" or "recorded device", the tangible medium upon which sounds or images are recorded or otherwise stored, and shall include any original phonograph record, disc, wire, tape, audio or video cassette, film or other medium now known or later developed on which sounds or images may be recorded or otherwise stored, or any copy or reproduction which duplicates, in whole or in part, the original.

"Audiovisual recording function", the capability to record or transmit visual images or soundtrack, including any portion thereof, from a motion picture.

"Motion picture theater", movie theater, screening room, or other venue if used primarily for the exhibition of motion pictures.

"Owner", the person or other entity who owns a master phonograph record, master disc, master tape, master film or other device used for reproducing recorded visual images or sounds on a phonograph record, disc, tape, film, video cassette or other article on which visual images or sound is recorded, and from which the transferred recorded images or sounds are directly or indirectly derived.

SECTION 143A
Unauthorized reproduction and transfer of sound recordings

Whoever directly or indirectly by any means, knowingly transfers or causes to be transferred any sound recorded on a phonograph record, disc, wire, tape, film, videocassette or other article on which such sound is recorded, with intent to sell, rent or transport, or cause to be sold, rented or transported, or to use or cause to be used for profit through public performance such article on which such sound is so transferred, without the consent of the owner, or whoever sells any such article with the knowledge that the sound thereon has been so transferred without the consent of the owner, shall be punished as provided in section 143E.

SECTION 143B
Unauthorized reproduction and sale of live performances

Whoever for commercial advantage or private financial gain records or causes to be recorded a live performance with knowledge that such recording is without the consent of the owner, or advertises, sells, rents, transports or causes to be advertised, sold, rented or transported, or possesses for any of such purposes, a recording of a live performance with the knowledge that the live performance was recorded without the consent of the owner, shall be punished as provided in section 143E.

SECTION 143C
Manufacture, rental, or sale of recorded devices in packaging not bearing reproducer's name and address

Whoever for commercial advantage or private financial gain knowingly manufactures, rents, sells, transports, or causes to be manufactured, rented, sold or transported, or possesses for purposes of sale, rental or transport, any recorded device the outside packaging of which does not clearly and conspicuously bear the true name and address of the transferor of the sounds or images contained thereon shall be punished as provided in section 143E.

SECTION 143D
Violations of Secs. 143–143C; punishment

(a) Nothing in sections 143A to 143C, inclusive, shall be construed to apply to any person lawfully entitled to use or who causes to be used such sound or images for profit through public performance, or who transfers or causes to be transferred any such sound or images as part of a radio or television broadcast or for archival preservation.

(b) Nothing in section 143A to 143C, inclusive, shall be construed to apply to local, state or federal law enforcement officers employing an audiovisual recording function during the lawful exercise of law enforcement duties.

SECTION 143E
Penalties

Whoever violates any provision of section 143A to section 143C, inclusive, shall be punished:

(i) by imprisonment for not more than 1 year in the house of correction or by a fine of not more than $25,000, or by both such fine and imprisonment;

(ii) by imprisonment in the house of correction for not more than 2 years or by a fine of not more than $100,000, or by both such fine and imprisonment if the offense involves less than 1,000 but not less than 100 unlawful sound recordings or less than 65 but not less than 7 unlawful audio visual recordings; or

(iii) by imprisonment in state prison for not more than 5 years or by a fine of not more than $250,000, or by both such fine and imprisonment if the offense involves not less than 1,000 unlawful sound recordings or not less than 65 unlawful audio visual recordings.

SECTION 143F
Unauthorized recording of motion picture in theater

(a) Any person, in a motion picture theater while a motion picture is being exhibited, who knowingly operates an audiovisual recording function, with the intent to unlawfully record the motion picture and without the consent of the owner or lessee of the motion picture theater, shall be punished for a first offense by imprisonment in the house of correction for not more than 2 years or by a fine of not more than $100,000, or by both such fine and imprisonment and for a second or subsequent conviction, by imprisonment in the state prison for not more than 5 years or by a fine of not more than $250,000, or by both such fine and imprisonment.

(b) Nothing in subsection (a) shall be construed to apply to local, state or federal law enforcement officers employing an audiovisual recording function during the lawful exercise of law enforcement duties.

SECTION 143G
Detaining of suspected violators of Sec. 143F permitted

In an action for false arrest or false imprisonment brought by any person, by reason of having been detained for questioning or awaiting the arrival of law enforcement, on or in the immediate vicinity of a motion picture theater, if such person was detained in a reasonable manner and for not more than a reasonable length of time by a person authorized to make arrests or by the owner or his agent or servant authorized for such purpose and if there were reasonable grounds to believe that the person so detained was committing or attempting to commit any violation of section 143F, it shall be a defense to such action.

SECTION 143H
Destruction of recordings and recording devices

Upon conviction of a person for a violation of sections 143A to 143C, inclusive, or section 143F, the court may order the forfeiture, destruction or other disposition of all recordings on which the conviction is based and all implements, devices and equipment used or intended to be used in the manufacture of the recordings on which the conviction is based. Such order shall be stayed pending any appeal.

SECTION 144
Carrying away or conversion of certain milk containers without permission of owners

Whoever, without permission of the owner, carries away or converts to his own use a plastic or wire milk case or a plastic or wire container for milk products which has been indelibly stamped with the name of a milk dealer or association of milk dealers shall be punished by a fine of not less than ten and not more than one hundred dollars.

SECTION 145
Theft of public records

Any person who intentionally conceals upon his person or otherwise any record of the commonwealth or a political subdivision thereof, as defined in section three of chapter sixty-six, with the intention of permanently depriving said commonwealth or said political subdivision of its use shall be punished by a fine of more than five hundred dollars.

A custodian of such records or his agent who has probable cause to believe that a person has violated the provisions of this section may detain such person in a reasonable manner and for a reasonable time.

A law enforcement officer may arrest without warrant any person he has probable cause to believe has violated the provisions of this section. The statement of a custodian of such records or his agent that a person has violated the provisions of this section shall constitute probable cause for arrest by a law enforcement officer authorized to make an arrest in such jurisdiction.

SECTION 146
Disposal of unlawful solid waste

For purpose of this section "solid waste" shall mean garbage, refuse, trash, rubbish, sludge, residue or by-products of processing or treatment of discarded material, and any other solid, semi-solid or liquid discarded material resulting from domestic, commercial, mining, industrial, agricultural, municipal, or other sources or activities, but shall not include solid or dissolved material in domestic sewage.

Whoever willfully and without right deposits solid waste in a commercial disposal container of another without the consent of the owner or other person who has legal custody, care or control thereof shall be punished by a fine of not less than one hundred dollars, nor more than one thousand dollars.

SECTION 147
Items or services bearing or identified by counterfeit mark; sales; penalties

(a) For purposes of this section, the following words shall have the following meanings:—

"Counterfeit mark", any unauthorized reproduction or copy of intellectual property, or intellectual property affixed to any item knowingly sold, offered for sale, manufactured or distributed, or identifying services offered or rendered, without the authority of the owner of the intellectual property.

"Intellectual property", any trademark, service mark, trade name, label, term, device, design or word that is (1) adopted or used by a person to identify such person's goods or services, and (2) registered, filed or recorded under the laws of the commonwealth or of any other state, or registered in the principal register of the United States Patent and Trademark Office.

"Retail value", the counterfeiter's regular selling price for the item or service bearing or identified by the counterfeit mark; provided, however, that in the case of items bearing a counterfeit mark which are components of a finished product, the retail value shall be the counterfeiter's regular selling price of the finished product on or in which the component would be utilized.

(b) Whoever willfully manufactures, uses, displays, advertises, distributes, offers for sale, sells or possesses with intent to sell or distribute any item or services bearing or identified by a counterfeit mark shall be punished as follows:

(1) if the violation involves 100 or fewer items bearing a counterfeit mark or the total retail value of all items bearing or of services identified b a counterfeit mark is $1,000 or less and is a first offense, by imprisonment in a jail or house of correction for not more than two and one-half years;

(2) if the violation involves more than 100 but fewer than 1,000 items bearing a counterfeit mark or the total retail value of all items bearing or of services identified by a counterfeit mark is more than $1,000 but less than $10,000 or is a second offense, by imprisonment in the state prison for not more than five years;

(3) if the violation involves 1,000 or more items bearing a counterfeit mark or the total retail value of all items bearing or of services identified by a counterfeit mark is $10,000 or more of if the violation involves the manufacture or production of items that pose a threat to the public health or safety or it is a third or subsequent offense, by imprisonment in the state prison for not more than ten years.

2

(c) For the purposes of this section, the quantity or retail value of items or services shall include the aggregate quantity or retail value of all items bearing or of services identified by every counterfeit mark the defendant manufactures, uses, displays, advertises, distributes, offers for sale, sells or possesses.

(d) A person having possession, custody or control of more than 25 items bearing a counterfeit mark shall be presumed to possess said items with the intent to sell or distribute. Any state or federal certificate of registration of any intellectual property shall be prima facie evidence of the facts stated therein.

(e) Any person convicted under this section shall, in addition to any penalty imposed pursuant to subsection (b), be punished by a fine in an amount not to exceed three times the retail value of the items bearing or of services identified by a counterfeit mark, unless extenuating circumstances are shown by the defendant.

(f) Any person convicted under this section shall, in addition to any penalty imposed pursuant to subsections (b) and

(e), be punished by a fine in an amount equal to 75 per cent of the retail value of the items bearing or of services identified by a counterfeit mark, when the items involved pose a threat to public health or safety.

(g) Any items bearing a counterfeit mark and all personal property including, but not limited to, any items, objects, tools, machines, equipment, instrumentalities or vehicles of any kind, employed or used in connection with a violation of this section shall be seized by any law enforcement office; provided, however, that all such seized personal property shall be forfeited in accordance with the provisions of chapter 257. Upon the request of the intellectual property owner, all seized items bearing a counterfeit mark shall be released to the intellectual property owner for destruction or disposition; provided, however, that if the intellectual property owner does not request release of seized items bearing a counterfeit mark, such items shall be destroyed unless the intellectual property owner consents to another disposition.

Chapter 267. Forgery and Crimes Against the Currency

Section

1	False or forged records; certificates, returns, attestations and other writings
2	Railroad or admission tickets; passes or badges
3	Seal of land court; stamping documents without authority
4	Forgery, or use without authority; railroad company stamp
5	Uttering false or forged records, deeds or other writings
6	Uttering a forged railroad or admission ticket, pass or badge
7	False or forged note, certificate or other bill of credit issued for debt of commonwealth
8	False, forged or counterfeited bank bill, note or traveller's check
9	Possession of ten or more of false, forged or counterfeited notes or bills
10	Uttering, passing or tendering false, forged or counterfeited note, certificate, bill or traveller's check
11	Common utterers of counterfeit bills
12	Possession of false, forged or counterfeit bills, notes or traveller's checks
13	Tools or material for making false, forged or counterfeited notes, certificates, bills or traveller's checks
14	Evidence relative to forged or counterfeited bank or institution bills or notes
15	Certificates of certain officials of the united states, a state or territory as evidence
16	Fictitious signatures of corporate officers or agents
17	Counterfeiting coin; possession of ten or more pieces of false money
18	Possession of less than ten pieces of counterfeit coin; uttering, passing or tendering in payment
19	Common utterers of counterfeit coin
20	Tools for making counterfeit coin
21	Notes, bills, orders or checks as currency
22	Notes, bills, orders or checks for less than five dollars, as currency
23	Bank notes or bills for a fraction of a dollar
24	Connecting parts of instruments
25	Damaging or impairing bank bills or notes
26	Gathering or retaining bank bill or notes
27	Possession of worthless bank bills or notes
28	Uttering, passing or tendering worthless bank bills or notes
29	Shop bills or advertisements similar to bank bills or treasury notes or other United States securities
30	Seizure of false, forged or counterfeit bills, notes or bonds or counterfeiter's tools; destruction; return
31	Compensation to prosecutors and officers

SECTION 1
False or forged records; certificates, returns, attestations and other writings

Whoever, with intent to injure or defraud, falsely makes, alters, forges or counterfeits a public record, or a certificate, return or attestation of a clerk or register of a court, public register, notary public, justice of the peace, town clerk or any other public officer, in relation to a matter wherein such certificate, return or attestation may be received as legal proof; or a charter, deed, will, testament, bond or writing obligatory, power of attorney, policy of insurance, bill of lading, bill of exchange or promissory note; or an order, acquittance or discharge for money or other property or a credit card or an instrument described as a United States Dollar Traveller's Check or Cheque, purchased from a bank or other financially responsible institution, the purpose of which is a source of ready money on cashing the instrument without identification other than the signature of the purchaser; or an acceptance of a bill of exchange, or an endorsement or assignment of a bill of exchange or promissory note for the payment of money; or an accountable receipt for money, goods or other property; or a stock certificate, or any evidence or muniment of title to property; or a certificate of title, duplicate certificate of title, certificate issued in place of a duplicate certificate, the registration book, entry book, or any indexes provided for by chapter one hundred and eighty-five, or the docket of the recorder; shall be punished by imprisonment in the state prison for not more than ten years or in jail for not more than two years.

NOTE 1   Definition. Forgery—"The false making, altering, forging or counterfeiting of any instrument described in [G.L. c. 267, § 1], or any instrument which, if genuine, would be a foundation for] or release of liability of the apparent maker." G.L. c. 277, § 39.

NOTE 2a   "False Making." Writing includes not only a forged handwriting, but also words which are printed, engraved, or lithographed. *Commonwealth v. Ray*, 69 Mass. (3 Gray) 441, 446–47 (1855).

NOTE 2b   "[If the writing] is done at the dictation or request of another, and for his purposes and use, and his designs are fraudulent so as to make it forgery if he had written it himself, then the instrument is a forged one . . . . If [one] signed it, without understanding its purpose, thoughtlessly, or from unfamiliarity with business matters, or being himself deceived, [that one] might not be guilty of a criminal offense, and yet the instrument might be a forgery, so [he] who procured it to be so made might be convicted of either the crime of forgery or of uttering a forged instrument." *Commonwealth v. Zaleski*, 3 Mass. App. Ct. 538, 542 (1975) (quoting *Commonwealth v. Foster*, 114 Mass. 311, 320–21 (1873)).

NOTE 2c   "[Forgery] may be the making of a false writing purporting to be that of another. It may be the alteration in some material particular of a genuine instrument by a change of its words or figures. It may be the addition of some material provision to an instrument otherwise genuine. It may be the appending of a genuine signature of another to an instrument for which it was not intended. The false writing, alleged to have been made, may purport to be the instrument of a person or firm existing, or of a fictitious person or firm. As a general rule however, to constitute forgery, the writing falsely made must purport to be the writing of another party than the person making it." *Commonwealth v. Baldwin*, 77 Mass. (11 Gray) 197, 198 (1858).

NOTE 3a   **Instrument.** Description of written instrument—G.L. c. 277, § 22.

NOTE 3b   Description of money—G.L. c. 277, § 23.

NOTE 3c   "The words 'notes, bank notes, checks, drafts [and] bills of exchange' generally suggest items with a certain character of negotiability or transferability deriving at least in part from an ability to be converted ultimately to 'cash'. Thus a note may be defined as a 'written unconditional promise to pay another a certain sum of money at a certain time, or at a time which must certainly arrive." *Commonwealth v. Baker*, 368 Mass. 58, 68 (1975) (quoting 11 Am.Jur. 2d, Bills and Notes, § 21 (1963)).

NOTE 3d   **Bank Signature Card.** "[A] bank signature card constitutes 'evidence or muniment of title to property' and, thus, is a document capable of being forged and altered under the statute . . . .

"A bank signature card is evidence of ownership of the account . . . capable of being forged under G.L. c. 267, § 1, and uttered under G.L. c. 267, § 5." *Commonwealth v. Murphy*, 59 Mass. App. Ct. 571, 577–78 (2003).

NOTE 4a   **Intent to injure or defraud.** *See* G.L. c. 277, § 30.

NOTE 4b   "The crimes of forgery and uttering both require proof of an intent to injure or defraud. The Commonwealth need not show that the defendant intended to injure or defraud a particular person. It is sufficient that he intended to injure or defraud someone. With respect to both crimes, proof of intent to injure or defraud may be inferred from the circumstances." *Commonwealth v. O'Connell*, 438 Mass. 658, 664 (2003) (citations omitted).

NOTE 4c   "[I]n prosecutions for forgery and for uttering forged paper, proof is admissible, in order to show an intent to defraud by forgery, and also to show knowledge on the part of the accused in reference to the particular document which he is charged with uttering, that at or near the time of committing the alleged offence he had passed or had in his possession other similar forged documents." *Commonwealth v. Russell*, 156 Mass. 196, 197 (1892).

NOTE 5a   **Defenses.** It is *no* defense that the forgery was made by the defendant in an honest belief that he was owed the money. *Commonwealth v. Peakes*, 231 Mass. 449, 456 (1918); *Commonwealth v. Zaleski*, 3 Mass. App. Ct. 538, 544 (1975).

NOTE 5b   It is *no* defense that the forged instrument was *not* presented or delivered to anyone. The false making, with intent to defraud is the gist of the offense. *Commonwealth v. Ladd*, 15 Mass. 526, 527 (1819).

NOTE 5c   It is *no* defense that the defendant intended and had the ability to pay the forged instrument when it became due. *Commonwealth v. Henry*, 118 Mass. 460, 462–63 (1875).

NOTE 5d   Lack of authority is not an essential element of forgery. "However, authority may be raised as a defense, and, if so raised, the Commonwealth then bears the burden of proving beyond a reasonable doubt the absence of authority." *Commonwealth v. O'Connell*, 438 Mass. 658, 664 (2003) (citations omitted).

NOTE 6   Upon a trial for forgery, the questions, "Did you sign that?" and "Did you authorize anyone to sign it?" asked by the prosecution, of the person whose name is alleged to have been forged, in reference to the paper, the genuineness of which is in issue, are questions unobjectionable as to both form and substance. *Commonwealth v. Kepper*, 114 Mass. 278, 280 (1873).

NOTE 7   **Jurisdiction.** The district court has jurisdiction, concurrent with that of the superior court, of forgery of a promissory note, or of an order for money or other property. G.L. c. 218, § 26.

NOTE 8a   **Related Statutes:** G.L. c. 46, § 30—Forgery of birth, marriage or death certificates.

Whoever falsely makes, alters, forges or counterfeits, or procures or assists another to falsely make, forge or counterfeit, a copy of a record of birth, marriage or death, or whoever forges or without authority uses the signature, facsimile of the signature, or validating signature stamp of a city or town clerk, or the secretary of state upon a genuine or falsely made, altered, forged or counterfeited copy of such a record, or whoever utters, publishes as true or in any way makes use of a falsely made, altered, forged or counterfeited copy of such a record, or whoever uses, attempts to use, with intent to defraud or deceive, a copy of a record of the birth or marriage of a person other than himself, shall be punished by a fine of not more than five hundred dollars or by imprisonment for not more than six months in a house of correction.

NOTE 8b   G.L. c. 64C, § 37—Forgery of cigarette excise stamps.

Whoever falsely or fraudulently makes, forges, alters or counterfeits, or causes or procures to be falsely or fraudulently made, forged, altered or counterfeited, any cigarette excise stamps prepared or prescribed by the commissioner under the authority of this chapter, or whoever knowingly and wilfully utters, publishes, passes or tenders as true, any such false, altered, forged or counterfeited stamp or makes a false affixation of or uses any stamp provided for by this chapter which has already once been used, for the purpose of evading the excise imposed by this chapter, shall be punished by a fine of not more than two thousand dollars or by imprisonment for not more than five years, or both.

If any person secures, manufactures or causes to be secured or manufactured, or has in his possession, any cigarette excise stamp or die or device not prescribed or authorized by the commissioner, or any counterfeit impression, such fact shall be prima facie evidence that such person has counterfeited stamps. Whoever wilfully removes or alters or knowingly permits to be removed or altered the canceling or defacing mark of any stamp provided for by this chapter with intent to use such stamp, or knowingly or wilfully buys, prepares for use, uses, has in possession, or suffers to be used, any metering machine without authority, or any washed, restored or counterfeit stamps, or whoever intentionally removes or causes to be removed, or knowingly permits to be removed, any stamps or meter impression affixed pursuant to this chapter, or whoever tampers with or causes to be tampered with any metering machine authorized to be used under the provisions thereof, shall be punished by a fine of not more than two thousand dollars or by imprisonment for not more than five years, or both.

Any stamps, metering machines or devices not prescribed or authorized by the commissioner shall be subject to seizure in the manner provided in section eight and shall be forfeited to the commonwealth and proceedings shall be had as provided in said section eight and in sections fifty to fifty-five, inclusive, of chapter one hundred and thirty-eight.

NOTE 8c   G.L. c. 266, § 37C—Forgery of credit cards (located in this book).

NOTE 8d   G.L. c. 131, § 33—Forgery of hunting and fishing license.

A person shall not alter, forge or counterfeit any license, permit, permit application, certificate, tag or seal issued under any

2

provisions of this chapter or any rule or regulation made under authority thereof, nor possess or use any such altered, forged or counterfeited license, permit, permit application, certificate, tag or seal, nor procure or attempt to procure a license, permit, permit application, certificate, tag or seal by fraud or false statements of any kind, nor use or attempt to use any license, permit, permit application, certificate, tag or seal of another, nor loan or allow another person to use his license, permit, permit application, certificate, tag or seal.

G.L. c. 131, § 34—Violation of § 33.

A license, permit, or certificate issued under a provision of this chapter . . . held by a person found guilty of, or convicted of, or assessed in any manner after a plea of nolo contendere, or penalized for, a violation of . . . § 33 . . . such particular license, permit, or certificate shall be void, and shall immediately be surrendered to an officer authorized to enforce this chapter. Said person or a person acting on his behalf shall not be given or make application for, that particular license, permit or certificate with respect to the violation for which said person was found guilty or penalized as aforesaid, during the period of one year from the date such person was found guilty or penalized, and such particular license, permit or certificate so issued shall be void and shall be surrendered to an officer authorized to enforce this chapter. Every license, permit, or certificate issued under a provision of this chapter, held by a person found guilty or assessed as aforesaid on three or more separate occasions for violations of a provision of this chapter, or a rule or regulation made under the authority thereof, shall be void and shall be immediately surrendered to an officer authorized to enforce this chapter. Said person or a person acting on his behalf shall not be given, or make application for, any license, permit or certificate under this chapter, during the period of one year from the date of his being found guilty or penalized as aforesaid, and such license, permit or certificate so issued shall be void and shall be surrendered to an officer authorized to enforce this chapter. No fee received for a license, permit or certificate made void under this section shall be refunded to the holder thereof.

NOTE 8e   G.L. c. 94, § 127—Forgery of livestock and poultry inspection certificate.

(d) No person shall: (1) cast, print, lithograph, or otherwise make any device containing any official mark or simulation thereof, or any label bearing any such mark or simulation, or any form of official certificate or simulation thereof, except as authorized by the commissioner; (2) forge any official device, mark, or certificate;

G.L. c. 94, § 128. Punishment—fine of not less than $1,000 nor more than $5,000, or by imprisonment for a term of not more than three years or by both such fine and imprisonment.

NOTE 8f   G.L. c. 90, § 24B—Forgery of motor vehicle license and sticker—located in this book.

NOTE 8g   G.L. c. 90B, § 4A—Forgery of motorboat certificate—located in this book.

NOTE 8h   G.L. c. 128A, § 10B—Forgery of pari-mutuel betting tickets.

Whoever, with intent to defraud, falsely makes, alters or forges a pari-mutuel betting ticket issued under the provisions of section five, or whoever, with intent to defraud, utters and publishes as true a false, forged or altered pari-mutuel betting ticket issued under the provisions of said section five, knowing the same to be false, forged or altered, shall be punished by a fine of not more than one thousand dollars or by imprisonment in the state prison for not more than five years or in a jail for not more than two years.

NOTE 8i   G.L. c. 101, § 31—Forgery of vendors', hawkers', and peddlers' licenses.

Whoever counterfeits or forges a license, or a certificate of registration issued pursuant to section thirty-four, or has a counterfeited or forged license or certificate in his possession with intent to utter or use the same as true, knowing it to be false or counterfeit, or attempts to sell under a license which has expired or has been revoked or canceled, or which has not been issued or transferred to him, or has in his possession another's license or certificate with intent to use the same, shall be punished by a fine of not

more than five hundred dollars or by imprisonment for not more than six months, or both such fine and imprisonment.

NOTE 8j   G.L. c. 10, § 30—Forgery of lottery tickets.

Whoever, with intent to defraud, falsely makes, alters, forges, utters, passes or counterfeits a state lottery ticket or share shall be punished by imprisonment in the state prison for not more than three years or in jail for not more than two years, or by a fine of not less than one hundred nor more than five hundred dollars.

NOTE 8k   G.L. c. 105, § 63—Forgery of warehouse receipts.

Whoever falsely makes, utters, forges or counterfeits, or whoever permits or is a party to the false making, uttering, forging or counterfeiting of, a warehouse receipt, certificate or other instrument, or of the signature of a warehouseman or of an endorser or other person to an instrument used to pass or to give title to property stored in a public warehouse, shall be punished by a fine of not more than five thousand dollars and by imprisonment in the state prison for not more than three years.

NOTE 9   Form of indictment—G.L. c. 277, § 79.

SECTION 2
Railroad or admission tickets; passes or badges

Whoever, with intent to injure or defraud, falsely makes, alters, forges or counterfeits a railroad ticket, railroad mileage book or railroad pass, or a ticket, badge, pass or any written or printed license purporting to entitle the holder or owner thereof to admission to any exhibition, entertainment, performance, match or contest of any kind, shall be punished by imprisonment in the state prison for not more than three years or in jail for not more than two years, or by a fine of not more than five hundred dollars.

SECTION 3
Seal of land court; stamping documents without authority

Whoever forges, procures to be forged or assists in forging, the seal of the land court, or, without lawful authority, stamps or procures to be stamped, or assists in stamping, any document with such forged seal or with the genuine seal of said court, shall be punished by imprisonment in the state prison for not more than ten years or in jail for not more than two years.

SECTION 4
Forgery, or use without authority; railroad company stamp

Whoever forges, procures to be forged or assists in forging, the stamp of any railroad company or of any railroad ticket agent, or, without lawful authority, stamps or procures to be stamped, or assists in stamping, any railroad ticket or railroad mileage book with such forged stamp, or with a genuine stamp of any railroad company or railroad ticket agent, shall be punished by imprisonment in the state prison for not more than three years or in jail for not more than two years, or by a fine of not more than five hundred dollars.

SECTION 5
Uttering false or forged records, deeds or other writings

Whoever, with intent to injure or defraud, utters and publishes as true a false, forged or altered record, deed, instrument or other writing mentioned in the four preceding sections, knowing the same to be false, forged or altered, shall be punished by imprisonment in the state prison for not more than ten years or in jail for not more than two years.

NOTE 1   See Notes following G.L. c. 267, § 1—Forgery.

NOTE 2   If it appears that the defendant knew that the check was false and asserted its genuineness for the purpose of getting money, it is not necessary to show that the check was made by the defendant or that the person whom the defendant sought to deceive was in fact misled. *Commonwealth v. Bond*, 188 Mass. 91 (1905).

NOTE 3   "The crimes of forgery and uttering both require proof of an intent to injure or defraud. The Commonwealth need not show that the defendant intended to injure or defraud a particular person. It is sufficient that he intended to injure or defraud someone. With respect to both crimes, proof of intent to injure or defraud may be inferred from the circumstances." *Commonwealth v. O'Connell*, 438 Mass. 658, 664 (2003) (citations omitted).

NOTE 4   Lack of authority is not an essential element of uttering. "However, authority may be raised as a defense, and, if so raised, the Commonwealth then bears the burden of proving beyond a reasonable doubt the absence of authority." *Commonwealth v. O'Connell*, 438 Mass. 658, 664 (2003) (citations omitted).

NOTE 5   Defendant prepared a forged check and delivered it to B, asking him to get a messenger to take it to the bank on which it was drawn and get it cashed. This was done, the messenger cashing the check, giving the cash to B who in turn gave it to defendant. Held, defendant's conviction of uttering the check affirmed. *Commonwealth v. Clune*, 162 Mass. 206 (1894).

NOTE 6   Uttering is *not* a lesser included offense of larceny (by false pretenses). "Uttering a forged instrument requires the use of a forged or altered commercial instrument; larceny by false pretenses (G.L. c. 266, § 30(1)) does not. Larceny by false pretenses requires a permanent taking of property caused by reliance on the defendant's false statement; uttering requires neither actual reliance nor any taking." *Commonwealth v. Crocker*, 384 Mass. 353, 358 (1981).

NOTE 7   Knowingly having in possession and uttering five false, forged and counterfeit notes may be charged as one offense in one count. *Commonwealth v. Thomas*, 76 Mass. (10 Gray) 483, 484 (1858).

NOTE 8   Related uttering statutes outside of this chapter include:

G.L. c. 90B, § 4A—Uttering false motorboat certificate number.
G.L. c. 94C, § 33(b)—Uttering a false drug prescription.
G.L. c. 266, § 37—Uttering a fraudulent check, draft, or order.
G.L. c. 266, § 43—Retention by printer of paper designated for bank bills.

NOTE 9   **Jurisdiction.** The district court has jurisdiction, concurrent with that of the Superior Court, of uttering a false note or order. G.L. c. 218, § 26.

NOTE 10   Form of indictment—G.L. c. 277, § 79.

SECTION 6
Uttering a forged railroad or admission ticket, pass or badge

Whoever, with intent to insure or defraud, utters and publishes as true a false, forged or altered railroad ticket, railroad mileage book or railroad pass, or a ticket, badge, pass or any written or printed license purporting to entitle the holder or owner thereof to admission to any exhibition, entertainment, performance, match or contest of any kind mentioned in section two, knowing the same to be false, altered or forged, shall be punished by imprisonment in the state prison for not more than three years or in jail for not more than two years, or by a fine of not more than five hundred dollars.

SECTION 7
False or forged note, certificate or other bill of credit issued for debt of commonwealth

Whoever, with intent to injure or defraud, falsely makes, alters, forges or counterfeits a note, certificate or other bill of credit issued by the state treasurer, or by any commissioner or other officer authorized to issue the same for a debt of this commonwealth, shall be punished by imprisonment in the state prison for life or for any term of years.

SECTION 8
False, forged or counterfeited bank bill, note or traveller's check

Whoever, with intent to injure or defraud, falsely makes, alters, forges or counterfeits a bank bill or promissory note payable to the bearer thereof or to the order of any person, issued by any incorporated banking company, or an instrument described as a United States Dollar Traveller's Check or Cheque, purchased from a bank or other financially responsible institution, the purpose of which is a source of ready money on cashing the instrument without identification other than the signature of the purchaser shall be punished by imprisonment in the state prison for life or for any term of years.

NOTE   Federal Reserve notes are "issued" by an "incorporated banking company" within this section and by a "bank" within G.L. c. 267, § 13; and the possession of ten or more counterfeit Federal Reserve notes with intent to "utter and pass" them, and the possession of certain equipment with intent to use it to make counterfeit notes, are crimes within G.L. c. 267, §§ 9 and 13 respectively. *Commonwealth v. Saville*, 353 Mass. 458, 461–64 (1968), upheld *Saville v. Scafati*, 297 F.Supp. 397 (D.Mass. 1969).

SECTION 9
Possession of ten or more of false, forged or counterfeited notes or bills

Whoever has in his possession at the same time ten or more similar false, altered, forged or counterfeit notes, bills of credit, band bills or notes, such as are mentioned in any of the preceding sections, payable to the bearer thereof or to the order of any person, knowing the same to be false, altered, forged or counterfeit, with intent to utter or pass the same as true, and thereby to injure or defraud, shall be punished by imprisonment in the state prison for life or for any term of years.

NOTE   See Note following G.L. c. 267, § 8.

SECTION 10
Uttering, passing or tendering false, forged or counterfeited note, certificate, bill or traveller's check

Whoever utters or passes or tenders in payment as true any such false, altered, forged or counterfeit note, certificate or bill of credit for any debt of the commonwealth, or a bank bill or promissory note payable to the bearer thereof or to the order of any person, issued as aforesaid, or an instrument described as a United States Dollar Traveller's Check or Cheque, purchased from a bank or other financially responsible institution, the purpose of which is a source of ready money on cashing the instrument without identification other than the signature of the purchaser, knowing the same to be false, altered, forged or counterfeit, with intent to injure or defraud, shall be punished by imprisonment in the state prison for not more than five years, or by a fine of not more than one thousand dollars and imprisonment in jail for not more than one year.

SECTION 11
Common utterers of counterfeit bills

Whoever, having been convicted of the crime mentioned in the preceding section, is again convicted of the like crime committed after the former conviction, and whoever is at the same sitting of the court convicted upon three distinct charges of such crime, shall be adjudged a common utterer of counterfeit bills, and be punished by imprisonment in the state prison for not more than ten years.

SECTION 12

Possession of false, forged or counterfeit bills, notes or traveller's checks

Whoever brings into this commonwealth or has in his possession a false, forged or counterfeit bill or note, in the similitude of the bills or notes, payable to the bearer thereof or to the order of any person, issued by or for any bank or banking company, or an instrument described as a United States Dollar Traveller's Check or Cheque, purchased from a bank or other financially responsible institution, the purpose of which is a source of ready money on cashing the instrument without identification other than the signature of the purchaser, with intent to utter or pass the same or to render the same current as true, knowing the same to be false, forged or counterfeit, shall be punished by imprisonment in the state prison for not more than five years, or by a fine of not more than one thousand dollars and imprisonment in jail for not more than one year.

SECTION 13

Tools or material for making false, forged or counterfeited notes, certificates, bills or traveller's checks

Whoever engraves, makes or mends, or begins to engrave, make or mend, a plate, block, press or other tool, instrument or implement, or makes or provides paper or other material adapted to and designed for the forging or making of a false and counterfeit note, certificate or other bill of credit, purporting to be issued by lawful authority for a debt of the commonwealth, or a false and counterfeit note or bill in the similitude of the notes or bills issued by any bank or banking company, or an instrument described as a United States Dollar Traveller's Check or Cheque, purchased from a bank or other financially responsible institution, the purpose of which is a source of ready money on cashing the instrument without identification other than the signature of the purchaser, and whoever has in his possession such a plate or block engraved in any part, or a press or other tool, instrument or implement, or paper or other material, adapted and designed as aforesaid, with intent to use the same or to cause or permit the same to be used in forging or making such false and counterfeit certificates, bills or notes, shall be punished by imprisonment in the state prison for not more than ten years, or by a fine of not more than one thousand dollars and imprisonment in jail for not more than two years.

NOTE   See Note following G.L. c. 267, § 8.

SECTION 14

Evidence relative to forged or counterfeited bank or institution bills or notes

In prosecutions for forging or counterfeiting notes or bills of the banks or institutions before mentioned, or for uttering, publishing or tendering in payment as true forged or counterfeit bank bills or notes, or for being possessed thereof with intent to utter and pass the same as true, the testimony of the president and cashier of any such bank may be dispensed with, if their place of residence is out of the commonwealth or more than forty miles from the place of trial; and the testimony of any person acquainted with the signature of such president or cashier, or who has knowledge of the difference in the appearance of the true and the counterfeit bills or notes of such banks, may be admitted to prove that such bills or notes are counterfeit.

SECTION 15

Certificates of certain officials of the United States, a state or territory as evidence

In prosecutions for forging or counterfeiting a note, certificate, bill of credit or other security issued on behalf of the United States, or on behalf of any state or territory, or for uttering, publishing or tendering in payments as true such forged or counterfeit note, certificate, bill of credit or security, or for being possessed thereof with intent to utter or pass the same as true, the certificate under oath of the secretary of the treasury, or of the treasurer of the United States, or of the secretary or treasurer of any state or territory, on whose behalf such note, certificate, bill of credit or security purports to have been issued, shall be admitted as evidence for the purpose of proving the same to be forged or counterfeit.

SECTION 16

Fictitious signatures of corporate officers or agents

If a fictitious or pretended signature, purporting to be the signature of an officer or agent of a corporation, is fraudulently affixed to an instrument or writing purporting to be a note, draft or other evidence of debt issued by such corporation, with intent to pass the same as true, it shall be a forgery, although no such person may ever have been an officer or agent of such corporation, or ever have existed.

SECTION 17

Counterfeiting coin; possession of ten or more pieces of false money

Whoever counterfeits any gold or silver coin current by law or usage within the commonwealth, or has in his possession at the same time ten or more pieces of false money, or coin counterfeited in the similitude of any gold or silver coin current as aforesaid, knowing the same to be false and counterfeit, and with intent to utter or pass the same as true, shall be punished by imprisonment in the state prison for life or for any term of years.

NOTE   Upon an indictment under this section, charging the defendant with having more than 10 pieces, proof of his having less than 10 pieces warrants a conviction, the defendant being sentenced under the following section. *Commonwealth v. Griffin*, 38 Mass. (21 Pick.) 523, 525–26 (1839).

SECTION 18

Possession of less than ten pieces of counterfeit coin; uttering, passing or tendering in payment

Whoever has in his possession less than ten pieces of the counterfeit coin mentioned in the preceding section, knowing the same to be counterfeit, with intent to utter or pass the same as true, or utters, passes or tenders in payment as true any such counterfeit coin, knowing the same to be false and counterfeit, shall be punished by imprisonment in the state prison for not more than ten years or by a fine of not more than one thousand dollars and imprisonment in jail for not more than two years.

NOTE   See Note following G.L. c. 267, § 17.

SECTION 19
Common utterers of counterfeit coin

Whoever, having been convicted of any of the crimes mentioned in the preceding section, is again convicted of the same crimes committed after the former conviction, and whoever is at the same sitting of the court convicted upon three distinct charges of said crimes, shall be adjudged a common utterer of counterfeit coin, and punished by imprisonment in the state prison for not more than twenty years.

SECTION 20
Tools for making counterfeit coin

Whoever casts, stamps, engraves, makes or mends, or knowingly has in his possession a mould, pattern, die, puncheon, engine, press or other tool or instrument, adapted to and designed for coining or making counterfeit coin, in the similitude of any gold or silver coin current by law or usage in the commonwealth, with intent to use or employ the same or to cause or permit the same to be used or employed in coining or making any such false and counterfeit coin as aforesaid, shall be punished by imprisonment in the state prison for not more than ten years or by a fine of not more than one thousand dollars and imprisonment in jail for not more than two years.

SECTION 21
Notes, bills, orders or checks as currency

Whoever issues or passes a note, bill, order or check, other than foreign bills of exchange, the notes or bills of a bank incorporated by the laws of the commonwealth, of the United States, of some one of the United States or of any of the British provinces of North America, with the intent that the same shall be circulated as currency, shall be punished by a fine of fifty dollars.

SECTION 22
Notes, bills, orders or checks for less than five dollars, as currency

Whoever issues or passes a note, bill, order or check, other than the notes or bills of a bank incorporated under the authority of this commonwealth, of the United States or of some one of the United States, for an amount less than five dollars, or whereon a less amount than five dollars is due at the time of such issuing or passing thereof, with intent that the same shall be circulated as currency, shall be punished by a fine of fifty dollars.

SECTION 23
Bank notes or bills for a fraction of a dollar

Whoever receives or puts in circulation as currency a bank note or bill which is, or a part of which is, for any fractional part of a dollar shall be punished by a fine of twenty-five dollars.

SECTION 24
Connecting parts of instruments

Whoever fraudulently connects different parts of several bank notes or other genuine instruments in such manner as to produce one additional note or instrument, with intent to pass all of them as genuine, shall be guilty of forgery, in like manner as if each of them had been falsely made or forged.

SECTION 25
Damaging or impairing bank bills or notes

Whoever wilfully and maliciously tears, cuts or in any manner damages and impairs the usefulness for circulation of a bank bill or note of a bank in this commonwealth shall be punished by a fine of not more than ten dollars; but the possession or uttering of a bill so injured shall not be evidence against a party charged, unless connected with other circumstances tending to prove that the bill or note was injured by him.

SECTION 26
Gathering or retaining bank bill or notes

Whoever maliciously gathers up or retains or maliciously aids in gathering up or retaining bills or notes of a bank or banking company, current by law or usage in the commonwealth, for the purpose of injuring or impeding the circulation or business of such bank or banking company, or of compelling it to do any act out of the usual course of its business, shall be punished by a fine of not more than five hundred dollars or by imprisonment for not more than two years; and in the prosecution of any such crime it shall not be necessary to set out and describe each bill, but it shall be sufficient to aver and prove any amount of the bills of any bank which have been so gathered up or retained.

SECTION 27
Possession of worthless bank bills or notes

Whoever has in his possession at the same time five or more bank bills or notes not current which are worthless as bank bills or notes, knowing the same to be worthless as aforesaid, or has papers not bank bills or notes, but made in the similitude thereof, or papers purporting to be the bills or notes of a bank which has never existed, knowing the character of such papers, with intent to pass, utter or circulate the same, or to procure any other person so to do, for the purpose of injuring or defrauding, shall be punished by imprisonment in the state prison for not more than five years, or by a fine of not more than five hundred dollars and imprisonment in the house of correction for not more than two and one half years.

SECTION 28
Uttering, passing or tendering worthless bank bills or notes

Whoever utters or passes or tenders in payment as true any such worthless bank bill or note not current, or any paper not a bank bill or note but made in similitude thereof, or any paper purporting to be the bill or note of a bank which has never existed, knowing the same to be worthless and not current, as aforesaid, with intent to injure and defraud, shall be punished by imprisonment in the state prison for not more than five years, or by a fine of not more than five hundred dollars and imprisonment in the house of correction for not more than two and one half years.

SECTION 29
Shop bills or advertisements similar to bank bills or treasury notes or other united states securities

Whoever engraves, prints, issues, utters or circulates a shop bill or advertisement, in similitude, form and appearance like a bank bill, on paper similar to paper used for bank bills, and with vignettes, figures or decorations used on bank bills, or having the general appearance of a bank bill, or in similitude, form and appearance, like a treasury note, note, certificate, bill or credit or other security issued by or on behalf of

2

the United States, on paper similar to paper used for the same, respectively, and with vignettes, figures or decorations used thereon, or having the general appearance of a treasury note, note, certificate, bill of credit or other security issued by or on behalf of the United States, shall be punished by a fine of not more than fifty dollars or by imprisonment in jail for not more than three months.

SECTION 30
Seizure of false, forged or counterfeit bills, notes or bonds or counterfeiter's tools; destruction; return

When false, forged or counterfeit bank bills or notes, or forged or counterfeit notes or bonds of any state or corporation, or plates, dies or other tools, instruments or implements used by counterfeiters, or designed for the forging or making of false or counterfeit notes, coin or bills, or worthless bank bills or notes not current described in sections twenty-seven and twenty-eight, come to the knowledge of a sheriff, consta-

ble, police officer or other officer of justice, he shall immediately seize and take possession of and deliver them into the custody of the superior court, which shall cause them to be destroyed by an officer of the court, who shall make return to the court of his doings in the premises.

SECTION 31
Compensation to prosecutors and officers

Upon a conviction of any crime mentioned in sections seven, eight, seventeen, eighteen, twenty or twenty-eight or upon forfeiture by persons prosecuted for any such crime of any recognizance for their appearance to answer to the same, the superior court may order compensation to the prosecutor and to the officer who has secured and kept the evidence of the crime, not exceeding their actual expenses, with a reasonable allowance for their time and trouble, which shall be paid by the county.

Chapter 267A. Money Laundering

Section
1   Definitions
2   Money laundering; penalties
3   Filing of reports by financial institutions; liability for making, filing or use of reports; disclosure
4   Forfeiture of monetary instruments or other property obtained in violation of sec. 2

SECTION 1
Definitions
(Added by 2011 Mass. Acts c. 194, § 48, effective Nov. 22, 2011.)

As used in this chapter, the following words shall have the following meanings unless the context clearly requires otherwise:

"Criminal activity", activity which constitutes a criminal offense punishable under the laws of the commonwealth by imprisonment in a state prison or a criminal offense committed in another jurisdiction punishable under the laws of that jurisdiction as a felony.

"Financial institution", (1) a bank as defined in section 1 of chapter 167; (2) a national banking association, bank, savings and loan association, savings bank, cooperative bank, building and loan or credit union organized under the laws of the United States; (3) a banking association, bank, savings and loan association, savings bank, cooperative bank, building and loan or credit union organized under the laws of any state; (4) an agency, agent or branch of a foreign bank; (5) a currency dealer or exchange; (6) a person or business engaged primarily in the cashing of checks; (7) a person or business regularly engaged in the issuing, selling or redeeming of traveler's checks, money orders or similar instruments; (8) a broker or dealer in securities or commodities; (9) a licensed transmitter of funds or other person or business regularly engaged in the transmission of funds to a foreign nation for others; (10) an investment banker or investment company; (11) an insurer; (12) a dealer in precious metals, stones or jewels; (13) a pawnbroker or scrap metal dealer; (14) a telegraph or other communications company; (15) a personal property or real estate broker; (16) a dealer in vehicles including, but not limited to, automobiles, aircraft and vessels; (17) an operator of a betting or gaming establishment; (18) a travel agent; (19) a thrift institution, as defined in section 1 of chap-

ter 167F; (20) an operator of a credit card system; or (21) a loan or finance company.

"Monetary instrument", the currency and coin of the United States or any foreign country; any bank check, money order, stock, investment security, or negotiable instrument in bearer form or otherwise in such form that title passes upon delivery; gold, silver or platinum bullion or coins; diamonds, emeralds, rubies or sapphires; any negotiable instrument including, bank checks, cashier's checks, traveler's checks or monetary orders made payable to the order of a named party that have not been endorsed or which bear restrictive endorsements; poker chips, vouchers or other tokens exchangeable for cash by gaming entities; and credit cards, debit cards, gift cards, gift certificates or scrips.

"Transaction", a purchase, sale, loan, pledge, gift, transfer, delivery or other disposition and, with respect to a financial institution, including, but not limited to, a deposit, withdrawal, bailment, transfer between accounts, exchange of currency, loan, extension of credit, purchase or sale of any stock, bond, certificate of deposit or other monetary instrument, use of a safe deposit box or any other payment, transfer or delivery by, through or to a financial institution, by whatever means effected.

SECTION 2
Money laundering; penalties
(Added by 2011 Mass. Acts c. 194, § 48, effective Nov. 22, 2011.)

Whoever knowingly:

(1) transports or possesses a monetary instrument or other property that was derived from criminal activity with the intent to promote, carry on or facilitate criminal activity;

(2) engages in a transaction involving a monetary instrument or other property known to be derived from criminal activity:

(i) with the intent to promote, carry on or facilitate criminal activity; or

(ii) knowing that the transaction is designed in whole or in part either to: (A) conceal or disguise the nature, location, source, ownership or control of the property derived from criminal activity; or (B) avoid a transaction reporting requirement of this chapter, of the United States, or of any other state; or

(3) directs, organizes, finances, plans, manages, supervises or controls the transportation of, or transactions in, monetary instruments or other property known to be derived from criminal activity or which a reasonable person would believe to be derived from criminal activity shall be guilty of the crime of money laundering and shall be punished by imprisonment in the state prison for not more than 6 years or by a fine of not more than $250,000 or twice the value of the property transacted, whichever is greater, or by both such imprisonment and fine. Whoever commits a second or subsequent such offense shall be punished by imprisonment in the state prison for not less than 2 years, but not more than 8 years or by a fine of not more than $500,000 or 3 times the value of the property transacted, whichever is greater, or by both such imprisonment and fine.

SECTION 3

Filing of reports by financial institutions; liability for making, filing or use of reports; disclosure

(Added by 2011 Mass. Acts c. 194, § 48, effective Nov. 22, 2011.)

(a) If the Financial Crimes Enforcement Network of the United States Department of the Treasury at any time no longer permits a law enforcement agency including, but not limited to, the attorney general, from entering into a memorandum of understanding to obtain reports required by the Currency and Foreign Transactions Act, set forth in 31 U.S.C. § 5311 to 5315, 31 C.F.R. chapter X, on a case-by-case basis, a financial institution, upon the request of the attorney general, shall file with the attorney general reports required by said Currency and Foreign Transactions Act, set forth in 31 U.S.C. § 5311 to 5315, 31 CFR chapter X.

(b) A financial institution, or an officer, employee or agent of a financial institution that provides any reports or information under this section shall not be liable to its customer, to a state or local agency or to any person for any loss or damage caused in whole or in part by the making, filing or governmental use of the report, or any information contained in the report. Nothing in this chapter shall give rise to a private cause of action for relief or damages. Nothing in this subsection shall preclude a financial institution, in its discretion, from instituting contact with, and then communicating with and disclosing customer financial records to appropriate federal, state or local law enforcement agencies if the financial institution has reason to suspect that the records or information demonstrate that the customer has violated this chapter.

(c) Any report, record or information obtained by the attorney general under this section shall not be a public record under clause Twenty-sixth of section 7 of chapter 4 or section 10 of chapter 66 and shall not be subject to disclosure, except to other state and federal law enforcement agencies.

SECTION 4

Forfeiture of monetary instruments or other property obtained in violation of sec. 2

(Added by 2011 Mass. Acts c. 194, § 48, effective Nov. 22, 2011.)

All monetary instruments or other property, real, intellectual or personal, obtained directly as a result of a violation of section 2, shall be subject to forfeiture to the commonwealth. Forfeiture proceedings shall be conducted as provided in subsections (b) to (j), inclusive, of section 47 of chapter 94C. For the purposes of subsection (d) of said section 47 of said chapter 94C, the investigations and enforcement bureau of the Massachusetts gaming commission established in chapter 23K shall be considered a police department and shall be entitled to a police department's distribution of forfeiture proceedings.

Chapter 268. Crimes Against Public Justice

Section

1	Perjury
1A	Statements containing declaration relative to penalties of perjury; verification; false statements
2	Subornation of perjury
3	Attempt to procure another to commit perjury
4	Testimony creating presumption of perjury; commitment; recognizance; witnesses bound over; notice to district attorney
5	Presumption of perjury; papers, books and documents detained for prosecution of perjury
6	False reports to, or false testimony before, state departments and commissioner; false entries in company books or statements; aiders or abettors
6A	False written reports by public officers or employees
6B	Process servers; false statements; penalty
7–8A	Repealed
8B	Compulsion or coercion to refuse appointment or promotion
9	Repealed
9A	Public officers or employees; solicitations regarding testimonial dinners
10–12	Repealed
13	Corrupting or attempting to corrupt masters, auditors, jurors, arbitrators, umpires or referees
13A	Picketing court, judge, juror, witness or court officer
13B	Intimidation of witnesses or jurors; penalties; "criminal investigator" defined
13C	Disruption of court proceedings
13D	Distributing transcript or description of grand jury testimony with intent to interfere with criminal proceedings
13E	Tampering with record, document or other object for use in an official proceeding
14	Receipt of gift by juror, arbitrator, umpire, referee, master or auditor
14A	Juror discharge from employment prohibited
14B	Witnesses in criminal proceedings; discharge, etc. from employment
15	Aiding escape from a correctional institution or jail; rescue
15A	Escapes from city or town jails; penalties
16	Escape or attempt to escape, or failure to return from temporary release or furlough
16A	Repealed
17	Aiding escape from officer or person having custody
18	Jailer or officer suffering prisoner to escape
19	Suffering or consenting to an escape from a penal institution
20	Negligently suffering prisoner to escape; refusal to receive prisoner
21	Suffering convict to be at large, visited, relieved or comforted
21A	Sexual relations with inmate
22	Delay of service of warrant
23	Refusal or delay to execute process resulting in escape
24	Neglect or refusal to assist officer or watchman
25	Refusal or neglect to obey order of justice of the peace to apprehend offender
26	Delivering alcoholic beverages to prisoners; possession
27	Delivering alcoholic beverages to patients of public institutions; possession
28	Delivering drugs or articles to prisoners in correctional institutions or jails; possession
29	Delivery, or permission of delivery, by officers, of alcoholic beverages, to prisoners; keeping together prisoners of different sexes or classes

2

30   Disturbing correctional institutions or jails; attracting attention of, or communicating with, inmates
31   Delivery or receipt of articles to or from inmates
32   Interference or tampering with police or fire signal systems, or motorist highway emergency aid call boxes; false alarms or calls
32A Interference with fire fighting operations
32B Resisting arrest
33   Falsely assuming to be justice of the peace or other officers
33A Unlicensed lead paint inspectors
34   Disguises to obstruct execution of law, performance of duties, or exercise of rights
34A Furnishing false name or social security number to law enforcement officer
35   Unauthorized use of town seal; making or possessing badge of town officer
36   Compounding or concealing felonies
37–38 Repealed
39   Perjury; statements alleging motor vehicle theft; penalty; subsequent offenses
40   Reports of crimes to law enforcement officials

SECTION 1
Perjury

Whoever, being lawfully required to depose the truth in a judicial proceeding or in a proceeding in a course of justice, wilfully swears or affirms falsely in a matter material to the issue or point in question, or whoever, being required by law to take an oath or affirmation, wilfully swears or affirms falsely in a matter relative to which such oath or affirmation is required, shall be guilty of perjury. Whoever commits perjury on the trial of an indictment for a capital crime shall be punished by imprisonment in the state prison for life or for any term of years, and whoever commits perjury in any other case shall be punished by imprisonment in the state prison for not more than twenty years or by a fine of not more than one thousand dollars or by imprisonment in jail for not more than two and one half years, or both such fine and imprisonment in jail.

An indictment or complaint for violation of this section alleging that, in any proceedings before or ancillary to any court or grand jury proceedings relating to an indictment or complaint for the commission of a violent crime, as defined in section 121 of chapter 140, the defendant under oath has knowingly made 2 or more declarations, which are inconsistent to the degree that 1 of them is necessarily false, need not specify which declaration is false if: (1) each declaration was material to the point in question and (2) each declaration was made within the period of the statute of limitations for the offense charged under this section. In any prosecution under this section, the falsity of a declaration set forth in the indictment or complaint shall be established sufficient for conviction by proof that the defendant, while under oath, made irreconcilably contradictory declarations material to the point in question. If, in the same continuous court or grand jury proceeding in which a declaration is made, the person making the declaration admits to such declaration to be false, such admission shall bar prosecution under this section if, at the time the admission is made, the declaration has not substantially affected the proceeding, or it has not become manifest that such falsity has been or will be exposed. It shall be a defense to an indictment or complaint made pursuant to this section that the defendant, at the time he made each declaration, believed each such declaration to be true or its falsity was the result of a good faith mistake or error.

NOTE 1a   **Materiality.** The falsity of the answer must be material to the matter under investigation. *Commonwealth v. Louis Constr. Co. Inc.*, 343 Mass. 600, 606–07 (1962).

NOTE 1b   "Materiality must not only be alleged but proven by the Commonwealth." *Commonwealth v. Louis Constr. Co. Inc.*, 343 Mass. at 607.

NOTE 1c   "Materiality in respect to perjury means relevance in the sense that the answer might tend in reasonable degree to affect some aspect or result of the inquiry." *Commonwealth v. Giles*, 350 Mass. 102, 110 (1966).

NOTE 1d   "[T]he test of relevancy and materiality is not whether the false testimony did in fact influence a pertinent determination. Instead it must be decided whether, viewed objectively, the testimony directly or circumstantially had a reasonable and natural tendency to do so." *Commonwealth v. Giles*, 350 Mass. at 111. *See also Commonwealth v. McDuffee*, 379 Mass. 353, 360 n.8 (1979).

NOTE 1e   Materiality issue is one for the jury to determine. *Commonwealth v. McDuffee*, 379 Mass. at 360–64.

NOTE 2   "[P]erjury alone does *not* constitute criminal contempt; there must be the further element of obstruction of the court in the performance of its duty." *Miaskiewicz v. Commonwealth*, 380 Mass. 153, 158 (1980). In *Miaskiewicz*, the petitioner, as an earlier plaintiff, initiated a civil action supported by a "tissue of fabrications." Twelve witnesses were called, the trial lasted 11 days, the cost for jurors was $2,240. The petitioner not only lied wilfully under oath, but enlisted judicial resources in a baseless, false and wasteful course. His conduct constituted both an affront to the court's dignity and a perversion of the court's purposes as an institution for just resolution of legitimate disputes. Accordingly, as both perjury and the additional element of court obstruction existed, a finding of criminal contempt was in order.

NOTE 3   **Form of Indictment.** G.L. c. 277, § 79.

NOTE 4   **Related Statute.** G.L. c. 268B, § 7.

NOTE 5   "Whether a defendant's sworn statement given during the course of an ongoing investigation to a Lieutenant of the State Police assigned to the District Attorney's Office may be properly characterized as given in a proceeding in a court of justice as required by G.L. c. 268, sec. 1?" The Supreme Judicial Court responded in the negative reasoning that "[t]he words 'proceeding in a course of justice' deal only with adjudicatory and not with investigative proceedings." *Commonwealth v. Dawson*, 399 Mass. 465, 467–68 (1987).

NOTE 6   "Since the early 1800s we have said that one may not be convicted of perjury except on the directly opposing testimony of either two witnesses or one witness and, in addition independent evidence [of] strong corroborating circumstances. This so-called 'quantitative rule' has been criticized strongly in recent years as inflexible and mechanical. [Accordingly] we today modify the quantitative rule. Hereafter, the Commonwealth may secure a conviction of perjury where it is able to offer evidence of perjury and corroboration of that evidence sufficient to establish the defendant's guilt beyond a reasonable doubt. In modifying the quantitative rule to eliminate the requirement that the Commonwealth introduce direct testimony in every perjury prosecution, we follow a number of other States which recently have determined that convictions for perjury may be based on evidence other than direct testimony. Where other kinds of evidence are substituted for the testimony of a live witness, however, that evidence must be of a highly reliable order and the necessity for corroboration is not eliminated. We adopt the statement of the Appeals Court that such evidence must be of a direct or clear and compelling character, objectively inconsistent with the innocence of the defendant. Moreover, just as in cases involving the direct testimony of a single witness, the corroboration requirement will be satisfied only with evidence that is independent of the principal evidence which it corroborates." *Commonwealth v. Silva*, 401 Mass. 318, 323–24 (1987) (citations and quotation marks omitted). *See also Commonwealth v. Knowlton*, 50 Mass. App. Ct. 266, 270 (2000) ("The policy behind the rule requiring evidence of 'a highly reliable order' is to prevent a conviction of perjury when there is no evidence other than the word of one witness against that of the defendant.") (citations and quotation marks omitted).

2

SECTION 1A
Statements containing declaration relative to penalties of perjury; verification; false statements

No written statement required by law shall be required to be verified by oath or affirmation before a magistrate if it contains or is verified by a written declaration that it is made under the penalties of perjury. Whoever signs and issues such a written statement containing or verified by such a written declaration shall be guilty of perjury and subject to the penalties thereof if such statement is wilfully false in a material matter.

NOTE 1   **Evidence.** "After our opinion, Pikul was indicted for and convicted of perjury in the post conviction proceedings based on his affidavit and his testimony. . . .

"The defendant argues that the Commonwealth's evidence was not sufficient to surmount the 'quantitative rule,' or, alternately, that it was not of a 'compelling character.' *See Commonwealth v. Silva*, 401 Mass. 318 (1987); *Commonwealth v. Coleman*, 20 Mass. App. Ct. 542 (1985), S.C., 397 Mass. . . The question whether Pikul was lying or 'simply mistaken' was an issue for the jury." *Commonwealth v. Pikul*, 407 Mass. 336, 336–37 (1990).

NOTE 2   **Sufficiency of Indictment.** "The defendant asserts that the indictment based on his affidavit is fatally defective because it alleged that the statement was made under the penalty of law and did not allege that the false statement was "made under the penalties of perjury." G.L. c. 268, § 1A (1988 ed.). To be sufficient, "[a]n indictment and a complaint shall contain . . . a plain, concise description of the act which constitutes the crime or an appropriate legal term descriptive thereof.' *See* Mass.R.Crim.P. 4 (a), 378 Mass. 849 (1979). The indictments contain a plain, concise description of the acts that constituted the crime. *Commonwealth v. Pikul*, 407 Mass. at 337–38.

NOTE 3   **Jurisdiction.** "The perjurious testimony and affidavit were [a]cts done outside Hampden County but intended to produce detrimental effects within it, and justify Hampden County in punishing the cause of the harm as if Pikul had been present at the effect." *Commonwealth v. Pikul*, 407 Mass. at 338 (quotation marks and citations omitted).

SECTION 2
Subornation of perjury

Whoever is guilty of subornation of perjury, by procuring another person to commit perjury, shall be punished as for perjury.

SECTION 3
Attempt to procure another to commit perjury

Whoever attempts to incite or procure another person to commit perjury, although no perjury is committed, shall be punished by imprisonment in the state prison for not more than five years or in jail for not more than one year.

SECTION 4
Testimony creating presumption of perjury; commitment; recognizance; witnesses bound over; notice to district attorney

If it appears to a court of record that a party or a witness who has been legally sworn and examined, or has made an affidavit, in any proceeding in a court or course of justice has so testified as to create a reasonable presumption that he has committed perjury therein, the court may forthwith commit him or may require him to recognize with sureties for his appearance to answer to an indictment for perjury; and thereupon the witnesses to establish such perjury may, if present, be bound over to the superior court, and notice of the proceedings shall forthwith be given to the district attorney.

NOTE   "[P]erjury alone does *not* constitute criminal contempt; there must be the further element of obstruction of the court in the performance of its duty." *Miaskiewicz v. Commonwealth*, 380 Mass. 153, 158 (1980). In *Miaskiewicz*, the petitioner, as an earlier plaintiff, initiated a civil action supported by a "tissue of fabrications." Twelve witnesses were called, the trial lasted 11 days, the cost for jurors was $2,240. The petitioner not only lied wilfully under oath, but enlisted judicial resources in a baseless, false and wasteful course. His conduct constituted both an affront to the court's dignity and a perversion of the court's purposes as an institution for just resolution of legitimate disputes. Accordingly as both perjury and the additional element of court obstruction existed, a finding of criminal contempt was in order.

SECTION 5
Presumption of perjury; papers, books and documents detained for prosecution of perjury

If perjury is reasonably presumed, as aforesaid, papers, books or documents which have been produced and are considered necessary to be used on a prosecution for such perjury may by order of the court be detained from the person who produces them so long as may be necessary for their use in such prosecution.

SECTION 6
False reports to, or false testimony before, state departments and commissioner; false entries in company books or statements; aiders or abettors

Except as provided in sections forty-eight and forty-nine of chapter one hundred and fifty-five, whoever shall wilfully make false report to the department of public utilities, the department of telecommunications and cable, the department of highways, the department of banking and insurance, the department of environmental protection, the board of registration of waste cleanup professionals, or the commissioner of revenue, or who before any such department, board or commissioner, shall testify or affirm falsely to any material fact in any matter wherein an oath or affirmation is required or authorized, or who shall make any false entry or memorandum upon any book, report, paper or statement of any company making report to any of the said departments or board or said commissioner, with intent to deceive the department or board or commissioner, or any agent appointed to examine the affairs of any such company, or to deceive the stockholders or any officer of any such company, or to injure or defraud any such company, and any persons who with like intent aids or abets another in any violation of this section shall be punished by a fine of not more than one thousand dollars or by imprisonment for not more than one year, or both such fine and imprisonment.

SECTION 6A
False written reports by public officers or employees

Whoever, being an officer or employee of the commonwealth or of any political subdivision thereof or of any authority created by the general court, in the course of his official duties executes, files or publishes any false written report, minutes or statement, knowing the same to be false in a material matter, shall be punished by a fine of not more than one thousand dollars or by imprisonment for not more than one year, or by both such fine and imprisonment.

NOTE 1   Statute requires that the Commonwealth prove that the public officer "knew his statement was false and that he knew it was false in a material matter." *Commonwealth v. Kelley*, 35 Mass. App. Ct. 745, 749 (1994).

2

NOTE 2   "A witness who is familiar with a person's handwriting may give an opinion as to whether the specimen in question was written by that person. Whether a witness is qualified to give such an opinion is a question, in the first instance, for the judge." *Commonwealth v. Ryan*, 355 Mass. 768, 770–71 (1969) (citations omitted).

SECTION 6B
Process servers; false statements; penalty

Any process server who returns to the court a writ or other official instrument of process on which he has willfully falsified either the fact that service has been made, or the fact that a particular kind of service has been made, shall be punished by a fine of not more than five hundred dollars or by imprisonment for not more than one year.

SECTIONS 7–8A
Repealed

SECTION 8B
Compulsion or coercion to refuse appointment or promotion

Any appointing authority or appointing officer, both as defined in chapter thirty-one, who, by himself or by some other person acting on his behalf, compels, or induces by the use of threats or other form of coercion, any person on an eligible list, as defined in chapter thirty-one, to refuse an appointment or promotion by such authority or officer to any position in the classified civil service shall be punished by a fine of not less than fifty nor more than two hundred dollars or imprisonment in a jail or house of correction for not more than two months, or by both such fine and imprisonment.

SECTION 9
Repealed

SECTION 9A
Public officers or employees; solicitations regarding testimonial dinners

No person shall sell, offer for sale, or accept payment for, tickets or admissions to, nor solicit or accept contributions for, a testimonial dinner or function, or any affair, by whatever name it may be called, having a purpose similar to that of a testimonial dinner or function, for any person, other than a person holding elective public office, whose office or employment is in any law enforcement, regulatory or investigatory body or agency of the commonwealth or any political subdivision thereof.

Whoever violates any provision of this section shall be punished by a fine of not more than five hundred dollars.

SECTIONS 10–12
Repealed

SECTION 13
Corrupting or attempting to corrupt masters, auditors, jurors, arbitrators, umpires or referees

Whoever corrupts or attempts to corrupt a master in chancery, master, auditor, juror, arbitrator, umpire or referee by giving, offering or promising any gift or gratuity whatever, with intent to influence his opinion or decision, relative to a cause or matter pending in a court, or before an inquest, or for the decision of which he has been chosen or appointed, shall be punished by imprisonment in the state prison for not more

than five years or by a fine of not more than one thousand dollars and imprisonment in jail for not more than one year.

SECTION 13A
Picketing court, judge, juror, witness or court officer

Whoever, with the intent of interfering with, obstructing, or impeding the administration of justice, or with the intent of influencing any judge, juror, witness, or court officer, in the discharge of his duty, pickets or parades in or near a building housing a court of the commonwealth, or in a building or residence occupied or used by such judge, juror, witness, or court officer, shall be punished by a fine of not more than five thousand dollars or by imprisonment for not more than one year, or both.

Nothing in this section shall interfere with or prevent the exercise by any court of the commonwealth of its power to punish for contempt.

SECTION 13B
Intimidation of witnesses or jurors; penalties; "criminal investigator" defined

(1) Whoever, directly or indirectly, willfully

(a) threatens, or attempts or causes physical injury, emotional injury, economic injury or property damage to;

(b) conveys a gift, offer or promise of anything of value to; or

(c) misleads, intimidates or harasses another person who is:

(i) a witness or potential witness at any stage of a criminal investigation, grand jury proceeding, trial or other criminal proceeding of any type;

(ii) a person who is or was aware of information, records, documents or objects that relate to a violation of a criminal statute, or a violation of conditions of probation, parole or bail;

(iii) a judge, juror, grand juror, prosecutor, police officer, federal agent, investigator, defense attorney, clerk, court officer, probation officer or parole officer;

(iv) a person who is furthering a civil or criminal proceeding, including criminal investigation, grand jury proceeding, trial, other criminal proceeding of any type, probate and family proceeding, juvenile proceeding, housing proceeding, land proceeding, clerk's hearing, court ordered mediation, any other civil proceeding of any type; or

(v) a person who is or was attending or had made known his intention to attend a civil or criminal proceeding, including criminal investigation, grand jury proceeding, housing proceeding, land proceeding, clerk's hearing, court-ordered mediation, any other civil proceeding of any type with the intent to impede, obstruct, delay, harm, punish or otherwise interfere thereby, or do so with reckless disregard, with such a proceeding shall be punished by imprisonment in a jail or house of correction for not more than 2 and one-half years or by imprisonment in a state prison for not more than 10 years, or by a fine of not less than $1,000 nor more than $5,000, or by both such fine and imprisonment.

(2) As used in this section, "investigator" shall mean an individual or group of individuals lawfully authorized by a department or agency of the federal government, or any political subdivision thereof, or a department or agency of the commonwealth, or any political subdivision thereof, to conduct or engage in an investigation of, prosecution for, or defense

of a violation of the laws of the United States or of the commonwealth in the course of his official duties.

(3) As used in this section, "harass" shall mean to engage in any act directed at a specific person or persons, which act seriously alarms or annoys such person or persons and would cause a reasonable person to suffer substantial emotional distress. Such act shall include, but not be limited to, an act conducted by mail or by use of a telephonic or telecommunication device or electronic communication device including but not limited to any device that transfers signs, signals, writing, images, sounds, data, or intelligence of any nature transmitted in whole or in part by a wire, radio, electromagnetic, photoelectronic or photo-optical system, including, but not limited to, electronic mail, internet communications, instant messages or facsimile communications.

(4) A prosecution under this section may be brought in the county in which the criminal investigation, grand jury proceeding, trial or other criminal proceeding is being conducted or took place, or in the county in which the alleged conduct constituting an offense occurred.

NOTE 1a   "General Laws c. 268, § 13B, does not require that a defendant specifically articulate a threat not to speak to the police or other criminal investigator. A fact-finder may evaluate that circumstances in which the statement was made, including its timing, to determine what the defendant in fact intended to intimidate the victim." *Commonwealth v. King*, 69 Mass. App. Ct. 113, 120 (2007).

NOTE 1b   "At issue is the March, 2006, amendment to the witness intimidation statute, G.L. c. 268, § 13B. . . . As we conclude that the elements of intimidation are defined, both before and after the amendment, by the acts, statements, and intentions of the defendant and their ordinary effects on a reasonable person, not the personal reaction of the particular, potential witness, we affirm." *Commonwealth v. Rivera*, 76 Mass. App. Ct. 530, 530–31 (2010).

NOTE 1c   "At best . . . the meaning of the verbs 'harm' and 'punish' in § 13B, as applied to a proceeding, is ambiguous, and we cannot interpret an ambiguous statute in a manner that disadvantages a criminal defendant. . . . We invite the Legislature to clarify G.L. c. 268, § 13B, particularly as it relates to retaliatory conduct." *Commonwealth v. Hamilton*, 459 Mass. 422, 437 (2011).

NOTE 2   "We have held that the purpose of the witness intimidation statute, in part, is to prevent interference with the administration of justice. To that end, the statute has two distinct branches—a 'witness' branch and a 'furnishing information' branch . . . "The statute may be applied either to witnesses and jurors in ongoing criminal proceedings, or to any person furnishing information to a criminal investigator relating to a crime." *Commonwealth v. Belle Isle*, 44 Mass. App. Ct. 226, 228 (1998) (citations and footnote omitted).

NOTE 3   The judge did *not* err in admitting into evidence bullets which had been fired at the victim one month prior to the shooting as the defendant could be tied to that earlier incident and it was relevant to the reality of defendant's threats and also relevant in that it corroborated earlier testimony that bullets had in fact been fired at the victim. *Commonwealth v. Orton*, 4 Mass. App. Ct. 593, 596 (1976).

NOTE 4   "It is not necessary that a defendant's statement or conduct refer directly to a pending court case in order to constitute intimidation. A jury can properly draw an inference from all of the circumstances that a defendant knew of the criminal proceedings." *Commonwealth v. Drumgoole*, 49 Mass. App. Ct. 87, 91 (2000).

NOTE 5   "In the circumstances of this case, we hold that the act of pointing of a cellular telephone camera at a witness waiting to testify in a criminal proceeding constitutes intimidation." *Commonwealth v. Casiano*, 70 Mass. App. Ct. 705, 705 (2007).

NOTE 6   Misleading Police Officer. "This interlocutory appeal presents the question whether the concealment and destruction of evidence can mislead a police officer within the meaning of G.L. c. 268, § 13B. On the facts presented here, we conclude that it can. . . . [T]he facts set forth in the complaint application give rise to a reasonable inference that the defendants affirmative act of picking up and swallowing the suspected heroin was a trick.

"Significantly, [the 2006 amendment of the statute] criminalized misleading conduct and added police officers to the list of victims protected. From this expansion of the statute we discern a legislative intent to arm law enforcement officers with additional tools to combat deliberate interference with criminal investigations and prosecutions, precisely the conduct alleged here." *Commonwealth v. Tejeda*, 89 Mass. App. Ct. 625, 625–26, 629–30 (2016).

NOTE 7   Misleading Parole Officer. "The issue presented on appeal is whether it is a crime under G.L. c. 268, § 13B, for a parolee to mislead a parole officer who is investigating the parolee's possible failure to comply with parole conditions. We conclude that it is." *Commonwealth v. Figueroa*, 464 Mass. 365, 365 (2013).

NOTE 8   Posttrial motion. "Under the plain language of the statute, there is no requirement that there be a pending criminal proceeding. Rather, it requires intent to interfere in a 'criminal proceeding of any type.' We conclude that a posttrial motion clearly falls under the statute's language." *Hrycenko v. Commonwealth*, 459 Mass. 503, 509–10 (2011).

NOTE 9   Post-Verdict Harassment. "In short, a trial does not end when the verdict is announced. Frequently, complex matters remain to be resolved before a judgment may be imposed . . . .

"[W]e conclude that the juvenile's threats here, made in court after the verdict was announced, but before any postconviction motions had been heard and before the conviction was reduced to a final judgment, amount to the requisite interference at a 'stage of a trial.'" *Commonwealth v. Cathy C.*, 64 Mass. App. Ct. 471, 474 (2005).

SECTION 13C
Disruption of court proceedings

Whoever causes or actively participates in the willful disruption of proceedings of any court of the commonwealth may be punished by a fine of not more than one thousand dollars or by imprisonment in a jail or house of correction for not more than one year, or both. Nothing in this section shall interfere with or prevent the exercise by any court of the commonwealth of its power of contempt.

NOTE   "[T]he Commonwealth must show some impact on at least one 'proceeding' in order to establish a violation of G.L. c. 268, § 13C . . . [T]here was ample evidence that Sholley's conduct was highly distracting and alarming. It certainly had the potential to disrupt proceedings that were underway in the various courtrooms at the Quincy District Court. However, the record is silent as to what impact—if any—this disturbance in the corridor actually had on any of those proceedings." *Commonwealth v. Sholley*, 432 Mass. 721, 731 (2000) (footnote omitted).

SECTION 13D
Distributing transcript or description of grand jury testimony with intent to interfere with criminal proceedings

(a) Whoever knowingly distributes or possesses with intent to distribute any transcript of grand jury testimony or any substantially verbatim description of grand jury testimony with the intent to impede, obstruct, delay or otherwise interfere with any criminal proceeding, or the participation of any victim, witness or juror in any stage of a trial, grand jury, or other criminal proceeding, or the continued participation of any person furnishing information to a criminal proceeding, or the continued participation of any person furnishing information to a criminal investigator relating to a violation of any criminal statute, shall be punished by imprisonment in a house of correction for not more than 2½ years or in the state prison for not more than 5 years, or by a fine of not more than $5,000, or both. Nothing in this subsection shall abridge any right protected by the First Amendment to the United States Constitution.

(b) Nothing in this section shall be construed so as to prohibit any person performing an official function in relation to the grand jury from disclosing a grand jury transcript or description thereof pursuant to Massachusetts Rules of Procedure or Federal Rule of Criminal Procedure 6.

(c) Any attorney representing a defendant in a criminal proceeding, including court appointed counsel, who receives a grand jury transcript or a description thereof related to such proceeding from a prosecutor, may provide the transcript or description to his client or any investigator employed by such attorney or another attorney employed by, or appointed by the court to represent, his client, unless such transfer would be in violation of a protective order from a court of competent jurisdiction. Such attorney may further disclose a grand jury transcript or description thereof related to such proceeding to assist in the legal defense of another defendant in a criminal proceeding, unless such transfer would be in violation of a protective order from a court of competent jurisdiction.

(d) Upon motion of the commonwealth and after hearing, a court may issue a protective order prohibiting defense counsel from distributing grand jury transcripts to a criminal defendant, if the commonwealth demonstrates that the defendant is accused of a violent crime, as defined in section 121 of chapter 140, and that there is a reason to believe, based on specific and articulable facts including, but not limited to, the defendant's past history of violence and the nature of the charges against the defendant, that the defendant poses a threat to a witness or victim. The defendant shall have a right to cross examine any commonwealth witness. In making a determination relative to the issuance of a protective order under this section, the court shall consider whether the defendant has an exceptional need to receive such grand jury transcripts.

(e) Any grand jury transcript or document citing or describing grand jury testimony filed with any court shall be filed and maintained under seal, unless the paper is filed in a criminal prosecution for perjury before a grand jury.

SECTION 13E
Tampering with record, document or other object for use in an official proceeding

(a) As used in this section the following word shall, unless the context clearly requires otherwise, have the following meaning:—

"Official proceeding", a proceeding before a court or grand jury, or a proceeding before a state agency or commission, which proceeding is authorized by law and relates to an alleged violation of a criminal statute or the laws and regulations enforced by the state ethics commission, the state secretary, the office of the inspector general, or the office of campaign and political finance, or an alleged violation for which the attorney general may issue a civil investigative demand.

(b) Whoever alters, destroys, mutilates, or conceals a record, document, or other object, or attempts to do so, with the intent to impair the record, document or object's integrity

or availability for use in an official proceeding, whether or not the proceeding is pending at that time, shall be punished, by (i) a fine of not more than $10,000, or by imprisonment in the state prison for not more than 5 years, or in a jail or house of correction for not more than 2½ years, or both, or (ii) if the official proceeding involves a violation of a criminal statute, by a fine of not more than $25,000, or by imprisonment in the state prison for not more than 10 years, or in a jail or house of correction for not more than 2½ years, or both.

(c) The record, document, or other object need not be admissible in evidence or free of a claim of privilege.

(d) A prosecution under this section may be brought in the county where the official proceeding was or would have been convened or where the alleged conduct constituting an offense occurred.

SECTION 14
Receipt of gift by juror, arbitrator, umpire, referee, master or auditor

Whoever, being summoned as a juror or chosen or appointed as an arbitrator, umpire or referee, or, being a master in chancery, master or auditor, corruptly takes anything to give his verdict, award or report, or corruptly receives any gift or gratuity from a party to a suit, cause or proceeding for the trial or decision of which such juror has been summoned, or for the hearing or determination of which such master in chancery, master, auditor, arbitrator, umpire or referee has been chosen or appointed, shall be punished by imprisonment in the state prison for not more than five years or by a fine of not more than one thousand dollars and imprisonment in jail for not more than one year.

SECTION 14A
Juror discharge from employment prohibited

No person shall be discharged from or deprived of his employment because of his attendance or service as a grand or traverse juror in any court. Violation of this section by an employer shall be a contempt of the court upon which such person is or has been in attendance or in which he is or has been serving as a grand or traverse juror, and such employer may be prosecuted upon complaint verified upon oath and be punished for such contempt.

SECTION 14B
Witnesses in criminal proceedings; discharge, etc. from employment

Any person who is a victim of a crime upon which an accusatory instrument is based, or is subpoenaed to attend a criminal action as a witness and who notifies his employer of such subpoena prior to the day of his attendance, shall not be subject to discharge or penalty by said employer on account of his absence from employment by reason of such witness service. An employer shall not subject an employee to discharge or penalty or the threat of discharge or penalty on account of the absence of such employee from employment by reason of his attendance as a witness at a criminal action. An employer who violates the provisions of this section shall be punished by a fine of not more than two hundred dollars or by imprisonment for not more than one month, or both such fine and imprisonment.

SECTION 15
Aiding escape from a correctional institution or jail; rescue

Whoever conveys into a correctional institution of the commonwealth or into a jail, house of correction, house of reformation or like place of confinement, a disguise, instrument tool, weapon or other thing which is adapted or useful to aid a prisoner in making his escape, with intent to aid the escape of a prisoner, or whoever, by any means, aids or assists such prisoner in endeavoring to escape therefrom, whether such escape is effected or attempted or not, and who ever forcibly or fraudulently rescues or attempts to rescue a prisoner held in custody upon a conviction or charge of crime, shall, if the person whose escape or rescue was effected or intended is a convict under sentence to the state prison or is charged with a felony, be punished by a fine of not more than five hundred dollars or by imprisonment in the state prison for not more than ten years; but if he is a convict under sentence to any other of said institutions, by imprisonment in the state prison for not more than seven years; and if he is charged with a misdemeanor, then by a fine of not more than five hundred dollars or by imprisonment in jail for not more than two years.

SECTION 15A
Escapes from city or town jails; penalties

Whoever, after lawfully being placed in custody in a jail of a city or town, escapes from any such jail shall be punished by imprisonment in a jail or house of correction for not more than two and one-half years, or by a fine of not more than five hundred dollars, or both.

SECTION 16
Escape or attempt to escape, or failure to return from temporary release or furlough

A prisoner of any penal institution including a prisoner who is held in custody for a court appearance or a person committed under the provisions of section five or six of chapter one hundred and twenty-three A to a treatment center or branch thereof described in sections two and four of said chapter one hundred and twenty-three A, or a prisoner committed to any jail or correctional institution under a lawful order of a court, who escapes or attempts to escape from any such institution or from land appurtenant thereto, or from any courthouse or from land appurtenant thereto or from the custody of any officer thereof while being conveyed to or from said institution, center or branch, or who knowingly disables or attempts to disable or defeat electronic monitoring of the prisoner, or fails to return from any temporary release from said institution under the provisions of section ninety A of chapter one hundred and twenty-seven, or fails to return from any temporary release from said institution, center or branch, may be pursued and recaptured and shall be punished by imprisonment in the state prison for not more than ten years or by imprisonment in a jail or house of correction for not more than two and one-half years.

NOTE 1   **Form of Indictment.** G.L. c. 277, § 79.

NOTE 2a   "We have no doubt that the law should provide a penalty for what the defendant did. No statute, or combination of statutes, however, does so. We suggest that the Legislature may wish to enact a comprehensive statute to embrace within the crime of escape the unauthorized departure or escape of a prisoner during any of the many circumstances under which prisoners (and perhaps others held in confinement) today may lawfully be outside the walls of an institution." *Commonwealth v. Boone*, 394 Mass. 851, 856 (1985).

NOTE 2b   "[W]e are asked to determine whether a person serving a house of correction sentence, which was ordered to be served on weekends, *see* G.L. c. 279, § 6A, who fails to report by 6:00 p.m. on a particular weekend, as required by the terms of his sentence, has 'escaped' within the meaning of § 16 because he 'fail[ed] to return from any temporary release from said institution.' . . . [W]e answer that question in the affirmative." *Commonwealth v. Porter*, 87 Mass. App. Ct. 676, 677 (2015).

NOTE 3   **Holding Cells.** "The use of the term 'and' in this definition is significant and can only be read to require that the facility must, at a minimum, maintain custody or control over committed offenders in order to qualify as a penal institution. Therefore, although a facility may also house a variety of other prisoners such as those who are held on bail, under an arrest warrant, in protective custody, or other forms of custody, it is the ability and the authority of the facility to house or care for committed prisoners that determines whether it is a 'penal institution' for purposes of escape. Because a cell block in a police station is only intended to hold prisoners who have not yet been committed to a correctional facility, it does not qualify as a penal institution." *Commonwealth v. Clay*, 65 Mass. App. Ct. 215, 217 (2005).

SECTION 16A
Repealed

SECTION 17
Aiding escape from officer or person having custody

Whoever aids or assists a prisoner in escaping or attempting to escape from an officer or person who has the lawful custody of such prisoner shall be punished by a fine of not more than five hundred dollars or by imprisonment for not more than two years.

SECTION 18
Jailer or officer suffering prisoner to escape

A jailer or officer who, except as provided in the following section, voluntarily suffers a prisoner in his custody upon conviction or upon a charge of crime to escape shall suffer the punishment and penalties to which the prisoner whom he suffered to escape was sentenced or would be liable to suffer upon conviction of the crime wherewith he stood charged.

SECTION 19
Suffering or consenting to an escape from a penal institution

An officer or other person, who, being employed in any penal institution, voluntarily suffers a convict confined therein to escape, or in any way consents to such escape, shall be punished by imprisonment in the state prison for not more than twenty years.

SECTION 20
Negligently suffering prisoner to escape; refusal to receive prisoner

A jailer or officer who, through negligence, suffers a prisoner in his custody upon conviction or upon a charge of crime to escape, or wilfully refuses to receive into his custody a prisoner lawfully directed to be committed thereto upon conviction, upon a charge of crime, or upon a lawful process, shall be punished by a fine of not more than five hundred dollars or by imprisonment for not more than two years.

2

SECTION 21
Suffering convict to be at large, visited, relieved or comforted
An officer or person who, being employed in the state prison, suffers a convict under sentence of solitary imprisonment to be at large or out of the cell assigned to him, or suffers any convict confined in the prison to be at large out of the prison, or to be visited, conversed with or in any way relieved or comforted, contrary to the regulations of the prison, shall be punished by a fine of not more than five hundred dollars.

SECTION 21A
Sexual relations with inmate
An officer or other person who is employed by or contracts with any penal or correctional institution in the commonwealth, and who, in the course of such employment or contract or as a result thereof, engages in sexual relations with an inmate confined therein, within or outside of such institution, or an inmate who is otherwise under the direct custodial supervision and control of such officer or other person, shall be punished by imprisonment for not more than five years in a state prison or by a fine of $10,000 or both. In a prosecution commenced under this section, an inmate shall be deemed incapable of consent to sexual relations with such person. For purposes of this section, sexual relations shall include intentional, inappropriate contact of a sexual nature, including, but not limited to conduct prohibited by section 22 or 24 of chapter 265 or section 2, 3, 35 or 53A of chapter 272.

SECTION 22
Delay of service of warrant
An officer who wilfully delays service of a warrant of arrest or a search warrant committed to him for service shall be punished by a fine of not more than fifty dollars.

SECTION 23
Refusal or delay to execute process resulting in escape
An officer who, being authorized to serve process, wilfully and corruptly refuses to execute a lawful process directed to him and requiring him to apprehend or confine a person convicted of or charged with crime, or wilfully and corruptly omits or delays to execute such process, whereby such person escapes, shall be punished by a fine of not more than five hundred dollars or by imprisonment for not more than one year.

SECTION 24
Neglect or refusal to assist officer or watchman
Whoever, being required in the name of the commonwealth by a sheriff, deputy sheriff, constable, police officer or watchman, neglects or refuses to assist him in the execution of his office in a criminal case, in the preservation of the peace or in the apprehension or securing of a person for a breach of the peace, or in a case of escape or rescue of persons arrested upon civil process, shall be punished by a fine of not more than fifty dollars or by imprisonment for not more than one month.

SECTION 25
Refusal or neglect to obey order of justice of the peace to apprehend offender
Whoever, being required by a justice of the peace, upon view of a breach of the peace or of any other offense proper for his cognizance, to apprehend the offender, refuses or neglects to obey such justice, shall be punished as provided in the preceding section; and no person to whom such justice is known or declares himself to be a justice of the peace shall plead any excuse on pretence of ignorance of his office.

SECTION 26
Delivering alcoholic beverages to prisoners; possession
Whoever gives, sells or delivers alcoholic beverages, as defined in section one of chapter one hundred and thirty-eight, to a person confined in any correctional institution or other place of confinement, or to a person in the custody of a sheriff, constable, police officer, superintendent of a correctional institution, or other superintendent or keeper of a place of confinement, or has in his possession, within the precincts of any prison or other place of confinement, any such beverages, with intent to convey or deliver them to any person confined therein, except under the direction of the physician appointed to attend such prisoner, shall be punished by a fine of not more than fifty dollars or by imprisonment for not more than two months.

SECTION 27
Delivering alcoholic beverages to patients of public institutions; possession
Whoever gives, sells or delivers any alcoholic beverages, as defined in section one hundred and thirty-eight, to any patient or inmate of any public institution, or to any patient or inmate under the control of any such institution, except under the direction of a physician authorized so to do, and whoever has in his possession within the precincts of any such institution any such beverages with intent to consume the same or to convey, give, sell or deliver the same to any patient or inmate thereof, except under direction as aforesaid, shall be punished by a fine of not more than fifty dollars or by imprisonment for not more than two months

SECTION 28
Delivering drugs or articles to prisoners in correctional institutions or jails; possession
Whoever gives or delivers to a prisoner in any correctional institution, or in any jail or house of correction, any drug or article whatever, or has in his possession within the precincts of any prison herein named with intent to give or deliver to any prisoner any such drug or article without the permission of the superintendent or keeper, shall be punished by imprisonment in the state prison for not more than five years, or in a jail or house of correction for not more than two years, or by a fine of not more than one thousand dollars.

SECTION 29
Delivery, or permission of delivery, by officers, of alcoholic beverages, to prisoners; keeping together prisoners of different sexes or classes
A sheriff, jailer, superintendent of a house of correction or officer of a correctional institution who, under any pretence, gives, sells or delivers or knowingly permits to be given, sold or delivered to a prisoner in his custody any alcoholic beverages, as defined in section one of chapter one hundred and thirty-eight, or cider, unless the physician of the penal institution certifies in writing that the health of the prisoner requires the same; or such sheriff, jailer, superintendent of a house of correction or officer of a correctional institution who

willingly or negligently suffers such prisoner to have or drink any alcoholic beverages, as so defined, or who places or keeps together prisoners in his custody of different sexes or classes, contrary to section twenty-two of chapter one hundred and twenty-seven, shall forfeit twenty five dollars for the first offense and fifty dollars for any offense committed subsequent to the first conviction, and upon second conviction, shall be removed from office, and be ineligible to hold the office of sheriff, deputy sheriff, jailer, superintendent or keeper of any correctional institution for five years thereafter. If the physician certifies that the health of the prisoner requires such liquor, the prisoner shall be allowed the quantity prescribed and no more.

SECTION 30
Disturbing correctional institutions or jails; attracting attention of, or communicating with, inmates

Whoever wilfully disturbs any correctional institution of the commonwealth, the Lyman school, industrial school for boys, industrial school for girls, or a jail or house of correction, or in any manner seeks to attract the attention of, or without the permission of the officer in charge has communication with, an inmate thereof, shall be punished by a fine of not more than fifty dollars or by imprisonment for not more than three months.

SECTION 31
Delivery or receipt of articles to or from inmates

Whoever delivers or procures to be delivered, or has in his possession with intent to deliver, to an inmate confined in any penal institution, or whoever deposits or conceals in or about the institution, or the dependencies thereof, or upon any land appurtenant thereto, or in any boat or vehicle going into the premises belonging to the institution, any article, with intent that an inmate shall obtain or receive it, and whoever receives from an inmate any article with intent to convey it out of the institution, contrary to the rules and regulations thereof, and without the knowledge and permission of the commissioner of correction or of the superintendent, keeper, sheriff or other officer in charge thereof shall be punished by a fine of not more than five hundred dollars or by imprisonment in the state prison for not more than three years or in jail for not more than two and one half years.

Any inmate of a correctional institution who, upon returning from furlough or a work program, brings or attempts to bring into said institution an illegal drug, gun, knife or other similar weapon as defined in section ten of chapter two hundred and sixty-nine of the General Laws, shall be punished by an additional sentence of not less than seven nor more than ten years in state prison.

SECTION 32
Interference or tampering with police or fire signal systems, or motorist highway emergency aid call boxes; false alarms or calls

Whoever opens a signal box connected with a police signal system for the purpose of giving, or causing to be given, a false alarm, or interferes in any way with such box by breaking, cutting, injuring or defacing the same; or whoever, without authority, opens, tampers or meddles with such box, or with any part or parts thereof, or with the police signal wires, or with anything connected therewith, or with such purpose, wantonly and without cause tampers or meddles with a signal box connected with a fire signal system or with any part or thing connected therewith, shall be subject to immediate arrest and shall be punished by a fine of not less than five hundred nor more than one thousand dollars, or by imprisonment for not more than two years, or both.

Whoever opens a motorist highway emergency aid call box on any state highway connected with a highway emergency signal system for the purpose of giving or causing to be given a false call for aid, or interferes in any way with such box by breaking, cutting, injuring or defacing the same; or, without authority, opens, tampers or meddles with such box, or with any part or parts thereof, or with anything connected therewith, or, with such purpose, wantonly and without cause tampers or meddles with a motorist highway emergency aid call box or with any part or thing connected therewith, shall be punished by a fine of not less than one hundred dollars nor more than five hundred dollars.

NOTE   **Related Statutes.**
   G.L. c. 266, § 11—Tampering with fire alarm system before fire.
   G.L. c. 266, § 12—Tampering with fire alarm system during fire.
   G.L. c. 269, § 13—False alarm of fires.

SECTION 32A
Interference with fire fighting operations

Whoever wilfully obstructs, interferes with or hinders a fire fighter in the lawful performance of his duty, or whoever wilfully obstructs, interferes with or hinders a fire fighting force in the lawful performance of its duty, shall be punished by a fine of not less than one hundred nor more than one thousand dollars or by imprisonment in a jail or house of correction for not less than thirty days nor more than two and one half years or by imprisonment in the state prison for not more than five years, or by both such fine and imprisonment in a jail or house of correction.

NOTE   See Note following G.L. c. 268, § 32 for related statutes.

SECTION 32B
Resisting arrest

(a) A person commits the crime of resisting arrest if he knowingly prevents or attempts to prevent a police officer, acting under color of his official authority, from effecting an arrest of the actor or another, by:

(1) using or threatening to use physical force or violence against the police officer or another; or

(2) using any other means which creates a substantial risk of causing bodily injury to such police officer or another.

(b) It shall not be a defense to a prosecution under this section that the police officer was attempting to make an arrest which was unlawful, if he was acting under color of his official authority, and in attempting to make the arrest he was not resorting to unreasonable or excessive force giving rise to the right of self-defense. A police officer acts under the color of his official authority when, in the regular course of assigned duties, he is called upon to make, and does make, a judgment in good faith based upon surrounding facts and circumstances that an arrest should be made by him.

(c) The term "police officer" as used in this section shall mean a police officer in uniform or, if out of uniform, one who has identified himself by exhibiting his credentials as such police officer while attempting such arrest.

(d) Whoever violates this section shall be punished by imprisonment in a jail or house of correction for not more

2

than two and one-half years or a fine of not more than five hundred dollars, or both.

NOTE 1   "Accordingly, we hold that the defendant was entitled to an instruction that his intoxication could be considered by the jury in determining whether the Commonwealth had proved beyond a reasonable doubt that the defendant both knew that the persons with whom he was engaged were police officers acting under the color of their authority and that he was preventing or attempting to prevent them from effecting an arrest." *Commonwealth v. Lawson*, 46 Mass. App. Ct. 627, 630 (1999).

NOTE 2a   When Committed. "[T]he resisting arrest statute states that the crime is committed, if at all, at the time of 'effecting' an arrest." *Commonwealth v. Grandison*, 433 Mass. 135, 145 (2001) ("a resisting arrest conviction can, in no way, rest on postarrest conduct").

NOTE 2b   Substantial risk of causing bodily injury. "The fact that the officers chose not to scale the fence and jump twenty feet into shallow water is not determinative of the question. . . . [T]he risk of bodily injury came from the fence located at the precipice of the canal, which presented a tripping hazard, especially in the dim light, as well as from the canal itself whose bottom had a 'pretty deep' layer of muck and mire and which was deep enough that the defendant had to tread water until his rescue." *Commonwealth v. Montoya*, 457 Mass. 102, 105–06 (2010).

NOTE 2c   A Charge of Resisting Arrest Is Inappropriate Where the Defendant's Resistance Occurred During a Protective Pat Frisk Rather than an Arrest Attempt. "The sweep of the statute applies only when police officers have attempted to seize or detain a person 'with the intention to effect an arrest.' *Commonwealth v. Grandison*, 433 Mass. 135, 145 (2001), quoting from *Commonwealth v. Cook*, 419 Mass. 192, 198 (1994). See *Commonwealth v. Smith*, 55 Mass. App. Ct. 569, 574 (2002) ('A stop for purposes of making a threshold inquiry is not an arrest')." *Commonwealth v. Pagan*, 63 Mass. App. Ct. 780, 784 (2005).

NOTE 3   Arrest. "[A]n arrest occurs when there is (1) an actual or constructive seizure or detention of the person, [2] performed with the intention to effect an arrest and [3] so understood by the person detained. . . . Whether a defendant understood that he was being arrested is determined with reference to an objective standard, what a reasonable man, innocent of any crime, would have thought had he been in the defendant's shoes. It is also established that an arrest may occur prior to the time police make a formal arrest, and that verbal notification to an individual that he is being arrested is not conclusive on the question of when an arrest occurs." *Commonwealth v. Montoya*, 73 Mass. App. Ct. 125, 127–28 (2008) (citations and quotation marks omitted).

NOTE 4   Self-Defense as a Defense. "Under the resisting arrest statute and general law, a person has a right to resist by reasonable force an arrest carried out by police with excessive or unreasonable force, see G.L. c. 268, § 32B; *Commonwealth v. Moreira*, 388 Mass. 596, 601–602 (1983), and this permitted exercise of self-defense does not turn upon the legality or illegality of the arrest itself, see *id.* at 601. . . .

"[T]he judge as fact finder should have been guided by an instruction as in *Commonwealth v. Graham*, 62 Mass. App. Ct. at 654 n.7:

'The gist of the instruction would provide as follows: If there is evidence of excessive or unnecessary force by police in making an arrest, the Commonwealth must prove beyond a reasonable doubt (1) that the arresting officer did not use excessive or unnecessary force in making the arrest. If the Commonwealth satisfies this burden, then the defendant has no right to engage in self-defense. If the Commonwealth fails to prove that excessive or unnecessary force was not used by police, and there is evidence of self-defense, then the Commonwealth must prove beyond a reasonable doubt (2) that the defendant did not act in self-defense, or (3) that force used by the defendant in self-defense was unreasonable or excessive in the circumstances. See *Commonwealth v.*

Kendrick, 351 Mass. 203, 211 (1966); *Commonwealth v. Rodriguez*, 370 Mass. [684,] 692 n.10 [(1976)]."
     Commonwealth v. Urkiel, 63 Mass. App. Ct. 445, 448, 452 (2005).

SECTION 33
Falsely assuming to be justice of the peace or other officers

Whoever falsely assumes or pretends to be a justice of the peace, notary public, sheriff, deputy sheriff, medical examiner, associate medical examiner, constable, police officer, probation officer, or examiner, investigator or other officer appointed by the registrar of motor vehicles, or inspector, investigator or examiner of the department of public utilities or the department of telecommunications and cable, or investigator or other officer of the alcoholic beverages control commission, or investigator or other official of the bureau of special investigations, or examiner, investigator or other officer of the department of revenue, and acts as such or requires a person to aid or assist him in a matter pertaining to the duty of such officer, shall be punished by a fine of not more than four hundred dollars or by imprisonment for not more than one year.

NOTE   Form of Indictment. G.L. c. 277, § 79—Assuming to be an officer.

SECTION 33A
Unlicensed lead paint inspectors

Whoever engages in or conducts a lead paint inspection without being licensed to do so, or holds himself out to the public as a licensed lead paint inspector and is not so licensed, shall be punished by a fine of not more than five thousand dollars or imprisonment in jail for not more than one year, or both.

SECTION 34
Disguises to obstruct execution of law, performance of duties, or exercise of rights

Whoever disguises himself with intent to obstruct the due execution of the law, or to intimidate, hinder or interrupt an officer or other person in the lawful performance of his duty, or in the exercise of his rights under the constitution or laws of the commonwealth, whether such intent is effected or not, shall be punished by a fine of not more than five hundred dollars or by imprisonment for not more than one year and may if imprisoned also be bound to good behavior for one year after the expiration of such imprisonment.

NOTE   "A person who gives a false name does not . . . disguise himself . . . and such conduct does not fall within the ambit of the statute." *Commonwealth v. Healey*, 17 Mass. App. Ct. 537, 539 (1984) (punctuation and quotation marks omitted).

SECTION 34A
Furnishing false name or social security number to law enforcement officer

Whoever knowingly and willfully furnishes a false name or Social Security number to a law enforcement officer or law enforcement official following an arrest shall be punished by a fine of not more than $1,000 or by imprisonment in a house of correction for not more than one year or by both such fine and imprisonment. Such sentence shall run from and after any sentence imposed as a result of the underlying offense. The court may order that restitution be paid to persons whose identity has been assumed and who have suffered monetary losses as a result of a violation of this section.

2

NOTE   Dishonest Purpose. "For purposes of G.L. c. 268, § 34A, a false name is one that a person has assumed for a dishonest purpose . . . . If a person previously has identified himself to any police department under a name that is different from the name he used following the arrest in question and failed to disclose his prior use of a different name, you are permitted to infer that his failure to make such disclosure was for a dishonest purpose. . . . The Commonwealth does not have to prove the defendant's true name." *Commonwealth v. Clark*, 446 Mass. 620, 630–31 (2006).

SECTION 35
Unauthorized use of town seal; making or possessing badge of town officer

Whoever, without being duly authorized thereto, prints, stamps, engraves or affixes, or causes to be printed, stamped, engraved or affixed to any paper or other article a representation of the seal of a town in the commonwealth, with intent to give to such paper or article an official character which it does not possess, or, without being duly authorized thereto, and with intent to assume an official character which he does not possess, casts, stamps, engraves, makes or has in his possession a badge or thing in the likeness of an official badge of a police officer, member of a fire department, or other officer appointed by a town in the commonwealth, or by any department of such town, shall be punished by a fine of not more than fifty dollars.

SECTION 36
Compounding or concealing felonies

Whoever, having knowledge of the commission of a felony, takes money, or a gratuity or reward, or an engagement therefor, upon an agreement or understanding, express or implied, to compound or conceal such felony, or not to prosecute therefor, or not to give evidence thereof, shall, if such crime is punishable with death or imprisonment in the state prison for life, be punished by imprisonment in the state prison for not more than five years or in jail for not more than one year; and if such crime is punishable in any other manner, by a fine of not more than five hundred dollars or by imprisonment in jail for not more than two years.

SECTIONS 37–38
Repealed

SECTION 39
Perjury; statements alleging motor vehicle theft; penalty; subsequent offenses

Whoever knowingly makes a false written statement on a form bearing notice that false statements made therein are punishable under the penalty of perjury, to a police officer, police department or the registry of motor vehicles alleging the theft or conversion of a motor vehicle, shall be punished by imprisonment for a first offense not less than five months, nor more than two years, or a fine of not less than two hundred and fifty dollars and not more than two thousand five hundred dollars, or both. A person found guilty of violating this section for a second or subsequent offense shall be punished by imprisonment not less than one, nor more than five years, or a fine of not less than five hundred dollars and not more than five thousand dollars, or both.

The sentence imposed upon a person convicted of violating this section for a second or subsequent offense shall not be reduced to less than one year.

A person convicted of a second or subsequent offense of violating the provisions of this section shall not be eligible for probation, parole, furlough or work release; provided, however that the commissioner of correction may, on the recommendation of warden, superintendent, or other person in charge of a correctional institution, or the administrator of a county correctional institution, grant to said offender a temporary release in the custody of an officer of such institution for the following purposes: to attend the funeral of next of kin or spouse; to visit a critically ill close relative or spouse; or to obtain emergency medical services unavailable at said institutions. A prosecution commenced under this section shall neither be continued without a finding nor placed on file.

NOTE   Defendant's signature on a stolen motor vehicle report constitutes a written statement, even when a police officer completed the remaining sections of the report. *Commonwealth v. Kelly*, 69 Mass. App. Ct. 751, 753 (2007).

"Compare G.L. c. 269, § 13A (criminalizing knowingly making false report of crime to police officer) with G.L. c. 268, § 39 (criminalizing knowingly making false written report under penalty of perjury to police officers)." *Commonwealth v. Kelly*, 69 Mass. App. Ct. at 753–54.

SECTION 40
Reports of crimes to law enforcement officials

Whoever knows that another person is a victim of aggravated rape, rape, murder, manslaughter or armed robbery and is at the scene of said crime shall, to the extent that said person can do so without danger or peril to himself or others, report said crime to an appropriate law enforcement official as soon as reasonably practicable. Any person who violates this section shall be punished by a fine of not less than five hundred nor more than two thousand and five hundred dollars.

Chapter 268A. Conduct of Public Officials and Employees

Section	
1	Definitions
2	Corrupt gifts, offers or promises to influence official acts; corruption of witnesses
3	Gifts, offers or promises for acts performed or to be performed; corruption of witnesses; solicitation of gifts
4	Other compensation; offer, gift, receipt or request; acting as agent or attorney for other than state; legislators; special state employees
5	Former state employees; acting as attorney or receiving compensation; partners of state employees or legislators
6	Financial interest of state employee, relative or associates; disclosure
6A	Conflict of interest of public official; reporting requirement
6B	Candidate for employment; disclosures
7	Financial interest in contracts of state agency; application of section
8	Public building or construction contracts
8A	Members of state commissions or boards; prohibited appointments to other positions
8B	Members of department of telecommunications and energy commission; prohibited employment within one year after service has ceased
9	Violations of Secs. 2–8; civil action for damages
10	Opinions of state ethics commission
11	County employees; receiving or requesting compensation from, or acting as agent or attorney for other than county agency

12   Former county employees; acting as attorney or receiving compensation from other than county; partners of employees or former employees; or legislators

13   Financial interest of county employees, relatives or associates; disclosure

14   County employees; financial interests in contracts of county agency

15   County agency; unfair advantage in relation to particular matter; additional remedies; civil action for damages

15A   Members of county commission or board; restrictions on appointments to certain positions

16   Repealed

17   Municipal employees; gift or receipt of compensation from other than municipality; acting as agent or attorney

18   Former municipal employee; acting as attorney or receiving compensation; from other than municipality; partners

19   Municipal employees, relatives or associates; financial interest in particular matter

20   Municipal employees; financial interest in contracts; holding one or more elected positions

21   Municipal agency; unfair advantage in relation to particular matter; additional remedies; civil action for damages

21A   Members of municipal commission or board; appointments to certain positions

21B   Prospective municipal appointees; demanding undated resignations prohibited

22   Opinions of corporation counsel, city solicitor or town counsel

23   Supplemental provisions; standards of conduct

23A   Trustees of public institutions of higher learning; prohibited positions

24   Disclosures and certifications; form; public inspection

25   Suspension of persons under indictment for misconduct in office; notice; compensation and fringe benefits; temporary replacements; reinstatement

26   Penalty for violations of clause (b)(2) or (b)(4) of Sec. 23

27   Publication of summaries of Chapter 268A; filing of acknowledgment by employees

28   Online training programs

29   Municipal liaisons to state ethics commission

SECTION 1
Definitions

In this chapter the following words, unless a different meaning is required by the context or is specifically prescribed, shall have the following meanings:—

(a) "Compensation", any money, thing of value or economic benefit conferred on or received by any person in return for services rendered or to be rendered by himself or another.

(b) "Competitive bidding", all bidding, where the same may be prescribed by applicable sections of the General Laws or otherwise, given and tendered to a state, county or municipal agency in response to an open solicitation of bids from the general public by public announcement or public advertising, where the contract is awarded to the lowest responsible bidder.

(c) "County agency", any department or office of county government and any division, board, bureau, commission, institution, tribunal or other instrumentality thereof or thereunder.

(d) "County employee", a person performing services for or holding an office, position, employment or membership in a county agency, whether by election, appointment, contract of hire or engagement, whether serving with or without compensation, on a full, regular, part-time, intermittent or consultant bias.

(e) "Immediate family", the employee and his spouse and their parents, children, brothers and sisters.

(f) "Municipal agency", any department or office of a city or town government and any council, division, board, bureau, commission, institution, tribunal or other instrumentality thereof or thereunder.

(g) "Municipal employee," a person performing services for or holding an office, position, employment or membership in a municipal agency, whether by election, appointment, contract of hire or engagement, whether serving with or without compensation on a full, regular, part-time, intermittent or consultant basis, but excluding (1) elected members of a town meeting and (2) members of a charter commission established under Article LXXXIX of the Amendments to the Constitution.

(h) "Official act", any decision or action in a particular matter or in the enactment of legislation.

(i) "Official responsibility", the direct administrative or operating authority, whether intermediate or final and either exercisable alone or with others and whether personal or through subordinates, to approve, disapprove or otherwise direct agency action.

(j) "Participate", participate in agency action or in a particular matter personally and substantially as a state, county or municipal employee, through approval, disapproval, decision, recommendation, the rendering of advice, investigation or otherwise.

(k) "Particular matter", any judicial or other proceeding, application, submission, request for a ruling or other determination, contract, claim, controversy, charge, accusation, arrest, decision, determination, finding, but excluding enactment of general legislation by the general court and petitions of cities, towns, counties and districts for special laws related to their governmental organizations, powers, duties, finances and property.

(l) "Person who has been selected", any person who has been nominated or appointed to be a state, county or municipal employee or has been officially informed that he will be so nominated or appointed.

(m) "Special county employee", a county employee who is performing services or holding an office, position, employment or membership for which no compensation is provided; or who is not an elected official and (1) occupies a position which, by its classification in the county agency involved or by the terms of the contract or conditions of employment, permits personal or private employment during normal working hours, provided that disclosure of such classification or permission is filed in writing with the State Ethics Commission and the office of the county commissioners prior to the commencement of any personal or private employment, or (2) in fact does not earn compensation as a county employee for an aggregate of more than eight hundred hours during the preceding three hundred and sixty-five days. For this purpose compensation by the day shall be considered as equivalent to compensation for seven hours per day. A special county employee shall be in such status on days for which he is not compensated as well as on days on which he earns compensation.

(n) "Special municipal employee", a municipal employee who is not a mayor, a member of a board of aldermen, a member of a city council or a selectman in a town with a population in excess of ten thousand persons, and whose position has been expressly classified by the city council, or board of aldermen if there is no city council, or the board of selectmen, as that of a special employee under the terms and provisions of this chapter; provided, however, that a selectman in a town with a population of ten thousand or fewer persons shall be a special municipal employee without being expressly so classified. All employees who hold equivalent offices, positions,

2

employment or membership in the same municipal agency shall have the same classification; provided, however, no municipal employee shall be classified as a "special municipal employee" unless he occupies a position for which no compensation is provided or which, by its classification in the municipal agency involved or by the terms of the contract or conditions of employment, permits personal or private employment during normal working hours, or unless he in fact does not earn compensation as a municipal employee for an aggregate of more than eight hundred hours during the preceding three hundred and sixty-five days. For this purpose compensation by the day shall be considered as equivalent to compensation for seven hours per day. A special municipal employee shall be in such status on days for which he is not compensated as well as on days on which he earns compensation. All employees of any city or town wherein no such classification has been made shall be deemed to be "municipal employees" and shall be subject to all the provisions of this chapter with respect thereto without exception.

(o) "Special state employee", a state employee:

(1) Who is performing services or holding an office, position, employment or membership for which no compensation is provided, or

(2) Who is not an elected official and

(a) occupies a position which, by its classification in the state agency involved or by the terms of the contract or conditions of employment, permits personal or private employment during normal working hours, provided that disclosure of such classification or permission is filed in writing with the state ethics commission prior to the commencement of any personal or private employment, or

(b) in fact does not earn compensation as a state employee for an aggregate of more than eight hundred hours during the preceding three hundred and sixty-five days. For this purpose compensation by the day shall be considered as equivalent to compensation for seven hours per day. A special state employee shall be in such status on days for which he is not compensated as well as on days on which he earns compensation.

(p) "State agency", any department of state government including the executive, legislative or judicial and all councils thereof and thereunder, and any division, board, bureau, commission, institution, tribunal or other instrumentality within such department, and any independent state authority, district, commission, instrumentality or agency, but not an agency of a county, city or town.

(q) "State employee", a person performing services for or holding an office, position, employment, or membership in a state agency, whether by election, appointment, contract of hire or engagement, whether serving with or without compensation, on a full, regular, part-time, intermittent or consultant basis, including members of the general court and executive council. No construction contractor nor any of their personnel shall be deemed to be a state employee or special state employee under the provisions of paragraph (o) or this paragraph as a result of participation in the engineering and environmental analysis for major construction projects either as a consultant or part of a consultant group for the commonwealth. Such contractors or personnel may be awarded construction contracts by the commonwealth and may continue with outstanding construction contracts with the commonwealth during the period of such participation; provided, that no such contractor or personnel shall directly or indirectly bid or be awarded a contract for any construction project if they have participated in the engineering or environmental analysis thereof.

SECTION 2
Corrupt gifts, offers or promises to influence official acts; corruption of witnesses

(a) Whoever, directly or indirectly, corruptly gives, offers or promises anything of value to any state, county or municipal employee, or to any person who has been selected to be such an employee, or to any member of the judiciary, or who offers or promises any such employee or any member of the judiciary, or any person who has been selected to be such an employee or member of the judiciary, to give any thing of value to any other person or entity, with intent

(1) to influence any official act or any act within the official responsibility of such employee or member of the judiciary or person who has been selected to be such employee or member of the judiciary, or

(2) to influence such an employee or member of the judiciary or person who has been selected to be such an employee or member of the judiciary, to commit or aid in committing, or collude in, or allow, any fraud, or make opportunity for the commission of any fraud on the commonwealth or a state, county or municipal agency, or

(3) to include such an employee or member of the judiciary or person who has been selected to be such an employee or member of the judiciary to do or omit to do any act in violation of his lawful duty; or

(b) Whoever, being a state, county or municipal employee or a member of the judiciary or a person selected to be such an employee or member of the judiciary, directly or indirectly, corruptly asks, demands, exacts, solicits, seeks, accepts, receives or agrees to receive anything of value for himself or for any other person or entity, in return for

(1) being influenced in his performance of any official act or any act within his official responsibility, or

(2) being influenced to commit or aid in committing, or to collude in, or allow any fraud, or make opportunity for the commission of any fraud, on the commonwealth or on a state, county or municipal agency, or

(3) being induced to do or omit to do any acts in violation of his official duty; or

(c) Whoever, directly or indirectly, corruptly gives, offers or promises anything of value to any person, or offers or promises such person to give anything of value to any other person or entity, with intent to influence the testimony under oath or affirmation of such first-mentioned person or any other person as a witness upon a trial, or other proceeding, before any court, any committee of either house or both houses of the general court, or any agency, commission or officer authorized by the laws of the commonwealth to hear evidence or take testimony, or with intent to influence such witness to absent himself therefrom; or

(d) Whoever, directly or indirectly, corruptly asks, demands, exacts, solicits, seeks, accepts, receives or agrees to receive anything of value for himself or for any other person or entity in return for influence upon the testimony under oath or affirmation of himself or any other person as a witness upon any such trial, hearing or other proceeding or in return for the absence of himself or any other person therefrom;— shall be punished by a fine of not more than $100,000, or by imprisonment in the state prison for not more than 10 years, or in a jail or house of correction for not more than 2½ years, or both; and in the event of final conviction shall be incapable of holding any office of honor, trust or profit under the commonwealth or under any state, county or municipal agency.

Clauses (c) and (d) shall not be construed to prohibit the payment or receipt of witness fees provided by law or the payment by the party upon whose behalf a witness is called and receipt by a witness of the reasonable cost of travel and subsistence incurred and the reasonable value of time lost in attendance at any such trial, hearing or proceeding, or, in the case of expert witnesses, involving a technical or professional opinion, a reasonable fee for time spent in the preparation of such opinion, in appearing or testifying.

NOTE   Defendant charged with illegal alcoholic sale to minor. Defendant offered bribe to officer after the minor had been apprehended, the alcohol confiscated, and the police report written. Defendant asserted that bribery conviction must fall as at the time the bribe was made it was impossible for the officer to alter course or outcome of any administrative action against defendant's liquor store. Conviction upheld as it was still possible for the officer to alter such cause or outcome. *Commonwealth v. Corey*, 10 Mass. App. Ct. 873, 874–75 (1980).

SECTION 3
Gifts, offers or promises for acts performed or to be performed; corruption of witnesses; solicitation of gifts

(a) Whoever knowingly, otherwise than as provided by law for the proper discharge of official duty, directly or indirectly, gives, offers or promises anything of substantial value to any present or former state, county or municipal employee or to any member of the judiciary, or to any person selected to be such an employee or member of the judiciary: (i) for or because of any official act performed or to be performed by such an employee or member of the judiciary or person selected to be such an employee or member of the judiciary; or (ii) to influence, or attempt to influence, an official action of the state, county or municipal employee or to any member of the judiciary; or

(b) Whoever knowingly, being a present or former state, county or municipal employee or member of the judiciary, or person selected to be such an employee or member of the judiciary, otherwise than as provided by law for the proper discharge of official duty, directly or indirectly, asks, demands, exacts, solicits, seeks, accepts, receives or agrees to receive anything of substantial value: (i) for himself for or because of any official act or act within his official responsibility performed or to be performed by him; or (ii) to influence, or attempt to influence, him in an official act taken; or

(c) Whoever knowingly, directly or indirectly, gives, offers or promises anything of substantial value to any person, for or because of testimony under oath or affirmation given or to be given by such person or any other person as a witness upon a trial, hearing or other proceeding, before any court, any committee of either house or both houses of the general court, or any agency, commission or officer authorized by the laws of the commonwealth to hear evidence or take testimony or for or because of his absence therefrom; or

(d) Whoever knowingly, directly or indirectly, asks, demands, exacts, solicits, seeks, accepts, receives or agrees to receive anything of substantial value for himself for or because of the testimony under oath or affirmation given or to be given by him or any other person as a witness upon any

such trial, hearing or other proceeding, or for or because of his absence therefrom; shall be punished by a fine of not more than $50,000, or by imprisonment in the state prison for not more than 5 years, or in a jail or house of correction for not more than 2½ years, or both.

(e) Clauses (c) and (d) shall not prohibit the payment or receipt of witness fees provided by law or the payment by the party upon whose behalf a witness is called and receipt by a witness of the reasonable cost of travel and subsistence incurred and the reasonable value of time lost in attendance at any such trial, hearing or proceeding, or, in the case of expert witnesses, involving a technical or professional opinion, a reasonable fee for time spent in the preparation of such opinion, in appearing or testifying.

(f) The state ethics commission shall adopt regulations: (i) defining "substantial value,"; provided, however, that "substantial value" shall be not less than $50; (ii) establishing exclusions for ceremonial gifts; (iii) establishing exclusions for gifts given solely because of family or friendship; and (iv) establishing additional exclusions for other situations that do not present a genuine risk of a conflict or the appearance of a conflict of interest.

SECTION 4
Other compensation; offer, gift, receipt or request; acting as agent or attorney for other than state; legislators; special state employees

(a) No state employee shall otherwise than as provided by law for the proper discharge of official duties, directly or indirectly receive or request compensation from anyone other than the commonwealth or a state agency, in relation to any particular matter in which the commonwealth or a state agency is a party or has a direct and substantial interest.

(b) No person shall knowingly, otherwise than as provided by law for the proper discharge of official duties, directly or indirectly give, promise or offer such compensation.

(c) No state employee shall, otherwise than in the proper discharge of his official duties, act as agent or attorney for anyone other than the commonwealth or a state agency for prosecuting any claim against the commonwealth or a state agency, or as agent or attorney for anyone in connection with any particular matter in which the commonwealth or a state agency is a party or has a direct and substantial interest.

Whoever violates any provision of this section shall be punished by a fine of not more than $10,000 or by imprisonment in the state prison for not more than 5 years, or in a jail or house of correction for not more than 2½ years, or both.

Neither a member of the general court nor a member of the executive council shall be subject to paragraphs (a) or (c). However, no member of the general court or executive council shall personally appear for any compensation other than his legislative or executive council salary before any state agency, unless:

(1) the particular matter before the state agency is ministerial in nature; or

(2) the appearance is before a court of the commonwealth; or

(3) the appearance is in a quasi-judicial proceeding.

For the purposes of this paragraph, ministerial functions include, but are not limited to, the filing or amendment of: tax returns, applications for permits or licenses, incorporation

2

papers, or other documents. For the purposes of this paragraph, a proceeding shall be considered quasi-judicial if:

(1) the action of the state agency is adjudicatory in nature; and

(2) the action of the state agency in appealable to the courts; and

(3) both sides are entitled to representation by counsel and such counsel is neither the attorney general nor the counsel for the state agency conducting the proceeding.

A special state employee shall be subject to paragraphs (a) and (c) only in relation to a particular matter (a) in which he has at any time participated as a state employee, or (b) which is or within one year has been a subject of his official responsibility, or (c) which is pending in the state agency in which he is serving. Clause (c) of the preceding sentence shall not apply in the case of a special state employee who serves on no more than sixty days during any period of three hundred and sixty-five consecutive days.

This section shall not prevent a state employee from taking uncompensated action, not inconsistent with the faithful performance of his duties, to aid or assist any person who is the subject of disciplinary or other personnel administration proceedings with respect to those proceedings.

This section shall not prevent a state employee, including a special employee, from acting, with or without compensation, as agent or attorney for or otherwise aiding or assisting members of his immediate family or any person for whom he is serving as guardian, executor, administrator, trustee or other personal fiduciary except in those matters in which he has participated or which are the subject of his official responsibility; provided, that the state official responsible for appointment to his position approves.

This section shall not prevent a present or former special state employee from aiding or assisting another person for compensation in the performance of work under a contract with or for the benefit of the commonwealth; provided, that the head of the special state employee's department or agency has certified in writing that the interest of the commonwealth requires such aid or assistance and the certification has been filed with the state ethics commission.

This section shall not prevent a state employee from giving testimony under oath or making statements required to be made under penalty for perjury or contempt.

This section shall not prohibit a state employee from holding an elective or appointive office in a city, town or district, nor in any way prohibit such an employee from performing the duties of or receiving the compensation provided for such office. No such elected or appointed official may vote or act on any matter which is within the purview of the agency by which he is employed or over which such employee has official responsibility.

This section shall not prevent a state employee, other than an employee in the department of revenue, from requesting or receiving compensation from anyone other than the commonwealth in relation to the filing or amending of state tax returns.

SECTION 5
Former state employees; acting as attorney or receiving compensation; partners of state employees or legislators
(Amended by 2011 Mass. Acts c. 194, § 49, effective Nov. 22, 2011.)

(a) A former state employee who knowingly acts as agent or attorney for, or receives compensation directly or indirectly from anyone other than the commonwealth or a state agency, in connection with any particular matter in which the commonwealth or a state agency is a party or has a direct and substantial interest and in which he participated as a state employee while so employed, or

(b) a former state employee who, within one year after his last employment has ceased, appears personally before any court or agency of the commonwealth as agent or attorney for anyone other than the commonwealth in connection with any particular matter in which the commonwealth or state agency is a party or has a direct and substantial interest and which was under his official responsibility as a state employee at any time within a period of two years prior to the termination of his employment, or

(b½) A former state, county or municipal employee who participated as such in general legislation on expanded gaming in the commonwealth or in the implementation, administration or enforcement of chapter 23K, and who becomes an officer or employee of, or who acquires a financial interest in, an applicant for a gaming license or a gaming licensee under said chapter 23K within one year after his last state, county or municipal employment has ceased, or

(c) a partner of a former state employee who knowingly engages, during a period of one year following the termination of the latter's employment by the commonwealth, in any activity in which the former state employee is himself prohibited from engaging in by clause (a), or

(d) a partner of a state employee who knowingly acts as agent or attorney for anyone other than the commonwealth in connection with any particular matter in which the commonwealth or a state agency is a party or has a direct and substantial interest and in which the state employee participates or has participated as a state employee or which is the subject of his official responsibility, or

(e) a former state employee or elected official, including a former member of the general court, who acts as legislative or executive agent, as defined in section thirty-nine of chapter three, for anyone other than the commonwealth or a state agency before the governmental body, as determined by the state ethics commission with which he has been associated, within one year after he leaves that body or

(f) a former state employee whose salary was not less than that in step one of job group M-VII in the management salary schedule in section forty-six C of chapter thirty, and who becomes an officer or employee of a business organization which is or was a party to any privatization contract as defined in section fifty-three of chapter seven in which contract he participated as such state employee, if he becomes such officer or employee while the business organization is such a party or within one year after he terminates his state employment, unless before the termination of his state employment the governor determines, in a writing filed with the state ethics commission, that such participation did not significantly affect the terms or implementation of such contract, shall be punished by a fine of not more than $10,000, or by imprisonment in the state prison for not more than 5 years, or in a jail or house of correction for not more than 2½ years, or both.

If a partner of a member of the general court or of a special state employee or of a former state employee is also a

2

member of another partnership in which the member of the general court or special or former employee has no interest, the activities of the latter partnership in which the member of the general court or special or former employee takes no part shall not thereby be subject to clause (c) or (d).

This section shall not prevent a present or former special state employee from aiding or assisting another person for compensation in the performance of work under a contract with or for the benefit of the commonwealth; provided, that the head of the special state employee's department or agency has certified in writing that the interest of the commonwealth requires such aid or assistance and the certification has been filed with the state ethics commission.

SECTION 6
Financial interest of state employee, relative or associates; disclosure

(a) Except as permitted by this section, any state employee who participates as such employee in a particular matter in which to his knowledge he, his immediate family or partner, a business organization in which he is serving as officer, director, trustee, partner or employee, or any person or organization with whom he is negotiating or has any arrangement concerning prospective employment, has a financial interest, shall be punished by a fine of not more than $10,000, or by imprisonment in the state prison for not more than 5 years, or in a jail or house of correction for not more than 2½ years, or both.

Any state employee whose duties would otherwise require him to participate in such a particular matter shall advise the official responsible for appointment to his position and the state ethics commission of the nature and circumstances of the particular matter and make full disclosure of such financial interest, and the appointing official shall thereupon either

(1) assign the particular matter to another employee; or

(2) assume responsibility for the particular matter; or

(3) make a written determination that the interest is not so substantial as to be deemed likely to affect the integrity of the services which the commonwealth may expect from the employee, in which case it shall not be a violation for the employee to participate in the particular matter. Copies of such written determination shall be forwarded to the state employee and filed with the state ethics commission by the person who made the determination. Such copy shall be retained by the commission for a period of six years.

SECTION 6A
Conflict of interest of public official; reporting requirement

Any public official, as defined by section 1 of chapter 268B, who in the discharge of his official duties would be required knowingly to take an action which would substantially affect such official's financial interests, unless the effect on such an official is no greater than the effect on the general public, shall file a written description of the required action and the potential conflict of interest with the state ethics commission established by said chapter 268B.

SECTION 6B
Candidate for employment; disclosures
(Added by 2011 Mass. Acts c. 93, § 118, effective July 1, 2011.)

Each candidate for employment as a state employee shall be required by the hiring authority as part of the application process to disclose, in writing, the names of any state employee who is related to the candidate as: spouse, parent, child or sibling or the spouse of the candidate's parent, child or sibling.

The contents of a disclosure received under this section from an employee when such employee was a candidate shall be considered public records under section 7 of chapter 4 and chapter 66.

All disclosures made by applicants hired by a state agency shall be made available for public inspection to the extent permissible by law by the official with whom such disclosure has been filed.

SECTION 7
Financial interest in contracts of state agency; application of section

A state employee who has a financial interest, directly or indirectly, in a contract made by a state agency, in which the commonwealth or a state agency is an interested party, of which interest he has knowledge or has reason to know, shall be punished by a fine of not more than $10,000, or by imprisonment in the state prison for not more than 5 years, or in a jail or house of correction for not more than 2½ years, or both.

This section shall not apply if such financial interest consists of the ownership of less than one per cent of the stock of a corporation.

This section shall not apply (a) to a state employee who in good faith and within thirty days after he learns of an actual or prospective violation of this section makes full disclosure of his financial interest to the contracting agency and terminates or disposes of the interest, or (b) to a state employee other than a member of the general court who is not employed by the contracting agency or an agency which regulates the activities of the contracting agency and who does not participate in or have official responsibility for any of the activities of the contracting agency, if the contract is made after public notice or where applicable, through competitive bidding, and if the state employee files with the state ethics commission a statement making full disclosure of his interest and the interests of his immediate family in the contract, and if in the case of a contract for personal services (1) the services will be provided outside the normal working hours of the state employee, (2) the services are not required as part of the state employee's regular duties, the employee is compensated for not more than five hundred hours during a calendar year, and (3) the head of the contracting agency makes and files with the state ethics commission a written certification that no employee of that agency is available to perform those services as a part of their regular duties, or (c) to the interest of a member of the general court in a contract made by an agency other than the general court or either branch thereof, if his direct and indirect interests and those of his immediate family in the corporation or other commercial entity with which the contract is made do not in the aggregate amount to ten per cent of the total proprietary interests therein, and the contract is made through competitive bidding and he files with the state ethics commission a statement making full disclosure of his interest and the interests of his immediate family, or (d) to a special state employee who does not participate in or have official responsibility for any of the activities of

2

the contracting agency and who files with the state ethics commission a statement making full disclosure of his interest and the interests of his immediate family in the contract, or (e) to a special state employee who files with the state ethics commission a statement making full disclosure of his interest and the interests of his immediate family in the contract, if the governor with the advice and consent of the executive council exempts him.

This section shall not apply to a state employee who provides services or furnishes supplies, goods and materials to a recipient of public assistance, provided that such services or such supplies, goods and materials are provided in accordance with a schedule of charges promulgated by the department of transitional assistance or the division of health care policy and finance and provided, further, that such recipient has the right under law to choose and in fact does choose the person or firm that will provide such services or furnish such supplies, goods and materials.

This section shall not prohibit a state employee from teaching or performing other related duties in an educational institution of the commonwealth; provided, that such employee does not participate in, or have official responsibility for, the financial management of such educational institution; and provided, further, that such employee is so employed on a part-time basis. Such employee may be compensated for such services, notwithstanding the provisions of section twenty-one of chapter thirty.

This section shall not prohibit a state employee from being employed on a part-time basis by a facility operated or designed for the care of mentally ill or mentally retarded persons, public health, correctional facility or any other facility principally funded by the state which provides similar services and which operates on an uninterrupted and continuous basis; provided that such employee does not participate in, or have official responsibility for, the financial management of such facility, that he is compensated for such part-time employment for not more than four hours in any day in which he is otherwise compensated by the commonwealth, and at a rate which does not exceed that of a state employee classified in step one of job group XX of the general salary schedule contained in section forty-six of chapter thirty, and that the head of the facility makes and files with the state ethics commission a written certification that there is a critical need for the services of the employee. Such employee may be compensated for such services, notwithstanding the provisions of section twenty-one of chapter thirty.

This section shall not preclude an officer or employee of the Massachusetts Port Authority from eligibility for any residential sound insulation program administered by said Authority, provided that any such officer or employee has no responsibility for the administration of said program.

SECTION 8
Public building or construction contracts
No state, county or municipal employee and no person acting or purporting to act on behalf of such employee, or any state, county or municipal agency, shall with respect to any public building or construction contract which is about to be or which has been competitively bid, require the bidder to make application to or furnish financial data to, or to obtain, or procure, any of the surety bonds or insurance specified in connection with such contract or specified by any law from

any particular insurance or surety company, agent, or broker. This section shall not prevent the exercise by such employee on behalf of a state, county, or municipal agency of its right to approve the form, sufficiency, or manner of execution of the surety bonds and insurance furnished by the insurance or surety company selected by the bidder to underwrite said insurance and bonds. Any provisions in any invitation for bids, or in any of the contract documents, in conflict with this section are hereby declared to be contrary to the public policy of this commonwealth. Whoever violates any provision of this section shall be punished by a fine of not more than $10,000, or by imprisonment in the state prison for not more than 5 years, or in a jail or house of correction for not more than 2½ years, or both.

SECTION 8A
Members of state commissions or boards; prohibited appointments to other positions
No member of a state commission or board shall be eligible for appointment or election by the members of such commission or board to any office or position under the supervision of such commission or board. No former member of such commission or board shall be so eligible until the expiration of thirty days from the termination of his service as a member of such commission or board.

SECTION 8B
Members of department of telecommunications and energy commission; prohibited employment within one year after service has ceased
No member of the commonwealth utilities commission, appointed pursuant to section 2 of chapter 25, or the commissioner of telecommunications and cable shall, within one year after his service has ceased or terminated on said commission, be employed by, or lobby said commission on behalf of, any company or regulated industry over which said commission had jurisdiction during the tenure of such member of the commission.

SECTION 9
Violations of Secs. 2–8; civil action for damages
(a) In addition to any other remedies provided by law, any violation of sections 2 to 8, inclusive, or section 23 which has substantially influenced the action taken by any state agency in any particular matter, shall be grounds for avoiding, rescinding or canceling the action on such terms as the interests of the commonwealth and innocent third persons shall require.

(b) In addition to the remedies set forth in subsection (a), the state ethics commission upon a finding pursuant to an adjudicatory proceeding that a person has acted to his economic advantage in violation of sections 2 to 8, inclusive, or section 23, may issue an order: (1) requiring the violator to pay the commission on behalf of the commonwealth damages in the amount of the economic advantage or $500, whichever is greater; and (2) requiring the violator to make restitution to an injured third party. If there has been no final criminal judgment of conviction or acquittal of the same violation, upon receipt of the written approval of the attorney general, the commission may order payment of additional damages in an amount not exceeding twice the amount of the economic advantage or $500, and payment of such additional damages shall bar any criminal prosecution for the same violation.

2

The maximum damages that the commission may order a violator to pay under this section shall be $25,000. If the commission determines that the damages authorized by this section exceed $25,000, it may bring a civil action against the violator to recover such damages.

(c) The remedies authorized by this section shall be in addition to any civil penalty imposed by the state ethics commission in accordance with clause (3) of subsection (j) of section 4 of chapter 268B.

SECTION 10
Opinions of state ethics commission

The state ethics commission shall issue opinions interpreting the requirements of this chapter, in accordance with clause (g) of section 3 of chapter 268B.

SECTION 11
County employees; receiving or requesting compensation from, or acting as agent or attorney for other than county agency

(a) No county employee shall, otherwise than as provided for the proper discharge of official duties, directly or indirectly receive or request compensation from anyone other than a county or a county agency in relation to any particular matter in which a county agency is a party or has a direct and substantial interest.

(b) No person shall knowingly, otherwise than as provided by law for the proper discharge of official duties, directly or indirectly give, promise or offer such compensation.

(c) No county employee shall, otherwise than as provided by law for the proper discharge of official duties, act as agent or attorney for anyone other than a county or a county agency in prosecuting any claim against a county or county agency, or as agent or attorney for anyone in connection with any particular matter in which a county or county agency is a party or has a direct and substantial interest.

Whoever violates any provision of this section shall be punished by a fine of not more than $10,000, or by imprisonment in the state prison for not more than 5 years, or in a jail or house of correction for not more than 2½ years, or both.

A county employee shall be subject to paragraphs (a) and (c) only in relation to the county of which he is an employee. A special county employee shall be subject to said paragraphs (a) and (c) only in relation to a particular matter (a) in which he has at any time participated as a county employee, or (b) which is or within one year has been a subject of his official responsibility, or (c) which is pending in the county agency in which he is serving. Clause (c) of the preceding sentence shall not apply in the case of a county employee who serves on no more than sixty days during any period of three hundred and sixty-five consecutive days.

This section shall not prevent a county employee from taking uncompensated action, not inconsistent with the faithful performance of his duties, to aid or assist any person who is the subject of disciplinary or other personnel administration proceedings with respect to those proceedings.

This section shall not prevent a county employee, including a special employee, from acting, with or without compensation, as agent or attorney for or otherwise aiding or assisting members of his immediate family or any person for whom he is serving as guardian, executor, administrator, trustee or other personal fiduciary except in those matters in which he

has participated or which are the subject of his official responsibility; provided, that the state or county official responsible for appointment to his position approves.

This section shall not prevent a present or former special county employee from aiding or assisting another person for compensation in the performance of work under a contract with or for the benefit of the county; provided, that the head of the special county employee's department or agency has certified in writing that the interest of the county requires such aid or assistance and the certification has been filed with the state ethics commission. The certification shall be open to public inspection.

This section shall not prevent a county employee from giving testimony under oath or making statements required to be made under penalty for perjury or contempt.

This section shall not prohibit a county employee from holding an elective or appointive office in a city, town or district nor in any way prohibit such an employee from performing the duties or receiving the compensation provided for such office. No such elected or appointed official may vote or act on any matter which is within the purview of the agency by which he is employed or over which such employee has official responsibility.

SECTION 12
Former county employees; acting as attorney or receiving compensation from other than county; partners of employees or former employees; or legislators

(a) A former county employee who knowingly acts as agent or attorney for or receives compensation directly or indirectly from anyone other than a county or a county agency in connection with any particular matter in which the county or a county agency of the same county is a party or has a direct and substantial interest and in which he participated as a county employee while so employed, or

(b) A former county employee who, within one year after his last employment has ceased, appears personally before any agency of the county as agent or attorney for anyone other than the county in connection with any particular matter in which the county or a county agency of the same county is a party or has a direct and substantial interest and which was under his official responsibility as a county employee at any time within a period of two years prior to the termination of his employment, or

(c) A partner of a former county employee who knowingly engages, during a period of one year following the termination of the latter's employment by the county, in any activity in which the former county employee is himself prohibited from engaging by clause (a), or

(d) A partner of a county employee who knowingly acts as agent or attorney for anyone other than the county in connection with any particular matter in which the county or a county agency of the same county is a party or has a direct and substantial interest and in which the county employee participates or has participated as a county employee or which is the subject of his official responsibility, shall be punished by a fine of not more than $10,000, or by imprisonment in the state prison for not more than 5 years, or in a jail or house of correction for not more than 2½ years, or both.

If a partner of a special county employee or of a former county employee is also a member of another partnership in which the special or former employee has no interest, activities of the latter partnership in which the special or former employee takes no part shall not thereby be subject to clause (c) or (d).

This section shall not prevent a present or former special county employee from aiding or assisting another person for compensation in the performance of work under a contract with or for the benefit of the county; provided, that the head of the special county employee's department or agency has certified in writing that the interest of the county requires such aid or assistance and the certification has been filed with the state ethics commission. The certification shall be open to public inspection.

SECTION 13
Financial interest of county employees, relatives or associates; disclosure

(a) Except as permitted by paragraph (b), a county employee who participates as such an employee in a particular matter in which to his knowledge he, his immediate family or partner, a business organization which he is serving as officer, director, trustee, partner or employee, or any person or organization with whom he is negotiating or has any arrangement concerning prospective employment, has a financial interest, shall be punished by a fine of not more than $10,000, or by imprisonment in the state prison for not more than 5 years, or in a jail or house of correction for not more than 2½ years, or both.

(b) Any county employee whose duties would otherwise require him to participate in such a particular matter shall advise the official responsible for appointment to his position and the state ethics commission of the nature and circumstances of the particular matter and make full disclosure of such financial interest, and the appointing official shall thereupon either

(1) assign the particular matter to another employee; or

(2) assume responsibility for the particular matter; or

(3) make a written determination that the interest is not so substantial as to be deemed likely to affect the integrity of the services which the county may expect from the employee, in which case it shall not be a violation for the employee to participate in the particular matter. Copies of such written determination shall be forwarded to the county employee and filed with the state ethics commission by the person who made the determination. Such copy shall be retained by the commission for a period of six years.

SECTION 14
County employees; financial interests in contracts of county agency

A county employee who has a financial interest, directly or indirectly, in a contract made by a county agency of the same county, in which the county or a county agency is an interested party of which financial interest he has knowledge or has reason to know, shall be punished by a fine of not more than $10,000, or by imprisonment in the state prison for not more than 5 years, or in a jail or house of correction for not more than 2½ years, or both.

This section shall not apply if such financial interest consists of the ownership of less than one percent of the stock of a corporation.

This section shall not apply (a) to a county employee who in good faith and within thirty days after he learns of an actual or prospective violation of this section makes full disclosure of his financial interest to the contracting agency and terminates or disposes of the interest, or (b) to a county employee who does not participate in or have official responsibility for any of the activities of the contracting agency, if the contract is made through competitive bidding and his direct and indirect interests and those of his immediate family in the corporation or other commercial entity with which the contract is made do not in the aggregate amount to ten per cent of the total proprietary interests therein, or (c) to a special county employee who does not participate in or have official responsibility for any of the activities of the contracting agency and who files with the state ethics commission a statement making full disclosure of his interest and the interests of his immediate family in the contract, if the county commissioners approve the exemption of his interest from this section.

SECTION 15
County agency; unfair advantage in relation to particular matter; additional remedies; civil action for damages

(a) In addition to any other remedies provided by law, a violation of section 2, 3, 8, or sections 11 to 14, inclusive, or section 23 which has substantially influenced the action taken by any county agency in any particular matter, shall be grounds for avoiding, rescinding, or canceling the action on such terms as the interests of the county and innocent third persons shall require.

(b) In addition to the remedies set forth in subsection (a), the commission may, upon a finding pursuant to an adjudicatory proceeding that a person has acted to his economic advantage in violation of section 2, 3, 8, sections 11 to 14, inclusive, or section 23, issue an order (1) requiring the violator to pay the commission on behalf of the county damages in the amount of the economic advantage or $500, whichever is greater; and (2) requiring the violator to make restitution to an injured third party. If there has been no final criminal judgment of conviction or acquittal of the same violation, upon receipt of the written approval of the attorney general and the district attorney, the commission may order payment of additional damages in an amount not exceeding twice the amount of the economic advantage or $500, and payment of such additional damages shall bar any criminal prosecution for the same violation.

The maximum damages that the commission may order a violator to pay under this section shall be $25,000. If the commission determines that the damages authorized by this section exceed $25,000, it may bring a civil action against the violator to recover such damages.

(c) The remedies authorized by this section shall be in addition to any civil penalty imposed by the commission in accordance with clause (3) of subsection (j) of section 4 of chapter 268B.

SECTION 15A
Members of county commission or board; restrictions on appointments to certain positions

No member of a county commission or board shall be eligible for appointment or election by the members of such commission or board to any office or position under the supervision of such commission or board. No former member of such commission or board shall be so eligible until the expiration of thirty days from the termination of his service as a member of such commission or board.

2

SECTION 16
Repealed

SECTION 17
Municipal employees; gift or receipt of compensation from other than municipality; acting as agent or attorney

(a) No municipal employee shall, otherwise than as provided by law for the proper discharge of official duties, directly or indirectly receive or request compensation from anyone other than the city or town or municipal agency in relation to any particular matter in which the same city or town is a party or has a direct and substantial interest.

(b) No person shall knowingly, otherwise than as provided by law for the proper discharge of official duties, directly or indirectly give, promise or offer such compensation.

(c) No municipal employee shall, otherwise than in the proper discharge of his official duties, act as agent or attorney for anyone other than the city or town or municipal agency in prosecuting any claim against the same city or town, or as agent or attorney for anyone in connection with any particular matter in which the same city or town is a party or has a direct and substantial interest.

Whoever violates any provision of this section shall be punished by a fine of not more than $10,000, or by imprisonment in the state prison for not more than 5 years, or in a jail or house of correction for not more than 2½ years, or both.

A special municipal employee shall be subject to paragraphs (a) and (c) only in relation to a particular matter (a) in which he has at any time participated as a municipal employee, or (b) which is or within one year has been a subject of his official responsibility, or (c) which is pending in the municipal agency in which he is serving. Clause (c) of the preceding sentence shall not apply in the case of a special municipal employee who serves on no more than sixty days during any period of three hundred and sixty-five consecutive days.

This section shall not prevent a municipal employee from taking uncompensated action, not inconsistent with the faithful performance of his duties, to aid or assist any person who is the subject of disciplinary or other personnel administration proceedings with respect to those proceedings.

This section shall not prevent a municipal employee, including a special employee, from acting, with or without compensation, as agent or attorney for or otherwise aiding or assisting members of his immediate family or any person for whom he is serving as guardian, executor, administrator, trustee or other personal fiduciary except in those matters in which he has participated or which are the subject of his official responsibility; provided, that the official responsible for appointment to his position approves.

This section shall not prevent a present or former special municipal employee from aiding or assisting another person for compensation in the performance of work under a contract with or for the benefit of the city or town; provided, that the head of the special municipal employee's department or agency has certified in writing that the interest of the city or town requires such aid or assistance and the certification has been filed with the clerk of the city or town. The certification shall be open to public inspection.

This section shall not prevent a municipal employee from giving testimony under oath or making statements required to be made under penalty for perjury or contempt.

This section shall not prevent a municipal employee from applying on behalf of anyone for a building, electrical, wiring, plumbing, gas fitting, septic system permit, nor from receiving compensation in relation to any such permit, unless such employee is employed by or provides services to the permit-granting agency or an agency that regulates the activities of the permit-granting agency.

SECTION 18
Former municipal employee; acting as attorney or receiving compensation; from other than municipality; partners

(a) A former municipal employee who knowingly acts as agent or attorney for or receives compensation, directly or indirectly from anyone other than the same city or town in connection with any particular matter in which the city or town is a party or has a direct and substantial interest and in which he participated as a municipal employee while so employed, or (b) a former municipal employee who, within one year after his last employment has ceased, appears personally before any agency of the city or town as agent or attorney for anyone other than the city or town in connection with any particular matter in which the same city or town is a party or has a direct and substantial interest and which was under his official responsibility as a municipal employee at any time within a period of two years prior to the termination of his employment, or (c) a partner of a former municipal employee who knowingly engages, during a period of one year following the termination of the latter's employment by the city or town, in any activity in which the former municipal employee is himself prohibited from engaging by clause (a), or (d) a partner of a municipal employee who knowingly acts as agent or attorney for anyone other than the city or town in connection with any particular matter in which the same city or town is a party or has a direct and substantial interest and in which the municipal employee participates or has participated as a municipal employee or which is the subject of his official responsibility, shall be punished by a fine of not more than $10,000, or by imprisonment in the state prison for not more than 5 years, or in a jail or house of correction for not more than 2½ years, or both.

If a partner of a former municipal employee or of a special municipal employee is also a member of another partnership in which the former or special employee has no interest, the activities of the latter partnership in which the former or special employee takes no part shall not thereby be subject to clause (c) or (d).

Notwithstanding the provisions of clause (b), a former town counsel who acted in such capacity on a salary or retainer of less than two thousand dollars per year shall be prohibited from appearing personally before any agency of the city or town as agent or attorney for any one other than the city or town only in connection with any particular matter in which the same city or town is a party or has a direct and substantial interest and in which he participated while so employed.

This section shall not prevent a present or former special municipal employee from aiding or assisting another person for compensation in the performance of work under a contract with or for the benefit of the city or town; provided, that the head of the special municipal employee's department or agency has certified in writing that the interest of the city or town requires such aid or assistance and the certification has been filed with the clerk of the city or town. The certification shall be open to public inspection.

SECTION 19
Municipal employees, relatives or associates; financial interest in particular matter

(a) Except as permitted by paragraph (b), a municipal employee who participates as such an employee in a particular matter in which to his knowledge he, his immediate family or partner, a business organization in which he is serving as officer, director, trustee, partner or employee, or any person or organization with whom he is negotiating or has any arrangement concerning prospective employment, has a financial interest, shall be punished by a fine of not more than $10,000, or by imprisonment in the state prison for not more than 5 years, or in a jail or house of correction for not more than 2½ years, or both.

(b) It shall not be a violation of this section (1) if the municipal employee first advises the official responsible for appointment to his position of the nature and circumstances of the particular matter and makes full disclosure of such financial interest, and receives in advance a written determination made by that official that the interest is not so substantial as to be deemed likely to affect the integrity of the services which the municipality may expect from the employee, or (2) if, in the case of an elected municipal official making demand bank deposits of municipal funds, said official first files, with the clerk of the city or town, a statement making full disclosure of such financial interest, or (3) if the particular matter involves a determination of general policy and the interest of the municipal employee or members of his immediate family is shared with a substantial segment of the population of the municipality.

SECTION 20
Municipal employees; financial interest in contracts; holding one or more elected positions

(a) A municipal employee who has a financial interest, directly or indirectly, in a contract made by a municipal agency of the same city or town, in which the city or town is an interested party of which financial interest he has knowledge or has reason to know, shall be punished by a fine of not more than $10,000, or by imprisonment in the state prison for not more than 5 years, or in a jail or house of correction for not more than 2½ years, or both.

This section shall not apply if such financial interest consists of the ownership of less than one per cent of the stock of a corporation.

This section shall not apply (a) to a municipal employee who in good faith and within thirty days after he learns of an actual or prospective violation of this section makes full disclosure of his financial interest to the contracting agency and terminates or disposes of the interest, or (b) to a municipal employee who is not employed by the contracting agency or an agency which regulates the activities of the contracting agency and who does not participate in or have official responsibility for any of the activities of the contracting agency, if the contract is made after public notice or where applicable, through competitive bidding, and if the municipal employee files with the clerk of the city or town a statement making full disclosure of his interest and the interest of his immediate family, and if in the case of a contract for personal services

(1) the services will be provided outside the normal working hours of the municipal employee, (2) the services are not required as part of the municipal employee's regular duties, the employee is compensated for not more than five hundred hours during a calendar year, (3) the head of the contracting agency makes and files with the clerk of the city or town a written certification that no employee of that agency is available to perform those services as part of their regular duties, and (4) the city council, board of selectmen or board of aldermen approve the exemption of his interest from this section, or (c) to a special municipal employee who does not participate in or have official responsibility for any of the activities of the contracting agency and who files with the clerk of the city or town a statement making full disclosure of his interest and the interests of his immediate family in the contract, or (d) to a special municipal employee who files with the clerk of the city, town or district a statement making full disclosure of his interest and the interests of his immediate family in the contract, if the city council or board of aldermen, if there is no city council, board of selectmen or the district prudential committee, approve the exemption of his interest from this section, or (e) to a municipal employee who receives benefits from programs funded by the United States or any other source in connection with the rental, improvement, or rehabilitation of his residence to the extent permitted by the funding agency, or (f) to a municipal employee if the contract is for personal services in a part time, call or volunteer capacity with the police, fire, rescue or ambulance department of a fire district, town or any city with a population of less than thirty-five thousand inhabitants; provided, however, that the head of the contracting agency makes and files with the clerk of the city, district or town a written certification that no employee of said agency is available to perform such services as part of his regular duties, and the city council, board of selectmen, board of aldermen or district prudential committee approve the exemption of his interest from this section or (g) to a municipal employee who has applied in the usual course and is otherwise eligible for a housing subsidy program administered by a local housing authority, unless the employee is employed by the local housing authority in a capacity in which he has responsibility for the administration of such subsidy programs or (h) to a municipal employee who is the owner of residential rental property and rents such property to a tenant receiving a rental subsidy administered by a local housing authority, unless such employee is employed by such local housing authority in a capacity in which he has responsibility for the administration of such subsidy programs.

This section shall not prohibit an employee or an official of a town from holding the position of selectman in such town nor in any way prohibit such employee from performing the duties of or receiving the compensation provided for such office; provided, however, that such selectman shall not, except as hereinafter provided, receive compensation for more than one office or position held in a town, but shall have the right to choose which compensation he shall receive; provided further, that no such selectman may vote or act on any matter which is within the purview of the agency by which he is employed or over which he has official responsibility; and provided further that no such selectman shall be eligible for appointment to any such additional position while he is still a member of the board of selectmen or for six months thereafter. Any violation of the provisions of this paragraph which

2

has substantially influenced the action taken by any municipal agency in any matter shall be grounds for avoiding, rescinding or canceling the action on such terms as the interest of the municipality and innocent third parties may require.

This section shall not prohibit any elected official in a town, whether compensated or uncompensated for such elected position, from holding one or more additional elected positions, in such town, whether such additional elected positions are compensated or uncompensated.

This section shall not prohibit an employee of a municipality with a city or town council form of government from holding the elected office of councillor in such municipality, nor in any way prohibit such an employee from performing the duties of or receiving the compensation provided for such office; provided, however, that no such councillor may vote or act on any matter which is within the purview of the agency by which he is employed or over which he has official responsibility; and provided further, that no councillor shall be eligible for appointment to such additional position while a member of said council or for six months thereafter. Any violation of the provisions of this paragraph which has substantially influenced the action taken by a municipal agency in any matter shall be grounds for avoiding, rescinding or canceling such action on such terms as the interest of the municipality and innocent third parties require. No such elected councillor shall receive compensation for more than one office or position held in a municipality, but shall have the right to choose which compensation he shall receive.

This section shall not prohibit an employee of a housing authority in a municipality from holding any elective office, other than the office of mayor, in such municipality nor in any way prohibit such employee from performing the duties of or receiving the compensation provided for such office; provided, however, that such elected officer shall not, except as otherwise expressly provided, receive compensation for more than one office or position held in a municipality, but shall have the right to choose which compensation he shall receive; provided further that no such elected official may vote or act on any matter which is within the purview of the housing authority by which he is employed; and provided further that no such elected official shall be eligible for appointment to any such additional position while he is still serving in such elective office or for six months thereafter. Any violation of the provisions of this paragraph which has substantially influenced the action taken by the housing authority in any matter shall be grounds for avoiding, rescinding, or canceling the action on such terms as the interest of the municipality and innocent third parties may require.

This section shall not prohibit an employee in a town having a population of less than three thousand five hundred persons from holding more than one appointed position with said town, provided that the board of selectmen approves the exemption of his interest from this section.

SECTION 21
Municipal agency; unfair advantage in relation to particular matter; additional remedies; civil action for damages

(a) In addition to any other remedies provided by law, a finding by the commission pursuant to an adjudicatory proceeding that there has been any violation of sections 2, 3, 8, 17 to 20, inclusive, or section 23, which has substantially

influenced the action taken by any municipal agency in any particular matter, shall be grounds for avoiding, rescinding or canceling the action of said municipal agency upon request by said municipal agency on such terms as the interests of the municipality and innocent third persons require.

(b) In addition to the remedies set forth in subsection (a), the commission may, upon a finding pursuant to an adjudicatory proceeding that a person has acted to his economic advantage in violation of sections 2, 3, 8, 17 to 20, inclusive, or section 23, may issue an order (1) requiring the violator to pay the commission on behalf of the municipality damages in the amount of the economic advantage or $500, whichever is greater; and (2) requiring the violator to make restitution to an injured third party. If there has been no final criminal judgment of conviction or acquittal of the same violation, upon receipt of the written approval of the district attorney, the commission may order payment of additional damages in an amount not exceeding twice the amount of the economic advantage or $500, and payment of such additional damages shall bar any criminal prosecution for the same violation. The maximum damages that the commission may order a violator to pay under this section shall be $25,000. If the commission determines that the damages authorized by this section exceed $25,000, it may bring a civil action against the violator to recover such damages.

(c) The remedies authorized by this section shall be in addition to any civil penalty imposed by the commission in accordance with clause (3) of subsection (j) of section 4 of chapter 268B.

SECTION 21A
Members of municipal commission or board; appointments to certain positions

Except as hereinafter provided, no member of a municipal commission or board shall be eligible for appointment or election by the members of such commission or board to any office or position under the supervision of such commission or board. No former member of such commission or board shall be so eligible until the expiration of thirty days from the termination of his service as a member of such commission or board.

The provisions of this section shall not apply to a member of a town commission or board, if such appointment or election has first been approved at an annual town meeting of the town.

SECTION 21B
Prospective municipal appointees; demanding undated resignations prohibited

No mayor, city manager, or town manager shall require a prospective appointee to a board, commission or position under his jurisdiction to submit as a condition precedent to said appointment an undated resignation from said board, commission or position. Whoever violates the provisions of this section shall be punished by a fine of not more than five hundred dollars.

SECTION 22
Opinions of corporation counsel, city solicitor or town counsel

Any municipal employee shall be entitled to the opinion of the corporation counsel, city solicitor or town counsel upon any question arising under this chapter relating to the duties, responsibilities and interests of such employee. All requests for such opinions by a subordinate municipal employee shall be made in confidence directly to the chief officer of the municipal agency in which he is employed, who shall in turn request in confidence such opinion of the corporation counsel, city solicitor or town counsel on behalf of such subordinate municipal employee, and all constitutional officers and chief officers or heads of municipal agencies may make direct confidential requests for such opinions on their own account. The town counsel or city solicitor shall file such opinion in writing with the city or town clerk and such opinion shall be a matter of public record; however, no opinion will be rendered by the town counsel or city solicitor except upon the submission of detailed existing facts which raise a question of actual or prospective violation of any provision of this chapter.

SECTION 23
Supplemental provisions; standards of conduct

(a) In addition to the other provisions of this chapter, and in supplement thereto, standards of conduct, as hereinafter set forth, are hereby established for all state, county, and municipal employees.

(b) No current officer or employee of a state, county or municipal agency shall knowingly, or with reason to know:

(1) accept other employment involving compensation of substantial value, the responsibilities of which are inherently incompatible with the responsibilities of his public office;

(2)(i) solicit or receive anything of substantial value for such officer or employee, which is not otherwise authorized by statute or regulation, for or because of the officer or employee's official position; or (ii) use or attempt to use such official position to secure for such officer, employee or others unwarranted privileges or exemptions which are of substantial value and which are not properly available to similarly situated individuals;

(3) act in a manner which would cause a reasonable person, having knowledge of the relevant circumstances, to conclude that any person can improperly influence or unduly enjoy his favor in the performance of his official duties, or that he is likely to act or fail to act as a result of kinship, rank, position or undue influence of any party or person. It shall be unreasonable to so conclude if such officer or employee has disclosed in writing to his appointing authority or, if no appointing authority exists, discloses in a manner which is public in nature, the facts which would otherwise lead to such a conclusion; or

(4) present a false or fraudulent claim to his employer for any payment or benefit of substantial value.

(c) No current or former officer or employee or a state, county or municipal agency shall knowingly, or with reason to know:

(1) accept employment or engage in any business or professional activity which will require him to disclose confidential information which he has gained by reason of his official position or authority;

(2) improperly disclose materials or data within the exemptions to the definition of public records as defined by section seven of chapter four, and were acquired by him in the course of his official duties nor use such information to further his personal interests.

(d) Any activity specifically exempted from any of the prohibitions in any other section of this chapter shall also be exempt from the provisions of this section. The state ethics commission, established by chapter two hundred and sixty-eight B, shall not enforce the provisions of this section with respect to any such exempted activity.

(e) Where a current employee is found to have violated the provisions of this section, appropriate administrative action as is warranted may also be taken by the appropriate constitutional officer, by the head of a state, county or municipal agency. Nothing in this section shall preclude any such constitutional officer or head of such agency from establishing and enforcing additional standards of conduct.

(f) The state ethics commission shall adopt regulations: (i) defining substantial value; provided, however, that substantial value shall not be less than $50; (ii) establishing exclusions for ceremonial privileges and exemptions; (iii) establishing exclusions for privileges and exemptions given solely because of family or friendship; and (iv) establishing additional exclusions for other situations that do not present a genuine risk of a conflict or the appearance of a conflict of interest.

SECTION 23A
Trustees of public institutions of higher learning; prohibited positions

No trustee of any public institution of higher education operated by the commonwealth shall be eligible to be appointed to or hold any other office or position with said institution for a period of three years next after the termination of his services as such trustee, or in the case of an elected student trustee at said institution, for a period of one year next after the termination of his services as such trustee; provided, however, that any such elected student trustee may accept and hold part-time employment at said institution while a student threat; and provided further, that a trustee may be appointed to or hold an unpaid office or position with said institution after his services as such trustee.

SECTION 24
Disclosures and certifications; form; public inspection

All disclosures and certifications provided for in this chapter and made in accordance with its provisions shall be made in writing and, unless otherwise specifically provided in this chapter, shall be kept open to inspection by the public by the official with whom such disclosure has been filed.

SECTION 25
Suspension of persons under indictment for misconduct in office; notice; compensation and fringe benefits; temporary replacements; reinstatement

An officer or employee of a county, city, town or district, howsoever formed, including, but not limited to, regional school districts and regional planning districts, or of any department, board, commission or agency thereof may, during any period such officer or employee is under indictment for misconduct in such office or employment or for misconduct in any elective or appointive public office, trust or employment at any time held by him, be suspended by the appointing authority, whether or not such appointment was subject to approval in any manner. Notice of said suspension shall be given in writing and delivered in hand to said person or his attorney, or sent by registered mail to said person at his residence, his place of business, or the office or place of employment from which he is being suspended. Such notice so given and delivered or sent shall automatically suspend the authority of such person to perform the duties of his office or employment until he is notified in like manner that his suspension is removed. A copy of any such notice together with an affidavit of service shall be filed as follows: in the case of a county, with the clerk of the superior court of the county in which the officer or employee is employed; in the case of a city, with the city clerk; in the case of a town, with the town clerk; in the case of a regional school district, with the secretary of the regional school district; and in the case of all other districts, with the clerk of the district.

Any person so suspended shall not receive any compensation or salary during the period of suspension, nor shall the period of his suspension be counted in computing his sick leave or vacation benefits or seniority rights, nor shall any person who retires from service while under such suspension be entitled to any pension or retirement benefits, notwithstanding any contrary provisions of law, but all contributions paid by him into a retirement fund, if any, shall be returned to him, subject to section 15 of chapter 32. The employer of a person so suspended shall immediately notify the retirement system of which the person is a member of the suspension and shall notify the retirement board of the outcome of any charges brought against the individual.

A suspension under this section shall not, in any way, be used to prejudice the rights of the suspended person either civilly or criminally. During the period of any such suspension, the appointing authority may fill the position of the suspended officer or employee on a temporary basis, and the temporary officer or employee shall have all the powers and duties of the officer or employee suspended.

Any such temporary officer or employee who is appointed as a member of a board, commission or agency may be designated as chairman.

If the criminal proceedings against the person suspended are terminated without a finding or verdict of guilty on any of the charges on which he was indicted, his suspension shall be forthwith removed, and he shall receive all compensation or salary due him for the period of his suspension, and the time of his suspension shall count in determining sick leave, vacation, seniority and other rights, and shall be counted as creditable service for purposes of retirement.

SECTION 26
Penalty for violations of clause (B)(2) or (B)(4) of Sec. 23

(a) Any person who, directly or through another, with fraudulent intent, violates clause (2) or (4) of subsection (b) of section 23, or any person who, with fraudulent intent, causes any other person to violate said clauses (2) or (4) of said subsection (b) of said section 23 or with fraudulent intent offers or gives any privileges or exemptions of substantial value in violation of said clause (2) or (4) of said subsection (b) of said section 23 , shall be punished by a fine of not more than $10,000, or by imprisonment in the state prison for not more than 5 years, or in a jail or house of correction for not more than 2½ years, or both, if the unwarranted privileges or exemptions have a fair market value in the aggregate of more than $1,000 in any 12 month period.

SECTION 27
Publication of summaries of Chapter 268A; filing of acknowledgment by employees

The commission shall prepare, and update as necessary, summaries of this chapter for state, county, and municipal employees, respectively, which the commission shall publish on its official website. Every state, county and municipal employee shall, within 30 days of becoming such an employee, and on an annual basis thereafter, be furnished with a summary of this chapter prepared by the commission and sign a written acknowledgment that he has been provided with such a summary. Municipal employees shall be furnished with the summary by, and file an acknowledgment with, the city or town clerk. Appointed state and county employees shall be furnished with the summary by, and file an acknowledgment with, the employee's appointing authority or his designee. Elected state and county employees shall be furnished with the summary by, and file an acknowledgment with, the commission. The commission shall establish procedures for implementing this section and ensuring compliance.

SECTION 28
Online training programs

The state ethics commission shall prepare and update from time to time the following online training programs, which the commission shall publish on its official website: (1) a program which shall provide a general introduction to the requirements of this chapter; and (2) a program which shall provide information on the requirements of this chapter applicable to former state, county, and municipal employees. Every state, county, and municipal employee shall, within 30 days after becoming such an employee, and every 2 years thereafter, complete the online training program. Upon completion of the online training program, the employee shall provide notice of such completion to be retained for 6 years by the appropriate employer.

The commission shall establish procedures for implementing this section and ensuring compliance.

SECTION 29
Municipal liaisons to state ethics commission

Each municipality, acting through its city council, board of selectmen, or board of aldermen, shall designate a senior level employee of the municipality as its liaison to the state ethics commission. The municipality shall notify the commission in writing of any change to such designation within 30 days of such change. The commission shall disseminate information to the designated liaisons and conduct educational seminars for designated liaisons on a regular basis on a schedule to be determined by the commission in consultation with the municipalities.

Chapter 268B. Financial Disclosure by Certain Public Officials and Employees

Section
1   Definitions
2   State ethics commission
3   Powers and duties of commission
4   Investigations by the commission
5   Statements of financial interests
6   Gifts from executive or legislative agents
7   Penalties for violation of confidentiality and for perjury
8   Discipline against employee or officer for filing complaint prohibited

SECTION 1
Definitions

As used in this chapter, the following words shall, unless the context clearly requires otherwise have the following meanings:

"Amount", a category of value, rather than an exact dollar figure, as follows: greater than $1,000 but not more than $5,000; greater than $5,000 but not more than $10,000; greater than $10,000 but not more than $20,000; greater than $20,000 but not more than $40,000; greater than $40,000 but not more than $60,000; greater than $60,000 but not more than $100,000; greater than $100,000.

"Business", any corporation, partnership, sole proprietorship, firm, franchise, association, organization, holding company, joint stock company, receivership, business or real estate trust or any other legal entity organized for profit or charitable purposes.

"Business with which he is associated", any business in which the reporting person or a member of his immediate family is a general partner, proprietor, officer or other employee, including one who is self-employed or serves as a director, trustee or in any similar managerial capacity and any business more than 1 per cent of any class of the outstanding equity of which is beneficially owned in the aggregate by the reporting person and members of his immediate family.

"Candidate for public office", any individual who seeks nomination or election to public office; provided, however, that , an individual shall be deemed to be seeking nomination or election to public office if he has: (1) received a political contribution or made an expenditure, or has given his consent for any other person or committee to receive a political contribution or make an expenditure, for the purpose of influencing his nomination or election to such office, whether or not the specific public office for which he will seek nomination or election is known at the time the political contribution is received or the expenditure is made; or (2) taken the action necessary under the laws of the commonwealth to qualify himself for nomination or election to such office.

"Commission", the state ethics commission established by section 2;

"Equity", any stock or similar ownership interest in a business.

"Executive agent", an executive agent as defined in section 39 of chapter 3.

"Gift", a payment, entertainment, subscription, advance, services or anything of value, unless consideration of equal or greater value is received; provided, however, that "gift" shall not include a political contribution reported as required by law, a commercially reasonable loan made in the ordinary course of business, anything of value received by inheritance or a gift received from a member of the reporting person's immediate family or from a relative within the third degree of consanguinity of the reporting person or of the reporting person's spouse or from the spouse of any such relative.

"Governmental body", a state or county agency, authority, board, bureau, commission, council, department, division or other entity, including the general court and the courts of the commonwealth.

"Immediate family", a spouse and any dependent children residing in the reporting person's household.

"Income", income from whatever source derived, whether in the form of a fee, salary, allowance, forebearance, forgiveness, interest, dividend, royalty, rent, capital gain or any other form of recompense or any combination thereof; provided, however, that interest from savings accounts or from government obligations other than those of the commonwealth or any political subdivision thereof or any public agency or authority created by the general court, alimony and support payments, proceeds from a life insurance policy, retirement or disability benefits and social security payments shall not be considered income for the purposes of this chapter.

"Legislative agent", a legislative agent as defined in section 39 of chapter 3.

"Major policymaking position", the executive or administrative head of a governmental body, all members of the judiciary, any person whose salary equals or exceeds that of a state employee classified in step 1 of job group XXV of the general salary schedule contained in section 46 of chapter 30 and who reports directly to said executive or administrative head, the head of each division, bureau or other major administrative unit within such governmental body and persons exercising similar authority.

"Person", a business, individual, corporation, union, association, firm, partnership, committee or other organization or group of persons.

"Political contribution", a contribution of money or anything of value to an individual, candidate, political committee or person acting on behalf of an individual, candidate or political committee, for the purpose of influencing the nomination or election of the individual or candidate or for the purpose of promoting or opposing a charter change, referendum question, constitutional amendment or other question submitted to the voters and shall include any: (1) gift, subscription, loan, advance, deposit of money, or thing of value, except a loan of money to a candidate by a national or state bank made in accordance with the applicable banking laws and regulations and in the ordinary course of business; (2) transfer of money or anything of value between political committees; (3) payment, by any person other than a candidate or political committee, or compensation for the personal services of another person which are rendered to such candidate or committee; (4) purchase from an individual, candidate or political committee, or person acting on behalf of an individual, candidate or political committee, whether through the device of tickets, advertisements, or otherwise, for fund-raising activities, including testimonials, held on behalf of said individual, candidate or political committee, to the extent that the purchase price exceeds the actual cost of the goods sold or services rendered; (5) discount or rebate not available to other candidates

2

for the same office and to the general public; and (6) forgiveness of indebtedness or payment of indebtedness by another person; provided, however, that political contribution shall not include the rendering of services by speakers, editors, writers, poll watchers, poll checkers or others, or the payment by those rendering such services of such personal expenses as may be incidental thereto, or the exercise of ordinary hospitality.

"Public employee", a person who holds a major policy-making position in a governmental body; provided, however, that a person who receives no compensation other than reimbursements for expenses, or any person serving on a governmental body that has no authority to expend public funds other than to approve reimbursements for expenses shall not be considered a public employee for the purposes of this chapter; provided, further, that the members of the board of bar examiners shall not be considered public employees for the purposes of this chapter.

"Public office", a position for which one is nominated at a state primary or chosen at a state election, excluding the positions of senator and representative in congress and the office of regional district school committee member elected district-wide.

"Public official", a person who holds a public office.

"Reporting person", a person required to file a statement of financial interest pursuant to section 5.

SECTION 2
State ethics commission

(a) There is established a state ethics commission composed of five members. At no time shall more than three members be from the same political party.

(b) Three members of the commission shall be appointed by the governor, one of whom shall be designated as chairman, and one member shall be appointed by the state secretary and one member shall be appointed by the attorney general. At no time shall more than two of the members to be appointed by the governor be from the same political party.

(c) Members of the commission shall serve for terms of five years.

(d) No person shall be appointed to more than one full five year term on the commission.

(e) Not less than thirty days prior to making any appointment to the commission, the appointing official shall give public notice that a vacancy on the commission exists.

(f) No member or employee of the commission shall:

(1) hold or be a candidate for any other public office while a member or employee or for one year thereafter;

(2) hold office in any political party or political committee;

(3) participate in or contribute to the political campaign of any candidate for public office.

(g) Members of the commission may be removed by a majority vote of the governor, state secretary, and attorney general, for substantial neglect of duty, inability to discharge the powers and duties of office, violation of subsection (f) of this section, gross misconduct, or conviction of a felony.

(h) Any vacancy occurring on the commission shall be filled within ninety days by the original appointing authority. A person appointed to fill a vacancy occurring other than by expiration of a term of office shall be appointed for the unexpired term of the member he succeeds, and shall be eligible for appointment to one full five year term.

(i) The commission shall elect a vice chairman. The vice chairman shall act as chairman in the absence of the chairman or in the event of a vacancy in that position.

(j) Three members of the commission shall constitute a quorum and three affirmative votes shall be required for any action or recommendation of the commission; the chairman or any three members of the commission may call a meeting; advance notice of all meetings shall be given to each member of the commission and to any other person who requests such notice;

(k) Members of the commission shall be compensated for work performed for the commission at such rate as the secretary of administration and finance shall determine, and shall be reimbursed for their expenses.

(l) The commission shall annually report to the general court and the governor concerning the action it has taken; the names and salaries and duties of all individuals in its employ and the money it has disbursed; and shall make such further reports on matters within its jurisdiction as may appear necessary;

(m) The commission shall employ an executive director, a general counsel, and, subject to appropriation, such other staff, including but not limited to clerks, accountants, and investigators, as are necessary to carry out its duties pursuant to this chapter and chapter 268A. The staff shall serve at the pleasure of the commission and shall not be subject to the provisions of chapter 31 or section 9A of chapter 30. The executive director shall be responsible for the administrative operation of the commission and shall perform such other tasks as the commission shall determine. The general counsel shall be the chief legal officer of the commission. The commission may employ, subject to appropriation, the services of experts and consultants necessary to carry out its duties. The colonel of state police, the state auditor, the comptroller, the attorney general, and the director of the office of campaign and political finance may make available to the commission personnel and other assistance as the commission may request.

SECTION 3
Powers and duties of commission
(Amended by 2016 Mass. Acts c. 121, § 15, effective Jan. 1, 2017 per 2016 Mass. Acts c. 121, § 22.)

The commission shall:

(a) prescribe and publish, pursuant to chapter 30A, rules and regulations: (1) to carry out this chapter, including rules governing the conduct of proceedings hereunder; and (2) to carry out chapter 268A; provided, however, that the rules and regulations shall be limited to providing exemptions from the provisions of sections 3 to 7, inclusive, sections 11 to 14, inclusive, sections 17 to 20, inclusive, and section 23 of said chapter 268A;

(b) prepare and publish, after giving the public an opportunity to comment, forms for the statements and reports required to be filed by this chapter and make such forms available to any and all persons required to file statements and reports pursuant to the provisions of this chapter;

(c) prepare and publish, pursuant to the provisions of chapter thirty A, methods of accounting and reporting to be used by persons required to file statements and reports by this chapter;

(d) make statements and reports filed with the commission available for public inspection and copying during regular office hours upon the written request of any individual who provides identification acceptable to the commission, including his affiliation, if any, at a charge not to exceed the actual administrative and material costs required in reproducing said statements and reports; provided, however, that the commission may make statements and reports filed with the commission available by electronic mail in a read-only format upon the written request of any individual that delivers the request by electronic mail and provides identification acceptable to the commission, including the individual's affiliation, if any; provided, however, that the commission shall be authorized, in its discretion, to exempt from public disclosure those portions of a statement of financial interest filed pursuant to section five which contain the home address of the filer; and provided, further, that the commission shall forward a copy of said request to the person whose statement has been examined;

(e) compile and maintain an index of all reports and statements filed with the commission to facilitate public access to such reports and statements;

(f) inspect all statements of financial interests filed with the commission in order to ascertain whether any reporting person has failed to file such a statement or has filed a deficient statement. If, upon inspection, it is ascertained that a reporting person has failed to file a statement of financial interests, or if it is ascertained that any such statement filed with the commission fails to conform with the requirements of section five of this chapter, then the commission shall, in writing, notify the delinquent; such notice shall state in detail the deficiency and the penalties for failure to file a statement of financial interests;

(g) upon written request from a person who is or may be subject to the provisions of this chapter or chapter two hundred and sixty-eight A, render advisory opinions on the requirements of said chapters. An opinion rendered by the commission, until and unless amended or revoked, shall be a defense in a criminal action brought under chapter two hundred and sixty-eight A and shall be binding on the commission in any subsequent proceedings concerning the person who requested the opinion and who acted in good faith, unless material facts were omitted or misstated by the person in the request for an opinion. Such requests shall be confidential; provided, however, that the commission may publish such opinions, but the name of the requesting person and any other identifying information shall not be included in such publication unless the requesting person consents to such inclusion;

(h) preserve all statements and reports filed with the commission for a period of six years from the date of receipt;

(i) act as the primary civil enforcement agency for violations of all sections of chapter two hundred and sixty-eight A and of this chapter;

(j) on or before February first of each year the executive director of the commission shall request a list of all major policymaking positions for the governmental bodies below from the persons listed below:

(1) the house of representatives, the speaker of the house;

(2) the senate, the president of the senate;

(3) the state secretary's office, the state secretary;

(4) the attorney general's office, the attorney general;

(5) the state auditor's office, the state auditor;

(6) the treasurer and receiver general's office, the state treasurer;

(7) for each court of the commonwealth, the chief judge of such court;

(8) for each executive office in the commonwealth and all governmental bodies within such executive office, the secretary for such executive office;

(9) the governor's office, the governor;

(10) the lieutenant governor's office, the lieutenant governor;

(11) for each county, the chairman of the county commissioners;

(12) for each authority or other governmental body not covered by clauses one through eleven above, the executive or administrative head of such authority or governmental body; and such persons shall furnish such lists within sixty days. The executive director may add any position that he determines to be a major policymaking position in such governmental body to such list. Any person aggrieved by such action of the executive director may appeal such action to the commission.

SECTION 4
Investigations by the commission

(a) Upon receipt of a sworn complaint signed under the penalties of perjury, or upon receipt of evidence which is deemed sufficient by the commission, the commission shall initiate a preliminary inquiry into any alleged violation of chapter 268A or 268B. At the commencement of a preliminary inquiry into any such alleged violation, the general counsel shall notify the attorney general in order to avoid overlapping civil and criminal investigations. All commission proceedings and records relating to a preliminary inquiry or initial staff review used to determine whether to initiate an inquiry shall be confidential, except that the general counsel may turn over to the attorney general, the United States Attorney or a district attorney of competent jurisdiction evidence which may be used in a criminal proceeding. The general counsel shall notify any person who is the subject of the preliminary inquiry of the existence of such inquiry and the general nature of the alleged violation within 30 days of the commencement of the inquiry.

(b) If a preliminary inquiry fails to indicate reasonable cause for belief that this chapter or said chapter two hundred and sixty-eight A has been violated, the commission shall immediately terminate the inquiry and so notify, in writing, the complainant, if any, and the person who had been the subject of the inquiry. All commission records and proceedings from any such preliminary inquiry, or from any initial staff review to determine whether to initiate an inquiry, shall be confidential.

(c) If a preliminary inquiry indicates reasonable cause for belief that this chapter or said chapter two hundred and sixty-eight A has been violated, the commission may, upon a majority vote, initiate an adjudicatory proceeding to determine whether there has been such a violation. The commission shall initiate such an adjudicatory proceeding within 5 years from the date the commission learns of the alleged violation, but no more than 6 years from the date of the last conduct relating to the alleged violation.

(d) The commission may require by summons the attendance and testimony of witnesses and the production of books, papers and other records relating to any matter being investigated by it pursuant to this chapter or said chapter two

2

hundred and sixty-eight A. Such summons may be issued by the commission only upon a majority vote of the commission and shall be served in the same manner as summonses for witnesses in civil cases, and all provisions of law relative to summonses issued in such cases, including the compensation of witnesses, shall apply to summonses issued by the commission. Such summonses shall have the same force, and be obeyed in the same manner, and under the same penalties in case of default, as if issued by order of a justice of the superior court and may be quashed only upon motion of the summonsed party and by order of a justice of the superior court.

(e) Any member of the commission may administer oaths and any member of the commission may hear testimony or receive other evidence in any proceeding before the commission.

(f) All testimony in a commission adjudicatory proceeding shall be under oath. All parties shall have the right to call and examine witnesses, to introduce exhibits, to cross-examine witnesses who testify, to submit evidence, and to be represented by counsel. Before testifying, all witnesses shall be given a copy of the regulations governing commission proceedings. All witnesses shall be entitled to be represented by counsel.

(g) Any person whose name is mentioned during an adjudicatory proceeding of the commission and who may be adversely affected thereby may appear personally before the commission on his own behalf, with or without an attorney, to give a statement in opposition to such adverse mention or file a written statement of such opposition for incorporation into the record of the proceeding.

(h) All adjudicatory proceedings of the commission carried out pursuant to the provisions of this section shall be public, unless the members vote to go into executive session.

(i) Within thirty days after the end of an adjudicatory proceeding pursuant to the provisions of this section, the commission shall meet in executive session for the purpose of reviewing the evidence before it. Within thirty days after completion of deliberations, the commission shall publish a written report of its findings and conclusions.

(j) The commission, upon a finding pursuant to an adjudicatory proceeding that there has been a violation of said chapter two hundred and sixty-eight A or a violation of this chapter, may issue an order requiring the violator to:

(1) cease and desist such violation of said chapter two hundred and sixty-eight A or this chapter;

(2) file any report, statement or other information as required by said chapter two hundred and sixty-eight A or this chapter; or

(3) pay a civil penalty of not more than $10,000 for each violation of this chapter or chapter 268A, with the exception of a violation of section 2 of chapter 268A, which shall be subject to a civil penalty of not more than $25,000.

The commission may file a civil action in superior court to enforce such order and any order issued by the commission in accordance with chapter 268A.

(k) Any final action by the commission made pursuant to chapter 268A or 268B shall be subject to review in superior court upon petition of any party in interest filed within thirty days after the action for which review is sought. The court shall enter a judgment enforcing, modifying or setting aside the order of the commission or it may remand the proceedings to the commission for such further action as the court may

direct. If the court modifies or sets aside the commission order or remands the proceedings to the commission, the court shall determine whether such modification, set aside or remand is substantial. If the court does find such modification, set aside or remand to be substantial, the employee shall be entitled to be reimbursed from the treasury of the commonwealth for reasonable attorneys' fees and all court costs incurred by him in the defense of the charges contained in said proceedings. The amount of such reimbursement shall be awarded by the court, but shall not exceed $30,000 per person, per case. Reimbursement of such costs shall be applicable to state, county or municipal employees whose conduct is so regulated by the provisions of chapter two hundred and sixty-eight A and this chapter.

(l) The superior court shall have concurrent jurisdiction to issue orders under paragraph (j) in a civil action brought by the attorney general. In any such action, an advisory opinion of the commission under clause (g) of section 3 shall be binding to the same extent as it is against the commission under that clause.

NOTE   Summons Under § 4(d). The commission may "compel an individual who is the subject of a preliminary inquiry into allegations of wrongdoing to appear before the commission and to testify, confidentially and under oath, regarding the allegations." *Doe v. State Ethics Comm'n*, 444 Mass. 269–70 (2005).

SECTION 5
Statements of financial interests

(a) Every candidate for public office shall file a statement of financial interest for the preceding calendar year with the commission on or before the date on which a certificate of nomination or nomination papers for such candidate are submitted to the state secretary. Every candidate for public office who has not filed nomination papers with the state secretary, but on whose behalf a statement of organization of a political committee has been filed with the director of campaign and political finance under section five of chapter fifty-five, and who is seeking public office by the so-called "write in" or "sticker" method, shall within three days after such filing file a statement of financial interest with the commission.

(b) Every public official shall file a statement of financial interest for the preceding calendar year with the commission on or before the last Tuesday in May of the year in which such public official first enters such public office and of each year that such public official holds such office, and on or before May first of the year after such public official leaves such office; provided, however, that no public official shall be required to file a statement of financial interests for the year in which he ceased to be a public official if he served for less than thirty days in such year.

(c) Every public employee shall file a statement of financial interest for the preceding calendar year with the commission within thirty days after becoming a public employee, on or before May first of each year thereafter that such person is a public employee and on or before May first of the year after such person ceases to be a public employee; provided, however, that no public employee shall be required to file a statement of financial interests for the year in which he ceased to be a public employee if he served less than thirty days in such year.

(d) The commission shall, upon receipt of a statement of financial interests pursuant to the provisions of this section, issue to the person filing such statement a receipt verifying the fact that a statement of financial interests has been filed and a receipted copy of such statement.

(e) No public employee shall be allowed to continue in his duties or to receive compensation from public funds unless he has filed a statement of financial interests with the commission as required by this chapter.

(f) The statement of financial interests filed pursuant to the provisions of this section shall be on a form prescribed by the commission and shall be signed under the penalty of perjury by the reporting person.

(g) Reporting persons shall disclose, to the best of their knowledge, the following information for the preceding calendar year, or as of the last day of said year with respect to the information required by clauses (2), (3) and (6) below; such persons shall also disclose the same information with respect to their immediate family provided, however, that no amount need be given for such information with regard to the reporting person's immediate family:

(1) the name and address of, the nature of association with, the share of equity in, if applicable, and the amount of income if greater than one thousand dollars derived from each business with which he is associated;

(2) the identity of all securities and other investments with a fair market value of greater than one thousand dollars which were beneficially owned, not otherwise reportable hereunder; and the amount of income if over one thousand dollars from any such security which is issued by the commonwealth or any political subdivision thereof or any public agency or authority created by the general court;

(3) the name and address of each creditor to whom more than one thousand dollars was owed and the original amount, the amount outstanding, the terms of repayment, and the general nature of the security pledged for each such obligation except that the original amount and the amount outstanding need not be reported for a mortgage on the reporting person's primary residence; provided, however, that obligations arising out of retail installment transactions, educational loans, medical and dental expenses, debts incurred in the ordinary course of business, and any obligation to make alimony or support payments, shall not be reported; and provided, further, that such information need not be reported if the creditor is a relative of the reporting person within the third degree of consanguinity or affinity;

(4) the name and address of the source, and the cash value of any reimbursement for expenses aggregating more than one hundred dollars in the calendar year if the source of such reimbursement is a legislative or executive agent; or if the recipient is a public official and the source of such reimbursement is a person having a direct interest in legislation, legislative action, or a matter before a governmental body; or if the recipient is a public employee and the source of such reimbursement is person having a direct interest in a matter before the governmental body by which the recipient is employed;

(5) the name and address of the donor, and the fair market value, if determinable, of any gifts aggregating more than one hundred dollars in the calendar year, if the recipient is a public official and the source of such gift(s) is a person having a direct interest in legislation, legislative action, or a matter before a governmental body; or if the recipient is a public employee and the source of such gift(s) is a person having a direct interest in a matter before the governmental body by which the recipient is employed.

(6) the description, as appearing on the most recent tax bill, and the amount of assessed value of all real property located within the commonwealth in which a direct or indirect financial interest was held, which has an assessed value greater than one thousand dollars; and, if the property was transferred during the year, the name and address of the person furnishing consideration to the reporting person or receiving it from him in respect to such transfer;

(7) the name and address of the source, and the fair market value, of any honoraria aggregating more than one hundred dollars if the source of such honoraria is a legislative agent; or if the recipient is a public official and the source of such honoraria is a person having a direct interest in legislation, legislative action, or a matter before a governmental body; or if the recipient is a public employee and the source of such honoraria is a person having a direct interest in a matter before the governmental body by which the recipient is employed;

(8) the name and address of any creditor who has forgiven an indebtedness of over one thousand dollars, and the amount forgiven; provided, however, that no such information need be reported if the creditor is a relative within the third degree of consanguinity or affinity of the reporting person, or the spouse of such a relative;

(9) the name and address of any business from which the reporting person is taking a leave of absence;

(10) the identity of any equity in a business with which the reporting person is associated which has been transferred to a member of the reporting person's immediate family; provided, however, that a member of the reporting person's family need not report any such transfer to the reporting person.

Nothing in this section shall be construed to require the disclosure of information which is privileged by law.

Failure of a reporting person to file a statement of financial interests within ten days after receiving notice as provided in clause (f) of section three of this chapter, or the filing of an incomplete statement of financial interests after receipt of such a notice, is a violation of this chapter and the commission may initiate appropriate proceedings pursuant to the provisions of section *four*.

SECTION 6
Gifts from executive or legislative agents
(Amended by 2011 Mass. Acts c. 194, § 50, effective Nov. 22, 2011.)

No executive or legislative agent shall knowingly and willfully offer or give to any public official or public employee or a member of such person's immediate family, and no public official or public employee or member of such person's immediate family shall knowingly and willfully solicit or accept from any executive or legislative agent, any gift of any kind or nature; provided, however, that the state ethics commission shall promulgate regulations: (i) establishing exclusions for ceremonial gifts; (ii) establishing exclusions for gifts given solely because of family or friendship; and (iii) establishing additional exclusions for other situations that do not present a genuine risk of a conflict or the appearance of a conflict of interest.

For the purposes of this section, a person who holds a license issued by the Massachusetts gaming commission, who was required to apply for that license pursuant to section 14 of chapter 23K, shall be considered a legislative agent.

2

SECTION 7
Penalties for violation of confidentiality and for perjury

Any person who violates the confidentiality of a commission inquiry under the provisions of paragraph (a) of section 4 of this chapter shall be punished by a fine of not more than one thousand dollars or by imprisonment for not more than one year, or both.

Any person who willfully affirms or swears falsely in regard to any material before a commission proceeding under paragraph (c) of section four of this chapter, or who willfully files a materially false statement of financial interests under section five of this chapter shall be punished by a fine of not more than $10,000, or by imprisonment in the state prison for not more than 5 years, or in a jail or house of correction for not more than 2½ years, or both.

NOTE   **Related Statute.** G.L. c. 268, § 1—Perjury.

SECTION 8
Discipline against employee or officer for filing complaint prohibited

No officer or employee of the commonwealth or of any county, city or town shall discharge an officer or employee, or change his official rank, grade or compensation, or deny him a promotion, or threaten so to do, for filing a complaint with or providing information to the commission or testifying in any commission proceeding.

Chapter 269. Crimes Against Public Peace

Section

1	Dispersing and suppressing unlawful assembly; arresting persons
2	Refusing or neglecting to depart or to assist in suppressing assembly or in arresting persons
3	Neglect or refusal to exercise authority to suppress assembly
4	Requiring aid; dispersing and suppressing assembly; seizure of persons
5	Armed forces obeying orders for suppressing riot and dispersing and arresting persons
6	Person killed or wounded as result of an assembly; guilt and responsibility
7	Injury to building or vessel by persons unlawfully assembled; punishment; liability
8	Destruction of or damage to property by persons riotously assembled; liability of town; recovery
9	Repealed
10	Penalty for unlawfully carrying dangerous weapons, possessing machine gun, etc.
10A	Selling, giving or using silencers; penalty; confiscation and destruction
10B	Repealed
10C	Use of tear gas, etc., in commission of crime; penalty
10D	Use or wearing of body armor in commission of crime; penalty
10E	Firearms sales; penalties; eligibility for probation, parole, furlough or work release
10F	Illegal sale, gifts or transfer of large capacity weapons or large capacity feeding devices; punishment
10G	Violations of Sec. 10 by persons previously convicted of violent crimes or serious drug offenses; punishment
10H	Carrying loaded firearm while under influence of liquor, marijuana, narcotic drugs, depressants or stimulant substances; punishment
11	Printing statutes for posters; sending copies to clerks and superintendents of schools in cities and towns; duties; costs
11A	Definitions
11B	Possession or control of firearm with serial or identification number removed or mutilated; while committing or attempting a felony; destruction
11C	Removal or mutilation of serial or identification numbers of firearms; receiving such firearm; possession or control as evidence; destruction
11D	Repealed
11E	Serial identification numbers on firearms; penalty
12	Manufacturing and selling knives, slung shots, swords, bludgeons and similar weapons; punishment
12A	Selling or furnishing air rifle to minor
12B	Possession of air rifle by minor under eighteen; shooting air rifle; disposition on conviction for violation
12C	Repealed
12D	Carrying rifle or shotgun having shells or cartridges therein on public way prohibited; exceptions; penalty
12E	Discharge of a firearm within 500 feet of a dwelling or other building in use; exceptions
12F	Cutting device in airport or airplane; penalties

13	False alarms of fire
13A	False reports to police officers
14	Explosives or other dangerous substance or contrivance; false reports as to location; punishment
14A	Annoying telephone calls or electronic communication
14B	False reports to emergency response services provider
15	Sale of stink bombs
16	Sale of broadheads, razorheads, or other hunting arrowheads
17	Hazing; organizing or participating; hazing defined
18	Failure to report hazing
19	Copy of Secs. 17–19; issuance to student and student groups, teams and organizations; report

SECTION 1
Dispersing and suppressing unlawful assembly; arresting persons

If five or more persons, being armed with clubs or other dangerous weapons, or if ten or more persons, whether armed or not, are unlawfully, riotously or tumultuously assembled in a city or town, the mayor and each of the aldermen of such city, each of the selectmen of such town, every justice of the peace living in any such city or town, any member of the city, town, or state police and the sheriff of the county and his deputies shall go among the persons so assembled, or as near to them as may be with safety, and in the name of the commonwealth command all persons so assembled immediately and peaceably to disperse; and if they do not thereupon immediately and peaceably disperse, each of said magistrates and officers shall command the assistance of all persons there present in suppressing such riot or unlawful assembly and arresting such person. For the purposes of this section, the University of Massachusetts at Amherst shall be considered a town.

SECTION 2
Refusing or neglecting to depart or to assist in suppressing assembly or in arresting persons

Whoever, being present and being so commanded to assist in arresting such rioters or persons so unlawfully assembled, or in suppressing such riot or unlawful assembly, refuses or neglects to obey such command, or, if required by such magistrate or officer to depart from the place, refuses or neglects so to do, shall be considered one of the rioters or persons unlawfully assembled, and shall be punished by imprisonment for not more than one year or by a fine of not less than one hundred dollars or more than five hundred dollars, or both.

SECTION 3
Neglect or refusal to exercise authority to suppress assembly

A mayor, alderman, selectman, justice of the peace, sheriff or deputy sheriff who, having notice of any such riotous or tumultuous and unlawful assembly in the city or town where he lives, neglects or refuses immediately to proceed to the place of such assembly, or as near thereto as he can with safety, or omits or neglects to exercise the authority conferred upon him by this chapter for suppressing such assembly and for arresting the offenders, shall be punished by a fine of not more than three hundred dollars.

SECTION 4
Requiring aid; dispersing and suppressing assembly; seizure of persons

If any persons who are so riotously or unlawfully assembled, and who have been commanded to disperse, as before provided, refuse or neglect to disperse without unnecessary delay, any two of the magistrates or officers before mentioned may require the aid of a sufficient number of persons, in arms or otherwise as may be necessary, and shall proceed, in such manner as they deem expedient, forthwith to disperse and suppress such assembly, and seize and secure the persons composing the same, so that they may be proceeded with according to law.

SECTION 5
Armed forces obeying orders for suppressing riot and dispersing and arresting persons

When an armed force, called out under chapter thirty-three to suppress a tumult or riot, or to disperse a body of men acting together by force and with intent to commit a felony, or to offer violence to persons or property, or with intent by force or violence to resist or oppose the execution of the laws of the commonwealth, arrives at the place of such unlawful, riotous or tumultuous assembly, its members shall obey such orders for suppressing the riot or tumult, and for dispersing and arresting all persons who are committing any of said offenses, as they have received from the governor, or a judge of a court of record, or the sheriff of the county, and also such orders as they there receive from any two of the magistrates or officers before mentioned.

SECTION 6
Person killed or wounded as result of an assembly; guilt and responsibility

If, by reason of the efforts made by any two or more of said magistrates or officers or by their direction to disperse such assembly, or to seize and secure the persons composing the same who have refused to disperse, though the number remaining may be less than five, any such person or any other person then present is killed or wounded, the magistrates and officers, and all persons acting by their order or under their direction, and all persons acting under the two preceding sections, shall be held guiltless, and fully justified in law; and if any of said magistrates or officers, or any person acting under or by the direction of any of the officers before mentioned, is killed or wounded, all persons so assembled, and all other persons who, when commanded or required, refused to aid and assist said magistrates or officers, shall be held answerable therefor.

SECTION 7
Injury to building or vessel by persons unlawfully assembled; punishment; liability

If any of the persons so unlawfully assembled demolishes, pulls down or destroys, or begins to demolish, pull down or destroy, a dwelling house or other building, or a ship or vessel, he shall be punished by imprisonment in the state prison for not more than five years or by a fine of not more than one thousand dollars and imprisonment in jail for not more than two years, and shall also be liable in tort to any person for all damages sustained by him thereby.

SECTION 8
Destruction of or damage to property by persons riotously assembled; liability of town; recovery

If property of the value of fifty dollars or more is destroyed or if property is damaged to that amount or to a value in excess thereof by fifteen or more persons who are riotously or tumultuously assembled and provided that the activities of such riotous or tumultuous group are observed and reported to the police during the period that such activities are occurring, the town within which the property was situated shall, if the owner of such property uses all reasonable diligence to prevent said destruction or damage and to procure the conviction of the offenders, be liable to indemnify the owner thereof in tort to the amount of three-fourth's of the value of the property destroyed or of the amount of such damage thereto, and may recover the same against any or all of the persons who so destroyed or damaged such property.

SECTION 9
Repealed

SECTION 10
Penalty for unlawfully carrying dangerous weapons, possessing machine gun, etc.
(Amended by 2014 Mass. Acts c. 284, §§ 89, 92, effective Aug. 11, 2014, 2014 Mass. Acts c. 284, § 90, effective Jan. 1, 2015. Bracketed text in subsection (m) deleted effective Jan. 1, 2021 by 2014 Mass. Acts c. 284, § 91.)

(a) Whoever, except as provided or exempted by statute, knowingly has in his possession; or knowingly has under his control in a vehicle; a firearm, loaded or unloaded, as defined in section one hundred and twenty-one of chapter one hundred and forty without either:

(1) being present in or on his residence or place of business; or

(2) having in effect a license to carry firearms issued under section one hundred and thirty-one of chapter one hundred and forty; or

(3) having in effect a license to carry firearms issued under section one hundred and thirty-one F of chapter one hundred and forty; or

(4) having complied with the provisions of sections one hundred and twenty-nine C and one hundred and thirty-one G of chapter one hundred and forty; or

(5) having complied as to possession of an air rifle or BB gun with the requirements imposed by section twelve B; and whoever knowingly has in his possession; or knowingly has under control in a vehicle; a rifle or shotgun, loaded or unloaded, without either:

(1) being present in or on his residence or place of business; or

2

(2) having in effect a license to carry firearms issued under section one hundred and thirty-one of chapter one hundred and forty; or

(3) having in effect a license to carry firearms issued under section one hundred and thirty-one F of chapter one hundred and forty; or

(4) having in effect a firearms identification card issued under section one hundred and twenty-nine B of chapter one hundred and forty; or

(5) having complied with the requirements imposed by section one hundred and twenty-nine C of chapter one hundred and forty upon ownership or possession of rifles and shotguns; or

(6) having complied as to possession of an air rifle or BB gun with the requirements imposed by section twelve B; shall be punished by imprisonment in the state prison for not less than two and one-half years nor more than five years, or for not less than 18 months nor more than two and one-half years in a jail or house of correction. The sentence imposed on such person shall not be reduced to less than 18 months, nor suspended, nor shall any person convicted under this subsection be eligible for probation, parole, work release, or furlough or receive any deduction from his sentence for good conduct until he shall have served 18 months of such sentence; provided, however, that the commissioner of correction may on the recommendation of the warden, superintendent, or other person in charge of a correctional institution, grant to an offender committed under this subsection a temporary release in the custody of an officer of such institution for the following purposes only: to attend the funeral of a relative; to visit a critically ill relative; or to obtain emergency medical or psychiatric service unavailable at said institution. Prosecutions commenced under this subsection shall neither be continued without a finding nor placed on file.

No person having in effect a license to carry firearms for any purpose, issued under section one hundred and thirty-one or section one hundred and thirty-one F of chapter one hundred and forty shall be deemed to be in violation of this section.

The provisions of section eighty-seven of chapter two hundred and seventy-six shall not apply to any person 18 years of age or older, charged with a violation of this subsection, or to any child between ages fourteen and 18 so charged, if the court is of the opinion that the interests of the public require that he should be tried as an adult for such offense instead of being dealt with as a child.

The provisions of this subsection shall not affect the licensing requirements of section one hundred and twenty-nine C of chapter one hundred and forty which require every person not otherwise duly licensed or exempted to have been issued a firearms identification card in order to possess a firearm, rifle or shotgun in his residence or place of business.

(b) Whoever, except as provided by law, carries on his person, or carries on his person or under his control in a vehicle, any stiletto, dagger or a device or case which enables a knife with a locking blade to be drawn at a locked position, any ballistic knife, or any knife with a detachable blade capable of being propelled by any mechanism, dirk knife, any knife having a double-edged blade, or a switch knife, or any knife having an automatic spring release device by which the blade is released from the handle, having a blade of over one and one-half inches, or a slung shot, blowgun, blackjack, metallic knuckles or knuckles of any substance which could be put to the same use with the same or similar effect as metallic knuckles, nunchaku, zoobow, also known as klackers or kung fu sticks, or any similar weapon consisting of two sticks of wood, plastic or metal connected at one end by a length of rope, chain, wire or leather, a shuriken or any similar pointed starlike object intended to injure a person when thrown, or any armband, made with leather which has metallic spikes, points or studs or any similar device made from any other substance or a cestus or similar material weighted with metal or other substance and worn on the hand, or a manrikigusari or similar length of chain having weighted ends; or whoever, when arrested upon a warrant for an alleged crime, or when arrested while committing a breach or disturbance of the public peace, is armed with or has on his person, or has on his person or under his control in a vehicle, a billy or other dangerous weapon other than those herein mentioned and those mentioned in paragraph (a), shall be punished by imprisonment for not less than two and one-half years nor more than five years in the state prison, or for not less than six months nor more than two and one-half years in a jail or house of correction, except that if the court finds that the defendant has not been previously convicted of a felony, he may be punished by a fine of not more than fifty dollars or by imprisonment for not more than two and one-half years in a jail or house of correction.

(c) Whoever, except as provided by law, possesses a machine gun, as defined in section one hundred and twenty-one of chapter one hundred and forty, without permission under section one hundred and thirty-one of said chapter one hundred and forty; or whoever owns, possesses or carries on his person, or carries on his person or under his control in a vehicle, a sawed-off shotgun, as defined in said section one hundred and twenty-one of said chapter one hundred and forty, shall be punished by imprisonment in the state prison for life, or for any term of years provided that any sentence imposed under the provisions of this paragraph shall be subject to the minimum requirements of paragraph (a).

(d) Whoever, after having been convicted of any of the offenses set forth in paragraph (a), (b) or (c) commits a like offense or any other of the said offenses, shall be punished by imprisonment in the state prison for not less than five years nor more than seven years; for a third such offense, by imprisonment in the state prison for not less than seven years nor more than ten years; and for a fourth such offense, by imprisonment in the state prison for not less than ten years nor more than fifteen years. The sentence imposed upon a person, who after a conviction of an offense under paragraph (a), (b) or (c) commits the same or a like offense, shall not be suspended, nor shall any person so sentenced be eligible for probation or receive any deduction from his sentence for good conduct.

(e) Upon conviction of a violation of this section, the firearm or other article shall, unless otherwise ordered by the court, be confiscated by the commonwealth. The firearm or article so confiscated shall, by the authority of the written order of the court be forwarded by common carrier to the colonel of the state police, who, upon receipt of the same, shall notify said court or justice thereof. Said colonel may sell or destroy the same, except that any firearm which may not be lawfully sold in the commonwealth shall be destroyed, and in the case of a sale, after paying the cost of forwarding the article, shall pay over the net proceeds to the commonwealth.

(f) The court shall, if the firearm or other article was lost by or stolen from the person lawfully in possession of it, order its return to such person.

(g) Whoever, within this commonwealth, produces for sale, delivers or causes to be delivered, orders for delivery, sells or offers for sale, or fails to keep records regarding, any rifle or shotgun without complying with the requirement of a serial number, as provided in section one hundred and twenty-nine B of chapter one hundred and forty, shall for the first offense be punished by confinement in a jail or house of correction for not more than two and one-half years, or by a fine of not more than five hundred dollars.

(h)(1) Whoever owns, possesses or transfers a firearm, rifle, shotgun or ammunition without complying with the provisions of section 129C of chapter 140 shall be punished by imprisonment in a jail or house of correction for not more than 2 years or by a fine of not more than $500. Whoever commits a second or subsequent violation of this paragraph shall be punished by imprisonment in a house of correction for not more than 2 years or by a fine of not more than $1,000, or both. Any officer authorized to make arrests may arrest without a warrant any person whom the officer has probable cause to believe has violated this paragraph.

(2) Any person who leaves a firearm, rifle, shotgun or ammunition unattended with the intent to transfer possession of such firearm, rifle, shotgun or ammunition to any person not licensed under section 129C of chapter 140 or section 131 of chapter 140 for the purpose of committing a crime or concealing a crime shall be punished by imprisonment in a house of correction for not more than 2½ years or in state prison for not more than 5 years.

(i) Whoever knowingly fails to deliver or surrender a revoked or suspended license to carry or possess firearms or machine guns issued under the provisions of section one hundred and thirty-one or one hundred and thirty-one F of chapter one hundred and forty, or firearm identification card, or receipt for the fee for such card, or a firearm, rifle, shotgun or machine gun, as provided in section one hundred and twenty-nine D of chapter one hundred and forty, unless an appeal is pending, shall be punished by imprisonment in a jail or house of correction for not more than two and one-half years or by a fine of not more than one thousand dollars.

(j) For the purposes of this paragraph, "firearm" shall mean any pistol, revolver, rifle or smoothbore arm from which a shot, bullet or pellet can be discharged.

Whoever, not being a law enforcement officer and notwithstanding any license obtained by the person pursuant to chapter 140, carries on the person a firearm, loaded or unloaded, or other dangerous weapon in any building or on the grounds of any elementary or secondary school, college or university without the written authorization of the board or officer in charge of the elementary or secondary school, college or university shall be punished by a fine of not more than $1,000 or by imprisonment for not more than 2 years or both. A law enforcement officer may arrest without a warrant and detain a person found carrying a firearm in violation of this paragraph.

Any officer in charge of an elementary or secondary school, college or university or any faculty member or administrative officer of an elementary or secondary school, college or university that fails to report a violation of this paragraph shall be guilty of a misdemeanor and punished by a fine of not more than $500.

[(k) *Deleted by 1983 Mass. Acts c. 516, § 3.*]

(l) The provisions of this section shall be fully applicable to any person proceeded against under section seventy-five of chapter one hundred and nineteen and convicted under section eighty-three of chapter one hundred and nineteen, provided, however, that nothing contained in this section shall impair, impede, or affect the power granted any court by chapter one hundred and nineteen to adjudicate a person a delinquent child, including the power so granted under section eighty-three of said chapter one hundred and nineteen.

(m) Notwithstanding the provisions of paragraph (a) or (h), any person not exempted by statute who knowingly has in his possession, or knowingly has under his control in a vehicle, a large capacity weapon or large capacity feeding device therefor who does not possess a valid [Class A or Class B] license to carry firearms issued under section 131 or 131F of chapter 140, except as permitted or otherwise provided under this section or chapter 140, shall be punished by imprisonment in a state prison for not less than two and one-half years nor more than ten years. The possession of a valid firearm identification card issued under section 129B shall not be a defense for a violation of this subsection; provided, however, that any such person charged with violating this paragraph and holding a valid firearm identification card shall not be subject to any mandatory minimum sentence imposed by this paragraph. The sentence imposed upon such person shall not be reduced to less than one year, nor suspended, nor shall any person convicted under this subsection be eligible for probation, parole, furlough, work release or receive any deduction from his sentence for good conduct until he shall have served such minimum term of such sentence; provided, however, that the commissioner of correction may, on the recommendation of the warden, superintendent or other person in charge of a correctional institution or the administrator of a county correctional institution, grant to such offender a temporary release in the custody of an officer of such institution for the following purposes only: (i) to attend the funeral of a spouse or next of kin; (ii) to visit a critically ill close relative or spouse; or (iii) to obtain emergency medical services unavailable at such institution. Prosecutions commenced under this subsection shall neither be continued without a finding nor placed on file. The provisions of section 87 of chapter 276 relative to the power of the court to place certain offenders on probation shall not apply to any person 18 years of age or over charged with a violation of this section.

The provisions of this paragraph shall not apply to the possession of a large capacity weapon or large capacity feeding device by (i) any officer, agent or employee of the commonwealth or any other state or the United States, including any federal, state or local law enforcement personnel; (ii) any member of the military or other service of any state or the United States; (iii) any duly authorized law enforcement officer, agent or employee of any municipality of the commonwealth; (iv) any federal, state or local historical society, museum or institutional collection open to the public; provided, however, that any such person described in clauses (i) to (iii), inclusive, is authorized by a competent authority to acquire, possess or carry a large capacity semiautomatic weapon and is acting within the scope of his duties; or (v) any gunsmith duly licensed under the applicable federal law.

2

(n) Whoever violates paragraph (a) or paragraph (c), by means of a loaded firearm, loaded sawed off shotgun or loaded machine gun shall be further punished by imprisonment in the house of correction for not more than 2½ years, which sentence shall begin from and after the expiration of the sentence for the violation of paragraph (a) or paragraph (c).

(o) For purposes of this section, "loaded" shall mean that ammunition is contained in the weapon or within a feeding device attached thereto.

For purposes of this section, "ammunition" shall mean cartridges or cartridge cases, primers (igniter), bullets or propellant powder designed for use in any firearm, rifle or shotgun.

NOTE 1   **Firearm**—pistol, revolver, or other weapon of any description, loaded or unloaded, from which a shot or bullet can be discharged and of which the length of barrel or barrels is less than 16 inches or 18 inches in the case of a shotgun. G.L. c. 140, § 121.

NOTE 2   **Statute Constitutional.** "[T]he defendant asserts that the Second Amendment bars any licensing system. The Court's decisions of *McDonald [v. Chicago*, 130 S. Ct. 3020 (2010)] and *District of Columbia v. Heller*, 554 U.S. 570 (2008) (Heller), however, do not support such a conclusion. To the contrary, the Court in Heller identified an individual right to carry and bear arms that is limited in scope. The Court explained that a citizen's Second Amendment right did not prohibit laws regulating who may possess and carry weapons or purchase them, or where such weapons may be carried. The Court stated: 'Although we do not undertake an exhaustive historical analysis today of the full scope of the Second Amendment, nothing in our opinion should be taken to cast doubt on longstanding prohibitions on the possession of firearms by felons and the mentally ill, or laws forbidding the carrying of firearms in sensitive places such as schools and government buildings, or laws imposing conditions and qualifications on the commercial sales of arms.' *Heller*, [554 U.S.] at 626–27. In *McDonald*, the Court cited to this specific language in *Heller* and stated: 'We repeat those assurances here. Despite . . . doomsday proclamations, incorporation does not imperil every law regulating firearms.' *McDonald*, [130 S. Ct.] at 3047. Thus, the requirement of 'prior approval by a government officer,' or a licensing system, does not by itself render the statute unconstitutional on its face." *Commonwealth v. Loadholt*, 460 Mass. 723, 726 (2011).

NOTE 3a   Violation of Section 10(a) occurred on the sidewalk in front of defendant's house in a location not within the exclusive control of the defendant. Conviction affirmed. *Commonwealth v. Samaras*, 10 Mass. App. Ct. 910 (1980) (rescript).

NOTE 3b   To be found guilty of possession of a firearm in an apartment not owned or rented by the defendant, there must be evidence to indicate that the defendant exercised dominion or control over the portion of the apartment in which the weapon was found. *Commonwealth v. Williams*, 3 Mass. App. Ct. 370, 371–72 (1975).

NOTE 4a   Despite there being no evidence that the revolver was tested and found operable, a "jury could find, without the aid of expert testimony, that the revolver was 'capable of discharging a bullet.'" *Commonwealth v. Stallions*, 9 Mass. App. Ct. 23, 25 (1980) (citing *Commonwealth v. Fancy*, 349 Mass. 196, 204 (1965)). In *Stallions* the jury had, as exhibits, the revolver and five cartridges taken from it.

NOTE 4b   The firearm itself need not be introduced into evidence; it may be described by a witness. *Commonwealth v. Lopez*, 10 Mass. App. Ct. 351, 354 (1980), aff'd, 393 Mass. 497 (1981).

NOTE 5a   "Whether a gun is a 'firearm' as defined is a question of fact for the jury." *Commonwealth v. Sperrazza*, 372 Mass. 667, 670 (1977).

NOTE 5b   Whether a certain weapon is a machine gun is a question of fact for the jury. *Commonwealth v. Bartholomew*, 326 Mass. 218, 222 (1950).

NOTE 5c   A weapon coming within the definition of a machine gun did *not* lose its character because its firing pin was missing, as it was easily replaceable. *Commonwealth v. Bartholomew*, 326 Mass. at 220.

NOTE 6a   **Knowledge.** "To convict under Section 10(a) it need *not* be shown that the accused knew of the necessity of a license nor that he possessed criminal scienter; it must however be established that the accused knew he was in possession of a firearm." *McQuoid v. Smith*, 556 F.2d 595, 598 (1st Cir. 1977). *See also Commonwealth v. Bacon*, 374 Mass. 358, 359 (1978).

NOTE 6b   "It is not enough to place the defendant and the weapon in the same car." *Commonwealth v. Boone*, 356 Mass. 85, 87 (1969). *See also Commonwealth v. Brown*, 401 Mass. 745, 747–48 (1988).

NOTE 6c   "Presence alone cannot show the requisite knowledge, power or intention to exercise control over the firearm, but presence, supplemented by other incriminating evidence 'will serve to tip the scale in favor of sufficiency.' The defendant's knowledge is personal to him; there is *no* substitute for personal knowledge." *Commonwealth v. Albano*, 373 Mass. 132, 134 (1977). In *Albano* the court found that the defendant had knowledge of the presence of a weapon when the evidence revealed: (a) the defendant drove without head lights or tail lights at 4 a.m. with the rear license plate obscured; (b) he drove slowly and stopped by a closed commercial establishment; (c) the butt of the gun protruded from beneath his seat; and (d) he appeared nervous.

NOTE 6d   "Knowledge may be inferred when the prohibited item is found in open view in an area over which the defendant has control." *Albano*, 373 Mass. at 135.

NOTE 6e   "An individual may be charged with possession of a gun or ammunition under a joint venture theory if the elements of a joint venture are met and there is sufficient evidence to support a conclusion that the defendant knew his joint venturer was armed." *Commonwealth v. Gonzalez*, 68 Mass. App. Ct. 91, 93 (2007).

NOTE 7a   **License.** "We repeatedly have held that in prosecutions under G. L. c. 269, §10 (a) and (h), the Commonwealth does not need to present evidence to show that the defendant did not have a license or FID card because the burden is on the defendant, under G. L. c. 278, § 7, to come forward with such evidence. *Commonwealth v. Colon*, 449 Mass. 207, 225–26 (2007), quoting *Commonwealth v. Tuitt*, 393 Mass. 801, 810 (1985), and *Commonwealth v. Jones*, 372 Mass. 403, 406 (1977). In *Commonwealth v. Jones*, supra, we explained that the absence of a license is not 'an element of the crime,' as that phrase is commonly used. We went on to conclude that G. L. c. 278, § 7, did not create an unconstitutional presumption because it did not shift to the defendant the burden of proof on an element of the crime. *Id.* at 409. We have refused to revisit these conclusions, *see Commonwealth v. Colon*, supra, and find no reason to do so now." *Commonwealth v. Powell*, 459 Mass. 572, 582 (2011).

NOTE 7b   **License—Joint Venture.** "We conclude that, where a defendant is charged with a possessory firearms offense on a theory of joint venture, the defendant does not bear the burden of producing evidence that his coventurer was licensed to possess a firearm before the burden shifts to the Commonwealth to prove the absence of that license beyond a reasonable doubt; however, the defendant must raise the defense of license before trial in accordance with Mass. R. Crim. P. 14(b)(3)." *Commonwealth v. Humphries*, 465 Mass. 762, 764 (2013) (footnote omitted).

NOTE 8a   **Variance.** "A defendant is not to be acquitted on the ground of a variance between the allegations and proof as long as the essential elements of the crime are correctly stated, unless the defendant is prejudiced in his defense." *Commonwealth v. Grasso*, 375 Mass. 138, 139 (1978). In *Grasso* the complaint referred to the weapon as a firearm when, in reality, the barrel was longer than 18 inches and therefore not a firearm under G.L. c. 140, § 121. The complaint however did say that the weapon was a .12 gauge shotgun. Conviction affirmed.

NOTE 8b "Gun found inside a closed console which divided the front seat of a borrowed car. The complaint stated 'carries on his person' and not 'under his control in a motor vehicle.' Conviction reversed as the factfinder "could only speculate whether the defendant had placed the gun in the console or whether the gun had been left there by the car's owner . . . . In short, there was no evidence that the defendant ever had the gun 'on his person.'" *Commonwealth v. Almeida*, 9 Mass. App. Ct. 813 (1980). *See also Doe v. Superintendent of Schs. of Worcester*, 421 Mass. 117 (1995).

NOTE 8c "As the defendant was both the owner and the driver of a car in which a revolver was found" under the back seat, his conviction was affirmed. *Commonwealth v. Moscatiello*, 257 Mass. 260, 262 (1926). *See also Commonwealth v. Crosby*, 6 Mass. App. Ct. 975 (1979).

NOTE 9 A flare device is not a firearm and one may not be convicted of unlawfully carrying it. *Commonwealth v. Sampson*, 383 Mass. 750, 758–59 (1981). Knives described as a "kitchen knife," a "folding knife" and a "swiss army knife" are not in the category of dangerous weapons. *Commonwealth v. Henry*, 37 Mass. App. Ct. 429 (1994).

NOTE 10a **BB Guns and Air Rifles.** G.L. c. 269, § 12B is "the exclusive statutory regulation of air rifles and BB guns." *Commonwealth v. Rhodes*, 389 Mass. 641, 647 (1983). *See also* G.L. c. 269, § 10(a)(5).

NOTE 10b "Possession of 'any type of air gun,' including a CO2 powered gun, by either an adult or a minor is regulated exclusively by G.L. c. 269, sec. 12B." *Commonwealth v. Fenton*, 395 Mass. 92, 95 (1985).

NOTE 10c **BB Gun on School Campus.** "The defendants in this case argue that because we said that § 12B is the 'exclusive regulatory language' governing BB gun possession, their compliance with § 12B insulates them from any criminal liability under § 10(j). We disagree. In the *Rhodes* case, we harmonized § 10(a), which regulates the possession of firearms, by requiring, inter alia, a license or compliance with other specified statutes in order to possess them outside of one's home, with § 12B, which sets forth the specific requirements for the possession of a BB gun in a public place. Section 10(j) is a provision of a different character. It specifically bans the possession of any firearm on school campuses, and it does so 'notwithstanding any license' that may provide a defense to a § 10(a) prosecution. G.L. c. 269, § 10(j). While compliance with § 12B is a defense to a prosecution under § 10(a), just as the possession of a firearm license would be, it provides no similar defense to a prosecution under § 10(j), assuming the other elements of the offense are present.

". . .

"Contrary to the defendants' assertion, our conclusion in this case with regard to the interplay among §§ 10(a), 12B, and 10(j) is not anomalous. As a matter of legislative intent, it would be perfectly reasonable for the Legislature to provide more freedom for the possession of a BB gun than for the carrying of other firearms in public, but then equate the two when it came to protecting the schools of the Commonwealth from violence. The possession of a BB gun by an adult or minor on school grounds, when not permitted by one of the exceptions outlined in § 10(j), thus violates that section." *Commonwealth v. Sayers*, 438 Mass. 238, 240–41 (2002).

NOTE 11 **Dagger.** "In light of the longstanding definitions of the terms and of the purpose of G.L. c. 269, § 10(b), we recognize that, under that section, a dagger is any blade of relatively short length primarily designed or modified for stabbing. This definition excludes common household items such as a steak knife which are designed primarily for utilitarian purposes.

". . .

"While the blade in question was referred to by the witness and the Commonwealth as a 'sword,' this does not preclude it from being considered a 'dagger' under the statute. There is not a bright line dividing longer daggers and shorter swords. *See* 3 Oxford English Dictionary 7 (1978) (defining dagger as '[a] short . . . weapon, like a small sword, used for thrusting and stabbing'); The Random House Dictionary of the English Language 364 (1973)

(defining dagger as 'a short, swordlike weapon'); *State v. Leatherman*, 100 Wash. App. 318, 323, 997 P.2d 929 (2000) (pointing out one of dictionary definitions of 'dagger' also 'a weapon resembling a short sword'). Our decision not to artificially create such a bright line is consistent with the legislative purpose, noted supra, of outlawing the possession of weapons primarily designed for stabbing human beings." *Commonwealth v. Garcia*, 82 Mass. App. Ct. 239, 247, 249 (2012) (footnote omitted).

NOTE 12a **Duplicative Charges.** "Although the defendants have not raised the point, we note that the sentence imposed under G.L. c. 269, § 10(a) (carrying or control in a motor vehicle) and under G.L. c. 140, § 129C (possession) are duplicative because the elements of the former include those of the latter." *Commonwealth v. DiMatteo*, 12 Mass. App. Ct. 547, 555 (1981).

NOTE 12b Defendant convicted of carrying a shotgun under his control in a motor vehicle (G.L. c. 269, § 10a) and of having a shotgun in his possession (G.L. c. 269, § 10h). "In the circumstances of this case it is clear that the charge of carrying under the defendant's control in a vehicle included all the elements of possession, and . . . there was (therefore) duplication of the charges." *Commonwealth v. Grasso*, 375 Mass. 138, 140 (1978).

NOTE 12c **Ammunition and Loaded Firearm.** "There was no evidence that the defendant possessed any ammunition apart from that found loaded in the revolver. All of the required elements of unlawful possession of ammunition were encompassed by the elements of unlawful possession of a loaded firearm, and, therefore, the former crime was a lesser included offense of the latter crime." *Commonwealth v. Johnson*, 461 Mass. 44, 53 (2011).

NOTE 12d "The verdict acquitting Charles of possession of ammunition did not preclude the verdict convicting him of possession of a loaded firearm. . . . Moreover, it is not accurate to say that the jury determined that Charles did not possess the ammunition that the Commonwealth sought to prove the pistol contained. On the contrary, the jury found beyond a reasonable doubt that Charles did possess the pistol containing the ammunition. That they acquitted him of possession of ammunition (which they might have assumed the power to do for 'any number of factors having nothing to do with the defendant's actual guilt,' including prejudice or compassion), does not dictate the entry of judgment for him on the charge of possession of a loaded firearm." *Commonwealth v. Charles*, 463 Mass. 1008, 1009 (2012) (citations omitted).

NOTE 13 **Separate Offenses.** Firearm possession and discharge offenses are *not* lesser included offenses of the charge of assault with intent to murder while armed with a deadly weapon. *Commonwealth v. Lopez*, 10 Mass. App. Ct. at 352 n.1.

NOTE 14 **New Resident.** "We acknowledge that the defendant was a 'new resident' of the Commonwealth within the meaning of G.L. c. 140, sec. 129C(j), at the time of his arrest. This status entitled the defendant to own or to possess a firearm during his first sixty days in the State, notwithstanding his noncompliance with the ordinary licensing requirements. This exemption does not allow the defendant, however, to 'carry' a firearm during this same time period. *See* G.L. c. 140, sec. 129C(j) (referring to possession)." *Commonwealth v. Wood*, 398 Mass. 135, 137 (1986).

NOTE 15a **Necessity as a Defense.** "The defense of necessity applies when (1) the defendant is faced with a clear and imminent danger, not one which is debatable or speculative; (2) the defendant can reasonably expect that his action will be effective as the direct cause of abating the danger; (3) there is no legal alternative which will be effective in abating the danger; and (4) the Legislature has not acted to preclude the defense by a clear and deliberate choice regarding the values at issue. It is well settled that the imminent danger may be faced by a third person rather than the defendant." *Commonwealth v. Power-Koch*, 69 Mass. App. Ct. 735, 739 (2007) (citations, quotation marks, and brackets omitted).

NOTE 15b "We are aware of no authority that would support a defense of necessity in circumstances in which a defendant takes possession of a weapon in his own home and carries it into public places, in anticipation of the possibility of a serious encounter with

2

a person who had threatened him at some earlier time." *Commonwealth v. Lindsey*, 396 Mass. 840, 845 (1986).

NOTE 15c   The Supreme Judicial Court noted that the following instruction is correct.

"Now very recently our Supreme Judicial Court has stated that the unlicensed temporary possession of a firearm in a public place might be lawful in certain necessitous circumstances. . . . Necessity is defined in terms of a balancing of harms where the criminal conduct represents the better choice. Now the rule of necessity allows a defendant to take from an assailant a firearm if the threat to that defendant is immediate, substantial and unavoidable and arises in circumstances in which action and self-defense are warranted. In other words, if a defendant was threatened by an assailant with a weapon and then the defendant seized that weapon from the assailant then the possession of that firearm in the midst of such an emergency by a defendant, that is not unlawful. Clearly, the taking of a firearm from an assailant during a struggle would not constitute an unlawful carrying or possession. . . . However, what is the law after the struggle is over? What about that period of time that exists after the struggle and until that gun is surrendered, if it was surrendered, later on?

"Remember—And I don't mean to suggest what the evidence is, it's for you to say—but there was some testimony in this case that some time after the shooting, if the shooting occurred, that this defendant brought that particular gun to the Worcester police station, so what you have to do is you must balance the particular harms. What would the better course of conduct for the defendant have been to follow? What would it have been the better for him to have done? Should he have dropped the weapon and left or waited for the police? Should he have discarded the weapon somewhere? Bear in mind this, that if he had disposed of a gun or left it at the scene some other person may have acquired it. Some other person or even a child could end up with it. It is for you to say what actually happened, and it's for you to say whether based upon the circumstances that were developed during the trial—whether the conduct of this defendant, if this is what he did, in carrying this weapon to the police station represented the better choice. In this regard, the Commonwealth bears the burden of proving beyond a reasonable doubt that the defendant did not act out of necessity when he acquired possession of this weapon and when he carried it to the police station, so that's entirely up to you."

Commonwealth v. Iglesia, 403 Mass. 132, 135–36 (1988).

NOTE 16   Assault weapons banned in Boston. *See* 1989 Mass. Acts c. 596, §§ 1–7.

NOTE 17   "i. Unlawful possession of a firearm in violation of G. L. c. 269, § 10 (h) (1). Under G. L. c. 140, § 129B (1) (v), only individuals under the age of fifteen are prohibited from obtaining an FID card. Significantly, the defendant does not contend that he ever attempted to obtain an FID card. The defendant, thus, has not demonstrated that a denial of the issuance of an FID card would have been rendered. Had he been denied an FID card, his recourse is set forth in G. L. c. 140, § 129B (5) ("Any applicant . . . aggrieved by a denial . . . of [an FID card] . . . may . . . [ninety] days after receipt of notice of such denial . . . file a petition to obtain judicial review in the district court having jurisdiction in the city or town wherein the applicant filed for . . . such card"). Instead of applying for an FID card, the defendant chose to violate the law. In these circumstances, we conclude that he may not challenge his conviction under G. L. c. 269, § 10(h)(1).

"ii. Unlawful carrying of a firearm in violation of G. L. c. 269, § 10 (a). With respect to his convictions of unlawfully carrying a loaded firearm, the defendant correctly points out that the licensing scheme, namely the age disqualification in G. L. c. 140, § 131 (d) (iv), barring the issuance of a § 131 license to carry to an applicant who 'at he time of the application [is] less than [twenty-one] years of age,' prohibits young adults between eighteen and twenty years of age from obtaining a § 131 license to carry a firearm. However, as was the case with an FID card, the defendant does not contend that he attempted to obtain a § 131 license to carry. As a consequence, the defendant has not demonstrated that a denial of the issuance of a § 131 license to him would have been rendered on

account of his age alone. We add that under the licensing scheme, had the defendant been denied a § 131 license to carry (for whatever reason), he could have appealed that decision pursuant to the provisions of the statutory licensing scheme. See G. L. c. 140, § 131 (f) ("Any applicant . . . aggrieved by a denial . . . of a license . . . may, within either [ninety] days after receiving notice of such denial . . . file a petition to obtain judicial review in the district court having jurisdiction in the city or town wherein the applicant filed for, or was issued, such license"). He chose instead (again) to violate the law. In these circumstances, we conclude that the defendant may not challenge his convictions under G. L. c. 269, § 10 (a)." *Commonwealth v. Powell*, 459 Mass. 572, 589–90 (2011) (citations omitted).

NOTE 18   **Ammunition.** In a G.L. c. 269, § 10(h) case, the Commonwealth "does not bear the burden of proving that particular ammunition is capable of being fired. . . . Rather, the government must show only that the putative ammunition is designed for that purpose." Factors to consider include physical appearance, manner of packaging and police testimony. *Commonwealth v. Mendes*, 44 Mass. App. Ct. 903, 904 (1997).

NOTE 19   **Broken Firing Pin.** "The Commonwealth's evidence showed that replacing the broken firing pin with a new one was a 'simple task,' requiring, in the opinion of an expert witness, only ten or fifteen minutes. The judge credited this testimony, and found that 'a slight repair, replacement, or adjustment could make this weapon effective as a firearm. . . .' On that basis, the judge found sufficient facts to warrant a finding of guilt. . . . There was no error." *Commonwealth v. Prevost*, 44 Mass. App. Ct. 398, 402–03 (1998) (citation omitted).

NOTE 20   **In Residence.** "The instruction and answer . . . correctly conveyed to the jury that a person is not in their residence for purposes of the statute if they are in a common area over which they do not have exclusive control.

". . .

"The facts of this case suggest that 'residence' here includes the entire apartment. Not only would Moore have to go through other parts of the apartment to answer the door, but the evidence contains indications that he had full use of the whole unit. . . .

"Our conclusion is buttressed by the fact that cases discussing the requirement that a common area be within the 'exclusive control' of the defendant for purposes of the exemption consistently involve areas outside of the defendant's apartment or home. *See Commonwealth v. Seay*, 376 Mass. at 743 (foyer or other common area of apartment building is not within residence exemption of G.L. c. 269, § 10); *Commonwealth v. Samaras*, 10 Mass. App. Ct. 910, 910 (1980) (violation of G.L. c. 269, § 10, which occurred on sidewalk in front of defendant's house, took place in location not within defendant's exclusive control); *Commonwealth v. Statham*, 38 Mass. App. Ct. [582, 584–585 (1995)] (whether backyard was under defendant's 'exclusive control' was question for jury); *Commonwealth v. Belding*, 42 Mass. App. Ct. at 440 (whether landlord was in area of 'exclusive control' when he stuck his arm out of his apartment and fired gun into hallway was question of fact for jury).

". . .

"A[n] . . . appropriate instruction, on the facts of this case, might have been: the Commonwealth has the burden of proving that the defendant was not within his residence or place of business when he possessed the gun; whether the Commonwealth has proven that the defendant was not within his residence is a question of fact for you to determine; in a dwelling with multiple units, a residence may be the entire unit if the person dwelling therein is not excluded from any part thereof and has access to all the rooms; a common area is an area outside the residence to which all of the tenants in a building have access and the landlord maintains control; an area outside of the residence will still fall within the exemption if it is an area over which the defendant maintains exclusive control alone or with other members of the residence. *See Commonwealth v. Statham*, 38 Mass. App. Ct. at 585 (approving jury instruction which stated exclusive control of backyard could be maintained by defendant and other members of household)." *Commonwealth v. Moore*, 54 Mass. App. Ct. 334, 344–46 (2002) (certain citations omitted).

NOTE 21   Mandatory Minimum Sentence—§ 10(m). "In general, a person convicted under § 10(m) who, at the time of the offense, did not possess a valid FID card, must be sentenced to a minimum sentence of two and one-half years in a State prison, but not more than ten years. Further, by its express terms, and consistent with G.L. c. 127, § 133, the so-called 'truth in sentencing act,' no portion of any sentence imposed under § 10(m) may be suspended. Finally, a person so convicted under § 10(m) must serve a minimum term of imprisonment in a State prison of not less than one year, and that term may not be reduced by any means, including (but not limited to) those enumerated in the statute (i.e., parole, furlough, and so forth)." *Commonwealth v. Semegen*, 72 Mass. App. Ct. 478, 480–81 (2008) (footnote omitted). *See also Commonwealth v. Lindsay*, 72 Mass. App. Ct. 485, 493–94 (2008).

NOTE 22   Weapon Manufactured Prior to 1900. "A firearm manufactured before 1900 is a 'firearm' within the definition of G.L. c. 140, § 121, which defines a '[f]irearm' as 'a pistol, revolver or other weapon of any description, loaded or unloaded, from which a shot or bullet can be discharged and of which the length of the barrel or barrels is less than 16 inches or 18 inches in the case of a shotgun as originally manufactured.' However, § 121 also provides that the 'provisions of [§§] 122 to 129D, inclusive, and [§§] 131, 131A, 131B and 131E shall not apply to . . . any firearm, rifle or shotgun manufactured in or prior to the year 1899.' Because G.L. c. 140, § 131, governs licenses to carry firearms, and because § 131 does not apply to firearms manufactured before 1900, a person does not need a license to carry a firearm made before 1900. The carrying of such an antique firearm, therefore, is exempted by § 131 from the prohibition in G.L. c. 269, § 10(a), against carrying a firearm without a license. . . . As a result, a defendant may not be convicted under § 10 (a) of carrying a firearm manufactured before 1900 without a license to carry because the defendant is permitted to carry such an antique firearm without a license to carry. . . .

"While firearms manufactured before 1900 are exempt from the licensing requirement in G.L. c. 140, § 131, a defendant may still be convicted of the unlawful possession of ammunition loaded in a firearm manufactured before 1900 if the defendant does not have a firearm identification card and the ammunition does not fall under some exemption. *See, e.g.*, G.L. c. 269, § 10(h) (crime to possess ammunition without firearm identification card); G.L. c. 140, § 129C (listing exemptions including 'so-called black powder rifles, shotguns, and ammunition therefor'). Therefore, a defendant in possession of a loaded firearm manufactured before 1900 may not be guilty of the unlawful carrying of a loaded firearm, but may still be guilty of the unlawful possession of ammunition. . . .

"In the future, where a defendant charged with the unlawful carrying of a firearm in violation of § 10(a) possesses evidence that the firearm was manufactured before 1900, the defendant shall provide the Commonwealth with pretrial notice of the affirmative defense of exemption as required by rule 14(b)(3). . . . Once a defendant gives proper notice to the Commonwealth, the defendant bears the burden of producing evidence of the affirmative defense that the firearm was manufactured before 1900. If such evidence is presented, the burden rests on the prosecution to prove beyond a reasonable doubt that the firearm was manufactured after 1899." *Commonwealth v. Jefferson*, 461 Mass. 821, 829–30, 832–34 (2012) (footnotes omitted).

SECTION 10A
Selling, giving or using silencers; penalty; confiscation and destruction
Any person, other than a federally licensed firearms manufacturer, an authorized agent of the municipal police training committee, or a duly authorized sworn law enforcement officer while acting within the scope of official duties and under the direct authorization of the police chief or his designee, or the colonel of the state police who sells or keeps for sale, or offers, or gives or disposes of by any means other than submitting to an authorized law enforcement agency, or uses or possesses any instrument, attachment, weapon or appliance for causing the firing of any gun, revolver, pistol or other firearm to be silent or intended to lessen or muffle the noise of the firing of any gun, revolver, pistol or other firearm shall be punished by imprisonment for not more than five years in state prison or for not more than two and one-half years in a jail or house of correction. Nothing contained herein shall be construed to prohibit a federally licensed firearms manufacturer from selling such instrument, attachment, weapon or appliance to authorized law enforcement agencies for law enforcement purposes or to the municipal police training committee for law enforcement training. Upon conviction of a violation of this section, the instrument, attachment or other article shall be confiscated by the commonwealth and forwarded, by the authority of the written order of the court, to the colonel of the state police, who shall destroy said article.

SECTION 10B
Repealed

SECTION 10C
Use of tear gas, etc., in commission of crime; penalty
Whoever uses tear gas cartridges, or any device or instrument which contains a liquid, gas, powder, or any other substance designed to incapacitate for the purpose of committing a crime shall be punished by imprisonment in the state prison for not more than seven years.

SECTION 10D
Use or wearing of body armor in commission of crime; penalty
Whoever, while in the commission or attempted commission of a felony, uses or wears any body armor, so-called, or any protective covering for the body or any parts thereof, made on resin-treated glass-fiber cloth, or of any other material or combination of materials, designed to prevent, deflect or deter the penetration thereof by ammunition, knives or other weapons, shall be punished by imprisonment in the state prison for not less than two and one-half years nor more than five years or for not less than one year nor more than two and one-half years in jail or house of correction.

SECTION 10E
Firearms sales; penalties; eligibility for probation, parole, furlough or work release
(Amended by 2014 Mass. Acts c. 284, § 93, effective Aug. 11, 2014.)
Whoever, except as provided by law, in a single transaction or occurrence or in a series of transactions within a 12 month period, knowingly or intentionally distributes, sells, or transfers possession of a quantity of firearms, rifles, shotguns, machine guns, or any combination thereof, shall, if the quantity of firearms, rifles, shotguns, machine guns, or any combination thereof is:

(1) 1 or more, but less than 3, be punished by a term of imprisonment of not more than 10 years in the state prison or by a fine of not more than $50,000, or by both such imprisonment and fine;

(2) 3 or more, but less than 10, be punished by a term of imprisonment, not to exceed 20 years in the state prison;

2

provided, however, that said sentence shall not be less than a mandatory minimum term of imprisonment of 5 years; and provided further, that said sentence may include and a fine of not more than $100,000, which shall not be in lieu of the mandatory minimum term of imprisonment;

(3) 10 or more, be punished by a term of imprisonment up to life imprisonment in the state prison; provided, that said sentence shall not be less than a mandatory minimum term of imprisonment of 10 years; and provided further, that said sentence may include a fine of not more than $150,000, which shall not be in lieu of the mandatory minimum term of imprisonment.

A prosecution commenced under this section shall not be placed on file or continued without a finding and the sentence imposed upon a person convicted of violating this section shall not be reduced to less than the mandatory minimum term of imprisonment, as established in the first paragraph, nor shall any sentence of imprisonment imposed upon any person be suspended or reduced until such person shall have served said mandatory minimum term of imprisonment.

A person convicted of violating this section shall not, until the individual has served the mandatory minimum term of imprisonment established herein, be eligible for probation, parole, furlough, work release or receive any deduction from his sentence for good conduct under sections 129C or 129D of chapter 127; provided, however, that the commissioner of corrections may, on the recommendation of the warden, superintendent or other person in charge of the correctional institution, grant to said offender a temporary release in the custody of an officer of such institution for the following purposes: to attend the funeral of a relative, to visit a critically ill relative or to obtain emergency medical or psychiatric services unavailable at said institution. Section 87 of chapter 276 shall not apply to any person, 18 years of age or over, charged with a violation of this section, or to any child between the age of 14 and 18, so charged, if the court is of the opinion that the interests of the public require that the child be tried for such offense instead of being dealt with as a child.

SECTION 10F
Illegal sale, gifts or transfer of large capacity weapons or large capacity feeding devices; punishment
(Amended by 2014 Mass. Acts c. 284, § 94, effective Aug. 11, 2014.)

(a) Any person who sells, keeps for sale, or offers or exposes for sale, gives or otherwise transfers any large capacity weapon or large capacity feeding device, both as defined in section 121 of chapter 140, to a person 18 years of age or over, except as permitted under this section or chapter 140, shall be punished by imprisonment in a state prison for not less than two and one-half years nor more than ten years. Any person who commits a second or subsequent such crime shall be punished by imprisonment in a state prison for not less than five years nor more than 15 years. The sentence imposed upon such person shall not be reduced to less than two and one-half years for a first offense, nor less than five years for a second or subsequent such offense, nor suspended, nor shall any person convicted under this subsection be eligible for probation, parole, furlough, work release or receive any deduction from his sentence for good conduct until he shall have served such minimum term of such sentence; provided, however, that the commissioner or other person in charge of a correctional institution or the administrator of a county cor-

rectional institution, grant to such offender a temporary release in the custody of an officer of such institution for the following purposes only: (i) to attend the funeral of a spouse or next of kin; (ii) to visit a critically ill close relative or spouse; or (iii) to obtain emergency medical services unavailable at such institution. Prosecutions commenced under this subsection shall neither be continued without a finding nor placed on file. The provisions of section 87 of chapter 276 relative to the power of the court to place certain offenders on probation shall not apply to any person 18 years of age or over charged with a violation of this subsection.

(b) Any person who transfers, sells, lends or gives a large capacity weapon or large capacity feeding device to a person under the age of 18, except as permitted under the provisions of chapter 140, shall be punished by imprisonment in a state prison for not less than five nor more than 15 years. The sentence imposed upon such person shall not be reduced to less than five years, nor suspended, nor shall any person convicted under this subsection be eligible for probation, parole, furlough, work release or receive any deduction from his sentence for good conduct until he shall have served such minimum term of such sentence; provided, however, that the commissioner or other person in charge of a correctional institution or the administrator of a county correctional institution, grant to such offender a temporary release in the custody of an officer of such institution for the following purposes only: (i) to attend the funeral of a spouse or next of kin; (ii) to visit a critically ill close relative or spouse; or (iii) to obtain emergency medical services unavailable at such institution. Prosecutions commenced under this subsection shall neither be continued without a finding nor placed on file. The provisions of section 87 of chapter 276 relative to the power of the court to place certain offenders on probation shall not apply to any person 17 years of age or over charged with a violation of this subsection.

SECTION 10G
Violations of Sec. 10 by persons previously convicted of violent crimes or serious drug offenses; punishment
(Amended by 2014 Mass. Acts c. 284, § 95, effective Aug. 11, 2014.)

(a) Whoever, having been previously convicted of a violent crime or of a serious drug offense, both as defined herein, violates the provisions of paragraph (a), (c) or (h) of section 10 shall be punished by imprisonment in the state prison for not less than three years nor more than 15 years.

(b) Whoever, having been previously convicted of two violent crimes, or two serious drug offenses or one violent crime and one serious drug offense, arising from separate incidences, violates the provisions of said paragraph (a), (c) or (h) of said section 10 shall be punished by imprisonment in the state prison for not less than ten years nor more than 15 years.

(c) Whoever, having been previously convicted of three violent crimes or three serious drug offenses, or any combination thereof totaling three, arising from separate incidences, violates the provisions of said paragraph (a), (c) or (h) of said section 10 shall be punished by imprisonment in the state prison for not less than 15 years nor more than 20 years.

(d) The sentences imposed upon such persons shall not be reduced to less than the minimum, nor suspended, nor shall persons convicted under this section be eligible for probation, parole, furlough, work release or receive any deduction from such sentence for good conduct until such person shall have served the minimum number of years of such sentence; provided, however, that the commissioner of correction may, on the recommendation of the warden, superintendent or other person in charge of a correctional institution for the following purposes only: (i) to attend the funeral of a spouse or next of kin; (ii) to visit a critically ill close relative or spouse; or (iii) to obtain emergency medical services unavailable at such institution. Prosecutions commenced under this subsection shall neither be continued without a finding nor placed on file. The provisions of section 87 of chapter 276 relative to the power of the court to place certain offenders on probation shall not apply to any person 18 years of age or over charged with a violation of this subsection.

(e) For the purposes of this section, "violent crime" shall have the meaning set forth in section 121 of chapter 140. For the purposes of this section, "serious drug offense" shall mean an offense under the federal Controlled Substances Act, 21 U.S.C. 801, et seq., the federal Controlled Substances Import and Export Act, 21 U.S.C. 951 et seq. or the federal Maritime Drug Law Enforcement Act, 46 U.S.C. App. 1901 et seq. for which a maximum term of imprisonment for ten years or more is prescribed by law, or an offense under chapter 94C involving the manufacture, distribution or possession with intent to manufacture or distribute a controlled substance, as defined in section 1 of said chapter 94C, for which a maximum term of ten years or more is prescribed by law.

NOTE 1   Juvenile Delinquency. "We conclude that the explicit incorporation in § 10G of the definition of violent crime detailed in G.L. c. 140, § 121, thereby expressly including certain acts of juvenile delinquency, was intended by the Legislature to encompass such acts within the term 'conviction' in § 10G." *Commonwealth v. Foreman*, 63 Mass. App. Ct. 801, 802 (2005).

NOTE 2   Knife as a Deadly Weapon. "The definition of violent crime in § 121 uses 'deadly weapon' in the general, common-law sense . . . in which a knife is commonly thought of as a deadly weapon. . . . In the context of the incorporating statute, G.L. c. 269, § 10G, the common-law definition of deadly weapon best comports with the statute's purpose of enhancing penalties for those who violate gun laws having previously been convicted of violent crimes or serious drug offenses." *Commonwealth v. Foreman*, 63 Mass. App. Ct. 801, 803 (2005).

NOTE 3   Pen is not a Deadly Weapon. "We first conclude that the term 'deadly weapon' in this context is distinct from the term 'dangerous weapon' as applied in our common law. We further hold that for the purposes of conviction under G.L. c. 269, § 10G, a deadly weapon is a weapon that is inherently deadly, and therefore conclude that a pen is not a deadly weapon under this statute." *Commonwealth v. Rezendes*, 88 Mass. App. Ct. 369, 370 (2015).

NOTE 4   Residual Clause Unconstitutionally Vague. "[T]he United States Supreme Court decided *Johnson v. United States*, 135 S. Ct. 2551, 2555–56, 2563 (2015), holding that the residual clause of the 'violent felony' provision of the Federal armed career criminal act (Federal ACCA) is unconstitutionally vague under the due process clause of the Fourteenth Amendment to the United States Constitution. In terms of its definitions of predicate crimes, the Massachusetts ACCA 'largely replicates' the Federal ACCA.

"Under the invalidated residual clause in the Federal ACCA, 18 U.S.C. § 924(e)(2)(B) (2012), a crime constituted a 'violent felony' if it was punishable by imprisonment for more than one year and 'otherwise involve[d] conduct that present[ed] a serious potential risk of physical injury to another.' The United States Supreme Court's decision in *Johnson, supra* at 2557, began by acknowledging the well-established rule that courts must use the 'categorical approach' to determine whether an offense constitutes a violent felony by 'pictur[ing] the kind of conduct that the crime involves in 'the ordinary case, and . . . judg[ing] whether that abstraction presents a serious potential risk of physical injury.' The Court then concluded, based largely on the arbitrariness of hypothesizing the 'ordinary case' of any given crime, that '[i]ncreasing a defendant's sentence under the clause denies due process of law' because 'the indeterminacy of the wide-ranging inquiry required by the residual clause both denies fair notice to defendants and invites arbitrary enforcement by judges.' *Id*. The Court was particularly concerned with the 'grave uncertainty' regarding 'how to estimate the risk posed by a crime' and 'how much risk it takes for a crime to qualify as a violent felony.' *Id*. at 2557–58. . . . The Court in *Johnson* thus invalidated the residual clause of the Federal ACCA. *Id*. at 2557.

"The language of the residual clause in the Massachusetts ACCA is almost identical to that in the Federal ACCA; the only difference is that the Federal ACCA uses the term 'potential' to qualify the level of risk required. . . . We think the additional term does not create a meaningful difference between the two provisions. We agree with the Court's analysis in *Johnson, supra*, and conclude that the residual clause of the Massachusetts ACCA is unconstitutionally vague." *Commonwealth v. Beal*, 474 Mass. 341, 349–51 (2016) (citations omitted).

NOTE 5   "[W]e interpret § 10G to mean that where the previous convictions of predicate offenses forming the basis of the sentence enhancement charge were all part of a single prosecution, they properly should be treated as a single predicate conviction." *Commonwealth v. Resende*, 474 Mass. 455, 456 (2016).

SECTION 10H
Carrying loaded firearm while under influence of liquor, marijuana, narcotic drugs, depressants or stimulant substances; punishment

Whoever, having in effect a license to carry firearms issued under section 131 or 131F of chapter 140, carries on his person, or has under his control in a vehicle, a loaded firearm, as defined in section 121 of said chapter 140, while under the influence of intoxicating liquor or marijuana, narcotic drugs, depressants or stimulant substances, all as defined in section 1 of chapter 94C, or the vapors of glue shall be punished by a fine of not more than $5,000 or by imprisonment in the house of correction for not more than two and one-half years, or by both such fine and imprisonment.

SECTION 10I
Transporting firearm into commonwealth
(Added by 2014 Mass. Acts c. 284, § 96, effective Jan. 1, 2015.)

(a) Whoever transports a firearm, rifle, shotgun, machine gun or sawed-off shotgun into the commonwealth to use the weapon for the commission of criminal activity shall be punished by imprisonment in the state prison for not less than 5 years nor more than 10 years.

(b) Whoever transports a firearm, rifle, shotgun, machine gun or sawed-off shotgun into the commonwealth to unlawfully distribute, sell or transfer possession of the weapon to a prohibited person, as defined in section 131 of chapter 140, shall be punished by imprisonment in the state prison for not less than 10 years nor more than 20 years.

(c) Whoever transports a firearm, rifle, shotgun, machine gun or sawed-off shotgun into the commonwealth to unlawfully distribute, sell or transfer the weapon to a prohibited person, as defined in section 131 of chapter 140, and if the weapon is subsequently used to cause the death of another, shall be punished by imprisonment in the state prison for not less than 20 years.

2

SECTION 10J
Breaking and entering to steal firearm
(Added by 2014 Mass. Acts c. 284, § 96, effective Jan. 1, 2015.)

(a) Whoever in the nighttime or the daytime breaks and enters a building, ship, vessel or vehicle to steal a firearm shall be punished by imprisonment in the state prison for not more than 5 years or by imprisonment in the house of correction for not more than 2½ years or by a fine of not more than $10,000, or by both such fine and imprisonment.

(b) Whoever in the nighttime or the daytime breaks and enters a building, ship, vessel or vehicle to steal a firearm to distribute to a prohibited person, as defined in section 131 of chapter 140 shall be punished by imprisonment in the state prison for not more than 10 years or by imprisonment in the house of correction for not more than 2½ years or by a fine of not more than $10,000, or by both such fine and imprisonment.

(c) Whoever in the nighttime or the daytime breaks and enters a building, ship, vessel or vehicle to steal a firearm and in the process causes injury of another shall be punished by imprisonment in the state prison for not more than 10 years or by imprisonment in the house of correction for not more than 2½ years or by a fine of not more than $10,000, or by both such fine and imprisonment.

Any motor vehicle lawfully owned or operated by any person convicted pursuant to this section shall be forfeited pursuant to section 24W of chapter 90. All proceeds from the auction of the vehicle shall be deposited into the Public Safety Training Fund established under section 2JJJJ of chapter 29.

SECTION 10K
Breaking and entering building in which firearm retailer, wholesaler or manufacturer conducts business
(Added by 2014 Mass. Acts c. 284, § 96, effective Jan. 1, 2015.)

(a) Whoever in the nighttime or the daytime breaks and enters any building in which a firearm retailer, wholesaler or manufacturer conducts business shall be punished by imprisonment in the state prison for not more than 10 years or by imprisonment in the house of correction for not more than 2½ years or by a fine of not more than $10,000, or by both such fine and imprisonment.

(b) Whoever in the nighttime or the daytime breaks and enters any building in which a firearm retailer, wholesaler or manufacturer conducts business with the intent to unlawfully obtain a firearm, rifle, shotgun, machine gun or ammunition shall be punished by imprisonment in the state prison for not more than 10 years or by imprisonment in the house of correction for not more than 2½ years or by a fine of not more than $10,000, or by both such fine and imprisonment.

(c) Whoever unlawfully obtains a firearm, rifle, shotgun, machine gun or ammunition by means of breaking and entering, in the nighttime or the daytime, any building in which a firearm retailer, wholesaler or manufacturer conducts business and who unlawfully distributes said firearm, rifle, shotgun, machine gun or ammunition shall be punished by imprisonment in the state prison for not more than 20 years or by imprisonment in the house of correction for not more than 2½ years or by a fine of not more than $10,000, or by both such fine and imprisonment.

SECTION 11
Printing statutes for posters; sending copies to clerks and superintendents of schools in cities and towns; duties; costs

The state secretary shall, annually, cause to be printed, in English and in such other languages as he may deem necessary, and in large letters so as to be easily read, for use as a poster, section one hundred and thirty-one of chapter one hundred and forty and sections ten, twelve B, and fourteen of this chapter. Sufficient copies of the said posters shall be sent to the clerks and to the superintendents of schools in all cities and towns for their use as herein provided. The city or town clerks shall cause posters received by them to be displayed in such places as they may select, and in such numbers, according to the population of the city or town, as its clerk may deem expedient. The superintendents of schools shall cause the posters received by them to be distributed among the schools within their jurisdiction, and in such numbers as they may deem necessary. The cost of preparing and printing the posters and of distributing them to the various cities and towns shall be paid by the commonwealth, and the cost of placing or affixing them in each city or town shall be paid by that city or town.

SECTION 11A
Definitions

For the purposes of this section and sections eleven B, eleven C and eleven D, the following words shall have the following meanings:—

"Firearm", a firearm as defined in section one hundred and twenty-one of chapter one hundred and forty, or a rifle or shotgun.

"Serial number", the number stamped or placed upon a firearm by the manufacturer in the original process of manufacture.

"Identification number", the number stamped or placed upon a firearm by the colonel of the state police under authority of section eleven D.

SECTION 11B
Possession or control of firearm with serial or identification number removed or mutilated; while committing or attempting a felony; destruction

Whoever, while in the commission or attempted commission of a felony, has in his possession or under his control a firearm the serial number or identification number of which has been removed, defaced, altered, obliterated or mutilated in any manner shall be punished by imprisonment in the state prison for not less than two and one half nor more than five years, or in a jail or house of correction for not less than six months nor more than two and one half years. Upon a conviction of a violation of this section, said firearm or other article, by the authority of the written order of the court, shall be forwarded to the colonel of the state police, who shall cause said weapon to be destroyed.

SECTION 11C
Removal or mutilation of serial or identification numbers of firearms; receiving such firearm; possession or control as evidence; destruction

Whoever, by himself or another, removes, defaces, alters, obliterates or mutilates in any manner the serial number or identification number of a firearm, or in any way participates therein, and whoever receives a firearm with knowledge that its serial number or identification number has been removed, defaced, altered, obliterated or mutilated in any manner, shall be punished by a fine of not more than two hundred dollars or by imprisonment for not less than one month nor more than two and one half years. Possession or control of a firearm the serial number or identification number of which has been removed, defaced, altered, obliterated or mutilated in any manner shall be prima facie evidence that the person having such possession or control is guilty of a violation of this section; but such prima facie evidence may be rebutted by evidence that such person had no knowledge whatever that such number had been removed, defaced, altered, obliterated or mutilated, or by evidence that he had no guilty knowledge thereof. Upon a conviction of a violation of this section said firearm or other article shall be forwarded, by the authority of the written order of the court, to the colonel of the state police, who shall cause said firearm or other article to be destroyed.

SECTION 11D
Repealed

SECTION 11E
Serial identification numbers on firearms; penalty

All firearms, rifles and shotguns of new manufacture, manufactured or delivered to any licensed dealer within the commonwealth shall bear serial numbers permanently inscribed on a visible metal area of said firearm, rifle or shotgun, and the manufacturer of said firearm, rifle or shotgun shall keep records of said serial numbers and the dealer, distributor or person to whom the firearm, rifle or shotgun was sold or delivered.

No licensed dealer shall order for delivery, cause to be delivered, offer for sale or sell within the commonwealth any newly manufactured firearm, rifle or shotgun received directly from a manufacturer, wholesaler or distributor not so inscribed with a serial number nor shall any licensed manufacturer or distributor of firearms, rifles or shotguns deliver or cause to delivered within the commonwealth any firearm, rifle or shotgun not complying with this section.

No licensed manufacturer within the commonwealth shall produce for sale within the United States, its territories or possessions any firearm, rifle or shotgun not complying with paragraph one of this section. Whoever violates this section shall be punished by a fine of five hundred dollars. Each such violation shall constitute a separate offense.

SECTION 12
Manufacturing and selling knives, slung shots, swords, bludgeons and similar weapons; punishment

Whoever manufactures or causes to be manufactured, or sells or exposes for sale, an instrument or weapon of the kind usually known as a dirk knife, a switch knife or any knife having an automatic spring release device by which the blade is released from the handle, having a blade of over one and one-half inches or a device or case which enables a knife with a locking blade to be drawn at a locked position, any ballistic knife, or any knife with a detachable blade capable of being propelled by any mechanism, slung shot, sling shot, bean blower, sword cane, pistol cane, bludgeon, blackjack, nunchaku, zoobow, also known as klackers or kung fu sticks, or any similar weapon consisting of two sticks of wood, plastic or metal connected at one end by a length of rope, chain, wire or leather, a shuriken or any similar pointed star-like object intended to injure a person when thrown, or a manrikigusari or similar length of chain having weighted ends; or metallic knuckles or knuckles of any other substance which could be put to the same use and with the same or similar effect as metallic knuckles, shall be punished by a fine of not less than fifty nor more than one thousand dollars or by imprisonment for not more than six months; provided, however, that sling shots may be manufactured and sold to clubs or associations conducting sporting events where such sling shots are used.

SECTION 12A
Selling or furnishing air rifle to minor

Whoever sells to a minor under the age of eighteen or whoever, not being the parent, guardian or adult teacher or instructor, furnishes to a minor under the age of eighteen an air rifle or so-called BB gun, shall be punished by a fine of not less than fifty nor more than two hundred dollars or by imprisonment for not more than six months.

SECTION 12B
Possession of air rifle by minor under eighteen; shooting air rifle; disposition on conviction for violation

No minor under the age of eighteen shall have an air rifle or so-called BB gun in his possession while in any place to which the public has a right of access unless he is accompanied by an adult or unless he is the holder of a sporting or hunting license and has on his person a permit from the chief of police of the town in which he resides granting him the right of such possession. No person shall discharge a BB shot, pellet or other object from an air rifle or so-called BB gun into, from or across any street, alley, public way or railroad or railway right of way, and no minor under the age of eighteen shall discharge a BB shot, pellet or other object from an air rifle or BB gun unless he is accompanied by an adult or is the holder of a sporting or hunting license. Whoever violates this section shall be punished by a fine of not more than one hundred dollars, and the air rifle or BB gun or other weapon shall be confiscated. Upon a conviction of a violation of this section the air rifle or BB gun or other weapon shall, by the written authority of the court, be forwarded to the colonel of the state police, who may dispose of said article in the same manner as prescribed in section ten.

NOTE   See Note 9a following G.L. c. 269, § 10.

SECTION 12C
Repealed

SECTION 12D
Carrying rifle or shotgun having shells or cartridges therein on public way prohibited; exceptions; penalty

(a) Except as exempted or provided by law, no person shall carry on his person on any public way a loaded rifle or shotgun having cartridges or shells in either the magazine or chamber thereof. For purposes of this section, "loaded shotgun or loaded rifle" shall mean any shotgun or rifle having ammunition in either the magazine or chamber thereof, such ammunition including a live cartridge, primer (igniter), bullet or propellant powder designed for use in any firearm, rifle or shotgun and, in the case of a muzzle loading or black powder shotgun or rifle, containing powder in the flash pan, a percussion cap and shot or ball; but the term "loaded shotgun or loaded rifle" shall not include a shotgun or rifle loaded with a

2

blank cartridge, which contains no projectile within such blank or within the bore or chamber of such shotgun or rifle.

Whoever violates the provisions of this subsection shall be punished by a fine of not less than $500 nor more than $5,000 or by imprisonment in the house of correction for not more than two years, or by both such fine and imprisonment, and may be arrested without a warrant; provided, however, that if such rifle or shotgun is a large capacity weapon, as defined in section 121 of chapter 140, such person shall be punished by a fine of not less than $1,000 nor more than $10,000 or by imprisonment for not less than one year nor more than ten years, or by both such fine and imprisonment, and may be arrested without a warrant.

(b) Except as exempted or provided by law, no person shall carry on his person on any public way an unloaded rifle or shotgun, unless such rifle or shotgun is enclosed in a case.

Whoever violates the provisions of this subsection shall be punished by a fine of not less than $100 nor more than $1,000, and may be arrested without a warrant; provided, however, that if such unloaded rifle or shotgun is a large capacity weapon and is carried simultaneously with a fully or partially loaded large capacity feeding device, such person shall be punished by a fine of not less than $1,000 nor more than $10,000 or by imprisonment for not less than one year nor more than ten years, or by both such fine and imprisonment, and may be arrested without a warrant.

This subsection shall not apply to drills, parades, military reenactments or other commemorative ceremonies, color guards or memorial service firing squads, so-called, as permitted by law.

(c) Upon a conviction of a violation of any provision of this section, such rifle or shotgun shall be confiscated by the commonwealth and, upon written order of the court, such weapon shall be forwarded to the colonel of the state police, who may dispose of such weapon in the manner prescribed in section 10.

(d) The provisions of this section shall not apply to the carrying of a loaded or unloaded rifle or shotgun on a public way by (i) any officer, agent or employee of the commonwealth or any other state or the United States, including any federal, state or local law enforcement personnel; (ii) any member of the military or other service of any state or the United States, including members of the national guard, reserves and junior reserve officer training corps; (iii) any duly authorized law enforcement officer, agent or employee of any municipality of the commonwealth; provided, however, that any such person described in clauses (i) to (iii), inclusive, shall be authorized by a competent authority to so carry a loaded or unloaded rifle or shotgun on a public way and such person is acting within the scope of his duties or training; or (iv) a person who is lawfully engaged in hunting and is the holder of a valid hunting or sporting license issued pursuant to chapter 131. This section shall not apply to the operation of a shooting gallery, licensed and defined under the provisions of section 56A of chapter 140, nor to persons using the same.

SECTION 12E
Discharge of a firearm within 500 feet of a dwelling or other building in use; exceptions

Whoever discharges a firearm as defined in section one hundred and twenty-one of chapter one hundred and forty, a rifle or shotgun within five hundred feet of a dwelling or oth-

er building in use, except with the consent of the owner or legal occupant thereof, shall be punished by a fine of not less than fifty nor more than one hundred dollars or by imprisonment in a jail or house of correction for not more than three months, or both. The provisions of this section shall not apply to (a) the lawful defense of life and property; (b) any law enforcement officer acting in the discharge of his duties; (c) persons using underground or indoor target or test ranges with the consent of the owner or legal occupant thereof; (d) persons using outdoor skeet, trap, target or test ranges with the consent of the owner or legal occupant of the land on which the range is established; (e) persons using shooting galleries, licensed and defined under the provisions of section fifty-six A of chapter one hundred and forty; and (f) the discharge of blank cartridges for theatrical, athletic, ceremonial, firing squad, or other purposes in accordance with section thirty-nine of chapter one hundred and forty-eight.

NOTE The definition of the term "discharges" in the statute includes the act of firing blank cartridges. *Commonwealth v. Stephens*, 67 Mass. App. Ct. 906, 907 (2006).

SECTION 12F
Cutting device in airport or airplane; penalties

(a) For the purposes of this section, the following words shall have the following meanings:—

"Airplane", an aircraft operated by an air carrier holding a certificate issued under 49 U.S.C. 41101 or any aircraft ordinarily used to transport passengers or cargo for hire.

"Cutting device", any knife, cutlery, straight razor, box cutter or other device containing a fixed, folding or retractable blade, which is not included in the list of weapons set forth in paragraph (b) of section 10.

"Prohibited weapon", any infernal machine as defined in section 102A of chapter 266, any stun gun as defined in section 131J of chapter 140, any rifle, shotgun or firearm as defined in section 121 of chapter 140 or any weapon included in the list of weapons set forth in paragraph (b) of section 10.

"Secure area", any area of an airport to which access is restricted through security measures by the airport authority or a public agency and the area beyond a passenger or property screening checkpoint at an airport.

"Airplane cabin", any passenger or flight crew area within an airplane while the airplane is on the ground in the commonwealth or over the commonwealth.

(b) Whoever occupies, or attempts to enter or occupy, a secure area of an airport or the cabin of an airplane, knowingly having in his possession or in his control and knowingly concealing, a cutting device or a prohibited weapon, notwithstanding any license to possess such a weapon or device, shall be punished by imprisonment in the house of correction for not more than 2 years or by imprisonment in the state prison for not more than 5 years or by a fine of not more than $5,000, or by both such fine and imprisonment.

(c) Whoever, with intent to commit a felony, occupies, or attempts to enter or occupy, a secure area of an airport or the cabin of an airplane knowingly having in his possession or in his control a cutting device or a prohibited weapon shall be punished by imprisonment in the house of correction for not more than 2 years or by imprisonment in the state prison for not more than 10 years or by a fine of not more than $10,000, or by both such fine and imprisonment.

2

(d) Whoever, with intent to commit a felony, places, attempts to place or attempts to have placed within a secure area of an airport or the cabin of an airplane, a prohibited weapon or cutting device, notwithstanding any license to possess such a weapon or device, shall be punished by imprisonment in the house of correction for not more than 2½ years or by imprisonment in the state prison for not more than 10 years or by a fine of not more than $10,000, or by both such fine and imprisonment.

(e) Whoever willfully and without regard for the safety of human life, or with reckless disregard for the safety of human life, violates subsection (b), (c) or (d) shall be punished by imprisonment in the state prison for not more than 20 years or by a fine of not more than $20,000, or by both such fine and imprisonment.

(f) This section shall not apply to:—

(1) any law enforcement officer of a state or political subdivision of a state, an officer or employee of the United States government or United States military personnel authorized to carry prohibited weapons or cutting devices in an official capacity;

(2) a duly licensed individual transporting an unloaded, lawful weapon or cutting device in baggage not accessible to a passenger in flight and, in the case of a lawful weapon, if the air carrier was informed of the presence of the weapon;

(3) a cutting device, which is otherwise lawfully possessed, ordinarily used in the course of the holder's employment, trade or occupation, while the holder is authorized to conduct such employment, trade or occupation within a secure area of an airport or airplane cabin.

SECTION 13
False alarms of fire

Whoever, without reasonable cause, by outcry or the ringing of bells, or otherwise, makes or circulates or causes to be made or circulated a false alarm of fire shall be punished by a fine of not less than one hundred dollars nor more than five hundred dollars, or by imprisonment in a jail or house of correction for not more than one year.

NOTE 1   Related Statutes.
G.L. c. 266, § 11—Tampering with fire alarm system or apparatus before fire.
G.L. c. 266, § 12—Tampering with fire alarm system or apparatus during fire; preventing fire extinction.
G.L. c. 268, § 32—Tampering with police or fire signal systems.
G.L. c. 268, § 32A—Interference with fire fighting operations.

NOTE 2   See note accompanying G.L. c. 268, § 39.

SECTION 13A
False reports to police officers

Whoever intentionally and knowingly makes or causes to be made a false report of a crime to police officers shall be punished by a fine of not less than one hundred dollars nor more than five hundred dollars or by imprisonment in a jail or house of correction for not more than one year, or both.

SECTION 14
Explosives or other dangerous substance or contrivance; false reports as to location; punishment

(a) For the purposes of this section, the following words shall have the following meanings:—

"Hijack", to commandeer or to take control without authority.

"School", any public or private preschool, headstart facility, elementary, vocational or secondary school, college or university.

"Serious bodily injury", bodily injury which results in a permanent disfigurement, protracted loss or impairment of a bodily function, limb or organ, or substantial risk of death.

(b) Whoever willfully communicates or causes to be communicated, either directly or indirectly, orally, in writing, by mail, by use of a telephone or telecommunication device including, but not limited to, electronic mail, Internet communications and facsimile communications, through an electronic communication device or by any other means, a threat:—

(1) that a firearm, rifle, shotgun, machine gun or assault weapon, as defined in section 121 of chapter 140, an explosive or incendiary device, a dangerous chemical or biological agent, a poison, a harmful radioactive substance or any other device, substance or item capable of causing death, serious bodily injury or substantial property damage, will be used at a place or location, or is present or will be present at a place or location, whether or not the same is in fact used or present; or

(2) to hijack an aircraft, ship, or common carrier thereby causing anxiety, unrest, fear, or personal discomfort to any person or group of persons shall be punished by imprisonment in the state prison for not more than 20 years or imprisonment in the house of correction for not more than 2½ years, or by fine of not more than $10,000, or by both such fine and imprisonment.

(c) Whoever willfully communicates or causes to be communicated such a threat thereby causing either the evacuation or serious disruption of a school, school related event, school transportation, or a dwelling, building, place of assembly, facility or public transport, or an aircraft, ship or common carrier, or willfully communicates or causes serious public inconvenience or alarm, shall be punished by imprisonment in the state prison for not less than 3 years nor more than 20 years or imprisonment in the house of correction for not less than 6 months nor more than 2½ years, or by fine of not less than $1,000 nor more than $50,000, or by both such fine and imprisonment.

(d) The court shall, after conviction, conduct a hearing to ascertain the extent of costs incurred, damages and financial loss suffered by an individual, public or private entity and the amount of property damage caused as a result of the defendant's crime. A person found guilty of violating this section shall, in all cases, in addition to any other punishment, be ordered to make restitution to the individual, public or private entity for any costs incurred, damages and financial loss sustained as a result of the commission of the crime. Restitution shall be imposed in addition to incarceration or fine, and not in lieu thereof, however, the court shall consider the defendant's present and future ability to pay in its determinations regarding a fine. In determining the amount, time and method of payment of restitution, the court shall consider the financial resources of the defendant and the burden restitution will impose on the defendant.

(e) Nothing in this section shall authorize the criminal prosecution of picketing, public demonstrations or other similar forms of expressing views.

NOTE1   "[T]he communication element of G.L. c. 269, § 14(b), may be proved by evidence that the threat was communicated to any person (other than a coconspirator or co-venturer), and the communication need not be made to an intended target or potential victim." *Commonwealth v. Kerns*, 449 Mass. 641, 643 (2007).

NOTE 2   Venue—G.L. c. 277, § 59A.

NOTE 3   Cross-reference G.L. c. 275, § 2. "G.L. c. 275, § 2, protects particular people and their possessions; G.L. c. 269, § 14(b), protects places or locations and, ultimately, the public." *Commonwealth v. Kerns*, 449 Mass. 641, 643 (2007).

SECTION 14A
Annoying telephone calls or electronic communication

Whoever telephones another person or contacts another person by electronic communication, or causes a person to be telephoned or contacted by electronic communication, repeatedly, for the sole purpose of harassing, annoying or molesting the person or the person's family, whether or not conversation ensues, or whoever telephones or contacts a person repeatedly by electronic communication and uses indecent or obscene language to the person, shall be punished by a fine of not more than $500 or by imprisonment for not more than 3 months, or by both such a fine and imprisonment.

For purposes of this section, "electronic communication" shall include, but not be limited to, any transfer of signs, signals, writing, images, sounds, data or intelligence of any nature transmitted in whole or in part by a wire, radio, electromagnetic, photo-electronic or photo-optical system.

NOTE   As "repeatedly" is alternately defined in dictionaries as "again and again" as well as "more than once", the defendant, who was charged with making two annoying phone calls, was given the benefit of the ambiguity, and his conviction was reversed. *Commonwealth v. Wotan*, 422 Mass. 740 (1996).

SECTION 14B
False reports to emergency response services provider

As used in this section, the following words shall have the following meanings:—

"Emergency response services provider", a police department, fire department, emergency medical service provider, PSAP, public safety department, private safety department or other public safety agency.

"PSAP", a facility assigned the responsibility of receiving 911 calls and, as appropriate, directly dispatching emergency response services or transferring or relaying emergency 911 calls to other public or private safety agencies or other PSAPs.

"Silent call", a call or other communication made to a PSAP in which the initiating party fails to provide information regarding his or her identity or location or the nature of the emergency. The initiating party shall not be considered to have provided any information that is automatically transmitted by a communication device or network upon connection with a PSAP including, but not be limited to, automatic location information and automatic number information.

(a) Whoever willfully and maliciously communicates with a PSAP, or causes a communication to be made to a PSAP, which communication transmits information which the person knows or has reason to know is false and which results in the dispatch of emergency services to a nonexistent emergency or to the wrong location of an actual emergency; or (b) whoever willfully and maliciously, makes or causes to be made 3 or more silent calls to any PSAP and thereby causes emergency services to be dispatched 3 or more times shall be punished by imprisonment in the house of correction for not more than 2½ years or by a fine of not more than $1,000.

Whoever commits a second or subsequent violation of this section shall be punished by imprisonment in the house of correction for not more than 2½ years or by imprisonment in the state prison for not more than 10 years or by a fine of not more than $5,000 dollars, or by both such fine and imprisonment.

(b) Upon any conviction of this section, the court shall conduct a hearing to ascertain the extent of costs incurred, and damages and financial loss sustained by any emergency response services provider as a result of the violation and shall order the defendant to make restitution to the emergency response services provider or providers for any such costs, damages or loss. Restitution shall not be waived and shall be imposed in addition to any imprisonment or fine, and not in lieu thereof, except that the court shall consider the defendant's present and future ability to pay restitution in its determinations relative to the imposition of a fine. In determining the amount, time and method of payment of restitution, the court shall consider the financial resources of the defendant and the burden restitution will impose upon the defendant.

SECTION 15
Sale of stink bombs

Whoever sells or offers for sale a stink bomb shall be punished by a fine of not less than ten nor more than two hundred dollars. As used in this section the words "stink bomb" shall mean a small bomb that gives off a foul odor on bursting or any compound or device prepared for the primary purpose of generating a foul odor and sold or offered for sale for such purpose.

SECTION 16
Sale of broadheads, razorheads, or other hunting arrowheads

Whoever sells or offers for sale devices known as broadheads, razorheads, or any other arrowhead used exclusively for hunting purposes to any person under fifteen years of age shall be punished by a fine of one hundred dollars upon conviction of the first offense, five hundred dollars upon conviction of the second offense, and one thousand dollars and not less than six months nor more than one year in a house of correction for the third and subsequent offenses.

SECTION 17
Hazing; organizing or participating; hazing defined

Whoever is a principal organizer or participant in the crime of hazing as defined herein shall be punished by a fine of not more than three thousand dollars or by imprisonment in a house of correction for not more than one year, or by both such fine and imprisonment.

The term "hazing" as used in this section and in sections eighteen and nineteen, shall mean any conduct or method of initiation into any student organization, whether on public or private property, which wilfully or recklessly endangers the physical or mental health of any student or other person. Such conduct shall include whipping, beating, branding, forced calisthenics, exposure to the weather, forced consumption of any food, liquor, beverage, drug or other substance, or any other brutal treatment or forced physical activity which is likely to adversely affect the physical health or safety of any such student or other person, or which subjects such student or other person to extreme mental stress, including extended deprivation of sleep or rest or extended isolation.

Notwithstanding any other provisions of this section to the contrary, consent shall not be available as a defense to any prosecution under this action.

SECTION 18
Failure to report hazing

Whoever knows that another person is the victim of hazing as defined in section seventeen and is at the scene of such crime shall, to the extent that such person can do so without danger or peril to himself or others, report such crime to an appropriate law enforcement official as soon as reasonably practicable. Whoever fails to report such crime shall be punished by a fine of not more than one thousand dollars.

SECTION 19
Copy of Secs. 17–19; issuance to student and student groups, teams and organizations; report

Each institution of secondary education and each public and private institution of post secondary education shall issue to every student group, student team or student organization which is part of such institution or is recognized by the institution or permitted by the institution to use its name or facilities or is known by the institution to exist as an unaffiliated student group, student team or student organization, a copy of this section and sections seventeen and eighteen; provided, however, that an institution's compliance with this section's requirements that an institution issue copies of this section and sections seventeen and eighteen to unaffiliated student groups, teams or organizations shall not constitute evidence of the institution's recognition or endorsement of said unaffiliated student groups, teams or organizations.

Each such group, team or organization shall distribute a copy of this section and sections seventeen and eighteen to each of its members, plebes, pledges or applicants for membership. It shall be the duty of each such group, team or organization, acting through its designated officer, to deliver annually, to the institution an attested acknowledgement stating that such group, team or organization has received a copy of this section and said sections seventeen and eighteen, that each of its members, plebes, pledges, or applicants has received a copy of sections seventeen and eighteen, and that such group, team or organization understands and agrees to comply with the provisions of this section and sections seventeen and eighteen.

Each institution of secondary education and each public or private institution of post secondary education shall, at least annually, before or at the start of enrollment, deliver to each person who enrolls as a full time student in such institution a copy of this section and sections seventeen and eighteen.

Each institution of secondary education and each public or private institution of post secondary education shall file, at least annually, a report with the board of higher education and in the case of secondary institutions, the board of education, certifying that such institution has complied with its responsibility to inform student groups, teams or organizations and to notify each full time student enrolled by it of the provisions of this section and sections seventeen and eighteen and also certifying that said institution has adopted a disciplinary policy with regard to the organizers and participants of hazing, and that such policy has been set forth with appropriate emphasis in the student handbook or similar means of communicating the institution's policies to its students. The board of higher education and, in the case of secondary institutions, the board of education shall promulgate regulations governing the content and frequency of such reports, and shall forthwith report to the attorney general any such institution which fails to make such report.

Chapter 270. Crimes Against Public Health

Section

1	Adulterating liquor; sale; forfeiture
1A	Sale of eyeglasses or sunglasses; specifications; flammable frames; penalty
2–2B	Repealed
3	Distribution of drugs or other substance injurious to users
3A	Placing poison for rodents where it may cause injury; enforcement officers
4	Food, drink or drug containing wood alcohol
5	Giving, selling or delivering alcoholic beverages or drugs to hospital patients; possession
6	Selling or giving tobacco to minors
6A	Selling cigarette rolling papers to minors
7	Posting copy of Sec. 6; removing copy
8	Selling candy containing alcohol
8A	Foods containing foreign injury-causing substances; distribution or sale
9	Feeding garbage or refuse; possession
10	Toys or confectionery containing or coated with material containing arsenic
11	Samples for analysis for arsenic
12	Fabric or paper containing arsenic; investigations; inspectors; chemists; regulations
13	Refusal or neglect to furnish water
14	Spitting
15	Arrest without warrant for spitting
16	Disposal of rubbish, etc. on or near highways and coastal or inland waters; penalties; enforcement; park rangers
16A	Alternative noncriminal disposition of violations of Sec. 16
17	Disposal of garbage or refuse in containers placed along highways
17A	Repealed
18	Substances having property of releasing toxic vapors; sale, possession and use
19	Sale of glue or cement to minors; smelling detergent ingredients; register
20	Burning of refuse, etc. within marine or shoreline boundaries
21	Repealed
22	Smoking in public places
23	Smoking at flea market
24	Sale of mercury thermometers
25	Ice cream truck vending; permit requirements

SECTION 1
Adulterating liquor; sale; forfeiture

Whoever, for the purpose of sale, adulterates any liquor used or intended for drink with Indian cockle, vitriol, grains of paradise, opium, alum, cochineal, capsicum, copperas, laurel water, logwood, Brazil wood, sugar of lead or any other substance poisonous or injurious to health, and whoever knowingly sells any such liquor so adulterated, shall be punished by imprisonment in the state prison for not more than three years; and the articles so adulterated shall be forfeited.

2

SECTION 1A
Sale of eyeglasses or sunglasses; specifications; flammable frames; penalty

No person shall distribute, sell or deliver any eyeglasses or sunglasses unless said eyeglasses or sunglasses are fitted with plastic lenses, laminated lenses, heat-treated glass lenses or lenses made impact-resistant by other methods. The provisions of this paragraph shall not apply if a physician or optometrist, having found that such lenses will not fulfill the visual requirements of a particular patient, directs in writing the use of other lenses and gives written notification thereof to the patient. Before they are mounted in frames, all impact-resistant eyeglass and sunglass lenses shall be capable of withstanding an impact test of a steel ball five-eighths of an inch in diameter weighing approximately fifty-six hundredths of an ounce dropped from a height of fifty inches. Raised ledge multifocal lenses shall be capable of withstanding said impact test but need not be tested beyond initial design testing. All prescription glass lenses shall withstand said impact test. To demonstrate that all nonprescription glass lenses, plastic lenses and laminated lenses are capable of withstanding said impact test, the manufacturer of such lenses shall subject to said impact test a statistically significant sampling of lenses from each production batch, and the lenses so tested shall be representative of the finished forms as worn by the wearer. Plastic prescription and plastic nonprescription lenses, tested on the basis of statistical significance, may be tested in uncut finished or semifinished form at the point of original manufacture.

No person shall distribute, sell, exchange or deliver or have in his possession with intent to distribute, sell, exchange or deliver any eyeglass or sunglass frame containing any form of cellulose nitrate or other highly flammable material.

Whoever violates any provision of this section shall be punished by a fine of not more than five hundred dollars for each violation.

SECTIONS 2–2B
Repealed

SECTION 3
Distribution of drugs or other substance injurious to users

Whoever distributes, delivers or gives away in any public way or from house to house or place to place, any bottle, box, envelope or package containing any liquid, medicine, pill, powder, tablet or other article composed of any drug, poison or other ingredient or substance which may be in any way injurious or harmful to any person who may taste, eat, drink or otherwise use the same, shall be punished by a fine of not less than fifty nor more than one hundred dollars.

SECTION 3A
Placing poison for rodents where it may cause injury; enforcement officers

Whoever negligently or maliciously places any poison or poisoned food for the control of rats, mice or other rodents in any place where it may cause injury to any human being or domestic animal shall be punished by a fine of twenty-five dollars. The officers charged with the enforcement of the laws relating to fish, birds and mammals under chapter one hundred and thirty-one shall take cognizance of violations of this section and enforce the provisions thereof, and they shall have all powers necessary therefor.

SECTION 4
Food, drink or drug containing wood alcohol

Whoever, himself, or by his servant or agent, or as the servant or agent of another, sells or exchanges, or has in his possession with intent to sell or exchange, or knowingly delivers or has in his possession with intent to deliver, any article of food or drink, or any drug intended for internal use, containing any wood alcohol, otherwise known as methyl alcohol, either crude or refined, under or by whatever name or trade mark the same may be called or known, shall be punished by a fine of not more than five thousand dollars or by imprisonment in a jail or house of correction for not more than two and one half years or in the state prison for not more than five years, or by both such fine and imprisonment.

SECTION 5
Giving, selling or delivering alcoholic beverages or drugs to hospital patients; possession

Whoever, except under the direction of a physician, gives, sells or delivers alcoholic beverages, as defined in section one of chapter one hundred and thirty-eight, or a narcotic drug to a patient in any hospital who is suffering from inebriety or from the effect of inebriety, or from excessive use of narcotic drugs or from the effect of such use, and whoever has in his possession within the precincts of any hospital any such beverage or drug with intent to convey or deliver it to any such patient, except under direction as aforesaid, shall be punished by a fine of not more than fifty dollars or by imprisonment for not more than two months.

SECTION 6
Selling or giving tobacco to minors

Whoever sells a cigarette, chewing tobacco, snuff or any tobacco in any of its forms to any person under the age of eighteen or, not being his parent or guardian, gives a cigarette, chewing tobacco, snuff or tobacco in any of its forms to any person under the age of eighteen shall be punished by a fine of not less than one hundred dollars for the first offense, not less than two hundred dollars for a second offense and not less than three hundred dollars for any third or subsequent offense.

SECTION 6A
Selling cigarette rolling papers to minors

Whoever sells cigarette rolling papers to any person under the age of eighteen shall be punished by a fine of not less than twenty-five dollars for the first offense, not less than fifty dollars for the second offense and not less than one hundred dollars for a third or subsequent offense.

Notwithstanding the provisions of any civil ordinance or by-law or regulation to the contrary, which is in effect on the effective date of this section, no city, town, department, board or other political subdivision or agency of the commonwealth may impose any requirements, restrictions or prohibitions pertaining to the sale of cigarette rolling papers, in addition to those in this section.

SECTION 7
Posting copy of Sec. 6; removing copy

A copy of the preceding section printed as therein specified shall be posted conspicuously by the owner or person in charge thereof in the shop or other place used to sell cigarettes at retail, and whoever violates this provision shall be punished by a fine of not more than fifty dollars. Any person unlawfully removing a copy so posted while said premises are used for the sale of cigarettes shall be punished by a fine of ten dollars.

SECTION 8
Selling candy containing alcohol

Whoever sells to a person any candy enclosing or containing liquid or syrup having more than one per cent of alcohol shall be punished by a fine of not more than one hundred dollars.

SECTION 8A
Foods containing foreign injury-causing substances; distribution or sale

Whoever sells, gives, or distributes to anyone candy or other food or food stuffs containing a foreign substance, which is intended or may reasonably be expected to cause injury to a person eating the same, shall be punished by imprisonment in the state prison for not more than five years.

SECTION 9
Feeding garbage or refuse; possession

Whoever knowingly feeds or has in his possession with intent to feed to a milch cow any garbage, refuse or offal collected by a town, or by any person having authority therefrom, shall be punished by a fine of not more than one hundred dollars or by imprisonment for not more than two months; and whoever knowingly feeds or has in his possession with intent to feed to any food animal, except swine, any garbage, refuse or offal collected by a city of more than thirty thousand inhabitants shall be punished by a fine of not more than fifty dollars or by imprisonment for not more than one month.

SECTION 10
Toys or confectionery containing or coated with material containing arsenic

Whoever, himself, or by his agent or servant, or as the agent or servant of another, manufactures, sells or exchanges, or has in his custody or possession with intent to sell or exchange, or exposes or offers for sale or exchange, any toys or confectionery, containing or coated wholly or in part with arsenic, shall be punished by a fine of not less than fifty nor more than one hundred dollars.

SECTION 11
Samples for analysis for arsenic

Whoever offers or exposes for sale or exchange any paper, fabric or other article shall furnish a sample thereof sufficient to ascertain by analysis the existence of arsenic therein, if such sample can be obtained without damage to the remaining portion, to any inspector, chemist or other agent or officer of the department of public health who applies therefor and tenders the value thereof; and for a violation of this section shall be punished as provided in the preceding section.

SECTION 12
Fabric or paper containing arsenic; investigations; inspectors; chemists; regulations

Whoever, himself, or by his agent or servant, manufactures, sells or exchanges, or has in his custody or possession with intent to sell or exchange, any woven fabric or paper containing arsenic in any form, or any article of dress or household use composed wholly or in part of such woven fabric or paper, shall be punished by a fine of not less than fifty nor more than two hundred dollars; but this section shall not apply to articles intended for the destruction of insects, having the word "POISON" plainly printed in uncondensed gothic letters not less than one inch long on both sides of each sheet and square foot of the fabric, or to dress goods or articles of dress containing not more than one-hundredth grain, or to other materials or articles containing not more than one tenth grain of arsenic for each square yard of the material. The department of public health shall make all necessary investigations as to the existence of arsenic in the aforesaid articles and materials, employ inspectors and chemists, and adopt such measures as are necessary to enforce this section.

SECTION 13
Refusal or neglect to furnish water

A corporation engaged in selling or distributing water, which refuses or neglects to furnish or supply water to or for any building or premises for the reason that a water bill remains unpaid by a previous owner or occupant of said building or premises shall, unless the person applying for water is in arrears to such corporation for water previously furnished to or for any building or premises, be punished by a fine of not less than ten nor more than twenty dollars.

SECTION 14
Spitting

Whoever expectorates or spits upon any public sidewalk, or upon any place used exclusively or principally by pedestrians, or, except in receptacles provided for the purpose, in or upon any part of any city or town hall, any court house or court room, any public library or museum, any church or theatre, any lecture or music hall, any mill or factory, any hall of any tenement building occupied by five or more families, any school building, any ferry boat or steamboat, any railroad car or elevated railroad car, except a smoking car, any street railway car, any railroad or railway station or waiting room, or on any track, platform or sidewalk connected therewith, and included within the limits thereof, shall be punished by a fine of not more than twenty dollars.

SECTION 15
Arrest without warrant for spitting

Any person detected in the act of violating the preceding section may, if his name is unknown to the officer, be arrested without a warrant by any officer authorized to serve criminal process in the place where the offense is committed and kept in custody until he can be taken before a court having jurisdiction of such offense.

SECTION 16
Disposal of rubbish, etc. on or near highways and coastal or inland waters; penalties; enforcement; park rangers

Whoever places, throws, deposits or discharges or whoever causes to be placed, thrown, deposited or discharged,

2

trash, bottles or cans, refuse, rubbish, garbage, debris, scrap, waste or other material of any kind on a public highway or within 20 yards of a public highway, or on any other public land, or in or upon coastal or inland waters, as defined in section 1 of chapter 131, or within 20 yards of such waters, or on property of another, or on lands dedicated for open space purposes, including lands subject to conservation restrictions and agricultural preservation restrictions as defined in chapter 184, shall be punished by a fine of not more than $5,500 for the first offense and a fine not to exceed $15,000 for each subsequent offense; provided, however, that 50 per cent of the fine imposed shall be deposited in the conservation trust established in section 1 of chapter 132A and the court may also require that the violator remove, at his own expense, the trash, refuse, rubbish, debris or materials. The permission of the owner of land to place, throw, deposit or discharge trash, refuse, rubbish, garbage, debris, scrap, waste or other material on the owner's land shall constitute a defense in any trial for such offense.

If a motor vehicle is used in committing such an offense where the offense involves the unlawful disposal of more than seven cubic feet of trash, bottles or cans, refuse, rubbish, garbage, debris, scrap, waste or any other materials and the motor vehicle is observed while the offense is in progress by an officer authorized to enforce this section, the officer may seize the vehicle and remove and store it or otherwise immobilize it by a mechanical device until (1) payment is made to the enforcing authority of a fine set by such enforcing authority up to the maximum fine which may be imposed under this section, (2) the illegally disposed of material is removed and legally disposed of, and (3) payment is made to the enforcing authority of its reasonable towing and storage charges, if any, for the seized vehicle. If, after payment of the above fine and towing and storage charges, the use of the seized vehicle is necessary to dispose of the material, the enforcing authority shall release the seized vehicle upon the posting of security sufficient to pay for the cost of legal disposal of the material. The security shall be returned to the person posting it upon proof of legal disposal of the material. Within five days of the payment of a fine to secure the release of a seized vehicle as provided for herein, the enforcing authority to whom the fine is paid shall deposit the fine in court along with an application for a criminal complaint regarding the offense, and the court shall hold the fine until judgment is entered on said complaint; provided, however, that at the discretion of the enforcing authority, the violation may be disposed of by the non-criminal disposition procedures pursuant to section twenty-one D of chapter forty, in which case the maximum fine shall be one thousand dollars. If a conviction is returned on the complaint the court shall award to any person or persons, other than an employee of the enforcing authority, whose information materially contributed to the identification of the convicted party, up to five hundred dollars, or forty percent of said fine, whichever is the greater, and the balance of the fine shall be equally divided between the enforcing authority and the court. If such violation is disposed of non-criminally, the balance of such fine, after payment of the award, if any, shall be deposited in the general fund of the enforcing authority. Vehicles seized under the provisions of this section which are not claimed or redeemed by their owners as provided for above within thirty days of the date of seizure, may after thirty days notice by certified mail to the vehicle's registered owner, be sold at auction and the proceeds be applied to the fines assessed herein, vehicle towing and storage costs and the costs for legal disposal of the material. Enforcing authorities shall adopt appropriate rules and regulations which provide for the orderly implementation of this section.

If a motor vehicle is used in committing such an offense, a conviction under this section shall forthwith be reported by the court to the registrar of motor vehicles, and the registrar may suspend the license of the operator of such vehicle for not more than thirty days, and if it appears from the records of the registrar of motor vehicles that the person so convicted is the owner of the motor vehicle so used, the registrar may suspend the certificate of registration of said vehicle for thirty days.

The provisions of this section shall not be applicable to any dumping ground approved under section one hundred and fifty A of chapter one hundred and eleven or by other appropriate public authority.

This section shall be enforced by natural resources officers, by the director of the division of motorboats or his authorized agents, by harbormasters and assistant harbormasters, by members of the state police and by city and town police officers. A city by majority vote of the city council, with the approval of the mayor, or in a town by a vote of its town meeting may enforce this section by designating its public health agents, health officers and health directors as enforcing officers. In the city of Boston this section shall also be enforced by the commissioner of health and hospitals, by the commissioner of housing inspection, and by the commissioner of public works, and their respective authorized agents, and in section sixteen A, the commissioner of health and hospitals, the commissioner of housing inspection, and the commissioner of public works shall be deemed to be the commanding officers of their respective authorized agents; provided, however, that any person observing a violation of this section may file a petition for issuance of a complaint pursuant to this section with the clerk of the district court having jurisdiction or, in the city of Boston, with the clerk of the Boston municipal court department, and upon determining that probable cause exists therefor, such clerk shall issue such complaint.

Chief park rangers and park rangers shall have the authority to enforce this section on state forests, reservations, parks, rinks, pools, piers and other facilities and properties under the jurisdiction of the department of environmental management. In addition to the fines imposed under this section, the violator may be held liable for costs associated with the identification, removal and disposal of said materials. The department of environmental management shall permanently post signs on all lands under its jurisdiction which identify: 1) the penalties applicable for the violations under this section; and 2) the proper authorities and contact information to report violations.

NOTE   **Related Statutes.**

G.L. c. 270, § 20—Burning of refuse, etc. within marine or shoreline boundaries.

G.L. c. 272, § 60—Refusal to remove rubbish, etc. placed on public way in violation of town regulations.

SECTION 16A
Alternative noncriminal disposition of violations of Sec. 16

If any officer empowered to enforce section sixteen takes cognizance of a violation thereof, he may request the offender to state his name and address. Whoever, upon such request, refuses to state his name and address, may be arrested without a warrant, or if he states a false name and address or a name and address which is not his name and address in ordinary use, he shall be punished by a fine or not less than fifty nor more than one hundred dollars. Such officer may, as an alternative to instituting criminal proceedings, forthwith give to the offender a written notice to appear before the clerk of the district court having jurisdiction at any time during office hours, not later than twenty-one days after the date of such violation. Such notice shall be made in triplicate, and shall contain the name and address of the offender and, if served with notice in hand at the time of such violation, the number of his license, if any, to operate motor vehicles; the registration number of the vehicle or motor boat involved, if any; the time and place of the violation; the specific offense charged; and the time and place for his required appearance. Such notice shall be signed by the officer, and shall be signed by the offender whenever practicable in acknowledgment that the notice has been received. The officer shall, if possible, deliver to the offender at the time and place of the violation a copy of said notice. Whenever it is not possible to deliver a copy of said notice to the offender at the time and place of the violation, said copy shall be mailed or delivered by the officer, or by his commanding officer or any person authorized by said commanding officer, to the offender's last known address, or in the case of a violation involving a motor vehicle or motor boat registered under the laws of this commonwealth, within five days of the offense, or in the case of any motor vehicle or motor boat registered under the laws of another state or country, within ten days thereof, exclusive, in either case, of Sundays and holidays, to the address of the registrant of the motor vehicle or motor boat involved, as appearing, in the case of a motor vehicle registered under the laws of this commonwealth, in the records of the registry of motor vehicles or the division of motor boats or, in the case of a motor vehicle or motor boat registered under the laws of another state or country in the records of the official in such state or country having charge of the registration of such motor vehicle or motor boat. Such notice mailed by the officer, his commanding officer, or the person so authorized to the last address of said registrant as appearing as aforesaid, shall be deemed a sufficient notice, and a certificate of the officer or person mailing such notice that it has been mailed in accordance with this section shall be deemed prima facie evidence thereof and shall be admissible in any court of the commonwealth as to the facts contained therein. At or before the completion of each tour of duty the officer shall give to his commanding officer those copies of each notice of such a violation he has taken cognizance of during such tour which have not already been delivered or mailed by him as aforesaid. Said commanding officer shall retain one of such copies and shall, at a time not later than the next court day after said delivery or mailing, deliver another copy to the clerk of the court before whom the offender has been notified to appear. The clerk of each district court shall maintain a separate docket of all such notices to appear.

Any person notified to appear before the clerk of a district court as hereinbefore provided may appear before such clerk and confess the offense charged, either personally or through an agent duly authorized in writing, or by mailing to such clerk, with the notice, the sum provided herein, such payment to be made only by postal note, money order or check. If it is the first, second or third offense subject to this section committed by such person within the jurisdiction of the court in the calendar year, payment to such clerk of the sum of twenty dollars shall operate as a final disposition of the case; if it is the fourth or subsequent such offense so committed in such calendar year, payment to such clerk of the sum of one hundred dollars shall operate as a final disposition of the case. Proceedings under this paragraph shall not be deemed criminal; and no person notified to appear before the clerk of a district court as provided herein shall be required to report to any probation officer, and no record of the case shall be entered in the probation records.

If any person notified to appear before the clerk of the district court fails to appear and pay the fine provided hereunder or, having appeared, desires not to avail himself of the procedure hereinbefore provided for the non-criminal disposition of the case, the clerk shall notify the officer concerned, who shall forthwith make application for a criminal complaint and follow the procedure established for criminal cases, and shall notify, if a motor vehicle is involved, the registrar of motor vehicles, or, if a motor boat is involved, the division of motor boats. If any person fails to appear in accordance with the summons issued upon such complaint the clerk shall send such person by certified mail, return receipt requested, a notice that the complaint is pending and that, if the person fails to appear within twenty-one days from the sending of such notice, a warrant for his arrest will be issued. If any person fails to appear within twenty-one days from the sending of such notice, the court shall issue a warrant for his arrest.

The notice to appear, provided herein, shall be printed in such form as the chief justice for the district court department and the chief justice for the Boston municipal court department may prescribe for their respective departments; provided, however, that a notice prepared pursuant to section twenty A or section twenty C of chapter ninety may be so revised or adapted that said notice may also be used for the notice provided for in this section.

SECTION 17
Disposal of garbage or refuse in containers placed along highways

Whoever disposes of household or commercial garbage or refuse by placing it in a trash barrel placed on a public highway by the commonwealth, or by any political subdivision thereof for the convenience of the traveling public shall be punished by a fine of not less than two hundred dollars. One-half of any fine paid into a court shall be paid over to the city or town where said offense occurred.

SECTION 17A
Repealed

SECTION 18
Substances having property of releasing toxic vapors; sale, possession and use

No person shall intentionally smell or inhale the fumes of any substance having the property of releasing toxic vapors,

2

for the purpose of causing a condition of intoxication, euphoria, excitement, exhilaration, stupefaction, or dulled senses or nervous system, nor possess, buy or sell any such substance for the purpose of violating or aiding another to violate this section.

This section shall not apply to the inhalation of anesthesia for medical or dental purposes.

Whoever violates the provisions of this section shall be punished by a fine of not more than two hundred dollars or by imprisonment for not more than six months, or both.

Any person who is discovered by a police officer or special police officer in the act of violating this section may be arrested without a warrant by such police officer or special police officer, and held in custody, in jail, or otherwise, until a complaint is made against him for such offense which complaint shall be made as soon as practicable and in any case within twenty-four hours, Sundays and legal holidays excepted.

SECTION 19

Sale of glue or cement to minors; smelling detergent ingredients; register

Any person who sells glue or cement to a minor shall require such minor to properly identify himself and write his name and address legibly in a permanently bound register. The seller shall keep such register available for police inspection for a period of six months after the last sale is recorded therein. No such glue or cement shall be sold to a minor unless it contains allyl isothiocyanate (oil of mustard) or some other equally effective and safe deterrent against smelling or inhaling the fumes of such glue or cement.

As used in this section, "glue" or "cement" shall mean any glue or cement that contains a solvent or chemical having the property of releasing toxic vapors.

Whoever violates the provisions of this section shall be punished by a fine of not more than two hundred dollars or by imprisonment for not more than six months, or both.

SECTION 20

Burning of refuse, etc. within marine or shoreline boundaries

No person shall burn refuse, rubbish or demolition debris within the marine boundaries of the commonwealth, or within twelve miles from the shoreline of the commonwealth, whichever is the shorter distance. Whoever violates any provision of this section shall be punished by a fine of not less than two hundred and fifty dollars nor more than one thousand dollars.

NOTE   Related Statutes.
G.L. c. 270, § 16—Disposal of rubbish, etc. on or near highways and coastal or inland waters.
G.L. c. 272, § 60—Refusal to remove rubbish, etc. placed on public way in violation of town regulations.

SECTION 21

Definitions—Repealed

SECTION 22

Smoking in public places

(a) As used in this section, the following words shall have the following meanings, unless the context requires otherwise:

"Business agent", an individual who has been designated by the owner or operator of any establishment to be the manager or otherwise in charge of the establishment.

"Compensation", money, gratuity, privilege, or benefit received from an employer in return for work performed or services rendered.

"Customer service area", an area of the workplace that a business invitee may access.

"Employee", an individual or person who performs a service for compensation for an employer at the employer's workplace, including a contract employee, temporary employee, and independent contractor who performs a service in the employer's workplace for more than a *de minimis* amount of time.

"Employer", an individual, person, partnership, association, corporation, trust, organization, school, college, university or other educational institution or other legal entity, whether public, quasi-public, private, or non-profit which uses the services of 1 or more employees at 1 or more workplaces, at any 1 time, including the commonwealth or its agencies, authorities or political subdivisions.

"Enclosed", a space bounded by walls, with or without windows or fenestrations, continuous from floor to ceiling and enclosed by 1 or more doors, including but not limited to an office, function room or hallway.

"Lodging home", a dwelling or part thereof which contains 1 or more rooming units in which space is let or sublet for compensation by the owner or operator to 4 or more persons. The residential portion of boarding houses, rooming houses, dormitories, and other similar dwelling places are included in this definition. Hospitals, sanitariums, jails, houses of correction, homeless shelters, and assisted living homes are not included in this definition.

"Membership association", a not-for-profit entity that has been established and operates, for a charitable, philanthropic, civic, social, benevolent, educational, religious, athletic, recreation or similar purpose, and is comprised of members who collectively belong to:

(i) a society, organization or association of a fraternal nature that operates under the lodge system, and having 1 or more affiliated chapters or branches incorporated in any state; or

(ii) a corporation organized under chapter 180; or

(iii) an established religious place of worship or instruction in the commonwealth whose real or personal property is exempt from taxation; or

(iv) a veterans' organization incorporated or chartered by the Congress of the United States, or otherwise, having 1 or more affiliated chapters or branches incorporated in any state.

Except for a religious place of worship or instruction, an entity shall not be a membership association for the purposes of this definition, unless individual membership is required for all members of the association for a period of not less than 90 days.

"Outdoor space", an outdoor area, open to the air at all times and cannot be enclosed by a wall or side covering.

"Public building", a building owned by the commonwealth or any political subdivision thereof, or in an enclosed indoor space occupied by a state agency or department of the commonwealth which is located in a building not owned by the commonwealth.

"Public transportation conveyance", a vehicle or vessel used in mass public transportation or in the transportation of the public, including a train, passenger bus, school bus or other vehicle used to transport pupils, taxi, passenger ferry boat, water shuttle or other equipment used in public transportation owned by, or operated under the authority of the Massachusetts Bay Transportation Authority, the Woods Hole, Martha's Vineyard & Nantucket Steamship Authority, Massachusetts Port Authority; state transportation department; or a vehicle or vessel open to the public that is owned by, or operated under the authority of a business, including tour vehicles or vessels, enclosed ski lifts or trams, passenger buses or vans regularly used to transport customers. Notwithstanding the foregoing, a private vehicle or vessel not open to the public or not used for the transportation of the public during the times of use, including a private passenger vehicle, a private charter or rental of a limousine, bus or van or the private rental of a boat or other vessel, shall not be considered a public transportation conveyance.

"Residence", the part of a structure used as a dwelling including without limitation: a private home, townhouse, condominium, apartment, mobile home; vacation home, cabin or cottage; a residential unit in a governmental public housing facility; and the residential portions of a school, college or university dormitory or facility. A residential unit provided by an employer to an employee at a place of employment shall be considered to be a residence; if the unit is an enclosed indoor space used exclusively as a residence, and other employees, excluding family members of the employee, or the public has no right of access to the residence. For the purposes of this definition, a hotel, motel, inn, lodge, bed and breakfast or other similar public accommodation, hospital, nursing home or assisted living facility shall not be considered a residence.

"Retail tobacco store", an establishment which is not required to possess a retail food permit whose primary purpose is to sell or offer for sale to consumers, but not for resale, tobacco products and paraphernalia, in which the sale of other products is merely incidental, and in which the entry of persons under the age of 18 is prohibited at all times, and maintains a valid permit for the retail sale of tobacco products as required to be issued by the appropriate authority in the city or town where the establishment is located.

"Smoking" or "smoke", the lighting of a cigar, cigarette, pipe or other tobacco product or possessing a lighted cigar, cigarette, pipe or other tobacco or non-tobacco product designed to be combusted and inhaled.

"Smoking bar", an establishment that occupies exclusively an enclosed indoor space and that primarily is engaged in the retail sale of tobacco products for consumption by customers on the premises; derives revenue from the sale of food, alcohol or other beverages that is incidental to the sale of the tobacco products; prohibits entry to a person under the age of 18 years of age during the time when the establishment is open for business; prohibits any food or beverage not sold directly by the business to be consumed on the premises; maintains a valid permit for the retail sale of tobacco products as required to be issued by the appropriate authority in the city or town where the establishment is located; and, maintains a valid permit to operate a smoking bar issued by the department of revenue.

"Workplace", an indoor area, structure or facility or a portion thereof, at which 1 or more employees perform a service for compensation for the employer, other enclosed spaces rented to or otherwise used by the public; and where the employer has the right or authority to exercise control over the space.

"Work space or work spaces", an enclosed area occupied by an employee during the course of his employment.

(b)(1) It shall be the responsibility of the employer to provide a smoke free environment for all employees working in an enclosed workplace.

(2) Smoking shall be prohibited in workplaces, work spaces, common work areas, classrooms, conference and meeting rooms, offices, elevators, hallways, medical facilities, cafeterias, employee lounges, staircases, restrooms, restaurants, cafes, coffee shops, food courts or concessions, supermarkets or retail food outlets, bars, taverns, or in a place where food or drink is sold to the public and consumed on the premise as part of a business required to collect state meals tax on the purchase; or in a train, airplane, theatre, concert hall, exhibition hall, convention center, auditorium, arena, or stadium open to the public; or in a school, college, university, museum, library, health care facility as defined in section 9C of chapter 112, group child care center, school age child care center, family child care center, school age day or overnight camp building, or on premises where activities are licensed under section 38 of chapter 10 or in or upon any public transportation conveyance or in any airport, train station, bus station, transportation passenger terminal, or enclosed outdoor platform.

(3) A person shall not smoke in the state house or in a public building or in a vehicle or vessel, owned, leased, or otherwise operated by the commonwealth or a political subdivision thereof, or in a space occupied by a state agency or department of the commonwealth which is located in another building, including a private office in a building or space mentioned in this sentence, or at an open meeting of a governmental body as defined in section 11A of chapter 30A, section 23A of chapter 39 and section 9F of chapter 34, or in a courtroom or courthouse. This subsection shall not apply to a resident or patient of a state hospital, the Soldiers' Home in Massachusetts located in the city of Chelsea or the Soldiers' Home in Holyoke.

(c) Notwithstanding subsection (b), smoking may be permitted in the following places and circumstances:

(1) Private residences; except during such time when the residence is utilized as part of a business as a group childcare center, school age child care center, school age day or overnight camp, or a facility licensed by the department of early education and care or as a health care related office or facility;

(2)(i) premises occupied by a membership association, if the premises is owned, or under a written lease for a term of not less than 90 consecutive days, by the association during the time of the permitted activity if the premises are not located in a public building; but no smoking shall be permitted in an enclosed indoor space of a membership association during the time the space is:

(A) open to the public; or

(B) occupied by a non-member who is not an invited guest of a member or an employee of the association; or

(C) rented from the association for a fee or other agreement that compensates the association for the use of such space.

(ii) Smoking may be permitted in an enclosed indoor space of a membership association at all times, if the space is restricted by the association to admittance only of its members, the invited guest of a member, and the employees of the membership association. A person who is a contract employee,

2

temporary employee, or independent contractor shall not be considered an employee of a membership association under this subsection. A person who is a member of an affiliated chapter or branch of a membership association that is fraternal in nature operating under the lodge system, and is visiting the affiliated association, shall be an invited guest for the purposes of this subsection.

(3) A guest room in a hotel, motel, inn, bed and breakfast or lodging home that is designed and normally used for sleeping and living purposes, that is rented to a guest and designated as a smoking room pursuant to paragraph (1) of subsection (g).

(4) A retail tobacco store, if the store maintains a valid permit for the sale of tobacco products issued by the appropriate authority in the city or town in which the retail tobacco store is located. All required permits shall be displayed in a conspicuous manner, visible at all times to patrons of the establishment.

(5) A smoking bar, if the smoking bar maintains a valid permit pursuant to this section. All required permits shall be displayed in a conspicuous manner, visible at all times to patrons of the establishment.

(6) By a theatrical performer upon a stage or in the course of a professional film production, if the smoking is part of a theatrical production, and if permission has been obtained from the appropriate local authority;

(7) By a person, organization or other entity that conducts medical or scientific research on tobacco products, if the research is conducted in an enclosed space not open to the public, in a laboratory facility at an accredited college or university, or in a professional testing laboratory as defined by regulation of the department of public health;

(8) Religious ceremonies where smoking is part of the ritual; and

(9) A tobacco farmer, leaf dealer, manufacturer, importer, exporter, or wholesale distributor of tobacco products, may permit smoking in the workplace for the sole purpose of testing said tobacco for quality assurance purposes; if the smoking is necessary to conduct the test.

[*There is no subsection (d.)*]

(e) If the outdoor space has a structure capable of being enclosed by walls or covers, regardless of the materials or the removable nature of the walls or covers, the space will be considered enclosed, when the walls or covers are in place. All outdoor spaces shall be physically separated from an enclosed work space. If doors, windows, sliding or folding windows or doors or other fenestrations form any part of the border to the outdoor space, the openings shall be closed to prevent the migration of smoke into the enclosed work space. If the windows, sliding or folding windows or doors or other fenestrations are opened or otherwise do not prevent the migration of smoke into the work space, the outdoor space shall be considered an extension of the enclosed work space and subject to this section.

(f)(1) A nursing home, licensed pursuant to section 71 of chapter 111 and any acute care substance abuse treatment center under the jurisdiction of the commonwealth, may apply to the local board of health having jurisdiction over the facility for designation of part of the facility as a residence.

(2) All applications shall designate the residential area of the facility. The residential area shall not contain an employee workspace, such as offices, restrooms or other areas used primarily by employees.

(3) The entire facility may not be designated as a residence.

(4) The designated residential area must be for the sole use of permanent residents of the facility. No temporary or short-term resident may reside in the residential portion of the facility.

(5) All areas in the designated residential area in which smoking is allowed shall be conspicuously designated as smoking areas and be adequately ventilated to prevent the migration of smoke to nonsmoking areas.

(6) The facility shall provide suitable documentation, acceptable to the local board of health, that the facility is the permanent domicile of the residents residing in that portion of the facility, that information on the hazards of smoking and second hand smoke have been provided to all residences and that smoking cessation aids are available to all residents who use tobacco products.

(7) The designated residential area shall be in conformance with the smoking restriction requirements of section 72X of chapter 111 and 105 CMR 150.015 (D)(11)(b). All residential areas shall be clearly designated as such and shall not be altered or otherwise changed without the express approval of the local board of health.

(8) All areas of a nursing home not designated as a residence shall comply with this section.

(9) The nursing home shall make reasonable accommodations for an employee, resident or visitor who does not wish to be exposed to tobacco smoke.

(10) Upon compliance with this section, submission of the required documentation and satisfactory inspection, the local board of health shall certify the designated portion of the facility as a residence. The certification shall be valid for 1 year from the date of issuance. No fewer than 30 days before the expiration of the certification, the facility may apply for re-certification. If the local board of health does not renew the certification before its expiration or provide notice that it has found sufficient cause to not recertify the residence portion of the nursing home as such, the certification shall be considered to continue until the time as the local board of health notifies the nursing home of its certification status.

(g)(1) A designated smoking room in a hotel, motel, inn, bed and breakfast and lodging home shall be clearly marked as a designated smoking room on the exterior of all entrances from a public hallway and public spaces; and in the interior of the room. Instead of marking each room, an establishment may designate an entire floor of residential rooms as smoking. The floor shall be conspicuously designated as smoking at each entranceway on to the floor. Smoking shall not be allowed in the common areas of the floor, such as halls, vending areas, ice machine locations and exercise areas and shall comply with paragraph (4).

(2) A retail tobacco store that permits smoking on the premises shall, pursuant to paragraph (4), post in a clear and conspicuous manner, a sign at each entrance warning persons entering the establishment that smoking may be present on the premises; of the health risks associated from second hand smoke; and, that persons under the age of 18 years of age may not enter the premises.

(3) A smoking bar shall, pursuant to paragraph (4), post in a clear and conspicuous manner signs at all entrances which warn persons entering the establishment that smoking may be present on the premises; and, of the health risks associated

from second hand smoke; and, that persons under the age of 18 years of age may not enter the premises.

(4) Every area in which smoking is prohibited by law shall have "no smoking" signs conspicuously posted so that the signs are clearly visible to all employees, customers, or visitors while in the workplace.

(5) Additional signs may be posted in public areas such as, the following areas: lobbies; hallways; cafeterias; kitchens; locker rooms; customer service areas; offices where the public is invited; conference rooms; lounges; waiting areas; and elevators.

(6) Approved signs and templates for signage design may be obtained from the department of public health or the local boards of health.

(7) It shall be the responsibility of the establishment to ensure that the appropriate signage is displayed and that an individual or group renting the space enforces the prohibition against smoking.

(h)(a)(1) A smoking bar operating in the commonwealth shall obtain a smoking bar permit from the department of revenue. A permit issued by the department shall be valid for a period of 2 years from date of issuance unless suspended or revoked. A valid permit that is not suspended at the time of its expiration may be renewed for consecutive 2-year periods.

(2) A non-refundable fee may be required with each permit and renewal application. Each permit issued by the department shall be non-transferable, for a specific location and business; and, only 1 permit may be issued to a business for a specific location during any permit period.

(3) The department shall not issue or renew a smoking bar permit to any business that has not filed all tax returns and paid all taxes due the commonwealth; or is delinquent in filing all declaration statements in connection with the smoking bar permit as required by the department.

(4) The department shall notify the local board of health or municipal health department in the city or town where the establishment is located of any permits issued, renewed, suspended, revoked or reinstated to a business.

(b) A smoking bar shall demonstrate on a quarterly basis that revenue generated from the sale of tobacco products are equal to or greater than 51 per cent of the total combined revenue generated by the sale of tobacco products, food and beverages. The department shall require each business that has been issued a smoking bar permit to submit a quarterly declaration for each 3 month period that the business is in operation; notwithstanding, the first declaration may include a period of not to exceed 4 months. A declaration submitted to the department in connection with a smoking bar permit shall be signed by the owner or business agent under the pains and penalties of perjury. A declaration received by the department shall be confidential and the financial information contained therein shall not be disclosed to the public or any other state governmental agency or department except the attorney general. In the event a business has not filed a required declaration statement, the department shall give written notice to the business that the statement is delinquent and, shall suspend the permit of a business that does not submit the required report after 21 days of the date of notice; but the department shall reinstate the suspended permit within 5 days after receiving the delinquent report.

(c) The department of revenue shall promulgate regulations to implement this section.

(i) Companies which sell ownership rights to owners of time share properties shall distinguish between smoking and non-smoking time share properties. Companies shall disclose to potential buyers whether the unit they are purchasing is a smoking or non-smoking property and post signs accordingly.

(j) Nothing in this section shall permit smoking in an area in which smoking is or may hereafter be prohibited by law including, without limitation: any other law or ordinance or by-law or any fire, health or safety regulation. Nothing in this section shall preempt further limitation of smoking by the commonwealth or any department, agency or political subdivision of the commonwealth.

(k) An individual, person, entity or organization subject to the smoking prohibitions of this section shall not discriminate or retaliate in any manner against a person for making a complaint of a violation of this section or furnishing information concerning a violation, to a person, entity or organization or to an enforcement authority. Notwithstanding the foregoing, a person making a complaint or furnishing information during any period of work or time of employment, shall do so only at a time that will not pose an increased threat of harm to the safety of other persons in or about such place of work or to the public.

(l) An owner, manager or other person in control of a building, vehicle or vessel who violates this section, in a manner other than by smoking in a place where smoking is prohibited, shall be punished by a fine of $100 for the first violation; $200 for a second violation occurring within 2 years of the date of the first offense; and $300 for a third or subsequent violation within 2 years of the second violation. Each calendar day on which a violation occurs shall be considered a separate offense. If an owner, manager or other person in control of a building, vehicle or vessel violates this section repeatedly, demonstrating egregious noncompliance as defined by regulation of the department of public health, the local board of health may revoke or suspend the license to operate and shall send notice of the revocation or suspension to the department of public health. The department of public health shall promulgate regulations to implement this section including, but not limited to notice, collection, and reporting of the fines or license action, and defining uniform standards that warrant license suspension or revocation.

(m)(1) The local board of health, the department of public health, the local inspection department or the equivalent, a municipal government or its agent, and the alcoholic beverages control commission shall enforce this section. In addition, in the city of Boston, the commissioner of health and his authorized agents shall enforce this section.

(2) An individual or person who violates this section by smoking in a place where smoking is prohibited shall be subject to a civil penalty of $100 for each violation. As an alternative to criminal prosecution, a violation of subsection (l) may also be considered a civil violation. Each enforcing agency under paragraph (1) shall dispose of a civil violation of this section by the non-criminal method of disposition procedures contained in section 21D of chapter 40, without an enabling ordinance or by-law, or by the equivalent of these procedures by a state agency under regulations of the department of public health. The disposition of fines assessed under this section shall be subject to section 188 of chapter 111. Fines assessed by the commonwealth or its agents shall be subject to section 2 of chapter 29. In a city or town having an

2

ordinance or by-law that imposes a fine greater than the fine imposed by this section, the ordinance or by-law shall prevail over this section.

(3) Any person may register a complaint to initiate an investigation and enforcement with the local board of health, the department of public health, or the local inspection department or the equivalent.

(4) The supreme judicial court or the superior court shall issue appropriate orders to enforce this section and any regulation under it, at the request of any agency mentioned in paragraph (1).

(5) A fine or fee collected by the commonwealth under this section shall be used for the enforcement or for educational programs on the harmful effects of tobacco.

(n) Each local board of health, each local inspection department or its equivalent, and the alcoholic beverages control commission shall report annually to the commissioner of public health, beginning January 1, 2006: the number of citations issued; the workplaces which have been issued citations and the number of citations issued to each workplace; the amount that each workplace has been fined; and the total amount collected in fines. The department of public health shall file a copy of the report with the clerks of the house of representatives and the senate.

(o) The department of public health may issue regulations to implement this section.

NOTE   **Related Statute.** G.L. c. 272, § 43A—Smoking in public conveyances and transportation facilities restricted.

SECTION 23
Smoking at flea market

(a) As used in this section, "flea market" shall mean that portion of a building then occupied by one or more vendors, other than retail stores, for sale to the public of new or used goods or products on a seasonal, limited or full schedule of operation. No person shall smoke in any building used for the purpose of operating a flea market, except as otherwise provided in this section. The owner, manager or other person in charge of such a building, shall post a notice in a conspicuous place at each entrance to such building indicating that smoking is prohibited therein, except in an area specifically designated as a smoking area. An area shall be designated as a smoking area only if nonsmoking areas of sufficient size and capacity are available to accommodate nonsmokers and if smoke from said smoking area is prevented from entering the no smoking area.

(b) Except as otherwise provided herein, no person shall smoke in any snack bar operated in conjunction with a flea market, except in such designated smoking area as may be provided. Said smoking area shall be physically separated from the no smoking area and separately ventilated to the outside to prevent smoke from entering the no smoking area. The owner, manager or other person in charge of a snack bar shall not permit the smoke from such smoking area to be vented to the no smoking area.

(c) The owner, manager or other person in charge of such snack bar shall post a notice or sign in a conspicuous place at each entrance to such snack bar indicating that smoking is prohibited therein except in specifically designated areas, shall post signs identifying the no smoking area and the smoking area, and shall make a reasonable effort to insure that no person shall smoke in a no smoking area. Said reason-

able effort shall include, but not be limited to, requesting that a person smoking in a no smoking area to either extinguish his cigarette, cigar or pipe, or move to a designated smoking area.

(d) Any person aggrieved by the willful failure or refusal to comply with any of the provisions of this section may complain in writing to a local health officer in the case of a snack bar or to the local building inspector in the case of all other facilities described in this section. Said authority shall respond in writing within 15 days to the complainant that the area described in the complaint has been inspected and said authority has enforced the provisions of this section. Said authority shall file a copy of the original complaint and its response thereto with the department of public health.

(e) No employer shall terminate or otherwise discriminate against any employee, independent contractor, or other worker for refusing to work in a smoking area or for exercising his rights under this section.

(f) Any person who violates this section by smoking where smoking is prohibited shall be subject to a civil fine not exceeding $25. Any person who violates this section in any way other than by smoking in an area where smoking is prohibited shall be subject to a civil fine of $50. Each day during which a violation of this section occurs shall be considered a separate violation.

(g) Fines assessed pursuant to this section shall be payable to the city or town in which the violation of this section occurs. A local board of health or health department shall enforce this section through noncriminal disposition.

(h) A city or town may, by ordinance or by-laws, establish a fund for the disposition of revenues received from fines levied in accordance with the provisions of this section. Said fund shall be expended under the authority of the municipal health department or local board of health for the purpose of public education on the hazards posed by secondhand smoke, also known as environmental tobacco smoke.

(i) Nothing in this section shall be construed to permit smoking in any area in which smoking is prohibited by law, including, without limiting the generality of the foregoing, any other provision of the law or ordinance or any fire, health, or safety regulation. This section shall not pre-empt the authority of any city or town to enact any ordinance, by-law or any fire, health, or safety regulation that limits or prohibits smoking in any place.

SECTION 24
Sale of mercury thermometers

No person shall sell or supply, including online, retail mercury fever thermometers, except in the case of a medical necessity as determined by a licensed physician or by prescription. Manufacturers of mercury fever thermometers sold or supplied in the commonwealth in such cases of medical necessity shall furnish clear instructions on the careful handling of thermometers to avoid breakage and proper cleanup should a breakage occur. This section shall not apply to digital thermometers using mercury-added button cell batteries. A violation of this section shall be punished by a fine of not more than $500.

SECTION 25
Ice cream truck vending; permit requirements
(Added by 2010 Mass. Acts c. 256, § 122, effective May 4, 2012.)

(a) For the purposes of this section, the following words shall have the following meanings:—

"Ice cream", any frozen dairy or frozen water-based food product.

"Ice cream truck", any motor vehicle used for selling, displaying or offering to sell ice cream.

"Ice cream truck vending", the selling, displaying or offering to sell ice cream or any other prepackaged food product from an ice cream truck.

"Permitting authority", the chief of police or the board or officer having control of the police in a city or town, or person authorized by them.

(b) No person shall engage in ice cream truck vending unless he shall have been issued a valid permit to do so by the permitting authority within the municipality wherein the applicant lives or intends to operate an ice cream truck. Such permit shall be conspicuously displayed and clearly visible on the windshield of any ice cream truck operated or from which ice cream or any other prepackaged food product is sold.

Whoever violates this section shall be assessed a fine of $500. Each day that such person is in operation in violation of this section may be considered a separate violation.

(c) The department of public safety shall adopt regulations relative to the annual permitting of ice cream truck vendors. Such regulations shall include, but not be limited to:

(i) a requirement that all applications for an ice cream truck vending permit or applications for renewal thereof shall include the applicant's fingerprints and a current photo of the applicant;

(ii) adoption of a uniform permit application and permit form, to be used by all municipalities;

(iii) a requirement that a permitting authority conduct an investigation into the criminal history of a permit applicant to determine eligibility therefore; and

(iv) a provision restricting a permitting authority from issuing an ice cream truck vending permit to any sex offender, as defined by section 178C of chapter 6 of the General Laws.

Chapter 271. Crimes Against Public Policy

Section

1	Gaming or betting; forfeiture; limitations
1A	"House", "building" and "place" includes ship or vessel
2	Gaming or betting in public conveyance or place or while trespassing in private place; arrest without warrant
3	Innholders and others keeping or suffering implements to be used for gaming or suffering a person to game; recognizance for good behavior
4	Gaming in inns and other occupied places; use of billiard table, bowling alley or other implement for gaming
5	Keeping, or playing or presence in, common gaming, lottery, pool or betting houses; keeping tables or apparatus for gaming
5A	Gambling devices; forfeiture; antique slot machines
5B	Unlawful possession of electronic machine or device for conducting or promoting sweepstakes through entertaining display; lawful exceptions; penalty
6	Gaming relative to cattle shows, military muster or public gathering; arrest without warrant
6A	Plans under which purchasers agree to obtain more purchasers; injunction; receivers
6B	Skilo and similar games
6C	Repealed
7	Lotteries; disposal of property by chance
7A	Raffles and bazaars; conduct by certain organizations; permit; reports; tax
8	Permitting lotteries, raffles and games of chance in buildings
9	Selling, exchanging or possessing lottery tickets or tokens or a share in a lottery
10	Conviction on subsequent offenses within five years
10A	Arrest without warrant
11	Advertising lottery tickets or tokens, inviting purchases or indicating where obtainable
12	Making, sale and possession of, or receipt of money for, false lottery tickets, tokens or share in lottery
13	Lottery tickets, tokens or shares deemed false
14	Forfeiture of money, prizes, or shares of lotteries or other property disposed of by chance; recovery
15	Aiding in setting up a lottery for money drawn out of commonwealth
16	Sale or possession of lottery ticket described in section 15
16A	Organizing or promoting gambling facilities or services
17	Keeping of, presence in, or permitting, a place for registering bets or dealing in pools; custodian or depository
17A	Telephones; use for gaming purposes; penalty
17B	Use of communications for unlawful purposes; demand of telephone company records by attorney general
18	Policy lotteries or shops; making, delivering or possessing a lottery ticket or token; receipt of money or thing of value
19	Making, advertising or delivering ticket or receipt of money or thing of value as prima facie evidence
20	Tickets, memoranda, books and sheets as nuisance; possession unlawful; possession and concealment as evidence
21	Words, figures or characters referring to horse, jockey or contest odds or bets as prima facie evidence; proof by copy or description
22	Delivery to or from a person engaged in a lottery or other gaming
22A	Whist or bridge for charitable and similar purposes
22B	Beano; sale of lottery tickets
23	Oath and warrant to enter a gaming or lottery place, arrest persons and seize implements and materials; disposal of articles
24	Owners, proprietors of, or persons present at, race tracks
25	Removal of obstructions barring access to gaming places; lien of expense
26	Subsequent obstructions; removal; punishment; lien
27	Judicial notice of methods and character of lotteries, policy games, pools and betting; tickets and other articles prima facie evidence
28	Complaints and indictments relative to lotteries or gaming; misnomer; sufficiency; variance
29	Representation that a thing other than subject of sale is to be delivered; stamps and other devices entitling purchaser to other property
30	Sale or delivery of trading stamps or similar devices
31	Racing horses for bets or stakes
31A	Racing results or information; transmission for unlawful purposes; penalty
32	Competing with horse disguised or different from one purported to be; horse in improper class
33	Race grounds in towns; consent; regulations; discontinuance; unlawful use
34	Race grounds as nuisance; abatement; punishment
35	Definition of words and phrases used in sections 35–38
36	Making contracts of bucketing; keeper of shop; dissolution of corporation; restraint from doing business
37	Quotations of prices for prohibited contracts
38	Written statements relative to purchases and sales of securities or commodities; refusal as prima facie evidence of bucketing
39	Gifts to influence business affairs; threats; penalty
39A	Gifts to influence action of participants in, and others connected with, a game or contest
40	Appointment, retention or discharge of employee of public service corporation or racing licensee on recommendation of public officer, officer elect or candidate
41	Offices not public offices under section 40

2

42   Betting or selling pools on boxing matches or exhibitions
43   Soliciting, disclosing, receiving or making use of information concerning public assistance
44   Settlement, release or statement by person in hospital; admissibility; reference to at trial; validity
45   Repealed
46   Removal of doors from discarded containers originally used for refrigerative purposes
47   Telephones; gambling; reinstallation; notices of convictions and removals
48   Schools or persons offering civil service preparatory courses; advertisement
49   Criminal usury
50   Sale of research papers, etc. and taking of examinations for another at educational institutions

SECTION 1

Gaming or betting; forfeiture; limitations
(Amended by 2011 Mass. Acts c. 194, § 51, effective Nov. 22, 2011.)

Whoever, on a prosecution commenced within eighteen months after the commission of the crime, is convicted of winning at one time or sitting, by gaming or betting on the sides or hands of those gaming, except as permitted under chapter 23K, money or goods to the value of five dollars or more, and of receiving the same or security therefor, shall forfeit double the value of such money or goods.

NOTE   A bet is the hazard of money or property upon an incident by which one or both parties stand to lose or win by chance. *Commonwealth v. Sullivan*, 218 Mass. 281, 283 (1914).

SECTION 1A

"House", "building" and "place" includes ship or vessel

The words "house", "building" and "place" used severally or together in this chapter shall mean and include a ship or vessel when it is within the territorial limits of the commonwealth.

NOTE   **Related Statute. Common Nuisances.**

G.L. c. 139, § 14—Buildings resorted to for illegal gaming or used for illegal keeping or sale of alcoholic beverages; nuisance.

Every building, place or tenement which is resorted to for illegal gaming, or which is used for the illegal keeping or sale of alcoholic beverages, as defined in section one of chapter one hundred and thirty-eight, shall be deemed a common nuisance.

G.L. c. 139, § 15—Penalty.

Whoever keeps or maintains such common nuisance shall be punished by a fine of not less than fifty nor more than one hundred dollars and by imprisonment for not less than three months nor more than one year.

Form of indictment for violation of G.L. c. 139, §§ 14–15, see G.L. c. 277, § 79.

SECTION 2

Gaming or betting in public conveyance or place or while trespassing in private place; arrest without warrant
(Amended by 2011 Mass. Acts c. 194, § 52, effective Nov. 22, 2011.)

Whoever, in a public conveyance or public place, or in a private place upon which he is trespassing, plays at cards, dice or any other game for money or other property, or bets on the sides or hands of those playing, except as provided in chapter 23K, shall forfeit not more than fifty dollars or be imprisoned for not more than three months; and whoever sets up or permits such a game shall be punished by a fine of not less than fifty nor more than one hundred dollars or by imprisonment for not less than three nor more than twelve months. If discovered in the act, he may be arrested without a warrant by a sheriff, deputy sheriff, constable or any officer qualified to serve criminal process, and held in custody, in jail or otherwise, for not more than twenty-four hours, Sunday and legal holidays excepted, until complaint may be made against him for such offense.

SECTION 3

Innholders and others keeping or suffering implements to be used for gaming or suffering a person to game; recognizance for good behavior
(Amended by 2011 Mass. Acts c. 194, § 53, effective Nov. 22, 2011.)

Except as permitted under chapter 23K, every innholder, common victualler or person keeping or suffering to be kept in any place occupied by him implements such as are used in gaming, in order that the same may for hire, gain or reward be used for amusement, who suffers implements of such kind to be used upon any part of such premises for gaming for money or other property, or who suffers a person to play at an unlawful game or sport therein, shall for the first offense forfeit not more than one hundred dollars or be imprisoned for not more than three months; and for a subsequent offense shall be imprisoned for not more than one year. In either case he shall further recognize with sufficient sureties in a reasonable sum for his good behavior, and especially that he will not be guilty of any offense against any of the provisions of sections one to six, inclusive, for three years from the date of the recognizance.

SECTION 4

Gaming in inns and other occupied places; use of billiard table, bowling alley or other implement for gaming

Whoever, in any place mentioned in the preceding section, for the purpose of gaming for money or other property, uses or takes part in using a billiard table, bowling alley or other implement of gaming, or there plays at an unlawful game or sport, or, for the purpose of such gaming, uses or takes part in using a billiard table or bowling alley kept by a person licensed under chapter one hundred and forty, shall forfeit not more than fifty dollars.

SECTION 5

Keeping, or playing or presence in, common gaming, lottery, pool or betting houses; keeping tables or apparatus for gaming
(Amended by 2011 Mass. Acts c. 194, § 54, effective Nov. 22, 2011.)

Whoever, except as permitted under chapter 23K, keeps or assists in keeping a common gaming house, or building or place occupied, used or kept for the purposes described in section twenty-three, or is found playing or present as provided in said section, or commonly keeps or suffers to be kept, in a building or place actually used and occupied by him, tables or other apparatus for the purpose of playing at an unlawful game or sport for money or any other valuable thing, shall be punished by a fine of not more than fifty dollars or by imprisonment for not more than three months.

SECTION 5A

Gambling devices; forfeiture; antique slot machines
(Amended by 2011 Mass. Acts c. 194, § 55, effective Nov. 22, 2011.)

Whoever manufactures, transports, sells, offers for sale, stores, displays, repairs, reconditions, possesses or uses any gambling device or parts for use therein shall be punished by a fine of not more than five thousand dollars; provided, however, that fifty percent of the said fine shall be remitted to the city or town in which the violation occurred. The remaining fifty percent shall be remitted to the general fund of the

Commonwealth. As used in this section, the term "gambling device" means any so called "slot machine" or any other machine or mechanical device an essential part of which is a drum or reel with insignia thereon, and which, when operated, may deal, as a result of the application of an element of chance, any money or property; or by the operation of which a person may become entitled to receive, as the result of the application of an element of chance, any money or property; or any sub-assembly or essential part intended to be used in connection with any such machine or mechanical device. Any gambling device or parts for use therein manufactured, transported, sold, offered for sale, stored, displayed, repaired, reconditioned, possessed or used in violation of this section shall be seized and be forfeited to the commonwealth and disposed of in the manner provided under the provisions of chapter two hundred and seventy-six. In respect to their constitutionality, the provisions of this section are hereby declared to be separable.

It shall be a defense to any prosecution under this section to show that the slot machine is an antique slot machine and was not operated for gambling purposes while in the defendant's possession. For the purposes of this section, a slot machine shall be presumed to be an antique slot machine, if it was manufactured at least thirty years prior to either the arrest of the defendant, or seizure of the machine.

This section shall not apply to persons who manufacture, transport, sell, offer for sale, store, display, repair, recondition, possess or use any gambling device or parts for use in such a device for licensed gaming conducted under chapter 23K.

NOTE   "Without a 'reel or drum,' it is not a 'gambling device' within G.L. c. 271, § 5A." *Commonwealth v. Frate*, 405 Mass. 52, 54 (1989).

SECTION 5B

Unlawful possession of electronic machine or device for conducting or promoting sweepstakes through entertaining display; lawful exceptions; penalty
(Added by 2012 Mass. Acts c. 187, effective Oct. 30, 2012; amended by 2013 Mass. Acts c. 3, § 9, effective Feb. 15, 2013.)

(a) As used in this section the following words shall, unless the context clearly requires otherwise, have the following meanings:—

"Electronic machine or device", a mechanically, electrically or electronically operated machine or device that is: (i) owned, leased or otherwise possessed by a sweepstakes sponsor or promoter, or any sponsors, promoters, partners, affiliates, subsidiaries or contractors thereof; (ii) intended to be used by a sweepstakes entrant; (iii) uses energy; and (iv) capable of displaying information on a screen or other mechanism; provided, that an electronic machine or device may, without limitation: (1) be server-based; (2) use a simulated game terminal as a representation of the prizes associated with the results of the sweepstakes entries; (3) utilize software such that the simulated game influences or determines the winning or value of the prize; (4) select prizes from a predetermined finite pool of entries; (5) utilize a mechanism that reveals the content of a predetermined sweepstakes entry; (6) predetermine the prize results and stores those results for delivery at the time the sweepstakes entry results are revealed; (7) utilize software to create a game result; (8) require deposit of any money, coin or token, or the use of any credit card, debit card, prepaid card or any other method of payment to activate the electronic machine or device; (9) require direct payment into the electronic machine or device, or remote activation of the electronic machine or device; (10) require purchase of a related product having legitimate value; (11) reveal the prize incrementally, even though it may not influence if a prize is awarded or the value of any prize awarded; (12) determine and associate the prize with an entry or entries at the time the sweepstakes is entered; (13) be a slot machine or other form of electrical, mechanical, or computer game; and provided further, that "electronic machine or device"' shall also include gambling devices as defined in section 5A.

"Enter" or "entry", the act or process by which a person becomes eligible to receive any prize offered in a sweepstakes.

"Entertaining display", any visual information, capable of being seen by a sweepstakes entrant, that takes the form of actual game play or simulated game play.

"Prize", any gift, award, gratuity, good, service, credit or anything else of value, which may be transferred to a person, whether possession of the prize is actually transferred, or placed on an account or other record as evidence of the intent to transfer the prize.

"Sweepstakes", any game, advertising scheme or plan, or other promotion, which, with or without payment of any consideration, a person may enter to win or become eligible to receive any prize, the determination of which is based upon chance.

(b) It shall be unlawful for any person to knowingly possess with the intent to operate, or place into operation, an electronic machine or device to: (1) conduct a sweepstakes through the use of an entertaining display, including the entry process or the reveal of a prize; or (2) promote a sweepstakes that is conducted through the use of an entertaining display, including the entry process or the reveal of a prize.

(c) Nothing in this section shall be construed to make illegal any activity which is lawfully conducted: (1) by the state lottery commission, under sections 24, 24A, 27, 27A, 37, 38, and 39A of chapter 10; (2) as pari-mutuel wagering on horse races, whether live or simulcast, under chapters 128A and 128C; (3) as the game of bingo conducted under chapters 10 and 271; (4) as charitable gaming, conducted under chapter 271; (5) under chapter 23K; or (6) by any retailer whose primary business is the sale of groceries, whereby the sweepstakes is directly related to the sale of groceries and the potential prize provided through the sweepstakes may not be redeemed for cash and may only be used as a discount to reduce the price of items purchased from the retailer.

(d) Any person who violates this section shall be punished by a fine of not more than $250,000 per electronic machine or device placed into operation or by imprisonment in state prison for not more than 15 years, or by both such fine and imprisonment.

SECTION 6

Gaming relative to cattle shows, military muster or public gathering; arrest without warrant
(Amended by 2011 Mass. Acts c. 194, 56, effective Nov. 22, 2011.)

Whoever, during or within twelve hours of the time of holding a cattle show, military muster or public gathering, within one mile of the place thereof, practices or engages in illegal gaming, shall forfeit not more than twenty dollars. If discovered in the act, he may be arrested without a warrant by any sheriff, deputy sheriff, constable or any officer qualified

2

to serve criminal process, and held in custody, in jail or otherwise, for not more than twenty-four hours, Sunday and legal holidays excepted, until a complaint may be made against him for such offense.

SECTION 6A
Plans under which purchasers agree to obtain more purchasers; injunction; receivers

Whoever sets up or promotes a plan by which goods or anything of value is sold to a person for a consideration and upon the further consideration that the purchaser agrees to secure one or more persons to participate in the plan by respectively making a similar purchase or purchases and in turn agreeing to secure one or more persons likewise to join in the said plan, each purchaser being given the right to secure money, credits, goods or something of value, depending upon the number of persons joining in the plan, shall be held to have set up and promoted a lottery and shall be punished as provided in section seven. The supreme judicial court shall have jurisdiction in equity upon a petition filed by the attorney general to enjoin the further prosecution of any such plan and to appoint receivers to secure and distribute the assets received thereunder.

SECTION 6B
Skilo and similar games

Whoever, except as provided in section twenty-two B, sets up or promotes the game commonly known as skilo or any similar game regardless of name, shall be held to have set up and promoted a lottery and shall be punished as provided in section seven.

SECTION 6C
Repealed

SECTION 7
Lotteries; disposal of property by chance
(Amended by 2011 Mass. Acts c. 194, 57, effective Nov. 22, 2011.)

Whoever sets up or promotes a lottery for money or other property of value, or by way of lottery disposes of any property of value, or under the pretext of a sale, gift or delivery of other property or of any right, privilege or thing whatever disposes of or offers or attempts to dispose of any property, with intent to make the disposal thereof dependent upon or connected with chance by lot, dice, numbers, game, hazard or other gambling device that is not taking place in a gaming establishment licensed pursuant to chapter 23K, whereby such chance or device is made an additional inducement to the disposal or sale of said property, and whoever aids either by printing or writing, or is in any way concerned, in the setting up, managing or drawing of such lottery, or in such disposal or offer or attempt to dispose of property by such chance or device, shall be punished by a fine of not more than three thousand dollars or by imprisonment in the state prison for not more than three years, or in jail or the house of correction for not more than two and one half years.

NOTE 1   "There are three elements in a lottery, (1) the payment of a price for (2) the possibility of winning a prize, depending upon (3) hazard or chance." *Commonwealth v. Lake*, 317 Mass. 264, 267 (1944); *Mobil Oil Corp. v. Attorney General*, 361 Mass. 401, 406 (1972).

NOTE 2   "A game is now considered a lottery if the element of chance predominates and not a lottery if the element of skill predominates." *Commonwealth v. Lake*, 317 Mass. at 267.

NOTE 3   "[P]rice means something of value and not merely the formal or technical consideration, such as registering one's name or attending a certain place, which might be sufficient consideration to support a contract . . . and that the price must come from participants in the game in part at least as payments for their chances and that the indirect advantage to the one conducting a game at his place of business is not in itself a price paid by participants." *Mobil Oil Corp. v. Attorney General*, 361 Mass. at 406 (citations and quotation marks omitted).

NOTE 4   "[W]hether or not a particular scheme amounts to a lottery depends upon the particular facts and circumstances of each case." *Mobil Oil Corp. v. Attorney General*, 361 Mass. at 406 (citations and quotation marks omitted).

NOTE 5   **Evidence.** Commonwealth, over defendant's objection, was permitted to introduce testimony that on December 29, 1956, about 10 days prior to the offense date (January 7, 1957), there was the commission of an offense separate from, but similar to, that of January 7, 1957. Held, evidence admissible. "The consistency of the defendant's conduct on two occasions . . . tended to show (a) relevant background, (b) that the unlawful payment on January 7 was intentional, not accidental, and (c) that it was part of a general purpose and course of operations having an intent and character violative of § 7." *Commonwealth v. Butynski*, 339 Mass. 151, 152 (1959) (citations omitted).

NOTE 6   **Form of Indictment.** G.L. c 277, § 79.

NOTE 7   **Additional Penalty.** G.L. c. 271, § 14 (Forfeiture of prizes).

NOTE 8   **Prima Facie Evidence.** *See* G.L. c. 271, §§ 19–21 and 27.

NOTE 9   **Variance.** *See* G.L. c. 271, § 28.

SECTION 7A
Raffles and bazaars; conduct by certain organizations; permit; reports; tax
(Amended by 2014 Mass. Acts c. 165, § 178, effective July 15, 2014.)

In this section the following words shall have the following meanings:

"Raffle", an arrangement for raising money by the sale of tickets, certain among which, as determined by chance after the sale, entitle the holders to prizes.

"Bazaar", a place maintained by the sponsoring organization for disposal by means of chance of one or both of the following types of prizes: (1) merchandise, of any value, (2) cash awards, not to exceed $250 each.

Notwithstanding any other provisions of law, raffles and bazaars may be promoted, operated and conducted under permits issued in accordance with provisions of this section.

No organization, society, church or club which conducts a raffle or bazaar under the provisions of this section shall be deemed to have set up and promoted a lottery and nothing in this chapter shall authorize the prosecution, arrest or conviction of any person connected with the operation of any such raffle or bazaar; provided, however, that nothing contained in this section shall be construed as permitting the game commonly known as "beano" or any similar game regardless of name.

No raffle or bazaar shall be promoted, operated or conducted by any person or organization, unless the same is sponsored and conducted exclusively by (a) a veterans' organization chartered by the Congress of the United States or included in clause (12) of section five of chapter forty of the General Laws; (b) a church or religious organization; (c) a fraternal or fraternal benefit society; (d) an educational or charitable organization; (e) a civic or service club or organization; and (f) clubs or organizations organized and operated exclusively for pleasure, recreation and other nonprofit purposes, no part of the net earnings of which inures to the benefit of any member or shareholder. Such organization shall have been organized and actively functioning as a nonprofit organization in the commonwealth for a period of not less than two years before it may apply for a permit. The promotion and operation of the raffle or bazaar shall be confined solely to the qualified members of the sponsoring organization and no such member shall receive remuneration in any form for time or effort devoted to the promotion or operation of such raffle or bazaar. All funds derived from any raffle or bazaar shall be used exclusively for the purposes stated in the application of the sponsoring organization which purposes shall be limited to educational, charitable, religious, fraternal or civic purposes or for veterans' benefits. An organization which meets the qualifications required by this section and which desires to conduct or operate a raffle or bazaar within the commonwealth shall apply for a permit to conduct raffles and bazaars from the clerk of the city or town in which the raffle will be drawn or the bazaar held. The application form shall be approved by the commissioner of public safety and shall include the name and address of the applicant, the evidence on which the applicant relies in order to qualify under this section, the names of three officers or members of the organization who shall be responsible for the operation the raffle or bazaar, and the uses to which the net proceeds will be applied. Unless otherwise established in a town by town meeting action and in a city by city council action, and in a town with no town meeting by town council action, by adoption of appropriate by-laws and ordinances to set such fees, a fee of ten dollars shall accompany each such application and shall be retained by the city or town, but in no event shall any such fee be greater than fifty dollars. Upon receipt of such application, the clerk shall determine whether it is in conformity with this section. If the clerk so determines, he shall forward the application to the chief of police of the city or town, who shall determine whether the applicant is qualified to operate raffles and bazaars under this section. If the chief of police so determines, he shall endorse the application and return it to the clerk, who shall forthwith issue a permit, which shall be valid for one year from the date of its issuance. The clerk shall retain a copy of the application and shall send a copy to the commissioner of public safety. If there is any change in the facts set forth in the application for a permit subsequent to the making of such application, the applicant shall forthwith notify the authority granting such permit of such change, and such authority shall issue such permit if the applicant is qualified, or, if a permit has already been issued and the change in the facts set forth in the application disqualify the applicant revoke such permit.

If an application is not acted upon within thirty days after it is submitted, or if the organization is refused a permit, or if a permit is revoked, any person named on the application may obtain judicial review of such refusal or revocation by filing within ten days of such refusal or revocation or within ten days of the expiration of such thirty day period a petition for review in the district court having jurisdiction in the city or town in which such application was filed. A justice of said court, after a hearing, may direct that such permit be issued, if he is satisfied that there was no reasonable ground for refusing such permit, and that the applicant was not prohibited by law from holding raffles or bazaars.

An organization issued a permit under this section shall within thirty days of the expiration of its permit submit a report on a form to be approved by the commissioner of public safety. Such form shall require information concerning the number of raffles and bazaars held, the amount of money received, the expenses connected with the raffle or bazaar, the names of the winners of prizes exceeding $250 in value, the net proceeds of the raffles and bazaars, and the uses to which the net proceeds were applied. The organization shall maintain and keep such books and records as may be necessary to substantiate the particulars of such report, which books and records shall be preserved for at least one year from the date of such report and shall be available for inspection. Such report shall be certified to by the three persons designated in the permit application as being responsible for such raffle or bazaar and by an accountant. Two copies of said report shall be filed with city or town clerk. The clerk shall send one copy to the commissioner of public safety. Failure to file said report shall constitute sufficient grounds for refusal to renew a permit to conduct raffles or bazaars. The fee for renewal of such permit shall be ten dollars.

The authority granting any permit under this section shall immediately revoke the same for a violation of any provision of this section and shall not issue any permit to such permittee within three years from the date of such violation. Any person aggrieved by the action of such authority revoking such permit may appeal to the district court having jurisdiction in the city or town where the permit was issued; provided that such appeal shall be filed in such court within twenty days following receipt of notification by said authority. The court shall hear all pertinent evidence and determine the facts and upon the facts so determined annul such action or make such decision as equity may require. The foregoing remedy shall be exclusive.

Any organization conducting or operating a raffle or bazaar under this section shall file a return with the state lottery commission, on a form prepared by it, within ten days after the raffle or bazaar is held and shall pay therewith a tax of five per cent of the gross proceeds derived from such raffle or bazaar.

All sums received by said commission from the tax imposed by this section as taxes, interest thereon, fees, penalties, forfeitures, costs of suits or fines, less all amounts refunded thereon, together with any interest or costs paid on account of such refunds, shall be paid into the treasury of the commonwealth.

Whoever violates any provision of this section or submits false information on an application or report required under this section shall be punished by a fine of not more than one thousand dollars or by imprisonment in the house of correction for not more than one year, or both.

No person who prints or produces tickets, cards or any similar article used in the conduct of a bazaar or raffle pursuant to a permit issued under the provisions of this section shall be subject to any penalty therefor, provided that a certified copy of such permit was presented to him prior to his undertaking to print or produce such tickets or cards.

No organization issued a permit under this section shall conduct more than three bazaars in any single calendar year nor shall such organization conduct more than one bazaar in any single calendar day. The operation of a bazaar shall be limited to five consecutive hours.

2

SECTION 8
Permitting lotteries, raffles and games of chance in buildings
(Amended by 2011 Mass. Acts c. 194, § 58, effective Nov. 22, 2011.)

Whoever owns, occupies or is in control of a house, shop or building and knowingly permits the establishing, managing or drawing of a lottery, or the disposal or attempt to dispose of property, or the sale of a lottery ticket or share of a ticket, or any other writing, certificate, bill, token or other device purporting or intended to entitle the holder, bearer or any other person to a prize or to a share of or an interest in a prize to be drawn in a lottery, or in the disposal of property, and whoever knowingly allows money or other property to be raffled for or won by throwing or using dice or by any other game of chance that is not being conducted in a gaming establishment licensed under chapter 23K, shall be punished by a fine of not more than $2,000 or by imprisonment in the house of correction for not more than 1 year.

SECTION 9
Selling, exchanging or possessing lottery tickets or tokens or a share in a lottery

Whoever, for himself or for another, sells or offers for sale or has in his possession with intent to sell or offer for sale, or to exchange or negotiate, or aids or assists in the selling, exchanging, negotiating or disposing of a ticket in such lottery, or a share of a ticket, or any such writing, certificate, bill, token or other device, or a share or right in such disposal or offer, as is mentioned in section seven, shall be punished by a fine of not more than two thousand dollars or by imprisonment for not more than one year.

SECTION 10
Conviction on subsequent offenses within five years

Whoever, within five years after being convicted of any offense mentioned in section five, seven, eight, nine, eleven, fifteen, sixteen, seventeen or seventeen A, commits the like offense, or any other of the offenses therein mentioned, shall, in addition to the fine therein provided, be punished by imprisonment for not less than three months nor more than one year, and the sentence imposing such fine and such imprisonment shall not be suspended.

SECTION 10A
Arrest without warrant

Any person who is discovered by a police officer in the act of violating section seven, eight, nine, twelve, sixteen, seventeen, seventeen A, eighteen or twenty-two, while such officer is lawfully at or within the place where such violation occurred, may be arrested without a warrant by such police officer, and held in custody, in jail or otherwise, until a complaint be made against him for such offense, unless previously admitted to bail, which complaint shall be made as soon as practicable and in any case within twenty-four hours, Sundays and legal holidays excepted.

SECTION 11
Advertising lottery tickets or tokens, inviting purchases or indicating where obtainable

Whoever, himself or by another, advertises a lottery ticket or a share in such ticket for sale, or sets up or exhibits, or devises or makes for the purpose of being set up or exhibited, any sign, symbol or emblematic or other representation of a lottery or the drawing thereof, in any way indicating where a lottery ticket or a share thereof or such writing, certificate, bill, token or other device before mentioned may be obtained, or in any way invites or entices, or attempts to invite or entice, any other person to purchase or receive the same, shall be punished by a fine of not more than two thousand dollars or by imprisonment for not more than one year.

SECTION 12
Making, sale and possession of, or receipt of money for, false lottery tickets, tokens or share in lottery

Whoever makes or sells, or has in his possession with intent to sell, exchange or negotiate, or by printing, writing or otherwise assists in making or selling, or in attempting to sell, exchange or negotiate, a false or fictitious lottery ticket, or any share thereof, or any writing, certificate, bill, token or other device before mentioned, or any ticket or share thereof in a fictitious or pretended lottery, knowing the same to be false or fictitious, or receives any money or other thing of value for such ticket or share of a ticket, writing, certificate, bill, token or other device purporting that the owner, bearer or holder thereof shall be entitled to receive any prize, or share of a prize, or other thing of value, that may be drawn in a lottery, knowing the same to be false or fictitious, shall be punished by imprisonment in the state prison for not more than three years.

SECTION 13
Lottery tickets, tokens or shares deemed false

Upon the trial of a person charged with any of the crimes mentioned in the preceding section, a ticket or share of a ticket, or other writing or thing before mentioned, which the defendant has sold or offered for sale, or for which he has received a valuable consideration, shall be deemed false, spurious or fictitious, unless the defendant proves that the same was true and genuine, duly issued by the authority of some legislature within the United States, that such lottery was existing and undrawn and that such ticket or share thereof, or other writing or thing before mentioned, was issued by lawful authority and is binding upon the person who issued the same.

SECTION 14
Forfeiture of money, prizes, or shares of lotteries or other property disposed of by chance; recovery
(Amended by 2011 Mass. Acts c. 194, § 59, effective Nov. 22, 2011.)

Money or other thing of value drawn as a prize or share thereof in a lottery, and all property disposed of or offered to be disposed of by illegal gaming under the pretext mentioned in section seven, by an inhabitant of or a resident within the commonwealth, and all money or other thing of value received by such person by reason of his being the owner or holder of a ticket or share of a ticket in a lottery or pretended lottery, or of a share or right in any such scheme of chance or such device, contrary to this chapter, shall be forfeited, and may be recovered by an information filed or by an action for money had and received brought by the attorney general or a district attorney in the name and on behalf of the commonwealth.

SECTION 15
Aiding in setting up a lottery for money drawn out of commonwealth

Whoever except as provided in section five of chapter one hundred and twenty-eight A, aids, either by printing or

2

writing, or is in any way concerned in setting up, promoting, managing or drawing a lottery for money, set up, promoted, managed or drawn out of the commonwealth, shall be punished by a fine of not more than two thousand dollars or by imprisonment for not more than one year.

SECTION 16
Sale or possession of lottery ticket described in Sec. 15

Whoever sells, for himself or another, or offers for sale or has in his possession with intent so to do or to exchange or negotiate, or aids or assists in selling, negotiating, exchanging or disposing of a ticket, or a share of a ticket, in a lottery described in the preceding section, shall be punished by a fine of not more than two thousand dollars or by imprisonment for not more than one year.

SECTION 16A
Organizing or promoting gambling facilities or services
(Amended by 2011 Mass. Acts c. 194, § 60, effective Nov. 22, 2011.)

Whoever knowingly organizes, supervises, manages or finances at least four persons so that such persons may provide facilities or services or assist in the provision of facilities or services for the conduct of illegal lotteries, or for the illegal registration of bets or the illegal buying or selling of pools upon the result of a trial or contest of skill, speed or endurance of man, beast, bird or machine, or upon the happening of any event, or upon the result of a game, competition, political nomination, appointment or election, or whoever knowingly receives from at least four such persons compensation or payment in any form as a return from such lotteries, such registration or such buying or selling shall be punished by imprisonment in the state prison for not more than fifteen years or by a fine of not more than ten thousand dollars, or by both such fine and imprisonment. As used in this section the word "persons" shall not include bettors or wagerers or persons who organize, supervise, manage or finance persons for the purpose of gaming conducted under chapter 23K who merely avail themselves of such facilities or services for the purpose of making a bet or wager and do not otherwise provide or assist in the provision of such facilities or services. This section shall not apply to such bettors or wagerers.

SECTION 17
Keeping of, presence in, or permitting, a place for registering bets or dealing in pools; custodian or depository
(Amended by 2011 Mass. Acts c. 194, § 61, effective Nov. 22, 2011.)

Whoever keeps a building or room, or any part thereof, or occupies, or is found in, any place, way, public or private, park or parkway, or any open space, public or private, or any portion thereof, with apparatus, books or any device, for registering bets, or buying or selling pools, upon the result of a trial or contest of skill, speed or endurance of man, beast, bird or machine, or upon the result of a game, competition, political nomination, appointment or election, or whoever is present in such place, way, park or parkway, or any such open space, or any portion thereof, engaged in such business or employment; or, being such keeper, occupant, person found or person present, as aforesaid, registers such bets, or buys or sells such pools, or is concerned in buying or selling the same; or being the owner, lessee or occupant of a building or room, or part thereof, or private grounds, knowingly permits the same to be used or occupied for any such purpose, or therein keeps, exhibits, uses or employs, or knowingly permits to be therein kept, exhibited, used or employed, any device or apparatus for registering such bets, or for buying or selling such pools, or whoever becomes the custodian or depository for hire, reward, commission or compensation in any manner, of any pools, money, property or thing of value, in any manner staked or bet upon such result, shall be punished by a fine of not more than three thousand dollars or by imprisonment in the state prison for not more than three years, or in jail or the house of correction for not more than two and one half years. This section shall not apply to a person who organizes, supervises, manages or finances another person for the purpose of gaming conducted in accordance with chapter 23K.

NOTE 1   **Place.** "[T]he hallway was a 'place' within the meaning of the statute. . . . The intention seems to have been to make punishable the possession of [gambling] apparatus and devices anywhere." *Commonwealth v. Carlson*, 331 Mass. 449, 450–51 (1954).

NOTE 2a   **Apparatus.** "[A]rticles (taping, pens and pencils) which could be used for innocent purposes may, when used with items designed for betting purposes, be found to be 'apparatus.'" *Commonwealth v. Cosolito*, 359 Mass. 467, 469 (1971) (quoting *Commonwealth v. Demogenes*, 349 Mass. 585, 587–88 (1965)).

NOTE 2b   Racing publications may become "apparatus" even when not used with other items specially designed for betting purposes, if a person registering bets supplies the publications for use in placing the bets. *Commonwealth v. Cosolito*, 359 Mass. 467, 469 (1971).

NOTE 2c   Betting slips found on the defendant are apparatus and devices despite the fact that they related to horse races held on the day before. *Commonwealth v. Carlson*, 331 Mass. 449, 451 (1954).

NOTE 2d   A telephone is apparatus within the meaning of the statute. *Commonwealth v. Jensky*, 318 Mass. 350, 352 (1945).

NOTE 3a   **Registering Bets.** "[T]he 'receiving of a bet upon a horse race and making a memorandum of it on the slip of paper delivered to the one making the bet is in fact the registering of a bet.'" *Commonwealth v. Pasquale*, 334 Mass. 669, 670–71 (1956) (quoting *Sullivan v. Vorenberg*, 241 Mass. 319, 321 (1922)).

NOTE 3b   "[A] bet is also registered if the memorandum is made out by the bettor and delivered to the person receiving the bet." The identity of the bettor may be unknown. *Commonwealth v. Pasquale*, 334 Mass. 669, 670–71 (1956).

NOTE 3c   One may register a bet by committing it to memory. *Commonwealth v. Cosolito*, 359 Mass. 467, 470 (1971).

NOTE 4   **Expert Testimony.** The nature of slips of paper found in the defendant's possession and the meaning of entries on the slips were proper subjects of expert testimony by a police officer qualified as an expert. "Nor was there error in permitting [the witness] to characterize slips as 'bookie' slips related to the 'number pool.'" *Commonwealth v. Boyle*, 346 Mass. 1, 4 (1963).

NOTE 5a   **Evidence.** On a telephone kept in a concealed location on the premises managed by the defendant, a police officer had within 30 minutes twelve conversations with persons calling who asked him to place bets on a horse race. Although the identities of the persons calling were unknown, no bets were placed, and two of the persons calling asked for someone by a name not the defendant's, the evidence is relevant and admissible. "Its relevancy was to show that the room where the defendant was found contained apparatus, in this case a telephone, which was used, or intended to be used, for registering bets upon horse races." *Commonwealth v. Jensky*, 318 Mass. 350, 352 (1945).

NOTE 5b   **Prima Facie Evidence.** *See* G.L. c. 271, §§ 19–21 and 27.

NOTE 5c   **Variance.** G.L. c. 271, § 28.

2

SECTION 17A
Telephones; use for gaming purposes; penalty
(Bracketed text deleted by 2011 Mass. Acts c. 77, § 12; 2011 Mass. Acts c. 194, § 84, effective July 31, 2014.)

Whoever uses a telephone or, being the occupant in control of premises where a telephone is located or a subscriber for a telephone, knowingly permits another to use a telephone so located or for which he subscribes, as the case may be, for the purpose of accepting wagers or bets, or buying or selling of pools, or for placing all or any portion of a wager with another, upon the result of a trial or contest of skill, speed, or endurance of man, beast, bird, or machine, or upon the result of an athletic game or contest, or upon the lottery called the numbers game, or for the purpose of reporting the same to a headquarters or booking office, or who under a name other than his own or otherwise falsely or fictitiously procures telephone service for himself or another for such purposes, shall be punished by a fine of not more than two thousand dollars or by imprisonment for not more than one year[; provided, however, that this section shall not apply to use of telephones or other devices or means to place wagers authorized pursuant to the provisions of section 5C of chapter 128A].

SECTION 17B
Use of communications for unlawful purposes; demand of telephone company records by attorney general

Except as otherwise prohibited under section 2703 of Title 18 of the United States Code, whenever the attorney general or a district attorney has reasonable grounds to believe that records in the possession of: (i) a common carrier subject to the jurisdiction of the department of telecommunications and cable, as provided in paragraph (d) of section 12 of chapter 159; or (ii) a provider of electronic communication service as defined in subparagraph (15) of section 2510 of Title 18 of the United States Code; or (iii) a provider of remote computing service as defined in section 2711 of Title 18 of the United States Code, are relevant and material to an ongoing criminal investigation, the attorney general or district attorney may issue an administrative subpoena demanding all such records in the possession of such common carrier or service, and such records shall be delivered to the attorney general or district attorney within 14 days of receipt of the subpoena. No such common carrier or service, or employee thereof, shall be civilly or criminally responsible for furnishing any records or information in compliance with such demand. Nothing in this section shall limit the right of the attorney general or a district attorney to otherwise obtain records from such a common carrier or service pursuant to a search warrant, a court order or a grand jury or trial subpoena.

No subpoena issued pursuant to this section shall demand records that disclose the content of electronic communications or subscriber account records disclosing internet locations which have been accessed including, but not limited to, websites, chat channels and newsgroups, but excluding servers used to initially access the internet. No recipient of a subpoena issued pursuant to this section shall provide any such content or records accessed, in response to such subpoena.

NOTE   "[A] defendant may move to suppress telephone records acquired by administrative subpoena and a judge should allow such a motion if it is shown that a district attorney had no reasonable grounds for belief that the target was using the telephone for an unlawful purpose. In so holding, we emphasize that the statute does not provide the district attorney with a free hand

to issue routine administrative subpoenas for telephone records absent the reasonable grounds called for in the statute." *Commonwealth v. Vinnie*, 428 Mass. 161, 178 (1999).

SECTION 18
Policy lotteries or shops; making, delivering or possessing a lottery ticket or token; receipt of money or thing of value

Whoever keeps, sets up, promotes or is concerned as owner, agent, clerk or in any other manner, in managing a policy lottery or policy shop, or writes, prints, sells, transfers or delivers a ticket, certificate, slip, bill, token or other device, purporting or designed to guarantee or assure to a person, or to entitle him to a chance of drawing or obtaining a prize or thing of value in a lottery or in the game or device commonly known as policy lottery or policy, whether drawn or determined, or remaining to be drawn or determined, or who receives from a person any money or other thing of value for such article or chance; or for himself or another writes, prints, sells, transfers or delivers or has in his possession for the purpose of sale, transfer or delivery, or in any way aids in selling, exchanging, negotiating, transferring or delivering a chance or ticket in a lottery, or in the game or device commonly known as policy lottery or policy, whether drawn or to be drawn, or any such bill, slip, certificate, token or other device, shall be punished by a fine of not more than five hundred dollars or by imprisonment for not more than one year.

SECTION 19
Making, advertising or delivering ticket or receipt of money or thing of value as prima facie evidence
(Amended by 2011 Mass. Acts c. 194, § 62, effective Nov. 22, 2011.)

The printing, writing, advertising, issuing or delivery of any ticket, paper, document or other article or material representing or purporting to represent the existence of or any chance or interest in any lottery, policy lottery or policy game, pool or pools, registered or other bet or other game or hazard, whether drawn or determined, or remaining to be drawn or determined, or the receiving of money or other thing of value for such article or chance, shall be prima facie evidence of the existence, location and drawing of such lottery, policy lottery or policy game, and of the act or event upon which such pool or pools, bet, game or hazard depends or may depend, and of the unlawful character of such lottery, policy lottery, pool, bet, game or hazard, and the issuing or delivery of such ticket, paper, document or other article or material shall be prima facie evidence of value received therefor by the person, company or corporation issuing or delivering the same, or aiding or abetting therein, and that such person, company or corporation is concerned in keeping, managing or promoting such lottery, pool, bet, game or hazard. This section shall not apply to advertising of gaming conducted pursuant to chapter 23K.

SECTION 20
Tickets, memoranda, books and sheets as nuisance; possession unlawful; possession and concealment as evidence
(Amended by 2011 Mass. Acts c. 194, § 63, effective Nov. 22, 2011.)

All lottery, policy or pool tickets, slips or checks, memoranda of any combination or other bet, manifold or other policy or pool books or sheets, are hereby declared a common nuisance and the possession thereof unlawful; and the possession of any such article, or of any other implements, apparatus or materials of any other form of gaming, shall be prima facie evidence of their use, by the person having them in possession, in the form of gaming in which like articles are commonly used. Any such article found upon the person of one lawfully arrested for violation of any law relative to lotteries, policy lotteries or policy, the buying or selling of pools or registering of bets or other form of gaming shall be competent evidence upon the trial of a complaint or indictment to which it may be relevant. If a person so arrested in a building or structure or part thereof conceals or attempts to conceal such articles upon his person or elsewhere, the possession and concealment or attempt at concealment thereof shall be prima facie evidence that the place in which the same occurs is kept, maintained, used or occupied for the form of gaming in which like articles are commonly used. Nothing in this section shall prohibit a gaming establishment licensed under chapter 23K from posting, advertising or displaying materials relevant to its gaming operations.

SECTION 21
Words, figures or characters referring to horse, jockey or contest odds or bets as prima facie evidence; proof by copy or description

In a prosecution or proceeding relative to lotteries, policy lotteries or policy, buying and selling pools or registered bets, any words, figures or characters, written, printed or exposed upon a blackboard, placard or otherwise, in a place alleged to be used or occupied for such business, purporting or appearing to be a name of a horse or jockey, or a description of or reference to a trial or contest of skill, speed or endurance of man, beast, bird or machine, or game, competition, political nomination, appointment or election, or other act or event, or any odds, bet, combination bet or other stake or wager, or any code, cipher or substitute therefor, shall be prima facie evidence of the existence of the race, game, contest or other act or event so purporting or appearing to be referred to, and that such place is kept or occupied for gaming; and in all cases the same may be proved by a copy or by oral description thereof.

SECTION 22
Delivery to or from a person engaged in a lottery or other gaming
(Amended by 2011 Mass. Acts c. 194, § 64, effective Nov. 22, 2011.)

Whoever receives a letter, package or parcel for delivery to or transportation from a person, or delivers or transports the same to or from a person, having reasonable cause to believe that such person is engaged or in any way concerned in the management or promotion of or agency for a lottery, or the game known as policy lottery or policy, or the buying or selling of pools or registering of bets, or other form of illegal gaming, and that such letter, package or parcel has relation to such business, shall be punished by a fine of not less than fifty nor more than five hundred dollars; but this section shall not apply to the receipt, carriage or delivery of United States mail matter by an officer or employee thereof.

SECTION 22A
Whist or bridge for charitable and similar purposes

Nothing in this chapter shall authorize the prosecution, arrest or conviction of any person for conducting or promoting, or for allowing to be conducted or promoted, a game of cards commonly called whist or bridge, in connection with which prizes are offered to be won by chance; provided, that

the entire proceeds of the charges for admission to such game are donated solely to charitable, civic, educational, fraternal or religious purposes.

SECTION 22B
Beano; sale of lottery tickets

Nothing in this chapter shall authorize the prosecution, arrest or conviction of any person for conducting or promoting, or for allowing to be conducted, promoted or played, the game commonly called beano, or substantially the same game under another name in connection with which prizes are offered to be won by chance or for selling lottery tickets or shares; provided, said game or sales are conducted under a license issued by the director of the state lottery, under the provisions of sections thirty-seven or thirty-eight of chapter ten.

SECTION 23
Oath and warrant to enter a gaming or lottery place, arrest persons and seize implements and materials; disposal of articles
(Amended by 2011 Mass. Acts c. 194, § 65, effective Nov. 22, 2011.)

If a person makes oath before a district court or justice of the peace authorized to issue warrants in criminal cases that he suspects or has probable cause to suspect that a house or other building, room or place is used as and for a common gaming house, for gaming for money or other property, or is occupied, used or kept for promoting a lottery, or for the sale of lottery tickets, or for promoting the game known as policy lottery or policy, or for the buying or selling of pools or registering of bets upon any race, game, contest, act or event, and that persons resort thereto for any such purpose, such court or justice, whether the names of the persons last mentioned are known to the complainant or not, shall, if satisfactory evidence is presented, issue a warrant commanding the sheriff or his deputy or any constable or police officer to enter such house, building, room or place, and to arrest the keepers thereof, all persons in any way assisting in keeping the same, whether as janitor, doorkeeper, watchman or otherwise, all persons who are there found participating in any form of gaming and all persons present whether so participating or not, if any lottery, policy or pool tickets, slips, checks, manifold books or sheets, memoranda of any bet, or other implements, apparatus or materials of any form of gaming are found in said place, and to take into their custody all the implements, apparatus or materials of gaming, as aforesaid, and all the personal property, including money, furniture and fixtures there found, and to keep said persons, implements, apparatus or materials, property, including money, furniture and fixtures so that they may be forthcoming before some court or magistrate to be dealt with according to law. The provisions of chapter two hundred and seventy-six relative to disposal of gaming articles seized upon search warrants shall apply to all articles and property seized as herein provided for; provided, however, that such provision shall not apply to gaming conducted pursuant to chapter 23K.

SECTION 24
Owners, proprietors of, or persons present at, race tracks

This chapter shall not authorize the arrest or conviction of the owner or proprietor of a race track or trotting course for the reason that another person has without his knowledge or consent violated any of its provisions relative to the buying and selling of pools or the registering or making of bets or to

2

any offense mentioned in the preceding section; nor the arrest or conviction of a person for being present on a race track or trotting course where pools are sold or bets registered or made on trials of speed or endurance between horses or trials of speed or endurance between horses or other animals; but this exception shall not apply to a person in any way participating or assisting in the buying or selling of pools or registering of bets.

SECTION 25
Removal of obstructions barring access to gaming places; lien of expense

If a captain of police in Boston or marshal or chief of police in any other city or town in the commonwealth finds that access to any building, apartment or place which he has reasonable cause to believe is resorted to for the purpose of unlawful gaming is barred by any obstruction, such as a door, window, shutter, screen, bar or grating of unusual strength, other than what is usual in ordinary places of business, or any unnecessary number of doors, windows or obstructions, he shall order the same removed by the owner or agent of the building where such obstruction exists, and if any of said officers cannot find either of the persons mentioned, so as to make personal service, said notice shall be posted upon the outside of the apartments and on the outside of said building, and upon the neglect to remove such obstruction for seven days from the date of said order or posting of said notices, any of said officers shall cause such obstruction to be removed from such building, and the expense of such removal shall be a lien on said building and be collected by the officer removing such obstruction, in the manner in which a mechanic's lien is collected.

SECTION 26
Subsequent obstructions; removal; punishment; lien

If, within one year after removal of said obstruction, the premises are again obstructed as above defined, the captain of police or marshal or chief of police shall have the same power of removal as provided in the preceding section, and in addition the owner or agent when such second order of removal is given, either by personal service or by posting on the building, shall be punished by a fine of not less than two hundred and fifty nor more than five hundred dollars, and the amount of said fine shall be a lien upon said building and be collected in like manner as provided in the preceding section. And for every subsequent obstruction as above defined, at any time within two years of the giving of the second notice, as above provided, said officers shall have the same powers as provided in the preceding section for removing the obstructions, and the owner or agent at the time such third or subsequent order of removal is given, either by personal service or by posting on the building, shall be punished by a fine of not less than five hundred nor more than one thousand dollars or may be punished by imprisonment for one year, and the amount of said fine shall be a lien upon the said building, and shall be collected in like manner as above provided. Obstructions as above defined, erected more than two years after the giving of the notice of the third offense, shall be construed to be a first offense under this section.

SECTION 27
Judicial notice of methods and character of lotteries, policy games, pools and betting; tickets and other articles prima facie evidence

Any court or magistrate having criminal jurisdiction may take judicial notice of the general methods and character of lotteries, policy lotteries or the game called policy, pools or combination bets, and the buying and selling of pools and registering of bets. In the trial of a complaint or indictment to which it may be relevant, any lottery, policy or pool ticket, certificate, slip or check, manifold or other policy or pool book or sheet, or memorandum of any pool or sale of pools, or of a bet or odds, or combination bet, or any other implement, apparatus, materials or articles of a character commonly employed in or in connection with lotteries, policy lotteries or policy, the buying or selling of pools or registering of bets, or other form of gaming shall be prima facie evidence of the existence and unlawful character of a lottery, policy lottery or game, pool or pools, bet, game or hazard, or other form of gaming in which like articles are commonly used, and that such article has relation thereto.

SECTION 28
Complaints and indictments relative to lotteries or gaming; misnomer; sufficiency; variance
(Amended by 2011 Mass. Acts c. 194, § 66, effective Nov. 22, 2011.)

No plea of misnomer shall be received to a complaint or indictment for violation of any law relative to lotteries, policy lotteries or policy, the selling of pools or registering of bets, or any form of illegal gaming; but the defendant may be arraigned, tried, sentenced and punished under any name by which he is complained of or indicted. No such complaint or indictment shall be abated, quashed or held insufficient by reason of any alleged defect, either of form or substance, if the same is sufficient to enable the defendant to understand the charge and to prepare his defence. No variance between such complaint or indictment and the evidence shall be deemed material, unless in some matter of substance essential to the charge under the rule above prescribed.

SECTION 29
Representation that a thing other than subject of sale is to be delivered; stamps and other devices entitling purchaser to other property

Whoever sells, exchanges or disposes of any property, or offers or attempts so to do, upon a representation, advertisement, notice or inducement that anything other than what is specifically stated to be the subject of the sale or exchange is or is to be delivered or received, or is in any way connected with or is a part of the transaction, or whoever gives a stamp, coupon or other device which entitles a purchaser to demand or receive from a person or company other than the merchant dealing in the goods purchased or the manufacturer thereof, any other property than that actually sold or exchanged, or whoever delivers by any person or company other than the merchant dealing in the goods purchased, or the manufacturer thereof, goods, wares or merchandise upon the presentation of such stamp, coupon or other device, shall be punished by a fine of not less than ten nor more than five hundred dollars.

SECTION 30
Sale or delivery of trading stamps or similar devices

Whoever, in connection with the sale of any article or any merchandise whatsoever, sells, gives or delivers any trading stamps, checks, coupons or similar devices to be exchanged for, or to be redeemed by the giving of, any indefinite or undescribed article, the nature and value of which are not stated, or to be exchanged for, or to be redeemed by the giving of, any article not distinctly bargained for at the time when such trading stamps or other devices as aforesaid were sold, given or delivered, shall be punished by a fine of not less than ten nor more than fifty dollars.

SECTION 31
Racing horses for bets or stakes
(Amended by 2011 Mass. Acts c. 194, § 67, effective Nov. 22, 2011.)

Whoever, except in trials of speed of horses for premiums offered by legally constituted agricultural societies, or by corporations authorized thereto by section fourteen of chapter one hundred and eighty, engages in racing, running, trotting or pacing a horse or other animal of the horse kind for a bet, wager of money or other thing of value or a purse or stake made within the commonwealth, or whoever aids or abets therein, shall be punished by a fine of not more than one thousand dollars or by imprisonment for not more than one year, or both. This section shall not apply to racing conducted pursuant to chapter 23K.

SECTION 31A
Racing results or information; transmission for unlawful purposes; penalty

Whoever transmits the results of a race, or information as to the progress of a race during the running thereof, in a racing meeting as defined in section one of chapter one hundred and twenty-eight A, by any means to another knowing that such results or information is to be used or intended to be used for unlawful purposes or in furtherance of unlawful gambling, shall be punished by a fine of not more than five thousand dollars or by imprisonment in a jail or house of correction for not more than two and one half years or in the state prison for not more than five years, or by both such fine and imprisonment.

This section shall not be construed as prohibiting a newspaper from printing such results for publication as news, or a television or radio station from telecasting or broadcasting such results or information as news.

SECTION 32
Competing with horse disguised or different from one purported to be; horse in improper class

Whoever, for the purpose of competing for a purse or premium offered by an agricultural society, or by a person or association in the commonwealth, knowingly and designedly enters or drives a horse that is painted or disguised, or is a different horse from the one that purports to be entered or driven, or knowingly and designedly, for the purpose of competing for a premium or purse, enters or drives a horse in a class to which it does not belong, shall be punished by a fine of not more than five hundred dollars or by imprisonment for not more than six months.

SECTION 33
Race grounds in towns; consent; regulations; discontinuance; unlawful use

No land within a town shall be laid out or used as a race ground or trotting park without the previous consent of and location by the mayor and city council, the town council in a town having a town council or the selectmen in any other town, who may regulate and alter the terms and conditions under which the same shall be laid out, used or continued in use and may discontinue the same when in their judgment the public good so requires; and no land shall be used for any of the purposes declared unlawful in section thirty-one.

SECTION 34
Race grounds as nuisance; abatement; punishment

Every race ground or trotting park established, laid out, used or continued in use contrary to this chapter is declared a common nuisance and may be abated as such; and all persons owning, keeping, using or permitting to be used such race ground or trotting park, or aiding or abetting therein, shall be punished by a fine of not more than one thousand dollars or by imprisonment for not more than one year, or both.

SECTION 35
Definition of words and phrases used in Secs. 35–38

The following words and phrases used in this and the three following sections of this chapter shall, unless a different meaning is required by the context, have the following meanings:

"Person", an individual, partnership, corporation or association, whether acting in his or their own right or as the officer, agent, servant, correspondent or representative of another.

"Contract", any agreement, trade or transaction.

"Securities", all evidences of debt or property and options for the purchase and sale thereof, shares in any corporation, joint stock company or association, bonds, coupons, scrip, rights, choses in action and other evidences of debt or property and options for the purchase or sale thereof.

"Commodities", anything movable that is bought and sold.

"Bucket shop", any room, office, store, building or other place where any contract prohibited by the following section is made or offered to be made.

"Keeper", any person owning, keeping, managing, operating or promoting a bucket shop, or assisting to keep, manage, operate or promote a bucket shop.

"Bucketing" or "Bucket-shopping",

(a) The making of, or offering to make, any contract respecting the purchase or sale, either upon credit or upon margin, of any securities or commodities, wherein both parties thereto intend, or such keeper intends, that such contract shall be, or may be, terminated, closed or settled according to, or upon the basis of, the public market quotations of prices made on any board of trade or exchange upon which said securities or commodities are dealt in, and without a bona fide purchase or sale of the same; or

(b) The making of, or offering to make, any contract respecting the purchase or sale, either upon credit or upon margin, of any securities or commodities, wherein both parties intend, or such keeper intends, that such contract shall be, or may be, deemed terminated, closed or settled, when such public market quotations of prices for the securities or commodities named in such contract shall reach a certain figure without bona fide purchase or sale of the same; or

2

(c) The making of, or offering to make, any contract respecting the purchase or sale, either upon credit or upon margin, of any securities or commodities, wherein both parties do not intend, or such keeper does not intend, the actual or bona fide receipt or delivery of such securities or commodities, but do intend, or such keeper does intend, a settlement of such contract based upon the differences in such public market quotations of prices at which said securities or commodities are, or are asserted to be, bought and sold.

SECTION 36
Making contracts of bucketing; keeper of shop; dissolution of corporation; restraint from doing business

Whoever makes, or offers to make, any contract of bucketing or bucket-shopping, or who is the keeper of any bucket shop, shall be punished by a fine of not more than one thousand dollars or by imprisonment for not more than one year. Whoever shall be convicted of a second offence shall be punished by imprisonment for not more than five years. The continuing of the keeping of a bucket shop, by any person, after the first conviction therefor, shall be deemed a second offense hereunder. If a domestic corporation shall be convicted of a second offence, the supreme judicial court may, upon an information in equity in the name of the attorney general, at the relation of the commissioner of revenue, dissolve the corporation; and if a foreign corporation shall be convicted of a second offense, the supreme judicial court may, in the same manner, restrain it from doing business in the commonwealth.

SECTION 37
Quotations of prices for prohibited contracts

Whoever shall communicate, receive, exhibit or display in any manner any statement of quotations of prices of any securities or commodities with an intent to make, of offer to make, or to aid in making, or offering to make, any contract prohibited by the preceding section shall be punished as provided therein.

SECTION 38
Written statements relative to purchases and sales of securities or commodities; refusal as prima facie evidence of bucketing

Every person shall furnish, upon demand, to any customer or principal for whom such person has executed any order for the actual purchase or sale of any securities or commodities, either for immediate or future delivery, a written statement containing the names of the persons from whom such property was bought, or to whom it has been sold, as the fact may be, the time when, place where and the price at which the same was either bought or sold; and if such person refuses or neglects to furnish such statement within twenty-four hours after such demand, such refusal or neglect shall be prima facie evidence that such purchase or sale was bucketing or bucketshopping.

SECTION 39
Gifts to influence business affairs; threats; penalty

(a) Whoever, in relation to any transaction or matter concerning the business affairs of an employer, principal or beneficiary (1) offers, gives or agrees to give an agent or fiduciary of another person any benefit or anything of value with intent to influence the recipient's conduct, or (2) as an agent or fiduciary, solicits, accepts or agrees to accept any benefit or anything of value from another person who is not an employee, principal, or beneficiary upon an agreement or understanding that such benefit or thing of value will influence his conduct, shall be punished by imprisonment in the state prison for not more than five years, or by a fine of not more than ten thousand dollars, or both.

(b) Whoever, verbally or by a written or printed communication: threatens an economic injury to another, or threatens to deprive another of an economic opportunity, with intent to compel that person to do any act, involving the use or disposition of anything of value against his will, shall be punished by imprisonment in the state prison for not more than five years, or in the house of correction for not more than two years, or by a fine of not more than five thousand dollars, or both. The provisions of this paragraph shall not apply to any labor disputes as defined in section two of chapter one hundred and fifty A.

SECTION 39A
Gifts to influence action of participants in, and others connected with, a game or contest

Whoever gives, promises or offers to any professional or amateur baseball, football, hockey, polo, tennis or basketball player or any boxer or any player who participates or expects to participate in any professional or amateur game or sport or any jockey, driver or groom or any person participating or expecting to participate in any horse race, including owners of race tracks and their employees, stewards, trainers, judges, starters or special policemen, or to any manager, coach or trainer of any team or participant or prospective participant in any such game, contest or sport, any valuable thing with intent to influence him to lose, or try to lose, or cause to be lost, or to limit his or his team's margin of victory in, a baseball, football, hockey or basketball game, boxing, tennis or polo match or a horse race or any professional or amateur sport, or game, in which such player or participant or jockey or driver, is taking part or expects to take part, or has any duty or connection therewith, or whoever, being a professional or amateur baseball, football, hockey, basketball, tennis or polo player, boxer, or jockey, driver, or groom or participant or prospective participant in any sport or game or a manager, coach or trainer of any team or individual participant or prospective participant in any such game, contest or sport, solicits or accepts any valuable thing to influence him to lose, or try to lose, or cause to be lost, or to limit his or his team's margin of victory in, a baseball, football, hockey or basketball game or boxing, tennis or polo match, or horse race or any game of sport in which he is taking part, or expects to take part, or has any duty or connection therewith, shall be punished by a fine of not more than one thousand dollars or by imprisonment for not more than two years, or both.

SECTION 40
Appointment, retention or discharge of employee of public service corporation or racing licensee on recommendation of public officer, officer elect or candidate

No railroad, street railway, electric light, gas, telegraph, telephone, water or steamboat company, and no licensee conducting a horse or dog racing meeting under chapter one hundred and twenty-eight A, shall appoint, promote, reinstate, suspend or discharge any person employed or seeking employment by any such company or licensee at the request of the governor, lieutenant governor, or any member or member elect of the council or of the general court, or candidate there-for, justice of the supreme judicial court, justice of the superi-or court, judge of probate, judge of the land court, justice of a district court, district attorney, member or member elect of a board of county commissioners, or candidate for county commissioner, mayor or mayor elect of a city, or candidate therefor, member or member elect of board of aldermen, or selectmen, or city council, or any executive, administrative or judicial officer, clerk or employee of any branch of the gov-ernment of the commonwealth or of any county, city or town; nor shall any such public officer or body, or any member or member elect thereof or candidate therefor, directly or indi-rectly advocate, oppose or otherwise interfere in, or make any request, recommendation, endorsement, requirement or certif-icate relative to, and the same, if made, shall not be required as a condition precedent to, or be in any way regarded or permitted to influence or control, the appointment, promotion, reinstatement or retention of any person employed or seeking employment by any such company or licensee, and no such person shall solicit, obtain, exhibit, or otherwise make use of any such official request, recommendation, certificate or en-dorsement in connection with any existing or desired em-ployment by a public service corporation or by any such li-censee. Any person or corporation violating any provision of this section shall be punished by a fine of not less than fifty nor more than one hundred dollars.

SECTION 41
Offices not public offices under Sec. 40

The offices of probation officer, notary public, justice of the peace, prison officer, agent of the commissioner of cor-rection and agent of the department of public welfare shall not be considered public offices within the meaning of the preceding section.

SECTION 42
Betting or selling pools on boxing matches or exhibitions

Whoever bets or wagers or sells pools on any boxing or sparring match or exhibition shall be punished by imprison-ment for not less than three months or by a fine of not less than fifty dollars, or both.

SECTION 43
Soliciting, disclosing, receiving or making use of information concerning public assistance

Any person who, except for purposes directly connected with the administration of general public assistance, old age assistance, aid to the blind, or aid to families with dependent children, and in accordance with the rules and regulations of the department of transitional assistance made under authority of section ten of chapter eighteen, or of the commission for the blind made under authority of section one hundred and forty-nine of chapter six, as the case may be, shall solicit, disclose, receive, make use of, or authorize, knowingly per-mit, participate in, or acquiesce in the use of, any list of, or names of, or any information concerning, persons applying for or receiving general public assistance, old age assistance, aid to families with dependent children or aid to the blind, directly or indirectly derived from the records, papers, files or communications of the department of transitional assistance, any city or town welfare department or bureau of old age assistance, or the commission for the blind, as the case may be, or acquired in the course of the performance of official

duties, shall be punished by a fine of not more than one hun-dred dollars. Nothing herein shall be construed to prevent the disclosure by the commissioner of revenue to the commis-sioner of transitional assistance or to the IV-D agency set forth in chapter one hundred and nineteen A, in concert with a wage reporting system, of such information as may be neces-sary to ascertain or confirm the existence of fraud, abuse or improper payments to an applicant, for or recipient of, public assistance; and nothing herein shall be construed to prevent the disclosure to said IV-D agency of information necessary for setoff debt collection pursuant to chapter sixty-two D or any other child support enforcement purpose.

SECTION 44
Settlement, release or statement by person in hospital; admissibility; reference to at trial; validity

Except as provided below, no settlement or general re-lease or statement in writing signed by any person confined in a hospital or sanitarium as a patient with reference to any personal injuries for which said person is confined in said hospital or sanitarium shall be admissible in evidence, used or referred to in any manner at the trial of any action to recover damages for personal injuries or consequential damages, so called, resulting therefrom, which statement, settlement or general release was obtained within fifteen days after the injuries were sustained and such settlement or release shall be null and void unless at least five days prior to the obtaining or procuring of such general release or statement such injured party had signified in writing his willingness that such gen-eral release or statement be given. This section shall not apply to statements or releases obtained by police officers or in-spectors of motor vehicles in the performance of their duty, members of the family of such person or by or on behalf of his attorney. The provisions of this section shall not apply to chapter one hundred and fifty-two.

SECTION 45
Repealed

SECTION 46
Removal of doors from discarded containers originally used for refrigerative purposes

Whoever fails to remove the door or doors from a con-tainer originally used for refrigerative purposes before dis-carding it, or setting it aside for failure to use such container, or before keeping it out of doors for sale or any other purpose in a place accessible to unattended children, shall be punished by a fine of not more than one thousand dollars.

SECTION 47
Telephones; gambling; reinstallation; notices of convictions and removals

A telephone shall not be installed for a person convicted of an illegal gaming activity under this chapter without the approval in writing of the head of both the police department of the municipality in which such telephone would be in-stalled and the head of the criminal information section of the state police, and a telephone shall not be reinstalled without such approval for a period of one year from the date of re-moval in any premises from which it has been removed for such illegal activity, whether or not there has been a convic-tion. The criminal information section shall notify the tele-phone companies of convictions in such cases, and telephone companies doing business in the commonwealth shall notify the criminal information section of the state police of any such removals.

SECTION 48
Schools or persons offering civil service preparatory courses; advertisement

Any school or person offering courses in preparation for civil service examinations shall cause to be printed in bold type on all its advertisements and circulars and all contracts to be entered into with prospective students a statement that disabled veterans who qualify for appointment must be given preference for appointment over veterans and non-veterans and that veterans must be given preference over non-veterans. Whoever violates the provisions of this section shall be punished by a fine of not less than fifty nor more than five hundred dollars.

SECTION 49
Criminal usury

(a) Whoever in exchange for either a loan of money or other property knowingly contracts for, charges, takes or receives, directly or indirectly, interest and expenses the aggregate of which exceeds an amount greater than twenty per centum per annum upon the sum loaned or the equivalent rate for a longer or shorter period, shall be guilty of criminal usury and shall be punished by imprisonment in the state prison for not more than ten years or by a fine of not more than ten thousand dollars, or by both such fine and imprisonment. For the purposes of this section the amount to be paid upon any loan for interest or expenses shall include all sums paid or to be paid by or on behalf of the borrower for interest, brokerage, recording fees, commissions, services, extension of loan, forbearance to enforce payment, and all other sums charged against or paid or to be paid by the borrower for making or securing directly or indirectly the loan, and shall include all such sums when paid by or on behalf of or charged against the borrower for or on account of making or securing the loan, directly or indirectly, to or by any person, other than the lender, if such payment or charge was known to the lender at the time of making the loan, or might have been ascertained by reasonable inquiry.

(b) Whoever, with knowledge of the contents thereof, possesses any writing, paper, instrument or article used to record a transaction proscribed under the provisions of paragraph (a) shall be punished by imprisonment in a jail or house of correction for not more than two and one half years, or by a fine of not more than five thousand dollars, or by both such fine and imprisonment.

(c) Any loan at a rate of interest proscribed under the provisions of paragraph (a) may be declared void by the supreme judicial or superior court in equity upon petition by the person to whom the loan was made.

(d) The provisions of paragraph (a) to (c), inclusive, shall not apply to any person who notifies the attorney general of his intent to engage in a transaction or transactions which, but for the provisions of this paragraph, would be proscribed under the provisions of paragraph (a) providing any such person maintains records of any such transaction. Such notification shall be valid for a two year period and shall contain the person's name and accurate address. No lender shall publicly advertise the fact of such notification nor use the fact of such notification to solicit business, except that such notification may be revealed to an individual upon his inquiry. Illegal use of such notification shall be punished by a fine of one thousand dollars. Such records shall contain the name and address of the borrower, the amount borrowed, the interest and expenses to be paid by the borrower, the date the loan is made and the date or dates on which any payment is due. Any such records shall be made available to the attorney general for the purposes of inspection upon his request. Such records and their contents shall be confidential but may be used by the attorney general, or any district attorney with the approval of the attorney general, for the purposes of conducting any criminal proceeding to which such records or their contents are relevant.

(e) The provisions of this section shall not apply to any loan the rate of interest for which is regulated under any other provision of general or special law or regulations promulgated thereunder or to any lender subject to control, regulation or examination by any state or federal regulatory agency.

SECTION 50
Sale of research papers, etc. And taking of examinations for another at educational institutions

Whoever, alone or in concert with others, sells to another, or arranges for or assists in such sale for another, a theme, term paper, thesis or other paper or the written results of research, knowing or having reason to know that such theme, term paper, thesis or other paper or research results or substantial material therefrom will be submitted or used by some other person for academic credit and represented as the original work of such person at an educational institution in the commonwealth or elsewhere without proper attribution as to source, or whoever takes an examination for another at any educational institution in the commonwealth, shall be punished by a fine of not more than one hundred dollars or by imprisonment for not more than six months, or both.

Chapter 271A. Enterprise Crime

Section
1   Definitions
2   Enterprise crime, penalties
3   Seizure and forfeiture of proceeds or property obtained as result of violation of chapter

SECTION 1
Definitions
(Added by 2011 Mass. Acts c. 194, § 68, effective Nov. 22, 2011.)

As used in this chapter, the following words shall have the following meanings unless the context clearly requires otherwise:

"Criminal enterprise activity", the commission, attempt to commit or conspiracy to commit or the solicitation, coercion, aiding, abetting or intimidation of another to commit any of the following criminal activities under the laws of the commonwealth or equivalent crimes under the laws of any other jurisdiction: a violation of any criminal provision of chapter 23K; a felony offense under chapter 271; distributing, dispensing, manufacturing or possessing with intent to distribute, dispense or manufacture a controlled substance in violation of chapter 94C; murder; rape; manslaughter, not including motor vehicle homicide; assault; assault and battery; assault and battery in order to collect a loan; assault with intent to rob or murder; poisoning; mayhem; robbery; extortion; stalking; criminal harassment; kidnapping; arson; burglary; malicious destruction of property; commission of a felony for hire; breaking and entering; child exploitation; assault and battery on a child; rape of a child; rape and abuse of a child; enticement of a child under 16; human trafficking; violation of constitutional rights under section 37 of chapter 265; usury; uttering; misuse or fraudulent use of credit cards under section 37C of chapter 266; identity fraud; misappropriation of funds; gross fraud under section 76 of chapter 276; insurance fraud; unlawful prize fighting or boxing matches; counterfeiting; perjury; subornation of perjury; obstruction of justice; money laundering; witness intimidation; bribery; electronic eavesdropping; prostitution under sections 2, 3, 4A, 4B, 6, 7, 12 and 13 of chapter 272; receiving stolen property; larceny over $250; larceny by false pretenses or embezzlement; forgery; procurement fraud; false claims; tax evasion; filing false tax returns; or any conduct defined as a racketeering activity under Title 18, U.S.C. s. 1961(1)(A)(B) and (D).

"Enterprise", an entity including any individual, sole proprietorship, partnership, corporation, association, trust or other legal entity and any unchartered union or group of persons associated in fact although not a legally-recognized entity.

"Gaming establishment", an establishment licensed under chapter 23K.

"Pattern of criminal enterprise activity", engaging in at least 3 incidents of criminal enterprise activity that have the same or similar pattern, intents, results, accomplices, victims or methods of commission or are otherwise interrelated by distinguishing characteristics and are not isolated incidents; provided, however, that at least 1 of the incidents shall have occurred after the effective date of this chapter and the last incident shall have occurred within 5 years of another incident of criminal enterprise activity.

"Unlawful debt", a debt which was incurred or contracted in an illegal gambling activity or business or which is unenforceable under state or federal law, in whole or in part, as to principal or interest under the law relating to usury.

SECTION 2
Enterprise crime; penalties
(Added by 2011 Mass. Acts c. 194, § 68, effective Nov. 22, 2011.)

Whoever knowingly: (1) through a pattern of criminal enterprise activity or through the collection of an unlawful debt acquires or maintains, directly or indirectly, an interest in or control of an enterprise which is engaged in, or the ac-

tivities of which affect, licensed gaming under chapter 23K or ancillary industries which do business with a gaming establishment; (2) having received proceeds derived, directly or indirectly, from a pattern of criminal enterprise activity or through the collection of an unlawful debt, uses or invests, directly or indirectly, part of the proceeds, including proceeds derived from the investment, in the acquisition of an interest in real property to be used in connection with licensed gaming, or in the establishment or operation of an enterprise which is engaged in, or the activities of which affect, licensed gaming operations or ancillary industries which do business with a gaming establishment; (3) is employed by or associated with an enterprise to conduct or participate, directly or indirectly, in the conduct of the enterprise's affairs or activities which affect licensed gaming operations or ancillary industries which do business with a gaming establishment by engaging in a pattern of criminal enterprise activity or through the collection of an unlawful debt; or (4) conspires or attempts to violate clauses (1), (2), or (3) or attempts to so conspire; shall be guilty of enterprise crime and shall be punished by imprisonment in the state prison for not more than 15 years or by a fine of not more than $25,000 or by both such imprisonment and fine.

Nothing in this chapter shall prohibit the purchase of securities on the open market for purposes of investment made without the intention of controlling or participating in the control of the issuer, or of assisting another to do so, if the securities of the issuer held by the: (i) purchaser; (ii) members of the purchaser's immediate family; or (iii) the purchaser's accomplices in any pattern of criminal activity for the collection of an unlawful debt after such purchase do not amount, in the aggregate, to 1 per cent of the outstanding securities of any 1 class and do not confer, either in law or in fact, the power to elect 1 or more directors of the issuer.

SECTION 3
Seizure and forfeiture of proceeds or property obtained as result of violation of chapter
(Added by 2011 Mass. Acts c. 194, § 68, effective Nov. 22, 2011.)

All monetary proceeds or other property, real, intellectual or personal, obtained directly as a result of a violation of this chapter, shall be subject to seizure and forfeiture to the commonwealth. Forfeiture proceedings shall be conducted as provided in subsections (b) to (j), inclusive of section 47 of chapter 94C. For the purposes of subsection (d) of said section 47 of said chapter 94C, the investigation and enforcement bureau of the Massachusetts gaming commission established in chapter 23K shall be considered a police department and shall be entitled to a police department's distribution of forfeiture proceedings.

Chapter 272. Crimes Against Chastity, Morality, Decency and Good Order

Section
1   Enticing away a person under 16 for marriage
2   Enticing away a person for prostitution or sexual intercourse
3   Drugging persons for sexual intercourse
4   Inducing person under 18 to have sexual intercourse
4A   Inducing minor into prostitution; penalties
4B   Living off or sharing earnings of minor prostitute; penalties
5   Repealed
6   One controlling a place, inducing or suffering a person to resort there for sexual intercourse
7   Support or sharing, earnings of prostitute
8   Soliciting for prostitute
9   Oath and warrant to enter place for prostitution; detention of person in control and prostitute; recognizance to appear as witness
10   Arrest without warrant
11   Corroboration of one witness; limitations

2

12   Procuring person to practice, or enter a place for, prostitution; employment office procuring person

13   Detaining, or drugging to detain, person in place for prostitution

14   Adultery

15   Polygamy

16   Open and gross lewdness and lascivious behavior

17   Incestuous marriage or intercourse

18   Fornication

19   Procuring miscarriage

20   Advertising relative to miscarriage or prevention of pregnancy

21   Instrument or other articles for self-abuse, prevention of conception or abortion, in general

21A   Furnishing drugs, articles or information for prevention of pregnancy or conception

21B   Privately controlled hospital or health facility not required to perform abortion or sterilization procedures, or to furnish contraceptive devices or information or family planning services

22   Concealment of death of child born out of wedlock

23   Joinder of charges of murder and offense under Sec. 22

24   Keeping house of ill fame

25   Enclosures in restaurants or taverns closed by devices obstructing view of patrons; barricaded entrances impeding access by officers

26   Resorting to restaurant or taverns for immoral purposes; engaging in such acts therein

27   Copy of record of convictions under Secs. 25 and 26 sent to licensing officers

28   Matter harmful to minors, dissemination; possession; defenses

28A–B Repealed

28C   Information or petition against obscene books; order of notice to show cause; notice of order; interlocutory adjudication; defense

28D   Answer to notice; right to jury trial

28E   Order of default; adjudication

28F   Hearing; evidence; adjudication

28G   Objection that mere judgment sought and no relief claimed on issue of knowledge

28H   Proceeding under Sec. 28C as evidence in trial under Sec. 28B; presumptions as to knowledge

28I   Certain procedures as condition precedent to institution of proceedings for dissemination of obscene books

29   Dissemination or possession of obscene matter; punishment; defense

29A   Posing or exhibiting child in state of nudity or sexual conduct; punishment

29B   Dissemination of visual material of child in state of nudity or sexual conduct; punishment

29C   Purchasing or possessing child pornography

30   Injunctive relief against dissemination of obscene matter; jurisdiction; procedures; appeal

30A–C Repealed

30D   Jurisdiction to enjoin dissemination of visual material of child in state of nudity or sexual conduct

31   Definitions applicable to Secs. 28, 28C, 28D, 28E, 29, 29A, 29B, 30 and 30D

32   Motion picture theater managers or operators; applicability of Secs. 28, 29 and 29A

33   Exhibition of deformities

34   Crime against nature

35   Unnatural and lascivious acts

35A   Unnatural and lascivious acts with child under 16

36   Blasphemy

36A   Sporting events, penalty for abuse of participants and officials

37   Repealed

38   Disturbance of assembly for worship

39   Selling goods and provisions, caring for horses, gaming, horse racing or exhibits near camp meetings

40   Disturbance of schools or assemblies

40A   Alcoholic beverages; gift, sale, delivery or possession on public school premises

41   Disturbance of libraries

42   Disturbance of funerals

42A   Disturbance of funeral services

42B   Disturbance of military funeral services

43   Disorderliness in public conveyances; disturbance of travelers

43A   Smoking in public conveyances and transportation terminals

44–52 Repealed

53   Penalty for certain offenses

53A   Engaging in sexual conduct for a fee; penalty

54   Apprehension for offenses mentioned in Sec. 53, without warrant; custody

55   Repealed

56   Commission of subsequent offense as breach of recognizance on appeal

57   Discharge upon recognizance and paying expenses of prosecutions under Secs. 53, 66 and 68

58   Employing or permitting employment of minor under 15 to beg

59   Violation of regulations relating to streets, reservations, or parkways; alcoholic beverages; profanity; arrest without warrant

60   Refusal to remove substance placed on public way in violation of town regulations; arrest without warrant until identity ascertained

61   Conviction after discharge from sentence under Sec. 53

62   Third conviction of being a common nightwalker

63   Tramps; begging or riding freight trains as prima facie evidence

64   Punishment of tramps; entering buildings; injuries to or threats against persons or property; carrying weapons

65   Arrest of tramps without warrant; making complaint

66   Vagrants

67   Arrest of vagrants without warrant; taking before court; making complaint

68   Vagabonds

69   Arresting vagabonds without warrant; taking before court; making complaint

70   Taking dead body on process or execution

71   Disinterring human bodies

72   Buying, selling or possessing dead bodies

73   Tombs, graves, memorials, trees, plants; injuring, removing

73A   Removal of gravestones and other memorials for repair or reproduction

73B   Sale of or attempt to sell stolen commemorative grave marker; receipt, retention or disposal of stolen commemorative grave marker

74   Desecrating place of burial; use and occupation as evidence of title

75   Removal of flowers, flags or memorial tokens from burial lot

76   Ways, railroads, canals or public easements through burial grounds

77   Cruelty to animals

77A   Wilfully injuring police dogs and horses

77B   Exhibition of wild animals

78   Selling, leading or using horses not fit for work; forfeiture of auctioneer's license

78A   Sale of foals under five months; penalty

79   Corporation's responsibility under Secs. 77 and 78

79A   Cutting bones or muscles to dock or set tail of horse; wound as evidence

79B   Exhibiting horse with tail cut under Sec. 79A; affidavit as to cutting in state where not prohibited; inspection

80   Repealed

80½   Devocalization of dogs or cats; definitions; penalty; exceptions; records

80A   Cropping or cutting off ear of dog; wound as prima facie evidence

80B   Exhibiting dogs with ears cropped or cut off

80C   Taking cat, dog or bird to exhibit it, subject it to experimentation or mutilation, or to sell it for such purposes; application of law

80D   Sale, etc. of living rabbits, baby chickens, ducklings or other fowl

80E   Use of decompression chambers for putting animals to death

80F   Giving away live animals as prize or award

80G   Experiments on vertebrates; vivisection, dissection of animals; care

80H   Motor vehicles; striking, injuring or killing dogs or cats

80I   Prohibition against the rental or leasing of dogs

81   Rest, water and feed for transported animals; lien; liability for detention

82   Arrest without warrant for violation of Sec. 77 or 81; notice to owner; care of animals; lien

83   Complaint, warrant and search relative to cruelty to animals

84   Prosecutions under Secs. 77 to 81

85   Repealed

85A   Injuring, taking away or harboring domesticated animals or birds; removal of dog license tag, collar or harness; imitation tag

85B   Assistance animals stolen or attacked; actions for economic and non-economic damages

86   Stabling horses or mules on second or higher floors, in places other than cities

86A	Stabling horses and mules above first floor or exceeding six in cities; use of exits
86B	Stabling horses or mules exceeding fifteen
86C	Smoking in buildings used for stabling horses or mules
86D	Pails of water and sand in buildings used for stables
86E	Entry upon premises to enforce Secs. 86A to 86D; ordering conditions remedied; service
86F	Punishment for violation of Secs. 86 to 86E or for neglect to comply with orders under Sec. 86E
87	Keeping or using birds to be shot at; shooting them; permitting premises to be used for shooting
88	Complaints and warrants relative to fighting animals; searches; arrests
89	Entering without warrant place for exhibition of fighting animals; seizure of animals
90	Custody of arrested persons; taking before court; proceedings
91	Application for decree of forfeiture; notice; hearing; adjudication; returning or killing animals; claimant
92	Appeal; recognizance; custody and disposition of animals
92A	Advertisement, book, notice or sign relative to discrimination; definition of place of public accommodation, resort or amusement
93	Expenses of care and destruction of fighting animals
94	Owning, possessing or training fighting animals; establishing or promoting exhibition
95	Aiding or being present at exhibition of fighting animals
96	False notice of birth, marriage or death
97	Repealed
97A	Demands, notices or other documents resembling court process; complaint; order to discontinue
98	Discrimination in admission to, or treatment in, place of public accommodation; punishment; forfeiture; civil right
98A	Accommodations and privileges of handicapped persons with guide dogs
98B	Discrimination in employment on public works or in public relief or transitional assistance
98C	Libel relative to groups of persons; punishment; prosecutions; defenses
99	Interception of wire and oral communications
99A	Overhearing deliberations of jury by using devices
100–103	Repealed
104	Security for seizure and impoundment of animals relating to cruelty to animals or animal fighting
105	Photographing, videotaping or electronically surveilling partially nude or nude person; exceptions; punishment
106	Stolen valor; penalty

SECTION 1

Enticing away a person under 16 for marriage

Whoever fraudulently and deceitfully entices or takes away an unmarried person under sixteen from the house of such person's parents or elsewhere, without the consent of the parent or guardian, if any, under whose care and custody such person is living, for the purpose of effecting a clandestine marriage of such person without the consent of such parent or guardian, shall be punished by imprisonment for not more than one year or by a fine of not more than one thousand dollars, or both.

NOTE   Form of indictment—G.L. c. 277, § 79 (Abduction (1)).

SECTION 2

Enticing away a person for prostitution or sexual intercourse

Whoever fraudulently and deceitfully entices or takes away a person from the house of his parent or guardian or elsewhere, for the purpose of prostitution or for the purpose of unlawful sexual intercourse, and whoever aids and assists in such abduction for such purpose, shall be punished by imprisonment in the state prison for not more than three years or in jail for not more than one year or by a fine of not more than

one thousand dollars, or by both such fine and imprisonment in jail.

NOTE 1   Form of indictment—G.L. c. 277, § 79 (Abduction (2)).

NOTE 2   Corroborating evidence necessary—G.L. c. 272, § 11.

NOTE 3   Statute of limitations—one year G.L. c. 272, § 11.

NOTE 4   DNA Database. A conviction of an offense under this section or of an attempt or conspiracy to commit such an offense results in the defendant being required to submit a DNA sample to the state's DNA database. *See* G.L. c. 22E, § 3.

NOTE 5   Sex Offender Registry. A conviction or adjudication of delinquency of an offense under this section or of an attempt to commit such an offense (*see* G.L. c. 274, § 6) renders the defendant subject to the requirements of the sex offender registry law. *See* G.L. c. 6, §§ 178C–178Q.

SECTION 3

Drugging persons for sexual intercourse

Whoever applies, administers to or causes to be taken by a person any drug, matter or thing with intent to stupefy or overpower such person so as to thereby enable any person to have sexual intercourse or unnatural sexual intercourse with such person shall be punished by imprisonment in the state prison for life or for any term or years not less than ten years.

NOTE 1   Related Statute. G.L. c. 265, § 22—Rape.

NOTE 2   DNA Database. A conviction of an offense under this section or of an attempt or conspiracy to commit such an offense results in the defendant being required to submit a DNA sample to the state's DNA database. *See* G.L. c. 22E, § 3.

NOTE 3   Sex Offender Registry. A conviction or adjudication of delinquency of an offense under this section or of an attempt to commit such an offense (*see* G.L. c. 274, § 6) renders the defendant subject to the requirements of the sex offender registry law. *See* G.L. c. 6, §§ 178C–178Q.

NOTE 4   Sexually Dangerous Person Commitment. A conviction or adjudication of delinquency of an offense under this section or of an attempt to commit such an offense (*see* G.L. c. 274, § 6) can serve as a predicate "sexual offense" for civil commitment as a "sexually dangerous person". *See* G.L. c. 123A, §§ 1–15.

SECTION 4

Inducing person under 18 to have sexual intercourse

Whoever induces any person under 18 years of age of chaste life to have unlawful sexual intercourse shall be punished by imprisonment in the state prison for not more than three years or in a jail or house of correction for not more than two and one-half years or by a fine of not more than $1,000 or by both such fine and imprisonment.

NOTE 1   Related Statutes.
         G.L. c. 265, § 22A—Rape of a child under 16.
         G.L. c. 265, § 23—Statutory rape.

NOTE 2   Corroborating evidence necessary—G.L. c. 272, § 11.

NOTE 3   Statute of limitations—one year—G.L. c. 272, § 11.

SECTION 4A

Inducing minor into prostitution; penalties

Whoever induces a minor to become a prostitute, or who knowingly aids and assists in such inducement, shall be punished by imprisonment in the state prison for not more than five, nor less than three years, and by a fine of five thousand dollars. The sentence of imprisonment imposed under this section shall not be reduced to less than three years, nor suspended, nor shall any person convicted under this section be eligible for probation, parole or furlough or receive any deduction

2

from this sentence for good conduct or otherwise until he shall have served three years of such sentence. Prosecutions commenced under this section shall not be continued without a finding nor placed on file.

NOTE 1   "We think that the language of the statute is plain and unambiguous and that it clearly expresses the Legislature's intent to penalize a person for inducing a minor, who is not then so engaged, to engage in the commercial enterprise of prostitution by offering for hire his or her body for indiscriminate sexual activity. We are hard pressed to locate in the wording of § 4A any Legislative intent to make it a crime to induce a minor to engage in a single act of sex for a fee. The Legislature rationally could have decided that inducing a minor who is not currently a prostitute to become one warrants separate punishment." *Commonwealth v. Matos*, 78 Mass. App. Ct. 578, 586–87 (2011).

NOTE 2   DNA Database. A conviction of an offense under this section or of an attempt or conspiracy to commit such an offense results in the defendant being required to submit a DNA sample to the state's DNA database. *See* G.L. c. 22E, § 3.

NOTE 3   Sex Offender Registry. A conviction or adjudication of delinquency of an offense under this section or of an attempt to commit such an offense (*see* G.L. c. 274, § 6) renders the defendant subject to the requirements of the sex offender registry law. *See* G.L. c. 6, §§ 178C–178Q.

SECTION 4B
Living off or sharing earnings of minor prostitute; penalties

Whoever lives or derives support or maintenance, in whole or in part, from the earnings or proceeds of prostitution committed by a minor, knowing the same to be earnings or proceeds of prostitution, or shares in such earnings, proceeds or monies, shall be punished by imprisonment in the state prison for not less than five years and by a fine five thousand dollars. The sentence imposed under this section shall not be reduced to less than five years, nor suspended, nor shall any person convicted under this section be eligible for probation, parole or furlough or receive any deduction from his sentence for good conduct or otherwise until he shall have served five years of such sentence. Prosecutions commenced under this section shall not be continued without a finding nor placed on file.

NOTE 1   DNA Database. A conviction of an offense under this section or of an attempt or conspiracy to commit such an offense results in the defendant being required to submit a DNA sample to the state's DNA database. *See* G.L. c. 22E, § 3.

NOTE 2   Sex Offender Registry. A conviction or adjudication of delinquency of an offense under this section or of an attempt to commit such an offense (*see* G.L. c. 274, § 6) renders the defendant subject to the requirements of the sex offender registry law. *See* G.L. c. 6, §§ 178C–178Q.

SECTION 5
Repealed

SECTION 6
One controlling a place, inducing or suffering a person to resort there for sexual intercourse

Whoever, being the owner of a place or having or assisting in the management or control thereof induces or knowingly suffers a person to resort to or be in or upon such place, for the purpose of unlawfully having sexual intercourse for money or other financial gain, shall be punished by imprisonment in the state prison for a period of five years and a five thousand dollar fine.

The sentence of imprisonment imposed under this section shall not be reduced to less than two years, nor suspended, nor shall any person convicted under this section be eligible for probation, parole, or furlough or receive any deduction from his sentence for good conduct or otherwise until he shall have served two years of such sentence. Prosecutions commenced under this section shall not be continued without a finding nor placed on file.

NOTE 1   Corroborating evidence necessary—G.L. c. 272, § 11.

NOTE 2   Statute of limitations—one year—G.L. c. 272, § 11.

NOTE 3   Related Statutes.
G.L. c. 272, § 24—Keeping house of ill fame.
Common Nuisances.
G.L. c. 139, § 4—Buildings used for prostitution, assignation or lewdness; nuisance.
Every building, part of a building, tenement or place used for prostitution, assignation or lewdness, and every place within or upon which acts of prostitution, assignation or lewdness are held or occur, shall be deemed a nuisance.
G.L. c. 139, § 5—Penalty.
Whoever keeps or maintains such a nuisance shall be punished by a fine of not less than one hundred nor more than one thousand dollars and by imprisonment for not less than three months nor more than three years.
G.L. c. 139, § 6—Enjoining nuisance.
Whenever there is reason to believe that such a nuisance is kept or maintained or exists in any town, either the district attorney for the district, or the attorney general, in the name of the commonwealth, or a citizen in his own name, may bring a civil action perpetually to enjoin the person conducting or maintaining the same, and the owner, lessee or agent of the building or place in or upon which such nuisance exists and their assignees from directly or indirectly maintaining or permitting such nuisance.
The procedures for implementing these sections are found in Sections 7–13 of G.L. c. 139, which are not contained in this book.

NOTE 4   Elements. "Conviction of owning, or assisting in the management or control of, a place for unlawful sexual intercourse requires the Commonwealth to show: (1) that the defendant owned, managed, or assisted in the management or control of certain premises; (2) that a person was present on those premises for the purpose of unlawfully having sexual intercourse; (3) that the defendant induced or knowingly suffered the person's presence on the premises for that purpose; and (4) that the purpose of sexual intercourse was for financial gain. . . .
"The statute does not require the Commonwealth to show that sexual intercourse took place on the premises. The Commonwealth need only show that the 'purpose' of the person's presence on the premises was unlawfully to have sexual intercourse." *Commonwealth v. Mullane*, 445 Mass. 702, 714–15 (2006).

NOTE 5   Definition of Sexual Intercourse. "The term 'sexual intercourse,' as used in G.L. c. 272, § 6, encompasses only penile-vaginal penetration." *Mullane*, 445 Mass. at 717.

SECTION 7
Support or sharing, earnings of prostitute

Whoever, knowing a person to be a prostitute, shall live or derive support or maintenance, in whole or in part, from the earnings or proceeds of his prostitution, from moneys loaned, advanced to or charged against him by any keeper or manager or inmate of a house or other place where prostitution is practiced or allowed, or shall share in such earnings, proceeds or moneys, shall be punished by imprisonment in the state prison for a period of five years and by a fine of five thousand dollars.

The sentence of imprisonment imposed under this section shall not be reduced to less than two years, nor suspended, nor shall any person convicted under this section be eligible for probation, parole, or furlough or receive any deduction from his sentence for good conduct or otherwise until he shall have served two years of such sentence. Prosecutions commenced under this section shall not be continued without a finding nor placed on file.

NOTE   District courts have jurisdiction over felonies punishable by imprisonment for not more than five years. G.L. c. 218, § 26.

SECTION 8
Soliciting for prostitute
(Stricken & replaced by 2011 Mass. Acts c. 178, § 24, effective Nov. 21, 2011.)

Whoever solicits or receives compensation for soliciting for a prostitute shall be punished by imprisonment in a house of correction for not more than 2 and one-half years, or by a fine of not less than $1,000 and not more than $5,000 or by both such imprisonment and fine.

SECTION 9
Oath and warrant to enter place for prostitution; detention of person in control and prostitute; recognizance to appear as witness

If a person makes oath before a district court that he has probable cause to suspect that a house, building, room or place is kept or resorted to for prostitution and that a certain person owning or having or assisting in the management or control of such house, building, room or place knowingly suffers another person to be in or upon such place for the purpose of unlawfully having sexual intercourse, said court shall, if satisfied that there is probable cause thereof, issue a warrant commanding the sheriff or his deputy, or any constable or police officer, to enter such house, building, room or place and search for such owner or person in control, and take into custody both the owner or person in control and such other person as may be in or upon such place for such purpose. Said owner or person in control shall be detained for not more than twenty-four hours until complaint may be made against him, and any such other person for a reasonable time until brought before said court to be recognized with or without sureties at the discretion of said court to appear as witnesses before the next or any succeeding sitting of said court. This section shall be in addition to and not in derogation of the common law.

SECTION 10
Arrest without warrant

Nothing in the preceding section shall prevent the arrest and detention without a warrant of any person who, the officer serving said process may have reasonable cause to believe, is violating any provision of this chapter, or is keeping a house, room or place resorted to for prostitution or lewdness, and said officer may upon such search arrest without a warrant any such person, and detain him until complaint may be made against him.

SECTION 11
Corroboration of one witness; limitations

A person shall not be convicted under sections 2, 4 and 6, upon the evidence of one witness only, unless his testimony is corroborated in a material particular, and prosecution for a violation of any of said sections shall not be commenced more than one year after the commission of the crime.

NOTE   "While we have not heretofore attempted to define 'material particular' as used in G.L. c. 272, sec. 11, the cases suggest that the term applies to some specific testimonial fact, which, in the context of the case, is probative on an element of the crime." *Commonwealth v. Helfant*, 398 Mass. 214, 219 (1986).

"In essence, the defendant would have us read the requirement of corroboration of a material particular as corroboration of a 'disputed issue of material fact' as that phrase is used and understood in the consideration of summary judgment motions in civil practice. However, G.L. c. 272, sec. 11, does not require that the material particular be disputed, and we decline to read such a requirement into the plain words of the statute." *Helfant*, 398 Mass. at 220 (citations omitted).

SECTION 12
Procuring person to practice, or enter a place for, prostitution; employment office procuring person

Whoever knowingly procures, entices, sends, or aids or abets in procuring, enticing or sending, a person to practice prostitution, or to enter as an inmate or a servant a house of ill fame or other place resorted to for prostitution, whether within or without the commonwealth, shall be punished by a fine of not less than one hundred nor more than five hundred dollars or by imprisonment for not less than three months nor more than two years. Whoever as a proprietor or keeper of an employment agency, either personally or through an agent or employee, procures or sends a person to enter as aforesaid a house of ill fame or other place resorted to for prostitution, the character of which on reasonable inquiry could have been ascertained by him, shall be punished by a fine of not less than fifty nor more than two hundred dollars.

SECTION 13
Detaining, or drugging to detain, person in place for prostitution

Whoever, for any length of time, unlawfully detains or attempts to detain, or aids or abets in unlawfully detaining or attempting to detain, or provides or administers or aids or abets in providing or administering any drug or liquor for the purpose of detaining a person in a house of ill fame or other place where prostitution is practiced or allowed, shall be punished by imprisonment in the state prison for not more than five years or in the house of correction for not less than one nor more than two and one half years or by a fine of not less than one hundred nor more than five hundred dollars.

SECTION 14
Adultery

A married person who has sexual intercourse with a person not his spouse or an unmarried person who has sexual intercourse with a married person shall be guilty of adultery and shall be punished by imprisonment in the state prison for not more than three years or in jail for not more than two years or by a fine of not more than five hundred dollars.

NOTE 1   Definition—G.L. c. 277, § 39.

NOTE 2   Form of indictment—G.L. c. 277, § 79 (Adultery).

SECTION 15
Polygamy

Whoever, having a former husband or wife living, marries another person or continues to cohabit with a second husband or wife in the commonwealth shall be guilty of polygamy, and be punished by imprisonment in the state prison for not more than five years or in jail for not more than two and

2

one half years or by a fine of not more than five hundred dollars; but this section shall not apply to a person whose husband or wife has continually remained beyond sea, or has voluntarily withdrawn from the other and remained absent, for seven consecutive years, the party marrying again not knowing the other to be living within that time, nor to a person who has been legally divorced from the bonds of matrimony.

NOTE   Form of indictment—G.L. c. 277, § 79 (Polygamy).

SECTION 16
Open and gross lewdness and lascivious behavior

A man or woman married or unmarried, who is guilty of open and gross lewdness and lascivious behavior, shall be punished by imprisonment in the state prison for not more than three years or in a jail for not more than two years or by a fine of not more than three hundred dollars.

NOTE 1   **Elements.** "The Commonwealth must prove beyond a reasonable doubt: (1) the defendant exposed his or her, genitals, buttocks, or female breasts to one or more persons; (2) the defendant did so intentionally; (3) the defendant did so "openly," that is, either he or she intended public exposure, or he or she recklessly disregarded a substantial risk of public exposure, to others who might be offended by such conduct; (4) the defendant's act was done in such a way as to produce alarm or shock; and (5) one or more persons were in fact alarmed or shocked by the defendant's exposing himself or herself." *Commonwealth v. Quinn,* 439 Mass. 492, 501 (2003). *See also Commonwealth v. Poillucci,* 46 Mass. App. Ct. 300, 302 (1999).

NOTE 2   **Statute constitutional.** "The defendant . . . was arrested and charged with open and gross lewdness in violation of G.L. c. 272, § 16, for dancing nude at an 'anti-Christmas' protest in the kiosk area of Harvard Square, Cambridge. A judge in the District Court allowed the defendant's motion to dismiss the complaint against her, concluding that G.L. c. 272, § 16, is facially unconstitutional because it is '[a] blanket prohibition against public nudity,' and thus proscribes expressive conduct protected by the First Amendment to the United States Constitution and art. 16 of the Massachusetts Declaration of Rights. . . . We conclude that the judge erred in ruling that the statute is facially unconstitutional. Our decisional law has narrowed the application of G.L. c. 272, § 16, so that it does not impermissibly prohibit protected expressive conduct. We have held that the statute cannot be constitutionally applied to public displays of lewdness and nudity unless they are imposed upon an unsuspecting or unwilling audience, and that conviction under the statute requires the display of nudity to be intentional, done in a manner to produce alarm or shock, and actually producing alarm or shock. These restrictions both limit the reach of the statute to conduct that the State is permitted to prohibit and minimize infringement of expressive conduct. Accordingly, we reverse the dismissal of the complaint. . . .

"We . . . determine that the statute is a legitimate content neutral restriction on expressive activity. The State has power to 'enact rules to regulate conduct, to the extent that such laws are "necessary to secure the health, safety, good order, comfort, or general welfare of the community."' Section 16 is within the Commonwealth's power to regulate conduct; it furthers the important State interest in preventing fright or intimidation from intentional lewd and lascivious conduct imposed on unsuspecting or unwilling persons, particularly children. This governmental interest is unrelated to the suppression of free expression. Neither the language of the statute nor its legislative history suggests that the statute targets any expressive message contained in any display of nudity. Furthermore, judicial construction . . . has limited the statute's application to be no greater than is essential to the furtherance of the important government interest in lewd or lascivious conduct." *Commonwealth v. Ora,* 451 Mass. 125, 125–26, 129–30 (2008) (citations and footnotes omitted).

NOTE 3a   **Exposure of Genitalia Not an Essential Element.** "Exposure or attempted exposure of genitalia is not an essential element of an open and gross lewdness offense prosecuted under G.L. c. 272, § 16." *Commonwealth v. Quinn,* 439 Mass. 492, 502 (2003).

NOTE 3b   **Exposure of Buttocks.** "[A] defendant may be convicted under G.L. c. 272, § 16, for exposing his buttocks provided, of course, that the other elements of that crime are proved beyond a reasonable doubt." *Commonwealth v. Quinn,* 439 Mass. 492, 495 (2003) ("[T]he exposure of buttocks may in some circumstances alarm or shock in violation of G.L. c. 272, § 16.").

"The sudden exposure of buttocks by dropping one's pants in front of children in an area (school) where such conduct would be wholly unexpected may alarm or shock, as surely as revealing one's penis." *Commonwealth v. Quinn,* 439 Mass. at 497–98.

"While the exposure of buttocks can be prosecuted under G.L. c. 272, § 16, we agree with the defendant that he was not provided with fair notice that deliberately exposing his thong-clad buttocks may be illegal. The statute is therefore unconstitutionally vague as applied to him." *Commonwealth v. Quinn,* 439 Mass. at, 499.

NOTE 4   **Open.** "To be 'open,' under G.L. c. 272, § 16, the conduct need not occur in a public place, but must occur in the presence of another person who can be alarmed or shocked." *Commonwealth v. Quinn,* 439 Mass. 492, 496 n.9 (2003) (citation omitted).

NOTE 5a   "The kind of activity obviously within the purview of Section 16 is the imposition of lewdness or nudity on an unsuspecting or unwilling person." *P.B.I.C., Inc. v. Byrne,* 313 F. Supp. 757, 764 (D. Mass. 1970), *stay denied,* 398 U.S. 916 (1970), *judgment vacated to consider mootness,* 401 U.S. 987 (1971), *judgment vacated for further consideration,* 413 U.S. 905 (1973) (enjoining application of Section 16 to performers of the musical "Hair").

NOTE 5b   Accordingly Section 16 *not* applicable to live theatrical production. *P.B.I.C., Inc. v. Byrne,* 313 F. Supp. at 764 n.11.

NOTE 5c   Section 16 unconstitutional as applied to nude "go-go" dancers in bars. *City of Revere v. Aucella,* 369 Mass. 138 (1975), *appeal dismissed,* 429 U.S. 877 (1976).

NOTE 6   **Indecent Exposure.** "Although the two statutes, 'open and gross lewdness,' G.L. c. 272, § 16, and 'indecent exposure,' G.L. c. 272, § 53, are similar, they have different elements, reflecting (in part) their different origins. . . .

"The two statutes prohibit different conduct. Any intentional exposure of genitalia may be prosecuted as a misdemeanor under G.L. c. 272,§ 53. Conviction of 'open and gross lewdness,' G.L. c. 272, § 16, on the other hand, requires the Commonwealth to prove, among other elements, intention, manner (done in such a way as to produce alarm or shock), and impact (does in fact alarm or shock). The requirement that the defendant must engage in conduct such as actually to alarm or shock another has remained unchanged since 1880. Whichever private parts of one's body is intentionally exposed, the fact finder must be persuaded beyond a reasonable doubt that the defendant acted in such a way as to alarm or shock. In contrast, to sustain a conviction of indecent exposure, G.L. c. 272, § 53, the Commonwealth is not required to prove the elements of alarm or shock." *Commonwealth v. Quinn,* 439 Mass. 492, 495–96 (2003) (citations and quotation marks omitted).

NOTE 7   **Unit of Prosecution.** "We recognize that G. L. c. 272, § 16, has been construed by our case law to require, among other things, that one or more persons in fact be shocked or alarmed by the defendant's conduct. This impact requirement has remained unchanged since 1880. However, it has no apparent bearing on the unit of prosecution. . . . Moreover, we observe that, although it is not directly reflective of the Legislature's intent, § 16 routinely is applied in a manner consistent with the view that the unit of prosecution is conduct-based and not victim-based. Furthermore, as the defendant points out, a contrary application of the statute could have absurd results, e.g., if a person were to run onto the field at Fenway Park during a game and intentionally expose himself in a way that produced shock or alarm, he conceivably could be charged with as many as 37,000 counts of open and gross lewdness. We decline to view the statute as permitting such an unreasonable result." *Commonwealth v. Botev*, 79 Mass. App. Ct. 281, 287–89 (2011) (footnotes and citations omitted).

NOTE 8   Exposure to a Child. Model Jury Instruction 5.42 includes a supplementary instruction if the defendant exposed himself or herself to a child of "tender years." The Court of Appeals held that the instruction is confusing and should not be given. *Commonwealth v. Kessler*, 442 Mass. 770, 777 (2004).

NOTE 9   Sex Offender Registry. A second or subsequent conviction or adjudication of delinquency of an offense under this section or of an attempt to commit such an offense (*see* G.L. c. 274, § 6) renders the defendant subject to the requirements of the sex offender registry law. *See* G.L. c. 6, §§ 178C–178Q.

NOTE 10   DNA Database. A conviction of an offense under this section or of an attempt or conspiracy to commit such an offense results in the defendant being required to submit a DNA sample to the state's DNA database. *See* G.L. c. 22E, § 3.

NOTE 11   Form of indictment—G.L. c. 277, § 79 (Lewd and lascivious cohabitation; exposure of person).

NOTE 12   Related Statutes.

G.L. c. 272, § 35—Unnatural and lascivious acts (see Notes there).

G.L. c. 272, § 53—Common night walkers, disorderly persons, etc. (see Notes there).

SECTION 17
Incestuous marriage or intercourse

Persons within degrees of consanguinity within which marriages are prohibited or declared by law to be incestuous and void, who intermarry or have sexual intercourse with each other, or who engage in sexual activities with each other, including but not limited to, oral or anal intercourse, fellatio, cunnilingus, or other penetration of a part of a person's body, or insertion of an object into the genital or anal opening of another person's body, or the manual manipulation of the genitalia of another person's body, shall be punished by imprisonment in the state prison for not more than 20 years or in the house of correction for not more than 2½ years.

NOTE 1   Sexual Intercourse. The term "sexual intercourse" as used in the incest statute is limited to penile-vaginal penetration, with or without emission. *Commonwealth v. Smith*, 431 Mass. 417 (2000).

NOTE 2   Form of indictment—G.L. c. 277, § 79 (Incest).

NOTE 3   DNA Database. A conviction of an offense under this section or of an attempt or conspiracy to commit such an offense results in the defendant being required to submit a DNA sample to the state's DNA database. *See* G.L. c. 22E, § 3.

NOTE 4   Sex Offender Registry. A conviction or adjudication of delinquency of an offense under this section or of an attempt to commit such an offense (*see* G.L. c. 274, § 6) renders the defendant subject to the requirements of the sex offender registry law. *See* G.L. c. 6, §§ 178C–178Q.

SECTION 18
Fornication

Whoever commits fornication shall be punished by imprisonment for not more than three months or by a fine of not more than thirty dollars.

NOTE 1   Definition—G.L. c. 277, § 39.

NOTE 2   Form of indictment—G.L. c. 277, § 79 (Fornication).

SECTION 19
Procuring miscarriage

Whoever, with intent to procure the miscarriage of a woman, unlawfully administers to her, or advises or prescribes for her, or causes any poison, drug, medicine or other noxious thing to be taken by her or, with the like intent, unlawfully uses any instrument or other means whatever, or, with like intent, aids or assists therein, shall, if she dies in consequence thereof, be punished by imprisonment in the state prison for not less than five nor more than twenty years; and, if she does not die in consequence thereof, by imprisonment in the state prison for not more than seven years and by a fine of not more than two thousand dollars.

NOTE   Form of indictment—G.L. c. 277, § 79 (Abortion).

SECTION 20
Advertising relative to miscarriage or prevention of pregnancy

Except as provided in section twenty-one A, whoever knowingly advertises, prints, publishes, distributes or circulates, or knowingly causes to be advertised, printed, published, distributed or circulated, any pamphlet, printed paper, book, newspaper, notice, advertisement or reference containing words or language giving or conveying any notice, hint or reference to any person, or to the name of any person, real or fictitious, from whom, or to any place, house, shop or office where any poison, drug, mixture, preparation, medicine or noxious thing, or any instrument or means whatever, or any advice, direction, information or knowledge may be obtained for the purpose of causing or procuring the miscarriage of a woman pregnant with child or of preventing, or which is represented as intended to prevent, pregnancy shall be punished by imprisonment in the state prison for not more than three years or in jail for not more than two and one half years or by a fine of not more than one thousand dollars.

NOTE   A similar state statute was found to be an unconstitutional infringement of one's First Amendment rights by the U.S. Supreme Court in *Bigelow v. Virginia*, 421 U.S. 809 (1975).

SECTION 21
Instrument or other articles for self-abuse, prevention of conception or abortion, in general

Except as provided in section twenty-one A, whoever sells, lends, gives away, exhibits or offers to sell, lend or give away an instrument or other article intended to be used for self-abuse, or any drug, medicine, instrument or article whatever for the prevention of conception or for causing unlawful abortion, or advertises the same, or writes, prints, or causes to be written or printed a card, circular, book, pamphlet, advertisement or notice of any kind stating when, where, how, of whom or by what means such article can be purchased or obtained, or manufactures or makes any such article shall be punished by imprisonment in the state prison for not more than five years or in jail or the house of correction for not more than two and one half years or by a fine of not less than one hundred nor more than one thousand dollars.

NOTE   The Supreme Court held that this statute (along with Section 21A) violated the equal protection clause of the Constitution. *Eisenstadt v. Baird*, 405 U.S. 438 (1972).

2

SECTION 21A
Furnishing drugs, articles or information for prevention of pregnancy or conception

A registered physician may administer to or prescribe for any married person drugs or articles intended for the prevention of pregnancy or conception. A registered pharmacist actually engaged in the business of pharmacy may furnish such drugs or articles to any married person presenting a prescription from a registered physician.

A public health agency, a registered nurse, or a maternity health clinic operated by or in an accredited hospital may furnish information to any married person as to where professional advice regarding such drugs or articles may be lawfully obtained.

This section shall not be construed as affecting the provisions of sections twenty and twenty-one relative to prohibition of advertising of drugs or articles intended for the prevention of pregnancy or conception; nor shall this section be construed so as to permit the sale or dispensing of such drugs or articles by means of any vending machine or similar device.

NOTE   See Note following Section 21 of this chapter.

SECTION 21B
Privately controlled hospital or health facility not required to perform abortion or sterilization procedures, or to furnish contraceptive devices or information or family planning services

No privately controlled hospital or other health facility shall be required to admit any patient for the purpose of performing an abortion, performing any sterilization procedure, or receiving contraceptive devices or information.

No privately controlled hospital or other privately controlled health facility shall be required to permit any patient to have an abortion, or any sterilization procedure performed in said hospital or other health facility, or to furnish contraceptive devices or information to such patient, nor shall such a hospital or other health facility be required to furnish any family planning services within or through said hospital or any other health facility or to make referrals to any other hospital or health facility for such services when said services or referrals are contrary to the religious or moral principles of said hospital or said health facilities as expressed in its charter, by-laws or code of ethics, or vote of its governing body.

Any such hospital or other health facility exercising the rights granted in this section shall not on account of the exercise thereof, be disciplined or discriminated against in any manner or suffer any adverse determination by any person, firm, corporation, or other entity, including but in no way limited to any political subdivision, board, commission, department, authority, or agency of the commonwealth.

SECTION 22
Concealment of death of child born out of wedlock

A parent who conceals the death of the issue of such parent, which if born alive would be a child born out of wedlock, so that it cannot be ascertained whether it was born alive or, if born alive, whether it was murdered, shall be punished by a fine of not more than one hundred dollars or by imprisonment for not more than one year.

SECTION 23
Joinder of charges of murder and offense under Sec. 22

A parent indicted for murder of the infant child born out of wedlock of such parent may also be charged in the same indictment with the crime described in the preceding section, and if acquitted of murder, such parent may be convicted of the concealment.

SECTION 24
Keeping house of ill fame

Whoever keeps a house of ill fame which is resorted to for prostitution or lewdness shall be punished by imprisonment for not more than two years.

NOTE 1   Form of indictment—G.L. c. 277, § 79 (House of ill fame).

NOTE 2   **Related Statute.** G.L. c. 272, § 6—Maintaining a house for prostitution (see common nuisances at Note 3).

NOTE 3   Where it appeared that the house was one of ill fame, and that the defendant lived and had the power to exercise control there, he may be found guilty of the charge notwithstanding the fact that the house was owned by his wife, who also lived there and who carried on the business and received all of the profits. *Commonwealth v. Wood*, 97 Mass. 225, 228–29 (1867).

NOTE 4   **Elements.** "Conviction for keeping a house of ill fame requires the Commonwealth to show (1) that the defendant owned, managed, or maintained the premises; and (2) that the premises were resorted to for sexual activity for hire." *Commonwealth v. Mullane*, 445 Mass. 702, 715–16 (2006).

SECTION 25
Enclosures in restaurants or taverns closed by devices obstructing view of patrons; barricaded entrances impeding access by officers

Any person owning, managing or controlling a restaurant, tavern or other place in any town, where food or drink is sold to the public to be consumed upon the premises or required to be licensed under chapter one hundred and thirty-eight, and any employee of such person, who provides, maintains, uses or permits the use of a booth, stall or enclosure of any description whatever which is so closed by curtains, screens or other devices that the persons within cannot at any time plainly be seen by other persons in such restaurant, tavern or other place, or in any division thereof, unless the enclosure is approved by the licensing authorities, and any person conducting such an establishment who maintains barred or barricaded entrances or exits thereto or other devices or appliances designed to impede access thereto by police officers, official inspectors and other officers entitled to enter the same, shall be punished by a fine of not less than fifty nor more than five hundred dollars or by imprisonment for not more than six months, or both.

SECTION 26
Resorting to restaurant or taverns for immoral purposes; engaging in such acts therein

Whoever, for the purpose of immoral solicitation or immoral bargaining, shall resort to any cafe, restaurant, tavern, as defined in section one of chapter one hundred and thirty-eight, or other place where food or drink is sold or served to be consumed upon the premises, and whoever shall resort to any such place for the purpose of, in any manner, inducing another person to engage in immoral conduct, and whoever, being in or about any such place, shall engage in any such acts, and any person owning, managing or controlling such place and any employee of such person who induces or knowingly suffers any person to resort to, or be in such place for the purpose of immoral solicitation or immoral bargaining, shall be punished by a fine of not less than twenty-five nor more than five hundred dollars or by imprisonment for not more than one year, or both.

SECTION 27
Copy of record of convictions under Secs. 25 and 26 sent to licensing officers

The clerk of the court in which any person is convicted of a violation of either of the two preceding sections shall forthwith send a copy of the record of such conviction to the officer or board issuing any license or licenses under which the place where the offense was committed is conducted.

SECTION 28
Matter harmful to minors, dissemination; possession; defenses
(Amended by 2011 Mass. Acts c. 9, § 19, effective Apr. 11, 2011.)

Whoever purposefully disseminates to a person he knows or believes to be a minor any matter harmful to minors, as defined in section 31, knowing it to be harmful to minors, or has in his possession any such matter with the intent to disseminate the same to a person he knows or believes to be a minor, shall be punished by imprisonment in the state prison for not more than 5 years or in a jail or house of correction for not more than 2½ years, or by a fine of not less than $1000 nor more than $10,000 for the first offense, not less than $5000 nor more than $20,000 for the second offense, or not less than $10,000 nor more than $30,000 for a third or subsequent offenses, or by both such fine and imprisonment. A person who disseminates an electronic communication or possesses an electronic communication with the intent to disseminate it shall not be found to have violated this section unless he specifically intends to direct the communication to a person he knows or believes to be a minor. A prosecution commenced under this section shall not be continued without a finding or placed on file. It shall be a defense in a prosecution under this section that the defendant was in a parental or guardianship relationship with the minor. It shall also be a defense in a prosecution under this section if the evidence proves that the defendant was a bona fide school, museum or library, or was acting in the course of his employment as an employee of such organization or of a retail outlet affiliated with and serving the educational purpose of such organization.

NOTE 1   **Definitions of Terms.** G.L. c. 272, § 31.

NOTE 2   **Sex Offender Registry**. A conviction or adjudication of delinquency of an offense under this section or of an attempt to commit such an offense (*see* G.L. c. 274, § 6) renders the defendant subject to the requirements of the sex offender registry law. *See* G.L. c. 6, §§ 178C–178Q.

SECTIONS 28A–B
Repealed

SECTION 28C
Information or petition against obscene books; order of notice to show cause; notice of order; interlocutory adjudication; defense

Whenever there is reasonable cause to believe that a book which is being disseminated, or is in the possession of any person who intends to disseminate the same, is obscene, the attorney general, or any district attorney within his district, shall bring an information or petition in equity in the superior court directed against said book by name. Upon the filing of such information or petition in equity, a justice of the superior court shall, if, upon a summary examination of the book, he is of opinion that there is reasonable cause to believe that such book is obscene, issue an order of notice, returnable in or within thirty days, directed against such book by name and addressed to all persons interested in the dissemination thereof, to show cause why said book should not be judicially determined to be obscene. Notice of such order shall be given by publication once each week for two successive weeks in a daily newspaper published in the city of Boston and, if such information or petition be filed in any county other than Suffolk county, then by publication also in a daily newspaper published in such other county. A copy of such order of notice shall be sent by registered mail to the publisher of said book, to the person holding the copyrights, and to the author, in case the names of any such persons appear upon said book, fourteen days at least before the return day of such order of notice. After the issuance of an order of notice under the provisions of this section, the court shall, on motion of the attorney general or district attorney, make an interlocutory finding and adjudication that said book is obscene, which finding and adjudication shall be of the same force and effect as the final finding and adjudication provided in section twenty-eight E or section twenty-eight F, but only until such final finding and adjudication is made or until further order of the court. It shall be an affirmative defense under this section if the evidence proves that the defendant was a bona fide school, museum or library, or as acting in the course of his employment as an employee of such organization or of a retail outlet affiliated with and serving the educational purpose of such organization.

NOTE   Definitions of terms for this section through Section 28I, see G.L. c. 272, § 31.

SECTION 28D
Answer to notice; right to jury trial

Any person interested in the dissemination of said book may appear and file an answer on or before the return day named in said notice or within such further time as the court may allow, and may claim a right to trial by jury on the issue whether said book is obscene.

SECTION 28E
Order of default; adjudication

If no person appears and answers within the time allowed, the court may at once upon motion of the petitioner, or of its own motion, no reason to the contrary appearing, order a general default and if the court finds that the book is obscene, may make an adjudication against the book that the same is obscene.

2

SECTION 28F
Hearing; evidence; adjudication

If an appearance is entered and answer filed, the case shall be set down for speedy hearing, but a default and order shall first be entered against all persons who have not appeared and answered, in the manner provided in section twenty-eight E. Such hearing shall be conducted in accordance with the usual course of proceedings in equity including all rights of exception and appeal. At such hearing the court may receive the testimony of experts and may receive evidence as to the literary, artistic, political or scientific character of said book and as to the manner and form of its dissemination. Upon such hearing, the court may make an adjudication in the manner provided in said section twenty-eight E.

SECTION 28G
Objection that mere judgment sought and no relief claimed on issue of knowledge

An information or petition in equity under the provisions of section twenty-eight C shall not be open to objection on the ground that a mere judgment, order or decree is sought thereby and that no relief is or could be claimed thereunder on the issue of the defendant's knowledge as to the obscenity.

SECTION 28H
Proceeding under Sec. 28C as evidence in trial under Sec. 29; presumptions as to knowledge

In any trial under section twenty-nine on an indictment found or a complaint made for any offense committed after the filing of a proceeding under section twenty-eight C, the fact of such filing and the action of the court or jury thereon, if any, shall be admissible in evidence. If prior to the said offense a final decree had been entered against the book, the defendant, if the book be obscene, shall be conclusively presumed to have known said book to be obscene, or if said decree had been in favor of the book he shall be conclusively presumed not to have known said book to be obscene, or if no final decree had been entered but a proceeding had been filed prior to said offense, the defendant shall be conclusively presumed to have had knowledge of the contents of said book.

SECTION 28I
Certain procedures as condition precedent to institution of proceedings for dissemination of obscene books

The procedures set forth in sections twenty-eight C, twenty-eight D, twenty-eight E, twenty-eight G and twenty-eight H shall be a condition precedent to the institution of any proceedings pursuant to section twenty-nine or thirty for dissemination of obscene books.

SECTION 29
Dissemination or possession of obscene matter; punishment; defense

Whoever disseminates any matter which is obscene, knowing it to be obscene, or whoever has in his possession any matter which is obscene, knowing it to be obscene, with the intent to disseminate the same, shall be punished by imprisonment in the state prison for not more than five years or in a jail or house of correction for not more than two and one-half years or by a fine of not less than one thousand nor more than ten thousand dollars for the trust offense, not less than five thousand nor more than twenty thousand dollars for the second offense, or not less than ten thousand nor more than

thirty thousand dollars for the third and subsequent offenses, or by both such fine and imprisonment. A prosecution commenced under this section shall not be continued without finding nor placed on file. It shall be a defense under this section if the evidence proves that the defendant was a bona fide school, museum or library, or was acting in the course of his employment as an employee of such organization or of a retail outlet affiliated with and serving the educational purpose of such organization.

NOTE 1   Definitions of terms for this section and Section 29A see G.L. c. 272, § 31.

NOTE 2   **DNA Database.** A conviction of an offense under this section or of an attempt or conspiracy to commit such an offense results in the defendant being required to submit a DNA sample to the state's DNA database. *See* G.L. c. 22E, § 3.

SECTION 29A
Posing or exhibiting child in state of nudity or sexual conduct; punishment

(a) Whoever, either with knowledge that a person is a child under eighteen years of age or while in possession of such facts that he should have reason to know that such person is a child under eighteen years of age, and with lascivious intent, hires, coerces, solicits or entices, employs, procures, uses, causes, encourages, or knowingly permits such child to pose or be exhibited in a state of nudity, for the purpose of representation or reproduction in any visual material, shall be punished by imprisonment in the state prison for a term of not less than ten nor more than twenty years, or by a fine of not less than ten thousand nor more than fifty thousand dollars, or by both such fine and imprisonment.

(b) Whoever, either with knowledge that a person is a child under eighteen years of age or while in possession of such facts that he should have reason to know that such person is a child under eighteen years of age, hires, coerces, solicits or entices, employs, procures, uses, causes, encourages, or knowingly permits such child to participate or engage in any act that depicts, describes, or represents sexual conduct for the purpose of representation or reproduction in any visual material, or to engage in any live performance involving sexual conduct, shall be punished by imprisonment in the state prison for a term of not less than ten nor more than twenty years, or by a fine of not less than ten thousand nor more than fifty thousand dollars, or by both such fine and imprisonment.

(c) In a prosecution under this section, a minor shall be deemed incapable of consenting to any conduct of the defendant for which said defendant is being prosecuted.

(d) For the purposes of this section, the determination whether the person in any visual material prohibited hereunder is under eighteen years of age may be made by the personal testimony of such person, by the testimony of a person who produced, processed, published, printed or manufactured such visual material that the child therein was known to him to be under eighteen years of age, or by expert medical testimony as to the age of the person based upon the person's physical appearance, by inspection of the visual material, or by any other method authorized by any general or special law or by any applicable rule of evidence.

NOTE 1   "After this court's opinion in *Commonwealth v. Oakes*, 401 Mass. 602 (1988), reversing the defendant's conviction for violation of G.L. c. 272, § 29A (1986 ed.), because of constitutional overbreadth under the First Amendment, the Legislature amended G.L. c. 272, § 29A. As a result of the legislative amendment to

G.L. c. 272, § 29A, and after oral argument, a plurality of the United States Supreme Court decided that the overbreadth issue was moot and remanded the case to us for further proceedings on the remaining 'live' issue, an as-applied Federal constitutional attack on the statute. *See Massachusetts v. Oakes*, 109 S.Ct. 2633, 2639 (1989). For the reasons stated in this opinion, we affirm the defendant's conviction.

"[T]he harm sought to be proscribed by Section 29A is the conduct involved in photographing a child nude or seminude, not the photographs themselves. Thus, the fact that the pictures are not child pornography under *New York v. Ferber*, 458 U.S. 747 (1982), is irrelevant. What is made criminal under § 29A is photographing minors nude or seminude. Accordingly, under Federal constitutional law, the Commonwealth's interest in protecting children permits the application of Section 29A to the defendant's conduct."

Commonwealth v. Oakes, 407 Mass. 92, 93, 97–98 (1990) (footnotes omitted).

NOTE 2   "Whether the defendant 'knowingly permitted' John to pose in a state of nudity is a question of fact. The question of a defendant's knowledge is exclusively within the province of the fact finder, and the fact finder is free to draw an inference of guilty knowledge if the inferences drawn from the circumstances are reasonable and possible." *Commonwealth v. Provost*, 418 Mass. 416, 419 (1994) (punctuation omitted). The Supreme Judicial Court also ruled that G.L. c. 272, §§ 29A and 31 were constitutional.

NOTE 3   Mere Nudity Not Enough. "The depiction of mere nudity is not enough to support a conviction under c. 272, § 29A." *Commonwealth v. Bean*, 435 Mass. 708, 715 n.17 (2002) (citations omitted).

NOTE 4a   Lascivious Intent. "'Lascivious intent' is defined as 'a state of mind in which the sexual gratification or arousal of any person is an objective.'" *Commonwealth v. Bean*, 435 Mass. 708, 709 (2002) (quoting G.L. c. 272, § 31).

NOTE 4b   "It is sufficient that the pose of the child be in a state of nudity as broadly defined by the statute, as long as the posing is done with 'lascivious intent.' *Commonwealth v. Provost*, [418 Mass. 416, 421 (1994)]. Absent the element of 'lascivious intent,' the statute is constitutionally overbroad. *Commonwealth v. Oakes*, 401 Mass. 602, 604–605 (1988) (*Oakes I*), vacated and remanded, 491 U.S. 576 (1989)." *Commonwealth v. Bean*, 435 Mass. 708, 711 (2002).

NOTE 4c   "In examining the four photographs, it is apparent that they are neither obscene nor pornographic. While this fact is not relevant on the question whether the nudity depicted falls within the scope of the statutory definition, *see Oakes II, supra* at 97–98, it may be relevant on the question of lascivious intent. In addition, consistent with the testimony of Bean's expert in art history and theory, the photographs appear intended to have an artistic quality independent of their specific subject matter. In other words, they appear to be more than mere snapshots intended to titillate potential viewers. A review of the other photographs taken by police from Bean's home and admitted in evidence at trial also provides a useful context for analyzing the intent behind the poses at issue. Many of these photographs were taken with black and white film and depict the minor (both by herself and with her boy friend) in a variety of poses and settings containing no elements suggestive of sexuality or lascivious intent.

"An analysis of the photographs in the context of the Dost factors does not lead us to conclude, as the Commonwealth urges, that the photographs themselves are lascivious or sufficient evidence of lascivious intent. Leaving aside the partial nudity of the subjects, the photographs (1) do not show sexual behavior or depict a sexually oriented display (factor [1]); (2) are not in a setting generally associated with sexual activity (factor [3]); (3) do not evince sexual suggestiveness or a willingness to engage in sexual activity (factor [5]). Factor (2), whether the breast is the focal point of the pose, is, in this case, a subjective assessment of little relevance." *Commonwealth v. Bean*, 435 Mass. 708, 715–16 (2002).

NOTE 4d   "The gist of the § 29A(a) offense is not the depiction, but rather the posing of the child for the purpose of depiction, with the requisite intent—a crime which would seem to be complete even if no depiction materializes, due to a lack of film, for example, or a malfunctioning camera." *Commonwealth v. Lawrence*, 68 Mass. App. Ct. 103, 105 (2007).

NOTE 5   "Artistic" Works. "We do not suggest that 'artistic' works cannot be posed with lascivious intent or that an artistic purpose is conclusive on the issue of lascivious intent. *New York v. Ferber*, 458 U.S. 747, 761 & n.12 (1982) (work that contains artistic value may nevertheless be sexually exploitative of its child subject). However, the artistic nature of the composition may be relevant evidence of an intention other than 'sexual gratification.'" *Commonwealth v. Bean*, 435 Mass. 708, 716 n.16 (2002).

NOTE 6   Definitions of Terms. Terms in Section 29A are defined in G.L. c. 272, § 31.

NOTE 7   DNA Database. A conviction of an offense under this section or of an attempt or conspiracy to commit such an offense results in the defendant being required to submit a DNA sample to the state's DNA database. See G.L. c. 22E, § 3.

NOTE 8   Sex Offender Registry. A conviction or adjudication of delinquency of an offense under this section or of an attempt to commit such an offense (*see* G.L. c. 274, § 6) renders the defendant subject to the requirements of the sex offender registry law. *See* G.L. c. 6, §§ 178C–178Q.

SECTION 29B
Dissemination of visual material of child in state of nudity or sexual conduct; punishment

(a) Whoever, with lascivious intent, disseminates any visual material that contains a representation or reproduction of any posture or exhibition in a state of nudity involving the use of a child who is under eighteen years of age, knowing the contents of such visual material or having sufficient facts in his possession to have knowledge of the contents thereof, or has in his possession any such visual material knowing the contents or having sufficient facts in his possession to have knowledge of the contents thereof, with the intent to disseminate the same, shall be punished in the state of prison for a term of not less than ten nor more than twenty years of by a fine of not less than ten thousand nor more than fifty thousand dollars or three times the monetary value of any economic gain derived from said dissemination, whichever is greater, or by both such fine and imprisonment.

(b) Whoever with lascivious intent disseminates any visual material that contains a representation or reproduction of any act that depicts, describes, or represents sexual conduct participated or engaged in by a child who is under eighteen years of age, knowing the contents of such visual material or having sufficient facts in his possession to have knowledge of the contents thereof, or whoever has in his possession any such visual material knowing the contents or having sufficient facts in his possession to have knowledge of the contents thereof, with the intent to disseminate the same, shall be punished in the state prison for a term of not less than ten nor more than twenty years or by a fine of not less than ten thousand nor more than fifty thousand dollars or three times the monetary value of any economic gain derived from said dissemination, whichever is greater, or by both such fine and imprisonment.

(c) For the purposes of this section, the determination whether the child in any visual material prohibited hereunder is under eighteen years of age may be made by the personal testimony of such child, by the testimony of a person who

2

produced, processed, published, printed or manufactured such visual material that the child therein was known to him to be under eighteen years of age, by testimony of a person who observed the visual material, or by expert medical testimony as to the age of the child based upon the child's physical appearance, by inspection of the visual material, or by any other method authorized by any general or special law or by any applicable rule of evidence.

(d) In a prosecution under this section, a minor shall be deemed incapable of consenting to any conduct of the defendant for which said defendant is being prosecuted.

(e) Pursuant to this section, proof that dissemination of any visual material that contains a representation or reproduction of sexual conduct or of any posture or exhibition in a state of nudity involving the use of a child who is under eighteen years of age was for a bona fide scientific, medical, or educational purpose for a bona fide school, museum, or library may be considered as evidence of a lack of lascivious intent.

NOTE 1   **"Visual Material."** See Notes following G.L. c. 272, § 31.

NOTE 2   **Definitions of Terms.** Terms in Section 29B are defined in G.L. c. 272, § 31.

NOTE 3   "Rather than creating two separate crimes, paragraphs (a) and (b) of § 29B describe different means of committing the same offense. We reach this conclusion because the language, structure, purpose, and history of the statute indicate that the Legislature intended to create a single crime that could be effectuated by various means, depending on the content of the visual materials at issue. . . . Here, the two paragraphs are identical with the exception of the fact that paragraph (a) pertains to depictions of children in a state of nudity, and paragraph (b) pertains to depictions of children engaged in sexual conduct. Each paragraph requires the same mental state (i.e., 'lascivious intent'), proscribes the same acts (possession with intent to distribute and distribution), assigns the same sentencing range (imprisonment for 'not less than ten nor more than twenty years'), and imposes the same range of monetary fines. The fact that the two paragraphs are identical except as to the content of the images demonstrates that the crime can be committed by two means, i.e., by distributing images of nudity or distributing images of sexual conduct. The elements of the two paragraphs are the same; the crime can simply be carried out by two different means." *Commonwealth v. Dingle*, 73 Mass. App. Ct. 274, 279 (2008).

NOTE 4   **Sex Offender Registry.** A conviction or adjudication of delinquency of an offense under this section or of an attempt to commit such an offense (*see* G.L. c. 274, § 6) renders the defendant subject to the requirements of the sex offender registry law. *See* G.L. c. 6, §§ 178C–178Q.

SECTION 29C
Purchasing or possessing child pornography

Whoever knowingly purchases or possesses a negative, slide, book, magazine, film, videotape, photograph or other similar visual reproduction, or depiction by computer, of any child whom the person knows or reasonably should know to be under the age of 18 years of age and such child is:

(i) actually or by simulation engaged in any act of sexual intercourse with any person or animal;

(ii) actually or by simulation engaged in any act of sexual contact involving the sex organs of the child and the mouth, anus or sex organs of the child and the sex organs of another person or animal;

(iii) actually or by simulation engaged in any act of masturbation;

(iv) actually or by simulation portrayed as being the object of, or otherwise engaged in, any act of lewd fondling, touching, or caressing involving another person or animal;

(v) actually or by simulation engaged in any act of excretion or urination within a sexual context;

(vi) actually or by simulation portrayed or depicted as bound, fettered, or subject to sadistic, masochistic, or sadomasochistic abuse in any sexual context; or

(vii) depicted or portrayed in any pose, posture or setting involving a lewd exhibition of the unclothed genitals, pubic area, buttocks, or, if such person is female, a fully or partially developed breast of the child; with knowledge of the nature or content thereof shall be punished by imprisonment in the state prison for not more than five years or in a jail or house of correction for not more than two and one-half years or by a fine of not less than $1,000 nor more than $10,000, or by both such fine and imprisonment for the first offense, not less than five years in a state prison or by a fine of not less than $5,000 nor more than $20,000, or by both such fine and imprisonment for the second offense, not less than 10 years in a state prison or by a fine of not less than $10,000 nor more than $30,000, or by both such fine and imprisonment for the third and subsequent offenses.

A prosecution commenced under this section shall not be continued without a finding nor placed on file.

The provisions of this section shall not apply to a law enforcement officer, licensed physician, licensed psychologist, attorney or officer of the court who is in possession of such materials in the lawful performance of his official duty. Nor shall the provisions of this section apply to an employee of a bona fide enterprise, the purpose of which enterprise is to filter or otherwise restrict access to such materials, who possesses examples of computer depictions of such material for the purposes of furthering the legitimate goals of such enterprise.

NOTE 1   **Statute Constitutional.** *Commonwealth v. Kenney*, 449 Mass. 840, 852 (2007), held this section constitutional.

NOTE 2   **"Depiction by Computer."** The language "'depiction by computer' includes graphic computer images stored in the form of data." *Commonwealth v. Hinds*, 437 Mass. 54, 64 (2002). *See also Commonwealth v. Kenney*, 449 Mass. 840 (2007) ("We conclude that the term 'depiction by computer' refers to the method by which the image is possessed and not its content.").

NOTE 3   "[S]even photocopies of photographs of naked children" did not violate G.L. c. 272, § 29C.

"Based on our de novo review of the photocopies, it is plainly apparent that their only notable feature is the nudity of the children. In none of the photocopies is the focal point of the visual depiction a child's genitals, and the children are not shown in any unnatural poses. Rather, the children are portrayed either simply standing around or engaging in ordinary activities in unremarkable settings. The visibility of the children's genitals is merely an inherent aspect of the fact that they are naked. There is nothing remotely sexual, either explicitly or implicitly, in any of the photocopies. The demeanor, facial expressions, and body language of the children suggest nothing inappropriate. In the photocopies depicting more than one child, the children appear to be comfortable in their surroundings and enjoying each other's company in a non-sexual manner. Nothing about the photocopies indicates in any way that they were derived from the sexual exploitation of the children depicted therein, such that their possession would result in the continuing victimization of those children." *Commonwealth v. Rex*, 469 Mass. 36, 37, 47–48 (2014).

NOTE 4   **Unit of Prosecution.** "[A] defendant's possession of a single cache of one hundred offending photographs in the same place at the same time gives rise to a single unit of prosecution pursuant to § 29C. The imposition of multiple punishments for such a singular possession is contrary to the defendant's guaranty against double jeopardy. Importantly, the meaning of 'punishment' for double jeopardy purposes is not limited to consecutive sentences, but extends also to concurrent sentences and multiple convictions.

"Yet, double jeopardy principles do not necessarily extend to simultaneous prosecutions. Thus, the Commonwealth may elect to prosecute a single violation of § 29C by way of multiple counts. Should that procedure result in multiple guilty verdicts for the same offense, the duplicative convictions must be vacated and merged into a single conviction for sentencing purposes.

"Nonetheless, . . . if the evidence presented to the jury would warrant a conviction on one ground, but not on another, and it is impossible to tell on which ground the jury relied, the verdict must be set aside on appeal."

FN5 "We do not . . . opine on the question . . . whether the possession of distinct formats of child pornography enumerated in § 29C (photographs, computer discs, and a computer hard drive) could constitute distinct units of prosecution if found in the same location at the same time. Nor do we opine whether the Commonwealth could, in another case, distinguish units of prosecution for possession of child pornography of the same format by establishing different periods of possession."

Commonwealth v. Rollins, 470 Mass. 66, 74–75, 78 & n.5 (2014) (citations omitted).

NOTE 5   Defense of Reasonable Mistake. "A defendant may, if he or she so chooses, present evidence indicating that he or she was honestly mistaken with regard to (or reasonably did not know) the age of the child depicted in the material. . . . Cases raising the defense of reasonable mistake will, we expect, be rare, because as is the situation here, the children involved in the pornography will ordinarily be readily ascertainable as children." *Commonwealth v. Kenney*, 449 Mass. 840, 857–58 (2007).

NOTE 6   Sex Offender Registry. A conviction or adjudication of delinquency of an offense under this section or of an attempt to commit such an offense (*see* G.L. c. 274, § 6) renders the defendant subject to the requirements of the sex offender registry law. *See* G.L. c. 6, §§ 178C–178Q.

SECTION 30
Injunctive relief against dissemination of obscene matter; jurisdiction; procedures; appeal

The superior court shall have jurisdiction to enjoin the dissemination of any matter which is obscene. The attorney general or a district attorney within his district may request an injunction against any person, firm, or corporation which disseminates or is about to disseminate any matter which is obscene.

The person, firm, or corporation sought to be enjoined shall be entitled to a trial on the merits within one day after filing of responsive pleadings and a decision shall be rendered by the court within two days of the conclusion of the trial.

A justice of the superior court may issue a preliminary injunction pending the trial on the merits against such person, firm, or corporation which disseminates or is about to disseminate any matter which is obscene.

No preliminary injunction shall be issued without notice to the adverse party.

In any action brought as herein provided the attorney general or a district attorney shall not be required to furnish security before the issuance of any injunction provided for in this section and neither the commonwealth nor any county, shall be liable for costs or for damages sustained by reason of the injunction in cases where judgment is rendered in favor of the person, firm, or corporation sought to be enjoined.

If the court finds that the person, firm, or corporation is disseminating or is about to disseminate any obscene matter, it shall issue a permanent injunction prohibiting the dissemination of that matter. The court's order shall direct the person, firm or corporation to surrender to a sheriff or a police officer the matter found obscene and a sheriff or police officer shall be directed to seize and destroy the same.

Appeals shall be as otherwise provided by law in civil proceedings, but any party or intervenor shall have the right to an expedited appeal to the appeals court.

The procedures set forth in this section are in addition to criminal proceedings initiated under any provisions of the General Laws, and not a condition precedent thereto.

NOTE   Definitions of Terms. G.L. c. 272, § 31.

SECTIONS 30A–C
Repealed

SECTION 30D
Jurisdiction to enjoin dissemination of visual material of child in state of nudity or sexual conduct

The superior court shall also have jurisdiction to enjoin the dissemination of any visual material that contains a representation or reproduction of any posture or exhibition in a state of nudity or of any act that depicts, describes, or represents sexual conduct participated or engaged in by a child who is under eighteen years of age. The procedures for issuance of such injunction shall be the same as those provided in section thirty, and are in addition to other criminal proceedings initiated under any provisions of the General Laws, and not a condition precedent thereto.

NOTE   Definitions of Terms. G.L. c. 272, § 31.

SECTION 31
Definitions applicable to Secs. 28, 28C, 28D, 28E, 29, 29A, 29B, 30 and 30D

As used in sections twenty-eight, twenty-eight C, twenty-eight D, twenty-eight E, twenty-nine, twenty-nine A, twenty-nine B, thirty and thirty D, the following words shall, unless the context requires otherwise, have the following meanings:

"Disseminate", to import, publish, produce, print, manufacture, distribute, sell, lease, exhibit or display.

"Harmful to minors", matter is harmful to minors if it is obscene or, if taken as a whole, it (1) describes or represents nudity, sexual excitement, so as to appeal predominantly to the prurient interest of minors; (2) is patently contrary to prevailing standards of adults in the county where the offense was committed as to suitable material for such minors; and (3) lacks serious literary, artistic, political or scientific value for minors.

"Knowing", a general awareness of the character of the matter.

"Lascivious intent", a state of mind in which the sexual gratification or arousal of any person is an objective. For the purposes of prosecution under this chapter, proof of lascivious intent may include, but shall not be limited to, the following:

(1) whether the circumstances include sexual behavior, sexual relations, infamous conduct of a lustful or obscene nature, deviation from accepted customs and manners, or sexually oriented displays;

(2) whether the focal point of a visual depiction is the child's genitalia, pubic area, or breast area of a female child;

2

(3) whether the setting or pose of a visual depiction is generally associated with sexual activity;

(4) whether the child is depicted in an unnatural pose or inappropriate attire, considering the child's age;

(5) whether the depiction denotes sexual suggestiveness or a willingness to engage in sexual activity;

(6) whether the depiction is of a child engaging in or being engaged in sexual conduct, including, but not limited to, sexual intercourse, unnatural sexual intercourse, bestiality, masturbation, sado-masochistic behavior, or lewd exhibition of the genitals.

"Minor", a person under eighteen years of age.

"Nudity", uncovered or less than opaquely covered human genitals, pubic areas, the human female breast below a point immediately above the top of the areola, or the covered male genitals in a discernible turgid state. For purposes of this definition, a female breast is considered uncovered if the nipple or areola only are covered.

"Matter", any handwritten or printed material, visual representation, live performance or sound recording including but not limited to, books, magazines, motion picture films, pamphlets, phonographic records, pictures, photographs, figures, statues, plays, dances, or any electronic communication including, but not limited to, electronic mail, instant messages, text messages, and any other communication created by means of use of the Internet or wireless network, whether by computer, telephone, or any other device or by any transfer of signs, signals, writing, images, sounds, data, or intelligence of any nature transmitted in whole or in part by a wire, radio, electromagnetic, photo-electronic or photo-optical system.

"Performance", any play, dance, exhibit, or such similar activity performed before one or more persons.

"Obscene", matter is obscene if taken as a whole it (1) appeals to the prurient interest of the average person applying the contemporary standards of the county where the offense was committed; (2) depicts or describes sexual conduct in a patently offensive way; and (3) lacks serious literary, artistic, political or scientific value.

"Sexual conduct", human masturbation, sexual intercourse, actual or simulated, normal or perverted, any lewd exhibitions of the genitals, flagellation or torture in the context of a sexual relationship, any lewd touching of the genitals, pubic areas, or buttocks of the human male or female, or the breasts of the female, whether alone or between members of the same or opposite sex or between humans and animals, and any depiction or representation of excretory functions in the context of a sexual relationship. Sexual intercourse is simulated when it depicts explicit sexual intercourse which gives the appearance of the consummation of sexual intercourse, normal or perverted.

"Sexual excitement", the condition of human male or female genitals or the breasts of the female while in a state of sexual stimulation or the sensual experiences of humans engaging in or witnessing sexual conduct or nudity.

"Visual material", any motion picture film, picture, photograph, videotape, book, magazine, pamphlet that contains pictures, photographs or similar visual representations or reproductions, or depiction by computer, telephone or any other device capable of electronic data storage or transmission. Undeveloped photographs, pictures, motion picture films, videotapes and similar visual representations or reproductions may be visual materials notwithstanding that processing, development or similar acts may be required to make the contents thereof apparent.

NOTE   **"Visual Material" Includes Computer Images.** "In this case, we are asked to decide whether the term '[v]isual material,' as defined in G.L. c. 272, § 31, encompasses computer images for purposes of a prosecution for dissemination, or possession with intent to disseminate, what is commonly called child pornography. G.L. c. 272, § 29B(a) and (b). We hold that it does . . . . We conclude that the statutory definition of "visual material" includes the computer images that underlie the defendant's indictments. Statutory language is given effect consistent with its plain meaning and the intent of the Legislature. *E.g., Chandler v. County Comm'rs of Nantucket County*, 437 Mass. 430, 435 (2002); *Sullivan v. Brookline*, 435 Mass. 353, 360 (2001). The scope of §§ 29B and 31 reflect the Legislature's obvious intent to include any visual image created by use of a camera or similar device, regardless of how or where the image is stored. This is clear from the plain language of the statute, interpreted in a commonsense manner.

". . .

"Any lingering doubt whether § 31 included computer images of the type at issue here is dispelled by the use of the word 'picture' and the context of the remainder of the section. This convinces us that the Legislature intended the section to reach images produced by any method of photography: conventional, 'instant,' electronic, digital, or some means as yet not invented. Because § 31 includes visual material even if undeveloped and even if it requires some sort of processing in order to be developed, the means used to store or display the visual material are of no relevance. The bytes of a computer image can be likened to conventional negatives. The Legislature was unconcerned with how the photographically created image is stored or communicated. So, too, it would not matter to the child whose humiliation is captured and permanently preserved on the Internet that the image is digital rather than conventional; indeed, this same permanence and the ease of transmission make the activity all the more pernicious for such a child. . . .

". . .

"Our conclusion is . . . unchanged by the recent amendment to § 31 itself. In 2002, the Legislature added 'depiction by computer' to the definition of '[v]isual material[ ]' . . . . By inserting 'depiction by computer,' the Legislature reaffirmed what was already evident. The statute, before the recent amendment, was broad enough to encompass the computer images here at issue. The fact that the Legislature revised the statute to include a specific reference to a particular technological advance does not mean that such material was not embraced by the prior statutory language. Statutory changes must be interpreted in context. In the present context, the 2002 amendment was not an effort to expand previously narrower coverage, but was instead an effort to modernize the language to keep it current with today's technology." *Perry v. Commonwealth*, 438 Mass. 282, 282–88 (2002).

SECTION 32
Motion picture theater managers or operators; applicability of Secs. 28, 29 and 29A

The provisions of sections twenty-eight, twenty-nine and twenty-nine A shall not apply to a manager or a motion picture operator or assistant operator licensed under sections seventy-five and seventy-six, respectively, of chapter one hundred and forty-three, who is employed in a motion picture theatre licensed under section one hundred and eighty-one of chapter one hundred and forty and the provisions of the state building code, in connection with a motion picture show exhibited in said theatre; provided that such manager, operator or assistant operator has no financial interest in the motion picture theatre wherein he is so employed; and provided, further, that such manager has no authority in determining which motion picture films are to be presented in said theatre.

SECTION 33
Exhibition of deformities

Whoever exhibits for hire an albino person, a minor or mentally ill person who is deformed or a person who has an appearance of deformity produced by artificial means shall be punished by a fine of not more than five hundred dollars.

SECTION 34
Crime against nature

Whoever commits the abominable and detestable crime against nature, either with mankind or with a beast, shall be punished by imprisonment in the state prison for not more than twenty years.

NOTE 1   Not Applicable to Private Consensual Conduct. "The defendants—the Attorney General and the district attorneys for the Northern and Suffolk districts—stipulated that their offices will not prosecute anyone under the challenged laws absent probable cause to believe that the prohibited conduct occurred either in public or without consent. This stipulation comports with the law: *Commonwealth v. Balthazar*, 366 Mass. 298, 302 (1974), established that 'consensual conduct in private between adults is not prohibited by § 35.' *Commonwealth v. Ferguson*, 384 Mass. 13, 16 (1981), quoting *Commonwealth v. Scagliotti*, 373 Mass. 626, 628 (1977), explained that the purpose of § 35 is 'to prevent the 'possibility that the defendant's conduct might give offense to persons present in a place frequented by members of the public' . . . . However, the statute is not designed to punish persons who desire privacy and who take reasonable measures to secure it.' This rationale applies equally to the 'crime against nature,' and we now clarify that our holdings in the *Balthazar* and *Ferguson* cases concerning acts conducted in private between consenting adults extend to § 34, as well." *Gay & Lesbian Advocates & Defenders v. Attorney General*, 436 Mass. 132, 133–34 (2002).

NOTE 2   Determining Whether Acts Occur In Public Place. "Because a 'place may be public at some times and under some circumstances, and not at others,' *Commonwealth v. Ferguson*, [384 Mass. 13, 16 (1981)], such determinations are for a fact finder. See *Commonwealth v. Scagliotti*, 373 Mass. 626, 628–629 (1977). The 'essential query' for determining whether the prohibited acts occur in public is 'whether the defendant intended public exposure or recklessly disregarded a substantial risk of exposure to one or more persons. . . . Conduct is not established as public merely because another person actually observes the conduct. . . . The Commonwealth must prove that the likelihood of being observed by casual passersby must have been reasonably foreseeable to the defendant, or stated otherwise, that the defendant acted upon an unreasonable expectation that his conduct would remain secret.' *Commonwealth v. Ferguson*, *supra*." *Gay & Lesbian Advocates & Defenders v. Attorney General*, 436 Mass. 132, 135 (2002).

NOTE 3   Form of indictment—G.L. c. 277, § 79 (Sodomy).

SECTION 35
Unnatural and lascivious acts

Whoever commits any unnatural and lascivious act with another person shall be punished by a fine of not less than one hundred nor more than one thousand dollars or by imprisonment in the state prison for not more than five years or in jail or the house of correction for not more than two and one half years.

NOTE 1a   "[T]he words 'unnatural and lascivious act' are 'words of common usage and indicate with reasonable clarity the kind and character of conduct which the Legislature intended to prohibit and punish,' and [we have] defined them to mean 'irregular indulgence in sexual behavior, illicit sexual relations, and infamous conduct which is lustful, obscene, and in deviation of accepted customs and manners.'" *Commonwealth v. Gallant*, 373

Mass. 577, 585 (1977) (citing *Commonwealth v. Balthazar*, 366 Mass. 298, 302 (1974), and quoting *Jaquith v. Commonwealth*, 331 Mass. 439, 442 (1954)).

NOTE 1b   "[T]he fondling of the victim's breasts or the touching of her pelvic area" are *not* an unnatural and lascivious act. *Commonwealth v. Zeitler*, 7 Mass. App. Ct. 543, 550 (1979).

NOTE 2   "[U]nnatural sexual intercourse must be taken to include oral and anal intercourse, including fellatio, cunnilingus, and other intrusions of a part of a person's body or other object into the genital or anal opening of another person's body." *Commonwealth v. Gallant*, 373 Mass. 577, 584 (1977), discussing a statute similar to Section 35, to wit, G.L. c. 265, § 23 (Statutory rape: "Whoever unlawfully has . . . unnatural sexual intercourse . . .").

NOTE 3   This section is inapplicable to private acts between consenting adults. *Commonwealth v. Balthazar*, 366 Mass. 298, 302 (1974); *Balthazar v. Superior Court*, 573 F.2d 698 (1st Cir. 1978).

NOTE 4a   Public Area. The burden is upon the Commonwealth to prove that the act took place in a public area. *Commonwealth v. Balthazar*, 366 Mass. 298, 302 (1974).

NOTE 4b   It cannot be ruled as a matter of law that a cubicle for two persons in a minitheatre is either a public or a private place. *Commonwealth v. Scagliotti*, 373 Mass. 626, 628–29 (1977).

NOTE 4c   "The rationale of . . . § 35 is to prevent the open flaunting of community standards regarding sexual matters . . . . [T]he statute is not designed to punish persons who desire privacy and who take reasonable measures to secure it . . . . A place may be public at some times and under some circumstances, and not public at others. The essential query is whether the defendant intended public exposure or recklessly disregarded a substantial risk of exposure to one or more persons. Conduct is not established as public merely because another person actually observes the conduct. The Commonwealth must prove that the likelihood of being observed by casual passersby must have been reasonably foreseeable to the defendant, or stated otherwise, that the defendant acted upon an unreasonable expectation that his conduct would remain secret." *Commonwealth v. Ferguson*, 384 Mass. 13, 16 (1981) (citations omitted). *See also Commonwealth v. Nicholas*, 40 Mass. App. Ct. 255 (1996).

NOTE 5a   Consent. The Commonwealth also has the burden of showing a lack of consent. *Commonwealth v. Reilly*, 5 Mass. App. Ct. 435, 437 (1977).

NOTE 5b   "Minors are presumed to be incapable of giving consent to unnatural and lascivious acts, in much the same manner that [certain] minors are unable to consent to intercourse." *Commonwealth v. Fleurant*, 6 Mass. App. Ct. 846 (1978) (quoting from trial court opinion).

NOTE 6   Public may be excluded at trials of certain crimes involving minors under the age of 18. G.L. c. 278, § 16A.

NOTE 7   Related Statutes.
    G.L. c. 265, § 22—Rape.
    G.L. c. 265, § 22A—Rape of child under sixteen.
    G.L. c. 265, § 23—Statutory rape.
    G.L. c. 265, § 24—Assault with intent to rape.
    G.L. c. 265, § 24B—Assault of a child with intent to commit rape.
    G.L. c. 272, § 16—Open and gross lewdness.
    G.L. c. 272, § 53—Lewd, wanton and lascivious persons.

NOTE 8   Form of indictment—G.L. c. 277, § 79 (Unnatural act).

NOTE 9   DNA Database. A conviction of an offense under this section or of an attempt or conspiracy to commit such an offense results in the defendant being required to submit a DNA sample to the state's DNA database. *See* G.L. c. 22E, § 3.

2

SECTION 35A
Unnatural and lascivious acts with child under 16

Whoever commits any unnatural and lascivious act with a child under the age of sixteen shall be punished by a fine of not less than one hundred dollars nor more than one thousand dollars or by imprisonment in the state prison for not more than five years or in jail or the house of correction for not more than two and one half years, and whoever over the age of eighteen commits a second or subsequent such offense shall be sentenced to imprisonment in the state prison for a term of not less than five years.

NOTE 1   **Consent.** See Note relating to consent following G.L. c. 272, § 35.

NOTE 2   **Related Statutes.** See Note 8 following G.L. c. 272, § 35.

NOTE 3   Section 35A is a lesser included offense of G.L. c. 265, § 23 (statutory rape). *Commonwealth v. Leo*, 379 Mass. 34 (1979).

NOTE 4   **Sex Offender Registry.** A conviction or adjudication of delinquency of an offense under this section or of an attempt to commit such an offense (*see* G.L. c. 274, § 6) renders the defendant subject to the requirements of the sex offender registry law. *See* G.L. c. 6, §§ 178C–178Q.

NOTE 5   **DNA Database.** A conviction of an offense under this section or of an attempt or conspiracy to commit such an offense results in the defendant being required to submit a DNA sample to the state's DNA database. *See* G.L. c. 22E, § 3.

NOTE 6   **Sexually Dangerous Person Commitment.** A conviction or adjudication of delinquency of an offense under this section or of an attempt to commit such an offense (*see* G.L. c. 274, § 6) can serve as a predicate "sexual offense" for civil commitment as a "sexually dangerous person". *See* G.L. c. 123A, §§ 1–15.

SECTION 36
Blasphemy

Whoever wilfully blasphemes the holy name of God by denying, cursing or contumeliously reproaching God, his creation, government or final judging of the world, or by cursing or contumeliously reproaching Jesus Christ or the Holy Ghost, or by cursing or contumeliously reproaching or exposing to contempt and ridicule, the holy word of God contained in the holy scriptures shall be punished by imprisonment in jail for not more than one year or by a fine of not more than three hundred dollars, and may also be bound to good behavior.

SECTION 36A
Sporting events, penalty for abuse of participants and officials

Whoever, having arrived at the age of sixteen years, directs any profane, obscene or impure language or slanderous statement at a participant or an official in a sporting event, shall be punished by a fine of not more than fifty dollars.

SECTION 37
Repealed

SECTION 38
Disturbance of assembly for worship

Whoever wilfully interrupts or disturbs an assembly of people met for worship of God shall be punished by imprisonment for not more than one year or by a fine of not more than one thousand dollars.

SECTION 39
Selling goods and provisions, caring for horses, gaming, horse racing or exhibits near camp meetings
(Amended by 2011 Mass. Acts c. 194, § 69, effective Nov. 22, 2011.)

Whoever, during the time of holding a camp or field meeting for religious purposes, and within one mile of the place thereof, hawks or peddles goods, wares or merchandise, or establishes or maintains a tent, booth or building for vending provisions or refreshments, or furnishes shelter and food for or has the care of horses for pay, without permission from the authorities or officers having the charge or direction of such meeting, or engages in illegal gaming or horse racing, or exhibits or offers to exhibit any show or play, shall forfeit not more than twenty dollars; provided, that the time of holding such meeting shall not exceed thirty consecutive days in any one year; and that a person having a regular, usual and established place of business within such limits need not suspend his business.

SECTION 40
Disturbance of schools or assemblies

Whoever wilfully interrupts or disturbs a school or other assembly of people met for a lawful purpose shall be punished by imprisonment for not more than one month or by a fine of not more than fifty dollars; provided, however, that whoever, within one year after being twice convicted of a violation of this section, again violates the provisions of this section shall be punished by imprisonment for one month, and the sentence imposing such imprisonment shall not be suspended.

NOTE   The Commonwealth need not show that the defendant possessed a specific intent to disturb the school proceedings. "The wilfulness requirement of G.L. c. 272, § 40 demands, however, only that the acts of the defendants be wilfully performed; so long as the acts were intentional and not due to accident or inadvertence, the requirement is satisfied." *Commonwealth v. Bohmer*, 374 Mass. 368, 377 (1978). *See also Commonwealth v. Sholley*, 432 Mass. 721, 731 (2000) (citing and quoting, in part, *Bohner*) ("G.L. c. 272, § 40, prohibiting interruption or disruption of schools extends only to 'activity that so significantly disrupts their functioning as to impair the accomplishment of their educational goals.'").

SECTION 40A
Alcoholic beverages; gift, sale, delivery or possession on public school premises

Whoever gives, sells, delivers or has in his possession any alcoholic beverage, except for medicinal purposes, in any public school building, or on any premises used for public school purposes and under the charge of a school committee or other public board or officer, shall be punished by imprisonment for not more than thirty days or by a fine of not more than one hundred dollars, or both provided, however, that a school committee of a city, town or district may authorize a public or nonprofit organization using a public school building with its permission during non school hours to possess and sell alcoholic beverages therein provided such nonprofit organization is properly licensed under the provisions of section fourteen of chapter one hundred and thirty-eight.

SECTION 41
Disturbance of libraries

Whoever wilfully disturbs persons assembled in a public library, or a reading room connected therewith, by making a noise or in any other manner during the time when such library or reading room is open to the public shall be punished as provided in the preceding section.

SECTION 42
Disturbance of funerals

Whoever wilfully interrupts or by fast driving or otherwise in any way disturbs a funeral assembly or procession shall be punished as provided in section forty.

SECTION 42A
Disturbance of funeral services

Whoever pickets, loiters or otherwise creates a disturbance within five hundred feet of a funeral home, church or temple or other building where funeral services are being held, shall be punished by a fine of not more than one thousand dollars or by imprisonment for not more than one year in a house of correction, or both.

SECTION 42B
Disturbance of military funeral services
(Added by 2014 Mass. Acts c. 62, § 26, effective July 2, 2014.)

Whoever willfully pickets, loiters or otherwise creates a disturbance within 500 feet of a funeral home, church, temple, burial or other building where military funeral services are being held, shall be punished by a fine of not more than $2,000 or by imprisonment for not more than 2 years in a house of correction, or both.

SECTION 43
Disorderliness in public conveyances; disturbance of travelers

Whoever, in or upon a railroad carriage, steamboat or other public conveyance, is disorderly, or disturbs or annoys travelers in or upon the same by profane, obscene or indecent language, or by indecent behavior, shall be punished as provided in section forty.

SECTION 43A
Smoking in public conveyances and transportation terminals

Whoever, in or upon a railroad carriage, steamboat, or other public conveyance, or in a terminal or other facility of the Massachusetts Bay Transportation Authority, smokes or carries an open flame or lighted match, cigar, cigarette, or pipe shall be punished by imprisonment for not more than ten days or by a fine of not more than one hundred dollars, or both such fine and imprisonment.

NOTE **Related Statute.** G.L. c. 270, § 22—Smoking in certain public places restricted.

SECTIONS 44–52
Repealed

SECTION 53
Penalty for certain offenses
(Amended by 2014 Mass. Acts c. 417, effective Mar. 24, 2015.)

(a) Common night walkers, common street walkers, both male and female, persons who with offensive and disorderly acts or language accost or annoy another person, lewd, wanton and lascivious persons in speech or behavior, keepers of noisy and disorderly houses, and persons guilty of indecent exposure shall be punished by imprisonment in a jail or house of correction for not more than 6 months, or by a fine of not more than $200, or by both such fine and imprisonment.

(b) Disorderly persons and disturbers of the peace, for the first offense, shall be punished by a fine of not more than $150. On a second or subsequent offense, such person shall be punished by imprisonment in a jail or house of correction for not more than 6 months, or by a fine of not more than $200, or by both such fine and imprisonment.

NOTE 1a **Common Night Walkers.** The common night walking provision of this section punishes "persons abroad at night who solicit others to illicit sexual acts." *Commonwealth v. King*, 374 Mass. 5, 13 (1977).

NOTE 1b **Evidence.** "The time, place, and frequency of the defendant's conduct warrant an inference that on each occasion [he or she] was soliciting [ ] for illicit sexual intercourse. Section 53 . . . does not require proof of past convictions for prostitution to sustain a conviction for common night walking." *King*, 374 Mass. at 14.

NOTE 1c Form of indictment—G.L. c. 277, § 79 (Common night walker).

NOTE 1d Third conviction for being a common night walker— G.L. c. 272, § 62.

NOTE 2a **Lewd, Wanton and Lascivious Persons.** The lewd, wanton and lascivious persons provision prohibits "'only the commission of conduct in a public place, or the public solicitation of conduct to be performed in a public place, when the conduct committed or solicited involves the touching of the genitals, buttocks, or female breasts, for purposes of sexual arousal, gratification, or offense, by a person who knows or should know of the presence of a person or persons who may be offended by the conduct.' *Commonwealth v. Sefranka*, 382 Mass. 108 (1980)." See also *Commonwealth v. Templema*, 376 Mass. 533 (1978).

NOTE 2b "In *Commonwealth v. Ferguson*, 384 Mass. 13 (1981) we construed the term 'public place' in a closely-related statute, G.L. c. 272, § 35. 'The essential query is whether the defendant intended public exposure or recklessly disregarded a substantial risk of exposure to one or more persons. . . . The Commonwealth must prove that the likelihood of being observed by casual passerby must have been reasonably foreseeable to the defendant, or stated otherwise, that the defendant acted upon an unreasonable expectation that his conduct would remain secret.' (Citations omitted). *Id.* at 16. One incident took place in a car parked in a supermarket parking lot during the day in the midst of a snowstorm which was sufficiently heavy to cause the schools to close. The other took place in a teachers' faculty room during a weekend debate meet when both the complainant and Beauchemin were alone. There is no evidence in the record warranting a finding that the complainant and Beauchemin were observed.

"Neither the parking lot nor the faculty lounge was a public place in the circumstances because there was little 'likelihood of [sexual conduct on the part of the complainant and the defendant] being observed by a casual passerby.' *Id.* Therefore, the motion for a required finding of not guilty should have been allowed." *Commonwealth v. Beauchemin*, 410 Mass. 181, 183, 183–84 (1991).

NOTE 2c **Related Statutes.**

G.L. c. 272, § 35—Unnatural and lascivious acts.
G.L. c. 272, § 16—Open and gross lewdness.
G.L. c. 265, § 22–24B—Rape laws.

NOTE 2d **Open and Gross Lewdness v. Indecent Exposure.** "Although the two statutes, 'open and gross lewdness,' G.L. c. 272, § 16, and 'indecent exposure,' G.L. c. 272, § 53, are similar, they have different elements, reflecting (in part) their different origins . . . .

"The two statutes prohibit different conduct. Any intentional exposure of genitalia may be prosecuted as a misdemeanor under G.L. c. 272, § 53. Conviction of 'open and gross lewdness,' G.L. c. 272, § 16, on the other hand, requires the Commonwealth to prove, among other elements, intention, manner (done in such a way as to produce alarm or shock), and impact (does in fact alarm or shock). The requirement that the defendant must engage in

2

conduct such as actually to alarm or shock another has remained unchanged since 1880. Whichever private parts of one's body is intentionally exposed, the fact finder must be persuaded beyond a reasonable doubt that the defendant acted in such a way as to alarm or shock. In contrast, to sustain a conviction of indecent exposure, G.L. c. 272, § 53, the Commonwealth is not required to prove the elements of alarm or shock." *Commonwealth v. Quinn*, 439 Mass. 492, 495–96 (2003) (citations and quotation marks omitted).

NOTE 3   Form of Indictment. G.L. c. 272, § 79 (Lewdness). Caveat—The indictment form recommended in G.L. c. 277, § 79 may well be unconstitutionally vague. *See Commonwealth v. Sefranka*, 382 Mass. 108 (1980).

NOTE 4a   Offensive Acts. "Offensive acts are those that cause 'displeasure, anger or resentment; esp., repugnant to the prevailing sense of what is decent or moral.' Black's Law Dictionary 1113 (8th ed. 2004). The defendant's act of grabbing the victim from behind 'really tight' around her shoulders, while she was attending to customers, was offensive, particularly when considered in the context of the defendant's other behaviors toward the victim in the workplace." *Commonwealth v. Cahill*, 446 Mass. 778, 781 (2006) (citation omitted).

NOTE 4b "We interpret the 'offensive' acts or language element of G.L. c. 272, § 53, as requiring proof of sexual conduct or language, either explicit or implicit. Explicit behavior is self-explanatory. By implicit sexual conduct or language, we mean that which a reasonable person would construe as having sexual connotations." *Commonwealth v. Sullivan*, 469 Mass. 621, 625–26 (2014).

NOTE 5   Accosting or Annoying. "Whereas disorderly conduct under the disorderly person provision must have a public impact, the crime of accosting or annoying a person of the opposite sex evinces a legislative intent to criminalize offensive and disorderly conduct or language that has a personal and private, rather than a necessarily public, impact." *Commonwealth v. Chou*, 433 Mass. 229, 233 (2001).

NOTE 6   Disorderly Acts. "[F]or purposes of this § 53 offense, 'disorderly' acts or language are those that involve fighting or threatening, violent or tumultuous behavior, or that create a hazardous or physically offensive condition for no legitimate purpose of the actor, whether the resulting harm is suffered in public by the public, or in private by an individual." *Commonwealth v. Chou*, 433 Mass. 229, 233 (2001).

NOTE 7a   Speech. The mere fact that the conduct of the defendant is accompanied by speech does not preclude a conviction. Section 53 embraces "activities which intentionally tend to disturb the public tranquility, or alarm or provoke others." *Commonwealth v. Carson*, 10 Mass. App. Ct. 920, 922 (1980) (rescript).

NOTE 7b   Sexually Explicit Language. "Sexually explicit language, when directed at particular individuals in settings in which such communications are inappropriate and likely to cause severe distress, may be inherently threatening." *Commonwealth v. Chou*, 433 Mass. 229, 234 (2001) (citation omitted).

NOTE 8 "The provision against 'disturbers of the peace' proscribes conduct which tends to annoy all good citizens and does in fact annoy anyone present not favoring it. This definition applies a two-pronged standard to disruptive conduct. It proscribes activities which, first, most people would find to be unreasonably disruptive, and second, did in fact infringe someone's right to be undisturbed." *Commonwealth v. Orlando*, 371 Mass. 732, 734–35 (1977) (citations omitted).

NOTE 9a   Indecent Exposure. "Indecent exposure requires 'an intentional act of lewd exposure, offensive to one or more persons.' *Commonwealth v. Broadland*, 315 Mass. 20, 21–22 (1943), quoting from *Commonwealth v. Bishop*, 296 Mass. 459, 462 (1937). . . . The judge could reasonably conclude that the defendant lewdly exposed himself to Nathan by using the urinal designed for shorter boys when higher urinals were available and by standing farther away from the urinal than was necessary to urinate.

Testimony that the defendant had an erection while standing at the urinal further supports the judge's finding." *Commonwealth v. Swan*, 73 Mass. App. Ct. 258, 261–62 (2008).

NOTE 9b   Indecent Exposure—Genitalia. "The exposure of genitalia has been defined by judicial interpretation as an essential element of the offense of indecent exposure." *Commonwealth v. Quinn*, 439 Mass. 492, 494 (2003) (citing *Commonwealth v. Arthur*, 420 Mass. 535, 540–41 (1995)).

NOTE 9c   Genitalia v. Genital Area or Pubic Hair. Is exposure of the genital area or pubic hair indecent within the meaning of the statute? No. "Neither G.L. c. 72, § 53, nor the related provisions of G.L. c. 272, § 16 have been construed by judicial decision to apply to an intentional exposure of the genital area or the pubic hair." *Commonwealth v. Arthur*, 420 Mass. 535, 541 (1995).

NOTE 10   Peeping Tom. "[T]he disorderly person statute may lawfully be applied to a 'Peeping Tom,' an activity that may cause alarm to the person peered at, . . . , and thereby makes a breach in the public peace. . . . Conduct that is disorderly by reason of its physically offensive nature does not, however, require that the object of the offensive conduct be aware of it." *Commonwealth v. LePore*, 40 Mass. App. Ct. 543, 548–49 (1996).

SECTION 53A

Engaging in sexual conduct for a fee; penalty

(Stricken & replaced by 2011 Mass. Acts c. 178, § 25, effective Nov. 21, 2011.)

(a)Whoever engages, agrees to engage or offers to engage in sexual conduct with another person in return for a fee, shall be punished by imprisonment in the house of correction for not more than 1 year or by a fine of not more than $500, or by both such imprisonment and fine, whether such sexual conduct occurs or not.

(b) Whoever pays, agrees to pay or offers to pay another person to engage in sexual conduct, or to agree to engage in sexual conduct with another person, shall be punished by imprisonment in the house of correction for not more than 2 and one-half years or by a fine of not less than $1,000 and not more than $5,000, or by both such imprisonment and fine, whether such sexual conduct occurs or not.

(c) Whoever pays, agrees to pay or offers to pay any person with the intent to engage in sexual conduct with a child under the age of 18, or whoever is paid, agrees to pay or agrees that a third person be paid in return for aiding a person who intends to engage in sexual conduct with a child under the age of 18, shall be punished by imprisonment in the state prison for not more than 10 years, or in the house of correction for not more than 2 and one-half years and by a fine of not less than $3,000 and not more than $10,000, or by both such imprisonment and fine, whether such sexual conduct occurs or not; provided, however, that a prosecution commenced under this section shall not be continued without a finding or placed on file.

NOTE 1 "[A] prostitute is one who permits common indiscriminate sexual activity for hire, in distinction from sexual activity confined exclusively to one person. . . .

"This conduct traditionally has included both performance of sexual acts as a business and public solicitation for such business."

Commonwealth v. King, 374 Mass. 5, 12–13 (1977).

NOTE 2   Form of indictment—G.L. c. 277, § 79 (Prostitute).

NOTE 3   Related Statutes. G.L. c. 272, §§ 4A–13, 24.

NOTE 4   DNA Database. A conviction of an offense under this section or of an attempt or conspiracy to commit such an offense results in the defendant being required to submit a DNA sample to the state's DNA database. *See G.L. c. 22E, § 3.*

2

SECTION 54
Apprehension for offenses mentioned in section 53, without warrant; custody

Whoever is found in a public way or other public place, committing any offense or disorder set forth in sections fifty-three and fifty-three A, may be apprehended by a sheriff, deputy sheriff, constable or police officer or by any other person by the order of a magistrate or any of said officers, without a warrant and be kept in custody for not more than twenty-four hours, Sundays and legal holidays excepted, until he can be taken before a court or trial justice having jurisdiction of such offense.

SECTION 55
Repealed

SECTION 56
Commission of subsequent offense as breach of recognizance on appeal

If a person convicted under section fifty-three appeals from the sentence, the commission of any like offense by him before judgment on the appeal shall be a breach of the condition of the recognizance, if any was taken upon allowing the appeal.

SECTION 57
Discharge upon recognizance and paying expenses of prosecutions under Secs. 53, 66 and 68

When a person is brought before a magistrate upon a charge of any offense mentioned in sections fifty-three, sixty-six and sixty-eight, such magistrate, or the court before which the case may be carried on appeal, may at any stage of the proceedings direct the defendant or appellant to be discharged, upon his entering into a recognizance, with sufficient sureties, in such sum as the magistrate or court orders, for his good behavior for not less than six months nor more than two years, and paying the expenses of prosecution or such part thereof as the magistrate or court orders.

SECTION 58
Employing or permitting employment of minor under 15 to beg

A parent or other person who employs a minor under fifteen in begging or who, having the care or custody of such minor, permits him to engage in such employment shall be punished by a fine of not more than two hundred dollars or by imprisonment for not more than six months.

SECTION 59
Violation of regulations relating to streets, reservations, or parkways; alcoholic beverages; profanity; arrest without warrant

Whoever remains in a street or elsewhere in a town in wilful violation of an ordinance or by-law of such town or of any rule or regulation for the government or use of any public reservation, parkway or boulevard made under authority of law by any department, officer or board in charge thereof, whoever is in a street or elsewhere in a town in wilful violation of an ordinance or by-law of such town or of any rule or regulation for the government of use of any public reservation, parkway or boulevard made under authority of law by any department, officer or board in charge thereof, the substance of which is the drinking or possession of alcoholic beverage, and whoever in a street or other public place ac-

costs or addresses another person with profane or obscene language, in wilful violation of an ordinance or by-law of such town, may be arrested without a warrant by an officer authorized to serve criminal process in the place where the offense is committed and kept in custody until he can be taken before a court having jurisdiction of the offense.

SECTION 60
Refusal to remove substance placed on public way in violation of town regulations; arrest without warrant until identity ascertained

Whoever commits a misdemeanor, as defined by a by-law, regulation or ordinance of a town or authority therein, in the presence of a police officer or an officer authorized to serve criminal process, the substance of which misdemeanor is the placing on or in or throwing into a public way, the sidewalk of a public way or a public alley, filth, rubbish or other substance, and, being requested by such officer forthwith to remove it, refuses or neglects so to do, and if the identity of such person is unknown to the officer, may be arrested by such officer and detained in a safe place without a warrant until his identity is ascertained. Reasonable diligence shall be exercised by the arresting officer in ascertaining the identity of the offender and when identified he shall be released from arrest unless a warrant has issued against him.

NOTE **Related Statutes.**
G.L. c. 270, § 16—Disposal of rubbish, etc. on or near highways and coastal or inland waters.
G.L. c. 270, § 20—Burning of refuse, etc. within marine or shoreline boundaries.

SECTION 61
Conviction after discharge from sentence under Sec. 53

Whoever, having been discharged under section one hundred and forty of chapter one hundred and twenty-seven, is afterward convicted of any offense mentioned in section fifty-three committed after the former conviction, either in the same or a different county, may be sentenced to hard labor in the house of correction for not more than one year.

SECTION 62
Third conviction of being a common nightwalker

If a complaint charges a person with being a common nightwalker, and it is proved at the trial that such person has been twice before convicted of the same offense, such person may be sentenced to the house of correction for not more than two and one half years or if a male, to the Massachusetts reformatory, or if a female, to the reformatory for women.

SECTION 63
Tramps; begging or riding freight trains as prima facie evidence

Whoever, not being under seventeen, or a person asking charity within his own town, roves about from place to place begging, or living without labor or visible means of support, shall be deemed a tramp. An act of begging or soliciting alms, whether of money, food, lodging or clothing, by a person having no residence in the town within which the act is committed, or the riding upon a freight train of a railroad, whether within or without any car or part thereof, without a permit from the proper officers or employees of such railroad or train, shall be prima facie evidence that such person is a tramp.

2

NOTE 1   Section unconstitutional, insofar as it makes it an offense to rove about living without a visible means of support, as it seeks to punish a status rather than the commission of an act. *Alegata v. Commonwealth*, 353 Mass. 287 (1967).

NOTE 2   See Notes (Idle and Disorderly) following G.L. c. 272, § 53.

SECTION 64
Punishment of tramps; entering buildings; injuries to or threats against persons or property; carrying weapons

A tramp shall be punished by imprisonment in the house of correction for not more than thirty days; and if he enters a dwelling house or other building without the consent of the owner or occupant thereof, or wilfully or maliciously injures or threatens to injure any person therein, or threatens to do any injury to any person, or to the property of another, or is found carrying a firearm or other dangerous weapon, he shall be punished by imprisonment in the house of correction for not less than one nor more than two and one half years, but notwithstanding the foregoing a tramp found carrying a firearm or other dangerous weapon in violation of section ten of chapter two hundred and sixty-nine may be prosecuted and punished thereunder.

NOTE   See Note 1 following G.L. c. 272, § 63.

SECTION 65
Arrest of tramps without warrant; making complaint

A sheriff, deputy sheriff, constable or police officer, upon view or information of an offense described in the two preceding sections, may, without a warrant, arrest the offender, and make complaint against him therefor; and the state police shall make such arrests and complaints. Mayors and selectmen shall appoint special police officers, who shall also make such arrests and complaints in their respective towns.

NOTE   See Note 1 following G.L. c. 272, § 63.

SECTION 66
Vagrants

Persons wandering abroad and begging, or who go about from door to door or in public or private ways, areas to which the general public is invited, or in other public places for the purpose of begging or to receive alms, and who are not licensed or who do not come within the description of tramps as contained in section sixty-three, shall be deemed vagrants and may be punished by imprisonment for not more than six months in the house of correction.

NOTE   Section declared unconstitutional. See Note 1 following G.L. c. 272, § 63.

SECTION 67
Arrest of vagrants without warrant; taking before court; making complaint

Sheriffs, deputy sheriffs, constables and police officers, acting on the request of any person or upon their own information or belief, shall without a warrant arrest and carry any vagrant before a district court for the purpose of an examination, and shall make complaint against him.

NOTE   See Note 1 following G.L. c. 272, § 63.

SECTION 68
Vagabonds

A person known to be a pickpocket, thief or burglar, if acting in a suspicious manner around any steamboat landing,

railroad depot, or any electric railway station, or place where electric railway cars stop to allow passengers to enter or leave the cars, banking institution, broker's office, place of public amusement, auction room, store, shop, crowded thoroughfare, car or omnibus, the dwelling place of another, or at any public gathering or assembly, shall be deemed a vagabond, and shall be punished by imprisonment in the house of correction for not less than four nor more than twelve months.

NOTE   Section unconstitutional as it prescribes conduct which does *not* constitute a crime. *Alegata v. Commonwealth*, 353 Mass. 287, 301 (1967).

SECTION 69
Arresting vagabonds without warrant; taking before court; making complaint

Sheriffs, deputy sheriffs, constables and police officers shall take any such vagabond into custody without a warrant and shall, within twenty-four hours after such arrest, Sundays and legal holidays excepted, take him before a district court, and shall make complaint against him.

NOTE   See Note following G.L. c. 272, § 68.

SECTION 70
Taking dead body on process or execution

A sheriff, deputy sheriff or constable who takes the body of a deceased person on mesne process or execution shall be punished by a fine of not more than five hundred dollars or by imprisonment for not more than six months.

SECTION 71
Disinterring human bodies

Whoever, not being lawfully authorized by the proper authorities, wilfully digs up, disinters, removes or conveys away a human body, or the remains thereof, or knowingly aids in such disinterment, removal or conveying away, and whoever is accessory thereto either before or after the fact, shall be punished by imprisonment in the state prison for not more than three years or in jail for not more than two and one half years or by a fine of not more than four thousand dollars.

NOTE   It is not necessary to allege or prove ownership of the cemetery from where the body was removed. *Commonwealth v. Cooley*, 27 Mass. (10 Pick.) 37 (1830).

SECTION 72
Buying, selling or possessing dead bodies

Whoever buys or sells, or has in his possession for the purpose of buying, selling or trafficking in, the dead body of a human being shall be punished by a fine of not less than fifty nor more than one thousand dollars or by imprisonment for not less than three months nor more than two and one half years.

SECTION 73
Tombs, graves, memorials, trees, plants; injuring, removing
(Amended by 2015 Mass. Acts c. 130, effective Feb. 21, 2016; 2015 Mass. Acts c. 131, effective Feb. 21, 2016.)

Whoever wilfully destroys, mutilates, defaces, injures or removes a tomb, monument, gravestone, American flag, veteran's grave marker, metal plaque, veteran's commemorative flag holder, commemorative flag holder representing service in a police or fire department, veteran's flag holder that commemorates a particular war, conflict or period of service, or flag, or other structure or thing which is placed or designed for a memorial of the dead, or a fence railing, curb or other thing which is intended for the protection or ornament of a structure or thing before mentioned or of an enclosure for the burial of the dead, or wilfully removes, destroys, mutilates, cuts, breaks or injures a tree, shrub or plant placed or being within such enclosure, or wantonly or maliciously disturbs the contents of a tomb or a grave, shall be punished by imprisonment in the state prison for not more than five years or by imprisonment in the jail or house of correction for not more than two and one-half years and by a fine of not more than five thousand dollars. In addition, the court shall order any person convicted of an offense pursuant to this section to pay restitution to the owner of the property that was damaged, destroyed, mutilated, defaced, injured or removed.

NOTE   Related Statutes.
   G.L. c. 266, § 113—Injury to timber, wood, or shrubs.
   G.L. c. 266, § 114—Injury to gate, bars or fence.
   G.L. c. 266, §§ 115, 117—Injury to orchards or gardens.
   G.L. c. 266, § 116A—Protection of certain flowers.
   G.L. c. 266, § 120—Trespass.
   G.L. c. 266, § 126—Injury to natural scenery.
   G.L. c. 266, § 127—Wilful and malicious destruction of personal and real property; wanton destruction.

SECTION 73A
Removal of gravestones and other memorials for repair or reproduction

In any city or town which accepts this section, the provisions of section seventy-three shall not prohibit the removal, in accordance with rules and regulations promulgated by the state secretary, of a gravestone or other structure or thing which is placed or designed as a memorial for the dead, for the purpose of repair or reproduction thereof by community sponsored, educationally oriented, and professionally directed repair teams.

SECTION 73B
Sale of or attempt to sell stolen commemorative grave marker; receipt; retention or disposal of stolen commemorative grave marker
(Added by 2015 Mass. Acts c. 129, effective Feb. 21, 2016.)

(a) For purposes of this section, "commemorative grave marker" shall mean a grave marker, headstone, monument, structure, medallion or other object designed to commemorate the grave of a veteran, police officer or firefighter.

(b) Whoever sells or attempts to sell a commemorative grave marker that has been stolen and the person knows or should know the commemorative grave marker to be stolen, shall be punished by a fine of not more than $5,000 for a first offense and for a second or subsequent offense by imprisonment in a state prison for not more than 5 years or by imprisonment in a jail or house of correction for not more than 2½ years and by a fine of not more than $5,000.

(c) Whoever receives, retains or disposes of a commemorative grave marker that the person knows or should know to be stolen, shall be punished by a fine of not more than $5,000; provided, however, that no such penalty shall be imposed upon: (i) a person who receives or retains the commemorative grave marker with the intent to return it to a cemetery, a member of law enforcement, a member of a fire department, a member of the department of veterans' services, a non-profit veterans' services group or a veterans' agent of a city or town; or (ii) a person who in fact disposes of the commemorative grave marker by returning it to a cem-

etery, a member of law enforcement, a member of a fire department, a member of the department of veterans' services, a non-profit veterans' services group or a veterans' agent of a city or town.

SECTION 74
Desecrating place of burial; use and occupation as evidence of title

Whoever wrongfully, and by any act not included in the preceding section, destroys, injures or removes a building, fence, railing or other thing lawfully erected in or around a place of burial or cemetery, or a tree, shrub or plant within its limits, or wrongfully injures a walk or path, or places rubbish or offensive matter or commits a nuisance therein, or in any way desecrates or disfigures the same, shall forfeit not less than five nor more than one hundred dollars. Upon the trial of a complaint hereunder, use and occupation for the purposes of burial shall be sufficient evidence of title.

NOTE   Related Statute. See Note following G.L. c. 272, § 73.

SECTION 75
Removal of flowers, flags or memorial tokens from burial lot

Whoever, without authority, removes flowers, flags or memorial tokens from any grave, tomb, monument or burial lot in any cemetery or other place of burial shall be punished by a fine of not more than one thousand dollars or by imprisonment for not more than six months.

NOTE   Related Statutes. G.L. c. 266, § 30—Larceny. See Note following G.L. c. 272, § 73.

SECTION 76
Ways, railroads, canals or public easements through burial grounds

Whoever lays out, opens, or makes a highway or town way, or constructs a railroad or canal, or any other thing in the nature of a public easement, over, through, in or upon any part of an enclosure, which is the property of a city, town, parish, religious society or of private proprietors and is used or appropriated for the burial of the dead, unless authority for that purpose is specially granted by law, or unless the consent of such city, town, parish, religious society or proprietors, respectively, is first obtained, shall be punished by a fine of not more than two thousand dollars or by imprisonment for not more than one year.

SECTION 77
Cruelty to animals
(Amended by 2012 Mass. Acts c. 193, § 49, effective Oct. 31, 2012; 2014 Mass. Acts c. 293, §§ 3–4, effective Nov. 18, 2014.)

Whoever overdrives, overloads, drives when overloaded, overworks, tortures, torments, deprives of necessary sustenance, cruelly beats, mutilates or kills an animal, or causes or procures an animal to be overdriven, overloaded, driven when overloaded, overworked, tortured, tormented, deprived of necessary sustenance, cruelly beaten, mutilated or killed; and whoever uses in a cruel or inhuman manner in a race, game, or contest, or in training therefor, as lure or bait a live animal, except an animal if used as lure or bait in fishing; and whoever, having the charge or custody of an animal, either as owner or otherwise, inflicts unnecessary cruelty upon it, or unnecessarily fails to provide it with proper food, drink, shelter, sanitary

2

environment, or protection from the weather, and whoever, as owner, possessor, or person having the charge or custody of an animal, cruelly drives or works it when unfit for labor, or willfully abandons it, or carries it or causes it to be carried in or upon a vehicle, or otherwise, in an unnecessarily cruel or inhuman manner or in a way and manner which might endanger the animal carried thereon, or knowingly and willfully authorizes or permits it to be subjected to unnecessary torture, suffering or cruelty of any kind shall be punished by imprisonment in the state prison for not more than 7 years in state prison or imprisonment in the house of correction for not more than 2½ years or by a fine of not more than $5,000 or by both fine and imprisonment; provided, however, that a second or subsequent offense shall be punished by imprisonment in the state prison for not more than 10 years or by a fine of not more than $10,000 or by both such fine and imprisonment. Notwithstanding section 26 of chapter 218 or any other general or special law to the contrary, the district courts and the divisions of the Boston municipal court department shall have original jurisdiction, concurrent with the superior court, of a violation of this section.

In addition to any other penalty provided by law, upon conviction for any violation of this section or of sections seventy-seven A, seventy-eight, seventy-eight A, seventy-nine A, seventy-nine B, eighty A, eighty B, eighty C, eighty D, eighty F, eighty-six, eighty-six A, eighty-six B or ninety-four the defendant shall forfeit to the custody of any society, incorporated under the laws of the commonwealth for the prevention of cruelty to animals or for the care and protection of homeless or suffering animals, the animal whose treatment was the basis of such conviction.

A person convicted of a crime of cruelty to an animal shall be prohibited from working in any capacity that requires such person to be in contact with an animal, including a commercial boarding or training establishment, shelter, animal control facility, pet shop, grooming facility, commercial breeder service, veterinary hospital or clinic or animal welfare society or other nonprofit organization incorporated for the purpose of providing for and promoting the welfare, protection and humane treatment of animals.

NOTE 1   "[W]here, as here, the terms of the statute are sufficiently defined so as to alert a pet owner that he or she may not throw a dog on its leash onto a deck with force enough to cause the animal to fall off the deck, twelve feet to its death, we perceive no constitutional infirmity." *Commonwealth v. Daly*, 90 Mass. App. Ct. 48, 51–52 (2016).

NOTE 2   Form of indictment—G.L. c. 277, § 79 (Cruelty to animals).

NOTE 3   Arrest without warrant—G.L. c. 272, § 82.

NOTE 4   Search warrants—G.L. c. 272, § 83.

SECTION 77A
Wilfully injuring police dogs and horses

Whoever wilfully tortures, torments, beats, kicks, strikes, mutilates, injures, disables or otherwise mistreats, a dog or horse owned by a police department or police agency of the commonwealth or any of its political subdivisions or whoever, wilfully by any action whatsoever, interferes with the lawful performance of such dog or horse shall be punished by a fine of not less than one hundred dollars and not more than five hundred dollars or by imprisonment for not more than two and one-half years or both. Persons violating this section

may be arrested without a warrant by any officer qualified to serve criminal process provided said offense is committed in his presence.

SECTION 77B
Exhibition of wild animals

No person shall exhibit or sponsor an exhibition of any wild animal for the purpose of attracting trade at or for any place of amusement, recreation or entertainment. This section shall not be deemed to prevent the exhibition of any wild animal in a zoological garden or in connection with any theatrical exhibition or circus or by any educational institution or wild animal farm, whether on or off the premises of such educational institution or wild animal farm. Whoever violates the provisions of this section shall be punished by a fine of not more than two hundred dollars or by imprisonment for not more than thirty days.

SECTION 78
Selling, leading or using horses not fit for work; forfeiture of auctioneer's license

No person holding an auctioneer's license shall receive or offer for sale or sell at public auction, nor shall any person sell at private sale, or lead, ride or drive on any public way, for any purpose except that of conveying the horse to a proper place for its humane keeping or killing, or for medical or surgical treatment, any horse which, by reason of debility, disease or lameness, or for other cause, could not be worked in the commonwealth without violating the laws against cruelty to animals. This section shall not prohibit the purchase of horses by humane societies incorporated under the laws of the commonwealth for the purpose of humanely killing the same. Violation of this section shall be punished by a fine of not less than five nor more than one hundred dollars or by imprisonment for not more than six months. If a licensed auctioneer violates this section, he shall also forfeit his license.

SECTION 78A
Sale of foals under five months; penalty

No person shall sell, offer for sale or otherwise dispose of any foal under five months of age other than for the purpose of immediate slaughter or humane killing unless such foal is accompanied by its dam. Violation of this section shall be punished by a fine of not more than one hundred dollars or by imprisonment for not more than six months.

SECTION 79
Corporation's responsibility under Secs. 77 and 78

A corporation violating either of the two preceding sections shall be punished by a fine as therein provided, and shall be responsible for the knowledge and acts of its agents and servants relative to animals transported, owned or used by it or in its custody.

SECTION 79A
Cutting bones or muscles to dock or set tail of horse; wound as evidence

Whoever cuts the bone of the tail of a horse for the purpose of docking the tail, or whoever causes or knowingly permits the same to be done upon premises of which he is the owner, lessee, proprietor or user, or whoever assists in or is present at such cutting, shall be punished by imprisonment for not more than one year or by a fine of not less than one hundred nor more than three hundred dollars; and whoever cuts the muscles or tendons of the tail of a horse for the purpose of setting up the tail, or whoever causes or knowingly permits the same to be done upon premises of which he is the owner, lessee, proprietor or user, or whoever assists in or is present at such cutting, shall be punished by a fine of not more than two hundred and fifty dollars. If a horse is found with the bone of its tail cut as aforesaid or with the muscles or tendons of its tail cut as aforesaid, and with the wound resulting from such cutting unhealed, upon the premises or in the charge and custody of any person, such fact shall be prima facie evidence of a violation of this section by the owner or user of such premises or the person having such charge or custody, respectively.

SECTION 79B
Exhibiting horse with tail cut under Sec. 79A; affidavit as to cutting in state where not prohibited; inspection

Whoever shows or exhibits at any horse show or exhibition in the commonwealth a horse with its tail cut in either manner prohibited in section seventy-nine A shall be punished by a fine of not more than two hundred and fifty dollars; provided, that this section shall not apply to the showing or exhibiting at such a show or exhibition of a horse with its tail cut in either manner prohibited by section seventy-nine A, if the owner of such horse furnishes to the manager or other official having charge of the horse show or exhibition at which such horse is shown or exhibited an affidavit by the owner, in a form approved by the director of the division of animal health of the department of food and agriculture, that the tail of such horse was so cut in a state wherein such cutting was not then specifically prohibited by the laws thereof and while the horse was actually owned by a legal resident of such state. Said affidavit shall state the year of such cutting, the name of the state wherein the cutting was done, and the sex and age of the horse, shall describe the markings of the horse, if any, and shall be subject to inspection by any officer or agent mentioned in section eighty-four.

SECTION 80
Repealed

SECTION 80½
Devocalization of dogs or cats; definitions; penalty; exceptions; records

(a) For the purposes of this section, the following words shall have the following meanings:—

"Board", the board of registration in veterinary medicine.

"Devocalization", a procedure on the larynx or vocal cords of an animal which causes the reduction or elimination of vocal sounds produced by that animal.

(b) Whoever performs, or causes to be performed, the surgical devocalization of a dog or cat shall be punished by imprisonment in the state prison for not more than 5 years or imprisonment in a house of correction for not more than 2½ years, or by a fine of not more than $2,500 or by both such fine and imprisonment. In addition to this penalty, the court may order that any person who violates this section shall successfully complete a course of instruction relative to the humane treatment of animals or be barred from owning or keeping a dog or cat or sharing a residence with another who owns or keeps a dog or cat for a period of time as determined by said court.

(c) Subsection (b) shall not apply if:

(1) the person performing such devocalization is licensed under section 55 of chapter 112; and

(2) surgical devocalization of a dog or cat is medically necessary to treat or relieve an illness, disease or injury or to correct a congenital abnormality that is causing or may cause the animal physical pain or harm; or

(3) the person who causes a devocalization procedure to be performed is relying upon the opinion of a person licensed under section 55 of chapter 112 that surgical devocalization of the dog or cat is medically necessary to treat or relieve an illness, disease or injury or to correct a congenital abnormality that is causing or may cause the animal physical pain or harm.

(d) A veterinarian who performs a surgical devocalization procedure on a dog or cat shall keep a record of the procedure for a period of 4 years after the last contact with the animal. This record shall include: the name and address of the animal's owner; the name and address of the person from whom payment is received for the procedure; a description of the animal, including its name, species, breed, date of birth, sex, color, markings and current weight; the license number and municipality that issued the license for the animal; the date and time of the procedure; the reason the procedure was performed; and any diagnostic opinion, analysis or test results to support the diagnosis. These records shall be subject to audit by the board.

Any person who performs a devocalization procedure on a dog or cat shall report the number of all such procedures to the board annually on or before March 30. The board shall maintain all notices received under this subsection for 4 years from the date of receipt.

Records maintained under this subsection shall not be considered a public record, as defined in clause twenty-sixth of section 7 of chapter 4 or section 10 of chapter 66, and these records shall not be publicly disseminated.

(e) The board shall, annually on or before March 1, report to the joint committee on the environment, natural resources and agriculture the number of animals that were the subject of devocalization notices received under subsection (d).

(f) Whoever being licensed under section 55 of chapter 112 violates any provision of this section shall be subject to the suspension or revocation of such license under section 59 of said chapter 112 and 256 C.M.R. 7.00.

SECTION 80A
Cropping or cutting off ear of dog; wound as prima facie evidence

Whoever, not being a veterinarian duly registered under chapter one hundred and twelve, crops or cuts off the whole or any part of the ear of a dog shall be punished by a fine of not more than two hundred and fifty dollars. If a dog with an ear cropped or cut off in whole or in part and with the wound resulting therefrom unhealed is found confined upon the premises or in the charge or custody of any person other than such veterinarian, or a dog officer of a city or town duly appointed under section one hundred and fifty-one of chapter one hundred and forty, such fact shall be prima facie evidence of a violation of this section by the person in control of such premises or the person having such charge or custody.

2

SECTION 80B
Exhibiting dogs with ears cropped or cut off

Whoever shows or exhibits or procures to be shown or exhibited at any dog show or exhibition in the commonwealth a dog with an ear or ears cropped or cut off, except when and as certified to be reasonably necessary by a veterinarian duly registered under the laws of the state of his residence, shall be punished by a fine of not more than two hundred and fifty dollars.

SECTION 80C
Taking cat, dog or bird to exhibit it, subject it to experimentation or mutilation, or to sell it for such purposes; application of law

Whoever, without the consent of the owner, takes a cat, dog or bird, with intent to exhibit or cause it to be exhibited or to subject it or cause it to be subjected to experimentation or mutilation while alive, or with intent to sell it or cause it to be sold for the purpose of being exhibited or subjected to experimentation or mutilation as aforesaid, shall be punished by a fine of not less than one hundred dollars nor more than the maximum fine permitted by law for the larceny of an article of the same value as such cat, dog or bird. This section shall not apply to an institution acquiring a cat, dog or bird under provisions of chapter forty-nine A.

SECTION 80D
Sale, etc. of living rabbits, baby chickens, ducklings or other fowl

No person shall sell, offer for sale, barter or give away as premiums living baby chickens, ducklings or other fowl under two months of age.

No person shall sell, offer for sale, barter, display or give away living rabbits, chickens, ducklings or other fowl which have been dyed, colored or otherwise treated so as to impart to them an artificial color.

Nothing in this section shall be construed to prohibit the sale or display of baby chickens, ducklings or other fowl under two months of age by breeders or stores engaged in the business of selling for purposes of commercial breeding and raising; provided, however, that prior to May first in any year, such ducklings may be sold or purchased only in quantities of twenty-four or more.

This section shall not prohibit, however, the sale or donation of such chickens, ducklings or fowl to schools for use in classroom instruction.

Whoever violates the provisions of this section shall be punished by a fine of not more than one hundred dollars.

SECTION 80E
Use of decompression chambers for putting animals to death

Whoever puts any animal to death by the use of a decompression chamber shall be punished by a fine of not less than one hundred dollars.

SECTION 80F
Giving away live animals as prize or award

No person shall offer or give away any live animal as a prize or an award in a game, contest or tournament involving skill or chance. The provisions of this section shall not apply to awards made to persons participating in programs relating to animal husbandry.

Whoever violates the provisions of this section shall be punished by a fine of not more than one hundred dollars.

SECTION 80G
Experiments on vertebrates; vivisection, dissection of animals; care

No school principal, administrator or teacher shall allow any live vertebrate to be used in any elementary or high school under state control or supported wholly or partly by public money of the state as part of a scientific experiment or for any other purpose in which said vertebrates are experimentally medicated or drugged in a manner to cause painful reactions or to induce painful or lethal pathological conditions, or in which said vertebrates are injured through any other type of treatment, experiment or procedure including but not limited to anesthetization or electric shock, or where the normal health of said animal is interfered with or where pain or distress is caused.

No person shall, in the presence of a pupil in any elementary or high school under state control or supported wholly or partly by public money of the state, practice vivisection, or exhibit a vivisected animal. Dissection of dead animals or any portions thereof in such schools shall be confined to the class room and to the presence of pupils engaged in the study to be promoted thereby, and shall in no case be for the purpose of exhibition.

Live animals used as class pets or for purposes not prohibited in paragraphs one and two hereof in such schools shall be housed or cared for in a safe and humane manner. Said animals shall not remain in school over periods when such schools are not in session, unless adequate care is provided at all times.

The provisions of the preceding three paragraphs shall also apply to any activity associated with or sponsored by the school.

Whoever violates the provisions of this section shall be punished by a fine of not more than one hundred dollars.

SECTION 80H
Motor vehicles; striking, injuring or killing dogs or cats

The operator of a motor vehicle that strikes and injures or kills a dog or cat shall forthwith report such an accident to the owner or custodian of said dog or cat or to a police officer in the town wherein such accident has occurred. A violation of this section shall be punished by a fine of not more than fifty dollars.

SECTION 80I
Prohibition against the rental or leasing of dogs

(a) As used in this section, the following words shall have the following meanings unless the context clearly requires otherwise:—

"Assistance and service dog", a canine specifically trained to help persons with disabilities or a canine trained to help a person with a disability in life; provided, however, that "assistance and service dog" shall also include a canine trained for search and rescue and a medical response dog.

"Canine foster care", an organization that places canines in a temporary home while awaiting pet adoption.

"Earth dog", a canine breed used as a hunting dog to track game above and below ground.

"Farm dog", a canine that works on a farm to assist humans or other animals.

"Pet adoption", the permanent ownership of and responsibility for a pet that a previous owner has abandoned or otherwise abdicated its responsibility.

"Renting and leasing", the practice of renting a dog for a fee or a cost which will knowingly result in a temporary possession of the animal by another party.

"Therapy dog", a canine that is used under the ownership and care of its handler that visits people for educational, medical or mental purposes.

(b) No person shall engage in the business of leasing or renting a dog. A dog held for such leasing or renting may be seized or impounded by an organization or agent thereof that is authorized to seize or impound animals under the General Laws. A violation of this section shall be punished by a fine of not less than $100 for the first violation, not less than $500 for the second violation and $1,000 for subsequent violations. Fines may be levied on both the business that is leasing a dog and the person that has entered into a rental agreement. Nothing in this section shall prohibit service animal businesses or organizations, pet adoption and foster care services, and working animals for the following purposes including, but not limited to: service animal businesses or organizations, pet adoption and foster care services, farming and agriculture, working dog activities, dogs working in entertainment and shows which are authorized to do so under the General Laws, dogs participating in performance sports or activities including, but not limited to, sporting, hunting, earth dog and racing dog activities and people engaged in breeding, training and showing dog, and dogs used for medical or scientific purposes so long as such use is lawful. This section shall not prohibit a pet store, kennel, pet adoption service or other entity authorized to sell pets under the General Laws for a fee or a cost from taking back a pet that it may have sold if the owner is unable to keep or handle that pet.

SECTION 81
Rest, water and feed for transported animals; lien; liability for detention

Railroad corporations shall not permit animals carried or transported by them to be confined in cars longer than twenty-eight consecutive hours without unloading them for at least five consecutive hours for rest, water and feeding, unless prevented by storm or accident. In estimating such confinement, the time during which the animals have been confined without such rest on connecting roads from which they are received shall be included. Animals so unloaded shall during such rest be properly fed, watered and sheltered by the owner or person having the custody of them, or, in case of his default, by the railroad corporation transporting them, at the expense of said owner or person in custody thereof. In such case the corporation shall have a lien upon such animals for food, care and custody furnished, and shall not be liable for such detention. A corporation, owner or custodian of such animals failing to comply with this section shall be punished by a fine of not less than one hundred nor more than five hundred dollars. This section shall not apply to animals carried in cars in which they can and do have proper food, water, space and opportunity for rest.

NOTE　　Arrest without warrant—see Section 82, below.

SECTION 82
Arrest without warrant for violation of Sec. 77 or 81; notice to owner; care of animals; lien

A person found violating any provision of section seventy-seven or eighty-one may be arrested and held without a warrant as provided in section fifty-four; the person making an arrest with or without a warrant shall use reasonable diligence to give notice thereof to the owner of animals found in the charge or custody of the person arrested, shall properly care and provide for such animals until the owner thereof takes charge of them, not, however, exceeding sixty days from the date of said notice, and shall have a lien on said animals for the expense of such care and provision.

SECTION 83
Complaint, warrant and search relative to cruelty to animals

If complaint is made to a court or magistrate authorized to issue warrants in criminal cases that the complainant has reasonable cause to believe that the laws relative to cruelty to animals have been or are violated in any particular building or place, such court or magistrate, if satisfied that there is reasonable cause for such belief, shall issue a search warrant authorizing any sheriff, deputy sheriff, constable or police officer to search such building or place; but no such search shall be made after sunset, unless specially authorized by the magistrate upon satisfactory cause shown.

SECTION 84
Prosecutions under Secs. 77 to 81

Sheriffs, deputy sheriffs, constables and police officers shall prosecute all violations of sections seventy-seven to eighty-one, inclusive, which come to their notice.

SECTION 85
Repealed

SECTION 85A
Injuring, taking away or harboring domesticated animals or birds; removal of dog license tag, collar or harness; imitation tag

Whoever with wrongful intent kills, maims, entices or carries away a dog or other domesticated animal or bird shall be liable in tort to its owner for three times its value. Any person who removes from the dog of another its license tag, collar or harness, or who, without the authorization of the owner or keeper, holds or harbors a dog or other domesticated animal of another, or who holds or harbors a lost or strayed dog or other domesticated animal for more than forty-eight hours after such animal comes into his possession without reporting or taking it to the police station or dog officer nearest to the place where it was found and informing the police officer or dog officer in charge where such dog or other animal was found, the name, color, age, size and pedigree, as fully as possible, of such animal and the person's own name and address, or who shall cause a dog to wear an imitation or counterfeit of the official tag prescribed by section one hundred and thirty-seven, one hundred and thirty-seven A or one hundred and thirty-seven B of chapter one hundred and forty, shall be punished by a fine of not more than one hundred dollars.

NOTE　　Related Statutes.

2

G.L. c. 266, § 47—Theft or abuse of dogs; removing collar of dog.

G.L. c. 266, § 132—Killing or frightening pigeons.

G.L. c. 272, § 87—Bird shooting.

SECTION 85B
Assistance animals stolen or attacked; actions for economic and non-economic damages

(a) A physically impaired person who uses an assistance animal or the owner of the assistance animal, may bring an action for economic and non-economic damages against a person who steals or attacks the assistance animal. The action authorized by this subsection may be brought by the physically impaired person or owner notwithstanding that the assistance animal was in the custody or under the supervision of another person when the theft or attack occurred. If any other non-assistance animal should attack an assistance animal, the owner of the assistance animal may seek compensation from the owner or custodian of the non-assistance animal found to have caused harm to the assistance animal.

(b) If the theft or attack of an assistance animal as described in subsection (a) results in the death of the animal or the animal is not returned or if injuries sustained prevent the assistance animal from returning to service, the measure of economic damages shall include, but are not limited to, the veterinary medical expenses and the replacement cost of an equally trained assistance animal, without any differentiation for the age or the experience of the animal.

(c) A cause of action shall not arise under this section if the physically impaired individual, owner or the individual having custody or supervision of the assistance animal was engaged in the commission of a crime at the time of injury sustained by the assistance animal.

SECTION 86
Stabling horses or mules on second or higher floors, in places other than cities

No person shall stable a horse or mule on the second or any higher floor of any building, unless there are two means of exit therefrom, at opposite ends of the building, to the main or street floor, unless such building is equipped with an automatic sprinkler system. This section shall not apply to cities.

NOTE   Punishment—G.L. c. 272, § 86F.

SECTION 86A
Stabling horses and mules above first floor or exceeding six in cities; use of exits

No person shall stable a horse or mule above the first or ground floor of any building not equipped with an automatic sprinkler system, or horses or mules exceeding six in all on the first or ground floor of any building not so equipped, unless there are two unobstructed means of exit from each floor whereon it or they are stabled, as far apart as practicable and so constructed as to grade that the said animal or animals can quickly and safely leave the building in case of fire and approved as to situation, arrangement and utility by the chief of the fire department. The person in charge of horses and mules stabled in any building not equipped with such a system and requiring two exits as aforesaid shall cause each such animal to use each such exit at least once a week. This and the four following sections shall apply only to cities.

NOTE   Punishment—G.L. c. 272, § 86F.

SECTION 86B
Stabling horses or mules exceeding fifteen

No person shall stable horses or mules exceeding fifteen in all at any one time in a building not equipped with an automatic sprinkler system unless a watchman is employed constantly on the premises to guard against fire.

NOTE   Punishment—G.L. c. 272, § 86F.
Applies to cities only—G.L. c. 272, § 86A.

SECTION 86C
Smoking in buildings used for stabling horses or mules

No person shall have a lighted cigarette, cigar or pipe in his possession in any building in which by the provisions of section eighty-six A two unobstructed means of exit are required or in which by the provisions of section eighty-six B the employment of a watchman is required, except in a room in said building made fire-resisting.

NOTE   Punishment—G.L. c. 272, § 86F.
Applies to cities only—G.L. c. 272, § 86A.

SECTION 86D
Pails of water and sand in buildings used for stables

On every floor of a building not equipped with an automatic sprinkler system, where horses or mules are stabled, there shall be kept in accessible locations and filled at all times, four pails of water and one pail of sand, for each one thousand square feet of floor space, to be used for no other purpose than extinguishing fires and to be so marked.

NOTE   Punishment—G.L. c. 272, § 86F.
Applies to cities only—G.L. c. 272, § 86A.

SECTION 86E
Entry upon premises to enforce Secs. 86A to 86D; ordering conditions remedied; service

The chief of the fire department or any person designated by him may, at all reasonable hours, enter into buildings within their jurisdiction where horses or mules are stabled, or upon premises adjacent thereto, for the purpose of enforcing sections eighty-six A to eighty-six D, inclusive, and if any such official or person so authorized finds the existence of conditions likely to cause a fire in such buildings or on such premises, he shall order such conditions to be remedied. Such order shall be served by delivering the same in hand or by posting the same in a conspicuous place on the building or premises affected thereby.

NOTE   Punishment—G.L. c. 272, § 86F.
Applies to cities only—G.L. c. 272, § 86A.

SECTION 86F
Punishment for violation of Secs. 86 to 86E or for neglect to comply with orders under Sec. 86E

Whoever violates any provision of sections eighty-six to eighty-six D, inclusive, shall be punished by a fine of not more than two hundred dollars or by imprisonment for not more than one month, or both. Whoever refuses or unreasonably neglects to comply with any order issued under section eighty-six E shall be punished by a fine of not more than ten dollars for each day during which such refusal or neglect continues after service of said order.

SECTION 87
Keeping or using birds to be shot at; shooting them; permitting premises to be used for shooting

Whoever keeps or uses any live bird, to be shot at either for amusement or as a test of skill in marksmanship, or shoots at a bird kept or used as aforesaid, or is a party to such shooting, or lets any building, room, field or premises, or knowingly permits the use thereof, for the purpose of such shooting, shall be punished by a fine of not more than fifty dollars or by imprisonment for not more than one month, or both. Nothing herein contained shall apply to the shooting of wild game.

NOTE   Related Statutes.
> G.L. c. 266, § 132—Killing or frightening pigeons.
> G.L. c. 272, § 85A—Injury to birds, etc.

SECTION 88
Complaints and warrants relative to fighting animals; searches; arrests

If complaint is made to a court or magistrate authorized to issue warrants in criminal cases that the complainant has reasonable cause to believe that preparations are being made for an exhibition of the fighting of birds, dogs or other animals, or that such exhibition is in progress, or that birds, dogs or other animals are kept, owned, possessed, trained, bred, loaned, sold, exported or otherwise transferred in violation of section 94 at any place or in any building or tenement, such court or magistrate, if satisfied that there is reasonable cause for such belief, shall issue a search warrant authorizing any sheriff, deputy sheriff, constable or police officer, or special police officer duly appointed by the colonel of the state police at the request of the Massachusetts Society for the Prevention of Cruelty to Animals or at the request of the Animal Rescue League of Boston, to search such place, building or tenement at any hour of the day or night and take possession of all such animals and all paraphernalia, implements, equipment or other property used or employed, or intended to be used or employed, in violation of section 94 there found, and arrest all persons there present.

SECTION 89
Entering without warrant place for exhibition of fighting animals; seizure of animals

Any officer authorized to serve criminal process, or any special police officer duly appointed by the colonel of the state police at the request of the Massachusetts Society for the Prevention of Cruelty to Animals, or any municipal officer involved with animal control may, without a warrant, enter any place or building in which there is an exhibition of any fighting birds, dogs or other animals, preparations are being made for such an exhibition, or birds, dogs or other animals are owned, possessed, kept, trained, bred, loaned, sold, exported or otherwise transferred in violation of section 94. Any such officer may arrest all persons there present and take possession of and remove from the place of seizure such animals there found in violation of said section 94, and hold the same in custody subject to the order of court as hereinafter provided.

SECTION 90
Custody of arrested persons; taking before court; proceedings

Persons arrested under either of the two preceding sections shall be kept in jail or other convenient place not more than twenty-four hours, Sundays and legal holidays excepted, at or before the expiration of which time they shall be taken before a district court and proceeded against according to law.

SECTION 91
Application for decree of forfeiture; notice; hearing; adjudication; returning or killing animals; claimant

After seizure and removal of animals or property used or employed, or intended to be used or employed, in violation of section 94, application shall be made to a district court for a decree of forfeiture of the animals or property. If, after hearing on the application, notice thereof having been previously given as the court orders, it shall be found that the animals, at the time of seizure, were engaged, or were intended to be engaged, in fighting at an exhibition thereof or the animals were owned, possessed, kept, trained, bred, loaned, sold, exported or otherwise transferred in violation of section 94, such animals shall be adjudged forfeited and the court shall thereupon, unless an appeal is taken as provided in the following section, issue an order for killing them. The order shall be directed to any officer authorized to serve criminal process and the officer receiving such order shall cause the animals to be killed within 24 hours thereafter. Animals or property seized as hereinbefore provided, which are not adjudged forfeited, shall be delivered to the owner or person entitled to the possession thereof. Any person shall be allowed to appear as claimant in the proceeding upon the application for a decree of forfeiture.

SECTION 92
Appeal; recognizance; custody and disposition of animals

An owner or claimant aggrieved by such judgment may, within twenty-four hours after the entry thereof and before its execution, appeal therefrom to the superior court; and all proceedings upon and after such appeal, including the right of exception, shall conform, so far as may be, to those in criminal cases, except that before such appeal is allowed the appellant shall recognize to the commonwealth in the sum of two hundred dollars, with sufficient sureties, to prosecute his appeal and to pay such expenses of the prosecution as the court may order and such expenses as may be thereafter incurred in the care and keeping of the birds, dogs or other animals claimed by such appellant if final judgment is rendered against them, and to abide the judgment of the court thereon. Upon the final judgment, the birds, dogs or other animals held in custody to abide such judgment shall be disposed of, under the direction of the superior court, in like manner as the court or justice might have disposed of them if no appeal had been taken. During the pendency of the appeal, all birds, dogs or other animals adjudged forfeited shall be kept in custody in a place other than that from which they were taken.

SECTION 92A
Advertisement, book, notice or sign relative to discrimination; definition of place of public accommodation, resort or amusement
(Amended by 2016 Mass. Acts c. 134, § 1, effective July 8, 2016, § 2 effective Oct. 1, 2016.)

No owner, lessee, proprietor, manager, superintendent, agent or employee of any place of public accommodation, resort or amusement shall, directly or indirectly, by himself or another, publish, issue, circulate, distribute or display, or cause to be published, issued, circulated, distributed or displayed, in

2

any way, any advertisement, circular, folder, book, pamphlet, written or painted or printed notice or sign, of any kind or description, intended to discriminate against or actually discriminating against persons of any religious sect, creed, class, race, color, denomination, sex, gender identity, sexual orientation, which shall not include persons whose sexual orientation involves minor children as the sex object, nationality, or because of deafness or blindness, or any physical or mental disability, in the full enjoyment of the accommodations, advantages, facilities or privileges offered to the general public by such places of public accommodation, resort or amusement.

A place of public accommodation, resort or amusement within the meaning hereof shall be defined as and shall be deemed to include any place, whether licensed or unlicensed, which is open to and accepts or solicits the patronage of the general public and, without limiting the generality of this definition, whether or not it be (1) an inn, tavern, hotel, shelter, roadhouse, motel, trailer camp or resort for transient or permanent guests or patrons seeking housing or lodging, food, drink, entertainment, health, recreation or rest; (2) a carrier, conveyance or elevator for the transportation of persons, whether operated on land, water or in the air, and the stations, terminals and facilities appurtenant thereto; (3) a gas station, garage, retail store or establishment, including those dispensing personal services; (4) a restaurant, bar or eating place, where food, beverages, confections or their derivatives are sold for consumption on or off the premises; (5) a rest room, barber shop, beauty parlor, bathhouse, seashore facilities or swimming pool, except such rest room, bathhouse or seashore facility as may be segregated on the basis of sex; (6) a boardwalk or other public highway; (7) an auditorium, theatre, music hall, meeting place or hall, including the common halls of buildings; (8) a place of public amusement, recreation, sport, exercise or entertainment; (9) a public library, museum or planetarium; or (10) a hospital, dispensary or clinic operating for profit; provided, however, that with regard to the prohibition on sex discrimination, this section shall not apply to a place of exercise for the exclusive use of persons of the same sex which is a bona fide fitness facility established for the sole purpose of promoting and maintaining physical and mental health through physical exercise and instruction, if such facility does not receive funds from a government source, nor to any corporation or entity authorized, created or chartered by federal law for the express purpose of promoting the health, social, educational vocational, and character development of a single sex; provided, further, that with regard to the prohibition of sex discrimination, those establishments which rent rooms on a temporary or permanent basis for the exclusive use of persons of the same sex shall not be considered places of public accommodation and shall not apply to any other part of such an establishment. An owner, lessee, proprietor, manager, superintendent, agent or employee of any place of public accommodation, resort or amusement that lawfully segregates or separates access to such place of public accommodation, or a portion of such place of public accommodation, based on a person's sex shall grant all persons admission to, and the full enjoyment of, such place of public accommodation or portion thereof consistent with the person's gender identity.

Any person who shall violate any provision of this section, or who shall aid in or incite, cause or bring about, in whole or in part, such a violation shall be punished by a fine of not more than one hundred dollars, or by imprisonment for not more than thirty days, or both.

NOTE   Related Statute. G.L. c. 272, § 98.

SECTION 93
Expenses of care and destruction of fighting animals

The necessary expenses incurred in the care and destruction of such birds, dogs and other animals may be allowed and paid in the same manner as expenses in criminal prosecutions.

SECTION 94
Owning, possessing or training fighting animals; establishing or promoting exhibition

Whoever: (i) owns, possesses, keeps or trains any bird, dog or other animal, with the intent that it shall be engaged in an exhibition of fighting; (ii) establishes or promotes an exhibition of the fighting of any birds, dogs or other animals; (iii) loans, sells, exports or otherwise transfers any bird, dog or other animal for the purpose of animal fighting; or (iv) owns, possesses or keeps any bird, dog or other animal for the purpose of breeding such animal with the intent that its offspring be used for animal fighting shall be punished by imprisonment in the state prison for not more than 5 years or in the house of correction for not more than 1 year, or by a fine of not more than $1,000 or by both such fine and imprisonment.

SECTION 95
Aiding or being present at exhibition of fighting animals

Whoever is present at any place, building or tenement where preparations are being made for an exhibition of the fighting of birds, dogs or other animals, with intent to be present at such exhibition, or is present at, aids in or contributes to such exhibition, shall be punished by a fine of not more than $1,000 or by imprisonment in the state prison for not more than 5 years or imprisonment in the house of correction for not more than 2½ years or by both such fine and imprisonment.

SECTION 96
False notice of birth, marriage or death

Whoever wilfully sends to the publisher of a newspaper for publication a false notice of a birth, marriage or death shall be punished by a fine of not more than one hundred dollars.

SECTION 97
Repealed

SECTION 97A
Demands, notices or other documents resembling court process; complaint; order to discontinue

Forms of demands or notices or other documents drawn to resemble court process shall not be used by attorneys at law, persons conducting collection agencies or others in the collection of bills, accounts or other indebtedness. A district court, on complaint of any person exhibiting and filing therewith such a form or document or copy thereof, alleging that a person who resides or has a place of business within the judicial district of such court has used or is using such form or document in violation of this section, may issue an order of notice to the person complained of to show cause why he should not be ordered to discontinue such use on penalty of contempt.

SECTION 98

Discrimination in admission to, or treatment in, place of public accommodation; punishment; forfeiture; civil right
(Amended by 2016 Mass. Acts c. 134, § 3, effective Oct. 1, 2016.)

Whoever makes any distinction, discrimination or restriction on account of race, color, religious creed, national origin, sex, gender identity, sexual orientation, which shall not include persons whose sexual orientation involves minor children as the sex object, deafness, blindness, or any physical or mental disability or ancestry relative to the admission of any person to, or his treatment in any place of public accommodation, resort or amusement, as defined in section ninety-two A, or whoever aids or incites such distinction, discrimination or restriction, shall be punished by a fine of not more than twenty-five hundred dollars or by imprisonment for not more than one year, or both, and shall be liable to any person aggrieved thereby for such damages as are enumerated in section five of chapter one hundred and fifty-one B; provided, however, that such civil forfeiture shall be of an amount not less than three hundred dollars; but such person so aggrieved shall not recover against more than one person by reason of any act of distinction, discrimination or restriction. All persons shall have the right to the full and equal accommodations, advantages, facilities and privileges of any place of public accommodation, resort or amusement subject only to the conditions and limitations established by law and applicable to all persons. This right is recognized and declared to be a civil right.

NOTE 1   **Related Statute.** G.L. c. 272, § 92A.

NOTE 2   "Provisions like these are well within the State's usual power to enact when a legislature has reason to believe a given group is the target of discrimination, and they do not as a general matter, violate the First or Fourteenth Amendments." However, the provision could not be applied to the private organizers of a parade. The organization could preclude groups from participating since each participating group affects the message conveyed by the parade organizers and "use of the State's power [to force participation of a particular group] violates the fundamental rule of protection under the First Amendment, that a speaker has the autonomy to choose the content of his own message." *Hurley v. Irish-American Gay Lesbian & Bisexual Group of Boston*, 515 U.S. 557, 572 (1995).

SECTION 98A

Accommodations and privileges of handicapped persons with guide dogs

Notwithstanding any other provision of law, any blind person, or deaf or hearing handicapped person, or other physically handicapped person accompanied by a dog guide, shall be entitled to any and all accommodations, advantages, facilities and privileges of all public conveyances, public amusements and places of public accommodation, within the commonwealth, to which persons not accompanied by dogs are entitled, subject only to the conditions and limitations applicable to all persons not accompanied by dogs, and no such blind person, or deaf or hearing handicapped, or other physically handicapped person shall be required to pay any charge or fare for or on account of the transportation on any public conveyance for himself and such dog so accompanying him in addition to the charge or fare lawfully chargeable for his own transportation. Whoever deprives any blind person, or deaf or hearing handicapped person, or other physically handicapped person of any right conferred by this section shall be punished by a fine of not more than three hundred dollars and shall be liable to any person aggrieved thereby for such damages as are set forth in section five of chapter one hundred and fifty-one B; provided, however, that such civic forfeiture shall be of an amount not less than one hundred dollars.

SECTION 98B

Discrimination in employment on public works or in public relief or transitional assistance

Whoever, knowingly and wilfully, employs discriminatory practices in the administration or giving of employment on public works or projects, or in the dispensing or giving of public relief or transitional assistance or any public benefit, because of race, color, religion or nationality, shall be punished by a fine of not more than one hundred dollars.

SECTION 98C

Libel relative to groups of persons; punishment; prosecutions; defenses

Whoever publishes any false written or printed material with intent to maliciously promote hatred of any group of persons in the commonwealth because of race, color or religion shall be guilty of libel and shall be punished by a fine of not more than one thousand dollars or by imprisonment for not more than one year, or both. The defendant may prove in defense that the publication was privileged or was not malicious. Prosecutions under this section shall be instituted only by the attorney general or by the district attorney for the district in which the alleged libel was published.

SECTION 99

Interception of wire and oral communications

Interception of wire and oral communications.—

A. Preamble.

The general court finds that organized crime exists within the commonwealth and that the increasing activities of organized crime constitute a grave danger to the public welfare and safety. Organized crime, as it exists in the commonwealth today, consists of a continuing conspiracy among highly organized and disciplined groups to engage in supplying illegal goods and services. In supplying these goods and services organized crime commits unlawful acts and employs brutal and violent tactics. Organized crime is infiltrating legitimate business activities and depriving honest businessmen of the right to make a living.

The general court further finds that because organized crime carries on its activities through layers of insulation and behind a wall of secrecy, government has been unsuccessful in curtailing and eliminating it. Normal investigative procedures are not effective in the investigation of illegal acts committed by organized crime. Therefore, law enforcement officials must be permitted to use modern methods of electronic surveillance, under strict judicial supervision, when investigating these organized criminal activities.

The general court further finds that the uncontrolled development and unrestricted use of modern electronic surveillance devices pose grave dangers to the privacy of all citizens of the commonwealth. Therefore, the secret use of such devices by private individuals must be prohibited. The use of such devices by law enforcement officials must be conducted under strict judicial supervision and should be limited to the investigation of organized crime.

B. Definitions. As used in this section—

2

1. The term "wire communication" means any communication made in whole or in part through the use of facilities for the transmission of communications by the aid of wire, cable, or other like connection between the point of origin and the point of reception.

2. The term "oral communication" means speech, except such speech as is transmitted over the public air waves by radio or other similar device.

3. The term "intercepting device" means any device or apparatus which is capable of transmitting, receiving, amplifying, or recording a wire or oral communication other than a hearing aid or similar device which is being used to correct subnormal hearing to normal and other than any telephone or telegraph instrument, equipment, facility, or a component thereof, (a) furnished to a subscriber or user by a communications common carrier in the ordinary course of its business under its tariff and being used by the subscriber or user in the ordinary course of its business; or (b) being used by a communications common carrier in the ordinary course of its business.

4. The term "interception" means to secretly hear, secretly record, or aid another to secretly hear or secretly record the contents of any wire or oral communication through the use of any intercepting device by any person other than a person given prior authority by all parties to such communication; provided that it shall not constitute an interception for an investigative or law enforcement officer, as defined in this section, to record or transmit a wire or oral communication if the officer is a party to such communication or has been given prior authorization to record or transmit the communication by such a party and if recorded or transmitted in the course of an investigation of a designated offense as defined herein.

5. The term "contents", when used with respect to any wire or oral communication, means any information concerning the identity of the parties to such communication or the existence, contents, substance, purport, or meaning of that communication.

6. The term "aggrieved person" means any individual who was a party to an intercepted wire or oral communication or who was named in the warrant authorizing the interception, or who would otherwise have standing to complain that his personal or property interest or privacy was invaded in the course of an interception.

7. The term "designated offense" shall include the following offenses in connection with organized crime as defined in the preamble: arson, assault and battery with a dangerous weapon, extortion, bribery, burglary, embezzlement, forgery, gaming in violation of section seventeen of chapter two hundred and seventy-one of the general laws, intimidation of a witness or juror, kidnapping, larceny, lending of money or things of value in violation of the general laws, mayhem, murder, any offense involving the possession or sale of a narcotic or harmful drug, perjury, prostitution, robbery, subornation of perjury, any violation of this section, being an accessory to any of the foregoing offenses and conspiracy or attempt or solicitation to commit any of the foregoing offenses.

8. The term "investigative or law enforcement officer" means any officer of the United States, a state or a political subdivision of a state, who is empowered by law to conduct investigations of, or to make arrests for, the designated offenses, and any attorney authorized by law to participate in the prosecution of such offenses.

9. The term "judge of competent jurisdiction" means any justice of the superior court of the commonwealth.

10. The term "chief justice" means the chief justice of the superior court of the commonwealth.

11. The term "issuing judge" means any justice of the superior court who shall issue a warrant as provided herein or in the event of his disability or unavailability any other judge of competent jurisdiction designated by the chief justice.

12. The term "communication common carrier" means any person engaged as a common carrier in providing or operating wire communication facilities.

13. The term "person" means any individual, partnership, association, joint stock company, trust, or corporation, whether or not any of the foregoing is an officer, agent or employee of the United States, a state, or a political subdivision of a state.

14. The terms "sworn" or "under oath" as they appear in this section shall mean an oath or affirmation or a statement subscribed to under the pains and penalties of perjury.

15. The terms "applicant attorney general" or "applicant district attorney" shall mean the attorney general of the commonwealth or a district attorney of the commonwealth who has made application for a warrant pursuant to this section.

16. The term "exigent circumstances" shall mean the showing of special facts to the issuing judge as to the nature of the investigation for which a warrant is sought pursuant to this section which require secrecy in order to obtain the information desired from the interception sought to be authorized.

17. The term "financial institution" shall mean a bank, as defined in section 1 of chapter 167, and an investment bank, securities broker, securities dealer, investment adviser, mutual fund, investment company or securities custodian as defined in section 1.165-12(c)(1) of the United States Treasury regulations.

18. The term "corporate and institutional trading partners" shall mean financial institutions and general business entities and corporations which engage in the business of cash and asset management, asset management directed to custody operations, securities trading, and wholesale capital markets including foreign exchange, securities lending, and the purchase, sale or exchange of securities, options, futures, swaps, derivatives, repurchase agreements and other similar financial instruments with such financial institution.

C. Offenses.

1. Interception, oral communications prohibited.

Except as otherwise specifically provided in this section any person who—

willfully commits an interception, attempts to commit an interception, or procures any other person to commit an interception or to attempt to commit an interception of any wire or oral communication shall be fined not more than ten thousand dollars, or imprisoned in the state prison for not more than five years, or imprisoned in a jail or house of correction for not more than two and one half years, or both so fined and given one such imprisonment.

Proof of the installation of any intercepting device by any person under circumstances evincing an intent to commit an interception, which is not authorized or permitted by this section, shall be prima facie evidence of a violation of this subparagraph.

2. Editing of tape recordings in judicial proceeding prohibited.

Except as otherwise specifically provided in this section any person who willfully edits, alters or tampers with any tape, transcription or recording of oral or wire communications by any means, or attempts to edit, alter or tamper with any tape, transcription or recording of oral or wire communications by any means with the intent to present in any judicial proceeding or proceeding under oath, or who presents such recording or permits such recording to be presented in any judicial proceeding or proceeding under oath, without fully indicating the nature of the changes made in the original state of the recording, shall be fined not more than ten thousand dollars or imprisoned in the state prison for not more than five years or imprisoned in a jail or house of correction for not more than two years or both so fined and given one such imprisonment.

3. Disclosure or use of wire or oral communications prohibited.

Except as otherwise specifically provided in this section any person who—

a. willfully discloses or attempts to disclose to any person contents of any wire or oral communication, knowing that the information was obtained through interception; or

b. willfully uses or attempts to use the contents of any wire or oral communication, knowing that the information was obtained through interception, shall be guilty of a misdemeanor punishable by imprisonment in a jail or a house of correction for not more than two years or by a fine of not more than five thousand dollars or both.

4. Disclosure of contents of applications, warrants, renewals, and returns prohibited.

Except as otherwise specifically provided in this section any person who—

willfully discloses to any person, any information concerning or contained in, the application for, the granting or denial of orders for interception, renewals, notice or return on an ex parte order granted pursuant to this section, or the contents of any document, tape, or recording kept in accordance with paragraph N, shall be guilty of a misdemeanor punishable by imprisonment in a jail or a house of correction for not more than two years or by a fine of not more than five thousand dollars or both.

5. Possession of interception devices prohibited.

A person who possesses any intercepting device under circumstances evincing an intent to commit an interception not permitted or authorized by this section, or a person who permits an intercepting device to be used or employed for an interception not permitted or authorized by this section, or a person who possesses an intercepting device knowing that the same is intended to be used to commit an interception not permitted or authorized by this section, shall be guilty of a misdemeanor punishable by imprisonment in a jail or house of correction for not more than two years or by a fine of not more than five thousand dollars or both.

The installation of any such intercepting device by such person or with his permission or at his direction shall be prima facie evidence of possession as required by this subparagraph.

6. Any person who permits or on behalf of any other person commits or attempts to commit, or any person who participates in a conspiracy to commit or to attempt to commit, or any accessory to a person who commits a violation of sub-

paragraphs 1 through 5 of paragraph C of this section shall be punished in the same manner as is provided for the respective offenses as described in subparagraphs 1 through 5 of paragraph C.

D. Exemptions.

1. Permitted interception of wire or oral communications.

It shall not be a violation of this section—

a. for an operator of a switchboard, or an officer, employee, or agent of any communication common carrier, whose facilities are used in the transmission of a wire communication, to intercept, disclose, or use that communication in the normal course of his employment while engaged in any activity which is a necessary incident to the rendition of service or to the protection of the rights or property of the carrier of such communication, or which is necessary to prevent the use of such facilities in violation of section fourteen A of chapter two hundred and sixty-nine of the general laws; provided, that said communication common carriers shall not utilize service observing or random monitoring except for mechanical or service quality control checks.

b. for persons to possess an office intercommunication system which is used in the ordinary course of their business or to use such office intercommunication system in the ordinary course of their business.

c. for investigative and law enforcement officers of the United States of America to violate the provisions of this section if acting pursuant to authority of the laws of the United States and within the scope of their authority.

d. for any person duly authorized to make specified interceptions by a warrant issued pursuant to this section.

e. for investigative or law enforcement officers to violate the provisions of this section for the purposes of ensuring the safety of any law enforcement officer or agent thereof who is acting in an undercover capacity, or as a witness for the commonwealth; provided, however, that any such interception which is not otherwise permitted by this section shall be deemed unlawful for purposes of paragraph P.

f. for a financial institution to record telephone communications with its corporate or institutional trading partners in the ordinary course of its business; provided, however, that such financial institution shall establish and maintain a procedure to provide semi-annual written notice to its corporate and institutional trading partners that telephone communications over designated lines will be recorded.

2. Permitted disclosure and use of intercepted wire or oral communications.

a. Any investigative or law enforcement officer, who, by any means authorized by this section, has obtained knowledge of the contents of any wire or oral communication, or evidence derived therefrom, may disclose such contents or evidence in the proper performance of his official duties.

b. Any investigative or law enforcement officer, who, by any means authorized by this section has obtained knowledge of the contents of any wire or oral communication, or evidence derived therefrom, may use such contents or evidence in the proper performance of his official duties.

c. Any person who has obtained, by any means authorized by this section, knowledge of the contents of any wire or oral communication, or evidence derived therefrom, may disclose such contents while giving testimony under oath or affirmation in any criminal proceeding in any court of the

United States or of any state or in any federal or state grand jury proceeding.

d. The contents of any wire or oral communication intercepted pursuant to a warrant in accordance with the provisions of this section, or evidence derived therefrom, may otherwise be disclosed only upon a showing of good cause before a judge of competent jurisdiction.

e. No otherwise privileged wire or oral communication intercepted in accordance with, or in violation of, the provisions of this section shall lose its privilege character.

E. Warrants: when issuable;

A warrant may issue only:

1. Upon a sworn application in conformity with this section; and

2. Upon a showing by the applicant that there is probable cause to believe that a designated offense has been, is being, or is about to be committed and that evidence of the commission of such an offense may thus be obtained or that information which will aid in the apprehension of a person who the applicant has probable cause to believe has committed, is committing, or is about to commit a designated offense may thus be obtained; and

3. Upon a showing by the applicant that normal investigative procedures have been tried and have failed or reasonably appear unlikely to succeed if tried.

F. Warrants: application.

1. Application. The attorney general, any assistant attorney general specially designated by the attorney general, any district attorney, or any assistant district attorney specially designated by the district attorney may apply ex parte to a judge of competent jurisdiction for warrant to intercept wire or oral communications. Each application ex parte for a warrant must be in writing, subscribed and sworn to by the applicant authorized by this subparagraph.

2. The application must contain the following:

a. A statement of facts establishing probable cause to believe that a particularly described designated offense has been, is being, or is about to be committed; and

b. A statement of facts establishing probable cause to believe that oral or wire communications of a particularly described person will constitute evidence of such designated offense or will aid in the apprehension of a person who the applicant has probable cause to believe has committed, is committing, or is about to commit a designated offense; and

c. That the oral or wire communications of the particularly described person or persons will occur in a particularly described place and premises or over particularly described telephone or telegraph lines; and

d. A particular description of the nature of the oral or wire communications sought to be overheard; and

e. A statement that the oral or wire communications sought are material to a particularly described investigation or prosecution and that such conversations are not legally privileged; and

f. A statement of the period of time for which the interception is required to be maintained. If practicable, the application should designate hours of the day or night during which the oral or wire communications may be reasonably expected to occur. If the nature of the investigation is such that the authorization for the interception should not automatically terminate when the described oral or wire communications have been first obtained, the application must specifically state facts establishing probable cause to believe that additional oral or wire communications of the same nature will occur thereafter; and

g. If it is reasonably necessary to make a secret entry upon a private place and premises in order to install an intercepting device to effectuate the interception, a statement to such effect; and

h. If prior application has been submitted or a warrant previously obtained for interception of oral or wire communications, a statement fully disclosing the date, court, applicant, execution, results, and present status thereof; and

i. If there is good cause for requiring the postponement of service pursuant to paragraph L, subparagraph 2, a description of such circumstances, including reasons for the applicant's belief that secrecy is essential to obtaining the evidence or information sought.

3. Allegations of fact in the application may be based either upon the personal knowledge of the applicant or upon information and belief. If the applicant personally knows the facts alleged, it must be so stated. If the facts establishing such probable cause are derived in whole or part from the statements of persons other than the applicant, the sources of such information and belief must be either disclosed or described; and the application must contain facts establishing the existence and reliability of any informant and the reliability of the information supplied by him. The application must also state, so far as possible, the basis of the informant's knowledge or belief. If the applicant's information and belief is derived from tangible evidence or recorded oral evidence, a copy or detailed description thereof should be annexed to or included in the application. Affidavits of person other than the applicant may be submitted in conjunction with the application if they tend to support any fact or conclusion alleged therein. Such accompanying affidavits may be based either on personal knowledge of the affiant or information and belief, with the source thereof, and reason therefor, specified.

G. Warrants: application to whom made.

Application for a warrant authorized by this section must be made to a judge of competent jurisdiction in the county where the interception is to occur, or the county where the office of the applicant is located, or in the event that there is no judge of competent jurisdiction sitting in said county at such time, to a judge of competent jurisdiction sitting in Suffolk County; except that for these purposes, the office of the attorney general shall be deemed to be located in Suffolk County.

H. Warrants: application how determined.

1. If the application conforms to paragraph F, the issuing judge may examine under oath any person for the purpose of determining whether probable cause exists for the issuance of the warrant pursuant to paragraph E. A verbatim transcript of every such interrogation or examination must be taken, and a transcription of the same, sworn to by the stenographer, shall be attached to the application and be deemed a part thereof.

2. If satisfied that probable cause exists for the issuance of a warrant the judge may grant the application and issue a warrant in accordance with paragraph I. The application and an attested copy of the warrant shall be retained by the issuing judge and transported to the chief justice of the superior court in accordance with the provisions of paragraph N of this section.

3. If the application does not conform to paragraph F, or if the judge is not satisfied that probable cause has been shown sufficient for the issuance of a warrant, the application must be denied.

I. Warrants: form and content.

A warrant must contain the following:

1. The subscription and title of the issuing judge; and

2. The date of issuance, the date of effect, and termination date which in no event shall exceed thirty days from the date of effect. The warrant shall permit interception of oral or wire communications for a period not to exceed fifteen days. If physical installation of a device is necessary, the thirty-day period shall begin upon the date of installation. If the effective period of the warrant is to terminate upon the acquisition of particular evidence or information or oral or wire communication, the warrant shall so provide; and

3. A particular description of the person and the place, premises or telephone or telegraph line upon which the interception may be conducted; and

4. A particular description of the nature of the oral or wire communications to be obtained by the interception including a statement of the designated offense to which they relate; and

5. An express authorization to make secret entry upon a private place or premises to install a specified intercepting device, if such entry is necessary to execute the warrant; and

6. A statement providing for service of the warrant pursuant to paragraph L except that if there has been a finding of good cause shown requiring the postponement of such service, a statement of such finding together with the basis therefor must be included and an alternative direction for deferred service pursuant to paragraph L, subparagraph 2.

J. Warrants: renewals.

1. Any time prior to the expiration of a warrant or a renewal thereof, the applicant may apply to the issuing judge for a renewal thereof with respect to the same person, place, premises or telephone or telegraph line. An application for renewal must incorporate the warrant sought to be renewed together with the application therefor and any accompanying papers upon which it was issued. The application for renewal must set forth the results of the interceptions thus far conducted. In addition, it must set forth present grounds for extension in conformity with paragraph F, and the judge may interrogate under oath and in such an event a transcript must be provided and attached to the renewal application in the same manner as is set forth in subparagraph 1 of paragraph H.

2. Upon such application, the judge may issue an order renewing the warrant and extending the authorization for a period not exceeding fifteen (15) days from the entry thereof. Such an order shall specify the grounds for the issuance thereof. The application and an attested copy of the order shall be retained by the issuing judge to be transported to the chief justice in accordance with the provisions of subparagraph N of this section. In no event shall a renewal be granted which shall terminate later than two years following the effective date of the warrant.

K. Warrants: manner and time of execution.

1. A warrant may be executed pursuant to its terms anywhere in the commonwealth.

2. Such warrant may be executed by the authorized applicant personally or by any investigative or law enforcement officer of the commonwealth designated by him for the purpose.

3. The warrant may be executed according to its terms during the hours specified therein, and for the period therein authorized, or a part thereof. The authorization shall terminate upon the acquisition of the oral or wire communications, evidence or information described in the warrant. Upon termination of the authorization in the warrant and any renewals thereof, the interception must cease at once, and any device installed for the purpose of the interception must be removed as soon thereafter as practicable. Entry upon private premises for the removal of such device is deemed to be authorized by the warrant.

L. Warrants: service thereof.

1. Prior to the execution of a warrant authorized by this section or any renewal thereof, an attested copy of the warrant or the renewal must, except as otherwise provided in subparagraph 2 of this paragraph, be served upon a person whose oral or wire communications are to be obtained, and if an intercepting device is to be installed, upon the owner, lessee, or occupant of the place or premises, or upon the subscriber to the telephone or owner or lessee of the telegraph line described in the warrant.

2. If the application specially alleges exigent circumstances requiring the postponement of service and the issuing judge finds that such circumstances exist, the warrant may provide that an attested copy thereof may be served within thirty days after the expiration of the warrant or, in case of any renewals thereof, within thirty days after the expiration of the last renewal; except upon a showing of important special facts which set forth the need for continued secrecy to the satisfaction of the issuing judge, said judge may direct that the attested copy of the warrant be served on such parties as are required by this section at such time as may be appropriate in the circumstances but in no event may he order it to be served later than three (3) years from the time of expiration of the warrant or the last renewal hereof. In the event that the service required herein is postponed in accordance with this paragraph, in addition to the requirements of any other paragraph of this section, service of an attested copy of the warrant shall be made upon any aggrieved person who should reasonably be known to the person who executed or obtained the warrant as a result of the information obtained from the interception authorized thereby.

3. The attested copy of the warrant shall be served on persons required by this section by an investigative or law enforcement officer of the commonwealth by leaving the same at his usual place of abode, or in hand, or if this is not possible by mailing the same by certified or registered mail to his known place of abode. A return of service shall be made to the issuing judge, except, that if such service is postponed as provided in subparagraph 2 of paragraph L, it shall be made to the chief justice. The return of service shall be deemed a part of the return of the warrant and attached thereto.

M. Warrant: return.

Within seven days after termination of the warrant or the last renewal thereof, a return must be made thereon to the judge issuing the warrant by the applicant therefor, containing the following:

a. a statement of the nature and location of the communications facilities, if any, and premises or places where the interceptions were made; and

b. the periods of time during which such interceptions were made; and

2

c. the names of the parties to the communications intercepted if known; and

d. the original recording of the oral or wire communications intercepted, if any; and

e. a statement attested under the pains and penalties of perjury by each person who heard oral or wire communications as a result of the interception authorized by the warrant, which were not recorded, stating everything that was overheard to the best of his recollection at the time of the execution of the statement.

N. Custody and secrecy of papers and recordings made pursuant to a warrant.

1. The contents of any wire or oral communication intercepted pursuant to a warrant issued pursuant to this section shall, if possible, be recorded on tape or wire or other similar device. Duplicate recordings may be made for use pursuant to subparagraphs 2 (a) and (b) of paragraph D for investigations. Upon examination of the return and a determination that it complies with this section, the issuing judge shall forthwith order that the application, all renewal applications, warrant, all renewal orders and the return thereto be transmitted to the chief justice by such persons as he shall designate. Their contents shall not be disclosed except as provided in this section. The application, renewal applications, warrant, the renewal order and the return or any one of them or any part of them may be transferred to any trial court, grand jury proceeding of any jurisdiction by any law enforcement or investigative officer or court officer designated by the chief justice and a trial justice may allow them to be disclosed in accordance with paragraph D, subparagraph 2, or paragraph O or any other applicable provision of this section.

The application, all renewal applications, warrant, all renewal orders and the return shall be stored in a secure place which shall be designated by the chief justice, to which access shall be denied to all persons except the chief justice or such court officers or administrative personnel of the court as he shall designate.

2. Any violation of the terms and conditions of any order of the chief justice, pursuant to the authority granted in this paragraph, shall be punished as a criminal contempt of court in addition to any other punishment authorized by law.

3. The application, warrant, renewal and return shall be kept for a period of five (5) years from the date of the issuance of the warrant or the last renewal thereof at which time they shall be destroyed by a person designated by the chief justice. Notice prior to the destruction shall be given to the applicant attorney general or his successor or the applicant district attorney or his successor and upon a showing of good cause to the chief justice, the application, warrant, renewal, and return may be kept for such additional period as the chief justice shall determine but in no event longer than the longest period of limitation for any designated offense specified in the warrant, after which time they must be destroyed by a person designated by the chief justice.

O. Introduction of evidence.

1. Notwithstanding any other provisions of this section or any order issued pursuant thereto, in any criminal trial where the commonwealth intends to offer in evidence any portions of the contents of any interception or any evidence derived therefrom the defendant shall be served with a complete copy of each document and item which make up each application, renewal application, warrant, renewal order, and

return pursuant to which the information was obtained, except that he shall be furnished a copy of any recording instead of the original. The service must be made at the arraignment of the defendant or, if a period in excess of thirty (30) days shall elapse prior to the commencement of the trial of the defendant, the service may be made at least thirty (30) days before the commencement of the criminal trial. Service shall be made in hand upon the defendant or his attorney by any investigative or law enforcement officer of the commonwealth. Return of the service required by this subparagraph including the date of service shall be entered into the record of trial of the defendant by the commonwealth and such return shall be deemed prima facie evidence of the service described therein. Failure by the commonwealth to make such service at the arraignment, or if delayed, at least thirty days before the commencement of the criminal trial, shall render such evidence illegally obtained for purposes of the trial against the defendant; and such evidence shall not be offered nor received at the trial notwithstanding the provisions of any other law or rules of court.

2. In any criminal trial where the commonwealth intends to offer in evidence any portions of a recording or transmission or any evidence derived therefrom, made pursuant to the exceptions set forth in paragraph B, subparagraph 4, of this section, the defendant shall be served with a complete copy of each recording or a statement under oath of the evidence overheard as a result of the transmission. The service must be made at the arraignment of the defendant or if a period in excess of thirty days shall elapse prior to the commencement of the trial of the defendant, the service may be made at least thirty days before the commencement of the criminal trial. Service shall be made in hand upon the defendant or his attorney by any investigative or law enforcement officer of the commonwealth. Return of the service required by this subparagraph including the date of service shall be entered into the record of trial of the defendant by the commonwealth and such return shall be deemed prima facie evidence of the service described therein. Failure by the commonwealth to make such service at the arraignment, or if delayed at least thirty days before the commencement of the criminal trial, shall render such service illegally obtained for purposes of the trial against the defendant and such evidence shall not be offered nor received at the trial notwithstanding the provisions of any other law or rules of court.

P. Suppression of evidence.

Any person who is a defendant in a criminal trial in a court of the commonwealth may move to suppress the contents of any intercepted wire or oral communication or evidence derived therefrom, for the following reasons:

1. That the communication was unlawfully intercepted.

2. That the communication was not intercepted in accordance with the terms of this section.

3. That the application or renewal application fails to set forth facts sufficient to establish probable cause for the issuance of a warrant.

4. That the interception was not made in conformity with the warrant.

5. That the evidence sought to be introduced was illegally obtained.

6. That the warrant does not conform to the provisions of this section.

Q. Civil remedy.

Any aggrieved person whose oral or wire communications were intercepted, disclosed or used except as permitted or authorized by this section or whose personal or property interests or privacy were violated by means of an interception except as permitted or authorized by this section shall have a civil cause of action against any person who so intercepts, discloses or uses such communications or who so violates his personal, property or privacy interest, and shall be entitled to recover from any such person—

1. actual damages but not less than liquidated damages computed at the rate of $100 per day for each day of violation or $1000, whichever is higher;

2. punitive damages; and

3. a reasonable attorney's fee and other litigation disbursements reasonably incurred. Good faith reliance on a warrant issued under this section shall constitute a complete defense to an action brought under this paragraph.

R. Annual report of interceptions of the general court.

On the second Friday of January, each year, the attorney general and each district attorney shall submit a report to the general court stating (1) the number of applications made for warrants during the previous year, (2) the name of the applicant, (3) the number of warrants issued, (4) the effective period for the warrants, (5) the number and designation of the offenses for which those applications were sought, and for each of the designated offenses the following: (a) the number of renewals, (b) the number of interceptions made during the previous year, (c) the number of indictments believed to be obtained as a result of those interceptions, (d) the number of criminal convictions obtained in trials where interception evidence or evidence derived therefrom was introduced. This report shall be a public document and be made available to the public at the offices of the attorney general and district attorneys. In the event of failure to comply with the provisions of this paragraph any person may compel compliance by means of an action of mandamus.

NOTE 1a   Eavesdropping in Private Home. "Warrantless electronic surveillance of conversations with the consent of just one of the parties does not violate the Constitution of the United States. *United States v. White*, 401 U.S. 745, 751 (1971). However, such surveillance, at least of conversations occurring in private homes, in the absence of evidence that the participants intended the contents to be broadcast, does violate art. 14 of the Massachusetts Declaration of Rights. *Commonwealth v. Blood*, 400 Mass. 61, 68–71 (1987). Furthermore, because such surveillance violates art. 14, the tapes and any testimony derived from them or from the transmissions is inadmissible in the Commonwealth's case-in-chief. *Id.* at 77.

"The sole issue in this case is whether, if the defendant should testify, the Commonwealth may introduce relevant portions of the tapes to impeach his testimony.

"[W]e answer the reported questions, 'No; the Commonwealth may not use the recorded conversations for impeachment purposes irrespective of whether the conversations dealt with collateral matters or directly with the crimes charged.' Of course, as in *Commonwealth v. Blood, supra*, the informant himself may testify to the conversations."

Commonwealth v. Fini, 403 Mass. 567, 568–69, 573–74 (1988) (footnote omitted).

NOTE 1b   Eavesdropping on Telephone Extension. "The troopers persuaded Disorbo to make two calls to the defendant at his home. Without the defendant's knowledge, but with Disorbo's consent, the troopers listened to these calls on an extension telephone."

Held, evidence admissible. "Unlike the defendant in the *Blood* case, he had no reason to assume that the conversation would not be heard by a third party. . . . Any expectation of privacy in a telephone conversation is not objectively reasonable, because a person is not reasonably entitled to assume that no one is listening in on an extension telephone."

Commonwealth v. Eason, 427 Mass. 595, 596, 600 (1998).

NOTE 2   Civil Ramifications. Defendants (management) clandestinely tape recorded parts of a meeting held by the plaintiff (tenants union).

Held,

1. "To be actionable under § 99(Q), then, an interception need not rise to the level of criminal conduct covered by the penal provisions of the law."

2. "'[C]oncurrent wrongdoers are independently liable under [this statute].'"

3. The plaintiffs were limited to statutory, not punitive, damages, especially since no actual harm was suffered.

4. The award of attorney fees was allowable.

Pine v. Rust, 404 Mass. 411, 414–17 (1989).

NOTE 3a "After the judge admitted the evidence, the defendant moved to strike it because the Commonwealth failed to comply with the mandatory provisions of the Massachusetts wiretap statute (act), G.L. c. 272, § 99. The pertinent provisions of the act require law enforcement officials of the Commonwealth to serve the defendant at least 30 days before trial with various documents and copies of intercepted conversations that the Commonwealth intends to use as evidence against the defendant at trial. G.L. c. 272, § 99(O)(1) (1986 ed.). . . .

"The failure of the Commonwealth to make service on the defendant rendered the evidence 'illegally obtained for purposes of the trial against the defendant.' G.L. c. 272, § 99(O)(1). Such illegally-obtained evidence may be suppressed by filing a timely motion to suppress. See § 99(P). . . .

"[D]espite the defendant's failure to file a timely motion to suppress, the Commonwealth is barred from offering the evidence [due to the language in G.L. c. 272, § 99(O)(1)]."

Commonwealth v. Picardi, 401 Mass. 1008, 1008–09 (1988) (rescript).

NOTE 3b   Federal Wiretaps. "While we reserved our opinion on a similar issue in [*Picardi*], we now consider whether the discovery provision of the wiretap statute is applicable to interceptions made by the Federal government, authorized by order of a Federal court. We are persuaded that §§ 99(O)(1) does not apply to such evidence." *Commonwealth v. Anguilo*, 415 Mass. 502, 517 (1993).

NOTE 4a   Wiretap by Private Person. "A private individual, apparently engaged in unlawful activity himself, recorded the defendant's conversations in violation of § 99. No deterrent purpose would be served by suppressing the intercepted conversations. The exclusionary rule was not designed to protect persons from the consequences of the unlawful seizure of evidence by their associates in crime. See § 99 A (preamble)." *Commonwealth v. Santoro*, 406 Mass. 421, 423 (1990); *see also Commonwealth v. Crowley*, 43 Mass. App. Ct. 919, 920 (1997) (Boarder made secret tape recordings of defendants beating their 7 year old child. Conviction affirmed. "The Legislature has left it to the courts to decide whether unlawfully intercepted communications must be suppressed. . .' 99(P) alone does not provide a mechanism for suppression" (quoting *Commonwealth v. Santoro*, 406 Mass. at 423)).

NOTE 4b "Here, following *Santoro*, [406 Mass. 421 (1990),] two factors compel denial of the motion to suppress. First, the police had no part in making, inducing, soliciting, or otherwise encouraging or abetting the making of the surveillance tape. The tape, evidence of a grave crime, fell into their hands. . . .

"Second . . . While the law bars all clandestine audio recording by private individuals, it was not intended to penalize the State when individuals with evidence pertaining to an ongoing murder investigation voluntarily disclose what they know to law enforcement authorities.

2

"Finally, had the Legislature intended the suppression of audio evidence in the circumstances present here (the use by police of a recording not of their making in an ongoing murder investigation), it has had ample opportunity to amend the statute accordingly. Since the *Santoro* decision, the Legislature twice has amended the wiretap statute but has not disturbed the statutory construction we established in that case." *Commonwealth v. Rivera*, 445 Mass. 119, 124, 126–27 (2005).

NOTE 5a   Issuance of Search Warrant. "[A]ny defect in the issuance of the search warrants was irrelevant because, under G.L. c. 272, § 99(B)(4) (1988 ed.), the consensual recording was not an 'interception' and thus no search warrant was needed. The authorization by the informant to record and transmit the communications, coupled with the fact that the recording and transmitting occurred 'in the course of an investigation of a designated offense as defined' in § 99(B)(4), meant that the secret hearing and recording of conversations by the police was not an 'interception.'

"The statutory procedures of § 99 concerning 'interceptions' had no application to this situation because, as the judge initially ruled, under § 99(B)(4), there was no 'interception.'" *Commonwealth v. Davis*, 407 Mass. 1001, 1002 (1990) (rescript).

NOTE 5b   Probable Cause. "[W]e conclude that a motion judge should make a de novo probable cause determination based on the affidavit accompanying an application for a wiretap warrant and any omitted tangible or recorded oral evidence, regardless of whether the failure to include that evidence in the warrant application was intentional or reckless." *Commonwealth v. Long*, 454 Mass. 542, 554 (2009).

NOTE 6 "General Laws c. 272, § 99E3, provides that a warrant authorizing a wiretap may issue only on 'a showing by the applicant that normal investigative procedures have been tried and have failed or reasonably appear unlikely to succeed if tried.'

"In meeting its statutory burden of establishing necessity, '[t]he Commonwealth need not show that traditional investigative techniques were wholly unsuccessful or that the police had exhausted all other investigative procedures before filing its application for a warrant authorizing a wiretap.' The necessity requirement is meant to 'assure that wiretapping is not resorted to in situations where traditional investigative techniques would suffice to expose the crime.' The affidavit will be adequate if it indicates a reasonable likelihood that normal investigative techniques have failed in gathering evidence or would fail if attempted. In determining whether the Commonwealth has met its burden, the affidavit should be read in a 'practical and common sense manner.'" *Commonwealth v. Fenderson*, 410 Mass. 82, 83–84 (1991) (citations omitted).

NOTE 7   Seven Day Return Requirement. "On appeal, the defendant . . . claims that suppression of all of the wiretap evidence was automatically required because of the Commonwealth's failure to comply with the statutory seven-day period. The statute, however, has not been construed so stringently. A slight delay in complying with the seven-day period will not require the suppression of wiretap evidence where, as here, the Commonwealth has acted in good faith and has not obtained any tactical advantage from the delay, and where there is no evidence that the tapes have been compromised. The short three-day delay by the Commonwealth in filing the return did not require suppression of the wiretap evidence." *Commonwealth v. Ricci*, 57 Mass. App. Ct. 155, 162 (2003) (citations omitted). *See also Commonwealth v. Vitello*, 367 Mass. 224, 275–76 (1975) (two days beyond seven day requirement did not warrant suppression).

NOTE 8   Prison Calls. "The issue in this interlocutory appeal is whether an audiotape recording by the Department of Correction (department) of a three-way telephone conversation among an inmate at the Plymouth County house of correction, the defendant and a codefendant must be suppressed pursuant to G.L. c. 272,§ 99P, where the inmate and the codefendant knew that the conversation was being recorded, but the defendant did not. We conclude that the recording need not be suppressed." *Common-*

wealth v. Ennis, 439 Mass. 64, 64–65 (2003) ("Certainly the department did not 'secretly record' any part of the resulting conversation wilfully. The department informed all of the anticipated parties to the collect telephone call that their communications would be recorded. The wiretap act is not so broad as to impose liability each time an additional party is added to a two-party conversation in circumstances beyond the recorder's knowledge, direction, or control.").

NOTE 9   Wireless Telephones. "It is clear that the exclusionary provision of Title III [18 U.S.C.S. § 2510 et seq.] 'now applies to the interception of conversations over both cellular and cordless phone.'" *Commonwealth v. Damiano*, 444 Mass. 444, 449 (2005) (quoting *Bartnicki v. Vopper*, 532 U.S. 514, 524 (2001)).

NOTE 10   Circumstantial Evidence. "Despite the lack of a tape, there was ample circumstantial evidence that the defendant made an unlawful secret recording, including (1) his possession of a device, together with the microphone secreted in his jacket, (2) the fact that the microphone was pointed in the direction of the officers during their conversation with the defendant, (3) the odd manner in which the defendant put his questions to police, and (4) the tapes he discarded into the crowd." *Commonwealth v. Manzelli*, 68 Mass. App. Ct. 691, 694 (2007) (footnote omitted).

NOTE 11   Authority to Issue Warrants. "Based on the language of the Massachusetts wiretap statute and the legislative history surrounding the Federal wiretap statute, we conclude that a Superior Court judge possesses the authority under the Massachusetts wiretap statute to issue warrants permitting the interception of cellular telephone calls and text messages." *Commonwealth v. Moody*, 466 Mass. 196, 198 (2013).

SECTION 99A
Overhearing deliberations of jury by using devices

Whoever secretly overhears, or attempts secretly to overhear or to have any other person overhear the deliberations of a jury by use of a device commonly known as a dictograph or dictaphone, or however otherwise described, or by any similar device or arrangement with intent to procure any information relative to the conduct of such jury or any of its members, shall be punished by imprisonment for not more than five years or by a fine of not more than five thousand dollars, or both.

SECTIONS 100–103
Repealed

SECTION 104
Security for seizure and impoundment of animals relating to cruelty to animals or animal fighting

(a) As used in this section the word "Authority" shall mean an organization or authorized agent thereof that seizes or impounds an animal pursuant to the General Laws.

(b) If an animal is lawfully seized or impounded pursuant to the General Laws relating to cruelty to animals or animal fighting, the owner, custodian or person claiming an interest in the animal, shall be given a show cause hearing within 30 days after application for the complaint.

(c) If an animal is lawfully seized and impounded, the authority may file a petition with the court requesting that the person from whom an animal is seized or a person claiming an interest in the seized animal, be ordered to post a security. The authority shall serve a copy of the petition on the person from whom the animal was seized, or if the person cannot be found, by posting of copy at the place where the animal was taken into custody. The authority shall also serve a copy of the petition on the district attorney. The court may order that person to post a security.

(d) The security shall be in an amount sufficient to secure payment for all reasonable expenses to be incurred by the authority having custody of the seized animal for a temporary period of at least 30 days. The amount of the security shall be determined by the court upon the recommendation of the authority. Reasonable expenses shall include, but shall not be limited to, estimated medical care, shelter, and board.

(e) When security is posted in accordance with this section, the authority may draw from the security the actual reasonable costs incurred for medical care, shelter, and board.

(f) If the court orders the posting of security, the security shall be posted with the clerk within 10 business days of the show cause hearing. The court shall order the immediate forfeiture of the seized animal to the authority if the person fails to post security as ordered. The court may waive the security requirement or reduce the amount of the security for good cause shown.

(g) Posting of the security shall not prevent the authority from disposing of the seized or impounded animal before the expiration of the period covered by the security, if the court rules in favor of the authority.

(h) The authority may humanely dispose of the animal at the end of the period for which expenses are covered by the security, if the court orders the disposition. If the disposition order is denied, the court may require the owner or custodian or any other person claiming interest in the animal, to provide additional security to secure payment of reasonable expenses and to extend the period of time pending adjudication by the court of the charges against the person from whom the animal was seized.

(i) The owner or custodian of an animal humanely killed pursuant to this section shall not be entitled to recover damages or the actual value of the animal if the owner or custodian failed to post security.

(j) The court may direct a refund to the person who posted the security in whole or part for any expenses not incurred by the authority. The court may direct a refund to the person who posted security upon acquittal of the charges.

SECTION 105
Photographing, videotaping or electronically surveilling partially nude or nude person; exceptions; punishment
(Amended by 2014 Mass. Acts c. 43, effective Mar. 7, 2014.)

(a) As used in this section, the following words shall have the following meanings unless the context clearly requires otherwise:

"Electronically surveils" or "electronically surveilled", to view, obtain or record a person's visual image by the use or aid of a camera, cellular or other wireless communication device, computer, television or other electronic device.

"Partially nude", the exposure of the human genitals, buttocks, pubic area or female breast below a point immediately above the top of the areola.

"Sexual or other intimate parts", human genitals, buttocks, pubic area or female breast below a point immediately above the tip of the areola, whether naked or covered by clothing or undergarments.

(b) Whoever willfully photographs, videotapes or electronically surveils another person who is nude or partially nude, with the intent to secretly conduct or hide such activity, when the other person in such place and circumstance would have a reasonable expectation of privacy in not being so photographed, videotaped or electronically surveilled, and without that person's knowledge and consent, shall be punished by imprisonment in the house of correction for not more than 2½ years or by a fine of not more than $5,000, or by both such fine and imprisonment.

Whoever willfully photographs, videotapes or electronically surveils, with the intent to secretly conduct or hide such activity, the sexual or other intimate parts of a person under or around the person's clothing to view or attempt to view the person's sexual or other intimate parts when a reasonable person would believe that the person's sexual or other intimate parts would not be visible to the public and without the person's knowledge and consent, shall be punished by imprisonment in the house of correction for not more than 2½ years or by a fine of not more than $5,000, or by both fine and imprisonment.

Whoever willfully photographs, videotapes or electronically surveils, with the intent to secretly conduct or hide such activity, the sexual or other intimate parts of a child under the age of 18 under or around the child's clothing to view or attempt to view the child's sexual or other intimate parts when a reasonable person would believe that the person's sexual or other intimate parts would not be visible to the public shall be punished by imprisonment in the house of correction for not more than 2½ years, by imprisonment in the state prison for not more than 5 years, or by a fine of not more than $10,000, or by both such fine and imprisonment.

(c) Whoever willfully disseminates the visual image of another person, with knowledge that such visual image was unlawfully obtained in violation of the first and second paragraphs of subsection (b) and without consent of the person so depicted, shall be punished by imprisonment in the house of correction for not more than 2½ years or in the state prison for not more than 5 years or by a fine of not more than $10,000, or by both such fine and imprisonment.

Whoever willfully disseminates the visual image of the sexual or other intimate parts of a child under the age of 18, with knowledge that such visual image was unlawfully obtained in violation of the third paragraph of subsection (b) shall be punished by imprisonment in the house of correction for not more than 2½ years or in the state prison for not more than 10 years or by a fine of not more than $10,000, or by both such fine and imprisonment.

(d) This section shall not apply to a merchant that electronically surveils a customer changing room, provided that signage warning customers of the merchant's surveillance activity is conspicuously posted at all entrances and in the interior of any changing room electronically surveilled.

(e) This section shall not apply to a law enforcement officer acting within the scope of the officer's authority under applicable law, or by an order or warrant issued by a court.

(f) A sheriff, deputy sheriff or police officer may arrest without a warrant, a person whom he has probable cause to believe has violated this section.

(g) A photograph, videotape or other recorded visual image, depicting a person who is nude or partially nude or which depicts a person's sexual or other intimate parts that is part of any court record arising from a prosecution under this section, shall not be open to public inspection and shall only be made available by court personnel to a law enforcement officer, prosecuting attorney, defendant's attorney, defendant, or victim connected to such prosecution for inspection, unless otherwise ordered by the court.

2

(h) In a prosecution under this section, a justice of the superior court or district court may issue appropriate orders to restrain or prevent the unlawful dissemination of a person's visual image in violation of this section.

SECTION 106
Stolen valor; penalty
(Added by 2015 Mass. Acts c. 128, effective Feb. 21, 2016.)

(a) A person commits the crime of stolen valor if that person knowingly, with the intent to obtain money, property or any other tangible benefit:

(i) fraudulently represents such person to be an active member or veteran of the United States Navy, Army, Air Force, Marines or Coast Guard, including armed forces reserves and National Guard through the unauthorized manufacture, sale or use of military regalia or gear, including the

wearing of military uniforms, or the use of falsified military identification and obtains money, property or another tangible benefit through such fraudulent representation; or

(ii) fraudulently represents such person to be a recipient of the Congressional Medal of Honor, Distinguished Service Cross, Navy Cross, Air Force Cross, Silver Star, Purple Heart, Combat Infantryman Badge, Combat Action Badge, Combat Medical Badge, Combat Action Ribbon or Air Force Combat Action Medal and obtains money, property or another tangible benefit through such fraudulent representation.

(b) Any person who commits the crime of stolen valor shall be punished by imprisonment in a house of correction for not more than 1 year or by a fine of $1,000, or both such fine and imprisonment.

Chapter 273. Desertion, Non-Support and Illegitimacy

Section

1	Abandonment and nonsupport; failure to comply with order for support; decree establishing rights of spouse as prima facie evidence
2	Jurisdiction; venue; supervision of parent by municipal or district court probation officers
3	Fines paid to probation officer or state treasurer
4–5	Repealed
6	Recognizance on release on probation; compliance with judgment or order for support; forfeiture
7	Evidence of marriage and parentage; husband and wife as witnesses; self-incrimination; evidence of wilfulness; confidential communications
8	Lack of custody as defense; duty to support child
9	Repealed
10	Uniform construction
11–12	Repealed
12A	Repealed
13–14	Repealed
15	Duty to support child born out of wedlock; conclusiveness of adjudication or acknowledgment of paternity
15A	Abandonment and willful nonsupport; penalties; alternative sentencing; restitution
15B	Concealing assets of another for purpose of avoiding payment of order of judgment for support; punishment
16	Application of Secs. 2, 6, 7, and 10
17	Dismissal of case
18	Money forfeited or recovered upon recognizance or deposit used for support
18A	Support obligations under prior law; enforcement; insurance coverage; amended orders
19	Repealed
20	Neglect or refusal to support parent
21	Venue; complainants
22	Orders under Sec. 5, and practice under Secs. 1 to 10 of this chapter
23	Needy disabled persons; neglect or refusal of parents to support; penalty

SECTION 1
Abandonment and nonsupport; failure to comply with order for support; decree establishing rights of spouse as prima facie evidence

A spouse or parent shall be guilty of a felony and shall be subject to the penalties set forth in section fifteen A if:

(1) he abandons his spouse or minor child without making reasonable provisions for the support of his spouse or minor child or both of them; or

(2) he leaves the commonwealth and goes into another state without making reasonable provisions for the support of his spouse or minor child or both of them; or

(3) he enters the commonwealth from another state without making reasonable provisions for the support of his spouse or minor child, or both of them, domiciled in another state; or

(4) wilfully and while having the financial ability and earning capacity to have complied, he fails to comply with an order or judgment for support which has been entered pursuant to chapter one hundred and nineteen, two hundred and seven, two hundred and eight, two hundred and nine, two hundred and nine C or two hundred and seventy-three, or received, entered or registered pursuant to chapter two hundred and nine D, or entered pursuant to similar laws of other states. No civil proceeding in any court shall be held to be a bar to a prosecution hereunder but the court shall not enter any order pursuant to section fifteen A which would directly or indirectly result in a decrease in the amount paid for current support pursuant to an order or judgment on behalf of the child or spouse to who, or on whose behalf, support is owed.

In a prosecution hereunder a decree or judgment of a probate court in a proceeding in which the defendant or spouse appeared or was personally served with process, establishing the right of his spouse to live apart or the freedom of such spouse to convey and deal with property, or the right to the custody of the children, shall be admissible and shall be prima facie evidence of such right.

NOTE 1a   Both parents have a duty to support their children. *Silvia v. Silvia*, 9 Mass. App. Ct. 339 (1980).

NOTE 1b   **Related Statute.** G.L. c. 208, § 19—Care, maintenance and support of minor children.

NOTE 2   "There is a presumption of legitimacy in the case of a child born in wedlock which can be overcome only by facts which prove beyond reasonable doubt that the husband could not have been the father. Proof of the impotency of the husband or no access to his wife is held to be sufficient." Likewise, exclusion determined by a blood test is also sufficient. *Commonwealth v. Stappen*, 336 Mass. 174, 177 (1957) (citations omitted).

NOTE 3   Section 12A providing for blood grouping tests in "any proceeding to determine the question of paternity" is inapplicable to a proceeding brought for nonsupport of a minor child under Section 1. *Commonwealth v. Stappen*, 336 Mass. 174, 175 (1957).

NOTE 4   Under the provisions of G.L. c. 273, § 7, proof of neglect by a husband to make reasonable provision for the support of his wife was sufficient to warrant a conviction of nonsupport under Section 1, although no evidence was offered of his ability to provide for her. *Commonwealth v. Truczinskas*, 318 Mass. 298 (1945).

NOTE 5   Evidence that (1) the defendant was able to work but made little effort to find employment and (2) he did not provide support for his wife and children warranted conviction. *Commonwealth v. Marino*, 343 Mass. 725 (1962).

NOTE 6   The test of criminal responsibility for failure to support a wife is unreasonableness. "That necessitates an inquiry into the matrimonial conduct of the wife, the comparative means, responsibilities and needs of both husband and wife, and all the circumstances that a fair minded person would consider in apportioning the income of the disrupted family." *Commonwealth v. Whiston*, 306 Mass. 65, 66 (1940).

NOTE 7   "There is no requirement that the provision for support be made on a weekly or monthly basis rather than by some other financial arrangement which relates to the period in question [two months]." *Commonwealth v. Zarilli*, 5 Mass. App. Ct. 518, 520 (1977).

NOTE 8   Complaint brought in June, 1980, alleged nonsupport of the defendant's wife and children from October 10, 1974, to the present. Lower court judge dismissed the complaint on the ground of excessive delay by the commonwealth in instituting the complaint. The appellate court reversed. There was no evidence of prejudice to the defendant, nor evidence of an intentional undertaking to gain a tactical advantage, nor a reckless disregard of known risks to the defendant's ability to mount a defense, nor evidence of gross governmental unfairness. *Commonwealth v. Geoghegan*, 12 Mass. App. Ct. 575 (1981).

SECTION 2
Jurisdiction; venue; supervision of parent by municipal or district court probation officers

Proceedings under section one shall be begun if in the superior court, in the county in which is situated the place where the husband and wife last lived together or where the husband or wife or parent of the child is living, and, if begun in a district court, in the court having such place within its judicial district; provided, that such a proceeding for an offense committed within the territorial limits of the Boston, the Worcester, Bristol county or the Springfield juvenile court, as designated by section fifty-seven of chapter two hundred and eighteen, if founded upon the same allegations as a proceeding under sections twenty-four to twenty-seven, inclusive, of chapter one hundred and nineteen, may be brought, heard and disposed of in said juvenile courts. Such a proceeding for an offense committed within the territorial limits prescribed for the criminal jurisdiction of any court other than the courts within the territorial limits of the Boston, the Worcester, Bristol county and the Springfield juvenile courts, if founded upon the same allegations as a proceeding under said sections twenty-four to twenty-seven, inclusive, of chapter one hundred and nineteen, may be heard and disposed of in the juvenile session of the court. Any parent placed on probation in such a proceeding in any of said juvenile courts shall at the request of the justice thereof be supervised by the probation officers of the municipal or district courts located within the territorial limits of that juvenile court.

SECTION 3
Fines paid to probation officer or state treasurer

The court imposing a fine under section fifteen A may at any time order it paid in whole or in part to a probation of-

ficer, to be paid by him to the spouse or to the city, town, corporation, society or person actually supporting the spouse, child or children, or to the state treasurer for the use of the department of children and families if the child has been committed to said department.

SECTION 4
Repealed

NOTE   For subject matter of former Section 4, see G.L. c. 209C, §§ 15, 19 (not in this book).

SECTION 5
Repealed

NOTE   For subject matter of former Section 5, see Section 18A of this chapter.

SECTION 6
Recognizance on release on probation; compliance with judgment or order for support; forfeiture

The court shall also have the power to release the defendant from custody on probation for a period so fixed, upon his or her entering into a recognizance, with or without surety, in such sum as the court may order and approve. The condition of the recognizance shall be such that if the defendant shall make his personal appearance in court whenever ordered to do so, and shall further comply with the terms of any currently enforceable judgment or order for support entered pursuant to any civil action, including an action for annulment, divorce, separate support, or paternity and support, under chapters two hundred and seven, two hundred and eight, two hundred and nine or two hundred and nine C, then such recognizance shall be void, otherwise of full force and effect. An order or judgment for support entered against the defendant in any such civil proceeding shall be deemed to be currently enforceable if the defendant is currently able to comply with said order or judgment and it is or would be enforceable pursuant to an action for contempt or otherwise as provided under said chapter in case of forfeiture of recognizance, and enforcement therefor by execution, the sum recovered may, in the discretion of the court, be paid in whole or in part, to the spouse or parent of the child or to the person entitled to receive support.

SECTION 7
Evidence of marriage and parentage; husband and wife as witnesses; self-incrimination; evidence of wilfulness; confidential communications

No other or greater evidence shall be required to prove the marriage of the husband and wife, or that the alleged father is the parent of the child, than may be required to prove the same facts in a civil action. In any prosecution begun under section one, both husband and wife shall be competent witnesses to testify against each other to any relevant matters, including the fact of their marriage and the parentage of the child; provided, that neither shall be compelled to give evidence incriminating himself. Proof of the desertion of the spouse or child, or of the neglect or refusal to make reasonable provision for their support and maintenance, shall be prima facie evidence that such desertion, neglect or refusal is wilful and without just cause. In no prosecution under sections one to ten, inclusive, shall any existing statute or rule of law prohibiting the disclosure of confidential communications between husband and wife apply.

2

NOTE   See Notes following G.L. c. 273, § 1.

SECTION 8
Lack of custody as defense; duty to support child

In proceedings under sections one or fifteen against a parent, relative to any minor child, it shall not of itself be a defense that the defendant has ceased to have custody or the right to custody of such child on his own acquiescence or by judicial action. The legal duty of the parent or parents to support a minor child shall continue notwithstanding the absence of a court decree ordering them or either of them to pay for the support of said child and notwithstanding any court decree granting custody of such child to another.

SECTION 9
Repealed

SECTION 10
Uniform construction

Sections one to eight, inclusive, shall be so interpreted and construed as to effectuate their general purpose to make uniform the law of those states enacting their provisions.

ILLEGITIMACY

SECTION 11
Repealed

SECTION 12
Repealed

NOTE   For subject matter of former Section 12, see G.L. c. 209C, §§ 3, 4, 8 and 12 (not in this book).

SECTION 12A
Repealed

NOTE   For subject matter of former Section 12A, see G.L. c. 209C, § 17 (not in this book).

SECTION 13
Repealed

NOTE   For subject matter of former Section 13, see G.L. c. 209C, § 9 (not in this book).

SECTION 14
Repealed

NOTE   For subject matter of former Section 14, see G.L. c. 209C, §§ 9 and 20 (not in this book).

SECTION 15
Duty to support child born out of wedlock; conclusiveness of adjudication or acknowledgment of paternity

A parent of a minor child born out of wedlock whether or not the child was born in the commonwealth who wilfully neglects or refuses to contribute reasonably to the support of the child or who leaves the commonwealth and goes into another state without making reasonable provision for the support of the child, or who enters the commonwealth from another state without making reasonable provision for the support of the child domiciled in another state, or who, wilfully and while having the financial ability or earning capacity to have complied, fails to comply with an order or judgment for support which has been entered pursuant to chapter one hundred and nineteen, two hundred and seven, two hundred and nine C or two hundred and seventy-three, or received, entered or registered pursuant to chapter two hundred and nine D, or

entered pursuant to similar laws of other states, shall be guilty of a felony and shall be subject to the penalties provided under section fifteen A. No civil proceeding in any court shall be held to be a bar to the prosecution hereunder but the court shall not enter any order pursuant to section fifteen A which would directly or indirectly result in a decrease in the amount paid for current support pursuant to an order or judgment on behalf of the child to whom, or on whose behalf, support is owed.

If there has been a voluntary acknowledgement of parentage or an adjudication of paternity under chapter two hundred and nine C or under any provision of this chapter in effect immediately prior to the effective date of this section or other law in this or any other jurisdiction, such acknowledgement or adjudication shall be conclusive on all persons in proceedings under this section. If there has been no adjudication or acknowledgement of paternity, proceedings under this section shall be stayed pending the conclusion of an action to establish paternity under chapter two hundred and nine C, which shall be commenced forthwith.

SECTION 15A
Abandonment and willful nonsupport; penalties; alternative sentencing; restitution

(1) The penalty for violation of sections one and fifteen of this chapter shall be by fine or by imprisonment or by both fine and imprisonment as specified below.

(2) A person who abandons his spouse or minor child without making reasonable provisions for the support of either or both of them or who is subject to an order or judgment for support pursuant to chapters one hundred and nineteen, two hundred and seven, two hundred and eight, two hundred and nine, two hundred and nine C, two hundred and seventy-three, or two hundred and nine D, or pursuant to similar laws of other states, who, wilfully and while having the financial ability or earning capacity to have complied, fails to comply with that order or judgment, shall be punished by imprisonment in the state prison for not more than five years or by imprisonment in jail or the house of correction for not more than two and one-half years, or by a fine of not more than five thousand dollars, or by both such fine and imprisonment.

(3) A person who leaves the commonwealth and goes into another state without making reasonable provisions for the support of a spouse or child, or who enters the commonwealth from another state without making reasonable provision for the support of a spouse or child domiciled in another state, shall be punished by imprisonment in the state prison for not more than ten years or by imprisonment in jail or the house of correction for not more than two and one-half years, or by a fine of not more than ten thousand dollars, or by both such fine and imprisonment.

(4) In a prosecution under this chapter, the court may, upon conviction of the defendant, provide for alternative sentencing including (a) the suspension of the sentence upon and during the compliance by the defendant with any order for the support as already made or as thereafter modified, or (b) notwithstanding the provision of section six of chapter two hundred and seventy-nine, the imprisonment of the defendant only on designated weekends, evenings or holidays, provided, that such defendant retains employment and complies with such support orders.

(5) In a prosecution under this chapter the defendant may be ordered to make restitution to the spouse or the custodial parent or to the person or agency, including the department of public welfare, who is supporting or has supported the spouse or child for all sums expended on behalf of such spouse or child, provided that if the defendant establishes a lesser ability to have provided support, the amount of any liability imposed by this section shall be consistent with the defendant's prior ability to have paid support.

SECTION 15B
Concealing assets of another for purpose of avoiding payment of order of judgment for support; punishment

Whoever receives or conceals an asset of another knowing that said asset is being transferred for the purpose of concealing it to avoid payment of an order or judgment for support issued pursuant to the provisions of chapter 119, 207, 208, 209, 209A, 209C, 209D, or 273, or pursuant to any similar laws of other states, shall be punished by a fine of not more than $5,000 or by imprisonment in a jail or house of correction for not more than two and one-half years, or by both such fine and imprisonment; and whoever transfers an asset for the purpose of concealing it to avoid payment of an order or judgment for support issued pursuant to said chapter 119, 207, 208, 209, 209A, 209C, 209D, or 273, or pursuant to any similar laws of other states shall be punished by a fine of not more than $5,000 or by imprisonment in a jail or house of correction for not more than two and one-half years, or both such fine and imprisonment. The court may in the alternative to the foregoing punishment divert the defendant to a program as defined in section 1 of chapter 276A.

SECTION 16
Application of sections 2, 6, 7, and 10

The provisions of sections two, six, seven and ten shall apply in proceedings under sections one and fifteen.

SECTION 17
Dismissal of case

If the court having jurisdiction of a case under sections fifteen to eighteen, inclusive, becomes satisfied that the alleged father and the mother have married each other and the child has become or will be the legitimate child of the alleged father or that it is for the best interest of the child, the case may be dismissed and if the court certifies that it is for the best interests of the child, no further prosecution shall be maintained under any of said sections.

SECTION 18
Money forfeited or recovered upon recognizance or deposit used for support

If money is forfeited or recovered upon a recognizance or deposit in lieu thereof given in proceedings under sections fifteen to eighteen, inclusive, or any of them, the court in which such proceedings are pending may order such money paid to the probation officer and expended by him, under the direction of the court, for the support of the child.

SECTION 18A
Support obligations under prior law; enforcement; insurance coverage; amended orders

(a) Any order issued by a court pursuant to sections one, five, or fifteen as those sections appeared prior to the effective date of this section directing the defendant to pay certain sums periodically to the probation officer as a condition of releasing the defendant from custody on probation, shall continue in full force and effect, subject to the jurisdiction of said court and to change from time to time as circumstances may require, for a period not exceeding six years from said date. A voluntary agreement relating to the support of a spouse or child or children previously executed by the defendant may be admitted as evidence of the defendant's support obligation. If the court finds that the obligation imposed by such agreement is reasonable in the circumstance, and that the defendant has failed to comply with its terms, the court may include in any subsequent order the payment of any part or all of the arrears which accrued under such agreement if the complaint includes the period of such arrearage; provided, however, that when such agreement is executed with the department of public welfare or with any official of the court, such agreement shall not be enforceable unless the defendant was informed in writing at the time he executed the agreement that the failure to comply with the support order would result in the commencement of criminal nonsupport proceedings under this chapter against him. The probation officer subject to the direction of the court, shall pay over payments received by him to the IV-D agency, as set forth in chapter one hundred and nineteen A, which shall in turn make payments to the spouse or guardian or custodian of the child, or to the city, town, corporation, society or person supporting the spouse or child, or to the state treasurer for the use of the department of children and families when the payments are for the support of a child committed to it. If the court is satisfied by due proof under oath that at any time the defendant has violated the terms of the order for payments, it may proceed to try the defendant upon the original charge, or sentence him under the original plea or conviction, or enforce the suspended sentence, as the case may be.

(b) When the court reviews or modifies an order for support on behalf of a spouse or child, said court shall determine whether the obligor under such order has health insurance or other health coverage available to him through an employer or organization or has health insurance or other health coverage available to him at reasonable cost that may be extended to cover the spouse or child for whom support is ordered. When said court has determined that the obligor has such insurance or coverage available to him, said court shall include in the support order a requirement that the obligor exercise the option of additional coverage in favor of the spouse and child or obtain coverage for the spouse and child.

(c) Each order for support reviewed, modified, or otherwise brought before the court pursuant to this section shall be amended so as to conform to and shall thereafter be enforced in accordance with the provisions of section twelve of chapter one hundred and nineteen A.

SECTION 19
Repealed

DESTITUTE PARENTS

SECTION 20
Neglect or refusal to support parent

Any person, over eighteen, who, being possessed of sufficient means, unreasonably neglects or refuses to provide for the support and maintenance of his parent, whether father or

2

mother, residing in the commonwealth, when such parent through misfortune and without fault of his own is destitute of means of sustenance and unable by reason of old age, infirmity or illness to support and maintain himself, shall be punished by a fine of not more than two hundred dollars or by imprisonment for not more than one year, or both. No such neglect or refusal shall be deemed unreasonable as to a child who shall not during his minority have been reasonably supported by such parent, if such parent was charged with the duty so to do, nor as to a child who, being one of two or more children, has made proper and reasonable contribution toward the support of such parent.

SECTION 21
Venue; complainants

Proceedings under the preceding section shall be begun, if in the superior court, in the county in which is situated the place where the defendant or the parent lives, and, if begun in a district court, in the court having such place within its judicial district. Complaints in district courts under the preceding section may be made by any such parent, by any child of such parent or by the department of public welfare.

NOTE   The Department of Public Welfare is now called the Department of Transitional Assistance.

SECTION 22
Orders under Sec. 5, and practice under Secs. 1 to 10 of this chapter

Before trial, with the consent of the defendant, or after entry of a plea of guilty or nolo contendere, or after conviction, the court may make for the benefit of such destitute parent orders similar to those provided by section five; and the practice established by the first ten sections of this chapter shall, so far as applicable, apply to proceedings under this and the two preceding sections.

SECTION 23
Needy disabled persons; neglect or refusal of parents to support; penalty

The father or mother of any needy disabled person who unreasonably neglects or refuses to provide for the support and maintenance of such person shall be punished by a fine of not more than five hundred dollars or by imprisonment for not more than two years, or both.

Chapter 274. Felonies, Accessories and Attempts to Commit Crimes

Section
1   Felonies and misdemeanors
2   Aiders; accessories before fact; punishment
3   Counseling or procuring felony; prosecution as accessory before fact or principal; punishment; venue
4   Accessories after fact; punishment; relationship as defence; cross-examination; impeachment
5   Felon's conviction or amenability to justice; venue
6   Attempts to commit crimes; punishment
7   Conspiracy; penalties

SECTION 1
Felonies and misdemeanors

A crime punishable by death or imprisonment in the state prison is a felony. All other crimes are misdemeanors.

SECTION 2
Aiders; accessories before fact; punishment

Whoever aids in the commission of a felony, or is accessory thereto before the fact by counselling, hiring or otherwise procuring such felony to be committed, shall be punished in the manner provided for the punishment of the principal felon.

NOTE 1   "General Laws c. 274, §§ 2 and 3, are complementary statutes that seek to punish a defendant who 'aids in the commission of a felony, or is accessory thereto before the fact by counseling, hiring or otherwise procuring such felony to be committed. . . . Section 2 defines the core offense, and [section] 3 states when and how an accessory before the fact may be tried. As we concluded in *Commonwealth v. Ortiz*, [424 Mass. 853, 858 (1997)], the 'practical effect of [G.L. c. 274, §§ 2 and 3] is to hold the criminal actor who participates in a felony liable as a principal without regard to whether the felony is completed or committed by another.' . . .

"There is no significance in the fact that the Commonwealth proceeded against the defendant as an accessory under § 2 of G.L. c. 274, instead of directly on the substantive felony under § 3 of the statute." *Commonwealth v. Moure*, 428 Mass. 313, 317–18 (1998).

NOTE 2   "Accomplice and conspiratorial liability are not synonymous, and one can be an accomplice aiding in the commission of a substantive offense without necessarily conspiring to commit it . . . . [T]he gist of conspiracy rests in the agreement between the conspirators to work in concert for the criminal or corrupt or unlawful purpose and it is that agreement which constitutes the criminal act and which generally serves to manifest the requisite criminal intent. On the other hand, accomplice liability has a broader application, making the defendant a principal when he consciously shares in a criminal act, regardless of the existence of a conspiracy. Accomplice liability is based on the defendant's desire to make the crime succeed and is usually established by proof that the defendant was present at the scene, that he assented to the crime occurring, and that he put himself in a position where he could render aid to the perpetrator if it should become necessary. Absent from the formulation of accomplice liability is the necessity of establishing an agreement or consensus in the same sense as those terms are used in describing the agreement or combination which hallmarks a conspiracy." *Commonwealth v. Cook*, 10 Mass. App. Ct. 668, 673–74 (1980) (citations and quotation marks omitted).

NOTE 3   "[A]n accessory is not bound by the verdict or judgment against the principal." *Commonwealth v. DiStasio*, 298 Mass. 562, 565 (1937). See also Section 3 of this chapter.

NOTE 4   "[W]hether a person may be found guilty of being an accessory before the fact (G.L. c. 274, § 2 [1990 ed.]) to rape (G.L. c. 265, § 2 [1990 ed.]) and to indecent assault and battery on a mentally retarded person (G.L. c. 265, § 13F [1990 ed.]), where the victim is a minor, the defendant is the minor's parent and the defendant failed to take reasonable steps to prevent the sexual attacks by a third person."

The Supreme Judicial Court answered "no."

"A person cannot be found guilty as an accessory before the fact simply because she knows a crime is going to be committed, even when this knowledge is coupled with her subsequent concealment of the completed crime. *Commonwealth v. Perry*, 357 Mass. 149, 151 (1970). *Commonwealth v. Murphy*, [1 Mass. App. Ct. 71] at 77. Therefore, it is clear that what is required to be convicted as an accessory before the fact is not only knowledge of the crime and a shared intent to bring it about, but also some sort of act that contributes to its happening. . . .

"By its very terms, G.L. c. 274, § 2, requires more than an omission to act. As our case law makes clear, in order to be punished as an accessory before the fact, the defendant must have actually aided in the commission of the felony or counseled, hired or otherwise procured someone to commit it."

Commonwealth v. Raposo, 413 Mass. 182, 184–85, 188 (1992).

NOTE 5   **New joint venture instruction.** "We, therefore, now adopt the language of aiding and abetting rather than joint venture for use in trials that commence after the issuance of the rescript in this case." *Commonwealth v. Zanetti*, 454 Mass. 449, 467 (2009).

NOTE 6   Form of indictment—G.L. c. 277, § 79.

NOTE 7   See Notes following Section 3 of this chapter.

SECTION 3

Counseling or procuring felony; prosecution as accessory before fact or principal; punishment; venue

Whoever counsels, hires or otherwise procures a felony to be committed may be indicted and convicted as an accessory before the fact, either with the principal felon or after his conviction; or may be indicted and convicted of the substantive felony, whether the principal felon has or has not been convicted, or is or is not amenable to justice; and in the last mentioned case may be punished in the same manner as if convicted of being an accessory before the fact. An accessory to a felony before the fact may be indicted, tried and punished in the same county where the principal felon might be indicted and tried, although the counselling, hiring or procuring the commission of such felony was committed within or without the commonwealth or on the high seas.

NOTE 1   The purpose of this section is "to furnish a method for the prosecution of any accessory before the fact, irrespective of the nature of the principal felony." *Commonwealth v. Bloomberg*, 302 Mass. 349, 353 (1939).

NOTE 2   Counselling, hiring or otherwise procuring means something more than mere acquiescence in the commission of the substantive crime but does not require physical participation, if there is association with the venture and any significant participation in it. *Commonwealth v. French*, 357 Mass. 356, 391 (1970), *vacated on other grounds*, 408 U.S. 936 (1972).

NOTE 3   "One who has advised, aided or abetted another to commit a felony, and is absent when the crime is committed or if present is not acting, may be found to be an accessory before the fact, but one who is present at the commission of a felony and is aiding and assisting the one who is actually committing the offense is a principal." *Commonwealth v. Mannos*, 311 Mass. 94, 109 (1942).

NOTE 4   See Notes following Section 2 in this chapter.

SECTION 4

Accessories after fact; punishment; relationship as defence; cross-examination; impeachment

Whoever, after the commission of a felony, harbors, conceals, maintains or assists the principal felon or accessory before the fact, or gives such offender any other aid, knowing that he has committed a felony or has been accessory thereto before the fact, with intent that he shall avoid or escape detention, arrest, trial or punishment, shall be an accessory after the fact, and, except as otherwise provided, be punished by imprisonment in the state prison for not more than seven years or in jail for not more than two and one half years or by a fine of not more than one thousand dollars. The fact that the defendant is the husband or wife, or by consanguinity, affinity or adoption, the parent or grandparent, child or grandchild, brother or sister of the offender, shall be a defense to a prosecution under this section. If such a defendant testifies solely as to the existence of such relationship, he shall not be subject to cross examination on any other subject matter, nor shall his criminal record, if any, except for perjury or subornation of perjury, be admissible to impeach his credibility.

NOTE 1   The offense requires the "purpose to hinder the apprehension, prosecution, conviction, or punishment of another for crime." *Commonwealth v. Kelly*, 1 Mass. App. Ct. 441, 448 (1973) (quoting The Model Penal Code § 242.3 (Proposed Official Draft)).

NOTE 2   "The crime has evolved from one in which the offender is considered in some sense an accomplice in the original crime into an independent crime the gravamen of which is the obstruction of justice." *Commonwealth v. Kelly,* 1 Mass. App. Ct. at 448.

NOTE 3   Intent must be proven since specific intent is an element of the crime. While not necessarily susceptible of proof by direct evidence, inferences from all of the facts and circumstances may be utilized. "Knowledge of a crime and an act, such as hiding a gun which could reasonably assist the principal ordinarily presents a jury question of whether the act was done with a purpose to obstruct justice." *Commonwealth v. Kelly,* 1 Mass. App. Ct. at 448–49.

NOTE 4   "[O]ne cannot be both a principal in a crime and an accessory after the fact to the same crime." *Commonwealth v. Berryman*, 359 Mass. 127, 129 (1971).

NOTE 5   The burden of going forward on the issue of family relationships is upon the defendant. *Commonwealth v. Valleca*, 358 Mass. 242, 245 (1970).

NOTE 6   **Mass. Statute Distinct from Model Penal Code.** "We recognize that commentators now recommend, and many States have taken, an approach to this crime that focuses on the defendant's conduct in obstructing justice or impeding law enforcement, rather than treating the defendant as an accomplice of the principal with a form of derivative liability for the principal's crimes. The offense as defined in the Model Penal Code 'covers the common law category of accessory after the fact but breaks decisively with the traditional concept that the accessory's liability derives from that of his principal. Thus, under the Model Code provision [§ 242.3], one who harbors a murderer is not made a party to the original homicide but is convicted, as he should be, for an independent offense of obstruction of justice.' Model Penal Code, Explanatory Note for §§ 242.1–242.8, 10A U.L.A. 639 (Master ed. 2001). That approach dispenses with many of the common-law elements (knowledge of the identity of the perpetrator, knowledge of the underlying felony, and even the requirement that a felony actually have been committed) and focuses instead on whether the defendant purposely hindered law enforcement. Under that approach, this defendant could only be charged in one indictment, as his obstruction of justice was perpetrated by means of a single course of conduct.

"Our statute, however, remains in the common-law form. In *Commonwealth v. Devlin*, [366 Mass. 132, 138–39 (1974)], citing Model Penal Code §§ 242.1, 242.3 (Proposed Official Draft 1962), and Proposed Criminal Code of Massachusetts, c. 268, §§ 9, 11 (1972), we recognized the alternative 'obstruction of justice' approach to such crimes. Yet, constrained by our statute's common-law form, this court imposed the traditional common-law requirements that an accessory must know both the identity of the felon he is assisting and the 'substantial facts' concerning the crime the felon committed. *Id.* at 136. Despite the suggestion of an alternative approach in *Commonwealth v. Devlin*, *supra* at 138–139, the Legislature has not amended the statute to transform the crime of being an accessory after the fact into the more modern articulation of the crime as an obstruction of justice. Our statute remains consistent with the common-law approach to the crime of being an accessory after the fact, and, unless and until the statute is amended, we must continue to construe it consistent with its common-law roots." *Commonwealth v. Perez*, 437 Mass. 186, 192–94 (2002) (some citations omitted).

NOTE 7   Form of indictment—G.L. c. 277, § 79.

SECTION 5
Felon's conviction or amenability to justice; venue

An accessory to a felony after the fact may be indicted, convicted and punished, whether the principal felon has or has not been previously convicted, or is or is not amenable to justice, either in the county where he became an accessory or in the county where the principal felony was committed.

SECTION 6
Attempts to commit crimes; punishment

Whoever attempts to commit a crime by doing any act toward its commission, but fails in its perpetration, or is intercepted or prevented in its perpetration, shall, except as otherwise provided, be punished as follows:

First, by imprisonment in the state prison for not more than ten years, if he attempts to commit a crime punishable with death.

Second, by imprisonment in the state prison for not more than five years or in a jail or house of correction for not more than two and one half years, if he attempts to commit a crime, except any larceny under section thirty of chapter two hundred and sixty-six, punishable by imprisonment in the state prison for life or for five years or more.

Third, by imprisonment in a jail or house of correction for not more than one year or by a fine of not more than three hundred dollars, if he attempts to commit a crime, except any larceny under said section thirty, punishable by imprisonment in the state prison for less than five years or by imprisonment in a jail or house of correction or by a fine.

Fourth, by imprisonment in a jail or house of correction for not more than two and one half years or by a fine, or by both such fine and imprisonment, if he attempts to commit any larceny punishable under said section thirty.

NOTE 1a   "A charge of an attempt should set forth in direct terms that the defendant attempted to commit the crime, and should allege the act or acts done toward its commission." "Overt acts not alleged may not be relied on to satisfy this requirement." "The overt acts alleged must approach the achievement of the substantive crime attempted near enough to warrant criminal liability in view of such circumstances as the gravity of the crime, the uncertainty of the result, and the seriousness of any threatened danger." *Commonwealth v. Gosselin*, 365 Mass. 116, 121 (1974).

NOTE 2   "[A] charge of a completed crime logically includes a charge of an attempt to commit it." *Commonwealth v. Gosselin*, 365 Mass. at 121.

NOTE 3   "The elements of attempt, whether general attempt or attempted murder, are (1) the specific intent to commit the substantive crime at issue, and (2) an overt act toward completion of the substantive crime . . . [but] nonachievement of murder is not an element of attempted murder." *Commonwealth v. LaBrie*, 473 Mass. 754, 764–65 (2016).

NOTE 4   If a defendant is acquitted on a complaint charging a completed crime, with no overt act alleged, there is *no* double jeopardy bar to a subsequent charge of attempt. *Commonwealth v. Gosselin*, 365 Mass. at 122.

NOTE 5   "Does an [i]ndictment alleging an [a]ttempt to [c]ommit the [c]rime of [i]ndecent [a]ssault and [b]attery charge a felony offense that is cognizable under the laws of the Commonwealth?" The court answered "Yes." *Commonwealth v. Marzilli*, 457 Mass. 64, 65 (2010).

NOTE 6   Form of indictment—G.L. c. 277, § 79 (Attempt).

SECTION 7
Conspiracy; penalties

Any person who commits the crime of conspiracy shall be punished as follows:

First, if the purpose of the conspiracy or any of the means for achieving the purpose of the conspiracy is a felony punishable by death or imprisonment for life, by a fine of not more than ten thousand dollars or by imprisonment in the state prison for not more than twenty years or in jail for not more than two and one half years, or by both such fine and imprisonment.

Second, if clause first does not apply and the purpose of the conspiracy or any of the means for achieving the purpose of the conspiracy is a felony punishable by imprisonment in the state prison for a maximum period exceeding ten years, by a fine of not more than ten thousand dollars or by imprisonment in the state prison for not more than ten years or in jail for not more than two and one half years, or by both such fine and imprisonment.

Third, if clauses first and second do not apply and the purpose of the conspiracy or any of the means for achieving the purpose of the conspiracy is a felony punishable by imprisonment in the state prison for not more than ten years, by a fine of not more than five thousand dollars or by imprisonment in the state prison for not more than five years or in jail for not more than two and one half years, or by both such fine and imprisonment.

Fourth, if clauses first through third do not apply and the purpose of the conspiracy or any of the means for achieving the purpose of the conspiracy is a crime, by a fine of not more than two thousand dollars or by imprisonment in jail for not more than two and one half years, or both.

If a person is convicted of a crime of conspiracy for which crime the penalty is expressly set forth in any other section of the General Laws, the provisions of this section shall not apply to said crime and the penalty therefore shall be imposed pursuant to the provisions of such other section.

NOTE 1   See Note 1 following G.L. c. 274, § 2.

NOTE 2   "To warrant a conviction for conspiracy the evidence must disclose something further than participating in the offense which is the object of the conspiracy; there must be proof of the unlawful agreement, either express or implied, and participation with knowledge of the agreement." *Commonwealth v. Cook*, 10 Mass. App. Ct. 668, 675 (1980) (citation omitted).

NOTE 3   "[C]onspiracy to commit an offense and the subsequent commission of the crime normally do not merge into a single punishable act . . . . [C]ommission of a substantive offense and a conspiracy to commit it are distinct and a plea of double jeopardy is no defense to a conviction for both unless the substantive offense and the conspiracy are identical." *Commonwealth v. Cook*, 10 Mass. App. Ct. 668, 676 n.6 (1980) (citations omitted and punctuation altered).

NOTE 4   "Imminence" is *not* a requirement of criminal conspiracy, as it is of criminal attempt. *Commonwealth v. Dellinger*, 10 Mass. App. Ct. 549, 556, *aff'd in part and rev'd in part on other grounds*, 383 Mass. 780 (1981).

NOTE 5   Form of indictment—G.L. c. 277, § 79 (Conspiracy).

NOTE 6   "[W]e have held as relevant that evidence which relates to the entire history of a conspiracy though the specific evidence predates the conspiracy." *Commonwealth v. Pero*, 402 Mass. 476, 481 (1988).

NOTE 7   "The crime of conspiracy 'is complete upon the formation of an agreement and a combination to commit, or cause[d]

2

to be committed, a crime or an unlawful act.' *Commonwealth v. Nighelli*, 13 Mass. App. Ct. 590, 593–594 (1982), and cases cited. 'A conspiracy may be proved by circumstantial evidence, and this is the usual mode of proving it, since it is not often that direct evidence can be had. The acts of different persons who are shown to have known each other, or to have been in communication with each other, directed towards the accomplishment of the same object . . . may be satisfactory proof of a conspiracy.' *Commonwealth v. Smith*, 163 Mass. 411, 417–18 (1895)." *Commonwealth v. Pratt*, 407 Mass. 647, 653 (1990).

NOTE 8   Renunciation. "The American Law Institute's Model Penal Code § 5.03(6) (1985) provides: 'Renunciation of Criminal Purpose. It is an affirmative defense [to a charge of conspiracy] that the actor, after conspiring to commit a crime, thwarted the success of the conspiracy, under circumstances manifesting a complete and voluntary renunciation of his criminal purpose.'" *Commonwealth v. Nee*, 458 Mass. 174, 175 n.4 (2010).

NOTE 9   Collateral Estoppel. "[T]ypically acquittal of a substantive offense does not preclude subsequent prosecution of

charges of conspiracy to commit that offense, and, conversely, acquittal of the conspiracy do not preclude subsequent prosecution on a charge of the substantive offense that was the object of the alleged conspiracy. As general rule, . . . the agreement that must be shown to prove a conspiracy is a meeting of the minds of the conspirators separate and distinct from and prior to the common intent that is implicit in the commission of the substantive crime." *Commonwealth v. DeCillis*, 41 Mass. App. Ct. 312, 314 (1996).

NOTE 10   Jury Instruction. "The commonsensical view is that if the offense which was the object of the conspiracy were some technical or unusually complex offense of which the trier of fact has no general impression, a suitable instruction explaining such an offense would be mandatory, but not so where the jury as ordinary laymen have a general knowledge of what constitutes armed robbery [the target offense involved in the case] which is self-defining." *Commonwealth v. Stack*, 49 Mass. App. Ct. 227, 236 (2000) (citation, quotations, and punctuation marks omitted). *See also Commonwealth v. Jordan*, 49 Mass. App. Ct. 802, 815 (2000).

Chapter 275. Proceedings to Prevent Crimes

Section
1   Justices keeping public peace; security
2   Threats
3   Warrant to apprehend accused
4   Punishment; appeal; recognizance to keep the peace
5   Commitment on refusal or neglect to recognize
6   Discharge of accused; complainant paying expenses
7   Accused paying expenses
8   Appeal from order to recognize
9   Witnesses to recognize for appearance
10   Proceedings on appeal
11   Failure to prosecute appeal; recognizance remaining in force
12   Discharge from commitment upon giving security
13   Recognizance; filing; breach of condition
14   Affray, threats or disturbance of peace in presence of justice; recognizance to keep peace
15   Repealed
16   Remission of portion of forfeited penalty
17   Right of surety to surrender principal; discharge from liability; new recognizance
18   Lifetime parole hearings

SECTION 1
Justices keeping public peace; security

The justices of the supreme judicial court, of the superior court, and of the district courts may cause all laws made for the preservation of the public peace to be kept; and in the execution of that power may require persons to give security to keep the peace, or for their good behavior, or both, as provided in this chapter.

SECTION 2
Threats

If complaint is made to any such court or justice that a person has threatened to commit a crime against the person or property of another, such court or justice shall examine the complainant and any witnesses who may be produced, on oath, reduce the complaint to writing and cause it to be subscribed by the complainant.

**NOTE 1   ** "In law, "threatened" has universally been interpreted to require more than the mere expression of intention. The elements of threatening a crime include an expression of intention to inflict a crime on another and an ability to do so in circumstances that would justify apprehension on the part of the recipient of the threat. While in this case the words 'drop the charges' of themselves do not constitute an expression of intention to do bodily harm or to

inflict any other evil, injury or damage, they must be interpreted in the context of the actions and demeanor which accompanied them; when viewed together they may constitute the requisite expression, and may indicate additionally, in the circumstances, ability and apprehension." *Commonwealth v. Elliffe*, 47 Mass. App. Ct. 580, 582 (1999) (citations and quotation marks omitted).

**NOTE 2   ** "The elements of threatening a crime include an expression of intention to inflict a crime on another and an ability to do so in circumstances that would justify apprehension on the part of the recipient of the threat." *Commonwealth v. Robicheau*, 421 Mass. 176, 183 (1995).

**NOTE 3   ** Defendant charged with assault and battery, kidnapping and threats to kill. Victim testified that defendant told her, "When I was in jail, the guards and everyone treated us like animals. Now you get an idea of what it's like." Held, admissible: (1) statement occurred during the crime; and (2) it bore directly on the victim's frame of mind, her apprehension as to the defendant's intentions, which went to the proof of the crimes of kidnapping and threats to kill. *Commonwealth v. Chalifoux*, 362 Mass. 811 (1973).

**NOTE 4   ** "[G]iven recent highly publicized incidents of school violence, a drawing that depicts a student pointing a gun at his teacher constitutes a threat." *Commonwealth v. Milo M.*, 433 Mass. 149, 150 (2001).

NOTE 5   Indirect Threat - Communication. "The Commonwealth must also prove that the threat was communicated in some manner to the defendant's intended victim, directly or through an intermediary. Mere proof that threatening words reach their target is insufficient to prove a statutory violation. 'The Commonwealth must [also] prove, beyond a reasonable doubt, that the defendant intended that [his] threats be communicated to [the victim].' *Commonwealth v. Meier*, 56 Mass. App. Ct. 278, 282 (2002). Evidence of the defendant's intent need not be express, but 'may be proved by circumstantial evidence.' *Ibid*. When a defendant utters a threat to a third party who would likely communicate it to the ultimate target, the defendant's act constitutes evidence of his intent to communicate the threat to the intended victim." *Commonwealth v. James*, 73 Mass. App. Ct. 383, 385–86 (2008) (some citations and quotations marks and footnote omitted).

NOTE 6   Sentencing. "The defendant argues that the threats statute, G.L. c. 275, § 4, prohibits a judge from imposing a probationary term greater than six months. He argues, as well, that to the extent the specific provisions of the threats statute conflict with the terms of the probation statute, G.L. c. 276, § 87, the more specific terms of the threats statute must prevail. Neither contention correctly interprets the relevant statutes. The threats statute does not prohibit a sentencing judge from imposing a probationary term of greater than six months. Nor is there a conflict between the provisions of the threats statute and those of the probation statute as to the permissible length of a probationary term." *Commonwealth v. Powers*, 73 Mass. App. Ct. 186, 186–87 (2008).

NOTE 7   Related Statutes. G.L. c. 265, § 13A—Assault; G.L. c. 209A—Abuse prevention.

SECTION 3
Warrant to apprehend accused

If, upon such examination, it is found there is just cause to fear that such crime may be committed, such court or justice shall issue a warrant, reciting the substance of the complaint, and requiring the officer to whom it is directed forthwith to apprehend the person complained of and take him before such justice or some other justice or court having jurisdiction of the cause. Such warrant, if issued by a justice, shall be under his hand.

SECTION 4
Punishment; appeal; recognizance to keep the peace

If the person complained of is convicted, he may be punished by a fine of not more than one hundred dollars or by imprisonment for not more than six months. Instead of imposing sentence, the court or justice may order the person complained of to enter into a recognizance, with sufficient sureties, in such sum as the court or justice orders, to keep the peace toward all the people of the commonwealth, and especially toward the person requiring such security, for such term, not exceeding six months, as the court or justice may order. The court or justice may, for good cause, revoke such order or reduce the amount of the recognizance, or order that it be taken without surety.

SECTION 5
Commitment on refusal or neglect to recognize

If the person complained of so recognizes, he shall be discharged, but if he refuses or neglects so to do, he shall be committed to the jail or house of correction during the period for which he was required to give security, or until within that time he so recognizes, stating in the warrant the cause of commitment and the sum and time for which security was required.

SECTION 6
Discharge of accused; complainant paying expenses

If, upon such examination, it is found that there is not just cause to fear that such crime will be committed by the person complained of, he shall be forthwith discharged; and if it is found that the complaint is unfounded, frivolous or malicious, the complainant may be ordered to pay the expenses of prosecution.

NOTE   Phrase "just cause" may be equated with "clear and present danger" or its variants. *Robinson v. Bradley*, 300 F.Supp. 665, 669 (D. Mass. 1969). See Note 1 following G.L. c. 275, § 2.

SECTION 7
Accused paying expenses

If a person is required to give security to keep the peace or for his good behavior, the court or justice may order him to pay the expenses of prosecution, or any part thereof, and that he shall stand committed until they are paid or he is otherwise legally discharged.

SECTION 8
Appeal from order to recognize

Whoever having waived jury trial in accordance with the provisions of section twenty-six A of chapter two hundred and eighteen is aggrieved by an order of the Boston municipal court or the district court, requiring him to recognize as provided aforesaid, may, upon giving the security required, appeal to the jury session designated pursuant to section twenty-seven A of chapter two hundred and eighteen for the conduct of jury trials in cases brought in the court wherein said order was made.

SECTION 9
Witnesses to recognize for appearance

The court or justice shall require such witnesses as may be necessary to support the complaint to recognize for their appearance at the jury session.

SECTION 10
Proceedings on appeal

The justice sitting in the jury session may affirm the order or discharge the appellant, or may require him to enter into a new recognizance, with sufficient sureties, in such sum and for such time as it may order, and may make such order relative to the expenses of prosecution as is just and reasonable.

SECTION 11
Failure to prosecute appeal; recognizance remaining in force

If the appellant fails to prosecute his appeal of an order of recognizance, his recognizance shall remain in full force and effect as to any breach of the condition, without an affirmation of the judgment or order of the court or justice, and shall also stand as security for any expenses of prosecution which the justice in the jury session may order the appellant to pay.

SECTION 12
Discharge from commitment upon giving security

A person committed for not finding sureties, or for refusing to recognize as required, may be discharged upon giving such security.

SECTION 13
Recognizance; filing; breach of condition

Upon a breach of the condition of a recognizance taken pursuant to the provisions of sections four to eleven, inclusive, an action thereon shall be commenced by the district attorney in the court in which the recognizance is then on file.

SECTION 14
Affray, threats or disturbance of peace in presence of justice; recognizance to keep peace

Whoever, in the presence of a justice named in section one or before a court of record, makes an affray, or threatens to kill or beat another, or to commit any violence or outrage against the person or property of another, or contends with hot and angry words, to the disturbance of the peace, may be ordered, without process or any other proof, to recognize to keep the peace or be of good behavior for not more than three months, and in case of refusal may be committed as provided in section five.

NOTE   Related Rules.
Mass.R.Crim.P. 43—Summary Contempt Proceedings.
Mass.R.Crim.P. 44—Contempt.
Mass.R.Crim.P. 45—Removal of the Disruptive Defendant.

2

SECTION 15
Repealed

SECTION 16
Remission of portion of forfeited penalty

If, upon a suit brought on such recognizance, the penalty thereof is adjudged forfeited, the court may, upon petition of a defendant, remit such portion of it as it finds ought to be remitted.

SECTION 17
Right of surety to surrender principal; discharge from liability; new recognizance

A surety in a recognizance to keep the peace, or for good behavior, or both, shall have the same authority and right to take and surrender his principal as if he were bail for him in a civil cause; and after such surrender shall be discharged from all liability for any act of the principal subsequent to such surrender which would be a breach of the condition of the recognizance. The person so surrendered may recognize anew with sufficient sureties for the residue of the term, and shall thereupon be discharged.

SECTION 18
Lifetime parole hearings

Whenever a person is convicted of a first offense under section 13B, 13F or 13H of chapter 265 or for a first offense for the attempt of any of the aforementioned crimes under section 6 of chapter 274, the district attorney, upon motion to the court, may request a hearing after conviction and before sentencing, to determine whether or not such person shall be committed, in addition to any term of imprisonment or probation authorized by said sections, to community parole supervision for life, to be served under the jurisdiction of the parole board as set forth in section 133D of chapter 127. Whenever a person is convicted of a first offense under section 22, 22A, 23, 24, 24B or 26 of said chapter 265, section 3 or 35A of chapter 272 or for a first offense for the attempt of any of the aforementioned crimes under said section 6 of said chapter 274, the elements of which are mitigated by certain circumstances, the defendant, upon motion to the court, may request a hearing after conviction and before sentencing to determine whether or not such person shall receive, in addition to a term of imprisonment or probation authorized by such sections, community parole supervision for life, to be served under the jurisdiction of the parole board as set forth in said section 133D of said chapter 127.

At such hearing, the defendant shall have the right to be represented by counsel, and, if financially unable to retain adequate representation, to have counsel appointed to him. The defendant shall be afforded an opportunity to testify, to present witnesses, to cross-examine witnesses who appear at the hearing and to present information. The rules concerning admissibility of evidence in criminal trials shall not apply to the presentation and consideration of information at the hearing. A finding by the court that such person shall be committed to community parole supervision for life shall be supported by clear and convincing evidence.

In making a determination the judge shall, on the basis of any information which he can reasonably obtain, consider any mitigating or aggravating circumstances including, but not limited to, the defendant's character, propensities, criminal record, the nature and seriousness of the danger posed to any person or the community and the nature and circumstances of the offense for which the defendant is convicted. If the judge finds, by clear and convincing evidence, that no reasons for community parole supervision for life to be served under the jurisdiction of the parole board, as set forth in section 133D of chapter 127, exist, the judge shall not impose community supervision for life on such first offender.

Whenever a person is convicted of a first offense under section 22, 22A, 23, 24, 24B or 26 of chapter 265, or section 3 or 35A of chapter 272 or for a first attempt of any of the aforementioned crimes under the provisions of section 6 of chapter 274, the district attorney may file a motion with the sentencing judge requesting that the defendant not receive community parole supervision for life, and upon receipt of such motion, the sentencing judge shall not impose community parole supervision for life on such first offender.

NOTE 1   **CPSL Is Unconstitutional.** "The issue presented on appeal is whether community parole supervision for life (CPSL) violates our separation of powers doctrine, articulated in art. 30 of the Massachusetts Declaration of Rights, by improperly delegating to the parole board, an entity of the executive branch, the exercise of the judicial power to impose sentences. We conclude that CPSL grants to the parole board a quintessential judicial power, the power to determine whether a defendant should be sentenced to additional terms of imprisonment, and therefore violates art. 30. *Commonwealth v. Cole*, 468 Mass. 294, 295 (2014).

NOTE 2   **CPSL Sentences Must Be Vacated.** "Therefore, we strike [G.L. c. 127,] § 133D in its entirety and order that CPSL sentences, whether imposed pursuant to G.L. c. 6, § 178H(a), or G.L. c. 265, § 45, be vacated." *Commonwealth v. Cole*, 468 Mass. 294, 295, 308–09 (2014).

NOTE 3   See Notes following G.L. c. 265, § 45.

Commentary on Chapter 276 Search and Seizure

General Laws c. 276, §§ 1–8 deal with search warrants. Ironically, while the statutes only occupy a few pages, the case law generated by this section is voluminous and invites a special commentary on general principles that cut across various statutory situations. Basically, all searches and seizures are conducted either

- with a warrant or
- with no warrant.

This special commentary is a rudimentary subject breakdown of the very basic principles.

1. WARRANTS

General Principles	Medical Marijuana
Administrative Fire Warrants	Motion to Suppress
Affidavits	Motor Vehicles
Anticipatory Warrants	Nexus with Home
Article 14	Nighttime
Attenuation	No Knock
Cellular Phones	Particularity
Copy of Warrant	Plain View
Curtilage	Return of Warrant
Execution of Warrant	Securing Premises

Expectation of Privacy   Staleness
Franks   Standing
Global Positioning System   Third-Party Residence
(GPS)
Identification of Confidential
Informant

General Principles

The following is reprinted (with some changes) with permission from Kantrowitz & Witkin, Criminal Defense Motions, Massachusetts Practice Series, § 10.21 (West).

Under the Fourth Amendment of the United States Constitution, which is applicable to the states by virtue of *Mapp v. Ohio*, 367 U.S. 643 (1961), and Article Fourteen of the Constitution of the Commonwealth of Massachusetts' Declaration of Rights, no search warrant may issue unless probable cause is shown.

G.L. c. 276, § 1 requires that a search warrant be issued only upon a showing of probable cause. Evidence seized without the requisite showing of probable cause is inadmissible at trial. *See Commonwealth v. Upton*, 394 Mass. 363, 367–68 (1985).

The standard of probable cause has been defined as "facts and circumstances . . . such as to warrant a man of reasonable prudence and caution in believing that an offense has been committed." *Carroll v. United States*, 267 U.S. 132, 161 (1925). *See also United States v. Watson*, 423 U.S. 411, 431 n.4 (1976) (Powell, J. concurring).

Corroboration. "The *Aguilar-Spinelli* safeguards are satisfied when, as here, multiple informants provide the police with mutually corroborative and complementary tips, and independent police investigation confirms the tips in significant detail." *Commonwealth v. Russell*, 46 Mass. App. Ct. 513, 519 (1999) (citations omitted).

Crediting hearsay. When, as here, hearsay from an unnamed informant is the basis of the action by the police, the police must have a substantial basis for crediting the hearsay. *Jones v. United States*, 362 U.S. 257, 269 (1960); *United States v. Harris*, 403 U.S. 573, 581 (1971).

There are two firmly established requirements which must be met in order to establish the credibility of the hearsay information. The so-called Aguilar-Spinelli test, see *Aguilar v. Texas*, 378 U.S. 108 (1964) and *Spinelli v. United States*, 393 U.S. 410 (1969), is the standard to be used to establish the credibility of hearsay information under Article 14 of the Massachusetts Declaration of Rights. *See Commonwealth v. Upton*, 394 Mass. 363 (1985) wherein the Massachusetts Supreme Judicial Court rejected the modified Aguilar-Spinelli test adopted by the United States Supreme Court in *Illinois v. Gates*, 462 U.S. 213 (1983). *See also Commonwealth v. Reddington*, 395 Mass. 315 (1985).

The Aguilar-Spinelli test requires that (1) there must be some underlying circumstances on which the police officer concluded that the contraband was where it was claimed to be (the basis of knowledge prong); and (2) there must be some underlying facts and circumstances to conclude that the informant was credible or that his information was reliable (the veracity prong).

Each of the two prongs must be separately considered and satisfied or they must be supplemented in some manner. If there is a deficiency in either or both prongs, independent police corroboration may make up for the deficiency. *Commonwealth v. Upton*, 394 Mass. at 375.

Sufficiency of affidavit. "In order to establish probable cause, an affidavit must 'contain enough information for the issuing magistrate to determine that the items sought are related to the criminal activity under investigation, and that they may reasonably be expected to be located in the place to be searched.' *Commonwealth v. Cefalo*, 381 Mass. 319, 328 (1980). 'In each case, the basic question for the magistrate is whether he has a substantial basis for concluding that any of the articles described in the warrant are probably in the place to be searched.' *Commonwealth v. Upton*, 394 Mass. 363, 370 (1985). In evaluating an affidavit, a magistrate may apply his or her common knowledge, while drawing reasonable inferences from the factual information contained in the document. *Commonwealth v. Taglieri*, 378 Mass. 196, 198, *cert. denied*, 444 U.S. 937 (1979)." *Commonwealth v. Fenderson*, 410 Mass. 82, 87–88 (1991).

Citizen-informants. "[Citizen informants] are subject to much less stringent credibility verification requirements than ordinary police informants, since the former generally lack the ulterior motives of the latter. Unlike the anonymous informer, the eyewitness students could be presumed reliable. If the citizen or victim informant is an eyewitness, this will be enough to support probable cause even without specific corroboration of reliability. In addition to citizen-informers' first-hand basis of knowledge and presumed credibility, their reports usually arise in urgent situations requiring a prompt response, so that a leisurely investigation of the report is seldom feasible." *Commonwealth v. Carey*, 407 Mass. 528, 534–35 n.4 (1990) (citations and quotation marks omitted).

Excluding illegally seized evidence. "[A]s a general rule, the mere fact that an unlawful search and seizure has occurred should not automatically result in the exclusion of any illegally seized evidence. Accordingly, the decision whether to exclude such evidence should properly turn on: (1) the degree to which the violation undermined the principles underlying the governing rule of law; and (2) the extent to which exclusion will tend to deter such violations from being repeated in the future." *Commonwealth v. Grimshaw*, 413 Mass. 73, 78 (1992) (citations and quotation marks omitted).

Administrative Fire Warrants

"To obtain an administrative warrant, in addition to showing that a fire of undetermined origin has occurred, officials must show that the scope of the proposed search is reasonable and will not intrude unnecessarily on the fire victim's privacy, and that the search will be conducted at a reasonable and convenient time. The proper scope of an administrative warrant issued to conduct an investigation pursuant to G.L. c. 148, § 2, is limited by the purpose for which the warrant is ought (to determine the cause and circumstances of a fire) and any warrant that is issued should limit the search in keeping with that purpose. [There is] a lesser standard of probable cause required to obtain an administrative search warrant linked to the limited scope of the administrative search)." *Commonwealth v. Jung*, 420 Mass. 675, 685 (1995) (citations and quotation marks omitted).

Affidavits

See Notes following G.L. c. 276, § 2B.

Anticipatory Warrants

"In *Commonwealth v. Soares*, 384 Mass. 149, 154–155 (1981), we concluded that anticipatory warrants were not per se unconstitutional under the Fourth Amendment to the United States Constitution and rejected the contention that the authorizing statute, G.L. c. 276, § 1, requires that explicit directions concerning the triggering event appear on the warrant. We reaffirm our holding in *Soares*, and, to the extent that *Callahan*[, 41 Mass. App. Ct. 420 (1996),] states a constitutional compulsion, we extend our holding in *Soares* to conclude that we discern no such compulsion under either the Federal or State Constitution." *Commonwealth v. Gauthier*, 425 Mass. 37, 41–42 (1997).

"We conclude that the execution of a search is authorized by an anticipatory search warrant once there is equivalent compliance, albeit not strict compliance, with the triggering conditions in the affidavit." *Commonwealth v. Colondres*, 471 Mass. 192, 198 (2015).

Article 14

"We conclude that art. 14 [of the Massachusetts Declaration of Rights] provides more substantive protection to criminal defendants than does the Fourth Amendment in the determination of probable cause." *Commonwealth v. Upton*, 394 Mass. 363 (1985).

Attenuation

"The question in this case is whether [the] attenuation doctrine applies when an officer makes an unconstitutional investigatory stop; learns during that stop that the suspect is subject to a valid arrest warrant; and proceeds to arrest the suspect and seize incriminating evidence during a search incident to that arrest. We hold that the evidence the officer seized as part of the search incident to arrest is admissible because the officer's discovery of the arrest warrant attenuated the connection between the unlawful stop and the evidence seized incident to arrest." *Utah v. Strieff*, 136 S. Ct. 2056, 2059 (2016).

Cellular Phones

"The judge concluded that, although the Commonwealth had obtained the CSLI [cell site location information] from the defendant's cellular service provider pursuant to a valid Superior Court order issued under 18 U.S.C. § 2703(d) (2006) of the Federal Stored Communications Act (SCA), the Commonwealth's access to the CSLI constituted a search within the meaning of art. 14 of the Massachusetts Declaration of Rights, and therefore a search warrant based on probable cause was required.

. . .

"We conclude, like the motion judge, that although the CSLI at issue here is a business record of the defendant's cellular service provider, he had a reasonable expectation of privacy in it, and in the circumstances of this case—where the CSLI obtained covered a two-week period—the warrant requirement of art. 14 applies." *Commonwealth v. Augustine*, 467 Mass. 230, 231–32 (2014).

"Returning to an issue briefly touched on in *Augustine*, 467 Mass. at 255 n.37, we conclude that a defendant's reasonable expectation of privacy protected under art. 14 of the Massachusetts Declaration of Rights is not violated where the Commonwealth requests up to six hours of historical CSLI without obtaining a search warrant." *Commonwealth v. Estabrook*, 472 Mass. 852, 854 (2015).

"We . . . decline to extend [principles regarding a search incident to arrest] to searches of data on cell phones, and hold instead that officers must generally secure a warrant before conducting such a search." *Riley v. California*, 134 S. Ct. 2473, 2485 (2014).

In *Riley v. California*, 134 S. Ct. 2473, 2494 (2014), "the Court held that 'the search incident to arrest exception does not apply to cell phones.'" *Commonwealth v. Sheridan*, 470 Mass. 752, 763 (2015).

"[W]here there was probable cause that evidence of communications relating to and linking the defendant to the crimes under investigation would be found in the electronic files on the iPhone, and because such communications can be conveyed or stored in photographic form, a search of the photograph files was reasonable." *Commonwealth v. Dorelas*, 473 Mass. 496, 497 (2016).

Copy of Warrant

"The Fourth Amendment does not require that an individual be given a copy of the warrant before the commencement of a search of his or her property. Although it is established that Art. 14 does require police officers to have a copy of a search warrant with them at the time they conduct a search, we have never required that the entire warrant be shown, read to, or understood by an individual who may be present and whose property is about to be searched . . . . Rather, it is intended to notify that person that the officers have been authorized to be in that particular place and to search for that particular thing." *Commonwealth v. Valerio*, 449 Mass. 562, 571–72 (2007) (citations omitted).

Curtilage

"*United States v. Dunn*, [480 U.S. 294, 301 (1987)] set out four factors to consider in deciding if a particular area is within the curtilage: (1) the proximity of the area to the home, (2) whether the area is included within an enclosure surrounding the home, (3) the nature of the uses to which the area is put, and (4) the steps taken by the resident to protect the area from observations by people passing by. These factors are not intended as a 'finely tuned formula'; rather, they provide a framework to aid in analyzing the relevant facts and deciding the core issue—whether the area in question 'harbors those intimate activities associated with domestic life and the privacies of the home.' [*United States v. Dunn*, 480 U.S.] at 301 and n.4." *Commonwealth v. McCarthy*, 428 Mass. 871, 874 (1999).

Parking space. "As the parking space was beyond the curtilage of the defendant's apartment, the search warrant for the defendant's apartment did not extend to it." *Commonwealth v. McCarthy*, 428 Mass. 871, 876 (1999).

Search of automobile. "In *Commonwealth v. Signorine*, 404 Mass. 400, 403–404 (1989), we acknowledged the well-settled principle 'under both Federal law and the law of other jurisdictions that the scope of a warrant authorizing the search of a particularly described premises, includes automobiles owned or controlled by the owner thereof, which are found on the premises.' We held that the same principle applies under art. 14 of the Massachusetts Declaration of Rights. [*Commonwealth v. Signorine*, 404 Mass.] at 404–405. We upheld a search of the automobile of the defendant's wife. We so ruled even though the police lacked independent probable cause to search the automobile, because the police had obtained a warrant based on probable cause to search the defendant's residence generally, and since the automobile was parked within the curtilage of the premises at the time the warrant was executed.

2

"The critical difference between Signorine and the case at bar is that, here, the defendant's automobile was parked on public street and not on private property constituting the curtilage of the premises described in the warrant. We decline to expand the definition of curtilage or to extend the holding in Signorine so as to justify, in this context, the search of an automobile parked on a public street." *Commonwealth v. Santiago*, 410 Mass. 737, 740–41 (1991) (footnote omitted).

Search of land. "Pratt claims that the affidavit failed to establish probable cause to search the land behind the Pratt residence because it purportedly demonstrated no nexus between the evidence sought and the land. We disagree.

"An affidavit must contain enough information for the issuing magistrate to determine that the items sought are related to the criminal activity under investigation, and that they reasonably may be expected to be found in the place to be searched. *Commonwealth v. Cefalo*, 381 Mass. 319, 328–29 (1980). A nexus between the items to be seized and the place to be searched need not be based on direct observation and may be found 'in the type of crime, the nature of the missing items, the extent of the suspect's opportunity for concealment, and normal inferences as to where a criminal would be likely to hide stolen property.'" *Commonwealth v. Burt*, 393 Mass. 703, 715 (1985) (quoting *Commonwealth v. Cinelli*, 389 Mass. 197, 213 (1983)).

"The affidavit provided sufficient information to show a nexus between the items to be seized and the land behind the defendant's house." *Commonwealth v. Pratt*, 407 Mass. 647, 661 (1990).

Execution of Warrant

See Notes following G.L. c. 276, § 2A.

Expectation of Privacy

Scope of constitutional right. "When a defendant has standing under our rule for State constitutional purposes, we then determine whether a search in the constitutional sense has taken place. This determination turns on whether the police conduct has intruded on a constitutionally protected reasonable expectation of privacy. The measure of the defendant's expectation of privacy is (1) whether the defendant has manifested a subjective expectation of privacy in the object of the search, and (2) whether society is willing to recognize that expectation as reasonable. The defendant bears the burden of establishing both elements. In examining the expectation of privacy question under art. 14, we do not necessarily reach the same result as under Fourth Amendment analysis.

"Conceding for present purposes that the defendant may have had a subjective expectation of privacy in the space above the hallway ceiling, we concluded that expectation was not reasonable. In evaluating the reasonableness of an individual's expectation of privacy, we look to a number of factors, including the character of the location involved. Thus, we consider whether the defendant owned the place involved; whether the defendant controlled access to the area; and whether the area was freely accessible to others. We have stated that an individual can have only a very limited expectation of privacy with respect to an area used routinely by others. One writer has suggested that 'the fundamental inquiry is whether [the] practice, if not subjected to Fourth Amendment restraints, would be intolerable because it would either encroach too much upon the 'sense of security' or impose unreasonable burdens upon those who wished to maintain that

security.' W.R. LaFave, Search and Seizure § 2.1(d), at 313 (2d ed. 1987). . . .

"We conclude, therefore, that the defendant had no constitutionally protected reasonable expectation of privacy in the area above the hallway ceiling not leased or controlled by him nor subject to any agreement or understanding with the landlord as to its use. The police conduct, therefore, did not constitute a search in the constitutional sense. Consequently, it is unnecessary to reach the defendant's arguments that the 'search' exceeded the scope of the warrant."

Commonwealth v. Montanez, 410 Mass. 290, 301–03 (1991) (citations omitted).

"In short, regardless of whether the juvenile resided in a palatial mansion or a single room in a transitional shelter, regardless of whether he owned the residence or was allowed to remain without paying rent, and regardless of whether his landlord or shelter director had a master key and could enter to ensure that he was abiding by the rules of the house, the juvenile had a reasonable expectation of privacy in his home." *Commonwealth v. Porter P.*, 456 Mass. 254, 261 (2010).

"Whether the government's activity amounted to a search depends on whether the activity intruded on the defendant's reasonable expectation of privacy. For a search to have taken place, the defendant must have had a subjective expectation of privacy, and that expectation must have been one that society recognizes as objectively reasonable. . . .

"[W]e are satisfied that the judge's conclusion that no 'search' had taken place, . . ."

"This court has considered various factors in determining whether an individual has an objectively reasonable expectation of privacy. These factors include whether the police had a lawful right to be where they were; whether the public had access to, or might be expected to be in, the area from which the surveillance was undertaken; the nature of the intrusion; and the character of the area (or object) which was the subject of the surveillance. The inquiry is one highly dependent on the particular facts and circumstances of the case." *Commonwealth v. One 1985 Ford Thunderbird Automobile*, 416 Mass. 603, 607 (1993) (citations omitted).

Commonwealth v. Pina, 406 Mass. 540, 544–45 (1990) (citations omitted).

Jail calls. "We conclude that, where the sheriff's policy of monitoring and recording detainees' and inmates' telephone calls is preceded by notice to all parties, and further, where the recording and monitoring is justified by legitimate penological interests, no privacy interest exists in the recorded conversations such that they cannot be obtained by a grand jury subpoena." *In re Grand Jury Subpoena*, 454 Mass. 685, 688 (2009).

Franks

See Notes following G.L. c. 276, § 2B.

Global Positioning System (GPS)

"[W]e conclude that the monitoring and use of data from GPS devices requires a warrant under art. 14." *Commonwealth v. Connolly*, 454 Mass. 808, 824 (2009).

Identification of Confidential Informant

"Where the disclosure of a [confidential] informer's identity, or of the contents of his communication, is relevant and helpful to the defense of an accused, or is essential to a fair determination of a cause, the [government's] privilege [against disclosure] must give way. However, the government is not required to disclose the identity of an informant who is not an active participant in the offense charged." *Commonwealth v. Clarke*, 44 Mass. App. Ct. 502, 511 (1998) (citations and quotation and punctuation marks omitted).

"The analysis of whether an informant's identity should be kept confidential or disclosed may best be described as generally occurring in two stages. The first stage involves preliminary determinations as to (a) whether the Commonwealth has properly asserted an informant privilege, and (b) whether the defendant has adequately challenged the assertion of the privilege as an impermissible interference with his or her right to present a defense. The second stage of the analysis then involves a balancing test, introduced by the United States Supreme Court in [*Roviaro v. United States*, 353 U.S. 53, 59 (1957)], in which the interest of the public in protecting the anonymity of informants is weighed against the defendant's right to defend himself." *Commonwealth v. Bonnett*, 472 Mass. 827, 846–47 (2015).

Medical Marijuana

"In accord with cases relating to other types of license regimes, we conclude that, if police seek a warrant to search such a property [where they suspect an individual is cultivating marijuana] for evidence of illegal marijuana possession or cultivation, they must offer information sufficient to provide probable cause to believe the individual is not properly registered under the act [for the humanitarian use of medical marijuana] to possess or cultivate the suspected substance." *Commonwealth v. Canning*, 471 Mass. 341, 342 (2015).

Motion to Suppress

Hearing. "In sum, we conclude that a defendant's voluntary absence from a scheduled suppression hearing, like a defendant's failure to appear after trial has commenced, may constitute waiver of the defendant's right to be present at that hearing. This does not, however, constitute waiver of any other rights the defendant may have, including the right to the hearing itself." *Robinson v. Commonwealth*, 445 Mass. 280, 290 (2005).

Motor Vehicles

Location of search. "Lugo had no right to require that the police search his automobiles, the object of a valid search warrant, in front of his apartment rather than at the police station. The right protected by the prohibition against unreasonable searches and seizures is a privacy right, not a proprietary one. . . . Privacy is disturbed no more by a search of the [van] at the police station than by a search at the apartment building." *Commonwealth v. Lugo*, 64 Mass. App. Ct. 12, 15 (2005) (citations omitted).

Nexus with Home

"[S]pecial protections are extended to a person's home under both the Federal and State Constitutions. We therefore have rejected the claim that a magistrate may reasonably infer that drugs are being stored in a home based solely on the fact that the defendant lives there, and have held that police must provide particularized information based on police surveillance or otherwise, that would permit a reasonable inference that the defendant likely kept a supply of drugs in the home.

"We have not defined the precise contours of what constitutes 'particularized information' because each case pre-

sents its own facts and must be considered in light of a unique set of circumstances. No bright line rule can establish whether there is a nexus between suspected drug dealing and a defendant's home. Police may rely on a variety of investigatory sources in making the necessary showing, including police surveillance and statements from credible informants. Observations by police of a suspect on multiple occasions leaving his residence and proceeding directly to a prearranged location to sell drugs can support a reasonable inference that the suspect is a drug dealer who stores drugs or packages drugs for resale in his residence.

"A single observation of a suspect leaving his home for a drug deal may also support an inference that drugs will be found in the home where it is coupled with other information, such as statements from credible informants.

"Where police do rely on a single observation of a suspected drug dealer leaving his residence and proceeding to the location of a drug sale, the suspect's location immediately prior to the sale is of greater significance to the nexus determination than are his activities after the sale. Before a sale, the drug dealer either is in possession of drugs, or must proceed to a location to obtain the drugs. The inference that drugs will be found in the house is less strong if based solely on police observations of a suspected dealer returning home after a sale. Nevertheless, 'there need not be definite proof that the seller keeps his supply at his residence. . . . [I]t will suffice if there are some additional facts [that] would support the inference that the supply is probably located there.' 2 W.R. LaFave, *Search and Seizure* § 3.7(d), at 420–421 (4th ed. 2004).

"Here, probable cause to search the apartment was established by Stanton's affidavit, which sets forth particularized information from which it may be inferred that the defendant was using his apartment as a base of operations for a drug delivery business. Stanton described the defendant's pattern, in each of the four controlled purchases, of arriving at the prearranged location, taking the informant for a short drive during which the sale would occur, and then returning to the apartment building. Although police only once observed the defendant leave from the apartment building to meet the informant, they twice observed him engage in the same pattern of behavior with others, on different days. Based on these observations, it reasonably may be inferred that the defendant engaged in six drug transactions. Before three of these transactions, the defendant departed from his apartment and drove directly to the location where an apparent drug deal took place; he returned to the apartment building after all six. The affidavit also provided information that the defendant could deliver drugs in variable quantities on short notice, further supporting the inference that the defendant kept a supply of drugs in his home. The information provided a substantial basis for concluding that drugs, as well as contraband related to an illegal drug distribution enterprise, would be found in the defendant's apartment.

"We reject the defendant's argument that his use of or access to the Toyota during three of the observed transactions provided 'affirmative evidence' that drugs were not being stored in his apartment. A warrant application 'need not establish to a certainty that the items to be seized will be found in the specified location, nor exclude any and all possibility that the items might be found elsewhere. The test is probable cause, not certainty.' That evidence of the defendant's drug

2

sales might also have been found in the defendant's vehicle does not detract from the conclusion that there was probable cause to search the apartment." *Commonwealth v. Escalera*, 462 Mass. 636, 643–46 (2012) (citations, quotations marks, and footnotes omitted).

"In March, 2008, police observed three controlled purchases of heroin by the informant from the defendant. During each purchase, the informant placed a telephone call to the number he associated with Nana, responded to the arranged meeting location under 'constant surveillance' by Brockton police officers, and purchased a quantity of heroin from the defendant, who arrived in the same black 2005 Honda Accord automobile on each occasion. After the first two controlled purchases, police followed the defendant from the site of the transaction; she drove directly to 957 Warren Avenue. Before the third controlled purchase, officers stationed outside that address observed the same black Honda Accord, operated by the defendant, leave the driveway and head in the direction of the prearranged meeting location. Communication from the officers at the location of the purchase confirmed that the same car arrived moments later. After that purchase, the officers who remained at the residence observed the Honda Accord returning to the apartment '[w]ithin two minutes of the transaction taking place,' and moments after its arrival, they 'observed a light turn on in the third floor apartment.'

"Using their police computer records, the officers identified Nana as the defendant. The registered owner of the Honda Accord was listed as the defendant's mother, but the defendant's name was in the record of a motor vehicle stop initiated by the Brockton police department. The defendant's address in the records was listed as '957 Warren Ave Apt. #3 Brockton, Massachusetts.'" . . .

"Given both the police observations of three drug purchases and the informant's tip, considered in light of Commonwealth v. Escalera, supra, there was a sufficient nexus between the defendant's drug-selling activities and her residence to establish probable cause to search that residence." *Commonwealth v. Tapia*, 463 Mass. 721, 723–26 (2012) (citations and footnotes omitted).

Nighttime

"The peculiar and special meaning of nighttime in G.L. c. 278, § 10, is applicable to the crimes of burglary and breaking and entering. There is no indication that the Legislature intended that statutory definition to apply to the procedural law regarding search warrants. *Commonwealth v. Garcia*, 23 Mass. App. Ct. 259, 263 n.7 (1986). . . .

"Henceforth, for warrant purposes, nighttime begins at 10 p.m. and ends at 6 a.m."
Commonwealth v. Grimshaw, 413 Mass. 73, 81 (1992).

No Knock

"Before attempting forcibly to enter a private dwelling to execute a warrant, police must knock, announce their identity, and state their purpose, unless the circumstances justify dispensing with one or all of these requirements. . . . The policies underlying the announcement rule at common law include decreasing the potential for violence, the protection of privacy, and the prevention of unnecessary damage to homes. This court has recognized certain exceptions that may excuse noncompliance with the rule, such as (a) where the police have reason to fear for their own safety or for the safety of people within the location to be entered; (b) where police are

reasonably acting to prevent destruction of evidence or a suspect's escape; and (c) where the person inside the dwelling to be entered has knowledge of the officers' purpose and presence. [This so-called "useless gesture" exception holds that] law enforcement officers should be relieved of having to engage in meaningless procedural formalities that do nothing to further the policies behind the knock and announce rule." *Commonwealth v. Antwine*, 417 Mass. 637, 638–39 (1994) (citations and quotation marks omitted).

Necessary showing to support. "Although not constitutionally required, the so-called 'knock and announce' rule has long featured prominently in our common law. . . . We have expressly held that police officers, when seeking a 'no-knock' warrant, must convince the issuing magistrate that probable cause exists to believe that the evidence will be destroyed if the 'knock and announce' rule is not dispensed with. The fact that drugs are involved is, by itself, insufficient to provide the necessary showing." *Commonwealth v. Gomes*, 408 Mass. 43, 45 (1990) (citations omitted); *see also Commonwealth v. Rodriguez*, 415 Mass. 447 (1993).

Consensual entry by ruse. "Our knock and announce rule is one of common law which is not constitutionally compelled. The reasons supporting the rule are the desirability of decreasing the potential for violence initiated by residents in response to a sudden and unexpected invasion of their premises, provoking further retaliatory violence by the police, damage to homes. A consensual entry by the police, even if obtained by ruse or trickery, will not violate the rule.

"The use of the 'Somerville Pop Warner' ruse by the police to have the door opened was not improper. Although the defendant on opening the door may have been surprised to see a group outside, the identity of the police should have been immediately obvious to her from the badges around their necks. Further, as the judge found, '[b]efore stepping into the apartment the police [formally] announced their identity, authority and purpose.' The reasons behind the rule were satisfied—there was no real likelihood of violence, no unwarranted intrusion on privacy, and no damage to the apartment." *Commonwealth v. Goggin*, 412 Mass. 200, 202 (1992) (citations and quotation marks omitted). *See also Commonwealth v. Villar*, 40 Mass. App. Ct. 742, 743–47 (1996).

Drugs. "The mere fact that drugs are involved and that they are, by their nature, readily disposable or destructible, is insufficient to provide the necessary showing [that the drugs would be destroyed, thus allowing a no knock warrant]." *Commonwealth v. Macias*, 429 Mass. 698, 702 (1999).

No knock not warranted. "The warrant was executed after dark, there was no lookout, and the suspects were not at the windows of the apartment. Every indication was that the officers would not be and were not observed approaching the building. In addition, the locked door on the first floor merely opened when pushed and did not present any obstacle or delay to entering the building, or provide any apparent notice to the suspects three floors above. In sum, when the police arrived at the threshold of the apartment to be searched, there was no basis to believe that the occupants might have notice of their presence and might therefore be destroying evidence. The most relevant concerns set forth in the affidavit, the likelihood of being observed approaching the building and the delay likely to be encountered in breaking through the locked door on the first floor, proved not to be present at the time of execution. These are precisely the type of circumstances that require a reappraisal of the legitimacy of a no-knock entry. On these facts, such entry was no longer warranted and was therefore unlawful." *Commonwealth v. Jimenez*, 438 Mass. 213, 222 (2002).

Particularity

See Notes following G.L. c. 276, § 2.

Plain View

"[T]he police may seize evidence that they inadvertently find in plain view during the course of a search pursuant to a warrant, if they recognize the evidence to be plausibly related to proof of criminal activity of which they are already aware." *Commonwealth v. Wilson*, 427 Mass. 336, 343–44 (1998).

Return of Warrant

See Notes following G.L. c. 276, § 3A.

Securing Premises

"Securing a dwelling, on the basis of probable cause, to prevent the destruction or removal of evidence while a search warrant is being sought is not itself an unreasonable seizure of the dwelling or its contents. *Segura v. United States*, 468 U.S. 796, 810 (1984). Police officers may secure an area to be searched before a warrant is procured as long as the search does not commence before issuance of the warrant." *Commonwealth v. Blake*, 413 Mass. 823, 829–30 (1992) (footnote omitted).

Staleness

"Factors such as the nature of the criminal activity under investigation and the nature of the evidence sought have a bearing on what constitutes excessive remoteness." *Commonwealth v. Scanlan*, 9 Mass. App. Ct. 173, 181 (1980).

In *Scanlan*, 10 months had gone by between the informant seeing the evidence, a sledge hammer, and the date of the affidavit. Court found this *not* to be stale as (1) the tool "had been used in a continuing pattern of criminal conduct;" and (2) it was the sort of item which "'would likely remain in the possession of the suspect in connection with his business or personal affairs.'" *Id.* (quoting 1 LaFave, *Search and Seizures* § 3.7 at 688 (1978)).

See also Commonwealth v. Russell, 46 Mass. App. Ct. 513, 519 (1999) ("[W]hen the information indicates engagement in protracted and continuous drug distribution, precise time is of less significance.") (citation and quotation marks omitted).

Standing

Automatic standing. "In *Commonwealth v. Amendola*, 406 Mass. 592, 601 (1990), we adopted an 'automatic standing' rule for one who seeks to contest the legality of the search and seizure of evidence if possession of that seized evidence is an essential element of the crime charged. . . . The automatic standing rule does not aid the defendant here because the items he seeks to suppress (the videotapes) are not contraband with whose unlawful possession he is charged. In *Commonwealth v. Manning*, 406 Mass. 425, 429 (1990), we discussed the theory of 'target standing' whereby an individual would gain standing to challenge the search of another, not to protect any reasonable expectation of privacy, but to deter police misconduct. We did not decide whether to recognize target standing in the *Manning* case because the record did not show that the police had intentionally engaged in a violation of someone else's constitutional rights in order to obtain evidence against the defendants.

"This case does not present any reasonable basis for granting the defendant standing to challenge the admission of the videotapes, even though he lacked standing on the basis of a reasonable expectation of privacy. A recognition of standing in other circumstances must have a foundation in serious police misconduct (such as described in the *Manning* opinion) or in fundamental unfairness (such as is discussed in the *Amendola* opinion). No police misconduct or basic unfairness is involved here."

Commonwealth v. Price, 408 Mass. 668, 673 (1990).

Possession as essential element of guilt. "The dispositive issue in determining whether a defendant has automatic standing is whether possession of the seized evidence at the time of the contested search is an essential element of guilt. Possession implies control and power, exclusive or joint, or, in the case of constructive possession, knowledge coupled with the ability and intention to exercise dominion and control. . . .

"[W]e conclude that possession is an essential element of the trafficking charge brought against Johnson. Therefore, he has standing to challenge the search of Frazier's handbag as it relates to the trafficking indictment.

"We now turn to the conspiracy charge. The heart of a conspiracy is the formulation of the unlawful agreement or combination. The law of the Commonwealth does not require an overt act to complete a conspiracy. The Commonwealth, however, must prove that the defendant combined with another with the intention to [commit the object crime]. Possession of the cocaine is not an essential element of the conspiracy charge, and, therefore, Johnson does not have standing to challenge the search as it relates to the alleged conspiracy."

Commonwealth v. Frazier, 410 Mass. 235, 243, 245–46 (1991) (citations and quotation marks omitted).

Derivative standing. "Derivative standing permits a defendant to object to the admission of evidence obtained in violation of the Fourth Amendment rights of a codefendant. The principle has been rejected by the Supreme Court of the United States and has no greater vitality in this Commonwealth." *Commonwealth v. Montes*, 49 Mass. App. Ct. 789, 794 n.6 (2000) (citations and quotation marks omitted).

Target standing. "[T]arget standing . . . allows a defendant to challenge the violation of a third party's constitutional rights when that violation was ultimately aimed at getting information to be used against the defendant. Target standing is not recognized as a matter of Federal constitutional law, *see Rakas v. Illinois*, 439 U.S. [128,] 133–138, and, unlike automatic standing, Massachusetts has not explicitly adopted target standing as a matter of State constitutional law. *See Commonwealth v. Manning*, 406 Mass. [425,] 429; *Commonwealth v. Scardamaglia*, 410 Mass. 375, 377–380 (1991)." *Commonwealth v. Montes*, 49 Mass. App. Ct. 789, 794 n.6 (2000).

Expectation of privacy.

Rule. "[I]n analyzing a search by a State actor, we look to whether the defendant had a subjective expectation of privacy in the place searched or the item seized, and whether as an objective matter society would recognize that expectation as reasonable." *Commonwealth v. Cabral*, 69 Mass. App. Ct. 68, 72 (2007).

"Where the defendant has automatic standing, the defendant need not show that he has a reasonable expectation of

2

privacy in the place searched. The practical consequence of automatic standing is that, if a defendant is charged with illegally possessing drugs or firearms that were seized during a search, the defendant may succeed in suppressing such evidence where the search was unconstitutional, regardless of whether he has a subjective or objectively reasonable expectation of privacy in the place where the drugs or firearms were found.

"The defendant, however, still must show that there was a search in the constitutional sense, that is, that someone had a reasonable expectation of privacy in the place searched, because only then would probable cause, reasonable suspicion, or consent be required to justify the search.

. . .

"Where, as here, automatic standing is applied to the search of an automobile, whether a person's expectation of privacy in a vehicle is reasonable turns on the degree of visibility of the automobile's interior from the outside. *See Commonwealth v. Connolly*, 454 Mass. 808, 819 (2009). A reasonable expectation of privacy in a vehicle 'clearly exists in those areas which would be otherwise free from observation except by physical intrusion of some sort.' *Commonwealth v. Podgurski*, 386 Mass. 385, 389 (1982), *cert. denied*, 459 U.S. 1222 (1983). 'In the typical passenger vehicle, these places must include at least the trunk, the glove compartment, closed containers in the interior, and in most cases, the area under the seats.' *Id.*

"Here, the police entered a parked automobile where the defendant had been sitting in the driver's seat, and inspected areas in the automobile, including the center console where the marijuana was found, that could not be seen without entering the automobile. As a result, the search of the center console inside the automobile, even if conducted during a protective sweep for weapons, was a search in the constitutional sense, and the defendant, because he is charged with possessing the marijuana found in the center console, has automatic standing to challenge the constitutionality of the search. In fact, even without the automatic standing rule, the defendant, who at a minimum was a passenger in the parked automobile, would have standing to challenge the search of the automobile in this case." *Commonwealth v. Mubdi*, 456 Mass. 385, 392–94 (2010) (footnotes and citations omitted).

Exception to automatic standing. "There is an exception to automatic standing where the defendant had no right to be in the house or automobile where the evidence was found. *See Commonwealth v. Carter*, 424 Mass. 409 (1997). While in *Commonwealth v. Carter*, *supra* at 412, we concluded that the defendant, who was charged with possession of cocaine found on a porch, could not challenge the constitutionality of the search of the porch because the defendant had been there only in an attempt to avoid apprehension and had no reasonable expectation of privacy in the porch, our holding reflects an exception to the automatic standing rule in circumstances where the defendant was unlawfully on the property searched and where it would be inappropriate to grant him standing to challenge a search of the property." *Commonwealth v. Mubdi*, 456 Mass. 385, 393 n.8 (2010).

Third-Party Residence

"We conclude that a person who is the subject of a valid arrest warrant and is arrested by police while in the residence of a third party has a right under the Fourth Amendment and art. 14 to insist that the police have a reasonable belief at the time they enter the residence that the person would be present. However, at least where, as in this case, the person has disclaimed any connection to the third party's residence, he does not have a constitutional right to insist that the police obtain a search warrant to search for him in the third party's residence or, where a search warrant is obtained, to challenge the basis on which the warrant issued." *Commonwealth v. Tatum*, 466 Mass. 45, 46 (2013).

2. WARRANTLESS SEARCHES

General Principles	Incident-to-Forfeiture
Abandonment	Inevitable Discovery
Accomplice Sweep	Informant's Tip
Administrative Searches	Intervening Action
Auto Body Shops and Used	Dissipating Taint
Car Businesses	of Illegality
Community Caretaking	Inventory Searches
Function	Motor Vehicles
Consent	Plain Feel
Consent by Another	Plain View
(Common Authority)	Presence
Consent by Another	Private Party Search
(Apparent Authority)	Probationer/Parolee Search
Destruction of Evidence	Protective Sweep
DNA Profile	Roadblocks
Emergency Exception	Ruse
Exclusionary Rule	School Searches
Exigent Circumstances	Search Incident to Arrest
"Free to Leave" Standard	Seizure
Furtive Gesture	Stop and Frisk

General Principles

Per se unreasonable. "'It is a cardinal principle that searches conducted outside the judicial process, without prior approval by judge or magistrate, are per se unreasonable [under both the Fourth Amendment and art. 14]—subject only to a few specifically established and well-delineated exceptions.'' *Commonwealth v. Anderson*, 406 Mass. 343, 346 (1989), quoting *United States v. Ross*, 456 U.S. 798, 825 (1982)."

"A warrantless search is inherently suspect unless it falls within one of the exceptions to the warrant requirement." *Commonwealth v. Frazier*, 410 Mass. 235, 239 (1991).

Burden of proof. "[I]t is the Commonwealth's burden to prove that a warrantless search falls within a permissible exception to the warrant requirement and is, therefore, reasonable[. I]t is equally well-settled that that burden only attaches to the Commonwealth after the defendant has first demonstrated that a 'search and seizure' in the constitutional sense has occurred." *Commonwealth v. McCambridge*, 44 Mass. App. Ct. 285, 289 (1998) (citation omitted).

While the burden of justifying the reasonableness of a warrantless search is on the Commonwealth, the burden of going forward with the evidence on the defendant's motion to suppress is on the defendant as the moving party. *Commonwealth v. Ferrara*, 10 Mass. App. Ct. 818 (1980).

Authority. Article 14 provides greater protection against unlawful searches of seizures than the Fourth Amendment. *Commonwealth v. Cast*, 407 Mass. 891, 907 (1990).

Counsel is wise to base motions to suppress evidence on G.L. c. 276, § 1, the Fourth Amendment of the United States

Constitution and article 14 of the Massachusetts Declaration of Rights.

Pursuit. "It is true that law enforcement personnel must have reasonable suspicion for pursuit to begin. But pursuit begins only when action by police would communicate to the reasonable person an attempt to capture or otherwise intrude on an individual's freedom of movement. It occurs when police attempt to stop an individual to effectuate a threshold inquiry. Following or observing someone without more, such as using a siren or lights, attempting to block or control an individual's path, direction, or speed, or commanding the individual to halt, is not pursuit. Following someone for the purpose of surveillance is not pursuit." *Commonwealth v. Grandison*, 433 Mass. 135, 138 (2001) (internal citations and quotation and punctuation marks omitted).

Seizures. See "Seizure" section below.

Strip searches. "Strip searches are not as intrusive as manual body cavity searches so as to require something more than probable cause before they can be deemed reasonable. However, strip searches are more intrusive than 'pat-downs,' which require police to have only a reasonable suspicion before conducting one. Thus, we conclude that probable cause is the appropriate standard to apply to strip and visual body cavity searches." *Commonwealth v. Thomas*, 429 Mass. 403, 408 (1999).

"Although we did not provide an express definition of a strip search in the *Thomas* case, we noted that '[a] strip search generally refers to an inspection of a naked individual, without any scrutiny of his body cavities. A visual body cavity search extends to a visual inspection of the anal and genital areas.' [*Commonwealth v. Thomas*, 429 Mass. 403,] 407 n.4 . . . The Appeals Court provided a correct and useful characterization of a strip search in *Commonwealth v. Ramirez*, 56 Mass. App. Ct. 317 (2002), when it stated that under the *Thomas* rule: 'before police may command removal of an arrested person's last layer of clothing, they must have probable cause to believe—i.e., "the facts and circumstances within the[ir] knowledge . . . [must be] enough to warrant a prudent person in believing," . . . —that they will find a weapon, contraband, or the fruits or instrumentalities of criminal activity that they could not reasonably expect to discover without forcing the arrested person to discard all of his or her clothing.' *Id.* at 323 . . . We approve of the Appeals Court's interpretation of *Thomas* and now adopt its implicit definition of a strip search as one in which a detainee is commanded to remove the last layer of his or her clothing. Here, the defendant was ordered to remove his shirt, his shoes, his socks, and his pants. In the last analysis, however, he was not told to remove the last layer of his clothing, and, thus, he was not subjected to a strip search." *Commonwealth v. Prophete*, 443 Mass. 548, 556–57 (2005) (citations omitted).

EXCEPTIONS TO WARRANT REQUIREMENT

Abandonment

Control relinquished. "Abandonment occurs only when . . . a defendant has voluntarily given up all control over the property." *Commonwealth v. Ferguson*, 410 Mass. 611, 615 (1991).

Trash Bag. The defendant contended "that he had a reasonable expectation of privacy in the contents of the trash bag. We disagree . . .

"The bag was placed three feet from the street near the driveway in front of Pratt's residence. It sat exposed to the public, waiting to be gathered up by the trash collector the following morning. This is not a case where police officers went to the defendant's back porch to seize garbage which had not yet been placed at the curbside for collection. *See People v. Edwards*, 71 Cal.2d 1096 (1969). Rather, in this case the defendant can be said to have abandoned his privacy interests in his garbage through the placement of his trash bags at the curb for collection. *See Commonwealth v. Chappee*, 397 Mass. 508, 512–513 (1986) (same result under Fourth Amendment to the United States Constitution)."

Commonwealth v. Pratt, 407 Mass. 647, 660 (1990).

Briefcase. *Commonwealth v. Straw*, 422 Mass. 756 (1996) (police needed warrant to search locked briefcase thrown by the defendant from his second floor window onto the fenced in curtilage of his house as he still had an expectation of privacy).

Saliva. "In the present case, although the defendant had a reasonable expectation of privacy in his saliva (and other bodily fluids), when he expectorated on to a public street and did not retrieve the fluid, he voluntarily abandoned that protection; he assumed the risk of the public witnessing his action and thereafter taking possession of his bodily fluids." *Commonwealth v. Cabral*, 69 Mass. App. Ct. 68, 72 (2007) (citations and quotation marks omitted).

Accomplice Sweep

"[T]he Commonwealth urges the application of the accomplice sweep exception to the warrant requirement. Although this exception has not been considered in Massachusetts, it has considerable appeal, assuming it has reasonable limits. The doctrine, for instance, could be an alternative to the protective sweep exception if there is a basis to seek out accomplices but not a basis for acting in the interest of self-protection. The standard applied by courts recognizing this exception appears to parallel the protective sweep, in that, once police have lawfully entered a premises and made an arrest therein, something less than the usual quantum of probable cause suffices to justify a limited additional intrusion to investigate the possible presence of accomplices.

". . . [W]e do not have occasion on the present record to adopt or reject an accomplice sweep exception."

Commonwealth v. Dubois, 44 Mass. App. Ct. 294, 297–98 n.4 (1998) (citations omitted).

Administrative Searches

"There is no question that area-entry inspections at court house entrances, for safety and security purposes, are permissible without a warrant or individualized suspicion of wrongdoing or danger . . . . The juvenile implicitly demonstrated his consent to such an inspection when he approached the security checkpoint area, placed his bag on the table, and passed through the metal detector. . . . We conclude that the juvenile was not entitled to withdraw his consent after the inspection had commenced, at the time he became aware that a manual search of his bag would in fact take place." *Commonwealth v. Roland R.*, 448 Mass. 278, 281 (2007).

"Thus, in the absence of any prior notice or warning to motorists, the State police failed to minimize the intrusiveness of the stop and search procedures at the reservoir. On that basis alone, the suspicionless stop of vehicles along Cobble Mountain Road fails to meet the standards required of a

2

constitutionally permissible administrative search." *Commonwealth v. Carkhuff*, 441 Mass. 122, 130 (2004) (footnote omitted).

"Where a search of persons entering a public place is necessary to protect a sensitive facility from a real danger of violence, an 'administrative search' without a warrant may be justified. The search must be limited and no more intrusive than necessary to protect against the danger to be avoided, but nevertheless reasonably effective to discover the materials sought. The inspection must be conducted for a purpose other than the gathering of evidence for criminal prosecutions." *Commonwealth v. Harris*, 383 Mass. 655, 657 (1981) (citations and quotation marks omitted).

Auto Body Shops and Used Car Businesses

"The principal issue is whether police officers constitutionally were entitled to conduct a warrantless inspection of the defendant's licensed auto body shop and used car business pursuant to G.L. c. 140, § 66. We hold that they were and thus affirm the defendant's conviction for refusal to permit the inspection."

The Supreme Judicial Court did note however that "a fair reading of §§ 66 and 67 requires that warrantless inspections be conducted only when the premises are open for business."

Commonwealth v. Eagleston, 402 Mass. 199, 200, 205 (1988).

Community Caretaking Function

"[T]he cases are literally legion in which police action involving a search or seizure is justified not by any reference to a law enforcement function but under this community caretaking rationale." Examples include "entry to quell loud and disruptive noise in residential neighborhood"; "break[ing] down a door to enter a burning home to rescue occupants or extinguish a fire, to prevent a shooting or to bring emergency aid to an injured person." *Commonwealth v. Smigliano*, 427 Mass. 490, 496–97 (1998) (concurring opinion) (citations omitted). *See also Smigliano Appendix* at 501–03, for numerous other examples and *Commonwealth v. Murdough*, 44 Mass. App. Ct. 736, 737–38 (1998) ("About one and one-half hours later, as they were driving past the same rest area [at 8 a.m.], the troopers noticed that the Capri was in the same spot, and that there were no other vehicles at the rest area. Its brake lights were on. [The engine was not running] . . . After two to three minutes of knocking, the defendant awoke . . . [appearing disheveled and not wearing shoes.]"). Unable to find the registration, the defendant in mid conversation became incoherent and fell asleep. Concerned about his condition, the defendant was asked to step from the car. He was unsteady on his feet and appeared dazed. In plain view the police saw drugs. Search valid although the defendant despite: (1) not being able to produce the registration, correctly named the owner of the car; and (2) a belief on the part of the police that drugs might be involved. The troopers acted reasonably in ascertaining the medical condition of the defendant.

"Several reasons justify an officer's actions in requesting a driver's license when performing community caretaking responsibilities. In many cases, police officers are required to make a written report of contacts with citizens. An officer needs to know whom he or she is assisting in the event a citizen later complains about improper behavior on the part of the officer or makes any kind of legal claim against the officer. Moreover, even seemingly innocent activity, such as

refueling a disabled car, could later turn out to be theft of a car that was left on the shoulder of a highway.

"Given the length of time it took for the trooper to rouse the defendant by knocking on the car window, the defendant's response to the trooper's question, and the fact that the defendant's car was parked in a breakdown lane late at night on a rural stretch of road, with no indication from the defendant that he was having car trouble . . . , it was reasonable for the trooper to ascertain the defendant's identity. This request for the defendant's license and registration was a minimal intrusion on the defendant's rights, outweighed by the trooper's responsibility to protect the public, through the community caretaking function, from a driver who may be unfit to continue driving." *Commonwealth v. Evans*, 436 Mass. 369, 375–76 (2002) (citations and quotation marks omitted).

Consent

Voluntariness. "When the Commonwealth relies on consent as the basis for a warrantless search, it must demonstrate consent unfettered by coercion, express or implied, which is something more than mere acquiescence to a claim of lawful authority. Voluntariness of consent is a question of fact to be determined in the circumstances of each case." *Commonwealth v. Cantalupo*, 380 Mass. 173, 177 (1980) (citations and quotation and punctuation marks omitted).

Ruse used to obtain. "It makes no difference that the defendant's consent to police entry was obtained by a ruse . . .

"[W]e hold that the common law of Massachusetts does not require officers to announce their identity and purpose before executing a search warrant at a residence to which they have access by consent of the resident."

Commonwealth v. Sepulveda, 406 Mass. 180, 182–83 (1989).

Consent by Another (Common Authority)

"A third party does not have the authority to consent to a warrantless entry into a building merely because he has a proprietary interest in the premises. . . . ([A] landlord does not generally have the authority to consent to a search of house rented to another.) Nevertheless, a person who has 'common authority' over the property to be searched may properly consent to a search.

"The 'common authority' that is required for a third party's consent to a warrantless entry into a building rests on mutual use of the property by persons generally having joint access or control for most purposes, so that it is reasonable to recognize that any of the co-inhabitants has the right to permit the inspection in his own right and that the others have assumed the risk that one of their number might permit the common area to be searched. (When third party persons have broad rights to access and use of one's property, one assumes the risk that they may consent to a search of those areas.)"

Commonwealth v. Ploude, 44 Mass. App. Ct. 137, 140 (1998) (citations and quotations marks omitted).

"Antagonism that may spring up between the occupants does not invalidate the consent, for the relevant analysis in consent cases focuses on the relationship between the consenter and the property searched, not the relationship between the consenter and the defendant. . . . What has been said needs the qualification that an occupant may have been excluded specifically from a particular part of the premises and so could not properly search it or give consent to its search." *Commonwealth v. Noonan*, 48 Mass. App. Ct. 356, 362 (1999).

2

"We understand that the police need clear guidance as to who has common authority over a residence and therefore who is entitled to give actual consent, because, as here, they rely on such consent in deciding to conduct a warrantless search, as opposed to securing the residence and applying for a search warrant. Therefore, we declare under art. 14 that a person may have actual authority to consent to a warrantless search of a home by the police only if (1) the person is a coinhabitant with a shared right of access to the home, that is, the person lives in the home, either as a member of the family, a roommate, or a houseguest whose stay is of substantial duration and who is given full access to the home; or (2) the person, generally a landlord, shows the police a written contract entitling that person to allow the police to enter the home to search for and seize contraband or evidence. No such entitlement may reasonably be presumed by custom or oral agreement." *Commonwealth v. Porter P.*, 456 Mass. 254, 264–265 (2010) (footnotes omitted).

Consent by Another (Apparent Authority)

"Apparent authority is 'judged against an objective standard: would the facts available to the officer at the moment . . . 'warrant a man of reasonable caution in the belief' that the consenting party had authority over the premises?'" *Commonwealth v. Porter P.*, 456 Mass. 254, 267 (2010) (citations omitted). "Even before the United States Supreme Court decided [*Illinois v. Rodriguez*, 497 U.S. 177 (1990)] . . . we suggested that apparent authority may justify a warrantless search where the person giving consent lacks actual authority, but we have never approved a warrantless search exclusively on apparent authority. Consistent with these past decisions but for the first time today, we explicitly adopt under art. 14 the doctrine of apparent authority." *Commonwealth v. Porter P.*, 456 Mass. at 269.

"While we conclude that a search of a home does not violate art. 14 if the police officer has the voluntary consent of an individual with the apparent authority to give such consent, we do so only if the reasonable mistake of fact occurs despite diligent inquiry by the police as to the consenting individual's common authority over the home. To conduct a diligent inquiry, a police officer must take two basic steps. First, the police officer must base his conclusion of actual authority on facts, not assumptions or impressions. He must continue his inquiry until he has reliable information on which to base a finding of actual authority to consent. . . .

"Second, even when the consenting individual explicitly asserts that he lives there, if the surrounding circumstances could conceivably be such that a reasonable person would doubt its truth, the police officer must make further inquiry to resolve the ambiguity. The police officer owes a duty to explore, rather than ignore, contrary facts tending to suggest that the person consenting to the search lacks actual authority. Police must not only thoroughly question the individual consenting to the search with respect to his or her actual authority, but also pay close attention to whether the surrounding circumstances indicate that the consenting individual is truthful and accurate in asserting common authority over the premises." *Commonwealth v. Porter P.*, 456 Mass. at 271–72 (citations, footnotes, and quotation marks omitted).

Destruction of Evidence

A warrantless entry into a house may be justified by the principle of destruction of evidence, particularly in illegal drug cases, "when entry is reasonably believed to be necessary to prevent the imminent destruction or removal of incriminating evidence." *Commonwealth v. DiGeronimo*, 38 Mass. App. Ct. 714, 725–26 (1995).

DNA Profile

"We conclude that where . . . DNA analysis is limited to the creation of a DNA profile from lawfully seized evidence of a crime, and where the profile is used only to identify its unknown source, the DNA analysis is not a search in the constitutional sense. Therefore, no search warrant was required to conduct the DNA analysis of the bloodstain from the defendant's clothing that revealed that the victim was the source of the blood." *Commonwealth v. Arzola*, 470 Mass. 809, 820 (2015).

Emergency Exception

"The emergency exception will justify what would otherwise be an illegal, warrantless entry when there is an immediate need for assistance for the protection of life or property." *Commonwealth v. Allen*, 54 Mass. App. Ct. 719, 721 (2002).

Standard. "'In justifying action under this doctrine the Commonwealth has the burden of showing . . . that "the authorities had reasonable grounds to believe that an exigency existed, and . . . that the action [of the police] . . . were reasonable under the circumstances . . . . [W]hether an exigency existed, and whether the response of the police was reasonable and therefore lawful, are matters to be evaluated in relation to the scene as it could appear to the officers at the time, not as it may seem to a scholar after the event with the benefit of leisured retrospective analysis.'" *Commonwealth v. Davis*, 63 Mass. App. Ct. 88, 89–90 (2005) (quoting *Commonwealth v. Young*, 382 Mass. 448, 456 (1981)) (citations omitted).

Drunk driving. Where an anonymous caller warned police that a drunk driver was heading in a particular direction and offered a detailed description of the driver and her vehicle and its license plate number, "[the evidence] was, under the circumstances, sufficient to conclude that an emergency existed, requiring immediate action for the protection of life and property of both the operator and the general public. By motioning the driver to pull over, the officer acted reasonably and proportionally given the situation." *Commonwealth v. Davis*, 63 Mass. App. Ct. 88, 90–91 (2005).

Exclusionary Rule

"The general rule is that evidence is to be excluded if it is found to be the 'fruit' of a police officer's unlawful actions. *See Wong Sun v. United States*, 371 U.S. 471, 484 (1963). 'In order to make effective the fundamental constitutional guarantees of sanctity of the home and inviolability of the person, [the United States Supreme] Court held nearly half a century ago that evidence seized during an unlawful search could not constitute proof against the victim of the search.' *Id.*, citing *Boyd v. United States*, 116 U.S. 616 (1886), and *Weeks v. United States*, 232 U.S. 383 (1914). 'The exclusionary prohibition extends as well to the indirect as the direct products of such invasions.' *Wong Sun v. United States*, *supra*, citing *Silverthorne Lumber Co. v. United States*, 251 U.S. 385 (1920)." *Commonwealth v. Balicki*, 436 Mass. 1, 15–16 (2002).

"However, the *Wong Sun* case also reaffirmed that the exclusionary rule does not apply when the government learned about the evidence 'from an independent source' or when the connection between the police officer's conduct and the discovery of the evidence has 'become so attenuated as to dissipate the taint.' *Wong Sun v. United States*, *supra*, quoting *Silverthorne Lumber Co. v. United States*, *supra*, and *Nardone v. United States*, 308 U.S. 338, 341 (1939). Over time, the inevitable discovery rule has evolved as an exception to the exclusionary rule. *See Nix v. Williams*, 467 U.S. 431 (1984); *Commonwealth v. O'Connor*, 406 Mass. 112, 115–116 (1989)." *Commonwealth v. Balicki*, 436 Mass. 1, 16 (2002).

Exigent Circumstances

"Exigencies which may justify a procedure without warrant are a narrow category and must be established by the Commonwealth which bears the burden of proof. Some factors which would tend to support a finding of exigency include: 'a showing that the crime was one of violence or that the suspect was armed, a clear demonstration of probable cause, strong reason to believe that the suspect was in the dwelling, and a likelihood that the suspect would escape if not apprehended. Additional considerations testing the reasonableness of police conduct are whether the entry is peaceable and whether the entry is in the nighttime. . . .

"In addition, since the entry into the apartment was consensual, no showing exigency to justify that entry is required." *Commonwealth v. Viriyahiranpaiboon*, 412 Mass. 224, 227 (1992).

Limit of "protective sweep" at murder scene. "In a murder case, the police may make a prompt warrantless search of the area to see if there are other victims or if a killer is still on the premises. The scope of such a search, sometimes characterized as a protective sweep, is limited to a cursory inspection for victims or suspects. Items of possible evidence found in plain view during the course of this limited protective search may be seized.

"[A]ny exigency ends with the conclusion of the protective sweep." A "more extended police presence" may be justified under an "exigency of perishable evidence." *Commonwealth v. Lewin (No. 1)*, 407 Mass. 617, 621–22, 624, 626 n.3 (1990) (citations and quotation marks omitted).

See *Couture* and *McCauley* cites following Stop and Frisk.

Defendant armed. "'When a tip . . . concerns the possession of a firearm, it deserves the immediate attention of law enforcement officials.' *Commonwealth v. Stoute*, 422 Mass. 782, 790 (1996)." *Commonwealth v. Manning*, 44 Mass. App. Ct. 695, 700 (1998) ("police were responding to a tip that the defendant had fired gunshots and was in possession of a firearm").

"Free to Leave" Standard

"[Under article 14, i]n the context of a police pursuit, . . . a person being pursued is seized when the circumstances, objectively considered, indicate to that person that 'he would not be free to leave the area (or to remain there) without first responding to a police officer's inquiry.'" *Commonwealth v. Ramos*, 430 Mass. 545, 548 (2000) (quoting *Commonwealth v. Stoute*, 422 Mass. 782, 789 (1996)).

Specific scenario considered. "Officer Peck pulled to the curb on the wrong side of the street, hailed the man (later identified as the defendant), and asked to speak to him. The defendant ignored Peck and continued walking at a faster pace. Zollo, who was not driving, got out of the cruiser, followed the defendant, and again asked to speak with him. Zollo told the defendant to stop, but the defendant ignored the command. When Zollo got to within two feet of the defend-

ant, the defendant removed the bulky object from his coat and threw it at Zollo. The object, a video cassette recorder (VCR), struck the officer in the leg. The defendant ran but was captured by the officers.

". . . The judge concluded that there was no constitutional violation in Peck's initial attempt to talk to the defendant. We agree. '[Peck] remained in [the] cruiser while asking to speak to the defendant, and he did not impede or restrict the defendant's freedom of movement.' *Commonwealth v. Barros*, 435 Mass. 171, 174 (2001).

"He then ruled that Zollo's action in getting out of the cruiser, following the defendant, and telling him to 'stop,' 'constituted pursuit and a seizure.' The case law supports this conclusion. *See Commonwealth v. Stoute*, 422 Mass. [782, 783 (1996)] ('a person is seized, for purposes of art. 14 [of the Declaration of Rights of the Massachusetts Constitution], when a police officer initiates a pursuit with the obvious intent of requiring the person to submit to questioning'); *Commonwealth v. Barros*, 435 Mass. [171, 175–76 (2001)] ('fact that the officer pursued the defendant by leaving his cruiser and walking up to him after being rebuffed is highly relevant in determining whether a reasonable person, in view of all the circumstances, would have felt free to terminate the encounter and leave')." *Commonwealth v. Mock*, 54 Mass. App. Ct. 276, 277–79 (2002) (certain quotation marks omitted).

Furtive Gesture

"The phrase 'furtive gesture' appears in many decisions where the issue is whether a patfrisk or a search of a vehicle is justified. The gestures are interpreted by the police (and by the courts) as demonstrating the hiding of contraband or as threatening the officers' safety." *Commonwealth v. Holley*, 52 Mass. App. Ct. 659, 664–65 (2001) (citation omitted).

"Strange, furtive, or suspicious behavior or movements can infuse otherwise innocent activity with an incriminating aspect. . . . [W]hether a gesture is furtive (and indicative of criminal activity or danger to police officers) or innocent depends on the factual context." *Commonwealth v. Pagan*, 63 Mass. App. Ct. 780, 782–83 (2005) (citations omitted).

"A lunge or other furtive gesture is usually insufficient, by itself, to render a search reasonable. Such movements, however, are a relevant factor to consider in determining the reasonableness of a patfrisk." *Commonwealth v. Holley*, 52 Mass. App. Ct. at 663 (citations and quotation marks omitted).

"The fact that a motorist, when in the process of being stopped, leans over to the passenger side visor, cannot be considered as a threatening gesture, or one that can be considered as hiding contraband. To hold otherwise, would mean that any gesture, no matter how innocent or trivial, could be interpreted as a furtive gesture." *Commonwealth v. Holley*, 52 Mass. App. Ct. at 665.

"That the defendant moved his upper shoulders and appeared to place something on the seat is neither indicative of criminality nor a ground for reasonable apprehension. He did not duck out of sight, lean forward, or move back and forth in his seat. In the circumstances here, moving his shoulders did not amount to strange, furtive, or suspicious behavior." *Commonwealth v. Hooker*, 52 Mass. App. Ct. 683, 687 (2001) (citations omitted).

Incident-to-Forfeiture

"The relevant provision of the Massachusetts forfeiture statute, G.L. c. 94C, § 47(f)(1), . . . shows that, unlike under the Federal forfeiture statute, an owner's property rights are not extinguished on the Commonwealth's seizure of property, the Commonwealth must follow statutory procedures subsequent to seizure, and, by specific reference to G.L. c. 276, procedures for securing search warrants are made applicable to forfeiture proceedings." *Commonwealth v. Agosto*, 428 Mass. 31, 35–36 (1998).

Inevitable Discovery

"In *Commonwealth v. O'Connor*, 406 Mass. 112 (1989), we adopted an inevitable discovery rule which complied with art. 14 of the Massachusetts Declaration of Rights. We indicated that application of the rule requires a two-step analysis which focuses, first, in the question of inevitability, and second, on the character of the police misconduct. *Id.* at 117. . . .

"In our view, the case turns on the resolution of the first part of the test—whether the pocketbook would have been inevitably discovered by lawful means. . . .

"It had not been found by anyone in the ten days that had elapsed after the commission of the crimes.

"Even though the police had some general leads on the pocketbook's whereabouts, the over-all situation as to its eventual discovery was characterized by a measure of doubt and uncertainty. At best, the findings indicate to us a probability that the pocketbook might have been found. This is insufficient to satisfy the demanding test of inevitability. The evidence should have been excluded."

Commonwealth v. Perrot, 407 Mass. 539, 546–47 (1990).

Informant's Tip

***Aguilar-Spinelli* two-prong test.** "To comport with art. 14 of the Massachusetts Declaration of Rights, an arrest and search executed in response to an informant's tip must meet the two-pronged standard of probable cause set forth in *Aguilar v. Texas*, 378 U.S. 108 (1964), and *Spinelli v. United States*, 393 U.S. 410 (1969). We require the Commonwealth to demonstrate (1) some underlying circumstances from which the law enforcement officials could have concluded that the information was reliable (the veracity test); and (2) some underlying circumstances which demonstrate a basis of the informant's knowledge (basis of knowledge test). . . .

"Addressing the second prong of the *Aguilar-Spinelli* test, we agree with the motion judge that the informant failed to provide information which would have established the basis of his knowledge of the defendant's drug possession. However, '[i]n the absence of a statement detailing the manner in which the information was gathered, it is especially important that the tip describe the accused's criminal activity in sufficient detail that the magistrate may know that he is relying on something more substantial than a casual rumor circulating in the underworld or an accusation based merely on an individual's general reputation. The detail provided by the informant in *Draper v. United States*, 358 U.S. 307 (1959), provides a suitable benchmark.' *Spinelli v. United States*, 393 U.S. 410, 416 (1969). Relying on *Spinelli*, we have stated that independent police corroboration can compensate for deficiencies in either or both prongs of the *Aguilar-Spinelli* test. . . .

"In this case, the informant accurately described the defendant's approximate age and height, as well as the details of his clothing. The informant also predicted the defendant's arrival time and place.[2]"

In footnote 2 the Court stated that "[t]his case is distinguishable from *Commonwealth v. Borges*, [395 Mass. 788 (1985)] because in this case, the informant described not only the defendant's physical appearance, but also his expected behavior, that is, his arrival in Boston on a particular bus from a particular point of departure. In *Borges*, the informant described only the defendant's physical appearance, and although she had recently been present with the defendant at a particular location, she did not state whether the defendant still could be found there. Indeed, the defendant's whereabouts were determined by a police officer who had seen the defendant five minutes before his arrest. Thus, the informant's tip in *Borges* did not indicate to police any expected behavior. *See Borges, supra* at 789."

Commonwealth v. Robinson, 403 Mass. 163, 164–66 (1988). *See also Commonwealth v. Santana*, 403 Mass. 167 (1988); *Commonwealth v. Gonzalez*, 403 Mass. 172 (1988); *Commonwealth v. Farrow*, 403 Mass. 176 (1988); *Commonwealth v. Spence*, 403 Mass. 179 (1988) ("Unlike the informants in the prior cases who described both the appearance and the expected behavior of the defendants, this informant failed to describe the defendant's appearance, with the requisite detail to satisfy the reliability prong of Aguilar-Spinelli." *Id.* at 182 (citation and footnote omitted)).

Relevance of informant's reliability. An informant told two police officers that drugs could be purchased by calling a specific telephone number. One officer called the number, and made arrangements to make a buy in fifteen minutes.

When the buy was made, an arrest was made.

A motion to suppress was allowed as the veracity and reliability of the informant was never established.

Held, the trial judge was wrong in allowing the motion to suppress. "[T]he veracity and reliability of the informant is irrelevant because the evidence was seized pursuant to a valid arrest."

Commonwealth v. Borden, 403 Mass. 1008, 1009 (1988) (rescript).

Circumstances insufficient to establish probable cause. "The circumstances that, sometime in 1979, police officers found the defendant's name in a ledger used by a subsequently convicted drug offender to record illegal drug sales, that in January, 1982, police officers had been told by a reliable informant that he had witnessed drug transactions in the defendant's home, that during the next seven months police officers had received tips respecting the defendant's drug dealing from various informants of unknown reliability, that in August, 1982, a reliable informant, revealing no source for his information, had told police officers that he had heard of a large amount of drugs in the defendant's home, and that, shortly after a police-arranged telephone call in which the defendant was told that police were about to search his home, a police officer had observed the defendant back his automobile up to the house, a second man place 'something' in the trunk of the automobile, and the defendant drive away did not, under the test enunciated in *Commonwealth v. Upton*, 394 Mass. 363 (1985), establish probable cause for the subsequent warrantless search by police officers of the trunk of the defendant's automobile, in which they found a fifty-pound bale and nine one-pound plastic bags of marihuana." *Commonwealth v. Reddington*, 395 Mass. 315 (1985) (quote from syllabus).

2

Reliability of anonymous informant. "[I]n order to conclude that a tip from an anonymous caller is reliable, the tip must provide some specificity of nonobvious facts which show familiarity with the suspect or specific facts which predict behavior." *Commonwealth v. Bakoian*, 412 Mass. 295, 300–01 (1992).

"By providing information to the police after knowing that her call was being recorded, and that the number she was calling from had been identified, we conclude that the caller placed her anonymity sufficiently at risk such that her reliability should have been accorded greater weight than that of an anonymous informant. Although at the end of the conversation the caller appeared anxious to terminate the telephone call, and did not leave her name, it is apparent from the tape recording of the conversation that she was principally concerned about the defendant (not the police) knowing her identity if she were to be observed on the cell phone." *Commonwealth v. Costa*, 448 Mass. 510, 517 (2007) (footnotes omitted). "While it is possible that the caller was using a borrowed cell phone or a prepaid cell phone to which she may not have been directly traceable, she would be potentially identifiable through the owner of the cell phone." *Id.* at n.11.

Reliability of ordinary citizen. Unlike an anonymous informer, an ordinary citizen who witnesses a violent crime can be regarded as reliable without any prior demonstration of his reliability. *Commonwealth v. Bowden*, 379 Mass. 472 (1980).

911 Call. In *Navarette v. California*, 134 S. Ct. 1683 (2014), the Supreme Court "concluded that because of technological and regulatory developments, 'a reasonable officer could conclude that a false tipster would think twice before using [the 911] system,' and therefore its use is 'one of the relevant circumstances that, taken together, [can justify an] officer's reliance on the information reported in the 911 call.' *Id.* at 1690. We . . . consider whether the police had reasonable suspicion to conduct an investigative stop of his vehicle, and whether, under art. 14 of the Massachusetts Declaration of Rights, we would afford weight similar to that afforded by the Supreme Court to the reliability of anonymous 911 telephone callers.

"We decline to endorse the Supreme Court's reliance on the use of the 911 system as an independent indicium of reliability for an anonymous tip." *Commonwealth v. Depiero*, 473 Mass. 450, 451–52 (2016).

Weapons. "We conclude that reasonable suspicion justifying an investigatory stop cannot be founded on an anonymous tip concerning a concealed weapon made by a person whose reliability is not established where there is no indication (in the tip or otherwise) of a threat to anyone's physical well being or of the commission of a crime (other than the possibility of the possession of an unlicensed weapon). *Commonwealth v. Alvarado*, 423 Mass. 266, 274 (1996).

Intervening Action Dissipating Taint of Illegality

"A woman living at the address reported that a 'heavier-set black male' attempted to enter the rear door of her [apartment], but was unsuccessful. After searching the immediate area without success, the officers resumed their routine patrol. Minutes later they saw a black man walking north on Federal Street toward the address from which the police had recently come. The man had a bulky object concealed under his coat. Although it had rained earlier, it was not raining at the time of this observation.

"Officer Peck pulled to the curb on the wrong side of the street, hailed the man (later identified as the defendant), and asked to speak to him. The defendant ignored Peck and continued walking at a faster pace. Zollo, who was not driving, got out of the cruiser, followed the defendant, and again asked to speak with him. Zollo told the defendant to stop, but the defendant ignored the command. When Zollo got to within two feet of the defendant, the defendant removed the bulky object from his coat and threw it at Zollo. The object, a video cassette recorder (VCR), struck the officer in the leg. The defendant ran but was captured by the officers.

". . .

"In his memorandum of decision the judge noted that '[s]tanding alone [the fact that the defendant threw the VCR and fled] might have provided reason to pursue and arrest him.' He concluded, however, that because that action 'was preceded by police conduct which violated art. 14 of the Declaration of Rights, it did not justify the arrest and search, or the recovery of the VCR.' On the facts of this case we disagree. The defendant's independent and intervening action of attacking [Zollo] . . . broke the chain of causation and dissipated the taint of the prior illegality.

". . . While an act by a defendant, which may in some sense be considered 'voluntary,' will not necessarily break the causal chain, an unprovoked physical assault on a police officer must have that effect. The defendant's action was more than an attempt to dispose of stolen property in response to being chased by an officer who lacked reasonable suspicion for his interest in the defendant. The defendant could have dropped the VCR and continued running. Instead, as the judge found, he threw it at Zollo, who was struck in the leg. Although we must be vigilant to protect Fourth Amendment rights, the privileges of the police in the specific circumstances of this case should not be measured on too fine a scale. Extending the fruits doctrine to immunize a defendant from arrest for new crimes gives a defendant an intolerable carte blanche to commit further criminal acts so long as they are sufficiently connected to the chain of causation started by the police misconduct. This result is too far reaching and too high a price for society to pay in order to deter police misconduct." *Commonwealth v. Mock*, 54 Mass. App. Ct. 276, 277–84 (2002) (citations and quotation marks omitted).

Inventory Searches

Inventory v. Investigative. "The distinction between an inventory search and an investigatory search is found in the objective of each. The objective of an investigatory search is to gather evidence, whereas and inventory search is conducted for the purposes of 'safeguarding the car or its contents, protecting the police against unfounded charges of misappropriation, protecting the public against the possibility that the car might contain weapons or other dangerous instrumentalities that might fall into the hands of vandals, or a combination of such reasons.' *Commonwealth v. Muckle*, 61 Mass. App. Ct. 678, 682–83 (2004)." *Commonwealth v. Baptiste*, 65 Mass. App. Ct. 511, 516 (2006).

"As the Appeals Court recognized in the *Sullo* case, enforcement of the Fourth Amendment and art. 14 requires a distinction between an inventory search and an investigatory search. If, during an inventory search, a police officer views material that is obvious, such as the writing on the card here that indicates that it is issued by Shawmut Bank, it is not realistic to expect the officer to forget what he has seen; and no purpose is served by requiring him to do so. The officer therefore may utilize the information so acquired. There is a substantial difference, however, between observing the 'Shawmut Bank' lettering and logo on the front of the card and examining the card closely enough to comprehend (and record) the multi-digit account numbers that were written on the back of the card. In this case, no valid inventory purpose would be served by recording the detailed information. It may be, however, that in some situations, recording the numbers on a card in a wallet may serve a valid inventory purpose. For example, there may be legitimate reasons (such as protecting the police against claims of theft or misuse) to record in an inventory search the identifying numbers of cards that can be used to obtain items of value, such as credit cards, charge cards or cash cards.

"[As] the United States Supreme Court has stated: 'The individual police officer must not be allowed so much latitude that inventory searches are turned into "a purposeful and general means of discovering evidence of crime."'

"Finally, the American Law Institute Model Code of Pre-Arraignment Procedure 530 (1975), provides: 'Generally speaking, none of [the legitimate purposes of a custodial search] will justify reading the accused's papers, except for the limited purposes specified in subsection (2) [of Section SS 230.6].' Subsection 2 of Section SS 230.6 states in part: 'Documents or other records may be read or otherwise examined only to the extent necessary for such [custodial] purposes, including identity checking and ensuring the arrestee's physical well-being.' *Id.* at 146.

"What the police may not do is hunt for information by sifting and reading materials taken from an arrestee which do not so declare themselves. Nor would there be any need for the police to record the account numbers on an inventory list, given that this particular card was of no value. Recording this information would not serve any of the generally accepted objectives of an inventory search preceding incarceration.

"The information on the back of the card was not overtly incriminating. It most likely became useful as an investigative tool at a later point during the investigation. As the Appeals Court concluded . . . : 'In making an inventory . . . the police are to act more or less mechanically, according to a set routine, for to allow then a range of discretion in going about a warrantless search would be to invite conduct which by design or otherwise would subvert constitutional requirements.' The police need not 'blind themselves' to information visible during an inventory search; what they may not do is investigate the information in the wallet without obtaining a search warrant." *Commonwealth v. Vuthy Seng*, 436 Mass. 537, 551–54 (2002) (citations and quotation marks omitted).

Standard procedures required. "[W]e have held that art. 14 of the Massachusetts Declaration of Rights requires that evidence seized during an inventory search must be suppressed unless the search was conducted pursuant to standard police procedures. Police procedures can be considered 'standard' only if they are set forth in writing. *Commonwealth v. Bishop*, 402 Mass. 449, 451 (1988)." *Commonwealth v. Garcia*, 409 Mass. 675, 681 (1991).

"There may be some question whether an inventory or storage search of the locked trunk of a vehicle impounded on a public way must be conducted pursuant to standard police procedures in order to meet the requirements of the Fourth Amendment. We, therefore, state, as a separate, adequate, and independent ground, that such a search must at least be made pursuant to such procedures in order to satisfy art. 14 of the Declaration of Rights.

'We are thus holding that art. 14 of the Declaration of Rights requires the exclusion of evidence seized during a storage search not conducted pursuant to standard police procedures."

Commonwealth v. Ford, 394 Mass. 421, 426 (1985); *see also Commonwealth v. Peters*, 48 Mass. App. Ct. 15, 21 (1999) ("First, the search must follow a [written] standard or routine procedure adopted and recognized by the police force. Second, it may not extend beyond the custodial necessities which are its sole justification. Third, it may not become a cover or pretext for an investigative search." [citation, footnote and quotation marks omitted]).

"[A]ny defect in the vehicle inventory report or the prisoner property inventory would not invalidate the inventory search." *Commonwealth v. Baptiste*, 65 Mass. App. Ct. 511, 518 (2006).

Closed containers. Written police policy mandated "a search of all arrestees and the making of an inventory of all items collected. The policy did not specifically indicate the procedure to be followed in the case of closed containers carried by the arrestee upon his or her person."

Held, inventory search of arrestee's handbag improper.

Commonwealth v. Rostad, 410 Mass. 618, 620, 622 (1991).

"[W]hether art. 14 is violated when a closed container is opened during an inventory search, even when the written procedures for conducting the inventory search direct that the closed container be opened."

Held, "[t]he opening of the closed but unlocked container and the seizure of the cocaine did not violate art. 14." *Commonwealth v. Caceres*, 413 Mass. 749, 755 (1992).

Motor Vehicles

General rule. "When there is probable cause to search an automobile stopped on a highway, an immediate search is constitutionally permissible. The inherent mobility of an automobile is the exigent circumstance that justifies a warrantless search at the time of a vehicular stop. The warrantless search continues to be permissible if the police, in the interest of their safety, wait to search a vehicle until after it has been seized and secured and removed to the safe environs of the police station, even though no exigent circumstances then prevail. Nonetheless, we have not endorsed giving the police carte blanche to search without a warrant any time subsequent to a valid stop. Rather, we have made clear that an unreasonable delay at the police station will render invalid an otherwise valid search." *Commonwealth v. Agosto*, 428 Mass. 31, 34 (1998) (21 days unreasonable) (citations and quotation marks omitted).

Probable cause to suspect particular automobile. "[F]or the automobile exception to be triggered, the police must have probable cause to believe a particular automobile contains contraband, not just probable cause regarding a specific container whose relationship to an automobile is 'purely coincidental.'" *Commonwealth v. Cast*, 407 Mass. 891, 902–03 (1990) (citing *United States v. Ross*, 456 U.S. 798, 813 (1982) (quoting *Arkansas v. Sanders*, 442 U.S. 753, 767 (1979) (Burger, C.J., concurring))).

Reasonable belief of danger. "[T]he Commonwealth argues that the initial search was a reasonably necessary lawful protective search. We agree. . . .

"The issue is whether a reasonably prudent [person] in the circumstances would be warranted in the belief that his safety or that of others was in danger. The defendants do not contest the judge's implicit ruling that the stop was justified. If the stop was justified, the officers could take reasonable precautions for their own protection. Such precautions may include ordering occupants out of a car for questioning. They also may include a search extending into the interior of an automobile, but they are confined to what is minimally necessary to learn whether the suspect is armed and to disarm him once the weapon is discovered. . . .

"A *Terry* type of search may extend into the interior of an automobile so long as it is limited in scope to a protective end. . . . The issue is the reasonableness of the troopers' action in initiating the limited search." *Commonwealth v. Robbins*, 407 Mass. 147, 151–52 (1990) (quotation marks and citations omitted). *See also Commonwealth v. Vasquez*, 426 Mass. 99 (1997).

Extent of search. "[I]f probable cause justifies the search of a lawfully stopped vehicle, it justifies the search of every part of the vehicle *and its contents* that may conceal the object of the search." *Commonwealth v. Bakoian*, 412 Mass. 295, 305 (1992) (citations omitted). *See also Commonwealth v. Cast*, 407 Mass. 891, 906–08 (1990) ("[A] lawful warrantless search of a motor vehicle, based on probable cause to search the vehicle, extends to all containers, open or closed, found within.") (footnote omitted); *Commonwealth v. Wunder*, 407 Mass. 909 (1990).

Time of search. "A search of an automobile incident to an arrest must be made contemporaneous with the arrest of any occupant of the vehicle." *Commonwealth v. Alvarado*, 420 Mass. 542, 554 (1995) (citations and quotation marks omitted).

Pretext. "No matter the judge's belief that the stop of the [car] was a pretext, the law is that the officers' motive for stopping the vehicle is irrelevant, and all that need be shown is that they had a reasonable suspicion that the driver of the [car] had [committed a motor vehicle infraction]." *Commonwealth v. Avellar*, 70 Mass. App. Ct. 608, 613 (2007).

Posting a guard. "The juvenile also contends that the police could have posted a guard while officers left to apply for a warrant. That argument has been rejected by the United States Supreme Court. For constitutional purposes, we see no difference between on the one hand seizing and holding an automobile before presenting the probable cause issue to a magistrate and on the other hand carrying out an immediate search without a warrant. Given probable cause to search, either course is reasonable under the Fourth Amendment.

"The leeway now allowed the police to conduct immediate searches of automobiles in lieu of holding them pending a warrant is based on Supreme Court cases emphasizing the special nature of automobiles and the lesser expectation of privacy one may have with respect to them." *Commonwealth v. A Juvenile (No. 2)*, 411 Mass. 157, 165 (1991) (citations and quotation marks omitted).

Exigent circumstances. If the police have probable cause to search a motor vehicle, which is parked in a public place and capable of being moved, a warrantless search may be conducted, no further exigency being required. *Commonwealth v. Gajka*, 425 Mass. 751, 752 (1997).

See Note accompanying Search Incident to Arrest.

Valid license/registration. "If the driver produces a valid license and registration, there is ordinarily no reason for an officer to probe further. The officer should give the driver a citation for the traffic offense and then permit the vehicle to proceed on its way.

"[However] an officer making a stop for a traffic violation [should not] ignore what he sees, smells or hears. The sight of a half empty bottle of gin, of a firearm, or of a furtive movement, the smell of liquor, or the sound of slurred speech . . . invites further inquiry." *Commonwealth v. Bartlett*, 41 Mass. App. Ct. 468, 471 (1996).

Exit orders. "[T]o permit an officer, in the absence of any specific and articulable facts, to order the driver of a vehicle [and a passenger or passengers] to step out of the vehicle would be to invite random and unequal treatment of motorists. . . . [O]nce a stopped driver has produced the necessary papers and they are found to be in order, he and his passengers are to be promptly released." *Commonwealth v. Gonsalves*, 429 Mass. 658, 664, 668 (1999).

"In Gonsalves . . . we held that art. 14 requires that, before ordering a driver out of a car, a police officer must have a reasonable belief that the officer's safety or the safety of others is in danger. The holding in that case was expressly limited to routine traffic stops. [*Commonwealth v. Gonsalves*, 429 Mass. 658, 662–663 (1999)] (art. 14 'requires that a police officer, in a routine traffic stop, must have a reasonable belief that the officer's safety, or the safety of others, is in danger before ordering a driver out of a motor vehicle'). *See id.* at 665–666 n.5 ('To the extent that a bright-line rule is needed, our conclusions today establish one: No exit order may be given to the driver or any passenger in a routine traffic stop without the police officer's having an objective reasonable basis to justify the order'); *id.* at 668 ('we conclude that, under art. 14, the balancing of interests requires that Massachusetts citizens should not be subjected to unjustified exit orders during routine traffic stops')." *Commonwealth v. Bostock*, 450 Mass. 616, 619–620 (2008).

"[I]t does not take much for a police officer to establish a reasonable basis to justify an exit order . . . based on safety concerns." *Commonwealth v. Goewey*, 452 Mass. 399, 407 (2008) (quoting *Commonwealth v. Gonsalves*, 429 Mass. at 664).

Article 14 of the Declaration of Rights requires, "after a proper stop, that there be a showing of justification for an exit order, whether addressed to a driver or a passenger. Thus it is possible for an exit order to be defensible in respect to a driver, but not so as to another occupant of the car." *Commonwealth v. Riche*, 50 Mass. App. Ct. 830, 833 (2001).

High-crime area. "[T]he fact that a routine traffic violation takes place in a high-crime area does not allow the police, without more, to order a driver out of a vehicle or to conduct a patfrisk." *Commonwealth v. Holley*, 52 Mass. App. Ct. 659, 663, 755 N.E.2d 811, 815 (2001) (citation omitted).

Recognition of vehicle. "[T]he police may, in the absence of any contrary evidence, reasonably conclude that a vehicle is likely being driven by its registered owner." *Commonwealth v. Deramo*, 436 Mass. 40, 43 (2002).

Smell of marijuana. "Given our conclusion that G.L. c. 94C, §§ 32L–32N, has changed the status of possessing one ounce or less of marijuana from a crime to a civil violation, without at least some other additional fact to bolster a reasonable suspicion of actual criminal activity, the odor of burnt marijuana alone cannot reasonably provide suspicion of criminal activity to justify an exit order." *Commonwealth v. Cruz*, 459 Mass. 459, 472 (2011).

"[W]e hold that [the] odor [of unburnt marijuana], standing alone, does not provide probable cause to search an automobile.

"In sum, we are not confident, at least on this record, that a human nose can discern reliably the presence of a criminal amount of marijuana, as distinct from an amount subject only to a civil fine." *Commonwealth v. Overmyer*, 469 Mass. 16, 17, 23 (2014).

"The Commonwealth maintains that the signs of recent use of marijuana, and the presence in the vehicle of less than an ounce of what the officer believed to be marijuana, gave the trooper probable cause to search for additional contraband elsewhere in the vehicle. In *Commonwealth v. Daniel*, [464 Mass. 746, 752 (2013)], on similar facts, we determined that an officer smelling freshly burnt marijuana inside a stopped vehicle, and an occupant surrendering a noncriminal amount of marijuana, did not, without more, support probable cause to believe that a criminal amount of marijuana would be found in the vehicle. 'Absent articulable facts supporting a belief that [any occupant of the vehicle] possessed a criminal amount of marijuana, the search was not justified by the need to search for contraband.' *Id.*

"The Commonwealth argues that the trooper properly searched the vehicle because he reasonably could have believed that the vehicle's occupants had been sharing marijuana, and thus had probable cause to believe that they were engaged in criminal distribution of marijuana in violation of G.L. c. 94C, § 32C (a). However, the social sharing of marijuana does not constitute distribution in violation of G.L. c. 94C, § 32C(a). *See Commonwealth v. Jackson*, [464 Mass. 758, 765 (2013)]. Because the trooper did not have probable cause to believe that the occupants of the vehicle were engaged in the distribution of marijuana, he was not permitted to search the trunk for evidence thereof." *Commonwealth v. Pacheco*, 464 Mass. 768, 771–72 (2013).

Reasonable Suspicion Not Enough for Motor Vehicle Stop. "[W]e conclude that in a case such as the present one, where the only factor leading an officer to conclude that an individual possesses marijuana is the smell of burnt marijuana, this factor supports a reasonable suspicion that that individual is committing the civil offense of possession of a small quantity of marijuana, but not probable cause to believe that he or she is committing the offense. Therefore, the question in this case is whether the Fourth Amendment and art. 14 permit police to stop a vehicle where they have reasonable suspicion, but not probable cause, to believe that a civil, infractionary offense of marijuana possession is occurring or has occurred." The court answered in the negative. *Commonwealth v. Rodriguez*, 472 Mass. 767, 775 (2015).

Federal Prohibition of Marijuana. "Where the 2008 initiative decriminalized possession of one ounce or less of marijuana under State law, and accordingly removed police authority to arrest individuals for civil violations, see G.L. c. 94C, § 32N, it also must be read as curtailing police authority to enforce the Federal prohibition of possession of small amounts of marijuana." *Commonwealth v. Craan*, 469 Mass. 24, 33 (2014).

"Dog sniff." "[W]e conclude that a dog sniff of a properly stopped vehicle is not a search under art. 14." *Commonwealth v. Feyenord*, 445 Mass. 72, 82–83 (2005).

Racial profiling. "[W]e conclude that evidence of racial profiling is relevant in determining whether a traffic stop is the product of selective enforcement violative of the equal protection guarantee of the Massachusetts Declaration of Rights; and that evidence seized in the course of a stop violative of equal protection should, ordinarily, be excluded at trial. We also conclude that statistical evidence demonstrating disparate treatment of persons based on their race may be offered to meet the defendant's burden to present sufficient evidence of impermissible discrimination so as to shift the burden to the Commonwealth to provide a race-neutral explanation for such a stop. Finally, we conclude that the evidence proffered by the defendant fell short of what is necessary to overcome the presumption that a law enforcement officer making a traffic stop, based on probable cause, has acted in good faith and without intent to discriminate."

In footnote 1 the court explained: "Racial profiling, as defined by St. 2000, c. 228, § 1, is 'the practice of detaining [or stopping] a suspect based on a broad set of criteria which casts suspicion on an entire class of people without any individualized suspicion of the particular person being stopped.' Racial profiling 'is generally understood to mean the improper use of race as a basis for taking law enforcement action.' *Chavez v. Illinois State Police*, 251 F.3d 612, 620 (7th Cir. 2001). In the context of traffic enforcement, officers who engage in racial profiling 'utilize impermissible racial classifications in determining [which motorists] to stop, detain, and search.' *Id.* at 635." *Commonwealth v. Lora*, 451 Mass. 425, 426 & n.1 (2008) (some footnotes and citations omitted).

"[V]alid statistical evidence of . . . impermissible profiling may be relevant and material to demonstrate that a particular traffic stop was unlawful. . . .

In *Commonwealth v. Betances*, [451 Mass.] 457, 462 n.6 (2008), . . . we suggest that a properly presented and documented motion under Mass. R. Crim. P. 14(a)(2) . . . may be an appropriate vehicle by which a defendant, who has reason to believe that he or she was subjected to a discriminatory traffic stop, may obtain statistical evidence . . . to demonstrate that the traffic stop was made on the basis of race or ethnicity." *Commonwealth v. Thomas*, 451 Mass. 451, 455 (2008).

"The preliminary showing required of a defendant seeking this type of discovery must contain reliable information in affidavit form demonstrating a reasonable basis to infer that profiling, and not a traffic violation alone, may have been the basis for the vehicle stop. It is not sufficient, as is the case here, to aver speculation that profiling may be occurring on the part of the arresting officer or his department. Even though the reports requested were within the possession, custody, and control of [the state trooper] (as the arresting officer and an anticipated prosecution witness), the motion seeking such material should not have been allowed in the absence of supporting information indicating that Trooper Maher, at the time he stopped the defendant's vehicle, may have been engaging in selective enforcement of the traffic laws." *Commonwealth v. Betances*, 451 Mass. 457, 461–462 (2008).

Plain Feel

The United States Supreme Court recognized a plain feel exception in *Minnesota v. Dickerson*, 508 U.S. 366 (1993).

2

"If a police officer lawfully pats down a suspect's outer clothing and feels an object whose contour or mass makes its identity immediately apparent, there has been no invasion of the suspect's privacy beyond that already authorized by the officer's search for weapons; if the object is contraband, its warrantless seizure would be justified by the same practical considerations that inhere in the plain-view context." *Minnesota v. Dickerson*, 508 U.S. at 375.

Plain View

"'Under the plain view doctrine, if police are lawfully in a position from which they view an object, if its incriminating character is immediately apparent, and if the officers have a lawful right of access to the object, they may seize it without a warrant.' *Commonwealth v. Santana*, 420 Mass. 205, 211 (1995). Our cases also have required that the police come across the item inadvertently. In the case of contraband and fruits and instrumentalities of crime, the nexus to criminal activity is obvious. 'Mere evidence', on the other hand, may be seized only if the officers recognize it as plausibly related to criminal activity of which they already were aware." *Commonwealth v. D'Amour*, 428 Mass. 725, 730–31 (1999) (citations and footnote omitted).

Inadvertence exception. "We have described the inadvertence element of the plain view doctrine as requiring that police lack probable cause before entering the room to believe the items would be there. The Commonwealth urges us to follow the United States Supreme Court and abandon the inadvertence requirement of the plain view doctrine.

"We decline to eliminate the inadvertence requirement from our art. 14 jurisprudence. The inadvertence requirement lends credibility to the plain view doctrine by ensuring that only evidence which the police did not anticipate or know to be at the locus of a search will be seized without a warrant. The rationale behind the inadvertent discovery requirement is that we will not excuse officers from the general requirement of a warrant to seize if the officers know the location of evidence, have probable cause to seize it, intend to seize it, and yet do not bother to obtain a warrant particularly describing that evidence. . . . [A]ttention must be paid also to seeing that the police, in full possession of probable cause to believe that incriminating evidence is present in a particular place, have not waited until an opportune moment to place themselves in a position to gain a plain view of the evidence . . . .

"Although the [Supreme] Court . . . may have been correct that the inadvertent discovery requirement furthers no privacy interests, we find that it continues to protect the possessory interests conferred on our citizens by art. 14. The inadvertent discovery requirement is essential if we are to take seriously the Fourth Amendment's protection of possessory interests as well as privacy interests. For these reasons, we decline to abandon the inadvertence requirement of the plain view exception to the warrant requirement. We do, however, take this opportunity to clarify that the inadvertence requirement means only that the police lacked probable cause to believe, prior to the search, that specific items would be discovered during the search." *Commonwealth v. Balicki*, 436 Mass. 1, 8–10 (2002) (citations and quotation and punctuation marks omitted).

Presence

"[W]e test the evidence to see if it supports inferences of sufficient 'plus' factors in addition to presence and awareness to warrant a finding that the defendant was involved in drug dealing." If "plus" factors are missing a conviction cannot stand. "Plus" factors, which were sufficient in this case, included evidence that (1) the defendant was acting as a lookout; (2) he and others were trying to protect or secret the drugs; and (3) he was present during numerous drug sales. People do not ordinarily engage in repetitive crimes in the presence of someone who is not a collaborator." *Commonwealth v. DeJesus*, 48 Mass. App. Ct. 911, 912 (1999).

Private Party Search

"There is no violation of the Fourth Amendment to the United States Constitution and art. 14 of the Massachusetts Declaration of Rights when evidence is seized by private parties who are not acting as agents of the police and subsequently turned over to police." *Commonwealth v. McCambridge*, 44 Mass. App. Ct. 285, 289 (1998) (citing *Commonwealth v. Jung*, 420 Mass. 675, 686 (1995)).

Probationer/Parolee Search

"We agree that both art. 14 of the Massachusetts Declaration of Rights and the Fourth Amendment to the Constitution of the United States forbid the search of a probationer or her premises unless the probation officer has at least a reasonable suspicion that a search might produce evidence of wrongdoing.

"We conclude that art. 14 bars the imposition on probationers of a blanket threat of warrantless searches . . .

"We suggest that an appropriate condition of probation, reflecting conclusions stated in this opinion, could read as follows: 'On the basis of a reasonable suspicion that a condition of the probationer's probation has been violated, a probation officer, or any law enforcement officer acting on the request of the probation office, may search the probationer, her property, her residence, and any place where she may be living, and may do so with or without a search warrant depending on the requirements of law.'"

Commonwealth v. LaFrance, 402 Mass. 789, 790, 795–96 (1988). *See also* G.L. c. 276, § 85B.

"We conclude that art. 14 offers greater protection to parolees than does the Fourth Amendment. Article 14 does not, however, offer as much protection to parolees as it affords to probationers. Therefore, where a parole officer has reasonable suspicion to believe that there is evidence in the parolee's home that the parolee has violated, or is about to violate, a condition of his parole, such suspicion is sufficient to justify a warrantless search of the home." *Commonwealth v. Moore*, 473 Mass. 481, 482–83 (2016).

Protective Sweep

"[I]n order to conduct even a cursory search of areas beyond the immediate arrest site (the so-called 'lunge area,' which defines the limits of a search incident to arrest, *see* G.L. c. 276, § 1), there must be 'articulable facts' that 'would warrant a reasonably prudent officer in believing that the area to be swept harbors an individual posing a danger to those on the arrest scene.'" *Commonwealth v. Nova*, 50 Mass. App. Ct. 633, 635 (2000) (quoting *Maryland v. Buie*, 494 U.S. 325, 334 (1990)).

"Here, police knocked on the defendant's door and received no reply. A few minutes later they heard a person climb the steps toward the defendant's apartment. When the police knocked again, the defendant answered. This sequence of events strongly suggests that the defendant was alone in the apartment. Such an inference is bolstered by the fact that police saw no other person as they ran through the apartment, and no one tried to intercede on the defendant's behalf from within the apartment at any time during the defendant's arrest.

"In these circumstances, there were no 'articulable facts' to support an inference that anyone was in the apartment at the time of the sweep—let alone anyone who posed a danger to the police." *Commonwealth v. Nova*, 50 Mass. App. Ct. 633, 635 (2000).

Roadblocks

"In order to assure that a roadblock seizure of a citizen without even individualized suspicion is 'reasonable' under the Fourth Amendment and art. 14 of the Declaration of Rights, the court has demanded that the roadblock meet standard, neutral guidelines, and be conducted pursuant to a plan devised in advance by law enforcement supervisory personnel. *Commonwealth v. McGeoghegan*, [389 Mass. 137, 143–144 (1983)].

"This court has also specifically pointed to the importance of the requirement that the roadblock be planned in advance by supervisory personnel and such plans must include date, location, time, duration, and set patterns of cars to be stopped. *Commonwealth v. Trumble*, [396 Mass. 81, 89 (1985)]."

Commonwealth v. Anderson, 406 Mass. 343, 347, 350 (1989) (punctuation and quotation marks omitted). (In *Anderson*, the court held a stop, made 15 minutes after the roadblock was to have ended, invalid.)

Commonwealth v. Rodriguez, 430 Mass. 577, 584–585 (2000) (footnote omitted) ("We have held that art. 14 may provide greater protection than the Fourth Amendment against searches and seizures. We determine that roadblocks for the purpose of searching for evidence of drug trafficking and other contraband violate art. 14.").

Ruse

See "Consent" above.

"Ruses must be designed to elicit 'consensual entry.'" Otherwise, attempted police ruses run the risk of provoking violence, unwarranted intrusion on privacy, and damage to the residence. *Commonwealth v. Ramos*, 430 Mass. 545, 550 (2000) (citation omitted).

"The roadblock was conducted pursuant to State police General Order TRF-15. . . . We conclude that TRF-15 falls within constitutional parameters, because its guidelines permit a vehicle to be diverted to secondary screening only when the officer has a reasonable suspicion, based on articulable facts, that the driver has committed an OUI violation or another violation of law. . . . [A]s a result of the orders and instructions in the operations plan that governed this sobriety checkpoint and supplemented the guidance provided by TRF-15, the discretion provided to the initial screening officers in greeting motorists was appropriately limited to pass constitutional muster." *Commonwealth v. Murphy*, 454 Mass. 318, 319–320 (2009); *see also Commonwealth v. Swartz*, 454 Mass. 330 (2009).

School Searches

Warrantless locker search. "[W]e pass over the expectation of privacy issue because we conclude that the warrantless search of the locker was in any event justified under the Fourth Amendment.

"In *New Jersey v. T.L.O.*, 469 U.S. 325 (1985), the United States Supreme Court held that school officials need not obtain a warrant, nor meet the standard of probable cause, in order to search a student under their authority. *Id.* at 340–341. Rather, the Court held such a search would pass Fourth Amendment muster if it were reasonable in all the circumstances. *Id.* at 341. . . .

"The search here not only clearly met such a lesser test, but the facts suggest strongly that probable cause existed as well. . . .

"On the basis of school administrators' preexisting knowledge of the defendant's Friday afternoon brawl and the two students' eyewitness report of a gun in the defendant's hands said to be linked to the Friday altercation, together with the failure to find the gun on the person of the defendant or at his most recent whereabouts, housemaster DeLuca's search of Carey's locker was clearly based on common sense, and was reasonable both at its inception and in its scope. . . .

"We affirm the judge's denial of the defendant's motion to suppress the sawed-off rifle found within the locker."

Commonwealth v. Carey, 407 Mass. 528, 533, 534, 535–36 (1990).

Reasonable suspicion. "Reasonable suspicion of wrongdoing is a common-sense conclusion about human behavior upon which practical people—including government officials—are entitled to rely. A student's direct statement to a person in authority, indicating personal knowledge of facts which establish that another student is engaging in illegal conduct, may provide school authorities reasonable grounds to search the second student's locker." *Commonwealth v. Carey*, 407 Mass. 528, 534, (1990) (citations and quotations marks omitted).

Probable cause for locker search. "The test under the Fourth Amendment for school administrators is whether the search of the locker was reasonable in all the circumstances. . . .

"In deciding whether the search of the locker and the seizure of the marihuana was constitutionally unreasonable, we need not determine whether the requirements of art. 14 of the Declaration of Rights impose a stricter standard than does the Fourth Amendment. The uncontroverted evidence at the hearing on the defendant's motion to suppress shows that the school officials had probable cause to search the defendant's locker and, once they found the book bag, to search the bag and the video cassette holder. Certainly, art. 14 imposes no higher standard than probable cause. *Cf. Commonwealth v. Upton*, 394 Mass. 363, 370 (1985). Thus, if there was probable cause to search the locker when it was searched, the requirements of art. 14 were met."

Commonwealth v. Snyder, 413 Mass. 521, 527, 529 (1992).

Public v. Private School Searches. "The Fourth Amendment applies to searches by school officials in public schools. Fourth Amendment protection does not apply to searches conducted by persons who are not State Agents . . . . Because, as a private entity, the school's activities cannot be fairly attributable to the State, there is no State action to serve as a predicate for application of either the Fourth Amendment or art. 14 . . . . Our reasoning for determining that the school officials are not State agents applies as well to the head of

2

2

security for the hotel. Acting in a private capacity, he responded to a call from school officials, entering the room at their request. . . . The fact that the head of security was also a part-time Cheshire police officer is irrelevant; he was not acting in that capacity at the time of this incident and, in any case, he was outside his jurisdiction." *Commonwealth v. Considine*, 448 Mass. 295, 298-301 (2007) (citations and footnotes omitted).

Search Incident to Arrest

Probable cause to arrest. "The fact that a search precedes a formal arrest is not important, as long as probable cause [to arrest] existed independent of the results of the search. . . .

"The purpose, long established, of a search incident to an arrest is to prevent an individual from destroying or concealing evidence of the crime for which the police have probable cause to arrest, or to prevent an individual from acquiring a weapon to resist arrest or to facilitate an escape. A search incident to arrest, similar to the search of a person pursuant to a warrant, generally is limited for purposes of both the Fourth Amendment to the United States Constitution and art. 14 of the Massachusetts Declaration of Rights, to the body of the person arrested and the area and items within his or her immediate possession and control at the time. In the case at bar, the defendant already had left his automobile by the time the officers approached and apprehended him. He was taken inside his apartment before the seizure of the contraband from his automobile. The automobile was no longer within the defendant's immediate control. There obviously was no danger that he could draw a weapon from the vehicle or attempt to conceal or destroy contraband which remained in it. The automobile was well out of his reach at the time."

Commonwealth v. Santiago, 410 Mass. 737, 742–43 (1991) (citations and footnote omitted).

"To be valid, an arrest must be based on probable cause. Evidence seized as the result of an illegal arrest is to be suppressed." "To constitute an arrest there must be either a physical seizure by the arresting officer, or a submission to his authority and control." *Commonwealth v. Bottari*, 395 Mass. 777, 782–83 (1985) (citations omitted).

"[P]robable cause exists where, at the moment of arrest, the facts and circumstances within the knowledge of the police are enough to warrant a prudent person in believing that the individual arrested has committed or was committing an offense. Were we to scrutinize in isolation each of the remaining facts and circumstances known at the time to the officer, we may conclude that no individual fact or circumstance made it probable that a crime had occurred or was occurring. We look, however, at the whole 'silent movie' disclosed to the eyes of an experienced narcotic investigator." *Commonwealth v. Kennedy*, 426 Mass. 703, 708 (1998) (citations and certain quotation marks omitted).

Degree of restraint determines standard. "'In determining whether a particular restraint is an arrest or tantamount to an arrest, thus requiring probable cause, or instead is a restraint short of an arrest, thus calling for analysis under a reasonableness standard, the degree of restraint must be analyzed. When no formal arrest has been made, several factors must be considered. In particular, courts have considered the amount of force used by the police, the extent of the intrusion, and the extent to which the individual's freedom of

movement is restrained. . . . In cases involving stops of cars, we have considered the number of police officers and cars used to effect the stop; whether the police blocked the car in motion or otherwise completely impeded its movement, or whether they merely pulled up near it; and whether the police officers had their guns drawn and in view.' (Citations omitted.)" *Commonwealth v. Bottari*, 395 Mass. at 781 (quoting *United States v. Marin*, 669 F.2d 73, 81 (2d Cir. 1982)) (citations omitted).

Area to be searched. "There is no determinative rule limiting the physical scope of a search incident to arrest to a particular number of feet. . . . In evaluating whether a search incident to arrest exceeded the area within the defendant's immediate control, we note that a police officer's decision how and where to conduct the search is a quick ad hoc judgment. A search incident to arrest may be valid even though a court, operating with the benefit of hindsight in an environment well removed from the scene of the arrest doubts that the defendant could have reached the items seized during the search." *Commonwealth v. Elizondo*, 428 Mass. 322, 324 (1998) (citations and quotation marks omitted).

Containers. "We are concerned with the admissibility of evidence found during a warrantless search of a gym bag that the defendant was carrying when the police lawfully arrested him. The defendant argues that the search was unreasonable in violation of the Fourth and Fourteenth Amendments to the Constitution of the United States and art. 14 of the Declaration of Rights of the Constitution of the Commonwealth. We affirm the defendant's conviction of trafficking in heroin. . . .

"The search of the gym bag was not an unreasonable search under the Fourth Amendment. Since *New York v. Belton*, 453 U.S. 454 (1981), courts have generally accepted as proper for Fourth Amendment purposes the search incident to an arrest of any container carried by a lawfully arrested person. . . .

"[I]t seems established, for now at least, that the Fourth Amendment is not violated when the police make a contemporaneous search of a container that a person is carrying at the time of his lawful arrest, even if the police have taken exclusive control of the container and even if it is unlikely that the search will disclose a weapon or evidence of the crime for which the arrest was made."

Commonwealth v. Madera, 402 Mass. 156, 157–58 (1988); *Commonwealth v. Clermy*, 421 Mass. 325, 328–31 (1995). See also *Commonwealth v. Elizondo*, 428 Mass. 322, 325 n.4 (1998) ("search incident to arrest may justify the opening of containers found within the physical area covered by the search") (citation and quotation marks omitted).

Search of companion. Patdown of companion of individual lawfully arrested permissible if specific and articulable facts exist indicating that companion is armed or a threat to officer or others. *Commonwealth v. Ng*, 420 Mass. 236 (1995). See also *Commonwealth v. Calderon*, 43 Mass. App. Ct. 228 (1997).

"We [recognize] . . . that there is no automatic right to search a companion of a person validly arrested, and that that principle has been extended to benefit a person who is merely present in a suspected car. Such a person does not lose 'immunities from search of his person to which he would otherwise be entitled.'" *Commonwealth v. Prevost*, 44 Mass. App. Ct. 398, 400 (1998) (citation omitted) (holding search of

2

companion in that case justified by circumstances confronting police).

Seizure

See "Free to Leave" Standard above.

What is not a seizure. "[N]ot all personal intercourse between policemen and citizens involves 'seizures' of persons. Only when the officer, by means of physical force or show or authority, has in some way restrained the liberty of a citizen may we conclude that a 'seizure' has occurred." *Commonwealth v. McHugh*, 41 Mass. App. Ct. 906, 907 (1996).

"The police do not effect a seizure merely by asking questions unless the circumstances of the encounter are sufficiently intimidating that a reasonable person would believe he was not free to turn his back on his interrogator and walk away." *Commonwealth v. Thomas*, 429 Mass. 403, 406 (1999).

The following did not amount to a "seizure"—"The officers were driving an unmarked cruiser when they turned to follow the defendants. They did not activate the cruiser's blue lights or sirens. The officers followed the defendants for 150 feet until the defendants voluntarily stopped running. One officer left the cruiser, identified himself, and said, 'Guys, can I talk to you for a second?' One officer stepped between the two defendants." *Commonwealth v. Rock*, 429 Mass. 609, 611–12 (1999).

"[W]e consistently have held no seizure was effected by a request to speak with a citizen." *Commonwealth v. Lopez*, 451 Mass. 608, 614 (2008). Thus, in *Lopez*, a police officer's statement "Can I speak with you?" constituted neither an order nor a seizure. *Id.* at 610.

Likewise, there was no seizure where the officer said "hold up a minute." *Commonwealth v. Stoute*, 422 Mass. 782, 789 (1996).

No seizure where police followed running defendant in their police cruiser as police conduct would not have communicated to the reasonable person an attempt to capture or otherwise intrude on the defendant's freedom of movement. *Commonwealth v. Williams*, 422 Mass. 111, 116–17 (1996).

No seizure where officer approached and asked questions about identity in unconfined public space, and did not indicate that subjects could not terminate encounter. *Commonwealth v. Thinh Van Cao*, 419 Mass. 383, 388, *cert. denied*, 515 U.S. 1146 (1995).

Encounter becomes a seizure. "In the instant case, when Officer McDermott initially confronted the defendant with the request, 'Hey you . . . I wanna speak with you,' the defendant was not seized. That was a request to engage in conversation and within the realm of 'personal intercourse' described by *Terry v. Ohio* . . . as not implicating constitutional rights. The defendant was free to decline the officer's request to converse and continue on his way, and he did precisely that. . . .

"But when Officer McDermott, rebuffed, followed up— 'Hey you. I wanna talk to you. Come here.'—the defendant was seized; he reasonably would have thought that he was not free to leave. It is instructive to recall the details accompanying that command. Officer McDermott was in uniform, had stepped out of his marked cruiser, and had pointed at the defendant. The command had been delivered in the presence of two other policemen, who arrived on the scene as back-up. Objectively, a reasonable person in those circumstances

would not have felt free to leave." *Commonwealth v. Barros*, 49 Mass. App. Ct. 613, 618 (2000).

"The defendant here correctly acknowledges that there was no 'pursuit' and, therefore, no seizure when the police officers initially pulled their vehicle alongside the defendant's bicycle on Bird Street and asked if he would speak with them. The officers did not restrict the defendant's movements, and plainly the defendant felt free to leave, because his response to the officers' inquiry was to pedal away quickly. *See Commonwealth v. Barros*, [435 Mass. 171, 174–176 (2001)]. Once that occurred, the officers merely followed the defendant in their cruiser, keeping him under surveillance. They did not turn on their blue lights, flashers, or sirens. There was no evidence that the officers blocked or impeded the defendant's path, direction, or speed. They did not demand that he stop and answer any questions. Such action (or inaction) by the police simply did not constitute a pursuit, and, therefore, was not a seizure of the defendant. It was the subsequent actions of the officers that constituted 'an intrusion of constitutional dimensions requiring justification.' *Commonwealth v. Stoute*, [422 Mass. 782, 789 (1996)]."

When a seizure occurred. "Seizure of the defendant for constitutional purposes occurred when the officers left their cruiser and began to chase the defendant immediately after he collided with a tree, abandoned his bicycle, and ran away from them, grabbing at his waistband. At this point, objectively, the police intended to stop the defendant to effectuate a threshold inquiry. *See* [*Stoute*, 422 Mass.] at 783, 788–790; *Commonwealth v. Williams*, [422 Mass. 111, 117 (1996)]; *Commonwealth v. Wilson*, 52 Mass. App. Ct. 411, 413–415 (2001)." *Commonwealth v. Sykes*, 449 Mass. 308, 313–314 (2007).

"The defendant, in this case, was seized within the meaning of art. 14, when the police notified her that they would not leave until she came out of the apartment and that if she continued to refuse, they would have the fire department break down the door. At that moment, the defendant was not free to leave the apartment or to remain there without responding to police inquiry. She was deprived of all available options to avoid the police. The police tactics violated the defendant's freedom of movement guaranteed by art. 14." *Commonwealth v. Ramos*, 430 Mass. 545, 549 (2000).

"The defendant was seized when, immediately after asking the defendant what he was doing, Officer Walsh conducted a patfrisk. At that moment, a reasonable person would have believed that he was not free to leave." *Commonwealth v. Gomes*, 453 Mass. 506, 510 (2009) (citations omitted).

"[T]he defendant's flight was not prompted by anything the police did, and, indeed, began before the officers got out of their vehicle. There was no evidence that the police exercised any show of authority or commanded the defendant to stop. *See Commonwealth v. Grandison*, [433 Mass. 135 (2001)] at 138. Nor did they block or impede his path. *See Commonwealth v. Sykes*, 449 Mass. 308, 313 (2007). Accordingly, the judge's conclusion that the defendant was seized when the police left their vehicle and began to run after him was incorrect." *Commonwealth v. Franklin*, 456 Mass. 818, 822–23 (2010).

Stop and Frisk

Handgun. "[U]ntil the Legislature says otherwise, carrying a gun in Massachusetts is not a crime. Carrying a firearm without a license (or other authorization) is. G.L. c. 269,

2

§ 10(a). A report that someone is carrying a gun does not by itself constitute reasonable suspicion to conduct a stop and frisk of that individual.

"What we are left with in the instant case is that the defendant showed a handgun to his friends, laughed, and tucked it back on his person. There is no evidence that the defendant was about to commit a crime with the handgun. The [*Commonwealth v.*] *Alvarado*[, 423 Mass. 266, 270–71 (1996)] opinion is explicit that the police may not stop and frisk on the basis of the statistical likelihood that the person carrying the weapon is unlicensed so to do." *Commonwealth v. Barros*, 49 Mass. App. Ct. 613, 619 (2000) ("Were the defendant and his friends so apparently young that the police could reasonably assume they were not of age to obtain a license to carry a firearm, that would be an objectively reasonable suspicion that the defendant was carrying unlawfully").

Two-fold inquiry. "Today we mark the end of *Fraser's* [*Commonwealth v. Fraser*, 410 Mass. 541, 544 n.4 (1991)] role as an exception, and we state expressly that police officers may not escalate a consensual encounter into a protective frisk absent a reasonable suspicion that an individual has committed, is committing, or is about to commit a criminal offense *and* is armed and dangerous. However, this is not to say that such suspicions must arise sequentially; it is clear that they may occur simultaneously. In such cases, a reasonable belief that an individual has a weapon and appears inclined to use it acts to satisfy both prongs of the *Terry* analysis. When an individual appears to be ready to commit violence, either against police officers or bystanders, it is reasonable to believe that he is 'about to commit a crime,' thus satisfying *Terry's* first prong. *Commonwealth v. Wilson*, 441 Mass. 390, 394 (2004). *See Terry* [*v. Ohio*, 392 U.S. 1 (1968)] at 30 (criminal activity 'afoot'). Moreover, the individual's conduct simultaneously gives rise to a reasonable belief that he is armed and dangerous, satisfying the second." *Commonwealth v. Narcisse*, 457 Mass. 1, 10 (2010) (footnotes and citation omitted).

"In 'stop and frisk' cases our inquiry is two-fold: first, whether the initiation of the investigation by the police was permissible in the circumstances, and, second, whether the scope of the search was justified by the circumstances." *Commonwealth v. Silva*, 366 Mass. 402, 405 (1974). *See Terry v. Ohio*, 392 U.S. 1, 21 (1968). "A police officer may stop a vehicle in order to conduct a threshold inquiry if he has a reasonable suspicion that the occupants have committed, are committing, or are about to commit, a crime. His suspicion must be based on specific, articulable facts and reasonable inferences drawn therefrom. A hunch will not suffice."

Stop legitimate here as (1) area was a high crime one; (2) upon seeing the police all four men quickly dispersed in two different directions; and (3) one man in the car, upon seeing the police, "ducked under the dashboard, completely out of [the officer's] sight."

Commonwealth v. Moses, 408 Mass. 136, 140 (1990).

Stop or arrest? "The question, stop or arrest, is fact bound, and as the court said in *Commonwealth v. Willis*, 415 Mass. 814, 819–820 (1993), In deciding whether this encounter [between police and suspect] was an arrest or merely a stop, we do not apply a bright line test. The answer depends on the proportional relationship of the degree of intrusiveness on the defendant to the degree of suspicion that prompted the intrusion. We should consider the degree to which the de-

fendant's movement is restrained, the degree of force used by the police and the extent of the intrusion. Specific factors include the length of the encounter, the nature of the inquiry, the possibility of flight, and, most important, the danger to the safety of the officers or the public or both." *Commonwealth v. Martinez*, 44 Mass. App. Ct. 513, 516 (1998) (quotation marks omitted).

Completed Misdemeanor. "'[T]he police are not automatically shorn of authority to stop a suspect in the absence of probable cause merely because the criminal has completed his crime and escaped from the scene.' [*United States v. Hensley*, 469 U.S. 221 (1985)] at 228. As the Court reasoned: '[W]here police have been unable to locate a person suspected of involvement in a past crime, the ability to briefly stop that person, ask questions, or check identification in the absence of probable cause promotes the strong government interest in solving crimes and bringing offenders to justice. Restraining police action until after probable cause is obtained would not only hinder the investigation, but might also enable the suspect to flee in the interim and to remain at large. Particularly in the context of felonies or crimes involving a threat to public safety, it is in the public interest that the crime be solved and the suspect detained as promptly as possible.' *Id.* at 229." *Commonwealth v. Edwards*, 71 Mass. App. Ct. 716, 720–21 (2008).

Adequate specific, articulable facts—flight. Flight alone cannot justify a stop and frisk. As "a stop starts when pursuit begins." *Commonwealth v. Thibeau*, 384 Mass. 762, 764 (1981), the police must have specific and articulable facts prior to the pursuit. In *Commonwealth v. Stoute*, 422 Mass. 782 (1996), the police, while patrolling a very high crime area, where told by a young girl in a crowd that the boy in the "hoody" had a gun. The police followed the defendant and his companion. Asking them to stop, the companion did (he was searched and had no gun) and the defendant fled. It was permissible for the police to pursue the defendant. It should be noted that "no *Terry*-type stop occurred when [the police officer] initially asked the defendant and his companion to 'hold up a minute.'" *Id.* at 789.

"If a defendant flees after having consented to a search, the officers are justified in pursuing him for the purpose of subjecting him to an initial investigatory inquiry. 'A police officer is warranted in making a threshold inquiry "where suspicious conduct gives the officer reason to suspect that a person has committed, is committing, or is about to commit a crime."' *Commonwealth v. Bacon*, 381 Mass. 642, 643 (1980) (quoting *Commonwealth v. Silva*, 366 Mass. 402, 405 (1974)). 'In following the constitutional standards of *Terry v. Ohio, supra*, we have required that the police officer's action be based on specific and articulable facts and the specific reasonable inferences which follow from such facts in light of the officer's experience.' *Commonwealth v. Silva, supra* at 406. A flight from police, after an initial consent to a search and before any pursuit by the police, provides a reasonable and articulable suspicion justifying an investigatory stop.

"The defendant relies on *Commonwealth v. Thibeau*, 384 Mass. 762, (1981), for the proposition that 'the defendant's flight from the officer's pursuit cannot be considered' to justify the investigatory stop. *Id.* at 764. The defendant's reliance is misplaced. In *Thibeau*, we said that 'a stop starts when pursuit begins.' *Id.* Because the police in that case began pursuing the defendant before he fled, they could not use his subsequent flight to justify the stop. Here, however, the defendant broke away from the police before they pursued him, thus providing the police with a reasonable and articulable suspicion before the stop. Also, here the defendant's actions caused further suspicion because he fled after an initial consent to a search. In *Commonwealth v. Thibeau*, there had been no initial conversation between the police and the defendant, and certainly no consent to a search." *Commonwealth v. Sanchez*, 403 Mass. 640, 645–46 (1988).

Defendant drove at high rate of speed, almost hitting unmarked police car, and tried to evade pursuing police officers. When forced to stop, seen reaching into his pants. Held, frisk valid under *Terry*. Further, seizure of drugs from defendant's pants also valid as incident to arrest, the police having probable cause to arrest the defendant for operating to endanger. G.L. c. 90, § 24. *Commonwealth v. Johnson*, 413 Mass. 598, 599–603 (1992).

Police radio call. "[I]f the police conduct an investigatory stop based on a police radio call, under both Federal and State law, the Commonwealth must present evidence at the hearing on the motion to suppress on the factual basis for the police radio call in order to establish its indicia of reliability. Independent police corroboration may make up for deficiencies in either or both the reliability or basis of knowledge factors. Because the standard is reasonable suspicion rather than probable cause, a less rigorous showing in each of these areas is permissible." *Commonwealth v. Butterfield*, 44 Mass. App. Ct. 926, 927 (1998) (rescript) (citations and quotation and punctuation marks omitted).

"The police radio call in this case was from an ordinary, known citizen, not an informant. . . . Unlike the anonymous informer, the caller in this case was an ordinary citizen who stated he had witnessed a crime and as such could be regarded as reliable without any prior demonstration of his reliability." *Commonwealth v. Butterfield*, 44 Mass. App. Ct. 926, 927 (1998) (rescript) (citation and quotation and punctuation marks omitted).

Soft object felt. A lump of white powder and six small paper folds were seized from the defendant. Search held to be valid notwithstanding the fact that the object felt was clearly not a weapon. "The court held that the dangerous circumstances facing the officer, his police experience, and the need for taking swift measures to discover the true facts and neutralize the threat of harm if it materialized permitted the police to find out what the defendant had concealed inside his pants. . . The trooper was not required to gamble with his personal safety." *Commonwealth v. Dedomenicis*, 42 Mass. App. Ct. 76, 80 (1997) (citing and quoting *Commonwealth v. Johnson*, 413 Mass. 598, 600–02 (1992)).

High crime area. "We caution that while the character of a neighborhood as a 'high crime area' can be considered as part of the aggregate circumstances that provide reasonable suspicion to justify a protective frisk, *see Commonwealth v. Fisher*, 54 Mass. App. Ct. 41, 45 (2002), 'this factor must be considered with some caution because many honest, law-abiding citizens live and work in high-crime areas. Those citizens are entitled to the protections of the Federal and State Constitutions, despite the character of the area.' *Commonwealth v. Holley*, 52 Mass. App. Ct. 659, 663 (2001)." *Commonwealth v. Gomes*, 453 Mass. 506, 512 (2009).

Inadequate specific, articulable facts—broadcast description. Radio broadcast of stabbing suspect was that of a black male wearing a black length goose, known as Angelo of the Humboldt group.

Defendant stopped mile from stabbing, wearing a dark-colored length goose. Asked his name he said either "Zan" or "Ann." A frisk revealed a handgun and drugs.

Held, search invalid as the officers "did not possess sufficient specific and articulable facts to establish a reasonable suspicion that the defendant had committed the crime."

The "'black male with a black length goose' could have fit a large number of men" who reside in that area. That he was found mile from the stabbing is insufficient to support a reasonable suspicion. Lastly, "a 'high crime area' is not persuasive [as it contributed] nothing to the officers' ability to distinguish the defendant from any other black male [in that area]." The police may not conduct a broad sweep of an area known as a high crime one.

Commonwealth v. Cheek, 413 Mass. 493–97 (1992).

Inadequate specific, articulable facts—drug transaction. Although the police had reasonable suspicion that the defendant was engaging in drug activity, "the police lacked particular facts from which a reasonable inference could be drawn that the defendant was armed and presented a danger to the officers or others. There was no evidence that the defendant's criminal history included any weapons-related offenses. Officer Walsh gave no testimony that the police observed anything suggesting that the defendant had a weapon. There was no evidence that the defendant made particular gestures or used any body language that would cause the officers to believe that he was carrying a weapon. Further, there was no evidence that the defendant attempted to flee from the officers when they approached his location. Although the incident at issue occurred around 4 a.m. in a high crime area, Officer Walsh was not alone or outnumbered during his interaction with the defendant where he was accompanied by two other officers, all in uniform, and the defendant's only companion was Bates. . . . In the circumstances here, the degree of police intrusion was not proportionate to the articulable risk to officer safety and, therefore, was constitutionally impermissible." *Commonwealth v. Gomes*, 453 Mass. 506, 511–514 (2009) (citations and quotation marks omitted).

Inadequate specific, articulable facts—jacket lost during flight. The defendant, while fleeing the police, "ran out of his jacket" as the police officer grabbed it. The officer patted down the jacket, which he noticed was heavy, and saw a plastic bag sticking out from the pocket. The bag contained cocaine.

Held, cocaine should have been suppressed. The justification for the intrusion leading to the discovery of the cocaine had ended before the discovery was made. Further held, statement that the officer had "busted [his] business" also suppressed.

Commonwealth v. Ferguson, 410 Mass. 611, 616 (1991).

Inadequate specific, articulable facts—removal of shoes. "We conclude that, although the officers may have had a reasonable suspicion that the defendant had committed a crime which would warrant an investigatory stop, the initial seizure of the defendant, i.e., the officer's request that the defendant remove his shoes,[1] exceeded the scope of investigatory stops outlined in *Terry, supra*, and its progeny. Moreover, the initial seizure was unsupported by probable cause. Thus, the seizure violated the defendant's rights under art. 14 of the Declaration of Rights and the Massachusetts Constitution. . . .

2

"At the outset we note that the officer's request that the defendant remove his shoes clearly constituted a seizure within the meaning of art. 14. An objective standard is used to determine when a seizure has occurred: 'a person has been 'seized' . . . if, in view of all of the circumstances surrounding the incident, a reasonable person would have believed that he was not free to leave.' *United States v. Mendenhall*, 446 U.S. 544, 554 (1980)."

"'The officer testified that he made the request to prevent the defendant's flight. The officer knew that the defendant was on parole and believed that the defendant might run if confronted by police officers."

Commonwealth v. Borges, 395 Mass. 788, 790–91 (1985) (footnote and citations omitted).

Inadequate specific, articulable—store clerk's description. "[A] clerk at a convenience store in Lowell telephoned the local police and informed them that a man inside the store had a small handgun protruding from his right rear pocket.

"In the case at hand, the judge's findings and the record make clear that the police had no probable cause to believe that the defendant was or had been engaged in any criminal activity. There is no evidence to suggest, and the Commonwealth does not claim, that the defendant was acting suspiciously when he was seen by the clerk at the convenience store. There is no indication that the gun which was seen was used in any manner to threaten or intimidate the store clerk. There is no suggestion that the defendant lingered for an unusual period of time at the store or that he was 'casing the joint' in preparation for a robbery. *See Terry v. Ohio*, 392 U.S. 1, 6 (1986). Rather, the police only knew that a man had been seen in public with a handgun. Under *Toole*, [389 Mass. 159 (1983)] this unadorned fact, without any additional information suggesting criminal activity, does not give rise to probable cause."

Commonwealth v. Coutore, 407 Mass. 178, 179–81 (1990).

Cf. Police officers received information from their dispatcher, shortly before midnight, that an anonymous caller reported that an armed man, whom he described in detail, was present in a nearby cafe. Police went to the cafe, spotted the man described, patted him down, and found a gun. Held, motion to suppress the weapon properly denied. "There are exigencies affecting life, limb, or grave property damage in which the police receive information of crime, not sufficient to establish probable cause for arrest and incidental search, and yet which, to any reasonable man, demand the taking of police action to prevent serious harm. In such cases it is not enough to say that nothing should be done, or that if something is done, the resultant evidence should be suppressed." *Commonwealth v. McCauley*, 11 Mass. App. Ct. 780, 783–84 (1981) (rescript) (quoting from *People v. Taggart*, 20 N.Y.2d 335, 339–40, 283 N.E.2d 1 (1967), *modified*, 21 N.Y.2d 729, *appeal dismissed*, 392 U.S. 667 (1968)).

Inadequate specific, articulable fact. "In the absence of a traffic violation or visible unlawful vehicular defect, we do not think that a broken window and missing trunk lock on a generally old dilapidated car add up to a basis for a threshold stop." *Commonwealth v. Kimball*, 37 Mass. App. Ct. 604, 606

(1994) (footnote omitted) (different result if a "popped-out" trunk lock).

"In the present case, the Commonwealth can point to nothing more than the officer's testimony that the defendant was acting suspiciously, moving around, and appeared extremely nervous. These general descriptions fall short of the specific and articulable facts which are required to demonstrate reasonableness." *Commonwealth v. Williams*, 46 Mass. App. Ct. 181, 184 (1999).

Chart. The chart on the next page [below] is intended as a brief overview for determining whether the event was an investigatory inquiry, a *Terry* stop or a full blown arrest. It was originally written by Judge George Jacobs of the Massachusetts Appeals Court and has been updated for the 2016 edition. Its brevity is both its greatest asset and liability. Positively, by a relatively quick glance one can easily and quickly frame the important issues. On the negative side, it is impossible to do justice to this area of the law short of LaFave's five volume treatise on the subject. Short of securing LaFave's work, one is directed to Joseph A. Grasso, Jr. & Christine M. McEvoy, *Suppression Matters under Massachusetts Law* (LexisNexis 2016 [forthcoming Dec. 2015]).

3. MOTION TO SUPPRESS
General Principles
Evidence Affidavit

General Principles

Burden of Proof. "[I]t is the Commonwealth's burden to prove that a warrantless search falls within a permissible exception to the warrant requirement and is, therefore, reasonable[. I]t is equally well-settled that that burden only attaches to the Commonwealth after the defendant has first demonstrated that a 'search and seizure' in the constitutional sense has occurred." *Commonwealth v. McCambridge*, 44 Mass. App. Ct. 285, 289 (1998) (citation omitted).

While the burden of justifying the reasonableness of a warrantless search is on the Commonwealth, the burden of going forward with the evidence on the defendant's motion to suppress is on the defendant as the moving party. *Commonwealth v. Ferrara*, 10 Mass. App. Ct. 818 (1980).

Integration with Trial. "[T]he seamless integration of a hearing on a motion to suppress with a trial on the merits should be avoided." *Commonwealth v. Powell*, 72 Mass. App. Ct. 22, 27 (2008).

Evidence Affidavit

"Rule 13(a)(2) codifies the standard requirements for a defendant's . . . motion to suppress evidence alleged to be the product of an unreasonable search or seizure. The motion papers must contain: (1) a pretrial motion stating 'the grounds on which it is based' and including 'in separately numbered paragraphs all reasons, defenses, or objections then available, which shall be set forth with particularity'; and (2) an affidavit giving in detail 'all facts relied upon in support of the motion and signed by a person with personal knowledge of the factual basis of the motion.'

Type of Police Encounter	Field Interrogation/ Observation (FIO)	Investigative Stop	Arrest
What Constitutes	Consensual encounter; individual approached remains free to leave (*Commonwealth v. Narcisse*, 457 Mass. 1, 6 (2010))	Seizure (*Terry v. Ohio*, 392 U.S. 1 (1968)); police exercise of authority by words or conduct, leading reasonable person to believe that he/she is not free to leave (*Commonwealth v. Stoute*, 422 Mass. 782, 786 (1996))	Requires: 1) Actual or constructive seizure or detention; 2) Performed with the intention to effect an arrest; and 3) So understood by the person detained (*Commonwealth v. Borges*, 395 Mass. 788, 792 n.2 (1985))
Requisite Justification	None (*Narcisse*, 457 Mass. 1, 6 (2010))	A <u>reasonable suspicion</u>, based on specific, articulable facts and reasonable inferences therefrom, that a suspect has committed, was committing, or was about to commit a crime. (*Commonwealth v. Alvarado*, 423 Mass. 266, 268 (1996)) Not subject to <u>Miranda</u> (*Berkemer v. McCarthy*, 468 U.S. 420, 439-40 (1984)).	<u>Probable cause</u> to arrest: "where, at the moment of arrest, the facts and circumstances within the knowledge of the police are enough to warrant a prudent person in believing that the individual arrested has committed or was committing an offense." (*Commonwealth v. Jewett*, 471 Mass. 624, 629 (2015))
What May Police Do?	Engage in conversation; ask questions; take photograph (*Commonwealth v. Van Cao*, 419 Mass. 383, 390 (1995))	Pat frisk for weapons only with reasonable suspicion that person is committing a crime <u>and</u> that he/she is armed and dangerous (*Narcisse*, 457 Mass. 1,9 (2010))	Search incident to arrest, under G.L. c. 276, § 1 only (1) for the purpose of seizing evidence of the crime for which the arrest has been made in order to prevent its destruction or concealment or (2) for the purpose of removing any weapon the person arrested might use to resist arrest or to escape. (*Commonwealth v. Blevines*, 438 Mass. 604, 607 (2003)) Inventory search according to written police inventory policy (*Commonwealth v. Vuthy Seng*, 436 Mass. 537, 550-51 (2002))

SEIZURES Prepared by Hon. George Jacobs, updated by Helle Sachse

"Where a defendant has filed a motion to suppress alleging an unconstitutional search or seizure, the detail required in the motion and accompanying affidavit under rule 13(a)(2) must be sufficient to accomplish two practical purposes. First, it must be sufficient to enable a judge to determine whether to conduct an evidentiary hearing. An evidentiary hearing is necessary only when the defendant has alleged facts that, if true, would establish (1) that evidence was obtained through a search or seizure for which the Commonwealth must prove probable cause, reasonable suspicion, or consent to search; and (2) that the defendant has standing to challenge the constitutionality of the search or seizure. Second, the affidavit required under rule 13(a)(2) must be sufficiently detailed to give fair notice to the prosecution of the particular search or seizure that the defendant is challenging, so that the prosecution may determine which witnesses it should call and what evidence it should offer to meet its burden of proving probable cause, reasonable suspicion, or consent." *Commonwealth v. Mubdi*, 456 Mass. 385, 388–89 (2010) (internal citations omitted).

Chapter 276. Search Warrants, Rewards, Fugitives from Justice, Arrest, Examination, Commitment and Bail, Probation Officers and Board of Probation

Section
1　Complaint; warrant for designated property or articles; search incident to arrest; documentary evidence subject to privilege
1A　Articles belonging to subversive organizations
1B　Definitions
2　Requisites of warrant
2A　Form of warrant
2B　Affidavit in support of application for warrant; contents and form
2C　Manner of issuing warrants; application of Secs. 2, 2A and 2B
3　Seizure, custody and disposition of articles; exceptions
3A　Time for return of warrant
4　Notice before forfeiture of property
5　Service of notice
6　Postponement of trial; further notice
7　Sale or destruction of property seized; disposition of proceeds
8　Appeal; recognizance; conformity to criminal cases; disposition of articles
9　Rewards offered by governor; determination of claims
10　Rewards offered for detecting or securing persons committing certain offenses; determination of claims
10A　Authority of officer of another state to arrest felon

10B　Proceedings after arrest
10C　Partial invalidity
10D　Citation of law; uniform construction
11　Definitions
12　Arrest and delivery of accused to executives of another state; governor's authority
13　Surrendering accused not in demanding state at time of crime or leaving demanding state involuntarily
14　Written demand; allegations; accompanying papers; charge of crime; authentication of copies of papers
15　Investigation of demand and report to governor
16　Governor's warrant of arrest; recital of facts
17　Arrest and delivery of accused; commanding aid
18　Authority to command assistance; penalties for refusal
19　Rights of arrested person; habeas corpus; notice; penalty
20　Confinement of accused; expense; evidence of transportation to demanding state; new requisition
20A　Warrant to apprehend accused on oath or affidavit; copies of papers attached
20B　Arrest without warrant; taking accused before court or justice; complaint

506

Chapter 276

Massachusetts Criminal Law Sourcebook & Citator 2017

2

20C   Commitment to permit arrest under warrant of governor on requisition
20D   Bail
20E   Discharge; recommitment; bail
20F   Forfeiture of bail
20G   Prosecution pending in commonwealth
20H   Inquiry into guilt or innocence
20I   Recall of warrant or issuance of another
20J   Waiver of warrant and procedure, etc.
20K   Warrant to receive accused and convey him to proper county; proceedings pending in another state
20L   Application for requisition
20M   Payment of agent's expenses
20N   Service of process in civil action or accused; immunity
20O   Trying for crimes; immunity
20P   Waiver by commonwealth
20Q   Partial validity
20R   Citation of law; uniform construction
21   Justices may issue process
22   Warrants, procedure for issuance
23   Service of warrants and other processes
23A   Persons arrested on warrants issued because of forfeit or default on bail bond or recognizance; fee
23B   Annual list of persons registered with licensing authorities; criminal history systems board; outstanding warrants; notification of license suspension; hearing
24   Summons instead of warrant
25   Summons fixing time for trial; service
26   Failure to appear and abide orders as contempt
27   Recognizance
28   Arrest without warrant
29   Recognizance in county of arrest; misdemeanor
30   Certifying bail on warrant; delivery of papers to court clerk; summoning witnesses
31   Default warrant for failure to make certain payments; additional fee; waiver; discharge upon payment
32   Conveying accused felon to county where warrant issued
33   Physical examination of and report on persons arrested
33A   Use of telephone in places of detention
34   Repealed
35   Adjournments of examinations and trials
36   Failure to appear; subsequent proceedings
37   Failure to recognize; subsequent proceedings
37A   Assignment of counsel
38   Examination; assistance of counsel; waiver of indictment
39   Repealed
40   Testimony reduced to writing; signing by witnesses
41   Discharge of prisoner
42   Bail or commitment
42A   Personal recognizance; terms and conditions to protect persons suffering physical abuse
43   Conveying prisoner through another county
44   Fees and expenses in district court in record sent to superior court
45   Witnesses bound by recognizance
46   Witnesses bound by recognizance on adjournment
47   Sureties with recognizance
48   Recognizances by minor witnesses
49   Commitment of witnesses; discharge upon recognizance
50   Repealed
51   Release of committed witnesses; proceedings
52   Rules regulating treatment of committed witnesses; removal to another county
52A   Removal of accused persons to another county or to a correctional institution; return; proceedings; cost of support
53   Transporting male and female prisoners
54   Handcuffing committed witnesses to accused persons; transporting together
55   Discharge upon acknowledgment of satisfaction for injury
56   Filing of order; delivery to jail keeper; discharge as bar to civil action
56A   Written ruling that abuse is alleged when judge releases, discharges or admits person to bail
57   Officials authorized to admit to bail; rules governing persons taking bail, etc.
58   Release on personal recognizance or unsecured appearance bond; determination; fees; refusal; petition for review

58A   Conditions of pretrial release of persons accused of felonies involving use of physical force, violation of an order, or abuse; detention hearing, order; review
58B   Revocation of release and detention order following violation of release conditions
59   Admission to bail by master in chancery
60   Bail in Suffolk County; proceedings
61   Bail taken out of court; certificate or recognizance and deposit by surety; presence of persons; monthly statements by person taking bail
61A   Disposition or encumbrance of real estate of bail or surety; violation of section
61B   Bond of professional bondsman; arrest bond certificates; conditions of acceptance; regulation
62   Notice to district attorney of application to accept bail in Suffolk County
63   Compensation for taking bail
64   Admission to bail on Sunday
65   Condition of recognizance
66   Return of recognizance and examination taken by magistrate; order compelling; contempt
67   Repealed
68   Surrender of principal; notice; exoneration of bail; return of deposits; subsequent bail
69   Surrender of principal after default; remission of penalty
70   Inability to surrender principal; exoneration of bail
71   Default on recognizance
72   Surety paying amount for which bound; costs
73   Award of portion of penalty to person entitled to forfeiture
74   Judgment for whole or part of penalty
75   Neglect, omissions or defects as defeating action
76   Review and rehearing of case after judgment on recognizance
77   Service of notice and copy of petition; return day
78   Proceedings if former judgment diminished, etc.; costs
79   Personal recognizance and deposit instead of sureties for release from custody
80   Forfeiture of deposit on default; sale of bonds; collection on bank books; payments to state treasurer
81   Defendant surrendering self; return of deposit, etc.
82   Bail commissioner or special magistrate authorized to admit to bails
82A   Failure to appear in court after release on bail or recognizance; penalty
83   Appointment and removal of probation officers
83A   Repealed
83B–84 Repealed
85   Powers and duties
85A   Support and maintenance enforcement
85B   Delinquent payments, collection, contempt
86   Appointment of deputy probation officers by Boston juvenile court; creditable service
87   Placing certain persons in care of probation officer
87A   Conditions of probation; probation fees
88   Clerical assistance
89   Temporary probation officers
89A   Counsellors to juvenile offenders
90   Powers of probation officers; reports; records; inspection
91   Power of probation officers appointed by Boston juvenile court to serve process
92   Restitution or reparation to injured person through probation officer
92A   Restitution in cases involving motor vehicle theft or fraudulent claims
93   Payment to treasurer of unclaimed money collected by probation officer
94   Expenses of probation officers
95   Temporary support or transportation of probationers
96   Refusal or neglect of duties by probation officer
97   Interference with duties of department of youth services
98   Commissioner of probation; appointment
98A   Advisory board
99   Powers and duties of commissioner of probation
99A   Repealed
99B   Probation officers; compensation
99C   Repealed
99D   Repealed

99E	Proof of indigency
99F	Performance measurement system
100	Detailed reports of probation work; records; accessibility of information
100A	Requests to seal files; conditions; application of section; effect of sealing of records
100B	Requests to seal delinquency files or records; conditions; sealing by commissioner; notice for compliance; effect of sealing; limited disclosure
100C	Sealing of records or files in certain criminal cases; effect upon employment reports; enforcement
100D	Availability of sealed criminal record information
101	Annual report of commissioner to general court
101A	Establishment of uniform forms of blanks and records for use in district court probation offices
102	Authority of courts to require keeping of probation records as affected by Secs. 98 to 101A
103	Notice to commissioner of appointment, removal, etc., of probation officer

SEARCH WARRANTS

SECTION 1
Complaint; warrant for designated property or articles; search incident to arrest; documentary evidence subject to privilege

A court or justice authorized to issue warrants in criminal cases may, upon complaint on oath that the complainant believes that any of the property or articles hereinafter named are concealed in a house, place, vessel or vehicle or in the possession of a person anywhere within the commonwealth and territorial waters thereof, if satisfied that there is probable cause for such belief, issue a warrant identifying the property and naming or describing the person or place to be searched and commanding the person seeking such warrant to search for the following property or articles:

First, property or articles stolen, embezzled or obtained by false pretenses, or otherwise obtained in the commission of a crime;

Second, property or articles which are intended for use, or which are or have been used, as a means or instrumentality of committing a crime, including, but not in limitation of the foregoing, any property or article worn, carried or otherwise used, changed or marked in the preparation for or perpetration of or concealment of a crime;

Third, property or articles the possession or control of which is unlawful, or which are possessed or controlled for an unlawful purpose; except property subject to search and seizure under sections forty-two through fifty-six, inclusive, of chapter one hundred and thirty-eight;

Fourth, the dead body of a human being.

Fifth, the body of a living person for whom a current arrest warrant is outstanding.

A search conducted incident to an arrest may be made only for the purposes of seizing fruits, instrumentalities, contraband and other evidence of the crime for which the arrest has been made, in order to prevent its destruction or concealment; and removing any weapons that the arrestee might use to resist arrest or effect his escape. Property seized as a result of a search in violation of the provisions of this paragraph shall not be admissible in evidence in criminal proceedings.

The word "property", as used in this section shall include books, papers, documents, records and any other tangible objects.

Nothing in this section shall be construed to abrogate, impair or limit powers of search and seizure granted under other provisions of the General Laws or under the common law.

Notwithstanding the foregoing provisions of this section, no search and seizure without a warrant shall be conducted, and no search warrant shall issue for any documentary evidence in the possession of a lawyer, psychotherapist, or a clergyman, including an accredited Christian Science practitioner, who is known or may reasonably be assumed to have a relationship with any other person which relationship is the subject of a testimonial privilege, unless, in addition to the other requirements of this section, a justice is satisfied that there is probable cause to believe that the documentary evidence will be destroyed, secreted, or lost in the event a search warrant does not issue. Nothing in this paragraph shall impair or affect the ability, pursuant to otherwise applicable law, to search or seize without a warrant or to issue a warrant for the search and seizure of any documentary evidence where there is probable cause to believe that the lawyer, psychotherapist, or clergyman in possession of such documentary evidence has committed, is committing, or is about to commit a crime. For purposes of this paragraph, "documentary evidence" includes, but is not limited to, writings, documents, blueprints, drawings, photographs, computer printouts, microfilms, X-rays, files, diagrams, ledgers, books, tapes, audio and video recordings, films or papers of any type or description.

NOTE 1   Counsel should base motions to suppress on G.L. c. 276, § 1, the Fourth Amendment, and article 14 of the Massachusetts Declaration of Rights.

NOTE 2   "'Mere evidence' may be seized only if the officers recognize it to be plausibly related as proof to criminal activity of which they were already aware. . . .

"There is other material that may be taken not only in the circumstances just described, but also when it bespeaks the likelihood of some criminal conduct of which the officer may have had no prior awareness . . . , [i.e.,] 'contraband, the fruits of crime, or things otherwise unlawfully possessed' and 'weapons or other things used or likely to be used as means of committing crime' (often called instrumentalities of crime)."

Commonwealth v. Bond, 375 Mass. 201, 206, 207 (1978).

NOTE 3   **Blood Samples.** Issue: "[May a judge order] a person not charged with a criminal offense nor the subject of a grand jury investigation to have blood extracted from his body?" Yes, "[if probable cause exists] for believing that the person whose blood the Commonwealth seeks has committed the crime . . . and that the blood found at the scene of the [crime] is relevant in the Commonwealth's investigation of the crime, that is, that the identity of the source of the blood would aid in its investigation of [the crime]." *In the Matter of Lavigne*, 418 Mass. 831, 832, 835, 836 (1994). See Blood Samples in Alphabetical References to Evidence section for discussion of grand jury or post-indictment obtaining of blood samples.

NOTE 4   Police officers were authorized by G.L. c. 276, § 1 to conduct a contemporaneous weapons search of a defendant whom they had arrested pursuant to a warrant. *Commonwealth v. Clermy*, 421 Mass. 325 (1995).

NOTE 5   "As a general proposition, G.L. c. 276, § 1, is more restrictive than the Fourth Amendment, as expounded in *United States v. Robinson*, 414 U.S. 218, 234–235 (1973), and *New York v. Belton*, 453 U.S. 454, 460 (1981). See *Commonwealth v. Rose*, 25 Mass. App. Ct. 905, 905 (1987); *Commonwealth v. Pacheco*, 51 Mass. App. Ct. 736, 742 n.5 (2001). *Compare Commonwealth v. Bongarzone*, 390 Mass. 326, 351–352 & n.18 (1983). A search under G.L. c. 276, § 1, is limited to seizure of the 'fruits and instrumentalities' of the crime, as well as contraband related to the crime, *Commonwealth v. Elizondo*, 428 Mass. 322, 323 (1998),

2

and for the purpose of 'removing any weapons that the arrestee might use to resist arrest or effect his escape.'" *Commonwealth v. Blevines*, 54 Mass. App. Ct. 89, 93–94 (2002).

SECTION 1A
Articles belonging to subversive organizations

A justice of the superior court, upon application of the attorney general or a district attorney, and upon complaint on oath that the complainant believes that any of the property or articles hereinafter named are concealed in a particular house or place, if satisfied that there is a reasonable cause for such belief, may issue a warrant to search for the following property or articles: books, records, files, membership lists, funds, referred to in sections eighteen and twenty-one of chapter two hundred and sixty-four, or written or printed documents, paper or pictorial representations, referred to in section eleven of said chapter two hundred and sixty-four, belonging to a subversive organization as defined in said section eighteen, or used, provided for, or intended to be used for, the purposes specified in said section eleven.

SECTION 1B
Definitions

(a) As used in this section, the following words shall have the following meanings:—

"Adverse result", occurs when notification of the existence of a search warrant results in:—

(1) danger to the life or physical safety of an individual;

(2) a flight from prosecution;

(3) the destruction of or tampering with evidence;

(4) the intimidation of a potential witness or witnesses; or

(5) serious jeopardy to an investigation or undue delay of a trial.

"Electronic communication services", shall be construed in accordance with sections 2701 to 2711 Title 18, of the United States Code. This definition shall not apply to corporations that do not provide electronic communication services to the general public.

"Foreign corporation", any corporation or other entity that makes a contract or engages in a terms of service agreement with a resident of the commonwealth to be performed in whole or in part by either party in the commonwealth. The making of the contract or terms of service agreement shall be considered to be the agreement of the foreign corporation that a search warrant or subpoena which has been properly served on it has the same legal force and effect as if served personally within the commonwealth.

"Massachusetts corporation", any corporation or other entity that is subject to chapter 155 or chapter 156B.

"Properly served", delivery of a search warrant or subpoena by hand, by United States mail, by commercial delivery service, by facsimile or by any other manner to any officer of a corporation or its general manager in the commonwealth, to any natural person designated by it as agent for the service of process, or if such corporation has designated a corporate agent, to any person named in the latest certificate filed pursuant to section 15.03 of chapter 156D.

"Remote computing services", shall be construed in accordance with sections 2701 to 2711, inclusive, of Title 18, of the United States Code. This definition shall not apply to corporations that do not provide those services to the general public.

"Subpoena", a grand jury or trial subpoena issued in the course of a criminal proceeding or an administrative subpoena issued pursuant to section 17B of chapter 271.

(b) A court or justice authorized to issue warrants in criminal cases may, upon complaint on oath that the complainant believes that any of the records hereinafter named are actually or constructively possessed by a foreign corporation that provides electronic communication services or remote computing services, if satisfied that probable cause has been established for such belief, issue a warrant identifying those records to be searched for and commanding the person seeking such warrant to properly serve the warrant upon the foreign corporation:—

(1) those records which would reveal the identity of a customer using those services;

(2) data stored by or on behalf of a customer;

(3) records of a customer's usage of those services;

(4) records of the source of communications sent to or the recipient or destination of communications sent from a customer; or

(5) the content of those communications stored by an electronic communication or remote commuting service.

(c) The following provisions shall apply to any search warrant issued pursuant to this section and to any subpoena issued in the course of a criminal investigation or proceeding directed to a foreign corporation that provides electronic communication services or remote computing services:

(1) when properly served with a search warrant issued by any court of the commonwealth or justice pursuant to this section or a subpoena, a foreign corporation subject to this section shall provide all records sought pursuant to that warrant or subpoena within 14 days of receipt, including those records maintained or located outside the commonwealth;

(2) if the applicant makes a showing and the court or justice finds that failure to produce records within less than 14 days would cause an adverse result, a warrant may require production of records within less than 14 days;

(3) a court or justice may reasonably extend the time required for production of the records upon finding that the foreign corporation has shown good cause for that extension and that an extension of time would not cause an adverse result;

(4) a foreign corporation seeking to quash a warrant or subpoena served on it pursuant to this section shall seek relief from the court that issued the warrant or the court which has jurisdiction over the subpoena within the time required for production of records pursuant to this section. The court shall hear and decide such motion not later than 14 days after the motion is filed;

(5) in the case of an administrative subpoena issued by the attorney general, the superior court of Suffolk county shall have jurisdiction and in the case of an administrative subpoena issued by a district attorney, the superior court in any county in which the district attorney maintains an office shall have jurisdiction; and

(6) the foreign corporation shall verify the authenticity of records that it produces by providing an affidavit from the person in custody of those records certifying that they are true and complete.

(d) A Massachusetts corporation that provides electronic communication services or remote computing services, when served with a warrant or subpoena issued by another state to produce records that would reveal the identity of the customers using those services, data stored by, or on behalf of the customer, the customer's usage of those services, the recipient or destination of communications sent to or from those customers, or the content of those communications, shall produce those records as if that warrant or subpoena had been issued under the law of the commonwealth.

(e) No cause of action shall lie against any foreign or Massachusetts corporation subject to this section, its officers, employees, agents or other persons for providing records, information, facilities or assistance in accordance with the terms of a warrant or subpoena issued pursuant to this section. A search conducted incident to an arrest may be made only for the purposes of seizing fruits, instrumentalities, contraband and other evidence of the crime for which the arrest has been made, in order to prevent its destruction or concealment; and removing any weapons that the arrestee might use to resist arrest or effect his escape. Property seized as a result of a search in violation of the provisions of this paragraph shall not be admissible in evidence in criminal proceedings.

SECTION 2
Requisites of warrant

Search warrants shall designate and describe the building, house, place, vessel or vehicle to be searched and shall particularly describe the property or articles to be searched for. They shall be substantially in the form prescribed in section two A of this chapter and shall be directed to the sheriff or his deputy or to a constable or police officer, commanding him to search in the daytime, or if the warrant so directs, in the nighttime, the building, house, place, vessel or vehicle where the property or articles for which he is required to search are believed to be concealed, and to bring such property or articles when found, and the persons in whose possession they are found, before a court having jurisdiction.

NOTE 1   Particularity.

a. General Purpose. "[T]he dual purposes of the particularity requirements of G.L. c. 276, § 2, and Art. 14 are (1) to protect individuals from general searches and (2) to provide the Commonwealth the opportunity to demonstrate, to a reviewing court, that the scope of the officers' authority to search was properly limited." *Commonwealth v. Valerio*, 449 Mass. 562, 566–67 (2007).

b. Technical defect. "Even though a search has been conducted pursuant to a warrant that is technically defective, suppression of the evidence does not automatically follow. There are times when a warrant, insufficient on its face, incorporates by reference an extrinsic document (usually an affidavit) that is physically attached to the warrant and present when the search is executed. In such circumstances, we have held that the affidavit cures the particularity deficiency in the warrant and, essentially, validates the warrant . . . . The relevant inquiry in determining whether exclusion is warranted under art. 14 and G.L. c. 276, § 2, is whether the affidavit is incorporated by, and attached to, the warrant (thus becoming an integral part of the warrant) and whether the affidavit is present during the execution of the search." *Commonwealth v. Valerio*, 449 Mass. 562, 567–68 (2007) (citations omitted).

NOTE 2a   Plain View Seizure. "When items in plain view are seized but are not described in the warrant the Commonwealth bears the burden of showing at the hearing on the motion to suppress that, at the time of seizure, it was apparent that the items bore a nexus to the crime committed." *Commonwealth v. Cefalo*, 381 Mass. 319, 330 (1980).

In addition to the "nexus" requirement, there are two additional prongs which must be met to allow the seizure of items in plain view: (1) the police must be lawfully on the premises: and (2)

the discovery of the evidence must be "inadvertent." *Commonwealth v. Cefalo*, 381 Mass. at 331.

"Mere Evidence". "[T]he Fourth Amendment . . . does not require a distinction prohibiting the seizure of items of evidential value only (mere evidence), as opposed to the seizure of contraband or of the instrumentalities or fruits of a crime. The [Supreme Judicial Court] is in accord. Evidence not described in a valid search warrant but inadvertently discovered and having a nexus with the crime under investigation may be seized at the same time as the material described in the warrant. The two-pronged test in the case of 'mere evidence' (as distinct from contraband or instrumentalities used to perpetuate a crime) is whether the officers recognize it to be plausibly related as proof of criminal activity of which they were already aware and whether the evidence sought will aid in a particular apprehension or conviction." *Commonwealth v. Halsey*, 41 Mass. App. Ct. 200, 202 (1996) (citations omitted).

NOTE 2b   Items to Be Seized Not Listed.

"The warrant made no reference to the items listed in [the police officer's] affidavit in support of the application. It neither listed them, nor incorporated them by reference; nor was the affidavit attached to the warrant. . . . The warrant at issue here clearly failed to meet these statutory requirements [for particularity]."

However, since (1) the deficiency was not as to probable cause, but as to particularity; (2) "the defect in the warrant did not lead to a general search of the premises"; (3) the police "officers in no way exploited, or attempted to exploit, the illegality of the warrant"; (4) "the defendant was not deprived of the opportunity to challenge the scope of the search, since there was a 'writing' in the form of an affidavit, which the officers had with them throughout the search and which was available to the defendant at his trial; the evidence should not be suppressed.

"Although there were violations of both art. 14 and G.L. c. 276, exclusion of the evidence seized is not required because there was no prejudice to the defendant, and thus the violations were not substantial."

Commonwealth v. Sheppard, 394 Mass. 381, 384, 387, 389–91 (1985).

NOTE 2c   "We conclude that the evidence should have been suppressed in response to the principles underlying art. 14 of the Declaration of Rights and G.L. c. 276, § 2. The violation of law here was substantial and not technical. Contrast *Commonwealth v. Sheppard*, 394 Mass. 381, 390–391 (1985). The police proceeded under a general search warrant prepared by a State trooper. There was no detailed involvement of a judge in the crafting of the warrant nor any explicit assurance from a judge (or any other magistrate) that the search warrant was in proper form. The police did not have with them any description of the items for which they were searching. Indeed, in this case the police could have only been proceeding in complete disregard of the detailed descriptions of the stolen property because only an accompanying list would have made the firearms' identification numbers available and furnished the intricate details of the sketches of the stolen jewelry. There is no finding that the police believed that their search was limited in scope to the items set forth in the affidavit and that they acted accordingly." *Commonwealth v. Rutkowski*, 406 Mass. 673, 677 (1990).

NOTE 3   Computers/disks. "[A] warrant that authorizes a search warrant for records (properly delineated in a warrant) permits the seizure of computers and disks that electronically may hide and store such records." *Commonwealth v. McDermott*, 448 Mass. 750, 770–71 (2007).

NOTE 4   Description of Premises.

"The issue here is whether the description is sufficient to enable the executing officer to locate and identify the premises with reasonable effort, and whether there is any reasonable probability that another premises might be mistakenly searched which is not the one intended to be searched under the search warrant. *Commonwealth v. Treadwell*, 402 Mass. 355, 359 (1988) (citations and footnote omitted).

2

"The only question in this case is whether the omission of the street address and town of the house to be searched was fatal to the warrant's validity . . . . It is well established that, when a description in a warrant facially contains adequate particulars, but, in application to a particular situation, the description is ambiguous, the knowledge of the executing officers may be sufficient to overcome the ambiguity." *Commonwealth v. Walsh*, 409 Mass. 642, 645 (1991). The court also noted that "a residence may be described with reference to its occupants." *Commonwealth v. Walsh*, 409 Mass. at 645.

NOTE 5   Motor Vehicles. "It is a well-settled principle under both Federal law and the law of other jurisdictions that the scope of a warrant authorizing the search of a particularly described premises, includes automobiles owned or controlled by the owner thereof, which are found on the premises . . .

"It is clear that a valid search may include any area, place, or container reasonably capable of containing the object of the search. *Commonwealth v. Wills*, 398 Mass. 768, 774 (1986). *Commonwealth v. Lett*, 393 Mass. 141, 147–148 (1984). There is nothing in art. 14 or the particularity requirement of G.L. c. 276, § 2 (1986 ed.), that requires that automobiles found on the premises be treated differently. 'Although a car is less fixed than a closet or cabinet . . . it is no less fixed than a suitcase or handbag found on the premises, both of which can be readily searched under [*United States v. Ross*, 456 U.S. 798 (1982)] if capable of containing the object of the search.' *United States v. Percival*, [756 F.2d 600, 612 (7th Cir. 1985)]. Here, the object of the search was moveable contraband that could be secreted in innumerable places, including the defendant's automobile. Requiring law enforcement officers to establish independent probable cause before they may search places within the curtilage (including automobiles), but beyond the four walls of the residence, would be unduly burdensome on police without providing defendants any significant additional constitutional protection."

Commonwealth v. Signorine, 404 Mass. 400, 403, 405 (1989) (footnotes omitted).

NOTE 6   "In *Groh v. Ramirez*, 540 U.S. 551 (2004), the Supreme Court explained that the language of the Fourth Amendment requires that the warrant itself—not the supporting documents—identify particularly the place to be searched and the persons or things to be seized. The reasons for this are twofold: it prevents general searches, and it assures the individual whose property is searched or seized of the lawful authority of the executing officer, his need to search, and the limits of his power to search. That the affidavit or application adequately described the things to be seized does not save the warrant from its facial invalidity (emphasis in original)." *Commonwealth v. Brown*, 68 Mass. App. Ct. 261, 268 (2007) (quotations and citations omitted).

NOTE 7   Assuming that the burden of persuasion remains on the defendant throughout, once he has made out a prima facie case by showing a defect in the warrant, it is up to the Commonwealth to present offsetting evidence. *Commonwealth v. Taylor*, 383 Mass. 272, 281 n.10 (1981)

SECTION 2A
Form of warrant

The warrant shall be in substantially the following form:

THE COMMONWEALTH OF MASSACHUSETTS
    (COUNTY), ss.   (NAME) COURT.

To the Sheriffs of our several counties, or their deputies, any State Police Officer, or any Constable or Police Officer of any city or town, within our said Commonwealth.

Proof by affidavit having been made this day before (name of person authorized to issue warrant) by (names of person or persons whose affidavits have been taken) that there is probable cause for believing that (certain property has been stolen, embezzled, or obtained by false pretenses; certain property is intended for use or has been used as the

means of committing a crime; certain property has been concealed to prevent a crime from being discovered; certain property is unlawfully possessed or kept or concealed for an unlawful purpose).

We therefore command you in the daytime (or at any time of the day or night) to make an immediate search of (identify premises) (occupied by A. B.) and (of the person of A. B.) and of any person present who may be found to have such property in his possession or under his control or to whom such property may have been delivered, for the following property:

(description of property)

and if you find any such property or any part thereof to bring it and the persons in whose possession it is found before (court having jurisdiction) at (name of court and location).

Dated at (city or town) this _____ day of _____, (insert year).

                                          Clerk.

NOTE 1   "[General Laws c. 276,] § 2A requires execution of search warrants within a reasonable time after issuance. Execution of a search warrant which is delayed more than seven days is per se invalid without regard to prejudice. Even if a delay of no more than seven days is shown to be unreasonable, evidence seized pursuant to the warrant need be suppressed only if the defendant sustains the burden of proving legal prejudice attributable to the delay." *Commonwealth v. Cromer*, 365 Mass. 519, 525–26 (1974).

NOTE 2   "The defendant does argue that the judge's failure to sign the warrant rendered the warrant a nullity and that therefore the search was a warrantless search not justified by exigent circumstances. The Commonwealth argues that the inadvertent failure of the judge to sign the warrant was a ministerial error which did not nullify the warrant. We agree with the Commonwealth." *Commonwealth v. Pellegrini*, 405 Mass. 86, 88 (1989).

NOTE 3   Warrant in Hand. "[U]nder art. 14 of the Declaration of Rights of the Massachusetts Constitution, law enforcement officials are required to possess a copy of the warrant in hand when executing a search warrant[.]" *Commonwealth v. Guaba*, 417 Mass. 746, 747 (1994).

SECTION 2B
Affidavit in support of application for warrant; contents and form

A person seeking a search warrant shall appear personally before a court or justice authorized to issue search warrants in criminal cases and shall give an affidavit in substantially the form hereinafter prescribed. Such affidavit shall contain the facts, information, and circumstances upon which such person relies to establish sufficient grounds for the issuance of the warrant. The person issuing the warrant shall retain the affidavit and shall deliver it within three days after the issuance of the warrant to the court to which the warrant is returnable. Upon the return of said warrant, the affidavit shall be attached to it and shall be filed therewith, and it shall not be a public document until the warrant is returned.

The affidavit in support of the application for a search warrant shall be in substantially the following form:

THE COMMONWEALTH OF
MASSACHUSETTS
(COUNTY), ss.   (NAME) COURT.
            _____, (insert year).

I, (name of applicant) being duly sworn, depose and say:
1. I am (describe position, assignment, office, etc.)

2. I have information, based upon (describe source, facts indicating reliability of source and nature of information; if based on personal knowledge and belief, so state).

3. Based upon the foregoing reliable information (and upon my personal knowledge) there is probable cause to believe that the property hereinafter described (has been stolen, or is being concealed, etc.) and may be found (in possession of A.B. or any other person) at premises (identity).

4. The property for which I seek the issuance of a search warrant is the following: (here describe the property as particularly as possible).

Wherefore, I respectfully request that the court issue a warrant and order of seizure, authorizing the search of (identify premises and the persons to be searched) and directing that if such property or evidence or any part thereof be found that it be seized and brought before the court; together with such other and further relief that the court may deem proper.

_____ Name.

Then personally appeared the above named _____ and made oath that the foregoing affidavit by him subscribed is true.

Before me this _____ day of _____, (insert year).

Justice or Special Justice, Clerk or Assistant Clerk of the _____ Court.

NOTE 1a   General. "The purpose of [an] affidavit is to provide the magistrate issuing the search warrant with information from which he can decide whether there is probable cause to issue the search warrant." *Commonwealth v. Cefalo*, 381 Mass. 319, 328 (1980).

NOTE 1b   "In the case of a search warrant, as distinguished from an arrest warrant, the affidavit must, in order to establish probable cause, contain enough information for the issuing magistrate to determine that the items sought are related to the criminal activity under investigation, and that they may reasonably be expected to be located in the place to be searched." *Cefalo*, 381 Mass. at 328.

NOTE 1c   "The nexus between the items sought and the place to be searched may be based on the type of crime, the nature of the missing items, the extent of the suspect's opportunity for concealment, and normal inferences as to where a criminal would be likely to hide evidence of the crime." *Commonwealth v. Wilson*, 427 Mass. 336, 342 (1998).

NOTE 1d   "[T]he affidavit is to be interpreted in a common sense fashion and not subjected to hypertechnical scrutiny. It must be examined as a whole to determine if probable cause existed to issue the warrant; not if there was evidence of guilt beyond a reasonable doubt." *Commonwealth v. Scanlan*, 9 Mass. App. Ct. 173, 179 (1980) (citations omitted).

NOTE 1e   **Personal Appearance.** "Under art. 14, and G. L. c. 276, § 2B, the oath and personal appearance are required to support the affidavit that establishes probable cause for the warrant. We conclude that, in the rare case where an officer must rely on communication by telephone and facsimile transmission to obtain an otherwise valid search warrant, the motion judge must make an express finding that the officer exhausted all reasonable efforts to find a judge before whom he could personally appear. Requiring such a finding ensures that an officer, whose attempt to obtain a proper warrant is thwarted by a failure of the system of on-call judges, is not penalized, while acting as a deterrent to police misconduct so that warrants are issued on probable cause. We hold that, if the motion judge finds that the officer did not make every reasonable effort, the evidence seized must be suppressed." *Commonwealth v. Nelson*, 460 Mass. 564, 573 (2011).

NOTE 2   **The *Aguilar/Spinelli* Standard.** "We conclude instead that the principles developed under *Aguilar v. Texas*, 378 U.S. 108 (1964), and *Spinelli v. United States*, 393 U.S. 410

(1969), if not applied hypertechnically, provide a more appropriate structure for probable cause inquiries under art. 14. Under the *Aguilar-Spinelli* standard, if an affidavit is based on information from an unknown informant, the magistrate must 'be informed of (1) some of the underlying circumstances from which the informant concluded that the contraband was where he claimed it was (the basis of knowledge test), and (2) some of the underlying circumstances from which the affiant concluded that the informant was 'credible' or his information 'reliable' (the veracity test). *Aguilar v. Texas, supra* at 114. If the informant's tip does not satisfy each aspect of the *Aguilar* test, other allegations in the affidavit that corroborate the information could support a finding of probable cause. *Spinelli v. United States, supra* at 415'. *Commonwealth v. Upton*, 390 Mass. [562, 566 (1983)]." *Commonwealth v. Upton*, 394 Mass. 363, 373, 374–75 (1985) (footnote omitted).

NOTE 3a   **The Veracity Test (Reliability).** "A naked assertion that in the past the informant had provided information which led to a prior arrest is insufficient by itself to establish an informant's veracity. The magistrate must be furnished with more detail regarding the circumstances of the prior arrest in order to make a meaningful determination of the informant's veracity. . . .

For an informant's tip to be considered reliable, despite failing to satisfy the requirements of the veracity prong, it must contain a high degree of specificity. In this case, the informant did not provide particularized distinguishing characteristics of the defendant's apartment, possessions, or activities. . . .

"In order for independent, unnamed informants' statements to corroborate each other, they must correspond in 'significant, detailed respects."

Commonwealth v. Rojas, 403 Mass. 483, 486–88 (1988).

NOTE 3b   "The fact that the informant gave information on one occasion in the past which led to the arrest of two individuals is insufficient to satisfy the veracity test. *Commonwealth v. Rojas*, 403 Mass. 483, 486 (1988)." *Commonwealth v. Melendez*, 407 Mass. 53, 59 (1990).

NOTE 3c   "*Commonwealth v. Rojas*, 403 Mass. 483, 486 (1988) held that, '[a] naked assertion that in the past the informant had provided information which led to a prior arrest is insufficient by itself to establish an informant's veracity.'

"We agree that should the affidavit's reference to convictions be struck, the affidavit would fail to establish probable cause. But in order to strike any false statements from the affidavit, the defendant has the burden of showing by a preponderance of the evidence that the statement was made 'knowingly and intentionally, or with reckless disregard for the truth.' A negligent misrepresentation by the affiant would not warrant a redaction of the false statement."

Commonwealth v. Brzezinski, 405 Mass. 401, 407 (1989) (citations omitted).

NOTE 3d   "In *Commonwealth v. Rojas*, 403 Mass. 483 [(1988)], we held that an affidavit which recites only that an informant previously provided information leading to an arrest is not sufficient to satisfy the reliability test. *Id.* at 486.

"Arrests resulting from an informant's tips may be reported in such number in an affidavit as to be construed as self-verifying without any additional indications of reliability. As we suggested in [*Commonwealth v. Melendez*, 407 Mass. 53, 54 (1990)] three arrests, standing alone, do not rise to this level of self-verification."

Commonwealth v. Mejia, 411 Mass. 108, 111, 114 (1991) (citations and quotation marks omitted).

NOTE 3e   "In *Rojas* this court held that '[a] naked assertion that in the past the informant had provided information which led to a prior arrest is insufficient by itself in establish an informant's veracity.' *Id.* at 486. We said, in effect, that a clerk-magistrate was not entitled to infer from such a statement that a prior tip had proved to be accurate. In this case, however, the affidavit recited that the prior tip had led not only to arrests, but also to seizure of cocaine. This distinction is critical." *Commonwealth v. Perez-Baez*, 410 Mass. 43, 46 (1991).

2

NOTE 3f   "In this case, the warrant affidavit informed the magistrate that the informant had 'given information in the past leading to the arrest and conviction of subjects for similar offenses' (emphasis added). This factual assertion provided sufficient basis for the magistrate to determine independently that the informant was reliable." *Commonwealth v. Amral*, 407 Mass. 511, 515 (1990).

NOTE 3g   "In contrast [to *Rojas*], the affidavit at issue here indicates that the informant's prior information had indeed proven to be correct. The mere fact that there has been no conviction will not disqualify an arrest based on an informant's tip from forming part of that informant's 'track record' so long as the significant information contained in the prior tip was shown to be accurate. In *Rojas, supra*, there was simply not enough information in the affidavit from which the magistrate could infer the informant's reliability. In this case, the magistrate was furnished with details regarding the informant's prior tip and its accuracy and was thus able to make a meaningful determination as to the informant's credibility. The veracity prong of the test is therefore met." *Commonwealth v. Lapine*, 410 Mass. 38, 41–42 (1991) (footnote omitted).

NOTE 4a   Statement Against Penal Interest. The affidavit in this case failed to satisfy the veracity test.

"In order for a statement to be considered by the magistrate to be a statement against penal interest, there must be information in the affidavit which tends to show that the informant would have had a reasonable fear of prosecution at the time that he made the statement. . . .

"For example, in *Commonwealth v. Parapar*, 404 Mass. 319 (1989), immediately after being arrested for cocaine trafficking and after the police had made three undercover cocaine purchases, the informant told the police where he had obtained the cocaine. In these circumstances, one could infer that the informant had an actual fear of being prosecuted. Similarly, in *Commonwealth v. Vynorius*, 369 Mass. 17 (1975), the affiant police officer caught the informant red-handed, his pockets stuffed with marijuana. After the informant confessed his drug purchase, he turned over the contraband to the police officer and gave him the information that the officer used as the basis for the affidavit.

"In contrast, the statement in this case did not indicate any circumstances which would cause the informant to have a reasonable fear of prosecution. The statement was unaccompanied by any physical evidence. Indeed, it is likely that the uncorroborated confession, in and of itself, would have been insufficient to prove guilt. *Commonwealth v. Leonard*, 401 Mass. 470, 472 (1988). The likelihood of prosecution was rather remote. One might infer in a case like this that the informant was a 'protected stool pigeon' whose inaccuracies or indiscretions are tolerated on a continuing basis in exchange for information."

Commonwealth v. Melendez, 407 Mass. 53, 56, 57 (1990) (citations and footnote omitted).

NOTE 4b   Although informant C stated that he purchased drugs, this was not a statement against penal interest as it was not clear from the affidavit whether the police/affiant knew the identity of the informant. *Commonwealth v. Allen*, 406 Mass. 575, 579 (1990).

NOTE 5   Informant Named. "The specificity of information supplied, the affiant's occasion to question the informant, and the fact that the informant was named and was not a paid informer may supply sufficient indicia of reliability." *Commonwealth v. Scanlan*, 9 Mass. App. Ct. 173, 179 (1980) (quoting *Commonwealth v. Fleurant*, 2 Mass. App. Ct. 250, 253 (1974)) (quotation marks omitted).

NOTE 6   The Basis of Knowledge Test. The Supreme Judicial Court ruled that the warrant was issued without probable cause in *Commonwealth v. Allen*, 406 Mass. 575 (1990).

"There was nothing in the affidavit to indicate that the undetailed information from the informants A and B was anything more than a casual rumor or a mere reflection of the reputation of the supposed actor." *Commonwealth v. Allen*, 406 Mass. at 578 (quotation marks and citation omitted).

NOTE 7a   Corroboration. Anonymity of informant not fatal to validity of warrant as information "was corroborated by the police officer's observations of the defendant's house and by his telephone conversation with the defendant about placing [an illegal bet in a sporting event]." *Commonwealth v. Carl*, 10 Mass. App. Ct. 906 (1980) (rescript).

NOTE 7b   Even if an informant's tip cannot meet the *Aguilar* criteria, the "constitutional requirements are met if the tip is corroborated by other sources." *Commonwealth v. Bowden*, 379 Mass. 472, 477 (1980); *see also Commonwealth v. Lee*, 10 Mass. App. Ct. 518, 527 (1980).

NOTE 7c   "A defendant's criminal history may be factored into a probable cause determination as corroboration of an informant's tip, but only if the history is sufficiently recent and similar to the crime charged to demonstrate that the defendant was not averse to committing such a crime." *Commonwealth v. Allen*, 406 Mass. 575, 579 (1990) (quotation marks and citation omitted).

NOTE 7d   The information from the three informants was not mutually corroborative. "[I]n order for this to be considered in a magistrate's probable cause determination the informants must provide detailed statements corroborating each other in significant, detailed respects." *Allen*, 406 Mass. at 580 (quotation marks and footnote omitted).

NOTE 7e   Controlled Buy. "A controlled purchase of narcotics, supervised by the police, provides probable cause to issue a search warrant. [Typically] the police either have seen the informant enter the defendant's apartment or dwelling or have seen the informant and the defendant together at the time of the buy." *Commonwealth v. Warren*, 418 Mass. 86, 89 (1994). (In *Warren*, the officer "made sure the informant had no drugs or money before entering the building with three apartments." The officer could not see however "the informant enter the particular apartment to make the controlled buy." The Supreme Judicial Court held that "[i]t is not fatal to the warrant application that police did not observe which of the three apartments the informant entered." *Commonwealth v. Warren*, 418 Mass. at 90). *See also Commonwealth v. Desper*, 419 Mass. 163 (1994).

NOTE 8a   Franks. "Under *Franks*, a hearing is constitutionally required if the defendant makes a substantial preliminary showing that: (1) the affiant made a false statement, either knowingly or intentionally, or with reckless disregard for its truth, and (2) at least in the case of reckless falsehood, the misstatement is necessary to the existence of probable cause." *Commonwealth v. Blake*, 413 Mass. 823, 825–26 (1992).

NOTE 8b   "Following his arrest, the defendant filed a motion for a hearing pursuant to *Franks v. Delaware*, 438 U.S. 154 (1978). Under *Franks*, where a defendant makes a preliminary substantial showing that an affidavit contains intentionally false statements, or statements made with reckless disregard for the truth, which were necessary to the determination of probable cause, he is entitled to a full hearing on the issue. If intentionally false statements, or statements made with reckless disregard of the truth, are found to exist in the affidavit, and such statements were material to the finding of probable cause, they are excised. If the affidavit as redacted fails to establish probable cause, then any evidence seized pursuant to a warrant issued on the basis of the affidavit is suppressed. *Franks, supra* at 155–156 . . .

"In his memorandum in support of the motion of a *Franks* hearing, the defendant pointed out a number of misstatements in the affidavit."

The Supreme Judicial Court found that the misstatements "were at most negligent misrepresentations and cannot form the basis of suppression under *Franks* or art. 14."

Commonwealth v. Valdez, 402 Mass. 65, 67, 70 (1988). *See also Commonwealth v. Ramos*, 402 Mass. 209, 214–15 (1988).

NOTE 8c   "In *Commonwealth v. Douzanis*, 384 Mass. 434 (1981), we noted that, '[a]lthough the defendants did not make a sufficient showing to require the holding of a *Franks*-type hearing as a matter of constitutional right, we have acknowledged the right of a trial judge, in his discretion, "to hold a hearing merely on a showing that an affidavit contained misstatements of fact, particularly material misstatements."' *Id.* at 439 (quoting *Commonwealth* *v. Nine Hundred & Ninety-two Dollars*, 383 Mass. 764, 775 n.12 (1981))." *Commonwealth v. Signorine*, 404 Mass. 400, 406–07 (1989).

NOTE 8d   "Material omission. Pratt claims that a material omission of fact from the affidavit in support of the warrant rendered its contents unworthy of credence by the magistrate. The affidavit, submitted on October 16, 1987, contained ten paragraphs which had been previously submitted in April of that year in an affidavit accompanying an application in another court for a warrant to search Pratt. The search pursuant to the April warrant uncovered no contraband. In the October affidavit, the affiant did not mention the unsuccessful search and stated that he had 'not previously submitted the same application.' The October affidavit included additional paragraphs relating to events which transpired in October, 1987. Pratt claims that the omission from the October affidavit that a substantial portion of its contents had previously been submitted to another court, and that the execution of the resulting warrant had not revealed any contraband, requires that portion of the affidavit be struck.

"The motion judge held a hearing pursuant to *Franks v. Delaware*, 438 U.S. 154 (1978), and *Commonwealth v. Nine Hundred & Ninety-two Dollars*, 383 Mass. 764 (1981). The burden at such a hearing is on the defendant to show by a preponderance of the evidence that the affiant made false statements in the warrant affidavit, 'knowingly and intentionally, or with reckless disregard for the truth,' *Franks, supra* at 155, misstatements which 'bespeak bad faith,' *Nine Hundred & Ninety-two Dollars, supra* at 771.

"The motion judge concluded that the affiant did not act in bad faith, and the evidence introduced at the hearing supported his determination. The motion judge could conclude that the affiant believed, in good faith, that he had 'not previously submitted the same application,' because the October affidavit contained significant new information relating to Pratt's alleged drug-dealing. Furthermore, the motion judge found that the police executed the April search warrant 'prematurely' and that the affiant 'attributed the failure on his actions and not on the information received from the informant.' Considering that the affiant never doubted the existence of probable cause to support the April warrant, the motion judge properly could conclude that the affiant acted in good faith when he omitted references to the aborted search in the October affidavit. There was no error."

Commonwealth v. Pratt, 407 Mass. 647, 658–59 (1990) (footnote omitted).

NOTE 8e   Informer's Privilege. "The United States Supreme Court has stated that: 'A genuine privilege, on . . . fundamental principle . . . , must be recognized for the *identity of persons supplying the government with information concerning the commission of crimes* . . . .' (Emphasis in original.) *McCray v. Illinois*, 386 U.S. 300, 308–309 (1967) (quoting 8 J. Wigmore, Evidence § 2374 (McNaughton rev. ed. 1961)).

"Today, we hold that the public interest in deterring police misconduct requires the trial judge to exercise his or her discretion to order an in camera hearing where the defendant by affidavit asserts facts which cast a reasonable doubt on the veracity of material representations made by the affiant concerning a confidential informant. Mere suspicion that there was no informant, or that the informant's 'reliability' credentials have been misstated, or that his information was other than as recited by the affiant, is not enough to trigger an in camera hearing, but an assertion of facts tending to confirm such a suspicion is sufficient. Otherwise, the very falsity that the defendant seeks to expose may forever be hidden as a result of the defendant's inability to establish who the informant was.

"The purpose of the in camera hearing would be to enable the judge through interrogating the affiant, and, if necessary, the informant to determine whether there is a substantial preliminary showing that the affiant has made false statements intentionally or recklessly. In other words, the purpose of the in camera hearing is to determine whether the defendant has a right to a *Franks* hearing. If the showing is not made, there shall be no *Franks* hearing. If the showing is made, a *Franks* hearing is held at which point the

judge may order disclosure. If the judge orders disclosure at the *Franks* hearing and the Commonwealth declines, the motion to suppress should be allowed. . . .

"In structuring the in camera hearing, the judge is to follow these procedural guidelines. The judge may conduct an in camera hearing without counsel or he may, in his discretion, permit the prosecutor, but not defense counsel, to attend the in camera hearing. Counsel who will not be present at the hearing may submit a limited number of questions which the judge may ask. A transcript of the in camera hearing shall be made and sealed for possible appellate review. Moreover, precautions shall be taken to protect the identity of the informant, including holding the in camera hearing at a place other than the courthouse if deemed necessary to guarantee the informant's anonymity.

"The substance of the in camera hearing we leave to the discretion of the trial judge. We emphasize, however, that if the judge determines following the in camera hearing that the defendant has failed to make the 'showing' required for a *Franks* hearing, the judge shall inform the defendant only that the required showing has not been made. The judge shall neither reveal the informant's identity nor reveal whether any person named by the defendants was the informant."

Commonwealth v. Amral, 407 Mass. 511, 515, 516–17, 522–23, 525 (1990) (footnote and citations omitted).

SECTION 2C
Manner of issuing warrants; application of Secs. 2, 2A and 2B

Search warrants issued pursuant to section two hundred and thirteen of chapter ninety-four, sections twenty and twenty-five of chapter one hundred and ten, section ten of chapter one hundred and thirty, shall be issued in the manner provided in sections two, two A and two B, in so far as they are applicable.

NOTE 1   G.L. c. 94, § 213. Repealed.

NOTE 2   G.L. c. 110—Labels, trade marks, names and registration thereof. Registered bottles. Section 20—Search warrant.

G.L. c. 110—Registration of milk cans and ice cream cans, tubs and cabinets. Section 25—Search warrant.

NOTE 3   G.L. c. 94—Regulation of trade. Section 146—Inspection of meat; seizure and condemnation; appeal market limits.

SECTION 3
Seizure, custody and disposition of articles; exceptions

If an officer in the execution of a search warrant finds property or articles therein described, he shall seize and safely keep them, under the direction of the court or justice, so long as necessary to permit them to be produced or used as evidence in any trial. As soon as may be, thereafter, all property seized under clause First of section one shall be restored to the owners thereof; and all other property seized in execution of a search warrant shall be disposed of as the court or justice orders and may be forfeited and either sold or destroyed, as the public interest requires, in the discretion of the court or justice, except:

(a) Diseased animals or carcasses thereof, or any tainted, diseased, corrupt, decayed or unwholesome meat, fish, vegetables, produce, fruit or provisions of any kind, or the meat of any calf killed when less than two weeks old, or any product thereof kept or concealed with intent to kill, sell or offer the same for sale for food, shall be destroyed or disposed of in accordance with section one hundred and forty-six of chapter ninety-four by the board of health or by an officer designated by the court or justice; and diseased animals found to have been kept or concealed in a particular building, place or enclosure shall be destroyed or disposed of by the division of

2

animal health and department of food and agriculture without compensation to the owners thereof.

(b) Rifles, shotguns, pistols, knives or other dangerous weapons which have been found to have been kept, concealed or used unlawfully or for an unlawful purpose shall be forfeited to the commonwealth and delivered forthwith to the colonel of the state police for destruction or preservation in the discretion of the colonel of the state police.

(c) Money seized under clause Third of section one shall be forfeited and paid over to the state treasurer.

(d) Any property, including money seized under section one, the forfeiture and disposition of which is specified in any general or special law shall be disposed of in accordance therewith.

NOTE   Regulation of Trade. G.L. c. 94, § 146—Inspection of meat; seizure and condemnation; appeal; market limits.

SECTION 3A
Time for return of warrant

Every officer to whom a warrant to search is issued shall return the same to the court by which it was issued as soon as it has been served and in any event not later than seven days from the date of issuance thereof, with a return of his doings thereon; provided, however, that a justice of the superior court may at any time receive complaints and issue search warrants returnable in seven days before a district court named in such warrant and in that event the officer shall make his return to such district court as directed.

NOTE 1   The omission of a reference on the return of the search warrant to approximately two ounces of cocaine that were seized does not require suppression of those drugs. "[R]equired warrant return procedures are ministerial, and failure to comply therewith is not ground for voiding an otherwise valid search." *Commonwealth v. Torres*, 45 Mass. App. Ct. 915, 916 (1998). *See also Commonwealth v. Cromer*, 365 Mass. 519, 521 (1974) (same reasoning for failure to return warrant to court within seven days as required by this section).

NOTE 2   "In this case, the critical question is whether the search warrant was executed within seven days of its issuance. Under similar provisions and rules in other jurisdictions, courts have held that the police do not need to complete forensic analysis of a seized computer and other electronic data storage devices within the prescribed period for executing a search warrant. Because a written return listing the devices to-be examined was filed seven days after the search warrant issued, there was no violation of G.L. c. 276, § 3A." *Commonwealth v. Kaupp*, 453 Mass. 102, 115 (2009) (citations omitted).

SECTION 4
Notice before forfeiture of property

Before a decree of forfeiture of property seized under a search warrant is issued, the court or justice shall, unless otherwise expressly provided, issue a notice under seal, signed by the clerk of the court or by the justice, setting forth the substance of the complaint, and commanding the persons, if any, in whose possession the articles were found, and the owner, if alleged, and all other persons who claim an interest therein, to appear at a time and place therein named to show cause why the articles seized should not be forfeited.

SECTION 5
Service of notice

The notice shall, not less than fourteen days before the time appointed for trial, be served upon the person, if any, alleged to be the owner of the articles seized, by an officer

authorized to serve criminal process, by leaving an attested copy thereof with him personally or at his usual place of abode and by posting an attested copy thereof on the house or building in which the articles were seized, if they were found in a house or building; otherwise, in a public place in the town where they were seized.

SECTION 6
Postponement of trial; further notice

If, at the time appointed for the trial, such notice has not been duly served, or if it appears necessary that any of the articles so seized should be kept longer for the purpose of being produced or used as evidence on any trial, or if other sufficient cause appears, the trial may be postponed to another day and place and further notice issued.

SECTION 7
Sale or destruction of property seized; disposition of proceeds

If upon trial the property is adjudged forfeited, it shall forthwith be disposed of as provided by law. So much thereof as is ordered to be sold by the court or justice shall be sold by the sheriff and the proceeds paid to the county. All moneys seized shall be paid over forthwith to the state treasurer. The court or justice may order any article not found to have been unlawfully used without the knowledge of its owner, lessor or mortgagee to be delivered to the party legally entitled to its possession.

SECTION 8
Appeal; recognizance; conformity to criminal cases; disposition of articles

A person aggrieved by a decree of forfeiture of a district court may appeal therefrom to the superior court; but before his appeal is allowed, he shall recognize to the commonwealth in the sum of two hundred dollars, with sufficient surety or sureties, to prosecute his appeal and to pay all such expenses as may thereafter arise, if final judgment is rendered against the articles adjudged forfeited, and to abide the judgment of the superior court thereon; and upon such appeal, any question of fact shall be tried by a jury. All proceedings in the superior court, including the right of exception, shall conform so far as may be to proceedings in criminal cases; and if, upon final judgment, the articles are adjudged forfeited, they shall be disposed of under the direction of the superior court as they might have been disposed of had no appeal been taken.

REWARDS

SECTION 9
Rewards offered by governor; determination of claims

The governor, if he deems the public good so requires, may offer a suitable reward of not more than ten thousand dollars in any one case to be paid by the commonwealth to any person who, in consequence of such offer, apprehends, brings back and secures a person who is convicted of or charged with a felony, who has escaped from prison in the commonwealth, or to any person who, in consequence of such offer, apprehends and secures a person charged with such crime, or for information that shall lead to the arrest and conviction of any person who has committed a felony, if the person cannot be arrested and secured in the common course of proceedings. If more than one claimant applies for the payment of such reward, the governor shall determine to whom it shall be paid, and if to more than one person, in what proportion to each, and his determination shall be final.

SECTION 10
Rewards offered for detecting or securing persons committing certain offenses; determination of claims

The aldermen or the selectmen, if in their opinion the public good so requires, may offer a suitable reward of not more than five hundred dollars in any one case, to be paid by the town to any person who, in consequence of such offer, detects or secures a person who has committed a felony in such place, either before or after he has been charged therewith, and such reward shall be paid by the treasurer upon the warrant of the aldermen or selectmen. If more than one claimant applies for the payment of such reward, the aldermen or selectmen shall determine to whom it shall be paid, and if to more than one person, in what proportion to each, and their determination shall be final.

The aldermen or the selectmen may offer a reward of five hundred dollars for information leading to the arrest and conviction of a person making or circulating or causing to be made or circulated a false alarm or fire.

In a city, the mayor, with the approval of the city council or, in a town, the selectmen, may offer a reward of not more than five thousand dollars, in any one case, to be paid by the town or city to any person who, in consequence of such offer, detects or secures the arrest and conviction of a person who assassinates or attempts to assassinate a police officer employed by such city or town. Such reward shall be paid by the treasurer upon the warrant of the mayor or selectmen. If more than one claimant applies for the payment of such reward, the mayor or selectmen shall determine to whom it shall be paid, and if to more than one person, in what proportion to each, and said determination shall be final.

EXTRA-TERRITORIAL ARREST ON FRESH PURSUIT

SECTION 10A
Authority of officer of another state to arrest felon

Any member of a duly organized state, county or municipal peace unit of another state of the United States the laws of which contain provisions substantially equivalent to the provisions of this and the following section, who enters this commonwealth in fresh pursuit, and continues herein in such fresh pursuit, of a person in order to arrest him on the ground that he has committed a felony in such other state shall have the same authority to arrest and hold in custody a person on the ground that he has committed a felony in this commonwealth. This section shall not be construed so as to make unlawful any arrest in this commonwealth which would otherwise be lawful.

NOTE   See Notes on "Fresh and Continued Pursuit Outside Jurisdiction" et seq. following G.L. c. 90, § 24.

SECTION 10B
Proceedings after arrest

If an arrest is made in this commonwealth by an officer of another state in accordance with the provisions of the preceding section he shall without unnecessary delay take the person arrested before a justice, associate justice or special justice of a court of record in the county in which the arrest was made, who shall conduct a hearing for the purpose of determining the lawfulness of the arrest. If such justice, associate justice or special justice determines that the arrest was lawful he shall commit the person arrested to await for a reasonable time the issuance of a rendition warrant by the governor of the state from which he fled. If such justice, associate justice or special justice determines that the arrest was unlawful he shall discharge the person arrested.

SECTION 10C
Partial invalidity

If any part of sections ten A and ten B is for any reason declared void, it is declared to be the intent of said sections that such invalidity shall not affect the validity of the remaining portions of said sections.

SECTION 10D
Citation of law; uniform construction

Sections ten A to ten C, inclusive, may be cited as the uniform extraterritorial arrest on fresh pursuit law, and shall be so interpreted and construed as to effectuate their general purpose to make uniform the law of the states which enact similar laws.

PROCEDURE ON INTERSTATE RENDITION

SECTION 11
Definitions

Wherever appearing in sections eleven to twenty R, inclusive, the term "governor" includes any person performing the functions of governor by authority of the law of this commonwealth, the term "executive authority" includes the governor, and any person performing the functions of governor, in any other state, the term "surrender" refers to the arresting and delivering up of a person in this commonwealth to the executive authority of another state, and the term "state", referring to a state other than this commonwealth, refers to any other state or territory, organized or unorganized, of the United States.

SECTION 12
Arrest and delivery of accused to executives of another state; governor's authority

Subject to the provisions of sections eleven to twenty R, inclusive, the controlling provisions of the constitution of the United States, and any and all acts of congress enacted in pursuance thereof, the governor may cause to be arrested and delivered up to the executive authority of any other state any person charged in such other state with treason, felony or other crime, or with having been convicted of a crime in such other state and having escaped from confinement or having broken the terms of his bail, probation or parole, who is found in this commonwealth.

SECTION 13
Surrendering accused not in demanding state at time of crime or leaving demanding state involuntarily

The governor may also surrender, on demand of the executive authority of any other state, any person in this commonwealth charged in such other state in the manner provided in section fourteen with committing an act in this commonwealth, or in a third state, intentionally resulting in a crime in the state whose executive authority is making the demand, hereafter in this section and in sections fourteen to twenty P, inclusive, referred to as the demanding state, and the provisions of sections eleven to twenty R inclusive, not otherwise inconsistent shall apply to such cases, even though the accused was not in the demanding state at the time of the commission of the crime.

The governor may surrender, on demand of the executive authority of any other state, any person in this commonwealth charged in the demanding state in the manner provided in section fourteen with having violated its laws, even though such person left such state involuntarily.

SECTION 14
Written demand; allegations; accompanying papers; charge of crime; authentication of copies of papers

No demand for the interstate rendition of a person charged with crime in another state shall be recognized by the governor unless it be in writing alleging either that the person demanded was present in the demanding state at the time of the commission of the alleged crime, or that such person committed in this commonwealth or in a third state an act intentionally resulting in a crime in the demanding state, or that such person has escaped from confinement or has broken the terms of his bail, probation or parole, nor unless such demand is accompanied by a copy of an indictment found, or of an information supported by affidavit, in the demanding state, or by a copy of an affidavit made before a magistrate of such state, and by a copy of the warrant which was issued thereon, or by a copy of a judgment of conviction or of a sentence imposed in execution thereof in the demanding state. The indictment or information, or the affidavit made before the magistrate who issued the warrant, shall substantially charge the person demanded with having committed a crime under the law of the demanding state, and the copy of the indictment, information, affidavit, judgment of conviction or sentence shall be authenticated by the executive authority of such state.

NOTE 1   A demand from the governor of a foreign state need not expressly state that the suspect was in that state at the time of the crime so long as "it plainly appears from the demand that [the suspect] was charged with a crime, the nature of which required his presence at the time and place where the offense occurred, and that thereafter he fled to this Commonwealth."
In re Baker, 310 Mass. 724, 728 (1942).

NOTE 2   This section does *not* require "sworn evidence in addition to the demand and a properly authenticated copy of the indictment." *In re Baker*, 310 Mass. at 728.

NOTE 3   "[D]oes a court of a sending State (here, Massachusetts) have jurisdiction to grant a habeas corpus petition predicated on the apparent failure of a receiving State (here, California) to comply with the Agreement?

"We therefore conclude that Gay remains a fugitive from California law, even assuming that California has violated the Agreement by not disposing of his pending burglary charge within 180 days. Because he remains a fugitive, Gay has no basis upon which to challenge the issuance of the Governor's warrant providing for his extradition to California." *Petition of Gay*, 406 Mass. 471, 474, 476–77 (1990).

SECTION 15
Investigation of demand and report to governor

When a demand shall be made upon the governor by the executive authority of another state for the surrender of a person so charged with crime, the governor may call upon the attorney general or any other prosecuting officer to investigate or assist in investigating the demand, and to report to him the situation and circumstances of the person so demanded, and whether he ought to be surrendered.

SECTION 16
Governor's warrant of arrest; recital of facts

If the governor decides that the demand should be complied with, he shall sign a warrant of arrest, sealed with the state seal and directed to an officer authorized to serve warrants in criminal cases or other person whom the governor may think fit to entrust with the execution thereof. Such warrant shall substantially recite the facts necessary to the validity of its issue.

SECTION 17
Arrest and delivery of accused; commanding aid

Such warrant shall authorize the person to whom it is directed to arrest the accused at any time and any place where he may be found within this commonwealth and to command the aid of all officers authorized to serve warrants in criminal cases or other persons in the execution thereof, and to deliver the accused, subject to the provisions of said sections eleven to twenty R, inclusive, to the duly authorized agent of the demanding state.

SECTION 18
Authority to command assistance; penalties for refusal

Every such person empowered to make an arrest shall have the same authority, in arresting the accused, to command assistance therein, as officers have by law in the execution of any criminal process directed to them, with like penalties against those who refuse their assistance.

SECTION 19
Rights of arrested person; habeas corpus; notice; penalty

No person arrested upon such a warrant shall be delivered over to the agent whom the executive authority of the demanding state shall have appointed to receive him unless such person shall first be taken forthwith before a justice or special justice of a court of record of this commonwealth, who shall inform such person of the demand made for his surrender and of the crime with which he is charged, and that he has the right to demand and procure legal counsel; and, if the prisoner or his counsel shall state that he desires to test the legality of his arrest, such justice or special justice shall fix a reasonable time to be allowed the prisoner within which to apply for a writ of habeas corpus. When such writ is applied for, notice thereof, and of the time and place of hearing thereon, shall be given to the attorney general and to the district attorney for the district in which the arrest is made and for the district in which the accused is in custody, and to said agent of the demanding state.

Any officer who shall deliver to said agent of the demanding state a person in his custody under the warrant of the governor, in wilful disobedience of the provisions of this section, shall be punished by a fine of not more than one thousand dollars or by imprisonment for not more than six months, or both.

SECTION 20
Confinement of accused; expense; evidence of transportation to demanding state; new requisition

The officer or other person executing the governor's warrant of arrest, or the agent of the demanding state to whom the prisoner shall have been delivered, may when necessary confine the prisoner in a jail or other place of detention in any county, city or town through which he may pass; and the keeper of such jail or place of detention shall receive and safely keep the prisoner until the officer or person having charge of him is ready to proceed on his journey, such officer or person being chargeable with the expense of keeping.

The officer or agent of a demanding state to whom a prisoner shall have been delivered following interstate rendition proceedings in another state, or to whom a prisoner shall have been delivered after waiving interstate rendition in another state, and who is passing through this commonwealth with such a prisoner for the purpose of immediately returning such prisoner to the demanding state may, when necessary, confine the prisoner in a jail or other place of detention in any county, city or town through which he may pass; and the keeper of such jail or other place of detention shall receive and safely keep the prisoner until the officer or agent having charge of him is ready to proceed on his journey, such officer or agent being chargeable with the expense of keeping; provided, that such officer or agent shall produce and show to such keeper satisfactory written evidence that he is actually transporting such prisoner to the demanding state pursuant to a requisition by the executive authority thereof, or that such prisoner has waived interstate rendition. No prisoner being transported pursuant to such a requisition or waiver shall be entitled to demand a new requisition while in this commonwealth.

SECTION 20A
Warrant to apprehend accused on oath or affidavit; copies of papers attached

Whenever any person within this commonwealth shall be charged, on the oath of any credible person before any court or justice in this commonwealth authorized to issue warrants in criminal cases, with the commission of any crime in any other state, including cases arising under section thirteen, or with having been convicted in such other state and having escaped from confinement or having broken the terms of his bail, probation or parole, or whenever complaint shall have been made before any such court or justice in this commonwealth setting forth, on the affidavit of any credible person in another state, that a crime has been committed in such other state and that a person has been charged in such state with the commission of a crime, including cases arising under section thirteen, or with having been convicted of a crime in that state and having escaped from confinement or having broken the terms of his bail, probation or parole, and is believed to be in this commonwealth, such court or justice may issue a warrant directed to any officer authorized to serve warrants in criminal cases commanding him to apprehend the person named therein, wherever he may be found in this commonwealth, and bring him before the same or any other such court or justice convenient of access to the place where the arrest may be made, to answer the charge or complaint and affidavit; and a certified copy of the sworn charge or complaint and affidavit upon which the warrant is issued shall be attached to the warrant.

SECTION 20B
Arrest without warrant; taking accused before court or justice; complaint

The arrest of a person may be lawfully made also by any officer authorized to serve warrants in criminal cases, without a warrant, upon reasonable information that the accused stands charged in another state with a crime punishable by death or by imprisonment for a term exceeding one year, but when so arrested the accused shall be taken with all practicable speed before a court or justice authorized to issue warrants in criminal cases and complaint shall be made against him under oath setting forth the ground for the arrest as in the preceding section; and thereafter his answer shall be heard as if he had been arrested on a warrant.

NOTE   "We are deciding this case under the United States Constitution under which, absent exigent circumstances, police may not make a warrantless entry into a person's dwelling to arrest him or seize evidence. It is true that the defendant was not in his own dwelling. He was a visitor lawfully in the home of his mother. Our law is clear that in these circumstances, absent exigency or consent, a search or arrest warrant must first be obtained before police may enter the home of a third person in search of a suspect.

"In this case, there were no exigent circumstances to justify a warrantless entry into the dwelling of the defendant's mother. The provision for a warrantless arrest in G.L. c. 276, § 20B (1986 ed.), does not advance the Commonwealth's position because the statute does not authorize an entry into a dwelling to effectuate a warrantless arrest."

Commonwealth v. Derosia, 402 Mass. 284, 286 (1988) (footnote and citations omitted).

SECTION 20C
Commitment to permit arrest under warrant of governor on requisition

If from the examination before such court or justice it appears that the person held is the person charged with having committed the crime alleged, including cases arising under section thirteen, or is the person charged with having been convicted of a crime and having escaped from confinement or having broken the terms of his bail, probation or parole, such court or justice shall, by a warrant reciting the accusation, commit him to a jail or house of correction for such time, not exceeding thirty days and specified in the warrant, as will enable the arrest of the accused to be made under a warrant of the governor, on a requisition of the executive authority of the state having jurisdiction of the crime, unless the accused gives bail as provided in the following section, or until he shall be legally discharged.

SECTION 20D
Bail
(Amended by 2014 Mass. Acts c. 260, § 25, effective Aug. 8, 2014.)

Unless the offense with which the person arrested is charged is shown to be an offense punishable by death or life imprisonment under the laws of the state in which it was committed, such court or justice may admit such person to bail by bond or undertaking, with sufficient sureties, and in such sum as such court or justice deems proper, conditioned for his appearance before such court or justice, at a time specified in such bond or undertaking, and for his surrender to be arrested upon the warrant of the governor; provided, however, that if such person is arrested for a crime committed in the commonwealth, any bail by bond or undertaking shall be assessed pursuant to sections 42, 42A, 57, 58 and 58A.

SECTION 20E
Discharge; recommitment; bail

If the accused has not been arrested under warrant of the governor at the expiration of the time specified in such warrant, bond or undertaking, such court or justice may discharge him or may recommit him for a further period of sixty days, or may again take bail for his appearance and surrender, as provided in the preceding section, but within a period not to exceed sixty days following the date of such new bond or undertaking.

SECTION 20F
Forfeiture of bail

If the accused is admitted to bail, and fails to appear and surrender himself according to the conditions of his bond or undertaking, such court or justice, by proper order, shall declare the bond or undertaking forfeited and order his immediate arrest without warrant if he be within this commonwealth. Recovery may be had on such bonds or undertakings in the name of the commonwealth as in the case of other bonds or undertakings given by persons accused in criminal proceedings within this commonwealth.

SECTION 20G
Prosecution pending in commonwealth

If a criminal prosecution has been instituted against such person under the laws of this commonwealth and is still pending, the governor, in his discretion, may either surrender him on the demand of the executive authority of another state, or hold him until the final disposition of such prosecution or, if convicted and sentenced, until his discharge from imprisonment.

SECTION 20H
Inquiry into guilt or innocence

The guilt or innocence of the accused as to the crime of which he is charged may not be inquired into by the governor, or in any proceeding after the demand for interstate rendition accompanied by a charge of crime in legal form as provided in section fourteen shall have been presented to the governor, except as it may be involved in identifying the person held as the person charged with the crime.

SECTION 20I
Recall of warrant or issuance of another

The governor, whenever he deems proper, may recall his warrant of arrest or may issue another warrant.

SECTION 20J
Waiver of warrant and procedure, etc.

Any person arrested in this commonwealth charged with having committed any crime in another state or with having been convicted in another state and having escaped from confinement or having broken the terms of his bail, probation or parole, may waive the issuance and service of the warrant provided for in sections sixteen and seventeen and all other procedure incidental to interstate rendition proceedings, by executing or subscribing in the presence of any court or justice of this commonwealth authorized to issue warrants in criminal cases a writing which states that he consents to return to the demanding state; provided, that if such waiver shall be executed or subscribed by such person it shall be the duty of such court or justice to inform such person of his rights to the issuance and service of a warrant in interstate rendition and to obtain a writ of habeas corpus as provided in section nineteen. If and when such consent has been duly executed it shall forthwith be forwarded to the office of the governor and filed therein. Such court or justice shall direct the officer having such person in custody to deliver forthwith such person to the duly accredited agent of the demanding state, and shall deliver or cause to be delivered to such agent a copy of such consent; provided, that nothing in this section shall be deemed to limit the right of the accused person to return voluntarily and without formality to the demanding state, nor shall the foregoing waiver procedure be deemed to be an exclusive procedure or to limit the powers, rights or duties of the officers of the demanding state or of this commonwealth.

SECTION 20K
Warrant to receive accused and convey him to proper county; proceedings pending in another state

Whenever the governor shall demand a person charged with crime in this commonwealth, or one charged with having been convicted in this commonwealth and having escaped from confinement or having broken the terms of his bail, probation or parole, from the chief executive of any other state, or from the chief justice or an associate justice of the supreme court of the District of Columbia authorized to receive such demand under the laws of the United States, he may issue a warrant, under the seal of this commonwealth, to some agent, commanding him to receive the person so charged if delivered to him, and convey him to the proper officer of the county in which the crime was committed.

Whenever it is desired to have returned to this commonwealth a person charged herein with a crime, or with having been convicted in this commonwealth and having escaped from confinement or having broken the terms of his bail, probation or parole, and such person is imprisoned or is held under criminal proceedings then pending against him in another state, the governor may agree with the executive authority of such other state for the interstate rendition of such person before the conclusion of such proceedings or of his term of sentence in such other state, upon such conditions relative to the return of such person to such other state at the expense of this commonwealth as may be agreed upon between the governor and the executive authority of such other state.

SECTION 20L
Application for requisition

(a) Whenever the return to this commonwealth of a person charged with crime herein is required, the attorney general, or the district attorney for the district in which the crime is alleged to have occurred, shall present to the governor his written application for a requisition for the return of the person charged, in which application there shall be included a statement of the name of the person so charged and the crime charged against him, the approximate time, place and circumstances of its commission, the state in which he is believed to be, including the location of the accused therein, at the time the application is made, and a certificate that, in the opinion of the said attorney general or district attorney, the ends of justice require the arrest and return of the accused to this commonwealth for trial, and that the proceeding is not instituted to enforce a private claim.

(b) Whenever the return to this commonwealth is required of a person who has been convicted of a crime herein and has escaped from confinement or has broken the terms of his bail, probation or parole, the district attorney for the district in which the crime is alleged to have occurred, the parole board or the warden or superintendent of the institution from

2

which escape was made, shall present to the governor a written application for a requisition for the return of such person, in which application shall be stated the name of the person, the crime of which he was convicted, the circumstances of his escape from confinement or of the breach of the terms of his bail, probation or parole, and the state in which he is believed to be, including the location of the person therein, at the time the application is made.

(c) The application shall be verified by affidavit, shall be executed in duplicate and shall be accompanied by two certified copies of the indictment returned, or of the complaint made to a court or justice, stating the offense with which the accused is charged, or of the judgment of conviction or of the sentence. The attorney general, district attorney, parole board, warden or superintendent may also attach such further affidavits or other documents in duplicate as he or it may deem proper to be submitted with such application. One copy of the application, with the action of the governor indicated by endorsement thereon, and one of the certified copies of the indictment or complaint, or of the judgment of conviction or of the sentence shall be filed in the office of the state secretary to remain of record in that office. The other copies of all such papers shall be forwarded with the requisition of the governor.

SECTION 20M
Payment of agent's expenses

If the application for a requisition for the return to this commonwealth of a person charged with crime herein, or for the return of a person who has been convicted of a crime herein and has escaped from confinement or has broken the terms of his bail, probation or parole, is complied with and an agent appointed, the account of such agent shall be paid like other expenses in criminal cases by the commonwealth.

SECTION 20N
Service of process in civil action or accused; immunity

A person brought into this commonwealth on, or after waiver of, interstate rendition based on a criminal charge shall not be subject to service of personal process in civil actions arising out of the same facts as the criminal proceeding to answer which he is being or has been returned, until he has been convicted or acquitted in the criminal proceeding, and, if acquitted, until he has had reasonable opportunity to return to the state from which he was brought by interstate rendition proceedings or upon waiver thereof.

SECTION 20O
Trying for crimes; immunity

After a person has been brought into this commonwealth by interstate rendition proceedings or upon waiver thereof he may be tried herein for other crimes which he may be charged with having committed herein, as well as that specified in the requisition for his interstate rendition or in the waiver thereof.

SECTION 20P
Waiver by commonwealth

Nothing in sections eleven to twenty O, inclusive, shall be deemed to constitute a waiver by this commonwealth of its right, power or privilege to try any person demanded of it for a crime committed herein, or of its right, power or privilege to regain custody of such a person by interstate rendition proceedings or otherwise for the purpose of trial, sentence or punishment for any crime committed herein, nor shall any

proceeding under said sections which result in, or fail to result in, interstate rendition be deemed a waiver by this commonwealth of any of its rights, privileges or jurisdiction in any way whatsoever.

SECTION 20Q
Partial validity

If any part of sections eleven to twenty P, inclusive, is for any reason declared void, such invalidity shall not affect the validity of the remaining portions of said sections.

SECTION 20R
Citation of law; uniform construction

Sections eleven to twenty R, inclusive, may be cited as the uniform criminal interstate rendition law, and shall be so interpreted and construed as to effectuate their general purpose to make uniform the law of those states enacting similar laws.

ARREST, EXAMINATION, COMMITMENT AND BAIL

SECTION 21
Justices may issue process

Justices of the supreme judicial, superior or district courts, may issue process for the apprehension of persons charged with crime and to carry into effect sections twenty-two to eighty-two, inclusive.

SECTION 22
Warrants, procedure for issuance

Upon complaint made to any justice that a crime has been committed, he shall examine on oath the complainant and any witnesses produced by him, reduce the complaint to writing, and cause it to be subscribed by the complainant, and, if it appears that a crime has been committed, shall issue a summons or warrant in compliance with the provisions of the Massachusetts Rules of Criminal Procedure.

SECTION 23
Service of warrants and other processes

Warrants and other processes issued for the apprehension of persons charged with crime and child support warrants issued pursuant to section 34A of chapter 215 may be directed to and served in any part of the commonwealth by an officer authorized to serve criminal process in any county. Such officer may command aid and exercise the same authority as if in his own county.

SECTION 23A
Persons arrested on warrants issued because of forfeit or default on bail bond or recognizance; fee

Whenever a court is requested to issue a warrant, the requesting authority shall provide to the court the person's name, last known address, date of birth, gender, race, height, weight, hair and eye color, the offense or offenses for which the warrant is requested, a designation of the offense or offenses as felonies or misdemeanors, any known aliases and any such information as shall be required for a warrant to be accepted by the criminal justice information system maintained by the department of criminal justice information services. A warrant which contains the above information as provided by the individual for whom the warrant is being issued shall not be nullified if such information is later found to be inaccurate. An individual or law enforcement official

2

seeking issuance of a warrant which does not contain all of the above required fields may apply to the clerk of the court for an exemption from this requirement. Such exemption shall be automatically granted upon the request of any law enforcement official or agency. No rights regarding the validity of a warrant may arise from such requirements not being met. Such information and the name of the police department responsible for serving the warrant shall be entered by the clerk's office into a computer system to be known as the warrant management system. All warrants appearing in the warrant management system shall be accessible through the criminal justice information system, maintained by the department of criminal justice information services to law enforcement agencies and the registry of motor vehicles. The warrant shall consist of sufficient information electronically appearing in the warrant management system, and a printout of the electronic warrant from the criminal justice information system shall constitute a true copy of the warrant. Such warrants appearing electronically in the warrant management system and, in turn, in the criminal justice information system, shall constitute notice and delivery of said warrants to the police department responsible for serving the warrant. Whenever a warrant is recalled or removed, the clerk's office shall, without any unnecessary delay, enter the same in the warrant management system which entry shall be electronically transmitted to the criminal justice information system.

No law enforcement officer, who in the performance of his duties relies in good faith on the warrant appearing in the warrant management system and, in turn, the criminal justice information system, shall be liable in any criminal prosecution or civil action alleging false arrest, false imprisonment, or malicious prosecution or arrest by false pretense.

The issuing court shall provide notification, either before the issuance of a default or arrest warrant or no later than 30 days after the issuance of the warrant, to the subject of the warrant. Such notice shall contain the following information: the name and address of the issuing court, a description of the charge for which the warrant is being issued, a description of the method by which the individual may clear the warrant and a summary of the consequences the individual may face for not responding to the warrant. Such notice shall be deemed satisfactory if notice is mailed to the address stated on the warrant.

SECTION 23B
Annual list of persons registered with licensing authorities; criminal history systems board; outstanding warrants; notification of license suspension; hearing

(a) Any agency, department, commission, division or authority of the commonwealth that issues a professional license, certificate, permit or authorization to engage in a profession, trade, or business shall ensure that such license, certificate, permit or authorization is suspended for a person who has a default or arrest warrant outstanding against him.

(b) In order to determine if a person has an outstanding warrant against him, the licensing authorities referenced in subsection (a) shall transmit to the department of criminal justice information services, in an electronic format and reporting schedule approved by the executive director of the department of criminal justice information services, a list of persons who are registered with such licensing authorities on an annual basis. The department of criminal justice information services shall, subject to appropriation, remit to each licensing authority a list of persons who have received a license, certificate, permit or authorization to engage in a profession, trade, or business against whom there is an outstanding default or arrest warrant issued by any court of the commonwealth. Evidence of the outstanding default or arrest warrant appearing in the warrant management system as established by section 23A shall be sufficient grounds for such suspension.

(c) Each licensing authority shall notify persons against whom there is a default or arrest warrant outstanding that their license, certificate, permit or authorization shall be suspended unless the person furnished proof within 30 days that such warrant has been recalled or that there is no such warrant outstanding against the person. Such notification shall be deemed sufficient if the notice is mailed to the address listed on the license, certificate, permit or authorization or application for the license, certificate, permit or authorization. If no such proof is furnished within 30 days, the person shall be notified that such license, certificate, permit or authorization is suspended subject to the opportunity for a hearing. After such notice to the person has been delivered or mailed by the licensing authority, the person may request a hearing within 90 days with respect to the existence of an outstanding warrant. If a hearing is requested within ten days from the time the notice that the license, certificate, permit or authorization is suspended is mailed or delivered, the license, certificate, permit or authorization shall not be suspended until a finding following the hearing. If a hearing is requested as provided for in this chapter, the law enforcement agency responsible for the warrant shall be notified of the time, place, date of hearing and the subject of the warrant. An affidavit from the law enforcement agency responsible for the warrant or from the colonel of the state police may be introduced as prima facie evidence of the existence of a warrant without the need for members of that law enforcement agency to attend any hearings held under this section. The licensing authority shall issue a finding within 45 days of conducting the hearing as to the existence of a warrant. If there is a warrant outstanding, the license, certificate, permit or authorization shall be suspended. Said license shall not be renewed or reinstated without sufficient proof that the warrant has been cleared.

(d) For the purposes of this section, a professional license shall mean any license, permit, certificate, registration, authority or similar form of permission necessary to engage in a trade or profession issued by an agency, department, commission, division or authority of the commonwealth.

(e) The licensing authorities referenced in this section shall promulgate regulations to implement this section. Implementation of this section shall be subject to appropriation.

SECTION 24
Summons instead of warrant

Upon a complaint or indictment for an offense, a summons shall issue instead of a warrant, unless, in the judgment of the court or justice, there is reason to believe that the defendant will not appear upon summons.

SECTION 25
Summons fixing time for trial; service

A summons shall require the defendant to appear before the court at a stated time and place on the return day and shall be served by an officer authorized to serve criminal process by giving to the defendant in hand or by leaving at his dwelling house or last and usual place of abode with some person of suitable age and discretion then residing therein an attested copy not less than twenty-four hours before the return day, or by mailing an attested copy to the defendant's last known address.

SECTION 26
Failure to appear and abide orders as contempt

If a defendant so summoned fails, without reasonable cause, to appear and abide the orders of the court or justice, he shall be considered in contempt of court, and may be punished by a fine of not more than twenty dollars. A warrant, if necessary, may be issued at any time after the issue of such summons, whether it has been served or not.

SECTION 27
Recognizance

If a defendant so summoned duly appears, he may be ordered to recognize for his further appearance but shall not be required to give surety upon his recognizance at any stage of the prosecution without a special order.

SECTION 28
Arrest without warrant

Any officer authorized to serve criminal process may arrest, without a warrant, and detain a person found in the act of stealing property in the presence of the officer regardless of the value of the property stolen and may arrest, without a warrant, and detain a person whom the officer has probable cause to believe has committed a misdemeanor by violating a temporary or permanent vacate, restraining, suspension and surrender, or no-contact order or judgment issued pursuant to section eighteen, thirty-four B or thirty-four C of chapter two hundred and eight, section three, three B, three C, four or five of chapter two hundred and nine A, section thirty-two of chapter two hundred and nine, or section fifteen or twenty of chapter two hundred and nine C. Said officer may arrest, without a warrant, and detain a person whom the officer has probable cause to believe has committed a misdemeanor involving abuse as defined in section one of chapter two hundred and nine A or has committed an assault and battery in violation of section thirteen A of chapter two hundred and sixty-five against a family or household member as defined in section one of chapter two hundred and nine A. Said officer may arrest and detain a person charged with a misdemeanor, without having a warrant for such arrest in his possession, if the officer making such arrest and detention shall have actual knowledge that a warrant then in full force and effect for the arrest of such person has in fact issued.

NOTE   **Related Statute.** G.L. c. 94C, § 41—Warrantless arrests in drug cases.

SECTION 29
Recognizance in county of arrest; misdemeanor

Before a court releases, discharges or admits to bail any person brought before said court, in any criminal matter, the court shall first check the warrant management system to determine whether any warrant has been issued against the person in any jurisdiction of the commonwealth. If the warrant management system indicates that any warrant is outstanding, said court shall, if the outstanding offense is bailable pursuant to section fifty-seven, fifty-eight or fifty-eight A of this chapter, make a determination of bail as provided by said sections for each outstanding warrant.

If such person is released on bail or recognizance for an outstanding warrant, said court shall confer with the court that issued the outstanding warrant and, based thereon, specify in the warrant management system the date on which the person must appear before the issuing court and so notify the person. If such person is not released on bail or recognizance for an outstanding warrant, the person shall be transported by an officer, or in accordance with section twenty-four of chapter thirty-seven, or in accordance with any other law of the commonwealth, to the court that issued the warrant, or if the issuing court is not in session, to the jail in the county of the issuing court, and thereafter, to the next regular sitting of the court that issued the warrant.

A person arrested on a default warrant for a felony or a misdemeanor punishable by imprisonment for more than one hundred days may be released on bail or recognizance only by a justice of the court having jurisdiction over the place where the person was arrested or is being held, or by a justice of the court that issued the warrant.

No person authorized to admit to bail, including but not limited to judges or court personnel, and no sheriff or police officer shall release a person from custody before he determines by checking the warrant management system whether any warrant is outstanding in the commonwealth against said person; provided, however, that no person authorized to admit to bail, including but not limited to judges or court personnel, and no sheriff or police officer, who in the performance of his duties acts in good faith, shall be liable in any criminal prosecution or civil action where a person is released from custody before determining by checking the warrant management system whether a warrant is outstanding against said person in the commonwealth.

If a warrant is outstanding for a felony charge, or a misdemeanor punishable by imprisonment for more than one hundred days, the person being held shall be brought before the court having jurisdiction over the place where the person is held, or to the court that issued the warrant, and a justice, clerk or assistant clerk of said court shall make a determination of bail as provided in the first and second paragraphs of this section.

If a warrant is outstanding for a misdemeanor punishable by imprisonment for one hundred days or less, the person may be released on bail or recognizance by a person authorized to admit to bail. Such person authorized to admit to bail shall, without unnecessary delay, provide the clerk of the court that issued the warrant with notice of the fact that the person was admitted to bail. If the person held on such misdemeanor warrant is not released, the person shall be brought before the next session of the court having jurisdiction over the place where the person is held, or to the court that issued the warrant, and such court shall make a determination of bail as provided in the first and second paragraphs of this section.

SECTION 30
Certifying bail on warrant; delivery of papers to court clerk; summoning witnesses

Notwithstanding any law, rule or regulation to the contrary, whenever a default warrant, issued in any jurisdiction in the commonwealth against any person, is recalled by a court,

2

the court shall assess a fee of fifty dollars against the person in payment of the costs of recalling the warrant, except that upon a finding of good cause by the court the fee may be waived.

Any person arrested on a warrant issued because such person has forfeited or defaulted on his bail bond or recognizance or has been surrendered by a probation officer shall be required by the court to pay a fee of $75 payable to the city or town in which such arrest was effected, unless the judge finds that such person is indigent, in which case such person shall be required to perform one day of community service, unless the judge further finds that such person is physically or mentally unable to perform such service.

SECTION 31
Default warrant for failure to make certain payments; additional fee; waiver; discharge upon payment

Whenever a court issues a default warrant solely due to the person's failure to pay a fine, assessment, court cost, restitution, support payment or other amount as ordered by the court or required by law, the court shall specify the amount owed, including an additional assessment of $50 which assessment may be waived by the court upon a finding of good cause, with a statement that the warrant against the person may be discharged upon payment of the amount and the assessment, if any, and shall note the same in the warrant management system. The administrative office of the trial court shall accept payment of such fine, assessment, court cost, restitution, support payment or other amount as ordered by the court, along with any assessment, to be remitted by mail, telephone or other electronic means, in any form deemed acceptable by the trial court. Upon receipt of payment, the warrant against the person shall be discharged, the discharge shall be noted in the warrant management system and the individual shall receive notice of the discharge within seven days.

SECTION 32
Conveying accused felon to county where warrant issued

Whenever a person, brought before a court, against whom an outstanding warrant was issued, solely due to the failure of the person brought before the court to pay a fine assessment, court cost, restitution, support payment, or other amount, the court may accept payment of such amount and assess an additional fifty dollars which assessment may be waived by the court upon a finding of good cause and if the person is not being held on other process, the court may direct that the person be released from custody and shall notify the jurisdiction in which the warrant was issued of the payment and the assessment, if any. Upon notice of the release the court that issued the warrant shall recall the warrant and cause such information to be entered in the warrant management system.

SECTION 33
Physical examination of and report on persons arrested

Whenever a person is arrested for a crime and is taken to or confined in a jail, police station or lockup, the officer in charge thereof shall immediately examine the prisoner, and if he finds any bruises, cuts or other injuries shall forthwith make a written report thereof to the chief of police of the town concerned, or in Boston to the police commissioner, and in towns where there is no chief of police to the selectmen. The requirement that the prisoner be examined shall not be deemed to compel the removal of clothing. When a person is

transferred from one place of confinement to another prior to his arraignment in court or to his release, the requirement that he shall be examined shall apply only to the place to which he is first taken after his arrest. Whoever violates this section shall be punished by a fine of not more than ten dollars.

SECTION 33A
Use of telephone in places of detention

The police official in charge of the station or other place of detention having a telephone wherein a person is held in custody, shall permit the use of the telephone, at the expense of the arrested person, for the purpose of allowing the arrested person to communicate with his family or friends, or to arrange for release on bail, or to engage the services of an attorney. Any such person shall be informed forthwith upon his arrival at such station or place of detention, of his right to so use the telephone, and such use shall be permitted within one hour thereafter.

NOTE 1   "It is settled that suppression is only an appropriate remedy for a violation of § 33A when the evidence demonstrates that law enforcement officers intentionally withheld the defendant's telephone right in order to coerce the defendant or to gain an advantage in the investigation. *See Commonwealth v. LeBeau*, 451 Mass. 244, 257 (2008). The defendant bears the burden of establishing an intentional violation of the statute." *Commonwealth v. Haith*, 452 Mass. 409, 413–14 (2008).

NOTE 2   Defendant given timely notice that he could call "anybody." "Although it would have been preferable if the police had recited the purposes for which such a call could be made, there was sufficient compliance with the purpose of the statute so that evidence of [the defendant's] confession need not be suppressed." *Commonwealth v. Daniels*, 366 Mass. 601, 610 (1975).

NOTE 3   "[S]uppression of evidence obtained as a result of an unintentional deprivation of a defendant's right to make a telephone call is not required." *Commonwealth v. Painten*, 429 Mass. 536, 542 (1999).

NOTE 4   As the defendants were not harmed by a violation of this section, their motions for directed verdicts were properly denied. *Commonwealth v. McGaffigan*, 352 Mass. 332, 336 (1967).

NOTE 5   **Police Outside Massachusetts Not Bound.** "While it is true that, in Massachusetts, unfavorable evidence derived from an intentional denial of a suspect's statutory right to a postarrest telephone call must be suppressed, *Commonwealth v. Johnson*, 422 Mass. 420, 429 (1996), the police departments in South Carolina are not bound by Massachusetts law." *Commonwealth v. Scoggins*, 439 Mass. 571, 578 (2003).

SECTION 34
Repealed

SECTION 35
Adjournments of examinations and trials

The court or justice may adjourn an examination or trial from time to time, and to the same or a different place in the county. In the meantime, if the defendant is charged with a crime that is not bailable, he shall be committed; otherwise, he may recognize in a sum and with surety or sureties to the satisfaction of the court or justice, or without surety, for his appearance for such examination or trial, or for want of such recognizance he shall be committed. While the defendant remains committed, no adjournment shall exceed thirty days at any one time against the objection of the defendant.

NOTE 1   "Dismissal does not occur as a matter of right where the time limitation of this section is violated even though . . . a continuance in excess of that limitation triggers an examination as to whether the delay was excusable and whether the defendant was prejudiced thereby." *Commonwealth v. Boyer*, 6 Mass. App. Ct. 938, 939 (1978) (rescript).

NOTE 2   "Although delays are not excusable merely because they are unintentional, such delays are to be weighed less heavily than prosecutorial attempt to frustrate the defense. 'Absent a demonstration of culpability on the part of the Commonwealth in delaying the trial, the burden . . . [is] on the defendant to show that the government unreasonably caused a prejudicial delay.'" *Commonwealth v. Conant*, 12 Mass. App. Ct. 287, 290 (1981) (quoting *Commonwealth v. Jackson*, 3 Mass. App. Ct. 511, 517 (1975)) (citations and some quotation marks omitted).

NOTE 3   "A continuance in violation of G.L. c. 276, § 35, does not automatically provide the defendant with the right to have the case against him dismissed. However, such a statutory violation does enter into the consideration whether the defendant's right to a speedy trial has been infringed." *Commonwealth v. Ludwig*, 370 Mass. 31, 34 n.1 (1976).

NOTE 4   No violation of Section 35 when the judge continued the trial from November 4 until December 8, over objections by the defendant, when the defendant was indicted seven days later, November 11. *Commonwealth v. Xiarhos*, 2 Mass. App. Ct. 225 (1974).

SECTION 36
Failure to appear; subsequent proceedings

If the recognizor does not appear according to his recognizance, the court or justice may issue process to bring him into court for trial. After his failure so to appear, the court or justice may at any time order his default recorded; but it may be removed for good cause at any time to which the case may be continued. If such default is not removed, the recognizance shall be certified with a record of such default to the superior court, and like proceedings shall be had thereon as upon a breach of the condition of a recognizance for appearance before said superior court, except in cases where bank books, bonds or money have been deposited at the time of the recognizance.

NOTE   See Note following G.L. c. 276, § 71.

SECTION 37
Failure to recognize; subsequent proceedings

If the defendant fails to recognize, he may be committed to jail by an order stating concisely that he is committed for further examination on a future day to be named in the order, and on the day named he may be brought before the court or justice by a verbal order to the officer who made the commitment, or by a written order to a different person.

SECTION 37A
Assignment of counsel

If a person is charged with a capital crime and brought before a district court for the initial appearance, the superior court may assign counsel upon his petition and upon certification of the charge to the superior court by the clerk of the district court. The examination shall thereupon be continued until the assignment of counsel has been made, and certification thereof received by the clerk of the district court, or until the petition for assignment of counsel has been otherwise disposed of. Upon a determination that a person accused of murder in the first or second degree is indigent, the chief counsel of the committee for public counsel services, or his designee, may assign the case to either the public counsel division or the private counsel division.

NOTE   An indigent defendant has no constitutional right to have private counsel of his own choice appointed to him at public expense when "a public defender or other comparable public counsel is available to the defendant and there is no special reason or circumstance which disqualifies or otherwise prevents public counsel from handling the case." *Costarelli v. Mun. Court*, 367 Mass. 35, 45 (1975).

SECTION 38
Examination; assistance of counsel; waiver of indictment

The court or justice before whom a person is taken upon a charge of crime shall, as soon as may be, examine on oath the complainant and the witnesses for the prosecution, in the presence of the defendant, relative to any material matter connected with such charge. After the testimony to support the prosecution, the witnesses for the prisoner, if any, shall be examined on oath, and he may be assisted by counsel in such examination and in the cross examination of the witnesses in support of the prosecution. Nothing contained herein shall be construed to prohibit the enforcement of the waiver provisions of Rule 3 of the Massachusetts Rules of Criminal Procedure. A defendant charged with an offense as to which he has the right to be proceeded against by indictment may elect a probable cause hearing in accordance with Rule 3 of the Massachusetts Rules of Criminal Procedure, but in such event shall be deemed to have waived his right to be proceeded against by indictment.

NOTE 1   The primary purpose of this section is to screen out "an erroneous or improper prosecution." *Myers v. Commonwealth*, 363 Mass. 843, 850 (1973) (quoting *Coleman v. Alabama*, 399 U.S. 1, 9 (1970)).

NOTE 2a   "Section 38 grants all defendants, who have not been indicted by a grand jury, a right to an adversary hearing where they may confront their accusers and present testimony in their own behalf on the question whether there is probable cause to bind them over for trial. Defendants are held for trial only if it appears to the examining magistrate (1) 'that a crime has been committed' *and* (2) 'that there is probable cause to believe the prisoner guilty.' C. 276, § 42." *Corey v. Commonwealth*, 364 Mass. 137, 140–41 (1973) (footnote and citation omitted).

NOTE 2b   Murder in the First Degree. "This case raises the question whether a defendant who is charged initially by complaint with murder in the first degree is entitled to a preliminary or probable cause hearing in the District Court pursuant to the provisions of G.L. c. 276, § 38 (§ 38), and, if so, when the probable cause hearing described in § 38 must be held. We conclude that § 38 is applicable to such a defendant and provides the defendant with the right to a probable cause hearing as soon as practicable in the circumstances. . . . [W]e decline to adopt a bright-line rule that would require the Commonwealth to conduct the probable cause hearing within thirty days or another definite time frame, but we conclude that because the probable cause hearing is an important stage in a criminal proceeding, the Commonwealth must demonstrate good cause to justify any request by the Commonwealth to continue it." *Commonwealth v. Perkins*, 464 Mass. 92, 92–93 (2013) (footnotes omitted).

NOTE 3   This section "does not apply to a hearing on the issuance of process on a complaint." *Commonwealth v. Riley*, 333 Mass. 414, 416 (1956).

NOTE 4   "[W]e hold that c. 276, § 38, grants defendants mandatory statutory rights to cross-examine prosecution witnesses and present testimony in their own behalf *before* the examining magistrate determines whether there is sufficient legally admissible evidence of the defendant's guilt to justify binding him over for trial." *Myers v. Commonwealth*, 363 Mass. 843, 856 (1973) (footnote omitted).

2

NOTE 5   "[A] district court judge should announce, *before the hearing commences*, whether he is conducting a probable cause hearing or a full trial on the merits." *Corey v. Commonwealth*, 364 Mass. 137, 141 n.7 (1973).

NOTE 6   "The Commonwealth has no duty to present its entire case at the hearing . . . but simply enough to allow a reliable determination of probable cause." *Commonwealth v. Look*, 379 Mass. 893, 904 (1980), *cert. denied*, 449 U.S. 827 (1980).

NOTE 7   "[A] grand jury may indict a defendant after a finding of no probable cause by a District Court judge even if the indictment is based on the same evidence that was presented to the District Court judge." *Burke v. Commonwealth*, 373 Mass. 157, 162 (1977).

SECTION 39
Repealed

SECTION 40
Testimony reduced to writing; signing by witnesses

The testimony of the witnesses examined shall be reduced to writing by, or under the direction of, the court or justice, if he considers it necessary, and shall, if required by him, be signed by the witnesses.

SECTION 41
Discharge of prisoner

If it appears, upon the whole examination, that no crime has been committed or that there is not probable cause for charging the prisoner therewith, he shall be discharged.

SECTION 42
Bail or commitment
(Amended by 2014 Mass. Acts c. 260, § 26, effective Aug. 8, 2014.)

If it appears that a crime has been committed and that there is probable cause to believe the prisoner guilty, the court or justice shall, if final jurisdiction is not exercised, admit the prisoner to bail, if the crime is bailable and sufficient bail is offered; otherwise, except as provided for in section sixteen of chapter one hundred and twenty-five, such prisoner shall be committed to jail for trial; provided, however, that if a person is arrested for a violation of an order issued pursuant to section 18 or 34B of chapter 208, section 32 of chapter 209, section 3, 4 or 5 of chapter 209A or section 15 or 20 of chapter 209C or any act that would constitute abuse, as defined in section 1 of chapter 209A, or a violation of sections 13M or 15D of chapter 265, any bail shall be assessed pursuant sections 42A, 57, 58 and 58A.

NOTE   See Notes following G.L. c. 276, § 38.

SECTION 42A
Personal recognizance; terms and conditions to protect persons suffering physical abuse
(Amended by 2014 Mass. Acts c. 260, §§ 27–28, effective Aug. 8, 2014.)

Whenever a court issues a criminal complaint and the crime involves assault and battery, trespass, threat to commit a crime, nonsupport, or any other complaint which involves the infliction, or the imminent threat of infliction, of physical harm upon a person by such person's family or household member as defined in section one of chapter two hundred and nine A, the court may, in lieu of or in addition to any terms of bail or personal recognizance, and after a hearing and finding, impose such terms as will insure the safety of the person allegedly suffering the physical abuse or threat thereof, and will prevent its recurrence.

Except where prohibited by section 57, for any violation of an order issued pursuant to section 18 or 34B of chapter 208, section 32 of chapter 209, section 3, 4 or 5 of 209A or section 15 or 20 of chapter 209C or any act that would constitute abuse, as defined in section 1 of said chapter 209A, or a violation of sections 13M or 15D of chapter 265, a person arrested, who has attained the age of 18 years, shall not be admitted to bail sooner than 6 hours after arrest, except by a judge in open court. Any person authorized to take bail for such violation under this section may impose conditions on a person's release in order to ensure the appearance of the person before the court and the safety of the alleged victim, any other individual or the community; provided, however, that the person authorized to take bail shall prior to admitting the person to bail, modifying an existing order of bail or imposing such conditions, have immediate access to all pending and prior criminal offender record information, board of probation records and police and incident reports related to the person detained, upon oral, telephonic, facsimile or electronic mail request, to the extent practicable, and shall take into consideration the following: the nature and circumstances of the offense charged, the potential penalty the person faces, the person's family ties, employment record and history of mental illness, the person's reputation, the risk that the person will obstruct or attempt to obstruct justice or threaten, injure or intimidate or attempt to threaten, injure or intimidate a prospective witness or juror, the person's record of convictions, if any, any illegal drug distribution or present drug dependency, whether the person is on bail pending adjudication of a prior charge, whether the acts alleged involve abuse, as defined in said section 1 of said chapter 209A, a violation of a temporary or permanent order issued pursuant to said sections 18 or 34B of said chapter 208, said section 32 of said chapter 209, said sections 3, 4 or 5 of said chapter 209A or said sections 15 or 20 of said chapter 209C, whether the person has any history of issuance of such orders pursuant to the aforesaid sections, whether the person is on probation, parole or other release pending completion of sentence for any conviction and whether the person is on release pending sentence or appeal for any conviction.

The person shall, prior to admittance to bail, with or without conditions, be provided with informational resources related to domestic violence by the person admitting the arrestee to bail, which shall include, but not be limited to, a list of certified batterer intervention programs located within or near the court's jurisdiction. If the defendant is released on bail from the place of detention, a reasonable attempt shall be made to notify the victim of the defendant's release by the arresting police department. If the defendant is released on bail by order of a court, a reasonable attempt shall be made to notify the victim of the defendant's release by the district attorney.

The commonwealth shall be the only party permitted to move for arraignment, within 3 hours of a complaint being signed by a magistrate or a magistrate's designee, for a person charged with violation of said sections 18 or 34B of said chapter 208, said section 32 of said chapter 209, said sections 3, 4 or 5 of said chapter 209A or said sections 15 or 20 of said chapter 209C or was a violation of said sections 13M or 15D of said chapter 265.

Such terms and conditions shall include reasonable restrictions on the travel, association or place of abode of the defendant as will prevent such person from contact with the person abused.

As part of the disposition of any criminal complaint, the court may establish such terms and conditions of probation as will insure the safety of the person who has suffered such abuse or threat thereof, and will prevent the recurrence of such abuse or threat thereof.

Such terms and conditions shall include reasonable restrictions on the travel, association or place of abode of the defendant as will prevent such person from all contact with the person abused; or the payment by the defendant to the person abused of monetary compensation for losses suffered as a direct result of the crime. Compensatory loss shall include, but not be limited to, loss of earnings or support, out-of-pocket losses for injuries sustained, moving expenses and reasonable attorneys fees.

In addition, the terms and conditions of either the probation or the disposition of the complaint may include, but not be limited to, referral of the defendant to a clinic, facility or professional for one or more examinations, diagnoses, counseling or treatment; requiring the defendant to report periodically to a probation officer; or release of the defendant to the custody of a residential treatment facility.

NOTE   "Threat" as used in this section includes nonintentional threats. *Commonwealth v. A Juvenile*, 10 Mass. App. Ct. 385, 390 (1980).

SECTION 43
Conveying prisoner through another county

If the journey from the town where the prisoner is held to the town where he is to be committed on the service of a mittimus can be made by railroad, the officer may convey the prisoner through any portion of another county in the prosecution of such journey.

SECTION 44
Fees and expenses in district court in record sent to superior court

If the defendant is held to appear before the superior court, the copies and record of proceedings sent to the superior court shall contain the details of all fees and expenses allowed or paid in the district court.

SECTION 45
Witnesses bound by recognizance

If the prisoner is admitted to bail or is committed, the court or justice shall bind by recognizance the material witnesses against the prisoner to appear and testify at the next sitting of the court having jurisdiction of the crime and in which the prisoner is held to answer.

SECTION 46
Witnesses bound by recognizance on adjournment

If the examination or trial of a defendant charged with a felony is adjourned under section thirty-five, the court or justice may bind by recognizance the principal witnesses against the prisoner to appear and testify at the time and place to which the trial or examination is adjourned.

SECTION 47
Sureties with recognizance

The court, if satisfied that there is good cause to believe that a witness will not perform the condition of his recognizance unless other security is given, may order the witness to enter into a recognizance with such sureties as the court deems necessary for his appearance at court; provided that the witness shall be entitled to be present and to be represented by counsel at a hearing before the court, at which hearing the witness shall be entitled to be heard on the issue of the alleged materiality of his testimony, and on the issue of recognizance with or without surety.

SECTION 48
Recognizances by minor witnesses

If a minor is a material witness, any other person may be allowed to recognize for his appearance; or, in the discretion of the court or justice, he may recognize in a sum not exceeding fifty dollars, which shall be valid and binding in law, notwithstanding his minority.

SECTION 49
Commitment of witnesses; discharge upon recognizance

A witness who, when required, refuses to recognize, either with or without sureties, shall, except as provided in the following section, be committed to jail until he complies with such order or is otherwise discharged; but if the court or justice finds that the witness, unless he is the prosecutor or an accomplice, is unable to procure sureties when so ordered, he shall, except in cases of felony, be discharged upon his own recognizance. Upon a complaint or indictment for a felony, against a defendant not in custody, a material witness committed for failure to furnish sureties upon his own recognizance may be held in custody for a reasonable time, pending the pursuit and apprehension of the defendant.

SECTION 50
Repealed

SECTION 51
Release of committed witnesses; proceedings

If a witness has been committed because of his inability to furnish sureties for his appearance before the superior court, the jailer shall forthwith give notice to the chief justice of the superior court, who shall direct the district attorney to inquire as to the importance of his testimony and the necessity for detaining him in jail, and the district attorney, if in his opinion the public interest will not suffer by the release of the witness on his own recognizance, shall so report to the chief justice, who may thereupon order the witness to be released upon his own recognizance.

SECTION 52
Rules regulating treatment of committed witnesses; removal to another county

The commissioner of correction shall from time to time make such rules relative to the diet, size of cells, amount of liberty and exercise, correspondence, visits and such other matters as he considers necessary regulating the treatment of witnesses held in jail as will secure their clear distinction and separation from other prisoners so far as possible, consistent with their safe custody and the prevention of tampering with their testimony. Said commissioner may, with the approval of the district attorney, remove such witnesses from the jail where they are confined to a jail in another county, and shall, at the request of the district attorney, cause them to be returned to the jail whence they were removed. The proceedings for such removal shall be the same as for the removal of prisoners from one jail or house of correction to another. The cost of support of a witness so removed and of both removals shall be paid by the county whence he is removed.

SECTION 52A
Removal of accused persons to another county or to a correctional institution; return; proceedings; cost of support

Persons held in jail for trial may, with the approval of the district attorney, and shall, by order of a justice of the superior court, be removed by the commissioner of correction to a jail in another county, and said commissioner shall, at the request of the district attorney, cause them to be returned to the jail whence they were removed. In addition, such persons, if they have been previously incarcerated in a correctional institution of the commonwealth under sentence for a felony, may, with the approval of the district attorney, be removed by the commissioner of correction to a correctional institution of the commonwealth, and said commissioner shall, at the request of the district attorney, cause them to be returned to the jail where they were awaiting trial. The proceedings for such removals shall be the same as for the removal of prisoners from one jail or house of correction to another. The cost of support of a person so removed and of the removals shall be paid by the county whence he is originally removed.

SECTION 53
Transporting male and female prisoners

An officer who, having the custody or control of prisoners, causes or permits male and female prisoners to be transported together to or from a court in a vehicle, in a city of more than thirty thousand inhabitants according to the latest census, shall be punished by a fine of not more than twenty dollars.

SECTION 54
Handcuffing committed witnesses to accused persons; transporting together

An officer who, having the custody of a witness committed because of his failure to furnish sureties, causes or permits him to be handcuffed to a person, held in custody, charged with or sentenced for crime, or to be transported within a city to or from any court or prison in a vehicle with such person, shall be punished by a fine of not more than twenty dollars.

SECTION 55
Discharge upon acknowledgment of satisfaction for injury
(Amended by 2014 Mass. Acts c. 260, § 29, effective Aug. 8, 2014.)

If a person committed to jail is under indictment or complaint for, or is under recognizance to answer to, a charge of assault and battery or other misdemeanor for which he is liable in a civil action, unless the offense was committed by or upon a sheriff or other officer of justice, or riotously, or with intent to commit a felony, or is a violation of an order issued pursuant to section 18 or 34B of chapter 208, section 32 of chapter 209, section 3, 4 or 5 of chapter 209A or section 15 or 20 of chapter 209C, a violation of sections 13M or 15D of chapter 265 or would otherwise constitute abuse, as defined in section 1 of said chapter 209A, and the person injured appears before the court or justice who made the commitment or took the recognizance, or before which the indictment or complaint is pending, and acknowledges in writing that he has received satisfaction for the injury, the court or justice may in its or his discretion, upon payment of such expenses as it or he shall order, discharge the recognizance or supersede the commitment, or discharge the defendant from the indictment or complaint, and may also discharge all recognizances and supersede the commitment of all witnesses in the case.

SECTION 56
Filing of order; delivery to jail keeper; discharge as bar to civil action

Such order discharging the recognizance, indictment or complaint of the person or the recognizance of witnesses shall be filed in the office of the clerk before the sitting of the court at which they are bound to appear; and such order superseding the commitment of the person charged or of a witness shall be delivered to the keeper of the jail where he is confined, who shall forthwith discharge him; and such order so filed and delivered, shall forever bar a civil action for such injury.

SECTION 56A
Written ruling that abuse is alleged when judge releases, discharges or admits person to bail
(Added by 2014 Mass. Acts c. 260, § 30, effective Aug. 8, 2014.)

Before a judge of the superior court, district court or Boston municipal court releases, discharges or admits to bail any person arrested and charged with a crime against the person or property of another, the judicial officer shall inquire of the commonwealth as to whether abuse, as defined in section 1 of chapter 209A, is alleged to have occurred immediately prior to or in conjunction with the crime for which the person was arrested and charged. The commonwealth shall file a preliminary written statement if it is alleged that abuse has so occurred. The judicial officer shall make a written ruling that abuse is alleged in connection with the charged offense. Such preliminary written statement shall be maintained within the statewide domestic violence record keeping system. Such preliminary written statement shall not be considered criminal offender record information or public records and shall not be open for public inspection. Such preliminary written statement shall not be admissible in any investigation or proceeding before a grand jury or court of the commonwealth related to the crime for which the person was brought before the court.

If the defendant has been found not guilty by the court or jury, or a no bill has been returned by the grand jury or a finding of no probable cause has been made by the court, the court shall remove the preliminary written statement from the statewide domestic violence record keeping system; provided however, that a dismissal shall not be eligible for removal from the statewide domestic record keeping system.

Nothing in this section shall be construed as modifying or limiting the presumption of innocence.

NOTE   "[W]e interpret § 56A to mean that before a judge makes a 'written ruling that abuse is alleged in connection with the charged offense,' the judge must inquire into and be satisfied that there is an adequate factual basis for the allegations of abuse made by the Commonwealth." *Commonwealth v. Dossantos*, 472 Mass. 74, 75 (2015).

SECTION 57
Officials authorized to admit to bail; rules governing persons taking bail, etc.
(Amended by 2014 Mass. Acts c. 260, § 31, effective Aug. 8, 2014.)

A justice of the supreme judicial or superior court, a clerk of courts or the clerk of the superior court for criminal business in the county of Suffolk, a standing or special commissioner appointed by either of said courts or, in the county of Suffolk, by the sheriff of said county with the approval of the superior court, a justice or clerk of a district court, a master in chancery, upon application of a prisoner or witness held under arrest or committed, either with or without a warrant, or held in the custody of an officer under a mittimus, may inquire into the case and admit such prisoner or witness to bail if he determines that such release will reasonably assure the appearance of the person before the court and will not endanger the safety of any other person or the community; and may admit to bail any person committed for not finding sureties to recognize for him. All persons authorized to take bail under this section shall be governed by the rules established by the supreme judicial or superior court. No person offering himself as surety shall be deemed to be insufficient if he deposits money of an amount equal to the amount of the bail required of him in such recognizance, or a bank book of a savings bank, credit union or of a savings account in a trust company or national bank, or a passbook or paid-up shares of a cooperative bank doing business in the commonwealth, properly assigned to the clerk with whom the same is or is to be deposited, and his successors, and satisfactory to the person so authorized to take bail, or deposits non-registered bonds of the United States or of the commonwealth or of any county, city or town within the commonwealth equal at their face value to the amount of the bail required of him in such recognizance. The sheriff of Suffolk county may, with the approval of the superior court, appoint standing or special commissioners to take bail to a number not exceeding twenty and may, with like approval, remove them.

Except where prohibited by this section, for any violation of an order issued pursuant to section 18 or 34B of chapter 208, section 32 of chapter 209, section 3, 4 or 5 of 209A or section 15 or 20 of chapter 209C or any act that would constitute abuse, as defined in section 1 of said chapter 209A, or a violation of sections 13M or 15D of chapter 265, a person arrested, who has attained the age of 18 years, shall not be admitted to bail sooner than 6 hours after arrest, except by a judge in open court. Any person authorized to take bail for such violation may impose conditions on a person's release in order to ensure the appearance of the person before the court and the safety of the alleged victim, any other individual or the community; provided, however, that the person authorized to take bail shall, prior to admitting the person to bail, modifying an existing order of bail or imposing such conditions, have immediate access to all pending and prior criminal offender record information, board of probation records and police and incident reports related to the person detained, upon oral, telephonic, facsimile or electronic mail request, to the extent practicable, and shall take into consideration the following: the nature and circumstances of the offense charged, the potential penalty the person faces, the person's family ties, employment record and history of mental illness, the person's reputation, the risk that the person will obstruct or attempt to obstruct justice or threaten, injure or intimidate or attempt to threaten, injure or intimidate a prospective witness or juror, the person's record of convictions, if any, any illegal drug distribution or present drug dependency, whether the person is on bail pending adjudication of a prior charge, whether the acts alleged involve abuse, as defined in said section 1 of said chapter 209A, a violation of a temporary or permanent order issued pursuant to said sections 18 or 34B of said chapter 208, said section 32 of said chapter 209, said sections 3, 4 or 5 of said chapter 209A or said sections 15 or 20 of said chapter 209C, whether the person has any history of issuance of such orders pursuant to the aforesaid sections, whether the person is on probation, parole or other release pending completion of sentence for any conviction and whether the person is on release pending sentence or appeal for any conviction.

The person shall, prior to admittance to bail, with or without conditions, be provided with informational resources related to domestic violence by the person admitting the arrestee to bail, which shall include, but not be limited to, a list of certified batterer intervention programs located within or near the court's jurisdiction. If the defendant is released on bail from the place of detention, a reasonable attempt shall be made to notify the victim of the defendant's release by the arresting police department. If the defendant is released on bail by order of a court, a reasonable attempt shall be made to notify the victim of the defendant's release by the district attorney.

The commonwealth shall be the only party permitted to move for arraignment, within 3 hours of a complaint being signed by a magistrate or a magistrate's designee, for a person charged with violation of said sections 18 or 34B of said chapter 208, said section 32 of chapter 209, said sections 3, 4 or 5 of said chapter 209A or said sections 15 or 20 of said chapter 209C or was a violation of said sections 13M or 15D of said chapter 265.

Notwithstanding the foregoing, a person arrested and charged with a violation of an order or judgment issued pursuant to section eighteen, thirty-four B or thirty-four C of chapter two hundred and eight, section thirty-two of chapter two hundred and nine, section three, four or five of chapter two hundred and nine A, or section fifteen or twenty of chapter two hundred and nine C, or arrested and charged with a misdemeanor or felony involving abuse as defined in section one of said chapter two hundred and nine A while an order of protection issued under said chapter two hundred and nine A was in effect against said person, shall not be released out of court by a clerk of courts, clerk of a district court, bail commissioner or master in chancery.

Before the amount of bail of a prisoner charged with an offence punishable by imprisonment for more than one year is fixed in court, the court shall obtain from its probation officer all available information relative to prior criminal prosecutions, if any, of the prisoner and the disposition of each of such prosecutions. If the offence with which such a prisoner is charged is a violation of any provision of sections twenty-two to twenty-four, inclusive, of chapter two hundred and sixty-five or section thirty-four or thirty-five of chapter two hundred and seventy-two, and it appears from such information or otherwise that he had been previously prosecuted for a violation of any such provision, the court shall, before the amount of bail is fixed, obtain from the department of mental health a report containing all information in its possession

2

relative to the prisoner, particularly with respect to any mental disease or defect with which he may have been afflicted; and said department shall furnish any such report to the court promptly upon its request.

No person arrested for violating any provision of section thirty-three or thirty-five of chapter fifty-six shall be admitted to bail unless there is deposited not less than five hundred dollars in cash, or there is offered real estate of the fair market value of not less than one thousand dollars, over and above all encumbrances, as security.

NOTE 1a   Section 57 versus Section 58. "We have held that [G.L. c. 276, § 57], rather than G.L. c. 276, § 58, is applicable to the setting of bail in the Superior Court." *Querubin v. Commonwealth*, 440 Mass. 108, 111 (2003) (citing *Serna v. Commonwealth*, 437 Mass. 1003 (2002); *Commesso v. Commonwealth*, 369 Mass. 368, 372 (1975)).

NOTE 1b "The order in question was entered in the Superior Court. The defendant contends that the order violates G.L. c. 276, § 58, under which he claims he has a statutory right to have bail set while awaiting trial. That statute, however, has no application because, by its terms, it does not address, or purport to govern, the setting of bail in the Superior Court. Rather, § 58 applies only to bail determinations by a 'justice or a clerk or assistant clerk of the *district court*, a bail commissioner or master in chancery' (emphasis added).

"The order was entered under G.L. c. 276, § 57, which applies to a 'justice of the supreme judicial court or superior court, a clerk of courts or the clerk of the superior court for criminal business in the county of Suffolk, a standing or special commissioner appointed by either of said courts or, in the county of Suffolk, by the sheriff of said county with the approval of the superior court, a justice or clerk of a district court, [or] a master in chancery.' Unlike § 58, which is limited to the District Court, § 57 applies to justices of the Supreme Judicial Court, the Superior Court and the District Court." *Serna v. Commonwealth*, 437 Mass. 1003, 1003 (2002) (rescript).

NOTE 2 "[A] defendant does not have a constitutional right to be released on bail prior to trial. There is no provision in the United States Constitution or the Constitution of Massachusetts as to the right to bail of a person accused of a crime. The Government has a substantial interest in ensuring that persons accused of crimes are available for trials and, ultimately, for service of their sentences, and confinement of such persons pending trial is a legitimate means of furthering that interest." *Querubin v. Commonwealth*, 440 Mass. 108, 112–13 (2003) (citations and quotation marks omitted).

NOTE 3a   Serious Flight Risk. "The essential purpose of bail is to secure the presence of a defendant at trial to ensure that, if the defendant is guilty, justice will be served.

"A judge may admit a defendant to bail if the judge determines that the release of the defendant 'will reasonably assure the appearance of the person before the court.' The statute also incorporates by reference 'rules established by the supreme judicial or superior court.' . . . [R]elevant factors include familial status, roots in the community, employment, prior criminal record, and general attitude and demeanor. These considerations involve determinations of fact and the exercise of sound, practical judgment, and common sense. The exercise of discretion by the trial judge will be upheld unless it is shown that he abused that discretion." *Querubin v. Commonwealth*, 440 Mass. 108, 113, 115–16 (2003) (citing § 57; other citations and quotation and punctuation marks omitted).

NOTE 3b See Rule 2 of the Rules Governing Persons Authorized to Take Bail for the factors to be considered in determining whether to grant bail.

NOTE 3c "The inquiry at a bail proceeding under § 57 where the only issue is the amount of bail that will reasonably assure the defendant's presence at trial involves the presentation of evidence

that, in the vast majority of cases, is undisputed, a matter of public record, or readily explained. It also involves the application of factors, previously noted, that are familiar, straightforward, and relatively simple. The necessary determination can be adequately presented and decided based on documents (e.g., police reports, witness statements, letters from employers and others, and probation records) and the representations of counsel. *Cf. Snow v. Commonwealth*, 404 Mass. 1007 (1989) (judge may rely on hearsay statements and representations of counsel). Of course, the evidence must be sufficiently reliable to avoid any significant risk of an erroneous deprivation of liberty. A bail proceeding under § 57 is not intended to be a mini-trial, and the rules of evidence do not apply. A full-blown evidentiary hearing that includes the right to present and cross-examine witnesses is not needed or required. However, such a hearing, or some variation, may be held in the discretion of the judge when the circumstances of a particular case warrant." *Querubin v. Commonwealth*, 440 Mass. 108, 118 (2003) (some citations omitted).

NOTE 3d "[T]he appropriate standard is preponderance of the evidence." *Querubin v. Commonwealth*, 440 Mass. 108, 119–20 (2003) (citations omitted).

NOTE 4   Bail Hearing for Person Incompetent to Stand Trial. "In answer to the reported question, it is generally permissible to proceed with a bail hearing pursuant to G.L. c. 276, § 57, in a case where the defendant has been found incompetent to stand trial, in the absence of circumstances that suggest that, because of that incompetency, the judge will be unable to obtain adequate information to make a reliable bail determination." *Commonwealth v. Torres*, 441 Mass. 499, 507 (2004).

SECTION 58
Release on personal recognizance or unsecured appearance bond; determination; fees; refusal; petition for review
(Amended by 2014 Mass. Acts c. 260, § 32, effective Aug. 8, 2014.)

A justice or a clerk or assistant clerk of the district court, a bail commissioner or master in chancery, in accordance with the applicable provisions of section fifty-seven, shall, when a person is held under arrest or committed either with or without a warrant for an offense other than an offense punishable by death, or, upon the motion of the commonwealth, for an offense enumerated in section fifty-eight A or for any offense on which a warrant of arrest has been issued by the superior court, hold a hearing in which the defendant and his counsel, if any, may participate and inquire into the case and shall admit such person to bail on his personal recognizance without surety unless said justice, clerk or assistant clerk, bail commissioner or master in chancery determines, in the exercise of his discretion, that such a release will not reasonably assure the appearance of the person before the court. In his determination under this section as to whether release will reasonably assure the appearance of the person before the court, said justice, clerk or assistant clerk, bail commissioner or master in chancery shall, on the basis of any information which he can reasonably obtain, take into account the nature and circumstances of the offenses charged, the potential penalty the person faces, the person's family ties, financial resources, employment record and history of mental illness, his reputation and the length of residence in the community, his record of convictions, if any, any illegal drug distribution or present drug dependency, any flight to avoid prosecution or fraudulent use of an alias or false identification, any failure to appear at any court proceeding to answer to an offense, whether the person is on bail pending adjudication of a prior charge, whether the acts alleged involve abuse as defined in section one of chapter two hundred and nine A, or violation of a temporary or permanent order issued pursuant to sections eighteen or thirty-four B of chapter two hundred and eight, section thirty-two of chapter two hundred and nine, sections three, four or five of chapter two hundred and nine A, or sections fifteen or twenty of chapter two hundred and nine C, whether the person has any history of orders issued against him pursuant to the aforesaid sections, whether he is on probation, parole, or other release pending completion of sentence for any conviction, and whether he is on release pending sentence or appeal for any conviction. The person authorized to admit the person to bail shall provide as an explicit condition of release for any person admitted to bail pursuant to this section or section fifty-seven that, should said person be charged with a crime during the period of his release, his bail may be revoked in accordance with the third paragraph of this section. If the justice or clerk or assistant clerk of the district court, the bail commissioner or master in chancery determines that a cash bail is required, the person shall be allowed to provide an equivalent amount in a surety company bond. If the justice or clerk or assistant clerk of the district court, the bail commissioner, or master in chancery determines it to be necessary, the defendant may be ordered to abide by specified restrictions on personal associations or conduct including, but not limited to, avoiding all contact with an alleged victim of the crime and any potential witness or witnesses who may testify concerning the offense, as a condition of release.

Except where prohibited by section 57, for any violation of an order issued pursuant to section 18 or 34B of chapter 208, section 32 of chapter 209, section 3, 4 or 5 of 209A or section 15 or 20 of chapter 209C or any act that would constitute abuse, as defined in section 1 of said chapter 209A, or a violation of sections 13M or 15D of chapter 265, a person arrested, who has attained the age of 18 years, shall not be admitted to bail sooner than 6 hours after arrest, except by a judge in open court. Any person authorized to take bail for such violation may impose conditions on a person's release in order to ensure the appearance of the person before the court and the safety of the alleged victim, any other individual or the community; provided, however, that the person authorized to take bail shall, prior to admitting the person to bail, modifying an existing order of bail or imposing such conditions, have immediate access to all pending and prior criminal offender record information, board of probation records and police and incident reports related to the person detained, upon oral, telephonic, facsimile or electronic mail request, to the extent practicable.

The person shall, prior to admittance to bail, with or without conditions, be provided with informational resources related to domestic violence by the person admitting the arrestee to bail, which shall include, but is not limited to, a list of certified batterer intervention programs located within or near the court's jurisdiction. If the defendant is released on bail from the place of detention, a reasonable attempt shall be made to notify the victim of the defendant's release by the arresting police department. If the defendant is released on bail by order of a court, a reasonable attempt shall be made to notify the victim of the defendant's release by the district attorney.

The commonwealth shall be the only party permitted to move for arraignment, within 3 hours of a complaint being signed by a magistrate or a magistrate's designee, for a person charged with violation of said sections 18 or 34B of said chapter 208, said section 32 of chapter 209, said sections 3, 4 or 5 of said chapter 209A or said sections 15 or 20 of said chapter 209C or was a violation of said sections 13M or 15D of said chapter 265.

A person, before being released on personal recognizance without surety, shall be informed by the person authorized to admit such person to bail of the penalties provided by section eighty-two A if he fails without sufficient excuse to appear at the specified time and place in accordance with the terms of his recognizance. A person authorized to take bail may charge the fees authorized by section twenty-four of chapter two hundred and sixty-two, if he goes to the place of detention of the prisoner to make a determination provided for in this section although said person is released on his personal recognizance without surety. Said fees shall not be charged by any clerk or assistant clerk of a district court during regular working hours.

A person aforesaid charged with an offense and not released on his personal recognizance without surety by a clerk or assistant clerk of the district court, a bail commissioner or master in chancery shall forthwith be brought before the next session of the district court for a review of the order to recognize in accordance with the standards set forth in the first paragraph of this section. The court shall provide as an explicit condition of release for any person admitted to bail pursuant to this section or section fifty-seven that should said person be charged with a crime during the period of his release, his bail may be revoked in accordance with this paragraph and the court shall enter in writing on the court docket that the person was so informed and the docket shall constitute prima facie evidence that the person was so informed. If a person is on release pending the adjudication of a prior charge, and the court before which the person is charged with committing a subsequent offense after a hearing at which person shall have the right to be represented by counsel, finds probable cause to believe that the person has committed a crime during said period of release, the court shall then determine, in the exercise of its discretion, whether the release of said person will seriously endanger any person or the community. In making said determination, the court shall consider the gravity, nature and circumstances of the offenses charged, the person's record of convictions, if any, and whether said charges or convictions are for offenses involving the use or threat of physical force or violence against any person, whether the person is on probation, parole or other release pending completion of sentence for any conviction, whether he is on release pending sentence or appeal for any conviction, the person's mental condition, and any illegal drug distribution or present drug dependency. If the court determines that the release of said person will seriously endanger any person or the community and that the detention of the person is necessary to reasonably assure the safety of any person or the community, the court may revoke bail on the prior charge and may order said person held without bail pending the adjudication of said prior charge, for a period not to exceed sixty days. The hearing shall be held upon the person's first appearance before the court before which the person is charged with committing an offense while on release pending adjudication of a prior charge, unless that person, or the attorney for the commonwealth, seeks and the court allows,

2

a continuance because a witness or document is not immediately available. Except for good cause, a continuance on motion of the person shall not exceed seven days and on motion of the attorney for the commonwealth may not exceed three business days. During such continuance, the person may be detained consistent with the provisions of this section. Said order shall state in writing the reasons therefor and shall be reviewed by the court upon the acquittal of the person, or the dismissal of, any of the cases involved. A person so held shall be brought to trial as soon as reasonably possible. A person aggrieved by the denial of a district court justice to admit him to bail on his personal recognizance without surety may petition the superior court for a review of the order of the recognizance and the justice of the district court shall thereupon immediately notify such person of his right to file a petition for review in the superior court. When a petition for review is filed in the district court or with the detaining authority subsequent to petitioner's district court appearance, the clerk of the district court or the detaining authority, as the case may be, shall immediately notify by telephone, the clerk and probation officer of the district court, the district attorney for the district in which the district court is located, the prosecuting officer, the petitioner's counsel, if any, and the clerk of courts of the county to which the petition is to be transmitted. The clerk of the district court, upon the filing of a petition for review, either in the district court or with the detaining authority, shall forthwith transmit the petition for review, a copy of the complaint and of the record of the court, including the appearance of the attorney, if any is entered, and a summary of the court's reasons for denying the release of the defendant on his personal recognizance without surety to the superior court for the county in which the district court is located, if a justice thereof is then sitting, or to the superior court of the nearest county in which a justice is then sitting; the probation officer of the district court shall transmit forthwith to the probation officer of the superior court, copies of all records of the probation office of said district court pertaining to the petitioner, including the petitioner's record of prior convictions, if any, as currently verified by inquiry of the commissioner of probation. The district court or the detaining authority, as the case may be, shall cause any petitioner in its custody to be brought before the said superior court on the same day the petition shall have been filed, unless the district court or the detaining authority shall determine that such appearance and hearing on the petition cannot practically take place before the adjournment of the sitting of said superior court for that day and in which event, the petitioner shall be caused to be brought before said court for such hearing during the morning of the next business day of the sitting of said superior court. The district court is authorized to order any officer authorized to execute criminal process to transfer the petitioner and any papers herein above described from the district court or the detaining authority to the superior court, and to coordinate the transfer of the petitioner and the papers by such officer. The petition for review shall constitute authority in the person or officer having custody of the petitioner to transport the petitioner to said superior cur without the issuance of any writ or other legal process, provided, however, that any district or superior court is authorized to issue a writ of habeas corpus for the appearance forthwith of the petitioner before the superior court.

The superior court shall in accordance with the standards set forth in the first paragraph of this section, hear the petition for review as speedily as practicable and except for unusual circumstances, on the same day the petition is filed; provided, however, that the court may continue the hearing to the next business day if the required records and other necessary information are not available. The justice of the superior court may, after a hearing on the petition for review, order that the petitioner be released on bail on his personal recognizance without surety, or, in his discretion, to reasonably assure the effective administration of justice, make any other order of bail or recognizance or remand the petitioner in accordance with the terms of the process by which he was ordered committed by the district court.

If a defendant has posted bail in the district court and has subsequently been arraigned in the superior court for the same offense, the superior court clerk shall notify the district court clerk holding the defendant's bail of such arraignment. Upon such notification, the amount of any bail bond posted by a defendant in the district court shall be carried over to a bail bond required by the superior court. The superior court justices' discretion in setting the amount of bail shall not be affected by the provisions of this paragraph.

Except where the defendant has defaulted on his recognizance or has been surrendered by a probation officer, an order of bail or recognizance shall not be revoked, revised or amended by the district court, because the defendant has been bound over to the superior court; provided, however, that if any court, in its discretion, finds that changed circumstances or other factors not previously known or considered, make the order of bail or recognizance ineffective to reasonably assure the appearance of said defendant before the court, the court may make a further order of bail, either by increasing the amount of the recognizance or requiring sufficient surety or both, which order will not revoke the order of bail or recognizance previously in force and effect. The court may also review such changed circumstances or other factors not previously known or considered in accordance with the third paragraph of this section.

The chief justice of the district court department and the chief justice of the Boston municipal court department shall prescribe forms for use in their respective courts, for the purpose of notifying a defendant of his right to file a petition for review in the superior court, forms for a petition for review and forms for the implementation of any other procedural requirements. The clerk of courts shall forthwith notify the district court of all orders or judgments of the superior court on petitions for review. Costs or expenses of services and transportation under this section shall be ordered paid in the amount determined by the superior court out of the state treasury.

For an offense enumerated in section fifty-eight A, and upon the motion of an attorney for the commonwealth for an order of pretrial detention or imposition of conditions of release based on dangerousness, a justice of the district or superior court shall hold a hearing pursuant to the provisions of subsection (5) of said section fifty-eight A and shall admit such person to bail on his personal recognizance without surety or subject to conditions of release unless said justice, determines, in the exercise of his discretion, that such release will endanger the safety of any other person or the community.

2

NOTE 1a   Section 57 versus Section 58. "We have held that [G.L. c. 276, § 57], rather than G.L. c. 276, § 58, is applicable to the setting of bail in the Superior Court." *Querubin v. Commonwealth*, 440 Mass. 108, 111 (2003) (citing *Serna v. Commonwealth*, 437 Mass. 1003 (2002); *Commesso v. Commonwealth*, 369 Mass. 368, 372 (1975)).

NOTE 1b   "The order in question was entered in the Superior Court. The defendant contends that the order violates G.L. c. 276, § 58, under which he claims he has a statutory right to have bail set while awaiting trial. That statute, however, has no application because, by its terms, it does not address, or purport to govern, the setting of bail in the Superior Court. Rather, § 58 applies only to bail determinations by a 'justice or a clerk or assistant clerk of the district court, a bail commissioner or master in chancery' (emphasis added).

"The order was entered under G.L. c. 276, § 57, which applies to a 'justice of the supreme judicial court or superior court, a clerk of courts or the clerk of the superior court for criminal business in the county of Suffolk, a standing or special commissioner appointed by either of said courts or, in the county of Suffolk, by the sheriff of said county with the approval of the superior court, a justice or clerk of a district court, [or] a master in chancery.' Unlike § 58, which is limited to the District Court, § 57 applies to justices of the Supreme Judicial Court, the Superior Court and the District Court." *Serna v. Commonwealth*, 437 Mass. 1003, 1003 (2002) (rescript).

NOTE 2   Absence of Defendant. Issue: "[W]hether a District Court judge may set bail in a defendant's absence and order him committed to a house of correction pending a postponed arraignment when medical necessity precludes his immediate appearance in court. We conclude that the defendant's right to participate in his bail hearing and his right to a prompt initial court appearance were violated by such a practice." *Commonwealth v. Perito*, 417 Mass. 674, 675 (1994).

NOTE 3   Warrantless Arrest/Bail. "A warrantless arrest must be followed by a judicial determination of probable cause no later than reasonably necessary [24 hours] to process the arrest and to reach a magistrate. . . . An arrestee promptly released on bail is not entitled to a prompt postarrest determination of probable cause. Such determination, when constitutionally required is governed by the same legal standards as apply to the issuance of a warrant. A magistrate who is sufficiently 'neutral and detached' may make the probable cause determination; there is no requirement that a judge make such determination. The probable cause determination may be made at an ex parte hearing, at which the arrestee is not entitled to the assistance of counsel. The arresting officer's documentation of probable cause may be oral or written, and must satisfy the explicit 'oath' or 'affirmation' requirement or art. 14. The determination of probable cause need not be reviewed at arraignment." *Jenkins v. Chief Justice of the District Court Dep't*, 416 Mass. 221, 232, 239 (1993).

NOTE 4   "The preferred result under G.L. c. 276, § 58, is release on personal recognizance. This statute was not intended to give the courts discretion to deny bail but rather to establish the right of the accused, in most circumstances, to be admitted to bail." *Paquette v. Commonwealth*, 440 Mass. 121, 126 (2003) (citations and quotation marks omitted).

NOTE 5a   Conditions. "We conclude, therefore, that no explicit statutory authority exists under G.L. c. 276, § 58, to make a defendant's pretrial release subject to conditions." *Commonwealth v. Dodge*, 428 Mass. 860, 865 (1999).

NOTE 5b   However, "other provisions of c. 276, namely §§ 42A, 58A, and 87, give a judge authority to set conditions of release. In particular, § 87 enables a judge, with the defendant's consent, to place the defendant on pretrial probation and then to set conditions, again with his consent, for release on personal recognizance or bail." *Jake J. v. Commonwealth*, 433 Mass. 70, 70–71 (2000) (citations omitted).

NOTE 6   Murder. "The provisions of the bail reform act, G.L. c. 276, § 58, which apply the concept of changed circumstances to the revision of bail do not apply to bail for a person charged with murder in the first degree. Since the statute does not apply, the question of bail for a person charged with murder in the first degree is a matter of discretion." *Magraw v. Commonwealth*, 429 Mass. 1004, 1004 (1999) (citations and quotation marks omitted).

NOTE 7a   Juvenile. "[A] Juvenile Court judge presiding in a delinquency matter may release a juvenile on bail pursuant to § 58 and at the same time place him, with his consent, on pretrial probation under § 87, subject to specific, agreed-on conditions of release." *Jake J. v. Commonwealth*, 433 Mass. 70, 71 (2000).

NOTE 7b   Revocation of Juvenile's Bail and Placement in DYS. "If the juvenile has consented to placement on pretrial supervised probation, with specific conditions, then the judge may surrender him and order him held in the custody of the department if he violates those conditions. We further conclude that the judge may do so by following the general criteria for revoking bail set forth in § 58B—even if that section does not apply specifically—where doing so would not prejudice the juvenile's rights in any way." *Jake J. v. Commonwealth*, 433 Mass. 70, 71 (2000).

NOTE 8a   Revocation/Third Paragraph of Section 58. "We conclude that the third paragraph of G.L. c. 276, § 58, is narrowly tailored to further the Commonwealth's legitimate and compelling interests in assuring compliance with its laws, and in preserving the integrity of the judicial process by exacting obedience to its lawful orders which, in this case, established conditions of the defendant's pretrial release. It does not violate principles of substantive due process." *Paquette v. Commonwealth*, 440 Mass. 121, 131 (2003).

NOTE 8b   "The first inquiry at a bail revocation proceeding under § 58 is whether, after a hearing at which the defendant shall have the right to be represented by counsel, there is probable cause to believe that the defendant committed a crime during the period of his release. [T]he probable cause to arrest standard, rather than the standard of probable cause to bind over ('directed verdict') set forth in *Myers v. Commonwealth*, 363 Mass. 843 (1973), is appropriate to a bail revocation hearing. . . . Probable cause exists where, at the moment of arrest, the facts and circumstances within the knowledge of the police are enough to warrant a prudent person in believing that the individual arrested has committed or was committing an offense.

"If probable cause has been established as to the new offense, the next inquiry is whether the release of such person will seriously endanger any person or the community. The Legislature has committed the second inquiry to the discretion of the judge. The criteria for making the second determination are expressly set forth in the third paragraph of § 58. They are straightforward and easily understood, and are not unconstitutionally vague. As such, the statute does not violate principles of procedural due process.

"The determinations of probable cause and dangerousness can be made without a full-blown evidentiary hearing and without significant risk of an erroneous deprivation of liberty. The detention is temporary, and a defendant so held shall be brought to trial as soon as reasonably possible. A bail revocation proceeding is not intended to be a mini-trial, and the rules of evidence do not apply. These determinations can be adequately presented and decided based on documents (e.g., police reports) and the representations of counsel. Nevertheless, an evidentiary hearing with the right to present and cross-examine witnesses, or some variation, may be held in the judge's discretion when the circumstances of a particular case warrant." *Paquette v. Commonwealth*, 440 Mass. 121, 131–33 (2003) (citations and quotation and punctuation marks omitted).

NOTE 8c   "The police report, which was offered for the truth of what it asserted, namely, that the defendant had committed a crime, was hearsay. While a judge's determination of probable cause to bind a defendant over for trial must be based on competent testimony that would be admissible at trial, determinations of probable cause to arrest can be based solely on hearsay testimony. Statements of victims to police are sufficiently reliable for the

2

purpose of establishing probable cause to arrest. Statements of police officers concerning their own observations and a description of their own activities, as well as those of other officers, are similarly reliable for purposes of establishing probable cause. Here, the judge could properly rely on the information in the police report to make a determination of probable cause to believe that the defendant had committed a crime while free on bail." *Paquette v. Commonwealth*, 440 Mass. 121, 134 (2003).

NOTE 8d   "[A] defendant 'on release' pursuant to G.L. c. 276, § 58, who defaults for failing to appear and later is charged with committing a new crime is subject to having his bail revoked." *Commonwealth v. Morales*, 473 Mass. 1019, 1021 (2016).

NOTE 9a   Commission of New Offense While on Bail. " If a defendant is charged with committing a new offense during the period of his release on a prior charge, the third paragraph of G.L. c. 276, § 58, requires a judge before whom the new charge is pending to make two inquiries in determining whether the defendant's bail on the prior charge may be revoked and the defendant held without bail. First, the judge must ascertain whether there is 'probable cause to believe that the person has committed a crime during said period of release.' G.L. c. 276, § 58, third par. Second, the court 'shall then determine, in the exercise of its discretion, whether the release of said person will seriously endanger any person or the community.' *Id.* A judge making this second determination must consider the factors set forth in the statute. If the probable cause and dangerousness inquiries are satisfied, then the judge 'may revoke bail on the prior charge and may order said person held without bail pending the adjudication of said prior charge, for a period not to exceed sixty days.' *Id.*" *Paquette v. Commonwealth*, 440 Mass. 121, 126–27 (2003).

NOTE 9b   "There is no authority for the Commonwealth's assertion that it can 'reserve' its right to a bail hearing on the subsequent charge until some future date." *Paquette v. Commonwealth*, 440 Mass. 121, 135 (2003).

NOTE 9c   "We shall clarify the statute's application on the particular facts of each case, concluding generally that, when none of the charges against the defendant has been dismissed or has resulted in acquittal, and where no manifest injustice exists, a District Court judge may not, under G.L. c. 276, § 58, third par., vacate a bail revocation order. We also conclude that once a bail revocation order enters, it is valid for a period of sixty days, and that, by mittimus returnable on the sixtieth day, the defendant shall be brought back to the court with jurisdiction over the charges to which the bail order relates (the original pending charges) for a new bail hearing on those charges." *Commonwealth v. Pagan*, 445 Mass. 315, 316 (2005).

NOTE 10   "Equivalent Amount"/Bond of Ten Times Cash Amount. "In light of the statute's history and purpose, we conclude that the words 'equivalent amount' contained in the last sentence of the first paragraph of G.L. c. 276, § 58, mean an amount equal in effect. In the bail context, we conclude that a surety bond set at an amount ten times the amount of a cash bail is equal in effect to that cash bail. . . . The practice of setting the amount of the surety bond at ten times the amount of cash bail or, otherwise stated, of providing for a ten per cent cash equivalent to the surety bond, is therefore permitted by the statute." *Commonwealth v. Ray*, 435 Mass. 249, 258 (2001).

SECTION 58A

Conditions of pretrial release of persons accused of felonies involving use of physical force, violation of an order, or abuse; detention hearing, order; review

(Amended by 2014 Mass. Acts c. 260, §§ 33–38, effective Aug. 8, 2014; 2014 Mass. Acts c. 284, § 97, effective Jan. 1, 2015.)

(1) The commonwealth may move, based on dangerousness, for an order of pretrial detention or release on conditions for a felony offense that has an element of the offense the use, attempted use or threatened use of physical force against the person of another or any other felony that, by its

nature, involves a substantial risk that physical force against the person of another may result, including the crimes of burglary and arson whether or not a person has been placed at risk thereof, or a violation of an order pursuant to section 18, 34B or 34C of chapter 208, section 32 of chapter 209, section 3, 4 or 5 of chapter 209A or section 15 or 20 of chapter 209C, or arrested and charged with a misdemeanor or felony involving abuse as defined in section 1 of said chapter 209A or while an order of protection issued under said chapter 209A was in effect against such person, an offense for a which a mandatory minimum term of 3 years or more is prescribed in chapter 94C, arrest and charged with a violation of section 13B of chapter 268 or a third or subsequent conviction for a violation of section 24 of chapter 90, or convicted of a violent crime as defined in said section 121 of said chapter 140 for which a term of imprisonment was served and arrested and charged with a second or subsequent offense of felony possession of a weapon or machine gun as defined in section 121 of chapter 140, or arrested and charged with a violation of paragraph (a), (c) or (m) of section 10 of chapter 269; provided, however, that the commonwealth may not move for an order of detention under this section based on possession of a large capacity feeding device without simultaneous possession of a large capacity weapon; or arrested and charged with a violation of section 10G of said chapter 269.

(2) Upon the appearance before a superior court or district court judge of an individual charged with an offense listed in subsection (1) and upon the motion of the commonwealth, the judicial officer shall hold a hearing pursuant to subsection (4) issue an order that, pending trial, the individual shall either be released on personal recognizance without surety; released on conditions of release as set forth herein; or detained under subsection (3).

If the judicial officer determines that personal recognizance will not reasonably assure the appearance of the person as required or will endanger the safety of any other person or the community, such judicial officer shall order the pretrial release of the person

(A) subject to the condition that the person not commit a federal, state or local crime during the period of release; and

(B) subject to the least restrictive further condition, or combination or conditions, that such judicial officer determines will reasonably assure the appearance of the person as required and the safety of any other person and the community that the person

(i) remain in the custody of a designated person, who agrees to assume supervision and to report any violation of a release condition to the court, if the designated person is able reasonably to assure the judicial officer that the person will appear as required and will not pose a danger to the safety of any other person or the community;

(ii) maintain employment, or, if unemployed, actively seek employment;

(iii) maintain or commence an educational program;

(iv) abide by specified restrictions on personal associations, place of abode or travel;

(v) avoid all contact with an alleged victim of the crime and with potential witness who may testify concerning the offense;

(vi) report on regular basis to a designated law enforcement agency, pretrial service agency, or other agency;

(vii) comply with a specified curfew;

(viii) refrain from possessing a firearm, destructive device, or other dangerous weapon;

(ix) refrain from excessive use of alcohol, or any use of a narcotic drug or other controlled substance, without a prescription by a licensed medical practitioner;

(x) undergo available medical, psychological, or psychiatric treatment, including treatment for drug or alcohol dependency and remain in a specified institution if required for that purpose;

(xi) execute an agreement to forfeit upon failing to appear as required, property of a sufficient unencumbered value, including money, as is reasonably necessary to assure the appearance of the person as required, and shall provide the court with proof of ownership and the value of the property along with information regarding existing encumbrances as the judicial office may require;

(xii) execute a bail bond with solvent sureties; who will execute an agreement to forfeit in such amount as is reasonably necessary to assure appearance of the person as required and shall provide the court with information regarding the value of the assets and liabilities of the surety if other than an approved surety and the nature and extent of encumbrances against the surety's property; such surety shall have a net worth which shall have sufficient unencumbered value to pay the amount of the bail bond;

(xiii) return to custody for specified hours following release for employment, schooling, or other limited purposes; and

(xiv) satisfy any other condition that is reasonably necessary to assure the appearance of the person as required and to assure the safety of any other person and the community.

The judicial officer may not impose a financial condition that results in the pretrial detention of the person.

The judicial officer may at any time amend the order to impose additional or different conditions of release.

(3) If, after a hearing pursuant to the provisions of subsection (4), the district or superior court justice finds by clear and convincing evidence that no conditions of release will reasonably assure the safety of any other person or the community, said justice shall order the detention of the person prior to trial. A person detained under this subsection shall be brought to a trial as soon as reasonably possible, but in absence of good cause, the person so held shall not be detained for a period exceeding 120 days excluding any period of delay as defined in Massachusetts Rules of Criminal Procedure Rule 36(b)(2). A justice may not impose a financial condition under this section that results in the pretrial detention of the person. Nothing in this section shall be interpreted as limiting the imposition of a financial condition upon the person to reasonably assure his appearance before the courts.

(4) When a person is held under arrest for an offense listed in subsection (1) and upon a motion by the commonwealth, the judge shall hold a hearing to determine whether conditions of release will reasonably assure the safety of any other person or the community.

The hearing shall be held immediately upon the person's first appearance before the court unless that person, or the attorney for the commonwealth, seeks a continuance. Except for good cause, a continuance on motion of the person may not exceed seven days, and a continuance on motion of the attorney for the commonwealth may not exceed three business days. During a continuance, the individual shall be detained upon a showing that there existed probable cause to arrest the person. At the hearing, such person shall have the right to be represented by counsel, and, if financially unable to retain adequate representation, to have counsel appointed. The person shall be afforded an opportunity to testify, to present witnesses, to cross-examine witnesses who appear at the hearing, and to present information. Prior to the summons of an alleged victim, or a member of the alleged victim's family, to appear as a witness at the hearing, the person shall demonstrate to the court a good faith basis for the person's reasonable belief that the testimony from the witness will be material and relevant to support a conclusion that there are conditions of release that will reasonably assure the safety of any other person or the community. The rules concerning admissibility of evidence in criminal trials shall not apply to the presentation and consideration of information at the hearing and the judge shall consider hearsay contained in a police report or the statement of an alleged victim or witness. The facts the judge uses to support findings pursuant to subsection (3), that no conditions will reasonably assure the safety of any other person or the community, shall be supported by clear and convincing evidence. In a detention order issued pursuant to the provisions of said subsection (3) the judge shall (a) include written findings of fact and a written statement of the reasons for the detention; (b) direct that the person be committed to custody or confinement in a corrections facility separate, to the extent practicable, from persons awaiting or serving sentence or being held in custody pending appeal; and (c) direct that the person be afforded reasonable opportunity for private consultation with his counsel. The person may be detained pending completion of the hearing. The hearing may be reopened by the judge, at any time before trial, or upon a motion of the commonwealth or the person detained if the judge finds that: (i) information exists that was not known at the time of the hearing or that there has been a change in circumstances and (ii) that such information or change in circumstances has a material bearing on the issue of whether there are conditions of release that will reasonably assure the safety of any other person or the community.

(5) In his determination as to whether there are conditions of release that will reasonably assure the safety of any other individual or the community, said justice, shall, on the basis of any information which he can reasonably obtain, take into account the nature and seriousness of the danger posed to any person or the community that would result by the person's release, the nature and circumstances of the offense charged, the potential penalty the person faces, the person's family ties, employment record and history of mental illness, his reputation, the risk that the person will obstruct or attempt to obstruct justice or threaten, injure or intimidate or attempt to threaten, injure or intimidate a prospective witness or juror, his record of convictions, if any, any illegal drug distribution or present drug dependency, whether the person is on bail pending adjudication of a prior charge, whether the acts alleged involve abuse as defined in section one of chapter two hundred and nine A, or violation of a temporary or permanent order issued pursuant to section eighteen or thirty-four B of chapter two hundred and eight, section thirty-two of chapter two hundred and nine, sections three, four or five of chapter two hundred and nine A, or sections fifteen or twenty of chapter two hundred and nine C, whether the prisoner has any history of orders issued against him pursuant to the aforesaid sections, whether he is on probation, parole or other release

pending completion of sentence for any conviction and whether he is on release pending sentence or appeal for any conviction; provided, however, that if the person who has attained the age of 18 years is held under arrest for a violation of an order issued pursuant to section18 or 34B of chapter 208, section 32 of chapter 209, section 3, 4 or 5 of chapter 209A or section 15 or 20 of chapter 209C or any act that would constitute abuse, as defined in section 1 of said chapter 209A, or a violation of sections 13M or 15D of chapter 265, said justice shall make a written determination as to the considerations required by this subsection which shall be filed in the domestic violence record keeping system.

(6) Nothing in this section shall be construed as modifying or limiting the presumption of innocence.

(7) A person aggrieved by the denial of a district court justice to admit him to bail on his personal recognizance with or without surety may petition the superior court for a review of the order of the recognizance and the justice of the district court shall thereupon immediately notify such person of his right to file a petition for review in the superior court. When a petition for review is filed in the district court or with the detaining authority subsequent to petitioner's district court appearance, the clerk of the district court or the detaining authority, as the case may be, shall immediately notify by telephone, the clerk and probation officer of the district court, the district attorney for the district in which the district court is located, the prosecuting officer, the petitioner's counsel, if any, and the clerk of courts of the county to which the petition is to be transmitted. The clerk of the district court, upon the filing of a petition for review, either in the district court or with the detaining authority, shall forthwith transmit the petition for review, a copy of the complaint and the record of the court, including the appearance of the attorney, if any is entered, and a summary of the court's reasons for denying the release of the defendant on his personal recognizance with or without surety to the superior court for the county in which the district court is located, if a justice thereof is then sitting or to the superior court of the nearest county in which a justice is then sitting; the probation officer of the district court shall transmit forthwith to the probation officer of the superior court, copies of all records of the probation office of said district court pertaining to the petitioner, including the petitioner's record of prior convictions, if any, as currently verified by inquiry of the commissioner of probation. The district court or the detaining authority, as the case may be, shall cause any petitioner in its custody to be brought before the said superior court within two business days of the petition having been filed. The district court is authorized to order any officer authorized to execute criminal process to transfer the petitioner and any papers herein above described from the district court or the detaining authority to the superior court, and to coordinate the transfer of the petitioner and the papers by such officer. The petition for review shall constitute authority in the person or officer having custody of the petitioner to transport the petitioner to said superior court without the issuance of any writ or other legal process; provided, however, that any district or superior court is authorized to issue a writ of habeas corpus for the appearance forthwith of the petitioner before the superior court.

The superior court shall in accordance with the standards set forth in section fifty-eight A, hear the petition for review under section fifty-eight A as speedily as practicable and in any event within five business days of the filing of the petition. The justice of the superior court hearing the review may consider the record below which the commonwealth and the person may supplement. The justice of the superior court may, after a hearing on the petition for review, order that the petitioner be released on bail on his personal recognizance without surety, or, in his discretion, to reasonably assure the effective administration of justice, make any other order of bail or recognizance or remand the petitioner in accordance with the terms of the process by which he was ordered committed by the district court.

(8) If after a hearing under subsection (4) detention under subsection (3) is ordered or pretrial release subject to conditions under subsection (2) is ordered, then: (A) the clerk shall immediately notify the probation officer of the order; and (B) the order of detention under subsection (3) or order of pretrial release subject to conditions under subsection (2) shall be recorded in (i) the defendant's criminal record as compiled by the commissioner of probation under section 100 and (ii) the domestic violence record keeping system.

NOTE 1a   This section is constitutional. Concerning subsection (4) however, for a defendant to be held for the three days, good cause must be shown by the Commonwealth. *Mendoza v. Commonwealth*, 423 Mass. 771 (1996).

NOTE 1b   "We conclude that where a criminal defendant has been arrested or is subject to an outstanding arrest warrant for an enumerated offense, the defendant may be subject to pretrial detention under G.L. c. 276, § 58A(4), even if the defendant is not held in custody following the arrest, so long as the dangerousness hearing takes place 'immediately upon the person's first appearance before the court.'

"Given [the statute's] explicitly articulated purpose to protect the public, it is unlikely that the Legislature intended to draw arbitrary distinctions between individuals who have been released on bail by a magistrate, those who are arrested and in physical custody, and those for whom an arrest warrant has issued, but has not been executed.

"In sum, the phrase 'held under arrest,' within the meaning of G.L. c. 276, § 58A(4), refers to any person who has been arrested or for whom an arrest warrant has issued in connection with one of the enumerated offenses in G.L. c. 276, § 58A(1)." *Commonwealth v. Diggs*, 475 Mass. 79, 80, 84, 85 (2016).

NOTE 2   **Incompetence.** "[W]e conclude that it is not a per se violation of due process to hold a hearing under § 58A to determine an incompetent person's dangerousness, regardless whether the person is an adult defendant or a juvenile." *Abbott A. v. Commonwealth*, 458 Mass. 24, 33 (2010).

NOTE 3a   **Juveniles.** Section 58A applies to juveniles as well as adults. *Victor V. v. Commonwealth*, 423 Mass. 793 (1996).

NOTE 3b   "May the juvenile be held beyond ninety days if he remains incompetent to stand trial? . . .

"While an incompetent defendant or juvenile potentially may be detained indefinitely awaiting trial under § 58A, his detention is limited by constitutional requirements of due process. The due process limitation is three-fold. First, an incompetent defendant or juvenile may not be held in criminal custody awaiting trial 'more than the reasonable period of time necessary to determine whether there is a substantial probability that he will attain [competency] in the foreseeable future.' *Jackson v. Indiana*, 406 U.S. 715, 733, 738 (1972). . . . n14

"n14 We . . . hold here that under art. 12 of the Massachusetts Declaration of Rights, the 'rule of reasonableness' applies to an incompetent adult criminal defendant or juvenile who is detained before trial on grounds of dangerousness under § 58A.

"Second, even if it is determined that the adult defendant or juvenile 'probably soon will be able to stand trial, his continued commitment must be justified by progress toward that goal.' *Jackson, supra.* . . .

"Third, even where there is a substantial probability that an adult defendant or juvenile will be restored to competency in the foreseeable future and there is progress toward achieving competency, due process requires that an incompetent defendant or juvenile not be detained under § 58A for an unreasonable period of time. . . .

"[O]nce an incompetent defendant's or juvenile's pretrial detention under § 58A violates the 'rule of reasonableness' in *Jackson* or fails to result in progress toward achieving competency or has become unreasonable in duration, due process requires that the Commonwealth either move for civil commitment under G.L. c. 123, § 8(d), and prove the individual's dangerousness by the more demanding beyond a reasonable doubt standard, or release the individual on bail. . . .

"If, after [a] hearing, the judge determines that the juvenile remains incompetent to stand trial but that due process does not yet require his release from pretrial detention, we exercise our superintendence power under G.L. c. 211, § 3, to require that, until the juvenile is declared competent to stand trial or released from pretrial detention, a hearing be conducted no less than every ninety days to determine whether he continues to be incompetent to stand trial and, if so, whether due process requires his release from pretrial detention." *Abbott A. v. Commonwealth*, 458 Mass. 24, 36–42 & n.14 (2010).

NOTE 3c   See Notes addressing Juveniles following G.L. c. 276, § 58.

NOTE 4   Hearsay. "May the Commonwealth satisfy its burden of proof at a § 58A hearing by relying solely on hearsay evidence, such as police reports and videotapes of police interrogations of codefendants and witnesses?" The court answered "Yes," applying "the same due process principles to a § 58A hearing" as announced in *Commonwealth v. Durling*, 407 Mass. 108, 114–120 (1996) with regard to probation revocation hearings. *Abbott A. v. Commonwealth*, 458 Mass. 24, 33–36 (2010).

NOTE 5   "[A] person previously subject to detention under § 58A based on an order of the District Court is entitled to a hearing on the subject upon arraignment in the Superior Court, but that the transcript and record of the earlier hearing may be considered by the Superior Court judge and given whatever weight he deems appropriate." *Commonwealth v. Murchison*, 428 Mass. 303, 308 (1998).

NOTE 6   Continuance Hearing. "We conclude that the Commonwealth may show probable cause by a complaint issued in accordance with court rules or by reading the police report to the judge; that the continuance determination may be made after a hearing where a defendant is represented by counsel with the opportunity to make representations and arguments before the court, but without a right to cross-examine witnesses or present evidence; and that such a defendant must be detained pending a dangerousness hearing on the grant of a continuance." *Commonwealth v. Lester L.*, 445 Mass. 250, 251 (2005).

NOTE 7   Predicate Offense. "The threshold question in every case is whether the defendant has committed a predicate offense under § 58A(1), thereby triggering the Commonwealth's right to move for a § 58A hearing. . . . Unlicensed possession of a firearm does not, by its nature, involve a substantial risk that physical force against another may result. That a person possesses a firearm without a valid license does not itself pose a substantial risk that physical force against another may result. Rather, it is the unlawful use of a firearm that involves a substantial risk that physical force against another may result. While we are cognizant that unlicensed possessors of firearms may use firearms unlawfully, unlicensed possession of a firearm itself is a regulatory crime. It is passive and victimless. It does not even require proof that a defendant knowingly failed to acquire or maintain a license, *see Commonwealth v. Jackson*, 369 Mass. 904, 917 (1976), and thus may occur regardless whether an individual has acquired a firearm

for an illicit or lawful purpose, or simply allowed a license to lapse. . . . [U]unlicensed possession of a firearm does not manifest a disregard for the safety and well-being of others, and therefore lacks the 'menace of dangerousness' inherent in the crimes specifically included in § 58A(1)." *Commonwealth v. Young*, 453 Mass. 707, 711, 714, 716 (2009) (citation omitted).

NOTE 8   Review and Modification. "[W]e consider whether a Superior Court judge has the authority to review and modify pretrial conditions of release imposed on a defendant by a District Court judge pursuant to G.L. c. 276, § 58A. . . . [W]e conclude that a Superior Court judge does have such authority." *Commonwealth v. Madden*, 458 Mass. 607, 607 (2010).

SECTION 58B
Revocation of release and detention order following violation of release conditions
(Amended by 2014 Mass. Acts c. 260, § 38, effective Aug. 8, 2014.)

A person who has been released after a hearing pursuant to sections 42A, 58, 58A or 87 and who has violated a condition of his release, shall be subject to a revocation of release and an order of detention. The judicial officer shall enter an order of revocation and detention if after hearing the judicial officer finds (1) that there is probable cause to believe that the person has committed a federal or state crime while on release, or clear and convincing evidence that the person has violated any other condition of release; and (2) the judicial officer finds that there are no conditions of release that will reasonably assure the person will not pose a danger to the safety of any other person or the community; or the person is unlikely to abide by any condition or combination of conditions of release.

If there is probable cause to believe that, while on release, the person committed a federal felony or an offense described in clause (1), a rebuttable presumption arises that no condition or combination of conditions will assure that the person will not pose a danger to the safety of any other prisoner or the community. If the judicial officer finds that there are conditions of release that will assure that the person will not pose a danger to the safety of any other person or the community, and that the person will abide by such conditions, the judicial officer shall treat the person in accordance with the provisions of this section and may amend the conditions of release accordingly. Upon the person's first appearance before the judicial officer in the court which will conduct proceedings for revocation of an order of release under this section, the hearing concerning revocation shall be held immediately unless that person or the attorney for the commonwealth seeks a continuance. During a continuance the person shall be detained without bail unless the judicial officer finds that there are conditions of release that will reasonably assure that the person will not pose a danger to the safety of any other person or the community and that the person will abide by conditions of release. If the person is detained without bail, except for good cause, a continuance on motion of the person shall not exceed seven days, a continuance on motion of the attorney for the commonwealth or probation shall not exceed three business days. A person detained under this subsection, shall be brought to trial as soon as reasonably possible, but in the absence of good cause, a person so held shall not be detained for a period exceeding ninety days excluding any period of delay as defined in Massachusetts Rules of Criminal Procedure Rule 36(b)(2).

2

NOTE   See Notes addressing Juveniles following G.L. c. 276, § 58.

SECTION 59
Admission to bail by master in chancery

After a person is committed to jail to await the action of the grand jury, he shall not be admitted to bail by a master in chancery who does not reside or have a usual place of business within the county where the jail is situated, except upon proof that written notice of the proposed application has been duly served upon the district attorney, or one of the assistant district attorneys, for the district, at least twenty-four hours before a hearing on the application, specifying the name of the person, the crime with which he is charged, the time and place of hearing, and the name, occupation and residence of the proposed sureties, or upon proof that the district attorney, or one of the assistant district attorneys, for the district has waived notice of the hearing on such proposed application.

SECTION 60
Bail in Suffolk county; proceedings

After a conviction or a plea of guilty or of nolo contendere in the superior court in Suffolk county, the prisoner shall not be admitted to bail except in open court; but when said court is not in session, bail may be taken by any judge of a court of record or by any commissioner appointed under section fifty-seven, upon proof that written notice of the proposed application has been duly served upon the district attorney, or one of the assistant district attorneys for the Suffolk district, at least twenty-four hours before the hearing of such application, specifying the name of the prisoner, the crime of which he has been convicted, the time and place of hearing, and the name, occupation and residence of the proposed sureties. No person who has been once offered and rejected as surety shall afterward be accepted as surety for the same person in the same case.

SECTION 61
Bail taken out of court; certificate or recognizance and deposit by surety; presence of persons; monthly statements by person taking bail

If bail is taken out of court, the person authorized to admit to bail in criminal cases shall cause a certificate to be signed and sworn to by each surety, which shall contain his name, his residence, including the name of the street and number, if any, of the dwelling house thereon, his occupation and place of business, a statement of the nature, location, purchase price, assessed value and fair market value of his property, and of the encumbrances, if any, thereon, the amount of his indebtedness, the amount and number of other bonds or recognizances on which he is or may be liable and all other matters pertinent to the amount and value of such property, each and all of which statements shall be deemed to be material statements in prosecutions for perjury, and shall return such certificate or certificates and a proper recognizance to the proper court. A surety may, instead of making such certificate, give his personal recognizance as surety and deposit money, bonds or a properly assigned bank book of the kind and in the amount and under the conditions set forth in section fifty-seven for making deposit of like nature. A person authorized to take bail shall take such bail in the presence of the person to be bailed and the surety or sureties, except as otherwise provided in section one hundred and five of chapter one hundred and seventy-five.

On the second Monday of each calendar month, every person taking bail out of court shall transmit to the chief justice of the superior court a written statement, setting forth each separate occasion, as defined in section sixty-one B, on which each bail or surety was accepted as aforesaid during the preceding calendar month, the name and address of each bail or surety, the date of such acceptance, the name of the defendant or defendants, the offense or offenses charged, and the court before which the defendant was required to appear.

SECTION 61A
Disposition or encumbrance of real estate of bail or surety; violation of section

Whenever a person becomes bail or surety in a criminal case and has offered real estate as his qualification for his acceptance as such bail or surety, and subsequently and while the case in which he has qualified as bail or surety is pending, desires to dispose of or encumber such real estate, he shall in writing notify the court in which the case is then pending of his desire, and shall, unless expressly authorized by the court to continue as such bail or surety, terminate his liability as such bail or surety before he disposes of or encumbers such real estate. Any person violating any provision of this section shall be punished by a fine of not more than one thousand dollars or by imprisonment in the house of correction for not more than one year, or both. Nothing in this section shall in any wise affect the title to such real estate.

SECTION 61B
Bond of professional bondsman; arrest bond certificates; conditions of acceptance; regulation

No person proposing to become bail or surety in a criminal case for hire or reward, either received or to be received, shall be accepted as such unless he shall have been approved and registered as a professional bondsman by the superior court or a justice thereof. No person proposing to become bail or surety in a criminal case in any calendar year after having become bail or surety in criminal cases on five separate occasions in said year shall be accepted thereafter during said year as bail or surety unless he shall have been approved and registered as a professional bondsman as aforesaid. A person who has been accepted as bail or surety, contrary to the provisions of this section, shall nevertheless be liable on his obligation as such bail or surety. Such approval and registration may be revoked at any time by such court or a justice thereof, and shall be revoked in case such a bondsman fails for thirty days after demand to satisfy in full a judgment recovered under section seventy-four or a new judgment entered on review under section seventy-six. The district attorney or prosecuting officer obtaining any such judgment which is not satisfied in full as aforesaid shall, forthwith upon the expiration of such period of thirty days, notify in writing the chief justice of such court. All professional bondsmen shall be governed by rules which shall be established from time to time by the superior court. Any unregistered person receiving hire or reward for his services as bail or surety in any criminal case, and any unregistered person becoming bail or surety in any criminal case in any calendar year after having become bail or surety in criminal cases on five separate occasions in said year, and any professional bondsman violating any provision of the rules established hereunder for such bondsmen, shall be punished by a fine of not more than one thousand dollars or by imprisonment for not more than one year, or both. The provisions of this section shall not apply to probation officers.

A guaranteed arrest bond certificate presented by the person whose signature appears thereon shall be accepted in lieu of cash or a bail bond in an amount not to exceed five hundred dollars to guarantee the appearance of such person in any court of the commonwealth, at the time required by such court, when such person is arrested for violation of any law or of any ordinance or by-law of any municipality therein relating to the operation of a motor vehicle. A guaranteed arrest bond certificate so presented in lien of a bail bond is subject to the same forfeiture and enforcement provisions as a bail bond or cash bail. Such guaranteed arrest bond certificate may only be used where the alleged violation is committed prior to the expiration date shown thereon. A guaranteed arrest bond certificate may not be accepted when a person is arrested for the offense of driving under the influence of intoxicating liquor or of drugs or narcotics. As used in this section, "guaranteed arrest bond certificate" shall mean a printed card or other certificate issued by a licensed automobile association or travel club to any of its members, which is signed by the member and contains a printed statement that such automobile association or travel club and a surety company licensed to do business shall, in the event of the failure of such person to appear in court at the time set for appearance, pay any fine or forfeiture imposed upon such person in an amount not to exceed five hundred dollars.

Whenever a domestic or foreign company licensed to do a surety business in the commonwealth becomes surety in an amount not to exceed five hundred dollars with respect to any guaranteed arrest bond certificates issued in such year by an automobile association or travel club by filing with the office of bail administration in undertaking to become surety, such undertaking shall state: (1) The name and address of the automobile or travel club or association with respect to guaranteed arrest bond certificates of which the surety company undertakes to be surety; (2) The unqualified obligation of the surety company to pay the fine or forfeiture in an amount not to exceed five hundred dollars of any person who, after posting a guaranteed arrest bond certificate with respect to which the surety company has undertaken to be surety, fails to make the appearance for which the guaranteed arrest bond certificate was posted. Such undertaking shall be filed with the office of bail administration ten days prior to its effective date. If such undertaking is terminated, the office of bail administration shall be notified promptly as possible but not later than the effective date of such termination.

Any such licensed automobile association, travel club or association and any licensed surety company, and its attorneys-in-fact, guaranteeing arrest bond certificates for members of such automobile association, travel club, or association with respect to motor vehicle violations hereunder, pursuant to the provisions of this section, shall not be required to obtain any additional license and compliance herewith shall be deemed to be in lieu of any such additional licensing.

A person shall be deemed to have become bail or surety on a separate occasion within the meaning of this section if he becomes such: (1) for a person in respect to a single offense; or (2) for a person in respect to two or more offenses wherefor he at one and the same time offers bail or surety, or in respect to two or more offenses committed at the same time or arising out of the same transaction or course of conduct wherefor he at different times offers bail or surety; or (3) for two or more persons at the same time offering bail or surety in respect to offenses committed jointly or in common course of conduct. Becoming bail or surety for the same person or persons in subsequent proceedings in connection with prosecution for the same offense or offenses shall not be deemed an additional occasion or occasions.

SECTION 62
Notice to district attorney of application to accept bail in Suffolk county

If application is made to a person authorized to take bail in criminal cases in Suffolk county to accept bail out of court in a case in which no amount has been fixed, he shall, if the crime charged is not within the jurisdiction of the municipal court of the city of Boston, before fixing bail, cause notice of such application to be given to the district attorney or one of the assistant district attorneys for the Suffolk district, if any of said attorneys is at the time within said district.

SECTION 63
Compensation for taking bail

No justice of any court, except a special justice of a district court, shall receive any fee or compensation for taking and approving bail in criminal cases, and no person authorized to admit to bail in criminal cases shall receive from any source in connection with the admitting to bail anything of value in excess of the statutory fees therefor. No person shall act as attorney in any case in which he has admitted a prisoner or witness to bail.

SECTION 64
Admission to bail on Sunday

Persons held in custody or committed upon a criminal charge, if entitled to be released upon bail, may, in the discretion of the magistrate, be admitted to bail on Sunday.

SECTION 65
Condition of recognizance

The condition of a recognizance of a person, either with or without surety, binding him to appear before a court or justice to answer to a charge against him or to prosecute an appeal shall be so framed as to bind him personally to appear at the time so expressed, and at any subsequent time to which the case may be continued, unless previously surrendered or discharged, and so from time to time, until the final decree, sentence or order of the court or justice thereon, and to abide such final sentence, order or decree, and not depart without leave. The condition of a recognizance of a person held to answer to a charge before a district court shall be further so framed as to bind him to appear before the district court to answer to the charge or to answer to any indictment which may be returned against him. The superior court shall by rule provide for the forms of recognizances and bail bonds. A recognizance of a person held to answer to a complaint before a district court which is required by law to sit in more than one municipality may, with his consent or at his request, be conditioned for his appearance at the next sitting of the court at any one of said municipalities.

2

SECTION 66
Return of recognizance and examination taken by magistrate; order compelling; contempt

A recognizance and examination taken by a magistrate under this chapter shall be certified and returned by him to the district attorney or to the clerk of the court before which the person charged is bound to appear, on or before the first day of the sitting thereof; and if he refuses or neglects to return the same, he may be compelled to do so forthwith by order of court, and, in case of disobedience, may be proceeded against as for contempt.

SECTION 67
Repealed

SECTION 68
Surrender of principal; notice; exoneration of bail; return of deposits; subsequent bail

Bail in criminal cases may be exonerated at any time before default upon their recognizance by surrendering their principal into court or to the jailer in the county where the principal is held to appear, or by such voluntary surrender by the principal himself, and in either event, in all cases where bank books, money or bonds are deposited by the surety, the court shall thereupon order the bank books, money or bonds so deposited to be returned to the surety or his order, and to be reassigned to the person entitled thereto. They shall deliver to the jailer their principal, with a certified copy of the recognizance, and he shall be received and detained by the jailer, but may again be bailed in the same manner as if committed for not finding sureties to recognize for him, provided that the surety making the surrender shall not be accepted as bail if the person surrendered shall again be bailed. The jailer shall forthwith notify the clerk or justice of the court where the proceeding is pending of such surrender.

SECTION 69
Surrender of principal after default; remission of penalty

Bail may surrender their principal at any time after default made upon the recognizance, or the principal may surrender himself, in the manner provided in the preceding section; and the court where the default is recorded may, upon application, remit the whole or any part of the penalty, if satisfied that the default of the principal was not with the connivance or consent of the bail.

NOTE   See Note following Section 71 in this chapter.

SECTION 70
Inability to surrender principal; exoneration of bail

If, by the act of God, of the government of the United States, of any state or by sentence of law, bail are unable without their fault to surrender their principal, they shall, upon motion before final judgment on scire facias, be exonerated and discharged by the court, with or without costs as the court deems equitable.

NOTE   "There is no indication in G.L. c. 276, § 70, that the Legislature intended to distinguish 'bail' from 'recognizance.' . . . G.L. c. 276, § 70, applies equally to both sureties and principals who post their own bail. Regardless of who posts bail, forfeiture is not appropriate when defendants are unable to appear in court, as required by the terms of their bail, due to the fact that they are being held in government custody." *Commonwealth v. Gomez*, 78 Mass. App. Ct. 569, 573, 576 (2011).

SECTION 71
Default on Recognizance

If a person under recognizance to appear and answer or to prosecute an appeal in a criminal case fails to appear according to his recognizance, and if a person under recognizance to testify in a criminal prosecution fails to perform the condition of his recognizance, his default shall be recorded, his obligation and that of his sureties forfeited, and process issued against them or such of them as the prosecuting officer directs; but in such suit no costs shall be taxed for travel. No such process shall issue in cases where bank books, bonds or money have been deposited at the time of such recognizance.

NOTE   "In assuming the position of bail, the surety enters into a contract with the Commonwealth by which the surety guarantees that the principal will appear and answer. If the surety fails to produce its principal at the appointed time, a default will be entered against the principal and surety and the principal's obligation and that of his surety will be forfeited. After the default has been entered, the Commonwealth must initiate proceedings to obtain a judgment on the forfeiture of the bonds. Default does not necessarily compel the surety or the principal to pay the Commonwealth the full face amount of the bonds, however. A judge may remove the default for 'good cause' (G.L. c. 276, § 36), 'remit the whole or any part of the penalty' (G.L. c. 276, § 69), or render judgment for part of the face amount of the bonds (G.L. c. 276, § 74)." *Commonwealth v. The Stuyvesant Ins. Co.*, 366 Mass. 611, 614–15 (1975).

SECTION 72
Surety paying amount for which bound; costs

A surety in such recognizance may, by leave of the court, after default, and either before or after process has been issued against him, pay to the county treasurer or clerk of the court the amount for which he was bound as surety, with such costs as the court shall direct, and shall be thereupon forever discharged.

SECTION 73
Award of portion of penalty to person entitled to forfeiture

If, in a suit on a recognizance to prosecute an appeal, the penalty is adjudged forfeited, or if by leave of court such penalty has been paid without suit or before judgment as provided in the preceding section, and any forfeiture accrues by law to a person by reason of the crime of which the appellant was convicted, the court may award to such person the portion of the amount paid to which he is entitled.

SECTION 74
Judgment for whole or part of penalty

If the penalty of a recognizance of a party or witness in a criminal prosecution is adjudged forfeited, the court may render judgment, upon such terms as it may order, against the principal or surety, or both, for the whole of the penalty with interest, or, in its discretion, for a part thereof, upon the filing in the case of a certificate of the district attorney or prosecuting officer stating that the interests of justice would be furthered thereby and setting forth specifically the reasons therefor; and no person shall, on behalf of the commonwealth, accept in satisfaction of any such judgment or any new judgment entered on review under section seventy-six any sum less than the full amount thereof.

NOTE   See Note following Section 71 in this chapter.

SECTION 75
Neglect, omissions or defects as defeating action

Such action shall not be barred or defeated, nor shall judgment be arrested, by reason of neglect or omission to note or record the default of any principal or surety at the time when it happens, nor by reason of a defect in the form of the recognizance, if it sufficiently appears from the tenor thereof at what court the party or witness was bound to appear, and that the court or magistrate before whom it was taken was authorized to require and take such recognizance.

SECTION 76
Review and rehearing of case after judgment on recognizance

A court which has rendered judgment on a recognizance may, upon petition of any person interested, stating the ground relied upon and filed in said court, grant a review and a rehearing of the case, upon the surrender or recaption of the prisoner who was released, or for any sufficient cause which has occurred or been ascertained by the person interested after the rendition of such judgment, or at such time as not to have afforded opportunity for presenting the same in evidence.

SECTION 77
Service of notice and copy of petition; return day

Notice of the petition and a copy thereof shall be given to or served upon the district attorney for the county where the petition is pending fourteen days at least before the return day expressed therein, and such notice shall be returnable on the first Monday of the first or second month after the filing of the petition.

SECTION 78
Proceedings if former judgment diminished, etc.; costs

If the court finds that a part of the judgment has been actually paid to or for the commonwealth upon the recognizance or judgment and orders the judgment to be reversed or entered for a less amount than has been so actually paid, it may order the amount of the difference between the payment and the new judgment to be repaid to the person who made the payment or to his legal representatives. The state treasurer shall, upon presentation of a copy of the order certified by the clerk of the court, make said repayment. If, upon such petition, the review is not granted or the original judgment is not altered, the court may award reasonable costs against the petitioner.

SECTION 79
Personal recognizance and deposit instead of sureties for release from custody

A person held in custody or committed upon a criminal charge, if entitled to be released on bail, or a person held in custody or committed as a witness to a crime, may, instead of giving surety or sureties, at any time give his personal recognizance to appear before the court and deposit the amount of the bail which he is ordered to furnish, or bonds or a properly assigned bank book, of the kind and in the amount and under the conditions set forth in section fifty-seven for making deposit of like nature, with the court, clerk of the court or magistrate authorized to take such recognizance, who shall give him a certificate thereof, and upon delivering said certificate to the officer in whose custody he is, shall be released. The court or magistrate shall forthwith, upon receipt of such amount, deposit it with the clerk of the court.

SECTION 80
Forfeiture of deposit on default; sale of bonds; collection on bank books; payments to state treasurer

At any time after default of the defendant, the court may order forfeited the money, bonds or bank books deposited at the time of the recognizance and the court or clerk of the court with whom the deposit was made shall thereupon pay to the state treasurer any money so deposited. The clerk of the court shall immediately proceed to sell any bonds so deposited either at public or private sale, and shall forthwith pay the proceeds thereof, after deducting all expenses connected with such sale, to the state treasurer and if bank books are so deposited, the said clerk shall collect the amount of bail from the depository, and pay the same, less the expense of collection, to the state treasurer.

SECTION 81
Defendant surrendering self; return of deposit, etc.

The defendant may surrender himself at any time before a default, in the same manner as sureties in criminal cases may surrender their principal, and the court shall thereupon order the bank books to be reassigned and the money or bonds so deposited to be returned to the person in whose name the deposit is made or to his order. At any time after default, on the surrender or recaption of the defendant, the court may order the whole or any part of the money so deposited or of the bonds, or of the amount of the net proceeds of the sale of said bonds, or the bank books, or the whole or any part of the amount collected from the depository thereunder, to be returned to the person in whose name the deposit is made or to his order. If the amount realized by sale or collection pursuant to the preceding section exceeds the amount of the recognizance, the court shall, on an application made at any time, order such excess to be returned to the party found by the court to be entitled thereto. The foregoing provisions shall apply to cases in which forfeiture has been ordered.

SECTION 82
Bail commissioner or special magistrate authorized to admit to bails

The term "magistrate", in any section of the statutes which provides for admitting persons to bail in criminal cases, shall be construed to include a bail commissioner or special magistrate, so far as to give him authority to admit prisoners to bail.

SECTION 82A
Failure to appear in court after release on bail or recognizance; penalty

A person who is released by court order or other lawful authority on bail or recognizance on condition that he will appear personally at a specified time and place and who fails without sufficient excuse to so appear shall be punished by a fine of not more than ten thousand dollars or by imprisonment in a house of correction for not more than one year, or both, in the case of a misdemeanor, and by a fine of not more than fifty thousand dollars and imprisonment in a state prison for not more than five years, or a house of correction for not more than two and one-half years, or by fine and imprisonment, in the case of a felony.

A term of imprisonment imposed under this section shall be consecutive to any other sentence of imprisonment for the offense for which the prisoner failed to appear.

PROBATION OFFICERS

SECTION 83
Appointment and removal of probation officers
(Stricken & replaced by 2011 Mass. Acts c. 93, § 119, effective July 1, 2011; amended by 2011 Mass. Acts c. 93, § 120, effective July 1, 2012.)

(a) Each applicant for initial appointment as a probation officer within the office of the commissioner of probation shall pass a written examination established and administered by the court administrator, after consultation with the personnel administrator, who shall determine the form, method and subject matter of such examination. The examination shall test the knowledge, skills and abilities which can be objectively and reliably measured and which are required to perform the duties of the position of probation officer. The court administrator, in consultation with the personnel administrator, shall establish a uniform minimum score needed for further consideration of the applicant for consideration as a probation officer.

(b) The name of each applicant for initial appointment as a probation officer within the office of the commissioner of probation who has successfully completed the examination under subsection (a) shall be forwarded to the court administrator or a designee who shall objectively screen the applicant to determine whether the applicant meets the minimum criteria for appointment as a probation officer.

(c) Those applicants who have passed the examination under subsection (a) and deemed by the court administrator to have met the minimum criteria for appointment under subsection (b) shall be subject to an investigative and interview process conducted by the commissioner of probation in consultation with the CJAM/Court Administrator, which shall include, but not be limited to: (i) inquiry into and review of the applicant's education, prior work history and other accomplishments to ensure that the applicant is well suited for the culture of the organization and will further the organization's stated goals; (ii) behaviorally-based interviews; and (iii) candidate assessments, including case study, presentation and writing assessments; provided, however, that the candidate assessments shall focus on the specific requirements of the position.

(d) Recommendations for employment submitted in support of candidates applying for employment by the trial court shall not be considered by a hiring authority until the applicant has passed the examination under subsection (a), been deemed by the court administrator to have met the minimum criteria for appointment under subsection (b) and has successfully completed the interview and investigative processes under subsection (c); provided, however, that the hiring authority may, in accordance with the trial court's regular practice for conducting reference checks, contact and speak with a reference provided to it by a candidate, or contact and speak with any person who has submitted a written recommendation on behalf of a candidate.

(e) Notwithstanding any general or special law, rule or regulation to the contrary, recommendations for employment submitted in support of candidates who are hired as probation officers shall be considered public records under section 7 of chapter 4 and chapter 66; provided, however that this shall not apply to internal communications.

(f) Those applicants who have passed the examination under subsection (a) and were deemed by the court administrator to have met the minimum criteria for appointment under subsection (b), and who have successfully completed the interview and investigative processes under subsection (c) shall be eligible for appointment by the commissioner as a probation officer. The commissioner may appoint probation officers to the several sessions of the trial court as the commissioner deems necessary, with the approval of the court administrator.

(g) A probation officer seeking a promotion within the office of the commissioner of probation shall pass a written examination established and administered by the court administrator, after consultation with the personnel administrator, who shall determine the form, method and subject matter of such examination. The examination shall test the knowledge, skills, and abilities which can be objectively and reliably measured and which are required to perform the duties of the position being applied for. The court administrator, in consultation with the personnel administrator, shall establish a uniform minimum score needed for further consideration of the applicant for consideration for promotion.

(h) The name of each applicant for promotion within the office of the commissioner of probation who has successfully completed the examination under subsection (g) shall be forwarded to the court administrator or a designee who shall objectively screen the applicant to determine whether the applicant meets the minimum criteria for promotion.

(i) Those applicants passed the examination under subsection (g) and were deemed by the court administrator to have met the minimum criteria for promotion under subsection (h) shall be subject to an investigative and interview process which shall include, without limitation: (i) inquiry into and review of the applicant's education, prior work history and other accomplishments to ensure that the applicant is well suited for the culture of the organization and will further the organization's stated goals; (ii) behaviorally-based interviews; and (iii) candidate assessments, including case study, presentation and writing assessments; provided, however, that the candidate assessments shall focus on the specific requirements of the position.

(j) Recommendations for promotion submitted in support of candidates applying for a promotion by the trial court shall not be considered by a hiring authority until the applicant has passed the examination under subsection (g), been deemed by the court administrator to have met the minimum criteria for appointment under subsection (h) and has successfully completed the interview and investigative processes under subsection (i); provided, however, that hiring authority may, in accordance with the trial court's regular practice for conducting reference checks, contact and speak with a reference provided to it by a candidate, or contact and speak with any person who has submitted a written recommendation on behalf of a candidate.

(k) Notwithstanding any general or special law, rule or regulation to the contrary, recommendations for employment submitted in support of candidates who are promoted as probation officers shall be considered public records under section 7 of chapter 4 and chapter 66; provided, however that this shall not apply to internal communications.

(l) Those applicants who have passed the examination under subsection (g) and were deemed by the court administrator to have met the minimum criteria for appointment under subsection (h) and successfully completed the interview and investigative processes under subsection (i) shall be eligible for promotion under subsection (m).

(m) In any court having 2 or more probation officers, the first justice, subject to the approval of the court administrator and the commissioner of probation, may designate 1 probation officer to serve as chief probation officer and may designate other probation officers to serve as assistant chief probation officers, as the first justice deems necessary for the effective administration of justice.

A first justice may recommend to the commissioner of probation the initiation of disciplinary proceedings against a probation officer so promoted under this section; provided, however, that such probation officer shall receive a hearing by the commissioner of probation prior to being discharged; and provided further, that such probation officer may appeal any suspension, discipline or discharge to the court administrator.

(n) The compensation of probation officers in the trial court shall be paid by the commonwealth according to schedules established in section 99B or in a provision of an applicable collective bargaining agreement.

(o) All probation officers shall devote their full time and attention to the duties of their office during regular business hours.

(n) all personnel standards developed under this section shall ensure that all appointments, promotions and increases in compensation of personnel within the trial court are merit based and maintain internal and external integrity with regard to their processes. Such standards shall be made available to the public and promulgated prominently on the website of the trial court.

SECTION 83A
Repealed

SECTIONS 83B–84
Repealed

SECTION 85
Powers and duties

Each person who receives an appointment as a probation officer shall, within six months of the date of his appointment, attend a basic orientation training course conducted by the commissioner of probation pursuant to section ninety-nine. All probation officers shall attend at least every three years an in-service training course pursuant to this section. In addition to the other duties imposed upon him, each probation officer shall, as the court may direct, inquire into the nature of every criminal case brought before the court under the appointment of which he acts, and inform the court, so far as is possible, whether the defendant has previously been convicted of crime and in the case of a criminal prosecution before said court charging a person with an offense punishable by imprisonment for more than one year the probation officer shall in any event present to the court such information as the commissioner of probation has in his possession relative to prior criminal prosecutions, if any, of such person and to the disposition of each such prosecution, and all other available information relative thereto, before such person is admitted to bail in court and also before disposition of the case against

him by sentence, or placing on file or probation. Such record of the probation officer presented to the court shall not contain as part thereof any information of prior criminal prosecutions, if any, of the defendant wherein the defendant was found not guilty by the court or jury in said prior criminal prosecution. Prior to the aforesaid disposition such record of the probation officer shall be made available to the defendant and his counsel for inspection. When it comes to the knowledge of a probation officer that the defendant in a criminal case before his court charged with an offense punishable by imprisonment is then on probation in another court or is then at liberty on parole or on a permit to be at liberty, such probation officer shall forthwith certify the fact of the presence of the defendant before his court to the probation officer of such other court or the parole authorities granting or issuing such parole or permit to be at liberty, as the case may be. He may recommend to the justice of his own court that any person convicted be placed on probation. He shall perform such other duties as the court requires. He shall keep full records of all cases investigated by him or placed in his care by the court, and of all duties performed by him. Every person released upon probation shall be given by the probation officer a written statement of the terms and conditions of the release.

NOTE 1   While the terms and conditions and any future modifications of probation should be put in writing, an individual may nonetheless be surrendered even if this procedure is not followed. The court will determine whether the defendant violated the terms of the original recognizance or of the oral arrangement made between him and the Commonwealth. *Commonwealth v. McGovern*, 183 Mass. 238, 240 (1903).

NOTE 2   Issue: "'Did [the] court have jurisdiction, on March 13, 1975, . . . to extend the term of or to revoke the defendant's probation on the basis of violations of conditions of his probation which occurred during the term of probation, in view of the fact that the defendant's term of probation had expired on September 4, 1974 and in view of the fact that he had not been brought before the court by his probation officer until over four months after that date?'" The Supreme Judicial Court answered in the affirmative. *Commonwealth v. Sawicki*, 369 Mass. 377, 379 (1975).

NOTE 3   "If the act alleged to be a violation of probation is made the subject of a criminal complaint, the commencement of the criminal prosecution does not preclude the revocation of the earlier probation nor does it require that the revocation proceedings be deferred until the completion of the new criminal proceeding.

"Further, if the act relied on as a violation of an earlier probation results in a criminal conviction, the fact that the conviction is awaiting appellate review does not prevent it from forming the basis for the revocation of probation." *Rubera v. Commonwealth*, 371 Mass. 177, 181 (1976) (citations omitted).

NOTE 4   "In general, when imposing a sentence, the judge should consider several goals: punishment, deterrence, protection of the public, and rehabilitation. . . . Generally, probationers do not have a right to be free from conditions that severely restrain their freedom of action." *Commonwealth v. Power*, 420 Mass. 410, 414, 416 (1995) (citations and quotation marks omitted).

SECTION 85A
Support and maintenance enforcement

In addition to other duties, a probation officer of the probate court may, when ordered to do so by the court, examine all records and files in divorce, legal separation, annulment, custody and paternity cases in which orders or decrees have been entered to ascertain whether the persons to whom payments of money should have been made regularly received the various and definite amounts provided for in the orders or

2

decrees of the court and, where there are dependent minor children, that the same are applied for the support, maintenance, education and betterment of said dependent minor children, and that said dependent minor children are properly cared for by their custodian. Said officers shall bring into court when necessary, by citation or otherwise, all persons who are delinquent in making payments ordered or decreed by the court and shall ascertain in the case of dependent minor children whether they are receiving proper maintenance and education and whether they are liable to become public charges. Consistent with these and other duties, a probation officer shall assist the IV-D agency, as set forth in chapter one hundred and nineteen A to enforce child support orders.

SECTION 85B
Delinquent payments, collection, contempt

Said probation officer shall have full power, by citation or other order duly issued by the probate court, to compel the attendance of witnesses to take testimony and do each and every thing necessary, including initiating contempt proceedings, to collect any and all delinquent payments due to any person entitled under order or decree of said court to receive payments, to make recommendations to the probate court, where there are dependent minor children, for the betterment of the conditions of said dependent minor children and to ascertain when requested to do so by the court the moral and general conditions surrounding said dependent minor children and shall report the result of such findings to said court.

SECTION 86
Repealed
(2011 Mass. Acts c. 93, § 121, effective July 1, 2011.)

SECTION 87
Placing certain persons in care of probation officer
(Amended by 2011 Mass. Acts c. 178, § 26, effective Nov. 21, 2011; 2013 Mass. Acts c. 84, § 30A, effective Sept. 18, 2013.)

The superior court, any district court and any juvenile court may place on probation in the care of its probation officer any person before it charged with an offense or a crime for such time and upon such conditions as it deems proper, with the defendant's consent, before trial and before a plea of guilty, or in any case after a finding or verdict of guilty; provided, that, in the case of any child under the age of 18 placed upon probation by the superior court, he may be placed in the care of a probation officer of any district court or of any juvenile court, within the judicial district of which such child resides; and provided further, that no person convicted under section twenty-two A, 22B, 22C, 24B or subsection (b) of section 50 of chapter two hundred and sixty-five or section thirty-five A of chapter two hundred and seventy-two shall, if it appears that he has previously been convicted under said sections and was eighteen years of age or older at the time of committing the offense for which he was so convicted, be released on parole or probation prior to the completion of five years of his sentence.

NOTE 1a   Surrender Hearings. "Today, both probation and the suspension of sentences are governed by statute. *See* G.L. c. 279, § 1–2, (power to suspend sentences and place defendants on probation); G.L. c. 276, § 87 (power of District [Superior and juvenile] Courts to place defendants on probation). . . .

"If the judge determines that the defendant is in violation, he can either revoke the probation and sentence the defendant or, if

appropriate, modify the terms of his probation. How best to deal with the probationer is within the judge's discretion. . . .

"*Morrissey* [*v. Brewer*, 408 U.S. 471 (1972)] and *Gagnon* [*v. Scarpelli*, 411 U.S. 778 (1973)] establish that the minimum requirements of due process include "'(a) written notice of the claimed violations of [probation or] parole; (b) disclosure to the [probationer or] parolee of the evidence against him; (c) opportunity to be heard in person to present witnesses and documentary evidence; (d) the right to confront and cross-examine adverse witnesses (unless the hearing officer specifically finds good cause for not allowing confrontation); (e) a 'neutral and detached' hearing body such as a traditional parole board, members of which need not be judicial officers or lawyers; and (f) a written statement by the factfinders as to the evidence relied on and reasons for revoking [probation or] parole." *Morrissey v. Brewer*, supra at 489.' *Gagnon v. Scarpelli*, supra at 786. . . .

"In this case we are squarely presented with the questions (1) whether hearsay may be utilized in probation revocation hearings; and (2) if so, when and to what extent. The first question, in our view, is easily resolved. The second requires careful consideration.

"This court has always allowed the use of hearsay at probation revocation hearings. . . .

"When hearsay evidence *is* reliable, however, then it *can* be the basis of a revocation. In our view, a showing that the proffered evidence bears substantial indicia of reliability and is substantially trustworthy is a showing of good cause obviating the need for confrontation. . . . We caution, however, that when hearsay is offered as the only evidence of the alleged violation, the indicia of reliability must be substantial (*see Brown v. State*, 317 Md. 417, 425–426 [1989]) because the probationer's interest in crossexamining the actual source (and hence testing its reliability) is greater when the hearsay is the only evidence offered. Thus, the hearsay must be substantially reliable to overcome that interest."

In this case, the court found that two police reports met this test of "substantial reliability."

"Both of the police reports relate facts observed by the police officers personally. Both reports are factually detailed rather than general statements or conclusions. We think the factual detail is indicative of reliability. Moreover, the fact that two different police officers from different police departments each reported finding the defendant in similar circumstances indicates that neither report is without a basis in fact. The similarity of the reports is indicative of their reliability. It should also be noted that it is a crime for police officers to file false reports. G.L. c. 268, § 6A. In our view, this significantly bolsters the reliability of the reports."

Commonwealth v. Durling, 407 Mass. 108, 111, 113, 114, 118, 121 (1990) (citations and footnote omitted).

NOTE 1b   Suppressed Statements. "The sole issue on appeal is whether, under Federal law, a trial judge may revoke probation on the basis of statements suppressed at trial for failure to comply with *Miranda v. Arizona*, 384 U.S. 436 (1966). We conclude that there was no error in admitting Vincente's inculpatory statements at the probation revocation hearing. We therefore affirm the order revoking probation." *Commonwealth v. Vincente*, 405 Mass. 278–79 (1989) (footnotes omitted).

NOTE 2   Unlawfully Obtained Evidence. "[W]here the police who unlawfully obtained the evidence neither knew nor had reason to know of the probationary status of the person whose property was seized, the evidence is admissible in a proceeding to revoke probation." *Commonwealth v. Olsen*, 405 Mass. 491, 491 (1989).

NOTE 3   Notice. "[T]he adequacy of an attempt or attempts to serve notice must be determined on a case-by-case basis, and the court particularly should examine the adequacy of the attempts in light of the information possessed by the authority charged with giving notice. . . . [T]he probation officer has the burden to show that notice was properly sent, in light of the information possessed by the officer. Where, as here, there was no evidence that the defendant in fact had changed his address, and the defendant raises nonreceipt of notice, the probation officer had the burden of showing that notice was properly sent." *Commonwealth v. Faulkner*, 418 Mass. 352, 363–64 (1994).

NOTE 4   Collateral Estoppel/Burden of Proof. "Principles of collateral estoppel do not bar the Commonwealth from revoking probation based on evidence of a violation of law of which a probationer has been found not guilty. The reason for this result lies in the difference in the burden of proof in the two proceedings. In a criminal case, [the standard is proof beyond a reasonable doubt; in a probation surrender, it is proof by a preponderance of the evidence.]" *Commonwealth v. Holmgren*, 421 Mass. 224, 225–26 (1995).

NOTE 5 "May a defendant be subjected to a probation revocation based upon criminal conduct occurring *after* the imposition of the sentence to probation but *before* the commencement of the probationary period?' . . . 'Yes.'" *Commonwealth v. Phillips*, 40 Mass. App. Ct. 801, 801 (1996).

NOTE 6a   Juvenile. "[A] Juvenile Court judge presiding in a delinquency matter may release a juvenile on bail pursuant to § 58 and at the same time place him, with his consent, on pretrial probation under § 87, subject to specific, agreed-on conditions of release." *Jake J. v. Commonwealth*, 433 Mass. 70, 71 (2000).

NOTE 6b   Revocation of Juvenile's Bail and Placement in DYS. "If the juvenile has consented to placement on pretrial supervised probation, with specific conditions, then the judge may surrender him and order him held in the custody of the department if he violates those conditions. We further conclude that the judge may do so by following the general criteria for revoking bail set forth in § 58B—even if that section does not apply specifically—where doing so would not prejudice the juvenile's rights in any way." *Jake J. v. Commonwealth*, 433 Mass. 70, 71 (2000).

NOTE 7 "[Section] 87 enables a judge, with the defendant's consent, to place the defendant on pretrial probation and then to set conditions, again with his consent, for release on personal recognizance or bail." *Jake J. v. Commonwealth*, 433 Mass. 70, 71 (2000) (citations omitted).

NOTE 8   Conditions of Probation. "Random drug and alcohol testing constitutes a search and seizure for constitutional purposes under art. 14 of the Massachusetts Declaration of Rights. Although a probationary condition is not necessarily invalid simply because it affects constitutional rights, the condition must be reasonably related to legitimate probationary goals in order to withstand constitutional scrutiny. Ordering a defendant to submit to random drug or alcohol testing as a condition of probation, therefore, is not permissible unless it is reasonably related to one or more of the goals of probation: punishment, deterrence, retribution, protection of the public, or rehabilitation." *Commonwealth v. Gomes*, 73 Mass. App. Ct. 857, 859 (2009) (citations omitted).

NOTE 9   No Pretrial Probation Over Objection of Commonwealth. "The first reported question asks whether a judge may, over the Commonwealth's objection, order a lengthy period of pretrial probation under G.L. c. 276, § 87, with the objective of dismissal at the end of the probationary period, utilizing the *Brandano* procedures to address the Commonwealth's objections to such a dismissal. We conclude that G.L. c. 276, § 87, cannot be used to dispose of the case in this manner." *Commonwealth v. Tim T.*, 437 Mass. 592, 594 (2002).

SECTION 87A
Conditions of probation; probation fees
(Bracketed text added by 2014 Mass. Acts c. 165, § 179, effective June 1, 2015.)

The conditions of probation imposed by a court upon a person pursuant to section eighty-seven of this chapter, section fifty-eight of chapter one hundred and nineteen or section one or section one A of chapter two hundred and seventy-nine, may include, but shall not be limited to, participation by said person in specified rehabilitative programs or performance by said person of specified community service work for a stated period of time. [If the court requires as a condition of probation that the defendant reside in alcohol and drug

free housing within the commonwealth, the judge issuing the order shall require the probation officer to refer the defendant only to alcohol and drug free housing certified under section 18A of chapter 17 and the probation officer shall require the defendant to reside in such certified housing in order to satisfy such condition. If accredited alcohol and drug free housing is not available, the judge issuing the order may permit the probation officer to refer the person placed on supervised probation to alcohol and substance free housing that is available and that, in the judge's discretion, appropriately supports the recovery goals of the person. If the court imposes as a condition of probation that the person reside in alcohol and drug free housing in another state, the judge issuing the order may permit the probation officer to refer the person to alcohol and drug free housing that, in the judge's discretion, appropriately supports the recovery goals of the person.]

The court shall assess upon every person placed on supervised probation, including all persons placed on probation for offenses under section 24 of chapter 90, a monthly probation supervision fee, hereinafter referred to as "probation fee", in the amount of $60 per month. Said person shall pay said probation fee once each month during such time as said person remains on supervised probation. The court shall assess upon every person placed on administrative supervised probation a monthly administrative probation supervision fee, hereinafter referred to as "administrative probation fee", in the amount of $45 per month. Said person shall pay said administrative probation fee once each month during such time as said person remains on administrative supervised probation. Notwithstanding the foregoing, said fees shall not be assessed upon any person accused or convicted of a violation of section 1 or 15 of chapter 273, where compliance with an order of support for a spouse or minor child is a condition of probation.

The court may not waive payment of either or both of said fees unless it determines after a hearing and upon written finding that such payment would constitute an undue hardship on said person or his family due to limited income, employment status or any other factor. Following the hearing and upon such written finding that either or both of said fees would cause such undue hardship then: (1) in lieu of payment of said probation fee the court shall require said person to perform unpaid community work service at a public or nonprofit agency or facility, as approved and monitored by the probation department, for not less than one day per month and (2) in lieu of payment of said administrative probation fee the court shall require said person to perform unpaid community work service at a public or nonprofit agency or facility, as approved and monitored by the probation department, for not less than four hours per month. Such waiver shall be in effect only during the period of time that said person is unable to pay his monthly probation fee.

The court may waive payment of either or both of said fees in whole or in part if said person is assessed payment of restitution. In such cases, said fees may be waived only to the extent and during the period that restitution is paid in an amount equivalent to said fee.

Said probation fee shall be collected by the several probation offices of the trial court and transmitted to the state treasurer for deposit into the General Fund. The state treasurer shall account for all such fees received and report said fees annually, itemized by court division, to the house and senate committees on ways and means.

The court shall also assess upon every person placed on supervised probation, including all persons placed on probation for offenses under section 24 of chapter 90, a monthly probationers' victim services surcharge, hereinafter referred to as "victim services surcharge", in the amount of $5 per month. Said person shall pay said victim services surcharge once each month during such time as said person remains on supervised probation. The court shall assess upon every person placed on administrative supervised probation a monthly administrative probationer's victim services surcharge, hereinafter referred to as "administrative victim services surcharge" in the amount of $5 per month.

Said person shall pay said administrative victim services surcharge once each month during such time as said person remains on administrative supervised probation. Notwithstanding the foregoing, said fees shall not be assessed upon any person accused or convicted of a violation of section 1 or 15 of chapter 273, where compliance with an order of support for a spouse or minor child is a condition of probation.

The court may not waive payment of either or both of said fees unless it has determined, after a hearing and upon written finding, that such payment would constitute an undue hardship on said person or his family due to limited income, employment status or any other factor. Such waiver shall be in effect only during the period of time that said person is unable to pay his monthly probation fee.

Said probation fee shall be collected by the several probation offices of the trial court and shall be transmitted to the state treasurer for deposit into the General Fund of the commonwealth. The state treasurer shall account for all such fees received and report said fees annually, itemized by court division, to the house and senate committees on ways and means.

SECTION 88
Clerical assistance
(Amended by 2011 Mass. Acts c. 93, § 122, effective July 1, 2012.)

Every court appointing probation officers may employ such clerical assistance as it deems necessary to keep, index and consolidate the records required to be kept by probation officers and for such other work in connection with its probation service as the court may determine. The compensation for such service, together with such other necessary expenses as the court shall incur in connection with such work, shall be paid by the commonwealth upon vouchers approved by said court.

The administrative justices for the district court and juvenile court departments, in consultation with the commissioner of probation, may designate and redesignate such divisions thereof, including in such term the Boston juvenile court, the Worcester juvenile court, the Bristol county juvenile court and the Springfield juvenile court, within each of the counties of the commonwealth as in the opinion of said administrative justices should join in the establishment of a probation district office for the clerical service of the probation officers of the divisions thereof so designated or redesignated and said divisions so designated or redesignated shall thereupon consult with the court administrator of the trial court and the commissioner of probation as to the establishment of such a probation district office, and shall join in the employment of such clerical assistance as is necessary to

keep, index and consolidate the records in such form as may be required by the commissioner of probation in connection with the probation service of the said courts. The compensation for such service, together with such other necessary expenses as the courts shall incur in connection with such work, shall be paid by the commonwealth upon vouchers approved by one of the justices of said courts, designated by said administrative justices.

SECTION 89
Temporary probation officers
(Amended by 2011 Mass. Acts c. 93, § 123, effective July 1, 2012.)

The superior court or the justice of a district court, including in such term the Worcester juvenile court, the Boston juvenile court, the Bristol county juvenile court and the Springfield juvenile court, may, in the case of a vacancy in the position of probation officer or in the absence of a probation officer, appoint a temporary probation officer, who shall have the powers and perform the duties of such probation officer and shall receive as compensation for each day's service an amount equal to the rate by the day of the minimum compensation of a regular probation officer according to the salary schedule established under section eight of chapter two hundred and eleven B. Compensation so paid to a temporary probation officer for service rendered in the absence of a probation officer, in excess of thirty days in any one year, shall be deducted from the compensation of the probation officer in whose place such service is rendered; provided, however, that if a probation officer is absent, due to his illness or physical disability, for a period not exceeding thirty days in any year, in addition to said thirty days, he shall be deemed to be on sick leave and no such deduction shall be made. Such thirty days' sick leave or any portion thereof not used in any year may be accumulated, but shall, in any event, not exceed ninety days in any consecutive three year period. If the person so appointed holds an office or position, the salary or compensation for which is paid out of the treasury of the commonwealth, or of a county, or of a municipality, he shall not receive the salary of both offices or positions during the period of such temporary service.

The justices of a probate court for any county, except the county of Dukes County and the counties of Nantucket and Franklin, may, in the absence of a probation officer, appoint a temporary probation officer in the same manner and upon the same conditions, with the same powers and duties and the same rate of compensation as is provided in the first paragraph.

The justice of a district court, with the approval of the administrative justice of district courts, may, in the case of the death, removal, resignation or retirement of a probation officer, appoint a temporary probation officer for a single term not to exceed ninety days. Such temporary probation officer shall receive as compensation from the commonwealth an amount equal to that which would have been paid, for a like period of service, to a regular probation officer receiving the minimum compensation according to the salary schedule as established under section eight of chapter two hundred and eleven B. No temporary probation officer appointed under this section shall serve for more than ninety days unless his appointment to such temporary office has been approved by the court administrator of the trial court upon recommendation of the commissioner of probation.

SECTION 89A
Counsellors to juvenile offenders
(Amended by 2011 Mass. Acts c. 93, § 124, effective July 1, 2012; 2013 Mass. Acts c. 84, § 31, effective Sept. 18, 2013.)

The superior court or the justice of a district court may appoint deputy probation officers who shall serve without compensation as counsellors to children under the age of 18 who have been placed in the care of probation officers under section eighty-seven in order that such children may receive to a greater degree individual attention and guidance. Deputy probation officers shall perform their services under the direction of probation officers. Deputy probation officers may be reimbursed by the commonwealth upon voucher approved by the court to which they are assigned for necessary expenses incurred by them in the course of their duties.

The court administrator, in consultation with the commissioner of probation, may apply for and accept federal grants or assistance for the purpose of defraying the costs of additional clerical assistance, equipment, books, materials and other expenses incident to the services which such deputy probation officers perform.

SECTION 90
Powers of probation officers; reports; records; inspection

A probation officer shall not be an active member of the regular police force, but so far as necessary in the performance of his official duties shall, except as otherwise provided, have all the powers of a police officer, and if appointed by the superior court may, by its direction, act in any part of the commonwealth. He shall report to the court, and his records may at all times be inspected by police officials of the towns of the commonwealth; provided, that his records in cases arising under sections fifty-two to fifty-nine, inclusive, of chapter one hundred and nineteen shall not be open to inspection without the consent of a justice of his court.

SECTION 91
Power of probation officers appointed by Boston juvenile court to serve process

Probation officers appointed by the Boston juvenile court may serve such process as may be directed to them by the court.

SECTION 92
Restitution or reparation to injured person through probation officer

If a person is placed on probation upon condition that he make restitution or reparation to the person injured by him in the commission of his offense, and payment is not made at once, the court may order that it shall be made to the probation officer, who shall give receipts for and keep record of all payments made to him, pay the money to the person injured and keep his receipt therefor, and notify the clerk of the court whenever the full amount of the money is received or paid in accordance with such order or with any modification thereof.

SECTION 92A
Restitution in cases involving motor vehicle theft or fraudulent claims

A person found guilty of violating the provisions of sections twenty-seven, twenty-eight, one hundred and eleven B and one hundred and thirty-nine of chapter two hundred and sixty-six shall, in all cases, upon conviction, in addition to any other punishment, be ordered to make restitution to any person whom the court deems appropriate for any financial loss sustained by the victim of his crime, his dependents or an insurer as a result of the commission of the crime. The term "financial loss" shall be interpreted to include but shall not be limited to, loss of earnings, out-of-pocket expenses, and replacement costs. Losses due to pain and suffering are not financial loss. Restitution shall be interpreted to include monetary reimbursement, work or service, or a combination thereof, provided to any person, organization, corporation, or governmental entity, the court determines has suffered said damage or financial loss, or to perform such work or service for any other person, organization, corporation or governmental entity as the court may determine. Restitution shall be imposed in addition to incarceration or fine, but not in lieu thereof. In an extraordinary case such as indigency, the court may determine that the interests of the victim and justice would not be served by ordering restitution. In such a case, the court shall make and enter specific written findings on the record concerning the extraordinary circumstances presented which militated against the imposition of restitution.

The court shall, after conviction, conduct an evidentiary hearing to ascertain the extent of the damages or financial loss suffered as a result of the defendant's crime. The court may then determine the amount and method of restitution. In so determining, the court shall consider the financial resources of the defendant and the burden restitution will impose on the defendant. The defendant's present and future ability to make such restitution shall be considered.

A defendant ordered to make restitution may petition the court for remission from any payment of restitution or from any unpaid portion thereof. If the court finds that the payment of restitution due will impose an undue financial hardship on the defendant or his family, the court may grant remission from any payment of restitution or modify the time and method of payment.

If a defendant who is required to make restitution defaults in any payment of restitution or installment thereof, the court may hold him in contempt unless said defendant has made a good faith effort to make restitution. If the defendant has made a good faith effort to make restitution, the court may, upon motion of the defendant, modify the order requiring restitution by:

(a) providing for additional time to make any payment in restitution;

(b) reducing the amount of any payment in restitution or installment thereof;

(c) granting a remission from any payment of restitution or part thereof.

Restitution shall not be authorized to a party whom the court determines to be aggrieved, without that party's consent.

SECTION 93
Payment to treasurer of unclaimed money collected by probation officer

Except as provided by section one of chapter two hundred and seventy-nine, money collected by a probation officer under order of the court by which he is appointed, if unclaimed after one year from the time of its collection, shall, upon further order of the court, be paid to the treasurer provided, that any part of the said money may be paid to persons establishing before the comptroller a lawful claim thereto

2

within five years of its payment to said treasurer, unless sooner paid over by order of the said commissioners.

SECTION 94
Expenses of probation officers

The reasonable expenses, including supplies and equipment, incurred by probation officers of the superior court and the probate court in the performance of their duties shall be approved and apportioned by the court, and paid by the commonwealth. Such reasonable expenses shall include the traveling expenses necessarily incurred by such a probation officer in connection with attendance at sessions of said court outside of the town in which the principal office of such probation officer is maintained, such expenses to be computed from and to said town. Money to be used for the necessary expenses to be incurred by such a probation officer in going outside the commonwealth for the purpose of bringing back for surrender to the court a person who is on probation shall be advanced by the treasurer of the commonwealth, upon presentation of a certificate signed by the probation officer and approved by said court. After his return such probation officer shall account for such money by filing with said state treasurer itemized vouchers, duly sworn to, approved by said court, setting forth the necessary expenses so incurred and any unexpended balance of such money shall be paid to said state treasurer. Subject to section eighty-one of chapter two hundred and eighteen, probation officers of district courts and of the Boston, Worcester, Bristol county and Springfield juvenile courts shall be reimbursed by the commonwealth for their actual disbursements for necessary expenses incurred while in the performance of their duties, including their reasonable traveling expenses in attending conferences authorized by section ninety-nine, not exceeding four hundred dollars to each in any one year, on vouchers approved by the court by which they are appointed.

SECTION 95
Temporary support or transportation of probationers

The superior courts or the Boston, Springfield, Bristol county and Worcester juvenile courts or a district court, except the municipal court of the city of Boston, may authorize a probation officer to expend such amount as the court considers expedient for the temporary support or transportation, or both, of a person placed on probation. A record of any amount so authorized shall be entered on the clerk's docket of the case.

The chief probation officer of the municipal court of the city of Boston may provide for the temporary support or transportation, or both, of a person placed on probation in said court, or for the relief of the immediate distress of such person, in any manner which he may deem proper, and for these purposes may annually expend a sum not exceeding two thousand dollars for all such cases of relief. At the end of each month said chief probation officer shall submit to the administrative justice of said court a list of the expenses so incurred, with proper vouchers, and upon approval of the administrative justice the amount thereof shall be paid to the chief probation officer by the commonwealth.

SECTION 96
Refusal or neglect of duties by probation officer

Any probation officer who refuses or neglects to perform any of the duties required of him shall forfeit two hundred dollars to the use of the commonwealth.

SECTION 97
Interference with duties of department of youth services

Sections eighty-three to ninety-six, inclusive, shall not authorize a probation officer to interfere with any of the duties required of the department of youth services under the law relative to juvenile offenders.

SECTION 98
Office of probation; commissioner of probation
(Stricken & replaced by 2011 Mass. Acts c. 93, § 124A, effective July 1, 2011, until appointment of a court administrator under G.L. c. 211B, § 12. See 2011 Mass. Acts c. 93, § 133.)

There shall be an office of probation which shall be under the supervision, direction and control of a commissioner of probation. The commissioner shall be appointed, and may be removed, by the chief justice for administration and management, with the advice of the chief justice of the juvenile court, the chief justice of the superior court, the chief justice of the district court, the chief justice of the probate and family court and the chief justice of the Boston municipal court. The commissioner shall be a person of skill and experience in the field of criminal justice. The commissioner shall be the executive and administrative head of the office of probation and shall be responsible for administering and enforcing the laws relative to the office of probation and to each administrative unit of the office. The commissioner shall serve a term of 5 years and may be reappointed. The commissioner shall receive such salary as may be determined by law and shall devote full time to the duties of the office. In the case of an absence or vacancy in the office of the commissioner or in the case of disability as determined by the chief justice for administration and management, the chief justice may designate an acting commissioner to serve as commissioner until the vacancy is filled or the absence or disability ceases. The acting commissioner shall have all of the powers and duties of the commissioner and shall have similar qualifications as the commissioner.

Subject to the approval and consent of the chief justice for administration and management, the commissioner may appoint such deputies, supervisors and assistants as may be necessary for the performance of the commissioner's duties. The deputies, supervisors and assistants shall, subject to appropriation, receive salaries to be fixed by the chief justice for administration and management. The commissioner shall perform such duties and responsibilities as otherwise provided by law or as designated from time to time by the chief justice for administration and management. The commissioner shall make recommendations to the chief justice for administration and management on:

(i) the supervision and evaluation of all probation programs within the trial court;

(ii) the evaluation of the probation service in each court of the commonwealth;

(iii) the compilation, evaluation and dissemination of statistical information on crime, delinquency and appropriate probate and family court matters available in the commissioner's records;

(iv) the recruitment, training and educational development of probation officers;

(v) the evaluation of the work performance of probation officers; and

(vi) planning, initiation and development of volunteer, diversion and other programs in consultation with probation officers throughout the commonwealth.

[*Section 98 as amended by 2011 Mass. Acts c. 93, § 124B, effective upon appointment of a court administrator under G.L. c. 211B, § 12, see 2011 Mass. Acts c. 93, § 132:*]

There shall be an office of probation which shall be under the supervision, direction and control of a commissioner of probation. The commissioner shall be appointed, and may be removed, by the chief justice of the trial court and the court administrator, with the advice of the chief justice of the juvenile court, the chief justice of the superior court, the chief justice of the district court, the chief justice of the probate and family court and the chief justice of the Boston municipal court. The commissioner shall be a person of skill and experience in the field of criminal justice. The commissioner shall be the executive and administrative head of the office of probation and shall be responsible for administering and enforcing the laws relative to the office of probation and to each administrative unit of the office. The commissioner shall serve a term of 5 years and may be reappointed. The commissioner shall receive such salary as may be determined by law and shall devote full time to the duties of the office. In the case of an absence or vacancy in the office of the commissioner, or in the case of disability as determined by the chief justice of the trial court, said chief justice may designate an acting commissioner to serve as commissioner until the vacancy is filled or the absence or disability ceases. The acting commissioner shall have all of the powers and duties of the commissioner and shall have similar qualifications as the commissioner.

Subject to the approval and consent of the court administrator, the commissioner may appoint such deputies, supervisors and assistants as may be necessary for the performance of the commissioner's duties. The deputies, supervisors and assistants shall, subject to appropriation, receive salaries to be fixed by the court administrator. Subject to the approval and direction of the court administrator, the commissioner shall perform such duties and responsibilities as otherwise provided by law or as designated from time to time by the chief justice of the trial court and the court administrator. The commissioner shall make recommendations to the chief justice of the trial court and the court administrator on:

(i) the supervision and evaluation of all probation programs within the trial court;

(ii) the evaluation of the probation service in each court of the commonwealth;

(iii) the compilation, evaluation and dissemination of statistical information on crime, delinquency and appropriate probate and family court matters available in the commissioner's records;

(iv) the recruitment, training and educational development of probation officers;

(v) the evaluation of the work performance of probation officers; and

(vi) planning, initiation and development of volunteer, diversion and other programs in consultation with probation officers throughout the commonwealth.

SECTION 98A
Advisory board to commissioner of probation and chief justice for administration and management
(Added by 2011 Mass. Acts c. 93, § 124A, effective July 1, 2011, until the appointment of a court administrator. See 2011 Mass. Acts c. 93, § 133.)

There shall be a board to advise the commissioner of probation and the chief justice for administration and management. The board shall make recommendations on the management of the office of probation. The board shall consist of 9 members to be appointed by the supreme judicial court: 2 persons who have significant experience in criminal justice, 2 persons who have significant experience in public policy, 2 persons who have significant experience in management, 1 person who has significant experience in human resources management, 1 person who is a member of the Massachusetts bar with active status and 1 person with significant experience as a probation officer. Upon the expiration of the term of any appointive member, the member's successor shall be appointed in a like manner for a term of 3 years. In making their initial appointments, the supreme judicial court shall appoint 2 members to serve for a term of 1 year, 4 members to serve for a term of 2 years and 3 members to serve for a term of 3 years.

A person appointed to fill a vacancy on the board shall be appointed in like manner and shall serve for only the unexpired term of the former member. No member shall serve for more than 2 full terms. The board shall annually elect 1 of its members to serve as chair and 1 of its members to serve as vice-chair. The chair shall hold regular meetings and shall notify the board members of the time and place of the meetings.

Members of the board shall serve without compensation but shall be reimbursed for their expenses actually and necessarily incurred in the discharge of their official duties. The chief justice for administration and management shall serve as the executive secretary of the board and the office of probation shall provide, at the request of the board, detailed reports regarding the work of probation in the court.

The board shall advise the commissioner of probation and the chief justice for administration and management on all matters of probation reform. The board shall make recommendations to the commissioner of probation and the chief justice for administration and management and shall forward such recommendations to the house and senate committees on ways and means.

[*Section 98 as amended by 2011 Mass. Acts c. 93, § 124B, effective upon appointment of a court administrator under G.L. c. 211B, § 12, see 2011 Mass. Acts c. 93, § 132:*]

There shall be a board to advise the commissioner of probation and the court administrator. The board shall make recommendations on the management of the office of probation. The board shall consist of 9 members to be appointed by the supreme judicial court: 2 persons who have significant experience in criminal justice, 2 persons who have significant experience in public policy, 2 persons who have significant experience in management, 1 person who has significant experience in human resources management, 1 person who is a member of the Massachusetts bar with active status and 1 person with significant experience as a probation officer. Upon the expiration of the term of any appointive member, the member's successor shall be appointed in a like manner for a term of 3 years. In making their initial appointments, the supreme judicial court shall appoint 2 members to serve for a term of 1 year, 4 members to serve for a term of 2 years and 3 members to serve for a term of 3 years.

A person appointed to fill a vacancy on the board shall be appointed in like manner and shall serve for only the unexpired term of the former member. No member shall serve for more than 2 full terms. The board shall annually elect 1 of its members to serve as chair and 1 of its members to serve as vice-chair. The chair shall hold regular meetings and shall notify the board members of the time and place of the meetings.

Members of the board shall serve without compensation but shall be reimbursed for their expenses actually and necessarily incurred in the discharge of their official duties. The court administrator shall serve as the executive secretary of the board and the office of probation shall provide, at the request of the board, detailed reports regarding the work of probation in the court.

The board shall advise the commissioner of probation and the court administrator on all matters of probation reform. The board shall make recommendations to the commissioner of probation and the court administrator and shall forward such recommendations to the house and senate committees on ways and means.

SECTION 99
Powers and duties of commissioner of probation
(Stricken & replaced by 2011 Mass. Acts c. 93, § 124A, effective July 1, 2011 until appointment of a court administrator under G.L. c. 211B, § 12. See 2011 Mass. Acts c. 93, § 133.)

The commissioner shall have executive control and supervision of the probation service and shall have the power to:

(1) supervise the probation work in all of the courts of the commonwealth and, for such purposes, the commissioner and the commissioner's staff shall have access to all probation records of those courts;

(2) subject to the approval of the chief justice for administration and management, establish reports and forms to be maintained by probation officers, establish procedures to be followed by probation officers and establish standards and rules of probation work, including methods and procedures of investigation, mediation, supervision, case work, record keeping, accounting and caseload and case management;

(3) promulgate rules and regulations concerning probation officers or offices; provided, however, that such rules and regulations shall be approved in writing by the chief justice for administration and management subject to chapter 150E;

(4) assist the chief justice for administration and management in developing standards and procedures for the performance evaluation of probation officers and assist each first justice in evaluating the work performance of probation officers; provided, however, that in the event of any conflict between this clause and a term of an applicable collective bargaining agreement, the term of the collective bargaining agreement shall take precedence;

(5) receive all notices of intended disciplinary action against a probation officer or supervising probation officer, including reprimand, fine, suspension, demotion or discharge, that may be initiated by a first justice, supervisor or chief probation officer;

(6) develop and conduct basic orientation and in-service training programs for probation officers, such programs to be held at such times and for such periods as the commissioner shall determine;

(7) conduct research studies relating to crime and delinquency; provided, however, that the commissioner may participate with other public and private agencies in joint research studies;

(8) annually submit written budget recommendations for the probation service to the chief justice for administration and management, which shall be in addition to the budget requests submitted by the first justices on behalf of their respective courthouse or courthouses, including probation offices;

(9) annually conduct regional meetings with chief probation officers to discuss the budget needs of the local probation offices; and

(10) hold conferences on probation throughout the commonwealth; provided, however, that the traveling expenses of trial court justices or probation officers authorized by the chief justice for administration and management to attend any such conference shall be paid by the commonwealth.

[Section 99 as amended by 2011 Mass. Acts c. 93, § 124A, effective upon appointment of a court administrator under G.L. c. 211B, § 12. See 2011 Mass. Acts c. 93, § 132:]

The commissioner shall have executive control and supervision of the probation service and shall have the power to:

(1) supervise the probation work in all of the courts of the commonwealth and, for such purposes, the commissioner and the commissioner's staff shall have access to all probation records of those courts;

(2) subject to the approval of the chief justice of the trial court, establish reports and forms to be maintained by probation officers, establish procedures to be followed by probation officers and establish standards and rules of probation work, including methods and procedures of investigation, mediation, supervision, case work, record keeping, accounting and caseload and case management;

(3) promulgate rules and regulations concerning probation officers or offices; provided, however, that such rules and regulations shall be approved in writing by the court administrator subject to chapter 150E;

(4) assist the court administrator in developing standards and procedures for the performance evaluation of probation officers and assist each first justice in evaluating the work performance of probation officers; provided, however, that in the event of any conflict between this clause and a term of an applicable collective bargaining agreement, the term of the collective bargaining agreement shall take precedence;

(5) receive all notices of intended disciplinary action against a probation officer or supervising probation officer, including reprimand, fine, suspension, demotion or discharge, that may be initiated by a first justice, supervisor or chief probation officer;

(6) develop and conduct basic orientation and in-service training programs for probation officers, such programs to be held at such times and for such periods as the commissioner shall determine;

(7) conduct research studies relating to crime and delinquency; provided, however, that the commissioner may participate with other public and private agencies in joint research studies;

(8) annually submit written budget recommendations for the probation service to the court administrator, which shall be in addition to the budget requests submitted by the first justices on behalf of their respective courthouse or courthouses, including probation offices;

(9) annually conduct regional meetings with chief probation officers to discuss the budget needs of the local probation offices; and

(10) hold conferences on probation throughout the commonwealth; provided, however, that the traveling expenses of trial court justices or probation officers authorized by the

court administrator to attend any such conference shall be paid by the commonwealth.

SECTION 99A
Repealed

SECTION 99B
Probation officers; compensation

(1) In those courts or regions having fewer than fifteen probation officers, all persons serving as chief probation officer or acting chief probation officer shall be allocated to the title of Chief or Acting Probation Officer I, and in those courts or regions having fifteen or more probation officers, all persons so-serving shall be allocated to the title of Chief or Acting Chief Probation Officer II.

(2) All probation officers, except the chief probation officer, shall be compensated in accordance with the provisions of the applicable collective bargaining agreement, pursuant to the provisions of chapter one hundred and fifty E. The salaries of chief probation officers and acting chief probation officers shall be paid by the commonwealth in accordance with a schedule of salaries as recommended in writing by the chief administrative justice of the trial court and filed with the house and senate committees on ways and means.

(3) Upon initial appointment, a probation officer shall be compensated at the minimum of said salary schedule for his group or, if he shall have had prior service as a probation officer or shall, in the judgment of the committee on probation, have had years of similar service in allied fields, the step for such group to which his years of prior service entitle him.

(4) Upon completion of each year of service, a probation officer shall be compensated at the next higher step, if any, of said salary schedule for his group.

(5) Upon promotion (including, in the case of a chief probation officer, a change in his class due to an increase in the number of probation officers his probation office has), a probation officer shall be compensated at the lowest step of his new group which is at least one increment of his new group, but less than two such increments, higher than his salary immediately prior to such promotion, and upon the completion of each year of service in his new group, shall be compensated at the next higher step, if any, of said salary schedule for such new group. Notwithstanding any other provision of this section, no chief probation officer shall receive a salary less than the next increment greater than the salary received by the first assistant chief probation officer in the same court.

SECTION 99C
Repealed

SECTION 99D
Repealed
NOTE   See Section 99B of this chapter.

SECTION 99E
Proof of indigency

(a) The commissioner of probation shall enter into an interagency service agreement with the department of revenue to verify income data and other information relevant to the determination of indigency of recipients of counsel pursuant to section 2 of chapter 211D.

(b) The commissioner of probation shall enter into an interagency service agreement with the department of transi-

tional assistance to verify income data and other information relevant to the determination of indigency of recipients of counsel pursuant to section 2 of chapter 211D.

(c) The commissioner of probation shall enter into an interagency service agreement with the department of medical assistance to verify income data and other information relevant to the determination of indigency of recipients of counsel pursuant to section 2 of chapter 211D.

(d) The commissioner of probation shall enter into an interagency service agreement with the registry of motor vehicles to verify the statements on motor vehicle ownership or nonownership by recipients of counsel pursuant to section 2 of chapter 211D.

SECTION 99F
Performance measurement system
(Added by 2011 Mass. Acts c. 93, § 125, effective July 1, 2011.)

(a) The commissioner of probation shall establish a performance measurement system for the office of probation and any private organizations under contract with the commonwealth to perform services as part of a probationary sentence. The commissioner shall annually establish program goals, measure program performance against those goals and report publicly on the progress to improve the effectiveness of probation programs. The commissioner shall determine the appropriate measures and standards of performance in all categories and reporting on performance trends. Clear measurements shall be developed and effectuated while ensuring that no undue administrative burden is placed on agencies and organizations subject to this section. The performance measurement system shall require each division to develop a strategic plan for program activities and performance goals.

(b) Performance measurements shall include, but not be limited to, the recidivism and violation rate for probationers, probationers' compliance with court orders, the effectiveness of the probation departments' provision of information to the court and any other measurements established by the commissioner of probation.

(c) The commissioner shall annually re-evaluate the goals and measures established by the office and monitor the results that the divisions and contractors report. The office shall recommend changes to proposed goals and measures as are appropriate to enhance public safety.

(d) The commissioner shall use the performance measurements established under this section to determine the quality of service of all private entities. The results of such performance measures shall be criteria used in negotiating any contracts, and contracts with private organizations not meeting their performance goals shall be publicly bid upon their expiration. Renewal contracts may also provide incentives to reward reporting in compliance with performance measurements and to reward achievement of specific performance goals.

(e) The commissioner may consider applications for rehabilitative pilot programs that incorporate evidence based correctional practices. Said applications shall encourage partnerships with the state and can demonstrate an ability to leverage federal and/or private grant opportunities.

(f) The results of such performance measures shall be considered in conducting performance evaluations of staff.

(g) The commissioner shall report regularly to the public on the progress the office and its divisions are making at achieving stated goals. The report on performance measurements shall be published annually and made available to the public not later than December 31. The report shall also be filed annually with the clerks of the house of representatives and the senate, the chairs of the house and senate committees on ways and means, the house and senate chairs of the joint committee on public safety and homeland security and the house and senate chairs of the joint committee on the judiciary. The commissioner shall be responsible for reporting publicly and transparently and making all reports available.

(h) The commissioner shall, to the extent practicable, develop partnerships with research institutions to further analyze performance management data.

SECTION 100
Detailed reports of probation work; records; accessibility of information

Every probation officer, or the chief or senior probation officer of a court having more than one probation officer, shall transmit to the commissioner of probation, in such form and at such times as he shall require, detailed reports regarding the work of probation in the court, and the commissioner of correction, the penal institutions commissioner of Boston and the county commissioners of counties other than Suffolk shall transmit to the commissioner, as aforesaid, detailed and complete records relative to all paroles and permits to be at liberty granted or issued by them, respectively, to the revoking of the same and to the length of time served on each sentence to imprisonment by each prisoner so released specifying the institution where each such sentence was served; and under the direction of the commissioner a record shall be kept of all such cases as the commissioner may require for the information of the justices and probation officers. Police officials shall cooperate with the commissioner and the probation officers in obtaining and reporting information concerning persons on probation. The information so obtained and recorded shall not be regarded as public records and shall not be open for public inspection but shall be accessible to the justices and probation officers of the courts, to the police commissioner for the city of Boston, to all chiefs of police and city marshals, and to such departments of the state and local governments as the commissioner may determine. Upon payment of a fee of three dollars for each search, such records shall be accessible to such departments of the federal government and to such educational and charitable corporations and institutions as the commissioner may determine. The commissioner of correction and the department of youth services shall at all times give to the commissioner and the probation officers such information as may be obtained from the records concerning prisoners under sentence or who have been released. The commissioner may use systems operated by the department of criminal justice information services, pursuant to sections one hundred sixty-seven to one hundred seventy-eight, inclusive, of chapter six, for any record-keeping lawfully required by him provided that such records remain subject to the regulations of said department.

NOTE   Related Rule. Mass.R.Crim.P. 28(d)—Presentence Investigation.

SECTION 100A
Requests to seal files; conditions; application of section; effect of sealing of records
(Amended by 2010 Mass. Acts c. 256, §§ 128–30, effective May 4, 2012.)

Any person having a record of criminal court appearance and dispositions in the commonwealth on file with the office of the commissioner of probation may, on a form furnished by the commissioner and signed under the penalties of perjury, request that the commissioner seal the file. The commissioner shall comply with the request provided that: (1) the person's court appearance and court disposition records, including any period of incarceration or custody for any misdemeanor to be sealed occurred not less than 5 years before the request; (2) the person's court appearance and court disposition records, including any period of incarceration or custody for any felony record to be sealed occurred not less than 10 years before the request; (3) the person had not been found guilty of any criminal offense within the commonwealth in the case of a misdemeanor, 5 years before the request, and in the case of a felony, 10 years before the request, except motor vehicle offenses in which the penalty does not exceed a fine of $50; (4) the form includes a statement by the petitioner that he has not been convicted of any criminal offense in another state, United States possession or in a court of federal jurisdiction, except said motor vehicle offenses, as aforesaid, and has not been imprisoned in any state or county in the case of a misdemeanor, within the preceding 5 years, and in the case of a felony, within the preceding 10 years; and (5) the person's record does not include convictions of offenses other than those to which this section applies. This section shall apply to court appearances and dispositions of all offenses; provided, however, that this section shall not apply in case of convictions for violations of sections 121 to 131H, inclusive, of chapter 140 or violations of said chapter 268 or chapter 268A.

In carrying out the provisions of this section, notwithstanding any laws to the contrary:

1. Any recorded offense which was a felony when committed and has since become a misdemeanor shall be treated as a misdemeanor.

2. Any recorded offense which is no longer a crime shall be eligible for sealing forthwith, except in cases where the elements of the offense continue to be a crime under a different designation.

3. In determining the period for eligibility, any subsequently recorded offenses for which the dispositions are "not guilty", "dismissed for want of prosecution", "dismissed at request of complainant", "nol prossed", or "no bill" shall not be held to interrupt the running of the required period for eligibility.

4. If it cannot be ascertained that a recorded offense was a felony when committed said offense shall be treated as a misdemeanor.

5. Any violation of section 7 of chapter 209A or section 9 of chapter 258E shall be treated as a felony.

6. Sex offenses, as defined in section 178C of chapter 6, shall not be eligible for sealing for 15 years following their disposition, including termination of supervision, probation or any period of incarceration, or for so long as the offender is under a duty to register in the commonwealth or in any other state where the offender resides or would be such a duty if residing in the commonwealth, whichever is longer; provided,

however, that any sex offender who has at any time been classified as a level 2 or level 3 sex offender, pursuant to section 178K of chapter 6, shall not be eligible for sealing of sex offenses.

When records of criminal appearances and criminal dispositions are sealed by the commissioner in his files, he shall notify forthwith the clerk and the probation officer of the courts in which the convictions or dispositions have occurred, or other entries have been made, of such sealing, and said clerks and probation officers likewise shall seal records of the same proceedings in their files.

Such sealed records shall not operate to disqualify a person in any examination, appointment or application for public service in the service of the commonwealth or of any political subdivision thereof; nor shall such sealed records be admissible in evidence or used in any way in any court proceedings or hearings before any boards or commissions, except in imposing sentence in subsequent criminal proceedings, and except that in any proceedings under sections 1 to 39I, inclusive, of chapter 119, sections 2 to 5, inclusive, of chapter 201, chapters 208, 209, 209A, 209B, 209C, or sections 1 to 11A, inclusive, of chapter 210, a party having reasonable cause to believe that information in a sealed criminal record of another party may be relevant to (1) an issue of custody or visitation of a child, (2) abuse, as defined in section 1 of chapter 209A or (3) the safety of any person may upon motion seek to introduce the sealed record into evidence. The judge shall first review such records in camera and determine those records that are potentially relevant and admissible. The judge shall then conduct a closed hearing on the admissibility of those records determined to be potentially admissible; provided, however, that such records shall not be discussed in open court and, if admitted, shall be impounded and made available only to the parties, their attorneys and court personnel who have a demonstrated need to receive them.

An application for employment used by an employer which seeks information concerning prior arrests or convictions of the applicant shall include the following statement: "An applicant for employment with a sealed record on file with the commissioner of probation may answer 'no record' with respect to an inquiry herein relative to prior arrests, criminal court appearances or convictions. An applicant for employment with a sealed record on file with the commissioner of probation may answer 'no record' to an inquiry herein relative to prior arrests or criminal court appearances. In addition, any applicant for employment may answer 'no record' with respect to any inquiry relative to prior arrests, court appearances and adjudications in all cases of delinquency or as a child in need of services which did not result in a complaint transferred to the superior court for criminal prosecution." The attorney general may enforce the provisions of this paragraph by a suit in equity commenced in the superior court.

The commissioner, in response to inquiries by authorized persons other than any law enforcement agency, any court, or any appointing authority, shall in the case of a sealed record or in the case of court appearances and adjudications in a case of delinquency or the case of a child in need of services which did not result in a complaint transferred to the superior court for criminal prosecution, report that no record exists.

NOTE 1   "[T]he sealed records statute does not operate to erase the fact of a prior conviction; it seeks simply to ensure confidentiality. The information is in fact maintained and is accessible to law enforcement agencies, courts, and appointing authorities under G.L. c. 276, § 100A." *Rzeznik v. Chief of Police*, 374 Mass. 475, 482 (1978) (citations omitted).

NOTE 2   Records sealed pursuant to this section may be considered by the police when issuing or revoking a gun license under G.L. c. 140, §§ 122, 122B and 131. *Rzeznik v. Chief of Police*, 374 Mass. at 480.

NOTE 3   Defendant, who had been pardoned, moved to compel the commissioner of probation to seal his record. Held, commissioner need *not* so act. A pardon is *not* the equivalent of the dispositions described in G.L. c. 276, §§ 100A or 100C. *Commonwealth v. Vickey*, 381 Mass. 762 (1980).

NOTE 4   Sealing Versus Expungement. While both "serve the same purpose, ensuring the confidentiality of a person's record," they are nonetheless different. "As we noted in *Police Comm'r of Boston v. Municipal Court of the Dorchester Dist.*, 374 Mass. 640, 648 (1978), 'the distinction between expungement of a record and sealing of a record is important. The former term refers to . . . an order to remove and destroy record 'so that no trace of the information remains.' The latter term refers to those steps taken to segregate certain records from the generality of records and to ensure their confidentiality to the extent specified in the controlling statute.'" *Commonwealth v. Balboni*, 419 Mass. 42, 45 n.6 (1994).

NOTE 5   Time Limits/Appeal. One has 30 days from the entry of the order of expungement to file a motion to reconsider and vacate the order. *Commonwealth v. Balboni*, 419 Mass. 42, 44 (1994).

NOTE 6   Discovery. "Based on our interpretation of the language of the relevant statutes and the Legislature's intent in prioritizing the policy interests promoted by the sealing statute, the mandatory discovery provisions of G.L. c. 218, § 26A, and Mass. R. Crim. P. 14(a)(1)(D) do not apply to a criminal record sealed under G.L. c. 276, § 100A." *Wing v. Commissioner of Probation*, 473 Mass. 368, 378 (2015).

SECTION 100B
Requests to seal delinquency files or records; conditions; sealing by commissioner; notice for compliance; effect of sealing; limited disclosure

Any person having a record of entries of a delinquency court appearance in the commonwealth on file in the office of the commissioner of probation may, on a form furnished by the commissioner, signed under the penalties of perjury, request that the commissioner seal such file. The commissioner shall comply with such request provided (1) that any court appearance or disposition including court supervision, probation, commitment or parole, the records for which are to be sealed, terminated not less than three years prior to said request; (2) that said person has not been adjudicated delinquent or found guilty of any criminal offense within the commonwealth in the three years preceding such request, except motor vehicle offenses in which the penalty does not exceed a fine of fifty dollars nor been imprisoned under sentence or committed as delinquent within the commonwealth within the preceding three years; and (3) said form includes a statement by the petitioner that he has not been adjudicated delinquent or found guilty of any criminal offense in any other state, United States possession or in a court of federal jurisdiction, except such motor vehicle offenses as aforesaid, and has not been imprisoned under sentence or committed as a delinquent in any state or county within the preceding three years.

When records of delinquency appearances and delinquency dispositions are sealed by the commissioner in his files, the commissioner shall notify forthwith the clerk and

2

the probation officer of the courts in which the adjudications or dispositions have occurred, or other entries have been made, and the department of youth services of such sealing, and said clerks, probation officers, and department of youth services likewise shall seal records of the same proceedings in their files.

Such sealed records of a person shall not operate to disqualify a person in any future examination, appointment or application for public service under the government of the commonwealth or of any political subdivision thereof; nor shall such sealed records be admissible in evidence or used in any way in any court proceedings or hearings before any boards of commissioners, except in imposing sentence for subsequent offenses in delinquency or criminal proceedings.

Notwithstanding any other provision to the contrary, the commissioner shall report such sealed delinquency record to inquiring police and court agencies only as "sealed delinquency record over three years old" and to other authorized persons who may inquire as "no record". The information contained in said sealed delinquency record shall be made available to a judge or probation officer who affirms that such person, whose record has been sealed, has been adjudicated a delinquent or has pleaded guilty or has been found guilty of and is awaiting sentence for a crime committed subsequent to sealing of such record. Said information shall be used only for the purpose of consideration in imposing sentence.

NOTE 1   A record of a juvenile, sealed pursuant to G.L. c. 276, § 100B, "may not be used to impeach credibility generally, but may be used only in cases in which it bears directly on the witness's bias or motive. . . .

"We think it only reasonable that a defendant seeking to use a sealed record for impeachment 'be expected to make some explanation as to how he expects to show bias.' *Commonwealth v. Cheek*, 374 Mass. 613, 615 (1978)."

Commonwealth v. Santos, 376 Mass. 920, 926 & n.7 (1978).

NOTE 2   **Juvenile Justice Lacks Authority to Order Expungement of Probation Records.** "We conclude that Juvenile Court judges lack the authority to order the expungement of probation records . . . ." *Commonwealth v. Gavin G.*, 437 Mass. 470, 471 (2002).

SECTION 100C

Sealing of records or files in certain criminal cases; effect upon employment reports; enforcement

(Amended by 2010 Mass. Acts c. 256, §§ 131–132, effective May 4, 2012.)

In any criminal case wherein the defendant has been found not guilty by the court or jury, or a no bill has been returned by the grand jury, or a finding of no probable cause has been made by the court, the commissioner of probation shall seal said court appearance and disposition recorded in his files and the clerk and the probation officers of the courts in which the proceedings occurred or were initiated shall likewise seal the records of the proceedings in their files. The provisions of this paragraph shall not apply if the defendant makes a written request to the commissioner not to seal the records of the proceedings.

In any criminal case wherein a nolle prosequi has been entered, or a dismissal has been entered by the court, and it appears to the court that substantial justice would best be served, the court shall direct the clerk to seal the records of the proceedings in his files. The clerk shall forthwith notify the commissioner of probation and the probation officer of the

courts in which the proceedings occurred or were initiated who shall likewise seal the records of the proceedings in their files.

Such sealed records shall not operate to disqualify a person in any examination, appointment or application for public employment in the service of the commonwealth or of any political subdivision thereof.

An application for employment used by an employer which seeks information concerning prior arrests or convictions of the applicant shall include in addition to the statement required under section one hundred A the following statement: "An applicant for employment with a sealed record on file with the commissioner of probation may answer 'no record' with respect to an inquiry herein relative to prior arrests or criminal court appearances." The attorney general may enforce the provisions of this section by a suit in equity commenced in the superior court.

The commissioner or the clerk of courts in any district or superior court or the Boston municipal court, in response to inquiries by authorized persons other than any law enforcement agency or any court, shall in the case of a sealed record report that no record exists. After a finding or verdict of guilty on a subsequent offense such sealed record shall be made available to the probation officer and the same, with the exception of a not guilty, a no bill, or a no probable cause, shall be made available to the court.

NOTE 1   See Note 3 following Section 100A of this chapter

NOTE 2   "[W]e no longer will require that a defendant seeking sealing under G.L. c. 276, § 100C, second par., prove 'that the value of sealing . . . clearly outweighs the constitutionally-based value of the record remaining open to society.' *Commonwealth v. Doe*, 420 Mass. 142, 151 (1995). Instead, we interpret the legislative directive that 'substantial justice [will] best be served' by sealing to mean that the defendant must establish that good cause exists for sealing. See G.L. c. 276, § 100C." *Commonwealth v. Pon*, 469 Mass. 296, 312 (2014).

NOTE 3   **Expungement vs. sealing.** "[W]e are asked to decide whether a judge has the authority to order the Commissioner of Probation (commissioner) to expunge a defendant's record where the criminal complaint was dismissed because its issuance was premised on a mistake. We conclude that a judge does not have such authority, but the judge may order that such a defendant's record be sealed pursuant to G.L. c. 276, § 100C." *Commonwealth v. Boe*, 456 Mass. 337, 337–38 (2010).

NOTE 4   "In all cases governed by G.L. c. 276, § 100C, sealing a criminal record is the exclusive remedy, and a judge lacks authority to allow a motion to expunge. This case falls into that narrow and exceptional class of cases in which the person originally charged with the crime was not only factually innocent, but was never the intended target of law enforcement. The presence of these factors takes the case outside the scope of the sealing statute because there is no public policy that favors the retention of such spurious records." *Commonwealth v. Alves*, 86 Mass. App. Ct. 210, 215 (2014).

SECTION 100D

Availability of sealed criminal record information

(Added by 2010 Mass. Acts c. 256, § 133, effective May 4, 2012.)

Notwithstanding any provision of section 100A, 100B, or 100C of this chapter, criminal justice agencies as defined in section 167 of chapter 6 shall have immediate access to, and be permitted to use as necessary for the performance of their criminal justice duties, any sealed criminal offender record information as defined in section 167 of chapter 6 and any sealed information concerning criminal offenses or acts of delinquency committed by any person before he attained the age of 17.

SECTION 101
Annual report of commissioner to general court

The commissioner of probation shall make an annual report to the general court of the probation work of the courts for the year ending on December thirty-first preceding. The report shall include such information as the commissioner may consider useful, with his suggestions or recommendations.

SECTION 101A
Establishment of uniform forms of blanks and records for use in district court probation offices

The commissioner of probation shall establish uniform forms of blanks and records for use in the probation offices of the district courts, and, upon receipt of competitive bids, the state purchasing agent shall order, at the expense of the commonwealth, and maintain such supply of said forms as the commissioner of probation shall determine to be necessary to meet the requirements of all such offices. The commissioner of probation shall from time to time distribute to the district and juvenile courts such quantities of such forms as he shall, with the probation officers of those courts, determine to be necessary. No forms of blanks and records other than those established and furnished hereunder shall be used in such probation offices unless approved by said commissioner.

SECTION 102
Authority of courts to require keeping of probation records as affected by Secs. 98 to 101A

Sections ninety-eight to one hundred and one A, inclusive, shall not affect the authority of the courts to require the keeping by their probation officers of probation records in addition to those necessary to conform to forms of records and reports prescribed by the commissioner of probation nor the authority of the courts to approve expenses and disbursements relating to the probation system.

SECTION 103
Notice to commissioner of appointment, removal, etc., of probation officer

Upon the appointment, removal, retirement, resignation, death, or leave of absence of a probation officer, the clerk of the court by which said probation officer was appointed shall notify forthwith the commissioner of probation of such appointment, removal, retirement, resignation, death, or leave of absence.

Chapter 276A. District Court Pretrial Diversion of Selected Offenders

Section
1   Definitions
2   Jurisdiction of court to divert persons charged with offenses to programs of community supervision and services
3   Screening of defendants for court's determination at arraignment of eligibility for diversion to program; continuance; directing defendant to program
4   Inapplicability of chapter to otherwise eligible persons charged with violation of controlled substances act, certain sex offenses or certain crimes against persons sixty-five or over
5   Report of assessment by director of program to court; recommendations; final determination; stay of criminal proceedings; consent of defendant; waiver of right to speedy trial; admissibility as evidence; disclosure restricted
6   Reports of progress or violations by director of program to court; hearing; termination of stay of criminal proceedings
7   Report by director of program to court upon expiration of stay of proceedings; disposition as to defendant; final report
8   Commissioner to certify, monitor and aid programs; court approval of certification; powers and duties of commissioner
9   Advisory board; members; expenses; duties
10   Confirmation of defendant's status as veteran; jurisdiction to divert to a program
11   14-day continuance

SECTION 1
Definitions
(Amended by 2014 Mass. Acts c. 165, § 180, effective July 15, 2014.)

The following words, as used in this chapter, unless the context otherwise requires, shall have the following meanings:

"Assessment", a thorough and complete measurement of the needs of an individual in, but not limited to, the following areas: education, vocational training, job placement, mental and physical health, family and social services, and an analysis of a defendant's commitment to participate in a program of community supervision and services.

"Commissioner", the commissioner of probation.

"Director", the person in charge of the operation of a program of community supervision and services.

"Official designee", a representative of a program of community supervision and service who has been approved by the presiding justice of a district court to work in conjunction with that court's probation office to screen defendants who may be eligible for diversion.

"Plan of service", a comprehensive and cohesive set of recommended programs and specific services to meet the needs of individuals as determined through assessment.

"Program", any program of community supervision and services certified or approved by the commissioner of probation under the provisions of section eight, including, but not limited to, medical, educational, vocational, social, substance use disorder treatment and psychological services, corrective and preventive guidance, training, performance of community service work, counselling, provision for residence in a halfway house or other suitable place, and other rehabilitative services designed to protect the public and benefit the individual.

SECTION 2
Jurisdiction of court to divert persons charged with offenses to programs of community supervision and services
(Amended by 2013 Mass. Acts c. 84, § 32, effective Sept. 18, 2013.)

The district courts, and in Boston, the municipal court of the city of Boston, shall have jurisdiction to divert to a program, as defined in section one, any person who is charged with an offense or offenses against the commonwealth for which a term of imprisonment may be imposed and over which the district courts may exercise final jurisdiction and who has reached the age of 18 years but has not reached the age of twenty-two, who has not previously been convicted of a violation of any law of the commonwealth or of any other state or of the United States in any criminal court proceeding after having reached the age of 18 years, except for traffic violations for which no term of imprisonment may have been imposed, who does not have any outstanding warrants, continuances, appeals or criminal cases pending before any courts of the commonwealth or any other state or of the United States, and who has received a recommendation from a program that he would, in light of the capacities of and guidelines governing it, benefit from participation in said program.

SECTION 3
Screening of defendants for court's determination at arraignment of eligibility for diversion to program; continuance; directing defendant to program

The probation officers of a district or municipal court, or their official designee, when gathering information in accordance with section eighty-five of chapter two hundred and seventy-six, shall also screen each defendant for the purpose of enabling the judge at arraignment to consider the eligibility of the defendant for diversion to a program.

Any defendant who is qualified for consideration for diversion to a program may, at his arraignment, be afforded a fourteen-day continuance for assessment by the personnel of a program to determine if he would benefit from such program.

If a defendant chooses to accept the offer of a continuance for the purpose of such an assessment, he shall so notify the judge at arraignment. Upon receipt of such notification, the judge shall grant a fourteen-day continuance. The judge, through the probation office or its official designee, shall direct the defendant to a program and shall inform said program of such action.

The judge may, in his discretion, grant a defendant who is preliminarily determined not to be eligible because of a failure to satisfy all the requirements of section two, a like fourteen-day continuance for assessment. In arriving at such a decision the opinion of the prosecution should be taken into consideration. Such a continuance may be granted upon the judge's own initiative or upon request by the defendant.

SECTION 4
Inapplicability of chapter to otherwise eligible persons charged with violation of controlled substances act, certain sex offenses or certain crimes against persons sixty-five or over

In the event that an individual who is eligible under the provisions of section two is charged with a violation of chapter ninety-four C, nothing in this chapter shall be construed to limit the effect or operation of sections thirty-eight to fifty-five, inclusive, of chapter one hundred and twenty-three.

In the event that an individual who is eligible under the provisions of section two is charged with a violation of one or more of the offenses enumerated in section three of chapter one hundred and twenty-three A, the provisions of this chapter shall not be applicable for said defendant.

A person charged with violating the provisions of subsection (a) of section fifteen A, subsection (a) of section fifteen B, subsection (a) of section eighteen and subsection (a) of section nineteen of chapter two hundred and sixty-five or subsection (a) of section twenty-five of chapter two hundred and sixty-six shall, for the second or subsequent such offense, not be diverted to a program as provided in section two.

SECTION 5
Report of assessment by director of program to court; recommendations; final determination; stay of criminal proceedings; consent of defendant; waiver of right to speedy trial; admissibility as evidence; disclosure restricted

Upon the expiration of a fourteen-day continuance granted pursuant to section three, the director of the program to which the defendant has been referred shall submit to the court a written report of its assessment. The report shall contain the information obtained through the program's assessment, the program's recommendation as to whether the defendant would benefit from diversion to the program, and a plan of services for the defendant if it has been determined that the defendant would so benefit.

The judge, upon receipt of the report, shall provide an opportunity for a recommendation by the prosecution regarding the diversion of the defendant. After receiving the report and having provided an opportunity for the prosecution to make its recommendation, the judge shall make a final determination as to the eligibility of the defendant for diversion to the program. The criminal proceedings of a defendant who qualifies for diversions under section two and who agrees to abide by the terms and conditions contained in the plan of services approved by the judge, shall be stayed for a period of ninety days, unless the judge in his discretion considers that the interest of justice would best be served by a hearing of the facts, after which the case may be continued without a finding for ninety days. No appeal shall be allowed from such final determination.

A defendant who has been determined to be ineligible by reason of his failure to satisfy certain provisions of section two, but who, in the judge's discretion, received a fourteen-day continuance for assessment, may on the basis of the report submitted by a program, be granted a like stay of proceedings.

In no event shall a stay of proceedings be granted pursuant to this section unless the defendant consents in writing to the terms and conditions of the stay of proceedings and knowingly executes a waiver of his right to a speedy trial on a form approved by the chief justice of the district courts, and, in Boston, the chief justice of the municipal court of the city of Boston. Such consent shall be with the advice of defendant's counsel. Any request for assessment, or a decision by the defendant not to enter such a program, or a determination by the program that the defendant would not benefit from it, or any statement made by the defendant during the course of assessment, shall not be admissible against the defendant in any criminal proceedings; nor shall any consent by the defendant to the stay of proceedings or any act done or statement made in fulfillment of the terms and conditions of such stay of proceedings be admissible as an admission, implied or otherwise, against the defendant, should the stay of proceedings be terminated and criminal proceedings resumed on the original charge or charges. No statement or other disclosure or records thereof made by a defendant during the course of assessment or during the stay of proceedings shall be at any time disclosed to a prosecutor or other law enforcement officer in connection with the charge or charges pending against said defendant or any codefendant.

2

SECTION 6
Reports of progress or violations by director of program to court; hearing; termination of stay of criminal proceedings

During a stay of proceedings or a continuance without a finding, as provided in section five, the director of a program shall submit periodic reports to the court relative to the progress of the defendant. The direct or shall also report violations of program conditions or subsequent arrests immediately upon notice thereof.

If the defendant during the stay of proceedings or a continuance without a finding violates a condition of the program or is charged with a subsequent offense, a judge in the court that entered the stay of proceedings may issue such process as is necessary to bring the defendant before the court. When the defendant is brought before the court, the judge shall afford him an opportunity to be heard. If the judge finds that the defendant has committed a violation of a condition of the program or that he has been charged with a subsequent offense, the judge may order, when appropriate, that the stay of proceedings be terminated and that the commonwealth proceed on the original charges as provided by law. No appeal shall be allowed from such an order.

SECTION 7
Report by director of program to court upon expiration of stay of proceedings; disposition as to defendant; final report

Upon the expiration of the initial ninety-day stay of proceedings or a continuance without a finding, the program director shall submit to the court a report indicating the successful completion of the program by a defendant or recommending an extension of the stay of proceedings or a continuance without a finding for not more than an additional ninety days, so that the defendant may complete the program successfully.

If the report indicates the successful completion of the program by a defendant, the judge may dismiss the original charges pending against the defendant. If the report recommends an extension of the stay of proceedings or a continuance without a finding, the judge may, on the basis of the report and any other relevant evidence, take such action as he deems appropriate, including the dismissal of the charges, the granting of an extension of the stay of proceedings or a continuance without a finding, or the resumption of criminal proceedings. In the event that an extension of the stay of proceedings or a continuance without a finding is granted, the program director shall submit a final report upon the expiration of such stay of proceedings.

SECTION 8
Commissioner to certify, monitor and aid programs; court approval of certification; powers and duties of commissioner

The office of the commissioner shall, in its discretion, certify, monitor and aid all programs to which defendants may be diverted pursuant to this chapter. The certification of programs shall be subject to the approval of the presiding justice of the individual court which would be the beneficiary of such services. The office of the commissioner shall, in its discretion, (a) issue for a term of two years, and may renew for like terms, a certification, subject to revocation for cause, to any person, partnership, corporation, society, association or other agency or entity of any kind, other than a licensed general hospital or a department, agency or institution of the federal government, the commonwealth or any political subdivision thereof, deemed to be responsible and suitable to establish and maintain such a program and to meet applicable certification standards and requirements; and in the case of a department, agency or institution of the commonwealth or any political subdivision thereof, grant approval to establish and maintain a program for a term of two years, and may renew such approval for like terms, subject to revocation for cause; (b) promulgate, in consultation with the advisory board established in section nine, rules and regulations establishing certification and approval standards and requirements; (c) establish limits for caseloads and enrollment so that programs are able to provide high quality intensive individualized service to those defendants participating in such programs; (d) procure, where appropriate, by contract, the personnel, facilities, services, and materials necessary to carry out the purposes of this act, subject to all applicable laws and regulations; (e) prepare reports for said advisory board showing the progress of all programs in fulfilling the purposes set forth; (f) notify the appropriate presiding justice of the individual court that adequate facilities and personnel are available to fulfill a plan of community supervision and services for that court; (g) provide technical assistance to such program as may be certified hereunder; (h) provide for the audit of any funds expended by the office for the support of programs certified hereunder; (i) promote the cooperation of all agencies which provide education, training, counseling, legal, employment, or other services to assure that eligible individuals released to programs may benefit to the maximum extent practicable; (j) prepare and submit an annual report to the chief justices of the supreme judicial, appeals, superior and district courts and to all justices in the district court system evaluating the performance of all programs.

SECTION 9
Advisory board; members; expenses; duties

There shall be an advisory board to the office of the commissioner for the overseeing of programs. The members of the advisory board shall be the attorney general, the commissioners of education, mental health, rehabilitation and welfare, a district court judge, the deputy director of the division of employment and training, the president of the Massachusetts District Attorney's Association, or their respective designees, and seven experts in the area of human services to the sociologically and economically disadvantaged through community based programs to be appointed by the governor for terms of two years, one of whom shall be an ex-offender. The members of the advisory board shall serve without compensation but shall be reimbursed for their expenses actually and necessarily incurred in the discharge of their duties. The advisory board shall annually select its chairman from among its members.

The advisory board shall assist the commissioner in coordinating the efforts of all public agencies and private organizations and individuals within the commonwealth concerned with the providing of services to defendants by said programs.

2

SECTION 10
Confirmation of defendant's status as veteran; jurisdiction to divert to a program
(Added by 2012 Mass. Acts c. 108, § 16, effective May 31, 2012.)

A probation officer of a district court, in Boston, the municipal court of the city of Boston or the officer's official designee, when gathering information in accordance with section 85 of chapter 276, shall, at or prior to arraignment of a defendant on a criminal complaint, use best efforts to confirm the defendant's status as a veteran, as defined in clause Forty-third of section 7 of chapter 4, a person on active service in the armed forces of the United States, as defined in said clause Forty-third of said section 7 of said chapter 4 or a person with a history of military service in the armed forces of the United States.

The district courts, and in Boston, the municipal court of the city of Boston, shall have jurisdiction to divert to a program any person who is a veteran, as defined in said clause Forty-third of said section 7 of said chapter 4, on active service in the armed forces of the United States, as defined in said clause Forty-third of said section 7 of said chapter 4, or who has history of military service in the armed forces of the United States who is charged with an offense against the commonwealth for which a term of imprisonment may be imposed, regardless of age, who has not previously been convicted of a violation of any law of the commonwealth or of any other state or of the United States in any criminal court proceeding after having reached the age of 18 years, except for traffic violations for which no term of imprisonment may have been imposed, who does not have any outstanding warrants, continuances, appeals or criminal cases pending before any courts of the commonwealth or any other state or of the United States and who has received a recommendation from a program that such person would, in light of the capacities of and guidelines governing it, benefit from participation in said program.

SECTION 11
14-day continuance
(Added by 2012 Mass. Acts c. 108, § 16, effective May 31, 2012.)

A defendant who is determined to be a veteran, on active service or has a history of military service in the armed forces of the United States and who is eligible for diversion or treatment under section 10 may, at arraignment, be afforded a 14-day continuance by the court to seek an assessment by the United States Department of Veterans Affairs, the department of veterans' services or another state or federal agency with suitable knowledge and experience of veterans affairs to provide the court with treatment options available to the defendant, including diversion programs, if appropriate. If the defendant has demonstrated symptomatology suggestive of a mental illness, a qualified psychiatrist, clinical psychologist or physician shall, in consultation with the United States Department of Veterans Affairs, the department of veterans' services or another federal or state agency, provide a written report to the court to assist in sentencing or diversion. The court may consider the recommendations of any diagnosing or treating licensed mental health professional for the defendant for pre-trial diversion or the imposition of a sentence. Prior to offering a continuance, the court shall inquire into the circumstances of the charge.

If the court offers a 14-day continuance to seek an assessment and a defendant chooses to accept the offer of a continuance, the defendant shall notify the court at arraignment. Upon receipt of such notification, the judge may grant a 14-day continuance. The court, through the probation office or the officer's official designee, shall direct the defendant to an assessment program, shall inform the program of the action and shall require that the program provide the probation department and court with its findings. A court may grant a defendant who is preliminarily determined not to be eligible for pre-trial diversion a 14-day continuance for assessment. The court shall consider the opinion of the commonwealth on the merits of granting or denying the continuance. A court may grant a continuance sua sponte or upon motion by the defendant.

Chapter 277. Indictments and Proceedings Before Trial

Section

1	Issuance of writs of venire facias for grand jurors; attendance at sittings of court
1A	Completion of investigations by grand juries; notice; order
2	Suffolk county; issuance of writs of venire facias for grand jurors
2A	Issuance of writs of venire facias for special grand jury
2B	Middlesex county; issuance of letters of venire for grand jurors
2C	Hampden county; issuance of writs of venire facias for grand jurors
2D	Plymouth county; issuance of writs of venire facias for grand jurors
2E	Worcester county; issuance of writs of venire facias for veniremen
2F	Norfolk county; issuance of writs of venire facias for grand jurors
2G	Essex county; issuance of writs of venire facias for grand jurors
2H	Bristol county; issuance of writs of venire facias for grand jurors
3	Drawing and summoning of grand jurors
3A	Suffolk county; impanelling grand jurors
4	Deficiency of grand jurors
5	Impanelling and oath
6	Affirmation in lieu of oath
7–10	Repealed
11	Re-summoning at same sitting
12–13	Repealed
14	Grand juror serving as traverse juror
14A	Right to counsel; grand jury proceedings
15	Discharge of accused person not indicted
16–17	Repealed
18	Circumstances of the act
19	Name of accused person; description by fictitious name; entry of true name
20	Time and place of commission of crime
21	Means
22	Description of written instrument; variance
23	Description of money
24	Description of value or price
25	Description of ownership
26	Description of public place
27	Description of animal
28	Description of judicial proceedings
29	Criminal responsibility
30	Intent to injure or defraud; general allegation
31	Alternative allegations
32	Continuing offenses
33	Unnecessary and immaterial allegations
34	Immaterial defects
35	Variance; prejudice
35A	Repealed
36	Scope of word "oath"
37	Negativing excuses, exceptions or provisos

38	Allegations, bill of particulars, presumption and proof in prosecutions involving controlled substances
39	Construction of words used in indictment
40	Repealed
41	Indictment for criminal dealing with personal property
42	Prosecutions for buying, receiving or aiding in concealment of stolen property
43	Indictment for perjury
44	Indictment for subornation of perjury
45	Indictment for unnatural and lascivious acts
46	Repealed
47	Arraignment; sentence; assignment of counsel
47A	Defenses or objections
48–52	Repealed
53	District attorneys; authority and duty as to transferred cases
54	Custody and delivery of prisoner
55	Compensation of counsel of prisoner
56	Expenses of counsel of prisoner
57	Prosecutions of crimes committed near boundary line of counties, etc.; crimes committed on sea
57A	Venue in cases where crime was committed without county or territorial jurisdiction of court
58	Larceny
58A	Buying, receiving, concealing or aiding in concealment of stolen or embezzled property
58 ½	Crimes involving electronically processed or stored data; place of prosecution
58B	Embezzlement or fraudulent conversion or appropriation by fiduciaries
59	Obtaining money or personal chattel by false pretenses
59A	Transmission of false reports, location of explosives, etc.
60	Homicide if injury is in one county and death in another
61	Crime committed at sea, etc., resulting in death in county
62	Crime committed in commonwealth resulting in death outside commonwealth
62A	Jurisdiction for criminal violations of chapter 209A
62B	Jurisdiction for stalking
62C	Jurisdiction for violations Sec. 35A of chapter 266
63	Limitations of criminal proceedings; general provisions
64	Limitation of new indictment against corporation after abatement or defeat of former indictment
65	Service of copy of indictment for murder on prisoner, etc.
66	List of jurors to prisoner; process for witnesses
67	Furnishing person in custody, etc., with copy of indictment
68	Issuance of subpoenas by attorney general and district attorneys
69	Repealed
70	Recognizance of witnesses
70A	Repealed
70B	Placing cases on file; statement of reasons
70C	Treating criminal offenses as civil infractions
71–72A	Repealed
73	Compensation for confinement of persons discharged
74–77	Repealed
78	Criminal proceedings as no bar to civil action
79	Application of annexed forms; schedule

SECTION 1
Issuance of writs of venire facias for grand jurors; attendance at sittings of court

The clerk of the courts for each county, except Suffolk, Middlesex, Essex, Norfolk, Plymouth and Worcester shall, not less than twenty-eight days before the commencement of the first sitting of the superior court for criminal business in each year, issue writs of venire facias for forty-five veniremen, from whose numbers the court shall select twenty-three grand jurors who shall serve in said court until the first regular sitting in the year next after they have been impanelled and until another grand jury has been impanelled in their stead. In counties where sittings of the court are established for the transaction of criminal business, they shall be required to attend only at such sittings.

SECTION 1A
Completion of investigations by grand juries; notice; order

Upon a written notice by the attorney general or any district attorney made to any justice of the superior court that public necessity requires further time by a grand jury to complete an investigation then in progress, the court may order such grand jury to continue to serve until said investigation has been completed and shall take up no new matter.

This section shall not be construed to prevent the issuance of writs of venire facias authorized by section one for impanelling a grand jury whose duty shall include all business not then before the grand jury continued under authorization of this section.

SECTION 2
Suffolk county; issuance of writs of venire facias for grand jurors

The clerk of the superior court for criminal business in Suffolk county shall, not less than twenty-eight days before the first Mondays of January and July, respectively, issue writs of venire facias for forty-five veniremen of whom thirty-nine shall be from Boston and two each from Chelsea, Revere and Winthrop. From these forty-five veniremen the court shall then select twenty-three grand jurors to serve in said court, who shall serve for each sitting thereof for six months and until another grand jury has been impanelled in their stead.

SECTION 2A
Issuance of writs of venire facias for special grand jury

The clerk of the courts in any county, or in Suffolk county the clerk of the superior court for criminal business, shall, upon written request of the attorney general accompanied by a certificate that public necessity requires such action, signed by the chief justice of the superior court, issue writs of venire facias for forty-five veniremen of whom the court shall select twenty-three for service as a special grand jury to hear, consider and report on such matters as the attorney general may present. Said jurors shall serve for a period of six months, unless sooner discharged by the attorney general or by the said chief justice, and shall be drawn, summoned and returned in the same manner, and shall have the same powers and receive the same compensation, as grand jurors summoned for service under sections one and two, and the provisions of sections three to fourteen, so far as apt, shall apply to such jurors. In Middlesex county, the clerk of the courts shall send a letter of venire to the jury commissioner as set forth in section twelve of chapter two hundred and thirty-four A.

SECTION 2B
Middlesex county; issuance of letters of venire for grand jurors

The clerk of courts in Middlesex county shall, not less than seventy days before the first Monday of January and July, respectively, issue letters of venire to the jury commissioner for thirty-five prospective grand jurors from whom the court shall select twenty-three grand jurors who shall serve in said court for each sitting thereof for six months and until another grand jury has been impanelled in their stead.

2

SECTION 2C
Hampden county; issuance of writs of venire facias for grand jurors

The clerk of the court for Hampden county shall, not less than twenty-eight days before the first Mondays of January and May, and the second Monday of September respectively, issue writs of venire facias for forty-five veniremen from whom the court shall select twenty-three grand jurors to serve in said court, who shall serve for each sitting thereof for four months and until another grand jury has been impanelled in their stead.

SECTION 2D
Plymouth county; issuance of writs of venire facias for grand jurors

The clerk of the court for Plymouth county shall not less than twenty-eight days before the first Mondays of January and May, and the second Monday of September respectively, issue writs of venire facias for forty-five veniremen from whom the court shall select twenty-three grand jurors to serve in said court, who shall serve for each sitting thereof for four months and until another grand jury has been impanelled in their stead.

SECTION 2E
Worcester county; issuance of writs of venire facias for veniremen

The clerk of the court for Worcester county shall, not less than twenty-eight days before the first Mondays of January and May, and the second Monday of September, respectively, issue writs of venire facias for fifty veniremen from whom the court shall select twenty-three grand jurors to serve in said court, who shall serve for each sitting thereof for four months and until another grand jury has been impanelled in their stead.

SECTION 2F
Norfolk county; issuance of writs of venire facias for grand jurors

The clerk of the court for Norfolk county shall, not less than twenty-eight days before the first Mondays of January and July respectively, issue writs of venire facias for fifty veniremen from whom the court shall select twenty-three grand jurors to serve in said court, who shall serve for each sitting thereof for six months and until another grand jury has been impanelled in their stead.

SECTION 2G
Essex county; issuance of writs of venire facias for grand jurors

The clerk of the court for Essex county shall, not less than twenty-eight days before the first Mondays of January and May, and second Monday of September respectively, issue writs of venire facias for forty-five veniremen from whom the court shall select twenty-three grand jurors to serve in said court, who shall serve for each sitting thereof for four months and until another grand jury has been impanelled in their stead.

SECTION 2H
Bristol county; issuance of writs of venire facias for grand jurors

The clerk of the court of Bristol county shall, not less than twenty-eight days before the first Mondays of January and July respectively, issue writs of venire facias for fifty veniremen from whom the court shall select twenty-three grand jurors to serve in said court, who shall serve for each sitting thereof for six months and until another grand jury has been impanelled in their stead.

SECTION 3
Drawing and summoning of grand jurors

Grand jurors shall be drawn, summoned and returned in the same manner as traverse jurors; and, if drawn at the same time with traverse jurors, the number of persons required whose names are first drawn shall be returned as grand jurors, and those whose names are afterward drawn shall be returned as traverse jurors. In Middlesex county, the selection and management of grand jurors shall be governed by chapter two hundred and thirty-four A and other applicable provisions of the General Laws.

SECTION 3A
Suffolk county; impanelling grand jurors

On the day when veniremen are summoned pursuant to section one, section two, section two A, section two B, section two C, section two D, section two E or section two F to attend court for the formation of a grand jury, the clerk of courts in any county, or in Suffolk county the clerk of the superior court for criminal business, shall cause the name of each person so summoned, and who appears and who has not been excused or set aside, to be written on separate ballots, substantially of uniform size, and shall cause such ballots to be placed in a box provided therefor. The clerk in open court, after shaking the ballots thoroughly, shall draw them out in succession until he has drawn the names of twenty-three grand jurors.

SECTION 4
Deficiency of grand jurors

If there is a deficiency of grand jurors, writs of venire facias may be issued to the constables of such towns as the court orders to return forthwith the further number of grand jurors required. In Middlesex county, letters of venire shall be issued to the jury commissioner as set forth in chapter two hundred and thirty-four A.

SECTION 5
Impanelling and oath

The clerk of the court shall prepare an alphabetical list of the names of all persons returned as grand jurors, and, when they are to be impanelled, the first two persons named thereon shall be first called, and the following oath shall be administered to them:

You, as grand jurors of this inquest for the body of this county of _____, do solemnly swear that you will diligently inquire, and true presentment make, of all such matters and things as shall be given you in charge; the commonwealth's counsel, your fellows' and your own, you shall keep secret; you shall present no man for envy, hatred or malice, neither shall you leave any unpresented for love, fear, favor, affection or hope of reward; but you shall present things truly, as they come to your knowledge, according to the best of your understanding; so help you God.

The other jurors shall then be called in such divisions as to the court considers proper, and the following oath shall be administered to them:

The same oath which your fellows have taken on their part, you and each of you on your behalf shall well and truly observe and keep; so help you God.

SECTION 6
Affirmation in lieu of oath
If a person who is returned as a grand juror is conscientiously scrupulous of taking the oath prescribed, he may affirm.

SECTIONS 7–10
Repealed

SECTION 11
Re-summoning at same sitting
If the grand jury are dismissed before the court is adjourned without day, they may be summoned to attend again in the same sitting, at such time as the court orders.

SECTIONS 12–13
Repealed

SECTION 14
Grand juror serving as traverse juror
No member of the grand jury which has found an indictment shall serve upon the jury for the trial thereof.

SECTION 14A
Right to counsel; grand jury proceedings
Any person shall have the right to consult with counsel and to have counsel present at every step of any criminal proceeding at which such person is present, including the presentation of evidence, questioning, or examination before the grand jury; provided, however, that such counsel in a proceeding before a grand jury shall make no objections or arguments or otherwise address the grand jury or the district attorney. No witness may refuse to appear for reason of unavailability of counsel for that witness.

NOTE   "The Commonwealth argued that this statute is violated only if a grand jury witness is prohibited from having an attorney in the grand jury room or is prevented from consulting with an attorney during questioning. In analyzing a right to counsel granted by statute in a different context, however, this court held that '[a] right to counsel is of little value unless there is an expectation that counsel's assistance will be effective.' *Care and Protection of Stephen*, 401 Mass. 144, 149 (1987). Thus, G.L. c. 277, § 14A, is violated if the person invoking it is denied the effective assistance of counsel." *Commonwealth v. Griffin*, 404 Mass. 372, 374–75 (1989).

INDICTMENTS AND COMPLAINTS

SECTION 15
Discharge of accused person not indicted
The grand jury shall, during its session, make daily return to the court of all cases wherein it has finally determined not to present an indictment against an accused person held in custody pending its action, and such person shall thereupon forthwith be discharged by order of the court unless he is held on other process. Whoever is held in custody on a charge of crime shall be discharged if he is not indicted before the end of the second sitting of the court at which he is held to an-

swer, unless the court finds that the witnesses for the prosecution have been enticed or kept away, or are detained and prevented from attending the court by illness or accident, and except as provided in the following section.

SECTIONS 16–17
Repealed

SECTION 18
Circumstances of the act
The circumstances of the act may be stated according to their legal effect, without a full description thereof.

SECTION 19
Name of accused person; description by fictitious name; entry of true name
If the name of an accused person is unknown to the grand jury, he may be described by a fictitious name or by any other practicable description, with an allegation that his real name is unknown. An indictment of the defendant by a fictitious or erroneous name shall not be ground for abatement; but if at any subsequent stage of the proceedings his true name is discovered, it shall be entered on the record and may be used in the subsequent proceedings, with a reference to the fact that he was indicted by the name or description mentioned in the indictment.

SECTION 20
Time and place of commission of crime
The time and place of the commission of the crime need not be alleged unless it is an essential element thereof. The allegation of time in the caption shall, unless otherwise stated, be considered as an allegation that the act was committed before the finding of the indictment, after it became a crime, and within the period of limitations. The name of the county and court in the caption shall, unless otherwise stated, be considered as an allegation that the act was committed within the territorial jurisdiction of the court. All allegations of the indictment shall, unless otherwise stated, be considered to refer to the same time and place.

NOTE 1   "The difference of about eight months between the original date of the offense specified in the indictment and the amended date does [*not* change the substantive offense charged.] . . . The date . . . is not an essential element of the crime." *Commonwealth v. Gallo*, 2 Mass. App. Ct. 636, 639–40 (1974).

NOTE 2   "There was no error in the allowance of the Commonwealth's motion to amend the indictment to change the termination date of the alleged conspiracy from February 26, 1975, the date of the robbery, to March 11, 1975. The duration of the conspiracy was not an essential element of the crime. G.L. c. 277, §§ 20, 79. The amendment made no change of substance. The defendant was not prejudiced in his defense. See G.L. c. 277, § 35A." *Commonwealth v. Liebman*, 379 Mass. 671, 676 (1980) (citations omitted).

NOTE 3   The defendant alleged that "at the time of the alleged incidents, Paul [who was 15 years old] was a relatively mature teenager who lived with his own family and held a steady job and that he could be expected to note the dates of the alleged incidents with greater specificity than was evident from the indictments [which alleged the incidents occurred between January and April]."

The Commonwealth countered that the "Appeals Court [has] allowed relatively imprecise dates in indictments for the sexual molestation of young victims."

The SJC, bothered by this on due process, not statutory grounds (G.L. c. 277, § 20), ruled "it best to leave the issue . . . to the sound discretion of the trial judge."

Commonwealth v. Montanino, 409 Mass. 500, 511–13 (1991).

SECTION 21
Means

The means by which a crime is committed need not be alleged in the indictment unless an essential element of the crime.

NOTE 1   Robbery committed with a gun. Indictment alleged a knife. Held, conviction affirmed. "The particular type of weapon with which the armed robbery was committed was not an essential element of the crime." *Commonwealth v. Harris*, 9 Mass. App. Ct. 708, 712 (1980).

NOTE 2   Murder indictment described weapon as "a certain blunt object, the name and more particular description of which is to the jurors aforesaid unknown." Held, indictment sufficient, as it enables the defendant to understand the charge and to prepare his defense. Also, the defendant was free to file a bill of particulars. *Commonwealth v. Snell*, 189 Mass. 12, 18 (1905).

SECTION 22
Description of written instrument; variance

If an allegation relative to a written instrument consisting wholly or in part of writing, print or figures is necessary, it may describe such instrument by any name or designation by which it is usually known, or by the purport thereof, without setting out a copy or facsimile of the whole or of any part thereof; and no variance between such recital or description and the instrument produced at the trial shall be material, if the identity of the instrument is evident and the purport thereof is so described as not to prejudice the defendant.

NOTE   This section does *not* apply to criminal proceedings in the federal courts (in Massachusetts). *United States v. Phelan*, 250 F. 927 (D. Mass. 1917).

SECTION 23
Description of money

If an allegation relative to any bullion, money, notes, bank notes, checks, drafts, bills of exchange, obligations or other securities for money of any country, state, county, city, town, bank, corporation, partnership or person is necessary, it may describe it as money, without specifying any particulars thereof; and such descriptive allegation shall be sustained by proof of any amount of bullion, money, notes or other securities for money as aforesaid, although the particular nature thereof shall not be proved.

SECTION 24
Description of value or price

The value or price of property need not be stated, unless an essential element of the crime. If the nature, degree or punishment of a crime depends upon the fact that the property exceeds or does not exceed a certain value, it may be described, as the case may be, of more than that value, or of not more than that value.

NOTE   **Related Statute.**
G.L. c. 266, § 30—Larceny.
G.L. c. 266, § 60—Receiving stolen goods.

SECTION 25
Description of ownership

If an indictment for a crime involving the commission or attempted commission of an injury to property describes the property with sufficient certainty in other respects to identify the act, it need not allege the name of the owner.

NOTE   Indictment failed to allege owner of car defendant attempted to steal. Owner's name given to the defendant, however, via a bill of particulars. Defendant moved to quash due to defects in the indictment. Held, motion rightly denied. *Commonwealth v. Kozlowsky*, 238 Mass. 379, 383 (1921).

SECTION 26
Description of public place

If one element of the criminality of an act is its commission in a public place, and if such place is not more particularly defined in the statute, the act may be alleged generally to have been committed "in a public place".

SECTION 27
Description of animal

In an indictment for the larceny of an animal, or for any other crime in respect thereof, it may be described by the name by which it is commonly known, without stating its age or sex or whether it is alive or dead.

SECTION 28
Description of judicial proceedings

If it is necessary to set forth the judicial proceedings in any case then or formerly pending in any court, civil or military, or any proceedings before a justice of the peace or any other magistrate, only the substance of said proceedings or such part thereof as all constitute in whole or in part the crime charged need be alleged.

SECTION 29
Criminal responsibility

An allegation that the defendant committed the act charged shall be a sufficient allegation that he was criminally responsible therefor.

SECTION 30
Intent to injure or defraud; general allegation

If an intent to injure or defraud is an essential element of a crime, an intent to injure or defraud may be alleged generally, without naming the person, corporation or government intended to be injured or defrauded. Proof of an intent to injure or defraud any person or body corporate shall be competent to support the allegation.

SECTION 31
Alternative allegations

Different means or different intents by or with which a crime may be committed may be alleged in the same count in the alternative.

SECTION 32
Continuing offenses

An allegation that a crime was committed or that certain acts were done during a certain period of time next before the finding of the indictment shall be a sufficient allegation that the crime alleged was committed or that the acts alleged were done on divers days and times within that period.

SECTION 33
Unnecessary and immaterial allegations

Presumptions and conclusions of law, matters of which judicial notice is taken and allegations not required to be proved need not be alleged. An indictment shall not be considered defective or insufficient because it omits to allege that the crime was committed, or the act was done "traitorously", "feloniously", "burglariously", "wilfully", "maliciously", "negligently", "unlawfully" or otherwise similarly to describe the crime, unless such description is an element of the crime charged, or because it omits to allege that the crime was committed or done with "force and arms", or "against the peace", or against the form of the statute or statutes, or against a by-law, ordinance, order rule or regulation of any public authority, or because it omits to state or misstates the title, occupation, estate or degree of the defendant or of any other person named in the indictment, or of the name of the county, city, town or place of his residence, unless such omission or misstatement tends to the prejudice of the defendant, or by reason of describing a fine or forfeiture as enuring to the use of the commonwealth instead of the use of the county, city or town, or by reason of any misstatement as to the appropriation of any fine or forfeiture, or by reason of its failure to allege or recite a special statute or a by-law or ordinance of a city or town or order of the mayor and aldermen or selectmen or rules or regulations of any public board of officers.

SECTION 34
Immaterial defects

An indictment shall not be dismissed or be considered defective or insufficient if it is sufficient to enable the defendant to understand the charge and to prepare his defense; nor shall it be considered defective or insufficient for lack of any description or information which might be obtained by requiring a bill or particulars.

NOTE   "[I]f the defendant wished to question the sufficiency of the complaint because it was not framed in the language of one of the forms found in G.L. c. 277, § 79, or wished to be apprised of a particular felony intended to be committed [the defendant was charged with breaking and entering with intent to commit a felony], or believed that the complaint was deficient for failure to allege intent to commit a felony inside the building broken into, he should have availed himself of the remedy of a motion for a bill of particulars." *Commonwealth v. Wainio*, 1 Mass. App. Ct. 866, 867 (1974) (citation and parenthetic material omitted).

SECTION 35
Variance; prejudice

A defendant shall not be acquitted on the ground of variance between the allegations and proof if the essential elements of the crime are correctly stated, unless he is thereby prejudiced in his defense. He shall not be acquitted by reason of an immaterial misnomer of a third party, an immaterial mistake in the description of property or the ownership thereof, failure to prove unnecessary allegations in the description of the crime or any other immaterial mistake in the indictment.

NOTE   Indictment date read January 3, when it should have been December 31. Held, conviction affirmed as the variance was not material. *Commonwealth v. Soper*, 133 Mass. 393, 394 (1882).

SECTION 35A
Repealed

SECTION 36
Scope of word "oath"

The word "oath" as used in an indictment shall include an "affirmation".

SECTION 37
Negativing excuses, exceptions or provisos

An excuse, exception or proviso not stated in the enacting clause of a statute creating a crime or stated only by refer-

ence to other provisions of the statute need not be negatived in the indictment unless necessary for a complete definition of the crime. If any statute shall prescribe a form of indictment in which an excuse, exception or proviso is not negatived, it shall be taken that it is not necessary to a complete definition of the crime that they should be negatived. If a statute creating a crime permits an act, therein declared to be criminal, to be performed without criminality under stated conditions, such conditions need not be negatived.

SECTION 38
Allegations, bill of particulars, presumption and proof in prosecutions involving controlled substances

In a prosecution under any provision of chapter ninety-four C, for unlawfully manufacturing, dispensing or distributing a controlled substance in violation of any provision of said chapter, it shall be sufficient to allege that the defendant did unlawfully manufacture, dispense or distribute, as the case may be, such alleged substance, without any further allegations, without naming the person to whom it dispensed or distributed, or quantity of the substance; but the defendant shall be entitled to a bill of particulars. In such a prosecution, a defendant relying upon a prescription, written order, receipt, registration, appointment or authority, or exemption as a defense or justification shall prove the same, and until he has proved it the presumption shall be that he is not so justified or authorized.

NOTE   "The indictments did not have to allege in the words of [G.L. c. 94C], § 32 that the defendant 'knowingly or intentionally' dispensed a controlled substance unlawfully." *Commonwealth v. Comins*, 371 Mass. 222, 224–25 (1976).

SECTION 39
Construction of words used in indictment

The words used in an indictment may, except as otherwise provided in this section, be construed according to their usual acceptation in common language; but if certain words and phrases are defined by law, they shall be used according to their legal meaning.

The following words, when used in an indictment, shall be sufficient to convey the meaning herein attached to them:

Adultery.—Sexual intercourse by a married person with a person not his spouse or by an unmarried person with a married person.

Affray.—Fighting together of two or more persons in a public place to the terror of the persons lawfully there.

Aggravated Rape.—Sexual intercourse or unnatural sexual intercourse by a person with another person who is compelled to submit by force and against his will or by threat of bodily injury; and either such sexual intercourse or unnatural sexual intercourse results in or is committed with acts resulting in serious bodily injury, or is committed by a joint enterprise, or is committed during the commission or attempted commission of an offense defined in section fifteen A, fifteen B, seventeen, nineteen or twenty-six of chapter two hundred and sixty-five, section fourteen, fifteen, sixteen, seventeen or eighteen of chapter two hundred and sixty-six, or section ten of chapter two hundred and sixty-nine.

False Pretenses.—False representations made by word or act of such a character, or made under such circumstances and in such a way, with the intention of influencing the action of another, as to be punishable.

2

Forgery.—The false making, altering, forging or counterfeiting of any instrument described in section one of chapter two hundred and sixty-seven, or any instrument which, if genuine, would be a foundation for or release of liability of the apparent maker.

Fornication.—Sexual intercourse between an unmarried male and an unmarried female.

Murder.—The killing of a human being, with malice aforethought.

Rape.—Sexual intercourse or unnatural sexual intercourse by a person with another person who is compelled to submit by force and against his will or by threat of bodily injury, or sexual intercourse or unnatural sexual intercourse with a child under sixteen years of age.

Robbery.—The taking and carrying away of personal property of another from his person and against his will, by force and violence, or by assault and putting in fear, with intent to steal.

Stealing. Larceny.—The criminal taking, obtaining or converting of personal property, with intent to defraud or deprive the owner permanently of the use of it; including all forms of larceny, criminal embezzlement and obtaining by criminal false pretenses.

NOTE 1   Affray. "We discern nothing in the legislative definition of 'affray' that requires the 'fighting together of two or more person' be by agreement or design of all the participants, including those who may be set upon. Rather, it is also sufficient that the 'fighting together' be by agreement of two or more individuals who undertake to set upon others. No less now than historically, affray is an injury to the public peace rather than to parties engaged in the fighting, and so long as two or more persons are engaged in the same combat, whether they are fighting on the same or opposing sides is immaterial to the terror caused to the public. The promiscuous attack by the defendant and his group upon Monaco, Pitt, and Marks satisfies the 'fighting together of two or more persons' element.

"We reject the defendant's contention that Monaco, Marks, and Pitt were not 'lawfully present' in the park because they followed the group intending to extract revenge for the earlier assault upon Monaco. The defendant mistakenly conflates the lawfulness of Monaco's, Marks's, and Pitt's presence with the alleged unlawfulness of their purpose. 'Lawfully present' for purposes of affray encompasses the lawful right to be present in the public place, not the purposes of those lawfully present there. It was undisputed that Monaco, Pitt, and Marks were lawfully in a public park, and nothing in the evidence raised a reasonable doubt as to the lawfulness of their presence on that evening." *Commonwealth v. Nee*, 83 Mass. App. Ct. 441, 446-47 (2013) (citations and footnotes omitted).

NOTE 2   Sex Offender Registry. A conviction or adjudication of delinquency of an offense of aggravated rape or of an attempt to commit such an offense (*see* G.L. c. 274, § 6) renders the defendant subject to the requirements of the sex offender registry law. *See* G.L. c. 6, §§ 178C–178Q.

SECTION 40
Repealed

SECTION 41
Indictment for criminal dealing with personal property

In an indictment for criminal dealing with personal property with intent to steal, an allegation that the defendant stole said property shall be sufficient; and such indictment may be supported by proof that the defendant committed larceny of the property, or embezzled it, or obtained it by false pretenses.

NOTE   "The effect of this statute . . . is to put it beyond a doubt that the former crimes of larceny, embezzlement, and the obtaining of property by false pretenses, are now merged into the one crime of larceny . . . . [T]he crime of larceny . . . may be proved by evidence which would have warranted a conviction upon any one of the three charges that formerly would have been needed. . . . This legislation was intended to do away with the possibility of a criminal indicted for one of the three crimes mentioned escaping punishment by reason of its being afterwards found that his crime was technically one of the other two." The Commonwealth may not be required to elect among the three. *Commonwealth v. Corcoran*, 348 Mass. 437, 440–41 (1965) (quoting *Commonwealth v. King*, 202 Mass. 379, 387–89 (1909)).

SECTION 42
Prosecutions for buying, receiving or aiding in concealment of stolen property

In prosecutions for buying, receiving or aiding in the concealment of stolen property known to have been stolen, it shall not be necessary to allege or prove that the person who stole the property has been convicted.

NOTE   Receiving stolen goods—G.L. c. 266, § 60; Receiving stolen motor vehicle—G.L. c. 266, § 28.

SECTION 43
Indictment for perjury

In an indictment for perjury alleged to have been committed in a criminal case an allegation of the substance of the crime shall be sufficient; if alleged to have been committed in a civil case, an allegation of the nature of the controversy in general terms shall be sufficient. In both cases, the court or magistrate before whom the oath or affirmation was taken shall be alleged, but no part of the proceeding in which, or the commission or authority of the court or person before whom, the perjury was committed need be alleged.

SECTION 44
Indictment for subornation of perjury

If, in an indictment for subornation of perjury or for attempting to incite or procure another person to commit perjury, it is alleged that perjury has been committed, an allegation of perjury as provided in the preceding section and an allegation that the defendant wilfully incited or procured said person to commit said perjury shall be sufficient. If it is not alleged that such perjury has been committed, an allegation of the substance of the crime with which the defendant is charged shall be sufficient, without allegations as to matters or things which by the preceding section are declared to be unnecessary.

SECTION 45
Indictment for unnatural and lascivious acts

In an indictment under section thirty-five of chapter two hundred and seventy-two, an allegation that the defendant committed an unnatural and lascivious act with the person named or referred to in the indictment shall be sufficient.

SECTION 46
Repealed

PROCEEDINGS UPON ARRAIGNMENT IN CAPITAL CASES

SECTION 47
Arraignment; sentence; assignment of counsel

If a prisoner, under indictment for a capital crime, pleads guilty, upon being arraigned, the court shall award sentence against him; if he does not plead guilty, the court may assign him counsel and take all other measures preparatory to a trial, which shall, subject to the Massachusetts Rules of Criminal Procedure, be held as soon after the finding of the indictment as the other official duties of the justices will admit and the circumstances of the case require.

PLEADINGS AND MOTIONS BEFORE TRIAL

SECTION 47A
Defenses or objections

In a criminal case, any defense or objection based upon defects in the institution of the prosecution or in the complaint or indictment, other than a failure to show jurisdiction in the court or to charge an offense, shall only be raised prior to trial and only by a motion in conformity with the requirements of the Massachusetts Rules of Criminal Procedure. The failure to raise any such defense or objection by motion prior to trial shall constitute a waiver thereof, but a judge or special magistrate may, for cause shown, grant relief from such waiver. A defense or objection based upon a failure to show jurisdiction in the court or the failure to charge an offense may be raised by motion to dismiss prior to trial, but shall be noticed by the court at any time.

SECTIONS 48–52
Repealed

SECTION 53
District attorneys; authority and duty as to transferred cases

If a case is transferred for plea or trial and sentence pursuant to the Massachusetts Rules of Criminal Procedure, the district attorney for the county to which the case is transferred or the district attorney for the county from which the case is transferred shall have the same authority and duty in the case as if it had not been transferred, depending upon which of the district attorneys is to try the case.

SECTION 54
Custody and delivery of prisoner

If a change of venue is ordered, the sheriff having custody of the prisoner shall forthwith deliver him to the sheriff of the county to which the venue has been changed, who shall receive and safely keep him as if the indictment had been found in such county.

SECTION 55
Compensation of counsel of prisoner

A justice of the court, sitting at the trial or other proceedings upon an indictment for murder, may allow reasonable compensation for the services of counsel assigned to defend the prisoner if he is otherwise unable to procure counsel, and such compensation shall be paid by the county where the indictment is found.

SECTION 56
Expenses of counsel of prisoner

The reasonable expenses incurred and paid by counsel assigned by the court for the defense of a person indicted for murder, who is otherwise unable to procure counsel, shall be paid by the commonwealth after approval by a justice sitting at the trial or other proceedings of the case.

VENUE OF SPECIFIC CRIMES

SECTION 57
Prosecutions of crimes committed near boundary line of counties, etc.; crimes committed on sea

A crime committed on or within one hundred rods of the boundary line of two counties may be alleged to have been committed, and may be prosecuted and punished, in either county; and if committed on or within fifty rods of the boundary line of two judicial districts, it may be alleged to have been committed, and may be prosecuted and punished, in either district. A crime committed upon the sea within one league of the shore may be prosecuted and punished in an adjacent county.

SECTION 57A
Venue in cases where crime was committed without county or territorial jurisdiction of court

A defendant shall not be discharged for want of jurisdiction if the evidence discloses that the crime with which he is charged was actually committed without the county or the territorial jurisdiction of the court in which he is being tried; provided, that the attorney general or the district attorney petitions to the court before proceeding with the trial for leave to proceed, stating that he is in doubt from the state of the evidence then in his possession as to whether or not the crime was committed within the county or the territorial jurisdiction of the court, and the court after hearing said petition orders the trial to proceed.

SECTION 58
Larceny

Larceny, whether at common law or as defined by section thirty of chapter two hundred and sixty-six, may be prosecuted and punished in any county where the defendant had possession of the property alleged to have been stolen.

SECTION 58A
Buying, receiving, concealing or aiding in concealment of stolen or embezzled property

The crime of buying, receiving or concealing a stolen motor vehicle or trailer, as defined in section twenty-eight of chapter two hundred and sixty-six, and the crime of buying, receiving or aiding in the concealment of stolen or embezzled property, as defined in section sixty of said chapter two hundred and sixty-six, may be prosecuted and punished in the same jurisdiction in which the larceny or embezzlement of any property involved in the crime may be prosecuted and punished.

SECTION 58A½
Crimes involving electronically processed or stored data; place of prosecution

The crimes described in sections thirty-three A and one hundred and twenty F of chapter two hundred and sixty-six and section one hundred and twenty-seven of said chapter two hundred and sixty-six when the personal property involved is electronically processed or stored data, either tangible or intangible, and data while in transit, may be prosecuted and punished in any county where the defendant was physically located at the time of the violation, or where the electronic data was physically located at the time of the violation.

2

SECTION 58B
Embezzlement or fraudulent conversion or appropriation by fiduciaries

The crime of embezzlement or fraudulent conversion or appropriation by a fiduciary of money, goods or property held or possessed by him, as set forth in section fifty-seven of chapter two hundred and sixty-six, including the fraudulent disposition or destruction of such property, may be prosecuted and punished in the county wherein is located the probate court which appointed the fiduciary or in any county where the deed or other instrument in writing creating the trust under which he served or acted was recorded or in any county where he had held or possessed the property as aforesaid after embezzling or fraudulently converting or appropriating the same, as well as in any county where he committed the act of embezzlement or fraudulent conversion or appropriation or other fraudulent disposition or destruction of property held or possessed by him as aforesaid.

SECTION 59
Obtaining money or personal chattel by false pretenses

The crime of obtaining money or a personal chattel by a false pretence, and the crime described in section thirty-one of chapter two hundred and sixty-six, may be alleged to have been committed, and may be prosecuted and punished, in any county where the false pretence was made, written or used, or in or through which any of the property obtained was carried, sent, transported or received by the defendant.

SECTION 59A
Transmission of false reports, location of explosives, etc.

The crime described in section fourteen of chapter two hundred and sixty-nine may be prosecuted and punished in the territorial jurisdiction in which the communication originates or is received.

SECTION 60
Homicide if injury is in one county and death in another

If a mortal wound is given, or if other violence or injury is inflicted, or if poison is administered, in one county, by means whereof death ensues in another county, the homicide may be prosecuted and punished in either county.

SECTION 61
Crime committed at sea, etc., resulting in death in county

If a mortal wound is given, or if other violence or injury is inflicted, or if poison is administered, on the high seas or on land either within or without the commonwealth, by means whereof death ensues in any county thereof, the homicide may be prosecuted and punished in the county where the death happens.

SECTION 62
Crime committed in commonwealth resulting in death outside commonwealth

If a mortal wound is given, or if other violence or injury is inflicted, or if poison is administered, in any county of the commonwealth, by means whereof death ensues without the commonwealth, the homicide may be prosecuted and punished in the county where the act was committed.

NOTE   "Section 62 makes clear that jurisdiction may exist here if a death ensued elsewhere because of non-mortal violence or injury inflicted in Massachusetts. Thus § 62 prescribes that the causal connection between the violence or injury and the death need not be immediate, direct, or proximate. The key words in § 62 for our purposes are 'by means whereof death ensues.' They cannot fairly be interpreted simply to mean 'follows' in a chronological sense . . . the death must be one that would not have occurred but for the violence or injury that was inflicted in Massachusetts." *Commonwealth v. Lent*, 420 Mass. 764, 768 (1995).

SECTION 62A
Jurisdiction for criminal violations of chapter 209A

Any criminal violation of chapter two hundred and nine A may be prosecuted and punished in the territorial jurisdiction in which the violation was committed or in which the original order under said chapter two hundred and nine A was issued.

SECTION 62B
Jurisdiction for stalking

The crime of stalking, as set forth in section forty-three of chapter two hundred and sixty-five, may be prosecuted and punished in any territorial jurisdiction of the commonwealth wherein an act constituting an element of the crime was committed.

SECTION 62C
Jurisdiction over violations of Sec. 35A of chapter 266

A violation of section 35A of chapter 266 may be prosecuted and punished in:

(1) the county in which the residential property for which a mortgage loan is being sought is located;

(2) the county in which any act was performed in furtherance of the violation;

(3) the county in which any person alleged to have violated this section had control or possession of any proceeds of, or other funds received as a result of the violation;

(4) the county in which a closing on the mortgage loan occurred; or

(5) the county in which a document containing a deliberate misstatement, misrepresentation or omission is filed with a registrar of deeds.

LIMITATIONS OF CRIMINAL PROSECUTIONS

SECTION 63
Limitations of criminal proceedings; general provisions
(Amended by 2011 Mass. Acts c. 178, §§ 27–29, effective Nov. 21, 2011.)

An indictment for murder may be found at any time after the death of the person alleged to have been murdered. An indictment or complaint for an offense set forth in section 13B, 13B½, 13B¾, 13F, 13L, 22A, 22B, 22C, 23, 23A, 23B, 24B or subsection (b) of section 50 of chapter 265, for conspiracy to commit any of these offenses, as an accessory thereto, or any 1 or more of them may be found and filed at any time after the date of the commission of such offense; but any indictment or complaint found and filed more than 27 years after the date of commission of such offense shall be supported by independent evidence that corroborates the victim's allegation. Such independent evidence shall be admissible during trial and shall not consist exclusively of the opinions of mental health professionals. An indictment for an offense set forth in sections 22, 24 or subsection (a) of section 50 of chapter 265, or for conspiracy to commit either of these offenses or as an accessory thereto or any 1 or more of them may be found and filed within 15 years of the date of commission of such offense. An indictment for an offense set forth in sections 17, 18, 19 and 21 of said chapter 265 or section 17 of chapter 272, for conspiracy to commit any such crime, as an accessory thereto, or any 1 or more of them may be found and filed within 10 years after the date of commission of such offense. An indictment for any other crime shall be found and filed within 6 years after such crime has been committed. Any period during which the defendant is not usually and publicly a resident within the commonwealth shall be excluded in determining the time limited.

Notwithstanding the first paragraph, if a victim of a crime set forth in section 13B, 13F, 13H, 22, 22A, 23, 24B, 26A or 50 of chapter 265, or section 1, 2, 3, 4, 4A, 4B, 5, 6, 7, 8, 12, 13, 17, 26, 28, 29A, 29B, 33, 34, 35 or 35A of chapter 272 is under the age of 16 at the time the crime is committed, the period of limitation for prosecution shall not commence until the victim has reached the age of 16 or the violation is reported to a law enforcement agency, whichever occurs earlier.

NOTE 1   "The defendant moved to dismiss the indictments, arguing that the statute of limitations had run and that a subsequent amendment extending the statutory period did not apply retroactively to the charges. . . .

"[G.L. c. 277, § 63] imposed a six-year limitation period for violations of G.L. c. 265, § 23 . . . G.L. c. 277, § 63, however, was amended . . . which extended the limitation period to ten years. . . .

"Thus, the statute of limitations was extended by an amendment more than seven months *after* the indictments were time-barred under the then effective statute of limitations. The indictments cannot stand."

Commonwealth v. Rocheleau, 404 Mass. 129, 129–30 (1989) (footnote omitted).

NOTE 2   "Assault with intent to rape is one of the many crimes governed by the statute of limitations set forth in G.L. c. 277, § 63 (1986 ed.). On the dates of the alleged offenses, § 63 provided a six-year period of limitations. However, in July, 1985, by force of St. 1985, c. 123, § 63 was amended, effective September 30, 1985, and the period of limitations for these crimes was extended from six years to ten years. This amendment became effective on September 30, 1985, a date within six years of the alleged commission of the crimes. To contest the vitality of the indictment and the applicability of the amendment of § 63 to the indictment, the defendant filed a motion to dismiss." *Commonwealth v. Bargeron*, 402 Mass. 589, 590 (1998).

The Supreme Judicial Court held that "there is no constitutional or statutory barrier to the application of the amendment to § 63 to this indictment and the motion to dismiss should be denied."

Commonwealth v. Bargeron, 402 Mass. at 594. *See also Commonwealth v. Pellegrino*, 402 Mass. 1003 (1988) (rescript).

NOTE 3   DNA Indictment. "We conclude that the criminal prosecution of the defendant . . . is not time barred. In reaching this conclusion, we hold that: (1) the description of 'John Doe' in the indictment, primarily consisting of his genetic identity, comported with the particularity requirements of art. 12 of the Declaration of Rights of the Massachusetts Constitution; and (2) the return of such an indictment tolled the fifteen-year statute of limitations for aggravated rape and rape as set out in G.L. c. 277, § 63." *Commonwealth v. Dixon*, 458 Mass. 446, 447 (2010).

NOTE 4   Tolling. "This case requires us to decide whether the filing of a criminal complaint tolls the statute of limitations set forth in G.L. c. 277, § 63, which states that '[a]n indictment for [armed robbery under G.L. c. 265, § 17] . . . may be found and filed within [ten] years after the date of commission of such offense.' We conclude that § 63 requires the filing of an indictment within the ten-year limitations period for armed robbery, G.L. c. 265, § 17, and that the filing of a complaint within the limitations period, and the return of an indictment outside of that period, does

not constitute timely commencement of the criminal proceeding." *Commonwealth v. Perella*, 464 Mass. 274, 274–75 (2013).

NOTE 5   Affirmative Defense. "Massachusetts treats the statute of limitations as an affirmative defense that is waived if not raised." *Commonwealth v. Bougas*, 59 Mass. App. Ct. 368, 372 (2003) (citing *Commonwealth v. Steinberg*, 404 Mass. 602, 606 (1989); *Commonwealth v. Barrett*, 418 Mass. 788, 792 (1994)) (other citations omitted).

NOTE 6   Ineffective Assistance of Counsel. Failure of trial counsel to move to dismiss twelve indictments charging indecent assault and battery on a child under 14, which were time barred was ineffective assistance of counsel. *Commonwealth v. Barrett*, 418 Mass. 788 (1994).

SECTION 64
Limitation of new indictment against corporation after abatement or defeat of former indictment

If an indictment, duly found and returned within the time limited by law against a corporation to recover a pecuniary penalty, is abated or otherwise avoided or defeated by reason of any matter of form, or if after a verdict against such corporation judgment is arrested, or if a judgment against such corporation is reversed on writ of error, a new indictment for the same cause may be found and filed within one year after the abatement of the former indictment of the reversal of the judgment as aforesaid.

ARREST, ARRAIGNMENT AND OTHER PROCEEDINGS

SECTION 65
Service of copy of indictment for murder on prisoner, etc.

After the finding of an indictment for murder, the defendant, if in custody, shall forthwith be served by the sheriff or his deputy with a copy thereof and with an order of the court notifying him that the indictment will be entered forthwith upon the docket of the superior court for the county where found.

SECTION 66
List of jurors to prisoner; process for witnesses

A prisoner indicted for a crime punishable with death or imprisonment for life, upon demand by him or his counsel upon the clerk, shall have a list of the jurors who have been returned and process to summon witnesses who are necessary to his defense, at the expense of the commonwealth.

SECTION 67
Furnishing person in custody, etc., with copy of indictment

Whoever, having been indicted for felony, is under recognizance or in custody to answer therefor shall be entitled to a copy of the indictment and of all endorsements thereon without charge.

SECTION 68
Issuance of subpoenas by attorney general and district attorneys

The attorney general and district attorneys may issue subpoenas under their hands for witnesses to appear and testify on behalf of the commonwealth, and such subpoenas shall have the same force, and be obeyed in the same manner, and under the same penalties, in case of default, as if issued by the clerk of the court.

2

NOTE 1   While it was improper for the prosecutor to subpoena in a witness on a nontrial day and question her, this does *not* warrant reversal of the defendant's conviction. *Commonwealth v. Smallwood*, 379 Mass. 878, 887–88 (1980).

NOTE 2   "We consider whether the Commonwealth, in a criminal case, may seek the production of records from a third party in advance of trial or an evidentiary hearing by issuing a subpoena duces tecum directly to the party under G.L. c. 277, § 68, or whether it must first obtain judicial approval, pursuant to Mass. R. Crim. P. 17 (a) (2), as construed by *Commonwealth v. Lampron*, 441 Mass. 265, 268–71 (2004). We conclude that it must first obtain judicial approval." *Commonwealth v. Odgren*, 455 Mass. 171, 172 (2009) (citation omitted).

SECTION 69
Repealed

SECTION 70
Recognizance of witnesses

A justice of a court of record may at any time order a witness for the commonwealth in a criminal case or in a case under sections fifty-two to sixty-four, inclusive, of chapter one hundred and nineteen, pending in such court to recognize, with or without sureties, to appear and testify at the next or any succeeding sitting of said court, and may issue a warrant to bring such witness before him to recognize as aforesaid; but a witness unable to procure sureties shall not on that account be committed to jail except in cases of felony.

SECTION 70A
Repealed

SECTION 70B
Placing cases on file; statement of reasons

Except as otherwise provided by law, a criminal case shall not be placed on file, on motion of a district attorney or assistant district attorney, unless such motion is accompanied by a written statement of the reasons for such disposition, signed by the district attorney or assistant district attorney, which shall be filed with the pleadings, and also accompanied by a statement of any previous criminal record of the accused.

SECTION 70C
Treating criminal offenses as civil infractions

Upon oral motion by the commonwealth or the defendant at arraignment or pretrial conference, or upon the court's own motion at any time, the court may, unless the commonwealth objects, in writing, stating the reasons for such objection, treat a violation of a municipal ordinance, or by-law or a misdemeanor offense as a civil infraction. The provisions of this section shall not apply to the offenses in sections 22F, 24, 24D, 24G, 24L, and 24N of chapter 90, sections 8, 8A, and 8B of chapter 90B, chapter 119, chapter 119A, chapter 209, chapter 209A, chapter 265, sections 1, 2, 3, 6, 6A, 6B, 8B, 13, 13A, 13B, 13B½, 13B¾, 13C, 14, 14B, 15, 15A, 16, 17, 18, 19, 20, 22A, 22B, 22C, 23, 23A, 23B, 28, 31 and 36 of chapter 268, chapter 268A, sections 10, 10A, 10C, 10D, 10E, 11B, 11C, 11E, 12, 12A, 12B, 12D and 12E of chapter 269 and sections 1, 2, 3, 4, 4A, 4B, 6, 7, 8, 12, 13, 16, 28, 29A and 29B of chapter 272. If a motion to proceed civilly is allowed, the court shall not appoint counsel. If counsel has already been appointed, the court shall revoke the appointment. A person complained of for such civil infraction shall be adjudicated responsible upon such finding by the court and shall not be sentenced to any term of incarceration. The common-

wealth shall maintain a copy of all objections filed under this section and shall report the number of such objections, delineated by divisions of the district court, every 6 months to the house and senate committees on ways and means.

When the court has treated a violation of a municipal ordinance or by-law or a misdemeanor offense as a civil infraction under this section and the ordinance, by-law or misdemeanor in question does not set forth a civil fine as a possible penalty, the court may impose a fine of not more than $5,000. An adjudication of responsibility shall neither be used in the calculation of second and subsequent offenses under any chapter, nor as the basis for the revocation of parole or of a probation surrender. An adjudication of responsibility under this section may include an order of restitution.

SECTIONS 71–72A
Repealed

SECTION 73
Compensation for confinement of persons discharged

Any person in the commonwealth kept in confinement awaiting trial for more than six months after having been indicted, and finally acquitted or discharged without trial, if the delay in trial was not at his request or with his consent, or at the request or with the consent of his attorney of record, may receive compensation for the period of his confinement after the lapse of said six months and until his acquittal or discharge; provided, that the payment of compensation is approved by the justice who presided at the trial, or in the case of a discharge without trial, by a justice of the superior court sitting at a session for criminal business in and for the county where the indictment was found. Such compensation shall be paid by the commonwealth and shall be equivalent to the amount which the indicted person earned or received from his regular employment for any period of equal length during the two years immediately preceding his confinement; and if he had no employment, the compensation shall be such reasonable sum as shall be determined by the justice who presided at the trial, or, in the case of a discharge without trial, by a justice of the superior court sitting at a session for criminal business in and for the county where the indictment was found. The justice, upon application by the person acquitted or discharged shall give a hearing at which such person or his representative may be present, if he so desires, and the district attorney or other officer representing the commonwealth may also be present, and the person acquitted or discharged and the commonwealth may offer testimony as in any civil case. The decision of the justice shall be final.

NOTE   "The sole issue on appeal is whether the defendant is entitled to compensation pursuant to G.L. c. 277, § 73, because the charges against him were dismissed pursuant to Mass.R. Crim.P. 36 . . . "

In this case, the Supreme Judicial Court ruled against the defendant. "A defendant's failure to object to delay and failure to press for trial constitutes implied consent to delay and bars recovery under § 73."

Commonwealth v. Bunting, 401 Mass. 687, 687–88, 690 (1988) (citations and footnotes omitted).

SECTIONS 74–77
Repealed

SECTION 78
Criminal proceedings as no bar to civil action

No proceedings against a person for a crime shall bar a civil action which might otherwise be maintained by a person aggrieved by the commission of the crime.

SECTION 79
Application of annexed forms; schedule

The provisions of this chapter, and the forms hereto annexed, shall apply as well to complaints as to indictments, and such forms shall be sufficient in cases to which they are applicable. In other cases, forms as nearly like the forms hereto annexed as the nature of the cases and the provisions of law will allow may be used; but any other form of indictment or complaint authorized by law may be used.

SCHEDULE OF FORMS
OF PLEADINGS

CAPTION AND COMMENCEMENT OF INDICTMENT

COMMONWEALTH OF
MASSACHUSETTS

(Suffolk,) to wit:

At the Superior Court holden at (Boston,) within and for the County of (Suffolk,) for the transaction of criminal business, on the _____ day of _____ in the year of our Lord one thousand, etc.

The jurors for the said Commonwealth on their oath present CAPTION AND COMMENCEMENT OF COMPLAINT (To a Police, District or Municipal Court) COMMONWEALTH OF MASSACHUSETTS

(Suffolk,) to wit:

To the _____ court of _____ holden at _____ for the transaction of criminal business, within the County of _____, A.B. of _____ in behalf of the Commonwealth of Massachusetts on the _____ day of _____ in the year _____, on oath complains that

(TO A TRIAL JUSTICE)

To A.B., a Trial Justice in and for the County of _____ and Commonwealth of Massachusetts, C. D. of _____ (etc. as in form above).

(To a Justice of the Peace commissioned to issue Warrants)

To A.B., Justice of the Peace in and for the County of _____ and Commonwealth of Massachusetts, designated and commissioned to issue warrants in criminal cases, C.D. of _____ (etc. as in form above.)

(If the statute requires a particular person to make complaint, this should be alleged.)

Abduction. (Under Chap. 272, §§ 1, 2.)

(1) That A.B. did fraudulently and deceitfully entice (and take away) one C.D., an unmarried person under the age of sixteen years, from the house of the father (*or* guardian, etc., as the case may be), without the consent of the said father (*or* guardian, etc., as the case may be), under whose care and custody said C.D. was living, for the purpose of effecting a clandestine marriage of said C.D. without the consent of said father (*or* guardian, etc., as the case may be).

(2) That A.B. did fraudulently and deceitfully entice (and take away) C.D. from his house (or, if a minor, from his father's or guardian's house; or if elsewhere, state it as the case may be), for the unlawful purpose of prostitution (or for the purpose of unlawful sexual intercourse).

Abortion. (Under Chap. 272, § 19.)

(1) That A.B., with intent to procure the miscarriage of C.D., did unlawfully administer to her (*or* advise, *or* prescribe for her, *or* cause to be taken by her) a certain drug (*or* medicine or other noxious thing, as the case may be).

If the woman dies, add "and in consequence thereof said C. D. died".

(2) That A.B., with intent to procure the miscarriage of C.D., did unlawfully use a certain instrument upon the body of said C.D., and in consequence thereof said C.D. died.

(3) That A.B., with intent to procure the miscarriage of C.D., did unlawfully do certain things (*naming them*) to (*or* upon the body of) said C.D.

Accessory before the fact. (Under Chap. 274, § 2.)

Charge principal felony and proceed: That A.B., before the said felony was committed, did incite, procure, aid, counsel, hire or command the said (principal) the said felony to do and commit.

Accessory after the fact. (Under Chap. 274 § 4.)

Charge principal felony and proceed: That A.B. afterwards, well knowing the said C.D. to have committed the felony aforesaid, did harbor, (conceal, maintain,) or assist said C.D., with intent that said C.D. should avoid or escape (detention, arrest,) trial, or punishment.

Adultery. (Under Chap. 272 § 14.)

(1) That A.B., a married person, did commit adultery with C.D., a person not his spouse.

(2) That A.B., an unmarried person, did commit adultery with C.D., a married person.

Affray. [See G.L. c. 279, § 5]

That A.B. and C.D. did make an affray.

Aggravated rape. (Under Chap. 265, § 22(a))

That A.B. did assault C.D., with intent to commit aggravated rape; and did commit aggravated rape upon said C.D.

Alcoholic beverages. (Under Chap. 138, § 2.)

That A.C. did expose and keep for sale alcoholic beverages, as defined in section one of chapter one hundred and thirty-eight, with intent unlawfully to sell the same.

Alcoholic beverages—Sale. (Under Chap. 138, § 2.)

That A.B. unlawfully did sell alcoholic beverages, as defined in section one of chapter one hundred and thirty-eight, to C.C.

Alcoholic beverages—Nuisance. (Under Chap. 139, § 15.)

That A.B., during the three months next before the finding of this indictment, without legal authority, did keep and maintain a certain tenement in said (Boston), by him used for the illegal sale and illegal keeping for sale of alcoholic beverages, as defined in section one of chapter one hundred and thirty-eight, to the common nuisance of all the people.

Armed with dangerous weapon when arrested.

(Under Chap. 269, § 9.)

(1) That A.B., while being lawfully arrested on a sufficient warrant on a criminal charge, was armed with a dangerous weapon, to wit, a slung shot (or other dangerous weapon, as the case may be).

2

(2) That A.B., while committing the crime of (*here state crime*), was lawfully arrested by C.D., sheriff of said county, and when so arrested was armed with, and had on his person, a certain dangerous weapon (a slung shot, etc., as the case may be).

Arson. (Under Chap. 266, §§ 1, 2, 4.)

(1) That A.B. wilfully and maliciously did burn the dwelling house of C.D. in _____ in said county.

(2) That A.B. wilfully and maliciously did burn a building adjoining the dwelling house of C.D. in _____ in said county.

(3) That A.B. wilfully and maliciously did set fire to a building in _____ by the burning whereof the dwelling house of C.D. was burned.

(4) That A.B. wilfully and maliciously, in the night time, did burn

(a) A meeting house (*or* church, town house, etc.) in _____ in said county, erected for public use.

(b) A banking house (*or* warehouse, etc.) of C.D. in _____ in said county, of the value, with the property therein, of one thousand dollars and not the property of (the defendant).

(c) A barn (*or stable or* shop *or* office) of C.D., in _____ in said county, the same being there within the curtilage of the dwelling house of said C.D.

(5) That A.B. wilfully and maliciously did burn a building, by the burning whereof [(a) (b), *or* (c)] was burned in the night time.

(6) That A.B. wilfully and maliciously did burn a banking house (*or other structure mentioned in the statute, as the case may be*) of C.D., in _____ in said county.

Assault and battery.

That A.B. did assault and beat C.D.

Assault to maim, etc., (Under Chap. 265, § 15.)

That A.B. did assault C.D., with the malicious intent to maim (*or* disfigure) said C.D. by cutting out his tongue (*or other facts required by the nature of the case*).

Assault to murder. (Under Chap. 265, § 15.)

That A.B. did assault C.D., with intent to murder him.

Assault to rape. (Under Chap. 265, § 24.)

(1) That A.B. did assault C.D., with intent to commit rape.

(2) That A.B. did assault C.D., a child under the age of sixteen years, with intent unlawfully and carnally to know and abuse.

Assault with dangerous weapon, with intent to rob, etc. (Under Chap. 265, § 18.)

That A.B., being armed with a dangerous weapon, did assault C.D., with intent to rob him (*or* to murder him).

Assault upon an officer.

That A.B. did assault and beat C.D., who was a police officer of the (city of Boston) (*or whatever the fact may be*), and who was also in the lawful discharge of his duties as such officer, as said (defendant) well knew, (and knowingly resisted and obstructed him in the discharge of his lawful duties). *This clause may be added if facts require.*

Assuming to be an officer. (Under Chap. 268, § 33.)

That A.B. did falsely assume and pretend to one C.D. that he, said A.B., was a police officer of (the city of _____) (*or* a constable of the city of _____), and did take upon himself to act as such officer, and did (*state what he did if desired.*)

Attempt to break and enter. (Under Chap. 274, § 6.)

That A.B. did attempt to break and enter a certain building in said (Boston) of one C.D., in the (night) time, with intent

therein to commit larceny, and in such attempt did (*set out the overt act relied on*); but did fail in the perpetration of said attempted offense (*or* was intercepted and prevented in the execution of said attempted offense).

Attempt to commit crime. (Under Chap. 274, § 6.)

That A.B. did attempt to commit larceny of the property of (another), (*or such other crime as may be intended to be charged*), and in such attempt did (set out the overt act relied on); but did fail in the perpetration of said attempted offense (*or* was intercepted and prevented in the execution of said attempted offense).

Attempt to steal from person. (Under Chap. 274, § 6.)

That A.B. did attempt to steal from the person of C.D., and in such attempt did put his hand against the person and into the pocket of the said C.D.; but did fail in the perpetration of said attempted offense (*or* was intercepted and prevented in the execution of said attempted offense).

Breaking, entering, etc. (Under Chap. 266, §§ 16–19.)

(1) That A.B. did break and enter in the night time the building (*or* ship or vessel) of one X., situated in said (Boston), with intent therein to commit murder (*or* rape, robbery, etc.).

(2) That A.B. did break and enter (*or* entered in the night time without breaking) a building (*or* ship or vessel) of one X., in said (Boston), with intent (*as above*), the said X. (*or other person*), who was lawfully therein, being put in fear.

(3) That A.B. did break and enter (*or* entered in the night time without breaking) a railroad car situated in said (Boston), of the (*name of the railroad*), with intent therein to commit larceny (*or* murder, etc., as the case may be).

(4) That A.B. did enter in the night time the dwelling house of one X., in said (Boston), with intent therein to commit larceny (*or* murder, etc., as the case may be).

(5) That A.B. did break and enter a building (*or* ship or vessel) of one X., in said (Boston), with intent therein (*etc. as above*).

Breaking glass. (Under Chap. 266, § 114.)

That A.B. did wantonly (*or* maliciously) break certain panes of glass in and part of a certain building, the property of C.D. in said (Boston).

Burglarious implements. (Under Chap. 266, § 49.)

That A.B. knowingly did have in his possession certain machines, tools and implements adapted and designed for cutting through, forcing and breaking open buildings, rooms, vaults, safes (and other depositories), in order to steal therefrom such money and other property as might be found therein, said A.B. knowing said machines, tools and implements to be adapted and designed for the purpose aforesaid, and intending to use and employ them therefor.

Burglary, etc. (Under Chap. 266, §§ 14, 15.)

(1) That A.B. in the night time did break and enter the dwelling house of C.D., situated in said (Boston), with intent therein to commit larceny (*or* murder, rape or robbery, as the case may be).

(*If desired add actual larceny in the building.*)

(2) That A.B. did enter the dwelling house of one X., situated in said (Boston), with intent therein to commit larceny, and after having so entered with said intent did break said dwelling house in the night time, X. being lawfully therein, and said A.B. being armed with a dangerous weapon at the time of such entry (*or* such breaking) (*or* arming himself with a dangerous weapon in said house) (*or* did make an assault on said X., who was lawfully therein).

(3) That A.B. did break and enter the dwelling house of one X., in said (Boston), in the night time, with intent therein to commit larceny (*or* murder, etc., as the case may be).

Burning to defraud insurance company. (Under Chap. 266, § 10.)

That A.B. did burn a certain building in _____ in said county, [*or* certain goods, wares and merchandise (*or other chattels—name the property*)] which was (*or* were) at the time of such burning insured in the _____ Insurance Company, a corporation duly established by law, against loss or damage by fire, with the intent thereby to injure the said insurer.

Common drunkard. (Under Chap. 272, § 53.)

That A.B., during the three months next before the making of this complaint, was a common drunkard.

Common nightwalker. (Under Chap. 272, § 53.)

That A.B., during the three months next before the making of this complaint, was a common nightwalker, habitually walking in the streets in the night time for the purpose of prostitution.

Concealing mortgaged personal property. (Under Chap. 266, § 82.)

That A.B. did mortgage to X. in due form of law certain personal property (*setting out the mortgaged property*), and that afterward, the said mortgage being in full force and effect, and the said X. remaining the owner thereof (*if such be the fact*), said A.B. did remove and conceal the said property with fraudulent intent to place the same beyond the control of the said X.

Conspiracy.

(1) That A.B. and C.D. conspired together to murder one E.F.

(2) That A.B. and C.D. conspired together to commit rape upon E.F.

(3) That A.B. and C.D. conspired together to steal the property, money, etc., of E.F.

Cruelty to animals. (Under Chap. 272, § 77.)

(1) That A.B. did overdrive (overload) (drive when overloaded) (overwork) (torture) (torment) (deprive of necessary sustenance) (cruelly beat) (cruelly mutilate) (cruelly kill) a certain horse (*or* dog, etc.).

(2) That A.B. did cause and procure one C.D. to overdrive (etc.) a certain horse (etc.).

(3) That A.B., having the charge and custody of a certain horse (etc.), did inflict unnecessary cruelty upon it.

(4) That A.B., having the charge and custody of a certain horse (etc.), did unnecessarily fail to provide it with proper food (*or* drink *or* shelter *or* protection from the weather).

Disorderly house. (Under Chap. 219, § 27.)

That A.B., during the three months next before the finding of this indictment, at said (Boston) did keep and maintain a certain and common, noisy, ill-governed and disorderly house, resorted to for the purpose of drinking, quarrelling, making great noises, and breaking and disturbing the peace, to the common nuisance of all the people.

Drunkenness. (Under Chap. 272, § 48.)

That A.B. was, by the voluntary use of intoxicating liquor, drunk.

Eavesdropping. (Under Chap. 272, § 99.)

That A.B. did commit the crime of eavesdropping.

Escape. (Under Chap. 268, § 16.)

That A.B., being lawfully imprisoned in the house of correction (*or* the Massachusetts correctional institution) in said county, did break therefrom and escape.

Exposure of person.

That A.B., in a public place in said (Boston), wherein were great numbers of people, indecently did expose to the view of the said people his body and person naked and uncovered.

Forged endorsement.

That A.B. did forge a certain endorsement in and upon the back of, and as a part of, a certain promissory note, with intent to injure and defraud. (*The purport or substance of the note and endorsement may be set forth.*)

Forgery. (Under Chap. 267, § 1.)

That A.B., with intent to injure and defraud, did forge a certain instrument purporting to be, etc. (give the name of the instrument, description, tenor or substance as the pleader chooses).

Fornication. (Under Chap. 272, § 18.)

That A.B., an unmarried person, did commit fornication with C.D., an unmarried person.

Gaming. (Under Chap. 139, § 15.)

That A.B., during the three months next before the finding of this indictment, at said (Boston), did keep and maintain a certain common nuisance, to wit, a tenement resorted to and used for illegal gaming.

House of ill fame. (Under Chap. 272, § 24.)

That A.B., during the three months next before the finding of this indictment, did keep at said (Boston) a certain house of ill fame, resorted to for purposes of prostitution and lewdness.

House of ill fame—Nuisance. (Under Chap. 139, § 15.)

That A.B., during the three months next before the finding of this indictment, at said (Boston), did keep and maintain a certain tenement used for prostitution, assignation and lewdness (or in which acts of prostitution, assignation and lewdness occurred), to the common nuisance of all the people.

Idle and disorderly person. (Under Chap. 272, § 53.)

That A.B., during the three months next before the making of this complaint, was an idle and disorderly person, and neglected all lawful business and habitually misspent his time by frequenting houses of ill fame, gaming houses or tippling shops.

Illegitimacy. Stricken by statute in 1978.

Incest. (Under Chap. 272, § 17.)

That A.B., being the father of C.D. (*or* state such relationship as will show the parties to be within the degree of consanguinity within which marriages are prohibited or declared by law to be incestuous and void), did have carnal knowledge of the body of said C.D.

(A.B. being married to another woman than said C.D., *if such be the fact, and it be desired to cover adultery*.)

Larceny. (Under Chap. 266, § 30.)

(1) That A.B. did steal one horse of the value of more (*or* less, as the case may be) than one hundred dollars, of the property of C.D.

(2) That A.B. did steal six cows, each of the value of twenty dollars, of the property of C.D.

Larceny from a conveyance. (Under Chap. 266, § 30.)

That A.B. did steal from a certain conveyance, to wit, the wagon of one C.D., one book of the value, etc., of the property of C.D., the said C.D. being a common carrier (*or* a person

2

carrying on the express business), and said conveyance being used by the said C.D. in said business.

Larceny from realty. (Under Chap. 266, § 44.)

That A.B., by a trespass, with intent to steal, did take and carry away from the realty, to wit, from the building of C.D., in said (Boston), ten pounds of lead pipe, each of the value of (etc.), of the property of C.D., against his will, the said pipe being annexed to and a part of said building.

Larceny in building. (Under Chap. 266, § 20.)

That A.B. did steal (one coat of the value of more than _____ or less than _____), of the property of X., in a certain building (*or* ship *or* vessel *or* railroad car) of the said X., situated in said (Boston).

Larceny of beast or bird. (Under Chap. 266, § 46.)

That A.B. did steal a certain domesticated animal (*or* bird which was ordinarily kept in confinement), which was the property of C.D.

Lewd and lascivious cohabitation. (Under Chap. 272, § 16.)

That A.B. and C.D., not being married to each other, did during one month next before the finding of this indictment (or such time as the evidence requires), lewdly and lasciviously associate and cohabit together.

Lewdness. (Under Chap. 272, § 53.)

That A.B., during the three months next before the finding of this indictment, was a lewd, wanton and lascivious person in speech and behavior.

Lord's Day. (Under Chap. 136, § 5.)

That A.B., on the _____ day of _____, in the year of our Lord one thousand, etc., that day being the Lord's Day, did keep open his shop in said (Boston), for the purpose of doing business therein (*or* did labor *or* business *or* work), the same not being a work of necessity or charity.

Lottery. (Under Chap. 271, § 7.)

(1) That A.B. did set up and promote a lottery for money.

(2) That A.B. was concerned in the setting up (*or* managing *or* drawing) of a certain lottery for money.

(3) That A.B. did dispose of a certain horse of the value of ten dollars to C.D., by way of a lottery.

(4) That A.B., under the pretext of the sale of certain property, to wit: (*state the property*) to C.D., did dispose of to said C.D. certain other personal property, to wit: (*state the property*), with intent of said A.B. to make the said disposal of said (property) dependent upon a chance by lot, and that such chance was made an additional inducement to the disposal and sale of said (property).

Maiming, etc. (Under Chap. 265, § 14.)

That A.B. did assault C.D., and, with malicious intent to maim and disfigure said C.D., did cut out his tongue.

Malicious injury. (Under Chap. 266, § 127.)

That A.B. did wilfully and maliciously injure (or destroy) certain personal property (*name it and allege value*) of C.D.

Malicious injury to real property. (Under Chap. 266, § 104.)

That A.B. did wilfully (*or* maliciously) destroy (*or* deface *or* mar) a certain building of C.D. in said (Boston).

Manslaughter. (Under Chap. 265, § 13.)

That A.B. did assault and beat C.D., and by such assault and beating did kill C.D.

Manslaughter by negligence.

That A.B., being under the legal duty, and being of sufficient ability to provide C.D., who was his spouse, with sufficient food and drink for sustenance and maintenance, did neglect and refuse so to do; by reason whereof said C.D., being unable to provide sufficient food and drink, became and was mortally sick and died.

Murder. (Under Chap. 265, § 1.)

That A.B. did assault and beat C.D., with intent to murder him (by striking him over the head with an axe), and by such assault and beating did (kill and) murder C.D. (and the jurors further say that the defendant is guilty of murder in the second degree and not in the first degree). *This may be added if murder in the first degree is not alleged.*

Neglect of Spouse or Minor Child. (Under Chap. 273, § 1.)

That A.B., during the three months next before the making of this complaint, being of sufficient ability, did unreasonably neglect to provide for the support of C.D., his lawful spouse (and E.D., his minor child).

Obtaining signature by false pretenses. (Under Chap. 266, § 31.)

That A.B. designedly and with intent to defraud did falsely pretend to C.D. that, etc., and by means of said false pretenses, which said C.D. believed and relied upon, did obtain the signature of said C.D. to a certain written instrument, the false making whereof would be punishable as forgery, to wit, a certain promissory note (*describe as in forgery*) that the pretenses so made to C.D. were false and were known to be false by the said A.B. at the time when he so made them.

Open and gross lewdness. (Under Chap. 272, § 16.)

That A.B. was guilty of open and gross lewdness and lascivious behavior in the presence of C.D.

Prostitute. (Under Chap. 272, § 53.)

That A.B. was a prostitute, offering his or her body indiscriminately to others for hire.

Perjury. (Under Chap. 268, § 1.)

That in a proceeding in the course of justice before the (*set forth the tribunal*), on an issue within the jurisdiction of said court duly joined, and tried before a jury of the county between X. as plaintiff and Y. as defendant, A.B. was lawfully sworn as a witness.

Whereupon it became and was material to said issue whether (*say what*), and to this the said A.B. did wilfully and corruptly testify and say in substance and effect that (*say what*); all his said testimony as above set forth being false, as he well knew.

Polygamy. (Under Chap. 272, § 15.)

(1) That A.B. unlawfully married C.D., the said A.B. having at the time he so unlawfully married a lawful spouse living other than said C.D.

(2) That A.B., having a lawful spouse living, to wit: X., did at (*state place*) unlawfully marry and have for his spouse one C.D., after which the said A.B. did, while said X., was still living, on, at, etc., unlawfully cohabit and continue to cohabit in (Boston) with the said C.D.

Rape. (Under Chap. 265, §§ 22(b), 23.)

(1) That A.B. did assault C.D. with intent to commit rape; and did commit rape upon said C.D.

(2) That A.B. did assault C.D., a child under the age of sixteen years, with the intent to unlawfully have sexual intercourse or unnatural sexual intercourse with and abuse said

C.D.; and did unlawfully have sexual intercourse or unnatural sexual intercourse with and abuse said C.D.

Receiving stolen property. (Under Chap. 266, § 60.)

That A.B., one watch of the value _____ dollars, the property of one C.D., then lately before stolen, did buy, receive, and aid in the concealment of, the said A.B. well knowing the said property to have been stolen as aforesaid.

Rescue. (Under Chap. 265, § 15.)

That A.B. did forcibly rescue and take out of the lawful custody of E.F. one C.D., the said C.D. being a prisoner arrested by and held in the lawful custody of E.F., upon the charge of the crime of (larceny), the said E.F. being a police officer of (said city), duly authorized to arrest and hold in custody the said C.D. upon the charge aforesaid.

Robbery. (Under Chap. 265, § 19.)

That A.B. did assault C.D. with intent to rob him, and thereby did rob and steal from the person of said C.D. (*mention the property*) of the property of said C.D.

Sodomy, etc. (Under Chap. 272, § 34.)

That A.B. did commit the abominable and detestable crime against nature with a (*state the person or beast*).

Stubborn child. (Under Chap. 272, § 53.)

That A.B., a minor, during the three months next before the making of this complaint, was a stubborn child, and stubbornly refused to submit to the lawful and reasonable commands of C.D., whose commands said A.B. was bound to obey.

Threats to extort. (Under Chap. 265, § 25.)

That A.B. did verbally (*or by a written or printed communication*) maliciously threaten one C.D., to accuse him of the crime of (*name it*), with the intent thereby to extort money from the said C.D.

Unlawful appropriation. (Under Chap. 266, § 63.)

That A.B. did wilfully, mischievously and without right take, drive and use a certain horse, the property of one C.D., without the consent of the said owner of said horse, or any person having the legal custody, care or control of the same.

Unnatural act. (Under Chap. 272, § 35.)

That A.B. did commit an unnatural and lascivious act with one C.D.

Uttering. (Under Chap. 267, § 5.)

That A.B., with intent to injure and defraud, did utter and publish as true a certain forged instrument (*describe as in forgery*), well knowing the same to be forged.

Vagabond. (Under Chap. 272, §§ 53, 68.)

That A.B., for three months next before the making of this complaint, was a vagabond, and wandered about from place to place, neglecting all lawful calling and employment, and not having any home or means of support.

Vagrant. (Under Chap. 272, § 66.)

That A.B., during the three months next before the making of this complaint was an idle person who, not having visible means of support, lived without lawful employment (and wandered abroad and visited tippling shops, and lodged in outhouses, and in the open air, and did not give a good account of himself, and wandered abroad and begged, and went about from door to door and placed himself in public places to beg and to receive alms).

The complaint may stop at the word "employment", or such part of the matter in parentheses may be added as the case requires.

(Under Chapter 94, Sections 197–213.)

Common nuisance.

That A.B., during the three months next before the finding of this indictment, at said (Boston), did keep and maintain a certain tenement resorted to by habitual users of narcotic drugs for the purpose of using narcotic drugs.

Unlawful possession.

That A.B. did have in his possession unlawfully certain narcotic drugs, to wit, morphine (*or cocaine or heroin or the name of the drug as it is commonly known*).

Unlawful possession with intent to sell.

That A.B. did have in his possession, with intent unlawfully to sell and deliver, a certain narcotic drug (*naming the drug*).

Conspiracy.

That A.B. and C.D. conspired together to engage in unlawful traffic in narcotic drugs.

Sale and delivery.

That A.B. did unlawfully sell (*or give away or deliver*) a narcotic drug, to wit, morphine (*or name drug is commonly known by*).

Unlawful prescribing and delivery, etc., by physician, etc.

That A.B., a physician (*or pharmacist or dentist or veterinarian, etc.*), did unlawfully prescribe (*or sell, give away, furnish or deliver*) a certain narcotic drug, to wit, (*naming it*).

False making of prescription.

That A.B. did falsely make (*or alter*) a prescription for a narcotic drug.

Uttering a false prescription.

That A.B. did utter and publish as true a certain false prescription for a narcotic drug, well knowing the same to be falsely made (*or altered*).

Misrepresentation.

That A.B. did falsely represent to C.D. (a physician, or dentist, veterinarian, pharmacist, etc.), for the purpose of obtaining a narcotic drug, that (*state the substance of the statements claimed to be representations*).

Chapter 278. Trials and Proceedings Before Judgment

Section	
1	Trial list of criminal cases; adding cases to list
2	Trial of issues of fact
2A–3	Repealed
4	Oaths of jurors
5	Affirmation of jurors
6	Repealed
6A	Testimony concerning ownership in cases involving motor vehicle theft or fraudulent claims; preservation of testimony
7	Burden to prove license or admission to practice as attorney at law
8	Justification in libel cases
8A	Killing or injuring a person unlawfully in a dwelling; defense
9	Proof of ownership of property
10	Night time; definition
11	Directed verdict; setting aside verdict; new trial or finding of guilty of included offense
11A	Habitual criminals; separate trial on issue of prior conviction
12	Acquittal of part of crime and conviction of residue
13	Repealed
14	Liability for fees of person acquitted

2

15   Discontinuance of prosecution under by-laws, ordinances, etc.
16   Assignment of counsel for inmates of institutions for reformation of juvenile offenders
16A   Exclusion of public from trial for sex offenses involving minors under age of eighteen
16B   Exclusion of public from trial of criminal proceeding involving husband and wife
16C   Exclusion of public from trial involving crime of incest or rape
16D   Child witness testimony; videotaping or transmission by simultaneous electronic means in certain cases
16E   Repealed
16F   Scheduling of trial where victim is a child
17   Repealed
18   Pleas and pretrial motions in the district court
18A   Repealed
19–22 Repealed
23   Certain acts or omissions by defendant not admissible against him in criminal trial
24–27 Repealed
28   Appeal to supreme judicial court
28A   Appellate division of superior court for review of sentences
28B   Right of appeal to appellate division; time limit; stay of execution of sentence; jurisdiction; review of judgment, etc.; disposition
28C   Amendment of judgment; resentencing or other disposition
28D   Repealed
28E   Appeals by commonwealth
29–29A Repealed
29B   Withdrawal of uncounseled guilty plea
29C   Repealed
29D   Conviction upon plea of guilty or nolo contendere; motion to vacate
30–33D Repealed
33E   Capital cases; review by supreme judicial court
33F–H Repealed
34   Motions in arrest of judgment
35   Trial of male and female prisoners

SECTION 1
Trial list of criminal cases; adding cases to list

At each session of the superior court for criminal business, the district attorney, before trials begin, shall make and deposit with the clerk, for the inspection of parties, a list of all cases to be tried at that session, and the cases shall be tried in the order of such trial list, unless otherwise ordered by the court for cause shown. Cases may be added to such list by direction of the court, on its own motion or upon motion of the district attorney or of the defendant.

SECTION 2
Trial of issues of fact

Issues of fact joined upon an indictment or complaint shall, in the superior court, be tried by a jury drawn and returned in the manner provided for the trial of issues of fact in civil causes, unless the person indicted or complained against elects to be tried by the court as provided by law.

NOTE 1   **Related Statute.** G.L. c. 263, § 6—Waiver of right to trial by jury.

NOTE 2   Defendant cannot waive jury trial in capital case. *Commonwealth v. Smith*, 357 Mass. 168, 175 (1970).

SECTIONS 2A–3
Repealed

SECTION 4
Oaths of jurors

The following oath shall be administered to the jurors for the trial of all criminal cases which are not capital:

You shall well and truly try the issue between the commonwealth and the defendant, (or the defendants, as the case may be,) according to your evidence; so help you God.

The following oath shall be administered to the jurors for the trial of capital cases:

You shall well and truly try, and true deliverance make, between the Commonwealth and the prisoner at the bar, whom you shall have in charge, according to your evidence; so help you God.

SECTION 5
Affirmation of jurors

A juror who is conscientiously scrupulous of taking either of the oaths above prescribed shall be allowed to affirm.

SECTION 6
Repealed

SECTION 6A
Testimony concerning ownership in cases involving motor vehicle theft or fraudulent claims; preservation of testimony

At the arraignment of a defendant charged with violating the provisions of sections twenty-seven A, twenty-eight, twenty-nine, one hundred and eleven A and one hundred and thirty-nine of chapter two hundred and sixty-six, the court shall upon a showing of need by the commonwealth, and after granting adequate time to defense counsel to consult with the defendant, allow testimony from the owner or person in control of such vehicle, solely on the issue of ownership and unauthorized use, and such testimony shall be taken and preserved and shall be admissible at trial.

In the prosecution of a person charged with violating the provisions of sections twenty-seven A, twenty-eight, twenty-eight A, twenty-nine, one hundred and eleven A and one hundred and thirty-nine of chapter two hundred and sixty-six, the court shall order, as a condition of granting a continuance, that the testimony of a witness then present in court be taken and preserved for subsequent use at trial or any other proceeding. The witness shall be examined in open court by the party on whose behalf he is present and the adverse party shall have the right to cross-examination. The expenses of taking and preserving the testimony shall be assessed as costs against the party requesting the continuance.

SECTION 7
Burden to prove license or admission to practice as attorney at law

A defendant in a criminal prosecution, relying for his justification upon a license, appointment, admission to practice as an attorney at law, or authority, shall prove the same; and, until so proved, the presumption shall be that he is not so authorized.

NOTE 1   **Gun Licenses.** "[U]nder G.L. c. 278, § 7, the burden is on a defendant to come forward with evidence of his license to carry a firearm; that, if he does, 'the burden is on the prosecution to persuade the trier of facts beyond a reasonable doubt that the defense does not exist'; and that, if he does not, there is no jury issue as to licensing or authority." *Commonwealth v. Jefferson*, 377 Mass. 716, 718 (1979) (citing and quoting *Commonwealth v. Jones*, 372 Mass. 403, 406 (1977)).

NOTE 2   **Hypodermic Needles and Syringes.** The same principles as enunciated above apply to prosecutions under G.L. c. 94C, § 27. Thus, a defendant charged with unlawfully possessing hypodermic needles and syringes has the burden of justifying such possession. *Commonwealth v. Jefferson*, 377 Mass. 716, 718 (1979).

NOTE 3   **Uninsured Motor Vehicle.** G.L. c. 278, § 7 is *inapplicable* to prosecutions under G.L. c. 90, § 34J (operating an uninsured motor vehicle). "In a prosecution under G.L. c. 90, § 34J, the Commonwealth must prove as an element of the crime charged that the motor vehicle was in fact uninsured. The defendant cannot be under any obligation to aid the Commonwealth in its proof of this central element of the case against him." *Commonwealth v. Munoz*, 384 Mass. 503, 507 (1981).

NOTE 4   **Liquor.** The defendant, in order to escape conviction for the unlawful sale of liquor, must prove his license for such sale. *Commonwealth v. Nickerson*, 236 Mass. 281, 305 (1920) (citing *Commonwealth v. Regan*, 182 Mass. 22, 25 (1902)).

SECTION 8
Justification in libel cases

The defendant in a prosecution for writing or publishing a libel may introduce in evidence the truth of the matter contained in the publication charged as libellous, and the truth shall be a justification, unless actual malice is proved.

SECTION 8A
Killing or injuring a person unlawfully in a dwelling; defense

In the prosecution of a person who is an occupant of a dwelling charged with killing or injuring one who was unlawfully in said dwelling, it shall be a defense that the occupant was in his dwelling at the time of the offense and that he acted in the reasonable belief that the person unlawfully in said dwelling was about to inflict great bodily injury or death upon said occupant or upon another person lawfully in said dwelling, and that said occupant used reasonable means to defend himself or such other person lawfully in said dwelling. There shall be no duty on said occupant to retreat from such person unlawfully in said dwelling.

NOTE 1   "The defendant asserts that the Legislature, in enacting G.L. c. 278, § 8A from which the judge drew the instructions on duty to retreat, intended to permit a person to respond to a life-threatening assault from a lawful visitor in one's home. The language of G.L. c. 278, § 8A, does not support the defendant's claim. Nothing in the statute eliminates the duty to retreat from a person *lawfully* on the premises." *Commonwealth v. Lapointe*, 402 Mass. 321, 328–29 (1988) (footnote omitted).

NOTE 2a   For purposes of this section a dwelling does not include its driveway. *Commonwealth v. Bennett*, 41 Mass. App. Ct. 920 (1996). *See also Commonwealth v. Carlino*, 449 Mass. 71, 76 (2007).

NOTE 2b   "[W]e conclude that G.L. c. 278, § 8A, does not include an open porch or outside stairs of a house . . ." *Commonwealth v. McKinnon*, 446 Mass. 263, 264 (2006).

SECTION 9
Proof of ownership of property

In the prosecution of crimes which relate to or affect real or personal estate, it shall be sufficient, and shall not be a variance, if it is proved on the trial that, at the time when the crime was committed, either the actual or constructive possession or the general or special property in the whole or any part of such real or personal estate was in the person or community alleged to be the owner thereof.

NOTE   "The purpose of this section is not to compel the Commonwealth to name correctly, at its peril, the true owner of the property allegedly stolen, but rather to avoid the effect of objections as to the allegation of ownership. An averment and a show-

ing that a possessory or other property interest in the thing stolen is in someone other than the thief and proof that the thief knew that he had no right to the property taken are sufficient." *Commonwealth v. Kiernan*, 348 Mass. 29, 50 (1964) (quotation marks and citation omitted).

SECTION 10
Night time; definition

If a crime is alleged to have been committed in the night time, night time shall be deemed the time between one hour after sunset on one day and one hour before sunrise on the next day; and the time of sunset and sunrise shall be ascertained according to mean time in the place where the crime was committed.

NOTE 1   **Related Statute.** G.L. c. 266, § 1—Burglary, etc.

NOTE 2   Nighttime definition different in search and seizure cases. See Nighttime in "Chapter 276—Search and Seizure Special Commentary."

SECTION 11
Directed verdict; setting aside verdict; new trial or finding of guilty of included offense

If a motion for a directed verdict of not guilty is denied and the case is submitted to the jury and a verdict of guilty is returned, the judge may on a renewed motion for a directed verdict of not guilty pursuant to the Massachusetts Rules of Criminal Procedure set aside the verdict and order a new trial, or order the entry of a finding of guilty of any offense included in the offense charged in the indictment or complaint.

NOTE 1   "[A] judge cannot be required to direct a verdict on an opening." *Commonwealth v. Baker*, 368 Mass. 58, 80–81 (1975) (citations omitted).

NOTE 2   **Related Rule.** Mass.R.Crim.P. 25—Motion for Required Finding of Not Guilty.

SECTION 11A
Habitual criminals; separate trial on issue of prior conviction

If a defendant is charged with a crime for which more severe punishment is provided for second and subsequent offenses, and the complaint or indictment alleges that the offense charged is a second or subsequent offense, the defendant on arraignment shall be inquired of only for a plea of guilty or not guilty to the crime charged, and that portion of the indictment or complaint that charges, or refers to a charge that, said crime is a second or subsequent offense shall not be read in open court. If such defendant pleads not guilty and is tried before a jury, no part of the complaint or indictment which alleges that the crime charged is a second or subsequent offense shall be read or shown to the jury or referred to in any manner during the trial; provided, however, that if a defendant takes the witness stand to testify, nothing herein contained shall prevent the impeachment of his credibility by evidence of any prior conviction, subject to the provisions of section twenty-one of chapter two hundred and thirty-three. If a defendant pleads guilty or if there is a verdict or finding of guilty after trial, then before sentence is imposed, the defendant shall be further inquired of for a plea of guilty or not guilty to that portion of the complaint or indictment alleging that the crime charged is a second or subsequent offense. If he pleads guilty thereto, sentence shall be imposed; if he pleads not guilty thereto, he shall be entitled to a trial by jury of the issue of conviction of a prior offense, subject to all of the

2

provisions of law governing criminal trials. A defendant may waive trial by jury. The court may, in its discretion, either hold the jury which returned the verdict of guilty of the crime, the trial of which was just completed, or it may order the impaneling of a new jury to try the issue of conviction of one or more prior offenses. Upon the return of a verdict, after the separate trial of the issue of conviction of one or more prior offenses, the court shall impose the sentence appropriate to said verdict.

NOTE 1   Sentencing under common and notorious thief statute, G.L. c. 266, § 40, is different from sentencing under habitual criminal statutes, G.L. c. 278, § 11A and G.L. c. 279, § 25. In the former a defendant may be sentenced without notice of the possibility appearing in the indictments. The sentencing scheme contained in the habitual criminal statutes, however, differs in that it authorizes maximum punishment for the felony currently charged only upon allegation and proof of prior felonies for which a defendant earlier had been convicted and sentenced. *Commonwealth v. Crocker*, 384 Mass. 353, 355 (1981).

NOTE 2   "Because of the guilty verdict on the underlying offense, the defendant was entitled to have the judge inquire whether she intended to plead guilty or not guilty to the portion of the complaint . . . alleging previous convictions on two or more occasions for [OUI]. According to the statute, a plea of not guilty would entitle her to a separate trial." *Commonwealth v. Zuzick*, 45 Mass. App. Ct. 71, 72 (1998).

SECTION 12
Acquittal of part of crime and conviction of residue

If a person indicted for a felony is acquitted by the verdict of part of the crime charged, and is convicted of the residue, such verdict may he received and recorded by the court, and thereupon the defendant shall be adjudged guilty of the crime, if any, which appears to the court to be substantially charged by the residue of the indictment, and shall be sentenced and punished accordingly.

NOTE   "This statute apparently contemplates a single verdict which . . . would commonly be returned in the form 'Guilty of so much of the indictment as charges . . . .'" *Commonwealth v. Burke*, 342 Mass. 144, 148 (1961).

SECTION 13
Repealed

SECTION 14
Liability for fees of person acquitted

No prisoner or person under recognizance, acquitted by verdict or discharged because no indictment has been found against him, or for want of prosecution, shall be liable for any costs or fees or for any charge for subsistence while he was in custody.

SECTION 15
Discontinuance of prosecution under by-laws, ordinances, etc.

In a prosecution before a district court under the by-laws, ordinances, orders, rules or regulations of a city or town, the city solicitor, town counsel or other person appointed to represent such city or town may enter a nolle prosequi or do anything relative to such prosecution which may be done by the district attorney.

SECTION 16
Assignment of counsel for inmates of institutions for reformation of juvenile offenders

The court may assign counsel to an inmate of any institution for the reformation of juvenile offenders who is to be tried for an offense alleged to have been committed therein; and shall, upon application, order the superintendent or other officer of such institution to produce at the trial such inmates thereof as, in the opinion of the counsel for the defense, certified in writing, or of the judge, in the absence of counsel, are material witnesses for the defence; and such officer shall obey the order and provide for the custody and safe return of such inmates.

SECTION 16A
Exclusion of public from trial for sex offenses involving minors under age of eighteen

At the trial of a complaint or indictment for rape, incest, carnal abuse or other crime involving sex, where a minor under eighteen years of age is the person upon, with or against whom the crime is alleged to have been committed, or at the trial of a complaint or indictment for getting a woman with child out of wedlock, or for the non-support of a child born out of wedlock, the presiding justice shall exclude the general public from the court room, admitting only such persons as may have a direct interest in the case.

NOTE 1   The mandatory-closure rule contained in this section, as construed by the Supreme Judicial Court violates the First Amendment. *Globe Newspaper Co. v. Superior Court*, 457 U.S. 596, 610–11 (1982), *reversing* 383 Mass. 838 (1981).

NOTE 2a   "A trial court can determine on a case-by-case basis whether closure is necessary to protect the welfare of a minor victim. Among the factors to be weighed are the minor victim's age, psychological maturity, and understanding, the nature of the crime, the desires of the victim, and the interests of parents and relatives." *Globe Newspaper Co. v. Superior Court*, 457 U.S. 596, 608 (1982) (footnotes omitted), *reversing* 383 Mass. 838 (1981).

NOTE 2b   "Further, the determination must satisfy four requirements articulated by the Supreme Court: '[1] the party seeking to close the hearing must advance an overriding interest that is likely to be prejudiced, [2] the closure must be no broader than necessary to protect that interest, [3] the trial court must consider reasonable alternatives to closing the proceeding, and [4] it must make findings adequate to support the closure.'" *Commonwealth v. Martin*, 417 Mass. 187, 194 (1994) (quoting *Waller v. Georgia*, 467 Mass. 39, 48 (1984)).

NOTE 2c   "[E]ven in a partial closure context, the remaining *Waller* factors must be satisfied." *Commonwealth v. Cohen*, 456 Mass. 94, 113 (2010).

NOTE 3   There is a guaranteed right of the public under the First and Fourteenth Amendments to attend a criminal trial. "Absent an overriding interest articulated in findings, the trial of a criminal case must be open to the public." *Richmond Newspapers, Inc. v. Virginia*, 448 U.S. 555, 580–81 (1980).

NOTE 4   "Because we conclude that counsel may waive a defendant's right to a public trial during jury selection without express consent and, in the circumstances here, that counsel's decision was a reasonable tactical decision, we affirm the denial of the defendant's motion for a new trial." *Commonwealth v. Lavoie*, 464 Mass. 83, 84 (2013).

SECTION 16B
Exclusion of public from trial of criminal proceeding involving husband and wife

The presiding justice of a district court may exclude the general public from the court room during the trial of any criminal proceeding involving husband and wife.

NOTE   See Notes following Section 16A of this chapter.

SECTION 16C
Exclusion of public from trial involving crime of incest or rape

To protect the parties involved at a trial arising from a complaint or indictment for incest or rape, the trial judge may exclude all spectators from the courtroom in which such trial is being held, or from said courtroom during those portions of such trial when direct testimony is to be presented; provided, that either of the parties requests that all spectators be so excluded at the trial or portions thereof; and provided further, that the defendant in such trial by a written statement waives his right to a public trial for those portions from which spectators are so excluded.

NOTE   See Notes following Section 16A of this chapter.

SECTION 16D
Child witness testimony; videotaping or transmission by simultaneous electronic means in certain cases
(Amended by 2011 Mass. Acts c. 178, § 30, effective Nov. 21, 2011.)

(a) For the purposes of this section, the following words shall have the following meanings:

"Child witness", a person who is under the age of fifteen years and who is alleged to have been a victim of, or a witness to an alleged violation of section thirteen B, 13 B½, 13B¾, thirteen F, thirteen H, twenty-two, twenty-two A, 22B, 22C, twenty-three, 23A, 23B, twenty-four, 24B or 50 of chapter two hundred and sixty-five, or section two, three, four, four A, four B, five, six, seven, eight, twelve, thirteen, sixteen, seventeen, twenty-four, twenty-eight, twenty-nine, twenty-nine A, twenty-nine B, thirty-three, thirty-four or thirty-five A of chapter two hundred and seventy-two.

"Simultaneous electronic means," any device capable of projecting a live visual and aural transmission such as closed-circuit television.

(b)(1) At any time after the issuance of a complaint or indictment alleging an offense punished by any of the statutes listed herein, the court on its own motion or on motion of the proponent of a child witness, and after a hearing, may order the use of a suitable alternative procedure for taking the testimony of the child witness, in proceedings pursuant to said complaint or indictment, provided that the court finds by a preponderance of the evidence at the time of the order that the child witness is likely to suffer psychological or emotional trauma as a result of testifying in open court, as a result of testifying in the presence of the defendant, or as a result of both testifying in open court and testifying in the presence of the defendant. If the court orders the use of a suitable alternative for taking the testimony of a child witness pursuant to this section, the court shall make and enter specific findings upon the record describing with particularity the reasons for such order.

(2) An order issued under paragraph (1) shall provide that the testimony of the child witness be recorded on videotape or film to be shown in court at a later time or that the

testimony be transmitted to the courtroom by simultaneous electronic means.

(3) Testimony taken by an alternative procedure pursuant to an order issued under paragraph (1) shall be taken in the presence of the judge, the prosecutor, defense counsel and such other persons as the court may allow. The defendant shall also have the right to be present unless the court's order under paragraph (1) is based wholly or in part upon a finding that the child witness is likely to suffer trauma as a result of testifying in the presence of the defendant. If the order is based on such a finding, the testimony of the child witness shall not be taken in the presence of the defendant except as provided in paragraph (4).

(4) Testimony taken by an alternative procedure pursuant to an order issued under paragraph (1) shall be taken in a suitable setting outside the courtroom, except that an order based only on a finding that the child witness is likely to suffer trauma as a result of testifying in the presence of the defendant may provide that the testimony be taken in a suitable setting inside the courtroom in a manner so that the child witness is not able to see or hear the defendant.

(5) When testimony is taken by an alternative procedure pursuant to an order issued under paragraph (1), counsel shall be given the opportunity to examine or cross-examine the child witness to the same extent as would be permitted at trial, and the defendant shall be able to see and hear the child witness and to have constant private communication with the defense counsel.

(6) The film, videotape or transmission of testimony taken by an alternative procedure pursuant to an order issued under paragraph (1) shall be admissible as substantive evidence to the same extent as and in lieu of live testimony by the child witness in any proceeding for which the order is issued or in any related criminal proceeding against the same defendant when consistent with the interests of justice, provided that such an order is entered or re-entered based on current findings at the time when or within a reasonable time before the film, videotape or transmission is offered into evidence. Subsequent testimony of a child witness in any such proceeding shall also be taken by a suitable alternative procedure pursuant to this section.

(7) Whenever pursuant to an order issued under paragraph (1), testimony is recorded on videotape or film or is transmitted to the courtroom by simultaneous electronic means, the court shall ensure that:

(a) The recording or transmitting equipment is capable of making an accurate recording or transmission and is operated by a competent operator;

(b) The recording or transmission is in color and the witness is visible at all times;

(c) Every voice on the recording or transmission is audible and identified;

(d) The courtroom is equipped with monitors which permit the jury and others present in the courtroom to see and hear the recording or transmission;

(e) In the case of recorded testimony, the recording is accurate and has not been altered;

(f) In the case of recorded testimony, each party is afforded the opportunity to view the recording before it is shown in the courtroom.

(8) Nothing in this section shall be deemed to prohibit the court from using other appropriate means, consistent with

this section and other laws and with the defendant's rights, to protect a child witness from trauma during a court proceeding.

NOTE 1   "After this case was tried, this court held G.L. c. 278, § 16D, which allows the presentation of a sexually abused child's testimony by videotape or simultaneous transmission, to be unconstitutional to the extent that it violated a defendant's right to confrontation by allowing a child witness to testify outside the physical presence of the defendant. *Commonwealth v. Bergstrom*, 402 Mass. 534, 547 (1988). This court also held that, in instances where testimony is videotaped outside the presence of the jury, the Commonwealth must establish a compelling need by showing that the procedure is necessary to avoid severe and long lasting emotional trauma to the child. *Id.* at 550–51.

"Unlike *Bergstrom*, the defendant here was present in the room when the child's testimony was videotaped. The defendant's challenge is that the judge failed to make a finding of 'compelling need' before allowing the videotaped testimony. Although the judge did not use the term 'compelling need,' it is clear to us, from the judge's findings and in light of all the circumstances, that the judge considered the need to be compelling.

"We stated in *Bergstrom* that, 'in constitutional terms, a videotape should be required to convey to the jury . . . the totality of the circumstances involved in the giving of testimony.' *Id.* at 549 n.16 . . . Ideally, all persons present in the room during the taping would be visible in the videotape. It is not, however, a fatal flaw to an otherwise satisfactory videotape. See *Bergstrom* . . . (criticizing videotape for poor color, poor sound, distracting background noises, obstructed view of the child witness, and disembodied voices)."   *Commonwealth v. Amirault*, 404 Mass. 221, 241, 242–43 (1989) (footnote omitted).

NOTE 2   "[W]hether, during the course of a criminal trial, child witnesses may, through electronic means, testify outside the physical presence of the defendant and of the jury consonant with the confrontation guarantees of the Sixth Amendment to the United States Constitution and of art. 12 of the Massachusetts Declaration of Rights. We resolve this issue solely under art. 12." *Commonwealth v. Bergstrom*, 402 Mass. 534, 535 (1988).

SECTION 16E
Repealed

SECTION 16F
Scheduling of trial where victim is a child

In any criminal proceeding involving an alleged sex crime perpetrated upon a minor child, or in which a minor child is expected to testify as a witness to a sex crime, the court shall, in order to minimize stress on such child, take action to expedite the trial and give precedence to the case over any other case; provided, however, that nothing in this section shall be construed to mean that trial should be expedited if it is not in the best interests of the child.

When a motion or a request for a continuance is made the prosecutor shall file an impact statement which specifies whether the commonwealth agrees to the request for continuance, whether the child or the child's representative agrees to such request, and the effect, if any, the granting of the continuance will have on the child. In ruling on any motion or request for continuance or other delay, the court shall consider and give weight to any possible adverse impact that a delay or continuance may have on the child. Prior to issuing an order on a motion for continuance or delay, the court shall make written findings of fact concerning the impact on the child of continuing or delaying the case.

SECTION 17
Repealed

SECTION 18
Pleas and pretrial motions in the district court

A defendant who is before the Boston municipal court or a district court or a district court sitting in a juvenile session or a juvenile court on a criminal offense within the court's final jurisdiction shall plead not guilty or guilty, or with the consent of the court, nolo contendere. Such plea of guilty shall be submitted by the defendant and acted upon by the court; provided, however, that a defendant with whom the commonwealth cannot reach agreement for a recommended disposition shall be allowed to tender a plea of guilty together with a request for a specific disposition. Such request may include any disposition or dispositional terms within the court's jurisdiction, including, unless otherwise prohibited by law, a dispositional request that a guilty finding not be entered, but rather the case be continued without a finding to a specific date thereupon to be dismissed, such continuance conditioned upon compliance with specific terms and conditions or that the defendant be placed on probation pursuant to the provisions of section eighty-seven of chapter two hundred and seventy-six. If such a plea, with an agreed upon recommendation or with a dispositional request by the defendant, is tendered, the court shall inform the defendant that it will not impose a disposition that exceeds the terms of the agreed upon recommendation or the dispositional request by the defendant, whichever is applicable, without giving the defendant the right to withdraw the plea.

If a defendant, notwithstanding the requirements set forth hereinbefore, attempts to enter a plea or statement consisting of an admission of facts sufficient for finding of guilt, or some similar statement, such admission shall be deemed a tender of a plea of guilty for purposes of the procedures set forth in this section.

Any pretrial motion filed in a criminal case pending in the Boston municipal court or district court or a district court sitting in a juvenile session or a juvenile court and decided before entry of defendant's decision on waiver of the right to jury trial shall not be refiled or reheard thereafter, except in the discretion of the court as substantial justice requires. Any such pretrial motion not filed or filed but not decided prior to entry of the defendant's decision on waiver of the right to jury trial may be filed thereafter but not later than twenty-one days after entry of said decision on waiver of the right to jury trial, except for good cause shown.

NOTE 1   Decision to Prosecute Rests with Executive Branch. "The defendant did not follow the procedure required by G.L. c. 278, § 18. He tendered neither a plea of guilty nor an admission to sufficient facts coupled with a request for an alternative disposition such as a continuance without a finding. Therefore, no purpose would be served by remanding for a *Brandano* hearing. The governing principle in this case is that the decision whether or not to prosecute the complaint rests within the sole discretion of the executive branch." *Commonwealth v. Everett*, 88 Mass. App. Ct. 902, 904 (2015).

NOTE 2   Pretrial Probation after an Admission to Sufficient Facts. "[W]e conclude that there is no legally cognizable disposition of 'pretrial probation' after an 'admission to sufficient facts' distinct from a 'continu[ance] without a finding' conditioned on probation, a disposition authorized by G.L. c. 278, § 18." *Commonwealth v. Sebastian S.*, 444 Mass. 306, 307 (2005).

NOTE 3   For related statute see G.L. c. 218, § 27A—jury sessions. *See also* Kaplan, W.J., "Sentencing Advocacy in the Massachusetts District Courts," 80 *Mass. L. Rev.* 22 (1995).

SECTION 18A–22
Repealed

SECTION 23
Certain acts or omissions by defendant not admissible against him in criminal trial

At the trial of a criminal case in the superior court, upon indictment, or in a district court, the fact that the defendant did not testify at any preliminary hearing in the first court, or that at such hearing he waived examination or did not offer any evidence in his own defense, shall not be used as evidence against him, nor be referred to or commented upon by the prosecuting officer.

NOTE 1a   Improper for prosecutor to ask five of six defense witnesses whether they had testified in previous court proceedings. *Commonwealth v. Palmarin*, 378 Mass. 474, 476–78 (1979).

NOTE 1b   *Cf. Commonwealth v. Stokes*, 10 Mass. App. Ct. 434, 438 (1980). "[O]ne isolated question, asked of one alibi witness [as to whether she had ever testified in any other proceeding in the case] (and not of the defendant or the other alibi witness) which elicited the response that she had not testified previously, and which was not referred to again, would not have influenced the jury to speculate whether the defendant had failed to offer any evidence in his defense in a preliminary hearing. The question would therefore not be a violation of § 23."

NOTE 2a   Prosecutor cross-examined the defendant's witnesses as to their presence at a probable cause hearing, their not testifying, and that the case had been held before a judge and the defendant was represented by counsel. Held, this was an improper method of impeachment and it brought to the jury's attention that the defendant had failed to testify or to offer any evidence in the district court in violation of Section 23. *Commonwealth v. Morrison*, 1 Mass. App. Ct. 632, 635–37 (1973).

NOTE 2b   *Cf. Commonwealth v. Cefalo*, 381 Mass. 319, 337–38 (1980). Two defense witnesses testified that they witnessed an argument about drugs between the victim and Shamberger on the evening of the victim's death. On cross, the prosecutor attempted to show recent fabrication by eliciting the fact that neither witnesses had gone to the police. In so doing the prosecutor asked one witness whether he had been at the probable cause hearing (answered yes), and whether he had spoken to representatives of the Commonwealth at that time (response no). Held, *no* violation of Section 23. The defendant's theory was that Shamberger committed the crime. The two defense witnesses supported that theory. The thrust of the questioning by the prosecutor was to suggest that the two witnesses both had prior opportunity to tell their stories to Commonwealth representatives and did not. This was a proper mode of impeaching the witnesses by showing recent contrivance or bias in favor of the defendant. The assistant district attorney did not ask one witness directly if he had testified at the probable cause hearing. The other witness was not asked the question at all. "In the absence of questions or comment suggesting that the defendant did not call any witnesses at the probable cause hearing there was no § 23 violation."

NOTE 3   "Section 23 must be read in conjunction with art. 12 of the Declaration of Rights of the Constitution of the Commonwealth ('No subject shall be . . . compelled to accuse, or furnish evidence against himself'), and the Fifth Amendment to the Constitution to the United States, made applicable to the States by the Fourteenth Amendment ('No person shall be . . . compelled in any criminal case to be a witness against himself')." *Commonwealth v. Palmarin*, 378 Mass. 474, 478 (1979).

NOTE 4   **Related Statute.** G.L. c. 233, § 20—Competency of witnesses; defendant in a criminal case.

SECTION 24–27
Repealed

SECTION 28
Appeal to supreme judicial court

A defendant aggrieved by a judgment of the district court or of the superior court in any criminal proceeding may appeal therefrom to the supreme judicial court.

NOTE   "We conclude that a defendant who is found not guilty by reason of mental illness may appeal under G.L. c. 278, § 28." *Commonwealth v. Bruneau*, 472 Mass. 510, 511 (2015).

SECTION 28A
Appellate division of superior court for review of sentences

There shall be an appellate division of the superior court for the review of sentences to the state prison imposed by final judgments in criminal cases, except in any case in which a different sentence could not have been imposed, and for the review of sentences to the reformatory for women for terms of more than five years imposed by final judgments in such criminal cases. Said appellate division shall consist of three justices of the superior court to be designated from time to time by the chief justice of said court and shall sit in Boston or at a Massachusetts correctional institution or at such other place as may be designated by the chief justice and at such times as he shall determine. No justice shall sit or act on an appeal from a sentence imposed by him. Two justices shall constitute a quorum to decide all matters before the appellate division.

A designation by the chief justice of the members of the appellate division shall be recorded by the clerk of the appellate division who shall forthwith send copies thereof to the several clerks of the superior court.

The clerk of the superior court for criminal business in Suffolk county shall be the clerk of the appellate division of the superior court. The first assistant clerk of superior court for criminal business in Suffolk county shall be the first assistant clerk of the appellate division of the superior court; the second assistant clerk of the superior court for criminal business in Suffolk county shall be the second assistant clerk of the appellate division of the superior court.

The clerk or an assistant clerk of the appellate division of the superior court shall attend all sittings of the appellate division wherever such sittings are held and shall record the proceedings thereof. The clerk shall have the care and custody of all records, books and papers which pertain to said appellate division. The clerk and the assistant clerks of the appellate division shall have all the power and authority of a clerk of courts in any county of the commonwealth in any and all matters pertaining to the appellate division or to any criminal case in which an appeal for a review of a sentence imposed in any county has been filed.

NOTE 1   "[W]e conclude that an eligible criminal defendant should first address to the Appellate Division a complaint regarding the severity of his sentence." *Commonwealth v. Brown*, 394 Mass. 394, 398 (1985).

NOTE 2   *See Commonwealth v. Alfonso*, 449 Mass. 738 (2007) (court rejected female defendant's claim that Appellate Division lacked jurisdiction to review her sentence, concluding that defendant's sentence to MCI-Framingham was a "state prison" sentence under G.L. c. 125, § 1(o)).

2

SECTION 28B
Right of appeal to appellate division; time limit; stay of execution of sentence; jurisdiction; review of judgment, etc.; disposition

A person aggrieved by a sentence which may be reviewed may appeal to the appellate division for a review of such sentence. Upon the imposition of a sentence which may be reviewed, the clerk of the court shall notify the person sentenced of his right to appeal. The appeal shall be filed with the clerk of the court for the county where the judgment was rendered within ten days after the imposition of said sentence. An appeal shall not stay the execution of a sentence. The clerk of the court shall notify the chief justice, the justice who imposed the sentence and the clerk of the appellate division of filing of an appeal. The justice who imposed the sentence appealed from may transmit to the appellate division a statement of his reasons for imposing the sentence and shall make such a statement within seven days if requested to do so by the appellate division.

The appellate division shall have jurisdiction to consider an appeal with or without a hearing, review the judgment so far as it relates to the sentence imposed and also any other sentence imposed when the sentence appealed from was imposed, notwithstanding the partial execution of any such sentence, and shall have jurisdiction to amend the judgment by ordering substituted therefor a different appropriate sentence or sentences or any other disposition of the case which could have been made at the time of the imposition of the sentence or sentences under review, but no sentence shall be increased without giving the defendant an opportunity to be heard. If the appellate division decides that the original sentence or sentences should stand, it shall dismiss the appeal. Its decision shall be final. The clerk of the appellate division shall forthwith notify the appellant, the superintendent of the correctional institution in which the appellant is confined, the clerk of the court in which judgment was rendered, the justice who imposed the sentence appealed from and the chief justice of the final action of the appellate division on an appeal. The appellate division may require the production of any records, documents, exhibits or other things connected with the proceedings. The superior court shall by rule establish forms for appeals hereunder and may by rule make such other regulations of procedure relative thereto, consistent with law, as justice may require.

NOTE "The Appellate Division of the Superior Court has authority to review a judgment only insofar as it relates to the sentence imposed. It has no authority over the judgment of conviction. . . . Furthermore, had the motion been timely, the judge would not have had the authority to revise the sentence imposed by the Appellate Division. The order of the Appellate Division is final." *Commonwealth v. Callahan*, 419 Mass. 306, 308–09 (1995).

SECTION 28C
Amendment of judgment; resentencing or other disposition

If the judgment is amended by an order substituting a different sentence or sentences or disposition of the case, the appellate division or any member thereof shall resentence the defendant or make any other disposition of the case in accordance with the order of said appellate division. Time served on a sentence appealed from shall be deemed to have been served on a substituted sentence.

SECTION 28D
Repealed

SECTION 28E
Appeals by commonwealth

An appeal may be taken by and on behalf of the commonwealth by the attorney general or a district attorney from the district court to the appeals court in all criminal cases and in all delinquency cases from a decision, order or judgment of the court (1) allowing a motion to dismiss an indictment or complaint, (2) allowing a motion to suppress evidence, or (3) denying a motion to transfer pursuant to section sixty-one of chapter one hundred and nineteen.

An appeal may be taken by and on behalf of the commonwealth by the attorney general or a district attorney from the superior court to the supreme judicial court in all criminal cases from a decision, order or judgment of the court (1) allowing a motion to dismiss an indictment or complaint, or (2) allowing a motion of appropriate relief under the Massachusetts Rules of Criminal Procedure.

An application for an appeal from a decision, order or judgment of the superior court determining a motion to suppress evidence prior to trial may be filed in the supreme judicial court by a defendant or by and on behalf of the commonwealth by the attorney general or a district attorney. If such application is denied, or if such application is granted but the interlocutory appeal is heard by a single justice, the determination of the motion to suppress evidence shall be open to review by the full court after trial in the same manner and to the same extent as determinations of such motions not appealed under the interlocutory procedure herein authorized.

Rules of practice and procedure with respect to appeals authorized by this section shall be the same as those applicable to criminal appeals under the Massachusetts Rules of Appellate Procedure.

NOTE 1 After the jury returned a verdict of guilty, the trial judge allowed the defendant's motion for a finding of not guilty. "The Commonwealth may appeal from the allowance of a defendant's renewed motion for a finding of not guilty presented pursuant to Mass.R.Crim.P. 25(b)(1)." *Commonwealth v. Therrien*, 383 Mass. 529, 532–33 (1981) (footnote omitted).

NOTE 2 "Double jeopardy principles require that there be no appellate review of the allowance of a defense motion for a finding of not guilty after jeopardy attaches and before the jury return their verdict. In such a case, review is to be denied because, even if the Commonwealth were successful on appeal, double jeopardy principles would bar a second trial." *Commonwealth v. Therrien*, 383 Mass. 529, 535–36 (1981).

NOTE 3 "[A]n appeal by the Commonwealth from an order or decision dismissing an indictment in the Superior Court must first be entered in the Appeals Court." *Commonwealth v. Friend*, 393 Mass. 310, 314 (1984).

So, too, an appeal by the Commonwealth from a Superior Court order allowing a motion for a new trial pursuant to Rule 25 of the Mass.R.Crim.P. should be docketed in the Appeals Court. *Commonwealth v. Preston*, 393 Mass. 318, 321 (1984).

SECTIONS 29–29A
Repealed

SECTION 29B
Withdrawal of uncounseled guilty plea

If a defendant having a right to counsel in a criminal proceeding has not been represented by counsel or has not properly waived his right to counsel and has entered a plea of guilty, such defendant may withdraw such plea as a matter of right at any time prior to imposition of sentence by the court.

SECTION 29C
Repealed

SECTION 29D
(Alien warnings) conviction upon plea of guilty or nolo contendere; motion to vacate

The court shall not accept a plea of guilty, a plea of nolo contendere, or an admission to sufficient facts from any defendant in any criminal proceeding unless the court advises such defendant of the following: "If you are not a citizen of the United States, you are hereby advised that the acceptance by this court of your plea of guilty, plea of nolo contendere, or admission to sufficient facts may have consequences of deportation, exclusion from admission to the United States, or denial of naturalization, pursuant to the laws of the United States." The court shall advise such defendant during every plea colloquy at which the defendant is proffering a plea of guilty, a plea of nolo contendere, or an admission to sufficient facts. The defendant shall not be required at the time of the plea to disclose to the court his legal status in the United States.

If the court fails so to advise the defendant, and he later at any time shows that his plea and conviction may have or has had one of the enumerated consequences, even if the defendant has already been deported from the United States, the court, on the defendant's motion, shall vacate the judgment, and permit the defendant to withdraw the plea of guilty, plea of nolo contendere, or admission of sufficient facts, and enter a plea of not guilty. Absent an official record or a contemporaneously written record kept in the court file that the court provided the advisement as prescribed in this section, including but not limited to a docket sheet that accurately reflects that the warning was given as required by this section, the defendant shall be presumed not to have received advisement. An advisement previously or subsequently provided the defendant during another plea colloquy shall not satisfy the advisement required by this section, nor shall it be used to presume the defendant understood the plea of guilty, or admission to sufficient facts he seeks to vacate would have the consequence of deportation, exclusion from admission to the United States, or denial of naturalization.

NOTE 1a   "A defendant need not show that any of the enumerated consequences has actually resulted, nor, contrary to the Commonwealth's intimation, that he would have pleaded differently to the criminal charges against him, had he received the statutory warning." *Commonwealth v. Mahadeo*, 397 Mass. 314, 318 (1986).

NOTE 1b   **Failure to Warn About Immigration Consequences Ineffective Assistance of Counsel.** "We agree with Padilla that constitutionally competent counsel would have advised him that his conviction for drug distribution made him subject to automatic deportation. Whether he is entitled to relief depends on whether he has been prejudiced, a matter that we do not address.

"When the law is not succinct and straightforward . . . a criminal defense attorney need do no more than advise a noncitizen client that pending criminal charges may carry a risk of adverse immigration consequences. But when the deportation consequence is truly clear, as it was in this case, the duty to give correct advice is equally clear." *Padilla v. Kentucky*, 559 U.S. 356, 369 (2010) (footnote omitted).

"[D]eportation consequences are often unclear. Lack of clarity in the law, however, does not obviate the need for counsel to say something about the possibility of deportation, even though it will affect the scope and nature of counsel's advice." *Padilla v. Kentucky*, 559 U.S. at 369 n.10.

NOTE 1c   **Defendant's Burden.** "The issue on appeal is what the defendant must show to establish that his conviction 'may have' the consequence of exclusion from admission to the United States. We conclude that a defendant satisfies this burden by showing (1) that he has a bona fide desire to leave the country and reenter, and (2) that, if the defendant were to do so, there would be a substantial risk that he or she would be excluded from admission under Federal immigration law because of his or her conviction." *Commonwealth v. Valdez*, 475 Mass. 178, 179 (2016).

NOTE 2a   **Retroactivity.** "We granted certiorari . . . to resolve a split among federal and state courts on whether *Padilla* [*v. Kentucky*, 559 U.S. 356 (2010)] applies retroactively. [The Court held] that it does not." *Chaidez v. United States*, 133 S. Ct. 1103, 1107 (2013).

NOTE 2b   "We conclude, as a matter of Massachusetts law and consistent with our authority as provided in *Danforth v. Minnesota*, 552 U.S. 264, 282 (2008), that the Sixth Amendment right enunciated in *Padilla* was not a 'new' rule and, consequently, defendants whose State law convictions were final after April 1, 1997, may attack their convictions collaterally on *Padilla* grounds. We thus affirm our decision in [*Commonwealth v. Clarke*, 460 Mass. 30 (2011)]." *Commonwealth v. Sylvain*, 466 Mass. 422, 423–24 (2013).

NOTE 2c   "[T]he enactment of the Antiterrorism and Effective Death Penalty Act (effective Apr. 24, 1996) (AEDPA), made deportation for noncitizens convicted of certain criminal offenses virtually inevitable.

"Thus, . . . the retroactivity affirmed in the *Sylvain* case should extend back to the effective date of AEDPA, April 24, 1996, for convictions of offenses for which AEDPA eliminated the then available protections (or discretionary waivers) for noncitizens." *Commonwealth v. Mercado*, 474 Mass. 80, 81–82 (2016).

NOTE 3a   "[T]he explicit language of the statute unambiguously manifests a legislative intent to place on the Commonwealth the burden of proving that the requirements of G.L. c. 278, § 29D, have been satisfied, irrespective of the amount of time that may have passed between a conviction and a defendant's motion to withdraw his plea or his admission to sufficient facts." *Commonwealth v. Jones*, 417 Mass. 661, 664 (1994).

NOTE 3b   For a different result than *Jones, see Commonwealth v. Pryce*, 429 Mass. 556, 559 (1999) ("[W]e have a record that the defendant received a hearing [six years prior when he entered a guilty plea at the BMC] augmented by a judge's finding that it is standard practice to give the alien warning at such hearing [the recording of which was destroyed 2.5 years later pursuant to BMC court rule]. We know that the defendant was aware when he entered his plea that it could result in his deportation. Furthermore, the statutory presumption which he seeks to invoke has no apparent application when his motion for a new trial comes after deportation. Nor has he satisfied the statutory requirement that he show that this conviction caused him to be deported.").

NOTE 4   "[T]he statute mandates that all three warnings must be given[. As the judge] omitted the consequence of 'exclusion from admission to the United States,' we conclude the motion to withdraw the plea should have been allowed." *Commonwealth v. Soto*, 47 Mass. App. Ct. 914, 916 (1999).

NOTE 5   **Orally.** "[T]he statute requires the judge to deliver the alien warnings orally as part of the colloquy, and, where the warnings given during that colloquy fail to meet the statutory requirements, the defendant's signature on the court's standard form containing the warnings does not suffice to avoid the consequences mandated by the statute." *Commonwealth v. Hilaire*, 437 Mass. 809, 810 (2002).

NOTE 6   "While nothing in the statute prevents judges from taking steps to avoid any misunderstanding as to the consequences of an admission to sufficient facts followed by a continuance without a finding (i.e., by telling defendants receiving that disposition that immigration authorities may treat their admission to sufficient facts as a 'conviction' notwithstanding the later dismissal of

2

the charge), judges are not required to expand upon the warnings prescribed by the Legislature." *Commonwealth v. Villalobos,* 437 Mass. 797, 804 (2002).

NOTE 7   Record. "Record" includes the official record or transcript or tape recording or "docket sheet on which a box has been checked indicating that the deportation advisement was given" or, in reconstructing a record of a plea hearing, the judge's reliance on his "customary practice in taking guilty pleas". *Commonwealth v. Rzepphiewski,* 431 Mass. 48, 52–55 (2000).

SECTIONS 30–33D
Repealed

SECTION 33E
Capital cases; review by supreme judicial court
(Amended by 2012 Mass. Acts c. 192, §§ 43–44, effective Aug. 2, 2012.)

In a capital case as hereinafter defined the entry in the supreme judicial court shall transfer to that court the whole case for its consideration of the law and the evidence. Upon such consideration the court may, if satisfied that the verdict was against the law or the weight of the evidence, or because of newly discovered evidence, or for any other reason that justice may require (a) order a new trial or (b) direct the entry of a verdict of a lesser degree of guilt, and remand the case to the superior court for the imposition of sentence. For the purpose of such review a capital case shall mean: (i) a case in which the defendant was tried on an indictment for murder in the first degree and was convicted of murder in the first degree, or (ii) the third conviction of a habitual offender pursuant to subsection (b) of section 25 of chapter 279. After the entry of the appeal in a capital case and until the filing of the rescript by the supreme judicial court motions for a new trial shall be presented to that court and shall be dealt with by the full court, which may itself hear and determine such motions or remit the same to the trial judge for hearing and determination. If any motion is filed in the superior court after rescript, no appeal shall lie from the decision of that court upon such motion unless the appeal is allowed by a single justice of the supreme judicial court on the ground that it presents a new and substantial question which ought to be determined by the full court.

NOTE 1   *See Commonwealth v. L'Abbe,* 421 Mass. 262 (1995).

NOTE 2   "Hereinafter, in the interests of consistency and finality, we shall require that a gatekeeper petition pursuant to G.L. c. 278, § 33E, be filed within thirty days of the denial of a motion for a new trial." *Mains v. Commonwealth,* 433 Mass. 30, 36 n.10 (2000).

SECTIONS 33F–H
Repealed

SECTION 34
Motions in arrest of judgment

No motion in arrest of judgment shall be allowed for a cause existing before verdict, unless it affects the jurisdiction of the court.

SECTION 35
Trial of male and female prisoners

In all trials in district courts, male and female prisoners shall not be placed at the same time in the same dock unless they are complained of jointly.

Chapter 278A. Post Conviction Access to Forensic and Scientific Analysis

Section

1	Definitions
2	Conditions for filing motion for forensic or scientific analysis; effect of chapter upon analysis under other circumstances
3	Filing of motion; contests; motion for discovery; affidavit of factual innocence; expeditious review of motion
4	Jurisdiction over motion; service of motion; response by prosecuting attorney
5	Appointed counsel
6	Hearing
7	Findings of fact and conclusions of law; criteria for allowing requested analysis; orders for discovery
8	Conditions of analysis; selection of forensic service provider; equal access to personnel and information; retention of material evidence; cooperation with laboratory
9	Time for performing analysis
10	Cost of analysis
11	Effect of proceedings on terms of sentence imposed
12	Disclosure of analysis results; orders to produce data, documents and notes
13	Additional analysis ordered upon inconclusive findings
14	Victim notification
15	Waiver of right to file motion prohibited
16	Retention and preservation of evidence or biological material by government entities; regulations
17	Civil or criminal liability of government officials; will or wanton misconduct or gross negligence by government entities; damages
18	Appeals

SECTION 1
Definitions
(Added by 2012 Mass. Acts c. 38, effective May 17, 2012.)

As used in this chapter, the following words shall, unless the context clearly requires otherwise, have the following meanings:—

"Analysis", the process by which a forensic or scientific technique is applied to evidence or biological material to identify the perpetrator of a crime.

"Biological material", a sexual assault forensic examination kit, semen, blood, saliva, hair, skin tissue or other identified biological substance.

"Conviction", a verdict or finding of guilty, a plea of guilty, a plea of nolo contendere or an adjudication of delinquency as a juvenile entered by the trial court.

"Exhaustive testing", analysis of a particular item of evidence or biological material that precludes replicate analysis of the evidence or biological material.

"Factually innocent", a person convicted of a criminal offense who did not commit that offense.

"Governmental entity", an official body of the commonwealth, or of a county, city or town within the commonwealth.

"Identity", the moving party's identity as the perpetrator of the offense for which the moving party was convicted in the underlying case.

"Moving party", a person who files a motion under this chapter.

"Post conviction", indicates any time after which a conviction has been entered.

"Prosecuting attorney", the district attorney for the district in which the moving party was convicted or the attorney general of the commonwealth.

"Replicate analysis", the duplication of an analysis performed on a particular item of evidence or biological material.

"Underlying case", the trial court proceedings that resulted in the conviction of the moving party.

"Victim", any natural person who suffered direct or threatened physical, emotional or financial harm as the result of the commission or attempted commission of the crime or delinquency case that is the subject of the underlying case; "victim" shall also include the parent, guardian, legal representative or administrator or executor of the estate of such person if that person is a minor, incompetent or deceased.

NOTE   "[T]he purpose of the legislation was to remedy the injustice of wrongful convictions of factually innocent persons by allowing access to analyses of biological material with newer forensic and scientific techniques." *Commonwealth v. Wade*, 467 Mass. 496, 504 (2014) (citations omitted).

SECTION 2
Conditions for filing motion for forensic or scientific analysis; effect of chapter upon analysis under other circumstances
(Added by 2012 Mass. Acts c. 38, effective May 17, 2012.)

A person may file a motion for forensic or scientific analysis under this chapter if that person: (1) has been convicted of a criminal offense in a court of the commonwealth; (2) is incarcerated in a state prison, house of correction, is on parole or probation or whose liberty has been otherwise restrained as the result of a conviction; and (3) asserts factual innocence of the crime for which the person has been convicted.

This chapter shall not be construed to prohibit the performance of forensic or scientific analysis under any other circumstances, including by agreement between the person convicted of a criminal offense and the prosecuting attorney.

NOTE   "In 2012, the Legislature enacted G.L. c. 278A, . . . in the wake of national recognition that 'DNA testing has an unparalleled ability both to exonerate the wrongly convicted and to identify the guilty,' *District Attorney's Office for the Third Judicial Dist. v. Osborne*, 557 U.S. 52, 55 (2009)[. It] permits access to forensic and scientific evidence on the filing of a motion by an individual who has been convicted of a criminal offense, who consequently has been incarcerated, and who asserts factual innocence." *Commonwealth v. Wade*, 467 Mass. 496, 497 (2014).

SECTION 3
Filing of motion; contests; motion for discovery; affidavit of factual innocence; expeditious review of motion
(Added by 2012 Mass. Acts c. 38, effective May 17, 2012.)

(a) A person seeking relief under this chapter shall file a motion in the court in which the conviction was entered, using the same caption and docket number as identified the underlying case.

(b) The motion shall include the following information, and when relevant, shall include specific references to the record in the underlying case or to affidavits that are filed in support of the motion that are signed by a person with personal knowledge of the factual basis of the motion:

(1) the name and a description of the requested forensic or scientific analysis;

(2) information demonstrating that the requested analysis is admissible as evidence in courts of the commonwealth;

(3) a description of the evidence or biological material that the moving party seeks to have analyzed or tested, including its location and chain of custody if known;

(4) information demonstrating that the analysis has the potential to result in evidence that is material to the moving party's identification as the perpetrator of the crime in the underlying case; and

(5) information demonstrating that the evidence or biological material has not been subjected to the requested analysis because:

(i) the requested analysis had not yet been developed at the time of the conviction; (ii) the results of the requested analysis were not admissible in the courts of the commonwealth at the time of the conviction; (iii) the moving party and the moving party's attorney were not aware of and did not have reason to be aware of the existence of the evidence or biological material at the time of the underlying case and conviction; (iv) the moving party's attorney in the underlying case was aware at the time of the conviction of the existence of the evidence or biological material, the results of the requested analysis were admissible as evidence in courts of the commonwealth, a reasonably effective attorney would have sought the analysis and either the moving party's attorney failed to seek the analysis or the judge denied the request; or (v) the evidence or biological material was otherwise unavailable at the time of the conviction.

(c) If the moving party is unable to include for filing with the motion any of the items or information described in subsection (b), or if the moving party lacks items or information necessary to establish any of the factors listed in subsection (b) of section 7, the moving party shall include a description of efforts made to obtain such items and information and may move for discovery of such items or information from the prosecuting attorney or any third party.

(d) The moving party shall file with the motion an affidavit stating that the moving party is factually innocent of the offense of conviction and that the requested forensic or scientific analysis will support the claim of innocence. A person who pleaded guilty or nolo contendere in the underlying case may file a motion. The court shall not find that identity was not or could not have been a material issue in the underlying case because of the plea. A person who is alleged to have, or admits to having, made a statement that is or could be incriminating may file a motion under this chapter. The court shall not find that identity was not or should not have been a material issue in the underlying case because the moving party made, or is alleged to have made, an incriminating statement. If the moving party entered a plea of guilty or nolo contendere to the offense of conviction or made an incriminating statement, the moving party shall state in the affidavit that the claim of factual innocence is made notwithstanding the plea or incriminating statement.

(e) The court shall expeditiously review all motions filed and shall dismiss, without prejudice, any such motion without a hearing if the court determines, based on the information contained in the motion, that the motion does not meet the requirements set forth in this section. The prosecuting attorney may provide a response to the motion, to assist the court in considering whether the motion meets the requirement under this section. The court shall notify the moving party and the prosecuting attorney as to whether the motion is sufficient to proceed under this chapter or is dismissed.

NOTE 1   "Chapter 278A creates a two-step procedure for requesting DNA testing or analysis. First, a threshold determination is made by the court in which the conviction was entered as to

2

whether the motion meets the preliminary criteria set forth in G.L. c. 278A, § 3. If those criteria are met, a hearing 'shall' be conducted pursuant to G.L. c. 278A, §§ 6 and 7, to determine whether a petitioner has established by a preponderance of the evidence sufficient facts for a judge to order DNA testing or further discovery.

"[T]he Legislature clearly intended that, to proceed to a hearing, a § 3 motion requires only the limited showing set forth explicitly in G.L. c. 278A, § 3(b) and (d), and review of the motion in order to determine whether a hearing will be conducted is confined to the assertions in the motion, the affidavits and supporting documents attached thereto, and any response that may be filed by the Commonwealth to assist the court." *Commonwealth v. Wade*, 467 Mass. 496, 501, 504 (2014).

NOTE 2 "In light of this legislative intent, we conclude that a § 3 motion should not be denied on the ground that the evidence sought to be tested has been subjected previously to a method of testing, if the accuracy of that testing has materially improved the test's ability to identify the perpetrator of a crime." *Commonwealth v. Donald*, 468 Mass. 37, 47 (2014).

NOTE 3 "[B]ecause Wade has demonstrated that 'the requested analysis had not yet been developed at the time of conviction,' G.L. c. 278A, § 3(b)(5)(i), he has met the requirement of the act to establish one of the five enumerated reasons explaining why the requested testing was not previously conducted. *See* G.L. c. 278A, § 3(b)(5)(i)–(v). It was therefore an abuse of discretion for the Superior Court judge to deny Wade's motion for scientific testing on the ground that Wade also was required to establish that the enumerated reason was the "primary reason" that his trial attorney did not seek the requested analysis, and that a reasonably effective attorney would have done so." *Commonwealth v. Wade*, 475 Mass. 54, 55–56 (2016).

NOTE 4 "[R]egardless whether a moving party proceeds under the reasonably effective attorney prong or any other prong of § 3(b)(5), whether his or her trial counsel made a strategic decision to forgo such testing is not relevant to that inquiry." *Commonwealth v. Wade*, 475 Mass. 54, 63 (2016).

SECTION 4
Jurisdiction over motion; service of motion; response by prosecuting attorney
(Added by 2012 Mass. Acts c. 38, effective May 17, 2012.)

(a) The moving party shall file a motion under section 3 with the court that adjudicated the underlying case and shall serve a copy of the motion on the prosecuting attorney.

(b) If the motion is not dismissed by the court under subsection (e) of section 3, the prosecuting attorney shall file a response with the court within 60 days after the date upon which the court issues notice under said subsection (e) of said section 3, and shall simultaneously serve the response on the moving party. The prosecuting attorney may request additional time in which to file the response, which the court may grant for good cause shown.

(c) The prosecuting attorney's response shall include any specific legal or factual objections that the prosecuting attorney has to the requested analysis.

SECTION 5
Appointed counsel
(Added by 2012 Mass. Acts c. 38, effective May 17, 2012.)

The court may assign or appoint counsel to represent a moving party who meets the definition of indigency under section 2 of chapter 211D in the preparation and presentation of motions filed under this chapter.

SECTION 6
Hearing
(Added by 2012 Mass. Acts c. 38, effective May 17, 2012.)

(a) The court shall order a hearing on the motion if the motion meets the requirements of section 3. The moving party shall be present for the hearing unless the moving party waives the party's presence at the hearing.

(b) The judge who conducted the trial or accepted the moving party's plea of guilty or nolo contendere in the underlying case shall conduct the hearing if possible.

SECTION 7
Findings of fact and conclusions of law; criteria for allowing requested analysis; orders for discovery
(Added by 2012 Mass. Acts c. 38, effective May 17, 2012.)

(a) After reviewing the motion, the prosecuting attorney's response and after holding a hearing, the court shall state findings of fact and conclusions of law on the record, or shall make written findings of fact and conclusions of law that support the decision to allow or deny a motion brought under section 3.

(b) The court shall allow the requested forensic or scientific analysis if each of the following has been demonstrated by a preponderance of the evidence:

(1) that the evidence or biological material exists;

(2) that the evidence or biological material has been subject to a chain of custody that is sufficient to establish that it has not deteriorated, been substituted, tampered with, replaced, handled or altered such that the results of the requested analysis would lack any probative value;

(3) that the evidence or biological material has not been subjected to the requested analysis for any of the reasons in clauses (i) to (v), inclusive, of paragraph (5) of subsection (b) of section 3; (4) that the requested analysis has the potential to result in evidence that is material to the moving party's identification as the perpetrator of the crime in the underlying case; (5) that the purpose of the motion is not the obstruction of justice or delay; and (6) that the results of the particular type of analysis being requested have been found to be admissible in courts of the commonwealth.

(c) The court on motion of any party, after notice to the opposing party and any third party from whom discovery is sought, and an opportunity to be heard, may authorize such discovery as provided for under Rule 30(c)(4) of the Massachusetts Rules of Criminal Procedure, from either party or any third party as is deemed appropriate, subject to appropriate protective orders or an order to the party seeking discovery to produce reciprocal discovery.

Such discovery may include items and biological materials from third parties, provided the party seeking discovery demonstrates that analysis of these items or biological material will, by a preponderance of the evidence, provide evidence material to the identification of a perpetrator of the crime.

If, in response to a motion made under subsection (c) of section 3, the court finds good cause for the moving party's inability to obtain items or information required under subsection (b) of said section 3 and subsection (b) of section 7, the court may order discovery to assist the moving party in identifying the location and condition of evidence or biological material that was obtained in relation to the underlying case, regardless of whether it was introduced at trial or would be admissible. The court, when considering such discovery requests, shall not require the establishment of a prima facie case for relief under Rule 30 of the Massachusetts Rules of Criminal Procedure.

NOTE 1   "Given its compelling interest in remedying wrongful convictions of factually innocent persons, the Legislature intended to permit access to DNA testing 'regardless of the presence of overwhelming evidence of guilt in the underlying trial. [*Commonwealth v. Wade*, 467 Mass. 496, 511 (2014)]. As such, it is entirely appropriate that we construe the language of G.L. c. 278A, § 7(b), in a manner that is generous to the moving party." *Commonwealth v. Clark*, 472 Mass. 120, 136 (2015).

NOTE 2   "[A] moving party satisfies § 7(b) upon establishing that 'any of the reasons' set forth in § 3(b)(5) are applicable to the facts of the party's case." *Commonwealth v. Wade*, 475 Mass. 54, 62–63 (2016).

SECTION 8
Conditions of analysis; selection of forensic service provider; equal access to personnel and information; retention of material evidence; cooperation with laboratory
(Added by 2012 Mass. Acts c. 38, effective May 17, 2012; 2014 Mass. Acts c. 165, §§ 182–183, effective July 15, 2014.)

(a) In allowing a motion under section 3, the court shall specify conditions on the analysis, including, but not limited to, the transportation, handling and return of evidence or biological materials, to protect the integrity of the evidence or biological material and the analysis.

(b) The prosecuting attorney and the moving party shall agree on a forensic services provider accredited by an accreditation body that is a signatory to the International Laboratory Accreditation Cooperation Mutual Recognition Agreement and offers forensic laboratory accreditation service to conduct the analysis, which, except in the case of exhaustive testing, may include the forensic and technology center of the state police crime laboratory or the Boston police department crime laboratory units.

(c) If the prosecuting attorney and the moving party are unable to agree on a forensic services provider, the prosecuting attorney and the moving party shall submit to the court a list of not more than 3 forensic services providers who are accredited by an accreditation body that is a signatory to the International Laboratory Accreditation Cooperation Mutual Recognition Agreement and offers forensic laboratory accreditation services and have the capability to perform the requested analysis. The court shall select a forensic services provider from either list. For purposes of this section, "laboratory" shall refer to the forensic services provider selected under this subsection or subsection (b).

(d) The laboratory shall give equal access to its personnel, opinions, conclusions, reports and other documentation to the prosecuting attorney and the moving party.

(e) The laboratory shall retain and maintain the integrity of a sufficient portion of the evidence or biological material for replicate analysis. If, after initial examination of the evidence or biological material, but before the actual analysis, the laboratory determines that there is insufficient material for replicate analysis, it shall simultaneously notify in writing the prosecuting attorney, the moving party and the court. Exhaustive testing shall not occur except by specific order of the court. In the event that exhaustive testing is so authorized, upon request of either party, the court shall make such orders to ensure that representatives of the moving party and the

prosecuting attorney have the opportunity to observe the analysis, unless such observation is inconsistent with the practices or protocols of the laboratory conducting the analysis.

(f) The moving party shall cooperate with the laboratory. At the laboratory's or the prosecuting attorney's request and upon court order, the moving party shall provide biological samples to the laboratory or to law enforcement personnel. If the moving party unreasonably fails to cooperate with such orders, the court may deny the motion with prejudice.

SECTION 9
Time for performing analysis
(Added by 2012 Mass. Acts c. 38, effective May 17, 2012.)

Upon allowance of a motion under section 3, analysis shall take place as soon as practicable.

SECTION 10
Cost of analysis
(Added by 2012 Mass. Acts c. 38, effective May 17, 2012.)

The costs of the analysis shall be paid:

(1) by the moving party if the moving party does not meet the definition of indigency under section 2 of chapter 211D and has sufficient means to make such payment;

(2) if the moving party meets the definition of indigency under said section 2 of said chapter 211D, as an extra fee or cost under sections 27A through 27G, inclusive, of chapter 261; or

(3) if a person is indigent, but has the ability to pay a reduced fee as defined under said section 2 of said chapter 211D, by the moving party to the maximum feasible amount possible given the financial resources of the moving party as the court deems equitable.

SECTION 11
Effect of proceedings on terms of sentence imposed
(Added by 2012 Mass. Acts c. 38, effective May 17, 2012.)

Proceedings under this chapter shall not stay or otherwise interfere with a term of incarceration, parole, probation or other sentence imposed.

SECTION 12
Disclosure of analysis results; orders to produce data, documents and notes
(Added by 2012 Mass. Acts c. 38, effective May 17, 2012.)

(a) The results of the analysis shall be simultaneously disclosed to the moving party, the prosecuting attorney and the court.

(b) The court shall, at the request of a party or on its own initiative, order production of the underlying laboratory data, documents and notes.

SECTION 13
Additional analysis ordered upon inconclusive findings
(Added by 2012 Mass. Acts c. 38, effective May 17, 2012.)

If the analysis is inconclusive, the court may order any additional analysis requested if the court concludes that the requirements of subsection (b) of section 7 are met.

SECTION 14
Victim notification
(Added by 2012 Mass. Acts c. 38, effective May 17, 2012.)

(a) If a motion is filed under section 3, the prosecuting attorney shall notify the victim of the crime in the underlying case.

(b) The prosecuting attorney shall notify the victim if the court allows a motion for forensic or scientific analysis and, if the victim is notified of the allowance of the motion, shall promptly notify the victim of the result of the analysis.

SECTION 15
Waiver of right to file motion prohibited
(Added by 2012 Mass. Acts c. 38, effective May 17, 2012.)

The right to file a motion under this chapter shall not be waived. This prohibition of any waiver includes, but is not limited to, any stated or unstated waiver that is or is alleged to be part of any agreement or understanding related to any plea of guilty or of nolo contendere or to any sentencing or appellate proceeding or to any correctional placement or conditions.

SECTION 16
Retention and preservation of evidence or biological material by government entities; regulations
(Added by 2012 Mass. Acts c. 38, effective May 17, 2012.)

(a) Any governmental entity that is in possession of evidence or biological material that is collected for its potential evidentiary value during the investigation of a crime, the prosecution of which results in a conviction, shall retain such evidence or biological material for the period of time that a person remains in the custody of the commonwealth or under parole or probation supervision in connection with that crime, without regard to whether the evidence or biological material was introduced at trial. Each governmental entity shall retain all such evidence or biological material in a manner that is reasonably designed to preserve the evidence and biological material and to prevent its destruction or deterioration. The evidence or biological material need not be preserved if it is to be returned to a third party or if it is of such a size, bulk or physical character as to render retention impracticable.

(b) The director of the crime laboratory within the department of state police, in consultation with the forensic sciences advisory board established by section 184A of chapter 6, shall promulgate regulations governing the retention and preservation of evidence or biological material by any governmental entity. The regulations shall include standards for maintaining the integrity of the materials over time, the designation of officials at each governmental entity with custodial responsibility and requirements for contemporaneously recorded documentation of individuals having and obtaining custody of any evidence or biological material.

SECTION 17
Civil or criminal liability of government officials; will or wanton misconduct or gross negligence by government entities; damages
(Added by 2012 Mass. Acts c. 38, effective May 17, 2012.)

(a) Governmental officials and employees acting in good faith shall not be liable in a civil or criminal proceeding for any act under this chapter.

(b) If a governmental entity responsible for the preservation of evidence or biological material engages in willful or wanton misconduct or gross negligence, which results in the deterioration or destruction of evidence or biological material so that a laboratory is unable to perform adequate or proper analysis, that entity shall be subject to proceedings for contempt.

(c) Nothing in this chapter shall create any cause of action for damages against the commonwealth or any of its subdivisions or officers, employees, agents or subdivisions, except as provided in this section.

SECTION 18
Appeals
(Added by 2012 Mass. Acts c. 38, effective May 17, 2012.)

An order allowing or denying a motion for forensic or scientific analysis filed under this chapter shall be a final and appealable order. If the moving party appeals an order denying a motion for forensic or scientific analysis the moving party shall file a notice of appeal with the court within 30 days after the entry of the judgment.

Chapter 279. Judgment and Execution

Section
1	Suspension of execution; payment of fine, etc.; revocation of suspension; exceptions
1A	Suspension of execution of sentence; probation
1B	Funds collection and disbursement
2	DYS suspended sentences
3	Arrest without warrant of person on probation; warrant for arrest of persons already imprisoned; application for disposition
3A	Motion of district attorney for sentence
4	Imposition of sentence; stay of execution
4A	Repealed
4B	Notice to victim of sentencing proceedings; oral or written statements
5	Sentence if no punishment is provided by statute
6	Sentence to jail or house of correction
6A	Special sentence of imprisonment (weekend sentences); eligible offenders; revocation or rescission of special sentence; subsequent crimes
7	Sentence to jail or house of correction for nonpayment of fine
8	Commitments upon two or more sentences
8A	Determinations of time of taking effect of sentence; "from and after" sentence
8B	Commission of crime while released on personal recognizance; consecutive sentences
9	Second sentence for nonpayment of fine
10	Conditional sentence
11	Punishment by imprisonment only or by fine only when law prescribes both
12	Recognizance of husband convicted of assault upon wife
13	Recognizance to keep the peace or to be of good behavior
14	Recognizance; filing; proceedings on breach of condition
15	Sentence to jail or house of correction in any county
16	Sentencing of female to Massachusetts correctional institution, Framingham
17–18	Repealed
19	Place of imprisonment of females convicted of felony
20	Execution of sentence of imprisonment of females sentenced to confinement at hard labor
21–22	Repealed
23	Limitation of sentences of males to jails or houses of correction
24	Indeterminate sentence to state prison
25	Punishment of habitual criminals
26	Further sentence of convict in state prison
27	Immediate execution of sentence to state prison of convict sentenced to jail or house of correction
28–29	Repealed
30	Vacation of office from time of sentence to state prison
31–33	Repealed
33A	Credit for days of confinement awaiting and during trial

34	Delivery to sheriff of certified transcript from minutes of court of conviction and sentence; execution of sentence
35	Transmission of complaint or indictment to correctional institution
36	Sentences to state farm
37	Setting out statutory name of crime in warrant for commitment
38	Powers of sheriff or constable in execution of warrant of commitment
39	Return of precept to magistrate
40	Service of new warrant of commitment upon convict
41	Default of corporation
42	Warrant of distress to compel payment of penalty or assessment
43–56	Repealed
57	Warrant of conviction and sentence of death
58	Confinement of prisoners under death sentence; psychiatric examinations; transfer to general prison population; court order
59	Time of execution of sentence of death
60	Infliction of death penalty
61	Sentencing of insane persons or pregnant women
62	Respite of execution where convict under sentence of death has become insane or pregnant
63	Respite for opportunity to investigate and consider case for pardon
64	Stay of execution of sentence of death
65	Witnesses of execution of sentence of death
66	Post mortem examination
67	Return of warrant
68	Presentence hearing in cases in which death penalty may be imposed; evidence considered; instructions; verdict; sentence; mistrial
69	Aggravating and mitigating circumstances in cases in which death penalty may be authorized
70	Necessity of jury findings to impose sentence of death
71	Review of sentence of death

SECTION 1
Suspension of execution; payment of fine, etc.; revocation of suspension; exceptions

When a person convicted before a court is sentenced to imprisonment, the court may direct that the execution of the sentence, or any part thereof, be suspended and that he be placed on probation for such time and on such terms and conditions as it shall fix. When a person so convicted is sentenced to pay a fine and to stand committed until it is paid, the court may direct that the execution of the sentence, or any part thereof, be suspended for such time as it shall fix and in its discretion that he be placed on probation on condition that he pay the fine within such time. If the fine does not exceed two hundred dollars and the court finds that the defendant is unable to pay it when imposed, the execution of the sentence shall be suspended and he may in its discretion be placed on probation, unless the court shall find that he will probably default, or that such suspension will be detrimental to the interests of the public. If he is committed for nonpayment of a fine, the order of commitment shall contain a recital of the findings of the court on which suspension is refused. The fine shall be paid in one payment, or in part payments, to the probation officer, and when fully paid the order of commitment shall be void. The probation officer shall give a receipt for every payment so made, shall keep a record of the same, shall pay the fine, or all sums received in part payment thereof, to the sheriff if such fine is imposed in the superior court, or to the clerk of the court if such fine is imposed in the district court, at the end of the period of probation or any extension thereof, and shall keep on file the sheriff's or clerk's receipt therefor. If during or at the end of said period the probation officer shall report that the fine is in whole or in part unpaid, and in his opinion the person is unwilling or unable to pay it, the court may either extend said period, place the case on file or revoke the suspension of the execution of the sentence.

When such suspension is revoked, in a case where the fine has been paid in part, the defendant may be committed for default in payment of the balance.

The provisions of this section shall not permit the suspension of the execution of the sentence of a person convicted of a crime punishable by death or imprisonment for life. In granting probation under this section, the court shall include in its terms and conditions of probation that the person convicted shall pay any child support due under a support order, as defined in section 1A of chapter 119A, including payment toward any arrearage of support that accrues or has accrued or compliance with any payment plan between the person convicted and the IV-D agency as set forth in said chapter 119A.

When a person is sentenced by a court upon conviction of any crime, he shall be informed by the probation department on a form provided by the department of criminal justice information services. that he will have a criminal record that may be accessible to the public under certain conditions, and of his rights pertaining thereto, as provided in sections one hundred and sixty-seven through one hundred and seventy-eight of chapter six.

NOTE 1   "We conclude . . . that the prohibition against suspension of execution of sentences found in G.L. c. 279, § 1, is inapplicable to crimes that carry the possibility of life imprisonment or imprisonment for a term of years . . . ." *Aldoupolis v. Commonwealth*, 386 Mass. 260, 267 (1982).

NOTE 2   See Notes following G.L. c. 276, § 85 (Probation officers' duties).

SECTION 1A
Suspension of execution of sentence; probation

When a person convicted before a court is sentenced to fine and imprisonment, the court may direct that the execution of the sentence, or any part thereof, be suspended, and that he be placed on probation for such time and on such terms and conditions as it shall fix. The court may direct, as one of such terms and conditions, that payment of the fine may be made to the probation officer in one payment, or in part payments, during the period of probation or any extension thereof, and when such fine shall have been fully paid the order of commitment as to the fine shall be void, but the order of commitment as to imprisonment shall not be affected by such payment. The probation officer shall give receipt for every payment so made, shall keep a record of the same, shall pay the fine, or all sums received in part payment thereof, to the clerk of the court at the end of the period of probation or any extension thereof, and shall keep on file the clerk's receipt therefor. If during or at the end of said period the probation officer shall report that the fine is in whole or in part unpaid, and in his opinion the person is unwilling or unable to pay it, the court may either extend said period, place the case on file or revoke the suspension of the execution of the sentence. When such suspension is revoked, in a case where the fine has been paid in part, the defendant may be committed for default in payment of the balance, and may also be committed for the term of imprisonment fixed in the original sentence. This section shall not permit the suspension of the execution of the sentence of any person convicted of a crime punishable by imprisonment for life or of a crime an element of which is being armed with a dangerous weapon, or of any person convicted of any other felony if it shall appear that he has been previously convicted of any felony. In granting probation

2

under this section, the court shall include in its terms and conditions of probation that the person convicted shall pay any child support due under a support order, as defined in section 1A of chapter 119A, including payment toward any arrearage of support that accrues or has accrued or compliance with any payment plan between the person convicted and the IV-D agency as set forth in said chapter 119A.

NOTE   See Notes following Section 1 of this chapter.

SECTION 1B
Funds collection and disbursement

Notwithstanding any other provision of law, the administrative justice of a department of the trial court may direct that both the clerk-magistrate's office and the probation office of one or more court divisions are to utilize a single funds collection and disbursement point within the courthouse.

SECTION 2
DYS suspended sentences

In all cases the execution of orders of commitment to any training school or reformatory, however named, the department of youth services, or the department of public welfare may be suspended, and such suspension continued or revoked, in the same manner and with the same effect as the execution of sentences in criminal cases.

SECTION 3
Arrest without warrant of person on probation; warrant for arrest of persons already imprisoned; application for disposition

At any time before final disposition of the case of a person placed under probation supervision in the custody or care of a probation officer, the probation officer may arrest him without a warrant and take him before the court, or the court may issue a warrant for his arrest. When taken before the court, it may, if he has not been sentenced, sentence him or make any other lawful disposition of the case, and if he has been sentenced, it may continue or revoke the suspension of the execution of his sentence; provided however, that in all cases where the probationer is served with notice of surrender and at least one of the underlying crimes for which he is on probation is a felony, then the probation officer shall provide a duplicate copy of the notice of surrender to the district attorney, and the court shall provide to the district attorney the opportunity to be heard and present evidence at the surrender hearing. If such suspension is revoked, the sentence shall be in full force and effect. If a warrant has been issued by the court for the arrest of such a person and he is a prisoner in any correctional institution, jail or house of correction, the commissioner of correction, the sheriff, master or keeper of said house of correction, or in Suffolk county, the penal institutions commissioner of the city of Boston, as the case may be, having such prisoner under his supervision or control, upon receiving notice of such warrant, shall notify such prisoner that he has the right to apply to the court for prompt disposition thereof. Such an application shall be in writing and given or sent by such prisoner to the commissioner of correction, or such sheriff, master, keeper, or penal institutions commissioner, who shall promptly forward it to the court from which the warrant issued, by certified mail, together with a certificate of said commissioner of correction, sheriff, master, keeper, or penal institutions commissioner,

stating (a) the term of commitment under which such prisoner is being held, (b) the amount of time served, (c) the amount of time remaining to be served, (d) the amount of good time earned, (e) the time of parole eligibility of such prisoner, and (f) any decisions of the board of parole relating to such prisoner. Said commissioner of correction, sheriff, master, keeper, or penal institutions commissioner shall notify the appropriate district attorney by certified mail of such application to the court. Any such prisoner shall, within six months after such application is received by the court, be brought into court for sentencing or other lawful disposition of his case as herein before provided.

In no case where a provision of this chapter provides for a finding, disposition or other order to be made by the court, or for a warrant to be issued, shall such be made or issued by any person other than a justice, special justice or other person exercising the powers of a magistrate.

Notwithstanding any restriction in the preceding paragraph, if a probation officer has probable cause to believe that a person placed under probation supervision or in the custody or care of a probation officer pursuant to sections 42A, 58A or 87 of chapter 276 or any other statute that allows the court to set conditions of release, has violated the conditions set by the court, the probation officer may arrest the probationer or may issue a warrant for the temporary custody of the probationer for a period not to exceed 72 hours or until the next sitting of the court, during which period the probation officer shall arrange for the appearance of the probationer before the court pursuant to the first paragraph of this section.

NOTE 1   See Notes following G.L. c. 276, § 85. Probation officers' duties.

NOTE 2   "[E]ven if an incarcerated defendant properly requests a speedy disposition of an outstanding probation matter pursuant to G.L. c. 279, § 3, that statute does not require, in the absence of prejudice, automatic dismissal, if such disposition does not occur within the six-month period set forth in the statute." *Commonwealth v. Whooley*, 419 Mass. 421, 423–24 (1995).

SECTION 3A
Motion of district attorney for sentence

Not later than seven days after a plea of guilty or after a verdict of guilty and in any event before adjournment of the sitting at which such plea or verdict has been taken and recorded in a case of felony wherein no question of law has been reported for decision by the supreme judicial court, the district attorney shall move for sentence; provided, that nothing herein shall preclude the district attorney from again making such a motion in any case where the imposition of sentence is delayed under section forty-seven.

NOTE   "[T]here is nothing in . . . G.L. c. 279, § 3A . . . which entitles a defendant to an automatic dismissal of an indictment against him upon expiration of the time periods mentioned therein." *Commonwealth v. McInerney*, 380 Mass. 59, 63 (1980).

SECTION 4
Imposition of sentence; stay of execution

Sentence shall be imposed upon conviction of a crime, regardless of whether an appeal has been taken, except as otherwise provided in section sixty-one in case of a conviction of a capital crime.

If sentence is imposed upon conviction of a crime punishable by death, the justice imposing the sentence shall at the same time stay the execution of the sentence, such stay to be effective until revoked by the superior court department of the trial court, which is hereby granted full powers of revocation in the premises. The clerk of such court shall, forthwith upon the revocation by the court of any such stay of execution of sentence, certify that said stay has been revoked and cause said certificate to be served upon the superintendent of the state prison, or the officer performing his duties, by any officer qualified to serve criminal process; and the officer serving the same shall forthwith make due return of service to the clerk.

NOTE 1a   This section "confers discretionary power to stay the execution of sentence pending appeal." *Commonwealth v. Allen*, 378 Mass. 489, 496 (1979).

NOTE 1b   "Where a defendant seeks a stay of execution of sentence, and both the judge in the trial court and a single justice of the Appeals Court deny the stay, 'the presumptive avenue for review is before a panel of the Appeals Court.'" *Christian v. Commonwealth*, 446 Mass. 1003, 1004 (2006) (quoting *Duong v. Commonwealth*, 434 Mass. 1006, 1008 (2004)) (footnote omitted).

NOTE 2   "[T]he same factors specified in [G.L. c. 276] § 58 [governing bail] may properly be considered under § 4. In addition, consideration should be given to danger to any other person or to the community and to the possibility of further acts of criminality during the pendency of the appeal. Finally, the judge or Justice should consider the likelihood of success on the merits of the appeal. There is no requirement, however, that he give a statement of reasons or make any particular finding or certification in order to grant or deny the stay." *Commonwealth v. Allen*, 378 Mass. 489, 498 (1979) (citations, footnotes, and quotation marks omitted).

NOTE 3   A single justice of the Supreme Judicial Court is not required to make an independent exercise of discretion on the question of whether a stay of execution is proper and may rule merely on whether the trial judge abused his discretion by granting the stay. *Commonwealth v. Hodge*, 380 Mass. 851, 853–54 (1980).

NOTE 4   See Note following G.L. c. 265, § 2.

SECTION 4A
Repealed

SECTION 4B
Notice to victim of sentencing proceedings; oral or written statements

Before disposition in any case where a defendant has been found guilty of any felony or any crime against the person or crime where physical injury to a person results excluding any crime for which a sentence of death may be imposed, and which involves an identified victim whose whereabouts are known, the district attorney shall give the victim actual notice of the time and place of sentencing and of the victim's right to make a statement to the court, orally or in writing at the victim's option, as to the impact of the crime and as to a recommended sentence. Before disposition, the court shall allow any victim who elects to make such an oral statement the opportunity to do so in the presence of the defendant. Before disposition, the district attorney shall file any such written statement with the court and shall make it available to the defendant.

If the victim is unable to make an oral or written statement because of his mental, emotional, or physical incapacity or his age, his attorney or a designated family member shall be provided the notice and the opportunity to make a statement prescribed in this paragraph.

Before said disposition the office of the district attorney shall cause to be prepared a written statement as to the impact of the crime on the victim, which shall be filed with the court as part of the presentence report and made available to the defendant. The statement shall include the following: (1) the name of the victim; (2) documentation of the net financial loss, if any, suffered by the victim or a family member as a result of the crime; (3) in cases where the crime has had an impact on the victim's personal welfare or family relationship or has had a psychological impact on the victim or his family, a statement of such impact.

The court shall allow the defendant to have the opportunity to rebut the victim's oral or written statement and the district attorney's written statement if the court decides to rely upon such statements or parts thereof in imposing sentence.

No sentence shall be invalidated because of failure to comply with the provisions of this section. This section shall not be construed to create any cause of action or any right of appeal on behalf of any person.

SECTION 5
Sentence if no punishment is provided by statute

If no punishment for a crime is provided by statute, the court shall impose such sentence, according to the nature of the crime, as conforms to the common usage and practice in the commonwealth. If a person is convicted of a misdemeanor punishable by imprisonment, he may, unless otherwise expressly provided, be sentenced to imprisonment either in the jail or in the house of correction.

SECTION 6
Sentence to jail or house of correction

Whoever is convicted of a crime punishable wholly or in part by imprisonment in jail may be sentenced to such imprisonment in the house of correction or to confinement at hard labor either in the jail or house of correction; and if convicted of a crime punishable by imprisonment in the house of correction may be sentenced to such imprisonment in a jail.

SECTION 6A
Special sentence of imprisonment (weekend sentences); eligible offenders; revocation or rescission of special sentence; subsequent crimes

When a person is sentenced on a first offense to imprisonment in a jail or house of correction for a term which does not exceed one year, the court may order the sentence to be served in whole or in part on weekends and legal holidays, or such other periodic interval as the court may order. Such a sentence shall be known as a special sentence of imprisonment. If the offender receives a special sentence of imprisonment under this section, he shall, unless otherwise provided by the sentence of the court, report to the institution to which he has been sentenced no later than 6:00 pm on Friday and shall be released at 7:00 am on the succeeding Monday; provided, however, that if the succeeding Monday is a holiday, the offender shall not be released until 7:00 am on Tuesday; and provided further, that the total time served shall be equal to the sentence imposed.

On application of the offender, of the department of correction or the director of the institution to which the offender is committed, or on its own motion, the court may after a hearing rescind or modify an order under the first paragraph, and may direct that the balance of the sentence of imprisonment shall be served consecutively. Before a special sentence is rescinded or modified, the court shall cause the notification thereof to be given to the district attorney and the offender.

2

If while serving such a special sentence, such person is convicted of a subsequent crime other than a non-moving motor vehicle violation, the terms of said special sentence shall be rescinded and said person shall complete the balance of his original sentence consecutively in the jail or house of correction in which he has been serving said special sentence.

SECTION 7
Sentence to jail or house of correction for nonpayment of fine

Whoever is convicted of a crime punishable by a fine, and is liable to imprisonment in the jail for its nonpayment, may be sentenced to such imprisonment in the house of correction, or to confinement at hard labor either in the jail or house of correction.

NOTE "The Illinois statute involved in *Williams* authorized both a fine and imprisonment. Williams was given the maximum sentence for petty theft of one year's imprisonment and a $500 fine, plus $5 in court costs. The judgment, as permitted by the Illinois statute, provided that if, when the one-year sentence expired, Williams did not pay the fine and court costs, he was to remain in jail a sufficient length of time to satisfy the total amount at the rate of $5 per day. We held that the Illinois statute as applied to Williams worked an invidious discrimination solely because he was too poor to pay the fine, and therefore violated the Equal Protection Clause.

"Although the instant case involves offenses punishable by fines only, petitioner's imprisonment for nonpayment constitutes precisely the same unconstitutional discrimination, since, like Williams, petitioner was subjected to imprisonment solely because of his indigency."

Tate v. Short, 401 U.S. 395, 397–98 (1971) (citing *Williams v. Illinois*, 399 U.S. 235 (1970)).

SECTION 8
Commitments upon two or more sentences

A convict upon whom two or more sentences to imprisonment are imposed may be fully committed upon all such sentences at the same time, and shall serve them in the order named in the mittimuses upon which he is committed; but when fine and imprisonment are named in one of the sentences the prisoner shall always be committed upon the term sentence first.

SECTION 8A
Determinations of time of taking effect of sentence; "from and after" sentence

For the purpose only of determining the time of the taking effect of a sentence which is ordered to take effect from and after the expiration of a previous sentence, such previous sentence shall be deemed to have expired when a prisoner serving such previous sentence shall have been released therefrom by parole or otherwise. Nothing in this section shall be construed to alter or control any provision of section one hundred and thirty-one or one hundred and forty-nine of chapter one hundred and twenty-seven.

NOTE "Whenever a sentence is ordered 'to take effect from and after the expiration' of concurrent sentences, it takes effect from and after the expiration of the longer sentence." *Carlino v. Comm'r of Correction*, 355 Mass. 159, 162 (1969). "General Laws c. 279, § 8A, is clear and unambiguous. It provides that a from and after sentence 'takes effect' when a prisoner is released from an earlier sentence 'by parole or otherwise.'" *Crooker v. Chairman of the Massachusetts Parole Bd.*, 38 Mass. App. Ct. 915, 916 (1995).

SECTION 8B
Commission of crime while released on personal recognizance; consecutive sentences

If a defendant on release subject to the provisions of section fifty-eight of chapter two hundred and seventy-six, commits a crime, the sentence imposed for such a crime shall run consecutively to the earlier sentence for the crime for which he was on release.

SECTION 9
Second sentence for nonpayment of fine

Except as provided in section one hundred and forty-six of chapter one hundred and twenty-seven, if a convict is sentenced to pay a fine in more than one case and has been committed to a jail, house of correction or other prison or other correctional institution for refusing to pay such fine, the subsequent sentence shall take effect upon the expiration of the imprisonment under the former sentence.

SECTION 10
Conditional sentence

If a person has been convicted of a crime punishable, at the discretion of the court, by fine or imprisonment in the jail or house of correction or by fine or imprisonment in the state prison, the court may impose upon him a conditional sentence, and order him to pay a fine within a limited time which shall be expressed in the sentence, and in default thereof to suffer such imprisonment as is provided by law. He shall be forthwith committed to the custody of an officer in court or to the jail, to be detained until the sentence is complied with; and if he does not within the time limited pay the fine imposed, the sheriff shall cause the other part of the sentence to be executed forthwith.

SECTION 11
Punishment by imprisonment only or by fine only when law prescribes both

Whoever is convicted of a crime, punishable by fine and imprisonment either in the jail or house of correction, except a person convicted under section thirty G of chapter one hundred and thirty-eight, may at the discretion of the court, be sentenced to be punished by imprisonment only, or by a fine only, if he shows to the satisfaction of the court that he has not before been convicted of a similar crime.

SECTION 12
Recognizance of husband convicted of assault upon wife

Except as provided in section twenty-eight of chapter two hundred and eighteen and in section twenty of chapter two hundred and nineteen, if a husband is convicted of an assault upon his wife, the court may, in addition to the other penalties imposed, or in lieu thereof, order him to recognize with surety or sureties to keep the peace for any term of not more than two years, and may at any time revoke such order or reduce the amount required or order that the recognizance be taken without surety.

SECTION 13
Recognizance to keep the peace or to be of good behavior

Except as provided in section twenty-eight of chapter two hundred and eighteen and in section twenty of chapter two hundred and nineteen, whoever is convicted of a misdemeanor may, in addition to the punishment prescribed by law, be required to recognize, with sufficient sureties, in a reasonable sum to keep the peace, or to be of good behavior, or both, for any term of not more than two years, and to stand committed until he so recognizes.

SECTION 14
Recognizance; filing; proceedings on breach of condition

Such recognizance shall be filed of record in the superior court for the county, and, upon a breach of the condition thereof, the proceedings shall be as provided in chapter two hundred and seventy-five relative to recognizances to keep the peace and be of good behavior.

SECTION 15
Sentence to jail or house of correction in any county

Whoever is convicted of a crime, punishable by imprisonment in the jail or house of correction, may be sentenced to a jail or house of correction of any county, and the master or keeper shall receive and detain him in the same manner as if he had been sentenced by a court sitting in the county where such jail or house of correction is situated.

SECTION 16
Sentencing of female to Massachusetts correctional institution, Framingham

A female, convicted of a crime punishable by imprisonment in a jail or house of correction, may be sentenced to the Massachusetts Correctional Institution, Framingham.

SECTIONS 17–18
Repealed

SECTION 19
Place of imprisonment of females convicted of felony

The sentence to imprisonment of a female convicted of a felony shall be executed in the Massachusetts Correctional Institution, Framingham; or the court imposing sentence in such a case may impose the sentence in a jail or house of correction provided by law in the case of male prisoners, if it does not exceed two and one half years.

SECTION 20
Execution of sentence of imprisonment of females sentenced to confinement at hard labor

Subject to the preceding section, a sentence of a female convict of whatever age to confinement at hard labor shall be executed in a jail or house of correction or the Massachusetts Correctional Institution, Framingham as the court orders.

SECTIONS 21–22
Repealed

SECTION 23
Limitation of sentences of males to jails or houses of correction

No sentence of a male convict to imprisonment or confinement for more than two and one half years shall be executed in any jail or house of correction.

SECTION 24
Indeterminate sentence to state prison
(Amended by 2012 Mass. Acts c. 192, §§ 45–46, effective Aug. 2, 2012; 2014 Mass. Acts c. 189, § 6, effective July 25, 2014.)

If a convict is sentenced to the state prison, except as an habitual criminal, the court shall not fix the term of imprisonment, but shall fix a maximum and a minimum term for which he may be imprisoned. The maximum term shall not be longer than the longest term fixed by law for the punishment of the crime of which he has been convicted, and the minimum term shall be a term set by the court, except that, where an alternative sentence to a house of correction is permitted for the offense, a minimum state prison term may not be less than one year. In the case of a sentence to life imprisonment, except in the case of a sentence for murder in the first degree, and in the case of multiple life sentences arising out of separate and distinct incidents that occurred at different times, where the second offense occurred subsequent to the first conviction, the court shall fix a minimum term which shall be not less than 15 years nor more than 25 years.

In the case of a sentence of life imprisonment for murder in the first degree committed by a person on or after the person's fourteenth birthday and before the person's eighteenth birthday, the court shall fix a minimum term of not less than 20 years nor more than 30 years; provided, however, that in the case of a sentence of life imprisonment for murder in the first degree with extreme atrocity or cruelty committed by a person on or after the person's fourteenth birthday and before the person's eighteenth birthday, the court shall fix a minimum term of 30 years; and provided further, that in the case of a sentence of life imprisonment for murder in the first degree with deliberately premeditated malice aforethought committed by a person on or after the person's fourteenth birthday and before the person's eighteenth birthday, the court shall fix a minimum term of not less than 25 years nor more than 30 years.

NOTE 1   The defendant received a 19- to 20-year sentence. On appeal he argued that "the time span between his minimum and maximum sentences is de minimis, amounting, in effect, to a prohibited determinate sentence."

Conviction and sentence affirmed.

Commonwealth v. Foley, 402 Mass. 703, 706 (1988).

NOTE 2   See notes following G.L. c. 265, § 2.

SECTION 25
Punishment of habitual criminals
(Stricken & replaced by 2012 Mass. Acts c. 192, § 47, effective Aug. 2, 2012.)

(a) Whoever is convicted of a felony and has been previously twice convicted and sentenced to state prison or state correctional facility or a federal corrections facility for a term not less than 3 years by the commonwealth, another state or the United States, and who does not show that the person has been pardoned for either crime on the ground that the person was innocent, shall be considered a habitual criminal and shall be punished by imprisonment in state prison or state correctional facility for such felony for the maximum term provided by law.

(b) Whoever: (i) has been convicted 2 times previously of 1 or more of the following offenses: section 1, section 13, section 13½, clause (i) of subsection (b) of section 13A, section 13B, subsection (a) of section 13B½, section 13B¾, section 13F, committing an assault and battery upon a child and by such assault and battery causing bodily injury or substantial bodily injury under subsection (b) of section 13J, section 14, section 15, clause (i) of subsection (c) of section 15A, section 16, sections 17 and 18 if armed with a firearm, shotgun, rifle, machine gun, or assault weapon, section 18A, section 18B, section 18C, section 21, section 22, section 22A, section 22B, section 22C, section 23A, section 23B, section

2

24, section 24B, section 26, section 26B, section 26C, section 28, and subsection (b) of section 39 of chapter 265, section 14 or section 102C of chapter 266, section 4A, section 17, subsection (b) of section 29A, subsection (b) of section 29B, section 29C, section 35A and subsection (b) of section 53A of chapter 272, or has been convicted 2 times previously of a like violation of the laws of another state, the United States or a military, territorial or Indian tribal authority, arising out of charges separately brought and tried, and arising out of separate and distinct incidents that occurred at different times, where the second offense occurred subsequent to the first conviction; (ii) has been sentenced to incarceration at a state prison or state correctional facility or federal correction facility for at least 3 years to be served for each of the prior 2 convictions; and (iii) does not show that he has been pardoned for either prior offense on the ground that he was innocent shall, upon conviction of 1 of the enumerated offenses in clause (i), where the offense occurred subsequent to the second conviction, shall be considered a habitual offender and shall be imprisoned in the state prison or state correctional facility for the maximum term provided by law for the offense enumerated in clause (i). No sentence imposed under this subsection shall be reduced or suspended nor shall such person so sentenced be eligible for probation, parole, work release or furlough or receive any deduction from such person's sentence for good conduct. A sentence imposed on a habitual offender under this subsection, if such habitual offender is incarcerated at a state prison or state correctional facility, shall commence upon the conclusion of the sentence such habitual offender is serving at the time of sentencing.

(c) No person shall be considered a habitual offender under subsection (b) based upon any offense for which such person was adjudicated a youthful offender, a delinquent child, or a like violation of the laws of another state, the United States or a military, territorial or Indian tribal authority for which a person was treated as a juvenile.

(d) Upon sentencing a defendant to a qualifying term of incarceration, or prior to accepting a guilty plea for any qualifying offense listed in subsection (b), the court shall inform the defendant that a conviction or plea of guilty for such an offense implicates the habitual offender statute and that upon conviction or plea of guilty for the third or subsequent of said offenses: (1) the defendant may be imprisoned in the state prison for the maximum term provided by law for such third or subsequent offense; (2) no sentence may be reduced or suspended; and (3) the defendant may be ineligible for probation, parole, work release or furlough, or to receive any deduction in sentence for good conduct. No otherwise valid plea or conviction shall be vacated based upon the failure to give such warnings.

NOTE 1 **Double Jeopardy.** The use of prior convictions to enhance penalties under G.L. c. 279, § 25 does not run afoul of the double jeopardy prohibitions of the Fifth Amendment to the Constitution of the United States or G.L. c. 263, § 7. *Commonwealth v. Burston*, 35 Mass. App. Ct. 355, 358–59 (1993) ("Although it is obnoxious to the Constitution and the statute to subject a person to successive trials for the same offense, it is rational and inoffensive to provide for cumulative penalties based on conviction of separate offenses.") (footnote omitted).

NOTE 2 "[T]he defendant had [earlier] pleaded guilty to two separate indictments drawn under G.L. c. 266, § 15, which alleged separate and distinct offenses committed at different times and places; . . . the defendant received concurrent sentences . . . on both indictments; . . . those sentences were ordered to take effect forthwith and notwithstanding a sentence which the defendant was then serving in a house of correction; and . . . a separate mittimus issued on each indictment. Those facts, when taken together with the further conviction under G.L. c. 266, § 15, which the defendant suffered in this case, warranted a finding that he was an habitual criminal within the meaning of G.L. c. 279, § 25." *Commonwealth v. Hall*, 19 Mass. App. Ct. 1004 (1985) (citation omitted) (rescript).

NOTE 3 **Related Statutes.**
G.L. c. 266, § 40—Common and notorious thief.
G.L. c. 278, § 11A—Habitual criminals (see Note there).

SECTION 26
Further sentence of convict in state prison

A convict under sentence of imprisonment in the state prison may be further sentenced for a maximum term not longer than the longest term fixed by law for the punishment of the crime for which he has been convicted, and a minimum term not less than one year.

SECTION 27
Immediate execution of sentence to state prison of convict sentenced to jail or house of correction

If a convict serving a sentence of imprisonment in a jail or house of correction is convicted of a felony, the court may impose sentence of imprisonment in the state prison and order it to take effect forthwith, notwithstanding the former sentence. The convict shall thereupon be removed to the reception center established under section twenty of chapter one hundred and twenty-seven, and shall be discharged at the expiration of his sentence thereto.

SECTIONS 28–29
Repealed

SECTION 30
Vacation of office from time of sentence to state prison

If a convict sentenced by a court of the commonwealth or of the United States to imprisonment in the state prison or by a court of the United States to a federal penitentiary for a felony holds an office under the constitution or laws of the commonwealth at the time of sentence, it shall be vacated from the time of sentence. If the judgment against him is reversed upon writ of error, he shall be restored to his office with all its rights and emoluments; but, if pardoned, he shall not by reason thereof be restored, unless it is so expressly ordered by the terms of the pardon.

SECTIONS 31–33
Repealed

SECTION 33A
Credit for days of confinement awaiting and during trial

The court on imposing a sentence of commitment to a correctional institution of the commonwealth, a house of correction, or a jail, shall order that the prisoner be deemed to have served a portion of said sentence, such portion to be the number of days spent by the prisoner in confinement prior to such sentence awaiting and during trial.

NOTE 1 **Related Statute.** G.L. c. 127, § 129B—Confinement while awaiting trial; reduction of sentence.

NOTE 2 **Inpatient Drug Treatment Program.** "Thus, at least for the purpose of determining credit for time spent in confinement, an inpatient drug treatment program as a condition of probation does not equal incarceration. This is not to say that there are no circumstances in which a condition of probation might be the equivalent of incarceration for which a defendant would be entitled to credit. Restrictions on a probationer's fundamental rights are not without limits. However, in such a case, there must be a showing that the deprivation of liberty to which the defendant was subjected approached incarceration." *Commonwealth v. Speight*, 59 Mass. App. Ct. 28, 32 (2003) (further noting that the provisions of G.L. c. 127, § 129B, and G.L. c. 279, § 33A had no application to the case) (citations omitted).

NOTE 3   Pretrial Probation. "[W]e conclude that the defendant's conditions of pretrial probation were not the equivalent of 'confinement' for purposes of G.L. c. 279, § 33A . . ." *Commonwealth v. Morasse*, 446 Mass. 113, 114 (2006).

SECTION 34
Delivery to sheriff of certified transcript from minutes of court of conviction and sentence; execution of sentence

When a convict is sentenced to pay a fine or to be imprisoned, the clerk of the court shall forthwith make out and deliver to the sheriff or to some officer in court a duly certified transcript from the minutes of the court of the conviction and sentence, which shall authorize the officer to execute such sentence, and he shall execute it accordingly. When such convict is sentenced to be imprisoned in a correctional institution of the commonwealth, except the Massachusetts Correctional Institution, Bridgewater and the Massachusetts Correctional Institution, Framingham, the officer authorized to execute such sentence shall deliver him to the reception center established in accordance with the provisions of section twenty of chapter one hundred and twenty-seven for examination and classification.

SECTION 35
Transmission of complaint or indictment to correctional institution

When a person is committed to any correctional institution of the commonwealth or to any other public penal institution, on conviction of felony, the clerk of the court shall, without charge, transmit with the mittimus an attested copy of the complaint or indictment under which such person was convicted and, if such complaint or indictment does not contain a reference to the chapter and section of the General Laws under which such person was convicted, a statement designating such chapter and section, and the names and addresses of the witnesses who testified for and against such person at the trial, together with a record containing the names and addresses of the presiding justice, district attorney and of the attorney for the defendant.

SECTION 36
Sentences to state farm

Except for commitments under sections thirty-five or forty-eight of chapter one hundred and twenty-three, no person shall be sentenced to the state farm except for drunkenness. Whoever is sentenced to the state farm for drunkenness may be there held in custody for not more than six months.

NOTE   General Laws c. 272, § 48, which dealt with drunkenness, was repealed in 1977. General Laws c. 123, § 48 also was repealed in 1981.

SECTION 37
Setting out statutory name of crime in warrant for commitment

Every warrant for the commitment of a person sentenced by a district court shall set forth the statutory name, if any, of the crime of which the person was convicted, and shall contain a citation of the statute, if any, under which the complaint was drawn.

SECTION 38
Powers of sheriff or constable in execution of warrant of commitment

A sheriff, deputy sheriff or constable, when engaged in the execution of a warrant for the commitment of a person to a penal institution which is not in his own county, shall have the same powers in any county through which he may pass as he would have in his own county in the performance of a similar duty.

SECTION 39
Return of precept to magistrate

The officer serving the precept in a criminal case shall, without charging travel therefor, return it with his doings and fees endorsed thereon to the court or magistrate issuing it, who shall tax, allow and certify the fees as a part of the expenses in the case. In case of commitment, the officer shall leave with the superintendent, jailer or keeper of the prison an attested copy of the precept, with his return thereon, which shall authorize the detention of the person committed.

SECTION 40
Service of new warrant of commitment upon convict

If a convict imprisoned under sentence is again sentenced to confinement in a prison other than that in which he is then held, the warrant for his commitment in pursuance of the second sentence shall be placed in the hands of the superintendent or keeper of the prison where the convict is held, and said superintendent or keeper, upon the expiration of the first sentence, shall commit the convict in obedience to said warrant.

SECTION 41
Default of corporation

If a corporation, after being duly served with process, fails to appear and answer to an indictment or complaint brought against it under the laws of the commonwealth, its default shall be recorded, the charges in the indictment or complaint taken to be true, and judgment rendered accordingly.

SECTION 42
Warrant of distress to compel payment of penalty or assessment

If judgment is rendered against a corporation upon an indictment or complaint under the laws of the commonwealth, the court may issue a warrant of distress to compel payment of the penalty or assessment, as the case may be, as prescribed by law, together with interest thereon if so ordered by the court.

If the records of the registrar of motor vehicles indicate that a corporation has failed to pay an assessment for a civil motor vehicle infraction as provided in section three of chapter ninety C, the registrar may issue a warrant of distress to compel payment of the assessment, plus any late fees or other administrative fees which the registrar is required or authorized by law or regulation to impose, unless such fees are waived in whole or in part by the registrar.

SECTIONS 43–56
Repealed

SECTIONS 57–71
NOTE   Death penalty statute, G.L. c. 279, §§ 57–71, unconstitutional. *Commonwealth v. Colon-Cruz*, 393 Mass. 150 (1984).

SECTION 57
Warrant of conviction and sentence of death

Immediately upon the pronouncing of the sentence of death upon a person convicted of a capital crime, and immediately upon the revocation under section four of the stay of execution of such a sentence, the clerk shall make, sign and deliver to the sheriff of the county where the conviction is had a warrant under the seal of the court stating the conviction and sentence, and that a stay of execution of the sentence has been granted under section four, and that such stay has been revoked under said section, and shall at the same time transmit to the superintendent of the state prison a certified copy of the warrant. Such warrant shall be directed to said superintendent commanding him to cause execution to be done in accordance with the provisions of such sentence. The clerk of the court shall, upon revocation under section four of the stay of execution of the sentence, make out and deliver to the governor a certified copy of the whole record of the conviction and sentence, including any rescripts from the supreme judicial court.

SECTION 58
Confinement of prisoners under death sentence; psychiatric examinations; transfer to general prison population; court order

The sheriff of the county in a jail whereof a prisoner sentenced to the punishment of death is confined, or a deputy designated by the sheriff, within ten days after receipt by the sheriff of the warrant for the execution of such sentence shall, at a time chosen by the sheriff, convey such prisoner to the state prison and deliver him, with the warrant in either case, to the superintendent thereof or to the officer performing his duties and such prisoner shall be placed in a cell provided for the purpose. Within fourteen days thereafter, the superintendent or officer performing his duties shall cause said prisoner to be examined by a psychiatrist for the purpose of rendering a written and signed opinion as to whether or not said prisoner is psychologically fit to be transferred from special confinement to confinement with the general prison population, and in the case of a female, to the general prison population at the reformatory for women, with full participation in the educational and work programs, within the prison, afforded prisoners under sentence other than the punishment of death. Upon receipt of said psychiatric opinion, and other pertinent information, the superintendent or officer performing his duties may transfer said prisoner to confinement with the general prison population with the right of full participation in the privileges afforded other prisoners as aforesaid. If the superintendent, or officer performing his duties, does not so transfer said prisoner, he shall notify said prisoner of his decision forthwith, whereupon said prisoner may appeal said decision within ten days of said notification by giving notice to the superintendent, or officer performing his duties, on a form

provided him at the time of the receipt of the notification of the adverse decision. Upon receipt of such notice, the superintendent or officer performing his duties shall notify the commissioner of correction forthwith whereupon the commissioner shall hold a hearing on said appeal within fifteen days of receipt of notice that such appeal has been made. The commissioner or his appointee shall conduct said hearing and shall render a decision granting or denying said appeal within five days following the date of the hearing. A prisoner who is denied such transfer by the superintendent, or officer performing his duties, shall remain in a cell for the purpose of the execution of his sentence, and shall thereafter be kept therein, unless an appeal made by him of the adverse decision is granted, until the sentence of death is executed upon him, and no person shall be allowed access to him without an order of the court, except the officers and employees of the prison, his counsel, such physicians, priest, or minister of religion as the superintendent may approve and members of the prisoner's family who are identified to the satisfaction of the superintendent. Any prisoner confined to a cell for the purpose of the execution of his sentence shall have his record reviewed annually for the purpose of determining whether or not said prisoner should be placed in the general population, and shall be entitled to a hearing, as provided above, on each adverse decision.

Notwithstanding the foregoing, the superior court may make any order relative to the custody of a prisoner confined in the state prison or the reformatory for women under this section in case said prisoner is granted a new trial.

SECTION 59
Time of execution of sentence of death

The sentence of death shall be executed by the superintendent of the state prison, or by a person acting under his direction, not earlier than twenty days nor later than thirty days after service upon said superintendent, or officer performing his duties, of a certificate of the clerk of the court that the stay of the execution of the sentence has been revoked under section four, unless the governor pardons the crime, commutes the punishment therefor or respites the execution or said execution is otherwise delayed by process of law. If the execution is respited or stayed by process of law, the sentence of death shall be executed within the week beginning on the day next after the day on which the term of respite or stay expires. The sentence of death shall be executed upon such day within the limits of time provided in this section as the superintendent elects; but no previous announcement thereof shall be made, except to such persons as may be permitted to be present in accordance with section sixty-five.

SECTION 60
Infliction of death penalty

The punishment of death shall be inflicted by causing a current of electricity of sufficient intensity to cause death to pass through the body of the prisoner, the application of said current to be continuous until he is dead or, at the election of the prisoner, by intravenous injection of a substance or substances in a lethal quantity sufficient to cause death and until such prisoner is dead. The sentence shall be executed within an enclosure or building for that purpose at the state prison and the company which furnishes the electric power or light to the state prison shall provide all necessary electricity for executions by electrocution at such times as the superintendent orders.

2

SECTION 61
Sentencing of insane persons or pregnant women

If a person convicted of a capital crime is, at the time when sentence is to be imposed, found by the court to be insane, it may cause such person to be removed to one of the state hospitals for such term and under such limitations as it may order. If a person convicted of a capital crime is, at the time when sentence is to be imposed, found by the court to be pregnant, the court shall not pass sentence upon her until it finds that she is no longer pregnant.

SECTION 62
Respite of execution where convict under sentence of death has become insane or pregnant

After examination by two psychiatrists designated by the commissioner of mental health, if it appears that a prisoner under sentence of death has become insane, the governor, with the advice and consent of the council, may, from time to time for a stated period, respite the execution of said sentence until it appears to their satisfaction that the prisoner is no longer insane. Upon such respite, the governor may order the removal of such prisoner to the hospital at the Massachusetts Correctional Institution, Bridgewater. Within ten days prior to the termination date of said respite, the medical director of said hospital shall have the said prisoner examined by two psychiatrists designated by the commissioner of mental health. If, after said examination, the said medical director is of the opinion that the prisoner is no longer insane, he shall so certify to the superintendent of the state prison, accompanied by a written statement regarding the mental condition of said prisoner. The superintendent shall thereupon cause the prisoner to be reconveyed to the state prison and to be kept there pursuant to the sentence of the court, and shall notify the governor of the return of said prisoner, and of his mental condition. If, however, in the opinion of the said medical director of said hospital the said prisoner is still insane, he shall so certify to the governor, accompanied by a written statement regarding the mental condition of the prisoner. Thereupon, the governor, with the advice and consent of the council, may further respite the execution of the sentence from time to time for a stated period, until it is determined that the prisoner is no longer insane, as herein provided.

If it appears to the satisfaction of the governor and council that a prisoner under sentence of death is pregnant, the governor, with the advice and consent of the council, shall from time to time respite the execution of said sentence for stated periods until it appears to their satisfaction that she is no longer pregnant.

SECTION 63
Respite for opportunity to investigate and consider case for pardon

The governor, with the advice and consent of the council, may from time to time respite the execution of a sentence of death for stated periods so long as he may consider it necessary to afford him, with the advice and consent of the council, an opportunity to investigate and consider the facts of the case for the purpose of considering whether or not to pardon the prisoner.

SECTION 64
Stay of execution of sentence of death

The execution of a sentence of death may be stayed from time to time for stated periods by the supreme judicial court, or a justice thereof, pending the final determination of any judicial question arising in or out of the case in which the sentence is imposed.

SECTION 65
Witnesses of execution of sentence of death

There shall be present at the execution of the sentence of death, in addition to the superintendent, deputy and such officers of the state prison as the superintendent deems necessary, the commissioner of correction or his representative, the person performing the execution under the direction of the superintendent, if any, and the following physicians: the prison physician, the state surgeon, and a medical examiner for Norfolk county, or if any or all are unable to be present, such physicians as the superintendent approves. The physicians present shall be the legal witnesses of the execution. There may also be present, upon the request of the prisoner who is to be executed, the immediate members of the family of the prisoner. There may also be present, upon the request of said prisoner, a priest, minister, or other representative of religion. There may also be present the sheriff of the county where the prisoner was convicted, or his deputy, and, with the approval of the superintendent, not more than three other persons.

SECTION 66
Post mortem examination

There shall be a post mortem examination by a medical examiner for Norfolk county of the body of every prisoner executed in conformity with the sentence of a court.

SECTION 67
Return of warrant

When the superintendent has executed the sentence of death upon a prisoner in obedience to a warrant from the court, he shall forthwith make return thereof under his hand, with the doings thereon, to the office of the clerk of said court.

SECTION 68
Presentence hearing in cases in which death penalty may be imposed; evidence considered; instructions; verdict; sentence; mistrial

In all cases in which a sentence of death may be imposed, the court shall submit to the jury special questions concerning the issue of murder in the first degree. If the jury determines beyond a reasonable doubt that the defendant is guilty of murder in the first degree, the jury shall specify whether the defendant is guilty of murder with deliberate premeditation, murder with extreme atrocity or cruelty, or murder in the commission or attempted commission of a crime punishable by imprisonment for life, or two or more of these. Upon a verdict of guilty of murder in the first degree with deliberate premeditation, or murder in the first degree with extreme atrocity or cruelty, a presentence hearing shall be conducted, unless the commonwealth stipulates that none of the aggravating circumstances as defined in paragraph (a) of section sixty-nine exists, before the jury before which the case was tried; provided, however, that if in the opinion of the judge presiding at the presentence hearing, it is impossible or impracticable for the trial jury to sit at the presentence hearing, a new jury shall be impanelled to sit at the presentence hearing. The selection of that jury shall be according to the laws and rules governing the selection of a jury for the trial of a capital case. During the presentence hearing, the only issue shall be the determination of the punishment to be imposed. During such hearing the jury shall hear all additional relevant evidence presented by either the commonwealth or defendant in mitigation of punishment regardless of its admissibility under the rules governing the admission of evidence at criminal trials. During such hearing, the jury shall also hear such evidence in aggravation of punishment as is relevant to the statutory aggravating circumstance or statutory aggravating circumstances as defined in said paragraph (a) of said section sixty-nine; provided, however, that only such evidence in aggravation of punishment as the commonwealth has made known to the defendant prior to his trial shall be admissible, and provided further, that said evidence is otherwise admissible according to the rules governing the admission of evidence at criminal trials. The jury shall also hear arguments by the defendant or his counsel or both and by the commonwealth regarding the punishment to be imposed. The commonwealth and the defendant or his counsel shall be allowed to make opening statements and closing arguments at the presentence hearing. The order of those statements and arguments and the order of presentation of evidence shall be the same as at trial. Upon the conclusion of evidence and arguments at the presentence hearing, the court shall instruct the jury orally and shall provide to the jury in writing the statutory aggravating circumstance or statutory aggravating circumstances as determined by the court to be warranted by the evidence, and also any and all statutory mitigating circumstance or statutory mitigating circumstances for its deliberation. The judge shall also instruct the jury to consider any other relevant mitigating circumstance or mitigating circumstances. The judge shall also instruct the jury that they may not find that the penalty of death shall be imposed unless they shall first make a unanimous determination of the existence of one or more statutory aggravating circumstances beyond a reasonable doubt, and make a unanimous determination that the statutory aggravating circumstance or statutory aggravating circumstances outweigh the statutory or other mitigating circumstance or statutory or other mitigating circumstances beyond a reasonable doubt.

The jury shall then retire to determine whether any statutory aggravating circumstance or statutory aggravating circumstances, as defined by said paragraph (a) of said section sixty-nine or any mitigating circumstance or mitigating circumstances, including but not limited to those defined by paragraph (b) of said section sixty-nine, exist. The jury shall further determine whether the statutory aggravating circumstance or statutory aggravating circumstances it finds to exist outweigh the statutory or other mitigating circumstance or statutory or other mitigating circumstances it finds to exist. The jury shall be instructed that: (1) it may choose to find that the penalty of death shall be imposed upon the defendant or (2) it may choose not to find that the penalty of death shall be imposed upon the defendant. The jury, if its unanimous verdict is to impose the penalty of death, shall designate in writing, signed by the foreman of the jury, the statutory aggravating circumstance or statutory aggravating circumstances which it unanimously found existed beyond a reasonable doubt, and that the statutory aggravating circumstance or statutory circumstances it so unanimously found outweighed any statutory mitigating circumstance or other mitigating circumstance or statutory circumstances or other mitigating circumstances beyond a reasonable doubt. The process of weighing the statutory aggravating circumstance or statutory aggravating circumstances and statutory mitigating circumstance or statutory mitigating circumstances or other mitigating circumstance or other mitigating circumstances to determine the sentence, shall not be a mere tallying of statutory aggravating circumstance or statutory aggravating circumstances and statutory or other mitigating circumstance or statutory or other mitigating circumstances for the purpose of numerical comparison. Instead, it shall be a process by which the statutory aggravating circumstance or statutory aggravating circumstances and statutory mitigating circumstance or other mitigating circumstance or statutory mitigating circumstances or other mitigating circumstances relevant to sentence are considered for the purpose of determining whether the sentence, in view of all the relevant circumstances in an individual case, shall be life imprisonment without parole, or death.

After the jury has made its findings, the court shall set a sentence in accordance with section seventy.

The declaration of a mistrial during the course of the presentence hearing or any error in the presentence hearing determined on final appeal or otherwise shall not affect the validity of the conviction.

SECTION 69
Aggravating and mitigating circumstances in cases in which death penalty may be authorized

(a) In all cases in which the death penalty may be authorized, the statutory aggravating circumstances are:

(1) the murder was committed on a victim who was killed while serving in the performance of his official duties as one or more of the following: police officer, special police officer, state or federal law enforcement officer, firefighter, officer or employee of the department of correction, officer or employee of a sheriff's department, officer or employee of a jail or officer or employee of a house of correction;

(2) the murder was committed by a defendant who was at the time incarcerated in a jail, house of correction, prison, state prison or a correctional or penal institution or a facility used for the housing or treatment or housing and treatment of prisoners;

(3) the murder was committed on a victim who was killed while engaged in the performance of his official duties as a judge, prosecuting attorney, juror, or witness;

(4) the murder was committed by a defendant who had previously been convicted of murder in the first degree, or of an offense in any other federal, state or territorial jurisdiction of the United States which is the same as or necessarily includes the elements of the offense of murder in the first degree;

(5) the murder was committed by the defendant pursuant to a contract, agreement or understanding by which he was to receive money or anything of value in return for committing the murder;

(6) the murder was committed by the defendant for the purpose of avoiding, interfering with, or preventing a lawful arrest of the defendant or another, or the murder was committed by the defendant for the purpose of effectuating an escape or attempting to effectuate an escape of the defendant or another from custody in a place of lawful confinement;

(7) the murder involved torture to the victim or the intentional infliction of extreme pain prior to death demonstrating a total disregard to the suffering of the victim;

(8) the murder was committed as part of a course of conduct involving the killing of or causing serious bodily injury to or the attempted killing of or the attempted causing of serious bodily injury to more than one person by the defendant;

(9) the murder was committed by means of a destructive device, bomb, or explosive planted, hidden, mailed, delivered, or concealed in any place, area, dwelling, building, or structure by the defendant or the murder was committed by means such that the defendant knew or reasonably should have known that his act or acts would create a grave risk of death or serious bodily injury to more than one person; or

(10) the murder was committed by the defendant and occurred during the commission or attempted commission or flight after committing or flight after attempting to commit aggravated rape, rape, rape of a child, indecent assault and battery on a child under fourteen, assault with intent to rape, assault on a child under sixteen years of age with intent to rape, kidnapping for ransom, kidnapping, armed robbery, unarmed robbery, breaking and entering with intent to commit a felony, armed assault in a dwelling, arson, confining or putting in fear or otherwise harming another for the purpose of stealing from depositories, or the murder occurred while the defendant was in possession of a sawed-off shotgun or a machine gun.

(b) In all cases in which the death penalty may be authorized, the mitigating circumstances shall be any factors proffered by the defendant or the commonwealth which are relevant in determining whether to impose a sentence less than death, including, but not limited to, any aspect of the defendant's character, propensities, or record and any of the circumstances of the murder, including but not limited to the following:

(1) the defendant has no significant history of prior criminal convictions;

(2) the victim was a participant in the defendant's conduct or had consented to it;

(3) the murder was committed while the defendant was under extreme duress or under the domination or control of another;

(4) the offense was committed while the capacity of the defendant to appreciate the criminality of his conduct or to conform his conduct to the requirements of the law was impaired as a result of a mental disease or defect, organic brain damage, emotional illness brought on by stress or prescribed medication, intoxication, or legal or illegal drug use by the defendant which was insufficient to establish a defense to the murder but which substantially affected his judgment;

(5) the defendant was over the age of seventy-five at the time of the murder, or any other relevant consideration regarding the age of the defendant at the time of the murder;

(6) the defendant was battered or otherwise physically, sexually, or mentally abused by the victim in connection with or immediately prior to the murder for which the defendant was convicted;

(7) the defendant was experiencing post-traumatic stress syndrome caused by military service during a declared or undeclared war.

SECTION 70
Necessity of jury findings to impose sentence of death

Where, upon a trial by jury, a person is convicted of a crime which is punishable by death, a sentence of death shall not be imposed unless findings in accordance with section sixty-eight are made. Where such findings are made and the jury finds that the death penalty shall be imposed, the court shall sentence the defendant to death. Where such findings are not made or not unanimously made or where a sentence of death is not a unanimous finding by the jury, the court shall sentence the defendant to life imprisonment as provided in section two of chapter two hundred and sixty-five.

SECTION 71
Review of sentence of death

In addition to review of the entire case pursuant to section thirty-three E of chapter two hundred and seventy-eight, the supreme judicial court shall review the sentence of death imposed pursuant to sections sixty-eight, sixty-nine and seventy of chapter two hundred and seventy-nine. If the supreme judicial court determines that (1) the sentence of death was imposed under the influence of passion, prejudice or any other arbitrary factor or (2) the evidence does not support the jury's finding of a statutory aggravating circumstance or statutory aggravating circumstances as defined in section sixty-nine or (3) the evidence does not support the jury's finding that the statutory aggravating circumstance or statutory aggravating circumstances defined in section sixty-nine outweigh the statutory or other mitigating circumstance or statutory or other mitigating circumstances or (4) the sentence of death is excessive or disproportionate to the penalty imposed in other similar cases of one or more jurisdictions legally authorized to impose said penalty of death, with the greater weight of such comparison to be given to similar Massachusetts cases in which the death penalty will have been imposed, with due consideration of both those cases in which a sentence of life imprisonment was imposed and those cases in which a sentence of death was imposed, or in the event that the court determines any or all of the four factors as enumerated in this section exist, the court shall (1) reverse the sentence of death and remand for a new presentence hearing pursuant to section sixty-eight of chapter two hundred and seventy-nine, or (2) reverse the sentence of death and remand to the superior court department of the trial court for sentence of imprisonment in the state prison for life. The court shall also have the authority to affirm the sentence of death.

Chapter 280. Fines and Forfeitures

Section
1   Recovery of fines and forfeitures
2   Payment of certain fines and forfeitures
3   Appointment of counsel to conduct proceedings for penalties
4   Payment of expenses in criminal prosecutions by commonwealth
5   Expense of briefs in criminal cases appealed to supreme judicial court
6   Cost as penalty for crime; expenses of prosecution
6A   Special cost assessments
6B   Criminal assessments
6C   Assessment proceeds
7   Certificates of fines
8   Payment of fines to state treasurer
9   Payment of fines to state treasurer by clerks of courts in Suffolk county
10   Payment of witness fees; certificate
11   Certification of fines and forfeitures; payment to commonwealth
12   Escape of prisoner; payment of fines, etc., by sheriff
13   Neglect of sheriff to make payment of fines, etc., remedy
14   Payments to jailer or superintendent of house of correction
15   Quarterly returns of jailer or superintendent of house of correction; account
16   Payment of expenses or fees by county treasurer if demanded in three years

SECTION 1
Recovery of fines and forfeitures

Fines and forfeitures exacted as punishments for offenses or violation or neglect of any duty imposed by statute may, unless otherwise provided, be prosecuted for and recovered by indictment or complaint or by an action of tort in the name of the commonwealth in a court having jurisdiction of the offence or action.

SECTION 2
Payment of certain fines and forfeitures

A fine or forfeiture imposed by a court shall, except as otherwise provided, be paid over to the state treasurer. Twenty per cent of the fines imposed under the provisions of chapter three hundred and fifty-four of the acts of nineteen hundred and fifty-two shall be paid over to the state treasurer. If the whole or any part of a fine is by law payable to a complainant or informant or to a person or corporation as beneficiary, the court may apportion the fine or forfeiture between such complainant, informant or other beneficiary and the commonwealth, respectively.

Fines imposed under the provisions of chapters eighty-nine and ninety, including fines, penalties and assessments imposed under the provisions of chapter ninety C for the violation of the provisions of chapters eighty-nine and ninety, fines assessed by a hearing officer of a city or town as defined in sections twenty A and twenty A of chapter ninety and forfeitures imposed under the provisions of section one hundred and forty-one of chapter one hundred and forty, shall be paid over to the treasury of the city or town wherein the offense was committed; provided, however, that only fifty percent of the amount of fines, penalties and assessments collected for violations of section seventeen of chapter ninety or of a special speed regulation lawfully made under the authority of section eighteen of said chapter ninety shall be paid over to the treasury of the city or town wherein the offense was committed and the remaining fifty percent shall be paid over to the state treasurer and credited to the Highway Fund.

SECTION 3
Appointment of counsel to conduct proceedings for penalties

In proceedings in the name of the commonwealth for the recovery of fines, forfeitures or penalties, the whole or any part of which do not enure to the benefit of the commonwealth, the court may, upon motion of the district attorney, appoint an attorney to conduct the cause under his direction; but such attorney so appointed shall have no right to control the cause or receive compensation from the commonwealth.

SECTION 4
Payment of expenses in criminal prosecutions by commonwealth

Expenses arising in a criminal prosecution, including fees of grand and traverse jurors for travel and attendance therein, shall be paid by the commonwealth.

Fees and costs of indigent defendants in criminal prosecutions except attorneys' fees, shall or may be waived or substituted by the court or paid by the commonwealth in accordance with the provisions of sections twenty-seven A to twenty-seven G, inclusive, of chapter two hundred and sixty-one.

SECTION 5
Expense of briefs in criminal cases appealed to supreme judicial court

In a criminal case in which questions of law are carried to the supreme judicial court, the attorney general or district attorney may have necessary copies of the brief for the commonwealth printed, and the expense thereof shall be paid in the same manner as other expenses in the case.

SECTION 6
Cost as penalty for crime; expenses of prosecution

Costs shall not be imposed by a justice as a penalty for a crime. A justice may, as a condition of the dismissal or placing on file of a complaint or indictment, or as a term of probation, order the defendant to pay the reasonable and actual expenses of the prosecution. A justice may impose reasonable costs as a result of a default by a criminal defendant that was intentional or negligent and without good cause.

NOTE   Judge imposed court costs of $500 in addition to a fine. Held, "costs imposed here constituted a penalty of the sort prohibited by G.L. c. 280, § 6. The costs were not imposed as a 'condition of the dismissal or filing of a complaint or indictment' or as a 'term of probation' as provided by the statute." *Commonwealth v. Scagliotti*, 373 Mass. 626, 629 (1977).

SECTION 6A
Special cost assessments

Before imposing a fine or forfeiture as a punishment or part punishment for a crime, the court or justice shall levy as a special cost assessment an equal amount to twenty-five per cent of the fine or forfeiture; provided however, that no special cost assessment shall be levied on fines or forfeitures for minor motor vehicle offenses, and juvenile offenses or acts of delinquency. Minor motor vehicle offenses shall be defined as those not punishable by incarceration.

When a fine is suspended, in whole or in part, the special cost assessment shall be computed on the fine remaining to be paid. In any case where a person convicted of any offense to which this section applies is imprisoned until the fine is satisfied, the court or justice may in his discretion waive all or any part of said cost assessment the payment of which would work a hardship on the person convicted or his immediate family.

Said cost assessment shall be accounted for by the clerk of the court and forwarded to the state treasurer who shall deposit such assessment in the General Fund.

SECTION 6B
Criminal assessments
(Amended by 2013 Mass. Acts c. 84, § 33, effective Sept. 18, 2013.)

The court shall impose an assessment of not less than thirty-five dollars nor more than one hundred dollars against any person who has attained the age of 18 years and who is convicted of a misdemeanor or against whom a finding of sufficient facts for a conviction is made on a complaint charging a misdemeanor under sections thirty-two C, thirty-two D, and thirty-two G and thirty-five of chapter ninety-four C. The court shall impose an assessment of not less than one hundred and fifty dollars nor more than five hundred dollars against any person who is convicted of a felony or against whom a finding of sufficient facts for a conviction is made on a complaint charging a felony under sections thirty-two, thirty-two A, thirty-two B, thirty-two E, thirty-two F and thirty-four of chapter ninety-four C. When multiple criminal offenses arising from a single incident are charged, the total assessment shall not exceed five hundred dollars. In the discretion of the court, any assessment imposed pursuant to this section which would cause the person against whom the assessment is made an undue hardship may be reduced or waived.

All such assessments made shall be collected by the court and shall be transmitted monthly to the state treasurer. The assessment from any conviction which is subsequently overturned on appeal shall be refunded by the court to the person whose conviction is overturned. Said court shall deduct such funds from the assessments transmitted to the state treasurer. Assessments pursuant to this section shall be in addition to any other fines or restitution imposed in any disposition.

SECTION 6C
Assessment proceeds
Any assessment imposed pursuant to section six B shall be deposited in the Drug Analysis Fund established by section fifty-one of chapter ten. The proceeds of the fund shall be made available, subject to appropriation, to the department of public health for services provided to analyse samples used in the prosecution of controlled substances.

SECTION 7
Certificates of fines
At the end of every sitting of the superior court for the transaction of criminal business, the clerk shall make and deliver to the state treasurer certificates of all fines imposed by the court, to the use of the commonwealth or to the treasurer of a city or town under the provisions of section two of this chapter.

SECTION 8
Payment of fines to state treasurer
The clerk of the superior court for the transaction of criminal business for Suffolk county, the clerks of the municipal courts in Boston, the sheriff, superintendent of the house of correction or other officer, except those named in the following section, upon receiving fines, fees or other money in any criminal proceedings, payable to the commonwealth or to a city or town shall, before the tenth day of every month, pay over to the state treasurer and account, on oath, for all fines, fees or other money so received during the preceding calendar month, and make the detailed statements required by law.

SECTION 9
Payment of fines to state treasurer by clerks of courts in Suffolk county
The clerks of all courts in Suffolk county, except those named in the preceding section, who are required to account to the commonwealth shall, on or before the tenth day of each month, pay over to the state treasurer and account, on oath, for all fines, fees and other money received by them in any criminal proceedings during the preceding calendar month remaining after the payments therefrom allowed by law.

SECTION 10
Payment of witness fees; certificate
The state treasurer shall pay to the persons entitled therein all witnesses fees or other money due for services rendered or expenses incurred in any of the courts named in section eight, or for any of the aforesaid officers, upon presentation to him of a certificate stating the name of the claimant, of the court and of the case, the nature of the services rendered or expenses incurred and the amount due therefor, signed by the clerk of the court or by the officer for whom the service was rendered.

SECTION 11
Certification of fines and forfeitures; payment to commonwealth
Except as otherwise provided in section eighty of chapter two hundred and seventy-six, fines and forfeitures imposed in criminal prosecutions by the superior court to the use of the commonwealth, and all amounts found to be due on forfeited recognizances, shall under the direction of the court, be certified by the clerk and paid to the commonwealth.

SECTION 12
Escape of prisoner; payment of fines, etc., by sheriff
A sheriff who, having a person in his custody by virtue of the sentence of a court, voluntarily or negligently suffers him to escape shall be held to have received the fines, forfeitures or forfeited recognizances described in the preceding section, at the time of the escape, and shall be liable for the same, with interest and costs, as if he had received them.

SECTION 13
Neglect of sheriff to make payment of fines, etc., remedy
If a sheriff neglects to make such payment for thirty days, the state treasurer shall recover of him in contract the amount of such fines, forfeitures and forfeited recognizances, with interest at the rate of twelve per cent from the time he is held to have received the same and costs.

SECTION 14
Payments to jailer or superintendent of house of correction
A person committed to a jail or house of correction in default of payment of a fine may pay it to the keeper of the jail or superintendent of the house of correction, and the warrant

for his commitment shall designate the town where the offense for which the fine was imposed was committed and the uses to which such fine is payable by the officer receiving it.

SECTION 15
Quarterly returns of jailer or superintendent of house of correction; account

Every keeper of a jail and superintendent of a house of correction shall, on the first days of January, April, July and October, pay over to the state treasurer all money received by him under the preceding section during the preceding three months, and render to said state treasurer an account, on oath, showing the names of prisoners by whom payments have been so made, the court by which each was committed and the amount received from each.

SECTION 16
Payment of expenses or fees by county treasurer if demanded in three years

The state treasurer shall pay over to the persons entitled thereto all amounts allowed to them for expenses of fees in criminal prosecutions, or allowed by the courts as rewards or compensations to prosecutors, which have been duly certified by the clerks, if demanded within three years after the allowance thereof; but he shall pay no such amounts to a clerk of a district court, until the clerk has rendered a written account of all fines received by him since his last return, and of all fees which have remained in his hands for one year after their allowance.

PART 3

Massachusetts Rules of Criminal Procedure

Rule
1   Title; Scope
2   Purpose; Construction; Definition of Terms
3   Complaint and Indictment: Waiver of Indictment; Probable Cause Hearing
3.1 Determination of Probable Cause for Detention
4   Form and Contents of Complaint or Indictment; Amendment
5   The Grand Jury
6   Summons to Appear; Arrest Warrant
7   Initial Appearance and Arraignment
8   Assignment of Counsel
9   Joinder of Offenses or Defendants
10   Continuances
11   Pretrial Conference and Pretrial Hearing
12   Pleas and Plea Agreements
13   Pretrial Motions
14   Pretrial Discovery
15   Interlocutory Appeal
16   Dismissal by the Prosecution
17   Summonses for Witnesses
18   Presence of Defendant
19   Trial by Jury or by the Court
20   Trial Jurors
21   Sequestration of Witnesses
22   Objections
23   Stipulations
24   Opening Statements; Arguments; Instructions to Jury
25   Motion for Required Finding of Not Guilty
26   Requests for Rulings
27   Verdict
28   Judgment
29   Revision or Revocation of Sentence
30   Post Conviction Relief
31   Stay of Execution; Relief Pending Review
32   Filing and Service of Papers
33   Counsel for Defendants Indigent and Indigent But Able to Contribute
34   Report
35   Depositions to Perpetuate Testimony
36   Case Management
37   Transfer of Cases
38   Disability of Judge
39   Records of Foreign Proceedings and Notice of Foreign Law
40   Proof of Official Records
41   Interpreters and Experts
42   Clerical Mistakes
43   Summary Contempt
44   Contempt
45   Removal of the Disruptive Defendant
46   Time
47   Special Magistrates
48   Sanctions

RULE 1

Title; Scope

(Amended effective Sept. 7, 2004 and applicable to those cases initiated (by indictment or complaint) on or after the effective date.) (Applicable to District Court and Superior Court.)

(a) Title.

These rules may be known and cited as the Massachusetts Rules of Criminal Procedure. (Mass.R.Crim.P.)

(b) Scope.

These rules govern the procedure in all criminal proceedings in the District Court, in all criminal proceedings in the Superior Court, in all delinquency and youthful offender proceedings in the Juvenile Court, District Court and Superior Court consistent with the General Laws, and in proceedings for post-conviction relief.

RULE 2

Purpose; Construction; Definition of Terms
(Applicable to District Court and Superior Court.)

(a) Purpose; Construction.

These rules are intended to provide for the just determination of every criminal proceeding. They shall be construed to secure simplicity in procedure, fairness in administration, and the elimination of expense and delay.

(1) Words or phrases importing the singular number may extend and be applied to several persons or things, words importing the plural number may include the singular, and words importing the masculine gender may include the feminine and neuter.

(2) When in these rules reference is made to a subdivision of a rule, that reference is to that subdivision and to any subdivisions thereof.

(b) Definition of Terms.

In construing these rules the following words and phrases shall have the following meanings unless a contrary intent clearly appears from the context in which they are used:

(1) "Indigent" means any defendant who is unable to procure counsel with his funds as defined in Supreme Judicial Court Rule 3:10.

(2) "Indigent but able to contribute" means any defendant who is unable to procure counsel with his funds but is able to contribute funds for the cost of counsel as defined in Supreme Judicial Court Rule 3:10.

(3) "Capital Crime" means a charge of murder in the first degree.

(4) "Commonwealth" includes the prosecuting office or agency and all officers or agents responsible thereto.

(5) "Court" includes a judge, special magistrate, or clerk.

(6) "District Attorney" or "Attorney General" include assistant district attorneys or assistant attorneys general and other attorneys specially appointed to aid in the prosecution of a case.

(7) "District Court" includes all divisions of the District Court Department of the Trial Court, the Boston Municipal Court Department of the Trial Court, and the Juvenile Court Department of the Trial Court, or sessions thereof for holding court.

(8) "Interested Person" includes the adverse party, a co-defendant, and a witness who is to be deposed.

(9) "Judge" includes a judge of a court or one properly assigned to a court or a special magistrate when in the performance of those duties imposed and authorized by these rules.

(10) "Juvenile Court" means a division of the Juvenile Court Department of the Trial Court, or a session thereof for holding court.

(11) "Mailing" means the use of regular mail and shall not require registered or certified mail.

(12) "Prosecuting Attorney" means the attorney general or assistant attorneys general, district attorney, assistant district attorneys, special assistant district attorneys, or legal assistants to the district attorney, or other attorneys specially appointed to aid in the prosecution of a case.

(13) "Prosecutor" means any prosecuting attorney or prosecuting officer, and shall include a city solicitor, a police prosecutor, or a law student approved for practice pursuant to and acting as authorized by the rules of the Supreme Judicial Court.

(14) "Related Offense" means one of two or more offenses which are based on the same criminal conduct or episode or arise out of a course of criminal conduct or series of criminal episodes connected together or constituting parts of a single scheme or plan.

(15) "Return Day" means the day upon which a defendant is ordered by summons to first appear or, if under arrest, does first appear before a court to answer to the charges against him, whichever is earlier.

(16) "Special Magistrate" means any person who is appointed pursuant to, and empowered to administer those functions authorized by, rule forty-seven of these rules.

(17) "Summons" means

(A) criminal process issued to a person requiring him to appear at a stated time and place to answer to criminal charges; or

(B) process issued to a person requiring him to appear at a stated time and place to give testimony in a criminal proceeding; or

(C) process issued to a person requiring him to appear and produce at a stated time and place books, designated papers, documents, or other objects for use in a criminal proceeding.

(18) "Superior Court" means Superior Court Department of the Trial Court, or a session thereof for holding court.

RULE 3
Complaint and Indictment: Waiver of Indictment; Probable Cause Hearing
(Amended effective Sept. 7, 2004 and applicable to those cases initiated (by indictment or complaint) on or after the effective date.) (Applicable to District Court and Superior Court.)

(a) Commencement of Criminal Proceeding.

A criminal proceeding shall be commenced in the District Court by a complaint and in the Superior Court by an indictment, except that if a defendant is charged in the District Court with a crime as to which the defendant has the right to be proceeded against by indictment and the defendant has waived the right to an indictment pursuant to subdivision (c), the Commonwealth may proceed in the Superior Court upon the complaint.

(b) Right to Indictment.

A defendant charged with an offense punishable by imprisonment in state prison shall have the right to be proceeded against by indictment except when the offense charged is within the concurrent jurisdiction of the District and Superior Courts and the District Court retains jurisdiction.

(c) Waiver of Indictment.

(1) *Right to Waive Indictment.* A defendant charged in a District Court with an offense as to which the defendant has the right to be proceeded against by indictment shall have the right, except when the offense charged is a capital crime, to waive indictment, unless the Commonwealth proceeds by indictment pursuant to subdivision (e) of this rule.

(2) *Procedure for Waiving Indictment.* The defendant may waive the right to be proceeded against by indictment by filing a written waiver of that right in the District Court prior to the determination to bind the case over to the Superior Court for trial. The District Court may for cause shown grant relief from that waiver. After the determination by the District Court to bind the case over to the Superior Court for trial, the defendant may waive the right to be proceeded against by indictment by filing a written waiver of that right, with the consent of the prosecutor, in the Superior Court.

(d) Transmission of Papers.

If the defendant is bound over to the Superior Court for trial after a finding of probable cause or after the defendant waives a probable cause hearing, the clerk of the District Court shall transmit to the clerk of the Superior Court a copy of the complaint and of the record; the original recognizances; a list of the witnesses; a statement of the expenses and the appearance of the attorney for the defendant, if any is entered; the waiver of the right to be proceeded against by indictment, if any is executed; the pretrial conference report, if any has been filed; and the report of the department of mental health as to the mental condition of the defendant, if such report has been filed under the provisions of the General Laws.

(e) Indictment after Waiver.

Notwithstanding the defendant's waiver of the right to be proceeded against by indictment, the prosecuting attorney may proceed by indictment.

(f) Probable Cause Hearing.

Defendants charged in a District Court with an offense as to which they have the right to be proceeded against by indictment and defendants charged in a District Court with an offense within the concurrent jurisdiction of the District and Superior Courts for which the District Court will not retain jurisdiction, have the right to a probable cause hearing, unless an indictment has been returned for the same offense. If the District Court finds that there is probable cause to believe that the defendant committed the crime or crimes alleged in the complaint, the court shall bind the defendant over to the Superior Court. If the District Court finds that there is no probable cause to believe that the defendant committed the crime or crimes alleged in the complaint, the court shall dismiss the complaint.

(g) The Complaint Process.

(1) *Procedure for Obtaining a Complaint.* Any person having knowledge, whether first hand or not, of the facts constituting the offense for which the complaint is sought may be a complainant. The complainant shall convey to the court the facts constituting the basis for the complaint. The complainant's account shall be either reduced to writing or recorded. The complainant shall sign the complaint under oath, before an appropriate judicial officer.

(2) *Probable Cause Requirement.* The appropriate judicial officer shall not authorize a complaint unless the information presented by the complainant establishes probable

cause to believe that the person against whom the complaint is sought committed an offense.

RULE 3.1
Determination of Probable Cause for Detention
(Added effective Sept. 7, 2004 and applicable to those cases initiated (by indictment or complaint) on or after the effective date.)

(a) No person shall be held in custody more than twenty-four hours following an arrest, absent exigent circumstances, unless:

(i) a warrant or other judicial process authorizes the person's detention,

(ii) a complaint has been authorized under Rule 3(g), or

(iii) a determination of probable cause for detention has been made pursuant to subsection (b).

(b) A determination of probable cause for detention shall be made by an appropriate judicial officer. The appropriate officer shall consider any information presented by the police, whether or not known at the time of arrest. The police shall present the information under oath or affirmation, or under the pains and penalties of perjury. The police may present the information orally, in person or by any other means, or in writing. If presented in writing, the information may be transmitted to the appropriate judicial officer by facsimile transmission or by electronic mail or by such other electronic means as may be found acceptable by the court. The determination of probable cause for detention shall be an ex parte proceeding. The person arrested has no right to appear, either in person or by counsel.

(c) Where subsection (a) requires a determination of probable cause for detention, the police shall present the information necessary to obtain such determination to the appropriate judicial officer as soon as reasonably possible after the arrest, but no later than twenty-four hours after arrest, absent exigent circumstances.

(d) The judicial officer shall promptly reduce to writing his or her determination as to probable cause and notify the police. A copy of the written determination shall be transmitted to the police, by facsimile transmission or other means, as soon as possible.

(e) The judicial officer shall apply the same standard in making the determination of probable cause for detention as in deciding whether an arrest warrant should issue. If the judicial officer determines that there is probable cause to believe the person arrested committed an offense, the judicial officer shall make a written determination of his or her decision which shall be filed with the record of the case together with all the written information submitted by the police.

(f) If there is not probable cause to believe that the person arrested committed an offense, the judicial officer shall order the person's prompt release from custody. The order and a written determination of the judicial officer shall be filed in the District Court having jurisdiction over the location of the arrest, together with all the written information submitted by the police. These documents shall be filed separately from the records of criminal and delinquency cases, but shall be public records.

RULE 4
Form and Contents of Complaint or Indictment; Amendment
(Applicable to District Court and Superior Court.)
(a) Contents of Indictment or Complaint.

An indictment and a complaint shall contain a caption as provided by law, together with a plain, concise description of the act which constitutes the crime or an appropriate legal term descriptive thereof.
(b) Subscription of Application for Issuance of Process.

An application for issuance of process may be subscribed by the arresting officer, the police chief, or any police officer within the jurisdiction of a crime, a prosecutor, or a private person.
(c) Indictment Based Upon Secondary Evidence.

An indictment shall not be dismissed on the grounds that the evidence presented before the grand jury consisted in whole or in part of the record from the defendant's probable cause hearing or that other hearsay evidence was presented before the grand jury.
(d) Amendment.

Upon his own motion or the written motion of either party, a judge may allow amendment of the form of a complaint or indictment if such amendment would not prejudice the defendant or the Commonwealth.

NOTE 1   *See* G.L. c. 268, § 1A.

NOTE 2   **Description of Defendant.** "We conclude that the criminal prosecution of the defendant . . . is not time barred. In reaching this conclusion, we hold that: (1) the description of 'John Doe' in the indictment, primarily consisting of his genetic identity, comported with the particularity requirements of art. 12 of the Declaration of Rights of the Massachusetts Constitution; and (2) the return of such an indictment tolled the fifteen-year statute of limitations for aggravated rape and rape as set out in G.L. c. 277, § 63." *Commonwealth v. Dixon*, 458 Mass. 446, 447 (2010).

RULE 5
The Grand Jury
(Amended effective Sept. 7, 2004 and applicable to those cases initiated (by indictment or complaint) on or after the effective date.) (Applicable to Superior Court.)
(a) Summoning Grand Juries.

As prescribed by law, the appropriate number of jurors shall be summoned in the manner and at the time required, from among whom the court shall select not more than twenty-three grand jurors to serve in said court as long as and at those specific times required by law, or as required by the court.

The regular grand jury shall be called upon and directed to sit by the Chief Justice of the Superior Court Department whenever within his or her discretion the conduct of regular criminal business and timely prosecution within a particular county so dictate. Notwithstanding the foregoing, special grand juries shall be summoned in the manner prescribed by the General Laws.
(b) Foreperson, Foreperson Pro Tem, Clerk, Clerk Pro Tem.

After the grand jurors have been impaneled they shall retire and elect one of their number as foreperson. The foreperson and the prosecuting attorney shall have the power to administer oaths and affirmations to witnesses who appear to testify before the grand jury, and the foreperson shall, under his or her hand, return to the court a list of all witnesses sworn before the grand jury during the sitting. If the foreperson is unable to serve for any part of the period the grand jurors are required to serve, a foreperson pro tem shall be elected in the same manner as provided herein for election of the foreperson. The foreperson pro tem shall serve until the foreperson returns or for the remainder of the term if the foreperson is unable to return. The grand jury may also appoint one of their number as clerk to be charged with keeping a record of their proceedings, and, if the grand jury so directs, to deliver such record to the attorney general or district attorney. If the clerk is unable to serve for any part of the period the grand jurors are required to serve, a clerk pro tem may be appointed.

(c) Who May be Present.

Attorneys for the Commonwealth who are necessary or convenient to the presentation of the evidence, the witness under examination, the attorney for the witness, and such other persons who are necessary or convenient to the presentation of the evidence may be present while the grand jury is in session. The attorney for the witness shall make no objections or arguments or otherwise address the grand jury or the prosecuting attorney. No witness may refuse to appear because of unavailability of counsel for that witness.

(d) Secrecy of Proceedings and Disclosures.

The judge may direct that an indictment be kept secret until after arrest. In such an instance, the clerk shall seal the indictment and no person may disclose the finding of the indictment except as is necessary for the issuance and execution of a warrant. A person performing an official function in relation to the grand jury may not disclose matters occurring before the grand jury except in the performance of his or her official duties or when specifically directed to do so by the court. No obligation of secrecy may be imposed upon any person except in accordance with law.

(e) Finding and Return of Indictment.

An indictment may be found only upon the concurrence of twelve or more jurors. The indictment shall be returned by the grand jury to a judge in open court.

(f) No Bill; Discharge of Defendant.

The grand jury shall during its session make a daily return to the court of all cases as to which it has determined not to present an indictment against an accused. Each such complaint shall be endorsed "no bill" and shall be filed with the court.

If upon the filing of a no bill the accused is held on process, he or she shall be discharged unless held on other process.

(g) Deliberation.

The prosecuting attorney shall not be present during deliberation and voting except at the request of the grand jury.

(h) Discharge.

A grand jury shall serve until the first sitting of the next authorized grand jury unless it is discharged sooner by the court or unless its service is extended to complete an investigation then in progress.

NOTE 1   "In order to sustain his claim of impairment of the integrity of the grand jury proceedings, the defendant bears a heavy burden. Under *Commonwealth v. Mayfield*, 398 Mass. 615, 621 (1986), the defendant must show that the prosecutor knowingly introduced false or deceptive evidence. In addition, the defendant must demonstrate that the evidence probably influenced the grand jury to return an indictment. *Id.*" *Commonwealth v. Shea*, 401 Mass. 731, 734 (1988).

NOTE 2   "Unlike the case of *Commonwealth v. O'Dell* [392 Mass. 445 (1984)], the omissions here did not distort the material that was presented to the grand jury, and we have repeatedly held that the mere withholding of exculpatory evidence without more is not a proper ground for dismissal of an indictment. *Commonwealth v. McGahee*, 393 Mass. 743, 746–747 (1985). *Commonwealth v. O'Dell*, supra at 447." *Commonwealth v. Pina*, 406 Mass. 540, 549

(1990). *See also Commonwealth v. O'Dell*, 392 Mass. 445, 447 (1984) (Commonwealth does not have obligation to present all potentially exculpatory evidence to the grand jury); *Commonwealth v. Levesque*, 436 Mass. 443, 455–56 (2002) (same).

NOTE 3   "As a general rule, a court will not inquire into the quality of evidence heard by a grand jury unless 'extraordinary circumstances' are present. The court has previously identified two such extraordinary circumstances where judicial inquiry is warranted: (1) when it is unclear that sufficient evidence was presented to the grand jury to support a finding of probable cause to believe that the defendant committed the offense charged in the indictment; and (2) when the defendant contends that the integrity of the grand jury proceedings somehow has been impaired. The defendant's claim implicates the second of these situations.

"Reference to a defendant's criminal record before a grand jury is clearly undesirable, and, in some circumstances, such reference may involve serious risk of prejudice. This is not such a case. The disputed comments were made in response to a grand juror's question; they were not offered gratuitously by the police officer or by the prosecutor. The reference to the past warrant was generally responsive to the grand juror's question, and did not exceed the scope of that question. The information furnished was not false or deceptive, and there is nothing to show that it was furnished with the intention of obtaining the indictments. Further, the prosecutor curtailed the line of questioning shortly after it had commenced. We do not discern here any blatant attempt to whet the jurors' appetite with information which could not serve as a basis for an indictment.

"In addition, the defendant has not proved that the disputed statements, viewed in the context of all the evidence presented to the grand jury, 'probably made a difference' in their decision to indict him."

Commonwealth v. Freeman, 407 Mass. 279, 282–83 (1990) (quotation marks, citations, and footnotes omitted).

NOTE 4   The prosecutor used a grand jury subpoena to obtain records of the defendant. The evidence was not presented to the grand jury, but was used at trial.

Held, while this was "an abuse of the grand jury subpoena power . . . the improper action of the district attorney did not 'seriously impair' the integrity of the grand jury, and did not prejudice the defendant in the proceedings before that body."

Commonwealth v. Cote, 407 Mass. 827, 831 (1990) (citation omitted).

NOTE 5   Elements of Crime. "The Commonwealth is not required to inform a grand jury of the elements of the offense for which it seeks an indictment or of any lesser included offenses." *Commonwealth v. Noble*, 429 Mass. 44, 48 (1999).

NOTE 6   Grand Jurors Voting to Indict Need Not Hear All Evidence Presented Against Defendant. "The defendant's discovery motion is predicated on the argument that the requirement in Mass. R. Crim. P. 5(e), 378 Mass. 850 (1979), of a 'concurrence' of at least twelve grand jurors to return an indictment, mandates that 'a core of at least twelve grand jurors heard all of the evidence and voted to indict.' He asserts that the word 'concurrence' 'presumes that a grand juror has been present to hear all of the evidence presented before joining in a decision to indict,' and, that such an obligation is necessitated by the grand jurors' oath, see G.L. c. 277, § 5. The defendant urges us to follow '[t]he better-reasoned decisions from other jurisdictions' that 'recognize that an informed grand jury that truly concurs to indict, based on hearing all of the evidence, ensures the integrity of the grand jury process.' We decline to add such a requirement to rule 5." *Commonwealth v. Wilcox*, 437 Mass. 33, 34–35 (2002).

RULE 6

Summons to Appear; Arrest Warrant
(Applicable to District Court and Superior Court.)

(a) Issuance of Process.

(1) *Summons.* A defendant not under arrest or otherwise in custody shall, except as provided in subdivision (a)(2) of

this rule, be notified of the criminal proceedings against him and of the date of the return day by means of a summons. A copy of the complaint or indictment shall accompany the summons. If the accused is a juvenile, a summons and copy of the complaint or indictment shall also be served upon the parent or legal guardian of the juvenile or upon the person with whom the juvenile resides. Such notice shall also advise the defendant to report in person to the probation department before the return day.

(2) *Warrant.* The District Court may authorize the issuance of a warrant in any case except where the accused is a juvenile less than twelve years of age. Upon the return of an indictment against a defendant, the Superior Court may authorize the issuance of a warrant. The decision to issue a warrant may be based upon the representation of a prosecutor made to the court that the defendant may not appear unless arrested. If a defendant fails to appear in response to a summons or for any reason is not amenable to service, the prosecutor may request that a warrant issue or may resummon the defendant.

(b) Form.

(1) *Warrant.* An arrest issued pursuant to this rule shall be signed by the official issuing it and shall contain the name of the defendant or, if his name is unknown, any name or description by which he can be identified with reasonable certainty. The warrant shall recite the substance of the offense charged in the complaint or indictment. It shall command that the defendant be arrested and brought before the court.

(2) *Summons.* A summons shall be in the same form as a warrant except that it shall summon the defendant to appear before the court at a stated time and place.

(c) Service or Execution; Return.

(1) *By Whom.* A summons may be served in the manner provided by subdivision (c)(3) of this rule by any person authorized by the General Laws to serve criminal process. A warrant shall be directed to and executed by an officer authorized by the General Laws to serve criminal process.

(2) *Territorial Limits.* A summons may be served or a warrant executed at any place within the Commonwealth.

(3) *Manner.* A summons shall be served upon a defendant by delivering a copy to him personally, or by leaving it at his dwelling house or usual place of abode with some person of suitable age and discretion then residing therein, or by mailing it to the defendant's last known address. A warrant shall be executed by the arrest of the defendant. The officer need not have the warrant in his possession at the time of the arrest, but upon request he shall show the warrant to the defendant as soon as possible. If the officer does not have the warrant in his possession at the time of the arrest, he shall then inform the defendant that a warrant has issued and of the offense charged, but if the officer does not then know of the offense charged, he shall inform the defendant thereof within a reasonable time after arrest.

(4) *Return.* On or before the return day, the person to whom a summons was delivered for service shall make return thereof to the issuing court. The clerk shall maintain a list of those summonses returned unserved which shall include a statement of the efforts made by the person to whom the summonses were delivered for service to serve them. If a summons is mailed pursuant to subdivision (c)(3) of this rule and returned, the clerk shall record that fact upon the list. The officer executing a warrant shall make return thereof to the

issuing court. At the request of the prosecutor any unexecuted warrant shall be returned to the issuing court and may be canceled by that court upon its own motion or upon the motion of the prosecutor. At the request of the prosecutor made at any time while a complaint or an indictment is pending, a summons returned unserved or a warrant returned unexecuted and not cancelled may be delivered to an authorized person for service or execution.

(d) Default.

(1) *Costs.* A judge may order that expenses incurred as a result of the entry of a default against a defendant are to be assessed as costs against the defendant.

(2) *Preservation of Testimony.* If counsel for a defendant is present upon the entry of a default against the defendant and if the judge finds that to require the attendance at a later time of a witness then present in court would constitute a hardship upon the witness because of age, infirmity, illness, profession or other sufficient reason, the judge may order that the testimony of the witness be taken and preserved for subsequent use at trial or any other proceeding. The witness shall be examined in open court by the party on whose behalf he is present and the adverse party shall have the right of cross-examination. The expense of taking and preserving the testimony may be assessed as costs against the defendant.

NOTE   "The defendant argues that the assessment of $50 in costs against him when he failed to appear on June 3 was improper. We agree. . . . The Reporters' Notes to the rule [6(d)(1)] indicate that '[w]hile the assessment is discretionary, it is intended to be exercised only upon the willful default of a defendant and as to those costs which directly result therefrom'. . . . No hearing was held to determine whether the defendant's default was wilful or 'solid.' Thus, the costs were improperly assessed because there was no basis on which the judge could determine whether the defendant's default was wilful.

"The assessment also was improper because it does not reflect any actual expenses resulting directly from the defendant's default."

Lastly, the court noted that the defendant "was entitled to a hearing on the default" and "the right to be represented by counsel."

Commonwealth v. Gomes, 407 Mass. 206, 209–11 (1990) (citations omitted).

RULE 7

Initial Appearance and Arraignment
(Amended effective Sept. 7, 2004 and applicable to those cases initiated (by indictment or complaint) on or after the effective date; further amended effective June 1, 2012.) (Applicable to District Court and Superior Court.)

(a) Time of Arraignment; Probation Interview; Indigency and Bail Reports.

(1) *Upon Arrest or Summons.* A defendant who has been arrested and is not released shall be brought for arraignment before a court if then in session; and if not, at its next session. A defendant who receives a summons or who has been arrested but is thereupon released shall be ordered to appear before the court for arraignment on a date certain.

(2) *Arrest of a Juvenile.* Upon the arrest of a juvenile, the arresting officer shall notify the parent or guardian of the juvenile and the probation office.

(3) *Probation Interview.* On the day of the arraignment, the probation department shall interview the defendant; the probation department shall report to the court the pertinent information reasonably necessary to determine the issues of bail and indigency.

(b) Arraignment Procedure.

(1) *Notice; Plea; and Bail.* The court shall:

(A) read the charges to the defendant in open court, except that the reading of the charges in open court may be waived by the defendant if he or she is represented by counsel;

(B) enter the defendant's plea to the charges;

(C) inform the defendant of all warnings and advisories required by law; and,

(D) determine the conditions of the defendant's release, if any.

(2) *Appointment of Counsel.* If the court finds that the defendant is indigent or indigent but able to contribute and has not knowingly waived the right to counsel under the procedures established in Supreme Judicial Court Rule 3:10, the Committee for Public Counsel Services shall be assigned to provide representation for the defendant.

(3) *Provision of Criminal Record; Preservation of Evidence.* The court shall ensure that at or before arraignment, (i) a copy of the defendant's criminal record, if any, as compiled by the Commissioner of Probation is provided to the defense and to the prosecution, and (ii) the parties are afforded an opportunity to move for the preservation of evidence pursuant to Rule 14(a)(1)(E).

(4) *Order Scheduling Pretrial Proceedings.* At a District Court arraignment on a complaint which is outside of the District Court's final jurisdiction or on which jurisdiction is declined, the court shall schedule the case for a probable cause hearing. In all other District and Superior Court cases the court shall issue an order at arraignment requiring the prosecuting attorney and defense counsel to (1) engage in a pretrial conference on a date certain, and (2) appear at a pretrial hearing on a specified subsequent date.

(c) Appearance of Counsel.

(1) *Filing.* An appearance shall be entered by the attorney for the defendant and the prosecuting attorney on or before the arraignment. The appearance may be entered either by personally appearing before the clerk or by submitting an appearance slip, which shall include the name, Board of Bar Overseers number, address, and telephone number of the attorney. An attorney appearing on behalf of an organization shall also file with the court proof of the attorney's authorization to represent the organization.

(2) *Effect; Withdrawal.* An appearance shall be in the name of the attorney who files the appearance and shall constitute a representation that the attorney shall represent the defendant for trial or plea or shall prosecute the case, except that, if at the arraignment such a representation cannot be made and no contrary legal restriction applies, (1) the court may permit an appearance to be entered by an attorney to represent the defendant or prosecute the case for such time as the court may order, and (2) the court shall permit an appearance in the name of the prosecuting agency, which shall constitute representations that the agency will prosecute the case, will ensure that throughout the duration of the appearance a prosecutor is assigned to the case, and upon request of the court or a party will identify the prosecutor assigned to the case. If the attorney who files an appearance for the defendant on or before the arraignment wishes to withdraw the appearance, he or she may do so within fourteen days of the arraignment, provided that the attorney who shall represent the defendant at trial files an appearance simultaneously with such withdrawal; thereafter no appearance shall be withdrawn

without permission of the court. The appearance of the prosecuting officer shall be withdrawn only with permission of the court.

(3) *Notice.* A copy of all appearances and withdrawals of appearance shall be filed and shall be served upon the adverse party pursuant to Rule 32.

Reporter's Notes (2012). In 2012, Rule 7 was amended in several respects. These revisions are discussed below.

Subdivision (a)(1). Defendants who are released on bail prior to the issuance of a complaint or those who receive a summons must be ordered to appear in court for their arraignment on a date certain. Courts may establish their own policy on whether that date falls on the same day of every week or within a particular time frame. The 2012 amendments eliminated the separate event of an initial appearance prior to arraignment. The widespread availability of counsel to represent defendants at arraignment made this separate event unnecessary. The 2012 amendments also eliminated the procedure that allowed a summonsed defendant who had retained counsel to be excused from appearing until the pretrial conference or trial.

Subdivision (b)(1). By referring to "the court" as the responsible agency for conducting all of the activities surrounding the arraignment, this subdivision is meant to include judges, special magistrates, and any Superior Court clerk-magistrates authorized to conduct arraignments.

Subdivision (b)(1)(A). This provision requires that the arraignment take place in open court. It restates accepted practice, reflected in the mandate of *Foley v. Commonwealth*, 429 Mass. 496, 498 (1999). The concept of an open court means that the public must be allowed access absent "'an overriding interest based on findings that closure is essential to preserve higher values arid is narrowly tailored to serve that interest.'" *Boston Herald v. Superior Court*, 421 Mass. 502, 505 (1995), quoting *Press-Enter. Co. v. Superior Court*, 464 U.S. 501, 510 (1984). Arraignments may take place outside of a courtroom, in settings such as correctional facilities, *see Foley, supra,* or hospitals, *see Boston Herald, supra,* so long as the public's right of access to the proceedings is as free as in a courthouse, subject to the same considerations that might lead a judge to close a courtroom to the public.

Subdivision (b)(1)(C). This provision is intended to alert all the participants at the arraignment of the provisions for notice that appear outside the Rules of Criminal Procedure, such as the bail warning mandated by G.L. c. 276, § 58, and the requirement of G.L. c. 111E, § 10, that defendants charged with drug offenses have a right to request an examination concerning drug dependency.

Subdivision (c)(1). When an attorney in a criminal case appears for an organization, whether incorporated or not, he or she must present the court with proof of authority to act on behalf of the defendant. The proof of authority that this subdivision requires can come in the form of a resolution by a board of directors in the case of a corporate defendant or a similar statement from the person or group authorized to make litigation decisions on behalf of an unincorporated organization. SJC Rule 1:21 already requires corporate defendants in criminal cases to file a disclosure form revealing the identity of any parent corporation or any publicly listed company that owns 10 percent or more of its shares.

NOTE 1   "We adopt for the future, with respect to police questioning of an arrested person, a rule similar to those in the Federal and the Pennsylvania systems discussed above. An otherwise admissible statement is not to be excluded on the ground of unreasonable delay in arraignment, if the statement is made within six hours of the arrest (day or night), or if (at any time) the defendant made an informed and voluntary written or recorded waiver of his right to be arraigned without unreasonable delay." *Commonwealth v. Rosario*, 422 Mass. 48, 56 (1996).

NOTE 2   "The goal of *Rosario's* safe harbor rule will not be furthered by automatic suppression of volunteered, unsolicited statements made by this defendant after the expiration of the six-hour safe harbor rule." *Commonwealth v. McWilliams*, 473 Mass. 606, 615 (2016).

RULE 8
Assignment of Counsel
(Applicable to District Court and Superior Court.)

If a defendant charged with a crime for which a sentence of imprisonment or commitment to the custody of the Department of Youth Services may be imposed initially appears in any court without counsel, the judge shall follow the procedures established in G.L. c. 211D and in Supreme Judicial Court Rule 3:10.

RULE 9
Joinder of Offenses or Defendants
(Applicable to District Court and Superior Court.)

(a) Joinder of Offenses.

(1) *Related Offenses.* Two or more offenses are related offenses if they are based on the same criminal conduct or episode or arise out of a course of criminal conduct or series of criminal episodes connected together or constituting parts of a single scheme or plan.

(2) *Joinder of Related Offenses in Complaint or Indictment.* If two or more related offenses are of the same or similar character, they may be charged in the same indictment or complaint, with each offense stated in a separate count.

(3) *Joinder of Related Offenses for Trial.* If a defendant is charged with two or more related offenses, either party may move for joinder of such charges. The trial judge shall join the charges for trial unless he determines that joinder is not in the best interests of justice.

(4) *Joinder of Unrelated Offenses.* Upon the written motion of a defendant, or with his written consent, the trial judge may join for trial two or more charges of unrelated offenses upon a showing that failure to try the charges together would constitute harassment or unduly consume the time or resources of the parties. The trial judge shall join the charges for trial unless he determines that the joinder is not in the best interests of justice.

(b) Joinder of Defendants.

Two or more defendants may be joined in the same indictment or complaint if the charges against them arise out of the same criminal conduct or episode or out of a course of criminal conduct or series of criminal episodes so connected as to constitute parts of a single scheme, plan, conspiracy or joint enterprise. The defendants may be charged separately or together in one or more counts; all of the defendants need not be charged in each count.

(c) Consolidation of Offenses or Defendants on Motion of Court.

The trial judge may order two or more indictments or complaints to be tried together if the offenses and the defendants, if more than one, could have been joined in a single indictment or complaint. The procedure shall be the same as if the prosecution were under a single indictment or complaint.

(d) Relief from Prejudicial Joinder.

(1) *In General.* If it appears that a joinder of offenses or of defendants is not in the best interests of justice, the judge may upon his own motion or the motion of either party order an election of separate trials of counts, grant a severance of defendants, or provide whatever other relief justice may require.

(2) *Motion by the Defendant.* A motion of the defendant for relief from prejudicial joinder shall be in writing and made before trial and shall be supported by an affidavit setting forth the grounds upon which any alleged prejudice rests, except that a motion for severance may be made before or at the close of all the evidence if based upon a ground not previously known.

(e) Conspiracy.

An indictment or complaint for conspiracy to commit a substantive offense shall not be tried simultaneously with an indictment or complaint for the commission of the substantive offense, unless the defendant moves for joinder of such charges pursuant to subdivision (a) of this rule.

NOTE 1　Joinder of Defendants. "More importantly, no matter how inconsistent or antagonistic the defenses or trial strategies of the two defendants, there is no compelling prejudice and therefore no requirement of severance where the jury were warranted in finding Raposo guilty of the crime of aggravated rape on the basis of the eyewitness testimony of the bartender and Raposo's own properly admitted confession. *Commonwealth v. Sinnott*, 399 Mass. 863, 874–75 (1987). *See United States v. Palow*, 777 F.2d 52, 55 (1st Cir. 1985), *cert. denied*, 475 U.S. 1052 (1986) ('severance not required when joinder has resulted in the admission of evidence that would have been admissible in a separate trial')." *Commonwealth v. Cordeiro*, 401 Mass. 843, 853 (1988).

NOTE 2　"Defendant MacLean claims that the trial judge erred in denying his motion to sever the trials under *Bruton v. United States*, 391 U.S. 123 (1968). According to *Bruton*, severance is constitutionally required where: a codefendant's extrajudicial statements are offered in evidence at a joint trial; the statements are 'clearly inadmissible' as against the defendant; the codefendant is not subject to cross-examination because he does not testify; and finally, there is a substantial possibility that, in determining the defendant's guilt, the jury relied on the codefendant's 'powerfully incriminating extrajudicial statements' notwithstanding any limiting instructions from the judge. *Id.* at 128 & n.3, 135–36." *Commonwealth v. Pontes*, 402 Mass. 311, 314 (1988) (citations omitted).

NOTE 3　"At a joint trial of two or more defendants, therefore, the admission in evidence of the extra-judicial statement of a nontestifying codefendant which inculpates another defendant is violative of the latter's right to confrontation under the Sixth Amendment to the United States Constitution. . . .

"[The Supreme Court in *Cruz v. New York*, 481 U.S. 186, 193 (1987)] held that a limiting instruction could not validate the admission of 'interlocking' confessions at a joint trial." *Commonwealth v. Dias*, 405 Mass. 131, 135–36 (1989).

NOTE 4　"The appropriate standard, set out in *Cruz v. New York*, 481 U.S. 186 (1987), is that, unless a nontestifying codefendant's statement incriminating the defendant is directly admissible against the defendant, the confrontation clause bars its admission at their joint trial. *Id.* at 193.

"The *Cruz* case holds that a violation of the confrontation clause in this manner may, in some instances, be harmless error beyond a reasonable doubt. *Id.* at 194. This court has decided that it will apply a stringent test to determine if a *Bruton* error is harmless beyond a reasonable doubt. The test is whether the 'spillover,' which is created by those portions of statements that do not perfectly interlock, was without effect on the jury and did not contribute to the verdict." *Commonwealth v. Cunningham*, 405 Mass. 646, 649 (1989) (citations and quotation marks omitted).

NOTE 5　Joinder of Offenses. "In particular, the propriety of joining any one of the six indictments turns, in large measure, on whether evidence of the other five offenses would have been admissible at a separate trial on each indictment. It is settled that evidence of other criminal conduct is inadmissible to prove the propensity of the defendant to commit the indicted offense. Such evidence can be used, however, to show a common scheme, pattern of operation, absence of accident or mistake, identity, intent, or motive." *Commonwealth v. Mamay*, 407 Mass. 412, 417 (1990) (citations and quotation marks omitted).

NOTE 6   "Joinder is a matter committed to the sound discretion of the trial judge. The defendant bears the burden of showing that joinder was improper." *Commonwealth v. Wilson*, 427 Mass. 336, 345 (1998) (citations and quotation marks omitted).

NOTE 7a   **Related Offenses.** "Offenses are 'related' when the evidence in its totality shows a common scheme and pattern of operation that tends to prove all the indictments." *Commonwealth v. Simpson*, 434 Mass. 570, 575–76 (2001) (citations and quotation marks omitted).

NOTE 7b   "Factors such as time and location play an important role in determining whether offenses are related. However, our cases have allowed considerable differences with respect to these factors and other factual circumstances. [For example,], joinder [was] proper where multiple offenses occurred in different locations over [a] period of three months [and] where offenses involved six different victims and other factual differences over [a] period of eight months." *Commonwealth v. Wilson*, 427 Mass. 336, 345–46 (1998) (citations omitted).

NOTE 8   **Undue Prejudice.** The question whether the failure to sever the indictments resulted in undue prejudice must be decided in the context of the guarantee of a fair trial for every defendant. The question turns, in large measure, on whether evidence of the defendant's other offenses would have been admissible at a separate trial on each set of indictments. However, this is not dispositive. Nonetheless, a defendant must show that any prejudice resulting from a joint trial is so compelling that it prevented him from obtaining a fair trial. It is not enough for the defendant to show merely that his chances for acquittal would have been better had the indictments been tried separately. Nor is it enough for the defendant simply to claim that he wanted to testify regarding some charges, but not others." *Commonwealth v. Wilson*, 427 Mass. 336, 346 (1998) (citations and quotation marks omitted).

RULE 10
Continuances
(Amended effective Dec. 1, 1997.) (Applicable to District Court and Superior Court.)

(a) Continuances.

(1) After a case has been entered upon the trial calendar, a continuance shall be granted only when based upon cause and only when necessary to insure that the interests of justice are served.

(2) The factors, among others, which a judge shall consider in determining whether to grant a continuance in any case are:

(A) Whether the failure to grant a continuance in the proceeding would be likely to make a continuation of the proceeding impossible, or result in a miscarriage of justice.

(B) Whether the case taken as a whole is so unusual or so complex, because of the number of defendants or the nature of the prosecution or otherwise, that it is unreasonable to expect adequate preparation of the case at the time it is scheduled for trial.

(C) Whether the overall caseload of defense counsel routinely prohibits his making scheduled appearances, whether there has been a failure of diligent preparation by a party, and whether there has been a failure by a party to use due diligence to obtain available witnesses.

(3) An attorney who is to be otherwise engaged in a trial, evidentiary hearing, or appellate argument so as to require a continuance shall notify the court and the adverse party or the attorney for the adverse party of such conflicting engagement not less than twenty-four hours before the scheduled appearance, or within such other time as is reasonable under the circumstances.

(4) A motion for a continuance may include a request that the court rule on the motion without a hearing. If such a motion is filed at least three court days prior to the scheduled appearance or trial date and indicates that all parties have agreed to the continuance, the court shall, prior to the scheduled date, rule on the motion without a hearing unless it deems a hearing to be necessary. In any other case, the court may in its discretion rule on a continuance motion without a hearing, provided that all parties have had an adequate opportunity to file an opposition to the motion. If the court continues the case without a hearing, defendant's counsel shall inform the defendant of the revised date. Any motion filed pursuant to this subdivision shall provide one or more proposed continuance dates and state all supporting grounds, and any factual allegations shall be supported by affidavit.

(b) Assessment of Costs.

When a continuance is granted upon the motion of either the Commonwealth or the defendant without adequate notice to the adverse party, causing the adverse party to incur unnecessary expenses, a judge may in his discretion assess those expenses as costs against the party or counsel requesting the continuance.

(c) Preservation of Testimony.

A judge may order as a condition upon the granting of a continuance that the testimony of a witness then present in court be taken and preserved for subsequent use at trial or any other proceeding. The witness shall be examined in open court by the party on whose behalf he is present and the adverse party shall have the right of cross-examination. The expense of taking and preserving the testimony shall be assessed as costs against the party requesting the continuance.

NOTE 1   "Ordinarily, the granting of a continuance rests in the sound discretion of the trial judge, and a denial of a continuance will not constitute error absent an abuse of that discretion. In considering a request for a continuance, a trial judge should balance the movant's need for additional time against the possible inconvenience, increased costs, and prejudice which may be incurred by the opposing party if the motion is granted. He must also give due weight to the interest of the judicial system in avoiding delays which would not measurably contribute to the resolution of a particular controversy." *Commonwealth v. Mamay*, 407 Mass. 412, 419–20 (1990) (quotation marks and citations omitted).

RULE 11
Pretrial Conference and Pretrial Hearing
(Amended effective Sept. 7, 2004 and applicable to those cases initiated (by indictment or complaint) on or after the effective date.) (Applicable to District Court and Superior Court.)

(a) The Pretrial Conference.

At arraignment, except on a complaint regarding which the court will not exercise final jurisdiction, the court shall order the prosecuting attorney and defense counsel to attend a pretrial conference on a date certain to consider such matters as will promote a fair and expeditious disposition of the case. The defendant shall be available for attendance at the pretrial conference. The court may require the conference to be held at court under the supervision of a judge or clerk-magistrate.

(1) *Conference Agenda.* Among those issues to be discussed at the pretrial conference are:

(A) Discovery and all other matters which, absent agreement of the parties, must be raised by pretrial motion. All motions which cannot be agreed upon shall be filed pursuant to Rule 13(d).

(B) Whether the case can be disposed of without a trial.

(C) If the case is to be tried, (i) the setting of a proposed trial date which shall be subject to the approval of the court and which when fixed by the court shall not be changed without express permission of the court; (ii) the probable length of trial; (iii) the availability of necessary witnesses; and (iv) whether issues of fact can be resolved by stipulation.

(2) *Conference Report.*

(A) Filing. A conference report, subscribed by the prosecuting attorney and counsel for the defendant, and when necessary to waive constitutional rights or when the report contains stipulations as to material facts, by the defendant, shall be filed with the clerk of the court pursuant to subdivision (b)(2)(i). The conference report shall contain a statement of those matters upon which the parties have reached agreement, including any stipulations of fact, and a statement of those matters upon which the parties could not agree which are to be the subject of pretrial motions. Agreements reduced to writing in the conference report shall be binding on the parties and shall control the subsequent course of the proceeding.

(B) Failure to File. If a party fails to participate in a pretrial conference or to cooperate in the filing of a conference report, the adverse party shall notify the clerk of such failure. If a conference report is not filed and a party does not appear at the pretrial hearing, no request of that party for a continuance of the trial date as scheduled shall be granted and no pretrial motion of that party shall be permitted to be filed, except by leave of court for cause shown. If the parties fail to file a conference report or do not appear at the pretrial hearing, the case shall be presumed to be ready for trial and shall be scheduled for trial at the earliest possible time. The parties shall be subject to such other sanctions as the judge may impose.

(b) The Pretrial Hearing.

At arraignment, except on a complaint regarding which the court will not exercise final jurisdiction, the court shall order the prosecuting attorney and defense counsel to appear before the court on a date certain for a pretrial hearing. The defendant shall be available for attendance at the hearing. The pretrial hearing may include the following events:

(1) *Tender of Plea.* The defendant may tender a plea, admission or other requested disposition, with or without the agreement of the prosecutor.

(2) *Pretrial Matters.* Unless the Court declines jurisdiction over the case or disposes of the case at the pretrial hearing, the pretrial hearing shall include the following events:

(i) Filing of Pretrial Conference Report. The prosecuting attorney and defense counsel shall file the pretrial conference report with the clerk of court.

(ii) Discovery and Pretrial Motions. The court shall hear all discovery motions pending at the time of the pretrial hearing. Other pending pretrial motions may be heard at the pretrial hearing, continued to a specified date for a hearing, or transmitted for hearing and resolution by the trial session.

(iii) Compliance and Trial Assignment. The court shall determine whether the pretrial conference report is complete, all discovery matters have been resolved, and compliance with all discovery orders has been accomplished. If so, the court shall obtain the defendant's decision on waiver of the right to a jury trial, and assign a trial date or trial assignment date. If completion of either the pretrial conference report or discovery is still pending, the court shall schedule and order the parties to appear for a compliance hearing pursuant to

Rule 11(c) unless the aggrieved party waives the right to a compliance hearing.

(iv) The court may issue such additional orders as will promote the fair, speedy and orderly disposition of the case.

(c) Compliance Hearing.

A compliance hearing ordered pursuant to Rule 11(b)(2)(iii) shall be limited to the following court actions:

(1) determining whether the pretrial conference report and discovery are complete and, if necessary, hearing and deciding discovery motions and ordering appropriate sanctions for non-compliance;

(2) receiving and acting on a tender of plea or admission; and

(3) if the pretrial conference report and discovery are complete, obtaining the defendant's decision on waiver of the right to a jury trial, and scheduling the trial date or trial assignment date.

NOTE 1   **Late Disclosure of Exculpatory Evidence.** "As we stated in *Commonwealth v. Lam Hue To*, 391 Mass. 301, 308 (1984), where there is 'an agreement with the force of a court order to disclose all exculpatory evidence, three factors are considered in determining whether the prosecutor violated his constitutional duty in failing to disclose exculpatory evidence *prior to trial* and whether remedial action is required. We consider the exculpatory and material nature of the evidence, and whether the delay in disclosing it prejudiced the defendant' (emphasis supplied). At the outset, we note that the alleged exculpatory evidence in this case was revealed prior to trial, albeit after the agreed date of October 15, 1984. In a similar case, we stated: In determining the consequences of late disclosure, a court should consider whether, given a timely disclosure, the defense would have been able to prepare and present its case in such a manner as to create a reasonable doubt that would not otherwise have existed." *Commonwealth v. Paradise*, 405 Mass. 141, 150 (1989) (citations and internal quotation marks omitted).

NOTE 2   "The defendant claims that the judge's refusal to grant permission to call Sergeant Mann, a witness not listed on the pretrial conference report, violated the defendant's State and Federal due process rights to present a defense. . . .

"A trial judge has the power to enforce agreements contained in a pretrial conference report, and can take remedial action to remedy a violation of these agreements. *Commonwealth v. Chappee*, [397 Mass. 508 (1986)] at 517. *Commonwealth v. Gliniewicz*, 398 Mass. 744, 747 (1986). This remedial power has been held to allow the exclusion of witnesses not listed on a pretrial conference report, subject to a balancing of the 'the Commonwealth's interest in enforcing its procedural rules against the defendant's constitutional right to present evidence in his behalf.' *Commonwealth v. Chappee*, [397 Mass.] at 517–518.

"In *Commonwealth v. Chappee*, supra, we laid out the factors which must be taken into account in assessing such a balance. They include: (1) prevention of surprise; (2) evidence of bad faith in the violation of the conference report; (3) prejudice to the other party caused by the testimony; (4) the effectiveness of less severe sanctions; and (5) the materiality of the testimony to the outcome of the case."

Commonwealth v. Durning, 406 Mass. 485, 494–96 (1990).

NOTE 3   **Disclosure of Expert Testimony Required by PTC Report.** "The pretrial conference report required disclosure of every expert opinion to be produced at trial. The defendant claims that the Commonwealth failed to disclose that its serologist would opine that 'blood spatter' on the defendant's shirt indicated that 'some force' was used to deliver the blow. The judge should not have allowed this testimony. The prosecutor's proffer that, because the serologist was an 'expert,' she could testify to her observations and opinions, was an inadequate response. The defendant was entitled to notice that the serologist would give an opinion as to blood spatter." *Commonwealth v. Garrey*, 436 Mass. 422, 440 (2002).

RULE 12
Pleas and Plea Agreements

(Amended effective Sept. 7, 2004 and applicable to those cases initiated (by indictment or complaint) on or after the effective date. Further amended effective May 11, 2015.) (Applicable to District Court and Superior Court.)

(a) Pleas In General.

(1) *Pleas That May Be Entered and by Whom.* A defendant may plead not guilty, or guilty, or with the consent of the judge, nolo contendere, to any crime with which the defendant has been charged and over which the court has jurisdiction. A plea of guilty or nolo contendere shall be received only from the defendant personally except pursuant to the provisions of Rule 18(b). Pleas shall be received in open court and the proceedings shall be recorded. If a defendant refuses to plead or if the judge refuses to accept a plea of guilty or nolo contendere, a plea of not guilty shall be entered.

(2) *Admission to Sufficient Facts.* In a District Court, a defendant may, after a plea of not guilty, admit to sufficient facts to warrant a finding of guilty.

(3) *Acceptance of Plea of Guilty, a Plea of Nolo Contendere, or an Admission to Sufficient Facts.* A judge may accept a plea of guilty or a plea of nolo contendere or an admission to sufficient facts only after first determining that it is made voluntarily with an understanding of the nature of the charge and the consequences of the plea or admission. A judge may refuse to accept a plea of guilty or a plea of nolo contendere or an admission to sufficient facts.

(b) Plea Discussions; Pleas Without Plea Agreement and With Plea Agreement.

(1) *In General.* The defendant may tender a guilty plea, a plea of nolo contendere, or an admission to sufficient facts to warrant a finding of guilty without entering into a plea agreement with the prosecutor. Alternatively, if the defendant intends to tender a plea of guilty or an admission to sufficient facts, the prosecutor and the defendant may enter into a plea agreement pursuant to Rule 12(b)(5).

(2) *Plea Discussions.* The judge may participate in plea discussions at the request of one or both of the parties if the discussions are recorded and made part of the record.

(3) *Inquiry as to the Existence of a Plea Agreement.* After being informed that a defendant intends to plead guilty or to admit to sufficient facts, the judge shall inquire as to the existence of a plea agreement.

(4) *Pleas Without an Agreement.* If the defendant intends to plead guilty or nolo contendere or to admit to sufficient facts and there is no agreement under Rule 12(b)(5), the judge shall follow the procedures set forth in Rule 12(c).

(5) *Pleas Conditioned Upon an Agreement.* The defendant may enter into a plea agreement with the prosecutor if the defendant intends to plead guilty or admit to sufficient facts but not if the defendant intends to plead nolo contendere.

(A) A plea agreement may specify both that the parties agree on a specific sentence, including the length of any term of probation, and that the prosecutor will make one or more of the following charge concessions: amend an indictment or complaint; dismiss, reduce, or partially dismiss charges; not seek an indictment; or not bring other charges. The judge shall follow the procedures set forth in Rule 12(d) when the parties enter into a plea agreement that includes both an agreement to a specific sentence and a charge concession. If the judge accepts the plea agreement and the defendant's plea, Rule 12(d) requires the judge to sentence the defendant according to the terms of the plea agreement.

(B) When the plea is conditioned on a plea agreement other than one described in Rule 12(b)(5)(A), the judge shall follow the procedures set forth in Rule 12(c).

(c) Procedure If No Plea Agreement or If Plea Agreement Does Not Include Both a Specific Sentence and a Charge Concession.

(1) *Disclosure of the Terms of Any Plea Agreement.* If the parties have entered into a plea described in Rule 12(b)(5)(B), the parties shall disclose the terms of that agreement on the record in open court unless the judge for good cause allows the parties to disclose the terms of the plea agreement in camera on the record.

(2) *Tender of Plea.* The defendant's plea or admission shall be tendered to the judge.

(3) *Colloquy.* The judge shall:

(A) Provide notice to the defendant of the consequences of a plea. The judge shall inform the defendant:

(i) that by a plea of guilty or nolo contendere, or an admission to sufficient facts, the defendant waives the right to trial with or without a jury, the right to confrontation of witnesses, the right to be presumed innocent until proved guilty beyond a reasonable doubt, and the privilege against self-incrimination;

(ii) of the maximum possible sentence on the charge, and, if applicable,

(a) any different or additional punishment based upon subsequent offense provisions of the General Laws;

(b) that the defendant may be subject to adjudication as a sexually dangerous person and required to register as a sex offender;

(c) the mandatory minimum sentence on the charge; and

(d) that a conviction or plea of guilty for an offense listed in G.L. c. 279, § 25(b) implicates the habitual offender statute, and that upon conviction or plea of guilty for the third or subsequent of said offenses: (1) the defendant may be imprisoned in the state prison for the maximum term provided by law for such third or subsequent offense; (2) no sentence may be reduced or suspended; and (3) the defendant may be ineligible for probation, parole, work release or furlough, or to receive any deduction in sentence for good conduct;

(iii) of the following potential immigration consequences of the plea:

(a) that, if the defendant is not a citizen of the United States, the guilty plea, plea of nolo contendere, or admission may have the consequence of deportation, exclusion of admission, or denial of naturalization; and

(b) that, if the offense to which the defendant is pleading guilty, nolo contendere, or admitting to sufficient facts is under federal law one that presumptively mandates removal from the United States and federal officials decide to seek removal, it is practically inevitable that this conviction would result in deportation, exclusion from admission, or denial of naturalization under the laws of the United States.

(B) Factual basis for the charge. The prosecutor shall present the factual basis of the charge.

(C) Rights of Victims and Witnesses of Crimes. If applicable, the judge shall inquire of the prosecutor as to compliance with the requirements of G.L. c. 258B, Rights of Victims and Witnesses of Crimes. At any time prior to imposing sentence, the judge shall give any person entitled under G.L. c. 258B to make an oral and/or written victim impact statement the opportunity to do so.

(4) *Disposition Requests.*

(A) When there is no agreed-upon recommendation as to sentence. The judge shall give both parties the opportunity to recommend a sentence to the judge. In the District Court, the judge shall inform the defendant that the disposition imposed will not exceed the terms of the defendant's request without first giving the defendant the right to withdraw the plea. In the Superior Court, the judge shall inform the defendant that the disposition imposed will not exceed the terms of the prosecutor's recommendation without first giving the defendant the right to withdraw the plea. At any time prior to accepting the plea or admission, the judge may continue the hearing on the judge's own motion to ensure that the judge has been provided with, and has had an opportunity to consider, all of the facts pertinent to a determination of a just disposition in the case.

(B) Where there is an agreed-upon recommendation as to disposition. The judge shall inform the defendant that the sentence imposed will not exceed the terms of the agreement without first giving the defendant the right to withdraw the plea. At any time prior to accepting the plea or admission, the judge may continue the hearing on the judge's own motion to ensure that the judge has been provided with, and has had an opportunity to consider, all of the facts pertinent to a determination of a just disposition in the case.

(5) *Findings of Judge; Acceptance of Plea.* The judge shall inquire whether the defendant still wishes to plead guilty or nolo contendere or admit to sufficient facts. If so, the judge will then make findings as to whether the plea or admission is knowing and voluntary, and whether there is an adequate factual basis for the charge. The defendant's failure to acknowledge all aspects of the factual basis shall not preclude a judge from accepting a guilty plea or admission. At the conclusion of the hearing, the judge shall accept or reject the tendered plea or admission.

(6) *Sentencing.* After acceptance of a plea of guilty or nolo contendere or an admission, the judge shall sentence the defendant.

(A) Conditions of Probation. If the judge's disposition includes a term of probation, the judge, with the assistance of probation where appropriate and after considering the recommendations of the parties, shall impose appropriate conditions of probation.

(B) Intent to Impose Sentence Exceeding Requested Disposition. In District Court, if the judge decides to impose a sentence that will exceed the defendant's request for disposition under Rule 12(c)(4)(A) or the parties' request for disposition under Rule 12(c)(4)(B), the judge shall, on the record, advise the defendant of that intent and shall afford the defendant the opportunity to withdraw the plea or admission. In Superior Court, if the judge decides to impose a sentence that will exceed the prosecutor's request for disposition under Rule 12(c)(4)(A) or the parties' request for disposition under Rule 12(c)(4)(B), the judge shall, on the record, advise the defendant of that intent and shall afford the defendant the opportunity to withdraw the plea or admission. In both District and Superior Court, the judge may indicate to the parties what sentence the judge would impose.

(d) Procedure If Plea Agreement Includes Both a Specific Sentence and a Charge Concession.

(1) *Disclosure of the Terms of the Plea Agreement.* The parties shall disclose the terms of the plea agreement on the record in open court unless the judge for good cause allows the parties to disclose the terms of the plea agreement in camera on the record.

(2) *Tender of Plea.* The defendant's plea or admission shall be tendered to the judge.

(3) *Colloquy.* The judge shall:

(A) Provide notice to the defendant of the consequences of a plea. The judge shall inform the defendant:

(i) that by a plea of guilty or an admission to sufficient facts, the defendant waives the right to trial with or without a jury, the right to confrontation of witnesses, the right to be presumed innocent until proved guilty beyond a reasonable doubt, and the privilege against self-incrimination;

(ii) of the maximum possible sentence on the charge, and, if applicable,

(a) any different or additional punishment based upon subsequent offense provisions of the General Laws;

(b) that the defendant may be subject to adjudication as a sexually dangerous person and required to register as a sex offender;

(c) the mandatory minimum sentence on the charge; and

(d) that a conviction or plea of guilty for an offense listed in G.L. c. 279, § 25(b) implicates the habitual offender statute, and that upon conviction or plea of guilty for the third or subsequent of said offenses: (1) the defendant may be imprisoned in the state prison for the maximum term provided by law for such third or subsequent offense; (2) no sentence may be reduced or suspended; and (3) the defendant may be ineligible for probation, parole, work release or furlough, or to receive any deduction in sentence for good conduct;

(iii) of the following potential immigration consequences of the plea:

(a) that, if the defendant is not a citizen of the United States, the guilty plea or admission may have the consequence of deportation, exclusion from admission, or denial of naturalization; and

(b) that, if the offense to which the defendant is pleading guilty or admitting to sufficient facts is under federal law one that presumptively mandates removal from the United States and federal officials decide to seek removal, it is practically inevitable that this conviction would result in deportation, exclusion from admission, or denial of naturalization under the laws of the United States.

(B) Factual basis for the charge. The prosecutor shall present the factual basis of the charge.

(C) Rights of Victims and Witnesses of Crimes. If applicable, the judge shall inquire of the prosecutor as to compliance with the requirements of G.L. c. 258B, Rights of Victims and Witnesses of Crimes. The judge shall give any person entitled under G.L. c. 258B to make an oral and/or written victim impact statement the opportunity to do so.

(4) *Review; Acceptance or Rejection of Plea Agreement.* The judge must accept or reject the plea agreement before the judge accepts a guilty plea or admission. The judge should not accept a plea agreement without considering whether the proposed disposition is just. At any time prior to the acceptance or rejection of the plea agreement, the judge may continue the plea hearing on the judge's own motion to ensure

that the judge has been provided with, and has had an opportunity to consider, all of the facts pertinent to a determination whether the plea agreement provides for a just disposition in the case.

(A) Accepted Plea Agreement. If the judge accepts the plea agreement, the judge shall inform the defendant that the judge will impose the sentence, including the length of any term of probation, provided in the plea agreement.

(B) Rejected Plea Agreement. If the judge rejects the plea agreement, the judge shall, on the record and in open court (or, for good cause, in camera on the record):

(i) inform the parties that the judge rejects the plea agreement, but the judge may indicate to the parties what sentence the judge would impose or what additional information the judge will require before the judge may make this determination;

(ii) allow either party to withdraw from the plea agreement; and

(iii) allow the defendant to withdraw his or her plea or admission.

(5) *Findings of Judge as to Plea Agreement and Plea; Acceptance of Plea.* If the judge has accepted the plea agreement, the judge shall inquire whether the defendant still wishes to plead guilty or admit to sufficient facts. If so, the judge will then make findings as to whether the plea agreement and plea or admission are knowing, voluntary, and supported by an adequate factual basis. The defendant's failure to acknowledge all aspects of the factual basis shall not preclude a judge from accepting a guilty plea or admission. At the conclusion of the hearing, the judge shall accept or reject the tendered plea or admission.

(6) *Sentencing.* After accepting the plea agreement and the plea or admission, the judge shall impose sentence according to the terms of the plea agreement. If the plea agreement includes a term of probation, the judge, with the assistance of probation where appropriate and after considering the recommendations of the parties, shall impose appropriate conditions of probation.

(e) Availability of Criminal Record and Presentence Report.

Prior to sentencing under Rule 12(c)(6) or to the judge's decision to accept or reject a plea agreement under Rule 12(d)(4), the judge, prosecutor, and counsel for the defendant shall have an opportunity to review the defendant's criminal record and any report of the presentence investigation as described in Rule 28(d)(2). In extraordinary cases, the judge may except from disclosure to the parties parts of the report which are not relevant to a proper sentence, diagnostic opinion which might seriously disrupt a program of rehabilitation, sources of information obtained upon a promise of confidentiality, or any other information which, if disclosed, might result in harm, physical or otherwise, to the defendant or other persons. If the report is not made fully available, the portions thereof which are not disclosed shall not be relied upon in determining sentence. No party may make any copy of the presentence report.

(f) Inadmissibility of Pleas, Offers of Pleas, and Related Statements.

Except as otherwise provided in this subdivision, evidence of a plea of guilty, or a plea of nolo contendere, or an admission, or of an offer to plead guilty or nolo contendere or an admission to the crime charged or any other crime, later withdrawn, or statements made in connection with, and rele-

vant to, any of the foregoing pleas or offers, is not admissible in any civil or criminal proceedings against the person who made the plea or offer. However, evidence of a statement made in connection with, and relevant to, a plea of guilty, later withdrawn, or a plea of nolo contendere, or an admission or an offer to plead guilty or nolo contendere or an admission to the crime charged or any other crime, is admissible in a criminal proceeding for perjury if the statement was made by the defendant under oath, on the record, and in the presence of counsel, if any.

Reporter's Notes (2015).
Rule 12 Pleas and Plea Agreements

As the title of Rule 12 suggests, the 2015 revision of the rule resulted in a more carefully delineated and somewhat expanded role for plea agreements in the process of a judge's consideration and acceptance of a proffered guilty plea. The rule's amendment was in response to the Supreme Judicial Court's interpretation of Rule 12 in *Commonwealth v. Rodriguez*, 461 Mass. 256 (2012), and *Commonwealth v. Dean-Ganek*, 461 Mass. 305 (2012), holding that former Rule 12 permitted a judge to impose a sentence more lenient than the sentence agreed to in a plea agreement accepted by the judge. The Court further held that jeopardy attaches when the judge accepts a plea, *see Dean-Ganek*, 461 Mass. at 312–313, thus preventing the prosecution's withdrawal in such a case, even when the plea agreement included negotiated charge concessions.

As amended, Rule 12 provides that, if (1) the parties enter a plea agreement which includes both a specific, agreed sentence and a prosecutorial charge concession and (2) the judge accepts that agreement, then the judge is bound to impose the agreed sentence. If, on the other hand, the judge rejects such an agreement, either party may withdraw. In all other pleas or admissions, whether conditioned on a plea agreement or not, the amended rule provides that the judge is not bound by the sentencing recommendations of the parties. However, in such cases, the amended rule permits the defendant to withdraw the plea if the judge indicates an intent to impose a sentence more severe than (1) an agreed recommendation (but without charge concessions), (2) the prosecutor's recommendation if there is no agreed sentencing recommendation, or (3) in District Court, the disposition requested by the defendant. Finally, in order to promote fair and efficient plea bargaining and to establish rules to govern the previously unregulated and widely varying practice of lobby conferences, amended Rule 12 provides for judicial participation in plea negotiations at the request of a party and requires that plea discussions with judicial participation be recorded.
Rule 12(a) Pleas in General

The 2015 amendments made no substantive changes to Rule 12(a). The only changes were stylistic, designed to make the rule more specific and clear.
Rule 12(b) Plea Discussions; Pleas Without Plea Agreement and With Plea Agreement
Rule 12(b)(1) In General

Rule 12(b)(1) makes it clear that the defendant may tender a guilty plea, a nolo contendere plea, or, in District Court, an admission to sufficient facts, without entering into a plea agreement. *See* Rule 2(b)(7) (defining "District Court" to include all divisions of the District Court, Boston Municipal Court, and Juvenile Court). However, the rule also provides that the parties may condition a guilty plea (or, in District Court, an admission to sufficient facts) on a plea agreement under Rule 12(b)(5), discussed below. Rule 12(b)(1) omits nolo contendere pleas from those that can be conditioned on a plea agreement, an omission that Rule 12(b)(5) makes explicit, thus limiting the benefits of a plea agreement to those defendants who take responsibility for the crimes to which they are pleading.
Rule 12(b)(2) Plea Discussions

Rule 12(b)(2) provides that the judge may participate in plea discussions at the request of either party provided that any such discussions are recorded and made part of the record. Such limited judicial participation in plea negotiations facilitates fair and efficient case management, particularly in courts with crowded dockets, and it has been a longstanding though largely unregulated practice in many courts. The rule maintains the recognized benefits of this practice while providing important safeguards to curb its potential for abuse.

Recognizing that judicial participation in plea negotiations can be coercive and leave the impression of unfairness, this provision addresses these concerns by conditioning such participation on the request of one or both parties and further requiring that these discussions be recorded and made a part of the record. See *Murphy v. Boston Herald, Inc.*, 449 Mass. 42, 57 n.15 (2007) (stressing the importance of recording lobby conferences). The rule does not, however, preclude a judge's uninvited announcement that he or she is willing to participate in plea discussions if invited to do so by either party. The rule's requirement that the discussions be recorded and made part of the record is not meant to require that they invariably be conducted in open court. As with other potentially sensitive matters, judges have discretion under the appropriate circumstances to conduct plea discussions in a manner that restricts immediate public access, most likely at sidebar, provided they are recorded. Judges are experienced in determining when sidebars or other such restrictions are appropriate, and the rule anticipates that they will continue to apply that experience in judiciously exercising this discretion.

Rule 12(b)(3) Inquiry as to the Existence of a Plea Agreement

Rule 12(b)(3) provides that, when a defendant indicates an intent to plead guilty or to admit to sufficient facts, the judge shall inquire if there is a plea agreement. Because plea procedures vary depending on whether there is an agreement that will bind the judge if accepted, such an inquiry is necessary in order to determine which procedure is applicable. Because Rule 12 does not permit a nolo contendere plea to be conditioned on a plea agreement, the rule does not require the judge to ask if there is a plea agreement in such a case. However, it may make sense for the judge nevertheless to make this preliminary inquiry in the case of a nolo plea, if only to ensure that the parties understand that any such plea agreement is outside the rule, constituting at best a joint recommendation that the judge is free to disregard.

Rule 12(b)(4) Pleas Without an Agreement

If there is no plea agreement under Rule 12(b)(5), Rule 12(b)(4) provides that the procedure for taking a plea or admission set forth in Rule 12(c) applies. In such a case, the parties are each free to make any dispositional request permitted by law.

Rule 12(b)(5) Pleas Conditioned Upon an Agreement

Rule 12(b)(5) provides that a defendant may condition an intended guilty plea or admission on a plea agreement with the prosecutor. As noted, the rule explicitly precludes a plea agreement if the intended plea is nolo contendere. The rule divides plea agreements into two categories. Rule 12(b)(5)(A) provides for a type of plea agreement that, if accepted by the judge, binds the judge to sentence in accordance with the agreement, and Rule 12(b)(5)(B) provides, in effect, that no other plea agreement binds the judge to impose a particular sentence.

Under Rule 12(b)(5)(A), an accepted plea agreement will bind the judge if the parties have agreed both to a particular charge concession(s) by the prosecutor and to a specific sentence, including the length of any probationary term. Rule 12(b)(5)(A)'s reach is intentionally narrow. The rule carves out an exception to judicial sentencing discretion, an exception applicable only to a plea bargain that expressly includes both a prosecutorial charge concession and an agreed sentence to a specific term of incarceration, to a specific period of probation, or to a specific term of incarceration coupled with a specific period of probation (e.g., a term of probation to be served in lieu of a suspended sentence of incarceration, or a term of probation to be served on and after a term of incarceration). If the parties enter into such an agreement, the rule requires the judge to follow the plea procedures set forth in Rule 12(d), noting that those procedures mandate imposition of the agreed sentence if the judge accepts the plea agreement and the

plea. See Rule 12(d)(4)(A) and (6), discussed below. As discussed below, Rule 12(d) further provides that, if the judge rejects such a plea agreement, either party may withdraw from the agreement and thus from the plea. See Rule 12(d)(4)(B).

Even though Rule 12(b)(5)(A) permits the parties to include a specific period of probation within a binding plea agreement, the rule does not permit the parties to bind the judge to impose specific conditions of probation. Any agreement by the parties concerning conditions of probation is treated as a non-binding recommendation for the judge to consider, with the assistance of probation, in deciding what probationary conditions are appropriate in the case. See Rule 12(d)(6), discussed below. Finally, nothing in Rule 12 is intended to limit a judge's lawful discretion to modify probationary conditions during the course of probation or to adjust the probationary term upon a finding of a probation violation. In short, a plea agreement containing a charge concession and an agreed-upon period of probation will bind a judge who accepts that agreement to impose the agreed term of probation, but the parties may not by agreement trench upon the longstanding prerogative of the judge to determine and subsequently to modify any conditions of probation during that probationary term. See *Commonwealth v. Goodwin*, 458 Mass. 11, 17–19 (2010).

Under Rule 12(b)(5)(B), pleas conditioned on plea agreements other than those described in Rule 12(b)(5)(A) are governed by the procedures set forth in Rule 12(c), the procedures that also govern pleas in which there is no plea agreement. As discussed below, Rule 12(c) treats any agreement contained in a Rule 12(b)(5)(B) plea agreement as a non-binding, joint recommendation. For example, if the parties agree to a specific sentence unaccompanied by a charge concession, to a charge concession unaccompanied by an agreement to a specific sentence, or to some other dispositional alternative such as incarceration in a particular facility, that agreement would not bind the judge in imposing sentence. As was true under former Rule 12(b), the parties are free to enter into an agreement to recommend any disposition, or kind of disposition, permitted by law in the case in question. However, unless the agreement provides for both a charge concession and a specific sentence, the judge cannot be bound to follow that recommendation.

Rule 12(c) Procedure If No Plea Agreement or If Plea Agreement Does Not Include Both a Specific Sentence and a Charge Concession

Rule 12(c) provides for the plea procedure in cases in which the parties have not entered a binding plea agreement under Rule 12(b)(5)(A). Rule 12(c)'s procedure is parallel to that set forth in Rule 12(d), which is applicable to pleas and admissions when there is a Rule 12(b)(5)(A) binding plea agreement. The two sections diverge in their respective timing of receipt of victim impact statements, compare Rule 12(c)(3)(C) with Rule 12(d)(3)(C), treatment of the parties' sentencing recommendations, compare Rule 12(c)(4) with Rule 12(d)(4), and sentencing, compare Rule 12(c)(6) with Rule 12(d)(6). Otherwise, the two plea procedures are substantively identical.

Rule 12(c)(1) Disclosure of Terms of Plea Agreement

As discussed above, if the plea is conditioned on a plea agreement, the applicability of Rule 12(c)'s procedures depends on the provisions of that agreement. If the agreement provides for both a prosecutorial charge concession and an agreed specific sentence, the procedures under Rule 12(d) apply; if not, Rule 12(c) applies. It is thus important for the parties and the judge to be clear about the terms of any agreement before the plea procedure begins.

Rule 12(c)(2) Tender of Plea

Because Rule 12(c) applies to pleas in which there is no agreement as well as to pleas conditioned on an agreement, Rule 12(c)(2) moves the tender of plea or admission to the beginning of the plea procedure so that from the outset the terms of the plea or admission are clear even if there is no agreement. Although the plea tender precedes Rule 12(c)(3)'s colloquy, which includes the notice of the consequences of the plea, Rule 12(c)(5) permits the defendant to withdraw the tendered plea or admission subsequent

3

to the colloquy but prior to the judge's acceptance of the plea or admission. In a District-Court plea in which there will be a recommendation of probation, whether unagreed or agreed, the party(ies) must consult with the probation department before tendering the plea so that probation will be in a position to provide any assistance that the judge may require in sentencing. *See* Dist./ Mun. Ct. R. Crim. P. 4(c).

Rule 12(c)(3) Colloquy

Rule 12(c)(3)(A) requires the judge to begin the plea colloquy by notifying the defendant of the consequences of the tendered plea or admission. The notice of consequences is substantively identical to former Rule 12(c)(3)'s required notice of consequences with two exceptions. First, unlike its predecessor, Rule 12(c)(3)(A)(ii)(d) requires the notice mandated by the 2012 amendments to the habitual-offender statute. *See* G.L. c. 279, § 25(d) (requiring notice of potential habitual-offender consequences "prior to accepting a guilty plea for any qualifying offense listed in subsection (b) [of the statute]" but further providing that the failure to give such notice is not a basis to vacate an otherwise valid plea or conviction).

Second, Rule 12(c)(3)(A)(iii) expands former Rule 12(c)(3)(C)'s required noncitizen warning. As did former Rule 12(c)(3)(C), Rule 12(c)(3)(A)(iii)(a) requires the warning mandated by G.L. c. 278, § 29D, advising a defendant that, if he or she is a noncitizen, his or her plea or admission may result in deportation, exclusion from admission, or denial of naturalization. Rule 12(c)(3)(A)(iii)(b) advises further that, if (1) the offense to which the defendant is pleading is under federal law one that "presumptively mandates removal from the United States" (a so-called "removable offense," *see Padilla v. Kentucky*, 559 U.S. 356, 363–364 (2010)) and (2) federal officials seek removal, it is "practically inevitable that [defendant's] conviction would result in deportation, exclusion from admission, or denial of naturalization."

This additional warning recognizes that under federal immigration law there are a substantial number of crimes—including "all controlled substances convictions except for the most trivial of marijuana possession offenses," *see Padilla*, 559 U.S. at 368; 8 U.S.C. § 1227(a)(2)(B)(i) (2008)—the conviction for which make "deportation practically inevitable" if federal officials seek the defendant's removal. *See Commonwealth v. DeJesus*, 468 Mass. 174, 181 & n. 5 (2014). *See also Moncrieffe v. Holder*, 133 S. Ct. 1678, 1682 (2013) (cited in *DeJesus*, noting that the federal Immigration and Nationality Act prohibits discretionary relief for deportations based on convictions for a wide range of crimes no matter how compelling the circumstances). Further, as the warning states, once deported due to such a conviction, a defendant would almost certainly be denied both re-admission to the United States and naturalization. *See, e.g.*, L. Rosenberg, D. Kanstroom & J. Smith, *Immigration Consequences of Criminal Proceedings*, Massachusetts Criminal Practice § 42.2 (E. Blumenson & A. Leavens eds., 4th ed. 2012). It is important to appreciate that Rule 12(c)(3)(A)(iii)(b)'s warning is limited to the consequences of a conviction for a "removable offense." The narrow focus of this enhanced warning is purposeful and should not be read to suggest that convictions for other crimes would have no serious immigration consequences. Under federal law, conviction for—or even an admission to conduct constituting—a broader range of crimes than those presumptively mandating removal can also result in denial of re-admission and of naturalization. *Id.* §§ 42.2–42.3.

Finally, as Rule 12(c)(3)(A)(iii)'s warning provides, under federal immigration law, "convictions" include admissions to sufficient facts even when the result is a continuance without a finding (CWOF), if the continuance is conditioned on "some form of punishment, penalty or restraint" such as payment of costs or restitution. *See DeVaga v. Gonzalez*, 503 F.3d 45, 49 (1st Cir. 2007) (holding that a CWOF conditioned on payment of restitution satisfies 8 U.S.C. § 1101(a)(48)(A)(ii)'s provision that an admission to sufficient facts constitutes a "conviction" if the admission results in "some form of punishment, penalty or restraint"); *Matter of Cabrera*, 24 I. & N. Dec. 459, 462 (BIA 2008) (holding that imposition of costs and surcharges following a plea is a "penalty" or "punishment" for purposes of § 1101(a)(48)(A)(ii)).

This noncitizen warning is not meant to displace the critical role of counsel in providing more particular advice concerning the immigration consequences of a particular plea. Quite the contrary, the warning is meant to trigger that advice if, under circumstances best known by counsel, a defendant is risking serious immigration consequences by pleading guilty or admitting to sufficient facts. *See Padilla v. Kentucky*, 559 U.S. 356, 368–369 (2010); *Commonwealth v. Clarke*, 460 Mass. 30, 45–46, 48–49 & n.20 (2011) (noting that then-Rule 12's requirement of "[immigration] warnings is not an adequate substitute for defense counsel's professional obligation to advise her client of the likelihood of specific and dire immigration consequences that might arise from such a plea"), *partially abrogated on other grounds, Chaidez v. United States*, 133 S. Ct. 1103 (2013); *DeJesus*, 468 Mass. at 182 (holding that counsel's advice to a noncitizen defendant that he would be "eligible for deportation" and would "face deportation" if he pled guilty to possession of cocaine with intent to distribute (a removable offense under the immigration statute) was constitutionally inadequate).

Rule 12(c)(3)(B) requires the prosecutor to present the factual basis of the charge. Unlike former Rule 12(c)(5)(A), Rule 12(c)(3)(B) does not exclude nolo contendere pleas from the requirement that the prosecutor present a factual basis for the tendered plea or admission. The factual basis of a nolo plea provides information essential to crafting an appropriate sentence, but, because the defendant is not called upon to acknowledge or admit those facts, they will not be admissible in any subsequent proceeding against the defendant. *See, e.g.*, Mass. Guide to Evidence § 803(22) (2014) (explicitly excluding judgments based on nolo contendere pleas from the hearsay exception generally applicable to judgments of conviction).

The prosecutor can present the factual basis in the traditional manner, stating the facts that he or she expects to prove if the case goes to trial, but the rule also permits presenting sworn testimony, at the request of the judge or otherwise, as a way to satisfy this requirement. If the plea is an Alford plea, i.e., one in which the defendant declines to admit one or more elements of the offense to which he or she is nevertheless pleading guilty, the Supreme Court requires "strong evidence of [the defendant's] guilt." *See North Carolina v. Alford*, 400 U.S. 25, 37–38 (1970). In such a case, the prosecutor should give particular attention to this testimonial option. *See* E. Cypher, Procedure if Defendant pleads Guilty or Nolo Contendere but does not admit Participation in Crime, 30A Mass. Prac., Criminal Practice & Procedure, § 24:78 n.4 (2014) ("[I]f an *Alford* plea is offered, the Commonwealth should . . . [offer] sworn testimony to show the case is strong against the defendant, his defense is non-existent, and the defendant has presented reasons why the plea should be accepted").

As the final part of the colloquy, Rule 12(c)(3)(C) requires the judge to inquire of the prosecutor as to compliance with G.L. c. 258B. However, the judge is granted discretion concerning when to hear any victim-impact statements. The judge does not need this input until deciding whether to accept or reject the plea and then to impose sentence. However, hearing victim-impact statements at this stage of the proceeding—just before hearing the parties' respective sentencing recommendations and arguments—may provide the judge with the proper perspective for considering those recommendations and deciding what is a just disposition in the case.

Rule 12(c)(4) Disposition Requests

Rule 12(c)(4) gives the parties the opportunity to make their respective sentencing recommendations. This section has two subdivisions: Rule 12(c)(4)(A) applies to cases in which there is no agreed-upon sentence recommendation, and Rule 12(c)(4)(B) applies to cases in which there is. Rule 12(c)(4)(A) requires a District Court judge to inform a defendant of the statutory right to withdraw the plea if the judge imposes a sentence that exceeds the defendant's request, *see* G.L. c. 278, § 18, and a Superior Court judge to inform a defendant of the right to withdraw the plea if the disposition imposed exceeds the prosecutor's recommendation. If the parties have agreed on a sentence recommendation, Rule 12(c)(4)(B) requires the judge to inform the defendant that the plea may be withdrawn if the sentence imposed exceeds the agreed-upon recommendation. However, unlike Rule 12(d)(4)(B)(ii), which applies to binding plea agreements, Rule 12(c)(4)(B) does not give the prosecution the right to withdraw from the plea agreement and the plea if the judge announces an intent to impose a sentence more lenient than the sentence jointly recommended.

If in considering the parties' joint or respective recommendations the judge decides that he or she needs more information or time to determine a just disposition in the case, both subsections of Rule 12(c)(4) allow the judge to continue the plea hearing for that purpose. Among the factors pertinent to the judge's sentencing decision are the nature of the offense committed, the manner in which it was committed, the impact that the offense had on any victims, the defendant's criminal history, and the defendant's circumstances (e.g., his or her mental health, substance abuse, and/or psychological issues). The judge, in consultation with probation where appropriate, should take the time and consider the facts necessary to craft a sentence, including any term and conditions of probation, that is fair, appropriate to the crime, and designed to diminish the risk of recidivism.

Rule 12(c)(5) Findings of Judge; Acceptance of Plea

Rule 12(c)(5) requires the judge to inquire if the defendant still wishes to plead guilty or admit to sufficient facts. At this point, the defendant has received the notice of consequences of the plea or admission, has heard the factual basis for the charged offense(s), and is aware of the respective sentencing recommendations of the parties. The defendant may have also heard the victim-impact statement(s), if any. The defendant must now elect to go forward with his or her tendered plea or admission, or choose to withdraw it and go to trial. If the defendant elects to go forward, the judge then makes the necessary inquiries to ensure that the plea or admission is knowing and voluntary. The amended rule is intended to make no change to former Rule 12(c)(5)'s provision for this voluntariness hearing, either in its form or substance.

The rule also requires the judge to find that there is an adequate factual basis for the plea or admission. As did its predecessor, Rule 12(c)(5) provides that the defendant's failure to acknowledge all aspects of the factual basis shall not preclude a judge from accepting a guilty plea. The rule is not intended to work any change to former Rule 12(c)(5)(A) in this regard.

If the judge is satisfied that the plea or admission is knowing, voluntary, and supported by an adequate factual basis, the judge is then in a position to accept the tendered plea or admission. Of course, if the judge is not satisfied in this regard, or, if for some other reason the judge determines that the plea or admission would not result in a just disposition of the case, the judge is permitted to reject the plea or admission. Nothing in the rule is meant to deprive the judge of this longstanding discretion. *See Commonwealth v. Dilone*, 385 Mass. 281, 285 (1982) (acceptance of a guilty plea is "wholly discretionary with the judge"), *citing Santobello v. New York*, 404 U.S. 257 (1971); E. Cypher, 30A Mass. Prac., Criminal Practice & Procedure, Judge may refuse to accept guilty plea, plea of nolo contendere or admission to sufficient facts, § 24:60 (4th ed. 2014).

Rule 12(c)(6) Sentencing

If the judge accepts the plea or admission, the judge then imposes sentence under Rule 12(c)(6). As required by G.L. c. 278, § 18, Rule 12(c)(6)(B) explicitly permits a District Court defendant to withdraw his or her tendered plea or admission if the intended sentence exceeds the defendant's requested disposition. Similarly, in Superior Court a defendant may withdraw his or her plea if the intended sentence exceeds the parties' agreed-upon recommendation or, if there is no agreed-upon recommendation, the recommendation of the prosecutor. In either event, the judge may indicate to the parties what sentence the judge would impose if the plea were to go forward.

Rule 12(d) Procedure If Plea Agreement Includes Both a Specific Sentence and a Charge Concession

The procedure set out in Rule 12(d) applies to pleas and admissions conditioned on a plea agreement that includes both an agreed charge concession by the prosecutor and an agreement to a specific sentence. *See* Rule 12(b)(5)(A), discussed above. Under Rule 12(d)(6), discussed below, if the judge accepts such a plea agreement, the judge is bound to impose the agreed sentence. If, however, the judge rejects the plea agreement, either party may withdraw from the agreement. *See* Rule 12(d)(4)(B), discussed below. Because jeopardy attaches when the judge accepts a tendered plea or admission, at that point foreclosing the prosecutor's withdrawal from any plea agreement, *see Commonwealth v. Dean-Ganek*, 461 Mass. 305, 312–313 (2012), the rule requires that the judge accept or reject a Rule 12(b)(5)(A) plea agreement prior to accepting the plea or admission. And, because such a plea agreement binds the judge if accepted, Rule 12(d) is structured to ensure that, at the time the judge must accept or reject the agreement, the judge has the necessary information to determine if the agreed disposition would be just and appropriate for the case.

Rule 12(d)(1) Disclosure of the Terms of the Plea Agreement

Rule 12(d)(1) requires disclosure of the plea agreement at the beginning of the plea hearing. Because acceptance of the agreement binds the judge to sentence according to its terms, it is essential that this disclosure include a clear explanation on the record of those terms.

Rule 12(d)(2) Tender of Plea

Rule 12(d)(2) moves the tender of plea to the beginning of the plea procedure so that the terms of the plea or admission are clear at the outset. In District Court, if the plea agreement includes any probationary terms or conditions, the parties must consult with the probation department before tendering the plea so that probation will be in a position to provide any assistance that the judge may require in considering the plea or the plea agreement. *See* Dist./Mun. Ct. R. Crim. P. 4(c). The plea tender precedes Rule 12(d)(3)'s colloquy, which includes the notice of the consequences of the plea or admission, but Rule 12(d)(5) permits the defendant to withdraw the tendered plea or admission subsequent to being informed of its consequences and prior to the judge's acceptance of it.

Rule 12(d)(3) Colloquy

Rule 12(d)(3)(A) provides for the notice of consequences in terms substantively identical to those of 12(c)(3)(A). The above discussion of Rule 12(c)(3)(A) thus applies here with equal force.

Rule 12(d)(3)(B) and (C) respectively require the prosecutor's presentation of the factual basis for the charge and any victim-impact statements mandated by G.L. c. 258B. As with Rule 12(c)(3)(B), the prosecutor can satisfy this obligation to inform the judge of the factual basis of the charge in the traditional manner, stating the facts that he or she expects to prove if the case goes to trial, but the rule also permits presenting sworn testimony, at the request of the judge or otherwise. Rule 12(d)(3)(C) provides for the receipt of any victim-impact statements at this time. While in some instances it may not be necessary for the judge to hear the victim-impact statements before deciding whether to accept the plea agreement, the judge should not defer hearing from the victims absent the most unusual circumstances. Victim-impact statements delivered after the judge accepts the plea agreement can have no effect on the sentence.

Rule 12(d)'s placement of the facts describing the offense and its impact on the victims at this point in the procedure is necessary because, as noted, the rule requires that the judge accept or reject the plea agreement prior to accepting the plea itself, and that, if accepted, the plea agreement binds the judge to sentence according to the agreement. It is thus essential that a judge have access to all of the facts pertinent to a just and appropriate disposition in the case prior to deciding whether to accept or reject the plea agreement under Rule 12(d)(4).

Rule 12(d)(4) Review; Acceptance or Rejection of Plea Agreement

As noted, to avoid the double-jeopardy bar to the prosecutor's withdrawal from a rejected plea agreement, the judge must accept or reject the plea agreement before accepting the plea or admission. *See Dean-Ganek*, 461 Mass. at 312–313. Rule 12(d)(4) imposes that timing requirement. At this point in the procedure, the judge has heard the facts of the charged offense and its impact on any victims. Moreover, in reviewing the plea agreement, the judge

3

will hear from the parties concerning the agreed disposition and will have access to the probation department concerning the defendant, including any criminal history. *See* Rule 12(e), discussed below. However, if the judge believes that there might be other information pertinent to a just disposition in the case, the rule permits the judge sua sponte to continue the plea hearing in order to obtain and consider that information. Once the judge accepts the agreement, he or she is bound by its terms, and it is therefore essential that at this point the judge be fully satisfied that the agreed-upon sentence is fair, appropriate to the crime, and designed to diminish the risk of recidivism. The only timing requirement imposed by Rule 12(d)(4) is that the judge accept or reject such a plea agreement prior to accepting the guilty plea.

If the judge accepts the plea agreement, Rule 12(d)(4)(A) requires the judge to inform the defendant that the judge will impose the sentence provided in the agreement. If the judge rejects the agreement, Rule 12(d)(4)(B) requires that the judge so inform the parties and permit either party to withdraw from the plea agreement and further permit the defendant to withdraw the tendered plea. Rule 12(d)(4)(B)(i) here gives the judge discretion to inform the parties what sentence he or she would impose if the plea were to go forward. The judge's doing so gives the parties the opportunity to proceed on that basis without agreement under Rule 12(c), to re-fashion their plea agreement to conform to the judge's suggestion (thus binding the judge if the judge accepts that amended agreement), or to forego the plea and try the case. If the judge has doubts concerning the wisdom or fairness of the agreed disposition and believes that additional information might help to resolve those doubts, Rule 12(d)(4)(B)(i) permits the judge so to inform the parties. This gives the parties the opportunity, if one or the other has the requested information and is in a position to divulge it, to do so before the judge decides whether to accept or reject the agreement.

Rule 12(d)(5) Findings of Judge as to Plea Agreement and Plea; Acceptance of Plea

If the judge accepts the plea agreement, Rule 12(d)(5) provides that the judge ask the defendant if the defendant wishes to go forward with the tendered plea or admission. At this point, the judge has informed the defendant of the consequences of the plea, including what the sentence will be, and the defendant has heard the factual basis of the charged offense and any victim statements as to its impact. If the defendant elects to go forward with the plea, the judge must then make the necessary inquiries to satisfy the judge that the plea agreement and the plea or admission are knowing and voluntary. Rule 12(d)(5) is intended to make no change to former Rule 12(c)(5)'s provision for a voluntariness hearing except that the hearing also applies to the plea agreement on which the plea or admission is conditioned.

Rule 12(d)(5) requires the judge to find that there is an adequate factual basis for the plea or admission. Rule 12(d)(5) preserves the former Rule 12(c)(5)(A)'s provision that the defendant's failure to acknowledge all aspects of the factual basis shall not preclude a judge from accepting a guilty plea, and the rule is not intended to work any change on its predecessor in this regard.

Once satisfied that the plea agreement and the plea or admission are knowing and voluntary, and that the plea or admission is supported by an adequate factual basis, the judge is in a position to accept the tendered plea or admission. Of course, if the judge is not satisfied in this regard, or, if for some other reason the judge determines that the plea or admission is not just, the judge is permitted to reject the plea or admission. Rule 12(d)(5) is not intended to deprive the judge of this longstanding discretion, even if the judge has accepted the plea agreement on which the plea or admission is conditioned. *See Commonwealth v. Dilone*, 385 Mass. 281, 285 (1982) (acceptance of a guilty plea is "wholly discretionary with the judge"), citing *Santobello v. New York*, 404 U.S. 257 (1971); E. Cypher, 30A Mass. Prac., Criminal Practice & Procedure, Judge may refuse to accept guilty plea, plea of nolo contendere or admission to sufficient facts, § 24:60 (4th ed. 2014).

Rule 12(d)(6) Sentencing

If the judge accepts the plea or admission, the judge must impose a sentence according to the terms of the plea agreement, including any agreed-upon probationary term. It lies with the judge, however, in consultation with probation where appropriate, to decide what conditions of probation are appropriate. To the extent that the plea agreement contains agreed-upon recommended conditions of probation, they are not binding on the judge; rather, they are to be considered as joint recommendations for the judge to consider, and neither party has the right to withdraw the plea or from the agreement if the judge declines to follow such recommendations. Unlike Rule 12(c)(6), Rule 12(d)(6) does not provide for the defendant's right to withdraw his or her plea in District Court. That right, afforded by G.L. c. 278, § 18, does not here apply. Under Rule 12(b)(5), the defendant agreed to and thus requested the sentence set forth in the plea agreement. A sentence that comports with that agreement therefore cannot exceed the defendant's requested disposition.

Rule 12(e) Availability of Criminal Record and Presentence Report

Rule 12(e) is amended to recognize an admission to sufficient facts in District Court as the equivalent of a guilty plea, see, e.g., Rule 12(a)(2), and to omit the requirement that the parties must file a written motion to obtain a presentence report. The former amendment conforms Rule 12(e) to Rule 12(a)(2) as it was amended in 2004, and the latter amendment achieves consistency between Rule 12(e) and Rule 28(d)(2). Further, the rule is amended to ensure that a judge considering whether to accept a binding plea agreement under Rule 12(d)(4) has both an updated record of the defendant's criminal record and any presentence report prepared by probation under Rule 28(d)(2).

Rule 12(f) Inadmissibility of Pleas, Offers of Pleas, and Related Statements

The 2015 amendments made no changes to Rule 12(f).

NOTE 1   Affidavit. "Whether an affidavit must accompany a new trial motion that relies solely on the contemporaneous record of the guilty plea proceeding has not been explicitly decided previously. We conclude that the rule does not impose such a requirement." *Commonwealth v. Sherman*, 68 Mass. App. Ct. 797, 800 (2007), *aff. on other grounds*, 451 Mass. 332 (2008).

NOTE 2   Tactics. "[A] defendant attacking a conviction based upon a guilty plea has a choice between two tactics. He may stand on the contemporaneous record, the record made in the case through the stage of the colloquy and conviction. If the defendant chooses this route, it is not open to the Commonwealth to introduce extraneous evidence tending to show that the defendant in fact acted freely and intelligently in tendering the plea. . . . Alternatively, the defendant may offer extraneous evidence to supplement (or contradict) the record, but in that event the Commonwealth has a like right to offer evidence. When a defendant has received a constitutionally inadequate plea colloquy, he is entitled to withdraw that plea. Consequently, a defendant who challenges the intelligence or voluntariness of his plea and relies solely on the contemporaneous record of the proceeding for that challenge need do no more than file with his motion a copy of the record of the plea proceeding being challenged. The record will then establish the constitutional adequacy or inadequacy of the colloquy." *Commonwealth v. Sherman*, 68 Mass. App. Ct. 797, 800 (2007) (quotations and citations omitted).

NOTE 3   Timing. "[T]he presiding justice argues that the statute is silent as to when a plea may be tendered and that, as a consequence, the timing of the tender is a matter left to the court's discretion and may be governed by court management rules. The presiding justice further argues that the court may impose a reasonable limitation on the right to tender a defendant-capped plea, as a means of improving court efficiency. We are not persuaded by the presiding justice's arguments and conclude that G.L. c. 278, § 18, and rule 12 preclude the imposition of a time limitation, as set forth in the standing order, on the tender of a guilty plea.

"While we acknowledge that neither G.L. c. 278, § 18, nor rule 12 contains express language governing the timing of a plea tender, we disagree that the absence of such language permits a judicially imposed time limitation. Applying familiar rules of statutory construction, we conclude that the Legislature's failure to include a time limit for the plea tender cannot justify an interpretation that undermines the purpose of the statute." *Charbonneau v. Presiding Justice of the Holyoke Div. of the Dist. Court Dep't*, 473 Mass. 515, 519 (2016).

NOTE 4 "A slip in the protocol prescribed by rule 12 does not entitle a defendant to withdraw a guilty plea if it did not significantly affect the substance of the particular requirement." *Commonwealth v. Sherman*, 68 Mass. App. Ct. 797, 805 (2007) (quotations and citations omitted).

NOTE 5 **Vacating Plea.** "This case presents the . . . question whether the Commonwealth has the authority to require a judge to vacate a defendant's guilty plea where the Commonwealth made a charge concession as part of the plea agreement and the judge imposes a sentence less severe than the agreed sentence recommendation. We conclude that the Commonwealth does not have this authority under Mass. R. Crim. P. 12 . . . or G.L. c. 278, § 18. We further conclude that if the guilty plea were to be vacated at the prosecution's request and over the objection of the defendant, double jeopardy would bar further prosecution on that charge." *Commonwealth v. Dean-Ganek*, 461 Mass. 305, 305–06 (2012).

RULE 13
Pretrial Motions
(Amended effective Sept. 7, 2004 and applicable to those cases initiated (by indictment or complaint) on or after the effective date.) (Applicable to District Court and Superior Court.)

(a) In General.

(1) *Requirement of Writing and Signature; Waiver.* A pretrial motion shall be in writing and signed by the party making the motion or the attorney for that party. Pretrial motions shall be filed within the time allowed by subdivision (d) of this rule.

(2) *Grounds and Affidavit.* A pretrial motion shall state the grounds on which it is based and shall include in separately numbered paragraphs all reasons, defenses, or objections then available, which shall be set forth with particularity. If there are multiple charges, a motion filed pursuant to this rule shall specify the particular charge to which it applies. Grounds not stated which reasonably could have been known at the time a motion is filed shall be deemed to have been waived, but a judge for cause shown may grant relief from such waiver. In addition, an affidavit detailing all facts relied upon in support of the motion and signed by a person with personal knowledge of the factual basis of the motion shall be attached.

(3) *Service and Notice.* A copy of any pretrial motion and supporting affidavits shall be served on all parties or their attorneys pursuant to Rule 32 at the time the originals are filed. Opposing affidavits shall be served not later than one day before the hearing. For cause shown the requirements of this subdivision (3) may be waived by the court.

(4) *Memoranda of Law.* The judge or special magistrate may require the filing of a memorandum of law, in such form and within such time as he or she may direct, as a condition precedent to a hearing on a motion or interlocutory matter. No motion to suppress evidence, other than evidence seized during a warrantless search, and no motion to dismiss may be filed unless accompanied by a memorandum of law, except when otherwise ordered by the judge or special magistrate.

(5) *Renewal.* Upon a showing that substantial justice requires, the judge or special magistrate may permit a pretrial motion which has been heard and denied to be renewed.

(b) Bill of Particulars.

(1) *Motion.* Within the time provided for the filing of pretrial motions by this rule or within such other time as the judge may allow, a defendant may request or the court upon its own motion may order that the prosecution file a statement of such particulars as may be necessary to give both the defendant and the court reasonable notice of the crime charged, including time, place, manner, or means.

(2) *Amendment.* If at trial there exists a material variance between the evidence and bill of particulars, the judge may order the bill of particulars amended or may grant such other relief as justice requires.

(c) Motion to Dismiss or to Grant Appropriate Relief.

(1) All defenses available to a defendant by plea, other than not guilty, shall only be raised by a motion to dismiss or by a motion to grant appropriate relief.

(2) A defense or objection which is capable of determination without trial of the general issue shall be raised before trial by motion.

(d) Filing.

Only pretrial motions the subject matter of which could not be agreed upon at the pretrial conference shall be filed with the court.

(1) *Discovery Motions.* Any discovery motions shall be filed prior to the conclusion of the pretrial hearing, or thereafter for good cause shown. A discovery motion filed after the conclusion of the pretrial hearing shall be heard and considered only if (A) the discovery sought could not reasonably have been requested or obtained prior to the conclusion of the pretrial hearing, (B) the discovery is sought by the Commonwealth, and the Commonwealth could not reasonably provide all discovery due to the defense prior to the conclusion of the pretrial hearing, or (C) other good cause exists to warrant consideration of the motion.

(2) *Non-discovery Pretrial Motions.* A pretrial motion which does not seek discovery shall be filed before the assignment of a trial date pursuant to Rule 11(b) or (c) or within 21 days thereafter, unless the court permits later filing for good cause shown.

(e) Hearing on Motions.

The parties shall have a right to a hearing on a pretrial motion. The opposing party shall be afforded an adequate opportunity to prepare and submit a memorandum of law prior to the hearing.

(1) *Discovery Motions.* All pending discovery motions shall be heard and decided prior to the defendant's election of a jury or jury-waived trial. Any discovery matters pending at the time of the pretrial hearing or the compliance hearing shall be heard at that hearing. Discovery motions filed pursuant to subdivision (d)(1) after the defendant's election shall be heard and decided expeditiously.

(2) *Non-Discovery Pretrial Motions.* A non-discovery motion filed prior to the pretrial hearing may be heard at the pretrial hearing, at a hearing scheduled to address the motion, or at the trial session. A non-discovery motion filed at or after the pretrial hearing shall be heard at the next scheduled court date unless otherwise ordered.

(3) Within seven days after the filing of a motion, or if the motion is transmitted to the trial session within seven days after the transmittal, the clerk or the judge shall assign a date for hearing the motion, but the judge or special magistrate for cause shown may entertain such motion at any time before trial. If the parties have agreed to a mutually convenient time

for the hearing of a pretrial motion, and the moving party so notifies the clerk in writing at the time of the filing of the motion, the clerk shall mark up the motion for hearing at that time subject to the approval of the court. The clerk shall notify the parties of the time set for hearing the motion.

3

NOTE 1a   Suggestive Identification Procedure. "On a motion to suppress a pretrial photographic identification, the question is whether 'the procedures employed in the showing of the photographic arrays . . . were so unnecessarily suggestive and conducive to mistaken identification as to deny the defendant due process of law. *Stovall v. Denno*, 388 U.S. 293, 301–302 (1965). *Commonwealth v. Venios*, 378 Mass. 24, 26–27 (1979). *Should such a showing be made*, the burden then on the Commonwealth, if it wishes to use evidence of the identification at trial, is that "of establishing by 'clear and convincing evidence' that the proffered identification has a source independent of the suggestive confrontation." *Commonwealth v. Botelho*, 369 Mass. 860, 865–868 (1976). *Venios*, supra (emphasis added). *Commonwealth v. Correia*, 381 Mass. 65, 77–78 (1980). It also may be that a pretrial identification following an impermissively suggestive procedure would be made admissible by a clear and convincing demonstration that the proffered identification is 'reliable' within the less strict standard of *Manson v. Brathwaite*, 432 U.S. 98 (1977). We need not decide that question. In any event, the independent source and reliability tests are no part of the judicial inquiry where, as here, the procedures in showing the photographic arrays were not suggestive. When the procedures are not suggestive, the pretrial identifications are admissible without a further showing. 'The question raised by a motion to suppress identification testimony is not whether the witness was or might be mistaken but whether any possible mistake was or would be the product of improper suggestions made by the police.' *Commonwealth v. Paszko*, 391 Mass. 164, 172 (1984) (quoting *Commonwealth v. Gordon*, 6 Mass. App. Ct. 230, 237 (1978)). See *Commonwealth v. Bowie*, 25 Mass. App. Ct. 70, 75 (1987)." *Commonwealth v. Warren*, 403 Mass. 137, 139 (1988).

NOTE 1a(1) The Supreme Judicial Court answered the question posed in *Warren*. "Only a rule of per se exclusion can ensure the continued protection against the danger of mistaken identification and wrongful convictions. Accordingly, we reject *Brathwaite* and affirm our confidence in the *Botelho* approach." *Commonwealth v. Johnson*, 420 Mass. 458, 472 (1995).

"In deciding whether a particular confrontation was unnecessarily suggestive, the judge is to consider the totality of the circumstances. Additionally, in determining whether a separate identification has a source independent of the unnecessarily suggestive identification, the judge considers the following factors: (1) The extent of the witness's opportunity to observe the defendant at the time of the crime; prior errors, if any, (2) in description, (3) in identifying another person or (4) in failing to identify the defendant; (5) the receipt of other suggestions; and (6) the lapse of time between the crime and the identification." *Commonwealth v. Johnson*, 420 Mass. at 463–64 (citations and quotation marks omitted).

NOTE 1b "Once the judge concluded that the police photographic identification procedures were valid, the witnesses' reliability was no longer at issue on the motion to suppress." *Commonwealth v. Smith*, 403 Mass. 1002, 1003 (1988) (rescript).

NOTE 1c   In-court Identification. "A Wakefield police officer showed a photograph of the juvenile to the victim after his arrest and told her that the juvenile was charged with the assault on her. This act was impermissibly suggestive, and the Commonwealth does not argue otherwise. It does argue, however, that the victim's identification is admissible because it has shown by clear and convincing evidence that the identification had a source independent of the suggestive confrontation or was otherwise reliable. In effect the Commonwealth is arguing that, as a matter of law, the evidence shows clearly and convincingly that the victim's identification testimony would be free from the taint of the improper con-

frontation." The court rejected this argument. *Commonwealth v. A Juvenile*, 402 Mass. 275, 280 (1988) (citations omitted).

NOTE 1d   Identification (Show-Ups). The Supreme Judicial Court in *Commonwealth v. Santos*, 402 Mass. 775 (1988), was faced with two separate show-ups. One was found permissible, the other not.

Concerning the impermissible show-up, the court stated:

"With regard to one-on-one confrontations, we have said that, while disfavored, such identifications are not subject to a per se rule of exclusion. *Commonwealth v. Storey*, 378 Mass. 312, 317 (1979), *cert. denied*, 446 U.S. 955 (1980). See *Commonwealth v. Torres*, 367 Mass. 737, 740 (1975). 'Although such confrontations pose particularly serious dangers of suggestiveness, we would consider it ill advised to exclude as constitutionally unacceptable all evidence that has been derived from single person confrontations simply because these identification procedures might have taken place just as easily in the form of lineups.' *Storey*, supra. See *Commonwealth v. Barnett*, 371 Mass. 87, 91, 92 (1976), *cert. denied*, 429 U.S. 1049 (1977). Our test is simply whether, in light of the 'totality of the circumstances,' the identification procedure was so unnecessarily suggestive and conducive to irreparable mistaken identification" as to deny the defendant due process of law.' *Commonwealth v. Venios*, 378 Mass. 24, 27 (1979) (quoting *Stovall v. Denno*, 388 U.S. 293, 301–302 (1967))." *Commonwealth v. Santos*, 402 Mass. at 781.

The show-up was unnecessarily suggestive as the witness, who had Down syndrome, gave no indication from his description "that he saw the defendant for a sufficient length of time to enable him to make a subsequent identification of the defendant." *Santos*, 402 Mass. at 781. Additionally, "at the stationhouse Santos was the only nonuniformed black person in the office at the time of Bartick's identification." *Commonwealth v. Santos*, 402 Mass. at 782.

"[T]estimony corroborating the unconstitutional identification must be excluded as well." *Commonwealth v. Santos*, 402 Mass. at 784.

As for the permissible identification, the court noted that "the identification was made immediately following the defendant's apprehension, and after both witnesses had been shown another suspect whom they both determined was not involved in Maxwell's murder." *Commonwealth v. Santos*, 402 Mass. at 783.

"'[T]he police procedure of arranging these showups is recognized as usual and natural and justified by the need for efficient investigation in the immediate aftermath of crime. . . . To have the witness view the suspect while his recollection or mental image of the offender is still fresh, before other images crowd in or his attempts to verbalize his impressions can themselves distort the original picture, provides the witness with good opportunity for an accurate identification. . . . A further consideration is that prompt confrontation yielding a negative result, besides freeing the innocent, informs the police that a possible predisposition on their part is or may be in error and releases them quickly to follow another track.' (Citations omitted.) *Commonwealth v. Barnett*, 371 Mass. 87, 92 (1976)." *Commonwealth v. Santos*, 402 Mass. at 784.

NOTE 1e   Photo Identification. "We disapprove of an array of photographs which distinguishes one suspect from all the others on the basis of some physical characteristic." *Commonwealth v. Thornley*, 406 Mass. 96, 100 (1989) (quotation marks and citations omitted).

NOTE 1e(1) "We reject the defendant's argument . . . that the inclusion of the defendant's photograph in the March 21 array after the same photograph (different print) had been included in the first, two hundred photograph array, requires suppression. See *Commonwealth v. Paszko*, 391 Mass. 164, 169–71 (1984), and cases collected there." *Commonwealth v. Dinkins*, 415 Mass. 715, 721 (1993).

NOTE 2a   *Miranda*, Motion to Dismiss. "After the officer had handcuffed the wounded defendant, but before any *Miranda* warnings had been given, he asked the defendant where his partner was. The defendant answered, 'I don't know. I fell and became weak.'

"After a voir dire hearing during trial, the judge denied the defendant's motion to suppress his admittedly custodial statement. The judge did so on the basis of *New York v. Quarles*, 467 U.S. 649, 657 (1984), in which the Court stated that 'the need for answers to questions in a situation posing a threat to the public safety outweighs the need for the prophylactic rule protecting the Fifth Amendment's privilege against self-incrimination.' We need not decide whether the rule of the *Quarles* case applies (or would be extended) to a situation in which the safety of police and not of the public generally (as in the *Quarles* case) is threatened,[2] because in this case the defendant introduced his own statement during the cross-examination of the Pembroke police sergeant. That appears to have been a tactical choice.

[2] "Although the *Quarles* opinion speaks generally of 'public safety' (*id.* at 651, 656, 657), there is some suggestion in the opinion that objectively warranted concerns for police safety as well as for public safety might also justify not applying the *Miranda* rule. See *id.* at 658–659. Compare *United States v. Eaton*, 676 F. Supp. 362, 366 (D. Me. 1988), ('the safety of the arresting officers was at high risk'), with *State v. Hazley*, 428 N.W.2d 406, 411 (Minn. Ct. App. 1988) ('[m]issing accomplices cannot be equated with missing guns in the absence of evidence that the accomplice presents a danger to the public' requiring immediate police action)."

Commonwealth v. Bourgeois, 404 Mass. 61, 66 & n.2 (1989).

NOTE 2b   "*Miranda* warnings are only necessary for 'custodial interrogations.' *Commonwealth v. Bryant*, 390 Mass. 729, 736 (1984). The judge could conclude that the defendant was not in custody when the police asked, 'What happened?' This simple question, posed to the defendant by the police on discovery of a dead body, 'was a proper preliminary inquiry not requiring Miranda warnings.' *Commonwealth v. Podlaski*, 377 Mass. 339, 343 (1979). It was directed to discovering generally what the defendant knew about the circumstances of the victim's death. See *id.*; *Commonwealth v. Borodine*, 371 Mass. 1, 4–5 (1976), *cert. denied*, 429 U.S. 1049 (1977); *Commonwealth v. Doyle*, 12 Mass. App. Ct. 786, 793–794 (1981). Suspicion had not focused on the defendant, and the questioning was neither aggressive nor overbearing. *Commonwealth v. Podlaski, supra.* See *Commonwealth v. Bryant, supra* at 738–739. The fact that the police probably would not have allowed the defendant to leave until he talked to them does not by itself make the situation custodial. See *id.*; *Commonwealth v. Podlaski, supra.* Thus, there was no error in the judge's determination that the defendant was not in custody when the police asked him, 'What happened?'" *Commonwealth v. Callahan*, 401 Mass. 627, 630 (1988) (footnote omitted).

NOTE 2c   Right to Remain Silent. "There should be no comments on the defendant's claim of his rights under the Fifth Amendment to the United States Constitution. Where such statements have been presented to the jury in order to prejudice the defendant for exercising his rights, reversible error has been found." *Commonwealth v. Habarek*, 402 Mass. 105, 110 (1988).

NOTE 2d   Police Promises. "The judge did not find that any promise had been made, and the evidence was conflicting. Even if the judge had found that Detective Scire told Carey it would be 'better' for him to admit to ownership if the jacket and gun were his, the conclusion that the defendant's admissions were involuntary would not be required. Initiation by the police interrogator of a discussion regarding leniency or a deal for the defendant, if the latter is forthcoming, is one of the many factors taken into consideration in assessing the voluntariness of a defendant's confession or self-criminating statement. A police officer may not assure the defendant that cooperation 'will aid the defense or result in a lesser sentence.' *Commonwealth v. Shine*, 398 Mass. 641, 652 (1986). That is not the same as a broad suggestion that it would be 'better' for the defendant to tell the truth. *Id.*"

Commonwealth v. Carey, 407 Mass. 528, 538 (1990) (citation omitted).

NOTE 2e   Suppression of Statement. The defendant was charged with murder. He told two court officers, at the early stages of the case, probable cause, "'Tell them I'll plead guilty to man-

slaughter. I don't give a shit what happens to me. They can kill me. I don't care.'"

The Supreme Judicial Court ruled that the trial judge was correct in suppressing the statement, as "in an exercise of discretion [he found that] the probative value of the evidence was clearly outweighed by its likely prejudicial effect. . . .

"We have consistently held that a judge has discretion to exclude a particular piece of evidence if the judge concludes that the probative worth of the evidence is outweighed by the prejudicial effect it may have on the jury. . . .

"The evidence here had little unambiguous probative value. The defendant's statement—'Tell them I'll plead guilty to manslaughter'—did not amount to a confession because it is neither 'a direct acknowledgement of guilt of the precise crime charged [n]or of all facts necessary to establish guilt of that crime.' P.J. Liacos, Massachusetts Evidence, 296–97 (5th ed. 1981). See *Commonwealth v. Haywood*, 247 Mass. 16, 18 (1923). The statement is not clearly an admission either. 'An admission in a criminal case is a statement by the accused, direct or implied, of facts pertinent to the issue, which although insufficient in itself to warrant a conviction tends in connection with proof of other facts to establish his guilt.' *Commonwealth v. Bonomi*, 355 Mass. 327, 347 (1957)."

Commonwealth v. Lewin (No. 2), 407 Mass. 629, 630–31 (1990).

NOTE 2f   "On appeal, the defendant argues only that because he chose not to answer certain questions during interrogation, the officers should have asked him if he wanted to stop the interrogation. He contends that his refusal to reply to certain questions was a reassertion of his right to silence, and that the failure of the officers to ask him whether he wanted to stop the interrogation requires suppression of his statements. We do not agree." *Commonwealth v. Roberts*, 407 Mass. 731, 733 (1990).

NOTE 2g   "[E]ven if the judge accepted as a fact that a defendant was suffering from mental retardation and mental impairment, it does not follow that the judge must rule that the statements were involuntary per se. A statement is inadmissible if it would not have been obtained but for the effects of the confessor's mental disease. After a hearing, the judge concluded that any mental impairment that the defendant suffered did not impede his ability to waive his Miranda rights and make a voluntary statement. . . .

"In reviewing a judge's determination that a voluntary waiver was made, the judge's subsidiary findings will not be disturbed unless there is clear error."

Commonwealth v. Libran, 405 Mass. 634, 638–39 (1989) (citations omitted).

NOTE 2h   Intoxication. "The defendant testified that he had ingested four or five mescaline pills and smoked seven or eight marihuana cigarettes on the day of the interrogation. He testified that he was not able to think clearly and that he had no recollection of being advised of his rights. The defendant stated that during the questioning 'everything is like cloudy.'

"'Intoxication alone is not sufficient to negate an otherwise voluntary act.' *Commonwealth v. Doucette*, 391 Mass. 443, 448 (1948). The defendant spoke coherently with the police, signed a waiver form, and appeared sober to the officers. See *Commonwealth v. Lanoue*, 392 Mass. 583, 589 (1984) (police entitled to rely on defendant's outward behavior). The defendant was able to explain the details of the murder in his confession, which is indicative of the fact that his 'mind was not overtaken by drugs.' *Id.* In short, the question was one of credibility for the finder of fact and we shall not substitute our judgment for that of the trial judge."

Commonwealth v. Bousquet, 407 Mass. 854, 861–62 (1990) (citation omitted).

NOTE 2i   Invocation of right to remain silent. "While being held for custodial interrogation, and without having first waived the Miranda rights of which he had been advised, the defendant shook his head from side to side in response to the question, 'So you don't want to speak?' The police then posed further questions and, after a time, the defendant made incriminating statements. . . . The question for decision is whether the defendant, by his conduct, had invoked the right to remain silent guaranteed under the Fifth Amendment to the United States Constitution and art. 12 of the Massachusetts Declaration of Rights and, if so, whether the police sufficiently honored that right. We conclude that, under both the Fifth Amendment and art. 12, the right to remain silent was invoked but was not 'scrupulously honored,' and that suppression of the subsequent incriminating statements was accordingly warranted. *Commonwealth v. Jackson*, 377 Mass. 319, 326 (1979), quoting *Michigan v. Mosley*, 423 U.S. 96, 104 (1975). In so concluding, we hold that, in the prewaiver context, art. 12 does not require a suspect to invoke his right to remain silent with the utmost clarity, as required under Federal law. *See Berghuis v. Thompkins*, 130 S.Ct. 2250, 2263 (2010)." *Commonwealth v. Clarke*, 461 Mass. 336, 336–37 (2012).

NOTE 3a   Bill of Particulars. "'A defendant in a criminal proceeding is not entitled by a motion for a bill of particulars to secure a resume of the evidence that the Commonwealth intends to introduce at the trial, or to have such a motion treated in all respects as if it were a set of interrogatories.' *Commonwealth v. Hayes*, 311 Mass. 21, 25 (1942). A bill of particulars should give a defendant reasonable notice of the nature and character of the crimes charged. *Id.* at 24–25. Here, the Commonwealth's bill of particulars provided the defendant with such notice. The defendant had reasonable knowledge of the crimes charged, with adequate notice to prepare his defense. *See Commonwealth v. Tavares*, 385 Mass. 140, 157, *cert. denied*, 457 U.S. 1137 (1982) (defendant charged with murder in the first degree was not prejudiced by variance between bill of particulars, which suggested proof of premeditation and felony-murder but not extreme atrocity or cruelty, and proof at trial of extreme atrocity or cruelty, because victim's autopsy report put defendant on notice). The defendant here was not surprised by the proof offered by the Commonwealth at trial. *Id.*" *Commonwealth v. Amirault*, 404 Mass. 221, 233–34 (1989).

NOTE 3b   "[A] bill of particulars is a matter of sound judicial discretion." *Commonwealth v. Allison*, 434 Mass. 670, 677 (2001) (citations omitted).

NOTE 4a   Requirements for Suppression Motion. "Mass.R. Crim.P. 13(a)(2), 378 Mass. 871 (1979), imposes two essential prerequisites on a defendant who seeks to suppress evidence alleged to be the product of an illegal search or seizure: (1) a motion setting forth with particularity, in numbered paragraphs, the grounds, *see Commonwealth v. Robie*, 51 Mass. App. Ct. 494, 499 (2001); and (2) an affidavit based on personal knowledge of the facts relied on in support of the motion. *See Commonwealth v. Santosuosso*, 23 Mass. App. Ct. 310, 313 (1986); *Commonwealth v. Santiago*, 30 Mass. App. Ct. 207, 212–213 (1991). The purpose of the affidavit requirement is 'to give the judge considering the motion a statement of anticipated evidence, in reliable form, to meet the defendant's initial burden of establishing the facts necessary to support his motion . . . and . . . to provide the Commonwealth with fair notice of the specific facts relied on in support of the motion set forth in a form, i.e., under oath, which is not readily subject to change by the affiant.' *Commonwealth v. Santosuosso*, *supra*." *Commonwealth v. Clegg*, 61 Mass. App. Ct. 197, 203 (2004).

NOTE 4b   The failure to file an affidavit "alone would have warranted *denial* of the motion to suppress without a hearing, *see Commonwealth v. Smallwood*, 379 Mass. 878, 888 (1980); *Commonwealth v. Chase*, 14 Mass. App. Ct. 1032, 1034 (1982), or at the very least, the insistence on a proper affidavit before scheduling the motion for hearing. *See Commonwealth v. McColl*, 375 Mass. 316, 322 (1978)." *Commonwealth v. Clegg*, 61 Mass. App. Ct. at 203–04.

NOTE 4c   "In view of the ambiguity as to whether the defendant was limiting his motion to the search of his person, the Commonwealth, before the evidentiary hearing, could have asked for a more particularized affidavit or moved that the motion to suppress be denied without a hearing for failing to provide the Commonwealth fair notice as to the search he was challenging. The Commonwealth, however, made no such motion and challenges

the particularity of the affidavit only on appeal. By failing to have made such a motion, the Commonwealth waived any objection to the particularity of the defendant's affidavit pursuant to rule 13(a)(2)." *Commonwealth v. Mubdi*, 456 Mass. 385, 390–91 (2010) (footnote and citation omitted).

NOTE 4d   Timing of Suppression Hearing and Trial. Combining a suppression hearing with a trial is improper. *Commonwealth v. Love*, 452 Mass. 498, 508 (2008); *Commonwealth v. Healy*, 452 Mass. 510, 516 (2008).

NOTE 5a   Lost or Destroyed Evidence. "The loss and destruction of highly relevant evidence by the Commonwealth and its agents defeated the defendant's opportunity effectively to present a defense." Accordingly, the Supreme Judicial Court reversed the defendant's conviction for murder in the first degree. *Commonwealth v. Olszewski*, 401 Mass. 749, 756 (1988).

NOTE 5b   "When potentially exculpatory evidence is lost or destroyed, the court must perform a balancing test to determine what remedial action, if any, is necessary. *Commonwealth v. Willie*, 400 Mass. 472, 432 (1987). Those factors to be considered include the culpability of the Commonwealth, the materiality of the evidence and the potential for prejudice to the defendant. *Id.* See *Arizona v. Youngblood*, 109 S.Ct. 333, 334–337 (1988) (failure to preserve potentially useful evidence not denial of due process absent bad faith by government)." *Commonwealth v. Troy*, 405 Mass. 253, 261 (1989) (footnote omitted).

NOTE 5c   "We seek to clarify and resolve the somewhat different approaches taken in our cases. When a defendant makes a claim that the government has lost or destroyed potentially exculpatory evidence, it makes sense that he or she should bear the initial burden of demonstrating the exculpatory nature of that evidence, using the *Neal* 'reasonable possibility, based on concrete evidence' formulation. [*Commonwealth v. Neal*, 392 Mass. 1 (1984)] at 12. We therefore hold that the defendant will be required to meet this threshold burden in order to advance a claim for relief. If the defendant does meet the burden, then . . . the judge, or the court on appeal, must proceed to balance the Commonwealth's culpability, the materiality of the evidence, and the prejudice to the defendant in order to determine whether the defendant is entitled to relief." *Commonwealth v. Williams*, 455 Mass. 706, 718 (2010) (citations omitted).

NOTE 6a   Egregious Misconduct. "'Absent egregious misconduct or at least a serious threat of prejudice, the remedy of dismissal infringes too severely on the public interest in bringing guilty persons to justice.' *Commonwealth v. Cinelli*, 389 Mass. 197, 210, *cert. denied*, 464 U.S. 860 (1983).

"This court has declined to adopt a per se rule mandating dismissal of complaints in cases in which government agents intentionally violate the attorney-client relationship and the right to a fair trial."

Commonwealth v. Fontaine, 402 Mass. 491, 495, 498 (1988) (citations omitted).

NOTE 6b   Defendant was arraigned March 16 and the case was continued until April 10. On April 10, the defense moved to continue, which was granted. The case was continued until May 8. On that date the police officer failed to appear and the judge dismissed the case. "Where a dismissal is without prejudice, the judge's action should be upheld in the absence of an abuse of discretion. Where, as here, the dismissals are with prejudice, there must be a showing of egregious misconduct or at least a serious threat of prejudice. Although we do not excuse the prosecutor's failure to ensure that the police officer would be present on May 8, we conclude that such conduct does not rise to the level of 'egregious conduct.'" *Commonwealth v. Connelly*, 418 Mass. 37, 38 (1994).

NOTE 7   Statute of Limitations. See G.L. c. 277, § 63.

NOTE 8   Preindictment Delay. "The judge found that the exercise of reasonable diligence by either the Fall River or the Providence police in all probability would have resulted in the defendant's being informed of the allegations against him shortly after the incident. However, the judge held that the defendant did not present sufficient evidence to meet his burden of proving that he is entitled to dismissal of the indictment. We agree with the judge's conclusions.

"The defendant bears the heavy burden of showing that there was prejudice and that the delay has been intentionally undertaken to gain a tactical advantage over the accused or has been incurred in reckless disregard of known risks to the putative defendant's ability to mount a defense." *Commonwealth v. Fayerweather*, 406 Mass. 78, 86 (1989) (quotation marks and citations omitted).

NOTE 9   Motion to Dismiss. "In *Commonwealth v. Brandano*, [359 Mass. 332, 337 (1971)], we stated that, when the defendant seeks dismissal of a complaint over the Commonwealth's objection, each party should submit affidavits in support of its position and there should be a hearing on any disputed matter. In *Commonwealth v. Clark*, 393 Mass. 361, 365 (1984), we held that the judge's use of the *Brandano* procedure when hearing the defendant's pretrial motion to dismiss, because of the insufficiency of the Commonwealth's contemplated evidence, was inappropriate since the Commonwealth's stipulations and offers of proof indicated that there was additional evidence. *See Rosenberg v. Commonwealth*, 372, Mass. 59, 63 (1977). Clearly these principles do not apply where the Commonwealth willingly participates in pretrial procedures potentially dispositive of the case, raising no objection nor making any attempt to inform the judge of its desire to offer additional evidence." *Commonwealth v. Black*, 403 Mass. 675, 678 (1989); *Commonwealth v. Thurston*, 419 Mass. 101 (1994) ("The reasons advanced by the judge [the inability of the Commonwealth to prove its case] do not amount to a justification for a dismissal in the 'interests of public justice' over objection of the Commonwealth [because the Commonwealth clearly does have evidence by which it might present a prima facie case]." *Id.* at 105.).

NOTE 10   Commonwealth Remedies. "The Commonwealth had ample remedies for the allegedly improper dismissal of a criminal complaint for lack of prosecution. It could have sought reconsideration of the dismissal of the complaint. It could have appealed the ruling. It could have proceeded by way of indictment. What it could not do was simply ignore the judge's ruling and refile the same complaints in the same court." *Commonwealth v. Williams*, 431 Mass. 71, 76–77 (2000) (citations, quotation marks and brackets omitted).

NOTE 11   Power to Reconsider. "Rule 13(a)(5) . . . permits a judge to reconsider if 'substantial justice requires.' This rule is not limited to instances where there are allegations of new or additional grounds that could not have been reasonably known when the original motion was filed. *Commonwealth v. Haskell*, 438 Mass. 790, 792 (2003). 'A judge's power to reconsider his own decisions during the pendency of a case is firmly rooted in the common law, and the adoption of Rule 13 was not intended to disturb this authority.' *Id.*" *Commonwealth v. Lugo*, 64 Mass. App. Ct. 12, 14 (2005).

RULE 14
Pretrial Discovery

(Amended effective Sept. 7, 2004 and applicable to those cases initiated (by indictment or complaint) on or after the effective date; amended by court order Apr. 4, 2005, effective May 1, 2005; Dec. 17, 2008, effective Apr. 1, 2009; June 26, 2012, effective Sept. 17, 2012; Nov. 5, 2015, effective Jan. 1, 2016.) (Applicable to trials in the District Court and Superior Court.)

(a) Procedures for Discovery.

(1) *Automatic Discovery.*

(A) Mandatory Discovery for the Defendant. The prosecution shall disclose to the defense, and permit the defense to discover, inspect and copy, each of the following items and information at or prior to the pretrial conference, provided it is relevant to the case and is in the possession, custody or control of the prosecutor, persons under the prosecutor's direction and control, or persons who have participated in investigating or evaluating the case and either regularly report to the prosecutor's office or have done so in the case:

(i) Any written or recorded statements, and the substance of any oral statements, made by the defendant or a codefendant.

(ii) The grand jury minutes, and the written or recorded statements of a person who has testified before a grand jury.

(iii) Any facts of an exculpatory nature.

(iv) The names, addresses, and dates of birth of the Commonwealth's prospective witnesses other than law enforcement witnesses. The Commonwealth shall also provide this information to the Probation Department.

(v) The names and business addresses of prospective law enforcement witnesses.

(vi) Intended expert opinion evidence, other than evidence that pertains to the defendant's criminal responsibility and is subject to subdivision (b)(2). Such discovery shall include the identity, current curriculum vitae, and list of publications of each intended expert witness, and all reports prepared by the expert that pertain to the case.

(vii) Material and relevant police reports, photographs, tangible objects, all intended exhibits, reports of physical examinations of any person or of scientific tests or experiments, and statements of persons the party intends to call as witnesses.

(viii) A summary of identification procedures, and all statements made in the presence of or by an identifying witness that are relevant to the issue of identity or to the fairness or accuracy of the identification procedures.

(ix) Disclosure of all promises, rewards or inducements made to witnesses the party intends to present at trial.

(B) Reciprocal Discovery for the Prosecution. Following the Commonwealth's delivery of all discovery required pursuant to subdivision (a)(1)(A) or court order, and on or before a date agreed to between the parties, or in the absence of such agreement a date ordered by the court, the defendant shall disclose to the prosecution and permit the Commonwealth to discover, inspect, and copy any material and relevant evidence discoverable under subdivision (a)(1)(A) (vi), (vii) and (ix) which the defendant intends to offer at trial, including the names, addresses, dates of birth, and statements of those persons whom the defendant intends to call as witnesses at trial.

(C) Stay of Automatic Discovery; Sanctions. Subdivisions (a)(1)(A) and (a)(1)(B) shall have the force and effect of a court order, and failure to provide discovery pursuant to them may result in application of any sanctions permitted for non-compliance with a court order under subdivision 14(c). However, if in the judgment of either party good cause exists for declining to make any of the disclosures set forth above, it may move for a protective order pursuant to subdivision (a)(6) and production of the item shall be stayed pending a ruling by the court.

(D) Record of Convictions of the Defendant, Codefendants, and Prosecution Witnesses. At arraignment the court shall order the Probation Department to deliver to the parties the record of prior complaints, indictments and dispositions of all defendants and of all witnesses identified pursuant to subdivisions (a)(1)(A)(iv) within 5 days of the Commonwealth's notification to the Department of the names and addresses of its witnesses.

(E) Notice and Preservation of Evidence. (i) Upon receipt of information that any item described in subparagraph

3

(a)(1)(A)(i)–(viii) exists, except that it is not within the possession, custody or control of the prosecution, persons under its direction and control, or persons who have participated in investigating or evaluating the case and either regularly report to the prosecutor's office or have done so in the case, the prosecution shall notify the defendant of the existence of the item and all information known to the prosecutor concerning the item's location and the identity of any persons possessing it. (ii) At any time, a party may move for an order to any individual, agency or other entity in possession, custody or control of items pertaining to the case, requiring that such items be preserved for a specified period of time. The court shall hear and rule upon the motion expeditiously. The court may modify or vacate such an order upon a showing that preservation of particular evidence will create significant hardship, on condition that the probative value of said evidence is preserved by a specified alternative means.

(2) *Motions for Discovery.* The defendant may move, and following its filing of the Certificate of Compliance the Commonwealth may move, for discovery of other material and relevant evidence not required by subdivision (a)(1) within the time allowed by Rule 13(d)(1).

(3) *Certificate of Compliance.* When a party has provided all discovery required by this rule or by court order, it shall file with the court a Certificate of Compliance. The certificate shall state that, to the best of its knowledge and after reasonable inquiry, the party has disclosed and made available all items subject to discovery other than reports of experts, and shall identify each item provided. If further discovery is subsequently provided, a supplemental certificate shall be filed with the court identifying the additional items provided.

(4) *Continuing Duty.* If either the defense or the prosecution subsequently learns of additional material which it would have been under a duty to disclose or produce pursuant to any provisions of this rule at the time of a previous discovery order, it shall promptly notify the other party of its acquisition of such additional material and shall disclose the material in the same manner as required for initial discovery under this rule.

(5) *Work Product.* This rule does not authorize discovery by a party of those portions of records, reports, correspondence, memoranda, or internal documents of the adverse party which are only the legal research, opinions, theories, or conclusions of the adverse party or its attorney and legal staff, or of statements of a defendant, signed or unsigned, made to the attorney for the defendant or the attorney's legal staff.

(6) *Protective Orders.* Upon a sufficient showing, the judge may at any time order that the discovery or inspection be denied, restricted, or deferred, or make such other order as is appropriate. The judge may alter the time requirements of this rule. The judge may, for cause shown, grant discovery to a defendant on the condition that the material to be discovered be available only to counsel for the defendant. This provision does not alter the allocation of the burden of proof with regard to the matter at issue, including privilege.

(7) *Amendment of Discovery Orders.* Upon motion of either party made subsequent to an order of the judge pursuant to this rule, the judge may alter or amend the previous order or orders as the interests of justice may require. The judge may, for cause shown, affirm a prior order granting discovery to a defendant upon the additional condition that the material to be discovered is to be available only to counsel for the defendant.

(8) A party may waive the right to discovery of an item, or to discovery of the item within the time provided in this Rule. The parties may agree to reduce or enlarge the items subject to discovery pursuant to subsections (a)(1)(A) and (a)(1)(B). Any such waiver or agreement shall be in writing and signed by the waiving party or the parties to the agreement, shall identify the specific items included, and shall be served upon all the parties.

(b) Special Procedures.

(1) *Notice of Alibi.*

(A) Notice by Defendant. The judge may, upon written motion of the Commonwealth filed pursuant to subdivision (a)(2) of this rule, stating the time, date, and place at which the alleged offense was committed, order that the defendant serve upon the prosecutor a written notice, signed by the defendant, of his or her intention to offer a defense of alibi. The notice by the defendant shall state the specific place or places at which the defendant claims to have been at the time of the alleged offense and the names and addresses of the witnesses upon whom the defense intends to rely to establish the alibi.

(B) Disclosure of Information and Witness. Within seven days of service of the defendant's notice of alibi, the Commonwealth shall serve upon the defendant a written notice stating the names and addresses of witnesses upon whom the prosecutor intends to rely to establish the defendant's presence at the scene of the alleged offense and any other witnesses to be relied on to rebut testimony of any of the defendant's alibi witnesses.

(C) Continuing Duty to Disclose. If prior to or during trial a party learns of an additional witness whose identity, if known, should have been included in the information furnished under subdivision (b)(1)(A) or (B), that party shall promptly notify the adverse party or its attorney of the existence and identity of the additional witness.

(D) Failure to Comply. Upon the failure of either party to comply with the requirements of this rule, the judge may exclude the testimony of any undisclosed witness offered by such party as to the defendant's absence from or presence at the scene of the alleged offense. This rule shall not limit the right of the defendant to testify.

(E) Exceptions. For cause shown, the judge may grant an exception to any of the requirements of subdivisions (b)(1)(A) through (D) of this rule.

(F) Inadmissibility of Withdrawn Alibi. Evidence of an intention to rely upon an alibi defense, later withdrawn, or of statements made in connection with that intention, is not admissible in any civil or criminal proceeding against the person who gave notice of that intention.

(2) *Mental Health Issues*

(A) Notice. If a defendant intends at trial to raise as an issue his or her mental condition at the time of the alleged crime, or if the defendant intends to introduce expert testimony on the defendant's mental condition at any stage of the proceeding, the defendant shall, within the time provided for the filing of pretrial motions by Rule 13(d)(2) or at such later time as the judge may allow, notify the prosecutor in writing of such intention. The notice shall state:

(i) whether the defendant intends to offer testimony of expert witnesses on the issue of the defendant's mental condition at the time of the alleged crime or another specified time;

(ii) the names and addresses of expert witnesses whom the defendant expects to call; and

(iii) whether those expert witnesses intend to rely in whole or in part on statements of the defendant as to his or her mental condition.

The defendant shall file a copy of the notice with the clerk. The judge may for cause shown allow late filing of the notice, grant additional time to the parties to prepare for trial, or make such other order as may be appropriate.

(B) Examination.

If the notice of the defendant or subsequent inquiry by the judge or developments in the case indicate that statements of the defendant as to his or her mental condition will be relied upon by a defendant's expert witness, the court, on its own motion or on motion of the prosecutor, may order the defendant to submit to an examination consistent with the provisions of the General Laws and subject to the following terms and conditions:

(i) The examination shall include such physical, psychiatric, and psychological tests as the court-appointed examiner (examiner) deems necessary to form an opinion as to the mental condition of the defendant at the relevant time. No examination based on statements of the defendant may be conducted unless the judge has found that (a) the defendant then intends to offer into evidence expert testimony based on his or her own statements or (b) there is a reasonable likelihood that the defendant will offer that evidence.

(ii) No statement, confession, or admission, or other evidence of or obtained from the defendant during the course of the examination, except evidence derived solely from physical examinations or tests, may be revealed to the prosecution or anyone acting on its behalf unless so ordered by the judge.

(iii) The examiner shall file with the court a written report as to the mental condition of the defendant at the relevant time.

Unless the parties mutually agree to an earlier time of disclosure, the examiner's report shall be sealed and shall not be made available to the parties unless (a) the judge determines that the report contains no matter, information, or evidence which is based upon statements of the defendant as to his or her mental condition at the relevant time or which is otherwise within the scope of the privilege against self-incrimination; or (b) the defendant files a motion requesting that the report be made available to the parties; or (c) after the defendant expresses the clear intent to raise as an issue his or her mental condition, the judge is satisfied that (1) the defendant intends to testify, or (2) the defendant intends to offer expert testimony based in whole or in part on statements made by the defendant as to his or her mental condition at the relevant time.

At the time the report of the examiner is disclosed to the parties, the defendant shall provide the Commonwealth with a report of the defense psychiatric or psychological expert(s) as to the mental condition of the defendant at the relevant time.

The reports of both parties' experts must include a written summary of the expert's expected testimony that fully describes: the defendant's history and present symptoms; any physical, psychiatric, and psychological tests relevant to the expert's opinion regarding the issue of mental condition and their results; any oral or written statements made by the defendant relevant to the issue of the mental condition for which the defendant was evaluated; the expert's opinions as to the defendant's mental condition, including the bases and reasons for these opinions; and the witness's qualifications.

If these reports contain both privileged and nonprivileged matter, the court may, if feasible, at such time as it deems appropriate prior to full disclosure of the reports to the parties, make available to the parties the nonprivileged portions.

(iv) If a defendant refuses to submit to an examination ordered pursuant to and subject to the terms and conditions of this rule, the court may prescribe such remedies as it deems warranted by the circumstances, which may include exclusion of the testimony of any expert witness offered by the defense on the issue of the defendant's mental condition or the admission of evidence of the refusal of the defendant to submit to examination.

(C) Discovery for the purpose of a court-ordered examination under Rule 14(b)(2)(B).

(i) If the judge orders the defendant to submit to an examination under Rule 14(b)(2)(B), the defendant shall, within fourteen days of the court's designation of the examiner, make available to the examiner the following:

(a) All mental health records concerning the defendant, whether psychological, psychiatric, or counseling, in defense counsel's possession;

(b) All medical records concerning the defendant in defense counsel's possession; and

(c) All raw data from any tests or assessments administered to the defendant by the defendant's expert or at the request of the defendant's expert.

(ii) The defendant's duty of production set forth in Rule 14(b)(2)(C)(i) shall continue beyond the defendant's initial production during the fourteen-day period and shall apply to any such mental health or medical record(s) thereafter obtained by defense counsel and to any raw data thereafter obtained from any tests or assessments administered to the defendant by the defendant's expert or at the request of the defendant's expert.

(iii) In addition to the records provided under Rule 14(b)(2)(C)(i) and (ii), the examiner may request records from any person or entity by filing with the court under seal, in such form as the Court may prescribe, a writing that identifies the requested records and states the reason(s) for the request. The examiner shall not disclose the request to the prosecutor without either leave of court or agreement of the defendant.

Upon receipt of the examiner's request, the court shall issue a copy of the request to the defendant and shall notify the prosecutor that the examiner has filed a sealed request for records pursuant to Rule 14(b)(2)(C)(iii). Within thirty days of the court's issuance to the defendant of the examiner's request, or within such other time as the judge may allow, the defendant shall file in writing any objection that the defendant may have to the production of any of the material that the examiner has requested. The judge may hold an ex parte hearing on the defendant's objections and may, in the judge's discretion, hear from the examiner. Records of such hearing shall be sealed until the report of the examiner is disclosed to the parties under Rule 14(b)(2)(B)(iii), at which point the records related to the examiner's request, including the records of any hearing, shall be released to the parties unless the court, in its discretion, determines that it would be unfairly prejudicial to the defendant to do so.

If the judge grants any part of the examiner's request, the judge shall indicate on the form prescribed by the Court the particular records to which the examiner may have access,

3

and the clerk shall subpoena the indicated record(s). The clerk shall notify the examiner and the defendant when the requested record(s) are delivered to the clerk's office and shall make the record(s) available to the examiner and the defendant for examination and copying, subject to a protective order under the same terms as govern disclosure of reports under Rule 14(b)(2)(B)(iii). The clerk's office shall maintain these records under seal except as provided herein. If the judge denies the examiner's request, the judge shall notify the examiner, the defendant, and the prosecutor of the denial.

(iv) Upon completion of the court-ordered examination, the examiner shall make available to the defendant all raw data from any tests or assessments administered to the defendant by the Commonwealth's examiner or at the request of the Commonwealth's examiner.

(D) Additional discovery. Upon a showing of necessity, the Commonwealth and the defendant may move for other material and relevant evidence relating to the defendant's mental condition.

(3) *Notice of Other Defenses.* If a defendant intends to rely upon a defense based upon a license, claim of authority or ownership, or exemption, the defendant shall, within the time provided for the filing of pretrial motions by Rule 13(d)(2) or at such later time as the judge may direct, notify the prosecutor in writing of such intention and file a copy of such notice with the clerk. If there is a failure to comply with the requirements of this subdivision, a license, claim of authority or ownership, or exemption may not be relied upon as a defense. The judge may for cause shown allow a late filing of the notice or grant additional time to the parties to prepare for trial or make such other order as may be appropriate.

(4) *Self Defense and First Aggressor.*

(A) Notice by Defendant. If a defendant intends to raise a claim of self defense and to introduce evidence of the alleged victim's specific acts of violence to support an allegation that he or she was the first aggressor, the defendant shall no later than 21 days after the pretrial hearing or at such other time as the judge may direct for good cause, notify the prosecutor in writing of such intention. The notice shall include a brief description of each such act, together with the location and date to the extent practicable, and the names, addresses and dates of birth of the witnesses the defendant intends to call to provide evidence of each such act. The defendant shall file a copy of such notice with the clerk.

(B) Reciprocal Disclosure by the Commonwealth. No later than 30 days after receipt of the defendant's notice, or at such other time as the judge may direct for good cause, the Commonwealth shall serve upon the defendant a written notice of any rebuttal evidence the Commonwealth intends to introduce, including a brief description of such evidence together with the names of the witnesses the Commonwealth intends to call, the addresses and dates of birth of other than law enforcement witnesses and the business address of law enforcement witnesses.

(C) Continuing Duty to Disclose. If prior to or during trial a party learns of additional evidence that, if known, should have been included in the information furnished under subdivision (b)(4)(A) or (B), that party shall promptly notify the adverse party or its attorney of such evidence.

(D) Failure to Comply. Upon the failure of either party to comply with the requirements of this rule, the judge may exclude the evidence offered by such party on the issue of the identity of the first aggressor.

(c) Sanctions for Noncompliance.

(1) *Relief for Nondisclosure.* For failure to comply with any discovery order issued or imposed pursuant to this rule, the court may make a further order for discovery, grant a continuance, or enter such other order as it deems just under the circumstances.

(2) *Exclusion of Evidence.* The court may in its discretion exclude evidence for noncompliance with a discovery order issued or imposed pursuant to this rule. Testimony of the defendant and evidence concerning the defense of lack of criminal responsibility which is otherwise admissible cannot be excluded except as provided by subdivision (b)(2) of this rule.

(d) Definition.

The term "statement", as used in this rule, means:

(1) a writing made, signed, or by a person having percipient knowledge of relevant facts and which contains such facts, other than drafts or notes that have been incorporated into a subsequent draft or final report; or

(2) a written, stenographic, mechanical, electrical, or other recording, or transcription thereof, which is a substantially verbatim recital of an oral declaration except that a computer assisted real time translation, or its functional equivalent, made to assist a deaf or hearing impaired person, that is not transcribed or permanently saved in electronic form, shall not be considered a statement.

Reporter's Notes (2015). *Rule 14(b)(2)(C) Discovery for the purpose of a court-ordered examination under Rule 14(b)(2)(B).* In *Commonwealth v. Hanright*, 465 Mass. 639, 648 (2013), the Supreme Judicial Court held that, when a judge orders a defendant under Rule 14(b)(2)(B) to submit to a forensic mental evaluation, the judge may also require the defendant to disclose to the court-appointed examiner ("Commonwealth's examiner" or "examiner") treatment records necessary to conduct that forensic evaluation. Rule 14(b)(2)(C) sets out the scope and sequence of that disclosure and the procedure by which it is implemented. Under the rule, both experts—the Commonwealth's examiner and the defendant's expert—must be given equal access to the information they collectively deem necessary to conduct an effective forensic examination and produce a competent report. The rule achieves this result, without involving the prosecutor, through a reciprocal discovery process that makes available to each expert (1) the defendant's pertinent medical and mental-health records and (2) the raw data from tests or assessments of the defendant administered during the course of the experts' respective examinations of the defendant. By ensuring that the experts are working from a common, comprehensive set of records and objective, test-generated data, the rule advances the reliability and fairness of the examinations and the ensuing reports, and it promotes efficiency in the examination process.

Rule 14(b)(2)(C)(i). Rule 14(b)(2)(C)(i) outlines the defendant's disclosure obligation. The rule requires that the defendant make available to the Commonwealth's examiner, within 14 days of the examiner's appointment, three categories of information: (a) the defendant's mental-health records, broadly defined, that are possessed by defense counsel, (b) the defendant's medical records that are possessed by defense counsel, and (c) the raw data from any tests or assessments administered to the defendant in the course of the defense expert's examination of the defendant. This discovery obligation is intended to provide equal and full access for both parties to the defendant's pertinent mental-health and medical history at the time each expert is conducting his or her examination of the defendant. Full discovery of pertinent source material at this point, when the examiners are forming their respective opinions concerning the defendant's mental health without yet having access to the opinions of the other, promotes the truth-seeking function of the trial, see *Hanright*, 465 Mass. at 644–645, while making the examination process more efficient.

In defining the scope of the mental-health and medical records to be produced as those possessed by defense counsel, the rule intends as wide a reach as is reasonably possible, covering every such record that the defense collected in the course of considering whether to assert this defense. At this point in the process, the defendant has waived any privilege that might preclude producing his statements and records to the Commonwealth's examiner, see *Hanright*, 465 Mass. at 645–648, and the rule means to give both experts access to every record reasonably available, relying on the experts independently to decide which records are relevant to the inquiry. If, in examining the defendant and the records that the defendant produced, the Commonwealth's examiner identifies a mental-health or medical record that the defense overlooked, or chose not to collect, and thus did not produce, Rule 14(b)(2)(C)(iii), discussed below, provides for a process by which the examiner can seek that record. Any such records would, under the rule, be available to both experts.

The raw testing data that Rule 14(b)(2)(C)(i) requires the defendant to produce consists of objective, uninterpreted test results, for example, multiple-choice, bubble outputs from a psychological test with quantification on various scales. As discussed below, Rule 14(b)(2)(C)(iv) requires the same disclosure from the Commonwealth's examiner. The intent is to provide both experts with all of the relevant, objective testing data available at the time each writes his or her report, thus avoiding the need for supplemental reports or evaluations that consider pertinent testing data first revealed in the other expert's report. Not only would the necessity of such supplemental reports or evaluations extend the examination process, but these reports would necessarily be written after reviewing the opposing expert's report, thus putting in question the independence of this supplemental evaluation of these testing data. The rule's discovery obligation reaches only raw testing data; it does not apply to the defense expert's work product, such as notes interpreting this raw testing data or notes relating to a clinical interview of the defendant. This mandatory disclosure of raw testing data generated by the experts during the course of their respective examinations works no unfair advantage to either side. The discovery obligation is mutual. As with defendant's mental-health and medical records, the raw data resulting from tests administered to the defendant are essential to determining the defendant's mental-health at the time in question, and all of these data must be considered by both examiners if their respective reports are to serve their truth-seeking function. Finally, the test results will ultimately be released with the final reports under Rule 14(b)(2)(B)(iii); the only question Rule 14(b)(2)(C)(i) & (iv) address is the timing of that release.

Rule 14(b)(2)(C)(ii). As noted, Rule 14(b)(2)(C)(i) requires the defendant to produce the mental-health and medical records and raw testing data within 14 days after the judge appoints the Commonwealth examiner. Under Rule 14(b)(2)(C)(ii), the defendant's duty to disclose records and raw testing data continues throughout the examination period provided under Rule 14(b)(2)(B). If the defendant discovers records or raw testing data that was subject to production under Rule 14(b)(2)(C)(i) but was not produced, those records or data must be produced as soon as they are discovered. Moreover, if subsequent to the initial production under Rule 14(b)(2)(C)(i) defense counsel obtains records covered by the rule or the defense expert generates test data covered by the rule, Rule 14(b)(2)(C)(ii) requires that these materials be promptly produced to the Commonwealth's examiner.

Rule 14(b)(2)(C)(iii). As noted, this subsection anticipates the possibility that the Commonwealth's examiner will learn of additional medical or mental-health records that he or she believes necessary to conducting a professionally competent examination. For example, a record provided by the defendant, or a comment by the defendant during the court-ordered examination, might refer to an earlier hospitalization of the defendant for which the defendant did not produce records. If the examiner concludes that there is a reasonable possibility that such records exist and should be reviewed, Rule 14(b)(2)(C)(iii) provides for a procedure by which

the examiner can file with the court a prescribed form under seal identifying the requested records (with as much specificity as circumstances reasonably permit) and stating the reason(s) for the request. Because at this point the court has yet to find sufficient evidence of privilege waiver by the defendant to permit the prosecutor's involvement in the examination process, see Rule 14(b)(2)(B)(iii), under Rule 14(b)(2)(C)(iii), the examiner may not inform the prosecutor of the document request or its contents, absent permission from either the defense or the court.

Upon receiving the sealed request, the court must issue a copy to the defendant, notifying the Commonwealth only that a sealed request for additional records has been filed. The defendant has 30 days to file ex parte a written objection to the requested production. If the defendant timely files such an objection, the judge has the discretion to hold an ex parte hearing on it, including, again in the judge's discretion, permitting the Commonwealth's examiner to participate. If the judge grants any part of the examiner's request, the judge must inform the clerk to which records the examiner may have access, and the clerk must then subpoena those records. When the records arrive at the clerk's office, the clerk must notify the examiner and the defendant of the records' availability for examination and copying, subject to a protective order forbidding their disclosure to the prosecutor unless the judge determines that the conditions set forth in Rule 14(b)(2)(B)(iii) for permitting prosecutorial access to the examiners' reports are met. The clerk's office must maintain the records under seal.

When the report of the Commonwealth's examiner is disclosed to the parties under Rule 14(b)(2)(B)(iii), the records related to the examiner's Rule 14(b)(2)(C)(iii) request for additional records shall also be released to the parties, subject to the judge's narrow discretion to forbid such release. At this point in the process, the defendant has effectively waived any claim of privilege concerning evidence relating to the mental-health defense. See *Hanright*, 465 Mass. at 645–647. The only reason for withholding from the prosecutor information concerning the examiner's request for additional records would presumably be a concern that information there set forth would have little or no relevance to the mental-health defense and would cause unfair prejudice to the defendant in conducting the mental-health defense, a balancing of interests with which judges are quite familiar. As is so with the release of the examiners' reports and supporting records, the release of records relating to a request for additional records would be confined to the parties; these records would remain sealed to the public. Granting the prosecutor access to the records relating to a denial of an examiner's request for records would not only permit full communication between the prosecutor and the examiner in preparing for trial, but it would also allow the Commonwealth to weigh the possibility, however remote, of seeking appellate review of the denial.

Rule 14(b)(2)(C)(iv). As noted above, once the Commonwealth's examiner completes his or her examination of the defendant, the examiner must disclose to the defendant all raw data from any tests or assessments that the examiner conducted or requested. This ensures full reciprocity between the parties. Presumably, the only mental-health or medical records available to the examiner would be those provided by the defendant or produced in response to a court order under Rule 14(b)(2)(C)(iii), making any reciprocal discovery of such records unnecessary. The production of raw testing data by the court-ordered examiner would result in both experts having full access to the same records and raw testing data before they complete and file their respective reports.

Reporter's Notes (2012). In 2012, Rule 14 was amended in several respects. These revisions are discussed below.

Subdivision (b)(2). Mental health issues. This amendment responds to the Supreme Judicial Court's expansion of the *Blaisdell* procedure to analogous situations such as defenses based on an inability to form the requisite intent for an element of the crime, see *Commonwealth v. Dias*, 431 Mass. 822, 829 (2000), on an inability to premeditate, see *Commonwealth v. Contos*, 435 Mass. 19, 24

3

n.7 (2001), and where the defendant places at issue his or her mental ability voluntarily to waive Miranda rights, *see Commonwealth v. Ostrander*, 441 Mass. 344, 352 (2004). In addition, the Court has indicated in dicta that the same would hold true in the case of a defense based on battered woman syndrome, *see Ostrander*, 441 Mass. at 355 (2004).

There are two different dimensions to the problem that this subsection addresses. One concerns giving notice to the Commonwealth of a complex issue that the prosecutor otherwise would have no reason to expect to litigate. The other deals with redressing the unfairness of allowing a defense expert to testify based on statements obtained from the defendant without giving the prosecution an opportunity to obtain equivalent access for its expert.

The proposed amendment addresses the first concern by expanding the scope of the notice provision beyond the context of *Blaisdell* to include all mental health defenses. A mental health defense is one that places in issue the defendant's mental condition at the time of the alleged crime, based on a claim that some mental disease or defect or psychological impairment, such as battered woman syndrome, affected the defendant's cognitive ability. These are complex issues for which the prosecutor should have time to prepare, whether an expert testifies for the defense or not. As used in this subsection, the term "mental health defense" does not include a claim that the defendant's cognitive ability was affected by intoxication, an issue that arises more frequently and does not present the same level of complexity as do the former examples.

The proposed amendment addresses the second concern by requiring notice whenever the defendant intends to rely on expert testimony concerning the defendant's mental condition at any stage of the process on any issue, whether it related to culpability, competency or because it concerns the admission of evidence. Thus, for example, if the defendant intends to introduce expert testimony in support of a claim that a confession was not voluntary, as in *Ostrander*, the notice would specify that the witness would testify as to the defendant's mental condition at the time of the confession. If it appears that the expert will rely on statements of the defendant as to his or her mental condition, then the judge may order the defendant to submit to an examination pursuant to subsection 14(b)(2)(B).

Subdivision (b)(2)(B)(i). The proposed amendment deletes "physiological tests" from those that may be included in a court-ordered examination. This deletion is not intended to work any substantive change to the rule but rather to eliminate a superfluous term. Under the rule, "physical tests" is meant to include "physiological tests," including but not limited to neurological tests and examinations such as magnetic resonance imaging (MRI) and positron emission tomography (PET) scans.

Subdivision (b)(2)(B)(iii). The Rule applies not only to experts who are psychiatrists, but to psychologists as well.

The regime for disclosure of expert reports has been amended in light of *Commonwealth v. Sliech-Brodeur*, 457 Mass. 300 (2010). The timing of the release of the Commonwealth's expert's report was altered only to make clear that the parties can agree on its disclosure at a time earlier than previously set out in the Rule. *See Sliech-Brodeur*, 457 Mass. at 325 n.34 (2010). As required by *Sliech-Brodeur*, defense experts as well as the prosecution's must prepare and disclose reports. In order to avoid infringing on the defendant's privilege against self-incrimination, the defense expert's report is released to the prosecution at the same time that the defendant receives the report of the Commonwealth's expert. The Rule also has been amended to address the timing of the exchange of reports. The latest date of exchange would be when the defendant expresses a "clear intent" to rely on mental impairment as an issue in the case, relying in part on the defendant's statements or testimony. This will often occur at the final pretrial conference or comparable event. The Rule attempts to avoid the delay and inconvenience of disclosing the reports only after the defendant's expert offers testimony on direct examination. Finally, the rule as amended makes clear the judge's discretion to review any expert report filed with and sealed by the court, and, if feasible and appropriate, to release to the parties any unprivileged material contained in the report prior to the report's full disclosure to the parties.

Once the reports have been released to the parties, they may be shared with the respective experts for each side.

The Rule has been amended to require more detail in the content of the report that both prosecution and defense experts must file. This portion of the Rule is patterned after 18 U.S.C.S. § 4247(c). In one major respect, however, the Rule goes beyond the federal model by requiring the report to contain a complete account of the statements of the defendant that are relevant to the issue of his or her mental condition. This includes both statements relating to the underlying incident as well as any statements prior to or following it that are relevant to the defendant's mental condition. If the examiner considered written statements of the defendant, the report should contain the relevant portions. If the examiner considered oral statements of the defendant, the report should include the substance of what the defendant said that bears on the question of his or her mental condition. In reporting on the defendant's statements, examiners should not withhold relevant evidence contrary to their own position.

The protection of the work product doctrine and the principle that notes or preliminary drafts are not discoverable if they are incorporated into a final report, applicable elsewhere in the discovery regime that Rule 14 establishes, apply as well in this context.

Subdivision (b)(2)(C). This provision gives trial judges the flexibility to require the parties to provide additional discovery beyond the information contained in the notice that the defendant must give and the reports that the experts must file. It is a very limited grant of discretion and should be reserved for cases presenting discovery issues that are out of the ordinary. In this respect, it is more restrictive than the analogous discovery provision in Rule 14(a)(2).

Subdivision (b)(4). Self-Defense and First Aggressor. This amendment implements the discovery obligation created by *Commonwealth v. Adjutant*, 443 Mass. 649 (2005). The procedure it mandates applies only to situations such as those in *Adjutant*, where the defendant intends to rely on self-defense claiming that the victim was the first aggressor. The notice procedure established in this amendment does not apply to other instances where prior violent conduct by the victim may be admissible, such as where the defendant intends to introduce evidence of a violent act by the victim of which he or she was aware at the time of the incident that is the subject of the criminal case before the court. *See Commonwealth v. Fontes*, 396 Mass. 733, 735–36 (1986). However, in a case where the defendant wishes to introduce evidence of an act of prior violence by the victim to support a claim based on both *Adjutant* and *Fontes*, the notice provision of this subsection would apply.

Beyond notice of an intent to raise the issue of prior violent acts by the alleged victim as it bears on the identity of the first aggressor, the amendment also requires the defendant to provide specific information about each incident. Where the defendant lacks specific details as to the time and place of a prior incident, the notice should contain as much information as is available, subject to a continuing duty to supplement the notice as counsel becomes aware of further facts.

The reciprocal obligation on the Commonwealth extends to all evidence that it intends to introduce to rebut the defendant's claim that the victim was the first aggressor. This may concern the victim's role in the incidents of prior violence upon which the defendant may rely, or any other evidence the Commonwealth may introduce in rebuttal.

Nothing in this amendment is intended to derogate from the discovery obligations of Rule 14(a)(1)(A)–(B) concerning physical evidence or documents that either party may rely on with respect to prior acts of violence by the victim.

This subsection does not affect the ultimate decision the judge must make on the admissibility of the evidence contained in the defendant's notice, or of any rebuttal evidence the prosecution might offer. The rule does contemplate, however, that failure to provide notice in advance may bar a party from offering evidence that might otherwise be admissible.

Subdivision (d). Definition. In 2012, Rule 23 was eliminated because the 2004 revision of Rule 14 largely made it irrelevant. Almost all of the statements that Rule 23 required a party to produce after a witness testified were made part of the automatic pretrial discovery mechanism of Rule 14. Because a small class of statements covered by Rule 23 was not included in the definition of a statement in the 2004 revision of Rule 14(d), an amendment to this subsection was made. The amendment brings within the confines of Rule 14 the remaining class of statements that were subject to the discovery provision of the former Rule 23.

Section 14(d)(1) was amended to include not only writings made by a witness, but also writings made by another and signed or otherwise adopted by the witness. A person otherwise adopts a statement when he or she approves it or accepts it as accurate. *See, e.g., Smith v. United States*, 31 F.3d 1294,1301 (4th Cir. 1994) ("[n]otes taken by prosecutors and other government agents during a pretrial interview of a witness may qualify as a 'statement' . . . if the witness has reviewed them in their entirety—either by reading them himself or by having them read back to him—and formally and unambiguously approved them—either orally or in writing—as an accurate record of what he said during the interview.")

Section 14(d)(2) was amended to remove the requirement that a witness's statement has been recorded contemporaneously. This is an issue that will only be relevant with respect to written accounts of what the witness said, since by their nature stenographic, mechanical, electrical or other means of recordings must be made contemporaneously. With respect to written accounts, Rule 14(d) includes substantially verbatim statements of a witness that are contained in a document written by someone else, whether the document consists solely of the witness's statement or the witness's statements appear only in part of the document. In the latter case, only that portion of the document that consists of the substantially verbatim account of the witness's statement must be produced. This provision is intended only to require the production of statements that can "fairly be deemed to reflect fully and without distortion" what the witness said. *See Palermo v. United States*, 360 U.S. 343, 352–53 (1959); *United States v. Hodges*, 556 F.2d 366 (5th Cir. 1977) *cert. den.* 434 US 1016 (1978) (that investigators' notes contained occasional verbatim recitation of phrases used by the person interviewed did not make such notes discoverable).

NOTE 1a   Recording Psychiatric Examination/Presence of Counsel. It is within the judge's discretion to allow or deny the (1) videotaping/recording of a psychiatric examination; and (2) presence of counsel at the examination. *Commonwealth v. Baldwin*, 426 Mass. 105 (1997).

NOTE 1b   "We have recently addressed the issue of whether a defendant's failure to provide notice of his intention to present a defense of lack of criminal responsibility precludes him from introducing testimony on that issue. In *Commonwealth v. Guadalupe*, 401 Mass. 372 (1987), we examined Mass.R.Crim.P. 14 and concluded that failure to notify the Commonwealth of the intention to present an insanity defense may preclude the defendant from introducing expert opinion 'only in circumstances where the defendant has refused to submit to a court-ordered psychiatric examination.' *Id.* at 375. Our holding in *Guadalupe* is dispositive of this appeal.

"Pursuant to a court order, the defendant in the instant case was examined by a psychiatrist at Bridgewater State Hospital to determine his criminal responsibility. At no time did he refuse to undergo an examination. Therefore, despite the defendant's noncompliance with the controlling notice provision, the trial judge should not have precluded the defendant from offering expert testimony on his lack of criminal responsibility. We recognize that there are inherent difficulties whenever a trial judge orders a continuance midway through the trial. However, a continuance would have provided the Commonwealth with sufficient time to secure rebuttal evidence, while allowing the defendant to introduce expert testimony."

Commonwealth v. Dotson, 402 Mass. 185, 188–89 (1988) (footnotes omitted).

NOTE 1c   Expert Opinion. "The judge, as trier of fact, could pick and choose on which witnesses and what portions of their testimony he would rely in making his determination of guilt. . . .

'[E]ven in the absence of expert opinion from the Commonwealth, the trier of fact is not required to conclude that a defendant lacks criminal responsibility."

Commonwealth v. Goulet, 402 Mass. 299, 306–09 (1988) (footnotes omitted).

NOTE 2a   Exculpatory Evidence. "Ordinarily, due process requires that the prosecution make timely disclosure to a defendant of exculpatory material evidence in its possession. Exculpatory evidence includes 'evidence which provides some significant aid to the defendant's case, whether it furnishes corroboration of the defendant's story, calls into question a material, although not indispensable, element of the prosecution's version of the events, or challenges the credibility of a key prosecution witness.' *Commonwealth v. Ellison*, 376 Mass. 1, 22 (1978).

"Undisclosed exculpatory evidence is material if evaluated in the context of the entire record, it creates a reasonable doubt that did not otherwise exist. When a defendant makes a specific request for reasonably identified evidence, the evidence is deemed material even if it only provides a substantial basis for claiming materiality exists.

"In this case, the prosecution disclosed Johnson's oral statement and his identity, but the disclosure was delayed until late in the trial. Where the defense has not made a specific request for the evidence whose disclosure is delayed, the question becomes whether, given a timely disclosure, the defense would have been able to prepare and present its case in such a manner as to create a reasonable doubt that would not otherwise have existed. On the other hand, where a specific request has been made, the appropriate question is whether, given a timely disclosure, the defense would have been able to prepare and present its case in such a manner as to create a substantial basis for claiming materiality exists."

Commonwealth v. Gregory, 401 Mass. 437, 441–42 (1988) (citations and quotation marks omitted).

NOTE 2b   Failure to Perform Bloodtyping Analysis. "The defendant asserts that the Commonwealth's failure to perform blood identification tests on the semen samples detected during the autopsy procedure constituted a suppression of evidence in violation of his due process rights. The Commonwealth maintains that it had no affirmative duty to pursue potentially exculpatory evidence for the benefit of the defendant. We conclude that there was no suppression of evidence in this matter.

"We have held that the Commonwealth's failure to conduct certain tests or produce certain evidence was a permissible ground on which to build a defense and that the defendant may argue such a defense. However, the failure to conduct blood typing tests does not constitute suppression of evidence in violation of due process within the doctrine of *Brady v. Maryland*, 373 U.S. 83 (1963)."

Commonwealth v. Richenburg, 401 Mass. 663, 669 (1988) (citations omitted).

NOTE 3   Reciprocal Discovery. "The defendant argues he had no obligation to turn over impeachment evidence to be used against a Commonwealth witness. . . .

"We conclude that the pretrial report, on its face, required the disclosure of the impeachment evidence. . . .

"Once it was discovered that the defendant violated the discovery order, it was incumbent on the judge to fashion an appropriate remedy. We have not reviewed the exclusion of statements sought to be used for impeachment as a remedy for a discovery violation. However, the factors taken into account in reviewing the exclusion of an undisclosed witness are applicable to this situation as well. Those factors are: (1) prevention of surprise; (2) evidence of bad faith in the violation of the conference report; (3) prejudice to the other party caused by the testimony; (4) the effectiveness of less severe sanctions; and (5) the materiality of the statements to the outcome of the case. In imposing the severest sanction of preclusion of the evidence, the judge must make clear that all these factors have been considered in balancing enforcement of the rules against the defendant's right to present a defense." *Commonwealth v. Reynolds*, 429 Mass. 388, 397–98 (1999) (citations omitted). *See also Commonwealth v. Lewis*, 48 Mass. App. Ct. 343, 348 (1999).

NOTE 4   Rebuttal Evidence. "[T]he defendant made a detailed motion for discovery regarding the Commonwealth's experts, which [was allowed]. There is nothing on the record before us to suggest that the Commonwealth sought to limit discovery to its case-in-chief. Moreover, the defendant disclosed the content of [his expert's] anticipated testimony to the Commonwealth. Where the accused has made a request for evidence sufficiently specific to place the prosecution on notice as to what the defense desires, the evidence must be disclosed. The Commonwealth, in violation of a discovery order." *Commonwealth v. Giontzis*, 47 Mass. App. Ct. 450, 459 (1999) (citations and quotation marks omitted).

NOTE 5   Criminal Records of Witnesses. "The proper route for the defendant to obtain prior convictions of prospective witnesses for the Commonwealth is by requesting the judge to order the probation department to produce them." *Commonwealth v. Martinez*, 437 Mass. 84, 95 (2002).

NOTE 6a   Notice of Defense of Acting Under Authority. "[A]uthority may be raised as a defense, and, if so raised, the Commonwealth then bears the burden of proving beyond a reasonable doubt the absence of authority. To raise the defense of acting under authority, the defendant must so notify the prosecutor and file a copy of the claim with the clerk of the court where the case is pending. Failure to do so renders the claim of authority unavailable as a defense." *Commonwealth v. O'Connell*, 438 Mass. 658, 664–65 (2003) (citations omitted).

NOTE 6b   *See* G.L. c. 278, § 7 for statute regarding defense of authority.

NOTE 7   Foreign Language Statements. "We hold that where the Commonwealth intends in its case-in-chief to offer at trial statements made by a defendant in a foreign language in a tape-recorded interview, it is within the judge's discretion to require the Commonwealth to provide defense counsel in advance of trial with an English-language transcript of the interview, and to exclude the statements where the Commonwealth declines to do so." *Commonwealth v. Portillo*, 462 Mass. 324, 326 (2012).

NOTE 8   Notice of Defense: Firearm Manufactured Before 1900. "In the future, where a defendant charged with the unlawful carrying of a firearm in violation of § 10(a) possesses evidence that the firearm was manufactured before 1900, the defendant shall provide the Commonwealth with pretrial notice of the affirmative defense of exemption as required by rule 14(b)(3). . . . Once a defendant gives proper notice to the Commonwealth, the defendant bears the burden of producing evidence of the affirmative defense that the firearm was manufactured before 1900. If such evidence is presented, the burden rests on the prosecution to prove beyond a reasonable doubt that the firearm was manufactured after 1899." *Commonwealth v. Jefferson*, 461 Mass. 821, 833–34 (2012) (footnote omitted).

NOTE 9a   Lost or Destroyed Evidence. "The loss and destruction of highly relevant evidence by the Commonwealth and its agents defeated the defendant's opportunity effectively to present a defense." Accordingly, the Supreme Judicial Court reversed the defendant's conviction for murder in the first degree. *Commonwealth v. Olszewski*, 401 Mass. 749, 756, (1988).

NOTE 9b   "When potentially exculpatory evidence is lost or destroyed, the court must perform a balancing test to determine what remedial action, if any, is necessary. *Commonwealth v. Willie*, 400 Mass. 472, 432 (1987). Those factors to be considered include the culpability of the Commonwealth, the materiality of the evidence and the potential for prejudice to the defendant. *Id.* See *Arizona v. Youngblood*, 109 S.Ct. 333, 334–337 (1988) (failure to preserve potentially useful evidence not denial of due process absent bad faith by government)." *Commonwealth v. Troy*, 405 Mass. 253, 261 (1989) (footnote omitted).

NOTE 10   Defense access to crime scene in private residence. "We conclude that the judge had authority to allow the motion and order access to a crime scene in a private residence, on the basis of a showing that the information obtainable at the scene was evidentiary and relevant to the defense, provided that the owner of the residence was served with notice of the motion and had an opportunity to be heard." *Commonwealth v. Matis*, 446 Mass. 632, 633 (2006).

NOTE 11   Protective Order. "Rule 14(a)(6) permits the entry of protective orders . . . where circumstances require. . . . The decision to enter such an order lies within a trial judge's discretion. The defendants first contend that the Commonwealth was required to make a factual showing of a specific threat to witness safety, and that such a showing was not made in this case, either by affidavit or sworn testimony, before the protective order issued. Although the Commonwealth bears the burden of demonstrating that the safety of a witness would be put at risk if information, otherwise required to be disclosed, was made available to the defendant in the absence of a protective order, we have previously held that it need not demonstrate a specific or actual threat to the safety of a witness when the danger to witness safety is inherent in the situation." *Commonwealth v. Holliday*, 450 Mass. 794, 803 (2008) (citations and footnotes omitted).

NOTE 12   Punitive Sanctions. "[S]anctions pursuant to rule 14(c) are designed to protect a defendant's right to a fair trial. To that end, such sanctions, tailored to cure any prejudice to the defendant resulting from a discovery violation, are remedial, not punitive, in nature. Here, however, the judge imposed a $5,000 sanction on the Commonwealth, the purpose of which was not to ensure that the defendant received a fair trial, but as the judge stated, to penalize the Commonwealth for its misconduct. While punitive monetary sanctions are permitted in some instances under the Massachusetts Rules of Criminal Procedure, they are not contemplated under rule 14(c)(1), given its remedial purpose." *Commonwealth v. Frith*, 458 Mass. 434, 442 (2010) (citations omitted).

NOTE 13   Sealed Criminal Records. "Based on our interpretation of the language of the relevant statutes and the Legislature's intent in prioritizing the policy interests promoted by the sealing statute, the mandatory discovery provisions of G.L. c. 218, § 26A, and Mass. R. Crim. P. 14(a)(1)(D) do not apply to a criminal record sealed under G.L. c. 276, § 100A." *Wing v. Commissioner of Probation*, 473 Mass. 368, 378 (2015).

RULE 15
Interlocutory Appeal
(Amended June 8, 2016, effective Aug. 1, 2016.) (Applicable to District Court and Superior Court.)

(a) Right of Interlocutory Appeal.

(1) *Right of Appeal Where Pretrial Motion to Dismiss or for Appropriate Relief Granted.* The Commonwealth shall have the right to appeal to the Appeals Court a decision by a judge granting a motion to dismiss a complaint or indictment or a motion for appropriate relief made pursuant to the provisions of Rule 13(c).

(2) *Right of Appeal Where Motion to Suppress Evidence Determined.* A defendant or the Commonwealth shall have the right and opportunity to apply to a single justice of the Supreme Judicial Court, in the form and manner prescribed by a standing order of that court, for leave to appeal an order determining a motion to suppress evidence prior to trial. If the single justice determines that the administration of justice would be facilitated, the justice may grant that leave and may hear the appeal or may order it to the full Supreme Judicial Court or to the Appeals Court for determination.

(3) *(Reserved)*

(4) *Probable Cause Hearings.* No interlocutory appeal or report may be taken of matters arising out of a probable cause hearing.

(b) Procedural Requirements.

(1) *Time for Filing Appeal.* An appeal under Rule 15(a)(1) shall be taken by filing a notice of appeal in the trial court within thirty days of the date of entry of the order being appealed. An application for leave to appeal under Rule 15(a)(2) shall be made by filing within thirty days of the date of entry of the order being appealed, or such additional time as either the trial judge or the single justice of the Supreme Judicial Court shall order, (a) a notice of appeal in the trial court, and (b) an application to the single justice of the Supreme Judicial Court for leave to appeal.

(2) *Record.* The record for an interlocutory appeal shall be defined and assembled pursuant to Massachusetts Rule of Appellate Procedure 8.

(3) *Findings.* The judge shall make all findings of fact relevant to the appeal or the application for leave to appeal within the period specified in Rule 15(b)(1) for filing the notice of appeal.

(c) Determination of Motions.

Any motion the determination of which may be appealed pursuant to this rule shall be decided by the judge before the defendant is placed in jeopardy under established rules of law.

(d) Costs upon Appeal.

If an appeal or application therefor is taken by the Commonwealth, the appellate court, upon the written motion of the defendant supported by affidavit, shall determine and approve the payment to the defendant of his or her costs of appeal together with reasonable attorney's fees to be paid on the order of the trial court upon the entry of the rescript or the denial of the application.

(e) Stay of the Proceedings.

If the trial court issues an order which is subject to the interlocutory procedures herein, the trial of the case shall be stayed and the defendant shall not be placed in jeopardy until interlocutory review has been waived or the period specified in Rule 15(b)(1) for instituting interlocutory procedures has expired. If an appeal is taken or an application for leave to appeal is granted, the trial shall be stayed pending the entry of a rescript from or an order of the appellate court. If an appeal or application therefor is taken by the Commonwealth, the defendant may be released on personal recognizance during the pendency of the appeal.

Reporter's Notes (2016). The 2016 amendments to Rule 15 respond to the Supreme Judicial Court's decision in *Commonwealth v. Jordan*, 469 Mass. 134 (2014), a case in which the Commonwealth sought interlocutory review of a suppression order through a late-filed notice of appeal and application for leave to appeal. In agreeing to consider the appeal in spite of the late filings, the Court acknowledged that the procedures governing the timeliness of such appeals lacked clarity, *id.* at 145, a problem that the Court addressed by announcing specific procedures prospectively applicable to Rule 15 filings seeking leave to appeal suppression orders. *Id.* at 147–148. In addition to this clarification of Rule 15 filing procedures, the Court expressed concern that then-Rule 15(b)(1)'s ten-day filing period for such appeals might be insufficient. *Id.* at 149–150. As discussed below, amended Rule 15 implements the procedural framework mandated in Jordan and expands to thirty days the time for filing a notice of appeal and an application for leave to appeal from an order determining a motion to suppress evidence. Amended Rule 15 also includes non-substantive changes that clarify its mandate and update it to reflect current law.

Rule 15(a)(1) Right of Appeal Where Pretrial Motion to Dismiss or for Appropriate Relief Granted. Amended Rule 15(a)(1) reflects longstanding case law, making it clear that the Appeals Court is the court to which the Commonwealth may appeal the allowance of a motion to dismiss or of a motion for appropriate relief other than to suppress evidence. See *Commonwealth v. Friend*, 393 Mass. 310, 314 (1984) (Commonwealth's appeal from allowance of a motion to dismiss must be to the Appeals Court).

Rule 15(a)(2) Right of Appeal Where Motion to Suppress Evidence Determined. Amended Rule 15(a)(2) implements the late-filing procedures mandated by the Supreme Judicial Court in *Commonwealth v. Jordan*, 469 Mass. 134 (2014) for interlocutory appeals of an order determining a motion to suppress. Former Rule 15(a)(2) did not specify what showing an applicant for such relief must make concerning the timeliness of the necessary filings, hampering the efforts of single justices to be consistent in addressing the threshold issue of whether the notice of appeal and application for leave to appeal were timely filed and, if not, whether they should nevertheless be considered. See *Jordan*, 469 Mass. at 145 (acknowledging a "lack of clarity" in the single justices' application of procedural rules governing timeliness of Rule 15(a)(2) filings).

Amended Rule 15(a)(2) cures this deficiency, incorporating by reference the Supreme Judicial Court's standing order prescribing with specificity the form and manner for making an application to a single justice for leave to appeal a suppression order. This standing order, Supreme Judicial Court Order Regarding Applications to A Single Justice Pursuant to Mass. R. Crim. P. 15(a)(2) (2016), in effect codifies Jordan's procedural framework for addressing timeliness issues, including a requirement that an application for leave to appeal a suppression order contain an affirmative representation that the application and notice to appeal are, or are not, timely under Rule 15(b)(1). If the appeal or application is untimely, the standing order requires that the application be accompanied by a motion to enlarge time for filing, supported by an affidavit providing "in meaningful detail the reasons for the delay." See Supreme Judicial Court Order Regarding Applications to A Single Justice Pursuant to Mass. R. Crim. P. 15(a)(2), § (a)(7) (2016). See also *Commonwealth v. Jordan*, 469 Mass. 134, 147–148 (2014) (setting out "Rule 15 procedure in future cases").

The purpose of this provision is to permit the single justice to whom the application is made to decide (1) whether the application satisfies Rule 15's timing requirements, and, if it does not, (2) whether the application should nevertheless be considered, before proceeding to the merits of the application and, if appropriate, the appeal. This threshold determination by the single justice is intended to be final, foreclosing further consideration of this procedural issue by the full court or the Appeals Court if the single justice refers the appeal to either for determination. See *Jordan*, 469 Mass. at 148 (2014).

Rule 15(a)(3) Right of Appeal Where Transfer of Delinquency Proceeding is Denied. Rule 15(a)(3), permitting the Commonwealth to appeal a judge's denial of a requested transfer of a delinquency proceeding to Superior or District Court for criminal prosecution, is deleted. G.L. c. 119, § 61, which provided for such transfers, was repealed, making Rule 15(a)(3) obsolete. This section is reserved for possible amendment to reflect current law.

Rule 15(b)(1) Time for Filing Appeal. Rule 15(b)(1), as amended, increases the time to file a notice of appeal and an application for leave to appeal a suppression order to thirty days, clarifying that the starting point for that time period is the date that the order being appealed is entered by the lower court. This filing period is meant to balance the need for adequate time to consider and prepare an application for interlocutory review of a suppression order against the potential for unnecessary, widespread delays in resolving the many criminal cases which involve suppression orders. Thirty days, the filing period applicable to other interlocutory appeals under Rule 15 and presumptively applicable to all appeals in criminal cases, see Rule 4(b), Mass. R. A P., as amended, 431 Mass. 1601 (2000), should ordinarily suffice. However, if in a particular case a party can demonstrate with specificity that thirty days is insufficient, the rule provides for leave to seek additional time from either the trial judge or single justice. If there is a timely motion to reconsider the suppression order in question, the thirty-day time period for filing an application for interlocutory review does not commence until the trial court enters its order deciding the motion to reconsider. See *Jordan*, 469 Mass. at 147 n. 24.

The SJC's standing order incorporated in amended Rule 15(a)(2) provides that the party opposing interlocutory appeal of the suppression order may file a memorandum in opposition to that application within fourteen days after the application for leave to appeal is entered. Supreme Judicial Court Order Regarding Applications to A Single Justice Pursuant to Mass. R. Crim. P. 15(a)(2), § (c) (2016). The order further permits the single justice to extend or shorten the time to file such opposition and provides that a party deciding not to file an opposition must serve notice of that intention within the time allowed for filing the opposition. *Id.*

Rule 15(b)(2) Record; Rule 15(b)(3) Findings. Rule 15(b)(2) and Rule 15(b)(3) contain the provisions of former Rule 15(b)(2), renumbered to separate former Rule 15(b)(2) into two parts, Rule 15(b)(2) providing for definition and assembly of the record and Rule 15(b)(3) requiring timely findings by the trial judge.

NOTE 1   "Litigants must be offered the opportunity to seek interlocutory review as provided in Mass. R. Crim. P. 15." *Commonwealth v. Love*, 452 Mass. 498, 507 (2008).

NOTE 2   "[T]he notice of appeal for an interlocutory appeal from an order, under Mass.R.A.P. 4(b), must be filed within thirty days after the order is filed." *Commonwealth v. Guaba*, 417 Mass. 746, 751 (1994).

NOTE 3   Procedure. "Going forward, we shall require a party (the Commonwealth or a defendant) seeking to take an interlocutory appeal from an order on a motion to suppress to demonstrate, to the satisfaction of the single justice, that there has been compliance with the rules concerning timeliness. Pursuant to rule 15(b)(1), the applicant must file a notice of appeal in the trial court and an application for leave to appeal in the county court within ten days of issuance of notice of the suppression order.[24] The applicant shall affirmatively represent in the application that both the notice of appeal and the application have been filed within ten days, as the rule requires, or that the applicant has previously obtained, from the trial court judge or the single justice, the necessary extension(s) of time in which to file.[25] If the applicant cannot make this representation—because the notice of appeal, the application, or both, are not timely and an extension has not previously been secured—then the applicant must file along with the application a motion to enlarge or suspend the time or times for filing, together with an affidavit setting forth in meaningful detail the reasons for the delay. These steps will help to ensure that any questions concerning the timeliness of the notice of appeal and the application are put squarely before the single justice. If the applicant fails to meet these requirements, the single justice may deny the application because of the noncompliance.

"If a single justice is presented with both an application for leave to appeal and a motion to enlarge or suspend the time for filing the notice of appeal, the application, or both, he or she will first rule on the threshold procedural motion. If that motion is denied, the application for leave to appeal will then be summarily denied as well, because of the noncompliance with the timing requirements. The single justice will proceed to rule on the substantive merits of the application for leave to appeal if, and only if, he or she first allows the motion to enlarge or suspend time. The single justice will then determine, as Mass. R. Crim. P. 15(a)(2) requires, whether allowing the interlocutory appeal 'will facilitate the administration of justice.' *Commonwealth v. Cavanaugh*, 366 Mass. 277, 279 (1974)."

---

[24] The filing of a motion for reconsideration, accompanied by all necessary supporting material, within ten days of issuance of notice of the order stays the time for filing the notice of appeal and the application. The notice of appeal and application must then be filed within ten days of the trial court's ruling on the reconsideration motion. *See Commonwealth v. Powers*, 21 Mass. App. Ct. 570, 573–74 (1986) (discussing effect of motions for reconsideration on timeliness of appeals generally); *Commonwealth v. Mandile*, 15 Mass. App. Ct. 83, 85–91 (1983). *See also Commonwealth v. Montanez*, 410 Mass. 290, 294 nn.4, 5 (1991).

[25] If the applicant filed a motion for reconsideration in the trial court within ten days of issuance of notice of the order, the applicant shall so indicate in the application and must affirmatively represent that the notice of appeal and application have been filed within ten days of the ruling on the reconsideration motion or that the applicant has previously obtained the necessary extensions.

Commonwealth v. Jordan, 469 Mass. 134, 147–48 (2014).

NOTE 3a   Rule 15(d). "[R]ule 15(d) reflects the Legislature's intent, once stated in G.L. c. 278, § 28E, that a defendant be reimbursed for attorney's fees and costs associated with defending a claim on which he or she has already succeeded." *Commonwealth v. Gonsalves*, 432 Mass. 613, 620 (2000).

NOTE 3b   "We therefore conclude that, after the date of this opinion, a defendant shall file a rule 15(d) request within thirty days of either the denial of the Commonwealth's application for leave to file an interlocutory appeal, or the issuance of the rescript from the appellate court that decides the appeal, unless the defendant on motion shows good cause why an enlargement of time should be allowed." *Commonwealth v. Ennis*, 441 Mass. 718, 720 (2004).

NOTE 3c   "In seeking an award of attorney's fees, the defendant shall file with the clerk of the court a motion and affidavits detailing and supporting the attorney's fees and costs sought. Because rule 15(d) is mandatory, the Justices will determine only the amount of the award. The Commonwealth shall be afforded thirty days to respond to the defendant's request, and the court will then enter an appropriate order. Any party aggrieved by the order may request reconsideration from the court." *Commonwealth v. Ennis*, 441 Mass. 718, 721 n.3 (2004) (citations omitted).

NOTE 3d   "The defendant shall file a motion and supporting affidavit with the clerk of the court within thirty days after the denial of leave to file the appeal. The Commonwealth shall be afforded thirty days to respond to the defendant's request, and the single justice shall then enter an appropriate order. Any party aggrieved by the order may request reconsideration from the single justice. Appellate review of the order of the single justice is generally not available." *Commonwealth v. Ennis*, 441 Mass. 718, 721 n.4 (2004) (citation and quotation marks omitted).

RULE 16
Dismissal by the Prosecution
(Applicable to District Court and Superior Court.)

(a) Entry of a Nolle Prosequi.

A prosecuting attorney may enter a nolle prosequi of pending charges at any time prior to the pronouncement of sentence. A nolle prosequi shall be accompanied by a written statement, signed by the prosecuting attorney, setting forth the reasons for that disposition.

(b) Entry of Nolle Prosequi During Trial.

After jeopardy attaches, a nolle prosequi entered without the consent of the defendant shall have the effect of an acquittal of the charges contained in the nolle prosequi.

RULE 17
Summonses for Witnesses
(Applicable to District Court and Superior Court.)

(a) Summons.

(1) *For Attendance of Witness; Form; Issuance.* A summons shall be issued by the clerk or any person so authorized by the General Laws. It shall state the name of the court and the title, if any, of the proceeding and shall command each person to whom it is directed to attend and give testimony at the time and place specified therein.

(2) *For Production of Documentary Evidence and of Objects.* A summons may also command the person to whom it is directed to produce the books, papers, documents, or other objects designated therein. The court on motion may quash or modify the summons if compliance would be unreasonable or

oppressive or if the summons is being used to subvert the provisions of Rule 14. The court may direct that books, papers, documents, or objects designated in the summons be produced before the court within a reasonable time prior to the trial or prior to the time when they are to be offered in evidence and may upon their production permit the books, papers, documents, objects, or portions thereof to be inspected and copied by the parties and their attorneys if authorized by law.

(b) Defendants Unable to Pay.

At any time upon the written ex parte application of a defendant which shows that the presence of a named witness is necessary to an adequate defense and that the defendant is unable to pay the fees of that witness, the court shall order the issuance of an indigent's summons. The witness so summoned shall be paid in accordance with the provisions of subdivision (c) of this rule. If the court so orders, the costs incurred shall be assessed to the defendant in accordance with the General Laws or the provisions of these rules.

(c) Payment of Witnesses.

Expenses incurred by a witness summoned on behalf of a defendant determined to be indigent under this rule as well as expenses incurred by a witness summoned on behalf of the Commonwealth, as such expenses are determined in accordance with the General Laws, shall be paid after the witness certifies in a writing filed with the court the amount of his travel and attendance.

(d) Service.

(1) *By Whom; Manner.* A summons may be served by any person authorized to serve a summons in a civil action or to serve criminal process. A summons shall be served upon a witness by delivering a copy to him personally, by leaving it at his dwelling house or usual place of abode with some person of suitable age and discretion then residing therein, or by mailing to the witness' last known address.

(2) *Place of Service.*

(A) Within the Commonwealth. A summons requiring the attendance of a witness at a hearing or a trial may be served at any place within the Commonwealth.

(B) Outside the Commonwealth or Abroad. A summons directed to a witness outside the Commonwealth or abroad shall issue and be served in a manner consistent with the General Laws.

(3) Return. The person serving a summons pursuant to this rule shall make a return of service to the court.

(e) Failure to Appear.

If a person served with a summons pursuant to this rule fails to appear at the time and place specified therein and the court determines that such person did receive actual notice to appear, a warrant may issue to bring that person before the court.

NOTE 1a   Standard for production of documentary evidence and of objects. "A judge's task in reviewing a defendant's request for Rule 17(a)(2) summonses is to balance the defendant's right to mount a defense with the Commonwealth's right to prevent unnecessary delay of the trial and unwarranted harassment of witnesses and third parties. . . . In *Lampron*, we adopted the standards articulated by the Federal courts regarding the issuance of a subpoena for production of documentary evidence because our rule was modeled after Fed. R. Crim. P. 17(c) and is intended to address the same circumstances. . . . *Id.* Accordingly, the party moving to subpoena documents to be produced before trial must establish good cause, satisfied by showing (1) that the

documents are evidentiary and relevant; (2) that they are not otherwise procurable reasonably in advance of trial by exercise of due diligence; (3) that the party cannot properly prepare for trial without such production and inspection in advance of trial and that the failure to obtain such inspection may tend to unreasonably delay the trial; and (4) that the application [was] made in good faith and is not intended as a general fishing expedition. *Id.* at 269." *Commonwealth v. Lam*, 444 Mass. 224, 229–30 (2005) (quoting *Commonwealth v. Lampron*, 441 Mass. 265 (2004)) (citation and punctuation omitted).

NOTE 1b "We consider whether the Commonwealth, in a criminal case, may seek the production of records from a third party in advance of trial or an evidentiary hearing by issuing a subpoena duces tecum directly to the party under G.L. c. 277, § 68, or whether it must first obtain judicial approval, pursuant to Mass. R. Crim. P. 17 (a) (2), as construed by *Commonwealth v. Lampron*, 441 Mass. 265, 268–71 (2004). We conclude that it must first obtain judicial approval." *Commonwealth v. Odgren*, 455 Mass. 171, 172 (2009) (citation omitted).

NOTE 2   Order allowing defense access to crime scene in private residence. *See* Mass.R.Crim.P. 14, note 8. "The Commonwealth and the complainant's family must have notice of the defendant's motion for pretrial access and the opportunity to be heard, and the order must be carefully tailored to protect the legitimate privacy interests involved." *Commonwealth v. Matis*, 446 Mass. 632, 635 (2006).

NOTE 3   Civil contempt for failure to produce. Judgment of civil contempt warranted where third party refused to produce summonsed documents and neither filed motion to quash nor asserted privilege. *Commonwealth v. Caceres*, 63 Mass. App. Ct. 747, 751 (2005).

NOTE 4   Ex parte motions for issuance of summons. "We conclude that, in rare instances, an ex parte motion may be an appropriate procedure by which to obtain a court order compelling the pretrial production of 'books, papers, documents, or other objects,' Mass. R. Crim. P. 17(a)(2), in the custody of a third party.

"An ex parte motion for a rule 17(a)(2) summons should be filed, therefore, only after the pretrial conference has occurred and the Commonwealth has furnished its discovery. The moving party first should file a motion requesting that summonses for documents returnable prior to the trial be issued ex parte and under seal and explaining, in specific terms and in detail, why it is necessary to proceed ex parte. An ex parte motion will be entertained only in circumstances where the defendant has demonstrated (1) a reasonable likelihood that the prosecution would be furnished with information incriminating to the defendant which it otherwise would not be entitled to receive; or (2) a reasonable likelihood that notice to a third party could result in the destruction or alteration of the requested documents. . . . An ex parte motion for the pretrial production of documents cannot be made on the basis that notice to the Commonwealth will reveal trial strategy or work product or might disclose client confidences.

"The judge should, whenever feasible, seal the defendant's motion and affidavit, in whole or in part, and allow the Commonwealth to be heard on the defendant's request for ex parte consideration. In such a circumstance, the judge should seal or impound only as much of the motion and affidavit as is absolutely necessary to protect the defendant's interests.

"In sum, although the process set forth in rule 17(a)(2) will normally be of an adversary nature, there is nothing in the rule, or in our cases interpreting the rule, that forecloses the availability of an ex parte process in extraordinary circumstances." *Commonwealth v. Mitchell*, 444 Mass. 786, 787–801 (2005) (citation omitted).

NOTE 5   Jail calls. "We conclude that, where the sheriff's policy of monitoring and recording detainees' and inmates' telephone calls is preceded by notice to all parties, and further, where the recording and monitoring is justified by legitimate penological interests, no privacy interest exists in the recorded conversations such that they cannot be obtained by a grand jury subpoena." *In re Grand Jury Subpoena*, 454 Mass. 685, 688 (2009).

RULE 18
Presence of Defendant
(Applicable to District Court and Superior Court.)
(a) Presence of Defendant.

In any prosecution for crime the defendant shall be entitled to be present at all critical stages of the proceedings.

(1) *Defendant Absenting Himself.* If a defendant is present at the beginning of a trial and thereafter absents himself without cause or without leave of court, the trial may proceed to a conclusion in all respects except the imposition of sentence as though the defendant were still present.

(2) *Waiver of Presence in Misdemeanor Cases.* A person prosecuted for a misdemeanor may at his own request, with leave of court, be excused from attendance if represented by counsel or an agent authorized by law and may be excused from attendance without leave of court if so authorized by the General Laws.

(3) *Presence Not Required.* A defendant need not be present at a revision or revocation of sentence pursuant to Rule 29 or at any proceeding where evidence is not to be taken.

(b) Presence of Corporation.

A corporation may appear by a duly authorized agent for the purposes of this rule.

NOTE 1 "The defendant [incorrectly] asserts that a jury-waived trial begins when jeopardy attaches. . . . [Rule 18(a)(1)], however, refers to 'the beginning of a trial,' not to the attachment of jeopardy. . . . The defendant's trial began when he was placed at the bar for trial." *Commonwealth v. Elizondo*, 428 Mass. 322, 325 (1998) (citations omitted).

NOTE 2 Defense Counsel to Continue In Absence of Defendant. "However much counsel may have chafed at going forward in the absence of the defendant, and whatever her motivation, it was a serious lapse in judgment to refuse to participate for more than a day as the Commonwealth proceeded with its case." *Commonwealth v. Vickers*, 60 Mass. App. Ct. 24, 33–34 (2003).

RULE 19
Trial by Jury or by the Court
(Applicable to Superior Court and jury sessions in District Court.)
(a) General.

A case in which the defendant has the right to be tried by a jury shall be so tried unless the defendant waives a jury trial in writing with the approval of the court and files the waiver with the clerk, in which instance he shall be tried by the court instead of by a jury. If there is more than one defendant, all must waive the right to trial by jury, and if they do not so waive, there must be a jury trial unless the court in its discretion severs the cases. The court may refuse to approve such a waiver for any good and sufficient reason provided that such refusal is given in open court and on the record.

(b) Less Than a Full Jury.

If after jeopardy attaches there is at any time during the progress of a trial less than a full jury remaining, a defendant may waive his right to be tried by a full jury and request trial by the remaining jurors by signing a written waiver which shall be filed with the court. If there is more than one defendant, all must sign and file a waiver unless the court in its discretion severs the cases.

NOTE 1 Codefendants. One wants jury trial, other does not. "The right to a trial by jury is constitutionally guaranteed. By contrast, the right of a defendant to waive a jury trial and proceed instead with a bench trial is not constitutionally guaranteed. . . . Therefore, a judge acting within his or her sound discretion may properly deny a defendant's written waiver of a jury trial and order

the defendant to stand trial before a jury—either alone, or with codefendants who have not waived their right to a jury trial." *Commonwealth v. Collado*, 42 Mass. App. Ct. 464, 466 (1997).

NOTE 2 Individual Voir Dire Required. (1) Interracial rape. *Commonwealth v. Sanders*, 383 Mass. 637, 640–41 (1981); (2) Interracial assault and sexual abuse of a child. *Commonwealth v. Hobbs*, 385 Mass. 863, 873 (1982); (3) Sexual offenses against minors. *Commonwealth v. Flebotte*, 417 Mass. 348, 353 (1994); (4) Interracial murder. *Commonwealth v. Young*, 401 Mass. 390, 398 (1987); (5) Insanity. *Commonwealth v. Seguin*, 421 Mass. 243, 249 (1995); *Commonwealth v. Biancardi*, 421 Mass. 251, 254–55 (1995); (6) Overwhelming pretrial publicity. *Commonwealth v. James*, 424 Mass. 770, 776 (1997); (7) Juror affected by extraneous issues. G.L. c. 234, § 28; Mass.R.Crim.P. 20(b)(2).

NOTE 3 Individual Voir Dire Not Required. (1) Hispanic defendant/white murder victim. *Commonwealth v. De La Cruz*, 405 Mass. 269 (1989); (2) Interracial robbery. *Commonwealth v. Grice*, 410 Mass. 586 (1991); (3) Racial/ethnic bias. *Commonwealth v. Ramirez*, 407 Mass. 553, 557 (1990).

NOTE 4a Waiver. "There is no constitutional requirement of a particular means of demonstrating the legality of a jury waiver. In this Commonwealth, a signed written waiver is required, as well as an oral colloquy. In the District Court there is also a defense counsel certificate confirming that trial counsel has explained to the defendant the characteristics of a jury trial forgone by executing a waiver.

"The judge's task in an oral colloquy is to satisfy himself that any waiver by the defendant is made voluntarily and intelligently.

" . . .

"In evaluating the colloquy, we keep in mind that in addition to considering the defendant's answers to the questions posed during the colloquy, a judge may also rely upon the information contained in the jury waiver form signed by the defendant and in defense counsel's certificate when making a determination whether the defendant's jury waiver is made voluntarily and intelligently. To hold otherwise would be to render the Legislature's mandate of a certificate from defense counsel meaningless. This is so even when the colloquy is sparse" *Commonwealth v. Ridlon*, 54 Mass. App. Ct. 146, 147–49 (2002) (citations and quotation and punctuation marks omitted).

NOTE 4b Written jury trial waiver. "The defendant's illiteracy does not, by any means, render the exercise of signing a written waiver meaningless." *Commonwealth v. Johnson*, 79 Mass. App. Ct. 903, 904 (2011) (rescript).

NOTE 4c Guilty Plea. "There is no requirement that, when accepting a defendant's tender of a guilty plea, a defendant's waiver of the right to a trial with or without a jury be in writing. . . . The absence of a written jury trial waiver does not violate G.L. c. 263, § 6, or rule 19(a), and does not provide a basis to invalidate the defendant's pleas. . . . The rule, by its express terms, applies only in circumstances where a defendant chooses to be tried by a judge instead of a jury." *Commonwealth v. Hubbard*, 457 Mass. 24, 26, 28 (2010).

NOTE 5 Rule 19(b). A defendant may constitutionally waive his right to a verdict rendered by fewer than six jurors. *Commonwealth v. Nicoll*, 452 Mass. 816, 818 (2008). *See also Commonwealth v. Dery*, 452 Mass. 823, 824 (2008).

NOTE 6 Related Statutes. G.L. c. 218, § 26A (Trial by jury of six; discovery; jury-waived trial; record of proceedings; probation); G.L. c. 263, § 6 (Conviction; manner; waiver of jury trial); G.L. c. 278, § 29D ((Alien Warnings) Conviction upon plea of guilty or nolo contendere; motion to vacate).

RULE 20
Trial Jurors
(Applicable to Superior Court and jury sessions in District Court.)
(a) Motion for Appropriate Relief.

Either party may challenge the array by a motion for appropriate relief pursuant to Rule 13(c). A challenge to the array shall be made only on the ground that the prospective jurors were not selected or drawn according to law. Challenges to the array shall be made and decided before any individual juror is examined unless otherwise ordered by the court. A challenge to the array shall be in writing supported by affidavit and shall specify the facts constituting the ground of the challenge. Challenges to the array shall be tried by the court and may in the discretion of the court be decided on the basis of the affidavit filed with the challenge. Upon the hearing of a challenge to the array, a witness may be examined on oath by the court and may be so examined by either party. If the challenge to the array is sustained, the court shall discharge the panel.

(b) Challenge for Cause.

(1) *Examination of Juror.* The court shall, or upon motion, the parties or their attorneys may under the direction of the court, examine on oath a person who is called as a juror in a case to learn whether he is related to either party, has any interest in the case, has expressed or formed an opinion, or is sensible of any bias or prejudice. The objecting party may, with the approval of the court, introduce other competent evidence in support of the objection.

(2) *Examination upon Extraneous Issues.* The court shall examine or cause a juror to be examined upon issues extraneous to the case if it appears that the juror's impartiality may have been affected by the extraneous issues. The examination may include a brief statement of the facts of the case, to the extent the facts are appropriate and relevant to the issues of such examination, and shall be conducted individually and outside the presence of other persons about to be called or already called as jurors.

(3) *Challenge of Juror.* Either party may challenge an individual prospective juror before the juror is sworn to try the case. The court may for cause shown permit a challenge to be made after the juror is sworn but before any evidence is presented. When a juror is challenged for cause, the ground of the challenge shall be stated. A challenge of a prospective juror and the statement of the grounds thereof may be made at the bench. The court shall determine the validity of each such challenge.

(c) Peremptory Challenges.

(1) *Number of Challenges.* Upon the trial of an indictment for a crime punishable by imprisonment for life, each defendant shall be entitled to twelve peremptory challenges of the jurors called to try the case; in any other criminal case tried before a jury of twelve, each defendant shall be entitled to four peremptory challenges; and in a case tried before a jury of six, each defendant shall be entitled to two peremptory challenges. Each defendant in a trial of an indictment for a crime punishable by imprisonment for life in which additional jurors are impaneled under subdivision (d) of this rule shall be entitled to one additional peremptory challenge for each additional juror. Each defendant in a case in which several indictments or complaints are consolidated for trial shall be entitled to no more peremptory challenges than the greatest number to which he would have been entitled upon trial of any one of the indictments or complaints alone. In every criminal case the Commonwealth shall be entitled to as many peremptory challenges as equal the whole number to which all the defendants in the case are entitled.

(2) *Time of Challenge.* Peremptory challenges shall be made before the jurors are sworn and may be made after the

determination that a person called to serve as a juror stands indifferent in the case.

(d) Alternate Jurors.

(1) *Impanelling Jury with Alternate Jurors.* If a jury trial is likely to be protracted, the judge may impanel a jury of not more than sixteen members and the court shall have jurisdiction to try the case with that jury.

(2) *Selection of Twelve Jurors.* If at the time of the final submission of the case to the jury more than twelve members of the jury who have heard the whole case are alive and not incapacitated or disqualified, the judge shall direct the clerk to place the names of all the remaining jurors except the foreman in a box and draw the names of a sufficient number to reduce the jury to twelve members. Those jurors whose names are drawn shall not be discharged, but shall be known as alternate jurors and shall be kept separate and apart from the other jurors in some convenient place, subject to the same rules and regulations as the other jurors, until the jury has agreed upon a verdict or has been otherwise discharged.

(3) *Disabled Juror: Selection of Alternate.* If, at any time after the final submission of the case by the court to the jury but before the jury has agreed on a verdict, a juror dies, becomes ill, or is unable to perform his duty for any other cause, the judge may order him to be discharged and shall direct the clerk to place the names of all the remaining alternate jurors in a box and draw the name of an alternate who shall take the place of the discharged juror on the jury, which shall renew its deliberations with the alternate juror.

(e) Regulation and Separation of Jurors.

(1) *Sequestration.* After the jurors have been sworn they shall hear the case as a body and, within the discretion of the trial judge, may be sequestered.

(2) *After Submission of the Cause.* Unless the jurors have been sequestered for the duration of the trial, the judge after the final submission of the case, may order that the jurors be permitted to separate for a definite time to be fixed by the judge and then reconvene in the courtroom before retiring for consideration of their verdict.

(3) *After Commencement of Deliberations.* After final submission of the case to the jury and after deliberations have commenced, the judge may allow the jurors, under proper instructions, to separate for a definite time to be fixed by the judge and to reconvene in the courtroom before retiring for further deliberation of their verdict.

NOTE 1   **Challenge for Cause.** The judge refused to challenge for cause a juror, who had been a policeman for 26 years.

The Supreme Judicial Court upheld that decision. "We decline to adopt a rule that the mere fact that a prospective juror is a police officer, in the absence of a showing of prejudice or partiality, or connection with the particular facts involved at trial, would form the basis to sustain a challenge for cause."

Commonwealth v. Ascolillo, 405 Mass. 456, 460–61 (1989).

NOTE 2   "We stated in *Commonwealth v. Sanders*, 383 Mass. 637, 640–641 (1981), that, in cases of interracial rape, prospective jurors must be interrogated individually in accordance with the statute, rather than as a group because, as a matter of law, 'interracial rape cases present a substantial risk that extraneous issues will influence the jury.' In *Commonwealth v. Hobbs*, 385 Mass. 863, 875 (1982), we extended the Sanders rule to the interracial assault and sexual abuse of a child. We extended the rule as to interracial murder in *Commonwealth v. Young*, 401 Mass. 390, 398 (1987). In each case, we held that the trial judge must question each juror individually, out of the hearing of the venire, about possible racial bias and prejudice. These decisions rested not on constitutional grounds but, rather, on our superintendency power to implement the statutory policy set forth in G.L. c. 234, § 28. *Commonwealth v. Young, supra* at 398 n.8. We have clearly stated that cases involving a black defendant and white victim, *Commonwealth v. Sanders, supra; Commonwealth v. Hobbs,* supra; or a black defendant and Hispanic victim, *Commonwealth v. Young, supra,* are 'interracial.' The issue before us now is whether sexual assault of a white child by an Hispanic defendant is an 'interracial' crime and, if not technically so, whether nevertheless it should be treated that way."

The Supreme Judicial Court answered in the negative. *Commonwealth v. De La Cruz,* 405 Mass. 269, 272 (1989).

NOTE 2a   Sexual Abuse. In cases involving sexual abuse against a minor, individual voir dire concerning whether or not a potential juror has been a victim of childhood abuse is mandated. *Commonwealth v. Flebotte,* 417 Mass. 348, 353 (1994).

NOTE 2b   Insanity. At a murder trial, the judge's individual questioning of each prospective juror was sufficient to ensure that no juror was biased against the defendant's reliance on the defense of insanity. *Commonwealth v. Seguin,* 421 Mass. 243 (1995). *See also Commonwealth v. Biancardi,* 421 Mass. 251 (1995).

NOTE 3a   Procedure. If a challenge is made, the judge must first determine whether or not a prima facie showing of impropriety has been made. If the judge asks the ADA the reasons for the challenge, the judge has in effect made that preliminary determination of impropriety. After the prosecutor offers an explanation for the challenge, the judge must then determine whether the reason is bona fide or a mere sham. *Commonwealth v. Seguin,* 421 Mass. 243 (1995). *See also Commonwealth v. Calderon,* 431 Mass. 21 (2000); *Commonwealth v. Calderon,* 46 Mass. App. Ct. 483, 486 (1999).

NOTE 3b   Procedure. "When the issue of improper peremptory challenges is raised, the trial judge should make a finding as to whether the requisite prima facie showing or impropriety has been made. . . . Once a defendant makes a sufficient showing of impropriety, the burden shifts to the prosecutor to provide a group-neutral reason for challenging the venire person in question. Although the prosecutor's explanation does not have to rise to the level of specificity required for a removal for cause, general assertions are not enough. The prosecutor must give a clear and reasonably specific explanation of his legitimate reasons for exercising the challenges. The reasons must be personal to the juror and not based on the juror's group affiliation. After hearing the prosecutor's explanations, the judge must then decide whether the challenges were exercised improperly because they were based on the juror's membership in a discrete group. Once the judge decides that an adequate reason exists for exercising the challenge, an appellate court will accord substantial deference to the decision if it is supported by the record." *Commonwealth v. Burnett,* 418 Mass. 769, 771, 642 (1994). *See also Commonwealth v. Carleton,* 418 Mass. 773 (1994) (prosecutor improperly struck potential jurors with Irish or Italian sounding surnames); *Commonwealth v. Caldwell,* 418 Mass. 777 (1994) (prosecutor struck four potential black jurors; proper reasons include: (1) if a juror lives in a neighborhood in which the prosecutor had investigated a multiple homicide; (2) if a juror had a very limited education and therefore would be unable to grasp some of the concepts which were central to the case; (3) if the juror had a trip planned; (4) if a police officer involved with the case indicates to the prosecutor that he is familiar with the juror's family with whom he may have had some dealings; (5) if the juror lives or used to live within a few streets of where the defendant lives with his parents; (6) a juror's demeanor and reactions during the voir dire (reason must not be vague and general). *Carleton,* 418 Mass. at 779–81.)

NOTE 3c   Different race. "The defendant, a minority person [Hispanic], was entitled to a jury representing a fair cross section of the community, which would include African-Americans as well as Hispanics." *Commonwealth v. Calderon,* 431 Mass. 21, 25 (2000).

NOTE 3d   Gender. "Gender is among the group affiliations on which peremptory challenges cannot be based." *Commonwealth v.*

Rodriguez, 431 Mass. 804, 807 (2000) (citations and quotation marks omitted).

NOTE 3e   Presumption. "There is a presumption that peremptory challenges are being used properly. . . . In deciding whether a party has made the requisite prima facie showing, the makeup of the entire venire can be taken into account. . . . If the judge decides that the presumption has been rebutted, the burden is shifted to the party who exercised the challenges to show some group neutral ground for the challenges. It is then for the judge to determine whether the proffered neutral explanation is legitimate." *Commonwealth v. LeClair,* 429 Mass. 313, 319–20 (1999) (citations omitted).

NOTE 3f   Removal of only minority juror. "If the peremptory challenge of juror X had left the jury with no minority jurors, a prima facie case of discrimination would have been established." *Commonwealth v. Serrano,* 48 Mass. App. Ct. 163, 165 (1999).

NOTE 3g   Once opportunity for peremptory challenge declined . . . "Once a party has declined an opportunity to exercise a peremptory challenge as to a particular juror, a peremptory challenge to that juror is no longer available. Rule 6 [of the Rules of the Superior Court] then expressly provides: 'No other challenging, except for cause shown, shall be allowed.' We have previously held that deviation from the procedures outlined in Rule 6 constitutes reversible error, even in the absence of prejudice. *Commonwealth v. Brown,* 395 Mass. 604, 606–607 (1985)." *Commonwealth v. Daye,* 435 Mass. 463, 471 (2001).

NOTE 3h   Number of Peremptory Challenges in Bifurcated Trial. In a bifurcated trial "where . . . the same jury is to be used for both phases, absent some reason to think the jury will not be fair and impartial for the second phase, neither our cases nor § 11A appears to require that additional voir dire be conducted before the second phase. In other words, the full number of peremptory challenges required by rule 20 must be allotted ab initio because, in the ordinary course, there will be no additional voir dire before the second phase." *Commonwealth v. Berardi,* 88 Mass. App. Ct. 466, 471 (2015) (citations omitted).

NOTE 3i   Bias. "The question before us is whether the protections against the improper use of peremptory challenges extend to groups delineated not just by one of the affiliations protected in *Commonwealth v. Soares,* [377 Mass. 461 (1979)], but by the intersection of two of them: race and gender. In other words, is the use of a peremptory challenge to exclude a juror solely on the basis of bias presumed to derive from that juror being, for example, a white male or a black female forbidden by the principles enunciated in *Commonwealth v. Soares.* . . . We conclude that it is." *Commonwealth v. Jordan,* 439 Mass. 47, 59 (2003).

NOTE 4   Questions Asked by Jurors. "We observe that the practice of allowing jurors to question witnesses has the potential for introducing prejudice, delay, and error into the trial, and should be utilized infrequently and with great caution." Such questions should not be oral, but handwritten and passed to the judge. *Commonwealth v. Urena,* 417 Mass. 692, 701–02 (1994).

RULE 21
Sequestration of Witnesses
(Applicable to District Court and Superior Court.)

Upon his own motion or the motion of either party, the judge may, prior to or during the examination of a witness, order any witness or witnesses other than the defendant to be excluded from the courtroom.

**NOTE 1   ** Although it is generally undesirable to have a testifying police officer sit at counsel table, it is within the judge's discretion to allow it. *Commonwealth v. Perez,* 405 Mass. 339 (1989). *See also Commonwealth v. Salcedo,* 405 Mass. 346 (1989).

**NOTE 2   ** The judge refused "to preclude a witness, who was under a sequestration order, from sitting in the courtroom after his testimony had concluded. The judge inquired into the likelihood that the witness would be recalled, and implicitly concluded that there was none. The witness was not mentioned on the defendant's witness list, and counsel made no showing of a need to exclude the witness from the courtroom. The witness was never recalled. There is no indication that the witness violated the sequestration order by disclosing his testimony to any witness, or otherwise. It was within the judge's discretion to modify the sequestration order as she did." *Commonwealth v. Croken*, 432 Mass. 266, 269 (2000) (citations omitted).

RULE 22
Objections
(Applicable to Superior Court and jury sessions in District Court.)

Exceptions to rulings or orders of the court are unnecessary and for all purposes for which an exception has heretofore been necessary, it is sufficient that a party, at the time the ruling or order of the court is made or sought, makes known to the court the action which he desires the court to take or his objection to the action of the court, but if a party has no opportunity to object to a ruling or order, the absence of an objection does not thereafter prejudice him.

If a party objects to a ruling or order of the court, he may state the precise legal grounds of his objection, but he shall not argue or further discuss such grounds unless the court calls upon him for such argument or discussion.

NOTE   Cross-Examination/Bias. "The defendant argues only one issue in this court. He challenges the trial judge's refusal to permit him to test the possible bias of a key prosecution witness by cross-examining the witness concerning his interest and involvement in a pending Federal forfeiture proceeding involving the defendant's house. We agree with the defendant that the cross-examination was erroneously and prejudicially excluded. . . .

"Because bias is intimately related to credibility, a defendant has the right to cross-examine a prosecution witness in order to reveal bias. As we recently said, a judge may not restrict cross-examination of a material witness by foreclosing inquiry into a subject that could show bias or prejudice on the part of the witness."
Commonwealth v. Koulouris, 406 Mass. 281, 285 (1989) (quotation marks and citations omitted).

RULE 23
Stipulations
(Added effective July 2, 2015.)
(a) Essential Elements.

Any stipulation to an essential element of a charged offense entered by the parties before or during trial shall be in writing and signed by the prosecutor, the defendant, and defense counsel. Any such stipulation shall be read to the jury before the close of the Commonwealth's case and may be introduced into evidence.

(b) Other Stipulations.

Any other stipulation shall be placed on the record before the close of evidence and may be read or otherwise communicated to the jury or introduced into evidence in the discretion of the court.

Reporter's Notes (2015). Rule 23 is intended to fill a gap in the Rules of Criminal Procedure identified by the Supreme Judicial Court in *Commonwealth v. Ortiz*, 466 Mass. 475 (2013). The rule provides for the manner in which stipulations of fact agreed to by the parties before or during trial are to be memorialized and used at trial. Rule 11 governs stipulations of fact agreed to at the pretrial conference, but prior to Rule 23 there were no rules that applied to such stipulations reached after the filing of the pretrial conference report at the pretrial hearing. Rule 23 remedies that deficiency, supplementing Rule 11's provisions concerning stipulations of fact.

Rule 23(a) Essential Elements
Rule 23(a) is modeled on Rule 11 in its treatment of stipulations of fact, but its coverage is narrower. Rule 11(a)(2)(A) re-

quires that the pretrial conference report include "any stipulations of fact" agreed to by the parties at the pretrial conference and further provides that the report be "subscribed by the prosecuting attorney and counsel for the defendant, and . . . when the report contains stipulations as to material facts, by the defendant." Rule 11(a)(2)(A) requires the parties to file the pretrial conference report with the clerk of court and provides that agreements contained in the report, including stipulations, "shall be binding on the parties and shall control the subsequent course of the proceeding." These requirements for binding stipulations of fact are consistent with such rules of other states. See, e.g., Ark. R. Cr. P. 20.4, Pretrial Conference; Vt. R. Cr. P. 17.1, Pretrial Conference; Ia. R. Cr. P. 2.16, Pretrial Conference; Haw. R. Cr. P. 17.1, Pretrial Conference.

Unlike Rule 11, Rule 23(a) is limited to stipulations to "an essential element of a charged offense," that is, a fact that the Commonwealth must prove beyond a reasonable doubt in order to secure a conviction. To take a common example, in a trial for operating a motor vehicle while under influence of intoxicating liquor, G.L. c. 90, § 24(1)(a)(1), the Commonwealth must prove three elements, one of which is "that the defendant operated a motor vehicle." *Commonwealth v. Cabral*, 77 Mass. App. Ct. 909, 909, *rev. denied*, 458 Mass. 1107 (2010). See Criminal Model Jury Instruction for Use in the District Court 5.310, Operating Under the Influence of Intoxicating Liquor pdf format of 5310-Operating Under the Influence (2013). If the parties stipulate to such operation, the Commonwealth's burden of production for that element is satisfied, foreclosing the need for further proof in that regard. *See Commonwealth v. Ortiz*, 466 Mass. 475, 481 (2013). Rule 23(a) thus requires that a stipulation subject to its coverage be memorialized, that the defendant formally express his or her agreement to the stipulation, and that it be made a matter of record. Moreover, because the stipulated fact constitutes sufficient evidence, maybe the only evidence, of the element in question, the rule requires that the stipulation be read to the jury before the prosecution rests, affording the judge the discretion to decide whether it should further be entered into evidence and given to the jury as an exhibit. The model jury instructions for the charged crime set out its constituent elements, providing a ready reference for the facts subject to Rule 23(a).

Although a stipulated element under Rule 23(a) relieves the Commonwealth of its burden of producing evidence to prove that element, *Ortiz*, 466 Mass. at 481, it is distinct from a so-called stipulated trial, in which a defendant stipulates to all of the facts conclusive of guilt in order to preserve his or her right to appeal the judge's rulings on one or more pretrial issues. *See, e.g., Commonwealth v. Brown*, 55 Mass. App. Ct. 440 (2002). Because a stipulated trial is tantamount to a guilty plea, the defendant is entitled to the safeguards applicable in a guilty plea or admission to sufficient facts, informing him or her of the consequences of the stipulation and providing a hearing to ensure that the stipulation was entered into knowingly and voluntarily. *Id.* at 448–49. See Rule 12. In contrast, a stipulated element under Rule 23(a) occurs in the context of a contested trial, and it represents a considered, tactical decision by the defendant and defense counsel which is a part of the defendant's litigation strategy. In the ordinary case, Rule 23(a)'s requirement, following that of Rule 11(a)(2)(A), that the stipulation be written and signed by the defendant should adequately demonstrate that the defendant understands and agrees with the decision to stipulate. Requiring in addition a colloquy such as that required for a guilty plea or an admission to sufficient facts seems unnecessary. *Cf. Commonwealth v. Ramsey*, 466 Mass. 489, 496 n.8 (2013) (observing that plea colloquies required for stipulated trials had no application to a defendant's trial concession, as part of a litigation strategy, that he possessed crack and powder cocaine). Of course, if the judge thinks it appropriate in the circumstances of a particular case to inquire, on the record out of the presence of the jury, in order to make the record clear that the defendant understands the evidentiary consequences of the stipulation and/or that the defendant's agreement to the stipulation is voluntary, the judge has the discretion to do so. *See, e.g., Commonwealth v. Walorz*, 79 Mass. App. Ct. 132, 135–36, *rev. denied*, 460 Mass. 1103 (2011) (noting trial judge's detailed explanation to

3

defendant of the effect of a stipulation to two elements of the charged offense in holding that a colloquy was not required).

A stipulated element subject to Rule 23(a) is also distinct from a defendant's concession that an essential element will be proved or that he or she is guilty of a lesser included offense. Unlike a stipulation of fact agreed to by the parties, the Commonwealth is not a participant in a defendant's strategic decision to concede that the evidence is sufficient to satisfy a portion of the charged offense. Nor does such a concession relieve the Commonwealth of its burden to prove every element of the charged offense beyond a reasonable doubt. *See Commonwealth v. Charles*, 456 Mass. 378, 383 (2010) (in a narcotics case, defense counsel's concession in opening and closing that defendant possessed "drugs" neither amounted to a tacit stipulation of that fact nor relieved the Commonwealth of its burden to prove each element beyond a reasonable doubt). Rather, a defendant's concession that some part of the Commonwealth's case is beyond dispute is a recognized trial tactic that, like other defense tactics, ordinarily requires no confirmation that the defendant understands its risks and agrees with its employment. The Supreme Judicial Court accordingly has declined to exercise its supervisory authority to require a colloquy to confirm that a defendant understands, and agrees with, a trial concession that he is guilty of a lesser included offense, deferring instead to the sound discretion of the trial judge concerning the need for any such inquiry. *See Commonwealth v. Evelyn*, 470 Mass. 765, 770 (2015). Similarly, Rule 23, including Rule 23(a)'s requirement of a signed writing, does not apply to a defendant's concession of some fact, element, or guilt of a lesser included offense.

Rule 23(b) Other Stipulations

The purpose of limiting Rule 23(a) to facts constituting an essential element of a charged offense is to avoid requiring a formal writing, subscribed by counsel and the defendant, to the variety of other factual stipulations that have long been a non-problematic part of criminal trials. Those stipulations are treated by the less formal provisions of Rule 23(b), which applies to stipulations during trial to evidentiary facts, such as those necessary to authenticate a document or to qualify a witness as an expert, and to facts that, while material, are not sufficient to prove an essential element of a charged offense. For example, in the above-hypothesized trial for operating under the influence, the fact that the defendant had told the police that he was driving a car at the time in question would certainly be material in determining whether he had operated a motor vehicle. However, standing alone, that confession would not be sufficient to prove the element of operation, *see Commonwealth v. Leonard*, 401 Mass. 470, 473 (1988), and the parties' stipulation that the defendant had so confessed would not be subject to Rule 23(a)'s requirements. Such stipulations of evidentiary and material facts have long been utilized to expedite trials where—in the judgment of the parties—nothing would be gained by insisting on a formal mode of proof. Requiring a subscribed, written stipulation in such circumstances would undercut its utility without any apparent gain. Rule 23(b) does not require that stipulations subject to its coverage be written, mandating only that they be placed on the record before the close of evidence. The rule leaves it to the judge to decide how that is done and, for stipulations of a material fact, how the stipulation should be communicated to the jury. Nothing in the rule prohibits a judge, as a matter of discretion, from requiring that a particular stipulation of fact be reduced to writing, whether because of its complexity or for any other good cause.

NOTE "[W]hen the defendant and the Commonwealth have agreed to stipulate to the existence of an element in a case, the stipulation should be placed before the jury before the close of the evidence." *Commonwealth v. Ortiz*, 466 Mass. 475, 484 (2013).

RULE 24
Opening Statements; Arguments; Instructions to Jury.
(Applicable to Superior Court and jury sessions in District Court.)
(a) Opening and Closing Statements; Arguments.

(1) *Order of Presentation.* The Commonwealth shall present its opening statement first. The defendant may present an opening statement of his defense after the opening statement of the Commonwealth or after the close of the Commonwealth's evidence. The defendant shall present his closing argument first.

(2) *Time Limitation.* Counsel for each party shall be allowed fifteen minutes for an opening statement and thirty minutes for argument; but before the opening or the argument commences, the judge on motion or sua sponte, may reasonably reduce or extend the time.

(b) Instructions to Jury; Objection.

At the close of the evidence or at such earlier time during the trial as the judge reasonably directs, any party may file written requests that the judge instruct the jury on the law as set forth in the requests. The judge shall inform counsel of his proposed action upon requests prior to their arguments to the jury. No party may assign as error the giving or the failure to give an instruction unless he objects thereto before the jury retires to consider its verdict, specifying the matter to which he objects and the grounds of his objection. Upon request, reasonable time shall be given to each party to object to the charge before the jury retires. Where either party wishes to object to the charge or to request additional instructions, the objection or the request shall be made out of the hearing of the jury, or where appropriate, out of the presence of the jury.

NOTE 1 **Double Jeopardy.** The defendants successfully moved for a mistrial after the Assistant District Attorney's opening statement to the jury.

"The second trial began immediately. Just prior to the empanelment of the second jury, the defendants moved to dismiss the indictments based on double jeopardy grounds. That motion was denied.

"Under Federal law, a defendant who moves for a mistrial must show that the prosecutor intended to provoke a mistrial or otherwise engaged in 'overreaching' or 'harassment.' *Oregon v. Kennedy*, 456 U.S. 667, 683 (1982) (Stevens, J., concurring). *Commonwealth v. Lam Hue To*, 391 Mass. 301, 310–312 (1984). As we have noted, the standard for barring a retrial based on double jeopardy principles is substantially the same under Massachusetts law. *Commonwealth v. Andrews*, 403 Mass. 441, 447 n.6, 449 (1988). *Gallinaro v. Commonwealth*, 362 Mass. 728, 736 (1973). There was no finding by the judge that the prosecutor had intended to provoke a mistrial, nor does the record reveal such intent. See *Andrews, supra* at 448."

Commonwealth v. Smith, 404 Mass. 1, 4–5 (1989).

See also Note 1 accompanying G.L. c. 263, § 7 in Part 2 of this book.

NOTE 2 **Retraction of Jury Instruction.** "The defendant also asserts that the judge invaded the province of the jury by not only refusing to give the manslaughter charge, but also by explaining to them why he would now have to retract the earlier charge he had given them concerning self-defense. He reminded the jurors that he had instructed them at great length about self-defense, but had concluded that was not an option available to them, because 'the evidence would not support any inference that Santiago started the trouble; that would be beyond reasonable inference and as a matter of law, speculation and conjecture.' The method and extent of a jury charge is within the discretion of the trial judge. It was within his discretion to correct the impression he may have left with the jurors regarding self-defense where there was no evidence to support such a theory." *Commonwealth v. Carrion*, 407 Mass. 263, 268–69 (1990) (citations omitted).

NOTE 3 "A trial judge must inform counsel of his proposed instructions before final argument." *Commonwealth v. Degro*, 432 Mass. 319, 332 (2000).

RULE 25
Motion for Required Finding of Not Guilty
(Applicable to District Court and Superior Court.)

(a) Entry by Court.

The judge on motion of a defendant or on his own motion shall enter a finding of not guilty of the offense charged in an indictment or complaint or any part thereof after the evidence on either side is closed if the evidence is insufficient as a matter of law to sustain a conviction on the charge. If a defendant's motion for a required finding of not guilty is made at the close of the Commonwealth's evidence, it shall be ruled upon at that time. If the motion is denied or allowed only in part by the judge, the defendant may offer evidence in his defense without having reserved that right.

(b) Jury Trials.

(1) *Reservation of Decision on Motion.* If a motion for a required finding of not guilty is made at the close of all the evidence, the judge may reserve decision on the motion, submit the case to the jury, and decide the motion before the jury returns a verdict, after the jury returns a verdict of guilty, or after the jury is discharged without having returned a verdict.

(2) *Motion after Discharge of Jury.* If the motion is denied and the case is submitted to the jury, the motion may be renewed within five days after the jury is discharged and may include in the alternative a motion for a new trial. If a verdict of guilty is returned, the judge may on motion set aside the verdict and order a new trial, or order the entry of a finding of not guilty, or order the entry of a finding of guilty of any offense included in the offense charged in the indictment or complaint.

(c) Appeal.

(1) *Right of Appeal where Motion for Relief under Subdivision (b) Is Allowed After a Jury Verdict of Guilty.* The Commonwealth shall have the right to appeal to the appropriate appellate court a decision of a judge granting relief under the provisions of subdivisions (b)(1) and (2) of this rule on a motion for required finding of not guilty after the jury has returned a verdict of guilty or on an order for the entry of a finding of guilt of any offense included in the offense charged in the indictment or complaint.

(2) *Costs Upon Appeal.* If an appeal or application therefor is taken by the Commonwealth, the appellate court, upon the written motion of the defendant supported by affidavit, may determine and approve the payment to the defendant of his costs of appeal together with reasonable attorney's fees, if any, to be paid on the order of the trial court upon the entry of the rescript or the denial of the application.

NOTE 1   **Standard.** "In reviewing the denial of the defendant's motions for required findings of not guilty, the 'question is whether, after viewing the evidence in the light most favorable to the prosecution, *any* rational trier of fact could have found the essential elements of the crime beyond a reasonable doubt' (emphasis in original). *Commonwealth v. Salemme,* 395 Mass. 594, 595 (1985), quoting *Commonwealth v. Latimore,* 378 Mass. 671, 677 (1979). See Mass.R.Crim.P. 25(a)." *Commonwealth v. Cordle,* 404 Mass. 733, 739 (1989). "We consider 'whether the evidence received, viewed in a light most favorable to the Commonwealth, is sufficient so that the jury "might properly draw inferences, not too remote in the ordinary course of events, or forbidden by any rule of law, and conclude upon all the established circumstances and warranted inferences that the guilt of the defendant was proved beyond a reasonable doubt.' *Commonwealth v. Clary,* 388 Mass. 583, 588 (1983), quoting *Commonwealth v. Vellucci,* 284 Mass. 443, 445 (1933). 'The inferences cannot be too remote but "allowable inferences need not be necessary or inescapable.'" *Commonwealth v. Lanoue,* 392 Mass. 583, 589–590 (1984), quoting *Commonwealth v. Rojas,* 388 Mass. 626, 630 (1983)." *Commonwealth v. Cordle,* 404 Mass. at 739.

NOTE 2   "Although the motion judge did not make a finding that there was insufficient evidence to warrant the jury's verdict, she did state that 'a motion for a required finding of not guilty based upon the evidence in this case was of arguable merit. It has more than a minimal chance of success.' The motion judge granted Cardenuto a new trial. We agree with the motion judge's conclusion that trial counsel's failure to appeal the denial of the motions for required findings of not guilty amounted to ineffective assistance of counsel. In so doing, we conclude that there was insufficient evidence to sustain the jury's verdict. Accordingly, we hold that trial counsel's failure to appeal the denial of the motions for a required finding of not guilty amounted to ineffective assistance of counsel."

Furthermore, "because the evidence introduced by the Commonwealth was insufficient to sustain the defendant's conviction, retrial is barred by the principles of double jeopardy." *Commonwealth v. Cardenuto,* 406 Mass. 450, 453, 457 (1990).

NOTE 3   "We consider only the evidence introduced up to the time that the Commonwealth rested its case and the defendant first filed his motions for directed verdicts. The defendant's rights became fixed at the time that the Commonwealth rested. In reviewing the denial of motions for required findings of not guilty in criminal cases, we have frequently said that we must consider and determine whether the evidence, in its light most favorable to the Commonwealth, notwithstanding the contrary evidence presented by the defendant, is sufficient to permit the jury to infer the existence of the essential elements of the crime charged." *Brown v. Commonwealth,* 407 Mass. 84, 85 (1990) (quotation marks, citations and footnote omitted).

NOTE 4   **Deterioration.** "Deterioration occurs, for purposes of deciding whether to allow a motion for required finding of not guilty at the close of all the evidence, if, after the defendant's case, the Commonwealth's prima facie case has been shown to be 'incredible or conclusively incorrect.' Deterioration does not occur simply because the defendant presented evidence that contradicted the Commonwealth's case." *Commonwealth v. Nhut Huynh,* 452 Mass. 481, 485 (2008) (citations omitted). *See also Commonwealth v. Gomez,* 450 Mass. 704, 710 (2008).

NOTE 5   **Constitutional Challenge.** "Generally, a challenge to the constitutionality of a statute as applied should be preserved in a motion for a required finding of not guilty under Mass.R. Crim.P. 25, as amended, 389 Mass. 1107 (1983). See *Commonwealth v. Jasmin,* 396 Mass. 653, 655 (1986) ('a challenge to . . . a statute as applied might properly be raised before trial, but it need not be raised until the Commonwealth has presented its evidence showing the circumstances in which the statute would be applied to a defendant')." *Commonwealth v. Oakes,* 407 Mass. 92, 94 (1990).

NOTE 6a   **Rule 25(b)(2).** "The judge's option to reduce a verdict offers a means to rectify a disproportionate verdict, among other reasons, short of granting a new trial. The judge's power under 25(b)(2), like our power under G.L. c. 278, § 33E, may be used to ameliorate injustice caused by the Commonwealth, defense counsel, the jury, the judge's own error, or, as may have occurred in this case, the interaction of several causes." *Commonwealth v. Woodward,* 427 Mass. 659, 667 (1998) (citation omitted).

NOTE 6b   "A judge's discretion to reduce a verdict pursuant to rule 25(b)(2) is appropriately exercised where the weight of the evidence in the case, although technically sufficient to support the jury's verdict, points to a lesser crime. . . . What is not justified, however, is reduction to a lesser verdict that would be inconsistent with the weight of the evidence, or reduction based solely on factors irrelevant to the level of offense proved." *Commonwealth v. Rolon,* 438 Mass. 808, 821–22 (2003) (citations omitted).

NOTE 7   Standard. "In deciding a Rule 25(b)(2) motion using the required finding standard set out in [*Commonwealth v. Latimore*, 378 Mass. 671 (1979)], the judge cannot weigh the evidence or assess the credibility of the witness." *Commonwealth v. Shabo*, 47 Mass. App. Ct. 923, 924 (1999) (quotation marks and citation omitted).

NOTE 8   Jury Instruction After Allowance of Required Finding Motion. "After the judge allowed the required finding motion on the charge, he told the jury, 'I'll tell you now that that indictment has been withdrawn from further consideration by you, the jury. The jury is advised that you should not speculate about the reason for the withdrawal. . . .' The judge's instruction followed our suggestion in *Commonwealth v. Pasciuti*, 12 Mass. App. Ct. 833, 840 & n.7 (1981)." *Commonwealth v. Kalhauser*, 52 Mass. App. Ct. 339, 347 (2001).

NOTE 9   Double Jeopardy. "Massachusetts Rule of Criminal Procedure 25(a) directs the trial judge to enter a finding of not guilty 'if the evidence is insufficient as a matter of law to sustain a conviction.' An order entering such a finding thus meets the definition of acquittal that our double jeopardy cases have consistently used: It 'actually represents a resolution, correct or not, of some or all of the factual elements of the offense charged.'" *Smith v. Massachusetts*, 543 U.S. 462, 467–68 (2005) (citations omitted).

RULE 26

Requests for Rulings

(Applicable to jury-waived trials in District Court and Superior Court.)

Requests for rulings in the trial of a case shall be in writing and shall be presented to the court before the beginning of closing arguments, unless consent of the court is given to present requests later.

NOTE   "Although case law regarding requests for rulings of law generally has arisen in the context of civil litigation, the rule also applies to criminal cases." *Commonwealth v. Szewczyk*, 89 Mass. App. Ct. 711, 714 (2016).

RULE 27

Verdict

(Applicable to jury trials in District Court and Superior Court.)

(a) Return.

The verdict shall be unanimous. It shall be a general verdict returned by the jury to the judge in open court. The jury shall file a verdict slip with the clerk upon the return of the verdict.

(b) Several Offenses or Defendants.

If there are two or more offenses or defendants tried together, the jury may, with the consent of the judge at any time during its deliberations return or be required by the judge to return a verdict or verdicts with respect to the defendants or charges as to which a verdict has been reached; and thereafter the jury may in the discretion of the judge resume deliberation. The judge may declare a mistrial as to any charges upon which the jury cannot agree upon a verdict; provided, however, that the judge may first require the jury to return verdicts on those charges upon which the jury can agree and direct that such verdicts be received and recorded.

(c) Special Questions.

The trial judge may submit special questions to the jury.

(d) Poll of Jury.

When a verdict is returned and before the verdict is recorded, the jury may be polled in the discretion of the judge. If after the poll there is not a unanimous concurrence, the jury may be directed to retire for further deliberations or may be discharged.

NOTE 1   Verdict and Postverdict Juror/Jury Interview. "The verdict is the formal decision of the jury, empaneled and sworn to try the case, as reported to the court. 'The verdict which determines the rights of the parties, and is admitted of record, and upon which judgment is rendered, is the verdict received from the lips of the foreman in open court.' . . .

"We agree with the judge that it was not essential to the validity of the verdict to have the clerk make a notation of it on the back of the complaint."

"We have said that '[p]ostverdict interview should be initiated only if the court finds some suggestion that there were extraneous matters in the jury's deliberations.' *Commonwealth v. Fidler*, 377 Mass. 192, 203 (1979). Faced with such suggestions, a trial judge properly may conduct a neutral, noncoercive interview with the juror. See *Commonwealth v. Hebert*, 379 Mass. 752, 754–755 (1980). However, the scope of that interview is strictly confined to the issue of whether any extraneous materials or statements might have come to the jury's attention before they delivered their verdict. See *Commonwealth v. Fidler*, supra at 196; *Woodward v. Leavitt*, 107 Mass. 453, 466 (1871). The judge is precluded from inquiring into the internal decision making process of the jury as a whole or of the individual juror being questioned." *Commonwealth v. Martell*, 407 Mass. 288, 292–95 (1990).

NOTE 2   Postverdict Juror Communication. "[I]n adopting [Rule 3.5 of the Massachusetts Rules of Professional Conduct], this court implicitly overruled the prohibition against attorney-originated communications with jurors set forth in [*Commonwealth v. Fidler*, 377 Mass. 192, 203 (1979)]."

"Going forward, on request of any party, the trial judge shall instruct the jury regarding an attorney's right to contact and communicate with jurors after trial and a juror's right to decline to speak with an attorney postverdict." *Commonwealth v. Moore*, 474 Mass. 541, 547, 551 (2016).

NOTE 3a   Polling the Jury. For different issues concerning polling the jury, see *Commonwealth v. Nettis*, 418 Mass. 715 (1994). *See also Commonwealth v. Wilson*, 427 Mass. 336, 356 (1998) ("The decision to poll the jurors is within the trial judge's discretion. We have concluded that the better practice is to obtain a clear sign of each juror's assent to the announced verdict, by polling the jurors or otherwise. However, we have never required the judge to poll the jurors unless there is specific evidence that the verdicts are not unanimous. Absent such evidence, the judge may properly deny an explicit request by the defendant for a poll.") (citations and quotation marks omitted).

NOTE 3b   Timing of Request to Poll Jury. "Any request to poll the jury must be made before the verdict is recorded, and judges should not allow untimely requests for polling." *Commonwealth v. Reaves*, 434 Mass. 383, 395 (2001).

NOTE 3c   Resuming Deliberations if Not Unanimous. Where polling of the jury reveals that the verdict was not unanimous, "[a] judge does not need the jury's agreement to resume deliberations. Nothing in Rule 27(d) makes such a step mandatory." *Commonwealth v. Reaves*, 434 Mass. 383, 396 n.18 (2001).

NOTE 4   Jury Colloquy. "The colloquy is a ritual that has developed for the return and recording of a verdict in a criminal case. The colloquy itself is not required by rule or statute. Its purpose is to allow jurors to express dissent to the court because such an affirmation is the only evidence the court can receive of the free and unanimous assent of the jury to the verdict. [In this case] we conclude that there was ample opportunity for members of the jury to indicate any lack of assent, and that the failure of the clerk precisely to follow the ritual did not create a substantial likelihood of a miscarriage of justice." *Commonwealth v. Fowler*, 431 Mass. 30, 34–36 (2000) (citations, footnotes, quotations, and punctuation marks omitted).

RULE 28
Judgment
(Amended Dec. 17, 2008, effective Apr. 1, 2009.) (Applicable to District Court and Superior Court.)

(a) Judgment.

If the defendant has been determined to be guilty, a verdict or finding of guilty shall be rendered, or if he has been determined to be not guilty, a verdict or finding of not guilty shall be rendered, in open court, and shall be entered on the court's docket.

(b) Imposition of Sentence.

After a verdict, finding, or plea of guilty, or a plea of nolo contendere, or an admission to sufficient facts, the defendant shall have the right to be sentenced without unreasonable delay. Pending sentence the court may commit the defendant or continue or alter the bail as provided by law. Before imposing sentence the court shall afford the defendant or his counsel an opportunity to speak on behalf of the defendant and to present any information in mitigation of punishment.

(c) Notification of Right to Appeal.

After a judgment of guilty is entered, the court shall advise the defendant of his right to appeal. In the District Court, upon the request of the defendant, the clerk of the court shall prepare and file forthwith a notice of appeal.

(d) Presentence Investigation.

(1) *Criminal Record.* The probation officer shall inquire into the nature of every criminal case or juvenile complaint brought before the court and report to the court information concerning all prior criminal prosecutions or juvenile complaints, if any, and the disposition of each such prosecution, except where the defendant was found not guilty. Such information is to be presented before a defendant is admitted to bail in court, and also before disposition of the case against him.

(2) *Report.* The report of the presentence investigation shall contain any prior criminal or juvenile prosecution record of the defendant, but shall not contain any information relating to criminal or juvenile prosecutions in which the defendant was found not guilty. In addition, the report shall include such other available information as may be helpful to the court in the disposition of the case.

(3) *Availability to Parties.* Prior to the disposition the presentence report shall be made available to the prosecutor and counsel for the defendant for inspection. In extraordinary cases, the judge may except from disclosure parts of the report which are not relevant to a proper sentence, diagnostic opinion which might seriously disrupt a program of rehabilitation, sources of information obtained upon a promise of confidentiality, or any other information which, if disclosed, might result in harm, physical or otherwise, to the defendant or other persons. If the report is not made fully available, the portions thereof which are not disclosed shall not be relied upon in determining sentence. No party may make any copy of the presentence report.

(e) Filing.

The court may file a case after a guilty verdict or finding without imposing a sentence if the defendant and the Commonwealth both consent. With the consent of both parties, the judge may specify a time limit beyond which the case may not be removed from the file, and may specify any events that may cause the case to be removed from the file. The defendant shall file a written consent with the court as to both the filing of the case and any time limit or events regarding removal from the file. Prior to accepting the defendant's consent, the court shall inform the defendant on the record in open court:

(i) that the defendant has a right to request sentencing on any or all filed case(s) at any time;

(ii) that subject to any time limit imposed by the court, the prosecutor may request that the case be removed from the file and sentence imposed if a related conviction or sentence is reversed or vacated or upon the prosecutor's establishing by a preponderance of the evidence either that the defendant committed a new criminal offense or that an event occurred on which the continued filing of the case was expressly made contingent by the court; and

(iii) that if the case is removed from the file the defendant may be sentenced on the case.

In sentencing the defendant after the removal of a case from the file, the court shall consider the over-all scheme of punishment employed by the original sentencing judge.

NOTE 1 "The sentence imposed by the judge was within the statutory limits of G.L. c. 265, § 13A (1988 ed.). 'The judge is permitted great latitude in sentencing, provided the sentence does not exceed statutory limits.'" *Commonwealth v. O'Connor*, 407 Mass. 663, 674 (1990) (quotation marks and citations omitted).

NOTE 2 At the close of the Commonwealth's case-in-chief, the judge informed the defendant that he could take the same sentence as he had originally received at the bench trial. The defendant declined and was ultimately found guilty by the jury. The judge increased the sentence.

Held, conviction affirmed, the Supreme Judicial Court finding neither impropriety nor vindictive sentencing by the judge.

Commonwealth v. Morse, 402 Mass. 735, 738–40 (1988).

NOTE 3 See Note 1 accompanying Mass.R.Crim.P. 27.

RULE 29
Revision or Revocation of Sentence
(Amended June 8, 2016, effective Sept. 1, 2016.) (Applicable to District Court and Superior Court.)

(a) Revision or Revocation.

(1) *Illegal Sentences.* The trial judge, upon the judge's own motion, or the written motion of the prosecutor, filed within sixty days after imposition of a sentence, may revise or revoke such sentence if the judge determines that any part of the sentence was illegal.

(2) *Unjust Sentences.* The trial judge, upon the judge's own motion, or the written motion of a defendant, filed within sixty days after the imposition of a sentence or within sixty days after issuance of a rescript by an appellate court on direct review, may, upon such terms and conditions as the judge shall order, revise or revoke such sentence if it appears that justice may not have been done.

(b) Affidavits.

If a party files a motion pursuant to this rule, the party shall file and serve, and the other party may file and serve, affidavits in support of their respective positions. The judge may deny a motion filed pursuant to this rule on the basis of facts alleged in the affidavits without further hearing.

(c) Notice.

The moving party shall serve the other party with a copy of any motion and affidavit filed pursuant to this rule. If the judge orders that a hearing be held on the motion, the court shall give the parties reasonable notice of the time set for the hearing.

(d) Place of Hearing.

A motion filed pursuant to this rule may be heard by the trial judge wherever the judge is then sitting.

(e) Appeal.

An appeal from a final order under this rule may be taken to the Appeals Court, or the Supreme Judicial Court in an appropriate case, by either party.

Reporter's Notes (2016). This amendment to Rule 29 is intended to fill a gap in the Rules of Criminal Procedure identified by the Supreme Judicial Court in *Commonwealth v. Selavka*, 469 Mass. 502 (2014), in which the Court upheld the Commonwealth's authority to move to correct an illegal sentence. After noting that neither former Rule 29(a) nor Rule 30(a) permitted a Commonwealth motion to revise or revoke an illegal sentence, the Court concluded that "rule 29(a), with its sixty-day time frame, is the proper vehicle by which the Commonwealth may challenge illegal sentences." *Selavka*, 469 Mass. at 508. This amendment to Rule 29 permits the Commonwealth to seek such relief.

Rule 29(a) Revision or Revocation. Rule 29(a)(1), Illegal Sentences, provides that, within 60 days after a trial judge imposes a sentence, either the Commonwealth or the judge may move to revise or revoke that sentence if any part of the sentence is illegal. While Rule 29(a) has long authorized a trial judge to increase a sentence under Rule 29(a), either because the sentence imposed is illegal or, on reflection, unjust, see *Commonwealth v. Aldoupolis*, 386 Mass. 260, 268–270 (1982), former Rule 29 did not authorize the Commonwealth to seek revision or revocation of a sentence for any purpose. See *Selavka*, 469 Mass. at 506. Rule 29(a)(1) makes it clear that the judge's authority to correct an illegal sentence remains unchanged, but the rule further permits the Commonwealth to seek such relief. This narrow provision for a Commonwealth motion to revise or revoke a sentence is intentionally limited to correcting an illegal sentence; it does not permit a motion to increase a legal sentence that the prosecutor considers to be legal but unduly lenient.

Rule 29(a)(1)'s authority to challenge an illegal sentence within 60 days of sentencing is limited to the Commonwealth and the trial judge for two reasons. First, the defendant is already authorized to file such a motion. Rule 29(a)(2), Unjust Sentences, leaves unchanged the defendant's right to challenge a sentence "if it appears that justice may not have been done," which includes a sentence imposing punishment not permitted by law. See *Selavka*, 469 Mass. 508 n.7. Quite apart from Rule 29(a), Rule 30(a) gives the defendant the right to challenge an illegal sentence at any time.

Second, a successful prosecution or judicial motion to revise or revoke an illegal sentence that is too lenient would result in additional punishment, which, if unduly belated, would implicate the defendant's double-jeopardy interest in sentence finality even though the original sentence was illegal. See *Selavka*, 469 Mass. at 509. The Court in *Selavka* concluded that limiting the potential for such upward adjustment of an illegal sentence to Rule 29(a)'s 60-day timeframe marks a reasonable balance between a defendant's interest in sentence finality and society's interest in enforcement of the sentencing laws. *Selavka*, 469 Mass. at 508. Rule 29(a)(1) thus provides for a 60-day time limit for the Commonwealth to file a motion seeking, or for the judge to initiate consideration of, the revision or revocation of an illegal sentence. After that, any motion to revise or revoke an illegal sentence must come from the defendant under Rule 30(a), which would raise no double-jeopardy problems.

Rule 29(a)(1) includes revocation as a potential remedy for an illegal sentence that is too lenient, in part because that sentence might have been the result of a guilty plea from which the defendant could have withdrawn had the sentence been more harsh than it was. See Rule 12(c)(4) (permitting defendant to withdraw (1) from a District-Court plea if the judge intends to impose a sentence in excess of defendant's request and (2) from a Superior-Court plea if the judge intends to sentence in excess of either the agreed recommendation or the prosecutor's recommendation); Rule 12(d)(4) (requiring a judge who accepts a plea agreement

providing for both a charge concession and a specific sentence to impose the agreed sentence and permitting the defendant to withdraw if the judge rejects the plea agreement); former Rule 12(c)(2) (permitting defendant to withdraw (1) from a District-Court plea if the judge intends to impose a sentence in excess of defendant's request and (2) from a Superior-Court plea if the judge intends to sentence in excess of an agreed recommendation on which the plea was contingent). At the very least, such a case would require re-sentencing, with the defendant presumably having the right to withdraw the plea if Rule 12 would have afforded that right at the plea hearing and initial sentencing. See *Selavka*, 469 Mass. at 514–515.

Rule 29(a)(2), Unjust Sentences, clarifies former Rule 29(a)'s provision for filing a motion to revise or revoke an unjust sentence following appellate review.

First, the rule makes clear that, other than the imposition of sentence, the only event that triggers the sixty-day period to file a Rule 29(a)(2) motion is the appellate court's issuance of the rescript in a case on direct review. If the conviction is affirmed, the issuance of the rescript marks the point at which the conviction becomes final, see *Foxworth v. St. Amand*, 457 Mass. 200, 206 (2010), making it an appropriate time for filing a motion to revise or revoke the sentence based on that conviction. Although on its face the rule does not limit such motions to cases in which the conviction is affirmed, as a practical matter, a conviction's reversal would result in vacation of the sentence, leaving nothing to revise or revoke.

Pegging the beginning of the sixty-day filing period to the rescript's issuance permits a defendant whose conviction is affirmed by the Appeals Court to seek either rehearing or further appellate review without impinging on the time period for filing a motion to revise and revoke. Rule of Appellate Procedure 23 requires the Appeals Court, after deciding an appeal and mailing the decision to the parties, to wait twenty-eight days before issuing the rescript, see Mass. R.A.P. 23, thereby affording the parties time to file for rehearing or further review. See Mass. R.A.P. 27 (petition for rehearing to be filed within fourteen days of decision); Mass. R.A.P. 27.1 (application for further review to be filed within twenty days of decision). If either is granted, the rescript's issuance is stayed pending disposition of that proceeding. See Mass. R.A.P. 23. Finally, the appellate court's issuance of the rescript, finalizing a conviction which is affirmed, is a procedural event of which the defendant would surely be aware and thus a fair time for the sixty-day filing period to begin. The amendment eliminates the uncertainty caused by basing the time period on the trial court's receipt of the rescript, which was subject to the vagaries of mail delivery and clerical document processing.

Second, by confining the extension of the sixty-day filing period to cases on direct review, Rule 29(a)(2) clarifies the reach of its predecessor. Former Rule 29(a) did not specify whether a rescript on appellate review of a collateral attack on a sentence would allow a Rule 29 motion, though the Appeals Court found in an unpublished opinion that it would not. *Commonwealth v. White*, No. 08-P-766, 74 Mass. App. Ct. 1115, 2009 Mass. App. Unpub. LEXIS 788, at *3–*6 (Mass. App. Ct. June 4, 2009). The rule's purpose is to permit the trial judge to revise or revoke a sentence that, based on the facts existing at the time of sentencing, appears in retrospect to have been unjust. See *Commonwealth v. Rodriguez*, 461 Mass. 256, 260 (2012); *Commonwealth v. DeJesus*, 440 Mass. 147, 152 (2003). This purpose is best served if the sentence review prompted by the motion occurs reasonably soon after the sentence's imposition. See *Commonwealth v. Barclay*, 424 Mass. 377, 380 (1997) (holding Rule 29 motion must be decided within reasonable time of its filing); *Commonwealth v. Layne*, 386 Mass. 291, 295-296 (1982) (noting that, with "the passage of time from the date of sentencing, it becomes increasingly difficult for a trial judge to make the determination called for by [then Rule 29(a)] without improperly considering postsentencing events"). Rule 29(a)(2) accordingly limits the filing time to sixty days from the imposition of sentence or from the issuance of the rescript in any direct appeal, the latter filing period commencing as soon as the conviction becomes final. The former rule's provision permitting filing within sixty days of any appellate court order or judgment "denying review of, or having the effect of upholding, a judgment of conviction" has been deleted as being either redundant (if the order or judgment in question is part of the rescript concluding a direct appeal), or not sufficiently clear.

Finally, Rule 29(a)(2) achieves gender neutrality.

Rule 29(b) Affidavits. Rule 29(b), Affidavits, is amended to accommodate the Commonwealth's narrow authority to file a motion to revise or revoke an illegal sentence under the rule, authorizing both parties to file appropriate affidavits in that event. Consistent with Rule 18(a)(3), the amended rule further provides that the judge may deny a motion filed under Rule 29(a) without a hearing, based solely on the affidavits. Mass. R. Cr. P. 18(a)(3), Presence [of Defendant] Not Required, 378 Mass. 887 (1979) ("A defendant need not be present at a revision or revocation of sentence pursuant to Rule 29 or at any proceeding where evidence is not to be taken)." However, any revision or revocation of a sentence under Rule 29, whether because the sentence imposed is illegal or unjust, must be predicated on a hearing. See E. B. Cypher, Revise or Revoke of Sentence Hearings, 30A Criminal Practice and Procedure, § 30:27 (4th ed. Mar. 2015). See also *Thompson v. United States*, 495 F.2d 1304, 1307 (1st Cir. 1974) (vacating post-trial sentence imposed in absentia to correct an illegal sentence, holding defendant must be present for re-sentencing; cited by Reporter's Notes to Mass. R. Cr. P. 18(a), Presence of Defendant, as example of sentencing requiring defendant's presence). Although the defendant does not have the right to present evidence at this hearing, see *Commonwealth v. Coggins*, 324 Mass. 552, 556-557, cert. denied, 338 U.S. 881 (1949), he or she has the right to be present and to be heard. See *Aldoupolis v. Commonwealth*, 386 Mass. 260, 275–276 (1982); E. B. Cypher, Presence of the Defendant at the [Rule 29] Hearing, 30B Criminal Practice and Procedure, §41:12 (4th ed. Mar. 2015). Further, any victim(s) covered by G.L. c. 258B , Rights of Victims and Witnesses of Crime, may present a victim-impact statement at such a hearing. See *Commonwealth v. Doucette*, 81 Mass. App. Ct. 740, 742, rev. denied, 463 Mass. 1103 (2012) (upholding judge's discretion under G.L. c. 258B, § 3(p) to permit victims to be heard on Rule 30(a) motion for a new trial, adding that "[t]he victim's family was also entitled [under the statute] to make a victim impact statement at sentencing or disposition").

Rule 29(c) Notice – (d) Place of Hearing. Rule 29(c), Notice, and Rule 29(d), Place of Hearing, are amended (1) to recognize the Commonwealth's narrow authority to file a motion to revise or revoke an illegal sentence, and (2) to achieve gender neutrality.

Rule 29(e) Appeal. Rule 29(e) provides that either party may appeal from a final order under the rule. This provision clarifies that the Commonwealth may appeal a denial of its motion to revise or revoke an illegal sentence. Prior to Rule 29(e), a defendant's right to appeal the denial of a motion to revise or revoke a sentence was well established, see *Commonwealth v. Richards*, 44 Mass. App. Ct. 478, 481 (1998), as was the Commonwealth's right to appeal the allowance of such a motion. See *Commonwealth v. Cowan*, 422 Mass. 546, 547 (1996) (recognizing Commonwealth's right under G.L. c. 211, § 3 to appeal District Court allowance of Rule 29 motion); Commonwealth v. Amirault , 415 Mass. 112, 115 (1993) (same under G.L. c. 278, § 28E for Superior Court motion). In contrast, while the Commonwealth had the right to move to correct an illegal sentence and presumably the attendant right to appeal the denial of such a motion, see *Commonwealth v. Selavka*, 469 Mass. 502, 507 & n.6 (2014), its avenue for pursuing that appeal was not clear. *Id.* Rule 29(e) cures that deficiency.

NOTE 1a   Judge's Authority. "[W]e consider whether a District Court judge had the authority pursuant to Mass.R.Crim.P. 29, 378 Mass. 899 (1979), to vacate his finding of guilt on a criminal complaint and enter a continuance without a finding conditioned on a defendant's payment of restitution. We conclude that the judge possessed no such authority under rule 29, or otherwise.

"When considering whether to allow a defendant's motion to revise or revoke, a judge may not take into account conduct of the defendant that occurs subsequent to the original sentencing. By

the explicit terms of rule 29, if a judge determines that justice has not been done, the judge may revise or revoke a sentence, not a finding of guilt. When the judge vacated the finding of guilt on the criminal complaint and entered a continuance without a finding subject to the payment of restitution, he effectively erased all vestiges of the criminal proceedings against the defendant. Such action was not within the purview of the judge's authority under rule 29. . . . The District Court judge's decision was motivated, as he acknowledged, by his concern for [the victim] which, while laudable, had nothing to do with the fairness of the defendant's sentence. Therefore, the defendant's rule 29 motion should not have been allowed." *Commonwealth v. McCulloch*, 450 Mass. 483, 487–88 (2008) (citations, footnotes, and quotation marks omitted).

NOTE 1b   "The issue in this case is whether a judge has the authority under Mass. R. Crim. P. 29(a) . . . to reduce a sentence after the defendant and the Commonwealth had entered into a plea agreement in which the Commonwealth agreed not to seek indictments against the defendant on the pending charges, the defendant had agreed to plead guilty to the charges and join the prosecutor's sentencing recommendation, and the judge had imposed the recommended sentence. We conclude that where, as here, a judge acts on his own timely motion to revise or revoke a sentence, the judge has the authority to reduce a sentence where 'it appears that justice may not have been done' regardless whether a plea agreement includes an agreed sentence recommendation." *Commonwealth v. Rodriguez*, 461 Mass. 256, 256–57 (2012).

NOTE 1c   "There is no merit to the defendant's argument that the judge could not, in revising the sentences, increase their severity. Under Mass. R. Crim. P. 29 . . . a judge has the authority on his own motion to revoke and revise a sentence and increase its severity if it appears that justice may not have been done." *Commonwealth v. Carver*, 33 Mass. App. Ct. 378, 390 (1992) (footnote and citations omitted).

NOTE 2a   "This sixty-day time period established in the rule is absolute and may not be extended. . . . Furthermore . . . the judge would not have had the authority to revise the sentence imposed by the Appellate Division. The order of the Appellate Division is final. See G.L. c. 278, § 28B." *Commonwealth v. Callahan*, 419 Mass. 306, 308–09 (1995).

NOTE 2b   A motion to revise and revoke must be heard within a reasonable time. Six years is unreasonable. *Commonwealth v. Barclay*, 424 Mass. 377, 380 (1997).

NOTE 3   Commonwealth's Challenge: "[W]e determine that rule 29(a), with its sixty-day time frame, is the proper vehicle by which the Commonwealth may challenge illegal sentences." *Commonwealth v. Selavka*, 469 Mass. 502, 508 (2014).

NOTE 4   "By allowing a motion to revise and revoke sentences when the parole board does not act in accordance with a judge's expectations, the judge is interfering with the executive function. The judge cannot nullify the discretionary actions of the parole board." *Commonwealth v. Amirault*, 415 Mass. 112, 116–17 (1993) (footnote omitted).

NOTE 5   "If there is a finding of ineffective assistance of counsel based on counsel's failure to file in a timely manner, as he promised, a motion to revise and revoke sentence, the judge should vacate the sentence and reimpose it, thereby affording the defendant an opportunity to file timely a motion pursuant to Mass.R.Crim.P. 29(a) to revise the new sentence." *Commonwealth v. Stubbs*, 15 Mass. App. Ct. 955 (1983) (rescript). *See also Commonwealth v. McNulty*, 42 Mass. App. Ct. 955, 956–57 (1997).

NOTE 6   Appeal. "[W]e conclude that the order of the District Court judge that denied the defendant's motion to revise or revoke his sentence under rule 29 was immediately appealable." *Commonwealth v. Richards*, 44 Mass. App. Ct. 478, 481 & n.4 (1998) ("The better practice, of course, is for the defendant to file a motion for post-conviction relief pursuant to [Rule 30], and to take an appeal under subparagraph (e)(8) of that rule. It would be elevating form over substance, however, to hold that this is an exclusive remedy and that it is not open to the defendant to file an appeal directly from the denial of the motion to revise or revoke in order to correct an illegal sentence. In the future, therefore, a clerk should accept for filing a defendant's notice of appeal from a rule 29 order unless there is a rule 30 motion on file.") (citation omitted).

NOTE 7   "One cannot file a motion to revise or revoke without stating the grounds on which it is based. *Commonwealth v. De-Jesus*, 440 Mass. 147, 152 (2003)." *Commonwealth v. Fenton F.*, 442 Mass. 31, 39 (2004).

RULE 30
Post Conviction Relief
(Amended Sept. 6, 2001, effective Oct. 1, 2001.) (Applicable to District Court and Superior Court.)

(a) Unlawful Restraint.

Any person who is imprisoned or whose liberty is restrained pursuant to a criminal conviction may at any time, as of right, file a written motion requesting the trial judge to release him or her or to correct the sentence then being served upon the ground that the confinement or restraint was imposed in violation of the Constitution or laws of the United States or of the Commonwealth of Massachusetts.

(b) New Trial.

The trial judge upon motion in writing may grant a new trial at any time if it appears that justice may not have been done. Upon the motion the trial judge shall make such findings of fact as are necessary to resolve the defendant's allegations of error of law.

(c) Post Conviction Procedure.

(1) *Service and Notice.* The moving party shall serve the office of the prosecutor who represented the Commonwealth in the trial court with a copy of any motion filed under this rule.

(2) *Waiver.* All grounds for relief claimed by a defendant under subdivisions (a) and (b) of this rule shall be raised by the defendant in the original or amended motion. Any grounds not so raised are waived unless the judge in the exercise of discretion permits them to be raised in a subsequent motion, or unless such grounds could not reasonably have been raised in the original or amended motion.

(3) *Affidavits.* Moving parties shall file and serve and parties opposing a motion may file and serve affidavits where appropriate in support of their respective position. The judge may rule on the issue or issues presented by such motion on the basis of the facts alleged in the affidavits without further hearing if no substantial issue is raised by the motion or affidavits.

(4) *Discovery.* Where affidavits filed by the moving party under subdivision (c)(3) establish a prima facie case for relief, the judge on motion of any party, after notice to the opposing party and an opportunity to be heard, may authorize such discovery as is deemed appropriate, subject to appropriate protective order.

(5) *Counsel.* The judge in the exercise of discretion may assign or appoint counsel in accordance with the provisions of these rules to represent a defendant in the preparation and presentation of motions filed under subdivisions (a) and (b) of this rule. The court, after notice to the Commonwealth and an opportunity to be heard, may also exercise discretion to allow the defendant costs associated with the preparation and presentation of a motion under this rule.

(6) *Presence of Moving Party.* A judge may entertain and determine a motion under subdivisions (a) and (b) of this rule without requiring the presence of the moving party at the hearing.

(7) *Place and Time of Hearing.* All motions under subdivision (a) and (b) of this rule may be heard by the trial judge wherever the judge is then sitting. The parties shall have at least thirty days' notice of any hearing unless the judge determines that good cause exists to order the hearing held sooner.

(8) *Appeal.* An appeal from a final order under this rule may be taken to the Appeals Court, or to the Supreme Judicial Court in an appropriate case, by either party.

(A) If an appeal is taken, the defendant shall not be discharged from custody pending final decision upon the appeal; provided, however, that the defendant may, in the discretion of the judge, be admitted to bail pending decision of the appeal.

(B) If an appeal or application therefor is taken by the Commonwealth, upon written motion supported by affidavit, the Appeals Court or the Supreme Judicial Court may determine and approve payment to the defendant of his costs of appeal together with reasonable attorney's fees, if any, to be paid on the order of the trial court after entry of the rescript or the denial of the application. If the final order grants relief other than a discharge from custody, the trial court or the court in which the appeal is pending may, upon application by the Commonwealth, in its discretion, and upon such conditions as it deems just, stay the execution of the order pending final determination of the matter.

(9) *Appeal under G.L. c. 278, § 33E.* If an appeal or application for leave to appeal is taken by the Commonwealth under the provisions of Chapter 278, Section 33E, upon written notice supported by affidavit, the Supreme Judicial Court may determine and approve payment to the defendant of the costs of appeal together with reasonable attorney's fees to be paid on order of the trial court after entry of the rescript or the denial of the application.

NOTE 1   **General Rule.** "The judge is to apply the standard set out in rule 30 'rigorously,' and may grant a motion to withdraw a guilty plea only if it appears that justice may not have been done. The motion is addressed to the sound discretion of the judge. . . .

"As a general rule, a judge may decide a motion for a new trial based solely on affidavits, and additional testimony need not be heard. . . . However, when a defendant attacks a conviction based upon a guilty plea, she has the choice between two tactics. She may stand on the contemporaneous record, the record made in the case through the stage of the colloquy and conviction. If the defendant chooses this route, it is not open to the Commonwealth to introduce extraneous evidence tending to show that the defendant in fact acted freely and intelligently in tendering the plea. Alternatively, the defendant may offer extraneous evidence to supplement (or contradict) the record, but in that event the Commonwealth has a like right to offer evidence."

Commonwealth v. Conaghan, 48 Mass. App. Ct. 304, 308–09 (1999).

NOTE 2   **Voluntariness.** "Where a defendant wishing to withdraw a guilty plea challenges the voluntary or intelligent nature of his plea, it is ordinarily the Commonwealth's burden to show by means of a contemporaneous or reconstructed record of the plea that it was entered understandably and voluntarily. . . . The concept of voluntariness requires that the defendant tender the plea free from coercion, duress, or improper inducements. To determine the voluntariness of the defendant's plea, the judge should conduct a real probe of the defendant's mind. The judge should also determine whether the plea was being extracted from the defendant under undue pressure, whether the defendant was being treated for or was aware of any mental illness from which he may be suffering, and whether the defendant was under the influence of alcohol or drugs." *Commonwealth v. Conaghan*, 48 Mass.

App. Ct. 304, 314–15 (1999) (citation, quotation, and punctuation marks omitted).

NOTE 3 "It is a very uphill battle for a party to establish that a judge acting on a motion for a new trial abused his discretion. Appellate courts give great deference to the judge's disposition of such a motion and rarely reverse." *Commonwealth v. Hammond*, 50 Mass. App. Ct. 171, 178 (2000).

NOTE 4 **Evidentiary Hearing.** "A judge may rule on a motion for a new trial without an evidentiary hearing if no substantial issue is raised by the motion or accompanying affidavits." *Commonwealth v. Vinton*, 432 Mass. 180, 183 n.2 (2000).

NOTE 5 **Discovery.** "To meet the prima facie case standard for discovery under a motion for a new trial based on newly discovered evidence, a defendant must make specific, not speculative or conclusory, allegations that the newly discovered evidence would have 'materially aid[ed] the defense against the pending charges,' *Commonwealth v. Tucceri*, 412 Mass. 401, 405 (1992), and that this evidence, if explored further through discovery, could yield evidence that might have 'played an important role in the jury's deliberation and conclusions, even though it is not certain that the evidence would have produced a verdict of not guilty.' *Id.* at 414." *Commonwealth v. Daniels*, 445 Mass. 392, 407 (2005).

NOTE 6 **Costs.** For a discussion of attorney fees and costs under this rule, see *Commonwealth v. Phinney*, 448 Mass. 621 (2007).

NOTE 7 **Green Sheet.** "The fact that neither the defendant nor his lawyer signed the green sheet to show that he accepted the disposition is neither dispositive nor sufficient to overcome the presumption of regularity." *Commonwealth v. Tokarev*, 87 Mass. App. Ct. 819, 822 (2015).

NOTE 8 **Predicate Offense.** "[W]e hold that where a judge improperly neglects to inform a defendant of the possibility that his or her conviction could serve as a predicate for civil confinement as a sexually dangerous person, the defendant must demonstrate a reasonable probability that but for the judge's error he or she would not have pleaded guilty and would have insisted on proceeding to trial. Where such a showing is made, the magnitude of the deprivation of liberty potentially arising from what the defendant was not told may be sufficient to raise a doubt as to whether justice has been done." *Commonwealth v. Roberts*, 472 Mass. 355, 364–65 (2015).

NOTE 9a **Immigration Consequences.** "We agree with Padilla that constitutionally competent counsel would have advised him that his conviction for drug distribution made him subject to automatic deportation. Whether he is entitled to relief depends on whether he has been prejudiced, a matter that we do not address." *Padilla v. Kentucky*, 559 U.S. 356, 360 (2010).

NOTE 9b **Retroactivity.** "We granted certiorari . . . to resolve a split among federal and state courts on whether *Padilla* [v. Kentucky, 559 U.S. 356 (2010)] applies retroactively. [The Court held] that it does not." *Chaidez v. United States*, 133 S. Ct. 1103, 1107 (2013).

NOTE 9c "We conclude, as a matter of Massachusetts law and consistent with our authority as provided in *Danforth v. Minnesota*, 552 U.S. 264, 282 (2008), that the Sixth Amendment right enunciated in *Padilla* was not a 'new' rule and, consequently, defendants whose State law convictions were final after April 1, 1997, may attack their convictions collaterally on *Padilla* grounds. We thus affirm our decision in [*Commonwealth v. Clarke*, 460 Mass. 30 (2011)]." *Commonwealth v. Sylvain*, 466 Mass. 422, 423–24 (2013).

NOTE 9d "[T]he enactment of the Antiterrorism and Effective Death Penalty Act (effective Apr. 24, 1996) (AEDPA), made deportation for noncitizens convicted of certain criminal offenses virtually inevitable.

"Thus, . . . the retroactivity affirmed in the *Sylvain* case should extend back to the effective date of AEDPA, April 24, 1996, for convictions of offenses for which AEDPA eliminated the then

available protections (or discretionary waivers) for noncitizens." *Commonwealth v. Mercado*, 474 Mass. 80, 81–82 (2016).

NOTE 9e "We conclude that, under art. 12 of the Massachusetts Declaration of Rights, constitutionally effective representation of a criminal defendant requires defense counsel to make a reasonable inquiry of the defendant to determine whether he or she is a citizen of the United States and, if the defendant is not, to make a reasonable inquiry into the defendant's immigration status, including whether the defendant was admitted into this country as a refugee or has been granted asylum.

"We also conclude that, in determining whether a defendant suffered prejudice from counsel's deficient performance, 'special circumstances' regarding immigration consequences, as contemplated in *Commonwealth v. Clarke*, 460 Mass. 30, 47–48 (2011), should be given substantial weight in determining, based on the totality of the circumstances, whether there is a reasonable probability that the defendant would have rejected the plea offer and insisted on going to trial had counsel provided competent advice regarding the immigration consequences of the guilty plea." *Commonwealth v. Lavrinenko*, 473 Mass. 42, 43 (2015).

RULE 31
Stay of Execution; Relief Pending Review
(Amended June 24, 2009, effective Oct. 2, 2009.) (Applicable to Superior Court and de novo trials in District Court.)

(a) Imprisonment.

If a sentence of imprisonment is imposed upon conviction of a crime, the entry of an appeal shall not stay the execution of the sentence unless the judge imposing it or, pursuant to Mass. R. App. P. 6, a single justice of the court that will hear the appeal, determines in the exercise of discretion that execution of said sentence shall be stayed pending the determination of the appeal. If execution of a sentence of imprisonment is stayed, the judge or justice may at that time make an order relative to the custody of the defendant or for admitting the defendant to bail.

(b) If the application for a stay of execution of sentence is allowed, the order allowing the stay may state the grounds upon which the stay may be revoked and, in any event, shall state that upon release by the appellate court of the rescript affirming the conviction, stay of execution automatically expires unless extended by the appellate court. Any defendant so released shall provide prompt written notice to the clerk of the trial court regarding the defendant's current address and promptly notify the clerk in writing of any change thereof. The clerk shall notify the appellate court that will hear the appeal that a stay of execution of sentence has been allowed. At any time after the stay expires, the Commonwealth may move in the trial court to execute the sentence. The court shall schedule a prompt hearing and issue notice thereof to the defendant unless the prosecutor requests, for good cause shown, that a warrant shall issue.

(c) Fine.

If a reservation, filing, or entry of an appeal is made following a sentence to pay a fine or fine and costs, the sentence shall be stayed by the judge imposing it or by a single justice of the court that will hear the appeal if there is a diligent perfection of appeal.

(d) Probation or Suspended Sentence.

An order placing a defendant on probation or suspending a sentence may be stayed if an appeal is taken.

NOTE "[T]he same factors specified in [G.L. c. 276,] § 58 [governing bail] may properly be considered under § 4. In addition, consideration should be given to danger to any other person or to the community and to the possibility of further acts of criminality during the pendency of the appeal. Finally, the judge or Justice should consider the likelihood of success on the merits of the appeal. There is no requirement, however, that he give a statement of reasons or make any particular finding or certification in order to grant or deny the stay." *Commonwealth v. Allen*, 378 Mass. 489, 498 (1979).

RULE 32
Filing and Service of Papers
(Applicable to District Court and Superior Court.)

(a) Service: When Required.

Written motions other than those which are heard ex parte, written notices, and similar papers shall be served upon each of the parties.

(b) Service: How Made.

Whenever under these rules or by order of court service is required or permitted to be made upon a party represented by an attorney, service shall be made upon the attorney, unless service upon the party himself is ordered by the court. Service upon the attorney or upon a party shall be made in the manner provided for in civil actions.

(c) Notice of Orders and Judgments.

If upon the entry of a judgment or order made on a written motion either or both of the parties are not present in court, the clerk shall immediately mail to the absent party or parties a notice of that entry and shall record the mailing in the docket.

(d) Filing.

Papers required to be served shall be filed with the court. Papers shall be filed in the manner provided for in civil actions.

(e) Additional Time after Service by Mail.

Whenever a party has the right or is required to do an act within a prescribed period after the service of a notice or other paper upon him and the notice or other paper is served upon him by mail, three days shall be added to the prescribed period.

RULE 33
Counsel for Defendants Indigent and Indigent but Able to Contribute
(Applicable to District Court and Superior Court.)

The assignment of counsel for defendants determined to be indigent or indigent but able to contribute shall be governed by the provisions of G.L. c. 211D and Supreme Judicial Court Rule 3:10.

NOTE 1   Burden of Proof. "[W]e hold that a defendant seeking appointment of counsel at public expense bears the burden of proving her indigency by a preponderance of the evidence. We further hold that S.J.C. Rule 3:10, § 1 (b) (ii), does not violate any guarantee of the Federal or State Constitution." *Commonwealth v. Porter*, 462 Mass. 724, 736 (2012).

NOTE 2a   Constitutionality and Contribution by Spouse, Girlfriend, Parent. "Requiring the defendant to prove his indigency is not unconstitutional. *See [Commonwealth v.] Porter,* [462 Mass. 724, 733 (2012)]. Consideration of the available funds of a defendant's spouse or the substantial equivalent (here, girl friend), or a defendant's parent, under S.J.C. Rule 3:10, § 1 (b) (ii) or (iii), in determining whether a defendant is indigent does not infringe on or violate the right to counsel afforded by the Sixth Amendment or art. 12." *Commonwealth v. Fico*, 462 Mass. 737, 748 (2012).

NOTE 2b   "[A] spouse has a duty to contribute to the cost of necessaries for the support and maintenance of the other spouse. G.L. c. 209, § 1. . . . Although occasionally a spouse or parent meeting the criteria of § 1(b)(ii) may refuse to pay, this fact does not in itself reduce the presumption to an arbitrary mandate." *Commonwealth v. Porter*, 462 Mass. 724, 735–36 (2012) (footnote omitted).

NOTE 3   IRA Funds. "[W]e conclude that a judge applying S.J.C. Rule 3:10 may properly consider funds held in IRAs to be available funds in the indigency determination, at least absent evidence demonstrating that a Federal statute or federally regulated retirement plan structure makes such funds in a particular case completely unavailable to a defendant as a matter of law, a burden the defendant has not met here." *Commonwealth v. Mortimer*, 462 Mass. 749, 759 (2012).

RULE 34
Report

If, prior to trial, or, with the consent of the defendant, after conviction of the defendant, a question of law arises which the trial judge determines is so important or doubtful as to require the decision of the Appeals Court, the judge may report the case so far as necessary to present the question of law arising therein. If the case is reported prior to trial, the case shall be continued for trial to await the decision of the Appeals Court.

RULE 35
Depositions to Perpetuate Testimony
(Applicable to District Court and Superior Court.)

(a) General Applicability.

Whenever due to exceptional circumstances, and after a showing of materiality and relevance, it is deemed to be in the interest of justice that the testimony of a prospective witness of the defendant or the Commonwealth be taken and preserved, the judge may at any time after the filing of a complaint or return of an indictment, upon his own motion or the motion of either party with notice to all interested persons, order that the testimony of the witness be taken by deposition and that any designated book, paper, document, record, recording, or other material not privileged be produced at the same time and place. If a witness is committed for failure to give bail to appear to testify at a trial or hearing, the judge may direct that his deposition be taken. A copy of a deposition ordered upon the judge's own motion shall be transmitted to the court by the person administering the deposition. In determining a motion filed pursuant to this rule, the judge may order a hearing or may determine whether exceptional circumstances exist and the materiality and relevance of the testimony on the basis of the supporting affidavit.

(b) Summonses.

An order to take a deposition shall authorize the issuance by the clerk of summonses pursuant to Rule 17 for the persons and objects named or described in such order. A witness whose deposition is to be taken may be required to attend at any place designated by the trial court, taking into account the convenience of the witness and the parties.

(c) Notice of Taking of Deposition.

The party on whose motion a deposition is to be taken shall give all interested persons reasonable written notice of the time and place for the taking of the deposition. If a defendant is in custody, the officer having custody of the defendant shall be notified by the court of the time and place set for taking of the deposition and shall produce the defendant at that time and place and keep him in the presence of the witness during the taking of the deposition. A defendant not in custody shall have the right to be present at the taking of a deposition, but his failure to appear after notice and without cause shall constitute a waiver of the right to be present and of all objections based upon that right.

(d) Payment of Expenses.

Whenever a deposition is taken upon motion of the Commonwealth, the court shall direct that the reasonable expenses of travel and subsistence of the defendant and his counsel and the witness be paid for by the Commonwealth. Expenses for a deposition taken upon motion of a defendant may be assessed to the defendant to be paid forthwith or in such other manner as the judge may determine.

(e) Scope of Examination.

Subject to such additional conditions as the judge may specify and except as otherwise provided in these rules, the taking of depositions in criminal cases shall be in the manner provided for in civil actions. The scope and manner of examination and cross-examination at the taking of the deposition shall be such as would be allowed in the trial itself.

(f) Objections to Deposition Testimony.

Objections to deposition testimony or evidence or parts thereof and the grounds for the objections shall be stated at the time of the taking of the deposition.

(g) Admissibility.

At a trial or upon any hearing, a part or all of a deposition, so far as it is otherwise admissible under the law of evidence, may be used as substantive evidence if the judge finds that the deponent is unavailable or if the deponent gives testimony at the trial or hearing which is inconsistent with his deposition. Any deposition may be used by any party for the purpose of contradicting or impeaching the testimony of the deponent as a witness. "Unavailable" as a witness includes situations in which the deponent:

(1) is exempt by a ruling of the judge on the ground of privilege from testifying concerning the subject matter of his deposition;

(2) persists in refusing to testify concerning the subject matter of his deposition despite an order of the judge to do so;

(3) lacks memory of the subject matter of his deposition;

(4) is unable to be present or to testify at the trial or hearing because of death or physical or mental illness or infirmity;

(5) is absent from the trial or hearing and the proponent of the deposition has been unable to procure the deponent's attendance by process or other reasonable means; or

(6) is absent from the trial or hearing and his testimony was ordered taken and preserved pursuant to Rule 6(d)(2).

A deponent is not unavailable as a witness if his exemption, refusal, claim of lack or memory, inability, or absence is due to the procurement or wrongdoing of the proponent of his deposition for the purpose of preventing the deponent from attending or testifying.

(h) Notice.

(1) *District Court.* All interested parties shall be given reasonable notice by the clerk of the time set for hearing motions filed under this rule.

(2) *Superior Court.* The moving party shall notify all interested parties of the time set for hearing motions filed under this rule at least seven days prior to the hearing.

(i) Deposition by Agreement Not Precluded.

Nothing in this rule shall preclude the taking of a deposition, orally or upon written questions, by agreement of the parties with the consent of the judge.

RULE 36
Case Management
(Applicable to District Court and Superior Court.)

(a) General Provisions.

(1) *Order of Priorities.* The trial of defendants in custody awaiting trial and defendants whose pretrial liberty is reasonably believed to present unusual risks to society shall be given preference over other criminal cases.

(2) *Function of the Court.*

(A) District Court. The court shall determine the sequence of the trial calendar.

(B) Superior Court. The court shall determine the sequence of the trial calendar after cases are selected for prosecution by the district attorney.

(b) Standards of a Speedy Trial.

The time limitations in this subdivision shall apply to all defendants as to whom the return day is on or after the effective date of these rules. Defendants arraigned prior to the effective date of these rules shall be tried within twenty-four months after such effective date.

(1) *Time Limits.* A defendant, except as provided by subdivision (d)(3) of this rule, shall be brought to trial within the following time periods, as extended by subdivision (b)(2) of this rule:

(A) during the first twelve-month period following the effective date of this rule, a defendant shall be tried within twenty-four months after the return day in the court in which case is awaiting trial.

(B) during the second such twelve-month period, a defendant shall be tried within eighteen months after the return day in the court in which the case is awaiting trial.

(C) during the third and all successive such twelve-month periods, a defendant shall be tried within twelve months after the return day in the court in which the case is awaiting trial.

(D) If a retrial of the defendant is ordered, the trial shall commence within one year after the date the action occasioning the retrial becomes final, as extended by subdivision (b)(2) of this rule. The order of an appellate court requiring a retrial is final upon the issuance by the appellate court of the rescript. In the event that the clerk of the appellate court fails to issue the rescript within the time provided for in Massachusetts Rule of Appellate Procedure 23, retrial shall commence within one year after the date when the rescript should have issued.

If a defendant is not brought to trial within the time limits of this subdivision, as extended by subdivision, (b)(2), he shall be entitled upon motion to a dismissal of the charges.

(2) *Excluded Periods.* The following periods shall be excluded in computing the time within which the trial of any offense must commence:

(A) Any period of delay resulting from other proceedings concerning the defendant, including, but not limited to:

(i) delay resulting from an examination of the defendant, and hearing on, his mental competency, or physical incapacity;

(ii) delay resulting from a stay of the proceedings due to an examination or treatment of the defendant pursuant to section 47 of chapter 123 of the General Laws;

(iii) delay resulting from a trial with respect to other charges against the defendant, which period shall run from the commencement of such other trial until fourteen days after an acquittal or imposition of sentence;

(iv) delay resulting from interlocutory appeals

(v) delay resulting from hearings on pretrial motions;

(vi) delay resulting from proceedings relating to transfer to or from other divisions or counties pursuant to Rule 37;

(vii) delay reasonably attributable to any period, not to exceed thirty days, during which any proceeding concerning the defendant is actually under advisement.

(B) Any period of delay resulting from the absence or unavailability of the defendant or an essential witness. A defendant or an essential witness shall be considered absent when his whereabouts are unknown and he is attempting to avoid apprehension or prosecution or his whereabouts cannot be determined by due diligence. A defendant or an essential witness shall be considered unavailable whenever his whereabouts are known but his presence for trial cannot be obtained by due diligence or he resists appearing at or being returned for trial.

(C) Any period of delay resulting from the fact that the defendant is mentally incompetent or physically unable to stand trial.

(D) If the complaint or indictment is dismissed by the prosecution and thereafter a charge is filed against the defendant for the same or a related offense, any period of delay from the date the charge was dismissed to the date the time limitation would commence to run as to the subsequent charge.

(E) A reasonable period of delay when the defendant is joined for trial with a codefendant as to whom the time for trial has not run and there is no cause for granting a severance.

(F) Any period of delay resulting from a continuance granted by a judge on his own motion or at the request of the defendant or his counsel or at the request of the prosecutor, if the judge granted the continuance on the basis of his findings that the ends of justice served by taking such action outweighed the best interests of the public and the defendant in a speedy trial. No period of delay resulting from a continuance granted by the court in accordance with this paragraph shall be excludable under this subdivision unless the judge sets forth in the record of the case, either orally or in writing, his reasons for finding that the ends of justice served by the granting of the continuance outweigh the best interests of the public and the defendant in a speedy trial.

(G) Any period of time between the day on which a defendant or his counsel and the prosecuting attorney agree in writing that the defendant will plead guilty or nolo contendere to the charges and such time as the judge accepts or rejects the plea arrangement.

(H) Any period of time between the day on which the defendant enters a plea of guilty and such time as an order of the judge permitting the withdrawal of the plea becomes final.

(3) *Computation of Time Limits.* In computing any time limit other than an excluded period, the day of the act or event which causes a designated period of time to begin to run shall not be included. Computation of an excluded period shall include both the first and the last day of the excludable act or event.

(c) Dismissal for Prejudicial Delay.

Notwithstanding the fact that a defendant is not entitled to a dismissal under subdivision (b) of this rule, a defendant shall upon motion be entitled to a dismissal where the judge after an examination and consideration of all attendant circumstances determines that: (1) the conduct of the prosecuting attorney in bringing the defendant to trial has been unreasonably lacking in diligence and (2) this conduct on the part

of the prosecuting attorney has resulted in prejudice to the defendant.

(d) Special Procedures: Persons Serving Term of Imprisonment.

(1) *General Provisions.* A person serving a term of imprisonment either within or without the prosecuting jurisdiction is entitled to all safeguards afforded him under subdivisions (a), (b), and (c) of this rule in the conduct of any criminal proceeding, subject to the limitations stated herein.

(2) *Persons Detained Within the Commonwealth.* Any person who is detained within the Commonwealth upon the unexecuted portion of a sentence imposed pursuant to a criminal proceeding is entitled to be tried upon any untried indictment or complaint pending against him in any court in this Commonwealth within the time prescribed by subdivision (b) of this rule.

(3) *Persons Detained Outside the Commonwealth.* Any person who is detained outside the Commonwealth upon the unexecuted portion of a sentence imposed pursuant to a criminal proceeding, and against whom an untried indictment or complaint is pending within the Commonwealth shall, subsequent to the filing of a detainer, be notified by the prosecutor by mail of such charges and of his right to demand a speedy trial. If the defendant pursuant to such notification does demand trial, the person having custody shall so certify to the prosecutor, who shall promptly seek to obtain the presence of the defendant for trial. If the prosecutor has unreasonably delayed (A) in causing a detainer to be filed with the official having custody of the defendant, or (B) in seeking to obtain the defendant's presence for trial, and the defendant has been prejudiced thereby, the pending charges against the defendant shall be dismissed.

(e) Effect of a Dismissal.

A dismissal of any charge ordered pursuant to any provision of this rule shall apply to all related offenses.

(f) Case Status Reports.

(1) *District Court.* The First Justice of each division of the District Court shall be advised periodically by the clerk of the status of all cases which have been pending in that court for six months or longer. The report shall be transmitted to the Administrative Justice for the District Court Department.

(2) *Superior Court.* The Administrative Justice for the Superior Court Department shall be notified by the clerk for each county of the status of all cases which have been pending in that court for six months or longer within the following time periods:

(A) for the first twelve-month period following the effective date of this rule, sixty days after the last day of a sitting;

(B) for the second such twelve-month period, forty-five days after the last day of a sitting;

(C) for the third and all successive such twelve-month periods, thirty days after the last day of a sitting.

Such notice shall include the number of the case, the name of the defendant, the offense charged, the name of the defense counsel, if any, and the name of the prosecutor.

NOTE 1a   Speedy Trial Clock. "We conclude that a defendant's right to a speedy trial, at least under art. 11, attaches when a criminal complaint issues. Therefore, arrest, indictment, or a criminal complaint issued pursuant to Massachusetts law, whichever comes first, will start the speedy trial clock. Any cases to the contrary are no longer good law. *See, e.g., Commonwealth v. Gove,* [366 Mass. 351 (1974)]. The constitutional right to a speedy trial attaches because the subject of a criminal complaint is undoubtedly an 'accused,' and is not merely in 'the preaccusation period when a police investigation is ongoing.' *Commonwealth v. Gove, supra* at 357, citing *Commonwealth v. Jones*, 360 Mass. 498 (1971). A criminal complaint is a formal charging document in Massachusetts. *See* Mass. R. Crim. P. 3(a). The fact that a complaint may be followed by an indictment, *see* Mass. R. Crim. P. 3(b), does not render a complaint any less of a formal accusation. Moreover, art. 11 does not distinguish between the types of cases (misdemeanor or felony; within the jurisdiction of the District or Superior Court) to which the right to a speedy trial attaches; it states that the right to a speedy trial applies to '[e]very subject of the [C]ommonwealth.' Art. 11 of the Massachusetts Declaration of Rights. *See Jacobson v. Winter*, 91 Idaho 11, 14, 415 P.2d 297 (1966) (same, as to Idaho constitution). Of perhaps greatest significance, the subject of a criminal complaint typically faces the same 'anxiety, concern, economic debilitation, public scorn and restraint on liberty' that the right to a speedy trial is intended to guard against. *Commonwealth v. Gove, supra* at 360. *See Commonwealth v. Look*, [379 Mass. 893, 903 (1980)]. For these reasons, 'no logical conclusion can be reached other than that the time within which an accused is to be secured in his right to a speedy trial must be computed from the time the complaint is filed against him.' *Jacobson v. Winter, supra.* Therefore, the clock on the defendant's art. 11 right to a speedy trial began running on September 16, 1991, the date on which the District Court issued the criminal complaint charging him with rape and unarmed burglary. *See Commonwealth v. Willis*, [21 Mass. App. Ct. 963, 964(1986)]" (footnotes omitted). *Commonwealth v. Butler*, 464 Mass. 706, 712–13 (2013).

NOTE 1b "Delay in which the defendant acquiesces or from which he benefits should be excluded in measuring the length of any delay. A failure to object to a continuance or other delay constitutes acquiescence." *Commonwealth v. Tanner*, 417 Mass. 1, 3 (1994) (citation omitted). *See also Commonwealth v. Marable*, 427 Mass. 504 (1998).

NOTE 1c "Certainly the fifty-three month span between the defendant's arraignment and his trial is sufficient to invoke a constitutionally-based speedy trial analysis. . . . [T]he defendant agreed to various continuances and sought others. The record does not indicate the defendant's zealous pursuit of his right to a speedy trial. Most important is the fact that the defendant cannot show that he was significantly prejudiced by the delay." *Commonwealth v. Lanigan*, 419 Mass. 15, 18–19 (1994).

NOTE 1d "Rule 36(b), as it applies to this case, requires that a defendant shall be tried within twelve months after the 'return day,' and if the defendant is not tried within that period, as it may be extended by subdivision (b)(2) of the rule, the defendant 'shall be entitled upon motion to a dismissal of the charges.' Rule 36(b)(1). "'Return Day' means the day upon which a defendant is ordered by summons to first appear or, if under arrest, does first appear before a court to answer to the charges against him, whichever is earlier.' Mass.R.Crim.P. 2(b)(15), 378 Mass. 844 (1979). Since this defendant was under arrest, the date of his arraignment, August 30, 1983, was the return day, see *Barry v. Commonwealth*, 390 Mass. 285, 291 (1983), and he was entitled to be tried within twelve months of that date unless the Commonwealth established that further delay was justified. The burden of proof relative to justification is on the Commonwealth. *Commonwealth v. Campbell*, 401 Mass. 698, 702, 704 (1988). *Barry v. Commonwealth, supra* at 291, 294.

"The commencement of trial after the expiration of the twelve-month period may be justified not only by the provision in rule 36(b)(2) for '[e]xcluded [p]eriods,' but also by the Commonwealth's demonstration that the defendant acquiesced in other periods of delay, or they benefited him or he was responsible for them. *Commonwealth v. Campbell, supra* at 702 (citing *Commonwealth v. Farris*, 390 Mass. 300, 305 (1983), and *Barry v. Commonwealth, supra* at 295)."

Commonwealth v. Mattos, 404 Mass. 672, 674–75 (1989).

NOTE 1e **Judicial Dismissal versus Nolle Prosequi.** "[W]e recognize a relevant distinction between a judicial dismissal and an entry of a nolle prosequi. A nolle prosequi is a strategic decision by the Commonwealth to cease pursuing charges. Its entry is thus an affirmative exercise of a prosecutorial tool to discontinue prosecution. In contrast, a judicial dismissal, even one without prejudice, signals that the Commonwealth has not met its prosecutorial burden. . . . The delay that results from the dismissal and subsequent rearraignment is attributable to the Commonwealth. The defendant's relief from criminal charges is only temporary, and the prolonging of the process is in part due to the Commonwealth's failure to fulfil its own rule 36 obligations to move the matter along diligently. We cannot permit the Commonwealth to earn itself more time simply by being unprepared." *Commonwealth v. Denehy*, 466 Mass. 723, 734 (2014) (citations omitted).

NOTE 1f **Resetting versus Resuming.** "We conclude that, as a general rule, the speedy trial clock 'resumes' once a defendant is indicted following the dismissal of formal charges such that time between an initial, formal charge (or other triggering event such as an arrest) and dismissal counts against the government for speedy trial purposes after charges are reinstated." *Commonwealth v. Butler*, 464 Mass. 706, 713 (2013).

NOTE 2 **Appellate Procedure.** "This appeal [by the Commonwealth] was not entered in the Appeals Court for more than two years after the notice of appeal was filed. . . . [While] it is clear that the glacial pace with which this case proceeded toward appellate resolution is not what is contemplated by the rules of appellate procedure [the defendant's motion to dismiss should not be allowed]. . . .

"The guaranty of a speedy trial set forth in the Sixth Amendment to the United States Constitution (and art. 11 of the Massachusetts Declaration of Rights) is not read as applying to the appellate process. . . .

"[T]o prevail on his constitutional due process argument, the defendant must show that the delay, which was clearly inordinate, was significantly prejudicial."

Commonwealth v. Hudson, 404 Mass. 282, 283–84, 285 (1989) (citations and quotation marks omitted).

NOTE 3 "Where a criminal defendant charged with first degree murder was led reasonably to believe she would not be tried by the prosecutor's unconditional promises not to oppose her plea of guilty to manslaughter and to recommend no incarceration beyond time served, she was held not to have acquiesced, when the promises were withdrawn, to a nearly three-year delay in her trial, and thus her motion to dismiss under Mass.R.Crim.P. 36 (b) was correctly allowed." *Commonwealth v. Campbell*, 401 Mass. 698 (1988) (syllabus).

RULE 37
Transfer of Cases
(Applicable to District Court and Superior Court.)
(a) Transfer for Plea and Sentence.

(1) *District Court.* A defendant against whom a complaint is pending and who appears in District Court, whether under arrest or pursuant to a summons, and against whom a complaint is pending in a division other than that in which he appears, may state in writing that he wishes to plead guilty or nolo contendere, to waive trial in the division in which the other complaint is pending, and to consent to disposition of the case in the division in which he appears. The District Court in which the defendant appears may order that the other complaint be transferred for disposition, subject to the written approval of the prosecutor in each division.

(2) *Superior Court.* A defendant against whom a complaint or indictment is pending and who appears in Superior Court, whether under arrest or pursuant to a summons, and against whom a complaint or indictment is pending in a county other than that in which he appears, may state in writing

that he wishes to plead guilty or nolo contendere, to waive trial in the county in which the other complaint or indictment is pending, and to consent to disposition of the case in the county in which he appears. The Superior Court in which the defendant appears may order that the other complaint or indictment be transferred for disposition, subject to the written approval of the prosecuting attorney in each county.

(3) *Effect of Not Guilty Plea.* If after a proceeding has been transferred pursuant to subdivision (a) of this rule the defendant pleads not guilty, the clerk shall return the papers transmitted pursuant to subdivision (c) of this rule to the court in which the prosecution was commenced, and the proceeding shall be restored to the docket of that court.

(b) Transfer for Trial.

(1) *Transfer for Prejudice.* A judge upon his own motion or the motion of a defendant or the Commonwealth made prior to trial may order the transfer of a case to another division or county for trial if the court is satisfied that there exists in the community where the prosecution is pending so great a prejudice against the defendant that he may not there obtain a fair and impartial trial.

(2) *Transfer of Other Cases.* A judge, upon motion of a defendant made pursuant to subdivision (3) or (4) of Rule 9(a), and after taking into account the convenience of the court, the parties, and their witnesses, may with the written approval of the prosecuting attorney in each division or county order the transfer and consolidation for trial of any or all charges pending against the defendant in the several divisions or counties of the Commonwealth.

(c) Proceedings on Transfer.

Upon receipt of the defendant's statement and the written approval of the prosecutor required by this rule, the clerk of the court in which a complaint or indictment is pending shall transfer the papers in the case and any bail taken to the clerk of the court to which the case is transferred. The clerk of the transferee court shall make immediate entry of the case upon the docket of that court and shall so notify the clerk of the transferor court so that the case may be closed on the docket of that court. The prosecution shall continue in the transferee court.

RULE 38
Disability of Judge
(Applicable to Superior Court and jury sessions in District Court.)

(a) During Trial.

If by reason of death, sickness, or other disability the judge before whom a jury trial has commenced is unable to proceed with the trial, any other judge of that court or properly assigned to that court, upon certifying in writing that he has familiarized himself with the record of the trial, may proceed with and finish the trial.

(b) Receipt of Verdict.

Any judge of a court or any judge properly assigned to that court may receive a verdict of the jury.

(c) After Verdict or Finding of Guilt.

If by reason of absence, unavailability, death, sickness, or other disability the judge before whom the defendant has been tried is unable to perform the duties to be performed by the judge after a verdict or finding of guilt, any other judge of that court or properly assigned to that court may perform those duties; but if the other judge is satisfied that he cannot perform those duties because he did not preside at the trial or

for any other reason, he may, in his discretion or upon motion of the defendant, order a new trial.

NOTE   **Rule 38(c).** "In reliance upon Mass. R. Crim. P. 38(c), 378 Mass. 916 (1979), Baro argues that the sentencing judge committed reversible error because he did not certify in writing his familiarity with the trial record, had not reviewed the trial transcript (still uncompleted), and did not discuss the reason for the unavailability of the trial judge. Rule 38(c) does not require the new judge to certify his familiarity with the trial record; it allows substitution for a trial judge who 'is unable to perform [his] duties' not only by reason of 'death, sickness, or other disability,' but also 'by reason of absence [or] unavailability'; and vests the newly assigned judge with the 'discretion' to order a new trial if he 'is satisfied that he cannot perform [his] duties because he did not preside at the trial or for any other reason.'" *Commonwealth v. Baro*, 73 Mass. App. Ct. 218, 224 (2008).

RULE 39
Records of Foreign Proceedings and Notice of Foreign Law
(Applicable to District Court and Superior Court.)

(a) Records of Courts of Other States or of the United States.

The records and judicial proceedings of a court of another state or of the United States shall be competent evidence in this Commonwealth if authenticated by the attestation of the clerk or other officer who has charge of the records of such court under its seal.

(b) Notice of Foreign Law.

The court shall upon request take judicial notice of the law of the United States or of any state, territory, or dependency thereof or of a foreign county whenever it shall be material.

RULE 40
Proof of Official Records
(Applicable to District Court and Superior Court.)

(a) Authentication.

(1) *Domestic.* An official record kept within the Commonwealth, or any entry therein, when admissible for any purpose, may be evidenced by an official publication thereof or by a copy attested by the officer having legal custody of the record, or by his deputy. If the record is kept in any other state, district, commonwealth, territory or insular possession of the United States, or within the Panama Canal Zone or the Trust Territory of the Pacific Islands, any such copy shall be accompanied by a certificate that such custodial officer has the custody. This certificate may be made by a judge of a court of record of the district or political subdivision in which the record is kept, authenticated by the seal of the court, or may be made by any public officer having a seal of office and having official duties in the district or political subdivision in which the record is kept, authenticated by the seal of his office.

(2) *Foreign.* A foreign official record, or an entry therein, when admissible for any purpose, may be evidenced by an official publication thereof, or a copy thereof, attested by a person authorized to make the attestation, and accompanied by a final certification as to the genuineness of the signature and official position (i) of the attesting person, or (ii) of any foreign official whose certificate of genuineness of signature and official position relates to the attestation or is in a chain of certificates of genuineness of signature and official position relating to the attestation. A final certification may be made by a secretary of embassy or legation, consul general, consul, vice consul, or consular agent of the United States, or a diplomatic or consular official of the foreign country assigned or accredited

to the United States. If reasonable opportunity has been given to all parties to investigate the authenticity and accuracy of the documents, the court may, for good cause shown, (i) admit an attested copy without final certification, or (ii) permit the foreign official record to be evidenced by an attested summary with or without a final certification.

(b) Lack of Record.

A written statement that after diligent search no record or entry of a specified tenor is found to exist in the records designated by the statement, authenticated as provided in subdivision (a)(1) of this rule in the case of a domestic record, or complying with the requirements of subdivision (a)(2) of this rule for a summary in the case of a foreign record, is admissible as evidence that the records contain no such record or entry.

(c) Other Proof.

This rule does not prevent the proof, by any other method authorized by law, of the existence of, or the lack of, an official record, or of entry, or lack of entry therein.

NOTE "We take this opportunity, however, to recommend strongly that copies of GPS records offered in future revocation proceedings be properly attested and certified by an appropriate custodial officer. *See* Mass. R. Crim. P. 40 (a), 378 Mass. 917 (1979). Such a certification will reduce, if not completely eliminate, some of the legitimate concerns with regard to the authenticity of the GPS records that were well raised during the revocation proceeding in this case." *Commonwealth v. Thissell*, 457 Mass. 191, 199 (2010) (citation omitted).

RULE 41

Interpreters and Experts

(Applicable to District Court and Superior Court.)

The judge may appoint an interpreter or expert if justice so requires and may determine the reasonable compensation for such services and direct payment therefor.

NOTE "Appointment of an interpreter lies within the sound discretion of the trial judge and will not be disturbed on appeal unless there was an abuse of that discretion. If two or more parties require an interpreter in the same language, the better practice is to have one interpreter and to pace the examination of the witnesses to allow time for the translation, thereby preventing parties from receiving differing versions of the testimony. . . . [Lastly,] the *jury* should be instructed that it is the interpreted testimony in English that is evidence and not their own translations." *Commonwealth v. Esteves*, 46 Mass. App. Ct. 339, 345 (1999), *rev'd on other grounds*, 429 Mass. 636 (1999) (citations and quotation marks omitted).

RULE 42

Clerical Mistakes

(Applicable to District Court and Superior Court.)

Clerical mistakes in judgments, orders, or other parts of the record and errors therein arising from oversight or omission may be corrected by the court at any time of its own initiative or on the motion of any party and after such notice, if any, as the court orders. During the pendency of an appeal, such mistakes may be corrected before the appeal is docketed in the appellate court, and thereafter while the appeal is pending may be corrected with leave of the appellate court.

RULE 43

Summary Contempt

(Amended effective Jan. 1, 2014.) (Applicable to District Court and Superior Court.)

(a) When Warranted.

A criminal contempt may be punished summarily when

(1) summary punishment is necessary to maintain order in the courtroom;

(2) the contemptuous conduct occurred in the presence of, and was witnessed by, the presiding judge;

(3) the presiding judge enters a preliminary finding at the time of the contemptuous conduct that a criminal contempt occurred; and

(4) the punishment for each contempt does not exceed three months imprisonment and a fine of $2,000.

(b) Procedure.

(1) Upon making a preliminary finding that a criminal contempt occurred, the presiding judge shall give the alleged contemnor notice of the charges and shall hold a hearing to provide at least a summary opportunity for the alleged contemnor to produce evidence and argument relevant to guilt or punishment. For good cause shown, the presiding judge may continue the hearing to enable the contemnor to obtain counsel or evidence.

(2) The presiding judge may order the alleged contemnor held, subject to bail and/or conditions of release, pending the hearing provided for in subsection (b)(1) if the judge finds it necessary to maintain order in the courtroom or to assure the alleged contemnor's appearance.

(3)(i) If, after the hearing provided for in subsection (b)(1), the presiding judge determines that summary contempt is not appropriate because the appropriate punishment for the alleged contempt exceeds three months imprisonment and a fine of $2,000, the judge shall refer the alleged contemnor for prosecution under Rule 44. If necessary to maintain order in the courtroom or to assure the alleged contemnor's appearance, the judge may order the alleged contemnor held, subject to bail and/or conditions of release, for a reasonable period of time, not to exceed 15 days absent good cause shown, pending the issuance of a complaint or indictment under Rule 44(a).

(ii) If, after the hearing, the presiding judge determines that summary contempt is not appropriate because one or more of the requirements in subsection (a)(1), (a)(2), or (a)(3) is not satisfied, or for another reason, the judge shall discharge the alleged contemnor. The judge, in his or her discretion, may refer the matter to the government for investigation and possible prosecution, and nothing in this subsection shall preclude such investigation or prosecution, whether undertaken in response to the judge's referral or independently.

(iii) If, after the hearing, the presiding judge determines that summary contempt is appropriate, the judge shall make a finding on the record of summary contempt, setting forth the facts upon which that finding is based. The court shall further announce a judgment of summary contempt in open court, enter that judgment on the court's docket, and notify the contemnor of the right to appeal. The judge may defer sentencing, or the execution of any sentence, where the interests of orderly courtroom procedure and substantial justice require. If necessary to maintain order in the courtroom or to assure the contemnor's appearance, the judge may order the contemnor held, subject to bail and/or conditions of release, pending sentencing.

(c) Appeal.

A contemnor may appeal a judgment of summary contempt to the Appeals Court.

Reporter's Notes (2014). This amendment to Rule 43 is intended to clarify the procedures by which a judge can impose summary punishment for criminal contempt or, alternatively, refer an alleged contemnor for prosecution by complaint or indictment under Rule 44. *See Vizcaino v. Commonwealth*, 462 Mass. 266, 279 n.11 (2012) (suggesting a need for clarification in the operation of Rule 43). Amended Rule 43 resolves ambiguities concerning the prerequisites for summary punishment of contempt and the procedural steps in a summary-contempt proceeding. Further, amended Rule 43(b) explicitly recognizes discretionary authority that judges have presumably enjoyed in summary contempt proceedings, principally the common-law authority to hold an accused contemnor if necessary to maintain courtroom order or to assure his or her appearance at any subsequent proceeding. The amended rule also increases the maximum fine permitted from $500 to $2,000.

Rule 43(a) When Warranted

Amended Rule 43(a), like its predecessor, provides for the four conditions necessary to warrant summary punishment for contempt. Such punishment must be necessary to maintain courtroom order; the contemptuous conduct must occur in the presence of and be witnessed by the judge; the judge must enter a finding of contempt at the time it occurs; and the punishment cannot exceed three months' imprisonment and a fine of $2,000. As discussed below, amended Rule 43(a)(3) clarifies an ambiguity in former Rule 43(a), the amended rule expressly providing that this threshold, contemporaneous finding of contempt be preliminary. As such, it gives notice to the alleged contemnor of the charges, but it is subject to reconsideration after affording the alleged contemnor an opportunity to be heard as required under Rule 43(b)(1).

Former Rule 43(a)(2) referred to the threshold, contemporaneous finding as a "judgment of contempt," leading to possible confusion between it and the final "judgment of contempt" which, under former Rule 43(b), the judge could make only after "giv[ing] the contemnor notice of the charges and at least a summary opportunity to adduce evidence or argument relevant to guilt or punishment." Mass. R. Crim. P. 43, 378 Mass. 919 (1979). *See Vizcaino v. Commonwealth*, 462 Mass. 266, 276 (2012) (holding that an opportunity to be heard followed by entry of the judgment on docket are necessary predicates to a Rule 43 judgment of summary contempt); *Commonwealth v. Segal*, 401 Mass. 95, 99–100 (1987) (same). Amended Rule 43(a)(3) makes it clear that the judge's threshold, contemporaneous finding of contempt is preliminary. While the Supreme Judicial Court had read former Rule 43(a)(2) to provide that this preliminary "judgment of contempt" be written, *see Vizcaino v. Commonwealth*, 462 Mass. 266, 272 & n.7 (2012) (interpreting Rule 43(a)'s contemporaneity requirement to permit reasonable, minor delays in preparing Rule 43(a)(2)'s written judgment of contempt), amended Rule 43(a)(2) neither provides nor contemplates that the preliminary finding of contempt be written. Such a requirement seems unnecessary given that the judge's finding is in open court and presumably subject to transcription if necessary. Moreover, requiring a written finding could delay both the alleged contemnor's opportunity to be heard and the trial in which the contemptuous conduct occurred. Finally, as noted, the amended rule increases the maximum fine for summary contempt from $500 to $2,000, an increase that partially accounts for the inflation that has occurred since the rule's adoption in 1979. This maximum fine is well within the punishment that may be imposed without implicating the Sixth Amendment right to a jury trial. *See Blanton v. City of N. Las Vegas, Nev.*, 489 U.S. 538, 544–45 (1989) (holding no Sixth Amendment right to jury trial for offense the maximum punishment for which was six months imprisonment and $1,000 fine, noting the possible fine was "well below" the $5,000 federal benchmark utilized in identifying petty offenses that can be tried without a jury); *Furtado v. Furtado*, 380 Mass. 137, 142 n.5 (1980) (noting Supreme Judicial Court has not interpreted article 12 to impose a stricter jury-trial requirement).

Rule 43(b) Procedure

As did former Rule 43(b), amended Rule 43(b)(1) provides that, following the preliminary finding of contempt under Rule 43(a)(3), the judge must conduct a hearing, affording the accused contemnor at least a summary opportunity to produce evidence and/or argument relevant to guilt or punishment. The amended rule further gives the judge discretion, for good cause shown, to continue the hearing so that the accused contemnor can obtain evidence or counsel.

Rule 43(b)(2) authorizes the judge to hold the accused contemnor, subject to bail and/or conditions of release, pending the summary-contempt hearing if necessary to maintain courtroom order or to assure the contemnor's appearance. Judges presumably had such common-law authority under former Rule 43, *see In re Terry*, 128 U.S. 289, 307–13 (1888) (recognizing longstanding judicial authority to apprehend, commit, and summarily punish one who engages in contemptuous conduct in the judge's presence); *see also* G.L. c. 276, § 57 (authorizing justices of the superior and district courts to admit a committed prisoner to bail upon finding that such release will reasonably assure the prisoner's future appearance before the court), but the amended rule makes it explicit.

Amended Rule 43(b)(3) sets out the respective procedures for the three possible results of the Rule 43(b)(1) hearing.

First, under Rule 43(b)(3)(i), if the judge determines that summary contempt is not appropriate because the accused contemnor deserves greater punishment than that permitted for summary contempt, the judge must refer the alleged contemnor for prosecution by complaint or indictment under Rule 44. In that event, if necessary to maintain courtroom order or the appearance of the accused, the rule recognizes the judge's common-law authority to hold the alleged contemnor subject to bail and/or conditions of release for up to 15 days, extendable for 3 good cause shown, pending issuance of the contempt complaint or indictment under Rule 44(a). Although the judge has wide discretion in determining what constitutes good cause to extend the 15-day limitation, it would ordinarily include a superior court referral in which there is no grand jury in session during that 15-day period.

Second, Rule 43(b)(3)(ii) covers the case in which, after considering the facts and arguments presented in the summary-contempt hearing, the judge decides for whatever reason that summary contempt is not appropriate. This possibility, although inferable under former Rule 43(b), is here explicit. Under Rule 43(b)(3)(ii), such a decision to forgo further proceedings and to discharge the alleged contemnor does not bar the alleged contemnor's prosecution for the alleged contempt. The rule explicitly provides that, in spite of this termination of summary-contempt proceedings, the judge has discretion to refer the matter to the government for investigation and possible prosecution, and that, even in the absence of such a judicial referral, the government may investigate and prosecute the alleged contempt. *Cf. Vizcaino*, 462 Mass. at 274–75 (holding that, where judge had not entered summary contempt judgment on the court's docket as required by Rule 43(b), further prosecution for nonsummary contempt under Rule 44 not barred by double jeopardy).

Third, Rule 43(b)(3)(iii) sets out the procedure if, after the hearing, the judge decides that summary punishment for the contempt is appropriate. The judge must make a finding of summary contempt on the record, setting out the facts on which it is based. Unlike former Rule 43(b), this finding need not be written; a transcript of the factual finding provides an adequate record for purposes of appeal. The rule further provides that, as in any criminal conviction, the court must announce the summary-contempt judgment in open court, enter the judgment on the docket, and notify the contemnor of the right to appeal. *See* Mass. R. Crim. P. 28(a), 378 Mass. 898 (1979). As did former Rule 43(b), Rule 43(b)(3)(iii) allows the judge discretion to defer summary-contempt sentencing or its execution where orderly courtroom procedure and substantial justice require. Although the rule does not explicitly limit the purpose or length of such sentence deferral, as was so under former Rule 43(b), it ordinarily would be reserved for cases of summary contempt by one of the parties or lawyers in the trial, *see Taylor v. Hayes*, 418 U.S. 488, 497–98 (1974), and imposition or execution of sentence would be deferred until after the trial is completed. The rule further permits the judge, if necessary, to order the contemnor held, subject to bail and/or conditions of release, pending sentencing.

Rule 43(c), providing for the right of appeal to the Appeals Court, remains in substance unchanged.

3

NOTE 1   See G.L. c. 233, § 20H.

NOTE 2   Warning unnecessary in cases of flagrant conduct. "The Supreme Judicial Court has additionally held that unless the conduct is 'flagrant,' a prior warning is required as a prerequisite to treating the alleged contempt summarily. *Sussman v. Commonwealth*, 374 Mass. 692, 697 (1978). . . .

"A warning is not a condition precedent to criminal contempt in all cases . . . .

"We conclude here that the defendant's conduct, although not immediately interfering with the business of the court, was sufficiently flagrant so as to undermine the authority of the court to constitute contempt." *Commonwealth v. Brunnell*, 65 Mass. App. Ct. 423, 424–28 (2006) (summary contempt proceeding appropriate where defendant yelled, "F*** you, judge; f*** you . . . . You know what, judge? You can s*** my f***** d***" after denial of petition for bail).

RULE 44
Contempt
(Applicable to District Court and Superior Court.)
(a) Nature of the Proceedings.

All criminal contempts not adjudicated pursuant to Rule 43 shall be prosecuted by means of complaint, unless the prosecutor elects to proceed by indictment. Except as otherwise provided by these rules, the case shall proceed as a criminal case in the court in which the contempt is alleged to have been committed.

(b) Special Provisions for District Court.

The District Court shall have jurisdiction to try all contempts committed therein except those prosecuted by indictment. Whenever a contemnor asserts his right to a jury trial in District Court, the trial shall be held before a jury in District Court. The contemnor's only right of appeal shall be to the Appeals Court.

(c) Disqualification of the Judge.

The contempt charges shall be heard by a judge other than the trial judge whenever the nature of the alleged contemptuous conduct is such as is likely to affect the trial judge's impartiality.

RULE 45
Removal of the Disruptive Defendant
(Applicable to District Court and Superior Court.)
(a) Removal of Defendant.

Upon the direction of the trial judge, a defendant may be removed from the courtroom during his trial when his conduct has become so disruptive that the trial cannot proceed in an orderly manner. Gagging or shackling may be employed if the trial judge has found such restraint reasonably necessary to maintain order. If the trial judge orders such restraint, he shall enter into the record of the case the reasons therefor. Whenever physical restraint of a defendant or witness occurs in the presence of the jury trying the case, or whenever the defendant is removed, the judge, at the request of the defendant, shall instruct the jury that such restraint or removal is not to be considered in assessing the proof and determining guilt.

(b) Defendant's Rights After Removal.

A defendant once removed shall be required to be present in the court building while the trial is in progress. At the time of his removal he shall be advised that he has the right to be returned to the courtroom upon his request and assurances of good behavior. Notwithstanding the failure of a defendant to request to be returned to the courtroom, he shall be returned to the courtroom, at appropriate intervals in the absence of the jury, and shall be advised in open court that he will be permitted to remain upon the giving of assurances of good behavior.

RULE 46
Time
(Applicable to District Court and Superior Court.)
(a) Computation.

In computing any period of time prescribed or allowed by these rules, by order of court, or by any applicable statute or rule, the day of the act, event, or default after which the designated period of time begins to run shall not be included. The last day of the period so computed shall be included, unless it is a Saturday, a Sunday, or legal holiday, in which event the period runs until the end of the next day which is not a Saturday, a Sunday, or a legal holiday. When the period of time prescribed or allowed is less than seven days, intermediate Saturdays, Sundays, and legal holidays shall be excluded in the computation. As used in this rule, "legal holiday" includes any day appointed as a holiday by the President or the Congress of the United States or so designated by the laws of the Commonwealth.

(b) Enlargement.

When by these rules or by a notice given thereunder or by order or rule of court an act is required or allowed to be done at or within a specified time, the court for cause shown may at any time in its discretion (1) with or without motion or notice order the period enlarged if a request therefor is made before the expiration of the period originally prescribed or as extended by a previous order; or (2) upon motion made after the expiration of the specified period permit the act to be done where the failure to act was the result of excusable neglect; or (3) permit the act to be done by stipulation of the parties; but the court may not extend the time for taking any action under Rules 25 and 29 except to the extent and under the conditions stated herein.

(c) For Motions, Affidavits in Superior Court.

A written motion, other than one which may be heard ex parte, and notices of the hearing thereof shall be served on all interested parties not later than seven days prior to the hearing unless a different period is fixed by these rules or by order of the court. For cause shown, such an order may issue upon an ex parte application. When a motion is supported by affidavit, the affidavit shall be served with the motion. Opposing affidavits shall be served not later than one day before the hearing, unless the court permits them to be served at a later time.

RULE 47
Special Magistrates
(Applicable to Superior Court.)

The justices of the Superior Court may appoint special magistrates to preside over criminal proceedings in the Superior Court. Such special magistrates shall have the power to preside at arraignments, to set bail, to assign counsel, to supervise pretrial conferences, to mark up pretrial motions for hearing, to make findings and report those findings and other issues to the presiding justice or Administrative Justice, and to perform such other duties as may be authorized by order of the Superior Court. The doings of special magistrates shall be endorsed upon the record of the case. Special magistrates shall be compensated in the same manner as is provided by the General Laws for the compensation of masters in civil cases.

RULE 48
Sanctions
(Applicable to District Court and Superior Court.)

A wilful violation by counsel of the provisions of these rules or of an order issued pursuant to these rules shall subject counsel to such sanctions as the court shall deem appropriate, including citation for contempt or the imposition of costs or a fine.

PART 4

Rules of the Superior Court

Rule
1   Effect of These Rules
2   Appearances
3   Authority to Appear
4   Postponement
5   Jurors
6   Peremptory Challenges of Jurors
7   Openings; Use of Pleadings
8   Objections to Evidence
8A   Notes by Jurors
9   Motions and Interlocutory Matters
9A–E   Omitted
10   Extra Charges by Officers
11   Attorney Not to Become Bail or Surety
12   Attorneys as Witnesses
13   Hospital Records
14   Exhibits Other than Hospital Records
15   Eliminating Requirement for Verification by Affidavit
16   Writ of Protection
17   Recording Devices
18–52   Omitted
53   Assignment of Counsel
54   Experts in Criminal Cases
55   Experts in Criminal and Delinquent Children Cases
56   Conditions of Probation
57   Term of Probation
58   Term of Orders for Payment
59   Waiver of Indictment
60   Plea of Not Guilty
61   Motions for Return of Property and to Suppress Evidence
61A   Motions for Post-Conviction Relief
62   Withdrawal of Appearance
63   Court Reporter in Grand Jury Proceedings
64   Appellate Division Procedure and Forms
65   Claim of Appeal
66–67   Repealed
68   Arguments
69   Examination of Witnesses
70   Requests for Instructions or Rulings
71   Depositions—Commissions
72   Depositions—Manner of Taking
73–77   Omitted
Superior Court Standing Orders
1-15   Participation in Juror Voir Dire by Attorneys and Self-
        Represented Parties
2-15   Exceptions to Notice Requirement of Trial Court Rule VIII,
        Uniform Rules on Impoundment Procedure (URIP)
2-86   (Amended) Criminal Case Management
2-86   Criminal Case Management

General Provisions

RULE 1

Effect of These Rules

The provisions of these rules, so far as they are the same as those of existing rules, shall be construed as a continuation thereof, and not as new provisions.

Unless a contrary intent appears, the word plaintiff shall include petitioner or libellant, and in criminal cases the Commonwealth, and the word defendant shall include respondent, libellee or co-respondent, and the word attorney or the word counsel shall include a party appearing or acting for himself.

RULE 2

Appearances

The name, address, and telephone number of the attorney for every party, or of the party if no attorney appears for him, shall be entered on the docket as they appear upon the paper or papers constituting the appearance, or some paper transmitted to the clerk therewith. Where no address or telephone number of the attorney or party, as the case may be, appears upon the docket, notice to such party may be given by posting the same publicly in the clerk's office or in a room, hall or passage adjacent thereto. The clerk upon request shall post the same.

RULE 3

Authority to Appear

The right of an attorney to appear for any party shall not be questioned by the opposite party, unless the objection be taken in writing within ten days after the appearance of such attorney, but the court may permit the objection to be taken later. When the authority of any attorney to appear for any party is demanded, if such attorney declares that he has been duly authorized to appear, by an application made directly to him by such party, or by some person whom he believes to have been authorized to employ him, such declaration shall be evidence of such authority.

RULE 4

Postponement

The court need not entertain any motion for postponement, grounded on the want of material testimony, unless supported by an affidavit, which shall state (1) the name, and, if known, the residence, of the witness whose testimony is wanted, (2) the particular testimony which he is expected to give, with the grounds of such expectation, and (3) the endeavors and means that have been used to procure his attendance or deposition; to the end that the court may judge whether due diligence has been used for that purpose. The party objecting to the postponement shall not be allowed to contradict the statement of what the absent witness is expected to testify, but may disprove any other fact stated in such affidavit. Such motion will not ordinarily be granted if the adverse party will admit that the absent witness would, if present, testify as stated in the affidavit, and will agree that the same shall be received and considered as evidence at the trial or hearing as though the witness were present and so testified; and such agreement shall be in writing, upon the affidavit, and signed by such adverse party or his attorney. The same rule shall apply, *mutatis mutandis*, when the motion is grounded on the want of any material document, thing or other evidence. In all cases the granting or denial of a motion for postponement shall be discretionary, whether the foregoing provisions have been complied with or not.

The court will not ordinarily grant a motion for postponement grounded on the absence of a material witness whom it is in the power of the moving party to summon, unless such party has caused such witness to be regularly summoned and to be paid or tendered his travel and one day's attendance.

RULE 5
Jurors

Persons summoned as jurors, who are excused because of any statutory exemption, shall be entitled to their fees for travel and attendance; but if excused for any other cause, or if service is postponed, it shall be on condition that no fee shall be allowed where no service is rendered, unless in any special case the court otherwise directs.

When practicable, excuses of jurors shall be presented under oath to the presiding justice in the session to which such jurors are summoned, or, where jurors are held in a central pool, to the justice in charge thereof.

If it is necessary to present such excuses before the return day of the venire, they shall be submitted to the justice assigned to sit in said session, if available, or, where jurors are held in a central pool, to the justice in charge thereof, or to the chief justice; and, if unavailable, by jurors in Suffolk to the justice presiding in the first session without jury; and by jurors in other counties to a justice holding court or resident in such county or an adjoining county. If any juror is excused in any place other than in open court, the justice excusing him shall forthwith notify the clerk of his action and the ground thereof.

The word jurors in this rule shall include grand jurors.

RULE 6
Peremptory Challenges of Jurors

The procedure in the matter of peremptory challenges of jurors, except when an individual voir dire is conducted, shall be as follows, unless specially otherwise ordered in a particular case. The jurors shall first be called until the full number is obtained. If any examination on oath of the jurors is required, it shall be made, and any challenge for cause shall be acted on, and if any jurors shall be excused others shall be called to take their places. When it has been determined that all the jurors stand indifferent in the case, each plaintiff shall at one time exercise his right of peremptory challenge as to such jurors, and after others have been called to take the places of those challenged, and it has been determined that they stand indifferent in the case, shall at one time exercise his right of challenge of such others, and so on until he has exhausted his right of peremptory challenge or has ceased to challenge. Each defendant shall then exercise his right in the same manner. Each plaintiff, if his right of peremptory challenge has not been exhausted, shall then again exercise his right in the same manner, but only as to jurors whom he has not already had opportunity to challenge; and the parties shall likewise exercise the right in turn, until the right of peremptory challenge shall be exhausted or the parties shall cease to challenge. No other challenging, except for cause shown, shall be allowed.

RULE 7
Openings; Use of Pleadings
(Amended Sept. 24, 2015, effective Jan. 1, 2016.)

The opening statement shall be limited to fifteen minutes, unless the court for cause shown shall extend the time.

The court in its discretion may permit, or in a civil action require, a defendant to make an opening statement of his defense before any evidence is introduced.

The court may order that the pleadings be summarized in an opening statement but not be read to the jury. Pleadings shall not go to the jury except by authorization of the court.

RULE 8
Objections to Evidence

In civil actions, pursuant to the provisions of Mass.R. Civ.P. 46, and in criminal actions, pursuant to Mass.R. Crim.P. 22, if a party objects to the admission or exclusion of evidence, he may, if he so desires, state the precise grounds of his objection; but he shall not argue or further discuss such grounds unless the court then calls upon him for such argument or discussion.

RULE 8A
Notes by Jurors

In any case where the court, in its discretion, permits jurors to make written notes concerning testimony and other evidence, the trial judge shall precede the announcement of permission to make notes with appropriate guidelines. Upon the recording of the verdict or verdicts, the notes of the jurors shall be destroyed by direction of the trial judge. Jurors may also be granted permission by the trial judge to make notes during summation by counsel and during the judge's instructions to the jury on the laws.

RULE 9
Motions and Interlocutory Matters

All civil motions shall be governed, where applicable, by Superior Court Rules 9A through 9E.

Any criminal motion must be in writing and filed before being placed upon a list for hearing, unless otherwise ordered by the court, or otherwise provided for under Superior Court Rule 61.

In criminal cases the court need not hear any motion, or opposition thereto, grounded on facts, unless the facts are verified by affidavit. No motion to suppress evidence, other than evidence seized during a warrantless search, and no motion to dismiss may be filed unless accompanied by a memorandum of law, except when otherwise ordered by the court.

RULES 9A–E
Omitted

RULE 10
Extra Charges by Officers

When any officer claims extra compensation in serving a precept, the same shall not be allowed unless the officer return with his precept a bill of particulars of the expenses, with his affidavit that such expenses were actually incurred, and that the charges are reasonable.

RULE 11
Attorney Not to Become Bail or Surety

No attorney shall become bail or surety in any criminal proceeding in which he is employed, or in any civil action or proceeding whatever in this court except as an endorser for costs.

RULE 12
Attorneys as Witnesses

No attorney shall be permitted to take part in the conduct of a trial in which he has been or intends to be a witness for his client, except by special leave of the court.

RULE 13
Hospital Records
(Amended Sept. 24, 2015, effective Jan. 1, 2016.) (First paragraph applicable to civil actions only; remainder of rule applicable to all cases.)

Any party, or his attorney, in any action for personal injuries, may file an application for an order for a copy of any hospital records of a party, together with a copy of the proposed order and an affidavit that he has notified the other party, or his attorney, of his intention to file said application seven days at least prior to said filing and that he has not received any objections in writing thereto. The order shall issue as of course upon the receipt of such application.

In the event of an objection, no order shall issue unless the parties comply with Superior Court Rule 9A.

When a hospital record, or any part thereof, is received in evidence, the record shall be returned to the hospital upon the conclusion of the trial unless the court otherwise orders.

If the court orders the retention of the hospital record, it shall remain in the custody of the clerk, who shall give a receipt therefor. The record shall be released to the hospital, upon the giving of a receipt to the clerk.

RULE 14
Exhibits Other than Hospital Records

Exhibits other than hospital records, which are placed in the custody of the clerk shall be retained by him for three years after the trial or hearing at which they were used, subject to an order of confiscation or destruction, unless sooner delivered to the parties or counsel to whom they respectively belong or by whom they were respectively presented or introduced. If in doubt as to the party or counsel entitled to delivery, the clerk may require an agreement of parties or counsel or order of the court, before delivery. The clerk may destroy or discard such exhibits, but not earlier than thirty days after notice by the clerk to the party presenting or introducing such exhibits, requesting him to remove them, nor earlier than three years after such trial or hearing.

RULE 15
Eliminating Requirement for Verification by Affidavit

No written statement in any proceeding in this court required to be verified by affidavit shall be required to be verified by oath or affirmation if it contains or is verified by a written declaration that it is made under the penalties of perjury.

RULE 16
Writ of Protection

A writ of protection shall issue only upon the application of the person for whom the writ of protection is to be issued, or some person in his behalf, and upon order of the court, and then only in case it is made to appear to the court, by affidavit and any other evidence that the court may require, (1) that the application is made in good faith and for the purpose of enabling such person to attend this court as a party or witness in some specified case pending, (2) if such person is a party, that

such case has not been brought collusively to enable him to obtain a writ of protection, and (3) if such person is a witness, that he has not been required to attend as a witness by his own request or procurement to enable him to obtain a writ of protection.

RULE 17
Recording Devices
(Amended Sept. 24, 2015, effective Jan. 1, 2016.)

No person shall use or have in his possession or under his control in the chambers or lobby of a justice or justices of the court, or in any courtroom or other place provided for a hearing or proceeding of any kind on any action or matter pending before the court, or before any master, arbitrator, or any other person appointed by the court, any mechanical, electronic or other device, equipment, appliance or apparatus for recording, registering or otherwise reproducing sounds or voices, unless prior authorization for such use or possession is granted by the justice then having immediate supervision of such courtroom or other place. All recordings or transmissions must comply with Rule 1:19 of the Supreme Judicial Court ("Electronic Access to the Courts").

RULES 18–52
Omitted

Special Provisions for Criminal Cases

RULE 53
Assignment of Counsel
1. All Cases.

If any party appears in the court in a matter in which the laws of the Commonwealth or the rules of the Supreme Judicial Court establish a right to be represented by counsel, the judge shall follow the procedures established in Supreme Judicial Court Rule 3:10.

2. Murder Cases.

Upon the determination by a judge that a person accused of murder in the first or second degree is to be provided counsel by the Committee for Public Counsel Services pursuant to Supreme Judicial Court Rule 3:10 and G.L. c. 211D, § 8, the clerk shall notify the chief counsel of the Committee for Public Counsel Services for purposes of the assignment of the case to either the Public Counsel Division or Private Counsel Division, subject to the approval of the justice making the determination of indigency.

RULE 54
Experts in Criminal Cases

The court will not allow compensation for the services of an expert or expert witness for the defense in a criminal case unless an order of the court or a justice, naming such expert or expert witness and authorizing his employment, was made before he was employed. Such order shall not be made without notice to the district attorney in charge of the case, and an opportunity to be heard.

RULE 55
Experts in Criminal and Delinquent Children Cases

The court will not allow compensation as an expert witness to a salaried medical examiner or a salaried physician of a penal institution or place of detention, unless it appears by the certificate of the district attorney that he has testified as an expert.

The court will allow no fee to a salaried physician of a penal institution or place of detention for making an examination into the mental condition of a person held in custody therein or for a report or medical certificate as to such condition.

RULE 56
Conditions of Probation

The conditions of probation, unless otherwise prescribed, shall be as follows: That the defendant shall (1) comply with all orders of the court, including any order for the payment of money, (2) report promptly to the probation officer as required by him, (3) notify the probation officer immediately of any change of residence, (4) make reasonable efforts to obtain and keep employment, (5) make reasonable efforts to provide adequate support for all person dependent upon him, and (6) refrain from violating any law, statute, ordinance, by-law or regulation, the violation whereof is punishable. Any other condition shall be presumed to be in addition to the foregoing.

RULE 57
Term of Probation

The term of probation, unless otherwise prescribed, shall be until the regular sitting for or including criminal business within the county appointed to begin next after the expiration of the following periods after the day on which the defendant is placed on probation namely:—in cases under G.L. Chapter 273, five years and eleven months; and in other cases, eleven months. At the end of the term of probation, the probation officer shall make a written report to the court of the result of probation, which shall be filed in the case, and, if the court shall order, the probation officer shall bring the defendant before the court for an extension of probation or for other disposition.

RULE 58
Term of Orders for Payment

Orders for payment under G.L. Chapter 273, unless otherwise prescribed, shall be in force for six years from the day when made.

RULE 59
Waiver of Indictment

The form for an application to waive indictment under the provisions of G.L. Chapter 263, sec. 4A shall be as follows:

COMMONWEALTH OF MASSACHUSETTS
_____ ss.   _____ 20__
COMMONWEALTH
v.

_____

APPLICATION TO WAIVE INDICTMENT
To the Honorable the Justices of the Superior Court:
Respectively represents said defendant that on _____, 20__, he was (committed) (bound over) (complained of) for trial in the Superior Court under the provisions of (G.L. c. 218 § 30) (G.L. c. 219 § 20) (St. 1934 c. 358) by the (Court of _____) (Hon. _____, Trial Justice _____) (District Attorney for the _____ District) upon a complaint numbered _____ of 20__ charging him with a crime not punishable by death; that he desires to waive indictment upon said charge and now applies for leave to waive such indictment and for prompt arraignment on such complaint.

_____
I hereby consent to the foregoing application.

_____
District Attorney for the _____ District.
Approved by the Court _____ Clerk.

RULE 60
Plea of Not Guilty

A plea of not guilty, whether voluntarily made by the defendant or entered by order of the court, shall not be deemed to be a waiver of matters in bar or abatement or an admission of the validity of the indictment or complaint. A defendant at the time of the entry of such plea, or within ten days thereafter or within such further time as the court may order, may file such motions and other pleadings relating to matters in bar or abatement or to the validity of the indictment or complaint as he may desire without at any time retracting the plea of not guilty.

Lack of jurisdiction or the failure of the indictment or complaint to charge an offense may be raised at any time during the pendency of the proceedings.

RULE 61
Motions for Return of Property and to Suppress Evidence

Motions for the return of property and motions to suppress evidence shall be in writing, shall specifically set forth the facts upon which the motions are based, shall be verified by affidavit, and shall otherwise comply with the requirements of Mass.R.Crim.P. 13.

Such motions shall be filed within seven days after the date set for the filing of the pre-trial conference report pursuant to Mass.R.Crim.P. 11(a)(2), or at such other time as the court may allow.

RULE 61A
Motions for Post-Conviction Relief
(A) Contents of the Motion.

Motions for post-conviction relief filed under Mass.R. Crim.P. 30 shall contain (1) an identification by county and docket number of the proceeding in which the moving party was convicted, (2) the date the judgment of conviction entered, (3) the sentence imposed following conviction and (4) a statement of the facts and grounds on which the motion is based. The motion shall also contain (5) a statement identifying all proceedings for direct review of the conviction and the orders or judgment entered and (6) a statement identifying all previous proceedings for collateral review of the conviction and the orders or judgments entered.
(B) Docket of Proceedings and Transmission of Papers.

After docketing, the Clerk shall attach to all such motions a copy of the docket of the proceedings that resulted in the conviction and shall forward the motion, and accompanying papers, to the Justice who presided at the trial from which the conviction resulted and to the office of the District Attorney or to the Attorney General responsible for prosecuting the case. If the Justice who presided at the trial has retired, or is otherwise unavailable, the Clerk shall forward the motion and accompanying papers to the Regional Administrative Justice for the county in which the conviction occurred.
(C) Action on Motions.

Motions that do not comply with the requirements of paragraph (A) hereof may be summarily denied, without prejudice to renewal when filed in accordance with those requirements. For all motions that do comply with the requirements of paragraph (A), the court may direct the Commonwealth to file and serve an opposition, or may act thereon in the manner it deems appropriate and as authorized by Mass.R.Crim.P. 30.

RULE 62
Withdrawal of Appearance

An attorney who, before the return day, has entered an appearance in behalf of a defendant in a criminal case in the Superior Court, may withdraw his appearance within fourteen days after the return day, provided that the attorney who shall represent the defendant at trial files an appearance simultaneously with such withdrawal. An attorney shall not withdraw his appearance otherwise, except by express leave of court.

RULE 63
Court Reporter in Grand Jury Proceedings

Stenographic notes of all testimony given before any grand jury shall be taken by a court reporter, who shall be appointed by a justice of the superior court and who shall be sworn. Unless otherwise ordered by the court, the court reporter shall furnish transcripts of said notes only as required by the district attorney or attorney general.

RULE 64
Appellate Division Procedure and Forms

Appeals to the appellate division, under G.L. Chapter 278, as amended, shall be signed by the person sentenced, on forms herein established to be furnished by the clerk.

Upon the imposition of a sentence which may be reviewed, the clerk shall forthwith advise the person sentenced of his right, within ten days to appeal to the appellate division for a review of the sentence or sentences imposed, notwithstanding that the execution of such sentence or sentences is stayed pending appeal or suspended with a term of probation and shall make an entry on the docket that the person has been so advised.

The clerk shall forthwith notify the justice who imposed the sentence, of any appeal, and likewise shall notify the appellate division of any appeal.

If new process issues as a result of action by the appellate division, it shall recite the original sentence, sentences or dispositions and set forth any amendment thereof.

The clerk of the appellate division shall send notice of the final action by the appellate division to the appellant, the superintendent of the correctional institution in which the appellant is confined, the clerk of the court in which judgment was rendered, the justice who imposed the sentence appealed from and the chief justice.

The appellate division shall hear appeals for the review of sentences only in those cases in which a claim of appeal has been filed within ten days after the date of the imposition of sentence.

The forms for appeal under the provisions of G.L. Chapter 278, Section 28B, shall be as follows:

COMMONWEALTH OF MASSACHUSETTS
_____ ss.   Superior Court
COMMONWEALTH   No. _____
v.
_____

APPEAL FROM SENTENCE TO MASSACHUSETTS CORRECTIONAL INSTITUTION, CEDAR JUNCTION

The defendant hereby appeals to the Appellate Division of the Superior Court for a review of a sentence to the Massachusetts Correctional Institution, Cedar Junction, imposed in the Superior Court sitting within and for the County of _____ by Justice _____ on the _____ day of _____, 20__.

_____
Signature of defendant
_____, 20__

Note: This appeal must be filed within ten days of imposition of sentence.

In cases in which a sentence was imposed in accordance with a recommendation agreed to by or on behalf of the defendant, the Appellate Division will not normally hold a hearing but will consider the appeal solely on the basis of the record.

COMMONWEALTH OF MASSACHUSETTS
_____ ss.   Superior Court
COMMONWEALTH   No. _____
v.
_____

APPEAL FROM SENTENCE OF MORE THAN FIVE YEARS TO MASSACHUSETTS CORRECTIONAL INSTITUTION, FRAMINGHAM

The defendant hereby appeals to the Appellate Division of the Superior Court for a review of a sentence to the Massachusetts Correctional Institution, Framingham, imposed in the Superior Court sitting within and for the County of _____ by Justice _____ on the _____ day of _____, 20__.

_____
Signature of defendant
_____, 20__

Note: This appeal must be filed within ten days of imposition of sentence.

In cases in which a sentence was imposed in accordance with a recommendation agreed to by or on behalf of the defendant, the Appellate Division will not normally hold a hearing but will consider the appeal solely on the basis of the record.

RULE 65
Claim of Appeal

After imposing judgment and sentence in a case which has gone to trial on a plea of not guilty, the judge or clerk shall forthwith advise the defendant of his right to appeal, and the clerk shall execute a statement in writing to that effect.

The clerk shall have no duty to advise the defendant of any right of appeal after sentence is imposed following a plea of guilty or nolo contendere.

Defendant's counsel shall be responsible for perfecting and prosecuting the appeal unless such counsel is relieved of that responsibility, after a hearing on counsel's motion to withdraw.

An appeal under General Laws Chapter 278, Section 28 shall be claimed within thirty days after the judgment from which the appeal is taken.

RULES 66–67
Repealed

RULE 68
Arguments

In trials of criminal cases the arguments of each party shall be limited to thirty minutes; but the court may reasonably reduce or extend the time.

RULE 69
Examination of Witnesses

Unless otherwise permitted by the court, the examination and cross-examination of each witness shall be conducted by one counsel only for each party, and the counsel shall stand while so examining or cross-examining.

RULE 70
Requests for Instructions or Rulings

Requests for instructions or rulings in trials or hearings with or without jury shall be made in writing before the closing arguments unless special leave is given to present requests later.

The question whether the court should order a verdict shall be raised by a motion, and not by a request for instructions.

RULE 71
Depositions—Commissions

Upon application by a defendant, the court will grant commissions to take the depositions of witnesses residing out of the Commonwealth. Such a defendant may, on application to the clerk, obtain a commission, directed to any commissioner appointed by the governor of the Commonwealth to take depositions in any other of the United States, or to any justice of the peace, notary public or other officer legally empowered to take depositions or affidavits in the state or country where the deposition is to be taken, or to such other person as the court may order. Unless otherwise ordered, such depositions shall be taken upon interrogatories filed by such defendant, and upon cross-interrogatories, if any, filed by the Commonwealth, which interrogatories and cross-interrogatories shall be annexed to the commission. Such defendant shall file his interrogatories in the clerk's office, give notice thereof to the Commonwealth, with a copy of the interrogatories, and file an affidavit of such notice in the clerk's office. The cross-interrogatories, if any, shall be filed within seven days after the giving of such notice, or within such further time as the court may order, and a copy shall be given to such defendant. When a deposition is taken and certified by any person as an officer or person to whom the commission was directed, if it shall be objected that such person was not the one to whom the commission was directed, the burden of proof shall be on the party so objecting. But if an objection be made to the authority of a person taking the deposition without such commission, the burden of proof of such authority shall be on the party producing the deposition.

RULE 72
Depositions—Manner of Taking

Where a deposition is taken on interrogatories, the commissioner shall take such deposition in a place separate and apart from all other persons, and shall permit no person to be present during such examination except the deponent himself, and such disinterested person, if any, as he may think fit to appoint as clerk or stenographer to assist him in reducing the deposition to writing. The commissioner shall permit no person to communicate by interrogatories or suggestions with the deponent while giving his deposition. The commissioner shall put the several interrogatories and cross-interrogatories to the deponent in their order, and shall take the answer of the deponent to each, fully and clearly, before proceeding to the next; and shall not read to the deponent, nor permit the deponent to read, a succeeding interrogatory, until the answer to the preceding has been fully taken down. The clerk, on issuing a commission to take a deposition on interrogatories, shall insert the substance of this rule therein; or shall annex this rule, or the substances thereof, to the commission, by way of notice and instruction to the commissioner.

Depositions shall be opened and filed by the clerk when received.

RULES 73–77
Omitted

STANDING ORDER 1-15
Participation in Juror Voir Dire by Attorneys and Self-Represented Parties
(Adopted Dec. 5, 2014, effective Feb. 2, 2015)

A. Purpose.

The purpose of this Standing Order is to provide an interim procedure for the implementation of St. 2014, c. 254, § 2, pending completion of the work of the Supreme Judicial Court Committee on Juror Voir Dire. The Superior Court anticipates that this Standing Order may be superseded by, or may be modified in response to, such rules, protocols, or guidelines as the Supreme Judicial Court may hereafter adopt or approve, as well as in response to experience in the implementation of this Standing Order, including experience with the pilot project referred to in paragraph C(9) hereof. This Standing Order is adopted pursuant to Trial Court Rule V; shall take effect on February 2, 2015, coincident with the effective date of St. 2014, c. 254, § 2; and shall remain in effect until such time as it may be superseded or modified.

B. Preamble.

In enacting St. 2014, c. 254, § 2, the Legislature recognized and preserved the discretion of the trial judge to lead and supervise the process of juror voir dire, including oral examination of prospective jurors by attorneys and self-represented parties in the exercise of the right granted by the statute. The Superior Court recognizes that trial judges may properly exercise discretion to employ procedures for the examination of prospective jurors by attorneys and self-represented parties that may differ from those set forth herein, as well as to use written juror questionnaires where they deem appropriate in addition to the Confidential Juror Questionnaire required by G.L. c. 234A, § 22 (hereinafter, the "statutory Confidential Juror Questionnaire"). This Standing Order fully preserves the discretionary authority of the trial judge with respect to the examination and selection of jurors in each case, and provides a standard procedure that will apply in each civil and criminal case unless otherwise ordered by the trial judge, while permitting attorneys and self-represented parties a fair opportunity to participate in voir dire so as to identify inappropriate bias.

C. Procedure.

1. Any attorney or self-represented party who seeks to examine the prospective jurors shall serve and file a motion requesting leave to do so. In civil cases such motion shall follow the procedure provided by Superior Court Rule 9A,

and shall be filed with the Court, along with any opposition or other response received, not later than the earlier of (a) the final trial conference if such a conference is scheduled in the case, or (b) fourteen days prior to the date scheduled for trial. In criminal cases the motion shall be served on all parties at least one week before filing, and the motion and any opposition or other response shall be filed with the Court not later than two business days prior to the scheduled date of the final pretrial conference, or, in the event that no final pretrial conference is scheduled, five business days before the scheduled trial date.

2. The motion shall identify generally the topics of the questions the moving party proposes to ask the prospective jurors. Topics identified shall be interpreted to include reasonable follow-up questions. Any opposition or response to any such motion may address the proposed topics. The trial judge may, in the exercise of discretion, and after notice to the parties, require attorneys and self-represented parties to submit the specific language of the proposed questions for pre-approval. The motion and any responsive filing shall also include any proposed language for brief preliminary instructions on principles of law to be given pursuant to paragraph 5(b) hereof.

3. The trial judge shall approve or disapprove the topics of questions proposed, or, if the trial judge requires pre-approval of the specific language of the proposed questions, shall approve or disapprove each proposed question. In doing so the judge shall give due regard to the goals of: (a) selecting jurors who can and will decide the case based on solely the evidence and the law, fairly and impartially to all parties, without in the process exposing jurors to any extraneous matter that would undermine their impartiality; (b) conducting the selection process with reasonable expedition, in proportion to the nature and seriousness of the case and the anticipated length of the trial, and with due regard for the needs of other sessions that draw on the same jury pool for access to potential jurors; and (c) respecting the dignity and privacy of each potential juror.

4. (a) Questions that should generally be approved are:

(1) those seeking factual information about the prospective juror's background and experience pertinent to the issues expected to arise in the case, along with reasonable follow-up questions regarding whether and how such background or experiences might influence the juror in the case, provided that questions that would elicit sensitive personal information about a juror, or that specifically reference information provided in a juror's statutory Confidential Juror Questionnaire, shall be permitted only outside the presence or hearing of other jurors, so as to preserve the confidentiality required by G.L. c. 234A, s. 23.

(2) those regarding preconceptions or biases relating to the identity of the parties or the nature of the claims or issues expected to arise in the case.

(3) those inquiring about the prospective jurors' willingness and ability to accept and apply pertinent legal principles as instructed, after consultation with the judge regarding the principles of law on which the judge will instruct the jury.

(b) Questions that should generally be disapproved are those:

(1) that duplicate the questions that appear on the statutory Confidential Juror Questionnaire, or any other written juror questionnaire used in the case, but questions seeking further detail regarding information provided on a juror's questionnaire, or completion of any uncompleted answers on the questionnaire, should generally be approved, subject to the limitation stated in paragraph (a)(1) hereof;

(2) regarding the prospective juror's political views, voting patterns, party preferences, religious beliefs or affiliation, reading or viewing habits, patterns of charitable giving, opinions on matters of public policy, hobbies or recreational activities, or similar matters, or regarding insurance, except insofar as such matters may be relevant to issues expected to arise, or may affect the juror's impartiality in the case;

(3) regarding the outcome of any trial in which the prospective juror has previously served as a juror, or deliberations in or the prospective juror's vote in such trial;

(4) purporting to instruct jurors on the law;

(5) that make arguments on any issue of fact or law; that tend to indoctrinate or persuade; that encourage the juror to identify with a party, victim, witness, attorney, or other person or entity, or to send a message; or that encourage the juror to prejudge any issue in the case, to make a commitment to support a particular result, or to do anything other than remain impartial and follow the Court's instructions.

(6) that require a juror to guess or speculate about facts or law.

(7) that would tend to embarrass or offend jurors or unduly invade jurors' privacy.

5. Prior to any questioning by attorneys or self-represented parties, the trial judge shall:

(a) provide the venire with a brief description of the case, including the nature of the facts alleged and of the claims or charges, including the date and location of the pertinent alleged event(s), and the identity of persons or entities significantly involved;

(b) provide the venire with brief, preliminary instructions on significant legal principles pertinent to the case. Such instructions should include a brief recitation of: the burden and standard of proof; the elements of at least the primary civil claim or at least the most serious criminal charge, and, if appropriate to the case and requested by counsel or a self-represented party, the elements of any affirmative defense that will be presented to the jury; and, in criminal cases, the defendant's right not to testify.

(c) explain to the venire the empanelment process, including, in cases where attorneys and/or self-represented parties will pose questions, the nature and topics of the questions that will be posed, and that any juror who finds either a particular question or the process of questioning by attorneys or self-represented parties intrusive on the juror's privacy may request to be permitted to decline to answer and/or that steps be taken to protect the privacy of any information disclosed. Upon request, the judge may permit each party to make a brief introductory statement to the venire limited to explaining the process and purpose of the questioning of jurors by attorneys or self-represented parties.

(d) ask all questions required by statute or case law, and any additional questions the judge deems appropriate in light of the nature of the case and the issues expected to be raised. The judge may ask questions of the venire as a group, but should conduct at least part of the questioning of each prospective juror individually outside the presence or hearing of other jurors.

4

(e) as to each prospective juror questioned individually, excuse the juror if the judge determines that service would pose a hardship, or if the judge has doubt as to the juror's impartiality; otherwise find the juror indifferent and able to serve.

6. After the judge has found an individual juror indifferent and able to serve, the judge shall permit questioning by attorneys or self-represented litigants if and to the extent that the judge has previously approved such questioning upon motion submitted in the manner provided herein. Such questioning shall begin with the party having the burden of proof.

(a) Except as provided in paragraphs C(6)(b) and C(9) hereof, the judge may require that such questioning be conducted of each prospective juror individually, outside the presence or hearing of other jurors. Parties may assert challenges for cause based on the juror's responses to questions posed by attorneys or self-represented parties, notwithstanding that the judge has previously found the juror indifferent based on the judge's questioning and information provided in the statutory Confidential Juror Questionnaire. If the juror is not excused for cause upon such challenge, the judge may require the exercise of any peremptory challenge at that time, beginning with the party who has the burden of proof and, in civil cases, the judge may alternate sides thereafter. Alternatively, the judge may seat the juror subject to the parties' later exercise of peremptory challenges.

(b) Upon request of one or both parties, the trial judge may permit counsel or self-represented parties to question jurors as a group, in a so-called "panel voir dire" procedure. Such questioning shall occur of those jurors whom the judge has already questioned individually and found indifferent and able to serve, after the judge has so found with respect to at least the number of jurors that will be seated for trial. If questioning occurs in this form, the judge shall not permit any questions that would elicit sensitive personal information about an individual juror, or that would specifically reference information provided in a juror's statutory Confidential Juror Questionnaire. Jurors to whom questions are addressed, or who respond to questions, shall be identified on the record by juror number only. After completion of questioning the parties may assert challenges for cause based on responses to questions posed by attorneys or self-represented parties, although the judge has previously found the challenged juror indifferent. The judge shall require that such challenges for cause, as well as peremptory challenges, be asserted outside the hearing of other jurors. Upon any challenge for cause, the judge may allow opposing counsel further opportunity to question the juror.

7. Whether questioning of jurors by attorneys or self-represented parties occurs individually or in a group, any party may object to a question posed by another party by stating "objection," without elaboration or argument. The judge may rule on the objection in the presence of the juror or jurors, or may hear argument and rule on the objection outside the presence or hearing of the juror or jurors.

8. The trial judge may set a reasonable time limit for questioning of prospective jurors by attorneys or self-represented parties, giving due regard to (1) the objective of identification of inappropriate bias in fairness to all parties; (2) the interests of the public and of the parties in reasonable expedition, in proportion to the nature and seriousness of the case and the length of the anticipated evidence, and (3) the

needs of cases scheduled in other sessions drawing on the same jury pool for access to prospective jurors.

9. The Court will establish a pilot project, in which judges who volunteer to do so will conduct so-called "panel voir dire," according to a consistent procedure to be determined and described in a separate document. During the course of the pilot project, the Court will compile data regarding identified measures. Upon completion of the pilot project, the Court will issue a public report of such data.

Judith Fabricant
Chief Justice, Superior Court
Adopted: December 5, 2015
Effective: February 2, 2015

SUPERIOR COURT STANDING ORDER 2-15
Exceptions to Notice Requirement of Trial Court Rule VIII, Uniform Rules on Impoundment Procedure (URIP)
(Amended Sept. 17, 2015, effective Oct. 1, 2015)

A. Purpose.

This rule makes exceptions to the notice requirement of Rule 13(b) of the Uniform Rules on Impoundment Procedure (URIP), which ordinarily requires that when a person files impounded material, he or she also must file a notice alerting the clerk to that material.

B. Exceptions to Notice Requirement of URIP Rule 13(b).

Because the following materials are impounded by law, and the clerks' offices impound them in the normal course, no Rule 13(b) notice is necessary when filing any of them:

1. an Affidavit of Indigency and Request for Waiver, Substitution or State Payment of Fees & Costs, on the form prescribed by the Chief Justice of the Supreme Judicial Court under G.L. c. 261, § 27B;

2. a Petition for Abortion Authorization under G.L. c. 112, § 12S, or any materials in such matter;

3. an action for judicial review of a decision of the Sex Offender Registry Board, under G.L. c. 6, § 178M, or any materials in such matter; or

4. any confidential document or other material prepared especially for a pre-indictment judicial hearing concerning a grand jury proceeding.

C. Duty of the Clerk.

The clerk shall maintain the impounded material described above in accordance with the clerk's duties prescribed in URIP Rule 9.

Judith Fabricant
Chief Justice, Superior Court
Effective: October 1, 2015

STANDING ORDER 2-86 (AMENDED)
Criminal Case Management
(Amended June 1, 2009, effective Sept. 8, 2009. Applicable to all counties and to cases initiated by indictment on or after Sept. 8, 2009. The previous version of this standing order appears below.)

I. Purposes

To improve procedures in criminal cases in the Superior Court.

To promote uniformity in practice throughout the Commonwealth.

To insure compliance with the provisions and aims of the Rules of Criminal Procedure and Rules of the Superior Court.

To recognize that a defendant's right to speedy trial, and the public, including victims and witnesses, interest in a timely, fair and just resolution of criminal cases, is best achieved by application of uniform and consistent time standards for the conduct of criminal cases in Superior Court.

To encourage the cooperation between the court, the prosecuting attorneys and the defense bar with a view towards a just and efficient disposition of criminal cases.

To provide guidelines for application in the great majority of cases, recognizing that a judge, in the exercise of discretion, may adjust or extend time periods in individual cases to insure a defendant's right to fair trial and the effective assistance of counsel, as well as, the protection of public safety.

To identify non-trial cases at the earliest stage so as to encourage their timely disposition with consequent savings of public and private resources.

II. Arraignments

Arraignment will ordinarily take place in the first session by the judge presiding in that session, except in such counties utilizing a magistrate session pursuant to G.L. c. 221, §§ 62B and 62C in which case arraignment shall occur before the magistrate, or in a room list session in such counties utilizing a room list system for the assignment of cases.

An arraignment in Superior Court shall be conducted according to Mass.R.Crim.P. 7. After entry of the defendant's plea to the charges, the judge or magistrate shall schedule dates for a mandatory pre-trial conference and a mandatory pre-trial hearing, the latter to occur within 90 days of arraignment for an "A" track case, 135 days of arraignment for a "B" track case, and 180 days of arraignment for a "C" track case.

At arraignment, the clerk shall issue a Notice of Presumptive Track Designation in the form of a Scheduling Order, setting forth dates at or before which certain events shall occur. The presumptive track designation shall be determined based solely on the lead indictment or charge unless a judge, for good cause shown, determines that a different track designation shall apply. In addition, the judge or clerk shall set forth dates for the filing and hearing of discovery motions and shall set a date for the filing of the Certificate of Compliance under Mass.R.Crim.P. 14(a)(3).

III. Case Track Designations

Cases shall be assigned a presumptive case track at arraignment that will establish a presumptive time period for disposition of the case. Cases shall be designated "A", "B", or "C" track cases based on the offense charged in the indictment, and on consideration of any extenuating or special circumstances raised by the parties. In the event more than one charge exists, the case track shall be the longest track determined by reference to the charges.

There shall be three criminal case tracks as follows:

"A"

> Assaults and batteries (non-sexual)
> Breaking and entering
> Burglary
> Civil rights offenses
> Destruction of property
> Firearms offenses
> Larcenies
> Mayhem
> Narcotics offenses (other than Trafficking/Subsequent Offenses)
> Operating under the influence

"B"

> Arson

> Embezzlement
> Fraud
> Home invasion
> Larcenous scheme
> Robberies
> Sexual offenses other than rape
> Motor Vehicle Homicide
> Trafficking/Subsequent Offense Narcotics

"C"

> Kidnapping
> Manslaughter
> Murder
> Rape

Accessories to specific offenses, assaults with the specific intent to commit other offenses, attempts, cases carrying enhanced penalties, and conspiracies shall receive the same case track designations as provided for the underlying offenses.

The clerk shall enter the case track designation on the court's electronic docket, and shall enter the scheduled dates for pre-trial and trial proceedings in a Scheduling Order.

IV. Automatic Discovery

Automatic discovery, as defined by Mass.R.Crim.P. 14(a), shall be provided, or notice thereof given, at arraignment if possible, or thereafter at the earliest time possible, in the exercise of due diligence, in order to permit the Commonwealth and the defendant sufficient time in advance of the pre-trial conference to evaluate the case and meaningfully participate in a pre-trial conference.

V. The Pre-Trial Conference

The prosecuting attorney and defense counsel shall confer prior to the scheduled pre-trial hearing in order to conference the case and to prepare a written pre-trial conference report. In accordance with Mass.R.Crim.P. 11(a), the defendant shall be available for attendance at the pre-trial conference. Further, the court may require the conference to be held at court under the supervision of a judge or magistrate. The pre-trial conference may occur on the same day as the pre-trial hearing provided that the prosecution has furnished discovery to the defendant at least seven days prior to the pre-trial hearing.

The parties shall discuss those matters set forth in Mass.R.Crim.P. 11(a)(1), and shall reflect the results of the conference in the written conference report filed in accordance with Mass.R.Crim.P. 11(a)(2). Counsel shall also discuss whether the case can be disposed of by means of a plea and, if so, shall propose a date for change of plea within the conference report. Except where the parties have tentatively reached an agreement to resolve the case by change of plea, counsel shall set forth within the conference report proposed dates for any anticipated pre-trial events (motion filing and hearing dates, etc.) and a proposed trial date which shall be determined according to the designated case track for the lead charge of the indictment.

VI. The Pre-Trial Hearing

Counsel who are going to try the case *shall* attend the pre-trial conference *and* pre-trial hearing and shall personally sign the conference report. In all cases the defendant shall be available for the pre-trial hearing in the courthouse, and shall sign the completed conference report when necessary to waive constitutional rights or when the report contains stipulations as to material facts. The conference report shall be tendered to the first session judge for his examination and approval before the clerk accepts it for filing.

(7) Whether the defendant or any witness is in custody, and if so, where;

(8) Whether the defendant or any witness requires an interpreter or other similar needs and, if so, the language or service sought; and

(9) Estimated length of trial.

XI. Continuances of Trial Date

A motion to continue a trial date, once set or confirmed by the court, shall be in writing and supported by good cause in conformity with Mass.R.Crim.P. Rule 10. Such motion shall include the following:

(a) whether the motion is a joint motion; and if not a joint motion, state, if known, whether there is opposition;

(b) the defendant's custody status;

(c) the specific grounds for the requested continuance, including when counsel learned of the grounds necessitating the request;

(d) the date when the case was first assigned a trial date;

(e) whether the trial date has been previously continued and, if so, the number of such continuances and the reasons therefor. Special consideration for continuing a trial date shall be given when a motion to continue is jointly made by the prosecutor and defense attorney. If the judge denies any motion to continue the trial, the judge shall state the reasons for such denial.

XII. Procedures Applicable to the First Session

In counties utilizing a first session the following procedures shall apply. In counties utilizing a room list system of case assignments, the room list session shall perform the proceedings described below. The first session shall receive all presentments by the grand jury, shall conduct all arraignments, bail reviews, dangerousness hearings, and other pretrial hearings and proceedings. The first session judge may utilize a magistrate's session to conduct arraignments, bails and pre-trial proceedings as assigned by the first session judge, and may also transfer cases to available criminal sessions for discrete events (e.g. a pre-trial conference or pretrial hearing). All trial dates shall be set in the first session and all motions for continuance or amendment to the case track designation shall take place in the first session.

The first session judge shall assign cases scheduled for trial to the criminal trial sessions then sitting. Ordinarily, cases involving defendants in custody, defendants whose pretrial liberty is reasonably believed to present unusual risks to society, and cases given priority by statute (i.e., criminal proceedings for sex crimes involving child victims or witnesses), shall be given priority.

Once in every two months, the Regional Administrative Justice or his/her designee shall conduct a tracking review of all cases that have been scheduled but not reached for trial within the presumptive time, as amended or extended by the court. All such cases shall be prioritized for trial at the earliest available date.

XIII. Multi-Location, Single Session, and Specialized Session Counties

In those counties where from time to time there are only single judge criminal sessions or counties where there are specialized sessions, the duties imposed upon the first session judge by part XII may be modified as necessary.

XIV. Judicial Discretion

It is understood that specific situations may arise from time to time which require some variation from the procedures set forth above. In the interest of justice and to address specific concerns in unusual circumstances, and in the promotion of judicial efficiency, the first session judge, in his or her sound discretion, may extend the time periods and alter procedural requirements hereinbefore mandated.

XV. Effect of this Standing Order

The procedures set forth herein are intended to facilitate the timely, fair and accurate resolution of criminal cases and to ensure the efficient use of court resources. They do not supplant any existing rule of criminal procedure or statute. A defendant's statutory right to a speedy trial is determined by Mass.R.Crim.P. 36 and not by reference to this Standing Order.

Barbara J. Rouse
Chief Justice, Superior Court
Effective: September 8, 2009
Dated: June 1, 2009

4

STANDING ORDER 2-86
Criminal Case Management
(Applicable to all counties and only to cases initiated by indictment on or after Sept. 7, 2004. Effective through Sept. 7, 2009. The current version of this standing order appears above.)

I. Purposes

To improve procedures in criminal cases in the Superior Court.

To promote uniformity in practice throughout the Commonwealth.

To insure compliance with the provisions and aims of the Rules of Criminal Procedure and Rules of the Superior Court.

To recognize that a defendant's right to speedy trial, and the public, including victims and witnesses, interest in a timely, fair and just resolution of criminal cases, is best achieved by application of uniform and consistent time standards for the conduct of criminal cases in Superior Court.

To encourage the cooperation between the court, the prosecuting attorneys and the defense bar with a view towards a just and efficient disposition of criminal cases.

To provide guidelines for application in the great majority of cases; it being understood that as a matter of discretion, in specific situations, a judge may extend time periods and vary requirements in the interest of justice.

To identify non-trial cases at the earliest stage so as to encourage their timely disposition with consequent savings of public and private resources.

II. Arraignments

Arraignment will be accomplished in the first session by the judge presiding in that session, except in such counties utilizing a magistrate session pursuant to G.L. c. 221, §§ 62B and 62C in which case arraignment shall occur before the magistrate.

An arraignment in Superior Court shall be conducted according to Mass.R.Crim.P. 7. After entry of the defendant's plea to the charges, the judge or magistrate shall schedule dates for a mandatory pretrial conference and a mandatory pretrial hearing, the latter to occur within 90 days of arraignment for an "A" track case, 135 days of arraignment for a "B" track case, and 180 days of arraignment for a "C" track case.

At arraignment, the clerk shall issue a Notice of Presumptive Track Designation in the form of a Scheduling Order, setting forth dates at or before which certain events shall occur. The presumptive track designation shall be determined based solely on the lead indictment or charge unless a judge, for good cause shown, determines that a different track designation shall apply. In addition, the judge or clerk shall set forth dates for the filing and hearing of discovery motions and shall set a date for the filing of the Certificate of Compliance under Mass.R.Crim.P. 14(a)(3).

III. Case Track Designations

Cases shall be assigned a presumptive case track at arraignment that will establish a presumptive time period for disposition of the case. Cases shall be designated "A", "B", or "C" track cases based on the offense charged in the indictment, and on consideration of any extenuating or special circumstances raised by the parties. In the event more than one charge exists, the case track shall be the longest track determined by reference to the charges.

There shall be three Criminal Case Tracks as follows:

"A"

Assaults and batteries (non-sexual)
Breaking and entering
Burglary
Civil rights offenses
Destruction of property
Firearms offenses
Larcenies
Mayhem
Narcotics offenses
Operating under the influence

"B"

Arson
Embezzlement
Home invasion
Larcenous scheme
Robberies
Sexual offenses other than rape
Motor Vehicle Homicide

"C"

Kidnapping
Manslaughter
Murder
Rape

Accessories to specific offenses, assaults with the specific intent to commit other offenses, attempts, cases carrying enhanced penalties, and conspiracies shall receive the same case track designations as provided for the underlying offenses.

The Clerk shall enter the Case Track designation on the court's electronic docket, and shall enter the scheduled dates for pretrial and trial proceedings in a Scheduling Order.

IV. Automatic Discovery

Automatic discovery, as defined by Mass.R.Crim.P. 14(a), shall be provided, or notice thereof given, at arraignment if possible, or thereafter at the earliest time possible, in the exercise of due diligence, in order to permit the Commonwealth and the Defendant sufficient time in advance of the pretrial conference to evaluate the case and meaningfully participate in a pretrial conference.

V. The Pretrial Conference

The prosecuting attorney and defense counsel shall confer prior to the scheduled pretrial hearing in order to conference the case and to prepare a written pretrial conference report. In accordance with Mass.R.Crim.P. 11(a), the defendant shall be available for attendance at the pretrial conference. Further, the court may require the conference to be held at court under the supervision of a judge or magistrate. The pre-

trial conference may occur on the same day as the pretrial hearing provided that the prosecution has furnished discovery to the defendant at least 7 days prior to the pretrial hearing.

The parties shall discuss those matters set forth in Mass.R.Crim.P. 11(a)(1), and shall reflect the results of the conference in the written conference report filed in accordance with Mass.R.Crim.P. 11(a)(2). Counsel shall also discuss whether the case can be disposed of by means of a plea and, if so, shall propose a date for change of plea within the conference report. Except where the parties have tentatively reached an agreement to resolve the case by change of plea, counsel shall set forth within the conference report proposed dates for any anticipated pretrial events (motion filing and hearing dates, etc.) and a proposed trial date which shall be determined according to the designated case track for the lead charge of the indictment.

VI. The Pretrial Hearing

Counsel who are going to try the case shall attend the pretrial conference and pretrial hearing and shall personally sign the conference report. In all cases the defendant shall be available for the pretrial hearing in the courthouse, and shall sign the completed conference report when necessary to waive constitutional rights or when the report contains stipulations as to material facts. The conference report shall be tendered to the first session judge for his examination and approval before the clerk accepts it for filing.

The first session judge shall personally meet with counsel and examine the proposed conference report so as to bring it into conformity with the spirit and language of Mass.R.Crim.P. 11. The judge shall determine the likelihood of trial, its length, and the issues in dispute. At this hearing the first session judge has the responsibility to foster plea negotiations within constitutional parameters. The first session judge may, in her discretion, send the case to any available criminal session for a pretrial hearing, and the judge sitting in the receiving session shall conduct the pretrial hearing.

At the pretrial hearing, the judge shall confirm the case track designation assigned at arraignment or designate a different track in accordance with Section III. In the event the parties are unable to resolve the case and seek further dates, the judge shall thereafter establish dates for the filing of any disputed motions, hearing dates, a final pre-trial conference, and a trial date. In the event that such dates are scheduled in a session other than the first session, such dates shall be tentative until approved by the First Session Judge.

VII. Final Case Track Designation

At the pretrial hearing, the judge shall confirm the case track designation assigned at arraignment or designate a different track in accordance with Section III. In the event the parties are unable to resolve the case and seek further dates, the Judge shall thereafter establish dates for the filing of any disputed motions, hearing dates, a final pretrial conference, and a firm trial date. In the event that such dates are scheduled in a session other than the first session, such dates shall be tentative until approved by the First Session Judge.

In confirming the final case track designation applicable to the case, the Judge may consider whether any special circumstances exist to warrant placing the case on an alternate track. Special circumstances may be raised orally by counsel at the pretrial hearing or may be set forth in a written submission to the court. Special circumstances include, but are not limited to: unavailability of a victim or essential witness;

information relating to the victim's capacity to testify at trial within the time frame established by the case track; existence of multiple defendants; anticipated delays occasioned by necessary forensic or scientific testing (e.g. DNA testing, drug analysis of multiple samples, etc.); necessity for extended pretrial hearings such as *Daubert/Lanigan, Bishop/Fuller* or similar proceedings, but not including motions to dismiss or motions to suppress statements, evidence, search warrants, or identifications. Counsel shall be afforded an opportunity to be heard regarding the existence of any special circumstance.

After consideration of special circumstances, the Judge shall confirm the Final Case Track Designation applicable to the case and shall so designate on the record.

Cases designated on the "A" Track shall presumptively be tried within 180 days of arraignment. Cases designated on the "B" Track shall presumptively be tried within 270 days of arraignment. Cases designated on the "C" Track shall presumptively be tried within 360 days of arraignment.

Following the Court's determination of the Final Case Track Designation, the Judge, in consultation with counsel, shall schedule a trial date, falling within the presumptive time periods set forth above. The Judge shall also schedule dates for any contemplated pretrial proceedings as reflected in the pretrial conference report, and shall schedule a Final Pretrial Conference 14 days prior to the assigned trial date. The selection of a trial date by trial counsel, either as reflected in the pretrial conference report or following the pretrial hearing, shall be deemed to be the equivalent of the district attorney placing the case on the trial list under G.L. c. 278, § 1, and in accordance with Mass.R.Crim.P. 11(a)(1)(C), shall not be changed without express permission of the court.

VIII. Amendments to the Scheduling Order

The Court recognizes that there are cases which by their very nature and complexity require special tracking standards and, as well, that unanticipated events may delay the trial of a case or require that a previously determined date be extended or continued. Therefore, a Scheduling Order may, from time to time and for good cause shown, be amended upon oral motion of the parties. All requests for an enlargement or limitation of a scheduled event shall in the first instance, be made by oral motion to the judge sitting in the session where the case is assigned. If the session judge hearing the motion denies the motion to enlarge or amend the scheduling order, the aggrieved party may file a motion for reconsideration with the session judge who heard the oral motion. The motion for reconsideration shall be in writing and set forth a statement specifying in detail the facts upon which the moving party then relies in support of said motion. The motion for reconsideration, and any opposition thereto, shall be submitted on the briefs without personal appearance or oral argument by counsel within seven days of the denial or the oral motion.

In the event the scheduling order is amended, the clerk shall enter the amended dates in the court's electronic docket and shall revise the Scheduling Order accordingly.

IX. Early Disposition Procedure

At anytime within 45 days of the pretrial conference, counsel may advance the case for an early disposition by notifying the first session clerk who shall schedule the case for a hearing. An early disposition by way of a change of plea may occur in the first session or may be sent by the first session judge to any available criminal session for a plea.

X. Final Pretrial Conference

A final pretrial conference shall be held fourteen days prior to the scheduled trial date. Trial counsel shall attend the final pretrial conference. Prior to the conference, counsel shall meet for the purpose of preparing a Joint Pretrial Memorandum, which shall be filed with the Court at the time of said final pretrial conference. Unless all counsel agree otherwise, counsel for the Commonwealth shall be responsible for preparing and circulating the first draft of the memorandum which shall contain the following component parts:

(1) Agreed statement of facts to be read to the jury during impanelment. (If counsel are unable to agree, each attorney shall submit a proposed statement of facts);

(2) Proposed stipulations of the parties;

(3) List of names of prospective witnesses;

(4) List of proposed exhibits;

(5) Statement of disputed legal issues, including but not limited to evidentiary issues (i.e. privilege, immunity, fresh complaint testimony, rape-shield, etc.);

(6) List of anticipated pretrial or trial motions to be heard by the trial judge;

(7) Whether the defendant or any witness is in custody, and if so, where;

(8) Whether the defendant or any witness requires an interpreter or other similar needs and, if so, the language or service sought; and

(9) Estimated length of trial.

XI. Procedures Applicable to the First Session

The First Session shall receive all presentments by the grand jury, shall conduct all arraignments, bail reviews, dangerousness hearings, and other pretrial hearings and proceedings. The First Session Judge may utilize a Magistrate's Session to conduct arraignments, bails and pretrial proceedings as assigned by the First Session Judge, and may also transfer cases to available criminal sessions for discrete events (e.g. a pretrial conference or pretrial hearing). All trial dates shall be set in the First Session and all motions for continuance or amendment to the Case Track Designation shall take place in the First Session.

The First Session Judge shall assign cases scheduled for trial to the criminal trial sessions then sitting. Ordinarily, cases involving defendants in custody, defendants whose pretrial liberty is reasonably believed to present unusual risks to society, and cases given priority by statute (i.e., criminal proceedings for sex crimes involving child victims or witnesses), shall be given priority.

Once in every two months, the Regional Administrative Judge or his/her designee shall conduct a tracking review of all cases that have been scheduled but not reached for trial within the presumptive time, as amended or extended by the Court. All such cases shall be prioritized for trial at the earliest available date.

XII. Multi-Location and Single Session Counties

In those counties where from time to time there are only single judge criminal sessions, the duties imposed upon the first session judge by part XI may be modified as necessary.

XIII. Judicial Discretion

It is understood that specific situations may arise from time to time which require some variation from the procedures set forth above. In the interest of justice and to address specific concerns in unusual circumstances, and in the promotion of judicial efficiency, the first session judge, in his or her sound discretion, may extend the time periods and alter procedural requirements hereinbefore mandated.

XIV. Effect of this Standing Order

The procedures set forth herein are intended to facilitate the timely, fair and accurate resolution of criminal cases and to ensure the efficient use of court resources. They do not supplant any existing rule of criminal procedure or statute. A defendant's statutory right to a speedy trial is determined by Mass.R.Crim.P. 36 and not by reference to this Standing Order.

Suzanne V. DelVecchio
Chief Justice of the Superior Court
DATED: July 12, 2004

4

PART 5

District/Municipal Court Rules
of Criminal Procedure

(Effective January 1, 1996.)
Rule
1   Applicability
2   Issuance of Complaint; Police Statement
3   Arraignment
4   Pretrial Hearing
5   Hearing Date for Discovery Compliance and Jury Waiver Election
6   Pretrial Motions
7   Trials
8   [Reserved]
9   Sanctions
10   Title
Boston Municipal Court Standing Orders
1-09 For the Sealing of Three or More Dismissals and Non-Conviction
      Criminal Records

RULE 1
Applicability

Notwithstanding any other rule of court inconsistent herewith, the following rules shall govern procedure in all criminal cases commenced in the District Court and in the Boston Municipal Court on or after January 1, 1996. For the purpose of this provision, commencement of a criminal action shall occur on the date of arrest, or in cases not initiated by arrest, on the date of the issuance of a criminal complaint.

RULE 2
Issuance of Complaint; Police Statement
(a) Cases Commenced by Warrantless Arrest.

Prior to the issuance of a criminal complaint in a case commenced by warrantless arrest, the clerk-magistrate shall obtain from the police department responsible for the arrest a written statement describing the facts constituting the basis for the arrest. This requirement may be satisfied by providing to the clerk magistrate a copy of the arresting officer's police report at the time the Application for Complaint is filed or by setting forth the statement in the space provided on the Application for Complaint, with an additional sheet or sheets attached to the Application as may be needed.

(b) Cases Commenced by Issuance of a Criminal Complaint on Application by Police or Civilian.

Prior to the issuance of a criminal complaint in a case commenced by an application therefor filed by a police officer, rather than by a warrantless arrest, the clerk-magistrate shall obtain from the police officer the police report, if any, relating to the alleged crime. In all cases, each police and civilian complainant shall, on the Application for Criminal Complaint, provide the information to support the issuance of the complaint.

NOTE 1   "Here . . . , after a warrantless arrest, the defendant faults trial counsel for failure to request dismissal of the complaint because the application for the complaint and accompanying police report did not establish probable cause that the defendant had committed an assault with a dangerous weapon. Such a determination is not relevant to the issuance of a complaint following a warrantless arrest. In that circumstance, the arresting officer sub-sequently applies for a complaint, not process. The sole requirement is for the arresting officer to submit a written statement describing the facts constituting the basis for the arrest. An application for a complaint after a warrantless arrest is, in essence, a pro forma proceeding that does not require the clerk-magistrate to determine whether a crime has been committed. It does not call on the court to issue process, the arrest already being an accomplished fact." *Commonwealth v. Rumkin*, 55 Mass. App. Ct. 635, 637 (2002) (citations and quotation marks omitted).

NOTE 2   **Probable cause requirement.** Mass. R. Crim. P. 3(g)(2).

RULE 3
Arraignment
(a) Defendant's Criminal Record and Police Statement.

At or before arraignment, the court shall ensure (1) that a copy of the defendant's criminal record as compiled by the Commissioner of Probation pursuant to G.L. c. 276, s. 100, if any, is provided to the defense and to the prosecution, pursuant to Mass.R.Crim.P. 12(e), and (2) that a copy of the police statement required by Rule 2 is provided to the defense by the prosecution.

(b) Notice of Probation Revocation Hearing.

If a defendant against whom a criminal case is commenced in the Boston Municipal Court is on probation in that court, the defendant may be served at arraignment with a notice of a probation revocation hearing.

(c) Order for Pretrial Conference; Discovery; Pretrial Hearing.

At arraignment in the District Court, the judge shall issue a written order to the attorney representing the defendant and to the prosecutor to (1) engage in a conference between themselves prior to a pretrial hearing in accordance with Mass.R. Crim.P. 11 and (2) appear before the court on a date certain for the conduct of the pretrial hearing on the results of that conference. If the parties agree to a date for the pretrial conference, said date shall be recorded on the order.

At arraignment in the Boston Municipal Court, the judge shall issue an order to the attorney representing the defendant and to the prosecutor to (1) appear for a conference between themselves under the supervision of an Assistant Clerk-Magistrate designated by the Clerk-Magistrate for Criminal Business and certified by the Chief Justice of the Boston Municipal Court, to be conducted in accordance with Mass.R. Crim.P. 11, in a designated courtroom and (2) appear before the court on a date certain for a hearing on the results of that pretrial conference.

Such order issued by the District Court or Boston Municipal Court shall also require the parties to provide, permit and obtain discovery in accordance with G.L. c. 218, s. 26A, and Mass.R.Crim.P. 14, in advance of the scheduled pretrial hearing and to be prepared to submit either a tender of plea or admission at said hearing or, in lieu thereof, a pretrial conference report, completed and signed by both parties. Discovery that is not provided, permitted or obtained in accordance with

5

the arraignment order shall be the subject of a court order, a motion for relief, or sanctions at the pretrial hearing, as provided in Rule 4(b).

(d) Charges Not Within District Court Final Jurisdiction.

In cases involving one or more charges not within District Court or Boston Municipal Court final jurisdiction, as the case may be, the order issued at arraignment shall allow for a tender of plea, admission or other disposition on charges reduced by the prosecution so as to be within the court's final jurisdiction. The preliminary discovery required to be included in the arraignment order under section (c) of this rule shall apply only to cases within the court's final jurisdiction.

(e) Appearance of Defense Counsel; Lack of Counsel.

Defense counsel, privately engaged or appointed on the basis of defendant's indigency, as the case may be, shall file an appearance at arraignment. If private or publicly provided defense counsel is not before the court at arraignment, if counsel is appointed "for bail only," or if the defendant indicates the intention to engage private counsel, the matter shall be continued for a brief period of time sufficient to permit the defendant to obtain counsel and to reappear for (1) either the assignment or waiver of counsel or the appearance of private counsel, and (2) completion of the arraignment, provided, however, that counsel "for bail only" may also be appointed "for arraignment only" in order to complete the arraignment.

If the arraignment is completed at defendant's first appearance, and the defendant indicates a desire to engage private counsel, the court may continue the matter for the next court event (namely, pretrial hearing in the district court or pretrial conference in the Boston Municipal Court), set the date therefor and issue to the defendant to give to defense counsel the required arraignment order and other necessary documents. Such an approach shall be employed only when the court determines that the defendant will, in fact, secure private counsel sufficiently promptly for such counsel to prepare for and participate in any required pretrial conference and pretrial hearing.

RULE 4
Pretrial Hearing

(a) Appearance of Parties.

The parties shall appear as scheduled for a hearing on the results of their pretrial conference, in accordance with the terms of the order issued at arraignment under Rule 3(c). Cases in which the parties have not conferenced in accordance with the order shall be held so that said conference may be completed, and the pretrial hearing conducted, prior to the end of the court day, if possible.

(b) Discovery.

Failure of either party to have provided, permitted or obtained discovery in accordance with the order issued at arraignment may subject that party to the sanctions provided in Mass.R.Crim.P. 14(c).

Where it is determined that discoverable material should have been produced but was not, the court may, in lieu of sanctions, order such discovery to be provided without further delay, including a brief continuance of the matter to allow the party responsible to secure the item at issue and bring it before the court that same day.

In the District Court, discovery that is not provided or permitted in accordance with the arraignment order and is not ordered at the pretrial hearing may be requested by motion filed at or prior to the conclusion of the pretrial hearing.

(c) Guilty Plea, Admission, or Other Disposition.

At the pretrial hearing the defendant may tender to the court a plea, admission or other requested disposition conditioned on specific dispositional terms, with or without the agreement of the prosecutor. Such tender of plea, admission or other disposition shall be set forth on the form promulgated therefor by the Chief Justice of the District Court or the Chief Justice of the Boston Municipal Court, as the case may be. If the court rejects the dispositional terms agreed to by the parties, or requested by the defendant without the agreement of the prosecution, it shall so inform the defendant and the defendant shall be permitted to withdraw the plea or admission, in accordance with G.L. c. 278, s. 18. Prior to submission to the court of a tender of plea or admission or a request for other disposition, and if the proposed dispositional terms involve any probationary terms or conditions, the parties shall consult with the probation department, so as to enable the probation department to be heard as may be required by the court at the time the court considers the tendered plea or admission.

If the court rejects a tendered plea, admission or other disposition, the judge may indicate to the parties what disposition he or she would impose, as provided in Mass.R.Crim.P. 12(c)(6), and a pretrial disposition may be requested by the defendant on those terms.

(d) Pretrial Conference Report.

If a pretrial disposition is not requested, or is requested but rejected by the court at the pretrial hearing, the parties shall submit a completed and signed pretrial conference report in accordance with the order issued at arraignment. Said report shall be set forth on the form promulgated therefor by the Chief Justice of the District Court or the Chief Justice of the Boston Municipal Court, as the case may be.

(e) Jury or Jury-Waived Trial.

When the pretrial conference report is submitted, the court shall examine it for completeness, shall rule on any disputed discovery issues, and, unless discovery compliance is still pending, shall inquire if the defendant waives the right to jury trial.

The court shall not compel the defendant's decision on waiver of jury trial until all discovery issues have been resolved and compliance with any discovery orders has been completed. Compliance with discovery orders may require the scheduling of a "compliance/election hearing" as provided in Rule 5. However, the defendant may proceed to enter the decision on jury waiver and a trial date may be set prior to compliance with discovery orders, at the defendant's option.

A waiver of the right to jury trial shall be submitted by the defendant on the form promulgated therefor by the Supreme Judicial Court and shall be accepted only upon completion of the colloquy required by law and the certificate of counsel required by G.L. c. 218, s. 26A. The required certificate shall be submitted on the form promulgated therefor by the Chief Justice of the District Court or the Chief Justice of the Boston Municipal Court, as the case may be.

If a waiver of jury trial is accepted in a District Court in which jury trials are not available and in which only one judge regularly sits, and that judge has rejected defendant's tendered plea or admission, the defendant shall be asked if he or she waives the right to be tried by a different judge. If the right to be tried by a different judge is waived, the case shall be scheduled for jury-waived trial in that court. If the right to be tried by a different judge is not waived, the case shall be scheduled for jury-waived trial in the court in which a session has been designated for that purpose under G.L. c. 218, s. 27A.

If the right to jury trial is not waived when that issue is addressed by the Court, the case shall be scheduled as follows:

(1) in the District Court the case shall be scheduled for jury trial on a date certain, provided, however, that in the District Court such cases may be scheduled for a trial assignment date if that procedure is authorized by the Chief Justice of the District Court, and

(2) in the Boston Municipal Court the case shall be scheduled for a date certain for trial assignment.

(f) Charges Outside District Court and Boston Municipal Court Final Jurisdiction.

If the case involves one or more charges that are not within District Court or Boston Municipal Court final jurisdiction, as the case may be, or if the court declines final jurisdiction over the pending charges, the court shall schedule a probable cause ("bind-over") hearing in accordance with G.L. c. 218, s. 30 at the completion of the pretrial hearing.

If the prosecution reduces the charge to a crime within District Court or Boston Municipal Court final jurisdiction, but the case cannot be disposed of at the pretrial hearing in the District Court, or at the pretrial conference or pretrial hearing in the Boston Municipal Court, the court shall continue the matter for a further pretrial hearing on a date certain and shall issue such further discovery and pretrial conference orders as may be necessary.

RULE 5

Hearing Date for Discovery Compliance and Jury Waiver Election

In those cases in the District Court wherein a discoverable item is not produced or is not deemed waived at the pretrial hearing and the court issues a discovery order, a subsequent court hearing shall be scheduled at the request of the party seeking discovery to ensure compliance with such order. In those cases in the Boston Municipal Court wherein a discoverable item is not produced or is not deemed waived at the pretrial hearing and the court issues a discovery order, a subsequent hearing may be scheduled by the court. If required, said hearing in the District Court or Boston Municipal Court shall be scheduled for a date on or after the compliance date and shall be limited to the following court actions:

(1) determining discovery compliance and, if necessary, ordering appropriate sanctions for non-compliance;

(2) receiving and acting on a tender of plea or admission in accordance with Rule 4(c); and

(3) obtaining defendant's decision on waiver of the right to jury and scheduling the trial date or trial assignment date, as required by Rule 4(e).

RULE 6

Pretrial Motions

(a) In the District Court

(1) *Discovery Motions.* Discovery motions shall be filed in accordance with Rule 4(b) and shall be heard and decided prior to the defendant's initial decision on waiver of jury trial, provided, however, that motions for discovery may be filed within twenty-one days after the defendant's initial decision on waiver of jury trial, or later, for good cause shown. Discovery motions filed within said twenty-one day period or later shall be entertained only upon a preliminary showing (1) that the items or information sought could not reasonably

have been sought and obtained prior to the initial decision on waiver of jury trial or (2) of other grounds that the court determines reasonably justify the delay in having filed the discovery motion after completion of the pretrial hearing.

(2) *Non-discovery Pretrial Motions.* All pretrial motions other than those involving discovery may be filed before or after the defendant's initial decision on waiver of the right to jury trial.

Such motions filed before the defendant's initial decision on the waiver of jury trial shall be transmitted to the appropriate trial session and scheduled to be heard there on the trial date, provided, however, that the judge before whom any such motion is filed may, as a matter of his or her discretion, hear and decide said motion (1) prior to the trial date, or, (2) where the trial will be conducted in a different court, prior to transmission of the case to such other court.

Such motions filed after defendant's initial decision on waiver of jury trial shall be filed in the court wherein the trial is scheduled to be heard no later than twenty-one days after defendant's decision on waiver of jury trial, or later, for good cause shown. Notwithstanding the foregoing, the presiding justice of the court in which the pretrial hearing is conducted, if different from the court in which the trial will be conducted, may require that such motions be filed and heard in the former court. In such cases, transmission of the case file to the other court for trial should be deferred until after the motion is heard and decided.

Rulings on pretrial motions rendered prior to the transmission of a case to a trial session shall be final, as provided in G.L. c. 278, § 18.

(b) In the Boston Municipal Court

(1) *Discovery Motions.* Discovery motions timely filed must be heard and decided prior to the scheduling of the trial session assignment date. Discovery motions filed after the scheduling of a trial session assignment date shall be allowed only;

(A) if the discovery being sought could not reasonably have been sought or obtained prior to the scheduling of the trial session assignment date; or

(B) if other good cause can be shown.

(2) *Non-Discovery Pretrial Motions.* Pretrial motions other than those involving discovery may be filed at any time but no later than 21 days after the date of the filing of the Pretrial Conference Report.

Rulings on pretrial motions rendered prior to the transmission of a case to a trial assignment session shall be final, as provided in G.L. c. 278, § 18.

RULE 7

Trials

Jury-waived trials and jury trials shall proceed in accordance with the provisions of law applicable to such trials in Superior Court as provided by G.L. c. 218, §§ 26A and 27A(d) and (e), respectively.

RULE 8

[Reserved]

RULE 9

Sanctions

The provisions of Mass.R.Crim.P. 48 regarding sanctions for willful violation of those rules shall apply to willful violations of these rules.

RULE 10
Title

These rules may be known and cited as the District/Municipal Courts Rules of Criminal Procedure (Dist./Mun.Cts.R.Crim.P.).

BOSTON MUNICIPAL COURT STANDING ORDER 1-09 (AMENDED)
For the Sealing of Three or More Dismissals and Non-Conviction Criminal Records

(Adopted Apr. 10, 2009, effective May 15, 2009 to May 14, 2010. Effective date extended to May 14, 2012; made permanent effective May 14, 2012. Amended effective Sept. 2, 2014.)

I. Authority

This permanent Standing Order is promulgated and revised by the Chief Justice of the Boston Municipal Court Department pursuant to G.L. c. 211B, § 10 and G.L. c. 218, § 51A.

II. Purpose and Applicability

In recognition of the hardships faced by individuals of limited economic resources with criminal records, and the burdens they face when seeking to seal their criminal records at the various court divisions in this Department, and in an effort to alleviate these hardships and burdens while promoting judicial economy, this Standing Order was originally promulgated by the Boston Municipal Court Department to allow for the filing of a single petition to seal three or more dismissals and non-conviction criminal records pursuant to the provisions of G.L. c. 276, § 100C. This Standing Order established the procedures to be followed by all court divisions of this Department in those instances when a person seeks to seal three or more criminal records from two or more court divisions within this Department where a dismissal or nolle prosequi or finding of no probable cause has been entered, or the defendant was found not guilty. However, in light of the recent Supreme Judicial Court decision in *Commonwealth v. Pon*, SJC-11542 (August 15, 2014), 469 Mass. [296] (2014), this Standing Order is being revised as of the effective date below to conform to the new legal standard and analysis established by the SJC in *Pon*.

III. Required Protocols and Procedures

A. Petition to Seal Multiple Criminal Records; Venue; Filing. As of the effective date of this revised Standing Order, a person who resides within the territorial jurisdiction of the court divisions of the Boston Municipal Court Department, with three or more dismissals and/or non-conviction criminal records in the court divisions of this Department, may request that these criminal records be sealed in a single petition filed in the court division in whose territory the person resides. If a person with three or more dismissals and/or non-conviction criminal records in the court divisions of this Department does not reside within the territorial jurisdiction of this Department, then these criminal records may be sealed in a single petition filed in the court division of the most recent applicable criminal record. A person seeking to seal multiple criminal records in a single petition pursuant to this amended Standing Order should be sure to list all applicable criminal cases with docket numbers from all court divisions of the Boston Municipal Court Department. A modified petition form that conforms to the *Pon* decision is available on the Trial Court website.

The Clerk-Magistrate who receives for filing the original petition to seal multiple criminal records shall docket and file the petition in the corresponding criminal case(s) within three (3) business days, and shall provide a copy of the petition with notice of the preliminary hearing to the Probation Department.

B. Hearing. In *Pon*, the Supreme Judicial Court determined that a court has the discretion either to conduct a preliminary hearing and then a final hearing, or to conduct a single final hearing.

1. *Preliminary hearing:* Upon the filing of a petition for sealing multiple criminal records, a preliminary hearing may be held to determine whether the petitioner has made out a prima facie case in favor of sealing said records. The new legal standard for the petitioner's prima facie case was established by the SJC in *Commonwealth v. Pon*, SJC-11542 (August 15, 2014), 469 Mass. [296] (2014), and is specifically incorporated by this revised Standing Order. In his discretion, a judge hearing a petition for sealing multiple criminal records may request additional information or document(s) regarding the criminal case(s) listed in the petition from the Clerk-Magistrate and/or the Probation Department.

2. *Final hearing:* If a judge finds that the petitioner has shown a prima facie case for sealing, whether at the preliminary hearing described above or upon review of the petition and/or other papers submitted by the petitioner, a final hearing shall be scheduled for no earlier than thirty (30) days, but no later than forty-five (45) days, from the date of the preliminary hearing or the filing of the petition. The Clerk-Magistrate of the court division ordering a final hearing shall notify the Probation Department of said final hearing.

C. Public Notice of Final Hearing. The Clerk-Magistrate of the court division conducting the final hearing shall post for a minimum of seven (7) days public notice of the date, time, and location of the final hearing.

D. Notice to District Attorney of Final Hearing; Objection to Venue. The petitioner is required to send a copy of the petition to seal multiple criminal records to the Suffolk County District Attorney's Office at least thirty (30) days before the final hearing so as to permit the District Attorney's Office to notify the victim(s), if any, of the scheduled final hearing. Unless the petitioner has complied with this provision, or said District Attorney's Office has waived the full thirty (30) day notice, no criminal record(s) from other court division(s) shall be sealed at the final hearing.

The victim(s), if any, and/or the Assistant District Attorney(s) of criminal case(s) from other court division(s) shall have the right to object to venue. Upon the receipt or articulation of any such objection, a judge in the court division in which the petition was filed may for good cause decline to hear the petition to seal for those criminal case(s) from other court division(s), without prejudice to the petitioner's filing of a separate petition to seal in the court division(s) in which those criminal case(s) originated.

E. Order on Petition to Seal Multiple Criminal Records. The Clerk-Magistrate of the court division that issues an order on the original petition to seal multiple criminal records shall promptly docket and file said order in the corresponding criminal case(s), shall transmit a copy of said order to the Probation Department, and shall transmit a copy of said order to the Clerk-Magistrate(s) of the other court division(s) with criminal case(s) listed on the petition.

F. Notice to Office of the Commissioner of Probation. The Chief Probation Officer of the Probation Department of the court division that enters an order to seal criminal record(s) is responsible for notifying the Office of the Commissioner of Probation of the court's order.

PART 6

Massachusetts Rules of Appellate Procedure

Rule
1   Scope of Rules: Definitions
2   Suspension of Rules
3   Appeal—How Taken
4   Appeal—When Taken
5   Report of a Case for Determination
6   Stay or Injunction Pending Appeal
7   Disability of a Member of the Lower Court
8   The Record on Appeal
9   Assembly and Transmission of the Record: Exhibits
10   Docketing the Appeal
11   Direct Appellate Review
11.1   Transfer from Supreme Judicial Court
12   Proceedings in Forma Pauperis
13   Filing and Service
14   Computation and Extension of Time
15   Motions
16   Briefs
17   Brief of an Amicus Curiae
18   Appendix to the Briefs
19   Filing and Serving of Briefs and Motions
20   Form of Briefs, Appendices, and Other Papers
21   Prehearing Conference
22   Oral Argument
23   Issuance of Rescript: Stay of Rescript
24   Justices' Participation
24.1   Divided Vote on Further Appellate Review
25   Damages for Delay
26   Costs
27   Petition for Rehearing
27.1   Further Appellate Review
28   Entry of Judgment Following Rescript
29   Voluntary Dismissal
30   Substitution of Parties
31   Duties of Clerks
32   Title

RULE 1

Scope of Rules: Definitions

(a) Scope of Rules. These rules govern procedure in appeals to an appellate court.

(b) Rules Not to Affect Jurisdiction. These rules shall not be construed to extend or limit the jurisdiction, as established by law, of the Supreme Judicial Court or the Appeals Court. All proceedings related to any appeal from: (a) a decision of a single Justice of the Supreme Judicial Court, and (b) a decision of any tribunal, appeal from which must by law be brought in the Supreme Judicial Court, shall be had only before the full Supreme Judicial Court or a single justice thereof (unless transferred to the Appeals Court by order of the Supreme Judicial Court). But these rules shall govern such proceedings, except as provided in Supreme Judicial Court Rule 2:21.

(c) Definitions. As used in these rules:

"appeal" means an appeal to an appellate court and supersedes any procedure other than reservation and report by which matters have heretofore been brought before an appellate court for review.

"Appellate Court" means the full Supreme Judicial Court, the full Appeals Court, or a statutory quorum of either, as the case may be, whichever court is exercising statutory jurisdiction over the case at bar.

"child welfare case" means any case that is before a court of competent jurisdiction pursuant to G.L. c. 119, §§ 21–39J; G.L. c. 190B Parts 2 and 3; or G.L. c. 210, §§ 1–11.

"clerk" means "clerk," "register," "recorder," and their respective assistants or deputies; "clerk of the appellate division" means the clerk of the trial court from which the action was reported to the appellate division.

"first class mail" means use of first class postage prepaid, whether certified, registered, uncertified, or unregistered. Registration or certification shall not be required unless specifically stated to be necessary.

"lower court" means the single justice, court, appellate division, board, commission, or other body whose decision is the subject of an appeal; for the purpose of Rule 9, the term includes any member of the lower court.

"rescript" means the order, direction, or mandate of the appellate court disposing of the appeal. "single justice" means a single justice of whichever appellate court is exercising statutory jurisdiction over the case at bar.

(d) Construction. Words or phrases importing the singular number may extend and be applied to several persons or things, words importing the plural number may include the singular, and words importing the masculine gender may include the feminine and neuter.

Reporter's Notes (2009). The 2009 amendments reflect changes resulting from the adoption of the Massachusetts Uniform Probate Code.

RULE 2

Suspension of Rules

In the interest of expediting decision, or for other good cause shown, the appellate court or a single justice may, except as otherwise provided in Rule 14(b), suspend the requirements or provisions of any of these rules in a particular case on application of a party or on its own motion and may order proceedings in accordance with its direction. Such a suspension may be on reasonable terms.

RULE 3

Appeal—How Taken

(a) Filing the Notice of Appeal. An appeal permitted by law from a lower court shall be taken by filing a notice of appeal with the clerk of the lower court within the time allowed by Rule 4. Failure of an appellant to take any step other than the timely filing of a notice of appeal shall not affect the validity of the appeal, but shall be ground only for such action as the appellate court deems appropriate, which may include dismissal of the appeal. A party need not claim an appeal from an interlocutory order to preserve his right to have such order reviewed upon appeal from the final judgment; but for all purposes for which an appeal from an interlocutory order has heretofore been necessary, it is sufficient that the party comply with the requirement of Massachusetts Rules of Civil Procedure 46 or Massachusetts Rules of Criminal Procedure 22, whichever was applicable to the trial of the case in the lower court.

(b) Joint or Consolidated Appeals. If two or more persons are entitled to appeal from a judgment or order of a lower court and their interests are such as to make joinder practicable, they may file a joint notice of appeal, or may join in appeal after filing separate timely notices of appeal, and they may thereafter proceed on appeal as a single appellant. Appeals may be consolidated by order of the appellate court upon its own motion or upon motion of a party, or by stipulation of the parties to the several appeals.

(c) Content of the Notice of Appeal. The notice of appeal shall specify the party or parties taking the appeal and shall, in civil cases, designate the judgment, decree, adjudication, order, or part thereof appealed from. In child welfare cases, the notice of appeal and any request for a transcript, if required, shall be signed by the party or parties taking the appeal, unless the appellant is the minor subject of the action; a notice of appeal that is not so signed shall not be accepted for filing by the clerk.

(d) Service of the Notice of Appeal. The clerk of the lower court shall serve notice of the filing of a notice of appeal by mailing a copy thereof to counsel of record for each party other than the appellant, or, if a party is not represented by counsel, to the party at his last known address. The clerk shall note on each copy served the date on which the notice of appeal was filed. Failure of the clerk to serve notice shall not affect the validity of the appeal. Service shall be sufficient notwithstanding the death of a party or his counsel. The clerk shall note in the docket the names of the persons to whom he mails copies, with the date of mailing.

(e) Change of Counsel on Appeal in Criminal and Certain Non-criminal Cases. If the defendant in a criminal case or any party in any other proceeding, excluding child welfare cases, in which counsel is required to be made available to such party pursuant to Supreme Judicial Court Rule 3:10 was represented by counsel at trial, trial counsel shall continue to represent that party on appeal until the trial court permits him to withdraw his appearance and until an appearance is filed by substitute counsel. If trial counsel wishes to withdraw, he shall, on the day upon which the notice of appeal is filed, file a motion to withdraw. Any motion under this provision shall be marked up by the trial counsel for hearing no later than seven days after filing. If the motion to withdraw is allowed, the judge shall assign the Committee for Public Counsel Services to provide representation according to the procedures established in Supreme Judicial Court Rule 3:10.

(f) Appointment of Appellate Counsel in Child Welfare Cases. Any party to a child welfare case in which counsel was appointed pursuant to Supreme Judicial Court Rule 3:10 and who was represented by counsel at trial, shall continue to be represented by that counsel on appeal until either the trial court has appointed counsel for appellate purposes and an appearance has been filed by appellate counsel or the trial court has denied a motion to appoint counsel for appellate purposes. Trial counsel shall, on the day upon which the signed notice of appeal is filed, file, and request a hearing on, a motion to allow reasonable costs associated with the appeal. At the same time, if trial counsel is not appellate certified by the Committee for Public Counsel Services, counsel shall also

file, and request a hearing on, a motion to appoint counsel for appellate purposes. Subject to the provisions of Supreme Judicial Court Rule 3:10, § 7, trial counsel shall continue to represent the party at all trial court proceedings. If the motion to appoint counsel for appellate purposes is allowed, the Committee for Public Counsel Services shall be assigned to provide representation according to the procedures established in Supreme Judicial Court Rule 3:10.

RULE 4
Appeal—When Taken
(Amended effective May 1, 2013.)

(a) Appeals in Civil Cases. In a civil case, unless otherwise provided by statute, the notice of appeal required by Rule 3 shall be filed with the clerk of the lower court within thirty days of the date of the entry of the judgment appealed from; but if the Commonwealth or an officer or agency thereof is a party, the notice of appeal may be filed by any party within sixty days of such entry, except in child welfare cases, in which the notice of appeal shall be filed within thirty days from the date of the entry of the judgment, decree, order, or adjudication. If a notice of appeal is mistakenly filed in an appellate court, the clerk of such appellate court shall note the date on which it was received and transmit it to the clerk of the lower court from which the appeal was taken and it shall be deemed filed in such lower court on the date so noted. If a timely notice of appeal is filed by a party, any other party may file a notice of appeal within fourteen days of the date on which the first notice of appeal was filed, or within the time otherwise prescribed by this rule whichever period last expires.

If a timely motion under the Massachusetts Rules of Civil Procedure is filed in the lower court by any party: (1) for judgment under Rule 50(b); (2) under Rule 52(b) to amend or make additional findings of fact, whether or not an alteration of the judgment would be required if the motion is granted; (3) to alter or amend a judgment under Rule 59 or for relief from judgment under Rule 60, however titled, if either motion is served within ten days after entry of judgment; or (4) under Rule 59 for a new trial, the time for appeal for all parties shall run from the entry of the order denying a new trial or granting or denying any other such motion. A notice of appeal filed before the disposition of any of the above motions shall have no effect. A new notice of appeal must be filed within the prescribed time measured from the entry of the order disposing of the motion as provided above. No additional fees shall be required for such filing.

(b) Appeals in Criminal Cases. In a criminal case, unless otherwise provided by statute, the notice of appeal required by Rule 3 shall be filed with the clerk of the lower court within thirty days after entry of judgment or order appealed from; or entry of a notice of appeal by the Commonwealth; or the imposition of sentence. The running of the time for filing a notice of appeal shall be terminated as to the moving party by a motion for a new trial pursuant to Massachusetts Rules of Criminal Procedure 30 filed in the lower court within thirty days after the verdict or finding of guilt or within thirty days after imposition of sentence and the full time fixed by this rule shall commence to run and shall be computed from the date of entry of an order denying such motion.

(c) Extension of Time for Filing Notice of Appeal. Upon a showing of excusable neglect, the lower court may extend the time for filing the notice of appeal by any party for a period not to exceed thirty days from the expiration of the time otherwise prescribed by this rule. Such an extension may be granted before or after the time otherwise prescribed by this rule has expired; but if a request for an extension is made after such time has expired, it shall be made by motion with such notice as the lower court shall deem appropriate.

Reporter's Notes (2013). The 2013 amendment to Appellate Rule 4(a) changed item (3) to provide that, if served within ten days after entry of judgment, a motion under Mass. R. Civ. P. 59 to alter or amend a judgment or a motion under Mass. R. Civ. P. 60 for relief from judgment will toll the time period to claim an appeal from the underlying judgment.

The language "however titled" in the amended version is intended to make clear that the substance and not the title of the motion should control. *See Pentucket Manor Chronic Hospital, Inc. v. Rate Setting Commission*, 394 Mass. 233, 235–236 (1985). Thus a post-judgment motion under either Mass. R. Civ. P. 59 or 60, whether titled as a motion to alter, amend, or vacate, for relief from judgment, or for reconsideration, if served within ten days, will toll the time period to file a notice of appeal.

The 2013 amendment to Mass. R. A. P. 4(a) was intended to address the confusion that sometimes arose when a post-judgment motion, denominated a motion for "reconsideration," was served within ten days after entry of judgment. Since the text of the Massachusetts Rules of Civil Procedure does not refer to motions for reconsideration, a motion for reconsideration, if served within ten days of judgment, could have been treated as a motion under Rule 59 (for new trial or to alter or amend judgment) or as a motion under Rule 60(b) (for relief from judgment). If treated as a Rule 59 motion, the motion for reconsideration would have operated to toll the time period to claim an appeal. If treated as a Rule 60(b) motion, the motion for reconsideration would not have served to toll the time period to claim an appeal. Mass. R. A. P. 4(a), as it existed prior to the 2013 amendment. The 2013 amendment to Mass. R. A. P. 4(a) eliminates this potential for confusion by tolling the time period to claim an appeal where a motion for reconsideration is served within ten days after entry of judgment.

This amendment is not intended to provide a litigant with multiple opportunities to extend the time period to claim an appeal. Assume that the defendant serves a motion for relief from judgment within ten days of entry of judgment, thereby staying the time period to claim an appeal from the judgment. Two months later, the judge enters an order denying the motion for relief. Entry of that order starts the clock running to file a notice of appeal. If the defendant moves for reconsideration of the order denying relief from judgment, the motion for reconsideration should have no effect on the time period to claim appeal from the original judgment.

A 2009 amendment to Rule 4(a)(4)(a) of the Federal Rules of Appellate Procedure similarly recognized that a motion for relief from judgment under Rule 60 tolls the time period to file a notice of appeal.

RULE 5
Report of a Case for Determination

A report of a case for determination by an appellate court shall for all purposes under these rules be taken as the equivalent of a notice of appeal. Whenever a case or any part of it is reported after decision or verdict, the aggrieved party (as designated by the lower court) shall be treated as the appellant. Whenever a case or any part of it is reported without decision or verdict, the plaintiff in a civil action or the defendant in a criminal case shall be treated as the appellant. The clerk of the lower court shall serve notice of the filing of the report by mailing a copy thereof to counsel of record for each party; or if a party is not represented by counsel, to the party at his last known address.

RULE 6
Stay or Injunction Pending Appeal
(a) Civil Cases.

(1) Stay Must Ordinarily be Sought in the First Instance in Lower Court; Motion for Stay in Appellate Court. In civil cases, an application for a stay of the judgment or order of a lower court pending appeal, or for approval of a bond under subsection (a)(2) of this rule, or for an order suspending, modifying, restoring or granting an injunction during the pendency of an appeal must ordinarily be made in the first instance in the lower court. A motion for such relief may be made to the appellate court or to a single justice, but the motion shall show that application to the lower court for the relief sought is not practicable, or that the lower court has denied an application, or has failed to afford the relief which the applicant requested, with the reasons given by the lower court for its action. The motion shall also show the reasons for the relief requested and the facts relied upon, and if the facts are subject to dispute the motion shall be supported by affidavits or other statements signed under the penalties of perjury or copies thereof. With the motion shall be filed such parts of the record as are relevant. Reasonable notice of the motion shall be given to all parties. The motion shall be filed with the clerk of the appellate court to which the appeal is being taken (provided that if the court be the Supreme Judicial Court, the motion shall be filed with the clerk of the Supreme Judicial Court for Suffolk County).

(2) Stay May Be Conditioned Upon Giving of Bond; Proceedings Against Sureties. Relief available in the appellate court under this rule may be conditioned upon the filing of a bond or other appropriate security in the lower court. If security is given in the form of a bond or stipulation or other undertaking with one or more sureties, each surety thereby shall submit to the jurisdiction of the lower court and irrevocably appoint the clerk of the lower court as an authorized agent upon whom any papers affecting liability on the bond or undertaking may be served. A surety's liability may be entered against the surety on motion in the lower court without the necessity of an independent action. The motion and such notice of the motion as the lower court prescribes may be served on the clerk of the lower court, who shall forthwith mail copies to the sureties if their addresses are known.

(3) Terms. Relief available in the appellate court under this rule, or denial of such relief, may be conditioned on such reasonable terms as the appellate court or single justice may impose. For failure to observe such terms, the appellate court or single justice may make such further order as it or he deems just and appropriate.

(b) Criminal Cases. A motion for a stay of execution of a sentence shall be governed by paragraph (b) of this rule and by Massachusetts Rules of Criminal Procedure 31

(1) Stay Must Ordinarily be Sought in the First Instance in Lower Court; Motion for Stay in Appellate Court. In criminal cases, an application for a stay of execution of a sentence pending appeal must ordinarily be made in the first instance in the lower court. A motion for such relief may be made to the single justice of the appellate court to which the appeal is being taken, but the motion shall show that application to the lower court for the relief sought is not practicable, or that the lower court has previously denied an application for a stay or has failed to afford the relief which the applicant requested with the reasons given by the lower court for its action. The motion shall also show the reasons for the relief requested and the facts relied upon, and if the facts are subject to dispute the motion shall be supported by affidavits or other statements signed under the penalties of perjury or copies thereof. With the motion shall be filed such parts of the record as are relevant The motion shall be filed with the clerk of the appellate court to which the appeal is being taken (provided that if the court be the Supreme Judicial Court, the motion shall be filed with the clerk of the Supreme Judicial Court for Suffolk County).

(2) Reasonable Notice. Reasonable notice of the motion for a stay shall be given to the Commonwealth. If the motion is filed at least 30 days prior to the date the appellant's brief is due, the time for a response shall be governed by Rule 15. If the motion is filed at any other time, the Commonwealth shall have 30 days to respond. A single justice may shorten or extend the time for responding to any motion authorized by this Rule.

(3) Appealability of Single Justice Order. Finality. An order by the single justice allowing or denying an application for a stay may be appealed to the appellate court in which the appeal is pending. An order by the appellate court in which the appeal is pending, allowing or denying an application for a stay, shall be final.

(4) Revocation of Stay Pending Appeal. If a defendant fails at any time to take any measure necessary for the hearing of an appeal or report, a stay of execution of a sentence may, on motion of the Commonwealth, be revoked.

(5) Expiration of Stay. Upon the release of the rescript by the appellate court of a judgment affirming the conviction, the stay of execution of sentence automatically expires, unless extended by the appellate court.

(6) Notice of Expiration of Stay. Upon release of a rescript affirming the conviction, the clerk of the appellate court shall notify the clerk of the trial court and the parties that the conviction has been affirmed and that therefore, the stay of execution of sentence has automatically expired.

Reporter's Notes (2009). [The notes to the 2009 amendments were drafted by the Reporter for the Massachusetts Rules of Criminal Procedure]. This Rule was revised in 2009 to describe more fully the procedure for obtaining a stay of execution of a criminal sentence in an appellate court. It complements Rule 31 of the Rules of Criminal Procedure.

The 2009 amendment clarified the appellate process for stays of execution of a criminal sentence pending an appeal. As in civil cases, requests for a stay must first be presented to the trial court, unless such an application is not practicable. Either the defendant or the Commonwealth may seek relief from a single justice of the court that will hear the appeal concerning the trial judge's decision to deny, e.g., *Commonwealth v. Aviles*, 422 Mass. 1008 (1996), or grant, e.g., *Commonwealth v. Hodge*, 380 Mass. 851 (1980), a stay. Only the parties may do so. *See Hagen v. Commonwealth*, 437 Mass. 374, 375 (2002) (crime victim lacks standing to request revocation of stay). In the ordinary course of events, for all but first-degree murder cases a single justice of the Appeals Court is the appropriate forum. The single justice does not review the decision of the trial judge, but considers the matter de novo. *See Commonwealth v. Allen*, 378 Mass. 489, 497 (1979).

Rule 6(b)(2) recognizes that it is important to give the Commonwealth adequate time to prepare a response to a motion for a stay, since that will often require substantial effort in addressing the merits of the underlying appeal.

After the single justice decides the issue, there is only one further step in the process: an appeal to the panel of the Appeals Court that will decide the merits, or the full bench of the Supreme Judicial Court if the case will be decided there. This changes prior practice, which allowed a party aggrieved by the decision of a single justice of the Appeals Court the option of seeking relief both by appealing the decision in that court and asking a single justice of the Supreme Judicial Court to entertain the matter. *See e.g., Duong v. Commonwealth*, 434 Mass. 1006 (2001). The appeal from the decision of the single justice may be accompanied by a motion for an expedited ruling. *See e.g., Restucci v. Commonwealth*, 442 Mass. 1045 (2004).

As also provided in Mass. R. Crim. P. 31, a stay of execution of sentence automatically expires when the appellate court considering the appeal releases a rescript affirming the conviction, unless the appellate court decides to extend it. A rescript is "released" when it is announced to the public and the appellate court notifies the parties that the court has decided the case. Cf. Mass. R. App. P. 23 (requiring the clerk of the appellate court to mail the parties a copy of the rescript and the opinion, if any). In the ordinary course of events, the rescript "issues" twenty-eight days following the release date or upon the denial of any petition for rehearing or application for further appellate review, whichever is later. *Id.*

When a rescript is released affirming a conviction, the clerk of the appellate court, in addition to the obligation that Mass. R. App. P. 23 imposes, shall notify the parties and the trial court clerk that the stay of execution of sentence has automatically expired. If the defendant wishes to apply for a new stay, in order to seek a rehearing or further appellate review, such a request should go to the appellate court that decided the case (either the panel of the Appeals Court or the full bench of the Supreme Judicial Court).

The court that decided the appeal may exercise its discretion to extend a stay of execution pending a petition for rehearing, application for further appellate review, or petition for certiorari. Unless otherwise specified, an extended stay expires when the rescript issues. The appellate court may act sua sponte or pursuant to the defendant's motion, which may be filed before the appeal is decided or after the rescript is released.

RULE 7

Disability of a Member of the Lower Court

If by reason of death, sickness, resignation, removal, or other disability, the judge or judges whose decision has been appealed to the appellate court be unable to perform the duties to be performed under these rules by the lower court, then any other judge regularly sitting in or assigned to such lower court may, on assignment by the Chief Justice or presiding judge of such lower court, perform those duties.

RULE 8

The Record on Appeal

(a) Composition of the Record on Appeal. The original papers and exhibits on file, the transcript of proceedings, if any, and a certified copy of the docket entries prepared by the clerk of the lower court shall constitute the record on appeal in all cases. In a civil case, in an appeal from an appellate division, the original papers and exhibits shall include the report of the trial judge to the appellate division with any exhibits made a part of such report.

(b) The Transcript of Proceedings.

(1) Civil Cases, Except Child Welfare Cases: Duty of Appellant to Order; Notice to Appellee if Partial Transcript Is Ordered. Within ten days after filing the notice of appeal the appellant shall order from the court reporter a transcript of such parts of the proceedings not already on file as he deems necessary for inclusion in the record. If the appellant intends to urge on appeal that a finding or conclusion is unsupported by the evidence or is contrary to the evidence, he shall include in the record a transcript of all evidence relevant to such finding or conclusion. Unless the entire transcript is to be included, the appellant shall, within the time above provided, file and serve on the appellee a description of the parts of the transcript which he intends to include in the record and a statement of the issues he intends to present on the appeal. If the appellee deems a transcript of other parts of the proceedings to be necessary he shall, within 10 days after the service of the statement of the appellant, file and serve on the appellant a designation of additional parts to be included. If the appellant shall refuse to order such parts, the appellee shall either order the parts or apply to the lower court for an order requiring the appellant to do so. At the time of ordering, a party shall make satisfactory arrangements with the court reporter for payment of the cost of the transcript.

(2) Criminal Cases: Duty of Clerk; Duty of Court Reporter. Upon the filing of a notice of appeal, unless the parties file therewith a stipulation designating the parts of the proceedings which need not be transcribed, the clerk of the lower court, within ten (10) days, shall order from the court reporter a transcript of the proceedings and shall file a certificate of such order. The parties are encouraged to stipulate to those parts of the proceedings which are unnecessary to the appeal. Upon receipt of an order, the court reporter shall prepare one original typed transcript. The court reporter shall deliver the original typed transcript to the clerk of the lower court who shall, by means of xerography or other similar method which produces legible copies, prepare one copy thereof for each of the appellate court, the appellant, and the appellee. The clerk of the lower court shall deliver one copy each to the appellant and the appellee and shall certify that the copies of the appellant and appellee have been delivered. The clerk of the lower court shall retain custody of the original typed transcript and one copy thereof until the record is transmitted to the appellate court as provided by Rule 9(d). The Commonwealth shall pay the cost of the original of the typed transcript and a copy for the appellate court. Except as provided in Rule 8(b)(4), the cost of the copy for the appellant shall be paid for by the appellant.

(3) Electronically Recorded Proceedings, Except Child Welfare Cases.

(i) Applicability. Rule 8(b)(3) applies to proceedings which were recorded electronically on equipment under the control of the court and which were not recorded by an official court reporter. If, however, a complete transcript of the electronic recording has been produced for use by the trial court, and it or a copy is available to the parties, such transcript or copy shall be utilized in lieu of preparing another pursuant to this Rule 8(b)(3). Upon receipt of the notice of appeal in such cases, the clerk shall advise the parties of the name of the preparer of the transcript; the parties shall then follow the procedure under Rule 8(b)(1) in a civil case, or Rule 8(b)(2) in a criminal case, as if a court reporter had been present, except the appellant's time for ordering a transcript shall be extended to within ten days after appellant's receipt of the clerk's notification of the name of the preparer of the transcript.

(ii) Duties of the Appellant and of the Clerk; Selection of Transcriber. If the appellant deems all or part of the electronic recording necessary for inclusion in the record, the appellant shall, simultaneously with filing a notice of appeal, order from the clerk of the lower court, in accordance with any rule or established policy of the court, a cassette copy of the electronic recording, which is hereinafter called "the cassette." The clerk shall promptly provide the cassette, unless the provisions of the second paragraph of Rule 8(b)(3)(i) apply. If a portion of the electronic recording has already been transcribed for use by the trial court, and such transcript or a copy is available to the parties, the clerk shall, in addition to providing the cassette, at the same time advise the parties of the name of the preparer of the transcript.

Within fifteen days of receipt of the cassette from the clerk, appellant shall file in court and serve on each appellee a document which includes the date of receipt of the cassette; a designation of the parts of the cassette the appellant intends to include in the transcript; and the name, address, and telephone number of the individual or firm selected to prepare the transcript, provided that the appellant and each appellee have agreed to this choice and the appellant so states. If the appellant and appellees have not so agreed, said document shall also specifically notify the clerk to select the transcriber.

The designation of the parts of the cassette to be transcribed should be precise and include such details as the name of the witness whose testimony has been designated and the portions to be included, giving an exact quote of the beginning words and concluding words of each designated portion.

If such selection of an individual or firm to prepare the transcript is not included, or if the transcript is to be provided at the expense of the Commonwealth, the individual or firm shall be selected by the clerk. When the selection is made by the clerk, the individual or firm shall be selected in accordance with procedures promulgated by the Chief Administrative Justice. The clerk shall promptly notify all parties of any such selection made by the clerk. Any individual or firm selected to transcribe the record pursuant to Rule 8(b)(3) is hereinafter called "the transcriber."

If the appellant has designated the entire cassette for transcription, then within said fifteen days of receipt of the cassette from the clerk, appellant shall also send or deliver to the transcriber the cassette provided by the clerk and a written order designating the entire cassette for transcription. If the appellant has not designated the entire cassette, then after twenty days have expired from the service upon the appellee of appellant's designation of transcript, the appellant shall promptly send or deliver to the transcriber the cassette provided by the clerk and a written order which states those parts of the cassette designated by the parties for transcription. In addition, the order, whether for all or part of the transcript, shall include a statement that the original of the designated portions of the transcript should be sent to the clerk of the lower court, and shall indicate the number of copies if any, to be sent to the appellant. The appellant shall promptly file with the clerk and serve on the other parties a copy of the order placed with the transcriber. Unless the entire cassette is to be transcribed, the appellant shall, together with appellant's designation of transcript, file and serve on the appellee a statement of the issues the appellant intends to present on the appeal. The appellant shall cooperate with the transcriber by providing such information as is necessary to facilitate transcription, and, where the Commonwealth is not responsible for the cost of transcription, make satisfactory arrangements with the transcriber to pay for the trial court's original of the designated portions of the transcript and any copies ordered by the appellant for the appellant's own use.

(iii) Duties of the Appellee. If the appellee deems it necessary to have a cassette in order to consider counterdesignating, or for any other purpose, the appellee shall, after receipt of the notice of appeal, promptly order the cassette from the clerk or promptly arrange with the appellant to use appellant's cassette. If the appellant has not designated and ordered the entire transcript and if the appellee deems a transcript of other portions of the proceedings to be necessary, the appellee shall within fifteen days after receipt of the appellant's designation, file in court, and serve on the appellant, a designation of such additional parts. The designation of the parts of the cassette to be transcribed should be precise and include such details as the name of the witness whose testimony has been designated and the specific portions to be included, giving an exact quote of the beginning words and concluding words of each designated portion. If the appellant shall refuse to order such parts, the appellee shall either order the parts or apply to the lower court for an order requiring the appellant to do so. If the appellee desires a copy of designated portions of the transcript, the appellee shall promptly communicate to the transcriber the number of copies wanted and, in cases where the Commonwealth is not responsible for the cost of the transcript, make satisfactory arrangements with the transcriber for payment for the appellee's own copies.

The appellee shall cooperate with the transcriber by providing such information as is necessary to facilitate transcription.

(iv) Duties of the Transcriber. The transcriber shall prepare an original typed transcript of the designated portions and the requested number of copies, in accordance with the designations, and shall deliver said original to the clerk, with the following certificate of accuracy:

I, _____, do hereby certify that the foregoing is a true and accurate transcript, prepared to the best of my ability, of the designated portions of the cassette provided to me by the appellant or appellee of a trial or hearing of the _____ Division of the _____ Court Department in the proceedings of _____ v. _____, case(s) no.(s) _____ before Justice _____ on _____.

(Day and Date)
Date: _____

_____
Transcriber's Signature

The transcriber shall deliver legible copies to all parties who have so requested.

(v) Unintelligible Portions of the Cassette. If portions of the cassette cannot be transcribed because they are unintelligible, the parties shall promptly use reasonable efforts to stipulate their content. If agreement cannot be reached, the parties shall promptly present their differences as to such portions to the trial judge who heard the testimony. The trial judge shall, if possible, settle the content of the unintelligible portions, which shall then be included in the transcript.

(vi) Transcripts Paid for by the Commonwealth. In criminal cases, the Commonwealth shall pay the cost of the original of the designated portions of the typed transcript and a copy for the appellate court. Except as provided in Rule 8(b)(4), the cost of the copy for the appellant shall be paid for by the appellant who shall make arrangements with the transcriber to pay for such copy. Whenever the Commonwealth is to pay for an original or copy of the designated portions of the

transcript, each party designating any portion of the cassette for transcription shall, at the time of filing the designation, also file a certificate that the parts designated are necessary to permit full consideration of the issues on appeal. Unless one of the parties specifically requests otherwise, that part of the cassette dealing with impanelment of a jury shall not be transcribed.

(4) Cost of Transcripts for Indigents. In all cases in which counsel is required to be made available pursuant to Supreme Judicial Court Rule 3:10 the cost of any transcript for such a party shall be paid for by the Commonwealth.

(5) Child Welfare Cases

(i) Proceedings Recorded by an Official Court Reporter. On the filing of a notice of appeal, unless the parties file therewith a stipulation designating the parts of the proceedings which need not be transcribed, the clerk of the lower court on behalf of the appellant, shall order from the court reporter a transcript of the entire proceeding or of such parts of the proceeding not already on file. The clerk of the lower court shall notify all parties of the date the transcript was ordered by sending a copy of the order form to all parties. On receipt of the order the court reported shall prepare an original typed transcript for filing with the lower court and a copy for the appellant and any party who so requests. The court reporter shall deliver the original to the clerk of the lower court who shall immediately notify all parties of its receipt, and the court reporter shall deliver legible copies to the appellant and to any party who so requests.

(ii) Electronically Recorded Proceedings

(a) Applicability: Rule 8(b)(5)(ii) applies to child welfare cases which were recorded electronically on equipment under the control of the court ad which were not recorded by an official court reporter. If, however, a complete transcript of the electronic recording has been produced for use by the lower court, and it or a copy is available to the parties, that transcript or copy shall be used.

(b) Duties of the Appellant and Clerk. Upon the filing of a notice of appeal, the clerk of the lower court shall produce a cassette copy of the electronic recording. Within 10 days of production of the cassette, the clerk of the lower court shall, unless the parties file a stipulation designating the parts of the cassette which need not be transcribed, on behalf of the appellant order a transcription of the entire cassette from a transcriber selected by the clerk in accordance with procedures promulgated by the Chief Justice for Administration and Management. The clerk shall also notify all parties of the name of the transcriber and the date the cassette was sent for transcription by sending a copy of the order form to all parties.

On receipt of the order the transcriber shall prepare an original typed transcript for filing in the lower court and a copy for the appellant and any party who so requests. The transcriber shall deliver the original to the clerk of the lower court who shall immediately notify all parties of its receipt, and the transcriber shall deliver legible copies to the appellant and to any party who so requests. The appellant and appellee shall cooperate with the transcriber by providing information necessary to facilitate transcription. The transcriber shall certify the original transcript using the following certificate of accuracy:

I, _____, do hereby certify that the foregoing is a true and accurate transcript, prepared to the best of my ability, of the designated portions of the cassette provided to me by the clerk of the lower court of a trial or hearing of the _____

Division of the _____ Court Department in the proceedings of
_____, case(s) no(s). _____ before Justice _____ on _____.
Date: _____
_____
Transcriber's Signature

(iii) Unintelligible Portions of the Cassette. If portions of the cassette cannot be transcribed because they are unintelligible, the parties shall promptly use reasonable efforts to stipulate their content. If agreement cannot be reached, the parties shall promptly present their differences as to such portions to the trial judge who heard the testimony. The trial judge shall, if possible, settle the content of the unintelligible portions, which shall then be included in the transcript.

(iv) Costs. The appellant shall pay for the cost of the original transcript filed with the lower court and for any copies ordered by the appellant. If there is more than one appellant, the cost of the original and any copies shall be divided between the various appellants. Any other party who requested a copy of the transcript shall pay for its copy. For any party for whom counsel is made available pursuant to Supreme Judicial Court Rule 3:10, the cost of any transcript requested by, or on behalf of, such party shall be paid in accordance with G.L. c. 261.

(c) Statement of the Evidence or Proceedings When No Report Was Made or When the Transcript Is Unavailable. If no report of the evidence or proceedings at a hearing or trial was made, or if a transcript is unavailable, the appellant may, within thirty days after the notice of appeal is filed, file a statement of the evidence or proceedings from the best available means, including his recollection. The statement shall be served on the appellee, who may file objections or proposed amendments thereto within ten days after service. Thereupon the statement and any objections or proposed amendments thereto shall be submitted to the lower court for settlement and approval and as settled and approved shall be included by the clerk of the lower court in the record on appeal.

(d) Agreed Statement as the Record on Appeal. In lieu of the record on appeal as defined in subdivision (a) of this rule, the parties may, within thirty days after the notice of appeal is filed, prepare and sign a statement of the case showing how the issues presented by the appeal arose and were decided in the lower court and setting forth only so many of the facts averred and proved or sought to be proved as are essential to a decision of the issues presented. If the statement conforms to the truth, it, together with such additions as the court may consider necessary fully to present the issues raised by the appeal, shall be approved by the lower court, and as approved shall be retained in the lower court as the record on appeal.

Copies of the agreed statement shall be filed as the appendix required by Rule 18.

(e) Correction or Modification of the Record. If any difference arises as to whether the record truly discloses what occurred in the lower court, the difference shall be submitted to and settled by that court and the record made to conform to the truth. If anything material to either party is omitted from the record by error or accident or is misstated therein, the parties by stipulation, or the lower court, either before or after the record is transmitted to the appellate court, or the appellate court, or a single justice, on proper suggestion or on its own motion, may direct that the omission or misstatement be corrected, and if necessary that a supplemental record be certified and transmitted. All other questions as to the form and content of the record shall be presented to a single justice.

RULE 9
Assembly and Transmission of the Record: Exhibits

(a) Assembly. The clerk of the lower court as soon as may be after the filing of the notice of appeal shall place together all the original papers including the exhibits filed in the lower court, together with such other papers as thereafter become a part of the record pursuant to Rule 8. The papers shall be numbered in the order of filing and the exhibits shall be plainly marked with the number assigned in the lower court preceded by the letters "exh.". The clerk shall append to the record a list of the documents correspondingly numbered and identified with reasonable definiteness. The record so assembled by the clerk shall be suitably spindled, bound, or tied and retained by the clerk in this form until the final disposition of the appeal, except as the record or any part of it is ordered to be transmitted by the appellate court or a single justice.

(b) Exhibits. No exhibit need be reproduced for the record, except by order of an appellate court, a single justice, or the judge of the lower court. Any counsel may reproduce any exhibit in several copies for the convenience of the court. The lower court shall make such orders as it deems necessary for the preservation of exhibits, and for the reproduction of important exhibits which the appellate court should examine, and the clerk of the lower court shall transmit any exhibit to the appellate court at the request of any party made at any time after the filing of the record appendix. A party shall make advance arrangements with the clerk of the lower court for the transmission and receipt of exhibits of unusual bulk or weight. No exhibit consisting of currency, bearer securities, firearms, narcotics, or contraband articles shall be transmitted to an appellate court unless pursuant to an order of the full appellate court or a justice thereof.

(c) Appellant's Obligation.

(1) In General. In a civil or criminal case, upon request by the clerk of the lower court, the appellant shall forthwith perform any act reasonably necessary to enable the clerk to assemble the record and the clerk shall assemble a single record. The lower court or the appellate court or a single justice thereof may require the record to be assembled and the appeal to be docketed at any time.

(2) Civil Cases. Notwithstanding any other obligation which these rules may impose, but excepting electronically recorded proceedings governed by Rule 8(b)(3), each appellant in a civil case shall, within ten days after filing a notice of appeal, deliver to the clerk of the lower court either (i) a transcript of those portions of the transcript of the lower court proceedings which the appellant deems necessary for determination of the appeal, (ii) a signed statement certifying that the appellant has ordered such portions from the court reporter, or (iii) a signed statement certifying that the appellate has not ordered and does not intend to order the transcript or any portion thereof. Upon receiving the transcript, the appellant in a civil case shall forthwith deliver it to the clerk of the lower court.

(d) Duty of Clerk; Transmission. When the record is fully assembled, the clerk of the lower court shall notify the parties and the clerk of the appellate court and shall transmit to the appellate court two certified copies of the docket entries and, in a criminal case, the original and one copy of the transcript and a list of all the exhibits. In case of an order to transmit, transmission shall be effected when the clerk of the lower court mails or otherwise forwards the record to the clerk of the appellate court. The clerk of the lower court shall indicate, by endorsement on the face of the record or otherwise, the date upon which it is transmitted to the appellate court.

(e) Record for Preliminary Hearing in the Appellate Court. If prior to the time the record is assembled a party desires to make in the appellate court a motion for dismissal, for a stay pending appeal or for any intermediate order, the appellate court or a single justice may, on its own motion or on motion of any party, with or without notice, order the clerk of the lower court to transmit to the appellate court such parts of the original record as the appellate court or the single justice shall deem appropriate.

RULE 10
Docketing the Appeal

(a) Docketing the Appeal.

(1) Civil Cases. Within ten days after receiving from the clerk of the lower court notice of assembly of the record, or of approval by the lower court of an agreed statement, each appellant, including each cross-appellant, shall pay to the clerk of the appellate court the docket fee fixed by law, and the clerk shall thereupon enter the appeal of such appellant or cross-appellant upon the docket.

(2) Criminal Cases. Upon receipt of notice of assembly of the record, pursuant to Rule 9(d), or of approval by the lower court of an agreed statement, pursuant to Rule 8(d), the clerk of the appellate court shall enter the appeal upon the docket.

(3) In General. Upon docketing of the appeal, the clerk shall serve written notice thereof upon each party and the clerk of the lower court. Upon motion, the lower court or a single justice of the appellate court may, for cause shown, enlarge the time for docketing the appeal or permit the appeal to be docketed out of time. An appeal shall be docketed under the title given to the action in the lower court, with the appellant identified as such, but if such title does not contain the name of the appellant, his name, identified as appellant, shall be added to the title.

(b) Filing. The clerk of the appellate court shall file upon receipt any part of the record or any paper authorized to be filed in lieu of the record under any provisions of Rule 9, following timely docketing of the appeal. The clerk shall immediately give notice to all parties of the date of each such filing.

(c) Dismissal for Failure of Appellant in a Civil Case to Comply With Rule 9(c) or Rule 10(a). If any appellant in a civil case shall fail to comply with Rule 9(c) or Rule 10(a)(1) or (3), the lower court may, on motion with notice by any appellee, dismiss the appeal, but only upon a finding of inexcusable neglect; otherwise, the court shall enlarge the appellant's time for taking the required action. If, prior to the lower court's hearing such motion for noncompliance with Rule 9(c), the appellant shall have cured the noncompliance, the appellant's compliance shall be deemed timely.

RULE 11
Direct Appellate Review

(a) Application; When Filed; Grounds. An appeal within the concurrent appellate jurisdiction of the Appeals Court and Supreme Judicial Court shall be entered in the Appeals Court before a party may apply to the Supreme Judicial Court for direct appellate review. Within twenty days after the docketing of an appeal in the Appeals Court, any party to the case (or two or more parties jointly) may apply in writing to the Supreme Judicial Court for direct appellate review, provided the questions presented by the appeal are: (1) questions of first impression or novel questions of law which should be submitted for final determination to the Supreme Judicial Court; (2) questions of law concerning the Constitution of the Commonwealth or questions concerning the Constitution of the United States which have been raised in a court of the Commonwealth; or (3) questions of such public interest that justice requires a final determination by the full Supreme Judicial Court. Oral argument in support of an application will not be permitted except by order of court.

(b) Contents of Application; Form. The application for direct appellate review shall contain, in the following order: (1) a request for direct appellate review; (2) a statement of prior proceedings in the case, (3) a short statement of facts relevant to the appeal; (4) a statement of the issues of law raised by the appeal, together with a statement indicating whether the issues were raised and properly preserved in the lower court; (5) a brief argument thereon (covering not more than ten pages of typing) including appropriate authorities, in support of the applicant's position on such issues; and (6) a statement of reasons why direct appellate review is appropriate. A certified copy of the docket entries shall be appended to the application. The applicant shall also append a copy of any written decision, memorandum, findings, rulings, or report of the lower court relevant to the appeal. The application shall comply with the requirements of Rule 20.

(c) Opposition; Form. Within ten days after the filing of the application, any other party to the case may, but need not, file and serve an opposition thereto (covering not more than ten pages of typing) setting forth reason why the application should not be granted. The opposition shall not restate matters described in subdivision (b)(2) and (3) of this rule unless the opposing party is dissatisfied with the statement thereof contained in the application. The opposition shall comply with the requirements of Rule 20.

(d) Filing; Service. One copy of the application and one copy of each opposition shall be filed in the office of the clerk of the Appeals Court. An original and seventeen copies of the application and of each opposition shall be filed in the office of the clerk of the full Supreme Judicial Court. Filing and service of the application and of any opposition shall comply with Rule 13.

(e) Effect of Application Upon Appeal. The filing of an application for direct appellate review shall not extend the time for filing briefs or doing any other act required to be done under these rules.

(f) Vote of Direct Appellate Review; Certification. If any two justices of the Supreme Judicial Court vote for direct appellate review, or if a majority of the justices of the Appeals Court shall certify that direct appellate review is in the public interest, an order allowing the application (or transferring the appeal sua sponte) or the certificate, as the case may be, shall be transmitted to the clerk of the Appeals Court; upon receipt, direct appellate review shall be deemed granted. The clerk shall forthwith transmit to the clerk of the full Supreme Judicial Court all papers theretofore filed in the case and shall notify the clerk of the lower court that the appeal has been transferred.

(g) Cases Transferred for Direct Review; Time for Serving and Filing Briefs. In any appeal transferred to the full Supreme Judicial Court from the Appeals Court:

(1) If at the time of transfer all parties have served and filed briefs in the Appeals Court, no further briefs may be filed except that a reply brief may be served and filed on or before the last date allowable had the case not been transferred, or within ten days after the date on which the appeal is docketed in the full Supreme Judicial Court, whichever is later.

(2) If at the time of transfer only the appellant's brief has been served and filed in the Appeals Court the appellant may, but need not, serve and file an amended brief within twenty days after the date on which the appeal is docketed in the full Supreme Judicial Court. The appellee shall serve and file his brief within thirty days after service of any amended brief of the appellant, or within fifty days after the date on which the appeal is docketed in the full Supreme Judicial Court, whichever is later.

(3) Service and filing of a reply brief shall comply with Rule 19.

(4) If at the time of transfer to the full Supreme Judicial Court no party to the appeal has served or filed a brief, the appellant shall serve and file a brief within twenty days after the date on which the appeal is docketed in the full Supreme Judicial Court or within forty days after the date on which the appeal was docketed in the Appeals Court, whichever is later.

RULE 11.1
Transfer from Supreme Judicial Court

In the case of a direct appeal to the Supreme Judicial Court, within fourteen days after the appeal has been docketed, or such further time as a single justice upon motion for cause shown may allow, any party may serve and file a motion, on notice, to transfer the appeal to the Appeals Court. The motion: (a) shall not exceed five typewritten pages; (b) shall succinctly specify the grounds for transfer; and (c) shall conform to Rules 13, 14, 15, and 20(b). Within seven days after filing of the motion, any other party may serve and file an opposition to the transfer. The opposition: (a) shall not exceed five typewritten pages; (b) shall succinctly specify the reasons for opposing the transfer; and (c) shall conform to Rules 13, 14, 15, and 20(b).

No oral argument will be permitted.

RULE 12
Proceedings in Forma Pauperis

(a) Leave to Proceed on Appeal In Forma Pauperis From Lower Court to Appellate Court. Either a lower court or a single justice, for cause shown and after reasonable notice, may authorize an appeal to be prosecuted in forma pauperis, upon such reasonable terms as such court or justice may prescribe.

(b) Form of Briefs, Appendices and Other Papers. Parties allowed to proceed in forma pauperis may file briefs, appendices and other papers in typewritten form, and may

request that the appeal be heard on the original record without the necessity of reproducing parts thereof in any form.

RULE 13
Filing and Service

(a) Filing. Papers required or permitted to be filed in the appellate court shall be filed with the clerk. Filing may be accomplished by first class mail, either registered or unregistered, addressed to the clerk, but filing shall not be timely unless the papers are received by the clerk within the time fixed for filing, except that briefs and appendices shall be docketed on the date of receipt and shall be deemed timely filed if (i) received within the time fixed for filing or (ii) accompanied by an affidavit signed by counsel of record attesting that the day of mailing was within the time fixed for filing. If a motion requests relief which may be granted by a single justice, the justice may permit the motion to be filed with him, in which event he shall note thereon the date of filing and shall thereafter transmit it to the clerk.

(b) Service of All Papers Required. Copies of all papers filed by any party and not required by these rules to be served by the clerk shall, at or before the time of filing be served by a party or person acting for him on all other parties to the appeal or review. Service on a party represented by counsel shall be made on counsel.

(c) Manner of Service. Service may be personal or by first class mail. Personal service includes delivery of the copy to a clerk or other responsible person at the office of counsel. Service by first class mail is complete on mailing.

(d) Proof of Service. Papers presented for filing shall contain an acknowledgment of service by the person served or proof of service in the form of a statement under the penalties of perjury of the date and manner of service and of the name of the person served, signed by the person who made service. Proof of service may appear on or be affixed to the papers filed. The clerk may permit papers to be filed without acknowledgment or proof of service but shall require such acknowledgment or proof to be filed promptly thereafter.

RULE 14
Computations and Extensions of Time

(a) Computation of Time. In computing any period of time prescribed by these rules, by order of court, or by any applicable statute, the day of the act event, or default after which the designated period of time begins to run shall not be included. The last day of the period shall be included, unless it is a Saturday, Sunday or a legal holiday, in which event the period shall extend until the end of the next day which is not a Saturday, Sunday or a legal holiday. When the period of time prescribed or allowed is less than 7 days, intermediate Saturdays, Sundays and legal holidays shall be excluded in the computation. As used in this rule "legal holiday" means those days specified in G.L. c. 4, § 7 and any other day appointed as a holiday by the President or the Congress of the United States or so designated by the laws of the Commonwealth.

(b) Enlargement of Time. The appellate court or a single justice for good cause shown may upon motion enlarge the time prescribed by these rules or by its order for doing any act, or may permit an act to be done after the expiration of such time; but neither the appellate court nor a single justice may enlarge the time for filing a notice of appeal beyond one year from the date of entry of the judgment or order sought to be reviewed, or, in a criminal case, from the date of the verdict or finding of guilt or the date of imposition of sentence, whichever date is later.

(c) Additional Time After Service by Mail. Whenever a party is required or permitted to do an act within a prescribed period after service of a paper upon him and the paper is served by mail, 3 days shall be added to the prescribed period.

RULE 15
Motions

(a) Content of Motions; Response; Reply. Unless another form is elsewhere prescribed by these rules, an application for an order or other relief shall be made by filing a motion for such order or relief with proof of service on all other parties. The motion shall contain or be accompanied by any matter required by a specific provision of these rules governing such a motion, shall state with particularity the grounds on which it is based, and shall set forth the order or relief sought. If a motion is supported by briefs, affidavits, or other papers, they shall be served and filed with the motion. Any party may file a response in opposition to a motion other than one for a procedural order (for which see subdivision (b)) within 7 days after service of the motion, but motions authorized by Rule 6 may be acted upon after reasonable notice, and the appellate court or a single justice may shorten or extend the time for responding to any motion.

(b) Determination of Motions for Procedural Orders. Notwithstanding the provisions of the preceding paragraph as to motions generally, motions for procedural orders, including any motion under Rule 14(b), may be acted upon at any time, without awaiting a response thereto. Any party adversely affected by such action may request reconsideration, vacation, or modification of such action.

(c) Power of a Single Justice to Entertain Motions. In addition to the authority expressly conferred by these rules or by law, a single justice may entertain and may grant or deny any request for relief which under these rules may properly be sought by motion, except that a single justice may not dismiss or otherwise determine an appeal or other proceeding, and except that the appellate court may provide by order or rule that any motion or class of motions shall be acted upon by the appellate court. The action of a single justice may be reviewed by the appellate court.

(d) Motions for New Trial in Capital Cases. After the docketing of an appeal in a criminal case in which the defendant was convicted of murder in the first degree and until the filing of a rescript by the appellate court, a motion for a new trial pursuant to Massachusetts Rules of Criminal Procedure 30 shall be filed in the appellate court and may be remitted to the trial judge for hearing and determination at such time as the appellate court may direct.

RULE 16
Briefs

(a) Brief of the Appellant. The brief of the appellant shall contain under appropriate headings and in the order here indicated:

(1) In all briefs, a table of contents, with page references, and a table of cases (alphabetically arranged), statutes and other authorities cited, with references to the pages of the brief where they are cited.

(2) A statement of the issues presented for review.

(3) A statement of the case, which shall first indicate briefly the nature of the case, the course of proceedings, and its disposition in the court below. There shall follow a statement of the facts relevant to the issues presented for review, with appropriate references to the record (see subdivision (e)).

(4) The argument, which shall contain the contentions of the appellant with respect to the issues presented, and the reasons therefor, with citations to the authorities, statutes and parts of the record relied on. In a brief with more than twenty-four pages of argument, there shall be a short summary of argument, suitably paragraphed and with page references to later material in the brief dealing with the same subject matter, which should be a condensation of the argument actually made in the body of the brief, and not a mere repetition of the headings under which the argument is arranged. The appellate court need not pass upon questions or issues not argued in the brief. Nothing argued in the brief shall be deemed to be waived by a failure to argue orally.

(5) A short conclusion stating the precise relief sought.

(6) Any written or oral findings or memorandum of decision by the court pertinent to an issue on appeal included as an addendum to the brief.

(7) In cases where geographical facts are of importance, unless appropriate plans are reproduced in the printed record or record appendix, an outline plan or chalk (preferably based on exhibits in evidence) shall be included. This outline plan should be suitable for reproduction on one page of the printed law reports.

(8) The printed names, Board of Bar Overseers (BBO) numbers, addresses, and telephone numbers of individual counsel, and, if an individual counsel is affiliated with a firm, the firm name.

(b) Brief of the Appellee. The brief of the appellee shall conform to the requirements of subdivision (a)(1)-(4) and (7), except that a statement of the issues or of the case need not be made unless the appellee is dissatisfied with the statement of the appellant.

(c) Reply Brief. The appellant may file a brief in reply to the brief of the appellee, and if the appellee has cross-appealed, the appellee may file a brief in reply to the response of the appellant to the issues presented by the cross appeal. No further briefs may be filed except with leave of the appellate court. Reply briefs shall comply with the requirements of Rule 16(a)(1).

(d) References in Briefs to Parties. Counsel will be expected in their briefs and oral arguments to keep to a minimum references to parties by such designations as "appellant" and "appellee." It promotes clarity to use the designations used in the lower court, or the actual names of the parties, or descriptive term such as "the employee," "the injured person," "the taxpayer," "the landlord," etc. If the name of a party has been impounded or has been made confidential by statute, rule, or court order, counsel shall preserve confidentiality in briefs and oral arguments.

(e) References in Briefs to the Record. References in the briefs to parts of the record reproduced in an appendix filed with a brief (see Rule 18(a)) shall be to the pages of the appendix at which those parts appear. If the appendix is prepared after the briefs are filed, references in the briefs to the record shall be made by one of the methods allowed by Rule 18(c). If the record is reproduced in accordance with the provisions of Rule 18(f), or if references are made in the briefs to parts of the record not reproduced, the references shall be to the pages of the parts of the record involved; e.g., Answer p. 7, Motion for Judgment p. 2, Transcript p. 231. Intelligible abbreviations may be used. If reference is made to evidence the admissibility of which is in controversy, reference shall be made to the pages of the appendix or of the transcript at which the evidence was identified, offered, and received or rejected. No statement of a fact of the case shall be made in any part of the brief without an appropriate and accurate record reference.

(f) Reproduction of Statutes, Rules, Regulations, etc. If determination of the issues presented requires consideration of constitutional provisions, statutes, rules, regulations, etc. or relevant parts thereof, they shall be reproduced in the brief or in an addendum at the end.

(g) Massachusetts Citations. Massachusetts Reports between 17 Massachusetts and 97 Massachusetts shall be cited by the name of the reporter. Any other citation shall include, wherever reasonably possible, a reference to any official report of the case or to the official publication containing statutory or similar material. References to decisions and other authorities should include, in addition to the page at which the decision or section begins, a page reference to the particular material therein upon which reliance is placed, and the year of the decision; as, for example: 334 Mass. 593, 597–598 (1956). Quotations of Massachusetts statutory material shall include a citation to either the Acts and Resolves of Massachusetts or to the current edition of the General Laws published pursuant to a resolve of the General Court.

(h) Length of Briefs. Except by permission of the court, principal briefs shall not exceed fifty pages, exclusive of pages containing the table of contents, tables of citations and any addendum containing statutes, rules, regulations, etc. Except by permission of the court, reply briefs shall not exceed twenty pages. Permission of the court shall not be granted unless the moving party specifies the relevant issue or issues and why such issues merit additional pages. A motion of a party to exceed the page limits stated in this rule will not be granted except for extraordinary reasons.

(i) Briefs in Cases Involving Cross Appeals. If a cross appeal is filed, the plaintiff in the court below shall be deemed the appellant for the purposes of this rule and Rules 18 and 19, unless the parties otherwise agree or the court otherwise orders. The brief of the appellee shall contain the issues and argument involved in his appeal as well as the answer to the brief of the appellant.

(j) Briefs in Cases Involving Multiple Appellants or Appellees. In cases involving more than one appellant or appellee, including cases consolidated for purposes of the appeal, any number of either may join in a single brief, and any appellant or appellee may adopt by reference any part of the brief of another. Parties may similarly join in reply briefs.

(k) Required Certification; Non-complying Briefs. The last page of each brief shall include a certification by counsel, or, if a party is proceeding pro se, by the party, that the brief complies with the rules of court that pertain to the filing of briefs, including, but not limited to: Mass. R. A. P. 16(a)(6) (pertinent findings or memorandum of decision); Mass. R. A. P. 16(e) (references to the record); Mass. R. A. P. 16(f) (reproduction of statutes, rules, regulations); Mass. R. A. P. 16(h) (length of briefs); Mass. R. A. P. 18 (appendix to the briefs); and Mass. R. A. P. 20 (form of briefs, appendices,

and other papers). A brief not complying with these rules (including a brief that does not contain a certification) may be struck from the files by the appellate court or a single justice.

(l) Citation of Supplemental Authorities. When pertinent and significant authorities come to the attention of a party after his brief has been filed, or after oral argument but before decision, a party may promptly advise the clerk of the court, by letter, with a copy to all counsel, setting forth the citations. There shall be a reference either to the page of the brief or to a point argued orally to which the citations pertain, but the letter shall without argument state the reasons for the supplemental citations. Any response shall be made promptly and shall be similarly limited.

(m) References to Impounded Material. Upon the filing of any brief or other document containing references to matters that are impounded or have been made confidential by statute, rule, or order counsel (or a party if pro se), shall file a written notice with the clerk, with a copy to all parties, so indicating. Wherever possible, counsel shall not disclose impounded material. Where it is necessary to include impounded material in a brief, the cover of the brief shall clearly indicate that impounded information is included herein.

RULE 17
Briefs of an Amicus Curiae

A brief of an amicus curiae may be filed only (1) by leave of the appellate court or a single justice granted on motion or (2) at the request of the appellate court, except that consent or leave shall not be required when the brief is presented by the Commonwealth. The brief may be conditionally filed with the motion for leave. A motion for leave shall identify the interest of the applicant and shall state the reasons why a brief of an amicus curiae is desirable. Any amicus curiae shall file its brief within the time allowed the party whose position as to affirmance or reversal the amicus brief will support unless the appellate court or a single justice for cause shown shall grant leave for later filing, and shall specify within what period an opposing party may answer. A motion of an amicus curiae to participate in the oral argument will be granted only for extraordinary reasons. The same number of copies of the brief of an amicus curiae shall be filed with the clerk and served on counsel for each party separately represented as required by Rule 19(b).

RULE 18
Appendix to the Briefs

(a) Duty of Appellant to Prepare and File; Content of Appendix; Time for Filing; Number of Copies. The appellant shall prepare and file an appendix to the briefs. In civil cases, the appendix shall contain: (1) the relevant docket entries in the proceedings below; (2) any relevant portions of the pleadings, charge, findings, or opinion; (3) the judgment, order, or decision in question; and (4) any other parts of the record to which the parties wish to direct the particular attention of the court. Except where they have independent relevance, memoranda of law in the lower court should not be included in the appendix.

In criminal cases, the appendix need not contain relevant portions of the transcript, but shall contain: (1) the relevant docket entries in the proceedings below; (2) a copy of the complaint or indictment; and (3) any paper filed in the case relating to an issue which is to be argued on appeal. Any party

6

in a criminal case may include in an appendix to his brief any other parts of the record to which he wishes to direct the particular attention of the court.

The appendix shall include any order of impoundment or confidentiality from the lower court. The fact that parts of the record are not included in the appendix shall not prevent the parties or the court from relying on such parts, provided that the court may decline to permit the parties to refer to portions of the record omitted from the appendix, unless leave be granted prior to argument.

Unless filing is to be deferred pursuant to the provisions of subdivision (c) of this rule, any appendix shall be filed and served with the brief. If separately bound, the same number of copies of the appendix shall be filed with the clerk as required by Rule 19(b) for the filing of the brief, and two shall be served on counsel for each party separately represented, unless the court shall by rule or order direct the filing or service of a lesser number and except as otherwise provided in subdivision (e) of this rule.

(b) Determination of Contents of Appendix in Civil Cases; Cost of Producing. The parties are encouraged to agree as to the contents of the appendix. In the absence of agreement, the appellant shall, not later than ten days after the date on which the clerk notifies the parties that the record has been assembled, serve on the appellee a designation of the parts of the record which he intends to include in the appendix and a statement of the issues which he intends to present for review. If the appellee deems it necessary to direct the particular attention of the court to parts of the record not designated by the appellant, he shall, within ten days after receipt of the designation, serve upon the appellant a designation of those parts. The parties shall not engage in unnecessary designation and may refer to parts of the record not included in the appendix if permitted by the appellate court or a single justice pursuant to the provisions of Rule 18(a) or 18(f). However, this does not affect the responsibility of the parties to include materials necessary to their appeal, including exhibits, in the appendix.

Where a party designates as part of the record any matter that has been impounded or has been made confidential by statute, rule, or order, the designation shall so state.

Unless the parties otherwise agree, the cost of producing the appendix shall initially be paid by the appellant, but if the appellant considers that parts of the record designated by the appellee for inclusion are unnecessary for the determination of the issues presented he may so advise the appellee and the appellee shall advance the cost of including such parts. In the event of a dispute as to the parts to be included or the advance required to include them, the matter shall be settled by the lower court on motion and notice. The cost of producing the appendix shall be taxed as costs in the case, but if either party shall cause matters to be included in the appendix unnecessarily the court may impose the cost of producing such parts on the party.

(c) Alternative Method of Designating Contents of the Appendix in Civil Cases; How References to the Record May Be Made in the Briefs When Alternative Method Is Used. In civil cases, if the appellant shall so elect—with leave of the appellate court or a single justice—preparation of the appendix may be deferred until after the briefs have been filed and the appendix may be filed twenty-one days after service of the brief of the appellee. Notice of the election by

the appellant to defer preparation of the appendix shall be filed and served by him within ten days after the date on which the clerk notifies the parties that the record has been assembled. If the preparation and filing of the appendix is thus deferred, the provisions of subdivision (b) of this Rule 18 shall apply, except that the designations referred to therein shall be made by each party at the time his brief is served, and a statement of the issues presented shall be unnecessary.

If the deferred appendix authorized by this subdivision is employed, references in the briefs to the record may be to the pages of the parts of the record involved, in which event the original paging of each part of the record shall be indicated in the appendix by placing in brackets the number of each page at the place in the appendix where that page begins. Or if a party desires to refer in his brief directly to pages of the appendix, he may serve and file typewritten or page-proof copies of his brief within the time required by Rule 19(a), with appropriate references to the pages of the parts of the record involved. In that event, within fourteen days after the appendix is filed he shall serve and file copies of the brief in the form prescribed by Rule 20(a) containing references to the pages of the appendix in place of or in addition to the initial references to the pages of the parts of the record involved. No other changes may be made in the brief as initially served and filed, except that typographical errors may be corrected.

(d) Arrangement of the Appendix. The pages of the appendix shall be consecutively numbered and the parts of the record which are reproduced therein shall be set out in chronological order. The appendix shall commence with a chronologically ordered list of the parts of the record which it contains, with references to the pages of the appendix at which each part begins. When an appendix relates to two or more cases or to more than two parties, the appendix shall indicate the case to which each paper belongs and by whom it was filed. Unless the party filing the appendix reproduces the entire transcript of testimony, he shall, preceding each portion of testimony transcript reproduced, insert a concise statement identifying:

(1) the witness whose testimony is being reproduced;

(2) the party originally calling him;

(3) the party questioning him; and

(4) the classification of his examination (direct, cross, or other).

When matter contained in the reporter's transcript of proceedings is set out in the appendix, the page number of the original transcript at which such matter may be found may be indicated in brackets immediately before the matter which is set out, unless it already appears on the matter as set out. Omissions in the text of papers or of the transcript must be indicated by asterisks. Immaterial formal matters (captions, subscriptions, acknowledgments, etc.) may be omitted. A question and its answer may be contained in a single paragraph.

(e) Reproduction of Exhibits and Transcripts. Exhibits and transcripts or portions thereof in civil cases, designated for inclusion in the appendix, may be contained in separate volumes, suitable indexed.

(1) Appeals Court. On appeals to the Appeals Court, five copies of the exhibits volume or volumes, and two copies of the transcript volume or volumes, shall be filed with the appendix and one copy of each shall be served on counsel for each party separately represented.

(2) Supreme Judicial Court. On appeal to the Supreme Judicial Court, and on further appellate review, five copies of the exhibits volume or volumes and five copies of the transcript volume or volumes shall be filed with the appendix and one copy of each shall be served on counsel for each party separately represented.

(3) Appeals transferred to the Supreme Judicial Court from the Appeals Court. In any appeal transferred to the full Supreme Judicial Court, in which copies of the exhibits and transcripts have already been filed in the Appeals Court pursuant to this rule three additional copies of the transcript volume or volumes shall be promptly filed with the clerk of the Supreme Judicial Court, unless the court by order in a particular case shall direct a lesser or greater number.

(f) Hearing of Appeals on the Original Record Without the Necessity of an Appendix. On motion, the appellate court or a single justice may, in specific cases, dispense with the requirement of an appendix and permit appeals to be heard in whole or in part on the original record, with such copies of the record, or relevant parts thereof, as the court may require.

(g) Reproduction of Impounded Materials. If the entire case has been impounded, the cover of the appendix shall clearly indicate that the appendix is impounded. If the entire case has not been impounded, a separate appendix volume shall be filed containing the impounded material and the cover thereof shall clearly indicate that it contains impounded material.

RULE 19
Filing and Service of Briefs and Motions

(a) Time for Serving and Filing Briefs. Except as provided in section (d) of this rule, and in Rule 11(g)(4) concerning the filing of briefs on direct appellate review, and in Rule 27.1(f) concerning the filing of briefs on further appellate review, the appellant shall serve and file his brief within 40 days after the date on which the appeal is docketed in the appellate court. The appellee shall serve and file his brief within thirty days after service of the brief of the appellant. The appellant may serve and file a reply brief within fourteen days after service of the brief of the appellee, but, except by leave of the appellate court or a single justice, for good cause shown, a reply brief must be filed at least three days before the first day of the sitting at which the case is in order for argument.

(b) Number of Copies to Be Filed and Served.

(1) Appeals Court. On appeals to the Appeals Court, seven copies of each brief shall be filed with the clerk, unless the court by order in a particular case shall direct a lesser number, and two copies shall be served on counsel for each party separately represented.

(2) Supreme Judicial Court. On appeal to the Supreme Judicial Court, an original and seventeen copies of each brief shall be filed with the clerk, unless the court by order in a particular case shall direct a lesser or greater number, and two copies shall be served on counsel for each party separately represented.

(3) Appeals transferred to the Supreme Judicial Court from the Appeals Court. In any appeal transferred to the full Supreme Judicial Court, in which briefs have already been filed in the Appeals Court, eleven additional copies of each brief shall be promptly filed with the clerk of the Supreme Judicial Court, unless the court by order in a particular case shall direct a lesser or greater number.

(c) Consequence of Failure to File Briefs. If an appellant fails to file his brief within the time provided by this rule, or within the time as extended, an appellee may move for dismissal of the appeal. If an appellee fails to file his brief, he will not be heard at oral argument except by permission of the appellate court.

(d) Rule for Appeals Pursuant to Massachusetts General Laws Chapter 278, sec. 33E.

(1) In the case of a direct appeal by an appellant who has been convicted of first degree murder, the appellant shall within one hundred and twenty days after the date on which the appeal is docketed in the Supreme Judicial Court: (1) serve and file the appellant's brief; (2) serve and file a motion for new trial; or (3) for good cause shown, seek a further enlargement of time for filing a brief or a motion for new trial. The commonwealth shall serve and file its brief within ninety days after service of the brief of the appellant. The appellant may serve and file a reply brief within the thirty days after service of the brief of the Commonwealth.

(2) If a motion for new trial is remanded to the Superior Court, the direct appeal of the conviction shall be stayed pending decision on the motion for new trial. The matter shall be heard and determined expeditiously in the Superior Court. The appellant shall file with the Clerk of the Supreme Judicial Court for the Commonwealth status reports at thirty-day intervals. An appeal by the defendant from the denial of a motion for new trial shall be consolidated with the direct appeal. An appeal by the Commonwealth or by the defendant from the determination of a motion for new trial shall have the same docket number as the direct appeal. The Clerk of the Supreme Judicial Court for the Commonwealth shall establish a briefing schedule.

RULE 20
Form of Briefs, Appendices, and Other Papers
(Amended effective May 1, 2010.)

(a) Form of Briefs and the Appendix. Except on order of the appellate court or a single justice, or if filed on behalf of a party allowed to proceed in forma pauperis, all briefs and appendices shall be produced by any duplicating or copying process which produces a clear black image on white paper. However produced, the page shall be eight and one-half inches in width and eleven inches in height. Pages shall be firmly bound at the left by saddle-wiring, side-wiring, stapling, or sewing. If side-wired or sewn, a strong paper cover shall be used. A transcript of testimony or a report of evidence may be included as part of the appendix and may be reproduced by Xerography or a similar process. No single volume of the appendix shall be more than one and one-half inches thick. The text of appendices may appear on both sides of the page.

The following rules shall govern the format of text on a page for all briefs:

(1) The top and bottom margins shall be at least one inch. The left and right margins shall be at least one and one-half inches. Thus, the text area should not be more than five and one-half inches in width no more than nine inches in height. Page numbers may appear in the margin.

(2) The typeface shall be a monospaced font (such as pica type produced by a typewriter or a Courier font produced by a computer word processor) of 12 point or larger size and not exceeding 10.5 characters per inch.

(3) Text shall be double-spaced, except that argument headings, footnotes and indented quotations may be single-spaced. For purposes of this rule, single spacing means not more than six lines of text per vertical inch; double spacing means not more than three lines of text per vertical inch and not more than twenty-seven double-spaced lines on a page.

(4) The text may appear on both sides of the page.

Briefs or appendices not in substantial compliance with these rules shall not be received unless the appellate court or a single justice shall otherwise order. The cover of the brief of the appellant shall be blue; that of the appellee, red; that of an intervenor or amicus curiae, green; that of any reply brief, gray. The cover of the appendix, if separately bound, shall be white. The front covers of the briefs and appendices, if separately produced, shall contain: (1) the name of the court and the number of the case; (2) the title of the case (see Rule 10(a)); (3) the nature of the proceeding in the court (e.g., Appeal; Application for Review) and the name of the court, agency, or board below; (4) the title of the document (e.g., Brief for Appellant, Appendix); and (5) the names, Board of Bar Overseers (BBO) numbers, addresses, telephone numbers, and e-mail addresses if any of counsel representing the party on whose behalf the document is filed, and, if an individual counsel is affiliated with a firm, the firm name.

(b) Form of Other Papers. Petitions for rehearing shall be produced in a manner prescribed by subdivision (a). Motions and other papers may be produced in like manner, or they may be typewritten in pica type upon opaque, unglazed paper eight and one half by eleven inches in size. Lines of typewritten text shall be double spaced. Consecutive sheets shall be attached at the left margin. Carbon copies may be used for filing and service if they are legible.

A motion or other paper addressed to the court shall contain a caption setting forth the name of the court, the title of the case, the file number, and a brief descriptive title indicating the purpose of the paper; said caption shall appear on the first page, typed so as to be legible.

The cover of applications for direct appellate review and for further appellate review shall be white.

Such motion or paper shall contain, at the end thereof, the names, Board of Bar Overseers (BBO) numbers, addresses, and telephone numbers of counsel, if any, representing the party on whose behalf the motion or paper is filed, and, if an individual counsel is affiliated with a firm, the firm name.

Reporter's Notes (2010). Rule 20(a)(4) has been amended to require attorneys to include their e-mail addresses, if any, on the front cover of briefs and appendices. A similar amendment to Mass.R.Civ.P. 11(a) was adopted in 2010 requiring attorneys to include their e-mail addresses on pleadings.

RULE 21
Prehearing Conference

The appellate court may direct the attorneys for the parties to appear before the court or a single justice for a prehearing conference to consider the simplification of the issues and such other matters as may aid in the disposition of the proceeding by the court. The appellate court or single justice shall make an order which recites the action taken at the conference and the agreements made by the parties as to any of the matters considered and which limits the issues to those not disposed of by admissions or agreements of counsel, and

such order when entered shall control the subsequent course of the proceeding, unless modified to prevent manifest injustice.

RULE 22
Oral Argument

(a) Notice of Argument; Postponement. The clerk shall advise all parties of the time and place at which oral argument will be heard. A request for postponement of the argument must be made by motion filed reasonably in advance of the date fixed for hearing.

(b) Time Allowed for Argument. Unless otherwise enlarged or limited by the appellate court, each side will be allowed 15 minutes for argument, except in a criminal case in which the defendant is appealing a conviction of murder in the first degree, in which case each side will be allowed twenty minutes for argument. If counsel is of the opinion that additional time is necessary for the adequate presentation of the argument, counsel may request additional time for good cause shown. Requests may be made by letter addressed to the clerk reasonably in advance of the date fixed for the argument. The appellate court may terminate the argument whenever in its judgment further argument is unnecessary.

(c) Order and Content of Argument. Except as otherwise provided in Rule 27.1(g), the appellant will argue first and shall include a fair statement of the case. Counsel will not be permitted to read, except briefly, from briefs, records, prepared statements, records or authorities. The party making the opening argument on request may be allowed the opportunity to reply in writing to new matter in the arguments of his adversary.

(d) Cross and Separate Appeals. A cross or separate appeal shall be argued with the initial appeal at a single argument, unless the appellate court otherwise directs. If a case involves a cross appeal, the plaintiff in the action below shall be deemed the appellant for the purposes of this rule unless the parties otherwise agree or the court otherwise directs. If separate appellants support the same argument, care shall be taken to avoid duplication of argument.

(e) Non-appearance of Parties. If the appellee fails to appear to present argument, the appellate court will hear argument on behalf of the appellant, if present. If the appellant fails to appear, the court may hear argument on behalf of the appellee, if his counsel is present. If neither party appears, the case will be decided on the briefs unless the appellate court shall otherwise order.

(f) No Oral Argument by an Attorney Who Has Been a Witness Except by Leave of Court. No attorney shall be permitted to take part in the argument of a case in which he has been a witness for his client; except by special leave of court.

(g) Submission on Briefs. By agreement of the parties, a case may at any time be submitted for decision on the briefs, but the appellate court may direct that the case be argued. At any time, any party may, by written notice filed and served, waive his right to oral argument. No criminal case in which the defendant was convicted of murder in the first degree may be submitted for decision on the briefs without oral argument unless the full appellate court or a justice thereof shall have approved the submission prior to the week the case has been scheduled for argument.

(h) Use of Physical Exhibits at Argument; Removal. If physical exhibits other than documents or chalks are to be used at the argument, counsel shall arrange to have them placed in the court room before the court convenes on the date of the argument. After the argument, the exhibits shall be left with the clerk unless the court otherwise directs. If exhibits are not reclaimed by counsel within a reasonable time after notice is given by the clerk, they shall be destroyed or otherwise disposed of as the clerk shall think best.

RULE 23
Issuance of Rescript: Stay of Rescript

The clerk of the appellate court shall mail to all parties a copy of the rescript and the opinion, if one was written. The rescript of the court shall issue to the lower court twenty-eight days after the date of the rescript unless the time is shortened or enlarged by order. The timely filing of a petition for rehearing or of an application for further appellate review will stay the rescript until disposition of the petition or application unless otherwise ordered by the appellate court. If the petition or application is denied, the rescript shall issue forthwith unless the appellate court or a single justice orders otherwise. If an application for further appellate review is granted the rescript of the Appeals Court shall not issue to the lower court.

RULE 24
Justices' Participation

(a) Other Justices May Participate Without Reargument. Whenever the justices before whom a law question has been heard so desire, others of the justices may be called in to take part in the decision, upon a perusal of the record and briefs, without reargument.

(b) Justice May Review Own Ruling in Certain Cases. No justice shall sit on the hearing of any proceeding in the nature of a review of any judgment decree, order, or ruling made by him; provided, however, that this shall not apply where it is necessary to secure a quorum or where the other justices of the court shall be equally divided in opinion.

RULE 24.1
Divided Vote on Further Appellate Review

If, following allowance of an application for further appellate review, the justices of the Supreme Judicial Court are equally divided in opinion, unless a majority of the participating justices decides otherwise, the court shall issue an order noting such equal division, the effect of which shall be the same as if the court had denied the application for further appellate renew.

RULE 25
Damages for Delay

(Applicable to Civil Cases)

If the appellate court shall determine that an appeal is frivolous, it may award just damages and single or double costs to the appellee, and such interest on the amount of the judgment as may be allowed by law.

RULE 26
Costs

(Applicable to Civil Cases)

(a) To Whom Allowed. Except as otherwise provided by law, if an appeal is dismissed, costs shall be taxed against the appellant unless otherwise agreed by the parties or ordered by the appellate court; if a judgment is affirmed, costs shall be taxed against the appellant unless otherwise ordered; if a judgment is reversed, costs shall be taxed against the appellee unless otherwise ordered; if a judgment is affirmed on reversed in part, or is vacated, costs shall be allowed only as ordered by the appellate court.

(b) Costs For and Against the Commonwealth. In cases involving the Commonwealth or an agency or officer thereof, if an award of costs against the Commonwealth is authorized by law, costs shall be awarded in accordance with the provisions of subdivision (a); otherwise, costs shall not be awarded for or against the Commonwealth.

(c) Costs of Briefs, Appendices, and Copies of Records. The cost of printing or otherwise producing necessary copies of briefs, appendices, or copies of records authorized by Rule 18(f) shall be taxable in the lower court at rates not higher than those generally charged for such work in the Commonwealth. A party who desires such costs to be taxed shall state them in an itemized and verified bill of costs which he shall file with the clerk of the lower court, with proof of service, within fourteen days after the entry of judgment.

(d) Clerk to Insert Costs in Lower Court Judgment; Costs Taxable. The clerk of the lower court shall prepare and certify an itemized statement of costs for insertion in the lower court judgment. The statement shall include those costs taxable under subdivision (c) of this rule; costs incurred in the preparation and transmission of the record, the cost of the reporter's transcript, if necessary for the determination of the appeal, the premiums paid for cost of any bond to preserve rights pending appeal, and the fee for filing the notice of appeal shall be taxed in the lower court as costs of the appeal in favor of the party entitled to costs under this rule.

RULE 27
Petition for Rehearing

(a) Time for Filing; Content; Answer; Action by Court if Granted. A petition for rehearing should be filed with the clerk of the appellate court within fourteen days after the date of the rescript unless the time is shortened or enlarged by order. It shall state with particularity the points of law or fact which it is contended the court has overlooked or misapprehended and shall contain such argument in support of the petition as the petitioner desires to present. Oral argument in support of the petition will not be permitted, except by order of the quorum or panel which decided the appeal. No answer to a petition for rehearing will be received unless requested by the quorum or panel, but a petition for rehearing will ordinarily not be granted in the absence of such a request. A petition for rehearing shall be decided by the quorum or panel which decided the appeal. If a petition for rehearing is granted, the quorum or panel may make a final disposition of the cause without reargument or may restore it to the calendar for reargument or resubmission or may make such other orders as are deemed appropriate under the circumstances of the particular case. Action upon a petition is in the discretion of such quorum or panel, which may award costs, including a reasonable attorney's fee, to the prevailing party.

(b) Form of Petition; Length. The petition shall be in a form of a letter to the senior justice of the quorum or panel which decided the appeal with seven clear and legible copies, and additional copies shall be mailed by first class mail or delivered to all other counsel. Except by permission of the quorum or panel, a petition for rehearing shall not exceed ten pages of standard typewritten material.

6

(c) Revision of Decision. Upon consideration of a petition for rehearing, a quorum or panel may in writing order their decision to be reviewed and revised by a majority of the justices of the court. The petitioner shall notify the Supreme Judicial Court of any action taken on the petition if an application for further appellate review also has been filed.

RULE 27.1
Further Appellate Review

(a) Application; When Filed; Grounds. Within twenty days after the date of the rescript of the Appeals Court any party to the appeal may file an application for leave to obtain further appellate review of the case by the full Supreme Judicial Court. Such application shall be founded upon substantial reasons affecting the public interest or the interests of justice. Oral argument in support of an application shall not be permitted except by order of the court.

(b) Contents of Application; Form. The application for leave to obtain further appellate review shall contain, in the following order: (1) a request for leave to obtain further appellate review; (2) a statement of prior proceedings in the case (including whether any party is seeking a rehearing in the Appeals Court); (3) a short statement of facts relevant to the appeal (but facts correctly stated in the opinion, if any, of the Appeals Court shall not be restated); (4) a statement of the points with respect to which further appellate review of the decision of the appeals court is sought; and (5) a brief statement (covering not more than ten pages of typing), including appropriate authorities, indicating why further appellate review is appropriate. A copy of the rescript and opinion, if any, of the Appeals Court shall be appended to the application. In addition, if the Appeals Court entered a memorandum and order under Appeals Court Rule 1:28 which refers to another document, such as a brief or judge's findings and rulings, a copy of that document, or, if appropriate, the pertinent pages of that document, shall be appended to the application. The application shall comply with the requirements of Rule 20.

(c) Opposition; Form. Within ten days after the filing of the application, any other party to the appeal may, but need not, file and serve an opposition thereto (covering not more than ten pages of typing) setting forth reasons why the application should not be granted. The opposition shall not restate matters described in subdivision (b)(2) and (3) of this rule unless the opposing party is dissatisfied with the statement thereof contained in the application. An application shall comply with the requirements of Rule 20.

(d) Filing; Service. One copy of the application and one copy of each opposition shall be filed in the office of the clerk of the Appeals Court. An original and seventeen copies of the application and of each opposition shall be filed in the office of the clerk of the full Supreme Judicial Court. Filing and service of the application and of any opposition shall comply with Rule 13.

(e) Vote for Further Appellate Review; Certification. If any three justices of the Supreme Judicial Court shall vote for further appellate review for substantial reasons affecting the public interest or the interests of justice, or if a majority of the justices of the Appeals Court or a majority of the justices of the Appeals Court deciding the case shall certify that the public interest or the interests of justice make desirable a further appellate review, an order allowing the application or the certificate, as the case may be, shall be transmitted to the clerk of the Appeals Court; upon receipt, further appellate review shall be deemed granted. The clerk shall forthwith transmit to the clerk of the full Supreme Judicial Court all papers theretofore filed in the case and shall notify the clerk of the lower court that leave to obtain further appellate review has been granted.

(f) Briefs. Any party may apply to the Supreme Judicial Court within ten days after the date on which the appeal is docketed in the full Supreme Judicial Court for permission to file a new brief. If the application is granted, the new brief must be filed in accordance with the briefing schedule established by the Clerk of the Supreme Judicial Court, and the court may impose terms as to the length and filing of such brief and any response thereto. If a new brief is filed, it will be considered in lieu of the Appeals Court brief. If permission to file a new brief is denied or not sought, cases in which further appellate review has been granted shall be argued on the briefs filed in the Appeals Court.

(g) Order of Argument. The applicant for leave to obtain further appellate review will argue first unless the court directs or the parties agree otherwise.

RULE 28
Entry of Judgment Following Rescript
(Applicable to Civil Cases)

When the rescript from the appellate court sets forth the text of the judgment to be entered, the clerk of the lower court shall, upon receipt of the rescript, prepare, sign and enter the judgment which has been ordered. If the rescript orders settlement of the form of the judgment in the lower court, the clerk of the lower court shall sign and enter the judgment after settlement. Notation of a judgment in the lower court docket constitutes entry of the judgment.

RULE 29
Voluntary Dismissal

(a) Dismissal in the Lower Court. If an appeal has not been docketed, the appeal may be dismissed by the lower court upon the filing in that court of a stipulation for dismissal signed by all the parties, or upon motion and notice by the appellant.

(b) Dismissal in the Appellate Court. If the parties to an appeal or other proceeding shall sign and file with the clerk of the appellate court an agreement that the proceeding be dismissed, specifying the terms as to payment of costs, and shall pay whatever fees are due, the clerk shall enter the case as dismissed, but no rescript or other process shall issue without an order of the appellate court. An appeal may be dismissed on motion of the appellant upon such terms as may be agreed upon by the parties or fixed by the court. The clerk of the appellate court shall promptly notify the clerk of the lower court whenever an appeal in a criminal case is dismissed pursuant to this rule.

(c) Settlement; Obligation of Appellant. In the event a case is settled or otherwise disposed of while an appeal is pending, it shall be the duty of counsel for the appellant to notify the clerk of the appellate court forthwith.

RULE 30
Substitution of Parties

(Applicable to Civil Cases)

(a) Death of a Party. If a party dies after a notice of appeal is filed in the lower court or while a proceeding is pending in the appellate court, the personal representative of the deceased party may be substituted as a party on motion filed by the representative or by any party with the clerk of the appropriate court. The motion of a party shall be served upon the representative in accordance with the provisions of Rule 13. If the deceased party has no representative, any party may suggest the death on the record and proceedings shall then be had as the appellate court or a single justice may direct. If a party against whom an appeal may be taken dies after entry of a judgment or order in the lower court but before a notice of appeal is filed, an appellant may proceed as if death had not occurred. After the appeal is docketed, substitution shall be effected in the appellate court in accordance with this subdivision. If a party entitled to appeal shall die before filing a notice of appeal, the notice of appeal may be filed by his personal representative, or, if he has no personal representative, by his attorney of record within the time prescribed by these rules. After the appeal is docketed, substitution shall be effected in the appellate court in accordance with this subdivision.

(b) Substitution for Other Causes. If substitution of a party in the appellate court is necessary for any reason other than death, substitution shall be effected in accordance with the procedure prescribed in subdivision (a).

(c) Public Officers; Death or Separation from Office.

(1) When a public officer is a party to an appeal or other proceeding in an appellate court in his official capacity and during its pendency dies, resigns, or otherwise ceases to hold office, the action does not abate and his successor is automatically substituted as a party. Proceedings following the substitution shall be in the name of the substituted party, but any misnomer not affecting the substantial rights of the parties shall be disregarded. An order of substitution may be entered at any time, but the omission to enter such an order shall not affect the substitution.

(2) When a public officer is a party to an appeal or other proceeding in his official capacity he may be described as a party by his official title rather than by name; but the court may require his name to be added.

RULE 31
Duties of Clerks

(a) General Provisions. Any clerk of the appellate court shall take the oath and give the bond required by law. No clerk shall practice in any court as an attorney or as counselor while he continues in office. The Supreme Judicial Court and the Appeals Court shall be deemed always open for the pur-

pose of filing any proper paper, of issuing and returning process and of making motions and orders. The office of the clerk with a clerk in attendance shall be open during the hours from nine in the morning to four-thirty in the afternoon on all days except Saturdays, Sundays, and those days specified in G.L. c. 4, § 7, any other day appointed as a holiday by the President or the Congress of the United States, or designated by the laws of the Commonwealth, and except that either court may authorize closing of its clerk's office at four in the afternoon during the period between the Fourth of July and Labor Day.

(b) The Docket; Calendar; Other Records Required. The clerk shall keep a book known as the docket, in such form and style as may be prescribed by the appellate court, and shall enter therein each case. Cases shall be assigned consecutive file numbers. The file number of each case shall be noted on the folio of the docket whereon the first entry is made. All papers filed with the clerk and all process, orders and rescripts shall be entered chronologically in the docket on the folio assigned to the case. Entries shall be brief but shall show the nature of each paper filed or rescript or order entered. The entry of an order or rescript shall show the date the entry is made. The clerk shall keep a suitable index of cases contained in the docket. The clerk shall prepare, under the direction of the appellate court, a calendar of cases awaiting argument. In placing cases on the calendar for argument, he shall give preference to appeals in criminal cases and to appeals and other proceedings entitled to preference by law. The clerk shall keep such other books and records as may be required from time to time by law or by the appellate court.

(c) Notice of Orders or Rescripts. Immediately upon the entry of an order or rescript or upon receipt of notice of the grant of an application for direct or further appellate review the clerk shall serve a notice of entry by mail upon each party to the proceeding together with a copy of any opinion respecting the order or rescript, and shall make a note in the docket of the mailing. Service on a party represented by counsel shall be made on counsel.

(d) Custody of Records and Papers. The clerk shall have custody of the records and papers of the appellate court. He shall not permit any original record or paper to be taken from his custody except as authorized by the orders or instructions of the court or a single justice. Original papers transmitted as the record on appeal or review shall upon disposition of the case be returned to the lower court from which they were received.

RULE 32
Title

These rules may be known and cited as the Massachusetts Rules of Appellate Procedure.

6

6

PART 7

District/Municipal Courts Rules for Probation Violation Proceedings

(The District/Municipal Court Rules for Probation Violation Proceedings replace the District Court Rules for Probation Violation Proceedings effective Sept. 8, 2015.)

Rule

1 Scope and Purpose
2 Definition of Terms
3 Commencement of Violation Proceedings: Charged Criminal Conduct
4 Commencement of Violation Proceedings: Violations Other than a New Criminal Complaint
5 Probation Detention Hearings
6 Conduct of Violation Hearings
7 Hearsay Evidence
8 Findings and Disposition
9 Violation of Conditions of a "Continuance without a Finding"

RULE 1

Scope and Purpose

These rules prescribe procedures in the Boston Municipal Court and the District Court to be followed upon the allegation of a violation of an order of probation issued in a criminal case after a finding of guilty or after a continuance without a finding. These rules do not apply to an alleged violation of pretrial probation, as the latter term is defined herein.

The purpose of these rules is to ensure that judicial proceedings undertaken upon the allegation of a violation of probation are conducted in full compliance with all applicable law, promptly and with an appropriate degree of procedural uniformity.

2015 Commentary to District/Municipal Courts Rule 1

In recognition of the advisability of having uniform procedures, to the extent practical, within the Trial Court, a single set of Rules for Probation Violation Proceedings has been promulgated for use in both the Boston Municipal Court and the District Court. These rules are largely modeled on the District Court Rules for Probation Violation Proceedings, made effective in 2000, with changes made both to account for legal and technological developments since 2000 and to account for the respective needs of each department.

2000 Commentary to District Court Rule 1

Probation violation proceedings are among the most important matters within District Court jurisdiction. The timely and proper conduct of these proceedings is essential to protect the rights of probationers as set forth in federal and state law, as well as to maintain the credibility, and thus the effectiveness, of probation orders. Just as fundamentally, the proper and timely conduct of probation violation proceedings is necessary to vindicate the public trust. Failure of the court to take appropriate action when a convicted defendant who has been given the benefit of probation is then alleged to have violated that order erodes public confidence in the judicial system.

These rules are intended to codify the provisions of applicable case law and to provide clarity in areas of long-standing ambiguity. Their purpose is to provide a clear and predictable process whereby probation violation proceedings are to be commenced, conducted and completed.

One area of ambiguity involves terminology. These rules are entitled "Rules for Probation Violation Proceedings" and not "Rules for Probation Revocation Proceedings." This is an important distinction involving the essential difference between adjudication and disposition. Ambiguity concerning this distinction appears occasionally in the relevant case law, which almost uniformly refers to "probation revocation hearings." The problem is that when a probationer is alleged to have violated his or her probation order, the first purpose of the subsequent hearing is to adjudicate the factual question of whether that violation occurred. The decision to revoke probation, or order any other disposition, can proceed only if a violation is found. Most of the due process requirements that have evolved for these hearings relate to the process by which the court is to determine the factual issue. The nature of the alleged violation is essentially irrelevant to the factual determination of whether it occurred. In contrast, the issue of whether the probation order should be revoked (in many instances requiring the execution of a sentence of incarceration) focuses directly on the nature of the violation, among other factors. In addition, the issue of violation is essentially a *factual* matter, whereas the dispositional decision of whether to revoke probation is essentially one of discretion.

Confusion on this distinction can affect proceedings significantly. For example, the preponderance of the evidence test at a probation violation hearing has nothing to do with the revocation decision; it is the evidentiary test by which court must determine if a violation occurred. Conversely, the seriousness of the alleged violation has nothing to do with whether it occurred, but is an important consideration regarding revocation.

It is believed that often probation violation proceedings are not initiated because the Probation Department has no intention of recommending revocation and the incarceration it may require. As long as the proceeding is referred to, and believed to be for the purpose of, revocation and incarceration, there can be reluctance to allege a violation if the appropriate disposition is not revocation but rather the imposition of more stringent or intense probation requirements. The concept of a probation *revocation* hearing promotes a mistaken "all or nothing" perception. It implies that revocation is the purpose of the hearing and that if a violation is found, revocation must follow. In fact, the purpose of the hearing is to adjudicate the allegation, with the court having broad discretionary authority if a violation is found.

These rules seek to clarify the important difference between adjudicating the factual issue of whether a violation has occurred and the court's dispositional decision following

7

such adjudication, not only by referring to the proceedings as "probation *violation* proceedings," but also by requiring a two-step procedure (Rule 5) and expressly defining the different purpose and procedures required for each step (Rule 7).

Throughout these rules the person who is the subject of probation violation proceedings is usually referred to as the "probationer" rather than the "defendant." With respect to the probation proceedings, such a person is *not* a defendant; he or she has either been convicted, after trial or based on a plea of guilty, or has formally submitted an admission to the facts of a criminal charge. Use of the term "probationer" is intended to underscore the legal status of the individual charged with a probation violation, which is fundamentally distinct from the status of a person who is a criminal defendant, particularly in terms of procedural rights.

RULE 2
Definition of Terms

As used in these rules, the following terms shall have the following meanings:

"Continuance without a finding:" the order of a court, following a formal submission and acceptance of a plea of guilty or an admission to sufficient facts, whereby a criminal case is continued to a date certain without the formal entry of a guilty finding. A continuance without a finding may include conditions imposed in an order of probation (1) the violation of which may result in the revocation of the continuance, entry of a finding of guilty and imposition of sentence, and (2) compliance with which will result in dismissal of the criminal case.

"District Attorney:" the criminal prosecuting authority including the Attorney General if the criminal case in which probation was ordered was prosecuted by the Office of the Attorney General.

"General conditions of probation:" the conditions of probation that are imposed as a matter of course in every order of probation, as set forth in the official form promulgated for such orders.

"Probation order:" the formal, written court order whereby a defendant is placed on probation and which expressly sets forth the conditions of probation. A probation order is not a contract.

"Pretrial probation:" the probationary status of a defendant pursuant to a probation order issued prior to a trial or the formal submission and acceptance of a plea of guilty or an admission to sufficient facts, as provided in G.L. c. 276, § 87.

"Revocation of probation:" the revocation by a judge of an order of probation as a consequence of a determination that a condition of that probation order has been violated.

"Special conditions of probation:" any condition of probation other than one of the general conditions of probation.

"Surrender:" the procedure by which a probation officer requires a probationer to appear before the court for a judicial hearing regarding an allegation of probation violation.

2015 Commentary to District/Municipal Courts Rule 2

The "general conditions of probation" are set forth in standard probation forms, promulgated after consultation with the Office of the Commissioner of Probation. In the Boston Municipal Court, this is form BMCD-CR-104. In the District Court, this is form DGCR-27.

A sentence has been added to the definition of "probation order" that existed in the 2000 District Court Rule to address the recurring error of probation orders being referred to as probation "contracts." A probation order is not a contract. *Commonwealth v. MacDonald*, 435 Mass. 1005, 1007 (2001).

In the definition of "pretrial probation," a reference to the relevant statute has been added.

2000 Commentary to District Court Rule 2

This rule provides definitions for six terms that are important for a clear understanding of various provisions of these rules.

The definition of "continuance without a finding" is provided to make clear that, as used in these rules, the term presupposes that the defendant whose case has been so continued has formally submitted, and the court has accepted, a plea of guilty or an admission to sufficient facts. There is no "continuance without a finding" unless a guilty plea or admission has been properly tendered and accepted. This definition also makes clear that the conditions of the continuance may be set forth in an order of probation. Thus, upon violation of one or more conditions of probation, the court may proceed to enter a guilty finding and impose sentence, as provided in Rule 9. It may be possible for a court to continue a case without a finding *without* imposing the conditions of the continuance as probation conditions, but these rules have no application in such a circumstance. If the conditions of a continuance without a finding, whether or not imposed as conditions of probation, are *not* violated, the criminal case may be dismissed. *See Commonwealth v. Pyles*, 423 Mass. 717 (1996).

"Probation order" is defined as a written court order that specifies the conditions imposed. Fundamental fairness requires that if a probationer is to be subject to sanctions for failure to obey probation conditions, those conditions must be clearly specified. And proof of a violation will require evidence that the defendant was made aware of the conditions he or she allegedly violated. Conditions of probation must not be vague. *See Commonwealth v. Power*, 420 Mass. 410 (1995). A written order is conducive to clarity. The probation order also fulfills a statutory requirement for written conditions: "Every person released upon probation shall be given by the probation officer a written statement of the terms and conditions of the release." G.L. c. 276, § 85.

The definition of "pretrial probation" makes clear that this term includes probation orders issued before a trial, a plea or an admission. A defendant placed on pretrial probation under G.L. c. 276, § 87, is formally on probation, but violation of such probation would not appear to subject the probationer to any sanction other than the resumption of the criminal proceeding. Having not admitted guilt or been tried, and having waived no rights, such a probationer would not appear to be subject to any sentencing, let alone any loss of liberty, even if a violation of such probation were alleged and proved. As a result, the due process requirements that are the central focus of these procedural rules do not apply to an alleged violation of a pretrial probation order, and Rule 1 expressly so provides.

The definition of "revocation of probation" makes clear that this is an order that must be preceded by a judicial determination that a condition of a probation order has been violated.

Special conditions of probation are defined simply as any condition other than the "general conditions." A violation of such a special condition (or a general condition other than the prohibition against any violation of law) has traditionally, and perhaps unfortunately, been referred to as a "technical" violation.

"Surrender" is defined in accordance with *Commonwealth v. Durling*, 407 Mass. 108, 111 (1990):

> When a violation is alleged, the probation officer "surrenders" the defendant to the court, subjecting the defendant to possible revocation of his probation.

This definition is intended to clarify that surrender is the process by which the Probation Department brings the probationer before the court to answer for an alleged violation. It may be effected by arrest with or without a warrant under G.L. c. 279, § 3, or by a notice requiring the defendant to appear before the court. If a defendant is already before the court on a separate matter (for example, following an arrest on a new alleged crime, with or without a warrant, or on a summons on a new alleged crime), he or she may be notified at that time of the probation violation and ordered to appear at, or held in custody until, a probation violation hearing. In such cases no actual surrender by the Probation Department is required, since the defendant is before the court for a different reason when violation proceedings are commenced.

This definition of "surrender" clarifies any confusion caused by the use of the term to mean the process following a revocation of probation where a sentence is executed or imposed. *See, e.g., Commonwealth v. Duro*, No. 95-P-2186 (Appeals Court, March 28, 1997) (summary disposition) (court refers to "order revoking the defendant's probation and surrendering him to the custody of the State. . . .").

RULE 3
Commencement of Violation Proceedings: Charged Criminal Conduct

(a) General. This rule prescribes the procedures to be undertaken upon the issuance of a criminal complaint against a probationer.

(b) When Probation Order and New Criminal Charge Involve Same Court Division.

(i) *Issuance and Service of Notice of Violation; Termination of Proceedings; Withdrawal of Notice of Violation.* When a criminal complaint is issued by a court division against a defendant who is the subject of a probation order previously issued by that same court division, the Probation Department shall commence violation proceedings against that probationer. Such proceedings shall be commenced by the issuance by the Probation Department of a Notice of Probation Violation and Hearing at or before the arraignment on the criminal charge, or as soon thereafter as possible. The notice shall be served on the probationer in hand following the assignment of a date and time for a probation violation hearing, as provided in Rule 3(b)(ii), and such service shall be recorded on the case docket, provided that, if such in-hand service is not possible, the notice shall be served on the probationer by first-class mail, unless the court orders otherwise. Service of the notice by first-class mail shall be recorded on the case docket. Out-of-court service other than by mail shall require a written return of service. The Probation Department shall provide a copy of each notice of violation to the District Attorney forthwith upon its issuance.

At any time during violation proceedings, the court, upon review of the notice of violation and as a matter of its discretion, may order termination of the proceedings. A notice of violation may be withdrawn only with the permission of the court and such withdrawal and permission shall be set forth on the record and entered on the case docket.

(ii) *Contents of Notice of Violation.* The Notice of Probation Violation and Hearing shall set forth the criminal behavior alleged to have been committed by the probationer as indicated in the criminal complaint, and shall set forth any other conditions of the probation order that the Probation Department alleges have been violated with a description of each such alleged violation. The notice shall also state the date, time, and place of the hearing.

(iii) *Scheduling of Hearing.* The probation violation hearing shall be scheduled to be commenced on the date of the pretrial hearing for the criminal charge, unless the court expressly orders an earlier hearing. The hearing shall be scheduled for a date certain no less than seven days after service on the probationer of the notice of violation unless the probationer waives the seven-day notice period. The hearing date shall not be later than 30 days after service of the notice of violation, except in extraordinary circumstances. In scheduling the pretrial hearing on the new criminal charge together with the probation violation hearing, the court shall give primary consideration to the need for promptness in conducting the probation violation hearing.

(c) When Probation Order and New Criminal Charge Involve Different Court Divisions within the Same Court Department.

(i) *Issuance and Service of Notice of Violation.* When a criminal complaint is issued by a court division (hereinafter the "criminal court") against a defendant who is the subject of a probation order issued by a different division of the same court department (hereinafter a "probation court"), the Probation Department at the criminal court shall issue a Notice of Probation Violation and Hearing to the probationer at or before arraignment on the criminal charge, or as soon thereafter as possible. The notice shall be served on the probationer in hand and such service shall be recorded on the case docket. Nothing in this rule shall preclude the later issuance and service on the probationer of a notice of violation by the Probation Department of a probation court.

(ii) *Contents of Notice of Violation.* The notice of violation shall set forth the name of the court division at which the probationer is on probation and the criminal behavior alleged to have been committed by the probationer as indicated the criminal complaint and shall order the probationer to appear at a specific date and time at the probation court for the express purpose of appointment of counsel, if necessary, and scheduling of a probation violation hearing.

(iii) *Transmission of Notice of Violation and Other Documents to Probation Court.* Prior to the service of the notice of violation on the probationer, the Probation Department at the criminal court shall send to the Chief Probation Officer at the probation court, by electronic transmission, copies of the following documents: the notice of violation; the criminal complaint and related police report on the new criminal charge that constitutes the alleged probation violation; and a request for the following information: whether the probation court recommends that the probationer to be transported in custody, and, if not, the date and time for the non-custodial appearance of the probationer at the probation court.

(iv) *Response by the Probation Court.* At the probation court, the Chief Probation Officer, an Assistant Chief Probation Officer, or a probation officer designated by either shall respond by electronic transmission to the request for information no later than one hour from receipt thereof. The response shall include a recommendation on whether the probationer should be transported to the probation court in custody, and, if not, the date and time for the probationer's non-custodial appearance at the probation court.

(v) *The Decision to Transport.* A judge at the criminal court shall decide whether the probationer is to be transported in custody to the probation court. The judge shall provide the probationer an opportunity to be heard and, unless exceptional circumstances require otherwise, shall wait at least one hour for receipt of the recommendation from the probation court before making such decision. If the criminal court orders custodial transport, it shall issue a probation warrant on behalf of the probation court, and the probation court shall be so notified. The probationer promptly shall be transported in accordance with the warrant, provided that, if the probationer is held in custody in the criminal proceeding, the warrant shall be lodged with custodial authority to ensure that the probationer will be detained and transported to the probation court. The Probation Department at the criminal court shall so notify the Probation Department at the probation court.

If the criminal court decides not to order custodial transport, it shall enter the probation court appearance date and other required information on the notice of violation and serve it on the probationer in accordance with Rule 3(c)(i). For good cause, the criminal court may hold the probationer in custody pending its decision regarding custodial transport. Nothing in this rule shall preclude the issuance of a probation warrant by the probation court to secure the appearance of a probationer for a probation violation proceeding.

(vi) *Probationer's Appearance at Probation Court; Service of a New Notice.* Upon appearance of the probationer at the probation court, that court shall appoint counsel, if necessary, and shall schedule a probation violation hearing for a date certain, the date to be no less than seven days later unless the defendant waives the seven-day period. The hearing date shall not be later than 30 days after the appearance, except in extraordinary circumstances. If the probation department at the probation court alleges additional violations, it shall prepare and serve on the probationer a new notice of violation which shall set forth all alleged violations. A new notice of violation shall also include the date, time, and place of the violation hearing, and shall be served on the probationer in hand while the probationer is before the court, or as soon thereafter as possible. Such service shall be recorded on the case docket. The Probation Department shall provide a copy of the notice of violation to the District Attorney at the time of, or before, such service on the probationer. At any time during the proceedings, the probation court, upon review of the notice of violation and as a matter of its discretion, may order termination of the proceedings. A notice of violation may be withdrawn only with the permission of the court and such withdrawal and permission shall be set forth on the record and entered on the case docket.

(vii) *Procedure When a Defendant Is a Probationer at More than One Other Court Division within the Same Court Department.* When a defendant appearing in a court division on a new criminal charge is on probation at more than one

other court division within the same court department, the criminal court shall select one of the latter divisions to be the probation court and shall issue a notice of violation for that division. The criminal court shall interact as provided in this rule with the selected probation court. The other probation court or courts each shall be responsible for the issuance and service on the probationer of a notice of violation based on the new criminal charge, and for securing the presence of the probationer for a violation hearing by means of such notice or by means of a warrant or other process.

(viii) *Unified Proceedings Permitted by Standing Order.* Each department may provide, by standing order, for the hearing of probation violation matters pending in any of the several divisions of that department at any one division.

(d) When Probation Order and New Criminal Charge Involve Different Court Departments. When a criminal complaint is issued by a court against a defendant who is the subject of a probation order issued by a court in a different court department, the Probation Department at the criminal court shall notify the Probation Department at the probation court of the new complaint as soon as may be done, but in any event prior to the new matter being heard in the criminal court.

2015 Commentary to District/Municipal Courts Rule 3

This rule involves cases in which an alleged probation violation consists of a new criminal charge against the probationer. Such cases can arise in two contexts: where the probationer is on probation at the same court division that issued the new criminal complaint (the "same court" situation), and where the criminal complaint was issued by a court division or department other than the one where the probationer is on probation (the "different court" situation).

For both situations, this rule contains a provision not included in the 2000 District Court Rules by which a Notice of Probation Violation and Hearing may be "withdrawn." Such withdrawals have been a method by which probation violation proceedings maybe terminated. Withdrawal has been held to be within the discretion of a Probation Department. *Commonwealth v. Milton*, 427 Mass. 18, 21 (1998). There has been no requirement for court approval or permission. The new provision imposes two new requirements: (1) that such withdrawals must receive the permission of the court, and (2) that such permission and the fact of the withdrawal must be entered on the case docket. By requiring judicial permission and entry on the record, the new provision reflects the importance of a process by which a probation violation proceeding that has been formally commenced may be terminated without adjudication.

The new provision regarding withdrawal appears both in section (b)(i) (for the "same court" situation) and in section (c)(vi) (for the "different court" situation). Sections (b)(i) and (c)(vi) also now make clear that the Probation Department is responsible for providing a copy of the notice of violation to the District Attorney.

The last paragraph of section (b)(i) continues to authorize the termination of a probation violation proceeding as a matter of judicial discretion, on the court's own initiative or otherwise. The reference to such termination occurring "at arraignment" has been deleted because such termination may be ordered at any stage of the proceeding. A similar provision has been added to section (c)(vi) to address the "different court" situation.

New subsections (iii)–(v) have been added to section (c) of the rule that did not appear in the 2000 District Court Rule. Former section (iii) from the 2000 District Court Rule has been retained, but renumbered section (vi). See below. The purpose of the three new subsections is to provide a detailed process by which, in the "different court" situation, the "criminal court" must interact with the "probation court." The purpose of this interaction is to effect the transfer of the probation proceeding and, in some instances, the custodial transfer of the probationer, to the probation court.

Section (c)(iii) specifies the documents that must be sent by the criminal court to the probation court, including the request that the probation court make a recommendation on whether the probationer should be transported in custody. This section also provides that the criminal court may hold the probationer in custody pending this decision. This is important because, if not held on bail on the new criminal charge, the probationer may be otherwise free to leave the court. Such a departure would render moot the process of determining custody in the different-court situation. The legal bases for temporary custody of a probationer for good cause are set forth in the Commentary to Rule 6(h).

Section (c)(iv) describes the response required of the probation court to the criminal court. This response, including the recommendation regarding transport, is the responsibility of the Chief Probation Officer, an Assistant Chief Probation Officer, or a designated probation officer of the probation court and must be transmitted to the criminal court within one hour after receipt of the criminal court's request for information.

Section (c)(v) provides that the judge at the criminal court is responsible for the decision on whether the probationer will be transported to the probation court. The judge must give the probationer an opportunity to be heard and is not bound by the probation court's recommendation. The probation officer must provide the criminal court with a recommendation within one hour, and the judge must wait for that recommendation, absent exceptional circumstances. If a recommendation is not received within that hour, the judge at the criminal court may, but need not, wait longer before deciding whether to transport. If the decision is made to transport the probationer, the court will issue a probation warrant on behalf of the probation court. It is not necessary for the probation court to take any action in this regard. For this decision, the judge, for jurisdictional purposes, will be sitting at a session of the probation court held at the location of the criminal court, by designation of the Chief Justice of the relevant department under G.L. c. 211B, § 10 and G.L. c. 218, § 43A.

Under the former procedure, the decision to transport a probationer was to be made at the probation court and a warrant issued there and sent to the criminal court. This meant that a probation officer had to seek the issuance of a warrant by a judge of that court, a judge who was otherwise unaware of the matter and was usually engaged in that court's daily business. This would often delay the process, particularly in those cases where the judge at the probation court required a more detailed description of the underlying allegations before issuing the warrant.

This rule has been changed because the judge in the criminal court is in a superior position, both substantively and practically, to make the transport decision. That judge will be addressing an issue in a case that is before the court at that time, will be immediately aware of the criminal case which constitutes the alleged probation violation, and will have all relevant information regarding the probationer's criminal record and pending probation status.

Section (c)(vi) of the rule, corresponding to section (c)(iii) of the 2000 District Court Rule, has been amended to clarify and simplify the requirement that, if the probation court wishes to allege additional probation violations, it must issue and serve a new notice of violation.

Section (c)(vii) has been added to address a circumstance that the rules did not previously address, namely, where the defendant before the criminal court is currently on probation in more than one other court division within the same court department. It provides that in such cases the judge at the criminal court must decide the probation court with which the criminal court will interact. This decision will determine which of the probation courts will be "first in line" to address the probationer's alleged violation based on the new criminal charge. The rule provides that the other courts at which the individual is on probation are responsible for charging the new crime as an alleged violation, and initiating a violation proceeding by issuing a notice of violation and mailing it to the probationer or obtaining the appearance of the probationer by means of a probation warrant or other process such as a writ of habeas corpus.

Section (c)(viii) has been added to acknowledge the practice in Boston Municipal Court of allowing probation violation matters in several different divisions to be adjudicated in a single division. Each department may, by standing order, authorize and regulate such practices as will promote the orderly dispatch of probation matters in its department.

Section (d) addresses the circumstance where a defendant is on probation in one department (for example, the District Court or the Superior Court) and is arrested in another department (for example, the Boston Municipal Court). In such circumstances, the Probation Department in the criminal court must notify the Probation Department in the probation court as soon as possible and always before the case is heard in the criminal court. Such notification should ordinarily occur as soon as the Probation Department becomes aware that the defendant is on probation. Although the criminal court lacks the authority to issue a notice of violation or warrant for the probation court, the Probation Departments should coordinate, especially if the Probation Department in the probation court wishes to issue a warrant under G.L. c. 279, § 3.

2000 Commentary to District Court Rule 3

This rule sets forth procedures for a specific circumstance, namely, where a probationer is charged with a crime by the issuance of a criminal complaint. It is based on the premise that when a formal criminal charge is issued against a person on probation, this constitutes a basis for an alleged violation of the first general condition of every probation order (that the probationer must obey all local, state and federal laws) and the court must address such an alleged violation.

Note that it makes no difference whether the criminal complaint was issued after an arrest, or after a hearing on a criminal complaint application with no arrest having occurred. Note also that the rule does not apply to alleged criminal conduct that has not yet resulted in a criminal complaint. Probation violation proceedings based on alleged criminal conduct where no criminal complaint has yet issued are governed by Rule 4.

Commencement of Proceedings in Every Case

The rule requires the commencement of a probation violation proceeding in every case where a criminal complaint is issued against a probationer. No attempt is made to discriminate between those criminal charges that are "serious enough" to warrant violation proceedings and those that are not. The charge of a crime against a person who has been given the benefit of probation is serious enough per se to require action by the Probation Department. If the violation is found to have occurred, it is important to document that finding. The seriousness of the violation is properly addressed by the court's dispositional discretion, which is extremely flexible: a serious violation may result in revocation; a minor violation may result in simply a warning. *See* Rule 7(d). Nor must an alleged minor violation require protracted proceedings. In appropriate cases, the defendant may admit to the probation violation resulting in a simple continuance of the current probation terms and consent to a disposition at arraignment on the new charge. Of course, a defendant's rights to oppose any alleged violation and to demand trial on any criminal charge remain inviolate.

Whenever a new crime is charged, commencement of probation violation proceedings may not be delayed solely to await the conclusion of the new criminal case. Rules 5(e) and 7(a) similarly preclude such "tracking" of the new criminal case as a basis for delaying the conduct and conclusion of probation violation proceedings. The commentary to Rules 5(e) provides the rationale for the requirement. Continuances are available on specific grounds under Rules 5(e).

Where the court "treats" a criminal charge as a civil infraction, as provided by G.L. c. 277, § 70C, the rule requiring the initiation of probation proceedings does not apply since the criminal charge, as such, can be considered no longer to exist. However, the underlying alleged behavior may constitute a violation of probation subject to possible violation proceedings under Rule 4.

Judicial Discretion to Terminate Proceedings After Commencement

It should be noted that the rule acknowledges the court's discretion to terminate a proceeding once it has been commenced. That is, the rule provides that proceedings are commenced "by the issuance by the Probation Department of a Notice of Probation Violation and Hearing at or before arraignment on the criminal charge." Usually such "issuance" will consist of the probation officer tendering the notice form to the court before the arraignment begins. (The notice will not be formally served on the probationer until and unless a hearing date is determined and recorded on the form.) At that time the judge is free as a matter of discretion to order that the proceedings be terminated. Such an order must be entered on the probation record and on the docket of the case in which probation was ordered to ensure accountability. While alleged probation violations based on new criminal charges, even minor ones, generally should proceed to a factual conclusion to vindicate the credibility of probation and to establish a proper record, there may be circumstances where, in the opinion of the court, the violation proceedings should be terminated at the outset.

Where the court at which the probationer is on probation is different from the court where the new criminal charge is brought, the judicial authority to order no further proceedings resides at the former court, and section (c)(iii) so states.

Same Court

There are two different circumstances in which proceedings under the rule can arise: where the criminal complaint is issued (1) by the same court that issued the probation order, or (2) by a different court. These situations are addressed separately in sections (b) and (c).

Section (b), the "same court" circumstance, requires the probationer to be served in hand with the Notice of Probation Violation and Hearing when he or she appears before the court for arraignment whenever possible. This requires administrative attention by the Probation Department at each court so as to ensure each day that all new arrestees and others appearing for arraignment are screened for probation status. Notices for all those who are on probation must be prepared for in-court service. Where necessary, these defendants can be scheduled last for arraignment to ensure preparation of the Notice and in-hand service. The issuance of the Notice constitutes "commencement" of action by the Probation Department. The prepared Notice should include any other violations that can properly be alleged in addition to the charged criminal conduct. For example, a probationer charged with a new crime may also have a history of failure to report as ordered. The date, time and place of the violation hearing should be left blank, to be recorded on the form when the hearing is scheduled along with the pretrial hearing on the criminal charge, as required in section (b)(iii). After this information is added, the Notice is to be served in hand on the probationer.

If the probationer defaults at arraignment, the Notice can be prepared and left in the case file.

When the court fails to make in-hand service at arraignment, the rule provides for other methods of service. In such cases, the goal should be to schedule the hearing on the same date as the pretrial hearing on the criminal charge, assuming this will not violate the seven-day minimum notice requirement.

There is no requirement that counsel in the original criminal case represent the probationer at the violation hearing. On the contrary, if appointment of counsel is required, it is appropriate to appoint the same attorney for the violation hearing and for the new criminal charge that also constitutes the alleged probation violation.

Different Courts

Section (c) of the rule addresses the circumstance where a person against whom a criminal complaint has issued is on probation in a different court. Under section (c)(i) the Probation Department of the court that issued the complaint must prepare and serve a Notice of Probation Violation and Hearing on the probationer in hand at arraignment, just as in the "same-court" situation. However, in addition to specifying the alleged violation, the Notice will order the probationer to appear on a date certain at the court where he or she is on probation. The purposes of that appearance will be to appoint counsel and schedule the violation hearing. The Probation Department of the court where the defendant is on probation may amend the notice to include additional violation allegations. Presumably the court where the probationer is on probation will schedule a prompt hearing date, consistent with the seven-day minimum notice period for the probationer. (See below.)

The requirement that copies of the Notice, criminal complaint and police report be sent "forthwith" to the probation court is most effectively satisfied by the use of facsimile ("fax") transmission.

Scheduling

Notice of the probation violation hearing "must be given sufficiently in advance of scheduled court proceedings so that reasonable opportunity to prepare will be afforded." *Commonwealth v. Odoardi*, 397 Mass. 28, 31–32 (1986), quoting *In re Gault*, 387 U.S. 1, 33 (1967). The rule provides a minimum of seven days notice in both the same-court and different-court situations. This is the minimum notice period previously provided by regulations of the Office of the Commissioner of Probation and should be minimally adequate in most cases given the narrow focus of these hearings. If either party desires more time than is allowed by the scheduled date, a continuance may be sought under Rule 5(e) [now Rule 6(e)].

The rule also provides that the hearing may not be scheduled for a date more than 30 days after service of the Notice if the probationer objects to such date. This is to protect the probationer from undue delay, which is a particular concern if the probationer is being held in probation detention. Finally, the rule provides that even if the hearing date is beyond the 30-day limit and the probationer objects, such delay may nonetheless be justified on the basis of "extraordinary circumstances."

The purpose of requiring the probation violation hearing to be scheduled along with the pretrial hearing on the new criminal case in the same-court situation (section (b)(iii)) is not only to avoid delay of the probation hearing, but also to create an opportunity for a disposition of the criminal case that takes into account the probation disposition. Most criminal cases, in fact, are disposed of by plea or admission. It is appropriate to provide the defendant an opportunity to consider whether to submit a plea or admission that may take into account the outcome of the probation violation hearing. The defendant's right to a trial on the new criminal charge remains unaffected.

The last sentence of section (b)(iii) is intended to indicate that the prompt scheduling of the probation violation hearing should drive the scheduling of the pretrial hearing on the new charge. Thus, in a court in which the next regularly available date for a pretrial hearing is not consistent with the need for a prompt hearing on the alleged probation violation in terms of public safety implications, a prompt date (even a minimum seven-day date where appropriate) should be given even if this means scheduling the pretrial hearing on the new criminal charge prior to the date it would otherwise receive.

In the different-court situation, the date of the Pretrial Hearing on the criminal charge should be indicated on the copy of the Notice sent to the probation court. This will allow the probation court to schedule the violation hearing before that date.

Under G.L. c. 258B, § 3(o), victims have a right to be notified by a probationer's supervising probation officer if a probationer "seeks to modify a restitution order." This does not appear to require a supervising probation officer to send a copy of the Notice of Probation Violation and Hearing to a victim, even if modification of a restitution order is a possible outcome of the hearing.

Notice to District Attorney

In both the same-court and the different-court situations, the rule requires that a copy of the Notice of Probation Violation and Hearing be provided to the District Attorney. The relevant law, G.L. c. 279, § 3, gives the District Attorney the right to receive a copy of the notice and appear at such hearings only where the original conviction for which the probationer is on probation involves at least one felony. However, the rule reflects the position that the District Attorney should be allowed to appear at all such hearings. It allows the District Attorney to decide which hearings to attend and provides as an alternative the submission of a written statement. (Rule 5(f)) This is appropriate, given the fact that some misdemeanor charges may have greater public safety implications than felony charges, e.g., drunk driving, domestic assault and battery and violation of restraining orders. Also, the District Attorney has certain obligations to victims of crime regarding probation violation hearings that can be met only if the District Attorney is informed of the scheduling of such hearings. G.L. c. 258B, § 3. See Rule 5(f) and related commentary.

RULE 4

Commencement of Violation Proceedings: Violations Other than a New Criminal Complaint

(a) General. This rule prescribes the procedures to be undertaken regarding alleged violations of probation that do not involve or include criminal conduct charged in a criminal complaint.

(b) Issuance and Service of Notice; Termination of Proceedings; Withdrawal of Notice. When a probation officer of a court that has issued a probation order determines that a probationer has violated any condition of that order other than the alleged commission of a crime as charged in a criminal complaint, that probation officer shall decide whether to commence probation violation proceedings. Such decision shall be made in accordance with the rules and regulations of the Office of the Commissioner of Probation, provided, however, that probation violation proceedings shall be commenced (1) upon the issuance of an indictment, (2) when the judge issuing the probation order orders that such proceedings are to be commenced upon an alleged violation of one or more conditions of probation, or (3) when the commencement of such proceedings is required by statutory mandate. In any case, a judge of the court may order the commencement of violation proceedings.

Violation proceedings shall be commenced by the issuance by the Probation Department of a Notice of Probation Violation and Hearing, which shall be served on the probationer in hand or by first-class mail, unless the court orders otherwise. Service of the notice in hand or by first-class mail shall be noted in the court record. Out-of-court service other than by first-class mail shall require a written return of service. The Probation Department shall provide a copy of each notice of violation to the District Attorney forthwith upon its issuance.

If deemed appropriate, because of the seriousness of the alleged violation or for other good reason, the court may issue a violation of probation warrant. The clerk shall forthwith enter such warrant in the warrant management system. Upon the probationer's first appearance before the court, the probationer shall be served in hand with the notice of violation.

At any time during the proceedings, the court, upon review of a notice of the violation and as a matter of its discretion, may order termination of the proceedings. A notice of violation may be withdrawn only with the permission of the

7

court and such withdrawal and permission shall be set forth on the record and entered on the case docket.

(c) Contents of Notice. The Notice of Probation Violation and Hearing shall set forth the conditions of the probation order that the Probation Department alleges have been violated and shall order the probationer to appear at a specific date and time for the express purpose of the appointment of counsel, if necessary, and the scheduling of a probation violation hearing.

(d) Scheduling of Hearing. Upon appearance of the probationer in accordance with the Notice required by Rule 4(c), the court shall appoint counsel, if necessary, and schedule a probation violation hearing for a date certain, the date to be no less than seven days later unless the probationer waives the seven-day notice period. The hearing date shall not be later than 30 days after the appearance, except in extraordinary circumstances.

2015 Commentary to District/Municipal Courts Rule 4

Section (b) differs from the 2000 District Court Rule in the addition of the last paragraph, which is identical to the last paragraph of Rule 3(b)(i) and (c)(vi). This paragraph refers to the authority of the court to terminate a violation proceeding and adds new requirements governing the withdrawal of a notice of violation by the Probation Department. This paragraph has been added to ensure that the same provisions that apply to violation proceedings involving charged criminal conduct (the subject of Rule 3), also apply to proceedings covered by Rule 4, i.e., proceedings that do not involve a new criminal complaint. The purpose of the new provisions governing the withdrawal of a notice of violation are discussed in the Commentary to the Rule 3 amendments.

Section (b) also makes clear that the Probation Department is responsible for providing a copy of the notice of violation to the District Attorney.

Section (b) specifies that the judge may issue a violation of probation warrant if the seriousness of the alleged violation or other good reason makes that advisable. For example, a probationer convicted of a sex crime may remove a global positioning system bracelet, demanding immediate action despite the absence of a new crime. Nothing in this grant of authority detracts from the statutory power of a probation officer to issue a violation of probation warrant without court approval under G.L. c. 279, § 3. The careful exercise of that power is essential to effective and efficient probation supervision.

The title of section (b) differs from the 2000 District Court Rule in referring to the two new topics that have been added to that section.

2000 Commentary to District/Municipal Court Rule 4

This rule provides the procedures to be followed when it is alleged that a probationer has violated any probation conditions that do not include criminal behavior as alleged in a criminal complaint, that is, any violation not governed by Rule 3. This includes allegations of criminal acts that are not the subject of a criminal complaint, allegations of a crime set forth in an indictment, any alleged violation of general probation conditions 2 (to report to the probation officer as required), 3 (to notify the probation officer of any change of employment or address) or 4 (to obtain permission to leave the Commonwealth), and any alleged violation of any special condition of probation.

Section (b) of the rule defers to the Rules and Regulations of the Office of the Commissioner of Probation (OCP) regarding the commencement of such proceedings. Unlike charged criminal acts, it is appropriate that other alleged violations be the subject of violation proceedings only in accordance with professional probation policies and standards. These policies provide an appropriate degree of discretion and also provide a procedure for administrative proceedings where the alleged violation does not warrant the commencement of court proceedings. Such policies require collaboration with the Presiding Justice at each court. Notwithstanding a probation officer's decision, in accordance with Probation Department regulations, not to commence proceedings in a particular case, a judge may order such proceedings to be commenced.

There are three exceptions to the reliance on OCP regulations and policies under section (b). The first requires commencement of proceedings upon the issuance of an indictment. The rationale for this is the same as for the required commencement of proceedings upon the issuance of a criminal complaint. See commentary to Rule 3. The second allows the sentencing judge to require in the probation order that upon certain alleged violations, a probation violation hearing must be commenced. The third exception is that a violation hearing must be commenced if required by law. Perhaps the most notable example of the last is G.L. c. 209A, § 7, which provides as follows:

"If the defendant ordered to undergo treatment [after being convicted of a violation of a restraining order issued under G.L. c. 209A] has received a suspended sentence, the original sentence shall be reimposed if the defendant fails to participate in said program as required by the terms of his probation."

The statute would appear to require that probation violation proceedings be commenced upon an allegation of such a violation, and that revocation be ordered if the violation is found.

The rationale for providing a copy of each Notice of Probation Violation and Hearing to the District Attorney is the same as for notices in proceedings under Rule 3. It allows the District Attorney to decide which hearings to appear at and permits the District Attorney to fulfill certain legal obligations to victims and witnesses involved in the original criminal case in which the probation order was issued. See Rule 5(f) and related commentary.

Sections (c) and (d) provide for notice to the probationer of the alleged violation and ordering him or her to appear in court on a specific date and time so that the issue of counsel may be addressed and the violation hearing scheduled. The minimum notice period for the hearing is seven days, unless waived.

In cases where custody of a probationer is warranted pending the hearing, the probationer may be arrested with or without a warrant pursuant to G.L. c. 279, § 3, and held if probable cause is found at a preliminary violation hearing following the arrest. See Rule 8 [now Rule 5].

RULE 5
Probation Detention Hearings

(a) Purpose. A probation detention hearing may be conducted to determine whether a probationer shall be held in custody pending the conduct of a probation violation hearing.

The issues to be decided at a probation detention hearing are whether probable cause exists to believe that the probationer has violated a condition of the probation order, and, if so, whether the probationer should be held in custody.

(b) Notice of Hearing. The probationer shall be given a written notice indicating the purpose of the hearing and referring to the probation violations alleged in the notice of violation which is required to be served on the probationer under these rules. The detention proceeding shall be commenced by the service of such notice on the probationer. The court may, for good cause, order that the probationer be taken into custody pending the completion of the proceeding. The notice shall be served in hand when the probationer is before the court having been arrested on a new criminal charge, having been arrested for a probation violation, or for any other reason. The notice shall be prepared and served by the Probation Department at the discretion of a probation officer or as directed by the court.

(c) Conduct of Hearing. Probation detention hearings shall be conducted by a judge or, if there is no judge at the court, by a magistrate. When a magistrate conducts a probation detention hearing, a resulting custody order shall not extend beyond the date on which a judge will next be present at the court. On such date, the probationer shall be brought before the court and any further custody order will require the conduct of a detention hearing by a judge.

Probation detention hearings shall be conducted in a courtroom on the record. The probationer shall be entitled to counsel. Following service of notice, as provided in Rule 5(b), and the appointment of counsel, the appearance of private counsel, or the knowing and voluntary waiver of the right to counsel, the probationer shall be allowed a reasonable time to prepare for the hearing. At the hearing, the probation officer shall be required to present evidence to support a finding of probable cause. The District Attorney may assist in the presentation of such evidence. The probationer shall be entitled to be heard in opposition. Testimony, including testimony of a probation officer, shall be taken under oath. The court shall admit such evidence as it deems relevant and appropriate. The scope of the inquiry shall be limited to the issue of whether there is probable cause to believe that the alleged violation of probation has occurred.

If probable cause is found, the court may order the probationer to be held in custody pending the conduct and completion of the violation hearing. The court's decision whether to order such custody shall include, but not necessarily be limited to, consideration of the following:

i. the probationer's criminal record;

ii. the nature of the offense for which the probationer is on probation;

iii. the nature of the offense or offenses with which the probationer is newly charged, if any;

iv. the nature of any other pending alleged probation violations;

v. the likelihood of probationer's appearance at the probation violation hearing if not held in custody; and

vi. the likelihood of incarceration if a violation is found following the probation violation hearing.

If probable cause is found and the court does not order the probationer held in custody, the court may order the probationer released upon such conditions as maybe provided for in standing orders promulgated by that court's department.

If no probable cause is found, the court may terminate the proceedings or schedule a probation violation hearing, serving the probationer with notice thereof, but the probationer may not be held in custody pending the hearing based on the alleged probation violation.

2015 Commentary to District/Municipal Courts Rule 5

This rule differs from its antecedent, 2000 District Court Rule 8, both in its placement and the replacement throughout of the terms "preliminary probation hearing" and "final [or 'full'] probation hearing" with the terms "probation detention hearing" and "probation violation hearing," respectively. The purpose of these changes was to use terms that more accurately describe and clearly differentiate these proceedings.

Section (b) contains a new sentence indicating that a probation detention proceeding is commenced when the notice thereof is served on the probationer. Another new sentence indicates that the court has the authority to hold the probationer in custody pending the completion of the proceedings for good cause. The bases for the latter authority are the same as those set forth for the authority to hold a probationer in custody after the probationer's arrival at court pending the commencement and completion of a probation violation hearing. See the Commentary to Rule 6(h). Where an alleged probation violation consists of a new criminal charge, the probationer may already be in custody prior to the conduct of a detention hearing, e.g., while awaiting a bail hearing on that charge.

Section (b) contains a new, final sentence indicating that a probation detention hearing may be conducted at the direction of the court as well at the initiative of the Probation Department. In other words, the court may initiate a detention hearing.

The first paragraph of section (c) recognizes the authority of magistrates to conduct probation detention hearings. Such authority is specifically provided in G.L. c. 221, § 62C(g). The rule provides conditions for the exercise of this authority by requiring that it be used only when there is no judge at the court and by limiting the duration of any resulting custody order.

The first sentence of the second paragraph of section (c) corresponds to the first paragraph of section (c) in the 2000 District Court Rule 8. The second paragraph also contains a new, express reference to the requirement that a waiver by a probationer of the right to counsel at these hearings must be made knowingly and voluntarily.

The remainder of section (c) differs from its antecedent in the deletion of surplus language, especially references to the court's obligation to issue and serve a notice of violation and to schedule a violation hearing. These requirements are set forth in Rules 3 and 4.

One question that the rule does not address involves the effect, if any, on the probation detention probable cause determination when the alleged violation consists of a new criminal charge. In such cases, a probable cause determination will already have been made as a prerequisite for issuance of the criminal complaint for that charge. However, it would appear that a court conducting a probation detention hearing is not "bound" by the earlier probable cause ruling. While the same evidence that was considered for probable cause on the criminal complaint may also be presented to the court in the probation detention proceeding (e.g., a police report), new probable cause ruling is nonetheless required. Under the principle of res judicata and the doctrine of "issue preclusion," an earlier ruling on a legal issue is binding in a subsequent proceeding only if several requirements are met. These requirements are not met in the situation at issue. For example, the issue must have involved a final judgment on the merits in the prior proceeding. *See Kobrin v. Bd. of Registration in Medicine*, 444 Mass. 837, 843–44 (2005), and cases cited therein. A probable cause ruling for the issuance of a criminal complaint is not a final judgment on the merits. Moreover; the party against whom preclusion would be asserted must have had a meaningful opportunity to have been heard in the prior proceeding. Id. In criminal cases, the accused is not entitled to be heard on the issue of probable cause (except in those cases where a criminal complaint hearing precedes an arrest).

The 2000 District Court Rule 8(d) prohibited conditions of release, including bail. This provision i[s] not included in the District/Municipal Courts Rule. Instead, when probable cause is found, the court is authorized to impose conditions of release. Violation of such a condition would ordinarily result in detention until the violation hearing. Recognizing the differing needs of the various court departments in the orderly processing of probation detention matters, the rule permits each court department to specify the allowable conditions of release in a standing order applicable to that department. Although bail as authorized by G.L. c. 276, § 58 is not permissible, see *Commonwealth v. Puleio*, 433 Mass. 39, 42 (2000), a department, by standing order, may authorize release based on a monetary condition. A probationer released on a monetary condition would not be able to seek bail review under G.L. c. 276, § 58. *Puleio*, 433 Mass. at 42.

When the court does not find probable cause, the court must exercise its discretion whether to terminate proceedings or to schedule a probation violation hearing nonetheless. Because of the need for dispatch in conducting a detention hearing, the absence of evidence, witnesses, or assistance from the District Attorney may result in the probationer officer's being unable to establish probable cause for the. purpose of detention but still having a reasonable prospect of proving the probation violation at a full hearing. The court will decide whether further proceedings are in the interests of justice, but in no event may the probationer be held or subject to conditions of release on the probation matter pending a probation violation hearing.

2000 Commentary to District Court Rule 8 [Now Rule 5]

Preliminary probation hearings are required only when the probationer is to be held in custody for an alleged probation violation pending the conduct of a full hearing.

> The purpose of the preliminary hearing is to protect the rights of the . . . probationer who, being at liberty, is taken into custody for alleged violation of his . . . probation conditions, and detained pending a final revocation hearing.

Fay v. Commonwealth, 379 Mass. 498, 504 (1980) (citations omitted).

Thus, for example, there is no requirement of a preliminary hearing if the alleged probation violator already has received a probable cause hearing on the new crime and has been bound over to the grand jury. *Stefanik v. State Board of Parole*, 372 Mass. 726 (1977). *See also Commonwealth v.*

Odoardi, 397 Mass. 28, 33, 34 (1986) (no preliminary hearing where probationer already incarcerated at the time of the proceeding on the alleged violation).

The issue of whether a probationer should be held in custody pending the conduct of a probation violation hearing can arise when a defendant is before the court on a separate matter (e.g., on arrest for a new criminal charge) or having been arrested with or without a warrant for a violation of probation. G.L. c. 279, § 3.

The probationer is entitled to a preliminary hearing "at the time of his arrest and detention . . . ." *Commonwealth v. Odoardi*, 397 Mass. 28, 33 (1986). That arrest can take place while the probationer is at liberty or when a probation officer takes custody of a probationer who is before the court on another matter, such as the charge of a new crime. Written notice must be given to the probationer at that time and the probationer and counsel must be given time to prepare for this hearing. If a continuance is requested and allowed, the custody resulting from the arrest will continue until the preliminary hearing (or a final hearing if the preliminary hearing is waived) is conducted.

The rule does not provide for notice of a preliminary probation violation hearing to be served on a probationer who is at liberty. If it is believed that a probationer who is at liberty has violated probation and should be in custody pending a hearing on that violation, custody should be effected by an arrest with or without a warrant, under G.L. c. 279, § 3. If it is believed that a probationer who is at liberty has violated probation, but there is no need to hold him or her in custody pending a final hearing, there is no need to serve a notice of a preliminary hearing. Rather, a notice of a final hearing should be served.

At the preliminary probation violation hearing, the question of revocation or other disposition is not at issue, only the question of probable cause for the alleged violation. Of course, the preliminary hearing can be transformed into a "final" hearing if the defendant waives the minimum seven-day notice period and both the probationer and the Probation Department are willing to proceed immediately with either an admission or a hearing. Only in such instances will the issue of revocation or other disposition be appropriately addressed.

The rule provides no qualifications on the evidence that may be admitted at preliminary hearings, other than to state that the court may hear such evidence as it deems appropriate. The rules of evidence do not apply. There appears to be no law categorically disqualifying a judge who has conducted a preliminary hearing from conducting the subsequent final hearing. When no judge is available, a magistrate may conduct the preliminary hearing. See G.L. c. 221, §§ 62B and 62C(g), and Uniform Magistrate Rule 6.

Section (c) of the rule also provides that upon a finding of probable cause, the court may order the probationer to be held in custody pending the final hearing. A finding of probable cause does not require a custody order. The rule lists six factors that the court must consider when deciding whether to release the probationer notwithstanding the finding of probable cause on the alleged violation. The list is not exclusive and the rule does not attempt to assign relative weight to the factors.

Section (d) makes clear that bail and other terms of pretrial release have no application regarding a probationer's custody pending the conduct and completion of a final probation violation hearing. Bail and other conditions of pretrial release, including pretrial detention based on "dangerousness," under G.L. c. 276, §§ 58 and 58A, have no legal or conceptual relevance to custody on an alleged probation violation. They relate solely to a newly alleged crime. If the court finds probable cause for a probation violation, it may order the defendant into custody pending the final hearing on the violation. If the court does *not* find probable cause, the probationer cannot be held in custody *on the alleged violation.* Even if the probationer *is* held on the probation allegation, if he or she is also before the court on a new criminal charge, the court must address the terms of pretrial release. This issue is unrelated to custody on the probation charge. The prosecutor may want to be heard on the issue of bail or dangerousness because if the probation matter is promptly resolved, the defendant may be released from custody on the probation matter well before the criminal case is concluded.

Conversely, the issue of probation custody should be addressed regardless of whether or not the prosecutor plans to ask for high bail or pretrial detention based on dangerousness.

There appears to be no basis in statutory or case law for Superior Court review of a District Court probable cause decision resulting in custody pending a final probation violation hearing.

RULE 6
Conduct of Violation Hearings

(a) In General. Probation violation hearings shall be conducted by a judge, in open court, on the record. All testimony, including that of a probation officer, shall be taken under oath. The presentation of the case against the probationer shall be the responsibility of the probation officer assigned by the Chief Probation Officer of the court. The probationer shall be entitled to the assistance of counsel, including the appointment of counsel for probationers determined by the court to be indigent. A waiver by the probationer of the right to counsel shall be accepted by the court only if the court determines that such waiver is being made knowingly and voluntarily.

(b) Requirement of Two-Step Procedure. Probation violation hearings shall proceed in two distinct steps: the first to adjudicate the factual issue of whether the alleged violation or violations occurred, the second to determine the disposition of the matter if a violation of probation is found to have occurred.

(c) Adjudication of Alleged Violation. Probation violation hearings shall commence with a statement by the probation officer describing the violation or violations alleged in the notice of violation, and shall proceed with a presentation of the evidence supporting the allegations. The probationer shall be permitted to present evidence relevant to the issue of the alleged violation. Each party shall be permitted to cross-examine witnesses produced by the opposing party. Hearsay evidence shall be admitted by the court, in accordance with Rule 7, provided that the court shall enforce any statutory privileges and disqualifications. The probation officer shall have the burden of proving the alleged violations with or without the participation of the District Attorney as provided below. The standard of proof at such hearings shall be the preponderance of the evidence. After the presentation of evidence, both parties or their counsel shall be permitted to make a closing statement.

(d) Dispositional Decision. If the court finds that the probationer has violated one or more conditions of probation as alleged, the probation officer shall recommend to the court a disposition consistent with the dispositional options set forth in Rules 8(d) and 9(b) and may present argument and evidence in support of that recommendation: The probationer shall be permitted to present argument and evidence relevant to disposition and to propose a disposition.

(e) Continuances; "Tracking" Prohibited. Probation violation hearings shall be continued only by a judge and only for good cause shown. The reason for any continuance shall be stated by the judge and set forth on the record. No continuance shall be ordered other than to a date certain and for a specific purpose, and as provided in Rule 8(a). When a criminal charge is the basis for an alleged violation of probation, no continuance of the violation hearing or disposition shall be allowed solely to "track" or await the disposition of the criminal charge.

(f) Participation of the District Attorney.

(i) *In general.* The District Attorney may participate in probation violation hearings as provided in G.L. c. 279, § 3, and such participation shall be permitted in any such proceeding regardless of whether the criminal case in which the probation order was issued involved a felony charge.

(ii) *Coordination with the Probation Department.* If the District Attorney intends to appear at a probation violation hearing, he or she shall confer prior to the hearing with the probation officer responsible for presenting the matter to the court, for the purpose of coordinating the District Attorney's involvement in the hearing with the planned presentation of the probation officer.

(iii) *Presentation of Evidence.* The District Attorney may present and examine witnesses at the hearing, may examine witnesses presented by the probation officer, and may cross-examine witnesses presented by the probationer. The probationer may cross-examine all witnesses, whether presented by the District Attorney or the probation officer. The District Attorney shall be responsible for the attendance of every witness he or she wishes to present, and for the summoning of such witnesses.

(iv) *Finding and Disposition.* After the presentation of evidence, the District Attorney may be heard on the strength of that evidence in supporting a finding of violation. If the court finds that the probationer has violated one or more of the conditions of probation as alleged in the notice of violation, the District Attorney may be heard regarding the court's disposition of the matter. The District Attorney may present a recommendation on disposition orally or in writing.

(g) Admission to Violation and Waiver of Right to Hearing. The court may accept an admission to an alleged probation violation and a waiver of the right to a violation hearing only upon a determination that the admission and waiver have been made knowingly and voluntarily.

Such an admission and waiver shall not be accepted by the court subject to any condition regarding the disposition of such violation or the disposition of any other probation violation or any pending criminal charge. A probationer shall not be entitled to withdraw an admission as of right after it has been accepted by the court.

(h) Ensuring Probationer's Presence in Courtroom. For good cause, the court may order that the probationer be taken into custody pending the commencement and completion of the violation hearing.

2015 Commentary to District/Municipal Courts Rule 6

Section (a) differs from its antecedent, 2000 District Court Rule 5, in the deletion of the last portion of the first sentence. This provision referred to the permissible "flexibility and informality" of violation hearings. While accurate, this reference was deemed unnecessary and the possible source of inappropriate informality.

Section (a) also contains a requirement that a waiver by a probationer of the right to counsel at a probation violation hearing requires a judicial determination that such waiver is being made knowingly and voluntarily.

Section (e) contains a different last sentence than the 2000 District Court Rule. The new sentence is meant to clarify and emphasize the prohibition in the rule against "tracking," i.e., the delay of a probation violation proceeding in order to await the disposition of a criminal charge when the criminal behavior involved constitutes the alleged probation violation. The disposition of an underlying criminal case is irrelevant to the issue at the probation violation hearing, that is, whether a violation can be proved by a preponderance of the evidence. The rationale for this prohibition and the case law on which it is based are set forth in the original commentary to this rule. The rule also has been amended to expressly prohibit "tracking" as a means of delaying dispositions as well as hearings. *See also* Rule 8(d). The caption of section (e) also is different.

Section (f) is modified from the 2000 District Court Rule to clarify its meaning.

Section (g) is new. It addresses the procedure whereby a probationer offers to admit to an alleged violation. The rule refers to the two components of such an admission. First, the probationer must admit. to the commission of one or more of the violations charged in the notice of violation, and second, the probationer must waive the right to a violation hearing. *See Commonwealth v. Sayyid*, 86 Mass. App. Ct. 479, 489, *rev. denied*, 470 Mass. 1103 (2014). Although the term "stipulation" is commonly used, the rule uses the term "admission" because it more accurately and appropriately describes this legal event.

Section (g) also provides that, unlike a guilty plea or admission to sufficient facts to a *criminal* charge, an admission to a probation violation may not be accompanied by conditions which, if not accepted by the court, would allow the probationer to withdraw the admission. In other words, there is no equivalency to the "defendant-capped plea" which can be tendered in the context of a criminal proceeding. The court may *allow* a probationer to withdraw a probation violation admission based on the court's intended disposition as a matter of its discretion. The probationer may not withdraw an admission as a matter of right once an admission is submitted and accepted by the court. A defendant would be entitled to withdraw an admission that was not made knowing and voluntarily. *Sayyid*, 86 Mass. App. Ct. at 490–92.

The prohibition in section (g) against "conditioned" probation violation admissions also precludes admissions conditioned by proposed dispositions "agreed to" by the probation department or by a prosecutor. Such an agreement does not bind the court or permit the withdrawal of the admission if the court's disposition is other than that "agreed upon" by a

probation officer or prosecutor. The court may consult with probation regarding the disposition after finding a probation violation. See Rule 8(d). But for probation violation admissions there is no equivalent to the tender of criminal guilty pleas which may include dispositional terms agreed to by the prosecution.

It should also be noted that section (g) does not require the conduct of a specific colloquy as the means by which the court is to determine that a probationer's admission to a violation is being made knowingly and voluntarily. The colloquy required for the acceptance of a *guilty plea to a criminal charge* is not required for the acceptance of a probation violation admission. *See Sayyid*, 86 Mass. App. Ct. at 488–89, 492–93. Rather, the court is left to conduct such questioning of the probationer and his or her counsel as it deems adequate for this determination. *See Sayyid*, 86 Mass. App. Ct. at 489, 492–93.

Section (g) does not require that a probationer's admission to a violation and waiver of the right to a hearing be set forth on a particular form. However, an approved form is available for this purpose on the internet at www.mass.gov/courts/courtsandjudges/courts/districtcourt/forms.html. At a minimum, the court's questioning of a probationer on this issue and the probationer's responses should be memorialized on the audio recording of the proceedings, and the facts that the questioning occurred and that the court accepted the admission and waiver should be entered on the court's written record.

Section (h) is new. It refers to the court's authority to secure the presence of a probationer pending the commencement and completion of a probation violation hearing. This rule addresses the problem of a probationer who, having arrived in court for a violation hearing while not in custody (in response to a notice of violation or otherwise), simply decides to exit the courtroom and the court house. This can occur if a probationer, while awaiting his or her hearing, observes a hearing that results in a finding of violation, revocation, and immediate execution of sentence.

The basis of the court's authority to secure the presence of a probationer, which includes custody, if necessary, pending the conduct of his or her hearing is threefold:

1. First, as a matter of constitutional law, a person on probation has a conditional liberty interest. The restricted scope of this liberty interest is perhaps best illustrated by the statutory authority of a probation officer *to issue an arrest warrant or to arrest a probationer without a warrant* to bring him or her before the court to answer to a possible probation violation. G.L. c. 279, § 3. If a probationer maybe arrested by a probation officer without a warrant to be brought to court on an alleged violation, then it would appear to follow that a probationer charged with a violation may be held by the court for good cause upon his or her non-custodial arrival in court for a hearing on that alleged violation.

2. Such a custody order merely enforces the existing order requiring the probationer's presence at the court. A probationer who has arrived in court in response to a notice of violation has been formally accused in that notice of one or more specific probation violations and ordered to appear in court. The notice informs the probationer that he or she is "HEREBY ORDERED AS FOLLOWS: YOU MUST APPEAR IN THIS COURT" on a specific date at a specific time. Thus, the probationer is under court order to be in court

for the conduct of the violation hearing. He or she is not free to leave. Custody of the probationer pending the conduct and completion of the hearing ensures compliance with that court order.

3. The authority of the court to secure the presence of a probationer for the conduct of a scheduled hearing also has a constitutional ba[s]is in the court's inherent power. "Of necessity, a judge's inherent power must encompass the authority to exercise 'physical control over his courtroom.'" *Commonwealth v. O'Neil*, 418 Mass. 760, 764 (1994) (quoting *Chief Admin. Justice of the Trial Ct. v. Labor Relations Commission*, 404 Mass. 53 , 57 (1989)); *see id.* ("'[t]he power of the judiciary to control its own proceedings, the conduct of participants, the actions of officers of the court and the environment of the court is a power absolutely necessary for a court to function effectively and do its job of administering justice'") (quoting *Chief Admin. Justice of the Trial Ct.*, 404 Mass. at 57). Perhaps nothing could be viewed as more fundamental or essential to the court's ability to function than the power to prevent a probationer who has been ordered to appear for a hearing on an alleged violation from simply leaving the court prior to the conduct of that hearing.

In order to secure the presence of the probationer, the rule requires that the court have "good cause," that is, some reason to believe that the probationer may attempt to leave the courtroom to avoid the proceeding (e.g., the probationer's in-court behavior, history of defaults, and history of previous probation violations; the seriousness of the underlying crime; the potential sentence if revocation is ordered; etc.).

The custody provision in this rule is relevant only when the violation hearing will proceed that same day. If a probationer arrives at court and is seen as a flight risk, but the actual hearing will be scheduled for a later date, the probation department may immediately request a detention hearing under Rule 5 (formerly Rule 8). That rule also provides for custody of a probationer prior to the conduct of such a hearing. If detention is ordered, it will result in the probationer's continued custody until the conduct and completion of the violation hearing.

2000 Commentary to District Court Rule 5 [Now Rule 6]

Probation revocation hearings are not part of a criminal prosecution, and for this reason a probationer need not be provided with the full panoply of constitutional protections applicable at a criminal trial. *Gagnon v. Scarpelli*, 411 U.S. 778 (1973). Indeed, case law has sought to preserve the flexible, informal nature of probation revocation hearings. *See Black v. Romano*, 471 U.S. 606 (1985).

On the other hand, the probationer's liberty is potentially at stake in violation proceedings, and therefore certain due process protections are required. As set forth for parole revocation in *Morrissey v. Brewer*, 408 U.S. 471 (1972) and made applicable to probation revocation by *Gagnon v. Scarpelli*, 411 U.S. 778 (1973), there are six such fundamental due process requirements: (1) written notice of the claimed violations of probation, (2) disclosure to the probationer of the evidence against him, (3) opportunity to be heard in person and to present witnesses and documentary evidence, (4) the right to confront and cross-examine adverse witnesses (unless a hearing officer specifically finds good cause for not allowing confrontation), (5) a neutral and detached hearing body, members of which need not be judicial officers or lawyers, and (6) a

written statement by the fact finder as to the evidence relied on and reasons for revoking probation.

This rule is intended to provide an orderly, relatively informal and flexible procedure for probation violation hearings, but one in which all required and appropriate due process safeguards are ensured.

General Requirements

Section (a) requires several fundamental procedural elements: a judicial procedure in open court, testimony under oath and the creation of a record. With regard to the record, Rule 211 of the Special Rules of the District Courts of Massachusetts, "Recording of Court Proceedings," requires that such proceedings be electronically recorded. Any District Court judge may conduct the hearing; the original sentencing judge is not required.

One of the six fundamental due process requirements for probation violation hearings, as provided in *Gagnon v. Scarpelli*, 411 U.S. 778 (1973), is "a neutral and detached hearing body." This requirement would appear to preclude the model by which a judge would take the initiative in the proceeding, as in an inquest, and the probation officer remain essentially passive in the role of a witness. Accordingly, the rule requires the probation officer, who is the "accuser," to present the case, with the judge remaining in the traditional neutral role. This does not prevent the judge from asking appropriate questions, nor is it inconsistent with the role of the probation officer as witness. The probation officer must provide evidence under oath and is subject to cross-examination.

It should be noted that in probation violation hearings the exclusionary rule does not apply if the police were unaware that the defendant was a probationer. *Commonwealth v. Olsen*, 405 Mass. 491 (1989) (evidence seized in violation of Fourth Amendment was admissible in probation violation proceeding, where police who seized evidence neither knew nor had reason to know of probationary status of person whose property was seized). There is no Massachusetts decision on whether the exclusionary rule applies in these proceedings where police are aware that the person is on probation.

Regarding the right to counsel, the rule goes beyond current law by providing the right to counsel regardless of whether the probationer faces the possibility of imprisonment if probation is revoked. *See Commonwealth v. Faulkner*, 418 Mass. 352 (1994) (probationer at probation violation hearing has right to counsel if revocation might result in imprisonment).

Two-step Proceeding

Section (b) imposes the critical requirement of a two-stage proceeding. As observed by the Supreme Court of the United States,

> the decision to revoke probation typically involves two distinct components: (1) a retrospective factual question whether the probationer has violated a condition of probation; and (2) a discretionary determination by the sentencing authority whether violation of a condition warrants revocation of probation.

Black v. Romano, 471 U.S. 606, 611 (1985), as quoted in *Commonwealth v. Marvin*, 417 Mass. 291, 295 (1994) (Liacos, C.J., dissenting).

This dichotomy is further reflected in Massachusetts law:

> At the revocation hearing, the judge must determine, as a factual matter, whether the defendant has violated the conditions of his probation. If the judge deter-

7

mines that the defendant is in violation, he can either revoke the probation and sentence the defendant or, if appropriate, modify the terms of his probation.

Commonwealth v. Durling, 407 Mass. 108, 111 (1990).

This distinction is an important one. The factual decision that a probation violation has occurred in no way compels an order of revocation. The court has wide dispositional latitude if a violation is found. *See* Rule 7(d) [now Rule 8(d)]. However, even if an alleged violation is relatively minor and, in all likelihood will not warrant revocation, it is important that it be adjudicated. It is essential for effective probation that a record of compliance and noncompliance with probation orders be maintained.

In addition, the distinction between the factual determination and the disposition must be maintained because different legal requirements are invoked. For example, the factual issue of whether an alleged violation has occurred must be decided based on a preponderance of the evidence, *Commonwealth v. Holmgren*, 421 Mass. 224 (1995), while the dispositional decision is a matter of judicial discretion. *McHoul v. Commonwealth*, 365 Mass. 465, 469–470 (1974). Similarly, the "seriousness" of the alleged violation is irrelevant to whether it occurred, while it is relevant to the question of appropriate disposition.

Adjudication of Violation

Section (c) sets out the basic requirements for how the first step of the hearing, adjudication of the alleged violation, should proceed. It ensures both parties the right to present evidence and cross-examine adverse witnesses. The court has some discretion in limiting cross-examination involving irrelevant or redundant questioning. *See Commonwealth v. Odoardi*, 397 Mass. 28, 34 (1986). Section (c) also entitles both parties to make a closing statement. In *Commonwealth v. Marvin*, 417 Mass. 291, 295 (1994), the court declined "to impose a universal due process requirement that a defendant in a probation revocation hearing has an absolute right to make a closing argument." However, that case goes on to state that it would be a "better practice" to permit a probationer to present at least a brief closing argument. The provision in this rule is intended to ensure that this better practice is provided for both parties.

Disposition

Section (d) provides that both parties may be heard regarding disposition, assuming the court finds that one or more alleged violations was committed. The court's dispositional options are provided in Rule 7. The probationer's right to be heard and present evidence regarding disposition implicate due process considerations. *See Commonwealth v. Odoardi*, 397 Mass. 28 (1986).

Continuances

Section (e) sets out certain requirements for continuances. It expressly eliminates "tracking," i.e., continuing a probation violation hearing to await disposition of the criminal case involving the charge that is also the alleged probation violation. The reason for this rule is that, on the one hand, there is no basis in law or in terms of fairness to the probationer for such a continuance, and, on the other hand, proceeding without delay on the alleged violation is of great importance in terms of the primary goals of probation, which are rehabilitation of the probationer and protection of the public. *Commonwealth v. LaFrance*, 402 Mass. 789, 795 (1988) (citations

omitted). The rule does provide for continuances where good cause is shown and the reason for the continuance is stated by the judge and set forth on the record.

The Supreme Judicial Court has long made clear that there is no prerequisite that the probationer be convicted of a criminal charge to permit that criminal conduct to be used as the basis of a probation revocation.

> If the act alleged to be a violation of probation is made the subject of a criminal complaint, the commencement of the criminal prosecution does not preclude the revocation of the earlier probation nor does it require that the revocation proceedings be deferred until the completion of the new criminal proceeding.

Rubera v. Commonwealth, 371 Mass. 177, 181 (1976) and cases cited.

After analyzing the federal constitutional law relevant to the point and the precedents from other states, the court in *Rubera* went on to explain the policy reasons that favor proceeding with revocation proceedings and not awaiting the outcome of the criminal case:

> We are aware that the practice which was followed in revoking the petitioner's probation in this case was not in accord with the procedure suggested by the ABA Project on Standards for Criminal Justice, Standards Relating to Probation § 5.3, at 62–63 (Approved Draft 1970), that "[a] revocation proceeding based solely upon commission of another crime ordinarily should not be initiated prior to the disposition of that charge." [citation omitted] That standard seems to impose an unreasonable and unfair burden on law enforcement authorities by placing them in the dilemma of having to decide between (a) having to forgo criminal prosecution of a person who is on probation and who appears to have committed another offense until they have first pursued steps to revoke his probation on the basis of his conduct in ordinary proceedings without reliance on any subsequent criminal conviction, or (b) having to start criminal prosecution promptly on the later offense and then being prevented from trying to revoke his earlier probation until after the later prosecution has run its full course which, in the present state of our criminal dockets, would amount to arming the defendant with the weapon of potential delay with which he could forestall termination of the proceeding by endless appeals. We decline to impose the burden of such a choice on either probation officers or prosecutors.

Rubera v. Commonwealth, 371 Mass. at 184–185 (1976).

See also, Commonwealth v. Holmgren, 421 Mass. 224 (1995), which held that a probation violation hearing may proceed on a charge of a new crime, even if the defendant has been acquitted of that crime, because the standard of proof at a probation hearing is lower than the standard at a criminal trial. In other words, an acquittal, or the possibility of an acquittal, is irrelevant to a probation violation proceeding because failure to convict under the "reasonable doubt" standard neither precludes nor is inconsistent with a finding of a probation violation under the "preponderance of the evidence" standard.

The only legal relationship between a probation violation hearing and a criminal prosecution for the same alleged criminal conduct is that, if the criminal case does go forward before the probation hearing and results in a conviction, that conviction will be evidence of a probation violation and no independent finding of the underlying facts is required of the judge. *Commonwealth v. Maggio*, 414 Mass. 193 (1993).

District Attorney Participation

Section (f) addresses the subject of participation by the District Attorney. Rules 3 and 4 require the court to provide a copy of every Notice of Probation Violation and Hearing to the District Attorney. Section (t) of this rule is intended to clarify the involvement of the District Attorney in those cases where he or she decides to participate, consistent with the statutory provisions of G.L. c. 279, § 3.

It should be noted that as a constitutional matter, probation functions are within the judicial branch, and the office of the District Attorney is considered within the executive branch. *Commonwealth v. Tate*, 34 Mass. App. Ct. 446, 447–448 (1993) and cases cited. Under the Massachusetts Constitution, Pt. 1 Art. 30 , the branches must maintain a separation of governmental powers.

> That separateness does not, however, lead to the conclusion that a district attorney's office may not assist the probation service in presenting evidence in support of a position that the probation service had decided upon.
>
> * * *
>
> [P]robation officers are only aided, not interfered with, when district attorneys, upon invitation, conduct examination of witnesses and present evidence.

Id. at 448, and cases cited.

Thus the right of District Attorneys to present evidence and witnesses, and to examine and cross-examine witnesses at these proceedings would appear to be constitutionally acceptable as long as it does not fundamentally interfere with probation.

RULE 7
Hearsay Evidence

(a) Admissibility of Hearsay Evidence. Hearsay evidence shall be admissible at probation violation hearings.

(b) Legal Sufficiency of Hearsay Evidence. The court may rely on hearsay as evidence of a probation violation only if the court finds in writing that the hearsay is substantially reliable. In determining if hearsay evidence is substantially reliable, the court may consider, among any other relevant factors, whether that evidence

(1) is based on personal knowledge and/or direct observation, rather than on other hearsay;

(2) involves observations recorded close in time to the events in question;

(3) is factually detailed, rather than generalized and conclusory;

(4) is internally consistent;

(5) is corroborated by any evidence provided by the probationer;

(6) was provided by a disinterested witness; or

(7) was provided under circumstances that support the veracity of the source (e.g., was provided under the pains and

penalties of perjury or subject to criminal penalties for providing false information).

2015 Commentary to District/Municipal Courts Rule 7

Section (a) is the same as the 2000 District Court Rule 6(a). It provides that hearsay evidence "shall be admissible" in Boston Municipal Court and District Court probation violation hearings. In *Commonwealth v. Durling*, 407 Mass. 108, 114 (1990), the Supreme Judicial Court stated that only "reliable" hearsay is admissible in these proceedings. The rule does not impose reliability as a formal precondition to admission, but rather requires that, in effect, hearsay evidence be admitted de bene. This avoids the potential bifurcation of each proceeding into a preliminary "suppression" hearing followed, if necessary, by a separate hearing on the factual issue of the alleged violation. Instead, the court commences the violation hearing and receives all proffered evidence, including hearsay. As set forth in section (b), any hearsay challenged as, and found by the court to be, unreliable may not be used as evidence of a violation. Moreover, if the court finds hearsay to be reliable it must provide written reasons. After resolving any issue of hearsay reliability, the court then rules on the alleged violation based on any competent evidence. Thus, the rule provides appropriate procedural clarity and simplicity while ensuring compliance with the constitutionally-based limitation on the use of hearsay in these proceedings, as set forth in *Durling*.

Nothing in these Rules precludes the judge from allowing a continuance to give either party an opportunity to summons witnesses if the judge deems it necessary to resolve facts in dispute.

Section (b) has been amended to conform to case law decided after the rule was initially promulgated. That case law has made it clear that there is a "one-pronged" test for determining whether hearsay evidence is legally sufficient as proof of a violation. Specifically, such evidence must be found by the court, in writing, to be "substantially reliable." *Commonwealth v. Maggio*, 414 Mass. 193 (1993); *see also Commonwealth v. Negron*, 441 Mass. 685 (2004).

The previous version of this rule imposed a two-pronged test, namely, for evidence to be legally adequate as a basis for finding a probation violation the rule required that it be both "substantially reliable," and, when the alleged violation was new criminal behavior, there had to be "good cause" for the absence of the percipient witness, i.e., the source of the hearsay. Current case law holds that where the hearsay is substantially reliable, this satisfies the good cause requirement. This paragraph and the previous paragraph of this Commentary were cited with approval by the Supreme Judicial Court. in *Commonwealth v. Bukin*, 467 Mass. 516, 522 n.10 (2014).

The new rule also makes it clear that the single "substantial reliability" test applies regardless of whether the alleged violation consists of a new criminal charge.

Section (b) and its caption require that hearsay be found by the court to be "substantially reliable" before it can serve as evidence of a violation, *even when the court also has relied on non-hearsay evidence.* The previous rule imposed the substantial reliability test only when hearsay was the only evidence relied upon by the court. In doing so it followed case law, *Commonwealth v. Durling*, 407 Mass. 108 (1990). Under the rule as amended, the court need not attempt to distinguish between hearsay that is "reliable" (and thus may be used if other, non-hearsay evidence is also relied upon by the court), and hearsay that is "substantially reliable" (and thus may be used when it is the only evidence of a violation). *See Commonwealth v. Durling*, 407 Mass. 108, 117–19 (1990).

Finally, section (b) lists the seven indicia set forth in case law that the court may consider in determining whether the "substantial reliability" test has been met.

It should be noted that, even if the court finds that hearsay is "substantially reliable" and thus may be used as evidence of an alleged violation, this is not conclusive on the issue whether a violation has occurred. The court's finding on an alleged violation must be based on whether, based on all the competent evidence submitted by both parties, the violation has been proved by a preponderance of that evidence.

2000 Commentary to District Court Rule 6 [Now Rule 7]

Probation violation hearings often involve evidence in the form of records, documents and statements that constitute hearsay, that is, "an extrajudicial statement offered to prove the truth of the matter asserted." *Commonwealth v. Keizer*, 377 Mass. 264, 269 n.4 (1979). Common examples of hearsay evidence used at these hearings are police reports used as evidence of the probationer's criminal behavior, and correspondence from programs such as batterers' treatment programs used as evidence of the probationer's failure to complete the program in compliance with the probation order.

This rule is based almost exclusively on the opinion in *Commonwealth v. Durling*, 407 Mass. 108 (1990), the leading case on the use of hearsay evidence at probation violation hearings. It is divided into separate sections, one on the admissibility of hearsay, the other on the sufficiency of hearsay as a matter of law when it is the only evidence presented against the probationer.

Admissibility

Section (a) states simply that hearsay is admissible at probation violation hearings. The Supreme Judicial Court "has always allowed the use of hearsay at probation revocation hearings." *Commonwealth v. Durling*, 407 Mass. at 114. The admissibility of hearsay is based on the principles set forth in *Morrissey* and *Gagnon*. The revocation process "should be flexible enough to consider evidence including letters, affidavits, and other material that would not be admissible in an adversary criminal trial." *Morrissey v. Brewer*, 408 U.S. 471, 489 (1972). Similarly, the Supreme Court has sanctioned the "use where appropriate of the conventional substitutes for live testimony including affidavits, depositions and documentary evidence." *Gagnon v. Scarpelli*, 411 U.S. 778, 782 n.5 (1973).

It has been held that if hearsay evidence qualifies under any of the legal exceptions to the hearsay rule (e.g., business record, excited utterance, dying declaration) it is presumptively reliable. *Durling*, 407 Mass. at 118. However, in keeping with the informal nature of these hearings and the fact that the case against the probationer is the responsibility of a probation officer rather than a trained criminal prosecutor, it would appear that the court should make a determination of the reliability of any hearsay, rather than engage in an argument on whether the hearsay qualifies as an exception to the hearsay rule so as to merit presumptively reliable status. In other words, if the court determines that a record of a drug treatment center is reliable, it is irrelevant as to whether it qualifies as a "business record." An example of hearsay that

might be found unreliable, and thus not worthy of the court's consideration, would be a second- or thirdhand out-of-court statement, or a statement that is vague or internally contradictory or inconsistent.

Sufficiency

Section (b) of the rule addresses an issue quite different from admissibility, namely, the legal sufficiency of hearsay evidence where hearsay is the only evidence of the probationer's alleged violation. In such cases, the probationer has no opportunity to confront a witness with personal knowledge and test the reliability of that evidence by cross-examination. This deprivation of the right to confrontation of witnesses implicates due process considerations. However, the Supreme Court in *Durling* made clear that since a probationer's liberty interest is conditional, so too is the probationer's right to confront witnesses, and that right can be denied for "good cause."

The court's description of "good cause," in *Durling* is somewhat unclear. On the one hand, the court indicates that "good cause" for denying the probationer the right to confront witnesses "has thus far been defined in terms of difficulty and expense of procuring witnesses *in combination* with 'demonstrably reliable' or 'clearly reliable' evidence." *Durling*, 407 Mass. at 120 (emphasis added).

In fact, the court defines the question in *Durling* in terms of this two-pronged issue:

> The judge in this case relied solely on hearsay in revoking the defendant's probation. The judge did not make any express determination that there was good cause for denying the defendant the right to confront a witness with personal knowledge. Nor did the judge make any determination whether the proffered hearsay was reliable.

Durling, supra, at 115. However, in contrast to this two-pronged definition, the *Durling* court also defines "good cause" solely in terms of the reliability of the hearsay evidence:

> In our view, a showing that the proffered evidence bears substantial indicia of reliability and is substantially trustworthy is a showing of good cause obviating the need for confrontation.

Durling, supra, at 118. Despite this apparent conflict, the opinion appears to settle on the two-pronged definition of good cause:

> On the whole, the resolution of the confrontation issue depends on the totality of the circumstances in each case . . . . If the Commonwealth has "good cause" for not using a witness with personal knowledge, *and* instead offers reliable hearsay or other evidence, then the requirements of due process are satisfied.

Durling, supra, at 118–19 (emphasis added). Also,

> The substantial reliability of the police reports in this case, *coupled with* the practical difficulty of presenting live testimony, discussed earlier, convinces us that the District Court judge could properly base his order of revocation on the evidence presented.

Durling, supra, at 122 (emphasis added).

In *Commonwealth v. Calvo*, 41 Mass. App. Ct. 903 (1996) (rescript), the Appeals Court interpreted *Durling* to require only a showing that hearsay evidence bears substantial indicia of reliability and is substantially trustworthy in order to meet the "good cause" test, obviating the right to confrontation. In *Calvo*, "good cause" was held not to require any showing that a live witness was unavailable.

This rule takes a middle ground, requiring that in all cases where the only evidence of an alleged probation violation is hearsay there must be a finding that the hearsay is substantially trustworthy and demonstrably reliable, and requiring a showing of why a live witness is unavailable when the alleged probation violation is based on charged or uncharged criminal behavior.

Trustworthiness and Reliability of Hearsay

There are at least five criteria for the court's determination of whether a given piece of hearsay evidence is "substantially trustworthy" and "demonstrably reliable," namely, whether the out-of-court statement:

(1) is factually detailed, rather than generalized and conclusory;

(2) is based on personal knowledge and direct observation by the source;

(3) is corroborated by evidence submitted by the probationer;

(4) was provided under circumstances that support the veracity of the source (e.g., was provided under the pains and penalties of perjury or subject to criminal penalties for providing false information);

(5) was provided by a disinterested witness.

This list of factors for determining reliability is taken directly from *Durling*, except item (5), which is taken from *Commonwealth v. Delaney*, 36 Mass. App. Ct. 930, 932 n.4 (1994) (rescript), a case applying the *Durling* test.

Good Cause for Absence of Witness

There are three factors mentioned in *Durling* for determining good cause for the absence of a live witness, namely,

(1) the distance a witness would have to travel to get to court,

(2) the costs the witness (or his or her public or private employer) would have to incur if the witness were compelled to appear, and

(3) the difficulty in scheduling the probation violation hearing at a time convenient to the witness and all other participants.

Hearsay Test Where the Alleged Violation Is Criminal Conduct

One of the most common alleged violations of probation is alleged criminal conduct. In many of these cases, evidence of the alleged violation will be a police report. Under the rule, there are two issues if the police report is the only evidence presented: reliability of the report and the reason for the absence of a live witness.

In establishing the requisite reliability of the police reports in *Durling*, the Court stressed that the two police reports related facts observed by the officers personally, and were factually detailed rather than general statements or conclusions. "We think the factual detail is indicative of reliability." *Durling, supra*, at 121 (citation omitted). The Court also mentioned the similarity of the two reports and the fact that the two officers were from different departments. Thus, in *Durling*, the police reports corroborated each other.

The *Durling* Court also stressed that in determining "good cause" to justify a finding of violation solely on hearsay, the court had to balance the interests of the probationer and those of the Commonwealth and look to the "totality of the circumstances." It would appear that such balancing includes the concept that the more reliable the hearsay evidence, the less stringent the test regarding the practical reasons for absence of a live witness. Conversely, where the reliability of the hearsay is not as high as it was in *Durling*, (which involved the unusual circumstance of two separate police reports) it would appear that the justification for the absence of a witness would have to be that much stronger.

Hearsay Test Where the Alleged Violation Is Something Other Than Criminal Conduct

The rule does not require a showing of why the live witness is unavailable where the alleged violation is something other than criminal conduct. Thus, for example, if the alleged violation were failure to attend a rehabilitation program, a report from the program, though hearsay, would be sufficient evidence if it met the reliability test of *Durling*, without regard to why the live witness were not present.

For cases applying the *Durling* test, see *Commonwealth v. Delaney*, 36 Mass. App. Ct. 930 (1994) (finding of violation based on hearsay statement reversed; statement did not meet reliability standard comparable to police reports in *Durling* and witness was available to testify); and *Commonwealth v. Joubert*, 38 Mass. App. Ct. 943 (1995) (revocation order reversed because hearsay statements of a child were not sufficiently reliable and findings indicate judge may have relied on them as the basis of decision).

RULE 8
Finding and Disposition

(a) Requirement of Finding. Upon the completion of the presentation of evidence and closing arguments on the issue of whether the probationer has violated one or more conditions of a probation order, as alleged, the court shall make a determination of that issue. The court shall decide the matter promptly and shall not continue the proceeding generally.

(b) Finding of No Violation. If the court determines that probation has failed to prove by a preponderance of the evidence that the probationer committed a violation alleged in the notice of violation, the court shall expressly so find and the finding shall be entered on the record.

(c) Finding of Violation; Written Finding of Fact. If the court determines that probation has proved by a preponderance of the evidence that the probationer has violated a condition of probation as alleged in the notice of violation, or if the probationer waives the hearing and admits such violation and the court accepts such admission in accordance with Rule 6(g), the court shall expressly so find, and such finding shall be entered on the record. In a contested proceeding, the court shall make written findings of fact to support the finding of violation, stating the evidence upon which the court relied. A finding of violation based on an admission may be recorded as such.

(d) Disposition After Finding of Violation. After the court has entered a finding that a violation of probation has occurred, the court may order any of the following dispositions set forth below, as it deems appropriate. These dispositional alternatives shall be the exclusive options available to the court. The court shall proceed to determine disposition promptly following the entry of a finding of violation. General continuances are prohibited. Awaiting the disposition of an underlying criminal charge shall not constitute such good cause for any continuance. In determining its disposition, the court shall give such weight as it may deem appropriate to the recommendation of the Probation Department, the probationer, and the District Attorney, if any, and to such factors as public safety; the circumstances of any crime for which the probationer was placed on probation; the nature of the probation violation; the occurrence of any previous violations; and the impact of the underlying crime on any person or community, as well as any mitigating factors.

(i) *Continuance of Probation.* The court may decline to modify or revoke probation and, instead, issue to the probationer such admonition or instruction as it may deem appropriate.

(ii) *Termination.* The court may terminate the probation order.

(iii) *Modification.* The court may modify the conditions of probation. Such modification may include the addition of reasonable conditions and the extension of the duration of the probation order.

(iv) *Revocation, Statement of Reasons.* The court may order that the order of probation be revoked. If the court orders revocation, it shall state the reasons therefor in writing.

(e) Execution of Suspended Sentence; Stay of Execution. Upon revocation of a probation order, any sentence that was imposed for the crime involved, the execution of which was suspended, shall be ordered executed forthwith; provided, however, that such execution maybe stayed (1) pending appeal in accordance with Mass. R. Crim. P. 31, or (2) at the court's discretion, and upon the probationer's motion, to provide a brief period of time for the probationer to attend to personal matters prior to commencement of a sentence of incarceration. The execution of such sentence shall not be otherwise stayed.

(f) Imposition of Sentence Where No Sentence Previously Imposed. Upon revocation of probation in a case where no sentence was imposed following conviction, the court shall impose a sentence or other disposition as provided by law.

2015 Commentary to District/Municipal Courts Rule 8

Section (c) differs from its antecedent, 2000 District Court Rule 7(c), in the addition of a reference to a probationer's waiver of the violation hearing as being part of the violation admission procedure. The sentence also differs in the deletion of the term "stipulates." Although an admission of a violation is often referred to as a "stipulation," it was concluded that the latter term inadequately describes the legal event at issue, and that the term "admission" is preferable. These amendments are consistent with Rule 6(g), which specifically addresses the violation admission procedure. Section (c) includes a reference to Rule 6(g).

Section (c) makes it clear that written findings stating the evidence relied upon are not required when a finding of violation is based on an admission. Section (d) differs from its antecedent in the addition of its third sentence, which prohibits the "continuance for disposition" without good cause, and expressly eliminates delay to await the outcome of an underlying new criminal charge as constituting such good cause. The latter provision is intended to eliminate the possibility of post-finding "tracking." Delay in the form of "tracking" at the outset of a violation proceeding, before a violation is found, is expressly prohibited by Rule 6(e).

Section (d) contains some minor improvements in terminology that are of no critical legal or procedural significance.

Section (f) reflects the addition of the phrase "or other disposition" in recognition of the fact that, following the revocation of probation, the court's options where no sentence was imposed at the time probation was ordered are not limited to the imposition of a sentence. For example, where straight probation (which is not a "sentence") had been ordered, the court, after finding violation and revoking probation, may once again order straight probation.

2000 Commentary to District Court Rule 7 [Now Rule 8]
Requirement of a Finding

This rule addresses the court's two separate tasks upon completion of the violation hearing. Section (a) requires the court to adjudicate the factual issue of whether a violation has occurred. It expressly eliminates as an option a "general continuance."

The requirement that a finding be made on the issue of violation is based on several considerations. First, and most important, it is essential for the credibility of the probation order that the issue raised by the alleged violation be resolved. Even if the alleged violation involves a relatively minor matter, the likelihood of successful change in the probationer's behavior is diminished if the court temporizes in its role as finder of fact. If a violation has occurred, the probationer should be confronted with that fact. If no violation is found, the probationer is entitled to that finding on the record. No useful judicial or probation purpose is served by failure to adjudicate after the evidence has been presented. A failure by the court to decide the issue can foster the perception on the part of the probationer that if the court does not take the matter seriously, neither should he or she.

Second, adjudication of the violation charge does not limit the court's wide discretion regarding disposition. As addressed further in the rule, if a violation is found, the court's options range from a simple warning with the current terms of probation continued, to a revocation of probation, which in many instances will result in incarceration.

Third, the adjudication of a violation will establish an appropriate record of the probationer's non-compliance, which can be essential to an appropriate disposition if a subsequent violation occurs. Minor violations, even if they do not warrant significant sanctions in themselves, may provide important information in any subsequent proceedings.

It should be noted that the "seriousness" of the violation, its impact or lack of impact on any victim and the nature of the underlying crime are irrelevant to whether the alleged violation occurred. Those matters relate solely to the court's disposition if a violation is found.

In referring to the situation where the court finds no violation, section (b) of the rule reiterates three important points: the probation officer bears the burden of proof, the standard of proof is a preponderance of the evidence, and only a violation that has been formally alleged in the Notice of Probation Violation and Hearing maybe found.

Section (c) of the rule repeats these three points regarding the finding of a violation and adds that a violation may be found based on the probationer's admission. It also adds the requirements of findings of fact and a statement of the evidence relied on, which are due process requirements. *Morrissey v. Brewer*, 408 U.S. 471, 489 (1972). Failure to make findings and a statement of the evidence relied on appears to be reversible error. *See Fay v. Commonwealth*, 379 Mass. 498, 504–05 (1980). The Court in *Fay* also ruled that written findings were not required as a matter of due process, where such findings were announced orally on the record in the presence of the probationer and the probationer subsequently obtained a written copy in the form of a transcript. *Fay v. Commonwealth*, 379 Mass. at 504–05 (1980). The rule, however, requires that the findings and evidence relied on be stated in writing.

Disposition

Section (d) of the rule sets out four specific types of dispositions that are available to the court if a violation is found. These are expressly described as an exclusive list of the court's options, though they provide a comprehensive range of sanctions. The rule also provides factors that the court should consider on disposition, namely:

- the recommendation of the Probation Department.
- public safety.
- seriousness of the crime of which the probationer was found guilty.
- nature of the violation.
- record of any previous violation.
- impact on a victim of the underlying crime.

Counsel is free to argue, and the court is free to consider, any relevant mitigating factors.

Regarding the choice of disposition, two factors are essential: (1) disposition is a matter of the court's discretion. *McHoul v. Commonwealth*, 365 Mass. 465, 469–70 (1974); *Commonwealth v. Durling*, 407 Mass. 108, 111 (1990); and (2) disposition is not a punishment for the new crime, but rather relates to the underlying offense. *Commonwealth v. Odoardi*, 397 Mass. 28, 30 (1986).

Section (d)(i) provides for continuance of probation. This may be appropriate where the violation is minor and the probationer has no history of previous violations. It can be completely appropriate for a probation officer to commence and successfully prosecute a probation violation proceeding and then recommend that the current probation terms merely be continued. This may reflect the probation officer's judgment that, though minor, the offense should be adjudicated to impress upon the probationer the importance of compliance, that a warning from the court is necessary to prevent more serious violations and that the violation should be a matter of record. The continuance of current probation terms despite a finding of violation is sometimes referred to as "reprobating" the probationer.

Section (d)(ii), provides for termination of probation. This outcome can be appropriate where the offense is minor and the court determines that the purpose of probation has been accomplished. It can also be appropriate in conjunction with the disposition of a new offense, where the probationer is already serving a sentence, and where the probationer is on probation in another court.

Under section (d)(iii), the court has the dispositional option of modifying the probationary terms after a finding of violation. It has been held that it is "a matter of well-established common law, that courts do possess [the authority to modify probation conditions], and that conditions of probation maybe amended to serve 'the ends of justice and the best interests of both the public and the defendant.'" *Buckley v. Quincy Division of the District Court Dept.*, 395 Mass. 815, 817 (1985), citing *Burns v. United States*, 287 U.S. 216, 221 (1932).

The addition of reasonable conditions to an individual's probation does not constitute a revision or revocation of a sentence under Mass. R. Crim. P. 29. *Buckley, supra*, at 818–19. The Court did not "define that point at which the modification is so drastic that it becomes the revision of a sentence subject to the requirements of rule 29," noting that the modification in *Buckley* was a nonpunitive rehabilitative measure, designed to facilitate the successful reintegration of the plaintiff into the community. *Buckley, supra*, at 818–19 n.5.

It should be noted that the Court in *Buckley* was addressing a situation where conditions were added to a probation order without any finding of a violation, but rather based on an assessment by a probation officer. The Court ruled that a supervising court (as distinguished from a sentencing court) may not modify the conditions of probation without a material change in circumstances such as a violation of probation. It also indicated that a violation of probation is a material change in circumstances:

> Our holding does not limit whatever authority is held by the supervisory court to modify conditions where there has been a material change in circumstances (such as a violation of a condition of probation). Nor need we outline those situations in which the sentencing court might modify the terms of probation.

Buckley v. Quincy Div. of Dist. Court Dept., supra, at 820.

Section (d)(iii) addresses issues left unaddressed in *Buckley* by affirmatively authorizing the court conducting a probation violation hearing to modify the conditions of probation upon a finding of violation.

Revocation: Stay after Revocation

Section (d)(iv) provides for the most serious sanction upon a finding of probation violation, namely, revocation of probation. Under *Commonwealth v. Holmgren*, 421 Mass. 224 (1995), any sentence that was imposed, but its execution suspended pending probation, must be ordered executed in its entirety upon revocation of probation. This ruling was based on an unambiguous statutory requirement in G.L. c. 279, § 3.

The requirement of executing a suspended sentence upon revocation of probation is reflected in section (e), which also provides two specific bases for a stay of execution. This provision precludes any stay other than for (1) appeal or (2) a brief time for a probationer to attend to personal matters. A stay simply to avoid the execution of sentence, with or without the addition of new terms, is not allowed under the rule. There are several reasons for this. First, there appears to be no established legal basis for such a stay. Second, such a stay is inconsistent with the plain language of *Holmgren*. Third, the terms of such a stay are unenforceable. Conditions on the person's behavior during the stay cannot be ordered as probation—probation has been revoked. On the other hand, the court cannot condition the stay on unstated or vague conditions (e.g., "stay out of further trouble"), since a termination of the stay presumably requires incarceration, which, in turn, requires an opportunity for the person to be notified and heard regarding the factual issue of whether he or she violated the stay. One element of such a process would be specificity of the alleged violation. Even if conditions on such a stay were expressly stated in writing, they could not be enforced without a due process procedure similar to the same probation revocation procedure that has just been concluded. Since the person would not be on probation, there would be no one with authority to "prosecute" the alleged violation of the stay conditions. Perhaps most important, such a stay is impermissible because it implies that if the person successfully completes the stay, on whatever terms are imposed, written or unwritten, the sentence that had to be ordered executed pursuant to *Holmgren* somehow disappears.

Section (d)(iv) requires that, if the court decides to revoke probation, it must provide the reasons for that decision. A statement of reasons for deciding to revoke probation is a requirement of due process. *Gagnon v. Scarpelli*, 411 U.S. 778 (1973). While the reasons need not be put in writing to ensure due process, *Fay v. Commonwealth*, 379 Mass. 498 (1980), the rule requires them in writing to ensure a clear and accessible record.

Disposition Where No Sentence Originally Imposed

Section (f) addresses the situation where the probationer was sentenced with "straight probation" on the underlying conviction. On the one hand, this means that upon a revocation of probation, there is no suspended sentence to be executed. On the other hand, the probationer is subject to any sentence for the underlying crime that is provided by law. Though it may appear illogical, this would appear to include a sentence involving probation, even though the triggering event for the imposition of such a sentence is a violation and revocation of the "straight" probation originally ordered. Presumably, if such post-revocation probation is imposed, the conditions and the consequences for any violation will take into account the fact that probation has already been violated.

RULE 9
Violation of Conditions of a "Continuance Without a Finding"

(a) Notice, Conduct of Hearing, Adjudication. The procedures set forth in these rules regarding notice for, and the conduct and adjudication of, probation violation hearings shall also apply where the Probation Department alleges a violation of one or more conditions of probation imposed together with a continuance without a finding.

(b) Disposition. The dispositional options available to the court following a determination that one or more conditions of probation imposed together with a continuance without a finding have been violated shall be as follows:

(i) *Termination of Probation.* The court may terminate the order of probation and the continuance without a finding and enter a dismissal on the underlying criminal case.

(ii) *Continuation of the Continuance Without a Finding With No Probation Modification.* The court may continue the continuance without a finding and issue to the probationer such admonition or instruction as it may deem appropriate.

(iii) *Continuation of the Continuance Without a Finding With Modification of Probation.* The court may continue the continuance without a finding and modify the conditions of probation including the duration of the continuance.

(iv) *Termination of the Continuance Without a Finding and No Revocation of Probation.* The court may terminate the continuance without a finding without revoking probation and, if a finding of sufficient facts was entered at the time the continuance without a finding was ordered, shall proceed to enter a guilty finding. The order of probation, with or without

modifications, may thereupon constitute the disposition on the guilty finding if the probationer consents.

(v) *Termination of the Continuance Without a Finding and Revocation of Probation.* The court may terminate the continuance without a finding and revoke the order of probation. If the court orders revocation, it shall state the evidence relied upon in writing, and, if a finding of sufficient facts was entered at the time the continuance without a finding was ordered, the court shall enter a guilty finding and impose. a sentence or other disposition as provided by law.

2015 Commentary to District/Municipal Courts Rule 9

The order of sections (b)(i) and (b)(ii) differs the 2000 District Rule to more accurately reflect the increasingly severe "hierarchy" of this list of dispositional options. Other, minor changes exist as well.

Section (b)(iii) reflects the fact that, where a probation order is modified after a finding of violation, there is no need to mention in the rule that a "material change of circumstance" is a prerequisite to such modification. This is so because a violation of probation constitutes per se sufficient grounds for a modification. *See Buckley v. Quincy Div. of the Dist. Ct. Dep't*, 395 Mass. 815, 820 (1985).

New section (b)(iv) has been added to acknowledge the court's option of terminating a CWOF, *but not revoking probation*. In such cases, the court, if a finding of sufficient facts had been made at the time the CWOF was ordered, may enter a guilty finding with the probation order, with or without modification, serving as the criminal sentence.

Section (b)(v) is based on the 2000 District Court Rule 9(b)(iv) and includes the requirement that when the court orders a revocation of probation it *must state in writing the evidence relied upon*. This has been held to be a requirement of fundamental due process. *Morrissey v. Brewer*, 408 U.S. 471, 488–89 (1972) (due process requirements for parole revocation hearings); *accord Gagnon v. Scarpelli*, 411 U.S. 778, 782 (1973) (same due process rights apply in probation revocation hearings).

Section (b)(v) also indicates that, if a violation of probation is found in the context of a continuance without a finding and probation is then revoked, the entry of a guilty finding and sentencing in the underlying case is possible only if the court that ordered the CWOF had entered a finding of sufficient facts.

Section (b)(v) also reflects the addition of a reference to the court's obligation to "impose a sentence or other disposition as provided by law" when it finds a violation and orders revocation in the context of a CWOF. This phrase formerly appeared in 2000 District Court Rule 9(d), which has been deleted, as explained below.

Section (c) of the 2000 District Court Rule has been deleted. It limited stays of execution following the imposition of sentence upon revocation of probation and entry of a guilty finding. The only stays permitted by the rule were those provided by rule (stay pending appeal, Mass. R. Crim. P. 31) and stays to allow a defendant to attend to personal matters prior to commencement of an incarceration sentence, as provided under common law. It was concluded that, since there is no other legal ground for such stays, the express limitation in the rule was unnecessary.

Section (d) of the 2000 District Court Rule has also been deleted. It involved admissions to sufficient facts seeking a

CWOF tendered by defendants and accepted by the court with no sentencing conditions included in the tender. In such cases, the court that later revokes probation is free to impose any sentence provided by law. The implication in this provision was that, if sentencing terms *had been included* with the tender, the court that later found a violation of the CWOF and revoked probation would be limited to imposing a sentence consistent with the terms set forth in the tender. It was concluded that this provision was unnecessary because such conditioned tenders seeking CWOFs are, in fact, not made, or, if made, are not accepted by the courts. In any event, Rule 9(b)(v) adequately addresses the issue in general terms: when the court terminates a CWOF and revokes probation, "the court must impose a sentence or other disposition *as provided by law.*" (Emphasis added.) This obviates the need for these rules to resolve the question of whether the tender of a plea or admission seeking a CWOF may be conditioned on specific sentencing terms, and, if accepted by the sentencing court, whether such sentencing terms are "binding" on the court that subsequently revokes probation and terminates the CWOF.

2000 Commentary to District Court Rule 9
Continuance Without a Finding with Probation

This rule addresses the situation where the allegation of a probation violation involves a probation order issued together with a continuance without a finding. In such cases, the conditions of probation are also the conditions whereby the underlying criminal case has been continued without the entry of a finding of guilty, following submission and acceptance of a formal plea or admission.

The rule makes clear that the procedure in these cases for commencing, conducting and disposing of probation violation proceedings is the same as in cases where a finding of guilty has been entered following a plea, admission or trial. The only differences from the latter involve the court's dispositional options if a probation violation is found.

Specifically, if the court finds a probation violation and decides as a matter of its discretion to revoke probation, the continuance is thereby terminated, a finding of guilty must be entered and sentence must be imposed. The court will be bound by whatever dispositional terms were set by the probationer and accepted by the court as formal conditions of his or her plea or admission, if any.

The rule takes the position that upon revocation of probation in a case continued without a finding, a sentence that was conditioned on probation compliance should be ordered executed in its entirety. This is parallel to the ruling in *Commonwealth v. Holmgren*, 421 Mass. 224 (1995), a case which involved execution of a suspended sentence upon violation of probation.

In cases where the defendant submitted his or her plea or admission conditioned only by a requirement that the case be continued without a finding, with no sentencing terms specified in the tender of plea or admission, the court may have indicated what sentence should be imposed if probation is violated and revoked (sometimes referred to as "a Duquette alternative"). Such a sentence should be given great deference but is not binding on the judge who enters the guilty finding and then imposes sentence. This parallels the "straight probation" situation. That is, if a violation is found and the court decides to revoke probation, the sentence to be imposed following entry of the guilty finding may be any sentence provided by law.

Continuance Without a Finding Without Probation

This rule does not address the situation where the court has ordered a case continued without a finding, but has not placed the defendant on probation, that is, where the conditions of the continuance are not conditions of probation.

In *Commonwealth v. Rivera*, No. SJ-96-0578, (Supreme Judicial Court, Single Justice Decision, November 29, 1996), the Single Justice held that

> like the procedure for probation revocation, the procedure for revocation of a continuance without a finding may result in the loss of the defendant's liberty, [thus] for purposes of due process it is appropriate to analyze the revocation of a continuance without a finding the same as this court does a revocation of probation.

Apparently, in *Rivera* the defendant's case had been continued without a finding, but he had not been placed on probation.

One problem with such cases involves the need for conditions of the continuance to be set forth in writing and given to the defendant. Where a case is continued without a finding, but the defendant not placed on probation, it is not clear how and by whom those conditions are reduced to writing and given to the defendant. Similarly, if the defendant is not on probation, it is not clear who presents the allegation of an alleged violation of the conditions of the continuance. In any event, the Court in *Rivera*, applying the due process requirements of probation violation proceedings, found that the proceedings were inadequate in terms of notice of the alleged violation, time to prepare for the hearing, and the reliability of the hearsay evidence submitted, and vacated the revocation of the continuance.

7

PART 8

Issues in Probation and Probation Revocation Hearings

Nicola J. Pangonis

Updated for the 2017 Edition by Helle Sachse.

I. PREAMBLE. GUIDELINES FOR PROBATION VIOLATION PROCEEDINGS IN THE SUPERIOR COURT, effective February 1, 2016
Section One: Scope and Purpose
Section Two: Definitions
Section Three: Commencement of Violation Proceedings
Section Four: Service of a Notice of Surrender
Section Five: Initial Violation Hearing
Section Six: Final Violation Hearing
Section Seven: Special Provisions For Commencement of Violation Proceedings Based on a New Criminal Offense

II. PROBATION IN MASSACHUSETTS
A.   Introduction
        1. Historical Overview
        2. Pretrial and Dispositional Probation
        3. The Goals of Probation are Rehabilitation and Public Safety
B.   Statutory Bases
        1. "Pretrial Probation" and Conditions of Release
        2. Dispositional Probation/Post Conviction/Adjudication/
            Continuance Without a Finding/Statutory Authority
        3. Specific Statutory Provisions Relating to Juveniles
            on Dispositional Probation
        4. "Straight Probation" or Sentence Deferral as a Disposition

III. PROBATION CONDITIONS
A.   Mandatory Conditions
        1. Superior Court Rule 56 Provides Conditions of Probation
            for all Probationers
        2. Probation Supervision Fee; Administrative Supervision Fee;
            Waiver of Fee; Victim/Witness Surcharge
        3. Other Mandatory Conditions: Child Support, Motor Vehicle,
            Sex Offenders
B.   Statutory Discretionary Conditions
        1. Court Costs as a Condition of Probation
        2. Inpatient or Outpatient Treatment as a Condition of Probation
        3. Discretionary Conditions Include Restrictions on Travel,
            Abode, Contact with Abused Person(s), Payment
            of Compensation to Abused Person(s)
        4. The Court May Impose Reasonable Discretionary Conditions
            Before Trial with the Defendant's Consent under c. 276, § 87
        5. Pretrial Conditions May Be Imposed if the Court Finds
            the Defendant Is Dangerous
        6. Specific Juvenile Probation Provisions
        7. Defendant May Be Relieved of Requirement to Register
            as a Sex Offender
C.   Non-Statutory Conditions of Probation
        1. Conditions of Probation Must Be Reasonably Related
            to the Crime
        2. Conditions Must Be Doable
        3. Conditions Must Be Written
        4. Conditions Must Be Clear and Understandable
        5. Conditions Must Not Unreasonably Restrict Constitutional
            Rights
        6. Restitution: Properly Determined Restitution Is a Valid
            Condition of Probation
        7. Probation Conditions Must Be Accompanied by Enforcement
            Mechanism
        8. Probation Conditions Signed by a Defendant Do Not
            Constitute a Contract
        9. A "No Contact" Order Is Distinct from a "Stay Away" Order;
            the Terms Are Not Interchangeable
        10. Conditions of Probation Are Not Negotiable After a Judgment
            of Conviction
        11. Refusal to Sign Conditions of Probation Constitutes a Violation
            of Probation
        12. Batterer's Programs; Fifth Amendment Claims
D.   Length of Probationary Sentence Not Limited by Statute
E.   No Right to Counsel for Post Conviction Probationary Evaluation
F.   Modifying Probation Conditions
        1. Supervisory Court Must Find a Material Change in
            Circumstances or Violation to Modify Conditions of Probation
        2. Probation Officer Cannot Alter Probation Conditions Ordered
            by Sentencing Judge
        3. Amending Probation Conditions
        4. Interstate Compact for Adult Offender Supervision

IV. PROBATION REVOCATIONS
A.   Constitutional Standards for Revocation
        1. Minimum Requirements of Due Process for Revocation
            of Probation
B.   Revocation Practice in Massachusetts
        1. Statutory Authority
        2. Pretrial Probation May Be Revoked when a Judge Imposes
            Bail and Places a Defendant on Pretrial Probation Conditions
            Pursuant to G.L. c. 276, § 87
        3. Procedural Requirements for Probation Revocation Hearings
C.   Nature of the Evidence
        1. Probationers Are Not Entitled to the Full Panoply of
            Constitutional Protections at Revocation Hearings and
            the Strict Rules of Evidence Do Not Apply to Revocation
            Proceedings
        2. Hearsay May Be Admissible with Indicia of Reliability
        3. Regardless of the Fact the Evidence Has Been Suppressed,
            Illegally Obtained Evidence Is Usually Admissible
        4. Alleged Crimes, Indictments, Probable Cause or Appealed
            Conviction Cases May Form the Basis of Revocation
D.   Nature of the Hearing
        1. Right to Confront Witnesses
        2. District Attorney May Assist Probation Officer so Long
            as Assistance Does Not Interfere With Role of Probation
            Department
        3. Right to Counsel in Probation Revocation Hearings
E.   Necessity of Written Findings
        1. After the Judge Has Ruled that the Probationer Has Violated
            His Probation, the Judge Must Write His Findings and State
            Reasons for Revocation
F.   After Finding Defendant Violated Probation, Disposition Must
        Be Determined
        1. Reliable but Uncharged Evidence of Misconduct May be
            Considered Without Offending Due Process Principles
        2. In Determining Disposition After a Violation of Probation has
            been Found, the Judge has Discretion to Consider a Broad
            Range of Information in Imposing Sentence
G.   Sentencing Issues upon Revocation of Probation
        1. Where a Judge Sentences a Defendant to Concurrent Sentences
            on Multiple Charges and Probation is Later Revoked, the
            Judge May Not "Unbundle" the Sentencing Scheme by
            Committing the Probationer on One Complaint and Continuing
            Probation on Another
        2. When Two or More Sentences Are to be Served Concurrently,
            the Shorter Ones are Considered to be 'Absorbed' Within the
            Longer Sentence

8

3. "Straight Probation:" Concurrent Terms on Multiple Charges;
Original Orders for Concurrent Terms of Straight Probation
do not Create a Sentencing Scheme that Forecloses Imposition
of Consecutive Sentences After a Revocation
4. Probation Upon Resentencing
H.   Appeal of Probation Revocation Proceeding
V. CONCLUSION

I. Preamble: Guidelines for Probation Violation Proceedings in the Superior Court

Effective February 1, 2016
SECTION ONE: SCOPE AND PURPOSE

These guidelines prescribe procedures in the Superior Court to be followed upon the allegation of a violation of an order or condition of probation imposed in a criminal case after a finding of guilty or after a continuance without a finding. These guidelines do not apply to an alleged violation of pretrial probation or other conditions of pretrial release.

The purpose of the guidelines is to ensure that judicial proceedings undertaken on an allegation of a violation of probation are conducted in accordance with applicable law, and in a prompt, uniform and consistent manner.

SECTION TWO: DEFINITIONS

In construing these guidelines, the following terms shall have the following meanings:

"Continuance without a finding" means the order of a court, following a formal submission and acceptance of a plea of guilty upon the defendant's agreement to the Commonwealth's evidence or a finding of sufficient facts, whereby a criminal case is continued to a date certain without formal entry of a guilty finding.[1] A court, in imposing a continuance without a finding, may include a term of probation with conditions, the violation of which may result in a revocation of the continuance and the entry of a finding of guilty and imposition of sentence.

"District Attorney" means the criminal prosecuting authority responsible for the criminal case in which a term of probation was imposed, to include the Attorney General.

"General conditions of probation" means those conditions of probation that are imposed as a matter of course in every probation order, as set forth in the official form promulgated for such orders.

"Notice of Surrender" means the written form issued by the Probation Department alleging a violation of probation and setting forth the precise grounds for a violation proceeding.

"Probation order" means the formal, written court order whereby a defendant is placed on probation and which expressly sets forth general and/or special conditions of probation.

"Pretrial Probation" means the probationary status of a defendant pursuant to a probation order issued prior to an adjudication of a criminal case.

"Revocation of probation" means the revocation of a probation order by a judge following an adjudication of a violation of a probation order.

"Special condition of probation" means any condition of probation imposed by a judge as part of a probation order in addition to general conditions of probation.

"Stipulation to violation" means a knowing and voluntary admission by a probationer that he/she has violated the probation order as alleged in the Notice of Surrender.

"Surrender" means the procedure, consistent with the instant Guidelines, by which a probation officer requires a probationer to appear before the court on an allegation of probation violation.

SECTION THREE: COMMENCEMENT OF VIOLATION PROCEEDINGS
A. Procedure

Violation Proceedings shall commence upon the filing, by a probation officer, of a written Notice of Surrender.[2] A Notice of Surrender shall be prepared in advance of Violation Proceedings except where the probationer has been arrested by the probation officer in accordance with G.L. c. 279, § 3, in which case the Notice of Surrender shall be prepared, filed with the court, and served on the probationer when the probationer first appears before the court. The Notice of Surrender shall be in a form promulgated by the Probation Department and shall identify the probationer by name, the offense or offenses for which the probationer was placed on probation, and the court and county where the offense was adjudicated and probation imposed. It shall specifically describe the basis for an alleged violation, shall include all alleged violations of the probation order known to the probation officer, and shall notify the probationer of the date and time of the Initial Hearing in the probation court.

B. Mandatory Commencement of Violation Proceedings

The probation officer shall issue a Notice of Surrender (1) when a probationer has been charged with a new criminal offense by way of complaint or indictment; (2) where the judge issuing the probation order directed that a Notice of Surrender is to issue upon any alleged violation of one or more conditions of probation; or (3) when the commencement of such proceedings is required by statute.

C. Discretionary Commencement of Violation Proceedings

Except as set forth above, the probation officer may issue a Notice of Surrender for an alleged violation of a general and/or special condition of probation if, in the discretion of the Probation Department, the alleged violation is unlikely to be successfully resolved through an administrative hearing or other intermediate interventions.

D. Amendment and Withdrawal

A Notice of Surrender may be amended at any reasonable time before a final surrender hearing, provided service is made in accordance with these guidelines. A Notice of Surrender may be withdrawn only with leave of court, provided, however, that a judge or magistrate may order the termination of the proceedings at any time in the exercise of discretion, after giving the Probation Department an opportunity to be heard.

SECTION FOUR: SERVICE OF A NOTICE OF SURRENDER

A Notice of Surrender shall be served on the probationer by in-hand service or by first class mail to the last known residential address that the probationer has provided to his probation officer. When a probationer is brought before the court where the probationer is under supervision as the result of his arrest by the probation officer pursuant to G.L. c. 279, § 3, or is in custody as the result of a separate criminal case, service shall be made in-hand and an initial hearing conducted. The manner of service of the Notice of Surrender shall be noted in the court docket. Out-of-court service other than by first-class mail shall require a written return of service. Where a probationer appears on a new criminal offense in a court other than the court that imposed or is supervising the probationer, the issuance and service of a Notice of Surrender shall be governed by Section Seven, Special Provisions For Commencement of Violation Proceedings based on a New Criminal Offense.

SECTION FIVE: INITIAL VIOLATION HEARING

Except for good cause, an Initial Violation Hearing shall be scheduled not later than fourteen days after the issuance of a Notice of Surrender. Upon the probationer's initial appearance before the probation court based on the issuance of a Notice of Surrender, a judge or magistrate shall confirm that the probationer has received the written Notice of Surrender, shall appoint counsel in the event the probationer is indigent and the offense for which probation was imposed has a potential penalty of incarceration, shall schedule a date and time for a final Violation Hearing, and shall determine whether the probationer should be detained pending a final hearing, or whether bail or release on personal recognizance (with or without conditions) should be imposed.[3] The probationer shall have the right to counsel at the time any detention, bail or release determination is made. Nothing herein shall preclude a court, utilizing a HOPE/MORR model of probation supervision, from detaining a probationer for a discrete period of time in accordance with that model.

A probationer shall not be detained pending a final Violation Hearing unless a judge or magistrate finds probable cause to believe that the probationer has violated a condition of his probation.[4] A probationer shall be entitled upon request to a preliminary violation hearing, to be held not more than seven days after the initial appearance, unless the probationer consents to a later date. The issues to be determined at such hearing are whether probable cause exists to believe that the probationer has violated a condition of the probation order, and if so, whether the probationer should continue to be held on bail or without right to bail. Where the violation is based on the issuance of an indictment for a new criminal offense, the indictment shall constitute proof of probable cause.[5] The hearing shall be conducted by a judge or magistrate in open court and shall be recorded. At such hearing the probation officer shall present evidence to support a finding of probable cause, and the probationer or his counsel shall be entitled to be heard in opposition. The District Attorney may, upon request of the probation officer, assist the probation officer in the presentation of evidence. If probable cause is found, a final violation hearing shall be scheduled by the court and the probationer shall be given notice in open court of the final hearing date. If probable cause is not found, the judge or magistrate may terminate the proceedings or may schedule a final hearing, but the probationer shall not be held in custody pending the final hearing.

SECTION SIX: FINAL VIOLATION HEARING
A. Scheduling the Hearing

A final Violation Hearing shall be scheduled not earlier than seven days after the Initial Violation Hearing unless the probationer assents to an earlier hearing, and not later than thirty days thereafter unless good cause is shown. Where the

probation surrender involves an alleged commission of a new criminal offense, a continuance to permit resolution of the case involving such new offense shall not ordinarily constitute good cause.[6]

B. Adjudicatory Determination

A final violation hearing shall consist of two parts: (1) an evidentiary hearing to adjudicate whether the alleged violation has occurred; and (2) upon a finding of violation, a dispositional hearing. The probationer shall be entitled to the assistance of counsel, but may waive counsel upon a determination by the court that such waiver is made knowingly and voluntarily.

The probation officer shall have the burden of proving that a probationer has violated one or more conditions of probation by a preponderance of evidence. At the request of a probation officer, or when required by G.L. c. 279, § 3, the District Attorney may participate in the presentation of evidence or examination of witnesses. Hearsay evidence shall be admissible at a Violation Hearing as permitted under Sections 802 through 804 of the Massachusetts Guide to Evidence, or when determined by the judge to be substantially reliable.[7] The probationer shall have the right to cross examine any witnesses called by the probation officer, including the probation officer; the right to call witnesses; the right to present evidence favorable to the probationer; the right to testify; and the right to make closing argument on the issue of whether a violation has been proved by a preponderance of evidence.

The court may accept a probationer's stipulation to a violation of probation as alleged in the Notice of Surrender if the judge finds after colloquy that the probationer is tendering a knowing and voluntary stipulation. However, the court shall not be bound by any agreement between the probationer and probation officer or District Attorney regarding the disposition to be imposed. A probationer shall not be entitled, as a matter of right, to withdraw a stipulation after it has been accepted by the court.

Upon the completion of the evidence and closing arguments, the court shall promptly determine whether a violation of probation has been proved by a preponderance of evidence. If the court finds that no violation has been proved, the probationer shall be restored to probation according to the terms and conditions previously imposed. If the court finds that a violation has been proved the judge shall make findings on the record as to the condition or conditions that have been violated and the facts found in making the determination.[8]

C. Dispositional Determination

Upon a finding that the probationer has violated one or more conditions of probation, the judge shall permit the probation officer and probationer, and where required by statute, the District Attorney, to make a recommendation regarding the appropriate sanction to be imposed by the court. Thereafter, the court shall impose a disposition based on the circumstances of the crime for which the probationer was placed on probation and its impact on any person or on the community, the occurrence of any prior violations of probation, the probationer's overall performance while on probation, the public safety, the effect of a sentence on the probationer's chances for rehabilitation, and any other mitigating or aggravating facts or circumstances. The court may consider information that was available to the judge who issued the probation order as well as information that has become available since the order was issued. The court, however, may not punish the probationer for criminal conduct which forms the basis of the violation.[9] The court may: (1) restore the probationer to his existing probationary term with such admonition or instruction as it may deem appropriate; (2) terminate the probation order and discharge the probationer; (3) extend the term of probation and modify the terms or conditions of probation; or (4) revoke probation in whole or in part.[10] Where probation is revoked on an offense for which a sentence had been imposed, the execution of which was suspended, the original sentence shall be ordered executed forthwith,[11] subject to a stay granted pending an appeal in accordance with Mass. R. Crim. P. 31, or at the court's discretion upon a probationer's request for a brief period of time to attend to personal affairs prior to the commencement of a sentence of incarceration. In the event probation is revoked on an offense for which no suspended sentence had previously been imposed, the court shall impose a sentence or other disposition as provided by law.[12]

Upon a finding of a violation of a probation order resulting from a continuance without a finding, the judge may terminate the probation order and the continuance without a finding and enter a dismissal on the underlying case, return the probationer to the same terms and conditions of probation with such admonitions or instructions as the judge deems appropriate, modify the continuance without a finding and modify the conditions of probation including the duration of the continuance, or terminate the continuance without a finding and enter a guilty finding and impose a sentence or other disposition as provided by law.

SECTION SEVEN: SPECIAL PROVISIONS FOR COMMENCEMENT OF VIOLATION PROCEEDINGS BASED ON A NEW CRIMINAL OFFENSE.

Whenever a person on probation is charged with a new criminal offense, the probation officer in the criminal court where the new offense is pending ("criminal court") shall immediately notify the Probation Department in the court where the person is subject to probation supervision ("probation court"). Said notification shall be made in accordance with policies of the Commissioner of Probation, or any policy, administrative order or standing order of the Chief Justice of the Trial Court. In order to comply with the mandatory provisions of Section 3(B), the chief probation officer or his designee in the probation court may order the issuance of a Notice of Surrender in the form set forth herein, to be served on the probationer by a probation officer in the criminal court, ordering the probationer to appear for an Initial Violation Hearing in the probation court at a fixed date and time.

Alternatively, the chief probation officer or his designee in the probation court may also seek the issuance of a warrant from the probation court pursuant to G.L. c. 279, § 3. In the event a warrant issued by the probation court is lodged at the criminal court or, where the probationer has been held in detention or in lieu of posted bail at a jail or house of correction, the clerk of the probation court shall, upon request, promptly issue process to bring the probationer before the probation court for an Initial Violation Hearing.

Footnotes

1 *Commonwealth v. Powell*, 453 Mass. 320 (2009); G.L. c. 278, § 18.

2 *Commonwealth v. Wilcox*, 446 Mass. 61, 66 (2006); *Commonwealth v. Durling*, 407 Mass. 108, 111 (1990) ("When a violation is alleged, the probation officer 'surrenders' the defendant to the court, subjecting the defendant to possible revocation of his probation.")

3 No authority explicitly establishes that bail either may or may not be set in probation violation proceedings. *But see Commonwealth v. Ward*, 15 Mass. App. Ct. 388, 393 (1983); *Rubera v. Commonwealth*, 371 Mass. 177, 184 n.3 (1976) (both suggesting that the setting of bail is appropriate).

4 *Fay v. Commonwealth*, 379 Mass. 498, 504 (1980) (right to a hearing before detention pending a final hearing is ordered); *Commonwealth v. Odoardi*, 397 Mass. 28, 33 (1986).

5 *Stefanik v. State Board of Parole*, 372 Mass. 726 (1977).

6 The practice of a probation surrender proceeding "tracking" a new criminal case is discouraged by these guidelines. However, a judge or magistrate may decide that good cause exists to permit tracking, for example, when the new criminal case is particularly complex or sensitive, such that providing discovery or presenting evidence at a final hearing could compromise the integrity of the new case. Such a determination shall be made in open court and entered on the record.

7 *Commonwealth v. Durling*, 407 Mass. 108, 114–118 (1990); *Morrissey v. Brewer*, 408 U.S. 471, 489 (1972); *Gagnon v. Scarpelli*, 411 U.S. 778, 782 n.5 (1973).

8 *Fay v. Commonwealth*, 379 Mass. 498, 504–505 (1980) (findings of fact not required to be in writing provided that they are made and announced on the record in the probationer's presence).

9 *Commonwealth v. Doucette*, 81 Mass. App. Ct. 740, 745 (2012); *Commonwealth v. Rodriguez*, 52 Mass. App. Ct. 572, 577 n.8 (2001).

10 A partial revocation of probation occurs where the probationer has been placed on probation on multiple offenses and the court revokes probation and imposes a sentence as to one or more offenses, and continues probation as to other offenses, typically to run from and after the committed sentence.

11 *Commonwealth v. Holmgren*, 421 Mass. 224 (1995); *see also*, *Commonwealth v. Bruzzese*, 437 Mass. 606 (2002) (where defendant was subject to multiple suspended sentences as part of a single sentencing structure, revoking probation on less than all charges violates double jeopardy principles)

12 A sentence imposed upon the finding of a violation shall not be imposed as punishment for any new crime, but rather as punishment for the offense(s) on which probation was imposed. *Commonwealth v. Odoardi*, 397 Mass. 28, 30 (1986). However, a judge may consider the conduct alleged in the new offense on the issue of the probationer's capacity for rehabilitation.

What are the procedural and constitutional requirements with which the court and counsel must be aware in conducting probation revocation hearings?

II. Probation in Massachusetts

A. Introduction

1. HISTORICAL OVERVIEW

Probation began in the Commonwealth of Massachusetts; the first documented usage of probation was in 1841 in Lexington, by John Augustus, an evangelical temperance worker. His work proved so popular that in 1878, Massachusetts enacted the world's first probation statute. Since then, the rest of the United States and most of the western world has adopted the use of probation in some form.

2. PRETRIAL AND DISPOSITIONAL PROBATION

"Probation, whether 'straight' or coupled with a suspended sentence, may be ordered as a legal disposition of criminal charges after a finding, verdict or plea of guilty or nolo contendere, i.e., admits to sufficient facts, pursuant to c. 276, § 87. Further, the court may accept a plea of guilty or an admission to sufficient facts, withhold adjudication of guilt and continue the case without a finding pursuant to c. 278, § 18. Probation allows the criminal offender to remain in the community subject to certain conditions and under the supervision of the court." *Commonwealth v. Sheridan*, 51 Mass. App. Ct. 74, 76 (2001) (quoting *Commonwealth v. Durling*, 407 Mass. 108, 11 (1990)).

A defendant may also be placed on pretrial probation with his or her consent pursuant to c. 276, § 87. Coupled with the authority to release a person on bail or personal recognizance, contained in c. 276, § 58, pretrial probation permits the court to set conditions, often known as "conditions of release" pending trial, so that the accused may remain at liberty during that time while public safety is protected.

3. THE GOALS OF PROBATION ARE REHABILITATION AND PUBLIC SAFETY

The primary goals of probation are rehabilitation of the probationer and protection of the public. *Commonwealth v. La France*, 402 Mass. 789, 795 (1988). Other recognized goals include punishment, deterrence and retribution. *Id.* (citing *United States v. Tonry*, 605 F.2d 144, 148 (5th Cir. 1979)). Probation is granted "with the hope that the probationer will be able to rehabilitate himself or herself under the supervision of the probation officer." *Sheridan*, 51 Mass. App. Ct. at 77 (citing *Commonwealth v. Olsen*, 405 Mass. 491, 493 (1989)).

B. Statutory Bases

1. "PRETRIAL PROBATION" AND CONDITIONS OF RELEASE

a. General Condition of Release on Bail or Personal Recognizance Is that the Person Not Be Charged with a Subsequent Crime

The Massachusetts general bail statute, c. 276, § 58, requires that the court inform the defendant as an explicit condition of release that should s/he be charged with a crime during the period of release, bail may be revoked. *Id.* The court may also impose other conditions of pretrial release, discussed *infra*.

b. Special Conditions of Pretrial Release

The general bail statute, c. 276, § 58, does not provide for the imposition of conditions of release other than that if the person is charged with another offense bail may be re-

voked and the person held for trial for up to sixty days. *Id.* However, sections 42A, 58A and 87 of chapter 276 authorize the judge to impose other conditions of pretrial release commonly known as "pretrial probation."

i. Domestic Abuse or Threat: Chapter 276, § 42A, Probation Before and After Trial of Offenses Relating to Domestic Abuse or Threat

Whenever a court issues a criminal complaint and the crime involves assault and battery, trespass, threat to commit a crime, nonsupport, or any other complaint which involves the infliction, or the imminent threat of infliction, of physical harm upon a person by such person's family or household member as defined in section one of chapter two hundred and nine A, the court may, in *lieu of or in addition to any terms of bail or personal recognizance, and after a hearing and finding, impose such terms as will insure the safety of the person allegedly suffering the physical abuse or threat thereof, and will prevent its recurrence.*

* * *

Such terms and conditions shall include reasonable restrictions on the travel, association or place of abode of the defendant as will prevent such person from contact with the person abused.

As part of the disposition of any criminal complaint, the *court may establish such terms and conditions of probation as will insure the safety of the person* who has suffered such abuse or threat thereof, and will prevent the recurrence of such abuse or threat thereof.

Such terms and conditions shall include reasonable restrictions on the travel, association or place of abode of the defendant as will prevent such persons from all contact with the person abused; or the payment by the defendant to the person abused of monetary compensation for losses suffered as a direct result of the crime. Compensatory loss shall include, but not be limited to, loss of earnings or support, out-of-pocket losses for injuries sustained, moving expenses and reasonable attorneys fees.

In addition, the terms and conditions of either the probation or the disposition of the complaint may include, but not be limited to, referral of the defendant to a clinic, facility or professional for one or more examinations, diagnoses, counseling or treatment; requiring the defendant to report periodically to a probation officer; or release of the defendant to the custody of a residential treatment facility.

G.L. c. 276, § 42A (emphasis added).

ii. Chapter 276, § 58A, Conditions of Pretrial Release for a Felony Offense

(1) The commonwealth may move, based on dangerousness, for an order of pretrial detention or release on conditions for a felony offense that has as an element of the offense the use, attempted use or threatened use of physical force against the person of another, or any other felony that, by its nature, involves a substantial risk that physical force against the person of another may result, including the

crime of burglary and arson whether or not a person has been placed at risk thereof, or a violation of an order pursuant to section 18, 34B or 34C of chapter 208, section 32 of chapter 209, section 3, 4 or 5 of chapter 209 A or section 15 or 20 of chapter 209C, or arrested and charged with a misdemeanor or felony involving abuse as defined in section 1 of said chapter 209A or while an order of protection issued under said chapter 209A was in effect against such person, an offense for which a mandatory minimum term of 3 years or more is prescribed in chapter 94C, arrested and charged with a violation of section 13B of chapter 268 or a third or subsequent conviction for a violation of section 24 of chapter 90, or convicted of a violent crime as defined in said section 121 of said chapter 140 for which a term of imprisonment was served and arrested and charged with a second or subsequent offense of felony possession of a weapon or machine gun as defined in section 121 of chapter 140, or arrested and charged with a violation of paragraph (a), (c) or (m) of section 10 of chapter 269; provided, however, that the commonwealth may not move for an order of detention under this section based on possession of a large capacity feeding device without simultaneous possession of a large capacity weapon; or arrested and charged with a violation of section 10G of said chapter 269.

(2) Upon the appearance before a superior court or district court judge of an individual charged with an offense listed in subsection (1) and upon the motion of the commonwealth, the judicial officer shall hold a hearing pursuant to subsection (4) issue an order that, pending trial, the individual shall either be released on personal recognizance without surety; *released on conditions of release as set forth herein*; or detained under subsection (3).

If the judicial officer determines that personal recognizance will not reasonably assure the appearance of the person as required or will endanger the safety of any other person or the community, such judicial officer shall order the pretrial release of the person—

(A) subject to the condition that the person not commit a federal, state or local crime during the period of release; and

(B) subject to the least restrictive further condition, or combination of conditions, that such judicial officer determines will reasonably assure the appearance of the person as required and the safety of any other person and the community that the person—

(i) remain in the custody of a designated person, who agrees to assume supervision and to report any violation of a release condition to the court, if the designated person is able reasonably to assure the judicial officer that the person will appear as required and will not pose a danger to the safety of any other person or the community;

(ii) maintain employment, or, if unemployed, actively seek employment;

(iii) maintain or commence an educational program;

(iv) abide by specified restrictions on personal associations, place of abode or travel;

(v) avoid all contact with an alleged victim of the crime and with any potential witness or witnesses who may testify concerning the offense;

(vi) report on a regular basis to a designated law enforcement agency, pretrial service agency, or other agency;

(vii) comply with a specified curfew;

(viii) refrain from possessing a firearm, destructive device, or other dangerous weapon;

(ix) refrain from excessive use of alcohol, or any use of a narcotic drug or other controlled substance, without a prescription by a licensed medical practitioner;

(x) undergo available medical, psychological, or psychiatric treatment, including treatment for drug or alcohol dependency and remain in a specified institution if required for that purpose;

(xi) execute an agreement to forfeit upon failing to appear as required, property of a sufficient unencumbered value, including money, as is reasonably necessary to assure the appearance of the person as required, and shall provide the court with proof of ownership and the value of the property along with information regarding existing encumbrances as the judicial officer may require;

(xii) execute a bail bond with solvent sureties; who will execute an agreement to forfeit in such amount as is reasonably necessary to assure appearance of the person as required and shall provide the court with information regarding the value of the assets and liabilities of the surety if other than an approved surety and the nature and extent of encumbrances against the surety's property; such surety shall have a net worth which shall have sufficient unencumbered value to pay the amount of the bail bond;

(xiii) return to custody for specified hours following release for employment, schooling, or other limited purposes; and

(xiv) satisfy any other condition that is reasonably necessary to assure the appearance of the person as required and to assure the safety of any other person and the community.

The judicial officer may not impose a financial condition that results in the pretrial detention of the person.

The judicial officer may at any time amend the order to impose additional or different conditions of release.

(3) If, after a hearing pursuant to the provisions of subsection (4), the district or superior court justice finds by clear and convincing evidence that no conditions of release will reasonably assure the safety of any other person or the community, said justice shall order the detention of the person prior to trial. A person detained under this subsection shall be brought to a trial as soon as reasonably possible, but in absence of good cause, the person so held shall not be detained for a period exceeding 120 days excluding any period of delay as defined in Massachusetts Rules of Criminal Procedure Rule 36(b)(2). A

justice may not impose a financial condition under this section that results in the pretrial detention of the person. Nothing in this section shall be interpreted as limiting the imposition of a financial condition upon the person to reasonably assure his appearance before the courts.

(4) When a person is held under arrest for an offense listed in subsection (1) and upon a motion by the commonwealth, the judge shall hold a hearing to determine whether conditions of release will reasonably assure the safety of any other person or the community.

The hearing shall be held immediately upon the person's first appearance before the court unless that person, or the attorney for the commonwealth, seeks a continuance. Except for good cause, a continuance on motion of the person may not exceed seven days, and a continuance on motion of the attorney for the commonwealth may not exceed three business days. During a continuance, the individual shall be detained upon a showing that there existed probable cause to arrest the person. At the hearing, such person shall have the right to be represented by counsel, and, if financially unable to retain adequate representation, to have counsel appointed. The person shall be afforded an opportunity to testify, to present witnesses, to cross-examine witnesses who appear at the hearing, and to present information. Prior to the summons of an alleged victim, or a member of the alleged victim's family, to appear as a witness at the hearing, the person shall demonstrate to the court a good faith basis for the person's reasonable belief that the testimony from the witness will be material and relevant to support a conclusion that there are conditions of release that will reasonably assure the safety of any other person or the community. The rules concerning admissibility of evidence in criminal trials shall not apply to the presentation and consideration of information at the hearing and the judge shall consider hearsay contained in a police report or the statement of an alleged victim or witness. The facts the judge uses to support findings pursuant to subsection (3), that no conditions will reasonably assure the safety of any other person or the community, shall be supported by clear and convincing evidence. In a detention order issued pursuant to the provisions of said subsection (3) the judge shall (a) include written findings of fact and a written statement of the reasons for the detention; (b) direct that the person be committed to custody or confinement in a corrections facility separate, to the extent practicable, from persons awaiting or serving sentence or being held in custody pending appeal; and (c) direct that the person be afforded reasonable opportunity for private consultation with his counsel. The person may be detained pending completion of the hearing. The hearing may be reopened by the judge, at any time before trial, or upon a motion of the commonwealth or the person detained if the judge finds that: (i) information exists that was not known at the time of the hearing or that there has been a change in circumstances and (ii) that such information or change in circumstances has a material bearing on the issue of whether there are conditions of release that will reasonably assure the safety of any other person or the community.

(5) In his determination as to whether there are conditions of release that will reasonably assure the safety of any other individual or the community, said justice, shall, on the basis of any information which he can reasonably obtain, take into account the nature and seriousness of the danger posed to any person or the community that would result by the person's release, the nature and circumstances of the offense charged, the potential penalty the person faces, the person's family ties, employment record and history of mental illness, his reputation, the risk that the person will obstruct or attempt to obstruct justice or threaten, injure or intimidate or attempt to threaten, injure or intimidate a prospective witness or juror, his record of convictions, if any, any illegal drug distribution or present drug dependency, whether the person is on bail pending adjudication of a prior charge, whether the acts alleged involve abuse as defined in section one of chapter two hundred and nine A, or violation of a temporary or permanent order issued pursuant to section eighteen or thirty-four B of chapter two hundred and eight, section thirty-two of chapter two hundred and nine, sections three, four or five of chapter two hundred and nine A, or sections fifteen or twenty of chapter two hundred and nine C, whether the person has any history of orders issued against him pursuant to the aforesaid sections, whether he is on probation, parole or other release pending completion of sentence for any conviction and whether he is on release pending sentence or appeal for any conviction; provided, however, that if the person who has attained the age of 18 years is held under arrest for a violation of an order issued pursuant to section 18 or 34B of chapter 208, section 32 of chapter 209, section 3, 4 or 5 of chapter 209A or section 15 or 20 of chapter 209C or any act that would constitute abuse, as defined in section 1 of said chapter 209A, or a violation of sections 13M or 15D of chapter 265, said justice shall make a written determination as to the considerations required by this subsection which shall be filed in the domestic violence record keeping system.

(6) Nothing in this section shall be construed as modifying or limiting the presumption of innocence.

(7) A person aggrieved by the denial of a district court justice to admit him to bail on his personal recognizance with or without surety may petition the superior court for a review of the order of the recognizance and the justice of the district court shall thereupon immediately notify such person of his right to file a petition for review in the superior court. When a petition for review is filed in the district court or with the detaining authority subsequent to petitioner's district court appearance, the clerk of the district court or the detaining authority, as the case may be, shall immediately notify by telephone, the clerk and probation officer of the district court,

8

the district attorney for the district in which the district court is located, the prosecuting officer, the petitioner's counsel, if any, and the clerk of courts of the county to which the petition is to be transmitted. The clerk of the district court, upon the filing of a petition for review, either in the district court or with the detaining authority, shall forthwith transmit the petition for review, a copy of the complaint and the record of the court, including the appearance of the attorney, if any is entered, and a summary of the court's reasons for denying the release of the defendant on his personal recognizance with or without surety to the superior court for the county in which the district court is located, if a justice thereof is then sitting, or to the superior court of the nearest county in which a justice is then sitting; the probation officer of the district court shall transmit forthwith to the probation officer of the superior court, copies of all records of the probation office of said district court pertaining to the petitioner, including the petitioner's record of prior convictions, if any, as currently verified by inquiry of the commissioner of probation. The district court or the detaining authority, as the case may be, shall cause any petitioner in its custody to be brought before the said superior court within two business days of the petition having been filed. The district court is authorized to order any officer authorized to execute criminal process to transfer the petitioner and any papers herein above described from the district court or the detaining authority to the superior court, and to co-ordinate the transfer of the petitioner and the papers by such officer. The petition for review shall constitute authority in the person or officer having custody of the petitioner to transport the petitioner to said superior court without the issuance of any writ or other legal process; provided, however, that any district or superior court is authorized to issue a writ of habeas corpus for the appearance forthwith of the petitioner before the superior court.

The superior court shall in accordance with the standards set forth in section fifty-eight A, hear the petition for review under section fifty-eight A as speedily as practicable and in any event within five business days of the filing of the petition. The justice of the superior court hearing the review may consider the record below which the commonwealth and the person may supplement. The justice of the superior court may, after a hearing on the petition for review, order that the petitioner be released on bail on his personal recognizance without surety, or, in his discretion, to reasonably assure the effective administration of justice, make any other order of bail or recognizance or remand the petitioner in accordance with the terms of the process by which he was ordered committed by the district court.

(8) If after a hearing under subsection (4) detention under subsection (3) is ordered or pretrial release subject to conditions under subsection (2) is ordered, then: (A) the clerk shall immediately notify the probation officer of the order; and (B) the order of detention under subsection (3) or order of pretrial release subject to conditions under subsection (2) shall be recorded in (i) the defendant's criminal record as compiled by the commissioner of probation under section 100 and (ii) the domestic violence record keeping system.

G.L. c. 276, § 58A (emphasis added).

iii. Proceedings Governing Violation of § 58A Condition(s)

Section 58B of chapter 276 sets forth the procedure for a violation of condition(s) imposed pursuant to § 58A. Section 58B provides:

A person who has been released after a hearing pursuant to sections 42A, 58, 58A or 87 and who has *violated a condition of his release, shall be subject to a revocation of release* and an order of detention. The judicial officer shall enter an order of revocation and detention if after a hearing the judicial officer finds (1) that there is probable cause to believe that the person has committed a federal or state crime while on release, or clear and convincing evidence that the person has violated any other condition of release; and (2) the judicial officer finds that there are no conditions of release that will reasonably assure the person will not pose a danger to the safety of any other person or the community; or the person is unlikely to abide by any condition or combination of conditions of release.

If there is probable cause to believe that, while on release, the person committed a federal felony or an offense described in clause (1), a rebuttable presumption arises that no condition or combination of conditions will assure that the person will not pose a danger to the safety of any other person or the community. If the judicial officer finds that there are conditions of release that will assure that the person will not pose a danger to the safety of any other person or the community, and that the person will abide by such conditions, the judicial officer shall treat the person in accordance with the provisions of this section and may amend the conditions of release accordingly. Upon the person's first appearance before the judicial officer in the court which will conduct proceedings for revocation of an order of release under this section, the hearing concerning revocation shall be held immediately unless that person or the attorney for the commonwealth seeks a continuance. During a continuance the person shall be detained without bail unless the judicial officer finds that there are conditions of release that will reasonably assure that the person will not pose a danger to the safety of any other person or the community and that the person will abide by conditions of release. If the person is detained without bail, except for good cause, a continuance on motion of the person shall not exceed seven days, a continuance on motion of the attorney for the commonwealth or probation shall not exceed three business days. A person detained under this subsection, shall be brought to trial as soon as reasonably possible, but in the absence of good cause, a person so held shall not be detained for a period exceeding ninety days excluding any period of delay as defined in Massachusetts Rules of Criminal Procedure Rule 36(b)(2).

G.L. c. 276, § 58B.

iv. Chapter 276, § 87, Pretrial Conditions with the Defendant's Consent

The superior court, any district court and any juvenile court *may place on probation* in the *care of its probation officer* any person before it *charged with an offense* or a crime for such time and upon such conditions as it deems proper, *with the defendant's consent, before trial and before a plea* of guilty, *or in any case* after a finding or verdict of guilty; provided, that, in the case of any *child under the age of 18* placed upon probation by the superior court, *he may be placed in the care of a probation officer of any district court or of any juvenile court,* within the judicial district of which such child resides. . . . *Id.* (emphasis added).

2. DISPOSITIONAL PROBATION/POST CONVICTION/ ADJUDICATION/CONTINUANCE WITHOUT A FINDING/STATUTORY AUTHORITY

a. Suspension of a Sentence or Part Thereof, Imposition of Probation, c. 279, §§ 1, 1a

G.L. c. 279, §§ 1 and 1A, addressing suspension of execution of sentence and probation, provide in pertinent part:

When a person convicted before a court is sentenced to imprisonment, the court may direct that the *execution of the sentence, or any part thereof, be suspended* and that *he be placed on probation* for such time and on such terms and conditions as it shall fix . . . .

G.L. c. 279, § 1 (emphasis added).

See also Commonwealth v. Talbot, 444 Mass. 586, 596 (2005) ("We hereby direct that, if requested by the defendant or her attorney, probation officers must give the defendant's attorney notice and a reasonable opportunity to attend a presentence interview of the defendant.").

b. Continuances Without a Finding: G.L. c. 278, § 18. Pleas of Not Guilty, Guilty or Nolo Contendere; Requests for Specific Disposition; Pretrial Motions

A defendant who is before the Boston municipal court or a district court or a district court sitting in a juvenile session or a juvenile court on a criminal offense within the court's final jurisdiction shall plead not guilty or guilty, or with the consent of the court, nolo contendere. Such plea of guilty shall be submitted by the defendant and acted upon by the court; provided, however, that a defendant with whom the commonwealth cannot reach agreement for a recommended disposition shall be allowed to tender a plea of guilty together with a request for a specific disposition. Such request may include any disposition or dispositional terms within the court's jurisdiction, including, unless otherwise prohibited by law, a dispositional request that a guilty finding not be entered, but rather the case be continued without a finding to a specific date thereupon to be dismissed, such continuance conditioned upon compliance with specific terms and conditions or that the defendant be placed on probation pursuant to the

provisions of section eighty-seven of chapter two hundred and seventy-six. If such a plea, with an agreed upon recommendation or with a dispositional request by the defendant, is tendered, the court shall inform the defendant that it will not impose a disposition that exceeds the terms of the agreed upon recommendation or the dispositional request by the defendant, whichever is applicable, without giving the defendant the right to withdraw the plea.

If a defendant, notwithstanding the requirements set forth hereinbefore, attempts to enter a plea or statement consisting of an admission of facts sufficient for finding of guilt, or some similar statement, such admission shall be deemed a tender of a plea of guilty for purposes of the procedures set forth in this section.

Any pretrial motion filed in a criminal case pending in the Boston municipal court or district court or a district court sitting in a juvenile session or a juvenile court and decided before entry of defendant's decision on waiver of the right to jury trial shall not be refiled or reheard thereafter, except in the discretion of the court as substantial justice requires. Any such pretrial motion not filed or filed but not decided prior to entry of the defendant's decision on waiver of the right to jury trial may be filed thereafter but not later than twenty-one days after entry of said decision on waiver of the right to jury trial, except for good cause shown.

G.L. c. 278, § 18.

c. Section 1A of Chapter 279 Provides for the Imposition of Terms and Conditions of Probation

The court may direct, as one of such terms and conditions, that payment of the fine may be made to the probation officer in one payment, or in part payments, during the period of probation or any extension thereof, and when such fine shall have been fully paid the order of commitment as to the fine shall be void, but the order of commitment as to imprisonment shall not be affected by such payment . . . If during or at the end of said period the probation officer shall report that the fine is in whole or in part unpaid, and in his opinion the person is unwilling or unable to pay it, the court may either extend said period, place the case on file or revoke the suspension of the execution of the sentence. When such suspension is revoked, in a case where the fine has been paid in part, the defendant may be committed for default in payment of the balance, and may also be committed for the term of imprisonment fixed in the original sentence.

G.L. c. 279, § 1A.

d. Probation Not Available if the Person Has Been Convicted of a Capital Crime or a Crime Involving Being Armed with a Dangerous Weapon if the Person Has Previously Been Convicted of Any Felony

[Section 1A of chapter 279 does] not permit the suspension of the execution of the sentence of any person convicted of a crime punishable by imprisonment

8

for life or of a crime an element of which is being armed with a dangerous weapon, or of any person convicted of any other felony if it shall appear that he has been previously convicted of any felony.

G.L. c. 279, § 1A.

e. Continuance Without a Finding with Conditions of Probation as Disposition

The Legislature has enacted several statutes that mandate or permit pretrial disposition. See *Commonwealth v. Duquette*, 386 Mass. 834, 438 (1982) for a discussion of the mutual benefits of pretrial disposition by means of a continuance without a finding.

Unless the statutory language of the charged offense prohibits it, a judge may dismiss an indictment or complaint after a plea of guilt (or delinquency or as a youthful offender) or admission to sufficient facts and after the satisfaction of conditions by continuing the case without a finding. *Commonwealth v. Cheney*, 440 Mass. 568, 574 (2003). *See also Commonwealth v. Tim T.*, 437 Mass. 592, 596–597 (2002) (juvenile court judge could not dispose of case over the Commonwealth's objection by imposing probation conditions pursuant to c. 276, § 87 without first complying with c. 278, § 18, which requires a guilty plea (or plea of delinquency or youthful offender) or an admission to sufficient facts).

In *Commonwealth v. Pyles*, 423 Mass. 717 (1996), the defendant, who could not reach an agreement with the Commonwealth, entered a plea of guilty on the day his bench trial was scheduled to commence and requested the judge not enter a finding of guilt, but rather, a continuance without a finding (cwof) with specific conditions of probation over the Commonwealth's objection. *Id.* at 718. The court allowed the request and entered a continuance without a finding with specific conditions of probation. The Commonwealth appealed arguing the disposition over its objection constituted a violation of art. 30 of the Massachusetts Declaration of Rights by improperly intruding on the executive power of the district attorney. *Id.* at 719. The Supreme Judicial Court disagreed, declaring c. 278, § 18, flows from the Legislature's authority to classify criminal conduct, establish criminal penalties and adopt rules of practice and procedure. *Id.* at 722.

Similarly, in *Commonwealth v. Powell*, 453 Mass. 320 (2009), the Supreme Judicial Court held that the interests of public justice warranted dismissal of an indictment in Superior Court after a period of time, contingent on the defendant's compliance with conditions, even though the Commonwealth objected to the disposition. *Id.* at 321.

A request by the defendant for the court to enter a disposition of continuance without a finding after a bench trial (or a trial by jury), however, should be denied, as there is no statutory or other authority for such an action. *See Commonwealth v. Norrell*, 423 Mass. 725 (1996). In *Norrell*, the defendant, who was charged with assault and battery from an altercation at a rock concert, waived her right to a jury trial and the case was tried before a judge. *Id.* at 725. At the conclusion the judge found facts sufficient to support a guilty finding. *Id.* At the sentencing phase, the court allowed defense counsel's request that the court enter a continuance without a finding; the Commonwealth appealed. *Id.* at 726. Acknowledging it had "crept into the culture" when the case was heard, the *Norrell* Court announced the practice of withholding a finding of guilt after a trial over the Common-

wealth's objection, would no longer be permitted. *Id.* at 727. The court noted Mass. R. Crim. P. 28(a) makes no provision after a bench trial for entry of a continuance without a finding, calling instead for a finding of guilty or not guilty. *Id.* "A jury cannot return a verdict in a criminal trial other than guilt or innocence." *Id.* at 727–28.

f. Probation in Lieu of 20-year Minimum Mandatory Sentence was Available Under Home Invasion Statute, c. 265, § 18C

In *Commonwealth v. Zapata*, 455 Mass. 530 (2009), the Supreme Judicial Court analyzed the statutory history and construction of section 18C of chapter 265 and concluded the judge had the authority to sentence a defendant convicted of home invasion to a term of five years of probation despite the section's provision that a person convicted of it "shall be punished by imprisonment in the state prison for life or for any term of not less than twenty years." *Id.* at 535. The court noted that when the Legislature amended the section it had deleted a former provision that expressly prohibited probation as a disposition. The resulting statute had led to confusion and within the opinion, the court invited the Legislature to clarify it. *Id.* at 536.

3. SPECIFIC STATUTORY PROVISIONS RELATING TO JUVENILES ON DISPOSITIONAL PROBATION

a. Chapter 119, Section 58, Specifically Authorizes Probation for Juvenile Offenders

i. Adjudication of Delinquency

> If a child is adjudicated a delinquent child on a complaint, the court may place the case on file or may place the child in the care of a probation officer for such time and on such conditions as it deems appropriate or may commit him to the custody of the department of youth services.

G.L. c. 119, § 58.

In *Commonwealth v. Magnus M.*, 461 Mass. 459, 459 (2012), the court held that under G.L. c. 119, § 58, a Juvenile Court judge is empowered to "continue a delinquency case without a finding and place the juvenile under the supervision of the probation department, notwithstanding a jury's prior verdict of delinquency."

ii. Adjudication as a Youthful Offender

> If a child is adjudicated a youthful offender on an indictment, *the court may sentence him to such punishment as is provided by law* for the offense. The court shall make a written finding, stating its reasons therefor, that the present and long-term public safety would be best protected by:
>
> (a) a sentence provided by law; or
>
> (b) a combination sentence which shall be a commitment to the department of youth services until he reaches the age of twenty-one, and an adult sentence to a house of correction or to the state prison as is provided by law for the offense. *The adult sentence shall be suspended pending successful completion of a term of probation*, which shall include, but not be limited to, the successful completion of the aforementioned commitment to the department of youth services. Any juvenile receiving a combination sentence shall be under the sole custody and control of the department of youth services

unless or until discharged by the department or until the age of twenty-one, whichever occurs first, and thereafter under the supervision of the juvenile court probation department until the age of twenty-one and thereafter by the *adult probation department*; provided, however, that in no event shall the aggregate sentence imposed on the combination sentence exceed the maximum adult sentence provided by law; or

> (c) a commitment to the department of youth services until he reaches the age of twenty-one.

G.L. c. 119, § 58 (emphasis added).

As section 58, expressly provides, the court may, in its discretion, place a child who has been adjudicated *delinquent* on probation and with such conditions as the court deems appropriate. Section 58 of c. 119, permits the court, among other things, to sentence a child adjudicated a youthful offender to an adult sentence. As such, probation is available to a youthful offender in the same manner as it is available to adult offenders. It is also available in conjunction with a commitment to the Department of Youth Services pursuant to subsection (b) of § 58, the so-called "combination sentence." G.L. c. 119, § 58(b).

4. "STRAIGHT PROBATION" OR SENTENCE DEFERRAL AS A DISPOSITION

a. Where Not Specifically Prohibited by Law, a Judge May Impose a Term of "Straight Probation" Without Imposing Sentence, Deferring Actual Sentencing

In *Commonwealth v. Rodriguez*, 52 Mass. App. Ct. 572 (2001), the defendant pleaded guilty to receiving stolen motor vehicle and masked armed robbery. The judge sentenced him to two and one-half years in the House of Correction on the first charge and placed him on "straight probation" on the masked armed robbery charge. *Id.* at 573. After he had served his time and while still on probation, Rodriguez was found to be in violation of his probation for committing new felonies. The judge then sentenced him to a term of from five to seven years on the masked armed robbery charge for which the defendant had previously been given "straight probation." *Id.* The Appeals Court affirmed the judge's denial of Rodriguez's motion to withdraw his guilty plea, but noted that when a defendant pleads guilty to a period of straight probation, it is "appropriate" that the court advise him of the maximum and minimum mandatory sentence for which he is at risk if he violates the terms of his probation at some future date. *Id.* at 574 (citing Mass.R.Crim.P. 12(c)(3)).

b. Traditional Factors Are Considered when Imposing Sentence After Defendant Has Violated the Terms of His "Straight Probation"

If a judge has imposed "straight probation" and defendant violates the terms of his probation, the judge shall take into consideration the traditional factors relevant to any sentencing decision and impose an appropriate sentence which reflects the original offense. *Id.* at 577.

c. Commencement of Probation Period

i. Probation Generally Commences When the Person Is Released into the Community but the Court May Order That the Conditions Also Apply During a Term of Incarceration

In *Commonwealth v. Cory*, 454 Mass. 559 (2009), the court noted that Massachusetts cases have sometimes interpreted the statutory language "placed on probation" to "refer to the time that the defendant was sentenced . . . , *see, e.g., Commonwealth v. Bruzzese*, 437 Mass. 606, 610 (2002); and at other times have used the same phrase to refer to the time the defendant began serving a probationary sentence. *See, e.g., Commonwealth v. Delisle*, 440 Mass. 137, 138 (2003)." *Cory*, 454 Mass. at 563 n.7. However, in *Commonwealth v. Ruiz*, 453 Mass. 474 (2009), the court held that a defendant may be subject to probation revocation occurring after the imposition of the sentence to probation but before the commencement of the probationary period, i.e., while he or she is incarcerated with conditions of probation. *Id.* at 480 (citing *Commonwealth v. Juzba*, 44 Mass. App. Ct. 457, 459 (1998)). While a judge "is not barred from placing a defendant on probation during the period of his incarceration," there must be evidence that the judge in fact did so. *Ruiz*, 453 Mass. at 480.

In *Ruiz*, the Supreme Judicial Court reversed the defendant's revocation on the ground he was denied due process because it was not made clear to him at the sentencing hearing that the condition that he have no contact with the victim was to apply during his term of incarceration. *Id.* at 480–81. The victim was his former domestic partner. The trial court judge had imposed a period of probation to be served on and after his term of incarceration. A special condition was that he have "no contact" with the victim. During the period of incarceration, Ruiz sent four letters to her. One contained a diatribe about his belief and anger that she was interfering with his relationship with their daughter. The frightened victim brought the letters to the attention of the probation officer who sent Ruiz a notice of probation revocation that charged the defendant's "failure to comply with no contact order imposed by the Court." *Ruiz*, 71 Mass. App. Ct. at 581.

"[T]he Commonwealth may request, and a judge may order, a sentence of probation to run concurrently with the defendant's term of incarceration. *Ruiz*, 453 Mass. at 483 (citing *Commonwealth v. Juzba*, 44 Mass. App. Ct. 457, 459). A defendant must, however, have clear notice if any terms of probation are to be in effect while he is incarcerated. *Ruiz*, 453 Mass. at 483.

"[T]he probation component of a split sentence after a period of civil confinement that was later found to be in violation of the requirements set out in G.L. c. 123A, § 14(a), for proceedings to commit a defendant as a sexually dangerous person (SDP) . . . [may] be deemed to begin to run upon the defendant's release from the Massachusetts Treatment Center for Sexually Dangerous Persons." *Commonwealth v. Howard*, 81 Mass. App. Ct. 757, 758 (2012).

ii. Delay Between the Time Probation Is Ordered and the Time it Commences Does Not Violate Due Process

In *Commonwealth v. Sheridan*, 51 Mass. App. Ct. at 78, the Appeals Court rejected the defendant's claims of denial of due process and fundamental fairness, concluding he did not experience any adverse consequences with respect to his liberty due to the delay of the commencement of his probation resulting from his commitment to the treatment center as a sexually dangerous person. *Id.* Because he had been committed to the center for a period of one day to life, the probation department had no reason to take any affirmative steps to determine his probation status until, if ever, he became eligible for release. *Id.* Once the probation department received notice of his impending release, promptly requested a hearing regarding the status of his probation. *Id.*

III. Probation Conditions

A. Mandatory Conditions

Unlike many state and federal statutes, Massachusetts law provides for relatively few mandatory post-conviction conditions of probation. Mandatory conditions include that the probationer may not commit a new offense, either local, state or federal. If the probationer is charged with a new offense while on dispositional probation, the court may, after a hearing, revoke the order of probation and impose a sentence of incarceration. A probationer must report, as directed, to his or her probation officer. Further, a probationer must pay a probation fee pursuant to G.L. c. 276, § 87A, and may be ordered to pay child support pursuant to § 87A. In the latter case, the court should not assess probation supervision fees if compliance with a support order for a child or spouse is a condition of probation. *Id.*

1. SUPERIOR COURT RULE 56 PROVIDES CONDITIONS OF PROBATION FOR ALL PROBATIONERS

Rule 56 of the Superior Court Rules, *CONDITIONS OF PROBATION*, sets forth the general conditions for all probationers:

> The conditions of probation, unless otherwise prescribed, shall be as follows: That the defendant shall 1) comply with all orders of the court, including any order for the payment of money, 2) report promptly to the probation officer as required by him, 3) notify the probation officer immediately of any change of residence, 4) make reasonable efforts to obtain and keep employment, 5) make reasonable efforts to provide adequate support for all persons dependent upon him, and 6) refrain from violating any law, statute, ordinance, by-law or regulation, the violation whereof is punishable. Any other condition shall be presumed to be in addition to the foregoing. *Id.*

2. PROBATION SUPERVISION FEE; ADMINISTRATIVE SUPERVISION FEE; WAIVER OF FEE; VICTIM/WITNESS SURCHARGE

G.L. c. 276, § 87A provides that every person placed on supervised probation must pay a monthly probation supervision fee, "probation fee," in the amount of $60 per month. The court also must assess every person placed on administrative probation an "administrative probation fee," in the amount of $45 per month. G.L. c. 276, § 87A. The court may waive the probation fee in whole or in part if it determines *after a hearing* that such payment would constitute an undue hardship. If said fee is waived and the court determines that the person is able to work, then in lieu of payment the court shall require said person to perform unpaid community work service

at a public or nonprofit agency or facility, for not less than one day per month. *Id.* (emphasis added).

In lieu of payment for the "administrative probation fee" the court shall require said person perform unpaid community service at a public or nonprofit agency or facility for not less than four hours per month. Such waiver shall be in effect only during the period of time that said person is unable to pay his monthly probation fee. *Id.*

The court may waive said probation fee in whole or in part if said person is assessed payment of restitution. In such cases, said probation fee may be waived only to the extent and during the period that restitution is paid in an amount equivalent to said probation fee. *Id.*

The court shall also assess upon every person placed on supervised or administrative probation, including those offenses under section 24 of chapter 90, a monthly probationers' victim services surcharge in the amount of $5 per month. G.L. c. 276, § 87A.

a. Increase in Probation Fees Upheld

In *Doe, Sex Offender Registry Bd. No. 10800 v. Sex Offender Registry Bd.*, 459 Mass. 603 (2011), Doe's probation fee was changed from $50 a month to $65 a month, and Doe challenged that the increase violated the ex post facto clauses of the Federal and Massachusetts Constitutions. *Id.* at 617. The Supreme Judicial Court found that, while the fee had a retrospective application to Doe, it was a civil regulatory fee and not punitive in nature, upholding the increased fee. *Id.* at 618–22.

3. OTHER MANDATORY CONDITIONS: CHILD SUPPORT, MOTOR VEHICLE, SEX OFFENDERS

a. Child Support

When the court imposes probation pursuant to G.L. c. 279, section 1 or 1A, the court shall include in its terms and conditions of probation that the person convicted shall pay any child support due under a support order . . . including payment toward any arrearage of support. *Id.* However, pursuant to section 87A of chapter 276, probation supervision fees and administrative probation fees shall not be assessed on any person who has been ordered to pay spousal or child support as a condition of probation for a violation of §§ 1 or 15 of c. 273. G.L. c. 276, § 87A.

b. Motor Vehicle Offenses

There are also mandatory conditions pursuant to specific motor vehicle offenses. For example, in order to limit loss of driver's license, a driver convicted of operating under the influence must enter and complete alcohol education and treatment programs certified by the Division of Alcoholism pursuant to G.L. c. 90, § 24D.

c. Sex Offender Registration—Criminal Systems History Board

Pursuant to section 178E(b) and (c), of chapter 6 of the General Laws, any sex offender, as defined by G.L. c. 6, § 178C, must register himself or herself with the Criminal History Systems Board ("CHSB") within the times required by section 178E. Failure to register may be grounds for revocation of probation (or parole) as it constitutes a criminal offense. G.L. c. 6, § 178H.

i. Payment of fees resulting from sex offender registration and DNA collection

In *Doe, Sex Offender Registry Bd. No. 10800*, the Supreme Judicial Court upheld the requirement that the defendant pay the fees relating to registering as a sex offender and providing a DNA sample, as the exaction was determined to be a regulatory fee rather than a tax. *Doe, Sex Offender Registry Bd. No. 10800 v. Sex Offender Registry Bd.*, 459 Mass. 603, 608–15 (2011).

d. Sex offenders—GPS-Requirement that all persons placed on probation for sex offenses wear a Global Positioning System (GPS) Device

General Laws Chapter 265, § 47 requires that all persons "placed on probation" for any offense listed within the definition of "sex offense," "a sex offense involving a child," or "a sexually violent offense" as those terms are defined in G.L. c. 6, § 178C, must wear a GPS device for the term of his or her probation as a condition of probation "at all times for the length of his probation for any such offense." G.L. c. 265, § 47.

In *Commonwealth v. Guzman*, 469 Mass. 492 (2014), the Court concluded "that G.L. c. 265, § 47 affords judges no discretion to decide whether GPS monitoring should apply in any particular set of circumstances; where a defendant is convicted of a qualifying offense and is sentenced to a term of probation, the sentencing judge must impose GPS monitoring as a condition of that probation." *Id.* at 496.

Because, however, "the imposition of GPS monitoring is singularly punitive in effect . . . a defendant must receive actual notice from the sentencing judge that his probation will be conditioned on such a harsh requirement." *Commonwealth v. Selavka*, 469 Mass. 502, 505 (2014) (citations omitted).

The application of section 47 is limited to persons who have been convicted, pleaded to sufficient facts, or admitted guilt on an offense listed in c. 6, § 178C. *Commonwealth v. Raposo*, 453 Mass. 739 (2009); *Commonwealth v. Emelio E.*, 453 Mass. 1024 (2009). It does not apply to persons placed on pretrial probation unless specifically imposed with the consent of the defendant pursuant to c. 276, § 87. *Raposo*, 453 Mass. at 748 n.11. Application of section 47 is further limited to cases in which the offense was committed after the effective date of the GPS statute, December 20, 2006, because imposition of GPS monitoring has been held to be punitive in nature, implicating the ex post facto clause. *Commonwealth v. Cory*, 454 Mass. 559 (2009).

Pursuant to G.L. c. 265, § 47, the Commissioner of Probation is required to establish "defined geographic exclusion zones including, but not limited to, the areas in and around the victim's residence, place of employment and school and other areas defined to minimize the probationer's contact with children, if applicable." G.L. c. 265, § 47.

i. If a probationer enters an exclusion zone, his location shall immediately be transmitted to police and to the Commissioner of Probation.

Under G.L. c. 265, § 47, if a probationer wearing a GPS device enters an exclusion zone, the location data shall immediately be transmitted to the police department wherein the violation occurred and to the Commissioner of Probation. If the Commissioner or the probationer's probation officer have probable cause to believe the probationer has violated his probation, the probationer shall be arrested pursuant to G.L. c. 279, § 3; otherwise, a notice of surrender shall be issued. G.L. c. 265, § 47.

ii. Fees incurred by the installation, maintenance, and operation of the GPS shall be paid by the probationer unless waived by the court.

Section 47 also requires that probationers who are required to wear a GPS device must pay the "fees incurred by installing, maintaining and operating the global positioning system device, or comparable device." G.L. c. 265, § 47. However, the court may waive such fees if the probationer establishes his inability to pay and there is no requirement that the probationer perform community service in lieu of said fee. G.L. c. 265, § 47.

iii. Homeless persons who are required to register as sex offenders must now verify their registration data every forty-five days.

General Laws Chapter 6, § 178F provides that any sex offender required to register who lists a homeless shelter as his or her residence is required to verify his or her registration data every 30 days. The sex offender must provide his or her name, date of birth, primary address, work address and any secondary addresses. *Id.*

iv. Community parole supervision for life Under G.L. c. 6, § 178H is unconstitutional.

Section 178H provides penalties for failing to register, verify information or providing false information. Any Level 2 or 3 sex offender who fails to register shall be subject to community parole supervision for life, which begins at the end of the term of incarceration, or upon the person's release from postrelease supervision; or upon expiration of a continuance without a finding; or upon discharge for commitment to any treatment center pursuant to c. 123A, § 9, whichever occurs first. *Id.*

In *Commonwealth v. Cole*, 468 Mass. 294 (2014), the court held, however, that community parole supervision for life (CPLS) is unconstitutional because it violates the separation of powers doctrine in art. 30 of the Massachusetts Declaration of Rights by improperly delegating to the parole board (executive branch) the judicial power to impose sentences. *Id.* at 295. All CPSL sentences must be vacated. *Id.* at 308–09.

v. GPS monitoring requirement is not mandatory for juveniles on probation.

In *Commonwealth v. Hanson H.*, 464 Mass. 807 (2013), the court decided "whether a Juvenile Court judge is required under G.L. c. 265, § 47, to order a juvenile to wear a global positioning system device that will monitor his whereabouts (GPS monitoring) as a condition of probation where a juvenile is adjudicated delinquent and placed on probation for committing a 'sex offense,' a 'sex offense involving a child,' or a 'sexually violent offense,' as defined in G.L. c. 6, § 178C." *Id.* at 807–08. The court concluded "that, when § 47 is read in its entirety, it is not apparent that the Legislature intended to apply mandatory GPS monitoring to juveniles placed on probation as a result of having been adjudicated delinquent and thereby eliminate the discretion granted to Juvenile Court judges to render individualized dispositions consistent with the best interests of the child." *Id.* at 808. It further said "that, where the Legislature has established the statutory principle that, 'as far as practicable, [juveniles] shall be treated, not as criminals, but as children in need of aid, encouragement and guidance,' G.L. c. 119, § 53, we will not interpret a statute affecting the delinquency adjudications of juveniles to conflict with this principle in the absence of clear

8

legislative intent. Here, where such clear legislative intent is absent, we conclude that a Juvenile Court judge retains the discretion, based on the totality of the circumstances, to determine whether GPS monitoring should be imposed as a condition of probation for a juvenile who is adjudicated delinquent after committing a sex offense." *Id.*

B. Statutory Discretionary Conditions

The court may also impose various discretionary conditions, a few of which are specifically provided by Massachusetts General Laws:

1. COURT COSTS AS A CONDITION OF PROBATION

Chapter 280, § 6, provides for court costs as a condition of probation. Costs are to cover the "actual expenses of the prosecution." *Id.*

2. INPATIENT OR OUTPATIENT TREATMENT AS A CONDITION OF PROBATION

Chapter 111E, § 12 provides for treatment in a "facility as an inpatient or outpatient," provided appropriate treatment is available, and for a "periodic program of urinalysis . . . to determine the drug free status of the probationer." The costs of the tests are to be borne by the Commonwealth. "If the court requires as a condition of probation that the defendant shall reside in alcohol and drug free housing," the probationer shall be required to reside in certified alcohol and drug free housing, if available. G.L. c. 111E, § 12.

Chapter 276, § 87A also provides for "participation . . . in specified rehabilitative programs or performance . . . of specified community service work for a stated period of time." *Id.*

3. DISCRETIONARY CONDITIONS INCLUDE RESTRICTIONS ON TRAVEL, ABODE, CONTACT WITH ABUSED PERSON(S), PAYMENT OF COMPENSATION TO ABUSED PERSON(S)

Chapter 276, § 42A, provides for the imposition, including at pretrial as well as post conviction, of "such terms as will insure the safety of the person allegedly suffering the physical abuse . . . and will prevent its reoccurrence." Further, section 42A provides that "[s]uch terms and conditions shall include reasonable restrictions on the travel, association or place of abode of the defendant as will prevent such person from contact with the person abused. *Id.* As part of the disposition of any such criminal complaint alleging abuse or threat of infliction by a person's family or household member, the court may establish terms and conditions of probation as will insure the safety of the person who suffered the abuse and will prevent recurrence of such abuse or threat thereof. *Id.* The court may restrict the probationer's travel, place of abode and all contact with the person abused. The court may also order the probationer to pay the abused person monetary compensation which shall include, but not be limited to, losses suffered as a direct result of the crime and shall not be limited to loss of earnings or support, out-of-pocket losses for injuries sustained, moving expenses and reasonable attorneys' fees.

G.L. c. 276, § 42A.

4. THE COURT MAY IMPOSE REASONABLE DISCRETIONARY CONDITIONS *BEFORE TRIAL* WITH THE DEFENDANT'S CONSENT UNDER c. 276, § 87

Chapter 276, § 87 expressly permits the imposition of conditions both pretrial and after a conviction. The court may only impose pretrial conditions of probation if the defendant consents. Section 87 authorizes the superior court, any district court and any juvenile court to:

> place on probation in the care of its probation officer any person before it charged with an offense or a crime for such time and upon such conditions as it deems proper, with the defendant's consent, before trial and before a plea of guilty, or in any case after a finding or verdict of guilty; provided, that, in the case of any child under the age of 18 placed upon probation by the superior court, he may be placed in the care of a probation officer of any district court or of any juvenile court, within the judicial district of which such child resides.

G.L. c. 276, § 87.

a. Except Where Expressly Authorized, a Judge Cannot Impose Conditions as a Part of Pretrial Probation

Although G.L. c. 276, §§ 42A, 58A, and 87 expressly authorize the imposition of pretrial conditions for release on bail or personal recognizance, the general bail statute, G.L. c. 276, § 58, does not contain such authority to make a defendant's pretrial release subject to conditions. *Commonwealth v. Dodge*, 428 Mass. 860, 864 (1999).

In *Dodge*, a judge ordered a defendant, who was charged with operating a motor vehicle while under the influence of intoxicating liquor, to undergo drug and alcohol screening as determined by probation and to participate in any outpatient counseling as determined by probation including Alcoholics Anonymous, (A.A.), or Narcotics Anonymous, (N.A.), as conditions of his release at time of arraignment. *See Dodge*, 428 Mass. at 861. The defendant expressly refused to consent to these conditions and moved to vacate the conditions of his release. *See id.* The judge denied the motion and informed the defendant that his refusal to comply with the conditions would constitute contempt. *Id.* The defendant again, indicated that he understood the judge's order, but still refused to comply. *Id.* As a result, the judge entered a judgment of contempt. *Id.* The defendant appealed. The case was transferred to the Supreme Judicial Court on its own motion.

Because the defendant did not consent to the conditions of pre-trial probation, the Supreme Judicial Court held that the judge had neither statutory authority under the general bail statute, G.L. c. 276, § 58, nor under G.L. c. 276, § 87, nor under its inherent power, to subject the defendant's pretrial release to conditions. *Dodge*, 428 Mass. at 864. Accordingly, Supreme Judicial Court held that the judge erred in placing conditions on defendant prior to trial. *Id.*

b. Conditions as a Part of Pretrial Probation Are Permissible under G.L. c. 276, § 87, When Defendant Consents and Is Placed on Probation

In contrast, G.L. c. 276, § 87 allows a judge to place a juvenile on pre-trial, pre-dispositional probation subject to conditions with the juvenile's consent, for release on personal recognizance or bail. *See Jake J. v. Commonwealth*, 433 Mass. 70 (2000) (citing *Dodge*, 428 Mass. at 864–66).

In *Jake J.*, 433 Mass. at 70–71, the judge released a juvenile on bail pursuant to G.L. c. 276, § 58 and at the same time placed him, with his consent, on pretrial probation under G.L. c. 276, § 87, subject to specific, agreed-upon conditions of release. *See id.* After posting bail, the juvenile was released and placed on supervised pretrial probation subject to terms that included the specific conditions of his release on bail. *See id.* at 71–72. Those conditions were subsequently amended because the juvenile had violated conditions and after violating again, his bail was revoked. *See id.* at 73.

On appeal, "Jake" argued that he was never placed on pretrial probation, that the conditions to which he had agreed were not conditions of probation, but rather conditions of release, which arose under G.L. c. 276, § 58, not section 87. *Id.* at 73–74. Therefore, he argued, pursuant to G.L. c. 276, § 58, the only reason his bail could be revoked was if he were charged with another crime during the period of release. *Id.* Additionally, he contended that because of the *Dodge*, 428 Mass. 860, decision (holding that conditions of release could not be imposed under section 58 without the defendant's consent), the conditions imposed on him were impermissible and of no effect whatsoever. *Jake J.*, 433 Mass. at 73–74. The Supreme Judicial Court disagreed.

The Legislature "expressly authorized the imposition of pre-trial conditions for release on bail or personal recognizance under section 87 when the juvenile defendant consents and is placed on probation." *Id.* at 74. After analyzing the process by which the conditions were imposed, the court concluded that the juvenile "reasonably should have known that he was being placed on pretrial probation pursuant to section 87." *Id.* at 75. During the proceeding, the judge made the juvenile and his mother aware that a violation of conditions would result in revocation of bail and holding the juvenile in custody. *Id.* Both the juvenile and his mother signed an agreement with the probation department that provided for, among other conditions, reporting weekly to probation. In addition, the agreement contained several references to probation. *Id.* Furthermore, the judge's intent was to assist and supervise the juvenile on bail while he remained within the community in the custody of his mother, which was consistent with the Juvenile Court's overall mission to further the best interest of children who appear before the court on delinquency matters and whenever possible to offer rehabilitation as set forth in G.L. c. 119, § 53. *Id.* at 76. The *Jake J.* Court held that if the judge lacked authority to set and enforce conditions for releasing troubled juveniles into the community while awaiting trial, the judge would have little recourse but to order them held by the Department of Youth Services, which, the court held, is not what the Legislature intended when it enacted G.L. c. 119, § 53. *Id.*

c. Judge Needs to Be Clear on the Record if S/He Intends to Set Pretrial Conditions of Release and Simultaneously Places the Defendant on Probation

In *Jake, supra,* the Supreme Judicial Court suggested that in future proceedings where the court intends to set conditions of pretrial release, the judge must be clear on the record that the defendant is being released on bail or personal recognizance pursuant to G.L. c. 276, § 58, and that, with his consent and agreement, he is simultaneously being placed on probation

pursuant to section 87. The judge should also explain on the record that any agreed upon conditions of pretrial probation also constitute the conditions of his release. *Jake J.*, 433 Mass. at 76–77. The consequences of violating any of the agreed upon conditions should also be clear and on the record. *Id.*

d. Post-Conviction Probation Is Not Available to Certain Persons Convicted of Sexual Crimes Against Children

The availability of probation is restricted under section 87 of chapter 276 as to persons convicted of rape of a child by force (c. 265, §§ 22A, 22B, 22C); assault of a child with intent to commit rape, (c. 265, § 24B); human trafficking of a child (c. 265, § 50(b)); or unnatural and lascivious acts with a child under 16 (c. 272, § 35A), if that person has previously been convicted under those sections and was at least eighteen years old at the time the offense was committed. In such cases, the person may not be released on parole or probation prior to the completion of five years of his sentence.

G.L. c. 276, § 87.

5. PRETRIAL CONDITIONS MAY BE IMPOSED IF THE COURT FINDS THE DEFENDANT IS DANGEROUS

Chapter 276, § 58A expressly authorizes the court to enter an order of pretrial detention or an order of release on conditions, if, after a hearing, the Commonwealth demonstrates and the judge finds that the defendant is dangerous. *Id.* The Commonwealth may move for a finding of dangerousness if the person is charged with a felony offense which contains as an element, the use, attempted or threatened use of force against another person; or, if it is one of the felonies specifically enumerated in section 58A. *See* G.L. c. 276, § 58A.

If the Commonwealth does *not* request a so-called "dangerousness hearing" pursuant to section 58A of chapter 276, the judge may place the defendant on pretrial conditions only with the defendant's consent pursuant to c. 276, § 87. *Commonwealth v. Jake J.*, 433 Mass. 70, 71 (2000); *Commonwealth v. Dodge*, 428 Mass. 860, 864–66 (1999).

6. SPECIFIC JUVENILE PROBATION PROVISIONS

The General Laws contain the following statutes providing for specific discretionary conditions for *juvenile* probationers:

a. Chapter 119, § 58, Probation Available upon Adjudication of Delinquency

Chapter 119, § 58, provides that if a child is adjudicated delinquent on a complaint, the court may place the child on probation with the consent of the child and at least one of the child's parents or guardians. Said probation may include a requirement, subject to agreement by the child and at least one of the child's parents or guardians, that the child "do work or participate in activities of a type and for a period of time deemed appropriate by the court."

G.L. c. 119, § 58.

b. Chapter 119, § 62, Court May Order a Juvenile to Make Restitution

Chapter 119, § 62 provides that if a juvenile is adjudged delinquent, and the court finds, as an element of such delinquency, that he has committed an act involving liability in a civil action, the court may require, as a condition of probation, "that he make restitution or reparation to the injured person to

8

such an extent and in such sum as the court determines." G.L. c. 119, § 62.

7. DEFENDANT MAY BE RELIEVED OF REQUIREMENT TO REGISTER AS A SEX OFFENDER

In *Commonwealth v. Ventura*, 465 Mass. 202 (2013), the court said that where the "defendant is a sex offender who, after pleading guilty to one indictment charging possession of child pornography, was placed on probation by a judge in the Superior Court and relieved of his obligation to register as a sex offender with the Sex Offender Registry Board (SORB), pursuant to G.L. c. 6, § 178E(f)," a "second judge, after finding the defendant in violation of his probation," may not order the defendant to register on the basis and consistent with the Sex Offender Registry Act, G.L. c. 6, §§ 178C–178Q (act).

C. Non-Statutory Conditions of Probation

The court is not limited to mandatory or discretionary conditions prescribed by statute. However, several maxims have been developed by the case law. In *Buckley v. Quincy Division. of the District Court Dep't*, 395 Mass. 815 (1985), the Supreme Judicial Court held that the only limit on conditions of probation are that they serve "the ends of justice and the best interests of both the public and the defendant." *Id.* (citing *Burns v. United States*, 287 U.S. 216, 221 (1932)).

1. CONDITIONS OF PROBATION MUST BE REASONABLY RELATED TO THE CRIME

Appellate courts typically allow conditions of probation that are reasonably related to either the crime committed and/or to the prevention of future criminal behavior by the defendant. For instance, in *Malone v. United States*, 502 F.2d 554 (9th Cir. 1974), *cert. denied*, 419 U.S. 1124 (1975), the court upheld as a condition of probation, banishment from Irish Pubs. The probationer had been convicted of gun running for the Irish Republican Army. *Id.*

In *Commonwealth v. Power*, 420 Mass. 410 (1995), Supreme Judicial Court held that the special condition of probation, that the probationer not profit from the sale of her story to news media, did not violate her First Amendment rights. The court reasoned that the condition did not prohibit the probationer's free speech; it merely prohibited her from profiting financially from such speech, and that it reasonably served valuable punitive and deterrent purposes. *Id.* at 416–17.

In *Commonwealth v. Williams*, 60 Mass. App. Ct. 331 (2004), the defendant was placed on probation for violating a domestic restraining order (c. 209A). At a subsequent revocation hearing, the district attorney and defense counsel agreed that the defendant would enter an anger management program. *Id.* at 332. The judge also added a condition that the defendant refrain from consuming alcohol during his probation. The Appeals Court upheld the condition noting it was a small step for the judge to add alcohol abstention where anger management counseling was indicated. "The judge could reasonably conclude that the consumption of alcohol would not improve the defendant's chances of dealing successfully with his problems with anger and violence." *Id.* at 332–33. "The connection between anger, violence, and alcohol consumption in a person who has demonstrated a violent disposition that is hard for him to control is not speculative or unreasonable." *Id.* at 333.

On the other hand, appellate courts have not upheld conditions of probation which are not reasonably related to the crime committed. In *Commonwealth v. Gomes*, 73 Mass. App. Ct. 857 (2009), the court reversed the condition of probation that the probationer submit to random drug and alcohol testing. In *Gomes*, the defendant was convicted of a firearms offense and was under the age of twenty-one when he was placed on probation. The Appeals Court held the condition that he submit to random drug and alcohol testing was not lawful where there was no evidence that alcohol played a role in the firearms offense. *Id.* at 859. "Ordering a defendant to submit to random drug or alcohol testing as a condition of probation, therefore, is not permissible unless it is reasonably related to one or more of the goals of probation: punishment, deterrence, retribution, protection of the public, or rehabilitation." *Id.*

2. CONDITIONS MUST BE DOABLE

In addition to being reasonably related to the offense, the probation conditions must be doable. An unemployed, indigent probationer could not be order to pay restitution of $250 and a fine of $500 by a specific date as a condition of probation. *Bearden v. Georgia*, 461 U.S. 660 (1983). Nor could a borderline mentally retarded juvenile be ordered to maintain satisfactory grades at school. *In re Robert M.*, 209 Cal. Rptr. 657 (Cal. Ct. App. 1985).

Further, when the defendant acted reasonably and in good faith to comply with the GPS monitoring requirement and is not responsible for his inability to comply with a probation condition because the Probation Department failed to provide the equipment needed, the defendant is not in violation of a probation condition. *Commonwealth v. Poirier*, 458 Mass. 1014, 1016 (2010). In *Commonwealth v. Canadyan*, 458 Mass. 574, 578–79 (2010), the Supreme Judicial Court found no probation violation where the indigent defendant made a good faith effort to find alternative housing or technological solutions so that he could comply with the GPS monitoring.

3. CONDITIONS MUST BE WRITTEN

Chapter 276, § 85 provides that once probation orders are made by the court, they must be committed to writing and given to the probationer. "Every person released upon probation shall be given by the probation officer a written statement of the terms and conditions of the release." G.L. c. 276, § 85.

4. CONDITIONS MUST BE CLEAR AND UNDERSTANDABLE

In *Commonwealth v. Power*, 420 Mass. 410 (1995), the Supreme Judicial Court held that the constitutional rule against vague laws applies equally to probation conditions as it does to legislative enactments. *Id.* at 421 (citing *Griffin v. Wisconsin*, 483 U.S. 868, 875–76 n.3 (1987)).

a. Condition of "No Excessive Use of Alcohol" Upheld

In *Commonwealth v. Swanson*, 79 Mass. App. Ct. 902, 902 (2011), the Appeals Court upheld the revocation of a defendant's probation on the grounds that defendant violated the condition requiring that there be "no excessive use of alcohol." *Id.* at 902. The court acknowledged that the condition was somewhat vague, but held that sufficient testimony was provided such that the judge could find that under any fair understanding of the condition, the defendant was in violation. *Id.* The court declined to consider the breathalyzer tests, and did not decide whether the foundational requirements established by G.L. c. 90, § 24K, and 501 C.M.R. §§ 2.00 et seq. (2010) apply in probation revocation hearings as they do in criminal prosecutions for driving under the influence. *Id.* at 903.

5. CONDITIONS MUST NOT UNREASONABLY RESTRICT CONSTITUTIONAL RIGHTS

a. Probationary Conditions are Subject to Less Scrutiny than Other Rights

In *Commonwealth v. Power*, 420 Mass. 410 (1995), the court held that a special condition of probation is not subject to the same rigorous First Amendment scrutiny that is employed against a statute of general applicability. *Id.* at 418.

The *Powers* Court noted that many other conditions placing burdens on otherwise constitutionally protected First Amendment or other rights have been upheld when applied to probationers. *Id.* at 417 n.6.

b. Probation Officer to Set Timeframe for Completion of Probation Conditions

"The practice is that the probation officer, in consultation with the probationer, establishes the date by which time the probationer must be enrolled in or must have completed a required treatment program. If the defendant does not agree with the timetable established by his probation officer, the matter may be reviewed administratively, either by the chief probation officer or his designee, or in accordance with a procedure established by the Commissioner of Probation. If a satisfactory resolution is not achieved, the probationer may file a motion for a judicial review by the sentencing judge." *Commonwealth v. Bynoe*, 85 Mass. App. Ct. 13, 20 (2014).

c. Unconstitutional to Impose Condition that Probationer Submit to Warrantless Searches by Probation Officer without Reasonable Suspicion

In *Commonwealth v. LaFrance*, 402 Mass. 789 (1988), the court held that a condition that the probationer submit to searches of her person, possessions and any place she may be, with or without a search warrant, at the probation officer's request, to be unconstitutional. The court held that under both the Fourth Amendment of the United States Constitution and article 14 of the Massachusetts Declaration of Rights, a warrantless search of the probationer required at least a "reasonable suspicion that a search might produce evidence of wrongdoing." *Id.* at 790.

d. Condition Prohibiting Father from Residing with His Own Children or Any Other Children Held Constitutional

In *Commonwealth v. Lapointe*, 435 Mass. 455 (2001), the defendant was convicted of indecent assault and battery of his fifteen-year old daughter. He also had a previous conviction for indecent assault and battery on a minor. The judge sentenced him to thirty-six to forty-four months, twenty-four months to be served, balance suspended for twenty years under probation supervision. *Id.* at 456. In addition to the standard terms of probation, the judge imposed a "no contact" order as to the victim; required the defendant to complete sexual abuse perpetrator counseling; and imposed other terms applicable to the twenty years probation, including conditions that: a) prohibited him from performing any work that would result in his being in the presence of children; b) prohibited him from being alone with *any* minor children; c) prohibited him from residing with *any* minor children, including his *own* children, "M.L." and "S.L.", and any future children he might have with the exception of his seventeen year old son, C.L.; d) permitted him to have unsupervised contact with "M.L.",

including "sleep overs," only if "M.L." slept in the same room with another person not younger than seventeen (excluding him); e) permitted him to have contact with "S.L." only in the presence of an adult over age twenty-one; and f) permitted him to have contact with his grandchildren only in the presence of their mothers. *Id.* at 457–458. The judge expressly retained jurisdiction over the special conditions prohibiting the defendant from residing with any future children and ordered him to obtain the judge's "express authority" to reside with any such children. With respect to "M.L." and "S.L.," the condition was to last until their eighteenth birthdays. He instructed the Commonwealth and defendant that if future events require modification of any other probation condition, relief could be sought. *Id.*

The defendant argued the condition prohibiting him from residing with his minor son, M.L., was invalid because he had no history of any sexual relationships with males, adult or minor, and that his seventeen year-old son, "C.L.," had "thrived while residing with him." *Id.* at 460–461. The Supreme Judicial Court disagreed. Regardless of gender, "M.L." could be considered a potential target, and the judge reasonably provided "M.L." a measure of protection. *Id.* at 461. The residency prohibitions did not deprive the defendant of any "parenting right" nor infringe impermissibly on his constitutional rights. Rather, the terms struck a balance between the facts of the case and the goals of sentencing and probation, consistent with authority affirming probation conditions in similar circumstances. They did not impermissibly infringe on his right to marry or procreate. *Id.* The judge retained jurisdiction to revisit all conditions and reserved the right to reconsider the residency prohibitions as to future children. He crafted a suitable procedure for appropriate future orders based on changed circumstances. *Id.* The court disagreed with the defendant's contention that the special conditions, together with the twenty-year probationary period, constituted cruel and unusual punishment. Section 87 of c. 276 authorizes such conditions. *Id.* at 462. Considering defendant's prior conviction, that he may be a recidivist, and the victim's trauma, the twenty-year period did not "shock the conscience and offend fundamental notions of human dignity." *Id.*

e. Condition that Banishes Probationer from the Commonwealth Is Unconstitutional

A probation condition that infringes upon an individual's constitutional rights must be "reasonably related" to the goals of sentencing and probation. *See Commonwealth v. Pike*, 428 Mass. 393, 403 (1998). In *Pike*, the defendant was convicted of the lesser offense of unauthorized use of a motor vehicle on an indictment charging armed car jacking, and assault and battery by means of a dangerous weapon. *Id.* at 393. He was sentenced to a prison term of six to eight years for the assault and battery conviction, and a term of two years in a house of correction for the unauthorized use of a motor vehicle. *Id.* The two-year sentence was suspended with probation. *Id.* One of the conditions of his probation, barred the defendant from entering the Commonwealth at any time. *Id.* The defendant challenged the constitutionality of this condition. *Id.*

The Supreme Judicial Court held that a probation condition banishing a defendant from the state is invalid and unenforceable, because it infringes upon the defendant's constitutional right to interstate travel and is not reasonably related to the goals of probation. *Id.* at 403. The goals of probation are

8

best served if the conditions are tailored to address the particular characteristics of the defendant and the crime. *Id.* A condition that prohibits a defendant from a state does not serve any rehabilitative purpose nor a legitimate public safety goal. *Id.* at 404. In addition, such condition fails to serve a deterrent purpose. *Id.*

f. Conditions Limiting Movements May Be Constitutional

Not all probation conditions restricting an individual's movement are invalid, however. Conditions that prevent probationers from certain, small geographic areas have been upheld in several states when they serve the goals of probation. *See Commonwealth v. Pike*, 428 Mass. 393, 403–04 (1998).

g. Defendant's Due Process Rights were Not Violated When His Probation Conditions Continued After He Left the United States

In *Commonwealth v. Al Saud*, 459 Mass. 221 (2011), the defendant was a Saudi Arabian national who voluntarily left the United States immediately after his incarceration. *Id.* at 223–24. Nearly two years later the defendant was found to be in violation of numerous conditions of his probation and a motion was allowed issuing a default warrant for his arrest. *Id.* at 225. The defendant unsuccessfully sought to terminate his probation, then appealed on due process grounds, contending that it was impossible to satisfy his probation conditions after leaving the United States, that he had received no guidance on doing so, and that he had no notice that his probation would continue after his departure. *Id.* at 228–34. The Supreme Judicial Court held that due process was not violated because the conditions violated were not inconsistent with the defendant's departure, the Commonwealth provided ample notice of his probation requirements, and the Commonwealth did not have a duty to clarify the probation conditions in light of the defendant's departure from the United States. *Id.*

h. Restrictions on Computer Use May be Overbroad

In *Commonwealth v. Rousseau*, 465 Mass. 372 (2013), the court held that, where the Department of Correction had digitized its law library, the defendant was entitled to a modification of his conditions of probation "permitting him to use the prison library computers for the limited purpose of conducting legal research and other activity related to his case." However, he "can be barred from using the library computers for any other purpose." *Id.* at 390.

6. RESTITUTION: PROPERLY DETERMINED RESTITUTION IS A VALID CONDITION OF PROBATION

In *Commonwealth v. Nawn*, 394 Mass. 1 (1985), the Supreme Judicial Court held that "[t]here is no question that restitution is an appropriate consideration in a criminal sentencing. *Id.* at 6 (citation omitted).

a. The Procedure to Determine Amount of Restitution Must Be Reasonable and Fair

In *Nawn*, the defendant was convicted of stealing a victim's purse. The victim told the judge that the estimated value of the property stolen in her purse was $3,000, but then agreed to accept $2,000. She was neither under oath nor subject to cross-examination. The defendant was not permitted an opportunity to rebut this evidence. On appeal the court held that the procedure used to determine the amount of restitution or reparation must be reasonable and fair. The Supreme Judicial Court stated that "'[p]ersons forced to settle their claims of right and duty through the judicial process must be given a meaningful opportunity to be heard.'" *Commonwealth v. Nawn*, 394 Mass. at 7 (quoting *Boddie v. Connecticut*, 401 U.S. 371, 377 (1971)).

> If the record reveals an arbitrary method of determining the amount of restitution, the order cannot stand *(citation omitted).* Thus, the defendant's request for a hearing and an opportunity to cross-examine the victim as to the value of the items taken was appropriate.

Nawn, 394 Mass. at 7.

b. Restitution Hearing Must Afford Both Sides the Opportunity to Present and Challenge Evidence as to the Amount of Victim's Loss

The *Nawn* Court vacated the sentence because the defendant was not afforded any meaningful opportunity to challenge the amount of money ordered to be repaid, and remanded for a new sentencing proceeding. The court outlined the procedure for a restitution hearing. It stated that it "need not be elaborate; a forum for both sides to air their views and cross-examine is sufficient." *Nawn*, 394 Mass. at 7 The court stated that the recommended amount of restitution and the manner of its payment should be included in a probation report and disclosed, and the court should allow comment from the defendant regarding the amount of restitution before it is imposed as a part of a sentence. The defendant is entitled to rebut the victim's estimate of the value of her property with his own expert or other evidence. *Id.* (citations omitted); *see also Commonwealth v. Rescia*, 44 Mass. App. Ct. 909 (1998).

c. The Commonwealth Must Prove Victim's Losses by a Preponderance Standard

i. Cross-Examination of the Victim Should Be Limited to the Issue of Restitution

The Supreme Judicial Court stated in *Nawn*, 394 Mass. at 7–8, that the Commonwealth bears the burden of "proving *by a preponderance of the evidence* the amount of the victim's losses. . . . The victim, through the Commonwealth, may testify to the contents of her purse and the value of the items taken. Cross-examination of the victim is limited to the issue of restitution and does not extend to matters concerning guilt or innocence." *Id.* at 8; *see also Commonwealth v. Rescia*, 44 Mass. App. Ct. 909 (1998).

d. Defendant in a Restitution Hearing Is Not Entitled to a Jury Trial

In *dictum*, the *Nawn* Court also declared that a defendant is not entitled to a jury trial to determine the amount of restitution under article 15 of the Massachusetts Declaration of Rights. The court reasoned that the matter was at heart a criminal matter, focusing on the guilt or innocence of the defendant, rather than a civil adjudication of damages. Therefore, restitution was an appropriate condition of probation imposed by the court within its sentencing discretion. *Nawn*, 394 Mass. at 8–9 (citing *United States v. Satterfield*, 743 F.2d 827, 836 (11th Cir. 1984)).

e. Determining Amount of Restitution Requires Consideration of Value of Goods and Money Stolen as Well as the Defendant's Ability to Pay

The *Nawn* Court provided further guidance to courts in determining the amount of restitution. It held that the "amount of restitution is not merely the measure of the value of goods and money stolen from the victim by the defendant; in a criminal case, the judge must also decide the amount that the defendant is able to pay and how such payment is to be made. Further, the judge may consider the defendant's employment history and financial prospects." *Nawn*, 394 Mass. at 9 (1985).

"Because we have not previously had the opportunity to articulate the legal standard for determining the defendant's ability to pay restitution, we do so here for the first time. In determining the defendant's ability to pay, the judge must consider the financial resources of the defendant, including income and net assets, and the defendant's financial obligations, including the amount necessary to meet minimum basic human needs such as food, shelter, and clothing for the defendant and his or her dependents." *Commonwealth v. Henry*, 475 Mass. 117, 126 (2016).

f. Appellate Court Will Look to Whether Restitution Proceedings Were Fundamentally Fair

In *Commonwealth v. Yeshulas*, 51 Mass. App. Ct. 486 (2001), the defendant was sentenced to state prison to be followed by three years of probation with "a special condition of probation that she make restitution to the victims in the amount of $2,500 with the terms of repayment to be set by the probation officer in his or her own discretion. *Id.* at 492. After the judge received both the Commonwealth's request of $5,000 restitution based on the trial testimony of the fire chief of the value of furniture and household items destroyed in the fire, and defense counsel's recommendation of $2,000, based on the defendant's job, the judge rejected both and set restitution in the amount of $2,500. *Id.*

Relying on *Commonwealth v. Nawn*, 394 Mass. 1 (1985), the defendant argued on appeal that the hearing was fundamentally unfair, that there should have been an evidentiary hearing as to the value of the lost property with an opportunity for cross-examination. *Yeshulas*, 51 Mass. App. Ct. at 492. In addition, she argued the judge should have considered her financial circumstances in setting the amount of restitution. *Id.* The *Yeshulas* Court, however, distinguished the facts in that case from those in *Nawn*. In *Yeshulas*, the defendant did not object to the restitution order or request an evidentiary hearing; rather she made her own recommendation for the amount. In addition, the fire chief, who had no personal stake in the amount of restitution, had estimated the amount of the victim's loss, not the victim herself. *Id.* Moreover, the defendant and her attorney participated in the restitution decision, and further, the amount of restitution the judge ordered was one-half of what the Commonwealth had asked for and only twenty-five percent more than the defendant suggested. Accordingly, even though the hearing did not strictly comply with the requirements of *Nawn*, the Court found that the process was not fundamentally unfair. *Id.* at 493.

g. The Judge May Order the Probation Officer to Set the Defendant's Restitution Payment Schedule

The *Yeshulas* Court affirmed judge's special condition of probation which allowed the terms of repayment to be set by the probation officer in his or her discretion. *Yeshulas*, 51 Mass. App. Ct. at 493.

h. Length of Probation, Revocation, and Ability to Pay Restitution

In *Commonwealth v. Morris M.*, 70 Mass. App. Ct. 688 (2007), the Appeals Court held that even though the restitu-

tion judge failed to consider the juvenile's ability to pay the court-ordered restitution amount of $2,649, there was no risk of a miscarriage of justice because the restitution was a condition of his probation and the juvenile could raise his inability to pay at any future probation revocation hearing that should take place for his failure to pay. *Morris*, 70 Mass. App. Ct. at 698.

Similarly, in *Commonwealth v. Chase*, 70 Mass. App. Ct. 826 (2007), the Appeals Court found no abuse of discretion in the judge's denial of defendant's Rule 30(b) motion for a new trial on the ground the judge had not considered his ability to pay. At the restitution hearing no evidence had been presented on the issue; the focus was only on the amount owed. *Chase*, 70 Mass. App. Ct. at 837. The judge denied the Rule 30(b) motion because the defendant had been given a "full and fair opportunity to present evidence of his ability to pay at the original hearing." *Id.* In affirming the denial of the motion for new trial the court noted that if the defendant faces revocation for his failure to pay, he may raise his ability to pay at any future probation revocation hearing. 70 Mass. App. Ct. at 838 (citing *Morris M.*, 70 Mass. App. Ct. at 688, 698).

The court further "declare[d] that a judge may not extend the length of probation where a probationer violated an order of restitution due solely to an inability to pay." *Commonwealth v. Henry*, 475 Mass. 117, 124 (2016).

"For the same reasons, equal justice means that the length of probation supervision imposed at the time of sentence should not be affected by the financial means of the defendant or the ability of the defendant to pay restitution. . . . To ensure that a defendant does not face a longer probationary period because of his or her limited means, the ability to pay determination should be made only after the judge has determined the appropriate length of the probationary period based on the amount of time necessary to serve the twin goals of rehabilitating the defendant and protecting the public." *Henry*, 475 Mass. at 124–25.

7. PROBATION CONDITIONS MUST BE ACCOMPANIED BY ENFORCEMENT MECHANISM

"Probation, whether straight or coupled with suspended sentence, is a legal disposition which allows a criminal offender to remain in the community subject to certain conditions and under the supervision of the court." *Commonwealth v. Taylor*, 428 Mass. 623, 626 (1999); *Commonwealth v. Durling*, 407 Mass. 108, 111 (1990). Thus, imposing conditions without more does not constitute "probation." *Taylor*, 428 Mass. at 626. Rather, a judge must couple the conditions with a supervisory element to ensure that the probationer abides by the probationary terms. *Id.* In *Taylor*, a judge continued the case for one year subject to conditions, but because there was no enforcement mechanism, *i.e.*, condition that defendant report to probation during one year continuance, or other court supervision, the judge's action did not constitute placing the defendant on pretrial probation pursuant to G.L. c. 276, § 87.

8. PROBATION CONDITIONS SIGNED BY A DEFENDANT DO NOT CONSTITUTE A CONTRACT

In *Commonwealth v. MacDonald*, 50 Mass. App. Ct. 220 (2000), *aff'd*, 435 Mass. 1005 (2001), the defendant violated his probation and, therefore, his probation was extended, subject to certain additional conditions ordered by the judge, including attendance at a batterers' program, counseling for drug and alcohol abuse, and a "stay away" order from Cynthia

Evans. *Id.* at 220–21. The defendant signed a form containing the new conditions of probation prepared by his probation officer. *Id.* at 221. In addition to the standard conditions of probation which were pre-printed on the form, there were three "special conditions" which the probation officer wrote in by hand, including a provision that the defendant have "no contact" with Evans. *Id.* While incarcerated, the defendant wrote Evans a letter which she considered threatening. *Id.* Consequently, the probation officer issued a probation surrender notice alleging that the defendant had violated the "no contact" condition of probation. *Id.* The defendant filed a motion to dismiss arguing that the original sentencing judge had ordered him to "stay away" from Evans, but had never directed him to have "no contact" with her. *Id.* The District Court judge ruled that, although the docket entries, submitted by defendant in support of his claim, did not reflect the "no contact" provision, the signed conditions of probation constituted a contract whose terms were controlling. *Id.* at 221–22. Therefore, the judge denied the defendant's motion to dismiss. *Id.*

On appeal, the Commonwealth argued that regardless of the contents of the docket, the signed conditions of probation constitute a contract, a breach of which amounts to a violation of probation. *MacDonald*, 50 Mass. App. Ct. at 222. The Appeals Court disagreed and stated that "although conditions of probation signed by defendants are often referred to as probation 'contracts,' *see Commonwealth v. Power*, 420 Mass. 410, 413 (1995), . . . such instruments are not premised upon mutuality of agreement or obligation." *MacDonald*, 50 Mass. App. Ct. at 223. "'[T]he defendant, on one side, and the judge on the other, [are not] equal contracting partners.'" *Id.* (quoting *Commonwealth v. Christian*, 46 Mass. App. Ct. 477, 481 (1999)). The Appeals Court further stated that "the signature of the defendant on the conditions of probation does not constitute his assent to a negotiated agreement." *MacDonald*, 50 Mass. App. Ct. at 223. Furthermore, in cases where a defendant agrees to offer a plea pursuant to an agreement negotiated with the Commonwealth and accepted by the court, the terms of the plea bargain, which may include probation, may take on the "characteristics of a contract," but even so, the resulting sentence is enforceable as an order of the court. *Id.* at 224 n.8.

The enforceability of probation, therefore, is derived not from the agreement of the defendant, but from the force of the judge's order. *MacDonald*, 50 Mass. App. Ct. at 224, 435 Mass. at 1006. Since the Commonwealth could not demonstrate that the original sentencing judge ordered that the defendant have "no contact" with Evans, only that he should "stay away" from her, the Supreme Judicial Court remanded the case to the District Court to determine what conditions of probation were actually imposed by the sentencing judge to determine whether the defendant was in violation. *MacDonald*, 435 Mass. at 1007.

9. A "NO CONTACT" ORDER IS DISTINCT FROM A "STAY AWAY" ORDER; THE TERMS ARE NOT INTERCHANGEABLE

In *MacDonald*, the Appeals Court distinguished a "stay away" order from a "no contact" order. Specifically, the court stated that "there is a distinct difference between the two terms and they are not interchangeable." *MacDonald*, 50 Mass. App. Ct. at 222 n.7. A "stay away" order requires a probationer to "remain a certain, often specified, physical distance away from the subject of the order," whereas, a "no

contact" order requires the probationer "also not communicate by speech, writing, or other means with the individual who is named in the order, even if in doing so they remain physically apart." *Id.* Therefore, a "no contact" order is broader in scope than a "stay away" order. *Id.* (citing *Commonwealth v. Butler*, 40 Mass. App. Ct. 906, 907 (1996)).

10. CONDITIONS OF PROBATION ARE NOT NEGOTIABLE AFTER A JUDGMENT OF CONVICTION

In *Commonwealth v. Christian*, 46 Mass. App. Ct. 477, *affirmed in part and modified in part by Commonwealth v. Christian*, 429 Mass. 1022 (1999), the defendant pleaded guilty to a violation of G.L. c. 209A domestic abuse order in Quincy District Court. *See Christian*, 46 Mass. App. Ct. at 477. The District Court judge imposed a sentence of one year probation with conditions that included completion of a specified counseling program for domestic violence offenders, and to "stay away from and have no contact with" the complainant. *Id.* at 478. When Christian's probation officer met with him to obtain his signature on the conditions of probation form, she explained to him that he would face a revocation hearing if another 209A was issued against him. *See id.*

The defendant in *Christian* felt the conditions of probation were a "trap" and refused to sign them. *Id.* Consequently, his probation officer provided him with a notice informing him that his refusal to sign said probation conditions form constituted a violation of his probation and that a revocation hearing would be held. *See id.* After the revocation hearing, the District Court judge found Christian had violated his terms of probation by refusing to sign the conditions. *See id.* at 479. The Appeals Court affirmed. *Id.* at 482.

11. REFUSAL TO SIGN CONDITIONS OF PROBATION CONSTITUTES A VIOLATION OF PROBATION

The Appeals Court in *Christian*, stated that "probation after conviction is not an entitlement, but the result of a discretionary act of the sentencing judge, who employs probation for purposes of 'rehabilitation of the probationer and protection of the public.'" *Christian*, 46 Mass. App. Ct. at 481 (citing *Commonwealth v. Power*, 420 Mass. 410, 414 (1995)). Therefore, because an individual who is convicted is not entitled to probation, the *Christian* Court held that the same person is not in a position to negotiate the conditions of his probation. *Christian*, 46 Mass. App. Ct. at 481. The same is true in the plea bargain context where the trial judge accepts a plea bargain containing probation, the judge is bound to sentence in accordance with its terms. *See id.* at 482 n.4.

In *Christian*, the Appeals Court further found that it was not an abuse of discretion for a judge to conclude that a refusal to acknowledge probation conditions constitutes a violation of them and grounds for revocation. *Id.* at 482. Accordingly, the judge's order revoking probation based on that ground was not error.

12. BATTERER'S PROGRAMS; FIFTH AMENDMENT CLAIMS

In *Commonwealth v. Delisle*, 440 Mass. 137 (2003), the probationer was required, inter alia as a special condition to attend the Emerge batterers' program. *Id.* at 139. His probation officer surrendered him after the Emerge program terminated him because he had failed to write an essay concerning abuse of his wife, which had been a condition for readmission to the program, and had physically assaulted his wife. *Id.* at 142.

Delisle argued on appeal that revocation of his probation was improper because it amounted to the imposition of a substantial penalty for the exercise of his Fifth Amendment right against compelled self-incrimination. *Id.*

The Supreme Judicial Court rejected his argument, holding the judge revoked Delisle's probation not only because he was terminated from Emerge, but also because he was convicted of violent offenses against his wife in the Lynn District Court, and because he assaulted his wife on December 15, 1998, on returning from an Emerge session. *Id.* at 143. The court stated that "there is no sound basis for Delisle's claim that his Fifth Amendment privilege against self-incrimination, that is, his right not to be 'compelled in any criminal case to be a witness against himself,' was implicated in the circumstances of this case, where the letter he complains of was not sought by the Commonwealth. *Id.* The court also rejected the defendant's Fifth Amendment argument, noting the consequence for Delisle's not writing this letter was the possibility he would not be readmitted by Emerge. "This consequence is not an inducement or a penalty rising to the level of compulsion prohibited by the Fifth Amendment." *Id.* at 144.

D. Length of Probationary Sentence Not Limited by Statute

Chapter 276, § 87, does not limit probationary sentences, but rather, simply provides that the court may place a person "on probation for such time and on such terms and conditions as it shall fix." *Id.* The sentencing judge has substantial leeway in ordering the length and conditions of the probationary period. *See Commonwealth v. Juzba*, 44 Mass. App. Ct. 457, 461 (1998). Moreover, Massachusetts case authority supports the court's power to extend or revoke probation within a reasonable time after the expiration of the probationary term. *Commonwealth v. Collins*, 31 Mass. App. Ct. 679 (1991); *Commonwealth v. Odiari*, 397 Mass. 28, 35–36 (1986); *Commonwealth v. Sawicki*, 369 Mass. 377, 383–85 (1975); *but see Commonwealth v. Mitchell*, 46 Mass. App. Ct. 921 (1999) (unreasonable to extend defendant's probation two and one-half to three years after probationary term expired when defendant did not hinder compliance with probation or cause undue delay). What constitutes a reasonable amount of time is determined on a case-by-case basis in light of all the circumstances of the particular case, including the possibility of specific prejudice to the defendant resulting from delay in bringing matters to a head. *Sawicki*, 369 Mass. at 385; *Collins*, 31 Mass. App. Ct. at 681. While the court is not bound to the terms of a particular defendant's probation, and may, for good reason, extend the term of probation, the probation department itself, may not do so whether by inadvertence, policy or otherwise.

E. No Right to Counsel for Post Conviction Probationary Evaluation

In *Commonwealth v. Woods*, 427 Mass. 169 (1998), the defendant was convicted of open and gross lewdness in violation of G.L. c. 272, § 16. He received a six-month suspended sentence and was placed on probation for three years. *Id.* at 174. As a condition of his probation, he was required to participate in a sex offender evaluation and to be treated by a psychologist. *See id.* While his appeal of conviction was pending, he was surrendered and his probation was revoked for failure to participate in the probation evaluation. *See id.* He filed a separate appeal from the probation revocation, contending

that under the Fifth Amendment to the U.S. Constitution and art. 12 of the Massachusetts Declaration of Rights, he could not be compelled as a condition of probation, to discuss with the psychologist the crime of which he had been convicted. *See id.*

Even though the defendant's conviction was reversed, thereby vacating the surrender of his probation based on that conviction, the Supreme Judicial Court, in *dicta*, addressed the validity of the defendant's proposition that he had a right to have counsel present at a psychological evaluation conducted in accordance with the terms of a validly imposed condition of probation. The Supreme Judicial Court found it "doubtful." *See id.* The court concluded that since a post conviction probationary evaluation is not a criminal proceeding, let alone a critical stage entitling a defendant to protection under either the Sixth Amendment to the U.S. Constitution or art. 12 of the Massachusetts Declaration of Rights, right to counsel does not attach. *See id.* The Supreme Judicial Court further likened the condition of probation requiring an evaluation, to a psychiatric interview with a defendant who raises an insanity plea at trial. *See id.* In that analogous situation, there is no right to counsel. *See id.* Therefore, the *Woods* court implied that the defendant is not entitled to counsel during a psychological evaluation conducted as a part of the terms of validly imposed probation. *See id.*

F. Modifying Probation Conditions

1. SUPERVISORY COURT MUST FIND A MATERIAL CHANGE IN CIRCUMSTANCES OR VIOLATION TO MODIFY CONDITIONS OF PROBATION

In *Buckley v. Quincy Div. of the District Court Dep't*, 395 Mass. 815 (1985), the Supreme Judicial Court discussed modification of conditions of probation. The court held that judges possess the authority to modify conditions of probation. However, the *Buckley* Court limited the authority of the supervisory court to modify conditions set by a judge in the jury session unless there has been a material change in circumstances. *Id.*

In *Buckley*, the defendant pled guilty in Dedham District Court to the charge of operating to endanger. The plea was the product of negotiations between the defendant and the assistant district attorney, whereby the defendant would plead guilty in exchange for a recommendation that a two-year sentence would be imposed, twenty-one days to be served and the balance suspended. The defendant would also be placed on probation for two years. *Id.* The judge accepted the plea and recommended sentence, and also imposed certain conditions on the defendant's probation.

Upon his release from prison, Buckley reported to the probation department of the Quincy District Court. After several interviews, his probation officer concluded that Buckley "might have an alcohol problem." *Id.* Accordingly, the probation officer ordered Buckley to attend an alcohol abuse evaluation program. *Id.* Buckley refused. The probation officer then requested a hearing in Quincy District Court to determine new conditions for probation. After the hearing, the court ordered that the conditions of Buckley's probation be modified to require him to submit to the alcohol abuse evaluation program, and whatever follow-up treatment was required. *Id.* Buckley then commenced an action under c. 211, § 3 to revoke the order of the Quincy District Court. A single justice reserved and reported the question to the full court.

8

Buckley asserted that even if the court possesses the authority to modify the conditions of probation, such authority must be exercised in accordance with Mass. R. Crim. P. 29. *Id.* The Supreme Judicial Court disagreed, holding that rule 29 is unsuited as a device for the modification of the terms and conditions of probation. *Id.* However, the court then addressed whether the Quincy District Court, the supervisory court, had the power to modify the conditions set by the Dedham District Court judge, the sentencing judge. The court held that the supervisory court had no authority to modify the terms of probation under the circumstances of that case, *i.e.,* where there had been no material change in the probationer's circumstances since the time the terms of probation were initially imposed by the Dedham court. *Id.*

The *Buckley* Court reaffirmed the importance of flexibility in the operation of the probation system and declared that the holding does not limit the authority of the supervisory court to modify conditions of probation where there has been a material change in circumstances (such as a violation of a condition of probation). However, the *Buckley* Court concluded that where there had been no violation nor material change in Buckley's circumstances, the Quincy District Court had no authority to modify his conditions of probation under c. 218, § 27A(I). Accordingly, the court vacated the order of the Quincy District Court and reinstated the original terms of probation. *Id.*

a. Addition of GPS Monitoring and Exclusion Zones for Sex Offender Denied Where There Were No Material Changes in Circumstances; GPS Held to be Punitive, Not Regulatory, in Nature

In *Commonwealth v. Goodwin*, 458 Mass. 11 (2010), the defendant had pleaded guilty in 1990 to three indictments charging rape of a child by force and one indictment charging kidnapping. *Id.* at 12. The defendant was incarcerated, then civilly committed, for a total of nineteen years. *Id.* at 21. In 2009, the defendant was found no longer sexually dangerous and was released from the treatment center. *Id.* He began serving his probation, which the probation department sought to modify by requiring the defendant to comply with the Department of Mental Health's treatment plan and adding exclusion zones and GPS monitoring. *Id.* at 13. The judge found, and the Supreme Judicial Court agreed, that unless there is a finding of a probation condition violation, a judge does not have the discretion to impose GPS monitoring as a condition of probation where there are no material changes in the defendant's circumstances, and where pairing the GPS device with exclusion zones would be so punitive as to increase significantly the severity of the original probationary terms. *Id.* at 15–23.

2. PROBATION OFFICER CANNOT ALTER PROBATION CONDITIONS ORDERED BY SENTENCING JUDGE

"It is the function of the sentencing judge to set the conditions of probation." *Commonwealth v. MacDonald*, 50 Mass. App. Ct. 220, 223 (2000), *aff'd*, 435 Mass. 1005 (2001) (citing *A.L. v. Commonwealth*, 402 Mass. 234, 242 (1988)). The duties of the probation officer, in turn, are defined and informed by the specific instructions of the sentencing judge and are found in the judge's conditions of probation. *Id.* Therefore, a probation officer does not have discretion to modify or alter the terms of a defendant's probation. *Mac-*

Donald, 50 Mass. App. Ct. at 224 (citing *Buckley v. Quincy Div. of Dist. Court, Dept.*, 395 Mass. 815, 820 (1985)).

In *MacDonald*, because the defendant violated his probation, it was extended, and the judge added conditions, including attendance at a batterers' program, counseling for drug and alcohol abuse, and a "stay away" order from one Cynthia Evans. *MacDonald*, 50 Mass. App. Ct. at 220. The defendant then signed new conditions of probation form prepared by his probation officer. *Id.* at 221. In addition to the standard conditions of probation which were pre-printed on the form, there were three "special conditions" which the probation officer wrote in by hand, including a provision that the defendant could have "no contact" with Evans. *Id.* While incarcerated, the defendant wrote Cynthia Evans a letter, which she considered to be threatening. *Id.* Consequently, the probation officer issued a probation surrender notice alleging that the MacDonald had violated the "no contact" condition of probation. *Id.* The defendant filed a motion to dismiss arguing that the original sentencing judge had ordered him to "stay away" from Evans but had never directed him to have "no contact" with her. *Id.*

The District Court judge ruled that although the docket entries submitted by defendant in support of his claim did not reflect the "no contact" provision, the signed conditions of probation constituted a contract, the terms of which were controlling. *Id.* at 221–22. Therefore, she denied the defendant's motion to dismiss. *Id.* MacDonald appealed.

The Appeals Court disagreed with the District Court and found that to be found in violation of probation, a defendant must have violated one of the probationary terms ordered by the sentencing judge, not the probation officer. *Id.* at 223–24. "Even if, through the defendant's assent, he voluntarily undertakes to perform such conditions [imposed by the probation officer, not the sentencing judge], his later failure to comply with them is not a violation of the court's sentencing order." *Id.* at 224. The conditions of probation signed by the defendant have no viability independent of the court order that brought them into existence. *Id.* at 448. Consequently, the violation of conditions added by the probation officer but not ordered by the judge did not constitute a violation of a defendant's probation. *Id.* at 224, 435 Mass. at 1006–07.

3. AMENDING PROBATION CONDITIONS

"A probationer who is dissatisfied with a condition of probation is not without a remedy." *Commonwealth v. Christian*, 46 Mass. App. Ct. 477, 482 (1999). Acceptance of conditions of probation does not waive a probationer's right to move under Mass.R.Crim.P. 29, for an amendment to the conditions of probation. *Id.* (citing *Commonwealth v. LaFrance*, 402 Mass. 789, 791 n.3 (1988)).

4. INTERSTATE COMPACT FOR ADULT OFFENDER SUPERVISION.

"The compact regulates the interstate transfer of supervision of those individuals on probation or parole due to the commission of a criminal offense. Interstate Commission for Adult Offender Supervision, ICAOS Rules, Rule 1.101, at 6 (effective Mar. 1, 2014) (ICAOS Rules), http://www .interstatecompact.org/Portals/0/library/legal/ICAOS_Rules .pdf. . . . The compact has been enacted by statute in all fifty States as well as the District of Columbia, Puerto Rico, and the United States Virgin Islands. Interstate Commission for

Adult Offender Supervision, ICAOS Bench Book for Judges and Court Personnel, at 40–41 (2014), http://www.interstatecompact.org/Portals/0/library/publications/Benchbook.pdf [https://perma.cc/3DFZ-RUEQ]. It was enacted in Massachusetts in 2005." *Goe v. Commissioner of Probation*, 473 Mass. 815, 820–21 (2016).

"[W]e conclude that probationers whose supervision is transferred to Massachusetts pursuant to the compact may challenge a special condition of probation that was added by Massachusetts through an action in the nature of certiorari in Massachusetts Superior Court, where they may claim that the additional special condition is not mandated by law or is unconstitutional. We also conclude that the Massachusetts probation department may not add mandatory GPS monitoring as a special condition of probation for this probationer because it is not required by G.L. c. 265, § 47. Finally, we conclude that the travel restriction applied by the Massachusetts probation department to the defendant was not an additional condition of probation, and that the appropriate forum to challenge the constitutionality of the application of that condition is a Connecticut court, where it may be combined with the defendant's nonconstitutional claims for modification of this probation condition." *Goe*, 473 Mass. at 831.

IV. Probation Revocations

If the probationer violates any condition of probation, the probation officer may send him notice to appear in court or arrest him and bring him to court for a probation revocation hearing. Because the officer is surrendering the probationer to the court, it is often referred to as a "surrender hearing."

A. Constitutional Standards for Revocation

1. MINIMUM REQUIREMENTS OF DUE PROCESS FOR REVOCATION OF PROBATION

In *Morrissey v. Brewer*, 408 U.S. 471 (1972), the United States Supreme Court outlined the minimum requirements of due process for revocation of parole, which the Court extended to probation revocation in *Gagnon v. Scarpelli*, 411 U.S. 778 (1973). The minimum requirements to revoke probation are:

a) *written notice* of the claimed violations of probation;

b) *disclosure* to the probationer of evidence against him;

c) opportunity to be heard in person and present witnesses and documentary evidence;

d) the right to confront and cross-examine adverse witnesses (unless the hearing officer specifically finds *good cause* for not allowing confrontation);

e) a *neutral and detached hearing body* such as a traditional parole board, members of which need not be judicial officers or lawyers; and

f) a *written statement* by the fact finder as to the *evidence relied on and the reasons* for revoking probation. *Commonwealth v. Maggio*, 414 Mass. 193, 196 (1993) (citing *Morrissey*, 408 U.S. at 489 n.34; *Gagnon*, 411 U.S. at 786 n.5) (emphasis added); *Commonwealth v. MacDonald*, 53 Mass. App. Ct. 156 (2001).

g) *Error:* In revocation proceedings, the most stringent constitutional test applies: *harmless beyond a reasonable doubt. Commonwealth v. MacDonald*, 53 Mass. App. Ct. 156 (2001).

B. Revocation Practice in Massachusetts

1. STATUTORY AUTHORITY

a. Statutory Authority for Probation Revocation of Adult Probationers

The Massachusetts statute which addresses revocation of probation of adults is codified as G.L. c. 279, § 3. It provides:

At any time before final disposition of the case of a person placed under probation supervision or in the custody or care of a probation officer, the probation officer may arrest him without a warrant and take him before the court, or the court may issue a warrant for his arrest. When taken before the court, it may, if he has not been sentenced, sentence him or make any other lawful disposition of the case, and if he has been sentenced, it may continue or revoke the suspension of the execution of his sentence; provided however, that in all cases where the probationer is served with notice of surrender and at least one of the underlying crimes for which he is on probation is a felony, then the probation officer shall provide a duplicate copy of the notice of surrender to the district attorney, and the court shall provide to the district attorney the opportunity to be heard and present evidence at the surrender hearing. If such suspension is revoked, the sentence shall be in full force and effect. If a warrant has been issued by the court for the arrest of such a person and he is a prisoner in any correctional institution, jail or house of correction, the commissioner of correction, the sheriff, master or keeper of said house of correction, or in Suffolk county, the penal institutions commissioner of the city of Boston, as the case may be, having such prisoner under his supervision or control, upon receiving notice of such warrant, shall notify such prisoner that he has the right to apply to the court for prompt disposition thereof. Such an application shall be in writing and given or sent by such prisoner to the commissioner of correction, or such sheriff, master, keeper, or penal institutions commissioner, who shall promptly forward it to the court from which the warrant issued, by certified mail, together with a certificate of said commissioner of correction, sheriff, master, keeper, or penal institutions commissioner, stating (a) the term of commitment under which such prisoner is being held, (b) the amount of time served, (c) the amount of time remaining to be served, (d) the amount of good time earned, (e) the time of parole eligibility of such prisoner, and (f) any decisions of the board of parole relating to such prisoner. Said commissioner of correction, sheriff, master, keeper, or penal institutions commissioner shall notify the appropriate district attorney by certified mail of such application to the court. Any such prisoner shall, within six months after such application is received by the court, be brought into court for sentencing or other lawful disposition of his case as hereinbefore provided.

In no case where a provision of this chapter provides for a finding, disposition or other order to be made by the court, or for a warrant to be issued, shall such be made or issued by any person other

8

than a justice, special justice or other person exercising the powers of a magistrate.

Notwithstanding any restriction in the preceding paragraph, if a probation officer has probable cause to believe that a person placed under probation supervision or in the custody or care of a probation officer pursuant to sections 42A, 58A or 87 of chapter 276 or any other statute that allows the court to set conditions of release, has violated the conditions set by the court, the probation officer may arrest the probationer or may issue a warrant for the temporary custody of the probationer for a period not to exceed 72 hours or until the next sitting of the court, during which period the probation officer shall arrange for the appearance of the probationer before the court pursuant to the first paragraph of this section.

Such warrant shall constitute sufficient authority to a probation officer and to the superintendent, jailer, or any other person in charge of any jail, house of correction, lockup, or place of detention to whom it is exhibited, to hold in temporary custody the probationer detained pursuant thereto.

G.L. c. 279, § 3.

b. Statutory Authority for Probation Revocation of Juvenile Probationers

Chapter 119, § 59, addresses juvenile probation revocation. It provides:

If a child has been placed in care of a probation officer, said officer, at any time before the final disposition of the case, may arrest such child without a warrant and take him before the court, or the court may issue a warrant for his arrest. When such child is before the court, it may make any disposition of the case which it might have made before said child was placed on probation, or may continue or extend the period of probation. *Id.*

2. PRETRIAL PROBATION MAY BE REVOKED WHEN A JUDGE IMPOSES BAIL AND PLACES A DEFENDANT ON PRETRIAL PROBATION CONDITIONS PURSUANT TO G.L. c. 276, § 87

In *Jake J. v. Commonwealth*, 433 Mass. 70 (2000), discussed in section II.B.4.b, *supra*, the court found that the defendant juvenile had been placed pretrial probation with conditions for release pursuant to c. 276, § 87, as well as on bail pursuant to c. 276, § 58, and that his bail was properly revoked even though § 87 does not provide for revocation, and section 58, the bail statute, does not provide for revocation of bail unless the bailee is charged with another crime during the period of his bail. *Id.* at 77–78. The *Jake J.* Court reasoned that the Legislature would not authorize a judge to set conditions of release but withhold authority to enforce them. *Id.* at 74–75. Therefore, the court may impose pretrial conditions of probation pursuant to § 87 of c. 276, and may also set bail under § 58. The court has the inherent authority to revoke bail if the condition(s) are violated. *Jake J.*, 433 Mass. at 77.

Because there was no explicit procedure for revocation of bail for a violation of § 87 conditions, the hearing judge in *Jake J.* followed the procedure for revocation set for in c. 276, § 58B. Although that section is explicitly limited to conditions imposed pursuant to section 58A relative to dangerousness, the *Jake J.* Court held that in the absence of any other relevant procedure, the judge could seek guidance from that section *Id.* at 78–79. Section 58B contains relevant factors for the court to consider, and provides that the standard of proof required for a revocation is clear and convincing evidence, further, the judge must conclude the defendant was "unlikely to abide by any other condition or combination of conditions of release." *Id.* at 79.

In *Jake J.*, the juvenile had a hearing, was represented by counsel, and the court held there was sufficient evidence to warrant a finding that a probation condition has been violated. *Id.* There was no showing, the court held, that the defendant was prejudiced by the judge's application of § 58B in revoking his bail. *Id.* The Supreme Judicial Court did, however, suggest that the Legislature consider adopting a procedure for future bail revocation proceedings based on violations of § 87 conditions. *Id.*

3. PROCEDURAL REQUIREMENTS FOR PROBATION REVOCATION HEARINGS

a. Notice

i. Alleged violations of probation must be clear, not vague, but court may look beyond four corners of probation order in determining whether notice was fair.

"In addition to unambiguous guidance about the conduct prohibited, probationers are entitled to clear guidance as to when their actions or omissions will constitute a violation of their probation. A judge's inquiry whether a defendant has received the required 'fair notice' is not 'confined to the four corners of the probation order;' rather, the order's meaning may be illuminated by the judge's statements and other events that are part of the notification process." *Commonwealth v. Ruiz*, 453 Mass. 474, 479–80 (2009) (citations and quotation marks omitted).

In *Fay v. Commonwealth*, 379 Mass. 498 (1980), the probationer appealed from the order of a single justice of the Supreme Judicial Court, affirming an adjudication by a judge of the Superior Court that the defendant had, *inter alia*, violated the terms of her probation. *Id.* at 499. The probation department had sent her a letter which provided formal notification of the revocation hearing and set forth three alleged violations. Fay contended that the notification was invalid because, she contended, the alleged violations were unconstitutionally vague. *Id.* at 501, 503.

The *Fay* Court held that while the first two allegations were vague, the third was a very specific charge. Thus, any vagueness in the first two charges was immaterial in view of the third specific one, especially, the court noted, in light of the precise notice the judge gave to Fay in open court of the purpose of the revocation hearing more than a month prior to it. The court concluded that Fay had received proper notice of the revocation hearing. *Id.* at 503.

ii. Four days notice of revocation of probation hearing held sufficient.

A defendant's fundamental due process was not violated when he was given only a four-day notice before the probation revocation hearing, when counsel was appointed on the day of the hearing, and where the notice did not specify whether the hearing was a preliminary or final hearing. *Commonwealth v. Morse*, 50 Mass. App. Ct. 582 (2000). In *Morse*, the defendant argued that a probationer facing a probation revocation proceeding has a right to have a "reasonable opportunity to prepare" for the hearing and a "reasonable opportunity for counsel to aid him in his defense." *Id.* at 586 (citing *Commonwealth v. Faulkner*, 418 Mass. 352, 358–60 (quoting *Commonwealth v. Cavanaugh*, 371 Mass. 46, 50 (1976))). The Appeals Court rejected the defendant Morse's argument because neither he nor counsel had moved for a continuance, much less made an offer of proof or even a statement regarding what they would do, or what evidence they would present, if they had more time to prepare. *Morse*, 50 Mass. App. Ct. at 586. Moreover, the defendant and his counsel were informed of the right to request a continuance, were asked on the date of the hearing whether they were ready and they failed to indicate they were not. *Id.* The *Morse* Court concluded that even if the defense's unspecific comments were interpreted as requests for continuance, decisions on such requests were within the sound discretion of the judge. *Id.* at 587. Because the defendant did not demonstrate how the judge abused his discretion or how he was prejudiced by the four-day notice, the Appeals Court concluded the defendant's due process rights were not violated. *Id.* at 593–94.

iii. A probationer facing revocation must be made aware of evidence to be used against him.

In *Commonwealth v. Maggio*, 414 Mass. 193 (1993), the Supreme Judicial Court held that a probationer facing a final revocation hearing based on the return of an indictment by the grand jury, must be made aware of the evidence to be used against him. In that case, the court considered that unlike defendants who are present at probable cause hearings or trials and actually hear the evidence against them, the defendant, Maggio, was not present when the grand jury heard the evidence against him which caused them to return the indictments. *Id.* at 197. Nor was there any other showing that Maggio had been informed of any of the facts underlying the indictments. Thus, the court concluded that Maggio had not been properly notified of the evidence to be used against him, and therefore, the procedure did not comply with the minimum due process requirements as set forth in *Morrissey*, 408 U.S. 471 (1972), and *Gagnon*, 411 U.S. 778 (1973). Accordingly, the *Maggio* Court vacated the guilty findings and sentences on the larceny charges entered by the judge after the revocation hearing. *Maggio*, 414 Mass. at 199.

iv. Where a defendant is given adequate notice of the alleged violation, other unfavorable evidence may be introduced to assist in disposition, similar to a sentencing hearing.

The Appeals Court found notice to be adequate in *Commonwealth v. Herrera*, 52 Mass. App. Ct. 294 (2001), where the defendant received notice that he had violated his probation based on new drug use charges and failure to report to probation. In *Herrera*, the judge determined that the defendant had violated the terms of his probation due to the charge of heroin use contained in the notice of probation violation. After the judge determined Herrara had indeed violated his probation, he reviewed a police report and a restraining order regarding an incident in which the defendant allegedly slashed the tires of his former girlfriend's car. *Id.* at 294. The probation surrender notice did not mention the tire-slashing incident, and therefore, Herrara argued, the judge should not have considered it when determining disposition. The Appeals Court disagreed. It held that due process requires that a person threatened with a revocation of probation must be given written notice of any alleged violations for which revocation is sought. *Id.* at 295. Here, the notice gave defendant fair

warning of the drug use charges and of his failure to report to his probation officer. *Id.*

The judge's finding that Herrara violated his probation was based exclusively on those charges stated in the notice of probation violation. *Id.* The tire-slashing incident was not introduced until the judge had found the defendant to be in violation when he was considering disposition. *Id.* There was no error. After the judge finds the defendant to have violated his probation, s/he must consider whether to revoke probation or modify the terms of probation. In making the determination, the judge may consider reliable evidence of past, uncharged misconduct without offending due process principles, similar to the way a sentencing judge may consider past, uncharged misconduct after guilt has been established. *Id.*

v. Return of indictment, alone, is insufficient to provide notice of alleged violation of probation.

In *Commonwealth v. Maggio*, 414 Mass. 193 (1993), the Supreme Judicial Court held that the revocation of the defendant's probation did not comply with due process. In that case, the defendant admitted to sufficient facts to warrant a finding of guilty on three charges of larceny in November 1990, in Cambridge District Court. The cases were continued to November 1992, without a finding, and the defendant was placed on probation, under the supervision of a probation officer on terms which, among others, required that he "obey local, state and federal laws and court orders." The agreements signed by the defendant also provided that, if he failed to meet any conditions of the continuance, guilty findings could be entered on each charge and he would be sentenced to serve a total of ninety days in the house of correction. *Id.* In 1991, he was arraigned on charges of assault and battery with a dangerous weapon and assault with intent to murder in Cambridge District Court. *Id.* at 194. On the date of arraignment, April 19, 1991, the defendant was served with a "Request for Summons Form," which advised him that he was in non-compliance with the terms of his probation based on: "New Offense Attempted Murder." Thereafter, the district attorney entered a *nolle prosequi* in the District Court on the assault complaints and obtained grand jury indictments in the Superior Court for the offenses. On May 14, 1991, the defendant was arraigned on the indictments in the Superior Court.

Subsequently, a hearing was held in Cambridge District Court in reference to the larceny charges. The Commonwealth sought to have guilty findings entered and the prescribed sentencing imposed pursuant to the agreements the defendant had signed. *Id.* At the hearing, the probation officer testified that the defendant had been arraigned in Middlesex Superior Court for assault and battery with a dangerous weapon and stated that she had the bill confirming this. *Id.* The probation officer furnished the court with a copy of an indictment, but the officer had no personal knowledge of what evidence had been presented to the grand jury. No other witness testified and no other evidence was presented. *Id.* Over the objections of counsel, on the basis of the probation officer's testimony, the judge entered guilty findings on the larceny charges and ordered the sentences to the house of correction to be imposed. *Id.*

vi. Probation officer has burden of showing proper notice has been served when non-receipt is at issue.

In *Commonwealth v. Faulkner*, 418 Mass. 352 (1994), the Court reiterated the well-settled rule that as a matter of due process the defendant is entitled to written notice of the claimed violations of probation. *Id.* at 360 (citing *Commonwealth v. Durling*, 407 Mass. 108 (1990)). In *Faulkner*, the probation officer testified that the notice of the probation revocation hearing was sent to "Merts Street." The defendant actually lived on Myrtle Street (although the surrender notice itself contained the last known address correctly, as "Myrtle Street"). 418 Mass. at 363. The court concluded that it was possible that the notice was incorrectly addressed or lost in the mail. Additionally the probation officer had not made any showing that he had attempted to notify the defendant in any other way, such as by telephone, personal service or a visit to the defendant's address. *Id.* at 364. The *Faulkner* Court held that the probation officer had the burden to demonstrate that notice was properly sent where there was no evidence that the defendant had changed his residence, and had raised the issue of non-receipt of notice. As such, the *Faulkner* Court held that the defendant did not receive the notice required by due process. *Id.*

vii. Probation officer must serve district attorney with copy of notice of surrender if underlying crime is a felony.

In June 1996, the Massachusetts Legislature amended chapter 279, § 3, to provide that if a probationer is served with a notice of surrender, the probation officer must send a duplicate copy of the notice to the district attorney, if at least one of the underlying crimes is a felony, and the court shall provide to the district attorney the opportunity to be heard and present evidence at the surrender hearing. G.L. c. 279, § 3.

b. Probationer Has Due Process Right to Be Present at Revocation Hearing

A probationer has a due process right to be present at a probation revocation hearing. *Commonwealth v. Harrison*, 429 Mass. 866 (1999). In *Harrison*, the defendant's probation was revoked following a hearing at which he was not present because he was serving a one hundred fifty-one month sentence in Federal prison for bank robbery. *Id.* The Superior Court made several attempts to secure his presence at the probation revocation hearing by asking the U.S. Marshal, and the marshal's representative, but were unsuccessful. *Id.* at 867. At the revocation hearing, over counsel's objection, the judge determined that the defendant was in violation of his probation, revoked probation and imposed the original sentence, to be served from and after completion of his federal sentence. *Id.*

On appeal, the Supreme Judicial Court vacated the order revoking the defendant's probation because his constitutional right to be heard in person at the hearing was violated. *Harrison*, 429 Mass. at 867 (citing *Morrissey*, 408 U.S. at 489 (specifying requirements for parole revocation hearing) and *Gagnon*, 411 U.S. at 782). Because the defendant was absent from the revocation hearing, he had no chance to challenge the testimony of witnesses, nor could he testify to, or offer evidence of, changed or mitigating circumstances. Therefore, error was not harmless beyond a reasonable doubt and the court ordered the revocation vacated. *See Harrison*, 429 Mass. at 868.

c. Necessity of Holding Preliminary Hearing

i. Preliminary hearing is required only when probationer is taken into custody.

In *Fay v. Commonwealth*, 379 Mass. 498 (1980), Fay argued, *inter alia*, that the court erred in failing to hold a pre-

liminary hearing where her probation was at risk of revocation. *Id.* at 503. Fay asserted that the United States Supreme Court in *Morrissey*, 408 U.S. 489, and *Gagnon*, 411 U.S. 778, required a preliminary hearing. The Supreme Judicial Court disagreed on the ground that the defendant was not deprived, due to any of the alleged probation violations, of her liberty prior to the final revocation of her probation The court noted that the purpose of the preliminary hearing is to protect the rights of the parolee or probationer, who, being at liberty, is taken into custody for an alleged violation of probation or parole conditions and is detained pending a final revocation hearing. There was no constitutional violation in *Fay*, even though there was no preliminary hearing because the probationer was not denied any liberty interest prior to the final revocation proceeding. *Id.* at 504 (citations omitted).

In *Commonwealth v. Morse*, 50 Mass. App. Ct. 582 (2000), the defendant argued that his due process rights were violated because he was given only a final probation hearing and not a preliminary hearing to which he claimed he was entitled and which the record does not show he waived. *Id.* at 588. The Appeals Court rejected his argument because the defendant failed to demonstrate how he was prejudiced by a lack of a preliminary hearing. *Id.* The Notice of Surrender and Hearing(s) in *Morse*, expressly informed him that he could waive the preliminary hearing if he so desired. *Id.* at n.10. Moreover, the defendant and his counsel were immediately notified that they were involved in a formal evidentiary hearing to determine whether he had violated probation. *Id.* at 588. Neither the defendant, nor counsel, however, made any objection regarding the lack of a preliminary hearing. *Id.* The Appeals Court concluded that a preliminary hearing prior to the final hearing would not have provided any material benefit to the defendant "in light of the strength of the Commonwealth's evidence on the alleged violations combined with the want of any valid defense thereto on Morse's part" and his failure to make any showing of prejudice either below or on appeal. *Id.* at 590.

ii. Where a defendant/probationer is already in custody, no preliminary hearing is required.

In *Fay v. Commonwealth*, 379 Mass. 498 (1980), the probationer had remained at liberty on probation continuously until the completion of the hearing on the probation revocation and contempt charges. She was not arrested or otherwise taken into custody pending that hearing. Therefore, the court reasoned, having suffered no detention or loss of liberty, she was not entitled to a preliminary hearing. *Id.*

Similarly, in *Commonwealth v. Odoardi*, 397 Mass. 28 (1986), the defendant argued that he was denied his right to a preliminary hearing. However, in *Odoardi*, the defendant was already serving time on a prior sentence when he pled guilty to armed robbery at a final probation revocation hearing. *Id.* at 33. The court applied the rationale set forth in *Fay*, 379 Mass. 498, and determined that the defendant was not entitled to a preliminary hearing. It reasoned that, as in *Fay*, the defendant was not deprived, due to any of the alleged probation violations, of his liberty prior to the final revocation of his probation. Therefore, a probable cause hearing would have served no purpose. *Odoardi*, 397 Mass. at 34. The court also cited *United States v. Tucker*, 524 F.2d 77, 78 (5th Cir. 1975) for the proposition that the rationale requiring preliminary hearing does not apply where probationer is incarcerated at the time of attempted revocation. *Odoardi*, 397 Mass. at 33.

d. No Release on Bail After a Finding of Probable Cause of a Probation Violation Pursuant to the Rules of the District/Municipal Court

In *Commonwealth v. Puleio*, 433 Mass. 39 (2000), the court held that when probable cause is found to believe that the probationer has violated the terms and conditions or his probation, the judge may order the probationer to be held in custody pending the final probation revocation hearing. *Id.* If the judge decides to hold the probationer in custody, "the court shall not impose any terms of release such as bail . . . as an alternative to such custody." *Id.* at 41. Therefore, when a judge at the preliminary revocation hearing finds probable cause exists and decides to hold the probationer in custody, the judge may not consider bail or other pre-hearing release as a substitute for custody. *Id.* at 42.

While bail as authorized by G.L. c. 276, § 58 is nor permissible, a court department may, by standing order, authorize release based on a monetary condition. "A probationer released on a monetary condition would not be able to seek bail review under G.L. c. 276, § 58." *Commentary to Rule 5 of the District/Municipal Court Rules for Probation Violation Proceedings* (citing *Puleio*, 433 Mass. at 42).

e. Timing of the Hearing

Pursuant to Superior Court Guidelines, the District/Municipal Court Rules, and the Juvenile Court Standing Order addressing probation violation proceedings probationers must be given at least seven days notice prior to a revocation hearing, either preliminary or final. A final violation hearing shall be scheduled not earlier than seven days after the initial hearing, and no later than thirty days thereafter, except for good cause. "The practice of a probation surrender proceeding 'tracking' a new criminal case is discouraged." *Superior Court Guidelines for Probation Violation Proceedings* at n.6. Although the standards provide at least a seven-day notice prior to a revocation hearing, in *Commonwealth v. Morse*, 50 Mass. App. Ct. 582 (2000), the Appeals Court found that a probationer's due process rights were *not* violated when he received only *four* days notice and counsel was appointed on the day of the probation violation hearing.

f. Jurisdiction Continues after the Probationary Period Ends Until Court Enters an Order Terminating Supervision

In *Commonwealth v. Sawicki*, 369 Mass. 377 (1975), the probationer's stated probation term was to end on September 4, 1974. However, after September 1974, the probation officer learned about probation violations which had been committed during the probationary period. In November 1974, Sawicki sought an order of termination of his probation. However, on November 15, 1974, his probation officer presented the court with a report stating that he was an unsuccessful probationer whose probation should have been revoked. The judge ordered the necessary steps be taken to determine whether Sawicki should be surrendered for a violation of probation. *Id.* at 379. In March 1975, the judge entered an order extending the probation period for two more years from September 4, 1974. Sawicki appealed on the issue of "jurisdiction" of the court to extend or revoke his probation in view of the fact that his term of probation had expired on September 4, 1974 and he had not been brought into court by his probation officer until more than four months after that date. *Id.* The court held that the "termination of probation, or rather the court's power over the probationer, is not automatic when the stated period has

run even when no steps leading to revocation of probation have previously been taken." On the contrary, the court held, an order signaling the end of the court's supervision is required to terminate probation and this may occur after the close of the probation period originally set. *Id.* at 380. Although the *Sawicki* Court affirmed the court's power beyond the probationary period, it confined that power to action in respect to violations committed during the period, and, further, required that the hearing judge decide the question of extension or revocation within a reasonable time. What is reasonable, the court held, must be decided on a case-by-case basis. *Id.* at 384–85.

i. Although the court retains jurisdiction until probation is formally terminated, it may only penalize for conduct that occurs during the scheduled term of probation.

In *Commonwealth v. Aquino*, 445 Mass. 446 (2005), the Supreme Judicial Court made clear that the trial court lacked jurisdiction to revoke probation for conduct that occurred after the scheduled probation termination date. This was true even though the probationer was on notice that revocation proceedings had begun and the case had been continued at the probationer's request. The court rejected the Commonwealth's argument that because the defendant received notice of probation violations during the probationary period and revocation proceedings were continued at his request beyond the scheduled termination date, the probationer remained on probation and therefore could be penalized for offenses committed before the court actually terminated his probation. *Id.* at 574. The *Aquino* Court cited *Sawicki*, 369 Mass. 377 (1975), for the rule that although the court retains jurisdiction to act beyond the term of probation and could extend probation, the acts that constituted the basis for extension must have been violations that occurred during the probationary period. *Id.* (citing *Sawicki*, 369 Mass. at 384).

ii. The court's power over a probationer after expiration of the probationary period depends on the "reasonableness" of the delay.

In *Commonwealth v. Ward*, 15 Mass. App. Ct. 388 (1983), the Appeals Court held that the judge's power to extend or revoke probation after expiration of the original term depends on whether the probation officer and the judge acted with reasonable promptness in light of all the circumstances of the case, including the possibility of any prejudice to the defendant resulting from the delay. *Id.* at 392 (citing *Sawicki*, 369 Mass. at 380, 383, 384–87).

In *Ward*, the Appeals Court held that there was a question, in light of all the circumstances, whether the probation officer had acted with reasonable promptness in initiating surrender proceedings. The court noted that the judge had apparently assumed that under *Sawicki*, he continued to have the power to revoke the probation which had expired four months prior to surrender. The record indicated that the judge had made no determination of whether the probation officer had acted with reasonable promptness. As such, the Appeals Court held, it could not determine whether the judge continued to have the power to revoke probation at the time he purported to do so. *Id.* at 391–92. The *Ward* Court therefore vacated the sentence which the judge had imposed and remanded the matter to Superior Court for detailed findings of fact, together with a ruling of law, on the question of whether the

8

probation officer surrendered the defendant with reasonable promptness. *Id.* at 393.

ii. Revocation two years after expiration of probation period not unreasonable where the defendant caused or contributed to the delay.

In *Commonwealth v. Baillargeon*, 28 Mass. App. Ct. 16 (1989), the Appeals Court held that revocation of probation more than two years after the probationary period had expired was not unreasonable because the defendant was responsible for the delay or had at least contributed to it by failing to disclose his whereabouts. *Id.* at 20–21.

iv. Revocation three years after end of probation term was unreasonable where the defendant did not cause or contribute to the delay.

On the other hand, in *Commonwealth v. Mitchell*, 46 Mass. App. Ct. 921, *rev. denied*, 429 Mass. 1108 (1999), the Appeals Court held a delay of two and one-half years was unreasonable where the probation officer took no action until two and one-half years after, and the judge took no action until three years after, expiration of the probation period. *Id.* at 922. In *Mitchell*, the defendant was convicted of illegally transferring electronic funds over $100 in value from two banks. *See id.* at 921. The defendant was sentenced to one year in the house of corrections, suspended, with a three-year term of probation with the condition that he make restitution of $12,000 during this period. *See id.* By the end of the probationary term, the defendant had not made full restitution, but he had been making weekly payments of $46.15 ($2,400 per year). At that time, the probation officer did not move to revoke or extend probation. *See id.* Two and one-half years after expiration of the probationary term, the probation officer scheduled a probation surrender hearing. At said hearing, over the objection of counsel, the judge entered an order purporting to extend probation on the same condition, restitution, for a further two-year period. *See id.*

The Appeals Court held that the lapse of two and one-half years before action was taken by the probation officer, and almost three years before the judge took any action, constituted a lack of reasonable promptness. *Mitchell*, 46 Mass. App. Ct. at 922. The defendant had been making weekly payments and was not in any way attempting to delay compliance with his probation. *Id.* Accordingly, the Appeals Court held under the circumstances, the judge lacked jurisdiction to extend probation. Accordingly, the Appeals Court ordered that the judge's order extending probation, be vacated. *Id.*

g. Revocation Proceedings Based on the Commission of Subsequent Crime May Be Initiated Before or After Disposition of the New Charge

In *Commonwealth v. Odoardi*, 397 Mass. 28 (1986), the Supreme Judicial Court addressed the issue of the delay in holding the revocation hearing. The defendant's Norfolk County probation was revoked nearly six months after his probation was due to expire, and twenty-two months after he was indicted in Essex County. *Id.* at 35. The defendant maintained that under *Sawicki*, 369 Mass. 377, the delay was unreasonable and prejudicial to his rights. *Id.* The *Odoardi* Court, noting that while the Commonwealth might have commenced revocation proceedings immediately after the Essex County indictments were returned, it was not required to do so. *Id.* The court noted that while Massachusetts has not adopted the American Bar Association's standards in this

area, it is relevant that they recommend that where revocation is based on the commission of subsequent criminal acts by the probationer, revocation proceedings not be initiated until after disposition at the trial of the new criminal charge. *Id.* at 36.

In *Commonwealth v. Holmgren*, 421 Mass. 224 (1995), the Supreme Judicial Court affirmed an order revoking probation and imposing the original sentence of incarceration, where the revocation hearing was held after the probationary period had expired and after the defendant had been tried, and acquitted, on the subsequent charges. *Id.* at 226–28.

When revocation is sought because of probationer's commission of a crime, the Commonwealth must prove by a preponderance of the evidence that the probationer was in breach of his probation contract. *Holmgren*, 421 Mass. at 227; *Commonwealth v. Juzba*, 44 Mass. App. Ct. 457, *rev. denied*, 427 Mass. 1104 (1998).

h. A Probationer Is Not Entitled to Credit for Time Served While Incarcerated on an Unrelated Offense

i. A probationer may not "bank" credit for future crimes.

In *Commonwealth v. Milton*, 427 Mass. 18 (1998), the defendant was placed on two years probation in November 1993, after he was convicted of assault and battery on a police officer, assault and battery with a deadly weapon, being a disorderly person and possession of an open container of alcohol.

A few months later, he was arrested and charged with armed robbery. The following day, he was served with a notice of probation surrender and hearing for alleged violation of probation. Two weeks later, the grand jury returned an indictment charging him with armed robbery. The defendant did not post bail. At his request, the surrender hearing was postponed until disposition of the armed robbery charges.

Almost fifteen months after his arrest for armed robbery, the Commonwealth *"nolle prossed"* that portion of the indictment as alleged armed robbery. The next day, the defendant was acquitted of unarmed robbery and he was discharged. The probation department withdrew the notice of surrender.

Six months later, while still on probation, the defendant was arrested for being a disorderly person. He moved to dismiss the second probation surrender hearing, or, in the alternative, that if found to be in violation, requested that he be given credit for the 410 days he spent in pretrial incarceration on the robbery charge for which he did not make bail and was ultimately acquitted. *Id.* at 20. After a hearing, the district court judge found the defendant to be in violation of probation, and imposed the previously suspended sentence of 2 concurrent one-year terms and one 6-month term, pursuant to the November 1993, convictions. The judge denied the defendant's request for credit; he gave Milton no credit for the 410 days spent in pretrial incarceration awaiting trial on the unarmed robbery charge. *Id.*

Defendant Milton argued that he should have received credit against his sentence on the revoked probation, for the time served in pretrial incarceration on the subsequent, unrelated armed robbery charge. The Supreme Judicial Court disagreed. Under G.L. c. 127, § 129B, a judge may reduce the sentence of any prisoner who was held in custody awaiting trial, by the number of days spent in confinement. *Id.* at 24. However, the time spent in custody awaiting trial for one crime generally may not be credited against a sentence for an unrelated crime. *Id.* (citations omitted). The purpose of this rule is to prevent criminals from essentially having a 'line of credit for future crimes.' *Id.* (citation omitted). The court held that in some circumstances a defendant may be credited for time served on an unrelated case, if necessary to prevent a defendant from serving "dead time." In some circumstances, a defendant may be allowed to credit time in an unrelated case if necessary to prevent a defendant from serving "dead time." In *Manning v. Superintendent, Mass. Correctional Inst., Norfolk*, 372 Mass. 387 (1977), the Supreme Judicial Court allowed the defendant to credit time served on a first sentence, which had been vacated on appeal, against a second sentence which he was supposed to serve consecutively, because it was necessary to remedy the injustice of his serving time for which he otherwise would receive no credit. *Id.* at 395. However, the statutes do not permit defendants to "bank time" against future offenses. In *Manning*, for example, it was important to the holding that the defendant was convicted of the second crime prior to being discharged on the first. *See id.* at 392–94 (defendant may not receive credit for confinement against sentence imposed for crime committed after period of confinement).

In *Milton*, unlike in *Manning*, the defendant was discharged approximately six months prior to being convicted on the second crime. Although the time he served awaiting trial on the robbery charge constituted "dead time," the Supreme Judicial Court held that the need to prevent criminal defendants from "banking time" for use against future sentences outweighs any fairness issues normally applicable in such situations. To allow prisoners to "bank time" in such a manner would be a matter of great concern, because it could in effect grant prisoners a license to commit future criminal acts with immunity. *Milton*, 427 Mass. at 24 (citing *Manning*, 372 Mass. at 392–94). Therefore, the defendant in *Milton* was not entitled to credit for time he served awaiting trial on the robbery charge, to reduce the sentence imposed as the result of a crime he committed six months after his acquittal and discharge on the robbery charge.

ii. The Probation Department may commence revocation immediately after return of an indictment or may postpone surrender proceedings until after disposition of the new charge.

Milton also contended that his motion to dismiss should have been allowed because he was unfairly prejudiced by the probation department's handling of his case. *Milton*, 427 Mass. at 21. He claimed the department's withdrawal of its surrender notice without a hearing, following such a lengthy incarceration, and subsequent filing of a second surrender against him after he was arrested on a misdemeanor charge, resulted in him being "set free to face another year in jail." *Id.* He also claimed the alleged mishandling deprived him of due process under the 5th and 14th Amendments to the Federal Constitution and under article 12 of the Massachusetts Declaration of Rights. *Id.* The Supreme Judicial Court disagreed.

The court cited *Odoardi*, 397 Mass. at 35, and *Rubera*, 371 Mass. at 181, for the rule that the probation department may commence a surrender hearing immediately after return of an indictment of a defendant who is on probation, or, may postpone the surrender proceedings until after disposition of the new charge. *Milton*, 427 Mass. at 21. The court noted that although Milton had been charged with only a misdemeanor, being a disorderly person, it was nevertheless a violation of the conditions of his probation. *Id.* at 22. The Supreme Judicial Court concluded that Milton was not entitled to dismissal of the second probation surrender. It held that after Milton was acquitted of the unarmed robbery charge, it was within the discretion of the probation department to withdraw its notice of surrender without a hearing. *Id.* The court noted that while it was unfortunate that Milton served more time awaiting trial on charges for which he was acquitted than he would have served on the original sentences imposed in November 1993, the conduct of the probation department was not improper. *Id.* The court also rejected the defendant's contention that his due process rights were violated, as without merit. The defendant, Milton, was incarcerated for 410 days because he could not post bail. His probation was not revoked under the first notice of surrender because *he* moved for a continuance, which the judge allowed. Therefore, he was not deprived of a right to notice and an opportunity to be heard. *Id.*

i. No Separation of Powers Violation Where the District Attorney Represents the Probation Department, So Long as Their Activities Do Not Intrude into the Internal Functioning of the Court

The defendant in *Milton* also argued that his motion to dismiss his surrender should have been allowed because the district attorney's office represented the probation department, which, he contended, constituted a violation of the separation of powers embodied in art. 30 of the Massachusetts Declaration of Rights. *Milton*, 427 Mass. at 22. The *Milton* Court cited *Commonwealth v. Tate*, 34 Mass. App. Ct. 446, 447–48 (1993) for the rule that the voluntary coordination of activity between various branches of government does not violate art. 30 as long as the activities do not intrude into the internal functioning of either branch.

C. Nature of the Evidence

The standard for evidence at the preliminary hearing is *probable cause*; the standard at the final hearing is *preponderance* of the evidence. *Commonwealth v. Holmgren*, 421 Mass. 224, 226 (1995); *Commonwealth v. Juzba*, 44 Mass. App. Ct. 457, *rev. denied*, 427 Mass. 1104 (1998).

1. PROBATIONERS ARE NOT ENTITLED TO THE FULL PANOPLY OF CONSTITUTIONAL PROTECTIONS AT REVOCATION HEARINGS AND THE STRICT RULES OF EVIDENCE DO NOT APPLY TO REVOCATION PROCEEDINGS

Revocation hearings are not part of a criminal prosecution. *Durling*, 407 Mass. 108, 113 (1990) (citation omitted); *Commonwealth v. Hill*, 52 Mass. App. Ct. 147, 152 (2001). Thus, a probationer need not be provided with the full panoply of constitutional protections applicable at a criminal trial. *Id.* Strict rules of evidence do not apply to probation revocation hearings. *Id.* at 114. The court in *Durling* explained:

> The probationer has a liberty interest at stake in the probation revocation proceeding. He has been given the opportunity to rehabilitate himself . . . . But the probationer's liberty interest is conditional. It was given to him as a matter of grace when the State had the right to imprison him.

407 Mass. at 115.

8

2. HEARSAY MAY BE ADMISSIBLE WITH INDICIA OF RELIABILITY

a. Revocation Hearings Must Be Flexible in Nature and All Reliable Evidence Should Be Considered

i. Probationer's right to confrontation may be denied for good cause.

In *Durling*, 407 Mass. 108, the Supreme Judicial Court stated, "[t]his court has always allowed the use of hearsay at probation revocation hearings." *Id.* at 115. The court cited the two overriding principles identified regarding revocation proceedings: *1) the revocation proceedings must be flexible in nature; and 2) all reliable evidence should be considered. Id.* (citations omitted). In *Durling*, the court addressed the issue of when and to what extent a court may rely on hearsay in a probation revocation hearing. *Id.* The court noted that the United States Supreme Court in *Gagnon*, expressly conditioned the probationer's right to confrontation by adding that the right could be denied if the "hearing officer specifically finds *good cause* for not allowing confrontation." *Id.* (citing *Gagnon v. Scarpelli*, 411 U.S. at 786); *see also Hill*, 52 Mass. App. Ct. at 153.

In *Durling*, the defendant was convicted of four counts of OUI. The Stoughton District Court judge sentenced him to two years in the house of correction with all sentences to run concurrently. The court, however, suspended all but the first ninety days of the sentences. 407 Mass. at 110. Subsequently, the defendant was again arrested for OUI, and a revocation hearing was scheduled. At the hearing, the defendant's probation officer read to the court the two police reports relating to the two subsequent arrests for OUI. Defense counsel attempted to cross-examine the probation officer, but abandoned his effort when he established that the officer had no personal knowledge of the events recounted in the police reports. The judge, based on the police officer's reports, determined that the defendant had violated the conditions of his probation, revoked the probation and committed him to the house of correction for nine months, with the balance of the sentence to remain suspended. *Id.* at 110. The judge based his ruling solely on hearsay, the two police reports. The defendant appealed, alleging that the revocation hearing failed to comport with due process. *Id.* at 109.

ii. The court should apply a balancing test to evidence not subject to cross-examination.

In determining whether the judge properly revoked the defendant's probation, the *Durling* Court applied a balancing test between the various interests involved, and concluded that the requirements of the due process clause, where the Commonwealth seeks to rely on evidence not subject to cross-examination, is the touchstone of an accurate and reliable determination.

iii. Admission of hearsay statements of alleged victim does not bar probationer from calling the alleged victim.

In *Commonwealth v. Hartfield*, 474 Mass. 474 (2016), the Supreme Judicial Court concluded that a judge's decision in a probation violation hearing to admit in evidence hearsay statements of an alleged victim regarding a new criminal offense does not bar the probationer from calling the alleged victim to testify. *Id.* at 475.

iv. If evidence is inadmissible under standard evidentiary rules, court must look independently to the reliability of the proffered evidence.

The *Durling* Court discussed the proper focus of inquiry in situations where the reliability of evidence is presented. It held that even though standard evidentiary rules do not apply to probation revocation hearings, the first step in such a determination is to decide whether the evidence would be admissible under those rules, including the exceptions to those standard rules. Evidence which would be admissible under standard evidentiary rules is presumptively reliable. 407 Mass. at 117–18. If the proffered evidence is not admissible under standard evidentiary rules, the court must look independently to the reliability of that evidence. *Unsubstantiated and unreliable hearsay cannot, consistent with due process, be the entire basis of a revocation.* When hearsay evidence *is* reliable, however, then it *can* be the basis of a revocation. *Id.* at 118. The court held that a showing that the proffered evidence bears substantial indicia of reliability and is substantially trustworthy, constitutes a showing of good cause obviating the need for confrontation. The court cautioned however, that *when hearsay is offered as the only evidence of the alleged violation, the indicia of reliability must be substantial. Id.* (citation omitted). The court stated that on the whole, resolution of the confrontation issue depends on the totality of the circumstances in each case, and the court must balance the defendant's due process right to confront and cross-examine against the Commonwealth's reason for not presenting witnesses. *Id.*

Former Rule 6(b) of the District Court Rules "no longer reflect[ed] our current case law." Since the rules went into effect, "this court has resolved *Durling*'s ambiguity, concluding that a finding of substantial reliability is itself sufficient to demonstrate good cause in such circumstances." *Commonwealth v. Bukin*, 467 Mass. 516, 522 (2014). Rule 7(b) of the District/Municipal Courts Rules for Probation Violation Proceedings now reflects that the single "substantial reliability" test applies "regardless of whether the the alleged violation consists of a new criminal charge." *2015 Commentary to District/Municipal Courts Rule 7.*

In *Commonwealth v. Emmanuel E.*, 52 Mass. App. Ct. 451 (2001), the defendant juvenile "Emmanuel" pleaded delinquent to assault and battery with a dangerous weapon. The judge committed him to the Department of Youth Services, suspended the commitment and placed him on probation. Subsequently, he was charged with breaking and entering in the daytime; his probation officer surrendered him. At the probation revocation hearing, the Commonwealth's sole witness was a police officer. He testified largely from his "notes" that he had responded to a report of a breaking and entering in progress in a multi-unit dwelling. A resident, Maria C., told him she had seen two suspects enter the premises and had asked them what they were doing; they told her they were looking for her son. Ten minutes later, she saw them leave through the side basement door. She identified the defendant and another male who were part of a group of people standing outside the dwelling as the men who had "broken" into her apartment. Her son reported that a knife was missing from his room. Based on his conversations with Maria C. and her son, the officer took the defendant into custody. Later, at the police station, the officer received a phone call from a neighbor of Maria C. who stated she saw two black males, one named

"Emmanuel," leave the premises via the side basement door. Counsel argued the Commonwealth failed to demonstrate good cause for preventing the defendant from confronting the witnesses to whom the officer referred. The judge did not respond but summarily found Emmanuel in violation of his probation. *Id.* at 453. The judge ordered him committed to the Department of Youth Services. The juvenile appealed, claiming his due process rights were violated because the Commonwealth failed to produce any witnesses with first hand knowledge of the alleged crime. *Id.* at 451–52.

The Appeals Court held that the officer's testimony did not fall under any established exception to the hearsay rule and noted that it was the only evidence offered against the juvenile. *Id.* at 454. The Appeals Court held the testimony was "fatally devoid of factual detail or corroborating personal observations" sufficient to render it reliable or to establish by a preponderance that Emmanuel committed the crime charged. *Id.* Further, it was not buttressed by corresponding or consistent hearsay testimony of another witness at the hearing. *Id.* That the testimony attributed the accusatory statements to two persons provided a marginal increase in its reliability, but it still fell far short of establishing by a preponderance that Emmanuel committed the offense. Moreover, even if there had been evidence establishing the reliability of the officer's testimony, there was no evidence of a "breaking" and scant evidence of Emmanuel's intent. The court concluded there was no good cause shown to deny him the right to confront and cross-examine his accusers. The court noted judges are often overburdened and probationers' rights due process are flexible, however, the *Emmanuel* Court suggested that if a probation revocation hearing is based entirely on hearsay evidence of criminal conduct, the judge should place on the record a brief, reasoned statement of the reliability of the hearsay evidence and an express finding of good cause for the Commonwealth not producing a witness with personal knowledge of the probation violation. *Id.* at 455. Because the evidence on which the judge relied was held not to be reliable, the Appeals Court vacated the judge's order revoking his probation. *Id.*

v. The Crawford standard is not applicable to Probation Violation Proceedings.

In *Commonwealth v. Wilcox*, 446 Mass. 61 (2006), the Supreme Judicial Court rejected the application of *Crawford v. Washington*, 541 U.S. 36 (2004), to probation violation proceedings. The court held that *Durling*, 407 Mass. 108, continued to control revocation hearings. *Wilcox*, 446 Mass. at 62. The court also held that art. 12 of the Massachusetts Declaration of Rights presents "no absolute and inflexible right to confront witnesses against him as described in the *Crawford* case." *Id.* at 70.

vi. Substantial reliable hearsay generally encompasses affidavits, depositions and documentary evidence.

Substantial reliable hearsay generally falls into the category of "conventional substitutes for live testimony, including affidavits, depositions, and documentary evidence." *Commonwealth v. Podoprigora*, 48 Mass. App. Ct. 136, 138 (1999) (citing *Gagnon v. Scarpelli*, 411 U.S. 778 (1973)). In *Podoprigora*, the court noted that the following have been found as examples of reliable hearsay from other jurisdictions: reports from police, *U.S. v. Bell*, 785 F.2d 640, 644 (8th Cir. 1986); reports from probation departments, *Prellwitz v.*

Berg, 578 F.2d 190 (7th Cir. 1978); hospital reports, *U.S. v. Simmons*, 812 F.2d 561 (9th Cir. 1987), *State v. Nelson*, 103 Wash.2d 760, 697 P.2d 579 (1985); laboratory reports, *U.S. v. Bell, supra; U.S. v. Penn*, 721 F.2d 762 (11th Cir. 1983); and reports from drug program directors, *Marshall v. Commonwealth*, 638 S.W.2d 288 (Ky. Ct. App. 1982). *Podoprigora*, 48 Mass. App. Ct. at 138–39. Other examples of reliable hearsay include a recorded, unsworn interview where the interviewee was subsequently rendered incompetent to testify, *Egerstaffer v. Israel*, 726 F.2d 1231 (7th Cir. 1984), authenticated copies of criminal records, *U.S. v. Miller*, 514 F.2d 41 (9th Cir. 1975), and invoices signed by the probationer himself, *People v. Maki*, 704 P.2d 743 (Cal. 1985). *See id.*

vii. Police reports containing hearsay statements may be reliable.

In *Commonwealth v. Calvo*, 41 Mass. App. Ct. 903 (1996), police reports which contained sworn statements by the defendant's mother-in-law and wife, describing the defendant's entry and assault, were found to be reliable hearsay evidence upon which his probation could be revoked. In *Calvo*, the defendant was on probation from several criminal convictions when he was charged with assault and battery and malicious destruction of property. He allegedly went to his mother-in-law's residence and beat her and his wife. *Id.* at 903–904. The defendant was surrendered for a violation of probation. The sole evidence at the surrender hearing were two police reports, one of which contained statements, sworn to under penalties of perjury, by the defendant's mother-in-law and wife, describing the defendant's entry and assault. At the hearing, the wife appeared, and contrary to her sworn statement, denied that the defendant assaulted her. *Id.* at 904. The hearing judge revoked the defendant's probation based upon the police reports. The defendant appealed the revocation, arguing that it was based solely on hearsay, and therefore violated his right to confrontation. *Id.* The appellate court disagreed, and held that the evidence at issue, the police reports which contained the sworn statements, were constituted reliable hearsay evidence on which the probation could be validly revoked. *Id.* at 904.

Two police reports in *Commonwealth v. Mejias*, 44 Mass. App. Ct. 948 (1998), were also found to be sufficiently reliable hearsay evidence. *Id.* at 949. In *Mejias*, one police report contained statements from a witness that were corroborated by observations made by the reporting police officer. *See id.* The second police report was based on the police officer's observation of the defendant smoking cocaine which was corroborated by a report of the defendant's girlfriend that she had also seen defendant smoking cocaine. *See id.* A third report which was based largely upon observations made by the defendant's girlfriend which were not observed by the reporting officer was found to be generally unreliable. *See id.* Since the defendant's probation revocation was based on the reliable reports made by the police officer, the defendant's probation revocation was affirmed. *See id.*

viii. Hearsay statements in police report may not be substantially reliable.

The police reports in *Commonwealth v. Wilson*, 47 Mass. App. Ct. 924 (1999), however, and a letter from the defendant to an acquaintance, coupled with testimony of the acquaintance's attorney did not create substantially reliable and sufficiently detailed allegations. *Id.*

In *Wilson*, while the defendant was on probation, a complainant came forward alleging that the defendant had a sexual relationship with the complaining witness which began when the complainant was underage. *Id.* at 925–26. The details contained in the police report were entirely of the acquaintance's making and were not observed directly by the police officer or produced by the officer's investigation into the case. *See id.* at 925. In addition, several events during the probation revocation hearing suggested its unreliability. The police officer, when he testified at the probation revocation hearing, acknowledged on cross-examination that he had questions about the truthfulness of the statement. *See id.* Furthermore, the defendant's emotional letter to the acquaintance, confirmed a close relationship between the two, but did not contain or confirm a sexual relationship when the acquaintance was underage. *See id.* More importantly, because the acquaintance had been recently arrested for extorting the defendant, the complaining witness had every reason to retaliate by making accusations against the defendant, particularly since he was well aware of the defendant's prior convictions, as well as a prior incident with the police, and presumably the subsequent probation review. *See id.* at 926. In addition, the attorney for the acquaintance testified at the defendant's probation revocation hearing, but his testimony did not confirm that his client had talked about alleged sexual abuse with the prosecutor, which further suggested that the acquaintance's statement was nothing more than uncorroborated hearsay. *See id.* The attorney did not make any inquiry into the reliability of his client's statements. *See id.* On direct examination, the acquaintance refused to answer specific questions about his relationship with the defendant, and on cross-examination, refused to answer any of the questions posed by defense counsel. *See id.* Because the testimony upon which the probation revocation was based was held to be unreliable, the order revoking the defendant's probation was vacated. *See id.*

ix. Factual detail rather than conclusions are indicia of reliability.

The *Durling* Court, 407 Mass. 108 (1990), also addressed the question of whether the facts in that case presented a situation wherein the hearing court properly revoked probation based on the out-of-court declarations of two police officers contained in two police reports from different police departments. *Id.* The court noted that both police reports contained facts observed by the police officers personally, rather than general statements or conclusions. The court stated that factual detail is indicative of reliability. *Id.* at 121. Moreover, the court stated, the fact that two different police officers from different departments each reported finding the defendant in similar circumstances indicated that neither report was without a basis in fact. The court further noted that it is a crime for police officers to file false reports. *Id.* The *Durling* Court concluded that the substantial reliability of the police reports, coupled with the practical difficulty of presenting live testimony, led to the conclusion that the District Court judge properly based his order of revocation on the evidence presented. *Id.* at 122.

x. Where hearsay evidence has substantial indicia of reliability, finding of witness unavailability is unnecessary.

The defendant in *Commonwealth v. Calvo*, 41 Mass. App. Ct. 903 (1996), also argued that the Commonwealth was required to show that the mother-in-law was unavailable in

order to be able to admit her sworn statement. *Id.* at 904 (citing *Commonwealth v. Delaney*, 36 Mass. App. Ct. 930, 932 (1994)). The Appeals Court disagreed, and stated that:

> "[t]he *Delaney* decision does not enlarge on *Commonwealth v. Durling*, which indicates that a probation revocation proceeding the opportunity for confrontation may be denied for 'good cause,' as when the witnesses to the violation are unavailable, or where hearsay evidence has *substantial indicia of reliability.*"

Calvo, 41 Mass. App. Ct. at 904 (emphasis added; citations omitted).

xi. Judge must find good cause to abrogate probationer's right to confrontation and cross-examination.

In contrast, in *Commonwealth v. Maggio*, 414 Mass. 193 (1993), the hearing judge revoked the defendant's probation on the basis of the probation officer's testimony that the probationer had been indicted, (who was unaware of what evidence had been presented to the grand jury to support the indictments) and a copy of one indictment. *Id.* at 195. In vacating the revocation order, the court cited *Durling*, 407 Mass. 108 (1990), for the rule that probation may properly be revoked based solely on hearsay evidence of the violation, as long as the hearsay evidence bore *substantial indicia of reliability.* *Maggio*, 414 Mass. at 196. However, the *Maggio* Court concluded that where the only evidence presented to the judge was the bare fact of the indictment or indictments, as in that case, there were no *sufficient indicia of reliability* as those upon which the court relied in *Durling*. *Id.* at 197–98.

The *Maggio* Court reasoned that it knew nothing about what was presented to the grand jury (contrasting those facts to the facts in *Durling*, where the court knew about the detailed police reports) and therefore had no basis for determining whether the proof was sufficiently trustworthy to excuse the probation department from presenting a live witness who could have been cross-examined. The hearing judge identified no other *good cause* for abrogating the defendant's right of confrontation and cross-examination, and the court did not discern one. 414 Mass. at 197–98. Additionally, the court noted that the evidence before the judge must be such that he is *capable of making an independent finding*, at least to a reasonable degree of certainty, that the defendant violated a condition or conditions of probation. *Id.* (citations omitted). In *Maggio*, however, the judge received no evidence beyond the indictment, so an independent finding could not be made. *Id.*

xii. Child's hearsay statement not reliable where court made no express determination of good cause to deny right of confrontation nor of the statement's reliability.

In *Commonwealth v. Joubert*, 38 Mass. App. Ct. 943 (1995), the Appeals Court vacated an order revoking the defendant's probation because the judge's findings indicated that the judge relied on hearsay statements of a child which was not shown to be sufficiently reliable to overcome the defendant's interest in cross-examining the witness. *Id.* at 946–47 (citing *Durling*, 409 Mass. at 118).

In *Joubert*, the probationer received a Notice of Surrender which alleged that he had violated the conditions of his probation, specifically, that he had unlawfully touched his daughter and had committed an indecent assault upon his wife's friend. *Id.* at 943.

After a hearing on the allegations, the judge revoked the defendant's probation and imposed the previously suspended two and one-half year suspended sentences. *Id.*

On appeal, Joubert claimed, *inter alia*, that he was denied due process at the revocation hearing. *Id.* at 944. In the revocation hearing, the adult friend of the defendant's wife testified that the defendant had committed indecent assault and battery upon her. Although she had not reported the incidents, the Appeals Court held that the testimony showed a clear violation of c. 265, § 13H. It was one of the eight conditions of the defendant's probation that he "obey local, state or federal laws or court order." *Id.* at 944. However, in revoking probation, the judge also relied on the defendant's daughter's hearsay statement that he had unlawfully touched her. The child had made the statement to her aunt. Although the judge relied on the statement in revoking probation, he did not make any express determination that there was *good cause* for denying the defendant the right of confrontation. Nor did the judge make any determination whether the proffered hearsay was *reliable. Id.* at 944–945. Since there was nothing in the record to show the circumstances of the touching of the child when it occurred, there was no basis upon which the judge could have concluded that the statement was a reliable spontaneous utterance. *Id.* (citations omitted). Nor was the statement admissible under c. 233, § 81, since the judge made none of the requisite findings upon which that statute conditions the admissibility, in any criminal proceeding, of out-of-court statements 'of a child under the age of ten describing an act of sexual conduct performed on or with the child . . . .' *Id.* at 945. (citation omitted).

The *Joubert* court noted that under *Durling*, 407 Mass. 108, the hearsay could provide the basis for the revocation if shown to be substantially reliable. However, analyzing the particular facts of the case, the appellate court concluded that the circumstances did not contain sufficient *indicia of reliability. Joubert*, 38 Mass. App. Ct. at 945. The *Joubert* court concluded that although the judge **could** properly have based his order of revocation on the indecent assault upon the wife's friend, his findings indicated that he also relied upon the unsubstantiated claim of an unlawful touching of the child, in considering the revocation. As such, the appellate court reversed the order revoking probation and remanded the matter to the District Court for the hearing judge to render a new decision based solely upon the evidence apart from the hearsay statements. *Id.* at 947.

In *Commonwealth v. Podoprigora*, 48 Mass. App. Ct. 136 (1999), the Appeals Court also found that evidence did not bear "sufficient indicia of reliability to obviate the need for confrontation." *Id.* at 139. In *Podoprigora*, the defendant was convicted of violating an abuse prevention order based on his admission to sufficient facts. *Id.* at 136. A thirty-month sentence was imposed, fifteen months to be served with the balance suspended. *See id.* Probation was conditioned by a G.L. c. 209A domestic abuse prevention order which prohibited defendant from contacting his ex-wife or their twelve-year-old daughter. *See id.* Defendant's probation officer was contacted and informed that defendant had allegedly violated the domestic abuse prevention order by contacting his daughter. *See id.* The defendant's notice of surrender alleged violation of the abuse of prevention order. *Id.*

At the probation revocation hearing, a police officer testified that he interviewed the defendant's daughter in her mother's presence. *See id.* at 137. The child told him that the defendant had telephoned the house that morning looking for her brother's telephone number. *See id.* The officer also testified that the defendant, who was then in the custody of the Immigration and Naturalization Service, had access to a telephone at the time of the alleged call. *See id.* At the hearing, the daughter did not testify; rather, the police officer testified that the child was fidgety and occasionally evasive during the interview. *See id.* The judge made a written finding that her hearsay statements were reliable. *See id.* The defendant appealed.

On appeal, the Commonwealth attempted to distinguish the case from *Joubert*, 38 Mass. App. Ct. 943, and argued that sufficient indicia of reliability were provided by the police officer's description of the child's demeanor, the corroborative evidence that the defendant had access to a telephone, the sworn statement of the child's mother, and the absence of any suggestion that the phone call was fabricated. *See Podoprigora*, 48 Mass. App. Ct. at 138.

The Appeals Court disagreed and found the testimony of the police officer indicating that he had interviewed the defendant's daughter lacked sufficient indicia of reliability and was not admissible. *See id.* The officer's testimony regarding the child's demeanor, that the child was fidgety and occasionally evasive, did not aid in providing reliability to her statements. *Id.* In addition, the entire interview of the child took place in the presence of her mother. *See id.* The sworn statement of the girl's mother likewise did not provide reliability, because the mother had no personal knowledge of the events in question since she was not on the other end of the phone conversation while her daughter allegedly spoke to the defendant. *See id.* In addition, the corroborating evidence that the defendant had access to a telephone fell well below the corroboration presented in *Joubert*, 38 Mass. App. Ct. 943 (4-year-old's hearsay statement that father unlawfully touched her, was corroborated by a medical examination which found bruising consistent with statement). *See Podoprigora*, 48 Mass. App. Ct. at 138. Therefore, because the evidence that formed the basis of the defendant's probation revocation did not bear sufficient indicia of reliability, the order revoking probation was reversed. *Id.* at 139.

In *Commonwealth v. Bukin*, 467 Mass. 516, 520–21 (2014), the court held that the judge did not abuse his discretion when he determined that the recorded interview of a child witness with Asperger's syndrome constituted reliable hearsay.

xiii. Admission of a victim's grand jury testimony in a probation violation hearing does not violate the defendant's right to confrontation.

In *Commonwealth v. Hill*, 52 Mass. App. Ct. 147 (2001), the defendant argued that the judge's revocation order should be set aside because it was based in part on hearsay and other incompetent evidence, specifically the judge's admission of the victim's grand jury testimony and dog-tracking evidence, which violated his right to confront witnesses. *Id.* at 152. The Appeals Court held that under *Durling*, the Commonwealth may use hearsay evidence in revocation hearings so long as it is reliable and the Commonwealth has good cause for not using a witness with personal knowledge. *Hill*, 52 Mass. App. Ct. at 152–53. In *Hill*, the court found that the Commonwealth had good cause for not calling the victim of the alleged rape as a witness because of her relatively young age and the potential trauma of describing yet again what had happened to her. *Id.* The victim's grand jury testimony had

8

been given under oath and was factually detailed rather than general or conclusory. *Id.* It was also corroborated by "fresh complaint" evidence. *Id.* Under these facts, the Court concluded that the challenged evidence was sufficiently reliable so as to be admissible. *Id.*

xiv. The admission of dog-scenting evidence can be reliable and does not violate the defendant's due process right to confrontation.

The *Hill* Court also found that there was no due process violation in the judge's admission of "dog-tracking" or scenting evidence. A dog was used to track the scent of the unknown intruder who raped the victim. 52 Mass. App. Ct. at 150. The dog followed the scent from the victim's home to the defendant's home where it indicated the trail had ended. *Id.* The Court reasoned that it is well established in the Commonwealth that such evidence is admissible, provided a proper foundation is laid, due to its widely recognized reliability. *Id.* at 153; *see also Commonwealth v. Taylor*, 426 Mass. 189, 197–98 (1997); *Commonwealth v. LePage*, 352 Mass. 403, 418–19 (1967).

xv. GPS monitoring records do not constitute hearsay and are admissible at revocation hearing.

In *Commonwealth v. Thissell*, 457 Mass. 191 (2010), the Supreme Judicial Court, without deciding whether GPS records are properly characterized as nonhearsay or whether they fall under an exception to the hearsay rule, *id.* at 197, held that GPS are substantially reliable. *Id.* at 197–98. The court emphasized that GPS records offered in evidence at probation revocation heaings should be properly attested and certified, thus eliminating concerns about their authenticity. *Id.* at 199.

xvi. At revocation proceeding, probationer's criminal record is not admissible.

In *Commonwealth v. MacDonald*, 53 Mass. App. Ct. 156 (2001), the defendant claimed his criminal record was admitted into evidence over his objection. At his final revocation hearing the probation officer offered a certified copy of a police report. The probationer objected. The probation officer indicated to the judge that the victim was available to testify, and that he could either call her or "finish the surrender summary." The judge told him to finish the summary. *Id.* at 157. The probation officer then summarized the probationer's criminal record. He had a total of fifty-seven entries on his record and was, at that time, nineteen years of age. *Id.* Defense counsel objected to introduction of the criminal record. The judge then allowed the probation officer to call the victim to testify. The Appeals Court held that although a probationer's criminal record is not admissible at a revocation hearing, the evidence before the judge was "overwhelming." *Id.* at 160.

xvii. Subsequent recantation of victim's videotaped SAIN interview held not to deteriorate the Commonwealth's case.

In *Commonwealth v. Patton*, 458 Mass. 119 (2010), the probationer allegedly violated the conditions of his probation by committing the crimes of indecent assault and battery on a child under fourteen, and threatening to commit a crime. *Id.* at 121. The evidence of the violation was a videotaped SAIN interview; the child later recanted by means of written statements by her parents and the testimony of the probationer's private investigator. *Id.* at 122. Probationer argued that the evidence against him was insufficient to support a finding by a preponderance of the evidence that he violated his probation. *Id.* at 123–24. The Supreme Judicial Court upheld the judge's ruling that the videotaped SAIN interview was admissible under common law rules of evidence as substantially reliable hearsay and the Commonwealth's case did not deteriorate as a result of evidence that the child recanted. *Id.* at 130–34.

3. REGARDLESS OF THE FACT THE EVIDENCE HAS BEEN SUPPRESSED, ILLEGALLY OBTAINED EVIDENCE IS USUALLY ADMISSIBLE

In *Commonwealth v. Vincente*, 405 Mass. 278 (1989), the Supreme Judicial Court addressed the issue of whether probation may be revoked based on statements which have been suppressed at trial for failure to comply with *Miranda* requirements. *Id.* at 279. The court noted that most federal courts of appeal that have considered the question have concluded that the exclusionary rule is not applicable to probation revocation proceedings. *Id.* at 280 (citations omitted). The *Vincente* Court agreed with the rationale set forth in the federal cases cited therein, i.e., to deter future police misconduct. The Court agreed with the federal courts' conclusion that application of the exclusionary rule would likely have only a marginal deterrent effect on such police misconduct. As such, the court held that the statements suppressed at trial for failure to comply with *Miranda* were properly admissible at the revocation proceeding. *Id.* at 280. *See also Commonwealth v. Olsen*, 405 Mass. 491 (1989); *Commonwealth v. Simon*, 57 Mass. App. Ct. 80, 87 (2003).

In *Commonwealth v. Olsen*, 405 Mass. 491 (1989), the Supreme Judicial Court held that where police who unlawfully seized evidence neither knew or had reason to know of the probationary status of the person who owned the property, the evidence was admissible in a probation revocation hearing. *Id.* at 491. In that case, while on probation for drug-related offenses, the defendant was arraigned on three new drug-related indictments in Superior Court. On the same day the indictments were returned, a district court judge held a surrender hearing. At the hearing, a police officer testified that drugs and paraphernalia were seized pursuant to a search warrant. Olsen indicated that she intended to file a motion to suppress the evidence at trial on the new indictments. The judge found Olsen had violated the terms of probation but continued the disposition of the matter. *Id.* at 492.

At trial, the judge allowed Olsen's motion to suppress the illegally obtained evidence. The Commonwealth indicated that it would not appeal the suppression ruling, and that it had no other evidence on which to go forward against the defendant. The judge dismissed all three indictments with prejudice. *Id.* at 492. On that same afternoon, the district court judge revoked Olsen's probation on the basis of the evidence suppressed at trial. *Id.*

Citing *Vincente*, 405 Mass. 278 (1989), and cases cited therein, the *Olsen* court held that the district court judge properly admitted the evidence which had been suppressed at trial. .*Olsen*, 405 Mass. at 493. One of the factors the Court relied on in determining that the evidence was admissible was the fact that the police officers who had seized it knew nothing of the probationer's status. The Court expressly left open the question of whether the police officer's knowledge of the probationer's status would compel a different result. *Id.* at 496 (citations omitted).

The *Olsen* Court concluded that its holding would actually protect the availability of probation for offenders, reasoning that if it were to exclude such evidence from revocation hearings, there might be a disinclination to order probation in the first place. *Id.* (citations omitted). The court further noted its holding also protects the public interest in having all reliable evidence relevant to the probationer's conduct and rehabilitation. *Id.* (citing *Vincente*, 405 Mass. at 280).

4. ALLEGED CRIMES, INDICTMENTS, PROBABLE CAUSE OR APPEALED CONVICTION CASES MAY FORM THE BASIS OF REVOCATION

a. Probation May Be Revoked for Untried, New Crimes: Conviction Not Necessary

In *Rubera v. Commonwealth*, 371 Mass. 177 (1976), the Supreme Judicial Court held that any conduct by a person on probation that constitutes a violation of his probation may form the basis for revocation. *Such conduct may involve the violation of criminal laws, but there is no prerequisite that the probationer be convicted thereof to permit the violation to be used as the basis of the revocation. Id.* at 181; *see also Commonwealth v. Emmanuel E.*, 52 Mass. App. Ct. 451 (2001). Furthermore, if the act alleged to be a violation of probation is made the subject of a criminal complaint, the commencement of the prosecution does not preclude the revocation of the earlier probation nor does it require that the revocation proceedings be deferred until completion of the new criminal proceedings. *Rubera*, 371 Mass. at 181 (citations omitted).

i. That conviction of new offense is on appeal does not prevent it from forming the basis of a revocation proceeding.

The *Rubera* Court further held that if the act relied on as a violation of probation results in a criminal conviction, the fact that the conviction is awaiting appellate review does not prevent it from forming the basis for revocation. 371 Mass. at 181. (citations omitted).

The court cited *Roberson v. Connecticut*, 501 F.2d 305 (2d Cir. 1974), for the rule that, "[a]ll that is required for revocation of probation is that the court be satisfied that the probationer has abused the opportunity given him to avoid incarceration . . . ." *Rubera*, 371 Mass. at 181 (citing *Roberson*, 501 F.2d at 308).

Likewise, in *Durling*, the court affirmed revocation of the defendant's probation, even though the defendant had not been convicted of the alleged crimes (operating under the influence). *Durling*, 407 Mass. at 112.

ii. Revocation may properly be based on unreported crimes.

In *Joubert*, 38 Mass. App. Ct. at 944, the Appeals Court stated that the probation revocation hearing judge could properly revoke probation based on the testimony of the wife's friend, even though she had not reported the alleged incidents to the authorities.

iii. Bare, unsupported indictments cannot be the sole basis of revocation.

As discussed *supra*, an indictment or indictments, unsupported by any account of the facts underlying them, cannot play the same role in a final probation revocation hearing as does a criminal conviction. *Maggio*, 414 Mass. at 199.

b. It is Improper to Revoke Probation Based Solely on Revocation of Probation in Another Court, Without Knowing the Facts of that Revocation

In *Commonwealth v. Michaels*, 39 Mass. App. Ct. 646 (1996), the defendant pled guilty in Cambridge to violating a 209A order and was sentenced to one year in the house of

correction, sentence suspended for one year. Subsequently, the probation department issued a Notice of Surrender listing as violations: "Somerville Court A & B 209A Subsequent Convictions Conditions fail to comply with existing Court orders and stay away orders." *Id.* at 646. At the probation revocation hearing, the judge in Cambridge revoked the defendant's probation, vacated the suspended sentence and ordered him committed to the Middlesex House of Correction for one year. *Id.* In the written findings, using a standard form, the judge checked a box indicating "violation of the conditions of probation" and added: "Probationary status from Somerville Dist. Ct. Revoked & sent. placed in effect." *Id.* Under the printed words, "Included in the evidence upon which I rely is the following," the judge wrote:

> "Issuance of 209A order—violation of probation with subsequent commitment by Somerville Dist. Ct. (Aug. 23, 1994). Court Record. Additional commitment for probation violation Somerville (Aug. 23, 1994) See certified copies attached."

Id. at 647. The evidence at the Cambridge revocation hearing consisted of the testimony of the defendant's probation officer. He testified that while the defendant was on probation, another restraining order had been issued against him on the complaint of his grandmother. She was not the complainant who had obtained the Cambridge restraining order.

The papers introduced at the Cambridge revocation hearing indicated that the convictions in Somerville **preceded** the sentencing in Cambridge.[1] The only additional matter discussed at the revocation hearing was the judge's comment that the defendant had been defaulted in Somerville.

[1] The papers submitted to the judge did not indicate what the alleged violations of the Somerville probation were, nor when they occurred. *Michaels*, 39 Mass. App. Ct. at 647 n.2.

The Appeals Court concluded that there was no basis in the record to revoke the defendant's probation. The record did not show that the judge received any evidence bearing on the defendant's conduct, other than that another court (Somerville District Court) had revoked probation for unknown violations on unknown dates, and that the Somerville records contained a notation of a default. *Id.* at 649. "Without knowing the circumstances of the Somerville default, the Cambridge judge could not properly rely on it to revoke probation." *Id.* In addition, the default was not listed as one of the violations in the Notice of Surrender. Since the record contained no indication to make the defendant aware that this would be one of the grounds of revocation, the court concluded that the defendant did not have an adequate opportunity to present a meaningful defense on this ground. *Id.* at 649 (citing *Maggio*, 414 Mass. at 196, 197). Accordingly, the Appeals Court vacated the order revoking probation and remanded the case to Cambridge District Court for further proceedings to determine whether the defendant was in violation of his probation. *Id.* at 649–650.

c. Mere Issuance of a Restraining Order Is an Insufficient Basis on Which to Revoke Probation Without Further Facts

In *Commonwealth v. Michaels*, 39 Mass. App. Ct. 646, 648 (1996), the Appeals Court held that the mere issuance of a c. 209A restraining order, without further facts, is insufficient to justify revocation of probation. *Id.* However, in *Commonwealth v. Pickering*, 75 Mass. App. Ct. 1113 (2009) (Rule 1:28 decision), the Appeals Court affirmed a revocation of probation

8

where, at the hearing, the probation officer described the contents of the affidavit filed in the restraining order proceeding. In addition, the victim in the c. 209A case was the daughter of the victim in the assault and battery case for which the defendant was on probation and the same judge heard both the revocation and restraining order proceedings. *Id.* at n.2.

d. Double Jeopardy Issues

i. Double Jeopardy does not apply to revocation hearings.

In *Krochta v. Commonwealth*, 429 Mass. 711 (1999), the Supreme Judicial Court explained why double jeopardy protection does not apply to probation revocation:

> Since a probation revocation hearing does not put a defendant at risk of a second prosecution for the same offense after acquittal . . . a second prosecution for the same offense after conviction," does not impose multiple punishments for the same offense, "are proceedings in which jeopardy does not attach because the court is without power to make any determination regarding guilt or innocence," are not criminal prosecutions, and because "any consequent revocation does not punish the defendant for any crime charged subsequent to the imposition of probation," probation revocation hearings cannot be the basis for a claim of either multiple prosecution or multiple punishment.

See id. at 713. Therefore, the *Krochta* Court upheld the denial of the defendant's motions to dismiss larceny charges even after the probation revocation proceeding based upon those charges resolved in his favor. *See id.* at 719.

ii. There is no double jeopardy protection against revocation of probation and imposition of imprisonment.

In *Commonwealth Odoardi*, 397 Mass. 28 (1986), the Supreme Judicial Court addressed the double jeopardy issue. In that case, the defendant's Suffolk County probation was revoked as a result of his conviction for robbery and breaking and entering in Essex County. The Suffolk County Superior Court judge revoked his probation and sentenced him to two and one-half years incarceration, to be served concurrently with the Essex County sentence. *Id.* at 29–30. Subsequently, after hearing, the defendant's Norfolk County probation was also revoked, and he was sentenced to five to ten years at M.C.I., to be served on and after completion of his Essex County sentence. *Id.* at 30.

The defendant contended on appeal that the sentence of incarceration imposed on revocation of his Norfolk County probation essentially constituted the third punishment for his robbery conviction in Essex County, and that this action violated his constitutional right not to be put in double jeopardy. *Id.* The Supreme Judicial Court disagreed. It quoted the U.S. Supreme Court for the rule that, "there is no double jeopardy protection against revocation of probation and imposition of imprisonment." *Id.* (citing *United States v. DiFrancesco*, 449 U.S. 117, 137 (1980)). "This is true whether revocation is predicated on the probationer's conviction of a criminal offense or merely a finding that he has 'abused the opportunity given him to avoid incarceration.'" *Id.* (citing *Rubera*, 371 Mass. at 181).

iii. Failure to prove a violation of probation by a preponderance of the evidence at a revocation hearing does not bar prosecution of a new offense.

In *Commonwealth v. Reddix*, 429 Mass. 1015 (1999), the Commonwealth, at the defendant's probation revocation hearing, failed to prove by a preponderance that the defendant violated his probation by committing a new offense. *See id.* The judge then entered an order dismissing the pending criminal charges. *See id.* The Commonwealth appealed directly to the Supreme Judicial Court. *See id.* The Supreme Judicial Court held that the double jeopardy protection does not preclude prosecution of a defendant on charges that the Commonwealth failed to prove at an earlier probation revocation proceeding. *Id.* The defendant was not put in jeopardy for the pending criminal charges at his probation revocation hearing. *Id.* Consequently, the order dismissing the charges against the defendant was vacated. *Id.* at 1016.

iv. Acquittal on the new charges does not bar the finding of a probation violation.

In *Commonwealth v. Holmgren*, 421 Mass. 224 (1995), the defendant was found guilty of his second offense of OUI of a motorcycle. The judge imposed an eighteen month sentence to the house of correction, which he suspended for two years. *Id.* at 224. During the probationary period the defendant was charged with his third OUI offense. Thereafter, a notice of surrender was issued and served on him for the alleged probation violation of the new criminal offense. Action on the probation violation was deferred until after trial on the new charges. *Id.* at 225.

The jury found the defendant not guilty on the third OUI offense. Relying on that verdict, he moved to dismiss the revocation proceedings, or, in the alternative, that no evidence concerning the third alleged OUI be admitted. The judge denied both motions, and based on a *preponderance of the evidence*, found the defendant had committed a subsequent offense of OUI. *Id.* The judge, believing he had no alternative, imposed the entire original eighteen-month sentence. *Id.*

On appeal, Holmgren argued the Commonwealth was collaterally estopped at the revocation hearing from relying on evidence of his alleged subsequent violations. He contended that since he was acquitted of the subsequent charges, the Commonwealth was barred from thereafter relying on evidence concerning those charges, to revoke his probation. The defendant also challenged the judge's ruling that he lacked the authority to impose anything less than the original sentence. The court disagreed. *Id.* at 225.

The *Holmgren* Court declared that principles of collateral estoppel do not bar the court from revoking probation based on evidence of a violation of law on which the probationer has been found not guilty. The reason lies, the court explained, in the different burdens of proof required in the two proceedings. *See also Reddix*, 429 Mass. at 1015; *Krochta*, 429 Mass. at 716. Whereas in a criminal case the Commonwealth must prove the elements of the crime beyond a reasonable doubt, it must only prove a violation of probation by a preponderance of the evidence. As such, the doctrine of collateral estoppel is not available to a probationer in a revocation hearing to bar evidence of the alleged violation, even if he has been found not guilty in a criminal trial. *Holmgren*, 421 Mass. at 225–26; *Reddix*, 429 Mass at 1015; *Krochta*, 429 Mass. at 716.

e. Collateral Estoppel Is Not a Bar to Either New Criminal or Probation Revocation Proceedings, But Bars a Second Probation Revocation Proceeding on the Same Charged Misconduct

After a probation revocation proceeding resulted in his favor, the defendant, in *Krochta v. Commonwealth*, 429 Mass. 711 (1999), moved to dismiss three counts of larceny, arguing that trial was barred by the principles of collateral estoppel. *Krochta*, 429 Mass. at 712. Collateral estoppel requires that the shared, "common factual issue" between the two proceedings be decided using the same standards of proof. *Id.* Because the standard of proof at a probation revocation hearing differs from the standard of proof at trial, the collateral estoppel argument fails. *See id.* at 716.

In *Krochta*, the defendant argued that the facts of his case were the reverse of *Holmgren*, 421 Mass. 224 (1995), in which the court held that "the difference of a higher burden of proof in an earlier criminal prosecution and a lower burden of proof in a subsequent probation revocation proceeding precluded the defendant from raising collateral estoppel as a bar to an attempt by the Commonwealth to prove that the defendant had violated his probation by committing the offenses on which he had previously been acquitted." *Krochta*, 429 Mass. at 718. In *Krochta*, the Supreme Judicial Court found that this fact scenario was not the reverse of *Holmgren*, *supra*. Rather, *Krochta* was the same as *Holmgren* in that it was, "a criminal prosecution and a non-criminal judicial proceeding that presented common factual issues, but at which the issues must be decided on different standards of proof and under different procedural rules." *Krochta*, 429 Mass. at 718. Therefore, the doctrine of collateral estoppel does not bar prosecution of the defendant for new criminal offenses, even if the Commonwealth fails to prove the commission of those new offenses under the preponderance standard at the probation revocation hearing. *Id.*

But in *Kimbroughtillery v. Commonwealth*, 471 Mass. 507 (2015), the court held that "principles of collateral estoppel bar a second probation revocation proceeding on the same charged misconduct that was litigated in an earlier probation revocation proceeding in a different county and was resolved in favor of the petitioner." *Id.* at 508.

f. When Probation Is Revoked, the Original Suspended Sentence Must Be Imposed

In *Commonwealth v. Holmgren*, 421 Mass. 224 (1995), the Supreme Judicial Court stated that, whether or not it is desirable, *when probation is revoked, the original, suspended sentence must be imposed*, if the time has expired in which the sentence may be revised or revoked. *Id.* at 228 (citing Mass. R. Crim. P. 29(a)). The court stated that pursuant to G.L. c. 279, § 3 (1994), if the suspension of a sentence is revoked, "the sentence shall be in full force and effect." *Id.* The judge had no choice, once he decided to revoke suspension of the sentence, to impose the entire original one. *Id.*; *see also Commonwealth v. Herrera*, 52 Mass. App. Ct. 294 (2001).

The court in *Holmgren* noted that the federal practice is different, allowing the revoking judge the discretion to impose any sentence within the statutory permissible range for the particular offense. *Holmgren*, 421 Mass. at 228 (citing 18 U.S.C. § 3565 (1994)). Accordingly, the court affirmed the order imposing the original sentence. *Id.*

g. When a Defendant is Sentenced to Concurrent Sentences, a Revocation Judge May Not Impose a Higher Sentence than That Originally Imposed

In *Commonwealth v. Bruzzese*, 53 Mass. App. Ct. 152 (2001), *aff'd*, 437 Mass. 606 (2002), the defendant was sentenced on four complaints to four concurrent sentences of two and one-half years at the House of Correction, eighteen months to be served, balance suspended with probation until September 1992. Subsequently, his probation was extended to June 2, 1998. On that date, the judge found that he had violated his probation by committing another offense and by not paying restitution, as the original judge had ordered. *Id.* at 153. The hearing judge revoked his probation on *three* of the four complaints, committed him to the House of Correction for the one-year suspended sentence and extended his probation until December 2000 on the *fourth* complaint for the purpose of paying the restitution ordered. *Id.* In February 2000, he was again found to be in violation of his probation. The judge revoked his probation and imposed the one-year suspended sentence on the fourth complaint. *Id.* Defendant appealed, claiming the judge did not have the authority to essentially change the original two and one-half year sentence to three and one-half years, arguing that such a result was contrary to the rule established by *Commonwealth v. Holmgrem*, 421 Mass. 224, 228 (1995), and that the new sentence also violated his double jeopardy rights. *Bruzzese*, 53 Mass. App. Ct. at 154. The Appeals Court agreed. The court concluded the judge impermissibly altered the concurrent sentencing scheme—that the defendant serve the four sentences concurrently—by extending the defendant's probation on one complaint while simultaneously revoking his probation and imposing the one-year sentence on the remaining three complaints. *Id.* at 155. As a result, when the judge revoked Bruzzese's probation in February 2000, his sentence was improperly increased from the original two and one-half years to three and a half years and was therefore illegal. In addition, because Bruzzese had already served the one-year sentence which was to run concurrently with the suspended sentence on the complaint on which probation was revoked in February 2000, the defendant's right not to be placed in jeopardy twice was violated. Accordingly, the Appeals Court vacated the order imposing the one-year sentence. *Id.*

h. Probation May Be Revoked Even Before the Probationary Period Has Commenced

In *Commonwealth v. Phillips*, 40 Mass. App. Ct. 801 (1996), the defendant was convicted of assault of a child under the age of sixteen with intent to commit rape, and three counts of indecent assault and battery of a child under fourteen years of age. He was committed to MCI-Concord for twenty years, and in addition, he was sentenced to three concurrent terms of nine to ten years at MCI-Cedar Junction to be served after completion of the MCI-Concord sentence. Execution of the three concurrent terms was suspended and a nine-year probationary period was imposed, to commence upon the defendant's release from Concord. *Id.* at 802. On the day the sentences were imposed, the defendant signed an agreement as to the conditions of his probation. The conditions included, among other things, the usual requirement that he obey all local, state and federal laws, and court order. *Id.* at 802.

While incarcerated in Concord, the defendant solicited a "hit man" to murder his second wife. The "hit man" was ac-

8

tually an undercover police officer. The defendant was convicted of solicitation to commit murder and was sentenced to two and a half years to be served from and after the Concord sentence. *Id*. After his conviction for solicitation for murder, the Commonwealth commenced proceedings to revoke the nine-year probation which had been imposed with the suspension of the three concurrent nine to ten year sentences. *Id*.

The defendant argued that he could not violate his probation, as a matter of logic, before the probationary period had begun. The Superior Court judge reported the question to the Appeals Court. The Appeals Court disagreed with the defendant and held that "[T]here is nothing in chapter 279, section 1 or section 3, which precludes a judge from revoking a probationary term for a violation of its conditions after its imposition but prior to its commencement." *Id*. at 803. Nor, the court added, "is there anything in our public policy which would preclude, as a matter of law, the revocation of the defendant's probation when he violated its conditions before he even began his probationary term by seeking the murder of his wife." *Id*. at 804.

i. Probation May Be Revoked While a Defendant Is Still Incarcerated but Only if the Defendant Was Notified That the Condition Would Be in Effect During the Incarceration

In *Commonwealth v. Ruiz*, 453 Mass. 474 (2009), the defendant was convicted of rape and other offenses. He was sentenced to five to five and one half years incarceration on the rape conviction and three years probation on the remaining convictions, to commence from and after his incarceration. One of the special conditions of probation was that he have no contact with the victim, his former domestic partner. *Id*. at 475. The victim had also obtained a c. 209A restraining order against him which was in effect at the time of the defendant's plea and sentence, but which expired during his incarceration. *Id*. at 477.

While still incarcerated but after the restraining order had expired, the defendant sent four letters to the victim, one of which frightened her. She reported them to the Superior Court probation department. The probation officer issued a notice to the defendant charging him with a violation of the conditions of his probation, specifically, "failure to comply with no contact order imposed by the Court." After a hearing, the judge determined he had violated the special condition of probation that he not contact the victim. *Id*.

On further appellate review, the Supreme Judicial Court reversed the revocation on due process grounds because the defendant did not receive notice that the special condition of probation—that he not contact the victim—commenced while he was incarcerated. *Id*. at 478. While a judge "is not barred from placing a defendant on probation during the period of his incarceration," there must be evidence that the judge in fact did so. *Id*. at 480. The *Ruiz* Court rejected the Commonwealth's argument that the use of the "present tense" on the probation condition form "took immediate effect upon imposition of [the] sentences." *Id*. at 481. The Supreme Judicial Court noted that the defendant was repeatedly and expressly told that probation was to take effect "after" he had served his sentence of incarceration. Further, it was not clear that the phrase was in fact in the "present tense"; the tense was dependent on the context and surrounding language. "An isolated, arguable use of the present tense describing one of many conditions of probation is hardly the 'clear' guidance required

to put the defendant on notice that a particular condition of probation is to take effect immediately." *Id*.

Additionally, in *Commonwealth v. Bunting*, 458 Mass. 569 (2010), the Supreme Judicial Court held that the defendant was not in violation of his probation based on crimes committed while incarcerated before the probationary term had begun because the defendant had not received the proper notice that such actions might be deemed a probation violation with resulting sanctions. *Id*. at 572–73. In order to hold the defendant accountable for compliance with probation conditions during his incarceration and before the probation term began, trial court was required to notify him that commission of new crimes before his probationary term had begun might be deemed a violation of his probation with a resulting sanction. *Id*. Additionally, it was of no constitutional consequence whether the condition proscribed criminal or noncriminal conduct. *Id*.

j. Threats to Third Parties May Form the Basis of a Probation Violation

In *Commonwealth v. Simmons*, 69 Mass. App. Ct. 348 (2007), during court-ordered evaluation, when discussing his former girlfriend, the defendant told the therapist, "I'm going to kill that fucking bitch." He also stated he was going to kill her current boyfriend and said "you can write that down." The defendant also implied that they lived close by and that he would shoot the former girlfriend and her boyfriend. After the therapist concluded the evaluation she notified her superiors and the probation department of defendant's statements concerning his plan to shoot his former girlfriend and her boyfriend. The defendant was surrendered and found in violation of his probation.

The Appeals Court affirmed, rejecting the defendant's argument that the evidence was insufficient because there was no evidence he intended the therapist to communicate the threats to the former girlfriend and her boyfriend. "[T]he elements of a threat include an expression of intention to inflict a crime on another and an ability to do so in circumstances that would justify apprehension on the part of the recipient of the threat. There must be evidence that the person making the threat either communicated it to the person targeted or intended that it be communicated to the person targeted so as to cause fear or apprehension in the victim. Thus, where a defendant makes a threat to a third party who would likely communicate it to [the ultimate target] . . . the defendant's act constitutes evidence of [his] intent to communicate the threat to the intended victim." *Simmons*, 69 Mass. App. Ct. at 350 (citations and quotation marks omitted).

D. Nature of the Hearing

Although the formal rules of evidence do not apply, the probationer has the right to call witnesses on his behalf and to present evidence in mitigation of his alleged probation violation. He also has the right to cross-examine witnesses against him, although the court may limit such cross-examination in certain circumstances. Evidence of a non-testimonial nature may be received. Although not subject to the strict evidentiary discipline of a trial, such probation revocations must proceed along judicially drawn lines and are subject to judicial review. *Commonwealth v. Tate*, 34 Mass. App. Ct. 446, 448 (1993) (citing *Durling*, 407 Mass. at 113, and *Maggio*, 414 Mass. at 196–99).

1. RIGHT TO CONFRONT WITNESSES

a. The Court May Limit Cross-Examination When the Basis of the Revocation Is a Conviction

In *Odoardi*, 397 Mass. 28 (1986), the judge at the revocation hearing limited defense counsel's cross-examination of the Commonwealth's only witness, a probation officer, who recommended that the defendant's probation be revoked and an 'on and after' sentence be imposed. In that case, the violation of probation consisted of a conviction for a subsequent crime. *Id.* at 29–30. The defendant argued that the judge's actions deprived him of his right under *Gagnon v. Scarpelli*, 411 U.S. 778 (1973), to cross-examine adverse witnesses. *Id.* at 34. The Supreme Judicial Court disagreed. It held that there was no dispute that there was a sufficient basis for revocation, since the defendant's *subsequent conviction* in Essex County was a *matter of record*. For this reason, the court refused to allow 'protracted questioning' of the probation officer. The court noted that the judge had not limited the defendant's opportunity to call his own witnesses or to present evidence in mitigation of his probation violations. The court stated, "[w]e do not interpret *Gagnon* to mean that a judge is without discretion to limit or curtail irrelevant or redundant inquiries." *Id.*

The *Maggio* Court, 414 Mass. 193 (1993), similarly recognized that a criminal conviction, after trial or a guilty plea, establishes beyond a reasonable doubt based on evidence heard by the defendant which he has either contested or admitted. The court reasoned that because the probationer knows the evidence against him, and had the opportunity to contest it, his due process rights are adequately protected. *Id.* at 198 (citing *Rubera*, 371 Mass. at 181–82). As such, the court may limit defense counsel's cross-examination of an adverse witness when the basis of a revocation hearing is a subsequent criminal conviction.

b. The Court Must Apply Discretion in Determining the Probationer's Right to Confrontation

In *Durling*, 407 Mass. 108, the Supreme Judicial Court held the extent of a probationer's due process right to confrontation at a probation revocation hearing must be determined by the totality of the circumstances present in each case. The judge must balance the defendant's due process right to confront and cross-examine against the Commonwealth's reasons for not presenting witnesses. *Id.* at 119. The *Durling* Court held that in some cases, there will simply be no adequate alternative to live testimony, but in other cases, there will clearly be adequate alternatives and those alternatives are not prohibited by the due process clause. *Id.* As discussed *supra*, the *Durling* Court analyzed the facts of that particular case and concluded that the defendant was not denied due process even though his probation was revoked solely on the hearsay statements of two police officers, because the court determined that the particular hearsay at issue in that case contained sufficient indicia of reliability to satisfy due process. Therefore, the defendant was not denied due process even though he was not allowed to cross-examine the witnesses against him. *Id.* at 120–21.

c. The Judge Must Find Good Cause to Deny the Right to Confrontation at a Probation Revocation Hearing

In *Joubert*, 38 Mass. App. Ct. 943 (1995), the Appeals Court reversed the judge's order revoking probation because the judge had relied, at least partially, on hearsay statements without making any determination as to whether the hearsay was reliable, and therefore no determination was made that there was *good cause* to deny the defendant the right to confront a witness against him. *Id.* at 944.

d. Offenses Committed After the Probationary Period Cannot Be the Basis of a Revocation

In *Commonwealth v. Smith*, 38 Mass. App. Ct. 324 (1995), the Appeals Court held that revocation of probation based on convictions for offenses which were committed *after* the scheduled end of the probationary period could not, as a matter of due process, provide a basis for revocation. *Id.* at 326. "There can be no violation of probation unless committed during the probationary period, [although] probation may be revoked after that period." *Id.* (citing *Commonwealth v. Baillargeon*, 28 Mass. App. Ct. 16, 20 (1989)). In *Smith*, the probation surrender notice listed two alleged violations. The first was listed as "conditions." The Appeals Court understood this to mean that the probationer had not performed one hundred hours of community service as required by his order of probation. The second alleged violation stated "Subsequent convictions—Peabody, Lynn." 38 Mass. App. Ct. at 326. At the hearing, as to the first alleged violation, the probation officer testified that the defendant had failed to document his hours of community service performance. As to the second alleged violation, the probation officer produced *un*certified copies of three conviction records in Lynn and Peabody District Courts. *Id.* In addition, he mentioned two other convictions. The five convictions which the probation officer mentioned were all for offenses committed *after* the scheduled end of the probationary period. *Id.* Smith appealed.

e. Due Process Requires the Disclosure of Evidence, Opportunity to Confront By Explanation, Cross-Examination or Other Rebuttal, Unless the Court Finds Good Cause to Deny Such Right

After the defendant in *Smith* filed his brief in the Appeals Court, the Commonwealth filed a motion to clarify the record in the lower court. The judge allowed the motion, stating he had reviewed the defendant's criminal history during the revocation hearing. However, the Appeals Court held that it was clear from the transcript that there had been no mention during the hearing of the defendant's criminal history (other than the five convictions testified to by the probation officer) or of the judge's review thereof at the bench. 38 Mass. App. Ct. at 327. The allowance of the Commonwealth's motion to clarify could not "rescue the revocation." The only convictions introduced at the revocation hearing were for post-probationary offenses. Due process requires disclosure to the probationer of the evidence to be used against him and an opportunity to confront the evidence by explanation, cross-examination or other rebuttal. *Id.* "If the probationer is unaware of the evidence against him, then realistically he cannot defend himself." *Id.* (citing *Commonwealth v. Maggio*, 414 Mass. 193, 197 (1993)). While the Commonwealth may rely on a conviction without going into its factual basis, it must at least disclose to the probationer that it intends to rely on the conviction. The Smith Court held that the probationer should have had an opportunity to argue that the conviction did not warrant a revocation. Accordingly, the Appeals Court reversed the order revoking probation and imposing the one-year sentence. The court noted that the defendant had already served

8

the one-year sentence when the case was decided, but ordered that the reversal be entered on the docket. *Id.* at 328.

In *Commonwealth v. Kelsey*, 464 Mass. 315 (2013), the court decided the question "whether a defendant facing probation revocation due to an alleged new criminal offense is entitled to disclosure of the identity of an informant who was a participant in the alleged offense, the only nongovernment witness to the offense, and the only percipient witness to the entire alleged transaction." The court concluded "that, in such circumstances, disclosure may be appropriate, and that the judge erred in denying the defendant's motion on the ground that disclosure is never required in probation revocation proceedings." *Id.* at 316.

In *Commonwealth v. Hartfield*, 474 Mass. 474 (2016), the court recognized "that a probationer has a presumptive due process right to call witnesses in his or her defense, but that the presumption may be overcome by countervailing interests, generally that the proposed testimony is unnecessary to a fair adjudication of the alleged violation or unduly burdensome to the witness or the resources of the court. In determining whether the countervailing interests overcome the presumption after considering the totality of the circumstances, a judge should consider, at a minimum, the following factors: (1) whether the proposed testimony of the witness might be significant in determining whether it is more likely than not that the probationer violated the conditions of probation, *see Kelsey*, 464 Mass. at 322; (2) whether, based on the proffer of the witness's testimony, the witness would provide evidence that adds to or differs from previously admitted evidence rather than be cumulative of that evidence, *cf. Commonwealth v. Carroll*, 439 Mass. 547, 552–53 (2003); and (3) whether, based on an individualized assessment of the witness, there is an unacceptable risk that the witness's physical, psychological, or emotional health would be significantly jeopardized if the witness were required to testify in court at the probation hearing, *cf. Commonwealth v. Housewright*, 470 Mass. 665, 671 (2015). As to the third factor, we recognize the risk that an alleged sexual assault victim might suffer trauma from having to testify at a probation violation hearing. *See Durling*, 407 Mass. at 117 n.4; *Commonwealth v. Hill*, 52 Mass. App. Ct. 147, 153 (2001). But we reject a general rule that would prevent a probationer from ever calling such an alleged victim to testify in his or her defense. The assessment whether testifying will adversely affect the physical, psychological, or emotional health of an alleged sexual assault victim must be individualized and evidence-based. *See Durling*, 407 Mass. at 114 ('the requirements of due process depend on the circumstances of each case and an analysis of the various interests at stake')." *Hartfield*, 474 Mass. at 481.

2. DISTRICT ATTORNEY MAY ASSIST PROBATION OFFICER SO LONG AS ASSISTANCE DOES NOT INTERFERE WITH ROLE OF PROBATION DEPARTMENT

The district attorney may provide legal representation to the probation department at surrender hearings without interfering with the internal functions of the probation department. *Commonwealth v. Milton*, 427 Mass. 18, 23 (1998). In *Milton*, the defendant argued that the degree of participation by the assistant district attorney interfered with the internal functioning of the probation officer, when an assistant district attorney briefly addressed the court with respect to the de-

fendant's motion to dismiss and the defendant's alternative request for jail credit. *Id.* at 23. Once the defendant's motion to dismiss was denied, however, the probation officer conducted the entire probation surrender portion of the hearing on behalf of the probation department. *See id.* Thus, the assistant district attorney's participation in this hearing was merely to provide legal assistance and aided the probation officer in arguing substantial issues of law, rather than interfering with the duties of the probation officer. *Id.* Accordingly, the Supreme Judicial Court found that the appearance of the assistant district attorney at the defendant's probation surrender hearing did not violate art. 30 of the Massachusetts Declaration of Rights. *Id.*

3. RIGHT TO COUNSEL IN PROBATION REVOCATION HEARINGS

In *Commonwealth v. Patton*, 458 Mass. 119, 123 (2010), probationer argued ineffective assistance of counsel. The Supreme Judicial Court found that probationer was entitled to appointed counsel and effective assistance of counsel at his probation revocation hearing where the issues were complex and not capable of being presented or defended adequately by someone untrained in the law and the probability of imprisonment was high if a violation was found. *Id.* at 126, 129.

E. Necessity of Written Findings

1. AFTER THE JUDGE HAS RULED THAT THE PROBATIONER HAS VIOLATED HIS PROBATION, THE JUDGE MUST WRITE HIS FINDINGS AND STATE REASONS FOR REVOCATION

After the judge has ruled that the probationer has violated his probation, the judge must write his findings regarding the evidence upon which he relied and must provide the probationer with a statement of the judge's reasons for revoking probation. *Commonwealth v. MacDonald*, 53 Mass. App. Ct. 156, 160 (2001). This requirement, however, is "not an inflexible or invariably mandatory requirement and can be satisfied other ways." *Commonwealth v. Morse*, 50 Mass. App. Ct. at 593 (citing *Fay v. Commonwealth*, 379 Mass. 498, 504–05 (1980)); *Durling*, 407 Mass. at 113, 114 (transcription of revocation proceedings accurately reflecting the evidence relied on and reasons for revocation sufficient); *MacDonald*, 53 Mass. App. Ct. 156 (Although failure to make written findings regarding evidence upon which judge relied in revoking probation violated due process, the error was harmless beyond a reasonable doubt.).

In *Fay v. Commonwealth*, 379 Mass. 498 (1980), the petitioner was found guilty of contempt and her probation was revoked. In open court, and in the defendant's presence, the judge reviewed the evidence, stated his findings and his reasons for revoking her probation. Although he did not make written findings, a court stenographer recorded the findings and subsequently reduced them to writing in preparing a transcript. The defendant was given a copy of the transcript. Under these facts, the *Fay* Court held that the requirements of due process were satisfied. *Id.* at 505.

In *Commonwealth v. Marvin*, 417 Mass. 291 (1994), the Supreme Judicial Court held that it was *error for the judge to fail to make written findings of fact or to state his reasons* for his conclusions that the defendant violated the conditions of his probation. Unlike the facts in *Fay*, 379 Mass. 498, the defendant filed a request for findings and reasons, but no action was taken on the motion. On appeal however, the defendant did not challenge the judge's omissions. The court stated that the defendant could have argued that the judge erred in not making written findings of fact and in not setting forth his reasons for the revocation of probation. However, the court stated that the defendant's failure to press the point regarding his right to written findings and reasons therefor, led the court to conclude that it need not decide whether his due process rights were violated. *Marvin*, 417 Mass. at 293 n.1.

In *Commonwealth v. Morse*, 50 Mass. App. Ct. 582 (2000), discussed *supra*, the Appeals Court found that although the judge did not explicitly set forth the evidence he relied upon, the case was simple and straightforward and the entirety of the short transcript, (aside from Morse's discredited false alibi) was inculpatory evidence. *Morse*, 50 Mass. App. Ct. at 593. The *Morse* Court also found that the defendant "had actual knowledge of the evidence relied on and the reasons for revoking his probation." *Id.* at 593–94. Therefore, there was "no reasonable basis from which to claim unfair surprise or prejudice arising from the judge's reliance upon improper or inadequate evidence." *Id.* at 593. The record disclosed sufficient reliable evidence to warrant the judge's finding that the defendant violated his conditions of probation. *Id.* at 594. Accordingly, the court found the defendant had received "fair treatment." and that there was an accurate basis for determining that revocation was proper. "All that is [otherwise] required for revocation of probation is that the court be satisfied that the probationer has abused the opportunity given him to avoid incarceration." *Id.*

In *Commonwealth v. Michaels*, 39 Mass. App. Ct. 646 (1996), the Appeals Court held that the probation revocation hearing judge failed to make adequate written findings, since the only written findings he made referred to an alleged violation of probation in Somerville, the circumstances of which the Cambridge judge was not aware. The Appeals Court therefore vacated the order revoking probation. *Id.* at 649.

F. After Finding Defendant Violated Probation, Disposition Must Be Determined

Pursuant to the District Court Rules for Probation Violation Proceedings, a judge presiding over a revocation hearing must conduct a two-part inquiry. First, the judge must determine whether a violation of a condition of probation was committed. If a violation is found to have occurred, the judge must then determine an appropriate disposition. *Commonwealth v. Dubowski*, 58 Mass. App. Ct. 292 (2003). "A judge, after finding a defendant in violation of the conditions of his probation, must determine whether to 'revoke the probation and sentence the defendant or, if appropriate, modify the terms of his probation.'" If, after finding the defendant violated one or more conditions of probation, the judge determines that a term of incarceration should be imposed, the judge must impose the full original sentence pursuant to c. 279, § 3. The section provides no authority for the court to impose only a portion. *Commonwealth v. Holmgren*, 421 Mass. 224, 228 (1995).

1. RELIABLE BUT UNCHARGED EVIDENCE OF MISCONDUCT MAY BE CONSIDERED WITHOUT OFFENDING DUE PROCESS PRINCIPLES

In *Commonwealth v. Herrera*, 52 Mass. App. Ct. 294, 295 (2001), the defendant argued that the judge considered conduct imputed to him that was not mentioned in the proba-

tion surrender notice: in particular, that the judge reviewed a police report and restraining order detailing an incident in which the defendant allegedly slashed the tires on his former girlfriend's car. *Id.* at 294–95. On appeal, the court found that the defendant received proper notice and that the judge did not consider the tire-slashing incident until after he had found the defendant had violated his probation and was considering disposition. Likening the use of evidence of misconduct in the judge's discretionary determination of the disposition as a result of a probation violation to those matters where a judge can exercise discretion in considering such misconduct in sentencing a defendant after a finding of guilt, the Court affirmed the judge's order revoking the defendant's probation.

2. IN DETERMINING DISPOSITION AFTER A VIOLATION OF PROBATION HAS BEEN FOUND, THE JUDGE HAS DISCRETION TO CONSIDER A BROAD RANGE OF INFORMATION IN IMPOSING SENTENCE

Once a judge has determined the defendant has violated his or her probation, a wide range of information is available for consideration in imposing sentence. *Herrera*, 52 Mass. App. Ct. at 295. The judge may consider pending criminal charges, *Commonwealth v. LeBlanc*, 370 Mass. 217, 220 (1976); facts surrounding the commission of the crime, *Commonwealth v. Morse*, 402 Mass. 735, 740 (1988); past uncharged conduct, *Commonwealth v. Goodwin*, 414 Mass. 88, 92–93 (1993); the defendant's character, family life, and employment situation; and "indictments or evidence of similar or recurrent criminal conduct if it is relevant in assessing the defendant's character and propensity for rehabilitation," *Commonwealth v. Coleman*, 390 Mass. 797, 805 (1984).

Rule 8(d) of the District/Municipal Courts Rules for Probation Violation Proceedings (2015) enumerates seven factors that a judge may consider in arriving at a disposition, specifically: (1) the recommendation of the Probation Department, the probationer, and the District Attorney; (2) public safety; (3) the circumstances of any crime for which the probationer was placed on probation; (4) the nature of the probation violation; (5) the occurrence of any previous violations; and (6) the impact of the underlying crime on any person or community, as well as (7) any mitigating factors. *Id.*

G. Sentencing Issues upon Revocation of Probation

In *Commonwealth v. Bruzzese*, 437 Mass. 606 (2002), the Supreme Judicial Court addressed various sentencing options available to judges after a defendant's probation has been revoked on multiple charges, and specifically, how a concurrent sentencing scheme affects those options.

1. WHERE A JUDGE SENTENCES A DEFENDANT TO CONCURRENT SENTENCES ON MULTIPLE CHARGES AND PROBATION IS LATER REVOKED, THE JUDGE MAY NOT "UNBUNDLE" THE SENTENCING SCHEME BY COMMITTING THE PROBATIONER ON ONE COMPLAINT AND CONTINUING PROBATION ON ANOTHER

"When a judge orders sentences to be served concurrently, his order creates a sentencing scheme that establishes a relationship between, or among, the sentences. The concurrency order thus becomes part of the sentences themselves." *Bruzzese*, 437 Mass. at 613. "Because the concurrency order was part of the over-all sentence structure, it was subject to

8

the revise and revoke provisions of Mass. R. Crim. P. 29. As such, once the time expired within which the order could be revised or revoked, the concurrent sentencing scheme could not be changed." *Id.* at 614 (citing *Commonwealth v. Layne,* 386 Mass. 291, 294–95 (1982)). When, the judge revoked probation, after the time under Rule 29 had expired, the judge had no choice but to order execution of all four. *Id.* (citing *Holmgren,* 421 Mass. at 228). The judge could not order the defendant to serve the suspended portion of the sentence on three complaints and extended probation on the fourth. *See id.*

2. WHEN TWO OR MORE SENTENCES ARE TO BE SERVED CONCURRENTLY, THE SHORTER ONES ARE CONSIDERED TO BE 'ABSORBED' WITHIN THE LONGER SENTENCE

When a judge imposes concurrent sentences, "the shorter ones are considered to be 'absorbed' within the longer sentence." *Bruzzese,* 437 Mass. at 613 (quoting *Carlino v. Commissioner of Corr.,* 355 Mass. 159, 161 (1969)). The order of concurrent sentences creates a sentencing scheme that establishes a relationship between, or among, the sentences. The concurrency order thus becomes part of the sentences themselves. In *Bruzzese* it established that the defendant would serve no more than two and one-half years on all four complaints. *Id.*

"When the judge revoked Bruzzese's probation on the fourth complaint . . . Bruzzese had served two and one-half years on the first three complaints. Because the original concurrency order contemplated a maximum punishment of two and one-half years on all four complaints, the order that Bruzzese serve another year on the fourth complaint resulted in his serving three and one-half years on the four complaints. That order violated principles of double jeopardy because it required him to serve multiple punishments for the same offense." *Id.* at 614.

3. "STRAIGHT PROBATION:" CONCURRENT TERMS ON MULTIPLE CHARGES; ORIGINAL ORDERS FOR CONCURRENT TERMS OF STRAIGHT PROBATION DO NOT CREATE A SENTENCING SCHEME THAT FORECLOSES IMPOSITION OF CONSECUTIVE SENTENCES AFTER A REVOCATION

a. Where a judge has placed a defendant on straight probation on multiple charges, if the defendant is subsequently found to have violated the terms of probation, the judge may impose a term of incarceration on one charge and continue probation on the other charge(s).

b. Original orders for concurrent terms of straight probation did not create a sentencing scheme that foreclosed imposition of consecutive sentences after probation revocation.

c. A judge, upon a revocation of probation based on multiple charges, may continue probation on one or more of the charges and may impose a term of incarceration on one of the other charge(s).

d. A period of straight probation is not a sentence, therefore, concurrent terms of straight probation are not concurrent sentences that have been bundled together under a concurrent sentencing scheme for double jeopardy purposes.

e. Imposition of concurrent terms of straight probation does not create a reasonable expectation as to the type of sen-

tence or sentences a defendant might receive if his probation is revoked. *See Bruzzese,* 437 Mass. at 617–18.

4. PROBATION UPON RESENTENCING

"We conclude that, where a defendant sentenced to committed time on a conviction is resentenced to a term of probation, the new sentence violates double jeopardy where the defendant already has completed the original sentence on that conviction before the resentencing. But where the defendant has yet to complete the original sentence on a conviction, resentencing to a term of probation does not violate double jeopardy, provided that the total length of incarceration imposed on the defendant for that conviction is not increased. Consequently, if the defendant's probation were to be revoked, the defendant may not be sentenced to a term of incarceration longer than the time remaining on his original uncompleted sentence." *Commonwealth v. Sallop,* 472 Mass. 568, 572–69 (2015).

H. Appeal of Probation Revocation Proceeding

a. Direct appeal of a probation revocation proceeding is available to both the defendant and the Commonwealth. *Commonwealth v. Negron,* 441 Mass. 685, 686 (2004). The defendant can appeal any probation revocation order. *Commonwealth v. Woods,* 427 Mass. at 169 (1998); *Commonwealth v. Christian,* 429 Mass. 1022, 1023 (1999). In order to appeal, the defendant must file a notice of appeal within thirty days of the imposition of the previously suspended sentence. *Christian,* 429 Mass. at 1023 (citing *Commonwealth v. White,* 429 Mass. 258, 262 (1999)). *See Commonwealth v. Abreu,* 66 Mass. App. Ct. 795 (2006). The defendant may not use Rule 30(a) of the Massachusetts Rules of Criminal Procedure as an avenue to review his/her probation revocation order. *Christian,* 429 Mass. at 1023. Rule 30(a) is an appropriate avenue for relief only where the defendant is not challenging the probation revocation itself, but rather the sentence imposed in consequence of the order. *Id.*

b. Mootness. An appeal will be moot if the defendant pleads guilty to the crime on which the revocation was based and his claim of error pertains to the judge's factual findings that the defendant violated his probation. *Commonwealth v. Milot,* 462 Mass. 197, 201–02 (2012). Subsequent convictions, however, do not render moot a claim "that some aspect of the proceeding violated the probationer's constitutional rights, potentially impacting the second phase of the judge's probation determination, that pertaining to the disposition of the matter." *Commonwealth v. Pena,* 462 Mass. 183, 187–88 (2012).

V. Conclusion

The Massachusetts statutes providing for the imposition of probation provide the court with the authority to impose a wide range of conditions on probation. These conditions may include such items as a requirement that the probationer perform a certain amount of community service, as provided by statute. However, the court is not limited to conditions provided by statute, and may impose any condition which is reasonably related to the offense for which the probationer is on probation.

Conditions of probation, as well as the notice to the probationer that he has allegedly violated his probation, must be in writing, and must be clear, understandable, and doable.

Restitution is a valid condition of probation. The court must hold a restitution hearing in which the defendant is permitted to challenge the victim's claim of loss, in determining the amount of restitution to impose.

The length of a probationary sentence is not limited by statute, and Massachusetts courts have the authority to extend or revoke probation within a reasonable time after expiration of the stated probationary term. Reasonableness must be determined on a case-by-case basis.

Although a probationer is not entitled to the full panoply of constitutional protections concerning revocation, he must be given: written notice; disclosure of evidence against him; an opportunity to be heard, to present witnesses and documentary evidence in his favor; to confront and cross-examine adverse witnesses, *unless the court specifically finds good cause to deny this right*; a neutral body to hear the revocation matter; and a written statement as to the evidence relied on and the reasons for the revocation.

The burden of proof which the Commonwealth bears to revoke probation is preponderance of the evidence. Hearsay is admissible in a probation revocation hearing as long as the court finds it contains indicia of reliability. When hearsay serves as the sole basis for revocation, the court must find substantial indicia of reliability.

Probation may be revoked on the basis of untried, subsequent crimes. However, the bare fact that an indictment has been returned against the probationer for a subsequent crime is insufficient to revoke probation. The court may properly revoke probation based on the conviction of a subsequent crime.

The court should always enter written findings whenever it determines that probation should be revoked, setting forth the evidence relied on and the court's reasons for the revocation.

8

8

PART 9

Elements and Penalties of Selected Crimes

Abbreviations

CWOF	continued without a finding
HC	House of Corrections
NLT	not less than
NMT	not more than

ARMED ASSAULT IN A DWELLING HOUSE— G.L. c. 265, § 18A

(see also Burglary, Armed or Making an Assault—G.L. c. 266, § 14)

Elements

Whoever
- armed with a dangerous weapon
- enters a dwelling house
- while therein assaults another
- with intent to commit a felony.

Penalty

Life or any term of yrs. NLT 10 yrs. No person imprisoned under this section shall be eligible for parole in less than 5 yrs. If armed with a firearm, shotgun, rifle, or assault weapon, NLT 10 yrs. state prison. Not parole eligible until expiration of 10 yrs.

ARMED ROBBERY—see Robbery (Armed)

ARSON (BUILDING)—G.L. c. 266, § 2

Elements

Whoever
- wilfully and maliciously
- sets fire to, burns, or causes to be burned, or
- aids, counsels or procures the burning of
- a meeting house, church, court house, town house, college, academy, jail or other building which has been erected for public use, or
- a banking house, warehouse, store, manufactory, mill, barn, stable, shop, outhouse or other building or
- an office building, lumber yard, ship, vessel, street car or railway car, or
- a bridge, lock, dam, flume, tank, or
- any building or structure or contents thereof, not included or described in the preceding section.

Penalty

NMT 10 yrs. state prison or NMT 2½ yrs. jail or HC.

NOTE 1   Immaterial whether property is owned by defendant or another.

NOTE 2   Immaterial whether property is occupied or unoccupied.

ARSON (DWELLING)—G.L. c. 266, § 1

Elements

Whoever
- wilfully and maliciously
- sets fire to, burns or causes to be burned, or
- aids, counsels or procures the burning of
- a dwelling house, or
- building adjoining or adjacent to a dwelling house, or

- building by the burning whereof a dwelling house is burned.

Penalty

NMT 20 yrs. state prison or NMT 2½ yrs. jail or HC or fine NMT $10,000, or by fine and imprisonment.

NOTE 1   Immaterial whether property is owned by defendant or another.

NOTE 2   Immaterial whether property is occupied or unoccupied.

NOTE 3   "Dwelling house"—shall mean and include all buildings used as dwellings, such as apartment houses, tenement houses, hotels, boarding houses, dormitories, hospitals, institutions, sanatoria, or other buildings where persons are domiciled. G.L. c. 266, § 1.

ASSAULT—G.L. c. 265, § 13A

Penalty

2½ yrs. HC or fine NMT $1,000.

NOTE 1   If assault causes serious bodily injury, or is committed against someone who is pregnant, or against someone who has a vacate, restraining, or no contact order or judgment against the accused, NMT 2½ yrs. HC or NMT 5 yrs. state prison, and/or fine NMT $5,000.

NOTE 2   "Serious bodily injury" shall mean bodily injury that results in a permanent disfigurement, loss or impairment of a bodily function, limb or organ, or a substantial risk of death.

ASSAULT BY MEANS OF A DANGEROUS WEAPON—G.L. c. 265, § 15B

Elements

(a) Whoever
- by means of a dangerous weapon
- commits an assault
- upon a person 60 years or older.

Penalty

NMT 5 yrs. state prison or fine NMT $1,000 or NMT 2½ yrs. jail. Second or subsequent offense—NLT 2 yrs. (mandatory 1 yr. to be served). Conviction under Section 15A (ABDW) or Section 18(a) (assault with intent to rob) count as a prior conviction for purposes of prosecution and sentencing.

Elements

(b) Whoever
- by means of a dangerous weapon
- commits an assault upon another.

Penalty

NMT 5 yrs. state prison or fine NMT $1,000 or NMT 2½ yrs. jail.

ASSAULT ON A CHILD UNDER 16 WITH INTENT TO COMMIT RAPE—G.L. c. 265, § 24B

Elements

Whoever
- assaults a child under 16
- with intent to commit rape as defined in G.L. c. 277, § 39 ("Sexual intercourse or unnatural sexual intercourse by a person with another person who is com-

9

pelled to submit by force and against his will or by threat of bodily injury, or sexual intercourse or unnatural sexual intercourse with a child under sixteen years of age.")

Penalty

Life or any term of years in state prison. Second or subsequent offense by 18 year old or older—life or any term of years in state prison but NLT 5 years. If armed with a firearm, shotgun, rifle, machine gun or assault weapon, 1st offense—life or for any term of years, but NLT 10 yrs. state prison, second or subsequent offense (if over 18 yrs. of age)—life or for any term of years, but NLT 15 yrs. state prison.

NOTE 1   **Sex Offender Registry.** *See* G.L. c. 6, §§ 178C–178Q.

NOTE 2   **Lifetime Parole.** *See* G.L. c. 265, § 45; G.L. c. 275, § 18.

NOTE 3   **Sexually Dangerous Person Commitment.** *See* G.L. c. 123A, §§ 1–15.

ASSAULT WITH INTENT TO COMMIT A FELONY—G.L. c. 265, § 29

Elements

Whoever
- assaults another
- with intent to commit a felony.

Penalty

If not herein before provided: NMT 10 yrs. state prison or fine NMT $1,000 and imprisonment in jail NMT 2½ yrs.

ASSAULT WITH INTENT TO COMMIT RAPE—G.L. c. 265, § 24

Elements

Whoever
- assaults another person
- with intent to commit rape.

Penalty

NMT 20 yrs. in state prison or NMT 2½ yrs. jail or HC. Second or subsequent offense—life or any term of yrs. in state prison; 2/3 of aggregate of minimum sentences must be served. If armed with a firearm, shotgun, rifle, machine gun or assault weapon, 1st offense—NLT 5 yrs. state prison, second or subsequent offense—life or for any term of years, but NLT 20 yrs. state prison.

NOTE 1   **Sex Offender Registry.** *See* G.L. c. 6, §§ 178C–178Q.

NOTE 2   **Lifetime Parole.** *See* G.L. c. 265, § 45; G.L. c. 275, § 18.

NOTE 3   **Sexually Dangerous Person Commitment.** *See* G.L. c. 123A, §§ 1–15.

ASSAULT WITH INTENT TO MURDER, MAIM, ETC.—G.L. c. 265, § 15

Elements

Whoever
- assaults another
- with intent to commit murder or to maim or disfigure his person (as described in G.L. c. 265, § 14, mayhem).

Penalty

NMT 10 yrs. state prison or fine NMT $1,000 and NMT 2½ yrs. jail.

ASSAULT WITH INTENT TO ROB OR MURDER (ARMED)—G.L. c. 265, § 18

Elements

(a) Whoever
- being armed with a dangerous weapon
- assaults a person
- 60 yrs. or older
- with intent to rob or murder.

Penalty

NMT 20 yrs. state prison. Second or subsequent offense—NLT 2 yrs. (mandatory). If armed with a firearm, shotgun, rifle, machine gun or assault weapon, 1st offense—NLT 10 yrs. state prison, second or subsequent offense—NLT 20 yrs. state prison.

Elements

(b) Whoever
- being armed with a dangerous weapon
- assaults another
- with intent to rob or murder.

Penalty

NMT 20 yrs. state prison. If armed with a firearm, shotgun, rifle, machine gun or assault weapon, NLT 5 yrs. state prison, NMT 20 yrs. state prison.

ASSAULT WITH INTENT TO ROB (UNARMED)—G.L. c. 265, § 20

Elements

Whoever
- not armed with a dangerous weapon
- assaults another
- with force or violence
- with intent to rob or steal.

Penalty

NMT 10 yrs. state prison.

ASSAULT AND BATTERY—G.L. c. 265, § 13A

Penalty

NMT 2½ yrs. HC or fine NMT $1,000.

NOTE 1   If A & B causes serious bodily injury, or is committed against someone who is pregnant, or against someone who has a vacate, restraining, or no contact order or judgment against the accused, NMT 2½ yrs. HC or NMT 5 yrs. state prison, and/or fine NMT $5,000.

NOTE 2   "Serious bodily injury" shall mean bodily injury that results in a permanent disfigurement, loss or impairment of a bodily function, limb or organ, or a substantial risk of death.

NOTE 3   If A & B is on a person with an intellectual disability, see G.L. c. 265, § 13F, wherein penalty is NMT 2½ yrs. HC or NMT 5 yrs. state prison (first offense); Second and subsequent offense: NMT 10 yrs. state prison.

NOTE 4   If A & B is on an elderly or disabled person, see G.L. c. 265, § 13K, wherein penalty is NMT 2½ yrs. HC or NMT 3 yrs. state prison, or fine NMT $1,000; if causing bodily injury, 2½ yrs. HC or NMT 5 yrs. state prison or fine NMT $1,000; if causing serious bodily injury, 2½ yrs. HC or NMT 10 yrs. state prison or fine NMT $5,000.

NOTE 5   If A & B is upon a child (defined as someone under age 14), see G.L. c. 265, § 13J.

ASSAULT AND BATTERY UPON A PUBLIC EMPLOYEE—G.L. c. 265, § 13D

Elements:

- assault
- battery
- upon any public employee

9

- engaged in performance of his duties.

Penalty

NLT 90 days, NMT 2½ yrs. HC or fine NLT $500, NMT $5,000.

NOTE   See also G.L. c. 127, § 38B, assault and battery upon a correctional facility employee.

ASSAULT ON AN EMT, ETC.—G.L. c. 265, § 13I

Elements

- assault
- or assault and battery
- on EMT, ambulance operator/attendant, or health care provider
- while said EMT, ambulance operator/attendant, or health care provider is treating or transporting a person in line of duty.

Penalty

NLT 90 days; NMT 2½ yrs. HC; and/or fine NLT $500, NMT $5,000.

ASSAULT AND BATTERY UPON AN ELDERLY OR DISABLED PERSON—G.L. c. 265, § 13K

Elements

- assault
- battery
- upon an elder or person with a disability.

Penalty

NMT 3 yrs. state prison or fine NMT $1,000; NMT 2½ yrs. HC.

NOTE 1   If causing bodily injury, NMT 5 yrs. state prison; NMT 2½ yrs. HC; and/or fine NMT $1,000.

NOTE 2   If causing serious bodily injury, NMT 10 yrs. state prison; NMT 2½ yrs. HC and/or fine NMT $5,000.

NOTE 3   If wantonly or recklessly permitting bodily injury or permitting another to cause bodily injury, NMT 5 yrs. state prison, NMT 2½ yrs. HOC, and/or fine NMT $5,000; serious bodily injury, NMT 10 yrs. state prison, NMT 2½ HOC; and/or fine NMT $1,000.

NOTE 4   "Person with disability," shall mean "a person with a permanent or long-term physical or mental impairment that prevents or restricts the individual's ability to provide for his or her own care or protection." An "elder" means a person age 60 or older.

ASSAULT AND BATTERY ON A FAMILY OR HOUSEHOLD MEMBER—G.L. c. 265, § 13M

(Added by 2009 Mass. Acts c. 534, effective Jan. 16, 2009.)

Elements:

- assault
- battery
- upon a family or household member

Penalty

Second or Subsequent Offense: NMT 2½ yrs HC or NMT 5 yrs. state prison.

NOTE 1   "[F]amily or household member shall be limited to persons who: (a) are married to each other or were married to each other within the 5 years preceding the date of the alleged offense; (b) are residing together in the same household or were residing together in the same household within the 5 years preceding the date of the alleged offense; (c) are related by blood; (d) have a child in common; or (e) are or have been in a substantive dating or engagement relationship within the 5 years preceding the date of the alleged offense; provided, however, that in determining that relationship, the court shall consider the following factors: (1) the length of time of the relationship; (2) the type of relationship;

(3) the frequency of interaction between the parties; and (4) if the relationship has been terminated by either person, the length of time that has elapsed since the termination of the relationship."

ASSAULT AND BATTERY BY MEANS OF A DANGEROUS WEAPON—G.L. c. 265, § 15A

Elements (a)

- assault
- battery
- upon a person 60 yrs. or older
- by means of a dangerous weapon.

Penalty

NMT 10 yrs. state prison or fine NMT $1,000 or NMT 2½ yrs. jail. Second offense—NLT 2 yrs. (mandatory).

Elements (b)

- assault
- battery
- by means of a dangerous weapon.

Penalty

NMT 10 yrs. state prison or fine NMT $5,000 or NMT 2½ yrs. jail.

Elements (c)

- assault and battery
- causing serious bodily injury
- committed against someone who is pregnant or
- committed against someone who has a vacate, restraining, or no contact order or judgment against the accused or
- is committed by a person 17 years of age or older, against a child under the age of 14

Penalty

NMT 2½ yrs. HC or NMT 15 yrs. state prison or fine NMT $10,000.

NOTE 1   "Serious bodily injury" shall mean bodily injury that results in a permanent disfigurement, loss or impairment of a bodily function, limb or organ, or a substantial risk of death.

ATTEMPTED EXTORTION—G.L. c. 265, § 25

Elements

Whoever

- verbally, or
- by a written or printed communication
- maliciously
- threatens to accuse another of a crime or offense, or
- threatens an injury to the person or property of another
- with intent to extort money or any pecuniary advantage, or
- with intent to compel any person to do any act against his will.

Or

- Any police officer or one having such powers, or
- any officer or employee of any licensing authority
- verbally or by written or printed communication
- maliciously
- and unlawfully
- with intent to extort money or any pecuniary advantage, or
- with intent to compel any person to do any act against his will.

Penalty

NMT 15 yrs. state prison or NMT 2½ yrs. HC or fine NMT $5,000, or both.

9

AUTOMOBILE THEFT—see Motor Vehicle Theft

BEING PRESENT WHERE HEROIN IS KEPT—G.L. c. 94C, § 35

Elements:
- knowingly present
- at a place where heroin is kept or deposited, or
- in the company of a person
- knowing that person to be in the possession of heroin.

Penalty

NMT 1 yr. and/or fine NMT $1,000. If defendant is a 1st time drug offender, he may, after the successful completion of a probationary period have the charge dismissed and the records sealed.

Special additional fine: NLT $35, NMT $100 if defendant eighteen or older and convicted or sufficient facts. If multiple offenses from single incident, total fine NMT $500. Fine may be reduced or waived if under hardship. G.L. c. 280, § 6B.

BREAKING AND ENTERING (BUILDING, SHIP, VESSEL OR VEHICLE) (DAYTIME) (OCCUPIED)—G.L. c. 266, § 17

Elements
Whoever
- breaks
- enters
- daytime
- building, ship, vessel or vehicle
- with intent to commit a felony
- the owner or any other person lawfully there being put in fear.

Penalty

NMT 10 yrs. state prison. If armed with a firearm, shotgun, rifle, machine gun or assault weapon, 1st offense—NLT 5 yrs. state prison or NMT 2½ yrs. HC.

BREAKING AND ENTERING (BUILDING, SHIP, MOTOR VEHICLE OR VESSEL) (DAYTIME) (UNOCCUPIED)—G.L. c. 266, § 18

Elements
Whoever
- breaks
- enters
- daytime
- building, ship or motor vehicle or vessel
- with intent to commit a felony
- no person lawfully therein being put in fear.

Penalty

NMT 10 yrs. state prison or fine NMT $500 and NMT 2 yrs. jail. If armed with a firearm, shotgun, rifle, machine gun or assault weapon, 1st offense—NLT 5 yrs. state prison or NMT 2½ yrs. HC.

BREAKING AND ENTERING (BUILDING, SHIP, ETC.) (NIGHTTIME) WITH INTENT TO COMMIT A FELONY—G.L. c. 266, § 16

Elements:
- nighttime
- breaks
- enters
- building, ship or vessel
- with intent to commit a felony.

Penalty

NMT 20 yrs. state prison or NMT 2½ yrs. jail or HC.

NOTE   Nighttime—the time between 1 hr. after sunset on one day and 1 hr. before sunrise on the next day—G.L. c. 278, § 10.

BREAKING AND ENTERING (BUILDING, SHIP, VESSEL OR VEHICLE) WITH INTENT TO COMMIT A MISDEMEANOR—G.L. c. 266, § 16A

Elements:
- breaks
- enters
- building, ship, vessel or vehicle
- with intent to commit a misdemeanor.

Penalty

NMT 6 mos. imprisonment and/or fine NMT $200.

BURGLARY, ARMED OR MAKING AN ASSAULT—G.L. c. 266, § 14

(see also Armed Assault in a Dwelling House—G.L. c. 265, § 18A; Home Invasion—G.L. c. 265, § 18C)

Elements
Whoever
- breaks
- enters
- dwelling house
- nighttime
- with intent to commit a felony

or
- after having entered
- with intent to commit a felony
- breaks
- dwelling house
- nighttime
- any person then lawfully therein

and
- offender armed with a dangerous weapon
- at the time of such breaking or entry, or
- arming himself with a dangerous weapon in such house, or
- making an actual assault on a person lawfully therein.

Penalty

Life or any term NLT 10 yrs. state prison. Second and subsequent offenses: mandatory. If armed with a firearm, shotgun, rifle, machine gun or assault weapon, 1st offense—life or for any term of years, but NLT 15 yrs. state prison, subsequent offense—life or for any term of years, but NLT 20 yrs. state prison.

NOTE   Nighttime—the time between 1 hr. after sunset on one day and 1 hr. before sunrise on the next day. G.L. c. 278, § 10.

BURGLARY (UNARMED)—G.L. c. 266, § 15

Elements
Whoever
- breaks
- enters
- dwelling house
- nighttime
- with intent to commit a felony

or
- having entered
- with intent to commit a felony
- breaks
- dwelling house

- nighttime
- offender not armed nor arming himself in such house with a dangerous weapon nor making an assault upon a person lawfully therein.

Penalty

NMT 20 yrs. state prison. Second offense—NLT 5 yrs.

NOTE   Nighttime—the time between 1 hr. after sunset on one day and 1 hr. before sunrise on the next day. G.L. c. 278, § 10.

CARJACKING—G.L. c. 265, § 21A

Elements

Whoever

- with intent to steal a motor vehicle
- assaults, confines, maims or puts any person in fear
- for the purpose of stealing a motor vehicle.

Penalty

NMT 15 yrs. state prison or NMT 2½ yrs. jail/HC and fine NLT $1,000, NMT $15,000

If armed with a dangerous weapon, NMT 20 yrs. state prison or NLT 1 yr., NMT 2½ yrs. jail/HC and fine NLT $5,000, NMT $15,000. If armed with a firearm, shotgun, rifle, machine gun or assault weapon, NLT 5 yrs. state prison.

NOTE   Immaterial whether suspect succeeds or fails in the perpetration of stealing the motor vehicle.

CAR THEFT—see Motor Vehicle Theft

CARRYING A FIREARM—see Unlawfully Carrying a Firearm

DERIVING SUPPORT FROM THE EARNINGS OF A PROSTITUTE—G.L. c. 272, § 7

Elements

Whoever

- knowing a person to be a prostitute
- lives or derives support or maintenance, in whole or in part,
- from the earnings or proceeds of that person's prostitution or
- from moneys loaned, advanced to or charged against him by any keeper or manager or inmate of a house or other place where prostitution is practiced or allowed, or
- shares in such earnings, proceeds or moneys.

Penalty

5 yrs. state prison and fine of $5,000; 2 yr. mandatory minimum; CWOF and file prohibited; District Court has jurisdiction and may impose a penalty of from 2–5 yrs. (and a fine) to any correctional institution except MCI–Walpole.

DESTRUCTION OF PROPERTY—see Willful and Malicious Destruction of Property

DISCLOSURE OF IDENTITY OR LOCATION OF WITNESS—G.L. c. 263A, § 13(b)

Elements

Whoever

- without the express written authorization of the prosecuting officer
- knowingly discloses any information
- received from the prosecuting officer or generated in connection with witness protection services and which poses a risk of harm
  a. to a program participant
  b. of disclosure of any person's participation in such program
  c. or of jeopardizing the objectives of the program.

Penalty

NMT 2½ years HC and/or by a fine of not more than $5,000.

NOTE   This section is not applicable to any members of the witness protection board; members of the attorney general's office; members of the district attorneys' offices; law enforcement; or agents thereof, acting in the lawful discharge of their duties.

DISORDERLY PERSON—G.L. c. 272, § 53

Elements

Whoever

- with purpose to cause public inconvenience, annoyance, or alarm, or
- recklessly creates a risk thereof
- engages in fighting or threatening, violent or tumultuous behavior, or
- creates a hazardous or physically offensive condition by any act which serves no legitimate purpose.

Penalty

NMT 6 mos. HC or jail and/or fine NMT $200. First offense for disorderly persons or disturbers of the peace: fine NMT $150; second or subsequent offense: NMT 6 mos. HC or jail and/or fine NMT $200.

ENTERING WITHOUT BREAKING (BUILDING, SHIP, VESSEL OR VEHICLE) (NIGHTTIME) (OCCUPIED)—G.L. c. 266, § 17

Elements

Whoever

- nighttime
- enters without breaking
- building, ship, vessel or vehicle
- with intent to commit a felony
- the owner or any other person lawfully therein being put in fear.

Penalty

NMT 10 yrs. state prison. If offense committed while armed with a firearm, rifle, shotgun, machine gun or assault weapon, NLT 5 yrs. state prison or NMT 2½ yrs. HC.

NOTE   Nighttime—the time between 1 hr. after sunset on one day and 1 hr. before sunrise on the next day. G.L. c. 278, § 10.

ENTERING WITHOUT BREAKING (DWELLING) (NIGHTTIME) (UNOCCUPIED)—G.L. c. 266, § 18

Elements

Whoever

- nighttime
- enters without breaking
- dwelling house
- with intent to commit a felony
- no person lawfully therein being put in fear.

Penalty

NMT 10 yrs. state prison or fine NMT $500 and NMT 2 yrs. HC. If offense committed while armed with a firearm, rifle, shotgun, machine gun, or assault weapon, NLT 5 yrs. state prison or NMT 2½ yrs. HC.

NOTE   Nighttime—the time between 1 hr. after sunset on one day and 1 hr. before sunrise on the next day. G.L. c. 278, § 10.

9

ENTICEMENT OF CHILD UNDER 18 TO ENGAGE IN PROSTITUTION, HUMAN TRAFFICKING OR COMMERCIAL SEXUAL ACTIVITY— G.L. c. 265, § 26D

Elements

Whoever
- by electronic communication
- knowingly
- entices a child under 18
- to engage in prostitution in violation of c. 272, §§ 50 or 53A, or
- human trafficking in violation of c. 265, §§ 50, 51, 52 or 53, or
- commercial sexual activity in violation of c. 265, § 49, or
- attempts to do so.

Penalty

NMT than 2½ years HC or NMT than 5 years state prison and/or fine NLT $2,500. Second or subsequent offense: NLT 5 years state prison (mandatory) and fine NLT $10,000; no eligibility for probation, parole, work release, or deduction for good conduct until 5 years served.

ESCAPE—G.L. c. 268, § 16

Elements

- Prisoner of any penal institution including a prisoner who is held in custody for a court appearance, or
- a person committed under the provisions of G.L. c. 123A, §§ 5 or 6 to a treatment center or branch thereof described in G.L. c. 123A, §§ 2 and 4, or
- a prisoner committed to any jail or correctional institution under a lawful court order
- who escapes or attempts to escape
  - from any such institution or land appurtenant thereto, or
  - from any courthouse or from land appurtenant thereto, or
  - from the custody of any officer thereof while being conveyed to or from said institution, center or branch, or
- knowingly disables or attempts to disable or defeat electronic monitoring of the prisoner, or
- fails to return from temporary release granted under G.L. c. 127, § 90A, or
- fails to return from any temporary release from said institution, center or branch.

Penalty

NMT 10 yrs. state prison or NMT 2½ yrs. HC or jail.

NOTE   Purposes of temporary release under G.L. c. 127, § 90A, include (a) to attend the funeral of a relative; (b) to visit a critically ill relative; (c) to obtain medical, psychiatric, psychological or other social services when adequate services are not available at the facility and cannot be obtained by temporary placement in a hospital; (d) to contact prospective employers; (e) to secure a suitable residence for use upon release on parole or discharge; (f) for any reason consistent with the reintegration of a committed offender into the community.

ESCAPE FROM JAIL—G.L. c. 268, § 15A

Elements

Whoever
- after lawfully being placed in custody in a jail of a city or town

- escapes.

Penalty

NMT 2½ years jail or HC and/or fine NMT $500.

EXTORTION—see Attempted Extortion

FAILURE TO STOP AFTER CAUSING PERSONAL INJURY—G.L. c. 90, § 24(2)(a½)(1)

Elements

Whoever
- operates
- a motor vehicle
- upon any way or in any place to which the public has a right of access, or
- upon any way or in any place to which members of the public have access as invitees or licensees
- without stopping and making known his name, residence and motor vehicle registration number
- goes away
- after knowingly colliding with or otherwise causing injury to any person.

Penalty

Imprisonment NLT 6 mos. NMT 2 yrs. and fine NLT $500, NMT $1,000.

NOTE 1   If death results, penalty is NLT 2½ yrs. state prison, NMT 10 yrs. and fine NLT $1,000, NMT $5,000 or NLT 1 yr., NMT 2½ yrs. HC or jail and fine NLT $1,000, NMT $5,000. One year mandatory minimum. G.L. c. 90, § 24(2)(a½)(2).

NOTE 2   A conviction under this section will also result in the revocation of the defendant's license or right to operate by the Registry of Motor Vehicles. G.L. c. 90, § 24(2)(b)–(c).

NOTE 3   See G.L. c. 90, § 24P for certain license suspensions for defendants under the ages of 21 or 18.

FAILURE TO STOP AFTER CAUSING PROPERTY DAMAGE—G.L. c. 90, § 24(2)(a)

Elements

Whoever
- operates
- a motor vehicle
- upon any way or in any place to which the public has a right of access, or
- upon any way or in any place to which members of the public have access as invitees or licensees
- without stopping and making known his name, residence and motor vehicle registration number
- goes away
- after knowingly colliding with or otherwise causing injury to any other vehicle or property.

Penalty

Fine NLT $20; NMT $200; and/or imprisonment NLT 2 weeks; NMT 2 yrs.

NOTE 1   A conviction under this section will also result in the revocation of the defendant's license or right to operate by the Registry of Motor Vehicles. G.L. c. 90, § 24(2)(b)–(c).

NOTE 2   See G.L. c. 90, § 24P for certain license suspensions for defendants under the ages of 21 or 18.

FALSE REPRESENTATIONS TO PROCURE WELFARE—G.L. c. 18, § 5B

Elements

- any person or institution
- knowingly makes a false representation, or

- contrary to a legal duty to do so, knowingly fails to disclose any material fact affecting eligibility or level of benefits
- to department of public welfare or its agents
- for the purpose of causing any person, including the person making such representations, to be supported in whole or in part by the commonwealth or
- for the purpose of procuring a payment under any assistance program administered by the department.

Penalty

Fine NLT $200, NMT $500 or imprisonment NMT 1 yr.; payments wrongfully received returned to Commonwealth (G.L. c. 18, § 5E).

NOTE   The Department of Public Welfare is now called the Department of Transitional Assistance.

FORGERY AND COUNTERFEITING CERTIFICATE AND OTHER WRITINGS—G.L. c. 267, § 1

Elements

Whoever
- with intent to injure or defraud
- falsely makes, alters, forges or counterfeits
- an instrument described in this section.

Penalty

NMT 10 yrs. state prison or NMT 2 yrs. jail.

NOTE   "Forgery"—The false making, altering, forging or counterfeiting of any instrument described in section one of chapter two hundred and sixty-seven, or any instrument which, if genuine, would be a foundation for or release of liability of the apparent maker. G.L. c. 277, § 39.

GOING AWAY CAUSING PERSONAL INJURY— see Failure to Stop After Causing Personal Injury

GOING AWAY AFTER CAUSING PROPERTY DAMAGE—see Failure to Stop After Causing Property Damage

HOMICIDE—see Murder or Manslaughter

HOMICIDE BY MOTOR VEHICLE—see Vehicular Homicide

INDECENT ASSAULT AND BATTERY ON A CHILD UNDER 14—G.L. c. 265, § 13B

Elements
- indecent
- assault
- battery
- child under the age of 14.

Penalty

NMT 10 yrs. state prison or NMT 2½ yrs. HC. A prosecution commenced under this section shall neither be placed on file nor CWOF.

NOTE 1   **Sex Offender Registry.** See G.L. c. 6, §§ 178C–178Q.

NOTE 2   **Lifetime Parole.** See G.L. c. 265, § 45; G.L. c. 275, § 18.

NOTE 3   **Sexually Dangerous Person Commitment.** See G.L. c. 123A, §§ 1–15.

AGGRAVATED INDECENT ASSAULT AND BATTERY ON A CHILD UNDER 14— G.L. c. 265, § 13B½

Elements
- indecent
- assault
- battery
- child under the age of 14
- during the commission or attempted commission of:
  - armed burglary (G.L. c. 266, § 14)
  - unarmed burglary (G.L. c. 266, § 15)
  - breaking and entering (G.L. c. 266, § 16)
  - entering without breaking (G.L. c. 266, § 17)
  - breaking and entering a dwelling (G.L. c. 266, § 18)
  - kidnapping (G.L. c. 265, § 26)
  - armed robbery (G.L. c. 265, § 17)
  - unarmed robbery (G.L. c. 265, § 19)
  - ABDW or ADW (G.L. c. 265, §§ 15A, 15B)
  - home invasion (G.L. c. 265, § 18C)
  - posing or exhibiting child in state of nudity or sexual conduct (G.L. c. 272, § 29A); or
- if committed by a mandated reporter as defined in G.L. c. 119, § 21.

Penalty

Life or any term of years, but NLT 10 yrs. state prison. A prosecution commenced under this section shall neither be placed on file nor CWOF.

NOTE 1   **Sex Offender Registry.** See G.L. c. 6, §§ 178C–178Q.

NOTE 2   **Lifetime Parole.** See G.L. c. 265, § 45; G.L. c. 275, § 18.

NOTE 3   **Sexually Dangerous Person Commitment.** See G.L. c. 123A, §§ 1–15.

INDECENT ASSAULT AND BATTERY ON A CHILD UNDER 14, SUBSEQUENT OFFENSE— G.L. c. 265, § 13B¾

Elements
- indecent
- assault
- battery
- child under the age of 14
- prior conviction for, or adjudicated delinquent or as a youthful offender for:
  - indecent assault and battery on a child under 14 (G.L. c. 265, § 13B);
  - aggravated indecent assault and battery on a child under 14 (G.L. c. 265, § 13B½);
  - indecent assault and battery (G.L. c. 265, § 13H);
  - assault with intent to rape a child (G.L. c. 265, § 24B);
  - forcible rape of a child (G.L. c. 265, § 22A);
  - aggravated rape of a child by force (G.L. c. 265, § 22B);
  - rape of a child (G.L. c. 265, § 23);
  - aggravated rape of a child (G.L. c. 265, § 23A);
  - rape (G.L. c. 265, § 22); or
  - a like violation of the laws of another state, US or military, territorial or Indian tribal authority.

9

Penalty

Life or any term of years, but NLT 15 yrs. state prison. A prosecution commenced under this section shall neither be placed on file nor CWOF.

In any prosecution commenced pursuant to this section, introduction into evidence of a prior adjudication or conviction or a prior finding of sufficient facts by either certified attested copies of original court papers, or certified attested copies of the defendant's biographical and informational data from records of the department of probation, any jail or house of correction or the department of correction, shall be prima facie evidence that the defendant before the court has been convicted previously by a court of the commonwealth or any other jurisdiction. Such documentation shall be self-authenticating and admissible, after the commonwealth has established the defendant's guilt on the primary offense, as evidence in any court of the commonwealth to prove the defendant's commission of any prior conviction described therein. The commonwealth shall not be required to introduce any additional corroborating evidence or live witness testimony to establish the validity of such prior conviction.

NOTE 1   **Sex Offender Registry.** *See* G.L. c. 6, §§ 178C–178Q.

NOTE 2   **Lifetime Parole.** *See* G.L. c. 265, § 45; G.L. c. 275, § 18.

NOTE 3   **Sexually Dangerous Person Commitment.** *See* G.L. c. 123A, §§ 1–15.

INDECENT ASSAULT AND BATTERY ON A PERSON WITH AN INTELLECTUAL DISABILITY— G.L. c. 265, § 13F

Elements

Whoever
- indecent
- assault
- battery
- on a person with an intellectual disability
- knowing such person to have an intellectual disability.

Penalty

NLT 5 yrs. state prison, NMT 10 yrs. state prison; Second or subsequent offense—NLT 10 yrs. state prison.

NOTE 1   Section inapplicable to the commission of an (Indecent) Assault and Battery by one person with an intellectual disability upon another person with an intellectual disability.

NOTE 2   If person with intellectually disability is victim of an assault and battery, penalty is NMT 2½ yrs. HC or NMT 5 yrs. state prison (first offense); second and subsequent offense: NMT 10 yrs. state prison.

NOTE 3   **Sex Offender Registry.** *See* G.L. c. 6, §§ 178C–178Q.

NOTE 4   **Lifetime Parole.** *See* G.L. c. 265, § 45; G.L. c. 275, § 18.

NOTE 5   **Sexually Dangerous Person Commitment.** *See* G.L. c. 123A, §§ 1–15.

INDECENT ASSAULT AND BATTERY ON AN ELDER OR A PERSON WITH A DISABILITY— G.L. c. 265, § 13H

Elements

Whoever
- indecent
- assault
- battery
- on an elder or person with a disability as defined in G.L. c. 265, § 13K.

Penalty

NMT 10 yrs. state prison and NMT 2½ yrs. jail. Second or subsequent offense—NMT 20 yrs. state prison. A prosecution commenced under this section shall neither be placed on file nor CWOF.

INDECENT ASSAULT AND BATTERY ON A PERSON OVER 14—G.L. c. 265, § 13H

Elements

Whoever
- indecent
- assault
- battery
- 14 years old or older.

Penalty

NMT 5 yrs. state prison or imprisonment in jail or HC NMT 2½ yrs.

INTIMIDATION OF A WITNESS OR JUROR— G.L. c. 268, § 13B

Elements

Whoever
- directly or indirectly willfully
- threatens, or attempts or causes physical injury, emotional injury, economic injury, or property damage to
- conveys a gift, offer or promise of anything of value to, or
- misleads, intimidates, or harasses another person who is
- a witness, or potential witness at any stage of a criminal investigation, grand jury proceeding, trial, or other criminal proceeding of any type
- a person who is or was aware of information, records, documents, or objects that relate to a violation of a criminal statute, or a violation
- of conditions of probation, parole, or bail
- a judge, juror, grand juror, prosecutor, police officer, federal agent, investigator, defense attorney, clerk, court officer, probation officer, or parole officer
- a person who is or was furthering a criminal investigation, grand jury proceeding, trial, or other criminal proceeding of any type or
- a person who is or was attending or had made known his intention to attend a grand jury proceeding, trial, or other criminal proceeding of any type with the intent to impede, obstruct, delay, harm, punish, or otherwise interfere thereby with a criminal investigation, grand jury proceeding, trial, or other criminal proceeding of any type.

Penalty

NMT 2½ years jail or HC or NMT 10 yrs. state prison and/or fine NMT $5,000, NLT $1,000.

NOTE 1   "Criminal investigator"—an individual or a group of individuals lawfully authorized by a department or agency of the commonwealth or the federal government or any political subdivision thereof to conduct, or engage in, an investigation of, or prosecution for, a violation of the laws of the commonwealth in the course of his official duties.

NOTE 2   "Harass"—an act directed at a specific person or persons that seriously alarms or annoys and would cause a reasonable person to suffer substantial emotional distress, including, but not limited to acts conducted by mail or by use of a telephonic or telecommunication device or electronic communication device including but not limited to any device that transfers signs, signals, writing, images, sounds, data, or intelligence of any nature transmitted in whole or in part by a wire, radio, electromagnetic, photo-electric or photo-optical system, including, but not limited to e-mail, Internet communications, instant messages or facsimile communications.

KIDNAPPING—G.L. c. 265, § 26

Elements
Whoever without lawful authority
- forcibly or secretly
- confines or imprisons
- another person
- within this commonwealth
- against his will, or
- forcibly carries or sends such person out of this commonwealth

or
- forcibly
- seizes and confines or inveigles
- or kidnaps
- another person
- with intent either to cause him to be secretly confined or imprisoned in this commonwealth against his will, or to cause him to be sent out of this commonwealth against his will or in any way held to service.

Penalty
NMT 10 yrs. state prison or fine NMT $1,000 and imprisonment in jail NMT 2 yrs.

An offense committed under this section with intent to extort money or other valuable thing is punishable by life or any terms or years in state prison.

If armed with a firearm, shotgun, rifle, machine gun or assault weapon, 1st offense—NLT 10 yrs. state prison or NMT 2½ yrs. HC.

If armed with a firearm, shotgun, rifle, machine gun or assault weapon with intent to extort money or other valuable thing, life or for any term of years, but NLT 20 yrs. state prison.

If armed with dangerous weapon and inflict serious bodily injury or sexually assaults, NLT 25 yrs. state prison.

NOTE 1 This section is inapplicable to the parent of a child under 18 who takes custody of such child. Refer to G.L. c. 265, § 26A for the applicable statute.

NOTE 2 **Sex Offender Registry** (kidnapping or attempting to kidnap child under the age of 16). *See* G.L. c. 6, §§ 178C–178Q.

NOTE 3 **Lifetime Parole** (kidnapping or attempting to kidnap child under the age of 16). *See* G.L. c. 265, § 45; G.L. c. 275, § 18.

KIDNAPPING OF MINOR OR INCOMPETENT BY RELATIVE—G.L. c. 265, § 26A

Elements
- relative
- of child less than 18
- without lawful authority
- holds or intends to hold such child permanently or for a protracted period, or
- takes or entices such child from his lawful custodian

or
- takes or entices
- from lawful custody
- any incompetent person, or
- other person entrusted by authority of law to the custody of another person or institution.

Penalty
NMT 1 yr. HC and/or fine NMT $1,000.

If person taken or enticed from lawful custody is exposed to a risk which endangers his safety or if said child is held outside the commonwealth—NMT 5 yrs. state prison and/or fine NMT $5,000.

LARCENY—G.L. c. 266, § 30

Elements
- taking
- carrying away
- personal property
- of another
- with the intent unlawfully to deprive that other permanently of the use of it.

Penalty
If value exceeds $250 or is a firearm—NMT 5 yrs. state prison or fine NMT $25,000 and NMT 2 yrs. jail; if value is under $250—NMT 1 yr. jail or fine NMT $300; if property was stolen from a conveyance of a common carrier or of a person carrying on an express business—NLT 6 mos.; NMT 2½ yrs. or fine NLT $50 and NMT $600, or both (1st offense) and for second and subsequent offenses—NLT 18 mos., NMT 2½ yrs., fine NLT $150, NMT $600, or both.

LARCENY FROM THE PERSON—G.L. c. 266, § 25

Elements (a)
- taking
- carrying away
- from the person
- personal property of a person 65 yrs. or older
- with intent unlawfully to deprive that other permanently of the use of it.

Penalty
NMT 5 yrs. state prison or 2½ yrs. jail. Second or subsequent crime—NLT 2 yrs. (mandatory 1 yr.)

Elements (b)
- taking
- carrying away
- from the person of another
- personal property, etc.

Penalty
NMT 5 yrs. state prison or NMT 2½ yrs. jail.

NOTE See elements for larceny (G.L. c. 266, § 30).

LEAVING THE SCENE OF AN ACCIDENT—see Failure to Stop

LEWD AND LASCIVIOUS BEHAVIOR—see Unnatural and Lascivious Acts

LOTTERIES—G.L. c. 271, § 7

Elements
- payment of a price for
- the possibility of winning a prize, depending upon
- hazard or chance
- not taking place in a gaming establishment licensed pursuant to c. 23K.

Penalty
Fine NMT $3,000 or NMT 3 yrs. state prison or NMT 2½ yrs. HC or jail.

MANSLAUGHTER—G.L. c. 265, § 13

Elements
- unlawful killing

9

- of another
- without malice.

Voluntary—act committed with real design and purpose to kill, but through the violence of sudden passion, occasioned by some great provocation.

Involuntary—act committed in commission of unlawful act, malum in se, not amounting to felony nor likely to endanger life; or act constituting wanton or reckless conduct.

Penalty

NMT 20 yrs. state prison or fine NMT $1,000 and NMT 2½ yrs. HC or jail.

Penalty for manslaughter while violating G.L. c. 266, §§ 101–102B (explosives; molotov cocktails, etc.)—life or any term of years in state prison.

MAYHEM—G.L. c. 265, § 14

Elements

- malicious intent
- to maim or disfigure
- cuts out or maims the tongue, puts out or destroys an eye, cuts or tears off an ear, cuts, slits or mutilates the nose or lip, or cuts off or disables a limb or member, of another person.

Or, whoever

- is privy to such intent, or
- is present and aids in the commission of such crime.

Or, whoever

- with intent to maim or disfigure
- assaults another person
- with a dangerous weapon, substance or chemical
- and by such assault disfigures, cripples or inflicts serious or permanent physical injury.

Or, whoever

- is privy to such intent, or
- is present and aids in the commission of such crime.

Penalty

NMT 20 yrs. state prison or fine NMT $1,000 and NMT 2½ yrs. jail.

MOTOR VEHICLE THEFT—G.L. c. 266, § 28

Elements

Whoever

- steals a motor vehicle or trailer, or
- maliciously damages a motor vehicle or trailer, or
- buys, receives, possesses, conceals, or obtains control of a motor vehicle or trailer
- knowing or having reason to know the same to have been stolen.

Or, whoever

- takes a motor vehicle
- without the authority of the owner
- steals from it any of its part or accessories.

Penalty

NMT 15 yrs. state prison or NMT 2½ yrs. jail or HC or fine NMT $15,000, or both fine and imprisonment.

NOTE 1   Evidence that an identification number or numbers of a motor vehicle or trailer or part thereof has been intentionally and maliciously removed, defaced, altered, changed, destroyed, obliterated, or mutilated shall be prima facie evidence that the defendant knew or had reason to know that the motor vehicle, or trailer or part thereof had been stolen.

NOTE 2   Case cannot be filed or continued without a finding.

MURDER—G.L. c. 265, §§ 1, 2; c. 279, §§ 57–71

Elements

1st degree

- killing
- human being
- with deliberately premeditated malice aforethought
- or with extreme atrocity or cruelty
- or in the commission or attempted commission or a crime punishable with death or imprisonment for life.

Penalty

Life (not eligible for parole) or death. Juvenile defendants: Life.

Elements

2nd degree

- murder which does not appear to be in the first degree.

Penalty

Life.

NONSUPPORT OF A CHILD BORN OUT OF WEDLOCK—G.L. c. 273, §§ 15, 16

Elements

- parent
- of minor child
- born out of wedlock
- wilfully neglects or refuses to contribute reasonably to the support of the child, or
- leaves the commonwealth without making reasonable provision for the support of the child, or
- enters the commonwealth without making reasonable provision for the support of the child domiciled in another state, or
- wilfully, while having the financial ability and earning capacity to have complied, fails to comply with an order or judgment for support.

Penalty

NMT 2 yrs. imprisonment and/or fine NMT $500; support for child.

A misdemeanor

(a) abandonment of spouse or minor child without making reasonable provisions for the support of either or both who is subject to an order or judgment or pursuant to similar laws of other states, having ability to pay, fails to comply— NMT 5 yrs. state prison or NMT 2½ yrs. jail or HC and/or fine NMT $5,000.

(b) leaves commonwealth without making reasonable provisions or enters commonwealth without making reasonable provisions for out-of-commonwealth spouse/child—NMT 10 yrs. state prison or NMT 2½ yrs. jail or HC and/or fine NMT $10,000.

(c) alternative sentencing including (1) a suspended sentence; or (2) weekends, evenings or holiday imprisonment.

(d) restitution is also permissible.

NOTE   Immaterial whether child begotten within or without the commonwealth.

OPEN AND GROSS LEWDNESS—G.L. c. 272, § 16

Elements

- man or woman
- married or unmarried
- open and gross lewdness and lascivious behavior.

Penalty

NMT 3 yrs. state prison or NMT 2 yrs. jail or fine NMT $300.

NOTE **Sex Offender Registry.** A conviction of an offense under this section or of an attempt to commit such an offense results in the defendant's name, photograph, etc., being added to the sex offender registry, which, in turn, gives rise to certain registration and reporting requirements. *See* G.L. c. 6, §§ 178C–178Q. *But see Doe v. Attorney General (No. 2)*, 425 Mass. 217, 221 n.7, 222 (1997) (permitting a judge to enjoin the enforcement of G.L. c. 6, § 178I against a defendant convicted under this section).

OPERATING TO ENDANGER—G.L. c. 90, § 24(2)(a)

Elements

Whoever
- upon any way or in any place to which the public has a right of access, or
- upon any place to which members of the public have access as invitees or licensees
- operates
- motor vehicle
- recklessly or negligently
- so that the lives or safety of the public might be endangered.

Penalty

Fine NLT $20, NMT $200; and/or imprisonment NLT 2 weeks, NMT 2 yrs.

OPERATING UNDER THE INFLUENCE— G.L. c. 90, § 24(1)

Elements

Whoever
- upon any way or in any place to which the public has a right of access, or
- upon any way or in any place to which members of the public have access as invitees or licensees
- operates
- motor vehicle
- with a percentage by weight of alcohol in their blood of eight one-hundredths or greater; or
- under the influence of intoxicating liquor, or of marijuana, narcotic drugs, depressants or stimulant substances, all as defined in G.L. c. 94C, § 1, or the vapors of glue.

Penalty

A common disposition for first time offenders is found in G.L. c. 90, § 24D, which calls for a 45–90 day loss of license (210 days if under 21 years of age and alcohol treatment/rehabilitation program).

For first time offenders who do not go the 24D route, the penalty is a fine NLT $500, NMT $5,000 and/or by imprisonment NMT 2½ yrs. with a one year loss of license (after 3 mos. may apply for limited (employment or educational related) license; after 6 mos. may apply for hardship license).

Second conviction more than 10 years after the first. A defendant convicted for second time more than 10 years after the first conviction or assignment to an alcohol or controlled substance program can take advantage of the disposition available under G.L. c. 90, §§ 24D and 24E. Note, however, that a defendant can only take advantage of this favorable disposition once in a lifetime.

Otherwise, second convictions within 10 years and all other subsequent convictions, regardless of when they occur, are subject to the following penalties:

- OUI 2nd: Fine NLT $600, NMT $10,000 and imprisonment NLT 60 days, NMT 2½ yrs; mandatory minimum 30 (rather than 14) days; license revocation of 2 yrs. (after 6 mos. may apply for limited (employment or educational related) license; after 1 yr. may apply for hardship license).
- OUI 3rd: Fine NLT $1,000, NMT $15,000 and either imprisonment NLT 180 days, NMT 2½ yrs. or imprisonment in state prison NLT 2½, NMT 5 yrs.; Mandatory minimum 150 days; license revocation of 8 yrs. (after 2 yrs. may apply for limited (employment or educational related) license; after 4 yrs. may apply for hardship license).
- OUI 4th: fine NLT $1,500, NMT $25,000 and either imprisonment NLT 2 yrs., NMT 2½ yrs. or imprisonment in state prison NLT 2½ yrs., NMT 5 yrs.; mandatory minimum 12 mos.; license revocation of 10 yrs. (after 5 yrs. may apply for limited (employment or educational related) license; after 8 yrs. may apply for hardship license).
- OUI 5th: fine NLT $2,000, NMT $50,000 and either imprisonment NLT 2½ yrs. or imprisonment in state prison NLT 2½ yrs., NMT 5 yrs.; mandatory minimum 24 mos.; license revocation for life.

Breathalyzer Refusal:

a. 120 day loss of license;

b. If under 21 or second offense (within 10 yrs.): 180 day loss of license;

c. If under 18 (see G.L. c. 90, § 24P) or third or greater offense (within 10 yrs.): 1 yr. loss of license;

d. If the driver refuses the breathalyzer, the police shall (i) immediately take the driver's license; (ii) provide the driver with written notice of intent to suspend; (iii) issue the driver a temporary license good for 15 days unless (1) driver's license was already suspended, revoked or cancelled; (2) license invalid; (3) driver not entitled to driving privileges for any other reason; or (4) out-of-state license.

Breathalyzer taken:

a. .08 or above—permissible inference driver under the influence; Police shall (i) immediately take the driver's license; (ii) provide the driver with written notice of intent to suspend; (iii) issue the driver a temporary license good for 15 days unless (1) driver's license was already suspended, revoked or canceled; (2) license invalid; (3) driver not entitled to driving privileges for any other reason; or (4) out-of-state license. Suspension until case disposed; in no event however, to exceed 90 days.

b. .06–.07—no permissible inference;

c. .05 or less—permissible inference driver not under the influence; driver to be released from custody forthwith;

d. If driver is under 21 and breathalyzer reading is .02 or above, police shall (i) immediately take the driver's license; (ii) provide the driver with written notice of intent to suspend; (iii) issue the driver a temporary license good for 15 days unless (1) driver's license was already suspended, revoked or canceled; (2) license invalid; (3) driver not entitled to driving privileges for any other reason; or (4) out-of-state license. Suspension until case disposed; in no event however, to exceed 90 days. If under 21 years of age, suspension is for 180 days. G.L. c. 90, § 24P. If under 18 years of age, suspension is for one year. G.L. c. 90, § 24P.

G.L. c. 138, § 34A (purchase of alcohol by one under 21) and G.L. c. 138, § 34C (possession of alcohol by one under

9

21)—conviction hereunder shall result in a 90 day loss of license.

PERJURY—G.L. c. 268, § 1

Elements

Whoever
- being lawfully required to depose the truth in a judicial proceeding or a proceeding in a course of justice
- wilfully swears or affirms falsely
- in a matter material to the issue of point in question.

Or, whoever
- being required by law to take an oath or affirmation
- wilfully swears or affirms falsely
- in a matter relative to which such an oath or affirmation is required.

Penalty

NMT 20 yrs. state prison or fine NMT $1,000 or NMT 2½ yrs. jail or both fine and imprisonment in jail.

Capital cases—life or any term of yrs. state prison.

POSSESSION OF A CONTROLLED SUBSTANCE— G.L. c. 94C, § 34

Elements

- knowing or intentional
- possession
- controlled substance.

Penalty

1. NMT 1 yr. imprisonment and/or fine NMT $1,000.

2. Heroin—NMT 2 yrs. HC and/or fine NMT $2,000. Second offense—NLT 2½ yrs., NMT 5 yrs. or fine NMT $5,000 and NMT 2½ yrs. state prison, HC or jail.

3. More than 1 ounce marijuana (Cl.D) or Cl.E—NMT 6 mos. HC and/or fine of $500.

4. Second and subsequent drug offenses (except Cl.E)— NMT 2 yrs. HC and/or fine NMT $2,000.

5. Any person charged with a violation of this chapter and who has no previous drug convictions eligible to have case dismissed and record sealed if there are no violations during the probationary period.

6. First time conviction for marijuana or Cl.E and who has no prior drug conviction: probation unless such person does not consent thereto, or unless the court files a written memorandum stating the reason for not so doing. Upon successful completion of such probation, case dismissed and records sealed.

7. Special additional fine: NLT $150. NMT $500, if conviction or sufficient facts; if multiple criminal offenses, total fine NMT $500. May be reduced or waived if undue hardship. G.L. c. 280, § 6B.

POSSESSION OF A CONTROLLED SUBSTANCE WITH INTENT TO DISTRIBUTE, ETC.— G.L. c. 94C, §§ 32–32D

Elements

- knowingly or intentionally
- manufactures, distributes, dispenses, or possesses with intent to manufacture, distribute or dispense
- controlled substance.

Penalties

1. Cl.A—G.L. c. 94C, § 32—NMT 10 yrs. state prison or NMT 2½ yrs. jail or HC and/or fine NLT $1,000, NMT $10,000.

Second or subsequent offense—NLT 3½ yrs., NMT 15 yrs. state prison; mandatory minimum 3½ yrs. state prison; fine NLT $2,500, NMT $25,000 may also be imposed, but not in lieu of the mandatory term of imprisonment. Sections 32, 32H.

Special additional fine: NLT $150, NMT $500, if conviction or sufficient facts; if multiple criminal offenses, total fine NMT $500. May be reduced or waived if undue hardship. G.L. c. 280, § 6B.

2. Cl.B—G.L. c. 94C, § 32A—NMT 10 yrs. state prison or NMT 2½ yrs. jail or HC and/or fine NLT $1,000, NMT $10,000.

Second or subsequent offense—NLT 2 yrs., NMT 10 yrs., state prison; mandatory minimum 2 yrs. state prison; fine NLT $2,500, NMT $25,000 may also be imposed, but not in lieu of the mandatory prison sentence. Sections 32A, 32H.

Special additional fine: NLT $150, NMT $500, if conviction or sufficient facts; if multiple criminal offenses, total fine NMT $500. May be reduced or waived if undue hardship. G.L. c. 280, § 6B.

2a. Phencyclidine or a controlled substance defined in G.L. c. 94C, § 31(a)(4) ("Coca leaves and any salt, compound, derivative . . .")—G.L. c. 94C, § 32A(c).

NLT 2½, NMT 10 years state prison or NLT 1, NMT 2½ years HC or jail; mandatory minimum—1 year; fine NLT $1,000, NMT $10,000 may be imposed but not in lieu of 1 year mandatory minimum sentence. Sections 32A, 32H.

Second or subsequent offense—G.L. c. 94C, § 32A(d) NLT 3½ years, NMT 15 years and fine NLT $2,500, NMT $25,000. Fine may not be in lieu of the 3½ year mandatory minimum sentence. Sections 32A, 32H.

3. Cl.C—G.L. c. 94C, § 32B—NMT 5 yrs. state prison or NMT 2½ yrs. jail or HC and/or fine NLT $500, NMT $5,000.

Second or subsequent offense—NLT 2½ yrs., NMT 10 yrs., state prison or NLT 18 mos., NMT 2½ yrs. jail or HC; 18 mos. mandatory minimum sentence; fine NLT $1,000, NMT $10,000 imposed, but not in lieu of the mandatory minimum sentence. Sections 32A, 32H.

Special additional fine: NLT $150, NMT $500, if conviction or sufficient facts; if multiple criminal offenses, total fine NMT $500. May be reduced or waived if undue hardship. G.L. c. 280, § 6B.

4. Cl.D—G.L. c. 94C, § 32C—NMT 2 yrs. HC or jail and/or fine NLT $500, NMT $5,000.

Second or subsequent offense—NLT 1 yr., NMT 2½ yrs. jail or HC and/or fine NLT $1,000, NMT $10,000.

Special additional fine: NLT $35, NMT $100 if defendant eighteen or older and convicted or sufficient facts. If multiple criminal offenses from single incident, total fine NMT $500. Fine may be reduced or waived if undue hardship. G.L. c. 280, § 6B.

5. Cl.E—G.L. c. 94C, § 32D—NMT 9 mos. jail or HC and/or fine NLT $250, NMT $2,500.

Second or subsequent offense—NMT 1½ yrs. HC or jail and/or fine NLT $500, NMT $5,000.

Special additional fine: NLT $35, NMT $100 if defendant eighteen or older and convicted or sufficient facts. If multiple criminal offenses from single incident, total fine NMT $500. Fine may be reduced or waived if undue hardship. G.L. c. 280, § 6B.

DRUG SALE IN SCHOOL ZONE—G.L. c. 94C, § 32J

Elements

Whoever

- violates any of G.L. c. 94C. §§ 32–32F or 32I
- within 300 feet of the real property comprising a public or private accredited preschool, accredited headstart facility, elementary, vocational, or secondary school if the violation occurs between 5:00 a.m. and midnight or
- within 100 feet of a public park or playground.

Penalty

NLT 2½ yrs., NMT 15 yrs. state prison or NLT 2 yrs., NMT 2½ yrs. jail or HC. Mandatory minimum 2 yr. sentence. Fine NLT $1,000, NMT $10,000 but not in lieu of mandatory prison sentence.

NOTE 1   No difference whether school in or not in session.

NOTE 2   Lack of knowledge of school boundaries not a defense.

NOTE 3   Sentence to be served on and after sentence on G.L. c. 94C, §§ 32–32F or 32I.

USE OF MINORS IN DRUG SALES—G.L. c. 94C, § 32K

Elements

Whoever

- knowingly
- causes, induces or abets
- person under eighteen
- to distribute, dispense or possess with intent to distribute or dispense any controlled substance or
- to accept, deliver or possess money intended for use in procurement, manufacture, compounding, processing, delivery, distribution or sale of any controlled substance.

Penalty

NLT 5 yrs., NMT 15 yrs. Mandatory minimum 5 yr. sentence. Fine NLT $1,000 NMT $100,000 but not in lieu of mandatory prison sentence which must begin from and after expiration of sentences for violation of other drug laws.

POSSESSION OF A COUNTERFEIT SUBSTANCE WITH INTENT TO DISTRIBUTE—G.L. c. 94C, § 32G

Elements

Whoever

- knowingly or intentionally
- creates, distributes, dispenses, or possesses with intent to distribute or dispense
- a counterfeit substance
- knowing such substance to be counterfeit.

Penalty

NMT 1 yr. HC or jail and/or fine NLT $250, NMT $2,500.

Special additional fine: NLT $35, NMT $100 if defendant eighteen or older and convicted or sufficient facts. If multiple criminal offenses from single incident, total fine NMT $500. Fine may be reduced or waived if undue hardship. G.L. c. 280, § 6B.

POSSESSION OF A FIREARM—see Unlawfully Possessing a Firearm

POSSESSION OF BURGLARIOUS TOOLS—G.L. c. 266, § 49

Elements

Whoever

- makes or mends or begins to make or mend, or
- knowingly has in his possession
- an engine machine, tool or implement
- adapted and designed for cutting through, forcing or breaking open a
- building, room, vault, safe or other depository
- in order to steal therefrom money or other property, or
- to commit another crime
- knowing the same to be adapted and designed for the purpose aforesaid
- with intent to use it for such purpose.

Penalty

NMT 10 yrs. state prison or fine NMT $1,000 and NMT 2½ yrs. jail.

PRESENT WHERE HEROIN IS KEPT—see Being Present

PROMOTING A LOTTERY—see Lotteries

RAPE—G.L. c. 265, § 22

Elements (a)

- sexual intercourse, or
- unnatural sexual intercourse
- with a person
- compels such person to submit by force and against his will, or
- compels such person to submit by threat of bodily injury, and
- such sexual intercourse or unnatural intercourse results in or is committed with acts resulting in serious bodily injury, or
- is committed by a joint enterprise, or
- is committed during the commission or attempted commission of an offense defined in G.L. c. 265, §§ 15A (ABDW), 15B (ADW), 17 (armed robbery), 19 (unarmed robbery), 26 (kidnapping), G.L. c. 266, §§ 14, 15, 16, 17, 18 (burglary, breaking and entering, etc.) or G.L. c. 269, § 10 (carrying dangerous weapon).

Penalty

Life or any term of years in state prison.

Second or subsequent offenses—two-thirds of minimum sentence must be served.

If armed with a firearm, shotgun, rifle, machine gun or assault weapon, 1st offense—NLT 10 yrs. state prison, second or subsequent offense—life or for any term of years, but NLT 15 yrs. state prison.

Elements (b)

- sexual intercourse, or
- unnatural sexual intercourse
- with a person
- compels such person to submit by force and against his will, or
- compels such person to submit by threat of bodily injury.

Penalty

NMT 20 yrs. state prison.

9

Second or subsequent offense—life or any term of yrs. in the state prison, two-thirds of minimum sentence must be served.

If armed with a firearm, shotgun, rifle, machine gun or assault weapon, 1st offense—NLT 10 yrs. state prison, second or subsequent offense—life or for any term of years, but NLT 15 yrs. state prison.

NOTE 1 Note (b) is a lesser included offense of (a).

NOTE 2 **Sex Offender Registry.** *See* G.L. c. 6, §§ 178C–178Q.

NOTE 3 **Lifetime Parole.** *See* G.L. c. 265, § 45; G.L. c. 275, § 18.

NOTE 4 **Sexually Dangerous Person Commitment.** *See* G.L. c. 123A, §§ 1–15.

RAPE AND ABUSE OF A CHILD UNDER 16 (STATUTORY RAPE)—G.L. c. 265, § 23

Elements
- sexual intercourse, or
- unnatural sexual intercourse
- abuses child under 16.

Penalty
Life or any term of years in state prison or any term in jail or HC. A prosecution commenced under this section shall neither be placed on file nor CWOF.

NOTE 1 **Sex Offender Registry.** *See* G.L. c. 6, §§ 178C–178Q.

NOTE 2 **Lifetime Parole.** *See* G.L. c. 265, § 45; G.L. c. 275, § 18.

NOTE 3 **Sexually Dangerous Person Commitment.** *See* G.L. c. 123A, §§ 1–15.

AGGRAVATED RAPE AND ABUSE OF A CHILD UNDER 16 (STATUTORY RAPE)—G.L. c. 265, § 23A

Elements
- sexual intercourse, or
- unnatural sexual intercourse
- abuses child under 16, and
  - there exists more than a 5 year age difference between the defendant and the victim and the victim is under 12 years of age;
  - there exists more than a 10 year age difference between the defendant and the victim where the victim is between the age of 12 and 16 years of age; or
  - the defendant is a mandated reporter as defined by G.L. c. 119, § 21.

Penalty
Life or any term of years in state prison, but NLT 10 years in state prison. A prosecution commenced under this section shall neither be placed on file nor CWOF.

NOTE 1 **Sex Offender Registry.** *See* G.L. c. 6, §§ 178C–178Q.

NOTE 2 **Lifetime Parole.** *See* G.L. c. 265, § 45; G.L. c. 275, § 18.

NOTE 3 **Sexually Dangerous Person Commitment.** *See* G.L. c. 123A, §§ 1–15.

SUBSEQUENT RAPE AND ABUSE OF A CHILD UNDER 16 (STATUTORY RAPE)—G.L. c. 265, § 23B

Elements
- sexual intercourse, or
- unnatural sexual intercourse
- abuses child under 16, and

- prior conviction for, or adjudicated delinquent or as a youthful offender for:
  - indecent assault and battery on a child under 14 (G.L. c. 265, § 13B);
  - aggravated indecent assault and battery on a child under 14 (G.L. c. 265, § 13B½);
  - indecent assault and battery (G.L. c. 265, § 13H);
  - assault with intent to rape a child (G.L. c. 265, § 24B);
  - forcible rape of a child (G.L. c. 265, § 22A);
  - aggravated rape of a child by force (G.L. c. 265, § 22B);
  - rape of a child (G.L. c. 265, § 23);
  - aggravated rape of a child (G.L. c. 265, § 23A);
  - rape (G.L. c. 265, § 22); or
  - a like violation of the laws of another state, US or military, territorial or Indian tribal authority.

Penalty
Life or any term of years in state prison, but NLT 15 years in state prison. A prosecution commenced under this section shall neither be placed on file nor CWOF.

In any prosecution commenced pursuant to this section, introduction into evidence of a prior adjudication or conviction or a prior finding of sufficient facts by either certified attested copies of original court papers, or certified attested copies of the defendant's biographical and informational data from records of the department of probation, any jail or house of correction or the department of correction, shall be prima facie evidence that the defendant before the court has been convicted previously by a court of the commonwealth or any other jurisdiction. Such documentation shall be self-authenticating and admissible, after the commonwealth has established the defendant's guilt on the primary offense, as evidence in any court of the commonwealth to prove the defendant's commission of any prior conviction described therein. The commonwealth shall not be required to introduce any additional corroborating evidence or live witness testimony to establish the validity of such prior conviction.

NOTE 1 **Sex Offender Registry.** *See* G.L. c. 6, §§ 178C–178Q.

NOTE 2 **Lifetime Parole.** *See* G.L. c. 265, § 45; G.L. c. 275, § 18.

NOTE 3 **Sexually Dangerous Person Commitment.** *See* G.L. c. 123A, §§ 1–15.

RAPE OF CHILD UNDER 16—G.L. c. 265, § 22A

Elements
- sexual intercourse, or
- unnatural sexual intercourse
- with a child under 16
- compels said child to submit by force or threat of bodily injury.

Penalty
Life or any term of years in state prison. A prosecution commenced under this section shall neither be placed on file nor CWOF.

NOTE 1 **Sex Offender Registry.** *See* G.L. c. 6, §§ 178C–178Q.

NOTE 2 **Lifetime Parole.** *See* G.L. c. 265, § 45; G.L. c. 275, § 18.

NOTE 3 **Sexually Dangerous Person Commitment.** *See* G.L. c. 123A, §§ 1–15.

AGGRAVATED RAPE OF CHILD UNDER 16— G.L. c. 265, § 22B

Elements

- sexual intercourse, or
- unnatural sexual intercourse
- with a child under 16
- compels said child to submit by force or threat of bodily injury,
- during the commission or attempted commission of:
    - armed burglary (G.L. c. 266, § 14)
    - unarmed burglary (G.L. c. 266, § 15)
    - breaking and entering (G.L. c. 266, § 16)
    - entering without breaking (G.L. c. 266, § 17)
    - breaking and entering a dwelling (G.L. c. 266, § 18)
    - kidnapping (G.L. c. 265, § 26)
    - armed robbery (G.L. c. 265, § 17)
    - unarmed robbery (G.L. c. 265, § 19)
    - ABDW or ADW (G.L. c. 265, §§ 15A, 15B)
    - home invasion (G.L. c. 265, § 18C)
    - posing or exhibiting child in state of nudity or sexual conduct (G.L. c. 272, § 29A); or
- results in or is committed with by acts resulting in substantial bodily injury as defined in G.L. c. 265, § 13J;
- the sexual intercourse or unnatural sexual intercourse is committed while the victim is tied, bound or gagged;
- the sexual intercourse or unnatural sexual intercourse is committed after the defendant administered, or caused to be administered, alcohol or a controlled substance by injection, inhalation, ingestion, or any other means to the victim without the victim's consent;
- the sexual intercourse or unnatural sexual intercourse is committed by a joint enterprise; or
- the sexual intercourse or unnatural sexual intercourse was committed in a manner in which the victim could contract a sexually transmitted disease or infection of which the defendant knew or should have known he was a carrier.

Penalty

Life or any term of years in state prison but NLT 15 years. A prosecution commenced under this section shall neither be placed on file nor CWOF.

NOTE 1   **Sex Offender Registry.** *See* G.L. c. 6, §§ 178C–178Q.

NOTE 2   **Lifetime Parole.** *See* G.L. c. 265, § 45; G.L. c. 275, § 18.

NOTE 3   **Sexually Dangerous Person Commitment.** *See* G.L. c. 123A, §§ 1–15.

RAPE OF CHILD UNDER 16 BY FORCE— G.L. c. 265, § 22C

Elements

- sexual intercourse, or
- unnatural sexual intercourse
- with a child under 16
- compels said child to submit by force or threat of bodily injury
- prior conviction for, or adjudicated delinquent or as a youthful offender for:
    - indecent assault and battery on a child under 14 (G.L. c. 265, § 13B);

- aggravated indecent assault and battery on a child under 14 (G.L. c. 265, § 13B½);
- indecent assault and battery (G.L. c. 265, § 13H);
- assault with intent to rape a child (G.L. c. 265, § 24B);
- forcible rape of a child (G.L. c. 265, § 22A);
- aggravated rape of a child by force (G.L. c. 265, § 22B);
- rape of a child (G.L. c. 265, § 23);
- aggravated rape of a child (G.L. c. 265, § 23A);
- rape (G.L. c. 265, § 22); or
- a like violation of the laws of another state, US or military, territorial or Indian tribal authority.

Penalty

Life or any term of years, but NLT 20 yrs. state prison. A prosecution commenced under this section shall neither be placed on file nor CWOF.

In any prosecution commenced pursuant to this section, introduction into evidence of a prior adjudication or conviction or a prior finding of sufficient facts by either certified attested copies of original court papers, or certified attested copies of the defendant's biographical and informational data from records of the department of probation, any jail or house of correction or the department of correction, shall be prima facie evidence that the defendant before the court has been convicted previously by a court of the commonwealth or any other jurisdiction. Such documentation shall be self-authenticating and admissible, after the commonwealth has established the defendant's guilt on the primary offense, as evidence in any court of the commonwealth to prove the defendant's commission of any prior conviction described therein. The commonwealth shall not be required to introduce any additional corroborating evidence or live witness testimony to establish the validity of such prior conviction.

NOTE 1   **Sex Offender Registry.** *See* G.L. c. 6, §§ 178C–178Q.

NOTE 2   **Lifetime Parole.** *See* G.L. c. 265, § 45; G.L. c. 275, § 18.

NOTE 3   **Sexually Dangerous Person Commitment.** *See* G.L. c. 123A, §§ 1–15.

RECEIVING STOLEN GOODS—G.L. c. 266, § 60

(Amended by 2014 Mass. Acts c. 451, § 3, effective Apr. 6, 2015.)

Elements

Whoever

- buys, receives or aids in the concealment of
- stolen or embezzled property
- knowing it to have been stolen or embezzled

or

- with intent to defraud
- buys, receives or aids in the concealment of
- property
- knowing it to have been obtained from a person by a false pretense of carrying on business and dealing in the ordinary course of trade

or

- obtains or exerts control over property in the custody of any law enforcement agency, or any individual acting on behalf of a law enforcement agency
- which is explicitly represented to such person by any law enforcement officer or any individual acting on behalf of a law enforcement agency as being stolen
- intending to deprive its rightful owner permanently of the use and enjoyment of said property.

9

Penalty

Value $250 or less—NMT 2½ yrs. HC or fine NMT $1,000; second or subsequent offense: NMT 2½ yrs. HC or 5 yrs. state prison and/or fine NMT $5,000..

Value exceeds $250—NMT 2½ yrs. HC or NMT 5 yrs. state prison and/or fine NMT $5,000.

ROBBERY (ARMED)—G.L. c. 265, § 17

Elements

Whoever
- armed with a dangerous weapon
- assaults another
- robs, steals or takes from his person money or other property which may be the subject of larceny.

Penalty

Life or any term of years in state prison.

If armed with a firearm, shotgun, rifle, machine gun or assault weapon, 1st offense—NLT 5 yrs., subsequent offense—NLT 15 years.

Elements

- Masked
- any person who commits any offense described herein while masked or disguised or while having his features artificially distorted.

Penalty

1st offense—NLT 5 yrs. Subsequent offense—NLT 10 yrs.

If armed with a firearm, shotgun, rifle, machine gun or assault weapon, 1st offense—NLT 5 yrs., subsequent offense—NLT 15 years.

ROBBERY (UNARMED)—G.L. c. 265, § 19

Elements (a)

Whoever
- not being armed with a dangerous weapon
- by force and violence, or
- by assault and putting in fear
- robs, steals or takes from the person of a person 60 years or older, or from his immediate control
- money or other property which may be the subject of larceny.

Penalty

Life or any term of years in state prison. Subsequent offenses—NLT 2 yrs. (mandatory).

Elements (b)

Whoever
- not being armed with a dangerous weapon
- by force and violence, or
- by assault and putting in fear
- robs, steals and takes from the person of another money or other property which may be the subject of larceny.

Penalty

Life or any term of years in state prison.

SETTING UP A LOTTERY—see Lotteries

SEX OFFENDER REGISTRATION/VERIFICATION—G.L. c. 6, § 178H

Elements

A sex offender who
- knowingly
- fails to register or

- fails to verify registration information as required by law or
- fails to provide notice of address change or
- provides false information.

Penalty

1st offense—NLT 6 months HC or NMT 2½ yrs. HC or 5 yrs. state prison or fine of NMT $1,000 or by both fine and imprisonment.

2nd and subsequent offense—NLT 5 yrs. state prison.

SHOPLIFTING—G.L. c. 266, § 30A

Elements

Whoever
- intentionally
- takes possession of or carries away, transfers or causes to be carried away or transferred
- any merchandise displayed, held, stored or offered for sale by any store or other retail mercantile establishment
- with the intention or depriving the merchant of the possession, use or benefit of such merchandise or converting the same to the use of such person
- without paying to the merchant the value thereof

or
- intentionally
- conceals upon his person or otherwise
- any merchandise offered for sale by any store or other retail mercantile establishment
- with the intention of depriving the merchant of proceeds, use or benefit of such merchandise or converting the same to the use of such person
- without paying

or
- intentionally
- alters, transfers or removes any label, price tag, etc.
- affixed to merchandise offered for sale
- attempts to purchase such merchandise personally or in consort with another at less than full retail value
- with the intention of depriving the merchant of all or some part of the retail value thereof

or
- intentionally
- transfers
- merchandise offered for sale
- from one container to another
- with intent to deprive the owner of all or part of the retail value thereof

or
- intentionally
- records a value for the merchandise which is less than the actual retail value
- with the intention of depriving the merchant of the full retail value thereof

or
- intentionally
- removes
- shopping cart
- from the store's premises
- without the consent of the merchant given at the time of such removal
- with the intention of permanently depriving the merchant of the possession, use and benefit of such cart.

Penalty

If retail value is less than $100: First offense—fine NMT $250; Second offense—fine NLT $100, NMT $500; Third and subsequent offense—fine NMT $500 and/or NMT 2 yrs. jail. If retail value is $100 or more: fine NMT $1,000 and/or NMT 2½ yrs. HC.

STALKING—G.L. c. 265, § 43

Elements

Whoever
- willfully and maliciously
- engages in a knowing pattern of conduct or series of acts over a period of time which seriously alarms or annoys that person and would cause a reasonable person to suffer substantial emotional distress
- makes a threat with the intent to place that person in imminent fear of death or bodily injury.

Penalty

Section (a): NMT 5 yrs. state prison or NMT 2½ yrs. HC and/or fine NMT $1,000.

Section (b): If crime is committed in violation of restraining order, NLT one year (mandatory), NMT 5 yrs. state prison or jail. CWOF or file not allowed.

Section (c): Second or subsequent offense—NLT 2 yrs. (mandatory), NMT 10 yrs. state prison or jail CWOF or file not allowed.

NOTE The conduct described in this paragraph can include acts or threats conducted by mail, telephone, e-mail, Internet communication, and/or by fax.

STATUTORY RAPE—see Rape and Abuse of a Child Under 16

SUBORNATION OF PERJURY—G.L. c. 268, § 2

Elements

Whoever
- procures another person
- to commit perjury.

Penalty

NMT 20 yrs. state prison or fine NMT $1,000 or NMT 2½ yrs. jail or both fine and imprisonment in jail. Capital case—life or any term of years state prison. G.L. c. 268, § 1.

THEFT OF MOTOR VEHICLE—see Motor Vehicle Theft

THEFT OF SHOPPING CART—see Shoplifting

THREATS—G.L. c. 275, §§ 2, 4

Elements

Whoever
- threatens
- to commit a crime
- against the person or property of another.

Penalty

NMT 6 mos. imprisonment or fine NMT $100; instead of imposing sentence, court may order defendant to enter into a recognizance, with sufficient sureties, to keep the peace.

TRAFFICKING IN MARIJUANA, COCAINE, HEROIN, MORPHINE, OPIUM, ETC.—G.L. c. 94C, § 32E

Elements

Whoever
- traffics by

- knowingly or intentionally
- manufacturing, distributing, dispensing, or cultivating (marijuana), or possessing with intent to manufacture, distribute, cultivate (marijuana) or dispense, or by bringing into the commonwealth
- controlled substance.

Penalty

Section (a)(1) marijuana 50–<100 pounds: NLT 2½ yrs. and NMT 15 yrs. state prison or NLT 1 yr. and NMT 2½ yrs. HC or both imprisonment and fine NLT $500, NMT $1,000; no sentence below 1 yr. minimum.

(2) marijuana 100–<2,000 pounds: NLT 2 yrs. and NMT 15 yrs. state prison or both imprisonment and fine NLT $2,500, NMT $25,000; no sentence below 2 yr. minimum.

(3) marijuana 2,000–<10,000 pounds: NLT 3½ yrs. and NMT 15 yrs. state prison or both imprisonment and fine NLT $5,000, NMT $50,000; no sentence below 3½ yr. minimum.

(4) marijuana 10,000 pounds or more: NLT 8 yrs. and NMT 15 yrs. state prison or both imprisonment and fine NLT $2,500, NMT $25,000; no sentence below 8 yr. minimum.

Section (b)(1) cocaine 18–<36 grams: NLT 2 yrs. and NMT 15 yrs. state prison or both imprisonment and fine NLT $2,500, NMT $25,000; no sentence below 2 yr. minimum.

(2) cocaine 36–<100 grams: NLT 3½ yrs. and NMT 20 yrs. state prison or both imprisonment and fine NLT $5,000, NMT $50,000; no sentence below 3½ yr. minimum.

(3) cocaine 100–<200 grams: NLT 8 yrs. and NMT 20 yrs. state prison or both imprisonment and fine NLT $10,000, NMT $100,000; no sentence below 8 yr. minimum.

(4) cocaine 200 grams or more: NLT 12 yrs. and NMT 20 yrs. state prison or both imprisonment and fine NLT $50,000, NMT $500,000; no sentence below 12 yr. minimum.

Section (c)(1) heroin, morphine, opium 18–<36 grams: NLT 3½ yrs. and NMT 20 yrs. state prison or both imprisonment and fine NLT $5,000, NMT $50,000; no sentence below 3½ yr. minimum.

(2) heroin, morphine, opium 36–<100 grams: NLT 5 yrs. and NMT 20 yrs. state prison or both imprisonment and fine NLT $5,000, NMT $50,000; no sentence below 5 yr. minimum.

(3) heroin, morphine, opium 100–<200 grams: NLT 8 yrs. and NMT 20 yrs. state prison or both imprisonment and fine NLT $10,000, NMT $100,000; no sentence below 8 yr. minimum.

(4) heroin, morphine, opium 200 grams or more: NLT 12 yrs. and NMT 20 yrs. state prison or both imprisonment and fine NLT $50,000, NMT $500,000; no sentence below 12 yr. minimum.

NOTE Upon conviction of a violation under subsections (b), (c) or (c½) of this section, the Registry of Motor Vehicles is statutorily required to suspend the defendant's license or right to operate for a period of not more than five years. G.L. c. 90, § 22½. The defendant may apply for a hardship license after completion of any time served. G.L. c. 90, § 22½.

TRAFFICKING OF ORGANS—G.L. c. 265, § 53

Elements

Whoever
- recruits, entices, harbors, transports or obtains by any means,
- another person
- intending or knowing that an organ, tissue or other body part of such person will be removed for sale,

9

- against such person's will, or
- knowingly receives anything of value directly or indirectly as a result.

Penalty

NMT 15 years state prison and/or fine $50,000.

Victim under 18: 5 years state prison (mandatory). Sentence cannot be reduced to less than 5 years and no eligibility for probation, parole, work release, furlough, or deduction in sentence for good conduct until 5 years served.

TRAFFICKING OF PERSONS FOR FORCED SERVITUDE—G.L. c. 265, § 50

Elements

Whoever knowingly

- subjects, or attempts to subject,
- another person to forced services, or
- recruits, entices, harbors, transports, provides or obtains by any means, or
- attempts to recruit, entice, harbor, transport, provide or obtain by any means,
- another person
- intending or knowing that such person will be subjected to forced services,
- benefits financially or by receiving anything of value.

Penalty

NLT 5 years, NMT 20 years state prison and fine NMT $25,000. Sentence cannot be reduced to less than 5 years and no eligibility for probation, parole, work release, furlough, or deduction in sentence for good conduct until 5 years served. Cannot be CWOF or placed on file.

Victim under 18: life or NLT 5 years state prison. Sentence cannot be reduced to less than 5 years and no eligibility for probation, parole, work release, furlough, or deduction in sentence for good conduct until 5 years served.

Business entity: fine NMT $1,000,000.

Second or subsequent offense: life or NLT 10 years. Sentence cannot be reduced to less than 10 years and no eligibility for probation, parole, work release, furlough, or deduction in sentence for good conduct until 10 years served. Cannot be CWOF or placed on file. *See* G.L. c. 265, § 52.

TRAFFICKING OF PERSONS FOR SEXUAL SERVITUDE—G.L. c. 265, § 50

Elements

Whoever knowingly

- subjects, or attempts to subject, or
- recruits, entices, harbors, transports, provides or obtains by any means, or
- attempts to recruit, entice, harbor, transport, provide or obtain by any means,
- another person
- to engage in commercial sexual activity, a sexually-explicit performance or the production of unlawful pornography in violation of Chapter 272, or
- benefits financially or by receiving anything of value.

Penalty

NLT 5 years, NMT 20 years state prison and fine NMT $25,000. Sentence cannot be reduced to less than 5 years and no eligibility for probation, parole, work release, furlough, or deduction in sentence for good conduct until 5 years served. Cannot be CWOF or placed on file.

Victim under 18: life or NLT 5 years state prison. Sentence cannot be reduced to less than 5 years and no eligibility

for probation, parole, work release, furlough, or deduction in sentence for good conduct until 5 years served.

Business entity: fine NMT $1,000,000.

Second or subsequent offense: life or NLT 10 years.

Sentence cannot be reduced to less than 10 years and no eligibility for probation, parole, work release, furlough, or deduction in sentence for good conduct until 10 years served. Cannot be CWOF or placed on file. *See* G.L. c. 265, § 52.

TRESPASS—G.L. c. 266, § 120

Elements

Whoever

- without right
- enters or remains in or upon
- the dwelling house, buildings, boats or improved or enclosed land, wharf, or pier
- of another
- after having been forbidden to do so by the person who has lawful control of said premises either directly or by notice posted or in violation of a court order pursuant to G.L. c. 208, § 34B (order to vacate marital home) or G.L. c. 209A, § 4 (abuse prevention temporary order).

Penalty

Fine NMT $100 and/or imprisonment NMT 30 days.

NOTE 1   Proof that a court has given notice of such a court order to the alleged offender shall be prima facie evidence that the notice requirement of this section has been met.

NOTE 2   This section does not apply to tenants or occupants of residential premises who, having rightfully entered said premises at the commencement of the tenancy or occupancy, remain therein after such tenancy or occupancy has been or is alleged to have been terminated. The owner or landlord of said premises may recover possession thereof only through appropriate private civil proceedings.

UNARMED ROBBERY—see Robbery (Unarmed)

UNLAWFULLY CARRYING A FIREARM— G.L. c. 269, § 10(a), (d)

Elements

Whoever

- knowingly
- has in his possession, or
- has under his control in a vehicle
- a firearm (as defined in G.L. c. 140, § 121)
- loaded or unloaded
- without being present in or on his residence or place of business, or
- without a license to carry (as issued under G.L. c. 140, §§ 131 or 131F), or
- without complying with G.L. c. 140, §§ 129C and 131G, or
- without complying with G.L. c. 269, § 12B (in the case of an air rifle or BB gun).

Or, whoever

- knowingly
- has in his possession, or
- has under his control in a vehicle
- a rifle or shotgun
- loaded or unloaded
- without being present in or on his residence or place of business; or
- without a license to carry as issued under G.L. c. 140, §§ 131 or 131F, or

- without a FID card as issued under G.L. c. 140, § 129B, or
- without complying with G.L. c. 140, § 129C or G.L. c. 269, § 12B.

Penalty

NMT 5 yrs., NLT 2½ yrs. state prison; or NMT 2½ yrs. NLT 18 mos. HC or jail. Mandatory minimum 18 mo. sentence. CWOF and file prohibited.

Second offense—NLT 5 yrs., NMT 7 yrs. state prison.
Third offense—NLT 7 yrs., NMT 10 yrs. state prison.
Fourth offense—NLT 10 yrs., NMT 15 yrs. state prison.

For second and subsequent offenses, the sentence "shall not be suspended, nor shall any person so sentenced be eligible for probation or receive any deduction from his sentence for good conduct." G.L. c. 269, § 10(d).

Additional penalty if loaded: NMT 2½ yrs. HC.

NOTE "Firearm"—see G.L. c. 140, § 121.

UNLAWFULLY POSSESSING A FIREARM OR AMMUNITION—G.L. c. 269, § 10(h)(1)

Elements

Whoever
- owns, possesses, or transfers possession
- of a firearm, rifle, shotgun or ammunition
- without complying with the FID card requirements of G.L. c. 140, § 129C.

Penalty

NMT 2 yrs. HC or jail or fine NMT $500. Second or subsequent offense—NMT 2 yrs. HC or jail or fine NMT $1,000 or both.

A violation of this subsection shall not be considered a lesser included offense to a violation of subsection (a).

UNNATURAL AND LASCIVIOUS ACTS— G.L. c. 272, § 35

Elements
- unnatural and lascivious act
- with another person

Penalty

Fine NLT $100, NMT $1,000; or NMT 5 yrs. state prison or NMT 2½ yrs. HC or jail.

NOTE 1 Lifetime Parole. See G.L. c. 265, § 45; G.L. c. 275, § 18.

NOTE 2 Sexually Dangerous Person Commitment. See G.L. c. 123A, §§ 1–15.

USE WITHOUT AUTHORITY—G.L. c. 90, § 24(2)(a)

Elements

Whoever
- uses
- motor vehicle
- public way
- without authority
- knowing that such use is unauthorized.

Penalty

Fine NLT $50, NMT $500; and/or imprisonment NLT 30 days; NMT 2 yrs; second offense—NMT 5 yrs. state prison or NLT 30 days, NMT 2½ yrs. HC, or fine NMT $1,000, or both fine and imprisonment. Third offense committed within 5 yrs. of the earliest of his two most recent prior offenses—fine NLT $200, NMT $1,000 or imprisonment NLT

6 mos. NMT 2½ yrs. HC or NLT 2½ yrs. NMT 5 yrs. state prison, or both fine and imprisonment.

NOTE 1 A conviction under this section will also result in the revocation of the defendant's license or right to operate by the Registry of Motor Vehicles. G.L. c. 90, § 24(2)(b)–(c).

NOTE 2 See G.L. c. 90, § 24P for certain license suspensions for defendants under the ages of 21 or 18.

UTTERING FALSE OR FORGED RECORDS, DEEDS OR OTHER WRITINGS—G.L. c. 267, § 5

Elements

Whoever
- with intent to injure or defraud
- utters and publishes as true
- a false, forged or altered
- record, deed, instrument or other writing mentioned in G.L. c. 267, §§ 1–4
- knowing the same to be false, forged or altered.

Penalty

NMT 10 yrs. state prison or NMT 2 yrs. jail.

VEHICULAR HOMICIDE—G.L. c. 90, § 24G

(a) Homicide by a motor vehicle while under the influence of an intoxicating substance.

Elements

Whoever
- upon any way or in any place to which the public has a right to access, or
- upon any way or in any place to which members of the public have access as invitees or licensees
- with a percentage by weight of alcohol in their blood of eight one-hundredths or greater
- while under the influence of intoxicating liquor, or of marijuana, narcotic drugs, depressants, or stimulant substances, all as defined in G.L. c. 94C, § 1, or the vapors of glue
- operates
- motor vehicle
- recklessly or negligently
- lives and safety of the public might be endangered
- by such operation causes the death of another person.

Penalty

NLT 2½ yrs., NMT 15 yrs. state prison and fine NMT $5,000; or NLT 1 yr., NMT 2½ yrs. HC or jail and fine NMT $5,000. License revoked for fifteen years. Mandatory 1 yr. jail sentence. CWOF or file prohibited. Second offense: license revoked for life.

(b) Homicide by motor vehicle

Elements

Whoever
- upon any way or in any place to which the public has a right of access, or
- upon any way or in any place to which members of the public have access as invitees or licenses

either
- operates
- motor vehicle
- under the influence of intoxicating liquor, or of marijuana, narcotic drugs, depressants or stimulant substances, all as defined in G.L. c. 94C, § 1, or the vapors of glue;

or
- operates

- motor vehicle
- recklessly or negligently
- lives or safety of the public might be endangered

and

- by such operation causes the death of another person.

Penalty

NLT 30 days, NMT 2½ yrs. HC or jail and/or fine NLT $300, NMT $3,000. License revoked 10 yrs. Second offense: license revoked for life.

NOTE   See G.L. c. 90, § 24P for certain license suspensions for defendants under the ages of 21 or 18.

WANTON DESTRUCTION OF PROPERTY— see Willful and Malicious

WELFARE FRAUD—see False Representations to Procure Welfare

WILLFUL AND MALICIOUS DESTRUCTION OF PROPERTY—G.L. c. 266, § 127

Elements

Whoever

- destroys or injures
- personal property, dwelling house or building of another
- willfully and maliciously.

Penalty

NMT 10 yrs. state prison or fine of $3,000 or 3 times the value of the property so destroyed or injured, whichever is greater and imprisonment in jail NMT 2½ yrs.

If destruction is wanton—fine of $1,500 or 3 times the value of the property so destroyed or injured, whichever is greater, or by imprisonment NMT 2½ yrs.; if the value of the property so destroyed or injured is not alleged to exceed $250, the punishment shall be by a fine of 3 times the value of the damage or injury to such property or imprisonment NMT 2½ months.

NOTE   "[W]here a fine is levied pursuant to the value of the property destroyed or injured, the court shall, after conviction, conduct an evidentiary hearing to ascertain the value of the property so destroyed or injured." G.L. c. 266, § 127.

9

PART 10

Schedule of Assessments
for Civil Motor Vehicle Infractions

DISTRICT COURT ADMINISTRATIVE REGULATION

No. 2-86

(Amended October 23, 2013)

SCHEDULE OF ASSESSMENTS FOR CIVIL MOTOR VEHICLE INFRACTIONS
PROMULGATED PURSUANT TO G.L. c. 90C, § 1

Administrative Regulation No. 2-86 is hereby amended as follows, effective October 23, 2013.

Pursuant to G.L. c. 90C, § 1, "Scheduled assessment," the attached revised schedule of assessments for civil motor vehicle infractions is hereby promulgated jointly by the Registrar of Motor Vehicles and the Chief Justice of the District Court.

In accordance with G.L. c. 90C, § 1, a copy of this revised schedule shall be visibly posted in the office of the clerk-magistrate of each district court.

Paul C. Dawley
Chief Justice of the District Court

Effective: October 23, 2013

NOTE:

These amounts represent the pay-by-mail civil assessments to be paid by motorists who do not wish to challenge their responsibility for civil motor vehicle infractions. They also represent the amounts of the civil assessments that are to be made by a judge or magistrate who has found a person responsible for a civil motor vehicle infraction after hearing, except where a reduction in the amount is permissible in accordance with District Court Administrative Regulation No. 2-06.

COMMONWEALTH OF MASSACHUSETTS
DISTRICT COURT DEPARTMENT OF THE TRIAL COURT
& REGISTRY OF MOTOR VEHICLES

Table of Citable Motor Vehicle Offenses
effective October 23, 2013

- **CITABLE "AUTOMOBILE LAW VIOLATIONS."** The offenses in this table are citable on the Massachusetts Uniform Citation. Note that not every offense relating to motor vehicles must (or may) be cited on a citation, but only those in which one element of the offense involves the **"operation or control"** of a motor vehicle. G.L. c.90C, §1 defines a citable "automobile law violation" as "any violation of any statute, ordinance, by-law or regulation relating to the operation or control of motor vehicles other than" parking violations and c.159B motor carrier violations. "[T]he mere fact that an offense involves a motor vehicle does not ipso facto make it an automobile law violation [unless] the thrust of [the offense is] aimed at regulating the manner in which automobiles are operated on a public way." *Commonwealth v. Giannino,* 371 Mass. 700, 702-703, 358 N.E.2d 1008, 1010 (1977).

  For purposes of G.L. c.90C, recreation vehicles, snow vehicles, and motorized bicycles and scooters are motor vehicles.

- **CRIMINAL AUTOMOBILE LAW VIOLATIONS** citable under G.L. c.90C, § 3(B) are identified in this table with the word "CRIMINAL" in the "ASSESSMENT" column.

- **CIVIL MOTOR VEHICLE INFRACTIONS** (CMVIs) citable under G.L. c.90C, § 3(A) are identified in this table with an asterisk (*). A CMVI is "an automobile law violation for which the maximum penalty does not provide for imprisonment" except for:
  - Unlicensed Operation (G.L. c.90, §10, ¶1)
  - Operating After Suspension or Revocation (G.L. c.90, §23)
  - Refusing to Stop for an Officer (§25)
  - Uninsured Motor Vehicle (§34J)
  - Violations "committed by a juvenile under the age of seventeen who does not hold a valid operators license." G.L. c.90C, §1.

  The **scheduled assessment** for each CMVI is indicated in the "ASSESSMENT" column of this table. The scheduled assessment is the amount which the citing officer must enter on the citation (G.L. c.90C, §3[A][2]), which the motorist must pay unless he or she asks for a hearing (§3[A][3]), and which a magistrate or judge must impose after finding the motorist responsible after a hearing except where a reduction from the scheduled assessment is authorized by District Court guidelines (§3[A][4]). Those guidelines are contained in District Court Administrative Regulation 3-86. The scheduled assessment for each CMVI is established jointly by the Chief Justice of the District Court Department and the Registrar of Motor Vehicles, and may be less than, but may not exceed, the maximum amount authorized by statute. G.L. c. 90C, §1. In this table, a "■" next to the schedule assessment indicates that the assessment has been set at less than the potential maximum.

10

G.L. CHAPTER & SECTION	OFFENSE CODE	VIOLATION *(INCLUDED OFFENSES APPEAR IN ITALICS)*		ASSESSMENT
c40 §21	40/21/H	**TIRE WIDTH BY-LAW VIOLATION** * c40 §21(9)		$300
c64E §2	64E/2/A	**SPECIAL FUELS, USE WITHOUT LICENSE** * c64E §2		$100
c85 §2		*DEPT OF TRANSPORTATION REGS FOR DRIVING ON STATE HIGHWAYS — see 720 CMR §§9.05-9.07*		
c85 §2B		*DEPT OF TRANSPORTATION REGS FOR LIMITED ACCESS HIGHWAYS — see 720 CMR §9.08*		
c85 §2E	85/2E/A	**STATE HWAY—CLOSED TO TRAVEL, MV WHERE** * c85 §2E		$50
c85 §10	85/10/A	**ANIMAL OFFAL, VIOL BY-LAW ON TRANSPORT** * c85 §10		$100
	85/10/B	**MOTOR VEH BY-LAW VIOLATION** * c85 §10		$20
c85 §14B	85/14B	**FLARES VIOLATION BY COMMERCIAL VEHICLE** * c85 §14B *FLARES, COMMERCIAL VEH FAIL DEPLOY* *FLARES, COMMERCIAL VEH OPERATE WITHOUT*		$50
c85 §15	85/15/A	**LIGHTS VIOLATION** * c85 §15		$5
c85 §16	85/16/A	**NAME/ADDRESS, MV OP REFUSE GIVE AT NT** * c85 §15		
c85 §19	85/19/A	**ANIMAL, TRANSPORT DANGEROUS WILD** * c85 §15		$20
c85 §20	85/20	**SPEEDING ON COUNTY BRIDGE VIOL BY-LAW** * c85 §20		$2
c85 §23	85/23	**STATE HWAY—GUBERNATORIAL BY-LAW VIOLATION** * c85 §23		$50
c85 §30	85/30/A	**WEIGHT VIOLATION** c85 §30 *INJURE SURFACE OF WAY*	ON COUNTY WAY *	$100
	85/30/B		ON MUNIC WAY *	
	85/30/C		ON STATE HWAY *	
c85 §30A	85/30A/A	**WEIGHT VIOL ON COUNTY WAY & NO STICKER** * c85 §30A		
	85/30A/B	**WEIGHT VIOL ON MUNIC WAY & NO STICKER** * c85 §30A		
	85/30A/C	**WEIGHT VIOL ON STATE HWAY & NO STICKER** * c85 §30A		
c85 §31	85/31/A	**METAL TIRES +4 MPH** c85 §31	ON COUNTY WAY *	
	85/31/B		ON MUNIC WAY *	
	85/31/C		ON STATE HWAY *	
c85 §34	85/34	**WEIGHT VIOLATION ON BRIDGE** * c85 §34		$200
c85 §35	85/35	**WEIGHT VIOLATION ON HWAY BRIDGE** * c85 §35		
c85 §36	85/36	**LOAD UNSECURED/UNCOVERED** * c85 §36		
c89 §1	89/1	**KEEP RIGHT FOR ONCOMING MV, FAIL TO** * c89 §1		$100 *from 12/1/13:* *plus $5 public safety surcharge*
c89 §2	89/2	**PASSING VIOLATION** * c89 §2 *PASSING ON RIGHT* *GIVE WAY TO PASSING VEH, FAIL TO*		
c89 §4	89/4	**KEEP RIGHT ON HILL/OBSTRUCTED VIEW, FL** * c89 §4		
c89 §4A	89/4A	**MARKED LANES VIOLATION** * c89 §4A *MOTORCYCLE LANES VIOLATION* *PASSING VIOLATION*		
c89 §4B	89/4B/A	**BREAKDOWN LANE VIOLATION** * c89 §4B		
	89/4B/B	**RIGHT LANE, FAIL DRIVE IN** * c89 §4B		
c89 §4C	89/4C	**LEFT LANE RESTRICTION VIOLATION** * c89 §4C *RIGHT LANE, HEAVY COMM VEH FAIL DRIVE IN*		
c89 §7	89/7	**EMERGENCY VEHICLE, WILFULLY OBSTRUCT** c89 §7		CRIMINAL
	89/7/B	2ND OFFENSE		
	89/7/C	3RD OFFENSE		
c89 §7A	89/7A	**EMERGENCY VEHICLE, OBSTRUCT** * c89 §7A *EMERGENCY VEH, FAIL PULL OVER FOR* *EMERGENCY VEH, WITHIN 300 FT BEHIND* *FIRE HOSE, DRIVE OVER*		$100 *from 12/1/13:* *plus $5 public safety surcharge*

10

G.L. CHAPTER & SECTION	OFFENSE CODE	VIOLATION *(INCLUDED OFFENSES APPEAR IN ITALICS)*	ASSESSMENT
c89 §7C	89/7C	**EMERGENCY VEHICLE, OBSTRUCT STATIONARY *** c89 §7C	$100 *from 12/1/13:* plus $5 public safety surcharge
c89 §8	89/8	**YIELD AT INTERSECTION, FAIL *** c89 §8 *RIGHT-ON-RED VIOLATION* *YIELD ON LEFT TURN, FAIL*	$35 *from 12/1/13:* plus $5 public safety surcharge
c89 §9	89/9	**STOP/YIELD, FAIL TO *** c89 §9 *FLASHING RED LIGHT VIOLATION* *INTERSECTION, BLOCK* *STOP SIGN VIOLATION* *YIELD SIGN VIOLATION*	1ST OFF: $100 ■ *from 12/1/13:* plus $5 public safety surcharge SUBSQ. OFF: $150 *from 12/1/13:* plus $5 public safety surcharge
c89 §11	89/11	**CROSSWALK VIOLATION *** c89 §11 *CROSSWALK, BLOCK* *CROSSWALK, PASS MV STOPPED AT* *CROSSWALK, PEDESTRIAN IN*	$200 *from 12/1/13:* plus $5 public safety surcharge
c90 §1B	90/1B/A	**MOPED OPERATION BY UNLIC –17** c90 §1B	DELINQUENCY
	90/1B/B	2ND OFFENSE	
	90/1B/C	3RD OFFENSE	
	90/1B/D	**MOPED VIOLATION *** c90 §1B *MOPED HELMET VIOLATION* *MOPED ON RESTRICTED HWAY* *MOPED OPERATION +17 WITHOUT LIC* *MOPED SPEED VIOLATION* *MOPED MISCELLANEOUS TRAFFIC VIOL*	1ST OFF: $25 *from 12/1/13:* plus $5 public safety surcharge 2ND OFF: $50 *from 12/1/13:* plus $5 public safety surcharge 3RD OFF: $100 *from 12/1/13:* plus $5 public safety surcharge
c90 §1E	90/1E	**MOTORIZED SCOOTER VIOLATION *** c90 §1E	1ST OFF: $25 *from 12/1/13:* plus $5 public safety surcharge 2ND OFF: $50 *from 12/1/13:* plus $5 public safety surcharge 3RD OFF: $100 *from 12/1/13:* plus $5 public safety surcharge
c90 §1F	90/1F	**LOW-SPEED VEHICLE VIOLATION *** c90 §1F	1ST OFF: $75 *from 12/1/13:* plus $5 public safety surcharge SUBSQ. OFF: $150 *from 12/1/13:* plus $5 public safety surcharge
c90 §2	90/2/A	**REGISTRATION, FL SURRENDER ON TRANSFER *** c90 §2	1ST OFF: $35 *from 12/1/13:* plus $5 public safety surcharge 2ND OFF: $75 *from 12/1/13:* plus $5 public safety surcharge 3RD OFF: $150 *from 12/1/13:* plus $5 public safety surcharge

10

G.L. CHAPTER & SECTION	OFFENSE CODE	VIOLATION *(INCLUDED OFFENSES APPEAR IN ITALICS)*	ASSESSMENT
c90 §2, cont.	90/2/B	**HANDICAP PARKING PLATE/PLACARD MISUSE** * c90 §2	1ST OFF: $500 *from 12/1/13:* plus $5 public safety surcharge
			SUBSQ. OFF: $1000 *from 12/1/13:* plus $5 public safety surcharge
	90/2/C	**NUMBER PLATE, MISUSE OFFICIAL** * c90 §2	$25 *from 12/1/13:* plus $5 public safety surcharge
c90 §2B	90/2B	**REGISTRATION LEFT IN TRANSFERRED MV** * c90 §2B	1ST OFF: $35 *from 12/1/13:* plus $5 public safety surcharge
			2ND OFF: $75 *from 12/1/13:* plus $5 public safety surcharge
			3RD OFF: $150 *from 12/1/13:* plus $5 public safety surcharge
c90 §3	90/3/A	**REGISTER MV OPERATED +30 DAYS YEAR, FL** * c90 §3	$250 *from 12/1/13:* plus $5 public safety surcharge
	90/3/B	**STUDENT MOTOR VEH REGISTRATION VIOL** * c90 §3 *NONRESIDENT STUDENT DECAL, FAIL DISPLAY* *NONRESIDENT STUDENT FAIL REGISTER MV*	$200 *from 12/1/13:* plus $5 public safety surcharge
c90 §3½	90/312/A	**REGISTER MV IMPROPERLY TO AVOID TAXES/PREMIUMS** c90 §3½ (c)(¶1)	CRIMINAL
	90/312/B	**REGISTER MV IMPROPERLY TO AVOID TAXES/PREMIUMS** * c90 §3½ (c)(¶2)	$500 *from 12/1/13:* plus $5 public safety surcharge
c90 §5		*RMV REGS FOR DEALER/REPAIR PLATES—see 540 CMR §18.04*	
c90 §5A	90/5A/A	**NUMBER PLATE, MISUSE MILITARY** * c90 §5A	$50 *from 12/1/13:* plus $5 public safety surcharge
c90 §6	90/6	**NUMBER PLATE VIOLATION** * c90 §6 *NUMBER PLATE COVERED WITH GLASS/PLASTIC* *NUMBER PLATE MISSING* *NUMBER PLATE OBSCURED* *NUMBER PLATE UNLIT*	1ST OFF: $35 *from 12/1/13:* plus $5 public safety surcharge
			2ND OFF: $75 *from 12/1/13:* plus $5 public safety surcharge
			3RD OFF: $150 *from 12/1/13:* plus $5 public safety surcharge
		REGISTRATION STICKER MISSING—see 540 CMR §2.05	
c90 §7	90/7/A	**BRAKES VIOLATION, MV** * c90 §7	1ST OFF: $35 *from 12/1/13:* plus $5 public safety surcharge
			2ND OFF: $75 *from 12/1/13:* plus $5 public safety surcharge

10

G.L. CHAPTER & SECTION	OFFENSE CODE	VIOLATION (INCLUDED OFFENSES APPEAR IN ITALICS)	ASSESSMENT
c90 §7, cont.			3RD OFF: $150 *from 12/1/13:* plus $5 public safety surcharge
	90/7/B	**HORN VIOLATION, MV** * c90 §7	1ST OFF: $35 *from 12/1/13:* plus $5 public safety surcharge
			2ND OFF: $75 *from 12/1/13:* plus $5 public safety surcharge
			3RD OFF: $150 *from 12/1/13:* plus $5 public safety surcharge
	90/7/C	**LIGHTS VIOLATION, MV** * c90 §7 *FLASHING/ROTATING/OSCILLATING LIGHT VIOLATION* *HAZARD LIGHTS VIOLATION*	1ST OFF: $35 *from 12/1/13:* plus $5 public safety surcharge
			2ND OFF: $75 *from 12/1/13:* plus $5 public safety surcharge
			3RD OFF: $150 *from 12/1/13:* plus $5 public safety surcharge
	90/7/D	**EQUIPMENT VIOLATION, MISCELLANEOUS MV** * c90 §7 *AUDIBLE ALARM ON DUMP TRUCK, NO* *AUDIBLE ALARM ON FLAMMABLES TANKER, NO* *LOCK VIOLATION* *MIRROR VIOLATION* *MUD GUARDS VIOLATION ON COMMERCIAL MV* *MUFFLER VIOLATION* *OVERHANG +4 FT WITHOUT FLAG/LIGHT* *REFLECTOR VIOLATION ON COMMERCIAL MV* *SAFETY CHAINS VIOL ON TRAILER* *SEAT BELT MISSING* *SLOW MOVING EMBLEM VIOL*	1ST OFF: $35 *from 12/1/13:* plus $5 public safety surcharge
			2ND OFF: $75 *from 12/1/13:* plus $5 public safety surcharge
			3RD OFF: $150 *from 12/1/13:* plus $5 public safety surcharge
	90/7/E	**MOTORCYCLE EQUIPMENT VIOLATION** * c90 §7 *MOTORCYCLE EQUIP/OPERATION VIOLATION* *MOTORCYCLE GOGGLES/FACESHIELD VIOLATION* *MOTORCYCLE HELMET VIOLATION*	1ST OFF: $35 *from 12/1/13:* plus $5 public safety surcharge
			2ND OFF: $75 *from 12/1/13:* plus $5 public safety surcharge
			3RD OFF: $150 *from 12/1/13:* plus $5 public safety surcharge
	90/7/F	**MOTORCYCLE PASSENGER VIOLATION** * c90 §7 *MOTORCYCLE DRIVER BEHIND PASSENGER* *MOTORCYCLE CARRY PASSENGER, SOLO*	1ST OFF: $35 *from 12/1/13:* plus $5 public safety surcharge
			2ND OFF: $75 *from 12/1/13:* plus $5 public safety surcharge
			3RD OFF: $150 *from 12/1/13:* plus $5 public safety surcharge
c90 §7A	*See c90 §20*		

10

G.L. CHAPTER & SECTION	OFFENSE CODE	VIOLATION (*INCLUDED OFFENSES APPEAR IN ITALICS*)	ASSESSMENT
c90 §7B	90/7B/A	**SCHOOL BUS OPERATION/EQUIPMENT VIOL** * c90 §7B *SCHOOL BUS—ALCOHOL CONSUMED ON* *SCHOOL BUS—BOARD/DISCHARGE IMPROPERLY* *SCHOOL BUS—DOORS OPEN WHILE MOVING* *SCHOOL BUS—DRIVER WITHOUT SEATBELT ON* *SCHOOL BUS—EQUIPMENT NOT REMOVED* *SCHOOL BUS—EQUIPMENT VIOLATION* *SCHOOL BUS—FLASHERS MISUSED/UNUSED* *SCHOOL BUS—FUEL WHILE OCCUPIED* *SCHOOL BUS—PRETRIP INSPECTION, NO* *SCHOOL BUS—SMOKE ON* *SCHOOL BUS—UNLICENSED OPERATION*	1ST OFF: $35 *from 12/1/13:* *plus $5 public safety surcharge* 2ND OFF: $75 *from 12/1/13:* *plus $5 public safety surcharge* 3RD OFF: $150 *from 12/1/13:* *plus $5 public safety surcharge*
	90/7B/B	**SCHOOL BUS OVERCROWDED** c90 §7B	CRIMINAL
	90/7B/F	**SCHOOL BUS INSPECTION, FAIL PERFORM POST-TRIP** * c90 §7B(17)	$100 *from 12/1/13:* *plus $5 public safety surcharge*
	90/7B/G	**SCHOOL BUS, USE MOBILE PHONE WHILE OPERATING** * c90 §7B	1ST OFF: $35 *from 12/1/13:* *plus $5 public safety surcharge* 2ND OFF: $75 *from 12/1/13:* *plus $5 public safety surcharge* 3RD OFF: $150 *from 12/1/13:* *plus $5 public safety surcharge*
c90 §7D	90/7D/A	**PUPIL TRANSPORT VEHICLE VIOLATION** * c90 §7D	1ST OFF: $35 *from 12/1/13:* *plus $5 public safety surcharge* 2ND OFF: $75 *from 12/1/13:* *plus $5 public safety surcharge* 3RD OFF: $150 *from 12/1/13:* *plus $5 public safety surcharge*
	90/7D/B	**PUPIL TRANSPORT VEHICLE OVERCROWDED** c90 §7D	CRIMINAL
c90 §7D½	90/7D12/A	**VOC STUDENT TRANSPORT VIOLATION** * c90 §7D½	1ST OFF: $35 *from 12/1/13:* *plus $5 public safety surcharge* 2ND OFF: $75 *from 12/1/13:* *plus $5 public safety surcharge* 3RD OFF: $150 *from 12/1/13:* *plus $5 public safety surcharge*
c90 §7E	90/7E	**RED/BLUE LIGHT VIOLATION, MV** * c90 §7E	$300 *from 12/1/13:* *plus $5 public safety surcharge*
c90 §7I	90/7I	**SAMARITAN VEHICLE MISUSE SIREN/LIGHT** * c90 §7I	1ST OFF: $35 *from 12/1/13:* *plus $5 public safety surcharge* 2ND OFF: $75 *from 12/1/13:* *plus $5 public safety surcharge*

10

G.L. CHAPTER & SECTION	OFFENSE CODE	VIOLATION *(INCLUDED OFFENSES APPEAR IN ITALICS)*	ASSESSMENT
c90 §7I, cont.			3RD OFF: $150 *from 12/1/13:* plus $5 public safety surcharge
c90 §7J		*RMV REGS ON MOTORCYCLE HANDLEBAR HEIGHT VIOLATION — see 540 CMR §4.06*	
c90 §7L	90/7L	**SCHOOL BUS OPERATE WITH STANDEES** * c90 §7L	$500 *from 12/1/13:* plus $5 public safety surcharge
c90 §7P	90/7P/A	**HEIGHT, OPERATE MV WITH MODIFIED** * c90 §7P	1ST OFF: $35 *from 12/1/13:* plus $5 public safety surcharge
			2ND OFF: $75 *from 12/1/13:* plus $5 public safety surcharge
			3RD OFF: $150 *from 12/1/13:* plus $5 public safety surcharge
c90 §7Q	90/7Q	**TIRE TREAD DEPTH VIOLATION** * c90 §7Q	1ST OFF: $35 *from 12/1/13:* plus $5 public safety surcharge
			2ND OFF: $75 *from 12/1/13:* plus $5 public safety surcharge
			3RD OFF: $150 *from 12/1/13:* plus $5 public safety surcharge
c90 §7R	90/7R	**VEHICLE ID NUMBER NOT DISPLAYED** * c90 §7R	1ST OFF: $35 *from 12/1/13:* plus $5 public safety surcharge
			2ND OFF: $75 *from 12/1/13:* plus $5 public safety surcharge
			3RD OFF: $150 *from 12/1/13:* plus $5 public safety surcharge
c90 §7U	90/7U	**MOTORCYCLE, NOISY** * c90 §7U	1ST OFF: $35 *from 12/1/13:* plus $5 public safety surcharge
			2ND OFF: $75 *from 12/1/13:* plus $5 public safety surcharge
			3RD OFF: $150 *from 12/1/13:* plus $5 public safety surcharge
c90 §7AA	90/7AA/A	**CHILD UNDER 8 & UNDER 58 INCHES WITHOUT CARSEAT** * c90 §7AA	$25 *from 12/1/13:* plus $5 public safety surcharge
	90/7AA/B	**CHILD 8-12 OR OVER 57 INCHES WITHOUT SEAT BELT** * c90 §7AA	
c90 §7CC	90/7CC	**SPECIAL NEEDS STUDENTS VEH FL ID OWNER** * c90 §7CC	$100 *from 12/1/13:* plus $5 public safety surcharge

10

G.L. CHAPTER & SECTION	OFFENSE CODE	VIOLATION (INCLUDED OFFENSES APPEAR IN ITALICS)	ASSESSMENT
c90 §8	90/8/E	**JUNIOR OPERATOR WITH PASSENGER UNDER 18** * c90 §8	1ST OFF: $35 *from 12/1/13:* plus $5 public safety surcharge
			2ND OFF: $75 *from 12/1/13:* plus $5 public safety surcharge
			3RD OFF: $150 *from 12/1/13:* plus $5 public safety surcharge
		LICENSE CLASS/RESTRICTION, OPERATE MV IN VIOLATION OF — see c90 §10 *JUNIOR OPERATOR OPERATE 12-5 AM WITHOUT PARENT — see c90 §10*	
c90 §8A½	90/8A12	**PUPILS, TRANSPORT WITHOUT LICENSE** * c90 §8A½	1ST OFF: $35 *from 12/1/13:* plus $5 public safety surcharge
			2ND OFF: $75 *from 12/1/13:* plus $5 public safety surcharge
			3RD OFF: $150 *from 12/1/13:* plus $5 public safety surcharge
c90 §8B	90/8B	**LEARNERS PERMIT VIOLATION** * c90 §8B *LEARNERS PERMIT—OP MCYCLE AT NIGHT* *LEARNERS PERMIT—OP MCYCLE W/PASSENGER* *LEARNERS PERMIT—OP WITHOUT ADULT*	1ST OFF: $35 *from 12/1/13:* plus $5 public safety surcharge
			2ND OFF: $75 *from 12/1/13:* plus $5 public safety surcharge
			3RD OFF: $150 *from 12/1/13:* plus $5 public safety surcharge
c90 §8M	90/8M	**MOBILE PHONE, OPERATOR UNDER 18 USE** * c90 §8M	1ST OFF: $100 *from 12/1/13:* plus $5 public safety surcharge
			2ND OFF: $250 *from 12/1/13:* plus $5 public safety surcharge
			3RD OFF: $500 *from 12/1/13:* plus $5 public safety surcharge
c90 §9	90/9/A	**NUMBER PLATE MISSING** * c90 §9	1ST OFF: $100 *from 12/1/13:* plus $5 public safety surcharge
			SUBSQ OFF: $1000 *from 12/1/13:* plus $5 public safety surcharge
	90/9/B	**UNREGISTERED MOTOR VEHICLE** * c90 §9	1ST OFF: $100 *from 12/1/13:* plus $5 public safety surcharge
			SUBSQ OFF: $1000 *from 12/1/13:* plus $5 public safety surcharge

10

G.L. CHAPTER & SECTION	OFFENSE CODE	VIOLATION *(INCLUDED OFFENSES APPEAR IN ITALICS)*	ASSESSMENT
c90 §9A	90/9A	**SAFETY GLASS VIOLATION** * c90 §9A	1ST OFF: $35 *from 12/1/13:* plus $5 public safety surcharge
			2ND OFF: $75 *from 12/1/13:* plus $5 public safety surcharge
			3RD OFF: $150 *from 12/1/13:* plus $5 public safety surcharge
c90 §9D	90/9D	**WINDOW OBSTRUCTED/NONTRANSPARENT** * c90 §9D	$250 *from 12/1/13:* plus $5 public safety surcharge
c90 §10	90/10/A	**UNLICENSED OPERATION OF MV** c90 §10	CRIMINAL
	90/10/B	**LICENSE CLASS, OPERATE MV IN VIOLATION** c90 §10	
	90/10/C	**LICENSE RESTRICTION, OPERATE MV IN VIOL** c90 §10	
	90/10/D	**JUNIOR OPERATOR OP 12:30-5 AM W/O PARENT** c90 §10	DELINQUENCY OR CRIMINAL
		SUSPENDED LICENSE, OPERATE MV WITH — see c90 §23	
c90 §11	90/11/A	**LICENSE NOT IN POSSESSION** * c90 §11 *LICENSE, FAIL SHOW AFTER ACCIDENT*	1ST OFF: $35 *from 12/1/13:* plus $5 public safety surcharge
			2ND OFF: $75 *from 12/1/13:* plus $5 public safety surcharge
			3RD OFF: $150 *from 12/1/13:* plus $5 public safety surcharge
c90 §11, cont.	90/11/B	**REGISTRATION NOT IN POSSESSION** * c90 §11 *REGISTRATION, FAIL SHOW AFTER ACCIDENT*	1ST OFF: $35 *from 12/1/13:* plus $5 public safety surcharge
			2ND OFF: $75 *from 12/1/13:* plus $5 public safety surcharge
			3RD OFF: $150 *from 12/1/13:* plus $5 public safety surcharge
c90 §12	90/12/A	**UNLICENSED OPERATOR, EMPLOY** * c90 §12(a)	1ST OFF: $1,000 *from 12/1/13:* plus $5 public safety surcharge
	90/12/B	**UNLICENSED OPERATOR, EMPLOY, SUBSQ.OFF.** c90 §12(a)	CRIMINAL
	90/12/C	**UNLICENSED/SUSPENDED OPERATION OF MV, PERMIT** c90 §12(b)	
	90/12/D	**UNLICENSED/SUSPENDED OPERATION OF MV, PERMIT, SUBSQ.OFF.** c90 §12(b)	
	90/12/E	**IGNITION INTERLOCK, PERMIT OPERATION WITHOUT** c90 §12(c)	
	90/12/F	**IGNITION INTERLOCK, PERMIT OPERATION WITHOUT, SUBSQ.OFF.** c90 §12(c)	
c90 §12A	90/12A/A	**MOBILE PHONE, PUBLIC TRANSPORT MV OPERATOR USE** * c90 §12A(a)	$500 *from 12/1/13:* plus $5 public safety surcharge

10

G.L. CHAPTER & SECTION	OFFENSE CODE	VIOLATION (*INCLUDED OFFENSES APPEAR IN ITALICS*)	ASSESSMENT
c90 §13	90/13/A	**UNSAFE OPERATION OF MV** * c90 §13 *BRAKE NOT SET* *CHILD UNDER 12 IN BODY OF PICKUP TRUCK* *CHOCK BLOCKS NOT USED* *HEADPHONES ON OPERATOR* *IMPEDED OPERATION* *KEY NOT REMOVED FROM MV* *OUTSIDE OF MV, PERMIT PERSON HANG ON* *TELEVISION VISIBLE TO MV OPERATOR* *UNATTENDED RUNNING MOTOR VEH*	1ST OFF: $35 *from 12/1/13:* plus $5 public safety surcharge 2ND OFF: $75 *from 12/1/13:* plus $5 public safety surcharge 3RD OFF: $150 *from 12/1/13:* plus $5 public safety surcharge
	90/13/H	**MOBILE PHONE, OPERATOR USE IMPROPERLY** * c90 §13	1ST OFF: $35 *from 12/1/13:* plus $5 public safety surcharge 2ND OFF: $75 *from 12/1/13:* plus $5 public safety surcharge 3RD OFF: $150 *from 12/1/13:* plus $5 public safety surcharge
c90 §13A	90/13A	**SEAT BELT, FAIL WEAR** * c90 §13A	$25; operator subject to $25 assessment for each passenger in violation. *from 12/1/13:* plus $5 public safety surcharge
c90 §13B	90/13B	**ELECTRONIC MESSAGE, OPERATOR SEND/READ** * c90 §13B	1ST OFF: $100 *from 12/1/13:* plus $5 public safety surcharge 2ND OFF: $250 *from 12/1/13:* plus $5 public safety surcharge 3RD OFF: $500 *from 12/1/13:* plus $5 public safety surcharge
c90 §14	90/14/A	**SLOW, FAIL TO** * c90 §14 *SLOW AT INTERSECTION, FAIL* *SLOW FOR BICYCLIST, FAIL* *SLOW FOR PEDESTRIAN, FAIL* *SLOW FOR STOPPED STREET RAILWAY, FAIL* *SLOW WHEN VIEW OBSTRUCTED, FAIL* *STOP FOR FRIGHTENED COW/HORSE, FAIL*	1ST OFF: $35 *from 12/1/13:* plus $5 public safety surcharge 2ND OFF: $75 *from 12/1/13:* plus $5 public safety surcharge 3RD OFF: $150 *from 12/1/13:* plus $5 public safety surcharge
	90/14/B	**TURN, IMPROPER** * c90 §14 *BICYCLIST, FAIL YIELD ON TURN TO* *LEFT TURN, FAIL YIELD ON* *LEFT TURN, IMPROPER* *RIGHT TURN, IMPROPER*	1ST OFF: $35 *from 12/1/13:* plus $5 public safety surcharge 2ND OFF: $75 *from 12/1/13:* plus $5 public safety surcharge 3RD OFF: $150 *from 12/1/13:* plus $5 public safety surcharge

10

G.L. CHAPTER & SECTION	OFFENSE CODE	VIOLATION (INCLUDED OFFENSES APPEAR IN ITALICS)	ASSESSMENT
c90 §14, cont.	90/14/C	**SCHOOL BUS, FAIL STOP FOR** * c90 §14	1ST OFF: $250 *from 12/1/13:* plus $5 public safety surcharge
			2ND OFF: $1000 *from 12/1/13:* plus $5 public safety surcharge
			3RD OFF:$2000 *from 12/1/13:* plus $5 public safety surcharge
	90/14/D	**SCHOOL BUS, OPERATE WITHIN 100 FT OF** * c90 §14	1ST OFF: $35 *from 12/1/13:* plus $5 public safety surcharge
			2ND OFF: $75 *from 12/1/13:* plus $5 public safety surcharge
			3RD OFF:$150 *from 12/1/13:* plus $5 public safety surcharge
	90/14/E	**MOTOR VEH DOOR, NEGLIGENTLY OPEN** * c90 §14	$100 *from 12/1/13:* plus $5 public safety surcharge
c90 §14A	90/14A/A	**BLIND PEDESTRIAN, FAIL STOP FOR** * c90 §14A	$500 *from 12/1/13:* plus $5 public safety surcharge
c90 §14B	90/14B	**SIGNAL, FAIL TO** * c90 §14B *STOP, FAIL SIGNAL BEFORE* *TURN, FAIL SIGNAL BEFORE*	$25 *from 12/1/13:* plus $5 public safety surcharge
c90 §15	90/15/A	**RAILROAD CROSSING VIOLATION** * c90 §15 *RAILROAD CROSSING—INFLAMMABLE LOAD FAIL STOP* *RAILROAD CROSSING—SLOW, FAIL* *RAILROAD CROSSING—STOP FOR LIGHT/GATE, FAIL*	$200 *from 12/1/13:* plus $5 public safety surcharge
	90/15/E	**RAILROAD CROSSING VIOL W/SCHL BUS/EXPLOSIVES/FLAMMABLES** * c90 §15	$500 ▪ *from 12/1/13:* plus $5 public safety surcharge
c90 §16	90/16	**OPERATION OF MV, IMPROPER** * c90 §16 *CLOSED TO TRAVEL* *EXHAUST, ALTERED* *MUFFLER MISSING/NOISY* *NOISE, HARSH & OBJECTIONABLE* *SIREN, IMPROPER* *SMOKE/POLLUTANTS, UNNECESSARY* *SPOT LIGHT, IMPROPER* *TIRES, STUDDED*	$50 ▪ *from 12/1/13:* plus $5 public safety surcharge
c90 §16A	90/16A	**IDLE ENGINE OF STOPPED MV OVER 5 MINS** * c90 §16A	1ST OFF: $100 *from 12/1/13:* plus $5 public safety surcharge
			2ND OFF: $250 ▪ *from 12/1/13:* plus $5 public safety surcharge

10

G.L. CHAPTER & SECTION	OFFENSE CODE	VIOLATION (*INCLUDED OFFENSES APPEAR IN ITALICS*)	ASSESSMENT
c90 §16B	90/16B	**IDLE ENGINE OF STOPPED MV ON SCHOOL PROPERTY** * c90 §16B(b)	1ST OFF: $100 *from 12/1/13:* plus $5 public safety surcharge
			2ND OFF: $500 *from 12/1/13:* plus $5 public safety surcharge
c90 §17	90/17/A	**SPEEDING** * c90 §17 *SCHOOL BUS +40 MPH*	$50, plus $10 for each M.P.H. in excess of 10 M.P.H. over limit, plus $50 head injury surcharge *from 12/1/13:* plus $5 public safety surcharge
	90/17/B	**SPEEDING WHILE OVERWEIGHT VIOL PERMIT** * c90 §17	1ST OFF: $100 plus $50 head injury surcharge *from 12/1/13:* plus $5 public safety surcharge
			2ND OFF: $150 plus $50 head injury sucharge *from 12/1/13:* plus $5 public safety surcharge
			3RD OFF: $300 plus $50 head injury surcharge *from 12/1/13:* plus $5 public safety surcharge
	90/17/C	**SPEEDING IN CONSTRUCTION ZONE** * c90 §17	$100, plus $20 for each M.P.H. in excess of 10 M.P.H. over limit, plus $50 head injury surcharge *from 12/1/13:* plus $5 public safety surcharge
c90 §17B	90/17B/A	**RACING MOTOR VEHICLE** c90 §17B	CRIMINAL
	90/17B/B	**RACING MOTOR VEHICLE, SUBSQ. OFF.** c90 §17B	
	90/17B/C	**RACING MOTOR VEHICLE BY JR OPERATOR/LEARNER** * c90 §17B	1ST OFF: $500 *from 12/1/13:* plus $5 public safety surcharge
	90/17B/D	**RACING MOTOR VEHICLE BY JR OPERATOR/LEARNER, SUBSQ.OFF.** * c90 §17B	2ND OFF: $1000 *from 12/1/13:* plus $5 public safety surcharge
c90 §18	90/18/A	**SPEEDING IN VIOL SPECIAL REGULATION** * c90 §18	$50, plus $10 for each M.P.H. in excess of 10 M.P.H. over limit, plus $50 head injury surcharge *from 12/1/13:* plus $5 public safety surcharge

10

G.L. CHAPTER & SECTION	OFFENSE CODE	VIOLATION (INCLUDED OFFENSES APPEAR IN ITALICS)	ASSESSMENT
c90 §18, cont.	90/18/B	**MOTOR VEH IN AREA CLOSED TO TRAVEL** * c90 §18	1ST OFF: $35 *from 12/1/13:* plus $5 public safety surcharge
			2ND OFF: $75 *from 12/1/13:* plus $5 public safety surcharge
			3RD OFF: $150 *from 12/1/13:* plus $5 public safety surcharge
c90 §19	90/19/A	**OVERSIZE MV** * c90 §19 *HEIGHT MARKINGS, NO* *HEIGHT VIOLATION* *LENGTH VIOLATION* *OVERHANG +4 FT WITHOUT FLAG/LIGHT* *OVERHANG +15 FT WITHOUT FOLLOW CAR* *TOW MORE THAN ONE MV/TRAILER* *WEIGHT VIOLATION, TRAILER* *WIDTH VIOLATION*	$100 *from 12/1/13:* plus $5 public safety surcharge
	90/19/B	**TIRE OUTSIDE FENDER** * c90 §19	
c90 §19A	90/19A/A	**WEIGHT VIOLATION** * c90 §19A	$40 per 1000 lbs. or fraction thereof overweight up to 10,000 lbs; $80 per 1000 lbs or fraction overweight over 10,000 lbs. *from 12/1/13:* plus $5 public safety surcharge
	90/19A/B	**WEIGHT VIOLATION WITH IRREDUCIBLE LOAD** * c90 §19A	$10 per 1000 lbs. or fraction thereof overweight, but not more than $500 *from 12/1/13:* plus $5 public safety surcharge
	90/19A/C	**WEIGHED, REFUSE TO BE** * c90 §19A	$500 *from 12/1/13:* plus $5 public safety surcharge
c90 §19D	90/19D/A	**WEIGHT CERTIFICATE VIOLATION** * c90 §19D *GVW CERTIFICATE, FAIL PRODUCE* *REVOKED PERMIT STICKER, FAIL REMOVE*	1ST OFF: $35 *from 12/1/13:* plus $5 public safety surcharge
			2ND OFF: $75 *from 12/1/13:* plus $5 public safety surcharge
			3RD OFF: $150 *from 12/1/13:* plus $5 public safety surcharge
c90 §19E	90/19E	**WEIGHT VIOLATION IN VIOL FEDERAL LAW** * c90 §19E	1ST OFF: $35 *from 12/1/13:* plus $5 public safety surcharge
			2ND OFF: $75 *from 12/1/13:* plus $5 public safety surcharge
			3RD OFF: $150 *from 12/1/13:* plus $5 public safety surcharge

10

G.L. CHAPTER & SECTION	OFFENSE CODE	VIOLATION (*INCLUDED OFFENSES APPEAR IN ITALICS*)	ASSESSMENT
c90 §19K	90/19K	**SNOW PLOW/HITCH, FAIL REMOVE** * c90 §19K	1ST OFF: WARNING
			2ND OFF: $250 *from 12/1/13:* plus $5 public safety surcharge
			3RD OFF: $500 *from 12/1/13:* plus $5 public safety surcharge
c90 §20	90/20/A	**SAFETY STANDARDS, MV NOT MEETING RMV** * c90 §20	$25 *from 12/1/13:* plus $5 public safety surcharge
	90/20/B	**INSPECTION/STICKER, NO** * c90 §20 *INSPECTION STICKER NOT DISPLAYED* *SCHOOL BUS INSPECTION VIOLATION*	$50 *from 12/1/13:* plus $5 public safety surcharge
c90 §22H	90/22H	**ANIMAL, TRANSPORT UNPROTECTED** * c90 §22H	$50 ■ *from 12/1/13:* plus $5 public safety surcharge
c90 §23	90/23/A	**LICENSE, EXHIBIT ANOTHER'S** c90 §23	CRIMINAL
	90/23/B	SUBSEQUENT OFFENSE	
	90/23/C	**LICENSE REVOKED AS HTO, OPERATE MV WITH** c90 §23	
	90/23/D	**LICENSE SUSPENDED, OP MV WITH** c90 §23	
	90/23/E	SUBSEQUENT OFFENSE	
	90/23/F	**LICENSE SUSPENDED FOR OUI/CDL, OPER MV WITH** c90 §23	
	90/23/G	**NUMBER PLATE VIOLATION TO CONCEAL ID** c90 §23	
	90/23/H	**REGISTRATION SUSPENDED, OP MV WITH** c90 §23	
	90/23/I	SUBSEQUENT OFFENSE	
	90/23/J	**OUI-RELATED OFFENSE WHILE LICENSE SUSPENDED FOR OUI-RELATED OFFENSE** c90 §23	
c90 §24	90/24/A	**LEAVE SCENE OF PERSONAL INJURY** c90 §24(2)(a½)(1)	CRIMINAL
	90/24/B	**LEAVE SCENE OF PERSONAL INJURY & DEATH** c90 §24(2)(a½)(2)	
	90/24/C	**LEAVE SCENE OF PROPERTY DAMAGE** c90 §24(2)(a)	
	90/24/D	**LICENSE, ALLOW ANOTHER TO USE** c90 §24(2)(a)	
	90/24/E	**NEGLIGENT OPERATION OF MOTOR VEHICLE** c90 §24(2)(a)	
	90/24/F	**OUI—DRUGS** c90 §24(1)(a)(1)	
	90/24/G	2ND OFFENSE	
	90/24/H	3RD OFFENSE	
	90/24/I	4TH OFFENSE	
	90/24/U	5TH OFFENSE	
	90/24/J	**OUI—LIQUOR OR .08%** c90 §24(1)(a)(1)	
	90/24/K	2ND OFFENSE	
	90/24/L	3RD OFFENSE	
	90/24/M	4TH OFFENSE	
	90/24/V	5TH OFFENSE	
	90/24/N	**RACING MOTOR VEHICLE** c90 §24(2)(a)	
	90/24/O	**RECKLESS OPERATION OF MOTOR VEHICLE** c90 §24(2)(a)	
	90/24/W	**NEGLIGENT OPERATION & INJURY FROM MOBILE PHONE USE** c90 §24(2)(a)	
c90 §24A	90/24A	**MOTOR VEH IN FELONY/LARCENY** c90 §24A *This is not a separate offense. This code may be used to report such use of a vehicle to the RMV.*	

10

G.L. CHAPTER & SECTION	OFFENSE CODE	VIOLATION *(INCLUDED OFFENSES APPEAR IN ITALICS)*	ASSESSMENT
c90 §24G	90/24G/A	**MOTOR VEH HOMICIDE BY NEGLIGENT OP** c90 §24G(b)	CRIMINAL
	90/24G/B	**MOTOR VEH HOMICIDE BY RECKLESS OP** c90 §24G(b)	
	90/24G/C	**MOTOR VEH HOMICIDE OUI—DRUGS** c90 §24G(b)	
	90/24G/D	**MOTOR VEH HOMICIDE OUI—DRUGS & NEGLIG** c90 §24G(a)	
	90/24G/E	**MOTOR VEH HOMICIDE OUI—DRUGS & RECKLESS** c90 §24G(a)	
	90/24G/F	**MOTOR VEH HOMICIDE OUI—LIQUOR OR .08%** c90 §24G(b)	
	90/24G/G	**MOTOR VEH HOMICIDE OUI—LIQUOR OR .08% & NEGLIGENT** c90 §24G(a)	
	90/24G/H	**MOTOR VEH HOMICIDE OUI—LIQUOR OR .08% & RECKLESS** c90 §24G(a)	
c90 §24I	90/24I	**ALCOHOL IN MV, POSSESS OPEN CONTAINER OF** * c90 §24I	$500 *from 12/1/13:* plus $5 public safety surcharge
c90 §24L	90/24L/A	**OUI—DRUGS & SERIOUS INJURY** c90 § 24L(2)	CRIMINAL
	90/24L/B	**OUI—DRUGS & SERIOUS INJURY & NEGLIGENT** c90 § 24L(1)	
	90/24L/C	**OUI—DRUGS & SERIOUS INJURY & RECKLESS** c90 § 24L(1)	
	90/24L/D	**OUI—LIQUOR OR .08% & SERIOUS INJURY** c90 § 24L(2)	
	90/24L/E	**OUI—LIQUOR OR .08% & SERIOUS INJURY & NEGLIGENT** c90 § 24L(1)	
	90/24L/F	**OUI—LIQUOR OR .08% & SERIOUS INJURY & RECKLESS** c90 § 24L(1)	
c90 §24S	90/24S	**IGNITION INTERLOCK, OPERATE WITHOUT** c90 §24S(a)	CRIMINAL
c90 §24V	90/24V/A	**CHILD ENDANGERMENT WHILE OUI** c90 §24V	
	90/24V/B	**CHILD ENDANGERMENT WHILE OUI, SUBSQ. OFF.** c90 §24V	
c90 §25	90/25/A	**IDENTIFY SELF, MV OPERATOR REFUSE** c90 §25 *NAME/ADDRESS, GIVE POLICE FALSE* *NAME/ADDRESS, REFUSE GIVE POLICE*	CRIMINAL
	90/25/B	**LICENSE/REGIS/PLATES, REFUSE PRODUCE** c90 §25 *LICENSE, REFUSE PRODUCE* *NUMBER PLATE, REFUSE PRODUCE* *REGISTRATION, REFUSE PRODUCE*	
	90/25/C	**SIGN NAME, MV OPERATOR REFUSE** c90 §25	
	90/25/D	**STOP FOR POLICE, FAIL** c90 §25	
c90 §26	90/26	**ACCIDENT REPORT, FAIL FILE** * c90 §26	1ST OFF: $35 *from 12/1/13:* plus $5 public safety surcharge / 2ND OFF: $75 *from 12/1/13:* plus $5 public safety surcharge / 3RD OFF: $150 *from 12/1/13:* plus $5 public safety surcharge
c90 §26A	90/26A	**NAME/ADDRESS CHANGE, FL NOTIFY RMV OF** * c90 §26A	1ST OFF: $35 *from 12/1/13:* plus $5 public safety surcharge / 2ND OFF: $75 *from 12/1/13:* plus $5 public safety surcharge / 3RD OFF: $150 *from 12/1/13:* plus $5 public safety surcharge
c90 §31	*RMV REGULATIONS — see 540 CMR*		

G.L. CHAPTER & SECTION	OFFENSE CODE	VIOLATION *(INCLUDED OFFENSES APPEAR IN ITALICS)*	ASSESSMENT
c90 §32C	90/32C/A	**LEASE MV TO INTOXICATED DRIVER** c90 §32C	CRIMINAL
	90/32C/B	**LEASE MV WITHOUT SEEING DRIVERS LICENSE** c90 §32C	
c90 §32E	90/32E/A	**LEASE MV LESSOR FAIL MAINTAIN INSURANCE** c90 §32C	
c90 §32G	90/32G/A	**DRIVING SCHOOL EQUIPMENT VIOLATION** * c90 §32G *DRIVING SCHOOL NONCOMPLYING MV/SEMI* *DRIVING SCHOOL NO SEAT BELTS* *DRIVING SCHOOL STUDENT NO SEAT BELT*	1ST OFF: $35 *from 12/1/13:* plus $5 public safety surcharge
			2ND OFF: $75 *from 12/1/13:* plus $5 public safety surcharge
			3RD OFF: $150 *from 12/1/13:* plus $5 public safety surcharge
c90 §34J	90/34J	**UNINSURED MOTOR VEHICLE** c90 §34J	CRIMINAL
c90B §21	90B/21	**SNOW/REC VEH—UNREGISTERED** * c90B §21 *thru 1/31/11*	$25 ∎
	90B/21	**REC VEH—OPERATOR UNDER 18 WITHOUT SAFETY COURSE** * c90B §21 *from 2/1/11*	$500
c90B §22	90B/22/A	**SNOW/REC VEH—ADDRESS CHANGE, FAIL REPORT** * c90B §22	*thru 4/30/11:* $25 ∎ *from 5/1/11:* $250 ∎
	90B/22/B	**SNOW/REC VEH—UNREGISTERED** * c90B §22	*thru 4/30/11:* $25 ∎ *from 5/1/11:* $500
c90B §23	90B/23	**SNOW/REC VEH—TRANSFER UNREPORTED** * c90B §23	*thru 10/28/10:* $25 ∎ *from 10/29/10:* $250 ∎
c90B §24	90B/24/A	**SNOW/REC VEH—EQUIPMENT VIOLATION** * c90B §24	
	90B/24/B	**SNOW/REC VEH—FUMES, EXCESS** * c90B §24	
	90B/24/C	**SNOW/REC VEH—NOISE VIOLATION** * c90B §24	
c90B §25	90B/25	**SNOW/REC VEH—PUBLIC WAY VIOL** * c90B §25	*thru 10/28/10:* CRIMINAL *from 10/29/10:* 1ST OFF: $250 SUB.OFF: $1000 ∎
c90B §26	90B/26/A	**SNOW/REC VEH—FIREARM, OP WHILE CARRY** * c90B §26(g)	*thru 10/28/10:* $75 ∎ *from 10/29/10:* $1000
	90B/26/B	**SNOW/REC VEH—GROWING STOCK, DAMAGE** * c90B §26(f)	$250 ∎
	90B/26/C	**SNOW/REC VEH—HELMET VIOLATION** * c90B §26(d)	*thru 10/28/10:* $75 ∎ *from 10/29/10:* 1ST OFF: $250 SUB.OFF: $1000 ∎
	90B/26/D	**SNOW/REC VEH—OUI—DRUGS** * c90B §26 *thru 10/28/10*	$75 ∎
	90B/26/E	**SNOW/REC VEH—OUI—LIQUOR** * c90B §26 *thru 10/28/10*	
	90B/26/F	**SNOW/REC VEH—UNSAFE OPERATION** * c90B §26 *thru 10/28/10*	
	90B/26/G	**SNOW/REC VEH—WILDLIFE, HARASS** * c90B §26(f) *thru 10/28/10*	*thru 10/28/10:* $75 ∎ *from 10/29/10:* $250 ∎
	90B/26/H	**SNOW/REC VEH—UNDER 14 OPERATE UNSUPERVSD** c90B §26 *thru 10/28/10*	DELINQUENCY

10

G.L. CHAPTER & SECTION	OFFENSE CODE	VIOLATION (INCLUDED OFFENSES APPEAR IN ITALICS)	ASSESSMENT
c90B §26, cont.	90B/26/H	SNOW/REC VEH—ALLOW UNDER 18 OPERATE IMPROP* c90B §26 *from 10/29/10*	1ST OFF: $250
			SUB.OFF: $1000 ■
	90B/26/I	SNOW/REC VEH—UNDER 16½ CROSS HIGHWAY c90B §26 *thru 10/28/10*	DELINQUENCY
	90B/26/J	SNOW VEH—PRIVATE PROPERTY, ON * c90B §26(e)	*thru 10/28/10:* $75 ■ *from 10/29/10:* $250 ■
	90B/26/K	SNOW/REC VEH—PUBLIC PROPERTY, ON * c90B §26(e) *from 10/29/10*	$250 ■
	90B/26/L	SNOW/REC VEH—DAMAGE PROPERTY, ON * c90B §26(f) *from 10/29/10*	$500 ■
	90B/26/M	SNOW/REC VEH—REFUSE STOP FOR POLICE * c90B §26(c) *from 10/29/10*	1ST OFF: $250
			SUB.OFF: $1000 ■
	90B/26/N	SNOW/REC VEH—REGISTRATION REVOKED, OP WITH *c90B §26(h)*from 10/29/10*	$250 ■
	90B/26/P	ALL TERRAIN/REC UTILITY VEH, UNDERAGE OP c90B §26(a) *from 10/29/10*	DELINQUENCY
	90B/26/Q	ALL TERRAIN/REC UTILITY VEH, UNDERAGE OP, SUBSQ.OFF. c90B §26(a) *from 10/29/10*	
c90B §26A	90B/26A/A	SNOW/REC VEH—OUI BY +21—DRUGS c90B §26A(a) *from 10/29/10*	CRIMINAL
	90B/26A/B	SNOW/REC VEH—OUI BY +21—LIQUOR OR .08% c90B §26A(a) *from 10/29/10*	
	90B/26A/C	SNOW/REC VEH—OUI BY –21—DRUGS c90B §26A(b) *from 10/29/10*	
	90B/26A/D	SNOW/REC VEH—OUI BY –21—LIQUOR OR .02% c90B §26A(b) *from 10/29/10*	
c90B §26B	90B/26B/A	SNOW/REC VEH—LEAVE SCENE OF PERSONAL INJURY c90B §26B(c) *from 10/29/10*	CRIMINAL
	90B/26B/B	SNOW/REC VEH—LEAVE SCENE OF PROPERTY DAMAGE c90B §26B(b) *from 10/29/10*	
	90B/26B/C	SNOW/REC VEH—NEGLIGENT/RECKLESS OP c90B §26B(a) *from 10/29/10*	
	90B/26B/D	SNOW/REC VEH—NEGLIGENT/RECKLESS OP & DEATH c90B §26B(e) *from 10/29/10*	
	90B/26B/E	SNOW/REC VEH—NEGLIGENT/RECKLESS OP & SERIOUS INJURY c90B §26B(d)	
c90B §27	90B/27	SNOW/REC VEH—ACCIDENT, FAIL REPORT * c90B §27 *thru 10/28/10*	$50 ■
c90B §29		*DIV OF LAW ENFORCEMENT REGULATIONS FOR SNOW/REC VEH — see 323 CMR*	
c90B §32	90B/32	SNOW/REC VEH—STOP FOR POLICE, FAIL * c90B §32 *thru 10/28/10*	$50 ■
c90B §33	90B/33	SNOWMOBILE OPERATOR REFUSE ID/LEAVE * c90B §33 *thru 10/28/10*	$50
c90F §4	90F/4	OUT-OF-SVCE ORDER VIOL, EMPLOYER PERMIT * c90F §4(c)	$2500
c90F §9	90F/9	OUT-OF-SVCE ORDER VIOLATION * c90F §9(E½)(3)	$1000
c265 §13½	265/1312	MANSLAUGHTER WHILE OUI c265 §13½	CRIMINAL
c266 §121A	266/121A	TRESPASS WITH MOTOR VEHICLE * c266 §121A	$250
c272 §80H	272/80H	DOG/CAT, MOTORIST FL REPORT INJURY TO * c272 §80H	$50
DIVISION OF LAW ENFORCEMENT REGULATIONS FOR RECREATION & SNOW VEHICLES			
323 CMR §3.03	323CMR303	SNOW/REC VEHICLE VIOLATION * 323 CMR §3.03 *SNOW/REC VEH—150 FT OF RESIDENCE* *SNOW/REC VEH—ANIMAL, MOLEST* *SNOW/REC VEH—BEACH DUNE, DAMAGE* *SNOW/REC VEH—DAMAGE PROPERTY* *SNOW/REC VEH—KEEP RIGHT ON TRAIL, FAIL* *SNOW/REC VEH—NO SNOW COVER ON PUBLIC LAND* *SNOW/REC VEH—OPERATE UNDERAGE* *SNOW/REC VEH—PASSING VIOLATION* *SNOW/REC VEH—SPEEDING* *SNOW/REC VEH—WETLAND* *SNOW/REC VEH—WITHOUT LANDOWNER'S OK*	$100

10

G.L. CHAPTER & SECTION	OFFENSE CODE	VIOLATION (INCLUDED OFFENSES APPEAR IN ITALICS)	ASSESSMENT
323 CMR §3.05	323CMR305	**SNOW/REC VEH—NUMBER PLATE VIOLATION** * 323 CMR §3.05 *SNOW/REC VEH—NUMBER PLATE OBSCURED* *SNOW/REC VEH—REGIS NUMBER NOT DISPLAYED* *SNOW/REC VEH—STICKER/NUMBER PLATE,UNAUTH*	$100
323 CMR §3.07	323CMR307	**SNOW/REC VEH—EQUIPMENT VIOLATION** * 323 CMR §3.07 *SNOW/REC VEH—BRAKES VIOLATION* *SNOW/REC VEH—LIGHTS VIOLATION* *SNOW/REC VEH—MUFFLER VIOLATION* *SNOW/REC VEH—SPARK ARRESTOR VIOLATION*	$100
MDC REGULATIONS FOR RESERVATIONS & PARKS			
350 CMR §2.01	350CMR201/A	**MDC WAY/RESERV—ENTRY/EXIT, IMPROPER MV** * 350 CMR §2.01(2)(a)	$200
MDC TRAFFIC RULES FOR MDC WAYS			
see also 700CMR §§ 5.201–5.401			
350 CMR §4.01	350CMR401/A	**MDC WAY—$200 VIOLATION** * 350 CMR §4.01 *MDC WAY—+12 PERSON SEATING CAPACITY* *MDC WAY—STOP/POSITION AS DIRECTED, FAIL*	$200
	350CMR401/B	**MDC WAY—$100 VIOLATION** * 350 CMR §4.01 *MDC WAY—CROSSWALK, PASS MV STOPPED AT* *MDC WAY—CROSSWALK, PEDESTRIAN IN* *MDC WAY—RIGHT LANE, FAIL DRIVE IN* *MDC WAY—SIGNAL/SIGN/MARKINGS VIOLATION*	$100 ■
	350CMR401/C	**MDC WAY—$50 VIOLATION** * 350 CMR §4.01 *MDC WAY—RED LIGHT VIOLATION* *MDC WAY—STOP SIGN VIOLATION* *MDC WAY—YIELD SIGN VIOLATION*	$50 ■
	350CMR401/D	**MDC WAY—$25 VIOLATION** * 350 CMR §4.01 *MDC WAY—SIGNAL, FAIL BEFORE STOP/TURN/BACK*	$25 ■
	350CMR401/E	**MDC WAY—SPEEDING** * 350 CMR §4.01	$50, plus $10 for each M.P.H. in excess of 10 M.P.H. over limit, up to $200 maximum
	350CMR401/F	**MDC WAY—SPEEDING OVER POSTED LIMIT** * 350CMR§4.01	
MDC REGULATIONS FOR LAND WITHIN WATERSHED RESERVATIONS			
350 CMR §11.09	350CMR1109/A	**MDC WATERSHED—MV VIOLATION** 350 CMR §11.09	CRIMINAL
REGISTRY OF MOTOR VEHICLES REGULATIONS			
540 CMR §2.05	540CMR205	**REGISTRATION STICKER MISSING** * 540 CMR §2.05(6)(a)	1ST OFF: $35 2ND OFF: $75 3RD OFF: $150
540 CMR §2.22	540CMR222/A	**TRUCK FAIL DISPLAY OWNER'S NAME** * 540 CMR §2.22(1)	1ST OFF: $35 2ND OFF: $75 3RD OFF: $150
540 CMR §3.00	*MOTORCYCLE, NOISY — see 90/7U*		
540 CMR §4.06	540CMR406	**MOTORCYCLE HANDLEBAR VIOLATION** * 540 CMR §4.06(5)(e)	$25
540 CMR §14.03	540CMR1403/A	**HAZARDOUS MATERIALS TRANSPORT VIOL** * 540 CMR §14.03	$500
	540CMR1403/B	**MOTOR CARRIER SAFETY VIOLATION** * 540 CMR §14.03	1ST OFF: $35 2ND OFF: $75 3RD OFF: $150
540 CMR §17.05	*HANDICAP PARKING PLATE, MISUSE — see 90/2/B*		

10

G.L. CHAPTER & SECTION	OFFENSE CODE	VIOLATION (*INCLUDED OFFENSES APPEAR IN ITALICS*)	ASSESSMENT
540 CMR §18.04	540CMR1804	**NUMBER PLATE, MISUSE OF DEALER/REPAIR** 540 CMR §18.04(2)	CRIMINAL
540 CMR §22.02		*NUMBER PLATE COVERED WITH GLASS/PLASTIC — see 90/6*	
540 CMR §22.05	540CMR2205	**HEADLIGHTS, FAIL DIM** * 540 CMR §22.05(2)	1ST OFF: $35
			2ND OFF: $75
			3RD OFF: $150
540 CMR §22.05, cont.	540CMR2205/B	**HEADLIGHTS, ALTERNATING FLASHING** * 540 CMR §22.05(5)	1ST OFF: $35
			2ND OFF: $75
			3RD OFF: $150
		OTHER LIGHTS VIOLATIONS — see 85/15/A and 90/7/C	
540 CMR §22.06		*FLASHING/ROTATING/OSCILLATING AMBER/COLORED LIGHT — see 90/7/C*	
540 CMR §22.07	540CMR2207	**AFTERMARKET LIGHTING, NONCOMPLIANT** * 540 CMR §22.07	1ST OFF: $35
			2ND OFF: $75
			3RD OFF: $150
540 CMR §22.08		*MOTORCYCLE HELMET VIOLATION — see 90/7/E*	
540 CMR §22.10		*SAFETY CHAINS VIOL ON TRAILER — see 90/7/D*	
540 CMR §22.11		*SLOW MOVING EMBLEM VIOL — see 90/7/D*	
540 CMR §27.00		*IDLE ENGINE OF STOPPED MV ON SCHOOL PROPERTY — see 90/16B*	
		DEPT OF TRANSPORTATION REGULATIONS FOR FORMER MDC/DCR WAYS	
700 CMR §5.201	700CMR5201/A	**DOT WAY—ENTRY/EXIT, IMPROPER MV** * 700 CMR §5.201(2)(a)	
700 CMR §5.401	700CMR5401/A	**DOT WAY—CROSSWALK VIOLATION** * 700 CMR §5.401(8)	
	700CMR5401/B	**DOT WAY—FAIL KEEP RIGHT** * 700 CMR §5.401(4)	
	700CMR5401/C	**DOT WAY—FAIL SIGNAL TURN** * 700 CMR §5.401(4)	
	700CMR5401/D	**DOT WAY—PLEASURE VEH RESTRICTION VIOL** * 700 CMR §5.401(10)	$200
	700CMR5401/F	**DOT WAY—SIGN/SIGNAL VIOL** * 700 CMR §5.401(1), (6)-(7)	
	700CMR5401/H	**DOT WAY—SPEEDING** * 700 CMR §5.401(2)	
	700CMR5401/J	**DOT WAY—SPEEDING OVER POSTED LIMIT** * 700 CMR §5.401(2)	
		DEPT OF TRANSPORTATION REGULATIONS	
700 CMR §7.03	700CMR703/A	**MASS PIKE—TOLL BOOTH, FAIL STOP AT** * 700 CMR §7.03(2)	$50
	700CMR703/B	**MASS PIKE—TOLL, EVADE** * 700 CMR §7.03(3)	$250
700 CMR §7.04	700CMR704/A	**MASS PIKE—ETC SYSTEM/LANE, UNAUTH USE** * 700 CMR §7.04(1)	$50
	700CMR704/B	**MASS PIKE—ETC TOLL, AVOID** * 700 CMR §7.04(3)	$250
700 CMR §7.05	730CMR705/D	**MASS PIKE—BRAKES VIOLATION** * 700 CMR §7.05(4)(g)	1ST OFF: $35
			2ND OFF: $75
			3RD OFF: $150
	700CMR705/F	**MASS PIKE—CONSTRUCTION EQUIPMENT** * 700 CMR §7.05(4)(e)	$100
	700CMR705/G	**MASS PIKE—ENTER/EXIT, UNAUTHORIZED** * 700 CMR §7.05(3)	$50
	700CMR705/H	**MASS PIKE—EXPLOSIVE WITHOUT PERMIT** * 700 CMR §7.05(4)(k)	$100
	700CMR705/J	**MASS PIKE—FALLING DEBRIS** * 700 CMR §7.05(4)(f)	$100
	700CMR705/K	**MASS PIKE—HAZARDOUS MATERIAL W/O PERMIT** * 700 CMR §7.05(4)(m)	$500
	700CMR705/N	**MASS PIKE—PASSENGER OUTSIDE VEH** * 700 CMR §7.05(4)(a)	$100
	700CMR705/R	**MASS PIKE—SIZE VIOLATION** * 700 CMR §7.05(4)(i)	$500
	700CMR705/S	**MASS PIKE—SMOKING/ODOROUS VEH** * 700 CMR §7.05(4)(o)	$50
	700CMR705/U	**MASS PIKE—SPECIAL FUEL VEH IN TUNNEL** * 700 CMR §7.05(4)(j)	$500

10

G.L. CHAPTER & SECTION	OFFENSE CODE	VIOLATION *(INCLUDED OFFENSES APPEAR IN ITALICS)*	ASSESSMENT
700 CMR §7.05, cont.	700CMR705/V	**MASS PIKE—SPECIAL FUEL WITHOUT PERMIT** * 700 CMR §7.05(4)(l)	$100 ■
	700CMR705/W	**MASS PIKE—SPECIAL RISK VEH IN TUNNEL** * 700 CMR §7.05(4)(n)	$500
	700CMR705/X	**MASS PIKE—TIRE VIOLATION** * 700 CMR §7.05(4)(b)	$35
	700CMR705/Y	**MASS PIKE—TOW WITH NON-RIGID DEVICE** * 700 CMR §7.05(4)(o)	$50
	700CMR705/Z	**MASS PIKE—WEIGHT VIOLATION** * 700 CMR §7.05(4)(h)	$40 per 1000 lbs. or fraction up to 10,000 lbs. overweight; $80 per 1000 lbs or fraction over 10,000 lbs. overweight
	700CMR705/BB	**MASS PIKE—WINDOW OBSTRUCTED** * 700 CMR §7.05(4)(c)	$100
	700CMR705/CC	**MASS PIKE—WRONG WAY** * 700 CMR §7.05(1)	$50
	700CMR705/DD	**MASS PIKE—WRONG WAY IN TUNNEL** * 700 CMR §7.05(2)	$500
700 CMR §7.06	700CMR706/A	**MASS PIKE—EXPLOSIVES PERMIT, FAIL CARRY** * 700 CMR §7.06(5)(f)(2)	$100
	700CMR706/B	**MASS PIKE—EXPLOSIVES VEH OP TOO CLOSE** * 700 CMR §7.06(5)(f)(4)	
	700CMR706/C	**MASS PIKE—EXPLOSIVES VEH STOP IMPROP** * 700 CMR §7.06(5)(f)(5)	$500
	700CMR706/D	**MASS PIKE—EXPLOSIVES VEH VIOL LAW/REGUL** * 700 CMR §7.06(5)(f)(6)	$500
	700CMR706/E	**MASS PIKE—HEIGHT CLEARANCE, FAIL CHECK** * 700 CMR §7.06(4)(g)	
	700CMR706/F	**MASS PIKE—HEIGHT, FAIL DISPLAY** * 700 CMR §7.06(4)(f)	$100
	700CMR706/G	**MASS PIKE—OVERSIZE CONSTR VEH W/O PERMIT** * 700 CMR §7.06(4)(c)(2)	$100
	700CMR706/J	**MASS PIKE—PILOT CAR VIOLATION** * 700 CMR §7.06(4)(d)	$500
	700CMR706/K	**MASS PIKE—REDUC LOAD PERMIT, FL CARRY** * 700 CMR §7.06(3)(c)(3)	$100
	700CMR706/L	**MASS PIKE—SPECIAL FUEL CARGO SIGNS, NO** * 700 CMR §7.06(6)(e)(2)	
	700CMR706/M	**MASS PIKE—SPECIAL FUEL PERMIT, FAIL CARRY** * 700 CMR §7.06(6)(e)(2)	
	700CMR706/N	**MASS PIKE—SPECIAL FUEL VEH OP TOO CLOSE** * 700 CMR §7.06(6)(e)(4)	
	700CMR706/P	**MASS PIKE—SPECIAL FUEL VEH STOP IMPROP** * 700 CMR §7.06(6)(e)(5)	
	700CMR706/Q	**MASS PIKE—SPECIAL FUEL VEH VIOL LAW/REGUL** * 700 CMR §7.06(6)(e)(6)	$500
	700CMR706/R	**MASS PIKE—TANDEM IN TUNNEL** * 700 CMR §7.06(2)(m)	
	700CMR706/S	**MASS PIKE—TANDEM/SADDLEMOUNT IN TUNNEL** * 700 CMR §7.06(4)(e)	
700 CMR §7.07	700CMR707/A	**MASS PIKE—TANDEM ASSEMBLY VIOLATION** * 700 CMR §7.07(13)	
	700CMR707/B	**MASS PIKE—TANDEM AXLE VIOLATION** * 700 CMR §7.07(10)	$500
	700CMR707/C	**MASS PIKE—TANDEM BRAKES VIOLATION** * 700 CMR §7.07(9)	
	700CMR707/D	**MASS PIKE—TANDEM DOLLY/CHAIN/CABLE VIOL** * 700 CMR §7.07(14)	
	700CMR707/E	**MASS PIKE—TANDEM EMERGENCY EQUIP VIOL** * 700 CMR §7.07(11)	
	700CMR707/F	**MASS PIKE—TANDEM GROSS WEIGHT VIOL** * 700 CMR §7.07(4)&(5)	
	700CMR707/G	**MASS PIKE—TANDEM INSPECTION VIOLATION** * 700 CMR §7.07(17)	
	700CMR707/H	**MASS PIKE—TANDEM INSURANCE CERTIF NOT FILED** * 700 CMR §7.07(21)	
	700CMR707/J	**MASS PIKE—TANDEM LIGHTS VIOLATION** * 700 CMR §7.07(16)	
	700CMR707/K	**MASS PIKE—TANDEM MAKEUP/BREAKUP VIOLATION** * 700 CMR §7.07(28)	$500
	700CMR707/L	**MASS PIKE—TANDEM OFF TURNPIKE** * 700 CMR §7.07(2)	
	700CMR707/M	**MASS PIKE—TANDEM OPERATOR, UNREGISTERED** * 700 CMR §7.07(18)	
	700CMR707/N	**MASS PIKE—TANDEM PASSING VIOLATION** * 700 CMR §7.07(22)	
	700CMR707/P	**MASS PIKE—TANDEM REPORT/OBSERVATION VIOL** * 700 CMR §7.07(23)	
	700CMR707/Q	**MASS PIKE—TANDEM SINGLE-UNIT INDICATION VIOL** * 700 CMR §7.07(15)	
	700CMR707/R	**MASS PIKE—TANDEM SIZE VIOLATION** * 700 CMR §7.07(3)&(5)	
	700CMR707/S	**MASS PIKE—TANDEM SPEED VIOLATION** * 700 CMR §7.07(19)	

10

G.L. CHAPTER & SECTION	OFFENSE CODE	VIOLATION *(INCLUDED OFFENSES APPEAR IN ITALICS)*	ASSESSMENT
700 CMR §7.07, cont.	700CMR707/T	**MASS PIKE—TANDEM SUSPENDED OPERATION VIOL** * 700 CMR §7.07(27)	$500
	700CMR707/U	**MASS PIKE—TANDEM TOO CLOSE** * 700 CMR §7.07(20)	
	700CMR707/V	**MASS PIKE—TANDEM TOW VEH, UNAPPROVED** * 700 CMR §7.07(6)	
	700CMR707/W	**MASS PIKE—TANDEM TRACTOR, UNAPPROVED** * 700 CMR §7.07(7)	
	700CMR707/X	**MASS PIKE—TANDEM TRAILER, UNAPPROVED** * 700 CMR §7.07(8)	
	700CMR707/Y	**MASS PIKE—TANDEM VEH ID VIOLATION** * 700 CMR §7.07(12)	
	700CMR707/Z	**MASS PIKE—TANDEM WITHOUT PERMIT** * 700 CMR §7.07(2)	
700 CMR §7.08	700CMR708/A	**MASS PIKE—BREAKDOWN LANE VIOLATION** * 700 CMR §7.08(9)	$100
	700CMR708/B	**MASS PIKE—COASTING VIOLATION** * 700 CMR §7.08(16)	
	700CMR708/C	**MASS PIKE—COMMON CARRIER FL STOP FOR POLICE** * 700 CMR §7.08(30)	
	700CMR708/D	**MASS PIKE—COMMON CARRIER PLATE VIOLATION** * 700 CMR §7.08(31)	
	700CMR708/E	**MASS PIKE—CROSS-OVER VIOLATION** * 700 CMR §7.08(10)(b)	$50
			IN TUNNEL: $100
	700CMR708/F	**MASS PIKE—DISABLED VEH REPAIR/TOW VIOL** * 700 CMR §7.08(18)	$50
	700CMR708/G	**MASS PIKE—DUTY STATUS RECORD VIOLATION** * 700 CMR §7.08(32)	$50
	700CMR708/H	**MASS PIKE—ENTER/EXIT IMPROPERLY** * 700 CMR §7.08(7)	$50
			IN TUNNEL: $100
	700CMR708/J	**MASS PIKE—EQUIPMENT VIOLATON** * 700 CMR §7.08(27)	1ST OFF: $35
			2ND OFF: $75
			3RD OFF: $150
	700CMR708/K	**MASS PIKE—EXCLUDED AREA IN CONSTRUCTION ZONE** * 700 CMR §7.08(12)(b)	$100
	700CMR708/L	**MASS PIKE—FUEL, INADEQUATE** * 700 CMR §7.08(23)	$50
			IN TUNNEL: $100
	700CMR708/M	**MASS PIKE—HEADLIGHT HIGH BEAM VIOLATION** * 700 CMR §7.08(22)	$35
			IN TUNNEL: $50
	700CMR708/N	**MASS PIKE—HEIGHT WARNING SIGNAL, IGNORE** * 700 CMR §7.08(19)	$500
	700CMR708/P	**MASS PIKE—IDLING** * 700 CMR §7.08(28)	$100
			SUBSQ OFF.: $250 ∎
	700CMR708/Q	**MASS PIKE—INSPECTION STICKER, NO** * 700 CMR §7.08(26)	$50
	700CMR708/R	**MASS PIKE—LEFT LANE RESTRICTION** * 700 CMR §7.08(11)(b)	$100
	700CMR708/S	**MASS PIKE—LIQUOR, UNLAWFULLY TRANSPORT** * 700 CMR §7.08(29)	$100
	700CMR708/T	**MASS PIKE—LOADING, NEGLIGENT** * 700 CMR §7.08(5)(b)	$50
			IN TUNNEL: $100
	700CMR708/U	**MASS PIKE—MARKED LANES VIOLATION** * 700 CMR §7.08(8)	$50
			IN TUNNEL: $100
	700CMR708/V	**MASS PIKE—MEDIAN/EXCLUDED AREA VIOLATION** * 700 CMR §7.08(10)(a)	$50
			IN TUNNEL: $100
	700CMR708/W	**MASS PIKE—MINIMUM SPEED VIOLATION** * 700 CMR §7.08(6)(c)	$20
	700CMR708/X	**MASS PIKE—MUFFLER CUTOUT** * 700 CMR §7.08(20)	$35
	700CMR708/Y	**MASS PIKE—NEGLIGENT OPERATION** * 700 CMR §7.08(5)(a)	$50
			IN TUNNEL: $500
	700CMR708/Z	**MASS PIKE—NEGLIGENT OP IN CONSTRUCTION ZONE** * 700 CMR §7.08(12)(c)	$100
	700CMR708/AA	**MASS PIKE—NOISE VIOLATION** * 700 CMR §7.08(21)	$35
	700CMR708/FF	**MASS PIKE—PASSING VIOLATION** * 700 CMR §7.08(14)	$100

G.L. CHAPTER & SECTION	OFFENSE CODE	VIOLATION *(INCLUDED OFFENSES APPEAR IN ITALICS)*	ASSESSMENT
700 CMR §7.08, cont.	700CMR708/GG	**MASS PIKE—POLICE ORDERS, FAIL OBEY** * 700 CMR §7.08(1)(b)	$50
	700CMR708/JJ	**MASS PIKE—RESTRICTED AREA VIOLATION** * 700 CMR §7.08(11)(a)	$100
	700CMR708/KK	**MASS PIKE—RIGHT LANE, FAIL KEEP TO** * 700 CMR §7.08(13)	
	700CMR708/LL	**MASS PIKE—SIGN, FAIL OBEY** * 700 CMR §7.08(1)(a)	$50
	700CMR708/PP	**MASS PIKE—SPEEDING** * 700 CMR §7.08(6)(a)	
	700CMR708/QQ	**MASS PIKE—SPEEDING IN CONSTRUCTION ZONE** * 700 CMR §7.08(12)(a)	$100, plus fine may be double per G.L. c. 90, §17
	700CMR708/RR	**MASS PIKE—SPEEDING OVER POSTED LIMIT** * 700 CMR §7.08(6)(c)	$50, plus $10 for each M.P.H. in excess of 10 M.P.H. over speed limit, to a maximum of $500
	700CMR708/SS	**MASS PIKE—SPEEDING TO ENDANGER** * 700 CMR §7.08(6)(b)	$50
			IN TUNNEL: $500
	700CMR708/TT	**MASS PIKE—STOP/BACK/U-TURN** * 700 CMR §7.08(17)(a)&(b)	$50
			IN TUNNEL: $100
	700CMR708/UU	**MASS PIKE—STOP/TURN, FAIL SIGNAL** * 700 CMR §7.08(17)(c)	$25
	700CMR708/VV	**MASS PIKE—TOO CLOSE** * 700 CMR §7.08(15)	$100
	700CMR708/WW	**MASS PIKE—TRAFFIC LIGHT, FAIL OBEY** * 700 CMR §7.08(2)	$50
	700CMR708/XX	**MASS PIKE—TRASH, IMPROP DISPOSE OF MINOR** 700 CMR §7.08(24)(a)	CRIMINAL
	700CMR708/YY	**MASS PIKE—TRASH, IMPROP DISPOSE OF MAJOR** 700 CMR §7.08(24)(b)	
730 CMR §7.09	700CMR709	**MASS PIKE—MOTOR CARRIER SAFETY ACT VIOL** * 700 CMR §7.09	$50
730 CMR §7.10	700CMR710	**MASS PIKE—HAZARDOUS MATERIAL VIOLATION** * 700 CMR §7.10	$500
730 CMR §7.11	700CMR711	**MASS PIKE—DISABLED VEH REPAIR/TOW VIOL** * 700 CMR §7.11	$25
DEPT OF TRANSPORTATION REGULATIONS FOR THE TOBIN BRIDGE			
700 CMR §11.03	700CMR1103/A	**TOBIN BRIDGE—TOLL, FAIL PAY** * 700 CMR §11.03(3)	$100
	700CMR1103/B	**TOBIN BRIDGE—TOLL, EVADE** * 700 CMR §11.03(6)	
700 CMR §11.04	700CMR1104/A	**TOBIN BRIDGE—ETC SYSTEM, UNAUTHORIZED USE OF** * 700 CMR §11.04(3)	
	700CMR1104/B	**TOBIN BRIDGE—TOLL, USE DEVICE TO EVADE** *700 CMR §11.04(5)	
700 CMR §11.05	700CMR1105/A	**TOBIN BRIDGE—EQUIPMENT VIOL** * 700 CMR §11.05(4)(b)	1ST OFF: $ 50
			2ND OFF: $150
			3RD OFF: $250
	700CMR1105/E	**TOBIN BRIDGE—LOAD UNSECURED/UNCOVERED** * 700 CMR §11.05	$100
	700CMR1105/J	**TOBIN BRIDGE—PROHIBITED VEHICLE** * 700 CMR §11.05(3)	1ST OFF: $ 50
			2ND OFF: $150
			3RD OFF: $250
	700CMR1105/K	**TOBIN BRIDGE—SPEEDING OVER POSTED LIMIT** * 700 CMR §11.05(11)	$50, plus $10 for each M.P.H. in excess of 10 M.P.H. over speed limit
	700CMR1105/L	**TOBIN BRIDGE—TRAFFIC VIOLATION** * 700 CMR §11.05	1ST OFF: $ 50
			2ND OFF: $150
			3RD OFF: $250
	700CMR1105/T	**TOBIN BRIDGE—WEIGHT/SIZE/LOAD/HAZMAT VIOL** * 700 CMR §11.05(4)(a)	$100

10

G.L. CHAPTER & SECTION	OFFENSE CODE	VIOLATION *(INCLUDED OFFENSES APPEAR IN ITALICS)*	ASSESSMENT
	*DEPT OF TRANSPORTATION REGULATIONS FOR STATE HIGHWAYS*
720 CMR §9.05	720CMR905	**STATE HWAY—WRONG WAY** * 720 CMR §9.05 *STATE HWAY—WRONG WAY AT ROTARY*	
720 CMR §9.06	720CMR906/A	**STATE HWAY—SIGNAL/SIGN/MARKINGS VIOL** * 720 CMR §9.06 *STATE HWAY—CLOSED TO TRAVEL* *STATE HWAY—FLASHING RED LIGHT VIOLATION* *STATE HWAY—FLASHING YELLOW LIGHT VIOL* *STATE HWAY—ISLAND VIOLATION* *STATE HWAY—LANE CONTROL VIOLATION* *STATE HWAY—MARKED LANES VIOLATION* *STATE HWAY—PEDESTRIAN AT CROSSING LT* *STATE HWAY—RAMP VIOLATION* *STATE HWAY—RED LIGHT VIOL* *STATE HWAY—STOP SIGN VIOLATION* *STATE HWAY—TURN, PROHIBITED* *STATE HWAY—U-TURN VIOLATION* *STATE HWAY—WORKERS/EQUIP, FAIL SLOW FOR* *STATE HWAY—YELLOW LIGHT VIOLATION* *STATE HWAY—YIELD SIGN VIOLATION*	$20
	720CMR906/B	**STATE HWAY—TRAFFIC VIOLATION** * 720 CMR §9.06 *STATE HWAY—CARE IN STOP/TURN/BACK, LACK* *STATE HWAY—CROSSWALK, BLOCK* *STATE HWAY—CROSSWALK, PASS MV STOPPED AT* *STATE HWAY—CROSSWALK, PEDESTRIAN IN* *STATE HWAY—ENTER UNSAFELY* *STATE HWAY—FOLLOW SLOW MV WITHIN 200 FT* *STATE HWAY—FOLLOW TOO CLOSELY* *STATE HWAY—GIVE WAY, FAIL* *STATE HWAY—HORN, FAIL SOUND* *STATE HWAY—INTERSECTION, BLOCK* *STATE HWAY—MEDIAN, CROSS* *STATE HWAY—OBSTRUCT TRAFFIC* *STATE HWAY—PASSING VIOLATION* *STATE HWAY—PEDESTRIAN, ENDANGER* *STATE HWAY—RIGHT LANE, FAIL DRIVE IN* *STATE HWAY—SIDEWALK, DRIVE ON* *STATE HWAY—YIELD AT INTERSECTION, FAIL*	
720 CMR §9.07	720CMR907	**STATE HWAY—TRAFFIC VIOLATION** * 720 CMR §9.07 *STATE HWAY—POLICE OFFICER, FAIL OBEY* *STATE HWAY—SIGNAL/SIGN/MARKINGS VIOL*	
	*DEPT OF TRANSPORTATION REGULATIONS FOR LIMITED ACCESS HIGHWAYS*
720 CMR §9.08	720CMR908/A	**STATE HWAY—FITZGERALD TUNL CRANE VIOL** * 720 CMR §9.08 *CRANE W/O FOLLOW CAR* *CRANE TOO TALL*	$20
	720CMR908/B	**STATE HWAY—FITZGERALD TUNL HAZARD MATS** * 720 CMR §9.08 *HAZARD MATS EMPTY TANK*	$500
	720CMR908/C	**STATE HWAY—RAMP, BACK ON/OFF** * 720 CMR §9.08	$20
	720CMR908/G	**STATE HWAY—LEFT LANE RESTRICTION VIOL** * 720 CMR §9.08(5)(b)	
	720CMR908/H	**STATE HWAY—SOUTH BOSTON HAUL ROAD VIOL** * 720 CMR §9.08(6)(a)	$50

10

G.L. CHAPTER & SECTION	OFFENSE CODE	VIOLATION *(INCLUDED OFFENSES APPEAR IN ITALICS)*	ASSESSMENT
\multicolumn{4}{c}{*MASS PORT AUTHORITY REGULATIONS FOR LOGAN AIRPORT & HANSCOM FIELD*}			
740 CMR §21.51	740CMR2151/A	**LOGAN—SPEEDING OVER POSTED LIMIT** * 740 CMR §21.51	1ST OFF: $50
			2ND OFF: $150
			3RD OFF: $250
	740CMR2151/B	**LOGAN—TRAFFIC VIOLATION** * 740 CMR §21.51 *ACCIDENT, FAIL REPORT* *EQUIPMENT VIOLATION* *LICENSED, OPERATE WITHOUT BEING*	1ST OFF: $50
		NEGLIGENT OPERATION *FAIL REPORT ACCIDENT* *MPA PERMIT, NO*	2ND OFF: $150
		OUI *UNREGISTERED MV* *UNSAFE MV*	3RD OFF: $250
740 CMR §21.52	740CMR2152	**LOGAN—SIGNAL/SIGN/MARKINGS** * 740 CMR §21.52	1ST OFF: $50
			2ND OFF: $150
			3RD OFF: $250
Varies	555555	**MISCELLANEOUS MV MUNIC ORDINANCE/BYLAW VIOL**	Varies
\multicolumn{3}{l}{*ANY CMVI NOT LISTED ABOVE*}			MAXIMUM FINE SET BY STATUTE, ORDINANCE OR REGULATION

10

Alphabetical Index of Citable Motor Vehicle Offenses

A

ACCIDENT REPORT, FAIL FILE .... c90 §26
AFTERMARKET LIGHTING, NONCOMPLIANT ..... 540 CMR §22.07
ALCOHOL IN MV, POSSESS OPEN CONTAINER OF ...... c90 §24I
ALL TERRAIN/REC UTILITY VEH, UNDERAGE OP .... 90B §26
ANIMAL OFFAL, VIOL BY-LAW ON TRANSPORT ...... c85 §10
ANIMAL, TRANSPORT DANGEROUS WILD .... c85 §19
ANIMAL, TRANSPORT UNPROTECTED .... c90 §22H
AUDIBLE ALARM ON DUMP TRUCK, NO .... *c90 §7*
AUDIBLE ALARM ON FLAMMABLES TANKER, NO .... *c90 §7*

B

BICYCLIST, FAIL YIELD ON TURN TO .... c90 §14
BLIND PEDESTRIAN, FAIL STOP FOR .... c90 §14A
BRAKE NOT SET .... *c90 §13*
BRAKES VIOLATION, MV .... c90 §7
BREAKDOWN LANE VIOLATION .... c89 §4B

C

CARSEAT, CHILD UNDER 8 & UNDER 58 INCHES WITHOUT c90 §7AA
CHILD 8-12 OR OVER 57 INCHES WITHOUT SEAT BELT .. c90 §7AA
CHILD ENDANGERMENT WHILE OUI .... c90 §24V
CHILD UNDER 8 & UNDER 58 INCHES WITHOUT CARSEAT c90 §7AA
CHILD UNDER 12 IN BODY OF PICKUP TRUCK .... *c90 §13*
CHOCK BLOCKS NOT USED .... *c90 §13*
CLOSED TO TRAVEL .... *c90 §16*
CROSSWALK VIOLATION .... c89 §11
CROSSWALK, BLOCK .... *c89 §11*
CROSSWALK, PASS MV STOPPED AT .... *c89 §11*
CROSSWALK, PEDESTRIAN IN .... *c89 §11*

D

DOG/CAT, MOTORIST FL REPORT INJURY TO .... c272 §80H
DOOR, NEGLIGENTLY OPEN MV .... c90 §14
DRIVING SCHOOL EQUIPMENT VIOLATION .... c90 §32G
DRIVING SCHOOL NONCOMPLYING MV/SEMI .... *c90 §32G*
DRIVING SCHOOL NO SEAT BELTS .... *c90 §32G*
DRIVING SCHOOL STUDENT NO SEAT BELT .... *c90 §32G*

E

ELECTRONIC MESSAGE, OPERATOR SEND/READ ...... c90 §13B
EMERGENCY VEH, FAIL PULL OVER FOR .... *c89 §7A*
EMERGENCY VEH, WITHIN 300 FT BEHIND .... *c89 §7A*
EMERGENCY VEH, OBSTRUCT .... *c89 §7A*
EMERGENCY VEH, OBSTRUCT STATIONARY .... *c89 §7C*
EMERGENCY VEH, WILFULLY OBSTRUCT .... c89 §7
EQUIPMENT VIOLATION, MISCELLANEOUS MV .... c90 §7
EXHAUST, ALTERED .... *c90 §16*

F

FIRE HOSE, DRIVE OVER .... *c89 §7A*
FLARES VIOLATION BY COMMERCIAL VEHICLE .... c85 §14B
FLARES, COMMERCIAL VEH FAIL DEPLOY .... *c85 §14B*
FLARES, COMMERCIAL VEH OPERATE WITHOUT .... *c85 §14B*
FLASHING RED LIGHT VIOLATION .... *c89 §9*
FLASHING/ROTATING/OSCILLATING LIGHT VIOLATION .... *c90 §7*

G

GIVE WAY TO PASSING VEH, FAIL TO .... *c89 §2*
GVW CERTIFICATE, FAIL PRODUCE .... *c90 §19D*

H

HANDICAP PARKING PLATE MISUSE .... c90 §2
HAZARD LIGHTS VIOLATION .... *c90 §7*
HAZARDOUS MATERIALS TRANSPORT VIOL ..... 540 CMR §14.03
HEADLIGHTS, ALTERNATING FLASHING .... 540 CMR §22.05
HEADLIGHTS, FAIL DIM .... 540 CMR §22.05
HEADPHONES ON OPERATOR .... *c90 §13*
HEIGHT MARKINGS, NO .... *c90 §19*
HEIGHT VIOLATION .... *c90 §19*
HEIGHT, OPERATE MV WITH MODIFIED .... c90 §7P
HORN VIOLATION, MV .... c90 §7

I

IDENTIFY SELF, MV OPERATOR REFUSE .... c90 §25
IDLE ENGINE OF STOPPED MV OVER 5 MINS .... c90 §16A
IDLE ENGINE OF STOPPED MV ON SCHOOL PROPERTY c90 §16B
IGNITION INTERLOCK, OPERATE WITHOUT .... c90 §24S
IGNITION INTERLOCK, PERMIT OPERATION WITHOUT .... c90 §12
IMPEDED OPERATION .... *c90 §13*
INJURE SURFACE OF WAY .... c85 §30
INSPECTION STICKER NOT DISPLAYED .... *c90 §20*
INSPECTION/STICKER, NO .... c90 §20
INTERSECTION, BLOCK .... *c89 §9*

J

JUNIOR OPERATOR OP 12:30–5 AM W/O PARENT .... c90 §10
JUNIOR OPERATOR WITH PASSENGER UNDER 18 .... c90 §8

K

KEEP RIGHT FOR ONCOMING MV, FAIL TO .... c89 §1
KEEP RIGHT ON HILL/OBSTRUCTED VIEW, FL .... c89 §4
KEY NOT REMOVED FROM MV .... *c90 §13*

L

LEARNERS PERMIT VIOLATION .... c90 §8B
LEARNERS PERMIT—OP MCYCLE AT NIGHT .... *c90 §8B*
LEARNERS PERMIT—OP MCYCLE W/PASSENGER .... *c90 §8B*
LEARNERS PERMIT—OP NITE W/O PARENT .... *c90 §8B*
LEASE MV LESSOR FAIL MAINTAIN INSURANCE .... c90 §32E
LEASE MV TO INTOXICATED DRIVER .... c90 §32C
LEASE MV WITHOUT SEEING DRIVERS LICENSE ...... c90 §32C
LEAVE SCENE OF PERSONAL INJURY .... c90 §24
LEAVE SCENE OF PERSONAL INJURY & DEATH .... c90 §24
LEAVE SCENE OF PROPERTY DAMAG .... c90 §24
LEFT LANE RESTRICTION VIOLATION .... c89 §4C
LEFT TURN, FAIL YIELD ON .... *c90 §14*
LEFT TURN, IMPROPER .... *c90 §14*
LENGTH VIOLATION .... *c90 §19*
LICENSE CLASS, OPERATE MV IN VIOLATION .... c90 §10
LICENSE NOT IN POSSESSION .... c90 §11
LICENSE RESTRICTION, OPERATE MV IN VIOL .... c90 §10
LICENSE REVOKED AS HTO, OPERATE MV WITH .... c90 §23
LICENSE SUSPENDED FOR OUI, OPER MV WITH .... c90 §23
LICENSE SUSPENDED FOR OUI-RELATED OFFENSE,
    OUI-RELATED OFFENSE WHILE .... c90 §23
LICENSE SUSPENDED, OPERATE MV WITH .... c90 §23
LICENSE, ALLOW ANOTHER TO USE .... c90 §24
LICENSE, EXHIBIT ANOTHER'S .... c90 §23
LICENSE, FAIL SHOW AFTER ACCIDENT .... *c90 §11*
LICENSE, REFUSE PRODUCE .... *c90 §25*
LICENSE/REGIS/PLATES, REFUSE PRODUCE .... c90 §25
LIGHTS VIOLATION .... c85 §15
LIGHTS VIOLATION, MV .... c90 §7
LOAD UNSECURED/UNCOVERED .... c85 §36

10

LOCK VIOLATION . . . . *c90 §7*
LOGAN—ACCIDENT, FAIL REPORT . . . . *740 CMR §21.51*
LOGAN—FAIL REPORT ACCIDENT . . . . *740 CMR §21.51*
LOGAN—LICENSED, OPERATE WITHOUT BEING . . *740 CMR §21.51*
LOGAN—MPA PERMIT, NO . . . . *740 CMR §21.51*
LOGAN—NEGLIGENT OPERATION . . . . *740 CMR §21.51*
LOGAN—OUI . . . . *740 CMR §21.51*
LOGAN—SIGNAL/SIGN/MARKINGS . . . . *740 CMR §21.52*
LOGAN—SPEEDING OVER POSTED LIMIT . . . . *740 CMR §21.51*
LOGAN—TRAFFIC VIOLATION . . . . *740 CMR §21.51*
LOGAN—UNREGISTERED MV . . . . *740 CMR §21.51*
LOGAN—UNSAFE MV . . . . *740 CMR §21.51*
LOW-SPEED VEH VIOLATION . . . . *c90 §1F*

M

MANSLAUGHTER WHILE OUI . . . . *c265 §13½*
MARKED LANES VIOLATION . . . . *c89 §4A*
MASS PIKE—BRAKES VIOLATION . . . . 700 CMR §7.05
MASS PIKE—BREAKDOWN LANE VIOLATION . . . . . . 700 CMR §7.08
MASS PIKE—COASTING VIOLATION . . . . 700 CMR §7.08
MASS PIKE—COMMON CARRIER FL STOP FOR POLICE
. . . . 700 CMR §7.08
MASS PIKE—COMMON CARRIER PLATE VIOLATION 700 CMR §7.08
MASS PIKE—CONSTRUCTION EQUIPMENT . . . . 700 CMR §7.05
MASS PIKE—CROSS-OVER VIOLATION . . . . 700 CMR §7.08
MASS PIKE—DISABLED VEH REPAIR/TOW VIOL . . . . 700 CMR §7.08
MASS PIKE—DISABLED VEH REPAIR/TOW VIOL . . . 700 CMR §7.11
MASS PIKE—DUTY STATUS RECORD VIOLATION . . . 700 CMR §7.08
MASS PIKE—ENTER/EXIT, UNAUTHORIZED . . . . 700 CMR §7.05
MASS PIKE—ETC SYSTEM/LANE, UNAUTH USE . . . . 700 CMR §7.04
MASS PIKE—ETC TOLL, AVOID . . . . 700 CMR §7.04
MASS PIKE—EXCLUDED AREA IN CONSTRUCTION ZONE
. . . . 700 CMR §7.08
MASS PIKE—EXPLOSIVE WITHOUT PERMIT . . . . 700 CMR §7.05
MASS PIKE—EXPLOSIVES PERMIT, FAIL CARRY . . . . 700 CMR §7.06
MASS PIKE—EXPLOSIVES VEH OP TOO CLOSE . . . . 700 CMR §7.06
MASS PIKE—EXPLOSIVES VEH STOP IMPROP . . . . 700 CMR §7.06
MASS PIKE—EXPLOSIVES VEH VIOL LAW/REGUL . . 700 CMR §7.06
MASS PIKE—FALLING DEBRIS . . . . 700 CMR §7.05
MASS PIKE—HAZARDOUS MATERIAL VIOLATION . . 700 CMR §7.10
MASS PIKE—HAZARDOUS MATERIAL W/O PERMIT . 700 CMR §7.05
MASS PIKE—HEADLIGHT HIGH BEAM VIOLATION . . 700 CMR §7.08
MASS PIKE—HEIGHT CLEARANCE, FAIL CHECK . . . . 700 CMR §7.06
MASS PIKE—HEIGHT WARNING SIGNAL, IGNORE . . 700 CMR §7.06
MASS PIKE—HEIGHT, FAIL DISPLAY . . . . 700 CMR §7.06
MASS PIKE—IDLING . . . . 700 CMR §7.08
MASS PIKE—INSPECTION STICKER, NO . . . . 700 CMR §7.08
MASS PIKE—LEFT LANE RESTRICTION . . . . 700 CMR §7.08
MASS PIKE—LIQUOR, UNLAWFULLY TRANSPORT . . 700 CMR §7.08
MASS PIKE—LOADING, NEGLIGENT . . . . 700 CMR §7.08
MASS PIKE—MARKED LANES VIOLATION . . . . 700 CMR §7.08
MASS PIKE—MEDIAN/EXCLUDED AREA VIOLATION . 700 CMR §7.08
MASS PIKE—MINIMUM SPEED VIOLATION . . . . 700 CMR §7.08
MASS PIKE—MOTOR CARRIER SAFETY ACT VIOL . . 700 CMR §7.09
MASS PIKE—MUFFLER CUTOUT . . . . 700 CMR §7.08
MASS PIKE—NEGLIGENT OPERATION . . . . 700 CMR §7.08
MASS PIKE—NEGLIGENT OP IN CONSTRUCTION ZONE
. . . . 700 CMR §7.08
MASS PIKE—NOISE VIOLATION . . . . 700 CMR §7.08
MASS PIKE—OVERSIZE CONSTR VEH W/O PERMIT 700 CMR §7.06
MASS PIKE—PASSENGER OUTSIDE VEH . . . . 700 CMR §7.05
MASS PIKE—PASSING VIOLATION . . . . 700 CMR §7.08
MASS PIKE—PILOT CAR VIOLATION . . . . 700 CMR §7.06
MASS PIKE—POLICE ORDERS, FAIL OBEY . . . . 700 CMR §7.08
MASS PIKE—REDUC LOAD PERMIT, FL CARRY . . . . 700 CMR §7.06
MASS PIKE—RESTRICTED AREA VIOLATION . . . . . . 700 CMR §7.08
MASS PIKE—RIGHT LANE, FAIL KEEP TO . . . . 700 CMR §7.08
MASS PIKE—SIGN, FAIL OBEY . . . . 700 CMR §7.08
MASS PIKE—SIZE VIOLATION . . . . 700 CMR §7.08
MASS PIKE—SMOKING/ODOROUS VEH . . . . 700 CMR §7.05
MASS PIKE—SPECIAL FUEL CARGO SIGNS, NO . . . 700 CMR §7.06
MASS PIKE—SPECIAL FUEL PERMIT, FAIL CARRY . 700 CMR §7.06
MASS PIKE—SPECIAL FUEL VEH IN TUNNEL . . . . . . 700 CMR §7.05
MASS PIKE—SPECIAL FUEL VEH OP TOO CLOSE . . 700 CMR §7.06

MASS PIKE—SPECIAL FUEL VEH STOP IMPROP . . . 700 CMR §7.06
MASS PIKE—SPECIAL FUEL VEH VIOL LAW/REGUL . 700 CMR §7.06
MASS PIKE—SPECIAL RISK VEH IN TUNNEL . . . . 700 CMR §7.05
MASS PIKE—SPECIAL FUEL WITHOUT PERMIT . . . . 700 CMR §7.05
MASS PIKE—SPEEDING . . . . 700 CMR §7.08
MASS PIKE—SPEEDING IN CONSTRUCTION ZONE . 700 CMR §7.08
MASS PIKE—SPEEDING OVER POSTED LIMIT . . . . . 700 CMR §7.08
MASS PIKE—SPEEDING TO ENDANGER . . . . 700 CMR §7.08
MASS PIKE—STOP/BACK/U-TURN . . . . 700 CMR §7.08
MASS PIKE—STOP/TURN, FAIL SIGNAL . . . . 700 CMR §7.08
MASS PIKE—TANDEM ASSEMBLY VIOLATION . . . . . 700 CMR §7.07
MASS PIKE—TANDEM AXLE VIOLATION . . . . 700 CMR §7.07
MASS PIKE—TANDEM BRAKES VIOLATION . . . . 700 CMR §7.07
MASS PIKE—TANDEM DOLLY/CHAIN/CABLE VIOL . 700 CMR §7.07
MASS PIKE—TANDEM EMERGENCY EQUIP VIOL . . . 700 CMR §7.07
MASS PIKE—TANDEM GROSS WEIGHT VIOL . . . . . . 700 CMR §7.07
MASS PIKE—TANDEM IN TUNNEL . . . . 700 CMR §7.06
MASS PIKE—TANDEM INSPECTION VIOLATION . . . . 700 CMR §7.07
MASS PIKE—TANDEM INSURANCE CERTIF NOT FILED
. . . . 700 CMR §7.07
MASS PIKE—TANDEM LIGHTS VIOLATION . . . . 700 CMR §7.07
MASS PIKE—TANDEM MAKEUP/BREAKUP VIOLATION
. . . . 700 CMR §7.07
MASS PIKE—TANDEM OFF TURNPIKE . . . . 700 CMR §7.07
MASS PIKE—TANDEM OPERATOR, UNREGISTERED 700 CMR §7.07
MASS PIKE—TANDEM PASSING VIOLATION . . . . 700 CMR §7.07
MASS PIKE—TANDEM REPORT/OBSERVATION VIOL 700 CMR §7.07
MASS PIKE—TANDEM SINGLE-UNIT INDICATION VIOL
. . . . 700 CMR §7.07
MASS PIKE—TANDEM SIZE VIOLATION . . . . 700 CMR §7.07
MASS PIKE—TANDEM SPEED VIOLATION . . . . 700 CMR §7.07
MASS PIKE—TANDEM SUSPENDED OPERATION VIOL
. . . . 700 CMR §7.07
MASS PIKE—TANDEM TOO CLOSE . . . . 700 CMR §7.07
MASS PIKE—TANDEM TOW VEH, UNAPPROVED . . . 700 CMR §7.07
MASS PIKE—TANDEM TRACTOR, UNAPPROVED . . . 700 CMR §7.07
MASS PIKE—TANDEM TRAILER, UNAPPROVED . . . . 700 CMR §7.07
MASS PIKE—TANDEM VEH ID VIOLATION . . . . 700 CMR §7.07
MASS PIKE—TANDEM WITHOUT PERMIT . . . . 700 CMR §7.07
MASS PIKE—TANDEM/SADDLEMOUNT IN TUNNEL . . 700 CMR §7.06
MASS PIKE—TIRE VIOLATION . . . . 700 CMR §7.05
MASS PIKE—TOLL BOOTH, FAIL STOP AT . . . . 700 CMR §7.03
MASS PIKE—TOLL, EVADE . . . . 700 CMR §7.03
MASS PIKE—TOLL, FAIL PAY . . . . 700 CMR §7.03
MASS PIKE—TOO CLOSE . . . . 700 CMR §7.08
MASS PIKE—TOW WITH NON-RIGID DEVICE . . . . . . 700 CMR §7.05
MASS PIKE—TRAFFIC LIGHT, FAIL OBEY . . . . 700 CMR §7.08
MASS PIKE—TRASH, IMPROP DISPOSE OF MAJOR . 700 CMR §7.08
MASS PIKE—TRASH, IMPROP DISPOSE OF MINOR . 700 CMR §7.08
MASS PIKE—WEIGHT VIOLATION . . . . c81A §19
MASS PIKE—WEIGHT VIOLATION . . . . 700 CMR §7.05
MASS PIKE—WEIGHT VIOL WHILE SPEEDING . . . . c81A §19
MASS PIKE—WINDOW OBSTRUCTED . . . . 700 CMR §7.05
MASS PIKE—WRONG WAY . . . . 700 CMR §7.05
MASS PIKE—WRONG WAY IN TUNNEL . . . . 700 CMR §7.05
MDC WATERSHED—MV VIOLATION . . . . 350 CMR §11.09
MDC WAY—$25 VIOLATION . . . . 350 CMR §4.01
MDC WAY—$50 VIOLATION . . . . 350 CMR §4.01
MDC WAY—$100 VIOLATION . . . . 350 CMR §4.01
MDC WAY—$200 VIOLATION . . . . 350 CMR §4.01
MDC WAY—+12 PERSON SEATING CAPACITY . . . . . 350 CMR §4.01
MDC WAY—CROSSWALK, PASS MV STOPPED AT . . 350 CMR §4.01
MDC WAY—CROSSWALK, PEDESTRIAN IN . . . . 350 CMR §4.01
MDC WAY—RED LIGHT VIOLATION . . . . 350 CMR §4.01
MDC WAY—RIGHT LANE, FAIL DRIVE IN . . . . 350 CMR §4.01
MDC WAY—SIGNAL, FAIL BEFORE STOP/TURN/BACK
. . . . 350 CMR §4.01
MDC WAY—SIGNAL/SIGN/MARKINGS VIOLATION . . . 350 CMR §4.01
MDC WAY—SPEEDING . . . . 350 CMR §4.01
MDC WAY—SPEEDING OVER POSTED LIMIT . . . . . . 350 CMR §4.01
MDC WAY—STOP SIGN VIOLATION . . . . 350 CMR §4.01
MDC WAY—STOP/POSITION AS DIRECTED, FAIL . . . 350 CMR §4.01
MDC WAY—YIELD SIGN VIOLATION . . . . 350 CMR §4.01
MDC WAY/RESERV—ENTRY/EXIT, IMPROPER MV . . 350 CMR §2.01
METAL TIRES +4 MPH . . . . *c85 §31*

10

MIRROR VIOLATION . . . . *c90 §7*
MISCELLANEOUS MUNIC MV ORDINANCE/BY-LAW VIOL . . c85 §10
MISCELLANEOUS MUNIC MV ORDINANCE/BYLAW VIOL . . . 555555
MOBILE PHONE, OPERATOR UNDER 18 USE . . . . c90 §8M
MOBILE PHONE, OPERATOR USE IMPROPERLY . . . . c90 §13
MOBILE PHONE, PUB TRANSPORT MV OPERATOR USE . . c90 §12A
MOPED HELMET VIOLATION . . . . *c90 §1B*
MOPED MISCELLANEOUS TRAFFIC VIOL . . . . *c90 §1B*
MOPED ON RESTRICTED HWAY . . . . *c90 §1B*
MOPED OPERATION +17 WITHOUT LIC . . . . *c90 §1B*
MOPED OPERATION BY UNLIC -17 . . . . c90 §1B
MOPED SPEED VIOLATION . . . . *c90 §1B*
MOPED VIOLATION . . . . c90 §1B
MOTOR CARRIER SAFETY VIOLATION . . . . 540 CMR §14.03
MOTOR VEH ORDINANCE/BY-LAW VIOLATION . . . . c85 §10
MOTOR VEH ORDINANCE/BY-LAW VIOLATION 555555
MOTOR VEH DOOR, NEGLIGENTLY OPEN . . . . c90 §14
MOTOR VEH IN AREA CLOSED TO TRAVEL . . . . c90 §18
MOTOR VEH HOMICIDE BY NEGLIGENT OP . . . . c90 §24G
MOTOR VEH HOMICIDE BY RECKLESS OP . . . . c90 §24G
MOTOR VEH HOMICIDE OUI—DRUGS . . . . c90 §24G
MOTOR VEH HOMICIDE OUI—DRUGS & NEGLIG . . . . c90 §24G
MOTOR VEH HOMICIDE OUI—DRUGS & RECKLESS . . . . . c90 §24G
MOTOR VEH HOMICIDE OUI—LIQUOR . . . . c90 §24G
MOTOR VEH HOMICIDE OUI—LIQUOR & NEGLIG . . . . . . c90 §24G
MOTOR VEH HOMICIDE OUI—LIQUOR & RECKL . . . . c90 §24G
MOTOR VEH IN FELONY/LARCENY . . . . c90 §24A
MOTOR VEH HOMICIDE OUI—LIQUOR, SOLO . . . . c90 §24G
MOTORCYCLE CARRY PASSENGER, SOLO . . . . c90 §7
MOTORCYCLE DRIVER BEHIND PASSENGER . . . . c90 §7
MOTORCYCLE EQUIPMENT VIOLATION . . . . c90 §7
MOTORCYCLE EQUIP/OPERATION VIOLATION . . . . *c90 §7*
MOTORCYCLE GOGGLES/FACESHIELD VIOLATION . . . . *c90 §7*
MOTORCYCLE HANDLEBAR VIOLATION . . . . 540 CMR §4.06
MOTORCYCLE HELMET VIOLATION . . . . *c90 §7*
MOTORCYCLE LANES VIOLATION . . . . *c89 §4A*
MOTORCYCLE, NOISY . . . . c90 §7U
MOTORCYCLE PASSENGER VIOLATION . . . . c90 §7
MOTORIZED SCOOTER VIOLATION . . . . c90 §1E
MUD GUARDS VIOLATION ON COMMERCIAL MV . . . . *c90 §7*
MUFFLER MISSING/NOISY . . . . *c90 §16*
MUFFLER VIOLATION . . . . *c90 §7*
MUNICIPAL MV ORDINANCE/BY-LAW VIOL . . . . c85 §10
MUNICIPAL MV ORDINANCE/BY-LAW VIOL 555555

N

NAME/ADDRESS CHANGE, FL NOTIFY RMV OF . . . . c90 §26A
NAME/ADDRESS, GIVE POLICE FALSE . . . . *c90 §25*
NAME/ADDRESS, MV OP REFUSE GIVE AT NT . . . . c85 §16
NAME/ADDRESS, REFUSE GIVE POLICE . . . . *c90 §25*
NEGLIGENT OPERATION OF MOTOR VEH . . . . c90 §24
NEGLIGENT OPERATION & INJURY FROM MOBILE PHONE USE
. . . . c90 §24
NOISE, HARSH & OBJECTIONABLE . . . . *c90 §16*
NONRESIDENT STUDENT DECAL, FAIL DISPLAY . . . . *c90 §3*
NONRESIDENT STUDENT FAIL REGISTER MV . . . . *c90 §3*
NUMBER PLATE COVERED WITH GLASS/PLASTIC . . . . *c90 §6*
NUMBER PLATE MISSING . . . . *c90 §6*
NUMBER PLATE MISSING . . . . c90 §9
NUMBER PLATE OBSCURED . . . . *c90 §6*
NUMBER PLATE UNLIT . . . . *c90 §6*
NUMBER PLATE VIOLATION . . . . c90 §6
NUMBER PLATE VIOLATION TO CONCEAL ID . . . . c90 §23
NUMBER PLATE, MISUSE MILITARY . . . . c90 §5A
NUMBER PLATE, MISUSE OF DEALER/REPAIR . . . . 540 CMR §18.04
NUMBER PLATE, MISUSE OFFICIAL . . . . c90 §2
NUMBER PLATE, REFUSE PRODUCE . . . . *c90 §25*

O

OPERATION OF MV, IMPROPER . . . . c90 §16
OUI—DRUGS . . . . c90 §24
OUI—DRUGS & SERIOUS INJURY . . . . c90 §24L

OUI—DRUGS & SERIOUS INJURY & NEGLIGENT . . . . c90 §24L
OUI—DRUGS & SERIOUS INJURY & RECKLESS . . . . c90 §24L
OUI—LIQUOR . . . . c90 §24
OUI—LIQUOR & SERIOUS INJURY . . . . c90 §24L
OUI—LIQUOR & SERIOUS INJURY & NEGLIGENT . . . . . . c90 §24L
OUI—LIQUOR & SERIOUS INJURY & RECKLESS . . . . c90 §24L
OUI-RELATED OFFENSE WHILE LICENSE SUSPENDED
 FOR OUI-RELATED OFFENSE . . . . c90 §23
OUT-OF-SVCE ORDER VIOLATION . . . . c90F §9
OUT-OF-SVCE ORDER VIOL, EMPLOYER PERMIT . . . . . . c90F §4
OUTSIDE OF MV, PERMIT PERSON HANG ON . . . . *c90 §13*
OVERHANG +4 FT WITHOUT FLAG/LIGHT . . . . *c90 §7*
OVERHANG +4 FT WITHOUT FLAG/LIGHT . . . . *c90 §19*
OVERHANG +15 FT WITHOUT FOLLOW CAR . . . . *c90 §19*
OVERSIZE MV . . . . c90 §19

P

PASSING ON RIGHT . . . . *c89 §2*
PASSING VIOLATION . . . . c89 §2
PASSING VIOLATION . . . . *c89 §4A*
PUPIL TRANSPORT VEHICLE OVERCROWDED . . . . c90 §7D
PUPIL TRANSPORT VEHICLE VIOLATION . . . . c90 §7D
PUPILS, TRANSPORT WITHOUT LICENSE . . . . c90 §8A½

R

RACING MOTOR VEHICLE . . . . c90 §17B
RACING MOTOR VEHICLE . . . . c90 §24
RAILROAD CROSSING—INFLAMMABLE LOAD FAIL STOP . . *c90 §15*
RAILROAD CROSSING—SCHL BUS/EXPLOSIVES/FLAMMABLES
. . . . *c90 §15*
RAILROAD CROSSING—SLOW, FAIL . . . . *c90 §15*
RAILROAD CROSSING—STOP FOR LIGHT/GATE, FAIL . . . . *c90 §15*
RAILROAD CROSSING VIOLATION . . . . c90 §15
REC VEH—OPERATOR UNDER 18 WITHOUT SAFETY COURSE
. . . . c90B §21
RECKLESS OPERATION OF MOTOR VEHICLE . . . . c90 §24
RED/BLUE LIGHT VIOLATION, MV . . . . c90 §7E
RED/BLUE LIGHT WITHOUT AUTHORITY . . . . *c90 §7E*
RED/BLUE LIGHT WITHOUT PERMIT IN POSSESSION . . . . *c90 §7E*
REFLECTOR VIOLATION ON COMMERCIAL MV . . . . *c90 §7*
REGISTER MV IMPROPERLY TO AVOID TAXES/PREMIUMS   c90 §3½
REGISTER MV OPERATED +30 DAYS YEAR, FL . . . . c90 §3
REGISTRATION LEFT IN TRANSFERRED MV . . . . c90 §2B
REGISTRATION NOT IN POSSESSION . . . . *c90 §11*
REGISTRATION STICKER MISSING . . . . 540 CMR §2.05
REGISTRATION, REFUSE PRODUCE . . . . *c90 §25*
REVOKED PERMIT STICKER, FAIL REMOVE . . . . *c90 §19D*
RIGHT LANE, FAIL DRIVE IN . . . . *c89 §4B*
RIGHT LANE, HEAVY COMM VEH FAIL DRIVE IN . . . . *c89 §4C*
RIGHT TURN, IMPROPER . . . . *c90 §14*
RIGHT-ON-RED VIOLATION . . . . *c89 §8*
REGISTRATION SUSPENDED, OP MV WITH . . . . c90 §23
REGISTRATION, FAIL SHOW AFTER ACCIDENT . . . . c90 §11
REGISTRATION, FL SURRENDER ON TRANSFER . . . . c90 §2
REGISTRATION, REFUSE PRODUCE . . . . *c90 §25*
REVOKED PERMIT STICKER, FAIL REMOVE . . . . *c90 §19D*
RIGHT LANE, FAIL DRIVE IN . . . . *c89 §4B*
RIGHT LANE, HEAVY COMM VEH FAIL DRIVE IN . . . . *c89 §4C*
RIGHT TURN, IMPROPER . . . . *c90 §14*
RIGHT-ON-RED VIOLATION . . . . *c89 §8*

S

SAFETY CHAINS VIOL ON TRAILER . . . . *c90 §7*
SAFETY GLASS VIOLATION . . . . c90 §9A
SAFETY STANDARDS, MV NOT MEETING RMV . . . . c90 §20
SAMARITAN VEHICLE MISUSE SIREN/LIGHT . . . . c90 §7I
SCHOOL BUS +40 MPH . . . . *c90 §17*
SCHOOL BUS INSPECTION VIOLATION . . . . *c90 §20*
SCHOOL BUS INSPECTION, FAIL PERFORM POST-TRIP . . . c90 §7B
SCHOOL BUS OPERATE WITH STANDEES . . . . c90 §7L
SCHOOL BUS OPERATION/EQUIPMENT VIOL . . . . c90 §7B

10

SCHOOL BUS OVERCROWDED . . . . c90 §7B
SCHOOL BUS—ALCOHOL CONSUMED ON . . . . c90 §7B
SCHOOL BUS—BOARD/DISCHARGE IMPROPERLY . . . . c90 §7B
SCHOOL BUS—DOORS OPEN WHILE MOVING . . . . c90 §7B
SCHOOL BUS—DRIVER WITHOUT SEATBELT ON . . . . c90 §7B
SCHOOL BUS—EQUIPMENT NOT REMOVED . . . . c90 §7B
SCHOOL BUS—EQUIPMENT VIOLATION . . . . c90 §7B
SCHOOL BUS—FLASHERS MISUSED/UNUSED . . . . c90 §7B
SCHOOL BUS—FUEL WHILE OCCUPIED . . . . c90 §7B
SCHOOL BUS—OPERATE WITHIN 100 FT OF . . . . c90 §14
SCHOOL BUS—PRETRIP INSPECTION, NO . . . . c90 §7B
SCHOOL BUS—SMOKE ON . . . . c90 §7B
SCHOOL BUS—UNLICENSED OPERATION . . . . c90 §7B
SCHOOL BUS, FAIL STOP FOR . . . . c90 §14
SCHOOL BUS, OPERATE WITHIN 100 FT OF . . . . c90 §14
SCHOOL BUS, USE MOBILE PHONE WHILE OPERATING . . . c90 §2
SEAT BELT MISSING . . . . c90 §7
SEAT BELT, CHILD 8-12 OR OVER 57 INCHES WITHOUT . c90 §7AA
SEAT BELT, FAIL WEAR . . . . c90 §13A
SIGN NAME, MV OPERATOR REFUSE . . . . c90 §25
SIGNAL, FAIL TO . . . . c90 §14B
SIREN, IMPROPER . . . . c90 §16
SLOW AT INTERSECTION, FAIL . . . . c90 §14
SLOW FOR BICYCLIST, FAIL . . . . c90 §14
SLOW FOR PEDESTRIAN, FAIL . . . . c90 §14
SLOW FOR STOPPED STREET RAILWAY, FAIL . . . . c90 §14
SLOW MOVING EMBLEM VIOL . . . . c90 §7
SLOW WHEN VIEW OBSTRUCTED, FAIL . . . . c90 §14
SLOW, FAIL TO . . . . c90 §14
SMOKE/POLLUTANTS, UNNECESSARY . . . . c90 §16
SNOW PLOW/HITCH, FAIL REMOVE . . . . c90 §19K
SNOW/REC VEH—300 FT OF RESIDENCE . . . . 323 CMR §3.03
SNOW/REC VEH—ADDRESS CHANGE, FAIL REPORT . . . . c90B §22
SNOW/REC VEH—ALLOW UNDER 18 OPERATE IMPROP . . c90B §26
SNOW/REC VEH—ANIMAL, MOLEST . . . . 323 CMR §3.03
SNOW/REC VEH—BEACH DUNE, DAMAGE . . . . 323 CMR §3.03
SNOW/REC VEH—BRAKES VIOLATION . . . . 323 CMR §3.07
SNOW/REC VEH—DAMAGE LANDOWNER'S PROP . 323 CMR §3.03
SNOW/REC VEH—DAMAGE PROPERTY, ON . . . . c90B §26
SNOW/REC VEH—EQUIPMENT VIOLATION . . . . c90B §24
SNOW/REC VEH—EQUIPMENT VIOLATION . . . . 323 CMR §3.07
SNOW/REC VEH—FIREARM, OP WHILE CARRY . . . . c90B §26
SNOW/REC VEH—FUMES, EXCESS . . . . c90B §24
SNOW/REC VEH—GROWING STOCK, DAMAGE . . . . c90B §26
SNOW/REC VEH—HELMET VIOLATION . . . . c90B §26
SNOW/REC VEH—KEEP RIGHT, FAIL . . . . 323 CMR §3.03
SNOW/REC VEH—LEAVE SCENE OF PERSONAL INJURY c90B §26B
SNOW/REC VEH—LEAVE SCENE OF PROPERTY DAMAGEc90B §26B
SNOW/REC VEH—LIGHTS VIOLATION . . . . 323 CMR §3.07
SNOW/REC VEH—MUFFLER VIOLATION . . . . 323 CMR §3.07
SNOW/REC VEH—NEGLIGENT/RECKLESS OP . . . . c90B §26B
SNOW/REC VEH—NEGLIGENT/RECKLESS OP & DEATH . c90B §26B
SNOW/REC VEH—NEGLIGENT/RECKLESS OP & SERIOUS
   INJURY . . . . c90B §26B
SNOW/REC VEH—NO SNOW COVER . . . . 323 CMR §3.03
SNOW/REC VEH—NOISE VIOLATION . . . . c90B §24
SNOW/REC VEH—NUMBER PLATE OBSCURED . . . . 323 CMR §3.05
SNOW/REC VEH—NUMBER PLATE VIOLATION . . . . 323 CMR §3.05
SNOW/REC VEH—OPERATE 11PM—6AM . . . . 323 CMR §3.03
SNOW/REC VEH—OPERATE ON PUBLIC LAND . . . . 323 CMR §3.03
SNOW/REC VEH—OPERATE UNDERAGE . . . . 323 CMR §3.03
SNOW/REC VEH—OUI BY −21—DRUGS . . . . c90B §26A
SNOW/REC VEH—OUI BY +21—DRUGS . . . . c90B §26A
SNOW/REC VEH—OUI BY −21—LIQUOR OR .02% . . . . . c90B §26A
SNOW/REC VEH—OUI BY +21—LIQUOR OR .08% . . . . . c90B §26A
SNOW/REC VEH—PASSING VIOLATION . . . . 323 CMR §3.03
SNOW/REC VEH—PUBLIC PROPERTY, ON . . . . c90B §26
SNOW/REC VEH—PUBLIC WAY VIOL . . . . c90B §25
SNOW/REC VEH—RACE/RALLY . . . . 323 CMR §3.03
SNOW/REC VEH—REFUSE STOP FOR POLICE . . . . c90B §26
SNOW/REC VEH—REGIS NUMBER NOT DISPLAYED 323 CMR §3.05
SNOW/REC VEH—REGISTRATION REVOKED, OP WITH . c90B §26
SNOW/REC VEH—SPARK ARRESTOR VIOLATION . . 323 CMR §3.07
SNOW/REC VEH—SPEEDING . . . . 323 CMR §3.03
SNOW/REC VEH—STICKER/NUMBER PLATE, UNAUTH

. . . . 323 CMR §3.05
SNOW/REC VEH—TRANSFER UNREPORTED . . . . c90B §23
SNOW/REC VEH—UNREGISTERED . . . . c90B §22
SNOW/REC VEH—WETLAND . . . . 323 CMR §3.03
SNOW/REC VEH—WILDLIFE, HARASS . . . . c90B §26
SNOW/REC VEH—WITHOUT LANDOWNER'S OK . . . 323 CMR §3.03
SNOW/REC VEHICLE VIOLATION . . . . 323 CMR §3.03
SPECIAL FUELS, USE WITHOUT LICENSE . . . . c64E §2
SPECIAL NEEDS STUDENTS VEH FL ID OWNER . . . . c90 §7CC
SPEEDING . . . . c90 §17
SPEEDING IN CONSTRUCTION ZONE . . . . c90 §17
SPEEDING IN VIOL SPECIAL REGULATION . . . . c90 §18
SPEEDING ON COUNTY BRIDGE VIOL BY-LAW . . . . c85 §20
SPEEDING WHILE OVERWEIGHT VIOL PERMIT . . . . c90 §17
SPOT LIGHT, IMPROPER . . . . c90 §16
STATE HWAY—CARE IN STOP/TURN/BACK, LACK . 720 CMR §9.06
STATE HWAY—CLOSED TO TRAVEL . . . . 720 CMR §9.06
STATE HWAY—CLOSED TO TRAVEL, MV WHERE . . . . . . c85 §2E
STATE HWAY—CRANE TOO TALL . . . . 720 CMR §9.08
STATE HWAY—CRANE W/O FOLLOW CAR . . . . 720 CMR §9.08
STATE HWAY—CROSSWALK, BLOCK . . . . 720 CMR §9.06
STATE HWAY—CROSSWALK, PASS MV STOPPED AT

. . . . 720 CMR §9.06
STATE HWAY—CROSSWALK, PEDESTRIAN IN . . . . 720 CMR §9.06
STATE HWAY—ENTER UNSAFELY . . . . 720 CMR §9.06
STATE HWAY—FITZGERALD TUNL CRANE VIOL . . . 720 CMR §9.08
STATE HWAY—FITZGERALD TUNL HAZARD MATS . 720 CMR §9.08
STATE HWAY—FITZGERALD TUNL HAZARD MATS EMPTY TANK

. . . . 720 CMR §9.08
STATE HWAY—FLASHING RED LIGHT VIOLATION . . 720 CMR §9.06
STATE HWAY—FLASHING YELLOW LIGHT VIOL . . . . 720 CMR §9.06
STATE HWAY—FOLLOW SLOW MV WITHIN 200 FT . 720 CMR §9.06
STATE HWAY—FOLLOW TOO CLOSELY . . . . 720 CMR §9.06
STATE HWAY—GIVE WAY, FAIL . . . . 720 CMR §9.06
STATE HWAY—GUBERNATORIAL BY-LAW VIOLATION . . . . c85 §23
STATE HWAY—HORN, FAIL SOUND . . . . 720 CMR §9.06
STATE HWAY—INTERSECTION, BLOCK . . . . 720 CMR §9.06
STATE HWAY—ISLAND VIOLATION . . . . 720 CMR §9.06
STATE HWAY—LANE CONTROL VIOLATION . . . . 720 CMR §9.06
STATE HWAY—LEFT LANE RESTRICTION VIOL . . . . 720 CMR §9.08
STATE HWAY—MARKED LANES VIOLATION . . . . 720 CMR §9.06
STATE HWAY—MEDIAN, CROSS . . . . 720 CMR §9.06
STATE HWAY—OBSTRUCT TRAFFIC . . . . 720 CMR §9.06
STATE HWAY—PASSING VIOLATION . . . . 720 CMR §9.06
STATE HWAY—PEDESTRIAN AT CROSSING LT . . . . 720 CMR §9.06
STATE HWAY—PEDESTRIAN, ENDANGER . . . . 720 CMR §9.06
STATE HWAY—POLICE OFFICER, FAIL OBEY . . . . . 720 CMR §9.07
STATE HWAY—RAMP VIOLATION . . . . 720 CMR §9.06
STATE HWAY—RAMP, BACK ON/OFF . . . . 720 CMR §9.08
STATE HWAY—RED LIGHT VIOL . . . . 720 CMR §9.06
STATE HWAY—RIGHT LANE, FAIL DRIVE IN . . . . . . 720 CMR §9.06
STATE HWAY—SIDEWALK, DRIVE ON . . . . 720 CMR §9.06
STATE HWAY—SIGNAL/SIGN/MARKINGS VIOL . . . 720 CMR §9.06
STATE HWAY—SIGNAL/SIGN/MARKINGS VIOL . . . 720 CMR §9.07
STATE HWAY—SOUTH BOSTON HAUL ROAD VIOL . 720 CMR §9.08
STATE HWAY—STOP SIGN VIOLATION . . . . 720 CMR §9.06
STATE HWAY—TRAFFIC VIOLATION . . . . 720 CMR §9.06
STATE HWAY—TRAFFIC VIOLATION . . . . 720 CMR §9.07
STATE HWAY—TURN, PROHIBITED . . . . 720 CMR §9.06
STATE HWAY—U-TURN VIOLATION . . . . 720 CMR §9.06
STATE HWAY—WORKERS/EQUIP, FAIL SLOW FOR . 720 CMR §9.06
STATE HWAY—WRONG WAY . . . . 720 CMR §9.05
STATE HWAY—WRONG WAY AT ROTARY . . . . 720 CMR §9.05
STATE HWAY—YELLOW LIGHT VIOLATION . . . . 720 CMR §9.06
STATE HWAY—YIELD AT INTERSECTION, FAIL . . . . 720 CMR §9.06
STATE HWAY—YIELD SIGN VIOLATION . . . . 720 CMR §9.06
STOP FOR FRIGHTENED COW/HORSE, FAIL . . . . c90 §14
STOP FOR POLICE, FAIL . . . . c90 §25
STOP SIGN VIOLATION . . . . c89 §9
STOP, FAIL SIGNAL BEFORE . . . . c90 §14B
STOP/YIELD, FAIL TO . . . . c89 §9
STUDENT MOTOR VEH REGISTRATION VIOL . . . . c90 §3

T

TELEVISION VISIBLE TO MV OPERATOR . . . . *c90 §13*
TIRE OUTSIDE FENDER . . . . c90 §19
TIRE TREAD DEPTH VIOLATION . . . . c90 §7Q
TIRE WIDTH BY-LAW VIOLATION . . . . c40 §21
TIRES, STUDDED . . . . *c90 §16*
TOBIN BRIDGE—EQUIPMENT VIOL . . . . 700 CMR §1105
TOBIN BRIDGE—ETC SYSTEM, UNAUTH USE OF . . 700 CMR §11.04
TOBIN BRIDGE—LOAD UNSECURED/UNCOVERED . 700 CMR §11.04
TOBIN BRIDGE—PROHIBITED VEHICLE . . . . 700 CMR §11.05
TOBIN BRIDGE—SPEEDING OVER POSTED LIMIT . 700 CMR §11.05
TOBIN BRIDGE—TOLL, EVADE . . . . 700 CMR §11.03
TOBIN BRIDGE—TOLL, FAIL PAY . . . . 700 CMR §11.03
TOBIN BRIDGE—TOLL, USE DEVICE TO EVADE . . . 700 CMR §11.04
TOBIN BRIDGE—TRAFFIC VIOLATION . . . . 700 CMR §11.05
TOBIN BRIDGE—WEIGHT/SIZE/LOAD/HAZMAT . . . 700 CMR §11.05
TOW MORE THAN ONE MV/TRAILER . . . . *c90 §19*
TRESPASS WITH MOTOR VEHICLE . . . . c266 §121A
TRUCK FAIL DISPLAY OWNER'S NAME . . . . 540 CMR §2.22
TURN, FAIL SIGNAL BEFORE . . . . *c90 §14B*
TURN, IMPROPER . . . . c90 §14

U

UNATTENDED RUNNING MOTOR VEH . . . . *c90 §13*
UNINSURED MOTOR VEHICLE . . . . c90 §32J
UNLICENSED OPERATION OF MV . . . . c90 §10
UNLICENSED OPERATOR, EMPLOY . . . . c90 §12
UNLICENSED/SUSPENDED OPERATION OF MV, PERMIT . . c90 §12

UNREGISTERED MOTOR VEHICLE . . . . c90 §9
UNSAFE OPERATION OF MV . . . . c90 §13

V

VEHICLE ID NUMBER NOT DISPLAYED . . . . c90 §7R
VOC STUDENT TRANSPORT VIOLATION . . . . c90 §7D½

W

WEIGHED, REFUSE TO BE . . . . c90 §19A
WEIGHT CERTIFICATE VIOLATION . . . . c90 §19D
WEIGHT VIOL & NO STICKER . . . . c85 §30A
WEIGHT VIOLATION . . . . c85 §30
WEIGHT VIOLATION . . . . c90 §19A
WEIGHT VIOLATION IN VIOL FEDERAL LAW . . . . c90 §19E
WEIGHT VIOLATION ON BRIDGE . . . . c85 §34
WEIGHT VIOLATION ON HWAY BRIDGE . . . . c85 §35
WEIGHT VIOLATION WITH IRREDUCIBLE LOAD . . . . c90 §19A
WEIGHT VIOLATION, TRAILER . . . . *c90 §19*
WIDTH VIOLATION . . . . *c90 §19*
WINDOW OBSTRUCTED/NONTRANSPARENT . . . . c90 §9D

Y

YIELD AT INTERSECTION, FAIL . . . . c89 §8
YIELD ON LEFT TURN, FAIL . . . . *c89 §8*
YIELD SIGN VIOLATION . . . . *c89 §9*

10

PART 11

Alphabetical References to Evidence

It would be impossible to do the subject of evidence justice in a book this size. Accordingly, we have taken the liberty of highlighting, in easy-to-locate, alphabetical order, some of the more common evidentiary areas. As any trial lawyer knows, a working knowledge of evidence is essential for any type of success to be achieved. There are numerous books on evidence, any one of which will serve you well. See, for example, the following:

- Supreme Judicial Court Advisory Committee on Massachusetts Evidence Law, *Massachusetts Guide to Evidence* (2016 ed.);
- Hon. R. Marc Kantrowitz, *Massachusetts Evidence from A to Z* (Matthew Bender 2003);
- Harold W. Potter, Jr. & Hon. Paul E. Troy eds., *A Practical Guide to Introducing Evidence: Basic Foundations and Objections* (MCLE, Inc. 4th ed. 2013 & Supp. 2015);
- J.W. Carney, Jr., ed., *Massachusetts Evidence: A Courtroom Reference* (MCLE, Inc. 8th ed. 2016);
- Mark S. Brodin & Michael Avery eds., *Handbook of Massachusetts Evidence* (Wolters Kluwer 2016 ed.); and
- Hon. William G. Young et al., *Evidence*, Massachusetts Practice Series (Thomson West 3rd ed. 2016).

ABANDONMENT

"[W]ithdrawal and abandonment must be in a timely and effective manner and if . . . withdrawal comes so late that the crime cannot be stopped, then it is too late and it is not effective. . . . [A] withdrawal is effective only if it is communicated to the other persons in the joint venture." *Commonwealth v. Pucillo*, 427 Mass. 108, 116 (1998) (quotation marks omitted).

ADMISSIONS

"A confession (or admission), whether made to police or to a civilian, is admissible only if it is voluntarily made. Thus, a statement by someone who by dint of physical or mental impediments is incapable of withholding the information conveyed cannot be used as evidence against him. Statements that are attributable in large measure to a defendant's debilitated condition, such as insanity, intoxication or the concussion of a bullet shattering in his head are not the product of a rational intellect or free will and are involuntary.

"If the defendant raises the issue of the voluntariness of his [or her] confession, or admission, the trial judge must hold a hearing out of the jury's presence. The judge must determine that the confession or admission was voluntarily given before the jury hears it. Even if the defendant fails to request it, the trial judge may have an obligation in some circumstances to conduct a voir dire to determine the voluntariness of a confession or admission. Thus, . . . this court held that the defendant's testimony that he had been beaten by police created an independent obligation on the part of the trial judge to hold such a hearing.

"Generally a judge has no duty to ask the jury to pass on voluntariness unless it is made a live issue at trial."

Commonwealth v. Benoit, 410 Mass. 506, 511 (1991) (citations and quotation marks omitted).

In sum, "a confession or admission, in order to be considered by the jury, must be voluntary and the product of a rational intellect. If either voluntariness or the declarant's mental state is in question, the Commonwealth must prove the elements of admissibility beyond a reasonable doubt, first to a judge on voir dire . . . and second—if the issue is a live one at trial—to the jury. If the Commonwealth does not sustain its burden, the statement must be excluded by the judge. If the statement is admitted in evidence, the jury may consider it only if they too find that the Commonwealth has met its burden." *Commonwealth v. Hooper*, 42 Mass. App. Ct. 730, 733 (1997).

ADMISSION BY NONDEFENDANT

"An out-of-court statement made by a person that he, and not the defendant on trial, committed the crime is admissible [for substantive purposes] where: (1) the declarant's testimony is unavailable; (2) the statement tends so far to subject the declarant to criminal liability that a reasonable man would not have made the statement unless he believed it were true; and (3) the statement, if offered to exculpate the accused, is corroborated by circumstances clearly indicating its truthfulness." *Commonwealth v. Fryar*, 425 Mass. 237, 249 (1997) (quoting *Commonwealth v. Gagnon*, 408 Mass. 185, 193–94 (1990)).

ADMISSION BY SILENCE

"Brown remained silent in response to an accusation by another coworker. Actions and statements that indicate consciousness of guilt on the part of the defendant are admissible and, together with other evidence, may be sufficient to prove guilt. An admission may be [inferred] from conduct as well as from words." *Brown v. Commonwealth*, 407 Mass. 84, 90 (1990) (quotation marks, citations and footnote omitted).

ADMISSION OF EVIDENCE

"On cross-examination, Clarke's counsel was permitted to read the statements [showing prior inconsistencies] in their entirety, to the jury. He then moved to admit the statements in evidence. The judge refused to admit the statements as exhibits because he did not want 'to have them given any more weight than any other testimony.'" The SJC upheld the ruling. *Commonwealth v. Clarke*, 418 Mass. 207, 211 (1994).

ADOPTIVE ADMISSIONS

"Adoptive admissions are a well-established and firmly rooted exception to the hearsay rule. The exception applies to any statement made in the presence of the defendant to which the defendant's response—whether by oral declaration, by gesture, or by revealing silence—objectively denotes the defendant's acceptance of the statement." *Commonwealth v. Stewart*, 450 Mass. 25, 34 (2007) (citations omitted).

"Evidence of adoptive admissions is to be received with caution, especially in criminal cases, due to the fact that the meaning of a defendant's response, or lack thereof, to an accusatory statement is often ambiguous. As foundation for the

11

evidence, it must be apparent that the party has heard and understood the statement, that he had an opportunity to respond, and that the context was one in which he would have been expected to respond to an accusation." *Commonwealth v. Stevenson*, 46 Mass. App. Ct. 506, 511 (1999) (citations and quotation marks omitted).

Additionally, "the party must not be under arrest or have received the *Miranda* warnings." *Commonwealth v. Kruah*, 47 Mass. App. Ct. 341, 345 (1999).

ALFORD PLEA

"An individual accused of a crime may voluntarily, knowingly, and understandingly [plead guilty] even if he is unwilling or unable to admit his participation in the [crime]." The record before the judge should contain strong evidence of guilt. *North Carolina v. Alford*, 400 U.S. 25, 37 (1970). In practice, the defendant will be asked, among other things, to admit that the Commonwealth has sufficient evidence to convict him. *See, e.g., Commonwealth v. Nikas*, 431 Mass. 453, 455 (2000).

ANOTHER DID IT

"A defendant may introduce evidence that another person recently committed a similar crime by similar methods, since such evidence tends to show that someone other than the accused committed the particular crime. A defendant may do so, however, only where the acts of the other person are so closely connected in point of time and method of operation as to cast doubt upon the identification of the defendant as the person who committed the crime. In addition, the shared act must be particularly distinguishing, rather than commonplace or ordinary." *Commonwealth v. Hunter*, 426 Mass. 715, 716–17 (1998) (citations, quotation and punctuation marks omitted).

ARREST

"A person may not be arrested based on mere suspicion and association with another individual, even if there is probable cause to believe that the latter committed a crime." *Commonwealth v. Frazier*, 410 Mass. 235, 240 (1991).

"'To be valid, an arrest must be based on probable cause,' *Commonwealth v. Bottari*, 395 Mass. 777, 783 (1985) and evidence seized as a result of an unlawful arrest must be suppressed. *Ibid*. 'Probable cause to arrest exists when, at the moment of arrest, the facts and circumstances known to the police officers were sufficient to warrant a person of reasonable caution in believing that the defendant had committed or was committing a crime.' *Commonwealth v. Gullick*, 386 Mass. 278, 283 (1982)." *Commonwealth v. Wedderburn*, 36 Mass. App. Ct. 558, 562 (1994).

"It is well established that the undisclosed intentions of law enforcement officers, in and of themselves, are not controlling in determining whether an individual has been arrested. . . . Before an individual can be said to be "arrested" there must be (1) an actual or constructive seizure or detention of the person, (2) performed with the intention to effect an arrest and (3) so understood by the person detained. The United States Supreme Court has recently held that, before a seizure occurs under the Fourth Amendment . . . , there must either be physical force applied against the suspect or an assertion of authority by a law enforcement officer and submission by the suspect to that assertion of authority. In our determination of what constitutes a "seizure" under art. 14 . . . [the test is]: Whether, in view of all the surrounding circumstances, a reasonable person would have believed that he was not free to leave." *Commonwealth v. Cook*, 419 Mass. 192, 198–99 (1994) (citations omitted).

Warrant not required. "[A] warrantless arrest in a public place is permissible if the arresting officer has probable cause, even if there is ample time to obtain a warrant." *Commonwealth v. Celestino*, 47 Mass. App. Ct. 916, 917 (1999) (citation omitted).

Timing of arrest. While the police could have arrested the defendant on one day, they elected to wait a few more days and "bet on finding the defendant with a greater quantity of cocaine." This was held to be permissible. "The police are not required to make an arrest every time they have probable cause to believe someone has committed a crime." *Commonwealth v. Celestino*, 47 Mass. App. Ct. at 918 (citation omitted).

ARREST WARRANT

"[I]f an arrest warrant is issued on probable cause . . . the police may enter a suspect's dwelling if they have reason to believe that the suspect is there. The arresting officer need not have probable cause to believe the suspect is at home." *Commonwealth v. DiBenedetto*, 427 Mass. 414, 417–18 (1998) (citation omitted).

AUDIOTAPES

"No Massachusetts case has yet declared it to be reversible error to refuse playing of an audiotape to a jury, although there is a consistent theme in the decisions that to allow the playing of an audiotape is the wiser course, assuming authentication, ready availability of audio equipment in the courtroom, and identification of the salient portions of the tape." *Commonwealth v. Supplee*, 45 Mass. App. Ct. 265, 266–67 (1998).

BATTERED WOMAN SYNDROME

"[W]here the claim of self-defense is in issue, and there is evidence of a pattern of abuse of the defendant by the victim, expert testimony on common patterns in abusive relationships and the typical emotional and behavioral responses of persons who are battered may be admissible." *Commonwealth v. Rodriquez*, 418 Mass. 1, 7 (1994). *See also* G.L. c. 233, § 23F.

"Evidence of battered woman syndrome is material to the issue whether [Conaghan] could assist her counsel in preparing a defense that served her best interests. A common characteristic of battered woman is a learned helplessness which manifests itself in the inability to perceive herself as abused and to communicate abuse to others. Evidence of battered woman syndrome may be considered newly discovered evidence warranting a new trial because usually there is delay in coming forward with information on the abuse, even if there were some knowledge of the abuse at trial." *Commonwealth v. Conaghan*, 433 Mass. 105, 109 (2000) (citations omitted).

BEST EVIDENCE

"[The best evidence rule] requires that, where the contents of a document are to be proved, the party must either produce the original document or show a sufficient excuse for its failure to offer the original." *Commonwealth v. Lenahan*, 50 Mass. App. Ct. 180, 185 (2000).

BLOOD SAMPLES

Grand jury. "As long as we define a standard for the production of blood samples that meets the requirement of reasonableness of the Fourth Amendment to the United States Constitution and of at. 14 of the Massachusetts Declaration of Rights, the label of probable cause need not be used. A standard that requires that a grand jury request must be reasonable in light of the facts seems appropriate. Given that a grand jury

11

must find probable cause to indict, it would be peculiar to require them to demonstrate the same degree of probable cause to believe that a target of their investigation committed a crime before the grand jury could properly obtain evidence in aid of their investigation. A grand jury subpoena is thus much different from a subpoena issued in the context of a prospective criminal trial. The Government cannot be required to justify the issuance of a grand jury subpoena by presenting evidence sufficient to establish probable cause because the very purpose of requesting the information is to ascertain whether probable cause exists.

"A grand jury must have a reasonable basis for believing (have probable cause for believing, if you wish) that a blood sample will provide test results that will significantly aid ... the grand jury in their investigation of circumstances in which there is good reason to believe a crime has been committed."

In the Matter of a Grand Jury Investigation, 427 Mass. 221, 225–26 (1998) (citations, quotation and punctuation marks omitted).

The grand jury need not file an application for a search warrant in order to obtain a blood sample, but, rather, need only seek an order for the production of such a sample. *In the Matter of a Grand Jury Investigation*,427 Mass. at 226 n.4 ("Such a process provides greater protection to an individual's interests than would the issuance of a search warrant in an ex parte proceeding before a judge.") (citation omitted).

Ortho-tolidine. "[E]xpert testimony as to the results of ortho-tolidine testing [a test that screens for the presence of blood] is admissible in Massachusetts." *Commonwealth v. Duguay*, 430 Mass. 397, 401 (1999).

Prior to charge or grand jury. See Note 3 following G.L. c. 276, § 1 for a discussion of obtaining a blood sample from a person who is neither charged with a crime nor the subject of a grand jury investigation.

Post indictment. "[P]ost-indictment, hence after finding of probable cause, order that defendant provide blood sample may properly issue on showing that a sample of the defendant's blood will probably produce evidence relevant to the question of the defendant's guilt." *In the Matter of a Grand Jury Investigation*, 427 Mass. 221, 223–24 (1998) (citing and quoting *Commonwealth v. Trigones*, 397 Mass. 633, 640 (1986)) (quotation marks omitted).

BOOKING QUESTIONS

"We believe that, where an arrestee's employment status may prove incriminatory, the police must give Miranda warnings before asking questions about employment. ... Recognizing an exception to the Miranda requirement for 'routine booking question[s]' does not mean that *any* questions asked during the booking process falls within that exception. Unless they first give the arrestee Miranda warnings or obtain a waiver of those rights, the police may not ask questions, even during booking, that are designed to elicit incriminating admissions." *Commonwealth v. Woods*, 419 Mass. 366, 372–73 (1995).

BOWDEN

"[T]he presentation of a *Bowden* [*Commonwealth v. Bowden*, 379 Mass. 472 (1980),] defense can expand the usual evidentiary boundaries quite significantly, permitting, as it does, the admission of evidence concerning information conveyed to the police by a wide variety of sources that would not or might not otherwise be admitted on hearsay or relevance grounds. *See, e.g., Commonwealth v. Silva-Santiago*, 453 Mass. [782 (2009)] at 803-804; *Commonwealth v. Mathews*, 450 Mass. 858, 872 n.15 (2008). Certainly a trial

judge has broad discretion to admit or exclude evidence, including the discretion to exclude evidence on the ground that it is more prejudicial than probative. *Commonwealth v. Avila*, 454 Mass. 744, 757 (2009) (citation omitted).

"As we have stated on many occasions, 'a judge is not required to instruct on the claimed inadequacy of a police investigation. *Bowden* simply holds that a judge may not remove the issue from the jury's consideration.' *Commonwealth v. Boateng*, 438 Mass. 498, 507 (2003), quoting *Commonwealth v. O'Brien*, 432 Mass. 578, 590 (2000)." *Commonwealth v. Lao*, 460 Mass. 12, 23 (2011) (quotation marks omitted).

BRUTON

1. "The *Bruton* rule is concerned only with inculpatory statements of a codefendant who is unavailable for cross-examination. *Bruton v. United States*, 391 U.S. 123, 126 (1968). *See Commonwealth v. Keevan*, 400 Mass. 557, 568–69 (1987) (*Bruton* teaching involves situation where nontestifying codefendant's confession inculpates another defendant). Even though a codefendant's isolated statement by itself might not be inculpatory, there is the risk that a defendant can be inculpated 'by the content of the statement taken in connection with other evidence in the case.' *Commonwealth v. LeBlanc*, 364 Mass. 1, 8 (1973), and cases cited." *Commonwealth v. Johnson*, 412 Mass. 318, 322–23 (1992).

2. *Compare Commonwealth v. James*, 424 Mass. 770, 782 (1997). "In *Richardson v. Marsh*, 481 U.S. 200, 208 (1987), the Supreme Court substantially restricted the scope of its *Bruton* rule, limiting its application to cases where the codefendant's statement 'expressly implicates' the defendant, leaving no doubt that it would prove to be 'powerfully incriminating.' ... [T]here is no *Bruton* error where the statement becomes incriminating only, when linked with evidence introduced at trial. ... Where a nontestifying codefendant's statement inferentially inculpates another defendant, we have recognized that it is not constitutionally required to consider the evidentiary context of the codefendant's statement so long as there is an adequate limiting instruction. ... [A] statement that does nothing more than raise an association between the defendants is not sufficient to give rise to a *Bruton* challenge."

BUCCAL SWAB

1. "[T]o obtain a buccal swab at this stage, [where criminal charges have been brought,] the Commonwealth's burden is merely to show that the sample sought will probably provide evidence relevant to the question of the defendant's guilt.

"This burden can be met through the submission of affidavits and documentary evidence as may be necessary in the circumstances or required by the judge. While an adversary hearing must be held, the holding of an evidentiary hearing, beyond the submissions of the parties, is not required." *Commonwealth v. Maxwell*, 441 Mass. 773, 778-79 (2004) ("The Commonwealth's motion ... should be handled in the manner prescribed in *Commonwealth v. Trigones*, 397 Mass. 633 (1986)) (citations omitted).

In *In re Jansen*, the Supreme Judicial Court affirmed the lower court's order pursuant to Mass.R.Crim.P. 17(a)(2) to compel a nonparty to provide a buccal swab for DNA analysis. The court held that the order was proper as the buccal swab test was critical to the preparation of the defendant's defense, but that in all cases, the person from whom the sample is sought must be given notice and an opportunity to be heard. *In re Jansen*, 444 Mass. 112, 121 (2005). *See also Commonwealth v. Draheim*, 447 Mass. 113 (2006).

11

2. "DNA identification of arrestees is a reasonable search that can be considered part of a routine booking procedure. When officers make an arrest supported by probable cause to hold for a serious offense and they bring the suspect to the station to be detained in custody, taking and analyzing a cheek swab of the arrestee's DNA is, like fingerprinting and photographing, a legitimate police booking procedure that is reasonable under the Fourth Amendment." *Maryland v. King*, 133 S. Ct. 1958 (2013).

CERTIFICATE OF ANALYSIS

See also Drug Certificate, below.

"The documents at issue here, while denominated by Massachusetts law 'certificates,' are quite plainly affidavits: 'declaration[s] of facts written down and sworn to by the declarant before an officer authorized to administer oaths.' Black's Law Dictionary 62 (8th ed. 2004). . . . The 'certificates' are functionally identical to live, in-court testimony, doing 'precisely what a witness does on direct examination.' *Davis v. Washington*, 547 U.S. 813, 830 (2006). . . . Absent a showing that the analysts were unavailable to testify at trial and that petitioner had a prior opportunity to cross-examine them, petitioner was entitled to 'be confronted with' the analysts at trial. *Crawford [v. Washington*, 541 U.S. 36, 54 (2004)]." *Melendez-Diaz v. Massachusetts*, 557 U.S. 305, 310–11 (2009) (footnote and some citations and quotation marks omitted).

"Although it could be error to admit a certificate that characterized a defendant in a particular way (*Commonwealth v. Sheline*, 391 Mass. 279, 286 [1984] [error to attribute alias to defendant on certificate]), here the certificate simply told the jury that the defendant was a defendant or a suspect, a fact that the jury already knew." *Commonwealth v. Caceres*, 413 Mass. 749, 756 (1992).

Footnote 9 adds that "[t]he better course would have been, on objection, to delete the reference to 'defendant or suspect.'" *Commonwealth v. Caceres*, 413 Mass. at 756 n.9 (citing *Commonwealth v. Foley*, 12 Mass. App. Ct. 983, 984 (1981)). *See also Commonwealth v. Jones*, 42 Mass. App. Ct. 378, 381 (1997).

CHAIN OF CUSTODY

"Alleged defects in the chain of custody usually go to the weight of the evidence and not its admissibility." *Commonwealth v. Viriyahiranpaiboon*, 412 Mass. 224, 230 (1992).

CIRCUMSTANTIAL EVIDENCE

"Given the close connection between circumstantial evidence instructions and reasonable doubt, it is best for judges [when instructing the jury on circumstantial evidence] to avoid examples that have numeric or quantifiable implications." *Commonwealth v. Brooks*, 422 Mass. 574, 579 (1996) (quoting *Commonwealth v. Rosa*, 422 Mass. 18, 28 (1996)).

CLOSING ARGUMENT

Improper prosecutorial conduct and/or closing argument includes the following:

a. Referring to the defendant's failure to testify. *Commonwealth v. Kozec*, 399 Mass. 514, 516–17 n.1 (1987). ("[The better practice is for the judge to intervene on his own] and immediately instruct the jury on the defendant's right not to testify." *Commonwealth. v. Arroyo*, 49 Mass. App. Ct. 672, 675 (2000).)

b. Misstating the evidence or referring to facts not in evidence. *Commonwealth. v. Kozec*, 399 Mass. at 516 n.2; *Commonwealth v. Beaudry*, 445 Mass. 577, 580 (2005)

("Here, the prosecutor exceeded the scope of proper argument by referring to facts not supported by evidence and not within a juror's common knowledge and suggesting an inference that could not reasonably be drawn from the evidence. The inference that the prosecutor suggested was that the complainant's testimony was true because 'it was not plausible that a child would possess knowledge of [the] sexual [acts alleged] unless she had acquired it from the acts which the defendant was charged.' *Commonwealth v. Scheffer*, 43 Mass. App. Ct. 398, 401 (1997)").

c. Interjecting personal belief in the defendant's guilt; *Commonwealth v. Kozec*, 399 Mass. at 516-17 n.3.

d. Playing on racial, ethnic or religious prejudice. *Commonwealth v. Kozec*, 399 Mass. at 517 n.4; *Commonwealth v. Gallego*, 27 Mass. App. Ct. 714, 717–20 (1989) ("Columbian drug dealers"); *Commonwealth v. Kines*, 37 Mass. App. Ct. 540, 541 (1994) ("'It is improper for the prosecutor to invite the jury to impute racial animosity into a situation without evidence to support it.' *Commonwealth v. Phoenix*, 409 Mass. 408, 425 (1991).").

e. Playing on the jury's sympathy or emotions. *Commonwealth v. Kozec*, 399 Mass. at 517 n.5; (*Commonwealth v. Woods*, 414 Mass. 343, 358 (1993) (Improper to point out the victim's parents who are seated in the courtroom if done for the improper purpose of appealing to emotional or sympathy.); *Commonwealth v. Harris*, 11 Mass. App. Ct. 165, 176–77 (1981) (Don't let the victim down.); *Commonwealth v. Sanchez*, 405 Mass. 369, 375 (1989) (End the victim's nightmare by convicting the defendant). "The Commonwealth may [however] tell the jury something of the person whose life has been lost in order to humanize the proceedings and a photograph may be admitted for this purpose." *Commonwealth v. Degro*, 432 Mass. 319, 323 (2000) (citations, quotation and punctuation marks omitted). *See also Commonwealth v. Grinkley*, 75 Mass. App. Ct. 798, 807–11 (2009) (error for prosecutor to discuss difficulty and pain of victims' rape examination, closing argument was "overwrought and inflammatory").

f. Commenting on the consequences of the verdict. *Commonwealth v. Kozec*, 399 Mass. at 517 n.6.

g. Pointing out the defendant's less-than-admirable profession, if it is overly prejudicial. *Commonwealth v. Kozec*, 399 Mass. at 524–25 (jello wrestler).

h. Pointing out that the police are not the ones on trial. *Commonwealth v. Shea*, 401 Mass. 731, 738 n.3 (1988). *See also Commonwealth v. Grandison*, 433 Mass. 135, 143 (2001) ("It was improper for the prosecutor to suggest to the jury that it was impermissible for defense counsel to question the veracity of the police officers ('how dare they').").

i. Pointing out the jury's duty to confront and avenge street crime. *Commonwealth v. Ward*, 28 Mass. App. Ct. 292, 294 (1990); *Commonwealth v. Cobb*, 26 Mass. App. Ct. 283, 286 (1988) ("[The duty of the jury] will result in a verdict of guilty.").

j. "The invitation to the jury to put themselves in the position of the victim is usually improper." *Commonwealth v. Jordan*, 49 Mass. App. Ct. 802, 816 (2000).

k. "The prosecutor also should not have suggested that the Commonwealth expected guilty verdicts . . . nor that the jury must return a verdict." *Commonwealth v. Jordan*, 49 Mass. App. Ct. 802, 816–17 (2000) (citation and footnote omitted).

l. "The prosecutor should not . . . have asked the jury 'to do your job.'" *Commonwealth v. Degro*, 432 Mass. 319, 328 (2000).

11

m. It is "improper to ask jury to send a message-that this type of action, of behavior is not going to be tolerated; ... to ask jury to consider right of people in neighborhood to feel safe; ... to tell jury they had duty to confront crime in the streets bravely and to avenge the wrong done the victim[;] ... to ask the jury to hold a person accountable for taking the law into his own hands because ours is a society governed by law." *Commonwealth v. Roberts*, 433 Mass. 45, 54 (2000) (citations and quotation and punctuation marks omitted).

(Much of this list was taken from Kantrowitz & Witkin, *Criminal Defense Motions*, Massachusetts Practice Series, Vol. 42, § 16.84 (2d ed., West Publishing Group 1998).)

n. Commenting on excluded evidence. "Counsel may not, in closing, 'exploit[ ] the evidence that had been excluded at his request.' *Commonwealth v. Carroll*, 439 Mass. 547, 555 (2003). Such exploitation of absent, excluded evidence is 'fundamentally unfair' and 'reprehensible.' *Commonwealth. v. Haraldstad*, 16 Mass. App. Ct. 565, 568 (1983)." *Commonwealth v. Harris*, 443 Mass. 714, 732 (2005).

Standard. "The cumulative effect of all the errors in the context of the entire argument ... and the case as a whole is considered in making this determination. The following factors are considered: whether defense counsel seasonably objected to the arguments at trial; whether the judge's instructions mitigated the error; whether the errors in the arguments went to the heart of the issues at trial or concerned collateral matters; whether the jury would be able to sort out the excessive claims made by the prosecutor; and whether the Commonwealth's case was so overwhelming that the errors did not prejudice the defendant." *Commonwealth v. Santiago*, 425 Mass. 491, 500 (1997). *See also Commonwealth v. McLaughlin*, 431 Mass. 506, 511 (2000).

CO-COUNSEL

"[W]e discern no reason to withhold from a defendant protection from statements by a codefendant's counsel." *Commonwealth v. Russo*, 49 Mass. App. Ct. 579, 582 (2000).

COLLATERAL ESTOPPEL

"The doctrine of collateral estoppel means imply that when an issue of ultimate fact has once been determined by a valid and final judgment, that issue cannot again be litigated between the same parties in any future lawsuit. Collateral estoppel requires the concurrence of three circumstances: (1) a common factual issue; (2) a prior determination of that issue in litigation between the same parties; and (3) a showing that the determination was in favor of the party seeking to raise the estoppel bar.

"The doctrine of collateral estoppel may work in two ways. First, it may bar totally a subsequent prosecution if one of the issues necessarily decided at the first trial is an essential element of the alleged crime in the second trial. Second, even if a prosecutor may proceed to a second trial, the doctrine may bar the introduction of certain facts determined in the defendant's favor at the first trial." *Commonwealth v. Mendes*, 46 Mass. App. Ct. 581, 585 (1999) (quotation marks and citations omitted). *See also Commonwealth v. Williams*, 431 Mass. 71, 74 (2000) ("Issues precluded under this doctrine must have been actually litigated in the action and there must have been available some avenue for review of the prior ruling on the issue. Finally, issue preclusion usually applies only where there is mutuality of the parties." (citations, quotation and punctuation marks omitted)).

In *Commonwealth v. Dorazio*, 472 Mass. 535 (2015) "the defendant ... [sought] to use the doctrine of collateral estoppel in order to bar the introduction of certain facts determined in the defendant's favor at the first trial ... for which he was acquitted, at [a subsequent] trial. Application of the doctrine of collateral estoppel ... demonstrates that its essential components technically have not been met. First, the acquittal evidence was admitted pursuant to a lower standard of proof than that required for a conviction, and second, the defendant has not satisfied his burden of showing that the jury in the trial involving J.D. "necessarily decided" that he did not engage in unlawful sexual conduct with J.D. ... As noted by Justice Brennan in his dissenting opinion in [*Dowling v. United States*, 493 U.S. 342 (1990)], there are a number of inherent problems in admitting evidence of a crime for which a defendant was acquitted despite its relevance on issues other than propensity in a subsequent trial:

"'First, [o]ne of the dangers inherent in the admission of extrinsic offense evidence is that the jury may convict the defendant not for the offense charged but for the extrinsic offense. This danger is particularly great where ... the extrinsic activity was not the subject of a conviction; the jury may feel the defendant should be punished for that activity even if he is not guilty of the offense charged. ... Alternatively, there is the danger that the evidence may lead [the jury] to conclude that, having committed a crime of the type charged, [the defendant] is likely to repeat it. ... Thus, the fact that the defendant is forced to relitigate his participation in a prior criminal offense under a low standard of proof combined with the inherently prejudicial nature of such evidence increases the risk that the jury erroneously will convict the defendant of the presently charged offense.' *Dowling*, 493 U.S. at 361–62 (Brennan, J., dissenting). 'Moreover, because of the significance a jury may place on evidence of a prior criminal offense, presenting a defense against that offense may be as burdensome as defending against the presently charged offense.' *Id.* at 362 (Brennan, J., dissenting). '[Because] the lower standard of proof makes it easier for the jury to conclude that the defendant committed the prior offense, the defendant is essentially forced to present affirmative evidence to rebut the contention that he committed that offense.' *Id.* (Brennan, J., dissenting).

"Justice Brennan also observed that the use of acquittal evidence offends the established interests of preserving the finality of judgments and protecting individuals from governmental overreaching. *Id.* at 355 (Brennan, J., dissenting). Because of the nature of a 'not guilty' verdict, it is difficult, at best, for a defendant to prove what issues were "actually decided" in the earlier proceeding at which he was acquitted. *Id.* at 357–58 (Brennan, J., dissenting). The result is inconsistent with the Supreme Court's 'admonition in Ashe that an excessively technical approach to collateral estoppel would, of course, simply amount to a rejection of the rule of collateral estoppel in criminal proceedings, at least in every case where the first judgment was based upon a general verdict of acquittal. [*Ashe v. Swenson*, 397 U.S. 436, 444 (1970)]. Indeed, forcing defendants to choose between forgoing the protections of the Double Jeopardy Clause and abandoning the defense of a general denial raises grave due process concerns.' *Dowling*, [493 U.S.] at 358 (Brennan, J., dissenting). Justice Brennan also found fault with the fact that the majority applied its reasoning to a successive criminal prosecution (and not a civil remedial proceeding as done in past cases) 'in which the Government [sought] to punish the defendant and [based] that punishment at least in part on a criminal act for

11

which the defendant [was] acquitted.' *Id.* at 360 (Brennan, J., dissenting).

"We find the thoughtful and extensive considerations enunciated in the dissenting opinion in Dowling to be instructive, and we conclude that the collateral estoppel protections necessarily embraced by art. 12 warrant the exclusion of the acquittal evidence in the circumstances of this case, a subsequent criminal proceeding involving alleged unlawful sexual conduct with minors." *Commonwealth v. Dorazio*, 472 Mass. 535, 545–47 (2015) (citations and quotation marks omitted).

COMPACT DISC (CD)

"For similar reasons, we hold that digital images placed and stored in a computer hard drive and transferred to a compact disc are subject to the same rules of evidence as videotapes." *Commonwealth v. Leneski*, 66 Mass. App. Ct. 291, 294 (2006).

COMPETENCY

"Competency to stand trial requires that the defendant have the capacity to understand the nature and object of the proceedings against him, to consult with counsel, and to assist in preparing his defense. *Commonwealth v. Crowley*, 393 Mass. 393, 398 (1984), quoting *Dusky v. United States*, 326 U.S. 162, 171 (1975). The burden of proof is on the Commonwealth to show that the defendant is competent. A competency hearing must be held where there exists doubt as to whether the defendant satisfied the *Dusky* test."

"The judge's determination that the defendant was competent to stand trial was within her discretion. *See Commonwealth v. DeMinico*, 408 Mass. 230, 234–35 (1990) (defendant competent to stand trial despite testimony during trial that defendant experiencing psychotic episode); *Commonwealth v. Kostka*, 370 Mass. 516, 522 (1976) (defendant competent despite some psychiatric testimony to contrary). . . . A defendant's demeanor at trial and response to questioning by the judge are relevant to a decision on the merits of the competency issue." *Commonwealth v. L'Abbe*, 421 Mass. 262, 266–67 (1995).

See also Commonwealth v. Lyons, 426 Mass. 466, 468–69 (1998) ("Competency to stand trial requires that the defendant have (1) sufficient present ability to consult with his lawyer with a reasonable degree of rational understanding and (2) a rational as well as factual understanding of the proceedings against him. The Commonwealth has the burden to prove by a preponderance of the evidence that the defendant was competent. When reviewing the judge's finding of competency, we give substantial deference to his findings of fact.") (citations and quotation marks omitted).

Competency to testify. "[T]here is a two-pronged test for competency. The witness must (1) have the general ability or capacity to observe, remember and give expression to that which she has seen, heard, or experienced; and (2) have understanding sufficient to comprehend the difference between truth and falsehood, the wickedness of the latter and the obligation and duty to tell the truth, and, in a general way, belief that failure to perform the obligation will result in punishment. A trial judge has broad discretion to determine whether a competency hearing is required, and whether a witness is competent to testify. Whether the test is met is peculiarly for the trial judge, and his determination will be rarely faulted on appellate review." *Commonwealth v. Allen*, 40 Mass. App. Ct. 458, 461 (1996) (citations and quotation marks omitted).

COMPLAINT, REFUSAL TO ISSUE (DISTRICT COURT)

"If a judge declines to issue a complaint, the complainant has no constitutional right to challenge that determination. The rights asserted by the plaintiff are not private but are in fact lodged in the Commonwealth as it may proceed to enforce its laws. In American jurisprudence a private citizen lacks a judicially cognizable interest in the prosecution or nonprosecution of another. The plaintiff had no constitutional or statutory right to have criminal complaints issue." *Tarabolski v. Williams*, 419 Mass. 1001 (1994) (citations and punctuation omitted).

COMPLETENESS, DOCTRINE OF

"When a defendant's statement is put in evidence to show his guilt, he has the right to offer any other part of the same statement which tends to explain the admission. He may not introduce portions of the statement that are unrelated to the admission. Even in the interests of "completeness," a defendant does not have the right to introduce unrelated, self-serving statements." *Commonwealth v. Hanlon*, 44 Mass. App. Ct. 810, 823 (1998) (citation omitted).

CONFLICT OF INTEREST

"An 'actual' or 'genuine' conflict of interest arises where the 'independent professional judgment' of trial counsel is impaired, either by his own interests, or by the interests of another client. An actual conflict requires reversal of a defendant's conviction under art. 12 of the Massachusetts Declaration of Rights without the necessity of showing that the conflict resulted in any prejudice. However, where a defendant can show nothing more than a potential conflict, the conviction will not be reversed except on a showing of actual prejudice. Actual prejudice is measured against the standard . . . as in cases involving claims of ineffective assistance of counsel." *Commonwealth v. Croken*, 432 Mass. 266, 272 (2000) (citations, quotation and punctuation marks omitted).

CONSCIOUSNESS OF GUILT

Generally. "Although our comments speak in terms of evidence of flight or concealment, we note that they are for the most part applicable to other types of evidence offered to prove consciousness of guilt, for example, false statements made to police, destruction or concealment of evidence, or the bribery or threatening of a witness." *Commonwealth v. Toney*, 385 Mass. 575, 584 n.4 (1982). *See also Commonwealth v. Scanlon*, 412 Mass. 664, 676 (1992).

Other examples of consciousness of guilt include
- Altering one's physical appearance. *Commonwealth v. Carrion*, 407 Mass. 263, 275–77 (1990).
- Defendant's delay in opening the door for the police. *Commonwealth v. Pratt*, 407 Mass. 647, 649, 652 (1990).
- Violent behavior during an escape attempt. *Commonwealth v. Roberts*, 407 Mass. 731, 736 (1990).
- "Acts of a joint venturer amounting to consciousness of guilt may be attributed to another joint venturer if the acts occurred during the course of a joint venture and in furtherance of it." *Commonwealth v. Mahoney*, 405 Mass. 326, 330–31 (1989).
- Escape or attempted escape. *Commonwealth v. Ouen Lam*, 420 Mass. 615, 617 (1995).
- Threat to kill a potential witness. *Commonwealth v. Fernandes*, 427 Mass. 90, 94 (1998).

11

- Expressions of sympathy and regret. *Commonwealth v. Carapellucci*, 429 Mass. 579, 583 (1999).
- "[D]efendant's statements that he wished coventurer would stop talking about crime and that he did not want to go to jail" *Commonwealth v. Carapellucci*, 429 Mass. 579, 583 (1999). (original case cite omitted).
- Discussion about disposing of murder weapon. *Commonwealth v. Carapellucci*, 429 Mass. 579, 583 (1999).
- Statement that he never meant to hurt victim. *Commonwealth v. Carapellucci*, 429 Mass. 579, 583 (1999).
- False alibi. *Commonwealth v. Carapellucci*, 429 Mass. 579, 583 (1999).
- Lack of regret at victim's death. *Commonwealth v. Carapellucci*, 429 Mass. 579, 583 (1999).
- False statements to police. *Commonwealth v. Carapellucci*, 429 Mass. 579, 583 (1999).
- Begging complaining witness to recant. *Commonwealth v. Carapellucci*, 429 Mass. 579, 583 (1999).

Consciousness of guilt does *not* include

- "The defendant also argues that the fact that he registered under an assumed name at the YMCA prior to the crime should not have been admitted. The defendant is correct." *Commonwealth v. Roberts*, 407 Mass. 731, 736 (1990) (footnote omitted).
- "The defendant argues that the judge erroneously allowed the Commonwealth to introduce evidence of the defendant's refusal to have his hands swabbed. We agree . . . since its use we violated the defendant's privilege against self-incrimination secured by art. 12." *Commonwealth v. Lydon*, 413 Mass. 309, 313, 315 (1992).
- "[T]estimony regarding the defendant's action of staring at the floor should not have been admitted for purposes of proving consciousness of guilt." *Commonwealth v. Thompson*, 431 Mass. 108, 117 (2000).
- "[D]efendant's hanging his head and biting his lip not admissible as nontestimonial admission demonstrating consciousness of guilt." *Commonwealth v. Thompson*, 431 Mass. 108, 117 (2000) (citation omitted).

Flight. "The evidence of the defendant's flight was properly before the jury. We have held that whether a flight from the police shows consciousness of guilt of the offense on trial when the defendant is charged with another offense is a question of fact for the jury going to the weight of the evidence, rather than a question of law for the judge going to the admissibility of the evidence. It is also well-established that evidence tending to show consciousness of guilt will not be rendered inadmissible simply because it may reveal to the jury that the defendant has committed another offense." *Commonwealth v. Burke*, 414 Mass. 252, 260 (1993) (citations and quotation marks omitted). *See also Commonwealth v. Burston*, 35 Mass. App. Ct. 355, 357 (1993) (upholding judge's discretionary decision to admit evidence of defendant's flight from earlier trial on grounds of consciousness of guilt).

Alternative explanation. "When there are multiple possible explanations for a defendant's flight, it is for the jury to decide if the defendant's actions resulted from consciousness of guilt of some other reason." *Commonwealth v. Prater*, 431 Mass. 86, 97 (2000) (citation omitted).

CONTINUANCE WITHOUT A FINDING (CWOF)

"As we have noted in prior decisions, the Legislature has, by enacting G.L. c. 278, § 18, provided a statutory procedure available in the District, Juvenile, and Boston Munici-

pal Courts for the disposition of criminal cases by means of a CWOF, the imposition of conditions, and dismissal. In those courts, this statutory procedure replaced the practice of CWOF dispositions that followed in the wake of [*Commonwealth v. Brandano*, 359 Mass. 332 (1971)]. The procedure requires that the defendant tender a plea of guilty (or admit to sufficient facts) as a precondition to such a disposition. Although the Legislature did not make G.L. c. 278, § 18, applicable to criminal proceedings in the Superior Court, we do not infer that it intended to bar the imposition of such dispositions in cases pending there, unless otherwise prohibited by law. Rather, the Legislature has delineated expressly crimes, over which neither the District Court nor the Boston Municipal Court has jurisdiction, where such dispositions may not be utilized. The Legislature has thus acknowledged that the disposition of 'continued without a finding' remains available in the Superior Court for those offenses that do not prohibit such dispositions [to be placed on file]." *Commonwealth v. Powell*, 453 Mass. 320, 324–26 (2009) (footnotes and citation omitted).

Unless specifically authorized by the sentencing provisions of a particular crime, a judge cannot "CWOF" a case after trial. *Commonwealth v. Norrell*, 423 Mass. 725, 727 (1996). However, a judge may "CWOF" a case pretrial over the objection of the Commonwealth so long as *Brandano* procedures are followed. *Commonwealth v. Pyles*, 423 Mass. 717 (1996). *Commonwealth v. Brandano*, 359 Mass. 332, 337 (1971) mandates that if a CWOF is desired, over the objection of the Commonwealth, then the defendant must file an affidavit containing facts and law justifying the dismissal. The Commonwealth may file a counter–affidavit. The judge may either rely fully on the affidavits or hold a hearing to determine that the interests of public justice require dismissal, citing findings of fact and the reasons for the decision.

Appeal. "When the Commonwealth appeals from an order continuing a case without a finding, it may file a motion seeking to stay the probationary period pending appeal to prevent the appeal from becoming moot." *Commonwealth v. Resende*, 427 Mass. 1005, 1006 (1998) (rescript) (citation omitted).

CORROBORATION RULE

A conviction may not be based solely on evidence of an extrajudicial confession by the accused. The corroboration rule applies to the admissions as well as the confessions, and where the evidence offered in corroboration of an out-of-court admission is entirely ambiguous and speculative, it is error to deny a defendant's motion for a required finding on not guilty. "[T]he required corroboration [must] be some evidence, besides the confession, that the criminal act was committed by someone, that is, that the crime was real and not imaginary." *Commonwealth v. Manning*, 41 Mass. App. Ct. 18, 19–21 (1996). *See also Commonwealth v. Landenburg*, 41 Mass. App. Ct. 23 (1996).

COURTROOM CLOSURE

The mandatory-closure rule contained in this section, as construed by the Supreme Judicial Court, violates the First Amendment. *Globe Newspaper Co. v. Superior Ct.*, 457 U.S. 596, 610–11 (1982), reversing 383 Mass. 838 (1981).

There is a guaranteed right of the public under the First and Fourteenth Amendments to attend a criminal trial. "Absent an overriding interest articulated in findings, the trial of a criminal case must be open to the public." *Richmond Newspapers, Inc. v. Virginia*, 448 U.S. 555, 580–81 (1980).

11

"A trial court can determine on a case-by-case basis whether closure is necessary to protect the welfare of a minor victim. Among the factors to be weighed are the minor victim's age, psychological maturity, and understanding, the nature of the crime, the desires of the victim, and the interests of parents and relatives." *Globe Newspaper Co. v. Superior Ct.*, 457 U.S. 596, 608 (1982) (footnotes omitted), *rev'g* 383 Mass. 838 (1981).

Waller Factors. "Further, the determination must satisfy four requirements articulated by the Supreme Court: '[1] the party seeking to close the hearing must advance an overriding interest that is likely to be prejudiced, [2] the closure must be no broader than necessary Checked case. to protect that interest, [3] the trial court must consider reasonable alternatives to closing the proceeding, and [4] it must make findings adequate to support the closure.'" *Commonwealth v. Martin*, 417 Mass. 187, 194 (1994) (quoting *Waller v. Georgia*, 467 Mass. 39, 48 (1984)).

Partial Closure. "[E]ven in a partial closure context, the remaining Waller factors must be satisfied." *Commonwealth v. Cohen*, 456 Mass. 94, 113 (2010).

Jury Selection. "The right to a public trial extends to the jury selection process." *Commonwealth v. Morganti*, 467 Mass. 96, 101 (2014) (citing *Presley v. Georgia*, 558 U.S. 209, 213 (2010); *Owens v. United States*, 483 F.3d 48, 66 (1st Cir. 2007); *Commonwealth v. Cohen*, 456 Mass. 94, 106 (2010)).

Waiver. "Because we conclude that counsel may waive a defendant's right to a public trial during jury selection without express consent and, in the circumstances here, that counsel's decision was a reasonable tactical decision, we affirm the denial of the defendant's motion for a new trial." *Commonwealth v. Lavoie*, 464 Mass. 83, 84 (2013).

Sign-in Procedure. "Although we conclude that the conditions imposed by the judge of signing in and showing identification fell short of a constitutional closure, that does not mean that they may be imposed without justification or that they are exempt from judicial review. ... [A] spectator should be free to enter a court room where a criminal case against an adult is being adjudicated without first having to show identification or provide one's name. That presumption may be overcome and identification may be required of spectators only where a judge sets forth on the record the reasons that justify imposing this condition on entry based on the special circumstances of the case and only where the conditions are no broader than needed to accomplish their purpose." *Commonwealth v. Maldonado*, 466 Mass. 742, 751–52 (2014).

Rape Shield Hearings. "[W]e ... conclude that, before a judge may order the court room closed for a rape shield hearing, the judge must make a case-by-case determination in accordance with the four-prong framework articulated by the United States Supreme Court in *Waller* [v. Georgia, 467 U.S. 39, 48 (1984)]." *Commonwealth v. Jones*, 472 Mass. 707, 722 (2015).

CREDIBILITY OF WITNESS

It is improper to ask one witness whether another witness is lying. "It is a fundamental principle that a witness cannot be asked to assess the credibility of his testimony or that of other witnesses. The fact finder, not the witness, must determine the weight and credibility of testimony." *Commonwealth v. Triplett*, 398 Mass. 561, 567 (1986) (citations and quotation marks omitted). *Cf. Commonwealth v. Johnson*, 412 Mass. 318, 327–28 (1992) ("It was proper for the prosecutor to point out, through this line of questioning, that there were

inconsistencies between the defendant's testimony and that of the arresting officer, so long as the defendant was not asked to assess the credibility of the arresting officer's testimony.").

CRIMINAL PROFILES

"The use of criminal profiles or substantive evidence of guilt is inherently prejudicial to the defendant." *Commonwealth v. Day*, 409 Mass. 719, 723 (1991). See also Experts, below.

CROSS-EXAMINATION

Bias. "Evidence of bias is almost never a collateral issue. ... [E]vidence of police brutality may indicate bias of police witnesses [and is therefore admissible]". *Commonwealth v. Hall*, 50 Mass. App. Ct. 208, 212–13 (2000) (citations, quotation marks, and brackets omitted).

"A judge may not restrict cross-examination of a material witness by foreclosing inquiry into a subject that could show bias or prejudice on the part of the witness. If, on the facts, there is a possibility of bias, even a remote one, the judge has no discretion to bar all inquiry into the subject. Notwithstanding, this rule is not ironclad; weighed in addition is the correlative principle that the right of cross-examination is not infringed by reasonable limitations as, for example, where the matter sought to be elicited has been sufficiently aired." *Commonwealth v. Omonira*, 59 Mass. App. Ct. 200, 204 (2003) ("The judge did not err in allowing the prosecutor to cross-examine the defendant's wife, on a good faith basis, as to her knowledge of the defendant's possible deportation if convicted. There was at least a possibility of bias.") (citations and quotation marks omitted).

Evidence of drug use to attack credibility. "Evidence of the witness's use of illegal drugs, legally prescribed medication, or alcohol at the time of the events concerning which she was testifying, or evidence of a pattern of such drug or alcohol addiction, if it would impair the witness's ability to perceive and to remember correctly, is admissible on cross-examination to attack the witness's credibility. However, there is no apparent connection between the witness's possible use of drugs at Framingham and the witness's ability to perceive, remember, or testify to the events in question." *Commonwealth v. Carrion*, 407 Mass. 263, 273–74 (1990) (citation omitted).

Factors—Determining Unreasonable Limitations on Cross-Examinations. "There are two factors to be weighed in determining 'whether a defendant's constitutional right to cross-examine and thus to confront a witness against him has been denied because of an unreasonable limitation of cross-examination.' *Commonwealth v. Miles*, 420 Mass. 67, 72 (1995). The first is the 'materiality of the witness's direct testimony,' and the second is the 'degree of the restriction on cross-examination.' *Commonwealth v. Miles*, 420 Mass. 67, 72 (1995). There is no question that Kelley's direct testimony was material to the Commonwealth's case because she provided the only first-hand account of the murder. The judge did not improperly limit the defense's cross-examination of Kelley, however, because the jury were presented with sufficient evidence with which to assess her bias and credibility. She was extensively cross-examined about her drug use, prior convictions of forgery, larceny, and fraud, her plea agreement with the Commonwealth, and her fears about being convicted of murder and incarcerated for life." *Commonwealth v. Knight*, 437 Mass. 487, 496 (2002).

Improper questioning. "It is error for a prosecutor to communicate impressions by innuendo through questions which are answered in the negative when the questioner has no evidence to support the innuendo." *Commonwealth v. LaFaille*, 46 Mass. App. Ct. 144, 151, *rev'd on other grounds*, 430 Mass. 44 (1999) (citation, quotation marks, and punctuation omitted). It is also improper to ask a witness to comment on the credibility of another witness's testimony. *Commonwealth v. Alvarado*, 50 Mass. App. Ct. 419, 423 (2000).

Judge's discretion to limit. "Defense counsel then sought to probe the victim's relationship and the substance of her conversations with the district attorney's staff. The judge sustained the Commonwealth's objections to this line of inquiry. . . .

"[T]he judge ruled that, in the absence of any proof of the victim's being 'coached' beyond 'supposition or surmise,' the defendant could not inquire in further detail into the witness's contact with the 'system . . . a so-called victim witness advocate program.'

"A defendant is entitled as a matter of right to a reasonable cross-examination of a witness in order to show bias and prejudice. It is equally true, however, that the scope and contours of cross-examination are within the judge's sound discretion, and that he or she may limit 'to what extent the accuracy, veracity, and credibility of a witness may be tested. This discretion is not subject to reversal unless the defendant can show he was prejudiced by too narrow a restriction in his cross-examination rights."

Commonwealth v. O'Connor, 407 Mass. 663, 671 (1990) (citations omitted); *see also Commonwealth v. Smiledge*, 419 Mass. 156, 159 (1994) ("Where, as here, there has been extensive inquiry into a witness's bias and credibility in general, it was within the judge's discretion to exclude a specific inquiry . . . . The right to cross examine a witness on bias is not infringed on by curbing such inquiry . . . . The right to cross-examine a witness on bias is not infringed on by curbing such inquiry if the matter has been sufficiently aired" and *Commonwealth v. Wheeler*, 42 Mass. App. Ct. 933 (1997) ("If a party cross-examines a witness upon a collateral matter, he must take the answer as it is given, he cannot contradict it." *Commonwealth v. Wheeler*, 42 Mass. App. Ct. at 936 (quoting *Leone v. Doran*, 363 Mass. 1, 15 (1973)).

CRUEL AND UNUSUAL PUNISHMENT

Concerning cruel and unusual punishment, a "defendant . . . bears a heavy burden of showing that a particular punishment that has been established by the Legislature exceeds the limitations of art. 26 . . . or the Eighth Amendment. . . . Specifically, a defendant must persuade a reviewing court that the punishment is 'so disproportionate to the crime' that it shocks the conscience and offends fundamental notions of human dignity' . . . . '[T]hree factors [considered are:] (1) the nature of the offender and the offence in light of the degree of harm to society; (2) sentencing provisions in other jurisdictions for similar offenses; and (3) sentences for more severe offenses within the Commonwealth.'" *Commonwealth v. Dunn*, 43 Mass. App. Ct. 58, 62–63 (1997) (quoting *Commonwealth v. Alvarez*, 413 Mass. 224, 233–34 (1992)).

CUMULATIVE ERROR

"We do not consider whether each of the errors by itself would warrant reversal of the defendant's convictions. Instead, we take them in combination and conclude that [reversal is warranted]." *Commonwealth v. Jackson*, 45 Mass. App. Ct. 666, 672 (1998).

DANGEROUS WEAPON

"The essential question, when an object which is not dangerous per se is alleged to be a dangerous weapon, is whether the object, as used by the defendant, is capable of producing serious bodily harm . . . . Resolution of these questions is invariably for the fact finder and involves not only consideration of any evidence as to the nature and specific features of the object but also attention to the circumstances surrounding the assault and the use of the object, and the manner in which it was handled or controlled." *Commonwealth v. Fernandez*, 43 Mass. App. Ct. 313, 315 (1997) (citations and quotation marks omitted). The prosecution is not, however, required to "demonstrate an intent on the part of the perpetrator to employ the instrumentality as a weapon." *Commonwealth v. Tevlin*, 433 Mass. 305, 313 (2001).

DEFAULTING DEFENDANT

"[*Commonwealth v. Kane*, 19 Mass. App. Ct. 129, 135 (1984) advises] a vigorous effort to find an absconding defendant and some formality in presenting the evidence about her disappearance, if the jury were to be permitted to make any use of the circumstances of flight." *Commonwealth v. Stack*, 49 Mass. App. Ct. 227, 239 (2000).

DEFENDANT AT COUNSEL TABLE

"[O]rdinarily, a criminal defendant should be permitted to sit at counsel table unless upon inquiry, the judge finds that some security measures are necessary. If the judge denies a motion to sit at counsel table, the judge's reasons must be stated on the record." *Commonwealth v. Moyles*, 45 Mass. App. Ct. 350, 353 (1998) (citations and quotation marks omitted).

DEFENDANT AT SIDEBAR

"A defendant is entitled to be present at all critical stages of a criminal proceeding, including voir dire of an individual juror [at sidebar], if an appropriate request for his presence is made. The defendant made no such request in this case, the judge never 'excluded him', and his counsel never objected to the defendant's absence. In such circumstances, we consider the issue waived and will not address it on appeal." *Commonwealth v. Perry*, 432 Mass. 214, 238 (2000) (citations, brackets, and quotation and punctuation marks omitted).

DESTRUCTION OF EVIDENCE

"To obtain a dismissal of an indictment based on the destruction of evidence, a defendant has the initial burden of establishing a reasonable possibility, based on concrete evidence and not on mere speculation, that the Commonwealth's actions deprived him of evidence that would have been favorable to his case. Once the defendant meets this burden, a judge must then balance the culpability of the Commonwealth, the materiality of the evidence, and the potential prejudice to the defendant in order to determine the appropriate remedy, which, although rare, may include dismissal of an indictment." *Commonwealth v. McIntyre*, 430 Mass. 529, 537 (1999) (citations and quotation marks omitted.)

DIMINISHED CAPACITY

"There is no diminished capacity defense in this Commonwealth. *Commonwealth v. Parker*, 420 Mass. 242, 245 n.3 (1995). In *Commonwealth v. Gould*, 380 Mass. 672, 673 (1980), we said that a defendant 'may produce expert testimony on the issue whether or not the impairment of his mental processes precluded him from being able to deliberately premeditate,' and whether the defendant acted with extreme atrocity or cruelty. We have also said that evidence of a

11

defendant's mental impairment is relevant to the question 'whether the crime of murder was committed at all,' *Commonwealth v. Grey*, 399 Mass. 469 (1987), including issues of intent and knowledge, *Commonwealth v. Sires*, 413 Mass. 292, 299 (1992), and whether a murder was committed with extreme atrocity or cruelty. *Commonwealth v. Baldwin*, 426 Mass. 105 (1997)." *Commonwealth v. Hardy*, 426 Mass. 725, 729 n.5 (1998).

DISMISSAL

"[W]e have never ordered the dismissal of an indictment for misconduct in the absence of prejudice. ... We have sometimes remarked that outrageous police conduct, not shown to be prejudicial to a fair trial, may require the dismissal of charges, but we have never dismissed charges in such a circumstance (although we have upheld the suppression of evidence in such situations)." *Commonwealth v. Phillips*, 413 Mass. 50, 59 (1992) (citations and quotation marks omitted).

"We take this occasion to note that a judge has inherent authority to dismiss an indictment sua sponte. This is a necessary corollary of the judge's authority to process criminal cases. Because the allowance of a motion to dismiss ends the Commonwealth's prosecution, it has the right to appeal the allowance of a motion to dismiss." *Commonwealth v. Jenkins*, 431 Mass. 501, 504 (2000) (citations and quotation marks omitted).

DISMISSAL WITH PREJUDICE

"Dismissal with prejudice is appropriate in cases of egregious prosecutorial misconduct or on a showing of prejudice (or a substantial threat thereof), or irremediable harm to the defendant's opportunity to obtain a fair trial." *Commonwealth v. Hernandez*, 421 Mass. 272, 277 (1995).

DNA

Admissibility. DNA test results, if properly conducted, are admissible into evidence. *See Commonwealth v. Mathews*, 450 Mass. 858, 872 (2008); *Commonwealth v. Gaynor*, 443 Mass. 245, 264 (2005); *Commonwealth v. Vao Sok*, 425 Mass. 787 (1997); *Commonwealth v. Rosier*, 425 Mass. 807 (1997); *Commonwealth v. Fowler*, 425 Mass. 819 (1997); and *Commonwealth v. Lanigan*, 419 Mass. 15, 27 (1994). See also Experts, below.

Admissibility of Inconclusive DNA Evidence. "In *Commonwealth v. Mathews*, [450 Mass. 858, 871–72 (2008)], we stated that the admissibility of DNA results, even when those results are inconclusive, should be determined on a case-by-case basis. ... We ... stress here ... that for inconclusive DNA evidence to be admissible, it must be probative of an issue of consequence in the case." *Commonwealth v. Nesbitt*, 452 Mass. 236, 253–54 (2008).

Buccal swab. For notes regarding the Commonwealth's right to obtain a DNA sample, see Buccal Swab, above.

Constitutionality. DNA law, G.L. c. 22E, requiring convict to provide DNA sample for State DNA database, constitutional. *Landry v. Attorney General*, 429 Mass. 336 (1999); *see also Murphy v. Dep't of Correction*, 429 Mass. 736 (1999).

Statistical significance. "We have also held that in a criminal trial we will not permit the admission of test results showing a DNA match (a positive result) without telling the jury anything about the likelihood of that match occurring. *Commonwealth v. Curnin*, 409 Mass. 218, 222 n.7 (1991). We have explained our approach by stating that evidence of a match based on correctly used testing systems is of little or no

value without reliable evidence indicating the significance of the match, that is, evidence of the probability of a random match of [the victim's or] the defendant's DNA in the general population.

"The same reasoning applies to evidence that a DNA test, although resulting in less than a complete 'match,' could not exclude a particular individual as a potential contributor." *Commonwealth v. Mattei*, 455 Mass. 840, 850–51 (2010) (citations, footnote, and quotations marks omitted).

Not testimonial. "We conclude that the probability statistics [regarding a DNA match] are not testimonial." *Commonwealth v. Cole*, 473 Mass. 317, 330 (2015).

DOCKET SHEET

"[D]ocket sheets are part of the court records and may be presented as prima facie evidence of the facts recorded therein." *Commonwealth v. Podoprigora*, 46 Mass. App. Ct. 928, 929 (1999).

DREAMS

"In many circumstances, any relationship between testimony about a dream and a subsequent act may be speculative and therefore unreliable. ... [However] in the circumstances of this case, the defendant's recounting of a dream during which he stated he killed the victim just hours before the victim was stabbed in the car, could serve to explicate the defendant's later comment 'I just killed her. She just fucked up. I dreamed about it last night.'" Furthermore, any potential prejudice to the defendant was limited by the judge's sua sponte instruction ... limiting the evidence to the issue of motive and intent." *Commonwealth v. McIntyre*, 430 Mass. 529, 539 (1999).

DRUG CERTIFICATE

"There is little doubt that the documents at issue in this case fall within the 'core class of testimonial statements' thus described. ... The documents at issue here, while denominated by Massachusetts law 'certificates,' are quite plainly affidavits: 'declaration[s] of facts written down and sworn to by the declarant before an officer authorized to administer oaths.' Black's Law Dictionary 62 (8th ed. 2004). The 'certificates' are functionally identical to live, in-court testimony, doing 'precisely what a witness does on direct examination.' *Davis v. Washington*, 547 U.S. 813, 830 (2006). Here, moreover, not only were the affidavits 'made under circumstances which would lead an objective witness reasonably to believe that the statement would be available for use at a later trial,' but under Massachusetts law the sole purpose of the affidavits was to provide 'prima facie evidence of the composition, quality, and the net weight' of the analyzed substance, Mass. Gen. Laws, ch. 111, § 13. We can safely assume that the analysts were aware of the affidavits' evidentiary purpose, since that purpose—as stated in the relevant state-law provision—was reprinted on the affidavits themselves. In short, under our decision in *Crawford* the analysts' affidavits were testimonial statements, and the analysts were 'witnesses' for purposes of the Sixth Amendment. Absent a showing that the analysts were unavailable to testify at trial and that petitioner had a prior opportunity to cross-examine them, petitioner was entitled to 'be confronted with' the analysts at trial. *Crawford [v. Washington*, 541 U.S. 36], 54 [(2004)]." *Melendez-Diaz v. Massachusetts*, 557 U.S. 305, 310–11 (2009) (footnote and some citations and quotation marks omitted). *See also Commonwealth v. Charles*, 456 Mass. 378 (2010) (admission of drug certificates without analyst's testimony unconstitutional in light of *Melendez-Diaz*); *Commonwealth v. Vasquez*, 456 Mass. 350 (2010) (same).

DUPLICATIVE CONVICTIONS

The remedy for duplicative convictions "is to vacate both the conviction and the sentence on the lesser included offense, and to affirm the sentence on the more serious offense." *Commonwealth v. Raymond*, 424 Mass. 382, 396 (1997) (quoting *Commonwealth v. Berry*, 420 Mass. 95, 113 (1995)).

EAVESDROPPING

The chief of police entered a crawl space under the defendant's first-floor apartment with the permission of the owner of the property.

"[W]e conclude that the search and seizure of the defendant's conversations violated art. 14 of the Declaration of Rights of the Constitution of the Commonwealth. Society should honor the privacy interests that apartment dwellers and condominium owners have in being free from warrantless eavesdropping by police who have infiltrated crawl spaces and other areas to which neither the public nor any other occupant of the multiple dwelling has access. Because these conversations took place in the defendant's home, the fact that Chief Berkel was lawfully where he was and that the defendant had no legal interest in the crawl space cannot be dispositive of the question. Intrusions into the privacy of one's home raise classic search and seizure problems." *Commonwealth v. Panetti*, 406 Mass. 230, 234 (1989).

EGREGIOUS GOVERNMENT MISCONDUCT

"Egregious government conduct is similar to entrapment. The challenge under egregious conduct is a constitutional due process challenge and is reserved for only the most intolerable government conduct." *Commonwealth v. Monteagudo*, 427 Mass. 484, 485 n.1 (1998) (citations and quotation and punctuation marks omitted).

"In cases alleging egregious government conduct, the focus . . . is not on the propensities and predisposition of a specific defendant, but on whether the police conduct revealed in the particular case falls below standards, to which common feelings respond, for the proper use of governmental power. Under this approach, the determination of the lawfulness of the government's conduct must be made—as it is on all questions involving the legality of law enforcement methods—by the trial judge, not the jury." *Commonwealth v. Monteagudo*, 427 Mass. at 486 (citations and quotation marks omitted).

Drug Lab Scandal. In *Commonwealth v. Scott*, 467 Mass. 336, 346 (2014), the court

"adopted the two-pronged test in *Ferrara v. United States*, 456 F.3d 278, 290 (1st Cir. 2006), which requires a defendant who sought to vacate a guilty plea because of government misconduct to show 'both that egregiously impermissible conduct . . . by government agents . . . antedated the entry of his plea' and that 'the misconduct influenced his decision to plead guilty or, put another way, that it was material to that choice.' In considering whether the defendant in *Scott* had satisfied the first prong of this test, [the court] summarized the findings of the State police investigation of Dookhan's conduct at the Hinton drug lab. [The court] noted that, among other misconduct:

- She 'admitted to 'dry labbing' for two or three years prior to her transfer out of the lab in 2011, meaning that she would group multiple samples together from various cases that looked alike and then test only a few samples, but report the results as if she had tested each sample individually.' *Scott*, 467 Mass. at 339.

- She admitted to 'contaminating samples intentionally, including turning negative samples into positive samples on at least a few occasions.' *Id*.

- She admitted that she removed samples from the evidence locker in breach of lab protocols, postdated entries in the evidence log book, and forged an evidence officer's initials. *Id*.

- She falsified reports intended to verify that the gas chromatography-mass spectrometer machine used in 'confirmatory' drug testing was functioning properly before she ran samples through the machine. *Id*. at 339–40.

[The court] concluded that, because Dookhan 'made a number of affirmative misrepresentations by signing drug certificates and testifying to the identity of substances in cases in which she had not in fact properly tested the substances in question,' Dookhan's misconduct was 'egregious.' *Id*. at 348.

[The court] also concluded that, even though there was no indication that any prosecutor knew of her misconduct, *id*. at 350 n.7, her egregious misconduct was 'attributable to the government' for purposes of a motion for new trial, *id*. at 350 & n.7, because as a primary and secondary chemist she 'participated in the investigation or evaluation of the case' and 'reported to the prosecutor's office concerning the case.' *Id*. at 349 (quoting *Commonwealth v. Martin*, 427 Mass. 816, 824 (1998)).

[The court] also noted that Dookhan acknowledged 'that she may not be able to identify those cases in which she tested the samples properly and those in which she did not.' *Scott*, 467 Mass. at 339. 'Thus, even if Dookhan herself were to testify in each of the thousands of cases in which she served as primary or secondary chemist, it is unlikely that her testimony, even if truthful, could resolve the question whether she engaged in misconduct in a particular case.' *Id*. at 352. Because it was 'reasonably certain . . . that her misconduct touched a great number of cases,' *id*., but 'may be impossible' for any defendant to prove that the drug analysis in his or her case was tainted by her misconduct, *id*. at 351, [the court] recognized that her 'particularly insidious form of misconduct, which belies reconstruction,' resulted in 'a lapse of systemic magnitude in the criminal justice system,' *id*. at 352.

To protect 'the due process rights of defendants, the integrity of the criminal justice system, [and] the efficient administration of justice . . . in the wake of government misconduct that has cast a shadow over the entire criminal justice system,' [the court] exercised [its] superintendence power and held that, where Dookhan signed the drug certificate in a defendant's case as an assistant analyst, a defendant

11

who seeks to vacate his or her guilty plea after learning of Dookhan's misconduct 'is entitled to a conclusive presumption that egregious government misconduct occurred in [his or her] case.' *Id.*"

Commonwealth v. Francis, 474 Mass. 816, 821–23 (2016).

In *Francis*, the court decided that a "defendant [who] learned of Dookhan's misconduct after trial, and now moves for a new trial based on that misconduct. . . . is entitled to the same conclusive presumption. The consequence of the conclusive presumption is that we deem it error to have admitted the drug certificates or comparable evidence regarding Dookhan's drug analysis where the defendant had no knowledge of Dookhan's misconduct and therefore no opportunity to challenge the admissibility or credibility of that evidence. We further conclude that the appropriate standard to be applied to the erroneous admission of this evidence is the prejudicial error standard applied to preserved nonconstitutional errors." *Commonwealth v. Francis*, 474 Mass. at 817.

ENTRAPMENT

A defendant may claim entrapment and also deny committing the crime. "We conclude that, if the judge based his refusal to give an entrapment instruction on the ground that the defendant may not claim entrapment while also denying committing the crime, it was error." *Commonwealth v. Tracey*, 416 Mass. 528, 535 (1993).

"[W]hen evidence of inducement has been entered, the burden rests upon the Commonwealth to prove beyond a reasonable doubt the predisposition of the defendant to commit the crime. The Commonwealth may introduce a defendant's prior criminal acts to show predisposition. Those prior criminal acts, however, must be similar to the crimes for which the defendant is on trial. Only those crimes which are similar will have probative value sufficient to outweigh the strong likelihood of prejudice to the defendant."

"[T]he crime of possession [of cocaine], by itself, is not similar to the crime of distribution for purposes of proving a predisposition to distribute. A prior crime of possession with the intent to distribute, however, is sufficiently similar to the crime of distribution, such that it may be proved to show a defendant's predisposition to distribute [and traffic in cocaine]." *Commonwealth v. Vargas*, 417 Mass. 792, 795–96 (1994) (citations and quotation marks omitted).

EQUAL PROBABILITIES, Theory of

The theory is: "When the evidence tends equally to sustain either of two inconsistent propositions, neither of them can be said to have been established by legitimate proof."

However, "confusion as to the application and meaning of this frequently invoked principle is as widespread as its incantation. This is particularly so in the context of a motion for a required finding of not guilty, which must surmount the prosecution-friendly *Latimore* standard. In fact, the concept pertains only to situations in which any view of the Commonwealth's evidence, however favorable, still requires a leap of conjecture with respect to essential elements of the crime charged in order to obtain a conviction. . . ."

"Proof in a criminal trial need not exclude all possible exculpatory interpretations of the evidence. Along the same lines, it is not necessary for the Commonwealth to negate the possibility that someone other than the defendant might have committed the crime charged."

"The 'equal probabilities' asserted by the defendant were either entirely speculative and flamboyantly implausible . . . ;

inconsistent with reason and experience . . . ; or contrary to the evidence."

Commonwealth v. Latney, 44 Mass. App. Ct. 423, 425–26 (1998) (quotation marks and citations omitted).

ERROR

"An error is nonprejudicial only if the conviction is sure that the error did not influence the jury, or had but very slight effect. But if one cannot say, with fair assurance, after pondering all that happened without stripping the erroneous action from the whole, that the judgment was not substantially swayed by the error, it is impossible to conclude that substantial rights were not affected." *Commonwealth v. Flebotte*, 417 Mass. 348, 353 (1994) (citations and punctuation omitted).

EXCITED UTTERANCE

"The excited utterance exception to the hearsay rule "is based on the experience that, under certain external circumstances of physical shock, a stress of nervous excitement may be produced which stills the reflective faculties so that the utterance which then occurs is a spontaneous and sincere response to the actual sensations and perceptions already produced by the external shock. Since this utterance is made under the immediate and uncontrolled domination of the senses, and during the brief period when considerations of self-interest could not have been brought fully to bear by reasoned reflection, the utterance may be taken as particularly trustworthy and may therefore be received as testimony to those facts. The test to determine the admissibility of a statement under the excited utterance exception to the hearsay rule is as follows. The utterance must have been made before there has been time to contrive and misrepresent. The statements need not be strictly contemporaneous with the exciting cause; they may be subsequent to it, provided there has not been time for the exciting influence to lose its sway and to be dissipated. There can be no definite and fixed limit of time. Each case must depend upon its own circumstances. The trial judge in determining whether an utterance meets the tests of admissibility ought to be given broad discretion. Only in clear cases of an improper exercise of discretion should the judge's ruling be revised." *Commonwealth v. Grant*, 418 Mass. 76, 80–81 (1994) (citations and punctuation omitted).

The excited utterance exception and the treatment of out-of-court testimonial statements came under close scrutiny in *Commonwealth v. Gonsalves*, 445 Mass. 1 (2005) and its companion cases, *Commonwealth v. Foley*, 445 Mass. 1001 (2005) (rescript) and *Commonwealth v. Rodriguez*, 445 Mass. 1003 (2005) (rescript).

Contemporaneousness. "[W]hether the trial judge properly admitted in evidence under the spontaneous exclamation exception to the hearsay rule answers given by the three and one-half-year-old victim in response to two questions asked by a physician at Boston City Hospital [five hours after a scalding episode]."

Held: Evidence properly admitted.

"Precise contemporaneousness is not required so long as it appears that, notwithstanding the passage of some time, the statements were made under the stress of the exciting event, a circumstance which is present here."

Commonwealth v. Brown, 413 Mass. 693, 696 (1992).

Corroboration. "[W]e decline to add any requirement of corroboration to the spontaneous utterance exception to the hearsay rule." *Commonwealth v. Moquette*, 439 Mass. 697, 702 (2003).

"That other evidence at trial may controvert the facts alleged in a spontaneous utterance does not change the fact that the spontaneous utterance has been admitted for substantive purposes and that it is for the jury to determine what weight to give that substantive evidence. The declarant's recantation is simply one form of evidence that may be offered to try to detract from the weight of the spontaneous utterance. Or, the evidence refuting the content of the spontaneous utterance may come from a witness other than the declarant. The mere existence of such contrary evidence does not operate to add an additional requirement of corroboration in order for the spontaneous utterance to constitute evidence sufficient for conviction." *Commonwealth v. Moquette*, 439 Mass. 697, 703 (2003) (citations omitted).

911 call. A 911 call may qualify as an excited utterance so long as the call meets its requirements (see *Zagranski*, above). *Commonwealth v. Brown*, 46 Mass. App. Ct. 279, 281–83 (1999), *rev'd on other grounds*, 431 Mass. 772 (2000).

"Alicia was not in imminent personal peril at the time the 911 call was made because the defendant already had left the scene of the incident. Therefore, Alicia's 911 call was not the reporting of an emergency situation, but, rather, was a 'solemn declaration . . . made for the purpose of establishing . . . some fact,' namely that the defendant had tried to run her over with his car. Because the 911 call was not subject to cross-examination, we conclude that, in all likelihood, it would have been inadmissible pursuant to the principles enunciated in *Crawford*." *Commonwealth v. Lao*, 450 Mass. 215, 226 (2007) (citation omitted).

Fax. "[Can] a facsimile transmission ever [ ] be considered a spontaneous exclamation, qualifying as an exception to the hearsay rule[?] We have never addressed the question. We decline to establish a categorical rule, as we can envision rare circumstances in which a writing, whether in the form of a facsimile transmission or otherwise, could be considered a spontaneous exclamation made when a person is in an excited or agitated state." *Commonwealth v. DiMonte*, 427 Mass. 233, 236 (1998).

Writings. Examples where a writing may be admissible as a spontaneous exclamation include (1) murder victim scrawled defendant's name on floor 5–10 minutes before dying; (2) victim is held hostage and cannot communicate in any way other than writing; and (3) victim's vocalization is impaired." *Commonwealth v. DiMonte*, 427 Mass. at 238–39.

Text Message. Text message admissible as spontaneous utterance where "six minutes later the victim frantically telephoned 911 to report that her husband was stabbing her and, only a few minutes after that, she was found barely breathing and lying in a pool of blood." *Commonwealth v. Mulgrave*, 472 Mass. 170, 177 (2015). The court held that the "opportunity for instant communication by way of cellular telephone technology elevates text messages, at least on the spontaneity scale, beyond the level of an ordinary writing." *Commonwealth v. Mulgrave*, 472 Mass. at 178–79 (citations omitted).

EXCLUSIONARY RULE

Police reliance on clerical error. "[The defendant] asserts that his arrest for operating the automobile after his license had been suspended was constitutionally invalid because, in making the arrest, the police officer relied on erroneous information furnished by the registry of motor vehicles (registry) regarding the status of the defendant's driver's license.

". . . The defendant's contention that the arrest was invalid under the Fourth Amendment to the United States Constitution is foreclosed by the decision in *Arizona v. Evans*, 514 U.S. 1 (1995), in which the United States Supreme Court announced a categorical exception to the exclusionary rule for clerical errors of court employees. *See Arizona v. Evans*, 514 U.S. 1 at 16. Considering whether suppression was warranted of evidence seized pursuant to an arrest based on inaccurate information in a computer database, the Court reasoned that 'court clerks are not adjuncts to the law enforcement team engaged in . . . ferreting out crime [and] have no stake in the outcome of particular criminal prosecutions' (citations omitted). *Arizona v. Evans*, 514 U.S. 1 at 15. The Court found 'no indication that the arresting officer was not acting objectively reasonably when he relied upon the police computer record.' *Arizona v. Evans*, 514 U.S. 1 at 16–17. The Court concluded that, because responsibility for the error lay with court employees and not with police, 'the exclusion of evidence at trial would not sufficiently deter future errors so as to warrant such a severe sanction.' *Arizona v. Evans*, 514 U.S. 1 at 14.

". . . When the matter is grounded in police fault, then policy reasons for applying the exclusionary rule become more relevant . . . Police may not rely upon incorrect or incomplete information when they are at fault in permitting the records to remain uncorrected' or at fault in not informing themselves.

". . . The interest in deterring unlawful police conduct, which is the foundation of the exclusionary rule, is not implicated where police rely on records of an independent State agency, such as the registry, to make an otherwise proper arrest." *Commonwealth v. Wilkerson*, 436 Mass. 137, 138–42 (2002) (certain citations and quotation and punctuation marks omitted).

Warrant Management System. "[B]ecause the police violated an explicit departmental policy that requires them to check on the status of a warrant '[i]mmediately prior to' an arrest by contacting their operations center 'so that the computerized Warrant Management System [WMS] can be checked to determine if the outstanding warrant is still active,'" the motion to suppress was correctly allowed as the defendant was arrested and searched two hours after his default warrant had been recalled. *Commonwealth v. Maingrette*, 86 Mass. App. Ct. 691, 700 (2014) (Agnes, J. concurring).

EXCULPATORY EVIDENCE

"A rule that encourages prosecutors to make pretrial disclosures of obviously or even arguably exculpatory material would not only promote fair trials but would also help to avoid the difficulties of post-trial judicial review. Judges, therefore, should be sensitive to the allowance of motions for the disclosure of specific information claimed to be exculpatory. A prosecutor's duty, however, extends only to exculpatory evidence in the prosecutor's possession or in the possession of the police who participated in the investigation and presentation of the case. Third, when the omission of the prosecution is knowing and intentional or follows a specific request, a standard of prejudice more favorable to the defendant is justified in order to motivate prosecutors to be alert to defendants' rights to disclosure." *Commonwealth v. Tucceri*, 412 Mass. 401, 406–07 (1992) (citation and footnote omitted).

Delayed disclosure. "When dealing with a delayed disclosure of exculpatory evidence, it is the consequences of the delay that matters, not the likely impact on the nondisclosed evidence, and we ask whether the prosecution's disclosure was sufficiently timely to allow the defendant to make effective use of the evidence in preparing and presenting his case."

11

Commonwealth v. Smiledge, 419 Mass. 156, 158 (1994) (citations and quotation marks omitted).

Prosecutor's duty to inquire. "The duty to disclose exculpatory information does not require a prosecutor to make defense-directed inquiries to independent witnesses, including complainants." *Commonwealth v. Beal*, 429 Mass. 530, 531 (1999). *Compare Commonwealth v. Martin*, 427 Mass. 816, 823–24 (1998) ("The prosecution had a duty to inquire concerning the existence of scientific tests, at least those conducted by the Commonwealth's own crime laboratory. That obligation is inherent in the allowance of the motion to produce all scientific test results. The prosecutor's office obviously did not conduct scientific tests. It could not satisfy the production order by turning over test information that it had in its files. It had a duty of inquiry. *See Kyles v. Whitley*, 514 U.S. 419, 438 (1995). A prosecutor's obligations extend to information in possession of a person who has participated in the investigation or evaluation of the case and has reported to the prosecutor's office concerning the case.").

Exculpatory evidence to police. "A person ordinarily has no legal obligation to provide exculpatory information to the police. There are many situations, however, where the natural response of a person in possession of exculpatory information would be to come forward in order to avoid a mistaken prosecution of a relative or a friend. When a witness in such circumstances chooses to remain silent rather than provide the police or prosecutors with the exculpatory information, and discloses the information to the prosecution only when called by the defense to testify at trial, it may be a reasonable inference that the exculpatory information is not credible, either because it is a recent contrivance or because the witness is biased toward the defendant.

"There are some circumstances, though, in which it would not be natural for a witness to provide the police before trial with exculpatory information, such as when the witness does not realize she possesses exculpatory information, when she thinks that her information will not affect the decision to prosecute, or when she does not know how to furnish such information to law enforcement. In light of these circumstances, the Appeals Court . . . required prosecutors to lay a foundation for this type of cross-examination by first establishing that [1] the witness knew of the pending charges in sufficient detail to realize that he possessed exculpatory information, [2] that the witness had reason to make the information available, [3] that he was familiar with the means of reporting it to the proper authorities, and [4] that the defendant or his lawyer, or both, did not ask the witness to refrain from doing so. . . .

"We now abolish the fourth element: the prosecutor need not elicit from the witness that she was not asked by the defendant or the defense attorney to refrain from disclosing her exculpatory information to law enforcement authorities. The theory underlying this fourth element is that, when a witness complies with a request by the defendant or the defense attorney not to provide exculpatory information to the police, her credibility may not reasonably be questioned based on her failure to furnish this information to the police. This theory, however, is flawed. While adherence to such a request may not permit an inference of recent contrivance, it may permit an inference of bias in favor of the defendant, if only because such adherence reflects that the witness was willing to do what the defendant or defense attorney asked of her.

"Moreover, when a prosecutor seeks to elicit this information from the witness in front of the jury, the prosecutor faces an ethical dilemma. He is asking these questions simply to elicit a negative answer in order to meet the fourth foundational element, and has no good faith basis to believe that either the defendant or the defense attorney asked the witness not to speak to the police. Yet, generally, we do not permit an attorney to pursue a line of questioning when there is no reasonable expectation of being able to prove the matters to which the line refers. . . . This dilemma is made worse by the fact that, unless the witness is a relative, employee, or agent of the client, an attorney is barred by the Massachusetts Rules of Professional Responsibility from requesting 'a person other than a client to refrain from voluntarily giving relevant information to another party.' Mass. R. Prof. C. 3.4(f), 426 Mass. 1389 (1998). Consequently, in many cases, this fourth element would compel a prosecutor who seeks to impeach an alibi witness based on her failure to provide the exculpatory information to the police to ask the witness whether the defense attorney engaged in conduct that would constitute an ethical breach when the prosecutor has no good faith basis to believe that the defense attorney committed any such breach. . . .

"If a defense witness has been requested by a defendant or defense counsel not to provide law enforcement with the exculpatory information, and the defendant wishes to preclude the prosecutor from impeaching the witness for having failed to do so, defense counsel should inform the judge before the witness testifies so that the matter may be explored at a bench conference. The judge then may consider whether the probative weight of the impeachment is outweighed by the risk of confusion or of unfair prejudice. Even without such information, if a judge wishes to ascertain whether the witness will testify to any such request, the judge may conduct a voir dire examination of the witness. If the impeachment evidence is admitted, the defendant is free to elicit on redirect examination the witness's reason for prior silence." *Commonwealth v. Hart*, 455 Mass. 230, 238–42 (2009) (citations, footnotes, and quotation marks omitted).

EXCULPATORY EVIDENCE (GRAND JURY)

"'Prosecutors are not required in every instance to reveal all exculpatory evidence to a grand jury. . . . Evidence must be disclosed, however, if it would greatly undermine the credibility of evidence likely to affect the grand jury's decision to indict.' . . . The question, therefore, is whether the grand jury's decision to indict would have been different had they been aware of the existence of the [evidence]." *Commonwealth v. Garrity*, 43 Mass. App. Ct. 349, 352 (1997) (quoting *Commonwealth v. Trowbridge*, 419 Mass. 750, 753 (1995)) (citations, quotation marks, and punctuation omitted).

EXPERTS

Overview. "[A] party seeking to introduce scientific evidence may lay an adequate foundation either by establishing general acceptance in the scientific community or by showing that the evidence is reliable or valid through an alternate means." *Canavan's Case*, 432 Mass. 304, 310 (2000).

Standard. "The crucial issue in determining whether a witness is qualified to give an expert opinion is whether the witness has sufficient education, training, experience and familiarity with the subject matter of the testimony. . . . The admission of expert testimony lies largely within the discretion of the trial judge . . . [and] will be reversed on appeal only if it constituted an abuse of discretion or was otherwise tainted with error of law." *Commonwealth v. Richardson*, 423 Mass. 180, 182–83 (1996) (citations, quotation marks and punctuation omitted).

11

Standard of review. "[A]pplying an abuse of discretion standard on appellate review will allow trial judges the needed discretion to conduct the inherently fact-intensive and flexible *Lanigan* analysis, while preserving a sufficient degree of appellate review to assure that *Lanigan* determinations are consistent with the law and supported by a sufficient factual basis in the particular case." *Canavan's Case*, 432 Mass. 304, 312 (2000).

Gatekeeper function of judge. "The gatekeeping function pursuant to *Lanigan* is the same regardless of the nature of the methodology used: to determine whether the process or theory underlying a scientific expert's opinion lacks reliability such that the opinion should not reach the trier of fact." *Canavan's Case*, 432 Mass. 304, 313 (2000).

Daubert test applicable. "Our test for the admissibility of expert testimony based on scientific knowledge has usually been the *Frye* test, 'that is, whether the community of scientists involved generally accepts the theory or process. *Frye v. United States*, 293 F.2d 1013 (D.C. Cir. 1923).' . . . The ultimate test, however, is the reliability of the theory or process underlying the expert's testimony. . . . The general proposition set forth in the *Daubert* opinion [*Daubert v. Merrell Dow Pharmaceuticals, Inc.*, 509 U.S. 579 (1993)] seems sound. . . . The expert's opinion must 'have a reliable basis in the knowledge and experience of his discipline.' *Daubert v. Merrell Dow Pharmaceuticals, Inc.*, 509 U.S. at 2796. The overarching issue is 'the scientific validity and thus the evidentiary relevance and reliability of the principles that underlie a proposed submission.' *Daubert v. Merrell Dow Pharmaceuticals, Inc.*, 509 U.S. at 2797. The trial judge has a significant function to carry out in deciding on the admissibility of a scientific expert's opinion. If the process or theory underlying a scientific expert's opinion lacks reliability, that opinion should not reach the trier of fact. Consequently, the judge must rule first on any challenge to the validity of any process or theory underlying a proffered opinion. 'This entails a preliminary assessment of whether the reasoning or methodology underlying the testimony is scientifically valid and of whether that reasoning or methodology properly can be applied to the facts in issue.' *Daubert v. Merrell Dow Pharmaceuticals, Inc.*, 509 U.S. at 2796. The judge thus has a gatekeeper role. Of course, if the judge rules the opinion evidence admissible, that ruling is not final on the reliability of the opinion evidence, and the opponent of that evidence may challenge its validity before the trier of fact. . . . We suspect that general acceptance in the relevant scientific community will continue to be the significant, and often the only, issue. We accept the idea, however, that a proponent of scientific opinion evidence may demonstrate the reliability or validity of the underlying scientific theory or process by some other means, that is, without establishing general acceptance." *Commonwealth v. Lanigan*, 419 Mass. 15, 24–26 (1994).

"[T]he new *Daubert* standard, . . . set forth five factors that a judge should consider in determining the reliability of proposed scientific evidence. The five factors are whether the scientific theory or process (1) has been generally accepted in the relevant scientific community; (2) has been, or can be, subjected to testing; (3) has been subjected to peer review and publication; (4) has an unacceptably high known or potential rate of error; and (5) is governed by recognized standards." *Commonwealth v. Powell*, 450 Mass. 229, 238 (2007).

Daubert test exception. General Laws c. 123A, § 14(c), which makes admissible "the report of any qualified examiner" in a proceeding seeking the commitment of an individual as a sexually dangerous person, also provides for the admissibility of the opinion testimony of the qualified examiners at trial, without subjecting it to the more rigorous test of admissibility set forth in *Daubert v. Merrell Dow Pharmaceuticals, Inc.*, 509 U.S. 579 (1993), and *Commonwealth v. Lanigan*, 419 Mass. 15 (1994). *Commonwealth v. Bradway*, 62 Mass. App. Ct. 280 (2004).

Acceptance within scientific community. "[I]n most cases general acceptance will be the significant and often the only issue." *Canavan's Case*, 432 Mass. 304, 310 (2000) (citation and punctuation and quotation marks omitted).

Ballistics. "[W]e offer the following guidelines to ensure that expert forensic ballistics testimony appropriately assists the jury in finding the facts but does not mislead by reaching beyond its scientific grasp. First, before trial, the examiner must adequately document the findings or observations that support the examiner's ultimate opinion, and this documentary evidence, whether in the form of measurements, notes, sketches, or photographs, shall be provided in discovery, so that defense counsel will have an adequate and informed basis to cross-examine the forensic ballistics expert at trial.

"Second, before an opinion is offered at trial, a forensic ballistics expert should explain to the jury the theories and methodologies underlying the field of forensic ballistics. This testimony should include, but is not limited to, explanation of how toolmarks are imparted onto projectiles and cartridge casings; the differences between class, subclass, and individual characteristics of firearms; and the different types of resulting toolmarks that examiners look for and compare. Such testimony should also clearly articulate the differences between class and subclass characteristic toolmarks, which can narrow down the group of weapons that may have fired a particular projectile, and individual characteristic toolmarks, which potentially may permit an opinion that a particular firearm fired a projectile. Such background testimony is essential to assist the jury in evaluating any opinion offered by the expert.

"Third, in the absence of special circumstances casting doubt on the reliability of an opinion, and once these two things have been done, a forensic ballistics expert may present an expert's opinion of the toolmarks found on projectiles and cartridge casings. Where a qualified expert has identified sufficient individual characteristic toolmarks reasonably to offer an opinion that a particular firearm fired a projectile or cartridge casing recovered as evidence, the expert may offer that opinion to a 'reasonable degree of ballistic certainty.' Where the individual characteristic toolmarks are not so distinctive as to justify such an opinion, a qualified ballistics expert may still offer an opinion based on the class or subclass characteristics that narrow the scope of possible firearms or eliminate a class of possible firearms as the source of the spent projectiles or cartridge casings. . . .

"We conclude that, where defense counsel is furnished in discovery with the documentation needed to prepare an effective cross-examination, where a jury are provided with the necessary background regarding the theory and methodology of forensic ballistics, and where an opinion matching a particular firearm to recovered projectiles or cartridge casings is limited to a 'reasonable degree of ballistic certainty,' a jury will be assisted in reaching a verdict by having the benefit of the opinion, as well as the information needed to evaluate the limitations of such an opinion and the weight it deserves" *Commonwealth v. Heang*, 458 Mass. 827, 846–48, 850 (2011) (citations and footnotes omitted).

11

Electrophoresis. "The defendant claims that the judge erroneously admitted evidence of a genetic marker analysis performed upon bloodstains on the paper bag found at the crime scene because the Commonwealth failed to establish that the procedure employed to analyse the stain—electrophoresis—is generally accepted within the relevant scientific community. *Commonwealth v. Neal*, 392 Mass. 1, 12 (1984). *Commonwealth v. Fatalo*, 346 Mass. 266, 269 (1963). *See Frye v. United States*, 293 F. 1013, 1014 (D.C. Cir. 1923). There was no error." *Commonwealth v. Gomes*, 403 Mass. 258, 265–66 (1988) (footnote omitted).

Personal observations. "There is no logical reason why conclusions based on personal observations or clinical experience should not be subject to the *Lanigan* analysis. . . . If the proponent can show that the method of personal observation is either generally accepted by the relevant scientific community or otherwise reliable to support a scientific conclusion relevant to the case, such expert testimony is admissible." *Canavan's Case*, 432 Mass. 304, 313–14 (2000).

Hypothetical Questions. "A hypothetical question must be 'based on the facts in evidence,' *Commonwealth v. Federico*, 425 Mass. 844, 850 (1997), that is, 'facts . . . testified to by [the expert witness] or upon facts assumed in the questions put to [the witness] and supported either by admitted facts or by the testimony of other witnesses already given or to be given at the trial, or upon facts derived partly from one source and partly from the other.' *Department of Youth Servs. v. A Juvenile*, 398 Mass. 516, 527 (1986), quoting *Commonwealth v. Russ*, 232 Mass. 58, 73 (1919)." *Commonwealth v. Burgess*, 450 Mass. 422, 434 (2008).

Police officers. "The judge erred in allowing a police officer to testify as an expert witness 'within a reasonable degree of police certainty' that the chrome strip found at Great Plains Road originally came from the victim's automobile. The police officer was present when the strip was positioned on the vehicle, and he could state properly as a lay witness whether the strip fit the vehicle. The error here was that we do not recognize, as a standard, 'a reasonable degree of police certainty.' This error, however, was not prejudicial because the police officer was competent to give a shorthand expression in testifying to his observation. See P.J. Liacos, Massachusetts Evidence 100–103 (5th Ed. 1981)." *Commonwealth v. Olszewski*, 401 Mass. 749, 759 (1988).

Motor Vehicle Black Box. The defendant moved in limine to exclude evidence based on the motor vehicle's event data recorder (EDR), "based on her claim that the Commonwealth cannot establish the reliability and accuracy of the device.

"Here, the motion judge held an extensive hearing on the reliability of the data from the EDR. He concluded that the Commonwealth's expert, William Russell Haight, was qualified as an expert in EDRs and found the EDR to be an accurate device. The judge also determined that there was general acceptance in the scientific community of the validity of such data. In our review of his decision to allow the admission of the evidence, the standard is whether there was an abuse of discretion. There was no abuse of discretion.

"Haight's testimony, in sum, indicated that he was amply qualified as an expert, had conducted 200 tests on EDRs, had taught and published on the subject, and had testified as an expert on EDRs in other States; that the technology behind the EDR had been known for many years; that he and others had tested the speed of motor vehicles by other methods to compare information provided by the EDRs and had found

the EDRs to be reliable; that EDRs need no maintenance and calibration for ten years; and that his calculations based on the physical and other evidence in this case were consistent with the EDR data from the defendant's vehicle. Based on Haight's testimony—the defendant presented no expert at the motion hearing—the judge ruled that evidence from the EDR met the standard set forth in *Commonwealth v. Lanigan*, 419 Mass. [15, 26 (1994)], for reliability. . . .

"The judge also concluded that the alternative Lanigan ground—general acceptance of data from motor vehicle crash recorders in the relevant scientific community—applied in this case." *Commonwealth v. Zimmermann*, 70 Mass. App. Ct. 357, 359–60, 363–64 (2007).

Narcotics investigation. "The admission of such evidence is largely within the discretion of the trial judge and he will be reversed only where the admission constitutes an abuse of discretion or error of law [*Commonwealth v. Pilail*, 400 Mass. 550, 553 (1987)]. The use of narcotics investigators as experts in drug cases has an impressive history. *See Commonwealth v. Davis*, 376 Mass. 777, 788 (1978) (permissible for police officer to testify as to use of small manila envelopes for bagging heroin); *Commonwealth v. Sendele*, 18 Mass. App. Ct. 755, 759 (1984) (narcotics officers were permitted to testify as to their opinion that content of vial was for defendant's personal use but the cocaine in the valise was intended for distribution); *Commonwealth v. Fiore*, 9 Mass. App. Ct. 618, 624 (1980) (police officer properly testified as to street value of cocaine).

"In sum, there was no error in the admission of the police officer's expert testimony. . . ."

Commonwealth v. Johnson, 410 Mass. 199, 202 (1991).

"The use of narcotics investigators to testify in this manner [that the cocaine as packaged was consistent with an intent to distribute] as experts in drug cases has been consistently upheld. . . . The admission of such evidence is largely within the discretion of the judge, whose ruling will be reversed only where the admission constitutes an abuse of discretion or error of law." *Commonwealth v. Johnson*, 413 Mass. 598, 604 (1992) (citations omitted).

Police officer, even if qualified as an expert, may not give his opinion that "a drug transaction had taken place and that he believed that the defendant was selling crack cocaine." *Commonwealth v. Woods*, 36 Mass. App. Ct. 950, 951 (1994) (rescript), 419 Mass. 366, 374–76 (1995).

Cf. Commonwealth v. Santiago, 41 Mass. App. Ct. 916, 917 (1996) (permissible for ADA to ask police expert, in possession of drugs with intent to distribute cases, "Do you have an [and what is your] opinion as to whether or not the amount of heroin is consistent or inconsistent with personal use?" Improper to ask, however, "Do you have an [and what is your] opinion as to whether or not this amount of heroin packaged in this manner *was intended for* distribution or for personal use?" "Where a specific intent is an element of the crime, a witness's opinion as to what the defendant intended is improper.").

Specific qualification. "According to the defendants, while Pino was generally qualified in chemistry, he was not specifically qualified in the chemistry of residual stomach contents. . . ."

"Pino admitted that he had never analyzed residual stomach contents before this case, but stated that he was familiar with its chemical properties. . . ."

"A judge has wide discretion in qualifying a witness to offer an expert opinion on a particular question, and his

11

determination will not be upset on appeal if any reasonable basis appears for it. In qualifying an expert witness, the question for judicial decision is whether the witness has sufficient skill, knowledge, and experience in the area of his training to aid a jury. There is no requirement that testimony on a question of discrete knowledge come from an expert qualified in that subspecialty rather than from an expert more generally qualified. . . .”

“Based on Pino's education, training, and experience, and his use of proper methodology to study the subject before him, the judge was warranted in concluding that the jury would be helped by his testimony and that it was for them to determine the weight to be given to it. There was no abuse of discretion.” *Commonwealth v. Mahoney*, 406 Mass. 843, 852–53 (1990) (citations omitted).

See *Dockham* cite in notes accompanying G.L. c. 265, § 22A.

Sexual abuse/rape. While an expert may testify “relating generally to behavioral characteristics of sexual assault and sexual abuse victims,” the expert may not testify “that an alleged victim was in fact sexually assaulted.” *Commonwealth v. Colin C., a juvenile*, 419 Mass. 54, 60 (1994). “Although expert testimony on the general behavioral characteristics of sexually abused children is permissible, an expert may not refer or compare the child to those general characteristics. . . . Where there is no link between the expert testimony and the victim, the opinion is usually allowed.” *Commonwealth v. Richardson*, 423 Mass. 180, 185–86 (1996) (quotation marks and citations omitted). *See also Commonwealth v. Federico*, 425 Mass. 844 (1997).

Medical examiner. “To repeat, as we held in *Nardi*, the substitute medical examiner, as an expert witness, is not permitted on direct examination to recite or otherwise testify about the underlying factual findings of the unavailable medical examiner as contained in the autopsy report. *Nardi*, [452 Mass. 379 (2008)] at 394 (deeming statements in autopsy report testimonial hearsay barred by *Crawford*). The expert witness's testimony must be confined to his or her own opinions and, as to these, the expert is available for cross-examination.” *Commonwealth v. Avila*, 454 Mass. 744, 762–63 (2009).

The defendant “contends that our ordinary rule regarding the proper basis for expert testimony, as set out in *Commonwealth v. Markvart*, 437 Mass. 331, 337 (2002), which includes ‘facts or data not in evidence if the facts or data are independently admissible and are a permissible basis for an expert to consider in formulating an opinion’ should now be interpreted to require that facts or data that are ‘independently admissible’ actually must be admitted at trial through percipient witnesses in order to satisfy the defendant's right of confrontation.” The court rejected the defendant's argument. *Commonwealth v. Hensley*, 454 Mass. 721, 732 n.7 (2009).

EXPUNGEMENT OF RECORDS

The expungement or sealing of records involves many intricate questions. As a starting point, see Sealing of Records, G.L. c. 276, §§ 100A et seq. (this volume) and *Police Commissioner of Boston v. Municipal Court of the Dorchester District*, 374 Mass. 640 (1978).

EXTRANEOUS EVIDENCE

“[E]xtraneous evidence may have a gripping quality and asking the jury to disregard it may be tantamount to asking the jury to ignore that an elephant has walked through the jury box.” *Commonwealth v. Flebotte*, 34 Mass. App. Ct. 676, 680 (1993).

EYEWITNESS IDENTIFICATION

See Model Jury Instructions on Eyewitness Identification, 473 Mass. 1051 (2015).

“Where an eyewitness has not participated before trial in an identification procedure, we shall treat the in-court identification as an in-court showup, and shall admit it in evidence only where there is ‘good reason’ for its admission. The new rule we declare today shall apply prospectively to trials that commence after issuance of this opinion, and shall apply only to in-court identifications of the defendant by eyewitnesses who were present during the commission of the crime.”

“[W]e place the burden on the prosecutor to move in limine to admit the in-court identification of the defendant by a witness where there has been no out-of-court identification. Once the motion is filed, the defendant would continue to bear the burden of showing that the in-court identification would be unnecessarily suggestive and that there is not ‘good reason’ for it. Although we impose no restrictions on when such a motion must be filed, a prosecutor would be wise to file it in advance of trial, because, if the defendant were to prevail in suppressing the in-court identification as unnecessarily suggestive, the Commonwealth would still have time, if it chose, to conduct a less suggestive out-of-court identification procedure.” *Commonwealth v. Crayton*, 470 Mass. 228, 241–42, 243 (2014).

“In the future, where an eyewitness to a crime has not made an unequivocal positive identification of the defendant before trial but the prosecutor nonetheless intends to ask the eyewitness to make an in-court identification of the defendant, we impose the same burden on the prosecutor as we did in *Crayton* to move in limine to admit the in-court identification, preferably before trial.” *Commonwealth v. Collins*, 470 Mass. 255, 266 (2014).

“Until we are confident that we can materially aid the jury in their evaluation of a failure to identify based on principles that have attained near consensus in the relevant scientific community, we will not offer even a provisional model jury instruction regarding an eyewitness's failure to identify a defendant, where there is no positive or partial identification.” *Commonwealth v. Johnson*, 470 Mass. 389, 398 (2015).

In *Commonwealth v. Gomes*, 470 Mass. 352, 379–88 (2015), the court proposed a new provisional jury instruction regarding eyewitness identification, based on five “principles regarding eyewitness identification for which there is a near consensus in the relevant scientific community.” *Commonwealth v. Gomes*, 470 Mass. at 367.

i. Human memory does not function like a video recording but is a complex process that consists of three stages: acquisition, retention, and retrieval;

ii. An eyewitness's expressed certainty in an identification, standing alone, may not indicate the accuracy of the identification, especially where the witness did not describe that level of certainty when the witness first made the identification

iii. High levels of stress can reduce an eyewitness's ability to make an accurate identification

iv. Information that is unrelated to the initial viewing of the event, which an eyewitness receives before or after making an identification, can influence the witness's later recollection of the memory or of the identification; and

v. A prior viewing of a suspect at an identification procedure may reduce the reliability of a subsequent identification

11

procedure in which the same suspect is shown. *Commonwealth v. Gomes*, 470 Mass. at 369–75.

"[W]e shall direct that a cross-racial instruction be given unless all parties agree that there was no cross-racial identification. . . . Consequently, we amend our provisional instruction in *Gomes* to the extent that, in criminal trials that commence after the issuance of this opinion, the following instruction should be included when giving the model eyewitness identification instruction, unless all parties agree to its omission:

"If the witness and the person identified appear to be of different races, you should consider that people may have greater difficulty in accurately identifying someone of a different race than someone of their own race." *Commonwealth v. Bastaldo*, 472 Mass. 16, 27 (2015).

"Although not constitutionally required, we conclude that, moving forward, it is appropriate to require that the Commonwealth inquire directly of the alleged identifying witness about the alleged prior identification before introducing evidence of that alleged identification through a third-party witness. This sequence will provide the defendant specific notice of the prior identification, information that will permit the defendant to fully cross-examine the alleged declarant. The opportunity to recall the declarant witness after the statement has been introduced through a third party is too limited, and inappropriately places a strategic burden on the non-offering party. Further, the approach we adopt may reduce confusion for the jury by providing them with both versions of the events in a timely fashion, leaving it to the jury to resolve the conflicting claims concerning that prior identification." *Commonwealth v. Herndon*, 475 Mass. 324, 334 (2016).

FAILURE TO CALL WITNESS

"'Where a party has knowledge of a person who can be located and brought forward, who is friendly to, or at least not hostilely disposed toward, the party, and who can be expected to give testimony of distinct importance to the case, the party would naturally offer that person as a witness. If, then, without reasonable explanation, he does not do so, the jury may, if they think reasonable in the circumstances, infer that person, had he been called, would have given testimony unfavorable to the party.' [*Commonwealth v. Schatvet*, 23 Mass. App. Ct. 130, 134 (1986)].

"This is a delicate area, requiring caution. A jury may unfairly be led to draw improper conclusions from the failure of a defendant to call a witness."

Commonwealth v. Zagranski, 408 Mass. 278, 287 (1990). *See also Commonwealth v. Figueroa*, 413 Mass. 193, 198–99 (1992); *Commonwealth v. Anderson*, 411 Mass. 279 (1991).

FEAR OF TESTIFYING

"Generally, questions regarding a witness's fear of testifying, whether caused by the defendant or not, are allowable in the judge's discretion. . . . The questions put to Cawley and Johnson were relevant to explain why the two had not spoken candidly to the police on the night of the incident." It should also be noted that in this case the judge gave a strong jury instruction and the ADA did not argue that the defendant had made the threats. *Commonwealth v. Auguste*, 418 Mass. 643, 647 (1994).

FINGERPRINTS

"The mere fact that a fingerprint is found at the scene of the crime is insufficient to warrant submitting the case to the jury. There must also be further evidence linking the defendant to the crime enabling the prosecution to establish beyond a reasonable doubt that the fingerprints in fact were placed at the scene during the commission of the crime. It is the prosecution's burden to rebut the possibility that the fingerprints had been placed at the scene at a time other than that of the occurrence of the crime." *Commonwealth v. Estremera*, 37 Mass. App. Ct. 923, 924 (1994) (citations, punctuation and quotation marks omitted).

Scientific analysis. "Evidence of fingerprint individualization determined by application of the ACE-V method to single latent fingerprint impressions meets the *Lanigan-Daubert* reliability standard. The general acceptance of this application of ACE-V by the fingerprint examiner community leads us to this conclusion. However, the application of ACE-V to simultaneous impressions cannot rely on the more usual application of ACE-V for its admissibility, but must be independently tested against the *Lanigan-Daubert* standard. On the record before the motion judge, the Commonwealth has not yet established that the application of the ACE-V method to simultaneous impressions is generally accepted by the fingerprint examiner community or that a review of the other *Daubert* factors favors admission of evidence based on such an application." *Commonwealth v. Patterson*, 445 Mass. 626, 654–55 (2005).

"Testimony to the effect that a latent print matches, or is 'individualized' to, a known print, if it is to be offered, should be presented as an opinion, not a fact, and opinions expressing absolute certainty about, or the infallibility of, an 'individualization' of a print should be avoided." *Commonwealth v. Gambora*, 457 Mass. 715, 729 n.22 (2010).

FIRST COMPLAINT

The court in *Commonwealth v. King*, 445 Mass. 217 (2005), reconsidered both the scope of and continued necessity for the Massachusetts fresh complaint doctrine, and substantially revised the doctrine, changing its name to the "first complaint" doctrine. Under this doctrine, the recipient of a complainant's first complaint of an alleged sexual assault may testify about the facts and details of the first complaint and the circumstances surrounding the making of that first complaint. Testimony from additional complaint witnesses is not admissible. First complaint testimony is not relevant and therefore not admissible under the doctrine where neither the fact of the sexual assault nor the complainant's consent is at issue, as in cases where the identity of the assailant is the only contested issue.

"We stated in the King case that in certain circumstances a judge, in his discretion, could permit someone other than and 'in lieu of, the very "first" complaint witness' to testify, *Commonwealth v. King*, 445 Mass. 217, 243 (2005), and we provided some specific examples of when such substitutions could occur. For example, 'where the first person told of the alleged assault is unavailable, incompetent, or too young to testify meaningfully, the judge may exercise discretion in allowing one other complaint witness to testify.' *Id.* at 243–244. Thus, we left open the possibility that, on unusual occasions, the first person the victim informs of the incident may not be required to be the first complaint witness. We did not attempt to set forth an exhaustive list of appropriate substitutions. Other exceptions are permissible based on the purpose and limitations of the first complaint doctrine.

"The present case provides us an opportunity to detail two such additional exceptions. The first is when the encounter that the victim has with the first person does not constitute

11

a complaint, when, for example, the victim expresses to that person unhappiness, upset or other such feelings, but does not actually state that she has been sexually assaulted. The second is when there is such a complaint, but the listener has an obvious bias or motive to minimize or distort the victim's remarks.

"We endorse these exceptions because they are consistent with the purposes of the first complaint doctrine as enunciated in the King case. The exceptions permit the Commonwealth to rebut any suggestion that the victim's silence was indicative of fabrication, while still avoiding the 'piling on' of complaint witnesses. *Id.* at 243–245. On the other hand, always requiring the Commonwealth to proceed with the first complaint witness regardless of the content of the conversation or the motivation of the witness may undermine the purpose for which the hearsay is permitted. Testimony of a vague conversation that does not 'complain' that a sexual assault occurred or testimony by a hostile first complaint witness may communicate to the jury that the victim in fact did not complain at all and that, if she had indeed been assaulted, she would have complained with more force and in greater detail.

"By permitting these exceptions to the first complaint doctrine, we do not suggest a relaxation of that doctrine so that the Commonwealth may pick and choose among various complaint witnesses to locate the one with the most complete memory, the one to whom the complainant related the most details, or the one who is likely to be the most effective witness. We conclude only that a judge, in situations such as we have described, may substitute a later complaint witness as the first complaint witness. The substituted witness should in most cases be the next complaint witness, absent compelling circumstances justifying further substitution." *Commonwealth v. Murungu*, 450 Mass. 441, 445–46 (2008).

The first complaint doctrine does not permit "description of the investigative process. . . . The fact that the Commonwealth brought its resources to bear on this incident creates the imprimatur of official belief in the complainant. It is unnecessary and irrelevant to the issue of the defendant's guilt, and is extremely prejudicial." *Commonwealth v. Stuckich*, 450 Mass. 449, 457 (2008).

"The doctrine, however, is not intended to be used as a shield to bar the jury from obtaining a fair and accurate picture of the Commonwealth's case-in-chief. If testimony, other than that specifically and properly designated as first complaint testimony, serves no purpose other than to repeat the fact of a complaint and thereby corroborate the complainant's accusations, it is inadmissible. If, however, after careful balancing of the testimony's probative and prejudicial value, testimony is found by the judge to be relevant and admissible for reasons that are independent of the first complaint doctrine, in the context of a particular case, it is within the judge's discretion to admit the testimony. In this way, the jury will be able to make a fairer and more accurate assessment of the Commonwealth's case." *Commonwealth v. Arana*, 453 Mass. 214, 228–29 (2009).

"[W]here there was both ongoing abuse over a period of many years and escalating abuse during that period, with disclosures at two widely separated intervals, the judge's decision to allow two first complaint witnesses was appropriate." *Commonwealth v. Kebreau*, 454 Mass. 287, 296 (2009).

"Six years after the adoption of the first complaint doctrine . . . [w]e now conclude that the doctrine should be retained, but that the scope of appellate review of decisions on the admissibility of first complaint evidence should be modified.

"We remain concerned with the fact that sexual assault victims, particularly children, often do not promptly report or disclose such crimes for a variety of reasons, including fear, shame, psychological trauma, or concern that they will not be believed. *See [Commonwealth v.] King*, 445 Mass. 217, 237-238, 240 [(2005), *cert. denied*, 546 U.S. 1216 (2006)]. *See also Commonwealth v. Licata*, 412 Mass. 654, 657 (1992) ('It is not difficult to understand a rape victim's reluctance to discuss with others, particularly strangers, the uncomfortably specific details of a sexual attack'). The primary goals of the first complaint doctrine were, and still are, to 'refute any false inference that silence is evidence of a lack of credibility on the part of [sexual assault] complainants,' *King*, [445 Mass.] at 243, and 'to give the jury as complete a picture as possible of how the accusation of sexual assault first arose.' *Id.* at 247. We continue to believe that by allowing in evidence all the details of the first complaint, the doctrine gives the fact finder 'the maximum amount of information with which to assess the credibility of the . . . complaint evidence as well as the over-all credibility of the victim.' *Commonwealth v. Licata*, [412 Mass.] at 659, quoting Graham, *The Cry of Rape: The Prompt Complaint Doctrine and the Federal Rules of Evidence*, 19 Willamette L. Rev. 489, 511 (1983). The fact finder should not be left to speculate on the evidence or to draw erroneous inferences due to incomplete information. *See King*, [445 Mass.] at 244–45.

"Until now, we have considered the first complaint doctrine to be an 'evidentiary rule' that is designed 'to give support to a complainant's testimony of a sexual assault in cases where the credibility of the accusation is a contested issue at trial' (emphasis added). [*Commonwealth v.*] *Arana*, 453 Mass. [214, 228 (2009)]. The admission of evidence in violation of such evidentiary rule, that is, in violation of the established parameters of the first complaint doctrine, will always be deemed error. *See, e.g., id.* at 222–23; *Commonwealth v. Lyons*, 71 Mass. App. Ct. 671, 673–74 (2008). Where a defendant has objected to the admission of the evidence, an appellate court then will determine whether the error was prejudicial, *see Arana*, [453 Mass.] at 228, and where a defendant has not raised an objection, an appellate court will determine whether the error created a substantial risk of a miscarriage of justice. *See Commonwealth v. McCoy*, 456 Mass. 838, 850–52 (2010).

"As our post-King jurisprudence has developed, it has become apparent that trial judges need greater flexibility to deal with the myriad factual scenarios that arise in the context of purported first complaint evidence. Rules, because of their inherent inflexibility, tend to break down when it becomes necessary to address factual circumstances not yet contemplated by the established rubric. Rather than considering the first complaint doctrine as an evidentiary 'rule,' it makes greater sense to view the doctrine as a body of governing principles to guide a trial judge on the admissibility of first complaint evidence. . . . The judge who is evaluating the facts of a particular case is in the best position to determine the scope of admissible evidence, keeping in mind the underlying goals of the first complaint doctrine, our established first complaint jurisprudence, and our guidelines for admitting or excluding relevant evidence. *See* Mass. G. Evid. §§ 401–03 (2011). *See also Commonwealth v. Kebreau*, 454 Mass. 287, 296 (2009) ('Any determination concerning first complaint testimony is fact-specific and requires, in the first analysis, a careful evaluation of the circumstances by the trial judge'); *Commonwealth v. Murungu*, 450 Mass. 441, 445–47 (2008)

11

(judge warranted in determining whether witness other than very first person to whom victim spoke about sexual assault should be permitted to testify as substituted first complaint witness). Once a judge has carefully and thoroughly analyzed these considerations, and has decided that proposed first complaint evidence is admissible, an appellate court shall review that determination under an abuse of discretion standard.

"The modification we announce today in no way should be construed as a relaxation or erosion of our first complaint jurisprudence. Our observation in King, [445 Mass.] at 243, that '[t]he testimony of multiple complaint witnesses likely serves no additional corroborative purpose, and may unfairly enhance a complainant's credibility as well as prejudice the defendant by repeating for the jury the often horrific details of an alleged crime,' remains relevant and significant. The importance of maintaining a balance between the interests of a complainant (who still may be a child) 'in having her credibility fairly judged on the specific facts of the case' and the interests of a defendant 'in receiving a trial free from irrelevant and potentially prejudicial testimony' cannot be overstated.[10] *Arana*, [453 Mass. at 228].

"FN10 While the first complaint doctrine prohibits the 'piling on' of multiple complaint witnesses, *Commonwealth v. Murungu*, 450 Mass. 441, 442–43 (2008), it does not exclude testimony that is 'otherwise independently admissible' and serves a purpose 'other than to repeat the fact of a complaint and thereby corroborate the complainant's accusations.' *Commonwealth v. Arana*, 453 Mass. 214, 220–21, 229 (2009). The modification that we announce today does not impact the admissibility of such evidence because it is outside the scope of the first complaint doctrine. *See id.* at 220. *See also Commonwealth v. Dargon*, 457 Mass. 387, 399 (2010) (certain evidence may be admissible 'under an evidentiary rubric other than first complaint')." *Commonwealth v. Aviles*, 461 Mass. 60, 71–73 (2011).

"[T]he first complaint rule is a neutral rule of evidence that permits such testimony whenever the credibility of a sexual assault allegation is at issue." *Commonwealth v. Mayotte*, 475 Mass. 254, 255 (2016). "Although the issue has arisen solely in the context of a jury's assessment of the credibility of a complaining witness in a sexual assault prosecution, nothing in our jurisprudence precludes the application of the first complaint doctrine to a defendant in a sexual assault prosecution. As demonstrated by our cases, the first complaint rule owes its genesis to the confluence of two factors: (1) that the central issue is a sexual assault rather than some other nonsexual crime; and (2) the need to provide to the jury 'as complete a picture as possible of how the accusation of sexual assault first arose.' *King*, 445 Mass. at 247. At its core, therefore, the doctrine exists to facilitate credibility determinations where an allegation of sexual assault is at issue. This purpose is no less important when a jury is called upon to assess such an allegation made by a defendant." *Commonwealth v. Mayotte*, 475 Mass. at 260. Therefore, "a defendant may proffer first complaint evidence where the defendant claims to be the victim of sexual assault and that claim is a live issue in the case." *Commonwealth v. Mayotte*, 475 Mass. at 265.

See Notes following G.L. c. 265, § 22.

FORFEITURE BY WRONGDOING

"We hold that a defendant forfeits, by virtue of wrongdoing, the right to object to the admission of an unavailable witness's out-of-court statements on both confrontation and

hearsay grounds on findings that (1) the witness is unavailable; (2) the defendant was involved in, or responsible for, procuring the unavailability of the witness; and (3) the defendant acted with the intent to procure the witness's unavailability. A defendant's involvement in procuring a witness's unavailability need not consist of a criminal act, and may include a defendant's collusion with a witness to ensure that the witness will not be heard at trial . . . .

"[T]he causal link necessary between a defendant's actions and a witness's unavailability may be established where (1) a defendant puts forward to a witness the idea to avoid testifying, either by threats, coercion, persuasion, or pressure; (2) a defendant physically prevents a witness from testifying; or (3) a defendant actively facilitates the carrying out of the witness's independent intent not to testify." *Commonwealth v. Edwards*, 444 Mass. 526, 540–41 (2005).

Standard of proof. "We, like virtually all of the jurisdictions that have considered the issue, hold that the prosecution must prove by a preponderance of the evidence that the defendant procured the witness's unavailability. . . . While the Commonwealth must prove all the essential elements of a crime beyond a reasonable doubt . . . preliminary questions of fact and subsidiary facts need only be proved by a preponderance of the evidence. . . . Moreover, the admission of statements through the forfeiture by wrongdoing doctrine is functionally equivalent to the rule regarding the admission of co-conspirator and joint venturer statements." *Commonwealth v. Edwards*, 444 Mass. 526, 542–43 (2005).

Evidentiary hearing. "We are of the view that, prior to a determination of forfeiture, the parties should be given an opportunity to present evidence, including live testimony, at an evidentiary hearing outside the jury's presence. We note that the hearing is not intended to be a mini-trial and, accordingly, hearsay evidence, including the unavailable witness's out-of-court statements, may be considered." *Commonwealth v. Edwards*, 444 Mass. 526, 545 (2005).

Collusion. "A finding that a defendant somehow influenced a witness's decision not to testify is not required to trigger the application of the forfeiture by wrongdoing doctrine where there is collusion in implementing that decision or planning for its implementation. . . . Therefore, in collusion cases (the third category above), a defendant's joint effort with a witness to secure the latter's unavailability, regardless of whether the witness already decided 'on his own' not to testify, may be sufficient to support a finding of forfeiture by wrongdoing.

"Furthermore, that a defendant and a witness are ultimately unable to carry out their plan to engineer the witness's unavailability through the precise method intended does not necessarily preclude a finding of forfeiture in collusion cases. Where a defendant's goal in colluding with a witness is to deprive the Commonwealth of valuable testimony, the defendant may be no less successful where the desired result is achieved by means other than those originally contemplated (such as a witness's refusal to testify). As noted above, there must be some causal connection between the defendant's actions and the witness's ultimate unavailability. The method by which the witness becomes unavailable must, at the very least, be a logical outgrowth or foreseeable result of the collusion. Thus, where the defendant has had a meaningful impact on the witness's unavailability, the defendant may have forfeited confrontation and hearsay objections to the witness's out-of-court statements, even where the witness modified the initial strategy to procure the witness's silence.

11

"Finally, a defendant's intentional procurement of a witness's unavailability through collusion will constitute a per se wrongdoing sufficient to trigger the doctrine, even if the collusion is carried out through lawful means. As an initial matter, collusion with a witness implies some degree of improper or untoward interference with official process. More importantly, any action on the part of a defendant that satisfies all elements of the doctrine as set forth above will most certainly be sufficiently 'wrongful' to justify forfeiture. 'It is the fact that a defendant's conduct interferes with the interest in having witnesses testify at a public trial that makes a defendant's conduct wrongful[;] the nature of the defendant's conduct is not as important as the effect of that conduct on the witness's willingness to testify.' *State v. Hallum*, 606 N.W.2d 351, 356 (Iowa 2000)." *Commonwealth v. Edwards*, 444 Mass. 526, 540–42 (2005).

GENERAL CONTINUANCE

A general continuance, over the objection of the Commonwealth, is improper. *Commonwealth v. Taylor*, 428 Mass. 623 (1999).

HANDWRITING

"A witness who is familiar with a person's handwriting may give an opinion as to whether the specimen in question was written by that person. Whether a witness is qualified to give such an opinion is a question, in the first instance, for the judge." *Commonwealth v. Ryan*, 355 Mass. 768, 770-71 (1969) (citations omitted).

HEARSAY

Police testimony on action taken. "The prosecutor asked, 'What ultimately happened, Officer Foley, to [the defendant] as a result of your conversations?' Officer Foley answered, 'She was arrested.' The prosecutor then asked, 'What was she charged with?' Officer Foley answered, 'Breaking and entering in the nighttime, malicious destruction of personal property.'

"The defendant argues that this testimony should not have been admitted because it let in hearsay 'through the back door.' We do not agree. As an initial matter, the officer's testimony clearly was not hearsay. 'Hearsay is a statement, other than one made by the declarant while testifying at trial or hearing, offered in evidence to prove the truth of the matter asserted.' McCormick, Evidence § 246 at 729 (3d ed. 1984). See P.J. Liacos, *Handbook of Massachusetts Evidence* 262 (5th ed. 1981). No out of court statements were offered in this testimony. The defendant has not cited to us any authority for the proposition that a witness may not testify as to actions taken in response to inadmissible hearsay. Further, the officer's action was not based solely on his conversation with Anderson. He himself was able to observe the broken window and doors, Anderson in tears, and the defendant in a chair in the kitchen with her shoe in her hand and a large gash on her foot." *Commonwealth v. Cordle*, 404 Mass. 733, 743–44 (1989).

Statement not offered for truth. "Gary Grace testified that he heard the defendant tell Kathy that if anyone asked about the victim, to simply say that he left Kathy's apartment in a taxicab. One of the investigating officers testified at trial that Kathy told him that the victim left her apartment in a taxicab. The same officer testified that he checked with a number of taxicab companies, and that none of them had a record of any fares which would be consistent with the victim's being picked up at Kathy's apartment.

"Sullivan claims that the statement attributed to Kathy was impermissible hearsay. We disagree. Hearsay is an extrajudicial statement offered to prove the truth of the matter asserted. In this instance, the Commonwealth offered the statement not for its truth but rather to show that the statement was made. The fact that Kathy made that statement to the police officer tends to support Grace's testimony that Sullivan told Kathy to make such a statement. A statement by Sullivan to his sister that she ought to tell anyone who asked that the victim left in a taxicab, when that was not in fact the case, is evidence that he was conscious of his guilt and was attempting to cover up evidence of the crime. Such evidence is admissible against a criminal defendant. Because the statement was not offered to prove the truth of the matter it asserted, but rather only for the fact that it was made, it was not hearsay." *Commonwealth v. Sullivan*, 410 Mass. 521, 526 (1991) (citations and quotation marks omitted).

Probative effect. "'Absent objection, the hearsay evidence was properly admitted, and the jurors were entitled to give it such probative effect as they deemed appropriate.' *Abraham v. Woburn*, 383 Mass. 724, 726 n.1 (1981)." *Commonwealth v. Paniaqua*, 413 Mass. 796, 803 (1992).

Defendant denies crime. "If a defendant is charged with a crime and unequivocally denies it, and this is the whole conversation, that denial is not admissible in evidence. Unless it is admissible under a different theory, a criminal defendant's denial of an accusation should be excluded as hearsay." *Commonwealth v. Henry*, 37 Mass. App. Ct. 429, 432–33 (1994) (citations omitted).

Joint venture. "An extrajudicial statement of a joint venturer may be admitted against a criminal defendant if (a) the statement was made during the course of and in furtherance of a common criminal enterprise and (b) there is sufficient nonhearsay evidence to establish an adequate probability that the declarant and the defendant were engaged in the criminal enterprise. . . . The jury should [be] told that they could rely on [the] statement only if they first found, based on nonhearsay evidence, that a joint venture had existed." *Commonwealth v. Nascimento*, 421 Mass. 677, 681 (1995).

"The rule applies to statements made subsequent to the crime, including when the coventurers are attempting to evade arrest." *Commonwealth v. Freeman*, 430 Mass. 111, 117 (1999).

Drug conversation. Trooper Leon testified that he overheard his plainclothes partner, Trooper Thompson, and Rollins discuss a drug transaction within earshot of the defendant. The conversation was not hearsay and was relevant. "First, it put the drug transaction into context, enabling the jury to understand the complete occurrence. . . . Second, because the jury could have inferred that the defendant heard the conversation, it showed that he knew that a crime was being planned. The evidence of his knowledge was a link in the chain of proof that he was a joint venturer in the drug transaction. . . . [E]ven if considered hearsay, [it was admissible] under the well settled exception that out-of-court statements of coventurers are admissible against the others so long as the statements are made during and in furtherance of the joint criminal enterprise." *Commonwealth v. Ward*, 45 Mass. App. Ct. 901, 903 (1998) (rescript) (citations omitted).

Threat of non-defendant. "A declarant's state of mind to 'get' or kill someone is admissible to show that the declarant had a particular state of mind and that he carried out his intent. . . . Stix's [who was not the defendant] threat against Starks and his cousin showed Stix's state of mind at the time

11

and was admissible to show that Stix carried out his intent. Rather than imputing this state of mind to the defendant, the threat put the killing into the context of a narrative that was comprehensible to the jury and was relevant to the purpose of the joint venture." *Commonwealth v. Fernandes*, 427 Mass. 90, 95 (1998) (citations omitted).

Credibility. "[T]he credibility of the declarant of a hearsay statement may be impeached by any evidence that would have been admissible if the declarant had testified, even if the declarant has no opportunity to deny or explain any inconsistent statement or behavior." *Commonwealth v. Pina*, 430 Mass. 66, 75 (1999) (adopting Proposed Mass.R.Evid. 806, which is identical to Fed.R.Evid. 806).

Verbatim not required. "A witness rarely can recite an oral conversation verbatim. All that in reason he can be asked to do is to give the substance of the talks. . . . As Professor Wigmore states: 'The general rule, universally accepted, is therefore that the substance or effect of the actual words spoken will suffice, the witness stating this substance as best he can from the impression left upon his memory. He may give his 'understanding' or 'impression' as to the net meaning of the words heard.''" *Commonwealth v. Solomonsen*, 50 Mass. App. Ct. 122, 126 (2000) (citations omitted).

Admissible absent objection. "The defendant cites no authority for the proposition that a trial judge is required to strike, sua sponte, hearsay evidence to which there was no objection. On the contrary, . . . the trial judge's responsibility to conduct a fair trial does not require her to act as an attorney for a pro se litigant.

"Absent objection, jurors are entitled to give hearsay such probative effect as they deem appropriate." *Commonwealth v. Pimental*, 54 Mass. App. Ct. 325, 330 & n.5 (2002) (citations omitted).

Prior consistent statements. "It is well established that the prosecutor may ask a witness to explain inconsistencies between prior and present statements. *Commonwealth v. Dickinson*, 394 Mass. 702, 706 (1985), and cases cited. Moreover, 'the introduction of parts of statements on cross-examination generally allows detailed examination of the entire statements on redirect' (citation omitted). *Commonwealth v. Hoffer*. . . . [The witness]'s testimony that almost everything in his statement to the police was false was inaccurate. Rather, much of his [prior] version of events was reasonably consistent with his trial testimony, and it demonstrated that his trial testimony was not recently contrived.

"However, 'it is a fundamental principle that "a witness cannot be asked to assess the credibility of his testimony or that of other witnesses."' *Commonwealth v. Triplett*, 398 Mass. 561, 567 (1986). . . . Here, unlike in the *Triplett* case where the defendant was questioned about the credibility of his mother, [the witness] was not asked to assess the credibility of another witness, but was asked whether portions of his own prior statements were true. Thus, the prosecutor's questions 'did not create an issue of credibility between the defendant and other witnesses.' *Commonwealth v. Alphas*, 430 Mass. 8, 18 (1999). . . . Essentially, the prosecutor was asking whether the events mentioned in [the witness]'s prior statements actually occurred, which we have previously found was not prejudicial . . . .

"While the prosecutor should not have asked [the witness] to comment on the truthfulness of his previous statements, this does not require reversal. We are convinced from our review of the record that the prosecutor's questioning was more likely designed to clarify [the witness]'s testimony that

he 'lied about everything' in his previous statements to the police and to rebut the defendant's claim of recent contrivance, than to bolster [the witness]'s testimony." *Commonwealth v. Wright*, 444 Mass. 576, 583–84 (2005) (citations omitted).

Forfeiture of right to object on hearsay grounds by wrongdoing. See Forfeiture by Wrongdoing, above.

See also Spontaneous Utterance, State of Mind, and Unavailable Witness, below.

HUMANE PRACTICE

"Our humane practice requires that at a preliminary hearing in the absence of the jury, a judge must decide whether a defendant's incriminating statements were voluntary. Moreover, due process requires the Commonwealth to persuade the judge at the suppression hearing that the statement was voluntary before it is admitted in evidence at trial. A trial judge, therefore, has a constitutional obligation to conduct a voir dire examination in the absence of the jury where the voluntariness of a confession is in issue and to make an affirmative finding of voluntariness before the jury are allowed to consider it." *Commonwealth v. Crawford*, 429 Mass. 60, 65 (1999) (citations and quotation marks omitted).

Expert testimony. "The testimony of experts may provide invaluable help to judges and to juries in making a determination of voluntariness." *Commonwealth v. Crawford*, 429 Mass. 60, 65 (1999) (citations and quotation marks omitted).

Jury instruction. "[A jury instruction on humane practice] is not required unless the voluntariness of the defendant's statement is a live issue at trial." *Commonwealth v. O'Brien*, 432 Mass. 578, 590 (2000).

Statement prior to crime. "The humane practice instruction applies only to 'admissions or confessions made after the crime is committed' and not to statements made to an acquaintance prior to a killing." *Commonwealth v. Caputo*, 439 Mass. 153, 168 (2003) (quoting *Commonwealth v. LaCava*, 438 Mass. 708, 720 n.12 (2003)).

IDENTIFICATION

"The Commonwealth [may make] substantive use of pre-trial identification evidence, even if the witness testifies that he or she did not make such an identification, consistent with Federal decisions that have allowed substantive use of such identification evidence under Fed.R.Evid. 801(d)(1)(C). This court has approved of the identically worded Proposed Mass. R. Evid. 801(d)(1)(C), and [*Commonwealth v. Daye*, 393 Mass. 55 (1984)] no longer comports with Federal jurisprudence applying that same rule. . . . [W]e therefore overrule that portion of *Daye*." *Commonwealth v. Cong Duc Le*, 444 Mass. 431, 432 (2005).

Mistaken identification instruction. "'Fairness to a defendant compels the trial judge to give an instruction on the possibility of an honest but mistaken identification when the facts permit it and when the defendant requests it.' *Commonwealth v. Pressley*, 390 Mass. 617, 620 (1983). *See Commonwealth v. Odware*, 429 Mass. 231, 237 (1999) (failure of the judge to give a requested *Pressley* instruction constituted error where mistaken identification was part of the defendant's case); *Commonwealth v. Richards*, ante 333, 337–338 (2001) (error for the trial judge to refuse the defendant's proper request for a *Pressley* instruction).

"In future cases, the better course is to include in the *Rodriguez* instruction the language set forth in the *Pressley* case, that a witness might be 'honest but mistaken' in his identification of the defendant. There is no harm in including such language, when the evidence so warrants and when a defendant

11

requests the instruction, and it will help to ensure that the jury understand 'the thrust' of the *Rodriguez* instruction—i.e., that a witness might simply be mistaken." *Commonwealth v. Pires*, 453 Mass. 66, 69–72 (2009) (citation omitted).

"However, regardless of the efficacy of such an instruction, '[w]e know of no rule that requires the judge to give a Pressley instruction sua sponte, in the absence of a proper request.' *Commonwealth v. Traylor*, 43 Mass. App. Ct. 239, 247 (1997)." *Commonwealth v. Willard*, 53 Mass. App. Ct. 650, 659 (2002).

See also Eyewitness Identification, Photographic Identification, Suppression of Identification Testimony, and Voice Identification.

IDENTIFICATION CARDS

"Identification cards are common currency of everyday life. They are also portable objects that can be lost, stolen, or transplanted by others. . . . After a jury-waived trial in District Court, a judge found the defendant guilty of malicious destruction of property, breaking and entering in the daytime, and larceny over $250. The defendant argues on appeal that the judge erred in denying his motion for a required finding of not guilty made at the close of the Commonwealth's evidence. He contends that an identification card found at the scene of the crime was insufficient evidence to prove beyond a reasonable doubt that he was the person who had committed the charged crimes. We agree." *Commonwealth v. Renaud*, 81 Mass. App. Ct. 261, 261 (2012).

IMMUNITY

"The defendant next contends that she should have been able to obtain a grant of use immunity for a prospective witness. . . ."

Held, no error. "[B]arring unique circumstances, any inquiry into the question of immunity is foreclosed if the prospective witness is an actual or potential target of prosecution. . . . Although this court has stated in some unique circumstances due process may require the granting by a judge of a limited form of immunity, we have never defined what those 'unique circumstances' may entail."

Commonwealth v. Grimshaw, 412 Mass. 505, 511–12 (1992); *see also Commonwealth v. Cash*, 64 Mass. App. Ct. 812 (2005).

INCONSISTENT DEFENSES

"We have permitted defendants in criminal actions to raise 'inconsistent' defenses in other situations [including never entering a joint venture v. withdrawal; murder v. voluntary manslaughter; accident v. self-defense; entrapment v. denying committing the crime]." *Commonwealth v. Tracey*, 416 Mass. 528, 534–35 (1993).

INCONSISTENT VERDICTS

"The rule is well established in criminal cases that mere inconsistency in verdicts will not render the verdict of guilty erroneous even though such inconsistency may have indicated the possibility of compromise on the part of the jury. Accordingly, a defendant may be found not guilty by reason of insanity or impaired mental condition as to one charge, and guilty as to other charges, even where all arise out of the same criminal episode." *Commonwealth v. McLaughlin*, 431 Mass. 506, 508 (2000) (citations, brackets, and quotation and punctuation marks omitted).

"There is a distinction between verdicts that are impossible at law and those verdicts that are merely inconsistent. . . . [A]n internal inconsistency . . . is not fatal to the convictions

as long as the guilty verdicts are supported by the evidence." *Commonwealth v. Robinson*, 48 Mass. App. Ct. 329, 340–41 (1999) (citations omitted).

INEFFECTIVE ASSISTANCE OF COUNSEL

"[W]hat is required . . . is a discerning examination and appraisal of the specific circumstances of the given case to see whether there has been serious incompetency, inefficiency, or inattention of counsel—behavior of counsel falling measurably below that which might be expected from an ordinary fallible lawyer—and, if that is found, then, typically, whether it has likely deprived the defendant of an otherwise available, substantial ground of defense." *Commonwealth v. Urena*, 417 Mass. 692, 696 (1994) (quoting *Commonwealth v. Saferian*, 366 Mass. 89, 96 (1974)). For the federal standard, see *Lockhart v. Fretwell*, 506 U.S. 364, 369–70 (1993).

Insanity. "It is settled law in this Commonwealth that the failure to investigate an insanity defense falls below the level of competence demanded of attorneys if facts known to, *or accessible to*, trial counsel raised a reasonable doubt as to the defendant's mental condition." *Commonwealth v. Milton*, 49 Mass. App. Ct. 552, 560 (2000) (citations and quotation marks omitted).

Probation revocation. "We hold that a probationer is entitled to effective assistance of counsel at a probation violation hearing if his liberty is palpably at risk, or, alternatively, in all District Court cases. We further hold that a motion for a new trial under rule 30 (b) is the proper means to raise a claim of ineffective assistance of counsel at such a hearing." *Commonwealth v. Patton*, 458 Mass. 119, 120 (2010).

INFERENCES

"Inferences drawn by the jury need only be reasonable and possible and need not be necessary or inescapable." *Commonwealth v. Noble*, 417 Mass. 341, 346 (1994) (citations and punctuation omitted).

INSANITY/LACK OF CRIMINAL RESPONSIBILITY

1. "The standard for lack of criminal responsibility, set out in *McHoul*, [352 Mass. 544, 546–47 (1967)], provides: 'A person is not responsible for criminal conduct if at the time of such conduct as a result of mental disease or defect he lacks substantial capacity either to appreciate the criminality [wrongfulness] of his conduct or to conform his conduct to the requirements of [the] law.' We have held that neither alcoholism nor drug addiction is a disease or defect which, alone, can trigger the application of McHoul." *Commonwealth v. Blake*, 409 Mass. 146, 157 (1991).

2. "If voluntary consumption of a drug activated a latent mental disease or defect and, as a result of that mental disease or defect, the defendant lost the substantial capacity to understand the wrongfulness of his conduct or to conform his conduct to the requirements of the law, lack of criminal responsibility would be established, unless the defendant knew or had reason to know that the drug would activate the illness. . . .

"The weight of authority in this country recognizes an insanity defense that is based on a mental disease or defect produced by long-term substance abuse. We see no logical reason for rejecting a drug-induced mental disease or defect as a basis for the application of the *McHoul* test simply because the disease or defect is caused only by the drug ingestion." *Commonwealth v. Herd*, 413 Mass. 834, 839–41 (1992) (citations, punctuation marks and footnote omitted).

3. "The defendant's major defense, applicable to both charges, was that he had a mental disease or defect and, as a

11

result, lacked the substantial capacity to appreciate the wrongfulness of his conduct or to conform his conduct to the requirements of [the] law. The defendant's evidence tended to show that his drug consumption caused the epileptic seizure that allegedly existed at the time of the attack on the victim. In the circumstances, the requested instruction dealt with a significant dispute in the trial. The jury should have been told that they could consider the effects of any epileptic seizure that the defendant may have had even if induced by the defendant's drug consumption.⁴"

FN4 "Consistent with the instruction requested, in some other case such an instruction might have to include an exception if the defendant knew or reasonably should have known of the effect of his drug consumption on his mental disease or defect." *Commonwealth v. Angelone*, 413 Mass. 82, 87 & n.4 (1992).

4. "The law is clear that the 'defense' of the lack of criminal responsibility is not available to a defendant with a mental disease or defect who knows that his consumption of a substance will cause him to be substantially incapable of either appreciating the wrongfulness of his conduct or conforming his conduct to the requirements of the law (or both)."

The standard is a subjective, not objective, one. *Commonwealth v. Ruddock*, 428 Mass. 288, 290 (1998) (citations omitted).

5. "The Commonwealth had the burden of proving beyond a reasonable doubt that the defendant was criminally responsible at the time of the crime. The Commonwealth, however, may prove sanity without presenting expert testimony. A trier of fact may reject the testimony of experts that a defendant lacked criminal responsibility and may infer sanity from the defendant's conduct and the facts of the crime. We have also permitted the trier of fact to consider as evidence the so-called presumption of sanity. This inference of presumption is based on the trier of fact's common knowledge that a great majority of people are sane, and the probability that any particular person is sane. A jury instruction concerning the presumption of sanity should be given in every case in which the question of the defendant's criminal responsibility is raised." *Commonwealth v. Keita*, 429 Mass. 843, 846 (1999) (citations and quotation marks omitted).

6. "The *McHoul* case did not intend that questions about right versus wrong be prohibited in criminal responsibility cases, and it follows that there is no requirement that they be excluded when mental impairment is the issue." *Commonwealth v. Urrea*, 443 Mass. 530, 538 (2005).

Suicide. "An attempt at suicide, even when coupled with other self-destructive behavior, is not sufficient to support an insanity instruction." *Commonwealth v. Scott*, 430 Mass. 351, 356 (1999).

7. **Mental illness and drugs or alcohol.** "[W]e set forth an appropriate instruction that may be used in this case and in future homicide cases as warranted where there is evidence that a defendant had a mental disease or defect and consumed drugs or alcohol:

"'A defendant's lack of criminal responsibility cannot be solely the product of intoxication caused by her voluntary consumption of alcohol or another drug. *Commonwealth v. Sheehan*, 376 Mass. 765, 770 (1978). However, a defendant is not criminally responsible if you have a reasonable doubt as to whether, when the crime was committed, the defendant had a latent mental disease or defect that became activated by the voluntary consumption of drugs or alcohol, or an active mental disease or defect that became intensified by the voluntary

consumption of drugs or alcohol, which activated or intensified mental disease or defect then caused her to lose the substantial capacity to appreciate the wrongfulness of her conduct or the substantial capacity to conform her conduct to the requirements of the law. If you have a reasonable doubt as to whether the defendant was criminally responsible, you shall find the defendant not guilty by reason of lack of criminal responsibility. *Commonwealth v. Herd*, 413 Mass. 834, 841 (1992). *Commonwealth v. McGrath*, 358 Mass. 314 (1970).

"Where a defendant has an active mental disease or defect that caused her to lose the substantial capacity to appreciate the wrongfulness of her conduct or the substantial capacity to conform her conduct to the requirements of the law, the defendant's consumption of alcohol or another drug cannot preclude the defense of lack of criminal responsibility.'" *Commonwealth v. Berry*, 457 Mass. 602, 617–18 (2010) (footnote and quotation marks omitted).

The court further stated: "Where the Commonwealth offers evidence that the defendant knew or had reason to know of the effects of drugs or alcohol on her latent mental disease or defect, or on the intensification of her active mental disease or defect, the following instruction must be added: 'However, if the Commonwealth has proved beyond a reasonable doubt that the defendant consumed drugs or alcohol knowing or having reason to know that the drugs or alcohol would activate a latent mental disease or intensify an active mental disease, causing her to lose the substantial capacity to appreciate the wrongfulness of her conduct or the substantial capacity to conform her conduct to the requirements of the law, then you would be warranted in finding the defendant criminally responsible for a crime in which you find she knowingly participated. In deciding what the defendant had reason to know about the consequences of her consumption of drugs or alcohol, you should consider the question solely from the defendant's point of view, including her mental capacity and her past experience with drugs or alcohol.'" *Commonwealth v. Berry*, 457 Mass. 602, 617 n.9 (2010).

INTERNAL AFFAIRS

"We conclude that, on motion pursuant to [Mass.R. Crim.P.] 17, a judge should normally issue a subpoena to the internal affairs division of a police department directing it to produce any statements of percipient witnesses. No special showing of relevance or need is required for the production of statements of percipient witnesses. . . .

"A defendant [however] may not obtain information in the possession of an internal affairs division, other than statements of percipient witnesses, without seeking a summons for the production of that information and, if production is opposed, without making a showing to a judge (normally by affidavit) that there is a specific, good faith reason for believing that the information is relevant to a material issue in the criminal proceedings and could be of real benefit to the defense. . . .

"A judge who has been provided with both (a) a good faith, specific, and reasonable basis for believing that the records of an internal affairs investigation (beyond statements of percipient witnesses) will contain exculpatory evidence that is relevant and material to the issue of a defendant's guilt and (b) good reason to deny production of the records, may elect to conduct an in camera review of the records before deciding what records, if any, should be disclosed." *Commonwealth v. Wanis*, 426 Mass. 639, 644–45 (1998).

11

INTERNET MATERIALS

"With respect to the Internet materials, we conclude that the pages taken from two Web sites and used during the plaintiff's examination of the defendant did not qualify under the learned treatise exception to the hearsay rule." *Kace v. Liang*, 472 Mass. 630, 631 (2015).

INTOXICATION

1. "Voluntary intoxication instructions are not required where the evidence does not suggest a condition of 'debilitating intoxication' that could support a reasonable doubt as to whether a defendant was capable of forming the requisite criminal intent." *Commonwealth v. James*, 424 Mass. 770, 789 (1997) (quoting *Commonwealth v. Morgan*, 422 Mass. 373, 377 (1996)). *See also Commonwealth v. Brown*, 449 Mass. 747, 768 (2007) ("An instruction on voluntary intoxication is not required absent evidence of debilitating intoxication. Such evidence must support the inference that at the time of the killing, intoxication impaired the defendant's ability to form any requisite criminal intent." (citations and quotation marks omitted)).

2. If a jury instruction is required, all that is necessary is simply telling the jury that they "may consider credible evidence of the effects of the defendant's consumption of [alcohol] in deciding whether the Commonwealth [has] met its burden of proving the defendant's state of mind beyond a reasonable doubt." *Commonwealth v. Morgan*, 422 Mass. at 789–90 (quoting *Commonwealth v. Sires*, 413 Mass. 292, 300 (1992)).

3. "In *Commonwealth v. Delle Chiaie*, 323 Mass. 615, 617–18 (1949), we held that the instruction '[o]ne may be perfectly unconscious of what he is doing and yet be responsible for his conduct during drunkenness,' was a correct and accurate statement of the law." *Commonwealth v. Mello*, 420 Mass. 375, 387 (1995).

4. "[W]here there is no requirement of specific intent, a defendant is not entitled to an instruction on the effect intoxication may have on his ability to form intent." *Commonwealth v. Parzyck*, 44 Mass. App. Ct. 655, 662 (1998) (citations and brackets omitted).

5. "While police officers should be sensitive to a defendant's state of intoxication, they are ordinarily entitled to rely on a suspect's outward behavior and assurances of sobriety when deciding whether to proceed with an interrogation." *Commonwealth v. Pina*, 430 Mass. 66, 71 (1999) (citations and quotation marks omitted).

6. "The general rule is that where the cause of a mental condition that creates a lack of criminal responsibility is distinct from the effects of any voluntary consumption of alcohol, a defendant may still assert the defense—even if the voluntary use of alcohol triggered the diminished mental state. *See Commonwealth v. Brennan*, 399 Mass. 358, 362 (1987). However, a defendant may not assert lack of criminal responsibility where he had reason to know in advance that the use of alcohol would produce such a condition. *Ibid. See Commonwealth v. Sheehan*, [376 Mass. 765, 769]. Thus, in this case, if the defendant had reason to know that her use of alcohol might combine with her prescription medications to impair her mental faculties, and such a combined effect was in fact the cause of her diminished abilities, she would be deemed criminally responsible for her actions. If, on the other hand, she had no such foreknowledge, or if her mental defect existed wholly apart from any use of alcohol, the defense would be available." *Commonwealth v. Darch*, 54 Mass. App. Ct. 713, 715–16 (2002).

7. **Involuntary Intoxication.** "Examples of involuntary intoxication include situations in which a defendant is compelled to ingest intoxicants unwillingly, or where a defendant suffers intoxicating effects from prescription medication used as instructed. In the latter case, the defense is premised on the notion that a defendant, at least where not specifically told otherwise, is entitled to presume that an intoxicating dose of medication will not be prescribed." *Commonwealth v. Darch*, 54 Mass. App. Ct. 713, 715 (2002) (citing *Commonwealth v. Sheehan*, 376 Mass. 765, 771 n.6 (1978)).

8. See annotations following murder, G.L. c. 265, § 1, and manslaughter, G.L. c. 265, § 13.

JAIL CREDIT

"Criminal defendants have a right to have their sentences reduced by the amount of time they spend in custody awaiting trial, unless in imposing the sentence, the judge has already deducted such time or taken it into consideration in determining the sentence. *See* G.L. c. 127, § 129B; G.L. c. 279, § 33A. However, time spent in custody awaiting trial for one crime generally may not be credited against a sentence for an unrelated crime. The purpose of this rule is to prevent criminals from essentially having a line of credit for future crimes." *Commonwealth v. Milton*, 427 Mass. 18, 23–24 (1998) (footnote and citations omitted).

JAILHOUSE INFORMANT

"[U]nder the Sixth Amendment and art. 12, a jailhouse informant who has an agreement containing a specific benefit or promise thereof does not have to target an individual defendant specifically to be an agent of the government. In addition, we conclude that the jailhouse informant deliberately elicited incriminating statements from the defendant in violation of his right to counsel under the Sixth Amendment and that these statements were not harmless beyond a reasonable doubt." *Commonwealth v. Murphy*, 448 Mass. 452, 471–72 (2007).

JEOPARDY

"A defendant is not put in jeopardy within the meaning of the constitutional prohibition until he is put to trial before the trier of the facts, whether the trier be a jury or a judge. . . . In the case of a jury trial, jeopardy attached when a jury is empaneled and sworn. . . . In a nonjury trial, jeopardy attaches when the court begins to hear evidence." *Commonwealth v. Ludwig*, 370 Mass. 31, 33 (1976) (citations and quotation marks omitted).

"We adhere to the principle that jeopardy attaches at the time the first witness is sworn." *Commonwealth v. DeFuria*, 400 Mass. 485, 489 (1987) (citations omitted).

"[W]hen a defendant has been acquitted at trial he may not be retried on the same offense, even if the legal rulings underlying the acquittal were erroneous." *Commonwealth v. Lowder*, 432 Mass. 92, 105 (2000) (quotation marks and citations omitted).

JOINT DEFENSE AGREEMENT

Joint defense agreements were formally recognized in *Hanover Insurance Company v. Rapo & James Insurance Services, Inc.*, 449 Mass. 609 (2007).

JOINT VENTURE

New jury instruction. "[W]e address the traditional jury instruction on joint venture and conclude that our law on joint venture will be better understood, and ultimately more fair

11

and just, if in the future judges simply instruct juries in appropriate cases that a defendant is guilty of a crime if he knowingly participated in the commission of the crime charged, alone or with others, with the intent required for that crime. . . .

"We, therefore, now adopt the language of aiding and abetting rather than joint venture for use in trials that commence after the issuance of the rescript in this case. When there is evidence that more than one person may have participated in the commission of the crime, judges are to instruct the jury that the defendant is guilty if the Commonwealth has proved beyond a reasonable doubt that the defendant knowingly participated in the commission of the crime charged, alone or with others, with the intent required for that offense.

"We continue to permit the trial judge to furnish the jury with a general verdict slip even when there is differing evidence that the defendant committed the crime as a principal or as an accomplice. Now, however, on appeal after a conviction, we will examine whether the evidence is sufficient to permit a rational juror to conclude beyond a reasonable doubt that the defendant knowingly participated in the commission of the crime charged, with the intent required to commit the crime, rather than examine the sufficiency of the evidence separately as to principal and joint venture liability.

"This shift from the language of joint venture to the language of aiding and abetting does not enlarge or diminish the scope of existing joint venture liability. Nor should it be understood to interfere with a trial judge's ability to take steps to ensure that the jury's verdict rests on sufficient evidence. Rather, by abandoning the language of joint venture and returning to the more simple and appropriate language of aiding and abetting in the commission of a criminal act, we hope to provide clearer guidance to jurors and diminish the risk of juror confusion in cases where two or more persons may have committed criminal acts." *Commonwealth v. Zanetti*, 454 Mass. 449, 450, 467–68 (2009) (footnotes omitted).

Crawford. "[T]he confrontation clause does not bar the admission of statements that a reasonable person in the position of the declarant would not objectively foresee as being used in the investigation or prosecution of a crime. Certainly, just after the murder, in the privacy of an apartment, neither Cooper nor Taylor would have reasonably foreseen their statements being used in the investigation or prosecution of a crime. Many other jurisdictions have reached a similar conclusion, holding in general that statements of joint venturers (or coperpetrators or coconspirators) are the type of remarks that the *Crawford* Court deemed nontestimonial." *Commonwealth v. Burton*, 450 Mass. 55, 63–64 (2007) (citations omitted).

Mental state. "Under joint venture [in contrast to the crime of conspiracy] where no such meeting of the minds is required, proper instructions focus on the defendant's mental state and do not require the Commonwealth to prove the co-venturer's mental capacity." "The judge was not required to instruct that in order for a joint venture to be established there must be a prior agreement. There is no need to prove an anticipatory compact between the parties to establish joint venture and if at the climatic moment the parties consciously acted together in carrying out the criminal endeavor." *Commonwealth v. Springer*, 49 Mass. App. Ct. 469, 481–82 (2000) (citations and quotation marks omitted).

Motive. "There is no requirement that joint venturers share a motive for the success of the venture. Motive is not an element of proof under the theory of joint venture. Evidence of motive may be admitted if it 'tends to establish the issue'

or 'contradicts a link in the chain of proof.'" *Commonwealth v. Carroll*, 439 Mass. 547, 553 (2003) (quoting *Commonwealth v. Weichell*, 390 Mass. 62, 73 (1983)).

Sole principal actor. "[W]here . . . a defendant is the sole principal actor, he cannot be found guilty as a joint venturer." *Commonwealth v. Mackedon*, 60 Mass. App. Ct. 901, 902 (2003) (rescript) (citing *Commonwealth v. Green*, 420 Mass. 771, 778–81 (1995); *Commonwealth v. Berry*, 431 Mass. 326, 330–33 (2000)).

Withdrawal. "In order to support a theory of withdrawal or abandonment of a joint venture, there must be at least an appreciable interval between the alleged termination and the commission of the crime, a detachment from the enterprise before the crime has become so probable that it cannot reasonably be stayed, and such notice or definite act of detachment that other principles in the attempted crime have opportunity also to abandon it." *Commonwealth v. Cook*, 419 Mass. 192, 202 (1994).

Weapon. "Where a defendant is charged as an aider or abettor of an aggravated robbery, requiring proof of the use of a dangerous weapon, the government must show that the accomplice knew a dangerous weapon would be used or at least that he was on notice of the likelihood of its use." *Commonwealth v. Avery*, 44 Mass. App. Ct. 781, 783 (1998) (quotation marks and citation omitted).

Lookout. "[A] person who acts as a lookout while others are engaged in a criminal enterprise can be convicted on a joint enterprise theory. However, for the Commonwealth to withstand a motion for a required finding of not guilty, it cannot rely on evidence that merely places the defendant at the scene of the crime and shows him to be in association with the principals. Rather, the Commonwealth must present additional evidence which implicates the defendant in the crime." *Commonwealth v. McKay*, 50 Mass. App. Ct. 604, 606 (2000) (citations and quotation marks omitted).

Identity of other principals. "It is not necessary that the Commonwealth prove the identity of the other joint venturer or joint venturers, as long as the evidence supports the existence of some principal other than the defendant and that the defendant shared the other's intent and was available to help if needed." *Commonwealth v. Gonzalez*, 443 Mass. 799, 806 (2005).

JUDGE QUESTIONING WITNESS

"It is true that 'the effect on the jury of whatever a judge says or does may be significant' and therefore a judge should use restraint in interrogating witnesses. However, 'there may be occasions in which a trial judge quite appropriately asks questions to clarify a point, to prevent perjury or to develop trustworthy testimony.' Of course, the judge must be careful not to reveal partisanship or bias." *Commonwealth v. Marangiello*, 410 Mass. 452, 461 (1991) (citations omitted).

See also Commonwealth v. Hassey, 40 Mass. App. Ct. 806 (1996) (conviction reversed due to the judge's penetrating examination of a defense witness, which left the impression with the jury that the judge thought the witness was lying).

JUROR QUESTION

"The constitutional right to the assistance of counsel is of particular importance when a judge receives a communication of legal significance from a deliberating jury. The assistance of counsel at that stage requires the judge, before he or she responds to such a communication, to afford counsel the opportunity to assist in framing an appropriate answer and to place on record any objections they might have to the course chosen by the judge. Where possible, any messages or questions from the jury to the judge should be in writing; they should be shown to counsel and immediately placed on record; and any reply thereto by the judge to the jury should also be placed on record in the presence of counsel, if available." *Commonwealth v. Bacigalupo*, 49 Mass. App. Ct. 629, 632–33 (2000) (citations and quotation and punctuation marks omitted).

JURORS QUESTIONING WITNESSES

"It bears emphasizing that the decision to allow juror questioning and the manner of questioning rests in the sound discretion of the trial judge. It need not be limited to any particular type of case. The judge may permit questioning over the objection of all parties. We continue, however, to encourage judges to consult the parties on the matter, preferably before trial. *See Commonwealth v. Urena*, [417 Mass. 682 (1994)].

"We adhere to the other procedures recommended in *Commonwealth v. Urena*, [417 Mass.] at 702–703, which we now review, with some modifications based on the growing experience with the practice in this and other jurisdictions. (1) '[T]he judge should instruct [the jury] . . . that they will be given the opportunity to pose questions to witnesses.' We suggest that the jury also be instructed not to let themselves become aligned with any party, and that their questions should not be directed at helping or responding to any party. Rather, they must remain neutral and impartial, and not assume the role of investigator or of advocate. (2) Jurors' questions need not be limited to 'important matters,' as we stated in *Urena*, but may also seek clarification of a witness's testimony. Reining in excessive questioning may present the greatest challenge to a judge, as occurred in the instant case. (3) The judge should 'emphasize[ ] to jurors that, although they are not expected to understand the technical rules of evidence, their questions must comply with those rules, and so the judge may have to alter or to refuse a particular question.' (4) 'The judge further should emphasize that, if a particular question is altered or refused, the juror who poses the question must not be offended or hold that against either party.' (5) '[I]t is important that the jurors are told that they should not give the answers to their own questions a disproportionate weight.' We suggest that the judge also instruct jurors not to discuss the questions among themselves but, rather each juror must decide independently any questions he or she may have for a witness. (6) 'These instructions should be repeated during the final charge to the jury before they begin deliberations.' *Id.* (7) All questions should be submitted in writing to the judge. We suggest that the juror's identification number be included on each question. This will enable the judge to address problems unique to a juror, as by voir dire, or to give a curative instruction without exposing the entire jury to any potential prejudice. (8) On submission of questions, counsel should have an opportunity, outside the hearing of the jury, to examine the questions with the judge, make any suggestions, or register objections. This may be done at sidebar, or the jury may be removed at the judge's discretion. The judge should rule on any objections at this time, including any objection that the question touches on a matter that counsel purposefully avoided as a matter of litigation strategy, and that, if asked, will cause particular prejudice to the party. (9) Finally, counsel should be given the opportunity to reexamine a witness after juror interrogation. *See DeBenedetto v. Goodyear Tire & Rubber Co.*, 754 F.2d 512, 515 n.1 (4th Cir. 1985); *Rudolph v. Iowa Methodist Med.*

Ctr., 293 N.W.2d 550, 556 (Iowa 1980). The scope of the examination should ordinarily be limited to the subject matter raised by the juror question and the witness's answer. *See id.* The purpose of reexamination is two fold. First, it cures the admission of any prejudicial questions or answers; and second, it prevents the jury from becoming adversary in its interrogation." *Commonwealth v. Britto*, 433 Mass. 596, 613–14 (2001).

JURY NULLIFICATION

"[W]hile it is improper for a jury to take such action, in practice they have the power to accomplish such a result. Juries, however, are not to be instructed on their power of nullification." *Commonwealth v. Floyd P.*, 415 Mass. 826, 832 n.6 (1993) (citations omitted).

JURY'S DUTY

"The judge instructed the jury that it was their 'duty—if you conclude that the defendant is guilty of any offense . . . to return a verdict on the highest crime or crimes which have been proven by the Commonwealth beyond a reasonable doubt.' This was a correct instruction." *Commonwealth v. O'Brien*, 432 Mass. 578, 591 (2000).

JURY VENIRE

"A judge has discretion in determining whether to grant an evidentiary hearing on a motion to dismiss a jury venire. . . . In order to establish a prima facie case of unconstitutional jury selection under the Sixth Amendment, the defendant [is] required to demonstrate that (1) the group allegedly discriminated against is a 'distinctive' group in the community, (2) that the group is not fairly and reasonably represented in the venires in relation to its proportion of the community, and (3) that underrepresentation is due to systematic exclusion of the group in the jury selection process." *Commonwealth v. Prater*, 431 Mass. 86, 91 (2000) (citations and quotation marks omitted).

JURY WAIVER

To waive a jury, a written waiver and colloquy are mandated. *Commonwealth v. Wheeler*, 42 Mass. App. Ct. 933 (1997) (citing *Ciummei v. Commonwealth*, 378 Mass. 504, 509–11 (1979)).

"We hold that, in addition to considering the defendant's answers to questions posed during the colloquy, a judge may also rely upon the information contained in the jury waiver form signed by the defendant and in defense counsel's certificate when making a determination whether the defendant jury's jury waiver is made voluntarily and intelligently." *Commonwealth v. Hernandez*, 42 Mass. App. Ct. 780, 785 (1997).

"While the Commonwealth concedes that an effective and procedurally adequate jury trial waiver generally requires a colloquy and a written waiver, it argues that such safeguards are not required during the sentencing stage of a . . . bifurcated trial because the defendant is not facing a criminal conviction for a separate crime, but rather a sentencing enhancement (citations omitted). We disagree.

"It has been established clearly that, while a defendant may waive a jury trial on the subsequent offense portion of a trial, the procedural safeguards mandated under [*Ciummei v. Commonwealth*, 378 Mass. 504 (1979)] are required in the second portion of the bifurcated proceedings."

Commonwealth v. Dussault, 71 Mass. App. Ct. 542, 548 (2008).

11

KNOWINGLY

"'Knowingly' when used in a criminal statute commonly imports a perception of the facts requisite to make up the crime." *Commonwealth v. Lawson*, 46 Mass. App. Ct. 627, 629–30 (1999).

LEARNED TREATISE

"Proposed Mass. R. Evid. 803(18), which we adopted in *Commonwealth v. Sneed*, 413 Mass. 387, 396 (1992), provides in relevant part:

'The following are not excluded by the hearsay rule, even though the declarant is available as a witness: . . .

'(18) Learned Treatises. To the extent called to the attention of an expert witness upon cross-examination, statements contained in published treatises, periodicals, or pamphlets on a subject of history, medicine, or other science or art, established as a reliable authority by the testimony or admission of the witness or by other expert testimony or by judicial notice. If admitted, the statements may be read into evidence but may not be received as exhibits.'

"[T]he rule contemplates that an authored treatise, and not the statements contained therein, must be established as a reliable authority." *Brusard v. O'Toole*, 429 Mass. 597, 601–03 (1999).

LESSER INCLUDED OFFENSES

"[T]he test to determine if an instruction on a lesser included offense is required does not depend on whether there is an objection by the defendant or the Commonwealth but rather whether the evidence supports the giving of such an instruction. A judge should not instruct the jury on a lesser included offense of the crime charged unless an element which distinguishes the lesser and the greater is sufficiently in dispute. . . . The lesser-included offense is required if the evidence provides a rational basis for acquitting the defendant of the crime charged and convicting him of the lesser included offense." *Commonwealth v. Henry*, 37 Mass. App. Ct. 429, 439 (1994) (citations omitted).

"[T]he prosecution has a right to jury instructions on lesser included offenses, on request, if the evidence so warrants, in spite of a defendant's objection." *Commonwealth v. Woodward*, 427 Mass. 659, 664 (1998) (footnote omitted).

LOST OR DESTROYED EVIDENCE

See also Missing Evidence, below.

"We seek to clarify and resolve the somewhat different approaches taken in our cases. When a defendant makes a claim that the government has lost or destroyed potentially exculpatory evidence, it makes sense that he or she should bear the initial burden of demonstrating the exculpatory nature of that evidence, using the *Neal* 'reasonable possibility, based on concrete evidence' formulation. [*Commonwealth v. Neal*, 392 Mass. 1 (1984)] at 12. We therefore hold that the defendant will be required to meet this threshold burden in order to advance a claim for relief. If the defendant does meet the burden, then . . . the judge, or the court on appeal, must proceed to balance the Commonwealth's culpability, the materiality of the evidence, and the prejudice to the defendant in order to determine whether the defendant is entitled to relief. . . .

"Our cases indicate that where the Commonwealth has acted in bad faith or recklessly, resulting in the loss or destruction of evidence, the defendant may be independently entitled to a remedy even without meeting the *Neal* test. Moreover, even where the government's level of culpability

is no greater than negligence, the defendant may still be entitled at trial to make an argument that focuses on such negligence—such as, for example, that the negligence reflects an inadequate or incompetent investigation by the government that may give rise to a reasonable doubt as to the defendant's guilt. *See Commonwealth v. Bowden*, 379 Mass. 472, 485–486 (1980)." *Commonwealth v. Williams*, 455 Mass. 706, 718–19 (2010) (citations and footnote omitted).

The standard in federal court is stricter. "[U]nless a criminal defendant can show bad faith on the part of the police, failure to preserve potentially useful evidence does not constitute a denial of due process of law." *Arizona v. Youngblood*, 488 U.S. 51, 58 (1988).

COMMENTARY ON MELENDEZ-DIAZ

Commentary. In 2009, the United States Supreme Court decided *Melendez-Diaz v. Massachusetts*, 557 U.S. 305 (2009), and determined in a 5 to 4 decision that the admission of a narcotics certificate of analysis violated the Confrontation Clause of the U.S. Constitution. This decision overruled *Commonwealth v. Verde*, 444 Mass. 279 (2005), which held that these certificates were admissible as prima facie evidence of the weight and composition of a controlled substance. *Melendez-Diaz* has led to a plethora of decisions determining its reach, and its application not only to narcotics cases, but to a wide variety of cases involving records, reports, and forensic testing. As such we thought it important to include a section outlining the significant cases on this issue. The reader is cautioned, however, that the state of the law in this area is still very much in flux.

Narcotics Certificates. "There is little doubt that the documents at issue in this case fall within the 'core class of testimonial statements' thus described. . . . The documents at issue here, while denominated by Massachusetts law 'certificates,' are quite plainly affidavits: 'declaration[s] of facts written down and sworn to by the declarant before an officer authorized to administer oaths.' Black's Law Dictionary 62 (8th ed. 2004). The 'certificates' are functionally identical to live, in-court testimony, doing 'precisely what a witness does on direct examination.' *Davis v. Washington*, 547 U.S. 813, 830 (2006). Here, moreover, not only were the affidavits 'made under circumstances which would lead an objective witness reasonably to believe that the statement would be available for use at a later trial,' but under Massachusetts law the sole purpose of the affidavits was to provide 'prima facie evidence of the composition, quality, and the net weight' of the analyzed substance, Mass. Gen. Laws, ch. 111, § 13. We can safely assume that the analysts were aware of the affidavits' evidentiary purpose, since that purpose—as stated in the relevant state-law provision—was reprinted on the affidavits themselves. In short, under our decision in *Crawford* the analysts' affidavits were testimonial statements, and the analysts were 'witnesses' for purposes of the Sixth Amendment. Absent a showing that the analysts were unavailable to testify at trial and that petitioner had a prior opportunity to cross-examine them, petitioner was entitled to 'be confronted with' the analysts at trial. *Crawford [v. Washington*, 541 U.S. 36], 54 [(2004)]." *Melendez-Diaz v. Massachusetts*, 557 U.S. 305, 310-11 (2009) (footnote and some citations and quotation marks omitted).

Futility Exception Applicable To Cases Pending On Direct Appeal When Melendez-Diaz Decided. "[D]efense counsel's actions with regard to the admissibility of the drug certificates must be considered in light of our decision in

[*Commonwealth v. Verde*, 444 Mass. 279 (2005)] which unquestionably was binding on the judge. Because any objection to the admissibility of the drug certificates would have been futile, and because the constitutional issues at stake for the defendant are substantial, we review the constitutional error as though preserved by proper objection at trial." *Commonwealth v. Vasquez*, 456 Mass. 350, 352 (2010).

Melendez-Diaz Not Retroactive. "The question raised in this case is whether the rule announced in *Melendez-Diaz* applies retroactively to cases on collateral review. . . . *Melendez-Diaz* . . . broke new ground and announced a new rule. FN9 [W]e conclude that *Melendez-Diaz* is not retroactive."

FN9 "We limit our holding on the retroactivity of *Melendez-Diaz* to the category of records produced pursuant to G. L. c. 111, §§ 12 and 13 [narcotics analyses and certificates]. As to the retroactive effect of *Melendez-Diaz* in relation to other categories of records or reports, we reach no conclusions." *Commonwealth v. Melendez-Diaz*, 460 Mass. 238, 239, 246 & n.9, 248 (2011).

Substitute Analyst. "Donald Bullcoming was arrested on charges of driving while intoxicated (DWI). Principal evidence against Bullcoming was a forensic laboratory report certifying that Bullcoming's blood-alcohol concentration was well above the threshold for aggravated DWI. At trial, the prosecution did not call as a witness the analyst who signed the certification. Instead, the State called another analyst who was familiar with the laboratory's testing procedures, but had neither participated in nor observed the test on Bullcoming's blood sample. . . . The question presented is whether the Confrontation Clause permits the prosecution to introduce a forensic laboratory report containing a testimonial certification—made for the purpose of proving a particular fact—through the in-court testimony of a scientist who did not sign the certification or perform or observe the test reported in the certification. We hold that surrogate testimony of that order does not meet the constitutional requirement. The accused's right is to be confronted with the analyst who made the certification, unless that analyst is unavailable at trial, and the accused had an opportunity, pretrial, to cross-examine that particular scientist." *Bullcoming v. New Mexico*, 564 U.S. 180 (2011).

"A substitute analyst may accordingly be cross-examined on the data on which that analyst purports to have relied reasonably, the basis on which he or she concluded that such data were adequate and appropriate to the task, and the basis for concluding that the data had been prepared in conformity with relevant accepted professional standards, inquiries that implicate the manner in which the testing analyst performed his or her work." *Commonwealth v. Munoz*, 461 Mass. 126, 135 (2011).

Opinion Of Substitute Medical Examiner.
Commonwealth v. Nardi, 452 Mass. 379, 388–91 (2008) (post-*Crawford*, pre-*Melendez-Diaz*) (upholding admissibility of substitute medical examiner's opinion based in part upon unadmitted autopsy report).

Commonwealth v. Hensley, 454 Mass. 721, 731–34 (2009) (substitute medical examiner's opinion upon cause of death was admissible; additional references to autopsy information violated hearsay and confrontation standards but became harmless because the cause of death did not constitute a contested trial issue).

Commonwealth v. Durand, 457 Mass. 574, 581–88 (2010) (two substitute medical examiners' opinions of cause and manner of death, based on autopsy report prepared by nontestifying examiner, properly admissible, but testimony of graphic factual findings of autopsy violated hearsay and confrontation rights of defendant).

Commonwealth v. McCowen, 458 Mass. 461, 480–82 (2010) (substituted medical examiner presented observations, findings, and opinions in notes and reports of unavailable medical examiner who had performed autopsy; no objection; violations of hearsay and confrontation standards did not create a substantial likelihood of a miscarriage of justice because most of information cumulative of separate properly admitted evidence, and because absent examiner's noncumulative opinion assisted the defendant's exculpatory theory and closing argument).

Commonwealth v. Housen, 458 Mass. 702, 710 (2011) (substitute medical examiner should not have been permitted to testify about factual findings of autopsy report on direct examination; no substantial risk of a miscarriage of justice because facts of testimony undisputed).

Opinion Of Substitute DNA Analyst.
"We now conclude that [testimony of a local forensic specialist that she matched a DNA profile produced by an outside laboratory] does not violate the Confrontation Clause because that provision has no application to out-of-court statements that are not offered to prove the truth of the matter asserted. When an expert testifies for the prosecution in a criminal case, the defendant has the opportunity to cross-examine the expert about any statements that are offered for their truth. Out-of-court statements that are related by the expert solely for the purpose of explaining the assumptions on which that opinion rests are not offered for their truth and thus fall outside the scope of the Confrontation Clause. . . . [E]ven if the report produced by Cellmark had been admitted into evidence, there would have been no Confrontation Clause violation. The Cellmark report is very different from the sort of extrajudicial statements, such as affidavits, depositions, prior testimony, and confessions, that the Confrontation Clause was originally understood to reach. The report was produced before any suspect was identified. The report was sought not for the purpose of obtaining evidence to be used against petitioner, who was not even under suspicion at the time, but for the purpose of finding a rapist who was on the loose. And the profile that Cellmark provided was not inherently inculpatory. On the contrary, a DNA profile is evidence that tends to exculpate all but one of the more than 7 billion people in the world today. The use of DNA evidence to exonerate persons who have been wrongfully accused or convicted is well known. If DNA profiles could not be introduced without calling the technicians who participated in the preparation of the profile, economic pressures would encourage prosecutors to forgo DNA testing and rely instead on older forms of evidence, such as eyewitness identification, that are less reliable. *See Perry v. New Hampshire*, 565 U.S. __, 132 S. Ct. 716 (2012). The Confrontation Clause does not mandate such an undesirable development. This conclusion will not prejudice any defendant who really wishes to probe the reliability of the DNA testing done in a particular case because those who participated in the testing may always be subpoenaed by the defense and questioned at trial." *Williams v. Illinois*, 132 S. Ct. 2221, 2228 (2012).

Commonwealth v. Barbosa, 457 Mass. 773, 782–83, 789 (2010) (testifying analyst was supervisor of absent analyst; table showing results of original analyst's testing came into evidence without objection; information "was testimonial hearsay admitted in violation of the confrontation clause;" no substantial risk of a miscarriage of justice; court placed

11

particular emphasis upon the objective reliability of DNA analysis: "We conclude that the balance here [between the probative value of the admissible opinion of the testifying expert and the prejudicial effect of the inadmissible results produced by the absent expert] weighs heavily in favor of the admission of the opinion, and that the objective nature of the science underlying DNA analysis strengthens the opinion's probative weight and diminishes the risk of unfair prejudice.").

Commonwealth v. McCowen, 458 Mass. 461, 482–84 (2010) (successor DNA analyst's presentation of nontestifying predecessor's allele test results violated hearsay and confrontation standards; no substantial likelihood of miscarriage of justice because numbers alone had insignificant probative value and acquired such value only from independent opinion of witness properly admitted and exposed to cross-examination).

Ballistics Certificates. "[W]e recognize that the holding of [*Melendez-Diaz v. Massachusetts*] applies equally to the certificate at issue in this case, which certified that the revolver found near the defendant at the time of his arrest was a firearm from which a bullet could be discharged and that the ammunition was designed for use in a firearm. *See Morales v. Massachusetts*, 129 S. Ct. 2858 (2009) (vacating firearms convictions where ballistics certificate was admitted over defense objection, and remanding to Appeals Court 'for further consideration in light of [*Melendez-Diaz*]')." *Commonwealth v. Depina*, 456 Mass. 238, 248 (2010) (footnote omitted).

Proving Composition Of Controlled Substance Without Certificate Of Drug Analysis. "In a case involving a narcotics offense, the Commonwealth must prove beyond a reasonable doubt that the substance at issue 'is a particular drug because such proof is an element of the crime charged.' *Commonwealth v. Vasquez*, 456 Mass. 350, 361 (2010), quoting *Commonwealth v. McGilvery*, 74 Mass. App. Ct. 508, 511 (2009). That proof may be made by circumstantial evidence, including the testimony of experienced police officers. *Commonwealth v. Cantres*, 405 Mass. 238, 245–46 (1989), quoting *Commonwealth v. Dawson*, 399 Mass. 465, 467 (1987). An individual's familiarity with the properties of marijuana through past experience coupled with 'present observation' of the substance at issue is sufficient to establish its identity. *Commonwealth v. Cantres, supra* at 246–47, quoting *United States v. Harrell*, 737 F.2d 971, 978–79 (11th Cir. 1984). However, an officer's opinion as to the nature of the substance must not be conclusory, but must be based on objective criteria as well as on sufficient training or experience. *See, e.g., Commonwealth v. Charles*, 456 Mass. 378, 381–82 (2010) (where testimony of officers with no specialized training or experience with narcotics investigation was conclusory and equivocal concerning composition of substance at issue, it was insufficient to overcome prejudice caused by erroneous admission of certificates of drug analysis in violation of defendant's constitutional right to confrontation). In addition, although circumstantial evidence is sufficient to establish the composition of a substance, this court stated in *Dawson*, supra at 467, a case involving the identification of cocaine, that 'it would be a rare case in which a witness's statement that a particular substance looked like a controlled substance would alone be sufficient to support a conviction.' . . .

"*Melendez-Diaz* . . . explicitly rejected the idea that only an analyst's testimony would be sufficient to prove the chemical composition of a substance. The Court stated that its decision 'in no way alters the type of evidence (including circumstantial evidence) sufficient to sustain a conviction.'

[*Melendez-Diaz v. Massachusetts*, 557 U.S. 305, 329 n.14 (2009)]. Thus, *Melendez-Diaz* stands for the proposition that if a certificate of drug analysis is used, it must be accompanied by the testimony of an analyst so that the defendant's right to confrontation is preserved. However, nowhere does the decision state that where, as here, a prosecutor uses the opinion testimony of an expert to establish the composition of a drug, that testimony requires corroboration. Furthermore, the defendant's right to confrontation is preserved because the expert is subject to cross-examination. A prosecutor's decision to proceed without a certificate of drug analysis does not violate the holding in *Melendez-Diaz*." *Commonwealth v. MacDonald*, 459 Mass. 148, 153–56 (2011).

Notice Of License Suspension Mailed—Testimonial. "[W]e consider whether a District Court judge erred by admitting in evidence, pursuant to G. L. c. 90, § 22 (d) a certificate from the registry of motor vehicles (registry) attesting to the fact that a notice of license suspension or revocation was mailed to the defendant. . . . We conclude that the registry certificate, like a certificate of drug analysis, is testimonial in nature. It is a solemn declaration made by the registrar for the purpose of establishing the fact that a notice of license revocation was mailed to the defendant on May 2, 2007, and, by inference, was received by him. The registry certificate was dated July 24, 2009, nearly two months after the criminal complaint for operating a motor vehicle after license revocation had issued against the defendant. As such, it plainly was made for use at the defendant's trial as prima facie evidence that he was notified of his license revocation, an essential element of the charged crime that the Commonwealth was required to prove. The certificate did not simply attest to the existence and authenticity of records kept by the registry but made a factual representation based on those records that a particular action had been performed—notice had been mailed on a specified date. . . . [T]he actual notice of the defendant's license revocation . . . constitutes a business record of the registry, created and kept in the ordinary course of its affairs. However, there is no evidence of the existence of a contemporaneous business record showing that the notice was mailed on that date. If such a record had been created at the time the notice was mailed and preserved by the registry as part of the administration of its regular business affairs, then it would have been admissible at trial" (footnotes and citations omitted). *Commonwealth v. Parenteau*, 460 Mass. 1, 2, 9–10 (2011).

Probation Certification—Testimonial. "[T]here was error under *Melendez-Diaz* in the admission of the probation certification. This record does not qualify as a nontestimonial business record under *Melendez-Diaz*. Rather, this record . . . has every appearance of having been prepared in anticipation of litigation—the litigation being the defendant's criminal trial for OUI as a fourth offense . . . In fact, the certification is addressed, as if it were a memorandum, to the assistant district attorney who would be the prosecutor. A record such as this, even if generated in the ordinary course of probation department business, is 'prepared specifically for use at [the defendant's trial' and is testimonial, 'whether or not it qualifies as a business or official record.' *Melendez-Diaz*, 129 S. Ct. at 2540. The testimonial aspects embedded in the probation certification are discernible when it is considered that the certificate was prepared by a person who, in the writing thereof, engaged in certain deliberative decisions, and formulated evaluative statements and opinions in framing answers to the matters appearing on the pre-printed form lines of the probation certification, so that the certification could be used in litigation. . . . The compilation of such information required that the writer of this document review certain other documents (which are not specified in any way), engage in a deliberative process, and enter evaluative and opinion-based responses to the various certification line inquiries. Hence, there is a testimonial component which underlies what the writer did in reviewing documents and answering questions on the probation certification form. These actions and nonactions by the writer were ones that would be subject to interrogation in cross-examination. In sum, the 'Certification of Probation Information and Prior OUI Offense' implicates confrontation rights under *Melendez-Diaz*." *Commonwealth v. Ellis*, 79 Mass. App. Ct. 330, 333–34 (2011) (citations and footnote omitted).

Breathalizer Machines Certification—Not Testimonial. "The regulations promulgated pursuant to G.L. c. 90, § 24K, establish an office of alcohol testing (OAT) within the State police crime laboratory. 501 Code Mass. Regs. § 2.10. The OAT is charged with maintaining a list of approved breathalyzer machines, subject to several enumerated criteria. 501 Code Mass. Regs. § 2.38. In order to effectuate the requirement that all breathalyzer tests are conducted on certified devices, the regulations provide that OAT must annually certify that any breathalyzer machine in use is compliant with certain regulatory criteria. 501 Code Mass. Regs. §§ 2.39 and 2.40. . . . [W]e conclude that the OAT certification records are nontestimonial, and their admission without the live testimony of the technician who prepared them did not violate the confrontation clause of the Sixth Amendment." *Commonwealth v. Zeininger*, 459 Mass. 775, 779, 788–89 (2011).

Restraining Order Return Of Service—Not Testimonial. "We conclude that the primary purpose for which the return of service . . . was created is to serve the routine administrative functions of the court system, ensuring that the defendant received the fair notice to which he is statutorily and constitutionally entitled (*see* G. L. c. 209A, § 7, and the due process clause of the Fourteenth Amendment to the United States Constitution), establishing a time and manner of notice for purposes of determining when the order expires or is subject to renewal, and assuring the plaintiff that the target of the order knows of its existence. The return of service here was not created for the purpose of establishing or proving some fact at a potential future criminal trial. It is true that a return of service might be used in a later criminal prosecution to furnish proof that the defendant was on notice of the abuse prevention order entered against him. When so used, returns are the functional equivalent of the serving officer's live testimony. In this sense they bear some resemblance to the drug analysis certificates in *Melendez-Diaz*. Unlike the drug certificates at issue in *Melendez-Diaz*, however, a return of service is not created solely for use in a pending criminal prosecution. For this reason, it is not testimonial for purposes of the confrontation clause." *Commonwealth v. Shangkuan*, 78 Mass. App. Ct. 827, 833–34 (2011) (footnotes and citations omitted).

RMV Records—Not Testimonial. "[T]he RMV is an independent agency of State government charged with keeping complete records on the status of drivers' licenses and 'a record of all convictions of persons charged with violations of the laws relating to motor vehicles.' G. L. c. 90, § 30, as amended by St. 1990, c. 256, § 5. Unlike the certificates at issue in *Melendez-Diaz*, which are created solely to prove an element of the prosecution's case, RMV records are maintained independently of any prosecutorial purpose and are therefore admissible in evidence as ordinary business records

under G. L. c. 233, § 78, as well as pursuant to G. L. c. 233, § 76." *Commonwealth v. Martinez-Guzman*, 76 Mass. App. Ct. 167, 171 n.3 (2010).

Certified Records Of Convictions—Not Testimonial. "Certified records of convictions are created to establish the fact of adjudication, so as to promote accountability to the public regarding official proceedings and public knowledge of the outcomes of those proceedings. They are used for a number of administrative purposes, including background checks and parole records. *See* G. L. c. 6, §§ 172C, 172D, 172E, 172F. Unlike drug certificates, docket sheets are not prepared for an upcoming case and are not testimonial since the authors are not witnesses against the criminal defendant. Furthermore, the docket sheets are not testimonial under the two-part inquiry set forth in *Commonwealth v. Gonsalves*, 445 Mass. 1, 3 (2005), *cert. denied*, 548 U.S. 926 (2006). First, the docket sheets are not 'testimonial per se' because they are not 'made in a formal or solemnized form (such as a deposition, affidavit, confession, or prior testimony) or in response to law enforcement interrogation.' *See Commonwealth v. Simon*, 456 Mass. 280, 297 (2010). Second, the docket sheets are not 'testimonial in fact' because, as we have discussed above, given the purposes for which they are created, and in light of the fact that they are not created for the purpose of any pending litigation, it would not reasonably be anticipated that they would be used against an accused. In short, certified docket sheets of conviction are distinguishable from drug certificates and do not constitutionally require cross-examination." *Commonwealth v. Weeks*, 77 Mass. App. Ct. 1, 5–7 (2010) (citations and footnotes omitted).

Medical Records Generated For Evaluation And Treatment Purposes—Not Testimonial. "Medical records generated for evaluation and treatment purposes do not constitute testimonial evidence triggering a constitutional right of confrontation. The *Melendez-Diaz* Court expressly excluded medical records from 'this core class of testimonial statements.' [*Melendez-Diaz v. Massachusetts*, 557 U.S. 305, 312 n.2 (2009)] ('medical reports created for treatment purposes . . . would not be testimonial under our decision today'). With particular regard to medical records of blood alcohol level test results, Massachusetts courts have previously concluded that such information implicates no right of confrontation. *See Commonwealth v. Lampron*, 65 Mass. App. Ct. 340, 344–46 (2005) (finding certain medical record drug screening notations not testimonial because created for patient evaluation and treatment). Medical records do not have testimonial character because they are procured neither for litigation purposes nor through law enforcement interrogation, nor are they made in anticipation of use in the investigation or prosecution of a crime. . . . Since the right of confrontation presented no bar to the admission of the hospital's blood alcohol test result without confrontation of an analyst, it was admissible under G. L. c. 233, § 79. The statute, as appearing in St. 1957, c. 200, provides, 'Records kept by hospitals [as required by statute] . . . may be admitted . . . as evidence in the courts of the commonwealth so far as such records relate to the treatment and medical history of such cases.'" *Commonwealth v. Dyer*, 77 Mass. App. Ct. 850, 854–56 (2010) (citations and footnotes omitted).

Sex Offender Registry Board (SORB) Documents—Not Testimonial. "The Supreme Judicial Court has recently stated that a copy of a 'notice of the defendant's license revocation . . . created and kept in the ordinary course' of the registry of motor vehicles' affairs is not testimonial. [*Common-*

11

wealth v.] Parenteau, 460 Mass. 1, 10 (2011). . . . The same is true of the SORB documents at issue here. The documents were not created for the 'purpose of establishing an essential fact at trial.' *See Parenteau*, [460 Mass. at 10.] These records are maintained for administrative purposes, such as keeping an updated registry of biographical data regarding sex offenders, including their names, photographs, fingerprints, and addresses, so that the public may obtain information about dangerous sex offenders who live or work in each community, and so that law enforcement can access and distribute information about sex offenders to prevent further victimization. *See* G.L. c. 6, § 178D. Nor is 'the regularly conducted business activity' of SORB for which these documents were created 'the production of evidence for use at trial.' *Melendez-Diaz [v. Massachusetts*, 557 U.S. 305, 321] (2009). . . . The introduction of the SORB records at issue here in the absence of a SORB witness did not violate the Sixth Amendment." *Commonwealth v. Fox*, 81 Mass. App. Ct. 244, 245–46, *rev. denied*, 462 Mass. 1106 (2012).

MIRANDA

Admission to civilian. "An admission or a confession made to a civilian as much as to a police officer is admissible only if it is voluntarily made. . . . But the question of voluntariness must be raised by the defendant, and he must offer some proof to support his claim. . . . [A] judge has no duty to ask the jury to pass on voluntariness unless it is made a live issue at trial." *Commonwealth v. Smith*, 426 Mass. 76, 82 (1997) (quoting *Commonwealth v. Tavares*, 385 Mass. 140, 150 (1982)).

Assertion of right to counsel. "*Edwards v. Arizona*, 451 U.S. 477 (1981), teaches that, once a prospective defendant invokes his right to counsel, further interrogation without counsel is impermissible unless the defendant thereafter 'initiates further communications, exchanges, or conversations with the police.' *Id.* at 484–85. The police may ask routine booking questions, but not about the crime that is under investigation. If the defendant initiates further conversation about the subject matter under investigation, the police may interrogate further, but they may not construe unrelated questions by the defendant as indicative of a change of position on his part. Further statements by a defendant that are not the product of impermissible further interrogation need not be suppressed. Finally, in order to use a defendant's statement to the police, the Commonwealth must prove voluntariness beyond a reasonable doubt." *Commonwealth v. Chadwick*, 40 Mass. App. Ct. 425, 427 (1996).

"[A] mere inquiry regarding the need for an attorney does not require the police to cease an interrogation." *Commonwealth v. Scoggins*, 439 Mass. 571, 575 (2003) (citing *Commonwealth v. Jones*, 439 Mass. 249, 258–59 (2003); *Commonwealth v. Judge*, 420 Mass. 433, 450 (1995); *Commonwealth v. Todd*, 408 Mass. 724, 726 (1990)).

Assertion of right to remain silent. "Even if the defendant told Troopers Kelleher and Condon, after he denied his involvement in the armed robbery of Reilly, that 'he had nothing else he could say,' as testified to by Condon, that statement, supplemented by the defendant's 'thinking out loud' about whether he should talk or 'shut . . . up,' falls far short of constituting an expression of unwillingness to continue to be interviewed by the police. Those statements show no more than the defendant's reaffirmation of his noninvolvement in the robbery and his momentary indecision, later resolved, about whether to exercise his known right to silence. These statements are not enough to qualify as the invocation of a right to cut off enough questioning. *See Commonwealth v. Roberts*, 407 Mass. 731, 733–34 (1990) (defendant's refusal to reply to certain questions was not an assertion of his right to remain silent); *Commonwealth v. Pennellatore*, 392 Mass. 382, 386–88 (1984)] (in the context of the defendant's willingness to talk both immediately before and after a break in questioning, his words, 'Can we stop, please?' were not meant as an assertion of his right to remain silent or to stop the questioning permanently); *Commonwealth v. Bradshaw*, 385 Mass. 244, 265 (1982) (defendant's words, 'I don't want to talk,' were insufficient to establish an assertion of his right to halt further questioning when, without any more encouragement than the question, 'And then what?', the defendant continued speaking)." *Commonwealth v. Hussey (No. 1)*, 410 Mass. 664, 671–72 (1991).

"After the videotape equipment was set up, the police officer asked the defendant if he wanted to 'make a statement.' The defendant said, 'Nope.' The officer then asked him whether he wanted to talk about what happened. The defendant agreed to, and the interrogation proceeded.

"A defendant who has waived the Miranda warnings still retains the right to cut off interrogation but must indicate to the police the he or she is invoking the warning previously waived. To terminate questioning, there must be either an expressed unwillingness to continue or an affirmative request for an attorney. Once the defendant invokes his or her right to terminate questioning, that right must be 'scrupulously honored.' . . .

"By declining to make a formal statement, the defendant neither terminated questioning nor involved his right to remain silent."

Commonwealth v. James, 427 Mass. 312, 314–15 (1998) (citations and quotation marks omitted).

"While being held for custodial interrogation, and without having first waived the Miranda rights of which he had been advised, the defendant shook his head from side to side in response to the question, 'So you don't want to speak?' The police then posed further questions and, after a time, the defendant made incriminating statements. . . . The question for decision is whether the defendant, by his conduct, had invoked the right to remain silent guaranteed under the Fifth Amendment to the United States Constitution and art. 12 of the Massachusetts Declaration of Rights and, if so, whether the police sufficiently honored that right. We conclude that, under both the Fifth Amendment and art. 12, the right to remain silent was invoked but was not 'scrupulously honored,' and that suppression of the subsequent incriminating statements was accordingly warranted. *Commonwealth v. Jackson*, 377 Mass. 319, 326 (1979), quoting *Michigan v. Mosley*, 423 U.S. 96, 104 (1975). In so concluding, we hold that, in the pre-waiver context, art. 12 does not require a suspect to invoke his right to remain silent with the utmost clarity, as required under Federal law. *See Berghuis v. Thompkins*, 130 S.Ct. 2250, 2263 (2010)." *Commonwealth v. Clarke*, 461 Mass. 336, 336-37 (2012).

Attorney—When defendant in police custody. The Supreme Judicial Court, in *Commonwealth v. Mavredakis*, 430 Mass. 848, 861 (2000), recognized "a duty to inform a suspect of an attorney's efforts to provide legal services. . . . When an attorney identifies himself or herself to the police as counsel on a suspect's behalf, the police have a duty to stop questioning and to inform the suspect of the attorney's request immediately. The duty to inform applies whether the

11

attorney telephones or arrives at the station. The suspect can then choose whether to speak with the attorney, or whether to decline the offer of assistance. On the suspect's acceptance of this assistance, the police must suspend questioning until the suspect is afforded the opportunity to consult with the attorney either on the telephone or in person. If the attorney telephones and then informs the police that he or she will appear for the initial consultation, the suspension of questioning will apply only so long as the attorney appears at the station within a reasonable time." (citations and footnote omitted).

The Appeals Court, in a rescript opinion, subsequently discussed the scope of *Mavredakis*: "[T]he defendant relies on . . . *Mavredakis* . . . for the proposition that, under art. 12, a suspect in a police interrogation has the right to be notified when the police learn that someone, either a family member or an acquaintance, intends to retain legal counsel to act on the suspect's behalf. However, the holding in *Mavredakis* is not so expansive. . . . A promise made by a third party . . . is not the 'concrete offer of assistance' by an attorney envisioned by *Mavredakis*. The police, therefore, have no obligation to inform a suspect that a third party intends to retain legal counsel for the suspect." *Commonwealth v. Nelson*, 55 Mass. App. Ct. 911, 911–12 (2002) (rescript) (citations omitted).

In the subsequent case of *Commonwealth v. Collins*, 440 Mass. 475 (2003), the Supreme Judicial Court had to "determine the reach of the *Mavredakis* rule, and, in particular, whether suppression is required where the suspect retained and consulted with counsel prior to his arrest, was informed of his right to have counsel present when he waived his Miranda rights and spoke to the police, but was not informed that several days prior to the arrest his attorney had told the police that he wanted to be present during any interview of his client." 440 Mass. at 476. The court held that, [w]here, as here, a suspect has retained and consulted with an attorney concerning the matter under investigation, it cannot be said that the right to consult with counsel is 'abstract'; and where the police have done nothing to impede the contact or the flow of information or advice between lawyer and client (including, e.g., failing to notify the defendant of attempts by the lawyer to contact him), our concerns regarding interference with the attorney-client relationship are simply not present. In these circumstances, the *Mavredakis* rule does not apply, and to extend it would unduly burden law enforcement with responsibilities that firmly belong with attorneys and defendants." 440 Mass. at 480–81. In so ruling, the court noted that "[i]f, as here, a suspect volunteers that he has retained and consulted with an attorney regarding a police request to interview him, the conclusion that the suspect is fully cognizant of his right to consult with counsel is virtually inescapable. . . . Additionally, this is not a case in which a lawyer has been denied access to a client in custody or under interrogation. . . . Nor is it a case in which a suspect under interrogation, or about to be interrogated, has been kept unaware that a lawyer, purporting to act on his behalf, is attempting to render advice and assistance." 440 Mass. at 479–80 (citations omitted).

Building on *Mavredakis*, the court held that "because the police did not convey adequately to the defendant the substance of his attorney's telephone message and advice, the defendant's subsequent indication that he would continue to speak to the police did not constitute a knowing or intelligent waiver of his Miranda rights." *Commonwealth v. McNulty*, 458 Mass. 305, 318 (2010).

Concern for loved one. "Concern for a loved one may, in certain circumstances, render a confession involuntary." *Commonwealth v. Scott*, 430 Mass. 351, 355 (1999).

Confusion Due to Inconsistent Sets of Warnings. "We conclude that where two sets of warnings are given and one is defective or incomplete and the circumstances are such that the defendant would be confused by the discrepancy or omission, a waiver so obtained is not voluntary." *Commonwealth v. Vuthy Seng*, 436 Mass. 537, 547 (2002).

Court officers. "With respect to the statements made by the defendant to [the] court officer [ ], the motion judge held that [the court officer] was 'a government official in an enforcement status with respect to the defendant,' that her initial remarks to the defendant were not the functional equivalent of interrogation, but that [the court officer] should have known that her subsequent express questions about the fire were likely to elicit an incriminating response. . . .

"Once the Sixth Amendment right to counsel has attached, the *Massiah* line of cases more broadly prohibits '*government efforts* to elicit information from the accused" (emphasis added) . . . including interrogation by '*the government* or someone acting on its behalf' (emphasis added). . . .

"We . . . agree with the judge's assessment that, for purposes of a Sixth Amendment analysis, [the] court officer [ ] must be viewed as an agent of law enforcement. . . .

"[The court officer]'s subsequent questions to the defendant (asking her whether she had lit the fire, why she had done so, and whether she knew about the other occupants of the house) were specific questions about the crime, and . . . they were reasonably likely to elicit an incriminating response from the defendant. Those questions were posed in derogation of the defendant's Sixth Amendment rights, and her incriminating responses to those specific questions were properly suppressed." *Commonwealth v. Hilton*, 443 Mass. 597, 613, 615, 617, 619 (2005) (citations omitted).

Custodial interrogation. Defined by the Supreme Court "as questioning initiated by a law enforcement official after a suspect has been deprived of his freedom. The Supreme Court noted that not all statements made by a defendant after being taken into custody are to be considered the product of interrogation. [*Miranda v. Arizona*, 384 U.S. 436, 478 (1966).] 'Any statement given freely and voluntarily without any compelling influences is, of course, admissible in evidence.' *Miranda, supra*." *Commonwealth v. Chipman*, 418 Mass. 262 (1994) (citation omitted). *See also Commonwealth v. Jung*, 420 Mass. 675, 688 (1995), wherein the Supreme Judicial Court wrote that "Miranda warnings are only necessary for 'custodial interrogations.' 'By custodial interrogation, we mean questioning initiated by law enforcement officers after a person has been taken into custody or otherwise deprived of his freedom of action in any significant way.' *Miranda v. Arizona*, [384 U.S. at 444]. We have recognized that four factors in particular are helpful in determining whether an individual's freedom of action is sufficiently curtailed so as to require Miranda warnings: '(1) the place of the interrogation; (2) whether the investigation has begun to focus on the suspect, including whether there is probable cause to arrest the suspect; (3) the nature of the interrogation, including whether the interview was aggressive or, instead, informal and influenced in its contours by the suspect; and (4) whether, at the time the incriminating statement was made, the suspect was free to end the interview by leaving the locus of the interrogation or by asking the interrogator to leave, as evidenced by

11

whether the interview terminated with the defendant's arrest.' *Commonwealth v. Bryant*, 390 Mass. 729, 737 (1984)."

"The fact that the defendant was not free to leave (at least until the performance of field sobriety tests) did not render the interrogation custodial." *Commonwealth v. Cameron*, 44 Mass. App. Ct. 912, 915 (1998) (quoting *Commonwealth v. Ayre*, 31 Mass. App. Ct. 17, 20 (1991)).

Is defendant a suspect? The second Bryant factor has been reviewed in *Commonwealth v. Morse*, 427 Mass. 117 (1998). The SJC in *Morse* ruled that a "police officer's subjective view that the individual under questioning is a suspect, if undisclosed, does not bear upon the question whether the individual is in custody for purposes of Miranda." *Commonwealth v. Morse*, 427 Mass. at 124 (quoting *Stansbury v. California*, 511 U.S. 318, 324 (1994)).

For other *Miranda* cases, see *Commonwealth v. Blanchette*, 409 Mass. 99 (1991) and *Commonwealth v. Watson*, 409 Mass. 110 (1991); *Commonwealth v. Osachuk*, 418 Mass. 229 (1994).

For an example of a case in which a prisoner was found not to be in custody for Miranda purposes, *see Commonwealth v. Larkin*, 429 Mass. 426 (1999). The Supreme Judicial Court discussed *Larkin* in a later case: "The *Larkin* decision represents the general rule that Miranda warnings are only necessary where one is the subject of 'custody and official interrogation.' The mere fact that a person is incarcerated does not automatically render that person 'in custody' for Miranda purposes. Rather, in such circumstances, it must be determined, from the totality of the circumstances, whether the prisoner would reasonably believe himself to be in custody beyond that imposed by the confines of ordinary prison life. The defendant bears the burden of proving custody." *Commonwealth v. Girouard*, 436 Mass. 657, 665 (2002) (citations and quotation marks omitted).

"The defendant bears the burden of proving custody. Once the defendant satisfies that burden, the burden shifts to the government to demonstrate that the defendant knowingly and intelligently waived his privilege against self-incrimination and his right to counsel." *Commonwealth v. Alcala*, 54 Mass. App. Ct. 49, 53 (2002) (citations omitted).

Electronic recording of statement. "Proponents of electronic recording of interrogations ask that we . . . exercise our superintendence power to impose a bright-line rule refusing to admit in evidence statements and confessions obtained by way of unrecorded custodial interrogation. . . . Although appealing in its superficial simplicity (and unquestionably an effective method of convincing law enforcement officials to adopt recording as a standard practice), we still decline to impose such a rule. . . .

"We are not, however, satisfied with preservation of the status quo, which amounts only to repeated pronouncements from the court about the potential benefits of recording interrogations. . . .

"Thus, when the prosecution introduces evidence of a defendant's confession or statement that is the product of a custodial interrogation or an interrogation conducted at a place of detention (e.g., a police station), and there is not at least an audiotape recording of the complete interrogation, the defendant is entitled (on request) to a jury instruction advising that the State's highest court has expressed a preference that such interrogations be recorded whenever practicable, and cautioning the jury that, because of the absence of any recording of the interrogation in the case before them, they should weigh evidence of the defendant's alleged statement

with great caution and care. Where voluntariness is a live issue and the humane practice instruction is given, the jury should also be advised that the absence of a recording permits (but does not compel) them to conclude that the Commonwealth has failed to prove voluntariness beyond a reasonable doubt. . . .

"Where we now mandate a jury instruction, not a rule of exclusion, we think that the instruction is appropriate for any custodial interrogation, or interrogation conducted in a place of detention, without regard to the alleged reasons for not recording that interrogation. It is of course permissible for the prosecution to address any reasons or justifications that would explain why no recording was made, leaving it to the jury to assess what weight they should give to the lack of a recording. The mere presence of such reasons or justifications, however, does not obviate the need for the cautionary instruction." *Commonwealth v. DiGiambattista*, 442 Mass. 423, 447–49 (2004).

"[A] trial judge need only give a *DiGiambattista* instruction upon request." *Commonwealth v. Woods*, 466 Mass. 707, 721 (2014).

"In future cases, the judge should abstain from using the word 'waived' when referring to the factual circumstances surrounding the defendant's decision not to have his interrogation recorded. A slight modification of the judge's instruction provided in this case is all that would be required. For example, the judge might instruct the jury that 'in evaluating the significance of the lack of a recording in this case, you may also consider the evidence concerning whether the defendant was given an opportunity to have his interrogation recorded, and whether the defendant voluntarily elected not to have his interrogation recorded.'" *Commonwealth v. Rousseau*, 465 Mass. 372, 393 (2013).

"We now add that the better practice is not to instruct juries that defendants have a 'right' to refuse recording. Permission to record an interview is not required so long as the interviewee has actual knowledge of the recording." *Commonwealth v. Alleyne*, 474 Mass. 771, 785 (2016) (citations omitted).

"[T]he Commonwealth was entitled to introduce evidence of the defendant's refusal to inform the jury that the police followed proper procedures." *Commonwealth v. DaSilva*, 471 Mass. 71, 80 (2015).

"Fifth" Miranda warning not required. "We do not require that the defendant be informed of his right to terminate questioning, a so-called 'fifth' Miranda warning." *Commonwealth v. Silanskas*, 433 Mass. 678, 688 n.11 (2001) (citations omitted). *See also Commonwealth v. Novo*, 442 Mass. 262, 271 (2004) (quoting *Silanskas*).

"Nonetheless, the details of the interrogation, including the recitation of Miranda warnings, are relevant in determining whether a confession is voluntary. Put another way, although a police officer is not *required* to give the fifth Miranda warning, if the officer gives the warning and gets it wrong, the incorrect statement of rights may affect the voluntariness of the defendant's confession." *Commonwealth v. Novo*, 442 Mass. 262, 271 (2004) (citation omitted).

Grand jury target. "Because grand jury testimony is compelled, it ought to be ameliorated with an advisement of rights where there is a substantial likelihood that the witness may become an accused; that is, where the witness is a 'target' or is reasonably likely to become one. Accordingly, we adopt a rule that where, at the time a person appears to testify before a grand jury, the prosecutor has reason to believe that the witness is either a 'target' or is likely to become one, the

11

witness must be advised, before testifying, that (1) he or she may refuse to answer any question if a truthful answer would tend to incriminate the witness, and (2) anything that he or she does say may be used against the witness in a subsequent legal proceeding. The rule we adopt is meant to discourage the Commonwealth from identifying a person as a likely participant in the crime under investigation, compelling his or her appearance and testimony at the grand jury without adequate warnings, and then using that testimony in a criminal trial." *Commonwealth v. Woods*, 466 Mass. 707, 719–20 (2014) (footnote omitted).

Humane practice. "Such an instruction is not required unless the voluntariness of the defendant's statement is a live issue at trial." *Commonwealth v. O'Brien*, 432 Mass. 578, 590 (2000).

"The humane practice instruction applies only to 'admissions or confessions made after the crime is committed' and not to statements made to an acquaintance prior to a killing." *Commonwealth v. Caputo*, 439 Mass. 153, 168 (2003) (quoting *Commonwealth v. LaCava*, 438 Mass. 708, 720 n.12 (2003)).

Impeachment. A statement suppressed due to a Miranda violation may nonetheless still be used for impeachment purposes so long as it was voluntary. *Commonwealth v. Ferrer*, 47 Mass. App. Ct. 645, 647–48 (1999) (citing *Commonwealth v. Harris*, 364 Mass. 236, 238–40 (1973)).

Improper reinterrogation. "*Edwards v. Arizona*, 451 U.S. 477, 485 (1981), requires that, once a suspect invokes his right to counsel, police interrogation must cease immediately, unless the suspect 'initiates further communication, exchanges, or conversations with the police.' Where the suspect does so, reinterrogation may follow, but 'the burden remains upon the prosecution to show that subsequent events indicated a waiver of the Fifth Amendment right to have counsel present during the interrogation.' . . . Thus, before police may recommence interrogation in these circumstances, they must first obtain from the suspect a voluntary, knowing, and intelligent waiver." *Commonwealth v. Nom*, 426 Mass. 152, 156–57 (1997) (citations omitted).

Improper Testimony. The following testimony was found to be highly improper: "I went in and I gave him his Miranda rights. We were trying to speak to him to see if he would . . . cooperate, but he refused to cooperate." *Commonwealth v. DeLarosa*, 50 Mass. App. Ct. 623, 630–31 (2000).

"Interrogation." "For the purposes of Miranda, 'interrogation' means not only express questioning of a suspect but also its 'functional equivalent'. The 'functional equivalent' of interrogation includes any words or actions on the part of the police (other than those normally attendant to arrest and custody) that the police should know are reasonably likely to elicit an incriminating response from the suspect. The "functional equivalent" test does not turn on the subjective intent of the particular police officer but on an objective assessment as to whether the police statements and conduct could be perceived as an interrogation by a reasonable person in the same circumstances. Interrogation is present if an objective observer with the same knowledge of the suspect as the police officer would infer that the officer's speech or conduct was designed to elicit an incriminating response." *Commonwealth v. D'Entremont*, 36 Mass. App. Ct. 474, 478–79 (1994) (quotation marks, citations, footnote and punctuation omitted).

Intoxication. "A defendant's intoxication is one factor that bears on the voluntariness of a statement . . . but the fact that a defendant has consumed drugs and alcohol before his arrest does not necessarily mandate a finding that the defend-

ant's confession was involuntary." *Commonwealth v. Smith*, 426 Mass. 76, 81–82 (1997) (citations omitted).

Juveniles—Interested Adults. "[W]e take this opportunity to extend the [interested adult] rule, on a prospective basis, to seventeen year old defendants." *Commonwealth v. Smith*, 471 Mass. 161, 166 (2015).

"Whenever a criminal defendant's out-of-court statements are offered in evidence against him, the prosecution has a heavy burden to demonstrate that the defendant knowingly and intelligently waived his privilege against self-incrimination and his right to retained or appointed counsel. When the defendant is a juvenile, courts proceed with special caution. . . .

"We conclude that, for the Commonwealth successfully to demonstrate a knowing and intelligent waiver by a juvenile, in most cases it should show that a parent or an interested adult was present, understood the warnings, and had the opportunity to explain his rights to the juvenile so that the juvenile understands the significance of waiver of these rights. For the purpose of obtaining the waiver, in the case of juveniles who are under the age of fourteen, we conclude that no waiver can be effective without this added protection. This procedure reflects our assumption that an informed parent, or person standing in loco parentis, will be better able to understand the child's rights, rights which a child of such tender years is unlikely to comprehend fully without the assistance of such person. For cases involving a juvenile who has reached the age of fourteen, there should ordinarily be a meaningful consultation with the parent, interested adult, or attorney [or at least an opportunity for such consultation] to ensure that the waiver is knowing and intelligent. For a waiver to be valid without such a consultation [or opportunity] the circumstances should demonstrate a high degree of intelligence, experience, knowledge, or sophistication on the part of the juvenile."

Commonwealth v. Guyton, 405 Mass. 497, 500, 501–02 (1989) (citations and quotation marks omitted).

A foster parent may act as an interested adult. *Commonwealth v. Escalera*, 70 Mass. App. Ct. 729, 732 (2007).

Low intelligence. "The police, and ultimately judges, must give special attention to whether a person of low intelligence waived Miranda rights and voluntarily and knowingly made a statement to the police . . . . Here, the defendant had prior experience with law enforcement personnel. He had been living on his own, had a driver's license, and had held various part-time jobs. The Commonwealth's experts testified [contrary to the defense expert] that the defendant was not unduly vulnerable to coercion." Waiver of rights upheld, statements admissible. *Commonwealth v. Hartford*, 425 Mass. 378, 381 (1997) (citations omitted). *See also Commonwealth v. Jackson*, 432 Mass. 82, 85–87 (2000).

"While a low IQ is a factor in considering whether the defendant knowingly and voluntarily waived his Miranda rights or made a voluntary statement to police, it alone is not determinative. *See Commonwealth v. Jackson*, 432 Mass. 82, 86–87 (2000)." *Commonwealth v. Dingle*, 73 Mass. App. Ct. 274, 285–86 (2008).

Off hour questioning. "'Off hour questioning,' such as during the early morning hours, has been held in some Federal cases to be a coercive circumstance. We are unaware of any cases in which such off-hour questioning is the sole circumstance suggestive of coerciveness in the police interrogation. We view such police practice with disfavor, especially when a suspect's sleep is interrupted in the middle of the

11

night or in the early morning hours with no apparent necessity to do so at that time. We are mindful, however, that the six-hour rule of *Commonwealth v. Rosario*, [422 Mass. 48 (1996)], may supply the necessity for such questioning." *Commonwealth v. Hunter*, 426 Mass. 715, 722–23 n.3 (1998) (citations omitted). See discussion of Safe Harbor Rule, below.

Physical evidence resulting from voluntary unwarned statements. "Because we conclude that the Supreme Court's construction of the Miranda rule [in *United States v. Patane*, 542 U.S. 630 (2004)], which was intended to secure the privilege against compelled incrimination in the context of inherently coercive custodial interrogations, is no longer adequate to safeguard the parallel but broader protections afforded Massachusetts citizens by art. 12, we adopt a common-law rule governing the admissibility of physical evidence obtained in these circumstances. Such evidence, if derived from unwarned statements where Miranda warnings would have been required by Federal law in order for them to be admissible, is presumptively excludable from evidence at trial as 'fruit' of the improper failure to provide such warnings. . . .

"[The defendant] was questioned as to the whereabouts of a firearm that the police intended to use against him as evidence in a criminal investigation. . . . He was asked to communicate incriminating information to the police. Article 12 rights are directly implicated and would be imperiled if the product of such a communication—obtained in the presumptively coercive atmosphere of police custody, unmitigated by Miranda warnings—was routinely admissible in evidence. Suppression of the statement alone is an inadequate remedy." *Commonwealth v. Martin*, 444 Mass. 213, 215, 220 (2005).

Post-arrest/Post-Miranda silence. "[E]vidence of a criminal defendant's postarrest, post-Miranda silence cannot be used for the substantive purpose of permitting an inference of guilt." *Commonwealth v. Thompson*, 431 Mass. 108, 118 (2000). *See also Commonwealth v. Gonsalves*, 74 Mass. App. Ct. 910, 911 (2009) ("fact that the defendant's silence was in connection with booking questions makes no difference" regarding admissibility).

Public safety exception. Police officer arrested defendant for having very recently committed two murders and asked him, "Where's the gun?" *Miranda* not necessary due to "public safety doctrine of *New York v. Quarles*, 467 U.S. 649, 657–659 (1984)." *Commonwealth v. Waite*, 422 Mass. 792, 796 n.3, 798 (1996).

Remarks by Interrogators. "The defendant contends that his distraught emotional state, combined with the officer's recommendation that he be 'forthright' and 'clear a slate,' rendered his confession involuntary. Implicit in the judge's denial of the defendant's motion to suppress is a finding that the confession was voluntary. . . . That implicit finding is supported by the evidence. . . . [W]e see no meaningful distinction between that recommendation and the kind of remarks that we have found unobjectionable in other cases. *See Commonwealth v. Souza*, 428 Mass. 478, 481–482 n.3 (1998) (interrogating officers advised defendant that it was in his 'best interest to deal with [them] at this point, to set the record straight in regards to what happened'); *Commonwealth v. Raymond*, 424 Mass. 382, 395–396 (1997) (officer suggested that defendant should tell 'his side of the story'). 'An officer may suggest broadly that it would be 'better' for a suspect to tell the truth,' as long as there is no 'assurance, express or implied, that it will aid the defense or result in a lesser sentence.' *Commonwealth v. Meehan*, 377 Mass. 552, 564 (1979), *cert. dismissed*, 445 U.S. 39 (1980). The recom-

mendation at issue here was no more than a general admonition that the defendant tell the truth, and was devoid of any implication that doing so would result in more lenient treatment. As such, the officer's remark did not prevent the Commonwealth from satisfying its burden of proving voluntariness beyond a reasonable doubt." *Commonwealth v. Brandwein*, 435 Mass. 623, 633–34 (2002).

Re-Mirandizing. "We have repeatedly held that an accused need not continually be reminded of his or her Miranda rights once he or she has intelligently waived them. In this case, where no significant lapse of time occurred between the defendant's being given Miranda rights at the scene of her arrest and her booking procedure, we decide there was no error in the failure to readvise her of her Miranda warnings." *Commonwealth v. Dayes*, 49 Mass. App. Ct. 419, 421 (2000).

Safe harbor rule. Police questioning an arrested person. "An otherwise admissible statement is not to be excluded on the ground of unreasonable delay in arraignment, if the statement is made within six hours of the arrest (day or night) or if (at any time) the defendant made an informed and voluntary written or recorded waiver of his right to be arraigned without unreasonable delay." *Commonwealth v. Rosario*, 422 Mass. 48, 56 (1996). This rule also applies "to an arrested but unarraigned defendant's statements which concern matters relevant to a crime for which a complaint is pending against the defendant. . . . There is no reason to distinguish between police questioning about a crime as to which charges are pending against an arrestee and questioning about a crime as to which no complaint has yet been issued." *Commonwealth v. Ortiz*, 422 Mass. 64, 65, 69 (1996).

"The goal of *Rosario's* safe harbor rule will not be furthered by automatic suppression of volunteered, unsolicited statements made by this defendant after the expiration of the six-hour safe harbor rule." *Commonwealth v. McWilliams*, 473 Mass. 606, 615 (2016).

Same offense—specific rule. A defendant, charged and given counsel on one crime, may subsequently be questioned, without a lawyer, if the defendant waives his Miranda rights, on an unrelated, uncharged charge. *Commonwealth v. Rainwater*, 425 Mass. 540 (1997). *See also Texas v. Cobb*, 532 U.S. 162, 168 & n.1 (2001) (rejecting "inextricably intertwined" exception set forth in *Rainwater*).

Spontaneous and unprovoked statements. "[A]re admissible even if made after a defendant has invoked his right to remain silent." *Commonwealth v. Brum*, 438 Mass. 103, 115 (2002).

Trickery or ruse. "[T]rickery alone may not invalidate a waiver if there is evidence, in light of the other surrounding circumstances, that the waiver was made voluntarily." *Commonwealth v. Edwards*, 420 Mass. 666, 671 (1995); *see also Commonwealth v. Selby*, 420 Mass. 656 (1995).

"Even though the use of a ruse by the police is insufficient, by itself, to render a confession involuntary, a false statement concerning the strength of the Commonwealth's case, coupled with an implied promise that the defendant will benefit if he makes a confession, may undermine the defendant's ability to make a free choice. The specter of coercion arises in these circumstances from the possibility that an innocent defendant, confronted with apparently irrefutable (but false) evidence of his guilt, might rationally conclude that he was about to be wrongfully convicted and give a false confession in an effort to salvage the situation." *Commonwealth v. Scoggins*, 439 Mass. 571, 576 (2003) (citations and quotation marks omitted).

11

Voluntariness. Whenever a defendant makes statements to the police, two separate issues arise: *Miranda* and voluntariness. "The test for voluntariness of a confession is whether, in light of the totality of the circumstances surrounding the making of the statement, the will of the defendant was overborne to the extent that the statement was not the result of a free and voluntary act. There is no easy acid test for voluntariness. The traditional factors indicating voluntariness or lack thereof [include] promises or other inducements, conduct of the defendant, the defendant's age, education, intelligence and emotional stability, experience with and in the criminal justice system, physical and mental condition, the initiator of the discussion of a deal or leniency [whether the defendant or the police], and the details of the interrogation, including the recitation of Miranda warnings. . . ." *Commonwealth v. Carp*, 47 Mass. App. Ct. 229, 232–33 (1999) (quotation marks, parentheses, and citations omitted).

"A statement is voluntary if it is . . . not induced by physical or psychological coercion." *Commonwealth v. Caputo*, 439 Mass. 153, 157 (2003) (quoting *Commonwealth v. LeBlanc*, 433 Mass. 549, 554 (2001)).

"If the defendant is asserting a voluntariness objection, the Commonwealth must prove beyond a reasonable doubt that the statement was voluntary." *Commonwealth v. Burton*, 450 Mass. 55, 61 (2007).

"While a low IQ is a factor in considering whether the defendant knowingly and voluntarily waived his Miranda rights or made a voluntary statement to police, it alone is not determinative. *See Commonwealth v. Jackson*, 432 Mass. 82, 86–87 (2000)." *Commonwealth v. Dingle*, 73 Mass. App. Ct. 274, 285–86 (2008).

Waiver. "'In determining whether a waiver was made voluntarily, the court must examine the totality of the circumstances surrounding the making of waiver.' . . . The relevant factors include, but are not limited to, 'promises or other inducements, conduct of the defendant, the defendant's age, education, intelligence and emotional stability, experience with and in the criminal justice system, physical and mental condition, the initiator of the discussion of a deal or leniency (whether the defendant or the police), and the detail of the interrogation, including the recitation of Miranda warnings.'" *Commonwealth v. Rodriguez*, 425 Mass. 361, 366 (1997) (quoting *Commonwealth v. Edwards*, 420 Mass. 666, 670 (1995); *Commonwealth v. Mandile*, 397 Mass. 410, 413 (1986)).

MISCARRIAGE OF JUSTICE

For an explanation of the substantial risk of a miscarriage of justice test, see *Commonwealth v. Alphas*, 430 Mass. 8 (1999).

MISSING EVIDENCE

See also Lost or Destroyed Evidence, above.

Jury instruction. "Before [a missing evidence instruction] is given, the defendant must meet his initial burden of establishing a reasonable possibility, based on concrete evidence rather than a fertile imagination that access to the evidence would have produced evidence favorable to his cause. If the defendant meets this burden, the court must weigh the culpability of the Commonwealth, the materiality of the evidence and the potential prejudice to the defendant . . . . [W]hen it is determined that it is appropriate to give a missing evidence instruction, such instruction should generally permit, rather than require, a negative inference against the Commonwealth." *Commonwealth v. Kee*, 449 Mass. 550, 557–58 (2007) (citations, quotation marks, and brackets omitted).

MISSING WITNESS

"Where a defendant has knowledge of an available witness whose general disposition toward the defendant is friendly, or at least not hostile, and who could be expected to give testimony of distinct importance to the defendant's case, but the defendant, without explanation, fails to call that witness, the jury may permissibly infer that that witness would have given testimony detrimental to the defendant's case. The strength of the case against the defendant, whether the defendant would be expected to call the witness if the defendant were innocent, and the importance of the witness's likely testimony to the defense are important considerations in determining whether an adverse inference based on the defendant's failure to call a certain witness is appropriate. Where a witness's testimony would have been merely cumulative or unimportant, there is no basis for such an inference.

"Whether the adverse inference is permissible depends on the facts of each case, and whether to give a missing witness instruction is a decision that must be made on a case-by-case basis, in the discretion of the trial judge. That decision will be overturned on appeal only if it was 'manifestly unreasonable.'" *Commonwealth v. Thomas*, 429 Mass. 146, 150–51 (1999) (citations omitted). For a case in which a conviction was reversed due to the trial judge erroneously giving a missing witness instruction, *see Commonwealth v. Spencer*, 49 Mass. App. Ct. 383 (2000).

"Because the inference, when it is made, can have a seriously adverse effect on the non-calling party—suggesting, as it does, that the party has willfully attempted to withhold or conceal significant evidence—it should be invited only in clear cases, and with caution." *Commonwealth v. Figueroa*, 413 Mass. 193, 199 (1992) (citation omitted); *see also Commonwealth v. Giberti*, 51 Mass. App. Ct. 907, 907 (2001) (quoting *Figueroa*) (rescript).

Instruction. "A missing witness instruction from a judge and a missing witness argument by counsel go hand in hand. If a judge determines that the foundational requirements for the instruction are met, and that the adverse inference is warranted on the facts of the case, the instruction informs the jury that they may infer from a party's failure to call a witness that the witness would have testified unfavorably to that party. Counsel may then urge the jury in closing argument affirmatively to draw that inference. But before giving the instruction, and before permitting counsel to argue the point, the judge must be satisfied that the foundational requirements for the instruction and argument are in fact met and that the adverse inference is warranted in the circumstances. The same considerations apply in determining whether to permit the argument as apply in determining whether to give the instruction." *Commonwealth v. Salentino*, 449 Mass. 657, 670 (2007) (footnote omitted).

MISTRIAL

"[A] mistrial declared upon a defendant's request ordinarily does not present a bar to retrial on double jeopardy grounds." *Commonwealth v. Curtis*, 53 Mass. App. Ct. 636, 639 (2002).

Prosecutorial misconduct. "An order of a mistrial or of a dismissal based upon prosecutorial misconduct bars retrial only if the misconduct is of a specific character: some form of overreaching, harassment, or other intentional misconduct on the part of the prosecution aimed at provoking a mistrial. Unintentional prosecutorial mistakes, arising from negligence or inadvertence, although resulting in mistrials, do not bar a

11

second trial." *Commonwealth v. Curtis*, 53 Mass. App. Ct. 636, 639 (2002) (citations and quotation and punctuation marks omitted).

MISTAKEN IDENTIFICATION
See Identification, above.

MOTIONS IN LIMINE
"In the past, we have generally required a defendant to object to the admission of evidence at trial even where he or she has sought a pretrial ruling to exclude the evidence either through a motion in limine or by opposing a motion in limine. *See Commonwealth v. Whelton*, 428 Mass. 24, 25 (1998). . . .

"Going forward, we dispense with any distinction, at the motion in limine stage, between objections based on constitutional grounds and objections based on other grounds. We will no longer require a defendant to object to the admission of evidence at trial where he or she has already sought to preclude the very same evidence at the motion in limine stage." *Commonwealth v. Grady*, 474 Mass. 715, 718–19 (2016).

MOTIVE
"If there is evidence of motive, that evidence is admissible. Determination of the weight of such evidence is for the jury, and evidence which merely suggests rather than clearly shows a motive for the crime may still be ruled admissible. There is no requirement that evidence of motive be conclusive in order to be admissible." *Commonwealth v. Ashley*, 427 Mass. 620, 624–25 (1998) (citations, quotation marks and punctuation omitted).

"The Commonwealth need not prove motive." *Commonwealth v. Kappler*, 416 Mass. 574, 579 n.3 (1993).

MUGSHOTS
The use of the phrase "mugshot" is disfavored. Further, such photographs "should be sanitized to avoid calling the jury's attention to their source." *Commonwealth v. Cohen*, 412 Mass. 375, 382 (1992).

"'Admission of a defendant's mug shots in evidence, laden, as it is, with potential for characterizing the defendant as a careerist in crime, is inhibited by three criteria: (1) the prosecution must show some need to introduce the mug shots; (2) the mug shots, to the extent possible, should not indicate a prior record; and (3) the mug shots should not call attention their origins and implications.'" *Commonwealth v. Gee*, 36 Mass. App. Ct. 154, 157–58 (1994) (quoting *Commonwealth v. Smith*, 29 Mass. App. Ct. 449, 451 (1990)). *See also Commonwealth v. Picher*, 46 Mass. App. Ct. 409, 416 (1999).

NECESSITY (DEFENSE OF JUSTIFICATION BY)
"Under the common law defense of justification by necessity, a crime committed under the pressure of imminent danger may be excused if the harm sought to be avoided far exceeds the harm resulting from the crime committed. We have ruled that the application of the defense is limited to the following circumstances: (1) the defendant is faced with a clear and imminent danger, not one which is debatable or speculative; (2) the defendant can reasonably expect that his [or her] action will be effective as the direct cause of abating the danger; (3) there is [no] legal alternative which will be effective in abating the danger; and (4) the Legislature has not acted to preclude the defense by a clear and deliberate choice regarding the values at issue. A defendant is entitled to an instruction on necessity only if there is evidence that would warrant a reasonable doubt whether [the defendants' actions were] justified as a choice between evils. If the question is properly raised, the Commonwealth then has the burden to prove the absence of justification beyond a reasonable doubt." *Commonwealth v. Schuchardt*, 408 Mass. 347, 349 (1990) (citations and punctuation marks omitted). *See also Commonwealth v. Hutchins*, 410 Mass. 726, 730 (1991) ("It must be understood, however, that oft-repeated principle, that the necessity defense is limited to certain specified circumstances, does not mean that, whenever those circumstances obtain, the defense automatically applies.").

NEWLY DISCOVERED EVIDENCE
"A defendant seeking a new trial on the ground of newly discovered evidence must establish both that the evidence is newly discovered and that it casts real doubt on the justice of the conviction. The evidence said to be new not only must be material and credible but also must carry a measure of strength in support of the defendant's position. Thus, newly discovered evidence that is cumulative of evidence admitted at the trial tends to carry less weight than new evidence that is different in kind. Moreover, the judge must find there is a substantial risk that the jury would have reached a different conclusion had the evidence been admitted at trial." *Commonwealth v. Scanlon*, 412 Mass. 664, 679–80 (1992) (citation and punctuation marks omitted).

OFFER OF PROOF
"Since there was no offer of proof, there is no basis for us to conclude that the defendant has been harmed by the ruling." *Commonwealth v. Blake*, 409 Mass. 146, 159 (1991).

OPENING STATEMENTS
"An opening statement is to outline in a general way the nature of the case which counsel expects to prove." *Commonwealth v. Degro*, 432 Mass. 319, 322 (2000) (citations and quotation marks omitted).

"Generally, a prosecutor in a criminal action may state anything in her opening argument that she expects to be able to prove by evidence. The prosecutor may argue inferences from the evidence favorable to her case." *Commonwealth v. Johnson*, 429 Mass. 745, 748 (1999) (quotation marks, citations and punctuation omitted).

"The proper function of an opening is to outline in a general way the nature of the case which the counsel expects to be able to prove or support by evidence. This expectation must, of course, have been reasonable and grounded in good faith. It is not an opportunity for argument. Counsel in an opening statement may not vouch for the credibility of a key witness." *Commonwealth v. Croken*, 432 Mass. 266, 268 (2000) (citations and quotation marks omitted).

Failure to produce all promised evidence. "We recognize that failure to present critical evidence that has been announced in an opening statement can have drastic ramifications. See *Commonwealth v. Duran*, 435 Mass. 97, 109 (2001). . . . However, failure to produce evidence that counsel has predicted in an opening does not automatically amount to ineffective assistance of counsel. . . . Rather, we must look to whether the opening statement 'reflected inadequate preparation, incompetency, or inattention,' *Commonwealth v. Nardone*, 406 Mass. 123, 127 (1989), and whether the subsequent failure to produce the evidence was 'a decision forced upon [counsel] by events over which he had no control,' *id.*, or otherwise was supported by 'strategic justifications,' *Commonwealth v. Duran*, supra at 110." *Commonwealth v. McMahon*, 443 Mass. 409, 425 (2005) (citations omitted).

11

Mistrial. "The proper function of an opening is to outline in a general way the nature of the case which the counsel expects to be able to prove or support by evidence. A mistrial may be appropriate where the force of the prosecutor's opening remarks [are] overwhelmingly prejudicial and likely to leave an indelible imprint on the jurors' minds." *Commonwealth v. Hoilett*, 430 Mass. 369, 372 (1999) (citations and quotation marks omitted).

No opening. "Failure to make an opening statement is not sufficient to support a claim of ineffective assistance of counsel." *Commonwealth v. Scott*, 430 Mass. 351, 357 (1999).

Required finding. "We conclude that judges have inherent power to enter a finding of not guilty in a criminal case after the prosecutor's opening statement. . . ."

"The overwhelming majority of courts have held that motions to acquit a defendant made after an opening statement should be denied unless it clearly appears from the opening statement that the defendant cannot be lawfully convicted and then only after the prosecution has been made aware of the difficulty and fails or is otherwise unable to correct it. We adopt this standard. We foresee two circumstances in which the entry of a finding of not guilty after an opening statement might be warranted: (1) the statement clearly and deliberately admits a fact which must necessarily prevent a conviction and require an acquittal; and (2) the statement embraces all operative facts to be proven at trial and those facts are insufficient to sustain a claim for relief under any legal theory, showing unmistakably that the prosecutor's evidence cannot prove one or more elements of the offense charged. In either of these circumstances, the basic facts lead inescapably to a conclusion that the prosecution must fail regardless of the light in which the facts are viewed."

"Trial judges must adhere to this standard with strictness because the Commonwealth is otherwise barred from retrying the defendant. A judge who directs a verdict in violation of the standard abuses his or her discretion." *Commonwealth v. Lowder*, 432 Mass. 92, 99–101 (2000) (citations and quotation and punctuation marks omitted).

OUT-OF-COURT IDENTIFICATION

"There was no error in admitting [the police officer's] out-of-court identification of the defendant, which was admissible both as corroboration of Bly's testimony regarding that identification and of Bly's in-court identification of the defendant." *Commonwealth v. Thomas*, 429 Mass. 146, 159 (1999) (citations omitted).

"'Testimony by a third party, such as a police officer, regarding a witness's extrajudicial identification is substantively admissible if the identifying witness is unable or unwilling [to make an identification] in court and is available for cross-examination . . . . [I]t is immaterial that the identifying witness disavows having made a prior extrajudicial identification, or even denies having any basis for making an identification.'" *Commonwealth v. Spray*, 467 Mass. 456, 470 (2014) (quoting *Commonwealth v. Raedy*, 68 Mass. App. Ct. 440, 446–47 (2007) (citing *Commonwealth v. Cong Duc Le*, 444 Mass. 431, 441 (2005))).

PAST RECOLLECTION RECORDED

"Over objection, the Commonwealth was permitted to introduce the tape recording of [the witness's] June 3, 1990, statement to the police. The Commonwealth correctly argues that the statement was admissible, in the judge's discretion, as past recollection recorded, an established hearsay exception.

"A memorandum or recording may be admissible under this exception if (1) the witness has no revivable recollection of the subject, (2) the witness had firsthand knowledge of the facts recorded, (3) the witness can testify that the statement was truthful when made, and (4) the recording was made when the events were fresh in her memory. . . . A witness's inability to remember details of an event [even if she could remember other details] described in a statement can justify the discretionary admission of the statement if it otherwise meets the test for admissibility."

Commonwealth v. Nolan, 427 Mass. 541, 543–44 (1998).

PEREMPTORY CHALLENGES

"A single peremptory challenge can constitute a prima facie showing that rebuts the presumption of proper use. . . . This presumption is rebuttable . . . on a showing that (1) there is a pattern of excluding members of a discrete group and (2) it is likely that individuals are being excluded solely on the basis of their membership within this group. . . .

Confronted with a claim that a peremptory challenge is being used to exclude members of a discrete group, the judge must 'determine whether to draw the reasonable inference that peremptory challenges have been exercised so as to exclude individuals on account of their group affiliation.' If the judge so determines, the challenging party must give the judge reasons justifying his exercise of a peremptory challenge which pertain to the individual qualities of the prospective juror and not to that juror's group association. . . . [The judge must next determine] whether the proffered neutral reasons are bona fide or sham excuses belatedly contrived to avoid admitting facts of group discrimination."

[The judge must make] a finding as to whether an initial prima facie showing of impropriety was established and specifically to determine whether the reasons advanced by the exercising party were bona fide or a mere sham."

Commonwealth v. Curtiss, 424 Mass. 78, 79–81 (1997) (citations and punctuation omitted). *See also Commonwealth v. Benoit*, 452 Mass. 212, 213–26 (2008).

Different race. "The defendant, a minority person [Hispanic], was entitled to a jury representing a fair cross section of the community, which would include African-Americans as well as Hispanics." *Commonwealth v. Calderon*, 431 Mass. 21, 25 (2000).

Gender. "Gender is among the group affiliations on which peremptory challenges cannot be based." *Commonwealth v. Rodriguez*, 431 Mass. 804, 807 (2000) (citations and quotation marks omitted).

Presumption. "There is a presumption that peremptory challenges are being used properly. . . . In deciding whether a party has made the requisite prima facie showing, the makeup of the entire venire can be taken into account. . . . If the judge decides that the presumption has been rebutted, the burden is shifted to the party who exercised the challenges to show some group neutral ground for the challenges. It is then for the judge to determine whether the proffered neutral explanation is legitimate." *Commonwealth v. LeClair*, 429 Mass. 313, 319–20 (1999) (citations omitted).

Procedure. If a challenge is made, the judge must first determine whether or not a prima facie showing of impropriety has been made. If the judge asks the ADA the reasons for the challenge, the judge has in effect made that preliminary determination of impropriety. After the prosecutor offers an explanation for the challenge, the judge must then determine whether the reason is bona fide or a mere sham. *Common-*

11

wealth v. LeClair, 429 Mass. 313, 319–20 (1999) (citations omitted); *see also Commonwealth v. Calderon*, 431 Mass. 21, 25–27 (2000).

Removal of only minority juror. "If the peremptory challenge of juror X had left the jury with no minority jurors, a prima facie case of discrimination would have been established." *Commonwealth v. Serrano*, 48 Mass. App. Ct. 163, 165 (1999).

Once opportunity for peremptory challenge declined ... "Once a party has declined an opportunity to exercise a peremptory challenge as to a particular juror, a peremptory challenge to that juror is no longer available. Rule 6 [of the Rules of the Superior Court] then expressly provides: 'No other challenging, except for cause shown, shall be allowed.' We have previously held that deviation from the procedures outlined in Rule 6 constitutes reversible error, even in the absence of prejudice. *Commonwealth v. Brown*, 395 Mass. 604, 606–607 (1985)." *Commonwealth v. Daye*, 435 Mass. 463, 471 (2001).

PHOTOGRAPHS

"The law on the admissibility of photographs is clear. If the photographs possess evidential value on a material matter, they are not rendered inadmissible solely because they are gruesome or duplicative or may have an inflammatory effect on the jury."

It is a matter within the discretion of the judge. *Commonwealth v. Robertson*, 408 Mass. 747, 752 (1990) (citations and punctuation marks omitted).

Photo must be relevant/not overly prejudicial. "The defendant's photograph [which was "grossly offensive and inflammatory"] was not, directly or inferentially, relevant to any issue in the case. ... [E]ven where evidence is relevant, there must be a determination whether its probative value is outweighed by the unfairly prejudicial effect it might have on the factfinder." Interestingly, the defendant's conviction was reversed notwithstanding the fact that this was a jury waived trial. "Where a judge has not indicated whether he or she has considered improperly admitted evidence, we can only speculate upon the effect of that evidence. When we are not in a position to say that it had none ... such doubts as we entertain can only be resolved in favor of the defendant." *Commonwealth v. Darby*, 37 Mass. App. Ct. 650, 654–55 (1994) (citations and punctuation omitted); *see also Commonwealth v. Prashaw*, 57 Mass. App. Ct. 19, 26 (2003).

"The fact that a photograph is cumulative of other evidence has not required the exclusion of the photograph." *Commonwealth v. Allison*, 434 Mass. 670, 684 (2001) ("This is true even where the defendant agrees to stipulate to the facts that an offered photograph tends to prove.") (citations omitted).

"The photographs of the victim, showing all seventy-nine stab wounds and the gunshot to the head, supported the Commonwealth's theory of murder in the first degree based on extreme atrocity and cruelty." *Commonwealth v. Allison*, 434 Mass. 670, 684 (2001) (citations omitted).

Autopsy photographs. "While we agree with the defendant that the photographs were disturbing, we do not agree that they lacked relevance. A critical issue in the case was the amount of force used to shake the victim. As the nature of the injuries supported an inference concerning that amount of force used to inflict the injuries, the photographs were relevant to that issue. Additionally, the final photograph admitted, showing no injury to the back of the victim's head, was

relevant to contradict the defendant's testimony that the victim hit his head in the bathtub. Furthermore, the judge appropriately mitigated any potential prejudice by cautioning the jury not to be affected by the nature of the photographs, and by instructing them that the photographs were to be used only to draw attention to a clinical medical status or the nature and extent of the victim's injuries." *Commonwealth v. Lyons*, 444 Mass. 289, 298 (2005).

PHOTOGRAPHIC IDENTIFICATION

See also Suppression of Identification Testimony, below.

"A photographic identification procedure is constitutionally invalid if the procedures were 'so impermissibly suggestive as to give rise to a very substantial likelihood of irreparable misidentification.' The initial burden rests on the defendant to show, by a preponderance of the evidence, that, considering the totality of the circumstances attending the particular identification, the witness was subjected by the State to an identification so unnecessarily suggestive and conducive to irreparable misidentification as to deny the defendant due process of the law.

"If the defendant sustains this burden, the Commonwealth may offer evidence of subsequent identifications only if it can show by clear and convincing evidence that they were not the product of the suggestive identification, but had a source independent of the suggestive identification."

Footnote 6 indicated that "*Manson v. Braithwaite*, 432 U.S. 98, 109–14 (1977) ... allows use of an out-of court identification even where suggestive procedures have been employed, provided certain indicia of reliability exist to ensure that the identification is correct. We need not decide whether to adopt this analysis in this case, since we conclude that the procedures were not suggestive. *See, e.g., Commonwealth v. Melvin*, 399 Mass. 201, 205 n.6 (1987)."

Commonwealth v. Holland, 410 Mass. 248, 253 (1991) (citations omitted).

Protocol. "What is practicable in nearly all circumstances is a protocol to be employed before a photographic array is provided to an eyewitness, making clear to the eyewitness, at a minimum, that: he will be asked to view a set of photographs; the alleged wrongdoer may or may not be in the photographs depicted in the array; it is just as important to clear a person from suspicion as to identify a person as the wrongdoer; individuals depicted in the photographs may not appear exactly as they did on the date of the incident because features such as weight, head, and facial hair are subject to change; regardless of whether an identification is made, the investigation will continue; and the procedure requires the administrator to ask the witness to state, in his or her own words, how certain he or she is of any identification. ... We decline at this time to hold that the absence of any protocol or comparable warnings to the eyewitnesses requires that the identifications be found inadmissible, but we expect such protocols to be used in the future." *Commonwealth v. Silva-Santiago*, 453 Mass. 782, 797–98 (2009) (citations omitted).

"[W]e reiterate our expectation that the identification protocol set forth in *Commonwealth v. Silva-Santiago*, [453 Mass. 782 (2009)] at 797–798, will be employed in the regular course of administering photographic arrays." *Commonwealth v. Watson*, 455 Mass. 246, 252 (2009).

Minimum of Five Fillers. "We are not convinced that the rate of false positive identification is greater with all-suspect arrays, but we are persuaded that the danger that a false positive identification will result in a wrongful prosecution is

11

greater with an all-suspect array. . . [A]n all-suspect array significantly and needlessly increases the potentially unjust consequences that may arise from a false positive identification. Unless there are exigent or extraordinary circumstances, the police should not show an eyewitness a photographic array, whether simultaneous or sequential, that contains fewer than five fillers for every suspect photograph. *See State v. Henderson*, [27 A.3d 872, 898 (N.J. 2011)] ('lineups should include a minimum number of fillers . . . [and] there appears to be general agreement that a minimum of five fillers should be used'). We expect police to follow our guidance to avoid this needless risk." *Commonwealth v. Walker*, 460 Mass. 590, 603–04 (2011).

Multiple pictures of the defendant. "Duplication of a defendant's photograph in one or more arrays is not sufficient by itself to compel the suppression of a resulting identification." *Commonwealth v. Wallace*, 417 Mass. 126, 129 (1994) (citation and punctuation marks omitted).

Surveillance photographs. "In *Commonwealth v. Pleas*, 49 Mass. App. Ct. 321 (2000), this court described factors to be used in determining the admissibility of testimony purporting to identify individuals in surveillance photographs. The quality of the photographic images matters; if they are neither so unmistakably clear or so hopelessly obscure that the witness is not better-suited than the jury to make the identification, then lay opinion testimony may be admitted. . . . The level of familiarity of the witness with the person shown in the photograph is also a factor. . . . The courts also consider whether the defendant is disguised in the photograph or has changed his appearance since the time of the crime. In sum, a witness's opinion concerning the identity of a person depicted in a surveillance photograph is admissible if there is some basis for concluding that the witness is more likely to correctly identify the defendant from the photograph than is the jury. In addition, identification testimony from a police officer or other law enforcement official may create the risk of unfair prejudice." *Commonwealth v. Pearson*, 77 Mass. App. Ct. 95, 105 (2010) (citations and quotation marks omitted).

PLEA COLLOQUY

"Where a defendant wishing to withdraw a guilty plea challenges the voluntary or intelligent nature of his plea, it is ordinarily the Commonwealth's burden to show by means of a contemporaneous or reconstructed record of the plea that it was entered understandably and voluntarily. . . .

"A plea is intelligently made when the defendant has knowledge of the elements of the charges against him. . . . There must be an explanation by the judge or defense counsel of the elements of the crimes charged or an admission by the defendant to the facts constituting those crimes. . . . This requirement can be satisfied in one of several ways: (1) by the judge explaining to the defendant the elements of the crime; (2) by counsel's representation that she has explained to the defendant the elements he admits by his plea; or (3) by the defendant's stated admission to facts recited during the colloquy which constitute the unexplained elements. . . . The judge must ensure that the defendant is informed, on the record and in open court, of the three constitutional rights which are waived by a plea of guilty: the right to trial, the right to confront one's accusers, and the privilege against self-incrimination." *Commonwealth v. Correa*, 43 Mass. App. Ct. 714, 716–17 (1997) (citations and quotation marks omitted).

However, "[g]iven the long delay [10 years] in the defendant's attack on his guilty pleas, it is appropriate to accord the plea proceedings a presumption of regularity [thus putting the burden on the defendant] . . . to persuade the judge that he was without legal assistance at the time of the pleas." *Commonwealth v. Gonzales*, 43 Mass. App. Ct. 926 (1997). *See Commonwealth v. Lopez*, 426 Mass. 657 (1998); *Commonwealth v. Grant*, 426 Mass. 667 (1998). *See also Commonwealth v. Pingaro*, 44 Mass. App. Ct. 41, 49–50 (1997) ("A defendant's naked claim that he did not receive a constitutionally adequate guilty plea colloquy does not automatically thrust upon the Commonwealth the burden of proving the existence of a contemporaneous record establishing that the plea was entered knowingly and voluntarily. Rather, the initial burden is on the moving defendant to present some articulable reason which the motion judge deems a credible indicator that the presumptively proper guilty plea proceedings were constitutionally defective, above and beyond a movant's credulity straining contentions regarding questions the judge did not ask almost sixteen years earlier and reliance upon the mere nonexistence of a transcript of the plea proceedings." (citations, quotation marks, footnote and punctuation omitted)). *See also Commonwealth v. DeCologero*, 49 Mass. App. Ct. 93 (2000); *Commonwealth v. Andrews*, 49 Mass. App. Ct. 201 (2000).

Collateral consequences. "It is settled in Massachusetts that a defendant need not be advised of contingent or collateral consequences." *Commonwealth v. Hason*, 27 Mass. App. Ct. 840, 843 (1989); *see also Commonwealth v. Pingaro*, 44 Mass. App. Ct. 41, 55 n.18 (1997).

POLYGRAPH TEST

"In *Commonwealth v. Steward*, 422 Mass. 385, 389 (1996), we stated that, '[i]f polygraphic evidence is to be admissible in a given case, it seems likely that its reliability will be established by proof in a given case that a qualified tester who had conducted the test had in similar circumstances demonstrated, in a statistically valid number of independently verified and controlled tests, the high level of accuracy of the conclusions that the tester reached in those tests.'" *Commonwealth v. Duguay*, 430 Mass. 397, 402 (1999).

POSSESSION OF MEANS TO COMMIT CRIME

"The defendants contend that a mask taken from Ware at the time of his arrest had no connection to any of the crimes committed . . . , and that it was impermissibly introduced as evidence of Ware's propensity toward crime. *See Commonwealth v. Yelle*, 19 Mass. App. Ct. 465, 472 (1985).

"The absence of any evidence that the crimes were committed with the use of a mask is not determinative. Evidence of a defendant's possession of the means to commit a crime within a reasonable time of the crime charged is admissible without proof that that particular means was in fact the one used. *See Commonwealth v. O'Toole*, 326 Mass. 35, 39 (1950). In the *O'Toole* case a handgun found in the defendant's room was admitted in evidence because the handle was capable of causing the blunt trauma suffered by the victim. There was no direct evidence that the injuries were caused by that handgun, but it was relevant to show that the defendant had the means to commit the crime.

"Here, the mask was relevant to show that Ware had the intent and means to rob. The mask is a thermal type mask that covers the nose and lower half of the face, with velcro straps that hold it in place at the base of the skull. A flap covers the bridge of the nose but not the nostrils, and holes in the area covering the mouth permit ease in breathing and talking. As the temperature at about 9 P.M. on May 6, 1993, was seventy

11

degrees, the jury could reasonably infer that there was no apparent reason for Ware to have that type of mask, except to assist him in committing robberies, if necessary. There was no error." *Commonwealth v. Evans*, 438 Mass. 142, 151–52 (2002).

PRIMA FACIE EVIDENCE

1. "Prima facie evidence is evidence that, until its effect is overcome by other evidence, compels the conclusion that the evidence is true. When evidence is introduced that contradicts the prima facie evidence, however, the prima facie evidence loses its artificial force and a factual issue arises. In these circumstances, the prima facie evidence is no more significant than any other evidence, but must be weighed equally with all other evidence to determine whether a particular fact has been proved. Furthermore, the burden of persuasion always remains on the party who must prove the point, even though the party is aided by prima facie evidence." *Burns v. Commonwealth*, 430 Mass. 444, 450–51 (1999) (citations omitted).

2. "When instructing a jury on the use of so-called prima facie evidence, it is essential that the judge convey to the jury the sense that such evidence carries no particular presumption of validity. . . . Rather, the weight to be accorded prima facie evidence is a matter left entirely to the jury's discretion. . . . As a result, prima facie evidence, like other evidence adduced at trial, may be disregarded whether or not contradicted by any evidence offered by the opposing party." *Commonwealth v. Berrio*, 43 Mass. App. Ct. 836, 837–38 (1997).

PRIOR BAD ACTS

Other crimes, wrongs or acts. "Evidence of prior bad acts may not be introduced for the purpose of showing the accused's propensity to commit the crime charged. See *Commonwealth v. Helfant*, 398 Mass. 214, 224 (1986). Such evidence may be admissible, however, if relevant for some other probative purpose, including for the purpose of showing intent, motive, state of mind, or some other relevant issue at trial. See *Commonwealth v. Leonard*, 428 Mass. 782, 786 (1999); *Commonwealth v. Rodriguez*, 425 Mass. 361, 370–71 (1997), and cases cited. These determinations are left to the sound discretion of the judge, see *Commonwealth v. Marrero*, 427 Mass. 65, 67–68 (1998), whose decision to admit such evidence will be upheld absent clear error. See *Commonwealth v. Kater*, 432 Mass. 404, 415 (2000), and cases cited. Here, [the witness]'s testimony that the defendant had used cocaine in his apartment was relevant to prove the defendant's motive for breaking into [the witness]'s apartment on the night of the murder. Testimony that a probation officer accompanied police officers to the defendant's home with a default warrant was relevant to explain the sequence of events that took place on the day the defendant was arrested. Finally, the defendant's statement that he had been involved in other 'B and Es' was relevant to prove the defendant's intent and to support his admission that he had broken into the victim's house on the night of the murder. The challenged testimony in context, '[the defendant] stated that he had done a lot of B and Es but he had never killed anybody' was entirely consistent with the theory of defense, and, as a practical matter, even may have helped the defendant. We conclude that the above evidence properly was admitted, and, thus, his trial counsel cannot be faulted for failing to object." *Commonwealth v. DelValle*, 443 Mass. 782, 790–91 (2005).

"What is troubling here is that evidence of plan, prior pattern, etc., was already adequately, if not overwhelmingly,

established via the testimony of the eight victims, all of whose cases were appropriately joined for trial. It is thus difficult to discern how the probative value of the five prior bad act witnesses added anything consequence.

"That being said, it is also clear that the judge assiduously instructed the jury, see *Commonwealth v. McGeoghean*, 412 Mass. 839, 842 (1992), which took those instruction to heart, as evidenced by its split verdict. *See Commonwealth v. Walker*, 442 Mass. 185, 202–03 (2004). Under these circumstances, the defendant is unable to demonstrate sufficient prejudice to warrant reversal of his convictions." *Commonwealth v. Ramos*, 63 Mass. App. Ct. 379, 382 (2005).

Proposed Rules of Evidence 404(b). This states the current status of the law.

Judge's discretion. "The defendant argues that evidence concerning the May 28 break-in itself should not have been admitted, because it merely tended to smear the defendant's character. 'In Massachusetts, evidence of other criminal behavior may not be admitted to prove the propensity of the accused to commit the indicted offense but it is admissible for other relevant probative purposes.' *Commonwealth v. Gallison*, 383 Mass. 659, 672 (1981), citing *Commonwealth v. Chalifouz*, 362 Mass. 811, 815–16 (1973). The admission of such evidence generally is 'a matter on which the opinion of the trial judge will be accepted on review except for palpable error.' *Commonwealth v. Young*, 382 Mass. 448, 462–463 (1981)." *Commonwealth v. Cordle*, 404 Mass. 733, 744 (1989).

"While the Commonwealth is prohibited from introducing evidence of a defendant's criminal or wrongful behavior to show a tendency of bad character or propensity to commit the crime charged, such evidence is admissible for other relevant probative purposes. 'Furthermore, "[t]he admission of such evidence generally is 'a matter on which the opinion of the trial judge will be accepted on review except for palpable error' . . . .'"

"'Without the challenged evidence' the assault and battery 'could have appeared to the jury as an essentially inexplicable act of violence.' In this situation where a man is assaulted in the house of a female friend by her estranged boy friend, admitting evidence of such prior events enables the prosecutor to present a full picture of the incident. Since this evidence related to motive, intent, or state of mind, its admission was within the sound discretion of the judge. . . . [T]he law does not require a judge to give limiting jury instructions regarding the purpose for which evidence is offered unless so requested by the defendant."

Commonwealth v. Leonardi, 413 Mass. 757, 763–64 (1992) (citations omitted). *See also Commonwealth v. Montanino*, 409 Mass. 500, 505 (1991); *Commonwealth v. Robertson*, 408 Mass. 747, 750–51 (1990).

See note(s) on prior bad acts following G.L. c. 265, § 24.

PRIOR CONSISTENT STATEMENT

"Generally, a witness's prior consistent statement is inadmissible. However, a witness's prior statement is admissible where a claim is made that the witness's in-court statement is of recent contrivance or is the product of inducement or bias. The trial judge has a range of discretion in determining whether a suggestion of recent contrivance exists in the circumstances." *Commonwealth v. Fryar*, 425 Mass. 237, 252 (1997) (citations omitted).

See also Commonwealth v. Brookins, 416 Mass. 97, 102–03 (1993) ("The general rule is that a witness's prior consistent statement is not admissible, even though the witness's

11

prior inconsistent statement has already been admitted. The reason for that rule is that evidence that a witness has given an out-of-court account of an event or transaction that contradicts his in-court testimony fairly warrants an inference that the witness is unreliable, and that inference is not dissipated by the fact that the witness has also given another out-of-court statement that is consistent with his testimony. The contradiction and suggestion of unreliability remain. However, when a witness is sought to be impeached, by cross-examination or by independent evidence, tending to show that at the time of giving his evidence he was under a strong bias or in such a situation as to put him under a sort of moral duress to testify in a particular way . . . it is competent to rebut this ground of impeachment and to support the credit of the witness by showing that, when he was under no such bias, or when he was free from any influence or pressure, he made statements similar to those which he has given at the trial. The rule is based on logic. Of course, to be admissible, the witness's out-of-court statement that is consistent with his testimony must have been made before he became subject to the bias or pressure that is claimed to have influenced his testimony.") (citations and quotations marks omitted).

PRIOR CONVICTIONS
See notes following G.L. c. 233, § 21.

PRIOR INCONSISTENT STATEMENT
"That question is whether the trial judge erred by admitting in evidence for substantive purposes four questions among many that had been put to the alleged victim in the course of her testimony before the grand jury, and her answers to those four questions. In her testimony before the grand jury, the alleged victim had stated that the defendant had sexually abused her since she was about nine years old and on many occasions had sexual intercourse with her since she was twelve. However, at trial, having been called as a witness by the Commonwealth, she testified that the sexual abuse had never happened and that she had lied to the grand jury and others because she was angry with her father."

The Supreme Judicial Court affirmed the trial judge's decisions to admit the grand jury answers as probative evidence. *Commonwealth v. Berrio*, 407 Mass. 37, 44 (1990).

The Supreme Judicial Court relied on *Commonwealth v. Daye*, 393 Mass. 55 (1984), the case which "simply adopted proposed Mass. R. Evidence 801 (d)(1)(A) subject to [certain declared] conditions." *Commonwealth v. Berrio*, 407 Mass. at 45. Those conditions were outlined in the *Daye* holding:

"In summary, we hold that a prior inconsistent statement is admissible as probative if made under oath before a grand jury, provided the witness can be effectively cross-examined as to the accuracy of the statement, the statement was not coerced and was more than a mere confirmation or denial of an allegation by the interrogator, and other evidence tending to prove the issue is presented."

Commonwealth v. Daye, 393 Mass. at 75 (footnote omitted).

"Normally prior inconsistent statements are not admissible to establish the truth of the matter asserted. Where there is no objection, however, and no request for a limiting instruction, the statements may be considered as substantive evidence." *Commonwealth v. Ashley*, 427 Mass. 620, 627–28 (1998) (citations and quotation marks omitted).

"In this case, we determine that the *Daye* rule may appropriately be expanded to apply to c. 209A affidavits that

result in the issuance of an abuse protection order." *Commonwealth v. Belmer*, 78 Mass. App. Ct. 62, 65 (2010).

"[W]here prior inconsistent statements relate to a main issue at trial, the judge has 'no discretion to preclude their use for impeachment purposes.'" *Commonwealth v. Donnelly*, 33 Mass. App. Ct. 189, 197 (1992).

PRIOR INCONSISTENT STATEMENT (DEFENDANT'S PRETRIAL AFFIDAVIT)
"[A] defendant's testimony in support of a motion to suppress evidence . . . may not be admitted against him at trial on the issue of guilt. This rule, however, has not been applied to exclude the use of prior inconsistent statements for impeachment purposes . . . . [A] judge should conduct a voir dire on the question of impeaching a defendant with a pretrial affidavit and, if the evidence is admitted, on request the judge should instruct the jury to consider the omission of any facts from the affidavit only if they find that the witness naturally should have spoken up in the circumstances." *Commonwealth v. Rivera*, 425 Mass. 633, 637, 641 (1997).

PRIOR RECORDED STATEMENT
"In criminal cases, the admission of prior recorded testimony from an unavailable witness implicates the right of confrontation under the Sixth Amendment to the United States Constitution and art. 12 of the Massachusetts Declaration of Rights. Prior recorded testimony may be admitted in evidence where the witness is unavailable, if the prior testimony was given under oath in a proceeding where the issues are substantially the same as the current proceeding, and the party against whom it is being offered had a reasonable opportunity and similar motivation to cross-examine the witness. Before allowing the Commonwealth to introduce prior recorded testimony of an alleged unavailable witness, the judge must be satisfied that the Commonwealth has made a good faith effort to locate and produce the witness at trial. Whether the Commonwealth has been sufficiently diligent in attempting to obtain the witness's attendance depends upon what is a reasonable effort in light of the peculiar facts of the case." *Commonwealth v. Robinson*, 451 Mass. 672, 674–75 (2008) (citations, quotation marks, and footnote omitted).

"[A] witness is unavailable if there is an unacceptable risk that the witness's health would be jeopardized by testifying in court on the scheduled date and either (1) a continuance would not reduce the risk to an acceptable level, or (2) a continuance would make the risk acceptable but would not serve the interests of justice.

"In addition, before determining whether to admit prior recorded testimony of an unavailable witness, the judge should consider whether there would be an unacceptable risk that the witness's health would be jeopardized if the witness's testimony were obtained through a deposition at a suitable out-of-court location, such as an attorney's office, the witness's home, or a health facility.

"Where a witness is unavailable due to illness or infirmity, the 'good faith effort' required of the Commonwealth is to promptly inform the court and the defendant of the unavailability of the witness once the Commonwealth learns of it, so that they have an adequate opportunity to learn more about the witness's medical condition and to explore the alternative of a continuance or a deposition." *Commonwealth v. Housewright*, 470 Mass. 665, 672–73, 674 (2015) (citations omitted).

11

PROBABLE CAUSE

Arrest. "There is probable cause to arrest a suspect if at the moment of arrest, the facts and circumstances within the knowledge of the police are enough to warrant a prudent person in believing that the individual arrested has committed an offense. [O]r, to put it another way, probable cause to arrest requires more than mere suspicion but something less than evidence sufficient to warrant a conviction." *In the Matter of a Grand Jury Investigation*, 427 Mass. 221, 224 (1998) (citations, quotation and punctuation marks omitted).

Indictment. "There is probable cause to indict a suspect if there is sufficient evidence to establish the identity of the accused, and probable cause to arrest him or her." *In the Matter of a Grand Jury Investigation*, 427 Mass. 221, 224 (1998) (citations and quotation marks omitted).

Probable cause hearing. "The term imports a higher standard when a District Court judge at a probable cause hearing decides whether a criminal defendant should be held for trial. Probable cause to hold a defendant for trial requires the Commonwealth to present evidence sufficient to warrant a conviction (the 'directed verdict' rule)." *In the Matter of a Grand Jury Investigation*, 427 Mass. 221, 224 (1998) (citations and quotation marks omitted).

See Mass.R.Crim.P. 25 for discussion of directed verdict.

PROFILE EVIDENCE

"Profile evidence characteristically presents to the trier the description of a stereotypical offender—say a child batterer—and suggests that because the defendant conforms to the stylized description, he is by that token proved guilty. Such a line of inference is not permitted. . . . [T]he mere fact that a defendant fits the profile does not tend to prove that a particular defendant [committed the crime]. . . ." There is however a distinction between this type of testimony and modus operandi testimony, which is admissible. *Commonwealth v. Frias*, 47 Mass. App. Ct. 293, 296 (1999) (citations and quotation marks omitted).

PRO SE DEFENDANTS

See also Right to Counsel, below.

"[W]e have noted the importance of protecting the defendant's autonomy in decisions relating to his defense. Even in the face of the obvious truth that the average defendant lacks the skill necessary to protect oneself in a criminal proceeding, the United States Constitution and the Massachusetts Constitution protect a defendant's right to proceed pro se because it is the defendant who must suffer the personal consequences of a conviction. It is the defendant who must be free personally to decide whether in his particular case counsel is to his advantage. And although he may conduct his own defense ultimately to his own detriment, his choice must be honored out of that respect for the individual which is the lifeblood of the law." *Commonwealth v. Federici*, 427 Mass. 740, 744 (1998) (citations and quotation marks omitted).

Self representation. "A criminal defendant has a right to reject the appointment of counsel and represent himself at trial. The right to self-representation, however, is not absolute unless there is an unequivocal and timely invocation of the right accompanied by an adequate waiver of the right to counsel." *Commonwealth v. Lameire*, 50 Mass. App. Ct. 271, 275 n.2 (2000) (citations and quotation marks omitted).

Pro se litigants. "Pro se litigants are held to the same standards as practicing attorneys." *Jackson v. Commonwealth*, 430 Mass. 260, 264 (1999).

PSYCHIATRIC, PSYCHOLOGICAL, PRIVILEGED RECORDS

To secure these records in criminal cases, the protocol outlined in *Commonwealth v. Dwyer*, 448 Mass. 122 (2006) and *Commonwealth v. Lampron*, 441 Mass. 265 (2004) must be followed. *Dwyer* replaced the protocol originally set out in *Commonwealth v. Bishop*, 416 Mass. 169 (1993).

Duty of prosecutor. "The duty to disclose exculpatory information does not require a prosecutor to make defense-directed inquiries to independent witnesses, including complainants." *Commonwealth v. Beal*, 429 Mass. 530, 531 (1999).

Records unprivileged absent affirmative assertion by patient. "Absent an affirmative assertion [by the patient] of the privileges established by G.L. c. 233, § 20B, and G.L. c. 112, § 135B, the [trial] court must treat such records as if they [are] unprivileged." *Commonwealth v. Oliveira*, 438 Mass. 325, 337 (2002).

PSYCHOLOGICAL EVALUATIONS

Right of counsel (probation evaluation). "[W]e would regard as doubtful the validity of the proposition that the defendant has a right to have an attorney present at a psychological evaluation conducted in accordance with the terms of validly imposed probation. . . . A postconviction probationary evaluation is not a criminal proceeding, let alone a critical stage entitling a defendant to protection under either the Sixth Amendment or art. 12. Therefore, the right to counsel does not apply. A probationer is no longer considered a criminal defendant because he has already been convicted of a crime at trial." *Commonwealth v. Woods*, 427 Mass. 169, 174–75 (1998) (citations and footnote omitted).

Right to counsel (pre-trial evaluation). See Notes to Mass.R.Crim.P. 14 for a discussion of the right to counsel at a court-ordered pre-trial psychological evaluation.

RADIO TRANSMISSIONS

"Where probable cause is based on a radio message to police officers, the Commonwealth must demonstrate the reliability of the factual basis of the transmission. Evidence must be adduced demonstrating that the police officer responsible for issuing the radio communication had reliable information that a crime had occurred and that the instrumentalities or evidence of that crime would be found in the vehicle described in the broadcast." *Commonwealth v. White*, 422 Mass. 487, 496 (1996) (citations and quotation marks omitted). In *White*, the Commonwealth met its burden by showing that the broadcast was based on eyewitness accounts as well as on independent observations by the police verifying that information.

REBUTTAL EVIDENCE

"Where the accused has made a request for evidence sufficiently specific to place the prosecution on notice as to what the defense desires, the evidence must be disclosed. The Commonwealth, therefore, was in violation of a discovery order [and should have revealed a potential rebuttal witness]." *Commonwealth v. Giontzis*, 47 Mass. App. Ct. 450, 459 (1999).

REASONABLE DOUBT

"[G]oing forward, Massachusetts judges sitting on criminal trials are to instruct the jury as follows:

The burden is on the Commonwealth to prove beyond a reasonable doubt that the defendant is guilty of the charge(s) made against him (her).

11

What is proof beyond a reasonable doubt? The term is often used and probably pretty well understood, though it is not easily defined. Proof beyond a reasonable doubt does not mean proof beyond all possible doubt, for everything in the lives of human beings is open to some possible or imaginary doubt. A charge is proved beyond a reasonable doubt if, after you have compared and considered all of the evidence, you have in your minds an abiding conviction, to a moral certainty, that the charge is true. When we refer to moral certainty, we mean the highest degree of certainty possible in matters relating to human affairs—based solely on the evidence that has been put before you in this case.

I have told you that every person is presumed to be innocent until he or she is proved guilty, and that the burden of proof is on the prosecutor. If you evaluate all the evidence and you still have a reasonable doubt remaining, the defendant is entitled to the benefit of that doubt and must be acquitted.

It is not enough for the Commonwealth to establish a probability, even a strong probability, that the defendant is more likely to be guilty than not guilty. That is not enough. Instead, the evidence must convince you of the defendant's guilt to a reasonable and moral certainty; a certainty that convinces your understanding and satisfies your reason and judgment as jurors who are sworn to act conscientiously on the evidence.

This is what we mean by proof beyond a reasonable doubt.

In consequence of this decision, the traditional *Webster* charge should no longer be used as the instruction on reasonable doubt in this Commonwealth." *Commonwealth v. Russell*, 470 Mass. 464, 477–78 (2015).

RECUSAL

"The matter of recusal is generally left to the discretion of the trial judge . . . and an abuse of that discretion must be shown to reverse a decision not to allow recusal. A judge must consult first his own emotions and conscience to determine whether he possesses the capacity to rule fairly at trial. Then, a judge must also conduct an objective appraisal of whether his impartiality might reasonably be questioned. A judge's impartiality might reasonably be questioned in circumstances where he has a personal bias or prejudice concerning a party, or where he served as a lawyer in the matter of controversy, or a lawyer with whom he previously practiced law served during such association as a lawyer concerning the matter." *Commonwealth v. Daye*, 435 Mass. 463, 469–70 (2001) (citations and quotation marks omitted).

REDIRECT EXAMINATION

"'The scope of redirect examination of a witness is within the sound discretion of the trial judge. . . . A defendant who claims, on appeal, an abuse of discretion, assume a heavy burden.' *Commonwealth v. Maltais*, 387 Mass. 79, 92 (1982)." *Commonwealth v. D'Entremont*, 36 Mass. App. Ct. 474, 481–82 (1994).

"On redirect, a witness should have the opportunity to explain why he or she did or did not do certain things which were the subject of questioning on cross-examination." *Commonwealth v. Charles*, 47 Mass. App. Ct. 191, 192 (1999). *See also Commonwealth v. Emence*, 47 Mass. App. Ct. 299,

303 (1999) ("It is well established that a witness may explain, modify, or correct damaging testimony that was elicited on cross-examination.").

REDUCTION OF CHARGES

"Absent some legal basis for doing so, a judge may not reduce the charges against a defendant over the Commonwealth's objection. Enforcement of a prosecutor's promise which, on principles of contract law, would be an enforceable contract is one legal basis upon which such relief may be granted." *Commonwealth v. Doe*, 412 Mass. 815, 818 (1992) (citation omitted).

RELEVANCY

Issue: "Did the judge err by admitting in evidence knives found near the defendant at the time of his arrest ten weeks after Nicholson was assaulted?" *Commonwealth v. Marangiello*, 410 Mass. 452, 453 (1991) (citations and punctuation omitted).

Answer: No.

"Whether evidence is relevant in any particular instance and whether the evidence is so inflammatory in nature as to outweigh its probative value and thus preclude its admission are questions addressed to the sound discretion of the trial judge. The test of relevancy is a matter on which the opinion of the trial judge will be accepted on review except for palpable error. The fact that, at or about the time of a crime, a defendant had a weapon that could have been used in committing the crime is admissible in the judge's discretion. [I]t is commonly competent to show the possession by a defendant of an instrument capable of being used in the commission of the crime, without direct proof that particular instrument was in fact the one used. Also, whether the knives were discovered at a time too remote from the crime to be probative is a decision within the trial judge's discretion." *Commonwealth v. Marangiello*, 410 Mass. at 456. *See also Commonwealth v. Lora*, 43 Mass. App. Ct. 136, 142 (1997) ("Evidence is relevant if it renders the desired inference more probable than it would have been without it. As long as evidence tends to establish the issue or constitutes a link in the chain of proof, it may be sufficiently relevant.") (citations and quotation marks omitted).

REOPENING THE EVIDENCE

"The decision whether 'to admit additional evidence after a party has rested lies in the sound discretion of the trial judge.' *Jones v. Vappi & Co.*, 28 Mass. App. Ct. 77, 83 (1989) (while holding that no abuse of discretion occurred by denying motion to reopen, 'to admit additional evidence after the evidence has formally closed may be indulgently exercised to remedy an oversight discovered shortly thereafter, before parties have changed position and before the case has gone to a next phase' was implicit in judge's discretion)." *Weber v. Coast to Coast Med., Inc.*, 83 Mass. App. Ct. 478, 481 (2013).

REPUTATION

Victim. "A defendant who claims he killed in self-defense may offer evidence of a victim's reputation as a violent and quarrelsome person. The evidence of the victim's reputation is relevant even if the defendant did not know of the reputation at the time of the crime, if it is offered to prove that the victim and not the defendant was likely to be the 'first aggressor.' *Commonwealth v. Adjutant*, 443 Mass. 649, 660 (2005).

11

"After surveying the state of the law in jurisdictions throughout the country, we are persuaded that evidence of a victim's prior violent conduct may be probative of whether the victim was the first aggressor where a claim of self-defense has been asserted and the identity of the first aggressor is in dispute. Consequently, when such circumstances are present, we hold, as a matter of common-law principle, that trial judges have the discretion to admit in evidence specific incidents of violence that the victim is reasonably alleged to have initiated." *Commonwealth v. Adjutant*, 443 Mass. 649, 650 (2005).

"[E]vidence of the victim's experience as a boxer, trained fighter, or martial artist was inadmissible to prove he was the first aggressor." *Commonwealth v. Amaral*, 78 Mass. App. Ct. 557, 559 (2011).

"Once the defense has opened the door as to the issue of the victim's character, the prosecution can, on rebuttal, introduce evidence of the victim's reputation in the community for peacefulness."
Commonwealth v. Lapointe, 402 Mass. 321, 325 (1988) (citations omitted).

"When defense counsel told the judge that he was going to call witnesses who would testify to the reputation of the defendant for truthfulness, he asked the judge to rule that the Commonwealth not be permitted to cross-examine these witnesses about false statements made by the defendant regarding his military service record. . . .

"The language in the case of *Commonwealth v. Montanino*, 27 Mass. App. Ct. 130, 136 (1989), to the effect that a trial judge may permit cross-examination on matters that are 'inconsistent or conflict with the character trait to which the witness has testified' is in point.

"In *Montanino*, the Appeals Court said, *supra* at 137: 'The credibility of the witness is tested in the following manner—if the witness states that he has not heard of the report of prior misconduct, his professed knowledge of the defendant's reputation in the community may be doubted by the jury or, if he states that he has heard of the report but still testifies that the defendant's reputation is good in the community, the jury may consider whether the witness is fabricating or whether the community standards in regard to character are too low.'"
Commonwealth v. Brown, 411 Mass. 115, 117–18 (1991).

RESTITUTION

"An order of restitution must be supported by facts and evidence. The procedure for establishing an order of restitution must be fair and reasonable. The defendant must have an opportunity to be heard and to cross-examine witnesses. The defendant is entitled to rebut the victim's estimate of the injury with the defendant's own experts or witnesses. Finally, the Commonwealth bears the burden of proving the amount of the loss by a preponderance of the evidence." *Commonwealth v. McIntyre*, 436 Mass. 829, 834 (2002) (citations omitted).

"We adopt the less formulaic approach announced by the Supreme Court of Florida in *Glaubius v. State*, 688 So. 2d 913, 915 (Fla. 1997), and hold that the scope of restitution is limited to "loss or damage [that] is causally connected to the offense and bears a significant relationship to the offense." *Glaubius v. State*, 688 So. 2d 913, 915 (Fla. 1997) Furthermore, "we look to the underlying facts of the charged offense, not the name of the crime [of which the defendant was convicted, or] to which the defendant entered a plea." *State v. Landrum*, 66 Wash. App. 791, 799 (1992). *Commonwealth v. McIntyre*, 436 Mass. 829, 835 (2002).

"Whether an award of restitution that takes account of property damage as part of a criminal conviction of assault and battery by means of a dangerous weapon, in the absence of a conviction of a crime based on property damage, exceeds the proper scope of a restitution order. We answer the question in the negative . . . ." *Commonwealth v. McIntyre*, 436 Mass. 829, 829–30 (2002).

"[The judge should also] consider whether the defendant is financially able to pay the amount ordered. In that regard, the judge may take into consideration the defendant's employment history and financial prospects [and whether there is a payment schedule as opposed to an open ended order]." *Commonwealth v. Rescia*, 44 Mass. App. Ct. 909, 910 (1998) (citations and quotation marks omitted).

"We discern no requirement that strict evidentiary rules apply at restitution hearings." *Commonwealth v. Casanova*, 65 Mass. App. Ct. 750, 755 (2006) (citations omitted).

"[W]e treat restitution as an entirely judicially determined penalty, lacking any legislative parameters . . . Thus, restitution proceedings as they are currently conducted neither usurp the jury's fact-finding function nor deteriorate the constitutional protections afforded to criminal defendants.

. . .

"We now affirm what we stated in *McIntyre*, 436 Mass. at 833, . . . and elsewhere that a judge has the authority to conduct restitution hearings and, in so doing, make factual determinations relevant to the restitution award. As long as the proper procedural mechanisms are employed in the restitution hearing, we see no violation of the Sixth Amendment or art. 12 in this approach." *Commonwealth v. Denehy*, 466 Mass. 723, 737–38 (2014).

"Because we have not previously had the opportunity to articulate the legal standard for determining the defendant's ability to pay restitution, we do so here for the first time. In determining the defendant's ability to pay, the judge must consider the financial resources of the defendant, including income and net assets, and the defendant's financial obligations, including the amount necessary to meet minimum basic human needs such as food, shelter, and clothing for the defendant and his or her dependents." *Commonwealth v. Henry*, 475 Mass. 117, 126 (2016).

RIGHT TO COUNSEL
See also Pro Se Defendants, above.

Discharge. "A defendant's request to discharge counsel on the day trial is scheduled to begin is a matter left to the sound discretion of the trial judge. The defendant bears the burden of establishing good cause to discharge counsel. . . . [The] judge must allow [the] defendant to present reasons he moved to discharge counsel. [Here t]here was nothing in the defendant's response that raised even a suggestion for the kind of problems—conflict of interest, incompetence of counsel, an irreconcilable breakdown in communications—that might have outweighed the Commonwealth's interest in the expeditious trial of this case." *Commonwealth v. Ortiz*, 50 Mass. App. Ct. 304, 305–06 (2000) (citations and quotation marks omitted).

RULE 1:28
"A summary decision pursuant to rule 1:28, issued after the date of this opinion, [February 25, 2008 (ed.),] may be cited for its persuasive value but . . . not as binding precedent.

"In an effort to ensure that all litigants have equal access to rule 1:28 decisions their adversaries may cite, the court is proposing today a rule requiring, inter alia, inclusion of the rule 1:28 decision in an addendum to the brief in which the decision is cited. Until proceedings on that proposed rule are completed, litigants should include the full text of the decision as an addendum to the brief in which it is cited."

Chace v. Curran, 71 Mass. App. Ct. 258, 261 n.4 (2008).

RULE OF LENITY

"[The] rule [of lenity] may be applied when a statute can plausibly be found to be ambiguous to give the defendant the benefit of the ambiguity." *Commonwealth v. Roucoulet*, 413 Mass. 647, 652 (1992).

SCHOOL RECORDS

"There is no privilege which would prevent the introduction of relevant school records in evidence at a trial. School records are not subject to public disclosure under G.L. c. 66, § 10. See G.L. c. 4, § 7. Twenty-sixth(c). However, regulations issued by the Department of Education provide that third parties may gain access to school records upon service of a lawfully issued subpoena." *Commonwealth v. Beauchemin*, 410 Mass. 181, 185 (1991).

SEARCH AND SEIZURE

See commentary accompanying G.L. c. 276.

SELECTIVE PROSECUTION

"There is . . . a well-settled presumption that criminal prosecutions are undertaken in good faith, without intent to discriminate. As such, the defendant bears the initial burden of presenting evidence which raises at least a reasonable inference of impermissible discrimination. To be successful, the defendant must show (1) that a broader class of persons than those prosecuted has violated the law; (2) that failure to prosecute was either consistent or deliberate; and (3) that the decision not to prosecute was based on an impermissible classification such as race, religion, or sex. Once a defendant has raised a reasonable inference of selective prosecution, the Commonwealth must rebut that inference or suffer dismissal of the underlying complaint." *Commonwealth v. Lafaso*, 49 Mass. App. Ct. 179, 182 (2000) (citations and quotation marks omitted).

SELF-DEFENSE

"A person may defend himself with the use of nondeadly force if he reasonably fears for his personal safety. Deadly force may be used in defense of oneself only on a reasonable belief that one is in imminent danger of death or serious bodily harm, and that no other means will suffice to prevent such harm. Deadly force is . . . force intended or likely to cause death or great bodily harm." *Commonwealth v. Cataldo*, 423 Mass. 318, 321 (1996) (citations and quotation marks omitted).

"[I]t is a rule that where the issue of self-defense has been sufficiently raised by the evidence, the defendant is entitled to an instruction which places on the Commonwealth the burden of disproving the factor of self-defense beyond a reasonable doubt. To raise the issue sufficiently, the evidence viewed in the light most favorable to the defendant must permit a reasonable doubt whether the defendant (1) had reasonable ground to believe and actually did believe that he was in imminent danger of death or serious bodily harm, from which he could save himself only by using deadly force, (2) had availed himself of all proper means to avoid physical combat before resorting to the use of deadly force, and (3) used no more force than was reasonably necessary in all the circumstances of the case. . . . [W]here there was no evidence raising the issue of self-defense, a judge may so inform the jury."

Commonwealth v. Reed, 427 Mass. 100, 102–03 (1998) (citations and quotation marks omitted).

First Aggressor. "[W]e are persuaded that evidence of a victim's prior violent conduct may be probative of whether the victim was the first aggressor where a claim of self-defense has been asserted and the identity of the first aggressor is in dispute. Consequently, when such circumstances are present, we hold, as a matter of common-law principle, that trial judges have the discretion to admit in evidence specific incidents of violence that the victim is reasonably alleged to have initiated." *Commonwealth v. Adjutant*, 443 Mass. 649, 650 (2005) (footnote omitted).

"The principal question before us concerns the rule adopted by this court in *Commonwealth v. Adjutant*, 443 Mass. 649 (2005). The question is this: during a trial where the defendant raises a claim of self-defense and, pursuant to Adjutant, has been permitted to introduce evidence of the victim's prior violent acts on the issue of the identity of the first aggressor, may the Commonwealth introduce evidence of the defendant's prior violent acts on that same issue—to be followed by an instruction that the jury may consider the evidence of both parties' violent acts on the findings of who was the first aggressor? We answer the question 'Yes,' provided that the Commonwealth gives the defendant notice appropriately in advance of its intent to introduce such evidence and the trial judge determines that introduction of such evidence is more probative of its intended purpose than prejudicial to the defendant." *Commonwealth v. Morales*, 464 Mass. 302, 302–03 (2013).

"This is the first time that we have addressed whether *Adjutant* evidence is admissible where it is essentially undisputed that the victim provoked or initiated a nondeadly assault, but where it is disputed whether the defendant or the victim was the first to use or threaten deadly force. Where a victim's prior act or acts of violence demonstrate a propensity for violence, we conclude that *Adjutant* evidence is as relevant to the issue of who initiated the use or threat of deadly force as it is to the issue of who initiated an earlier nondeadly assault, and such evidence may be admitted to assist the jury where either issue is in dispute, because the resolution of both issues may assist the jury in deciding whether the prosecution has met its burden of proving that the defendant did not act in self-defense." *Commonwealth v. Chambers*, 465 Mass. 520, 529–30 (2013).

Trespasser. "A person may use no more force than reasonably necessary to remove a trespasser." *Commonwealth v. Haddock*, 46 Mass. App. Ct. 246 (1999).

SELF-INCRIMINATION

"A witness may refuse to testify unless it is perfectly clear, from a careful consideration of all the circumstances in the case, that the witness is mistaken, and that the answer[s] cannot possibly have such tendency to incriminate. The privilege afforded not only extends to answers that would in themselves support a conviction but likewise embraces those which would furnish a link in the chain of evidence needed to prosecute.

"Nonetheless, a witness may not rely on a bald assertion of his privilege if the circumstances do not clearly indicate a possibility of self-incrimination. It is for the judge, rather than a witness or his attorney, to decide whether a witness's silence is justified. A witness must show a real risk that his answers to questions will tend to indicate his involvement in illegal activity, and not a mere imaginary, remote or speculative

11

possibility of prosecution." In certain limited instances an in-camera examination may be permissible. *Commonwealth v. Martin*, 423 Mass. 496, 502 (1996) (punctuation, quotation and citations omitted); *see also Commonwealth v. King*, 436 Mass. 252, 258 (2002).

Testimonial communications. "Fifth Amendment protection is unavailable when the evidence sought from a witness is real or physical rather than testimonial. Therefore, a suspect may be compelled to submit to field sobriety tests, provide fingernail scrapings, provide a voice exemplar, stand in a lineup, and furnish a blood sample. In order to be testimonial, an accused's communication must itself, explicitly or implicitly, relate a factual assertion or disclose information. The Fifth Amendment privilege against self-incrimination applies not only to verbal communications, but, as the term implicitly suggests, also to nonverbal acts that imply assertions . . . . [I]f the evidence in question is nontestimonial, then a witness can be compelled to yield that evidence under the Fifth Amendment." *Commonwealth v. Burgess*, 426 Mass. 206, 210–11 (1997) (citations, quotation marks and punctuation omitted).

Waiver by testimony. "A witness who voluntarily testifies regarding an incriminating fact waives his privilege against self-incrimination as to subsequent questions seeking related facts . . . . [T]he waiver by testimony rule applies only to the proceeding in which the testimony is given and does not extend to subsequent proceedings . . . . [T]estimony before a grand jury should not be considered a waiver of a witness's privilege against self-incrimination for the purpose of offering testimony at a subsequent trial on an indictment returned by that grand jury." *Commonwealth v. Burgess*, 426 Mass. at 500–01 (punctuation, quotation and citations omitted).

Waiver after assertion of privilege (assertion not forever binding). "We have been presented with, and know of, no authority, decisional or statutory, to support the notion that a validly asserted claim of the Fifth Amendment privilege is forever binding and cannot be subsequently waived." *Commonwealth v. Barnes-Miller*, 59 Mass. App. Ct. 832, 834–35 (2003) ("Although the complainant's reliance on her Fifth Amendment privilege during her deposition made her unavailable in that proceeding, there is nothing in G.L. c. 258B, § 3(m), that supports the claim that she became, as matter of law, an 'unavailable' witness in all other proceedings involving the same or related facts. Rather, § 3(m) simply provides that when a witness is served with lawful process, the witness cannot refuse to appear and be questioned. The complainant complied with the statute; she appeared at the deposition and responded to questions with her claim of privilege. Nor is there anything in § 3(m) which states or even suggests that the complainant's reliance on her Fifth Amendment privilege at the deposition precluded the defendant from thereafter seeking to speak with her about the criminal proceedings. Any assumption by the defendant that the complainant might decline such an interview is irrelevant. . . . Whether she intended to waive her privilege and testify was not a matter to be determined on the basis of her deposition or the representations of the prosecutor. As just noted, the complainant was free to waive her Fifth Amendment privilege and testify during the proceedings on her criminal complaint, albeit with potentially adverse consequences, or to stand on her privileged right of refusal to testify and run the risk of a required finding of not guilty on her criminal complaint.").

Article 12. "There are two significant aspects to the prohibition in art. 12 that a person not 'be compelled to accuse, or furnish evidence against himself.' First, the evidence must

have a testimonial aspect. If evidence sought is real or physical evidence, such as hair and blood samples, voice exemplars, fingerprints, lineups, sobriety tests, or breathalyzer tests, art. 12 does not protect a person from having to provide such evidence. Although the production of such evidence is compelled, it is not testimonial and hence is not subject to art. 12 protection. By contrast, conduct offered to show a defendant's state of mind is testimonial. Conduct evidence admitted to show consciousness of guilt is always testimonial because it tends to demonstrate that the defendant knew he was guilty.

"The second consideration under art. 12 is whether the State compelled the production of the testimonial evidence. In instances of a false alibi, fleeing the vicinity of the crime, or making false exculpatory statements, for example, compulsion is absent, and art. 12 does not bar the admission of such evidence. If, however, as we have said, the defendant's conduct is testimonial and if the police, by their request, force the defendant to choose between two potentially inculpatory alternatives, the defendant's refusal to comply with that request may not be introduced against him over objection without violating art. 12.

"Evidence of a defendant's outright refusal to provide fingerprints to the police may not be admitted as evidence of consciousness of guilt because, as we have just discussed, art. 12 forbids it. This case involves such a refusal. The fact that the defendant first agreed to provide prints and then failed to do so does not eliminate compulsion. The defendant had only two alternatives, each of which could be adverse to his interests. Because there was governmental compulsion, admission of evidence that the defendant did not appear at the police station to be fingerprinted violated his art. 12 rights. The error cannot be fairly said to have been harmless." *Commonwealth v. Conkey*, 430 Mass. 139, 142–43 (1999).

Right to comment upon defendant's refusal to produce evidence. "[W]hen a criminal defendant refuses to produce evidence that is the subject of a warrant or court order, admission of evidence concerning that refusal does not violate his rights under art. 12 because he does not face the choice that was integral to our decision in *Opinion of the Justices*, 412 Mass. 1201, 1211 (1992). The choice either to produce incriminating evidence or be punished with an inference of guilt in refusal is absent when a defendant's decision to cooperate is foreclosed by order of a judge." *Commonwealth v. Bly*, 448 Mass. 473, 497 (2007) (citation omitted).

Appellate Review of Hearing. "A Martin hearing poses the unique situation of compelling potentially incriminating testimony from a reluctant witness for the sole purpose of determining whether the witness has a valid privilege against self-incrimination. Having compelled such testimony, the court has an obligation to ensure that the compelled testimony not be used in any way, directly or indirectly, against the witness in any criminal case. . . . We decide here that the more limited determination on appeal of whether the judge erred in finding a valid invocation of the privilege can adequately be made by the appellate Justices alone, without disclosure to the parties of the content of the Martin hearing." *Pixley v. Commonwealth*, 453 Mass. 827, 834, 836 (2009) (citation omitted).

SENTENCING

"A judge has considerable latitude within the framework of the applicable statute to determine the appropriate individualized sentence. That sentence should reflect the judge's careful assessment of several goals: punishment, deterrence, protection of the public, and rehabilitation. In making that assessment, the judge may consider many factors which would not be relevant at trial including hearsay information about the defendant's character, behavior, and background.

"Federal due process principles do not prevent consideration at sentencing of a defendant's past uncharged misconduct. There is no Federal constitutional bar against a sentencing judge considering a convicted defendant's record of arrests, unresolved criminal charges against him, or other evidence of criminal conduct by him for which there has been no conviction. Due process would require resentencing if the sentencing judge had relied on information which was inaccurate or misleading[,] a prior conviction later revealed to be constitutionally infirm[,] or allegations of other criminal conduct which were wholly unreliable. Of course, a sentencing judge may not undertake to punish the defendant for any conduct other than that for which the defendant stands convicted in the particular case. Massachusetts decisions have recognized the relevance at sentencing of reliable evidence of the defendant's prior misconduct[, such as] indictments or other evidence of similar criminal conduct [and a] prior sexual abuse charge which had been dismissed".

Commonwealth v. Goodwin, 414 Mass. 88, 92–93 (1998) (citations, quotation and punctuation marks omitted).

See also the notes to Mass.R.Crim.P. 28–29 for further discussion relative to sentencing.

Cases placed on file. A case placed on file may be brought forward for sentencing. *See Commonwealth v. Connolly*, 49 Mass. App. Ct. 424, 425 (2000).

"[A]lthough our appellate jurisprudence on the practice of removing a case from the file typically has included only instances where a defendant either successfully appealed from a parallel conviction or violated some express condition of the filing, no common-law rule has so limited the practice . . . .

"It is true that once removed from the file, the sentencing judge retains the same discretion in punishment as that afforded the original trial judge. This discretion, however, cannot be exercised in a vacuum. Rather, the sentencing judge must consider the over-all scheme of punishment employed by the trial judge. The sword of Damocles still properly hangs over a defendant who has consented to placing his case on file, but it should not be wielded without restraint . . . .

"Further, although today we uphold the practice of the placing of cases on file with the consent of the defendant, we recognize that Massachusetts now stands alone in this regard. We believe there are valid reasons for continuing this common-law tradition, namely the discretion and flexibility afforded to judges, prosecutors, and defendants. In light of this landscape, we believe it warrants referring the future of placing indictments on file, including the necessity of colloquy confirming consent and enunciating express expectations of good behavior, to the rules committee of this court." *Commonwealth v. Simmons*, 448 Mass. 687, 696–700 (2007) (citations omitted).

Coercion. "A judge's involvement in plea negotiations violates a defendant's constitutional rights if the judge forces a guilty plea by putting the defendant on notice that he could expect more severe punishment if he insisted on a trial by jury." *Commonwealth v. Carter*, 50 Mass. App. Ct. 902, 904 (2000) (citation and quotation marks omitted).

Concurrent sentences. "When two or more sentences are to be served concurrently, the shorter ones are considered to be 'absorbed' within the longer sentence and a prisoner will not be released until the expiration of the longer sen-

tence." *Commonwealth v. Burden*, 48 Mass. App. Ct. 232, 235 (1999) (citation and quotation marks omitted).

Mitigating factors. "If representatives of the district attorney's office permitted the defendant reasonably to believe that his successful cooperation in obtaining evidence of substantial drug violations would lead to a sentencing recommendation of 'street time' only and if the defendant, reasonably relying on that apparent opportunity in order to aid his sentencing prospects, engaged in dangerous undercover work that he would have eschewed without the prospect of a 'street time' recommendation, fairness obliges the Commonwealth to make the sought-after sentencing recommendation." *Commonwealth v. Mr. M.*, 409 Mass. 538, 543–44 (1991).

Perjury. "A trial judge may not consider a defendant's alleged perjury on the witness stand in determining the punishment to impose for a criminal conviction . . . [as] a prospective defendant's inclination to testify may be chilled due to a trial judge's imposition of a harsher penalty if he or she disbelieves the defense." *Commonwealth v. McFadden*, 49 Mass. App. Ct. 441, 443 (2000) (citations and quotation marks omitted).

Probation v. suspended sentence. "If a prison sentence has been imposed but suspended, violation and consequent revocation of probation requires imposition of the sentence of incarceration. If there has been no sentence of imprisonment and the sentence is one of probation, the judge, in the event the probationer has violated a condition of probation, has discretion to consider alternatives to incarceration." *Commonwealth v. Christian*, 46 Mass. App. Ct. 477, 478 n.1, *aff'd*, 429 Mass. 1022 (1999) (citation omitted).

"In arriving at a new sentence, the resentencing judge had authority to consider information concerning the defendant's good conduct while he was incarcerated following his original sentencing. When imposing a sentence, judges are permitted considerable latitude.

"It is established that, in resentencing, after a conviction and sentence have been vacated and the case has been retried, new information unfavorable to a defendant, including information concerning his conduct subsequent to his original sentencing, may be considered by a sentencing judge, subject to limitations safeguarding against retaliatory vindictiveness. It logically follows that, in resentencing following the invalidation of a sentence (where the underlying conviction has not been vacated), the resentencing judge has authority to consider favorable information about the defendant's good conduct subsequent to his original sentencing. . . .

"This principle does not grant a windfall to the defendant. Fairness dictates, that, in accordance with the common-law principle that we adopted in *Commonwealth v. Hyatt*, [419 Mass. 815, 823 (1995)], the resentencing judge may also consider information presented by the Commonwealth concerning a defendant's unfavorable conduct occurring subsequent to his original sentencing hearing." *Commonwealth v. White*, 436 Mass. 340, 343–45 (2002) (certain citations omitted).

Resentencing. "A successful challenge to one sentence imposed at the same time as other sentences opens up all the interdependent, lawful sentences for reconsideration without violating the double jeopardy clause, at least if the aggregate of the original sentences is not to be increased." *Commonwealth v. Burden*, 48 Mass. App. Ct. 232, 236 (1999) (citation and quotation marks omitted).

"Should the resentencing judge impose a punishment harsher than what the defendant originally received, his reasons for doing so must appear on the record and be based on

11

information not before the first sentencing judge." *Commonwealth v. Renderos*, 440 Mass. 422, 435 (2003) (citation omitted); *see also Commonwealth v. Pillai*, 445 Mass. 175, 194 (2005).

Sentencing Entrapment. "The court has previously declined to recognize sentencing entrapment as a defense." *Commonwealth v. Salentino*, 449 Mass. 657, 664 (2007).

Veracity of defendant's testimony. A judge, in sentencing, may not take into consideration the veracity of the defendant's testimony. *Commonwealth v. Juzba*, 46 Mass. App. Ct. 319, 325 (1999).

SEXUAL KNOWLEDGE (OF CHILDREN)

"We have held that in challenging the reliability of a child's testimony about sexual abuse, a defendant has a right to show that the child had personal knowledge of sexual acts and terminology from sexual abuse prior to the incidents alleged against the defendant. *Commonwealth v. Ruffen*, 399 Mass. 811, 815 (1987). The defendant must have a reasonable suspicion and a good faith basis for the inquiry. *Commonwealth v. Ruffen*, 399 Mass. 811, 815 (1987). We have suggested that a judge, given such reasonable suspicion and good faith basis, should permit a voir dire examination to determine whether a child had been a victim of sexual abuse in the past. *Commonwealth v. Ruffen*, 399 Mass. 811, 815 (1987). Before any such evidence is admitted, the judge should determine both that the past abuse is factually similar to the abuse in the case on trial and that the child victim displays knowledge of sexual matters beyond his or her years." *Commonwealth v. Walker*, 426 Mass. 301, 306 (1997).

"We hold, as did the Appeals Court, that 'where a prosecutor expressly urges in her closing that a child victim's sexual knowledge was derived from identified acts of abuse, there must be an adequate and specific basis in the record for such a claim that excludes other possible sources of such knowledge.'" *Commonwealth v. Beaudry*, 445 Mass. 577, 584 (2005) (citations omitted).

SHOW-UPS

See also Suppression of Identification Testimony, below.

"One-on-one pretrial identifications are generally disfavored because they are viewed as inherently suggestive. *Commonwealth v. Johnson*, 420 Mass. 458, 461 (1995); *Commonwealth v. Barnett*, 371 Mass. 87, 91–92 (1976), cert. denied, 429 U.S. 1049 (1977). But, as we stated in *Commonwealth v. Austin*, 421 Mass. 357, 361 (1995):

> [A] one-on-one pretrial identification raises no due process concerns unless it is determined to be unnecessarily suggestive. Whether an identification procedure is 'unnecessarily' or 'impermissibly' suggestive . . . involves inquiry whether good reason exists for the police to use a one-on-one identification procedure . . . bearing in mind that . . . [e]xigent or special circumstances are not a prerequisite to such confrontations (citations omitted).

Although stating that the analysis cannot be generalized, the *Austin* court went on to observe:

> Relevant to the good reason examination are the nature of the crime involved and corresponding concerns for public safety; the need for efficient police investigation in the immediate aftermath of a crime; and the usefulness of prompt confirmation of the accuracy of investigatory information, which, if in

error, will release the place quickly to follow another track.

Commonwealth v. Austin, 421 Mass. at 362.

"The identifications in this case were justified because they constituted parts of an efficient police investigation in the immediate aftermath of a crime." *Commonwealth v. Thompson*, 427 Mass. 729, 735 (1998).

SLEEPING JUROR

"'[A] judge's receipt of reliable information' that a juror was asleep during evidence requires prompt judicial intervention, which typically includes a voir dire of one or more of the jurors." *Commonwealth v. Gonzalez*, 86 Mass. App. Ct. 253, 254 (2014) (quoting *Commonwealth v. Beneche*, 458 Mass. 61, 78 (2010)).

SPONTANEOUS UTTERANCE

See Excited Utterance, above.

STATE OF MIND (OF DEFENDANT)

Relevance in murder charge. "When the officer asked the defendant to get out of the motor vehicle, the defendant instead drove off, dragging the officer to his death. . . . We have no question that the defendant should have been permitted to say what he was thinking at the time he drove off. Certainly, evidence of the defendant's state of mind was relevant on the charge of murder (which is now foreclosed by the jury's verdict) and, for the reasons given by the Appeals Court, that evidence was also relevant on the manslaughter charge. When a defendant's state of mind or his knowledge of mind or his knowledge is a factor in the proof of a crime, his proffered testimony concerning his state of mind or knowledge must be admitted." *Commonwealth v. Papadinis*, 402 Mass. 73, 74 (1988).

Existence of malice. "The trial judge did not abuse her discretion in admitting evidence, bearing only on the defendant's state of mind and intent, that tended to show that between six weeks and four months before her daughter's death, the defendant inflicted cigarette burns on Sarah's chest. . . .

"The evidence was probative of the defendant's state of mind toward her daughter and was relevant to her intent at the time Sarah was killed, issues that bore at least on the existence of malice. The cigarette burns were not too remote in time. *See Commonwealth v. Jordan (No. 1)*, [397 Mass. 489, 492 (1986) (five to seven months); *Commonwealth v. Little*, 376 Mass. 233, 238 (1978) (two years). Nor does the fact that the burns may have been inflicted in only a single incident bar the admission of evidence of the scars."

Commonwealth v. McGeoghean, 412 Mass. 839, 841 (1992) (some citations omitted).

STATE OF MIND (OF VICTIM)

Defendant's awareness of. "The Commonwealth called two coworkers of the victim, who testified at a voir dire hearing that the victim had told them on the day she disappeared that she was going to get the money that the defendant owed her or that she (the victim) would tell the police of the defendant's involvement in the 'Mobil robberies.' The judge ultimately ruled that the witnesses could mention the 'Mobil robberies,' and the witnesses testified accordingly. Immediately thereafter, the judge instructed the jury that the testimony was admitted only for the limited purpose of revealing the victim's state of mind. The judge's allowance of this testimony was erroneous and prejudicial. The witnesses' testimony was irrelevant because there was no showing by the Commonwealth that the victim's state of mind was ever transmitted to the defendant. Without this foundation, the statements were inadmissible and the judge's instructions were not curative. This evidence, absent a credible showing that the defendant was aware of the victim's statements, should not be admitted at the new trial." *Commonwealth v. Olszewski*, 401 Mass. 749, 758–59 (1988) (citation and footnote omitted). See also *Commonwealth v. Cyr*, 425 Mass. 89, 93 (1997) (Generally, a deceased's expressions of fear of the defendant are not relevant to or probative or the defendant's motive).

"A murder victim's attitude of contempt or hostility toward the defendant, when it is known to the defendant, would constitute some evidence which, if augmented by other evidence, might warrant a fact finder's determination that the defendant responded by killing the victim. However, a victim's contempt for the defendant or hostile attitude toward him, unknown to the defendant, would be irrelevant and inadmissible at the defendant's trial for murder. . . . A murder victim's statement that he feared the defendant, even if made known to the defendant, sheds no light on whether the defendant had a motive to kill him, and therefore is not admissible in the defendant's trial for murder." *Commonwealth v. Qualls*, 425 Mass. 163, 168–69 (1997). *But see Commonwealth v. Adjutant*, 443 Mass. 649, 660 (2005) (evidence of the victim's reputation is relevant even if the defendant did not know of the reputation at the time of the crime, if it is offered to prove that the victim and not the defendant was likely to be the "first aggressor").

STATE OF MIND (OF WITNESS)

"A witness's state of mind is not admissible unless it is relevant. In the circumstances of this case, a properly elicited answer to, 'why didn't you intervene in the fight?' would have been relevant to rebut the defendant's contention that the witness did not intervene because the fight was not serious. That is not, however, what happened in this case. On direct examination, [the witness] was asked what his state of mind was while he was riding to the party. . . . ['I felt there would be trouble . . .']. The witness's state of mind on his way to the party had no relevance to any contested issue, and served only to implicate the witness's fear of the defendant, and consequently, the defendant's bad character. The evidence should not have been admitted." *Commonwealth v. McIntyre*, 430 Mass. 529, 540 (1999) (footnote omitted).

STATEMENT AGAINST PENAL INTEREST

"A statement is admissible under the penal interest exception if (1) the declarant's testimony is unavailable; (2) the statement so far tends to subject the declarant to criminal liability that a reasonable person in his position would not have made the statement unless he believed it to be true; and (3) the statement, if offered to exculpate the accused, is corroborated by circumstances clearly indicating its trustworthiness." *Commonwealth v. Charles*, 428 Mass. 672, 677 (1999).

STATEMENTS OF JOINT VENTURERS

"It is well settled that out-of-court statements by joint criminal venturers are admissible against the others if the statements are made both during the pendency of the cooperative effort and in furtherance of its goal. This exception to the hearsay rule does not apply after the criminal enterprise has ended, as where a joint venturer has been apprehended and imprisoned. At that point, the joint venturers no longer share the commonality of interests which is some assurance that their statements are reliable.

"Statements may be introduced under this exception only if the existence of the joint criminal venture is shown by some other evidence. The judge need not make a preliminary finding that a joint criminal enterprise exists as a precondition to admitting the evidence. Evidence may be admitted subject to a later motion to strike if the prosecution fails to show that the defendant was part of a joint enterprise." *Commonwealth v. Colon-Cruz*, 408 Mass. 533, 543–44 (1990) (citations and punctuation marks omitted); *see also Commonwealth v. Clarke*, 418 Mass. 207, 218 (1994).

"[N]otwithstanding the fact that nearly two years had elapsed between the commission of the murders and Snow's statement to the defendant in his April 26, 2007, letter that the defendant had 'made [his] bones,' the two men remained actively engaged in an effort to conceal their involvement in the crimes and thereby evade arrest. In his December, 2006, letter to the defendant, Snow expressed his concerns that Burgess knew too much, was plotting against them, and 'need[ed] to be' buried. In his subsequent letter to the defendant in April, 2007, Snow provided Burgess's address and gave the defendant instructions to burn down her house. A month or two later, the defendant went to Burgess's home and told her roommate why he was there, although the defendant ultimately decided that he was unable to commit the act of arson. Based on these circumstances, we conclude that there was sufficient evidence to support the judge's determination that the joint venture remained ongoing at the time Snow wrote to the defendant that he (the defendant) had 'made [his] bones.' Although it was made a significant period of time after the murders of Chrapan and Lyon, this statement was not outside the scope of the joint venture." *Commonwealth v. Winquist*, 474 Mass. 517, 523–24 (2016).

STATE OF POLICE KNOWLEDGE

"We have permitted the use of carefully circumscribed extrajudicial statements in criminal trials to explain the state of police knowledge. We have explained that an arresting or investigating officer should not be put in the false position of seeming just to have happened upon the scene; he should be allowed some explanation of his presence and conduct. It goes without saying that the testimony may not be used for the truth of the statements that served as the basis for the officer's knowledge. . . . We have therefore permitted this evidence only through the testimony of a police officer who must testify only on the basis of his own knowledge. . . . Second, the testimony must be limited to the facts required to establish the officer's state of knowledge. Disclosure of the substance of the conversation ordinarily is not required, and should be curtailed because of its prejudicial value. . . . For this reason a statement that an officer acted 'upon information received,' or 'as a consequence of a conversation,' or words to that effect—without further detail—satisfy the purpose of explaining police conduct. . . . Third, the police action or state of police knowledge must be relevant to an issue in the case." *Commonwealth v. Rosario*, 430 Mass. 505, 508–10 (1999) (citations and quotation marks omitted).

STATEMENTS TO PRIVATE CITIZENS

When the voluntariness of a defendant's statements to private citizens is in issue, the judge must conduct a voir dire to determine the voluntariness of the statements. If the judge determines that the statements are voluntary the issue of voluntariness should be submitted to the jury for consideration. The Commonwealth has the burden of proving to both the judge and jury the voluntariness of the statements beyond a

11

reasonable doubt. A statement by someone who by dint of physical or mental impediments is incapable of withholding the information conveyed cannot be used as evidence against him. Statements that are attributable in large measure to a defendant's debilitated condition, such as insanity are not the product of a rational intellect or free will and are involuntary. *Commonwealth v. Hunter*, 416 Mass. 831, 834 (1994) (citations and quotation marks omitted). *See also Commonwealth v. Ferreira*, 417 Mass. 592, 600 (1994) ("The judge has no duty to pass on the voluntariness of the defendant's statements unless it is made a live issue at trial.").

STAY AWAY ORDER V. NO CONTACT ORDER

"There is a distinct difference between the two terms and they are not interchangeable. A 'stay away' order requires a probationer to remain a certain, often specified, physical distance away from the subject of the order. However, the parties involved can make contact, either written or oral, so long as there is no physical proximity between them. A 'no contact' order, on the other hand, requires that the probationer also not communicate by speech, writing, or other means with the individual who is named in the order, even if in doing so they remain physically apart. Accordingly, a 'no contact' order is broader in scope than a 'stay away' order." *Commonwealth v. MacDonald*, 50 Mass. App. Ct. 220, 222 n.7 (2000), *aff'd*, 435 Mass. 1005 (2001) (citation omitted).

STAY OF SENTENCE

"Execution of a sentence may be stayed in cases in which the defendant raises an issue which is worthy of presentation to an appellate court, one which offers some reasonable possibility of a successful decision in the appeal. A judge must find that the defendant presents no risk of flight or danger to the community, and that he is unlikely to commit additional criminal acts during the pendency of his appeal." *Commonwealth v. Senior*, 429 Mass. 1021, 1021–22 (1999) (quotation marks and citations omitted) (rescript).

"Sentences are to be executed forthwith unless suspended or stayed for the exceptional reasons permitted by law . . . [N]ormally this power should be exercised only with the consent of the defendant and for short periods of time. . . . Ordinarily, a judge would employ a stay only to allow a convicted person to arrange his or her affairs, or pending determination of an appeal." *Commonwealth v. McLaughlin*, 431 Mass. 506, 518–20 (2000) (sentences taken out of order, quotation marks and citations omitted).

STIPULATIONS

"[A] judge may admit relevant evidence even if a party has agreed to stipulate to the fact that the offered evidence tends to prove." *Commonwealth v. Worcester*, 44 Mass. App. Ct. 258, 262 (1998) (quoting *Commonwealth v. Benoit*, 389 Mass. 411, 425 (1993)).

"[W]hen the defendant and the Commonwealth have agreed to stipulate to the existence of an element in a case, the stipulation should be placed before the jury before the close of the evidence." *Commonwealth v. Ortiz*, 466 Mass. 475, 484 (2013).

STRIKING EVIDENCE

"In imposing the severest sanction, that of preclusion or striking of evidence [of the defendant], the judge should make clear that she has taken into account certain requisite factors in the course of balancing the vindication of the rules against a defendant's right to present witnesses. Those factors include:

(1) prevention of surprise; (2) evidence of bad faith in the violation of the conference report; (3) prejudice to the other party caused by the violation; (4) the effectiveness of less severe sanctions; and (5) the materiality of the testimony in issue to the outcome of the case." *Commonwealth v. Steinmeyer*, 43 Mass. App. Ct. 185, 190 (1997) (citations, quotation marks and brackets omitted).

STRUCTURAL DEFECT DOCTRINE

"A structural error is one that so infringes on a defendant's right to the basic components of a fair trial that it can never be considered harmless. Such errors include, for example, deprivation of the right to counsel, trial before a biased judge, and unlawful exclusion of members of the defendant's race from the jury." *Commonwealth v. Villanueva*, 47 Mass. App. Ct. 905, 906 (1999) (citation omitted) (rescript).

SUPPRESSION OF IDENTIFICATION TESTIMONY

See also Photographic Identification and Showups, above.

"In order to suppress identification testimony, the defendant must show by a preponderance of the evidence that the procedures employed, viewed in the totality of the circumstances, were so unnecessarily suggestive and conducive to mistaken identification as to deny the defendant due process of law. *See Commonwealth v. Thornley*, 400 Mass. 355, 363 (1987); *Commonwealth v. Correia*, 381 Mass. 65, 78 (1980). The crucial question is whether any possible mistake was the result of improper procedures on the part of the Commonwealth. *Commonwealth v. Paszko*, 391 Mass. 164, 172 (1984). If the defendant succeeds in showing that the pretrial identification was impermissibly suggestive, then the prosecution can offer other identification testimony only after demonstrating by clear and convincing evidence that the identification has an independent source. *Commonwealth v. Thornley*, [400 Mass.] at 363." *Commonwealth v. Colon-Cruz*, 408 Mass. 533, 541–42 (1990).

SURRENDER HEARINGS

"Whether it is a desirable rule or not, when probation is revoked, the original suspended sentence must be imposed, if the time has expired within which the sentence may be revised or revoked." *Commonwealth v. Holmgren*, 421 Mass. 224, 228 (1995).

SURVEILLANCE POST LOCATION

"We have distinguished between a demand for disclosure of privileged information at a pretrial hearing, such as a motion to suppress, and a demand for disclosure at trial, where the issue is the defendant's ultimate guilt or innocence. Disclosure has been required at trial where the material is relevant and helpful to the defense of an accused, or is essential to a fair determination of a cause." *Commonwealth v. Hernandez*, 421 Mass. 272, 275 (1995) (quoting *Commonwealth v. Lugo*, 404 Mass. 565 (1990)) (citations and quotation marks omitted).

TELEPHONE CONVERSATIONS

"A caller's mere self-identification, without more, is insufficient authentication to admit the substance of a telephone conversation." *Commonwealth v. Howard*, 42 Mass. App. Ct. 322, 324 (1997).

However, "[a] telephone conversation between a witness and a person the witness has never met may be admitted when confirming circumstances tend to authenticate the identity of the other person, even if . . . the witness does not recognize the voice." *Commonwealth v. Wojcik*, 43 Mass. App.

11

Ct. 595, 606–07 (1997) (quoting *Commonwealth v. Anderson*, 404 Mass. 767, 770 (1989)).

TENDER YEARS DOCTRINE

"At common law, a child under the 'tender years,' defined as a child under fourteen years of age, was incapable of consenting to kidnapping. We have long recognized that a child of tender years is incapable of assenting to forcible removal from the legal custody of his or her parents." *Commonwealth v. Colon*, 431 Mass. 188, 191 (2000) (citation and quotation marks omitted).

TENDER YEARS JURY INSTRUCTION

"The present 'tender years' Supplemental Instruction 5.42 of the Model Jury Instructions for Use in the District Court, which suggests that the age of the observer may obviate the need to establish the fifth element of the offense of open and gross lewdness, should not be given." *Commonwealth v. Kessler*, 442 Mass. 770, 777 (2005).

TESTIMONIAL v. NONTESTIMONIAL STATEMENTS

The excited utterance exception and the treatment of out-of-court testimonial statements are subject to the requirements set forth in *Crawford v. Washington*, 541 U.S. 36 (2004), and *Commonwealth v. Gonsalves*, 445 Mass. 1 (2005). Under the confrontation clause of the Sixth Amendment to the U.S. Constitution, regardless of the local rules of evidence, testimonial out-of-court statements are inadmissible "unless the declarant is available at trial or the declarant formally is unavailable to testify and the defendant had a prior opportunity to cross-examine the declarant." *Commonwealth v. Gonsalves*, 445 Mass. at 3. If an out-of-court statement is not testimonial, the confrontation clause does not apply and the admissibility of the statement depends solely on the rules of evidence. *Gonsalves*, 445 Mass. at 13.

Gonsalves employs a two-part test to determine whether a statement is "testimonial." First, the trial judge must decide whether the statement is testimonial per se, which includes statements made in affidavits, depositions, confessions, prior testimony at a preliminary hearing, before a grand jury, or at a former trial, and statements "procured through law enforcement interrogation" (not including "emergency questioning . . . to secure a volatile scene or determine the need for or provide medical care"). *Gonsalves*, 445 Mass. at 13. Second, if the statement is not testimonial per se, the judge must further consider "whether a reasonable person in the declarant's position would anticipate the statement's being used against the accused in investigating and prosecuting the crime." *Gonsalves*, 445 Mass. at 13. If so, or if the statement is testimonial per se, then the confrontation clause applies and requires either that the declarant testify at trial or, if he is formally unavailable, that he have been previously subject to cross examination. *Gonsalves*, 445 Mass. at 13.

"[T]he statements made by the victim to the 911 dispatcher were admissible because they were made in circumstances that objectively indicated that their primary purpose was to enable police to meet an ongoing emergency. Conversely, the statements the victim made to responding officers at her home when the emergency had passed were improperly admitted in evidence." *Commonwealth v. Galicia*, 447 Mass. 737, 739 (2006) (citation omitted).

In *Davis v. Washington*, 547 U.S. 813, 126 S.Ct. 2266, 165 L.Ed.2d 224 (2006), the Court indicated that "'[s]tatements are nontestimonial when made in the course of police interrogation under circumstances objectively indicating that the primary purpose of the interrogation is to enable police assistance to meet an ongoing emergency. They are testimonial when the circumstances objectively indicate that there is no such ongoing emergency. . . .' *Id*. at 2273–2274. In addition, the Court provided various indicia that help determine whether the 'primary purpose' of a statement obtained during interrogation may be seen as testimonial, including (1) whether the declarant was speaking about 'events as they were actually happening rather than describ[ing] past events'; (2) whether a reasonable interrogator would recognize that the declarant was facing an 'ongoing emergency'; (3) whether the question and answer were, viewed objectively, 'necessary to be able to resolve the present emergency, rather than simply to learn . . . what had happened in the past,' including whether it was necessary for the interrogator to know the identity of the alleged perpetrator; and (4) the 'level of formality' of the interview. *Id*. at 2276–2277 (emphasis in original). The Court noted that 'statements made in the absence of any interrogation are [not] necessarily nontestimonial,' *id*. at 2274, n.1, and that 'even when interrogation exists, it is in the final analysis the declarant's statements, not the interrogator's questions, that the [c]onfrontation [c]lause requires us to evaluate,' *id*." *Commonwealth v. Burgess*, 450 Mass. 422, 428 (2008).

THIRD-PARTY EVIDENCE

"'A defendant may introduce evidence that tends to show that another person committed the crime or had the motive, intent, and opportunity to commit it.' *Commonwealth v. Harris*, 395 Mass. 296, 300 (1985). Evidence of other crimes, committed by another person, is admissible if they 'are so closely connected in point of time and method of operation as to cast doubt upon the identification of [the] defendant as the person who committed the crime.' *Commonwealth v. Harris*, 395 Mass. 296, 300 (1985) (quoting *Commonwealth v. Keizer*, 377 Mass. 264, 267 (1979)). However, '[t]he evidence should not be too remote in time or too weak in probative quality, and it should be closely related to the facts of the case against the defendant.' *Commonwealth v. Harris, supra* (quoting *Commonwealth v. Graziano*, 368 Mass. 325, 329–30 (1975)). The judge has considerable discretion in determining whether the proffered evidence meets these conditions and thus whether to admit the evidence." *Commonwealth v. Lawrence*, 404 Mass. 378, 387 (1989) (footnote omitted); *see also Commonwealth v. Signorine*, 404 Mass. 400, 407–08 (1989).

"In view of the additional evidence offered by the defendant in this trial regarding the landlord's sexual aggression toward women, it simply cannot be said that the evidence of the landlord's prior incidents of sexual assaults was not relevant. The additional evidence provided sufficient similarity between all the prior incidents and the present crime to render the proffered evidence relevant. The evidence assumes even greater relevance given the fact that, according to the defendant, he has no connection with the victim. By contrast, the landlord had a relationship with the victim, possessed a key to her home, had been in her bedroom recently and even had opened her lingerie drawer. He had a history of sexual assault and anger when rejected by women and he had been rejected by the victim here. There was substantially more evidence of motive on the part of the landlord than on the part of this defendant." *Commonwealth v. Conkey*, 443 Mass. 60, 69–70 (2004).

11

Evidence of similar crime. "[T]o offer evidence of another similar crime, a defendant must also 'provide [a] basis for a conclusion that [he] was not the perpetrator of that crime.' *Commonwealth v. Perito*, 417 Mass. 674, 685 (1994). . . . [The defendant] provided no evidence of his lack of involvement in the earlier crime. Consequently, the judge properly found that evidence regarding the [other] murder was not relevant." *Commonwealth v. Dew*, 443 Mass. 620, 627 (2005) (defendant challenged denial of request to offer evidence of similar crime before grand jury around same time).

Exhibition of third party for identification. "We agree with the defendant that nothing in the presentation of [the third party] for an in-court identification of him as [the codefendant]'s supplier raised the problems posed by having a witness invoke the Fifth Amendment in front of the jury. A witness may not be called to the stand solely to assert the Fifth Amendment in front of the jury because there is no probative value to such an assertion of privilege (as it may be prompted by a variety of considerations, wholly unrelated to the case being tried), but there is a high potential for prejudice (as jurors are likely to treat such an assertion of privilege as an admission of guilt). . . . Here, by comparison, there was obvious probative value to the proposed display of [the third party] to the jury. . . . An in-court identification of [the third party] could not be dismissed as a false accusation of someone for whom the accusation could not be of any consequence. . . .

"To the extent the judge was concerned that jurors might speculate as to why [the third party] did not testify, that concern was no different from the customary concern that jurors might wonder about witnesses who are mentioned at trial but who do not testify. . . .

"Where there was no legitimate reason for restricting the defendant to the use of a photograph, it was an abuse of discretion for the judge to have done so." *Commonwealth v. Rosario*, 444 Mass. 550, 557–59, 561 (2005).

UNANIMITY INSTRUCTION

"If a defendant requests a specific unanimity instruction, and 'where evidence of separate incidents is offered to the jury and any one incident could support a conviction, a general unanimity instruction may not suffice to ensure that the jury actually does reach a unanimous verdict.'" *Commonwealth v. Julien*, 59 Mass. App. Ct. 679, 685 (2003) (quoting *Commonwealth v. Pimental*, 54 Mass. App. Ct. 325, 329–330 n.4 (2002)).

"One circumstance calling for a specific unanimity instruction is when, on a single charged offense, the prosecutor presents evidence of separate, discrete incidents, any one of which would suffice by itself to make out the crime charged. There, in order to find the defendant guilty of the charged offense, the jury must all agree as to at least one, specific incident. *See Commonwealth v. Conefrey*, 420 Mass. 508, 513–514 (1995) (where defendant was charged in single indictment alleging indecent assault and battery on child occurring "on divers dates and times," and child complainant testified to eight distinct episodes of sexual contact, it was error to refuse defendant's request for specific unanimity instruction). Unless the jury all agree that there is proof beyond a reasonable doubt as to one of the specific criminal acts alleged, there is not unanimous agreement that he has committed any crime. Absent a specific unanimity instruction, the jury might mistakenly believe that they could convict the defendant even if they disagreed as to which of the alleged criminal acts he had committed. Thus, if the evidence raises the possibility of this form of juror confusion, and the defendant requests a specific unanimity instruction, the instruction must be given. *Id.* at 514. *See Commonwealth v. Comtois*, 399 Mass. 668, 676–677 & n.11 (1987); *Commonwealth v. Lemar*, 22 Mass. App. Ct. 170, 172 (1986).

"However, if the offense is alleged to have been committed as part of a single episode, there is no such risk of juror confusion and no specific unanimity instruction need be given. The jury must be unanimous that the crime was committed on the occasion alleged, but they need not agree as to every detail concerning how the crime was committed. 'When a single count is charged and where the spatial and temporal separations between acts are short, that is, where the facts show a continuing course of conduct, rather than a succession of clearly detached incidents, a specific unanimity instruction is not required.' *Commonwealth v. Thatch*, 39 Mass. App. Ct. 904, 905 (1995) (judge not required to give specific unanimity instruction where rape was alleged to have occurred as part of single episode, despite victim's testimony as to multiple acts of penetration). The same is true if the prosecution presents evidence of a single criminal scheme or plan carried out consistently over time. In the absence of some distinguishing differences between the successive events, there is no reason to fear that the jury will pick and choose among the alleged incidents and convict the defendant while disagreeing as to which of them were committed. *See Commonwealth v. Sanchez*, 423 Mass. 591, 599–600 (1996) (where child victim described repeated identical pattern of sexual assaults, but did not describe particular incidents, specific unanimity instruction not required). *See also Commonwealth v. Pimental*, 54 Mass. App. Ct. 325, 327–328 (2002); *Commonwealth v. Lewis*, 48 Mass. App. Ct. 343, 350–352 (1999)." *Commonwealth v. Santos*, 440 Mass. 281, 284–86 (2003).

"Thus, while the court has adopted the requirement that the jury be unanimous as to the 'theory' of guilt when the Commonwealth has proceeded on 'alternate theories,' and the companion requirement that that 'theory' be identified on the verdict slip, the examples of what the court means by 'alternate theories' are the differing theories of murder in the first degree (deliberate premeditation, extreme atrocity or cruelty, or felony-murder) and the differing theories of manslaughter (voluntary or involuntary). In each case, these are separate, distinct, and essentially unrelated ways in which the same crime can be committed. (Indeed, with respect to manslaughter, voluntary and involuntary manslaughter are mutually exclusive—one cannot kill both intentionally and unintentionally at the same time.)" *Commonwealth v. Santos*, 440 Mass. 281, 287–88 (2003).

This "applies only in cases where the alternative 'theories' presented are substantively distinct or dissimilar. While it may be difficult to construct a precise definition identifying those alternate 'theories' that will require specific unanimity, it is clear that the rule does not automatically extend to every alternate method by which a single element may be established. . . . [T]hose alternatives are often closely related, and no purpose would be served by requiring the jury to dissect the evidence and agree as to which related, or even overlapping, variant of the same element had been proved. For example, while there are three prongs of 'malice,' we do not require juror unanimity as to which form of malice has been proved. Or, in rape cases, where there is evidence that the defendant both exerted 'force' on the victim and made a 'threat of bodily injury,' G.L. c. 265, § 22(a), we do not require

11

the jury to be unanimous as to whether it was the 'force' or the 'threat' that compelled the victim to submit—it would make no sense to acquit a defendant of rape (or to declare a mistrial) merely because the jury could not agree on whether the victim submitted because she had been hit or whether she submitted because the defendant threatened to strangle her. . . . The 'assault' element of robbery pertains to the conduct that is used to instill fear and overcome the victim's resistance to the taking. The methods of doing so--actual force or the threat of force—are closely related and, when both are present, will work in combination to subdue the victim. These alternative methods of establishing a required element are not distinct 'theories' of how the crime may be committed, but are merely similar, equivalent types of conduct any one (or more) of which will suffice to prove a single element." *Commonwealth v. Santos*, 440 Mass. 281, 289 (2003).

"Elsewhere we have rejected the notion that . . . the jury must be unanimous in their parsing of the details as to how a crime was committed. *See Commonwealth v. Laurore*, 437 Mass. 65, 82 (2002); *Commonwealth v. Cyr*, 433 Mass. 617, 623 (2001). . . . Indeed, . . . if we were to require unanimity down to this level of ostensible 'theory,' such a requirement would effectively require unanimity as to minute factual details within a single episode, a form of unanimity that we have never required." *Commonwealth v. Santos*, 440 Mass. 281, 289–90 (2003).

"We have also rejected the argument that the jury must be unanimous as to whether guilt is based on liability as a principal or as a joint venturer. *See Commonwealth v. Ellis*, 432 Mass. 746, 761 (2000); *Commonwealth v. Nolan*, 427 Mass. 541, 544 (1998). While we sometimes use the term 'theory' of principal liability or 'theory' of joint venture, those are not alternate, differing 'theories' of the crime that are to be subjected to . . . specific unanimity and verdict slip requirements. . . ." *Commonwealth v. Santos*, 440 Mass. 281, 290 (2003).

UNAVAILABLE WITNESS

"Prior recorded testimony may be admitted in evidence only when it is established that the witness is 'unavailable' to testify at trial and the prior testimony is deemed 'reliable.' *Commonwealth v. Bohannon*, 385 Mass. 733, 741 (1982). See *Commonwealth v. Salim*, 399 Mass. 227 (1987). We require proof of both necessity (shown by unavailability) and reliability because the introduction of previously recorded testimony directly implicates the defendant's Federal and State constitutional rights to confront witnesses against him. *Commonwealth v. Bohannon, supra* at 741."

"a. *Unavailability* . . . As we noted, the crucial inquiry is whether the witness is available to 'testify in person at the time [the] former testimony is to be admitted in evidence.' *Id.* at 744–745. . . .

"b. *Reliability* . . . The test for reliability involves two components. First, the testimony must be shown to be reliable when given. Second, it must be shown that the testimony was accurately preserved. *Commonwealth v. Bohannon,* supra at 746.

"Despite the defendant's implication to the contrary, he is not entitled under the confrontation clause to a cross-examination that is 'effective in whatever way, and to whatever extent, the defense might wish.' *Delaware v. Fensterer,* 474 U.S. 15, 20 (1985). In the instant case, the defendant was represented by counsel at the probable cause hearing. That hearing focused on the same issue subsequently presented at

trial. The transcript reveals that the witness, while under oath, underwent extensive cross-examination."

Commonwealth v. Siegfriedt, 402 Mass. 424, 427–29 (1988) (footnotes omitted).

Unavailability. In *Commonwealth v. Charles*, 428 Mass. 672 (1999), the Court noted that a witness may be unavailable in any one of the following circumstances: (1) the witness invokes his 5th Amendment rights; (2) the witness is a fugitive; (3) the witness "is absent from the hearing and the proponent of a statement has been unable to procure the declarant's attendance . . . by process or other reasonable means." *Commonwealth v. Charles*, 428 Mass. at 678 (quoting (#3) Federal Rules of Evidence 804(a)(5)).

Burden on Commonwealth. "The Commonwealth had the burden of proving that the witness was unavailable to testify at the time of trial. . . . The Commonwealth must exercise substantial diligence in order to meet its burden of showing a witness's unavailability. . . . The fact that the deponent was in another country is not, standing alone, sufficient under the common law of the Commonwealth to justify admission of her deposition testimony. . . . The possibility of a refusal is not the equivalent of asking and receiving a rebuff." *Commonwealth v. Ross*, 426 Mass. 555, 557–58 (1998) (citations and quotation marks omitted).

Crawford **and out-of-court testimonial statements.** The treatment of out-of-court testimonial statements from unavailable witnesses came under close scrutiny in *Commonwealth v. Gonsalves*, 445 Mass. 1 (2005).

In *Commonwealth v. Lao*, 450 Mass. 215, 224–27 (2007), the court held that while a 911 call and a statement to a police officer were not admissible under *Crawford*, statements to a relative were admissible because the declarant had no reasonable expectation that they would be used prosecutorially at a later point.

UNMEDICATED STATE

"On appeal, the defendant contends that the judge erred in preventing Dr. Profit from testifying as to the type and effect of the medications prescribed to and taken by the defendant at the time of the trial. More specifically, the defendant argues that the jury ought to have been informed that, during the trial, the defendant was under the influence of antipsychotic medication and his outward appearance was substantially affected thereby. This fact, the defendant states, should have been considered by the jury when assessing his character and credibility, as well as deciding whether he possessed the specific intent to commit the crimes charged. In support of his argument, the defendant relies on *Commonwealth v. Louraine*, 390 Mass. 28, 33–34 (1983), where this court held that the State and Federal Constitutions required that a defendant charged with murder, who was under the influence of antipsychotic medication at the time of trial, be afforded the opportunity to have the jury observe him in an unmedicated state."

The Supreme Judicial Court agreed.

Commonwealth v. Gurney, 413 Mass. 97, 101 (1992).

VERBAL COMPLETENESS

"Whenever statements of a person are put in evidence, all that was said or written by him at the same time and upon the same subject becomes admissible; but other statements, even though made at the same time, are not admissible unless they are upon the same subject matter." *Commonwealth v. Watson*, 377 Mass. 814, 828 (1979) (quoting Leach and Liacos,

11

Massachusetts Evidence 320 (4th ed. 1967)). *See also Commonwealth v. Slonka*, 42 Mass. App. Ct. 760, 771 (1997).

VIDEOTAPED SIMULATIONS

"A videotaped demonstration may be admitted in evidence provided it sufficiently resembles the actual event so as to be fair and informative. Whether the conditions were sufficiently similar to make the observation offered by the demonstration of any value in aiding the jury to pass upon the issue submitted to them is primarily for the trial judge to determine as a matter of discretion. The judge's decision in this respect will not be interfered with unless plainly wrong." *Commonwealth v. Chipman*, 418 Mass. 262, 270–71 (1994).

VIDEOTAPES

"Videotapes are admissible in evidence 'if they are relevant, they provide a fair representation of that which they purport to depict, and they are not otherwise barred by an exclusionary rule.'" *Commonwealth v. Lawson*, 425 Mass. 528, 533 (1997) (quoting *Commonwealth v. Mahoney*, 400 Mass. 524, 527 (1987)).

VOICE IDENTIFICATION

General rule. "[In *Chartrand v. Registrar of Motor Vehicles*, 345 Mass. 321, 325 (1963)] the court stated that a witness is competent to identify a voice over the telephone if the witness (1) is familiar with the caller's voice, (2) identified the voice at the time of the call, and (3) personally heard the conversation." *Commonwealth v. Carpinto*, 37 Mass. App. Ct. 51, 53 (1994).

Exception: "*Chartrand* and its progeny . . . all have dealt with instances in which a witness identified a person's voice heard but not recorded over a telephone line. Here, we are concerned with witnesses identifying a person's voice that has been recorded. . . . [W]here a recording of telephone conversations exists (provided it is deemed an accurate *representation*—a necessary prerequisite for admissibility, . . . a witness may offer identification testimony simply upon a showing that the first prong of the Chartrand test is met, i.e., that the witness is familiar with the speaker's voice." *Commonwealth v. Carpinto*, 37 Mass. App. Ct. at 54 (citations omitted).

Corroboration. "A telephone conversation between a witness and a person the witness had never met may be admitted when confirming circumstances tend to authenticate the identity of the other person, even if (unlike the case before us) the witness does not recognize the voice. In this case, there was voice recognition based on evidence of previous telephone calls and evidence that the defendant was the only male who lived at the apartment to which the calls were placed. Statements made by the man who answered the telephone tended themselves to confirm his identity as the defendant. The evidence was properly given to the jury." *Commonwealth v. Anderson*, 404 Mass. 767, 770 (1989) (citations omitted).

VOID FOR VAGUENESS

"It is a central tenet of our constitutional law that, as a matter of due process, a criminal statute that fails to give a person of ordinary intelligence fair notice that his contemplated conduct is forbidden should be deemed void for vagueness. *Opinion of the Justices*, 378 Mass. 822, 826 (1979). *See Commonwealth v. Williams*, 395 Mass. 302, 304 (1985)." *Commonwealth v. Kwiatkowski*, 418 Mass. 543, 547

(1994). *See also Commonwealth v. Dunn*, 43 Mass. App. Ct. 58, 59–62 (1997).

WARRANTS

See commentary accompanying G.L. c. 276.

WEAPON FOUND ON DEFENDANT

"The fact that the defendant, within four months of the crimes, had in his possession a weapon that could have been the one used by Pope, was admissible in the judge's discretion. *Commonwealth v. Toro*, 395 Mass. 354, 356 (1985).

'[I]t is commonly competent to show the possession by a defendant of an instrument capable of being used in the commission of a crime, without direct proof that particular instrument was in fact used.' *Id.*, quoting *Commonwealth v. O'Toole*, 326 Mass. 35, 39 (1950). Even if there are circumstances in which the prejudicial effect of the evidence outweighs its probative value, a judge can ameliorate such prejudice by a jury instruction, *id.* at 357. . . ." *Commonwealth v. Hamilton*, 411 Mass. 313, 322 (1991).

Similar looking weapon. "Under the circumstances, the judge did not abuse her discretion in allowing [the witness] to testify regarding a knife similar but not identical to the one used by the robber. The knife was illustrative of the knife used in the robbery, hence relevant to the question of whether a dangerous weapon was used, a requirement of the Commonwealth's case. It was also supportive of [the witness's] recollection of the event." *Commonwealth v. Johnson*, 46 Mass. App. Ct. 398, 404 (1999) (citations omitted).

WILLFUL BLINDNESS

A willful blindness instruction is appropriate when (1) 'a defendant claims a lack of knowledge,' (2) 'the facts suggest a conscious course of deliberate ignorance, and' (3) 'the instruction, taken as a whole, cannot be misunderstood [by a juror] as mandating an inference of knowledge' (citation omitted). *United States v. Hogan*, 861 F.2d 312, 316 (1st Cir. 1988)." *Commonwealth v. Mimless*, 53 Mass. App. Ct. 534, 544 (2002).

"After instructing that the Commonwealth must prove beyond a reasonable doubt that the defendant did not act because of ignorance, mistake or misunderstanding, the judge provided the following willful blindness instruction:

"'[I]f the Commonwealth has proved to you beyond a reasonable doubt that the defendant deliberately closed his eyes as to what would have been obvious to him, then, under such circumstances . . . that element [knowledge] you would be warranted in determining has been shown. So a finding beyond a reasonable doubt by the jury of an intent of the defendant to avoid knowledge or enlightenment would permit the jury to infer such knowledge. . . . Stated another way, a defendant's knowledge of a particular fact may be inferred from a deliberate or intentional ignorance or deliberate or intentional blindness to the existence of that fact.'"

Commonwealth v. Mimless, 53 Mass. App. Ct. 534, 545 n.9 (2002).

WITHDRAWAL

See Abandonment, above.

PART 12

Reference Tables

Table of Cases

A

A.L. v. Commonwealth, 730
Abbott A. v. Commonwealth, 534, 535
Abbott Eng'g, Inc., Commonwealth v., 324
Abraham v. Woburn, 823
Abreu, Commonwealth v., 750
Accetta, Commonwealth v., 275
Acevedo, Commonwealth v., 271
Adams, Commonwealth v., 64
Adjutant, Commonwealth v., 272, 624, 847, 848, 849, 853
Adoption of, *see* name of party
Agosto, Commonwealth v., 493, 495
Aguilar v. Texas, 482, 493, 511
Ahearn, Commonwealth v., 279
Al Saud, Commonwealth v., 726
Alano, Commonwealth v., 65, 260
Albano, Commonwealth v., 400
Albert A., Commonwealth v., 7
Alcala, Commonwealth v., 836
Aldoupolis v. Commonwealth, 585, 638, 639
Alegata v. Commonwealth, 454
Alfonso, Commonwealth v., 577
Ali, Commonwealth v., 314
Alicea v. Commonwealth, 107
Alisha A., Commonwealth v., 107
Allen, Commonwealth v. (1979), 587, 642, 672
Allen, Commonwealth v. (1990), 512
Allen, Commonwealth v. (1996), 808
Allen, Commonwealth v. (2002), 491
Alleyne, Commonwealth v., 836
Allison, Commonwealth v., 269, 618, 842
Almeida, Commonwealth v., 401
Alphas, Commonwealth v., 824, 839
Alvarado, Commonwealth v. (1995), 496
Alvarado, Commonwealth v. (1996), 494, 502, 505
Alvarado, Commonwealth v. (2000), 811
Alvarado, Commonwealth v. (2008), 169, 170
Alvarez, Commonwealth v., 113, 811
Alves, Commonwealth v., 552
Amaral, Commonwealth v., 68, 69, 848
Ambers, Commonwealth v., 269, 270
Amendola, Commonwealth v., 487
Ames, Commonwealth v., 67
Amirault, Commonwealth v. (1989), 576, 618
Amirault, Commonwealth v. (1993), 639
Amral, Commonwealth v., 512, 513
Anderson, Commonwealth v. (1923), 333
Anderson, Commonwealth v. (1989), 68, 488, 499, 855, 858
Anderson, Commonwealth v. (1991), 820
Andrade, Commonwealth v., 260
Andrews, Commonwealth v. (1988), 231, 634
Andrews, Commonwealth v. (2000), 843
Angelo Todesca Corp., Commonwealth v., 75

Angelone, Commonwealth v., 826
Anguilo, Commonwealth v., 469
Anolik, Commonwealth v., 314, 315
Antonmarchi, Commonwealth v., 291
Antwine, Commonwealth v., 486
Appleby, Commonwealth v., 284, 285
Aquino, Commonwealth v., 735
Arana, Commonwealth v., 293, 294, 821, 822
Arizona v. Evans, 815
Arizona v. Youngblood, 618, 626, 830
Arkansas v. Sanders, 495
Armand, Commonwealth v., 354
Armenia, Commonwealth v., 332
Arroyo, Commonwealth v., 806
Arruda, Commonwealth v., 66
Arthur, Commonwealth v., 452
Arzola, Commonwealth v., 491
Ascolillo, Commonwealth v., 296, 631
Ashe v. Swenson, 807
Ashley, Commonwealth v., 840, 845
Askew, Commonwealth v., 275
Atencio, Commonwealth v., 75
Attorney Gen. v. Tufts, 118
Aucella v. Commonwealth, 75, 261
Auguste, Commonwealth v., 820
Augustine, Commonwealth v., 483
Austin, Commonwealth v., 852
Austin A., Commonwealth v., 228
Avellar, Commonwealth v., 496
Avery, Commonwealth v., 828
Avila, Commonwealth v., 805, 819
Aviles, Commonwealth v., 294, 672, 822
Ayre, Commonwealth v., 67, 836

B

Bacigalupo, Commonwealth v., 829
Bacon, Commonwealth v. (1978), 400
Bacon, Commonwealth v. (1980), 502
Baez, Commonwealth v. (1997), 47
Baez, Commonwealth v. (1998), 270
Baillargeon, Commonwealth v., 736, 747
Baker, Commonwealth v. (1975), 323, 361, 573
Baker, Commonwealth v. (2006), 274
Baker, In re, 516
Bakoian, Commonwealth v., 494, 496
Balakin, Commonwealth v., 292
Balboni, Commonwealth v., 551
Baldwin, Commonwealth v. (1858), 361
Baldwin, Commonwealth v. (1997), 625, 812
Balicki, Commonwealth v., 491, 492, 498
Balthazar v. Superior Ct., 449
Balthazar, Commonwealth v., 449
Baptiste, Commonwealth v., 494, 495
Barbeau, Commonwealth v., 65
Barber, Commonwealth v., 285
Barbosa, Commonwealth v., 831
Barclay, Commonwealth v., 638, 639

Bargeron, Commonwealth v., 565
Barklow, Commonwealth v., 324
Barnes-Miller, Commonwealth v., 850
Barnett, Commonwealth v., 616, 852
Baro, Commonwealth v., 646
Barrett, Commonwealth v., 297, 565
Barros, Commonwealth v. (1997), 272
Barros, Commonwealth v. (2000), 501, 502
Barros, Commonwealth v. (2001), 492, 501
Barry v. Commonwealth, 645
Bartholomew, Commonwealth v., 400
Bartlett, Commonwealth v., 496
Bartley v. Illinois, 68
Bartnicki v. Vopper, 470
Bastaldo, Commonwealth v., 820
Bastarache, Commonwealth v., 271
Beal, Commonwealth v. (1999), 816, 846
Beal, Commonwealth v. (2016), 405
Beale, Commonwealth v., 354
Beals, Commonwealth v., 302
Bean, Commonwealth v., 445
Bearden v. Georgia, 724
Beauchemin, Commonwealth v., 451, 849
Beaudry, Commonwealth v., 806, 852
Beaulieu, Commonwealth v., 54, 274
Belding, Commonwealth v., 402
Bell, Commonwealth v., 114
Bell, United States v., 739
Belle Isle, Commonwealth v., 371
Belmer, Commonwealth v., 845
Beneche, Commonwealth v., 852
Bennett, Commonwealth v., 573
Benoit, Commonwealth v., 227, 803, 841, 854
Berardi, Commonwealth v., 632
Berggren, Commonwealth v., 75
Berghuis v. Thompkins, 618, 834
Bergstrom, Commonwealth v., 576
Berkemer v. McCarthy, 505
Bernard v. Commonwealth, 128
Bernbury, Commonwealth v., 147
Berrio, Commonwealth v. (1990), 227, 845
Berrio, Commonwealth v. (1997), 844
Berry v. Commonwealth, 261
Berry, Commonwealth v. (1995), 813
Berry, Commonwealth v. (2000), 828
Berry, Commonwealth v. (2010), 271, 826
Berryman, Commonwealth v., 477
Betances, Commonwealth v., 497
Biagiotti, Commonwealth v., 337
Biancardi, Commonwealth v., 630, 632
Bibbo, Commonwealth v., 306
Bibby, Commonwealth v., 302
Bigelow v. Virginia, 441
Birchfield v. N. Dakota, 66
Bishop, Commonwealth v. (1937), 452
Bishop, Commonwealth v. (1988), 495
Bishop, Commonwealth v. (1993), 846

Blache, Commonwealth v., 295
Black v. Romano, 699
Black, Commonwealth v., 172, 619
Blais, Commonwealth v., 66, 67
Blaisdell, Commonwealth v., 623
Blake, Commonwealth v. (1991), 825, 840
Blake, Commonwealth v. (1992), 487, 512
Blanchette, Commonwealth v. (1991), 836
Blanchette, Commonwealth v. (2002), 168, 169
Blanton v. City of N. Las Vegas, Nev., 648
Blevines, Commonwealth v., 505, 508
Blood, Commonwealth v., 469
Bloomberg, Commonwealth v., 477
Bly, Commonwealth v. (2005), 231
Bly, Commonwealth v. (2007), 850
Boateng, Commonwealth v., 284, 805
Boddie v. Connecticut, 726
Boe, Commonwealth v., 552
Bohannon, Commonwealth v., 295, 296, 857
Bohmer, Commonwealth v., 450
Bolden, Commonwealth v., 316
Bolling, Commonwealth v., 3
Bond, Commonwealth v. (1905), 363
Bond, Commonwealth v. (1978), 507
Bongarzone, Commonwealth v., 507
Bonnett, Commonwealth v., 485
Bonomi, Commonwealth v., 617
Boone, Commonwealth v. (1969), 67, 400
Boone, Commonwealth v. (1985), 373
Boos, Commonwealth v., 321
Borden, Commonwealth v., 493
Borges, Commonwealth v., 493, 504, 505
Boris, Commonwealth v., 321
Borodine, Commonwealth v., 617
Bostock, Commonwealth v., 496
Boston Herald v. Superior Ct., 604
Botelho, Commonwealth v., 616
Botev, Commonwealth v., 441
Bottari, Commonwealth v., 500, 804
Boucher, Commonwealth v. (1989), 271, 272
Boucher, Commonwealth v. (2002), 165
Bouchie v. Murray, 236
Bougas, Commonwealth v., 565
Bourgeois, Commonwealth v., 270, 289, 617
Bousquet, Commonwealth v., 617
Bouvier, Commonwealth v., 274
Bowden, Commonwealth v., 70, 494, 512, 805, 830
Bowie, Commonwealth v., 616
Boyd v. United States, 491
Boyer, Commonwealth v., 523
Boyle, Commonwealth v., 427
Bradley, Commonwealth v. (1974), 288, 323
Bradley, Commonwealth v. (2013), 113
Bradshaw, Commonwealth v., 834
Bradway, Commonwealth v., 817
Brady v. Maryland, 625
Braica, Commonwealth v., 306
Brailey, Commonwealth v., 314
Brandano, Commonwealth v., 543, 619, 809
Brandwein, Commonwealth v., 838
Brattman, Commonwealth v., 300
Brazelton, Commonwealth v., 65, 66
Brennan, Commonwealth v., 827
Bridges, Commonwealth v., 64
Britto, Commonwealth v., 829
Broadland, Commonwealth v., 452
Brookins, Commonwealth v., 844
Brooks, Commonwealth v. (1941), 269
Brooks, Commonwealth v. (1996), 806
Brown v. Commonwealth, 635, 803

Brown v. Genakos, 277, 291
Brown v. State, 542
Brown, Commonwealth v. (1985), 575, 632, 842
Brown, Commonwealth v. (1988), 400
Brown, Commonwealth v. (1991), 848
Brown, Commonwealth v. (1992), 814
Brown, Commonwealth v. (1998), 121
Brown, Commonwealth v. (1999), 815
Brown, Commonwealth v. (2002), 633
Brown, Commonwealth v. (2007), 510, 827
Brown, Commonwealth v. (2008), 230
Brown, Commonwealth v. (2013), 273
Brum, Commonwealth v., 838
Bruneau, Commonwealth v., 577
Brunell, Commonwealth v., 649
Bruno, Commonwealth v., 163, 164, 167, 168
Brusard v. O'Toole, 830
Brusgulis, Commonwealth v., 300
Bruton v. United States, 605, 805
Bruzzese, Commonwealth v., 712, 719, 745, 749, 750
Bryant, Commonwealth v., 617, 836
Brzezinski, Commonwealth v., 511
Buckley v. Quincy Div. of the Dist. Ct. Dep't, 705, 706, 724, 729, 730
Buckley, Commonwealth v., 301
Budreau, Commonwealth v., 335
Bukin, Commonwealth v., 701, 738, 741
Bullcoming v. New Mexico, 831
Bunting, Commonwealth v., 566, 746
Burbank, Commonwealth v., 272, 285
Burden, Commonwealth v., 851
Burgess, Commonwealth v., 164, 818, 850, 855
Burke v. Commonwealth, 524
Burke, Commonwealth v. (1866), 320
Burke, Commonwealth v. (1870), 295
Burke, Commonwealth v. (1961), 574
Burke, Commonwealth v. (1993), 809
Burkett, Commonwealth v. (1977), 288
Burkett, Commonwealth v. (1986), 289
Burnett, Commonwealth v., 632
Burno, Commonwealth v., 276
Burns v. Commonwealth, 844
Burns v. United States, 705, 724
Burns, Commonwealth v., 335
Burston, Commonwealth v., 590, 809
Burt, Commonwealth v., 484
Burton, Commonwealth v., 828, 839
Butler, Commonwealth v. (1996), 728
Butler, Commonwealth v. (2013), 645, 645
Butterfield, Commonwealth v., 503
Butynski, Commonwealth v., 424
Bynoe, Commonwealth v., 725
Bynum v. Commonwealth, 109

C

Cabot, Commonwealth v., 323, 335
Cabral, Commonwealth v., 487, 489, 633
Cabrera, Commonwealth v., 335
Cabrera, Matter of, 612
Caceres, Commonwealth v., 495, 629, 806
Cadwell, Commonwealth v., 233
Cahill, Commonwealth v., 73, 452
Calderon, Commonwealth v. (1997), 500
Calderon, Commonwealth v. (1999), 632
Calderon, Commonwealth v. (2000), 632, 841, 842
Caldwell, Commonwealth v., 632
Callahan v. Lach, 75
Callahan, Commonwealth v. (1988), 617

Callahan, Commonwealth v. (1989), 63
Callahan, Commonwealth v. (1995), 578, 639
Callahan, Commonwealth v. (1996), 483
Callahan, Commonwealth v. (1998), 69
Callahan, Commonwealth v. (2003), 169
Callen, Commonwealth v., 73
Calvo, Commonwealth v., 702–03, 739, 740
Camelio, Commonwealth v., 324
Cameron, Commonwealth v., 67, 836
Campbell, Commonwealth v. (1967), 274
Campbell, Commonwealth v. (1979), 261
Campbell, Commonwealth v. (1988), 645
Campbell, Commonwealth v. (2003), 321
Canadyan, Commonwealth v., 724
Canavan, Case of, 816, 817, 818
Canavan, Commonwealth v., 70
Canning, Commonwealth v., 485
Cantalupo, Commonwealth v., 490
Cantres, Commonwealth v., 118, 832
Canty, Commonwealth v., 64
Caparella, Commonwealth v., 324
Caplan v. Donovan, 214, 218, 219
Caputo, Commonwealth v., 824, 837, 839
Caracciola, Commonwealth v., 296
Carapellucci, Commonwealth v., 809
Cardenuto, Commonwealth v., 635
Care & Prot. of, *see* name of party
Carey, Commonwealth v., 482, 499, 617
Carkhuff, Commonwealth v., 490
Carl, Commonwealth v., 512
Carleton, Commonwealth v., 632
Carlino v. Comm'er of Corr., 588, 750
Carlino, Commonwealth v., 573
Carlson, Commonwealth v., 427
Carp, Commonwealth v., 839
Carpinto, Commonwealth v., 858
Carr v. Lanagan, 318
Carrion, Commonwealth v., 272, 634, 808, 810
Carroll v. United States, 482
Carroll, Commonwealth v., 748, 807, 828
Carson, Commonwealth v. (1980), 452
Carson, Commonwealth v. (2008), 65
Carter, Commonwealth v. (1940), 317
Carter, Commonwealth v. (1980), 280
Carter, Commonwealth v. (1997), 488
Carter, Commonwealth v. (2000), 851
Carter, Commonwealth v. (2016), 274
Carver, Commonwealth v., 639
Casale, Commonwealth v., 269, 324
Casanova, Commonwealth v., 70, 272, 848
Case of, *see* name of party
Cash, Commonwealth v., 825
Casiano, Commonwealth v., 371
Cass, Commonwealth v., 272
Cast, Commonwealth v., 488, 495, 496
Cataldo, Commonwealth v., 849
Cathy C., Commonwealth v., 371
Cavanaugh, Commonwealth v., 628, 733
Cedeno v. Commonwealth, 108
Cefalo, Commonwealth v., 482, 484, 509, 511, 577
Celestino, Commonwealth v., 804
Cextary, Commonwealth v., 316
Chace v. Curran, 849
Chadwick, Commonwealth v., 834
Chaidez v. United States, 579, 612, 641
Chaleumphong, Commonwealth v., 271
Chalifoux, Commonwealth v., 479, 844
Chambers, Commonwealth v. (2003), 276
Chambers, Commonwealth v. (2013), 849

Chandler v. County Comm'rs of Nantucket County, 448

Chappee, Commonwealth v., 489, 607

Charbonneau v. Presiding Justice of the Holyoke Div. of the Dist. Ct. Dep't, 615

Charland, Commonwealth v., 67

Charles, Commonwealth v. (1999), 847, 853, 857

Charles, Commonwealth v. (2010), 634, 812, 832

Charles, Commonwealth v. (2012), 401

Chartrand v. Registrar of Motor Vehicles, 858

Chase, Commonwealth v., 618, 727

Chavez v. Illinois State Police, 497

Cheek, Commonwealth v. (1978), 552

Cheek, Commonwealth v. (1992), 503

Cheney, Commonwealth v., 718

Chief Admin. Justice of the Trial Ct. v. Labor Relations Comm'n, 699

Chipman, Commonwealth v., 835, 858

Chou, Commonwealth v., 452

Christian v. Commonwealth, 587

Christian, Commonwealth v., 728, 730, 750, 851

Ciesla, Commonwealth v., 335

Cimino, Commonwealth v., 354

Cinelli, Commonwealth v., 484, 618

City of, *see* name of city

Ciummei v. Commonwealth, 69, 261, 829

Claiborne, Commonwealth v., 69

Clark, Commonwealth v. (1984), 619

Clark, Commonwealth v. (2006), 107, 377

Clark, Commonwealth v. (2015), 583

Clarke, Commonwealth v. (1926), 63

Clarke, Commonwealth v. (1994), 257, 803, 853

Clarke, Commonwealth v. (1998), 485

Clarke, Commonwealth v. (2011), 579, 612, 641

Clarke, Commonwealth v. (2012), 618, 834

Clary, Commonwealth v., 635

Claudio, Commonwealth v., 111, 270

Clay, Commonwealth v., 373

Cleary, Commonwealth v., 283

Clegg, Commonwealth v., 618

Clemens, Commonwealth v., 306

Clermy, Commonwealth v., 108, 500, 507

Cline, Commonwealth v., 320

Clint C., Commonwealth v., 142

Clune, Commonwealth v., 363

Cobb, Commonwealth v., 806

Coffee, Commonwealth v., 323

Coggins, Commonwealth v., 639

Cohen, Commonwealth v. (1992), 840

Cohen, Commonwealth v. (2002), 277

Cohen, Commonwealth v. (2010), 574, 810

Cole, Commonwealth v. (2014), 10, 307, 481, 721

Cole, Commonwealth v. (2015), 812

Colella, Commonwealth v., 335

Coleman v. Alabama, 523

Coleman, Commonwealth v. (1925), 67

Coleman, Commonwealth v. (1984), 749

Coleman, Commonwealth v. (1985), 369

Colin C., Commonwealth v., 238, 819

Collado, Commonwealth v., 630

Collier, Commonwealth v., 217, 218

Collins, Commonwealth v. (1991), 729

Collins, Commonwealth v. (2003), 835

Collins, Commonwealth v. (2014), 819

Colon, Commonwealth v., 302, 400, 855

Colon-Cruz, Commonwealth v. (1984), 273, 592

Colon-Cruz, Commonwealth v. (1990), 269, 853, 854

Colondres, Commonwealth v., 483

Colonial Motor Sales, Inc., Commonwealth v., 357

Colturi, Commonwealth v., 65

Comins, Commonwealth v., 561

Commesso v. Commonwealth, 528, 531

Commissioner of Prob. v. Adams, 218

Commissioner of Pub. Safety v. Treadway, 335

Commonwealth v., *see* name of party

Comtois, Commonwealth v., 856

Conaghan, Commonwealth v. (1999), 640

Conaghan, Commonwealth v. (2000), 804

Conant, Commonwealth v., 523

Conefrey, Commonwealth v., 856

Cong Duc Le, Commonwealth v., 824, 841

Conkey, Commonwealth v., 850, 855

Connelly, Commonwealth v., 618

Connolly, Commonwealth v., 64, 285, 484, 488, 851

Connor C., Commonwealth v., 224

Connors, Commonwealth v., 169

Conroy, Commonwealth v., 317, 332

Considine, Commonwealth v., 500

Constantino, Commonwealth v., 67, 68

Contos, Commonwealth v., 623

Cook, Commonwealth v. (1980), 476, 478

Cook, Commonwealth v. (1994), 376, 804, 828

Cooley, Commonwealth v., 454

Cooper, Commonwealth v. (1881), 325

Cooper, Commonwealth v. (1928), 314, 315

Corcoran, Commonwealth v. (1965), 325, 562

Corcoran, Commonwealth v. (2007), 335

Cordeiro, Commonwealth v., 231, 605

Cordle, Commonwealth v., 635, 823, 844

Corey v. Commonwealth, 523, 524

Corey, Commonwealth v., 380

Corrado v. Hedrick, 212

Correa, Commonwealth v., 843

Correia, Commonwealth v., 616, 854

Corridori, Commonwealth v., 189

Cortellesso v. Commonwealth, 333

Cory, Commonwealth v., 308, 719, 721

Cosolito, Commonwealth v., 427

Costa, Commonwealth v., 494

Costarelli v. Commonwealth, 68

Costarelli v. Mun. Ct., 523

Cote, Commonwealth v., 602

Coutore, Commonwealth v., 504

Coviello, Commonwealth v., 233

Cowan, Commonwealth v., 639

Craan, Commonwealth v., 110, 115, 497

Cramer v. Commonwealth, 261

Crawford v. Washington, 739, 806, 812, 815, 819, 830, 855

Crawford, Commonwealth v. (1999), 824

Crawford, Commonwealth v. (2000), 286

Crayton, Commonwealth v., 819

Crocker, Commonwealth v., 363, 574

Croken, Commonwealth v., 633, 808, 840

Cromer, Commonwealth v., 510, 514

Cromwell, Commonwealth v., 335

Crooker v. Chairman of the Mass. Parole Bd., 588

Crosby, Commonwealth v., 401

Crosscup, Commonwealth v., 54, 291

Crouse, Commonwealth v., 231

Crowell, Commonwealth v., 78

Crowley, Commonwealth v. (1897), 292

Crowley, Commonwealth v. (1984), 808

Crowley, Commonwealth v. (1997), 469

Cruz v. New York, 605

Cruz, Commonwealth v. (1992), 271

Cruz, Commonwealth v. (1999), 316, 319

Cruz, Commonwealth v. (2011), 109, 115, 497

Cruz, Commonwealth v. (2015), 282

Cruz, Commonwealth v. (2016), 114

Cruzado, Commonwealth v., 291

Cunneen, Commonwealth v., 269

Cunningham, Commonwealth v., 605

Curley, Commonwealth v., 65

Curnin, Commonwealth v., 812

Curtis, Commonwealth v., 839, 840

Curtiss, Commonwealth v., 841

Cyr, Commonwealth v. (1997), 853

Cyr, Commonwealth v. (2001), 272, 857

D

Dagenais, Commonwealth v., 269

Dale D., Commonwealth v., 142

Daley v. Bd. of Appeal on Motor Vehicle Liab. Policies & Bonds, 69, 78–79

Daley, Commonwealth v., 68, 456

Damiano, Commonwealth v., 470

D'Amour, Commonwealth v., 498

Danforth v. Minnesota, 579, 641

Daniel, Commonwealth v., 64, 497

Daniels, Commonwealth v., 522, 641

Darby, Commonwealth v., 842

Darch, Commonwealth v., 827

Dargon, Commonwealth v., 294, 822

Darnell D., Commonwealth v., 322

DaSilva, Commonwealth v., 836

Daubert v. Merrell Dow Pharm., Inc., 817, 820

Davidson, Commonwealth v., 278

Davis v. Alaska, 147

Davis v. Washington, 806, 812, 830, 855

Davis, Commonwealth v. (1978), 818

Davis, Commonwealth v. (1979), 291

Davis, Commonwealth v. (1980), 285

Davis, Commonwealth v. (1990), 470

Davis, Commonwealth v. (1991), 257

Davis, Commonwealth v. (1996), 323, 324

Davis, Commonwealth v. (2005), 491

Davis, Commonwealth v. (2007), 291

Dawson, Commonwealth v., 107, 368, 832

Day, Commonwealth v., 297, 810

Daye, Commonwealth v. (1984), 824, 845

Daye, Commonwealth v. (2001), 632, 842, 847

Dayes, Commonwealth v., 838

De Golyer v. Commonwealth, 260

De La Cruz, Commonwealth v., 630, 632

Dean, Commonwealth v., 302

Dean-Ganek, Commonwealth v., 610, 613, 615

DeBenedetto v. Goodyear Tire & Rubber Co., 829

Deberry, Commonwealth v., 231, 354

Debrosky, Commonwealth v., 228

DeCillis, Commonwealth v., 479

DeCologero, Commonwealth v., 843

Dedomenicis, Commonwealth v., 503

DeFuria, Commonwealth v., 827

Degro, Commonwealth v., 634, 806, 840

12

DeJesus, Commonwealth v. (1999), 498
DeJesus, Commonwealth v. (2003), 638, 640
DeJesus, Commonwealth v. (2014), 612
DeJoinville v. Commonwealth, 289
Delaney, Commonwealth v. (1994), 703, 740
Delaney, Commonwealth v. (1997), 217, 218
DeLarosa, Commonwealth v., 837
Delaware v. Fensterer, 857
Delgado, Commonwealth v., 276, 287
Delisle, Commonwealth v., 719, 728
Dellamano, Commonwealth v., 321
Delle Chiaie, Commonwealth v., 827
Dellinger, Commonwealth v., 332, 478
Dello Iacono, Commonwealth v., 286, 291
DeLuca v. Boston. Elev. Ry., 213
DelValle, Commonwealth v., 844
DelVerde, Commonwealth v. (1986), 157
DelVerde, Commonwealth v. (1988), 158, 225
DeMinico, Commonwealth v., 808
Demogenes, Commonwealth v., 427
Denehy, Commonwealth v., 645, 848
D'Entremont, Commonwealth v., 837, 847
Department of Youth Servs. v. A Juvenile, 818
Depiero, Commonwealth v., 494
Depina, Commonwealth v., 832
Deramo, Commonwealth v., 54, 70, 234, 496
DeRome, Commonwealth v., 318
Derosia, Commonwealth v., 518
Dery, Commonwealth v., 630
Desper, Commonwealth v., 512
DeVaga v. Gonzalez, 612
DeVincent, Commonwealth v., 301
Devlin, Commonwealth v., 477
Dew, Commonwealth v., 856
Dias, Commonwealth v (1988), 157
Dias, Commonwealth v (1989), 605
Dias, Commonwealth v. (2000), 623
Diatchenko v. Dist. Attorney for the Suffolk Dist., 273
Diaz, Commonwealth v., 107
DiBenedetto, Commonwealth v., 804
DiBennadetto, Commonwealth v., 224
Dickinson, Commonwealth v., 824
DiFrancesco, United States v., 744
DiGeronimo, Commonwealth v., 491
Diggs, Commonwealth v., 534
DiGiambattista, Commonwealth v., 836
Dilone, Commonwealth v., 613, 614
DiMarzo, Commonwealth v., 231
DiMatteo, Commonwealth v., 401
Dimond, Commonwealth v., 320
DiMonte, Commonwealth v., 815
Dingle, Commonwealth v., 446, 837, 839
Dinkins, Commonwealth v., 616
DiRoma, Commonwealth v., 147
Disler, Commonwealth v., 302
DiStasio, Commonwealth v., 476
District Attorney for the Northwestern Dist. v. Eastern Hampshire Div. of the Dist. Ct. Dep't, 121
District Attorney for the Suffolk Dist. v. Watson, 273
District Attorney's Office for the Third Judicial Dist. v. Osborne, 581
District of Columbia v. Heller, 400
Dixon, Commonwealth v., 565, 601
Dockham, Commonwealth v., 297
Dodge, Commonwealth v., 531, 722, 723
Doe v. Attorney Gen. (No. 1), 147

Doe v. Attorney Gen. (No. 2), 10, 763
Doe v. Police Comm'r of Boston, 14
Doe v. Sex Offender Registry Bd. (1998), 13, 14
Doe v. Sex Offender Registry Bd. (2006), 14, 15
Doe v. Sex Offender Registry Bd. (2007), 14
Doe v. Sex Offender Registry Bd. (2008), 14, 15
Doe v. Sex Offender Registry Bd. (2011), 16
Doe v. State Ethics Comm'n, 394
Doe v. Superintendent of Sch. of Worcester, 401
Doe, Commonwealth v. (1989), 1
Doe, Commonwealth v. (1992), 847
Doe, Commonwealth v. (1995), 552
Doe, Commonwealth v. (2005), 308
Doe, Sex Offender Registry Bd. No. 10800 v. Sex Offender Registry Bd., 720, 721
Donald, Commonwealth v., 582
Donnelly, Commonwealth v., 845
Donovan, Commonwealth v., 286, 323
Dorazio, Commonwealth v., 807, 808
Dorelas, Commonwealth v., 483
Dorvil, Commonwealth v., 277
Dossantos, Commonwealth v., 526
Dotson, Commonwealth v., 257, 625
Doucette, Commonwealth v., 290, 316, 317, 617, 639, 712
Douzanis, Commonwealth v., 512
Dow, Commonwealth v., 338
Dowler, Commonwealth v., 78
Dowling v. United States, 807
Downs, Commonwealth v., 65, 66
Doyle, Commonwealth v. (1981), 617
Doyle, Commonwealth v. (2008), 75
Draheim, Commonwealth v., 805
Draper v. United States, 493
Dresser, Commonwealth v., 170
Drew, Commonwealth v., 287
Drumgoole, Commonwealth v., 371
Dube, Commonwealth v., 70
Dubois, Commonwealth v. (1998), 489
Dubois, Commonwealth v. (2008), 257
Dubowski, Commonwealth v., 749
Duddie Ford, Inc., Commonwealth v., 327
Duguay, Commonwealth v., 805, 843
Dunn, Commonwealth v., 290, 811, 858
Dunn, United States v., 483
Duong v. Commonwealth, 587, 672
Duquette, Commonwealth v., 718
Duran, Commonwealth v., 840
Durand, Commonwealth v., 831
Durham, Commonwealth v., 285
Durling, Commonwealth v., 535, 542, 689, 700, 701, 702, 703, 705, 712, 713, 727, 734, 737, 738, 739, 740, 741, 743, 746, 748
Durning, Commonwealth v., 65, 607
Duro, Commonwealth v., 689
Dusky v. United States, 808
Dussault, Commonwealth v., 69, 70, 829
Dwyer, Commonwealth v., 227, 229, 846
Dyer, Commonwealth v., 336, 833
Dykens, Commonwealth v., 332

E

E.C.O. v. Compton, 211
Eagleston, Commonwealth v., 490
Eagle-Tribune Publ'g Co. v. Clerk-Magistrate of the Lawrence Div. of the Dist. Ct. Dep't, 224

Eason, Commonwealth v., 469
Eaton, Commonwealth v., 276, 277
Eaton, United States v., 617
Edge v. Commonwealth, 218, 282, 306
Edwards v. Arizona, 834, 837
Edwards, Commonwealth v. (1995), 838, 839
Edwards, Commonwealth v. (2005), 822, 823
Edwards, Commonwealth v. (2008), 502
Egerstaffer v. Israel, 739
Egerton, Commonwealth v., 278
Egleson, Commonwealth v., 349
Eisenstadt v. Baird, 441
Elizondo, Commonwealth v., 500, 507, 630
Elliffe, Commonwealth v., 479
Ellis, Commonwealth v. (1947), 299
Ellis, Commonwealth v. (1970), 107
Ellis, Commonwealth v. (2000), 857
Ellis, Commonwealth v. (2011), 833
Ellison, Commonwealth v., 625
Emence, Commonwealth v., 847
Emilio E., Commonwealth v., 721
Emmanuel E., A Juvenile, Commonwealth v., 738–39, 743
England, Commonwealth v., 323
Ennis, Commonwealth v (2003), 470
Ennis, Commonwealth v (2004), 628
Eppich, Commonwealth v., 317
Erdely, Commonwealth v., 271
Escalera, Commonwealth v., 486, 837
Estabrook, Commonwealth v., 483
Esteves, Commonwealth v., 647
Estremera, Commonwealth v., 820
Eugene, Commonwealth v., 272
Evans, Commonwealth v., 490, 844
Evelyn, Commonwealth v., 634
Everett, Commonwealth v., 576

F

Falvey, Commonwealth v., 354
Fancy, Commonwealth v., 400
Fano, Commonwealth v., 231
Farrell, Commonwealth v., 277, 283
Farris, Commonwealth v., 645
Farrow, Commonwealth v., 493
Fatalo, Commonwealth v., 818
Faulkner, Commonwealth v., 542, 699, 733, 734
Fay v. Commonwealth, 696, 705, 706, 712, 732, 734, 748
Fay, Commonwealth v., 165
Fayerweather, Commonwealth v., 226, 619
Federici, Commonwealth v., 846
Federico, Commonwealth v., 818, 819
Felix F., a Juvenile v. Commonwealth, 142
Fenderson, Commonwealth v., 470, 482
Fenton, Commonwealth v., 401
Fenton F., Commonwealth v., 640
Ferguson, Commonwealth v. (1981), 449, 451
Ferguson, Commonwealth v. (1991), 489, 503
Fernandes, Commonwealth v. (1997), 228
Fernandes, Commonwealth v. (1998), 808, 824
Fernandez, Commonwealth v., 811
Ferola, Commonwealth v., 66
Feroli, Commonwealth v., 231
Ferrara, Commonwealth v. (1975), 147
Ferrara, Commonwealth v. (1980), 488, 504
Ferreira, Commonwealth v., 67, 854

12

Ferrer, Commonwealth v., 837
Feyenord, Commonwealth v., 497
Fico, Commonwealth v., 642
Fidler, Commonwealth v., 636
Figueroa, Commonwealth v. (1992), 820, 839
Figueroa, Commonwealth v. (2002), 75
Figueroa, Commonwealth v. (2013), 371
Filopoulos, Commonwealth v., 302
Finase, Commonwealth v., 218
Finegan, Commonwealth v., 66
Fini, Commonwealth v., 469
Fiore, Commonwealth v., 818
Fisher, Commonwealth v., 503
Fitzgerald v. Lewis, 349
Fitzgerald, Commonwealth v. (1988), 296
Fitzgerald, Commonwealth v. (1992), 232
Flebotte, Commonwealth v., 297, 630, 632, 814, 819
Fleming, Commonwealth v., 289
Fleurant, Commonwealth v., 449, 512
Flowers, Commonwealth v., 288
Floyd P., Commonwealth v., 829
Fluker, Commonwealth v., 269
Flynn v. Warner, 218
Flynn, Commonwealth v., 288
Foley v. Commonwealth, 604
Foley, Commonwealth v. (1981), 806
Foley, Commonwealth v. (1988), 589
Foley, Commonwealth v. (2005), 814
Fontaine, Commonwealth v., 618
Fontes, Commonwealth v., 624
Ford, Commonwealth v. (1985), 495
Ford, Commonwealth v. (1986), 231
Ford, Commonwealth v. (1997), 276
Forde, Commonwealth v., 64
Foreman, Commonwealth v., 405
Fortune, Commonwealth v., 320, 325
Foss v. Commonwealth, 158
Foster, Commonwealth v. (1873), 361
Foster, Commonwealth v. (2015), 270
Fourteen Thousand Two Hundred Dollars, Commonwealth v., 121
Fowler, Commonwealth v. (1997), 812
Fowler, Commonwealth v. (2000), 293, 636
Fox, Commonwealth v., 4, 834
Foxworth v. St. Amand, 638
Francis, Commonwealth v. (2000), 245
Francis, Commonwealth v. (2016), 814
Franklin, Commonwealth v., 147, 501
Franks v. Delaware, 512, 513
Franks, Commonwealth v. (1971), 297
Franks, Commonwealth v. (1976), 297
Fraser, Commonwealth v., 502
Frate, Commonwealth v., 423
Frazier, Commonwealth v., 487, 488, 804
Freeman, Commonwealth v. (1968), 95
Freeman, Commonwealth v. (1990), 275, 602
Freeman, Commonwealth v. (1999), 823
Freeman, Commonwealth v. (2015), 142
French, Commonwealth v., 477
Frias, Commonwealth v., 846
Friend, Commonwealth v., 578, 627
Frith, Commonwealth v., 626
Frizado v. Frizado, 211, 213
Fryar, Commonwealth v., 274, 803, 844
Frye v. United States, 817, 818
Fuller, Commonwealth v., 268
Furtado v. Furtado, 648

G

Gagnon v. Scarpelli, 542, 699, 702, 706, 712, 731, 733, 734, 738, 739, 747
Gagnon, Commonwealth v., 1, 803
Gajka, Commonwealth v., 496
Galicia, Commonwealth v., 855
Gallant, Commonwealth v., 293, 449
Gallego, Commonwealth v., 806
Gallinaro v. Commonwealth, 634
Gallison, Commonwealth v., 844
Gallo, Commonwealth v., 559
Galvin, Commonwealth v., 108
Gambora, Commonwealth v., 820
Garabedian, Commonwealth v., 275
Garcia, Commonwealth v. (1986), 486
Garcia, Commonwealth v. (1991), 107, 495
Garcia, Commonwealth v. (1999), 281
Garcia, Commonwealth v. (2012), 401
Garcia-Echeverria v. United States, 109, 115
Garreffi, Commonwealth v., 333
Garrett, Commonwealth v., 288
Garrey, Commonwealth v., 240, 608
Garrity, Commonwealth v., 816
Gaulden, Commonwealth v., 275
Gault, In re, 693
Gauthier, Commonwealth v., 483
Gavin G., Commonwealth v., 552
Gay, Petition of, 516
Gay & Lesbian Advocates & Defenders v. Attorney Gen., 449
Gaynor, Commonwealth v., 812
Gee, Commonwealth v., 840
Geoghegan, Commonwealth v., 473
Giannino, Commonwealth v., 67, 68, 774
Giavazzi, Commonwealth v., 331
Giberti, Commonwealth v., 839
Gichel, Commonwealth v., 293
Giles, Commonwealth v., 368
Gill, Commonwealth v., 107
Gillis, Commonwealth v., 168
Giontzis, Commonwealth v., 626, 846
Girouard, Commonwealth v., 836
Given, Commonwealth v., 170
Glaubius v. State, 848
Gliniewicz, Commonwealth v., 607
Globe Newspaper Co. v. Superior Ct., 574, 809, 810
Glover v. Callahan, 299
Glover, Commonwealth v., 316
Goe v. Comm'r of Probation, 731
Goewey, Commonwealth v., 496
Goggin, Commonwealth v., 486
Goldenberg, Commonwealth v., 295
Goldman, Commonwealth v. (1977), 287
Goldman, Commonwealth v. (1986), 121
Goldoff, Commonwealth v., 316
Goldstein, Commonwealth v., 315
Gomes, Commonwealth v. (1988), 818
Gomes, Commonwealth v. (1990), 486, 603
Gomes, Commonwealth v. (2009), 501, 503, 543, 724
Gomes, Commonwealth v. (2015), 819, 820
Gomez, Commonwealth v., 538, 635
Gonsalves, Commonwealth v. (1999), 496
Gonsalves, Commonwealth v. (2000), 628
Gonsalves, Commonwealth v. (2002), 321, 322
Gonsalves, Commonwealth v. (2005), 814, 833, 855, 857
Gonsalves, Commonwealth v. (2009), 838
Gonzales, Commonwealth v. (1992), 113

Gonzales, Commonwealth v. (1997), 843
Gonzalez, Commonwealth v. (1988), 493
Gonzalez, Commonwealth v. (2005), 828
Gonzalez, Commonwealth v. (2007), 400
Gonzalez, Commonwealth v. (2014), 852
Goodwin, Commonwealth v., 611, 730, 749, 851
Gopaul, Commonwealth v., 114
Gorassi, Commonwealth v., 276
Gordon, Commonwealth v. (1978), 616
Gordon, Commonwealth v. (1996), 270, 286
Gordon, Commonwealth v. (1997), 290, 316
Goren, Commonwealth v., 329
Gorman, Commonwealth v., 95
Gosselin, Commonwealth v., 478
Gould, Commonwealth v., 811
Goulet, Commonwealth v., 625
Gove, Commonwealth v., 644, 645
Grace, Commonwealth v. (1928), 317
Grace, Commonwealth v. (1997), 118
Grady, Commonwealth v., 840
Graham, Commonwealth v., 376
Grand Jury Investigation, In the Matter of, 805, 846
Grand Jury Subpoena, In re, 484, 629
Grandison, Commonwealth v., 376, 489, 501, 806
Grant, Commonwealth v. (1994), 814
Grant, Commonwealth v. (1998), 843
Grasso, Commonwealth v., 400, 401
Gray, Commonwealth v., 82
Graziano, Commonwealth v., 855
Green, Commonwealth v. (1990), 66
Green, Commonwealth v. (1995), 828
Greenberg, Commonwealth v., 327
Gregory, Commonwealth v., 625
Grey, Commonwealth v., 268, 269, 812
Grice, Commonwealth v., 630
Griffen, Commonwealth v., 218
Griffin v. Wisconsin, 724
Griffin, Commonwealth v. (1839), 364
Griffin, Commonwealth v. (1989), 559
Griffith, Commonwealth v., 233
Grimshaw, Commonwealth v., 482, 486, 825
Grinkley, Commonwealth v., 806
Grise, Commonwealth v., 69
Groh v. Ramirez, 510
Gross, Commonwealth v., 170
Grossman, Commonwealth v., 334
Guaba, Commonwealth v., 510, 628
Guadalupe, Commonwealth v., 625
Guaman, Commonwealth v., 75
Guilfoyle, Commonwealth v., 17
Gullick, Commonwealth v., 804
Gurney, Commonwealth v., 67, 857
Guyton, Commonwealth v., 837
Guzman, Commonwealth v., 308, 721

H

Habarek, Commonwealth v., 617
Haddock, Commonwealth v., 849
Hagen v. Commonwealth, 672
Haith, Commonwealth v., 522
Hall, Commonwealth v. (1985), 590
Hall, Commonwealth v. (2000), 316, 810
Hallett v. Rimer, 64
Halsey, Commonwealth v., 509
Hamilton, Commonwealth v., 371, 858
Hammond, Commonwealth v., 641
Hanlon, Commonwealth v., 808
Hannaford, Commonwealth v., 277

12

Hanover Ins. Co. v. Rapo & James Ins. Servs., Inc., 827
Hanright, Commonwealth v., 622, 623
Hanson H., Commonwealth v., 308, 721
Haraldstad, Commonwealth v., 807
Harding v. Commonwealth, 336
Hardy, Commonwealth v., 812
Harrell, United States v., 832
Harrington, Commonwealth v., 272, 285
Harris, Commonwealth v. (1973), 837
Harris, Commonwealth v. (1980), 287, 560
Harris, Commonwealth v. (1981), 490, 806
Harris, Commonwealth v. (1985), 855
Harris, Commonwealth v. (2005), 232, 293, 807
Harris, United States v., 482
Harrison, Commonwealth v., 734
Hart, Commonwealth v., 63, 816
Hartfield, Commonwealth v., 738, 748
Hartford, Commonwealth v., 837
Hartman, Commonwealth v., 236
Haskell, Commonwealth v., 189, 619
Hason, Commonwealth v., 843
Hassey, Commonwealth v., 828
Hawkins, Commonwealth v. (1855), 270
Hawkins, Commonwealth v. (1986), 289
Hayes, Commonwealth v., 618
Haynes, Commonwealth v., 296
Hays, Commonwealth v., 324, 325
Haywood, Commonwealth v. (1923), 617
Haywood, Commonwealth v. (1979), 147
Healey, Commonwealth v., 376
Healy, Commonwealth v., 618
Heang, Commonwealth v., 817
Hebert, Commonwealth v. (1977), 275
Hebert, Commonwealth v. (1980), 636
Helfant, Commonwealth v., 295, 439, 844
Hendricks, Commonwealth v., 282
Henry, Commonwealth v. (1875), 361
Henry, Commonwealth v. (1994), 401, 823, 830
Henry, Commonwealth v. (2016), 325, 727, 848
Hensley, Commonwealth v., 819, 831
Hensley, United States v., 502
Henson, Commonwealth v. (1970), 286
Henson, Commonwealth v. (1985), 288, 289
Herd, Commonwealth v., 271, 825, 826
Hernandez, Commonwealth v., 812, 829, 854
Herndon, Commonwealth v., 820
Herrera, Commonwealth v., 733, 745, 749
Hilaire, Commonwealth v., 579
Hill, Commonwealth v. (2001), 737, 738, 741, 742, 748
Hill, Commonwealth v. (2003), 318
Hill, Petitioner, 168
Hilton, Commonwealth v., 835
Hinds, Commonwealth v., 446
Hines, Commonwealth v., 290
Hobbs, Commonwealth v., 630, 631, 632
Hodge, Commonwealth v., 587, 672
Hodges, United States v., 625
Hoffer, Commonwealth v., 824
Hogan, Commonwealth v. (1979), 283
Hogan, Commonwealth v. (1996), 332
Hogan, United States v., 858
Hoilett, Commonwealth v., 841
Holland, Commonwealth v., 842
Holley, Commonwealth v., 492, 496, 503
Holliday, Commonwealth v., 626

Holmgren, Commonwealth v., 543, 700, 705, 706, 707, 712, 736, 737, 744, 745, 749, 750, 854
Hooker, Commonwealth v., 492
Hooper, Commonwealth v., 803
Horsfall, Commonwealth v., 67, 68
Hosman, Commonwealth v., 354
Housen, Commonwealth v., 831
Housewright, Commonwealth v., 748, 845
Houston, Commonwealth v., 272
Howard, Commonwealth v. (1982), 287
Howard, Commonwealth v. (1997), 854
Howard, Commonwealth v. (2012), 719
Howe, Commonwealth v. (1882), 324
Howe, Commonwealth v. (1989), 69, 70
Hrycenko, Commonwealth v., 261, 296, 371
Hubbard, Commonwealth v., 261, 630
Hudson, Commonwealth v. (1989), 326, 645
Hudson, Commonwealth v. (1994), 296
Huffman, Commonwealth v., 118
Humberto H., Commonwealth v., 142
Humphries, Commonwealth v., 400
Hunter, Commonwealth v. (1994), 854
Hunter, Commonwealth v. (1998), 804, 838
Hurley v. Irish-American Gay Lesbian & Bisexual Group of Boston, 463
Hussey (No. 1), Commonwealth v., 834
Hutchins, Commonwealth v., 840
Hyatt, Commonwealth v., 851

I

Iamele v. Asselin, 213
Ierardi, Commonwealth v., 69
Iglesia, Commonwealth v., 402
Illinois v. Gates, 482
Illinois v. Rodriguez, 491
In re, *see* name of party
In the Matter of, *see* name of party

J

Jackson v. Commonwealth, 846
Jackson v. Indiana, 534
Jackson, Commonwealth v. (1975), 523
Jackson, Commonwealth v. (1976), 535
Jackson, Commonwealth v. (1979), 618, 834
Jackson, Commonwealth v. (1994), 300
Jackson, Commonwealth v. (1998), 811
Jackson, Commonwealth v. (2000), 269, 270, 837, 839
Jackson, Commonwealth v. (2013), 109, 115, 497
Jackson, Commonwealth v. (2015), 272
Jacobsen, Commonwealth v., 211, 216
Jacobson v. Winter, 645
Jake J. v. Commonwealth, 531, 543, 723, 732
James, Commonwealth v. (1997), 630, 805, 827
James, Commonwealth v. (1998), 834
James, Commonwealth v. (2008), 479
Jansen, In re, 805, 805
Jaquith v. Commonwealth, 449
Jasmin, Commonwealth v., 113, 635, 636
Jean-Pierre, Commonwealth v., 277
Jefferson, Commonwealth v. (1979), 572, 573
Jefferson, Commonwealth v. (2012), 403, 626
Jenkins v. Chief Justice of the Dist. Ct. Dep't, 168, 531
Jenkins, Commonwealth v., 812
Jensky, Commonwealth v., 427

Jewett, Commonwealth v., 295, 505
Jiles, Commonwealth v., 269
Jimenez, Commonwealth v., 487
Johnson v. MBTA, 235
Johnson v. United States, 405
Johnson, Commonwealth v. (1908), 333
Johnson, Commonwealth v. (1978), 68
Johnson, Commonwealth v. (1979), 287, 321, 323
Johnson, Commonwealth v. (1989), 111
Johnson, Commonwealth v. (1991), 818
Johnson, Commonwealth v. (1992), 107, 233, 503, 805, 810, 818
Johnson, Commonwealth v. (1995), 616, 852
Johnson, Commonwealth v. (1996), 522
Johnson, Commonwealth v. (1999), 840, 858
Johnson, Commonwealth v. (2002), 113
Johnson, Commonwealth v. (2011), 401, 630
Johnson, Commonwealth v. (2014), 306
Johnson, Commonwealth v. (2015), 819
Johnston, Commonwealth v., 284
Jones v. United States, 482
Jones v. Vappi & Co., 847
Jones, Commonwealth v. (1969), 332
Jones, Commonwealth v. (1971), 645
Jones, Commonwealth v. (1972), 291
Jones, Commonwealth v. (1977), 400, 572
Jones, Commonwealth v. (1978), 284
Jones, Commonwealth v. (1981), 75, 275
Jones, Commonwealth v. (1994), 579
Jones, Commonwealth v. (1997), 806
Jones, Commonwealth v. (2003), 314, 315, 834
Jones, Commonwealth v. (2015), 232, 810
Jordan, Commonwealth v. (No. 1) (1986), 852
Jordan, Commonwealth v. (2000), 479, 806
Jordan, Commonwealth v. (2003), 632
Jordan, Commonwealth v. (2014), 627, 628
Joubert, Commonwealth v., 703, 740, 741, 743, 747
Joyce, Commonwealth v., 232
Joyner, Commonwealth v., 288
Judge, Commonwealth v., 834
Julien, Commonwealth v., 856
Jung, Commonwealth v., 482, 498, 835
Juvenile, A, Commonwealth v. (1980), 525
Juvenile, A, Commonwealth v. (1981), 67
Juvenile, A, Commonwealth v. (1984), 286
Juvenile, A, Commonwealth v. (1987), 297
Juvenile, A, Commonwealth v. (1988), 616
Juvenile, A (No. 1), Commonwealth v. (1978), 349
Juvenile, A (No. 2), Commonwealth v. (1981), 147
Juvenile, A (No. 2), Commonwealth v. (1991), 496
Juzba, Commonwealth v., 19, 719, 729, 736, 737, 852

K

Kace v. Liang, 827
Kalhauser, Commonwealth v., 636
Kalinowski, Commonwealth v., 318
Kane, Commonwealth v., 811
Kaplan, Commonwealth v., 315
Kappler, Commonwealth v., 840
Kater, Commonwealth v., 844
Kaupp, Commonwealth v., 514
Kebreau, Commonwealth v., 294, 821
Kee, Commonwealth v., 839

Keefner, Commonwealth v., 109, 115
Keevan, Commonwealth v., 295, 805
Keita, Commonwealth v., 826
Keizer, Commonwealth v., 702, 855
Kelcourse, Commonwealth v., 270
Kelley, Commonwealth v. (1955), 335
Kelley, Commonwealth v. (1994), 369
Kelly, Commonwealth v. (1973), 477
Kelly, Commonwealth v. (2007), 377
Kelly, Commonwealth v. (2015), 304
Kelsey, Commonwealth v., 748
Kendrick, Commonwealth v. (1966), 272, 376
Kendrick, Commonwealth v. (2006), 217
Kennedy, Commonwealth v. (1998), 500
Kennedy, Commonwealth v. (2002), 168, 169
Kenney, Commonwealth v., 446, 447
Kepper, Commonwealth v., 361
Kerns, Commonwealth v., 410
Kerr, Commonwealth v., 301
Kessler, Commonwealth v., 441, 855
Kiernan, Commonwealth v., 573
Kimball, Commonwealth v., 504
Kimbroughtillery v. Commonwealth, 745
Kines, Commonwealth v., 806
King, Commonwealth v. (1909), 562
King, Commonwealth v. (1977), 451, 452
King, Commonwealth v. (1999), 260
King, Commonwealth v. (2002), 850
King, Commonwealth v. (2005), 293, 294, 297, 820, 821, 822
King, Commonwealth v. (2007), 371
Kingsbury, Commonwealth v., 316
Klusman, Commonwealth v., 113
Knap, Commonwealth v., 299
Kneram, Commonwealth v., 173
Knight, Commonwealth v., 810
Knowlton, Commonwealth v., 368
Kobrin v. Bd. of Registration in Med., 696
Koney, Commonwealth v., 54, 69
Kostka, Commonwealth v., 808
Koulouris, Commonwealth v., 633
Kozec, Commonwealth v., 806
Kozlowsky, Commonwealth v., 560
Krasner, Commonwealth v., 332, 349
Krochta v. Commonwealth, 744, 745
Kronick, Commonwealth v., 335
Kruah, Commonwealth v., 804
Kuklis v. Commonwealth, 107
Kuperstein, Commonwealth v., 335
Kwiatkowski, Commonwealth v., 858
Kyles v. Whitley, 816

L
Labare, Commonwealth v., 316, 317
L'Abbe, Commonwealth v., 580, 808
LaBrie, Commonwealth v., 287, 478
LaCava, Commonwealth v., 824, 837
Ladd, Commonwealth v., 361
LaFaille, Commonwealth v., 811
Lafaso, Commonwealth v., 849
LaFrance, Commonwealth v., 498, 700, 713, 725, 730
Lake, Commonwealth v., 424
Lam, Commonwealth v., 629
Lam Hue To, Commonwealth v., 607, 634
Lamarche v. Lussier, 218
Lamb, Commonwealth v., 225
Lameire, Commonwealth v., 846
Lamont L., Commonwealth v., 142
Lamothe, Commonwealth v., 314

Lampron, Commonwealth v., 566, 629, 833, 846
Landenburg, Commonwealth v., 809
Landry v. Attorney Gen., 20, 812
Lanigan, Commonwealth v., 645, 812, 817, 818, 820
Lanoue, Commonwealth v., 617, 635
Lao, Commonwealth v., 805, 815, 857
Lapine, Commonwealth v., 512
LaPlante, Commonwealth v., 302
Lapointe, Commonwealth v. (1988), 573, 848
Lapointe, Commonwealth v. (2001), 725
Larkin, Commonwealth v., 836
Laro, Commonwealth v., 113
Latimore, Commonwealth v., 261, 287, 324, 635, 636, 814
Latney, Commonwealth v., 317, 814
Laurore, Commonwealth v., 857
Lauzier, Commonwealth v., 354
Lavigne, Commonwealth v., 277
Lavigne, In the Matter of, 507
Lavoie, Commonwealth v., 574, 810
Lavrinenko, Commonwealth v., 641
Lawrence, Commonwealth v. (1989), 272, 855
Lawrence, Commonwealth v. (2007), 445
Lawson, Commonwealth v., 376, 830, 858
Layne, Commonwealth v., 638, 750
Leate, Commonwealth v., 274
LeBeau, Commonwealth v., 522
LeBlanc, Commonwealth v. (1973), 805
LeBlanc, Commonwealth v. (1975), 279
LeBlanc, Commonwealth v. (1976), 749
LeBlanc, Commonwealth v. (1990), 69
LeBlanc, Commonwealth v. (2001), 839
LeClair, Commonwealth v., 271, 632, 841–42
Lednum, Commonwealth v., 285
Lee, Commonwealth v. (1974), 107
Lee, Commonwealth v. (1980), 189, 512
Lemar, Commonwealth v., 856
Lenahan, Commonwealth v., 272, 804
Lender, Commonwealth v., 148
Leneski, Commonwealth v., 808
Lent, Commonwealth v., 302, 564
Leo, Commonwealth v., 450
Leonard, Commonwealth v. (1967), 324
Leonard, Commonwealth v. (1988), 64, 512, 634
Leonard, Commonwealth v. (1996), 70
Leonard, Commonwealth v. (1999), 844
Leonardi, Commonwealth v., 844
Leone v. Doran, 811
LePage, Commonwealth v., 742
LePore, Commonwealth v., 452
Lester L., Commonwealth v., 535
Lett, Commonwealth v., 510
Levesque, Commonwealth v., 274, 275, 602
Levia, Commonwealth v., 290
Lewin (No. 1), Commonwealth v., 492
Lewin (No. 2), Commonwealth v., 617
Lewinski, Commonwealth v., 274
Lewis, Commonwealth v. (1963), 316
Lewis, Commonwealth v. (1980), 272
Lewis, Commonwealth v. (1996), 68, 321
Lewis, Commonwealth v. (1999), 324, 626, 856
Libby, Commonwealth v. (1971), 300
Libby, Commonwealth v. (2015), 168
Libran, Commonwealth v., 617
Licata, Commonwealth v., 293, 821
Liebenow, Commonwealth v., 288, 325

Liebman, Commonwealth v., 559
Life Care Ctrs. of Am., Inc., Commonwealth v., 275
Lindner, Commonwealth v., 260
Lindsay, Commonwealth v., 403
Lindsey, Commonwealth v., 402
Liotti, Commonwealth v., 330
Little, Commonwealth v., 852
Loadholt, Commonwealth v., 400
Lockhart v. Fretwell, 825
Logan v. Goward, 42
Lojko, Commonwealth v., 205
Long, Commonwealth v., 470
Look, Commonwealth v., 524, 645
Lopez, Commonwealth v. (1981), 400, 401
Lopez, Commonwealth v. (1998), 843
Lopez, Commonwealth v. (2001), 295
Lopez, Commonwealth v. (2008), 501
Lora, Commonwealth v. (1997), 847
Lora, Commonwealth v. (2008), 497
Lord, Commonwealth v., 285
Louis Constr. Co., Inc., Commonwealth v., 368
Louraine, Commonwealth v., 857
Love, Commonwealth v., 618, 628
Lovelace, Commonwealth v., 68
Lovett, Commonwealth v., 317
Lowder, Commonwealth v., 827, 841
Lowrey, Commonwealth v., 317
Ludwig, Commonwealth v., 523, 827
Lugo, Commonwealth v., 485, 619, 854
Lupo, Commonwealth v., 117
Lydon, Commonwealth v., 809
Lyons, Commonwealth v. (1998), 157, 808
Lyons, Commonwealth v. (2005), 269, 842
Lyons, Commonwealth v. (2008), 293, 294, 821

M
MacDonald, Commonwealth v. (2000), 727, 728, 730, 731, 854
MacDonald, Commonwealth v. (2001), 688, 731, 742, 748
MacDonald, Commonwealth v. (2011), 832
Macias, Commonwealth v., 486
Mackedon, Commonwealth v., 828
Madden, Commonwealth v., 535
Madera, Commonwealth v., 1, 500
Maggio, Commonwealth v., 701, 731, 733, 740, 743, 743, 746, 747
Magnus M., Commonwealth v., 146, 718
Magraw v. Commonwealth, 531
Mahadeo, Commonwealth v., 579
Maher, Commonwealth v., 69
Mahoney, Commonwealth v. (1987), 67, 858
Mahoney, Commonwealth v. (1989), 808
Mahoney, Commonwealth v. (1990), 819
Maingrette, Commonwealth v., 815
Mains v. Commonwealth, 580
Maker, Commonwealth v., 10
Maldonado, Commonwealth v., 233, 810
Malone v. United States, 724
Maloney, Commonwealth v., 70
Maltais, Commonwealth v., 847
Mamacos, Commonwealth v., 75
Mamay, Commonwealth v. (1977), 297
Mamay, Commonwealth v. (1990), 296, 606
Mandell, Commonwealth v., 261
Mandile, Commonwealth v., 628, 839
Manning, Commonwealth v. (1990), 487
Manning, Commonwealth v. (1996), 64, 809
Manning, Commonwealth v. (1998), 492

12

Manning, Commonwealth v. (1999), 231
Manning v. Municipal Court, 223
Manning v. Superintendent, Mass. Corr. Inst., Norfolk, 737
Mannos, Commonwealth v., 477
Manson v. Brathwaite, 616, 842
Mantinez, Commonwealth v., 502
Manzelli, Commonwealth v., 470
Mapp v. Ohio, 482
Mara, Commonwealth v., 63
Marable, Commonwealth v., 645
Marangiello, Commonwealth v., 828, 847
Marin, United States v., 500
Marino, Commonwealth v., 473
Markvart, Commonwealth v., 170, 819
Marrero, Commonwealth v., 844
Marshall v. Commonwealth, 739
Martell, Commonwealth v., 636
Martin, Commonwealth v. (1976), 277
Martin, Commonwealth v. (1994), 574, 810
Martin, Commonwealth v. (1996), 850
Martin, Commonwealth v. (1997), 283
Martin, Commonwealth v. (1998), 816
Martin, Commonwealth v. (1999), 107
Martin, Commonwealth v. (2005), 838
Martin v. Commonwealth, 227, 229
Martinez, Commonwealth v. (2002), 626
Martinez, Commonwealth v. (2014), 291
Martinez-Guzman, Commonwealth v., 833
Marvin, Commonwealth v., 699, 700, 748–49
Maryland v. Buie, 498
Maryland v. King, 806
Marzilli, Commonwealth v., 478
Materia, Commonwealth v., 82
Mathews, Commonwealth v., 805, 812
Matis, Commonwealth v., 626, 629
Matos, Commonwealth v., 438
Matsos, Commonwealth v., 306
Mattei, Commonwealth v., 812
Matter of, *see* name of party
Mattos, Commonwealth v., 645
Mavredakis, Commonwealth v., 291, 834, 835
Maxwell, Commonwealth v., 805
Mayfield, Commonwealth v., 602
Mayotte, Commonwealth v., 822
McAfee, Commonwealth v., 233
McArthur, Commonwealth v., 322
McCaffery, Commonwealth v., 123
McCambridge, Commonwealth v., 488, 498, 504
McCan, Commonwealth v., 295
McCarthy, Commonwealth v. (1981), 94
McCarthy, Commonwealth v. (1999), 483
McCauley, Commonwealth v. (1969), 268
McCauley, Commonwealth v. (1981), 504
McColl, Commonwealth v., 618
McCourt, Commonwealth v., 296, 297
McCowen, Commonwealth v., 831, 832
McCoy, Commonwealth v., 293, 821
McCray v. Illinois, 513
McCulloch, Commonwealth v., 70, 639
McDermott v. W.T. Grant Co., 319
McDermott, Commonwealth v., 509
McDonald v. Chicago, 400
McDuffee, Commonwealth v., 368
McFadden, Commonwealth v., 851
McGaffigan, Commonwealth v., 522
McGahee, Commonwealth v., 602
McGeoghean, Commonwealth v., 231, 844, 852

McGeoghegan, Commonwealth v., 68, 69, 499
McGhee, Commonwealth v., 292, 309
McGillivary, Commonwealth v., 64
McGilvery, Commonwealth v., 832
McGovern, Commonwealth v., 541
McGowan, Commonwealth v., 205
McGrail, Commonwealth v., 66
McGrath, Commonwealth v., 271, 826
McGuirk, Commonwealth v., 270
McHoul v. Commonwealth, 700, 705, 826
McHugh, Commonwealth v., 501
McInerney, Commonwealth v., 586
McIntosh, Commonwealth v., 314
McIntyre, Commonwealth v. (1994), 260
McIntyre, Commonwealth v. (1999), 811, 812, 853
McIntyre, Commonwealth v. (2002), 70, 319, 848
McKay, Commonwealth v., 828
McKinnon, Commonwealth v., 573
McLaughlin, Commonwealth v., 807, 825, 854
McLeod, Commonwealth v., 168
McMahon, Commonwealth v., 157, 840
McNulty, Commonwealth v., 639, 835
McQuoid v. Smith, 400
McWilliams, Commonwealth v., 604, 838
Meehan, Commonwealth v., 838
Mehales, Commonwealth v., 314
Meier, Commonwealth v., 479
Mejia, Commonwealth v., 511
Mejias, Commonwealth v., 739
Melendez, Commonwealth v., 511, 512
Melendez-Diaz v. Massachusetts, 4, 806, 812, 830, 831, 832, 833, 834
Melendez-Diaz, Commonwealth v., 831
Mello, Commonwealth v., 827
Melton, Commonwealth v., 286, 290
Melvin, Commonwealth v., 842
Mendenhall, United States v., 504
Mendes, Commonwealth v. (1997), 402
Mendes, Commonwealth v. (1999), 807
Mendonca, Commonwealth v., 217, 218
Mendoza v. Commonwealth, 534
Mercado, Commonwealth v., 579, 641
Mercedes v. Commonwealth, 261
Miaskiewicz v. Commonwealth, 368, 369
Michaels v. Commonwealth, 743
Michaels, Commonwealth v., 743, 749
Michigan v. Mosley, 618, 834
Miles, Commonwealth v., 810
Miller v. Alabama, 152, 273
Miller, Commonwealth v., 301
Miller, Petitioner, 167
Miller, United States v., 739
Millican, Commonwealth v., 75
Mills, Commonwealth v., 325
Milo M., Commonwealth v., 479
Milot, Commonwealth v., 750
Milton, Commonwealth v., 690, 736, 737, 748, 825, 827
Mimless, Commonwealth v., 858
Minnesota v. Dickerson, 497–98
Miozza, Commonwealth v., 277, 278
Miranda v. Arizona, 67, 542, 835
Mitchell v. Mitchell, 213
Mitchell, Commonwealth v. (1999), 729, 736
Mitchell, Commonwealth v. (2005), 629
Mitchell, Commonwealth v. (2006), 276, 316
Mobil Oil Corp. v. Attorney Gen., 424
Mock, Commonwealth v., 492, 494

Moe v. Sex Offender Registry Bd., 4, 14
Mogelinski, Commonwealth v., 151
Moncrieffe v. Holder, 612
Montalvo, Commonwealth v., 114
Montanez, Commonwealth v., 294, 484, 628
Montanino, Commonwealth v., 560, 844, 848
Monteagudo, Commonwealth v., 813
Monterosso v. Gaudette, 349
Montes, Commonwealth v., 279, 487
Montgomery v. Louisiana, 273
Montoya, Commonwealth v., 376
Monzon, Commonwealth v., 225
Moody, Commonwealth v., 470
Moore, Commonwealth v. (1994), 276
Moore, Commonwealth v. (2002), 403
Moore, Commonwealth v. (2016), 498, 636
Moquette, Commonwealth v., 814, 815
Morales v. Massachusetts, 832
Morales, Commonwealth v. (2007), 274
Morales, Commonwealth v. (2013), 849
Morales, Commonwealth v. (2016), 532
Moran, Commonwealth v., 270
Morasse, Commonwealth v., 591
Moreira, Commonwealth v., 279, 376
Morgan, Commonwealth v., 268, 827
Morganti, Commonwealth v., 810
Morrill, Commonwealth v., 324
Morris v. Commonwealth, 65
Morris M., Commonwealth v., 68, 353, 727
Morrison, Commonwealth v., 577
Morrissey v. Brewer, 542, 699, 702, 704, 706, 712, 731, 732, 733, 734
Morrissey, Commonwealth v., 69
Morse, Commonwealth v. (1988), 637, 749
Morse, Commonwealth v. (1998), 836
Morse, Commonwealth v. (2000), 733, 734, 735, 748, 749
Mortimer, Commonwealth v., 642
Moscatiello, Commonwealth v., 401
Moses, Commonwealth v. (1990), 502
Moses, Commonwealth v. (2002), 269, 271
Mountry, Commonwealth v., 232, 295
Moure, Commonwealth v., 476
Moyles, Commonwealth v., 302, 811
Mr. M., Commonwealth v., 851
Mubdi, Commonwealth v., 488, 505, 618
Muckle, Commonwealth v., 494
Muir, Commonwealth v., 68
Mulgrave, Commonwealth v., 815
Mullane, Commonwealth v., 438, 442
Mullen, Commonwealth v., 69
Mullins, Commonwealth v., 94
Munoz, Commonwealth v. (1980), 107
Munoz, Commonwealth v. (1981), 83, 573
Munoz, Commonwealth v. (2011), 831
Murchison, Commonwealth v., 535
Murdough, Commonwealth v., 490
Murphy v. Boston Herald, Inc., 611
Murphy v. Dep't of Corr., 20, 812
Murphy, Commonwealth v. (1973), 476
Murphy, Commonwealth v. (1983), 69
Murphy, Commonwealth v. (1991), 54
Murphy, Commonwealth v. (2003), 361
Murphy, Commonwealth v. (2007), 54, 827
Murphy, Commonwealth v. (2009), 68, 499
Murray, Commonwealth v., 326
Murungu, Commonwealth v., 294, 821, 822
Musgrave, Commonwealth v., 286
Myers v. Commonwealth, 168, 523, 531

N

Nager v. Reid, 68

Nanny, Commonwealth v., 142, 151
Narcisse, Commonwealth v., 502, 505
Nardi, Commonwealth v., 819, 831
Nardone, Commonwealth v., 272, 840
Nardone v. United States, 492
Nascimento, Commonwealth v., 823
Nassar, Commonwealth v., 158
Navrette v. California, 494
Nawn, Commonwealth v., 325, 726, 727
Naylor, Commonwealth v., 277
Nazarro, Commonwealth v., 220
Neal, Commonwealth v., 618, 818, 830
Neary-French, Commonwealth v., 66
Nee, Commonwealth v. (2010), 479
Nee, Commonwealth v. (2013), 562
Negron, Commonwealth v., 289, 317, 701, 750
Nelson, Commonwealth v. (2002), 835
Nelson, Commonwealth v. (2009), 349
Nelson, Commonwealth v. (2011), 511
Nesbitt, Commonwealth v., 812
Nettis, Commonwealth v., 636
Neumyer, Commonwealth v., 229
New Jersey v. T.L.O., 499
New York v. Belton, 500, 507
New York v. Ferber, 445
New York v. Quarles, 617, 838
Ng, Commonwealth v., 500
Nhut Huynh, Commonwealth v., 635
Nicholas, Commonwealth v., 449
Nichols, Commonwealth v., 106, 107
Nichypor, Commonwealth v., 270
Nickerson, Commonwealth v., 573
Nicoll, Commonwealth v., 630
Niemic, Commonwealth v., 272
Nieves, Commonwealth v., 164
Nighelli, Commonwealth v., 479
Nikas, Commonwealth v., 804
Nine Hundred & Ninety-two Dollars, Commonwealth v., 512–13
Nissenbaum, Commonwealth v., 117
Nix v. Williams, 492
Noble, Commonwealth v., 602, 825
Nolan, Commonwealth v., 841, 857
Nom, Commonwealth v., 837
Noonan, Commonwealth v., 490
Norrell, Commonwealth v., 718, 809
North Carolina v. Alford, 612, 804
Nova, Commonwealth v., 498, 499
Novo, Commonwealth v., 836

O
Oakes, Commonwealth v. (1988), 444, 445
Oakes, Commonwealth v. (1990), 445, 635
Oakes, Massachusetts v. (1989), 445
Obershaw, Commonwealth v., 269
O'Brien, Commonwealth v. (1940), 325
O'Brien, Commonwealth v. (2000), 805, 824, 829, 837
Obshatkin, Commonwealth v., 335
O'Connell, Commonwealth v., 361, 363, 626
O'Connor, Commonwealth v. (1989), 492, 493
O'Connor, Commonwealth v. (1990), 637, 811
O'Connor, Commonwealth v. (1995), 64
O'Dell, Commonwealth v., 602
Odgren, Commonwealth v., 566, 629
Odiari, Commonwealth v., 729
Odoardi, Commonwealth v., 693, 696, 700, 705, 712, 734, 736, 737, 744, 747
Odware, Commonwealth v., 824

O'Hara, Commonwealth v., 69
Oliveira, Commonwealth v. (2000), 227, 229
Oliviera, Commonwealth v. (2002), 129, 227, 846
Olsen, Commonwealth v., 542, 699, 713, 742
Olszewski, Commonwealth v., 618, 626, 818, 853
Omonira, Commonwealth v., 810
One 1985 Ford Thunderbird Auto., Commonwealth v., 484
One 1986 Volkswagen GTI Auto., Commonwealth v., 121
One 2004 Audi Sedan Auto., Commonwealth v., 121
O'Neil, Commonwealth v., 699
Opinion of the Justices (1979), 858
Opinion of the Justices (1992), 65, 850
Opinion of the Justices (1996), 3
Ora, Commonwealth v., 440
Oregon v. Kennedy, 634
Orlando, Commonwealth v., 452
Ortiz, Commonwealth v. (1990), 270
Ortiz, Commonwealth v. (1995), 108
Ortiz, Commonwealth v. (1996), 838
Ortiz, Commonwealth v. (1997), 476
Ortiz, Commonwealth v. (2000), 848
Ortiz, Commonwealth v. (2013), 633, 634, 854
Orton, Commonwealth v., 371
Osachuk, Commonwealth v., 836
Osborne, Commonwealth v., 261
Ostrander, Commonwealth v., 624
Otmishi, Commonwealth v., 65
O'Toole, Commonwealth v., 843, 858
Ouen Lam, Commonwealth v., 808
Overmyer, Commonwealth v., 109, 115, 497
Owens v. United States, 810

P
P.B.I.C., Inc. v. Byrne, 440
Pacheco, Commonwealth v. (2001), 507
Pacheco, Commonwealth v. (2013), 497
Packer, Commonwealth v., 277
Padilla v. Kentucky, 579, 612, 641
Pagan, Commonwealth v., 376, 492, 532
Painten, Commonwealth v., 522
Palermo v. United States, 625
Palmarin, Commonwealth v., 577
Palmer, Commonwealth v., 110, 115
Palmer P., Commonwealth v., 319
Palow, Commonwealth v., 605
Panetti, Commonwealth v., 813
Paniaqua, Commonwealth v., 823
Papadinis, Commonwealth v., 852
Pappas, Commonwealth v., 94
Paquette v. Commonwealth, 531, 532
Paradise, Commonwealth v., 607
Parapar, Commonwealth v., 512
Parenteau, Commonwealth v., 4, 50, 832, 833–34
Parker, Commonwealth v. (1988), 275
Parker, Commonwealth v. (1995), 811
Parra, Commonwealth v., 169
Parsons, Commonwealth v., 275
Parzyck, Commonwealth v., 827
Pasciuti, Commonwealth v., 636
Pasquale, Commonwealth v., 427
Paszko, Commonwealth v., 616, 854
Patane, United States v., 838
Paton, Commonwealth v., 306
Patterson, Commonwealth v., 820

Patton, Commonwealth v., 742, 748, 825
Peakes, Commonwealth v., 361
Pearson, Commonwealth v., 843
Pease, Commonwealth v., 276
Pellegrini, Commonwealth v., 510
Pellegrino, Commonwealth v., 565
Pena, Commonwealth v., 750
Penn, United States v., 739
Pennellatore, Commonwealth v., 834
Pentucket Manor Chronic Hosp., Inc. v. Rate Setting Comm'n, 671
Pentz, Commonwealth v., 67
Peopcik, Commonwealth v., 335
People v. Bartley, 68
People v. Edwards, 489
People v. Maki, 739
People v. Miller, 276
People v. Taggart, 504
Percival, United States v., 510
Perella, Commonwealth v., 565
Perez, Commonwealth v. (1989), 632
Perez, Commonwealth v. (2002), 477
Perez-Baez, Commonwealth v., 511
Perito, Commonwealth v., 531, 856
Perkins, Commonwealth v., 523
Perl, Commonwealth v., 225
Pero, Commonwealth v., 478
Perron, Commonwealth v., 317
Perrot, Commonwealth v., 493
Perry v. Commonwealth, 448
Perry v. New Hampshire, 831
Perry, Commonwealth v. (1970), 476
Perry, Commonwealth v. (1994), 260
Perry, Commonwealth v. (2000), 811
Peruzzi, Commonwealth v., 354
Peters, Commonwealth v., 495
Peterson, Commonwealth v., 260
Pettingel, Commonwealth v., 325, 335
Phelan, United States v., 560
Phillips, Commonwealth v. (1992), 812
Phillips, Commonwealth v. (1996), 543, 745
Phinney, Commonwealth v., 641
Phoenix, Commonwealth v., 806
Picardi, Commonwealth v., 469
Picher, Commonwealth v., 840
Pickering, Commonwealth v., 743
Pierce, Commonwealth v., 268
Pierre, Commonwealth v., 66
Pike, Commonwealth v., 725, 726
Pikul, Commonwealth v., 369
Pillai, Commonwealth v., 852
Pillail, Commonwealth v., 818
Pimental, Commonwealth v., 285, 824, 856
Pina, Commonwealth v. (1973), 323
Pina, Commonwealth v. (1990), 484, 602
Pina, Commonwealth v. (1999), 824, 827
Pine v. Rust, 469
Pingaro, Commonwealth v., 843
Pires, Commonwealth v., 825
Pixley v. Commonwealth, 850
Pizzano, Commonwealth v., 95
Pleas, Commonwealth v., 843
Ploude, Commonwealth v., 314, 490
Podgurski, Commonwealth v., 488
Podlaski, Commonwealth v., 617
Podoprigora, Commonwealth v., 739, 741, 812
Poe v. Sex Offender Registry Bd., 14
Poillucci, Commonwealth v., 440
Poirier, Commonwealth v., 724

12

Police Comm'r of Boston v. Mun. Ct. of
    the Dorchester Dist., 551, 819
Pon, Commonwealth v., 552, 668
Pontes, Commonwealth v., 605
Poole, Commonwealth v., 107
Pope, Commonwealth v., 1, 270
Porges, Commonwealth v., 151
Porter, Commonwealth v., 316, 373, 642
Porter P., Commonwealth v., 484, 491
Portillo, Commonwealth v., 626
Powell, Commonwealth v. (1980), 317
Powell, Commonwealth v. (2007), 817
Powell, Commonwealth v. (2008), 504
Powell, Commonwealth v. (2009), 713,
    718, 809
Powell, Commonwealth v. (2011), 400, 402
Power, Commonwealth v., 541, 688, 724,
    725, 728
Power-Koch, Commonwealth v., 401
Powers, Commonwealth v., 480, 628
Prashaw, Commonwealth v., 842
Prater, Commonwealth v., 809, 829
Pratt, Commonwealth v., 107, 479, 484,
    489, 513, 808
Prellwitz v. Berg, 739
Presley v. Georgia, 810
Press-Enterprise Co. v. Superior Ct., 604
Pressley, Commonwealth v., 824
Preston, Commonwealth v., 578
Prevost, Commonwealth v., 402, 500
Price, Commonwealth v., 487
Prophete, Commonwealth v., 489
Provost, Commonwealth v., 445
Pryce, Commonwealth v., 579
Pucillo, Commonwealth v., 803
Puleio, Commonwealth v., 696, 735
Pyburn, Commonwealth v., 354
Pyles, Commonwealth v., 688, 718, 809

Q

Qualls, Commonwealth v., 853
Querubin v. Commonwealth, 528, 531
Quinn, Commonwealth v. (1916), 324
Quinn, Commonwealth v. (2003), 440, 452

R

Rabb, Commonwealth v., 290
Raedy, Commonwealth v., 841
Rahilly, Commonwealth v., 295
Rainwater, Commonwealth v., 838
Rajotte, Commonwealth v., 287
Rakas v. Illinois, 487
Ramirez, Commonwealth v., 489, 630
Ramos, Commonwealth v., 292, 492, 499,
    501, 512, 844
Ramsey, Commonwealth v., 633
Raposo, Commonwealth v. (1992), 477
Raposo, Commonwealth v. (2009), 308, 721
Rarick, Commonwealth v., 107
Ray, Commonwealth v. (1855), 360
Ray, Commonwealth v. (2001), 532
Raymond, Commonwealth v. (1997), 271,
    813, 838
Raymond, Commonwealth v. (2002), 217
Reading, Town of v. Murray, 97
Reaves, Commonwealth v., 636
Rebecca, Care & Prot. of, 238
Reddington, Commonwealth v., 482, 493
Reddix, Commonwealth v., 744
Reed, Commonwealth v., 275, 849
Regan, Commonwealth v., 573
Reilly, Commonwealth v., 449

Renaud, Commonwealth v., 825
Renderos, Commonwealth v., 852
Rescia, Commonwealth v., 726, 848
Resende, Commonwealth v. (1998), 809
Resende, Commonwealth v. (2016), 405
Restucci v. Commonwealth, 672
Revere, City of v. Aucella, 440
Rex, Commonwealth v., 446
Reynolds, Commonwealth v., 66, 318, 626
Rezendes, Commonwealth v., 405
Rhoades, Commonwealth v., 275
Rhodes, Commonwealth v., 401
Ricci, Commonwealth v., 470
Rich v. United Material Fire Ins. Co., 323
Richards, Commonwealth v. (1973), 276
Richards, Commonwealth v. (1998), 639
Richards, Commonwealth v. (2001), 824
Richardson v. Marsh, 805
Richardson, Commonwealth v. (1943), 349
Richardson, Commonwealth v. (1994), 107
Richardson, Commonwealth v. (1996),
    816, 819
Riche, Commonwealth v., 496
Richenburg, Commonwealth v., 625
Richmond Newspapers, Inc. v. Virginia,
    574, 809
Ridlon, Commonwealth v., 630
Riley v. California, 483
Riley, Commonwealth v., 523
Rivera, Commonwealth v., 371, 470, 707,
    845
Robbins, Commonwealth v., 496
Roberson v. Connecticut, 743
Robert M., In re, 724
Roberts, Commonwealth v. (1990), 617,
    808, 809, 834
Roberts, Commonwealth v. (2000), 807
Roberts, Commonwealth v. (2015), 641
Robertson, Commonwealth v. 842, 844
Robicheau, Commonwealth v., 214, 478
Robie, Commonwealth v., 618
Robinson v. Bradley, 480
Robinson v. Commonwealth, 485
Robinson, Commonwealth v. (1988), 493
Robinson, Commonwealth v. (1999), 269,
    270, 825
Robinson, Commonwealth v. (2005), 306,
    307
Robinson, Commonwealth v. (2008), 845
Robinson, United States v., 507
Rocheleau, Commonwealth v., 565
Rock, Commonwealth v., 501
Roderick, Commonwealth v., 231
Roderiques, Commonwealth v., 282
Rodriguez, Commonwealth v. (1976), 271,
    376
Rodriguez, Commonwealth v. (1981), 117
Rodriguez, Commonwealth v. (1993), 486
Rodriguez, Commonwealth v. (1997), 839,
    844
Rodriguez, Commonwealth v. (2000), 499,
    632, 841
Rodriguez, Commonwealth v. (2001), 712,
    719
Rodriguez, Commonwealth v. (2005), 115,
    497, 814
Rodriguez, Commonwealth v. (2012), 610,
    638, 639
Rodriquez, Commonwealth v., 804
Roe v. Attorney Gen., 7
Rogan v. Commonwealth, 318
Rojas, Commonwealth v. (1983), 635

Rojas, Commonwealth v. (1988), 511
Roland R., Commonwealth v., 489
Rollins, Commonwealth v., 447
Rolon, Commonwealth v., 635
Ronald R., Commonwealth v., 7
Ronchetti, Commonwealth v., 317
Rosa, Commonwealth v., 806
Rosario, Commonwealth v., 604, 838, 853,
    856
Rose, Commonwealth v., 507
Rosenberg v. Commonwealth, 619
Rosenberg, Commonwealth v., 227
Rosewarne, Commonwealth v., 260
Rosier, Commonwealth v., 812
Ross, Commonwealth v. (1998), 857
Ross, Commonwealth v. (2008), 82
Ross, United States v., 488, 495, 510
Rossi, Commonwealth v., 335
Rostad, Commonwealth v., 495
Rotonda, Commonwealth v., 70
Roucoulet, Commonwealth v. (1986), 231
Roucoulet, Commonwealth v. (1992), 113,
    849
Rourke, Commonwealth v., 323
Rousseau, Commonwealth v., 726, 836
Rovario v. United States, 485
Rubera v. Commonwealth, 541, 700, 712,
    737, 743, 744, 747
Ruci, Commonwealth v., 269
Ruddock, Commonwealth v., 826
Rudenko, Commonwealth v., 318
Rudolph v. Iowa Methodist Med. Ctr., 829
Ruffen, Commonwealth v., 852
Ruiz, Commonwealth v., 290, 719, 732, 746
Rumkin, Commonwealth v., 665
Russ, Commonwealth v., 818
Russell, Commonwealth v., (1892) 361
Russell, Commonwealth v., (1999) 482, 487
Russell v. Commonwealth, (2015), 847
Russin, Commonwealth v., 157
Russo, Commonwealth v., 807
Rutkowski, Commonwealth v., 509
Ryan v. Ryan, 225
Ryan, Commonwealth v. (1969), 370, 823
Ryan, Commonwealth v. (1981), 335
Rzepphiewski, Commonwealth v., 580
Rzeznik v. Chief of Police, 551

S

Saferian, Commonwealth v., 825
Salcedo, Commonwealth v., 632
Salemme, Commonwealth v., 635
Salentino, Commonwealth v., 840, 852
Salerno, Commonwealth v., 324
Salim, Commonwealth v., 857
Sallop, Commonwealth v., 750
Sama, Commonwealth v., 268
Samaras, Commonwealth v., 400, 402
Sampson, Commonwealth v., 401
Sanchez, Commonwealth v. (1988), 503
Sanchez, Commonwealth v. (1989), 277–
    78, 296, 806
Sanchez, Commonwealth v. (1996), 107,
    856
Sanders, Commonwealth v., 630, 631, 632
Sandler, Commonwealth v., 335
Sands, Commonwealth v., 66
Sandstrom v. Montana, 289
Santana, Commonwealth v., 493, 498
Santiago, Commonwealth v. (1991), 484,
    500, 618
Santiago, Commonwealth v. (1996), 818

12

Santiago, Commonwealth v. (1997), 807
Santobello v. New York, 613, 614
Santoro, Commonwealth v., 469
Santos, Commonwealth v. (1978), 147, 552
Santos, Commonwealth v. (1988), 616
Santos, Commonwealth v. (1999), 148
Santos, Commonwealth v. (2003), 856, 857
Santos, Petitioner, 166
Santosuosso, Commonwealth v., 618
Sargent, Commonwealth v., 169
Sarourt Nom, Commonwealth v., 272
Sasu, Commonwealth v., 82
Satterfield, United States v., 726
Sauer, Commonwealth v., 67
Saunders, Commonwealth v., 231
Saville v. Scafati, 363
Saville, Commonwealth v., 363
Sawicki, Commonwealth v., 541, 729, 735, 736
Sawyer, Commonwealth v., 279
Sayers, Commonwealth v., 401
Saylor, Commonwealth v., 302
Sayyid, Commonwealth v., 698
Scagliotti, Commonwealth v., 449, 596
Scanlan, Commonwealth v., 487, 511, 512
Scanlon, Commonwealth v., 808, 840
Scardamaglia, Commonwealth v., 487
Schatvet, Commonwealth v., 820
Scheffer, Commonwealth v., 806
Schraffa, Commonwealth v., 324
Schuchardt, Commonwealth v., 353, 354, 840
Scoggins, Commonwealth v., 522, 834, 838
Scott, Commonwealth v. (1971), 65
Scott, Commonwealth v. (1998), 270
Scott, Commonwealth v. (1999), 826, 835, 841
Scott, Commonwealth v. (2008), 318
Scott, Commonwealth v. (2013), 277
Seay, Commonwealth v., 402
Sebastian S., Commonwealth v., 576
Sefranka, Commonwealth v., 451, 452
Segal, Commonwealth v., 648
Seguin, Commonwealth v., 630, 632
Segura v. United States, 487
Selavka, Commonwealth v., 638, 639, 721
Selby, Commonwealth v. (1995), 838
Selby, Commonwealth v. (1997), 270
Semedo, Commonwealth v., 269, 272
Semegen, Commonwealth v., 403
Senedele, Commonwealth v., 818
Seney v. Morhy, 253
Senior, Commonwealth v., 854
Sepulveda, Commonwealth v., 107, 490
Serna v. Commonwealth, 528, 531
Serrano, Commonwealth v., 632, 842
Seth, Adoption of, 227
Seven Thousand Two Hundred Forty-six Dollars, Commonwealth v., 121
Sexton, Commonwealth v., 285
Shabo, Commonwealth v., 636
Shanahan, Commonwealth v., 268
Shangkuan, Commonwealth v., 218, 833
Shea, Commonwealth v. (1969), 65
Shea, Commonwealth v. (1988), 602, 806
Shea, Commonwealth v. (1995), 284, 285
Shea, Commonwealth v. (2014), 219
Sheehan, Commonwealth v., 117, 271, 287, 826, 827
Sheline, Commonwealth v., 806
Sheppard, Commonwealth v. (1985), 509

Sheppard, Commonwealth v. (1989), 275, 292
Sheridan, Commonwealth v., 164, 483, 713, 719
Sherman, Commonwealth v. (1870), 320
Sherman, Commonwealth v. (2007), 614, 615
Shields, Commonwealth v., 68, 69
Shine, Commonwealth v., 617
Shipps, Commonwealth v., 259
Sholley, Commonwealth v., 371, 450
Shore, Commonwealth v., 277
Siegfriedt, Commonwealth v., 260, 857
Signorine, Commonwealth v., 483, 510, 513, 855
Silanskas, Commonwealth v., 836
Silva, Commonwealth v. (1974), 502
Silva, Commonwealth v. (1983), 270
Silva, Commonwealth v. (1987), 368, 369
Silva, Commonwealth v. (2000), 217
Silva-Santiago, Commonwealth v., 805, 842
Silverthorne Lumber Co. v. United States, 491, 492
Silvia v. Silvia, 472
Simmons, Commonwealth v., 746, 851
Simmons, United States v., 739
Simon, Commonwealth v., 742, 833
Simpson, Commonwealth v. (2001), 606
Simpson, Commonwealth v. (2002), 287
Sinath IM v. Commonwealth, 257
Singh v. Capuano, 213, 218
Sinnott, Commonwealth v., 605
Sires, Commonwealth v., 812, 827
Sitko, Commonwealth v., 318
Slaney, Commonwealth v., 276
Sliech-Brodeur, Commonwealth v., 624
Slonka, Commonwealth v., 858
Smallwood, Commonwealth v., 566, 618
Smigliano, Commonwealth v., 490
Smiledge, Commonwealth v., 811, 816
Smith v. Massachusetts, 636
Smith v. Neibauer Bus Co., 42
Smith v. United States, 625
Smith, Commonwealth v. (1895), 479
Smith, Commonwealth v. (1970), 572
Smith, Commonwealth v. (1988), 231, 616
Smith, Commonwealth v. (1989), 261, 634
Smith, Commonwealth v. (1990), 840
Smith, Commonwealth v. (1995), 747
Smith, Commonwealth v. (1997), 834, 837
Smith, Commonwealth v. (1998), 292
Smith, Commonwealth v. (2000), 441
Smith, Commonwealth v. (2002), 376
Smith, Commonwealth v. (2015), 837
Smithson, Commonwealth v., 63
Sneed, Commonwealth v., 268, 830
Snell, Commonwealth v., 560
Snow v. Commonwealth, 528
Snow, Commonwealth v., 325
Snyder, Commonwealth v., 499
Soares, Commonwealth v., 270, 482, 483, 632
Soaris, Commonwealth v., 275
Solomonsen, Commonwealth v., 824
Soper, Commonwealth v., 561
Sostilio, Commonwealth v., 274, 276
Soto, Commonwealth v., 579
Souza v. Registrar of Motor Vehicles, 67
Souza, Commonwealth v. (1986), 324
Souza, Commonwealth v. (1998), 324, 838
Spano, Commonwealth v., 113
Sparks, Commonwealth v., 283

Speight, Commonwealth v., 591
Spence v. Gormley, 164
Spence, Commonwealth v., 493
Spencer, Commonwealth v., 839
Sperrazza, Commonwealth v. (1977), 400
Sperrazza, Commonwealth v. (1989), 261
Spinelli v. United States, 482, 493, 511
Spray, Commonwealth v., 841
Spring, Matter of, 276
Springer, Commonwealth v., 828
St. Hillaire, Commonwealth v., 325
St. Louis, Commonwealth v., 280
St. Pierre, Commonwealth v., 231
Stack, Commonwealth v., 479, 811
Stallions, Commonwealth v., 400
Stansbury v. California, 836
Stappen, Commonwealth v., 472
State v. Ghylin, 65
State v. Hallum, 823
State v. Hazley, 617
State v. Henderson, 843
State v. Jones, 68
State v. Landrum, 848
State v. Leatherman, 401
State v. Nelson, 739
State v. Pisano, 314
State v. Pritchett, 64
Statham, Commonwealth v., 402
Stathopoulos, Commonwealth v., 64
Steele, Commonwealth v., 66
Stefanik v. State Bd. of Parole, 696, 712
Steinberg, Commonwealth v., 228, 565
Steinmeyer, Commonwealth v., 854
Stephen, Care & Prot. of, 559
Stephens, Commonwealth v., 408
Stevenson, Commonwealth v., 804
Steward, Commonwealth v., 843
Stewart, Commonwealth v. (1996), 231
Stewart, Commonwealth v. (2007), 803
Stockhammer, Commonwealth v., 232, 297
Stoddard, Commonwealth v., 63
Stokes, Commonwealth v. (1978), 272
Stokes, Commonwealth v. (1980), 577
Stoltz, Commonwealth v., 217
Stone v. Hubbardston, 42
Storey, Commonwealth v., 616
Stoute, Commonwealth v., 492, 501, 502, 505
Stovall v. Denno, 616
Stovall, Commonwealth v., 325
Straw, Commonwealth v., 489
Stubbs, Commonwealth v., 639
Stuckich, Commonwealth v., 295, 821
Stuyvesant Ins. Co., Commonwealth v., 538
Suave, Commonwealth v., 165
Sudderth, Commonwealth v., 63, 64
Suliveres v. Commonwealth, 295
Sullivan v. Brookline, 448
Sullivan v. Vorenberg, 427
Sullivan, Commonwealth v. (1870), 323
Sullivan, Commonwealth v. (1914), 422
Sullivan, Commonwealth v. (1991), 823
Sullivan, Commonwealth v. (2014), 452
Supplee, Commonwealth v., 231, 804
Sussman v. Commonwealth, 649
Swahn, Commonwealth v., 318
Swan, Commonwealth v., 452
Swanson, Commonwealth v., 724
Swartz, Commonwealth v., 68, 499
Sykes, Commonwealth v., 501
Sylvain, Commonwealth v., 579, 641
Szewczyk, Commonwealth v., 636

12

T

Taglieri, Commonwealth v., 482
Talbot, Commonwealth v. (1977), 288, 301
Talbot, Commonwealth v. (2005), 717
Tanner, Commonwealth v., 645
Tapia, Commonwealth v., 486
Tarabolski v. Williams, 808
Tarrant, Commonwealth v., 287
Tate v. Short, 588
Tate, Commonwealth v., 701, 737, 746
Tatro v. Kervin, 17
Tatum, Commonwealth v., 488
Tavares, Commonwealth v., 618, 834
Taylor v. Hayes, 648
Taylor, Commonwealth v. (1981), 510
Taylor, Commonwealth v. (1992), 113
Taylor, Commonwealth v. (1997), 742
Taylor, Commonwealth v. (1999), 727, 823
Tejeda, Commonwealth v., 270, 288, 371
Templema, Commonwealth v., 451
Terry v. Ohio, 501, 502, 503, 504, 505
Terry, In re, 648
Tevlin, Commonwealth v., 285, 811
Texas v. Cobb, 838
Thatch, Commonwealth v., 856
Thayer, Commonwealth v., 297
Therriault, Commonwealth v., 75
Therrien, Commonwealth v., 578
Thibeau, Commonwealth v., 502, 503
Thibeault, Commonwealth v., 225
Thinh Van Cao, Commonwealth v., 501
Thissell, Commonwealth v., 647, 742
Thomas, Commonwealth v. (1858), 363
Thomas, Commonwealth v. (1987), 295
Thomas, Commonwealth v. (1999), 489, 501, 839, 841
Thomas, Commonwealth v. (2003), 231
Thomas, Commonwealth v. (2008), 114, 497
Thompson v. United States, 639
Thompson, Commonwealth v. (1998), 852
Thompson, Commonwealth v. (2000), 809, 838
Thompson, Commonwealth v. (2002), 279
Thompson, Commonwealth v. (2016), 331
Thornley, Commonwealth v. (1987), 854
Thornley, Commonwealth v. (1989), 616
Thurston, Commonwealth v., 619
Tilley, Commonwealth v. (1940), 332
Tilley, Commonwealth v. (1969), 316, 317
Tim T., Commonwealth v., 543, 718
Tirado, Commonwealth v., 272
Titus, Commonwealth v., 324
Tivnon, Commonwealth v., 332
Tobin, Commonwealth v., 279
Todd, Commonwealth v., 834
Tokarev, Commonweatlh v., 641
Toney, Commonwealth v., 808
Tonry, United States v., 713
Toro, Commonwealth v., 296, 858
Torres, Commonwealth v. (1975), 616
Torres, Commonwealth v. (1998), 514
Torres, Commonwealth v. (2004), 164, 528
Torres, Commonwealth v. (2014), 218, 277
Tracey, Commonwealth v., 814, 825
Traylor, Commonwealth v., 825
Traynor, Commonwealth v., 278
Treadwell, Commonwealth v., 509
Trigones, Commonwealth v., 805
Triplett, Commonwealth v., 810, 824
Tripolone, Commonwealth v., 224, 229

Trowbridge, Commonwealth v., 816
Troy, Commonwealth v., 270, 295, 618, 626
Truczinskas, Commonwealth v., 473
Trumble, Commonwealth v., 68, 69, 499
Tucceri, Commonwealth v. (1980), 283
Tucceri, Commonwealth v. (1992), 641, 815
Tucker, Commonwealth v., 269
Tucker, United States v., 734
Tuckerman, Commonwealth v., 325
Tuitt, Commonwealth v., 400

U

Ubilez,Commonwealth v., 54
Umina v. Malbica, 219
United States v., *see* name of party
Upton, Commonwealth v., 482, 483, 493, 499, 511
Urban, Commonwealth v., 295
Urena, Commonwealth v., 632, 825, 829
Urkiel, Commonwealth v., 376
Urrea, Commonwealth v., 826
Uski, Commonwealth v., 64
Utah v. Strieff, 483

V

Valdez, Commonwealth v. (1988), 512
Valdez, Commonwealth v. (2016), 579
Valerio, Commonwealth v., 483, 509
Valleca, Commonwealth v., 477
Van Cao, Commonwealth v., 505
Vanhouton v. Commonwealth, 66
Vao Sok, Commonwealth v., 812
Vargas, Commonwealth v., 814
Vartanian, Commonwealth v., 67
Vasquez, Commonwealth v. (1981), 301
Vasquez, Commonwealth v. (1997), 496
Vasquez, Commonwealth v. (2010), 813, 831, 832
Vasquez, Commonwealth v. (2012), 272
Vellucci, Commonwealth v., 635
Venios, Commonwealth v., 616
Ventura, Commonwealth v., 7, 724
Verde, Commonwealth v., 830, 831
Vickers, Commonwealth v., 630
Vickey, Commonwealth v., 551
Victor V. v. Commonwealth, 534
Vieira, Commonwealth v., 296
Villalobos, Commonwealth v., 580
Villanueva, Commonwealth v., 854
Villar, Commonwealth v., 486
Vincente, Commonwealth v., 542, 742, 743
Vinnicombe, Commonwealth v., 318
Vinnie, Commonwealth v., 428
Vinton, Commonwealth v., 641
Viriyahiranpaiboon, Commonwealth v., 492, 806
Vitello, Commonwealth v., 470
Vittone v. Clairmont, 211–12
Vives, Commonwealth v., 270, 288
Vizcaino v. Commonwealth, 648
Vuthy Seng, Commonwealth v., 495, 505, 835
Vynorius, Commonwealth v., 512

W

Wade, Commonwealth v. (2014), 582, 583
Wade, Commonwealth v. (2016), 582, 583
Wainio, Commonwealth v., 561
Waite, Commonwealth v. (1996), 838
Walczak, Commonwealth v., 272
Walker, Commonwealth v. (1987), 231
Walker, Commonwealth v. (1997), 852

Walker, Commonwealth v. (2004), 303, 844
Walker, Commonwealth v. (2011), 843
Wall, Commonwealth v., 236
Wallace, Commonwealth v. (1982), 66
Wallace, Commonwealth v. (1994), 843
Waller v. Georgia, 232, 574, 810
Walorz, Commonwealth v., 633
Walsh, Commonwealth v., 510
Walter R., Commonwealth v., 297
Walters, Commonwealth v. (1981), 354
Walters, Commonwealth v. (2015), 306
Wanis, Commonwealth v., 826
Ward, Commonwealth v. (1983), 712, 735
Ward, Commonwealth v. (1990), 806
Ward, Commonwealth v. (1998), 823
Ware, Commonwealth v., 302
Warren, Commonwealth v. (1988), 616
Warren, Commonwealth v. (1994), 512
Watson, Commonwealth v. (1979), 857
Watson, Commonwealth v. (1983), 270, 288
Watson, Commonwealth v. (1991), 836
Watson, Commonwealth v. (2009), 842
Watson, United States v., 482
Watts v. Commonwealth, 142
Weber v. Coast to Coast Med., Inc., 847
Wedderburn, Commonwealth v., 804
Weeks, Commonwealth v., 833
Weeks v. United States, 491
Weichell, Commonwealth v., 828
Weiner, Commonwealth v., 291
Welansky, Commonwealth v., 354
Welch, Commonwealth v., 306
Werner, Commonwealth v., 289
Wheeler, Commonwealth v., 811, 829
Whelan, Commonwealth v., 69
Whelton, Commonwealth v., 840
Whiston, Commonwealth v., 473
White, Commonwealth v. (1877), 336
White, Commonwealth v. (1967), 107
White, Commonwealth v. (1975), 233
White, Commonwealth v. (1996), 846
White, Commonwealth v. (1999), 750
White, Commonwealth v. (2002), 851
White, Commonwealth v. (2009), 638
White, United States v., 469
Whitehead, Commonwealth v., 293
Whooley, Commonwealth v., 586
Whynaught, Commonwealth v., 42
Wilcox, Commonwealth v. (2002), 602
Wilcox, Commonwealth v. (2006), 712, 739
Wilkerson, Commonwealth v., 815
Willard, Commonwealth v., 317, 324, 825
Williams v. Illinois, 588, 831
Williams, Commonwealth v. (1849), 319, 323
Williams, Commonwealth v. (1975), 400
Williams, Commonwealth v. (1985), 858
Williams, Commonwealth v. (1987), 270
Williams, Commonwealth v. (1996), 501
Williams, Commonwealth v. (1998), 269, 275
Williams, Commonwealth v. (1999), 504
Williams, Commonwealth v. (2000), 619, 807
Williams, Commonwealth v. (2002), 113
Williams, Commonwealth v. (2003), 245
Williams, Commonwealth v. (2004), 724
Williams, Commonwealth v. (2010), 618, 830
Willie, Commonwealth v., 618, 626
Willis, Commonwealth v., 502, 645
Wills, Commonwealth v., 510
Wilson, Commonwealth v. (1998), 487, 511, 606, 636

12

Wilson, Commonwealth v. (1999), 739
Wilson, Commonwealth v. (2001), 501
Wilson, Commonwealth v. (2004), 502
Wing v. Comm'r of Probation, 552, 626
Winquist, Commonwealth v., 221, 853
Winter, Commonwealth v., 301
Wojcik, Commonwealth v., 128, 854
Wong Sun v. United States, 491, 492
Wood, Commonwealth v. (1867), 442
Wood, Commonwealth v. (1927), 64
Wood, Commonwealth v. (1986), 401
Woods, Commonwealth v. (1993), 806
Woods, Commonwealth v. (1994), 818
Woods, Commonwealth v. (1995), 67, 805
Woods, Commonwealth v. (1998), 729, 750, 846
Woods, Commonwealth v. (2014), 836, 837
Woodward, Commonwealth v. (1869), 272
Woodward, Commonwealth v. (1998), 635, 830

Woodward v. Leavitt, 636
Worcester, Commonwealth v., 854
Wotan, Commonwealth v., 410
Wright, Commonwealth v. (2005), 824
Wright, Commonwealth v. (2015), 17
Wunder, Commonwealth v., 496
Wyatt, Petitioner, 168
Wygrzywalski, Commonwealth v., 317

X
Xiarhos, Commonwealth v., 523

Y
Yameen, Commonwealth v., 70
Yelle, Commonwealth v., 843
Yeshulas, Commonwealth v., 727
Young, Commonwealth v. (1950), 279
Young, Commonwealth v. (1981), 491, 844
Young, Commonwealth v. (1987), 630, 631, 632
Young, Commonwealth v. (2009), 535

Z
Zagranski, Commonwealth v., 815, 820
Zaleski, Commonwealth v., 361
Zanetti, Commonwealth v., 477, 828
Zangari, Commonwealth v., 291
Zapata, Commonwealth v., 291, 718
Zarilli, Commonwealth v., 473
Zawatsky, Commonwealth v., 304
Zeininger, Commonwealth v., 76, 833
Zeitler, Commonwealth v., 449
Zevitas, Commonwealth v., 65
Zezima, Commonwealth v., 288
Zimmerman, Commonwealth v., 818
Zirpolo, Commonwealth v., 69
Zorrilla, Commonwealth v., 36
Zullo v. Goguen, 218
Zuzick, Commonwealth v., 574
Zwickert, Commonwealth v., 108

Index

A

ABANDONMENT
Evidence, 803
Infant under ten, 131
Motor vehicles, 50–51
Nonsupport and, 472–73
    Penalties, 474–75
Warrantless searches, 489

ABORTION
Forms for indictment, 567
Instruments of, 441
Private hospital not obligated to perform, 442

ABUSE
Child victims, statements of, 237–38
Expert testimony, admissibility of, 234

ABUSE PREVENTION, 210–19
Address of plaintiff, exclusion from court documents, 219
Batterers' treatment program, assessment of participants, 219
Complaint, form of, 219
Confidentiality of records, 219
Court closed, granting relief when, 214
Criminal proceedings, information as to, 213
Definitions, 210–11
Domestic violence record search, 216–19
Firearms license
    Continuation or modification of, 214
    Order for suspension and surrender, 213–14
Intent, 217
Jurisdiction, 564
Nature of proceedings, 213
Orders, 216–19
    Contact, accidental, mistaken, etc., 217
    Expungement, 218
    Intent, 217
    Out-of-state defendant, 218–19
    Service of, 216–19
    Third-party acts, 218
    Violation, elements of, 217
Period of relief, 211–13
Pets, custody of, 219
Police powers, 215–17
Protection order by another jurisdiction, 215

Remedies, 211–13
Temporary orders, 214
Venue, 211

ACCESSORIES
See FELONIES, ACCESSORIES AND ATTEMPTS TO COMMIT CRIME

ACCIDENTS
Manslaughter as, 275
Motor vehicles
    License and registration, presentation of, 37–38
    Reports, 82

ACCUSED, RIGHTS OF, 259–62
Acquittal, effect on subsequent charges, 261
Conviction, manner of, 261
Counsel, right to, 260
Defective pleadings, acquittal on, 261–62
Double jeopardy, 261
Driving while intoxicated
    Lost blood sample, 260–61
    Medical examination, right to, 260–61
False imprisonment, limitation on action, 259
False pretenses, arrest on, 259
Fingerprinting and photographing, 259
Indictment, waiver of, procedure, 260
Jury trial waiver, 261
Juveniles, 259
Medical examination, DUI cases, right to, 260–61
Merits, acquittal on, 262
Nature of crime, right to be informed of, 259
Photographing, 259
Prosecution of crime, manner of, 259
Punishment, conditions precedent, 262
Subsequent indictments, 261–62

ACQUITTAL
Controlled substances, 118
Defective pleadings, on, 261–62
Effect on subsequent charges, 261
Fees, liability for, 574
Merits, on, 262
Part of crime only, 574

ADMISSIONS, 803–04

ADULTERY, 439, 561
Forms for indictment, 567

ADVERTISEMENTS
Deceptive, 341–42
Discriminatory, 461–62
False or exaggerated statements, 342
Firearms and weapons, 181
Lottery tickets, 426
Malicious injury to posted copy of, 352
Merchandise, commodities, and service, regulation of, 341
Procuring divorce, 209
Schools, by, 434
Similar to bank bills, 365–66
Untrue or misleading, 341

AGENTS AND BROKERS
Embezzlement by, 333
Interstate rendition, payment of expenses of, 519

AIRPORT OR AIRPLANE
Cutting device in, 408–09

ALCOHOLIC BEVERAGES
Adulteration of, 411
Analysis of, 174
    Certificate accompanying analysis, 174
Candy containing, sale of, 413
Driver alcohol education program, 71–73
Employment of persons under 172–73
Field sobriety tests, 66, 67, 123
Forms for indictment, 567
Hospital patients, furnishing to, 412
Identification cards for purchasing liquor, 173–74
Ignition interlock device, 38, 70–71, 79–80
Intoxication, evidence of, 826
Involuntary intoxication, evidence of, 826
Mental health commitment of alcoholics, 160–61
Minors
    Furnishing alcohol to, 172–73
    Operation of motor vehicle containing alcohol, 174
    Purchase by, 173
    Suspension of driver's license, 174

12

ALCOHOLIC BEVERAGES *(cont'd)*
Motorboats, operating under the influence of, 83–92
Patients, delivery to, 374
Prisoners, delivery to, 374
Reasonable suspicion standard, 123
School premises, on, 450
Treatment and rehabilitation programs, 71–73, 79
Weapons, carrying while under the influence, 405
Wood alcohol, consumables containing, 412

ALCOHOLISM
Incapacitation due to, police assistance, 122–23

ALFORD PLEA, 804

ALIENS
See NONRESIDENTS AND ALIENS

ANARCHY
Promotion of, 266

ANATOMICAL GIFTS, 129

ANIMALS
Abuse prevention
    Pets, custody of, 219
Appeals, 461
Arrest without a warrant, 459
Assistance animals, theft or attack of, 460
Baby rabbits and fowl, sale of, 458
Birds, kept for shooting, 461
Cats
    Devocalization of, 457
    Motor vehicle striking, injuring or killing, 458
Cruelty to, 455–56
    Arrest without a warrant, 459
    Complaint, warrant, arrest for, 459
    Department of Children and Families, reporting by, 152–53
    Forfeiture, 461
    Forms for indictment, 569
    Impoundment, security for, 470–71
    Seizure, security for, 470–71
Decompression chambers, 458
Dogs
    Assistance animals, theft or attack of, 460
    Cropping or cutting off ears, 457
    Devocalization of, 457
    Exhibiting with ears cropped or cut off, 458
    Guide dogs, accommodation, 463
    License, removal of, 459–60
    Motor vehicle striking, injuring or killing, 458
    Police dogs, willfully injuring, 456
    Rental or leasing of, 458–59
    Wrongful removal of collar, 332, 459–60
Domestic
    Malicious killing or injury of, 348
    Trespass on land, 348
Entering without a warrant, 460
Experimentation of, taking for purpose of, 458
False pedigree, 342
Fighting
    Aiding or being present at, 462
    Complaints and warrants relative to, 461
    Expenses related to care and destruction of, 462
    Owning, possessing, or training, 462
    Place of, entering without warrant, 461

Security for seizure and impoundment, 470–71
Foals under five months, sale of, 456
Forfeiture, 461
Garbage, feeding with, 413
Horses
    Docking tails of, 456–57
    Enforcement, 460
    Exhibiting with cut tail, 457
    Foals under five months, sale of, 456
    Penalties, 460
    Police horses, willfully injuring, 456
    Smoking in buildings used for stabling, 460
    Stable requirements, 460
    Stabling higher than second floor, 460
    Stabling more than 15, 460
    Use of when not fit, 456
    Water and sand, 460
Humane society, injury to property, 355
Impoundment, security for, 470–71
Indictment, description of, 560
Injuring, taking away or harboring, 459–60
Killing
    Decompression chamber, by use of, 458
    Motor vehicle, by, 458
Leghold traps prohibited, 171–72
Motor vehicle transport of, 52
Mules
    Enforcement, 460
    Penalties, 460
    Smoking in buildings used for stabling, 460
    Stable requirements, 460
    Stabling more than 15, 460
    Water and sand, 460
Pets, taking of, 459–60
Pigeons, killing or frightening, 355
Police dogs and horses, willful injury of, 456
Prizes, use of as, 458
Prosecutions, 459
Rental or leasing of dogs, 458–59
Research, unauthorized removal, 345
Rodent poison in inappropriate location, 412
Seizure, security for, 470–71
Service animals
    Privileges of persons with, 463
    Theft or attack of, 460
Transportation of, requirements for, 459
Traps, types of, 171–72
Vivisection of vertebrates, 458
Wild, exhibition of, 456

ANTIPSYCHOTIC MEDICATION
Treatment of committed persons with, 155–56

APPEAL
See also RULES OF APPELLATE PROCEDURE
Animal treatment offenses, 461
Appellate division of SJC, right of, 578
Child in need of services, 135
Commonwealth, by, 578
Court costs of indigent persons, 257
Forensic and scientific analysis, postconviction access, 584
Forfeiture of property, 514
Interlocutory, 626–28
Probation revocation hearings, 750
Sex Offender Registry classification and registration, 16
Sexually dangerous persons, 168–69

Supreme Judicial Court, 577
    Expenses related to, 596
Victims of violent crimes, claims for compensation, 250

ARMED FORCES
Military funeral services, disturbance of, 451
Motor vehicle licenses, 37
Riots, suppressing, 397
Veterans
    See VETERANS

ARMED ROBBERY, 287–87
Joint enterprise, 288
Masks, 288
Self-defense, 288

ARRAIGNMENT, 603–04
Capital cases, 562–63
Civil motor vehicle infractions
    Criminal proceeding no bar to, 567
    Treating criminal offenses as, 566

ARREST
Contempt; failure to appear and abide orders, 521
Controlled substances violations, 118
Counsel
    Assignment of, 523
    Assistance of, 523–24
Credit card offenses, 329–30
Criminal History Systems Board, 520
Default
    Arrest on warrants for default or forfeiture of, 519–20
    Warrants, 522
Discharge
    Acknowledgment of satisfaction for injury, 526
    Bar to civil action, 526
    Prisoner, 524
Evidence, 804
Examination of arrested person for injury, 522
Extraterritorial pursuit, 68–69, 515
Failure to appear
    Contempt, 521
    Subsequent proceedings, 523
Fees and expenses; records sent to Superior Court, 525
Handcuffing, 526
Interstate rendition, 515–19
Issuance of warrant, procedure for, 519
Justices, process issued by, 519
Licensing authorities, list of persons registered with, 520
Physical examinations, 522
Pretrial release, conditions of, 532–35
Prisoner
    Conveying through another county, 525
    Male and female, transporting, 526
    Removal to another county or correctional institution, 526
Pursuit outside jurisdiction, 69
Resisting, 375–76
Review, petition for, 528–32
Sex Offender Registry, failure to comply with registration requirements, 16
Summons
    Fixing time for trial, 520–21
    Instead of warrant, 520
Surrender of principal, 538
    After default, 538
Telephone, use of in places of detention, 522

12

ARREST *(cont'd)*
Violation of pretrial release conditions, 532–35
Certifying bail on, 521–22
Conveying accused to county where warrant issued, 522
Default warrants, 522
Issuance procedures, 519
Service of, 519
Warrants
See also as subhead to other topics

ARREST, ARRAIGNMENT, AND OTHER PROCEEDINGS
See also ARRAIGNMENT; ARREST; as subhead to other topics
Civil motor vehicle infractions, 773–802
Indictment, copy to person in custody, 565
List of jurors to prisoner, 565
Murder indictment, service of copy, 565
Placing cases on file, 566
Subpoenas, 565–66

ARSON
Attempted, 314
Building, 314, 753
Dwelling, 313–14, 753
Forms for indictment, 568
Wood and other property, 314

ASSAULT AND BATTERY
See ELEMENTS AND PENALTIES OF SELECTED CRIMES; PERSON, CRIMES AGAINST

ATTEMPTS
See FELONIES, ACCESSORIES AND ATTEMPTS TO COMMIT CRIME

ATTORNEY GENERAL
Constitutional rights violations, civil actions by, 16–17
Subpoenas, issuance of, 565–66
Subversive organizations, 266–67

ATTORNEYS
Appearance by, 651
Assignment of
Arrest, 523
Criminal procedure rules, 605
Inmates, for, 574
Juveniles, for, 574
Pretrial proceedings, 563
Superior Court rules, 653
Burden to prove admission to bar, 572–73
Children in need of services, right to, 133–34
Compensation of counsel of prisoner, 563
Fine and forfeiture cases, appointment of, 596
Forensic and scientific analysis, postconviction, appointment of counsel, 582
Ineffective assistance of, 825
Right to
Accused persons, 260
Evidence, 848
Generally, 260
Grand jury, 559
Interrogation, 837
Mental health commitment or retention hearings, 154
Probation, 729
Protection and care of children, 133–34
Sex offender classification hearings, 14–16
Sexually dangerous persons, 169–70

Witnesses, 227–28
State employees and, 381–82
Withdrawal of appearance by, 655

AUTOMOBILES
See MOTOR VEHICLES

B

BAIL
See also ARREST
Abuse allegation, written ruling of, 526
Admission to, master in chancery, 536
Arrest on warrants for default or forfeiture of, 519–20
Bail commissioner or special magistrate authorized to admit, 539
Commitment, or, 524
Compensation for taking, 537
Exoneration of, 538
Failure to appear after release on, 539–40
Justice of the peace, 224
Misdemeanor, 521
Officials authorized to admit, 527–28
Professional bondsman, 536–37
Real estate accepted as, disposition of, 536
Revocation, 531
Right to, 260
Serious flight risk, 528
Suffolk County, 536, 537
Sundays, taking on, 537
Surrender of principal after default, 538
Taken out of court, 536
Warrants certifying bail on, 521–22

BANK BILLS AND PAPER
Counterfeit, 365
Damaging, 365
Larceny of, 332
Retaining bank bills, 365

BANKS
Embezzlement or fraud by employees of, 333
Insolvent, receipt of deposits by, 334
Misconduct by employees of, 333

BATTERERS' TREATMENT PROGRAM
Assessment of participants, 219

BEANO, 429

BEGGING
Employing minor under 15 to, 453

BETTING
See GAMING OR BETTING; PUBLIC POLICY, CRIMES AGAINST

BICYCLES
Larceny of, 331
Motorized, 31, 33

BIOLOGICAL, CHEMICAL, NUCLEAR WEAPONS, 345

BIRTH CONTROL
Furnishing means of, 442

BLASPHEMY, 450

BLOOD SAMPLES, 507–08
Evidentiary use of, 625, 804–05

BODY ARMOR
Wearing in commission of crime, 403

BOSTON
Juvenile Court, probation officers to serve process, 545
Municipal Court, sealing of dismissals and nonconviction records, 668

Parking regulation in, 45–47
Probation officers, powers, 545

***BOWDEN* DEFENSE**, 805

BOXING MATCHES, 273–74
Betting on, 433

BREAKING AND ENTERING
See ELEMENTS AND PENALTIES OF SELECTED CRIMES; PROPERTY, CRIMES AGAINST

BRIDGE OR WHIST GAMES, 429

BRIDGES AND CANALS
Injury to, 346

***BRUTON* RULE**, 605, 805

BUCKETING, 431–32

BUILDINGS
Breaking and entering to commit misdemeanor, 318, 756
County, defacement of, 342
Destruction or injury to, 345
Oil of vitriol or other substance, throwing into, 345
School or church, defacement or injury to, 342–43
State property, defacement or injury to, 342
Unlawful assembly, injury to, 397

BURGLARY
See PROPERTY, CRIMES AGAINST

BURNING
Burning motor vehicle, 322
Reckless or willful, resulting in injury to firefighter, 279

C

CAMBRIDGE
Parking regulation in, 45–46

CAPITAL PUNISHMENT
See DEATH SENTENCE

CARGO INVOICE
False, 346

CARJACKING, 292, 757

CARSEATS, 36

CASE MANAGEMENT
Superior Court rules, 658–64

CHASTITY, CRIMES AGAINST
See DECENCY, MORALITY, GOOD ORDER, AND CHASTITY, CRIMES AGAINST

CHEMICAL WEAPONS, 345

CHILDREN
Air rifles, 407
Area directors, powers and duties of, 140
Arrest of, procedure following, 135
Begging, employing minor under 15 to, 453
Born out of wedlock, concealing death of, 442
Cigarette rolling papers, 412
Commitment of, held for examination or trial, 149–50
Controlled substances
Distribution to, 111–12
Found where such kept, protective custody of, 117
Criminal proceedings against, 152–53
Limitation on, 152
Warrant of commitment to Department of Youth Services, 152

12

CHILDREN *(cont'd)*
Delinquent children, 141–48
    Abetting violation of court order, 148
    Adjournment of proceedings, 144–45
    Adjudication, 145–46
    Admissibility of and effect, 146–47
    Aiding or abetting violation of court
        order, 148
    Commissioner of Probation, powers
        concerning, 148
    Complainant, 141–42
    Complaint of, procedure following, 142
    Definitions, 141
    Disposition request, 143–44
    Inducing or abetting delinquency, 148
    Inspection of records, 147
    Investigation by probation officer, 145
    Jury trial of, 143
    Liberal construction, 141
    Motor vehicle violations, 146–47
    Nature of proceedings against, 141
    Parent or guardian, summoning, 142–43
    Plea, tender of, 143–44
    Probation violations, 147
    Record of performance, 145
    Restitution or reparation, 148
    Summons, 141–42
    Warrant, 141–42
    Youthful offender, definition of, 141
Department of Youth Services
    Diagnostic study by, 150
    Probation officer duties and, 546
    Suspended sentences, 586
    Warrant of commitment to, 152
Discipline of, as assault and battery, 277
District Court cases, process for, 224
Drugs
    Found where such kept, protective
        custody, 117
    Rehabilitation of, after referral by
        Department of Children and
        Families, 127
    Sale in school zone, 765
Enticing, 302–03, 758
Exclusion of public, 148
Exclusion of public from trials for sex
    offenses, 574
Exploitation of
    Firearms and ammunition, furnishing to,
        190, 407
    Jurisdiction to enjoin dissemination of
        visual material, 447
    Purchasing or possessing child
        pornography, 446–47
Foster homes, 150
    Newborns, placement in, 131–32
Furnishing to, 190
Gaming or betting, 24
Glue or cement sales to, 416
Harmful to minors, definition, 447
Indecent assault and battery on child under
    14, 277–79
Information registry, 141
Injured
    Custody of, 139–40
    Physically or emotionally, 137–40
    Reports of, 137–39, 140–41
Kidnapping, 301–02
    By relative, 302, 761
Marriage, enticement of person under 16,
    437
Matters harmful to, 443

Motor vehicles
    Car seats, 36
    Endangerment of child, 80
    Passenger restraints, 36
Multidisciplinary service teams, 140
Police station, detention of child in, 148
Pornography
    Dissemination of, 447
    Purchasing or possessing, 446–47
Posing or exhibiting in state of nudity or
    sexual conduct
    Dissemination of child pornography, 447
    Punishment, 444–45
Presence of minors at juvenile sessions, 148
Proceedings against, 148–52
    Apprehension after 19th birthday, 151
    Arrest notice, 149
    Capias, 150
    Commitment of children held for
        examination or trial, 149–50
    Continuing jurisdiction, 150–51
    Crimes committed when between ages
        of 14 and 18, 151–52
    Detention homes, 150
    Detention of, 148–49
    Diagnostic study and services, 150
    Failure to appear, 150
    Foster homes, 150
    Murder adjudication, 151–52
    Parent or guardian, summoning, 150
    Probation officers, information of, 150
    Public excluded, 148
    School reports, 150
Prostitution, inducement into, 303, 437
Protection and care of, 130–41
    Appeal of need determination, 135
    Area directors, 140
    Arrest of child, 135
    Child in need of services, 132–33
    Confidentiality, 141
    Counsel, right to, 133–34
    Custody pending transfer, 139–40
    Definitions, 130–31
    Foster homes, 150
        Newborns placed in, 131–32
    Hearing on need for services, 134–35
    Information registry, 141
    Injured children, reports, 137–39, 140–
        41
    Jurisdiction, 132–33
    Multidisciplinary service teams, 140
    Newborns placed in foster care, 131–32
    Nightwalking or streetwalking, child in
        violation of, 136
    Petition seeking determination that child
        needs services, 132–33
    Physically or emotionally injured
        children, 137–40
    Protective alert, 141
    Right to counsel, 133–34
    Sexually exploited, 136
    Standing, 132–33
Protective alert, 141
Rape of child under 16, 766–67
Reckless endangerment to, 282
Sexually exploited, child welfare services,
    136
Tobacco, furnishing to, 412
Trafficking
    Enticing child to engage in prostitution,
        trafficking, sexual activity, 437–
        38, 758

    Forced servitude, 309
    Organ trafficking, 310
    Sexual servitude, for, 308–09
Unnatural and lascivious acts with child
    under 16, 450
Weapons
    Air rifles, 407
Witnesses, 225

**CHILDREN AND FAMILIES,
DEPARTMENT OF**
Animal cruelty, abuse or neglect, reporting,
    152–53
Children referred for drug rehabilitation, 127
Confidentiality of reports, 140–41

CHURCHES
Defacement of, 342–43
Destruction, 355
Worship assembly, disturbance of, 450

CIVIL RIGHTS
Action for civil rights violations, 355
Massachusetts Civil Rights Act, 17

COLLATERAL ESTOPPEL, 479, 543,
807–08

COLLATERAL SECURITY
Sale before debt due, 340

COMMON CARRIERS
Gross negligence by, 303

COMMON NIGHTWALKER
See NIGHTWALKING

COMMUNICATIONS AND EQUIPMENT
See also TELEPHONES
Used for unlawful purpose, 428
Wire and oral communications
    interceptions, 463–70

COMMUNIST PARTY, 266

COMMUNITY ACCESS PROGRAM
Sexually dangerous persons and, 165–66

COMPLAINT
See also INDICTMENT AND PRETRIAL
    PROCEEDINGS; as subhead to
    other topics
Harassment, 252, 255
Issuance of, 665
Refusal to issue, 808
Sexual assault, first complaint / fresh
    complaint, 293–94

COMPLETENESS
Doctrine of, 808

COMPUTER DATA AND PROGRAMS
Admissibility into evidence, 237
Intent to defraud service, 327–28
Unauthorized access to, 351–52
Venue, 563

CONFIDENTIALITY
See also as subhead to other topics
Clergy communications, 225
Department of Children and Families
    reports, 140–41
DNA Database records, 21
Domestic violence counselor, 229
Harassment prevention order records, 255
Human trafficking victim caseworkers,
    229–30
Juror questionnaires, 239
Mental health commitment, court records
    regarding, 162
Psychotherapist communications, 226–27

12

CONFIDENTIALITY *(cont'd)*
Rape victim's name, 300–01
Sex Offender Registry, 10, 16
Sexual assault counselor, 228–29
Social workers, communications by, 127–29
State Ethics Commission inquiries, 396

CONSPIRACY, 478–79
Controlled substances and, 118
Forms for indictment, 569

CONSTITUTIONAL ISSUES
DNA Database, 20
Sex Offender Registry, 3

CONSTITUTIONAL RIGHTS
Jury trial, 1
Search and seizure, unreasonable, 1
Search warrants, expectation of privacy, 484
Violations, 16–17, 304

CONTEMPT OF COURT
Criminal Procedure Rules, 647–49
Witness, 228

CONTINUANCE
Criminal procedure rules, 606
General, 823
Pretrial diversion, 556
Probation violation proceedings, 688, 707
Without a finding
    Evidence, 809, 823
    Probation violation proceedings, 688, 707

CONTROLLED SUBSTANCES, 99–122
Acquittal, dismissal, etc., 118
Arrest for offenses involving, without
        warrant, 118
Chemist's analysis of, 19, 121–22
Children, 765
    Protective custody, 117
    Rehabilitation of, after referral by
            Department of Children and
            Families, 127
Class A, 103–04, 106–07
    Beepers, 107
    Chain of custody, 107
    Complaint, 107
    Duplicative convictions, 107
    Expert testimony, 107
    Indictment, 107
    Intent to distribute, 106–07
    List of, 103
    Location of contraband, 107
    Minors, distribution to, 111–12
    Offenses involving, 106–07
    Unlawful manufacture, etc., 106–07
Class B, 104, 107–09
    Duplicative convictions, 108
    List of, 104
    Mandatory sentence, 108
    Minors, distribution to, 111–12
    Offenses involving, 107–09
Class C, 104–06
    List of, 104–06
    Minors, distribution to, 111–12
    Offenses involving, 109
Class D, 106, 109–10
    List of, 106
    Offenses involving, 109
Class E, 106, 110
    List of, 106
    Offenses involving, 110
Classes of, 103–10
Cocaine, trafficking in, 110–11, 769
Conspiracy and, 118

Controlled substance analogue, 100
Counterfeit substances, 100, 111–12, 765
Definitions, 99–102
Delivery to prisoners, 374
Depressant or stimulant substance, 100
Destruction of seized drugs, 121–22
Driving under the influence of
    See DRIVING UNDER THE INFLUENCE
Drug, defined, 100
Drug paraphernalia, 100–01, 112–13
Expert testimony, 107
Fingerprinting person charged with felony,
        118
Forfeiture of property, 118–21
    Burden of showing probable cause, 121
    Initiation of proceedings, 121
    Lawfulness of judgment, 121
    Monies seized as drug proceeds, 121
    Ownership defined, 121
Heroin
    Driving under influence of, 66
    Trafficking in, 110–11, 769
    Unlawful possession, 116–17
    Unlawful presence at place of, 117
Hypodermic syringes and needles
    Assault by means of, 286
    Disposal of, 102–03
    Sale of, 102
Immunity from prosecution for persons
        seeking medical assistance, 117
Indictment, 107, 561
Inspectors, analysts, and chemists, 122
Kidnapping, used to consummate, 302
Marijuana, 101
    Medical, 485
    Motor vehicle searches, 496–97
    One ounce or less, 114–15
    Smell of, 109, 115
    Trafficking in, 110–11, 769
    Unlawful possession, 116–17
Medical assistance, immunity from
        prosecution for persons seeking, 117
Mental health commitment of substance
        abusers, 160–61
Minors
    Inducing or abetting sale by, 114
    Unlawful distribution to, 111–12
Morphine, trafficking in, 110–11
Motorboats, operation of under influence
        of, 83–92
Narcotic drug, definition of, 101
Opium, trafficking in, 110–11, 769
Paraphernalia offenses, 112–13
Penalties, 113–15, 115–16, 118
Photographing person charged with felony
        involving, 118
Prosecution not to be continued or placed
        on file, 112
Registration numbers, unlawful use of, 116
Schools, violations in or near, 113–14
    Place of offense, 113
Sealing of records, 118
Seizure of, 121–22
Theft of from authorized dispenser, 117
Tobacco rolling papers, 112–13
Trafficking in marijuana, cocaine, heroin,
        etc., 110–11, 769
Unlawful distribution to minors, 111–12
Unlawful possession
    Criminal responsibility, 117
    Heroin, 116–17
    Marijuana, 115

Unlawful presence at place where heroin
        kept, 117
Violations, penalties, 118
Weapons, carrying while under the
        influence, 405

COPPER WIRE
Records of purchases, 357

CORRECTIONAL INSTITUTIONS
Delivering or receiving items from
        prisoners, 375
Disturbing, 375
Escape, aiding, 373
Injury to property, 355
Sentence to, 587, 589, 589

CORROBORATION RULE, 809

COSTS IN CIVIL ACTIONS, 255–58
Definitions, 255–56
Indigent persons
    Affidavit of, 256
    Appeal, 257
    Court costs of, 256–58
    Definition, 255–56
    Payment, 258
    Public record, 258
    Repayment, 257
    Report of expenditures, 258
    Speedy hearing, 257
    Substitute documents or objects at less
            cost, 257–58
Normal fees and costs, 256
Substitution or state payment of fees or
        costs, 257–58
Waiver, granting requests for, 256–57

COUNSEL
See ATTORNEYS

COUNTERFEIT MARK, 359–60

COUNTY EMPLOYEES
See PUBLIC OFFICIALS AND
        EMPLOYEES

**COURT PERSONNEL AND
PROCEEDINGS, CRIMES AGAINST**
Corruption of, 370
Disruption of, 371
Gifts given to, 372
Impersonation of justice of the peace,
        other officers, 376
Picketing of, 370

COURTS
See specific court

CREDIT CARDS
Fraudulent use of, 330
Misuse of, 329–30
    Definitions, 329
    Penalties, 329–30
Publishing number or coding system, 330

CRIMINAL HISTORY SYSTEMS BOARD,
4–7, 520

CRIMINAL RECORDS
Delinquent children, 147
DNA database, 20–22
Motor vehicle offenses, 97–98
Sex offender registry, 1–16
Witnesses, impeachment of, 232

CRIMINAL RESPONSIBILITY
Controlled substances, unlawful
        possession, 117
Indictment and proceedings before trial, 560

12

CROSS-EXAMINATIONS, 810–11

CRUEL AND UNUSUAL PUNISHMENT, 811

CUMULATIVE ERROR, 811

CURRENCY
See FORGERY AND CURRENCY CRIMES

D

DAGGERS, 401

DAMS OR RESERVOIRS
Malicious injury, 356

DANGEROUS PERSONS
See MENTAL HEALTH; SEXUALLY
      DANGEROUS PERSONS

DEAD BODIES
Buying, selling, or possessing, 454
Disinterring, 454
Taking on process or execution, 454

DEATH SENTENCE
Circumstances authorizing, 594–95
Confinement of prisoners under, 592
Execution of
      Stay of, 593
      Time for, 592
Infliction of, 592
Jury findings necessary for, 595
Mistrial, 593–94
Postmortem examination, 593
Presentence hearing where possibility of,
      593–94
Respite
      Pardon consideration investigation, 593
      Prisoner becomes insane or pregnant,
      593
Review of, 595
Stay of execution, 593
Warrant of conviction and sentence of
      death, 592
Warrant return, 593
Witnesses to, 593

**DECENCY, MORALITY, GOOD ORDER,
AND CHASTITY, CRIMES AGAINST**,
435–72
Abortion
      Instruments of, 441
      Private hospital not obligated to
      perform, 442
Adultery, 439, 561, 567
Alcohol on school premises, 450
Animals, treatment of
      See ANIMALS
Begging, employing minor under 15 to, 453
Birth control, furnishing means of, 442
Blasphemy, 450
Burial ground offenses, 454–55
Camp meeting, horse racing or gaming
      near, 450
Child born out of wedlock, concealing
      death of, 442
Child exploitation
      Computer images, 448
      Dissemination of child pornography, 447
      Harmful to minors, definition, 447
      Jurisdiction to enjoin dissemination of
      visual material, 447
      Posing or exhibiting in state of nudity or
      sexual conduct, 444–45
      Possessing child pornography, 446–47
      Purchasing child pornography, 446–47

Children
      Begging, employing minor under 15 to,
      453
      Harmful to minors, definition, 447
      Matters harmful to, 443
      Prostitution, inducement into, 303, 437–38
      Unnatural and lascivious acts with child
      under 16, 450
Common nightwalker, 451
      Third conviction, 453
Communications, interception of, 463–70
Dead bodies
      Buying, selling, or possessing, 454
      Disinterring, 454
      Taking on process or execution, 454
Definitions, 447–48
Deformities, exhibition of, 449
Demands, notices, official documents
      resembling court process, 462
Disabled persons
      Accommodations, 463
      Guide dogs, 463
Discrimination
      Advertisements with effect of, 461–62
      Civil rights, 463
      Employment and benefits, 463
      Hatred of groups, publishing, 463
      Public accommodations, in, 463
Drugging for sexual intercourse, 437
Eavesdropping in private home, 469
Exposure, indecent, 440, 452
False birth, marriage, or death certificates,
      462
Fornication, 441
Funerals, disturbance of, 451
House of ill fame, keeping, 442
Incest, 441
Indecent exposure, 440, 452
Jury, overhearing deliberations by using
      devices, 470
Lewd and lascivious behavior, 440–41
Libel related to hatred of group, 463
Libraries, disturbance of, 450–51
Marriage enticement of person under 16,
      437
Military funeral services, disturbance of,
      451
Miscarriage
      Advertising services concerning, 441
      Procuring, 441
Motion picture theaters, 448–49
Nature, crimes against, 449
      Conduct, private and consensual, 449
Nude persons, photographing or
      videotaping, 471–72
Obscene books, 443, 444
Penalties, 451–52
Polygamy, 439–40, 570
Pornography
      Child pornography, 445–47
      Dissemination or possession, 444
      Injunctive relief against, 447
Profanity, 453
Prostitution
      See PROSTITUTION
Public conveyances
      Disorderliness on, 451
      Smoking on, 451
Restaurants or taverns
      Hidden areas of used by customers, 442
      Immoral purposes, use for, 442–43
Schools

Alcohol on premises of, 450
      Disturbance of, 450
Sexual intercourse and conduct
      Definition of sexual conduct, 448
      Drugging persons for, 437
      Enticing for, 437
      For fee, engaging in, 452
      Inducing person under 18, 437
      Place of, prohibitions on, 438
Sporting events, abuse of participants and
      officials, 450
Streets, reservations, or parkways,
      violations of regulations relating to,
      453
Tombs, graves, memorials, desecrating,
      etc., 455
Tramps, vagrants, and vagabonds, 454
      Arrest of, without warrant, 454
      Begging or riding freight trains as
      evidence of being, 453–54
      Buildings, entering by, 454
Unnatural and lascivious acts, 449
      Child under 16, 450
Vagabonds, 454
Vagrants, 454
Wedlock, concealment of death of child
      born out of, 442
Wiretapping
      See WIRETAPPING
Worship assembly, disturbance of, 450

DEFECT, STRUCTURAL
Doctrine of, 854

DEFORMITIES
Exhibition of, 449

**DEPARTMENT OF CHILDREN
AND FAMILIES**
See CHILDREN AND FAMILIES,
      DEPARTMENT OF

**DEPARTMENT OF CRIMINAL JUSTICE
INFORMATION SERVICES**
Mental health commitment order, report of,
      162

**DEPARTMENT OF TRANSITIONAL
ASSISTANCE**
See TRANSITIONAL ASSISTANCE,
      DEPARTMENT OF

DEPARTMENT OF YOUTH SERVICES
See YOUTH SERVICES, DEPARTMENT
      OF

DEPOSITIONS
Perpetuation of testimony by, criminal
      procedure rules for, 642–43
Superior Court rules
      Commissions to take, 656
      Manner of taking, 656

**DESERTION, NONSUPPORT,
AND ILLEGITIMACY**, 472–76
Abandonment and nonsupport, 472–73
      Penalties, 474–75
Acknowledgment of paternity, 474
Concealing assets, 475
Destitute parents
      Neglect or refusal to support, 475–76
      Venue, 476
Disabled persons, parent refusal to
      support, 476
Duty to support
      Custody, lack of, 474
      Illegitimacy, 474

12

DESERTION, NONSUPPORT, AND ILLEGITIMACY *(cont'd)*
Elements of nonsupport, 762
Fines, payment to probation officer, 473
Illegitimacy
    Abandonment and willful nonsupport, 474–75
    Dismissal of case, 475
    Duty to support, 474
    Prior law obligations, 475
Insurance coverage, 475
Jurisdiction, 473
Lack of custody as defense, 474
Marriage and parentage, evidence of, 473
Money forfeited or recovered, 475
Needy disabled persons, parents' failure to support, 476
Penalties for nonsupport, 762
Prima facie evidence, 472–73
Recognizance on release on probation, 473

DIMINISHED CAPACITY, 811–12

DISABLED PERSONS
Assault and battery of, 281–82, 755
Assistance animals
    Privileges of persons with, 463
    Theft or attack of, 460
Blind pedestrians on crosswalks, 41
Discrimination, 463
Guide dogs, 463
Intellectually disabled persons
    Assault and battery of, 279–80, 760
    Witnesses, 233–34
Parent refusal to support, 476
Service animals
    Privileges of persons with, 463
    Theft or attack of, 460

DISCOVERY, 220–21
District and municipal criminal procedure rules concerning, 667
Forensic and scientific analysis, postconviction, 581–82
Pretrial, criminal procedure rules concerning, 619–26

DISCRIMINATION
Advertisements with effect of, 461–62
Civil rights, 463
Employment and benefits, 463
Handicapped persons, 463
Hatred of groups, publishing, 463
Public accommodations, in, 463

DISGUISES
Used to obstruct law enforcement, 376

DISORDERLY HOUSE, 569

DISORDERLY PERSON, 757

DISTRICT COURT RULES FOR PROBATION VIOLATION PROCEEDINGS, 687–707
Commencement of violation proceedings
    Charged criminal conduct (Rule 3), 689–93
    Violations other than charged criminal conduct (Rule 4), 693–94
Conduct of hearings (Rule 6), 697–701
Continuance without a finding (Rule 9), 706–07
Definition of terms (Rule 2), 688–89
Detention hearings, 694–97
Finding and disposition (Rule 8), 703–06
Hearings, conduct of, 697–701

Hearsay evidence (Rule 7), 701–03
Scope and purpose (Rule 1), 687–88
Surrender, 688

DISTRICT COURTS, 220–24
See also DISTRICT COURT RULES FOR PROBATION VIOLATION PROCEEDINGS; DISTRICT/MUNICIPAL COURT RULES OF CRIMINAL PROCEDURE
Arrest without warrant, 223
Binding over to Superior Court, 223
Complaints and warrants, 223
    Issuance on complaint for misdemeanors, 223–24
Criminal jurisdiction, 220–24
Defendants, process for, 224
Discovery, 220–21
Disqualification to hear case, 223
General provisions, 220
Jury of six, 220–21
Jury sessions, 221–23
Jury-waived trial, 220–21
Justice of the peace, taking bail, 224
Juvenile cases, process for, 224
Misdemeanor complaints, procedure on, 223–24
Penalty imposition, 221
Probation, 220–21
Process, 223–24
Prosecutor, role of, 223
Recognizances to keep peace, 223
Record of proceedings, 220–21
Warrants and process, 223
Witnesses, process for, 224

DISTRICT/MUNICIPAL COURT RULES OF CRIMINAL PROCEDURE, 665–68
Applicability, 665
Arraignment, 665–66
Boston Municipal Court, sealing of dismissals and nonconviction records, 668
Complaint, issuance of, 665
Discovery, 667
Hearing date for discovery compliance and jury waiver election, 667
Issuance of complaint, 665
Police statement, 665
Pretrial hearing, 666–67
Pretrial motions, 667
Sanctions, 667
Trials, 667

DIVERSION
See PRETRIAL DIVERSION

DIVISION OF VICTIM COMPENSATION AND ASSISTANCE, 249

DIVORCE, 207–09
Advertisement to procure, 209
Certificate of, unlawful issuance, 209
Cohabitation after divorce, 208
Criminal offenses, notice to district attorney, 209
Domestic violence record search, 208
Libels for divorce, 207
Marital home
    Order of restraint, 208
    Order to vacate, 208
Personal liberty of spouse, 207
Personation, 208–09
Restraint orders, 208
Unlawful, procurement of, 209

Vacate marital home, order to, 208
Warrants, outstanding, 208

DNA
See also DNA DATABASE
Evidence, 812

DNA DATABASE, 20–22
Analysis of samples and records, 21
Armed assault, 288, 289
Assault and battery, 278, 280, 284, 288, 289
Attempt to murder, 287
Burglary, 317
Collection of samples, 20–21
Confidentiality of records, 21
Constitutionality, 20
Definitions, 20
Director of, 20
Disclosure of records, unauthorized, 21–22
Drugging persons for sexual intercourse, 437
Enticing away for prostitution or sexual intercourse, 43
Expungement, application and grounds for, 22
Facilities, 21
Failure to provide sample, penalty, 21
Firearms used in committing felony, 289–90
Incestuous marriage or intercourse, 441
Indecent assault and battery on child under 14, 277–79
Inducing minor into prostitution, 437–38
Laboratories and facilities, 21
Living off or sharing earnings of minor prostitute, 438–39
Manslaughter, 275
Murder conviction, 273
Obscene matter, dissemination or possession of, 444
Offenses requiring sample, 20
Penalties, 22
Rape, 297
Release of information, 21–22
Submission of sample, 20
Tampering with records or samples, 22
Testing and analysis rules, 21

DOCKET SHEET
Evidentiary use of, 812

DOCUMENTARY EVIDENCE
Bank account statement and checks, 235
Bank and trust company records, 235
Business records, 235
Certification, 236
Certified copies of public and private records, 236
Child abuse victims, statements of, 237–38
Hospital records, 235–37, 653
Impeachment, 235
Medical records, 235–37
Newspapers, 236
Photographic copies, 236
Photographic film prints, 236
Private records, 236
Public records, 236
Public way, proof of, 236
Regular course of business, 235
Reproductions, business or public records, 236
Stenographic notes, 237

DOMESTIC VIOLENCE
Battered woman syndrome, 804
Counselor, confidentiality provisions for, 229

12

DOMESTIC VIOLENCE *(cont'd)*
Discharge or bail, written ruling of abuse allegation, 526
Harassment prevention orders, review and filing of records, 254–55
Record search, 208, 216–19
Victim programs, location, confidentiality of, 229

DOUBLE JEOPARDY, 261, 590, 634, 636

DRIVER ALCOHOL OR CONTROLLED SUBSTANCE EDUCATION PROGRAM, 71–73

DRIVING UNDER THE INFLUENCE, 55–70
Additional substances, 64
Admission, 64
Alcohol, 67
Amphetamines, 66
Blood test, 66
Breathalyzer, 65–66
Chain of custody, 70
Chemical breath test, 76
Child endangerment, 80
Closing argument, 70
Codeine, 66
Complaint, suspension of license on issuance of, 77–78
Deterrent trust fund, 80–81
Dismissal of charges, 73–74
Driver alcohol education program, 71–73
Driving to endanger, 67
Driving while drinking, 174
Drugs, 66, 67
Elements, 763
Endangerment of children, 80
Establishment serving alcohol, 76
Extraterritorial pursuit, 69
Factors, 64
Failure of proof, 66
Failure to stop after collision, 55–70
Field sobriety tests, 66, 67
Forfeiture of motor vehicle, 81
Heroin, 66
Horizontal gaze nystagmus test, 66
Ignition interlock device, 38, 70–71, 79–80
Law enforcement training regarding, 77
Lay opinion as to intoxication, 64
Leaving the scene, 68
Lifetime revocation of license or right to operate, 79
Lost or ill motorist, 70
Marijuana, 64
Medical examination, right to, 260–61
Medication, effect of, 66
Melanie's law, 70
Minors and, 79, 174
Miranda warnings, 67
Open container violations, 75–76, 174
Operation of vehicle, requirements for, 63–64
Penalty, 763–64
Posting notices of penalties, 174
Prescription drugs, 66
Probation, 71–73
Public way, proof of, 63
Purpose of statute, 64–65
Pursuit outside jurisdiction, 69
Reasonable suspicion standard, 66
Reckless and unauthorized driving, 55–70
Registration, cancellation of, 81–82
Restitution, 70
Roadblocks, 68

Second offense, 69
Selective traffic enforcement program, 77
Serious bodily injury while under influence, 76–77
Statement regarding further violations, 78
Subsequent offenses, 69
Suspension of license, 77–78, 79, 174
Third offense, 69
Training of law enforcement personnel, 77
Treatment and rehabilitation programs, 71–73
Treatment programs, 79
Use without authority, 67–68
Vehicular homicide, 74–75
Videotape of booking, 67

DRUG REHABILITATION, 123–27
Children referred by Department of Children and Families or Juvenile Court, 127
Defendant, charges against
Drug offense, 124–25
Other than drug offense, 125–26
Hearings, 124–26
Incapacitated persons, protective custody, 123–24
Juveniles and youthful offenders, 126–27
Probation, 126
Stay of proceedings, 124–25
Urinalysis, 126

DRUGS
See CONTROLLED SUBSTANCES; DRUG REHABILITATION

DRUNK DRIVING
See DRIVING UNDER THE INFLUENCE

DUEL
Accessory, 273
Foreign state conviction or acquittal, 273
Wound without and death within state, 273

DWELLING HOUSE
Armed assault within, 289, 753
Arson, 313–14, 753
Burglary, 316–17
Daytime entry, 318
Entry at night, 318
Entry by false pretenses, 319
Killing or injuring a person, 573

E

EAVESDROPPING, 469, 569, 813

EDUCATION
See SCHOOLS

ELDERLY PERSONS
Assault and battery of, 281–82, 755
Indecent assault and battery on, 760

ELECTRONIC COMMUNICATION
Annoying, 410

ELEMENTS AND PENALTIES OF SELECTED CRIMES, 753–72
Aggravated assault and battery on child under 14, 759
Armed assault in a dwelling house, 753
Arson
Building, 753
Dwelling, 753
Assault, 753
Battery, and, 754
Child under 16 with intent to commit rape, on, 753–54

Dangerous weapon, by means of, 753, 755
Elderly or disabled person, on, 755
EMT, etc., on, 755
Family or household member, on, 755
Felony, intent to commit, 754
Murder, maim, etc., intent to, 754
Public employee, on, 754–55
Rape, intent to commit, 754
Rob or murder, intent to, 754
Unarmed robbery, intent to commit, 754
Attempted extortion, 755
Breaking and entering (building, ship, etc.), 756
Intent to commit a misdemeanor, 756
Nighttime with intent to commit a felony, 756
Occupied, 756
Unoccupied, 756
Burglarious tools, possession of, 765
Burglary
Armed or making an assault, 756
Unarmed, 756–57
Carjacking, 757
Carrying a firearm, 770–71
Deriving support from the earning of a prostitute, 757
Disclosure of identity or location of witness, 757
Disorderly person, 757
Drug sale in a school zone, 765
Entering without breaking
Building, ship, etc. (nighttime) (occupied), 757
Dwelling (nighttime) (unoccupied), 757
Enticing child under 18 to engage in prostitution, trafficking, sexual activity, 758
Escape from jail, 758
Extortion, 758
Failure to stop
Personal injury, after causing, 758
Property damage, after causing, 758
False representation to procure welfare, 758–59
Forgery and counterfeiting certificate and other writings, 759
Heroin, being present where kept, 756
Homicide by motor vehicle, 771–72
Indecent assault and battery
Child under 14, on, 759–60
Elder, on, 760
Intellectually disabled person, on, 760
Person over 14, on, 760
Person with disability, on, 760
Intimidation of a witness or juror, 760–61
Kidnapping, 761
Minor or incompetent by a relative, 761
Larceny, 761
From the person, 761
Leaving the scene, 761
Lotteries, 761
Manslaughter, 761–62
Mayhem, 762
Motor vehicle theft, 762
Murder, 762
Nonsupport of a child born out of wedlock, 762
Open and gross lewdness, 762–63
Operating to endanger, 763
Operating under the influence, 763–64
Perjury, 764

ELEMENTS AND PENALTIES OF SELECTED CRIMES *(cont'd)*
Possession of a controlled substance, 764
  With intent to distribute, 764
Rape, 765–67
  Child under 16, 766–67
  Statutory rape, 766–67
Receiving stolen goods, 767–68
Robbery
  Armed, 768
  Unarmed, 754, 768
Sex offender registration verification, 768
Shoplifting, 768–69
Stalking, 769
Statutory rape, 769
Subornation of perjury, 769
Threats, 769
Trafficking in marijuana, cocaine, heroin, etc., 769
Trafficking of persons for forced or sexual servitude, 770
Trespass, 770
Unarmed robbery, 754, 768
Unlawfully carrying a firearm, 770–71
Unlawfully possessing a firearm or ammunition, 771
Unnatural and lascivious acts, 771
Use of minors in drug sales, 765
Use without authority (motor vehicle), 771
Uttering false or forged records, deeds, or other writings, 771
Vehicular homicide, 771–72
Willful and malicious destruction of property, 772

EMBEZZLEMENT
Bank employees, 333
Bank liquidating agent or receiver, 334
Brokers or agents, 334
Fiduciaries, 334, 564
Municipal officers, 333
Property at fire, 319
State treasury, 333
Transitional Assistance Department property, obtaining through, 18
Voluntary association, 334

EMERGENCY ASSISTANCE PERSONNEL
Assault and battery of, 280, 755

ENTERPRISE CRIME
Definitions, 434–35
Penalties, 435
Seizure and forfeiture of proceeds or property, 435

ENTRAPMENT, 814

EQUAL PROBABILITIES
Theory of, 814

ESCAPE
Aiding, 373
Attempt or failure to return, 373
City or town jail, from, 373
Consenting to, 373
Correctional institution, aiding escape from, 373
Elements of, 758
Forms for indictment, 569
Jailer allowing, 373
Negligently suffering, 373
Penalty for, 758
Person having custody, aiding escape from, 373

Prisoner, 597
Process server's refusal or delay resulting in, 374
Suffering convict to be at large, etc., 374

ESTATES
Taking from, 307

EVIDENCE, 803–58
Abandonment, 803
Abuse
  Admissibility of physical, sexual, etc., 234
  Expert testimony and, 234
Admissions, 803
  Adoptive, 803–04
  Nondefendant, by, 803
  Silence, by, 803
Alford plea, 804
Another did it, 804
Arrest, 804
Arrest warrant, 804
Assertion of rights, 834
Attorney, ineffective assistance of, 825
Audiotapes, 804
Battered woman syndrome, 804
Best evidence, 804
Blood samples, 804–05
  Grand jury, 804–05
  Ortho-talidine, 805
  Postindictment, 805
  Prior to charge, 805
Booking questions, 805
Bowden defense, 805
Bruton rule, 805
Buccal swab, 805–06
Certificate of analysis, 806
Chain of custody, 806
Circumstantial, 806
Closing argument, 806–07
Co-counsel, 807
Collateral estoppel, 807–08
Compact disc, 808
Competency, 808
Complaint, refusal to issue, 808
Completeness, doctrine of, 808
Computer data and programs, 237
Confession, 803
Conflict of interest, 808
Consciousness of guilt, 808–09
Continuance
  General, 823
  Without a finding, 809
Corroboration rule, 809
Court officers, statements to, 835
Courtroom closure, 809–10
Credibility of witness, 810
Criminal profiles, 810
Cross-examination, 810–11
  Bias, 810
  Drug use, 810
  Improper, 810–11
  Judge's discretion, 811
Cruel and unusual punishment, 811
Cumulative error, 811
Custodial interrogation, 835–36
Dangerous weapon, 811
Defaulting defendant, 811
Defendant
  Counsel table, at, 811
  Defaulting, 811
  Sidebar, at, 811
Destruction of, 811
Diminished capacity, 811–12

Dismissal, 812
  With prejudice, 812
DNA, 812
Docket sheet, 812
Dreams, 812
Drug certificate, 812–13
Duplicative convictions, 813
Eavesdropping, 813
Egregious government misconduct, 813–14
Electronic recording of statement, 836
Entrapment, 814
Equal probability, theory of, 814
Error, 814
Evidence affidavit, 504
Excited utterance, 814–15
Exclusionary rule, 815
Exculpatory, 815–16
  Delayed disclosure, 815–16
  Duty of prosecutor as to, 816
  Grand jury, 816
Experts, 816–19
  Abuse, admissibility of, 234
  Ballistics, 817
  Daubert test, 817
  Electrophoresis, 818
  Event data recorder, 818
  Hypothetical questions, 818
  Motor vehicle black box, 818
  Murder, 271
  Narcotics investigation, 818
  Police officers, 818
  Rape, 819
  Sexual abuse, 819
  Standard for, 816
  Superior Court rules concerning, 653
Expungement of records, 819
Extraneous evidence, 819
Eyewitness identification, 819–20
Failure to call witness, 820
Fear of testifying, 820
Fingerprints, 820
First complaint, 820–22
Foreign law, judicial notice of, 234
Forfeiture by wrongdoing, 822
Forgery and counterfeiting, evidence relative to, 364
General continuance, 823
Grand jury, 804–05, 816
Handwriting, 823
Hearsay, 823–24
  Admissible absent objection, 824
  Credibility, 824
  Drug conversation, 823
  Police testimony on action taken, 823
  Prior consistent statements, 824
  Statement not offered for truth, 823
Humane practice, 824
Identification, 824–25
  Out-of-court, 841
  Suppression of testimony, 854
  Voice identification, 858
Identification cards, 825
Immunity, 825
Impeachment of party's own witness, 233
Inconsistent defenses, 825
Inconsistent verdicts, 825
Inferences, 825
Insanity, 825–26
Internal affairs, 826
Internet materials, 827
Intoxication, 827
Involuntary intoxication, 827

12

EVIDENCE *(cont'd)*
Jail credit, 827
Jailhouse informants, 827
Jeopardy, 827
Joint defense agreements, 827
Joint ventures, 827–28
    Identity of other principals, 828
    Jury instructions, 827–28
    Lookout, 828
    Mental state, 828
    Motive, 828
    Sole principal actor, 828
    Statements, 853
    Weapons, 828
Judge questioning witness, 828–29
Judicial notice of foreign law, 234
Juror questions, 828–29
Jury
    Duty of, 829
    Nullification, 829
    Questions from, 828–29
    Venire, 829
    Waiver, 829
Justice, miscarriage of, 839
Knowingly, 830
Learned treatises, 830
Legislative and administrative bodies,
        admissibility of copies, 234
Lesser included offenses, 830
Lost or destroyed, 626, 830
Melendez-Diaz, 830–34
Miranda, 834–39
Miscarriage of justice, 839
Missing evidence, 839
Missing witness, 839
Mistrial, 839–40
Motions in limine, 840
Motive, 840
Mugshots, 840
Necessity, defense of justification, 840
Newly discovered, 840
Newspapers, 236
911 call, 815
No contact order, 854
Nontestimonial versus testimonial
        statements, 855
Offer of proof, 840
Opening statements, 840–41
Out-of-court identification, 841
Past recollection recorded, 841
Peremptory challenges, 841–42
Perjury, 851
Photographic copies, 236
Photographic films, 236
Photographs, 842–43
Plea colloquy, 843
Police knowledge test, 853
Polygraph test, 843
Possession of means to commit crime,
        843–44
Prima facie, 844
    Drugs, chemist's analysis of, 19
    Motor vehicle records, 19
    Sperm cells, chemist's analysis of, 19
Prior bad acts, 844
Prior consistent statement, 844–45
Prior convictions, 845
Prior inconsistent statement, 845
Prior recorded statement, 845
Pro se defendants, 846
Probable cause, 846
Profile, 846

Psychiatric examination
    Privileged records, 846
    Statement of accused while undergoing,
        233
Psychological evaluations, 846
    Privileged records, 846
Public way, proof of, 236
Radio transmissions, 846
Reasonable doubt, 846-7
Rebuttal, 846
Records of courts of other states or U.S., 234
Recusal, 847
Redirect examination, 847
Reduction of charges, 847
Relevancy, 847
Reopening, 847
Reproductions, business or public records,
        236
Reputation, 232, 847–48
Restitution, 848
Right to counsel, 848
Rule 1:28, 848–49
Rule of lenity, 849
Safe harbor rule, 838
School records, 849
Search and seizure, 849
Selective prosecutions, 849
Self-defense, 849
Self-incrimination, 849–50
Sentence, stay of, 854
Sentencing, 850–52
Sex crime victims' sexual conduct, 232
Sex Offender Registry hearings, 14
Sexual knowledge of children, 852
Show-ups, 852
Spontaneous utterance, 814–15
State of mind, 852–53
    Defendant, 852
    Victim, 852–53
    Witness, 853
Statements
    Against penal interest, 853
    Joint venturers, of, 853
    Opening, 840–41
    Prior recorded, 845
    Private citizens, to, 853–54
Statutes, proof of, 234–37
Stay away order, 854
Stay of sentence, 854
Stipulations, 633–34, 854
Striking, 854
Structural defect doctrine, 854
Suppression
    Identification testimony, 854
    Superior Court rules, 654
Surrender hearings, 854
Surveillance post location, 854
Telephone conversations, 854–55
Tender years doctrine, 855
Testimonial versus nontestimonial
        statements, 855
Third-party, 855–56
Unanimity instruction, 856–57
Unavailable witness, 857
Unmedicated state, 857
Verbal completeness, 857–58
Videotaped simulations, 858
Videotapes, 858
Voice identification, 858
Void for vagueness, 858
Weapon found on defendant, 858
Willful blindness, 858

EXAMINATIONS
Adjournment of, 522–23
Testimony reduced to writing, 524

EXCITED UTTERANCE, 814–15

EXECUTION OF SENTENCE
See JUDGMENT AND EXECUTION

EXPERT TESTIMONY
Abuse, admissibility of, 234
Ballistics, 817
Controlled substance offenses, 107
Criminal Procedure Rules about, 647
Daubert test, 817
Disclosure of, 607–08
Electrophoresis, 818
Event data recorder, 818
Hypothetical questions, 818
Motor vehicle black box, 818
Murder, 271
Narcotics investigation, 818
Police officers, 818
Rape, 819
Sex offender registry classification, 15
Sexual abuse, 819
Standard for, 816
Superior Court rules concerning, 653

EXPLOSIVES
False reports, 409–10, 564
Hoax explosives
    Definition, 344
    Possession of, 344
Incendiary devices, 344
Oil of vitriol and other substances, use of,
        345

EXPUNGEMENT
Abuse prevention orders, 218
DNA database records, 22
Evidence of, 819

EXTORTION
Attempted, 301, 755
Elements of, 755

EXTRATERRITORIAL ARREST, 515

EYEGLASSES
Sales of, 412

F

FAILURE TO APPEAR
Children, proceedings against, 150
Contempt, 521
Jury service, 240
Motor vehicle violations, 43–45
Release on bail or recognizance, after,
        539–40
Subsequent proceedings, 523

FALSE CLAIMS
Endorsement or approval, 341
Presentation of, 337

FALSE INFORMATION
Anatomical gifts, 129
Firearms and weapons purchases, 182–83
Juror questionnaires, 240
Mortgages, 328
Sex offender registry, 9–10
Transitional Assistance Department, to, 17

FALSE PRETENSES
Commercial transactions, 327
Dwelling house entry, by, 319
Money or membership by, 338
Money or personal chattel by, 564

FALSE PRETENSES *(cont'd)*
Obtaining goods by, 338
Signature by, 327, 338

FALSE REPORTS AND TESTIMONY
Emergency response services providers, to, 410
Explosives or other dangerous substances, 409–10
Fire alarms, 409
Governmental bodies, to, 369
Police officers, to, 409
Process servers, 370
Public officers and employees, by, 369–70

FAMILY MEMBERS
See also HUSBAND AND WIFE; PARENTS AND GUARDIANS
Assault and battery on, 283

FELONIES, ACCESSORIES AND ATTEMPTS TO COMMIT CRIME, 476–79
Accessories after fact, 477
    Relationship as defense, 477
Accessories before fact, 477
Aiders, 476–77
Attempts, punishment, 478
Conspiracy, 478–76
    Collateral estoppel, 479
    Jury instruction, 479
Conviction or amenability to justice, 478
Counseling or procuring, 477
Cross-examination, 477
Felonies and misdemeanors, 476
Prosecution of, 476–79
Punishment, 476–77, 478
Venue, 478

FETUS
Homicide of viable, 272

FINES AND FORFEITURES, 596–98
Certificates of fines, 597
Cost as penalty for crime, 596
Counsel appointed to conduct proceedings concerning, 596
County treasurer, payment of expenses or fees, 598
Criminal assessments, 597
Escape of prisoner, payment of fines by sheriff, 597
Expenses
    Briefs for cases appealed to Supreme Judicial Court, 596
    Criminal prosecutions, 596
Forfeiture by wrongdoing, 822
Jailer
    Payment to, 597–98
    Quarterly returns of, 598
Payment of, 596, 597
Proceeds from assessments, 597
Recovery of, 596
Sheriff, neglect of, 597
Special cost assessments, 596–97
State treasurer, payment to, 597
Witness fees, payment of, 597

FINGERPRINTING
Accused, rights of, regarding, 259
Controlled substance felonies, person charged with, 118
Evidentiary use of, 820

FIRE, INJURY BY
Negligent use, 315
Town, negligent use, 315

FIREARMS AND WEAPONS, 174–207
Abuse prevention proceedings, order for suspension and surrender of license, 213–14
Advertisement of, 181
Aliens
    Furnishing to, 190
    Ownership or possession, conditions, 203
    Temporary license, 201–03
Ammunition
    Defined, 175
    Fees, 177
    License to sell, 177
    Loaded firearms, 401
    Refusal to grant license, 177
    Sales, 177
Assault and battery, 286–87
Assault weapons, 175, 205
Basic firearm safety certificate, 205–06
Biological, possession, 345
Breaking and entering to steal firearm, 406
Broadheads, razorheads, other arrowheads, sale of, 410
Carrying or possessing as crime against public peace, 397–403
    BB guns and air rifles, 401
    Breaking and entering to steal firearm, 406
    Constitutionality of statute, 400
    Cutting device in airport or airplane, 408–09
    Discharge near dwelling, 408
    Duplicative charges, 401
    Elements and penalties, 770–71
    Identifying numbers, 406–07
    Knowledge, 400–01
    Machine guns, 397–403
    Necessity as defense, 401–02
    New resident, 401
    Public way, 407–08
    Retailer, wholesaler, or manufacturer, breaking and entering place of business, 406
    Rifle or shotgun, loaded, 407–08
    Separate offenses, 401
    Serial numbers, 406–07
    Silencers, offenses involving, 403
    Transporting into state, 405
    Under the influence, while, 405
    Variance, 400–01
Certificate by ballistics expert, 176
Chemical weapons, possession, 345
Covert weapons, 205
Criminal act, firearm used to carry out, 206
Daggers, 401
Deceptive weapon, possession of, 311
Definitions, 175–76
Electrical weapons, 203–04
Entry on land with, 352
False information given in regard to, 182–83
False license or identification card, 203
Felony, used in commission of, 289–90
Fictitious name or address, 182–83
Firearm defined, 175
Firearms Surrender Program, 205
Forms for indictment, 568
Gun Control Advisory Board, 199
Gunsmith, 175
Hearings by licensing review board, 190–91
Hunting arrowheads, sale of, 410
Identification cards, 183–87
    Falsification of, 203

Resident's right to purchase firearms and weapons, 200–01
Identification of, 176
Large capacity weapons and feeding devices
    Definitions, 175–76
    Offenses involving, 404
    Roster of certain weapons to be published, 199
    Without safety devices, liability, 204
License
    Abuse prevention proceedings, order for suspension and surrender of license, 213–14
    Carry or possess firearms, to, 191–99
    Conditions, 178–81
    Criminal act, firearm used to carry out, 206
    Falsification of, 203
    Fees, 176–77
    Forfeiture or suspension of, 181
    Licensing review board, 190–91
    Penalties, 177–78
    Record of, 177
    Refusal to grant, 176–77
    Requirements, 176–77
    Self-defense spray, 178–79
    Surrender of firearms and ammunition to licensing authority, 189–90
    Suspension of, 181
    Term of, 181
    Transfer of, 182
Licensing review board, 190–91
Loans secured by weapons, penalties, 200
Machine guns
    Carrying or possession, 397–403
    Prima facie evidence of sales, 181
    Sales, 182
Manufactured before 1900, 626
Mayhem, 283–84
Minors, furnishing to, 190
    Sales to, 190
Nonresidents, conditions on carrying, 203
Nuclear weapons, possession, 345
Ownership, rules as to, 187–89
Permits to purchase, rent, or lease, 199–200
Petitions to licensing review board, 190–91
Prima facie evidence of sale of firearms, 181
Resident's right to purchase, 200–01
    Identification card, 200–01
Retailer, wholesaler or manufacturer, breaking and entering place of business, 406
Rifle, 176
Roster of certain weapons to be published, 199
Safety certificate, 205–06
Sales record book, 177
Self-defense spray, 178–79
Statewide firearms surrender program, 205
Storage of, 204–05
Surrender of to licensing authority, 189–90
Theatrical productions, use of in, 203
Transfers, reporting of, 187–89
Unauthorized purchase of, 182
Vehicle transport of, 200
Violent crime, 176

FIREFIGHTING AND EQUIPMENT
Burning, reckless or willful, firefighter injured by, 279
Fire alarms, false, 409
Hotel manager duty to notify, 316

12

FIREFIGHTING AND EQUIPMENT *(cont'd)*
Injury before fire, 315
Injury during fire, 315
Interference with, 375
Wanton or malicious injury to fire engines or apparatus, 315

FIRST COMPLAINT, 293–94
Evidence, 820–22

FISH, GAME AND NATURAL RESOURCES
Leghold traps restricted, 171–72

FLAGS
Foreign
    Display, 265
    Misuse of, 265
Penalty for misuse, 265
Print use of, 265

FLEA MARKETS
Smoking at, 420

FLOWERS
Gardens, offenses involving, 348
Protection of, 348

FOOD STAMPS TRAFFICKING, 18

FORENSIC AND SCIENTIFIC ANALYSIS, POSTCONVICTION ACCESS, 580–84
Affidavit of factual innocence, 581–82
Appeals, 584
Conditions of analysis, 583
Contest of motion for, 581–82
Cost of, 583
Counsel, appointment of, 582
Criteria for allowing, 582–83
Data, documents, and notes, order to produce, 583
Definitions, 580–81
Disclosure of results, 583
Discovery
    Motion for, 581–82
    Orders for, 582–83
Findings of fact and conclusions of law, 582–83
Forensic service provider, selection of, 583
Government officials, civil or criminal liability, 584
Hearing, 582
Inconclusive, order for additional analysis, 583
Jurisdiction over motion, 582
Laboratory, cooperation with, 583
Misconduct or negligence by government entities, 584
Motion for, 581
Retention of material evidence, 584
Service of motion, 582
Term of sentence, effect on, 583
Time for performing, 583
Victim notification, 583–84
Waiver of right to file motion prohibited, 584

FORFEITURE
See also FINES AND FORFEITURES
Controlled substances offenses, 118–21
Forfeiture by wrongdoing, 822
Gaming devices or games, 24

FORGERY AND CURRENCY CRIMES, 360–66
Admission tickets, 362, 363
Advertisements similar to bank bills, 365–66
Bank bills, gathering or retaining, 365
Bank signature card, 361

Checks, fraudulent, 329
Coins, 364, 365
Compensation of officers and prosecutors regarding, 366
Connecting parts of instruments, 365
Counterfeited notes or bills, possession of ten or more, 363
Damaging bank bills, 365
Defenses, 361
Definition of forgery, 361
Elements of, 759
Evidence relative to, 364
False birth, marriage, or death certificates, 360–61
False or forged records, etc., 360–61
    Defenses, 361
Forms for indictment, 569
Government certificates, 364
Land Court seal, 362
Notes, bills, etc. as currency, 365
    Fraction of a dollar, 365
    Less than $5, 365
Penalty for, 759
Possession
    Counterfeit bills, 364
    Less than ten coins, 364
    Ten or more coins, 364
    Ten or more forged bills, 363
    Worthless bank bills, 365
Railroad company stamp, 362
Railroad tickets, 362, 363
Records, 360–61
Retaining bank bills, 365
Seizure of counterfeits and materials related thereto, 366
Signatures of corporate officers, 364
Tickets, 362, 363
Tools for making, 364
Uttering
    Counterfeit bills, 363–64
    Counterfeit coins, 365
    Elements and penalties, 771
    False or forged note, 363
    False or forged records, 362–63
    Forged railroad or admission ticket, 363
    Forms for indictment, 571
    Worthless bank bills, 365
Worthless bank bills, 365

FORNICATION, 441, 562, 569

FRAUD
Anatomical gifts, 129
Bank employees, 333
Checks, drawing or uttering, 329
Corporate books, false entries, 337
Corporate credit, 338
Credit card use, 330
Identity, 330–31
Jury processing or selection, 242
Labor union seal, trademark, insignia, 338
Municipal officers, 333
State treasury, 333
Transitional Assistance Department
    Hotline sign, 18
    Property obtained through, 18
Vessel captain, conversion of property by, 327

FRESH COMPLAINT, 293

FRESH PURSUIT, EXTRATERRITORIAL ARREST, 515
Authority of officer of another state, 515

Out-of-state officer's authority, 515
Postarrest proceedings, 515

FUNERALS
Disturbance of, 451

FURS
Imitation, offenses involving, 340

G

GAMBLING AND VENDING DEVICES
See GAMING OR BETTING

GAMING COMMISSION
Interference with commission agents or employees, 23

GAMING OR BETTING, 22–24
Cattle shows, relative to, 423–24
Cheating and swindling, 23
Children, 24
Complaints and indictments relative to, 430
Definitions, 22
Delivery to or from person engaged in, 429
Devices of, 422–23
Evidence, 427
Forfeiture, 422
Forms for indictment, 569
Gambling devices, 22, 422–23
    Fraudulent use, 338–39
Gifts for influence, 432
Hotels, etc., in, 422
Implements of, possession, 422
Inns, etc., in, 422
Interference with commission agents or employees, 23
Judicial notice concerning, 430
Lottery, pool or betting houses, 422
Manufacture of devices or games, 23–24
Obstructing entrance to place of, 430
Organizing or promoting, 427
Place to register bets, 427
Policy lotteries or shops, 428
Possession of devices or games, 23
Prima facie evidence, 428, 429, 430
Public place in, or while trespassing, 422
Seizure and forfeiture of devices or games, 23–24
Ship or vessel, 422
Skilo and similar games, 424
Sweepstakes, unlawful possession of electronic machine or device for conducting or promoting, 423
Telephones used for, 427, 428, 433–34
Unlawful acts, 22–23
Warrant to enter place of, 429

GANGS
Assault with intent to force membership in, 307

GIFT CERTIFICATES
Offenses involving, 339

GLOBAL POSITIONING SYSTEM (GPS) DEVICES
Homeless sex offender to wear device, 9
Sex offenders, to be worn by, 307–08

GOAL POSTS
Destruction of, 345

GOOD ORDER, CRIMES AGAINST
See DECENCY, MORALITY, GOOD ORDER, AND CHASTITY, CRIMES AGAINST

GOOD SAMARITANS
Liability of, 251

GOVERNMENTS, CRIMES AGAINST,
264–67
Anarchy, 266
Anthem, national, 265
Communist party, 266
Educational activities, 266
   Exchange teachers, 266
Flag
   Foreign, misuse of, 265
   Penalty for misuse, 265
   Print use of, 265
Misprision of treason, 264
National anthem, 265
Public office, ineligibility for, 267
Subversive organization
   Actions to enjoin, 266–67
   Attorney general, duty of, 266–67
   Books, destruction or concealment of, 267
   Buildings, permitting use by, 267
   Contributions to, 267
   Defined, 266
   Member, knowingly becoming or
      remaining, 267
   Prohibition, 267
   Public office, ineligibility to, 267
Treason
   Conviction, manner of, 265
   Defined, 264
   Misprision of, 264
   Penalty for, 264
Uniforms, unlawful use, 265–66

GOVERNOR
Rewards offered by, 514–15

GPS DEVICES
Search warrants, 484
Sex offenders, to be worn by, 9, 307–08

GRAND JURY, 557–59
Affirmation in lieu of oath, 559
Bristol County, 558
Completion of investigation by, 557
Court reporter, 655
Criminal Procedure Rule, 601–02
Deficiency of grand jurors, 558
Drawing and summoning of, 558, 601
Essex County, 558
Evidence, 804–05, 816
Exculpatory evidence, 816
Hampden County, 558
Impaneling and oath, 558–59
Investigation, completion of, 557
Issuance of writs of venire facias for, 557
Middlesex County, 557
Norfolk County, 558
Plymouth County, 558
Resummoning, 559
Right to counsel, 559
Secrecy of proceedings, 602
Special grand juries, 557
Suffolk County, 557, 558
   Impaneling, 558
Transcripts, distributing, 371–72
Traverse juror, serving as, 559
Witnesses, 227
Worcester County, 558

GUILTY PLEAS, 630
Not guilty, 654

GUN CONTROL ADVISORY BOARD, 199

GUNS
See FIREARMS AND WEAPONS

H

HABITUAL CRIMINALS
Punishment of, 589–90
Separate trial as to prior conviction, 573–74

HABITUAL TRAFFIC OFFENDER
Revocation and reinstatement of license,
   51–52

HANDICAPPED PERSONS
See DISABLED PERSONS

HANDWRITING EVIDENCE, 823

HARASSMENT
Constitutionality, 306
Criminal harassment, 306–07
Employee serving on jury, 241
Malice, 306
Pattern of conduct or series of acts, 306
Prevention orders, 251–55
   Assessment for treatment program, 255
   Complaint form, 255
   Confidentiality of records, 255
   Court records, review and filing, 254–55
   Criminal proceedings, availability, 252
   Definitions, 251–52
   Domestic violence recordkeeping
      system, 254–55
   Enforcement of order issued by other
      jurisdiction, 253
   Filing of complaint, 252
   Jurisdiction, 252
   Notice of nature of proceedings, 252
   Relief granted, without complaint filed,
      253
   Temporary orders, 252–53
   Warrants, execution of, 254–55
Speech as conduct, 306
Substantial emotional distress, 306–07

HAZING, 410–11

HEARINGS
See specific topics

HEARSAY, 823–24
Admissible absent objection, 824
Credibility, 824
Drug conversation, 823
Police testimony on action taken, 823
Prior consistent statements, 824
Statement not offered for truth, 823

HOAX EXPLOSIVES, 344

HOME INVASION, 290–91

HOMELESS PERSONS
Sex Offender Registry, 3, 8, 9

HOMICIDE
See also MURDER
Motor vehicle, by, 74–75, 771–72

HOSPITALS AND MEDICAL FACILITIES
Abortion, 442
Obstruction of entry, 350
Records of
   Admissibility in evidence, 235–37
      Superior Court rules, 653

HOUSE OF ILL FAME, 442, 569

HUMAN TRAFFICKING
See TRAFFICKING OF PERSONS

HUMANE PRACTICE, 824

HUSBAND AND WIFE, 209–10
Custody and maintenance orders, 209–10
Domestic violence record search, 208
Restraint of personal liberty of spouse,
   order prohibiting, 209–10
Support orders, 209–10
Witnesses, 225

**HYPODERMIC SYRINGES
AND NEEDLES**
See SYRINGES AND NEEDLES

I

ICE CREAM TRUCK VENDING
Public health requirements, 420–21
Sex offenders prohibited from, 308

IDENTIFICATION
Evidence, 825–26
   Out-of-court, 841
      Suppression of testimony, 854
      Voice identification, 858
Firearms, 176
In-court, 616
Motor vehicles, defacement of identifying
   numbers, 356
Motorboats, identification number
   violations, 84
Photographic, 616, 842–43
Show-ups, 616
Suggestive procedure, 616
Voice identification, 858

IDENTIFICATION CARDS
Alcohol, purchase of, 173–74
Evidence, 825
Firearms and weapons, 183–87
   Falsification of, 203
   Resident's right to purchase, 200–01

IDENTITY FRAUD, 330–31

IGNITION INTERLOCK DEVICES, 38, 70–
71, 79–80

ILLEGITIMACY
See DESERTION, NONSUPPORT
   AND ILLEGITIMACY

IMMUNITY
See also WITNESSES
Evidence, 825

IMPEACHMENT
Business records, 235
Criminal records of witness, 232
Party's own witness, 233

IMPOUNDED MATERIALS
Exception to notice requirement, 658

INCENDIARY DEVICES
Definitions, 343–44
Malicious explosion, 345
Notice of seizure of, 345
Possession or control of, 344
Throwing, secreting, launching, or placing
   of, 345

INCEST
Complaint form for, 569
Crime of, 441
Public, exclusion of at trial, 575

**INDICTMENT AND PRETRIAL
PROCEEDINGS,** 556–71
Accused person
   Discharge of person not indicted, 559
   Rights of, 260, 262
Affray, 561, 567

12

**INDICTMENT AND PRETRIAL
PROCEEDINGS** (cont'd)
Allegations, 561
    Alternative, 560
    Unnecessary and immaterial, 560–61
Animal, description of, 560
Arraignment in capital cases, 562–63
Bill of particulars, 561
Circumstances of act, 559
Compensation for confinement of persons
        discharged, 566
Construction of words used in indictment,
        561–62
    Adultery, 561
    Affray, 561
    Aggravated rape, 561
    False pretenses, 561
    Forgery, 562
    Fornication, 562
    Larceny, 562
    Murder, 562
    Rape, 562
    Robbery, 562
    Stealing, larceny, 562
Continuing offenses, 560
Controlled substance allegations, etc., 107,
        561
Counsel, assignment of, 562–63
Criminal dealing with personal property, 562
Criminal responsibility, 560
Discharge of accused person not indicted,
        559
Forms for indictment
    Abduction, 567
    Abortion, 567
    Accessory after the fact, 567
    Accessory before the fact, 567
    Adultery, 567
    Affray, 567
    Aggravated rape, 567
    Alcoholic beverages, 567
        Sale, nuisance, 567
    Armed with dangerous weapon when
        arrested, 567–68
    Arson, 568
    Assault to maim, 568
    Assault to murder, 568
    Assault to rape, 568
    Assault with dangerous weapon, with
        intent to rob, 568
    Assuming to be an officer, 568
    Attempt to break and enter, 568
    Attempt to commit a crime, 568
    Attempt to steal from person, 568
    Breaking, entering, etc., 568
    Breaking glass, 568
    Burglarious implements, 568
    Burglary, etc., 568–69
    Burning to defraud insurance company,
        569
    Common drunkard, 569
    Common nightwalker, 569
    Concealing mortgaged personal
        property, 569
    Conspiracy, 569
    Cruelty to animals, 569
    Disorderly home, 569
    Drunkenness, 569
    Eavesdropping, 569
    Escape, 569
    Exposure of person, 569
    Forgery, 569

    Fornication, 569
    Gaming, 569
    House of ill fame, 569
    Idle and disorderly person, 569
    Illegitimacy, 569
    Incest, 569
    Larceny, 569–70
    Lewd and lascivious cohabitation, 570
    Lewdness, 570
    Lord's Day, 570
    Lottery, 570
    Maiming, 570
    Malicious injury, 570
    Manslaughter, 570
    Misrepresentation to obtain drug, 571
    Murder, 570
    Neglect of spouse or minor child, 570
    Nuisance, 571
    Obtaining signature by false pretenses,
        570
    Open and gross lewdness, 570
    Perjury, 570
    Polygamy, 570
    Prescriptions, false, 571
    Prescriptions, unlawful, 571
    Prostitute, 570
    Rape, 571–71
    Receiving stolen property, 571
    Rescue, 571
    Robbery, 571
    Sale and delivery (drug), 571
    Sodomy, etc., 571
    Stubborn child, 571
    Threats to extort, 571
    Unlawful appropriation, 571
    Unnatural act, 571
    Uttering, 571
    Vagabond, 571
    Vagrant, 571
Gambling, 430
Grand jurors, 557–59
    Affirmation in lieu of oath, 559
    Bristol County, 558
    Completion of investigation by, 557
    Criminal Procedure Rule, 601–02
    Deficiency of, 558
    Drawing and summoning of, 558
    Essex County, 558
    Hampden County, 558
    Impaneling and oath, 558–59
    Investigation, completion of, 557
    Issuance of writs of venire facias for, 557
    Middlesex County, 557
    Norfolk County, 558
    Plymouth County, 558
    Resummoning, 559
    Right to counsel, 559
    Special grand jury, 557
    Suffolk County, 557, 558
        Impaneling, 558
    Transcripts, distributing, 371–72
    Traverse juror, serving as, 559
    Worcester County, 558
Immaterial defects in, 561
Intent to injure or defraud, 560
Judicial proceedings, description of, 560
Larceny
    Construction of words used in
        indictment, 562
    Forms for indictment, 569–70
Means of crime, 560
Money, description of, 560

Name of accused person, 559
Negative excuses, 561
Oath, 561
Ownership, description of, 560
Perjury, 368, 562, 570
Pleadings and motions before trial, 563
Prejudice, 561
Public place, description of, 560
Rape
    Construction of words used in
        indictment, 562
    Forms for indictment, 570–71
Robbery, 562, 570
Sentence, 562–63
Service of copy on prisoner, 565
Stalking, jurisdiction, 564
Stolen property, prosecutions involving,
        562, 571
Subornation of perjury, 562
Superior Court rules, 654
Time and place of commission of crime,
        559–60
Transmission of indictment, 591
Unnatural and lascivious acts, 562
Value or price, description of, 560
Variance, 561
    Venue of specific crimes, 563–64
Waiver of, 260, 600–01, 654
Words used in, construction of, 561–62
Written instrument, description of, 560

INDIGENT PERSONS
Affidavit, 256
Child in need of services, 133–34
Counsel for, 642
Court costs of, 256–58
Definition, 255–56, 599
Driver alcohol and controlled substance
        education program, 71–73
Proof of indigency, 549
Sex offenders, 16

INSANITY
See also MENTAL HEALTH
Evidence, 825–26
Jury trial, 632

INSIGNIA OF SOCIETIES
Labor union, 338
Unlawful use, 337–38
Veterans organizations, unlawful use, 337–
        38

INSURANCE
Forms for indictment; burning to defraud,
        569
Motor vehicles
    Fraudulent claims, 347
    Liability insurance, operating without,
        82–83
Policies
    Fraudulent claims, penalty for, 346–47
    Motor vehicle, fraudulent claims, 347

**INTELLECTUALLY DISABLED
PERSONS**
Assault and battery of, 279–80, 760
Witnesses, 233–34

INTERPRETERS
Criminal procedure rules concerning, 647

INTERSTATE RENDITION, 515–19
Agent's expenses, payment of, 519
Arrest and delivery of accused, 515
Arrest without warrant, 517

INTERSTATE RENDITION *(cont'd)*
Assistance, authority to command, 516
Bail, 517–18
    Forfeiture, 518
Confinement of accused, 516–17
Conveyance to proper county, 518
Definitions, 515
Discharge, 517–18
Forfeiture of bail, 518
Governor's warrant of arrest, 517
Habeas corpus, 517
Inquiry into guilt or innocence, 518
Investigation of demand, 516
Payment of agent's expenses, 519
Pending prosecution in Commonwealth, 518
Recall of warrant, 518
Requisition
    Application, 518–19
    Warrant of governor on, 517
Rights of arrested person, 516
Service of process, 519
Surrendering accused, 515–16
Waiver by Commonwealth, 519
Waiver of warrant procedure, 518
Warrant
    Apprehend on oath or affidavit, 517
    Convey to proper county, 518
    Governor's warrant of arrest, 517
    Recall of, 518
    Waiver of procedure, 518
Written demand, 516

INTIMIDATION
Assault with intent to, 304
Elements of, 760
Penalty for, 760–61
Witnesses or jurors, 370–71, 760–61

INTOXICATION, 617
See also ALCOHOLIC BEVERAGES;
    DRIVING UNDER THE INFLUENCE
Manslaughter, 275
Murder, defense to, 271
Rape, 295

IRRIGATION EQUIPMENT
Malicious injury, 356

J

JOINT VENTURES
Evidence, 827–28
Statements of joint venturers, 853

JUDGES
Disability of
    Appellate procedure rule concerning,
        672
    Criminal procedure rules concerning,
        646
Intimidation of, 370–71
Witness questioning, 828

JUDGMENT AND EXECUTION, 584–95
Arrest, persons on probation, 586
Commission of crime while released on
    personal recognizance, 588
Complaint or indictment, transmission of, 591
Conditional sentence, 588
Convict, service of new warrant of
    commitment, 591
Corporations, default by, 591
    Warrant of distress to compel payment,
        591–92
Credit for time in jail awaiting trial, 590–91
Death sentence

Circumstances authorizing, 594–95
Confinement of prisoners under, 592
Execution of
    Stay of, 593
    Time for, 592
Infliction of, 592
Jury findings necessary for, 595
Mistrial, 593–94
Postmortem examination, 593
Presentence hearing where possibility
    of, 593–94
Respite
    Pardon consideration investigation,
        593
    Prisoner becomes insane or
        pregnant, 593
Review of, 595
Stay of execution, 593
Warrant of conviction and sentence of
    death, 592
Warrant return, 593
Witnesses to, 593
District attorney motion for sentence, 586
DYS suspended sentences, 586
Execution
    Immediate, 590
    Stay of, 586–87
Females
    Hard labor, 589
    Imprisonment of, 589
    Pregnant, sentencing of, 593
    Sentencing, 589
Forensic and scientific analysis,
    postconviction, effect on, 583
"From and after" sentences, 588
Habitual criminals, punishment of, 589–90
Husband, assault on wife by, 588
Imposition of sentence, 586–87
Imprisonment and fine, 588
Indeterminate sentence of state prison, 589
Insane persons, sentencing of, 593
Jail or correctional institution, sentence to,
    587
Jail or house of correction, sentence to, 589
Judgment
    Amendment of, 578
    Motions in arrest of, 580
Magistrate, return of precept to, 591
Males, limitation of sentences to jails or
    houses of correction, 589
Multiple sentences, 588
Nonpayment of fine, sentence for, 588
Office holder, vacation of on sentencing,
    590
Pardon, 593
Public officers, effect of conviction on office
    held, 590
Recognizance
    Breach of condition, 589
    Good behavior or keeping the peace,
        588–89
    Husband convicted of assault on wife, 588
Sentence
    Execution of (certified transcript), 591
    Further sentence of convict in state
        prison, 590
    Immediate execution of, 590
    Imposition of, 586–87
    Limitation of sentences, 589
    No punishment provided by statute, 587
    Stay of, 854
    Weekend, 587–88

State farm, sentences to, 591
Statutory name of crime, 591
Stay of sentence, 854
Suspended sentences, 585–86
Two or more sentences, commitments
    upon, 588
Victim, notice to of sentencing
    proceedings, 587
Warrant of commitment
    Execution of by sheriff or constable, 591
    Statutory name of crime set out in, 591
Warrant of conviction and sentence of
    death, 592
Warrant of distress, 591–92
Weekend sentences, 587–88

JUDICIAL NOTICE
Foreign law, 234
Gaming or betting, 430

JUDICIAL OFFICERS
Stenographers, employment of by
    defendant, 224

JURIES
See also GRAND JURY
Additional jurors impaneled, 242
Affirmation of, 572
Alternate jurors, 242
Challenge of array, 242
Colloquy, 636
Criminal complaint for delinquent juror, 240
Death sentence imposed by, findings
    necessary, 595
Deferment of advancement of juror, 240
Delinquency notice for failure to appear for
    jury service, 240
Delinquent children, trial of, 143
Discharge from employment prohibited, 372
Dismissal or discharge of juror, 240
Disqualification from juror service, 239–40
District Courts, 221–23
Duty of, 829
Employer
    Harassment of employee, 241
    Liability for failure to pay salary of juror,
        241
Enforcement of provisions, 240
Examination of jurors, 241
Excused from juror service, 240
Failure to agree, 242
Failure to appear for jury service, 240
Foreperson, 242
Fraud in processing or selection, 242
Gifts given to, 372
Gratuities, 243
Instructions
    Conspiracy, 479
    Criminal procedure rules, 634
    Joint ventures, evidence, 827–28
    Manslaughter, 274
    Murder, 268
    Number of jurors to agree, 242
    Rape, 294
    Unanimity instruction, 856–57
    Vehicular homicide, 75
Intimidation, 370–71, 760–61
Interests of jurors, not disqualifying, 241
Juror service, 238
Jury Commissioner, Office of, 238–43
Jury pool, challenge of, 242
Mistrial or verdict to be set aside, 242–43
Notes by, 652
Nullification of, 829

12

JURIES *(cont'd)*
Number of jurors to agree, 242
Oath of, 572
Overhearing deliberations of by using
    devices, 470
Peremptory challenges of, 632, 652
Picketing juror, 370
Polling, 636
Postverdict communication, 636
Preemptory challenges, 241
Questionnaires, jurors', 239
    Use during voir dire, 239
    Willful misrepresentations, 240
Questions, 239, 632, 828–29
Right to, 1
Sleeping juror, 852
Superior Court rules concerning, 652
Talesmen, 239
Trial, right to, 1, 630
Venire, 829
View by, 242
Voir dire procedures, 241
Waiver of, 261, 630, 829

JURISDICTION
See also as subhead to other topics
Abuse, criminal violations, 564
Burglary, 317
Children, proceedings against, 152
Children's need for services, 132–33
Dangerous persons, proceedings to
    commit, 155
District Courts, 220–24
Forensic and scientific analysis,
    postconviction, 582
Harassment prevention orders, 252
Perjury, statements containing declaration
    regarding, 369
Stalking, 564
Stolen property, 336
Superior Court, 220

JUSTICE, CRIMES AGAINST, 367–77
Alcohol, delivery of
    Patients, to, 374
    Prisoners, to, 374
Appointment or promotion, compulsion or
    coercion, 370
Apprehension of offender, disregard of
    order to, 374
Arrest, resisting, 375–76
Assisting peace officer, neglect or refusal
    to, 374
Badge of town officer, making or
    possessing, 377
Coercion to refuse advancement, 370
Correctional institutions
    Delivering or receiving items from
        prisoners, 375
    Disturbing, 375
Corruption of jurors, masters, etc., 370
Court personnel and proceedings
    Corruption of, 370
    Disruption of, 371
    Gifts given to, 372
    Picketing of, 370
Crime, obligation to report, 377
Disguises used to obstruct law
    enforcement, 376
Disruption of court proceedings, 371
Emergency signal systems, tampering
    with, 375
Escape

Aiding escape, 373
Attempt or failure to return, 373
City or town jail, from, 373
Consenting to, 373
Correctional institution, aiding escape
    from, 373
Elements of, 758
Jailer allowing, 373
Negligently suffering, 373
Penalty for, 758
Person having custody, aiding escape
    from, 373
Process server's refusal or delay
    resulting in, 374
Suffering convict to be at large, etc., 374
False reports and testimony
    Emergency response services
        providers, to, 410
    Governmental bodies, to, 369
    Police officers, to, 409
    Process servers, 370
    Public officers and employees, by, 369–
        70
Felonies, compounding or concealing, 377
Firefighting or police boxes, interference
    with, 375
Impersonation of court officer, 376
Inmate, sexual relations with, 374
Intimidation of witness or juror, 370–71,
    760–61
Juror
    Corrupting or attempt to corrupt, 370
    Discharge from employment prohibited,
        372
    Gifts given to, 372
    Intimidation of, 370–71, 760–61
    Picketing, 370
Justice of the peace
    Falsely assuming to be, 376
    Order to aid in apprehension of
        offender, refusal to obey, 374
Lead paint inspectors, unlicensed, 376
Perjury, 368
    Complaint form for, 570
    Elements of, 764
    Evidence, 851
    False statements, 369
    Indictment, 562
    Materiality, 368
    Motor vehicle theft, alleging, 377
    Penalty for, 764
    Presumption of, 369
        Documents detained for prosecution
            of, 369
        Testimony creating, 369
    Procuring another to commit, attempt, 369
    State Ethics Commission, before, 396
    Statements containing declaration
        regarding
        Evidence, 369
        Indictment, sufficiency of, 369
        Jurisdiction, 369
        Penalties of perjury, 369
    Subornation of, 369, 769
Picketing judge, juror, etc., 370
Process servers
    False statements by, 370
    Refusal or delay, resulting in escape, 374
Public officers, false reports by, 369–70
Records, tampering with, 372
Reporting crimes to law enforcement, 377
Sexual relations with inmate, 374

Social Security number, using or giving
    false, 376–77
Tampering with records of official
    proceedings, 372
Testimonial dinners, solicitations by public
    employees, 370
Town seal, unauthorized use of, 377
Warrant, delay in service of, 374
Witness discharged from employment, 372

JUSTICE, MISCARRIAGE OF, 839

JUVENILE COURT
Drug rehabilitation referrals by, 126–27
Probation officers, Boston Juvenile Court,
    545

K

KEYS
Master, offenses involving, 357

KICKBOXING, 274

KIDNAPPING, 301–02
Drugging for purposes of, 302
Elements of, 761
Minor, by relative, 302, 761
Minor victim, 302
Penalty for, 761
Tender years doctrine, 302, 855
Venue, 303

L

LAND
Attached, conveyance without notice, 340
Encumbered, conveyance without notice,
    340

LARCENY, 322–26
Bank bill paper, 332
Bicycles, second conviction, 331
Continuing scheme, 325–26
Counterfeiting retail sales or return receipt,
    327
Defenses, 324, 325
Definition, 323
Elements of, 761
Embezzlement, 324–25
False pretenses, by, 324, 327
    Contracts, banking, credit, 327
False statement of fact, 324
Indictment, 562, 569–70
Inducement to part with property, 328
Intent, 323
Joint enterprise, 325
Leased or rented property, 340
Of another, 323–24
Organized retail crime, 327
Penalty for, 761
Permanently deprive, intent to, 324
Person, from, 320, 761
    Attempted, 320
    Elements of, 761
    Joint enterprise, 320
    Penalty for, 761
    Pickpocketing, 320
Personal property, 323
Restitution, 325
Stealing by confining or fear, 292
Taking, 323
Theft detection shielding device,
    distribution or possession of, 326–27
Threshold value of $250, 323
Venue, 563

12

LARCENY *(cont'd)*
Voluntary association, embezzlement from, 334
Wrongful detention of money by carriers, 331

LAW OF THE ROAD
See TRAFFIC, LAW OF THE ROAD

LEAD PAINT
Inspectors, unlicensed, 376

LEWD AND LASCIVIOUS BEHAVIOR, 440–41

LIBRARIES
Definitions, 343
Disturbance of, 450–51
Mutilation of property of, 343
Theft, etc., 343

LIFETIME PAROLE, 307, 481

LIMITATION OF PROSECUTIONS
Corporations, new indictments, 565
General provisions, 564–65
Tolling, 565

LITTERING
Motor vehicle license suspension for, 52
Public way, 303

LOANS
Assault and battery as means to collect, 278
Firearms or weapons, secured by, 200

LOTTERIES
See also PUBLIC POLICY, CRIMES AGAINST
Advertising sale of tickets, 426
Aiding in setting up, 426–27
Arrest without warrant, 426
Complaints and indictments relative to, 430
Delivery to or from person engaged in, 429
Disposal of property by chance, 424
Elements of, 761
False tickets, making, 426
Forfeiture of money, prizes, or shares of lotteries, 426
Forms for indictment, 570
Judicial notice concerning, 430
Penalties for, 761
Permitting in buildings, 426
Place of, 422
Policy lottery or shop, 428
Raffles and bazaars, 424–25
Selling, exchanging, or possessing tickets, 427
Subsequent offenses, 426
Tickets for, 426
Warrant to enter place of, 429

M

MACE
Assault and battery, 285

MANSLAUGHTER, 274–75
Accident, 275
Battery, 275
DNA database, 275
Elements of, 762–62
Forms for indictment, 570
Intoxication, 275
Involuntary, 274
Model jury instructions, 274
Motor vehicle, manslaughter while operating, 275–76
Omission/failure to act, 274
Penalty for, 762

Self-defense, 275
Verdict, 275
Wanton or reckless conduct, 275

MASSACHUSETTS CIVIL RIGHTS ACT, 17

MAYHEM, 283–84, 762

MEDICAL EXAMINATIONS
Mental health commitment or retention hearings, 154

MEDICAL RECORDS, 235–37

MELENDEZ-DIAZ, 830–34

MENTAL HEALTH, 153–62
Alcoholics, commitment of, 160–61
Antipsychotic medication as treatment, 155–56
Bridgewater State Hospital, retention of persons at, 154
Commitment or retention hearings, 154–55
  Counsel, right to, 154
Competence to stand trial, 156–57
Court records of examination or commitment, 161–62
Dangerous persons, 154–55
  Commitment and retention of, 154
  Potential victims, duty to warn, 162
  Proceedings to commit, 154–55
Definitions, 153–54
Delinquents, 156–57
Department of Criminal Justice Information Services, report of commitment order to, 162
Discharge from commitment, application for, 156
Evidence of insanity, 825–26
Expenses of apprehension, etc. of mentally ill person, 159–60
Hearings, 154–57, 158–59
Incompetent to stand trial/not guilty by reason of insanity
  Hospitalization because of, 157–58
  Review of determination, 158
Likelihood of serious harm, 153
Medical examination, 154
Mental health professionals, 154
  Duty to warn potential victim, 162
Mental illness defined, 158
Murder and, 271
Prisoners, mentally ill, hospitalization of, 159
Privacy of court records of examination or commitment, 161–62
Psychiatric nurse, 153
Psychiatrist, 153
Psychologist, 153
Reasonable precautions, 154
Retention of persons, 154
Review of matters of law, 156
Right to counsel, 154
Veterans Administration, transfer or commitment to, 160
Warning potential victims, duty to, 162
Witnesses or parties, determination of mental condition, 159

MILITARY
See ARMED FORCES

MILK CONTAINERS
Carrying away without permission, 359
Defacement of, 355

MILLS
Injury by raising of water, 356

MINORS
See CHILDREN; as subhead to other topics

MIRANDA WARNINGS, 834–39
Driving under the influence, 67

MISCARRIAGE
Advertising services concerning, 441
Procuring, 441

MISCARRIAGE OF JUSTICE, 839

MISPRISION OF TREASON, 264

MONEY LAUNDERING, 366–67
Definitions, 366
Financial institutions, reports by, 367
Forfeiture, 367
Penalties, 366–67

MONUMENTS AND MARKERS
Malicious destruction of, 342

MORALITY, CRIMES AGAINST
See DECENCY, MORALITY, GOOD ORDER, AND CHASTITY, CRIMES AGAINST

MORTGAGES
False statements, 328

MOTIONS, PRETRIAL, 615–19

MOTIONS IN LIMINE, 840

MOTOR VEHICLES, 24–83
See also DRIVING UNDER THE INFLUENCE; TRAFFIC, LAW OF THE ROAD
Abandonment of, 50–51
Accidents
  License and registration, presentation of, 37–38
  Reports, 82
Animals, transport of, 52
Armed forces, 37
Arrest without warrant, 47
Bicycles, motorized, 31, 33
Blind pedestrians, 40–41
Brakes, 34–36
Campus police, citations issued by, 95
Carjacking, 292, 757
Children
  Endangerment of child, 80
  Passenger restraints, 36
Citable offenses, table of, 773–802
Citations, issuance of, 95–97
Civil liability for unauthorized use of vehicle, 74
Concealment of vehicle identity, 53–55
Definitions, 28–33
Drag racing, 42
Driver alcohol or controlled substance education program, 71–73
Electronic messages, composing, sending, or reading during operation, 39–40
Emergency vehicles, 25–26
False documents for, 71
Farmer, definition of, 29
Felony, use of in commission of, 71
Firearms, transport of, 200
Fraudulent insurance claims, 347
Habitual traffic offender, 51–52
Homicide by, 74–75
Horns, 34–36
Ignition interlock device, 38, 70–71, 79–80
Illegal operation of, 41
Improperly equipped vehicles, operation of, 36–37

12

MOTOR VEHICLES (cont'd)
Indigents, driver alcohol and controlled
        substance education program, 71–73
Insurance
        Claims, fraudulent, 347
        Liability insurance, operating without,
            82–83
Junk yard owners, 75
Lane changes, 26
Liability insurance, operating without, 82–83
License
        Accident, presentation after, 37–38
        Changes, reporting, 82
        False, 71
        Lifetime revocation, 79
        Operation without, 37, 38
        Reinstatement, 51–52
        Suspension or revocation of, 37, 47–50,
            51–53, 174
License plates, display of, 33–34
Lights, 34–36
Littering, 52
Mobile telephone, use of, 38
Motorcycles
        Definition, 30–31
        Single-lane driving and passing, 25
Motorized bicycles, 31, 33
Mufflers, 34–36
Nonresidents, 37
Number plates, display of, 33–34
Odometer tampering, 357
Offensive or illegal operation, 41
Open container violations, 75–76, 174
Operation without license, 37, 38
        After suspension or revocation, 53–54
Parking regulations, 43–45
        Boston, 45–47
        Cambridge, 45–47
        Failure to appear, 43–45
        Fines, 47
        Safety precautions for, 38–39
        Tags, tampering or destruction of, 47
Parts of abandoned vehicle, removal of, 51
Pedestrians, blind, 40–41
Penalties, 38, 39–40, 42–43, 50–51
        Parking regulations, 47
        Title certificates, falsification of, 98
Permit
        Changes, reporting, 82
        Stealing or forging, 71
Police officers, refusing to submit to, 82
Probation, 71–74
Procedure for offenses, 92–98
        Access to records of offenders, 97–98
        Arrest without warrant, 97–98
        Audit sheets, 98
        Campus police, 95
        Citation books, 93–94, 98
        Citations
            Disposal of, 98
            Falsification, 98
            Issuance, 95–97
            Mutual agreements with other states,
                98
            Not writ, 98
            Printing and distribution of books, 98
        Civil motor vehicle infractions, 773–802
            Schedule of assessments, 773–802
        Criminal complaint, 97–98
        Definitions, 92–93
        Electronic communication between
            courts and registry, 98

Falsification of citation, 98
Hearing, 95–97
Issuance of citation and procedure
        following, 95–97
Mutual agreements with other states, 98
Police department requirements, 93–95
Printing and distribution of citation
        books, 98
Reciprocal agreements with other
        states, 98
Public places, removal from, 75
Radar devices, 42
Refusal to submit to police officer, 82
Registration
        Accident, presentation after, 37–38
        Cancellation for drunk driving offenders,
            81–82
        Carrying, 37–38
        Name and address changes, reporting,
            82
        Suspension or revocation, 47–50
Reinstatement of license, 51–52
Removal of abandoned vehicle's parts, 51
Safety standards
        Operation of vehicle, 38–39
        Requirements for vehicle, 34–36
        Seatbelt use, 39
        Travelers, precautions for, 40
Sale disclosures, 342
Salvage yards, 75
School buses, 40
Search and seizure, 75
Search warrants, 483–84, 485
Seatbelts, 39
Signaling, uniform use of for stopping
        and turning, 41
Speed limits, 41–42
Stickers and emblems, 34–36, 71
Stopping, 41
Suspension or revocation
        License, 37, 47–50, 51–53
        Operation of motor vehicle after, 53–55
        Registration, 47–50
Text messaging while driving, 39–40
Title, certificates of, 98–99
Transportation network company
        certificate, 207
Travelers, precautions for safety of, 40
Trespass with, 349, 352
Turning signals, 41
Unauthorized use of, liability to owner, 74
Unlicensed operator, 37, 38
Unregistered vehicles, operation of, 36–37
Use without authority, 771

MOTORBOATS AND OTHER VESSELS,
83–92
Alcohol, operating under influence of, 84–91
Altering, forging, or counterfeiting
        certificates, 84
Arrest for offenses without warrant, 92
Certificates of number, violations
        concerning, 84
Controlled substances, 84–92
Counterfeiting certificates, 84
Definitions, 83–84
Destruction or injury to defraud, 346
Drunk or drugged operation of, 84–91
Forging certificates, 84
Identification numbers, violations
        concerning, 84
Jet ski operation, 92

Oil of vitriol or other substance, throwing
        into, 345
Operating under the influence, 84–91
        Death, causing, 91–92
        Serious bodily injury, causing, 91
Penalties for violation of laws concerning,
        84, 92
Personal flotation devices, 84
Removal, defacing, etc. of identification
        numbers, 84
Surf jet operation, 92
Unlawful assembly, injury by, 397
Wetbike operation, 92

MUGSHOTS, 840

MUNICIPAL EMPLOYEES
See PUBLIC OFFICIALS AND EMPLOYEES

MURDER, 268–72
See also HOMICIDE
Armed robbery, 270
Assault with intent to, 284, 754
Atrocity/cruelty, 269
Attempt to, 287
Case-by-case, 270
Crime committed in Commonwealth, death
        outside, 564
Dangerous weapon, 269, 270
Deliberate premeditation, 269
DNA, 273
Elements of, 762
Expert testimony, 271
Felony murder, 269, 270
Frame of mind, 269
Human life, 270
Indictment, 570
Intervening act, 272
Intoxication, 270–71
Joint enterprise, 270, 272
Jury instructions, 268
Juvenile defendants, 272, 273
Malice, three prongs of, 268–69
Mental illness, 271
Mitigating circumstances, 272
Mode of commission, 272
Model jury instructions, 268
Motive, 272
Penalty for, 762
Predicate offenses, 269–70
Premeditation, 269
Probable cause hearing, 523–24
Provocation, 271
Punishment for, 272–73
Rape, 270
Self-defense, 271–72
Solicitation to commit, 272
Unarmed robbery, 270
Venue, 564
Viable fetus, 272

N

NAMES
Benevolent organizations, false use of, 338
Fraternal, use in publication, 338

NATIONAL ANTHEM
Manner of playing, 265

NATURAL SCENERY
Defacement of, 352–53

NECESSITY
Defense of, 401–02

12

NEEDLES
See SYRINGES AND NEEDLES

NEGLIGENCE
Common carriers, gross, 303

NEMANSKET CORRECTIONAL CENTER
Sexually dangerous persons, rehabilitation of, 165

NIGHTWALKING, 451
Child in violation of, 136
Indictment forms, 569
Third conviction, 453
Trafficking victim, affirmative defense, 311

NONRESIDENTS AND ALIENS
Abuse prevention orders, 218–19
Firearms and ammunition
   Carrying conditions, 203
   Furnishing to, 190
   Ownership or possession of, 203
   Temporary licenses for, 201–03
Motor vehicle licenses, 37

NONSUPPORT
See DESERTION, NONSUPPORT AND ILLEGITIMACY

NOTICE
Motor vehicle license suspension or revocation, 47–50

NUCLEAR WEAPONS, 345

O

OCCUPATIONS
See PROFESSIONS AND OCCUPA-TIONS, REGISTRATION OF

OPEN AND GROSS LEWDNESS, 440–41, 451–52, 570, 762–63

OPENING STATEMENTS, 634, 652, 840–41

ORCHARDS
See WOODS, TIMBER, ORCHARDS

ORGAN TRAFFICKING, 310, 769–70

P

PARDON
Stay of execution for investigation concerning, 593

PARENTS AND GUARDIANS
Delinquent children, of, summoning, 141–43
Destitute
   Neglect or refusal to support, 475–76
   Venue, 476
Proceedings against children, summons, 150
Witnesses, 225

PARK OR PLAYGROUND EQUIPMENT
Injury to, 343

PAROLE, LIFETIME, 10, 307, 481

PENALTIES
See also ELEMENTS AND PENALTIES OF SELECTED CRIMES; as subhead to other topics
Bank officers and employees, misconduct, 333
Controlled substances, 112–14
   Registration numbers, unlawful use of, 116
   Schools, violations in or near, 113–14
Copyrighted material, unauthorized reproduction, 358–59

Credit card misuse, 329–30
District Courts, imposition of, 221
DNA database violations, 22
Enterprise crime, 435
Firearms and weapons, license violations, 176–77
Foreign flag, misuse of, 265
Motor vehicles, 42–43, 50–51
   Parking regulations, 47
   Title certificates, falsification of, 98–99
Motorboats and other vessels, 84, 92
   Serious bodily injury, causing, 91
Murder, 272–73
Sex Offender Registry
   Failure to register or verify, 9–10
   Misuse of information, 16
Traffic violations, 25, 27
Trafficking of persons, 308–09
Transitional assistance
   Embezzlement, theft, or fraud to obtain department property, 18
   Father leaving family to obtain, 17
   Food stamps trafficking, 18–19
Transitional Assistance Department
   Electronic benefit transfer transactions, 17–18
Treason, 264
Uniforms, government, unlawful use, 265–66

PERFORMANCES
Live, unauthorized reproduction of, 358

PERJURY, 368
Complaint form for, 570
Elements of, 764
False statements, 369
Indictment, 369, 562
Materiality, 368
Motor vehicle theft, alleging, 377
Penalty for, 764
Presumption of, 369
   Documents detained for prosecution of, 369
   Testimony creating, 369
Procuring another to commit, attempt, 369
State Ethics Commission, before, 396
Statements containing declaration regarding
   Evidence, 369
   Indictment, sufficiency of, 369
   Jurisdiction, 369
   Penalties of perjury, 369
Subornation of, 369, 769

PERSON, CRIMES AGAINST, 267–311
Armed assault, 288–89
   Dwelling house, 753
Armed robbery, 287–88
   Joint enterprise, 288
   Masks, 288
   Self-defense, 288
Assault and battery, 276–82, 754, 755
   Actual physical injury requirement, 276
   Ambulance operator, 280
   Armed assault, 288–89
   Assault defined, 276
   Battery defined, 276
   Child
      Discipline, 277
      Liability of person having custody, 280–81
   Consent not a defense, 277
   Dangerous weapon, 284–86, 753, 755
      Consent, 285

Deceptive weapon, possession of, 311
Discharge of firearm, 286–87
Family member, attempted or threatened use against, 283
Firearm, 286–87
Household member, attempted or threatened use against, 283
Mayhem, 283
Self-defense, 285
Defenses, 277
Disabled person, 281–82, 755
Discharge of firearm, 286–87
DNA database, 278, 280, 284, 287, 288, 289
Dwelling house, in, 289
Elderly or disabled person, 281–82, 755
Emergency assistance personnel, 280, 755
Family or household member, on, 283, 755
Felony
   Assault with intent to commit, 303, 754
   Commission of for hire, 280
Firefighter, injury to, 279
Forms for indictment, 568
Gang membership as intent, 307
Hypodermic syringes and needles, by means of, 286
Indecent
   Child of 14 or older, 280, 760
   Child under 14, 277–79, 759–50
   Intellectually disabled person, 279–80, 760
Intellectually disabled person, 279–80, 760
Intimidation as intent, 304
Lesser included offenses, 276–77, 285
Loan collection, for purposes of, 279
Mace, 285
Murder or maiming as intent, 284, 754
Natural gas, 285
Police officers, on, 279
Psychological harm, 276
Public servants, on, 279, 754–55
Race, intimidation due to, 304
Rape as intent, 299–300, 754
Robbery as intent, 292, 754
Self-defense, 277, 285
Serious bodily injury, 277
Sexually dangerous person commitment, 278, 280
Sleeping victim, 276
Spitting, 277
Strangulation, 286
Suffocation, 286
Threatened battery, 276
Wanton/reckless conduct, 276
Words, 276
Boxing matches, 273–74
Burning, reckless or willful, resulting in injury, 279
Carjacking, 292, 757
Children, reckless endangerment of, 282
Common carrier, gross negligence, 303
Constitutional rights violations, 304
Deceptive weapon, possession of, 311
Duel
   Accessory, 273
   Conviction or acquittal in foreign state, 273
   Wound without and death within state, 273

12

PERSON, CRIMES AGAINST *(cont'd)*
Estate, taking from, 307
Extortion, attempted, 301, 755–56
Glass, throwing in street or beach, 303
Harassment, criminal, 306–07
Hired felony, commission of, 280
Home invasion, 290–91
Kickboxing, 274
Kidnapping, 301–02
    Drugging for purposes of, 302
    Elements of, 761
    Minor, by relative, 302, 761
    Minor victim, 302
    Penalty for, 761
    Tender years doctrine, 302, 855
    Venue, 303
Lifetime parole, 307
Littering, public way, 303
Manslaughter, 274–75
    Accident, 275
    Battery, 275
    DNA database, 275
    Elements of, 762
    Forms for indictment, 570
    Intoxication, 275
    Involuntary, 274
    Model jury instructions, 274
    Motor vehicle, manslaughter while
        operating, 275–76
    Omission/failure to act, 274
    Penalty for, 762
    Self-defense, 275
    Verdict, 275
    Wanton or reckless conduct, 275
Mayhem, 283–84, 762
Murder, 268–72
    Armed robbery, 270
    Assault with intent to, 284, 754
    Atrocity/cruelty, 269
    Attempt to, 287
    Case-by-case, 270
    Dangerous weapon, 269, 270
    Deliberate premeditation, 269
    DNA, 273
    Elements of, 762
    Expert testimony, 271
    Felony murder, 269, 270
    Frame of mind, 269
    Human life, 270
    Indictment, 570
    Intervening act, 272
    Intoxication, 271
    Joint enterprise, 270, 272
    Juvenile defendants, 272, 273
    Malice, three prongs of, 268–69
    Mental illness, 271
    Mode of commission, 272
    Motive, 272
    Penalty for, 762
    Predicate offenses, 269–70
    Premeditation, 269
    Provocation, 271
    Punishment for, 272–73
    Rape, 270
    Self-defense, 271–72
    Solicitation to commit, 272
    Unarmed robbery, 270
    Viable fetus, 272
Parole, lifetime, 307
Physical exercise training programs, bodily
    injury, 304
Poison, 303

Prize fighting
    Aiding or promoting, 273
    Boxing matches, 273
    Outside state, appointment made
        within, 273
Public way, throwing or dropping objects
    on, 303
Race, assault or battery due to, 304
Radio or boom box use in public, 305
Rape
    See RAPE
Sentencing for violations, 304
Sex offenders
    GPS devices, to be worn by, 9, 307–08
    Ice cream truck vending prohibited, 308
Sporting events, throwing objects during,
    303–04
Stalking, 305–06
Stealing by confining or fear, 292
Strangulation, 286
Suffocation, 286
Tattooing, 303
Trafficking of persons, 308–09
    Children under 18, 308–09
    Definitions, 308
    Fines, transmittal to state treasurer, 310
    Forced servitude, 309, 770
    Monies used in violations, forfeiture to
        Commonwealth, 310
    Nightwalking or streetwalking,
        affirmative defense, 311
    Organ trafficking, 310
    Property subject to forfeiture, 310–11
    Restitution, 310
    Sexual servitude, for, 308–09, 770
    Subsequent violations, 309
Unarmed robbery, 291–92
Venue, 300

PERSONALTY
Malicious or wanton injury, 353–55
Mortgaged, concealment of, 340
Sale by mortgagor without consent, 340

PESTS
Bringing into state, 348

PETS
See also ANIMALS
Custody of, 219

PHOTOGRAPHS
Accused, rights of, regarding, 259
Arrest and, 259
Controlled substance felonies, taking of
    person charged with, 118
Evidentiary use of, 842–43
Nude persons, 471–72

PHYSICAL EXERCISE PROGRAMS
Serious bodily injury caused to
    participants, 304

PICKPOCKETING, 320

**PLEADINGS AND MOTIONS BEFORE
TRIAL**
Compensation of counsel of prisoner, 563
Custody and delivery of prisoner, 563
Defenses or objections, 563
District attorneys, transferred cases and, 563
Expenses of counsel of prisoner, 563

PLEAS
Criminal court rules, 608–15
Guilty, 630
Not guilty, 654

POISON, 303
Arsenic
    Analysis of samples, 413
    Fabric containing, 413
    Toys or food containing, 413
Rodent poison in inappropriate location, 412

POLICE
See also as subhead to other topics;
    STATE POLICE
Abuse prevention powers, 215–17
Assault and battery on, 279
Assisting, neglect or refusal to, 374
False reports to, 409
Harassment prevention order, emergency
    response, 253–54
Sex Offender Registry, liability of, 16

POLLUTION
See also PUBLIC HEALTH
Littering, 303
Refuse, burning near shoreline, 416
Rubbish disposal, 413–15
Solid waste, unlawful disposal of, 359

PONDS
Ice, injury to, 346

PRECIOUS METALS
Dealer records, 357–58
Gold, false marking of, 339–40
Sterling and coin silver, false marking of, 339

PRETRIAL DIVERSION, 553–56
Advisory board, 555
Commissioner's duties regarding, 555
Continuance, fourteen days, 556
Definitions, 553
Director, report by, 554
Final report, 555
Inapplicability of chapter, sex offenses,
    etc., 554
Ineligible offenses, 554
Jurisdiction, 553–54
Progress reports, 555
Screening of defendants for, 554
Speedy trial, 554
Veteran status of defendant, 556

PRETRIAL PROCEEDINGS
See INDICTMENT AND PRETRIAL
    PROCEEDINGS
Grand jury
    See GRAND JURY
Venire facias writs for grand jurors,
    issuance of
    See VENIRE FACIAS WRITS
Venue
    See VENUE

PREVENTION OF CRIME, 479–81
Accused paying expenses, 480
Affray in presence of justice, 480
Discharge of accused
    Complainant pays expenses, 480
    Providing security, 480
Justices to keep public peace, 479
Lifetime parole hearings, 481
Proceedings on appeal, 480
    Failure to prosecute, 480
Recognizance to keep peace, 480
    Appeal, 480
    Commitment if no recognizance, 480
    Witnesses, 480
Remission of portion of forfeited penalty, 481
Surety, 481

PREVENTION OF CRIME *(cont'd)*
Threats, 479–80
Warrant to apprehend accused, 480

PRISONERS
Alcohol, delivery to, 374
Controlled substance, delivery to, 374
Counsel for, 563, 574
Death sentence, confinement of those
    under, 592
Delivering or receiving items from, 375
Discharge, 524
Escape, 597
Insane, 593
List of jurors, 565
Mentally ill, hospitalization of, 159
Murder indictment, 565
Pregnant, 593
Sexual relations with, 374
Transporting, 526

PRIVILEGE
Clergy communications, 225
Domestic violence victim counselor, 229
Psychotherapist-patient, 226–27
Self-incrimination, 227
Sexual assault counselor, 228–29

PRIZE FIGHTING
Aiding or promoting, 273
Boxing matches, 273
Outside state, appointment made within, 273

PROBATION
Advisory board, 547–48
Arrest of persons on probation, 586
Commissioner of
    Annual report of, 553
    Appointment, 546–47
    Notices to, concerning officers, 553
    Powers and duties of, 548–49
Conditions, 543–44, 720–31
    Length of probationary sentence, 729
    Mandatory conditions, 720–22
    Modifying probation conditions, 729–31
    Nonstatutory conditions of probation,
        722–24
    Right to counsel and, 729
Definitions, 710
Delinquent child, violation of, 147
Detailed reports of probation work, 550
District Court, 220–21
Drug dependent persons, 126
Fees for, 543–44
Forms, uniform, used in, 553
Hearings
    Guidelines, 710–12
    Massachusetts practice, 713–20
        Revocation, 731–51
        Youthful offender, 718–19
Indigency, proof of, 549
Introduction to, 713
Officers, 540–53
    Appointment and removal of, 540–41
    Boston Juvenile Court, 545
    Clerical assistance, 544
    Compensation of, 549
    Contempt power, 542
    Counselors to juvenile offenders, as, 545
    Delinquent payments, collection, 542
    Expenses of, 546
    Interference with Department of Youth
        Services, 546
    Persons in care of, placing, 542–43

Powers and duties of, 541, 545
Records and reports, 545
Refusal or neglect of duties by, 546
Restitution
    Injured persons, 545
    Motor vehicle theft or fraudulent
        claims, 545
Support and maintenance enforcement
    by, 541–42
Surrender hearings, 542
Temporary, 544
Unclaimed money collected by,
    disposition of, 545–46
Performance measurement system, 549–50
Reports and records concerning, 545, 550
Revocation, 731–51
    Appeal, 750
    Constitutional standards for, 731
    Disposition, 749
    Evidence, nature of, 737–46
    Hearings
        Nature of, 746–48
    Massachusetts practice, 731–37
    Sentencing, 749–50
    Written findings, necessity of, 748–49
Rules for violation proceedings, 687–707
    Charged criminal conduct, 689–93
        Conduct of hearings, 697–701
    Continuance without a finding, 706–07
    Definitions, 688–89
    Detention hearings, 694–97
    Findings and disposition, 703–06
    Guidelines, 710–12
    Hearings, conduct of, 697–701
    Hearsay evidence, 701–03
    Scope and purpose, 687–88
    Violations other than charged criminal
        conduct, 693–94
Sealing files, 550–51
    Availability of sealed information, 552–53
    Certain criminal cases, in, 552
    Expungement versus, 551
    Requests, 551–52
Statutory bases for, 713–20
Temporary support or transportation of
    probationers, 546
Transportation of probationers, 546
Uniform forms, 553

PROCEEDINGS BEFORE TRIAL
See INDICTMENT AND PRETRIAL
    PROCEEDINGS

PROCESS SERVERS
False statements by, 370
Refusal or delay in, resulting in escape, 374

**PROFESSIONS AND OCCUPATIONS,
REGISTRATION OF**, 127–29
Definitions, 127
Social workers
    Confidential communications, 127–28
    Testimonial privilege, 128–29
    Unlicensed, 128

PROOF
See also STATUTES, LAWS, AND
    GOVERNMENT DOCUMENTS,
    PROOF OF
Conviction of crime, credibility of witness,
    230–31
Criminal procedure rules, 646–47
Indigency, 549
Motor vehicle ownership, 321

Property ownership, 573
Public way, 63, 236
Victims of violent crimes, claims, 250

PROPERTY, CRIMES AGAINST, 312–60
Advertisements
    Deceptive, 341–42
    False or exaggerated statements, 342
    Merchandise, commodities, and
        service, regulation of, 341
    Show bill or advertisement, malicious
        injury to, 352
    Untrue or misleading, 341
Animals
    Domestic
        Malicious killing or injury of, 348
        Trespass on land, 348
    False pedigree, 342
    Humane society, injury to property, 355
    Pigeons, killing or frightening, 355
    Research, unauthorized removal, 345
Arson
    Attempted, 314
    Building, 314, 753
    Dwelling, 313–14, 753
        Malice, 314
    Wood and other property, 314
Attached land, conveyance without notice,
    340
Bank bill paper
    Larceny of, 332
    Retention by printer with intent to pass,
        332
Banks
    Embezzlement or fraud by employees
        of, 333
    Insolvent, receipt of deposits by, 334
    Liquidating agent or receiver,
        embezzlement by, 334
    Misconduct by employees of, 333
Biological, chemical, or nuclear weapons,
    possession, 345
Breaking and entering
    Buildings, 318
    Firearm, theft of, 406
    Railroad car, 319
    Restitution, 319
    Retailer, wholesaler or manufacturer of
        firearms, breaking and entering
        place of business, 406
    Trucks, tractors, trailers, freight
        containers, 319
    Vehicles, 318
    Vessels, 318
Bridges and canals, injury to, 346
Buildings
    Breaking and entering, 318, 756
        Daytime, 318
        Entering without breaking, 318
        Forms for indictment, 568
        Lesser included offenses, 317
        Ownership, 318
    Churches, defacement of, 342–43
    County, defacement of, 342
    Entering without breaking, nighttime, 318
    Schoolhouse, defacement or injury to,
        342–43
    State, defacement or injury to, 342
    Stealing in, 319
Burglary
    Armed assault on occupants, 316–17,
        756

12

PROPERTY, CRIMES AGAINST
Burglary *(cont'd)*
   Assault, 756
   Bike locks, 332–33
   Breaking, 316
   Dangerous weapon, 317
   DNA database, 317
   Dwelling house, 316
   Entering, 316
   Intent to commit felony, 317
   Jurisdiction, 317
   Lesser included offenses, 317
   Nighttime, 316, 317–18
   Recently stolen property, 317
   Self-defense, 317
   Tools, possession of, 332–33, 568, 765
   Unarmed, 317, 756–57
Capital facility construction projects; false
   entries, 337
Checks, fraudulent, 329
Chemical weapons, possession, 345
Collateral security, sale before debt due, 340
Common and notorious thief, 331
Computer systems, unauthorized access
   to, 351–52
Consignee or factor, fraudulent deposit or
   pledge of property, 341
Construction loan, misapplication, 331
Copper wire, records of purchases, 357
Corporate books as evidence, 337
Corporate credit, fraudulent use of, 338
Correctional institutions, injury to property,
   355
Counterfeit mark, 359–60
County building, defacement, 342
Credit cards
   Fraudulent use of, 330
   Misuse of, 329–30
      Definitions, 329
      Penalties, 329–30
   Publishing numbering or coding system,
      330
Dams or reservoirs, malicious injury, 356
Defacement
   Tagging, spraying, 353
   Walls, signs, gravestones, 353
Defraud
   Burning insured property with intent to,
      315
   Burning with intent to, 569
   Computer service, intent to defraud,
      327–28
Degrees, offenses involving issuance of, 341
Dogs, wrongful removal of collar, 332,
   459–60
Dwelling house
   Burglary, 316–17
   Daytime breaking and entering, 318
   Entry at night, 318
   Entry by false pretenses, 319
Embezzlement
   Bank employees, 333
   Bank liquidating agent or receiver, 334
   Brokers or agents, 334
   Fiduciaries, 334, 564
   Municipal officers, 333
   Property at fire, 319
   State treasury, 333
   Voluntary association, 334
Endorsement or approval, false claim of, 341
Explosives
   Hoax explosives, 344

Incendiary devices, 343–44
Malicious use of, 345
Oil of vitriol and other substances, use
   of, 345
False claims
   Endorsement or approval, 341
   Presentation of, 337
False pretenses
   Money or membership by, 338
   Obtaining goods by, 338
   Signature by, 327, 338
Fences
   Malicious injury, 348
   Removal, unauthorized, 345–46
Fire, injury by
   Negligent use, 315
   Town, negligent use in, 315
Firearms, entry on land with, 352
Firefighting equipment
   Fire alarms, false, 409
   Hotel manager duty to notify, 316
   Injury before fire, 315
   Injury during fire, 315
   Interference with, 375
   Wanton or malicious injury to fire
      engines or apparatus, 315
Flowers
   Gardens, offenses involving, 348
   Protection of, 348
Fraternal organization, obtaining money,
   etc. under false pretenses, 338
Fraud
   Bank employees, 333
   Checks, drawing or uttering, 329
   Corporate books, false entries, 337
   Corporate credit, 338
   Identity, 330–31
   Labor union seal, trademark, insignia,
      338
   Municipal officers, 333
   Procurement of supplies, 337
   State treasury, 333
   Vessel captain, conversion of property
      by, 327
Furs, imitation, 340
Gambling and vending devices, fraudulent
   use of, 338–39
Gift certificates, offenses involving, 339
Goal posts, destruction of, 345
Gross fraud or cheat at common law, 339
Hired property, intent to defraud in
   dealings with, 340
Historical monuments, malicious
   destruction of, 342
Hoax devices, possession, transportation,
   use of, 344
Hoax explosives
   Definition, 344
   Possession of, 344
Hospitals and medical facilities, obstruction
   of entry, 350
Humane society, injury to property, 355
Identity fraud, 330–31
Incendiary devices
   Definitions, 343–44
   Malicious explosion, 345
   Notice of seizure of, 345
   Possession or control of, 344
   Throwing, secreting, launching, or
      placing of, 345
Insignia of societies
   Unlawful use, 337–38

Veteran organizations, unlawful use,
   337–38
Insurance claims, fraudulent, 346–47
Insured property, burning with intent to
   defraud, 315, 569
Intellectual property
   Counterfeit mark, 359–60
   Violations of, 359
Irrigation equipment, malicious injury, 356
Keys, master, offenses involving, 357
Labor union seal, fraudulent use of, 338
Land
   Attached, conveyance without notice, 340
   Encumbered, conveyance without
      notice, 340
   Entry on adjoining lands not a trespass,
      349
   Entry on land by abutting property
      owner, 349
Larceny, 322–26
   Bank bill paper, 332
   Bicycles, second conviction, 331
   Continuing scheme, 325–26
   Defenses, 324, 325
   Definition, 323
   Elements of, 761
   Embezzlement, 324–25
   False pretenses, by, 324, 327
      Contracts, banking, credit, 327
   False statement of fact, 324
   Indictment, 562, 569–70
   Inducement to part with property, 328
   Intent, 323
   Joint enterprise, 325
   Leased or rented property, 340
   Of another, 323–24
   Organized retail crime, 327
   Penalty for, 761
   Permanently deprive, intent to, 324
   Person, from, 320, 761
      Attempted, 320
      Elements of, 761
      Joint enterprise, 320
      Penalty for, 761
      Pickpocketing, 320
   Personal property, 323
   Restitution, 325
   Taking, 323
   Threshold value of $250, 323
   Voluntary association, embezzlement
      from, 334
   Wrongful detention of money by
      carriers, 331
Leased or rented property, 340
Legal notices, malicious injury to, 352
Libraries
   Definitions, 343
   Disturbance of, 450–51
   Mutilation of property of, 343
   Theft, etc., 343
Loan, construction, misapplication, 331
Master keys, sale of, 357
Medical facility, obstruction of, 350
Milk containers
   Carrying away without permission, 359
   Defacement of, 355
Mills, injury by raising of water, 356
Monuments and markers, malicious
   destruction of, 342
Motor vehicles
   Burning motor vehicle, owner's
      statement, 322

12

PROPERTY, CRIMES AGAINST
Motor vehicles *(cont'd)*
  Defacement of identification numbers, 356
  Fraud, 320–21
  Fraudulent insurance claims, 347
  Machines, etc. to obliterate IDs, 357
  Odometer tampering, 357
  Parking on private way, 349
  Recovery of vehicle, 322
  Removal of motor vehicles from private
    way or property, 349
  Sale disclosures, 342
  Statement concerning theft, 322
  Stolen leased or rented motor vehicles,
    340–41
  Theft, 321–22
  Trespass with, 349, 352
Names
  Benevolent organizations, false use of,
    338
  Fraternal, use in publication, 338
Natural scenery, defacement of, 352–53
Nuclear weapons, possession, 345
Organized retail crime, 327
Park or playground equipment, injury to, 343
Performances, live, unauthorized
  reproduction of, 358
Personalty
  Malicious or wanton injury, 353–55
  Mortgaged, concealment of, 340
  Sale by mortgagor without consent, 340
Pests, bringing into state, 348
Ponds, ice, injury to, 346
Poultry thieves, detention by owner, 319
Precious metals
  Dealer records, 357–58
  Gold, false marking of, 339–40
  Sterling and coin silver, false marking
    of, 339
Procurement of supplies, fraudulent, 337
Railroad cars
  Breaking and entering, 319
  Stealing in, 319
Religious places of worship, destruction of,
  355
Reproduction of copyrighted material
  Definitions, 358
  Forfeiture or destruction of, 359
  Manufacture of, 358
  Penalties, 358
  Unauthorized recording of motion
    picture in theater, 358–59
  Unauthorized reproduction, 358
  Live performances, 358
Reproductive health-care facility, buffer
  zone, 350–51
Restitution for stolen property, 336
Retail receipt, counterfeiting, 327
Schoolhouse, defacement or injury to,
  342–43
Shoplifting, 326
Slugs, manufacture and sale, 339
Solid waste, unlawful disposal of, 359
Sound recordings, unauthorized
  reproduction of, 358
State building, defacement or injury to, 342
Stealing
  Fire, at, 319
  Trucks, tractors, trailers, freight
    containers, 319
Stock
  Fraudulent issue or transfer, 336

  Unauthorized issue, 336
Stolen property
  Arresting officer's duty to secure, 332
  Buying or receiving, 334–36
    Elements of, 334–35, 767–68
    Knowledge, 335
    Recency, 335
    Statute of limitations, 335
    Value, 335
  Common receiver, 336
  Indictment and pretrial proceedings,
    562, 571
  Jurisdiction, 336
  Leased or rented motor vehicles, 340–41
  Refusal to surrender, 319
  Restitution, effect of, 336
  Statute of limitations, 335
  Trade secrets, 336
  Transportation media, 336
Stone walls, unauthorized removal of,
  345–46
Sunday trespassers, 355
Theft
  Common and notorious thief, 331
  Contractor tools, 320
  Motor vehicle, 321–22
    Recovery of, 322
    Statement concerning, 322
  Public records, 359
Theft detection shielding device,
  distribution or possession of, 326–27
Transportation media
  Fraudulent hiring of, 336
  Unlawful taking or use of, 336
Trespass, 348–49
  Elements of, 770
  Entry on land by abutting property, 349
  Land of Commonwealth, 352
  Motor vehicle, 349, 352
  Notice against, defacement of, 352
  Penalty for, 770
  Private property, 349
  Public land, 352
  Sunday trespassers, 355
Trick, obtaining property by, 338
Vehicles
  Breaking and entering, 318
  Entering without breaking, nighttime, 318
Vessels
  Breaking and entering, 318
  Destruction or injury to defraud owner
    or insurer, 346
  Entering without breaking, nighttime, 318
  False affidavit or protest, 346
  False invoice of cargo, 346
  Fitting out with intent to destroy, 346
  Fraud by injury to, 346
  Mooring offenses, 356
  Stealing in, 319
Voluntary association, embezzlement from,
  334
Weapons, biological, chemical, or nuclear,
  possession, 345
Wills, destruction or concealment, 331
Woods, timber, orchards
  Entry with intent to injure, 348
  Injury or destruction by fire, 314
  Malicious injury, 348
  Protection of certain flowers, 348
  Trespass in, 348
  Willful cutting and destruction, 348
Wrongful detention of money by carriers, 331

PROSECUTION
Regulation of, 1

PROSTITUTION
See also NIGHTWALKING
Apprehension, 453
Arrest without warrant, 439
Discharge upon recognizance, 453
Drugging to detain person in place of, 439
Employment of persons for, 439
Engaging in for a fee, 452
Enticement, 437
Forms for indictment, 570
Inducing minor into, 437–38
Living off or sharing earnings from, 438–39
Minor, inducing, 437–38
Oath and warrant to enter place of, 439
Pimping, 438
Procuring, 439
Soliciting for, 439
Subsequent offense, 453
Warrant to enter place of, 439

PROTECTION OF WITNESSES, 262–64
See also WITNESSES

PSYCHIATRIC EXAMINATION
Record of, 625
Statements made under, admissibility of, 233

**PSYCHOTHERAPIST-PATIENT
PRIVILEGE**, 226–27

PUBLIC ASSISTANCE
See TRANSITIONAL ASSISTANCE,
  DEPARTMENT OF

PUBLIC HEALTH, 411–21
See also DNA DATABASE; POISON
Alcohol, furnishing to hospital patients, 412
Arsenic
  Analysis of samples, 413
  Fabric containing, 413
  Toys or food containing, 413
Candy containing alcohol, sale of, 413
Certificate of result of analysis, 806
Cigarette rolling papers, sale to minors, 412
Drugs, analysis of, 19
Drugs injurious to users, distribution of, 412
Foods containing injury-causing
  substances, 413
Garbage
  Disposal of, 413–14
  Feeding animals with, 413
  Highway containers for, 415
Glue or cement sales to minors, 416
Hospital patients, alcohol or drugs
  furnished to, 412
Ice cream truck vending, 420–21
Inspectors, analysts, and chemists, 122
Liquor adulteration, 411
Posting laws relating to minors and
  smoking, 413
Refuse, burning near shoreline, 416
Rodent poison in inappropriate location, 412
Rubbish disposal, 413–15
Smoking
  Flea market, at, 420
  Public places, in, 416–20
Spitting, 413
Thermometers, mercury, sale of, 420
Tobacco, furnishing to minors, 412
Toxic vapors, 415–16
Water, refusal or neglect to furnish, 413
Wood alcohol, consumables containing, 412

12

PUBLIC JUSTICE, CRIMES AGAINST
See JUSTICE, CRIMES AGAINST

PUBLIC OFFICIALS AND EMPLOYEES, 377–90
Appointments to other positions, 383
Assault and battery on, 279, 754–55
Attorneys
    Former county employees, 384–85
    Former state employee or partner of, 381–82
Bidding, 378
Candidates for employment, 382
Civil action for damages, 383–84
    County employees, 385
    Municipal employees, 388
Commission or board members, other positions prohibited, 383
Compensation other than by government, 380–81
    Municipal employees, 386–87
Conduct of, 377–90
    Conflict of interest, 382
    Definitions, 378–79
    Former employees, restrictions on activities of, 381–82
    Gifts to, 379–81
    Solicitation of gifts, 380
    Standards of, 389
Conflict of interest, 382
Corporation counsel, city solicitor, opinions of, 388–89
County
    Agent or attorney for other than county agency, 384–85
    Civil action for damages, 385
    Commission or board members, 385
    Compensation other than by government, 384
    Contracts of county, interest in, 385
    Financial interests of, 385
    Former, prohibitions on activities of, 384–85
    Prohibitions on activities of, 384–85
    Unfair advantage in particular matters, 385
Definitions, 378–79, 391–92
Discipline for filing complaint, 396
Disclosures and certifications, 389
Financial disclosure by, 391–96
    Complaint, filing of, effect, 396
    Confidentiality of state ethics commission inquiries, 396
    Definitions, 391–92
    Gifts from legislative agents, 395
    Perjury before state ethics commission proceedings, 396
Financial interests of, 382–83
    Contracts with state, 382–83
    County employees, 385
Forensic and scientific analysis, postconviction, liability, 584
Former state employees, 381–82
Gifts, corruption or solicitation of, 380
Institutions of higher learning, trustees of, 389
Municipal
    Appointments to certain positions, 388
    Civil action for damages, 388
    Commission or board members, 388
    Corporation counsel, city solicitor, opinions of, 388–89

Financial interests of, 387–88
Former, prohibitions on activities of, 386–87
Gifts or other compensation to, 386
One or more elected positions, holding, 387–88
Prospective appointees, undated resignations prohibited, 388
Relatives or associates, 387
Unfair advantage in particular matters, 388
Penalties, 390
Public building or construction contracts, 383
Sex Offender Registry, liability of regarding, 16
Standards of conduct, 389
State employees, 380–81
State Ethics Commission
    Confidentiality of inquiries, 396
    Discipline for filing complaint, 396
    Financial interest statements, 394–95
    Investigations, 393–94
    Members, 392
    Municipal liaisons, 390
    Online training programs, 390
    Opinions, 384
    Perjury before, 396
    Powers and duties of, 392–93
Suspension of persons under indictment for misconduct, 389–90
Telecommunications and energy commission, other positions prohibited, 383
Trustees of higher education institutions, 389
Witnesses, corruption of, 379–80

PUBLIC PEACE, CRIMES AGAINST, 396–411
Body armor, wearing in commission of crime, 403
Broadheads, sale of, 410
Electronic communications, annoying, 410
Explosives, false reports of, 409–10
Fire alarms, false, 409
Firearms sales, 403–04
Hazing offenses, 410–11
Hunting arrowheads, sale of, 410
Knives and similar weapons, offenses involving, 407
Large capacity weapons, 404
Minors, air rifles and, 407
Persons previously convicted of violent crimes, 404–05
Police officers, false reports to, 409
Poster, distributing to schools about laws, 406
Razorheads, sale of, 410
Riot, armed forces role in suppressing, 397
Statutes, printing for posting, 406
Stink bombs, sale of, 410
Tear gas, use of in crime, 403
Telephone calls, annoying, 410
Unlawful assembly
    Armed forces, use of, 397
    Assistance in dispersing, requiring, 397
    Building or vessel, injury to, 397
    Damage to property as result of, 397
    Death or injury as result of, 397
    Dispersing and suppressing, 396
    Person killed or wounded, 397
    Refusing or neglecting to depart, 396

Suppression of, refusal to exercise authority concerning, 397
Vessel, injury to, 397
Weapons, carrying or possessing, 397–403
    BB guns and air rifles, 401
    Breaking and entering to steal firearm, 406
    Constitutionality of statute, 400
    Cutting device in airport or airplane, 408–09
    Definitions, 406
    Discharge near dwelling, 408
    Duplicative charges, 401
    Identifying numbers, 406–07
    Knives and similar weapons, offenses involving, 407
    Knowledge, 400–01
    Machine gun or sawed-off shotgun, 397–403
    Necessity as defense, 401–02
    New resident, 401
    Public way, 407–08
    Retailer, wholesaler or manufacturer, breaking and entering place of business, 406
    Rifle or shotgun, loaded, 407–08
    Separate offenses, 401
    Serial numbers, 406–07
    Silencers, offenses involving, 403
    Transporting firearm into state, 405
    Under the influence, while, 405
    Variance, 400–01

PUBLIC POLICY, CRIMES AGAINST, 421–35
Beano, 429
Boxing matches, betting on, 433
Bridge or whist games, 429
Bucketing offenses, 431–32
Communications equipment used for unlawful purpose, 428
Definitions, 431–32, 434–35
Enterprise crime, 434–35
Gaming or betting
    Cattle shows, relative to, 423–24
    Complaints and indictments relative to, 430
    Delivery to or from person engaged in, 429
    Devices of, 422–23
    Evidence, 427
    Forfeiture, 422
    Forms for indictment, 569
    Gambling devices, 422–23
        Fraudulent use of, 338–39
    Gifts for influence, 432
    Implements of, possession, 422
    Inns and hotels, etc., in, 422
    Judicial notice concerning, 430
    Lottery, pool or betting houses, 422
    Organizing or promoting, 427
    Place to register bets, 427
    Policy lotteries or shops, 428
    Prima facie evidence, 428, 429, 430
    Public place in, or while trespassing, 422
    Ship or vessel, 422
    Skilo and similar games, 424
    Telephones used for, 427, 427, 433–34
    Warrant to enter place of, 429
Gifts for influence, 432
Horse-related words or figures as evidence, 429

12

PUBLIC POLICY, CRIMES AGAINST
(cont'd)
Lotteries
    Advertising sale of tickets, 426
    Aiding in setting up, 426–27
    Arrest without warrant, 426
    Complaints and indictments relative to, 430
    Delivery to or from person engaged in, 429
    Disposal of property by chance, 424
    Elements of, 761
    False tickets, making, 426
    Forfeiture of money, prizes, or shares of lotteries, 426
    Forms for indictment, 570
    Judicial notice concerning, 430
    Penalties for, 761
    Permitting in buildings, 426
    Place of, 422
    Policy lottery or shop, 428
    Selling, exchanging, or possessing tickets, 426
    Subsequent offenses, 426
    Tickets for, 426
    Warrant to enter place of, 429
Nuisance, race grounds as, 431
Oath and warrant to arrest, 429
Patients in hospital, settlement or release of claims, 433
Public assistance fraud, 433
Public office; appointment, discharge, etc., 432–33
Race track owners and proprietors at, 429–30
Race tracks
    Bets or stakes on horses, 431
    Disguising horse, 431
    Nuisance, as, 431
    Transmission of results of race, 431
    Urban location of, 431
Raffles and bazaars, 424–25
Refrigerator door removal, 433
Research papers, sale of, 434
Schools, advertising by, 434
Skilo and similar games, 424
Subject of sale, representation of delivery of thing other than, 430
Telephones, use for gaming, 427, 428
Tickets, as evidence, 428–29
    Trading stamps, sale or delivery of, 431
Usury, criminal, 434
Whist or bridge, 429

PUBLIC WAY
Littering, 303
Proof of, 63, 236

R

RACE TRACKS AND RACING
Bets or stakes on horses, 431
Disguising horse, 431
Nuisance, as, 431
Transmission of results of race, 431
Urban location of, 431

RACIAL PROFILING, 497

RAFFLES AND BAZAARS, 424–25

RAILROADS
Company stamp, forgery of, 362
Tickets, forgery of, 362, 363

RAPE, 292–300
Assault with intent to commit, 299–300, 754
    Aggravated rape of child under 16, 298, 767
    Assault of child with intent to commit, 300, 753–54
    Child under 16, 297–98, 766–67
    Prior bad acts, 300
Confidentiality of victim's name, 300–01
Consent, 295
DNA database, 297
Duplicative convictions, 296
Elements of, 765–67
Evidence, 296, 297, 819
Expert testimony, 296
First complaint, 293–94
Force, evidence of, 296
Fresh complaint, 293
Indictment
    Construction of words used in indictment, 562
    Forms for indictment, 570–71
Intoxication, 295
Investigative process, 294–95
Jury instructions, 294
Lesser included offense, 295
Penalty for, 765–67
Penetration, 293
Prior bad acts, 297, 300
Prior complaint of, 296
Public, exclusion of at trial, 574
Records, 297
Sex offender registry, 278, 297, 299
Sexually dangerous person commitment, 278, 297, 300
Statutory, 299, 766–67
Venue, 300
Weapon, evidence of, 296

REASONABLE DOUBT, 846–47

REBUTTAL EVIDENCE, 846

RECKLESS ENDANGERMENT TO CHILDREN, 282

RECOGNIZANCE, 521
Conditions of, 537
County of arrest, in, 521
Default, 538
    Forfeiture of deposit, 539
Defendant surrendering self, 539
Failure to appear after release on, 539–40
Failure to recognize, 523
Forfeiture, award to person entitled to, 538
Judgment
    Former judgment diminished, 539
    Whole or part of penalty, 538
Minor witnesses, 525
Neglect, omissions, or defects, 539
Paying amount for which bound, 538
Personal, 524–25, 528–32, 539
Release
    Personal, 528–32
    Revocation of, 535–36
Return of, 538
Review, petition for, 539
Revocation of bail, 531
Service of notice, 539
Sureties with, 525
Witnesses, 566

RECUSAL, 847

REOPENING EVIDENCE, 847

REPRODUCTIVE HEALTH-CARE FACILITY
Buffer zone, 350–51

REPUTATION
Evidence of, 847–48

RESISTING ARREST, 375–76

RESTAURANTS OR TAVERNS
Immoral purposes, use for, 442–43

RESTITUTION
Breaking and entering, 319
Delinquent children, 148
Driving under the influence, 70
Evidence, 848
Injured persons, 545
Larceny, 325
Motor vehicle theft or fraud cases, 322, 545
Stolen property, 336

REWARDS, 514–15

RIGHT TO COUNSEL
See ATTORNEYS

RIGHTS OF PERSONS ACCUSED OF CRIME
See ACCUSED, RIGHTS OF

RIOT
See also PUBLIC PEACE, CRIMES AGAINST
Armed forces role in suppressing, 397

ROAD, LAW OF
See TRAFFIC, LAW OF THE ROAD

ROBBERY
Armed, 270, 287–88, 768
Elements of, 768
Indictment, 562, 571
Penalty for, 768
Unarmed, 270, 291–92, 754, 768

RULES OF APPELLATE PROCEDURE, 669–85
Amicus curiae briefs (Rule 17), 679
Briefs (Rules 16–20), 678–82
    Amicus curiae (Rule 17), 679
    Appendix to (Rule 18), 679–81
    Filing (Rule 19), 681
    Form (Rule 20), 681–82
    Service (Rule 19), 681
Clerks (Rule 31), 685
Costs (Rule 26), 683
Damages for delay (Rule 25), 683
Definitions (Rule 1), 669
Delay, damages (Rule 25), 683
Direct review (Rule 11), 676–77
Disability of lower court judge (Rule 7), 672
Dismissal, voluntary (Rule 29), 684
Divided vote, further appellate review (Rule 24.1), 683
Docketing (Rule 10), 676
Exhibits (Rule 9), 675–76
Filing (Rule 13), 677
Further appellate review (Rule 27.1), 684
    Divided vote (Rule 24.1), 683
How taken (Rule 3), 669–70
In forma pauperis proceedings (Rule 12), 677
Injunction pending appeal (Rule 6), 671–72
Justices' participation (Rule 24), 683
Motions (Rule 15), 678
Oral argument (Rule 22), 682–83
Petition for rehearing (Rule 27), 683–84
Prehearing conference (Rule 21), 682

12

RULES OF APPELLATE PROCEDURE
(cont'd)
Record (Rule 8), 672–75
  Assembly and transmission (Rule 9),
    675–76
Rehearing, petition for (Rule 27), 683–784
Report of case for determination (Rule 5),
  671
Rescript (Rule 23), 683
  Entry of judgment following (Rule 28), 684
Scope (Rule 1), 669
Service (Rule 13), 677
Stay pending appeal (Rule 6), 671–72
Substitution of parties (Rule 30), 685
Suspension of rules (Rule 2), 669
Time, computations and extensions
  (Rule 14), 677–78
Transfer from Supreme Judicial Court
  (Rule 11.1), 677
Voluntary dismissal (Rule 29), 684
When taken (Rule 4), 670–71

RULES OF CRIMINAL PROCEDURE,
599–650
See also DISTRICT/MUNICIPAL COURT
    RULES OF CRIMINAL PROCEDURE
Arraignment, 603–04
Arrest warrant, 602–03
Assignment of counsel (Rule 8), 605
Case management (Rule 36), 643–45
Clerical mistakes (Rule 42), 647
Complaint and indictment (Rule 3), 600–01
  Form and contents of (Rule 4), 601
  Probable cause, determination of
    (Rule 3.1), 601
Construction of, 599
Contempt (Rule 44), 649
Continuances (Rule 10), 606
Counsel for indigent defendants (Rule 33),
  642
Definitions, 599–600
Depositions to perpetuate testimony
  (Rule 35), 642–43
Dismissal by prosecution (Rule 16), 628
Experts (Rule 41), 647
Filing and service of papers (Rule 32), 642
Foreign proceedings and foreign law
  (Rule 39), 646
Grand jury (Rule 5), 601–02
Indictment, waiver of, 600–01
Indigent defendants, counsel for (Rule 33),
  642
Initial appearance and arraignment
  (Rule 7), 603–04
Interlocutory appeal (Rule 15), 626–28
Interpreters and experts (Rule 41), 647
Joinder of offenses or defendants (Rule 9),
  605–06
Judge, disability of (Rule 38), 646
Judgment (Rule 28), 637
Jury instructions (Rule 24), 634
Motion for required finding of not guilty
  (Rule 25), 635–36
Objections (Rule 22), 633
Opening statements (Rule 24), 634
Pleas (Rule 12), 608–15
Postconviction relief (Rule 30), 640–41
Presence of defendant (Rule 18), 630
Pretrial
  Conference and hearing (Rule 11),
    606–08
  Discovery (Rule 14), 619–26

Hearing and conference (Rule 11),
    606–08
  Motions (Rule 13), 615–19
Probable cause, determination of
  (Rule 3.1), 601
Proof, official records (Rule 40), 646–47
Relief pending review (Rule 31), 641–42
Removal of disruptive defendant (Rule 45),
  649
Report (Rule 34), 642
Requests for rulings (Rule 26), 636
Revision or revocation of sentence
  (Rule 29), 637–40
Sanctions (Rule 48), 650
Service of papers (Rule 32), 642
Special magistrates (Rule 47), 649–50
Stay of execution (Rule 31), 641–42
Stipulations (Rule 23), 633–34
Summary contempt (Rule 43), 647–49
Summons
  Appear, to (Rule 6), 602–03
  Witnesses, for (Rule 17), 628–29
Time (Rule 46), 649
Transfer of cases (Rule 37), 645–46
Trial by jury or court (Rule 19), 630
Trial jurors (Rule 20), 630–32
Verdict (Rule 27), 636
Waiver of indictment, 600–01
Witnesses
  Sequestration of (Rule 21), 632–33
  Summons (Rule 17), 628–29

RULES OF SUPERIOR COURT
See SUPERIOR COURT

S

SCHOOLS
Advertising by, 434
Alcohol on premises of, 450
Animal vivisection or dissection, 458
Buses, 40
Controlled substance violations in or near,
  113–14
Defacement or injury, 342–43
Disturbance of, 450
Drug sale, 765
Examinations, taking for another, 434
Exchange teachers, 266
Hazing, 410–11
Locker searches, 499
Records as evidence, 849
Research papers, sale of, 434
Searches, warrantless, 499
Trustees of institutions of higher learning,
  389

SEARCH AND SEIZURE, 481–505
See also SEARCH WARRANTS;
    WARRANTLESS SEARCHES
Gaming devices or games, 23–24
Postponement of trial, 514
Unreasonable, freedom from, 1

SEARCH WARRANTS, 507–14
Administrative fire warrants, 482
Affidavit in support of application for
  warrant, 510–13
Aguilar-Spinelli standard, 511
Anticipatory warrants, 482–83
Appeal, 514
Article 14, Massachusetts Declaration of
  Rights, 1, 483
Basis of knowledge test, 512
Blood samples, 507–08

Cellular phones, 483
Citizen-informants, 482
Complaint, 507–08
Computers and disks, 509
Confidential informant, identity of, 484–85
Controlled buy, 512
Copy of, 483
Corroboration, 482, 512
Curtilage, 483–84
  Automobile search, 483–84
  Land, 484
  Parking space, 483
Definitions, 508–09
Description of premises, 509–10
Designated property or articles, 507–08
Documentary evidence subject to privilege,
  507–08
Forfeiture of property, notice before, 514
Form of, 510
Franks, 512–13
General principles, 482
  Affidavit, sufficiency of, 482
  Citizen-informants, 482
  Corroboration, 482
  Hearsay, crediting, 482
  Illegally seized evidence, excluding, 482
Global positioning system (GPS) devices,
  484
Hearsay, 482
Informant named, 512
Informer's privilege, 513
Issuance, manner of, 513
Items to be seized not listed, 509
Jail calls, 484
Location of search, 485
Medical marijuana, 485
Motion to suppress, 485
Motor vehicles, 485, 510
Nexus with home, 485–86
Nighttime, 486
No knock, 486–87
  Consensual entry by ruse, 486
  Drugs, 486
  Necessary showing, 486
  Not warranted, 486–87
Personal appearance, 511
Plain view, 487, 509
Postponement of trial, 514
Privacy, expectation of, 484, 487–88
Probable cause, 482
Requisites of, 509–10
Return of, time for, 514
Sale or destruction of property seized, 514
Securing premises, 487
Seizure of items, disposition of, 513–14
Service of notice, 514
Staleness, 487
Standing, 487
  Automatic, 487
  Derivative standing, 487
  Exception to automatic standing, 488
  Expectation of privacy, 487–88
  Possession as essential element of
    guilt, 487
  Target standing, 487
Statement against penal interest, 512
Subversive organizations, articles
  belonging to, 508
Technical defect, 509
Third-party residences, 488
Veracity test, 511–12

SECURITIES AND COMMODITIES
Bucketing offenses, 431–32

SELF-DEFENSE
Armed robbery, 288
Arrest, resisting, 376
Assault and battery, 277, 285
Burglary, 317
Evidence of, 849
Manslaughter, defense to, 275
Resisting arrest, 376

SELF-INCRIMINATION
Custodian of corporate records, 1
Privilege against, 227
Right to remain silent, 617–18
When refusal to testify allowed, 849–50

SENTENCING
See JUDGMENT AND EXECUTION

SEX OFFENDER REGISTRY, 1–16
Acts requiring registration, 297, 437, 438,
      446
Arrest for failure to comply with registration
      requirements, 16
Burden of proof, 7, 13–14
Classification hearing, 14–16
Confidentiality, 10, 16
Constitutionality of, 3
Criminal History Systems Board, 4–7
Definitions, 2–3
Drugging for sexual intercourse, 437
Due process and, 7, 14
Enticing away for prostitution or sexual
      intercourse, 437
Evidence, 14
Expert testimony, 15
Failure to register or verify information, 9–10
Fee for registration, 16–17
GPS device worn by homeless offender, 9
Homeless offenders, 3, 8, 9
Incestuous marriage or intercourse, 441
Inducing minor into prostitution, 437–38
Information disseminated, 10–11
Judicial review of classification and
      registration requirements, 16
Liability of public officers and employees
      regarding, 16
Living off or sharing earnings of minor
      prostitute, 438–39
Misuse of information, 16
Penalties
      Failure to register or verify information,
         9–10
      Misuse of information, 16
Personal appearance, 8–9
Police, local, offender's appearance at, 8–9
Registration data, 3–4
Registration requirements, 4–9
Request for information from, 10–11
Sex Offender Registry Board, 3, 11–14
Termination of registration obligation, 9
Transmission of data to law enforcement
      agencies, 4–7

SEX OFFENDERS
See also SEXUALLY DANGEROUS
      PERSONS
Global positioning system device to be
      worn by, 9, 307–08
Ice cream truck vending prohibited, 308

SEXUAL CRIME VICTIM
Children
      Child welfare service needs, 136

Enticing child under 18 to engage in
      prostitution, trafficking, sexual
      activity, 303, 758
Jury trial, 632
Nightwalking or streetwalking, child in
      violation of, 136
Posing or exhibiting in state of nudity or
      sexual conduct, 444–45
Trafficking, 308–09
Sexual conduct of, evidence of, 232
Trafficking of persons, 308–09

SEXUALLY DANGEROUS PERSONS,
162–71
Appeals, 168–69
Attorney, right to, 169–70
Attorney general, notice to, 167–69
Bruno directed verdict standard, 167–68
Definitions, 163–65
District attorney, notice to, 167–69
Drugging person for sexual intercourse, 437
Due process, 164
Evidence, 169–70
Ex post facto, 164
Examination and discharge petitions, 166–67
      Period of examination, 169
Examiners, qualified, 163, 169
Expert evidence, 168
Incompetent defendant, 164, 170
Jury waiver, 170
Nemansket Correctional Center, 165
Notice, 167–69
Personality disorder, 163
Petition
      Examination and discharge, 166–67
      Trial, 170
Probable cause hearing, 168
Reports, annual, 170–71
Right to counsel, 169–70
Security, appropriate levels of, 165–66
Sexual offense, 163
Supervised probation, 169
Temporary commitment, 169–70
Transfer to correctional institution, 165
Voluntary treatment services, 165

SHOPLIFTING, 326, 768–69

SHOW-UPS, 852

SLUGS
Manufacture and sale, 339

SMOKING
See TOBACCO

SOCIAL SECURITY NUMBER
Using or giving false, 376–77

SPERM CELLS
Chemical analysis, 19

SPITTING, 277, 413

SPORTING EVENTS
See also GAMING OR BETTING
Abuse of participants and officials, 450
Throwing objects at, 303–04

STALKING, 305–06
Elements of and penalties for, 769
Jurisdiction, 564

STANDING
Children's need for services, 132–33

STATE EMPLOYEES
See PUBLIC OFFICIALS AND EMPLOYEES

STATE ETHICS COMMISSION
See also PUBLIC OFFICIALS
      AND EMPLOYEES
Confidentiality of inquiries, 396
Discipline for filing complaint, 396
Financial interest statements, 394–95
Investigations, 393–94
Members, 392
Municipal liaisons, 390
Online training programs, 390
Opinions, 384
Perjury before, 396
Powers and duties of, 392–93

STATE POLICE, DEPARTMENT OF
Alcoholic beverages, analysis, 19
Drugs, chemical analysis, 19
Motor vehicle ownership records, 19
Sperm cells, analysis, 19

STATUTE OF LIMITATIONS
Stolen property, 335

**STATUTES, LAWS, AND GOVERNMENT
DOCUMENTS, PROOF OF**
Admissibility, 234
Court records, 234
Foreign law, 234
Governmental departments, records of,
      234–35
Legislative and administrative acts, 234

STENOGRAPHERS
Child abuse victims, statement of, 237–38
Defendant's employment of, 224
Transcripts, 224
      Evidence, as, 237

STIPULATIONS, 633–34, 854

STOCK
Fraudulent issue or transfer, 336
Unauthorized issue, 336

STOLEN PROPERTY
See LARCENY; PROPERTY, CRIMES
      AGAINST

STREETWALKING
Child in violation of, 136
Trafficking victim, affirmative defense, 311

STRUCTURAL DEFECT DOCTRINE, 854

SUBROGATION
Victim compensation, 251

SUBVERSIVE ORGANIZATIONS
See GOVERNMENTS, CRIMES AGAINST

SUMMONS
Arrest
      Fixing time for trial, 520–21
      Instead of warrant, 520
Criminal Procedure Rules
      Appear, summons to, 602–03
      Definition, 600
      Witnesses, 628–29

SUPERIOR COURT
Case management for criminal cases,
      658–64
Criminal case management, 658–64
Criminal jurisdiction, 220
District Courts, case bound over from, 223
Rules of, 651–64
      Affidavit, verification by, 653
      Appeal, claim of, 655
      Appearances, 651
      Appellate division procedure and forms,
         655

12

SUPERIOR COURT
Rules of *(cont'd)*
    Arguments, 656
    Attorneys
        Appearance by, 651
        Assignment of, 653
        Not to become bail or surety, 652–53
        Participation in voir dire, 656–58
        Withdrawal of appearance, 655
        Witnesses, as, 653
    Authority to appear, 651
    Court reporter, grand jury proceedings, 655
    Criminal cases, special provisions for, 653–58
    Depositions
        Commissions to take, 656
        Manner of taking, 656
    Evidence, objections to, 652
    Exhibits, 653
    Experts
        Criminal cases, 653
        Delinquent children cases, 653–54
    Extra charges by officers, 652
    Grand jury proceedings, court reporter at, 655
    Hospital records, 653
    Impounded materials, 658
    Indictment, waiver of, 654
    Instructions or rulings, request for, 656
    Interlocutory matters, 652
    Jurors, 652
        Notes by, 652
        Peremptory challenges of, 652
        Voir dire of, participation in, 656–58
    Motions, 652
        Postconviction relief, 654–55
        Return of property, 654
        Suppression of evidence, 654
    Not guilty plea, 654
    Objections to evidence, 652
    Opening statements, 652
    Payment orders, term of, 654
    Peremptory challenges of jurors, 652
    Postponements, 651–52
    Probation
        Conditions of, 654
        Term of, 654
    Property, return of, motion for, 654
    Recording devices, 653
    Self-represented parties, participation in voir dire, 656–58
    Waiver of indictment, 654
    Witnesses, examination of, 656
    Writ of protection, 653

SWEEPSTAKES
Unlawful possession of electronic machine or device for conducting or promoting, 423

SYRINGES AND NEEDLES
Assault by means of, 286
Disposal of, 102–03
Sale of, 102

T

TATTOOING, 303

TEAR GAS
Use in commission of crime, 403

TELEPHONES
See also WIRETAPPING

Annoying telephone calls, 410
Evidentiary use of conversations held by, 854–55
Gambling or betting, used for, 427, 428, 433–34
Unlawful purposes, use for, 428

THEATRICAL PRODUCTIONS
Firearms and weapons, use of in, 203

THREATS, 479–80, 571
Elements of, 769
Penalty for, 769

TICKETS
Admission tickets, forged, 362, 363
Forgery, 362, 363
License to sell, 207
Lottery tickets, 426
    Advertising, 426
    False, 426
Raffle, 424–25
Railroad, 362, 363
Resale, 207

TOBACCO
Cigarette rolling papers, 112–13, 412
Minors, furnishing to, 412
Smoking
    Flea market, at, 420
    Public places, at, 416–20

TRADING STAMPS
Sale or delivery of, 431

TRAFFIC, LAW OF THE ROAD, 24–27
See also MOTOR VEHICLES
Crosswalks, 27
Emergency vehicle right of way and operation, 25–26
Fire engines and apparatus, right of way of, 25–26
Heavy trucks, multilane highways, 25
Intersecting ways, right of way at, 26
Meeting vehicles, 24
Motorcycles, single-lane driving and passing, 25
Obstructed view, keeping right, 24–25
One-way traffic, 27
Passing vehicle going in same direction, 24
Pedestrians, 27
Penalties, 25, 27
Red signals, turning on, 26
Right lane travel, 25
Single lane driving, 25
Sleds or sleighs, bells on, 25
Street railway cars, 25
Through ways, designation of highways as, 27
Trucks, multilane highways, 25

TRAFFICKING IN CONTROLLED SUBSTANCES, 110–11, 769

TRAFFICKING OF ORGANS, 310, 769–70

TRAFFICKING OF PERSONS, 308–09
Children under 18, 308–09
    Enticing, 758
Definitions, 308
Fines, transmittal to state treasurer, 310
Forced servitude, 309, 770
Monies used in violations, forfeiture to Commonwealth, 310
Nightwalking or streetwalking, affirmative defense, 311
Organ trafficking, 310
Property subject to forfeiture, 310–11

Restitution, 310
Sexual servitude, for, 308–09, 770
Subsequent violations, 309
Victim caseworkers, witnesses, 229–30

TRAMPS, VAGRANTS, AND VAGABONDS, 454, 571

TRANSCRIPTS
Child abuse victims, statement of, 237–37
Evidence, as, 237

TRANSITIONAL ASSISTANCE, DEPARTMENT OF
Electronic benefit transfer transactions, 17
Embezzlement to obtain property, 18
False representations, 17
Father leaving family to obtain assistance, 17
Food stamps trafficking, 18
Fraud hotline sign, 18–19
Fraud to obtain property, 18
Theft to obtain property, 18
Unlawful payments, return of, 17

TRANSPORTATION MEDIA
Fraudulent hiring of, 336
Unlawful taking or use of, 336

TRANSPORTATION NETWORK COMPANIES
Title, 207

TRAVELER'S CHECKS
See FORGERY AND CURRENCY CRIMES

TREASON
Conviction, manner of, 265
Defined, 264
Misprision, 264
Penalty for, 264

TRESPASS
Boston Housing Authority, 349
Elements of, 770
Entry on land by abutting property owner, 349
Land of Commonwealth, 352
Motor vehicle, 349, 352
Notice against, defacement of, 352
Penalty for, 770
Private property, 349
Public land, 352
Sunday trespassers, 355
Water sources, 352

TRIALS AND PROCEEDINGS BEFORE JUDGMENT, 571–80
Acquittal
    Liability for fees of person acquitted, 574
    Part of crime and conviction on residue, 574
Adjournment of, 522–53
Appeals by Commonwealth, 578
Appellate Division
    Review of sentences, 577
    Right of appeal, 578
Attorney assigned to juvenile offenders, 574
Burden to prove admission to bar, 572–73
Child
    Scheduling trial, 576
    Witness, as, 575–76
Criminal cases, trial list of, 572
Defendant; admissibility of acts or omissions, 577
Directed verdict, 573
Discontinuance of prosecution
    Bylaws, ordinances, 574

TRIALS AND PROCEEDINGS BEFORE JUDGMENT *(cont'd)*
Guilty
   Conviction upon plea, 579–80
   Withdrawal of uncounseled plea, 578
Habitual criminal, separate trial as to prior conviction, 573–74
Issues of fact, trial of, 572
Judgment
   Amendment of, 578
   Motions in arrest of, 580
Jurors
   Affirmation of, 572
   Oaths of, 572
Killing or injuring a person in dwelling house, 573
Libel, justification of, 573
Male and female prisoners, trial of, 580
Motion to vacate, 579–80
Motor vehicle theft or fraudulent claims, testimony, 572
Nighttime, definition of, 573
Nolo contendere, conviction upon plea of, 579–80
Ownership of property, proof, 573
Pleas and pretrial motions in the District Court, 576
Public, exclusion of
   Husband and wife in criminal proceeding, 575
   Incest or rape, 575
   Minors, 574
Simultaneous electronic means, definition of, 575–76
Supreme Judicial Court
   Appeal to, 577
   Capital cases, 580
Vacate, motion to, 579–80

U

UNIFORMS
Government, unlawful use of, 265–66

UNLAWFUL ASSEMBLY
See PUBLIC PEACE, CRIMES AGAINST

UNNATURAL AND LASCIVIOUS ACTS, 449–50, 771
Child under 16, 450
Indictment, 562

URINALYSIS, 126

USURY, 434

UTTERING
See FORGERY AND CURRENCY CRIMES

V

VEHICLES
See MOTOR VEHICLES

VEHICULAR HOMICIDE, 74–75
Elements of and penalty for, 771–72

VENIRE FACIAS WRITS
Bristol County, 558
Essex County, 558
Grand jurors, 558
Hampden County, 558
Middlesex County, 557
Norfolk County, 558
Plymouth County, 558
Special grand jury, 557
Suffolk County, 557
Worcester County, 558

VENUE
See also as subhead to other topics
Abuse prevention, 211
Abuse violations, jurisdiction, 564
Boundary line cases, 563
Computer data cases, 563
Crime committed in Commonwealth, death outside, 564
Crime committed out of county, 563
Embezzlement by fiduciaries, 564
Explosives, false reports, 564
False pretenses, obtaining money or goods by, 564
False reports, 564
Larceny, 563
Sea, crimes committed on, 563, 564
Specific crimes, 563–64
Stalking, 564
Stolen or embezzled property, 563

VESSELS
See MOTORBOATS AND OTHER VESSELS; PROPERTY, CRIMES AGAINST

VETERANS
Mental health, transfer or commitment to Veterans Administration, 160
Organizations, unlawful use of insignia, 337–38
Pretrial diversions, 556

VICTIM AND WITNESS ASSISTANCE BOARD, 245–46

VICTIMS
Compensation of victims of violent crimes, 247–51
   Award or denial
      Notice, 250
   Change of address, 250
   Civil investigative demands, 250
   Definitions, 248
   Division of Victim Compensation and Assistance, 249
   Eligibility for, 248
   Filing and proof of claims, 250
   Good Samaritans, liability, 251
   Judicial review, 250–51
   Misrepresentation or concealment, effect, 251
   Offsets by amounts received from other sources, 251
   Payment, 250
   Restrictions, 248–49
   Subrogation, 251
Division of Victim Compensation and Assistance, 249
Forensic and scientific analysis, postconviction, notification, 583–84
Good Samaritans, liability, 251
Mental health professional's duty to warn, 162
Name of, confidentiality, 300–01
Rape, confidentiality of victim's name, 300–01
Restitution, 245
Rights of, 243–47
   Assessments imposed by court, 246–47
      Deposit of assessments, 247
   Assurance of, 247
   Criminal justice agencies, assistance by, 247
   Definitions, 243

District attorney programs, 246
Duration of, 247
Eligibility for services, 243
Enforcement of, 247
Failure to provide, 247
Interagency cooperation, 246
Nature of rights, 243–45
Program plan, 246
Restitution, 245
Victim and Witness Assistance Board, 245–46
Victim-witness advocate, 243
Victim and Witness Assistance Board, 245–46

VOICE IDENTIFICATION, 858

W

WARRANTLESS SEARCHES, 488–504
Abandonment, 489
   Briefcase, 489
   Control relinquished, 489
   Saliva, 489
   Trash bag, 489
Accomplice sweep, 489
Administrative searches, 489–90
Apparent authority, 491
Arrest, incident to, 500–01
   Area to be searched, 500
   Companion, search of, 500–01
   Containers, 500
   Degree of restraint determines standard, 500
   Probable cause to arrest, 500
Auto body shops and used car businesses, 490
Burden of proof, 504
Community caretaking function, 490
Consent
   By another (apparent authority), 491
   By another (common authority), 490–91
   Ruse used to obtain, 490
   Voluntariness, 490
Destruction of evidence, 491
Emergency exception, 491
   Drunk driving, 491
   Standard, 491
Evidence affidavit, 504
Exclusionary rule, 491–92
Exigent circumstances, 492
   Limit of "protective sweep" at murder scene, 492
Free to leave standard, 492
Furtive gesture, 492
General principles, 488–89
   Authority, 488–89
   Burden of proof, 488
   Per se unreasonable, 488
   Pursuit, 489
   Strip searches, 489
Incident to forfeiture, 492–93
Inevitable discovery, 493
Informant's tip, 493–94
   Aguilar-Spinelli two-prong test, 493
   Anonymous informant, reliability of, 494
   Circumstances insufficient to establish probable cause, 493
   Ordinary citizen, reliability of, 49
   Reliability of, 49
   Weapons, 494
Intervening action dissipating taint of illegality, 494

12

WARRANTLESS SEARCHES *(cont'd)*
Inventory searches, 494–95
    Closed containers, 495
    Standard procedures, 495
Motion to suppress and, 504–05
Motor vehicles, 495–97
    Danger, reasonable belief of, 496
    Exigent circumstances, 496
    Exit orders, 496
    Extent of search, 496
    General rule, 495
    High-crime area, 496
    License/registration valid, 496
    Marijuana, 497
    Posting a guard, 496
    Pretext, 496
    Probable cause to suspect particular
        vehicle, 495
    Racial profiling, 497
    Recognition of vehicle, 496
    Smell of marijuana, 496–97
    Time of search, 496
Plain feel, 497–98
Plain view, 498
    Inadvertence exception, 498
Presence, 498
Private party search, 498
Probation officer search, 498
Protective sweep, 498–99
Racial profiling, 497
Roadblocks, 499
Ruse, 499
Saliva, 489
School searches, 499–500
    Locker searches, 499
    Public versus private schools, 499–500
    Reasonable suspicion, 499
Seizure, 500
    Encounter becomes seizure, 501
    What is not a seizure, 501
    When seizure occurred, 501
Stop and frisk, 501–504
    Completed misdemeanor, 502
    Drug transaction, 503
    Flight, 502–03
    Handgun, 501–02
    High-crime area, 503
    Inadequate specific, articulable facts, 504
    Jacket lost during flight, 503
    Police radio call, 503
    Radio broadcast description, 503
    Shoes, removal of, 503–04
    Soft object felt, 503
    Stop versus arrest, 502
    Store clerk description, 504
    Two-fold inquiry, 502
Terry stop, 503, 504

WARRANTS
See ARREST; SEARCH WARRANTS;
    as subhead to other topics

WATER
Refusal or neglect to furnish, 413
Trespass upon water sources, 352

WEAPONS
See FIREARMS AND WEAPONS;
    PUBLIC PEACE, CRIMES AGAINST

WIFE AND HUSBAND
See HUSBAND AND WIFE

WILLS
Destruction or concealment, 331

WIRETAPPING, 463–70
Circumstantial evidence, 470
Civil remedy, 469
Definitions, 463–64
Eavesdropping in private home, 469
    Telephone extension, 469
Editing of tape recordings in judicial
    proceedings, 465
Exemptions, 465–66
Federal wiretaps, 469
Introduction of evidence, 468–69
Oral communications, 464
Prison calls, 470
Private person, by, 469–70
Probable cause, 470
Search warrant, 470
Warrants, 466–68
    Authority to issue, 470
Wireless telephones, 470

WITNESSES, 224–34
See also RULES OF CRIMINAL
    PROCEDURE; as subhead to other
    topics
Attorneys as, Superior Court rules
    concerning, 653
Competency of, 225
Contempt of court, 228
Credibility of, 810
    Proof of conviction of crime, 230–31
Criminal defendant, 225
Criminal records of, 626
Discharge from employment, 372
District Courts, 224
Domestic violence victim programs,
    confidentiality of, 229
    Location of, 229
Evidence
    See EVIDENCE
Grand jury proceedings, 227
Handcuffing, 526
Human trafficking victim caseworkers,
    229–30
Husband and wife, 225
Immunity
    Corroborating evidence needed for
        grant of, 228
    Crimes subject to, 227
    Prosecution, from, 227–28
    Protection of witnesses, 264
    Right to counsel, 227–28
    Scope of, 228
    Supreme Judicial Court application for,
        227–28
Impeachment of party's own, 233
Intellectually disabled persons, 233–34
Intimidation, 370–71, 760–61
Parent and child, 225

Privilege
    Clergy communications, 225
    Psychotherapist-patient, 226–27
    Self-incrimination, 227
Protection, 262–64
    Confidentiality of records, 264
    Critical witnesses, 262, 263
    Definitions, 262
    Disclosure of identity or location, 264, 757
    Governmental immunity, 264
    Memoranda of understanding, written,
        263
    Petition requesting, 262
    Public housing, relocation within, 263
    Public school, relocation to another, 263
    Refusal of, 263
    Temporary action, 262
    U.S. Marshall's Office, liaison with, 264
    Witness Protection Board, 262
Rape crisis centers, confidentiality of, 229
Release of committed witnesses, 525
Removal to another county, 526
Reputation, evidence of, 232
Rights of, 243–47
    Assessments imposed by court, 246–47
        Deposit of assessments, 247
    Definitions, 243
    District attorney programs, 246
    Enforcement of, 247
    Interagency cooperation, 246
    Nature of rights, 243–45
    Program plan, 246
    Victim and Witness Assistance Board,
        245–46
    Victim-witness advocate, 243
Sequestration of, 632–33
Sex crime victims' sexual conduct, 232
Sexual assault counselor, confidential
    communications, 228–29
Social worker home address, disclosure of,
    230
Summons, Criminal Procedure Rules,
    628–29
Supreme Judicial Court, application to for
    immunity, 227–28
Treatment of, rules regulating, 525–26
Unavailable, 857

WOMEN
Imprisonment of, 589
Pregnant, sentencing of, 593
Transporting with male prisoners, 526
Trial with male prisoners, 580

WOODS, TIMBER, ORCHARDS
Entry with intent to injure, 348
Fire, injury or destruction by, 314
Malicious injury, 348
Trespass in, 348
Willful cutting and destruction, 348

Y

YOUTH SERVICES, DEPARTMENT OF
Diagnostic study, 150
Suspended sentences, 586
Warrant of commitment to, 152